CW00920558

POCKET OXFORD THESAURUS

Pocket Oxford Thesaurus

SECOND EDITION

Edited by
Sara Hawker

OXFORD
UNIVERSITY PRESS

Great Clarendon Street, Oxford OX2 6DP

Oxford University Press is a department of the University of Oxford.
It furthers the University's objective of excellence in research, scholarship,
and education by publishing worldwide in

Oxford New York

Auckland Cape Town Dar es Salaam Hong Kong Karachi
Kuala Lumpur Madrid Melbourne Mexico City Nairobi
New Delhi Shanghai Taipei Toronto

With offices in

Argentina Austria Brazil Chile Czech Republic France Greece
Guatemala Hungary Italy Japan Poland Portugal Singapore
South Korea Switzerland Thailand Turkey Ukraine Vietnam

Published in the United States
by Oxford University Press Inc., New York

First edition 2004
Second edition 2008

British Library Cataloguing in Publication Data

Data available

Library of Congress Cataloging in Publication Data

Data available

Typeset in Frutiger and Parable
by Asiatype, Inc
Printed and bound in Italy
by L.E.G.O. S.p.A. Lavis (TN)

ISBN 978–0–19–953482–1

10 9

Contents

Introduction vii

Guide to the thesaurus viii

Pocket Oxford Thesaurus **1**

Wordfinder *central section*

Note on trademarks and proprietary status

This dictionary includes some words which have, or are asserted to have, proprietary status as trademarks or otherwise. Their inclusion does not imply that they have acquired for legal purposes a non-proprietary or general significance, nor any other judgement concerning their legal status. In cases where the editorial staff have some evidence that a word has proprietary status this is indicated in the entry for that word by the label trademark, but no judgement concerning the legal status of such words is made or implied thereby.

Contents

Introduction

This brand-new edition of the *Pocket Oxford Thesaurus* has been revised, updated, and redesigned to make it even clearer and easier to use than before. It benefits directly from our ongoing analysis of the Oxford English Corpus, an enormous database containing billions of words of real English taken from a wide variety of different written sources. This analysis enables us to monitor how words are really used and so provide better-matching and more useful groups of synonyms, giving you the best possible choice of alternative words. The synonym sets are arranged in order of their closeness in meaning to the main entry word, with the closest one given first and printed in bold type. Lots of example sentences are provided to help you pinpoint the exact sense you are looking for. Antonyms, words with opposite meanings, are also provided for many of the main entries in the thesaurus.

Extra vocabulary is provided in the special Word Link features. These contain a selection of terms that, while not being synonyms, are closely linked to a main entry word in some other way. At **bird**, for example, you will find the terms **ornithology** (the study of birds) and **avian** (relating to birds) in the Word Link panel. If you look up **steal** the Word Link panel gives you **kleptomania** (a recurrent urge to steal things). There are also dozens of notes giving straightforward guidance about words that are easily confused (e.g. **affect** and **effect**, or **flaunt** and **flout**).

The newly designed Wordfinder section in the centre of the thesaurus provides still more vocabulary to help with crosswords and puzzle-solving, in the form of handy quick-reference lists on a wide range of topics including animal breeds, plant species, musical instruments, and different types of food.

Guide to the thesaurus

This thesaurus is intended to be as easy to use and understand as possible. Here is an explanation of the main features that you will find.

1. STRUCTURE OF THE ENTRIES

Part of speech of the entry word

air noun **1** *hundreds of birds hovered in the air:* **sky**, atmosphere; ether; literary heavens. **2** *let's open the windows to get some air:* **ventilation**; breeze wind. **3** *an air of defiance:* **look**, appearance, impression, aspect, aura, mien, manner, bearing, tone; feel, ambience, atmosphere; informal vibe. **4** *a traditional Scottish air:* **tune**, melody, song.
• verb **1** *a chance to air your views:* **express**, voice, make public, articulate, state, declare, give expression/voice to; have your say. **2** *the windows were opened to air the room:* **ventilate**, freshen, refresh, cool; aerate. **3** *the film was aired nationwide:* **broadcast**, transmit, screen, show, televise.

Example of use to help distinguish different senses

Numbered sense of the entry word

Core synonym – the word closest in meaning to the entry word

Combined synonym group (= *give expression to* and *give voice to*)

Word links – extra vocabulary linked to the entry word

WORD LINKS
aerial relating to the air
aerodynamics the study of objects' movement through the air

flout verb *retailers have been flouting the law for years:* **defy**, refuse to obey, disobey, break, violate, fail to comply with, fail to observe, contravene, infringe, breach, commit a breach of, transgress against; ignore, disregard; informal cock a snook at.
– OPPOSITES observe.

Register label showing the level of English in which the following synonym is used

Word or words meaning the opposite of the entry word

Note giving extra information about the entry word

Don't confuse **flout** with **flaunt**, which means 'display something in a way intended to attract attention' (*they openly flaunted their wealth*).

Homonym number indicating a different word with the same spelling

case[2] **noun 1** *a cigarette case:* **container**, box, canister, holder. **2** *a seed case:* **casing**, cover, sheath, envelope, sleeve, jacket, shell, integument. **3** (Brit.) *she threw some clothes into a case:* **suitcase**, bag, valise, portmanteau; (**cases**) luggage, baggage. **4** *a glass display case:* **cabinet**, cupboard.

Geographical label showing where this sense of the entry word is used

Form of the entry word for which the following synonyms can be substituted

Subject label showing the specialist field in which the following synonym is used

spike noun prong, barb, point; skewer, stake, spit; tine, pin; spur; Mountaineering **piton**.
• **verb** (informal) **adulterate**, contaminate, drug, lace; informal dope, doctor, cut.

Register label showing the level of English of this sense of the entry word

imperturbable adjective self-possessed, composed, {cool, calm, and collected}; serene, phlegmatic; informal unflappable, laid-back.
– OPPOSITES excitable.

Curly brackets showing that the phrase they contain is one complete synonym

2. LABELS

Most of the synonyms in the *Pocket Oxford Thesaurus* are part of standard English, which means they are the kinds of words that can be used in every type of situation, whether at home, with friends, or in a formal environment. Some words, however, are only suitable for certain situations or types of writing. These are grouped together at the end of their sense, preceded by one or more of the following labels, as appropriate.

Register labels

Register labels refer to a particular level of use in language. They show that a term is informal, formal, old-fashioned, and so on. These are the register labels used in this thesaurus:

informal	normally used only in speech or informal writing or email (e.g. *barmy* or *gawp*)
formal	normally used only in writing, especially in official documents (e.g. *dwelling*)
dated	no longer used by most people (e.g. *victuals*)
old use	not in ordinary use today, though sometimes used to give an old-fashioned effect (e.g. *comely*)
historical	historical – only used today to refer to things that are no longer part of modern life (e.g. *alms*)
literary	found only or mainly in works of literature (e.g. *swoon*)
technical	normally used only in technical language (e.g. *occlude*)
derogatory	meant to convey a low opinion or to insult someone (e.g. *pleb*)

Geographical labels

English is spoken throughout the world, and while most of the words used in standard British English will be the same as those used in other varieties, there are some words which are only found in one type of English. If a word has the geographical label Brit. in this dictionary and thesaurus, this means that it is used in standard British English but not in American English, although it may be found in other varieties such as Australian English. The labels US and N. Amer., on the other hand, mean that the word is typically American and is not standard in British English, though it may be found elsewhere.

Subject labels

These are used to show that a word or sense is connected with a particular subject or specialist activity such as Medicine or Computing.

Aa

aback adverb.
■ **take someone aback**. See SURPRISE.

abandon verb **1** *the party abandoned policies that made it unelectable:* **renounce**, relinquish, dispense with, discard; give up, drop, jettison, do away with, axe; informal ditch, scrap, scrub, junk; formal forswear. **2** *by that stage, she had abandoned painting:* **give up**, stop, cease, have done with, outgrow; informal pack in, quit; Brit. informal jack in. **3** *he abandoned his wife and children:* **desert**, leave, turn your back on, cast aside, finish with; jilt, throw over; informal walk/run out on, dump, ditch; literary forsake. **4** *they abandoned the car and set off on foot:* **leave**, vacate, dump, quit, evacuate, discard, jettison. **5** *a vast expanse of territory was abandoned to the invaders:* **relinquish**, surrender, give up, cede, yield, leave. **6** *she abandoned herself to the sensuousness of the music:* **give way to,** give yourself up to, yield to, lose yourself to/in.
– OPPOSITES keep, retain, continue.
• **noun** *she danced with reckless abandon:* **uninhibitedness**, recklessness, lack of restraint, lack of inhibition.
– OPPOSITES self-control.

abandoned adjective **1** *abandoned vehicles:* **discarded**, empty, stranded; informal dumped, ditched. **2** *an abandoned tin mine:* **disused**, neglected, idle; deserted, unoccupied, uninhabited, derelict, empty.

abashed adjective **embarrassed**, ashamed, shamefaced, mortified, humiliated, humbled, chagrined, crestfallen, sheepish, red-faced, blushing, with your tail between your legs.

abate verb **1** *the storm had abated:* **subside**, die down, lessen, ease off, let up, decrease, diminish, fade, dwindle, recede, tail off, peter out, taper off, wane, ebb, weaken. **2** *nothing abated his crusading zeal:* **decrease**, lessen, diminish, reduce, ease, soothe, dampen, calm, tone down, allay, temper.
– OPPOSITES intensify, increase.

abatement noun **1** *the storm still rages with no sign of abatement:* **subsiding**, dying away, lessening, let-up. **2** *noise abatement:* **reduction**, control.

abattoir noun **slaughterhouse**; old use shambles.

abbreviate verb **shorten**, reduce, cut, contract, condense, compress, abridge, truncate, prune, shrink, telescope; summarize, abstract, precis, edit.
– OPPOSITES lengthen, expand.

abbreviated adjective **shortened**, reduced, cut, condensed, abridged, concise, compact, succinct; thumbnail.
– OPPOSITES long.

abbreviation noun **shortened form**, contraction, acronym; initialism.

abdicate verb **1** *the king abdicated in 1936:* **resign**, retire, stand down, step down, bow out, renounce the throne. **2** *the state abdicated all responsibility for their welfare:* **disown**, reject, renounce, give up, relinquish, abandon, turn your back on, wash your hands of; formal abjure; literary forsake.

abdication noun **1** *Edward VIII's abdication:* **resignation**, retirement. **2** *an abdication of responsibility:* **disowning**, renunciation, rejection, refusal, relinquishment, repudiation, abandonment.

abdomen noun **stomach**, belly, gut, middle, intestines; informal tummy, tum, insides, guts, pot, paunch.

WORD LINKS

abdominal, **ventral**, **coeliac** relating to the abdomen

laparotomy a surgical incision of the abdomen

abdominal adjective **gastric**, intestinal, stomach, duodenal, visceral, coeliac, ventral.

abduct verb **kidnap**, carry off, seize, capture, run away/off with, make off with, spirit away; informal snatch.

aberrant adjective **deviant**, abnormal, atypical, anomalous, irregular, rogue; strange, odd, peculiar, uncommon, freakish; twisted, warped, perverted.
– OPPOSITES normal, typical.

aberration noun **anomaly**, deviation, abnormality, irregularity, variation, freak, oddity, peculiarity, curiosity; mistake.

abet verb **assist**, aid, help, support, encourage; cooperate with, collaborate with, work with, collude with, side with; endorse, sanction; connive at.
– OPPOSITES hinder.

abeyance noun
■ **in abeyance** pending, suspended, deferred, postponed, put off, put to one side, unresolved, up in the air; informal in cold storage, on ice, on the back burner.

abhor verb **detest**, hate, loathe, despise, shrink from, recoil from, shudder at; formal abominate.
– OPPOSITES love, admire.

abhorrence noun **hatred**, loathing, detestation, revulsion, disgust, repugnance, horror, odium, aversion.

abhorrent adjective **detestable**, hateful, loathsome, abominable, repellent, repugnant, repulsive, revolting, disgusting, horrible, horrid, horrifying, awful, heinous, reprehensible, obnoxious, odious, nauseating.
– OPPOSITES admirable.

abide verb **1** *he expected everybody to abide by the rules:* **comply with**, obey, observe, follow, keep to, hold to, conform to, adhere to, stick to, stand by, act in accordance with, uphold, heed, accept, go along with, acknowledge, respect, defer to. **2** (informal) *I can't abide the smell of cigarettes:* **stand**, bear; Brit. informal stick. **3** *at least one memory will abide:* **continue**, remain, survive, last, persist, stay, live on.
– OPPOSITES flout, disobey.

abiding adjective **enduring**, lasting, lifelong, durable, everlasting, perpetual, eternal, unending, constant, permanent, unchanging, steadfast.
– OPPOSITES short-lived, ephemeral.

ability noun **1** *the ability to read and write:* **capacity**, capability, power, faculty, facility; wherewithal, means. **2** *the president's leadership ability:* **talent**, skill, expertise, aptitude, savoir faire, prowess, accomplishment; competence, proficiency; dexterity, deftness, cleverness, flair, finesse, gift, knack, genius; informal know-how.

abject adjective **1** *abject poverty:* **extreme**, acute, severe, appalling, atrocious, awful, terrible, dreadful; wretched, miserable, hopeless, pitiful, degrading, humiliating. **2** *an abject failure:* **catastrophic**, total, utter, complete, unmitigated, unreserved, unqualified. **3** *an abject apology:* **grovelling**, cringing, submissive, craven.

ablaze adjective **1** *several vehicles were ablaze:* **on fire**, alight, aflame, in flames, flaming, burning, blazing. **2** *every window was ablaze with light:* **lit up**, alight, gleaming, glowing, aglow, bright, shining, glittering, radiant, shimmering, sparkling, flashing, luminous, incandescent.

able adjective **1** *he will soon be able to resume his duties:* **capable of**, competent to, up to, fit to, qualified to; allowed to, free to, in a position to. **2** *an able student:* **intelligent**, clever, talented, skilful, skilled, accomplished, gifted; proficient, apt, good, adroit, adept; capable, competent, efficient, effective.
– OPPOSITES incompetent, incapable.

able-bodied adjective **healthy**, **fit**, in good health, strong, sound, hale and hearty; in good shape.
– OPPOSITES infirm, frail.

abnormal adjective **unusual**,

uncommon, atypical, untypical, unrepresentative, irregular, anomalous, deviant, aberrant, freak, freakish; strange, odd, peculiar, bizarre, weird; eccentric, unconventional, exceptional; unnatural, perverse, perverted, twisted, warped; informal funny, freaky, kinky.
– OPPOSITES normal, typical, common.

abnormality noun **oddity**, peculiarity, strangeness, irregularity, inconsistency, incongruity, aberration, anomaly, singularity; eccentricity, unconventionality.

abolish verb **put an end to**, get rid of, scrap, end, remove, dissolve, stop, ban; informal do away with, give something the chop, knock something on the head.
– OPPOSITES retain, create.

abolition noun **scrapping**, ending, dissolution, removal.

abominable adjective **loathsome**, detestable, hateful, odious, obnoxious, despicable, contemptible, diabolical; disgusting, revolting, repellent, repulsive, repugnant, abhorrent, reprehensible, atrocious, horrifying, foul, vile, wretched, horrible, awful, dreadful, appalling, nauseating; informal terrible, shocking, God-awful; Brit. informal beastly.
– OPPOSITES good, admirable.

abomination noun **atrocity**, disgrace, horror, obscenity, outrage, evil, crime, monstrosity.

abort verb **1** *the organism can cause pregnant ewes to abort:* **miscarry**, have a miscarriage. **2** *the crew aborted the take-off:* **halt**, stop, end, call off, abandon, discontinue, terminate, arrest; informal pull the plug on.

abortion noun **termination**; miscarriage.

abortive adjective **unsuccessful**, failed, vain, ineffective, ineffectual, unproductive.
– OPPOSITES successful, fruitful.

abound verb **1** *cafes abound in the narrow streets:* **be plentiful**, be abundant, be numerous, be thick on the ground; informal grow on trees, be two/ten a penny. **2** *a stream which abounded with trout:* **be full of**, overflow with, teem with, be packed with, be crowded with; be crawling with, swarm with, bristle with, be thick with; informal be stuffed with, be chock-a-block with.

about preposition **1** *a book about ancient Greece:* **regarding**, concerning, with reference to, referring to, with regard to, with respect to, relating to, on, touching on, dealing with, relevant to, connected with, in connection with, on the subject of. **2** *two hundred people were milling about the room:* **around**, round, throughout, over, through, on every side of.
• adverb *it cost about £15,000:* **approximately**, roughly, around, in the region of, circa, of the order of; or so, or thereabouts, more or less, give or take; N. Amer. informal in the ballpark of.
■ **about to** on the point of, on the verge of, ready to, all set to, preparing to, intending to.

about-turn noun (Brit.) *the government was forced to make an about-turn:* **volte-face**, U-turn, reversal, retraction, backtracking; change of heart, change of mind.

above preposition **1** *a tiny window above the door:* **over**; on top of, on, upon. **2** *those above the rank of Colonel:* **superior to**, senior to, over, higher than; in charge of, commanding. **3** *an increase above the rate of inflation:* **greater than**, more than, higher than, exceeding, in excess of, over, over and above, beyond, surpassing, upwards of.
– OPPOSITES below, under, beneath.
• adverb **1** *in the darkness above, something moved:* **overhead**, high up, on high, up above. **2** *the two cases described above:* **earlier**, previously, before, formerly.
• adjective *the above example:* **preceding**, previous, earlier, former, foregoing, prior, aforementioned, aforesaid.
■ **above all** most importantly, most of all, chiefly, primarily, first and foremost, essentially, in essence, at bottom; informal at the end of the day, when all is said and done.

abrade verb **wear away**, wear down, erode.

abrasion noun **1** *he had abrasions to*

his forehead: **graze**, cut, scrape, scratch, gash, laceration, injury, contusion; Medicine trauma. **2** *the metal is resistant to abrasion:* **erosion**, wearing away/down.

abrasive adjective **1** *abrasive kitchen cleaners:* **rough**, coarse, harsh, scratchy. **2** *her abrasive manner:* **curt**, brusque, sharp; harsh, rough.
– OPPOSITES kind, gentle.

abreast adverb
■ **abreast of** up to date with, up with, in touch with, informed about, acquainted with, knowledgeable about, conversant with, familiar with, au fait with.

abridge verb **shorten**, cut, abbreviate, condense, contract, compress, reduce; summarize, sum up, precis, edit; truncate, trim, crop, clip, prune.
– OPPOSITES lengthen.

abridged adjective **shortened**, cut, concise, condensed, abbreviated; bowdlerized, censored, expurgated; informal potted.

abroad adverb **1** *he regularly travels abroad:* **overseas**, out of the country, to foreign parts. **2** *rumours were abroad:* **in circulation**, circulating, in the air; about, around; at large.

abrupt adjective **1** *an abrupt halt* | *an abrupt change of subject:* **sudden**, unexpected, unanticipated, unforeseen, precipitate, surprising, startling; quick, swift, rapid. **2** *an abrupt manner:* **curt**, brusque, blunt, short, sharp, terse, brisk, crisp, unceremonious.
– OPPOSITES gradual, gentle.

abscess noun **swelling**, ulcer, ulceration, cyst, boil, blister, sore, pustule, carbuncle, pimple.

abscond verb **run away/off**, escape, bolt, flee, make off, take flight, take off, decamp; disappear, vanish, slip away, sneak away; informal clear out, skedaddle, skip, head for the hills, do a disappearing act, fly the coop, take French leave, scarper, vamoose; Brit. informal do a bunk, do a runner; N. Amer. informal take a powder.

absence noun **1** *his absence from the office:* **non-attendance**, absenteeism; truancy; leave, holiday, sabbatical; N. Amer. vacation. **2** *the absence of any other suitable candidate:* **lack**, want, non-existence, unavailability, shortage.
– OPPOSITES presence.

absent adjective **1** *she was absent from work:* **away**, off, out; off duty, on holiday, on leave; gone, missing, unavailable; informal AWOL. **2** *her eyes had an absent look:* **distracted**, preoccupied, inattentive, vague, absorbed, dreamy, far away; blank, empty, vacant.
– OPPOSITES present, attentive, alert.
• verb *Rose absented herself:* **stay away**, be absent, withdraw, retire, take your leave, remove yourself.

absent-minded adjective **forgetful**, distracted, scatterbrained, preoccupied, inattentive; informal having a mind/memory like a sieve.

absolute adjective **1** *absolute silence* | *an absolute disgrace:* **complete**, total, utter, out-and-out, outright, perfect, pure; thorough, thoroughgoing, unqualified, unadulterated, unalloyed, unreserved, downright, consummate, unmitigated, sheer. **2** *an absolute fact:* **definite**, certain, unconditional, categorical, unquestionable, incontrovertible, undoubted, unequivocal, conclusive, confirmed. **3** *absolute power:* **unlimited**, unrestricted, unrestrained, unbounded, boundless, infinite, ultimate, total, supreme, unconditional. **4** *absolute moral standards:* **universal**, fixed, unchanging.
– OPPOSITES partial, qualified, limited, conditional.

absolutely adverb *you're absolutely right:* **completely**, totally, utterly, perfectly, entirely, wholly, fully, quite, thoroughly, unreservedly; definitely, certainly, unquestionably, undoubtedly, without doubt, without question, in every way/respect, one hundred per cent.

absolution noun **release**, pardon, exoneration; deliverance.

absolve verb **exonerate**, discharge, acquit; release, relieve, free, deliver, clear, exempt, let off.
– OPPOSITES blame, condemn.

absorb verb **1** *a material which absorbs water:* **soak up**, suck up, draw up/in, take up/in, mop up, sop up. **2** *she absorbed the information in silence:* **assimilate**, digest, take in. **3** *the company was absorbed into the new concern:* **incorporate**, assimilate, integrate, subsume, include, co-opt, swallow up. **4** *these roles absorb most of his time:* **use up**, consume, take up, occupy. **5** *the girl was totally absorbed in her book:* **engross**, captivate, occupy, preoccupy, engage, rivet, grip, hold, immerse, involve, enthral, spellbind, fascinate.

absorbent adjective **porous**, spongelike, permeable.

absorbing adjective **fascinating**, interesting, captivating, gripping, engrossing, compelling, compulsive, enthralling, riveting, spellbinding, thrilling, exciting, intriguing; informal unputdownable.
– OPPOSITES boring, uninteresting.

absorption noun **1** *the absorption of water:* **soaking up**, sucking up. **2** *the company's absorption into a larger concern:* **incorporation**, assimilation, integration, inclusion. **3** *her total absorption in the music:* **involvement**, immersion, raptness, engrossment, preoccupation, engagement, captivation, fascination, enthralment.

abstain verb **1** *he abstained from wine:* **refrain**, desist, hold back, forbear; give up, renounce, avoid, shun, eschew, forgo, go/do without, deny yourself; refuse, decline; informal cut out; formal abjure. **2** *most pregnant women abstain, or drink very little:* **be teetotal**, take the pledge; informal be on the wagon.

abstemious adjective **self-denying**, temperate, moderate, self-disciplined, restrained, self-restrained, sober, austere, ascetic, puritanical, spartan.
– OPPOSITES self-indulgent.

abstinence noun **self-denial**, self-restraint; teetotalism, temperance, sobriety, abstemiousness.

abstract adjective **1** *abstract concepts:* **theoretical**, conceptual, intellectual, metaphysical, philosophical, academic. **2** *abstract art:* **non-representational**.
– OPPOSITES actual, concrete.
• noun *an abstract of her speech:* **summary**, synopsis, precis, résumé, outline; N. Amer. wrap-up.

abstracted adjective **absent-minded**, distracted, preoccupied, in a world of your own, with your head in the clouds, daydreaming, dreamy, inattentive, pensive, lost in thought, deep/immersed in thought, musing, brooding, absent; informal miles away.
– OPPOSITES attentive.

abstraction noun **1** *philosophical abstractions:* **concept**, idea, notion, thought, theory, hypothesis. **2** *she sensed his momentary abstraction:* **absent-mindedness**, distraction, preoccupation, inattentiveness, inattention, pensiveness.

abstruse adjective **obscure**, arcane, esoteric, rarefied, recondite, difficult, hard, cryptic, over/above your head, incomprehensible, unfathomable, impenetrable.

absurd adjective **preposterous**, ridiculous, ludicrous, farcical, laughable, risible, stupid, foolish, silly, pointless, senseless; informal crazy; Brit. informal barmy, daft.
– OPPOSITES reasonable, sensible.

absurdity noun **preposterousness**, ridiculousness, ludicrousness, stupidity, foolishness, silliness, inanity, pointlessness, senselessness; informal craziness.

abundance noun **profusion**; host, cornucopia, wealth; plenty, multitude; informal lots, heaps, masses, stacks, piles, loads, bags, mountains, tons, slew, oodles, millions; Brit. informal shedload; N. Amer. informal gobs.
– OPPOSITES lack, scarcity.

abundant adjective **plentiful**, copious, ample, large, huge, great, bumper, overflowing, teeming; in abundance; informal a gogo, galore.
– OPPOSITES scarce, sparse.
■ **be abundant** abound, be plentiful, be numerous, be in abundance, be thick on the ground; informal be two/ten a penny.

abuse verb **1** *the judge abused his power:* **misuse**; exploit, take advantage of. **2** *he was accused of abusing children:* **mistreat**, maltreat, ill-treat; molest, interfere with, assault. **3** *the referee was abused by players from both teams:* **insult**, revile, swear at, shout at; Brit. barrack.
• noun **1** *the abuse of power:* **misuse**;

exploitation. **2** *the abuse of children:* **mistreatment**, maltreatment, ill-treatment; molestation, assault. **3** *torrents of abuse:* **insults**, curses, expletives, swear words; swearing, cursing, name-calling; invective; old use contumely.

abusive adjective **insulting**, rude, offensive, derogatory, slanderous, libellous.

abysmal adjective (informal) *some of the teaching was abysmal:* **terrible**, dreadful, awful, frightful, atrocious, disgraceful, hopeless, lamentable; informal rotten, appalling, pathetic, pitiful, woeful, useless, lousy, dire, poxy, the pits; Brit. informal chronic, shocking.

abyss noun **chasm**, crevasse, gulf, pit, void.

academic adjective **1** *an academic institution:* **educational**, scholastic. **2** *his academic turn of mind:* **scholarly**, literary, intellectual, bookish, cerebral. **3** *the outcome is entirely academic:* **irrelevant**, beside the point; hypothetical, speculative, conjectural.
• noun *a group of Russian academics:* **scholar**, don, professor, fellow, man/woman of letters, thinker; informal egghead.

academy noun **educational institution**, school, college, university, institute, seminary, conservatory, conservatoire.

accede verb (formal) *he acceded to the government's demands:* **agree to**, consent to, accept, assent to, acquiesce in, comply with, go along with, concur with, surrender to, yield to, give in to, give way to, defer to.

accelerate verb **1** *the car accelerated:* **speed up**, go faster, gain momentum, increase speed, pick up speed, gather speed, put on a spurt. **2** *inflation started to accelerate:* **increase**, rise, go up, surge, escalate, spiral. **3** *the university accelerated the planning process:* **hasten**, speed up, step up; informal crank up.
– OPPOSITES decelerate, delay.

acceleration noun **1** *the acceleration of the industrial process:* **speeding up**, quickening, stepping up. **2** *an acceleration in the divorce rate:* **increase**, rise, leap, surge, escalation.

accent noun **1** *a Scottish accent:* **pronunciation**, intonation, enunciation, articulation, inflection, tone, modulation, cadence, timbre, delivery. **2** *the accent is on the first syllable:* **stress**, emphasis, accentuation; beat. **3** *the accent is on comfort:* **emphasis**, stress; priority, importance, prominence.

accentuate verb **focus attention on**, draw attention to, point up, underline, underscore, accent, highlight, spotlight, foreground, feature, bring to the fore, heighten, stress, emphasize.

accept verb **1** *he accepted £7000 in compensation:* **receive**, take, get, obtain, acquire. **2** *she was accepted as one of the family:* **welcome**, receive, embrace, adopt. **3** *he accepted her explanation:* **believe**; informal buy, swallow. **4** *we have to accept his decision:* **go along with**, concur with, comply with, abide by, follow, adhere to, act in accordance with, defer to, yield to, surrender to, bow to, give in to, submit to, respect. **5** *she will just have to accept the consequences:* **put up with**, take, swallow; reconcile yourself to, resign yourself to, get used to, adjust to, learn to live with, make the best of; face up to.
– OPPOSITES refuse, reject.

> ! Don't confuse **accept** with **except**, which means 'apart from' (*they work every day except Sunday*).

acceptable adjective **1** *an acceptable standard of living:* **satisfactory**, adequate, reasonable, fair, decent, good enough, sufficient, sufficiently good, tolerable, passable. **2** *an acceptable risk:* **bearable**, tolerable, allowable, admissible, sustainable; informal liveable with.

acceptance noun **1** *the acceptance of an award:* **receipt**, receiving, taking. **2** *the acceptance of responsibility:* **assumption**, acknowledgement, taking on. **3** *their acceptance of the decision:* **compliance**, acquiescence, deference, submission, respect. **4** *the acceptance of pain:* **toleration**, endurance, forbearance.

accepted adjective **recognized**, acknowledged, established, traditional, orthodox; usual, customary, normal, standard.

access noun **1** *the building has a side access:* **entrance**, entry, way in; door. **2** *they were denied access to the stadium:* **admission**, admittance, entry.
• verb *the program is used to access the data:* **retrieve**, obtain; read.

accessible adjective **1** *the village is only accessible on foot | an easily accessible reference tool:* **reachable**, attainable, approachable; obtainable, available; informal get-at-able. **2** *his accessible style of writing:* **understandable**, comprehensible, easy to understand, intelligible. **3** *Professor Cooper is very accessible:* **approachable**, friendly, congenial, affable, cordial, welcoming, pleasant.

accessorize verb **complement**, enhance, set off; go with, accompany; decorate, adorn, ornament.

accessory noun **1** *camera accessories:* **attachment**, add-on; supplement; paraphernalia, equipment, gear, stuff. **2** *an accessory to murder:* **accomplice**, collaborator, co-conspirator.

accident noun **1** *an accident at work:* **mishap**, misadventure; disaster, tragedy, catastrophe, calamity. **2** *an accident on the motorway:* **crash**, collision, smash, bump; derailment; N. Amer. wreck; informal smash-up, pile-up; Brit. informal prang, shunt.

accidental adjective **fortuitous**, chance, coincidental, serendipitous; unintentional, unintended, inadvertent, unwitting.
– OPPOSITES intentional, deliberate.

accidentally adverb **by accident**, by chance, unintentionally, inadvertently, unwittingly.

acclaim verb *the booklet has been acclaimed by teachers:* **praise**, applaud, cheer, commend, approve, welcome, hail; formal laud.
– OPPOSITES criticize.
• noun *she has won widespread acclaim:* **praise**, applause, cheers, tributes; approval, admiration, congratulations, commendation.
– OPPOSITES criticism.

acclaimed adjective **celebrated**, admired, highly rated, esteemed, exalted, well thought of, well received; eminent, renowned, distinguished, prestigious, illustrious, pre-eminent.

acclimatization noun **adjustment**, adaptation, accommodation, habituation, acculturation, familiarization; naturalization; N. Amer. acclimation.

acclimatize verb **adjust**, adapt, get used; familiarize yourself, find your feet, get your bearings; N. Amer. acclimate.

accolade noun **tribute**, honour, compliment, prize.

accommodate verb **1** *refugees were accommodated in army camps:* **lodge**, house, put up, billet, board. **2** *the cottages accommodate up to six people:* **hold**, take, have room for, sleep; seat. **3** *we made every effort to accommodate her:* **help**, assist, oblige, cater for, fit in with, satisfy.

accommodating adjective **obliging**, cooperative, helpful, amenable, hospitable; flexible.

accommodation noun **1** *the shortage of accommodation:* **housing**, lodgings, living quarters, rooms; place to stay, billet; shelter, a roof over your head; informal digs, pad; formal abode, residence, dwelling. **2** *an accommodation between the two parties was reached:* **arrangement**, understanding, settlement, accord, deal, compromise.

accompaniment noun **1** *a musical accompaniment:* **backing**, support, background, soundtrack, backing track. **2** *the wine makes a superb accompaniment to cheese:* **complement**, addition, adjunct.

accompany verb **1** *the driver accompanied her to the door:* **go with**, travel with, keep someone company, tag along with, partner, escort, chaperone, attend, show, see, usher, conduct. **2** *he accompanied the choir on the piano:* **back**, play along with, support.

accomplice noun **partner in crime**, associate, accessory, confederate, collaborator, fellow conspirator; henchman; informal sidekick.

accomplish verb **fulfil**, achieve, succeed in, realize, attain, manage,

a

bring about/off, carry out/through, execute, effect, perform, do, discharge, complete.

accomplished adjective **expert**, skilled, skilful, masterly, virtuoso, master, consummate, talented, gifted, able, capable; informal mean, nifty, crack, ace, wizard; N. Amer. informal crackerjack.

accomplishment noun **1** *a remarkable accomplishment:* **achievement**, act, deed, exploit, effort, feat, move, coup. **2** *her many accomplishments:* **talent**, skill, gift, ability.

accord verb **1** *the national assembly accorded him more power:* **give**, grant, present, award, vouchsafe; confer on, bestow on, invest with. **2** *his views accorded with mine:* **correspond**, agree, tally, match, concur, be consistent, be in harmony, be compatible, be in tune.
– OPPOSITES withhold, disagree, differ.
• noun **1** *a peace accord:* **pact**, treaty, agreement, settlement, deal, entente, protocol, contract. **2** *the two sides failed to reach accord:* **agreement**, consensus, unanimity, harmony.
■ **of your own accord** voluntarily, of your own free will, of your own volition, by choice; willingly, freely, readily.

accordance noun
■ **in accordance with** *a ballot held in accordance with trade union rules:* in agreement with, in conformity with, in line with, true to, in the spirit of, observing, following, heeding.

according adverb
■ **according to 1** *cook the rice according to the instructions:* in line with, as per, in accordance with. **2** *salary will be fixed according to experience:* in proportion to, proportional to, commensurate with, in relation to, relative to, in line with, corresponding to.

accordingly adverb **1** *they recognized the danger and acted accordingly:* **appropriately**, correspondingly. **2** *accordingly, he returned home:* **therefore**, for that reason, consequently, so, as a result, as a consequence, hence, that being the case.

accost verb **approach**, stop, confront, detain, speak to; informal buttonhole, collar.

account noun **1** *his account of the incident:* **description**, report, version, story, statement, explanation, tale; chronicle, history, record, log. **2** *the firm's quarterly accounts:* **financial record**, ledger, balance sheet, financial statement; (**accounts**) books. **3** *I pay the account off in full each month:* **bill**, invoice, tally; debt, charges; N. Amer. check; informal tab. **4** *his background is of no account:* **importance**, import, significance, consequence.
• verb *her visit can be accounted a success:* **consider**, regard as, reckon, hold to be, think, look on as, view as, see as, judge, count, deem, rate.
■ **account for 1** *they must account for the delay:* explain, answer for, justify, rationalize. **2** *excise duties account for over half the price:* constitute, make up, comprise, form, compose, represent. **on account of** because of, owing to, due to, as a consequence of, thanks to, by virtue of, in view of.

accountability noun **responsibility**, liability.

accountable adjective **responsible**, liable, answerable; to blame.

accoutrements plural noun **equipment**, paraphernalia, stuff, things, apparatus, tackle, kit, implements, rig, outfit, regalia, odds and ends, bits and pieces, bits and bobs, trappings, accessories.

accredit verb **1** *he was accredited with being one of the world's fastest sprinters:* **recognize as**, credit with. **2** *the discovery is usually accredited to the Arabs:* **ascribe**, attribute. **3** *professional bodies accredit these research degrees:* **recognize**, authorize, approve, certify, license.

accredited adjective **official**, appointed, recognized, authorized, approved, certified, licensed.

accretion noun **accumulation**, formation, collecting, accrual; growth, increase.

accrue verb **1** *financial benefits will accrue from restructuring:* **result**, arise, follow, ensue. **2** *interest is added to the account as it accrues:* **accumulate**, collect, build up, mount up, grow, increase.

accumulate verb **gather**, collect, build up, amass, stockpile, pile up, heap up, store, hoard, lay in/up; increase, accrue, multiply; run up.

accumulation noun **mass**, build-up, pile, collection, stock, store, stockpile, reserve, hoard.

accuracy noun **correctness**, precision, exactness; fidelity, faithfulness, truth, truthfulness, veracity, authenticity, realism, verisimilitude.

accurate adjective **1** *accurate information | an accurate representation of the situation:* **correct**, precise, exact, right; factual, literal, faithful, true, truthful, authentic, realistic; informal on the mark, on the beam, on the nail; Brit. informal spot on, bang on; N. Amer. informal on the money, on the button. **2** *an accurate shot:* **well aimed**, on target, unerring, deadly, lethal, sure, true.

accusation noun **allegation**, charge, claim, assertion, imputation.

accuse verb **1** *four people were accused of assault:* **charge with**, indict for, arraign for; N. Amer. impeach for. **2** *you accused the companies of causing job losses:* **blame for**, hold responsible for; condemn for, criticize for, denounce for; informal point the finger at.
– OPPOSITES absolve, exonerate.

accustom verb *I soon became accustomed to the heat:* **adapt**, adjust, acclimatize, habituate; become reconciled, get used to, come to terms with, learn to live with; N. Amer. acclimate.

accustomed adjective **customary**, usual, normal, habitual, regular, routine; literary wonted.

ace adjective (informal) *an ace tennis player:* **excellent**, first-rate, first-class, marvellous, wonderful, magnificent, outstanding, superlative, formidable, virtuoso, expert, champion, consummate; informal great, terrific, tremendous, superb, fantastic, sensational, fabulous, fab, crack, hotshot, A1, mean, demon, awesome, magic, tip-top, top-notch; Brit. informal smashing, brilliant, brill.
– OPPOSITES mediocre.

acerbic adjective **sharp**, sarcastic, sardonic, mordant, trenchant, cutting, razor-edged, biting, stinging, searing, scathing, caustic; N. Amer. informal snarky.

ache noun **1** *a stomach ache:* **pain**, cramp, twinge, pang; gnawing, stabbing, stinging, smarting; soreness, tenderness, irritation, discomfort. **2** *the ache in her heart:* **sorrow**, sadness, misery, grief, anguish, suffering, pain, agony, torture, hurt.
• verb *my legs were aching:* **hurt**, be sore, be painful, be in pain, throb, pound; smart, burn, sting; informal give someone gyp; Brit. informal play up.

achieve verb **attain**, reach; realize, bring off/about, pull off, accomplish, carry out/through, fulfil, complete; earn, win, gain, acquire, obtain, come by, get, secure, clinch, net; informal wrap up, wangle, swing.

achievement noun **1** *the achievement of a high rate of economic growth:* **attainment**, realization, accomplishment, fulfilment, implementation, completion. **2** *they were proud of their achievement:* **accomplishment**, feat, act, action, deed, effort, exploit; work, handiwork.

Achilles heel noun **weak spot**, weak point, weakness, shortcoming, failing, imperfection, flaw, defect, chink in your armour.
– OPPOSITES strength.

aching adjective **painful**, sore, stiff, tender, uncomfortable; in pain, throbbing, pounding, smarting, burning, stinging.

acid adjective **1** *a slightly acid flavour:* **acidic**, sour, tart, sharp, acerbic, vinegary. **2** *acid remarks:* **acerbic**, sarcastic, sharp, sardonic, scathing, cutting, biting, stinging, caustic, trenchant, mordant, astringent, harsh, vitriolic, waspish; N. Amer. acerb; informal bitchy, catty.
– OPPOSITES sweet, pleasant.

acknowledge verb **1** *the government acknowledged the need to begin talks:* **admit**, accept, grant, allow, concede, confess, own, recognize. **2** *few people acknowledged my letters:* **answer**, reply to, respond to. **3** *he did not acknowledge Colin:* **greet**, salute, address.
– OPPOSITES reject, deny, ignore.

acknowledged adjective **recognized**, accepted, confirmed, declared.

acknowledgement noun **1** *acknowledgement of the need to change:* **acceptance**, admission, recognition. **2** *he gave her a smile of acknowledgement:* **greeting**, welcome, salutation. **3** *she left without a word of acknowledgement:* **thanks**, gratitude, appreciation, recognition. **4** *I sent off the form, but there was no acknowledgement:* **answer**, reply, response.

acme noun **peak**, pinnacle, zenith, height, high point, crown, crest, summit, top, apex, apogee.
– OPPOSITES nadir.

acolyte noun **assistant**, helper, attendant; follower, disciple, supporter; informal groupie, hanger-on.

acquaint verb **familiarize** with, make familiar with, make aware of, inform of, advise of, apprise of, bring up to date on; informal fill in on, gen up on, clue in on.

acquaintance noun **1** *a business acquaintance:* **contact**, associate, colleague. **2** *my acquaintance with George:* **association**, relationship, contact. **3** *the pupils had little acquaintance with the language:* **familiarity with**, knowledge of, experience of, awareness of, understanding of, comprehension of, grasp of.

acquainted adjective **familiar**, conversant, at home, up to date, abreast, au fait, versed, knowledgeable, well informed; apprised; informal genned up, clued up; formal cognizant.

acquiesce verb *he acquiesced in the cover-up:* **accept**, consent to, agree to, allow, assent to, concur with, go along with, give the nod to.

acquiescence noun **consent**, agreement, acceptance, concurrence, assent.

acquiescent adjective **compliant**, willing, obliging, amenable, unprotesting, docile.

acquire verb **obtain**, come by, get, receive, gain, earn, win, come into; buy, purchase, procure, secure, pick up; informal get your hands on, get hold of, land, bag, score.
– OPPOSITES lose.

acquisition noun **1** *a new acquisition:* **purchase**, addition, investment, possession; informal buy. **2** *the acquisition of funds:* **obtaining**, gaining, earning, winning, procurement, collection.

acquisitive adjective **greedy**, avaricious, grasping, grabbing, predatory, rapacious, mercenary, materialistic; informal money-grubbing.

acquisitiveness noun **greed**, greediness, avarice, rapaciousness, rapacity, materialism.

acquit verb **1** *the jury acquitted her:* **clear**, exonerate, find innocent, absolve; discharge, release, free, set free; informal let off. **2** *the boys acquitted themselves well:* **behave**, conduct yourself, perform, act.
– OPPOSITES convict.

acquittal noun **clearing**, exoneration; discharge, release, freeing; informal letting off.
– OPPOSITES conviction.

acrid adjective **pungent**, bitter, sharp, harsh; stinging, burning.

acrimonious adjective **bitter**, angry, rancorous, harsh, vicious, nasty, bad-tempered, ill-natured.

acrimony noun **bitterness**, anger, rancour, resentment, ill feeling, bad blood, animosity, antagonism.
– OPPOSITES goodwill.

act verb **1** *the Government must act to remedy the situation:* **take action**, take steps, take measures, move, react. **2** *he was acting on the orders of the party leader:* **follow**, obey, comply with; fulfil, discharge. **3** *Alison began to act oddly:* **behave**, conduct yourself, react. **4** *the scents act as a powerful aphrodisiac:* **operate**, work, function, serve. **5** *he acted in a highly successful film:* **perform**, play, take part, appear.
• noun **1** *acts of kindness | a criminal act:* **deed**, action, feat, exploit, gesture. **2** *the act will raise taxes:* **law**, decree, statute, bill, edict, ruling; N. Amer. formal ordinance. **3** *a comedy act:* **performance**, turn, routine, number, sketch. **4** *it was all an act:* **pretence**, show, front, facade, masquerade, charade, pose, sham; informal a put-on.

acting noun *the theory and practice of acting:* **drama**, the theatre, the

stage, the performing arts, dramatics, stagecraft; informal treading the boards.
• adjective *the bank's acting governor:* **temporary**, interim, caretaker, pro tem, provisional, stopgap; deputy, stand-in; N. Amer. informal pinch-hitting.
– OPPOSITES permanent.

action noun **1** *there can be no excuse for their actions:* **deed**, act, undertaking, exploit, manoeuvre, endeavour, effort, exertion; behaviour, conduct, activity. **2** *the need for local action:* **measures**, steps, activism, campaigning; pressure. **3** *the action of hormones on the pancreas:* **effect**, influence, working; power. **4** *he missed all the action while he was away:* **excitement**, activity; informal goings-on. **5** *twenty-nine men died in action:* **battle**, combat, hostilities; fighting, active service. **6** *a civil action:* **lawsuit**, suit, case, prosecution, litigation, proceedings.

activate verb **operate**, switch on, turn on, start, set going, trigger, set in motion, actuate, energize; trip.

active adjective **1** *despite her illness she remained active:* **busy**, mobile; informal on the go, full of beans. **2** *an active member of the union:* **hard-working**, industrious, tireless, keen, committed, devoted. **3** *the watermill was active until 1960:* **operative**, working, functioning, operating, operational, in action, in operation, up and running; live.
– OPPOSITES listless, passive.

activity noun **1** *there was a lot of activity in the area:* **bustle**, action, movement, life; informal toing and froing, comings and goings. **2** *a wide range of activities:* **pursuit**, occupation, interest, hobby, pastime, recreation, diversion; venture, undertaking, enterprise, project, scheme; act, action, deed, exploit.

actor, actress noun **performer**, player, trouper, thespian; film star, star, starlet; Brit. informal luvvy.

> **WORD LINKS**
> **thespian**, **histrionic** relating to actors

actual adjective **real**, true, genuine, authentic, verified, attested, confirmed, definite, hard; informal real live.
– OPPOSITES notional.

actually adverb *I looked upset but actually I was rather excited:* **really**, in fact, in point of fact, as a matter of fact, in reality, in actuality, in truth, if truth be told, to tell the truth.

acumen noun **astuteness**, shrewdness, acuity, sharpness, smartness, brains; judgement, insight; informal nous, savvy, know-how; N. Amer. informal smarts; formal perspicuity.

acute adjective **1** *acute food shortages:* **severe**, dire, dreadful, terrible, awful, grave, serious, desperate. **2** *acute stomach pains:* **sharp**, severe, stabbing, excruciating, agonizing, racking, searing. **3** *his acute mind:* **astute**, shrewd, sharp, razor-sharp, quick, quick-witted, agile, nimble, intelligent, canny, discerning, perceptive, penetrating, insightful, incisive, piercing, discriminating; N. Amer. informal heads-up. **4** *an acute sense of smell:* **keen**, sharp, good, penetrating, discerning, sensitive; discriminating.
– OPPOSITES mild, dull.

acutely adverb **intensely**, very, severely, deeply, profoundly, keenly, painfully, thoroughly.
– OPPOSITES slightly.

adage noun **saying**, maxim, axiom, proverb, aphorism, saw, dictum, precept, motto, truism, platitude, cliché, commonplace.

adamant adjective **unshakeable**, immovable, unwavering, unswerving, resolute, resolved, determined, firm, steadfast; unrelenting, unyielding, unbending, dead set.

adapt verb **modify**, alter, change, adjust, convert, remodel, revamp, rework, rejig, reorganize; customize, tailor; amend, refine; informal tweak.

adaptable adjective **flexible**, versatile; accommodating.

adaptation noun **adjustment**, alteration, modification, change.

add verb **1** *the front porch was added later:* **attach**, build on, join, connect;

a

include, incorporate. **2** *they added all the figures up:* **total**, count, compute, reckon up, tally; Brit. tot up. **3** *the subsidies added up to £1700:* **amount to**, come to, run to, make, total, equal, number. **4** *her decision just added to his woe:* **increase**, magnify, amplify, augment, intensify, heighten, deepen; exacerbate, aggravate, compound, reinforce; add fuel to the fire, rub salt in the wound.
–OPPOSITES subtract.

addendum noun **appendix**, codicil, postscript, afterword, tailpiece, rider, coda, supplement; adjunct, appendage, addition, add-on, attachment.

addict noun **1** *a heroin addict:* **abuser**, user; informal junkie, druggy, -freak, -head, pill-popper; N. Amer. informal hophead. **2** (informal) *skiing addicts:* **enthusiast**, fan, lover, devotee, aficionado; informal freak, nut, fiend, fanatic, maniac.

addicted adjective **1** *he was addicted to tranquillizers:* **dependent on**; informal hooked on, using; US informal having a jones for. **2** *she became addicted to the theatre:* **devoted to**, obsessed with, fixated on, fanatical about, passionate about, a slave to; informal hooked on, mad on, crazy about.

addiction noun **1** *his heroin addiction:* **dependency**, dependence, habit. **2** *a slavish addiction to fashion:* **devotion to**, dedication to, obsession with, infatuation with, passion for, love of, mania for, enslavement to.

addictive adjective **habit-forming**; compulsive; Brit. informal moreish.

addition noun **1** *the soil is improved by the addition of compost:* **adding**, incorporation, inclusion, introduction. **2** *an addition to the existing regulations:* **supplement**, adjunct, appendage; add-on, extra; rider.
■ **in addition 1** *conditions were harsh and in addition some soldiers fell victim to snipers:* additionally, as well, what's more, furthermore, moreover, also, into the bargain, to boot. **2** *eight presidential candidates in addition to the General:* besides, as well as, on top of, plus, over and above.

additional adjective **extra**, added, supplementary, supplemental, further; auxiliary, ancillary; more, other, another, new, fresh.

additionally adverb **also**, in addition, as well, too, besides, on top of that, moreover, further, furthermore, over and above that, into the bargain, to boot.

addled adjective **muddled**, confused, muzzy, fuddled, befuddled, dazed, disoriented, disorientated, fuzzy; informal woozy.

address noun **1** *our officers called at the address:* **house**, flat, apartment, home; formal residence, dwelling, abode, domicile. **2** *his address to the European Parliament:* **speech**, lecture, talk, presentation, dissertation; sermon.
• verb **1** *the preacher addressed a crowded congregation:* **talk to**, speak to, make a speech to, lecture, hold forth to; preach to, give a sermon to. **2** *correspondence should be addressed to the Banking Ombudsman:* **direct**, send, communicate, convey. **3** *the minister failed to address the issue of subsidies:* **attend to**, apply yourself to, tackle, see to, deal with, confront, get to grips with, get down to, turn to, take in hand, concentrate on, focus on, devote yourself to.

adept adjective *an adept negotiator:* **expert**, proficient, accomplished, skilful, talented, masterly, consummate; adroit, dexterous, deft, artful.
–OPPOSITES inept.
• noun *kung fu adepts:* **expert**, master; maestro, doyen.
–OPPOSITES amateur.

adequacy noun **1** *the adequacy of the existing services:* **satisfactoriness**, acceptability; sufficiency. **2** *he had deep misgivings about his own adequacy:* **capability**, competence, ability; effectiveness, fitness; formal efficacy.

adequate adjective **1** *he lacked adequate financial resources:* **sufficient**, enough, requisite. **2** *the company provides an adequate service:* **acceptable**, passable, reasonable, satisfactory, tolerable, fair, decent, quite good, pretty good, goodish, moderate, unexceptional, unremarkable, undistinguished, ordinary, average, not bad, all right, middling; informal OK, so-so, fair-to-middling, nothing to write home about. **3** *the work-stations were small but seemed adequate to the task:* **equal to**, up to, capable of, suitable for, able to do, fit for, sufficient for.

adhere verb **1** *a dollop of cream adhered to her nose:* **stick**, cling, bond, attach; be stuck, be fixed, be glued. **2** *they adhere scrupulously to Judaic law:* **abide by**, stick to, hold to, comply with, live/act in accordance with, conform to, submit to; follow, obey, heed, observe, respect, uphold, fulfil.
– OPPOSITES flout, ignore.

adherent noun **follower**, supporter, upholder, defender, advocate, disciple, devotee, partisan, member; believer, worshipper.
– OPPOSITES opponent.

adhesion noun **traction**, grip, purchase, hold.

adhesive noun **glue**, fixative, gum, paste, cement; N. Amer. mucilage; N. Amer. informal stickum.
• adjective **sticky**, tacky, gluey, gummed; viscous; technical adherent.

ad infinitum adverb **forever**, for ever and ever, always, all the time, every time, endlessly; Brit. for evermore; informal until the cows come home.

adjacent adjective **adjoining**, neighbouring, next-door, abutting, contiguous; (**adjacent to**) close to, near, next to, by, by the side of, bordering on, beside, alongside, attached to, touching, cheek by jowl with.

adjoin verb **be next to**, be adjacent to, border, abut; join, connect with, touch, meet.

adjoining adjective **connecting**, connected, interconnecting, adjacent, neighbouring, bordering, next-door; contiguous; attached, touching.

adjourn verb **1** *the hearing was adjourned:* **suspend**, break off, discontinue, interrupt, recess. **2** *sentencing was adjourned until June 9:* **postpone**, put off/back, defer, delay, hold over. **3** *they adjourned to the sitting room:* **withdraw**, retire, retreat; formal repair, remove.

adjournment noun **suspension**, discontinuation, interruption, postponement, deferment, deferral, stay.

adjudicate verb **judge**, try, hear, examine, arbitrate; pronounce on, pass judgement on, decide, determine, settle, resolve.

adjudication noun **judgement**, decision, pronouncement, ruling, settlement, resolution, arbitration, finding, verdict, sentence.

adjudicator noun **judge**, arbitrator, arbiter; referee, umpire.

adjunct noun **supplement**, addition, extra, add-on, accessory, accompaniment, complement; attachment, appendage, addendum.

adjust verb **1** *Kate had adjusted to her new life:* **adapt**, become/get accustomed, get used, accommodate, acclimatize, orient yourself, reconcile yourself, habituate yourself, assimilate; come to terms with, blend in with, fit in with; N. Amer. acclimate. **2** *he adjusted the brakes:* **modify**, alter, regulate, tune, fine-tune, balance; arrange, rearrange, change, rejig, rework, revamp, remodel, reshape, tailor, improve, enhance, customize; repair, fix, correct, rectify, overhaul, put right; informal tweak.

adjustable adjective **alterable**, adaptable, modifiable, variable, multiway, versatile.

adjustment noun **1** *a period of adjustment:* **adaptation**, acclimatization, habituation, acculturation, naturalization, assimilation; N. Amer. acclimation. **2** *the car will run on unleaded petrol with no adjustment:* **modification**, alteration, adaptation, rearrangement, change, customization, refinement; repair, correction, amendment, overhaul, improvement.

ad-lib verb *she ad-libbed half the speech:* **improvise**, extemporize, speak impromptu, make it up as you go along; informal busk it, wing it.
• adverb *she spoke ad lib:* **impromptu**, extempore, spontaneously, extemporaneously; informal off the cuff, off the top of your head.

• adjective *an ad-lib speech:* **impromptu**, extempore, extemporary, improvised, unprepared, unrehearsed, unscripted, spontaneous; informal off-the-cuff, spur-of-the-moment.

administer verb **1** *the union is administered by a central executive:* **manage**, direct, control, operate, regulate, coordinate, conduct, handle, run, organize, supervise, superintend, oversee, preside over, govern, rule, lead, head, steer; be in control of, be in charge of, be responsible for, be at the helm of; informal head up. **2** *the lifeboat crew administered first aid:* **dispense**, issue, give, provide, apply, offer, distribute, hand out, dole out. **3** *a gym shoe was used to administer punishment:* **inflict**, mete out, deal out, deliver.

administration noun **1** *the day-to-day administration of the company:* **management**, direction, control, command, charge, conduct, operation, running, leadership, coordination, government, governing, superintendence, supervision, regulation, overseeing. **2** *the previous Labour administration:* **government**, cabinet, regime, executive, authority, directorate, council, leadership, management; parliament, congress, senate; term of office, incumbency.

administrative adjective **managerial**, executive, organizational, supervisory, regulatory.

administrator noun **manager**, director, executive, controller, coordinator, head, chief, leader, governor, superintendent, supervisor; informal boss.

admirable adjective **commendable**, praiseworthy, laudable, estimable, creditable, exemplary, honourable, worthy, deserving, respectable, worthwhile, good, sterling, fine.
– OPPOSITES deplorable.

admiration noun **respect**, approval, approbation, appreciation, high regard, esteem; commendation, acclaim, applause, praise, compliments, tributes, accolades, plaudits.
– OPPOSITES scorn.

admire verb **1** *I admire your courage:* **respect**, approve of, esteem, think highly of, rate highly, hold in high regard, applaud, praise, commend. **2** *Simon had admired her for a long time:* **adore**, love, worship, dote on, be enamoured of, be infatuated with; be taken with, be attracted to; informal carry a torch for, have a thing about.
– OPPOSITES despise.

admirer noun **fan**, devotee, enthusiast, aficionado; supporter, adherent, follower, disciple.

admissible adjective **valid**, allowable, allowed, permissible, permitted, acceptable, tenable, sound, legitimate; informal OK, legit, kosher, pukka.

admission noun **1** *membership entitles you to free admission:* **admittance**, entry, entrance, right of entry, access, right of access. **2** *admission is fifty pence:* **entrance fee**, entry charge, ticket. **3** *a written admission of liability:* **confession**, acknowledgement, acceptance, concession, disclosure, divulgence.

admit verb **1** *Paul admitted that he was angry:* **confess**, acknowledge, own, concede, grant, accept, allow; reveal, disclose, divulge. **2** *he admitted three offences of reckless driving:* **confess to**, plead guilty to, own up to. **3** *he was admitted as a scholar to Winchester College:* **accept**, take on, receive, enrol, enlist, register, sign up.
– OPPOSITES deny, exclude.

admittance noun **entry**, right of entry, admission, entrance, access, right of access.
– OPPOSITES exclusion.

admonish verb **reprimand**, rebuke, scold, reprove, reproach, upbraid, chastise, chide, berate, criticize, take to task, pull up, read the Riot Act to, haul over the coals; informal tell off, dress down, bawl out, rap over the knuckles, give someone hell; Brit. informal tick off, give someone a rocket, have a go at, carpet, tear someone off a strip; N. Amer. informal chew out; formal castigate.

adolescence noun **teenage years**, teens, youth; pubescence, puberty.

adolescent noun *an awkward adolescent:* **teenager**, youngster,

young person, youth, boy, girl; juvenile, minor; informal teen, teeny-bopper.
•**adjective 1** *an adolescent boy:* **teenage**, pubescent, young; juvenile; informal teen. **2** *adolescent silliness:* **immature**, childish, juvenile, infantile, puerile.
–OPPOSITES adult, mature.

adopt **verb 1** *they adopted local customs:* **embrace**, take on/up, espouse, assume, follow. **2** *the people adopted it as their mascot:* **choose**, select, pick, vote for, elect, decide on, opt for.
–OPPOSITES abandon.

adorable **adjective** **lovable**, appealing, charming, cute, sweet, enchanting, bewitching, captivating, engaging, endearing, dear, delightful, lovely, beautiful, attractive, gorgeous, winsome, winning, fetching; Scottish & N. English bonny.
–OPPOSITES hateful.

adoration **noun** **love**, devotion, care, fondness; admiration, awe, idolization, worship, hero-worship, adulation.

adore **verb** *he adored his mother:* **love**, be devoted to, dote on, hold dear, cherish, treasure, prize, think the world of; admire, hold in high regard, look up to, idolize, worship; informal put on a pedestal.
–OPPOSITES hate.

adorn **verb** **decorate**, embellish, ornament, enhance; beautify, prettify, grace, bedeck, deck out, dress, trim, swathe, wreathe, festoon, garland, array, emblazon.
–OPPOSITES disfigure.

adornment **noun** **decoration**, embellishment, ornamentation, ornament, enhancement; beautification, prettification; frills, accessories, trimmings, finishing touches.

adrift **adjective 1** (Brit. informal) *the pipe of my breathing apparatus came adrift:* **loose**, free; detached, unsecured, unfastened, untied, unknotted, undone. **2** *he was adrift in a strange country:* **lost**, off course; disorientated, disoriented, confused; drifting, rootless, unsettled.

adroit **adjective** **skilful**, adept, dexterous, deft, nimble, able, capable, skilled, expert, masterly, masterful, practised, polished, slick, proficient, accomplished, gifted, talented; quick-witted, quick-thinking, clever, smart, sharp, cunning, wily, resourceful, astute, shrewd, canny; informal nifty.
–OPPOSITES inept, clumsy.

adroitness **noun** **skill**, skilfulness, prowess, expertise, adeptness, dexterity, deftness, nimbleness, ability, capability, mastery, proficiency, accomplishment, artistry, art, facility, aptitude, flair, finesse, talent; quick-wittedness, cleverness, sharpness, cunning, astuteness, shrewdness, resourcefulness, savoir faire; informal know-how, savvy.

adulation **noun** **hero-worship**, worship, idolization, adoration, admiration, veneration, awe, devotion, glorification, praise, flattery.

adult **adjective 1** *an adult woman:* **mature**, grown-up, fully grown, full-grown, fully developed, of age. **2** *an adult movie:* **explicit**, erotic, sexy; pornographic, obscene; informal blue.

adulterate **verb** **dilute**, spoil, taint, contaminate, water down, weaken; informal cut.
–OPPOSITES purify.

adulterous **adjective** **unfaithful**, disloyal, deceiving, deceitful; extramarital; informal cheating, two-timing.
–OPPOSITES faithful.

adultery **noun** **infidelity**, unfaithfulness; affair, liaison, amour; informal carryings-on, hanky-panky, playing around; formal fornication.
–OPPOSITES fidelity.

advance **verb 1** *the battalion advanced rapidly:* **move forward**, proceed, press on, push on, push forward, make progress, make headway, gain ground, approach, come closer, draw nearer, near. **2** *the move advanced his career:* **promote**, further, forward, help, aid, assist, boost, strengthen, improve, benefit; fuel, foster. **3** *technology has advanced in the last few years:* **progress**, make progress, make headway, develop, evolve,

make strides, move forward in leaps and bounds; improve, thrive, flourish, prosper. **4** *a relative advanced him some money:* **lend**, loan, put up, come up with; Brit. informal sub.
–OPPOSITES retreat, hinder.
•noun **1** *the advance of the aggressors:* **progress**, forward movement; approach. **2** *a significant medical advance:* **breakthrough**, development, step forward, quantum leap; find, discovery, invention.
•adjective **1** *an advance party of settlers:* **preliminary**, first, exploratory; pilot, test, trial. **2** *advance warning:* **early**, prior.
■ **in advance** beforehand, before, ahead of time, earlier, previously; in readiness.

advanced adjective **1** *advanced manufacturing techniques:* **state-of-the-art**, new, modern, up to date, up to the minute, the newest, cutting-edge, the latest; pioneering, innovative, sophisticated. **2** *advanced further-education courses:* **higher-level**, higher, tertiary.
–OPPOSITES primitive.

advancement noun *there are opportunities for advancement:* **promotion**, career development, upgrading, a step up the ladder, progress, improvement, betterment, growth.

advantage noun **1** *the advantage of belonging to a union:* **benefit**, value, good/strong point, asset, plus, bonus, boon, blessing, virtue; attraction, beauty; convenience, profit. **2** *they appeared to be gaining the advantage:* **upper hand**, edge, lead, whip hand; superiority, dominance, ascendancy, supremacy, power, mastery. **3** *there is no advantage to be gained from delaying the process:* **benefit**, profit, gain, good; informal mileage.
–OPPOSITES disadvantage, drawback, detriment.

advantageous adjective **1** *an advantageous position:* **superior**, dominant, powerful; good, fortunate, lucky, favourable. **2** *the arrangement is advantageous to both sides:* **beneficial**, of benefit, helpful, of assistance, useful, of use, of value, profitable, fruitful; convenient, in everyone's interests.
–OPPOSITES disadvantageous, detrimental.

advent noun **arrival**, appearance, emergence, dawn, birth, rise, development; approach, coming.
–OPPOSITES disappearance.

adventure noun **1** *her recent adventures in Italy:* **exploit**, escapade, deed, feat, experience; stunt. **2** *they set off in search of adventure:* **excitement**, thrills, stimulation; risk, danger, hazard, peril, uncertainty, precariousness.

adventurer noun **daredevil**, hero, heroine; swashbuckler; entrepreneur; informal adrenalin junkie.

adventurous adjective **1** *an adventurous traveller:* **daring**, intrepid, bold, fearless, brave; informal gutsy, spunky. **2** *adventurous activities:* **risky**, dangerous, perilous, hazardous, precarious, uncertain; exciting, thrilling.
–OPPOSITES cautious.

adversary noun **opponent**, rival, enemy, antagonist, combatant, challenger, contender, competitor; opposition, competition; literary foe.
–OPPOSITES ally, supporter.

adverse adjective **1** *adverse weather conditions:* **unfavourable**, inclement, bad, poor, untoward. **2** *the drug's adverse side effects:* **harmful**, dangerous, injurious, detrimental, hurtful, deleterious. **3** *an adverse response from the public:* **hostile**, unfavourable, antagonistic, unfriendly, negative.
–OPPOSITES favourable, auspicious, beneficial.

> ! Don't confuse **adverse** with **averse**, which means 'strongly disliking' or 'very unwilling', e.g. *I'm not averse to helping out* (i.e. *I'm willing to help out*).

adversity noun **misfortune**, ill luck, bad luck, trouble, difficulty, hardship, distress, disaster, suffering, sorrow, misery, tribulation, woe, pain, trauma; mishap, misadventure, accident, upset, setback, crisis, catastrophe, tragedy, calamity; trial, burden, blow, vicissitude; hard times, trials and tribulations.

advertise verb **publicize**, make public, make known, announce, broadcast, proclaim, trumpet, call attention to, bill; promote, market, beat/bang the drum for, trail; informal push, plug, hype, boost; N. Amer. informal ballyhoo, flack.

advertisement noun **notice**, announcement, bulletin; commercial, promotion, blurb, write-up; poster, leaflet, pamphlet, flyer, handbill, handout, circular, brochure, sign, placard; informal ad, push, plug, puff; Brit. informal advert.

advice noun **guidance**, counselling, counsel, help, direction; information, recommendations, guidelines, suggestions, hints, tips, pointers, ideas.

advisable adjective **wise**, desirable, preferable, sensible, prudent, proper, appropriate, apt, suitable, fitting; expedient, politic, advantageous, beneficial, profitable, in your best interests.

advise verb **1** *she advised them about career possibilities:* **counsel**, give advice, guide, offer suggestions. **2** *he advised caution:* **advocate**, recommend, suggest, urge. **3** *you will be advised of our decision:* **inform**, notify, give notice, apprise, warn, acquaint with; informal fill in on.

adviser noun **counsellor**, mentor, guide, consultant, confidant, confidante; coach, teacher, tutor, guru.

advocacy noun **support**, backing, promotion, championing; recommendation; N. Amer. boosterism.

advocate noun **champion**, upholder, supporter, backer, promoter, proponent, exponent, spokesman, spokeswoman, spokesperson, campaigner, lobbyist, fighter, crusader; propagandist, apostle, apologist; N. Amer. booster.
– OPPOSITES critic.
• verb **recommend**, prescribe, advise, urge; support, back, favour, uphold, subscribe to; champion, campaign for, speak for, argue for, lobby for, promote.

aesthetic adjective **artistic**, tasteful, in good taste, pleasing.

affable adjective **friendly**, amiable, genial, congenial, cordial, warm, pleasant, nice, likeable, personable, charming, agreeable, sympathetic, good-humoured, good-natured, kindly, kind, approachable, accessible, amenable, sociable, outgoing, gregarious, clubbable, neighbourly, welcoming, hospitable, obliging; Scottish couthy.
– OPPOSITES unfriendly.

affair noun **1** *what you do is your affair:* **business**, concern, matter, responsibility, province, preserve; problem, worry; Brit. informal lookout. **2** **(affairs)** *his financial affairs:* **transactions**, concerns, matters, activities, dealings, undertakings, ventures, business. **3** *the board admitted responsibility for the affair:* **event**, incident, episode; case, matter, business. **4** *his affair with Anthea was over:* **relationship**, romance, fling, dalliance, liaison, involvement, intrigue, amour; informal hanky-panky; Brit. informal carry-on.

affect[1] verb **1** *this development may have affected the judge's decision:* **have an effect on**, influence, act on, work on, have an impact on; change, alter, modify, transform, form, shape, sway, bias. **2** *he was visibly affected by the experience:* **move**, touch, make an impression on; hit hard, upset, trouble, distress, disturb, agitate, shake.

> ! Don't confuse **affect** and **effect**. The main meaning of **affect** is 'make a difference to', while the main meaning of **effect** is 'a change which is the result of something' (*the effects of global warming*).

affect[2] verb *he affected an air of innocence:* **assume**, take on, adopt, feign.

affectation noun **1** *he had always abhorred affectation:* **pretension**, pretentiousness, affectedness, artificiality, posturing, posing; airs and graces; Brit. informal side. **2** *an affectation of calm:* **facade**, front, show, appearance, pretence.

affected adjective **pretentious**, artificial, contrived, unnatural, stagy, studied, mannered, ostentatious; insincere, unconvincing, feigned, false, fake, sham; informal phoney.
– OPPOSITES natural, unpretentious, genuine.

a

affecting adjective **touching**, moving, emotional; stirring, heart-warming; poignant, pitiful, piteous, tear-jerking, heart-rending, heartbreaking, disturbing, distressing, upsetting, haunting.

affection noun **fondness**, love, liking, tenderness, warmth, devotion, endearment, care, attachment, friendship.

affectionate adjective **loving**, fond, adoring, devoted, caring, doting, tender, warm, warm-hearted, soft-hearted, friendly; demonstrative; informal touchy-feely, lovey-dovey.
– OPPOSITES cold.

affiliate verb **associate with**, unite with, combine with, join up with, join forces with, link up with, ally with, align with, amalgamate with, merge with; incorporate into.

affiliated adjective **associated**, allied, related, connected, linked; in league, in partnership.

affiliation noun **association**, connection, alliance, alignment, link, attachment, tie, relationship, fellowship, partnership, coalition, union; amalgamation, incorporation, integration.

affinity noun **empathy**, rapport, sympathy, accord, harmony, relationship, bond, closeness, understanding; liking, fondness; informal chemistry.
– OPPOSITES aversion, dislike, dissimilarity.

affirm verb **declare**, state, assert, proclaim, pronounce, attest, swear, avow, guarantee, pledge; formal aver.
– OPPOSITES deny.

affirmation noun **declaration**, statement, assertion, proclamation, pronouncement, attestation; oath, avowal, guarantee, pledge; deposition.
– OPPOSITES denial.

affirmative adjective *an affirmative answer:* **positive**, assenting, consenting, favourable.
– OPPOSITES negative.
• noun *she took his grunt as an affirmative:* **agreement**, acceptance, assent, acquiescence, yes; informal OK.
– OPPOSITES disagreement.

affix verb **stick**, glue, paste, gum; attach, fasten, fix; clip, tack, pin; tape.
– OPPOSITES detach.

afflict verb **trouble**, burden, distress, beset, harass, worry, oppress; torment, plague, blight, bedevil, rack, curse.

affliction noun **1** *a herb reputed to cure a variety of afflictions:* **disorder**, disease, malady, complaint, ailment, illness. **2** *he bore his affliction with great dignity:* **suffering**, distress, pain, trouble, misery, hardship, misfortune, adversity, sorrow, torment, tribulation, woe.

affluence noun **wealth**, prosperity, fortune; riches, money, resources, assets, possessions, property, substance, means.
– OPPOSITES poverty.

affluent adjective **wealthy**, rich, prosperous, well off, moneyed, well-to-do; propertied, substantial, of means, of substance; informal well heeled, rolling in it, made of money, filthy rich, stinking rich, loaded, worth a packet.
– OPPOSITES poor, impoverished.

afford verb **1** *I can't afford a new car:* **pay for**; run to, stretch to, manage, spare. **2** *the rooftop terrace affords beautiful views:* **provide**, supply, furnish, offer, give, yield.

affront noun *an affront to public morality:* **insult**, offence, slight, snub, put-down, provocation, injury; outrage, atrocity, scandal; informal slap in the face, kick in the teeth.
• verb *she was affronted by his familiarity:* **insult**, offend, provoke, pique, wound, hurt; put out, irk, displease, bother, rankle, vex, gall; outrage, scandalize; informal put someone's back up, needle.

aficionado noun **connoisseur**, expert, authority, specialist, pundit; enthusiast, devotee; informal buff, freak, nut, fiend, maniac, fanatic, addict.

afoot adjective & adverb **in preparation**, on the way, brewing, looming, in the offing, in the air/wind, on the horizon; going on, happening, in progress; informal on the cards.

afraid adjective **1** *they ran away because they were afraid:* **frightened**, scared, terrified, fearful, petrified, shaking in your

shoes, shaking like a leaf; intimidated, alarmed; faint-hearted, cowardly; informal scared stiff, in a funk, in a cold sweat; N. Amer. informal spooked. **2** *don't be afraid to ask awkward questions:* **reluctant**, hesitant, unwilling, slow, chary, shy.
– OPPOSITES brave, confident.

afresh **adverb** **anew**, again.

after **preposition** **following**, subsequent to, as a result of, as a consequence of, in the wake of, post-.
– OPPOSITES before.

after-effect **noun** **repercussion**, aftermath, consequence.

aftermath **noun** **repercussions**, after-effects, consequences, results, fruits.

afterwards **adverb** **later**, later on, subsequently, then, next, after this/that; at a later time/date, in due course.

again **adverb** **1** *her spirits lifted again:* **once more**, another time, afresh, anew. **2** *this can add half as much again to the price:* **extra**, in addition, additionally, on top. **3** *again, evidence was not always consistent:* **also**, furthermore; moreover, besides.
■ **again and again** repeatedly, over and over again, time and time again, many times, many a time; often, frequently, continually, constantly.

against **preposition** **1** *a number of delegates were against the motion:* **opposed to**, in opposition to, hostile to, averse to, antagonistic towards, unsympathetic to, resistant to, at odds with, in disagreement with; informal anti, agin. **2** *his age is against him:* **disadvantageous to**, unfavourable to, damaging to, detrimental to, prejudicial to, deleterious to, harmful to, injurious to; a drawback.
– OPPOSITES for, pro.

age **noun** **1** *her hearing had deteriorated with age:* **elderliness**, old age, seniority, maturity; your advancing/declining years. **2** *the Elizabethan age:* **era**, epoch, period, time. **3** (informal) *you haven't been in touch with me for ages:* **a long time**, an eternity; informal ages and ages, donkey's years, a month of Sundays; Brit. informal yonks.
• **verb** *Cabernet Sauvignon ages well:* **mature**, mellow, ripen.

aged **adjective** **elderly**, old, mature, senior, advanced in years, long in the tooth, as old as the hills, past your prime, ancient, in your dotage, senescent; informal getting on, over the hill, no spring chicken.
– OPPOSITES young.

agency **noun** **business**, organization, company, firm, office, bureau.

agenda **noun** **list**, schedule, programme, timetable, line-up, plan.

agent **noun** **1** *the sale was arranged through an agent:* **representative**, emissary, envoy, go-between, proxy, negotiator, intermediary, broker, spokesperson, spokesman, spokeswoman; informal rep. **2** *a travel agent:* **agency**, business, organization, company, firm, bureau. **3** *a CIA agent:* **spy**, secret agent, undercover agent, operative, mole; N. Amer. informal spook, G-man.

agglomeration **noun** **collection**, mass, cluster, lump, clump, pile, heap; accumulation, build-up; miscellany, jumble, hotchpotch.

aggravate **verb** **1** *the new law could aggravate the situation:* **worsen**, make worse, exacerbate, inflame, compound; add fuel to the fire/flames, add insult to injury, rub salt in the wound. **2** (informal) *you don't have to aggravate people to get what you want:* **annoy**, irritate, exasperate, put out, nettle, provoke, antagonize, get on someone's nerves, ruffle someone's feathers, try someone's patience; Brit. rub up the wrong way; informal needle, bug, hack off, get someone's goat, get under someone's skin; Brit. informal wind up, nark, get on someone's wick; N. Amer. informal tick off.
– OPPOSITES alleviate, improve.

aggravation **noun** (informal) **nuisance**, annoyance, irritation, hassle, trouble, difficulty, inconvenience, bother; informal aggro.

aggregate **noun** **1** *an aggregate of rock and mineral fragments:* **collection**, mass, agglomeration; mixture, mix, combination, blend; compound, alloy, amalgam. **2** *he won with an aggregate of 325:* **total**, sum, grand total.
• **adjective** *an aggregate score:* **total**, combined, gross, overall, composite.

a

aggression noun **hostility**, belligerence, combativeness, aggressiveness, pugnacity, forcefulness, provocation; force, violence; militancy, warmongering.

aggressive adjective **1** *aggressive and disruptive behaviour:* **violent**, confrontational, antagonistic, truculent, pugnacious, macho; quarrelsome, argumentative. **2** *aggressive foreign policy:* **warmongering**, warlike, warring, belligerent, bellicose, hawkish, militaristic; expansionist; informal gung-ho. **3** *aggressive sales tactics:* **assertive**, forceful, vigorous, energetic, dynamic, strong; bold, audacious; informal in-your-face, feisty.
– OPPOSITES peaceable, peaceful.

aggressor noun **attacker**, assaulter, assailant; invader.

aggrieved adjective **resentful**, affronted, indignant, disgruntled, discontented, upset, offended, piqued, riled, nettled, vexed, irked, irritated, annoyed, put out; informal peeved, miffed, in a huff; Brit. informal cheesed off; N. Amer. informal sore, steamed.
– OPPOSITES pleased.

aghast adjective **horrified**, appalled, dismayed, thunderstruck, stunned, shocked, staggered; informal flabbergasted; Brit. informal gobsmacked.

agile adjective **1** *she was as agile as a monkey:* **nimble**, lithe, supple, acrobatic. **2** *an agile mind:* **alert**, sharp, acute, shrewd, astute, perceptive, quick.
– OPPOSITES clumsy, stiff.

agitate verb **1** *any mention of Clare agitates my grandmother:* **upset**, perturb, fluster, ruffle, disconcert, unnerve, disquiet, disturb, distress, unsettle; informal rattle, faze; N. Amer. informal discombobulate. **2** *she agitated for the appointment of more women:* **campaign**, push, press, lobby; demonstrate, protest. **3** *agitate the water to disperse the oil:* **stir**, whisk, beat, shake.

agitated adjective **upset**, perturbed, flustered, disconcerted, unnerved, disquieted, disturbed, distressed, unsettled; informal rattled, fazed, in a flap, in a state, jittery, in a tizz; Brit. informal having kittens, in a flat spin; N. Amer. informal discombobulated.
– OPPOSITES calm, relaxed.

agitation noun **anxiety**, disquiet, distress, concern, alarm, worry.

agitator noun **troublemaker**, rabble-rouser, agent provocateur, demagogue; insurgent, subversive; informal stirrer.

agnostic noun **sceptic**, doubter, doubting Thomas.
– OPPOSITES believer.

agog adjective **eager**, excited, impatient, keen, anxious, avid, in suspense, on tenterhooks, on the edge of your seat, on pins and needles, waiting with bated breath.

agonize verb **worry**, fret, fuss, brood, wrestle with yourself, be worried/anxious; informal stew.

agonizing adjective **excruciating**, harrowing, racking, searing, torturous, tormenting, piercing; informal hellish, killing.

agony noun torment, torture, anguish, affliction, trauma.

agree verb **1** *I agree with you:* **concur**, see eye to eye, be in sympathy, be united, be as one, be unanimous. **2** *they agreed to a ceasefire:* **consent**, assent, acquiesce, accept, approve, say yes, give your approval, give the nod; formal accede. **3** *the plan and the drawing do not agree with each other:* **match**, correspond, conform, coincide, fit, tally, be in harmony/agreement, be consistent; informal square. **4** *they agreed on a price:* **settle**, decide, arrive at, negotiate, come to terms, strike a bargain, make a deal, shake hands.
– OPPOSITES disagree, differ, contradict, reject.

agreeable adjective **1** *an agreeable atmosphere of rural tranquillity:* **pleasant**, pleasing, enjoyable, pleasurable, nice, appealing, relaxing, friendly. **2** *an agreeable fellow:* **likeable**, amiable, affable, pleasant, nice, friendly, good-natured, sociable, genial, congenial. **3** *we should get together for a talk, if you're agreeable:* **willing**, amenable, in agreement.
– OPPOSITES unpleasant, disagreeable.

agreement noun **1** *all heads nodded in agreement:* **accord**, concurrence,

consensus; assent, acceptance, consent, acquiescence. **2** *an agreement on imports:* **contract**, compact, treaty, covenant, pact, accord. **3** *there is some agreement between my view and that of the author:* **correspondence**, consistency, compatibility, accord; similarity, resemblance, likeness.
– OPPOSITES disagreement, discord.

agricultural adjective **farm**, farming, agrarian; rural, rustic, pastoral, countryside.
– OPPOSITES urban.

agriculture noun **farming**, cultivation, husbandry; agribusiness, agronomy.

> **WORD LINKS**
> **agrarian** relating to agriculture

aid noun **1** *with the aid of his colleagues:* **assistance**, support, help, backing, cooperation. **2** *humanitarian aid:* **relief**, assistance, support, subsidy, funding, donations, grants; historical alms.
– OPPOSITES hindrance.
• verb **1** *he provided an army to aid the King:* **help**, assist, support, relieve, back up. **2** *herbal remedies can aid restful sleep:* **facilitate**, promote, encourage, help, further, boost.
– OPPOSITES hinder.

aide noun **assistant**, helper, adviser, right-hand man/woman, man/girl Friday, adjutant, deputy, second in command; lieutenant.

ailing adjective **1** *the country's ailing economy:* **failing**, weak, poor, tottering, fragile. **2** *his ailing mother:* **sick**, ill, sickly, poorly, weak, in poor/bad health, infirm.
– OPPOSITES healthy.

ailment noun **illness**, disease, disorder, affliction, malady, complaint, infirmity; informal bug, virus.

aim verb **1** *he aimed the rifle:* **point**, direct, train, sight, line up. **2** *she aimed at the target:* **take aim**, fix on, zero in on, draw a bead on.
3 *undergraduates aiming for a first degree:* **work towards**, be after, set your sights on, try for, strive for, aspire to; formal essay. **4** *this system is aimed at the home entertainment market:* **target**, intend, direct, design, tailor, market, pitch. **5** *we aim to give you the best possible service:* **intend**, mean; plan, resolve, propose.
• noun *our aim is to develop gymnasts to the top level:* **objective**, object, goal, end, target, design, desire, intention, intent, plan, purpose, object of the exercise; ambition, aspiration, wish, dream, hope.

aimless adjective **purposeless**, directionless, undirected, random.
– OPPOSITES purposeful.

air noun **1** *hundreds of birds hovered in the air:* **sky**, atmosphere; ether; literary heavens. **2** *let's open the windows to get some air:* **ventilation**; breeze wind. **3** *an air of defiance:* **look**, appearance, impression, aspect, aura, mien, manner, bearing, tone; feel, ambience, atmosphere; informal vibe. **4** *a traditional Scottish air:* **tune**, melody, song.
• verb **1** *a chance to air your views:* **express**, voice, make public, articulate, state, declare, give expression/voice to; have your say. **2** *the windows were opened to air the room:* **ventilate**, freshen, refresh, cool; aerate. **3** *the film was aired nationwide:* **broadcast**, transmit, screen, show, televise.

> **WORD LINKS**
> **aerial** relating to the air
> **aerodynamics** the study of objects' movement through the air

airborne adjective **flying**, in flight, in the air, on the wing, up, aloft.

aircraft noun **plane**, airliner, jet; Brit. aeroplane; N. Amer. airplane.

> **WORD LINKS**
> **aeronautics** the science of aircraft flight
> **aviation** the activity of operating and flying aircraft

airily adverb **lightly**, breezily, flippantly, casually, nonchalantly, heedlessly.
– OPPOSITES seriously.

airing noun **1** *the airing of different views:* **expression**, voicing, articulating, stating, declaration, communication. **2** *I hope the BBC gives the play another airing:* **broadcast**, transmission, screening, showing, televising.

a

airless adjective **stuffy**, close, stifling, suffocating, oppressive; unventilated.
–OPPOSITES airy.

airtight adjective **1** *an airtight container:* **sealed**, hermetically sealed. **2** *an airtight alibi:* **indisputable**, cast-iron, solid, incontrovertible, incontestable, irrefutable, watertight.

airy adjective **1** *the conservatory is light and airy:* **well ventilated**, fresh; spacious, uncluttered; light, bright. **2** *an airy gesture:* **nonchalant**, casual, breezy, flippant, dismissive, insouciant. **3** *airy clouds:* **delicate**, soft, fine, feathery, insubstantial.
–OPPOSITES stuffy.

aisle noun **passage**, passageway, gangway, walkway.

akin adjective **similar**, related, close, near, comparable, equivalent; connected, alike, analogous.
–OPPOSITES unlike.

alacrity noun **eagerness**, willingness, readiness; enthusiasm, keenness; promptness, haste, swiftness, dispatch, speed.

alarm noun **1** *the girl spun round in alarm:* **fear**, anxiety, apprehension, nervousness, unease, distress, agitation, consternation, disquiet, fright, panic. **2** *a smoke alarm:* **detector**, sensor; siren, signal, bell.
–OPPOSITES calmness, composure.
•verb *the news had alarmed her:* **frighten**, scare, panic, unnerve, distress, agitate, upset, disconcert, shock, dismay, disturb; informal rattle, spook; Brit. informal put the wind up.

alarming adjective **frightening**, unnerving, shocking; distressing, upsetting, disconcerting, disturbing; informal scary.
–OPPOSITES reassuring.

alcohol noun **liquor**, spirits; informal booze, hooch, the hard stuff, firewater, rotgut, moonshine, grog, the demon drink, the bottle; Brit. informal gut-rot; N. Amer. informal juice; technical ethyl alcohol, ethanol.

> **WORD LINKS**
> **alcoholism**, **dipsomania** addiction to alcohol
> **temperance**, **teetotalism** the practice of never drinking alcohol

alcoholic adjective **intoxicating**, inebriating; strong, hard, stiff; formal spirituous.
•noun dipsomaniac, drunk, drunkard, heavy/hard/serious drinker, problem drinker, alcohol-abuser; inebriate; informal boozer, lush, alky, dipso, soak, wino, barfly; Austral./NZ informal hophead.

alcove noun **recess**, niche, nook, inglenook, bay.

alert adjective **1** *police have asked neighbours to keep alert:* **vigilant**, watchful, attentive, observant, wide awake; on the lookout, on your guard/toes; informal keeping your eyes open/peeled. **2** *she's still active and alert:* **quick-witted**, sharp, bright, quick, perceptive; informal on the ball, quick on the uptake, all there, with it.
–OPPOSITES inattentive.
•noun **1** *a state of alert:* **vigilance**, watchfulness, attentiveness, alertness. **2** *a flood alert:* **warning**, notification, notice; siren, alarm, signal.
•verb *police were alerted by a phone call:* **warn**, notify, apprise, forewarn, put on your guard; informal tip off.

alias noun *he is known under several aliases:* **assumed name**, false name, pseudonym, sobriquet; pen/stage name, nom de plume, nom de guerre.
•adverb *Cassius Clay, alias Muhammad Ali:* **also known as**, aka.

alien adjective **1** *alien cultures:* **foreign**, overseas, non-native. **2** *an alien landscape:* **unfamiliar**, unknown, strange, peculiar; exotic, foreign. **3** *a vicious role alien to his nature:* **incompatible**, opposed, conflicting, contrary, in conflict, at variance. **4** *alien beings:* **extraterrestrial**, unearthly.
–OPPOSITES native, familiar, earthly.
•noun **1** *an illegal alien:* **foreigner**, non-native, immigrant, émigré, incomer. **2** *the alien's spaceship crashed:* **extraterrestrial**, ET; informal little green man.

alienate verb **estrange**, distance, isolate, cut off; set against, turn away, drive apart, set at variance/odds, drive a wedge between.

alienation noun **isolation**,

detachment, estrangement, separation.

alight[1] verb **1** *he alighted from the train:* **get off**, step off, disembark, pile out. **2** *a swallow alighted on a branch:* **land**, come to rest, settle, perch.
– OPPOSITES get on, board.

alight[2] adjective *the stable was alight:* **burning**, ablaze, on fire, in flames, blazing.

align verb **1** *the desks are aligned with the wall:* **line up**, arrange, position, set, site; coordinate. **2** *he aligned himself with the workers:* **ally**, affiliate, associate, identify, join, side, join forces, team up, band together, throw in your lot.

alike adjective *all the doors looked alike:* **similar**, much the same, indistinguishable, identical, uniform, interchangeable, cut from the same cloth, like two peas in a pod; informal much of a muchness.
– OPPOSITES different.

alive adjective **1** *the synagogue has kept the Jewish faith alive:* **active**, in existence, functioning, in operation; on the map. **2** *teachers need to be alive to their pupils' needs:* **alert**, awake, aware, conscious, mindful, heedful, sensitive, familiar; formal cognizant. **3** *the place was alive with mice:* **teeming**, swarming, overrun, crawling, bristling, infested; crowded, packed.
– OPPOSITES dead, inanimate, inactive.

all determiner **1** *all the children went:* **each of**, every, each and every. **2** *the sun shone all week:* **the whole of the**, the complete, the entire.
• pronoun **1** *all of the cups were broken:* **each one**, the whole lot. **2** *they took all of it:* **everything**, every part, the lot, the entirety.
– OPPOSITES none, nothing.
• adverb *he was dressed all in black:* **completely**, fully, entirely, totally, wholly, utterly.
– OPPOSITES partly.

allay verb **reduce**, diminish, decrease, lessen, assuage, alleviate, ease, relieve, soothe, soften, calm.
– OPPOSITES increase, intensify.

allegation noun **claim**, assertion, charge, accusation, contention.

allege verb **claim**, assert, charge, accuse, contend.

alleged adjective **supposed**, so-called, claimed, professed, purported, ostensible, putative, unproven.

allegedly adverb **reportedly**, supposedly, reputedly, purportedly, ostensibly, apparently, so the story goes.

allegiance noun **loyalty**, faithfulness, fidelity, obedience, adherence, devotion.
– OPPOSITES disloyalty, treachery.

allegorical adjective **symbolic**, metaphorical, figurative, representative, emblematic.

allegory noun **parable**, analogy, metaphor, symbol, emblem.

alleviate verb **reduce**, ease, relieve, take the edge off, deaden, dull, diminish, lessen, weaken, lighten, allay, assuage, palliate, damp, soothe, help, soften.
– OPPOSITES aggravate.

alley noun **passage**, passageway, alleyway, back alley, backstreet, lane, path, pathway, walk.

alliance noun **association**, union, league, confederation, federation, confederacy, coalition, consortium, affiliation, partnership.

allied adjective *agriculture and allied industries:* **associated**, related, connected, interconnected, linked; similar, equivalent.
– OPPOSITES independent, unrelated.

all-important adjective **vital**, essential, indispensable, crucial, key, critical, life-and-death, paramount, pre-eminent, high-priority; urgent, pressing, burning.
– OPPOSITES inessential.

allocate verb **allot**, assign, distribute, apportion, share out, portion out, deal out, dole out, give out, dish out, parcel out, ration out, divide out/up; informal divvy up.

allocation noun **1** *the efficient allocation of resources:* **allotment**, assignment, distribution, sharing out, handing out, dealing out, doling out, giving out, dishing out, dividing out/up; informal divvying up. **2** *our annual allocation of funds:* **allowance**, allotment, quota, share, ration, grant, slice; informal cut; Brit. informal whack.

a

allot verb **allocate**, assign, apportion, distribute, issue, grant; earmark, designate, set aside; hand out, deal out, dish out, dole out, give out; informal divvy up.

allow verb **1** *the police allowed him to go home:* **permit**, let, authorize, give permission/authorization, license, entitle; consent, assent, give your consent/blessing, give the nod, acquiesce, agree, approve; informal give the go-ahead, give the thumbs up, OK, give the green light; formal accede. **2** *allow an hour or so for driving:* **set aside**, allocate, allot, earmark, designate, assign.
–OPPOSITES prevent, forbid.

allowable adjective *the maximum allowable number of users:* **permissible**, permitted, allowed, admissible, acceptable, legal, lawful, authorized, sanctioned, approved; informal OK, legit.
–OPPOSITES forbidden.

allowance noun **1** *your baggage allowance:* **allocation**, allotment, quota, share, ration, grant, limit. **2** *the elderly receive a heating allowance:* **payment**, contribution, grant, subsidy, maintenance.
■ **make allowances for 1** *you must make allowances for delays:* take into consideration, take into account, bear in mind, provide for, plan for, cater for, allow for, make provision for, be prepared for. **2** *she always made allowances for him:* excuse, make excuses for, forgive, indulge; overlook.

alloy noun **mixture**, mix, amalgam, fusion, blend, compound, combination, composite, union; technical admixture.

all-powerful adjective **omnipotent**, almighty, supreme, absolute, pre-eminent.
–OPPOSITES powerless.

all right adjective **1** *the tea was all right:* **satisfactory**, acceptable, adequate, passable, reasonable; informal so-so, OK. **2** *thankfully, the three boys are all right:* **unhurt**, uninjured, unharmed, in one piece, safe, safe and sound; well, fine, alive and well; informal OK. **3** *it's all right for you to go now:* **permissible**, permitted, allowed, acceptable, legal, lawful, authorized, approved, in order; safe; informal OK, legit, cool.
–OPPOSITES unsatisfactory.
•adverb *the system works all right:* **satisfactorily**, adequately, fairly well, passably, acceptably, reasonably well; informal OK.

allude verb **refer**, touch on, suggest, hint, imply, mention.

allure noun **attraction**, lure, draw, pull, appeal, enticement, temptation, charm, seduction, fascination.

alluring adjective **enticing**, tempting, attractive, appealing, inviting, captivating, seductive; enchanting, charming, fascinating.

allusion noun **reference**, mention, suggestion, hint, comment, remark.

ally noun *close political allies:* **associate**, colleague, friend, confederate, partner, supporter.
–OPPOSITES enemy, opponent.
•verb **1** *he allied his racing experience with business acumen:* **combine**, marry, couple, merge, amalgamate, join, fuse. **2** *the Catholic powers allied with Philip II:* **unite**, combine, join, join forces, band together, team up, collaborate, side, align yourself, form an alliance, throw in your lot.
–OPPOSITES split.

almighty adjective **1** *I swear by almighty God:* **all-powerful**, omnipotent, supreme. **2** (informal) *an almighty explosion.* See BIG sense 1.

almost adverb **nearly**, about, more or less, practically, virtually, all but, as good as, close to, not quite, to all intents and purposes, quasi-; approaching, bordering on, verging on; informal pretty well; literary well-nigh, nigh on.

alone adjective & adverb **1** *she was alone in the house:* **by yourself**, on your own, solitary, single, solo; unescorted, unchaperoned; Brit. informal on your tod, on your lonesome, on your Jack Jones. **2** *he had to manage alone:* **unaided**, unassisted, without help/assistance, single-handedly, solo, on your own. **3** *she felt terribly alone:* **lonely**, isolated, deserted, abandoned, friendless. **4** *a house standing alone:* **apart**, by itself/yourself, separate. **5** *you alone can inspire me:* **only**, solely, just.

aloof adjective **distant**, detached, unfriendly, remote, unapproachable, formal, stiff, austere, withdrawn, reserved, unforthcoming, uncommunicative; informal stand-offish.
– OPPOSITES familiar, friendly.

also adverb **too**, as well, besides, in addition, additionally, furthermore, further, moreover, into the bargain, on top of that, to boot, equally; old use withal.

alter verb **change**, adjust, adapt, amend, modify, revise, revamp, rework, redo, refine; informal tweak.

alteration noun **change**, adjustment, adaptation, modification, variation, revision, amendment; rearrangement, reordering, restyling, rejigging, reworking, revamping; sea change, transformation; humorous transmogrification.

altercation noun **argument**, quarrel, squabble, fight, shouting match, disagreement, difference of opinion, falling-out, dispute, wrangle, war of words; Brit. row; informal tiff, run-in, slanging match, spat, scrap; Brit. informal row, barney, ding-dong, bust-up.

alternate verb **1** *rows of trees alternate with dense shrub:* **be interspersed**, follow one another; take turns, take it in turns. **2** *we could alternate the two groups:* **rotate**; swap, exchange, interchange.
• adjective **1** *she attended on alternate days:* **every other**, every second. **2** (N. Amer.) *an alternate plan.* See **ALTERNATIVE** adjective sense 1.

alternative adjective **1** *an alternative route:* **different**, other, another, second, substitute, replacement; standby, emergency, reserve, backup, auxiliary, fallback; N. Amer. alternate. **2** *an alternative lifestyle:* **unorthodox**, unconventional, non-standard, unusual, out of the ordinary; radical, revolutionary, nonconformist, avant-garde; informal offbeat, way-out.
• noun *we have no alternative:* **option**, choice; substitute, replacement.

altitude noun **height**, elevation; distance.

> **WORD LINKS**
> **altimetry** the measurement of altitude

altogether adverb **1** *he wasn't altogether happy:* **completely**, totally, entirely, absolutely, wholly, fully, thoroughly, utterly, perfectly, one hundred per cent, in all respects. **2** *we have five offices altogether:* **in all**, all told, in total.

altruism noun **unselfishness**, selflessness, compassion, kindness, public-spiritedness; philanthropy, humanitarianism.
– OPPOSITES selfishness.

always adverb **1** *he's always late:* **every time**, each time, all the time, without fail, consistently, invariably, regularly, habitually, unfailingly. **2** *she's always complaining:* **continually**, continuously, constantly, forever; all the time, day and night, seven days a week; informal 24-7. **3** *I'll always love him:* **forever**, for good, for evermore, for ever and ever, until the end of time, eternally; informal for keeps, until the cows come home.
– OPPOSITES never, seldom, sometimes.

amalgamate verb **combine**, merge, unite, fuse, blend, meld; join, join forces, band together, link up, team up.
– OPPOSITES separate.

amalgamation noun **combination**, union, blend, mixture, fusion, synthesis, composite, amalgam.

amass verb **gather**, collect, assemble; accumulate, stockpile, store, accrue, lay in/up, garner; informal stash away.
– OPPOSITES dissipate.

amateur noun **1** *the crew were all amateurs:* **non-professional**, non-specialist, layman, layperson; dilettante. **2** *what a bunch of amateurs:* **incompetent**, bungler; Brit. informal bodger, cowboy, clown.
– OPPOSITES professional, expert.
• adjective **non-professional**, non-specialist, lay; dilettante.

amateurish adjective **incompetent**, inept, inexpert, amateur, clumsy, maladroit, bumbling; Brit. informal bodged.

amaze verb **astonish**, astound, surprise, stun, stagger, nonplus, shock, startle, stupefy, stop someone in their tracks, leave open-mouthed, leave aghast, take someone's breath away, dumbfound; informal bowl over, flabbergast; Brit. informal knock for six; (**amazed**) thunderstruck, at a loss for words, speechless; Brit. informal gobsmacked.

amazement noun **astonishment**, surprise, shock, stupefaction, incredulity, disbelief, speechlessness, awe, wonder, wonderment.

amazing adjective **astonishing**, astounding, surprising, stunning, staggering, stupefying, breathtaking; awesome, awe-inspiring, sensational, remarkable, spectacular, stupendous, phenomenal, extraordinary, incredible, unbelievable; informal mind-blowing; literary wondrous.

ambassador noun **envoy**, emissary, representative, diplomat.

ambience noun **atmosphere**, air, aura, climate, mood, feel, feeling, vibrations, character, quality, impression, flavour, look, tone; informal vibe.

ambiguity noun **ambivalence**, equivocation; vagueness.

ambiguous adjective **equivocal**, ambivalent, unclear, vague, doubtful, dubious, uncertain.
– OPPOSITES clear.

ambition noun **1** *young people with ambition:* **drive**, determination, enterprise, initiative, eagerness, motivation, a sense of purpose; informal get-up-and-go. **2** *her ambition was to become a model:* **aspiration**, intention, goal, aim, objective, object, purpose, intent, plan, desire, wish, target, dream.

ambitious adjective **1** *an energetic and ambitious politician:* **aspiring**, determined, enterprising, motivated, energetic, committed, purposeful, power-hungry; informal go-ahead, go-getting. **2** *an ambitious task:* **challenging**, exacting, demanding, formidable, difficult, hard, tough.
– OPPOSITES laid-back.

ambivalent adjective **equivocal**, uncertain, unsure, doubtful, indecisive, inconclusive, in two minds, undecided, torn, in a dilemma, in a quandary, on the fence, hesitating, wavering, vacillating, equivocating, blowing hot and cold; informal iffy.
– OPPOSITES unequivocal, certain.

amble verb **stroll**, saunter, wander, promenade, walk, take a walk; informal mosey, tootle; Brit. informal toddle, mooch.

ambush verb **surprise**, waylay, attack, jump on, pounce on; N. Amer. bushwhack.

amenable adjective **1** *an amenable child:* **compliant**, biddable, manageable, responsive, reasonable, easy. **2** *many cancers are amenable to treatment:* **susceptible**, receptive, responsive.
– OPPOSITES uncooperative.

amend verb **revise**, alter, change, modify, qualify, adapt, adjust; edit, rewrite, redraft, rephrase, reword, rework, revamp.

amends plural noun
■ **make amends** compensate, recompense, indemnify; atone for, make up for, make good, expiate.

amenity noun **facility**, service, convenience, resource.

America noun. See **UNITED STATES OF AMERICA**.

amiable adjective **friendly**, affable, cordial, amicable; engaging, good-natured, good-tempered, approachable, pleasant, agreeable, likeable, genial, good-humoured, companionable, personable, kind, obliging.
– OPPOSITES unfriendly, disagreeable.

amicable adjective **friendly**, good-natured, cordial, easy, neighbourly, harmonious, cooperative, civilized.
– OPPOSITES unfriendly.

ammunition noun **bullets**, shells, projectiles, missiles, rounds, shot, slugs, cartridges, munitions; informal ammo.

amnesty noun *an amnesty for political prisoners:* **pardon**, reprieve; release, discharge; informal let-off.

amok adverb
■ **run amok** go berserk, rampage, riot, run riot, go on the rampage; informal raise hell.

amoral adjective **unprincipled**, without standards/morals/scruples, unethical; mercenary.
– OPPOSITES principled.

amorous adjective **lustful**, sexual, erotic, amatory, ardent, passionate,

impassioned; in love, enamoured, lovesick; informal lovey-dovey; Brit. informal randy.
– OPPOSITES cold, unloving.

amorphous adjective **shapeless**, formless, structureless, indeterminate.
– OPPOSITES definite.

amount noun **quantity**, number, total, aggregate, sum, quota, group, size, mass, weight, volume.
■ **amount to 1** *the bill amounted to £50:* add up to, come to, run to, be, total; Brit. tot up to. **2** *the delays amounted to maladministration:* constitute, comprise, be tantamount, come down, boil down; signify, signal, indicate, suggest, denote, point to; literary betoken.

ample adjective **1** *there is ample time for discussion:* **enough**, sufficient, adequate, plenty of, more than enough. **2** *an ample supply of wine:* **plentiful**, abundant, copious, profuse, lavish, liberal, generous, bountiful; informal a gogo, galore; literary plenteous. **3** *the ample folds of her skirt:* capacious, voluminous, loose-fitting, baggy; spacious, roomy.
– OPPOSITES insufficient, meagre.

amplify verb **1** *speakers amplify the sound:* **make louder**, increase, boost, step up, raise, strengthen. **2** *these notes amplify our statement:* **expand**, enlarge on, elaborate on, develop, flesh out, fill out; add to, supplement.
– OPPOSITES lower, reduce.

amputate verb **cut off**, sever, remove, saw/chop off, take off.

amulet noun **lucky charm**, talisman, fetish, mascot, totem.

amuse verb **1** *he made faces to amuse her:* **entertain**, divert, cheer up, delight, please, charm, tickle; informal crack up; Brit. informal crease up. **2** *he amused himself by writing poetry:* **occupy**, engage, busy, absorb, engross, hold someone's attention; interest, entertain, divert.
– OPPOSITES bore.

amusement noun **1** *we looked with amusement at the cartoon:* **mirth**, merriment, hilarity, glee, delight; enjoyment, pleasure. **2** *I read the book for amusement:* **entertainment**, pleasure, leisure, relaxation, fun, enjoyment, interest; informal R & R; N. Amer. informal rec. **3** *a wide range of amusements:* **activity**, entertainment, diversion; game, sport.

amusing adjective **entertaining**, funny, comical, humorous, lighthearted, jocular, witty, droll, diverting; informal rib-tickling.
– OPPOSITES boring, solemn.

anaemic adjective **colourless**, bloodless, pale, pallid, wan, ashen, grey, sallow, pasty, sickly.

analogous adjective **comparable**, parallel, similar, like, equivalent, corresponding, related.
– OPPOSITES unrelated, dissimilar.

analogy noun **similarity**, parallel, correspondence, likeness, resemblance, correlation, relation, comparison.
– OPPOSITES dissimilarity.

analyse verb **examine**, inspect, survey, study, scrutinize; investigate, probe, research, review, evaluate, break down, dissect, anatomize.

analysis noun **examination**, investigation, inspection, survey, study, scrutiny; exploration, probe, research, dissection.

analytical, **analytic** adjective **systematic**, logical, scientific, methodical, well organized, ordered, orderly, meticulous, rigorous.
– OPPOSITES unsystematic.

anarchic adjective **lawless**, unruly, chaotic, turbulent.
– OPPOSITES ordered.

anarchist noun **troublemaker**, nihilist, anti-capitalist, agitator, subversive, insurrectionist.

anarchy noun **lawlessness**, nihilism, mobocracy, disorder, chaos, tumult.
– OPPOSITES government, order.

anathema noun *racism was anathema to him:* **abhorrent**, hateful, repugnant, repellent, offensive; an abomination, an outrage.

anatomy noun **structure**, make-up, composition, constitution, form, body, physique.

ancestor noun **1** *he could trace his ancestors back to King James I:* **forebear**, forefather, predecessor, antecedent, progenitor. **2** *the instrument is an ancestor of the lute:* **forerunner**, precursor, predecessor.
– OPPOSITES descendant, successor.

a

ancestral adjective **inherited**, hereditary, familial.

ancestry noun **ancestors**, forebears, forefathers, progenitors, antecedents; family tree; lineage, genealogy, roots, blood.

anchor verb **1** *the ship was anchored in the bay:* **moor**, berth, make fast, be at anchor. **2** *the fish anchors itself to the coral:* **secure**, fasten, attach, fix.

ancient adjective **1** *tales of ancient civilizations:* **early**, prehistoric, primeval, primordial, primitive. **2** *an ancient custom:* **old**, age-old, archaic, antediluvian, time-worn, time-honoured. **3** *I feel positively ancient:* **antiquated**, decrepit, antediluvian, geriatric; informal out of the ark; Brit. informal past its/your sell-by date.
– OPPOSITES recent, contemporary.

WORD LINKS

archaeology the study of ancient history by examining objects dug up from the ground

palaeography the study of ancient writing systems

ancillary adjective **additional**, auxiliary, supporting, helping, extra, supplementary, accessory.

anecdotal adjective unscientific, unreliable, based on hearsay, unofficial.

anecdote noun **story**, tale, narrative; informal yarn.

angel noun (informal) *she's an angel:* saint, gem, treasure, darling, dear; informal star; Brit. informal, dated brick.
– OPPOSITES devil.

angelic adjective **innocent**, pure, virtuous, saintly, cherubic.

anger noun **annoyance**, vexation, exasperation, irritation, irritability, indignation; rage, fury, wrath, outrage, ill temper/humour.
– OPPOSITES pleasure, good humour.
• verb **annoy**, irritate, exasperate, irk, vex, put out; enrage, incense, infuriate; informal aggravate, rile, hack off.
– OPPOSITES pacify, placate.

angle noun **1** *the wall is sloping at an angle of 33°:* **gradient**, slant, inclination. **2** *consider the problem from a different angle:* **perspective**, point of view, viewpoint, standpoint, position, aspect, slant, direction, approach, tack.
• verb *Anna angled her camera upwards:* **tilt**, slant, direct, turn, twist, swivel, lean, tip.

angry adjective **1** *angry customers:* **annoyed**, irate, cross, vexed, irritated, indignant, irked; furious, enraged, infuriated, in a temper, fuming, seething, outraged; informal hopping mad, hot under the collar, up in arms, foaming at the mouth, steamed up, in a lather/paddy; Brit. informal aerated, shirty; N. Amer. informal sore, bent out of shape, teed off, ticked off; literary wrathful. **2** *an angry debate:* **heated**, passionate, stormy, lively, full and frank; bad-tempered, ill-tempered, acrimonious, bitter. **3** *angry sores:* **inflamed**, red, swollen, sore, painful.
– OPPOSITES pleased, good-humoured.
■ **get angry** lose your temper, go berserk, flare up; informal go mad/crazy, go bananas, hit the roof, go up the wall, see red, go off the deep end, fly off the handle, blow your top, blow a fuse/gasket, lose your rag, flip your lid, have a fit, foam at the mouth, explode, go ballistic; Brit. informal go spare, do your nut; N. Amer. informal flip your wig, blow your lid/stack.

angst noun **anxiety**, fear, worry, trepidation, malaise, disquiet, unease, anguish.

anguish noun **agony**, pain, torment, torture, suffering, distress, angst, misery, sorrow, grief, heartache.
– OPPOSITES happiness.

anguished adjective **agonized**, tormented, tortured; grief-stricken, wretched, heartbroken, devastated.

angular adjective **1** *an angular shape:* **sharp**, pointed, pointy. **2** *an angular face:* **bony**, lean, rangy, spare, thin, gaunt.
– OPPOSITES rounded, curving.

animal noun **1** *endangered animals:* **creature**, beast, living thing; (**animals**) wildlife, fauna; N. Amer. informal critter. **2** *the man was an animal:* **beast**, brute, monster, devil, demon, fiend; informal swine, pig.
• adjective *animal passion:* **carnal**, fleshly, bodily, physical; brutish, animalistic.

WORD LINKS
zoological relating to animals or zoology
zoology the scientific study of animals

animate verb **enliven**, energize, invigorate, revive, liven up; inspire, thrill, excite, fire, rouse; N. Amer. light a fire under; informal buck up, pep up.
– OPPOSITES depress.
• adjective **living**, breathing, alive, live; sentient, aware.
– OPPOSITES inanimate.

animated adjective **lively**, spirited, high-spirited, energetic, full of life, excited, enthusiastic, eager, alive, vigorous, vibrant, vivacious, buoyant, exuberant, ebullient, effervescent, bouncy, bubbly, perky; informal bright-eyed and bushy-tailed, full of beans, bright and breezy, chirpy, chipper, peppy.
– OPPOSITES lethargic, lifeless.

animosity noun **antipathy**, hostility, friction, antagonism, enmity, bitterness, rancour, resentment, dislike, ill feeling/will, bad blood, hatred, loathing.
– OPPOSITES goodwill, friendship.

annals plural noun **records**, archives, chronicles.

annex verb **take over**, appropriate, seize, conquer, occupy, invade.
• noun (also **annexe**) **extension**, addition; wing; N. Amer. ell.

annexation noun **seizure**, occupation, invasion, conquest, takeover, appropriation.

annihilate verb **destroy**, wipe out, obliterate, wipe off the face of the earth; kill, slaughter, exterminate, eliminate, liquidate; informal take out, rub out, snuff out, waste, blow away.
– OPPOSITES create.

annotate verb **comment on**, gloss, interpret, explain, elucidate.

annotation noun **note**, comment, gloss, footnote; commentary, explanation, interpretation, exegesis.

announce verb **1** *the results were announced:* **make public**, make known, report, declare, state, give out, publicize, broadcast, publish, advertise, circulate, proclaim, release. **2** *Victor announced the guests:* **introduce**, present. **3** *strains of music announced her arrival:* **signal**, indicate, herald, proclaim; literary betoken.

announcement noun **1** *an announcement by the Minister:* **statement**, declaration, proclamation, pronouncement; bulletin, communiqué; N. Amer. advisory. **2** *the announcement of the decision:* **declaration**, notification, reporting, publishing, broadcasting.

announcer noun **presenter**, anchorman, anchorwoman, anchor; newsreader, newscaster, broadcaster.

annoy verb **irritate**, vex, anger, exasperate, irk, gall, pique, put out, antagonize, get on someone's nerves, ruffle someone's feathers, make someone's hackles rise, nettle, rankle; Brit. rub up the wrong way; informal aggravate, peeve, hassle, miff, rile, needle, bug, hack off, get up someone's nose, get someone's goat, get someone's back up, give someone the hump, drive mad/crazy, drive round the bend/twist, drive up the wall, get someone's dander up; Brit. informal wind up, nark, get on someone's wick; N. Amer. informal tee off, tick off; informal, dated give someone the pip.
– OPPOSITES please, gratify.

annoyance noun **1** *much to his annoyance, she didn't even notice:* **irritation**, exasperation, vexation, indignation, anger, displeasure, chagrin. **2** *the Council found him an annoyance:* **nuisance**, pest, bother, irritant, inconvenience, thorn in your flesh; informal pain, drag; N. Amer. informal nudnik, burr under someone's saddle.

annoyed adjective **irritated**, cross, angry, vexed, exasperated, irked, piqued, displeased, put out, disgruntled, nettled, in a bad mood, in a temper; informal aggravated, peeved, miffed, riled, hacked off, hot under the collar; Brit. informal narked, shirty; N. Amer. informal teed off, ticked off, sore, bent out of shape; Austral./NZ informal snaky, crook; old use wroth.

annoying adjective **irritating**, infuriating, exasperating, maddening, trying, tiresome, troublesome, bothersome, irksome, vexing, galling; informal aggravating.

annual adjective **yearly**, once-a-year; year-long, twelve-month.

a

annually adverb **yearly**, once a year, each year, per annum.

annul verb **declare invalid**, declare null and void, nullify, invalidate, void; repeal, reverse, rescind, revoke.
– OPPOSITES restore, enact.

anodyne adjective **bland**, inoffensive, innocuous, neutral, unobjectionable.

anomalous adjective **abnormal**, atypical, irregular, aberrant, exceptional, freak, freakish, odd, bizarre, peculiar, unusual, out of the ordinary.
– OPPOSITES normal, typical.

anomaly noun **oddity**, peculiarity, abnormality, irregularity, inconsistency, incongruity, aberration, quirk.

anonymous adjective **1** *an anonymous donor:* **unnamed**, nameless, unidentified, unknown. **2** *an anonymous letter:* **unsigned**, unattributed. **3** *an anonymous housing estate:* **characterless**, nondescript, impersonal, faceless; grey.
– OPPOSITES known, identified.

answer noun **1** *her answer was unequivocal:* **reply**, response, rejoinder, reaction; retort, riposte; informal comeback. **2** *a new filter is the answer:* **solution**, remedy, way out.
– OPPOSITES question.
• verb **1** *Steve was about to answer:* **reply**, respond; rejoin, retort, riposte. **2** *he has yet to answer the charges:* **rebut**, refute, defend yourself against. **3** *a man answering this description:* **match**, fit, correspond to.
■ **answer for** *he will answer for his crime:* pay for, be punished for, suffer for; make amends for, make reparation for, atone for.

answerable adjective **accountable**, responsible, liable; subject.

ant noun

WORD LINKS
formic relating to ants
myrmecology the study of ants

antagonism noun **hostility**, enmity, antipathy, opposition, dissension; bitterness, rancour, resentment, dislike, ill/bad feeling, ill will.
– OPPOSITES rapport, friendship.

antagonist noun **adversary**, opponent, enemy, rival.
– OPPOSITES ally.

antagonistic adjective **hostile**, against, dead set against, opposed, inimical, antipathetic, ill-disposed, resistant, in disagreement; informal anti.

antagonize verb **anger**, annoy, provoke, vex, irritate; Brit. rub up the wrong way; informal aggravate, rile, needle, rattle someone's cage, get someone's back up, get someone's dander up; Brit. informal nark.
– OPPOSITES pacify, placate.

antediluvian adjective **out of date**, outdated, outmoded, old-fashioned, antiquated, behind the times.

anteroom noun **antechamber**, vestibule, lobby, foyer.

anthem noun **hymn**, song, chorale.

anthology noun **collection**, selection, compendium, compilation, miscellany.

anticipate verb **1** *the police did not anticipate trouble:* **expect**, foresee, predict, be prepared for, bargain on, reckon on; N. Amer. informal figure on. **2** *warders can't always anticipate the actions of prisoners:* **pre-empt**, forestall, second-guess. **3** *her plays anticipated her film work:* **foreshadow**, precede, antedate, come/go before.

anticipation noun **expectation**, excitement, suspense.
■ **in anticipation of** in the expectation of, in preparation for, ready for.

anticlimax noun **let-down**, bathos, disappointment, comedown, non-event; disillusionment; Brit. damp squib; informal washout.

antics plural noun **capers**, pranks, larks, high jinks, skylarking; Brit. informal monkey tricks.

antidote noun *laughter is a good antidote to stress:* **remedy**, cure; solution; coping mechanism.

antipathetic adjective **hostile**, against, dead set against, opposed, antagonistic, ill-disposed, unsympathetic; informal anti, down on.

antipathy noun **hostility**, antagonism, animosity, aversion, enmity, dislike, distaste, hatred, abhorrence, loathing.
– OPPOSITES liking, affinity.

antiquated adjective **outdated**, out of date, outmoded, outworn, behind

the times, old-fashioned, anachronistic; informal out of the ark; N. Amer. informal horse-and-buggy, mossy, clunky.
– OPPOSITES modern, up to date.

antique noun **collector's item**, period piece, bygone, antiquity, object of virtu.
• adjective **old**, ancient; antiquarian, vintage, collectable.
– OPPOSITES modern, state-of-the-art.

antiquity noun **1** *the civilizations of antiquity:* **long ago**, the past, prehistory, classical/ancient times. **2** *Islamic antiquities:* **antique**, artefact, treasure, object, collector's piece.

antisocial adjective **1** *antisocial behaviour*: objectionable, offensive, unacceptable, disruptive, rowdy. **2** *I'm feeling a bit antisocial:* **unsociable**, unfriendly, uncommunicative, reclusive.

antithesis noun **direct opposite**, converse, reverse, inverse, obverse, the other side of the coin; informal the flip side.

antithetical adjective **directly opposed**, contrasting, contrary, contradictory, conflicting, incompatible, irreconcilable, inconsistent, poles apart, at variance/odds.
– OPPOSITES identical, like.

anxiety noun **worry**, concern, apprehension, apprehensiveness, uneasiness, unease, fearfulness, fear, disquiet, agitation, angst, nervousness, nerves, tenseness; informal butterflies (in your stomach), jitteriness, twitchiness, collywobbles.
– OPPOSITES serenity.

anxious adjective **1** *I'm anxious about her:* **worried**, concerned, apprehensive, fearful, uneasy, perturbed, troubled, bothered, disturbed, distressed, fretful, agitated, nervous, edgy, unquiet, on edge, tense, worked up, keyed up, jumpy; informal uptight, with butterflies in your stomach, jittery, twitchy, all of a dither, in a tizz/tizzy, het up; Brit. informal strung up, windy; N. Amer. informal antsy, spooky, squirrelly; Austral./NZ informal toey. **2** *she was anxious for news:* **eager**, keen, desirous, impatient.
– OPPOSITES carefree, serene, unconcerned.

apart adverb
■ **apart from** except for, but for, aside from, with the exception of, excepting, excluding, bar, barring, besides, other than; informal outside of; formal save.

apartment noun **1** *a rented apartment:* **flat**, penthouse; Austral. home unit; N. Amer. informal crib. **2** *the royal apartments:* **suite**, rooms, quarters, accommodation.

apathetic adjective **uninterested**, indifferent, unconcerned, unmoved, uninvolved, unemotional, emotionless, dispassionate, lukewarm; informal couldn't-care-less.

apathy noun **indifference**, lack of interest/enthusiasm, unconcern, unresponsiveness, impassivity, dispassion, dispassionateness, lethargy, languor.
– OPPOSITES enthusiasm, passion.

ape noun **primate**; technical anthropoid.
• verb *he aped Barbara's accent:* **imitate**, mimic, copy, do an impression of; informal take off, send up.

> **WORD LINKS**
> **simian** relating to apes and monkeys
> **primatology** the branch of zoology concerned with apes and monkeys

aperture noun **opening**, hole, gap, slit, slot, vent, crevice, chink, crack; technical orifice.

apex noun **1** *the apex of a pyramid:* **tip**, peak, summit, pinnacle, top, vertex. **2** *the apex of his career:* **climax**, culmination, apotheosis; peak, pinnacle, zenith, acme, apogee, highest point.
– OPPOSITES bottom, nadir.

aphorism noun **saying**, maxim, axiom, adage, epigram, dictum, gnome, proverb, saw, tag.

aplomb noun **poise**, self-assurance, self-confidence, calmness, composure, collectedness, levelheadedness, sangfroid, equilibrium, equanimity; informal unflappability.

apocryphal adjective **fictitious**, made-up, untrue, fabricated, false, spurious; unverified, unauthenticated, unsubstantiated.
– OPPOSITES authentic.

apologetic adjective **regretful**, sorry, contrite, remorseful,

penitent, repentant; conscience-stricken, shamefaced, ashamed.
– OPPOSITES unrepentant.

apologist noun **defender**, supporter, upholder, advocate, proponent, exponent, propagandist, champion, campaigner.
– OPPOSITES critic.

apologize verb **say sorry**, express regret, ask forgiveness, ask for pardon, eat humble pie.

apology noun **1** *I owe you an apology:* **expression of regret**, your regrets. **2** (informal) *an apology for a flat:* **travesty**, inadequate/poor example; informal excuse.

apoplectic adjective (informal) **furious**, enraged, infuriated, incensed, raging; incandescent, fuming, seething; informal hopping mad, livid, foaming at the mouth.

apostle noun **advocate**, apologist, proponent, exponent, promoter, supporter, upholder, champion; convert; N. Amer. booster.

apotheosis noun **culmination**, climax, peak, pinnacle, zenith, acme, apogee, highest point.
– OPPOSITES nadir.

appal verb **horrify**, shock, dismay, distress, outrage, scandalize; disgust, repel, revolt, sicken, nauseate, offend, make someone's blood run cold.

appalling adjective **1** *an appalling crime:* **shocking**, horrific, awful, horrifying, horrible, terrible, dreadful, ghastly, hideous, horrendous, frightful, atrocious, abominable, abhorrent, outrageous, gruesome, grisly, monstrous, heinous. **2** (informal) *your schoolwork is appalling:* **dreadful**, awful, terrible, frightful, atrocious, disgraceful, deplorable, hopeless, lamentable; informal rotten, crummy, pathetic, pitiful, woeful, useless, lousy, abysmal, dire; Brit. informal chronic, shocking.

apparatus noun **1** *laboratory apparatus:* **equipment**, gear, tackle, paraphernalia, accoutrements; appliances, instruments. **2** *the apparatus of government:* **machinery**, system, framework, organization.

apparent adjective **1** *their relief was all too apparent:* **evident**, plain, obvious, clear, manifest, visible, discernible, perceptible; unmistakable, crystal clear, palpable, patent, blatant, as plain as a pikestaff, writ large; informal as plain as the nose on your face, written all over your face. **2** *his apparent lack of concern:* **seeming**, ostensible, outward, superficial.
– OPPOSITES unclear.

apparently adverb **seemingly**, evidently, it seems, it appears, by all accounts; ostensibly, outwardly, on the face of it, so the story goes; allegedly, reputedly.

apparition noun **ghost**, phantom, spectre, spirit, wraith; informal spook; literary phantasm.

appeal verb **1** *police are appealing for information:* **ask**, call, plead. **2** *Andrew appealed to me to help them:* **implore**, beg, entreat, call on, plead with, exhort, ask, request, petition; literary beseech. **3** *the thought of travelling appealed to me:* **attract**, interest, take someone's fancy, fascinate, tempt, entice, allure, lure, draw, whet someone's appetite; informal float someone's boat.
• noun **1** *an appeal for help:* **plea**, request, entreaty, cry, call. **2** *the cultural appeal of the island:* **attraction**, attractiveness, allure, charm; fascination, magnetism, drawing power, pull.

appealing adjective **attractive**, engaging, alluring, enchanting, captivating, bewitching, fascinating, tempting, enticing, seductive, irresistible, winning, winsome, charming, desirable; Brit. informal tasty.
– OPPOSITES disagreeable, off-putting.

appear verb **1** *a cloud of dust appeared on the horizon:* **become visible**, come into view/sight, materialize, pop up. **2** *fundamental differences were beginning to appear:* **be revealed**, emerge, surface, manifest itself, become apparent/evident, come to light; arise, crop up. **3** (informal) *he eventually appeared after dinner:* **arrive**, turn up, put in an appearance, come, get here/there; informal show up, roll up. **4** *they appeared to be completely devoted:* **seem**, look, give the impression, come across as,

strike someone as. **5** *he appeared on Broadway:* **perform**, play, act.
– OPPOSITES vanish, disappear.

appearance noun **1** *her dishevelled appearance:* **looks**, air, aspect, mien. **2** *an appearance of respectability:* **impression**, air, show; semblance, facade, veneer, front, pretence. **3** *the sudden appearance of her daughter:* **arrival**, advent, coming, emergence, materialization. **4** *the appearance of these symptoms:* **occurrence**, manifestation, development.

appease verb **conciliate**, placate, pacify, propitiate, reconcile, win over; informal sweeten.
– OPPOSITES provoke, inflame.

appeasement noun **conciliation**, placation, pacification, propitiation, reconciliation; peacemaking, peacemongering.
– OPPOSITES provocation.

append verb **add**, attach, affix, tack on, tag on, join on.

appendage noun **protuberance**, projection; limb.

appendix noun *a three-page appendix was added:* **supplement**, addendum, postscript, codicil; coda, epilogue, afterword, tailpiece.

appetite noun **1** *a walk sharpens the appetite:* **hunger**, taste, palate. **2** *my appetite for learning:* **craving**, longing, yearning, hankering, hunger, thirst, passion; enthusiasm, keenness, eagerness, desire, yen.

appetizer noun **starter**, first course, hors d'oeuvre, amuse-gueule, antipasto.

appetizing adjective **mouth-watering**, inviting, tempting; tasty, delicious, flavoursome, toothsome, delectable; informal scrumptious, scrummy, yummy, moreish.
– OPPOSITES bland, unappealing.

applaud verb **1** *the audience applauded:* **clap**, give a standing ovation, put your hands together; informal give someone a big hand. **2** *police have applauded the decision:* **praise**, commend, salute, welcome, celebrate, approve of, sing the praises of, pay tribute to, speak highly of, take your hat off to.
– OPPOSITES boo, criticize.

applause noun **clapping**, standing ovation; cheering.

appliance noun **1** *domestic appliances:* **device**, machine, instrument, gadget, contraption, apparatus, implement, mechanism, contrivance, labour-saving device; informal gizmo. **2** *the appliance of science:* **application**, use, exercise, employment, implementation, utilization, practice, applying, discharge, execution, prosecution, enactment.

applicable adjective **relevant**, appropriate, pertinent, apposite, germane, material, significant, related, connected; fitting, suitable, apt.
– OPPOSITES inappropriate, irrelevant.

applicant noun **candidate**, interviewee, competitor, contestant, contender, entrant; claimant, petitioner; prospective student/employee, job-seeker.

application noun **1** *an application for an overdraft:* **request**, appeal, petition, entreaty, plea; approach, claim, demand. **2** *the application of anti-inflation policies:* **implementation**, use, exercise, employment, utilization, applying, discharge, execution, prosecution, enactment. **3** *the argument is clearest in its application to the theatre:* **relevance**, bearing, significance, aptness, importance. **4** *the job requires a great deal of application:* **hard work**, diligence, industriousness, commitment, dedication, devotion, conscientiousness, perseverance, persistence, tenacity, doggedness; concentration, attention, attentiveness, steadiness, patience, endurance; effort, labour, endeavour. **5** *a new graphics application:* **program**, software, routine.

apply verb **1** *300 people applied for the job:* **bid**, put in, try, petition, register, audition; request, seek, solicit, claim, ask. **2** *the Act did not apply to Scotland:* **be relevant**, have a bearing, pertain, relate, concern, affect, involve, cover, deal with, touch. **3** *she applied some ointment:* **put on**, rub in/on, work in, spread, smear on, slap on. **4** *a steady pressure should be applied:* **exert**, administer, use, exercise, employ, utilize, bring to bear.

a

■ **apply yourself** work hard, be industrious, show commitment, show dedication; exert yourself, make an effort, try hard, do your best, give your all, buckle down, put your shoulder to the wheel, keep your nose to the grindstone; strive, endeavour, struggle, labour, toil; pay attention, commit yourself, devote yourself; persevere, persist; informal put your back in it, knuckle down, get stuck in.

appoint verb **nominate**, name, designate, install as, commission, engage, co-opt; select, choose, elect, vote in.
–OPPOSITES reject.

appointed adjective **1** *I arrived at the appointed time:* **scheduled**, arranged, prearranged, specified, agreed, designated, allotted, set, fixed, chosen, established, settled, prescribed, decreed. **2** *a well appointed room:* **furnished**, decorated, fitted out, supplied.

appointment noun **1** *a six o'clock appointment:* **meeting**, engagement, interview, consultation, session; date, rendezvous, assignation; commitment, fixture. **2** *the appointment of directors:* nomination, naming, designation, installation, commissioning, engagement, co-option; selection, choosing, election. **3** *he held an appointment at the university:* **job**, post, position, situation, place, office.

apportion verb **share**, divide, allocate, distribute, allot, assign, give out, hand out, mete out, deal out, dish out, dole out; ration, measure out; split; informal divvy up.

apposite adjective **appropriate**, suitable, fitting, apt, befitting; relevant, pertinent, to the point, applicable, germane, material.
–OPPOSITES inappropriate.

appraisal noun **1** *an objective appraisal of the book:* **assessment**, evaluation, estimation, judgement, summing-up, consideration. **2** *a free insurance appraisal:* **valuation**, estimate, estimation, quotation.

appraise verb *your manager will appraise your performance:* **assess**, evaluate, judge, rate, gauge, review, consider; informal size up.

> Don't confuse **appraise** with **apprise**, which means 'inform' (*they apprised him of the situation*).

appreciable adjective **considerable**, substantial, significant, sizeable, goodly, fair, reasonable, marked; perceptible, noticeable, visible; informal tidy.
–OPPOSITES negligible.

appreciate verb **1** *I don't feel I'm appreciated here:* **value**, admire, respect, think highly of, recognize, esteem. **2** *I'd appreciate your advice:* **be grateful**, be thankful, be indebted. **3** *we appreciate the problems:* **recognize**, acknowledge, realize, know, be aware of, be conscious of, be sensitive to, understand. **4** *a home that will appreciate in value:* **increase**, gain, grow, rise, go up.
–OPPOSITES disparage, depreciate, decrease.

appreciation noun **1** *he showed his appreciation:* **gratitude**, thanks, gratefulness, thankfulness, recognition. **2** *her appreciation of literature:* **knowledge**, awareness, enjoyment, love; feeling, discrimination, sensitivity. **3** *an appreciation of the value of teamwork:* **acknowledgement**, recognition, realization, knowledge, awareness, consciousness, understanding, comprehension. **4** *the appreciation of the franc against the pound:* **increase**, gain, growth, rise, inflation, escalation. **5** *an appreciation of the professor's work:* **review**, critique, criticism, analysis, assessment, evaluation, judgement; Brit. informal crit.
–OPPOSITES ingratitude, unawareness, depreciation, decrease.

appreciative adjective **1** *we are appreciative of all your efforts:* **grateful**, thankful, obliged, indebted. **2** *an appreciative audience:* **supportive**, encouraging, sympathetic, responsive; receptive, enthusiastic, admiring, approving, complimentary.
–OPPOSITES ungrateful, disparaging.

apprehend verb **1** *the thieves were quickly apprehended:* **arrest**, catch, capture, seize; take prisoner, take into custody; informal collar, nab, nail, run in, bust, pick up, pull in, feel someone's collar; Brit. informal nick. **2** *they are slow to apprehend danger:* **appreciate**, recognize, discern, perceive, grasp, understand, comprehend.

apprehension noun **1** *he was filled with apprehension:* **anxiety**, worry, unease, nervousness, nerves, misgivings, disquiet, concern, tension, trepidation, consternation, angst, dread, fear, foreboding; informal butterflies (in your stomach), the heebie-jeebies. **2** *the apprehension of a perpetrator:* **arrest**, capture, seizure; detention; informal bust.
– OPPOSITES confidence.

apprehensive adjective **anxious**, worried, uneasy, nervous, concerned, agitated, tense, afraid, scared, frightened, fearful.
– OPPOSITES confident.

apprentice noun **trainee**, learner, probationer, novice, beginner, starter; pupil, student; informal rookie; N. Amer. informal tenderfoot, greenhorn.
– OPPOSITES veteran.

apprise verb *he was apprised of the situation:* **inform**, tell, notify, advise, brief, make aware, enlighten, update, keep posted; informal clue in, fill in, put wise, put in the picture.

> ! Don't confuse **apprise** with **appraise**, which means 'assess' (*your manager will appraise your performance*).

approach verb **1** *she approached the altar:* **move towards**, come/go towards, advance on, draw near, near; close in on, gain on, bear down on. **2** *the trade deficit is approaching £20 million:* **border on**, verge on, approximate, touch, nudge, get on for, near, come/be close to. **3** *she approached him about a pay rise:* **speak to**, talk to, sound out, proposition. **4** *he approached the problem in the best way:* **tackle**, address, manage, set about.
– OPPOSITES leave.
• noun **1** *the traditional British approach:* **method**, procedure, technique, modus operandi, style, way; strategy, tactic, system, means, line of action. **2** *he considered an approach to the High Court:* **proposal**, submission, application, appeal, plea, request. **3** *the dog barked at the approach of any intruder:* **advance**, arrival, appearance. **4** *the approach to the castle:* **driveway**, drive, road; way.

approachable adjective **1** *students found the staff approachable:* **friendly**, welcoming, pleasant, agreeable, congenial, affable, cordial; obliging, helpful. **2** *the south landing is approachable by boat:* **accessible**, reachable; informal get-at-able.
– OPPOSITES aloof, inaccessible.

approbation noun **approval**, acceptance, endorsement, appreciation, respect, admiration, commendation, praise, congratulations, acclaim, esteem, applause.
– OPPOSITES criticism.

appropriate adjective *this isn't the appropriate time:* **suitable**, proper, fitting, apt, right; relevant, apposite; convenient, opportune; seemly, befitting.
– OPPOSITES unsuitable, inappropriate .
• verb **1** *the barons appropriated church lands:* **seize**, commandeer, expropriate, annex, sequestrate, sequester, take over, hijack; steal, take; informal swipe, nab; Brit. informal pinch, half-inch, nick. **2** *his images have been appropriated by advertisers:* **plagiarize**, copy; poach, steal, swipe, 'borrow'; informal rip off, pinch, half-inch, nick.

approval noun **1** *their proposals went to the ministry for approval:* **acceptance**, agreement, consent, assent, permission, leave, the nod; rubber stamp, sanction, endorsement, ratification, authorization, validation; support, backing; informal the go-ahead, the green light, the OK, the thumbs up. **2** *Lily looked at him with approval:* **approbation**, appreciation, admiration, regard, esteem, respect.
– OPPOSITES disapproval, refusal.

approve verb **1** *his boss doesn't approve of his lifestyle:* **agree with**, hold with, endorse, support, be in favour of, favour, think well of, like, take kindly to; admire. **2** *the government approved the proposals:* **accept**, agree to, consent to, assent to, give your blessing to, bless,

rubber-stamp, give the nod; ratify, sanction, endorse, authorize, validate, pass; support, back; informal give the go-ahead, give the green light, give the OK, give the thumbs up.
– OPPOSITES condemn, refuse.

approximate adjective **estimated**, rough, imprecise, inexact, broad, loose; N. Amer. informal ballpark.
– OPPOSITES precise.
• verb **be/come close to**, be/come near to, approach, border on, verge on; resemble, be similar to.

approximately adverb **roughly**, about, around, circa, round about, more or less, in the neighbourhood of, in the region of, of the order of, give or take; near to, close to, circa, nearly, almost, approaching; N. Amer. informal in the ballpark of.
– OPPOSITES precisely.

approximation noun **1** *the figure is only an approximation:* **estimate**, estimation, guess, rough calculation; informal guesstimate; N. Amer. informal ballpark figure. **2** *an approximation to the truth:* **semblance**, resemblance, likeness, similarity, correspondence.

apt adjective **1** *a very apt description:* **suitable**, fitting, appropriate, relevant, applicable, apposite; Brit. informal spot on. **2** *they are apt to be a bit slipshod:* **inclined**, given, likely, liable, prone.
– OPPOSITES inappropriate, unlikely.

aptitude noun **talent**, gift, flair, bent, skill, knack, facility, ability, capability, potential, capacity, faculty, genius.

aquatic adjective **marine**, water, saltwater, freshwater, seawater, sea, oceanic, river.

arbiter noun **1** *an arbiter between Moscow and Washington.* See **ARBITRATOR**. **2** *the great arbiter of fashion:* **authority**, judge, controller, director; master, expert, pundit.

arbitrary adjective **capricious**, whimsical, random, chance, unpredictable; casual, wanton, motiveless, unreasoned, irrational, illogical, groundless, unjustified.
– OPPOSITES reasoned.

arbitrate verb **adjudicate**, judge, referee, umpire; mediate, intervene, intercede; settle, decide, resolve, pass judgement.

arbitration noun **adjudication**, judgement; mediation, conciliation, intervention.

arbitrator noun **adjudicator**, arbiter, judge, referee, umpire; mediator, intervenor, go-between.

arc noun **curve**, arch, crescent, semicircle, half-moon; curvature, convexity.

arcade noun **1** *a classical arcade:* **gallery**, colonnade, loggia, portico, cloister. **2** (Brit.) *a cafe in the arcade:* **shopping centre**, market, galleria; N. Amer. plaza, mall.

arcane adjective **mysterious**, secret, covert, clandestine; enigmatic, esoteric, obscure, abstruse, recondite, impenetrable, opaque.

arch[1] noun *a stone arch:* **archway**, vault.
• verb *she arched her eyebrows:* **curve**, arc; raise.

arch[2] adjective *an arch grin:* **mischievous**, teasing, knowing, playful, roguish, impish, cheeky.

arch- combining form *his arch-enemy:* **chief**, principal, foremost, leading, main, major, prime, premier, greatest; informal number-one.
– OPPOSITES minor.

archaic adjective **obsolete**, out of date, old-fashioned, outmoded, behind the times, bygone, anachronistic, antiquated, superannuated, antediluvian, olde worlde; ancient, old, extinct, defunct; informal out of the ark.
– OPPOSITES modern.

archetypal adjective **quintessential**, classic, typical, representative, model, exemplary, textbook, copybook; stock, stereotypical, prototypical.
– OPPOSITES atypical.

archetype noun **quintessence**, essence, representative, model, embodiment, prototype, stereotype; original, pattern, standard, paradigm, exemplar.

architect noun **originator**, author, creator, founder, founding father; engineer, inventor.

architecture noun **1** *modern architecture:* **building**, planning, design, construction. **2** *computer* *architecture:* **structure**, construction, organization, layout, design, build, make-up; informal set-up.

WORD LINKS
architectonic relating to architecture

archive noun **1** *she delved into the family archives:* **records**, annals, chronicles; papers, documents, files; history. **2** *the National Sound Archive:* **record office**, registry, repository, museum, library. • verb *the videos are archived for future use:* **file**, log, catalogue, document, record, register; store, cache.

arctic adjective **1** *Arctic waters:* **polar**, northern; literary hyperborean; technical boreal. **2** *arctic weather conditions:* **bitterly cold**, wintry, freezing, frozen, icy, glacial, sub-zero, polar, Siberian.
– OPPOSITES Antarctic, tropical.

ardent adjective **passionate**, fervent, zealous, wholehearted, intense; enthusiastic, keen, eager, avid, committed, dedicated.
– OPPOSITES apathetic.

ardour noun **passion**, fervour, zeal, intensity; enthusiasm, eagerness, keenness, dedication.

arduous adjective **onerous**, taxing, difficult, hard, heavy, laborious, strenuous, vigorous, back-breaking; demanding, tough, challenging, formidable; exhausting, tiring, punishing, gruelling; informal killing; Brit. informal knackering.
– OPPOSITES easy.

area noun **1** *an inner-city area:* **district**, region, zone, sector, quarter; locality, locale, neighbourhood, parish, patch; tract, belt; informal neck of the woods; Brit. informal manor; N. Amer. informal turf. **2** *specific areas of scientific knowledge:* **field**, sphere, realm, domain, sector, province, territory, line. **3** *the dining area:* **section**, space; place, room.

arena noun **1** *an ice-hockey arena:* **stadium**, amphitheatre; ground, field, ring, rink, pitch, court; N. Amer. bowl, park. **2** *the political arena:* **scene**, sphere, realm, province, domain, sector, forum, territory, world.

argot noun **jargon**, slang, cant, parlance, vernacular, patois; dialect, speech, language; informal lingo.

arguable adjective **debatable**, questionable, open to question, controversial, contentious, doubtful, uncertain, moot.
– OPPOSITES untenable, certain.

arguably adverb **possibly**, conceivably, feasibly, plausibly, probably, maybe, perhaps.

argue verb **1** *the children are always arguing:* **quarrel**, disagree, squabble, fall out, bicker, fight, wrangle, feud, have words, cross swords, lock horns, be at each other's throats; Brit. row. **2** *they argued that the government was to blame:* **contend**, assert, maintain, submit, insist, hold, claim, reason, swear, allege; formal aver, opine.

argument noun **1** *he had an argument with his brother:* **quarrel**, disagreement, squabble, fight, dispute, wrangle, clash, altercation, feud, contretemps, falling-out; Brit. row; informal tiff, slanging match; Brit. informal barney. **2** *arguments for the existence of God:* **reasoning**, justification, explanation, rationalization; case, defence, vindication; evidence, reasons, grounds.

argumentative adjective **quarrelsome**, disputatious, contrary, cantankerous, contentious; belligerent, bellicose, combative, antagonistic, truculent, pugnacious.

arid adjective **1** *an arid landscape:* **dry**, waterless, parched, scorched, baked, thirsty, desiccated, desert; barren, infertile. **2** *an arid documentary:* **dreary**, dull, drab, dry, sterile, colourless, uninspiring, flat, boring, uninteresting, lifeless.
– OPPOSITES wet, fertile.

arise verb **1** *many problems arose:* **come to light**, become apparent, appear, emerge, crop up, turn up, surface, spring up; occur; literary come to pass. **2** *injuries arising from defective products:* **result**, proceed, follow, ensue, derive, stem, originate.

aristocracy noun **nobility**, peerage, gentry, upper class, ruling class, elite, lords, ladies, peers (of the realm), nobles, noblemen, noblewomen; informal upper crust, top drawer, aristos; Brit. informal nobs, toffs.
– OPPOSITES working class.

aristocrat noun **nobleman, noblewoman**, lord, lady, peer (of the realm), peeress; informal aristo; Brit. informal toff, nob.
– OPPOSITES commoner.

aristocratic adjective **1** *an aristocratic family:* **noble**, titled, upper-class, blue-blooded, high-born; informal upper crust, top drawer; Brit. informal posh; old use gentle. **2** *an aristocratic manner:* **refined**, polished, courtly, dignified, decorous, gracious, fine, gentlemanly, ladylike; haughty, proud.
– OPPOSITES working-class, vulgar.

arm[1] noun *the political arm of the group:* **branch**, section, department, division, wing, sector.

arm[2] verb **1** *he armed himself with a revolver:* **equip**, provide, supply, furnish, issue, fit out. **2** *arm yourself against criticism:* **prepare**, make ready, brace, steel, fortify.

armada noun **fleet**, flotilla; literary navy.

armaments plural noun **arms**, weapons, weaponry, firearms, guns, ordnance, artillery, munitions, materiel.

armistice noun **truce**, ceasefire, peace, suspension of hostilities.

armoured adjective **armour-plated**, steel-plated, ironclad; bulletproof, bombproof; reinforced, toughened.

arms plural noun **weapons**, weaponry, firearms, guns, ordnance, artillery, armaments, munitions.

army noun **1** *the invading army:* **armed force**, military force, land force, military, soldiery, infantry, militia; troops, soldiers. **2** *an army of tourists:* **crowd**, swarm, horde, multitude, mob, gang, throng, mass, flock, herd, pack.

> **WORD LINKS**
> **military** relating to soldiers or armed forces

aroma noun **smell**, odour, fragrance, scent, perfume, bouquet, nose.

aromatic adjective **fragrant**, scented, perfumed, fragranced.

around preposition *the cost would be around £1,500:* **approximately**, about, round about, circa, roughly, more or less, in the region of, in the neighbourhood of, give or take; nearly, close to, approaching; N. Amer. informal in the ballpark of.

arouse verb **1** *the meeting had aroused suspicion:* **provoke**, trigger, stir up, kindle, engender, cause, foster. **2** *his ability to arouse the masses:* **stir up**, rouse, galvanize, excite, electrify, stimulate, inspire, move, fire up, whip up, get going, inflame, agitate, goad, incite. **3** *she was aroused from her sleep:* **wake**, awaken, bring to/round, rouse; literary waken.
– OPPOSITES allay, pacify.

arraign verb **indict**, prosecute, put on trial, bring to trial, take to court, summons, cite; accuse of, charge with; N. Amer. impeach.
– OPPOSITES acquit, praise.

arrange verb **1** *the figures are arranged in 12 rows:* **set out**, order, lay out, array, position, present, display, exhibit; group, sort, organize, tidy. **2** *they hoped to arrange a meeting:* **organize**, fix, plan, schedule, contrive, settle on, decide, determine, agree. **3** *he arranged the piece for a full orchestra:* **adapt**, set, score, orchestrate.

arrangement noun **1** *the arrangement of the furniture:* **positioning**, presentation; grouping, organization, alignment. **2** *the arrangements for my trip:* **preparation**, plan, provision; planning. **3** *we had an arrangement:* **agreement**, deal, understanding, bargain, settlement, pact. **4** *an arrangement of Beethoven's symphonies:* **adaptation**, orchestration.

array noun **range**, collection, selection, assortment, variety; line-up; display, exhibition.
• verb **arrange**, assemble, group, order, range, place, position, set out, lay out, spread out; display.

arrears plural noun **outstanding payments**, debts, liabilities, dues.
– OPPOSITES credit.
■ **in arrears** behind, late, overdue, in the red, in debt.

arrest verb **1** *police arrested him for murder:* **apprehend**, take into custody; informal pick up, pull in, pinch, bust, nab, do, collar; Brit. informal nick. **2** *the spread of the*

disease can be arrested: **stop**, halt, check, block, curb; prevent, obstruct.
– OPPOSITES release, start.
• noun **detention**, apprehension, seizure, capture.

arresting adjective *an arresting image:* **striking**, eye-catching, conspicuous, engaging, impressive, imposing, spectacular, dramatic, breathtaking, stunning, awe-inspiring; distinctive.
– OPPOSITES inconspicuous.

arrival noun **1** *they awaited Ruth's arrival:* **coming**, appearance, entrance, entry, approach. **2** *staff greeted the late arrivals:* **comer**, entrant, incomer; visitor, caller, guest. **3** *the arrival of democracy:* **emergence**, appearance, advent, coming, dawn, onset.
– OPPOSITES departure, end.

arrive verb **1** *more police arrived:* **come**, turn up, get here/there, make it, appear, enter, present yourself, come along, materialize; informal show up, roll in/up, blow in, show your face. **2** *we arrived at his house at 10.30:* **reach**, get to, come to, make, end up at. **3** *they arrived at an agreement:* **reach**, achieve, attain, gain, accomplish; work out, draw up, put together, strike, settle on; informal clinch. **4** *virtual reality had arrived:* **emerge**, appear, surface, dawn, be born, come into being, arise.
– OPPOSITES depart, leave.

arrogant adjective **haughty**, conceited, self-important, egotistic, full of yourself, superior; overbearing, pompous, bumptious, imperious, overweening; proud, immodest; informal high and mighty, too big for your boots, big-headed.
– OPPOSITES modest.

arrow noun **1** *a bow and arrow:* **shaft**, bolt, dart. **2** *the arrow pointed right:* **pointer**, indicator, marker, needle.

> **WORD LINKS**
> **fletcher** (in the past) a maker of arrows

arsenal noun **1** *Britain's nuclear arsenal:* **weapons**, weaponry, arms, armaments. **2** *mutineers broke into the arsenal:* **armoury**, arms depot, arms cache, ordnance depot, magazine, ammunition dump.

art noun **1** *he studied art:* **fine art**, design; aesthetics. **2** *the art of public speaking:* **skill**, craft, technique, knack; facility, ability.

artful adjective **sly**, crafty, cunning, wily, scheming, devious, Machiavellian, sneaky, tricky, conniving, designing, calculating; canny, shrewd; deceitful, duplicitous, underhand.
– OPPOSITES ingenuous.

article noun **1** *small household articles:* **object**, thing, item, artefact, commodity, product. **2** *an article in The Times:* **report**, account, story, write-up, feature, item, piece, column, review, commentary. **3** *the crucial article of the treaty:* **clause**, section, subsection, point, item, paragraph, part, portion.

articulate adjective *an articulate speaker:* **eloquent**, fluent, effective, persuasive, lucid, expressive, silver-tongued.
– OPPOSITES inarticulate.
• verb *they were unable to articulate their emotions:* **express**, voice, vocalize, put in words, communicate, state.

articulated adjective **hinged**, jointed, segmented.

artifice noun **trickery**, deceit, deception, duplicity, guile, cunning, artfulness, wiliness, craftiness, slyness, chicanery.

artificial adjective **1** *artificial flowers:* **synthetic**, fake, imitation, mock, ersatz, substitute, replica, faux, reproduction; man-made, manufactured, plastic; informal pretend. **2** *an artificial smile:* **insincere**, feigned, false, unnatural, contrived, put-on, exaggerated, forced, laboured, strained, hollow; informal pretend, phoney.
– OPPOSITES natural, genuine.

artisan noun **craftsman**, craftswoman, craftsperson, technician; smith, wright, journeyman; old use artificer.

artist noun **expert**, master, maestro, virtuoso, genius; informal pro, ace; Brit. informal dab hand.
– OPPOSITES novice.

artiste noun **entertainer**, performer, showman, artist; player, musician, singer, dancer, actor, actress; star.

a

artistic adjective **creative**, imaginative, inventive, expressive; sensitive, perceptive, discerning.
– OPPOSITES unimaginative.

artistry noun **creativity**, skill, art, talent, genius, brilliance, flair, proficiency, virtuosity, finesse, style; craftsmanship, workmanship.

artless adjective **natural**, ingenuous, naive, simple, innocent, childlike, guileless; candid, open, sincere, unaffected.
– OPPOSITES scheming.

ascend verb **climb**, go up/upwards, move up/upwards, rise; mount, scale, conquer.
– OPPOSITES descend.

ascendancy noun **dominance**, supremacy, superiority, predominance, primacy, dominion, hegemony, authority, control, command, power, rule, sovereignty.
– OPPOSITES subordination.

ascent noun **1** *the ascent of the Matterhorn:* **climbing**, scaling, conquest. **2** *the ascent grew steeper:* **slope**, incline, gradient.
– OPPOSITES descent, drop.

ascertain verb **find out**, discover, get to know, work out, learn, deduce, divine, discern, see; establish, determine, verify, confirm; informal figure out; Brit. informal suss out.

ascetic adjective **austere**, self-denying, abstemious, self-disciplined; puritanical, monastic, strict.
– OPPOSITES sybaritic.

ascribe verb **attribute**, assign, put down, accredit, credit, impute; blame on, lay at the door of; connect with, associate with.

ash noun **cinders**, ashes, clinker.

ashamed adjective **1** *the poor are made to feel ashamed:* **sorry**, shamefaced, sheepish, guilty, contrite, remorseful, repentant, penitent, regretful, apologetic; embarrassed, mortified. **2** *he was ashamed to admit it:* **reluctant**, loath, unwilling, disinclined, afraid.
– OPPOSITES proud, pleased.

ashen adjective **pale**, wan, pasty, grey, colourless, pallid, white, waxen, ghostly, bloodless.

asinine adjective **foolish**, stupid, brainless, mindless, idiotic, ridiculous, absurd, fatuous, silly, inane, witless, empty-headed; informal half-witted, dumb, moronic; Brit. informal daft; Scottish & N. English informal glaikit.
– OPPOSITES intelligent, sensible.

ask verb **1** *he asked what time we opened:* **enquire**, want to know; question, interrogate, quiz. **2** *they want to ask a few questions:* **put**, pose, raise, submit. **3** *we've asked for extra funds:* **request**, demand; solicit, seek, crave, apply, petition, call, appeal.
– OPPOSITES answer.

askew adjective **crooked**, lopsided, tilted, at an angle, awry, out of true, uneven, off-centre, asymmetrical; informal cockeyed, wonky; Brit. informal skew-whiff.
– OPPOSITES straight.

asleep adjective **sleeping**, napping, catnapping, dozing, drowsing; informal snoozing, dead to the world; Brit. informal kipping; humorous in the land of Nod; literary slumbering.
– OPPOSITES awake.

aspect noun **1** *the photos depict every aspect of life:* **feature**, facet, side, characteristic, particular, detail; angle, slant. **2** *his face had a sinister aspect:* **appearance**, look, air, cast, mien, demeanour, expression; atmosphere, mood, quality, feeling. **3** *a summer house with a southern aspect:* **outlook**, view, exposure; situation, position, location. **4** *the front aspect of the hotel:* **face**, elevation, facade, side.

asperity noun **harshness**, sharpness, abrasiveness, severity, acerbity.

aspersions plural noun
■ **cast aspersions on** vilify, disparage, denigrate, defame, run down, impugn, belittle, criticize, condemn; malign, slander, libel, discredit; informal pull apart, knock, bad-mouth; Brit. informal rubbish, slate, slag off.

asphyxiate verb **choke**, suffocate, smother, stifle; throttle, strangle.

aspiration noun **desire**, hope, dream, wish, longing, yearning; aim, ambition, expectation, goal, target.

aspire verb **desire**, hope, dream, long, yearn, set your heart on, wish, want; aim, seek, set your sights on.

aspiring adjective **would-be**, hopeful, budding; potential, prospective; informal wannabe.

assassin noun **murderer**, killer, gunman; executioner; informal hit man.

assassinate verb **murder**, kill; eliminate, liquidate, execute; N. Amer. terminate; informal hit.

assassination noun **murder**, killing; execution, elimination; N. Amer. termination; informal hit.

assault verb *he assaulted a police officer:* **attack**, hit, strike, punch, beat up, thump; informal clout, wallop, belt, clobber, deck, slug, plug, lay into, do over, rough up.
• noun **1** *he was charged with assault:* **violence**, battery; indecency, rape, molestation; Brit. grievous bodily harm, GBH, actual bodily harm, ABH. **2** *an assault on the city:* **attack**, strike, onslaught, offensive, charge, push, thrust, invasion, bombardment, sortie, incursion, raid, blitz.

assemblage noun **collection**, accumulation, conglomeration, gathering, group, grouping, cluster, aggregation, mass, number; assortment, selection, array.

assemble verb **1** *a crowd had assembled:* **gather**, collect, get together, congregate, convene, meet, muster, rally. **2** *he assembled the suspects:* **bring/call together**, gather, collect, round up, marshal, muster. **3** *the new machine is being assembled:* **construct**, build, erect, set up, put together, connect.
– OPPOSITES disperse, dismantle.

assembly noun **1** *an assembly of dockers:* **gathering**, meeting, congregation, convention, rally, convocation, group, body, crowd, throng, company; informal get-together. **2** *car assembly:* **construction**, manufacture, building, fabrication, erection.

assent noun *they are likely to give their assent:* **agreement**, acceptance, approval, consent, acquiescence; sanction, endorsement, confirmation; permission, leave, blessing; informal the go-ahead, the green light, the OK, the thumbs up.
– OPPOSITES dissent, refusal.
• verb *he assented to the change:* **agree to**, accept, approve, consent to, give your blessing to, give the nod; sanction, endorse, confirm; informal give the go-ahead, give the green light, give the OK, OK, give the thumbs up; formal accede to.
– OPPOSITES refuse.

assert verb **1** *they asserted that all aboard were safe:* **declare**, maintain, contend, argue, state, claim, announce, pronounce, swear, insist, avow; formal aver. **2** *we find it difficult to assert our rights:* **insist on**, stand up for, uphold, defend, press/push for.

assertion noun **declaration**, contention, statement, claim, opinion, announcement, pronouncement, protestation, avowal.

assertive adjective **confident**, self-confident, bold, decisive, assured, self-assured, self-possessed, strong-willed, forceful, insistent, determined, commanding, pushy; informal feisty.
– OPPOSITES timid.

assess verb **1** *the committee's power is hard to assess:* **evaluate**, judge, gauge, rate, estimate, appraise, get the measure of, determine, weigh up, analyse; informal size up. **2** *the damage was assessed at £5 billion:* **value**, calculate, work out, determine, cost, price, estimate.

assessment noun **1** *a teacher's assessment of the pupil's abilities:* **evaluation**, judgement, rating, estimation, appraisal, analysis, opinion. **2** *some assessments valued the estate at £2 million:* **valuation**, calculation, costing, pricing, estimate.

asset noun **1** *he sees his age as an asset:* **benefit**, advantage, blessing, good/strong point, strength, forte, virtue, recommendation, attraction, resource, boon, merit, bonus, plus, pro. **2** *the seizure of all their assets:* **property**, resources, estate, holdings, possessions, effects, goods, valuables, belongings.
– OPPOSITES liability.

assiduous adjective **diligent**, careful, meticulous, thorough, sedulous, attentive, conscientious, punctilious, painstaking, rigorous.

assign verb **1** *a young doctor was assigned the task:* **allocate**, allot, give, set; charge with, entrust with. **2** *she was assigned to a new post:* **appoint**, promote, delegate, commission, post, co-opt; Military detail. **3** *we assign large sums of money to travel budgets:* **earmark**, designate, set aside, reserve, appropriate, allot, allocate, apportion.

assignation noun **rendezvous**, date, appointment, meeting.

assignment noun **1** *I'm going to finish this assignment tonight:* **task**, job, duty, chore, mission, errand, undertaking, exercise, business, endeavour, enterprise; project, homework. **2** *the assignment of tasks:* **allocation**, allotment, designation; sharing out, apportionment, distribution, handing out.

assimilate verb **1** *the amount of information he can assimilate:* **absorb**, take in, acquire, pick up, grasp, comprehend, understand, learn, master; digest. **2** *many tribes were assimilated by Turkic peoples:* **subsume**, incorporate, integrate, absorb.

assist verb **1** *I spend my time assisting the chef:* **help**, aid, cooperate with, work with; support, back up. **2** *the exchange rates assisted the firm's expansion:* **facilitate**, aid, ease, expedite, spur, promote, boost, benefit, encourage, further.
– OPPOSITES hinder, impede.

assistance noun **help**, aid, support, backing, reinforcement, succour, relief; a helping hand.
– OPPOSITES hindrance.

assistant noun **subordinate**, deputy, second in command, number two, right-hand man/woman, aide, personal assistant, PA, attendant, mate, apprentice, junior, auxiliary; helper, man/girl Friday; informal sidekick, gofer; Brit. informal dogsbody, skivvy.

associate verb **1** *the colours that we associate with fire:* **link**, connect, relate, identify, equate. **2** *I was forced to associate with them:* **mix**, keep company, mingle, socialize, go around, rub shoulders, fraternize, consort; N. Amer. rub elbows; informal hobnob, hang out/around/round. **3** *the firm is associated with a local charity:* **affiliate**, align, connect, ally; merge, integrate.
• noun *his business associate:* **partner**, colleague, co-worker, workmate, collaborator, comrade, ally, confederate, acquaintance; informal crony; Austral./NZ informal offsider.

associated adjective **related**, connected, linked, similar, corresponding; attendant, accompanying, incidental.
– OPPOSITES unrelated.

association noun **1** *a trade association:* **alliance**, consortium, coalition, union, league, guild, syndicate, federation, confederation, confederacy, conglomerate, cooperative, partnership, affiliation. **2** *the association between man and environment:* **relationship**, relation, interrelation, connection, interconnection, link, bond, union, tie, attachment, interdependence.

assorted adjective **various**, miscellaneous, mixed, varied, varying, diverse, multifarious, sundry; literary divers.

assortment noun **mixture**, variety, array, mixed bag, mix, miscellany, selection, medley, diversity, ragbag, potpourri.

assuage verb **1** *a pain that could never be assuaged:* **relieve**, ease, alleviate, soothe, mitigate, allay, suppress, subdue, tranquillize; moderate, lessen, diminish, reduce. **2** *her hunger was quickly assuaged:* **satisfy**, gratify, appease, relieve, slake, sate, satiate, quench, check.
– OPPOSITES aggravate, intensify.

assume verb **1** *I assumed he wanted me to keep the book:* **presume**, suppose, take it, take for granted, take as read, conjecture, surmise, conclude, deduce, infer, reason, think, fancy, believe, understand, gather; N. Amer. figure. **2** *he assumed a Southern accent:* **affect**, adopt, put on. **3** *they are to assume more responsibility:* **accept**, shoulder, bear, undertake, take on/up. **4** *he assumed control of their finances:* **seize**, take, appropriate, wrest, usurp.

assumed adjective **false**, fictitious, invented, made-up, fake, bogus,

sham, spurious, make-believe; informal pretend, phoney; Brit. informal cod.
– OPPOSITES genuine.

assumption noun **1** *an assumption about his past:* **supposition**, presumption, conjecture, speculation. **2** *the assumption of power by revolutionaries:* **seizure**, appropriation, expropriation, commandeering, confiscation, hijacking, wresting.

assurance noun **1** *her sister's calm assurance:* **self-confidence**, confidence, self-assurance, self-possession, nerve, poise, level-headedness; calmness, composure, sangfroid, equanimity; informal cool. **2** *you have my assurance:* **word**, word of honour, promise, pledge, vow, oath, undertaking, guarantee, commitment. **3** *life assurance:* **insurance**, indemnity, protection, security, cover.
– OPPOSITES self-doubt, uncertainty.

assure verb **1** *we must assure him of our loyal support:* **reassure**, convince, satisfy, persuade. **2** *he wants to assure a favourable vote:* **ensure**, secure, guarantee, seal, clinch; informal sew up. **3** *they guarantee to assure your life:* **insure**, cover, indemnify.

assured adjective **1** *an assured voice:* **confident**, self-confident, self-assured, self-possessed, poised; calm, composed, imperturbable, unruffled; informal unflappable, together. **2** *an assured supply of weapons:* **guaranteed**, certain, sure, secure, reliable, dependable, sound; informal sure-fire.
– OPPOSITES doubtful, uncertain.

astonish verb **amaze**, astound, stagger, startle, stun, confound, dumbfound, nonplus, take aback, leave open-mouthed; informal bowl over, flabbergast; Brit. informal knock for six.

astonished adjective **amazed**, astounded, staggered, surprised, startled, stunned, thunderstruck, aghast, taken aback, dumbfounded, dumbstruck, stupefied, dazed, nonplussed, awestruck; informal flabbergasted; Brit. informal gob-smacked.

astonishing adjective **amazing**, astounding, staggering, surprising, breathtaking, remarkable, extraordinary, incredible, unbelievable, phenomenal; informal mind-boggling.

astonishment noun **amazement**, surprise, stupefaction, incredulity, disbelief, awe, wonder.

astound verb **amaze**, astonish, stagger, surprise, startle, stun, confound, dumbfound, stupefy, daze, take aback, leave open-mouthed; informal flabbergast, bowl over; Brit. informal knock for six.

astounding adjective **amazing**, astonishing, staggering, surprising, breathtaking, remarkable, extraordinary, incredible, unbelievable, phenomenal; informal mind-boggling.

astray adverb **1** *the shots went astray:* **off target**, wide of the mark, awry, off course. **2** *the older boys lead him astray:* **into wrongdoing**, into sin, away from the straight and narrow.

astringent adjective *her astringent comments:* **severe**, sharp, stern, harsh, acerbic, caustic, mordant, trenchant; scathing, cutting, incisive, waspish; N. Amer. acerb.

astronaut noun **spaceman/woman**, cosmonaut, space traveller, space cadet; N. Amer. informal jock.

astronomical adjective **1** *astronomical alignments:* **planetary**, stellar, sidereal; celestial. **2** (informal) *the sums he has paid are astronomical:* **huge**, enormous, prodigious, monumental, colossal, vast, gigantic, massive; substantial, considerable, sizeable, hefty; inordinate; informal astronomic, whopping, humongous; Brit. informal ginormous.
– OPPOSITES tiny.

astute adjective **shrewd**, sharp, acute, quick, clever, intelligent, bright, smart, canny, perceptive, insightful, incisive, sagacious, wise; informal on the ball, quick on the uptake, savvy; Brit. informal suss; N. Amer. informal heads-up.
– OPPOSITES stupid.

asylum noun *political asylum:* **refuge**, sanctuary, shelter, protection, immunity; a safe haven.

asymmetrical adjective **lopsided**, unsymmetrical, uneven, unbalanced, crooked, awry, askew, skew, squint, misaligned; disproportionate, unequal, irregular; informal cockeyed; Brit. informal skew-whiff, wonky.

athletic adjective **muscular**, muscly, sturdy, strapping, well built, strong, powerful, robust, hardy, lusty, hearty, brawny, burly, broad-shouldered, Herculean; fit, in good shape, in trim; informal sporty, hunky; N. Amer. informal buff.
– OPPOSITES puny.

atmosphere noun **1** *the gases present in the atmosphere:* **air**; sky; literary the heavens, the firmament, the ether. **2** *the hotel has a relaxed atmosphere:* **ambience**, air, mood, feel, feeling, character, tone, aura, quality, undercurrent, flavour; informal vibe.

> **WORD LINKS**
> **meteorology** the study of the atmosphere

atom noun *there isn't an atom of truth in the allegations:* **particle**, bit, piece, fragment; grain, iota, jot, whit, mite, scrap, shred, ounce, scintilla; informal smidgen.

atone verb **make amends**, make reparation, make up for, compensate, pay, recompense, expiate, make good, offset; do penance.

atrocious adjective **1** *atrocious cruelties:* **brutal**, barbaric, barbarous, savage, vicious; wicked, cruel, nasty, heinous, monstrous, vile, inhuman, fiendish, ghastly, horrible; abominable, disgusting, despicable, contemptible, loathsome, odious, abhorrent, sickening, horrifying, unspeakable, obscene. **2** *the weather was atrocious:* **appalling**, dreadful, terrible, unpleasant, miserable; informal abysmal, dire, rotten, lousy, God-awful; Brit. informal shocking, chronic.
– OPPOSITES admirable, superb.

atrocity noun **1** *press reports detailed a number of atrocities:* **outrage**, massacre; horror, violation, abuse; crime. **2** *scenes of atrocity:* **barbarity**, barbarism, brutality, savagery, inhumanity, cruelty, wickedness.

atrophy verb *their muscles atrophied:* **waste away**, become emaciated, wither, shrivel, shrink; decline, deteriorate, degenerate.
– OPPOSITES strengthen.
• noun *muscular atrophy:* **wasting**, emaciation, withering; decay, decline, deterioration, degeneration.

attach verb **1** *a weight is attached to the cord:* **fasten**, fix, affix, join, connect, link, secure, make fast, tie, bind, chain; stick, adhere, glue, fuse. **2** *he attached himself to the Liberal Party:* **affiliate**, associate, align, ally, join. **3** *they attach considerable importance to research:* **ascribe**, assign, attribute, accredit, impute. **4** *the medical officer attached to HQ:* **assign**, appoint, allocate, second; Military detail.
– OPPOSITES detach, separate.

attached adjective *she was very attached to her brother:* **fond of**, devoted to; informal mad about, crazy about.

attachment noun **1** *he has a strong attachment to his mother:* **bond**, closeness, devotion, loyalty; fondness for, love for, affection for, feeling for; relationship with. **2** *the shower had a massage attachment:* **accessory**, fitting, extension, add-on. **3** *the attachment of safety restraints:* **fixing**, fastening, linking, coupling, connection. **4** *he was on attachment from another regiment:* **assignment**, appointment, secondment, transfer; Military detail.

attack verb **1** *he had been brutally attacked:* **assault**, assail, set upon, beat, beat up; batter, punch; N. Amer. beat up on; informal do over, work over, rough up; Brit. informal duff up. **2** *the French had still not attacked:* **strike**, charge, pounce; bomb, shell, strafe, fire. **3** *the clergy attacked government policies:* **criticize**, censure, condemn, pillory, savage, revile, vilify; informal knock, slam, lay into; Brit. informal slate, slag off, rubbish; N. Amer. informal pummel. **4** *they have to attack the problem soon:* **address**, attend to, deal with, confront, apply yourself to, get to grips with, get to work on, embark on. **5** *the virus attacks the liver:* **affect**, have an effect on, strike; infect, damage, injure.

– OPPOSITES defend, praise, protect.
• **noun 1** *an attack on their home:* **assault**, onslaught, offensive, strike, blitz, raid, charge, rush, invasion, incursion. **2** *an outright attack on his style of leadership:* **criticism**, censure, rebuke, admonishment, reprimand, reproof; condemnation, denunciation, revilement, vilification; tirade, diatribe, polemic; informal roasting; Brit. informal slating, rollicking. **3** *an asthmatic attack:* **fit**, seizure, spasm, convulsion, paroxysm, outburst, bout, episode.
– OPPOSITES defence, commendation.

attacker **noun** **assailant**, assaulter, aggressor; mugger, rapist, killer, murderer.

attain **verb** **achieve**, accomplish, reach, obtain, gain, procure, secure, get, score, net, win, earn, acquire; realize, fulfil; informal clinch, bag, wrap up.

attainable **adjective** **achievable**, obtainable, accessible, within reach, realizable; practicable, workable, realistic, reasonable, viable, feasible, possible; informal doable, get-at-able.

attainment **noun 1** *the attainment of common goals:* **achievement**, accomplishment, realization, fulfilment, completion. **2** *educational attainment:* **achievement**, accomplishment, proficiency, competence; qualification; skill, aptitude, ability.

attempt **verb** *I attempted to answer the question:* **try**, strive, aim, venture, endeavour, seek, undertake, make an effort; have a go at, try your hand at; informal go all out, bend over backwards, bust a gut, have a crack at, have a shot at, have a stab at; formal essay.
• **noun** *an attempt to put the economy to rights:* **effort**, endeavour, try, venture, trial, bid; informal crack, go, shot, stab; formal essay.

attend **verb 1** *they attended a carol service:* **be present at**, sit in on, take part in; appear at, turn up at, visit, go to; informal show up at, show your face at. **2** *he had not attended to the needs of their clients:* **pay attention**, pay heed, be attentive, listen; concentrate, take note, bear in mind, take into consideration, heed, observe, mark. **3** *the wounded were attended to nearby:* **care for**, look after, minister to, see to; tend, treat, nurse, help, aid, assist. **4** *he attended to the boy's education:* **deal with**, see to, manage, organize, sort out, handle, take care of, take charge of, take in hand, tackle. **5** *the queen was attended by an usher:* **escort**, accompany, chaperone, lead, conduct, usher, shepherd; assist, help, serve, wait on. **6** *her giddiness was attended by a fever:* **be accompanied by**, occur with, be associated with, be connected with, be linked with.
– OPPOSITES miss, disregard, ignore, neglect.

attendance **noun 1** *you requested the attendance of a doctor:* **presence**, appearance; attention. **2** *their gig attendances grew:* **audience**, turnout, house, gate; crowd, congregation, gathering; Austral. informal muster.
– OPPOSITES absence.
■ **in attendance** present, here, there, near, nearby, at/on hand, available; assisting, supervising.

attendant **noun 1** *a sleeping car attendant:* **steward**, waiter, waitress, porter, servant; N. Amer. waitperson. **2** *a royal attendant:* **escort**, companion, retainer, aide, lady-in-waiting, equerry, chaperone; servant, manservant, valet, maidservant, maid; N. Amer. houseman; Brit. informal skivvy; Military, dated batman.
• **adjective** *new discoveries and the attendant excitement:* **accompanying**, associated, related, connected, concomitant; resultant, resulting, consequent.

attention **noun 1** *the issue needs further attention:* **consideration**, contemplation, deliberation, thought, study, observation, scrutiny, investigation, action. **2** *he tried to attract the attention of a policeman:* **awareness**, notice, scrutiny; eye, gaze. **3** *medical attention:* **care**, treatment, relief, aid, help, assistance.

attentive **adjective 1** *a bright and attentive scholar:* **alert**, perceptive, observant, acute, aware, heedful, vigilant; intent, focused,

committed, studious, diligent, conscientious, earnest; informal not missing a trick, on the ball. **2** *the most attentive of husbands:* **conscientious**, considerate, thoughtful, kind, caring, solicitous, understanding, sympathetic, obliging, accommodating, gallant, chivalrous; dutiful, responsible.
– OPPOSITES inattentive.

attenuated adjective **1** *his muscle activity was much attenuated:* **weakened**, reduced, lessened, decreased, diminished, impaired. **2** *his attenuated fingers:* **thin**, narrow, skinny, spindly, bony.

attest verb **certify**, corroborate, confirm, verify, substantiate, authenticate, evidence, demonstrate, show, prove; endorse, support, affirm, bear out, give credence to, vouch for; formal evince.
– OPPOSITES disprove.

attic noun **loft**, roof space, cock loft; garret.

attire noun *he preferred formal attire:* **clothing**, clothes, garments, dress, wear, garb, costume; informal gear, togs, duds, get-up; Brit. informal clobber; N. Amer. informal threads; formal apparel; old use raiment.
• verb *she was attired in black crêpe:* **dress**, clothe, garb, robe, array, costume, swathe, deck out, turn out, fit out, trick out/up, rig out; informal get up.

attitude noun **1** *you seem ambivalent in your attitude:* **view**, viewpoint, outlook, perspective, stance, standpoint, position, orientation, approach, reaction; opinion, ideas, convictions, feelings, thinking. **2** *an attitude of prayer:* **position**, pose, posture, stance.

attorney noun **lawyer**, member of the bar, counsel, barrister; Brit. Queen's Counsel, QC; Scottish advocate; N. Amer. counselor; informal brief.

attract verb **1** *positive ions are attracted to the negatively charged terminal:* **draw**, pull; suck. **2** *he was attracted by her smile:* **entice**, allure, lure, charm, win over, woo, engage, enchant, entrance, captivate, beguile, bewitch, seduce; excite, titillate, arouse; informal turn on.
– OPPOSITES repel.

attraction noun **1** *the stars are held together by gravitational attraction:* **pull**, draw, force. **2** *she had lost whatever attraction she had ever had:* **appeal**, attractiveness, desirability, seductiveness, allure, magnetism; charisma, charm, beauty, good looks. **3** *the park boasts many attractions:* **entertainment**, activity, diversion; amenity, service.
– OPPOSITES repulsion.

attractive adjective **1** *a more attractive career:* **appealing**, inviting, tempting; agreeable, pleasing, interesting. **2** *she has no idea how attractive she is:* **good-looking**, beautiful, pretty, handsome, lovely, stunning, striking, arresting, gorgeous, prepossessing, fetching, captivating, bewitching, beguiling, engaging, charming, enchanting, appealing, delightful; sexy, seductive, alluring, tantalizing, irresistible, ravishing, desirable; Scottish & N. English bonny; informal fanciable, tasty, hot, drop-dead gorgeous; Brit. informal fit; N. Amer. informal cute, foxy; Austral./NZ informal spunky; old use comely, fair.
– OPPOSITES unattractive, ugly.

attribute verb *they attributed their success to him:* **ascribe**, assign, accredit, credit, impute; put down, chalk up, pin on; connect with, associate with.
• noun **1** *he has all the attributes of a top player:* **quality**, characteristic, trait, feature, element, aspect, property, sign, hallmark, mark. **2** *the hourglass is the attribute of Father Time:* **symbol**, mark, sign, hallmark, trademark; signature, emblem.

attrition noun **1** *a gradual attrition of the market economy:* **wearing down/away**, weakening, enfeebling, sapping, attenuation. **2** *the attrition of the edges of the teeth:* **abrasion**, friction, erosion, corrosion, wearing away.

attune verb **accustom**, adjust, adapt, acclimatize, condition, accommodate, assimilate; N. Amer. acclimate.

atypical adjective **unusual**, untypical, uncommon, unconventional, unorthodox, irregular, abnormal,

aberrant, deviant, unrepresentative; strange, odd, peculiar, bizarre, weird, queer, freakish; exceptional, singular, rare, out of the way, out of the ordinary, extraordinary; informal funny, freaky.
– OPPOSITES normal, typical.

auburn adjective **reddish-brown**, russet, chestnut, copper, coppery.

audacious adjective **bold**, daring; daredevil, devil-may-care, reckless, madcap; informal gutsy, spunky, ballsy.
– OPPOSITES timid, polite.

audacity noun **1** *a traveller of extraordinary audacity:* **boldness**, daring, pluck; recklessness; spirit; informal guts, gutsiness, spunk; Brit. informal bottle; N. Amer. informal moxie. **2** *he had the audacity to contradict me:* **impudence**, impertinence, insolence, presumption, cheek, effrontery, nerve, gall, defiance, temerity; informal brass neck, chutzpah; Brit. informal sauce.

audible adjective **perceptible**, discernible, detectable; clear, distinct.
– OPPOSITES faint.

audience noun **1** *the audience applauded:* **spectators**, **listeners**, viewers, onlookers; crowd, throng, congregation, turnout; house, gallery, stalls; Brit. informal punters. **2** *the radio station has a teenage audience:* **public**, market, following, fans; fan base, demographic, readership. **3** *an audience with the Pope:* **meeting**, consultation, conference, hearing, reception, interview.

audit noun *an audit of the party accounts:* **inspection**, examination, scrutiny, probe, investigation, assessment, appraisal, evaluation, review, analysis; informal going-over, once-over.
• verb *we audited their accounts:* **inspect**, examine, survey, go through, scrutinize, check, probe, vet, investigate, enquire into, assess, appraise, evaluate, review, analyse, study; informal give something a/the once-over.

auditorium noun **theatre**, hall, assembly room; chamber, room.

au fait adjective **familiar**, acquainted, conversant, at home, up to date, in touch; abreast, apprised, in the know, well informed, knowledgeable, well versed, enlightened; informal clued-up, wise to, hip to, tuned in to, up to speed with.

augment verb **increase**, add to, supplement, enhance, build up, enlarge, expand, extend, raise, multiply, swell; magnify, amplify, escalate; improve, boost; informal up, jack up, hike up, bump up, soup up, beef up, turbocharge.
– OPPOSITES decrease.

augur verb *the development augurs a new era in politics:* **bode**, portend, presage, foreshadow, signal, be a sign of, promise, spell; warn of, forewarn of, be an omen of; predict, prophesy; literary betoken, foretoken.

august adjective **distinguished**, respected, eminent, venerable, hallowed, illustrious, prestigious, renowned, celebrated, honoured, acclaimed, esteemed, exalted; great, important, noble, stately, grand, dignified.

aura noun **atmosphere**, ambience, air, quality, character, mood, feeling, feel, flavour, tone; emanation, vibration; informal vibe.

auspices plural noun **patronage**, aegis, umbrella, protection, keeping, care; support, backing, guardianship, trusteeship, guidance, supervision.

auspicious adjective **favourable**, propitious, promising, good, encouraging; opportune, timely, lucky, fortunate, providential, felicitous, advantageous.

austere adjective **1** *an outwardly austere man:* **severe**, stern, strict, harsh, flinty, dour, grim, cold, frosty, unemotional, unfriendly; formal, stiff, reserved, aloof, forbidding; grave, solemn, serious, unsmiling, unsympathetic, unforgiving; hard, unyielding, unbending; informal hard-boiled. **2** *an austere life:* **ascetic**, self-disciplined, frugal, spartan, puritanical, abstemious, strict, temperate, sober, simple, restrained; chaste. **3** *the buildings were austere:* **plain**, simple, basic, functional, unadorned; bleak, bare, clinical, spartan, ascetic; informal no frills.
– OPPOSITES genial, self-indulgent, ornate.

Australia noun informal **Oz**, Aussie, down under.

authentic adjective **1** *an authentic document:* **genuine**, real, bona fide, true; legitimate, lawful, legal, valid; informal the real McCoy, the real thing, pukka, kosher; Austral./NZ informal dinkum. **2** *an authentic depiction of the situation:* **reliable**, dependable, trustworthy, authoritative, honest, faithful; accurate, factual, true, truthful; formal veracious.
– OPPOSITES fake, unreliable.

authenticate verb **1** *the evidence will authenticate his claim:* **verify**, validate, prove, substantiate, corroborate, confirm, support, back up, attest to, give credence to. **2** *a mandate authenticated by the popular vote:* **validate**, ratify, confirm, seal, sanction, endorse.

authenticity noun **1** *the authenticity of the painting:* **genuineness**, bona fides; legitimacy, legality, validity. **2** *the authenticity of this account:* **reliability**, dependability, trustworthiness, credibility; accuracy, truth, veracity, fidelity.

author noun **1** *modern Canadian authors:* **writer**, wordsmith; novelist, playwright, poet, essayist, biographer; columnist, reporter; informal scribe, scribbler. **2** *the author of the peace plan:* **originator**, creator, instigator, founder, father, architect, designer, deviser, producer.

authoritarian adjective **autocratic**, dictatorial, despotic, tyrannical, draconian, oppressive, repressive, illiberal, undemocratic; disciplinarian, domineering, overbearing, high-handed, peremptory, imperious, strict, rigid, inflexible; informal bossy.
– OPPOSITES democratic, liberal.
• noun **autocrat**, despot, dictator, tyrant; disciplinarian.

authoritative adjective **1** *authoritative information:* **reliable**, dependable, trustworthy, sound, authentic, valid, attested, verifiable; accurate. **2** *the authoritative edition:* **definitive**, most reliable, best; authorized, accredited, recognized, accepted, approved. **3** *his father's authoritative manner:* **assured**, confident, assertive; commanding, masterful; domineering, imperious, overbearing, authoritarian; informal bossy.
– OPPOSITES unreliable, timid.

authority noun **1** *a rebellion against those in authority:* **power**, jurisdiction, command, control, charge, dominance, rule, sovereignty, supremacy; influence; informal clout. **2** *the authority to arrest drug traffickers:* **authorization**, right, power, mandate, prerogative, licence. **3** *the money was spent without parliamentary authority:* **authorization**, permission, consent, leave, sanction, licence, dispensation, assent, acquiescence, agreement, approval, endorsement, clearance; informal the go-ahead, the thumbs up, the OK, the green light. **4** *the authorities:* **officials**, officialdom; government, administration, establishment; police; informal the powers that be. **5** *an authority on the stock market:* **expert**, specialist, pundit, doyen/doyenne, guru, sage, maven; informal boffin.

authorization noun **permission**, consent, leave, sanction, licence, dispensation, clearance, the nod; assent, agreement, approval, endorsement; authority, right, power, mandate; informal the go-ahead, the thumbs up, the OK, the green light.
– OPPOSITES refusal.

authorize verb **1** *they authorized further action:* **sanction**, permit, allow, approve, consent to, assent to; ratify, endorse, validate; informal give the green light, give the go-ahead, OK, give the thumbs up. **2** *the troops were authorized to fire:* **empower**, mandate, commission; entitle.
– OPPOSITES forbid.

authorized adjective **approved**, recognized, sanctioned; accredited, licensed, certified; official, lawful, legal, legitimate.
– OPPOSITES unofficial, unauthorized.

autobiography noun **memoirs**, life story, personal history.

autocrat noun **absolute ruler**, dictator, despot, tyrant.

autocratic adjective **despotic**,

tyrannical, dictatorial, totalitarian; undemocratic, one-party; domineering, draconian, overbearing, high-handed, peremptory, imperious; harsh, rigid, inflexible, illiberal, oppressive.

automatic adjective **1** *automatic garage doors:* **mechanized**, mechanical, automated, self-activating, computerized, electronic, robotic, light/heat/motion-sensitive. **2** *an automatic reaction:* **instinctive**, involuntary, reflex, knee-jerk, unconscious, instinctual, subconscious; spontaneous, impulsive, unthinking; mechanical; informal gut. **3** *he is the automatic choice for the team:* **inevitable**, unavoidable, inescapable, mandatory, compulsory; certain, definite, obvious, undoubted, assured.
– OPPOSITES manual, deliberate.

autonomous adjective **self-governing**, self-ruling, self-determining, independent, sovereign, free.

autonomy noun **self-government**, self-rule, home rule, self-determination, independence, sovereignty, freedom.

auxiliary adjective **1** *an auxiliary power source:* **additional**, supplementary, supplemental, extra, reserve, backup, emergency, fallback, second, other. **2** *auxiliary nursing staff:* **ancillary**, assistant, support.
• noun *a nursing auxiliary:* **assistant**, helper, ancillary, aid.

avail noun
■ **to no avail** in vain, without success, unsuccessfully, fruitlessly, for nothing.

available adjective **1** *refreshments will be available:* **obtainable**, accessible, to/at hand, at your disposal, handy, convenient; on sale; untaken, unsold, unused; informal up for grabs, on tap. **2** *I'll see if he's available:* **free**, unoccupied; present, here, in, around/about, at work, on duty; contactable.
– OPPOSITES unavailable, engaged.

avalanche noun **1** **snowslide**, icefall; rockslide, landslide, mudslide, landslip. **2** *an avalanche of press comment:* **barrage**, volley, flood, deluge, torrent, tide, wave.

avant-garde adjective **experimental**, left-field, modern, cutting-edge, progressive, unorthodox, unconventional; informal offbeat, way-out.
– OPPOSITES conservative.

avarice noun **greed**, acquisitiveness, cupidity, covetousness, rapacity, materialism, mercenariness; informal money-grubbing.
– OPPOSITES generosity.

avenge verb **requite**, punish, repay, pay back, take revenge for, get even for.

avenue noun **1** *tree-lined avenues:* **road**, street, drive, parade, boulevard, thoroughfare. **2** *possible avenues of research:* **line**, path; method, approach; angle, tack.

average noun *the price is above the national average:* **mean**, median, mode; norm, standard, rule, par.
• adjective **1** *the average temperature:* **mean**, median, modal. **2** *a woman of average height:* **ordinary**, standard, normal, typical, regular. **3** *a very average director:* **mediocre**, second-rate, undistinguished, ordinary, middle-of-the-road, unexceptional, unexciting, unremarkable, unmemorable, indifferent, pedestrian, lacklustre, forgettable; informal OK, so-so, fair-to-middling, no great shakes; Brit. informal not much cop; N. Amer. informal bush-league; NZ informal half-pie.
– OPPOSITES outstanding, exceptional.
■ **on average** normally, usually, ordinarily, generally, in general, for the most part, as a rule, typically; overall, by and large, on the whole.

averse adjective *I'm not averse to taking risks:* **opposed**, against, antipathetic, hostile, ill-disposed, resistant; disinclined, reluctant, loath; informal anti.
– OPPOSITES keen.

> ! Don't confuse **averse** with **adverse**, which means 'harmful' or 'unfavourable' (*the drug's adverse side effects*).

aversion noun **dislike**, antipathy, distaste, abhorrence, hatred, loathing, detestation, hostility; reluctance, disinclination.
– OPPOSITES liking.

a

avert verb **1** *she averted her gaze:* **turn aside**, turn away; shift, redirect. **2** *an attempt to avert political chaos:* **prevent**, avoid, stave off, ward off, head off, forestall, preclude.

avid adjective **keen**, eager, enthusiastic, ardent, passionate, zealous; devoted, dedicated, wholehearted, earnest.
– OPPOSITES apathetic.

avoid verb **1** *I avoid situations that cause me stress:* **keep away from**, steer clear of, give a wide berth to. **2** *he is trying to avoid responsibility:* **evade**, dodge, sidestep, escape, run away from, delegate; informal duck, wriggle out of, get out of, cop out of; Austral./NZ informal duck-shove. **3** *you've been avoiding me all evening:* **shun**, stay away from, evade, keep your distance, elude, hide from; ignore. **4** *he should avoid drinking alcohol:* **refrain from**, abstain from, desist from; steer clear of, eschew.
– OPPOSITES confront, face.

avoidable adjective **preventable**; stoppable, escapable.

avowed adjective **self-confessed**, self-declared, acknowledged, admitted; open, overt.

await verb **1** *Peter was still awaiting news:* **wait for**, expect, anticipate; hope for, look forward to. **2** *many dangers await them:* **be in store for**, lie ahead of, lie in wait for, be waiting for.

awake verb **1** *she awoke early the following morning:* **wake**, wake up, awaken, stir, come to, come round; literary waken. **2** *they finally awoke to the extent of the problem:* **realize**, become aware of, recognize, grasp, understand, comprehend, see; informal cotton on to; Brit. informal suss.
• adjective **1** *she was still awake:* **wakeful**, sleepless, restless, restive. **2** *too few are awake to the dangers:* **aware of**, conscious of, mindful of, alert to; formal cognizant of.
– OPPOSITES asleep, oblivious.

awaken verb **1** *I awakened early | the jolt awakened her.* See AWAKE verb. **2** *he had awakened strong emotions in her:* **arouse**, rouse, bring out, engender, evoke, trigger, stir up, stimulate, kindle; revive.

award verb *the society awarded him a medal:* **give**, grant, accord, assign; confer on, bestow on, present to, decorate with.
• noun **1** *an award for high-quality service:* **prize**, trophy, medal, decoration; reward; informal gong. **2** *a libel award:* **payment**, settlement, compensation. **3** *the Arts Council gave him an award of £1,500:* **grant**, scholarship, endowment; Brit. bursary.

aware adjective **1** *she is aware of the dangers:* **conscious of**, mindful of, informed about, acquainted with, familiar with, alive to, alert to, au fait with; informal wise to, in the know about, hip to; formal cognizant of. **2** *we need to be more environmentally aware:* **sensitive**, enlightened, knowledgeable, informed, au fait; correct; informal clued-up, genned-up, plugged-in; Brit. informal switched-on.
– OPPOSITES unaware, ignorant.

awareness noun **consciousness**, recognition, realization; understanding, grasp, appreciation, knowledge, insight; familiarity, sensitivity; formal cognizance.

awash adjective **1** *the road was awash:* **flooded**, under water, submerged. **2** *the city was awash with journalists:* **inundated**, flooded, swamped, teeming, swarming, overflowing, overrun; informal knee-deep in, buried in.

away adverb *we'll be away for two weeks:* **elsewhere**, abroad; absent; on holiday; N. Amer. on vacation.

awe noun **wonder**, wonderment; admiration, reverence, respect.

awe-inspiring adjective. See AWESOME.

awesome adjective **breathtaking**, awe-inspiring, magnificent, amazing, stunning, staggering, imposing; formidable, fearsome; informal mind-boggling, mind-blowing, brilliant; literary wondrous.
– OPPOSITES unimpressive.

awestruck adjective **awed**, wonderstruck, amazed, lost for words, open-mouthed; informal gobsmacked.

awful adjective **1** *the place smelled awful:* **disgusting**, terrible, dreadful, ghastly, horrible, vile,

foul, revolting, repulsive, repugnant, odious, sickening, nauseating; informal sick-making, gross; Brit. informal beastly; literary noisome. **2** *an awful book:* **dreadful**, terrible, frightful, atrocious; lamentable; informal crummy, pathetic, rotten, woeful, lousy, appalling, abysmal, dismal, dire, poxy; Brit. informal rubbish. **3** *an awful accident:* **serious**, bad, terrible, dreadful. **4** *you look awful—go and lie down:* **ill**, unwell, sick, nauseous; Brit. off colour, poorly; Brit. informal grotty, ropy; Austral./NZ informal crook. **5** *I felt awful for getting so angry with her:* **guilty**, ashamed, contrite, sorry, regretful, repentant; informal rotten.
– OPPOSITES wonderful.

awfully adverb **1** (informal) *an awfully nice man:* **very**, extremely, really, immensely, exceedingly, thoroughly, dreadfully, exceptionally, remarkably, extraordinarily; N. English right; informal terrifically, terribly, devilishly, seriously, majorly; Brit. informal jolly, dead, well; N. Amer. informal real, mighty, awful; informal, dated frightfully; old use exceeding. **2** *we played awfully:* **terribly**, dreadfully, atrociously, appallingly; informal abysmally, pitifully, diabolically.

awkward adjective **1** *the box was awkward to carry:* **difficult**, tricky; cumbersome, unwieldy; Brit. informal fiddly. **2** *an awkward time:* **inconvenient**, inappropriate, inopportune, difficult. **3** *he put her in a very awkward position:* **embarrassing**, uncomfortable, unpleasant, delicate, tricky, problematic, troublesome, thorny; humiliating, compromising; informal sticky, dicey, hairy; Brit. informal dodgy. **4** *she felt awkward when alone with him:* **uncomfortable**, uneasy, tense, nervous, edgy; self-conscious, embarrassed. **5** *his awkward movements:* **clumsy**, ungainly, uncoordinated, graceless, inelegant, gauche, gawky, wooden, stiff; unskilful, maladroit, inept, blundering; informal clodhopping, ham-fisted, cack-handed; Brit. informal all fingers and thumbs. **6** (Brit.) *you're being really awkward:* **unreasonable**, uncooperative, unhelpful, difficult, obstructive; contrary, perverse; stubborn, obstinate; Brit. informal bloody-minded, bolshie; N. Amer. informal balky; formal refractory.
– OPPOSITES easy, convenient, graceful, amenable.

awning noun **canopy**, shade, sunshade, shelter, cover; Brit. blind.

awry adjective **1** *something was awry:* **amiss**, wrong; informal up. **2** *his wig looked awry:* **askew**, crooked, lopsided, tilted, skewed, skew, squint, to one side, off-centre, uneven; informal cockeyed; Brit. informal skew-whiff, wonky.
– OPPOSITES straight.

axe noun **hatchet**, cleaver, adze; Brit. chopper.
• verb **1** *the show was axed:* **cancel**, withdraw, drop, scrap, discontinue, terminate, end; informal ditch, dump, pull the plug on. **2** *500 staff were axed:* **dismiss**, make redundant, lay off, let go, discharge, get rid of; informal sack, fire, give someone the sack, give someone their marching orders; Brit. informal give someone their cards.

axiom noun **accepted truth**, general truth, dictum, truism; maxim, adage, aphorism.

axis noun *an axis of evil:* **alliance**, coalition, bloc, union, confederation, confederacy, league.

axle noun **shaft**, spindle, rod.

Bb

babble verb 1 **prattle**, rattle on, gabble, chatter, jabber, twitter, go on, run on, prate, ramble, burble, blather; informal gab, yak, yabber, yatter, yammer, blabber, jaw, gas, shoot your mouth off; Brit. informal witter, rabbit, chunter, natter, waffle. 2 *a brook babbled gently:* **burble**, murmur, gurgle.

babel noun **clamour**, din, racket, tumult, uproar, hubbub; Brit. row; informal hullabaloo.

baby noun *a newborn baby:* **infant**, newborn, child, tot; Scottish & N. English bairn; technical neonate; informal sprog, tiny; literary babe, babe in arms.
• adjective *baby carrots:* **miniature**, mini, little, small, small-scale, scaled-down, toy, pocket, midget, dwarf; Scottish wee; N. Amer. vest-pocket; informal teeny, teensy, itsy-bitsy, tiddly, bite-sized; Brit. informal titchy; N. Amer. informal little-bitty.
– OPPOSITES large.
• verb **pamper**, mollycoddle, spoil, cosset, coddle, indulge, over-indulge.

babyish adjective **childish**, immature, infantile, juvenile, puerile.
– OPPOSITES mature.

back noun 1 **spine**, backbone, spinal column, vertebral column. 2 *the back of the house:* **rear**; Nautical stern. 3 *the back of the queue:* **end**, tail end, rear end; N. Amer. tag end. 4 *the back of a postcard:* **reverse**, other side, underside; informal flip side.
– OPPOSITES front, head, face.
• adverb 1 *he pushed his chair back:* **backwards**, behind you, to your rear; away. 2 *a few months back:* **ago**, earlier, previously, before.
– OPPOSITES forward.
• verb 1 *companies backed the scheme generously:* **sponsor**, finance, put up the money for, fund, subsidize, underwrite; informal foot the bill for, pick up the tab for. 2 *most people backed the idea:* **support**, endorse, sanction, approve of, give your blessing to, favour, advocate, promote, uphold, champion; informal throw your weight behind. 3 *he'd backed the winner:* **bet on**, gamble on. 4 *he backed away:* **reverse**, draw back, step back, move backwards, back off, pull back, retreat, withdraw.
– OPPOSITES oppose, advance.
• adjective 1 *the back seats:* **rear**, rearmost, hind, hindmost, posterior. 2 *a back copy:* **past**, old, previous, earlier.
– OPPOSITES front, future.
■ **back down** give in, concede defeat, surrender, yield, submit, climb down, concede. **back out of** renege on, withdraw from, pull out of, retreat from, fail to honour. **back something up** substantiate, corroborate, confirm, support, bear out, endorse, bolster, reinforce, lend weight to. **back someone up** support, stand by, side with, take someone's part. **behind someone's back** secretly, without someone's knowledge, on the sly, sneakily, covertly, surreptitiously.

WORD LINKS
dorsal, **lumbar** relating to the back
supine lying on your back

backbiting noun **malicious talk**, spiteful talk, slander, libel, defamation, abuse; informal bitching, cattiness, mud-slinging, bad-mouthing; Brit. informal slagging off, rubbishing.

backbone noun 1 **spine**, spinal column, vertebral column, vertebrae; back. 2 *infantry are the backbone of most armies:* **mainstay**, cornerstone, foundation. 3 *he has* *enough backbone to see us through:* **strength of character**, strength of will, firmness, resolution, resolve, grit, determination, fortitude, mettle, spirit; informal guts, spunk; Brit. informal bottle.

back-breaking adjective **gruelling**, arduous, strenuous, onerous, punishing, crushing, demanding, exacting, taxing, exhausting, draining; informal killing; Brit. informal knackering.
–OPPOSITES easy.

backer noun **1** *£3 million was provided by the project's backers:* **sponsor**, investor, underwriter, financier, patron, benefactor; informal angel. **2** *the backers of the proposition:* **supporter**, defender, advocate, promoter, proponent; seconder; N. Amer. booster.

backfire verb *Bernard's plan backfired on him:* **rebound**, boomerang, come back; fail; informal blow up in someone's face.

background noun **1** *a background of trees:* **backdrop**, backcloth, surroundings, setting, scene. **2** *students from different backgrounds:* **circumstances**, environment, class, culture, tradition. **3** *her nursing background:* **experience**, record, history, past, training, education.
–OPPOSITES foreground.
■ **in the background** behind the scenes, out of the public eye, out of the spotlight, out of the limelight, backstage.

backhanded adjective **indirect**, ambiguous, oblique, equivocal.
–OPPOSITES direct.

backing noun **1** *he has the backing of his colleagues:* **support**, help, assistance, aid; approval, endorsement. **2** *financial backing:* **sponsorship**, funding, patronage. **3** *musical backing:* **accompaniment**; harmony, obbligato.

backlash noun **adverse reaction**, counterblast, comeback; retaliation, reprisal.

backlog noun **accumulation**, logjam, pile-up.

back-pedal verb *the government has back-pedalled on its plans:* **change your mind**, go into reverse, backtrack, back down, climb down, do a U-turn, renege, go back on, back out of; Brit. do an about-turn.

backslide verb **relapse**, lapse, regress, retrogress, weaken, default.
–OPPOSITES persevere.

backup noun **help**, support, assistance, aid; reinforcements, reserves.

backward adjective **1** *a backward look:* **rearward**, to/towards the rear, to/towards the back, behind you, reverse. **2** *the decision was a backward step:* **retrograde**, retrogressive, regressive, for the worse, in the wrong direction, downhill, negative. **3** *the area is economically backward:* **underdeveloped**, undeveloped; primitive. **4** *he was not backward in displaying his talents:* **hesitant**, reticent, reluctant; shy, diffident, bashful, timid.
–OPPOSITES forward, progressive, advanced, confident.

backwards adverb **1** *she glanced backwards:* **towards the rear**, rearwards, backward, behind you. **2** *count backwards from twenty to ten:* **in reverse**, in reverse order.
–OPPOSITES forwards.

backwoods plural noun **the back of beyond**, the wilds, the hinterland, a backwater; N. Amer. the backcountry; informal the middle of nowhere, the sticks; N. Amer. informal the boondocks.

bacteria plural noun **microorganisms**, microbes, germs, bacilli, pathogens; informal bugs.

bad adjective **1** *bad workmanship:* **substandard**, poor, inferior, second-rate, second-class, unsatisfactory, inadequate, unacceptable, deficient, imperfect, defective, faulty, shoddy, amateurish, careless, negligent; informal crummy, rotten, pathetic, useless, woeful, bum, lousy, ropy; Brit. informal duff, rubbish. **2** *the alcohol had a bad effect:* **harmful**, damaging, detrimental, injurious, hurtful, destructive, ruinous, deleterious, nasty. **3** *the bad guys:* **wicked**, sinful, immoral, evil, corrupt, base, black-hearted, reprobate, amoral; informal crooked, bent. **4** *you bad girl!* **naughty**, badly behaved, disobedient, wayward, wilful, self-willed, defiant, unruly. **5** *bad news:* **unpleasant**, disagreeable, unwelcome; unfortunate; terrible, dreadful, awful, grim,

distressing. **6** *a bad time to arrive:* **inauspicious**, unfavourable, inopportune, unpropitious, unfortunate, disadvantageous, inappropriate, unsuitable. **7** *a bad accident:* **severe**, serious, grave, critical, acute; formal grievous. **8** *the meat's bad:* **rotten**, off, decayed, decomposed, decomposing, putrid. **9** *a bad knee:* **injured**, wounded, diseased; Brit. informal gammy, knackered; Austral./NZ informal crook. **10** *I felt bad about leaving them:* **guilty**, conscience-stricken, remorseful, guilt-ridden, ashamed, contrite.
– OPPOSITES good, beneficial, virtuous, minor.

badge noun **1** pin, brooch; N. Amer. button. **2** *a badge of success:* **sign**, symbol, indication, signal, mark; hallmark, trademark.

badger verb **pester**, harass, bother, plague, torment, hound, nag, chivvy, harry, keep on at, go on at; informal hassle, bug.

badinage noun **banter**, repartee, witty conversation, wordplay, cut and thrust; N. Amer. informal josh.

badly adverb **1** *the job had been very badly done:* **poorly**, incompetently, ineptly, inexpertly, inefficiently, imperfectly, deficiently, defectively, unsatisfactorily, inadequately, incorrectly, faultily, shoddily, amateurishly, carelessly, negligently; informal crummily, pitifully, woefully. **2** *try not to think badly of me:* **unfavourably**, ill, critically, disapprovingly. **3** *stop behaving badly:* **naughtily**, disobediently, wilfully, reprehensibly, mischievously. **4** *he had been badly treated:* **cruelly**, wickedly, unkindly, harshly, shamefully; unfairly, unjustly, wrongly, improperly. **5** *it turned out badly:* **unsuccessfully**, unfavourably, adversely, unfortunately. **6** *some of the victims are badly hurt:* **severely**, seriously, gravely, acutely, critically; formal grievously.
– OPPOSITES well, slightly.

bad-tempered adjective **irritable**, irascible, tetchy, testy, grumpy, grouchy, crotchety, in a bad mood, cantankerous, curmudgeonly, ill-tempered, ill-humoured, peevish, cross, fractious, pettish, crabby; informal snappish, on a short fuse; Brit. informal shirty, stroppy, ratty; N. Amer. informal cranky, ornery; Austral./NZ informal snaky.
– OPPOSITES good-humoured, affable.

baffle verb **perplex**, puzzle, bewilder, mystify, bemuse, confuse, confound, nonplus; informal flummox, faze, stump, beat, fox; N. Amer. informal discombobulate.
– OPPOSITES enlighten.

baffling adjective **puzzling**, **bewildering**, perplexing, mystifying, bemusing, confusing, unclear.
– OPPOSITES clear, comprehensible.

bag noun **suitcase**, case, valise, portmanteau, holdall, grip, overnighter; (**bags**) luggage, baggage.
• verb **1** *locals bagged the most fish:* **catch**, land, capture, trap, snare, ensnare. **2** *he bagged seven medals:* **get**, secure, obtain, acquire, pick up; win, achieve, attain; informal land, net.

baggage noun **luggage**, suitcases, cases, bags.

baggy adjective **loose-fitting**, loose, roomy, generously cut, full, ample, voluminous, billowing.
– OPPOSITES tight.

bail noun *he was released on bail:* **surety**, security, assurance, indemnity; bond, guarantee, pledge.
■ **bail out** *the pilot bailed out:* eject, parachute to safety. **bail someone/something out** rescue, save, relieve; finance, help, assist, aid.

bait noun **1** *the fish let go of the bait:* **lure**, decoy, fly. **2** *was she the bait to lure him into a trap?* **enticement**, lure, decoy, snare, trap, siren, carrot, attraction, draw, magnet; informal come-on.
• verb *he was baited at school:* **taunt**, tease, goad, pick on, torment, persecute, plague, harry, harass, hound; informal needle; Brit. informal wind up.

bake verb *the earth was baked by the sun:* **scorch**, burn, sear, parch, dry up, desiccate.

balance noun **1** *I tripped and lost my balance:* **stability**, equilibrium, steadiness, footing. **2** *political balance in broadcasting:* **fairness**, justice, impartiality; parity, equity, equilibrium, evenness, symmetry, uniformity, comparability. **3** *the*

food was weighed on a balance: **scales**, weighing machine, weighbridge. **4** *the balance of the rent:* **remainder**, outstanding amount, rest, residue, difference.
– OPPOSITES instability, imbalance, bias.
• verb **1** *she balanced the book on her head:* **steady**, stabilize, poise, level. **2** *he balanced his radical remarks with more familiar declarations:* **counterbalance**, offset, even out/up, counteract, compensate for, make up for. **3** *their income and expenditure do not balance:* **correspond**, agree, tally, match up, concur, coincide, be in agreement, be consistent. **4** *you need to balance cost against benefit:* **weigh**, compare, evaluate, consider, assess, appraise, judge.
■ **in the balance** uncertain, undetermined, unsettled, up in the air, unresolved, pending, in limbo, at a turning point, critical. **on balance** overall, all in all, all things considered, taking everything into consideration/account, by and large.

balanced adjective **1** *a balanced view:* **fair**, equitable, just, unbiased, unprejudiced, objective, impartial, dispassionate. **2** *a balanced diet:* **mixed**, varied; healthy, sensible. **3** *a balanced individual:* **level-headed**, well adjusted, mature, stable, sensible, practical, pragmatic, reasonable, rational, sane, even-tempered.
– OPPOSITES partial, unhealthy, neurotic.

bald adjective **1** *a bald head:* **hairless**, smooth, shaven, depilated. **2** *a few bald bushes:* **leafless**, bare, uncovered. **3** *a bald statement:* **plain**, simple, unadorned, unvarnished, unembellished, undisguised; informal upfront.
– OPPOSITES hairy, lush, vague.

baldness noun **hair loss**, hairlessness; Medicine alopecia.

bale[1] noun *a bale of cotton:* **bundle**, truss, bunch, pack, package, parcel.

bale[2] verb
■ **bale out**. See BAIL.

baleful adjective **menacing**, threatening, unfriendly, hostile, antagonistic, evil, evil-intentioned, vindictive, malevolent, malicious, malignant, malign, sinister.
– OPPOSITES benevolent, friendly.

balk verb. See BAULK.

ball[1] noun **sphere**, globe, orb, globule.

ball[2] noun *a fancy-dress ball:* **dance**, dinner dance, masquerade; N. Amer. hoedown, prom.

ballad noun **song**, folk song, shanty, ditty, canzone.

balloon verb **1** *her long skirt ballooned in the wind:* **swell**, puff out/up, bulge, bag, belly out, fill out, billow out. **2** *the company's debt has ballooned:* **increase rapidly**, soar, rocket, shoot up, escalate, mount, spiral; informal go through the roof, skyrocket.

ballot noun **vote**, poll, election, referendum, plebiscite.

balm noun **1** *a skin balm:* **ointment**, lotion, cream, salve, liniment, embrocation, rub, gel, emollient; technical demulcent, humectant. **2** *balm for troubled spirits:* **relief**, comfort, ease, succour, consolation, cheer, solace; literary easement.

balmy adjective **mild**, gentle, temperate, summery, calm, tranquil, clement, fine, pleasant.
– OPPOSITES harsh, wintry.

ban verb **1** *smoking was banned:* **prohibit**, forbid, veto, proscribe, disallow, outlaw, make illegal, embargo, bar, debar; Law enjoin, restrain. **2** *Gary was banned from the playground:* **exclude**, banish, expel, eject, evict, drive out, force out; informal boot out, kick out; Brit. informal turf out.
– OPPOSITES permit, admit.
• noun **1** *a ban on smoking:* **prohibition**, veto, proscription, embargo, bar, moratorium, injunction. **2** *a ban from international football:* **exclusion**, banishment, expulsion, ejection, eviction.
– OPPOSITES permission, admission.

banal adjective **trite**, hackneyed, clichéd, platitudinous, vapid, commonplace, ordinary, common, stock, conventional, stereotyped, overused, overdone, overworked, stale, worn out, time-worn, unimaginative, unoriginal; informal old hat, corny, played out.
– OPPOSITES original.

banality noun **1** *the banality of most sitcoms:* **triteness**, vapidity, staleness, unimaginativeness,

b

prosaicness. **2** *they exchanged banalities:* **platitude**, cliché, truism, commonplace.
– OPPOSITES originality, witticism.

band[1] noun **1** *a band round her waist:* **belt**, sash, girdle, strap, tape, ring, hoop, loop, circlet, circle, cord, tie; literary cincture. **2** *the green band round his pullover:* **stripe**, strip, streak, line, bar.

band[2] noun **1** *a band of robbers:* **group**, gang, mob, pack, troop, troupe, company, party, crew, body, posse; team, side, line-up; association, society, club, circle, fellowship, partnership, guild, lodge, order, fraternity, sorority, union, alliance, institution, league, federation, clique, set, coterie; informal bunch. **2** *the band played on:* **group**, ensemble, orchestra; informal outfit, combo.
• verb **join together**, team up, join forces, pool resources, club together, get together; amalgamate, unite, form an alliance.
– OPPOSITES split up.

bandage verb *she bandaged my knee:* **bind**, dress, strap up.

bandit noun **robber**, thief, raider, mugger; freebooter, outlaw, hijacker, looter, marauder, gangster; dated desperado; literary brigand; historical rustler, highwayman.

bandy[1] adjective *bandy legs:* **bowed**, curved, bent.
– OPPOSITES straight.

bandy[2] verb **1** *lots of figures were bandied about:* **spread about/ around**, put about, discuss, rumour, mention, repeat; literary bruit about/ abroad. **2** *I'm not going to bandy words with you:* **exchange**, swap, trade.

bane noun **scourge**, plague, curse, blight, pest, nuisance, headache, nightmare, trial, hardship, burden, thorn in your flesh/side.

bang noun **1** *the door slammed with a bang:* **thud**, thump, bump, crack, crash, smack, boom, clang, clap, knock, tap, clunk, clonk; stamp, stomp, clump, clomp; report, explosion, detonation. **2** *a nasty bang on the head:* **blow**, knock, thump, bump, hit, smack, crack; informal bash, whack.
• verb **1 hit**, strike, beat, thump, hammer, knock, rap, pound, thud, punch, bump, smack, crack, slap, slam, welt, cuff, pummel, buffet; informal bash, whack, clobber, clout, clip, wallop, belt. **2** *fireworks banged in the air:* **explode**, crack, detonate, burst, blow up.

bangle noun **bracelet**, wristlet, armlet.

banish verb **1** *he was banished for his crime:* **exile**, expel, deport, eject, expatriate, extradite, repatriate, transport; cast out, oust, evict, throw out, exclude, shut out, ban. **2** *he tried to banish his fear:* **dispel**, dismiss, disperse, scatter, dissipate, drive away, chase away, shut out.

banister noun **handrail**; baluster; balustrade.

bank[1] noun **1** *the banks of Lake Michigan:* **edge**, side, embankment, levee, border, verge, boundary. **2** *a grassy bank:* **slope**, rise, incline, gradient, ramp; mound, ridge, hillock, hummock, knoll; bar, reef, shoal, shelf; pile, heap, mass, drift. **3** *a bank of switches:* **array**, row, line, tier, group, series.
• verb **1** *they banked up the earth:* **pile up**, heap up, stack up; accumulate, amass. **2** *the aircraft banked:* **tilt**, lean, tip, slant, incline, angle, slope, list, camber, pitch, dip, cant.

> **WORD LINKS**
> **riparian**, **riverine** relating to or found on a riverbank

bank[2] noun **store**, reserve, accumulation, stock, stockpile, supply, pool, fund, cache, hoard, deposit; storehouse, reservoir.
• verb **deposit**, pay in; keep, save.

bankrupt adjective **1** *the company was declared bankrupt:* **insolvent**, failed, ruined; Brit. in administration, in receivership; informal bust, belly up; Brit. informal skint, stony broke, in Queer Street. **2** *this government is bankrupt of ideas:* **bereft**, devoid, empty, destitute; without, in need of, wanting; informal minus, sans.
– OPPOSITES solvent.
• verb **ruin**, impoverish, reduce to penury.

bankruptcy noun **insolvency**, liquidation, failure, financial ruin; Brit. administration, receivership.
– OPPOSITES solvency.

banner noun **1** *students waved banners:* **placard**, sign, poster, notice. **2** *banners fluttered above the troops:* **flag**, standard, ensign, colours, pennant, banderole.

banquet noun **feast**, dinner; informal spread, blowout; Brit. informal nosh-up, slap-up meal.
– OPPOSITES snack.

banter noun *a brief exchange of banter:* **repartee**, witty conversation, raillery, wordplay, cut and thrust, badinage.
• verb *sightseers were bantering with the guards:* **joke**, jest, quip; informal josh, wisecrack.

baptism noun **1** *the baptism ceremony:* **christening**, naming. **2** *his baptism as a politician:* **initiation**, debut, introduction, inauguration, launch, rite of passage.

baptize verb **1** *he was baptized Enoch:* **christen**, name, call. **2** *they were baptized into the church:* **admit**, initiate, enrol, recruit.

bar noun **1** *an iron bar:* **rod**, pole, stick, batten, shaft, rail, paling, spar, strut, crosspiece, beam. **2** *a bar of chocolate:* **block**, slab, cake, tablet, wedge, ingot. **3** *your drinks are on the bar:* **counter**, table, buffet. **4** *she had a drink in a bar:* **hostelry**, tavern, inn, taproom; Brit. pub, public house; informal watering hole; Brit. informal local, boozer; dated alehouse. **5** *a bar to promotion:* **obstacle**, impediment, hindrance, obstruction, block, hurdle, barrier. **6** (Brit.) *members of the Bar:* **barristers**, advocates, counsel.
– OPPOSITES aid.
• verb **1** *they have barred the door:* **bolt**, lock, fasten, secure, block, barricade, obstruct. **2** *I was barred from entering:* **prohibit**, debar, preclude, forbid, ban, interdict, inhibit; exclude; obstruct, hinder, block.
– OPPOSITES open, admit.
• preposition *everyone bar me already knew:* **except**, excluding, not including, excepting, omitting, not counting, but, besides, apart from, aside from, other than, saving; with the exception of; formal save.

barb noun **1 spike**, prong, spur, thorn, needle, prickle, spine, quill. **2** *the barbs from his critics:* **insult**, sneer, jibe, cutting remark, shaft, slight, brickbat, slur, jeer, taunt; (**barbs**) abuse, disparagement, scoffing, scorn, sarcasm, goading; informal dig, put-down.

barbarian noun *the city was besieged by barbarians:* **savage**, heathen, brute, beast; ruffian, thug, lout, vandal, hoodlum, hooligan; informal roughneck; Brit. informal yob, lager lout.
• adjective *the barbarian hordes:* **savage**, uncivilized, barbaric, primitive, heathen, wild, brutish, Neanderthal.
– OPPOSITES civilized.

barbaric adjective **1** *barbaric crimes:* **brutal**, barbarous, brutish, bestial, savage, vicious, wicked, cruel, ruthless, merciless, villainous, murderous, heinous, monstrous, vile, inhuman, infernal, dark, fiendish, diabolical. **2** *barbaric cultures:* **savage**, barbarian, primitive, heathen, wild, brutish, uncivilized.
– OPPOSITES civilized.

barbarity noun **1** *the barbarity of slavery:* **brutality**, brutalism, cruelty, bestiality, barbarism, barbarousness, savagery, viciousness, wickedness, villainy, baseness, inhumanity. **2** *the barbarities of the last war:* **atrocity**, crime, outrage, enormity.
– OPPOSITES benevolence.

barbarous adjective. See **BARBARIC** sense 1.

barbed adjective **hurtful**, wounding, cutting, stinging, mean, spiteful, nasty, cruel, vicious, unkind, snide, scathing, pointed, bitter, acid, caustic, sharp, vitriolic, venomous, poisonous, hostile, malicious, malevolent, vindictive; informal bitchy, catty.
– OPPOSITES kindly.

bare adjective **1** *he was bare to the waist:* **naked**, unclothed, undressed, uncovered, exposed, stripped, nude; informal without a stitch on, in your birthday suit, in the raw, in the altogether, in the buff; Brit. informal starkers; Scottish informal in the scud; N. Amer. informal buck naked. **2** *a bare room:* **empty**, unfurnished; stark, austere, spartan, unadorned, unembellished, unornamented,

b

plain. **3** *a cupboard bare of food:* **empty**, devoid, bereft; without, lacking. **4** *a bare landscape:* **barren**, bleak, exposed, desolate, stark, arid, desert. **5** *the bare facts:* **basic**, essential, fundamental, plain, straightforward, simple, pure, stark, bald, cold, hard, brutal, harsh.
– OPPOSITES dressed.
• verb **uncover**, strip, undress, unclothe, denude, expose.
– OPPOSITES cover.

! Don't confuse **bare** with **bear**. The main meaning of the verb **bear** is 'carry' (*he was bearing a tray of wine glasses*).

barefaced adjective **flagrant**, blatant, glaring, obvious, undisguised, unconcealed, naked; shameless, unabashed, unashamed, impudent, audacious, brazen, brass-necked.

barely adverb **hardly**, scarcely, only just, narrowly, by the skin of your teeth, by a hair's breadth; almost not; informal by a whisker.
– OPPOSITES easily.

bargain noun **1** *I'll make a bargain with you:* **agreement**, arrangement, understanding, deal; contract, pact; pledge, promise. **2** *this coat is a bargain at £50:* **good value**; informal good buy, cheap buy, snip, steal, giveaway.
• verb **haggle**, negotiate, discuss terms, deal, barter.
■ **bargain for/on** expect, anticipate, be prepared for, allow for, plan for, reckon with, take into account/consideration, contemplate, imagine, envisage, foresee, predict; count on, rely on, depend on, bank on, plan on, reckon on; N. Amer. informal figure on. **into the bargain** also, as well, in addition, besides, on top of that, over and above that, to boot, for good measure.

barge noun lighter, canal boat; Brit. narrowboat.
• verb **push**, shove, force, elbow, shoulder, jostle, bulldoze, muscle.
■ **barge in** burst in, break in, butt in, cut in, interrupt, intrude, encroach; gatecrash; informal horn in.

bark[1] verb **1** *the dog barked:* **woof**, yap, yelp, bay. **2** *'Okay, outside!' he barked:* snap; shout, bawl, cry, yell, roar, bellow, thunder; informal holler.
– OPPOSITES whisper.

bark[2] noun *the bark of a tree:* **rind**, skin, peel, covering.
• verb *he barked his shin:* **scrape**, graze, scratch, abrade, scuff, rasp, skin.

WORD LINKS
corticate relating to bark

barn noun **outbuilding**, shed, outhouse, shelter; stable, stall; Brit. byre.

baron noun **1** **lord**, noble, nobleman, aristocrat, peer. **2** *a press baron:* **magnate**, tycoon, mogul, captain of industry, nabob, mandarin.

baroque adjective **1** *the baroque exuberance of his printed shirts:* **ornate**, fancy, over-elaborate, extravagant, rococo, fussy, busy, ostentatious, showy. **2** *baroque prose:* **flowery**, florid, flamboyant, high-flown, magniloquent, grandiloquent; informal highfalutin, purple.
– OPPOSITES plain.

barrack verb (Brit. & Austral./NZ) **jeer**, heckle, shout at/down; interrupt, boo, hiss.
– OPPOSITES applaud.

barracks plural noun **garrison**, camp, encampment, depot, billet, quarters, fort, cantonment.

barrage noun **1** *an artillery barrage:* **bombardment**, cannonade; gunfire, shelling; salvo, volley, fusillade; historical broadside. **2** *a barrage of criticism:* **deluge**, stream, storm, torrent, onslaught, flood, spate, tide, avalanche, hail, blaze; abundance, mass, profusion. **3** *a barrage across the river:* **dam**, barrier, weir, dyke, embankment, wall.

barrel noun **cask**, keg, butt, vat, tun, drum, hogshead, kilderkin, pin, pipe; historical firkin.

WORD LINKS
cooper a person who makes barrels

barren adjective **1** *barren land:* **unproductive**, infertile, unfruitful, sterile, arid, desert. **2** *a barren exchange of courtesies:* **pointless**, futile, worthless, profitless, unrewarding, purposeless, useless, vain, aimless, hollow, empty, vacuous, vapid.
– OPPOSITES fertile.

barricade noun *a barricade across the street:* **barrier**, roadblock,

blockade; obstacle, obstruction.
• verb *they barricaded the building:* **seal**, close up, block off, shut off/up; defend, protect, fortify, occupy.

barrier noun **1** **fence**, railing, barricade, hurdle, bar, blockade, roadblock. **2** *a barrier to international trade:* **obstacle**, obstruction, hurdle, stumbling block, bar, impediment, hindrance, curb.

barring preposition **excepting**, with the exception of, discounting, short of, apart from, but for, other than, aside from, excluding, omitting, leaving out, saving; informal outside of.

barrister noun **counsel**, Queen's Counsel, QC, lawyer; Scottish advocate; N. Amer. attorney, counselor; informal brief; (**barristers**) Brit. the Bar.

barter verb **1** *they bartered grain for salt:* **trade**, swap, exchange, sell. **2** *you can barter for souvenirs:* **haggle**, bargain, negotiate, deal, dicker.
• noun *an economy based on barter:* **trading**, exchange, business, commerce, buying and selling, dealing.

base[1] noun **1** *the base of the tower:* **foundation**, bottom, foot, support, stand, pedestal, plinth. **2** *the system uses existing technology as its base:* **basis**, foundation, bedrock, starting point, source, origin, root, core, key component. **3** *the troops returned to their base:* **headquarters**, camp, site, station, settlement, post, centre.
– OPPOSITES top.
• verb **1** *he based his idea on a movie:* **found**, build, construct, form, ground, root; (**be based on**) derive from, spring from, stem from, originate in, issue from. **2** *the company was based in London:* **locate**, situate, position, install, station, site.

base[2] adjective *base motives:* **sordid**, ignoble, low, mean, immoral, improper, unseemly, unscrupulous, unprincipled, dishonest, dishonourable, shameful, bad, wrong, evil, wicked, iniquitous, sinful.
– OPPOSITES noble.

baseless adjective *baseless accusations:* **groundless**, unfounded, without foundation; unsubstantiated, unproven, unsupported, uncorroborated, unconfirmed, unverified, unattested; unjustified, unwarranted; speculative, conjectural; unsound, unreliable, spurious, specious, trumped up, fabricated, untrue.
– OPPOSITES valid.

basement noun **cellar**, vault, crypt, undercroft; Scottish dunny.

bashful adjective **shy**, reserved, diffident, inhibited, retiring, reticent, reluctant, shrinking; hesitant, timid, apprehensive, nervous, wary.
– OPPOSITES bold, confident.

basic adjective **1** *basic human rights:* **fundamental**, essential, primary, principal, cardinal, elementary, quintessential, intrinsic, central, pivotal, critical, key, focal; vital, necessary, indispensable. **2** *basic cooking facilities:* **plain**, simple, unsophisticated, straightforward, adequate; unadorned, undecorated, unornamented; spartan, stark, severe, austere, limited, meagre, rudimentary, patchy, sketchy, minimal; unfussy, crude, makeshift; informal bog-standard.
– OPPOSITES secondary, unimportant, elaborate.

basically adverb **fundamentally**, essentially, in essence; firstly, first and foremost, primarily; at heart, at bottom, au fond; principally, chiefly, above all, mostly, mainly, on the whole, by and large, substantially; intrinsically, inherently; informal at the end of the day, when all is said and done.

basics plural noun **fundamentals**, essentials, rudiments, first principles, foundations, preliminaries, groundwork; essence, basis, core; informal nitty-gritty, brass tacks, nuts and bolts, ABC.

basin noun **1** **bowl**, dish, pan. **2** *a basin among low hills:* **valley**, hollow, dip, depression.

basis noun **1** *the basis of his method:* **foundation**, support, base; reasoning, rationale, defence; reason, grounds, justification, motivation. **2** *the basis of discussion:* **starting point**, base, point of departure, beginning, premise, fundamental point/principle, principal constituent, cornerstone,

b

core, heart, thrust, essence, kernel, nub. **3** *she's employed on a part-time basis:* **footing**, condition, status, position; arrangement.

bask verb **1** *I basked in the sun:* **laze**, lie, lounge, relax, sprawl, loll. **2** *she's basking in all the glory:* **revel**, delight, luxuriate, wallow, take pleasure, rejoice, glory; enjoy, relish, savour, lap up.

basket noun **hamper**, pannier, punnet, trug, creel.

bass adjective **low**, deep, resonant, sonorous, rumbling, booming, resounding; baritone.
– OPPOSITES high.

bastardize verb **adulterate**, corrupt, contaminate, weaken, dilute, taint, pollute, debase, distort.

bastion noun **1** *the town wall and bastions:* **projection**, outwork, breastwork, barbican. **2** *a bastion of respectability:* **stronghold**, bulwark, defender, supporter, guard, protection, protector, defence, prop, mainstay.

batch noun **group**, quantity, lot, bunch, mass, cluster, raft, set, collection, bundle, pack; consignment, shipment.

bathe verb **1** *I bathed in the pool:* **swim**, take a dip. **2** *they bathed his wounds:* **clean**, wash, rinse, wet, soak. **3** *the room was bathed in light:* **suffuse**, permeate, pervade, envelop, flood, cover, wash, fill.

bathos noun **anticlimax**, let-down, disappointment, disillusionment; absurdity; informal comedown.

baton noun **1** *the conductor's baton:* **stick**, rod, staff, wand. **2** *police batons:* **truncheon**, club, cudgel, bludgeon, stick, mace, shillelagh; Brit. cosh; N. Amer. nightstick, blackjack.

battalion noun *a battalion of supporters.* See CROWD noun sense 1.

batten noun *a timber batten:* **bar**, bolt, rail, shaft; board, strip.
• verb *he was battening down the shutters:* **fasten**, fix, secure, clamp, lash, make fast, nail, seal.

batter verb **pummel**, pound, hit repeatedly, rain blows on, buffet, belabour, thrash, beat up; informal knock about/around, beat the living daylights out of, lay into, lace into, do over, rough up.

battered adjective **damaged**, shabby, run down, worn out, falling to pieces, falling apart, dilapidated, rickety, ramshackle, crumbling.

battery noun **1** *a gun battery:* **emplacement**, artillery unit; cannonry, ordnance. **2** *a battery of equipment:* **array**, set, bank, group, row, line, line-up, collection. **3** *a battery of tests:* **series**, sequence, cycle, string, succession. **4** *assault and battery:* **violence**, mugging; Brit. grievous bodily harm, GBH, actual bodily harm, ABH.

battle noun **1** *he was killed in the battle:* **fight**, armed conflict, clash, struggle, skirmish, engagement, fray, duel; war, campaign, crusade; warfare, combat, action, hostilities; informal scrap, dogfight, shoot-out. **2** *a legal battle:* **conflict**, clash, contest, competition, struggle; disagreement, argument, altercation, dispute, controversy.
• verb **1** *he has been battling against illness:* **fight**, combat, contend with; resist, withstand, stand up to, confront; war, feud; struggle, strive, work. **2** *Mark battled his way to the bar:* **force**, push, elbow, shoulder, fight; struggle, labour.

battle cry noun **1** *the army's battle cry:* **war cry**, war whoop, rallying call/cry. **2** *the battle cry of the feminist movement:* **slogan**, motto, watchword, catchphrase.

battlefield noun **battleground**, field of battle, field of operations, combat zone, front.

battlement noun **castellation**, crenellation, parapet, rampart, wall.

bauble noun **trinket**, knick-knack, ornament, frippery, gewgaw, gimcrack, bibelot.

baulk verb **1** *I baulk at paying that much:* **be unwilling to**, draw the line at, jib at, be reluctant to, hesitate over; eschew, resist, refuse to, take exception to; draw back from, flinch from, shrink from, recoil from, demur from. **2** *they were baulked by traffic:* **impede**, obstruct, thwart, hinder, prevent, check, stop, curb, halt, bar, block, forestall, frustrate.

bawdy adjective **ribald**, indecent, risqué, racy, rude, spicy, sexy, suggestive, titillating, naughty,

improper, indelicate, indecorous, off colour, earthy, broad, locker-room, Rabelaisian; obscene, vulgar, crude, coarse, gross, lewd, dirty, filthy, smutty, unseemly, salacious, prurient, lascivious, licentious; informal X-rated, blue, raunchy; euphemistic adult.
– OPPOSITES clean, innocent.

bawl verb **1** *'Come on!' he bawled:* **shout**, yell, roar, bellow, screech, scream, shriek, howl, whoop, bark, trumpet, thunder; informal yammer, holler. **2** *the children continued to bawl:* **cry**, sob, weep, shed tears, wail, whine, howl, squall, ululate; Scottish informal greet.
– OPPOSITES whisper.

bay[1] noun *ships were anchored in the bay:* **cove**, inlet, indentation, gulf, bight, basin, fjord, arm; natural harbour, anchorage.

bay[2] noun *there was a bay let into the wall:* **alcove**, recess, niche, nook, opening, hollow, cavity, inglenook.

bay[3] verb **1** *the hounds bayed:* **howl**, bark, yelp, yap, cry, bellow, roar. **2** *the crowd bayed for an encore:* **clamour**, shout, call, press, yell, scream, shriek, roar; demand, insist on.
■ **at bay** at a distance, away, off, at arm's length.

bazaar noun **1** *a Turkish bazaar:* **market**, souk, mart. **2** *the church bazaar:* **fete**, fair; fund-raiser, charity event; Brit. jumble sale, bring-and-buy sale, car boot sale; N. Amer. tag sale.

be verb **1** *there was once a king:* **exist**, have being, have existence; live, be alive, have life, breathe, draw breath, be extant. **2** *the trial is tomorrow:* **occur**, happen, take place, come about, arise, fall, materialize, ensue; literary come to pass, befall, betide. **3** *the bed is over there:* **be situated**, be located, be found, be present, be set, be positioned, be placed, be installed; sit, lie, live. **4** *it has been like this for hours:* **remain**, stay, last, continue, persist.

beach verb *they beached the boat:* **land**, ground, strand, run aground, run ashore.

beachcomber noun **scavenger**, forager, collector.

beached adjective **stranded**, grounded, aground, ashore, marooned, high and dry, stuck.
– OPPOSITES afloat.

beacon noun signal, danger signal, bonfire; lighthouse.

bead noun **1** *glass beads:* **ball**, globule, sphere, spheroid, oval, ovoid, orb, round; (**beads**) necklace, rosary, chaplet. **2** *beads of sweat:* **droplet**, drop, blob, dot.

beak noun **bill**, nib, mandible; Scottish & N. English neb.

beaker noun **cup**, tumbler, glass, mug, drinking vessel.

beam noun **1** *an oak beam:* **joist**, lintel, rafter, purlin; spar, girder, baulk, timber, plank; support, strut. **2** *a beam of light:* **ray**, shaft, stream, streak; flash, gleam, glow, glimmer, glint. **3** *the beam on her face:* **grin**, smile.
– OPPOSITES frown.
• verb **1** *the signal is beamed out:* **broadcast**, transmit, relay, send/put out, disseminate; direct, aim. **2** *the sun beamed down:* **shine**, radiate, glare, gleam. **3** *he beamed broadly:* **grin**, smile, smirk; informal be all smiles.
– OPPOSITES frown.

bear[1] verb **1** *she was bearing a tray of drinks:* **carry**, bring, transport, move, convey, take, fetch; informal tote. **2** *the bag bore my name:* **display**, exhibit, be marked with, show, carry, have. **3** *will it bear his weight?* **support**, carry, hold up, prop up, withstand. **4** *they can't bear the cost alone:* **sustain**, carry, support, shoulder, absorb, take on. **5** *she still bears a grudge:* **harbour**, foster, entertain, cherish, nurse, nurture. **6** *I can't bear his sarcasm any more:* **tolerate**, put up with, take, endure, stand, stomach; informal hack; Brit. informal stick, wear; formal brook. **7** *she bore a son:* **give birth to**, deliver, have, produce, spawn. **8** *a shrub that bears red berries:* **produce**, yield, give, grow, provide, supply. **9** *bear left at the junction:* **turn**, veer, fork, diverge, bend.
■ **bear yourself** conduct yourself, carry yourself, acquit yourself, act, behave, perform; formal comport yourself. **bear down on** advance on, close in on, move in on, converge

b

on. **bear something in mind** take into account, remember, consider, be mindful of, mark, heed. **bear on** relate to, affect, concern, be relevant to, apply to, be pertinent to; formal appertain to. **bear something out** confirm, corroborate, substantiate, endorse, vindicate, give credence to, support, ratify, warrant, uphold, justify, prove, authenticate, verify. **bear with** be patient with, make allowances for, tolerate, put up with, endure. **bear witness/testimony to** testify to, be evidence of, be proof of, attest to, vouch for; demonstrate, show, establish, indicate, reveal, bespeak.

> ! Don't confuse **bear** with **bare**, which means 'naked' (*her bare legs*) or 'uncover' (*he bared his chest*).

bear[2] **noun**

> **WORD LINKS**
> **ursine** relating to bears

bearable **adjective** **tolerable**, endurable, sustainable.

beard **noun** **facial hair**, whiskers, stubble, five o'clock shadow, bristles. • **verb** **confront**, face, challenge, brave, stand up against, square up to.

bearded **adjective** **unshaven**, whiskered; stubbly, bristly. – OPPOSITES clean shaven.

bearer **noun** **1** *a lantern-bearer:* **carrier**, porter. **2** *the bearer of bad news:* **messenger**, agent, conveyor, carrier, emissary. **3** *the bearer of the documents:* **holder**, possessor, owner.

bearing **noun** **1** *a man of military bearing:* **posture**, stance, carriage, gait; Brit. deportment; formal comportment. **2** *a rather regal bearing:* **demeanour**, manner, air, aspect, attitude, mien, style. **3** *this has no bearing on the matter:* **relevance**, pertinence, connection, appositeness, germaneness, importance, significance. **4** *a bearing of 015°:* **direction**, orientation, course, trajectory, heading, tack, path. **5** *I lost my bearings:* **orientation**, sense of direction; whereabouts, location, position.

beast **noun** **1** *the beasts of the forest:* **animal**, creature, brute; N. Amer. informal critter. **2** *he is a cruel beast:* **monster**, brute, savage, barbarian, animal, swine, pig, ogre, fiend, sadist, demon, devil.

beat **verb** **1** **hit**, strike, batter, thump, bang, hammer, punch, knock, thrash, pound, pummel, slap, rain blows on; assault, attack, abuse; cudgel, club, birch; informal wallop, belt, bash, whack, clout, clobber, slug, tan, biff, bop, sock, deck. **2** *the waves beat along the shore:* **break on/against**, dash against; lash, strike, lap, wash; splash, ripple, roll. **3** *we beat them 4–1:* **defeat**, conquer, win against, get the better of, trounce, rout, overpower, overcome; informal lick, thrash, whip, clobber; literary vanquish. **4** *he beat the record:* **surpass**, exceed, better, improve on, eclipse, transcend, top, trump, cap. **5** *her heart was still beating:* **pulsate**, pulse, palpitate, vibrate, throb; pump, pound, thump, thud, hammer, drum. **6** *the eagle beat its wings:* **flap**, flutter, thrash, wave, vibrate, oscillate. **7** *beat the cream into the mixture:* **whisk**, mix, blend, whip. **8** *the metal is beaten into a die:* **hammer**, forge, form, shape, mould, work, stamp, fashion, model. **9** *she beat a path through the grass:* **tread**, tramp, trample, wear, flatten. • **noun** **1** *the song has a good beat:* **rhythm**, pulse, metre, time, measure, cadence; stress, accent. **2** *the beat of her heart:* **pulse**, pulsating, vibration, throb, palpitation, reverberation; pounding, thump, thud, hammering, drumming. **3** *a policeman on his beat:* **circuit**, round, route, path.
■ **beat someone/something off** repel, fight off, fend off, stave off, repulse, drive away/back, force back, push back. **beat someone up** assault, attack, mug; informal knock about/around, do over, work over, rough up, fill in, lay into; Brit. informal duff someone up; N. Amer. informal beat up on.

beatific **adjective** **1** *a beatific smile:* **rapturous**, joyful, ecstatic, seraphic, blissful, serene, happy, beaming. **2** *a beatific vision:* **blessed**, exalted, sublime, heavenly, holy, divine, celestial, paradisiacal, glorious.

beatify **verb** **canonize**, bless, sanctify, hallow, consecrate.

beatitude noun **blessedness**, benediction, grace; bliss, ecstasy, exaltation, supreme happiness, divine joy/rapture; saintliness.

beautiful adjective **attractive**, pretty, handsome, good-looking, alluring, prepossessing; lovely, delightful, appealing, engaging, winsome; ravishing, gorgeous, stunning, arresting, glamorous, bewitching, beguiling; graceful, elegant, exquisite, magnificent; Scottish & N. English bonny; informal tasty, divine, knockout, drop-dead gorgeous, fanciable; Brit. informal smashing; N. Amer. informal cute, foxy; Austral./NZ informal beaut, spunky; literary beauteous.
–OPPOSITES ugly.

beautify verb **adorn**, embellish, enhance, decorate, ornament, garnish, gild, smarten, prettify, enrich, glamorize; informal get up, do up, do out, tart up.
–OPPOSITES spoil, uglify.

beauty noun **1 attractiveness**, prettiness, good looks, comeliness, allure, loveliness, appeal; winsomeness, grace, elegance, exquisiteness; splendour, magnificence, grandeur, impressiveness; gorgeousness, glamour; literary beauteousness, pulchritude. **2** *she is a beauty:* **beautiful woman**, belle, vision, Venus, goddess, picture; informal looker, lovely, stunner, knockout, bombshell, dish, cracker, peach, eyeful, bit of all right; Brit. informal smasher. **3** *the beauty of this plan:* **advantage**, attraction, strength, benefit, boon, good thing, strong point, virtue, merit.
–OPPOSITES ugliness, drawback.

becalmed adjective **motionless**, still, at a standstill, at a halt, unmoving.

because conjunction **since**, as, in view of the fact that, seeing that; literary for.
–OPPOSITES despite.
■ **because of** on account of, as a result of, as a consequence of, owing to, due to; thanks to, by/in virtue of; formal by reason of.

beckon verb **1** *the guard beckoned to Benny:* **gesture**, signal, wave, gesticulate, motion. **2** *the countryside beckons you:* **entice**, invite, tempt, coax, lure, charm, attract, draw, call.

become verb **1** *she became rich:* **grow**, get, turn, come to be, get to be; literary wax. **2** *he became a tyrant:* **turn into**, change into, develop into, evolve into. **3** *he became Foreign Secretary:* **be appointed**, be nominated, be elected, be made. **4** *the dress becomes her:* **suit**, flatter, look good on; set off, show to advantage; informal do something for. **5** *it ill becomes him to preach the gospel:* **befit**, suit; formal behove.
■ **become of** happen to, be the fate of, overtake; literary befall, betide.

becoming adjective **flattering**, fetching; attractive, lovely, pretty, handsome; stylish, elegant, chic, fashionable, tasteful.

bed noun **1** couch, berth, billet; informal the sack, the hay; Brit. informal your pit; Scottish informal your kip. **2** *a flower bed:* **patch**, plot, border, strip. **3** *the structure is built on a bed of stones:* **base**, foundation, support, prop, substructure, substratum. **4** *a river bed:* **bottom**, floor, ground.
•verb **1** *the tiles are bedded in mortar:* **embed**, set, fix, insert, inlay, implant, bury, base, plant, settle. **2** *it's time to bed out the seedlings:* **plant**, transplant.
■ **go to bed** retire; informal hit the sack, hit the hay, turn in.

bedeck verb **decorate**, adorn, ornament, embellish, furnish, garnish, trim, deck; swathe, wreathe, festoon; informal get up, do out.

bedevil verb **afflict**, torment, beset, assail, beleaguer, plague, blight, rack, oppress; harass, distress, trouble, worry, torture.

bedlam noun **uproar**, pandemonium, commotion, mayhem, confusion, disorder, chaos, anarchy, lawlessness; furore, upheaval, hubbub, hurly-burly, turmoil, riot, ruckus, rumpus, tumult; informal hullabaloo.
–OPPOSITES calm.

bedraggled adjective **dishevelled**, disordered, untidy, unkempt, tousled, disarranged; N. Amer. informal mussed.
–OPPOSITES neat, clean, dry.

bedridden adjective immobilized; informal laid up, flat on your back.

bedrock noun **core**, basis, base, foundation, roots, heart, backbone, principle, essence, nitty-gritty; informal nuts and bolts.

b

bedspread noun **bedcover**, coverlet, quilt, throw-over, blanket; Brit. eiderdown; N. Amer. throw, spread, comforter; dated counterpane.

bee noun

WORD LINKS
apian relating to bees
apiary a place where bees are kept

beefy adjective (informal) **muscular**, brawny, hefty, burly, hulking, strapping, well built, solid, strong, powerful, heavy, robust, sturdy.
– OPPOSITES puny.

beer noun **ale**, brew; Brit. informal wallop, pint, jar; Austral./NZ informal hop, sherbet.

beetling adjective **projecting**, protruding, prominent, overhanging, sticking out, jutting out.

befitting adjective *he couldn't have chosen a more befitting slogan:* **appropriate**, apt, fit, suitable, suited, proper, right.

before preposition **1** *he dressed up before going out:* **prior to**, previous to, earlier than, preparatory to, in preparation for, preliminary to, in anticipation of, in expectation of; in advance of, ahead of; pre-. **2** *he appeared before the judge:* **in front of**, in the presence of, in the sight of. **3** *death before dishonour:* **in preference to**, rather than, sooner than.
– OPPOSITES after.
• adverb **1** *she has ridden before:* **previously**, before now/then, until now/then, up to now/then; earlier, formerly, hitherto, in the past, in days gone by; formal heretofore. **2** *a small party went on before:* **ahead**, in front, in advance.
– OPPOSITES behind.

beforehand adverb **in advance**, in readiness, ahead of time; before, before now/then, earlier, previously, already, sooner.
– OPPOSITES afterwards.

befuddled adjective **confused**, muddled, addled, bewildered, disorientated, all at sea, fazed, perplexed, dazed, dizzy, stupefied, groggy, muzzy, foggy, fuzzy; informal mixed up, dopey, woozy; N. Amer. informal discombobulated.
– OPPOSITES clear.

beg verb **1** *he begged on the streets:* **ask for money**, seek charity, seek alms; informal sponge, cadge, scrounge, bum. **2** *we begged for mercy:* **ask for**, request, plead for, appeal for, call for, sue for, solicit, seek, press for. **3** *he begged her not to go:* **implore**, entreat, plead with, appeal to, supplicate, pray to, importune; ask, request, call on, petition; literary beseech.

beggar noun **tramp**, vagrant, vagabond, mendicant; N. Amer. hobo; informal scrounger, sponger, cadger, freeloader; Brit. informal dosser; N. Amer. informal bum; Austral./NZ informal bagman.

beggarly adjective *a beggarly sum:* **meagre**, paltry, pitiful, miserable, miserly, ungenerous, scant, inadequate, insufficient, insubstantial; informal measly, stingy, pathetic, piddling, piffling, mingy; formal exiguous.
– OPPOSITES considerable.

beggary noun **poverty**, penury, destitution, ruin, ruination, indigence, impecuniousness, impoverishment, need, privation, pauperism, mendicity, want, hardship, reduced circumstances.

begin verb **1** *we began work:* **start**, commence, set about, go about, embark on, launch into, get down to, take up; initiate, set in motion, institute, inaugurate; informal get cracking on. **2** *he began by saying hello:* **open**, lead off, get under way, get going, get off the ground, start, commence; informal start the ball rolling, kick off. **3** *when did the illness begin?* **appear**, arise, become apparent, spring up, crop up, turn up, come into existence, originate, start, commence, develop.
– OPPOSITES finish, end, disappear.

beginner noun **novice**, starter, raw recruit, newcomer, tyro, fledgling, neophyte, initiate, fresher, probationer; postulant, novitiate; informal rookie, new kid on the block; N. Amer. informal tenderfoot, greenhorn.
– OPPOSITES expert, veteran.

beginning noun **1** *the beginning of socialism:* **dawn**, birth, inception, conception, origination, genesis, emergence, rise, start, commencement, launch, onset, outset; day one; informal kick-off. **2** *the beginning of the article:* **opening**, start, commencement, first part,

introduction, preamble. **3** *the therapy has its beginnings in China:* **origin**, source, roots, starting point, birthplace, cradle, spring; genesis, creation.
– OPPOSITES end, conclusion.

begrudge verb **1** *she begrudged Brian his affluence:* **envy**; resent, be jealous of, be envious of. **2** *don't begrudge the cost:* **resent**, feel aggrieved about, be resentful of, mind, object to, take exception to.

beguile verb **1** *she was beguiled by his charming manner:* **charm**, attract, enchant, entrance, win over, woo, captivate, bewitch, spellbind, dazzle, hypnotize, mesmerize, seduce. **2** *they were beguiled into signing the treaty:* **trick**, dupe, deceive, hoodwink.
– OPPOSITES repel.

beguiling adjective **charming**, enchanting, entrancing, charismatic, captivating, bewitching, spellbinding, hypnotizing, mesmerizing, magnetic, alluring, enticing, tempting, inviting, seductive; informal come-hither.
– OPPOSITES unappealing.

behalf noun
■ **on behalf of/on someone's behalf** **1** *I am writing on behalf of my client:* as a representative of, as a spokesperson for, for, in the name of, in place of, on the authority of, at the behest of. **2** *a campaign on behalf of cycling:* in the interests of, in support of, for, for the benefit of, for the good of, for the sake of.

behave verb **1** *she behaved badly:* **conduct yourself**, act, acquit yourself, bear yourself; formal comport yourself. **2** *the children behaved themselves:* **be well mannered**, be well behaved, be good, be polite, mind your Ps and Qs.
– OPPOSITES misbehave.

behaviour noun **1** *his behaviour was inexcusable:* **conduct**, deportment, bearing, etiquette; actions, doings; manners, ways; formal comportment. **2** *the behaviour of these organisms:* **functioning**, action, performance, operation, working, reaction, response.

WORD LINKS

ethology the science or study of behaviour

behead verb **decapitate**, guillotine.

behind preposition **1** *he hid behind a tree:* **at the back/rear of**, beyond, on the far/other side of; N. Amer. in back of. **2** *a guard ran behind him:* **after**, following, hard on the heels of, in the wake of. **3** *he was behind the bombings:* **responsible for**, at the bottom of, the cause of, the source of; to blame for, culpable of, guilty of. **4** *they have the nation behind them:* **supporting**, backing, for, on the side of, in agreement with; financing; informal rooting for.
– OPPOSITES in front of, ahead of.
• adverb **1** *we're behind, so don't stop:* **late**, running late, behind schedule, behindhand, not on time. **2** *he was behind with his subscription:* **in arrears**, overdue; late, behindhand.

behindhand adjective **behind**, behind schedule/time; late, belated, slow, unpunctual.
– OPPOSITES ahead.

beholden adjective **indebted**, in someone's debt, obligated, under an obligation; grateful, owing a debt of gratitude.

beige adjective **fawn**, pale brown, buff, sand, sandy, oatmeal, biscuit, coffee-coloured, café au lait, camel.

being noun **1** *she is warmed by his very being:* **existence**, living, life, reality, actuality, lifeblood, vital force. **2** *God is alive in the being of man:* **soul**, spirit, nature, essence, inner self, psyche; heart, bosom, breast. **3** *an enlightened being:* **creature**, life form, living thing, individual, person, human.

belabour verb **attack**, beat, hit, strike, smack, batter, pummel, pound, buffet, rain blows on, thrash; N. Amer. beat up on; informal wallop, whack, clout, clobber, bop, biff, sock, plug.

belated adjective **late**, overdue, behindhand, delayed, tardy, unpunctual.
– OPPOSITES early.

belch verb **1** informal **burp**; Scottish & N. English informal rift. **2** *the furnace belched flames:* **emit**, give off, pour out, discharge, disgorge, spew out, spit out, vomit, cough up.

beleaguered adjective **1** *the beleaguered garrison:* **besieged**, blockaded, surrounded, encircled,

b

hemmed in, under attack. **2** *a beleaguered government:* **hard-pressed**, troubled, in difficulties, under pressure, under stress, in a tight corner; informal up against it.

belie verb **1** *his eyes belied his words:* **contradict**, be at odds with, call into question, give the lie to, disprove, debunk, discredit, controvert. **2** *his image belies his talent:* **conceal**, cover, disguise; misrepresent, falsify, give a false idea/account of.
– OPPOSITES testify to, reveal.

belief noun **1** *it's my belief that age is irrelevant:* **opinion**, view, conviction, judgement, thinking, idea, impression, theory, conclusion, notion. **2** *belief in God:* **faith**, trust, reliance, confidence, credence. **3** *traditional beliefs:* **ideology**, principle, ethic, tenet, canon; doctrine, teaching, dogma, article of faith, creed, credo.
– OPPOSITES disbelief, doubt.

believable adjective **credible**, plausible, tenable, conceivable, likely, probable, possible, feasible, reasonable.
– OPPOSITES inconceivable.

believe verb **1** *I don't believe you:* **trust**, have confidence in. **2** *do you believe that story?* **accept**, be convinced by, give credence to, credit, trust; informal swallow, buy, go for. **3** *I believe they've met before:* **think**, be of the opinion that, have an idea that, imagine, assume, presume, take it, conjecture, surmise, conclude, deduce, understand, gather; informal reckon, figure.
– OPPOSITES doubt.
■ **believe in 1** *they believed in his ability:* have faith in, pin your faith on, trust in, have every confidence in, cling to, set great store by, value; informal swear by. **2** *I don't believe in censorship of the arts:* approve of, subscribe to; be convinced by, be persuaded by.

believer noun **devotee**, adherent, disciple, follower, supporter, upholder, worshipper.
– OPPOSITES infidel, sceptic.

belittle verb **disparage**, denigrate, run down, deprecate, downgrade, play down, trivialize, minimize, make light of; informal do down, pooh-pooh; formal derogate.
– OPPOSITES praise.

bell noun

WORD LINKS
campanology bell-ringing

belle noun **beauty**, vision, picture, pin-up, beauty queen, goddess, Venus; informal looker, lovely, stunner, knockout, bombshell, dish, cracker, bobby-dazzler, peach, honey, eyeful, bit of all right; Brit. informal smasher.

bellicose adjective **belligerent**, aggressive, hostile, antagonistic, pugnacious, truculent, confrontational, contentious, militant, combative; informal spoiling for a fight; Brit. informal stroppy, bolshie.
– OPPOSITES peaceable.

belligerent adjective **1** *a loud, belligerent voice:* **hostile**, aggressive, threatening, antagonistic, pugnacious, bellicose, truculent, confrontational, contentious, militant, combative; informal spoiling for a fight; Brit. informal stroppy, bolshie; N. Amer. informal scrappy. **2** *the belligerent states:* **warring**, combatant, fighting, battling.
– OPPOSITES peaceable, neutral.

bellow verb **roar**, shout, bawl, thunder, trumpet, boom, bark, yell, shriek, howl, scream; informal holler.
– OPPOSITES whisper.

belly noun **stomach**, abdomen, paunch, middle, midriff, girth; informal tummy, gut, insides.
• verb *her skirt bellied out:* **billow out**, bulge, balloon out, fill out.

belong verb **1** *the house belongs to his mother:* **be owned by**, be the property of, be in the possession of, be in the hands of. **2** *I belong to a union:* **be a member of**, be affiliated to, be linked to, be an adherent of, be part of; be attached to, be an adjunct of.

belonging noun **affiliation**, acceptance, association, attachment, integration, closeness; rapport, fellow feeling, fellowship.
– OPPOSITES alienation.

belongings plural noun **possessions**, effects, worldly goods, chattels, property; informal gear, tackle, kit, things, stuff, bits and pieces; Brit. informal clobber, gubbins.

beloved adjective *his beloved wife:* **darling**, dear, precious, adored, much loved, cherished, treasured, prized, highly regarded, admired, esteemed, idolized.

below preposition **1** *the water rushed below them:* **beneath**, under, underneath. **2** *the sum is below average:* **less than**, lower than, under, smaller than. **3** *a captain is below a major:* **lower than**, under, inferior to, subordinate to, subservient to.
–OPPOSITES above, over.

belt noun **1** **girdle**, sash, strap, cummerbund, band; literary cincture, baldric. **2** *the commuter belt:* **region**, area, district, zone, sector, territory; tract, strip.
■ **below the belt** unfair, unjust, unacceptable, inequitable; unethical, unprincipled, immoral, unscrupulous, unsporting, sneaky, dishonourable, underhand; informal low-down, dirty; Brit. informal out of order, off, not cricket.

bemoan verb **lament**, bewail, mourn, grieve over, cry over; deplore, complain about.
–OPPOSITES rejoice at, applaud.

bemused adjective **bewildered**, confused, puzzled, perplexed, baffled, mystified, nonplussed, dumbfounded, at sea, at a loss, taken aback, disoriented, disconcerted; informal flummoxed, bamboozled, fazed; N. Amer. informal discombobulated.

bemusement noun **bewilderment**, confusion, puzzlement, perplexity, bafflement, befuddlement, stupefaction, mystification, disorientation; informal bamboozlement; N. Amer. informal discombobulation.

bench noun **1** *he sat on a bench:* **pew**, form, stall, settle. **2** *a laboratory bench:* **workbench**, work table, worktop, counter. **3** *the bench heard the evidence:* **judges**, magistrates, judiciary; court.

benchmark noun **standard**, point of reference, gauge, criterion, specification, canon, convention, guide, guideline, norm, touchstone, yardstick, barometer, indicator, measure, model, exemplar, pattern.

bend verb **1** *the frames can be bent to fit your face:* **curve**, crook, flex, angle, hook, bow, arch, buckle, warp, contort, distort, deform, twist. **2** *the highway bent to the left:* **turn**, curve, incline, swing, veer, deviate, diverge, fork, change course, curl, loop. **3** *he bent down to tie his shoe:* **stoop**, bow, crouch, hunch, lean down/over.
–OPPOSITES straighten.
•noun *he came to a bend in the road:* **curve**, turn, corner, kink, angle, arc, crescent, twist.
–OPPOSITES straight.

beneath preposition **1** *we sat beneath the trees:* **under**, underneath, below, at the foot of, at the bottom of. **2** *the rank beneath theirs:* **inferior to**, below, lower than, subordinate to, subservient to. **3** *such an attitude was beneath her:* **unworthy of**, unbecoming to, degrading to, below.
–OPPOSITES above.

benediction noun **1** *the priest said a benediction:* **blessing**, prayer, invocation; grace. **2** *he eventually achieved benediction:* **blessedness**, beatitude, bliss, grace.

benefactor, **benefactress** noun **patron**, supporter, backer, sponsor; donor, contributor, subscriber; informal angel.

beneficent adjective **benevolent**, charitable, altruistic, humanitarian, neighbourly, public-spirited, philanthropic; generous, magnanimous, munificent, unselfish, unstinting, open-handed, liberal, lavish, bountiful.
–OPPOSITES unkind, mean.

beneficial adjective **advantageous**, favourable, helpful, useful, of assistance, valuable, profitable, rewarding, gainful.
–OPPOSITES disadvantageous.

beneficiary noun **heir**, heiress, inheritor, legatee; recipient.

benefit noun **1** *for the benefit of others:* **good**, sake, welfare, well-being, advantage, comfort, ease, convenience; help, aid, assistance, service. **2** *the benefits of working for a large firm:* **advantage**, reward, merit, boon, blessing, virtue; bonus; value; informal perk; formal perquisite. **3** *state benefit:* **social security payments**, welfare; charity, financial assistance; informal the dole; Scottish informal the broo.
–OPPOSITES detriment, disadvantage.
•verb **1** *the deal benefited them both:* **be advantageous to**, be beneficial

to, profit, be of service to, serve, be useful to, be helpful to, aid, assist; better, improve, strengthen, boost, advance, further. **2** *they may benefit from drugs:* **profit**, gain, reap reward, make money; make the most of, exploit, turn to your advantage, put to good use, do well out of; informal cash in, make a killing.
– OPPOSITES damage, suffer.

benevolence noun **kindness**, kind-heartedness, goodness, goodwill, charity, altruism, humanitarianism, compassion, philanthropism; generosity, magnanimity, munificence, unselfishness, beneficence; literary bounty, bounteousness.
– OPPOSITES spite, miserliness.

benevolent adjective **1** *a benevolent patriarch:* **kind**, kindly, kind-hearted, good-natured, good, benign, compassionate, caring, altruistic, humanitarian, philanthropic; generous, magnanimous, munificent, unselfish, open-handed, beneficent; literary bounteous. **2** *a benevolent institution:* **charitable**, non-profit-making, not-for-profit.
– OPPOSITES unkind, miserly.

benighted adjective **ignorant**, unenlightened, uneducated, uninformed, backward, simple; primitive, uncivilized, unsophisticated, philistine, barbarian, barbaric, barbarous.
– OPPOSITES enlightened.

benign adjective **1** *a benign grandfatherly role:* **kindly**, kind, warm-hearted, good-natured, friendly, affectionate, agreeable, genial, congenial, cordial, approachable, tender-hearted, gentle, sympathetic, compassionate, caring, well disposed, benevolent. **2** *the benign climate of Southern California:* **temperate**, mild, gentle, balmy, soft, pleasant; healthy, wholesome, salubrious. **3** (Medicine) *a benign tumour:* **harmless**, non-malignant, non-cancerous, innocent.
– OPPOSITES unfriendly, hostile, unhealthy, malignant.

bent adjective **twisted**, crooked, warped, contorted, deformed, misshapen, out of shape, irregular; bowed, arched, curved, angled, hooked, kinked; N. Amer. informal pretzeled.
– OPPOSITES straight.
• noun *an artistic bent:* **inclination**, leaning, tendency; talent, gift, flair, aptitude, facility, skill, capability, capacity; predisposition, disposition, instinct, orientation, predilection, proclivity, propensity.
■ **bent on** intent on, determined on, set on, insistent on, resolved on; committed to, single-minded about, obsessed with, fanatical about, fixated on.

benumbed adjective **numb**, unfeeling, insensible, stupefied, groggy, foggy, fuzzy, muzzy, dazed, dizzy; befuddled, fuddled, disoriented, confused, bewildered, all at sea; informal dopey, woozy, mixed up; N. Amer. informal discombobulated.

bequeath verb **leave**, will, make over, pass on, hand on/down, entrust, grant, transfer; donate, give; bestow on, confer on, endow with; Law demise, devise, convey.

bequest noun **legacy**, inheritance, endowment, settlement; estate, heritage; bestowal, bequeathal; Law devise.

berate verb **scold**, rebuke, reprimand, reproach, reprove, admonish, chide, criticize, upbraid, take to task, pull up; informal tell off, give someone a talking-to, give someone a telling-off, give someone a dressing-down, give someone a roasting, rap over the knuckles, bawl out; Brit. informal tick off, have a go at, carpet, give someone a rocket, give someone a rollicking, tear someone off a strip; N. Amer. informal chew out, ream out; formal castigate.
– OPPOSITES praise.

bereaved adjective orphaned, widowed; mourning, grieving.

bereavement noun loss, death, demise; formal decease.

bereft adjective **deprived**, robbed, stripped, devoid, bankrupt; (**bereft of**) wanting, in need of, lacking, without; informal minus, clean out of; literary sans.

berserk adjective **mad**, crazy, insane, out of your mind, hysterical, frenzied, crazed, demented, maniacal, manic, frantic, raving, wild, out of control, amok, on the rampage; informal off your head, off the deep end, ape, bananas, bonkers, nuts, hyper; Brit. informal spare, crackers, barmy; N. Amer. informal postal.

berth noun **1** *a 4-berth cabin:* **bunk**, bed, cot, couch, hammock. **2** *the vessel left its berth:* **mooring**, dock.
•verb **1** *the ship berthed in London Docks:* **dock**, moor, land, tie up, make fast. **2** *the boats each berth six:* **accommodate**, sleep.
■ **give someone/something a wide berth** avoid, shun, keep away from, steer clear of, keep at arm's length, have nothing to do with; dodge, side-step, circumvent, skirt round.

beseech verb (literary) **implore**, beg, entreat, plead with, appeal to, call on, supplicate, importune, pray to, ask, request, petition.

beset verb **1** *he is beset by fears:* **plague**, bedevil, assail, beleaguer, afflict, torment, rack, oppress, trouble, worry, harass, dog.
2 *they were beset by enemy forces:* **surround**, besiege, hem in, shut in, fence in, box in, encircle, ring round.

beside preposition **1** *Kate walked beside him:* **alongside**, by/at the side of, next to, parallel to, abreast of; adjacent to, next door to; bordering, abutting, neighbouring. **2** *beside her sister, she felt clumsy:* **compared with/to**, in comparison with/to, next to, against, contrasted with.
■ **beside yourself** distraught, overcome, out of your mind, frantic, desperate, distracted, at your wits' end, frenzied, wound up, worked up; hysterical. **beside the point**. See POINT[1].

besides preposition *who did you ask besides Mary?* **in addition to**, as well as, over and above, above and beyond, on top of; apart from, other than, aside from, but for, save for, not counting, excluding, not including, except, with the exception of, leaving aside; N. Amer. informal outside of.
•adverb **1** *there's a lot more besides:* **in addition**, as well, too, also, into the bargain, on top of that, to boot. **2** *besides, he's a man:* **furthermore**, moreover, further; anyway, anyhow, in any case; informal what's more; N. Amer. informal anyways.

besiege verb **1** *fans besieged his hotel:* **surround**, mob, crowd round, swarm round, throng round, encircle; blockade. **2** *guilt besieged him:* **oppress**, torment, torture, rack, plague, afflict, haunt, harrow, beset, beleaguer, trouble, bedevil, prey on someone's mind. **3** *he was besieged with requests:* **overwhelm**, inundate, deluge, flood, swamp, snow under; bombard.

besotted adjective **infatuated**, smitten, in love, obsessed; doting on, greatly enamoured of; informal bowled over by, swept off your feet by, struck on, crazy about, mad about, wild about, gone on, carrying a torch for; Brit. informal potty about.

bespatter verb **splatter**, spatter, splash, speck, fleck, spot; dirty, soil; informal splotch, splodge.

bespeak verb **1** *a tree-lined road which bespoke money:* **indicate**, be evidence of, be a sign of, denote, point to, testify to, evidence, reflect, demonstrate, show, manifest, display, signify; reveal, betray; informal spell. **2** (formal) *he had bespoken a room:* **order**, reserve, book.
– OPPOSITES belie.

best adjective **1** *the best hotel in Paris:* **finest**, greatest, top, foremost, leading, pre-eminent, premier, prime, first, chief, principal, supreme, superlative, unrivalled, second to none, without equal, nonpareil, unsurpassed, peerless, matchless, unparalleled, unbeatable, optimum, ultimate, incomparable; highest, record-breaking; informal star, number-one, a cut above the rest, top-drawer; formal unexampled. **2** *do whatever you think best:* **most advantageous**, most useful, most suitable, most fitting, most appropriate; most prudent, most sensible, most advisable.
– OPPOSITES worst.
•noun **1** *only the best will do:* **finest**, choicest, top, cream, choice, prime, elite, crème de la crème, flower, jewel in the crown; informal tops, pick of the bunch. **2** *she dressed in her best:* **best clothes**, finery, Sunday best; informal best bib and tucker, glad rags.
■ **do your best** do your utmost, try your hardest, make every effort,

give your all; informal bend over backwards, go all out, pull out all the stops, bust a gut, break your neck, move heaven and earth.

bestial adjective 1 *Stan's bestial behaviour:* **savage**, brutish, brutal, barbarous, barbaric, cruel, vicious, violent, inhuman, subhuman; depraved, degenerate, perverted, immoral, warped. 2 *man's bestial ancestors:* **animal**, beast-like, animalistic.
– OPPOSITES civilized, humane.

bestow verb **confer on**, grant, accord, afford, endow someone with, vest in, present, award, give, donate, entrust with, vouchsafe.

bestride verb **straddle**, span, bridge, extend across.

best-seller noun brand leader; informal hit, smash, blockbuster, chart-topper, chartbuster.
– OPPOSITES failure, flop.

best-selling adjective **very successful**, very popular; informal number-one, chart-topping, hit, smash.

bet verb 1 *he bet £10 on the favourite:* **wager**, gamble, stake, risk, venture, hazard, chance; put/lay money, speculate; informal punt; Brit. informal have a flutter, chance your arm.
2 (informal) *I bet it was your idea:* **be certain**, be sure, be convinced, be confident; expect, predict, forecast, guess.
• noun 1 *a £20 bet:* **wager**, gamble, stake, ante; Brit. informal flutter, punt.
2 (informal) *my bet is that they'll lose:* **prediction**, forecast, guess; opinion, belief, feeling, view, theory.
3 (informal) *your best bet is to go early:* **option**, choice, alternative, course of action, plan.

bête noire noun **bugbear**, pet hate, bogey; a thorn in your flesh/side, the bane of your life; N. Amer. bugaboo.
– OPPOSITES favourite.

betray verb 1 *he betrayed his own brother:* be disloyal to, break faith with; inform on/against, give away, denounce, sell out, stab in the back, double-cross; informal stitch up, do the dirty on, sell down the river, split on, rat on, peach on, squeal on; Brit. informal grass on, shop, sneak on; N. Amer. informal rat out, drop a/the dime on, finger; Austral./NZ informal dob on, point the bone at. 2 *he betrayed a secret:* **reveal**, disclose, divulge, tell, give away, leak; unmask, expose; let slip, let out, let drop, blurt out; informal blab, spill.

betrayal noun **disloyalty**, treachery, bad faith, faithlessness, falseness; duplicity, deception, double-dealing; breach of faith, breach of trust, stab in the back; double-cross, sell-out.
– OPPOSITES loyalty.

betrayer noun **traitor**, back-stabber, Judas, double-crosser; renegade, double agent, collaborator, informer, mole, stool pigeon; turncoat, defector; informal snake in the grass, rat, scab; Brit. informal grass, supergrass, nark.

betrothal noun (dated) **engagement**, marriage contract; old use espousal.

betrothed adjective (dated) **engaged**; informal spoken for; literary affianced; old use plighted, espoused.

better adjective 1 *better facilities:* **superior**, finer; preferable; informal a cut above, streets ahead, head and shoulders above. 2 *are you better?* **healthier**, fitter, stronger; well, cured, healed, recovered; recovering, on the road to recovery, making progress, improving, on the mend.
– OPPOSITES worse, inferior.
• verb 1 *he bettered the record:* **surpass**, improve on, beat, exceed, outdo, top, cap, trump, eclipse.
2 *refugees who want to better their lot:* **improve**, ameliorate, raise, advance, further, lift, upgrade, enhance.
– OPPOSITES worsen.

betterment noun **improvement**, amelioration, advancement, furtherance, upgrading, enhancement.

between preposition 1 *he stood between his parents:* in the middle of; old use betwixt. 2 *the bond between her and her mother:* **connecting**, linking, joining; uniting, allying.

bevel noun **slope**, slant, angle, cant, chamfer.

beverage noun **drink**, liquid refreshment; humorous libation.

bevy noun **group**, crowd, herd, flock, horde, army, galaxy, assemblage, gathering, band, body, pack; knot, cluster; informal bunch, gaggle, posse.

bewail verb **lament**, bemoan, mourn, grieve over, sorrow over, cry over; deplore, complain about.
– OPPOSITES rejoice at, applaud.

beware verb **watch out**, look out, mind out, be alert, keep your eyes open/peeled, keep an eye out, be on the qui vive, take care, watch your step.

bewilder verb **baffle**, mystify, bemuse, perplex, puzzle, confuse, confound, nonplus; informal flummox, faze, stump, beat, fox, be all Greek to, floor, bamboozle; N. Amer. informal discombobulate.
– OPPOSITES enlighten.

bewildered adjective **baffled**, mystified, bemused, perplexed, puzzled, confused, nonplussed, at sea, at a loss, disorientated, taken aback; informal flummoxed, bamboozled; N. Amer. informal discombobulated.

bewitch verb **1** *that evil woman bewitched him:* **cast/put a spell on**, enchant; possess, witch, curse; N. Amer. hex, hoodoo; Austral. point the bone at. **2** *she was bewitched by her surroundings:* **captivate**, enchant, entrance, enrapture, charm, beguile, delight, fascinate, enthral.
– OPPOSITES repel.

beyond preposition **1** *beyond the trees:* **on the far side of**, on the other side of, behind, past, after. **2** *inflation beyond 10 per cent:* **greater than**, more than, exceeding, in excess of, above, upwards of. **3** *little beyond food was provided:* **apart from**, except, other than, besides; formal save.

bias noun **1** *he accused the media of bias:* **prejudice**, partiality, partisanship, favouritism, unfairness, one-sidedness; bigotry, intolerance, discrimination, a jaundiced eye; leaning, tendency, inclination, predilection. **2** *a dress cut on the bias:* **diagonal**, cross, slant, angle.
– OPPOSITES impartiality.
• verb *this may have biased the result:* **prejudice**, influence, colour, sway, weight, predispose; distort, skew, slant.

biased adjective **prejudiced**, partial, partisan, one-sided, blinkered; bigoted, intolerant, discriminatory; jaundiced, distorted, warped, twisted, skewed.
– OPPOSITES impartial.

bibliophile noun **book lover**, avid reader; informal bookworm.

bicker verb **squabble**, argue, quarrel, wrangle, fight, disagree, dispute, spar, have words, be at each other's throats, lock horns; informal scrap.
– OPPOSITES agree.

bicycle noun **cycle**, two-wheeler; informal bike, pushbike; historical penny-farthing.

bid[1] verb **1** *United bid £12 million for the striker:* **offer**, put up, tender, proffer, propose. **2** *she is bidding for a place in the England team:* **try to obtain**, try to get, make a pitch for.
• noun **1** *a bid of £3,000:* **offer**, tender, proposal. **2** *a bid to cut crime:* **attempt**, effort, endeavour, try; informal crack, go, shot, stab; formal essay.

bid[2] verb *she bid him farewell:* **wish**, utter.

biddable adjective **obedient**, acquiescent, compliant, tractable, amenable, complaisant, cooperative, dutiful, submissive.
– OPPOSITES disobedient, uncooperative.

bidding noun **command**, order, instruction, decree, injunction, demand, mandate, direction, summons, call; wish, desire; request; literary behest.

big adjective **1** *a big building:* **large**, sizeable, substantial, great, huge, immense, enormous, extensive, colossal, massive, mammoth, vast, tremendous, gigantic, giant, monumental, mighty, gargantuan, elephantine, titanic, mountainous, Brobdingnagian; towering, tall, high, lofty; outsize, oversized; goodly; capacious, voluminous, spacious; king-size, man-size, family-size; informal jumbo, whopping, bumper, mega, humongous, monster, astronomical, almighty, dirty great; Brit. informal whacking great, ginormous; formal commodious. **2** *a big man:* **well built**, sturdy, brawny, burly, broad-shouldered, muscular, muscly, rugged, lusty, Herculean, bulky, hulking, strapping, thickset, stocky, solid, hefty; tall, huge, gigantic;

b

fat, stout, portly, plump, fleshy, paunchy, corpulent, obese; informal hunky, beefy, husky. **3** *my big brother:* **grown-up**, adult, mature, grown; elder, older. **4** *a big decision:* **important**, significant, major, momentous, weighty, consequential, far-reaching, key, vital, critical, crucial. **5** (informal) *he has big plans:* **ambitious**, far-reaching, grandiose, on a grand scale. **6** *she's got a big heart:* **generous**, kind, kindly, caring, compassionate, loving. **7** (informal) *African bands are big in Britain:* **popular**, successful, in demand, sought-after, all the rage; informal hot, in, cool, trendy, now, hip; Brit. informal, dated all the go.
– OPPOSITES small, minor, modest.

big-headed adjective (informal) **conceited**, full of yourself, cocky, arrogant, cocksure, self-important; vain, self-satisfied, pleased with yourself, smug, swollen-headed, complacent; informal too big for your boots; literary vainglorious.
– OPPOSITES modest.

big-hearted adjective **generous**, magnanimous, munificent, open-handed, bountiful, unstinting, unselfish, altruistic, charitable, philanthropic, benevolent; kind, kindly, kind-hearted; literary bounteous.
– OPPOSITES mean.

bigot noun **dogmatist**, partisan, sectarian; racist, sexist, xenophobe, chauvinist, jingoist.

bigoted adjective **prejudiced**, biased, partial, one-sided, sectarian, discriminatory; opinionated, dogmatic, intolerant, narrow-minded, blinkered, illiberal; racist, sexist, homophobic, xenophobic, chauvinistic, jingoistic; jaundiced, warped, twisted, distorted.
– OPPOSITES open-minded.

bigotry noun **prejudice**, bias, partiality, partisanship, sectarianism, discrimination; dogmatism, intolerance, narrow-mindedness; racism, sexism, homophobia, xenophobia, chauvinism, jingoism.
– OPPOSITES open-mindedness.

bijou adjective **small**, little, compact, snug, cosy.

bilious adjective **1** *I felt bilious:* **nauseous**, sick, queasy, green about the gills; N. Amer. informal barfy. **2** *his bilious disposition:* **bad-tempered**, irritable, irascible, tetchy, testy, crotchety, ill-tempered, ill-natured, ill-humoured, peevish, fractious, pettish, crabby, waspish, prickly, crusty, shrewish, quick-tempered; N. Amer. informal cranky, ornery. **3** *a bilious green and pink colour scheme:* **lurid**, garish, loud, violent; sickly, nauseating.
– OPPOSITES well, good-humoured, muted.

bill[1] noun **1** *a bill for £60:* **invoice**, account, statement, list of charges; humorous the damage; N. Amer. check; N. Amer. informal tab. **2** *a parliamentary bill:* **draft law**, proposal, measure. **3** *she was top of the bill:* **programme**, line-up; N. Amer. playbill. **4** (N. Amer.) *a $10 bill:* **banknote**, note; US informal greenback. **5** *he had been posting bills:* **poster**, advertisement, public notice, announcement; flyer, leaflet, handbill; Brit. fly-poster; informal ad; Brit. informal advert.
• verb **1** *please bill me for the work:* **invoice**, charge, debit. **2** *the concert went ahead as billed:* **advertise**, announce; schedule, programme, timetable; N. Amer. slate. **3** *he was billed as the new Sean Connery:* **describe**, call, style, label, dub; promote, publicize, talk up; informal hype.

bill[2] noun *a bird's bill:* **beak**; Scottish & N. English neb.

billet noun *the troops' billets:* **quarters**, rooms; accommodation, lodging, housing; barracks, cantonment.
• verb *two soldiers were billeted here:* **accommodate**, quarter, put up, lodge, house; station, garrison.

billow noun *billows of smoke:* **cloud**, mass.
• verb **1** *her dress billowed around her:* **puff out**, balloon out, swell, fill out, belly out. **2** *smoke billowed from the chimney:* **swirl**, spiral, roll, undulate, eddy; pour, flow.

billowing adjective **rolling**, swirling, undulating, surging, heaving, billowy, swelling, rippling.

bin noun **container**, receptacle, holder; drum, canister, caddy, can, tin.

bind verb **1** *they bound her hands:* **tie**, fasten, hold together, secure, make fast, attach; rope, strap, lash,

truss, tether. **2** *Shelley bound up the wound with a dressing:* **bandage**, dress, cover, wrap; strap up, tape up. **3** *the experience had bound them together:* **unite**, join, bond, knit together, draw together, yoke together. **4** *we have not bound ourselves to join:* **commit yourself**, undertake, pledge, vow, promise, swear, give your word. **5** *the edges are bound in a contrasting colour:* **trim**, hem, edge, border, fringe; finish. **6** *they are bound by the agreement:* **constrain**, restrict, restrain, trammel, tie hand and foot, tie down, shackle; hamper, hinder, inhibit.
– OPPOSITES untie, separate.

binding adjective **irrevocable**, unalterable, inescapable, unbreakable, contractual; compulsory, obligatory, mandatory, incumbent.

binge noun (informal) **drinking bout**, debauch; informal bender, session, booze-up, blind; Scottish informal skite; N. Amer. informal jag, toot.

bird noun fowl; chick, fledgling, nestling; (**birds**) avifauna; informal feathered friend, birdie.

WORD LINKS
avian relating to birds
aviary a large enclosure for keeping birds
ornithology the study of birds

birth noun **1** *the birth of a child:* **childbirth**, delivery, nativity; technical parturition; dated confinement. **2** *the birth of science:* **beginning**, emergence, genesis, dawn, dawning, rise, start. **3** *he is of noble birth:* **ancestry**, lineage, blood, descent, parentage, family, extraction, origin, genealogy, heritage, stock, kinship.
– OPPOSITES death, demise, end.
■ **give birth to** have, bear, produce, be delivered of, bring into the world; N. Amer. birth; informal drop.

WORD LINKS
natal relating to a person's birth
antenatal during pregnancy; before birth
perinatal relating to the time immediately before and after a birth
post-natal relating to the period after a birth
obstetrics the branch of medicine concerned with childbirth

birthright noun **patrimony**, inheritance, heritage; right, due, prerogative, privilege; primogeniture.

biscuit (Brit.) noun **cracker**, wafer; N. Amer. cookie; informal bicky.

bisect verb **cut in half**, halve; divide, cut, split; cross, intersect.

bishop noun diocesan, metropolitan, suffragan; formal prelate.

WORD LINKS
episcopal relating to a bishop

bishopric noun **diocese**, see.

bit noun **1** *a bit of bread:* **piece**, portion, segment, section, part; chunk, lump, hunk, slice; fragment, scrap, shred, crumb, grain, speck; spot, drop, pinch, dash, soupçon, modicum; morsel, mouthful, bite, sample; iota, jot, tittle, whit, atom, particle, trace, touch, suggestion, hint, tinge; snippet, snatch; informal smidgen, tad. **2** *can you wait a bit?* **moment**, minute, second, while; informal sec, jiffy; Brit. informal mo, tick.
– OPPOSITES lot.
■ **a bit** rather, fairly, slightly, somewhat, quite, moderately; informal pretty, sort of, kind of. **bit by bit** gradually, little by little, in stages, step by step, piecemeal, slowly. **in a bit** soon, in a while, in a second, in a minute, in a moment, shortly; informal anon, in a jiffy, in two shakes; Brit. informal in a tick, in a mo; N. Amer. informal in a snap.

bitchy adjective (informal) **spiteful**, malicious, mean, nasty, hurtful, mischievous, cruel, unkind, vindictive, vengeful; informal catty.

bite verb **sink your teeth into**, chew, munch, nibble, crunch, champ, gnaw at.

biting adjective **1** *biting comments:* **vicious**, harsh, cruel, savage, cutting, sharp, bitter, scathing, caustic, acid, acrimonious, acerbic, stinging; vitriolic, hostile, spiteful, venomous; informal bitchy, catty. **2** *the biting wind:* **freezing**, icy, arctic, glacial; bitter, piercing, penetrating, raw, wintry.
– OPPOSITES mild.

bitter adjective **1** *bitter coffee:* **sharp**, acidic, acrid, tart, sour, biting, unsweetened, vinegary. **2** *a bitter woman:* **resentful**, embittered, aggrieved, begrudging,

b

rancorous, spiteful, jaundiced, ill-disposed, sullen, sour, churlish. **3** *a bitter blow:* **painful**, unpleasant, disagreeable, nasty, cruel, awful, distressing, upsetting, harrowing, heartbreaking, heart-rending, agonizing, traumatic, tragic; formal grievous. **4** *a bitter wind:* **freezing**, icy, arctic, glacial; biting, piercing, penetrating, raw, wintry. **5** *a bitter row:* **acrimonious**, virulent, angry, rancorous, spiteful, vicious, vitriolic, savage, ferocious, hate-filled, venomous, poisonous, acrid, nasty, ill-natured.
– OPPOSITES sweet, magnanimous, content, welcome, warm, amicable.

bitterness noun **1** *the bitterness of the medicine:* **sharpness**, acidity, acridity, tartness, sourness, harshness, vinegariness. **2** *his bitterness grew:* **resentment**, rancour, indignation, grudge, spite, sullenness, sourness, churlishness, moroseness, petulance, pique, peevishness. **3** *the bitterness of war:* **trauma**, pain, agony, grief; unpleasantness, nastiness; heartache, heartbreak, distress, desolation, despair, tragedy. **4** *there was no bitterness between them:* **acrimony**, hostility, antipathy, antagonism, enmity, animus, friction, rancour, vitriol, hatred, loathing, venom, poison, nastiness, ill feeling, bad blood.
– OPPOSITES sweetness, magnanimity, warmth, goodwill.

bizarre adjective **strange**, peculiar, odd, funny, curious, outlandish, outré, eccentric, unconventional, unorthodox, queer, extraordinary; informal weird, wacky, oddball, way out, freaky; Brit. informal rum; N. Amer. informal wacko.
– OPPOSITES normal.

black adjective **1** *a black horse:* **dark**, pitch-black, jet-black, inky. **2** *a black night:* **unlit**, dark, starless, moonless. **3** *the blackest day of the war:* **tragic**, dark, disastrous, calamitous, catastrophic, cataclysmic, fateful, wretched, woeful; formal grievous. **4** *Mary was in a black mood:* **miserable**, unhappy, sad, wretched, heartbroken, grief-stricken, sorrowful, anguished, desolate, despairing, disconsolate, downcast, dejected, cheerless, melancholy, morose, dark, gloomy, glum, mournful, doleful, funereal, forlorn, woeful; informal blue; literary dolorous. **5** *black humour:* **cynical**, macabre, weird, unhealthy, ghoulish, morbid, gruesome; informal sick. **6** *a black look.* See ANGRY sense 1.
– OPPOSITES white, clear, bright, joyful.
• verb **1** *the steps were neatly blacked:* **blacken**, darken; dirty, make sooty, stain, grime, soil. **2** *she blacked his eye:* **bruise**, contuse.
■ **black out** faint, lose consciousness, pass out; informal flake out; literary swoon. **black and white 1** *a black-and-white picture:* monochrome, greyscale. **2** *I wish to see the proposals in black and white:* in print, written down, set down, on paper, recorded, documented. **3** *in black-and-white terms:* categorical, unequivocal, absolute, uncompromising, unconditional, unqualified, unambiguous, clear.

blackball verb **reject**, debar, bar, ban, vote against, blacklist, exclude.
– OPPOSITES admit.

blacken verb **1** *they blackened their faces:* **black**, darken; dirty, make sooty, stain, grime, soil. **2** *the sky blackened:* **grow/become black**, darken, dim, cloud over. **3** *someone has blackened my name:* **sully**, tarnish, besmirch, drag through the mud/mire, stain, taint, smear, disgrace, dishonour, damage, ruin; slander, defame.
– OPPOSITES whiten, clean, lighten, brighten, clear.

blacklist verb **boycott**, ostracize, avoid, embargo, ignore; refuse to employ.

black magic noun **sorcery**, witchcraft, wizardry, necromancy, devilry.

blackmail noun *he was accused of blackmail:* **extortion**, demanding money with menaces; formal exaction.
• verb **1** *he was blackmailing the murderer:* **extort money from**, threaten, hold to ransom. **2** *she blackmailed me to work for her:* **coerce**, pressurize, pressure, force; informal lean on, put the screws on, twist someone's arm.

blackout noun **1** **power cut**, power failure, outage; N. Amer. brown-out.

2 fainting fit, loss of consciousness, collapse; literary swoon.

blame verb **1** *he always blames others:* **hold responsible**, hold accountable, condemn, accuse. **2** *they blame youth crime on unemployment:* **ascribe to**, attribute to, impute to, lay at the door of, put down to; informal pin.
– OPPOSITES absolve.
• noun *he was cleared of all blame:* **responsibility**, guilt, accountability, liability, culpability, fault.

blameless adjective **innocent**, guiltless, above reproach, unimpeachable, in the clear, exemplary, perfect, virtuous, pure, impeccable; informal squeaky clean.
– OPPOSITES blameworthy.

blameworthy adjective **culpable**, reprehensible, indefensible, inexcusable, guilty, wrong, evil, wicked; to blame, at fault, reproachable, responsible, answerable, erring, errant, in the wrong.
– OPPOSITES blameless.

blanch verb **1** *the sun blanches her hair:* **turn pale**, whiten, lighten, wash out, fade, blench, etiolate. **2** *his face blanched:* **pale**, whiten, lose its colour, lighten, fade, blench. **3** *blanch the spinach leaves:* **scald**, boil briefly.
– OPPOSITES colour, darken.

bland adjective **1** *bland food:* **tasteless**, flavourless, insipid, weak, watery, mild, wishy-washy. **2** *a bland film:* **uninteresting**, dull, boring, tedious, monotonous, dry, drab, dreary, wearisome; unexciting, unimaginative, uninspired, lacklustre, vapid, flat, stale, trite, vacuous, wishy-washy. **3** *a bland expression:* **unemotional**, emotionless, dispassionate, passionless; unexpressive, cool, impassive; expressionless, blank, wooden, stony, deadpan, hollow, undemonstrative, imperturbable.
– OPPOSITES tasty, interesting, expressive.

blandishments plural noun **flattery**, cajolery, coaxing, wheedling, persuasion, honeyed words, smooth talk, blarney; informal soft soap, buttering up.

blank adjective **1** *a blank sheet of paper:* **empty**, unmarked, unused, clear, free, bare, clean, plain. **2** *a blank face:* **expressionless**, deadpan, wooden, stony, impassive, unresponsive, vacuous, empty, glazed, fixed, lifeless, inscrutable. **3** *'What?' said Maxim, looking blank:* **baffled**, mystified, puzzled, perplexed, stumped, at a loss, stuck, bewildered, nonplussed, bemused, lost, uncomprehending, confused; informal flummoxed, bamboozled. **4** *a blank refusal:* **outright**, absolute, categorical, unqualified, complete, flat, straight, positive, certain, explicit, unequivocal, clear.
– OPPOSITES full, expressive, qualified.
• noun **space**, gap, lacuna.

blanket noun *a blanket of cloud:* **covering**, layer, coating, carpet, overlay, cloak, mantle, veil, pall, shroud.
• adjective *blanket coverage:* **complete**, total, comprehensive, overall, general, mass, umbrella, inclusive, all-round, wholesale, outright, across the board, sweeping, indiscriminate, thorough; universal, global, worldwide, international, nationwide, countrywide, coast-to-coast.
– OPPOSITES partial, piecemeal.
• verb **1** *snow blanketed the mountains:* **cover**, coat, carpet, overlay; cloak, shroud, swathe, envelop. **2** *double glazing blankets the noise:* **muffle**, deaden, soften, mute, silence, quieten, smother, dampen.
– OPPOSITES amplify.

blare verb *sirens blared:* **blast**, sound loudly, trumpet, clamour, boom, roar, thunder, bellow, resound.
– OPPOSITES murmur.

blarney noun **blandishments**, honeyed words, smooth talk, flattery, cajolery, coaxing, wheedling, persuasion; charm offensive; informal sweet talk, soft soap, smarm, buttering up.

blasé adjective **indifferent**, unconcerned, uncaring, casual, nonchalant, offhand, uninterested, apathetic, unimpressed, unmoved, unresponsive, phlegmatic; informal laid-back.
– OPPOSITES concerned, responsive.

blaspheme verb **swear**, curse, take the Lord's name in vain; informal cuss.

b

blasphemous adjective **sacrilegious**, profane, irreligious, irreverent, impious, ungodly, godless.
– OPPOSITES reverent.

blasphemy noun **profanity**, sacrilege, irreligion, irreverence, taking the Lord's name in vain, swearing, curse, impiety, desecration.
– OPPOSITES reverence.

blast noun **1** *he heard the blast and rushed outside:* **explosion**, detonation, discharge, bang. **2** *a sudden blast of cold air:* **gust**, burst, rush, gale, squall, wind, draught, waft, puff, flurry. **3** *the shrill blast of the trumpets:* **blare**, wail, roar, screech, shriek, hoot, honk, beep.
• verb **1** *bombers were blasting the airfields:* **blow up**, bomb, dynamite, explode; destroy. **2** *music blasted out at full volume:* **blare**, boom, roar, thunder, bellow, pump, shriek, screech. **3** *a motorist blasted his horn:* **honk**, beep, toot, sound.
■ **blast off** take off, lift off, be launched, leave the ground, become airborne, take to the air.

blast-off noun **launch**, lift-off, take-off, ascent, firing.
– OPPOSITES touchdown.

blatant adjective **flagrant**, glaring, obvious, undisguised, unconcealed, open; shameless, barefaced, unabashed, unashamed, unblushing, brazen, brass-necked.
– OPPOSITES inconspicuous, shamefaced.

blather verb **prattle**, babble, chatter, twitter, prate, go on, run on, rattle on, yap, maunder, ramble, burble, drivel; informal yak, yatter; Brit. informal witter, rabbit, chunter, waffle.

blaze noun **1** **fire**, flames, conflagration, inferno, holocaust. **2** *a blaze of light:* **glare**, gleam, flash, burst, flare, streak, radiance, brilliance, beam. **3** *a blaze of anger:* **outburst**, burst, eruption, flare-up, explosion, outbreak; blast, attack, fit, spasm, paroxysm, access, rush, storm.
• verb **1** *the fire blazed merrily:* **burn**, be alight, be on fire, be in flames. **2** *headlights blazed:* **shine**, flash, flare, glare, gleam, glint, dazzle, glitter, glisten. **3** *soldiers blazed away with sub-machine guns:* **fire**, shoot, blast, let fly.

blazon verb **1** *their name is blazoned across the sails:* **display**, exhibit, present, spread, emblazon, plaster. **2** *the newspapers blazoned the news abroad:* **publicize**, make known, make public, announce, report, communicate, spread, circulate, give out, publish, broadcast, trumpet, proclaim, promulgate.

bleach verb **turn white**, whiten, turn pale, blanch, lighten, fade; peroxide.
– OPPOSITES darken.

bleak adjective **1** *a bleak landscape:* **bare**, exposed, desolate, stark, desert, lunar, open, empty, windswept; treeless, without vegetation, denuded. **2** *the future is bleak:* **unpromising**, unfavourable, unpropitious, inauspicious; discouraging, disheartening, depressing, dim, gloomy, black, dark, grim, hopeless.
– OPPOSITES lush, promising.

bleary adjective **blurry**, unfocused; fogged, clouded, dull, misty, watery, rheumy.
– OPPOSITES clear.

bleat verb *don't bleat to me about fairness:* **complain**, moan, grouse; informal gripe, beef, whinge, bellyache; N. English informal mither; N. Amer. informal kvetch.

bleed verb **1** *his arm was bleeding:* **lose blood**, haemorrhage. **2** *one colour bled into another:* **flow**, run, seep, filter, percolate, leach. **3** *sap was bleeding from the trunk:* **flow**, run, ooze, seep, exude, weep. **4** *the country was bled dry by poachers:* **drain**, sap, deplete, milk, exhaust. **5** *my heart bleeds for them:* **grieve**, ache, sorrow, mourn, lament, feel, suffer; sympathize with, pity.

blemish noun **1** *not a blemish marred her skin:* **imperfection**, flaw, defect, fault, deformity, discoloration, disfigurement; bruise, scar, pit, pock, scratch, cut, gash; mark, spot, smear, speck, blotch, smudge; birthmark. **2** *his reputation is without blemish:* **fault**, failing, flaw, imperfection, foible; shortcoming, weakness, limitation; taint, stain.
– OPPOSITES virtue.
• verb **1** *nothing blemished the coastline:* **mar**, spoil, impair, disfigure, blight, deface, mark, scar; ruin. **2** *his reign has been blemished by contro-*

versy: **sully**, tarnish, besmirch, blacken, blot, taint; spoil, mar, ruin, disgrace, damage, undermine, degrade, dishonour; formal vitiate.
– OPPOSITES enhance.

blench verb **flinch**, start, shy away, recoil, shrink, pull back, cringe, wince, quail, cower.

blend verb **1** *blend the ingredients until smooth:* **mix**, mingle, combine, merge, fuse, meld, coalesce, integrate; stir, whisk, fold in. **2** *the new buildings blend with the older ones:* **harmonize**, go well, fit in, be in tune, be compatible; coordinate, match, complement.
• noun *a blend of bananas and ginger:* **mixture**, mix, combination, amalgamation, amalgam, union, marriage, fusion, meld, synthesis.

bless verb **1** *the Cardinal blessed the memorial plaque:* **consecrate**, sanctify, dedicate to God, make holy, make sacred; formal hallow. **2** *bless the name of the Lord:* **praise**, worship, glorify, honour, exalt, pay homage to, venerate, reverence, hallow. **3** *God blessed us with free will:* **endow**, bestow, furnish, accord, give, favour, grace; confer on.
– OPPOSITES curse.

blessed adjective **1** *a blessed place:* **holy**, sacred, hallowed, consecrated, sanctified; ordained, canonized, beatified. **2** *blessed are the meek:* **favoured**, fortunate, lucky, privileged, enviable. **3** *the fresh air made a blessed change:* **welcome**, pleasant, agreeable, refreshing, favourable, gratifying, heartening, much needed.
– OPPOSITES cursed, wretched, unwelcome.

blessing noun **1** *may God give us his blessing:* **protection**, favour. **2** *a special blessing from the priest:* **benediction**, invocation, prayer, intercession; grace. **3** *she gave the plan her blessing:* **sanction**, endorsement, approval, approbation, favour, consent, assent, agreement; backing, support; informal the thumbs up. **4** *it was a blessing they didn't have far to go:* **boon**, godsend, advantage, benefit, help, bonus, plus; stroke of luck, windfall.
– OPPOSITES condemnation, affliction.

blight noun **1** *potato blight:* **disease**, canker, infestation, fungus, mildew, mould. **2** *the blight of aircraft noise:* **affliction**, scourge, bane, curse, plague, menace, misfortune, woe, trouble, ordeal, trial, nuisance, pest.
– OPPOSITES blessing.
• verb **1** *a tree blighted by leaf curl:* **infect**, mildew; kill, destroy. **2** *scandal blighted the careers of several politicians:* **ruin**, wreck, spoil, mar, frustrate, disrupt, undo, end, scotch, destroy, shatter, devastate, demolish; informal mess up, foul up, put paid to, put the kibosh on, stymie; Brit. informal scupper.

blind adjective **1** *he has been blind since birth:* **sightless**, unsighted, visually impaired, unseeing. **2** *he's blind to her faults:* **unaware of**, oblivious to, unconscious of, ignorant of, impervious to, unconcerned about. **3** *blind acceptance of conventional opinion:* **uncritical**, unreasoned, unthinking, unquestioning, mindless, undiscerning, indiscriminate. **4** *a blind rage:* **wild**, uncontrolled, uncontrollable, unrestrained, furious, towering. **5** *a blind alley:* **blocked**, closed, barred, impassable; dead end.
– OPPOSITES sighted, aware.
• verb **1** *he was blinded in a car crash:* **make blind**, deprive of sight, render sightless; put someone's eyes out. **2** *they try to blind you with statistics:* **overawe**, intimidate, confuse, bewilder, confound, perplex, overwhelm; informal faze, psych out.
• noun **1** *a window blind:* **screen**, shade, sunshade, curtain, awning, canopy; louvre, jalousie, shutter. **2** *some crook had sent the card as a blind:* **trick**, ploy, ruse; deception, camouflage, smokescreen, front, facade, cover, pretext, feint.

blink verb **1** *his eyes did not blink:* **flutter**, flicker, wink, bat. **2** *several red lights began to blink:* **flash**, flicker, wink.

blinkered adjective **narrow-minded**, inward-looking, parochial, provincial, insular, small-minded, short-sighted; hidebound, inflexible, entrenched, prejudiced, bigoted; Brit. parish-pump.
– OPPOSITES broad-minded.

b

bliss noun **1** *a sigh of bliss:* **joy**, happiness, pleasure, delight, ecstasy, elation, rapture, euphoria. **2** *religions promise perfect bliss after death:* **blessedness**, benediction, beatitude, glory, heavenly joy, divine happiness; heaven, paradise.
– OPPOSITES misery, hell.

blissful adjective **ecstatic**, euphoric, joyful, elated, rapturous, on cloud nine, in seventh heaven; delighted, thrilled, overjoyed; informal over the moon, on top of the world; literary joyous.

blister noun *check for blisters in the roofing felt:* **bubble**, swelling, bulge, protuberance.

blistering adjective **1** *blistering heat:* **intense**, extreme, ferocious, fierce; scorching, searing, blazing, burning, fiery; informal boiling, baking, roasting, sweltering. **2** *a blistering attack:* **savage**, vicious, fierce, bitter, harsh, scathing, devastating, caustic, searing, vitriolic. **3** *a blistering pace:* **very fast**, breakneck; informal blinding.
– OPPOSITES mild, leisurely.

blithe adjective *a blithe disregard for the rules:* **casual**, indifferent, unconcerned, unworried, untroubled, uncaring, careless, heedless, thoughtless; nonchalant, blasé.
– OPPOSITES thoughtful.

blitz noun *the 1940 blitz on London:* **bombardment**, bombing, attack, onslaught, barrage; assault, raid, strike.
• verb *the town was blitzed in the war:* **bombard**, attack, bomb, shell, torpedo, strafe; destroy, devastate, ravage.

blizzard noun **snowstorm**, white-out.

bloated adjective **swollen**, distended, tumefied, bulging, inflated, enlarged, expanded, dilated.

blob noun **drop**, droplet, globule, bead, bubble; spot, blotch, blot, dot, smudge; informal splotch, splodge, glob.

bloc noun **alliance**, coalition, federation, confederation, league, union, partnership, axis, body, association, group.

block noun **1** *a block of cheese:* **chunk**, hunk, lump, wedge, cube, brick, slab, piece; Brit. informal wodge. **2** *an apartment block:* **building**, complex, structure, development. **3** *a block of shares:* **batch**, group, set, quantity, tranche. **4** *a sketching block:* **pad**, notepad, jotter, tablet. **5** *a block to development:* **obstacle**, bar, barrier, impediment, hindrance, check, hurdle, deterrent. **6** *a block in the pipe:* **blockage**, obstruction, stoppage, congestion, occlusion, clot.
• verb **1** *weeds can block drainage ditches:* **clog up**, stop up, choke, plug, bung up, obstruct, gum up, dam up, congest, jam, close; Brit. informal gunge up. **2** *picket lines blocked access to the factory:* **hinder**, hamper, obstruct, impede, inhibit, restrict, limit; halt, stop, bar, check, prevent. **3** *he blocked a shot on the goal line:* **parry**, stop, deflect, fend off, hold off, repel, repulse.
– OPPOSITES clear, facilitate.
■ **block something off** close up, shut off, seal off, barricade, bar, obstruct. **block something out 1** *trees blocked out the light:* conceal, keep out, blot out, exclude, obliterate, blank out, stop. **2** *block out an area in charcoal:* rough out, sketch out, outline, delineate, draft.

blockade noun **1** *a naval blockade of the island:* **siege**. **2** *they erected blockades:* **barricade**, barrier, roadblock; obstacle, obstruction.
• verb *rebels blockaded the capital:* **barricade**, block off, shut off, seal; besiege, surround.

blockage noun **obstruction**, stoppage, block, occlusion, congestion.

blonde, blond adjective **fair**, light, yellow, flaxen, tow-coloured, golden, platinum; bleached, peroxide.
– OPPOSITES dark.

blood noun *a woman of noble blood:* **ancestry**, lineage, bloodline, descent, parentage, family, birth, extraction, origin, genealogy, heritage, stock, kinship.

> **WORD LINKS**
> **haematology** the branch of medicine concerned with the blood

blood-curdling adjective **terrifying**, frightening, spine-chilling, hair-raising, horrifying, alarming; eerie, sinister, horrible; informal scary.

bloodless adjective **1** *a bloodless revolution:* **non-violent**, peaceful, peaceable, pacifist. **2** *his face was bloodless:* **anaemic**, pale, wan, pallid, ashen, colourless, chalky, waxen, white, grey, pasty, drained, drawn, deathly. **3** *a bloodless Hollywood mogul:* **heartless**, unfeeling, cruel, ruthless, merciless, pitiless, uncharitable; cold, hard, stony-hearted, cold-blooded, callous.
– OPPOSITES violent, ruddy.

bloodshed noun **slaughter**, massacre, killing, wounding; carnage, butchery, bloodletting, bloodbath; violence, fighting, warfare, battle.

bloodthirsty adjective **murderous**, homicidal, violent, vicious, barbarous, barbaric, savage, brutal, cut-throat; fierce, ferocious, inhuman.

bloody adjective **1** *his bloody nose:* **bleeding**. **2** *the bandages were bloody:* **bloodstained**, blood-soaked, gory. **3** *a bloody civil war:* **vicious**, ferocious, savage, fierce, brutal, murderous, gory.

bloom noun **1** *orchid blooms:* **flower**, blossom, floweret, floret. **2** *a girl in the bloom of youth:* **prime**, perfection, acme, peak, height, heyday; salad days. **3** *the bloom of her skin:* **radiance**, lustre, sheen, glow, freshness; blush, rosiness, pinkness, colour.
• verb **1** *the geraniums bloomed:* **flower**, blossom, open; mature. **2** *the children bloomed in the Devonshire air:* **flourish**, thrive, prosper, progress, burgeon; informal be in the pink.
– OPPOSITES wither, decline.

blossom noun *pink blossoms:* **flower**, bloom, floweret, floret.
• verb **1** *the snowdrops have blossomed:* **bloom**, flower, open, unfold. **2** *the whole region had blossomed:* **develop**, grow, mature, progress, evolve; flourish, thrive, prosper, bloom, burgeon.
– OPPOSITES fade, decline.
■ **in blossom** in flower, flowering, blossoming, blooming, in bloom, open, out.

blot noun **1** *an ink blot:* **spot**, dot, mark, blotch, smudge, patch, dab; informal splotch; Brit. informal splodge. **2** *the only blot on his record:* **blemish**, taint, stain, blight, flaw, fault; disgrace, dishonour. **3** *a blot on the landscape:* **eyesore**, monstrosity, carbuncle, mess; informal sight.
• verb **1** *the writing was messy and blotted:* **smudge**, smear, blotch, mark. **2** *he had blotted our family's name:* **tarnish**, taint, stain, blacken, sully, mar; dishonour, disgrace, besmirch.
■ **blot something out 1** *clouds were starting to blot out the stars:* conceal, hide, obscure, obliterate; shadow, eclipse. **2** *he urged her to blot out the memory:* erase, efface, eradicate, expunge, wipe out, blank out.

blotch noun *his clothes were covered in blotches of paint:* **patch**, mark, smudge, dot, spot, blot, dab, daub; informal splotch; Brit. informal splodge.

blotchy adjective **mottled**, dappled, patchy, spotty, smudged, marked; informal splotchy; Brit. informal splodgy.

blow[1] verb **1** *the icy wind blew around us:* **gust**, puff, flurry, blast, roar, bluster, rush, storm. **2** *his ship was blown on to the rocks:* **sweep**, carry, toss, drive, push, force. **3** *leaves blew across the road:* **drift**, flutter, waft, float, glide, whirl, move. **4** *he blew a smoke ring:* **exhale**, puff; emit, expel, discharge, issue. **5** *she was puffing and blowing:* **wheeze**, puff, pant, gasp. **6** *he blew a trumpet:* **sound**, blast, toot, pipe, trumpet; play. **7** *a rear tyre had blown:* **burst**, explode, blow out, split, rupture, puncture. **8** *the bulb had blown:* **fuse**, short-circuit, burn out, break, go. **9** *his cover was blown:* **expose**, reveal, uncover, disclose, divulge, unveil, betray.
• noun *we're in for a bit of a blow:* **gale**, storm, tempest, hurricane; wind, breeze, gust, draught, flurry.
■ **blow out 1** *the matches will not blow out in a strong wind:* be extinguished, go out, be put out, stop burning. **2** *the front tyre blew out.* See BLOW[1] verb sense 7. **3** *the windows blew out:* shatter, rupture, crack, smash, splinter, disintegrate; burst, explode, fly apart; informal bust. **blow something out** extinguish, put out, snuff, douse, quench, smother. **blow up**

b

a lorryload of shells blew up: explode, detonate, go off, ignite, erupt. **blow something up 1** *they blew the plane up:* bomb, blast, destroy; explode, detonate. **2** *blow up the balloons:* inflate, pump up, fill up, puff up, swell, expand, aerate.

blow² noun **1** *a blow on the head:* **knock**, bang, hit, punch, thump, smack, crack, rap; informal whack, thwack, bash, clout, sock, wallop. **2** *losing his job must have been a blow:* **shock**, surprise, bombshell, thunderbolt, jolt; calamity, catastrophe, disaster, upset, setback.

blowout noun *the steering is automatic in the event of blowouts:* **puncture**, flat tyre, burst tyre; informal flat.

blowsy adjective **untidy**, sloppy, scruffy, messy, dishevelled, unkempt, frowzy, slovenly.
– OPPOSITES tidy, respectable.

blowy adjective **windy**, windswept, blustery, gusty, breezy; stormy, squally.
– OPPOSITES still.

bludgeon noun *hooligans wielding bludgeons:* **cudgel**, club, stick, truncheon, baton; Brit. cosh; N. Amer. nightstick, blackjack.
• verb **1** *he was bludgeoned to death:* **batter**, cudgel, club, beat, thrash; informal clobber. **2** *I let him bludgeon me into marriage:* **coerce**, force, compel, pressurize, pressure, bully, browbeat, hector, dragoon, steamroller; informal strong-arm, railroad.

blue adjective sky-blue, azure, cobalt, sapphire, navy, ultramarine, aquamarine, cyan.

blueprint noun **1** *blueprints of the aircraft:* **plan**, design, diagram, drawing, sketch, map, layout, representation. **2** *a blueprint for similar measures in other countries:* **model**, plan, template, framework, pattern, example, guide, prototype, pilot.

bluff¹ noun *this offer was denounced as a bluff:* **deception**, subterfuge, pretence, sham, fake, deceit, feint, hoax, fraud, charade; trick, ruse, scheme, machination; informal put-on.
• verb **1** *they are bluffing to hide their guilt:* **pretend**, sham, fake, feign, lie, hoax, pose, posture, masquerade, dissemble. **2** *I managed to bluff the board into believing me:* **deceive**, delude, mislead, trick, fool, hoodwink, dupe, hoax, beguile, gull; informal con, kid, have on.

bluff² adjective *a bluff man:* **plain-spoken**, straightforward, blunt, direct, no-nonsense, frank, open, candid, forthright, unequivocal; hearty, genial, good-natured; informal upfront.

bluff³ noun **cliff**, promontory, headland, crag, bank, peak, escarpment, scarp.

blunder noun *he shook his head at his blunder:* **mistake**, error, gaffe, slip, oversight, faux pas; informal botch, slip-up, boo-boo; Brit. informal clanger, boob; N. Amer. informal blooper.
• verb **1** *the government admitted it had blundered:* **make a mistake**, err, miscalculate, bungle, trip up, be wrong; informal slip up, screw up, blow it, goof; Brit. informal boob. **2** *she blundered down the steps:* **stumble**, lurch, stagger, flounder, struggle, fumble, grope.

blunt adjective **1** *a blunt knife:* **unsharpened**, dull, worn. **2** *the leaf is broad with a blunt tip:* **rounded**, flat, obtuse, stubby. **3** *a blunt message:* **straightforward**, frank, plain-spoken, candid, direct, bluff, forthright, unequivocal, outspoken; brusque, abrupt, curt, terse, tactless, insensitive, stark, bald; informal upfront.
– OPPOSITES sharp, pointed, subtle.
• verb *age hasn't blunted my passion for life:* **dull**, take the edge off, deaden, dampen, numb, weaken, sap, cool, temper, allay, abate; diminish, reduce, decrease, lessen, deplete.
– OPPOSITES sharpen, intensify.

blur verb **1** *she felt tears blur her vision:* **cloud**, fog, obscure, dim, make hazy, soften. **2** *films blur the difference between villains and victims:* **obscure**, make vague, confuse, muddle, muddy, obfuscate, cloud, weaken. **3** *memories of the picnic had blurred:* **become dim**, dull, numb, deaden, mute; lessen, decrease, diminish.
– OPPOSITES sharpen, focus.
• noun *a blur on the horizon:* **indistinct shape**, smudge; haze, cloud, mist.

blurred adjective **indistinct**, fuzzy,

hazy, misty, foggy, shadowy, faint; unclear, vague, indefinite, unfocused, obscure, nebulous.

blurt verb
■ **blurt something out** burst out with, exclaim, call out; divulge, disclose, reveal, betray, let slip, give away; informal blab, let on, spill the beans.

blush verb *Joan blushed at the compliment:* **redden**, turn/go pink, turn/go red, flush, colour, burn up.
• noun *the darkness hid her fiery blush:* **flush**, rosiness, pinkness, bloom, high colour.

bluster verb **1** *he started blustering about the general election:* **rant**, thunder, bellow, sound off. **2** *storms bluster in from the sea:* **blast**, gust, storm, roar, rush.
• noun *his bluster turned to cooperation:* **ranting**, thundering, hectoring, bullying; bombast, bumptiousness, braggadocio.

blustery adjective **stormy**, gusty, blowy, windy, squally, wild, tempestuous, turbulent; howling, roaring.
– OPPOSITES calm.

board noun **1** *a wooden board:* **plank**, beam, panel, slat, batten, timber, lath. **2** *the board of directors:* **committee**, council, panel, directorate, commission, group. **3** *your room and board will be free:* **food**, meals, provisions, refreshments, table, bread; keep, maintenance; informal grub, nosh, eats, chow; Brit. informal scoff.
• verb **1** *he boarded the aircraft:* **get on**, go aboard, enter, mount, ascend; embark; catch. **2** *a number of students boarded with them:* **lodge**, live, reside, be housed; N. Amer. room; informal put up, have digs. **3** *they run a facility for boarding dogs:* **accommodate**, lodge, take in, put up, house; keep, feed, cater for.
■ **above board** legitimate, lawful, legal, honest; informal legit, kosher, pukka, by the book, fair and square, on the level, upfront. **board something up/over** cover up, close up, shut up, seal.

boast verb **1** *his mother had been boasting about him:* **brag**, crow, swagger, swank, gloat, show off; exaggerate, overstate; informal talk big, lay it on thick; Austral./NZ informal skite. **2** *the hotel boasts a fine restaurant:* **possess**, have, own, enjoy, pride yourself/itself on, offer.
• noun **1** *I said I'd win and it wasn't an idle boast:* **brag**, exaggeration, overstatement; Austral./NZ informal skite. **2** *the hall is the boast of the county:* **pride**, joy, wonder, delight, treasure, gem.

boastful adjective **bragging**, swaggering, bumptious, puffed up, full of yourself; cocky, conceited, arrogant, egotistical; informal swanky, big-headed.
– OPPOSITES modest.

boat noun *a rowing boat:* **vessel**, craft, watercraft, ship; literary keel, barque.
• verb *he insisted on boating into the lake:* **sail**, yacht, cruise.

bob verb **1** *their yacht bobbed about:* **move up and down**, bounce, toss, skip, dance, jounce; wobble, jiggle, joggle, jolt, jerk. **2** *she bobbed her head:* **nod**, incline, dip; wag, waggle. **3** *the maid bobbed and left the room:* **curtsy**, bow.

bode verb **augur**, portend, herald, be a sign of, warn of, foreshadow, be an omen of, presage, indicate, signify, promise, threaten, spell, denote, foretell; prophesy, predict.

bodily adjective *bodily sensations:* **physical**, corporeal, corporal, somatic; concrete, real, actual, tangible.
– OPPOSITES spiritual, mental.
• adverb *he hauled her bodily from the van:* **forcefully**, forcibly, violently; wholly, completely, entirely.

body noun **1** *the human body:* **figure**, frame, form, physique, anatomy, skeleton; informal bod. **2** *he was hit by shrapnel in the head and body:* **torso**, trunk. **3** *the bodies were put in the fire:* **corpse**, carcass, skeleton, remains; informal stiff; Medicine cadaver. **4** *the body of the article:* **main part**, core, heart, hub. **5** *the body of the ship:* **bodywork**, hull; fuselage. **6** *a body of water:* **expanse**, mass, area, stretch, tract, sweep, extent. **7** *a growing body of evidence:* **quantity**, amount, volume, collection, mass, corpus. **8** *the representative body of the employers:* **association**, organization,

b

group, party, company, society, circle, syndicate, guild, corporation, contingent. **9** *a heavenly body:* **object**, entity. **10** *add body to your hair:* **fullness**, thickness, substance, bounce, lift, shape.

■ **body and soul** completely, entirely, totally, utterly, fully, thoroughly, wholeheartedly, unconditionally.

WORD LINKS

corporal, **corporeal**, **somatic** relating to the body

bodyguard noun **minder**, guard, protector, guardian, defender; informal heavy.

bog noun **marsh**, swamp, mire, quagmire, morass, slough, fen, wetland; Brit. carr.

■ **bog someone/something down** mire, stick, entangle, ensnare, embroil; hamper, hinder, impede, obstruct, delay, stall, detain; swamp, overwhelm.

bogey noun **1** *bogeys and demons:* **evil spirit**, spectre, phantom, hobgoblin, demon; informal spook. **2** *the guild is the bogey of bankers:* **bugbear**, pet hate, bane, anathema, abomination, nightmare, horror, dread, curse; N. Amer. bugaboo.

boggy adjective **marshy**, swampy, miry, fenny, muddy, waterlogged, wet, soggy, sodden, squelchy; spongy, heavy, sloughy.
– OPPOSITES dry, firm.

bogus adjective **fake**, spurious, false, fraudulent, sham, deceptive; counterfeit, forged, feigned; make-believe, dummy, pseudo; informal phoney, pretend.
– OPPOSITES genuine.

bohemian noun *he is an artist and a real bohemian:* **nonconformist**, avant-gardist, free spirit, dropout; hippy, beatnik.
– OPPOSITES conservative.
• adjective *a bohemian student life:* **unconventional**, nonconformist, unorthodox, avant-garde, irregular, alternative; artistic; informal arty-farty, way-out, offbeat.
– OPPOSITES conventional.

boil[1] verb **1** *make the sauce while the lobsters are boiling:* **simmer**. **2** *a cliff with the sea boiling below:* **churn**, seethe, froth, foam, bubble.
• noun *bring the stock to the boil:* **boiling point**, 100 degrees centigrade.

■ **boil something down** condense, reduce, concentrate, thicken.

boil[2] noun *a boil on her neck:* **swelling**, spot, pimple, blister, pustule, eruption, carbuncle, wen, abscess.

boisterous adjective **1** *a boisterous game:* **lively**, animated, exuberant, spirited; rowdy, unruly, wild, uproarious, unrestrained, undisciplined, uninhibited, uncontrolled, rough, disorderly, riotous; noisy, loud, clamorous; informal rumbustious. **2** *a boisterous wind:* **blustery**, gusty, windy, stormy, wild, squally, tempestuous; howling, roaring; informal blowy.
– OPPOSITES restrained, calm.

bold adjective **1** *bold adventurers:* **daring**, intrepid, brave, courageous, valiant, valorous, fearless, dauntless, audacious, daredevil; adventurous, heroic, plucky, spirited, confident, assured; informal gutsy, spunky, feisty. **2** *a bold pattern:* **striking**, vivid, bright, strong, eye-catching, prominent; gaudy, lurid, garish. **3** *departure times are in bold type:* **heavy**, thick, pronounced.
– OPPOSITES timid, cowardly.

bolster noun **pillow**, cushion.
• verb *the fall in interest rates bolstered confidence:* **strengthen**, reinforce, boost, fortify, renew; support, buoy up, shore up, maintain, aid, help; augment, increase.
– OPPOSITES undermine.

bolt noun **1** *the bolt on the door:* **bar**, **lock**, catch, latch, fastener. **2** *nuts and bolts:* **rivet**, pin, peg, screw. **3** *a bolt whirred over my head:* **arrow**, dart, shaft. **4** *a bolt of lightning:* **flash**, shaft, streak, burst, flare. **5** *Mark made a bolt for the door:* **dash**, dart, run, sprint, leap, bound. **6** *a bolt of cloth:* **roll**, reel, spool.
• verb **1** *he bolted the door:* **lock**, bar, latch, fasten, secure. **2** *the lid was bolted down:* **rivet**, pin, peg, screw; fasten, fix. **3** *Anna bolted from the room:* **dash**, dart, run, sprint, hurtle, rush, fly, shoot, bound; flee; informal tear, scoot, leg it. **4** *he bolted down his breakfast:* **gobble**, gulp, wolf, guzzle, devour; informal demolish,

polish off, shovel down; N. Amer. informal scarf, snarf.

■ **a bolt from/out of the blue** shock, surprise, bombshell, thunderbolt, revelation; informal turn-up for the books. **bolt upright** straight, rigidly, stiffly.

bomb noun **explosive**, incendiary device; missile, projectile; dated bombshell.

• verb *their headquarters were bombed:* **bombard**, blast, shell, blitz, strafe, pound; attack, assault; blow up, destroy, demolish, flatten, devastate.

bombard verb **1** *gun batteries bombarded the islands:* **shell**, pound, blitz, strafe, bomb; assail, attack, assault, batter, blast, pelt. **2** *we were bombarded with information:* **inundate**, swamp, flood, deluge, snow under; besiege, overwhelm.

bombast noun **bluster**, pomposity, empty talk, turgidity, verbosity, verbiage; pretentiousness, ostentation, grandiloquence; informal hot air.

bombastic adjective **pompous**, blustering, turgid, verbose, high-flown, orotund, high-sounding, overwrought, pretentious, ostentatious, grandiloquent; informal highfalutin.

bona fide adjective **authentic**, genuine, real, true, actual; legal, legitimate, lawful, valid, proper; informal legit, pukka, the real McCoy.

– OPPOSITES bogus.

bonanza noun **windfall**, godsend, boon, blessing, bonus, stroke of luck; informal jackpot.

bond noun **1** *the women forged a close bond:* **friendship**, relationship, fellowship, partnership, association, affiliation, alliance, attachment. **2** *the prisoner struggled with his bonds:* **chains**, fetters, shackles, manacles, irons, restraints. **3** *a gentleman's word is his bond:* **promise**, pledge, vow, oath, word of honour, guarantee; agreement, contract.

• verb **join**, fasten, fix, affix, attach, secure, bind, stick, fuse.

bondage noun **slavery**, enslavement, servitude, subjugation, subjection, oppression, domination, exploitation, persecution.

– OPPOSITES liberty.

bone noun

> **WORD LINKS**
> **osseous** consisting of bone
> **orthopaedics** the branch of medicine concerned with bones

bonhomie noun **geniality**, affability, conviviality, cordiality, amiability, sociability, friendliness, warmth, joviality.

– OPPOSITES coldness.

bon mot noun **witticism**, quip, pun, pleasantry, jest, joke; informal wisecrack, one-liner.

bonny adjective (Scottish & N. English) **beautiful**, attractive, pretty, gorgeous, fetching, prepossessing; lovely, nice, sweet, cute, appealing, endearing, adorable, lovable, charming, winsome; informal divine; Austral./NZ informal beaut.

– OPPOSITES unattractive.

bonus noun **1** *the extra work's a real bonus:* **benefit**, advantage, boon, blessing, godsend, stroke of luck, asset, plus, pro, attraction; informal perk; formal perquisite. **2** *she's on a good salary and she gets a bonus:* **gratuity**, handout, gift, present, reward, prize; incentive, inducement; informal perk, sweetener; formal perquisite.

– OPPOSITES disadvantage.

bon viveur, bon vivant noun **hedonist**, pleasure-seeker, sensualist, sybarite, voluptuary; epicure, gourmet, gastronome.

– OPPOSITES puritan.

bony adjective **gaunt**, angular, skinny, thin, lean, spare, spindly, skin and bone, skeletal, emaciated, underweight.

– OPPOSITES plump.

book noun **1** *he published his first book in 1610:* **volume**, tome, publication, title; novel, treatise, manual. **2** *the council had to balance its books:* **accounts**, records; ledger, balance sheet.

• verb **1** *I've booked four tickets:* **reserve**, prearrange, order; informal bag; formal bespeak. **2** *we booked a number of events in the Festival:* **arrange**, programme, schedule, timetable, line up, lay on.

■ **by the book** according to the rules, within the law, lawfully, legally, legitimately; honestly,

b

fairly; informal on the level, fair and square. **book in** register, check in, enrol.

WORD LINKS
bibliography a list of books
bibliophile a person who collects or loves books

booking noun **reservation**, prearrangement; appointment, date.

bookish adjective **studious**, scholarly, academic, intellectual, highbrow, erudite, learned, educated, knowledgeable; cerebral, serious, earnest, thoughtful.

booklet noun **pamphlet**, brochure, leaflet, handbill, flyer, tract; N. Amer. folder, mailer.

boom noun **1** *the boom of the waves on the rocks:* **reverberation**, resonance, thunder, echoing, crashing, drumming, pounding, roar, rumble. **2** *an unprecedented boom in sales:* **upturn**, upsurge, upswing, increase, advance, growth, boost, escalation, improvement.
– OPPOSITES slump.
• verb **1** *thunder boomed overhead:* **reverberate**, resound, resonate; rumble, thunder, blare, echo; crash, roll, clap, explode, bang. **2** *a voice boomed at her:* **bellow**, roar, thunder, shout, bawl; informal holler. **3** *the market continued to boom:* **flourish**, burgeon, thrive, prosper, progress, improve, pick up, expand, mushroom, snowball.
– OPPOSITES whisper, slump.

boomerang verb **backfire**, recoil, rebound, come back, ricochet; be self-defeating; informal blow up in your face.

booming adjective **1** *a booming voice:* **resonant**, sonorous, ringing, resounding, reverberating, carrying, thunderous; strident, stentorian, strong, powerful. **2** *a booming construction business:* **flourishing**, burgeoning, thriving, prospering, prosperous, successful, strong, buoyant; profitable, fruitful, lucrative; expanding.

boon noun **blessing**, godsend, bonus, plus, benefit, advantage, help, aid, asset; stroke of luck; informal perk; formal perquisite.
– OPPOSITES curse.

boor noun **lout**, oaf, ruffian, thug, barbarian, Neanderthal, brute, beast; informal yahoo, roughneck, pig; Brit. informal yob, oik.

boorish adjective **coarse**, uncouth, rude, ill-bred, uncivilized, rough, unrefined, common, thuggish, loutish; vulgar, unsavoury, gross, brutish, Neanderthal; informal cloddish, plebby; Brit. informal yobbish; Austral. informal ocker.
– OPPOSITES refined.

boost noun **1** *a boost to one's morale:* **uplift**, lift, spur, encouragement, help, inspiration, stimulus, fillip; informal shot in the arm. **2** *a boost in sales:* **increase**, expansion, upturn, upsurge, upswing, rise, escalation, improvement, advance, growth, boom; informal hike.
– OPPOSITES decrease.
• verb **1** *he phones her to boost her morale:* **improve**, raise, uplift, increase, enhance, encourage, heighten, help, promote, foster, stimulate, invigorate, revitalize; informal buck up. **2** *they used advertising to boost sales:* **increase**, raise, escalate, improve, strengthen, inflate, push up, promote, advance, foster, stimulate; facilitate, help, assist, aid; informal hike, bump up.
– OPPOSITES decrease.

boot verb **1** *his shot was booted away by the goalkeeper:* **kick**, punt, tap; propel, drive, knock. **2** *boot up your computer:* **start up**, fire up.

booth noun **1** *booths for different traders:* **stall**, stand, kiosk. **2** *a phone booth:* **cubicle**, kiosk, box, enclosure, cabin.

bootleg adjective **illegal**, illicit, unlawful, unauthorized, unlicensed, pirated; contraband, smuggled, black-market.

booty noun **loot**, plunder, pillage, haul, spoils, ill-gotten gains, pickings; informal swag.

border noun **1** *the border of a medieval manuscript:* **edge**, **margin**, perimeter, circumference, periphery; rim, fringe, verge; sides. **2** *the French border:* **frontier**, boundary, borderline, perimeter.
• verb **1** *the fields were bordered by hedges:* **surround**, enclose, encircle, circle, edge, fringe, bound, flank. **2** *the straps are bordered with gold braid:* **edge**, fringe, hem; trim, pipe,

finish. **3** *the forest bordered on Broadmoor:* **adjoin**, abut, be next to, be adjacent to, be contiguous with, touch.

■ **border on** verge on, approach, come close to, be comparable to, approximate to, be tantamount to, be similar to, resemble.

borderline noun *the borderline between old and antique:* **dividing line**, division, line, cut-off point; threshold, margin, border, boundary.

• adjective *borderline cases:* **marginal**, uncertain, indefinite, unsettled, undecided, doubtful, indeterminate, unclassifiable, equivocal; questionable, debatable, controversial, contentious, problematic; informal iffy.

bore[1] verb *bore a hole in the wall:* **drill**, pierce, perforate, puncture, punch, cut; tunnel, burrow, mine, dig, gouge, sink.

• noun **1** *a well bore:* **borehole**, hole, well, shaft, pit. **2** *the canon has a bore of 890 millimetres:* **calibre**, diameter, gauge.

bore[2] verb *the news bored him:* **stultify**, pall on, stupefy, weary, tire, fatigue, send to sleep, leave cold; informal turn off.

– OPPOSITES interest.

• noun *you can be such a bore:* **tedious person/thing**, tiresome person/thing, bother, nuisance, pest, annoyance, trial, vexation, thorn in your flesh/side; informal drag, pain, headache, hassle.

boredom noun **weariness**, ennui, apathy, unconcern; frustration, dissatisfaction, restlessness, restiveness; tedium, dullness, monotony, repetitiveness, flatness, dreariness; informal deadliness.

boring adjective **tedious**, dull, monotonous, repetitive, unrelieved, unvaried, unimaginative, uneventful; characterless, featureless, colourless, lifeless, insipid, uninteresting, unexciting, uninspiring, unstimulating, jejune, flat, bland, dry, stale, tired, banal, lacklustre, stodgy, dreary, humdrum, mundane; mind-numbing, soul-destroying, wearisome, tiresome; informal deadly; Brit. informal samey; N. Amer. informal dullsville.

borrow verb **1** *we borrowed a lot of money:* **loan**; lease, hire; informal cadge, scrounge, bum; Brit. informal scab; N. Amer. informal mooch; Austral./NZ informal bludge. **2** *adventurous chefs borrow foreign techniques:* **adopt**, take on, acquire, embrace.

– OPPOSITES lend.

bosom noun **1** *the gown was set low over her bosom:* **bust**, chest; breasts. **2** *love was kindled within his bosom:* **heart**, breast, soul, core, spirit.

• adjective *bosom friends:* **close**, boon, intimate, inseparable, faithful, constant, devoted; good, best, firm, favourite.

boss (informal) noun *the boss of a large company:* **head**, chief, principal, director, president, chief executive, chair, manager; supervisor, foreman, overseer, controller; employer, owner, proprietor, patron; informal number one, kingpin, top dog, bigwig; Brit. informal gaffer, governor; N. Amer. informal head honcho.

• verb *you have no right to boss me about:* **order about/around**, dictate to, lord it over, bully, push around/about, domineer, dominate, pressurize, browbeat; call the shots, lay down the law; informal bulldoze, walk all over, railroad.

bossy adjective (informal) **domineering**, pushy, overbearing, imperious, officious, authoritarian, dictatorial; informal high and mighty.

– OPPOSITES submissive.

bother verb **1** *no one bothered her:* **disturb**, trouble, inconvenience, pester, badger, harass, plague, nag, hound, harry, annoy, upset, irritate; informal hassle, bug; N. English informal mither; N. Amer. informal ride. **2** *the incident was too small to bother about:* **mind**, care, concern yourself, trouble yourself, worry; informal give a damn, give a hoot. **3** *there was something bothering him:* **worry**, trouble, concern, perturb, disturb, disquiet, disconcert, unnerve; fret, upset, distress, agitate, gnaw at, weigh down; informal rattle.

• noun **1** *I don't want to put you to any bother:* **trouble**, effort, exertion, inconvenience, fuss, pains; informal hassle. **2** *the food was such a bother to cook:* **nuisance**, pest, palaver, rigmarole, job, trial, bind, bore, drag, inconvenience,

b

trouble, problem; informal hassle, headache, pain. **3** *a spot of bother in the public bar:* **disorder**, fighting, trouble, ado, disturbance, agitation, commotion, uproar; informal argy-bargy, kerfuffle.

bothersome adjective **annoying**, irritating, vexatious, maddening, exasperating; tedious, wearisome, tiresome; troublesome, trying, taxing, awkward; informal aggravating, pesky, pestilential.

bottle noun *a bottle of whisky:* **flask**, carafe, decanter, pitcher, flagon, carboy, demijohn.
■ **bottle something up** suppress, repress, restrain, withhold, hold in, rein in, inhibit, smother, stifle, contain, conceal, hide; informal keep a lid on.

bottleneck noun **traffic jam**, congestion, hold-up, gridlock, tailback; constriction, narrowing, restriction, obstruction, blockage; informal snarl-up.

bottom noun **1** *the bottom of the stairs:* **foot**, lowest part, base; foundation, substructure, underpinning. **2** *the bottom of the car:* **underside**, underneath, undersurface, undercarriage; underbelly. **3** *the bottom of Lake Ontario:* **floor**, bed, depths. **4** *the bottom of his garden:* **farthest point**, far end, extremity. **5** *they finally got to the bottom of the mystery:* **origin**, cause, root, source, basis, foundation; heart, kernel; reality, essence. **6** (Brit.) **rear end**, rump, seat; buttocks; informal behind, backside, derrière; Brit. informal bum; N. Amer. informal butt, fanny, tush; humorous fundament, posterior.
– OPPOSITES top, surface.
• adjective *she sat on the bottom step:* **lowest**, last, bottommost.
– OPPOSITES top.
■ **from top to bottom** thoroughly, fully, extensively, completely, comprehensively, rigorously, exhaustively.

bottomless adjective **1** *the bottomless pits of hell:* **fathomless**, endless, infinite, immeasurable. **2** *the media's bottomless appetite for celebrity gossip:* **unlimited**, boundless, infinite, inexhaustible, endless, everlasting; vast, huge, enormous.
– OPPOSITES limited.

bough noun **branch**, limb, arm, offshoot.

boulder noun **rock**, stone; Austral./NZ gibber.

boulevard noun **avenue**, street, road, drive, lane, parade, broadway, thoroughfare.

bounce verb **1** *the ball bounced:* **rebound**, spring back, ricochet, jounce; N. Amer. carom. **2** *William bounced down the stairs:* **bound**, leap, jump, spring, bob, hop, skip, trip, prance.
• noun **1** *he reached the door in a single bounce:* **bound**, leap, jump, spring, hop, skip. **2** *the pitch's uneven bounce:* **springiness**, resilience, elasticity, give. **3** *she had lost her bounce:* **vitality**, vigour, energy, vivacity, liveliness, animation, sparkle, verve, spirit, enthusiasm, dynamism; cheerfulness, happiness, buoyancy, optimism; informal get-up-and-go, pep, zing.
■ **bounce back** recover, revive, rally, pick up, be on the mend; perk up, cheer up, brighten up, liven up; informal buck up.

bouncing adjective **vigorous**, thriving, flourishing, blooming; healthy, strong, robust, fit, in fine fettle; informal in the pink.

bouncy adjective **1** *a bouncy surface:* **springy**, flexible, resilient. **2** *a rather bouncy ride:* **bumpy**, jolting, jerky, jumpy, jarring, rough. **3** *she was always bouncy:* **lively**, energetic, perky, frisky, jaunty, dynamic, vital, vigorous, vibrant, animated, spirited, buoyant, bubbly, sparkling, vivacious; enthusiastic, upbeat; informal peppy, zingy, chirpy.

bound[1] adjective **1** *he raised his bound wrists:* **tied**, chained, fettered, shackled, secured. **2** *she seemed bound to win:* **certain**, sure, very likely, destined. **3** *they are bound by the Official Secrets Act:* **obligated**, obliged, compelled, required, constrained. **4** *religion and morality are bound up with one another:* **connected**, linked, tied, united, allied.

bound[2] verb **leap**, jump, spring, bounce, hop; skip, bob, dance, prance, gambol, gallop.

bound[3] verb **1** *corporate freedom is bounded by law:* **limit**, restrict, confine, circumscribe, demarcate, delimit. **2** *the heath is bounded by a hedge:* **enclose**, surround, encircle, circle, border; close in/off, hem in. **3** *the garden was bounded by Mill Lane:* **border**, adjoin, abut; be next to, be adjacent to.

boundary noun **1** *the boundary between Israel and Jordan:* **border**, frontier, borderline, partition. **2** *the boundary between art and advertising:* **dividing line**, division, borderline, cut-off point. **3** *the boundary of his estate:* **bounds**, confines, limits, margins, edges, fringes; border, periphery, perimeter. **4** *the boundaries of accepted behaviour:* **limits**, parameters, bounds, confines.

boundless adjective **limitless**, untold, immeasurable, abundant; inexhaustible, endless, infinite, interminable, unfailing, ceaseless, everlasting.
–OPPOSITES limited.

bounds plural noun **1** *we keep rents within reasonable bounds:* **limits**, confines, proportions. **2** *land within the forest bounds:* **borders**, boundaries, confines, limits, margins, edges; periphery, perimeter.
■ **out of bounds** off limits, restricted; forbidden, banned, proscribed, illegal, illicit, unlawful, unacceptable, taboo; informal no go.

bountiful adjective **1** *their bountiful patron:* **generous**, magnanimous, munificent, open-handed, unselfish, unstinting, lavish; benevolent, beneficent, charitable. **2** *a bountiful supply of fresh food:* **abundant**, plentiful, ample, copious, bumper, superabundant, inexhaustible, prolific, profuse; lavish, generous, handsome, rich; informal whopping; literary plenteous.
–OPPOSITES mean, meagre.

bounty noun **1** *they offered a bounty for information leading to his arrest:* **reward**, prize, commission. **2** (literary) *thanks to his bounty I have a roof over my head:* **generosity**, magnanimity, munificence, bountifulness, largesse; benevolence, beneficence, charity, goodwill; blessings, favours.

bouquet noun **1** *her bridal bouquet:* posy, nosegay, spray, corsage. **2** *bouquets go to Ann for a well-planned event:* **compliment**, commendation, tribute, accolade; praise, congratulations, applause. **3** *the Chardonnay has a fine bouquet:* **aroma**, nose, smell, fragrance, perfume, scent, odour.

bourgeois adjective **1** *a bourgeois family:* **middle-class**, propertied; conventional, conservative, conformist; provincial, suburban, small-town. **2** *bourgeois decadence:* **capitalistic**, materialistic, money-oriented, commercial.
–OPPOSITES proletarian, communist.

bout noun **1** *a bout of exercise:* **spell**, period, time, stretch, stint, session; burst, flurry, spurt. **2** *a coughing bout:* **attack**, fit, spasm, paroxysm, convulsion, eruption, outburst. **3** *he is fighting only his fifth bout:* **contest**, match, round, heat, competition, event, meeting, fixture; fight, prizefight.

bovine adjective *she wore an expression of bovine contentment:* **stupid**, slow, unintelligent, half-baked, vacuous; sluggish, sleepy, torpid.
• noun **cow**, heifer, bull, bullock, calf, ox.

bow[1] verb **1** *the officers bowed:* nod, salaam, bob. **2** *the mast quivered and bowed:* **bend**, buckle, stoop, curve, flex, deform. **3** *the government bowed to foreign pressure:* **yield**, submit, give in, surrender, succumb, capitulate, defer, conform; comply with, accept, heed, observe. **4** *a footman bowed her in:* **usher**, conduct, show, lead, guide, direct, steer, shepherd.
• noun *a perfunctory bow:* **obeisance**, salaam, bob, nod.

bow[2] noun *the bow of the tanker:* **prow**, front, stem, nose, head, cutwater; Brit. humorous sharp end.

bow[3] noun **1** *she tied a bow in her hair:* **loop**, knot; ribbon. **2** *he bent the rod into a bow:* **arc**, curve, bend; crescent, half-moon.

bowdlerize verb **expurgate**, censor, blue-pencil, cut, edit; sanitize, water down, emasculate.

bowel noun **1** *a disorder of the bowels:* **intestine**, small intestine, large intestine, colon; informal guts, insides. **2** *the bowels of the ship:* **interior**, inside, core, belly; depths, recesses; informal innards.

b

bower noun *a rose-scented bower:* **arbour**, pergola, grotto, alcove, sanctuary.

bowl[1] verb **1** *he bowled a hundred or so balls:* **pitch**, throw, propel, hurl, toss, lob, loft, fling, launch, deliver; spin, roll; informal chuck, sling, bung. **2** *the car bowled along the roads:* **hurtle**, speed, shoot, sweep, career, hare, fly; informal belt, tear, scoot; Brit. informal bomb; N. Amer. informal clip.
■ **bowl someone over** *the explosion bowled us over:* knock down/over, fell, floor, prostrate.

bowl[2] noun **1 dish**, basin, pot, crock, crucible, mortar; container, vessel, receptacle. **2** *the town lay in a shallow bowl:* **valley**, hollow, dip, depression, trough, crater. **3** (N. Amer.) *the Hollywood Bowl:* **stadium**, arena, amphitheatre, coliseum; enclosure, ground; informal park.

box[1] noun **1 carton**, pack, packet; case, crate, chest, coffer, casket. **2** *a telephone box:* **booth**, cubicle, kiosk, cabin, hut; compartment, carrel, alcove, bay, recess.
• verb *Muriel boxed up his clothes:* **package**, pack, parcel, wrap, bundle, bale, crate.
■ **box something/someone in** hem in, fence in, close in, shut in; trap, confine, imprison, intern; surround, enclose, encircle, circle.

box[2] verb **1** *he began boxing professionally:* **fight**, prizefight, spar; battle, brawl; informal scrap. **2** *he boxed my ears:* **cuff**, smack, strike, hit, thump, slap, swat, punch, jab, wallop; informal belt, bop, biff, sock, clout, clobber, whack, plug, slug.

boxer noun **fighter**, pugilist, ringster, prizefighter; informal bruiser, scrapper.

boxing noun **pugilism**, the noble art, fighting, sparring, fisticuffs; prizefighting.

boy noun **lad**, schoolboy, male child, youth, young man; Scottish & N. English laddie; humorous stripling. See also **CHILD**.

boycott verb *they boycotted the election:* **spurn**, snub, shun, avoid, abstain from, reject, veto.
– OPPOSITES support.
• noun *a boycott on the use of tropical timbers:* **ban**, veto, embargo, prohibition, sanction, restriction; avoidance, rejection.

boyfriend noun **lover**, sweetheart, beloved, darling, man, escort, suitor; partner, significant other; informal fella, flame, fancy man; N. Amer. informal squeeze; dated beau.

boyish adjective **youthful**, young, childlike, adolescent, teenage; immature, juvenile, infantile, childish, babyish, puerile.

brace noun **1** *the aquarium is supported by wooden braces:* **prop**, beam, joist, batten, rod, post, strut, stay, support, stanchion, bracket. **2** *the brace on his right leg:* **support**, caliper. **3** *a brace of partridges:* **pair**, couple, duo, twosome; two.
• verb **1** *the plane's wing is braced by rods:* **support**, shore up, prop up, hold up, buttress, underpin; strengthen, reinforce. **2** *he braced his hand on the railing:* **steady**, secure, stabilize, fix, poise; tense, tighten. **3** *brace yourself for disappointment:* **prepare**, get ready, gear up, nerve, steel, galvanize, gird, strengthen, fortify; informal psych yourself up.

bracelet noun **bangle**, band, circlet, armlet, wristlet.

bracing adjective **invigorating**, refreshing, stimulating, energizing, exhilarating, reviving, restorative, rejuvenating, revitalizing, rousing, fortifying, strengthening.

bracket noun **1** *each speaker is fixed on a bracket:* **support**, prop, stay, batten, joist; rest, mounting, rack, frame. **2** *put the words in brackets:* **parenthesis**. **3** *a higher tax bracket:* **group**, category, grade, classification, set, division, order.
• verb *women were bracketed with minors:* **group**, classify, class, categorize, grade, list, sort, place, assign; couple, pair, twin; liken, compare.

brackish adjective **salty**, saline.

brag verb **boast**, crow, swagger, swank, bluster, gloat, show off; blow your own trumpet, sing your own praises; informal talk big, lay it on thick.

braggart noun **boaster**, bragger, swaggerer, poseur, egotist; informal big-head, loudmouth, show-off, swank; N. Amer. informal showboat, blowhard.

braid noun **1** *straps bordered with*

gold braid: **cord**, thread, tape, binding, rickrack, ribbon; cordon, torsade. **2** *his hair is in braids:* **plait**, pigtail, twist; cornrows, dreadlocks. •**verb 1** *she began to braid her hair:* **plait**, entwine, intertwine, interweave, weave, twist, twine. **2** *the sleeves are braided in scarlet:* **trim**, edge, border, pipe, hem, fringe.

brain noun **1** *the disease attacks cells in the brain:* **cerebrum**, cerebral matter, encephalon. **2** *success requires brains as well as brawn:* **intelligence**, intellect, brainpower, cleverness, wits, reasoning, wisdom, acumen, discernment, judgement, understanding, sense; informal nous, grey matter, savvy; N. Amer. informal smarts.

WORD LINKS

cerebral, **encephalic** relating to the brain

encephalitis inflammation of the brain

brainless adjective **stupid**, foolish, witless, unintelligent, ignorant, idiotic, simple-minded, empty-headed, half-baked; informal dumb, half-witted, brain-dead, moronic, cretinous, thick, dopey, dozy, birdbrained, pea-brained, dippy, wooden-headed; Brit. informal divvy; Scottish & N. English informal glaikit; N. Amer. informal chowderheaded.
–OPPOSITES clever.

brainwash verb **indoctrinate**, condition, re-educate, persuade, influence.

brake verb **slow down**, decelerate, reduce speed.
–OPPOSITES accelerate.

Don't confuse **brake** with **break**, which mainly means 'separate into pieces' or 'a pause or short rest' (*a tea break*).

branch noun **1** *the branches of a tree:* **bough**, limb, arm, offshoot. **2** *a branch of the river:* **tributary**, feeder, side stream. **3** *the judicial branch of government:* **division**, subdivision, section, subsection, department, sector, part, side, wing. **4** *the corporation's New York branch:* **office**, bureau, agency; subsidiary, offshoot, satellite. •**verb 1** *the place where the road branches:* **fork**, bifurcate, divide, subdivide, split. **2** *narrow paths branched off the road:* **diverge from**, deviate from, split off from; fan out from, radiate from.
■ **branch out** expand, open up, extend; diversify, broaden your horizons.

brand noun **1** *a new brand of margarine:* **make**, line, label, marque; type, kind, sort, variety; trade name, trademark, proprietary name. **2** *her particular brand of humour:* **type**, kind, sort, variety, class, category, genre, style, ilk; N. Amer. stripe. **3** *the brand on a sheep:* **identification**, marker, earmark. **4** *the brand of dipsomania:* **stigma**, shame, disgrace; taint, blot, mark. •**verb 1** *the letter M was branded on each animal:* **mark**, stamp, burn, sear. **2** *the scene was branded on her brain:* **engrave**, stamp, etch, imprint. **3** *the media branded us as communists:* **stigmatize**, mark out; denounce, discredit, vilify; label.

brandish verb **flourish**, wave, shake, wield; swing, swish; display, flaunt.

brash adjective **1** *a brash man:* **self-assertive**, pushy, cocksure, cocky, self-confident, arrogant, bold, audacious, brazen; forward, impudent, insolent, rude. **2** *brash colours:* **garish**, gaudy, loud, flamboyant, showy, tasteless; informal flashy, tacky.
–OPPOSITES meek, muted.

brassy adjective **1** **brazen**, forward, bold, self-assertive, pushy, cocksure, cocky, brash; shameless, immodest; loud, vulgar, showy, ostentatious; informal flashy. **2** *brassy music:* **loud**, blaring, noisy, deafening, strident; raucous, harsh, dissonant, discordant, cacophonous; tinny.
–OPPOSITES demure, soft.

brat noun (derogatory) **rascal**, wretch, imp; minx, chit; informal monster, horror, whippersnapper.

bravado noun **boldness**, swaggering, bluster; machismo; boasting, bragging, bombast, braggadocio; informal showing off.

brave adjective **courageous**, plucky, valiant, valorous, intrepid, heroic, lionhearted, bold, fearless, daring, audacious; unflinching, unshrinking, unafraid, dauntless, doughty, mettlesome, stout-hearted, spirited; informal game, gutsy, spunky.
–OPPOSITES cowardly.

b

• **noun** (dated) *an Indian brave:* **warrior**, soldier, fighter.
• **verb** *loyal fans braved freezing temperatures:* **endure**, put up with, bear, withstand, weather, suffer, go through; face, confront, defy.

bravery **noun** **courage**, pluck, valour, intrepidity, nerve, daring, fearlessness, audacity, boldness, stout-heartedness, heroism; backbone, grit, spine, spirit, mettle; informal guts, spunk; Brit. informal bottle; N. Amer. informal moxie.

bravo **exclamation** **well done**, congratulations; encore.

bravura **noun** *a display of bravura:* **skill**, brilliance, virtuosity, expertise, artistry, talent, ability, flair.
• **adjective** *a bravura performance:* **virtuoso**, masterly, outstanding, excellent, superb, brilliant, first-class; informal mean, ace, A1.

brawl **noun** **fight**, skirmish, scuffle, tussle, fray, melee, free-for-all, scrum; fisticuffs; informal scrap, dust-up, set-to; Brit. informal punch-up, ruck.

brawn **noun** **physical strength**, muscle, burliness, huskiness, toughness, power, might; informal beef.

brawny **adjective** **strong**, muscular, muscly, well built, powerful, mighty, Herculean, strapping, burly, sturdy, husky, rugged; bulky, hefty, meaty, solid; informal beefy, hunky, hulking.
– OPPOSITES puny, weak.

bray **verb** **1** *a donkey brayed:* **neigh**, whinny, hee-haw. **2** *Billy brayed with laughter:* **roar**, bellow, trumpet.

brazen **adjective** **bold**, shameless, unashamed, unabashed, unembarrassed; defiant, impudent, impertinent, cheeky; barefaced, blatant, flagrant; Brit. informal saucy.
– OPPOSITES timid.
■ **brazen it out** put on a bold front, stand your ground, be defiant, be unrepentant, be unabashed.

breach **noun** **1** *a breach of the regulations:* **contravention**, violation, infringement, infraction, transgression, neglect. **2** *a breach between government and Church:* **rift**, schism, division, gulf, chasm; disunion, estrangement, discord, dissension, disagreement; split, break, rupture, scission; Brit. informal bust-up. **3** *a breach in the sea wall:* **break**, rupture, split, crack, fracture; opening, gap, hole, fissure.
• **verb** **1** *the river breached its bank:* **break**, burst, rupture; informal bust. **2** *the changes breached union rules:* **break**, contravene, violate, infringe; defy, disobey, flout, fly in the face of.

breadth **noun** **1** *a breadth of 100 metres:* **width**, broadness, thickness; span; diameter. **2** *the breadth of his knowledge:* **range**, extent, scope, depth, reach, compass, scale, degree.

break **verb** **1** *the mirror broke:* **shatter**, smash, crack, snap, fracture, fragment, splinter; split, burst; informal bust. **2** *the bite had barely broken the skin:* **pierce**, puncture, penetrate, perforate; cut. **3** *the coffee machine's broken:* **stop working**, break down, give out, go wrong, malfunction, crash; informal go kaput, conk out, be on the blink, give up the ghost; Brit. informal pack up. **4** *traders who break the law:* **contravene**, violate, infringe, breach; defy, flout, disobey, fly in the face of. **5** *his concentration was broken:* **interrupt**, disturb, interfere with. **6** *the film broke box-office records:* **exceed**, surpass, beat, better, cap, top, outdo, outstrip, eclipse. **7** *old habits are very difficult to break:* **give up**, relinquish, drop; informal kick, shake, pack in, quit. **8** *the strategies used to break the union:* **destroy**, crush, quash, defeat, overcome, overpower, overwhelm, suppress; weaken, subdue, cow, undermine; literary vanquish. **9** *he tried to break the news gently:* **reveal**, disclose, divulge, impart, tell; announce, release. **10** *he broke the encryption code:* **decipher**, decode, decrypt, unravel, work out; informal crack, figure out. **11** *waves broke against the rocks:* **crash**, dash, beat, pound, lash. **12** *her voice broke as she relived the experience:* **falter**, quaver, quiver, tremble, shake.
– OPPOSITES mend, keep.
• **noun** **1** *the magazine has been published without a break since 1950:* **interruption**, interval, gap, hiatus; discontinuation, suspension, disruption, cut-off; stop, stoppage, cessation. **2** *we need a break:* **rest**,

respite, recess; stop, pause; interval, intermission; informal breather, time out. **3** *a weekend break:* **holiday**; N. Amer. vacation; Brit. informal vac. **4** *a break in diplomatic relations:* **rift**, schism, split, severance, rupture; Brit. informal bust-up. **5** *a break in the wall:* **gap**, opening, space, hole, breach, chink, crack, fissure; tear, split.

■ **break away** *they broke away from the main party:* leave, secede from, split off from, separate from, part company with, defect from; form a splinter group. **break down 1** *his van broke down on the M40.* See BREAK verb sense 3. **2** *pay negotiations broke down:* fail, collapse, founder, fall through, disintegrate; informal fizzle out. **3** *she broke down, sobbing loudly:* burst into tears; lose control, be overcome, go to pieces, crumble, disintegrate; informal crack up, lose it. **break something down** *graphs show how the information can be broken down:* analyse, categorize, classify, sort, itemize, organize, divide, separate; dissect. **break in/into 1** *thieves broke into her house:* burgle, rob; force your way into, burst into. **2** *'I don't want to interfere,' she broke in:* interrupt, butt in, cut in, interject, interpose, intervene, chime in; Brit. informal chip in. **break someone in** train, initiate; informal show someone the ropes. **break something off** *they threatened to break off diplomatic relations:* end, sever, terminate, stop, cease, call a halt to, finish, dissolve; suspend, discontinue; informal pull the plug on. **break out 1** *he broke out of the detention centre:* escape from, abscond from, flee from. **2** *fighting broke out:* flare up, erupt, burst out. **break up 1** *the meeting broke up:* end, finish, stop, terminate; adjourn; N. Amer. recess. **2** *the crowd began to break up:* disperse, scatter, disband. **3** *Danny and I broke up last year:* split up, separate, part company; divorce.

> ! Don't confuse **break** with **brake**, which means 'a device for slowing or stopping a vehicle' or 'slow or stop a vehicle' (*I braked to avoid the car in front*).

breakable adjective **fragile**, delicate, flimsy, insubstantial; destructible; formal frangible.

breakaway adjective *a breakaway group:* **separatist**, secessionist, schismatic, splinter; rebel, renegade.

breakdown noun **1** *the breakdown of the negotiations:* **failure**, collapse, disintegration, foundering. **2** *on the death of her father she suffered a breakdown:* **nervous breakdown**; informal crack-up. **3** *the breakdown of the computer system:* **malfunction**, failure, crash. **4** *a breakdown of the figures:* **analysis**, classification, examination, investigation, dissection.

breaker noun **wave**, roller, comber, white horse; informal boomer.

break-in noun **burglary**, robbery, theft, raid; informal smash-and-grab.

breakneck adjective *the breakneck pace of change:* **rapid**, speedy, high-speed, lightning, whirlwind.

■ **at breakneck speed** at full tilt, flat out; informal hell for leather, like the wind, like a bat out of hell, like greased lightning; Brit. informal like the clappers.

breakthrough noun **advance**, development, step forward, success, improvement; discovery, innovation, revolution.

–OPPOSITES setback.

break-up noun **1** *the break-up of negotiations:* **end**, dissolution; breakdown, failure, collapse, disintegration. **2** *their break-up was very amicable:* **separation**, split, parting, divorce; estrangement, rift; Brit. informal bust-up. **3** *the break-up of the Soviet Union:* **division**, partition.

breakwater noun **sea wall**, jetty, mole, groyne, pier.

breast noun **1** *the curve of her breasts:* **bosom**, bust, chest. **2** *feelings of frustration were rising up in his breast:* **heart**, bosom, soul, core.

> **WORD LINKS**
> **mastectomy** the surgical removal of a breast
> **mammogram** a breast X-ray

breath noun **1** *I took a deep breath:* **inhalation**, gulp of air; exhalation, expiration; Medicine respiration. **2** *a breath of wind:* **puff**, waft; breeze.

■ **take someone's breath away** astonish, astound, amaze, stun,

b

startle, stagger, shock, take aback, dumbfound, jolt, overawe, thrill; informal knock sideways, flabbergast, blow away, bowl over; Brit. informal knock for six.

breathe verb **1** *she breathed deeply:* **inhale**, **exhale**, respire, draw breath; puff, pant, blow, gasp, wheeze; Medicine inspire, expire. **2** *he would breathe new life into his firm:* **instil**, infuse, inject, impart. **3** *'Together at last,' she breathed:* **whisper**, murmur, purr, sigh, say.

WORD LINKS
respiratory relating to breathing

breathless adjective **1** *Will arrived flushed and breathless:* **out of breath**, panting, puffing, gasping, wheezing; winded; informal out of puff. **2** *the crowd were breathless with anticipation:* **agog**, open-mouthed, on the edge of your seat, on tenterhooks, in suspense.

breathtaking adjective **spectacular**, magnificent, wonderful, awe-inspiring, awesome, astounding, astonishing, amazing, stunning, incredible; informal sensational, out of this world; literary wondrous.

breed verb **1** *elephants breed readily in captivity:* **reproduce**, produce offspring, procreate, multiply; mate. **2** *she was born and bred in the village:* **bring up**, rear, raise, nurture. **3** *the political system bred discontent:* **cause**, bring about, give rise to, lead to, produce, generate, foster, result in; stir up; literary beget.
•noun **1** *a breed of cow:* **variety**, stock, strain; type, kind, sort. **2** *a new breed of journalist:* **type**, kind, sort, variety, class, genre, generation.

breeding noun **1** *individual birds pair for breeding:* **reproduction**, procreation; mating. **2** *the breeding of rats:* **rearing**, raising, nurturing. **3** *her aristocratic breeding:* **upbringing**, rearing; parentage, family, pedigree, blood, birth. **4** *people of rank and breeding:* **good manners**, gentility, refinement, cultivation, polish, urbanity; informal class.

breeding ground noun *the school is a breeding ground for communists:* **nursery**, cradle, nest, den; hotbed.

breeze noun **1 gentle wind**, puff of air, gust; literary zephyr. **2** (informal) *travelling through London was a breeze:* **easy task**, five-finger exercise, walkover; child's play, nothing; informal doddle, piece of cake, cinch, kids' stuff, cakewalk.

breezy adjective **1** *a breezy day:* **windy**, fresh, brisk, airy; blowy, blustery, gusty. **2** *his breezy manner:* **jaunty**, cheerful, cheery, brisk, carefree, easy, casual, relaxed, informal, light-hearted, lively, buoyant, sunny, upbeat.

brevity noun **1** *the report is notable for its brevity:* **conciseness**, succinctness, economy of language, pithiness, incisiveness, shortness, compactness. **2** *the brevity of human life:* **shortness**, briefness, transience, ephemerality, impermanence.
–OPPOSITES verbosity.

brew verb **1** *this beer is brewed in Frankfurt:* **make**, prepare, ferment; infuse. **2** *there's trouble brewing:* **develop**, loom, impend, be imminent, be on the horizon, be in the offing.
•noun **1** *a hot reviving brew | home brew:* **drink**, beverage, infusion. **2** *a dangerous brew of political turmoil and violent conflict:* **mixture**, mix, blend, combination, amalgam, cocktail.

bribe verb **buy off**, pay off, suborn; informal grease someone's palm, keep someone sweet, fix, square; Brit. informal nobble.
•noun **inducement**, incentive, carrot, douceur; informal backhander, pay-off, kickback, sweetener; Brit. informal bung.

bribery noun **subornation**; N. Amer. payola; informal palm-greasing, graft, hush money.

WORD LINKS
venal susceptible to bribery

bric-a-brac noun **ornaments**, knick-knacks, trinkets, bibelots, gewgaws, gimcracks; bits and bobs, odds and ends; informal junk.

brick noun *a brick of ice cream:* **block**, cube, bar, cake.

bridal adjective **wedding**, nuptial, marriage, matrimonial, marital, conjugal.

bride noun **wife**, bride-to-be; newly-wed.

bridge noun **1** *a bridge over the river:* **viaduct**, flyover, overpass,

aqueduct. **2** *a bridge between rival groups:* **link**, connection, bond, tie.
• verb **1** *a walkway bridged the motorway:* **span**, cross, extend across, traverse, arch over. **2** *an attempt to bridge the cultural gap:* **join**, link, connect, unite; straddle; overcome, reconcile.

WORD LINKS
pontine relating to bridges

bridle noun *a horse's bridle:* **harness**, headgear.
• verb **1** *she bridled at his tone:* **bristle**, take offence, take umbrage, be affronted, be offended, get angry. **2** *he bridled his indignation:* **curb**, restrain, hold back, control, check, rein in/back; suppress, stifle; informal keep a/the lid on.

brief adjective **1** *a brief account:* **concise**, succinct, short, pithy, incisive, abridged, condensed, compressed, abbreviated, compact, thumbnail, potted; formal compendious. **2** *a brief visit:* **short**, flying, fleeting, hasty, hurried, quick, cursory, perfunctory; temporary, short-lived, momentary, transient; informal quickie. **3** *a pair of brief shorts:* **skimpy**, scanty, short; revealing. **4** *the boss was rather brief with him:* **brusque**, abrupt, curt, short, blunt, sharp.
– OPPOSITES long, lengthy.
• noun **1** *my brief is to reorganize the project:* **instructions**, directions, directive, remit, mandate. **2** *a barrister's brief:* **case**, summary, argument, contention; dossier.
• verb *employees were briefed about the decision:* **inform**, tell, update, notify, advise, apprise; prepare, prime, instruct; informal fill in, clue in, put in the picture.

briefing noun **1** *a press briefing:* **conference**, meeting, interview, session; N. Amer. backgrounder. **2** *this briefing explains the systems:* **information**, rundown, guidance; instructions, directions, guidelines.

briefly adverb **1** *Henry paused briefly:* **momentarily**, temporarily, for a moment, fleetingly. **2** *briefly, the plot is as follows:* **in short**, in brief, in a word, in sum, in a nutshell, in essence.

brigade noun **1** *a brigade of soldiers:* **unit**, contingent, battalion, regiment, division, squadron, company, platoon, section, corps, troop. **2** *the volunteer ambulance brigade:* **squad**, team, group, band, party, crew, force, outfit.

bright adjective **1** *the bright surface of the metal:* **shining**, brilliant, dazzling, beaming, glaring; sparkling, flashing, glittering, gleaming, glowing, luminous, radiant; shiny, lustrous, glossy. **2** *a bright morning:* **sunny**, cloudless, clear, fair, fine. **3** *bright colours:* **vivid**, vibrant, brilliant, intense, strong, bold, glowing, rich; gaudy, lurid, garish; dated gay. **4** *a bright young graduate:* **clever**, intelligent, quick-witted, smart, canny, astute, intuitive, perceptive; ingenious, resourceful; informal brainy. **5** *a bright smile:* **happy**, cheerful, cheery, jolly, merry, sunny, beaming; lively, exuberant, buoyant, bubbly, bouncy, perky, chirpy. **6** *a bright future:* **promising**, rosy, optimistic, hopeful, favourable, propitious, auspicious, encouraging, good, golden.
– OPPOSITES dull, dark, stupid.

brighten verb **1** *sunshine brightened the room:* **illuminate**, light up, lighten, cast/shed light on. **2** *you can brighten up the shadiest of corners:* **enhance**, embellish, enrich, dress up, prettify, beautify; informal jazz up. **3** *Sarah brightened up as she thought of Emily's words:* **cheer up**, perk up, rally; be enlivened, feel heartened, be uplifted, be encouraged, take heart; informal buck up, pep up.

brilliance noun **1** *a philosopher of great brilliance:* **genius**, talent, ability, prowess, skill, expertise, aptitude, flair, finesse, panache; greatness, distinction; intelligence, wisdom, sagacity, intellect. **2** *the brilliance and beauty of Paris:* **splendour**, magnificence, grandeur, resplendence. **3** *the brilliance of the sunshine:* **brightness**, vividness, intensity; sparkle, glitter, glow, blaze, beam, luminosity, radiance.

brilliant adjective **1** *a brilliant student:* **gifted**, talented, able, adept, skilful; bright, intelligent, clever, smart, astute, intellectual; elite, superior, first-class, excellent; informal brainy. **2** *his brilliant career:* **superb**, glorious, illustrious,

b

impressive, remarkable, exceptional. **3** *a shaft of brilliant light:* **bright**, shining, blazing, dazzling, vivid, intense, gleaming, glaring, luminous, radiant; literary irradiant, coruscating. **4** *brilliant green:* **vivid**, intense, bright, bold, dazzling.
– OPPOSITES stupid, inglorious, dark.

brim noun **1** *the brim of his hat:* peak, visor, shield, shade. **2** *the cup was filled to its brim:* **rim**, lip, brink, edge.
• verb **1** *the pan was brimming with water:* **be full**; overflow, run over. **2** *her eyes were brimming with tears:* **fill**; overflow.

brimful adjective **full**, brimming, filled to capacity, overfull, running over; informal chock-full.
– OPPOSITES empty.

brindle, brindled adjective **tawny**, brownish; streaked, striped, dappled, mottled, speckled, flecked.

bring verb **1** *he brought her cases:* **carry**, fetch, bear, take; convey, transport. **2** *he brought them into the kitchen:* **escort**, conduct, guide, lead, usher, show, shepherd. **3** *economic decline brought pressure for change:* **cause**, produce, create, generate, precipitate, lead to, give rise to, result in; stir up, whip up, promote. **4** *the police contemplated bringing charges:* **put forward**, prefer, lay, submit, present, initiate, institute. **5** *this job brings him a regular salary:* **earn**, make, fetch, bring in, yield, net, gross, return, produce; command, attract.
■ **bring something about** cause, produce, give rise to, result in, lead to, occasion, bring on, bring to pass; provoke, generate, engender, precipitate; formal effectuate. **bring something back 1** *the smell brought back memories:* conjure up, evoke, summon up, put someone in mind of. **2** *they're unlikely to bring back capital punishment:* reintroduce, reinstate, re-establish, revive, resurrect. **bring something down 1** *we will bring down the price:* decrease, reduce, lower, cut, drop; informal slash. **2** *the unrest brought down the government:* unseat, overturn, topple, overthrow, depose, oust. **bring something forward** propose, suggest, advance, raise, table, present, move, submit, lodge. **bring something on**. See BRING SOMETHING ABOUT. **bring something out 1** *they were bringing out a new magazine:* launch, establish, begin, start, found, set up, instigate, inaugurate, market; publish, print, issue, produce. **2** *the shawl brings out the colour of your eyes:* accentuate, highlight, emphasize, accent, set off. **bring someone round** *we would have brought him round, given time:* persuade, convince, talk round, win over, sway, influence. **bring someone up** rear, raise, care for, look after, nurture, provide for. **bring something up** mention, allude to, touch on, raise, broach, introduce; voice, air, suggest, propose, submit, put forward, table.

brink noun **1** *the brink of the abyss:* **edge**, verge, margin, rim, lip; border, boundary, perimeter, periphery, limits. **2** *two countries on the brink of war:* **verge**, threshold, point, edge.

brio noun **vigour**, vivacity, gusto, verve, zest, enthusiasm, vitality, dynamism, animation, spirit, energy; informal pep, vim, get-up-and-go.

brisk adjective **1** *a brisk pace:* **quick**, rapid, fast, swift, speedy, hurried; energetic, lively, vigorous; informal nippy. **2** *the bar was doing a brisk trade:* **busy**, bustling, lively, hectic; good. **3** *his tone became brisk:* **no-nonsense**, decisive, businesslike; brusque, abrupt, short, sharp, curt, blunt, terse, gruff; informal snappy. **4** *a brisk breeze:* **bracing**, fresh, crisp, invigorating, refreshing, stimulating, energizing; biting, keen, chilly, cold; informal nippy.
– OPPOSITES slow, quiet.

bristle noun **1** *the bristles on his chin:* **hair**, whisker; (**bristles**) stubble, five o'clock shadow. **2** *a hedgehog's bristles:* **spine**, prickle, quill, barb.
• verb **1** *the hair on the back of his neck bristled:* **rise**, stand up, stand on end. **2** *she bristled at his tone:* **bridle**, take offence, take umbrage, be affronted, be offended; get angry, be irritated. **3** *the roof bristled with antennae:* **abound**, overflow, be full, be packed, be crowded, be jammed, be covered; informal be thick, be chock-full.

bristly adjective **1** *bristly bushes:* **prickly**, spiky, thorny, scratchy, brambly. **2** *the bristly skin of his cheek:* **stubbly**, hairy, fuzzy, unshaven, whiskery; scratchy, rough, coarse, prickly.
– OPPOSITES smooth.

brittle adjective **1** *a brittle material:* **breakable**, fragile, delicate; splintery; formal frangible. **2** *a brittle laugh:* **harsh**, hard, sharp, grating. **3** *a brittle woman:* **edgy**, nervy, anxious, unstable, highly strung, tense, excitable, jumpy, skittish, neurotic; informal uptight.
– OPPOSITES flexible, resilient, soft, relaxed.

broach verb **1** *I broached the matter with my parents:* **bring up**, raise, introduce, talk about, mention, touch on, air. **2** *he broached a barrel of beer:* **pierce**, puncture, tap; open, uncork; informal crack open.

broad adjective **1** *a broad flight of steps:* **wide**. **2** *the leaves are two inches broad:* **wide**, across, in breadth, in width. **3** *a broad expanse of prairie:* **extensive**, vast, immense, great, spacious, expansive, sizeable, sweeping, rolling. **4** *a broad range of opportunities:* **comprehensive**, inclusive, extensive, wide, all-embracing, eclectic, unlimited. **5** *this report gives a broad outline:* **general**, non-specific, rough, approximate, basic; loose, vague. **6** *a broad hint:* **obvious**, unsubtle, explicit, direct, plain, clear, straightforward, bald, patent, transparent, undisguised, overt. **7** *his broad humour:* **indecent**, coarse, indelicate, ribald, risqué, racy, rude, suggestive, naughty, off colour, earthy, smutty, dirty, filthy, vulgar; informal blue, near the knuckle. **8** *a broad Somerset accent:* **pronounced**, noticeable, strong, thick. **9** *he was attacked in broad daylight:* **full**, complete, total; clear, bright.
– OPPOSITES narrow, limited, detailed, subtle.

broadcast verb **1** *the show will be broadcast worldwide:* **transmit**, relay, air, beam, show, televise, telecast, screen. **2** *the result was broadcast far and wide:* **report**, announce, publicize, proclaim; spread, circulate, air, blazon, trumpet. **3** *broadcast the seed over the desired area:* **scatter**, sow, disperse, sprinkle, spread, distribute.
• noun **programme**, show, production, transmission, telecast, screening, videocast; informal prog.

broaden verb **1** *her smile broadened:* **widen**, expand, spread; deepen. **2** *the government tried to broaden its political base:* **expand**, enlarge, extend, stretch, widen, swell; increase, augment, add to, amplify; develop, enrich, improve, build on.

broadly adverb **1** *the pattern is broadly similar for men and women:* **in general**, on the whole, as a rule, in the main, mainly, predominantly; loosely, roughly, approximately. **2** *he was smiling broadly:* **widely**, openly, from ear to ear.

broad-minded adjective **liberal**, tolerant, freethinking, indulgent, progressive, permissive, unshockable; unprejudiced, unbiased.
– OPPOSITES intolerant.

broadside noun **1** (historical) *the gunners fired broadsides:* **salvo**, volley, cannonade, barrage, blast, fusillade. **2** *a broadside against the economic reforms:* **criticism**, censure, polemic, diatribe, tirade; attack, onslaught.

brochure noun **booklet**, prospectus, catalogue; pamphlet, leaflet, handbill, handout; N. Amer. folder.

broil verb (N. Amer.) **grill**, toast, barbecue; cook.

broken adjective **1** *broken glass:* **smashed**, shattered, fragmented, fractured, splintered, crushed, snapped; in bits, in pieces; destroyed, disintegrated; cracked, split; informal in smithereens. **2** *the TV's broken:* **damaged**, faulty, defective, not working, malfunctioning, in disrepair, inoperative, out of order, broken-down, down; informal on the blink, kaput, bust, conked out, acting up, done for; Brit. informal knackered. **3** *a broken marriage:* **failed**, ended, unsuccessful. **4** *he was left a broken man:* **defeated**, beaten, subdued; demoralized, dispirited, discouraged, crushed, humbled; dishonoured, ruined. **5** *a night of broken sleep:* **interrupted**, disturbed, fitful, disrupted, discontinuous, intermittent,

b

unsettled, troubled. **6** *she spoke in broken English:* **halting**, hesitating, disjointed, faltering, imperfect.
–OPPOSITES whole, working.

broken-down adjective **1** *an old, broken-down hotel:* **dilapidated**, run down, ramshackle, tumble-down, in disrepair, battered, crumbling, deteriorated, gone to rack and ruin. **2** *a broken-down car:* **defective**, faulty; not working, malfunctioning, inoperative; informal kaput, conked out, clapped out, done for; Brit. informal knackered.
–OPPOSITES smart.

broken-hearted adjective **heart-broken**, grief-stricken, desolate, devastated, inconsolable, miserable, depressed, melancholy, wretched, sorrowful, forlorn, heavy-hearted, woeful, doleful, downcast, woebegone; informal down in the mouth.
–OPPOSITES overjoyed.

broker noun **dealer**, agent; middleman, intermediary, mediator; factor, liaison; stockbroker.
• verb **arrange**, organize, orchestrate, work out, settle, clinch; negotiate, mediate.

bronzed adjective **tanned**, suntanned, brown.
–OPPOSITES pale.

brooch noun **breastpin**, pin, clip, badge.

brood noun **offspring**, young, progeny; family, hatch, clutch; formal progeniture.
• verb **1** *once the eggs are laid the male broods them:* **incubate**, hatch. **2** *he slumped in his armchair, brooding:* **worry**, fret, agonize, mope, sulk; think, ponder, contemplate, meditate, muse.

brook[1] noun *a babbling brook:* **stream**, streamlet, rill, runnel, gill; N. English beck; Scottish & N. English burn; S. English bourn; N. Amer. & Austral./NZ creek.

brook[2] verb (formal) *we brook no violence:* **tolerate**, allow, stand, bear, abide, put up with, endure; accept, permit, countenance; informal stomach, hack; Brit. informal stick.

brothel noun whorehouse; N. Amer. bordello; Brit. informal knocking shop; euphemistic massage parlour; Law disorderly house; old use bawdy house, house of ill repute.

brother noun **1** *she had a younger brother:* sibling. **2** *they were brothers in crime:* **colleague**, associate, partner, comrade, fellow, friend; informal pal, chum; Brit. informal mate. **3** *a brother of the Order:* **monk**, cleric, friar, religious, monastic.

WORD LINKS

fraternal relating to or like a brother
fratricide the killing of your brother or sister

brotherhood noun **1** *the ideals of justice and brotherhood:* **comradeship**, fellowship, fraternalism, kinship; camaraderie, friendship. **2** *a Masonic brotherhood:* **society**, fraternity, association, alliance, union, league, guild, order, body, community, club, lodge, circle.

brotherly adjective **1** *brotherly rivalry:* **fraternal**, sibling. **2** *brotherly love:* **friendly**, comradely; affectionate, amicable, kind, devoted, loyal.

brow noun **1** **forehead**, temple. **2** *the brow of the hill:* **summit**, peak, top, crest, crown, head, pinnacle, apex.

browbeat verb **bully**, hector, intimidate, force, coerce, compel, dragoon, bludgeon, pressure, pressurize, tyrannize, terrorize, menace; harass, harry, hound; informal bulldoze, railroad.

brown adjective **1** *brown eyes | brown hair:* hazel, chocolate-coloured, coffee-coloured; brunette, chestnut; sepia, mahogany, umber, burnt sienna; beige, buff, tan, fawn, camel, café au lait, caramel. **2** *his skin was brown from the summer sun:* **tanned**, suntanned, bronzed, weather-beaten; dark, swarthy, dusky.

browse verb **1** *I browsed among the shops:* **look around/round**, window-shop. **2** *she browsed through the newspaper:* **scan**, skim, glance, look, peruse; thumb, leaf, flick; dip into. **3** *cows were browsing in the meadow:* **graze**, feed, crop; ruminate.

bruise noun *a bruise on her forehead:* **contusion**, lesion, mark, injury; swelling, lump, bump, welt.
• verb **1** *her face was badly bruised:* **contuse**, injure, mark, discolour. **2** *every one of the apples is bruised:* **mark**, discolour, blemish; damage,

spoil. **3** *Eric's ego was bruised:* **upset**, offend, insult, affront, hurt, wound, injure, crush.

brunette adjective **brown-haired**, dark.

brunt noun **force**, impact, shock, burden, pressure, weight; effect, repercussions, consequences.

brush[1] noun **1** *a dustpan and brush:* **broom**, sweeper, besom, whisk. **2** *he gave the seat a brush with his hand:* **clean**, sweep, wipe, dust. **3** *the brush of his lips against her cheek:* **touch**, stroke, skim, graze, nudge, contact; kiss. **4** *a brush with the law:* **encounter**, clash, confrontation, conflict, altercation, incident; informal run-in, to-do; Brit. informal spot of bother.

• verb **1** *he spent his day brushing the floors:* **sweep**, clean, buff. **2** *she brushed her hair:* **groom**, comb, neaten, tidy, smooth, arrange, fix, do. **3** *she felt his lips brush her cheek:* **touch**, stroke, caress, skim, sweep, graze, contact; kiss. **4** *she brushed a wisp of hair away:* **push**, move, sweep, clear.

■ **brush something aside** disregard, ignore, dismiss, shrug off, wave aside; overlook, pay no attention to, take no notice of, neglect, forget about, turn a blind eye to; reject, spurn; laugh off, make light of, trivialize; informal pooh-pooh. **brush someone off** rebuff, dismiss, spurn, reject; slight, scorn, disdain; ignore, disregard, snub, cut, turn your back on, give someone the cold shoulder, freeze out; jilt, cast aside, discard, throw over, drop, leave; informal knock back.

brush[2] noun **undergrowth**, underwood, scrub, brushwood, shrubs, bushes; N. Amer. underbrush, chaparral.

brusque adjective **curt**, abrupt, blunt, short, sharp, terse, brisk, peremptory, gruff, bluff; offhand, discourteous, impolite, rude; informal snappy.
– OPPOSITES polite.

brutal adjective **1** *a brutal attack:* **savage**, cruel, vicious, ferocious, barbaric, barbarous, wicked, murderous, bloodthirsty, cold-blooded, callous, heartless, merciless, sadistic; heinous, monstrous, abominable, atrocious. **2** *brutal honesty:* **unsparing**, unstinting, unembellished, unvarnished, bald, naked, stark, blunt, direct, straightforward, frank, outspoken, forthright, plain-spoken; complete, total.
– OPPOSITES gentle.

brutalize verb **1** *the men were brutalized by life in the trenches:* **desensitize**, dehumanize, harden, toughen, inure. **2** *they were brutalized by the police:* **attack**, assault, beat, batter; abuse.

brute noun **1** *a callous brute:* **savage**, beast, monster, animal, barbarian, fiend, ogre; sadist; thug, lout, ruffian; informal swine, pig. **2** *the Alsatian was a vicious-looking brute:* **animal**, beast, creature; N. Amer. informal critter.

• adjective *brute strength:* **physical**, bodily; crude, violent.

bubble noun *bubbles of liquid:* globule, bead, blister, air pocket; (**bubbles**) sparkle, fizz, effervescence, froth, foam, suds.

• verb **sparkle**, fizz, effervesce, foam, froth.

bubbly adjective **1** *a bubbly wine:* **sparkling**, fizzy, effervescent, gassy, aerated, carbonated; spumante; frothy, foamy. **2** *she was bubbly and full of life:* **vivacious**, animated, ebullient, lively, high-spirited, zestful; sparkling, bouncy, buoyant, carefree; merry, happy, cheerful, perky, sunny, bright; informal upbeat, chirpy.
– OPPOSITES still, listless.

buccaneering adjective *a buccaneering businessman and politician:* **adventurous**, risk-taking, bold, daring, daredevil; high-risk.
– OPPOSITES cautious.

buck verb *it takes guts to buck the system:* **resist**, oppose, defy, fight, kick against.

bucket noun **pail**, scuttle, can, tub.

buckle noun *a belt buckle:* **clasp**, clip, catch, hasp, fastener.

• verb **1** *he buckled the belt round his waist:* **fasten**, do up, hook, strap, secure, clasp, clip. **2** *the front axle buckled:* **warp**, bend, twist, curve, distort, contort, deform; bulge, arc, arch; crumple, collapse, give way.

bucolic adjective **rustic**, rural, pastoral, country, countryside; literary Arcadian, sylvan, georgic.

b

budding adjective **promising**, up-and-coming, rising, in the making, aspiring, future, prospective, potential, fledgling, developing; informal would-be, wannabe.

budge verb **1** *the horses wouldn't budge:* **move**, shift, stir, go. **2** *I couldn't budge the door:* **dislodge**, shift, move, reposition. **3** *they refuse to budge on the issue:* **give way**, yield, change your mind, acquiesce, compromise, do a U-turn. **4** *our customers won't be budged on price alone:* **influence**, sway, convince, persuade, induce, entice, tempt, lure, cajole, bring round.

budget noun **1** *your budget for the week:* **financial plan**, forecast; accounts, statement. **2** *the defence budget:* **allowance**, allocation, quota; grant, award, funds, resources, capital.
• verb *we have budgeted £7,000 for the work:* **allocate**, allot, allow, earmark, designate, set aside.
• adjective *a budget hotel:* **cheap**, inexpensive, economy, low-cost, low-price, cut-price, discount, bargain.
– OPPOSITES expensive.

buff[1] adjective *a plain buff envelope:* **beige**, yellowish, yellowish-brown, light brown, fawn, sandy, wheaten, biscuit, camel.
• verb *he buffed the glass:* **polish**, burnish, shine, clean, rub.

buff[2] noun (informal) *a film buff:* **enthusiast**, fan, devotee, lover, admirer; expert, aficionado, authority, pundit; informal freak, nut, fanatic, addict.

buffer noun *a buffer against market fluctuations:* **cushion**, bulwark, shield, barrier, guard, safeguard.
• verb *a massage helped to buffer the strain:* **cushion**, absorb, soften, lessen, diminish, moderate, allay.
– OPPOSITES intensify.

buffet[1] noun **1** *a sumptuous buffet:* **cold table**, self-service meal, smorgasbord. **2** *a station buffet:* **cafe**, cafeteria, snack bar, canteen, restaurant. **3** *the plates are kept in the buffet:* **sideboard**, cabinet, cupboard.

buffet[2] verb *rough seas buffeted the coast:* **batter**, pound, lash, strike, hit; afflict, beset, bedevil.

buffoon noun *he regarded the man as a buffoon:* **fool**, idiot, dunce, ignoramus, simpleton, jackass; informal chump, blockhead, nincompoop, numbskull, dope, twit, nitwit, halfwit, clot, birdbrain, twerp.

bug noun **1** *bugs were crawling everywhere:* **insect**, minibeast; informal creepy-crawly, beastie. **2** *the bug planted on his phone:* **listening device**, hidden microphone, wire, wiretap, tap. **3** *the program developed a bug:* **fault**, error, defect, flaw; virus; informal glitch, gremlin.
• verb *her conversations were bugged:* **record**, eavesdrop on, spy on, overhear; wiretap, tap, monitor.

bugbear noun **pet hate**, bête noire, bogey; bane, irritation, vexation, anathema, thorn in your flesh/side; informal peeve, pain in the neck, hang-up; N. Amer. bugaboo.

build verb **1** *a supermarket had been built:* **construct**, erect, put up, assemble. **2** *they were building a snowman:* **make**, construct, form, create, fashion, model, shape. **3** *they are building a business strategy:* **establish**, found, set up, institute, inaugurate, initiate.
• noun *a man of slim build:* **physique**, frame, body, figure, form, shape, stature, proportions; informal vital statistics.
■ **build something in/into** incorporate in/into, include in, absorb into, subsume into, assimilate into. **build on** expand on, enlarge on, develop, elaborate, flesh out, embellish, amplify; refine, improve, perfect. **build up** increase, grow, mount up, intensify, escalate; strengthen. **build something up 1** *he built up a huge business:* establish, set up, found, institute, start, create; develop, expand, enlarge. **2** *he built up his stamina:* boost, strengthen, increase, improve, augment, raise, enhance, swell; informal beef up. **3** *I have built up a collection of prints:* accumulate, amass, collect, gather; stockpile, hoard.

builder noun **1** *a canal builder:* **designer**, planner, architect, deviser, creator, maker, constructor. **2** *the builders must finish the job in time:* **construction worker**, bricklayer, labourer; Brit. ganger.

building noun **1** *a brick building:* **structure**, construction, edifice, erection, pile; property, premises, establishment. **2** *the building of power stations:* **construction**, erection, fabrication, assembly.

WORD LINKS
architectural relating to building

build-up noun **1** *the build-up of military strength:* **increase**, growth, expansion, escalation, development, proliferation. **2** *the build-up of carbon dioxide:* **accumulation**, accretion. **3** *the build-up for the World Cup:* **publicity**, promotion, advertising, marketing; informal hype.

built-in adjective **1** *a built-in cupboard:* **fitted**, integral, integrated, incorporated. **2** *built-in advantages:* **inherent**, intrinsic, inbuilt; essential, implicit, basic, fundamental, deep-rooted.

bulb noun **tuber**, corm, rhizome.

bulbous adjective **bulging**, protuberant, round, fat, rotund; swollen, tumid, distended, bloated.

bulge noun **swelling**, bump, lump, protuberance, prominence.
• verb **swell**, stick out, puff out, balloon out, fill out, belly, distend; project, protrude, stand out.

bulk noun **1** *the sheer bulk of the ship:* **size**, volume, dimensions, proportions, mass, scale, magnitude, immensity, vastness. **2** *the bulk of entrants were British:* **majority**, generality, main part, lion's share, preponderance; most, almost all.
– OPPOSITES minority.
• verb *some meals are bulked out with fat:* **expand**, pad out, fill out, eke out; augment, increase.

bulky adjective **1** *bulky items:* **large**, big, sizeable, substantial, massive, outsize, oversized, considerable; cumbersome, unmanageable, unwieldy, ponderous, heavy, weighty; informal jumbo, whopping, hulking. **2** *a bulky man:* **heavily built**, stocky, thickset, sturdy, well built, burly, strapping, solid, heavy, hefty, meaty; stout, fat, plump, chubby, portly, rotund, round, chunky; overweight, obese, fleshy, corpulent; informal tubby, pudgy, roly-poly, beefy, porky, blubbery; Brit. informal podgy.
– OPPOSITES small, slight.

bull noun

WORD LINKS
taurine relating to a bull

bulldoze verb **1** *they plan to bulldoze the park:* **demolish**, knock down, tear down, pull down, flatten, level, raze, clear. **2** *he bulldozed his way through:* **force**, push, shove, barge, elbow, shoulder, jostle; plunge, crash, sweep.

bullet noun ball, shot; informal slug; (**bullets**) lead.

bulletin noun **1** *a news bulletin:* **report**, dispatch, story, press release, newscast, flash; statement, announcement, message, communication, communiqué. **2** *the society's monthly bulletin:* **newsletter**, newssheet, proceedings; newspaper, magazine, digest, gazette, review.

bullish adjective **confident**, positive, assertive, assured, bold, determined; optimistic, buoyant, sanguine; informal feisty, upbeat.

bully noun **persecutor**, oppressor, tyrant, tormentor, intimidator; tough guy, thug.
• verb **1** *the others bully him:* **persecute**, oppress, tyrannize, browbeat, intimidate, strong-arm, dominate; informal push around/about. **2** *she was bullied into helping:* **coerce**, pressure, pressurize, press, push; force, compel; badger, goad, prod, browbeat, bludgeon, intimidate, dragoon, strong-arm; informal bulldoze, railroad, lean on.

bulwark noun **1** *ancient bulwarks:* **wall**, rampart, fortification, parapet, stockade, palisade, barricade, embankment, earthwork. **2** *a bulwark of liberty:* **protector**, defender, protection, guard, defence, supporter, buttress; mainstay, bastion, stronghold.

bumbling adjective **blundering**, bungling, inept, clumsy, maladroit, awkward, muddled; oafish, clodhopping, lumbering; crude; informal botched, ham-fisted, cack-handed.
– OPPOSITES efficient.

bump noun **1** *I landed with a bump:* **jolt**, crash, smash, smack, crack, bang, thud, thump; informal whack, thwack, bash, wallop. **2** *I was woken by a bump:* **bang**, crack, boom, clang, knock, thud, thump, clunk,

crash, smash; stomp, clump, clomp. **3** *a bump in the road:* **hump**, lump, ridge, bulge, knob, protuberance. **4** *a bump on his head:* **swelling**, lump, bulge, injury, contusion; outgrowth, growth, carbuncle, protuberance.
• verb **1** *cars bumped into each other:* **hit**, crash, smash, slam, bang, knock, run, plough; ram, collide with, strike; N. Amer. impact. **2** *a cart bumping along the road:* **bounce**, jolt, jerk, rattle, shake.

bumper adjective **abundant**, rich, bountiful, good, fine; large, big, huge, plentiful, profuse, copious; informal whopping; literary plenteous, bounteous.
– OPPOSITES meagre.

bumpkin noun **yokel**, peasant, provincial, rustic, country cousin, countryman/woman; N. Amer. informal hayseed, hillbilly, hick; Austral. informal bushy.

bumptious adjective **self-important**, conceited, arrogant, self-assertive, pushy, swollen-headed, pompous, overbearing, cocky, swaggering; proud, haughty, egotistical; informal snooty, uppity.
– OPPOSITES modest.

bumpy adjective **1** *a bumpy road:* **uneven**, rough, rutted, pitted, potholed; lumpy, rocky. **2** *a bumpy ride:* **bouncy**, rough, uncomfortable, jolting, lurching, jerky, jarring, bone-shaking. **3** *a bumpy start:* **inconsistent**, variable, irregular, fluctuating, intermittent, erratic, patchy; rocky, unsettled, unstable, turbulent, chaotic.
– OPPOSITES smooth.

bunch noun **1** *a bunch of flowers:* **bouquet**, posy, nosegay, spray, corsage; wreath, garland. **2** *a bunch of keys:* **cluster**, clump, knot; group.
• verb **1** *he bunched the reins in his hand:* **bundle**, clump, cluster, group, gather; pack. **2** *his trousers bunched around his ankles:* **gather**, ruffle, pucker, fold, pleat. **3** *the runners bunched up behind him:* **cluster**, huddle, gather, congregate, collect, amass, group, crowd.

bundle noun *a bundle of clothes:* **bunch**, roll, clump, wad, parcel, sheaf, bale, bolt; pile, stack, heap, mass; informal load, wodge.
• verb **1** *she bundled up her things:* **tie**, pack, parcel, wrap, roll, fold, bind, truss, bale. **2** *she was bundled in furs:* **wrap**, envelop, clothe, cover, muffle, swathe, swaddle, shroud, drape, enfold.

bung noun **stopper**, plug, cork, spigot, spile, seal; N. Amer. stopple.

bungle verb **mishandle**, mismanage, mess up, spoil, ruin; informal botch, muff, fluff, make a hash of, foul up, screw up; Brit. informal make a pig's ear of, cock up; N. Amer. informal flub, goof up.

bungler noun **blunderer**, incompetent, amateur, bumbler, clown; Brit. informal bodger; N. Amer. informal jackleg.

bungling adjective **incompetent**, blundering, amateurish, inept, unskilful, clumsy, awkward, bumbling; informal ham-fisted, cack-handed.

bunk noun **berth**, cot, bed.

buoy noun *a mooring buoy:* **float**, marker, beacon.
• verb *the party was buoyed by an election victory:* **cheer**, hearten, rally, invigorate, uplift, lift, encourage, stimulate; informal pep up, perk up, buck up.
– OPPOSITES depress.

buoyancy noun **1** *the buoyancy of the market:* **vigour**, strength, resilience, growth, improvement, expansion. **2** *he radiated buoyancy and optimism:* **cheerfulness**, happiness, light-heartedness, joy, bounce, breeziness, jollity; liveliness, ebullience, high spirits, vivacity, vitality, verve, sparkle, zest.

buoyant adjective **1** *a buoyant substance:* floating, floatable. **2** *a buoyant mood:* **cheerful**, cheery, happy, light-hearted, carefree, bright, merry, joyful, bubbly, bouncy, sunny, jolly; lively, jaunty, high-spirited, perky; optimistic, confident, positive; informal peppy, upbeat. **3** *sales were buoyant:* **booming**, strong, vigorous, thriving; improving, expanding, mushrooming, snowballing.

burble verb **1** *the exhaust was burbling:* **gurgle**, bubble, murmur, purr, whirr, drone, hum, rumble. **2** *he burbled on:* **prattle**, blather, babble, gabble, prate, drivel, rattle, ramble, maunder, go on, run on; informal jabber, blabber, yatter, gab; Brit. informal rabbit, witter, waffle, chunter.

burden noun 1 *they shouldered their burdens:* **load**, cargo, weight; pack, bundle. 2 *a financial burden:* **responsibility**, onus, charge, duty, obligation, liability; trouble, care, problem, worry, difficulty, strain, encumbrance. 3 *the burden of his message:* **gist**, substance, drift, thrust, meaning, significance, essence, import.
• verb 1 *he was burdened with a heavy pack:* **load**, charge, weigh down, encumber, hamper; overload, overburden. 2 *avoid burdening them with guilt:* **oppress**, trouble, worry, harass, upset, distress; haunt, afflict, strain, stress, tax, overwhelm.

burdensome adjective **onerous**, oppressive, troublesome, weighty, worrisome, stressful; vexatious, irksome, trying, difficult; arduous, strenuous, hard, laborious, exhausting, tiring, taxing, demanding, punishing, gruelling.

bureau noun 1 *an oak bureau:* **desk**, writing table, secretaire, escritoire; Brit. davenport. 2 *a marriage bureau:* **agency**, service, office, business, company, firm. 3 *the intelligence bureau:* **department**, division, branch, section.

bureaucracy noun 1 *the ranks of the bureaucracy:* **civil service**, government, administration; establishment, system, powers that be; ministries, authorities. 2 *unnecessary bureaucracy:* **red tape**, rules and regulations, protocol, officialdom, paperwork.

bureaucrat noun **official**, administrator, civil servant, minister, functionary, mandarin; Brit. jack-in-office; derogatory apparatchik.

bureaucratic adjective 1 *bureaucratic structure:* **administrative**, official, governmental, ministerial, state, civic. 2 *current practice is far too bureaucratic:* **rule-bound**, rigid, inflexible, complicated.

burgeon verb **flourish**, thrive, prosper, improve; expand, escalate, swell, grow, boom, mushroom, snowball, rocket.

burglar noun **housebreaker**, robber, thief, raider, looter, safe-breaker/cracker; intruder.

burglary noun 1 *a sentence for burglary:* **housebreaking**, breaking and entering, theft, stealing, robbery, larceny, thievery, looting. 2 *a series of burglaries:* **break-in**, theft, robbery, raid; informal smash and grab; N. Amer. informal heist.

burgle verb **rob**, loot, steal from, plunder, rifle, pillage; break into; informal do.

burial noun **burying**, interment, committal, inhumation, entombment.
– OPPOSITES exhumation.

burial ground noun **cemetery**, graveyard, churchyard, necropolis; Scottish kirkyard; N. Amer. memorial park; informal boneyard.

burlesque noun **parody**, caricature, satire, lampoon, skit; informal send-up, take-off, spoof.

burly adjective **strapping**, well built, sturdy, brawny, strong, muscly, thickset, big, hefty, bulky, stocky, Herculean; informal hunky, beefy.
– OPPOSITES puny.

burn verb 1 *the whole city was burning:* **be on fire**, be alight, blaze, be in flames, be aflame; smoulder, glow. 2 *he burned the letters:* **set fire to**, set alight, set light to, ignite, touch off; incinerate, cremate; informal torch. 3 *I burned my dress with the iron:* **scorch**, singe, sear, char, blacken, brand; scald. 4 *her face burned:* **blush**, redden, flush, colour; be hot, be feverish, be on fire. 5 *Meredith burned to know the secret:* **yearn**, long, ache, desire, want, wish, hanker, crave, hunger, thirst; informal itch, be dying. 6 *the energy they burn up:* **consume**, use up, expend, get through, eat up; dissipate.

burning adjective 1 *burning coals:* **blazing**, flaming, fiery, ignited, glowing, red-hot, smouldering; raging, roaring. 2 *burning desert sands:* **extremely hot**, fiery, blistering, scorching, searing, sweltering, torrid; informal baking, boiling, roasting, sizzling. 3 *a burning desire:* **intense**, passionate, deep-seated, profound, wholehearted, strong, ardent, fervent, urgent, fierce, eager, frantic, consuming, uncontrollable. **4** *burning issues:* **important**, crucial, significant, vital, essential, pivotal; urgent, pressing, compelling, critical.

burnish verb **polish**, shine, buff up, rub.

burrow noun *a rabbit's burrow:* **warren**, tunnel, hole, dugout; lair, set, den, earth.
•verb *the mouse burrows a hole:* **tunnel**, dig, excavate, grub, mine, bore, channel; hollow out, gouge out.

burst verb **1** *one balloon burst:* **split**, rupture, break, tear. **2** *a shell burst:* **explode**, blow up, detonate, go off. **3** *smoke burst through the hole:* **break**, erupt, surge, gush, rush, stream, flow, pour, spill; spout, spurt, jet, spew. **4** *he burst into the room:* **charge**, barge, plough, hurtle, plunge, career, rush, dash, tear.
•noun **1** *mortar bursts:* **explosion**, detonation, blast, eruption, bang. **2** *a burst of gunfire:* **volley**, salvo, fusillade, barrage, discharge; hail, rain. **3** *a burst of activity:* **outbreak**, eruption, flare-up, blaze, attack, fit, rush, gale, storm, surge, upsurge, spurt.
■ **burst out** *'I don't care!' she burst out:* exclaim, blurt out, cry, shout, yell; dated ejaculate.

bury verb **1** *he was buried in the churchyard:* **inter**, lay to rest, entomb. **2** *the countryside was buried under several feet of snow:* **hide**, conceal, cover, blanket, engulf. **3** *he buried himself in his work:* **absorb**, engross, immerse, occupy, engage, busy, involve. **4** *the bullet buried itself in the wood:* **embed**, sink, implant, submerge; drive into; lodge.
–OPPOSITES exhume, disinter.

bush noun **1** *a rose bush:* **shrub**; (**bushes**) undergrowth, shrubbery. **2** *they were lost in the bush:* **wilds**, wilderness; backwoods, hinterlands; N. Amer. backcountry; Austral./NZ outback, backblocks; N. Amer. informal boondocks.

bushy adjective **thick**, shaggy, fuzzy, bristly, fluffy, woolly; informal jungly.
–OPPOSITES sleek, wispy.

busily adverb **actively**, energetically, vigorously, enthusiastically; industriously, purposefully, diligently.

business noun **1** *she has to smile in her business:* **work**, occupation, profession, career, employment, job, position; field, sphere, trade, craft; informal racket, game. **2** *who do you do business with?* **trade**, commerce, dealing, traffic, merchandising; dealings, transactions, negotiations. **3** *she started her own business:* **firm**, company, concern, enterprise, venture, organization, operation, undertaking; office, agency, franchise, practice; informal outfit, set-up. **4** *it's none of your business:* **concern**, affair, responsibility, duty, function, obligation; problem, worry; informal pigeon, bailiwick; Brit. informal lookout. **5** *an odd business:* **affair**, matter, thing, case, circumstance, situation, event, incident, happening, occurrence; episode.

businesslike adjective **professional**, efficient, slick, competent, methodical, disciplined, systematic, orderly, organized, structured, practical, pragmatic.

businessman, **businesswoman** noun **entrepreneur**, industrialist, manufacturer, tycoon, magnate, employer; dealer, trader, broker, merchant, buyer, seller, marketeer, merchandiser, vendor, tradesman, retailer, supplier.

bust noun **1** **chest**, bosom, breasts. **2** *a bust of Caesar:* **sculpture**, carving, effigy, statue; head and shoulders.

bustle verb **1** *people bustled about:* **rush**, dash, hurry, scurry, scuttle, scamper, scramble; run, tear, charge; informal scoot, beetle, buzz, zoom. **2** *she bustled us into the kitchen:* **hustle**, sweep, push, whisk; informal bundle.
•noun *the bustle of the market:* **activity**, action, liveliness, excitement; tumult, hubbub, whirl; informal toing and froing, comings and goings.

bustling adjective **busy**, crowded, swarming, teeming, thronged; buzzing, hectic, lively.
–OPPOSITES deserted.

busy adjective **1** *they are busy raising money:* **occupied with**, engaged in, involved in, employed in, working at, hard at work; rushed off your feet, hard-pressed; on the job, absorbed, engrossed, immersed, preoccupied; informal on the go, hard at it. **2** *she is busy at the moment:* **unavailable**, engaged, occupied; working; informal tied up. **3** *a busy day:* **hectic**, active, lively, full, eventful; energetic, tiring. **4** *the town was busy:* **crowded**, bustling, hectic, swarming, teeming, full, thronged. **5** *a busy design:* **ornate**, over-elaborate, overblown, overwrought, overdone, fussy, cluttered, overworked.

– OPPOSITES idle, free, quiet.

• **verb** *he busied himself with paperwork:* **occupy**, involve, engage, concern, absorb, engross, immerse, preoccupy; distract, divert.

busybody noun **meddler**, interferer, troublemaker; gossip, scandalmonger; eavesdropper, gawker; informal nosy parker, snoop, rubberneck; Brit. informal gawper.

but conjunction **1** *he stumbled but didn't fall:* **yet**, nevertheless, nonetheless, even so, however, still, notwithstanding, despite that, in spite of that, for all that, all the same; though, although. **2** *I am innocent but you aren't:* **whereas**, conversely, but then, then again, on the other hand, by/in contrast, on the contrary.

• **preposition** *everyone but him agreed:* **except**, apart from, other than, besides, aside from, with the exception of, bar, excluding, leaving out, save, saving.

• **adverb** *he is but a shadow of his former self:* **only**, just, simply, merely, no more than, nothing but; a mere.

■ **but for** except for, barring, notwithstanding.

butcher verb **1** *the goat was butchered:* **slaughter**, cut up, carve up, joint. **2** *they butchered 150 people:* **massacre**, murder, slaughter, kill, destroy, exterminate, assassinate; N. Amer. terminate; informal dispose of; literary slay. **3** *the studio butchered the film:* **spoil**, ruin, mutilate, mangle, mess up, wreck; informal make a hash of, screw up.

butchery noun *the rebellion ended in butchery and defeat:* **slaughter**, massacre, mass murder, carnage, a bloodbath; literary slaying.

butt[1] verb *she butted him in the stomach:* **ram**, headbutt, bunt; bump, buffet, push, shove; N. English tup.

butt[2] noun *the butt of a joke:* **target**, victim, object, subject; laughing stock.

butt[3] noun **1** *the butt of a gun:* **stock**, end, handle, hilt, haft, helve. **2** *a cigarette butt:* **stub**, end, stump, remnant; informal dog end.

buttocks plural noun **rear**, rump, seat; Brit. bottom; informal behind, backside, derrière; Brit. informal bum, jacksie; N. Amer. informal butt, fanny, tush, tail, buns, booty, heinie; humorous fundament, posterior.

button noun **1** *shirt buttons:* **fastener**, stud, toggle; hook, catch, clasp. **2** *press the button:* **switch**, knob, control; lever, handle.

buttress noun **1** *stone buttresses:* **prop**, support, abutment, shore, pier, reinforcement, stanchion. **2** *a buttress against social collapse:* **safeguard**, defence, protection, guard; support, prop; bulwark.

• **verb** **strengthen**, reinforce, fortify, support, bolster, shore up, underpin, cement, uphold, defend, back up.

buxom adjective **shapely**, ample, plump, rounded, full-figured, voluptuous, curvaceous, Rubenesque; informal busty, chesty, well endowed, curvy.

buy verb **1** **purchase**, acquire, obtain, get, pick up, snap up; take, procure, pay for; invest in; informal get hold of, score. **2** *he could not be bought:* **bribe**, buy off, suborn, corrupt; informal grease someone's palm, get at, fix, square; Brit. informal nobble.

– OPPOSITES sell.

buyer noun **purchaser**, customer, consumer, shopper, investor; (**buyers**) clientele, patronage, market; Law vendee.

buzz noun **1** *the buzz of the bees:* **hum**, murmur, drone. **2** *an insistent buzz from her control panel:* **warning sound**, purr, ring, note, tone, beep, alarm. **3** (informal) *I got such a buzz out of this competition:* **thrill**, feeling of excitement, feeling of euphoria; informal kick, lift, high; N. Amer. informal charge.

• **verb** **1** *above her head bees were buzzing:* **hum**, drone, bumble, murmur. **2** *the intercom soon*

b

buzzed: **purr**, warble, sound, ring, beep. **3** *the club is buzzing with excitement:* **hum**, throb, vibrate, pulse, bustle.

by preposition **1** *I broke it by forcing the lid:* **through**, as a result of, by dint of, by way of, via, by means of; with the help of, with the aid of, by virtue of. **2** *be there by midday:* **no later than**, at, before. **3** *a house by the lake:* **next to**, beside, alongside, by/at the side of, adjacent to; near, close to, neighbouring, adjoining, bordering, overlooking; connected to, contiguous with, attached to. **4** *go by the building:* **past**, in front of, beyond.
• adverb *people hurried by:* **past**, on, along.
■ **by and by** eventually, ultimately, finally, in the end, one day, sooner or later, in time, in a while, in the long run, in the future, in due course. **by yourself** alone, on your own, singly, separately, unaccompanied, unattended, unescorted, unchaperoned, solo; unaided, unassisted, without help, by your own efforts, under your own steam, independently, single-handed, off your own bat, on your own initiative; informal by your lonesome; Brit. informal on your tod, on your Jack Jones.

bygone adjective **past**, former, olden, earlier, previous, one-time, long-ago, of old, ancient, antiquated; departed, dead, extinct, defunct, out of date, outmoded; literary of yore.
– OPPOSITES present, recent.

by-law noun (Brit.) **local law**, regulation, rule.

bypass noun **ring road**, detour, diversion, alternative route; Brit. relief road.
• verb **1** *bypass the farm and continue to the main road:* **go round**, go past, make a detour round; avoid. **2** *an attempt to bypass the problem:* **avoid**, evade, dodge, escape, elude, circumvent, get round, skirt, sidestep, steer clear of; informal duck. **3** *they bypassed the regulations:* **ignore**, pass over, omit, neglect, go over the head of; informal short-circuit.

by-product noun **side effect**, consequence, corollary; ramification, repercussion, spin-off, fallout; fruits; Brit. knock-on effect.

bystander noun **onlooker**, passer-by, non-participant, observer, spectator, eyewitness; informal gawper, rubberneck.

byword noun **1** *the office was a byword for delay:* **perfect example**, classic case, model, exemplar, embodiment, incarnation, personification, epitome, typification. **2** *reality was his byword:* **slogan**, motto, maxim, mantra, catchword, watchword, formula; middle name.

Cc

cab noun **1** *she hailed a cab:* **taxi**, taxi cab; Brit. minicab, hackney carriage; N. Amer. hack. **2** *a truck driver's cab:* **compartment**, cabin.

cabal noun **clique**, faction, coterie, cell, sect; caucus, lobby, pressure group; Brit. ginger group.

cabaret noun **1** *the evening's cabaret:* **entertainment**, floor show, performance; revue. **2** *the cabarets of Montreal:* **nightclub**, club; informal nightspot, niterie.

cabin noun **1** *a first-class cabin:* **berth**, stateroom, deckhouse. **2** *a cabin by the lake:* **hut**, log cabin, shanty, shack; chalet; Scottish bothy; N. Amer. cabana; Austral. mia-mia. **3** *the driver's cabin:* **cab**, compartment.

cabinet noun *a walnut cabinet:* **cupboard**, bureau, chest of drawers.

cable noun **1** *a thick cable moored the ship:* **rope**, cord, line; Nautical hawser; N. Amer. choker. **2** *electric cables:* **wire**, lead, cord; power line; Brit. flex.

cache noun **hoard**, store, stockpile, stock, supply, reserve; arsenal; informal stash.

cachet noun **prestige**, status, standing, kudos, snob value, stature, pre-eminence, eminence; informal street cred.
– OPPOSITES stigma.

cackle verb **1** *the geese cackled at him:* **squawk**, honk, cluck. **2** *she cackled with glee:* **laugh**, guffaw, crow, chortle, chuckle.

cacophonous adjective **loud**, noisy, ear-splitting, raucous, discordant, unmelodious, tuneless.
– OPPOSITES harmonious.

cacophony noun **din**, racket, noise, discord, dissonance; informal bedlam.

cadaver noun (Medicine) **corpse**, body, remains, carcass; informal stiff.

cadaverous adjective **deathly pale**, pallid, ashen, grey, whey-faced, etiolated, corpse-like; as thin as a rake, bony, skeletal, emaciated, skin and bone, haggard, gaunt, drawn, pinched, hollow-cheeked, hollow-eyed; informal like a bag of bones; old use starveling.
– OPPOSITES plump.

cadence noun **rhythm**, tempo, metre, beat, pulse; intonation, modulation, lilt.

cadge verb (informal) **borrow**; informal scrounge, bum, touch someone for, sponge; N. Amer. informal mooch; Austral./NZ informal bludge.

cadre noun **corps**, body, team, group, unit.

cafe noun **snack bar**, cafeteria; coffee bar/shop, tea room/shop; bistro, brasserie; N. Amer. diner; informal eatery, noshery; Brit. informal caff.

cafeteria noun **restaurant**, canteen, cafe, buffet, refectory, mess hall.

cage noun **enclosure**, pen, pound; coop, hutch; birdcage, aviary.
• verb **confine**, shut in/up, pen, coop up, enclose, lock up.

cagey adjective (informal) **secretive**, guarded, non-committal, tight-lipped, reticent, evasive; informal playing your cards close to your chest.
– OPPOSITES open.

cajole verb **persuade**, wheedle, coax, talk into, prevail on; informal sweet-talk, soft-soap, twist someone's arm.

cake noun **1** *cream cakes:* **bun**, pastry, gateau, slice. **2** *a cake of soap:* **bar**, tablet, block, slab, lump, wedge, piece.
• verb *boots caked with mud:* **coat**, encrust, plaster, cover.

WORD LINKS
patissier a maker or seller of cakes
patisserie a shop selling cakes

C

calamitous adjective **disastrous**, catastrophic, cataclysmic, devastating, dire, tragic.

calamity noun **disaster**, catastrophe, tragedy, cataclysm, adversity, misfortune, misadventure.
–OPPOSITES godsend.

calculate verb **1** *the interest is calculated on a daily basis:* **compute**, work out, reckon, figure; add up/together, count up, tally, total; Brit. tot up. **2** *his words were calculated to wound her:* **intend**, mean, design. **3** *we had calculated on a quiet Sunday:* **expect**, anticipate, reckon, bargain; N. Amer. informal figure on.

calculated adjective **deliberate**, premeditated, planned, preplanned, preconceived, intentional, intended.
–OPPOSITES unintentional.

calculating adjective **cunning**, crafty, wily, shrewd, scheming, devious, designing, Machiavellian, disingenuous, contrived.
–OPPOSITES ingenuous.

calculation noun **1** *the calculation of the overall cost:* **computation**, reckoning, adding up, counting up, working out, figuring; Brit. totting up. **2** *political calculations:* **assessment**, judgement; forecast, projection, prediction.

calendar noun *my social calendar:* **schedule**, programme, diary; timetable, agenda.

calibre noun **1** *a man of his calibre:* **quality**, merit, distinction, stature, excellence, pre-eminence; ability, expertise, talent, capability, capacity, proficiency; standard, level. **2** *the calibre of a gun:* **bore**, diameter, gauge.

call verb **1** *'Wait for me!' she called:* **cry**, shout, yell, bellow, roar, bawl, scream; informal holler. **2** *I'll call you tomorrow:* **phone**, telephone, give someone a call; Brit. ring, give someone a ring; informal give someone a buzz; Brit. informal give someone a bell, get someone on the blower, give someone a tinkle. **3** *he called at Ashgrove Cottage:* **pay a visit to**, visit, pay a call on, drop in on, drop/stop by, pop into. **4** *the prime minister called a meeting:* **convene**, summon, assemble; formal convoke. **5** *they called their daughter Hannah:* **name**, christen, baptize; designate, style, term, dub. **6** *I would call him a friend:* **describe as**, regard as, look on as, think of as, consider to be.
• noun **1** *I heard calls from the auditorium:* **cry**, shout, yell, roar, scream, exclamation; informal holler. **2** *the call of the barn owl:* **cry**, song, sound. **3** *I'll give you a call tomorrow:* Brit. ring; informal **buzz**; Brit. informal bell. **4** *a call for party unity:* **appeal**, request, plea. **5** *there's no call for that kind of language:* **need**, necessity, reason, justification, excuse. **6** *there's no call for expensive wine here:* **demand**, desire, market. **7** *the call of the mountains:* **attraction**, appeal, lure, allure, spell, pull, draw.
▪ **call something off** cancel, abandon, scrap, drop, axe; informal scrub; N. Amer. informal redline. **call on 1** *I might call on her later:* visit, pay a visit to, look/drop in on; N. Amer. visit with; informal look up. **2** *he called on the government to hold a referendum:* appeal to, ask, request, urge. **call someone up 1** *they called up the reservists:* enlist, recruit, conscript; US draft. **2** *he was called up for the England team:* select, pick, choose; Brit. cap.

calling noun **profession**, occupation, vocation, career, work, employment, job, business, trade, craft, line of work.

callous adjective **heartless**, cold, unfeeling, uncaring, cold-hearted, hard, as hard as nails, hard-hearted, stony-hearted, insensitive, hard-bitten, unsympathetic.
–OPPOSITES kind, compassionate.

callow adjective **immature**, inexperienced, naive, green, raw, untried, unworldly, unsophisticated; informal wet behind the ears.
–OPPOSITES mature.

calm adjective **1** *she seemed very calm:* **serene**, tranquil, relaxed, unruffled, unperturbed, unflustered, untroubled; equable, even-tempered; placid, unexcitable, unemotional, phlegmatic; composed, {cool, calm, and collected}, cool-headed,

self-possessed; informal laid-back, unflappable, unfazed, together. **2** *the night was calm:* **windless**, still, quiet. **3** *the calm waters of the lake:* **tranquil**, still, smooth, glassy, like a millpond.
– OPPOSITES excited, nervous, stormy.
• noun **1** *calm prevailed:* **tranquillity**, stillness, calmness, quiet, quietness, peace, peacefulness. **2** *his usual calm deserted him:* **composure**, coolness, calmness, self-possession, sangfroid; serenity, tranquillity, equanimity, placidity; informal cool, unflappability.
▪ **calm down 1** *I tried to calm him down:* soothe, pacify, placate, mollify, appease, conciliate; Brit. quieten. **2** *she forced herself to calm down:* compose yourself, recover/regain your composure, control yourself, pull yourself together, simmer down, cool down/off, take it easy; Brit. quieten down; informal get a grip, keep your shirt on, wind down; N. Amer. informal chill out, hang/stay loose, decompress.

camaraderie noun **friendship**, comradeship, fellowship, companionship; mutual support, team spirit, esprit de corps.

camouflage noun **disguise**, concealment.
• verb **disguise**, hide, conceal, mask, screen, cover up.

camp noun **1** *an army camp:* **bivouac**, encampment; campsite, camping ground. **2** *the liberal and conservative camps:* **faction**, wing, group, lobby, caucus, bloc.
• verb *they camped in a field:* **pitch tents**, set up camp, encamp, bivouac.

campaign noun **1** *Napoleon's Russian campaign:* **operation**, manoeuvres; crusade, war, battle, offensive, attack. **2** *the campaign to reduce vehicle emissions:* **crusade**, drive, push, struggle; operation, strategy, battle plan.
• verb **1** *they are campaigning for political reform:* **crusade**, fight, battle, push, press, strive, struggle, lobby, agitate. **2** *she campaigned as a political outsider:* **run/stand for office**; canvass, electioneer, lobby; N. Amer. stump.

campaigner noun **crusader**, fighter, activist; champion, advocate, promoter.

can noun **tin**, canister.

cancel verb **1** *the match was cancelled:* **call off**, abandon, scrap, drop, axe; informal scrub; N. Amer. informal redline. **2** *his US visa has been cancelled:* **annul**, invalidate, nullify, declare null and void, void; revoke, rescind, retract, withdraw. **3** *rising unemployment cancelled out earlier economic gains:* **neutralize**, counterbalance, counteract, balance out; negate, nullify, wipe out.

cancer noun **1** *most skin cancers are curable:* **malignant growth**, tumour, malignancy; technical carcinoma, sarcoma, melanoma, lymphoma, myeloma. **2** *racism is a cancer:* **evil**, blight, scourge, poison, canker, plague; old use pestilence.

> **WORD LINKS**
> **carcinogen** a substance that can cause cancer
> **oncology** the branch of medicine dealing with cancer

candid adjective **1** *his responses were remarkably candid:* **frank**, forthright, blunt, open, honest, truthful, sincere, direct, plain-spoken, bluff; informal upfront; N. Amer. informal on the up and up. **2** *candid shots:* **unposed**, informal, uncontrived, impromptu, natural.
– OPPOSITES guarded.

candidate noun **1** *candidates should be computer-literate:* **applicant**, interviewee; contender, nominee, possible; Brit. informal runner. **2** *A-level candidates:* **examinee**, entrant; student.

candour noun **frankness**, openness, honesty, candidness, truthfulness, sincerity, forthrightness, directness, plain-spokenness, bluffness, bluntness; informal telling it like it is.

candy noun (N. Amer.) See CONFECTIONERY.

cane noun **1** *a silver-topped cane:* **walking stick**, staff; crook; Austral./NZ waddy. **2** *tie the shoot to a cane:* **stick**, stake, upright, pole.
• verb *he was caned for bullying:* **beat**, flog, thrash, lash, birch; informal give someone a hiding.

canker noun *racism remains a canker.* See CANCER sense 2.

C

cannabis noun **marijuana**, hashish, bhang, hemp, kif, ganja, sinsemilla; informal hash, dope, grass, skunk, pot, blow, draw, weed, reefer; Brit. informal wacky baccy; N. Amer. informal locoweed.

cannon noun **field gun**; mortar, howitzer; machine gun, chain gun.
• verb *the couple behind cannoned into us:* **collide with**, hit, run into, crash/smash/plough into.

canny adjective **shrewd**, astute, smart, sharp, sharp-witted, discerning, penetrating, discriminating, perceptive, perspicacious; cunning, crafty, wily; N. Amer. as sharp as a tack; informal savvy; Brit. informal suss, sussed; N. Amer. informal heads-up.
– OPPOSITES foolish.

canon noun **1** *the canons of fair play and equal opportunity:* **principle**, rule, law, tenet, precept; standard, convention, criterion, measure. **2** *the Shakespeare canon:* **works**, writings, oeuvre, body of work.

canopy noun **awning**, shade.

cant noun **1** *he challenged political and religious cant:* **hypocrisy**, sanctimoniousness, humbug; informal hot air. **2** *thieves' cant:* **slang**, jargon, idiom, argot, patois, speech, terminology, language; informal lingo, -speak, -ese.

cantankerous adjective **bad-tempered**, irascible, irritable, grumpy, grouchy, crotchety, tetchy, testy, crusty, curmudgeonly, ill-tempered, ill-humoured, peevish, fractious, pettish, crabby, prickly, touchy; informal snappy; Brit. informal shirty, narky, ratty; N. Amer. informal cranky, ornery; Austral./NZ informal snaky.
– OPPOSITES affable.

canteen noun **1** *the staff canteen:* **restaurant**, cafeteria, refectory, mess hall; N. Amer. lunchroom. **2** *a canteen of water:* **container**, flask, bottle.

canvass verb **1** *he's canvassing for the Conservative Party:* **campaign**, electioneer; N. Amer. stump; Brit. informal doorstep. **2** *they promised to canvass all members:* **poll**, question, ask, survey, interview, consult.

canyon noun **ravine**, gorge, gully, defile; chasm, abyss, gulf; N. Amer. gulch, coulee.

cap noun **1** *a white plastic cap:* **lid**, top, stopper, cork, bung; N. Amer. stopple. **2** *a cap on spending:* **limit**, ceiling; curb, check.
• verb **1** *mountains capped with snow:* **top**, crown, cover, coat, tip; sprinkle, dust, dot, pepper, wreath, ring, shroud. **2** *his innings capped a great day:* **round off**, crown, be a fitting climax/end/conclusion to. **3** *they tried to cap each other's stories:* **beat**, better, improve on, surpass, outdo, outshine, top. **4** (Brit.) *he was capped for England:* **choose**, select, pick. **5** *budgets will be capped:* **limit**, restrict; curb, control, peg.

capability noun **ability**, capacity, power, potential; competence, proficiency, accomplishment, adeptness, aptitude, faculty, experience, skill, talent, flair; informal know-how.

capable adjective *a very capable young woman:* **competent**, able, efficient, effective, proficient, accomplished, adept, handy, experienced, skilful, skilled, talented, gifted; informal useful.
– OPPOSITES incompetent.

capacious adjective **roomy**, spacious, ample, big, large, sizeable, generous.
– OPPOSITES cramped, small.

capacity noun **1** *the capacity of the freezer:* **volume**, size, dimensions, measurements, proportions. **2** *his capacity to inspire trust.* See CAPABILITY. **3** *in his capacity as Commander-in-Chief:* **position**, post, job, office; role, function.

cape[1] noun *a woollen cape:* **cloak**, mantle, cope, stole, poncho.

cape[2] noun *the ship rounded the cape:* **headland**, promontory, point, head; horn, mull.

caper verb *children were capering about:* **skip**, dance, romp, frisk, gambol, cavort, prance, frolic, leap, hop, jump.
• noun (informal) *I'm too old for this kind of caper:* **business**, stuff, thing; informal lark, scene.

capital noun **money**, finances, funds, the wherewithal, the means, assets, wealth, resources; informal dough, bread, loot; Brit. informal dosh, brass, lolly, spondulicks; US informal greenbacks; N. Amer. informal bucks.

capitalism noun **private enterprise**, free enterprise, the free market.
–OPPOSITES communism.

capitalize verb
■ **capitalize on** take advantage of, profit from, make the most of, exploit, develop; informal cash in on.

capitulate verb **surrender**, give in, yield, concede defeat, give up, submit; lay down your arms, raise/show the white flag, throw in the towel/sponge.
–OPPOSITES resist, hold out.

caprice noun **1** *his wife's caprices:* **whim**, fancy, fad, quirk, eccentricity, foible. **2** *the staff tired of his caprice:* **fickleness**, volatility, capriciousness, unpredictability.

capricious adjective **fickle**, changeable, variable, mercurial, volatile, unpredictable, temperamental; whimsical, fanciful, flighty, quirky, faddish.
–OPPOSITES consistent.

capsize verb **overturn**, turn over, turn upside down, upend, flip/tip/keel over, turn turtle.
–OPPOSITES right.

capsule noun **1** *he swallowed a capsule:* **pill**, tablet, lozenge, pastille; informal tab. **2** *a space capsule:* **module**, craft, probe.

captain noun **1** *the ship's captain:* **commander**, master; informal skipper. **2** *the team captain:* **leader**, head; informal boss, skipper.
• verb *a vessel captained by John Cabot:* **command**, run, control, manage, govern; informal skipper.

caption noun **title**, heading, wording, legend, rubric, slogan, byline.

captivate verb **enthral**, charm, enchant, bewitch, fascinate, beguile, entrance, enrapture, delight, attract, allure.
–OPPOSITES repel, bore.

captive noun **prisoner**, convict, detainee, inmate; prisoner of war, POW, internee.
• adjective **confined**, caged, incarcerated, locked up; jailed, imprisoned, in prison, interned, detained, in captivity, under lock and key, behind bars.

captivity noun **imprisonment**, confinement, internment, incarceration, detention.
–OPPOSITES freedom.

capture verb **1** *he was captured in Moscow:* **catch**, apprehend, seize, arrest; informal nab, collar, lift, pick up, pull in; Brit. informal nick. **2** *guerrillas have captured several towns:* **occupy**, invade, conquer, seize, take possession/control of. **3** *the music captured the atmosphere of a summer morning:* **express**, reproduce, represent, encapsulate, sum up. **4** *the tales of pirates captured their imagination:* **engage**, attract, catch, seize, hold, grip.
–OPPOSITES free.

car noun **1 vehicle**, automobile; informal wheels, motor; N. Amer. informal auto. **2** *the dining car:* **carriage**, coach; Brit. saloon.

carafe noun **flask**, jug, pitcher, decanter, flagon.

caravan noun **mobile home**; N. Amer. trailer.

carcass noun **corpse**, body, remains; Medicine cadaver; informal stiff.

cardinal adjective **fundamental**, basic, main, chief, primary, prime, principal, paramount, pre-eminent, highest, key, essential.
–OPPOSITES unimportant.

care noun **1** *the care of the child:* **safe keeping**, supervision, custody, charge, protection, control, responsibility; guardianship. **2** *handle with care:* **caution**, circumspection, respect. **3** *she chose her words with care:* **discretion**, sensitivity, thought; diplomacy, tact; accuracy, precision. **4** *the cares of the day:* **worry**, anxiety, trouble, concern, stress, pressure, strain; sorrow, woe, hardship. **5** *his constant care for others:* **concern**, consideration, thought, regard, solicitude.
–OPPOSITES neglect, carelessness.
• verb *the teachers didn't care about our work:* **be concerned**, worry, trouble/concern yourself, bother, mind, be interested; informal give a damn/hoot.
■ **care for 1** *he cares for his children:* love, be fond of, be devoted to, treasure, adore, dote on, think the world of, worship, idolize. **2** *would you care for a cup of coffee?* like, want, desire, fancy, feel like. **3** *the hospice cares for the terminally ill:*

C

look after, take care of, tend, attend to, minister to, nurse.

career noun **1** *a business career:* **profession**, occupation, vocation, calling, employment, line of work, walk of life, métier. **2** *a chequered career:* **history**, life, course, passage, path, existence.
•adjective *a career politician:* **professional**, permanent, full-time.
•verb *they careered down the hill:* **hurtle**, rush, shoot, race, speed, charge, hare, fly, pelt, go like the wind; informal belt, scoot, tear; Brit. informal bucket.

carefree adjective **unworried**, untroubled, blithe, airy, nonchalant, insouciant, happy-go-lucky, free and easy, easy-going, relaxed; informal laid-back.
–OPPOSITES careworn.

careful adjective **1** *be careful when you go up the stairs:* **cautious**, alert, attentive, watchful, vigilant, wary, on guard, circumspect. **2** *Roland was careful of his reputation:* **mindful**, heedful, protective, jealous. **3** *he's very careful with money:* **prudent**, thrifty, economical, sparing, frugal, scrimping, abstemious, mean; informal stingy. **4** *careful consideration of the facts:* **attentive**, conscientious, painstaking, meticulous, diligent, assiduous, scrupulous, methodical.
–OPPOSITES careless, extravagant.

careless adjective **1** *careless motorists:* **inattentive**, negligent, remiss; heedless, irresponsible, impetuous, reckless. **2** *careless work:* **shoddy**, slapdash, slipshod, scrappy, slovenly, sloppy, negligent, lax, slack, disorganized, hasty, hurried; informal slap-happy. **3** *a careless remark:* **thoughtless**, insensitive, indiscreet, unguarded, incautious, inadvertent.
–OPPOSITES careful, meticulous.

caress verb **stroke**, touch, fondle, brush, feel.

caretaker noun **janitor**, attendant, porter, custodian, concierge; N. Amer. superintendent.
•adjective *the caretaker manager:* **temporary**, short-term, provisional, substitute, acting, interim, pro tem, stand-in, fill-in, stopgap; N. Amer. informal pinch-hitting.
–OPPOSITES permanent.

careworn adjective **worried**, anxious, harassed, strained, stressed; drained, drawn, gaunt, haggard; informal hassled.
–OPPOSITES carefree.

cargo noun **freight**, load, haul, consignment, delivery, shipment; goods, merchandise.

caricature noun *a caricature of the Prime Minister:* **cartoon**, parody, satire, lampoon; informal send-up, take-off.
•verb *she has turned to caricaturing her fellow actors:* **parody**, satirize, lampoon, make fun of; informal send up, take off.

caring adjective **kind**, kind-hearted, warm-hearted, tender; concerned, attentive, thoughtful, solicitous, considerate; affectionate, loving, doting, fond; sympathetic, understanding, compassionate, feeling.
–OPPOSITES cruel.

carnage noun **slaughter**, massacre, butchery, bloodbath, bloodletting, mayhem.

carnal adjective **sexual**, sensual, erotic, lustful, lascivious, libidinous, lecherous, licentious; physical, bodily, corporeal, fleshly.
–OPPOSITES spiritual.

carnival noun **1** *the town's annual carnival:* **festival**, fiesta, fete, gala, jamboree, Mardi Gras. **2** (N. Amer.) *he worked at a carnival:* **funfair**, circus, fair, amusement show.

carouse verb **drink**, revel, celebrate, roister; informal paint the town red, party, go on the booze, go on a bender, whoop it up, make whoopee.

carp verb **complain**, grumble, grouse, whine, bleat, nag; informal gripe, grouch, beef, bellyache, moan, bitch, whinge; N. English informal mither; N. Amer. informal kvetch.
–OPPOSITES praise.

carpenter noun **joiner**, cabinet-maker; Brit. informal chippy.

carpet noun **1** *a Turkish carpet:* **rug**, mat. **2** *a carpet of wild flowers:* **covering**, blanket, layer, cover, cloak, mantle.
•verb *the ground was carpeted in moss:* **cover**, coat, overlay, blanket.

carriage noun **1** *a railway carriage:*

coach, car; Brit. saloon. **2** *a horse and carriage:* **wagon**, coach, trap; historical gig, hansom, hackney, landau. **3** *an erect carriage:* **posture**, bearing, stance, gait; attitude, manner, demeanour; Brit. deportment.

carrier noun **bearer**, conveyor, transporter; porter, courier, haulier.

carry verb **1** *she carried the box into the kitchen:* **convey**, bear, take, transfer, transport, move, bring, lug, fetch; informal cart, hump. **2** *satellites carry the signal over the Atlantic:* **transmit**, conduct, relay, communicate, convey, beam, send. **3** *the dinghy can carry two people:* **accommodate**, hold, take; sustain, support, bear. **4** *managers must carry most responsibility:* **undertake**, accept, assume, bear, shoulder, take on. **5** *she carried herself with assurance:* **conduct**, bear, hold; act, behave, acquit; formal comport. **6** *a resolution was carried:* **approve**, accept, endorse, pass, ratify; agree to, assent to, rubber-stamp; informal OK, give the thumbs up to. **7** *we carry a wide range of products:* **sell**, stock, keep in stock, offer, retail, supply.
■ **carry on** *they carried on with their work:* continue, proceed, keep on, go on, press on; persist in, persevere in; informal stick with/at. **carry something out 1** *we carried out a market-research survey:* conduct, perform, implement, execute. **2** *I carried out my promise:* fulfil, carry through, honour, make good; keep, observe, abide by, adhere to, stick to, keep faith with.

cart noun **1** *a horse-drawn cart:* **wagon**, carriage, dray. **2** *a man with a cart took their luggage:* **handcart**, pushcart, trolley, barrow.
• verb (informal) *he had the wreckage carted away:* **transport**, haul, move, shift, take; carry.

carton noun **box**, package, cardboard box, container, pack, packet.

cartoon noun **1** *a cartoon of the Prime Minister:* **caricature**, parody, lampoon, satire; informal take-off, send-up. **2** *he was reading cartoons:* **comic strip**, comic, graphic novel. **3** *detailed cartoons for a full-size portrait:* **sketch**, rough, outline.

cartridge noun **cassette**, magazine, canister, case, container.

carve verb **1** *he carved horn handles:* **sculpt**; cut, hew, whittle; form, shape, fashion. **2** *I carved my initials on the tree:* **engrave**, incise, score, cut. **3** *he carved the roast chicken:* **slice**, cut up, chop.
■ **carve something up** divide, partition, apportion, subdivide, split up, break up; share out, dole out; informal divvy up.

carving noun **sculpture**, model, statue, statuette, figure, figurine.

cascade noun **waterfall**, cataract, falls, rapids, white water; flood, torrent.
• verb *rain cascaded from the roof:* **pour**, gush, surge, spill, stream, flow, issue, spurt, jet.

case[1] noun **1** *a classic case of overreaction:* **instance**, occurrence, manifestation, demonstration; example, illustration, specimen, sample, exemplar. **2** *if that is the case I will have to find somebody else:* **situation**, position, state of affairs, the lie of the land; circumstances, conditions, facts, how things stand; Brit. state of play; informal score. **3** *the officers on the case:* **assignment**, job, project, investigation, exercise, enquiry, campaign, affair, examination. **4** *he lost his case:* **lawsuit**, legal action, suit, trial, legal/judicial proceedings, litigation. **5** *they presented a strong case for new research methods:* **argument**, defence, justification, vindication, exposition, thesis.

case[2] noun **1** *a cigarette case:* **container**, box, canister, holder. **2** *a seed case:* **casing**, cover, sheath, envelope, sleeve, jacket, shell, integument. **3** (Brit.) *she threw some clothes into a case:* **suitcase**, bag, valise, portmanteau; (**cases**) luggage, baggage. **4** *a glass display case:* **cabinet**, cupboard.

cash noun **1** *a wallet stuffed with cash:* **money**, currency, hard cash; banknotes, coins, change; N. Amer. bills; informal dough, bread, loot, moolah; Brit. informal dosh, readies, brass, lolly, spondulicks; US informal greenbacks; N. Amer. informal bucks, dinero. **2** *a lack of cash:* **finances**, money, resources, funds, assets, the means, the wherewithal.

•verb *the bank cashed her cheque:* **exchange**, change; honour, pay, accept; Brit. encash.
■ **cash in on** take advantage of, exploit, milk; make money from, profit from; informal make a killing out of.

cashier noun **clerk**, bank clerk, teller, banker, treasurer, bursar, purser.

casing noun **cover**, covering, case, shell, envelope, sheath, sleeve, jacket, housing, fairing.

cask noun **barrel**, keg, butt, tun, vat, drum, hogshead; historical firkin.

casket noun **1** *a small casket:* **box**, chest, case, container. **2** (N. Amer.) *the casket of a dead soldier.* See COFFIN.

cast verb **1** *he cast the stone into the stream:* **throw**, toss, fling, flick, pitch, hurl, lob; informal chuck, sling, bung. **2** *she cast a fearful glance over her shoulder:* **direct**, shoot, throw, send. **3** *each citizen cast a vote:* **register**, record, enter, file. **4** *the fire cast a soft light:* **emit**, give off, throw, send out, radiate; create, produce; project. **5** *the stags' antlers are cast each year:* **shed**, lose, discard, slough off.
•noun **1** *the cast of 'Hamlet':* **actors**, performers, players; dramatis personae, characters. **2** *a bronze cast of the sculpture:* **mould**, die, matrix, shape, casting, model.
■ **cast something aside** discard, reject, throw away/out, get rid of, dispose of, abandon, dump, jettison; informal ditch. **cast someone away** shipwreck, wreck; strand, maroon.

caste noun **social class**, level, stratum, echelon, status.

castigate verb (formal) **reprimand**, rebuke, admonish, chastise, chide, upbraid, reprove, reproach, scold, berate, take to task, lambaste, haul over the coals, censure; informal tell off, give someone an earful, give someone a roasting, dress down, bawl out, give someone hell, blow up at, pitch into, lay into, blast; Brit. informal carpet, tear someone off a strip, give someone what for, give someone a rocket; N. Amer. informal chew out.
–OPPOSITES praise, commend.

castle noun **fortress**, fort, stronghold, fortification, keep, citadel.

castrate verb **neuter**, geld, cut, desex, sterilize, fix; N. Amer. & Austral. alter; Brit. informal **doctor**; old use emasculate.

casual adjective **1** *a casual attitude to life:* **relaxed**, unconcerned, carefree, easy-going, free and easy, devil-may-care; blasé, nonchalant, insouciant, blithe, offhand, flippant; indifferent, uncaring, lackadaisical; informal laid-back. **2** *a casual remark:* **offhand**, spontaneous, unthinking, unconsidered, impromptu, throw-away, unguarded; informal off-the-cuff. **3** *a casual glance:* **cursory**, perfunctory, superficial, passing, fleeting; hasty, brief, quick. **4** *a casual acquaintance:* **slight**, superficial. **5** *casual work:* **temporary**, part-time, freelance, impermanent, irregular, occasional. **6** *a casual meeting changed his life:* **chance**, accidental, unplanned, unintended, unexpected, unforeseen, unanticipated, fortuitous, serendipitous, adventitious. **7** *a casual shirt:* **informal**, leisure, everyday; informal sporty. **8** *the inn's casual atmosphere:* **relaxed**, friendly, informal, easy-going, free and easy; informal laid-back.
–OPPOSITES careful, considered, formal.

casualty noun **victim**, fatality, loss; walking wounded.

cat noun **feline**, tomcat, tom, kitten; informal pussy cat, puss, kitty; Brit. informal moggie, mog; old use grimalkin.

> **WORD LINKS**
> **feline** relating to cats
> **ailurophobia** fear of cats

cataclysm noun **disaster**, catastrophe, calamity, tragedy, devastation, upheaval, convulsion.

cataclysmic adjective **disastrous**, catastrophic, calamitous, tragic, devastating, ruinous, terrible, violent, awful.

catalogue noun **1** *a library catalogue:* **directory**, register, index, list, listing, record, archive, inventory. **2** *a mail-order catalogue:* **brochure**; N. Amer. informal wish book.
•verb *the whole collection is fully catalogued:* **classify**, categorize, index, list, archive, inventory, record, itemize.

catapult noun **sling**, slingshot; historical ballista, trebuchet.
• verb *the explosion catapulted the car along the road:* **propel**, launch, hurl, fling, send flying; fire, shoot.

catastrophe noun **disaster**, calamity, cataclysm, ruin, tragedy.

catastrophic adjective **disastrous**, calamitous, cataclysmic, ruinous, tragic, fatal, dire, awful, terrible, dreadful.

catcall noun **whistle**, boo, hiss, jeer, raspberry, hoot, taunt; (**catcalls**) scoffing, abuse, taunting, derision; slow handclap.

catch verb **1** *he caught the ball:* **seize**, grab, snatch, grasp, grip, clutch, clench; receive, get, intercept. **2** *we've caught the thief:* **capture**, seize; apprehend, arrest, take prisoner/captive, take into custody; trap, snare, ensnare; net, hook, land; informal nab, collar, run in, bust; Brit. informal nick. **3** *her heel caught in a hole:* **become trapped**, become entangled, snag, jam, wedge, lodge, get stuck. **4** *she caught the 7.45 bus:* **be in time for**, make, get; board, get on, leave on. **5** *they were caught siphoning petrol:* **discover**, find, come upon/across, stumble on, chance on; surprise, catch red-handed. **6** *the scheme caught his imagination:* **engage**, capture, attract, draw, grab, grip, seize; hold, absorb, engross. **7** *she caught a whiff of aftershave:* **perceive**, get, pick up, notice, observe, discern, detect, note, make out, glimpse; Brit. informal clock. **8** *I couldn't catch what she was saying:* **hear**, perceive, discern, make out; understand, comprehend, grasp, apprehend; informal get, get the drift of, figure out; Brit. informal suss out. **9** *the film caught the flavour of the sixties:* **evoke**, conjure up, call to mind, recall, encapsulate, capture. **10** *the blow caught her on the side of her face:* **hit**, strike, slap, smack, bang. **11** *he caught malaria:* **contract**, get, be taken ill with, develop, come down with, be struck down with; Brit. go down with.
– OPPOSITES drop, release, miss.
• noun **1** *a fisherman's catch:* **haul**, net, bag, yield. **2** *I closed the door and slipped the catch:* **latch**, lock, fastener, clasp, hasp. **3** *he is always looking for the catch:* **snag**, disadvantage, drawback, stumbling block, hitch, fly in the ointment, pitfall, complication, problem, hiccup, difficulty; trap, trick, snare; informal con.
■ **catch on 1** *radio soon caught on:* become popular, take off, boom, flourish, thrive. **2** *I caught on fast:* understand, comprehend, learn, see the light; informal cotton on, latch on, get the picture/message, get wise, wise up.

catching adjective **infectious**, contagious, communicable; dated infective.

catchphrase noun **saying**, jingle, quotation, quote, slogan, catchword; N. Amer. informal tag line.

catchword noun **motto**, watchword, slogan, byword, catchphrase; informal buzzword.

catchy adjective **memorable**, unforgettable; appealing, popular.

categorical adjective **unqualified**, unconditional, unequivocal, absolute, explicit, unambiguous, definite, direct, downright, outright, emphatic, positive, point-blank, conclusive, out-and-out.
– OPPOSITES qualified, equivocal.

categorize verb **classify**, class, group, grade, rate, designate; order, arrange, sort, rank; file, catalogue, list, index.

category noun **class**, classification, group, grouping, bracket, heading, set; type, sort, kind, variety, species, breed, brand, make, model; grade, order, rank.

cater verb
■ **cater for 1** *a resort catering for older holidaymakers:* serve, provide for, meet the needs/wants of, accommodate. **2** *he seemed to cater for all tastes:* take into account/consideration, allow for, consider, bear in mind, make provision for.
cater to satisfy, indulge, pander to, gratify, accommodate, minister to, give in to.

catholic adjective **diverse**, wide, broad, broad-based, eclectic, liberal; comprehensive, all-encompassing, all-embracing, all-inclusive.
– OPPOSITES narrow.

cattle plural noun **cows**, oxen; livestock, stock.

WORD LINKS
bovine relating to cattle

catty adjective (informal) *a catty remark.* See SPITEFUL.

C

caucus noun **1** (in North America & NZ) *caucuses will be held in eleven states:* **meeting**, assembly, gathering, congress, conference, convention, rally, convocation. **2** (in the UK) *the right-wing caucus:* **faction**, camp, bloc, group, set, band, lobby, coterie, pressure group; Brit. ginger group.

cause noun **1** *the cause of the fire:* **source**, root, origin, beginnings, starting point; basis, foundation; originator, author, creator, agent. **2** *there is no cause for alarm:* **reason**, grounds, justification, call, need, necessity, occasion, excuse. **3** *the cause of human rights | a good cause:* **principle**, ideal, belief, conviction; object, end, aim, objective, purpose; charity.
– OPPOSITES effect, result.
• verb *this disease can cause blindness:* **bring about**, give rise to, lead to, result in, create, produce, generate, engender, spawn, bring on, precipitate, prompt, provoke, trigger, make happen, induce, inspire, promote, foster; literary beget.

caustic adjective **1** *a caustic cleaner:* **corrosive**. **2** *a caustic comment:* **sarcastic**, cutting, biting, mordant, sharp, scathing, derisive, sardonic, ironic, scornful, trenchant, acerbic, vitriolic; Brit. informal sarky.

caution noun **1** *proceed with caution:* **care**, attention, attentiveness, alertness, watchfulness, vigilance, circumspection, discretion, prudence. **2** *a first offender may receive a caution:* **warning**, admonishment, injunction; reprimand, rebuke, reproof; informal telling-off, dressing-down, talking-to; Brit. informal ticking-off.
• verb **1** *advisers cautioned against tax increases:* **advise**, warn, counsel, urge. **2** *he was cautioned by the police:* **warn**, admonish; reprimand; informal tell off, give someone a talking-to; Brit. informal give someone a ticking-off.

cautious adjective **careful**, attentive, circumspect, prudent, alert, watchful, vigilant.
– OPPOSITES reckless.

cavalcade noun **procession**, parade, motorcade, cortège; Brit. march past.

cavalier adjective *a cavalier disregard for danger:* **offhand**, indifferent, casual, dismissive, insouciant, unconcerned.

cave noun **cavern**, grotto, pothole, chamber.
■ **cave in 1** *the roof caved in:* collapse, fall in/down, give way, crumble, subside. **2** *the manager caved in to their demands:* yield, surrender, capitulate, give in, back down, make concessions, throw in the towel/sponge.

WORD LINKS
speleology (Brit. **potholing**; N. Amer. **spelunking**) the study or exploration of caves

cavern noun **cave**, grotto, chamber, gallery.

cavernous adjective **vast**, huge, immense, spacious, roomy, capacious, voluminous, extensive, deep; hollow, gaping, yawning.
– OPPOSITES small.

cavity noun **space**, chamber, hollow, hole, pocket; orifice, aperture; socket, gap, crater, pit, crack.

cavort verb **skip**, dance, romp, jig, caper, frisk, gambol, prance, frolic, lark; bounce, trip, leap, jump, bound, spring, hop.

cease verb **1** *hostilities had ceased:* **come to an end**, come to a halt, end, halt, stop, conclude, terminate, finish, draw to a close, be over. **2** *they ceased all military activity:* **bring to an end**, bring to a halt, end, halt, stop, conclude, terminate, finish, wind up, discontinue, suspend, break off.
– OPPOSITES start, continue.

ceaseless adjective **continual**, constant, continuous; incessant, unceasing, unending, endless, never-ending, interminable, non-stop, uninterrupted, unremitting, relentless, unrelenting, unrelieved, sustained, persistent, eternal, perpetual.
– OPPOSITES intermittent.

cede verb **surrender**, concede, relinquish, yield, part with, give up; hand over, deliver up, give over, make over, transfer; abandon, forgo, sacrifice.

ceiling noun *they imposed a wage ceiling of 3 per cent:* **upper limit**, maximum.

celebrate verb **1** *they were celebrating their wedding anniversary:* **commemorate**, observe, mark, keep, honour, remember. **2** *let's all celebrate!* **enjoy yourself**, make merry, have fun, have a good time, revel, carouse, roister; N. Amer. step out; informal party, whoop it up, make whoopee, live it up, have a ball. **3** *the priest celebrated mass:* **perform**, observe, officiate at.

celebrated adjective **acclaimed**, admired, highly rated, revered, honoured, esteemed, exalted, vaunted, well thought of; eminent, great, distinguished, prestigious, illustrious, pre-eminent, notable, of note, of repute.
– OPPOSITES unsung.

celebration noun **1** *the celebration of his 50th birthday:* **commemoration**, observance, marking, keeping. **2** *a cause for celebration:* **jollification**, merrymaking, enjoying yourself, revelry, revels, festivities; informal partying. **3** *a birthday celebration:* **party**, function, gathering, festivities, festival, fete, carnival, jamboree; informal do, bash, rave; Brit. informal rave-up, knees-up, beanfeast, bunfight, beano. **4** *the celebration of the Eucharist:* **observance**, performance, officiation, solemnization.

celebrity noun **1** *his celebrity grew:* **fame**, prominence, renown, eminence, pre-eminence, stardom, popularity, distinction, note, notability, prestige, stature, repute, reputation. **2** *a sporting celebrity:* **star**, superstar, household name, big name, VIP, personality; informal celeb, somebody, megastar.
– OPPOSITES obscurity.

celestial adjective **1** *a celestial body:* **extraterrestrial**, stellar, planetary. **2** *celestial beings:* **heavenly**, holy, saintly, divine, godly, godlike, ethereal; angelic.
– OPPOSITES earthly.

celibate adjective **unmarried**, single; chaste, virginal.

cell noun **1** *a prison cell:* **room**, cubicle, chamber; dungeon, lock-up. **2** *each cell of the honeycomb:* **compartment**, cavity, hole, hollow, section, unit. **3** *terrorist cells:* **unit**, squad, detachment, group.

cellar noun **basement**, vault; crypt; Scottish dunny.
– OPPOSITES attic.

cemetery noun **graveyard**, churchyard, burial ground, necropolis, garden of remembrance; mass grave; informal boneyard; Scottish kirkyard; N. Amer. memorial park; old use God's acre.

censor verb *letters home were censored:* **cut**; edit, expurgate, sanitize, bowdlerize; informal clean up.

censorious adjective **hypercritical**, overcritical, disapproving, condemnatory, denunciatory, deprecatory, disparaging, reproachful, reproving.
– OPPOSITES complimentary.

censure verb *he was censured for his conduct:* **reprimand**, rebuke, admonish, chastise, upbraid, berate, haul over the coals, criticize, condemn, attack; formal castigate.
• noun *a note of censure:* **condemnation**, criticism, attack; reprimand, rebuke, admonishment, reproof, upbraiding, disapproval, reproach, obloquy; formal excoriation, castigation.
– OPPOSITES approval.

central adjective **1** *a central position:* **middle**, centre, halfway, midway, mid. **2** *central London:* **inner**, innermost, middle, mid. **3** *their central campaign issue:* **main**, chief, principal, primary, leading, foremost, first, most important, predominant, key, crucial, vital, essential, basic, fundamental, core, prime, premier, paramount, major, overriding; informal number-one.
– OPPOSITES side, outer, subordinate.

centralize verb **concentrate**, consolidate, amalgamate, condense, unify, focus.
– OPPOSITES devolve.

centre noun *the centre of the town:* **middle**, nucleus, heart, core, hub.
– OPPOSITES edge.
• verb *the story centres on a doctor:* **focus**, concentrate, pivot, revolve, be based.

centrepiece noun **highlight**, main feature, high point/spot, climax;

focus of attention, focal point, centre of attention.

ceremonial adjective **formal**, official, state, public; ritualistic, ritual, stately, solemn.
–OPPOSITES informal.

ceremonious adjective **dignified**, majestic, imposing, impressive, solemn, stately, formal, courtly; regal, imperial, grand, glorious, splendid, magnificent.

ceremony noun **1** *a wedding ceremony:* **rite**, ritual, observance; service, sacrament, liturgy, celebration. **2** *the new Queen was proclaimed with due ceremony:* **pomp**, protocol, formalities, niceties, decorum, etiquette.

certain adjective **1** *I'm certain he's guilty:* **sure**, confident, positive, convinced, in no doubt, satisfied, assured, persuaded. **2** *it is certain that more changes are in the offing:* **unquestionable**, sure, definite, beyond question, not in doubt, indubitable, undeniable, indisputable; obvious, evident, undisputed. **3** *they are certain to win:* **sure**, bound, destined. **4** *certain defeat:* **inevitable**, assured; unavoidable, inescapable, inexorable. **5** *there is no certain cure for this:* **reliable**, dependable, foolproof, guaranteed, sure, infallible; informal sure-fire.
–OPPOSITES doubtful, possible, uncertain.

certainly adverb *this is certainly a late work:* **unquestionably**, surely, assuredly, definitely, beyond/without question, without doubt, undoubtedly, indubitably, undeniably, irrefutably, indisputably; unmistakably.
–OPPOSITES possibly.

certainty noun **1** *she knew with certainty that he was telling the truth:* **confidence**, sureness, conviction, certitude, assurance. **2** *he accepted defeat as a certainty:* **inevitability**, foregone conclusion; informal sure thing; Brit. informal dead cert.
–OPPOSITES doubt, possibility.

certificate noun **guarantee**, certification, document, authorization, authentication, accreditation, licence, diploma.

certify verb **1** *the aircraft was certified as airworthy:* **verify**, guarantee, attest, validate, confirm, substantiate, endorse, vouch for, testify to. **2** *a certified hospital:* **accredit**, recognize, license, authorize, approve.

cessation noun **end**, ending, termination, stopping, halting, ceasing, finish, stoppage, conclusion, winding up, discontinuation, abandonment, suspension, breaking off, cutting short.
–OPPOSITES start, resumption.

chafe verb **1** *the collar chafed his neck:* **rub**, graze, scrape, scratch; make sore. **2** *I chafed her feet:* **rub**, warm up.

chaff verb *rival supporters chaffed each other:* **tease**, make fun of, poke fun at, rag; informal take the mickey out of, rib, josh, kid, have on, pull someone's leg; Brit. informal wind up; N. Amer. informal goof on, rag on, razz; old use make sport of.
• noun *there was a fair amount of good-natured chaff:* **banter**, repartee, teasing, joking, jesting, raillery, badinage, wisecracks, witticisms; formal persiflage.

chagrin noun **annoyance**, irritation, vexation, exasperation, displeasure, dissatisfaction, discontent; anger, rage, fury, wrath, indignation, resentment; embarrassment, mortification, humiliation, shame.
–OPPOSITES delight.

chain noun **1** *he was held in chains:* **fetters**, shackles, irons, leg irons, manacles, handcuffs; informal cuffs, bracelets. **2** *a chain of events:* **series**, succession, string, sequence, train, course.
• verb *she chained her bicycle to the railings:* **secure**, fasten, tie, tether, hitch; restrain, shackle, fetter, manacle, handcuff.

chair verb *she chairs the economic committee:* **preside over**; lead, direct, run, manage, control, be in charge of, head.

chairman, **chairwoman** noun **chair**, chairperson, president, leader, convener; spokesperson, spokesman, spokeswoman.

chalk verb
■ **chalk something up** achieve, attain, accomplish, gain, earn, win, make, get, obtain, notch up, rack up.

WORD LINKS
calcareous containing chalk

chalky adjective *chalky skin:* **pale**, bloodless, pallid, colourless, wan, ashen, white, pasty.

challenge noun **1** *he accepted the challenge:* **dare**; summons, offer. **2** *a challenge to his leadership:* **test**, dispute, stand, opposition, confrontation. **3** *the journey was proving quite a challenge:* **problem**, difficult task, test, trial.
• verb **1** *we challenged their statistics:* **question**, disagree with, dispute, take issue with, protest against, call into question, object to. **2** *changes that would challenge them:* **test**, tax, strain, make demands on; stretch, stimulate, inspire, excite.

challenging adjective **demanding**, testing, taxing, exacting; difficult, tough, hard, formidable, onerous, arduous, strenuous, gruelling.
– OPPOSITES easy, uninspiring.

chamber noun **1** *a debating chamber:* **room**, hall, assembly room, auditorium. **2** (old use) *he entered her chamber and kissed her:* **bedroom**, boudoir; literary bower; old use bedchamber. **3** *the left chamber of the heart:* **compartment**, cavity; Anatomy auricle, ventricle.

champagne noun **sparkling wine**; mousseux, spumante, cava; informal champers, bubbly, fizz.

champion noun **1** *the 2007 world champion:* **winner**, title-holder, defending champion, gold medallist; prizewinner, victor; informal champ, number one. **2** *a champion of change:* **advocate**, proponent, promoter, supporter, defender, upholder, backer, exponent; campaigner, lobbyist, crusader; N. Amer. booster.
• verb *they championed the rights of tribal peoples:* **advocate**, promote, defend, uphold, support, back, stand up for; campaign for, lobby for, fight for, crusade for, stick up for.
– OPPOSITES oppose.

chance noun **1** *there was a chance he might be released:* **possibility**, prospect, probability, likelihood; risk, threat, danger. **2** *I gave her a chance to answer:* **opportunity**, opening, occasion, turn, time; N. Amer. & Austral./NZ show; informal shot, look-in. **3** *he took an awful chance:* **risk**, gamble, long shot, leap in the dark. **4** *we met by pure chance:* **accident**, coincidence, serendipity, fate, destiny, fortuity, providence, happenstance; good fortune, luck, fluke.
• adjective *it was a chance discovery:* **accidental**, fortuitous, fluky, coincidental, serendipitous; unintentional, unintended, inadvertent, unplanned.
– OPPOSITES intentional.
■ **by chance** fortuitously, by accident, accidentally, coincidentally, serendipitously; unintentionally, inadvertently. **chance on** come across, run across/into, happen on, light on, stumble on, find by chance; informal bump into.

change verb **1** *the customer may want to change the design:* **alter**, adjust, adapt, amend, modify, revise, refine; reshape, refashion, redesign, restyle, revamp, rework, remodel, reorganize, reorder; vary, transform, transfigure, transmute, metamorphose; informal tweak. **2** *he's changed his car:* **exchange**, substitute, swap, switch, replace, alternate.
– OPPOSITES preserve, keep.
• noun **1** *a change of plan:* **alteration**, modification, variation, revision, amendment, adjustment, adaptation; remodelling, reshaping, rearrangement, reordering, restyling, reworking; metamorphosis, transformation, evolution, mutation; humorous transmogrification. **2** *a change of government:* **replacement**, exchange, substitution, swap, switch. **3** *I haven't got any change:* **coins**, cash, silver, coppers.

changeable adjective **variable**, inconstant, varying, changing, fluctuating, irregular; erratic, inconsistent, unstable, unsettled, turbulent, changeful; fickle, capricious, temperamental, volatile, mercurial, unpredictable, blowing hot and cold; informal up and down.
– OPPOSITES constant.

changeless adjective **unchanging**, unvarying, timeless, static, fixed, permanent, constant, unchanged,

consistent, uniform, undeviating; stable, steady, unchangeable, unalterable, invariable, immutable.
– OPPOSITES variable.

channel noun **1** *the English Channel:* **straits**, sound, narrows, passage. **2** *the water ran down a channel:* **duct**, gutter, conduit, trough, culvert, sluice, race, drain. **3** *a channel for their extraordinary energy:* **use**, medium, vehicle; release, safety valve, vent. **4** *a channel of communication:* **means**, medium, instrument, mechanism, agency, vehicle, route, avenue.
• verb *many countries channel their aid through charities:* **convey**, transmit, conduct, direct, relay, pass on, transfer.

chant noun **shout**, cry, call, slogan; chorus, refrain.
• verb **shout**, chorus, repeat, call.

chaos noun **disorder**, disarray, disorganization, confusion, mayhem, bedlam, pandemonium, havoc, turmoil, tumult, commotion, disruption, upheaval, uproar; a muddle, a mess, a shambles; anarchy, lawlessness; informal hullabaloo, all hell broken loose.
– OPPOSITES order.

chaotic adjective **disorderly**, disordered, in disorder, in chaos, in disarray, disorganized, topsy-turvy, in pandemonium, in turmoil, in uproar; in a muddle, in a mess, messy, in a shambles; anarchic, lawless; Brit. informal shambolic.

chap[1] verb *my skin chapped in the wind:* **become raw**, become sore, become inflamed, chafe, crack.

chap[2] noun (Brit. informal) *he's a nice chap:* **man**, boy, fellow, character; informal guy, geezer; Brit. informal bloke, lad, bod; N. Amer. informal dude, hombre.

chapter noun **1** *the first chapter of the book:* **section**, part, division. **2** *a new chapter in our history:* **period**, phase, page, stage, epoch, era. **3** (N. Amer.) *a local chapter of the American Cancer Society:* **branch**, division, subdivision, section, department, lodge, wing, arm.

char verb **scorch**, burn, singe, sear, blacken; informal toast.

character noun **1** *her forceful character:* **personality**, nature, disposition, temperament, temper, mentality, make-up; features, qualities, properties, traits. **2** *we want to preserve the character of our town:* **distinctiveness**, individuality, identity, essence, spirit, ethos, complexion, tone, feel, feeling. **3** *a woman of character:* **integrity**, honour, moral strength/fibre, rectitude; fortitude, strength, backbone, resolve, grit, will power; informal guts; Brit. informal bottle. **4** *a stain on his character:* **reputation**, name, standing, stature, position, status. **5** (informal) *she's a bit of a character:* **eccentric**, oddity, madcap, crank, individualist, nonconformist; informal oddball. **6** *a boorish character:* **person**, man, woman, soul, creature, individual, customer; informal cookie; Brit. informal guy. **7** *written characters:* **letter**, figure, symbol, sign.

characteristic noun **attribute**, feature, quality, property, trait, aspect, element, facet; mannerism, habit, custom, idiosyncrasy, peculiarity, quirk, oddity, foible.
• adjective *his characteristic eloquence:* **typical**, usual, normal; distinctive, particular, special, especial, peculiar, idiosyncratic, singular, unique.

characterize verb **1** *the period was characterized by scientific advancement:* **distinguish**, mark, typify, set apart. **2** *the women are characterized as prophets of doom:* **portray**, depict, present, represent, describe; categorize, class, style, brand.

charade noun **farce**, pantomime, travesty, mockery, parody, act, masquerade.

charge verb **1** *they will charge an hourly fee:* **ask**, demand; bill, invoice. **2** *two men were charged with murder:* **accuse**, indict, arraign; prosecute, try, put on trial; N. Amer. impeach. **3** *they charged him with reforming the system:* **entrust**, burden, encumber, saddle, tax. **4** *demonstrators charged the barricades:* **attack**, storm, assault, assail, fall on, swoop on, descend on. **5** *we charged into the crowd:* **rush**, storm, stampede, push, plough, launch yourself, go headlong; informal steam; N. Amer. informal barrel. **6** *charge your glasses!* | *the* *guns were charged:* **fill**, top up; load, arm. **7** *his poetry is charged with emotion:* **suffuse**, pervade, permeate, saturate, infuse, imbue, fill.

• **noun 1** *all customers pay a charge:* **fee**, payment, price, tariff, amount, sum, fare, levy. **2** *he pleaded guilty to the charge:* **accusation**, allegation, indictment, arraignment; N. Amer. impeachment. **3** *an infantry charge:* **attack**, assault, offensive, onslaught, drive, push, thrust. **4** *the child was in her charge:* **care**, protection, safe keeping, control; custody, guardianship, wardship; hands.

■ **in charge of** responsible for, in control of, at the helm/wheel of, managing, running, administering, directing, supervising, overseeing, controlling; informal running the show.

charisma noun **charm**, presence, personality, strength of character; magnetism, appeal, allure.

charismatic adjective **charming**, fascinating; magnetic, captivating, beguiling, appealing, alluring.

charitable adjective **1** *charitable activities:* **philanthropic**, humanitarian, altruistic, benevolent, public-spirited; non-profit-making. **2** *charitable people:* **big-hearted**, generous, open-handed, free-handed, munificent, bountiful, beneficent; literary bounteous. **3** *he was charitable in his judgements:* **magnanimous**, generous, liberal, tolerant, sympathetic, lenient, indulgent, forgiving.

charity noun **1** *an Aids charity:* **charitable organization**, charitable institution; fund, trust, foundation. **2** *we don't need charity:* **financial assistance**, aid, welfare, relief; handouts, gifts, presents, largesse; historical alms. **3** *his actions are motivated by charity:* **philanthropy**, humanitarianism, humanity, altruism, public-spiritedness, social conscience, benevolence. **4** *show a bit of charity:* **goodwill**, compassion, consideration, concern, kindness, kind-heartedness, tenderness, tender-heartedness, sympathy, indulgence, tolerance, leniency.

charlatan noun **quack**, sham, fraud, fake, impostor, hoodwinker, hoaxer, cheat, deceiver, double-dealer, confidence trickster, swindler, fraudster; informal phoney, shark, con man/artist; Austral. informal illywhacker.

charm noun **1** *people were captivated by her charm:* **attractiveness**, beauty, glamour, loveliness; charisma, appeal, allure, seductiveness, animal magnetism; informal pulling power. **2** *these traditions retain a lot of charm:* **appeal**, attraction, allure, fascination. **3** *a lucky charm:* **talisman**, fetish, amulet, mascot, totem. **4** *magical charms:* **spell**, incantation, formula; N. Amer. mojo, hex.

• **verb 1** *he charmed them with his singing:* **delight**, please, win over, attract, captivate, lure, dazzle, fascinate, enchant, enthral, enrapture, seduce, spellbind. **2** *he charmed his mother into agreeing:* **coax**, cajole, wheedle; informal sweet-talk, soft-soap.

charming adjective **delightful**, pleasing, pleasant, agreeable, endearing, lovely, lovable, adorable, appealing, attractive, good-looking, prepossessing; alluring, delectable, ravishing, winning, winsome, fetching, captivating, enchanting, entrancing; informal heavenly, divine, gorgeous, easy on the eye; Brit. informal smashing; old use fair, comely.

– OPPOSITES repulsive.

chart noun *check your ideal weight on the chart:* **graph**, table, diagram, histogram; bar chart, pie chart, flow chart; Computing graphic.

• **verb 1** *the changes were charted accurately:* **tabulate**, plot, record, register, represent. **2** *the book charted his progress:* **follow**, trace, outline, describe, detail, record, document, chronicle, log.

charter noun **1** *a Royal charter:* **authority**, authorization, sanction, dispensation, consent, permission; permit, licence, warrant, franchise. **2** *the UN Charter:* **constitution**, code; principles.

• **verb** *they chartered a bus:* **hire**, lease, rent; book, reserve.

chase verb **1** *the dogs chased the fox:* **pursue**, run after, follow; hunt, track, trail; informal tail. **2** *she chased him out of the house:* **drive**, send; informal send packing. **3** *she chased*

C

away all thoughts of him: **dispel**, banish, dismiss, drive away, shut out, put out of your mind. **4** *photographers chased on to the runway:* **rush**, dash, race, speed, shoot, charge, scramble, scurry, hurry; informal scoot, belt; N. Amer. informal hightail.
• **noun** *they gave up the chase:* **pursuit**, hunt, trail.

chasm noun **1** *a deep chasm:* **gorge**, abyss, canyon, ravine, gully, gulf, crevasse, fissure, crevice; N. Amer. gulch. **2** *the chasm between their views:* **breach**, gulf, rift; difference, separation, division, schism.

chassis noun **framework**, frame, structure, substructure.

chaste adjective **1** *I have led a chaste life:* **celibate**, abstinent, self-denying; pure, virtuous, innocent, sinless; virginal. **2** *a chaste kiss:* **non-sexual**, platonic, innocent. **3** *a small, chaste bedroom:* **plain**, simple, bare, unadorned, undecorated, unembellished; functional, austere.
– OPPOSITES promiscuous, passionate.

chasten verb *both men were chastened by the experience:* **subdue**, humble, cow, squash, deflate, flatten, take down a peg or two, put someone in their place; informal cut down to size.

chastity noun **celibacy**, abstinence, self-denial; purity, virtue, innocence; virginity.

chat noun *I popped in for a chat:* **talk**, conversation, gossip, heart-to-heart, tête-à-tête; informal jaw, gas, confab; Brit. informal natter, chinwag.
• **verb** *they chatted with the guests:* **talk**, gossip; informal gas, jaw, chew the rag/fat; Brit. informal natter, have a chinwag; N. Amer. informal shoot the breeze/bull; Austral./NZ informal mag.

chatter noun *she tired him with her constant chatter:* **chat**, talk, gossip, chit-chat, patter, jabbering, prattle, babbling, tittle-tattle, blathering; informal yabbering, yammering, yattering, yapping; Brit. informal nattering, chuntering, rabbiting on.
• **verb** *she was chattering about her holiday:* **prattle**, rattle on, gabble, babble, jabber, go on, run on, ramble on, blather; informal gab, yak, yatter, jaw, gas, shoot your mouth off; Brit. informal witter, rabbit, chunter, natter, waffle.

chatty adjective **1** *he was a chatty person:* **talkative**, communicative, expansive, unreserved, gossipy, gossiping, garrulous, loquacious, voluble, verbose; informal mouthy, gabby, gassy. **2** *a chatty letter:* **conversational**, gossipy, informal, casual, familiar, friendly; informal newsy.
– OPPOSITES taciturn.

chauvinist adjective **jingoistic**, chauvinistic, flag-waving, xenophobic, racist, ethnocentric; sexist, misogynist.
• **noun sexist**, misogynist; informal male chauvinist pig, MCP.

cheap adjective **1** *the software is reliable and cheap:* **inexpensive**, low-priced, low-cost, economical, competitive, affordable, reasonable, budget, economy, bargain, cut-price, reduced, discounted, discount, rock-bottom, giveaway, bargain-basement; informal dirt cheap. **2** *it's plain without looking cheap:* **poor-quality**, second-rate, third-rate, substandard, inferior, vulgar, shoddy, trashy, tawdry; informal tacky, kitsch; Brit. informal naff; N. Amer. informal two-bit, dime-store. **3** *a cheap trick:* **despicable**, contemptible, immoral, unscrupulous, unprincipled, cynical.
– OPPOSITES expensive.

cheapen verb **1** *this would cheapen the cost of US exports:* **reduce**, lower, cut, mark down, discount; informal slash. **2** *she never cheapened herself:* **demean**, debase, degrade, lower, humble, devalue, compromise, discredit, disgrace, dishonour, shame.

cheat verb **swindle**, defraud, deceive, trick, dupe, hoodwink, double-cross, gull; informal diddle, rip off, con, fleece, shaft, sting, put one over on, pull a fast one on; N. Amer. informal sucker, stiff; Austral. informal pull a swifty on.
• **noun swindler**, cheater, fraudster, confidence trickster, deceiver, hoaxer, double-dealer, double-crosser, sham, fraud, fake, charlatan; informal con artist; N. Amer. informal grifter; Austral. informal illywhacker.

check verb **1** *troops checked all vehicles | I checked her background:*

examine, inspect, look at/over, scrutinize; study, investigate, research, probe, look into, enquire into; screen, vet; informal check out, give something a/the once-over. **2** *he checked that the gun was cocked:* **make sure**, confirm, verify. **3** *two defeats checked their progress:* **halt**, stop, arrest; bar, obstruct, foil, thwart, curb, block.
• **noun 1** *a check of the records:* **examination**, inspection, scrutiny, perusal, study, investigation; test, trial, monitoring; check-up; informal once-over, look-see. **2** *a check on the abuse of authority:* **control**, curb, restraint, constraint, limitation. **3** (N. Amer.) *the waitress arrived with the check:* **bill**, account, invoice, statement; N. Amer. informal tab.

check-up **noun** **examination**, inspection, evaluation, analysis, survey, test, appraisal; check; informal once-over, going-over.

cheek **noun** **impudence**, impertinence, insolence, cheekiness, impoliteness, disrespect, bad manners, rudeness, cockiness; answering back, talking back; informal brass neck, lip, mouth, chutzpah; Brit. informal backchat; N. Amer. informal sass, sassiness, back talk.

cheeky **adjective** **impudent**, disrespectful, impertinent, insolent, presumptuous, cocky, overfamiliar, discourteous, impolite, rude; informal brass-necked, lippy, mouthy, fresh, saucy; N. Amer. informal sassy, nervy.
– OPPOSITES respectful, polite.

cheer **verb 1** *they cheered their team:* **applaud**, hail, salute, shout for, clap, put your hands together for; bring the house down; informal holler for, give someone a big hand, big up; N. Amer. informal ballyhoo. **2** *my arrival seemed to cheer him:* **raise/lift someone's spirits**, brighten, buoy up, enliven, hearten, gladden, uplift, perk up, encourage; informal buck up.
– OPPOSITES boo, depress.
• **noun** *the cheers of the crowd:* **hurrah**, hurray, whoop, bravo, shout; (**cheers**) acclaim, clamour, applause, ovation.
– OPPOSITES boo.
■ **cheer up** perk up, brighten, liven up, rally, revive, bounce back, take heart; informal buck up. **cheer someone up**. See CHEER verb sense 2.

cheerful **adjective 1** *he arrived looking cheerful:* **happy**, jolly, merry, bright, glad, sunny, joyful, light-hearted, in good spirits, full of the joys of spring, exuberant, buoyant, ebullient, cheery, jaunty, animated, smiling; jovial, genial, good-humoured; carefree, unworried, untroubled, without a care in the world; informal chipper, chirpy, peppy, bright-eyed and bushy-tailed, full of beans; literary joyous. **2** *a cheerful room:* **pleasant**, attractive, agreeable, bright, sunny, happy, friendly, welcoming.
– OPPOSITES sad.

cheerless **adjective** **gloomy**, dreary, dull, dismal, bleak, drab, sombre, dark, dim, dingy, funereal; austere, stark, bare, comfortless, unwelcoming, uninviting; miserable, wretched, joyless, depressing, disheartening, dispiriting.

cheery **adjective**. See CHEERFUL sense 1.

cherish **verb 1** *a woman he could cherish:* **adore**, hold dear, love, dote on, be devoted to, revere, esteem, admire; think the world of, hold in high esteem; care for, look after, protect, preserve, keep safe. **2** *I cherish her letters:* **treasure**, prize, hold dear. **3** *they cherished dreams of glory:* **harbour**, entertain, cling to, foster, nurture.

chest **noun 1** *a bullet wound in the chest:* **breast**, upper body, torso, trunk; technical thorax. **2** *she had a large chest:* **bust**, bosom. **3** *an oak chest:* **box**, case, casket, crate, trunk, coffer, strongbox.

> **WORD LINKS**
> **pectoral**, **thoracic** relating to the chest

chew **verb** *Carolyn chewed a mouthful of toast:* **munch**, masticate, champ, crunch, gnaw, eat, consume.

chic **adjective** **stylish**, smart, elegant, sophisticated, dressy, dapper, dashing; fashionable, in vogue, up to date, up to the minute, à la mode; informal trendy, snappy, snazzy, natty; Brit. informal swish; N. Amer. informal fly, spiffy, kicky, tony.
– OPPOSITES unfashionable.

C

C

chicanery noun **trickery**, deception, deceit, deceitfulness, duplicity, dishonesty, deviousness, unscrupulousness, subterfuge, underhandedness, fraud, fraudulence, sharp practice, skulduggery, swindling, cheating, duping; informal crookedness, monkey business, hanky-panky, shenanigans; Brit. informal jiggery-pokery; N. Amer. informal monkeyshines; old use knavery.

chief noun **1** *a Highland chief:* **leader**, chieftain, head, headman, ruler, overlord, master, commander, potentate. **2** *the chief of the central bank:* **head**, principal, president, chief executive (officer), CEO, chair, chairman, chairwoman, chairperson, governor, director, manager, manageress; informal head honcho, boss; Brit. informal gaffer, guv'nor.
• adjective **1** *the chief rabbi:* **head**, leading, principal, premier, highest, supreme, arch. **2** *their chief aim:* **main**, principal, primary, prime, first, cardinal, central, key, crucial, essential, predominant, pre-eminent, overriding; informal number-one.
– OPPOSITES subordinate, minor.

chiefly adverb **mainly**, in the main, primarily, principally, predominantly, mostly, for the most part; usually, habitually, typically, commonly, generally, on the whole, largely, by and large, as a rule, almost always.

child noun **youngster**, boy, girl; baby, newborn, infant, toddler; schoolboy, schoolgirl, minor, junior; son, daughter, descendant; (**children**) offspring, progeny; Scottish & N. English bairn, laddie, lassie, lass; informal kid, kiddie, kiddiewink, nipper, tiny, tot, lad; Brit. informal sprog; N. Amer. informal rug rat; Austral./NZ informal ankle-biter; derogatory brat, guttersnipe.

> **WORD LINKS**
> **paediatrics** the branch of medicine dealing with children

childhood noun **youth**, early years/life, infancy, babyhood, boyhood, girlhood, prepubescence, minority.
– OPPOSITES adulthood.

childish adjective **1** *childish behaviour:* **immature**, babyish, infantile, juvenile, puerile; silly. **2** *a round childish face:* **childlike**, youthful, young, young-looking, girlish, boyish.
– OPPOSITES mature, adult.

childlike adjective **innocent**, artless, guileless, unworldly; unsophisticated, naive, trusting, unsuspicious; unaffected, uninhibited, natural, spontaneous.

chill noun **1** *a chill in the air:* **coldness**, chilliness, coolness, nip. **2** *he caught a chill:* **cold**; flu.
– OPPOSITES warmth.
• verb *his quiet tone chilled Ruth:* **scare**, frighten, petrify, terrify, alarm; make someone's blood run cold, chill to the bone/marrow, make someone's flesh crawl; informal scare the pants off; Brit. informal put the wind up; old use affright.
– OPPOSITES reassure.
• adjective *a chill wind:* **cold**, chilly, cool, fresh; wintry, frosty, icy, ice-cold, glacial, polar, arctic, bitter, biting, freezing; informal nippy; Brit. informal parky.
■ **chill out** (informal). See RELAX sense 1.

chilly adjective **1** *the weather had turned chilly:* **cold**, cool, crisp, fresh, wintry, frosty, icy; informal nippy; Brit. informal parky. **2** *a chilly reception:* **unfriendly**, unwelcoming, cold, cool, frosty; informal stand-offish.
– OPPOSITES warm.

chime verb **ring**, peal, toll, sound, clang; literary knell.
• noun **peal**, pealing, ringing, carillon, toll, tolling; tintinnabulation.

chimera noun **illusion**, fantasy, delusion, dream, fancy.

china noun **1** *a china cup:* **porcelain**. **2** *a table laid with the best china:* **dishes**, plates, cups and saucers, crockery, tableware, dinnerware, dinner service, tea service.

chink[1] noun *a chink in the curtains:* **opening**, gap, space, hole, aperture, crack, fissure, cranny, cleft, split, slit.

chink[2] verb *the glasses chinked:* **jingle**, jangle, clink, tinkle.

chip noun **1** *wood chips:* **fragment**, sliver, splinter, shaving, paring, flake. **2** *a chip in the glass:* **nick**, crack, scratch; flaw, fault.

3 *gambling chips:* **counter**, token; N. Amer. check.
• verb *the teacup was chipped:* **nick**, crack, scratch, break.
■ **chip in 1** *'He's right,' Gloria chipped in:* interrupt, interject, interpose, cut in, chime in, butt in. **2** *parents and staff chipped in to raise the cash:* contribute, club together, pay; informal fork out, shell out, cough up; Brit. informal stump up; N. Amer. informal kick in.

chirpy adjective (informal). See **CHEERFUL** sense 1.

chivalrous adjective **gallant**, gentlemanly, honourable, respectful, considerate; courteous, polite, gracious, well mannered.
– OPPOSITES rude, cowardly.

chivalry noun **gallantry**; courtesy, politeness, graciousness, good manners.
– OPPOSITES rudeness.

chivvy verb **nag**, badger, hound, harass, harry, pester, keep on at, go on at; informal hassle, bug, breathe down someone's neck; N. Amer. informal ride.

choice noun **1** *their choice of candidate | freedom of choice:* **selection**, choosing, picking; decision, say, vote. **2** *you have no other choice:* **option**, alternative, course of action; way out. **3** *an extensive choice of wines:* **range**, variety, selection, assortment. **4** *the perfect choice:* **appointee**, nominee, candidate, selection.
• adjective *choice plums:* **superior**, first-class, first-rate, prime, premier, grade A, best, finest, excellent, select, quality, top, top-quality, high-grade, prize, fine, special; informal A1, top-notch.
– OPPOSITES inferior.

choke verb **1** *the boy started to choke:* **gag**, retch, cough, fight for breath. **2** *she had been choked to death:* **strangle**, throttle; asphyxiate, suffocate, smother, stifle; informal strangulate. **3** *the guttering was choked with leaves:* **clog up**, bung up, stop up, block, obstruct; technical occlude.

choose verb **1** *we chose a quiet country hotel:* **select**, pick, opt for, plump for, settle on, decide on, fix on; appoint, name, nominate, vote for. **2** *I'll stay as long as I choose:* **wish**, want, desire, feel/be inclined, please, like, see fit.

choosy adjective (informal) **fussy**, finicky, fastidious, over-particular, difficult/hard to please, exacting, demanding; informal pernickety, picky; N. Amer. informal persnickety.

chop verb **cut**, cube, dice; hew, split; fell; N. Amer. hash.
■ **chop something off** cut off, sever, lop, shear; amputate.

choppy adjective **rough**, turbulent, heavy, heaving, stormy, squally, tempestuous.
– OPPOSITES calm.

chore noun **task**, job, duty, errand.

chortle verb **chuckle**, laugh, giggle, titter, tee-hee, snigger; guffaw.

christen verb **1** *she was christened Sara:* **baptize**, name, give the name of, call. **2** *a group who were christened 'The Magic Circle':* **call**, name, dub, style, term, designate, label, nickname.

Christmas noun **Noel**; informal Xmas; Brit. informal Chrimbo; old use Yule, Yuletide.

chronic adjective **1** *a chronic illness:* **persistent**, long-standing, long-term; incurable. **2** *chronic economic problems:* **constant**, continuing, ceaseless, persistent, long-lasting; severe, serious, acute, grave, dire. **3** *a chronic liar:* **inveterate**, dyed-in-the-wool, hardened, incorrigible; compulsive; informal pathological.
– OPPOSITES acute, temporary.

chronicle noun *a chronicle of the region's past:* **record**, account, history, annals, archives; log, diary, journal.
• verb *the events that followed have been chronicled:* **record**, put on record, write down, set down, document, report.

chronological adjective **sequential**, consecutive, in sequence, in order; linear.

chubby adjective **plump**, tubby, rotund, portly, dumpy, chunky, well upholstered, well covered, well rounded; informal roly-poly, pudgy, blubbery; Brit. informal podgy; N. Amer. informal zaftig, corn-fed.
– OPPOSITES skinny.

C

chuck verb (informal) **1** *he chucked the letter on to the table:* **throw**, toss, fling, hurl, pitch, cast, lob; informal sling, bung; Austral. informal hoy; NZ informal bish. **2** *I chucked the rubbish:* **throw away/out**, discard, dispose of, get rid of, dump, bin, jettison; informal ditch, junk; N. Amer. informal trash. **3** *I've chucked my job:* **give up**, leave, resign from; informal quit, pack in; Brit. informal jack in. **4** *Mary chucked him for another guy:* **leave**, finish with, break off with, jilt; informal dump, ditch, give someone the elbow; Brit. informal give someone the push, give someone the big E.

chuckle verb **chortle**, giggle, titter, snicker, snigger.

chum noun (informal) **friend**, companion, intimate; playmate, classmate, schoolmate, workmate; informal pal, crony; Brit. informal mate, china, mucker; N. Amer. informal buddy, amigo, compadre.
– OPPOSITES enemy, stranger.

chunk noun **lump**, hunk, wedge, block, slab, square, nugget, brick, cube, bar, cake; informal wodge; N. Amer. informal gob.

chunky adjective **1** *a chunky young man:* **stocky**, sturdy, thickset, heavily built, well built, burly, bulky, brawny, solid; Austral./NZ nuggety. **2** *a chunky sweater:* **thick**, bulky, heavy.
– OPPOSITES slight, light.

churchyard noun **graveyard**, cemetery, necropolis, burial ground, garden of remembrance; Scottish kirkyard; N. Amer. memorial park; old use God's acre.

churlish adjective **rude**, ill-mannered, discourteous, impolite; inconsiderate, uncharitable, surly, sullen; informal ignorant.
– OPPOSITES polite.

churn verb *the propellers churned up the water:* **disturb**, stir up, agitate.
■ **churn something out** produce, make, turn out; informal crank out, bang out.

chute noun **1** *a refuse chute:* **channel**, slide, shaft, funnel, conduit, tube. **2** *water chutes:* **slide**, flume.

cigarette noun informal ciggy, smoke, cancer stick; Brit. informal fag, snout.

circa preposition **approximately**, about, around, in the region of, roughly, or so, or thereabouts, more or less; N. Amer. informal in the ballpark of.
– OPPOSITES exactly.

circle noun **1** *a circle of gold stars:* **ring**, band, hoop, circlet; halo, disc; technical annulus. **2** *her circle of friends:* **group**, set, company, coterie, clique; crowd, band; informal gang, bunch, crew, posse. **3** *she moves in illustrious circles:* **sphere**, world, milieu; society.
• verb **1** *seagulls circled above:* **wheel**, revolve, rotate, whirl, spiral. **2** *satellites circle the earth:* **go round**, travel round, circumnavigate; orbit. **3** *the abbey was circled by a wall:* **surround**, encircle, ring, enclose, encompass; literary gird.

circuit noun **lap**, turn, round, circle.

circuitous adjective **roundabout**, indirect, winding, meandering, serpentine.
– OPPOSITES direct.

circular noun **leaflet**, pamphlet, handbill, flyer; N. Amer. mailer, folder, dodger.

circulate verb **1** *the news was widely circulated:* **spread**, communicate, disseminate, make known, make public, broadcast, publicize, advertise; distribute, give out, pass around. **2** *they circulated among the guests:* **socialize**, mingle; mix; wander, stroll.

circumference noun **perimeter**, border, boundary; edge, rim, margin, fringe.

circumspect adjective **cautious**, wary, careful, chary, guarded, on your guard; watchful, alert, attentive, heedful, vigilant, leery; informal cagey.
– OPPOSITES unguarded.

circumstances plural noun **1** *favourable economic circumstances:* **situation**, conditions, state of affairs, position; events, factors, context, background, environment. **2** *Jane explained the circumstances to him:* **the facts**, the details, the particulars, things, the lie of the land; Brit. the state of play; N. Amer. the lay of the land; informal the score.

circumvent verb **avoid**, get round/past, evade, bypass, sidestep, dodge; informal duck.

citadel noun **fortress**, fort, stronghold, fortification, castle; old use hold.

citation noun **1** *a citation from an eighteenth-century text:* **quotation**, quote, extract, excerpt, passage, line; reference, allusion; N. Amer. cite. **2** *a citation for gallantry:* **commendation**, honourable mention.

cite verb **1** *cite the passage in full:* **quote**, reproduce. **2** *he cited the case of Leigh v. Gladstone:* **refer to**, make reference to, mention, allude to, instance; specify, name.

citizen noun **1** *a British citizen:* **subject**, national, passport holder, native. **2** *the citizens of Edinburgh:* **inhabitant**, resident, native, townsman, townswoman, taxpayer, people; formal denizen; old use burgher.

city noun **town**, municipality, metropolis, megalopolis; conurbation; Scottish burgh; informal big smoke; N. Amer. informal burg.

> **WORD LINKS**
> **civic**, **metropolitan**, **urban** relating to a city

civic adjective **municipal**, city, town, urban, metropolitan; public, civil, community.

civil adjective **1** *a civil marriage:* **secular**, non-religious, lay; formal laic. **2** *civil aviation:* **non-military**, civilian. **3** *he behaved in a civil manner:* **polite**, courteous, well mannered, gentlemanly, chivalrous, gallant, ladylike.
– OPPOSITES religious, military, rude.

civilian noun **non-combatant**, ordinary/private citizen.

civility noun **courtesy**, politeness, courteousness, good manners, graciousness, consideration, respect.
– OPPOSITES rudeness.

civilization noun **1** *a higher stage of civilization:* **human development**, advancement, progress, enlightenment, culture, refinement, sophistication. **2** *ancient civilizations:* **culture**, society, nation, people.

civilize verb **enlighten**, improve, educate, instruct, refine, cultivate, polish, socialize, humanize; formal edify.

civilized adjective **polite**, courteous, well mannered, civil; cultured, cultivated, refined, polished, sophisticated; enlightened, educated, advanced, developed.
– OPPOSITES rude, unsophisticated.

clad adjective **dressed**, clothed, attired, got up, garbed, rigged out; wearing, sporting; old use apparelled.

C

claim verb **1** *he claimed that she was lying:* **assert**, declare, profess, maintain, state, hold, affirm, avow; argue, contend, allege; formal aver. **2** *you can claim compensation:* **request**, ask for, apply for; demand, exact.
• noun **1** *he accepted her claim that she had been raped:* **assertion**, declaration, profession, avowal, protestation; contention, allegation. **2** *a claim for damages:* **request**, application; demand, petition.

claimant noun **applicant**, candidate; petitioner, plaintiff, litigant, appellant.

clamber verb **scramble**, climb, scrabble.

clammy adjective **1** *his clammy hands:* **moist**, damp, sweaty, sticky; slimy, slippery. **2** *the clammy atmosphere:* **damp**, dank, wet; humid, close, muggy, heavy.
– OPPOSITES dry.

clamour noun **din**, racket, rumpus, uproar, tumult, shouting, yelling, screaming, baying, roaring; commotion, hubbub; Brit. row; informal hullabaloo.
• verb **demand**, call, press, push, lobby.

clamp noun *a clamp was holding the wood:* **brace**, vice, press.
• verb **1** *the sander is clamped on to the workbench:* **fasten**, secure, fix, attach; screw, bolt. **2** *a pipe was clamped between his teeth:* **clench**, grip, hold, press, clasp. **3** *his car was clamped:* **immobilize**, wheel-clamp; N. Amer. boot.
■ **clamp down on** suppress, prevent, stop, put a stop/end to, stamp out; crack down on, limit, restrict, control.

clampdown noun (informal) *a clampdown on crime:* **suppression**, prevention; crackdown, restriction, curb.

clan noun **family**, house, dynasty, tribe; Anthropology kinship group.

clandestine adjective **secret**, covert, furtive, surreptitious, stealthy, cloak-and-dagger; informal hush-hush.

C

clang noun **reverberation**, ring, peal, chime.
•verb **reverberate**, resound, ring, peal, chime, toll.

clank noun & verb **jangle**, rattle, clink, clang, jingle.

clannish adjective **cliquey**, cliquish, insular, exclusive; unfriendly, unwelcoming.

clap verb **1** *the audience clapped:* **applaud**, give someone a round of applause, put your hands together; informal give someone a big hand; N. Amer. informal give it up. **2** *he clapped Owen on the back:* **slap**, strike, hit, smack, thump; pat; informal whack.
•noun **1** *everybody gave him a clap:* **round of applause**, standing ovation; informal hand. **2** *a clap of thunder:* **crack**, crash, bang, boom; peal.

claptrap noun. See NONSENSE sense 1.

clarify verb **make clear**, shed/throw light on, illuminate, elucidate; explain, define, spell out, clear up.
–OPPOSITES confuse.

clarity noun **1** *the clarity of his explanation:* **lucidity**, clearness, coherence, transparency. **2** *the clarity of the image:* **sharpness**, clearness, crispness, definition. **3** *the clarity of the water:* **limpidity**, clearness, transparency, translucence.
–OPPOSITES vagueness, blurriness, opacity.

clash noun **1** *clashes between armed gangs:* **confrontation**, skirmish, fight, battle, engagement, encounter, conflict. **2** *an angry clash:* **argument**, altercation, confrontation, shouting match; contretemps, quarrel, disagreement, dispute; informal run-in, slanging match. **3** *the clash of cymbals:* **crash**, clang, bang.
•verb **1** *protesters clashed with police:* **fight**, battle, confront, skirmish, contend, come to blows, come into conflict. **2** *the prime minister clashed with union leaders:* **disagree**, differ, wrangle, dispute, cross swords, lock horns, be at loggerheads. **3** *the dates clash:* **conflict**, coincide, overlap. **4** *she clashed the cymbals together:* **bang**, strike, clang, crash.

clasp verb **1** *Ruth clasped his hand:* **grasp**, grip, clutch, hold tightly, squeeze; take hold of, seize, grab. **2** *he clasped Joanne in his arms:* **embrace**, hug, envelop; hold, squeeze.
•noun **1** *a gold clasp:* **fastener**, fastening, catch, clip, pin; buckle, hasp. **2** *his tight clasp:* **embrace**; grip, grasp.

class noun **1** *a hotel of the first class:* **category**, grade, rating, classification, group, grouping. **2** *a new class of heart drug:* **kind**, sort, type, variety, genre, brand; species, genus, breed, strain; N. Amer. stripe. **3** *other people of her own class:* **rank**, stratum, level, echelon, group, grouping; status, caste. **4** *there are 30 pupils in the class:* **form**, group, set, stream. **5** *a maths class:* **lesson**, period; seminar, tutorial, workshop. **6** (informal) *a woman of class:* **style**, elegance, chic, sophistication, taste, refinement, quality.
•verb *the 12-seater is classed as a commercial vehicle:* **classify**, categorize, group, grade; order, sort, codify; bracket, designate, label, pigeonhole.

classic adjective **1** *the classic work on the subject:* **definitive**, authoritative; outstanding, first-rate, first-class, best, finest, excellent, superior, masterly. **2** *a classic example of Norman design:* **typical**, archetypal, quintessential, vintage; model, representative, perfect, prime, textbook. **3** *a classic look:* **simple**, elegant, understated; traditional, timeless, ageless.
–OPPOSITES atypical.
•noun *a classic of the genre:* **definitive example**, model, epitome, paradigm, exemplar; masterpiece.

classical adjective **1** *classical mythology:* ancient Greek, Hellenic; Latin, Roman. **2** *a classical style:* **simple**, pure, restrained, plain, austere; harmonious, balanced, symmetrical, elegant.
–OPPOSITES modern.

classification noun **1** *the classification of diseases:* **categorization**, classifying, grouping, grading, ranking, organization, sorting, codification, systematization. **2** *a series of classifications:* **category**, class, group, grouping, grade, grading, ranking, bracket.

classify verb **categorize**, group,

grade, rank, order, organize, range, sort, type, codify, bracket; catalogue, list, file, index.

classy adjective (informal) **stylish**, high-class, superior, exclusive, chic, elegant, smart, sophisticated; Brit. upmarket; N. Amer. high-toned; informal posh, ritzy, plush, swanky; Brit. informal swish.

clatter verb **rattle**, clank, clang.

clause noun **section**, paragraph, article, subsection; condition, proviso, rider.

claw noun **1** *a bird's claw:* **talon**, nail. **2** *a crab's claw:* **pincer**, nipper.
•verb *her fingers clawed his shoulders:* **scratch**, lacerate, tear, rip, scrape, dig into.

clean adjective **1** *the room was clean and bright:* **washed**, scrubbed, cleansed; spotless, immaculate, pristine, dirt-free; hygienic, sanitary, disinfected, sterilized, sterile, aseptic; laundered. **2** *a clean sheet of paper:* **blank**, empty, clear, plain; unused, new, pristine, fresh, unmarked. **3** *clean air:* **pure**, clear, fresh; unpolluted, untainted, uncontaminated. **4** *a clean life:* **virtuous**, good, upright, upstanding; honourable, respectable, reputable, decent, righteous, moral, exemplary, blameless, guilt-free, above suspicion; innocent, pure, chaste, unsullied. **5** *a good clean fight:* **fair**, honest, sporting, sportsmanlike, honourable, by the rules/book; informal on the level. **6** *a clean cut:* **neat**, smooth, straight, precise. **7** *the clean lines of the design:* **simple**, elegant, graceful, streamlined, smooth.
–OPPOSITES dirty, polluted.
•verb **1** **wash**, cleanse, wipe, sponge, scrub, mop, rinse, scour, swab, hose down, sluice down, disinfect; shampoo, launder. **2** *she cleaned the fish:* **gut**, draw, dress; formal eviscerate.

cleanse verb **1** *the wound was cleansed:* **clean**, wash, bathe, rinse, disinfect. **2** *cleansing the environment of traces of lead:* **rid**, clear, free, purify, purge.

clear adjective **1** *clear instructions:* **understandable**, comprehensible, intelligible, plain, uncomplicated, explicit, lucid, coherent, simple, straightforward, unambiguous, clear-cut. **2** *a clear case of harassment:* **obvious**, evident, plain; sure, definite, unmistakable, manifest, indisputable, unambiguous, patent, incontrovertible, irrefutable, beyond doubt, beyond question; palpable, visible, discernible, conspicuous, overt, blatant, glaring. **3** *clear water:* **transparent**, limpid, translucent, crystal clear, pellucid. **4** *a clear sky:* **bright**, cloudless, unclouded; blue, sunny, starry. **5** *the road was clear | a clear view:* **unobstructed**, passable, open; unrestricted, unhindered. **6** *the algae were clear of toxins:* **free**, devoid, without, unaffected by; rid. **7** *two clear days' notice:* **whole**, full, entire, complete.
–OPPOSITES vague, opaque, cloudy, obstructed.
•verb **1** *the rain had cleared:* **disappear**, stop, die away, fade, wear off, lift, settle, evaporate, dissipate, decrease, lessen, shift. **2** *they cleared the table:* **empty**, unload, strip. **3** *staff cleared the building:* **evacuate**, empty; leave. **4** *I cleared the bar at my first attempt:* **jump**, vault, sail over, leap over, hurdle. **5** *he was cleared by the court:* **acquit**, declare innocent, find not guilty; absolve, exonerate; informal let off. **6** *they were cleared to work on the project:* **authorize**, permit, allow, pass, accept, endorse, license, sanction; informal OK, give the OK, give the thumbs up, give the green light, give the go-ahead. **7** *I cleared £50,000 profit:* **net**, make/realize a profit of, take home, pocket; gain, earn, make, get, bring in, pull in.
■ **clear off/out** (informal) go away, get out, leave; informal beat it, push off, shove off, scram, scoot, buzz off; Brit. informal hop it, sling your hook; Austral./NZ informal rack off; N. Amer. informal bug off, take a hike; literary begone. **clear something out 1** *we cleared out the junk room:* empty out; tidy, clear up. **2** *clear out the rubbish:* get rid of, throw out/away, discard, dispose of, dump, bin, scrap, jettison; informal chuck out/away, ditch. **clear something up 1** *staff cleared up the shop:* tidy, put in order, straighten up, clean up. **2** *we've cleared up the problem:*

solve, resolve, straighten out, find the answer to; get to the bottom of, explain; informal crack, figure out, fix, suss out.

C

clearance noun **1** *slum clearance:* **removal**, clearing, demolition. **2** *you must have Home Office clearance:* **authorization**, permission, consent, approval, leave, sanction, licence, dispensation, assent, agreement, endorsement; informal the green light, the go-ahead, the thumbs up, the OK, say-so. **3** *there is plenty of clearance:* **space**, room, headroom, margin, leeway.

clear-cut adjective **definite**, distinct, clear, well defined, precise, specific, explicit, unambiguous, unequivocal, black and white, cut and dried.
–OPPOSITES vague.

clearing noun **glade**, dell, gap, opening.

clearly adverb **1** *write clearly:* **intelligibly**, plainly, distinctly, comprehensibly; legibly, audibly. **2** *clearly, substantial changes are needed:* **obviously**, evidently, patently, unquestionably, undoubtedly, without doubt, plainly, undeniably, incontrovertibly, doubtless, it goes without saying, needless to say.

cleave verb
■ **cleave to** (literary) **1** *her tongue cleaved to the roof of her mouth:* stick to, adhere to, be attached to. **2** *they cleaved to their faith:* adhere to, hold to, abide by, be loyal/faithful to.

cleaver noun **chopper**, hatchet, axe, knife.

cleft noun **1** *a deep cleft in the rocks:* **split**, crack, fissure, crevice, rift, break, fracture, rent, breach. **2** *the cleft in his chin:* **dimple**.
• adjective *a cleft tail:* **split**, divided, cloven.

clemency noun **mercy**, pity, mercifulness, leniency, mildness, indulgence, quarter; compassion, humanity, sympathy.
–OPPOSITES ruthlessness.

clench verb **grip**, grasp, grab, clutch, clasp, clamp, hold tightly, seize, press, squeeze.

clergy noun **clergymen, clergywomen**, churchmen, churchwomen, clerics, priests, ecclesiastics, men/women of God; ministry, priesthood, holy orders, the church, the cloth.
–OPPOSITES laity.

WORD LINKS
clerical relating to the clergy

clergyman, clergywoman noun **priest**, churchman, churchwoman, man/woman of the cloth, man/woman of God; cleric, minister, preacher, chaplain, father, ecclesiastic, pastor, vicar, rector, parson, curate, deacon, deaconess; Scottish kirkman; N. Amer. dominie; informal reverend, padre, Holy Joe.

clerical adjective **1** *clerical jobs:* **office**, desk; administrative, secretarial; white-collar. **2** *a clerical matter:* **ecclesiastical**, church, priestly, religious, spiritual; holy.
–OPPOSITES secular.

clerk noun **office worker**, clerical worker, administrator; bookkeeper; cashier, teller; informal pen-pusher.

clever adjective **1** *a clever young woman:* **intelligent**, bright, smart, astute, quick-witted, shrewd; talented, gifted, capable, able, competent; educated, learned, knowledgeable, wise; informal brainy, savvy. **2** *a clever scheme:* **ingenious**, canny, cunning, crafty, artful, slick, neat; informal nifty. **3** *she was clever with her hands:* **skilful**, dexterous, adroit, adept, deft, nimble, handy; skilled, talented, gifted. **4** *a clever remark:* **witty**, amusing, droll, humorous, funny; facetious, sarcastic, cheeky.
–OPPOSITES stupid.

cliché noun **platitude**, hackneyed phrase, commonplace, banality, truism, stock phrase; informal old chestnut.

click verb (informal) **1** *that night it clicked:* **become clear**, fall into place, come home, make sense, dawn, register, get through, sink in. **2** *we just clicked:* **take to each other**, get along, be compatible, be like-minded, feel a rapport, see eye to eye, be on the same wavelength; informal hit it off. **3** *this issue hasn't clicked with the voters:* **go down well**, prove popular, be a hit, succeed, resonate, work, take off.

client noun **customer**, buyer, purchaser, shopper, consumer, user;

patient; patron, regular; (**clients**) clientele, patronage, public, market; Brit. informal punter.

clientele noun. See CLIENT.

cliff noun **precipice**, rock face, crag, bluff, ridge, escarpment, scar, scarp, overhang.

climactic adjective **final**, ending, closing, concluding, ultimate; exciting, thrilling, gripping, riveting, dramatic, hair-raising; crucial, decisive, critical.

climate noun **1** *a mild climate:* **weather conditions**, weather. **2** *they come from colder climates:* **region**, area, zone, country, place; literary clime. **3** *the political climate:* **atmosphere**, mood, feeling, ambience; ethos, attitude; milieu; informal vibes.

climax noun *the climax of his career:* **peak**, pinnacle, height, highest point, top; acme, zenith; culmination, crowning point, crown, crest; highlight, high spot.
– OPPOSITES nadir.
• verb *the event will climax with a concert:* **culminate**, peak, reach a pinnacle, come to a crescendo, come to a head.

climb verb **1** *we climbed the hill:* **ascend**, mount, scale, scramble up, clamber up, shin up; N. Amer. shinny up. **2** *the road climbs steeply:* **slope upwards**, rise, go uphill, incline. **3** *the shares climbed to 550 pence:* **increase**, rise, go up; shoot up, soar, rocket. **4** *he climbed through the ranks:* **advance**, rise, move up, progress, work your way.
– OPPOSITES descend, fall.
• noun *a steep climb:* **ascent**, route; walk.
– OPPOSITES descent.
■ **climb down** *the Government had to climb down:* back down, admit defeat, surrender, capitulate, yield, give in, give way, submit; retreat, backtrack; eat your words, eat humble pie; do a U-turn; Brit. do an about-turn; N. Amer. informal eat crow.

clinch verb **1** *he clinched the deal:* **secure**, settle, conclude, close, pull off, bring off, complete, confirm, seal, finalize; informal sew up, wrap up. **2** *these findings clinched the matter:* **settle**, decide, determine; resolve. **3** *they clinched the title:* **win**, secure.
– OPPOSITES lose.

cling verb *rice grains tend to cling together:* **stick**, adhere, hold.
■ **cling to 1** *she clung to him:* hold on, clutch, grip, grasp, clasp, hang on; embrace, hug. **2** *they clung to their beliefs:* adhere to, hold to, stick to, stand by, abide by, cherish, remain true to, have faith in; informal stick with.

clinic noun **medical centre**, health centre, surgery, doctor's; workshop, session.

clinical adjective **1** *he seemed so clinical:* **detached**, impersonal, dispassionate, uninvolved, distant, remote, aloof, removed, cold, indifferent, neutral, unsympathetic, unfeeling, unemotional. **2** *the room was very clinical:* **plain**, stark, austere, spartan, bleak, bare; functional, basic, institutional, impersonal, characterless.
– OPPOSITES emotional, luxurious.

clip[1] noun **1** *the clip on his briefcase:* **fastener**, clasp, hasp, catch, hook, buckle, lock. **2** *three clips of ammunition:* **magazine**, cartridge.
• verb *he clipped the pages together:* **fasten**, attach, fix, join; pin, staple, tack.

clip[2] verb **1** *I clipped the hedge:* **trim**, prune, cut, snip, crop, shear, pare; lop; neaten, shape. **2** *clip the coupon below:* **remove**, cut out, tear out, detach. **3** *his lorry clipped a van:* **hit**, strike, touch, graze, glance off, nudge, dent, scrape.
• noun *a film clip:* **extract**, excerpt, snippet, fragment; trailer.

clipping noun **cutting**, snippet, extract, excerpt; article, report, feature, review.

clique noun **coterie**, set, circle, ring, in-crowd, group; club, society, fraternity, sorority; cabal, caucus; informal gang, posse.

cloak noun **1** *the cloak over his shoulders:* **cape**, robe, mantle. **2** *a cloak of secrecy:* **cover**, veil, mantle, shroud, screen, mask, shield, blanket.
• verb *a peak cloaked in mist:* **conceal**, hide, cover, veil, shroud, mask, obscure, cloud; envelop, swathe, surround.

clock noun **timepiece**, timer,

C

chronometer, chronograph; pocket watch, hunter.

clod noun **lump**, clump, chunk, hunk, wedge, slab.

clog verb **block**, obstruct, congest, jam, choke, bung up, plug, stop up, fill up; Brit. informal gunge up.

C

cloister verb *they were cloistered at home:* **confine**, isolate, shut away, sequester, seclude, closet.

cloistered adjective **secluded**, sheltered, protected, insulated; shut off, isolated; solitary, monastic, reclusive, hermit-like.

close[1] adjective **1** *the town is close to Leeds:* **near**, adjacent; in the vicinity of, in the neighbourhood of, within reach of; neighbouring, adjoining, abutting, alongside, on the doorstep, a stone's throw away; nearby, at hand, at close quarters; informal within spitting distance. **2** *aircraft flying in close formation:* **dense**, compact, tight, solid. **3** *I was close to tears:* **near**, on the verge of, on the brink of, on the point of. **4** *a very close match:* **evenly matched**, even, neck and neck, nip and tuck. **5** *close friends | close family members:* **intimate**, bosom; close-knit, inseparable, devoted, faithful, fast, firm; informal as thick as thieves. **6** *a close resemblance:* **strong**, marked, distinct, pronounced. **7** *a close examination:* **careful**, detailed, thorough, minute, searching, painstaking, meticulous, rigorous, scrupulous, conscientious. **8** *the weather was close:* **humid**, muggy, stuffy, airless, heavy, sticky, sultry, oppressive, stifling.
–OPPOSITES far, distant.
• noun (Brit.) *a small close of houses:* **cul-de-sac**, street; courtyard.

close[2] verb **1** *she closed the door:* **shut**, pull to, push to, slam. **2** *close the hole with cotton wool:* **block up/off**, stop up, plug, seal, shut up/off; bung up. clog up, choke, obstruct. **3** *the enemy were closing fast:* **catch up**, creep up, near, approach, gain on someone. **4** *the gap is closing:* **narrow**, reduce, shrink, lessen, get smaller, diminish, contract. **5** *he closed the meeting:* **end**, conclude, finish, terminate, wind up. **6** *the factory has closed:* **shut down**, close down, cease production, cease trading, be wound up, go out of business, go bankrupt, go into receivership, go into liquidation; informal fold, go to the wall, go bust. **7** *he's closed the deal:* **clinch**, settle, secure, seal, confirm, establish; transact, pull off; complete, conclude, fix, agree, finalize; informal wrap up.
–OPPOSITES open, start, begin.
• noun *the close of the talks:* **end**, finish, conclusion.
–OPPOSITES beginning.
■ **close down.** See sense 6 above.

closeness noun **proximity**, propinquity, nearness.

closet noun *a clothes closet:* **cupboard**, wardrobe, cabinet, locker.
• adjective *a closet revolutionary:* **secret**, covert, private; surreptitious, clandestine.
• verb *David was closeted in his den:* **shut away**, sequester, seclude, cloister, confine, isolate.

closure noun **closing down**, shutdown, winding up.

clot noun **lump**, clump, mass; thrombosis, embolus; informal glob, gob.
• verb **coagulate**, set, congeal, thicken, solidify.

> **WORD LINKS**
> **embolectomy**, **thrombectomy** the surgical removal of a blood clot

cloth noun **1** *a maker of cloth:* **fabric**, material, textiles. **2** *a cloth to wipe the table:* **rag**, wipe, duster; flannel, towel; Austral. washer. **3** *a gentleman of the cloth:* **the clergy**, the priesthood, the ministry; clergymen, clerics, priests.

> **WORD LINKS**
> **draper** a person who sells cloth

clothe verb **dress**, attire, robe, garb, array, costume, swathe, deck out, turn out, fit out, rig out; informal get up.

clothes plural noun **clothing**, dress, garments, attire, garb, wear, costume; informal gear, togs, duds, get-up; Brit. informal clobber; N. Amer. informal threads; formal apparel; old use raiment.

> **WORD LINKS**
> **sartorial** relating to clothes
> **clothier**, **couturier**, **tailor** a maker or seller of clothes

clothing noun. See CLOTHES.

cloud noun *a cloud of exhaust smoke:* **mass**, billow; pall, mantle, blanket.
• verb **1** *the sand is churned up, clouding the water:* **dirty**, muddy. **2** *anger clouded my judgement:* **confuse**, muddle, obscure.

cloudy adjective **1** *a cloudy sky:* **overcast**, clouded; dark, grey, black, leaden, murky; sombre, dismal, heavy, gloomy; sunless, starless; hazy, misty, foggy. **2** *cloudy water:* **murky**, muddy, milky, dirty, turbid.
– OPPOSITES clear.

cloven adjective **split**, divided, cleft.

clown noun **1** *the class clown:* **joker**, comedian, comic, wit, jester, buffoon; informal wag; Austral./NZ informal hard case. **2** *a bunch of clowns:* **fool**, idiot, dolt, simpleton, ignoramus; informal ass, moron, numbskull, nincompoop, halfwit; Brit. informal prat, berk, twit, nitwit, twerp.

cloying adjective **sickly**, syrupy, saccharine; sickening, nauseating; mawkish, sentimental, mushy, slushy, sloppy; Brit. twee; informal over the top, OTT, gooey, cheesy, corny; N. Amer. informal cornball, sappy.

club[1] noun **1** *a canoeing club:* **society**, association, organization, institution, group, circle, band, body, ring, crew; alliance, league, union. **2** *the city has great clubs:* **nightclub**, bar; informal disco, niterie. **3** *the top club in the league:* **team**, squad, side.
▪ **club together** pool resources, join forces, team up, band together, get together, pull together, collaborate; informal have a whip-round.

club[2] noun *a wooden club:* **cudgel**, truncheon, bludgeon, baton, stick, mace, bat; Brit. cosh; N. Amer. blackjack, nightstick.
• verb *he was clubbed with an iron bar:* **cudgel**, bludgeon, bash, beat, hit, strike, batter, belabour; Brit. cosh; informal clout, clobber.

clue noun **1** *police are searching for clues:* **hint**, indication, sign, signal, pointer, trace, indicator; lead, tip; evidence, information. **2** *a crossword clue:* **question**, problem, puzzle, riddle, poser.

clump noun **1** *a clump of trees:* **cluster**, thicket, group, bunch. **2** *a clump of earth:* **lump**, clod, mass, chunk.
• verb **1** *galaxies clump together:* **cluster**, group, collect, gather, assemble, congregate, mass. **2** *they were clumping around upstairs:* **stamp**, stomp, clomp, tramp, lumber; thump, bang; informal galumph.

clumsy adjective **1** *she was terribly clumsy:* **awkward**, uncoordinated, ungainly, graceless, inelegant; inept, maladroit, unskilful, accident-prone, like a bull in a china shop, all fingers and thumbs; informal cack-handed, ham-fisted, butterfingered, having two left feet; N. Amer. informal klutzy. **2** *a clumsy contraption:* **unwieldy**, cumbersome, bulky, awkward. **3** *a clumsy remark:* **gauche**, awkward, graceless; unsubtle, crass; tactless, insensitive, thoughtless, undiplomatic, indelicate, ill-judged.
– OPPOSITES graceful, elegant, tactful.

cluster noun **1** *clusters of berries:* **bunch**, clump, mass, knot, group, clutch. **2** *a cluster of spectators:* **crowd**, group, knot, huddle, bunch, throng, flock, pack; informal gaggle.
• verb *they clustered around the television:* **congregate**, gather, collect, group, assemble; huddle, crowd.

clutch verb **grip**, grasp, clasp, cling to, hang on to, clench, hold, grab.
▪ **clutch at** reach for, snatch at, grab at, claw at, scrabble for.

clutches plural noun **power**, control; hands, hold, grip, grasp; custody.

clutter noun **disorder**, chaos, disarray, untidiness, mess, confusion; litter, rubbish, junk.
• verb **litter**, mess up; be strewn, be scattered; cover, bury.

coach[1] noun **1** *a journey by coach:* **bus**. **2** *a railway coach:* **carriage**, wagon, compartment, van, Pullman; N. Amer. car.

coach[2] noun *a football coach:* **instructor**, trainer; teacher, tutor, mentor, guru.
• verb *he coached Richard in maths:* **instruct**, teach, tutor, school, educate; drill; train.

coagulate verb **congeal**, clot, thicken, gel; solidify, harden, set, dry.

C

coal noun

WORD LINKS
colliery a coal mine
collier a coal miner

coalesce verb **merge**, unite, join/come together, combine, fuse, mingle, blend; amalgamate, consolidate, integrate, converge.

coalition noun **alliance**, union, partnership, bloc, caucus; federation, league, association, confederation, consortium, syndicate, combine; amalgamation, merger.

coarse adjective **1** *coarse blankets:* **rough**, scratchy, prickly, wiry, harsh. **2** *his coarse features:* **rough**, rough-hewn, heavy; ugly. **3** *a coarse boy:* **oafish**, loutish, boorish, uncouth, rough, rude, impolite, ill-mannered; vulgar, common, rough. **4** *a coarse remark:* **vulgar**, crude, rude, off colour, lewd, smutty, indelicate, improper, unseemly, crass, tasteless.
–OPPOSITES soft, delicate, refined.

! Don't confuse **coarse** with **course**, which means 'a direction' (*the plane changed course*), or 'a programme of study' (*a French course*).

coarsen verb **1** *hands coarsened by work:* **roughen**, toughen, harden, callus. **2** *I had been coarsened by the army:* **desensitize**, dehumanize, harden; dull, deaden.
–OPPOSITES soften, refine.

coast noun *the west coast:* **seaboard**, coastline, seashore, shore, shoreline, seaside, waterfront.
•verb *the car coasted down a hill:* **freewheel**, cruise, taxi, drift, glide, sail.

WORD LINKS
littoral relating to a coast or seashore

coat noun **1** *a winter coat:* overcoat, raincoat; parka, jacket. **2** *a dog's coat:* **fur**, hair, wool, fleece; hide, pelt, skin. **3** *a coat of paint:* **layer**, covering, coating, skin, film, wash; glaze, veneer, patina; deposit.
•verb *the tube was coated with wax:* **cover**, paint, glaze, varnish; surface, veneer, laminate, plate, face; daub, smear, cake, plaster.

coax verb **persuade**, wheedle, cajole, get round; beguile, seduce, inveigle, manoeuvre; informal sweet-talk, soft-soap, butter up, twist someone's arm.

cobble verb
■ **cobble something together** throw together; improvise, contrive, rig up, whip up; informal **rustle up**; Brit. informal **knock up**.

cock noun **rooster**, cockerel, capon.
•verb **1** *he cocked his head:* **tilt**, tip, angle, incline, dip. **2** *she cocked her little finger:* **bend**, flex, crook, curve; lift, raise, hold up.

cockeyed adjective (informal) **1** *that picture is cockeyed:* **crooked**, awry, askew, lopsided, tilted, off-centre, skewed, skew, squint, misaligned; Brit. informal skew-whiff, wonky. **2** *a cockeyed scheme:* **absurd**, ridiculous, idiotic, stupid, foolish, silly, half-baked, hare-brained; informal crazy; Brit. informal barmy, daft.

cocksure adjective **arrogant**, conceited, overconfident, cocky, proud, vain, self-important, swollen-headed, egotistical, presumptuous.
–OPPOSITES modest.

cocky adjective **arrogant**, conceited, overconfident, cocksure, swollen-headed, self-important, egotistical, presumptuous, boastful.
–OPPOSITES modest.

cocoon verb **protect**, shield, shelter, screen, cushion, insulate, isolate, cloister.

coddle verb **pamper**, cosset, molly-coddle; spoil, indulge, overindulge, pander to; mother, wait on hand and foot.
–OPPOSITES neglect.

code noun **1** *a secret code:* **cipher**. **2** *a strict social code:* **convention**, etiquette, protocol, ethic. **3** *the penal code:* **laws**, rules, regulations; constitution, system.

WORD LINKS
cryptography the art of writing or solving codes
encrypt, **encode**, **encipher** convert something into code
decrypt, **decipher**, **crack** make a coded message intelligible

codify verb **systematize**, organize, arrange, order, structure; tabulate, catalogue, list, sort, index, classify, categorize, file, log.

coerce verb **pressure**, pressurize, press, push, constrain; force, compel, oblige, browbeat, bludgeon, bully, threaten, intimidate, dragoon, twist someone's arm; informal railroad, squeeze, steamroller, lean on.

coercion noun **force**, compulsion, constraint, duress, oppression, enforcement, harassment, intimidation, threats, arm-twisting, pressure.

coffer noun **funds**, reserves, resources, money, finances, wealth, capital, purse.

coffin noun sarcophagus; N. Amer. casket; informal box; humorous wooden overcoat.

cogent adjective **convincing**, compelling, strong, forceful, powerful, potent, effective; valid, sound, plausible, telling; impressive, persuasive, eloquent, credible; conclusive; logical, reasoned, rational, reasonable, lucid, coherent, clear.

cognition noun **perception**, discernment, apprehension, learning, understanding, comprehension, insight; reasoning, thinking, thought.

cognizance noun (formal). See **AWARENESS**.

cognizant adjective (formal). See **AWARE** sense 1.

coherent adjective **logical**, reasoned, rational, sound, cogent, consistent; clear, lucid, articulate; intelligible, comprehensible.
–OPPOSITES muddled.

cohesion noun **unity**, togetherness, solidarity, bond, coherence; connection, linkage.

coil noun **loop**, twist, turn, curl; spiral.
• verb **wind**, loop, twist, curl, twine, wrap.

coin verb *he coined the term 'desktop publishing':* **invent**, create, make up, conceive, originate, think up, dream up.

> **WORD LINKS**
> **numismatics** the study or collection of coins and banknotes

coincide verb **1** *the events coincided:* **occur simultaneously**, happen together, co-occur, coexist. **2** *their interests do not always coincide:* **tally**, correspond, agree, accord, match up, fit, be consistent, be compatible, dovetail, mesh; informal square.
–OPPOSITES differ.

coincidence noun **accident**, chance, serendipity, providence, happenstance, fate, luck; fortune; a fluke.

coincidental adjective **accidental**, chance, fluky, random; fortuitous, adventitious, serendipitous.

coitus noun (technical). See **SEX** noun sense 1.

cold adjective **1** *a cold day:* **chilly**, chill, cool, freezing, icy, snowy, wintry, frosty, frigid; bitter, biting, raw; informal nippy, arctic; Brit. informal parky. **2** *I'm cold:* **freezing**, frozen, numb; chilly, shivery. **3** *a cold reception:* **unfriendly**, inhospitable, unwelcoming, cool, frigid, frosty; distant, formal, stiff.
–OPPOSITES hot, warm.

cold-blooded adjective **cruel**, callous, sadistic, inhuman, inhumane, pitiless, merciless, ruthless, unfeeling, uncaring, heartless.

cold-hearted adjective **unfeeling**, unloving, uncaring, unsympathetic, unemotional, unfriendly, uncharitable, unkind, insensitive; hard-hearted, stony-hearted, heartless, hard, cold.

collaborate verb **1** *they collaborated on the project:* **cooperate**, join forces, work together, combine; pool resources, club together. **2** *they collaborated with the enemy:* **fraternize**, conspire, collude, cooperate, consort.

collaborator noun **1** *his collaborator on the book:* **co-worker**, partner, associate, colleague, confederate; assistant. **2** *a wartime collaborator:* **sympathizer**; traitor, quisling, fifth columnist.

collapse verb **1** *the roof collapsed:* **cave in**, fall in, subside, fall down, give way, crumple, crumble, disintegrate. **2** *he collapsed last night:* **faint**, pass out, black out, lose consciousness, keel over; informal flake out, conk out. **3** *she collapsed in tears:* **break down**; go to pieces, be overcome; informal crack up. **4** *peace talks collapsed:* **break down**, fail, fall through, fold, founder; informal flop, fizzle out.

C

• **noun 1** *the collapse of the roof:* **cave-in**, disintegration. **2** *the collapse of the talks:* **breakdown**, failure.

collar verb (informal) *she collared me in the street:* **accost**, waylay, approach, detain, stop, halt, catch, confront, importune; informal buttonhole; Brit. informal nobble.

collate verb **collect**, gather, accumulate, assemble; combine, put together; arrange, organize.

collateral noun **security**, surety, guarantee, insurance, indemnity; backing.

colleague noun **co-worker**, fellow worker, workmate, teammate, associate, partner, collaborator, ally, confederate; Brit. informal oppo.

collect verb **1** *relief agencies are collecting supplies:* **gather**, accumulate, assemble; amass, stockpile, pile up, heap up, store, hoard, save; mass, accrue. **2** *a crowd soon collected:* **gather**, assemble, meet, muster, congregate, convene, converge. **3** *I must collect the children:* **fetch**, pick up, call for, meet. **4** *they collect money for charity:* **raise**, ask for, solicit; obtain, acquire, gather.
– OPPOSITES disperse, distribute.

collected adjective **calm**, cool, self-possessed, self-controlled, composed, poised; serene, tranquil, relaxed, unruffled, unperturbed, untroubled; placid, quiet, sedate, phlegmatic; informal unfazed, laid-back.
– OPPOSITES excited, hysterical.

collection noun **1** *a collection of stolen items:* **hoard**, pile, heap, stack, stock, store, stockpile; accumulation, reserve, supply, bank, pool, fund, mine, reservoir; informal stash. **2** *a collection of shoppers:* **group**, crowd, body, gathering; knot, cluster. **3** *his collection of Victorian dolls:* **array**, display; hoard. **4** *a collection of short stories:* **anthology**, selection, compendium, compilation, miscellany. **5** *a collection for famine relief:* appeal; informal whip-round.

collective adjective **common**, shared, joint, combined, mutual, communal, pooled; united, allied, cooperative, collaborative.
– OPPOSITES individual.

college noun **school**, academy, university, institute.

collide verb *the train collided with a lorry:* **crash**; hit, strike, run into, bump into, meet head-on.

collision noun **1** *a collision on the ring road:* **crash**, accident, smash; Brit. RTA (road traffic accident); N. Amer. wreck; informal pile-up; Brit. informal shunt. **2** *a collision between two ideas:* **conflict**, clash.

colloquial adjective **informal**, conversational, everyday; unofficial, idiomatic, slangy, vernacular, popular, demotic.
– OPPOSITES formal.

collude verb **conspire**, connive, collaborate, plot, scheme; informal be in cahoots.

colonize verb **settle in**, people, populate; occupy, take over, invade.

colony noun **1** *a French colony:* **territory**, dependency, protectorate, satellite, settlement, outpost, province. **2** *the British colony in New York:* **population**, community. **3** *an artists' colony:* **community**, commune; quarter, district, ghetto.

colossal adjective **huge**, massive, enormous, gigantic, giant, mammoth, vast, immense, monumental, prodigious, mountainous, titanic, towering, king-size; informal monster, whopping, humongous, jumbo; Brit. informal ginormous.
– OPPOSITES tiny.

colour noun **1** *a rich brown colour:* **hue**, shade, tint, tone; coloration. **2** *tubes of oil colour:* **paint**, pigment, colourant, dye, stain. **3** *she's got some colour back in her cheeks:* **redness**, pinkness, rosiness, ruddiness, blush, flush, bloom, glow, radiance. **4** *anecdotes add colour to the text:* **vividness**, life, liveliness, vitality, excitement, interest, richness, zest, spice, piquancy, impact, immediacy; informal oomph, pizzazz, punch, kick. **5** *the colours of the Oxford City club:* **strip**, kit, uniform, costume, livery, regalia. **6** *the regimental colours.* See FLAG noun.
• **verb 1** *the wood was coloured blue:* **tint**, dye, stain, paint, bleach. **2** *she coloured with embarrassment:* **blush**, redden, go pink, go red, flush. **3** *the experience coloured her outlook:* **influence**, affect, taint, skew, distort.

WORD LINKS
chromatic relating to colour

colourful adjective **1** *a colourful picture:* **brightly coloured**, vivid, vibrant, brilliant, radiant, rich; gaudy, glaring, garish; multi-coloured, multicolour, rainbow, psychedelic; informal jazzy. **2** *a colourful account:* **vivid**, graphic, lively, animated, dramatic, fascinating, interesting, stimulating, scintillating, evocative.

colourless adjective **1** *a colourless liquid:* **transparent**, clear; translucent. **2** *her colourless face:* **pale**, pallid, wan, anaemic, bloodless, ashen, white, waxen, pasty, sickly, drained, drawn, ghostly, deathly.
– OPPOSITES colourful, rosy.

column noun **1** *arches supported by massive columns:* **pillar**, post, support, upright, pier, pile, pilaster, stanchion. **2** *a column in the paper:* **article**, piece, feature, review, editorial, leader. **3** *we walked in a column:* **line**, file, queue, procession, train, convoy; informal crocodile.

columnist noun **writer**, contributor, journalist, correspondent, newspaperman, newspaperwoman, newsman, newswoman; wordsmith; critic, reviewer, commentator; informal scribbler, hack, journo.

comatose adjective **unconscious**, in a coma, insensible.

comb verb **1** *she combed her hair:* **groom**, brush, untangle, smooth, straighten, neaten, tidy, arrange. **2** *police combed the area:* **search**, scour, hunt through, explore, sweep, examine, check.

combat noun *he was killed in combat:* **battle**, fighting, action, hostilities, conflict, war, warfare.
• verb *they tried to combat the disease:* **fight**, battle, tackle, attack, counter, resist; impede, block; stop, halt, prevent, check, curb.

combative adjective **pugnacious**, aggressive, antagonistic, quarrelsome, argumentative, hostile, truculent, belligerent; informal spoiling for a fight.
– OPPOSITES conciliatory.

combination noun **amalgamation**, amalgam, merger, blend, mixture, mix, fusion, marriage, coalition, integration, incorporation, synthesis, composite.

combine verb **1** *he combines comedy with tragedy:* **amalgamate**, integrate, incorporate, merge, mix, fuse, blend; join, marry. **2** *teachers combined to tackle the problem:* **unite**, collaborate, join forces, get together, team up.

C

combustible adjective **inflammable**, flammable.

come verb **1** *don't come any closer:* **approach**, advance. **2** *they came last night:* **arrive**, get here/there, make it, appear; turn up, materialize; informal show up, roll in/up. **3** *they came to a stream:* **reach**, arrive at, get to; come across, run across, happen on, chance on, come upon, stumble on; end up at; informal wind up at. **4** *the dress comes to her ankles:* **extend**, stretch, reach, hang. **5** *she comes from Belgium:* **be from**, be a native of, hail from, originate in; live in, reside in. **6** *attacks came without warning:* **happen**, occur, take place, come about, fall, present itself, crop up, materialize, arise, arrive, appear.
– OPPOSITES go, leave.
■ **come about** happen, occur, take place, transpire, fall; arise; literary come to pass. **come across** *they came across some of his friends:* meet, run into, run across, come upon, chance on, stumble on, happen on; discover, encounter, find; informal bump into. **come along 1** *the building work is coming along nicely:* progress, make progress, develop, shape up. **2** *come along, I haven't got all day:* hurry up, be quick, get a move on, look lively, speed up; informal get moving, get cracking, step on it, move it, buck up, shake a leg, make it snappy; Brit. informal get your skates on; N. Amer. informal get a wiggle on; dated make haste. **come by** obtain, acquire, gain, get, find, pick up, procure, secure; buy, purchase; informal get your hands on, get hold of, bag, score, swing. **come in for** receive, experience, sustain, undergo, go through, encounter, face, be subjected to, bear, suffer. **come to 1** *the bill came to £17.50:* amount to, add up to, run to, total, equal. **2** *I came to in the hospital:*

regain consciousness, come round, awake, wake up. **come up with** produce, devise, think up; propose, put forward, submit, suggest, recommend, advocate, introduce.

C

comeback noun **return**, recovery, resurgence, rally, upturn; Brit. fightback.

comedian noun **comic**, comedienne, funny man/woman, humorist, stand-up; wit; informal wag.

comedienne noun. See **COMEDIAN**.

comedy noun *the comedy in their work:* **humour**, funny side, laughs, jokes.
–OPPOSITES tragedy.

comfort noun **1** *a rich family who lived in comfort:* **ease**, relaxation, repose; luxury, prosperity, a bed of roses. **2** *she offered words of comfort:* **consolation**, condolence, sympathy, commiseration; support, reassurance, cheer.
•verb *a friend tried to comfort her:* **console**; support, reassure, soothe, calm; cheer, hearten.
–OPPOSITES distress, depress.

comfortable adjective **1** *a comfortable lifestyle:* **pleasant**; affluent, well-to-do, luxurious, opulent. **2** *a comfortable room:* **cosy**, snug, warm, pleasant, agreeable; restful, homely; informal comfy. **3** *comfortable clothes:* **loose**, casual; informal comfy. **4** *a comfortable pace:* **leisurely**, unhurried, relaxed, easy, gentle, sedate, undemanding, slow; informal laid-back. **5** *they feel comfortable with each other:* **at ease**, relaxed, secure, safe, contented, happy.
–OPPOSITES hard, spartan, tense.

comforting adjective **soothing**, reassuring, calming; heartening, cheering.

comic adjective **humorous**, funny, amusing, hilarious; comical; zany; witty.
–OPPOSITES serious.
•noun **comedian**, comedienne, funny man/woman, humorist, wit; joker.

comical adjective **1** *he could be quite comical:* **funny**, humorous, droll, witty, amusing, entertaining; informal wacky, waggish. **2** *they look comical in those suits:* **silly**, absurd, ridiculous, laughable, ludicrous, preposterous, foolish; informal crazy.
–OPPOSITES sensible.

coming adjective *the coming general election:* **forthcoming**, imminent, impending, approaching.
•noun *the coming of spring:* **approach**, advance, advent, arrival, appearance, emergence, onset.

command verb **1** *he commanded his men to retreat:* **order**, tell, direct, instruct, call on, require. **2** *Jones commanded a tank squadron:* **be in charge of**, be in command of; head, lead, control, direct, manage, supervise, oversee; informal head up.
•noun **1** *officers shouted commands:* **order**, instruction, direction. **2** *he had 160 men under his command:* **authority**, control, charge, power, direction, dominion, guidance; leadership, rule, government, management, supervision, jurisdiction. **3** *a brilliant command of English:* **knowledge**, mastery, grasp, comprehension, understanding.

commandeer verb **seize**, take, requisition, appropriate, expropriate, sequestrate, sequester, confiscate, annex, take over, claim; hijack, help yourself to; informal walk off with.

commander noun **leader**, head, chief, overseer, controller; commander-in-chief, C.-in-C., commanding officer, CO, officer; informal boss, boss man, skipper, numero uno, number one, top dog, kingpin, head honcho; Brit. informal gaffer, guv'nor.

commanding adjective **1** *their commanding position:* **dominant**, superior, powerful, prominent, advantageous, favourable. **2** *a commanding voice:* **authoritative**, masterful, assertive, firm, emphatic.

commemorate verb **celebrate**, pay tribute to, pay homage to, honour, salute, toast; remember, recognize, acknowledge, observe, mark.

commence verb **begin**, start; get the ball rolling, get going, get under way, get off the ground, set about, embark on, launch into; open, initiate, inaugurate; informal kick off, get the show on the road.
–OPPOSITES conclude.

commencement noun **beginning**, start, opening, outset, onset, launch, inception; informal kick-off.

commend verb **1** *we should commend him:* **praise**, compliment,

congratulate, applaud, salute, honour; sing the praises of, pay tribute to, take your hat off to, pat on the back. **2** *I commend her to you without reservation:* **recommend**; endorse, vouch for, speak for, support, back. **3** (formal) *I commend them to your care:* **entrust**, trust, deliver, commit, hand over, give, turn over, consign, assign.
– OPPOSITES criticize.

commendable adjective **admirable**, praiseworthy, creditable, laudable, estimable, meritorious, exemplary, noteworthy, honourable, respectable, fine, excellent.
– OPPOSITES reprehensible.

commendation noun **1** *letters of commendation:* **praise**, congratulation, appreciation; recognition, tribute. **2** *a commendation for bravery:* **award**, prize, honour, citation.

commensurate adjective *a salary that is commensurate with your qualifications:* **appropriate to**, in keeping with, in line with, consistent with, corresponding to, according to, relative to; dependent on, based on.

comment noun **1** *their comments on her appearance:* **remark**, observation, statement; pronouncement, judgement, reflection, opinion, view; criticism. **2** *a great deal of comment:* **discussion**, debate; interest. **3** *a comment in the margin:* **note**, annotation, footnote, gloss, explanation.
• verb **1** *they commented on the food:* **remark on**, speak about, talk about, discuss, mention. **2** *'It will soon be night,' he commented:* **remark**, observe, say, state, declare, announce.

commentary noun **1** *the test match commentary:* **narration**, description, report, review. **2** *textual commentary:* **explanation**, elucidation, interpretation, exegesis, analysis; assessment, appraisal, criticism; notes, comments.

commentator noun **1** *a television commentator:* **narrator**, announcer, presenter, anchor, anchorman, anchorwoman; reporter, journalist, newscaster, sportscaster. **2** *a political commentator:* **analyst**, pundit, monitor, observer.

commerce noun **trade**, trading, business, dealing, traffic; financial transactions, dealings.

commercial adjective **1** *a vessel built for commercial purposes:* **trade**, trading, business, private enterprise, mercantile, sales. **2** *we turn good ideas into commercial products:* **lucrative**, moneymaking, money-spinning, profitable, remunerative, fruitful; viable, successful.
• noun *a TV commercial:* **advertisement**, promotion, display; informal ad, plug; Brit. informal advert.

commercialized adjective **profit-orientated**, money-orientated, commercial, materialistic, mercenary.

commiserate verb **sympathize**, offer your condolences, offer your sympathies; comfort, console.

commiseration noun **condolences**, sympathy, pity.

commission noun **1** *the dealer's commission:* **percentage**, share, portion, dividend, premium, fee, bonus; informal cut, take, rake-off, slice; Brit. informal whack, divvy. **2** *a commission to design a monument:* **contract**, engagement, assignment, booking; appointment, job. **3** *an independent commission:* **committee**, board, council, panel, body.
• verb **1** *he was commissioned to paint a portrait:* **engage**, contract, charge, employ, hire, recruit, retain, appoint, enlist, co-opt, book, sign up. **2** *they commissioned a sculpture:* **order**; authorize.
■ **out of commission** not in service, not in use, unserviceable; not working, inoperative, out of order; broken; informal knackered.

commit verb **1** *he committed a terrible crime:* **carry out**, do, perpetrate, engage in, execute; be responsible for, be guilty of. **2** *the EU has committed to support the government:* **pledge**, guarantee, promise, contract, undertake; vow. **3** *they have committed substantial funds to the project:* **set aside**, allocate, give, earmark; pledge, devote, dedicate; spend **4** *she was committed to their care:* **entrust**, consign, assign, deliver, give, hand

C

over, relinquish; formal commend. **5** *the judge committed him to prison:* **consign**, send, deliver.

commitment noun **1** *the pressure of his commitments:* **responsibility**, obligation, duty, tie, liability; task; engagement, arrangement. **2** *her commitment to her students:* **dedication**, devotion, allegiance, loyalty, faithfulness, fidelity. **3** *he made a commitment:* **vow**, promise, pledge, oath; contract, pact, deal; decision, resolution.

committed adjective **devout**, devoted, dedicated, loyal, faithful, staunch, firm, steadfast, unwavering, wholehearted, keen, passionate, ardent, fervent, sworn; informal card-carrying, true blue.
– OPPOSITES apathetic.

commodity noun **item**, material, product, article, object; import, export.

common adjective **1** *a very common occurrence:* **familiar**, ordinary, normal, routine, usual, regular, frequent, recurrent, everyday; standard, typical, conventional, commonplace, unexceptional, run-of-the-mill. **2** *a common belief:* **widespread**, general, universal, popular, prevalent, prevailing, rife, established, conventional, traditional, orthodox, accepted. **3** *the common good:* **collective**, communal, community, public, popular, general; shared, combined. **4** *they're so common:* **uncouth**, vulgar, coarse, rough, unladylike, ungentlemanly, uncivilized, unsophisticated, unrefined.
– OPPOSITES unusual, rare, uncommon, refined.

commonly adverb **often**, frequently, regularly, repeatedly, time and time again, all the time, routinely, habitually, customarily; N. Amer. oftentimes; informal lots.

commonplace adjective **1** *a commonplace occurrence:* **common**, normal, usual, ordinary, familiar, routine, standard, everyday, daily, regular, frequent, habitual, typical. **2** *a commonplace writing style:* **ordinary**, unremarkable, run-of-the-mill, unexceptional, average, mediocre, pedestrian, prosaic, lacklustre, dull, bland, uninteresting, mundane; hackneyed, trite, banal, clichéd, predictable, stale, tired, unoriginal; informal bog-standard, a dime a dozen; Brit. informal common or garden; N. Amer. informal bush-league.
– OPPOSITES original, unusual.

common sense noun **sense**, good sense, wit, judgement, level-headedness, prudence, discernment, astuteness, shrewdness, wisdom, insight, perception; practicality, capability, resourcefulness, enterprise; informal horse sense, gumption, nous, savvy; Brit. informal common; N. Amer. informal smarts.
– OPPOSITES folly.

commotion noun **disturbance**, uproar, tumult, rumpus, ruckus, furore, hue and cry, fuss, stir, storm; turmoil, disorder, confusion, chaos, mayhem, havoc, pandemonium; unrest, fracas, riot; Brit. row; Irish, N. Amer., & Austral. donnybrook; informal ructions, ballyhoo, kerfuffle, hoo-ha, to-do, hullabaloo; Brit. informal carry-on, argy-bargy.

communal adjective **1** *a communal kitchen:* **shared**, joint, common. **2** *they farm on a communal basis:* **collective**, cooperative, community.
– OPPOSITES private, individual.

commune noun *she lives in a commune:* **collective**, cooperative, kibbutz.
• verb **communicate**, be in contact, make contact; speak, talk.

communicable adjective **contagious**, infectious, transmittable, transmissible, transferable, spreadable; informal catching.

communicate verb **1** *he communicated the news to his boss:* **convey**, tell, impart, relay, transmit, pass on, announce, report, recount, relate, present; divulge, disclose, mention; spread, disseminate, broadcast. **2** *they communicate daily:* **liaise**, be in touch, be in contact, have dealings, interface, commune, meet; talk, speak. **3** *learn how to communicate better:* **get your message across**, explain yourself, express yourself, make yourself understood, get through to someone. **4** *the disease is communicated easily:* **transmit**, transfer, spread, carry, pass on.

communication noun **1** *the communication of news:* **transmission**, divulgence, disclosure; dissemination, promulgation, broadcasting. **2** *there was no communication between them:* **contact**, dealings, relations, connection, association, socializing, intercourse; correspondence, dialogue, talk, conversation, discussion; dated commerce. **3** *an official communication:* **message**, statement, announcement, report, dispatch, communiqué, letter, bulletin, correspondence. **4** *road and rail communications:* **links**, connections; services, routes; systems, networks.

communicative adjective **forthcoming**, expansive, expressive, unreserved, uninhibited, vocal, outgoing, frank, open, candid; talkative, chatty, loquacious; informal gabby.

communion noun **affinity**, fellowship, kinship, friendship, fellow feeling, togetherness, closeness, harmony, understanding, rapport, connection, communication, empathy, accord, unity.

communiqué noun **communication**, press release, bulletin, message, missive, dispatch, statement, report, announcement, declaration, proclamation; N. Amer. advisory; informal memo.

communism noun **collectivism**, state ownership; Bolshevism, Marxism, Maoism.

communist noun & adjective **collectivist**, leftist; Bolshevik, Bolshevist, Marxist, Maoist; informal, derogatory Commie, Bolshie, red, lefty; dated Soviet.

community noun **1** *work done for the community:* **population**, populace, people, citizenry, general public; residents, inhabitants, citizens. **2** *a monastic community:* **brotherhood**, fraternity; colony, order. **3** *a community of interests:* **similarity**, likeness, comparability, correspondence, agreement, closeness, affinity.

commute verb **1** *he commutes from Corby to Kentish Town:* **travel back and forth**, shuttle; informal straphang. **2** *his sentence was commuted:* **reduce**, lessen, lighten, shorten, cut.

compact[1] adjective **neat**, small, handy, petite; fiddly; pocket size, mini, bijou; Scottish wee; Brit. informal dinky.
– OPPOSITES bulky.
• verb **compress**, condense, pack down, press down, tamp down, flatten.

compact[2] noun *the warring states signed a compact:* **treaty**, pact, accord, agreement, contract, bargain, deal, settlement, covenant, concordat.

companion noun **1** *Harry and his companion:* **associate**, partner, escort; friend, intimate, confidant, confidante; compatriot, comrade; informal pal, chum, crony, sidekick; Brit. informal mate; N. Amer. informal buddy. **2** *the tape is a companion to the book:* **complement**; accompaniment, supplement, addition, adjunct, accessory. **3** *The Gardener's Companion:* **handbook**, manual, guide, reference book, ABC, primer; informal bible.

companionable adjective **friendly**, affable, cordial, genial, congenial, amiable, easy-going, good-natured; sociable, convivial, outgoing, gregarious; informal chummy, pally; Brit. informal matey; N. Amer. informal clubby.

companionship noun **friendship**, fellowship, closeness, togetherness, amity, intimacy, rapport, camaraderie, brotherhood, sisterhood.

company noun **1** *an oil company:* **firm**, business, corporation, establishment, agency, office, bureau, institution, organization, concern, enterprise; conglomerate, consortium, syndicate, multinational; informal outfit. **2** *I enjoy his company:* **companionship**, friendship, fellowship; society. **3** *I'm expecting company:* **guests**, visitors, callers, people; someone. **4** *a company of poets:* **group**, crowd, party, band, assembly, troupe, throng; informal bunch, gang. **5** *a company of infantry:* **unit**, section, detachment, corps, squad, platoon.

WORD LINKS
corporate relating to a company or business

C

C

comparable adjective **1** *comparable incomes:* **similar**, close, near, approximate, equivalent, commensurate, proportional, proportionate; like, matching. **2** *nobody is comparable with him:* **equal to**, as good as, in the same league as, able to hold a candle to, on a par with, on a level with; a match for.

compare verb **1** *we compared the two portraits:* **contrast**; examine, assess, weigh up. **2** *he was compared to Wagner:* **liken**, equate; class with, bracket with. **3** *the porcelain compares with Dresden china:* **be as good as**, be comparable to, bear comparison with, be the equal of, match up to, be on a par with, be in the same league as, come close to, hold a candle to; match, resemble, rival, approach.
■ **beyond compare** without equal, second to none, in a class of its own; peerless, matchless, unmatched, incomparable, inimitable, outstanding, consummate, unique, singular, perfect.

comparison noun *there's no comparison between them:* **resemblance**, likeness, similarity, correspondence.

compartment noun **section**, part, recess, chamber, cavity; pocket.

compartmentalize verb **categorize**, pigeonhole, bracket, group, classify, characterize, stereotype, label, brand; sort, rank, rate.

compass noun **scope**, range, extent, reach, span, breadth, ambit, limits, parameters, bounds.

compassion noun **pity**, sympathy, empathy, fellow feeling, care, concern, solicitude, sensitivity, warmth, love, tenderness, mercy, leniency, tolerance, kindness, humanity, charity.
– OPPOSITES indifference, cruelty.

compassionate adjective **sympathetic**, empathetic, understanding, caring, sensitive, warm, loving; merciful, lenient, tolerant, considerate, kind, humane, charitable, big-hearted.

compatibility noun **like-mindedness**, similarity, affinity, closeness, fellow feeling, harmony, rapport, empathy, sympathy.

compatible adjective **well suited**, well matched, like-minded, in tune, in harmony; informal on the same wavelength.

compatriot noun **fellow citizen**, fellow countryman/woman, comrade.

compel verb **force**, pressurize, pressure, press, push; oblige, require, make; informal lean on, put the screws on.

compelling adjective **1** *a compelling lead performance:* **enthralling**, captivating, gripping, riveting, spellbinding, mesmerizing, absorbing. **2** *a compelling argument:* **convincing**, persuasive, cogent, irresistible, powerful, strong.
– OPPOSITES boring, weak.

compendium noun **collection**, compilation, anthology, digest.

compensate verb **1** *we agreed to compensate him for his loss:* **recompense**, repay, pay back, reimburse, remunerate, recoup, indemnify. **2** *his flair compensated for his faults:* **balance out**, counterbalance, counteract, offset, make up for, cancel out.

compensation noun **recompense**, repayment, reimbursement, remuneration, indemnification, indemnity, redress; damages; N. Amer. informal comp.

compère noun **host**, presenter, anchor, anchorman/woman, master of ceremonies, MC, announcer; N. Amer. informal emcee.

compete verb **1** *they competed in a tennis tournament:* **take part**, participate, play, be involved; enter, go in for. **2** *they had to compete with other firms:* **contend**, vie, battle, jockey, go head to head, pit yourself against; challenge, take on. **3** *no one can compete with him:* **rival**, challenge, keep up with, keep pace with, compare with, match, be in the same league as, come near to, come close to, touch; informal hold a candle to.

competence noun **1** *my technical competence:* **capability**, ability, competency, proficiency, accomplishment, expertise, skill, prowess, talent; informal savvy, know-how. **2** *the competence of the system:* **adequacy**, suitability, fitness; effectiveness; formal efficacy. **3** *matters within the competence of the courts:* **authority**, power, control, jurisdiction, ambit, scope, remit.

competent adjective **1** *a competent carpenter:* **capable**, able, proficient, adept, accomplished, complete, skilful, skilled, gifted, talented, expert; good. **2** *the court was not competent to hear the case:* **fit**, suitable, suited, appropriate; qualified, empowered, authorized.
– OPPOSITES incompetent, unfit.

competition noun **1** *she won the competition by one point:* **contest**, tournament, match, game, heat, fixture, event; trial. **2** *I'm not interested in competition:* **rivalry**, competitiveness; conflict; informal keeping up with the Joneses. **3** *we must stay ahead of the competition:* **opposition**, other side, field; enemy; informal other guy; literary foe.

competitive adjective **1** *a very competitive player:* **ambitious**, zealous, keen, combative, aggressive; informal go-ahead. **2** *a highly competitive industry:* **ruthless**, aggressive, fierce; informal dog-eat-dog, cut-throat. **3** *competitive prices:* **reasonable**, moderate, keen; low, inexpensive, cheap, budget, bargain; rock-bottom, bargain-basement.
– OPPOSITES apathetic, exorbitant.

competitor noun **1** *the competitors in the race:* **contestant**, contender, challenger, participant, entrant; runner, player. **2** *our European competitors:* **rival**, challenger, opponent, adversary; competition, opposition.
– OPPOSITES ally.

compilation noun **collection**, selection, anthology, compendium, corpus.

compile verb **assemble**, put together, make up, collate, compose, organize, arrange; gather, collect.

complacency noun **smugness**, self-satisfaction, self-congratulation, self-regard.

complacent adjective **smug**, self-satisfied, self-congratulatory, self-regarding.

complain verb **protest**, grumble, whine, bleat, carp, cavil, grouse, make a fuss, object, speak out, criticize, find fault; informal whinge, gripe, bellyache, moan, beef, bitch, sound off; Brit. informal create; N. Amer. informal kvetch.

complaint noun **1** *they lodged a complaint:* **protest**, objection, grievance, grouse, quibble, grumble; charge, accusation, allegation, criticism; informal beef, gripe, whinge. **2** *a kidney complaint:* **disorder**, disease, infection, illness, ailment, sickness; condition, problem, upset, trouble; informal bug, virus.

complement noun **1** *the perfect complement to the food:* **accompaniment**, companion, addition, supplement, accessory. **2** *a full complement of lifeboats:* **amount**, contingent, capacity, allowance, quota.
• verb *her accessories complement her outfit perfectly:* **accompany**, go with, round off, set off, suit, harmonize with; enhance, complete.

> ! Don't confuse **complement** with **compliment**, which means 'politely congratulate or praise' (*I complimented her on her appearance*).

complementary adjective *complementary furnishings and decoration:* **harmonious**, compatible, corresponding, matching; reciprocal.
– OPPOSITES incompatible.

> ! Don't confuse **complementary** with **complimentary**, which means 'praising' (*complimentary reviews*), or 'given free of charge' (*a complimentary bottle of wine*).

complete adjective **1** *the complete interview:* **entire**, whole, full, total; uncut, unabridged, unexpurgated. **2** *their research was complete:* **finished**, ended, concluded, completed; discharged, settled, done; informal wrapped up, sewn up. **3** *a complete fool:* **absolute**, out-and-out, utter, total, real, downright, thoroughgoing, veritable, prize, perfect, unqualified, unmitigated, sheer; N. Amer. full-bore; Brit. informal right.
– OPPOSITES partial, unfinished.
• verb **1** *he had to complete his training:* **finish**, end, conclude,

finalize, wind up; informal wrap up. **2** *the outfit was completed with a veil:* **finish off**, round off, top off, crown, cap. **3** *complete the application form:* **fill in/out**, answer.

C

completely adverb **totally**, entirely, wholly, thoroughly, fully, utterly, absolutely, perfectly, unreservedly, unconditionally, quite, altogether, downright; in every way, in every respect, one hundred per cent, every inch, to the hilt.

completion noun **realization**, accomplishment, achievement, fulfilment, consummation, finalization, resolution; finish, end, conclusion.

complex adjective **1** *a complex situation:* **complicated**, involved, intricate, convoluted, elaborate; difficult, knotty, tricky, thorny; Brit. informal fiddly. **2** *a complex structure:* **compound**, composite, multiplex.
–OPPOSITES simple.
•noun **1** *a complex of roads:* **network**, system, nexus, web. **2** (informal) *he had a complex about losing his hair:* **obsession**, fixation, preoccupation; neurosis; informal hang-up, thing, bee in your bonnet.

complexion noun **1** *a very pale complexion:* **skin**, skin colour/tone. **2** *governments of all complexions:* **type**, kind, sort; colour, persuasion.

complexity noun **complication**, problem, difficulty, intricacy.

compliance noun **1** *compliance with international law:* **obedience to**, observance of, adherence to, conformity to, respect for. **2** *he mistook her silence for compliance:* **acquiescence**, agreement, assent, consent, acceptance.
–OPPOSITES violation, defiance.

compliant adjective **acquiescent**, amenable, biddable, tractable, accommodating, cooperative; obedient, docile, malleable, pliable; submissive, tame.
–OPPOSITES recalcitrant.

complicate verb *other factors are complicating the issue:* **make more difficult**, make matters worse, mix up, confuse, muddle, obscure, obfuscate.
–OPPOSITES simplify.

complicated adjective **complex**, intricate, involved, convoluted, tangled, impenetrable, knotty, tricky, thorny, labyrinthine, tortuous; confusing, bewildering, perplexing; Brit. informal fiddly.
–OPPOSITES straightforward.

complication noun **1** *a complication concerning ownership:* **difficulty**, problem, obstacle, hurdle, stumbling block; drawback, snag, catch, hitch; Brit. spanner in the works; informal headache. **2** *the complication of life in our society:* **complexity**, complicatedness, intricacy, convolutedness.

complicity noun **collusion**, involvement, collaboration, connivance; conspiracy.

compliment noun **1** *an unexpected compliment:* **tribute**, accolade, commendation, pat on the back; (**compliments**) praise, acclaim, congratulations, admiration, flattery, blandishments. **2** *she sends her compliments:* **greetings**, regards, respects, good wishes, best wishes.
–OPPOSITES insult.
•verb *they complimented his performance:* **praise**, pay tribute to, speak highly/well of, flatter, wax lyrical about, make much of, commend, acclaim, applaud, salute; congratulate.
–OPPOSITES criticize.

> ! Don't confuse **compliment** and **complement**. As a verb, **complement** means 'add to in a way that improves' (*her accessories complement her outfit perfectly*).

complimentary adjective **1** *complimentary remarks:* **flattering**, appreciative, congratulatory, admiring, approving, commendatory, favourable, glowing, adulatory. **2** *complimentary tickets:* **free**, gratis, for nothing; courtesy; informal on the house.
–OPPOSITES derogatory.

> ! Don't confuse **complimentary** with **complementary**, which means 'combining to form a whole or to improve each other'.

comply verb *Myra complied with his wishes:* **abide by**, observe, obey, adhere to, conform to, follow, respect; agree to, assent to, go along with, yield to, submit to, defer to.
–OPPOSITES ignore, disobey.

component noun **part**, piece, bit, element, constituent, ingredient; unit, module, section.
•adjective **constituent**; basic, essential.

compose verb **1** *a poem composed by Shelley:* **write**, devise, make up, think up, produce, invent, concoct; pen, author. **2** *composing a photograph is like painting a picture:* **organize**, arrange, set out. **3** *the congress is composed of ten senators:* **make up**, constitute, form, comprise.
■ **compose yourself** calm down, control yourself, regain your composure, pull yourself together, steady yourself, keep your head; informal get a grip, keep your cool; N. Amer. informal decompress.

composed adjective **calm**, collected, cool, self-controlled, self-possessed; serene, tranquil, relaxed, at ease, unruffled, unperturbed, poised, untroubled; equable, even-tempered, imperturbable; informal unflappable, together, laid-back.
–OPPOSITES excited.

composer noun melodist, symphonist, songwriter, songster; informal tunesmith, songsmith.

composite adjective **compound**, complex; combined, blended, mixed.
•noun **amalgamation**, amalgam, combination, compound, fusion, synthesis, mixture, blend; alloy.

composition noun **1** *the composition of the council:* **make-up**, constitution, configuration, structure, formation, form, fabric, anatomy, organization; informal set-up. **2** *a literary composition:* **work of art**, creation, opus, piece. **3** *the composition of a poem:* **writing**, creation, formulation, compilation. **4** *a school composition:* **essay**, paper, study, piece of writing; N. Amer. theme. **5** *the composition of the painting:* **arrangement**, layout; proportions, balance, symmetry.

composure noun **self-control**, self-possession, calm, equanimity, equilibrium, serenity, tranquillity; poise, presence of mind, sangfroid, placidness, impassivity; informal cool.

compound noun **amalgamation**, combination, composite, amalgam, blend, mixture, mix, fusion, synthesis.
•adjective *a compound substance:* **composite**, complex.
–OPPOSITES simple.
•verb **1** *a smell compounded of dust and mould:* **be composed of**, be made up of, be formed from. **2** *his illness compounds their problems:* **aggravate**, exacerbate, worsen, add to, augment, intensify, heighten, increase.
–OPPOSITES alleviate.

comprehend verb **understand**, grasp, take in, apprehend, follow, make sense of, fathom; informal work out, figure out, make head or tail of, get your head around, take on board, get the drift of, catch on to, get; Brit. informal twig, suss.

comprehensible adjective **intelligible**, understandable, accessible; lucid, coherent, clear, plain, straightforward.
–OPPOSITES opaque.

comprehension noun **understanding**, grasp, conception, apprehension, cognition, ken, knowledge, awareness.
–OPPOSITES ignorance.

comprehensive adjective **inclusive**, all-inclusive, complete; thorough, full, extensive, all-embracing, exhaustive, detailed, in-depth, encyclopedic, universal; radical, sweeping, across the board, wholesale; broad, wide-ranging; informal wall-to-wall.
–OPPOSITES limited.

compress verb **squeeze**, press, squash, crush, compact; informal scrunch.
–OPPOSITES expand.

comprise verb **1** *the country comprises twenty states:* **consist of**, be made up of, be composed of, contain, encompass, incorporate; include. **2** *this breed comprises half the herd:* **make up**, constitute, form, compose; account for.

compromise noun *they reached a compromise:* **agreement**, understanding, settlement, terms, deal, trade-off, bargain; middle ground, happy medium, balance.
–OPPOSITES intransigence.
•verb **1** *we compromised:* **meet each other halfway**, come to an

C

understanding, make a deal, make concessions, find a happy medium, strike a balance. **2** *his actions could compromise his reputation:* **undermine**, weaken, damage, harm; jeopardize, prejudice.

compulsion noun **1** *he is under no compulsion to go:* **obligation**, duress, pressure. **2** *a compulsion to tell the truth:* **urge**, impulse, need, desire, drive; obsession, fixation, addiction.

compulsive adjective **1** *a compulsive desire:* **irresistible**, uncontrollable, compelling, overwhelming, urgent. **2** *compulsive eating:* **obsessive**, obsessional, addictive, uncontrollable. **3** *a compulsive liar:* **inveterate**, chronic, incorrigible, incurable, hopeless, persistent, habitual; informal pathological. **4** *it's compulsive viewing:* **fascinating**, compelling, gripping, riveting, engrossing, enthralling, captivating.

compulsory adjective **obligatory**, mandatory, required, requisite, necessary, essential; imperative, unavoidable, enforced, prescribed.
– OPPOSITES optional.

compunction noun **scruples**, misgivings, qualms, worries, unease, doubts, reluctance, reservations.

compute verb **calculate**, work out, reckon, determine, evaluate, quantify; add up, count up, tally, total; Brit. tot up.

comrade noun **companion**, friend; colleague, associate, partner, co-worker, workmate; informal pal, chum, crony; Brit. informal mate; N. Amer. informal buddy.

con (informal) verb & noun. See SWINDLE.

concave adjective hollow, depressed, sunken; indented, recessed; curved.
– OPPOSITES convex.

conceal verb **1** *clouds concealed the sun:* **hide**, screen, cover, obscure, block out, blot out, mask, shroud. **2** *he concealed his true feelings:* **hide**, cover up, disguise, mask, veil; keep secret; suppress, repress, bottle up; informal keep a/the lid on.
– OPPOSITES reveal, confess.

concealed adjective **hidden**, out of sight, invisible, covered, disguised, camouflaged, obscured; private, secret.

concealment noun **1** *the concealment of the bushes:* **cover**, shelter, protection, screen; privacy, seclusion; secrecy. **2** *the deliberate concealment of facts:* **suppression**, hiding, covering up, hushing up.

concede verb **1** *I had to concede that I'd overreacted:* **admit**, acknowledge, accept, allow, grant, recognize, own, confess; agree. **2** *he eventually conceded the title to Ali:* **surrender**, yield, give up, relinquish, hand over.
– OPPOSITES deny, retain.

■ **concede defeat** capitulate, admit defeat, give in, surrender, yield, give up, submit, raise the white flag; back down, climb down, throw in the towel.

conceit noun **1** *his extraordinary conceit:* **vanity**, narcissism, conceitedness, egotism, self-admiration, self-regard; pride, arrogance, self-importance; informal big-headedness. **2** *the conceits of Shakespeare's verse:* **image**, imagery, metaphor, simile, trope.
– OPPOSITES humility.

conceited adjective **vain**, narcissistic, self-centred, egotistic, egocentric; proud, arrogant, boastful, full of yourself, self-important, immodest; self-satisfied; supercilious, haughty, snobbish; informal big-headed, too big for your boots, stuck-up, high and mighty.

conceivable adjective **imaginable**, possible; plausible, credible, believable, feasible.

conceive verb **1** *the project was conceived in 1977:* **think up**, think of, dream up, devise, formulate, design, originate, create, develop; hatch; informal cook up. **2** *I could hardly conceive what it must be like:* **imagine**, envisage, visualize, picture, think; grasp, appreciate.

concentrate verb **1** *the government concentrated its efforts on staying in power:* **focus**, direct, centre. **2** *she was concentrating on the film:* **focus on**, pay attention to, keep your mind on, devote yourself to; be absorbed in, be engrossed in, be immersed in. **3** *troops concentrated on the horizon:* **collect**, gather, congregate, converge, mass, rally. **4** *the liquid is filtered and concentrated:* **condense**, boil down, reduce.
– OPPOSITES disperse, dilute.

• noun *a fruit concentrate:* **extract**, distillation.

concentrated adjective **1** *a concentrated effort:* **strenuous**, concerted, intensive, all-out, intense. **2** *a concentrated solution:* **condensed**, reduced; undiluted; strong.
– OPPOSITES half-hearted, diluted.

concentration noun **1** *a task requiring concentration:* **close attention**, attentiveness, application, single-mindedness, absorption. **2** *the concentration of effort:* **focusing**, centralization. **3** *a high concentration of sodium:* **density**, level; presence; amount, volume.
– OPPOSITES inattention.

concept noun **idea**, notion, conception, abstraction; theory, hypothesis.

conception noun **1** *the fertility treatment resulted in conception:* pregnancy, fertilization, impregnation, insemination. **2** *the product's conception:* **inception**, genesis, origination, creation, invention; beginning, origin. **3** *his original conception:* **plan**, scheme, project, proposal; intention, aim, idea. **4** *my conception of democracy:* **idea**, concept, notion, understanding; perception, image, impression. **5** *they had no real conception of our problems:* **understanding**, comprehension, appreciation, grasp, knowledge; idea, inkling; informal clue.

concern verb **1** *the report concerns the war:* **be about**, deal with, cover; relate to, pertain to. **2** *that doesn't concern you:* **affect**, involve, be relevant to, apply to, have a bearing on, impact on; be important to, interest. **3** *one thing still concerns me:* **worry**, disturb, trouble, bother, perturb, unsettle.
• noun **1** *her voice was full of concern:* **anxiety**, worry, disquiet, apprehensiveness, unease, consternation. **2** *his concern for others:* **solicitude**, consideration, care, sympathy, regard. **3** *housing is the concern of the council:* **responsibility**, business, affair, charge, duty, job; province, preserve; problem, worry; informal bailiwick; Brit. informal lookout. **4** *issues of concern to women:* **interest**, importance, relevance, significance. **5** *a publishing concern:* **company**, business, firm, organization, operation, corporation, establishment, house, office, agency; informal outfit, set-up.
– OPPOSITES indifference.

concerned adjective **1** *her mother looked concerned:* **worried**, anxious, upset, perturbed, troubled, uneasy, apprehensive. **2** *all concerned parties:* **interested**, involved, affected; connected, related, implicated.

concerning preposition **about**, regarding, relating to, with reference to, referring to, with regard to, as regards, with respect to, respecting, dealing with, on the subject of, in connection with, re, apropos.

concert noun **performance**, show, production; recital; informal gig.
■ **in concert** together, jointly, in combination, in collaboration, in cooperation, in league, side by side; in unison.

concerted adjective **1** *a concerted effort:* **strenuous**, vigorous, intensive, all-out, intense, concentrated. **2** *concerted action:* **joint**, united, collaborative, collective, combined, cooperative.
– OPPOSITES half-hearted, individual.

concession noun **1** *the government had to make several concessions:* **compromise**; sop. **2** *tax concessions:* **reduction**, cut, discount, deduction, decrease; rebate; informal break. **3** *a logging concession:* **right**, privilege; licence, permit, franchise, warrant.

conciliate verb **1** *he tried to conciliate the workforce:* **appease**, placate, pacify, mollify, assuage, soothe, win over, make peace with. **2** *he conciliated in the dispute:* **mediate**, act as peacemaker, arbitrate.
– OPPOSITES provoke.

conciliator noun **peacemaker**, mediator, go-between, middleman, intermediary.
– OPPOSITES troublemaker.

conciliatory adjective **propitiatory**, placatory, appeasing, pacifying, mollifying, peacemaking.

concise adjective **succinct**, pithy, incisive, brief, short and to the point, short and sweet;

C

abridged, condensed, compressed, abbreviated, compact, potted; informal snappy.
– OPPOSITES lengthy, wordy.

C

conclude verb **1** *the meeting concluded at ten:* **finish**, end, draw to a close, stop, cease. **2** *he concluded the press conference:* **bring to an end**, close, wind up, terminate, dissolve; round off; informal wrap up. **3** *an attempt to conclude a deal:* **negotiate**, broker, agree, come to terms on, settle, clinch, finalize, tie up; bring about, arrange, effect, engineer. **4** *I concluded that he was rather unpleasant:* **deduce**, infer, gather, judge, decide, conjecture, surmise; N. Amer. figure.
– OPPOSITES commence.

conclusion noun **1** *the conclusion of his speech:* **end**, ending, finish, close. **2** *the conclusion of a trade agreement:* **negotiation**, brokering, settlement, completion, arrangement, resolution. **3** *his conclusions have been verified:* **deduction**, inference, interpretation, judgement, verdict.
– OPPOSITES beginning.
■ **in conclusion** finally, in closing, to conclude, last but not least; to sum up.

conclusive adjective **1** *conclusive proof of guilt:* **incontrovertible**, undeniable, indisputable, irrefutable, unquestionable, convincing, certain, decisive, definitive, definite, positive, categorical, unequivocal. **2** *a conclusive win:* **emphatic**, resounding, convincing; decisive.
– OPPOSITES unconvincing.

concoct verb **1** *this story she has concocted:* **make up**, dream up, fabricate, invent; formulate, hatch, brew; informal cook up. **2** *she concocted a salad:* **put together**, assemble; informal fix, rustle up; Brit. informal knock up, throw together.

concoction noun **1** *a concoction containing gin and vodka:* **mixture**, brew, preparation, potion. **2** *a strange concoction of styles:* **blend**, mixture, mix, combination, hybrid. **3** *her story is an improbable concoction:* **fabrication**, invention, falsification; informal fairy story, fairy tale.

concord noun (formal) **1** *council meetings rarely ended in concord:* **agreement**, harmony, accord, consensus, concurrence, unity. **2** *a concord was to be drawn up:* **treaty**, agreement, accord, pact, compact, settlement.
– OPPOSITES discord.

concourse noun **entrance**, foyer, lobby, hall.

concrete adjective **1** *concrete objects:* **solid**, material, real, physical, tangible, palpable, substantial. **2** *concrete proof:* **definite**, firm, positive, conclusive, definitive; real, genuine, bona fide.
– OPPOSITES abstract, imaginary.

concur verb **1** *we concur with this view:* **agree**, be in agreement, go along, fall in, be in sympathy; see eye to eye, be of the same mind, be of the same opinion. **2** *the two events concurred:* **coincide**, be simultaneous, co-occur.
– OPPOSITES disagree.

concurrent adjective **simultaneous**, contemporaneous, parallel.

condemn verb **1** *he condemned the suspended player's actions:* **censure**, criticize, denounce, deplore, revile, attack; informal slam, hit out at; Brit. informal slate. **2** *he was condemned to death:* **sentence**. **3** *his illness condemned him to a lonely childhood:* **doom**, destine, damn; consign, assign.
– OPPOSITES praise.

condemnation noun **censure**, criticism, denunciation, vilification; informal flak, a bad press.

condense verb **1** *the water vapour condenses:* **precipitate**, liquefy, become liquid; deliquesce. **2** *he condensed the story into a few paragraphs:* **abridge**, shorten, cut, abbreviate, edit.
– OPPOSITES vaporize, expand.

condensed adjective **1** *a condensed text:* **abridged**, shortened, cut, compressed, abbreviated, reduced, truncated, concise; informal potted. **2** *condensed soup:* **concentrated**, evaporated, reduced; strong, undiluted.
– OPPOSITES diluted.

condescend verb **1** *don't condescend to your reader:* **patronize**, talk down to, look down your nose at, look down on. **2** *he condescended to see us:* **deign**, stoop, lower yourself, demean yourself, consent.

condescending adjective **patronizing**, supercilious, superior, disdainful, lofty, haughty; informal snooty, stuck-up; Brit. informal toffee-nosed.

condition noun **1** *they are in excellent condition:* **state**, shape, order; health, fitness, form Brit. informal nick. **2** *they lived in appalling conditions:* **circumstances**, surroundings, environment, situation, set-up; habitat. **3** *a liver condition:* **disorder**, problem, complaint, illness, disease, ailment, sickness, affliction, infection, upset; informal bug, virus. **4** *a condition of employment:* **stipulation**, constraint, prerequisite, precondition, requirement, rule, term, specification, provision, proviso.
• verb **1** *their choices are conditioned by the economy:* **constrain**, control, govern, determine, decide; influence, affect, shape. **2** *our minds are conditioned by habit:* **train**, teach, educate, guide; accustom, adapt, habituate, mould. **3** *a product for conditioning leather:* **treat**, prepare, prime, process, season; improve, nourish.

conditional adjective **1** *their approval is conditional on success:* **subject to**, dependent on, contingent on, based on, determined by, controlled by, tied to. **2** *a conditional offer:* **qualified**, dependent, contingent, with reservations, limited, provisional, provisory.

condolences plural noun **sympathy**, commiserations.

condone verb **disregard**, accept, allow, let pass, turn a blind eye to, overlook, forget; forgive, pardon, excuse, let go.
– OPPOSITES condemn.

conducive adjective **favourable**, beneficial, advantageous, opportune, encouraging, promising, convenient, good, helpful, instrumental, productive, useful.
– OPPOSITES unfavourable.

conduct noun **1** *they complained about her conduct:* **behaviour**, performance; actions, activities, deeds, doings, exploits; habits, manners. **2** *the conduct of the elections:* **management**, running, direction, control, supervision, regulation, administration, organization, coordination, handling.
• verb **1** *the election was conducted lawfully:* **manage**, direct, run, administer, organize, coordinate, orchestrate, handle, control, oversee, supervise, regulate, carry out/on. **2** *he was conducted through the corridors:* **escort**, guide, lead, usher, show; shepherd, see, bring, take, help. **3** *aluminium conducts heat:* **transmit**, convey, carry, channel, relay.
■ **conduct yourself** behave, act, acquit yourself, bear yourself.

conduit noun **channel**, duct, pipe, tube, gutter, trench, culvert, sluice, chute.

confectionery noun **sweets**, chocolates, bonbons; N. Amer. candy; informal sweeties; old use sweetmeats.

confederacy noun **federation**, confederation, alliance, league, association, coalition, consortium, syndicate, group, circle; bloc, axis.

confederate adjective *confederate councils:* **federal**, federated, allied, associated, united.
– OPPOSITES split.
• noun *he met his confederate in the street:* **associate**, partner, accomplice, helper, assistant, ally, collaborator, colleague; Austral./NZ informal offsider.

confederation noun **alliance**, league, confederacy, federation, association, coalition, consortium, conglomerate, syndicate, group, circle; society, union.

confer verb **1** *she conferred a knighthood on him:* **bestow on**, present to, grant to, award to, decorate with, honour with, give to, endow with, extend to, vouchsafe to. **2** *she went to confer with her colleagues:* **consult**, talk, speak, converse, have a chat, have a tête-à-tête, parley.

conference noun **congress**, meeting, convention, seminar, colloquium, symposium, forum, summit.

confess verb **1** *he confessed that he had done it:* **admit**, acknowledge, reveal, disclose, divulge; own up;

C

informal fess up. **2** *they could not make him confess:* **own up**, plead guilty, accept the blame; tell the truth, tell all; informal come clean, spill the beans, let the cat out of the bag. **3** *I confess I don't know:* **acknowledge**, admit, concede, grant, allow, own.
–OPPOSITES deny.

confession noun **admission**, acknowledgement.

confidant, confidante noun **close friend**, bosom friend, best friend; intimate, familiar; informal chum, pal, crony; Brit. informal mate, mucker; N. Amer. informal buddy.

confide verb **reveal**, disclose, divulge, impart, declare, vouchsafe, tell; confess.

confidence noun **1** *I have little confidence in these figures:* **trust**, belief, faith. **2** *she's brimming with confidence:* **self-assurance**, self-confidence, self-possession, assertiveness, self-belief; conviction.
–OPPOSITES scepticism, doubt.

confident adjective **1** *we are confident that business will improve:* **optimistic**, hopeful; sure, certain, positive, convinced, in no doubt, satisfied. **2** *a confident girl:* **self-assured**, assured, self-confident, positive, assertive, self-possessed.

confidential adjective **private**, personal, intimate, quiet; secret, sensitive, classified, restricted, unofficial, undisclosed, unpublished; informal hush-hush.

confidentially adverb **privately**, in private, in confidence, between ourselves/themselves, off the record, quietly, secretly, in secret, behind closed doors.

configuration noun **arrangement**, layout, geography, design, organization, order, grouping, positioning, disposition, alignment; shape, form, array, formation, structure, format.

confine verb **1** *they were confined in the house:* **shut in/up**, coop up, keep, lock in/up; incarcerate, imprison, intern, impound, hold captive, trap; fence in, hedge in, enclose. **2** *he confined his remarks to the weather:* **restrict**, limit.

confined adjective **cramped**, constricted, restricted, limited, small, narrow, compact, tight, poky, uncomfortable, inadequate.
–OPPOSITES roomy.

confinement noun **imprisonment**, internment, incarceration, custody, captivity, detention, restraint; house arrest.

confines plural noun **limits**, margins, extremities, edges, borders, boundaries, fringes; periphery, perimeter.

confirm verb **1** *records confirm the latest evidence:* **corroborate**, verify, prove, validate, authenticate, substantiate, justify, vindicate; support, uphold, back up. **2** *he confirmed that help was on the way:* **affirm**, reaffirm, assert, assure someone, repeat. **3** *his appointment was confirmed by the President:* **ratify**, validate, sanction, endorse, formalize, authorize, warrant, accredit, approve, accept.
–OPPOSITES contradict, deny.

confirmation noun **1** *independent confirmation of the deaths:* **corroboration**, verification, proof, testimony, endorsement, authentication, substantiation, evidence. **2** *confirmation of your appointment:* **ratification**, approval, authorization, validation, sanction, endorsement, formalization, acceptance.

confirmed adjective **established**, long-standing, committed, dyed-in-the-wool, through and through; staunch, loyal, faithful, devoted, dedicated, steadfast; habitual, compulsive, persistent; unapologetic, unashamed, inveterate, chronic, incurable; informal card-carrying.

confiscate verb **impound**, seize, commandeer, requisition, appropriate, expropriate, sequester, sequestrate, take away.
–OPPOSITES return.

confiscation noun **seizure**, requisition, appropriation, expropriation, sequestration.

conflagration noun **fire**, blaze, flames, inferno, firestorm.

conflict noun **1** *industrial conflicts:* **dispute**, quarrel, squabble, disagreement, clash; discord, friction, strife, antagonism, hostility; feud, schism. **2** *the Vietnam conflict:* **war**, campaign, fighting, engagement, encounter, struggle, hostilities; warfare, combat. **3** *a conflict*

between work and home life: **clash**, incompatibility, friction; mismatch, variance, divergence, contradiction.
– OPPOSITES agreement, peace, harmony.
• verb *their interests sometimes conflict:* **clash**, be incompatible, vary, be at odds, be in conflict, differ, diverge, disagree, contrast, collide.

conflicting adjective **contradictory**, incompatible, inconsistent, irreconcilable, contrary, opposite, opposing, antithetical, clashing, divergent; at odds.

confluence noun **convergence**, meeting, junction.

conform verb **1** *visitors have to conform to our rules:* **comply with**, abide by, obey, observe, follow, keep to, stick to, adhere to, uphold, heed, accept, go along with, fall in with, respect, defer to; satisfy, meet, fulfil. **2** *they refuse to conform:* **fit/blend in**; behave, toe the line, obey the rules; informal play it by the book, play by the rules. **3** *goods must conform to their description:* **match**, fit, suit, answer, agree with, be like, correspond to, be consistent with, measure up to, tally with, square with.
– OPPOSITES flout, rebel.

conformist noun **traditionalist**, conservative, diehard, reactionary; informal stick-in-the-mud, stuffed shirt.
– OPPOSITES eccentric, rebel.

confound verb **1** *the figures confounded analysts:* **amaze**, astonish, dumbfound, stagger, surprise, startle, stun, nonplus; throw, shake, discompose, bewilder, baffle, mystify, bemuse, perplex, puzzle, confuse; take aback, catch off balance; informal flabbergast, flummox, faze, stump, beat; N. Amer. informal discombobulate. **2** *the data have confounded their economic theories:* **contradict**, counter, invalidate, negate, go against, explode, demolish, shoot down, destroy, disprove; informal shoot full of holes.

confront verb **1** *he confronted the intruder:* **challenge**, stand up to, square up to, face, come face to face with; accost. **2** *they must confront these issues:* **tackle**, address, face, face up to, get to grips with, grapple with, take on, attend to, see to, deal with. **3** *she confronted him with the evidence:* **present**, face.
– OPPOSITES avoid.

confrontation noun **conflict**, clash, fight, battle, encounter, head-to-head, face-off, engagement, skirmish; hostilities, fighting; informal set-to, run-in, dust-up, showdown.

confuse verb **1** *don't confuse students with too much detail:* **bewilder**, baffle, mystify, bemuse, perplex, puzzle, confound, nonplus; informal flummox, faze, stump; N. Amer. informal discombobulate. **2** *the authors have confused the issue:* **complicate**, muddle, blur, obscure, cloud. **3** *some confuse strokes with heart attacks:* **mix up**, muddle up, mistake for.
– OPPOSITES enlighten, simplify.

confused adjective **1** *they are confused about what is going on:* **bewildered**, bemused, puzzled, perplexed, baffled, mystified, muddled, dumbfounded, at sea, at a loss, taken aback, disoriented; informal flummoxed; N. Amer. informal discombobulated. **2** *her confused elderly mother:* **muddled**, addled, befuddled, disoriented, disorientated; senile. **3** *a confused recollection:* **vague**, unclear, indistinct, imprecise, blurred, hazy, dim; imperfect, sketchy. **4** *a confused mass of bones:* **disorderly**, disordered, disorganized, untidy, muddled, jumbled, mixed up, chaotic, topsy-turvy, tangled; informal higgledy-piggledy; Brit. informal shambolic.
– OPPOSITES lucid, clear, precise, neat.

confusing adjective **bewildering**, baffling, perplexing, puzzling, mystifying; ambiguous, misleading, inconsistent, contradictory.

confusion noun **1** *there is confusion about the new system:* **uncertainty**, doubt, ignorance. **2** *she stared in confusion:* **bewilderment**, bafflement, perplexity, puzzlement, befuddlement; N. Amer. informal discombobulation. **3** *her life was in utter confusion:* **disorder**, disarray, chaos, mayhem; turmoil, tumult, uproar, hurly-burly, muddle, mess;

informal shambles. **4** *a confusion of boxes:* **jumble**, muddle, mess, heap, tangle.
– OPPOSITES certainty, order.

congeal verb **coagulate**, clot, thicken, gel, cake, set.

congenial adjective **1** *very congenial people:* **sociable**, sympathetic, convivial, hospitable, genial, personable, agreeable, friendly, pleasant, likeable, amiable, nice. **2** *a congenial environment:* **pleasant**, pleasing, agreeable, enjoyable, pleasurable, nice, appealing, satisfying, relaxing, welcoming, hospitable, favourable.
– OPPOSITES unpleasant.

congenital adjective **1** *congenital defects:* **inborn**, innate, constitutional, inbuilt, natural, inherent. **2** *a congenital liar:* **inveterate**, compulsive, persistent, chronic, regular, habitual, obsessive, confirmed; incurable, incorrigible, irredeemable, hopeless; informal pathological.
– OPPOSITES acquired.

congested adjective **crowded**, overcrowded, full, overflowing, packed, jammed, thronged, teeming, swarming; obstructed, blocked, clogged, choked; informal snarled up, gridlocked, jam-packed.
– OPPOSITES clear.

congestion noun **crowding**, overcrowding; obstruction, blockage; traffic jam, bottleneck; informal snarl-up, gridlock.

conglomerate noun **1** *the conglomerate was broken up:* **corporation**, combine, group, consortium, partnership, federation, multinational. **2** *a conglomerate of disparate peoples:* **mixture**, mix, combination, amalgamation, union, composite, synthesis; miscellany, hotchpotch.

congratulate verb *they are to be congratulated:* **praise**, commend, applaud, salute, honour; pay tribute to, pat on the back, take your hat off to.
– OPPOSITES criticize.

congratulations plural noun best wishes, compliments; felicitations.

congregate verb **assemble**, gather, collect, come together, convene, rally, muster, meet, cluster, group.
– OPPOSITES disperse.

congregation noun **parishioners**, parish, churchgoers, flock, faithful, believers; audience.

congress noun **legislature**, assembly, parliament, council, senate, chamber, house.

conical adjective **cone-shaped**, tapered, tapering, pointed; informal pointy.

conjectural adjective **speculative**, theoretical, hypothetical, putative, notional; postulated, inferred, presumed, assumed.

conjecture noun **speculation**, guesswork, surmise, fancy, theory, supposition, a shot in the dark.
– OPPOSITES fact.
• verb **guess**, speculate, surmise, infer, assume, suppose.
– OPPOSITES know.

conjugal adjective **marital**, matrimonial, nuptial, marriage, bridal; literary connubial.

conjunction noun **co-occurrence**, concurrence, coincidence, coexistence, synchronicity, synchrony.

conjure verb **1** *he conjured a cigarette out of the air:* **produce**, magic, summon. **2** *the picture that his words conjured up:* **bring to mind**, call to mind, evoke, summon up, suggest.

conjuring noun **magic**, illusion, sleight of hand, legerdemain; formal prestidigitation.

conjuror noun **magician**, illusionist; formal prestidigitator.

connect verb **1** *electrodes were connected to the device:* **attach**, join, fasten, fix, link, secure, hitch; stick, pin, screw, bolt, clamp, clip, hook up. **2** *bonuses are connected to the firm's performance:* **link**, relate, associate, correlate.
– OPPOSITES detach, separate.

connection noun **1** *the connection between commerce and art:* **link**, relationship, relation, interconnection, interdependence, association; bond, tie, tie-in, correspondence, parallel, analogy. **2** *he has the right connections:* **contact**, friend, acquaintance, ally, colleague, associate; relation, relative.
■ **in connection with** regarding, concerning, with reference to, with regard to, with respect to, relating

to, in relation to, on, connected with, on the subject of, in the matter of, apropos, re.

connivance noun **collusion**, complicity, collaboration, involvement, assistance.

connive verb **1** *wardens connived at offences:* **ignore**, overlook, disregard, pass over, take no notice of, turn a blind eye to. **2** *the government connived with security forces:* **conspire**, collude, collaborate, plot, scheme.

conniving adjective **scheming**, cunning, calculating, devious, wily, sly, tricky, artful, guileful; manipulative, Machiavellian, deceitful, underhand, treacherous.

connoisseur noun **expert**, authority, specialist, pundit, aesthete; gourmet, epicure, gastronome; informal **buff**; N. Amer. informal maven.

connotation noun **overtone**, undertone, undercurrent, implication, nuance, hint, echo, association.

connote verb **imply**, suggest, indicate, signify, hint at, give the impression of, smack of.

conquer verb **1** *the Franks conquered the Visigoths:* **defeat**, beat, triumph over, be victorious over, get the better of; overcome, overwhelm, overpower, overthrow, subdue, subjugate, quell, quash, crush; literary vanquish. **2** *Peru was conquered by Spain:* **seize**, take, appropriate, subjugate, capture, occupy, invade, annex, overrun. **3** *the first men to conquer Mount Everest:* **climb**, ascend, mount, scale. **4** *she conquered her fear:* **overcome**, get the better of, control, master, deal with, cope with, rise above; quell, quash, beat, triumph over; informal lick.
– OPPOSITES lose.

conquest noun **1** *the conquest of the Aztecs:* **defeat**, overthrow, subjugation; victory over, triumph over. **2** *their conquest of the valley:* **seizure**, takeover, capture, occupation, invasion, acquisition, appropriation. **3** *the conquest of Everest:* **ascent**, climbing.
– OPPOSITES surrender.

conscience noun **sense of right and wrong**; morals, standards, values, principles, ethics, beliefs; scruples, qualms.

conscientious adjective **diligent**, industrious, punctilious, painstaking, sedulous, assiduous, dedicated, careful, meticulous, thorough, attentive, hard-working, studious, rigorous, particular; religious, strict.
– OPPOSITES casual.

conscious adjective **1** *the patient was conscious:* **aware**, awake; informal with us. **2** *a conscious decision:* **deliberate**, purposeful, knowing, considered, calculated, wilful, premeditated.
– OPPOSITES unconscious, unaware.

conscript verb *they were conscripted into the army:* **call up**, enlist, recruit; US draft.
• noun *an army conscript:* enlisted soldier/man/woman, recruit; US draftee.
– OPPOSITES volunteer.

consecrate verb **sanctify**, bless; dedicate, devote.

consecutive adjective **successive**, succeeding, in succession, running, in a row, one after the other, back-to-back, straight, uninterrupted; informal on the trot.

consensus noun **1** *there was consensus among delegates:* **agreement**, harmony, concurrence, accord, unity, unanimity, solidarity. **2** *the consensus was that they should act:* **general opinion**, common view.
– OPPOSITES disagreement.

consent noun *the consent of all members:* **agreement**, assent, acceptance, approval; permission, authorization, sanction, leave; backing, endorsement, support; informal go-ahead, thumbs up, green light, OK.
– OPPOSITES dissent.
• verb *she consented to surgery:* **agree**, assent, submit; allow, give permission, sanction, accept, approve, go along with.
– OPPOSITES refuse, forbid.

consequence noun **1** *a consequence of inflation:* **result**, effect, upshot, outcome, repercussion, ramification, corollary, concomitant; fruits, product, by-product, end result. **2** *the past is of no consequence:* **importance**, import,

significance, account, substance, note, value, concern, interest.
– OPPOSITES cause.

consequent adjective **resulting**, resultant, ensuing, consequential; following, subsequent, successive; attendant, accompanying, concomitant; collateral, associated, related.

consequential adjective **1** *a fire and the consequential smoke damage:* **resulting**, resultant, ensuing, consequent; subsequent; attendant, accompanying, concomitant; collateral. **2** *one of his more consequential initiatives:* **important**, significant, momentous.
– OPPOSITES insignificant.

consequently adverb **as a result**, as a consequence, so, thus, therefore, ergo, accordingly, hence, for this/that reason, because of this/that.

conservation noun **preservation**, protection, safeguarding, safe keeping; care, guardianship, husbandry, supervision; upkeep, maintenance, repair, restoration; ecology, environmentalism.

conservative adjective **1** *the conservative wing of the party:* **right-wing**, reactionary, traditionalist; Brit. Tory; US Republican. **2** *the conservative trade-union movement:* **traditionalist**, old-fashioned, dyed-in-the-wool, hidebound, unadventurous, reactionary, set in your ways; moderate, middle-of-the-road; informal stick-in-the-mud. **3** *a conservative suit:* **conventional**, sober, modest, sensible, restrained, low-key, demure; informal square, straight.
– OPPOSITES socialist, radical, ostentatious.
• noun *liberals and conservatives have found common ground:* **right-winger**, reactionary; Brit. Tory; US Republican.

conservatory noun *a teaching job at the Moscow Conservatory:* **conservatoire**, music school, drama school; academy.

conserve verb *fossil fuel should be conserved:* **preserve**, protect, save, safeguard, keep, look after; sustain, husband.
– OPPOSITES squander.
• noun *cherry conserve:* **jam**, preserve; US jelly.

consider verb **1** *Isabel considered her choices:* **think about**, contemplate, reflect on, examine, review; mull over, ponder, deliberate on, chew over, meditate on, ruminate on; assess, evaluate, weigh up, appraise; informal size up. **2** *I consider him irresponsible:* **deem**, think, believe, judge, rate, count, find; regard as, hold to be, reckon to be, view as, see as. **3** *he considered the ceiling:* **look at**, contemplate, observe, regard, survey, examine, inspect. **4** *the inquiry will consider those issues:* **take into consideration**, take account of, make allowances for, bear in mind, be mindful of, note.
– OPPOSITES ignore.

considerable adjective **sizeable**, substantial, appreciable, significant; informal tidy.
– OPPOSITES paltry.

considerably adverb **greatly**, much, a great deal, a lot, lots; significantly, substantially, appreciably, markedly, noticeably; informal plenty.

considerate adjective **attentive**, thoughtful, solicitous; kind, unselfish, caring; polite, sensitive.

consideration noun **1** *your case needs careful consideration:* **thought**, deliberation, reflection, contemplation; examination, inspection, scrutiny, analysis, discussion; attention. **2** *his health is the prime consideration:* **factor**, issue, matter, concern, aspect, feature. **3** *firms should show more consideration:* **attentiveness**, concern, care, thoughtfulness, solicitude; understanding, respect, sensitivity, tact, discretion, compassion, charity.

considering preposition **bearing in mind**, taking into consideration, taking into account, in view of, in the light of.

consign verb **send**, deliver, deposit, put; banish, exile, relegate; informal dump.

consignment noun **delivery**, shipment, load, boatload, truckload, cargo; batch.

consist verb **be composed**, be made up, be formed; comprise, contain, incorporate.

consistency noun **1** *the trend shows a degree of consistency:*

uniformity, constancy, regularity, evenness, steadiness; dependability, reliability. **2** *cream of pouring consistency:* **thickness**, density, viscosity; texture.

consistent adjective **1** *consistent opinion-poll evidence:* **constant**, regular, uniform, steady, stable, even, unchanging; dependable, reliable, predictable. **2** *her injuries were consistent with a knife attack:* **compatible**, in tune, in line; corresponding to, conforming to.
–OPPOSITES inconsistent, incompatible.

consolation noun **comfort**, solace, sympathy, pity, commiseration; relief, encouragement, reassurance.

console[1] verb *she tried to console him:* **comfort**, cheer up, encourage, hearten, reassure, soothe, help, support; commiserate with.
–OPPOSITES upset.

console[2] noun *a digital console:* **control panel**, instrument panel, dashboard, keyboard, array.

consolidate verb **1** *we consolidated our position in the market:* **strengthen**, secure, stabilize, reinforce, fortify. **2** *consolidate the results into an action plan:* **combine**, unite, merge, integrate, amalgamate, fuse, synthesize, bring together.

consonance noun **agreement**, accord, harmony, unison; compatibility, congruity, congruence.

consort noun *the queen and her consort:* **partner**, companion, mate; spouse, husband, wife.
•verb *he consorted with other women:* **associate**, keep company, mix, go around, spend time, socialize, fraternize, have dealings; informal run around, hang around/ round, hang out; Brit. informal hang about.

conspicuous adjective **easily seen**, clear, visible, noticeable, discernible, perceptible, detectable; obvious, manifest, evident, apparent, marked, pronounced, prominent; striking, eye-catching, overt, blatant, writ large; distinct, recognizable, unmistakable, inescapable; informal as plain as the nose on your face, standing out like a sore thumb, standing out a mile.

conspiracy noun **plot**, scheme, plan, machination, subterfuge, intrigue, collusion, connivance; ploy, trick, ruse.

conspire verb **1** *they admitted conspiring to steal cars:* **plot**, scheme, plan, intrigue. **2** *circumstances conspired against them:* **combine**, unite, join forces; informal gang up.

constancy noun **1** *constancy between lovers:* **fidelity**, faithfulness, loyalty, commitment, dedication, devotion; dependability, reliability, trustworthiness. **2** *the constancy of the tradition:* **continuity**, permanence, persistence, endurance, immutability.

constant adjective **1** *the constant background noise:* **continual**, continuous, persistent, sustained, round-the-clock; ceaseless, unceasing, perpetual, incessant, never-ending, eternal, endless, unabating, non-stop, unrelieved; interminable, unremitting, relentless, unflagging. **2** *a constant speed:* **consistent**, regular, steady, uniform, even, invariable, unvarying, unchanging, undeviating. **3** *a constant friend:* **faithful**, loyal, devoted, true, fast, firm, unswerving; steadfast, staunch, dependable, trustworthy, trusty, reliable.
–OPPOSITES fitful, variable, fickle.

constantly adverb **always**, all the time, continually, continuously, persistently; round the clock, night and day, {morning, noon, and night}; endlessly, non-stop, incessantly, unceasingly, perpetually, eternally, forever; interminably, unremittingly, relentlessly; Scottish aye; informal 24-7.
–OPPOSITES occasionally.

consternation noun **dismay**, distress, disquiet, discomposure; surprise; alarm, fear, fright, shock.
–OPPOSITES satisfaction.

constituent adjective *constituent parts:* **component**, integral; elemental, basic, essential.
•noun **1** *MPs must listen to their constituents:* **voter**, elector. **2** *the constituents of tobacco:* **component**, ingredient, element; part, piece, bit, unit; section, portion.

C

constitute verb **1** *farmers constituted 10 per cent of the population:* **amount to**, add up to, account for, form, make up, compose, comprise. **2** *this constitutes a breach of copyright:* **be equivalent to**, be, be tantamount to, be regarded as. **3** *the courts were constituted in 1875:* **inaugurate**, establish, initiate, found, create, set up, start, form, organize, develop; commission, charter, invest, appoint, install.

constitution noun **1** *the constitution guarantees our rights:* **charter**, social code, law; bill of rights; rules, regulations. **2** *the chemical constitution of the dye:* **composition**, make-up, structure, construction, configuration, formation, anatomy. **3** *she has the constitution of an ox:* **health**, physique; strength, stamina, energy.

constitutional adjective **1** *constitutional powers:* **legal**, lawful, legitimate, authorized, permitted; sanctioned, ratified, warranted, constituted, statutory, chartered, official. **2** *a constitutional weakness:* **inherent**, intrinsic, innate, fundamental, essential, inborn.

constrain verb **1** *he felt constrained to explain:* **compel**, force, drive, impel, oblige, require. **2** *prices were constrained by state controls:* **restrict**, limit, curb, check, restrain, contain, hold back, keep down.

constraint noun **1** *financial constraints:* **restriction**, limitation, curb, check, restraint, control; hindrance, impediment, obstruction, handicap. **2** *they were able to talk without constraint:* **inhibition**, uneasiness, embarrassment; self-consciousness, forcedness, awkwardness.

constrict verb **narrow**, tighten, compress, contract, squeeze, strangle; old use straiten.
– OPPOSITES expand, dilate.

constriction noun **tightness**, pressure, compression, contraction; obstruction, blockage, impediment; Medicine stricture.

construct verb **1** *a new motorway was being constructed:* **build**, erect, put up, set up, assemble, manufacture, fabricate, create, make. **2** *he constructed a faultless argument:* **formulate**, form, put together, create, devise, compose, work out; fashion, mould, shape, frame.
– OPPOSITES demolish.

construction noun **1** *the construction of a new airport:* **building**, erection, putting up, setting up, establishment; assembly, manufacture, fabrication, creation. **2** *the station was a spectacular construction:* **structure**, building, edifice, work.

constructive adjective **useful**, helpful, productive, positive, encouraging; practical, valuable, profitable, worthwhile.

construe verb **interpret**, understand, read, see, take, take to mean, regard.

consul noun **ambassador**, diplomat, chargé d'affaires, attaché, envoy, emissary.

consult verb **1** *you need to consult a solicitor:* **seek advice from**, see, call on, speak to, turn to, contact, get in touch with; informal pick someone's brains. **2** *the government must consult with interested parties:* **confer**, talk things over, communicate, parley, deliberate; informal put your heads together. **3** *she consulted her diary:* **refer to**, turn to, look at, check.

consultant noun **1** *an engineering consultant:* **adviser**, expert, specialist, pundit. **2** *a consultant at Guy's hospital:* **senior doctor**, specialist.

consultation noun **1** *the need for further consultation with industry:* **discussion**, dialogue, debate, negotiation, deliberation. **2** *a 30-minute consultation:* **meeting**, talk, discussion, interview, audience, hearing; appointment, session.

consume verb **1** *vast amounts of food and drink were consumed:* **eat**, devour, ingest, swallow, gobble up, wolf down, guzzle, feast on, snack on; drink, gulp down, imbibe, sup; informal tuck into, put away, polish off, dispose of, pig yourself on, down, neck, sink, swill; Brit. informal scoff, shift; N. Amer. informal scarf, snarf. **2** *natural resources are being consumed at an alarming rate:* **use up**, utilize, expend; deplete, exhaust. **3** *the fire consumed fifty houses:* **destroy**, demolish, lay waste, wipe out, annihilate, devastate, gut, ruin, wreck. **4** *she was consumed with guilt:* **eat up**, devour, grip, overwhelm; absorb, preoccupy.

consumer noun **purchaser**, buyer, customer, shopper; user, end-user; client; (**the consumer** or **consumers**) the public, the market, people.

consuming adjective **absorbing**, compelling, compulsive, obsessive, overwhelming; intense, powerful, burning, raging, profound, deep-seated.

consummate verb *the deal was finally consummated:* **complete**, conclude, finish, accomplish, achieve; execute, carry out, perform; informal sew up, wrap up.
• adjective *his consummate skill | a consummate politician:* **supreme**, superb, superlative, superior, accomplished, expert, proficient, skilful, skilled, masterly, master, first-class, polished, practised, perfect, ultimate; complete, total, utter, absolute, pure.

consumption noun **1** *food unfit for human consumption:* **eating**, drinking, ingestion. **2** *the consumption of fossil fuels:* **use**, using up, utilization, depletion.

contact noun **1** *a disease transmitted through contact with rats:* **touch**, touching; proximity, exposure, intimacy. **2** *diplomats were asked to avoid all contact with him:* **communication**, correspondence; association, connection, intercourse, relations, dealings. **3** *he had many contacts in Germany:* **connection**, acquaintance, associate, friend.
• verb *anyone with information should contact the police:* **get in touch with**, communicate with, approach, notify; telephone, phone, call, ring up, speak to, talk to, write to; informal get hold of.

contagious adjective **infectious**, communicable, transmittable, transmissible; informal catching; dated infective.

contain verb **1** *the archive contains much unpublished material:* **include**, comprise, take in, incorporate, involve, encompass, embrace; consist of, be made up of, be composed of. **2** *the boat contained four people:* **hold**, carry, accommodate, seat; sleep. **3** *he must contain his anger:* **restrain**, curb, rein in, suppress, repress, stifle, subdue, quell, swallow, bottle up, hold in, keep in check.

container noun **receptacle**, vessel, holder, repository; box, canister.

contaminate verb **pollute**; defile, debase, corrupt, taint, infect, spoil, soil, stain; poison.
– OPPOSITES purify.

contemplate verb **1** *she contemplated her image in the mirror:* **look at**, view, regard, examine, inspect, observe, survey, study, scrutinize, stare at, gaze at, eye. **2** *he contemplated his fate:* **think about**, ponder, reflect on, consider, mull over, muse on, dwell on, deliberate over, meditate on, ruminate on, chew over, brood on/about, turn over in your mind; formal cogitate. **3** *he was contemplating action for damages:* **consider**, think about, have in mind, intend, plan, propose.

contemplation noun **1** *the contemplation of beautiful objects:* **viewing**, examination, inspection, observation, survey, study, scrutiny. **2** *a time for contemplation:* **thought**, reflection, meditation, consideration, deliberation, introspection.

contemplative adjective **thoughtful**, pensive, reflective, meditative, ruminative, introspective, brooding, deep/lost in thought.

contemporary adjective
1 *contemporary sources:* **of the time**, of the day, contemporaneous, concurrent, coexisting.
2 *contemporary society:* **modern**, present-day, present, current. **3** *a very contemporary design:* **modern**, up to date, up to the minute, fashionable; modish, latest, recent; informal trendy, on-trend, hip.
– OPPOSITES old-fashioned, out of date.
• noun *Chaucer's contemporaries:* **peer**, fellow.

contempt noun **scorn**, disdain, derision; disgust, loathing, hatred, abhorrence.
– OPPOSITES respect.

contemptible adjective **despicable**, detestable, hateful, reprehensible, deplorable, unspeakable, disgraceful, shameful, ignominious, abject, low, mean, cowardly, discreditable, worthless, shabby, cheap; old use scurvy.
– OPPOSITES admirable.

contemptuous adjective **scornful**, disdainful, insulting, insolent, derisive, mocking, sneering, scoffing, withering, scathing; condescending, supercilious, haughty, superior, arrogant, dismissive, aloof; informal high and mighty, snotty, sniffy.
– OPPOSITES respectful.

contend verb **1** *the pilot had to contend with torrential rain:* **cope with**, face, grapple with, deal with, take on, handle. **2** *three main groups were contending for power:* **compete**, vie, contest, fight, battle, tussle; strive, struggle. **3** *he contends that the judge was wrong:* **assert**, maintain, hold, claim, argue, insist, state, declare, profess, affirm; allege; formal aver.

content[1] adjective *she seemed content with life:* **contented**, satisfied, pleased, fulfilled, happy, cheerful, glad; unworried, untroubled, at ease, at peace, tranquil, serene.
– OPPOSITES discontented, dissatisfied.
• verb *her reply seemed to content him:* **satisfy**, please; soothe, pacify, placate, appease, mollify.

content[2] noun **1** *foods with a high fibre content:* **amount**, proportion, level. **2** (**contents**) *the contents of a vegetarian sausage:* **constituents**, ingredients, components. **3** *the content of the essay:* **subject matter**, theme, argument, thesis, message, thrust, substance, text, ideas.

contented adjective *a contented man.* See CONTENT[1] adjective.

contention noun **1** *a point of contention:* **disagreement**, dispute, argument, discord, conflict, friction, strife, dissension, disharmony. **2** *the Marxist contention that capitalism equals exploitation:* **argument**, claim, submission, allegation, assertion, declaration; opinion, position, view, belief, thesis, case.
– OPPOSITES agreement.

contentious adjective **1** *a contentious issue:* **controversial**, debatable, disputed, open to debate, moot, vexed. **2** *a contentious debate:* **heated**, vehement, fierce, violent, intense, impassioned.

contentment noun **contentedness**, content, satisfaction, fulfilment, happiness, pleasure, cheerfulness; ease, comfort, well-being, peace, equanimity, serenity, tranquillity.

contest noun **1** *a boxing contest:* **competition**, match, tournament, game, meet, trial, bout, heat, fixture, tie, race. **2** *the contest for the party leadership:* **fight**, battle, tussle, struggle, competition, race.
• verb **1** *he intended to contest the seat:* **compete for**, contend for, vie for, fight for, go for. **2** *we contested the decision:* **oppose**, object to, challenge, take issue with, question, call into question. **3** *the issues have been hotly contested:* **debate**, argue about, dispute, quarrel over.

contestant noun **competitor**, participant, player, contender, candidate, aspirant, entrant.

context noun **circumstances**, conditions, factors, state of affairs, situation, background, scene, setting.

contingency noun **eventuality**, occurrence, event, incident, happening, juncture, possibility, accident, chance, emergency.

contingent adjective **1** *the merger is contingent on government approval:* **dependent on**, conditional on, subject to, determined by, hingeing on, resting on. **2** *contingent events:* **chance**, accidental, fortuitous, possible, unforeseeable, unpredictable, random, haphazard.
• noun **1** *a contingent of Japanese businessmen:* **group**, party, body, band, company, cohort, deputation, delegation; informal bunch. **2** *a contingent of marines:* **detachment**, unit, group.

continual adjective **1** *a service disrupted by continual breakdowns:* **frequent**, repeated, constant, recurrent, recurring, regular. **2** *she was in continual pain:* **constant**, continuous, unremitting, unrelenting, unrelieved, chronic, uninterrupted, unbroken, round-the-clock.
– OPPOSITES occasional, temporary.

continuance noun. See CONTINUATION.

continuation noun **carrying on**, continuance, extension, prolongation, protraction, perpetuation.
–OPPOSITES end.

continue verb **1** *he was unable to continue with his job:* **carry on**, proceed, pursue, go on, keep on, persist, press on, persevere, keep at; informal stick at. **2** *discussions continued throughout the year:* **go on**, carry on, last, extend, run on, drag on. **3** *we are keen to continue this relationship:* **maintain**, keep up, sustain, keep going, keep alive, preserve. **4** *his willingness to continue in office:* **remain**, stay, carry on, keep going. **5** *we continued our conversation after supper:* **resume**, pick up, take up, carry on with, return to, revisit.
–OPPOSITES stop, break off.

continuing adjective **ongoing**, continuous, sustained, persistent, steady, relentless, uninterrupted, unabating, unremitting, unrelieved, unceasing.
–OPPOSITES sporadic.

continuous adjective **continual**, uninterrupted, unbroken, constant, ceaseless, incessant, steady, sustained, solid, continuing, ongoing, unceasing, without a break, non-stop, round-the-clock, persistent, unremitting, relentless, unrelenting, unabating, unrelieved, endless, unending, never-ending, perpetual, everlasting, eternal, interminable; running; N. Amer. without surcease.
–OPPOSITES intermittent.

contort verb **twist**, bend out of shape, distort, misshape, warp, buckle, deform.

contour noun **outline**, shape, form; lines, curves; silhouette, profile.

contraband adjective **smuggled**, black-market, bootleg, under the counter, illegal, illicit, unlawful; prohibited, banned, proscribed, forbidden; informal hot.

contract noun *a legally binding contract:* **agreement**, commitment, arrangement, settlement, understanding, compact, covenant, bond; deal, bargain.
• verb **1** *the market for such goods began to contract:* **shrink**, get smaller, decrease, diminish, reduce, dwindle, decline; collapse. **2** *her stomach muscles contracted:* **tighten**, tense, flex, constrict, draw in, narrow. **3** *his name was soon contracted to 'Jack':* **shorten**, abbreviate, cut, reduce; elide. **4** *the company was contracted to build the stadium:* **engage**, take on, hire, commission; employ. **5** *she contracted German measles:* **develop**, catch, get, pick up, come down with, succumb to; Brit. go down with.
–OPPOSITES expand, relax, lengthen.

contraction noun **1** *the contraction of the industry:* **shrinking**, shrinkage, decline, decrease, diminution, dwindling; collapse. **2** *the contraction of muscles:* **tightening**, tensing, flexing. **3** *my contractions started at midnight:* **labour pains**, labour; cramps. **4** *'goodbye' is a contraction of 'God be with you':* **abbreviation**, short form, shortened form, elision, diminutive.

contradict verb **1** *he contradicted the government's account of the affair:* **deny**, refute, rebut, dispute, challenge, counter. **2** *nobody dared to contradict him:* **argue with**, go against, challenge, oppose; formal gainsay. **3** *this research contradicts previous computer models:* **conflict with**, be at odds with, be at variance with, be inconsistent with, run counter to, disagree with; challenge, undermine.
–OPPOSITES confirm, agree with.

contradiction noun **1** *the contradiction between his faith and his lifestyle:* **conflict**, clash, disagreement, opposition, inconsistency, mismatch, variance. **2** *a contradiction of his statement:* **denial**, refutation, rebuttal, countering.
–OPPOSITES confirmation, agreement.

contradictory adjective **opposed**, in opposition, opposite, antithetical, contrary, contrasting, conflicting, at variance, at odds, opposing, clashing, divergent, different; inconsistent, incompatible, irreconcilable.

contraption noun **device**, gadget, apparatus, machine, appliance, mechanism, invention, contrivance; informal gizmo, widget; Brit. informal gubbins.

contrary adjective **1** *contrary views:* **opposite**, opposing, opposed, contradictory, clashing, conflicting, antithetical, incompatible, irreconcilable. **2** *she was sulky and contrary:* **perverse**, awkward, difficult, uncooperative, unhelpful, obstructive, recalcitrant, wilful, self-willed, stubborn, obstinate, mulish, pig-headed, intractable; informal cussed; Brit. informal bloody-minded, bolshie, stroppy; N. Amer. informal balky; formal refractory.
– OPPOSITES compatible, accommodating.
• noun *in fact, the contrary is true:* **opposite**, reverse, converse, antithesis.
■ **contrary to** in conflict with, against, at variance with, at odds with, in opposition to, counter to, incompatible with.

contrast noun **1** *the contrast between rural and urban trends:* **difference**, dissimilarity, disparity, distinction, divergence, variance, variation, differentiation; contradiction, incongruity, opposition. **2** *Jane was a complete contrast to Sarah:* **opposite**, antithesis; foil, complement.
– OPPOSITES similarity.
• verb **1** *a view which contrasts with his earlier opinion:* **differ from**, be at variance with, be contrary to, conflict with, go against, be at odds with, be in opposition to, disagree with, clash with. **2** *people contrasted her with her sister:* **compare**, juxtapose; measure against; distinguish from, differentiate from.
– OPPOSITES resemble, liken.

contravene verb **break**, breach, violate, infringe; defy, disobey, flout.
– OPPOSITES comply with.

contravention noun **breach**, violation, infringement.

contribute verb **1** *the government contributed a million pounds:* **give**, donate, put up, grant, bestow, present, provide, supply, furnish; informal chip in, pitch in, fork out, shell out, cough up; Brit. informal stump up; N. Amer. informal kick in, ante up, pony up. **2** *an article contributed by Dr Clouson:* **supply**, provide, submit. **3** *numerous factors contribute to job satisfaction:* **play a part in**, be instrumental in, be a factor in, have a hand in, be conducive to, make for, lead to, cause.

contribution noun **1** *voluntary financial contributions:* **donation**, gift, offering, present, handout, grant, subsidy, allowance, endowment, subscription. **2** *contributions from local authors:* **article**, piece, story, item, paper, essay.

contributor noun **1** *the magazine's regular contributors:* **writer**, columnist, correspondent. **2** *campaign contributors:* **donor**, benefactor, subscriber, supporter, backer, subsidizer, patron, sponsor.

contrite adjective **remorseful**, repentant, penitent, regretful, sorry, apologetic, rueful, sheepish, hangdog, ashamed, chastened, shamefaced.

contrition noun **remorse**, remorsefulness, repentance, penitence, sorrow, sorrowfulness, regret, ruefulness, pangs of conscience; shame, guilt.

contrivance noun **1** *a mechanical contrivance:* **device**, gadget, machine, appliance, contraption, apparatus, mechanism, implement, tool, invention; informal gizmo, widget. **2** *her matchmaking contrivances:* **scheme**, stratagem, tactic, manoeuvre, move, plan, ploy, gambit, wile, trick, ruse, plot, machination.

contrive verb **bring about**, engineer, manufacture, orchestrate, stage-manage, create, devise, concoct, construct, plan, fabricate, plot, hatch; informal wangle, set up.

contrived adjective **forced**, strained, studied, artificial, affected, put-on, pretended, false, manufactured, unnatural; laboured, overdone.
– OPPOSITES natural.

control noun **1** *China retained control over the region:* **jurisdiction**, power, authority, command, dominance, government, mastery, leadership, rule, sovereignty, supremacy; charge, management, direction, supervision, superintendence. **2** *strict import controls:* **restraint**, constraint, limitation, restriction, check, curb; regulation. **3** *her control deserted her:* **self-control**, self-restraint, self-possession, composure, calmness; informal cool. •verb **1** *one family had controlled the company since its formation:* **be in charge of**, run, manage, direct, administer, head, preside over, supervise, steer; command, rule, govern, lead, dominate, hold sway over, be at the helm; informal head up, be in the driving seat. **2** *she struggled to control her temper:* **restrain**, keep in check, curb, check, contain, hold back, bridle, rein in, suppress, repress, master. **3** *public spending was controlled:* **limit**, restrict, curb, cap, constrain.

controversial adjective **contentious**, disputed, moot, disputable, debatable, arguable, vexed, tendentious.

controversy noun **disagreement**, dispute, argument, debate, conflict, contention, wrangling, quarrelling, war of words, storm; Brit. row.

conundrum noun **problem**, question, difficulty, quandary, dilemma.

convalesce verb **recuperate**, get better, recover, get well, get back on your feet.

convalescence noun **recuperation**, recovery, return to health, rehabilitation, improvement.

convene verb **1** *he convened a secret meeting:* **summon**, call, call together, order; formal convoke. **2** *the committee convened for its final session:* **assemble**, gather, meet, come together, congregate; formal foregather.

convenience noun **1** *the convenience of the arrangement:* **expedience**, advantageousness, advantage, propitiousness, timeliness; suitability, appropriateness. **2** *for convenience, the handset is wall-mounted:* **ease of use**, practicality, usefulness, utility, serviceability. **3** *the kitchen has all the modern conveniences:* **appliance**, labour-saving device, gadget; amenity, facility; informal mod con.

convenient adjective **1** *a convenient time:* **suitable**, appropriate, fitting, fit, suited, opportune, timely, favourable, advantageous, seasonable, expedient. **2** *a hotel that's convenient for the beach:* **near**, close to, within easy reach of, well situated for, handy for, not far from; informal a stone's throw from, within spitting distance of.

convent noun **nunnery**, priory, abbey.

convention noun **1** *social conventions:* **custom**, usage, practice, tradition, way, habit, norm; rule, code, canon; propriety, etiquette, protocol; formal praxis; (**conventions**) mores. **2** *a convention signed by 74 countries:* **agreement**, accord, protocol, compact, pact, treaty, concordat; contract, bargain, deal. **3** *the party's biennial convention:* **conference**, meeting, congress, assembly, gathering, summit, convocation, synod, conclave.

conventional adjective **1** *the conventional wisdom of the day:* **orthodox**, traditional, established, accepted, received, mainstream, prevailing, prevalent. **2** *a conventional railway:* **normal**, standard, regular, ordinary, usual, traditional, typical, common. **3** *a very conventional woman:* **conservative**, traditional, conformist, bourgeois, old-fashioned, of the old school, small-town; informal straight, square, stick-in-the-mud, fuddy-duddy. **4** *a conventional piece of work:* **unoriginal**, formulaic, predictable, unadventurous, unremarkable.
– OPPOSITES unorthodox, original.

converge verb **meet**, intersect, cross, connect, link up, coincide, join, unite, merge.
– OPPOSITES diverge.

conversant adjective **familiar**, acquainted, au fait, at home, well versed, well informed, knowledgeable, informed, abreast, up to date; informal up to speed, clued-up, genned-up; formal cognizant.

conversation noun **discussion**, talk, chat, gossip, tête-à-tête, heart-to-heart, head-to-head, exchange, dialogue; informal confab, jaw, chit-chat; Brit. informal chinwag, natter; N. Amer. informal gabfest, schmooze; Austral./NZ informal yarn; formal colloquy.

conversational adjective **informal**, colloquial, idiomatic, everyday; chatty, relaxed, friendly.

converse[1] verb *they conversed in low*

voices: **talk**, speak, chat, discourse, communicate; informal chew the fat, jaw; Brit. informal natter; N. Amer. informal visit, shoot the breeze/bull; Austral./NZ informal mag.

C

converse[2] noun *the converse is also true:* **opposite**, reverse, obverse, contrary, antithesis, other side of the coin; informal flip side.

conversion noun **1** *the conversion of waste into energy:* **change**, changing, transformation, metamorphosis, transmutation; humorous transmogrification. **2** *the conversion of the building:* **adaptation**, alteration, modification, redevelopment, redesign, renovation.

convert verb **1** *plants convert the sun's energy into chemical energy:* **change**, turn, transform, metamorphose, transfigure, transmute; humorous transmogrify. **2** *the factory was converted into flats:* **adapt**, turn, change, alter, modify, redevelop, redesign, restyle, revamp, renovate, rehabilitate; N. Amer. bring up to code; informal do up; N. Amer. informal rehab. **3** *they sought to convert sinners:* **proselytize**, evangelize, redeem, save, reform, re-educate.

convey verb **1** *taxis conveyed guests to the station:* **transport**, carry, bring, take, fetch, bear, move, ferry, shuttle, shift, transfer. **2** *he conveyed the information to me:* **communicate**, pass on, make known, impart, relay, transmit, send, hand on, relate, tell, reveal, disclose. **3** *it's impossible to convey how I felt:* **express**, communicate, get across/over, put across/over, indicate, say; articulate. **4** *he conveys an air of competence:* **project**, exude, emit, emanate.

convict verb **find guilty**, sentence; Brit. informal send down.
– OPPOSITES acquit.
• noun **prisoner**, inmate; criminal, offender, lawbreaker, felon; informal jailbird, con, old lag, crook; N. Amer. informal yardbird.

conviction noun **1** *his political convictions:* **beliefs**, opinions, views, persuasion, ideals, position, stance, values. **2** *she spoke with conviction:* **certainty**, certitude, assurance, confidence, sureness. **3** *his conviction for murder:* judgement, sentence.
– OPPOSITES uncertainty.

convince verb **1** *he convinced me that I was wrong:* **make certain**, persuade, satisfy, prove to; assure. **2** *I convinced her to marry me:* **persuade**, induce, prevail on, get, talk into, win over, cajole, inveigle.

convincing adjective **1** *a convincing argument:* **cogent**, persuasive, plausible, powerful, potent, strong, forceful, compelling, irresistible, telling, conclusive. **2** *a convincing 5–0 win:* **resounding**, emphatic, decisive, conclusive.

convivial adjective **friendly**, genial, affable, amiable, congenial, agreeable, good-humoured, cordial, warm, sociable, outgoing, gregarious, clubbable, companionable, cheerful, jolly, jovial, lively; enjoyable, festive; Scottish couthy.

conviviality noun **friendliness**, geniality, affability, amiability, bonhomie, congeniality, cordiality, warmth, good nature, sociability, gregariousness, cheerfulness, good cheer, joviality, jollity, gaiety, liveliness.

convocation noun **assembly**, gathering, meeting, conference, convention, congress, council, symposium, colloquium, conclave, synod.

convoluted adjective **complicated**, complex, involved, elaborate, serpentine, labyrinthine, tortuous, tangled, Byzantine; confused, confusing, bewildering, baffling.
– OPPOSITES straightforward.

convolution noun **1** *crosses adorned with elaborate convolutions:* **twist**, turn, coil, spiral, twirl, curl, helix, whorl, loop, curlicue. **2** *the convolutions of the plot:* **complexity**, intricacy, complication, twist, turn, entanglement.

convoy noun **group**, fleet, cavalcade, motorcade, cortège, caravan, line, train.

convulsion noun **1** *she had convulsions:* **fit**, seizure, paroxysm, spasm, attack. **2** (**convulsions**) *the audience collapsed in convulsions:* **fits of laughter**, paroxysms of laughter, uncontrollable laughter; informal hysterics. **3** *the political convulsions of the period:* **upheaval**, eruption, cataclysm, turmoil, turbulence, tumult, disruption, agitation, disturbance, unrest, disorder.

convulsive adjective **spasmodic**, jerky, paroxysmal, violent, uncontrollable.

cook verb **prepare**, make, put together; informal fix, rustle up; Brit. informal knock up.
■ **cook something up** (informal) concoct, devise, contrive, fabricate, trump up, hatch, plot, plan, invent, make up, think up, dream up.

cooking noun **cuisine**, cookery, baking; food.

> **WORD LINKS**
> **culinary** relating to cooking

cool adjective **1** *a cool breeze:* **chilly**, chill, cold, bracing, brisk, crisp, fresh, refreshing, invigorating; draughty; informal nippy; Brit. informal parky. **2** *a cool response:* **unenthusiastic**, lukewarm, tepid, indifferent, uninterested, apathetic, half-hearted; unfriendly, distant, remote, aloof, cold, chilly, frosty, unwelcoming, unresponsive, offhand, uncommunicative, undemonstrative; informal standoffish. **3** *his ability to keep cool in a crisis:* **calm**, composed, as cool as a cucumber, collected, level-headed, self-possessed, controlled, self-controlled, poised, serene, tranquil, unruffled, unperturbed, unmoved, untroubled, imperturbable, placid, phlegmatic; informal unflappable, together, laid-back. **4** (informal) *she thinks she's so cool:* **fashionable**, stylish, chic, up to the minute, sophisticated; informal trendy, funky, with it, hip, happening, groovy; N. Amer. informal tony, fly.
– OPPOSITES warm, enthusiastic, agitated.
• noun **1** *the cool of the evening:* **chill**, chilliness, coldness, coolness. **2** (informal) *Ken lost his cool:* **self-control**, control, composure, self-possession, calmness, equilibrium, calm; aplomb, poise, sangfroid.
– OPPOSITES warmth.
• verb **1** *cool the sauce in the fridge:* **chill**, refrigerate. **2** *her reluctance did nothing to cool his interest:* **lessen**, moderate, diminish, reduce, dampen. **3** *Simpson's ardour had cooled:* **subside**, lessen, diminish, decrease, abate, moderate, die down, fade, dwindle, wane. **4** *after a while, she cooled off:* **calm down**, recover/regain your composure, compose yourself, control yourself, pull yourself together, simmer down.
– OPPOSITES heat, inflame, intensify.

coop noun *a hen coop:* **pen**, run, cage, hutch, enclosure.
• verb *he hates being cooped up at home:* **confine**, shut in/up, cage in, pen up/in, keep, detain, trap, incarcerate, immure.

cooperate verb **1** *police and social services cooperated in the operation:* **collaborate**, work together, work side by side, pull together, join forces, team up, unite, combine, pool resources, liaise. **2** *he was happy to cooperate:* **be of assistance**, assist, help, lend a hand, be of service, do your bit; informal play ball.

cooperation noun **1** *cooperation between management and workers:* **collaboration**, joint action, combined effort, teamwork, partnership, coordination, liaison, association, synergy, give and take, compromise. **2** *thank you for your cooperation:* **assistance**, helpfulness, help, aid.

cooperative adjective **1** *a cooperative effort:* **collaborative**, collective, combined, common, joint, shared, mutual, united, concerted, coordinated. **2** *pleasant and cooperative staff:* **helpful**, eager to help, obliging, accommodating, willing, amenable.

coordinate verb **1** *exhibitions coordinated by a team of international scholars:* **organize**, arrange, order, synchronize, bring together; curate, manage, oversee. **2** *care workers coordinate at a local level:* **cooperate**, liaise, collaborate, work together, communicate, be in contact. **3** *floral designs coordinate with the decor:* **match**, complement, set off; harmonize, blend, fit in, go.

cope verb **1** *she couldn't cope on her own:* **manage**, survive, subsist, look after yourself, fend for yourself, shift for yourself, carry on, get by/through, bear up, hold your own, keep your end up, keep your head above water; informal make it, hack it. **2** *his inability to cope with the situation:* **deal with**, handle, manage, address, face up to, confront, tackle, get to grips with, get through, weather, come to terms with.

C

copious adjective **abundant**, plentiful, ample, profuse, extensive, full, generous, lavish, fulsome, liberal, overflowing, in abundance, many, numerous; informal a gogo, galore; literary plenteous.
–OPPOSITES sparse.

copse noun **thicket**, grove, wood, coppice, clump; Brit. spinney; N. Amer. & Austral./NZ brush; old use holt.

copy noun **1** *a copy of the report:* **duplicate**, facsimile, photocopy; transcript; reprint; trademark Xerox. **2** *a copy of a sketch by Leonardo da Vinci:* **replica**, reproduction, print, imitation, likeness; counterfeit, forgery, fake.
• verb **1** *each form had to be copied:* **duplicate**, photocopy, xerox, photostat, run off, reproduce. **2** *portraits copied from original paintings by Reynolds:* **reproduce**, replicate; forge, fake, counterfeit. **3** *their sound was copied by a lot of jazz players:* **imitate**, reproduce, emulate, follow, echo, mirror, parrot, mimic, ape; plagiarize, steal; informal rip off.

coquettish adjective **flirtatious**, flirty, provocative, seductive, inviting, kittenish, coy, arch, teasing, playful; informal come-hither, vampish.

cord noun **string**, thread, thong, lace, ribbon, strap, tape, tie, line, rope, cable, wire, ligature; twine, yarn, elastic, braid.

cordial adjective *a very cordial welcome:* **friendly**, warm, genial, affable, amiable, pleasant, fond, affectionate, warm-hearted, good-natured, gracious, hospitable, welcoming, hearty.
• noun *fruit cordial:* **squash**, crush, concentrate; juice.

cordon noun **barrier**, line, row, chain, ring, circle.
• verb **close off**, shut off, seal off, fence off, separate off, isolate, enclose, surround.

core noun **1** *the earth's core:* **centre**, interior, middle, nucleus; recesses, bowels, depths; informal innards. **2** *the core of the argument:* **heart**, heart of the matter, nucleus, nub, kernel, marrow, meat, essence, quintessence, crux, gist, pith, substance, basis, fundamentals; informal nitty-gritty, brass tacks.
–OPPOSITES periphery.
• adjective *the core issue:* **central**, key, basic, fundamental, principal, primary, main, chief, crucial, vital, essential; informal number-one.
–OPPOSITES peripheral.

cork noun **stopper**, stop, plug, bung, peg; N. Amer. stopple.

corn noun **grain**, cereal; wheat, barley, oats, rye; maize.

corner noun **1** *the cart lurched round the corner:* **bend**, curve, dog-leg; turn, turning, junction, fork, intersection; Brit. hairpin bend. **2** *a charming corner of Italy:* **district**, region, area, section, quarter, part; informal neck of the woods. **3** *he found himself in a bit of a corner:* **predicament**, plight, tight spot, mess, muddle, difficulty, problem, dilemma, quandary; informal pickle, jam, stew, fix, hole, hot water, bind.
• verb **1** *he was eventually cornered by police dogs:* **surround**, trap, hem in, pen in, enclose, isolate, cut off; capture, catch. **2** *crime syndicates have cornered the stolen car market:* **gain control of**, take over, control, dominate, monopolize; capture; informal sew up.

cornerstone noun **foundation**, basis, keystone, mainspring, mainstay, linchpin, bedrock, base, backbone, key, centrepiece, core, heart, centre, crux.

corny adjective (informal) **banal**, trite, hackneyed, clichéd, predictable, stereotyped, platitudinous, tired, stale, overworked, overused, well worn; mawkish, sentimental, mushy, slushy, sloppy, cloying, syrupy, sugary, saccharine; Brit. twee; informal cheesy, schmaltzy, cutesy, toe-curling; Brit. informal soppy; N. Amer. informal cornball, hokey.

corollary noun **consequence**, result, upshot, effect, repercussion, product, by-product; Brit. knock-on effect.

corporation noun **1** *the chairman of the corporation:* **company**, firm, business, concern, operation, organization, agency, trust, partnership; conglomerate, group, chain, multinational; informal outfit, set-up. **2** (Brit.) *the corporation refused two planning applications:* **council**, local authority.

corporeal adjective **bodily**, fleshly, carnal, human, mortal, earthly, physical, material.

corps noun **1** *an army corps:* **unit**, division, detachment, section, company, contingent, squad, squadron, regiment, battalion, brigade, platoon. **2** *a corps of trained engineers:* **group**, body, band, party, gang, pack; team, crew.

corpse noun **dead body**, body, carcass, remains; informal stiff; Medicine cadaver.

> **WORD LINKS**
> **necrophobia** extreme fear of death or dead bodies

corpulent adjective **fat**, obese, overweight, plump, portly, stout, chubby, paunchy, beer-bellied, heavy, bulky, chunky, well padded, well covered, meaty, fleshy, rotund, broad in the beam; informal tubby, pudgy, beefy, porky, roly-poly, blubbery; Brit. informal podgy; N. Amer. informal corn-fed.
– OPPOSITES thin.

correct adjective **1** *the correct answer:* **right**, accurate, true; informal on the mark, on the beam, on the nail; Brit. informal spot on, bang on; N. Amer. informal on the money, on the button. **2** *correct behaviour:* **proper**, seemly, decorous, decent, respectable, right, suitable, fit, fitting, befitting, appropriate; approved, accepted, conventional, customary, traditional, orthodox.
– OPPOSITES wrong, improper.
• verb **1** *correct any mistakes you have made:* **rectify**, put right, set right, amend, emend, remedy, repair. **2** *an attempt to correct the trade imbalance:* **counteract**, offset, counterbalance, compensate for, make up for, neutralize. **3** *the brakes need correcting:* **adjust**, fix, set, reset, standardize, normalize, calibrate, fine-tune.

correction noun **rectification**, righting, amendment, repair, remedy.

corrective adjective **remedial**, therapeutic, restorative, curative.

correlate verb **1** *social status often correlates with wealth:* **correspond**, match, parallel, agree, tally, tie in, be consistent, be compatible, coordinate, dovetail, relate, conform; informal square; N. Amer. informal jibe. **2** *fat intake was correlated with heart disease:* **connect**, link, associate, relate.
– OPPOSITES contrast.

correlation noun **connection**, association, link, tie-in, tie-up, relation, relationship, interrelationship, interdependence, interconnection, interaction; correspondence.

correspond verb **1** *their actions do not correspond with their statements:* **correlate**, agree, be in agreement, be consistent, be compatible, accord, be in tune, concur, coincide, tally, tie in, dovetail, fit in; match; informal square; N. Amer. informal jibe. **2** *a rank corresponding to the British rank of sergeant:* **be equivalent**, be analogous, be comparable, equate. **3** *Debbie and I corresponded for years:* **exchange letters**, write, communicate, keep in touch/contact.

correspondence noun **1** *there is some correspondence between the two variables:* **correlation**, agreement, consistency, compatibility, conformity, similarity, resemblance, parallel, comparability, accord, concurrence, coincidence. **2** *his private correspondence:* **letters**, messages, missives, mail, post; communication.

correspondent noun **reporter**, journalist, columnist, writer, contributor, commentator.

corresponding adjective **commensurate**, parallel, correspondent, matching, correlated, relative, proportional, proportionate, comparable, equivalent, analogous.

corridor noun **passage**, passageway, aisle, gangway, hall, hallway, gallery, arcade.

corroborate verb **confirm**, verify, endorse, ratify, authenticate, validate, certify; support, back up, uphold, bear out, bear witness

to, attest to, testify to, vouch for, substantiate, sustain.
– OPPOSITES contradict.

corrode verb **1** *the iron had corroded:* **rust**, tarnish; wear away, disintegrate, crumble, perish, rot; oxidize. **2** *acid rain corrodes buildings:* **wear away**, eat away at, consume, destroy; dissolve.

corrosive adjective **caustic**, burning, stinging; destructive, damaging, harmful, harsh.

corrugated adjective **ridged**, fluted, grooved, furrowed, crinkled, crinkly, puckered, creased, wrinkled, wrinkly, crumpled; technical striated.

corrupt adjective **1** *a corrupt official | corrupt practices:* **dishonest**, unscrupulous, unprincipled, unethical, amoral, untrustworthy, venal, underhand, double-dealing, fraudulent; criminal, illegal, unlawful, nefarious; informal crooked, shady, dirty, sleazy; Brit. informal bent, dodgy. **2** *he is utterly corrupt:* **immoral**, depraved, degenerate, vice-ridden, perverted, debauched, dissolute, dissipated, bad, wicked, evil, base, sinful, ungodly, profane, impious, impure; informal warped.
– OPPOSITES honest, ethical, pure.
• verb **deprave**, pervert, warp, lead astray, defile, pollute, sully.

corruption noun **1** *political corruption:* **dishonesty**, unscrupulousness, double-dealing, fraud, misconduct, crime, criminality, wrongdoing; bribery, subornation, venality, extortion, profiteering; N. Amer. payola; informal graft, crookedness, sleaze. **2** *his fall into corruption:* **immorality**, depravity, vice, degeneracy, perversion, debauchery, dissoluteness, decadence, wickedness, evil, sin, sinfulness, ungodliness; formal turpitude.
– OPPOSITES honesty, morality, purity.

cortège noun *the funeral cortège:* **procession**, parade, cavalcade, motorcade, convoy, train, column, file, line.

cosmetic adjective *most of the changes were merely cosmetic:* **superficial**, surface, skin-deep, outward, exterior, external.
– OPPOSITES fundamental.
• noun (**cosmetics**) *a new range of cosmetics:* **make-up**, beauty products; informal warpaint, paint, slap.

cosmic adjective **1** *cosmic bodies:* **extraterrestrial**, space, astral, planetary, stellar; sidereal. **2** *a tale on a cosmic scale:* **epic**, huge, immense, enormous, massive, colossal, prodigious; fathomless, measureless, infinite, limitless, boundless.

cosmonaut noun **astronaut**, spaceman/woman, space traveller, space cadet; N. Amer. informal jock.

cosmopolitan adjective **1** *the student body has a cosmopolitan character:* **multicultural**, multiracial, international, worldwide, global. **2** *a cosmopolitan audience:* **worldly**, worldly-wise, cultivated, cultured, sophisticated, suave, urbane, glamorous, fashionable; informal jet-setting.

cosset verb **pamper**, indulge, overindulge, mollycoddle, coddle, baby, pet, mother, nanny, pander to, feather-bed, spoil; wrap in cotton wool, wait on someone hand and foot.

cost noun **1** *the cost of the equipment:* **price**, fee, tariff, charge; expense, expenditure, outlay; humorous damage. **2** *the human cost of the conflict:* **sacrifice**, loss, expense, penalty, toll, price. **3** (**costs**) *we need to make £10,000 to cover our costs:* **expenses**, outgoings, overheads; expenditure, outlay, disbursements.
• verb **1** *the jacket costs £186:* **be priced at**, sell for, be valued at, come to, amount to; informal set someone back, go for. **2** *the proposal has not yet been costed:* **price**, put a price on, value, put a figure on.

costly adjective **1** *costly machinery:* **expensive**, dear, high-cost, overpriced; Brit. over the odds; informal steep, pricey. **2** *a costly mistake:* **catastrophic**, disastrous, calamitous, ruinous; damaging, harmful, injurious, deleterious.
– OPPOSITES cheap.

costume noun **clothes**, garments, robes, outfit, ensemble; dress, clothing, attire, garb, uniform, livery; informal get-up, gear, togs; Brit. informal clobber, kit; N. Amer.

informal threads; formal apparel; old use raiment.

cosy adjective **1** *a cosy country cottage:* **snug**, comfortable, warm, homey, homely, welcoming; safe, sheltered, secure; N. Amer. home-style; informal comfy. **2** *a cosy chat:* **intimate**, heart-to-heart, relaxed, informal, friendly.

coterie noun **clique**, set, circle, inner circle, crowd, in-crowd, band, community; informal gang, posse.

cottage noun **lodge**, chalet, cabin; shack, shanty; (in Russia) dacha; Scottish bothy, but and ben; Austral. informal weekender; literary bower.

couch noun *she seated herself on the couch:* **settee**, sofa, divan, chaise longue, chesterfield, love seat, settle, ottoman; Brit. put-you-up; N. Amer. daybed, davenport.
• verb *his reply was couched in deferential terms:* **express**, phrase, word, frame, put, formulate, style, convey, say, state, utter.

cough verb *he coughed loudly:* hack, hawk, bark; splutter, clear your throat.
• noun *a loud cough:* bark, splutter; informal frog in your throat.
■ **cough up** pay up, come up with, hand over, dish out, part with; informal fork out, shell out, lay out; Brit. informal stump up; N. Amer. informal ante up, pony up.

WORD LINKS
tussive relating to coughing

council noun **1** *the town council:* **local authority**, local government, municipal authority, administration, executive, chamber, assembly; Brit. corporation. **2** *the Schools Council:* **advisory body**, board, committee, commission, assembly, panel; synod. **3** *that evening, she held a family council:* meeting, gathering, conference, assembly.

! Don't confuse **council** with **counsel**, which means 'advice' or 'advise someone' (*we counselled him to see a solicitor*).

counsel noun **1** *his wise counsel:* **advice**, guidance, counselling, direction; recommendations, suggestions, guidelines, hints, tips, pointers, warnings. **2** *the counsel for the defence:* **barrister**, lawyer; Scottish advocate; N. Amer. attorney, counselor; informal brief.
• verb *he counselled the team to withdraw from the deal:* **advise**, recommend, direct, advocate, encourage, warn, caution; guide.

C

counsellor noun **adviser**, consultant, guide, mentor.

count verb **1** *she counted the money again:* **add up**, reckon up, figure up, total, tally, calculate, compute; Brit. tot up. **2** *a company with 250 employees, not counting overseas staff:* **include**, take into account, take account of, allow for, take into consideration. **3** *I count it a privilege to be asked:* **consider**, think, feel, regard, look on as, view as, hold to be, judge, deem, account. **4** *it's your mother's feelings that count:* **matter**, be of consequence, be of account, be significant, signify, be important, carry weight; informal cut any ice.
• noun *her white blood cell count:* **amount**, number, total; level, reading, index; density, concentration.
■ **count on 1** *you can count on me:* rely on, depend on, bank on, trust, be sure of, have confidence in, believe in, put your faith in, take for granted, take as read. **2** *they hadn't counted on Rangers' indomitable spirit:* expect, reckon on, anticipate, envisage, allow for, be prepared for, bargain for/on; N. Amer. informal figure on.

countenance noun *his strikingly handsome countenance:* **face**, features, physiognomy, profile; expression, look, appearance, aspect, mien; informal mug; literary visage.
• verb *he would not countenance the use of force:* **tolerate**, permit, allow, agree to, consent to, go along with, hold with, put up with, accept; informal stand for; formal brook.

counter[1] noun *a pile of counters:* **token**, chip, disc; piece, man, marker; N. Amer. check.

counter[2] verb **1** *workers countered accusations of dishonesty with claims of oppression:* **respond to**, parry, hit back at, answer, retort to. **2** *the second argument is more difficult to counter:* **oppose**, dispute,

argue against/with, contradict, controvert, negate, counteract; challenge, contest; formal gainsay.
– OPPOSITES support.
• adjective *a counter bid:* **opposing**, opposed; retaliatory, contrary.
■ **counter to** against, in opposition to, contrary to, at variance with, in defiance of, in contravention of, in conflict with, at odds with.

counteract verb **1** *new measures to counteract drug trafficking:* **prevent**, thwart, frustrate, foil, impede, curb, hinder, hamper, check, put a stop/end to, defeat. **2** *a drug to counteract the possible effect on her heart:* **offset**, counterbalance, balance out, cancel out, even out, countervail, compensate for, make up for, remedy; neutralize, nullify, negate, invalidate.
– OPPOSITES encourage, exacerbate.

counterbalance verb **compensate for**, make up for, offset, balance out, even out, counteract, equalize, neutralize; nullify, negate, undo.

counterfeit adjective *counterfeit cassettes:* **fake**, pirate, bogus, forged, imitation; informal phoney.
– OPPOSITES genuine.
• noun *the notes were counterfeits:* **fake**, forgery, copy, reproduction, imitation; fraud, sham; informal phoney.
– OPPOSITES original.
• verb *his signature was hard to counterfeit:* **fake**, forge, copy, reproduce, imitate.

countermand verb **revoke**, rescind, reverse, undo, repeal, retract, withdraw, quash, overturn, overrule, cancel, annul, invalidate, nullify, negate.
– OPPOSITES uphold.

counterpart noun **equivalent**, opposite number, peer, equal, parallel, complement, analogue, match, twin, mate, fellow, brother, sister.

countless adjective **innumerable**, numerous, untold, legion, without number, numberless, limitless, multitudinous, incalculable; informal umpteen, no end of, loads of, stacks of, heaps of, masses of, oodles of, zillions of; N. Amer. informal gazillions of; literary myriad.
– OPPOSITES few.

countrified adjective **rural**, rustic, pastoral, bucolic, country; idyllic, unspoilt; literary Arcadian, sylvan.
– OPPOSITES urban.

country noun **1** *foreign countries:* **nation**, state, kingdom, realm, territory, province, principality. **2** *he risked his life for his country:* **homeland**, native land, fatherland, motherland. **3** *the country took to the streets:* **people**, public, population, populace, citizenry, nation; electorate, voters, taxpayers, grass roots; Brit. informal Joe Public. **4** *thickly forested country:* **terrain**, land, territory; landscape, scenery, setting, surroundings, environment. **5** *she hated living in the country:* **countryside**, green belt, great outdoors; provinces, rural areas, backwoods, back of beyond, hinterland; Austral./NZ outback, bush, back country, backblocks; informal sticks, middle of nowhere; N. Amer. informal boondocks.
• adjective *country pursuits:* **rural**, countryside, outdoor, rustic, pastoral, bucolic; literary sylvan, Arcadian.
– OPPOSITES urban.

countryman, countrywoman noun **compatriot**, fellow citizen; brother, sister, comrade.

countryside noun **1** *beautiful unspoilt countryside:* **landscape**, scenery, surroundings, setting, environment; country, terrain, land. **2** *I was brought up in the countryside.* See COUNTRY noun sense 5.

county noun shire, province, territory, region, district, area.

coup noun **1** *a violent military coup:* coup d'état, overthrow, takeover; palace revolution, rebellion, revolt, insurrection, uprising. **2** *a major publishing coup:* **success**, triumph, feat, accomplishment, achievement, scoop.

coup de grâce noun **death blow**, final blow, kiss of death; informal KO, kayo.

coup d'état noun. See COUP sense 1.

couple noun **1** *a couple of girls:* **pair**, duo, twosome, two, brace. **2** *a honeymoon couple:* **husband and wife**, twosome, partners, lovers; informal item.
• verb **1** *a sense of hope is coupled*

with a sense of loss: **combine**, accompany, mix, incorporate, link, associate, connect, ally; add to, join to; formal conjoin. **2** *a cable is coupled to one of the wheels:* **connect**, attach, join, fasten, fix, link, secure, tie, bind, strap, rope, tether, truss, lash, hitch, yoke, chain, hook up.
– OPPOSITES detach.

coupon noun **voucher**, token, ticket, slip, form; N. Amer. informal comp, rain check.

courage noun **bravery**, courageousness, pluck, valour, fearlessness, nerve, daring, audacity, boldness, grit, heroism, gallantry; informal guts, spunk; Brit. informal bottle; N. Amer. informal moxie, cojones, sand.
– OPPOSITES cowardice.

courageous adjective **brave**, plucky, fearless, valiant, intrepid, heroic, undaunted, unflinching, unshrinking, unafraid, dauntless, indomitable, doughty, mettlesome, stout-hearted, gallant, death-or-glory; N. Amer. rock-ribbed; informal game, gutsy, spunky, ballsy, have-a-go.
– OPPOSITES cowardly.

courier noun **1** *the documents were sent by courier:* **messenger**, dispatch rider, runner. **2** *a courier for a package holiday company:* **representative**, tour guide; N. Amer. tour director; informal rep.

course noun **1** *the plane changed course:* **route**, direction, way, track, path, line, trail, trajectory, bearing, heading. **2** *the course of history:* **progression**, development, progress, advance, evolution, flow, movement, sequence, order, succession, rise, march, passage, passing. **3** *the best course to adopt:* **procedure**, plan, course/line of action, modus operandi, practice, approach, technique, way, means, policy, strategy, tactic, programme. **4** *a waterlogged course:* **racecourse**, racetrack, track, ground. **5** *a French course:* **course of study**, syllabus; classes, lectures, studies. **6** *a course of antibiotics:* **programme**, series, sequence, system, schedule, regime.
• verb *tears coursed down her cheeks:* **flow**, pour, stream, run, rush, gush, cascade, flood, roll.
■ **of course** naturally, as might be expected, needless to say, certainly, to be sure, as a matter of course, obviously, it goes without saying.

> **!** Don't confuse **course** with **coarse**, which means 'rough' (*my hair is coarse and wavy*).

court noun **1** *the court found him guilty:* **court of law**, law court; bench, bar, tribunal, chancery, assizes. **2** *the King's court:* **royal household**, retinue, entourage, train, suite, courtiers, attendants.
• verb **1** *a newspaper editor who was courted by senior politicians:* **cultivate**, curry favour with, make up to, ingratiate yourself with; wine and dine; informal butter up, suck up to. **2** *he was busily courting public attention:* **seek**, pursue, go after, strive for, solicit. **3** *he's often courted controversy:* **risk**, invite, attract, bring on yourself.

> **WORD LINKS**
> **forensic** relating to courts of law

courteous adjective **polite**, well mannered, civil, respectful, well behaved; gentlemanly, chivalrous, gallant; gracious, obliging, considerate.
– OPPOSITES rude.

courtesy noun **politeness**, courteousness, good manners, civility, respect; chivalry, gallantry; graciousness, consideration, thought.

courtier noun **attendant**, lord, lady, lady-in-waiting, steward, equerry, page, squire.

courtship noun **1** *a whirlwind courtship:* **romance**, love affair; engagement. **2** *his courtship of Emma:* **wooing**, courting, suit, pursuit.

courtyard noun **quadrangle**, cloister, square, plaza, piazza, close, enclosure, yard; informal quad.

cove noun *a small sandy cove:* **bay**, inlet, fjord; Scottish loch; Irish lough.

covenant noun **contract**, agreement, undertaking, commitment, guarantee, warrant, pledge, promise, bond, indenture; pact, deal, settlement, arrangement, understanding.

cover verb **1** *she covered her face with her hands:* **protect**, shield, shelter; hide, conceal, mask. **2** *his car was covered in mud:* **cake**, coat,

C

encrust, plaster, smother; daub, smear, splatter. **3** *snow covered the fields:* **blanket**, carpet, coat, shroud, smother. **4** *a course covering all aspects of the business:* **deal with**, consider, take in, include, involve, incorporate, embrace. **5** *the trial was covered by a range of newspapers:* **report on**, write about, describe, commentate on, deal with. **6** *he turned on the radio to cover the sound of their conversation:* **mask**, disguise, hide, camouflage. **7** *I'm covering for Jill:* **stand in for**, fill in for, deputize for, take over from, relieve, take the place of, sit in for, hold the fort; informal sub for; N. Amer. informal pinch-hit for. **8** *can you make enough to cover your costs?* **pay**, fund, finance; pay back, make up for, offset. **9** *your home is covered against damage and loss:* **insure**, protect, secure, underwrite, indemnify; Brit. assure. **10** *we covered ten miles each day:* **travel**, journey, go, do.
–OPPOSITES reveal, expose.
• **noun 1** *a protective cover:* **covering**, sleeve, wrapping, wrapper, envelope, sheath, housing, jacket, casing, cowling; awning, canopy, tarpaulin, fairing. **2** *a manhole cover:* **lid**, top, cap. **3** *a book cover:* **binding**, jacket, dust jacket, dust cover, wrapper. **4** (**covers**) *she pulled the covers over her head:* **bedclothes**, bedding, sheets, blankets. **5** *a thick cover of snow:* **coating**, coat, covering, layer, carpet, blanket; film, sheet, veneer, crust, skin, cloak, mantle, veil, pall, shroud. **6** *panicking onlookers ran for cover:* **shelter**, protection, refuge, sanctuary, haven, hiding place. **7** *the company was a cover for an international swindle:* **front**, facade, smokescreen, screen, blind, camouflage, disguise, mask, cloak. **8** (Brit.) *your policy provides cover against damage by subsidence:* **insurance**, protection, security, assurance, indemnification, indemnity.
■ **cover something up** conceal, hide, keep secret/dark, hush up, draw a veil over, suppress, sweep under the carpet, gloss over; informal whitewash, keep a/the lid on.

coverage **noun reporting**, description, treatment, handling, presentation, investigation, commentary; reports, articles, pieces, stories; portrayal.

covering **noun 1** *a canvas covering:* **awning**, canopy, tarpaulin, cowling, casing, housing, fairing; wrapping, wrapper, cover, envelope, sheath, sleeve, jacket, lid, top, cap. **2** *a covering of snow:* **layer**, coating, coat, carpet, blanket, overlay, topping, dusting, film, sheet, veneer, crust, skin, cloak, mantle, veil.
• **adjective** *a covering letter:* **accompanying**, explanatory, supplementary.

coverlet **noun bedspread**, bedcover, cover, throw, duvet, quilt; Brit. eiderdown; N. Amer. spread, comforter; dated counterpane.

covert **adjective secret**, furtive, clandestine, surreptitious, stealthy, cloak-and-dagger, backstairs, under-the-table, hidden, concealed, private, undercover, underground; informal hush-hush.
–OPPOSITES overt.

cover-up **noun whitewash**, concealment, facade, camouflage, disguise, mask.
–OPPOSITES exposé.

covet **verb desire**, yearn for, crave, have your heart set on, want, wish for, long for, hanker after/for, hunger after/for, thirst for.

covetous **adjective grasping**, greedy, acquisitive, desirous, possessive, envious, green with envy.

cow **verb intimidate**, daunt, browbeat, bully, tyrannize, scare, terrorize, frighten, dishearten, subdue; informal psych out, bulldoze, steamroller.

coward **noun weakling**, milksop, namby-pamby, mouse; informal chicken, scaredy-cat, yellow-belly, sissy, baby; Brit. informal big girl's blouse; N. Amer. informal pantywaist, pussy; Austral./NZ informal dingo, sook.
–OPPOSITES hero.

cowardly **adjective faint-hearted**, lily-livered, spineless, chicken-hearted, craven, timid, timorous, fearful, pusillanimous; informal yellow, chicken, weak-kneed, gutless, yellow-bellied, wimpish, wimpy; Brit. informal wet.
–OPPOSITES brave.

cowboy **noun cattleman**, cowhand, cowman, cowherd, herder, herdsman, drover, stockman, rancher, gaucho, vaquero; N. Amer. informal cowpuncher, cowpoke; N. Amer. dated buckaroo.

cower verb **cringe**, shrink, crouch, tremble, shake, quake, blench, quail, grovel.

coy adjective demure, shy, modest, bashful, reticent, diffident, self-effacing, shrinking, timid.
– OPPOSITES brazen.

crabbed adjective *her crabbed handwriting:* **cramped**, ill-formed, bad, illegible, unreadable, indecipherable; shaky, spidery.

crabby adjective **irritable**, cantankerous, irascible, bad-tempered, grumpy, grouchy, crotchety, tetchy, testy, crusty, curmudgeonly, ill-tempered, ill-humoured, peevish, cross, fractious, pettish, crabbed, prickly, waspish; informal snappy; Brit. informal shirty, stroppy, narky, ratty; N. Amer. informal cranky, ornery; Austral./NZ informal snaky.
– OPPOSITES affable.

crack noun **1** *a crack in the glass:* **split**, break, chip, fracture, rupture; crazing; flaw, imperfection. **2** *a crack between two rocks:* **space**, gap, crevice, fissure, cleft, breach, rift, cranny, chink. **3** *the crack of a rifle:* **bang**, report, explosion, detonation, pop; clap, crash. **4** *a crack on the head:* **blow**, bang, hit, knock, rap, punch, bump, smack, slap; informal bash, whack, thwack, clout, wallop, biff, bop. **5** (informal) *we'll have a crack at it:* **attempt**, try; informal go, shot, stab, bash. **6** (informal) *cheap cracks about her clothes:* **joke**, witticism, quip; jibe, taunt, sneer, insult; informal gag, wisecrack, dig.
• verb **1** *the glass cracked in the heat:* **break**, split, fracture, rupture, snap. **2** *she cracked him across the forehead:* **hit**, strike, smack, slap, beat, thump, knock, rap, punch; informal bash, whack, thwack, clobber, clout, clip, wallop, belt, biff, bop, sock; Brit. informal slosh; N. Amer. informal boff, bust, slug. **3** *he finally cracked:* **break down**, give way, cave in, go to pieces, crumble, lose control, yield, succumb. **4** (informal) *the code proved hard to crack:* **decipher**, interpret, decode, break, solve, work out; informal figure out, suss out.
• adjective *a crack shot:* **expert**, formidable, virtuoso, masterly, consummate, excellent, first-rate, first-class, marvellous, wonderful, magnificent, outstanding, superlative; deadly; informal great, superb, fantastic, ace, hotshot, mean, demon; Brit. informal brilliant; N. Amer. informal crackerjack.
– OPPOSITES incompetent.
■ **crack down on** suppress, prevent, stop, put a stop to, put an end to, stamp out, eliminate, eradicate; clamp down on, get tough on, come down hard on, limit, restrain, restrict, check, keep in check, control, keep under control.

cracked adjective **chipped**, broken, crazed, fractured, splintered, split; damaged, defective, flawed, imperfect.

crackle verb **sizzle**, fizz, hiss, crack, snap, sputter, splutter.

cradle noun **1** *the baby's cradle:* **crib**, Moses basket, cot, carrycot. **2** *the cradle of democracy:* **birthplace**, fount, fountainhead, source, spring, fountain, origin, place of origin, seat; literary wellspring.
• verb *she cradled his head in her arms:* **hold**, support, pillow, cushion, shelter, protect; rest, prop.

craft noun **1** *the historian's craft:* **activity**, occupation, trade, profession, work, line of work, job. **2** *she used craft and diplomacy:* **cunning**, craftiness, guile, wiliness, artfulness, deviousness, slyness, trickery, duplicity, dishonesty, deceit, deceitfulness, deception, intrigue, subterfuge; wiles, ploys, ruses, schemes, tricks. **3** *a sailing craft:* **vessel**, ship, boat.

craftsman, **craftswoman** noun **artisan**, artist, skilled worker; expert, master.

craftsmanship noun **workmanship**, artistry, art, handiwork, work; skill, expertise, technique.

crafty adjective **cunning**, wily, guileful, artful, devious, sly, tricky, scheming, calculating, sharp, shrewd, astute, canny; duplicitous, dishonest, deceitful; old use subtle.
– OPPOSITES honest.

crag noun **cliff**, bluff, ridge, precipice, height, peak, tor, escarpment, scarp.

C

craggy adjective **1** *the craggy cliffs:* **steep**, sheer, perpendicular; rocky, rugged. **2** *his craggy face:* **rugged**, rough-hewn, strong; weather-beaten, weathered.

cram verb **1** *wardrobes crammed with clothes:* **fill**, stuff, pack, jam, fill to overflowing, fill to the brim, overload; crowd, throng. **2** *they all crammed into the car:* **crowd**, pack, pile, squash. **3** *he crammed his clothes into a suitcase:* **thrust**, push, shove, force, ram, jam, stuff, pack, pile, squash, squeeze, wedge. **4** *most of the students are cramming for exams:* **revise**; informal swot, mug up, bone up.

cramp noun *stomach cramps:* **muscle/muscular spasm**, pain, shooting pain, pang.
• verb *tighter rules will cramp economic growth:* **hinder**, impede, inhibit, hamper, constrain, hamstring, interfere with, restrict, limit, shackle; slow down, check, arrest, curb, retard.

cramped adjective **1** *cramped accommodation:* **poky**, uncomfortable, confined, restricted, constricted, small, tiny, narrow; crowded, congested. **2** *cramped handwriting:* **small**, crabbed, illegible, unreadable, indecipherable.
– OPPOSITES spacious.

crane noun **derrick**, winch, hoist, windlass; block and tackle.

crank[1] verb *you crank the engine by hand:* **start**, get going.
■ **crank something up** (informal) increase, intensify, heighten, escalate, add to, augment, build up, expand, extend, raise; speed up, accelerate; informal up, jack up, hike up, step up, bump up, pump up.

crank[2] noun *a bunch of cranks:* **eccentric**, oddity, madman/madwoman, lunatic; informal oddball, freak, weirdo, crackpot, loony, nut, nutcase, head case, maniac; Brit. informal nutter; N. Amer. informal screwball, kook.

cranky adjective **1** (informal) *a cranky diet:* **eccentric**, bizarre, weird, peculiar, odd, strange, unconventional, left-field, unorthodox, outlandish; silly, stupid, mad, crazy, idiotic; informal wacky, crackpot, nutty; Brit. informal daft, potty. **2** (N. Amer. informal) *the children were tired and cranky.* See IRRITABLE.

cranny noun **chink**, crack, crevice, slit, split, fissure, rift, cleft, opening, gap, aperture, cavity, hole, hollow, niche, corner, nook.

crash verb **1** *the car crashed into a tree:* **smash into**, collide with, be in collision with, hit, strike, ram, cannon into, plough into, meet head-on, run into; N. Amer. impact. **2** *he crashed his car:* **smash**, wreck; Brit. write off; Brit. informal prang; N. Amer. informal total. **3** *waves crashed against the shore:* **dash**, batter, pound, lash, slam, thunder. **4** *thunder crashed overhead:* **boom**, crack, roll, explode, bang, blast, blare, resound, reverberate, rumble, thunder, echo. **5** (informal) *his company crashed:* **collapse**, fold, fail, go under, go bankrupt, cease trading, go into receivership, go into liquidation, be wound up; informal go broke, go bust, go to the wall, go belly up.
• noun **1** *a crash on the motorway:* **accident**, collision, smash, road traffic accident, RTA; derailment; N. Amer. wreck; informal pile-up; Brit. informal prang, shunt. **2** *a loud crash:* **bang**, smash, smack, crack, bump, thud, clatter, clang; report, detonation, explosion; noise, racket, din. **3** *the crash of her company:* **collapse**, failure, liquidation.

crass adjective **stupid**, insensitive, mindless, thoughtless, witless, oafish, boorish, asinine, coarse, gross, graceless, tasteless, tactless, clumsy, heavy-handed, blundering; informal ignorant.
– OPPOSITES intelligent.

crate noun **case**, chest, tea chest, box; container, receptacle.

crater noun **hollow**, bowl, basin, hole, cavity, depression; Geology caldera.

crave verb **long for**, yearn for, desire, want, wish for, hunger for, thirst for, sigh for, pine for, hanker after, have a yen for, covet, lust after, ache for, set your heart on, dream of, be bent on; informal itch for, be dying for.

craven adjective **cowardly**, lily-livered, faint-hearted, chicken-hearted, spineless, timid, timorous,

fearful, pusillanimous, weak, feeble; informal yellow, chicken, weak-kneed, gutless, yellow-bellied, wimpish; contemptible, abject, ignominious; Brit. informal wet.
–OPPOSITES brave.

craving noun **longing**, yearning, desire, want, wish, yen, hankering, hunger, thirst, appetite, greed, lust, ache, need, urge; informal itch.

crawl verb **1** *they crawled under the table:* **creep**, worm your way, go on all fours, go on hands and knees, wriggle, slither, squirm, scrabble. **2** (informal) *I'm not going to go crawling to him:* **grovel to**, kowtow to, pander to, toady to, bow and scrape to, dance attendance on, make up to, fawn on/over; informal suck up to, lick someone's boots, butter up. **3** *the place was crawling with soldiers:* **be full of**, overflow with, teem with, be packed with, be crowded with, be alive with, be overrun with, swarm with, be bristling with, be infested with, be thick with; informal be stuffed with, be jam-packed with, be chock-a-block with, be chock-full of.

craze noun **fad**, fashion, trend, vogue, enthusiasm, mania, passion, rage, obsession, compulsion, fixation, fetish, fancy, taste, fascination, preoccupation; informal thing.

crazed adjective **mad**, insane, deranged, demented, certifiable, lunatic, psychopathic; wild, raving, berserk, manic, maniac, frenzied; informal crazy, mental, off your head, out of your head, raving mad. See also CRAZY sense 1.
–OPPOSITES sane.

crazy adjective (informal) **1** *a crazy old man:* **mad**, insane, out of your mind, deranged, demented, not in your right mind, crazed, lunatic, non compos mentis, unhinged, mad as a hatter, mad as a March hare; informal mental, off your head, nutty, off your rocker, not right in the head, round the bend, raving mad, bats, batty, bonkers, cuckoo, loopy, loony, bananas, loco, with a screw loose, touched, gaga, doolally, not all there, out to lunch, away with the fairies; Brit. informal barmy, crackers, barking, potty, round the twist, off your trolley, not the full shilling; N. Amer. informal nutso, out of your tree, wacko, gonzo; Austral./NZ informal bushed. **2** *a crazy idea:* **stupid**, foolish, idiotic, silly, absurd, ridiculous, ludicrous, preposterous, farcical, laughable, nonsensical, imbecilic, hare-brained, half-baked, impracticable, unworkable, ill-conceived, senseless; informal cockeyed; Brit. informal barmy, daft. **3** *he's crazy about her:* **passionate about**, very keen on, enamoured of, infatuated with, smitten with, devoted to; very enthusiastic about, fanatical about; informal mad about.
–OPPOSITES sane, sensible.

creak verb **squeak**, squeal; groan; whine, complain.

cream noun **1** *skin cream:* **lotion**, ointment, moisturizer, emollient, unguent, cosmetic; salve, rub, embrocation, balm, liniment. **2** *the cream of the world's photographers:* **best**, finest, pick, flower, crème de la crème, elite.
–OPPOSITES dregs.
• adjective *a cream dress:* **off-white**, cream-coloured, creamy, ivory.

creamy adjective **smooth**, thick, velvety; rich, buttery.
–OPPOSITES lumpy.

crease noun **1** *trousers with knife-edge creases:* **fold**, line, ridge; pleat, tuck; furrow, groove, corrugation. **2** *the creases at the corners of her eyes:* **wrinkle**, line, crinkle, pucker; (**creases**) crow's feet.
• verb *her skirt was creased and stained:* **crumple**, wrinkle, crinkle, line, scrunch up, rumple.

create verb **1** *she has created a work of stunning originality:* **produce**, generate, bring into being, make, fashion, build, construct; design, devise, frame, develop, shape, form, forge. **2** *regular socializing creates a good team spirit:* **bring about**, give rise to, lead to, result in, cause, breed, generate, engender, produce, make for, promote, foster, sow the seeds of, contribute to. **3** *the governments planned to create a free-trade zone:* **establish**, found, initiate, institute, constitute, inaugurate, launch, set up, form, organize, develop. **4** *she was created a life peer in 1990:* **appoint**, make; invest as, install as.
–OPPOSITES destroy.

C

creation noun **1** *the creation of a coalition government:* **establishment**, formation, foundation, initiation, institution, inauguration, constitution; production, generation, fashioning, building, construction, development, setting up. **2** *the whole of creation:* **the world**, the universe, the cosmos; the living world, the natural world, nature, life, living things. **3** *Dickens's literary creations:* **work**, work of art, production, opus; achievement.
–OPPOSITES destruction.

creative adjective **inventive**, imaginative, innovative, experimental, original; artistic; inspired, visionary; enterprising, resourceful.

creativity noun **inventiveness**, imagination, innovation, innovativeness, originality, individuality; artistry, inspiration, vision; enterprise, initiative, resourcefulness.

creator noun *the creator of the series:* **author**, writer, designer, deviser, maker, producer; originator, inventor, architect, mastermind, prime mover.

creature noun **1** *the earth and its creatures:* **animal**, beast; living thing, living being; N. Amer. informal critter. **2** *you're such a lazy creature!* **person**, individual, human being, character, soul, wretch, customer; informal devil, beggar, sort, type. **3** *she was denounced as a creature of the liberals:* **lackey**, minion, hireling, servant, puppet, tool, cat's paw, pawn; informal stooge, yes-man; Brit. informal poodle.

credence noun **1** *the government placed little credence in the scheme:* **belief**, faith, trust, confidence, reliance. **2** *later reports lent credence to this view:* **credibility**, plausibility.

credentials plural noun **documents**, documentation, papers, identity papers, bona fides, ID, ID card, identity card, passport, proof of identity; certification.

credibility noun **1** *the whole tale lacks credibility:* **plausibility**, believability, credence; authority, cogency. **2** *the party lacked moral credibility:* **trustworthiness**, reliability, dependability, integrity.

credible adjective **believable**, plausible, tenable, able to hold water, conceivable, likely, probable, possible, feasible, reasonable, having a ring of truth, persuasive, convincing.

credit noun *he never got much credit for the show's success:* **praise**, commendation, acclaim, acknowledgement, recognition, kudos, glory, esteem, respect, admiration, tributes, bouquets, thanks, gratitude, appreciation; informal brownie points.
•verb **believe**, accept, give credence to, trust, have faith in; informal buy, swallow, fall for, take something as gospel.

creditable adjective **commendable**, praiseworthy, laudable, admirable, honourable, estimable, meritorious, worthy, deserving, respectable.
–OPPOSITES deplorable.

credulous adjective **gullible**, naive, easily taken in, impressionable, unsuspecting, unsuspicious, unwary, unquestioning; innocent, ingenuous, inexperienced, unsophisticated, unworldly, wide-eyed.
–OPPOSITES suspicious.

creed noun **1** *people of many creeds and cultures:* **faith**, religion, belief, persuasion, denomination, sect. **2** *his political creed:* **beliefs**, principles, articles of faith, ideology, credo, doctrine, teaching, dogma, tenets.

creek noun **inlet**, bay, estuary, bight, fjord, sound; Scottish firth, frith; (in Orkney & Shetland) voe.

creep verb **1** *Tim crept out of the house:* **tiptoe**, steal, sneak, slip, slink, pad, edge, inch; skulk, prowl. **2** (informal) *they're always creeping to the boss:* **grovel to**, ingratiate yourself with, curry favour with, toady to, kowtow to, bow and scrape to, pander to, fawn on/over, make up to; informal crawl to, suck up to, lick someone's boots, butter up.

creepy adjective (informal) **frightening**, eerie, disturbing, sinister, weird, hair-raising, menacing, threatening; Scottish eldritch; informal spooky, scary.

crescent noun **half-moon**, sickle; arc, curve, bow.

crest noun **1** *the bird's crest:* **comb**, plume, tuft. **2** *the crest of the hill:*

summit, peak, top, tip, pinnacle, brow, crown, apex. **3** *the Duke of Wellington's crest:* **insignia**, regalia, badge, emblem, coat of arms, arms.

crestfallen adjective **downhearted**, downcast, despondent, disappointed, disconsolate, disheartened, discouraged, dispirited, dejected, sad, dismayed, unhappy, forlorn.
–OPPOSITES cheerful.

crevasse noun **chasm**, abyss, fissure, cleft, crack, split, breach, rift, hole, cavity.

crevice noun **crack**, fissure, cleft, chink, cranny, nook, slit, split, rift, fracture, breach; opening, gap, hole.

crew noun **1** *the ship's crew:* **sailors**, mariners, hands, ship's company, ship's complement. **2** *a crew of cameramen and sound engineers:* **team**, company, unit, corps, party, gang.

crib noun **cot**, cradle, Moses basket, carrycot.
• verb (informal) *she cribbed the plot from a Shakespeare play:* **copy**, plagiarize, poach, appropriate, steal, 'borrow'; informal rip off, lift; Brit. informal nick, pinch.

crick verb **strain**, twist, rick, sprain, pull, wrench; injure, hurt, damage.

crime noun **1** *kidnapping is a very serious crime:* **offence**, unlawful act, illegal act, felony, misdemeanour, misdeed; Law tort. **2** *the increase in crime:* **lawbreaking**, delinquency, wrongdoing, criminality, misconduct, illegality, villainy; Law malfeasance.

WORD LINKS
felonious relating to or involved in crime
criminology the scientific study of crime

criminal noun *a convicted criminal:* **lawbreaker**, offender, villain, delinquent, felon, convict, miscreant; thief, burglar, robber, armed robber, gunman, gangster, terrorist; informal crook, con, jailbird, old lag; N. Amer. informal hood, yardbird; formal malefactor; Law malfeasant.
• adjective **1** *criminal conduct:* **unlawful**, illegal, illicit, lawless, felonious, delinquent, fraudulent, actionable, culpable; villainous, nefarious, corrupt, wrong; informal crooked; Brit. informal bent; Law malfeasant. **2** (informal) *a criminal waste of taxpayers' money:* **deplorable**, shameful, reprehensible, disgraceful, inexcusable, unforgivable, unpardonable, outrageous, monstrous, shocking, scandalous, wicked.
–OPPOSITES lawful.

crimp verb **pleat**, flute, corrugate, ruffle, fold, crease, crinkle, pucker, gather; pinch, compress, press/squeeze together.

cringe verb **1** *she cringed as he bellowed in her ear:* **cower**, shrink, recoil, shy away, flinch, blench; shake, tremble, quiver, quake. **2** *I cringe when I think of it:* **wince**, shudder, squirm, feel embarrassed, feel mortified.

crinkle verb **wrinkle**, crease, pucker, furrow, corrugate, line; rumple, scrunch up.

crinkly adjective **wrinkled**, wrinkly, crinkled, creased, crumpled, rumpled, crimped, corrugated, fluted, puckered, furrowed; wavy.

cripple verb *the company had been crippled by the recession:* **devastate**, ruin; paralyse, bring to a standstill, put out of action, put out of business, bankrupt, break, bring someone to their knees.

crisis noun **1** *the situation had reached a crisis:* **critical point**, turning point, crossroads, head, moment of truth, zero hour, point of no return, Rubicon; informal crunch. **2** *the current economic crisis:* **emergency**, disaster, catastrophe, calamity; predicament, plight, mess, trouble, dire straits, difficulty, extremity.

crisp adjective **1** *crisp bacon:* **crunchy**, crispy, brittle, breakable; dry. **2** *a crisp autumn day:* **invigorating**, brisk, fresh, refreshing, exhilarating; cool, chill, chilly; informal nippy; Brit. informal parky. **3** *her answer was crisp:* **brisk**, businesslike, no-nonsense, incisive, to the point, matter of fact, brusque; terse, succinct, concise, brief, short, short and sweet, laconic; informal snappy. **4** *crisp white bedlinen:* **smooth**, fresh, ironed; starched.
–OPPOSITES soft, sultry, rambling.

C

criterion noun **standard**, specification, measure, gauge, test, scale, benchmark, yardstick, touchstone, barometer; principle, rule, law, canon.

critic noun **1** *a literary critic:* **reviewer**, commentator, analyst, judge, pundit. **2** *critics of the government:* **detractor**, attacker, fault-finder.

critical adjective **1** *a highly critical report:* **censorious**, condemnatory; disparaging, disapproving, fault-finding, judgemental, negative, unfavourable; informal nit-picking, picky. **2** *a critical essay:* **analytical**, interpretative, expository, explanatory. **3** *the situation is critical:* **grave**, serious, dangerous, risky, perilous, hazardous, precarious, touch-and-go, in the balance, uncertain, desperate, dire, acute, life-and-death. **4** *the choice of materials is critical for product safety:* **crucial**, vital, essential, of the essence, all-important, paramount, fundamental, key, pivotal, decisive, deciding.
– OPPOSITES complimentary, unimportant.

criticism noun **1** *she was stung by his criticism:* **censure**, condemnation, denunciation, disapproval, disparagement, opprobrium, fault-finding, attack, brickbats, recrimination; informal flak, a bad press, panning; Brit. informal stick, slating; formal excoriation. **2** *literary criticism:* **evaluation**, assessment, appraisal, analysis, judgement; commentary, interpretation, explanation.

criticize verb **find fault with**, censure, denounce, condemn, attack, lambaste, pillory, rail against, inveigh against, cast aspersions on, pour scorn on, disparage, denigrate, give a bad press to, run down; informal knock, pan, slam, hammer, lay into, pull to pieces, pick holes in; Brit. informal slag off, slate, rubbish; N. Amer. informal trash; Austral./NZ informal monster; formal excoriate.
– OPPOSITES praise.

critique noun **analysis**, evaluation, assessment, appraisal, appreciation, criticism, review, study, commentary.

crock noun **pot**, jar; jug, pitcher, ewer; container, receptacle, vessel.

crockery noun **dishes**, crocks, china, tableware; plates, bowls, cups, saucers.

crony noun (informal) **friend**, companion, bosom friend, intimate, confidant, confidante, familiar, associate, comrade; cohort; informal pal, chum, sidekick; Brit. informal mate; N. Amer. informal buddy.

crook noun **1** (informal) *a small-time crook:* **criminal**, lawbreaker, villain, delinquent, felon, convict, wrongdoer; rogue, scoundrel, cheat, swindler, racketeer; thief, robber, burglar; informal old lag, shark, con man, con, jailbird; N. Amer. informal hood, yardbird; formal malefactor; Law malfeasant. **2** *the crook of a tree branch:* **bend**, fork, curve, angle.
• verb *he crooked his finger and called the waiter:* **cock**, flex, bend, curve, curl.

crooked adjective **1** *narrow, crooked streets:* **winding**, twisting, zigzag, meandering, tortuous, serpentine. **2** *a crooked spine:* **bent**, twisted, misshapen, deformed, malformed, contorted, warped, bowed, distorted; Scottish thrawn. **3** *the picture over the bed looked crooked:* **lopsided**, askew, awry, off-centre, uneven, out of true, out of line, at an angle, aslant, slanting, squint; Scottish agley; informal cockeyed; Brit. informal skew-whiff, wonky. **4** (informal) *a crooked cop* | *crooked deals:* **dishonest**, unscrupulous, unprincipled, untrustworthy, corrupt, venal; criminal, illegal, unlawful, nefarious, fraudulent; Brit. informal bent, dodgy.
– OPPOSITES straight, honest.

crop noun **1** *some farmers lost their entire crop:* **harvest**, yield; fruits, produce. **2** *a bumper crop of mail:* **batch**, lot, collection, supply, intake.
• verb **1** *she's had her hair cropped:* **cut short**, clip, shear, shave, lop off, chop off, hack off; dock. **2** *a flock of sheep were cropping the turf:* **graze on**, browse on, feed on, nibble, eat.
■ **crop up** happen, occur, arise, turn up, spring up, pop up, emerge, materialize, surface, appear, come to light, present itself; literary come to pass, befall.

WORD LINKS
agronomy the science of crop production

cross noun **1** *a bronze cross:* **crucifix**, rood. **2** *we all have our crosses to bear:* **burden**, trouble, worry, trial, tribulation, affliction, curse, misfortune, adversity, hardship, vicissitude; millstone, albatross, thorn in your flesh/side; misery, woe, pain, sorrow, suffering; informal hassle, headache. **3** *a cross between a yak and a cow:* **hybrid**, cross-breed, half-breed, mongrel; mixture, amalgam, blend, combination.
• verb **1** *they crossed the hills on foot:* **travel across**, traverse; negotiate, navigate, cover. **2** *the point where the two roads cross:* **intersect**, meet, join, connect, criss-cross. **3** *no one dared cross him:* **oppose**, resist, defy, obstruct; contradict, argue with, quarrel with, stand up to, take a stand against, take issue with. **4** *the breed was crossed with the similarly coloured Friesian:* **hybridize**, cross-breed, interbreed, cross-fertilize, cross-pollinate.
• adjective *he seemed to be very cross about something:* **angry**, annoyed, irate, irritated, in a bad mood, vexed, irked, piqued, put out, displeased; irritable, short-tempered, bad-tempered, snappish, crotchety, grouchy, grumpy, fractious, testy, tetchy, crabby; informal mad, hot under the collar, peeved, riled, snappy, up in arms, steamed up, in a paddy; Brit. informal aerated, shirty, stroppy, ratty; N. Amer. informal sore, bent out of shape, teed off, ticked off.
– OPPOSITES pleased.
■ **cross something out** delete, strike out, score out, put a line through, cancel, obliterate.

cross-examine verb **interrogate**, question, quiz, give someone the third degree; informal grill, pump, put someone through the wringer.

crossing noun **1** *a busy road crossing:* **junction**, crossroads, intersection, interchange; level crossing. **2** *a short ferry crossing:* **journey**, passage, voyage.

crosswise, **crossways** adverb **diagonally**, obliquely, transversely, aslant, cornerwise, at an angle, on the bias; N. Amer. cater-cornered, kitty-corner.

crotchety adjective **bad-tempered**, irascible, irritable, grumpy, grouchy, cantankerous, short-tempered, tetchy, testy, curmudgeonly, ill-tempered, ill-humoured, peevish, cross, fractious, pettish, waspish, crabbed, crabby, prickly, touchy; informal snappy; Brit. informal narky, ratty; N. Amer. informal cranky, ornery; Austral./NZ informal snaky.
– OPPOSITES good-humoured.

crouch verb **squat**, bend down, hunker down, hunch over, stoop, kneel down; duck, cower.

crow verb **1** *a cock crowed:* **cry**, squawk, screech, caw. **2** *try to avoid crowing about your success:* **boast**, brag, trumpet, swagger, swank, gloat.

crowd noun **1** *a crowd of people:* **throng**, horde, mass, multitude, host, army, herd, flock, drove, swarm, sea, troupe, pack, mob, rabble; collection, company, gathering, assembly, congregation; informal gaggle, bunch, gang, posse. **2** *he's been hanging round with Hurley's crowd:* **set**, group, circle, clique, coterie; camp; informal gang, crew, lot. **3** *the final attracted a capacity crowd:* **audience**, spectators, listeners, viewers; house, turnout, attendance, gate; congregation; Brit. informal punters.
• verb **1** *reporters crowded round her:* **cluster**, flock, swarm, mill, throng, huddle, gather, assemble, congregate, converge. **2** *the guests all crowded into the dining room:* **surge**, push your way, jostle, elbow your way; squeeze, pile, cram. **3** *the quayside was crowded with holidaymakers:* **throng**, pack, jam, cram, fill. **4** *stop crowding me:* **pressurize**, pressure; harass, hound, pester, harry, badger, nag; informal hassle, lean on.

crowded adjective **packed**, full, filled to capacity, full to bursting, congested, overflowing, teeming, swarming, thronged, populous, overpopulated; busy; informal jam-packed, stuffed, chock-a-block, chock-full, bursting at the seams, full to the gunwales, wall-to-wall, mobbed; Austral./NZ informal chocker.
– OPPOSITES deserted.

crown noun **1** *a jewelled crown:*

coronet, diadem, circlet. **2** *the world heavyweight crown:* **title**, award; trophy, cup, medal, plate, shield, belt, prize. **3** *loyal servants of the Crown:* **monarch**, sovereign, king, queen, emperor, empress; monarchy, royalty. **4** *the crown of the hill:* **top**, crest, summit, peak, pinnacle, tip, brow, apex.
•verb **1** *a teaching post at Harvard crowned his career:* **round off**, cap, be the climax of, be the culmination of, top off, complete. **2** *a steeple crowned by a gilded weathercock:* **top**, cap, tip, head, surmount.

crucial adjective **1** *negotiations were at a crucial stage:* **pivotal**, critical, key, decisive, deciding; life-and-death. **2** *confidentiality is crucial in this case:* **all-important**, of the utmost importance, of the essence, critical, pre-eminent, paramount, essential, vital.
–OPPOSITES unimportant.

crude adjective **1** *crude oil:* **unrefined**, unpurified, unprocessed, untreated; coarse, raw, natural. **2** *a crude barricade:* **primitive**, simple, basic, homespun, rudimentary, rough, rough and ready, rough-hewn, make-do, makeshift, improvised. **3** *crude jokes:* **vulgar**, rude, naughty, suggestive, bawdy, off colour, indecent, obscene, offensive, lewd, salacious, licentious, ribald, coarse, uncouth, indelicate, tasteless, smutty, dirty, filthy, scatological; informal blue.
–OPPOSITES refined, sophisticated.

cruel adjective **1** *a cruel man:* **brutal**, savage, inhuman, barbaric, barbarous, brutish, bloodthirsty, vicious, sadistic, wicked, fiendish, diabolical, monstrous; callous, ruthless, merciless, pitiless, remorseless, uncaring, heartless, stony-hearted, hard-hearted, cold-blooded, cold-hearted, unfeeling, unkind, inhumane. **2** *her death was a cruel blow:* **harsh**, severe, bitter, heart-breaking, heart-rending, painful, agonizing, traumatic; formal grievous.
–OPPOSITES compassionate.

cruelty noun **brutality**, savagery, inhumanity, barbarity, blood-thirstiness, barbarousness, brutishness, viciousness, sadism, wickedness; callousness, ruthlessness.

cruise noun *a cruise down the Nile:* **trip**, voyage, journey.
•verb **1** *she cruised across the Atlantic:* **sail**, voyage, journey. **2** *a taxi cruised past:* **drive slowly**, drift, sail; informal mosey, tootle; Brit. informal pootle.

crumb noun **fragment**, bit, morsel, particle, speck, scrap, shred, sliver, atom, grain, trace, tinge, mite, jot, ounce; informal smidgen, tad.

crumble verb **disintegrate**, fall apart, fall to pieces, fall down, break up, collapse, fragment; decay, fall into decay, deteriorate, degenerate, go to rack and ruin, decompose, rot, perish.

crumbly adjective **friable**, powdery, granular; short; soft.

crumple verb **1** *she crumpled the note in her fist:* **crush**, scrunch up, screw up, squash, squeeze. **2** *his trousers were dirty and crumpled:* **crease**, wrinkle, crinkle, rumple. **3** *her resistance crumpled:* **collapse**, give way, cave in, go to pieces, break down, crumble, be overcome.

crunch verb **munch**, chomp, champ, bite into; crush, grind, break, smash.

crusade noun **campaign**, drive, push, movement, effort, struggle; battle, war, offensive.
•verb **campaign**, fight, battle, take up arms, take up the cudgels, work, strive, struggle, agitate, lobby.

crusader noun **campaigner**, fighter, champion, advocate; reformer.

crush verb **1** *essential oils are released when the herbs are crushed:* **squash**, squeeze, press, compress; pulp, mash, mangle; flatten, trample on, tread on; informal squidge. **2** *your dress will get crushed:* **crease**, crumple, rumple, wrinkle, crinkle, scrunch up. **3** *crush the biscuits with a rolling pin:* **pulverize**, pound, grind, break up, smash, crumble; mill; technical comminute. **4** *he crushed her in his arms:* **hug**, squeeze, hold tight, embrace, enfold. **5** *the new regime crushed all opposition:* **suppress**, put down, quell, quash, stamp out, repress, subdue, extinguish. **6** *he was crushed by her words:* **mortify**, humiliate, chagrin, deflate, demoralize, flatten, squash; devastate, shatter.

•**noun 1** *the crush of people:* **crowd**, throng, horde, swarm, press, mob. **2** (informal) *a teenage crush:* **infatuation**, obsession, fixation; informal pash, puppy love, calf love. **3** *lemon crush:* **squash**, fruit juice, cordial, drink.

crust noun covering, layer, coating, cover, coat, sheet, thickness, film, skin, topping; encrustation, scab.

crusty adjective irritable, cantankerous, irascible, bad-tempered, ill-tempered, grumpy, grouchy, crotchety, short-tempered, tetchy, testy, crabby, curmudgeonly, peevish, cross, fractious, pettish, crabbed, prickly, waspish; informal snappy; Brit. informal narky, ratty; N. Amer. informal cranky, ornery; Austral./NZ informal snaky.
–OPPOSITES good-natured.

crux noun nub, heart, essence, central point, main point, core, centre, nucleus, kernel.

cry verb 1 *the girl started to cry:* **weep**, shed tears, sob, wail, bawl, howl, snivel, whimper; Scottish greet; informal blub, blubber, turn on the waterworks; Brit. informal grizzle. **2** *'Wait!' he cried:* **call**, shout, exclaim, sing out, yell, shriek, scream, screech, bawl, bellow, roar, squeal, yelp; informal holler.
–OPPOSITES laugh, whisper.
•**noun call**, shout, exclamation, yell, shriek, scream, screech, bawl, bellow, roar, howl; informal holler.
▪ **cry off** (informal) back out, pull out, cancel, withdraw, change your mind; informal get cold feet, cop out.

crypt noun tomb, vault, burial chamber, sepulchre, catacomb.

cryptic adjective enigmatic, mysterious, confusing, mystifying, puzzling, obscure, abstruse, arcane, elliptical, oblique.
–OPPOSITES clear.

cube noun block, lump, chunk, brick.

cuddle verb 1 *she picked up the baby and cuddled her:* **hug**, embrace, clasp, hold tight, hold in your arms. **2** *the pair were kissing and cuddling:* **embrace**, hug, caress, pet, fondle; informal canoodle, smooch; informal, dated spoon, bill and coo. **3** *I cuddled up to him:* **snuggle**, nestle, curl, nuzzle.

cuddly adjective huggable, cuddlesome; plump, curvaceous, buxom; soft, warm; N. Amer. informal zaftig.

cudgel noun club, bludgeon, truncheon, baton, shillelagh, mace; N. Amer. blackjack, nightstick; Brit. life preserver, cosh.
•**verb bludgeon**, club, beat, batter, bash; Brit. cosh.

cue noun signal, sign, indication, prompt, reminder.

cuff verb hit, strike, slap, smack, thump, beat, punch; informal clout, wallop, belt, whack, bash, clobber, bop, biff, sock; Brit. informal slosh; N. Amer. informal boff, slug.
▪ **off the cuff** (informal) *an off-the-cuff remark:* impromptu, extempore; unrehearsed, unscripted, unprepared, improvised, spontaneous, unplanned.

cuisine noun cooking, cookery; food.

cul-de-sac noun no through road, blind alley, dead end.

cull verb slaughter, kill, destroy; put down.

culminate verb *the festival culminated in a dramatic fire-walking ceremony:* **come to a climax**, come to a head, climax; build up to, lead up to; end with, finish with, conclude with.

culmination noun climax, pinnacle, peak, high point, height, summit, crest, zenith, crowning moment, apotheosis, apex, apogee; consummation.
–OPPOSITES nadir.

culpable adjective to blame, guilty, at fault, in the wrong, answerable, accountable, responsible, blameworthy.
–OPPOSITES innocent.

culprit noun guilty party, offender, wrongdoer, miscreant; criminal, lawbreaker, felon, delinquent; informal baddy, crook; formal malefactor.

cult noun 1 *a religious cult:* **sect**, group, movement. **2** *the cult of youth in Hollywood:* **obsession with**, fixation on, mania for, idolization of, devotion to, worship of, veneration of.

cultivate verb 1 *the peasants cultivated the land:* **till**, plough, dig, hoe, farm, work. **2** *they were encouraged to cultivate basic food*

C

crops: **grow**, raise, rear; plant, sow. **3** *Tessa tried to cultivate her:* **woo**, court, curry favour with, ingratiate yourself with; informal get in someone's good books, butter up, suck up to; N. Amer. informal shine up to. **4** *he wants to cultivate his mind:* **improve**, better, refine, elevate; educate, train, develop, enrich.

cultivated adjective **cultured**, educated, well read, civilized, enlightened, refined, polished; sophisticated, urbane, cosmopolitan.

cultural adjective **1** *cultural differences:* **social**, lifestyle; sociological, anthropological. **2** *cultural achievements:* **aesthetic**, artistic, intellectual; educational.

culture noun **1** *a lover of culture:* **the arts**, the humanities; high art. **2** *a man of culture:* **education**, cultivation, enlightenment, discernment, discrimination, taste, refinement, sophistication. **3** *Afro-Caribbean culture:* **civilization**, society, way of life, lifestyle; customs, traditions, heritage, habits, ways, conventions, values. **4** *a corporate culture of greed and envy:* **philosophy**, outlook, approach, modus operandi, ethic, rationale.

cultured adjective **cultivated**, artistic, enlightened, civilized, educated, well educated, well read, well informed, learned, knowledgeable, discerning, discriminating, refined, sophisticated; informal arty.
– OPPOSITES ignorant.

cumbersome adjective **1** *a very cumbersome diving suit:* **unwieldy**, unmanageable, awkward, clumsy, inconvenient; bulky, large, heavy, weighty; informal hulking, clunky. **2** *cumbersome procedures:* **complicated**, complex, involved, inefficient, unwieldy, slow.
– OPPOSITES manageable, straightforward.

cumulative adjective **increasing**, growing, mounting; collective, aggregate, amassed; Brit. knock-on.

cunning adjective *a cunning scheme:* **crafty**, wily, artful, devious, sly, scheming, designing, calculating, Machiavellian; shrewd, astute, clever, canny; deceitful, deceptive, duplicitous; old use subtle.
– OPPOSITES honest.
• noun *his political cunning:* **guile**, craftiness, deviousness, slyness, trickery, duplicity; shrewdness, astuteness.

cupboard noun **closet**, cabinet, armoire.

cupidity noun **greed**, avarice, avariciousness, acquisitiveness, covetousness, rapacity, materialism, mercenariness, Mammonism; informal money-grubbing.
– OPPOSITES generosity.

curable adjective **treatable**, operable.

curative adjective **healing**, therapeutic, medicinal, remedial, corrective, restorative, health-giving.

curator noun **custodian**, keeper, conservator, guardian, caretaker, steward.

curb verb **restrain**, hold back/in, keep back, repress, suppress, fight back, keep in check, check, control, rein in, contain, bridle, subdue; informal keep a/the lid on.
• noun **restraint**, restriction, check, brake, rein, control, limitation, limit, constraint; informal crackdown.

curdle verb **go off**, turn, sour, ferment.

cure verb **1** *he was cured of the disease:* **heal**, restore to health, make well/better. **2** *economic equality cannot cure all social ills:* **rectify**, remedy, put/set right, right, fix, mend, repair, heal, make better; solve, sort out; eliminate, end, put an end to. **3** *some farmers cured their own bacon:* **preserve**, smoke, salt, dry.
• noun **1** *a cure for cancer:* **remedy**, medicine, medication, antidote; treatment, therapy. **2** *interest rate cuts are not the cure for the problem:* **solution**, answer, antidote, panacea, cure-all.

curio noun **trinket**, knick-knack, ornament, bauble, oddity; objet d'art, rarity, curiosity, conversation piece.

curiosity noun **1** *his evasiveness roused my curiosity:* **interest**, inquisitiveness. **2** *the shop is full of curiosities:* **oddity**, curio; knick-knack, ornament, bauble, trinket; objet d'art, rarity; N. Amer. kickshaw.

curious adjective **1** *she was curious*

to know what had happened: **intrigued**, interested, eager/dying to know; inquisitive. **2** *her curious behaviour:* **strange**, odd, peculiar, funny, unusual, bizarre, weird, eccentric, queer, extraordinary, abnormal, out of the ordinary, anomalous, surprising, incongruous; informal offbeat; Scottish unco; Brit. informal rum.
– OPPOSITES uninterested, ordinary.

curl verb **1** *smoke curled up from his cigarette:* **spiral**, coil, wreathe, twirl, swirl; wind, curve, bend, twist and turn, loop, meander, snake, corkscrew, zigzag. **2** *Ruth curled her arms around his neck:* **wind**, twine, entwine, wrap. **3** *they curled up together on the sofa:* **nestle**, snuggle, cuddle; N. Amer. snug down.
• noun **1** *the tangled curls of her hair:* **ringlet**, corkscrew, kink. **2** *a curl of smoke:* **spiral**, coil, twirl, swirl, twist, corkscrew, curlicue; helix.

curly adjective **wavy**, curling, curled, frizzy, kinky, corkscrew.
– OPPOSITES straight.

currency noun **1** *foreign currency:* **money**, legal tender, cash, banknotes, notes, coins; N. Amer. bills. **2** *a term which has gained new currency:* **prevalence**, circulation, exposure; acceptance, popularity.

current adjective **1** *current events:* **contemporary**, present-day, modern, present, contemporaneous; topical, in the news, live, burning. **2** *the idea is still current:* **prevalent**, prevailing, common, accepted, in circulation, popular, widespread. **3** *a current driving licence:* **valid**, usable, up to date. **4** *the current prime minister:* **incumbent**, present, in office, in power; reigning.
– OPPOSITES past, former.
• noun **1** *a current of air:* **flow**, stream, slipstream; thermal, updraught, draught; undercurrent, undertow, tide. **2** *a new current of opinion:* **trend**, direction, tendency, movement.

curriculum noun **syllabus**, study programme; subjects.

curse noun **1** *the curse of racism:* **evil**, blight, scourge, plague, cancer, canker, poison. **2** *the curse of unemployment:* **affliction**, burden, bane. **3** *muffled curses:* **swear word**, expletive, oath, profanity, four-letter word, dirty word, obscenity; informal cuss, cuss word; formal imprecation.
• verb **1** *she was cursed with feelings of inadequacy:* **afflict**, trouble, plague, bedevil. **2** *drivers cursed and sounded their horns:* **swear**, take the Lord's name in vain; informal cuss, turn the air blue, eff and blind.

cursed adjective **damned**, doomed, ill-fated, ill-starred; informal jinxed; literary accursed, star-crossed.

cursory adjective **perfunctory**, desultory, casual, superficial, token; hasty, quick, hurried, rapid, brief, passing, fleeting.
– OPPOSITES thorough.

curt adjective **terse**, brusque, abrupt, clipped, blunt, short, monosyllabic, sharp; gruff, rude, impolite, discourteous.
– OPPOSITES expansive.

curtail verb **1** *economic policies designed to curtail spending:* **reduce**, cut, cut down, decrease, lessen, trim; restrict, limit, curb, rein in/back; informal slash. **2** *his visit was curtailed:* **shorten**, cut short, truncate.
– OPPOSITES increase, lengthen.

curtains noun N. Amer. drapes.

curvaceous adjective **shapely**, voluptuous, sexy, full-figured, buxom, full-bosomed, bosomy, Junoesque; informal curvy, well endowed, pneumatic, busty.
– OPPOSITES skinny.

curve noun *the serpentine curves of the river:* **bend**, turn, loop, curl, twist; arc, arch, bow, half-moon, undulation, curvature.
• verb *the road curved back on itself:* **bend**, turn, loop, wind, meander, undulate, snake, spiral, twist, coil, curl; arc, arch.

curved adjective **bent**, arched, bowed, crescent, curving, wavy, sinuous, serpentine, meandering, undulating, curvy.
– OPPOSITES straight.

cushion noun *a cushion against inflation:* **protection**, buffer, shield, defence, bulwark.
• verb **1** *she cushioned her head on her arms:* **support**, cradle, prop, rest. **2** *to cushion the blow, pensions were increased:* **soften**, lessen, diminish,

decrease, mitigate, alleviate, take the edge off; dull, deaden. **3** *residents are cushioned from the outside world:* **protect**, shield, shelter, cocoon.

C

cushy adjective (informal) **easy**, undemanding; comfortable.
– OPPOSITES difficult.

custodian noun **curator**, keeper, conservator, guardian, overseer, superintendent; caretaker, steward, protector.

custody noun *the parent who has custody of the child:* **care**, guardianship, charge, keeping, safe keeping, wardship, responsibility, protection, tutelage.
■ **in custody** in prison, in jail, imprisoned, incarcerated, locked up, under lock and key, interned, detained; on remand; informal behind bars, doing time, inside; Brit. informal banged up.

custom noun **1** *his unfamiliarity with local customs:* **tradition**, practice, usage, way, convention, formality, ceremony, ritual; shibboleth, sacred cow, unwritten rule; mores. **2** *it is our custom to visit the Lake District in October:* **habit**, practice, routine, way; policy, rule; formal wont.

customarily adverb **usually**, traditionally, normally, as a rule, generally, ordinarily, commonly; habitually, routinely.
– OPPOSITES occasionally.

customary adjective **1** *customary social practices:* **usual**, traditional, normal, conventional, familiar, accepted, routine, established, time-honoured, prevailing. **2** *her customary good sense:* **usual**, accustomed, habitual; literary wonted.
– OPPOSITES unusual.

customer noun **consumer**, buyer, purchaser, patron, client; shopper; Brit. informal punter.

customs plural noun. See **TAX** noun.

cut verb **1** *he cut his finger:* **gash**, slash, lacerate, slit, wound, injure; scratch, graze, nick, incise, score. **2** *cut the meat into small pieces:* **chop**, cut up, slice, dice, cube; carve; N. Amer. hash. **3** *a name had been cut into the stone:* **carve**, engrave, incise, etch, score; chisel, whittle. **4** *the government will cut public expenditure:* **reduce**, decrease, lessen, economize on, retrench, trim; rationalize, downsize; mark down, discount, lower; informal slash. **5** *the text has been substantially cut:* **shorten**, abridge, condense, abbreviate, truncate; edit; censor, expurgate. **6** *you need to cut ten lines per page:* **delete**, remove, take out, excise; informal chop. **7** *oil supplies had been cut:* **discontinue**, break off, suspend, interrupt; stop, end. **8** *the point where the line cuts the vertical axis:* **cross**, intersect, bisect; meet, join.
• noun **1** *a cut on his jaw:* **gash**, slash, laceration, incision, wound, injury; scratch, graze, nick. **2** *a cut of beef:* **piece**, joint, fillet, steak. **3** (informal) *they want their cut:* **share**, portion, bit, quota, slice, percentage; informal rake-off, piece of the action; Brit. informal whack. **4** *his hair was in need of a cut:* **haircut**, trim, clip. **5** *a cut in interest rates:* **reduction**, cutback, decrease, lessening; N. Amer. rollback. **6** *the cut of his jacket:* **style**, design; tailoring, line, fit.
■ **cut back** *companies cut back on foreign investment:* **1** reduce, decrease, lessen, retrench, economize on, trim, slim down, scale down; rationalize, downsize, pull/draw in your horns, tighten your belt; informal slash. **2** *cut back any new growth:* trim, snip, clip, crop, shear, shave; pare; prune, dock; mow. **cut something down** fell, chop down, lop. **cut in** interrupt, butt in, break in, interject, interpose, chime in; Brit. informal chip in. **cut someone/something off 1** *they cut off his finger:* sever, chop off, hack off; amputate. **2** *oil and gas supplies were cut off:* discontinue, break off, disconnect, suspend; stop, end, bring to an end. **3** *many people were cut off by the flood:* isolate, separate; trap, strand, maroon. **cut out** stop working, stop, fail, give out, break down; informal die, give up the ghost, conk out; Brit. informal pack up. **cut someone/something out 1** *cut out all the diseased wood:* remove, take out, excise, extract. **2** *it's best to cut out alcohol altogether:* give up, refrain from, abstain from, go without; informal quit, leave off, pack in, lay off, knock off. **3** *his mother*

cut him out of her will: exclude, leave out, omit, eliminate. **cut something short** break off, shorten, truncate, curtail, terminate, end, stop, abort, bring to an untimely end.

cutback noun **reduction**, cut, decrease; economy, saving; N. Amer. rollback.
– OPPOSITES increase.

cute adjective **endearing**, adorable, lovable, sweet, lovely, appealing, engaging, delightful, dear, darling, winning, winsome, attractive, pretty; informal twee; Brit. informal dinky.

cut-price adjective **cheap**, marked down, reduced, on offer, bargain-basement, discount; N. Amer. cut-rate.

cut-throat adjective **ruthless**, merciless, fierce, intense, aggressive, dog-eat-dog.

cutting noun *a newspaper cutting:* **clipping**; article, piece, column, paragraph.
• adjective *a cutting remark:* **hurtful**, wounding, barbed, pointed, scathing, acerbic, caustic, acid, sarcastic, sardonic, snide, spiteful, malicious, mean, nasty, cruel, unkind; informal bitchy, catty; Brit. informal sarky; N. Amer. informal snarky.
– OPPOSITES friendly, warm.

cycle noun **1** *the cycle of birth, death, and rebirth:* **circle**, round, rotation; pattern, rhythm; loop. **2** *the painting is one of a cycle of seven:* **series**, sequence, succession, run; set.

cyclical adjective **recurrent**, recurring, regular, repeated; periodic, seasonal, circular.

cyclone noun **hurricane**, typhoon, storm, tornado, whirlwind, tempest; Austral. willy-willy; N. Amer. informal twister.

cynic noun **sceptic**, doubter, doubting Thomas; pessimist, prophet of doom; informal doom and gloom merchant.
– OPPOSITES idealist.

cynical adjective **sceptical**, doubtful, distrustful, suspicious, disbelieving; pessimistic, negative, world-weary, disillusioned, disenchanted, jaundiced.
– OPPOSITES idealistic.

cynicism noun **scepticism**, doubt, distrust, mistrust, suspicion, disbelief; pessimism, negativity, world-weariness, disenchantment.
– OPPOSITES idealism.

cyst noun **growth**, lump; abscess, boil, carbuncle.

Dd

dab verb *she dabbed disinfectant on the cut:* **pat**, press, touch, swab; daub, apply, wipe.
• noun *a dab of glue:* **drop**, spot, smear, splash, bit; informal smidgen, lick.

dabble verb **1** *they dabbled their feet in the pool:* **splash**, dip, paddle, trail. **2** *he dabbled in politics:* **toy with**, dip into, flirt with, tinker with, play with.

dabbler noun **amateur**, dilettante.
– OPPOSITES professional.

daft adjective (Brit. informal) **1** *a daft idea:* **absurd**, preposterous, ridiculous, ludicrous, laughable; idiotic, stupid, foolish, silly, fatuous, hare-brained, half-baked; informal crazy, cockeyed; Brit. informal barmy. **2** *she's not as daft as she looks:* **stupid**, idiotic, empty-headed; informal thick, dim, dopey, dumb, dim-witted, half-witted, bird-brained, pea-brained, slow on the uptake, soft in the head, crazy, nuts, batty, bonkers; Brit. informal potty, barmy, crackers.
– OPPOSITES sensible.

daily adjective *a daily occurrence:* **everyday**, day-to-day, regular, routine, common, commonplace; quotidian, diurnal, circadian.

dainty adjective **1** *a dainty china cup:* **delicate**, fine, elegant, exquisite; Brit. informal dinky. **2** *a dainty eater:* **fastidious**, fussy, finicky; particular; informal choosy, pernickety, picky; Brit. informal faddy.
– OPPOSITES unwieldy, undiscriminating.

dais noun **platform**, stage, podium, rostrum, stand; soapbox.

dam noun **barrage**, barrier, wall, embankment, barricade, obstruction.
• verb **block**, obstruct, bung up, close; technical occlude.

damage noun **1** *bombing caused extensive damage to the area:* **harm**, destruction, ruin, havoc, devastation; injury, desecration; vandalism. **2** *she won £4,300 damages:* **compensation**, recompense, restitution, redress, reparation; indemnification, indemnity; N. Amer. informal comp.
• verb *the parcel had been damaged:* **harm**, deface, mutilate, mangle, impair, injure, disfigure, vandalize; tamper with, sabotage; ruin, destroy, wreck; N. Amer. informal trash.
– OPPOSITES repair.

damaging adjective **harmful**, detrimental, injurious, hurtful, inimical, dangerous, destructive, ruinous, deleterious; bad, malign, adverse, undesirable, prejudicial, unfavourable; unhealthy, unwholesome.
– OPPOSITES beneficial.

damn verb **condemn**, censure, criticize, attack, denounce, revile; find fault with, give something a bad press, deprecate, disparage; informal slam, lay into, blast; Brit. informal slate, slag off.
– OPPOSITES bless, praise.

damnation noun condemnation, eternal punishment, perdition, doom, hellfire; informal fire and brimstone.

damning adjective **1** *damning evidence:* **incriminating**, condemnatory, damaging; conclusive, strong. **2** *a damning indictment:* **fierce**, savage, scathing, devastating, searing, blistering.

damp adjective *her palms were damp | a damp evening:* **moist**; humid, steamy, muggy, clammy, sweaty, sticky, dank, wet, rainy, drizzly, showery, misty, foggy, dewy.
– OPPOSITES dry.

• **noun** *the damp in the air:* **moisture**, dampness, humidity, wetness, wet, water, condensation, steam, vapour; clamminess, dankness; rain, dew, drizzle, precipitation; perspiration, sweat.
– OPPOSITES dryness.

dampen verb **1** *the rain dampened her face:* **moisten**, damp, wet; literary bedew. **2** *nothing could dampen her enthusiasm:* **lessen**, decrease, diminish, reduce, moderate, damp, put a damper on, cool, discourage; suppress, extinguish, quench, stifle, curb, limit, check, restrain, inhibit, deter.
– OPPOSITES dry, heighten.

dampness noun. See DAMP noun.

dance verb **1** *they danced till dawn:* jive, pirouette, gyrate; informal bop, boogie, trip the light fantastic; N. Amer. informal get down. **2** *the girls danced round me:* **caper**, cavort, frisk, frolic, skip, prance, gambol; leap, jump, hop, bounce. **3** *flames danced in the fireplace:* **flicker**, leap, dart, play, flit, quiver; twinkle, shimmer, glitter.
• **noun** *the school dance:* **ball**; masquerade; N. Amer. prom, hoedown; informal disco, rave, hop, bop.

> **WORD LINKS**
> **terpsichorean** relating to dancing
> **choreography** the sequence of steps in a ballet or other dance

danger noun **1** *an element of danger:* **peril**, hazard, risk, jeopardy. **2** *he is a danger to society:* **menace**, hazard, threat, risk. **3** *a serious danger of fire:* **possibility**, chance, risk, probability, likelihood, prospect.
– OPPOSITES safety.

dangerous adjective **1** *a dangerous animal:* **menacing**, threatening, treacherous; savage, wild, vicious, murderous, desperate. **2** *dangerous wiring:* **hazardous**, perilous, risky, unsafe, unpredictable, precarious, insecure, touch-and-go, chancy, treacherous, unstable, volatile; informal dicey, hairy; Brit. informal dodgy.
– OPPOSITES harmless, safe.

dangle verb **1** *a chain dangled from his belt:* **hang**, droop, swing, sway, wave, trail, stream. **2** *he dangled the keys in front of her:* **wave**, swing, jiggle, brandish, flourish.

dangling adjective **hanging**, drooping, droopy, suspended, pendulous, trailing, flowing, tumbling.

dank adjective **damp**, musty, chilly, clammy, moist, wet, humid.
– OPPOSITES dry.

dapper adjective **smart**, spruce, trim, debonair, neat, well dressed, well groomed, well turned out, elegant, chic, dashing; informal snazzy, snappy, natty, sharp; N. Amer. informal spiffy, fly.
– OPPOSITES scruffy.

dappled adjective **speckled**, blotchy, spotted, spotty, dotted, mottled, marbled, flecked, freckled; piebald, brindle, brindled; patchy, variegated; informal splotchy, splodgy.

dare verb **1** *nobody dared to say a word:* **be brave enough**, have the courage; venture, have the nerve, have the temerity, be so bold as, have the audacity; risk, take the liberty of; N. Amer. take a flyer; informal stick your neck out, go out on a limb. **2** *she dared him to go:* **challenge**, defy, invite, bid, provoke, goad; throw down the gauntlet.
• **noun** *she accepted the dare:* **challenge**, invitation; wager, bet.

daredevil adjective *a daredevil skydiver:* **daring**, bold, intrepid, fearless, madcap; reckless, rash, impulsive, impetuous, foolhardy; Brit. tearaway.
– OPPOSITES cowardly, cautious.
• **noun** *a young daredevil crashed his car:* **madcap**, hothead, adventurer, exhibitionist; Brit. tearaway; informal show-off, adrenalin junkie.

daring adjective *a daring attack:* **bold**, audacious, intrepid, fearless, brave, valiant, heroic, dashing; madcap, rash, reckless, heedless; informal gutsy, spunky.
• **noun** *his sheer daring:* **boldness**, audacity, temerity, fearlessness, intrepidity, bravery, courage, valour, heroism, pluck, spirit, mettle; recklessness, rashness, foolhardiness; informal nerve, guts, spunk, grit; Brit. informal bottle; N. Amer. informal moxie, sand.

dark adjective **1** *a dark night:* **black**, pitch-black, jet-black, inky; starless, moonless; dingy, gloomy, shadowy, shady. **2** *a dark secret:* **terrible**, awful, dreadful, hideous, ghastly, gruesome; mysterious, secret, hidden, concealed, veiled, covert, clandestine. **3** *dark hair:* **brunette**, dark brown, sable, jet-black, ebony. **4** *dark skin:* **swarthy**, dusky, olive, black, ebony. **5** *dark days:* **difficult**, dangerous, challenging, hard, grim, desperate; dire, awful, terrible, dreadful, horrible, horrendous, atrocious, nightmarish, harrowing; wretched, woeful; tragic, disastrous, calamitous, catastrophic, cataclysmic. **6** *dark thoughts:* **gloomy**, dismal, negative, downbeat, bleak, grim, fatalistic, black; despairing, despondent, hopeless, cheerless, melancholy; glum, grave, morose, mournful, doleful. **7** *a dark look:* **moody**, brooding, sullen, dour, scowling, glowering, angry, forbidding, threatening, ominous. **8** *dark deeds:* **evil**, wicked, sinful, bad, iniquitous, ungodly, unholy, base; vile, unspeakable, foul, monstrous, shocking, atrocious, abominable, hateful, despicable, horrible, heinous, diabolical, fiendish, murderous, barbarous, black; sordid, degenerate, depraved; dishonourable, dishonest, unscrupulous; informal low-down, dirty, crooked, shady.

– OPPOSITES bright, blonde, pale, happy, good.

• **noun** *I hate cycling in the dark:* **night**, night-time, darkness; nightfall; blackout.

– OPPOSITES light, day.

■ **in the dark** (informal) unaware, ignorant, oblivious, uninformed, unenlightened, unacquainted.

darken **verb** **grow dark**, blacken, grow dim, cloud over, lour.

darkness **noun** **1** *lights shone in the darkness:* **dark**, blackness; gloom, dimness, murkiness, shadow, shade. **2** *darkness fell:* **night**, night-time, dark. **3** *the forces of darkness:* **evil**; wickedness, sin, ungodliness; the Devil.

darling **noun** *the darling of the media:* **favourite**, idol, hero, heroine; Brit. informal blue-eyed boy/girl.

• **adjective** **1** *his darling wife:* **dear**, dearest, precious, beloved; esteemed. **2** *a darling little hat:* **adorable**, charming, cute, sweet, enchanting, bewitching, dear, delightful, lovely, beautiful, attractive, gorgeous, fetching; Scottish & N. English bonny.

darn **verb** *he was darning his socks:* **mend**, repair; sew up, stitch, patch.

dart **noun** *she made a dart for the door:* **dash**, rush, run, bolt, break, charge, sprint, bound, leap, dive; scurry, scamper, scramble.

• **verb** **1** *Karl darted across the road:* **dash**, rush, tear, run, bolt, fly, shoot, charge, race, sprint, bound, leap, dive, gallop, scurry, scamper, scramble; informal scoot. **2** *he darted a glance at her:* **direct**, cast, throw, shoot, send, flash.

dash **verb** **1** *he dashed home:* **rush**, race, run, sprint, career, charge, shoot, hurtle, hare, fly, speed, zoom; informal tear, belt, pelt, zip, whip, hotfoot it, leg it; Brit. informal bomb, go like the clappers; N. Amer. informal barrel, hightail it. **2** *he dashed the glass to the ground:* **hurl**, smash, fling, slam, throw, toss, cast, propel, send; informal chuck, heave, sling, bung; N. Amer. informal peg. **3** *rain dashed against the walls:* **crash**, smash; batter, strike, beat, pound, lash, drum. **4** *her hopes were dashed:* **shatter**, destroy, wreck, ruin, crush, overturn, scotch, spoil, frustrate, thwart; informal put paid to; Brit. informal scupper.

– OPPOSITES dawdle.

• **noun** **1** *a dash for the door:* **rush**, race, run, sprint, bolt, dart, leap, charge, bound, break; scramble. **2** *a dash of salt:* **pinch**, touch, sprinkle, taste, spot, soupçon, drop, dab, speck, sprinkling, splash, bit, modicum, little; informal smidgen, tad, lick.

dashing **adjective** **1** *a dashing pilot:* **debonair**, devil-may-care, raffish, flamboyant, bold, swashbuckling; romantic, gallant. **2** *he looked very dashing:* **stylish**, smart, elegant, dapper, spruce, trim, debonair; informal snazzy, natty, swish; N. Amer. informal spiffy.

dastardly **adjective** (dated) **wicked**, evil, heinous, villainous, diabolical, fiendish, barbarous, cruel, dark, rotten, vile, monstrous, abominable, despicable, degenerate, sordid; bad, base, mean, low, dishonourable, dishonest, unscrupulous, unprincipled; informal low-down, dirty, shady, rascally, scoundrelly, crooked; Brit. informal beastly.

– OPPOSITES noble.

data noun **facts**, figures, statistics, details, particulars, specifics; information, intelligence, material, input; informal info, gen.

date noun **1** *it's the only date he has to remember:* **day**, occasion, time; year; anniversary. **2** *a later date seems likely for these structures:* **time**, age, period, era, epoch, century, decade, year. **3** *a lunch date:* **appointment**, meeting, engagement, rendezvous; commitment; literary tryst. **4** (informal) *have you got a date for tonight?* **partner**, escort, girlfriend, boyfriend.
• verb **1** *the building dates from the 16th century:* **originate in**, be built in, come from, belong to, go back to. **2** *the best films don't date:* **age**, grow old, become dated, show its age; be of its time.

WORD LINKS
chronological relating to dates

dated adjective **old-fashioned**, outdated, outmoded, passé, behind the times, archaic, obsolete, antiquated; unfashionable, unstylish; crusty, olde worlde, prehistoric, antediluvian; informal old hat, out, out of the ark.
– OPPOSITES modern.

daub verb *he daubed a rock with paint:* **smear**, plaster, splash, spatter, splatter, cake, cover, smother, coat.
• noun *daubs of paint:* **smear**, smudge, splash, blot, spot, patch, blotch; informal splodge, splotch.

daughter noun **female child**, girl; descendant, offspring.

WORD LINKS
filial relating to a son or daughter
filicide the killing of a son or daughter by one of their parents

daunt verb **discourage**, deter, demoralize, put off, dishearten, dispirit; intimidate, abash, throw, cow, overawe, awe; informal rattle, faze.
– OPPOSITES hearten.

dauntless adjective **fearless**, determined, resolute, indomitable, intrepid, doughty, plucky, spirited, mettlesome; informal gutsy.

dawdle verb **1** *they dawdled over breakfast:* **linger**, take your time, be slow, waste time, idle; delay, procrastinate, stall; informal dilly-dally; old use tarry. **2** *Ruth dawdled home:* **amble**, stroll, trail, move at a snail's pace; informal mosey, tootle; Brit. informal pootle, mooch.
– OPPOSITES hurry.

dawn noun **1** *we got up at dawn:* **daybreak**, sunrise, first light, daylight, cockcrow; N. Amer. sunup. **2** *the dawn of civilization:* **beginning**, start, birth, inception, genesis, emergence, advent, appearance, arrival, dawning, rise, origin, onset; unfolding, development, infancy.
– OPPOSITES dusk, end.
• verb **1** *Thursday dawned crisp and sunny:* **begin**, break, arrive, emerge. **2** *a bright new future has dawned:* **begin**, start, commence, be born, appear, arrive, emerge; arise, rise, break, unfold, develop. **3** *the reality dawned on him:* **occur to**, come to, strike, hit, register with, cross someone's mind, suggest itself.
– OPPOSITES end.

day noun **1** *I stayed for a day:* twenty-four hours. **2** *the animals hunt during the day:* **daytime**, daylight; waking hours. **3** *the leading architect of the day:* **period**, time, age, era, generation. **4** *in his day he had great influence:* **heyday**, prime, time; peak, height, zenith, ascendancy.
– OPPOSITES night, decline.
■ **day after day** repeatedly, again and again, over and over again, time and time again, frequently, often, time after time; {day in, day out}, night and day, all the time; persistently, recurrently, constantly, continuously, continually, relentlessly, regularly, habitually, unfailingly, always; N. Amer. oftentimes; informal 24-7. **day by day** gradually, slowly, progressively; bit by bit, inch by inch, little by little. **day in, day out**. See DAY AFTER DAY.

WORD LINKS
diurnal of or during the daytime

daybreak noun **dawn**, the crack of dawn, sunrise, first light, cockcrow; daylight; N. Amer. sunup.
– OPPOSITES nightfall.

daydream noun **1** *she was lost in a daydream:* **reverie**, trance, fantasy, vision, dream. **2** *a big house was*

one of her daydreams: **dream**, pipe dream, fantasy, castle in the air, castle in Spain, fond hope; wishful thinking; informal pie in the sky.
• verb **dream**, fantasize, be in cloud cuckoo land, build castles in the air, build castles in Spain.

d

daydreamer noun **dreamer**, fantasist, fantasizer, romantic, wishful thinker, idealist; visionary, theorizer, utopian, Walter Mitty.

day-to-day adjective **regular**, everyday, daily, routine, habitual, frequent, normal, standard, usual, typical.

daze verb **1** *he was dazed by his fall:* **stun**, confuse, disorient, stupefy; knock unconscious, knock out. **2** *she was dazed by the revelations:* **astound**, amaze, astonish, startle, dumbfound, stupefy, overwhelm, stagger, shock, confound, bewilder, take aback, nonplus, shake; informal flabbergast, knock sideways, bowl over, blow away; Brit. informal knock for six.
• noun *she is in a daze:* **stupor**, trance, haze; spin, whirl, muddle, jumble.

dazzle verb **1** *she was dazzled by the headlights:* **blind**; confuse, disorient. **2** *I was dazzled by the exhibition:* **overwhelm**, overcome, impress, move, stir, affect, touch, awe, overawe, leave speechless, take someone's breath away; spellbind, hypnotize; informal bowl over, blow away, knock out.
• noun *the dazzle of the limelight:* **sparkle**, glitter, brilliance, glory, splendour, magnificence, glamour; attraction, lure, allure, draw, appeal; informal razzle-dazzle, razzmatazz.

dazzling adjective **1** *the sunlight was dazzling:* **bright**, blinding, glaring, brilliant. **2** *a dazzling performance:* **remarkable**, extraordinary, outstanding, exceptional; incredible, amazing, astonishing, phenomenal, breathtaking, thrilling; excellent, wonderful, magnificent, marvellous, superb, first-rate, superlative, virtuoso; informal mind-blowing, out of this world, fabulous, fab, super, sensational, ace, A1, cool, awesome; Brit. informal smashing, brill.

dead adjective **1** *my parents are dead:* **passed on/away**, expired, departed, no more; late, lost; perished, fallen, slain, killed, murdered; lifeless, extinct; informal as dead as a doornail, six feet under, pushing up daisies; formal deceased. **2** *patches of dead ground:* **barren**, lifeless, bare, desolate, sterile. **3** *a dead language:* **obsolete**, extinct, defunct, disused, abandoned, discarded, superseded, vanished, forgotten; archaic, ancient. **4** *the phone was dead:* **out of order**, inoperative, inactive, broken, defective; informal kaput, conked out, on the blink, bust; Brit. informal knackered. **5** *a dead town:* **boring**, uninteresting, unexciting, uninspiring, dull, flat, quiet, sleepy, slow, lifeless; informal one-horse; N. Amer. informal dullsville.
– OPPOSITES alive, fertile, modern, lively.
• adverb **1** *he was dead serious:* **completely**, absolutely, totally, utterly, deadly, perfectly, entirely, quite, thoroughly, one hundred per cent. **2** *flares were seen dead ahead:* **directly**, exactly, precisely, immediately, right, straight, due, squarely; informal slap bang.

deadbeat noun (informal) **layabout**, loafer, idler, good-for-nothing; informal waster, slacker; Brit. informal skiver; N. Amer. informal bum; literary wastrel.

deaden verb **1** *drugs were used to deaden the pain:* **numb**, dull, blunt, suppress; alleviate, mitigate, diminish, reduce, lessen, ease, soothe, relieve, assuage. **2** *the wood panelling deadened any noise:* **muffle**, mute, smother, stifle, dull, damp down; soften; cushion, buffer, absorb.
– OPPOSITES intensify, amplify.

deadline noun **time limit**, limit, finishing date, target date, cut-off point.

deadlock noun **stalemate**, impasse, checkmate, stand-off; standstill, halt, stop, full stop, dead end, gridlock.

deadly adjective **1** *these drugs can be deadly:* **fatal**, lethal, mortal, life-threatening; dangerous, injurious, harmful, detrimental, deleterious, unhealthy; noxious, toxic, poisonous; literary deathly. **2** *deadly enemies:* **mortal**, irreconcilable, implacable; bitter, sworn. **3** *his aim is deadly:* **unerring**, unfailing,

perfect; sure, true, precise, accurate, exact; Brit. informal spot on, bang on.
– OPPOSITES harmless, mild, inaccurate.
• adverb *deadly serious:* **completely**, absolutely, totally, utterly, perfectly, entirely, wholly, quite, dead, thoroughly; one hundred per cent, to the hilt.

deadpan adjective **blank**, expressionless, unexpressive, impassive, inscrutable, poker-faced, straight-faced; stony, wooden, vacant, fixed, lifeless.
– OPPOSITES expressive.

deaf adjective **1** *she is deaf and blind:* **hard of hearing**, hearing impaired; informal as deaf as a post. **2** *she was deaf to their pleading:* **unmoved by**, untouched by, unaffected by, indifferent to, unresponsive to, unconcerned by; unaware of, oblivious to, impervious to.

deafening adjective **ear-splitting**, overwhelming, almighty, mighty, tremendous; booming, thunderous.
– OPPOSITES low, soft.

deal noun *the successful completion of the deal:* **agreement**, understanding, pact, bargain, covenant, contract, treaty; arrangement, compromise, settlement; terms; transaction, sale, account; Law indenture.
• verb **1** *how to deal with difficult children:* **cope with**, handle, manage, treat, take care of, take charge of, take in hand, sort out, tackle, take on; control; act/behave towards. **2** *the article deals with advances in biochemistry:* **concern**, discuss, consider, cover, treat; tackle, study, explore, investigate, examine, review, analyse. **3** *the company deals in high-tech goods:* **trade in**, buy and sell; sell, purvey, supply, stock, market, merchandise; traffic, smuggle; informal push; Brit. informal flog. **4** *the cards were dealt:* **distribute**, give out, share out, divide out, hand out, pass out, pass round, dispense, allocate; informal divvy up. **5** *the court dealt a blow to government reforms:* **deliver**, administer, inflict, give, impose; aim.

dealer noun **1** *an antique dealer:* **trader**, tradesman, tradesperson, merchant, salesman/woman, seller, vendor, purveyor, pedlar; buyer, merchandiser, distributor, supplier, shopkeeper, retailer, wholesaler; Brit. stockist. **2** *a dealer in a bank:* **stockbroker**, broker-dealer, broker, agent.

dealing noun **1** *dishonest dealing:* **business methods/practices**, business, commerce, trading, transactions; behaviour, conduct, actions. **2** *the UK's dealings with China:* **relations**, relationship, association, connections, contact, intercourse; negotiations, transactions; trade, trading, business, commerce, traffic; informal truck, doings.

dear adjective **1** *a dear friend:* **beloved**, loved, cherished, precious; esteemed, respected; close, intimate, bosom, boon, best. **2** *her pictures were too dear to part with:* **precious**, treasured, valued, prized, cherished, special. **3** *she's such a dear girl:* **endearing**, adorable, lovable, appealing, engaging, charming, captivating, winsome, lovely, nice, pleasant, delightful, sweet, darling. **4** *£20—that's a bit dear:* **expensive**, costly, high-priced, overpriced, exorbitant, extortionate; Brit. over the odds; informal pricey, steep, stiff.

dearly adverb *I love him dearly:* **very much**, a great deal, greatly, deeply, profoundly; to distraction.

dearth noun **lack**, scarcity, shortage, shortfall, want, deficiency, insufficiency, inadequacy, sparseness, scantiness, rareness; absence.
– OPPOSITES surfeit.

death noun **1** *her father's death:* **demise**, dying, end, passing, loss of life; murder, assassination, execution, slaughter, massacre; formal decease. **2** *the death of their dream:* **end**, finish, termination, extinction, extinguishing, collapse, destruction, obliteration.
– OPPOSITES life, birth.

> **WORD LINKS**
> **fatal**, **lethal**, **mortal** causing death
> **thanatology** the scientific study of death

deathless adjective **immortal**, undying, imperishable, indestructible; enduring, everlasting, eternal; timeless, ageless.
– OPPOSITES mortal, ephemeral.

d

d

deathly adjective **deadly**, ghostly, ghastly; ashen, chalky, white, pale, pallid, bloodless.

debacle noun **fiasco**, failure, catastrophe, disaster, mess, ruin; downfall, collapse, defeat; informal foul-up, screw-up, hash, botch, washout; Brit. informal cock-up, pig's ear, bodge; N. Amer. informal snafu.

debase verb **degrade**, devalue, demean, cheapen, prostitute, discredit, drag down, tarnish, blacken; disgrace, dishonour, shame; damage, harm, undermine.
–OPPOSITES enhance.

debased adjective **1** *their debased amusements:* **immoral**, debauched, dissolute, perverted, degenerate, wicked, sinful, vile, base, iniquitous, corrupt; lewd, lascivious, lecherous, prurient, indecent. **2** *the myth lives on in a debased form:* **corrupt**, corrupted, bastardized, adulterated, diluted, tainted.
–OPPOSITES honourable, pure.

debatable adjective **arguable**, disputable, questionable, open to question, controversial, contentious; doubtful, dubious, uncertain, unsure, unclear; borderline, inconclusive, moot, unsettled, unresolved, unconfirmed, undetermined, undecided, up in the air; informal iffy.

debate noun *a debate on the reforms:* **discussion**, discourse, parley, dialogue; argument, dispute, wrangle, war of words, dissension, disagreement, contention, conflict; negotiations, talks; informal confab, powwow.
• verb **1** *MPs will debate our future:* **discuss**, talk over/through, talk about, thrash out, argue, dispute; informal kick around/about. **2** *he debated whether to call her:* **consider**, think over/about, chew over, mull over, weigh up, ponder, deliberate, contemplate, muse, meditate; formal cogitate.

debauched adjective **dissolute**, dissipated, degenerate, corrupt, depraved, sinful, unprincipled, immoral; lascivious, lecherous, lewd, lustful, libidinous, licentious, promiscuous, loose, wanton, abandoned; decadent, profligate, intemperate, sybaritic.
–OPPOSITES wholesome.

debauchery noun **dissipation**, degeneracy, corruption, vice, depravity; immodesty, indecency, perversion, iniquity, wickedness, sinfulness, impropriety, immorality; lasciviousness, salaciousness, lechery, lewdness, lust, promiscuity, wantonness; decadence, intemperance; formal turpitude.

debilitate verb **weaken**, enfeeble, enervate, sap, drain, exhaust, weary, fatigue, prostrate; undermine, impair, indispose, incapacitate, lay low; informal knock out, do in.
–OPPOSITES invigorate.

debonair adjective **suave**, urbane, sophisticated, cultured, self-possessed, self-assured, confident, charming, gracious, courteous, gallant, gentlemanly, refined, polished, well bred, genteel, dignified, courtly; well groomed, elegant, stylish, smart, dashing; informal smooth, sharp; Brit. informal swish.
–OPPOSITES unsophisticated.

debrief verb **question**, quiz, interview, examine, cross-examine, interrogate, probe, sound out; informal grill, pump.

debris noun **detritus**, refuse, rubbish, waste, litter, scrap, dross, chaff, flotsam and jetsam; rubble, wreckage; remains, scraps, dregs; N. Amer. trash, garbage; informal junk.

debt noun **1** *he couldn't pay his debts:* **bill**, account, dues, arrears, charges; N. Amer. check; informal tab. **2** *his debt to the author:* **indebtedness**, obligation; gratitude, appreciation, thanks.
■ **in debt** owing money, in arrears, behind, overdrawn; insolvent, bankrupt, ruined; Brit. in liquidation; informal in the red, in Queer Street, on the rocks.

debtor noun **borrower**; bankrupt, insolvent, defaulter.
–OPPOSITES creditor.

debunk verb **explode**, deflate, quash, discredit, disprove, refute, contradict, controvert, invalidate, negate; challenge, call into question; informal shoot full of holes, blow sky-high; formal confute.
–OPPOSITES confirm.

debut noun **first appearance**, first performance, launch, entrance, premiere, introduction, inception, inauguration; informal kick-off.

decadence noun **dissipation**, degeneracy, debauchery, corruption, depravity, vice, sin, moral decay, immorality, amorality; intemperance, licentiousness, self-indulgence, hedonism.
–OPPOSITES morality.

decadent adjective **dissolute**, dissipated, degenerate, corrupt, depraved, sinful, unprincipled, immoral, amoral; licentious, abandoned, profligate, intemperate; sybaritic, hedonistic, pleasure-seeking, self-indulgent.

decant verb **pour out/off**, draw off, siphon off, drain, tap; transfer.

decay verb **1** *the body had begun to decay:* **decompose**, rot, putrefy, go bad, go off, spoil, fester, perish, deteriorate; break down, moulder, shrivel, wither. **2** *the city's infrastructure is decaying:* **deteriorate**, degenerate, decline, go downhill, slump, slide, go to rack and ruin, go to seed; disintegrate, fall to pieces, fall into disrepair; collapse; informal go to pot, go to the dogs; Austral./NZ informal go to the pack.
•noun **1** *signs of decay:* **decomposition**, putrefaction, rot; mould, mildew, fungus. **2** *the decay of the old industries:* **deterioration**, degeneration, debasement, degradation, decline, weakening, atrophy; crumbling, disintegration, collapse.

decayed adjective **decomposed**, decomposing, rotten, putrescent, putrid, bad, off, spoiled, perished; mouldy, festering, fetid, rancid, rank.

decaying adjective **1** *decaying fish:* **decomposing**, decomposed, rotting, rotten, putrescent, putrid, bad, off, perished; mouldy, festering, fetid, rancid, rank. **2** *a decaying city:* **declining**, degenerating, dying, crumbling; run down, tumbledown, ramshackle, shabby, decrepit.

deceased adjective (formal) **dead**, expired, departed, gone, no more, passed on/away; late, lost, late lamented; perished, fallen, slain, slaughtered, killed, murdered; lifeless, extinct; informal as dead as a doornail, six feet under, pushing up daisies.

deceit noun **deception**, deceitfulness, duplicity, double-dealing, lies, fraud, cheating, trickery, chicanery, deviousness, slyness, guile, bluff, lying, pretence, treachery; informal crookedness, monkey business, jiggery-pokery; N. Amer. informal monkeyshines.
–OPPOSITES honesty.

deceitful adjective **1** *a deceitful woman:* **dishonest**, untruthful, insincere, false, disingenuous, untrustworthy, unscrupulous, unprincipled, two-faced, duplicitous, double-dealing, underhand, crafty, cunning, sly, scheming, calculating, treacherous, Machiavellian; informal sneaky, tricky, crooked; Brit. informal bent. **2** *a deceitful allegation:* **fraudulent**, fabricated, invented, concocted, made up, trumped up, untrue, false, bogus, fake, spurious, fallacious, deceptive, misleading.
–OPPOSITES honest, true.

deceive verb *she was deceived by a con man:* **swindle**, defraud, cheat, trick, hoodwink, hoax, dupe, take in, mislead, delude, fool, outwit, lead on, inveigle, beguile, double-cross, gull; informal con, bamboozle, do, diddle, swizzle, rip off, shaft, pull a fast one on, take for a ride, pull the wool over someone's eyes, sell a pup to; N. Amer. informal sucker, snooker, stiff.

decelerate verb **slow down/up**, ease up, reduce speed, brake.
–OPPOSITES accelerate.

decency noun **1** *standards of taste and decency:* **propriety**, decorum, good taste, respectability, dignity, correctness, good form, etiquette; morality, virtue, modesty, delicacy. **2** *he didn't have the decency to tell me:* **courtesy**, politeness, good manners, civility; consideration, thoughtfulness.

decent adjective **1** *a decent burial:* **proper**, correct, appropriate, suitable; respectable, dignified, decorous, seemly; nice, right, tasteful; conventional, accepted, standard, traditional, orthodox; comme il faut; informal pukka.
2 (Brit. informal) *a very decent chap:* **honourable**, honest, trustworthy, dependable; respectable, upright, clean-living, virtuous, good; obliging, helpful, accommodating, generous, kind, thoughtful, considerate; neighbourly, hospitable,

d

pleasant, agreeable, amiable. **3** *a job with decent pay:* **satisfactory**, reasonable, fair, acceptable, adequate, sufficient; not bad, all right, tolerable, passable, suitable; informal OK, okay.
– OPPOSITES unpleasant, unsatisfactory.

deception noun **1** *they obtained money by deception:* **deceit**, deceitfulness, duplicity, double-dealing, fraud, cheating, trickery, chicanery, deviousness, guile, bluff, lying, pretence, treachery; informal crookedness, monkey business, jiggery-pokery; N. Amer. informal monkeyshines. **2** *it was all a deception:* **trick**, deceit, sham, fraud, pretence, hoax, fake, artifice; stratagem, device, ruse, scheme, dodge, machination, subterfuge; cheat, swindle; informal con, set-up, scam, flimflam; N. Amer. informal bunco.

deceptive adjective **1** *distances are very deceptive:* **misleading**; illusory; ambiguous. **2** *deceptive practices:* **deceitful**, duplicitous, fraudulent, counterfeit, underhand, scheming, treacherous, Machiavellian; disingenuous, untrustworthy, unscrupulous, unprincipled, dishonest, insincere, false; informal crooked, sharp, shady, sneaky, tricky; Brit. informal bent.

decide verb **1** *she decided to become a writer:* **resolve**, determine, make up your mind; elect, choose, opt, plan, aim, intend, have in mind, set your sights on. **2** *the court is to decide the case:* **adjudicate**, arbitrate, judge; hear, try, examine; sit in judgement on, pronounce on, give a verdict on, rule on, settle.

decided adjective **1** *they have a decided advantage:* **distinct**, clear, marked, pronounced, obvious, striking, noticeable, unmistakable, patent, manifest; definite, certain, positive, emphatic, undeniable, indisputable, unquestionable; assured, guaranteed. **2** *he was very decided:* **determined**, resolute, firm, strong-minded, strong-willed, emphatic, dead set, unwavering, unyielding, unbending, inflexible, unshakeable, unrelenting; N. Amer. rock-ribbed. **3** *our future is decided:* **settled**, established, resolved, determined, agreed, designated, chosen, ordained, prescribed; set, fixed; informal sewn up, wrapped up.

decidedly adverb **distinctly**, clearly, markedly, obviously, noticeably, unmistakably, patently, manifestly; definitely, certainly, positively, absolutely, downright, undeniably, unquestionably; extremely, exceedingly, exceptionally, particularly, especially, very; N. English right; informal terrifically, ultra, mega, majorly; Brit. informal jolly, dead, well; N. Amer. informal real, mighty, awful.

deciding adjective **determining**, decisive, conclusive, key, pivotal, crucial, critical, significant.

decipher verb **1** *he deciphered the code:* **decode**, decrypt, break, work out, solve, interpret, translate; make sense of, get to the bottom of, unravel; informal crack, figure out; Brit. informal twig, suss out. **2** *his writing was hard to decipher:* **make out**, discern, perceive, read, follow.
– OPPOSITES encode.

decision noun **1** *they came to a decision:* **resolution**, conclusion, settlement; choice, option, selection. **2** *the judge's decision:* **verdict**, finding, ruling, recommendation, judgement, pronouncement, adjudication; order, rule; result; Law determination; N. Amer. resolve.

decisive adjective **1** *a decisive man:* **resolute**, firm, strong-minded, strong-willed, determined; purposeful. **2** *the decisive factor:* **deciding**, conclusive, determining; key, pivotal, critical, crucial, significant, influential, major, chief, principal, prime.

deck verb **1** *the street was decked with bunting:* **decorate**, bedeck, adorn, ornament, trim, trick out, garnish, cover, hang, festoon, garland, swathe, wreathe; literary bedizen. **2** *Ingrid was decked out in blue:* **dress**, clothe, attire, garb, robe, drape, turn out, fit out, rig out, outfit, costume; informal doll up, get up, do up.

declaim verb **make a speech**, speak, hold forth, orate, preach, lecture, sermonize, moralize; speak out, rail, inveigh, fulminate, rage, thunder; rant; informal sound off, spout.

declaration noun **1** *they issued a declaration:* **announcement**, statement, communication, pronouncement, proclamation, communiqué, edict; N. Amer. advisory. **2** *a declaration of faith:* **assertion**, profession, affirmation, acknowledgement, revelation, disclosure, manifestation, confirmation, testimony, validation, certification, attestation; pledge, avowal, vow, oath, protestation.

declare verb **1** *she declared her political principles:* **proclaim**, announce, state, reveal, air, voice, articulate, express, vent, set forth, publicize, broadcast. **2** *he declared that they were guilty:* **assert**, maintain, state, affirm, contend, argue, insist, hold, profess, claim, avow, swear; formal aver.

decline verb **1** *she declined all invitations:* **turn down**, reject, brush aside, refuse, rebuff, spurn, repulse, dismiss; forgo, pass up; abstain from; informal give the thumbs down to, give something a miss, give someone the brush-off; Brit. informal knock back. **2** *the number of traders has declined:* **decrease**, reduce, lessen, diminish, dwindle, contract, shrink, fall off, tail off; drop, fall, go down, slump, plummet; informal nosedive, crash. **3** *standards steadily declined:* **deteriorate**, degenerate, decay, crumble, collapse, slump, slip, slide, go downhill, worsen; weaken, wane, ebb; informal go to pot, go to the dogs; Austral./NZ informal go to the pack.
–OPPOSITES accept, increase, rise.
•noun **1** *a decline in profits:* **reduction**, decrease, downturn, downswing, depreciation, diminution, ebb, drop, slump, plunge; informal nosedive, crash. **2** *habitat decline:* **deterioration**, degeneration, degradation, shrinkage; erosion.
■ **in decline** declining, decaying, crumbling, collapsing, failing; disappearing, dying, moribund; informal on its last legs, on the way out.

decode verb **decipher**, decrypt, work out, solve, interpret, translate; make sense of, get to the bottom of, unravel, find the key to; informal crack, figure out; Brit. informal twig, suss out.

decompose verb **decay**, rot, putrefy, go bad, go off, spoil, perish, deteriorate; degrade, break down.

decomposition noun **decay**, putrefaction, putrescence.

decontaminate verb **sanitize**, sterilize, disinfect, clean, cleanse, purify; fumigate.

decor noun **decoration**, furnishing; colour scheme.

decorate verb **1** *the door was decorated with a wreath:* **ornament**, adorn, trim, embellish, garnish, furnish, enhance, grace, prettify; festoon, garland, bedeck. **2** *he started to decorate his home:* **refurbish**, renovate, paint; informal do up, spruce up, fix up, give something a facelift, make over. **3** *he was decorated for outstanding bravery:* **honour**, cite, reward.

decoration noun **1** *a ceiling with rich decoration:* **ornamentation**, adornment, trimming, embellishment, gilding; beautification, prettification; enhancements, enrichments, frills, accessories, trimmings, finery, frippery. **2** *a Christmas tree decoration:* **ornament**, bauble, trinket, knick-knack. **3** *a decoration won on the battlefield:* **medal**, award, prize; Brit. informal gong.

decorative adjective **ornamental**; fancy, ornate, attractive, pretty, showy.
–OPPOSITES functional.

decorous adjective **proper**, seemly, decent, becoming, befitting, tasteful; correct, appropriate, suitable, fitting; restrained, modest, demure, ladylike.
–OPPOSITES indecorous.

decorum noun **1** *he had acted with decorum:* **propriety**, seemliness, decency, good taste, correctness; politeness, courtesy, good manners. **2** *a breach of decorum:* **etiquette**, protocol, good form, custom, convention.
–OPPOSITES impropriety.

decoy noun **lure**, bait, red herring; trap.
•verb **lure**, entice, tempt; lead away.

decrease verb **1** *pollution levels decreased:* **lessen**, reduce, drop, diminish, decline, dwindle, fall off; die down, abate, subside, tail off, ebb, wane; plummet, plunge. **2** *decrease the amount of fat in your*

body: **reduce**, lessen, lower, cut; slim down, tone down, deplete, minimize; informal slash.
– OPPOSITES increase.
• noun *a decrease in crime:* **reduction**, drop, decline, downturn, cut, cutback, diminution, ebb, wane.
– OPPOSITES increase.

d

decree noun **1** *a presidential decree:* **order**, edict, command, commandment, mandate, proclamation, dictum; law, statute, act; formal ordinance. **2** *a court decree:* **judgement**, verdict, adjudication, ruling, resolution, decision.
• verb *he decreed that a stadium should be built:* **order**, command, rule, dictate, pronounce, proclaim, ordain; direct, decide, determine.

decrepit adjective **1** *a decrepit old man:* **feeble**, infirm, weak, frail; incapacitated, doddering, tottering; old, elderly, aged, ancient, senile; informal past it, over the hill. **2** *a decrepit house:* **dilapidated**, rickety, run down, tumbledown, ramshackle, derelict, ruined, in disrepair, gone to rack and ruin; decayed, crumbling.
– OPPOSITES strong, sound.

decry verb **denounce**, condemn, criticize, censure, attack, rail against, run down, pillory, lambaste, vilify, revile; disparage, deprecate; informal slam, blast, knock; Brit. informal slate.
– OPPOSITES praise.

dedicate verb **1** *she dedicated her life to the sick:* **devote**, commit, pledge, give, sacrifice; set aside, allocate, consign. **2** *the chapel was dedicated to the Virgin Mary:* **devote**, assign; bless, consecrate, sanctify.

dedicated adjective **1** *a dedicated socialist:* **committed**, devoted, staunch, firm, steadfast, resolute, loyal, faithful, true, dyed-in-the-wool; wholehearted, single-minded, earnest, ardent, passionate, fervent; informal card-carrying. **2** *data is accessed by a dedicated search engine:* **exclusive**, custom built, customized, special, purpose built; built-in, inbuilt, on-board, in-house.
– OPPOSITES indifferent.

dedication noun **1** *sport requires dedication:* **commitment**, application, diligence, industry, resolve, enthusiasm, conscientiousness, perseverance, persistence, tenacity, drive, staying power; hard work, effort. **2** *her dedication to the job:* **devotion**, commitment, loyalty, allegiance. **3** *the book has a dedication to his wife:* **inscription**, message. **4** *the dedication of the church:* **blessing**, consecration, sanctification.
– OPPOSITES apathy.

deduce verb **conclude**, reason, work out, infer; glean, divine, intuit, understand, assume, presume, conjecture, surmise, reckon; informal figure out; Brit. informal suss out.

deduct verb **subtract**, take away, take off, debit, dock, discount; remove; informal knock off.
– OPPOSITES add.

deduction noun **1** *the deduction of tax:* **subtraction**, removal, debit. **2** *gross pay, before deductions:* **stoppage**, tax; expenses. **3** *she was right in her deduction:* **conclusion**, inference, supposition, hypothesis, assumption, presumption; suspicion, conviction, belief, reasoning.

deed noun **1** *heroic deeds:* **act**, action; feat, exploit, achievement, accomplishment, endeavour, undertaking, enterprise. **2** *unity must be established in deed and word:* **fact**, reality, actuality.

deem verb **consider**, regard as, judge, hold to be, view as, see as, take for, class as, count, find, esteem, suppose, reckon; think, believe, feel.

deep adjective **1** *a deep ravine:* **cavernous**, yawning, gaping, huge, extensive; bottomless, fathomless, unfathomable. **2** *his deep voice:* **low-pitched**, low, bass, rich, powerful, resonant, booming, sonorous. **3** *a deep red:* **dark**, intense, rich, strong. **4** *deep affection:* **intense**, heartfelt, wholehearted, deep-seated, deep-rooted; sincere, genuine, earnest, enthusiastic, great. **5** *a deep sleep:* **sound**, heavy. **6** *he was deep in concentration:* **rapt**, absorbed, engrossed, preoccupied, immersed, lost, gripped, intent, engaged. **7** *deep philosophical questions:* **obscure**, complex, mysterious, secret, unfathomable, opaque, abstruse, recondite, esoteric, enigmatic, arcane; puzzling, baffling, mystifying, inexplicable.
– OPPOSITES shallow, high, light.

deepen verb **1** *his love for her had deepened:* **grow**, increase, intensify, strengthen; informal step up; Brit. informal hot up. **2** *they deepened the hole:* **dig out**, dig deeper, excavate.

deeply adverb **profoundly**, greatly, enormously, extremely, very much; strongly, intensely, keenly, acutely; thoroughly, completely, entirely; informal well, seriously, majorly.

deep-rooted adjective **deep-seated**, deep, profound, fundamental, basic; established, ingrained, entrenched, unshakeable, inbuilt; persistent, abiding, lingering.
– OPPOSITES superficial.

deep-seated adjective. See **DEEP-ROOTED**.

deer noun

WORD LINKS
cervine relating to deer

deface verb **vandalize**, disfigure, spoil, ruin, damage; N. Amer. informal trash.

defamation noun **libel**, slander, calumny, character assassination, vilification; scandalmongering, aspersions, muckraking, abuse; disparagement, denigration; smear, slur; informal mud-slinging.

defamatory adjective **libellous**, slanderous, malicious, vicious, backbiting, muckraking; abusive, disparaging, denigrating, insulting; informal mud-slinging, bitchy, catty.

defame verb **libel**, slander, malign, cast aspersions on, smear, traduce, give someone a bad name, run down, speak ill of, vilify, besmirch, disparage, denigrate, discredit; informal do a hatchet job on, drag through the mud; N. Amer. slur; informal bad-mouth; Brit. informal slag off.
– OPPOSITES compliment.

defeat verb **1** *the army which defeated the Scots:* **beat**, conquer, win against, triumph over, get the better of; rout, trounce, overcome, overpower, crush, subdue; informal lick, thrash, wipe the floor with, make mincemeat of, clobber, slaughter, demolish, cane; literary vanquish. **2** *this defeats the original point of the plan:* **thwart**, frustrate, foil, ruin, scotch, derail; informal put the kibosh on, put paid to, stymie; Brit. informal scupper, nobble. **3** *the motion was defeated:* **reject**, overthrow, throw out, dismiss, outvote, turn down; informal give the thumbs down.
• noun **1** *a crippling defeat:* **loss**, conquest; rout, trouncing; informal thrashing, hiding, drubbing, licking, pasting, massacre, slaughter.
2 *the defeat of his plans:* **failure**, downfall, collapse, ruin; rejection, frustration, abortion, miscarriage; undoing.
– OPPOSITES victory, success.

defeatist adjective *a defeatist attitude:* **pessimistic**, fatalistic, negative, despondent, despairing, hopeless, gloomy.
– OPPOSITES optimistic.
• noun **pessimist**, fatalist, prophet of doom, doomster; misery, killjoy, worrier; informal quitter, wet blanket, loser.
– OPPOSITES optimist.

defect[1] noun *he spotted a defect in my work:* **fault**, flaw, imperfection, deficiency, weakness, inconsistency, weak spot, inadequacy, shortcoming, limitation, failing, deformity, blemish; mistake, error; informal glitch, gremlin, bug.

defect[2] verb *his chief intelligence officer defected:* **desert**, change sides, turn traitor, rebel, renege; Military go AWOL; literary forsake.

defection noun **desertion**, absconding, decamping, flight; treason, betrayal, disloyalty.

defective adjective **faulty**, flawed, imperfect, shoddy, inoperative, malfunctioning, out of order, unsound; broken; informal on the blink; Brit. informal knackered, duff.
– OPPOSITES perfect.

defector noun **deserter**, turncoat, traitor, renegade, Judas, quisling; informal rat.

defence noun **1** *the defence of the fortress:* **protection**, guarding, security, fortification; resistance, deterrent. **2** *more spending on defence was necessary:* **armaments**, weapons, weaponry, arms; the military, the armed forces. **3** *the prisoner's defence:* **vindication**, explanation, mitigation, justification, rationalization, excuse, alibi, reason; plea, pleading; testimony, declaration, case.

d

d

defenceless adjective **1** *defenceless animals:* **vulnerable**, helpless, powerless, weak. **2** *the country is wholly defenceless:* **undefended**, unprotected, unguarded, unarmed; vulnerable, exposed, insecure.
–OPPOSITES resilient.

defend verb **1** *a fort built to defend Ireland:* **protect**, guard, safeguard, secure, shield; fortify; uphold, support, watch over. **2** *he defended his policy:* **justify**, vindicate, argue for, support, make a case for, plead for; explain. **3** *the manager defended his players:* **support**, back, stand by, stick up for, stand up for.
–OPPOSITES attack, criticize.

defendant noun **accused**, prisoner at the bar; appellant, litigant, respondent; suspect.
–OPPOSITES plaintiff.

defender noun **1** *defenders of the environment:* **protector**, guard, guardian, preserver; custodian, watchdog, keeper, overseer, superintendent, caretaker. **2** *a defender of colonialism:* **supporter**, upholder, backer, champion, advocate, apologist, proponent, exponent, promoter; adherent, believer.

defensive adjective **1** *troops in defensive positions:* **defending**, protective. **2** *a defensive response:* **self-justifying**, oversensitive, prickly, paranoid, neurotic; informal uptight, twitchy.

defer[1] verb *the committee will defer their decision:* **postpone**, put off, delay, hold over/off, put back; shelve, suspend, stay, mothball; N. Amer. put over, table, take a rain check on; informal put on ice, put on the back burner, put in cold storage.

defer[2] verb *they deferred to Joseph's judgement:* **yield**, submit, give way, give in, surrender, capitulate, acquiesce.

deference noun **respect**, respectfulness; submissiveness, submission, obedience, accession, capitulation, acquiescence, compliance.
–OPPOSITES disrespect.

deferential adjective **respectful**, humble, obsequious; dutiful, obedient, submissive, subservient, yielding, acquiescent, compliant.

defiance noun **resistance**, opposition, non-compliance, disobedience, insubordination, dissent, recalcitrance, rebellion; contempt, disregard, scorn, insolence.
–OPPOSITES obedience.

defiant adjective **intransigent**, resistant, obstinate, uncooperative, non-compliant, recalcitrant; insubordinate, rebellious, mutinous; informal feisty; Brit. informal stroppy, bolshie.
–OPPOSITES cooperative.

deficiency noun **1** *a vitamin deficiency:* **insufficiency**, lack, shortage, want, deficit, shortfall; scarcity. **2** *the team's big deficiency:* **defect**, fault, flaw, imperfection, weakness, weak point, inadequacy, shortcoming, limitation, failing.
–OPPOSITES surplus, strength.

deficient adjective **1** *a diet deficient in vitamin A:* **lacking**, wanting, inadequate, insufficient, limited, poor; short of/on, low on. **2** *deficient leadership:* **defective**, faulty, flawed, inadequate, imperfect, shoddy, weak, inferior, unsound, substandard, poor; Brit. informal duff.

deficit noun **shortfall**, deficiency, shortage, undersupply; debt, arrears; loss.
–OPPOSITES surplus.

defile verb **desecrate**, profane, violate; contaminate, pollute, debase, degrade, dishonour.
–OPPOSITES sanctify.

definable adjective **determinable**, ascertainable, definite, clear-cut, precise, exact, specific.

define verb **1** *the dictionary defines it succinctly:* **explain**, expound, interpret, describe. **2** *he defined the limits of the middle class:* **determine**, establish, fix, specify, designate, decide, stipulate, set out.

definite adjective **1** *a definite answer:* **explicit**, specific, express, precise, exact, clear-cut, direct, plain, outright; fixed. **2** *definite evidence:* **certain**, sure, positive, conclusive, decisive, firm, concrete, unambiguous, unequivocal, clear, unmistakable, proven; guaranteed, assured, cut and dried. **3** *she had a definite dislike for Robert:* **unmistakable**, unequivocal, unambiguous, certain, undisputed, decided, marked, distinct. **4** *a*

definite geographical area: **fixed**, marked, specific, identifiable.
– OPPOSITES vague, ambiguous, indeterminate.

definitely adverb **certainly**, surely, for sure, unquestionably, without doubt, without question, undoubtedly, indubitably, positively, absolutely; undeniably, unmistakably, as sure as eggs is eggs.

definition noun **1** *the definition of 'intelligence':* **meaning**, sense; interpretation, explanation, description. **2** *the definition of the picture:* **clarity**, visibility, sharpness, crispness; resolution.

definitive adjective **1** *a definitive decision:* **conclusive**, final; unconditional, unqualified, absolute, categorical, positive, definite. **2** *the definitive guide:* **authoritative**, exhaustive, best, finest; classic, standard, recognized, accepted, official.

deflate verb **1** *he deflated the tyres:* **let down**, flatten; puncture. **2** *the news had deflated him:* **subdue**, humble, cow, chasten; dispirit, dismay, discourage, dishearten; squash, crush, bring down, take the wind out of someone's sails.
– OPPOSITES inflate.

deflect verb **1** *she wanted to deflect attention from herself:* **turn away**, divert, draw away; fend off, parry, stave off. **2** *the ball deflected off the wall:* **bounce**, glance, ricochet.

deform verb **disfigure**, bend out of shape, contort, buckle, warp; damage, impair.

deformed adjective **misshapen**, distorted, malformed, contorted, out of shape; twisted, crooked, warped, buckled, gnarled; disfigured, grotesque; injured, damaged, mutilated, mangled.

deformity noun **malformation**, misshapenness, distortion, crookedness; imperfection, abnormality, irregularity; disfigurement; defect, flaw, blemish.

defraud verb **swindle**, cheat, rob; deceive, dupe, hoodwink, double-cross, trick; informal con, do, sting, diddle, rip off, shaft, pull a fast one on, put one over on, sell a pup to; N. Amer. informal sucker, snooker, stiff; Austral. informal pull a swifty on.

deft adjective **skilful**, adept, adroit, dexterous, agile, nimble, handy; able, capable, skilled, proficient, accomplished, expert, polished, slick, professional, masterly; clever, shrewd, astute, canny, sharp; informal nifty, nippy.
– OPPOSITES clumsy.

defunct adjective **disused**, inoperative, non-functioning, unusable, obsolete, moribund; extinct.
– OPPOSITES working, extant.

defuse verb **1** *an attempt to defuse the situation:* **cool**, calm, settle, take the heat out of, relieve, smooth out, save. **2** *he tried to defuse the grenade:* **deactivate**, disarm, disable, make safe.
– OPPOSITES aggravate, activate.

> ! Don't confuse **defuse** with **diffuse**, which means 'spread over a wide area' (*new technologies diffuse rapidly*).

defy verb **1** *he defied European law:* **disobey**, go against, flout, fly in the face of, disregard, ignore; break, violate, contravene, breach, infringe; informal cock a snook at. **2** *he scowled, defying her to mock him:* **challenge**, dare.
– OPPOSITES obey.

degeneracy noun **corruption**, decadence, moral decay, dissipation, dissolution, profligacy, vice, immorality, sin, sinfulness, ungodliness; debauchery; formal turpitude.

degenerate adjective **1** *a degenerate form of classicism:* **debased**, degraded, corrupt, impure. **2** *her degenerate brother:* **corrupt**, decadent, dissolute, dissipated, debauched, reprobate, profligate; sinful, ungodly, immoral, unprincipled, amoral, dishonourable, disreputable, unsavoury.
– OPPOSITES pure, moral.
• noun *a bunch of degenerates:* **reprobate**, debauchee, profligate, libertine, roué.
• verb **1** *their quality of life had degenerated:* **deteriorate**, decline, slip, slide, worsen, lapse, slump, go downhill, regress; go to rack and ruin; informal go to pot, go to the dogs, hit the skids. **2** *the muscles started to degenerate:* **waste away**, atrophy, weaken, deteriorate.
– OPPOSITES improve.

d

degradation noun **1** *poverty brings with it degradation:* **humiliation**, shame, loss of self-respect, indignity, ignominy. **2** *the degradation of women:* **demeaning**, debasement.

degrade verb **1** *prisons should not degrade prisoners:* **demean**, debase, humiliate, dehumanize, brutalize. **2** *the polymer will not degrade:* **break down**, deteriorate, degenerate, decay.
– OPPOSITES dignify.

degrading adjective **humiliating**, demeaning, shameful, mortifying, ignominious, undignified.

degree noun **level**, standard, grade, mark; amount, extent, measure; magnitude, intensity, strength; proportion, ratio.
■ **by degrees** gradually, little by little, bit by bit, inch by inch, step by step, slowly; piecemeal.

deign verb **condescend**, stoop, lower yourself, demean yourself, humble yourself; consent, vouchsafe.

deity noun **god**, goddess, divine being, supreme being, divinity, immortal; creator, demiurge; godhead.

dejected adjective **downcast**, downhearted, despondent, disconsolate, dispirited, crestfallen, disheartened; depressed, crushed, desolate, heartbroken, in the doldrums, sad, unhappy, doleful, melancholy, miserable, woebegone, forlorn, wretched, glum, gloomy; informal fed up, blue, down in the mouth, down in the dumps.
– OPPOSITES cheerful.

delay verb **1** *we were delayed by the traffic:* **detain**, hold up, make late, slow up/down, bog down; hinder, hamper, impede, obstruct. **2** *don't delay:* **linger**, drag your feet, hold back, dawdle, waste time; stall, procrastinate, hang fire, mark time, hesitate, dither, shilly-shally; informal dilly-dally. **3** *he may delay the cut in interest rates:* **postpone**, put off, defer, hold over, shelve, suspend, stay; reschedule; N. Amer. put over, table; informal put on ice, put on the back burner, put in cold storage.
– OPPOSITES hurry, advance.
• noun **1** *drivers will face lengthy delays:* **hold-up**, wait. **2** *the delay of his trial:* **postponement**, deferral, deferment; adjournment.

delectable adjective **1** *a delectable meal:* **delicious**, mouth-watering, appetizing, flavoursome, toothsome; succulent, luscious, tasty; informal scrumptious, scrummy, yummy; N. Amer. informal finger-licking, nummy. **2** *the delectable Ms Davis:* **delightful**, lovely, captivating, charming, enchanting, appealing, beguiling; beautiful, attractive, ravishing, gorgeous, stunning, alluring, sexy, seductive, desirable, luscious; informal divine, heavenly, dreamy; Brit. informal tasty.
– OPPOSITES unpalatable, unattractive.

delegate noun *trade union delegates:* **representative**, envoy, emissary, commissioner, agent, deputy, commissary; spokesperson, spokesman/woman; ambassador.
• verb **1** *she must delegate routine tasks:* **assign**, entrust, pass on, hand on/over, turn over, devolve, transfer. **2** *they were delegated to negotiate with the States:* **authorize**, commission, appoint, nominate, mandate, empower, charge, choose, designate, elect.

delegation noun **1** *the delegation from South Africa:* **deputation**, diplomatic mission, commission; delegates, representatives, envoys, emissaries, deputies. **2** *the delegation of tasks to others:* **assignment**, entrusting, giving, devolution, transference.

delete verb **remove**, cut out, take out, edit out, expunge, excise, eradicate, cancel; cross out, strike out, ink out, scratch out, obliterate, white out; rub out, erase, efface, wipe out, blot out.
– OPPOSITES add.

deliberate adjective **1** *a deliberate attempt to provoke him:* **intentional**, calculated, conscious, intended, planned, studied, knowing, wilful, wanton, purposeful, purposive, premeditated, pre-planned; voluntary. **2** *small, deliberate steps:* **careful**, cautious; measured, regular, even, steady. **3** *a deliberate worker:* **methodical**, systematic, careful, painstaking, meticulous, thorough.
– OPPOSITES accidental, hasty, careless.
• verb *she deliberated on his words:*

think about/over, ponder, consider, contemplate, reflect on, muse on, meditate on, ruminate on, mull over, weigh up; brood over, dwell on; N. Amer. think on.

deliberately adverb **1** *he deliberately hurt me:* **intentionally**, on purpose, purposely, by design, knowingly, wittingly, consciously, purposefully; wilfully, wantonly; Law with malice aforethought. **2** *he walked deliberately down the aisle:* **carefully**, cautiously, slowly, steadily, evenly.

deliberation noun **1** *after much deliberation, I accepted:* **thought**, consideration, reflection, contemplation, meditation, rumination; formal cogitation. **2** *he replaced the glass with deliberation:* **care**, carefulness, caution.

delicacy noun **1** *the delicacy of the fabric:* **fineness**, delicateness, fragility; thinness, lightness, flimsiness, fragility. **2** *the delicacy of the situation:* **difficulty**, sensitivity, ticklishness, awkwardness. **3** *treat this matter with delicacy:* **care**, sensitivity, tact, discretion, diplomacy, subtlety, sensibility. **4** *an Australian delicacy:* **treat**, luxury; speciality.

delicate adjective **1** *delicate embroidery:* **fine**, intricate, dainty. **2** *a delicate shade of blue:* **subtle**, soft, muted; pastel, pale, light. **3** *delicate china cups:* **fragile**, frail. **4** *his wife is very delicate:* **sickly**, unhealthy, frail, feeble, weak; unwell, infirm. **5** *a delicate issue:* **difficult**, tricky, sensitive, ticklish, awkward, touchy; embarrassing; informal sticky, dicey. **6** *the matter required delicate handling:* **careful**, sensitive, tactful, diplomatic, discreet, kid-glove, softly-softly. **7** *a delicate mechanism:* **sensitive**, light, precision.
– OPPOSITES coarse, lurid, strong, robust, clumsy.

delicious adjective **delectable**, mouth-watering, appetizing, tasty, flavoursome, toothsome; succulent, luscious; informal scrumptious, scrummy, yummy; N. Amer. informal finger-licking, nummy.
– OPPOSITES unpalatable.

delight verb **1** *her manners delighted him:* **charm**, enchant, captivate, entrance, thrill; entertain, amuse, divert; informal send, tickle pink, bowl over. **2** *Fabia delighted in his touch:* **revel**, luxuriate, wallow, glory; adore, love, relish, savour, lap up; informal get a kick out of, get a buzz out of, get a thrill out of, dig; N. Amer. informal get a charge out of, get off on.
– OPPOSITES dismay, disgust, dislike.
• noun *she squealed with delight:* **pleasure**, happiness, joy, glee, gladness; excitement, amusement; bliss, rapture, elation.
– OPPOSITES displeasure.

delighted adjective **pleased**, glad, happy, thrilled, overjoyed, ecstatic, elated; on cloud nine, walking on air, in seventh heaven, jumping for joy; enchanted, charmed; amused, diverted; gleeful, cock-a-hoop; informal over the moon, tickled pink, as pleased as Punch, on top of the world, as happy as Larry; Brit. informal chuffed; N. English informal made up; Austral. informal wrapped.

delightful adjective **1** *a delightful evening:* **lovely**, enjoyable; amusing, entertaining; marvellous, wonderful, splendid, thrilling; informal great, super, fabulous, fab, terrific, heavenly, divine, grand; Brit. informal brilliant, brill, smashing; N. Amer. informal peachy, ducky; Austral./NZ informal beaut, bonzer. **2** *the delightful Sally:* **charming**, enchanting, captivating, bewitching, appealing; sweet, endearing, cute, lovely, adorable, delectable, delicious, gorgeous, ravishing, beautiful; Scottish & N. English bonny; informal divine.

delimit verb **determine**, establish, set, fix, demarcate, define, delineate.

delineate verb **1** *their powers are delineated by statute:* **describe**, set forth/out, present, outline, depict, represent; map out, define, specify, identify. **2** *a section delineated in red marker pen:* **outline**, trace, block in, mark out, delimit.

delinquency noun **crime**, wrongdoing, lawbreaking, lawlessness, misconduct, misbehaviour; misdemeanours, offences, misdeeds.

delinquent adjective **lawless**, lawbreaking, criminal; errant, badly

d

behaved, troublesome, difficult, unruly, disobedient, uncontrollable. • **noun offender**, wrongdoer, lawbreaker, criminal; hooligan, vandal, ruffian, hoodlum; young offender; informal tearaway; formal malefactor.

delirious adjective **1** *she was delirious most of the time:* **incoherent**, raving, babbling, irrational; feverish, frenzied; deranged, demented, out of your mind. **2** *the crowd was delirious:* **ecstatic**, elated, thrilled, overjoyed, beside yourself, walking on air, on cloud nine, in seventh heaven, transported, rapturous; hysterical, wild, frenzied; informal blissed out, over the moon.
– OPPOSITES lucid.

delirium noun **derangement**, madness, incoherence, irrationality, hysteria, feverishness, hallucination.
– OPPOSITES lucidity.

deliver verb **1** *the parcel was delivered to his house:* **bring**, take, convey, carry, transport; send, dispatch. **2** *the money was delivered up to the official:* **hand over**, turn over, make over, sign over; surrender, give up, yield, cede; consign, commit, entrust, trust. **3** *the court delivered its verdict:* **utter**, give, make, read, broadcast; pronounce, announce, declare, proclaim, hand down, return, set forth. **4** *he delivered the first ball:* **bowl**, pitch, hurl, throw, cast, lob. **5** *she delivered a blow to his head:* **administer**, deal, inflict, give; informal land. **6** *he was delivered from his enemies:* **save**, rescue, free, liberate, release, extricate, emancipate, redeem. **7** *we must deliver on our commitments:* **fulfil**, live up to, carry out, carry through, make good.

deliverance noun **liberation**, release, delivery, discharge, rescue, emancipation; salvation.

delivery noun **1** *the delivery of the goods:* **conveyance**, carriage, transportation, transport, distribution; dispatch, remittance; freightage, haulage, shipment. **2** *we get several deliveries a day:* **consignment**, load, shipment. **3** *her delivery was stilted:* **speech**, pronunciation, enunciation, articulation, elocution.

delude verb **mislead**, deceive, fool, take in, trick, dupe, hoodwink, gull, lead on; informal con, pull the wool over someone's eyes, lead up the garden path, take for a ride; N. Amer. informal sucker, snooker; Austral. informal pull a swifty on.

deluge noun **1** *homes were swept away by the deluge:* **flood**, torrent; tidal wave; Brit. spate. **2** *the deluge turned the pitch into a swamp:* **downpour**, torrential rain; thunderstorm, rainstorm, cloudburst. **3** *a deluge of complaints:* **barrage**, volley; flood, torrent, avalanche, stream.
• **verb 1** *homes were deluged by the rains:* **flood**, inundate, submerge, swamp, drown. **2** *we have been deluged with calls:* **inundate**, overwhelm, overrun, flood, swamp, snow under, engulf, bombard.

delusion noun **misapprehension**, misconception, misunderstanding, mistake, error, misconstruction, misbelief; fallacy, illusion, fantasy.

deluxe adjective **luxurious**, luxury, sumptuous, palatial, opulent, lavish; grand, high-class, quality, exclusive, choice, fancy; expensive, costly; Brit. upmarket; informal plush, posh, classy, ritzy, swanky; Brit. informal swish; N. Amer. informal swank.
– OPPOSITES basic, cheap.

delve verb **1** *she delved in her pocket:* **rummage**, search, hunt, scrabble, root about, ferret, fish about, dig; go through, rifle through. **2** *we must delve deeper into the matter:* **investigate**, enquire, probe, explore, research, look into, go into.

demand noun **1** *I gave in to her demands:* **request**, call, command, order, dictate. **2** *the demands of a young family:* **requirement**, need; claim; commitment, imposition. **3** *the big demand for such toys:* **market**, call, appetite, desire.
• **verb 1** *workers demanded wage increases:* **call for**, ask for, request, push for, hold out for; insist on, claim. **2** *Harvey demanded that I tell him the truth:* **order**, command, enjoin, urge, insist. **3** *'Where is she?' he demanded:* **ask**, inquire; say. **4** *an activity demanding detailed knowledge:* **require**, need, necessitate, call for, involve, entail. **5** *they demanded complete anonymity:* **insist on**, stipulate; expect, look for.
▪ **in demand** sought-after, desired,

coveted, wanted, desirable, popular, all the rage, at a premium, like gold dust; informal big, trendy, hot.

demanding adjective **1** *a demanding task:* **difficult**, challenging, taxing, exacting, tough, hard, onerous, formidable; arduous, rigorous, gruelling, back-breaking, punishing. **2** *a demanding child:* **nagging**, importunate; trying, tiresome, hard to please.
– OPPOSITES easy.

demarcation noun **1** *clear demarcation of function:* **separation**, distinction, differentiation, division, delimitation, definition. **2** *territorial demarcations:* **boundary**, border, borderline, frontier; dividing line, divide.

demean verb **discredit**, lower, degrade, debase, devalue; cheapen, abase, humiliate.
– OPPOSITES dignify.

demeaning adjective **degrading**, humiliating, shameful, mortifying, undignified.

demeanour noun **manner**, air, attitude, appearance, look; bearing, carriage; behaviour, conduct.

demented adjective **mad**, insane, deranged, out of your mind, crazed, lunatic, unbalanced, unhinged, disturbed, non compos mentis; informal crazy, mental, off your head, off your rocker, nutty, round the bend, raving mad, batty, cuckoo, loopy, loony, bananas, screwy, touched, gaga, not all there, out to lunch; Brit. informal barmy, bonkers, crackers, barking, round the twist, off your trolley, not the full shilling; N. Amer. informal nutso, wacko.
– OPPOSITES sane.

demise noun **1** *her tragic demise:* **death**, dying, passing, end; formal decease; old use expiry. **2** *the demise of the Ottoman Empire:* **end**, break-up, disintegration, fall, downfall, collapse.
– OPPOSITES birth.

demobilize verb **disband**, decommission, discharge; Brit. informal demob.

democratic adjective **elected**, representative, parliamentary, popular; egalitarian.

demolish verb **1** *they demolished a block of flats:* **knock down**, pull down, tear down, bring down, destroy, flatten, raze to the ground, level, bulldoze; blow up. **2** *he demolished her credibility:* **destroy**, ruin, wreck; overturn, explode, drive a coach and horses through; informal shoot full of holes.
– OPPOSITES construct, strengthen.

demolition noun **1** *the demolition of the building:* **destruction**, levelling, bulldozing, clearance. **2** *the demolition of his theory:* **destruction**, refutation.

demon noun **1** *demons from hell:* **devil**, evil spirit. **2** *the man was a demon:* **monster**, fiend, devil, brute, savage, beast, barbarian, animal. **3** *Surrey's fast-bowling demon:* **genius**, expert, master, virtuoso, maestro; star; informal hotshot, whizz, buff, pro, ace.
– OPPOSITES angel, saint.

demonic, demoniac, demoniacal adjective **1** *demonic powers:* **devilish**, fiendish, diabolical, satanic, hellish, infernal; evil. **2** *the demonic intensity of his playing:* **frenzied**, wild, feverish, frenetic, frantic, furious, manic, like one possessed.

demonstrable adjective **verifiable**, provable; verified, proven, confirmed; obvious, clear, clear-cut, evident, apparent, manifest, patent, distinct, noticeable; unmistakable, undeniable.

demonstrate verb **1** *his findings demonstrate that boys commit more crimes:* **show**, indicate, establish, prove, confirm, verify. **2** *she demonstrated various drawing techniques:* **show**, display; present, illustrate, exemplify. **3** *his work demonstrated an analytical ability:* **reveal**, bespeak, indicate, signify, signal, denote, show, display, exhibit; bear witness to, testify to. **4** *they demonstrated against the Government:* **protest**, rally, march; picket, strike.

demonstration noun **1** *a demonstration of woodcarving:* **exhibition**, presentation, display. **2** *his paintings are a demonstration of his talent:* **manifestation**, indication, sign, mark, token, embodiment; expression. **3** *an anti-racism demonstration:* **protest**, march, rally, lobby, sit-in; informal demo.

d

demonstrative adjective **expressive**, open, forthcoming, communicative, unreserved, emotional, effusive; affectionate, cuddly, loving, warm, friendly, approachable; informal touchy-feely, lovey-dovey.
– OPPOSITES reserved.

demoralize verb **dishearten**, dispirit, deject, cast down, depress, dismay, daunt, discourage, unnerve, crush, shake, throw, cow, subdue; break someone's spirit; informal knock the stuffing out of, knock sideways; Brit. informal knock for six.
– OPPOSITES hearten.

demoralized adjective **dispirited**, disheartened, downhearted, dejected, downcast, low, depressed; disconsolate, crestfallen, disappointed, dismayed, daunted, discouraged; crushed, humbled, subdued.

demote verb **downgrade**, relegate, reduce; depose, unseat, displace, oust; Military cashier.
– OPPOSITES promote.

demur verb **object**, take exception, take issue, protest; be unwilling, be reluctant, baulk.

demure adjective **modest**, reserved, shy, reticent; decorous, decent, seemly, ladylike, respectable, proper, virtuous, pure, innocent, chaste; sober, sedate, staid, prim, goody-goody, strait-laced; informal butter-wouldn't-melt.
– OPPOSITES brazen.

den noun **1** *the mink left its den:* **lair**, burrow, hole, shelter, hiding place, hideout. **2** *a den of violent crime:* **hotbed**, breeding ground, nest. **3** *the poet scribbled in his den:* **study**, private place, sanctum, retreat, sanctuary, hideaway; informal hidey-hole.

denial noun **1** *he issued a furious denial of her claims:* **contradiction**, refutation, rebuttal, repudiation, disclaimer; negation. **2** *the denial of insurance to certain people:* **refusal**, withholding; rejection, turndown; informal knock-back; N. Amer. formal declination.

denigrate verb **disparage**, belittle, deprecate, decry, cast aspersions on, criticize, attack; speak ill of, give someone a bad name, defame, slander, libel; run down, abuse, insult, revile, malign, vilify; N. Amer. slur; informal bad-mouth, pull to pieces; Brit. informal rubbish, slate, slag off.
– OPPOSITES extol.

denizen noun (formal) **inhabitant**, resident, townsman/woman, native, local; occupier, occupant, dweller.

denomination noun **1** *a Christian denomination:* **religious group**, sect, cult, movement, body, branch, order, school; church. **2** *banknotes in a number of denominations:* **value**, unit, size.

denote verb **1** *the headdress denoted high status:* **designate**, indicate, be a mark of, signify, signal, symbolize, represent, mean; distinguish, mark, identify. **2** *his manner denoted an inner strength:* **suggest**, point to, smack of, indicate, show, reveal, intimate, imply, convey, betray, bespeak; informal spell.

denouement noun **resolution**, outcome, ending, end, finish, close; culmination, climax, conclusion, solution.

denounce verb **1** *the pope denounced his critics:* **condemn**, criticize, attack, censure, decry, revile, damn; proscribe, rail against, run down; N. Amer. slur; informal slam, hit out at, lay into; Brit. informal slate, slag off; formal castigate. **2** *he was denounced as a traitor:* **expose**, betray, inform on; incriminate, implicate, cite, name, accuse.
– OPPOSITES praise.

dense adjective **1** *a dense forest:* **thick**, crowded, compact, solid, tight; overgrown, impenetrable, impassable. **2** *dense smoke:* **thick**, heavy, opaque, murky; concentrated, condensed. **3** (informal) *they were dense enough to believe me:* **stupid**, brainless, mindless, foolish, slow, simple-minded, empty-headed, idiotic; informal thick, dim, moronic, dumb, dopey, dozy; Brit. informal daft.
– OPPOSITES sparse, thin, clever.

density noun **solidity**, solidness, denseness, thickness, substance, mass; compactness, tightness, hardness.

dent noun **1** *a dent in the passenger door:* **knock**, indentation, dint, depression, hollow, crater, pit. **2** *a*

dent in their finances: **hole**; gap, reduction, cut.
– OPPOSITES increase.
• verb *the experience dented her confidence:* **diminish**, reduce, lessen, weaken, erode, undermine, sap, shake, damage.

deny verb **1** *the report was denied by witnesses:* **contradict**, repudiate, challenge, contest, reject, rebut. **2** *he denied the request:* **refuse**, turn down, reject, rebuff, repulse, decline, veto, dismiss; informal give the thumbs down to. **3** *she had to deny her faith:* **renounce**, repudiate, disavow, disown, wash your hands of, reject, discard, cast aside, abandon, give up; literary forsake.
– OPPOSITES confirm, accept.

depart verb **1** *they departed after lunch:* **leave**, go, withdraw, absent yourself, quit, exit, decamp, retreat, retire; set off/out, get under way, be on your way; informal make tracks, up sticks, take off; Brit. informal sling your hook. **2** *the budget departed from the norm:* **deviate**, diverge, digress, drift, stray, veer; differ, vary.
– OPPOSITES arrive.

departed adjective **dead**, expired, passed on/away; fallen; formal deceased.

department noun **1** *the public health department:* **division**, section, sector, unit, branch, wing; office, bureau, agency, ministry. **2** (informal) *the cooking is not my department:* **domain**, territory, province, area, line; responsibility, business, affair, charge, task, concern; informal pigeon, baby, bailiwick.

departure noun **1** *he tried to delay her departure:* **leaving**, going, leave-taking, withdrawal, exit. **2** *a departure from normality:* **deviation**, divergence, digression, shift; variation, change. **3** *an exciting departure for film-makers:* **change**, innovation, novelty.

depend verb **1** *her career depends on this reference:* **be dependent on**, hinge on, hang on, rest on, rely on. **2** *my family depends on me:* **rely on**, lean on; count on, bank on, trust in, have faith in, believe in; pin your hopes on.

dependable adjective **reliable**, trustworthy, trusty, faithful, loyal, stable; sensible, responsible.

dependant noun **child**, minor; ward, charge, protégé; relative; (**dependants**) offspring, children, progeny.

dependence noun. See **DEPENDENCY** senses 1, 2.

dependency noun **1** *her dependency on her husband:* **dependence**, reliance; need for. **2** *drug dependency:* **addiction**, dependence; reliance; craving, compulsion, fixation, obsession; abuse. **3** *a British dependency:* **colony**, protectorate, province, outpost; holding, possession.
– OPPOSITES independence.

dependent adjective **1** *your placement is dependent on her decision:* **conditional**, contingent, based; subject to, determined by, influenced by. **2** *the army is dependent on volunteers:* **reliant on**, relying on, counting on; sustained by, supported by. **3** *she is dependent on drugs:* **addicted to**, reliant on; informal hooked on. **4** *a UK dependent territory:* **subsidiary**, subject; ancillary.

depict verb **1** *the painting depicts the Last Supper:* **portray**, show, represent, picture, illustrate, reproduce, render. **2** *the process depicted by Darwin's theory:* **describe**, detail, relate; present, set forth, set out, outline, delineate; represent, portray, characterize.

depiction noun **1** *a depiction of Aphrodite:* **picture**, painting, portrait, drawing, sketch, study, illustration; image, likeness. **2** *the film's depiction of women:* **portrayal**, representation, presentation, characterization.

deplete verb **exhaust**, use up, consume, expend, drain, empty; reduce, decrease, diminish.
– OPPOSITES augment.

depletion noun **exhaustion**, use, consumption, expenditure; reduction, decrease, diminution; impoverishment.

deplorable adjective **1** *your conduct is deplorable:* **disgraceful**, shameful, inexcusable, unpardonable, atrocious, awful, terrible, dreadful, diabolical, unforgivable, despicable, abominable, contemptible, beyond the pale. **2** *the garden is in a*

d

deplorable state: **lamentable**, regrettable, unfortunate, wretched, atrocious, awful, terrible, dreadful, diabolical; sorry, poor; informal appalling, dire, abysmal, woeful, lousy; formal grievous.
– OPPOSITES admirable.

deplore verb **1** *we deplore violence:* **abhor**, find unacceptable, frown on, disapprove of, take a dim view of, take exception to; detest, despise; condemn, denounce. **2** *he deplored their lack of flair:* **regret**, lament, mourn, bemoan, bewail, complain about, grieve over, sigh over.
– OPPOSITES applaud.

deploy verb **1** *forces were deployed at strategic points:* **position**, station, post, place, install, locate, situate, site, establish; base; distribute. **2** *she deployed all her skills:* **use**, utilize, employ, take advantage of, exploit; bring into service, call on, turn to, resort to.

deport verb **expel**, banish, extradite, repatriate; throw out; informal kick out, boot out, send packing; Brit. informal turf out.
– OPPOSITES admit.

depose verb **overthrow**, unseat, dethrone, topple, remove, supplant, displace; dismiss, oust, throw out; informal chuck out, boot out, get rid of; Brit. informal turf out.

deposit noun **1** *a thick deposit of ash:* **accumulation**, sediment; layer, covering, coating, blanket. **2** *a copper deposit:* **seam**, vein, lode, layer, stratum, bed. **3** *they paid a deposit:* **down payment**, prepayment, instalment, retainer.
• verb **1** *she deposited her books on the table:* **put**, place, set, unload, rest; drop; informal dump, park, plonk; N. Amer. informal plunk. **2** *the silt deposited by flood water:* **leave**, precipitate, dump; wash up, cast up. **3** *the gold was deposited at the bank:* **lodge**, bank, house, store, stow, leave, put away; informal stash.

depot noun **1** *the bus depot:* **terminal**, terminus, station, garage; headquarters, base. **2** *an arms depot:* **storehouse**, warehouse, store, repository, depository, cache; arsenal, armoury, dump.

depraved adjective **corrupt**, perverted, deviant, degenerate, debased, immoral, unprincipled; debauched, dissolute, licentious, lecherous, prurient, indecent, sordid; wicked, sinful, vile, iniquitous, nefarious; informal warped, twisted, pervy, sick.

depravity noun **corruption**, vice, perversion, deviance, degeneracy, immorality, debauchery, dissipation, profligacy, licentiousness, lechery, prurience, obscenity, indecency; wickedness, sin, iniquity; informal perviness; formal turpitude.

depreciate verb **decrease in value**, lose value, fall in price.

depress verb **1** *the news depressed him:* **sadden**, dispirit, cast down, get down, dishearten, demoralize, crush, shake, weigh down on; upset, distress, grieve. **2** *new economic policies depressed sales:* **slow down**, reduce, lower, weaken, impair; inhibit, restrict. **3** *imports will depress farm prices:* **reduce**, lower, cut, cheapen, keep down, deflate, devalue, diminish. **4** *depress each key in turn:* **press**, push, hold down; tap.
– OPPOSITES encourage, raise.

depressed adjective **1** *he felt lonely and depressed:* **sad**, unhappy, miserable, gloomy, melancholy, dejected, disconsolate, downhearted, downcast, down, despondent, dispirited, low, heavy-hearted, morose, dismal, desolate; tearful, upset; informal blue, down in the dumps, down in the mouth, fed up. **2** *a depressed economy:* **weak**; inactive, flat, slow, slack, sluggish, stagnant. **3** *a depressed area:* **poverty-stricken**, poor, disadvantaged, deprived, needy, distressed; run down.
– OPPOSITES cheerful, strong, prosperous.

depressing adjective **1** *depressing thoughts:* **upsetting**, distressing, painful, heartbreaking; dismal, bleak, black, sombre, gloomy, grave, unhappy, melancholy, sad; wretched, doleful; informal morbid. **2** *a depressing place:* **gloomy**, melancholy, bleak, dreary, grim, drab, sombre, dark, dingy, funereal, cheerless, joyless, comfortless, uninviting.

depression noun **1** *she ate to ease her depression:* **unhappiness**, sadness, melancholy, melancholia, misery, sorrow, gloom, despondency, low spirits, heavy heart, despair, desolation, hopelessness. **2** *an economic depression:* **recession**, slump, decline, downturn, standstill; stagnation. **3** *a depression in the ground:* **hollow**, indentation, dent, dint, cavity, concavity, dip, pit, hole, trough, crater; basin, bowl.

deprivation noun **1** *unemployment and deprivation:* **poverty**, impoverishment, privation, hardship, destitution; need, want. **2** *deprivation of political rights:* **dispossession**, withholding, withdrawal, removal, expropriation, seizure.
–OPPOSITES wealth.

deprive verb **dispossess**, strip, divest, relieve; cheat out of; informal do out of.

deprived adjective **disadvantaged**, underprivileged, poverty-stricken, impoverished, poor, destitute, needy.

depth noun **1** *the depth of the well:* **deepness**, drop, vertical extent. **2** *the depth of his knowledge:* **extent**, range, scope, breadth, width. **3** *a work of great depth:* **complexity**, intricacy; profundity, weight, wisdom, understanding, intelligence, discernment, penetration, insight, awareness. **4** *depth of colour:* **intensity**, richness, deepness, vividness, strength, brilliance. **5** *the depths of the sea:* **bottom**, floor, bed.
–OPPOSITES shallowness, triviality, surface.
■ **in depth** thoroughly, extensively, comprehensively, rigorously, exhaustively, completely, fully; meticulously, scrupulously, painstakingly.

deputation noun **delegation**, commission, committee, diplomatic mission; contingent, group, party.

deputize verb **stand in**, sit in, fill in, cover, substitute, replace, take someone's place, relieve, take over; hold the fort, step into the breach; act for; informal sub.

deputy noun *he handed over to his deputy:* **second in command**, number two, assistant, aide, right-hand man/woman, man/girl Friday; substitute, stand-in, understudy; representative, proxy, agent, spokesperson; Scottish depute; informal sidekick, locum.
• adjective *her deputy editor:* **assistant**, substitute, acting, reserve, fill-in, caretaker.

deranged adjective **insane**, mad, disturbed, unbalanced, unhinged, unstable, irrational; crazed, demented, berserk, frenzied, lunatic; non compos mentis; informal touched, crazy, mental; Brit. informal barmy, barking, round the twist.
–OPPOSITES rational.

derelict adjective **1** *a derelict building:* **dilapidated**, ramshackle, run down, tumbledown, in ruins, falling down; disused, abandoned, deserted. **2** *he was derelict in his duty:* **negligent**, neglectful, remiss, lax, careless, sloppy, slipshod, slack, irresponsible.

dereliction noun **1** *buildings were reclaimed from dereliction:* **dilapidation**, disrepair, deterioration, ruin, rack and ruin; abandonment, neglect, disuse. **2** *dereliction of duty:* **negligence**, neglect, failure.

deride verb **ridicule**, mock, scoff at, jibe at, make fun of, poke fun at, laugh at, hold up to ridicule, pillory; disdain, disparage, denigrate, dismiss, slight; sneer at, scorn, insult; informal knock, pooh-pooh, take the mickey out of.
–OPPOSITES praise.

derision noun **mockery**, ridicule, jeers, sneers, taunts; disdain, disparagement, denigration, disrespect, insults; scorn, contempt.

derisive adjective **mocking**, jeering, scoffing, teasing, derisory, snide, sneering; disdainful, scornful, contemptuous, taunting, insulting; scathing, sarcastic; informal snidey; Brit. informal sarky.

derisory adjective **1** *a derisory sum:* **inadequate**, insufficient, tiny; trifling, paltry, pitiful, miserly, miserable; negligible; ridiculous, laughable, insulting; informal measly, stingy, lousy, pathetic, piddling, piffling, mingy, poxy. **2** *derisory calls from the crowd.* See DERISIVE.

derivation noun **origin**, etymology, root, provenance, source; origination, basis, cause.

derivative adjective *her poetry was*

derivative: **imitative**, unoriginal, uninventive, unimaginative, uninspired; plagiaristic; trite, hackneyed, clichéd, stale; informal copycat, cribbed, old hat.
– OPPOSITES original.
• noun **by-product**, extract; spin-off.

d

derive verb **1** *he derives consolation from his poetry:* **obtain**, get, take, gain, acquire, procure, extract. **2** *'coffee' derives from the Turkish word 'kahveh':* **originate in**, stem from, come from, descend from, spring from. **3** *his fortune derives from property:* **originate in**, be rooted in; stem from, come from, spring from, proceed from, issue from.

derogatory adjective **disparaging**, disrespectful, demeaning; critical, pejorative, negative, unfavourable, uncomplimentary, unflattering, insulting; offensive, personal, abusive, rude, nasty, mean, hurtful; defamatory, slanderous, libellous; informal bitchy, catty.
– OPPOSITES complimentary.

descend verb **1** *the plane started descending:* **go down**, come down; drop, fall, sink, dive, plummet, plunge, nosedive. **2** *she descended the stairs:* **climb down**, go down, come down; shin down, slide down. **3** *the road descends to a village:* **slope**, dip, slant, go down, fall away. **4** *she saw Leo descend from the bus:* **alight**, disembark, get down, get off, dismount. **5** *they would not descend to such mean tricks:* **stoop**, lower yourself, demean yourself, debase yourself; resort, be reduced. **6** *the situation descended into chaos:* **degenerate**, deteriorate, decline, sink, slide, slip. **7** *they descended on his house:* flock to, besiege, surround, take over, invade, swoop on, occupy.
– OPPOSITES ascend, climb, board.

descendant noun **successor**; heir; (**descendants**) offspring, progeny, family, lineage; Law issue.
– OPPOSITES ancestor.

descent noun **1** *a steep descent:* **slope**, incline, dip, drop, gradient, slant; hill. **2** *his descent into alcoholism:* **decline**, slide, fall, degeneration, deterioration. **3** *she is of Italian descent:* **ancestry**, parentage, ancestors, family; extraction, origin, derivation, birth; lineage, stock, blood; roots, origins. **4** *the sudden descent of the cavalry:* **attack**, assault, onslaught, charge, thrust, push, drive, incursion, foray.

describe verb **1** *he described his experiences in the war:* **report**, recount, relate, tell of, set out, chronicle; detail, catalogue, give a rundown of; explain, illustrate, discuss, comment on. **2** *she described him as a pathetic figure:* **designate**, pronounce, call, label, style, dub; characterize, class; portray, depict, brand, paint. **3** *the pen described a circle:* **delineate**, mark out, outline, trace, draw.

description noun **1** *a description of my travels:* **account**, report, rendition, explanation, illustration; chronicle, narrative, story; portrayal, portrait; details. **2** *the description of oil as 'black gold':* **designation**, labelling, naming, dubbing; characterization, classification, branding; portrayal, depiction. **3** *vehicles of every description:* **sort**, variety, kind, type, category, order, breed, class, designation, specification, genre, genus, brand, make, character, ilk; N. Amer. stripe.

descriptive adjective **illustrative**, expressive, graphic, detailed, lively, vivid, striking; explanatory.

desecrate verb **violate**, profane, defile, debase, degrade, dishonour; vandalize, damage, destroy, deface.

desert[1] verb **1** *his wife deserted him:* **abandon**, leave, turn your back on; throw over, jilt, break up with; leave high and dry, leave in the lurch, leave behind, strand, maroon; informal walk/run out on, drop, dump, ditch; literary forsake. **2** *his allies were deserting the cause:* **renounce**, repudiate, relinquish, wash your hands of, abandon, turn your back on, betray, disavow; literary forsake. **3** *soldiers deserted in droves:* **abscond**, defect, run away, make off, decamp, flee, turn tail, take French leave, depart, quit; Military go AWOL.

desert[2] noun *an African desert:* **wasteland**, wastes, wilderness; dust bowl.

deserted adjective **1** *a deserted*

wife: **abandoned**, jilted, cast aside; neglected, stranded, marooned; forlorn, bereft, dropped; literary forsaken. **2** *a deserted village:* **empty**, uninhabited, unoccupied, abandoned, evacuated, vacant; neglected; desolate, lonely, godforsaken.
–OPPOSITES populous.

deserter noun **absconder**, runaway, fugitive, truant, escapee; renegade, defector, turncoat, traitor.

deserve verb **merit**, earn, warrant, rate, justify, be worthy of, be entitled to, have a right to, qualify for.

deserved adjective **well earned**, merited, warranted, justified, justifiable; rightful, due, right, just, fair, fitting, appropriate, suitable, proper, apt.

deserving adjective **1** *a deserving cause:* **worthy**, commendable, praiseworthy, admirable, estimable, creditable; respectable, decent, honourable, righteous. **2** *a lapse deserving of punishment:* **meriting**, warranting, justifying, suitable for, worthy of.

design noun **1** *a design for the offices:* **plan**, blueprint, drawing, sketch, outline, map, plot, diagram, draft, representation, scheme, model. **2** *a Celtic design:* **pattern**, motif, device; style, theme, layout, form, shape.
• verb **1** *they designed a new engine:* **invent**, create, think up, come up with, devise, formulate, conceive; make, produce, develop, fashion; informal dream up. **2** *this paper is designed to provoke discussion:* **intend**, aim; mean.
■ **by design** deliberately, intentionally, on purpose, purposefully; knowingly, wittingly, consciously, calculatedly.

designate verb **1** *some firms designate a press officer:* **appoint**, nominate, depute, delegate; select, choose, pick, elect, name, identify, assign. **2** *the rivers are designated 'Sites of Special Scientific Interest':* **classify**, class, label, tag; name, call, term, dub.

designation noun **1** *the designation of a leader:* **appointment**, nomination, naming, selection, election. **2** *the designation 'Generalissimo':* **title**, name, epithet, tag; nickname, byname, sobriquet; informal moniker, handle; formal appellation.

desirability noun **1** *the desirability of the property:* **appeal**, attractiveness, allure; attraction. **2** *the desirability of a different approach:* **advisability**, advantage, benefit, merit, value, profitability. **3** *her obvious desirability:* **attractiveness**, sexual attraction, beauty, good looks; charm, seductiveness; informal sexiness.

desirable adjective **1** *a desirable location:* **attractive**, sought-after, in demand, popular, enviable; appealing, agreeable, pleasant; valuable, good, excellent; informal to die for, must-have. **2** *it is desirable that they should meet:* **advantageous**, advisable, wise, sensible, recommended; helpful, useful, beneficial, worthwhile, profitable, preferable. **3** *a very desirable woman:* **sexually attractive**, beautiful, pretty, appealing; seductive, alluring, enchanting, beguiling, captivating, bewitching, irresistible; informal sexy, beddable.
–OPPOSITES unattractive, undesirable.

desire noun **1** *his desire to see the world:* **wish**, aspiration, fancy, inclination, impulse; yearning, longing, craving, hankering, yen, hunger; eagerness, enthusiasm, determination; informal itch. **2** *his eyes glittered with desire:* **lust**, passion, sensuality, sexuality, hunger; lasciviousness, libidinousness.
• verb **1** *he never achieved the status he desired:* **want**, wish for, long for, yearn for, crave, hanker after, be bent on, have a yen for, covet, aspire to; fancy. **2** *there had been a time when he desired her:* **lust after**, yearn for; informal fancy, have the hots for.

desired adjective **1** *cut the cloth to the desired length:* **required**, necessary, proper, right, correct; appropriate, suitable; preferred, chosen, selected. **2** *the desired outcome:* **wished for**, wanted; sought-after, longed for.

desist verb **abstain**, refrain, forbear, hold back, keep; stop, cease, discontinue, give up, break off,

d

d

drop, dispense with, eschew; informal lay off, give over, quit, pack in.
– OPPOSITES continue.

desolate adjective **1** *desolate moorlands:* **bleak**, stark, bare, dismal, grim; wild, inhospitable; deserted, uninhabited, godforsaken, abandoned, empty; unfrequented, unvisited, isolated, remote. **2** *she is desolate:* **miserable**, despondent, depressed, disconsolate, devastated, despairing, inconsolable, broken-hearted, grief-stricken, bereft.
– OPPOSITES populous, joyful.

desolation noun **1** *the desolation of the Gobi Desert:* **bleakness**, starkness, barrenness; wildness; isolation, loneliness, remoteness. **2** *a feeling of utter desolation:* **misery**, sadness, unhappiness, despondency, sorrow, depression, grief, woe; broken-heartedness, wretchedness, dejection, devastation, despair, anguish, distress.

despair noun **hopelessness**, discouragement, desperation, distress, anguish, unhappiness; despondency, depression, disconsolateness, misery, wretchedness; defeatism, pessimism.
– OPPOSITES hope, joy.
• verb **lose hope**, give up, lose heart, be discouraged, be despondent, be demoralized, resign yourself; be pessimistic.

despairing adjective **hopeless**, in despair, dejected, depressed, despondent, disconsolate, gloomy, miserable, wretched, desolate, inconsolable; disheartened, discouraged, demoralized, devastated; defeatist, pessimistic.
– OPPOSITES hopeful, joyous.

despatch verb & noun. See DISPATCH.

desperate adjective **1** *a desperate look:* **despairing**, hopeless; anguished, distressed, wretched, desolate, forlorn, distraught; out of your mind, at your wits' end, beside yourself, at the end of your tether. **2** *a desperate attempt to escape:* **last-ditch**, last-gasp, eleventh-hour, do-or-die, final; frantic, frenzied, wild. **3** *a desperate shortage of teachers:* **grave**, serious, critical, acute; dire, awful, terrible, dreadful; urgent, pressing, drastic, extreme; informal chronic. **4** *they were desperate for food:* **eager**, longing, yearning, hungry, crying out; informal dying. **5** *a desperate act:* **violent**, dangerous, lawless; reckless, rash, hasty, impetuous, foolhardy, risky; do-or-die.

desperately adverb **1** *he screamed desperately for help:* **in desperation**, in despair, despairingly, in anguish, in distress; wretchedly, hopelessly, desolately, forlornly. **2** *they are desperately ill:* **seriously**, critically, gravely, severely, acutely, dangerously, perilously; very, extremely, dreadfully; hopelessly; informal terribly. **3** *he desperately wanted to talk:* **urgently**; intensely, eagerly.

desperation noun **hopelessness**, despair, distress; anguish, agony, torment, misery, wretchedness; discouragement.

despicable adjective **contemptible**, loathsome, hateful, detestable, reprehensible, abhorrent, abominable, awful, heinous; odious, vile, low, mean, abject, shameful, ignominious, shabby, ignoble, disreputable, discreditable, unworthy; informal dirty, rotten, low-down; Brit. informal beastly; old use scurvy.
– OPPOSITES admirable.

despise verb **detest**, hate, loathe, abhor, deplore; scorn, disdain, look down on, deride, sneer at, revile; spurn, shun.
– OPPOSITES adore.

despite preposition **in spite of**, notwithstanding, regardless of, in the face of, for all, even with.

despondency noun **hopelessness**, despair, discouragement, low spirits, wretchedness; melancholy, gloom, misery, desolation, disappointment, dejection, sadness, unhappiness; informal heartache.

despondent adjective **disheartened**, discouraged, dispirited, downhearted, downcast, crestfallen, down, low, disconsolate, despairing, wretched; melancholy, gloomy, morose, dismal, woebegone, miserable, depressed, dejected, sad; informal down in the mouth, down in the dumps.
– OPPOSITES hopeful, cheerful.

despot noun **tyrant**, oppressor, dictator, autocrat.

despotic adjective **autocratic**, dictatorial, totalitarian, absolutist,

undemocratic; one-party, tyrannical, tyrannous, oppressive, repressive, draconian, illiberal.
– OPPOSITES democratic.

dessert noun **pudding**, sweet; Brit. informal afters.

destabilize verb **undermine**, weaken, damage, subvert, sabotage, unsettle, upset, disrupt.
– OPPOSITES strengthen.

destination noun **journey's end**, end of the line; terminus, stop, stopping place, port of call; goal, target, end.

destined adjective **1** *he is destined to lead a troubled life:* **fated**, ordained, predestined, meant; doomed. **2** *computers destined for Pakistan:* **heading**, bound, en route, scheduled, headed; intended, meant, designated.

destiny noun **1** *he is the master of his own destiny:* **future**, fate, fortune, doom; lot. **2** *she was sent by destiny:* **fate**, providence; God, the stars; luck, fortune, chance; karma.

destitute adjective **penniless**, poor, impoverished, poverty-stricken, without a penny to your name, impecunious, indigent, ; Brit. on the breadline; informal hard up, broke, strapped for cash, without two pennies to rub together, without a bean, on your uppers; skint.
– OPPOSITES rich.

destitution noun **poverty**, impoverishment, penury, pennilessness, privation; hardship, need, want, straitened circumstances, dire straits, deprivation, financial distress.

destroy verb **1** *their offices were destroyed by bombing:* **demolish**, knock down, level, raze to the ground, fell; wreck, ruin, shatter; blast, blow up. **2** *illness destroyed his career chances:* **wreck**, ruin, spoil, undo, put an end to, put a stop to, terminate, frustrate, blight, crush, quash, dash, scotch; devastate, demolish, sabotage, wreak havoc on; informal put paid to, put the kibosh on; Brit. informal scupper. **3** *the horse had to be destroyed:* **kill**, put down, put to sleep, slaughter. **4** *we had to destroy the enemy:* **annihilate**, wipe out, obliterate, wipe off the face of the earth, eliminate, eradicate, liquidate; kill, slaughter, massacre, exterminate.
– OPPOSITES build, preserve.

destruction noun **1** *the destruction caused by allied bombers:* **devastation**, carnage, ruin, chaos; wreckage; mess, disorder. **2** *the destruction of the countryside:* wrecking, burning, digging up, pulling down, bombing, annihilation, obliteration, devastation, ruining. **3** *the destruction of cattle:* **slaughter**, killing, putting down, extermination, culling.

destructive adjective **devastating**, ruinous, disastrous, catastrophic, calamitous; damaging, crippling; violent, savage, fierce, brutal, deadly, lethal.

desultory adjective **perfunctory**, half-hearted, unenthusiastic, lackadaisical, aimless, apathetic.
– OPPOSITES purposeful.

detach verb **1** *he detached the lamp from its bracket:* **unfasten**, disconnect, disengage, separate, uncouple, remove, loose, unhitch, unhook, free; pull off, cut off, break off. **2** *he detached himself from the crowd:* **free**, separate; move away, split off; leave, abandon. **3** *he has detached himself from his family:* **dissociate**, divorce, alienate, separate, segregate, isolate, cut off; break away, disaffiliate; withdraw from, break with.
– OPPOSITES attach, join.

detached adjective **1** *a detached collar:* **unfastened**, disconnected, separated, separate, loosened; untied, unhitched, undone, unhooked, unbuttoned; free, severed, cut off. **2** *a detached observer:* **dispassionate**, disinterested, objective, uninvolved, outside, neutral, unbiased, unprejudiced, impartial, nonpartisan; indifferent, aloof, remote, distant, impersonal.

detachment noun **1** *she looked on with detachment:* **objectivity**, dispassion, disinterest, open-mindedness, neutrality, impartiality; indifference, aloofness. **2** *a detachment of soldiers:* **unit**, detail, squad, troop, contingent, outfit, task force, patrol, crew; platoon, company, corps, brigade, battalion.

d

d

detail noun **1** *the picture is correct in every detail:* **particular**, respect, feature, characteristic, specific, aspect, facet, part, constituent; fact, piece of information, point, element, circumstance, consideration. **2** *that's just a detail:* **triviality**, technicality, nicety, trifle, fine point, incidental, inessential. **3** *records with a considerable degree of detail:* **precision**, exactness, accuracy, thoroughness, carefulness, scrupulousness. **4** *a guard detail:* **unit**, detachment, squad, troop, contingent, outfit, task force, patrol.
• verb **1** *the report details our objections:* **describe**, explain, expound, relate, catalogue, list, spell out, itemize, identify, specify; state, declare, present, set out, frame; cite, quote, instance, mention, name. **2** *troops were detailed to prevent the escape:* **assign**, allocate, appoint, delegate, commission, charge; send, post; nominate, vote, elect, co-opt.
■ **in detail** thoroughly, in depth, exhaustively, minutely, closely, meticulously, rigorously, scrupulously, painstakingly, carefully; completely, comprehensively, fully, extensively.

detailed adjective **comprehensive**, full, complete, thorough, exhaustive, all-inclusive; elaborate, minute, intricate; explicit, specific, precise, exact, accurate, meticulous, painstaking; itemized, blow-by-blow.
– OPPOSITES general.

detain verb **1** *they were detained for questioning:* **hold**, take into custody, take in, confine, intern; arrest, apprehend, seize; informal pick up, run in, haul in, nab, collar; Brit. informal nick. **2** *don't let me detain you:* **delay**, hold up, make late, keep, slow up/down; hinder.
– OPPOSITES release.

detect verb **1** *I detected a note of urgency in her voice:* **notice**, perceive, discern, become aware of, recognize, pick up, register, distinguish, identify, note; catch, sense, see, make out, spot, smell, taste, feel, hear; Brit. informal clock. **2** *they are responsible for detecting fraud:* **discover**, uncover, find out, turn up, unearth, dig up, root out, expose, reveal. **3** *the hackers were detected:* **catch**, hunt down, track down, find, expose, reveal, unmask, smoke out; apprehend, arrest; informal nail.

detection noun **1** *the detection of methane:* **discernment**, perception, awareness, recognition, identification, diagnosis; sensing, sight, smelling, tasting, noticing. **2** *the detection of insider dealing:* **discovery**, uncovering, unearthing, exposure, revelation. **3** *he managed to escape detection:* **capture**, identification, exposure, discovery; arrest.

detective noun **investigator**, private investigator, private detective, operative; police officer; informal private eye, PI, sleuth, snoop; N. Amer. informal shamus, gumshoe.

detention noun **custody**, imprisonment, confinement, incarceration, internment, detainment, captivity; arrest; quarantine.

deter verb **1** *the high cost deterred many:* **discourage**, dissuade, put off, disincentivize; dishearten, demoralize, daunt, intimidate. **2** *the presence of a caretaker deters crime:* **prevent**, stop, avert, stave off, ward off.
– OPPOSITES encourage.

deteriorate verb **1** *his health deteriorated:* **worsen**, decline, degenerate; fail, slump, slip, go downhill, go backwards, wane, ebb; informal go to pot. **2** *these materials deteriorate if stored wrongly:* **decay**, degrade, degenerate, break down, decompose, rot, go off, spoil, perish.
– OPPOSITES improve.

deterioration noun **1** *a deterioration in law and order:* **decline**, collapse, failure, drop, downturn, slump, slip. **2** *deterioration of the roof structure:* **decay**, degradation, degeneration, breakdown, decomposition, rotting; weakening.
– OPPOSITES improvement.

determination noun **resolution**, resolve, will power, strength of character, single-mindedness, purposefulness; staunchness, perseverance, persistence, tenacity, staying power; strong-mindedness, backbone; stubbornness, doggedness, obstinacy; spirit, courage, pluck, grit, stout-heartedness; informal guts, spunk.

determine verb **1** *chromosomes determine the sex of the embryo:* **control**, decide, regulate, direct, dictate, govern; affect, influence. **2** *he determined to sell up:* **resolve**, decide, make up your mind, choose, elect, opt. **3** *the rent shall be determined by an accountant:* **specify**, set, fix, decide on, settle, assign, designate, arrange, choose, establish, ordain, prescribe, decree. **4** *an attempt to determine the composition of the fibres:* **ascertain**, find out, discover, learn, establish, calculate, work out, make out, deduce, diagnose, discern; check, verify, confirm; informal figure out.

determined adjective **1** *he was determined to have his way:* **intent on**, bent on, set on, insistent on, resolved to. **2** *a very determined man:* **resolute**, purposeful, adamant, single-minded, unswerving, unwavering, intent, insistent; persevering, persistent, tenacious; strong-minded, strong-willed, steely, four-square, dedicated, committed; stubborn, dogged, obstinate.

determining adjective **deciding**, decisive, conclusive, final, definitive, key, pivotal, crucial, critical, major, chief, prime.

deterrent noun **disincentive**, discouragement, damper, curb, check, restraint; inhibition.
– OPPOSITES incentive.

detest verb **loathe**, despise, abhor, hate, deplore, shrink from, be unable to bear; formal abominate.
– OPPOSITES love.

detestable adjective **abhorrent**, hateful, loathsome, despicable, abominable, repellent, repugnant, repulsive, revolting, disgusting, distasteful, horrible, horrid, awful.

detonate verb **1** *the charge detonated in deep water:* **explode**, go off, blow up; ignite. **2** *they detonated the bomb:* **set off**, explode, discharge, let off, touch off, trigger; ignite.

detonation noun **explosion**, discharge, blowing up; blast, bang, report.

detour noun **diversion**, roundabout route, indirect route, scenic route; bypass, ring road; digression, deviation; Brit. relief road.

detract verb **1** *my reservations should not detract from the book's excellence:* **belittle**, take away from, diminish, reduce, lessen, minimize, play down, trivialize, decry, devalue. **2** *the patterns will detract attention from each other:* **divert**, distract, draw away, deflect, avert, shift.

detractor noun **critic**, attacker, fault-finder; sceptic, cynic.

detriment noun **harm**, damage, injury, hurt, impairment, loss.
– OPPOSITES benefit.

detrimental adjective **harmful**, damaging, injurious, hurtful, inimical, deleterious, destructive, ruinous, disastrous, bad, malign, adverse, undesirable, unfavourable, unfortunate; unhealthy, unwholesome.
– OPPOSITES beneficial.

detritus noun **debris**, waste, refuse, rubbish, litter, scrap, flotsam and jetsam, rubble; remains, remnants, fragments, scraps, dregs, leavings, sweepings, dross; N. Amer. trash, garbage; informal dreck.

devalue verb **belittle**, disparage, denigrate, discredit, diminish, trivialize, reduce, undermine.

devastate verb **1** *the city was devastated by an earthquake:* **destroy**, ruin, wreck, lay waste, ravage, demolish, raze to the ground, level, flatten. **2** *he was devastated by the news:* **shatter**, shock, stun, daze, dumbfound, traumatize, crush, overwhelm, overcome, distress; informal knock sideways; Brit. informal knock for six.

devastating adjective **1** *a devastating cyclone:* **destructive**, ruinous, disastrous, catastrophic, calamitous, cataclysmic; damaging, injurious; crippling, violent, savage, fierce, dangerous, fatal, deadly, lethal. **2** *devastating news:* **shattering**, shocking, traumatic, overwhelming, crushing, distressing, terrible. **3** (informal) *a devastating critique:* **incisive**, highly effective, penetrating, cutting; withering, blistering, searing, scathing, fierce, savage, stinging, biting, caustic, harsh.

devastation noun **1** *the hurricane left a trail of devastation:* **destruction**, ruin, desolation,

d

havoc, wreckage; ruins. **2** *the devastation of Prussia:* **destruction**, wrecking, ruination; demolition, annihilation. **3** *the devastation you have caused the family:* **shock**, trauma, distress, stress, strain, pain, anguish, suffering, upset, agony, misery, heartache.

d

develop verb **1** *the industry developed rapidly:* **grow**, expand, spread; advance, progress, evolve, mature. **2** *a plan was developed:* **initiate**, instigate, set in motion; originate, invent, form, establish, generate. **3** *children should develop their talents:* **expand**, augment, broaden, supplement, reinforce; enhance, refine, improve, polish, perfect. **4** *a row developed:* **start**, begin, emerge, erupt, break out, arise, break, unfold, happen. **5** *he developed the disease last week:* **fall ill with**, be stricken with, succumb to; contract, catch, get, pick up, come down with.

development noun **1** *the development of the firm:* **evolution**, growth, expansion, enlargement, spread, progress; success. **2** *there have been a number of developments:* **event**, change, circumstance, thing; incident, occurrence. **3** *a housing development:* **estate**, complex, site.

deviant adjective **aberrant**, abnormal, atypical, anomalous, irregular, non-standard; nonconformist, perverse, uncommon, unusual; freakish, strange, odd, peculiar, bizarre, eccentric, idiosyncratic, unorthodox, exceptional; warped, perverted; informal kinky, quirky.
– OPPOSITES normal.
• noun **nonconformist**, eccentric, maverick, individualist; outsider, misfit; informal oddball, weirdo, freak; N. Amer. informal screwball, kook.

deviate verb **diverge**, digress, drift, stray, veer, swerve; get sidetracked, branch off; differ, vary.

deviation noun **divergence**, digression, departure; difference, variation, variance; aberration, abnormality, irregularity, anomaly, inconsistency, discrepancy.

device noun **1** *a device for measuring pressure:* **implement**, gadget, utensil, tool, appliance, apparatus, instrument, machine, mechanism, contrivance, contraption; informal gizmo, widget. **2** *an ingenious legal device:* **ploy**, tactic, move, stratagem, scheme, plot, trick, ruse, manoeuvre, dodge; Brit. informal wheeze. **3** *their shields bear his device:* **emblem**, symbol, logo, badge, crest, insignia, coat of arms, seal, mark, design, motif; monogram, trademark.

devil noun **1** *God and the Devil:* **Satan**, Beelzebub, Lucifer, the Prince of Darkness; informal Old Nick. **2** *they drove out the devils from their bodies:* **evil spirit**, demon. **3** *the man is a devil:* **brute**, beast, monster, fiend; villain, sadist, barbarian, ogre. **4** *a naughty little devil:* **rascal**, rogue, imp, fiend, monkey, wretch; informal monster, horror, scamp, tyke; N. Amer. informal varmint.

WORD LINKS
diabolical, **diabolic**, **satanic** relating to the Devil

devilish adjective **1** *devilish tortures:* **diabolical**, fiendish, demonic, satanic, wicked, evil, vile, foul, abominable, loathsome, monstrous, hideous, horrible, appalling, dreadful, awful, terrible, ghastly, despicable, depraved, dark, black, immoral; vicious, cruel, savage, barbaric. **2** *a devilish job:* **difficult**, tricky, ticklish, troublesome, thorny, awkward, problematic.

devil-may-care adjective **reckless**, rash, impetuous, impulsive, daredevil, hot-headed, wild, foolhardy; nonchalant, casual, breezy, flippant, insouciant, happy-go-lucky, easy-going, unworried, untroubled, unconcerned.

devious adjective **1** *the devious ways in which they bent the rules:* **underhand**, deceitful, dishonest, dishonourable, unethical, unprincipled, immoral, unscrupulous, unfair, treacherous, duplicitous; crafty, cunning, calculating, artful, conniving, scheming, sly, wily; sneaky, furtive, secret, clandestine, surreptitious, covert; N. Amer. snide, snidey; informal crooked, shady, dirty, low-down; Brit. informal dodgy. **2** *a devious route around the coast:* **circuitous**, roundabout, indirect, meandering, tortuous.
– OPPOSITES open, honest, direct

devise verb **conceive**, think up, dream up, work out, formulate, concoct; design, invent, coin, originate; compose, construct, fabricate, create, produce, develop; discover, hit on; hatch, contrive; informal cook up.

devoid adjective
■ **devoid of** empty of, free of, bereft of, denuded of, lacking, without, wanting; informal minus.

devolution noun **decentralization**, delegation; transfer; surrender, relinquishment.

devolve verb **delegate**, pass, hand over, transfer, transmit, assign, consign, convey, entrust, turn over, give, cede, surrender, relinquish, deliver; bestow, grant.

devote verb **allocate**, assign, allot, commit, give, apportion, consign, pledge; dedicate, consecrate; set aside, earmark, reserve.

devoted adjective **loyal**, faithful, true, staunch, steadfast, constant, committed, dedicated, devout; fond, loving.

devotee noun **1** *a devotee of rock music:* **enthusiast**, fan, lover, aficionado, admirer; informal buff, freak, nut, fiend, fanatic, addict. **2** *devotees thronged the temple:* **follower**, adherent, supporter, disciple, member; believer, worshipper.

devotion noun **1** *her devotion to her husband:* **loyalty**, faithfulness, fidelity, commitment, allegiance, dedication; fondness, love, care. **2** *a life of devotion:* **piety**, spirituality, godliness, holiness, sanctity.

devour verb **1** *he devoured the prawns with gusto:* **wolf down**, bolt, gobble, guzzle, gulp down, gorge yourself on, feast on, consume, eat up; informal pack away, demolish, dispose of, make short work of, polish off, shovel down, stuff yourself with, pig yourself on, put away; Brit. informal scoff. **2** *flames devoured the house:* **consume**, engulf, envelop.

devout adjective **dedicated**, devoted, committed, loyal, faithful, staunch, genuine, firm, steadfast, unwavering, sincere, wholehearted, keen, enthusiastic, zealous, passionate, ardent, fervent, active; pious, reverent, God-fearing, dutiful, churchgoing.

dexterity noun **deftness**, adeptness, adroitness, agility, ability, talent, skill, proficiency, expertise, experience, efficiency, mastery, finesse.

dexterous adjective **deft**, adept, adroit, agile, nimble, neat, handy, able, capable, skilful, skilled, proficient, expert, practised, polished; efficient, effortless, slick, professional, masterly; informal nifty, mean, ace.
–OPPOSITES clumsy.

diabolical, **diabolic** adjective **1** *diabolical forces:* **devilish**, satanic, demonic, hellish, infernal, evil, wicked, ungodly, unholy. **2** (informal) *a diabolical performance:* **dreadful**, awful, terrible, disgraceful, shameful, lamentable, deplorable, appalling, atrocious; informal crummy, dire, dismal, God-awful, abysmal, rotten, pathetic, pitiful, lousy; Brit. informal rubbish.

diagnose verb **identify**, determine, distinguish, recognize, detect, pinpoint.

diagnosis noun **1** *the diagnosis of coeliac disease:* **identification**, detection, recognition, determination, discovery, pinpointing. **2** *the results confirmed his diagnosis:* **opinion**, judgement, verdict, conclusion.

diagonal adjective **crosswise**, crossways, slanting, slanted, aslant, squint, oblique, angled, at an angle, cornerways, cornerwise; N. Amer. cater-cornered, kitty-corner.

diagram noun **drawing**, representation, plan, outline, figure.

dial verb **phone**, telephone, call, ring.

dialect noun **vernacular**, patois, idiom, speech; regionalisms, localisms; informal lingo.

dialogue noun **1** *a book consisting of a series of dialogues:* **conversation**, talk, discussion, interchange; chat, tête-à-tête; informal confab; formal colloquy. **2** *a serious political dialogue:* **discussion**, exchange, debate, exchange of views, talk, head-to-head, consultation, conference; talks, negotiations; informal powwow; N. Amer. informal skull session.

diameter noun **breadth**, width, thickness; calibre, bore, gauge.

d

diametrical, diametric adjective **direct**, absolute, complete, exact, extreme, polar.

diary noun **1** *he put the date in his diary:* **appointment book**, engagement book, personal organizer; trademark Filofax. **2** *her World War II diaries:* **journal**, memoir, chronicle, log, logbook, history, annal, record; N. Amer. daybook.

diatribe noun **tirade**, harangue, onslaught, attack, polemic, denunciation, broadside, fulmination; informal blast.

dictate verb **1** *his attempts to dictate policy:* **prescribe**, lay down, impose, set down, order, command, decree, ordain, direct, determine, decide, control, govern. **2** *you are in no position to dictate to me:* **order about/around**, lord it over; lay down the law; informal boss about/around, push around/about, throw your weight about/around. **3** *choice is often dictated by availability:* **determine**, control, govern, decide, influence, affect.
• noun *the dictates of his superior:* **order**, command, commandment, decree, edict, ruling, dictum, diktat, directive, direction, instruction, pronouncement, mandate, requirement, stipulation, injunction, demand; formal ordinance; literary behest.

dictator noun **autocrat**, despot, tyrant.
– OPPOSITES democrat.

dictatorial adjective **domineering**, autocratic, authoritarian, oppressive, imperious, officious, overweening, overbearing, peremptory; informal bossy, high-handed.

dictatorship noun **despotism**, tyranny, autocracy, authoritarianism, totalitarianism, fascism; oppression, repression.
– OPPOSITES democracy.

diction noun **1** *his careful diction:* **enunciation**, articulation, pronunciation, speech, intonation, inflection; delivery. **2** *the need for contemporary diction in poetry:* **phrasing**, turn of phrase, wording, language, usage, vocabulary, terminology, expressions, idioms.

dictionary noun **lexicon**, glossary.

> **WORD LINKS**
> **lexicography** the writing of dictionaries

didactic adjective **instructive**, instructional, educational, educative, informative, informational, edifying, moralistic.

die verb **1** *her father died last year:* **pass away**, pass on, lose your life, expire, breathe your last, meet your end, lay down your life, perish, go to meet your maker, cross the great divide; informal give up the ghost, kick the bucket, croak, buy it, turn up your toes, cash in your chips, shuffle off this mortal coil; Brit. informal snuff it, peg out, pop your clogs; N. Amer. informal bite the big one, buy the farm. **2** *the wind had died down:* **abate**, subside, drop, lessen, ease off, let up, moderate, fade, peter out, wane, ebb, relent, weaken; melt away, dissolve, vanish, disappear. **3** (informal) *the engine died:* **fail**, cut out, give out, stop; informal conk out, go kaput, give up the ghost; Brit. informal pack up. **4** (informal) *she's dying to meet you:* **long**, yearn, burn, ache; informal itch.
– OPPOSITES live.

diehard adjective **hard-line**, reactionary, ultra-conservative, traditionalist, dyed-in-the-wool, intransigent, inflexible, uncompromising, rigid, entrenched; staunch.

diet noun **food**, eating habits; nutrition; regimen.
• verb **be on a diet**, slim, watch your weight, count the calories; N. Amer. reduce; N. Amer. informal slenderize.

differ verb **1** *the second set of data differed from the first:* **contrast with**, be different/dissimilar to, be unlike, vary from, diverge from, deviate from, conflict with, run counter to, be incompatible with, be at odds with, go against, contradict. **2** *the two sides differed over this issue:* **disagree**, conflict, be at variance/odds, be in dispute, not see eye to eye.
– OPPOSITES resemble, agree.

difference noun **1** *the difference between the two sets of data:* **dissimilarity**, contrast, distinction, differentiation, variance, variation, divergence, disparity, deviation, polarity, gap, imbalance, contra-

diction. **2** *we've had our differences in the past:* **disagreement**, difference of opinion, dispute, argument, quarrel, wrangle, contretemps, altercation; Brit. row; informal tiff, set-to, run-in, spat. **3** *I am willing to pay the difference:* **balance**, remainder, rest.
–OPPOSITES similarity.

different adjective **1** *people with different lifestyles:* **dissimilar**, unlike, contrasting, divergent, differing, varying, disparate; poles apart, incompatible, mismatched, conflicting, clashing; informal like chalk and cheese. **2** *suddenly everything in her life was different:* **changed**, altered, transformed, new, unfamiliar, unknown, strange. **3** *two different occasions:* **distinct**, separate, individual, independent. **4** (informal) *he wanted to try something different:* **unusual**, out of the ordinary, unfamiliar, novel, new, fresh, original, unconventional, exotic, uncommon.
–OPPOSITES similar, related, ordinary.

differentiate verb **1** *he cannot differentiate between fantasy and reality:* **distinguish**, discriminate, make/draw a distinction, tell the difference, tell apart. **2** *this differentiates their business from all other booksellers:* **make different**, distinguish, set apart, single out, separate, mark out.

differentiation noun **distinction**, distinctness, difference; separation, demarcation, delimitation.

difficult adjective **1** *a very difficult job:* **hard**, strenuous, arduous, laborious, tough, demanding, punishing, gruelling, back-breaking, exhausting, tiring; informal hellish, killing, no picnic. **2** *she found maths very difficult:* **hard**, complicated, impenetrable, unfathomable, over/above your head, beyond one, puzzling, baffling, perplexing, confusing, mystifying; problematic, intricate, knotty, thorny, ticklish. **3** *a difficult child:* **troublesome**, tiresome, trying, exasperating, awkward, demanding, perverse, contrary, recalcitrant, unmanageable, obstreperous, unhelpful, uncooperative, disobliging; hard to please, fussy, finicky; formal refractory. **4** *you've come at a difficult time:* **inconvenient**, awkward, inopportune, unfavourable, unfortunate, inappropriate, unsuitable, untimely, ill-timed. **5** *the family have been through very difficult times:* **bad**, tough, grim, dark, black, hard, distressing, upsetting, traumatic.
–OPPOSITES easy, simple, accommodating.

difficulty noun **1** *the difficulty of balancing motherhood with a career:* **strain**, trouble, problems, struggle, laboriousness, arduousness; informal hassle, stress. **2** *practical difficulties:* **problem**, complication, snag, hitch, fly in the ointment, pitfall, handicap, impediment, hindrance, obstacle, hurdle, stumbling block, obstruction, barrier; Brit. spanner in the works; informal headache, hiccup. **3** *Charles got into difficulties:* **trouble**, predicament, plight, hard times, dire straits; quandary, dilemma; informal deep water, a fix, a jam, a hole.
–OPPOSITES ease.

diffidence noun **shyness**, bashfulness, modesty, self-effacement, meekness, unassertiveness, timidity, humility, hesitancy, reticence.

diffident adjective **shy**, bashful, modest, self-effacing, unassuming, meek, unconfident, unassertive, timid, timorous, humble, shrinking, reticent.
–OPPOSITES confident.

diffuse verb **spread**, spread around, disseminate, disperse, distribute, put about, circulate, communicate, purvey, propagate, transmit, broadcast, promulgate.

> Don't confuse **diffuse** with **defuse**, which means 'make a situation less tense or dangerous' (*an attempt to defuse the tension*).

diffusion noun **spread**, dissemination, scattering, dispersal, distribution, circulation, propagation, transmission, broadcasting, promulgation.

dig verb **1** *she began to dig the soil:* **turn over**, work, break up. **2** *he dug a hole:* **excavate**, dig out, quarry, hollow out, scoop out, gouge out; cut, bore, tunnel, burrow, mine. **3** *the bodies were hastily dug up:*

d

exhume, disinter, unearth. **4** *Winnie dug her elbow into his ribs:* **poke**, prod, jab, stab, shove, ram, push, thrust, drive, stick. **5** *he'd been digging into my past:* **delve**, probe, search, inquire, look, investigate, research, examine, scrutinize, check up on; informal check out. **6** *I dug up some disturbing information:* **uncover**, discover, find, unearth, dredge up, root out, ferret out, turn up, reveal, bring to light, expose.
• noun **1** *a dig in the ribs:* **poke**, prod, jab, stab, shove, push. **2** (informal) *they're always making digs at each other:* **snide remark**, cutting remark, jibe, jeer, taunt, sneer, insult, barb, insinuation; informal wisecrack, crack, put-down.

digest verb *Liz digested this information:* **assimilate**, absorb, take in, understand, comprehend, grasp; consider, think about, reflect on, ponder, contemplate, mull over.
• noun *a digest of their findings:* **summary**, synopsis, abstract, precis, résumé, summation; compilation; N. Amer. informal wrap-up.

digit noun **1** *the door code has ten digits:* **numeral**, number, figure, integer. **2** *our frozen digits:* **finger**, thumb, toe; extremity.

dignified adjective **stately**, noble, courtly, majestic, distinguished, proud, august, lofty, exalted, regal, lordly, imposing, impressive, grand; solemn, serious, grave, formal, ceremonious, decorous, sedate.

dignify verb **ennoble**, enhance, distinguish, add distinction to, honour, grace, exalt, magnify, glorify, elevate.

dignitary noun **worthy**, VIP, pillar of society, luminary, leading light, big name; informal heavyweight, bigwig, big gun, big shot.

dignity noun **self-respect**, pride, self-esteem, self-worth.

digress verb **deviate**, go off at a tangent, get off the subject, get sidetracked, lose the thread, diverge, turn aside/away, depart, drift, stray, wander.

digression noun **deviation**, detour, diversion, departure, divergence; aside.

dilapidated adjective **run down**, tumbledown, ramshackle, broken-down, in disrepair, shabby, battered, rickety, shaky, crumbling, in ruins, ruined, decayed, decaying, decrepit; neglected, uncared-for, untended, the worse for wear, falling to pieces, falling apart, gone to rack and ruin.

dilate verb **enlarge**, widen, expand, distend.
– OPPOSITES contract.

dilemma noun **quandary**, predicament, catch-22, vicious circle, plight, mess, muddle; difficulty, problem, trouble, perplexity, confusion, conflict; informal fix, tight spot/corner; Brit. informal sticky wicket.

dilettante noun **dabbler**, amateur, non-professional, non-specialist, layman, layperson.

diligence noun **conscientiousness**, assiduousness, hard work, application, concentration, effort, care, industriousness, rigour, meticulousness, thoroughness; perseverance, persistence, tenacity, dedication, commitment.

diligent adjective **industrious**, hard-working, assiduous, conscientious, particular, punctilious, meticulous, painstaking, rigorous, careful, thorough, sedulous; dedicated, committed.
– OPPOSITES lazy.

dilute verb **1** *strong bleach can be diluted with water:* **make weaker**, weaken, water down; thin out, thin; doctor, adulterate; informal cut. **2** *the original plans have been diluted:* **weaken**, moderate, tone down, water down, compromise.
– OPPOSITES concentrate.
• adjective *a dilute acid.* See DILUTED.

diluted adjective **weak**, dilute, thin, watered down, watery; adulterated.
– OPPOSITES concentrated.

dim adjective **1** *the dim light:* **faint**, weak, feeble, soft, pale, dull, subdued, muted, wishy-washy. **2** *long dim corridors:* **dark**, badly lit, dingy, dismal, gloomy, murky. **3** *a dim figure:* **indistinct**, ill-defined, unclear, vague, shadowy, nebulous, blurred, blurry, fuzzy. **4** *dim memories:* **vague**, imprecise, imperfect, unclear, indistinct, sketchy, hazy, blurred, shadowy. **5** *their prospects for the future looked dim:* **gloomy**, unpromising,

bleak, unfavourable, discouraging, disheartening, depressing, dispiriting, hopeless.
– OPPOSITES bright, distinct, encouraging.
• verb **1** *the lights were dimmed:* **turn down**, lower, dip, soften, subdue. **2** *my memories have not dimmed with time:* **fade**, dwindle.
– OPPOSITES brighten, sharpen, intensify.

dimension noun **1** *the dimensions of the room:* **size**, measurements, proportions, extent; length, width, breadth, depth, area, volume, capacity; footage, acreage. **2** *the dimension of the problem:* **size**, scale, extent, scope, magnitude; importance, significance. **3** *the cultural dimensions of the problem:* **aspect**, feature, element, facet, side.

diminish verb **1** *the pain will gradually diminish:* **decrease**, lessen, decline, reduce, subside, die down, abate, dwindle, fade, slacken off, let up, ebb, wane, recede, die away/out, peter out. **2** *new legislation diminished the courts' authority:* **reduce**, decrease, lessen, curtail, cut, cut down/back, constrict, restrict, limit, curb, check; weaken, blunt, erode, undermine, sap.
– OPPOSITES increase.

diminution noun **reduction**, decrease, lessening, decline, dwindling, fading, weakening, ebb.

diminutive adjective **tiny**, small, little, petite, elfin, minute, miniature, minuscule, compact, pocket, toy, midget, undersized, short; Scottish wee; informal teeny, teensy, tiddly, dinky, baby, pint-sized; Brit. informal titchy.
– OPPOSITES enormous.

dimple noun **indentation**, hollow, cleft, dint.

din noun **noise**, racket, rumpus, cacophony, babel, hubbub, tumult, uproar, commotion, clangour, clatter; shouting, yelling, screaming, caterwauling, clamour, outcry; Brit. row; informal hullabaloo.
– OPPOSITES silence.

dine verb **1** *we dined at a restaurant:* **have dinner**, have supper, eat; dated sup. **2** *they dined on lobster:* **eat**, feed on, feast on, banquet on, partake of; informal tuck into.

dingy adjective **gloomy**, dark, dull, badly/poorly lit, murky, dim, dismal, dreary, drab, sombre, grim, cheerless; dirty, grimy, shabby, faded, worn, dowdy, seedy, run down.
– OPPOSITES bright.

dinner noun **main meal**, supper; lunch; banquet, feast; Brit. tea; informal spread; formal repast.

dint noun **dent**, indentation, hollow, depression, dip, dimple, cleft, pit.
■ **by dint of** by means of, by virtue of, on account of, as a result of, as a consequence of, owing to, on the strength of, due to, thanks to, by; formal by reason of.

dip verb **1** *he dipped a rag in the water:* **immerse**, submerge, plunge, duck, dunk, lower, sink. **2** *the sun dipped below the horizon:* **sink**, set, drop, fall, descend; disappear, vanish. **3** *the president's popularity has dipped:* **decrease**, fall, drop, fall off, decline, diminish, dwindle, slump, plummet, plunge. **4** *you might have to dip into your savings:* **draw on**, use, make use of, have recourse to, spend. **5** *an interesting book to dip into:* **browse through**, skim through, look through, flick through, glance at, run your eye over.
– OPPOSITES rise, increase.
• noun **1** *a relaxing dip in the pool:* **swim**, bathe; paddle. **2** *chicken satay with peanut dip:* **sauce**, relish. **3** *the hedge at the bottom of the dip:* **slope**, incline, decline, descent; hollow, depression, basin. **4** *a dip in sales:* **decrease**, fall, drop, downturn, decline, falling-off, slump, reduction, diminution.

diplomacy noun **1** *diplomacy failed to win them independence:* **statesmanship**, statecraft, negotiation, discussion, talks, dialogue; international relations, foreign affairs. **2** *Jack's quiet diplomacy:* **tact**, tactfulness, sensitivity, discretion, delicacy, politeness, thoughtfulness, judiciousness, prudence.

diplomat noun **ambassador**, attaché, consul, chargé d'affaires, envoy, emissary, plenipotentiary.

diplomatic adjective **tactful**, sensitive, subtle, delicate, polite,

discreet, thoughtful, careful, judicious, prudent, politic.
–OPPOSITES tactless.

dire adjective **1** *the dire economic situation:* **terrible**, dreadful, appalling, frightful, awful, atrocious, grim, alarming; grave, serious, disastrous, ruinous, hopeless, wretched, desperate, parlous. **2** *he was in dire need of help:* **urgent**, desperate, pressing, crying, sore, grave, serious, extreme, acute. **3** *dire warnings:* **ominous**, gloomy, grim, dismal.

direct adjective **1** *the most direct route:* **straight**; short, quick. **2** *a direct flight:* **non-stop**, unbroken, uninterrupted, through. **3** *he is very direct:* **frank**, candid, straightforward, honest, open, blunt, plain-spoken, outspoken, forthright, no-nonsense, matter-of-fact, not afraid to call a spade a spade; informal upfront. **4** *direct contact with the president:* **face to face**, personal, head-on, first-hand, tête-à-tête. **5** *a direct quotation:* **verbatim**, word for word, to the letter, faithful, exact, precise, accurate, correct. **6** *the direct opposite:* **exact**, absolute, complete, diametrical.
•verb **1** *an economic elite directed the nation's affairs:* **manage**, govern, run, administer, control, conduct, handle, be in charge/control of, preside over, lead, head, rule; supervise, superintend, oversee, regulate, orchestrate, coordinate. **2** *was that remark directed at me?* **aim at**, target at, address to, intend for, mean for, design for. **3** *a man in uniform directed them to the hall:* **give directions**, show the way, guide, lead, conduct, accompany, usher, escort. **4** *the judge directed the jury to return a not guilty verdict:* **instruct**, tell, command, order, charge, require.

direction noun **1** *a northerly direction:* **way**, route, course, line, bearing, orientation. **2** *the newspaper's political direction:* **orientation**, inclination, leaning, tendency, bent, bias; tack, attitude. **3** *his direction of the project:* **administration**, management, conduct, handling, running, supervision, superintendence, regulation, orchestration; control, command, rule, leadership, guidance. **4** *explicit directions about nursing care:* **instruction**, order, command, rule, regulation, requirement.

directive noun **instruction**, direction, command, order, charge, injunction, rule, ruling, regulation, law, dictate, decree, dictum, edict, mandate, fiat; formal ordinance.

directly adverb **1** *they flew directly to New York:* **straight**, right, as the crow flies. **2** *I went directly after breakfast:* **immediately**, at once, instantly, right, straight, post-haste, without delay, forthwith; quickly, speedily, promptly; informal pronto. **3** *the houses directly opposite:* **exactly**, right, immediately; diametrically; informal bang. **4** *she spoke simply and directly:* **frankly**, candidly, openly, bluntly, forthrightly, without beating around the bush.

director noun **administrator**, manager, chairman, chairwoman, chairperson, chair, head, chief, principal, leader, governor, president; managing director, MD, chief executive, CEO; informal boss, kingpin, top dog, gaffer, head honcho, numero uno; N. Amer. informal Mister Big.

directory noun **index**, list, listing, register, catalogue, record, archive, inventory.

dirt noun **1** *his face was streaked with dirt:* **grime**, filth; dust, soot; muck, mud, mire, sludge, slime; smudges, stains; Brit. informal gunge. **2** *the packed dirt of the road:* **earth**, soil, clay; ground.

dirty adjective **1** *a dirty sweatshirt* | *dirty water:* **soiled**, grimy, grubby, filthy, mucky, stained, unwashed, greasy, muddy, dusty, sooty; unclean, sullied, impure, tarnished, polluted, contaminated, defiled, foul, unhygienic, insanitary, unsanitary; Brit. informal manky. **2** *a dirty joke:* **indecent**, obscene, rude, naughty, vulgar, smutty, coarse, crude, filthy, bawdy, suggestive, ribald, racy, salacious, risqué, offensive, off colour, lewd, pornographic, explicit, X-rated; informal blue; euphemistic adult. **3** *a dirty look:* **malevolent**, resentful, hostile, black, dark; angry, disapproving.
–OPPOSITES clean.

• verb **soil**, stain, muddy, blacken, mess, mark, spatter, smudge, smear, splatter; sully, pollute, foul, defile.

disable verb *the bomb squad disabled the device:* **deactivate**, defuse, disarm, make safe.

disadvantage noun **drawback**, snag, downside, stumbling block, fly in the ointment, catch, hindrance, obstacle, impediment; flaw, defect, weakness, fault, handicap, con, trouble, difficulty, problem, complication; informal minus.
– OPPOSITES benefit.

disadvantaged adjective **deprived**, underprivileged, depressed, in need, needy, poor, impoverished, indigent, hard up; Brit. on the breadline.

disadvantageous adjective **unfavourable**, bad; detrimental, prejudicial, deleterious, harmful, damaging, injurious.

disaffected adjective **dissatisfied**, disgruntled, discontented, frustrated, alienated, resentful, embittered.
– OPPOSITES contented.

disagree verb **1** *no one was willing to disagree with him:* **take issue**, challenge, contradict, oppose; be at variance/odds, not see eye to eye, differ, dissent, be in dispute, debate, argue, quarrel, wrangle, clash, be at loggerheads, cross swords, lock horns; formal gainsay. **2** *their accounts disagree on details:* **differ**, be dissimilar, be different, vary, diverge; contradict each other, conflict, clash. **3** *the spicy food disagreed with her:* **make ill**, make unwell, nauseate, sicken, upset.

disagreeable adjective **1** *a disagreeable smell:* **unpleasant**, nasty, offensive, off-putting, obnoxious, objectionable, horrible, horrid, dreadful, frightful, abominable, odious, repulsive, repellent, revolting, disgusting, foul, vile, nauseating, sickening, unpalatable. **2** *a disagreeable man:* **bad-tempered**, grumpy, sullen; unfriendly, unpleasant, nasty, mean, rude, surly, discourteous, impolite, brusque, abrupt.
– OPPOSITES pleasant.

disagreement noun **1** *there was some disagreement over possible solutions:* **dissent**, dispute, difference of opinion, controversy, conflict, discord, contention, division. **2** *a heated disagreement:* **argument**, debate, quarrel, wrangle, squabble, falling-out, altercation, dispute, war of words, contretemps; Brit. row; informal tiff, set-to, spat, ding-dong; informal barney; Scottish informal rammy. **3** *the disagreement between the results of the two assessments:* **difference**, dissimilarity, variation, variance, discrepancy, disparity, divergence, contradiction, conflict, clash, contrast.

disallow verb **reject**, refuse, dismiss; ban, bar, block, forbid, prohibit; cancel, invalidate, overrule, quash, overturn, countermand, reverse, throw out, set aside.

disappear verb **1** *by 4 o'clock the mist had disappeared:* **vanish**, be lost to view/sight, recede; fade away, melt away, clear, dissolve, disperse, evaporate. **2** *this way of life has disappeared:* **die out**, cease to exist, end, go, pass away, pass into oblivion, perish, vanish.
– OPPOSITES materialize.

disappoint verb **let down**, fail, dissatisfy; upset, dismay, sadden, disenchant, disillusion, shatter someone's illusions.
– OPPOSITES delight.

disappointed adjective **upset**, saddened, let down, cast down, disheartened, downhearted, downcast, dispirited, discouraged, despondent, dismayed, crestfallen; disenchanted, disillusioned; informal choked, miffed, cut up; Brit. informal gutted, as sick as a parrot.
– OPPOSITES delighted.

disappointing adjective **regrettable**, unfortunate, discouraging, disheartening, dispiriting, dismaying, unsatisfactory.

disappointment noun **1** *she tried to hide her disappointment:* **sadness**, regret, dismay, sorrow; disenchantment, disillusionment. **2** *the trip was a bit of a disappointment:* **letdown**, non-event, anticlimax; Brit. damp squib; informal washout.
– OPPOSITES delight.

disapproval noun **disapprobation**, objection, dislike; dissatisfaction,

disfavour, displeasure, distaste; criticism, censure, condemnation, denunciation, deprecation; informal the thumbs down.
– OPPOSITES approval, approbation.

disapprove verb **object to**, have a poor opinion of, look down your nose at, take exception to, dislike, take a dim view of, look askance at, frown on; deplore, criticize, censure, condemn, denounce, decry.
– OPPOSITES approve.

disapproving adjective **reproachful**, reproving, critical, censorious, condemnatory, disparaging, denigratory, deprecatory, unfavourable; hostile.

disarm verb **1** *the militia refused to disarm:* **lay down your arms/weapons**; surrender; demobilize, demilitarize. **2** *police disarmed the bomb:* **defuse**, disable, deactivate, make safe. **3** *the warmth in his voice disarmed her:* **win over**, charm, persuade; mollify, appease, placate, pacify, conciliate, propitiate.

disarmament noun **demilitarization**, demobilization, decommissioning; arms reduction, arms limitation, arms control.

disarming adjective **winning**, charming, irresistible, persuasive, beguiling; conciliatory, mollifying.

disarray noun **disorder**, confusion, chaos, untidiness, disorganization, dishevelment, a mess, a muddle, a shambles.
– OPPOSITES tidiness.

disaster noun **1** *a railway disaster:* **catastrophe**, calamity, cataclysm, tragedy, act of God; accident. **2** *a string of personal disasters:* **misfortune**, mishap, misadventure, setback, reversal, stroke of bad luck, blow. **3** (informal) *the film was a disaster:* **failure**, fiasco, catastrophe; informal flop, dud, washout, dead loss.
– OPPOSITES success, triumph.

disastrous adjective **catastrophic**, calamitous, cataclysmic, tragic; devastating, ruinous, dire, terrible, awful, shocking, appalling, dreadful; black, dark, unfortunate, unlucky, ill-fated, ill-starred, inauspicious.

disavow verb **deny**, disclaim, disown, wash your hands of, repudiate, reject, renounce.

disband verb **break up**, disperse, demobilize, dissolve, scatter, separate, go your separate ways, part company.
– OPPOSITES assemble.

disbelief noun **incredulity**, incredulousness, scepticism, doubt, doubtfulness, dubiousness; cynicism, suspicion, distrust, mistrust; formal dubiety.

disbelieving adjective **incredulous**, doubtful, dubious, unconvinced; distrustful, mistrustful, suspicious, cynical, sceptical.

disc, disk noun **1** *the sun was a huge scarlet disc:* **circle**, round. **2** *computer disks:* **diskette**, floppy disk, floppy; hard disk; CD-ROM. **3** *their new disc features a mix of styles:* **record**, album, CD.

discard verb **dispose of**, throw away/out, get rid of, toss out, jettison, scrap, dispense with, cast aside/off, throw on the scrap heap; reject, repudiate, abandon, drop, have done with, shed; informal chuck away/out, dump, ditch, bin, junk; Brit. informal get shot of; N. Amer. informal trash.
– OPPOSITES keep.

discern verb **perceive**, make out, pick out, detect, recognize, notice, observe, see, spot; identify, determine, distinguish; literary espy.

discernible adjective **visible**, detectable, noticeable, perceptible, observable, identifiable; apparent, evident, clear, obvious.

discerning adjective **discriminating**, judicious, shrewd, astute, intelligent, sharp, selective, sophisticated, tasteful, sensitive, perceptive, knowing.

discharge verb **1** *he was discharged from the RAF:* **dismiss**, eject, expel, throw out, make redundant; release, let go; Military cashier; informal sack, give someone the sack, fire, kick/boot out, give someone the boot, turf out, give someone their cards, give someone their marching orders, give someone the push. **2** *he was discharged from prison:* **release**, free, let out. **3** *oil is routinely discharged from ships:* **release**, eject, let out, pour out, void, give off, dump. **4** *the swelling will burst and discharge pus:* **emit**, exude, ooze,

leak, drip. **5** *he accidentally discharged a pistol:* **fire**, shoot, let off; set off, loose off, trigger, explode, detonate. **6** *they discharged their duties efficiently:* **carry out**, perform, execute, conduct, do; fulfil, accomplish, achieve, complete.
– OPPOSITES recruit, imprison, absorb.
• **noun 1** *his discharge from the service:* **dismissal**, release, removal, ejection, expulsion; Military cashiering; informal the sack, the boot. **2** *a discharge of diesel oil into the river:* **leak**, leakage, emission, release, outflow. **3** *a watery discharge from the eyes:* **emission**, secretion, excretion, suppuration; pus. **4** *the discharge of their duties:* **carrying out**, performance, performing, execution, conduct; fulfilment, accomplishment, completion.

disciple **noun** **follower**, adherent, believer, admirer, devotee, acolyte, apostle; pupil, student; supporter, advocate, proponent, apologist.

disciplinarian **noun** **martinet**, hard taskmaster, authoritarian; tyrant, despot; N. Amer. ramrod; informal slave-driver.

discipline **noun 1** *parental discipline:* **control**, training, teaching, instruction, regulation, direction, order, authority, rule, strictness, a firm hand. **2** *he was able to maintain discipline among his men:* **good behaviour**, order, control, obedience. **3** *sociology is a fairly new discipline:* **field of study**, branch of knowledge, subject, area; speciality.
• **verb 1** *she had disciplined herself to ignore the pain:* **train**, drill, teach, school, coach. **2** *he was disciplined by the management:* **punish**, penalize, bring to book; reprimand, rebuke, reprove, chastise, upbraid; informal dress down, give someone a dressing-down, give someone a roasting; Brit. informal carpet; formal castigate.

disclaim **verb** **deny**, refuse to accept/acknowledge, reject, wash your hands of.
– OPPOSITES accept.

disclose **verb 1** *the information must not be disclosed to anyone:* **reveal**, make known, divulge, tell, impart, communicate, pass on, vouchsafe; release, make public, broadcast, publish, report; leak, betray, let slip, let drop, give away. **2** *exploratory surgery disclosed an aneurysm:* **uncover**, reveal, show, bring to light.
– OPPOSITES conceal.

disclosure **noun 1** *she was embarrassed by this unexpected disclosure:* **revelation**, declaration, announcement, news, report, leak. **2** *the disclosure of official information:* **publishing**, broadcasting; revelation, communication, release, uncovering, unveiling, exposure; leaking.

discoloration **noun** **stain**, mark, patch, streak, spot, blotch, tarnishing; blemish, flaw, defect, bruise, contusion; birthmark; informal splodge, splotch.

discolour **verb** **stain**, mark, soil, dirty, streak, smear, spot, tarnish, spoil, blemish; blacken, char; fade, bleach.

discoloured **adjective** **stained**, marked, spotted, dirty, soiled, tarnished, blackened; bleached, faded, yellowed.

discomfort **noun 1** *discomfort caused by indigestion:* **pain**, aches and pains, soreness; aching, twinge, pang, throb, cramp; Brit. informal gyp. **2** *the discomforts of life at sea:* **inconvenience**, difficulty, problem, trial, tribulation, hardship; informal hassle. **3** *Ruth flushed and Thomas noticed her discomfort:* **embarrassment**, discomfiture, unease, awkwardness, discomposure, confusion, nervousness, distress, anxiety.
• **verb** *his purpose was to discomfort the Prime Minister:* **embarrass**, disconcert, nonplus, discomfit, take aback, unsettle, unnerve, ruffle, confuse, fluster; informal faze, rattle; N. Amer. informal discombobulate.

disconcerting **adjective** **unsettling**, unnerving, discomfiting, disturbing, perturbing, troubling, upsetting, worrying, alarming; confusing, bewildering, perplexing.

disconnect **verb 1** *the trucks were disconnected from the train:* **detach**, disengage, uncouple, decouple, unhook, unhitch, undo, unfasten,

d

unyoke. **2** *she felt as if she had been disconnected from the real world:* **separate**, cut off, divorce, sever, isolate, divide, part, disengage, dissociate, remove. **3** *an engineer disconnected the appliance:* **deactivate**, shut off, turn off, switch off, unplug, isolate.
– OPPOSITES attach, connect.

disconnected adjective **1** *a world that seemed disconnected from reality:* **detached**, separate, separated, divorced, cut off, isolated, dissociated, disengaged. **2** *a disconnected narrative:* **disjointed**, incoherent, garbled, confused, jumbled, mixed up, rambling, wandering, disorganized, uncoordinated, ill-thought-out.

disconsolate adjective **sad**, unhappy, doleful, woebegone, dejected, downcast, downhearted, despondent, dispirited, crestfallen, cast down, down, disheartened, discouraged, demoralized.
– OPPOSITES cheerful.

discontent noun **dissatisfaction**, disaffection, grievances, unhappiness, displeasure, bad feelings, resentment, envy; restlessness, unrest, uneasiness, unease, frustration, irritation, annoyance; informal a chip on your shoulder.
– OPPOSITES satisfaction.

discontented adjective **dissatisfied**, disgruntled, disaffected, unhappy, aggrieved, displeased, resentful, envious; restless, frustrated, irritated, annoyed; informal fed up.
– OPPOSITES satisfied.

discontinue verb **stop**, end, terminate, put an end/stop to, wind up, finish, call a halt to, cancel, drop, abandon, dispense with, do away with, get rid of, axe, abolish; suspend, interrupt, break off, withdraw; informal cut, pull the plug on, scrap, knock something on the head.

discontinuity noun **disconnectedness**, disconnection, break, disruption, interruption, disjointedness.

discontinuous adjective **intermittent**, sporadic, broken, fitful, interrupted, on and off, disrupted, erratic, disconnected.

discord noun **1** *stress resulting from family discord:* **strife**, conflict, friction, hostility, antagonism, antipathy, enmity, bad feeling, ill feeling, bad blood, argument, quarrelling, squabbling, bickering, wrangling, feuding, disagreement, dissension, dispute, disunity, division. **2** *the music faded in discord:* **dissonance**, discordance, disharmony, cacophony.
– OPPOSITES accord, harmony.

discordant adjective **inharmonious**, tuneless, off-key, dissonant, harsh, jarring, grating, jangling, jangly, strident, shrill, screeching, screechy, cacophonous; sharp, flat.
– OPPOSITES harmonious.

discount noun *students get a 10 per cent discount:* **reduction**, deduction, markdown, price cut, cut, concession; rebate.
• verb **1** *I'd heard rumours, but discounted them:* **disregard**, pay no attention to, take no notice of, dismiss, ignore, overlook, reject; informal take with a pinch of salt, pooh-pooh. **2** *the RRP is discounted in many stores:* **reduce**, mark down, cut, lower; informal knock down. **3** *top Paris hotels discounted 20 per cent off published room rates:* **deduct**, take off; informal knock off, slash.
– OPPOSITES believe, increase.

discourage verb **1** *we want to discourage children from smoking:* **deter**, dissuade, put off, talk out of; disincentivize. **2** *she was discouraged by his hostile tone:* **dishearten**, dispirit, demoralize, cast down, disappoint; put off, unnerve, daunt, intimidate. **3** *he sought to discourage further speculation:* **prevent**, stop, put a stop to, avert; inhibit, hinder, curb, put a damper on, throw cold water on.
– OPPOSITES encourage.

discouraged adjective **disheartened**, dispirited, demoralized, deflated, disappointed, let down, disconsolate, despondent, dejected, cast down, downcast, crestfallen, dismayed, low-spirited, gloomy, glum, unenthusiastic; put off, daunted, intimidated, cowed, crushed; informal down in the mouth, down in the dumps, fed up, unenthused.

discouraging adjective **depressing**,

demoralizing, disheartening, dispiriting, disappointing, gloomy, off-putting; unfavourable, unpromising, inauspicious.
– OPPOSITES encouraging.

discourse noun **1** *they prolonged their discourse outside the door:* **discussion**, conversation, talk, dialogue, conference, debate, consultation; parley, powwow, chat; informal confab; formal confabulation, colloquy. **2** *a discourse on critical theory:* **essay**, treatise, dissertation, paper, study, critique, monograph, disquisition, tract; lecture, address, speech, oration; sermon, homily.
• verb *he discoursed at length on his favourite topic:* **hold forth**, expatiate, pontificate; talk, speak, make a speech, lecture, sermonize, preach; informal spout, sound off.

discourteous adjective **rude**, impolite, ill-mannered, bad-mannered, disrespectful, uncivil, ungentlemanly, unladylike, ill-bred, boorish, crass, ungracious, uncouth; insolent, impudent, cheeky, audacious, presumptuous; curt, brusque, blunt, abrupt, offhand, short, sharp; informal ignorant.
– OPPOSITES polite, courteous.

discourtesy noun **rudeness**, impoliteness, ill manners, bad manners, incivility, disrespect, ungraciousness, boorishness, uncouthness; insolence, impudence, impertinence; curtness, brusqueness, abruptness.

discover verb **1** *firemen discovered a body in the debris:* **find**, locate, come across/upon, stumble on, chance on, uncover, unearth, turn up. **2** *eventually, I discovered the truth:* **find out**, learn, realize, ascertain, work out, fathom out, dig up/out, ferret out, root out; informal figure out, tumble to; Brit. informal twig, rumble, suss out; N. Amer. informal dope out. **3** *scientists discovered a new way of dating fossils:* **hit on**, find.

discovery noun **1** *the discovery of the body:* **finding**, location, uncovering, unearthing. **2** *the discovery that she was pregnant:* **realization**, recognition; revelation, disclosure. **3** *he failed to take out a patent on his discoveries:* **find**, finding, breakthrough, innovation.

discredit verb **1** *an attempt to discredit him:* **bring into disrepute**, disgrace, dishonour, damage the reputation of, blacken the name of, reflect badly on, compromise, smear, tarnish, taint; N. Amer. slur. **2** *that theory has been discredited:* **disprove**, invalidate, explode, refute; informal debunk.
• noun **dishonour**, disgrace, shame, humiliation, ignominy.
– OPPOSITES honour, glory.

discreditable adjective **dishonourable**, reprehensible, shameful, deplorable, disgraceful, disreputable, blameworthy, ignoble, shabby, regrettable.
– OPPOSITES creditable.

discreet adjective **1** *discreet enquiries:* **careful**, circumspect, cautious; tactful, diplomatic, judicious, strategic, sensitive. **2** *discreet lighting:* **unobtrusive**, inconspicuous, subtle, low-key, understated, subdued, muted, soft, restrained.

> Don't confuse **discreet** with **discrete**, which means 'separate' (*there are a number of discrete categories*).

discrepancy noun **difference**, disparity, variation, deviation, divergence, disagreement, inconsistency, dissimilarity, mismatch, discordance, incompatibility, conflict.
– OPPOSITES correspondence.

discrete adjective **separate**, distinct, individual, detached, unattached, disconnected, discontinuous.
– OPPOSITES connected.

discretion noun **1** *you can rely on his discretion:* **circumspection**, carefulness; tact, tactfulness, diplomacy, delicacy, sensitivity, prudence, judiciousness. **2** *honorary fellowships awarded at the discretion of the council:* **choice**, option, preference, disposition; pleasure, will, inclination.

discretionary adjective **optional**, voluntary, at your discretion.
– OPPOSITES compulsory.

discriminate verb **1** *he cannot discriminate between fact and opinion:* **differentiate**, distinguish, draw a distinction, tell the difference, tell apart; separate. **2** *policies* *that discriminate against women:* **be biased**, be prejudiced; treat differently, treat unfairly, put at a disadvantage, pick on.

discriminating adjective **discerning**, perceptive, astute, shrewd, judicious, insightful; selective, tasteful, refined, sensitive, cultivated, cultured, artistic, aesthetic.
– OPPOSITES indiscriminate.

d

discrimination noun **1** *racial discrimination:* **prejudice**, bias, bigotry, intolerance, partisanship; sexism, chauvinism, racism, racialism, anti-Semitism, ageism, classism; positive discrimination, affirmative action; (in S. Africa, historical) apartheid. **2** *a man with no discrimination:* **discernment**, judgement, perceptiveness, acumen, astuteness, shrewdness, judiciousness, insight; taste, refinement, sensitivity, cultivation.
– OPPOSITES impartiality.

discriminatory adjective **prejudicial**, biased, prejudiced, preferential, unfair, unjust, inequitable, weighted, one-sided, partisan; sexist, chauvinistic, chauvinist, racist, racialist, anti-Semitic, ageist, classist.
– OPPOSITES impartial.

discuss verb **1** *I discussed the matter with my wife:* **talk over**, talk about, talk through, converse about, debate, confer about, deliberate about, chew over, consider, weigh up, thrash out; informal kick around/about. **2** *chapter three discusses this topic in detail:* **examine**, explore, study, analyse, go into, deal with, treat, consider, concern itself with, tackle.

discussion noun **1** *a long discussion with her husband:* **conversation**, talk, dialogue, discourse, conference, debate, exchange of views, consultation, deliberation; powwow, chat, tête-à-tête, heart-to-heart; negotiations, parley; informal confab, chit-chat, rap; N. Amer. informal skull session, bull session; formal confabulation, colloquy. **2** *the book's candid discussion of sexual matters:* **examination**, exploration, analysis, study; treatment, consideration.

disdain noun *she looked at him with disdain:* **contempt**, scorn, scornfulness, contemptuousness, derision, disrespect; disparagement, condescension, superciliousness, hauteur, haughtiness, dismissiveness; distaste.
– OPPOSITES respect.
• verb *she disdained exhibitionism:* **scorn**, deride, pour scorn on, regard with contempt, sneer at, sniff at, curl your lip at, look down your nose at, look down on; despise.

disdainful adjective **contemptuous**, scornful, derisive, sneering, withering, disparaging, condescending, patronizing, supercilious, haughty, superior, arrogant, dismissive; informal high and mighty, sniffy, snotty.
– OPPOSITES respectful.

disease noun **illness**, sickness, ill health; infection, ailment, malady, disorder, condition, problem; pestilence, plague, cancer, canker, blight; informal bug, virus; Brit. informal lurgy; dated contagion.

> **WORD LINKS**
> **pathological** relating to or caused by disease

diseased adjective **unhealthy**, ill, sick, unwell, ailing, sickly, unsound; infected, septic, contaminated, blighted, rotten, bad.

disembark verb **get off**, alight, step off, leave; go ashore; land, arrive; N. Amer. deplane; informal pile out.

disembodied adjective **bodiless**, incorporeal, spiritual; intangible, insubstantial, impalpable; ghostly, spectral, phantom, wraithlike.

disembowel verb **gut**, draw; formal eviscerate.

disenchanted adjective **disillusioned**, disappointed, let down, discontented; informal fed up.

disenchantment noun **disillusionment**, disappointment, dissatisfaction, discontent.

disengage verb **1** *I disengaged his hand from mine:* **remove**, detach, disentangle, extricate, separate, release, free, loosen, loose, disconnect, unfasten, unclasp, uncouple, undo, unhook, unhitch, untie, unyoke, disentwine. **2** *American forces disengaged from the country:* **withdraw**, leave, pull out of, quit, retreat from.
– OPPOSITES attach, enter.

disentangle verb **1** *Allen was disentangling a coil of rope:* **untangle**, unravel, untwist, unwind, undo, untie, straighten out, smooth out. **2** *he disentangled his fingers from her hair:* **extricate**, extract, free, remove, disengage, disentwine, release, loosen, detach, unfasten, unclasp, disconnect.

disfigure verb **mar**, spoil, deface, scar, blemish; damage, mutilate, deform, maim, ruin; vandalize.
–OPPOSITES adorn.

disfigurement noun **1** *the disfigurement of Victorian buildings:* **defacement**, spoiling, scarring, mutilation, damaging, vandalizing, ruin. **2** *a facial disfigurement:* **blemish**, defect, discoloration, blotch; scar, pockmark; deformity, malformation, abnormality, injury, wound.

disgorge verb **pour out**, discharge, eject, throw out, emit, expel, spit out, spew out, belch forth, spout; vomit.

disgrace noun **1** *he brought disgrace on the family:* **dishonour**, shame, discredit, ignominy, degradation, disrepute, infamy, scandal, stigma, condemnation, vilification; humiliation, embarrassment, loss of face; Austral. strife. **2** *the unemployment figures are a disgrace:* **scandal**, outrage; affront, insult; informal crime, sin.
–OPPOSITES honour.
• verb **1** *you have disgraced the family name:* **bring shame on**, shame, dishonour, discredit, bring into disrepute, degrade, debase, defame, stigmatize, taint, sully, tarnish, besmirch, stain, blacken, drag through the mud/mire. **2** *he was publicly disgraced:* **discredit**, dishonour, stigmatize; humiliate, chasten, humble, demean, put someone in their place, take down a peg or two, cut down to size.
–OPPOSITES honour.
■ **in disgrace** out of favour, unpopular, under a cloud, disgraced; informal in someone's bad/black books, in the doghouse; NZ informal in the dogbox.

disgraceful adjective **shameful**, shocking, scandalous, deplorable, despicable, contemptible, beyond contempt, beyond the pale, dishonourable, discreditable, reprehensible, base, mean, low, blameworthy, unworthy, ignoble, shabby, inglorious, outrageous, abominable, atrocious, appalling, dreadful, terrible.
–OPPOSITES admirable.

disgruntled adjective **dissatisfied**, discontented, aggrieved, resentful, displeased, unhappy, disappointed, disaffected; annoyed, irked, put out; informal hacked off, browned off, peed off; Brit. informal cheesed off, narked; N. Amer. informal fed up, sore, teed off, ticked off.

disguise verb *he disguised his true feelings:* **camouflage**, conceal, hide, cover up, mask, screen, veil; paper over, gloss over.
–OPPOSITES expose.

disgust noun **revulsion**, repugnance, aversion, distaste, abhorrence, loathing, detestation.
–OPPOSITES delight.
• verb **revolt**, repel, repulse, sicken, horrify, appal, turn someone's stomach; N. Amer. informal gross out.

disgusting adjective **1** *the food was disgusting:* **revolting**, repulsive, sickening, nauseating, stomach-churning, stomach-turning, off-putting, unpalatable, distasteful, foul, abominable; N. Amer. vomitous; informal gross, sick-making. **2** *I find racism disgusting:* **abhorrent**, repellent, loathsome, offensive, appalling, outrageous, objectionable, shocking, horrifying, scandalous, monstrous, vile, odious, obnoxious, detestable, hateful, sickening, beyond the pale; informal gross, ghastly, sick.
–OPPOSITES delicious, delightful.

dish noun **1** *a china dish:* **bowl**, plate, platter, casserole. **2** *vegetarian dishes:* **recipe**, meal, course; (**dishes**) food; fare, cuisine.
■ **dish something out** distribute, dispense, issue, hand out/round, give out, pass out/round; deal out, dole out, share out, allocate, allot, apportion. **dish something up** serve, spoon out, ladle out.

disharmony noun **discord**, friction, strife, conflict, hostility, acrimony, bad blood, bad feeling, enmity, dissension, disagreement, feuding, quarrelling; disunity, division, divisiveness.

d

dishearten verb **discourage**, dispirit, demoralize, cast down, depress, disappoint, dismay; put off, deter, unnerve, daunt.
– OPPOSITES encourage.

disheartened adjective **discouraged**, dispirited, demoralized, deflated, disappointed, let down, despondent, dejected, cast down, downcast, depressed, crestfallen, dismayed; daunted; informal fed up, down in the mouth, down in the dumps.

dishevelled adjective **untidy**, unkempt, scruffy, messy, in a mess, disordered, disarranged, rumpled, bedraggled; uncombed, tousled, tangled, shaggy, straggly, windswept; N. Amer. informal mussed.
– OPPOSITES tidy.

dishonest adjective **fraudulent**, corrupt, swindling, cheating, double-dealing; underhand, crafty, cunning, devious, treacherous, unfair, unjust, dirty, unethical, immoral, unscrupulous, unprincipled; criminal, illegal, unlawful; false, untruthful, deceitful, deceiving, lying; informal crooked, shady, tricky, sharp; Brit. informal bent, dodgy; Austral./NZ informal shonky.

dishonesty noun **fraud**, fraudulence, sharp practice, corruption, cheating, chicanery, double-dealing, deceit, deception, duplicity, lying, falseness, falsity, falsehood, untruthfulness; trickery, underhandedness, subterfuge, skulduggery, treachery, unscrupulousness, criminality, misconduct; informal crookedness, dirty tricks, shenanigans; Brit. informal jiggery-pokery.
– OPPOSITES probity.

dishonour noun **disgrace**, shame, discredit; stigma.
• verb **disgrace**, shame, discredit, bring into disrepute, debase.

dishonourable adjective **disgraceful**, shameful, disreputable, discreditable, ignoble, reprehensible, shabby, shoddy, base, low, improper, unseemly, unworthy.

disillusion verb **disabuse**, enlighten, set straight, open someone's eyes; disenchant, shatter someone's illusions, disappoint.
– OPPOSITES deceive.

disillusioned adjective **disenchanted**, disappointed, let down, discouraged; cynical, sour, negative.

disincentive noun **deterrent**, discouragement; obstacle, impediment, hindrance, obstruction, block, barrier.

disinclined adjective **reluctant**, unwilling, unenthusiastic, hesitant.
– OPPOSITES willing.

disinfect verb **sterilize**, sanitize, clean, cleanse, purify, decontaminate.
– OPPOSITES contaminate.

disingenuous adjective **insincere**, dishonest, deceitful, duplicitous; hypocritical, cynical.

disinherit verb **cut someone out of your will**, cut off.

disintegrate verb **break up**, break apart, fall apart, fall to pieces, fragment, fracture, shatter, splinter; crumble, deteriorate, decay, decompose, collapse.

disinter verb **exhume**, unearth, dig up.

disinterest noun **1** *scholarly disinterest:* **impartiality**, neutrality, objectivity, detachment. **2** *he looked at us with complete disinterest:* **indifference**, lack of interest, unconcern, impassivity.
– OPPOSITES bias.

disinterested adjective **1** *disinterested advice:* **unbiased**, unprejudiced, impartial, neutral, non-partisan, detached, uninvolved, objective, dispassionate, impersonal, clinical; with no axe to grind. **2** *he looked at her with disinterested eyes:* **uninterested**, indifferent, incurious, unconcerned, impassive, detached; informal couldn't-care-less.

disjointed adjective **unconnected**, disconnected, discontinuous, fragmented, disordered, muddled, mixed up, jumbled, garbled.

dislike verb **find distasteful**, regard with distaste, have an aversion to, disapprove of, object to, take exception to, resent; hate, loathe, detest, despise, abhor.
– OPPOSITES like, love.
• noun **distaste**, aversion, disfavour, antipathy, resentment; disgust, hatred, loathing, detestation, repugnance, abhorrence.
– OPPOSITES liking, love, predilection.

dislodge verb **1** *replace any stones you dislodge:* **displace**, knock out of place, move, shift; knock over, upset. **2** *economic sanctions failed to dislodge the dictator:* **remove**, force out, drive out, oust, eject, get rid of, evict, unseat, depose, topple.

disloyal adjective **unfaithful**, false, untrue, inconstant; treacherous, subversive, seditious, unpatriotic, two-faced, double-dealing, double-crossing, deceitful; informal back-stabbing, two-timing; literary perfidious.

disloyalty noun **unfaithfulness**, infidelity, inconstancy, faithlessness, betrayal; duplicity, double-dealing, treachery, treason, subversion, sedition; informal back-stabbing, two-timing; literary perfidy, perfidiousness.

dismal adjective **1** *a dismal look:* **gloomy**, glum, melancholy, morose, doleful, woebegone, forlorn, dejected, dispirited, downcast, despondent, disconsolate, miserable, sad, unhappy, sorrowful, wretched; informal fed up, down in the dumps/mouth. **2** *a dismal hall:* **dingy**, dim, dark, gloomy, dreary, drab, dull, bleak, cheerless, depressing, uninviting, unwelcoming. **3** (informal) *a dismal performance.* See **POOR** sense 2.
– OPPOSITES cheerful, bright.

dismantle verb **take apart**, take to pieces/bits, pull to pieces, disassemble, break up, strip down.
– OPPOSITES assemble, build.

dismay verb **appal**, horrify, shock, shake; disconcert, take aback, alarm, unnerve, unsettle, throw off balance, discompose; disturb.
– OPPOSITES delight, please.
• noun **alarm**, shock, surprise, consternation, concern, perturbation, disquiet, discomposure.
– OPPOSITES pleasure, relief.

dismember verb **cut up**, chop up, carve up, joint; pull apart, butcher.

dismiss verb **1** *the president dismissed five ministers:* **give someone their notice**, get rid of, discharge; lay off, make redundant; informal sack, give someone the sack, fire, boot out, give someone the boot/elbow/push, give someone their marching orders, show someone the door; Brit. informal give someone their cards; Military cashier. **2** *the guards were dismissed:* **send away**, let go. **3** *he dismissed all morbid thoughts:* **banish**, set aside, put out of your mind; reject, deny, repudiate, spurn.
– OPPOSITES engage.

dismissal noun **1** *the threat of dismissal:* **your notice**, discharge; redundancy, laying off; informal the sack, sacking, firing, the push, the boot, the axe, the elbow, your marching orders; Brit. informal your cards, the chop. **2** *a condescending dismissal:* **rejection**, repudiation, repulse, non-acceptance.
– OPPOSITES recruitment.

dismissive adjective **contemptuous**, disdainful, scornful, sneering, disparaging; informal sniffy.
– OPPOSITES admiring.

disobedient adjective **insubordinate**, unruly, wayward, badly behaved, naughty, delinquent, troublesome, rebellious, defiant, mutinous, recalcitrant, wilful, intractable, obstreperous; Brit. informal bolshie.

disobey verb **defy**, go against, flout, contravene, infringe, transgress, violate; disregard, ignore, pay no heed to.

disorder noun **1** *he hates disorder:* **untidiness**, disorderliness, mess, disarray, chaos, confusion; clutter, jumble; a muddle, a shambles. **2** *incidents of public disorder:* **unrest**, disturbance, disruption, upheaval, turmoil, mayhem, pandemonium; violence, fighting, rioting, lawlessness, anarchy; breach of the peace, fracas, rumpus, melee; informal aggro. **3** *a blood disorder:* **disease**, infection, complaint, condition, affliction, malady, sickness, illness, ailment, infirmity.
– OPPOSITES tidiness, peace.

disordered adjective **1 untidy**, messy, in a mess, disorganized, chaotic, confused, jumbled, muddled; Brit. informal shambolic. **2 dysfunctional**, disturbed, unsettled, unbalanced.

disorderly adjective **1** *a disorderly desk:* **untidy**, disorganized, messy, cluttered; in disarray, in a mess,

jumbled, in a muddle, at sixes and sevens; informal higgledy-piggledy; Brit. informal shambolic. **2** *disorderly behaviour:* **unruly**, boisterous, rough, rowdy, wild, riotous; disruptive, troublesome, lawless.
– OPPOSITES tidy, orderly, peaceful.

d

disorganized adjective **1** *the campaign was hopelessly disorganized:* **unmethodical**, unsystematic, undisciplined, badly organized, inefficient; haphazard, hit-or-miss, careless, sloppy, slapdash, chaotic; Brit. informal shambolic. **2** *a disorganized tool box:* **disorderly**, disordered, jumbled, muddled, untidy, messy, topsy-turvy; in disorder, in disarray, in a mess, in a muddle, in a shambles; informal higgledy-piggledy.
– OPPOSITES organized.

disorientated, **disoriented** adjective **confused**, bewildered, at sea; lost, adrift, off-course, having lost your bearings.

disown verb **reject**, cast off/aside, abandon, renounce, deny; turn your back on, wash your hands of, have nothing more to do with.

disparage verb **belittle**, denigrate, deprecate, play down, trivialize; ridicule, deride, mock, scorn, scoff at, sneer at; run down, defame, discredit, speak badly of, cast aspersions on, impugn, vilify, traduce, criticize; N. Amer. slur; informal do down, pick holes in, knock, slam, pan, bad-mouth, pooh-pooh; Brit. informal rubbish, slate.
– OPPOSITES praise.

disparaging adjective **derogatory**, deprecatory, denigratory, belittling; critical, scathing, negative, unfavourable, uncomplimentary, uncharitable; contemptuous, scornful, snide, disdainful; informal bitchy, catty.
– OPPOSITES complimentary.

disparate adjective **contrasting**, different, differing, dissimilar; varying, various, diverse, diversified, heterogeneous, distinct, separate, divergent; literary divers.
– OPPOSITES homogeneous.

disparity noun **discrepancy**, inconsistency, imbalance; variance, variation, divergence, gap, gulf; difference, dissimilarity, contrast.
– OPPOSITES similarity.

dispassionate adjective **objective**, detached, neutral, disinterested, impartial, non-partisan, unbiased, unprejudiced; scientific, analytical.
– OPPOSITES biased.

dispatch verb **1** *all the messages were dispatched:* **send**, post, mail, forward. **2** *the business was dispatched in the morning:* **deal with**, finish, conclude, settle, discharge, perform; expedite, push through; informal make short work of. **3** *the good guy dispatched a host of villains:* **kill**, put to death; slaughter, butcher, massacre, wipe out, exterminate, eliminate; murder, assassinate, execute; informal bump off, do in, do away with, top, take out, blow away; N. Amer. informal ice, rub out, waste; literary slay.
• noun **1** *goods ready for dispatch:* **sending**, posting, mailing. **2** *the latest dispatch from the front:* **communication**, communiqué, bulletin, report, statement, letter, message; news, intelligence; literary tidings.

dispel verb **banish**, eliminate, drive away/off, get rid of; relieve, allay, ease, quell.

dispensable adjective **expendable**, disposable, replaceable, inessential, non-essential; unnecessary, redundant, superfluous, surplus to requirements.

dispense verb **1** *staff dispensed cooling drinks:* **distribute**, pass round, hand out, dole out, dish out, share out. **2** *the soldiers dispensed summary justice:* **administer**, deliver, issue, discharge, deal out, mete out. **3** *the product cannot be dispensed without a prescription:* **prepare**, make up; supply, provide, sell.
■ **dispense with 1** *let's dispense with the formalities:* waive, omit, drop, leave out, forgo; do away with; informal give something a miss. **2** *he dispensed with his crutches:* get rid of, throw away/out, dispose of, discard; informal ditch, scrap, dump, chuck out/away; Brit. informal get shot of.

disperse verb **1** *the crowd began to disperse | police dispersed the demonstrators:* **break up**, split up, disband, scatter, leave, go their separate ways; drive away/off, chase

away. **2** *the fog finally dispersed:* **dissipate**, dissolve, melt away, fade away, clear, lift. **3** *seeds dispersed by birds:* **scatter**, disseminate, distribute, spread.
– OPPOSITES assemble, gather.

dispirited adjective **disheartened**, discouraged, demoralized, downcast, low, low-spirited, dejected, downhearted, depressed, disconsolate; informal fed up.
– OPPOSITES heartened.

dispiriting adjective **disheartening**, depressing, discouraging, daunting, demoralizing.

displace verb **1** *roof tiles displaced by gales:* **dislodge**, dislocate, move, shift, knock out of place. **2** *English displaced the local language:* **replace**, take the place of, supplant, supersede.

display noun **1** *a display of dolls and puppets | a motorcycle display:* **exhibition**, exposition, array, arrangement, presentation, demonstration; spectacle, show, parade, pageant, spectacle. **2** *his display of concern:* **manifestation**, expression, show.
• verb **1** *the Crown jewels are displayed in London:* **exhibit**, show, put on show; arrange, array, present, lay out, set out, dispose. **2** *she proudly displayed her diamond wedding band:* **show off**, parade, flourish, flaunt. **3** *she displayed a vein of sharp humour:* **manifest**, reveal; demonstrate, show; formal evince.
– OPPOSITES conceal.

displease verb **annoy**, irritate, anger, irk, vex, pique, gall, nettle; put out, upset.

displeasure noun **annoyance**, irritation, crossness, anger, vexation, pique; dissatisfaction, discontent, disgruntlement, disapproval.
– OPPOSITES satisfaction.

disposable adjective **throwaway**, single-use; biodegradable.

disposal noun **throwing away**, discarding; removal; collection; informal dumping, chucking away.

dispose verb *material considerations may dispose them to compromise:* **incline**, encourage, persuade, predispose, make willing, prompt, lead, motivate; sway, influence.
■ **dispose of** throw away/out, get rid of, discard, jettison, scrap; informal dump, ditch, chuck out/away; Brit. informal get shot of; N. Amer. informal trash.

disposed adjective **1** *they are philanthropically disposed:* **inclined**, predisposed, minded. **2** *we are not disposed to argue:* **willing**, inclined, prepared, ready, minded, in the mood.

disposition noun **1** *a nervous disposition:* **temperament**, nature, character, constitution, make-up, mentality. **2** *the disposition of the armed forces:* **arrangement**, positioning, placement, configuration; set-up, line-up, layout.

dispossess verb **divest**, strip, rob, cheat out of, deprive; informal do out of.

disproportionate adjective **out of proportion**, inappropriate, incommensurate; inordinate, unreasonable, excessive, undue.

disprove verb **refute**, prove false, rebut, falsify, debunk, negate, invalidate; informal shoot full of holes, blow out of the water.

disputable adjective **debatable**, open to debate/question, arguable, contentious, contestable, moot, questionable, doubtful; informal iffy.

dispute noun **1** *a subject of dispute:* **debate**, discussion, disputation, argument, controversy, disagreement, dissension, conflict, friction, strife, discord. **2** *they have settled their dispute:* **quarrel**, argument, altercation, squabble, falling-out, disagreement, difference of opinion, clash, wrangle; Brit. row; informal tiff, spat, scrap; Brit. informal barney, ding-dong.
– OPPOSITES agreement.
• verb **1** *George disputed with him:* **debate**, discuss, exchange views; quarrel, argue, disagree, clash, fall out, wrangle, bicker, squabble. **2** *they disputed his findings:* **challenge**, contest, question, call into question, impugn, quibble over, contradict, argue about, disagree with, take issue with.
– OPPOSITES accept.

disqualified adjective **banned**, barred, debarred; ineligible.
– OPPOSITES allowed.

d

disquiet noun *grave public disquiet:* **unease**, uneasiness, worry, anxiety, anxiousness, concern; consternation, upset, angst; agitation, restlessness, fretfulness; informal jitteriness.
– OPPOSITES calm.
• verb *I was disquieted by the news:* **perturb**, agitate, upset, disturb, unnerve, unsettle, discompose, disconcert; make uneasy, worry, make anxious; trouble, concern, make fretful, make restless.

disregard verb *Annie disregarded the remark:* **ignore**, take no notice of, pay no attention/heed to; overlook, turn a blind eye to, turn a deaf ear to, shut your eyes to, gloss over, brush off/aside, shrug off.
– OPPOSITES heed.
• noun *blithe disregard for the rules:* **indifference**, non-observance, inattention, heedlessness, neglect.
– OPPOSITES attention.

disrepair noun **dilapidation**, decrepitude, shabbiness, ricketiness, collapse, ruin, neglect, disuse.

disreputable adjective **bad**, unwholesome, villainous; unsavoury, slippery, seedy, sleazy; informal crooked, shady, shifty; Brit. informal dodgy.
– OPPOSITES respectable.

disrepute noun **disgrace**, shame, dishonour, infamy, notoriety, ignominy, bad reputation.
– OPPOSITES honour.

disrespect noun **1** *disrespect for authority:* **contempt**, lack of respect, scorn, disregard, disdain. **2** *he meant no disrespect to anybody:* **discourtesy**, rudeness, impoliteness, incivility, ill/bad manners; insolence, impudence, impertinence.
– OPPOSITES esteem.

disrespectful adjective **discourteous**, rude, impolite, uncivil, ill-mannered, bad-mannered; insolent, impudent, impertinent, cheeky, flippant, insubordinate.
– OPPOSITES polite.

disrupt verb **disturb**, interfere with, upset, unsettle, destabilize, play havoc with, damage; obstruct, hinder, impede, hold up, delay, interrupt.

disruptive adjective **troublesome**, unruly, badly behaved, rowdy, disorderly, undisciplined, wild; unmanageable, uncontrollable, uncooperative, out of control, obstreperous, truculent; formal refractory.
– OPPOSITES well behaved.

dissatisfaction noun **discontent**, discontentment, disaffection, disquiet, unhappiness, disgruntlement, vexation, annoyance, irritation.

dissatisfied adjective **discontented**, malcontent, unsatisfied, disappointed, disaffected, unhappy, displeased; disgruntled, aggrieved, vexed, annoyed, irritated.
– OPPOSITES contented.

dissect verb **1** *the body was dissected:* **cut up/open**, dismember. **2** *the text of the gospels was dissected:* **analyse**, examine, study, scrutinize, pore over, investigate, go over with a fine-tooth comb.

dissection noun **1** *the dissection of the body:* **cutting up/open**, dismemberment; autopsy, postmortem. **2** *a thorough dissection of their policies:* **analysis**, examination, study, scrutiny, investigation; evaluation, assessment.

disseminate verb **spread**, circulate, distribute, disperse, promulgate, propagate, publicize, communicate, pass on, put about, make known.

dissent verb **differ**, disagree, demur, fail to agree, be at variance/odds, take issue; protest, object.
– OPPOSITES agree, conform.
• noun **disagreement**, difference of opinion, argument, dispute; disapproval, objection, protest, opposition; friction, strife.
– OPPOSITES agreement.

dissenter noun **dissident**, objector, protester, disputant; rebel, renegade, maverick, independent; heretic.

dissertation noun **essay**, thesis, treatise, paper, study, discourse, tract, monograph.

disservice noun **unkindness**, bad/ill turn, disfavour; injury, harm, hurt, damage, wrong, injustice.
– OPPOSITES favour.

dissident noun **dissenter**, objector, protester; rebel, revolutionary,

subversive, agitator, insurgent, insurrectionist, refusenik.
– OPPOSITES conformist.
• adjective **dissenting**, disagreeing; opposing, objecting, protesting, rebellious, rebelling, revolutionary, nonconformist.
– OPPOSITES conforming.

dissimilar adjective **different**, differing, unalike, variant, diverse, divergent, heterogeneous, disparate, unrelated, distinct, contrasting.

dissimilarity noun **difference**, variance, diversity, heterogeneity, disparateness, disparity, distinctness, contrast, non-uniformity, divergence.

dissipate verb **1** *his anger dissipated:* **disappear**, vanish, evaporate, dissolve, melt away, melt into thin air, be dispelled; disperse, scatter. **2** *he dissipated his fortune:* **squander**, fritter away, misspend, waste, be prodigal with, spend like water; use up, consume, run through, go through; informal blow, splurge.

dissipated adjective **dissolute**, debauched, decadent, intemperate, profligate, self-indulgent, wild, depraved; licentious, promiscuous; drunken.
– OPPOSITES ascetic.

dissipation noun **1** *tales of drunken dissipation:* **debauchery**, decadence, dissoluteness, dissolution, intemperance, excess, profligacy, self-indulgence, wildness; depravity, degeneracy; licentiousness, promiscuity; drunkenness. **2** *the dissipation of our mineral wealth:* **squandering**, frittering away, waste, misspending.

dissociate verb *the word 'spiritual' has become dissociated from religion:* **separate**, detach, disconnect, sever, cut off, divorce; isolate, alienate.
– OPPOSITES relate.

dissociation noun **separation**, disconnection, detachment, severance, divorce, split; segregation, division; literary sundering.
– OPPOSITES union.

dissolute adjective **dissipated**, debauched, decadent, intemperate, profligate, self-indulgent, wild, depraved; licentious, promiscuous; drunken.
– OPPOSITES ascetic.

dissolution noun **1** *the dissolution of parliament:* **cessation**, conclusion, end, ending, termination, winding up/down, discontinuation, suspension, disbanding. **2** *a life of dissolution.* See DISSIPATION sense 1.

dissolve verb **1** *his hopes dissolved:* **disappear**, vanish, melt away, evaporate, disperse, dissipate; dwindle, fade away, wither. **2** *the crowd dissolved:* **disperse**, disband, break up, scatter. **3** *the assembly was dissolved:* **disband**, bring to an end, end, terminate, discontinue, close down, wind up/down, suspend; adjourn. **4** *their marriage was dissolved:* **annul**, nullify, void, invalidate, revoke.

dissonant adjective **inharmonious**, discordant, unmelodious, atonal, off-key, cacophonous.
– OPPOSITES harmonious.

dissuade verb **discourage**, deter, prevent, divert, stop; talk out of, persuade against, advise against, argue out of.
– OPPOSITES encourage.

distance noun **1** *they measured the distance:* **interval**, space, span, gap, extent; length, width, breadth, depth; range, reach. **2** *a mix of warmth and distance:* **aloofness**, remoteness, detachment, unfriendliness; reserve, reticence, restraint, formality; informal stand-offishness.
■ **distance yourself from** *he distanced himself from Hollywood:* dissociate yourself from, reject, withdraw from, turn your back on, have nothing more to do with, keep your distance from, sever connections with, disown.

distant adjective **1** *distant parts of the world:* **faraway**, far-off, far-flung, remote, out of the way, outlying. **2** *a distant memory:* **vague**, faint, dim, indistinct, unclear, indefinite, sketchy, hazy. **3** *a distant family connection:* **remote**, indirect, slight. **4** *my father was always very distant:* **aloof**, reserved, remote, detached, unapproachable; withdrawn, taciturn, uncommunicative, undemonstrative, unforthcoming, unresponsive, unfriendly; informal stand-offish. **5** *a distant look in his eyes:* **distracted**, absent, faraway, detached, vague.
– OPPOSITES near, close, clear.

d

distaste noun **dislike**, aversion, disapproval, disapprobation, disdain, repugnance.
–OPPOSITES liking.

distasteful adjective **unpleasant**, disagreeable, displeasing, undesirable; objectionable, offensive, unsavoury, unpalatable, obnoxious.
–OPPOSITES agreeable.

distended adjective **swollen**, bloated, dilated, engorged, enlarged, inflated, expanded, extended, bulging, protuberant.

distil verb **purify**, refine, filter, treat, process; produce.

distinct adjective **1** *two distinct categories:* **discrete**, separate, different, unconnected; distinctive, contrasting. **2** *the tail has distinct black tips:* **clear**, well defined, unmistakable, easily distinguishable; recognizable, visible, obvious, pronounced, prominent, striking.
–OPPOSITES overlapping, indefinite.

distinction noun **1** *distinctions that we observed:* **difference**, contrast, variation; division, differentiation, dividing line, gulf, gap. **2** *a painter of distinction:* **importance**, significance, note, consequence; renown, prominence, eminence, pre-eminence, repute, reputation; merit, worth, greatness, excellence, quality. **3** *he had served with distinction:* **honour**, credit, excellence, merit.
–OPPOSITES similarity, mediocrity.

distinctive adjective **distinguishing**, characteristic, typical, individual, particular, peculiar, unique, exclusive, special.
–OPPOSITES common.

distinctly adverb **1** *there's something distinctly odd about him:* **decidedly**, markedly, definitely; unmistakably, manifestly, patently; Brit. informal dead. **2** *Laura spoke quite distinctly:* **clearly**, plainly, intelligibly, audibly.

distinguish verb **1** *he is capable of distinguishing reality from fantasy:* **differentiate**, tell apart, discriminate between, tell the difference between. **2** *he could distinguish shapes in the dark:* **discern**, see, perceive, make out; detect, recognize, identify. **3** *this is what distinguishes history from other disciplines:* **separate**, set apart, make distinctive, make different; single out, mark off, characterize.

distinguishable adjective **discernible**, recognizable, identifiable, detectable.

distinguished adjective **eminent**, famous, renowned, prominent, well known; esteemed, respected, illustrious, acclaimed, celebrated, great; notable, important, influential.
–OPPOSITES unknown, obscure.

distinguishing adjective **distinctive**, differentiating, characteristic, typical, peculiar, singular, unique.

distorted adjective **1** *a distorted face:* **twisted**, warped, contorted, buckled, deformed, malformed, misshapen, disfigured, crooked, awry, out of shape. **2** *a distorted version:* **misrepresented**, perverted, twisted, falsified, misreported, misstated, garbled, inaccurate; biased, prejudiced, slanted, coloured, loaded, weighted.

distract verb **divert**, sidetrack, draw away, disturb, put off.

distracted adjective **preoccupied**, inattentive, vague, abstracted, absent-minded, faraway, in a world of your own; bemused, confused, bewildered; troubled, harassed, worried; informal miles away, not with it.
–OPPOSITES attentive.

distracting adjective **disturbing**, unsettling, intrusive, disconcerting, bothersome, off-putting.

distraction noun **1** *a distraction from the real issues:* **diversion**, interruption, disturbance, interference, hindrance. **2** *frivolous distractions:* **amusement**, entertainment, diversion, recreation, leisure pursuit.

distraught adjective **worried**, upset, distressed, fraught; overcome, overwrought, beside yourself, out of your mind, desperate, hysterical, worked up, at your wits' end; informal in a state.

distress noun **1** *she concealed her distress:* **anguish**, suffering, pain, agony, torment, heartache, heartbreak; sorrow, sadness, unhappiness. **2** *a ship in distress:* **danger**,

peril, difficulty, trouble, jeopardy, risk.
– OPPOSITES happiness, safety.
• verb *he was distressed by the trial:* **upset**, pain, make miserable; trouble, worry, bother, perturb, disturb, disquiet, agitate; informal cut up.
– OPPOSITES calm, please.

distressing adjective **upsetting**, worrying, disturbing, disquieting, painful, traumatic, agonizing, harrowing; sad, saddening, heart-breaking, heart-rending.
– OPPOSITES comforting.

distribute verb **1** *the proceeds were distributed among his creditors:* **give out**, deal out, dole out, dish out, hand out/round; share out, divide out/up, parcel out. **2** *the newsletter is distributed free:* **circulate**, issue, hand out, deliver, disseminate. **3** *a hundred and thirty different species are distributed worldwide:* **disperse**, scatter, spread.
– OPPOSITES collect.

distribution noun **1** *the distribution of aid:* **giving out**, dealing out, doling out, handing out/round, issuing; allocation, sharing out, dividing up/out; supply, delivery, transportation. **2** *the geographical distribution of plants:* **spread**, dissemination, arrangement; placement, position, location. **3** *the statistical distribution of the problem:* **frequency**, prevalence, incidence, commonness.

district noun **neighbourhood**, area, region, locality, locale, community, quarter, sector, zone, territory; ward, parish; informal neck of the woods.

distrust noun **mistrust**, suspicion, wariness, chariness, lack of trust, lack of confidence; scepticism, doubt, doubtfulness, cynicism; misgivings, qualms, disbelief.
• verb **mistrust**, be suspicious of, be wary/chary of, be leery of, regard with suspicion, suspect; be sceptical of, have doubts about, doubt, be unsure of/about, have misgivings about.

disturb verb **1** *I hope we won't be disturbed:* **interrupt**, intrude on, butt in on, barge in on; distract, disrupt, bother, trouble, pester, harass; informal hassle. **2** *don't disturb his papers:* **move**, rearrange, mix up, interfere with, mess up, muddle. **3** *waters disturbed by winds:* **agitate**, churn up, stir up; cloud, muddy. **4** *he wasn't disturbed by the allegations:* **perturb**, trouble, concern, worry, upset; agitate, fluster, discomfit, disconcert, dismay, distress, discompose, unsettle, ruffle.

disturbance noun **1** *a disturbance to local residents:* **disruption**, distraction, interference; bother, trouble, inconvenience, upset, annoyance, irritation, intrusion; informal hassle. **2** *disturbances in the town centre:* **riot**, fracas, upheaval, brawl, street fight, melee, free-for-all, ruckus, rumpus; informal ructions. **3** *emotional disturbance:* **trouble**, perturbation, distress, worry, upset, agitation, discomposure, discomfiture.

disturbed adjective **1** *disturbed sleep:* **disrupted**, interrupted, fitful, intermittent, broken. **2** *disturbed children:* **troubled**, distressed, upset, distraught; unbalanced, unstable, disordered, dysfunctional, maladjusted, neurotic, unhinged, damaged; informal screwed up, mixed up.

disturbing adjective **worrying**, troubling, upsetting; distressing, discomfiting, disconcerting, disquieting, unsettling, dismaying, alarming, frightening.

disunity noun **disagreement**, dissent, dissension, argument, arguing, quarrelling, feuding; conflict, strife, friction, discord.

disuse noun **neglect**, abandonment, desertion; formal desuetude.

disused adjective **unused**, idle; abandoned, deserted, vacated, unoccupied, uninhabited.

ditch noun **trench**, trough, channel, dyke, drain, gutter, gully, watercourse, conduit.

dither verb **hesitate**, falter, waver, vacillate, change your mind, be in two minds, be indecisive, be undecided; Brit. haver; informal shilly-shally, dilly-dally.

dive verb **1** *they dived into the clear water | the plane was diving towards the ground:* **plunge**, nosedive, jump head first, bellyflop; plummet, fall,

drop, pitch. **2** *they dived for cover:* **leap**, jump, lunge, throw/fling yourself, go headlong, duck.
•noun **1** *a dive into the pool:* **plunge**, nosedive, jump, bellyflop; fall, drop, swoop, pitch. **2** *a sideways dive:* **lunge**, spring, jump, leap.

d

diverge verb **1** *the two roads diverged:* **separate**, part, fork, divide, split, bifurcate. **2** *areas where our views diverge:* **differ**, be different, be dissimilar; disagree, be at variance/odds, conflict, clash.
– OPPOSITES converge, agree.

divergence noun **1** *the divergence of the human and ape lineages:* **separation**, dividing, parting, forking, bifurcation. **2** *a marked political divergence:* **difference**, dissimilarity, variance, disparity; disagreement, incompatibility, mismatch.

divergent adjective **differing**, varying, different, dissimilar, unalike, disparate, contrasting, contrastive; conflicting, incompatible, contradictory, at odds, at variance.
– OPPOSITES similar.

diverse adjective **various**, sundry, manifold, multiple; varied, varying, miscellaneous, assorted, mixed, diversified, divergent, heterogeneous; different, differing, distinct, unlike, dissimilar; literary divers, myriad.

diversify verb **branch out**, expand, enlarge, grow, develop, restructure, modernize; vary, modify, alter, change, transform.

diversion noun **1** *the diversion of 19 rivers:* **re-routing**, redirection, deflection, deviation, divergence. **2** *traffic diversions:* **detour**, deviation, alternative route. **3** *the noise created a diversion:* **distraction**, disturbance, smokescreen; informal red herring. **4** *a city full of diversions:* **entertainment**, amusement, pastime, delight; fun, recreation, pleasure.

diversity noun **variety**, miscellany, assortment, mixture, mix, melange, range, array, multiplicity; variation, variance, diverseness, diversification, heterogeneity, difference.
– OPPOSITES uniformity.

divert verb **1** *a plan to divert Siberia's rivers:* **re-route**, redirect, change the course of, deflect, channel. **2** *he diverted her from her studies:* **distract**, sidetrack, disturb, draw away, put off. **3** *the story diverted them:* **amuse**, entertain, distract, delight, enchant, interest, fascinate, absorb, engross, rivet, grip, hold the attention of.

diverting adjective **entertaining**, amusing, enjoyable, pleasing, agreeable, delightful, appealing; interesting, fascinating, intriguing, absorbing, riveting, compelling; humorous, funny, witty, comical.
– OPPOSITES boring.

divest verb **deprive**, strip, dispossess, rob, cheat/trick out of.

divide verb **1** *he divided his kingdom into four:* **split**, cut up, carve up; dissect, bisect, halve, quarter. **2** *a curtain divided her cabin from the galley:* **separate**, segregate, partition, screen off, section off, split off. **3** *the stairs divide at the mezzanine:* **diverge**, separate, part, branch, fork, split, bifurcate. **4** *they divided the cash between them:* **share out**, portion out, ration out, parcel out, deal out, dole out, dish out, distribute, dispense; informal divvy up. **5** *he aimed to divide his opponents:* **disunite**, drive apart, drive a wedge between, break up, split, set at variance/odds; separate, isolate, estrange, alienate. **6** *living things are divided into three categories:* **classify**, sort, categorize, order, group, arrange, grade, rank.
– OPPOSITES unify, join, converge.
•noun *the sectarian divide:* **breach**, gulf, gap, split; borderline, boundary, dividing line.

dividend noun **1** *an annual dividend:* **share**, portion, premium, return, gain, profit; informal cut, rake-off; Brit. informal divvy. **2** *the research will produce dividends in the future:* **benefit**, advantage, gain; bonus.

divination noun **fortune telling**, divining, prophecy, prediction, soothsaying; clairvoyance.

divine[1] adjective **1** *a divine being:* **godly**, angelic; heavenly, celestial, holy. **2** *divine worship:* **religious**, holy, sacred, sanctified, consecrated, blessed, devotional.
– OPPOSITES mortal, infernal.

divine[2] verb *he somehow divined that the man was bluffing:* **guess**, surmise, conjecture, deduce, infer; discern, intuit, perceive, recognize, see, realize, appreciate, understand, grasp, comprehend; informal figure out; Brit. informal twig, suss.

divinity noun **1** *they denied Christ's divinity:* **divine nature**, divineness, godliness, deity, godhead. **2** *the study of divinity:* **theology**, religious studies, religion, scripture. **3** *a female divinity:* **deity**, god, goddess, divine being.

division noun **1** *the division of the island | cell division:* **dividing**, break-up, carving up, splitting, dissection, bisection; partitioning, separation, segregation. **2** *the division of his estates:* **sharing out**, parcelling out, allocation, apportionment. **3** *the division between nomadic and urban cultures:* **dividing line**, divide, boundary, borderline, border, demarcation line; gap, gulf. **4** *each class is divided into nine divisions:* **section**, subsection, subdivision, category, class, group, grouping, set. **5** *an independent division of the executive:* **department**, branch, arm, wing, sector, section, subsection, subdivision, subsidiary. **6** *the causes of social division:* **disunity**, disunion, conflict, discord, disagreement, alienation, isolation.

divisive adjective **alienating**, estranging, isolating, schismatic.
– OPPOSITES unifying.

divorce noun **1** **dissolution of marriage**, annulment, official separation. **2** *a growing divorce between the church and people:* **separation**, division, split, disunity, estrangement, alienation; schism, gulf, chasm.
• verb *religion cannot be divorced from morality:* **separate**, disconnect, divide, dissociate, detach, isolate, alienate, set apart, cut off.

divulge verb **disclose**, reveal, tell, communicate, pass on, publish, broadcast, proclaim; expose, uncover, make public, give away, let slip; informal spill the beans about, let on about.
– OPPOSITES conceal.

dizzy adjective **giddy**, light-headed, faint, unsteady, shaky, muzzy, wobbly; informal woozy.

do verb **1** *she did most of the work herself:* **carry out**, undertake, discharge, execute, perform, accomplish, achieve; bring about, engineer; informal pull off; formal effectuate. **2** *they can do as they please:* **act**, behave, conduct yourself, acquit yourself. **3** *regular coffee will do:* **suffice**, be adequate, be satisfactory, fill/fit the bill, serve your purpose, meet your needs. **4** *the company is doing a new range this spring:* **make**, create, produce, work on, design, manufacture. **5** *each room was done in a different style:* **decorate**, furnish, deck out, finish; Brit. informal do out. **6** *her maid did her hair:* **style**, arrange, adjust, prepare; informal fix. **7** *show me how to do these equations:* **work out**, figure out, calculate; solve, resolve. **8** *she's doing archaeology:* **study**, read, learn; N. Amer. major in.
• noun (Brit. informal) *he invited us to a do:* **party**, reception, gathering, celebration, function; informal bash, shindig; Brit. informal knees-up, beanfeast, bunfight.
■ **do away with 1** *they want to do away with the old customs:* abolish, get rid of, discard, remove, eliminate, discontinue, stop, end, terminate, put an end/stop to, dispense with, drop, abandon, give up; informal scrap, ditch, dump. **2** (informal) *she tried to do away with her husband.* See KILL verb sense 1. **do something up 1** *she did her shoelace up:* fasten, tie, lace, knot; make fast, secure. **2** (informal) *he's had his house done up:* renovate, refurbish, refit, redecorate, decorate, revamp, make over, modernize, improve, spruce up, smarten up; informal give something a facelift; N. Amer. informal rehab. **do without** forgo, dispense with, abstain from, refrain from, eschew, give up, cut out, renounce, manage without; formal forswear.

docile adjective **compliant**, obedient, pliant, submissive, deferential, unassertive, cooperative, amenable, accommodating, biddable.
– OPPOSITES disobedient, wilful.

dock[1] noun *his boat was moored at the dock:* **harbour**, marina, port; wharf, quay, pier, jetty, landing stage.

d

d

• **verb** *the ship docked:* **moor**, berth, put in, tie up, anchor.

dock² **verb 1** *they docked the money from his salary:* **deduct**, subtract, remove, debit, take off/away; informal knock off. **2** *workers had their pay docked:* **reduce**, cut, decrease. **3** *the dog's tail was docked:* **cut off**, cut short, shorten, crop, lop; remove, amputate, detach, sever, chop off, take off.

docket (Brit.) **noun document**, chit, coupon, voucher, certificate, counterfoil, bill, receipt, ticket; Brit. informal chitty.

doctor **noun physician**, clinician; general practitioner, GP, consultant, registrar; Brit. house officer, houseman; N. Amer. intern, extern; informal doc, medic; Brit. informal quack.
• **verb 1** *the reports have been doctored:* **falsify**, tamper with, interfere with, alter, change; forge, fake; Brit. informal fiddle. **2** *he denied doctoring Stephen's drink:* **adulterate**, tamper with, lace; informal spike, dope.

doctrinaire **adjective dogmatic**, rigid, inflexible, uncompromising; authoritarian, intolerant, fanatical, zealous, extreme.

doctrine **noun creed**, credo, dogma, belief, teaching, ideology; tenet, maxim, canon, principle, precept.

document **noun paper**, certificate, deed, contract, agreement.
• **verb record**, register, report, log, chronicle, put on record, write down; detail, note, describe.

documentary **adjective 1** *documentary evidence:* **recorded**, documented, registered, written, chronicled, archived, on record/paper, in writing. **2** *a documentary film:* **factual**, non-fictional.

doddery **adjective tottering**, staggering, shuffling, shambling, shaky, unsteady, wobbly; feeble, frail, weak.

dodge **verb 1** *she dodged into a telephone booth:* **dart**, bolt, dive, slip. **2** *he managed to dodge the two men:* **elude**, evade, avoid, escape, run away from, lose, shake off; informal give someone the slip. **3** *the minister tried to dodge the debate:* **avoid**, evade, get out of, back out of, sidestep; informal duck, wriggle out of; Austral./NZ informal duck-shove.
• **noun** *a clever dodge | a tax dodge:* **ruse**, ploy, scheme, tactic, stratagem, subterfuge, trick, hoax, wile, cheat, deception, blind; swindle, fraud; informal scam, con trick; Brit. informal wheeze; N. Amer. informal grift.

dodgy **adjective** (Brit. informal) **1** *a dodgy second-hand car salesman.* See DISHONEST. **2** *dodgy champagne:* **second-rate**, third-rate, substandard, inferior, low-quality; poor, cheap.

dog **noun hound**, canine, mongrel; pup, puppy; informal pooch, mutt.
• **verb** *the scheme was dogged by bad weather:* **plague**, beset, bedevil, beleaguer, blight, trouble.

> **WORD LINKS**
> **canine** relating to dogs

dogged **adjective tenacious**, determined, resolute, resolved, purposeful, persistent, persevering, single-minded, tireless; strong-willed, steadfast, staunch.
– OPPOSITES half-hearted.

dogma **noun teaching**, belief, tenet, principle, precept, maxim, article of faith, canon; creed, credo, doctrine, ideology.

dogmatic **adjective opinionated**, assertive, insistent, emphatic, adamant, doctrinaire, authoritarian, imperious, dictatorial, uncompromising, unyielding, inflexible, rigid.

dogsbody **noun** (Brit. informal) **drudge**, menial, factotum, servant, slave, lackey, minion, man/girl Friday; informal gofer; Brit. informal skivvy.

doing **noun 1** *the doing of the act constitutes the offence:* **performance**, performing, carrying out, execution, implementation, implementing, achievement, accomplishment, realization, completion. **2** *an account of his doings in Paris:* **exploit**, activity, act, action, deed, feat, achievement, accomplishment. **3** *that would take some doing:* **effort**, exertion, hard work, application, labour, toil, struggle.

doldrums **plural noun depression**, melancholy, gloom, down-heartedness, dejection, despondency, low spirits, despair; inertia, apathy, listlessness; informal blues. ■ **in the doldrums** *the housing market had been in the doldrums:* inactive, quiet, slow, slack, sluggish, stagnant.

dole verb
■ **dole something out** deal out, share out, divide up, allocate, distribute, dispense, hand out, give out, dish out/up; informal divvy up.

doleful adjective **mournful**, woeful, sorrowful, sad, unhappy, depressed, gloomy, melancholy, miserable, forlorn, wretched, woebegone, despondent, dejected, disconsolate, downcast, downhearted; informal blue, down in the mouth/dumps.
–OPPOSITES cheerful.

dollop noun (informal) **blob**, lump, spoonful, scoop, serving, helping, portion.

dolt noun. See IDIOT.

doltish adjective. See STUPID sense 1.

domain noun **1** *they extended their domain:* **realm**, kingdom, empire, dominion, province, territory, land. **2** *the domain of art:* **field**, area, sphere, discipline, province, world.

domestic adjective **1** *domestic commitments:* **family**, home, household. **2** *small domestic animals:* **domesticated**, tame, pet, household. **3** *the domestic car industry:* **national**, home, internal. **4** *domestic plants:* **native**, indigenous.

domesticated adjective
1 *domesticated animals:* **tame**, tamed, pet, domestic, trained, house-trained. **2** *domesticated crops:* **cultivated**, naturalized. **3** *I'm quite domesticated really:* home-loving, house-proud; Brit. homely.
–OPPOSITES wild.

dominance noun **supremacy**, superiority, ascendancy, pre-eminence, domination, dominion, mastery, power, authority, rule, command, control, sway.

dominant adjective **1** *the dominant classes:* **presiding**, ruling, governing, controlling, commanding, ascendant, supreme, authoritative. **2** *he has a dominant personality:* **assertive**, authoritative, forceful, domineering, commanding, controlling, pushy. **3** *the dominant issues in psychology:* **main**, principal, prime, premier, chief, foremost, primary, predominant, paramount, prominent; central, key, crucial, core; informal number-one.
–OPPOSITES subservient.

dominate verb **1** *the party dominated politics for four decades:* **control**, command, be in command of, be in charge of, monopolize, rule, lead, govern, direct, shape, influence; hold sway, be in the ascendancy, be in the driver's seat, be at the helm; literary sway. **2** *the Puritan work ethic still dominates:* **predominate**, prevail, reign, be prevalent, be paramount, be pre-eminent. **3** *the village is dominated by the viaduct:* **overlook**, command, tower above/over, loom over.

domination noun **rule**, government, sovereignty, control, command, authority, power, dominion, dominance, mastery, supremacy, superiority, ascendancy, sway.

domineering adjective **overbearing**, authoritarian, imperious, high-handed, autocratic; masterful, dictatorial, despotic, oppressive, strict, harsh; informal bossy.

dominion noun **supremacy**, ascendancy, dominance, domination, superiority, predominance, pre-eminence, hegemony, authority, mastery, control, command, power, sway, rule, government, jurisdiction, sovereignty.

don[1] noun *an Oxford don:* **university teacher**, university lecturer, fellow, professor, reader, academic, scholar.

don[2] verb *he donned an overcoat:* **put on**, get dressed in, dress yourself in, get into, slip into/on.

donate verb **give**, contribute, gift, subscribe, grant, bestow; bequeath; informal chip in, pitch in; Brit. informal stump up; N. Amer. informal kick in.

donation noun **gift**, contribution, subscription, present, handout, grant, offering.

donnish adjective **scholarly**, studious, academic, bookish, intellectual, learned, highbrow.

donor noun **giver**, contributor, benefactor, benefactress, subscriber; supporter, backer, patron, sponsor.

doom noun **destruction**, downfall,

ruin, ruination; extinction, annihilation, death, nemesis.
•verb **destine**, fate, predestine, preordain, mean; condemn, sentence.

doomed adjective **ill-fated**, ill-starred, cursed, jinxed, damned.

d

door noun **doorway**, portal, opening, entrance, entry, exit.
■ **out of doors** outside, outdoors, in the open air, alfresco.

dope noun (informal) **drugs**, narcotics.
•verb **drug**, tamper with, interfere with, contaminate, lace; sedate; Brit. informal spike, doctor, nobble.

dopey adjective (informal) **1** *I'm feeling a bit dopey:* **groggy**, dazed, sleepy, drowsy, stupefied, confused, muddled, befuddled, disorientated, muzzy; informal woozy. **2** *he's really dopey.* See STUPID sense 1.
–OPPOSITES alert, intelligent.

dormant adjective **sleeping**, resting; inactive, passive, inert, latent, idle, quiescent.
–OPPOSITES awake, active.

dose noun **measure**, portion, dosage; informal hit.

dossier noun **file**, report, case history; account, notes, documents, documentation, data, information, evidence.

dot noun *a pattern of tiny dots:* **spot**, speck, fleck, speckle; full stop, decimal point.
•verb **1** *spots of rain dotted his shirt:* **spot**, fleck, mark, spatter.
2 *restaurants are dotted around the site:* **scatter**, pepper, sprinkle, strew; spread, disperse, distribute.

dote verb
■ **dote on** adore, love dearly, be devoted to, idolize, treasure, cherish, worship, hold dear.

doting adjective **adoring**, loving, besotted, infatuated; affectionate, fond, devoted, caring.

double adjective *a double garage | double yellow lines:* **dual**, duplex, twin, binary, duplicate, in pairs, coupled, twofold.
–OPPOSITES single.
•noun **1** *if it's not her, it's her double:* **lookalike**, twin, clone, duplicate, exact likeness, replica, copy, facsimile, doppelgänger; informal spitting image, dead ringer, dead spit.
2 *she used a double for the stunts:* **stand-in**, substitute.
•verb **1** *they doubled his salary:* **multiply by two**, increase twofold.
2 *the bottom sheet had been doubled up:* **fold back**, turn back, tuck under.
■ **at/on the double** very quickly, as fast as your legs can carry you, at a run, at a gallop, fast, swiftly, rapidly, speedily, at full speed, at full tilt, as fast as possible; informal double quick, like lightning, like the wind, like a scalded cat, like a bat out of hell; Brit. informal like the clappers, at a rate of knots; N. Amer. informal lickety-split.

double-cross verb **betray**, cheat, defraud, trick, hoodwink, mislead, deceive, swindle, be disloyal to, be unfaithful to, play false; informal do the dirty on, sell down the river.

double-dealing noun **duplicity**, treachery, betrayal, double-crossing, unfaithfulness, untrustworthiness, infidelity, bad faith, disloyalty, fraud, underhandedness, cheating, dishonesty, deceit, deceitfulness, deception, falseness; informal crookedness.
–OPPOSITES honesty.

doubt noun **1** *a weak leader racked by doubt:* **uncertainty**, indecision, hesitation, insecurity, unease, apprehension; hesitancy, vacillation, irresolution. **2** *there is some doubt about their motives:* **scepticism**, distrust, mistrust, suspicion, cynicism, uneasiness, apprehension, wariness; reservations, misgivings, suspicions, queries, questions; confusion.
–OPPOSITES certainty, conviction.
•verb *they doubted my story:* **disbelieve**, distrust, mistrust, suspect, be suspicious of, have misgivings about; query, question, challenge.
–OPPOSITES trust.
■ **in doubt 1** *the issue was in doubt:* doubtful, uncertain, open to question, unconfirmed, unknown, undecided, unresolved, in the balance, up in the air; informal iffy.
2 *if you are in doubt, ask for advice:* irresolute, hesitant, ambivalent; doubtful, unsure, uncertain, in two minds, undecided, in a quandary/dilemma. **no doubt** doubtless, undoubtedly, indubitably, without doubt; unquestionably, undeniably, incontrovertibly, irrefutably;

unequivocally, clearly, plainly, obviously, patently.

doubter noun **sceptic**, doubting Thomas, non-believer, unbeliever, disbeliever, cynic, scoffer, dissenter.
– OPPOSITES believer.

doubtful adjective **1** *I was doubtful about going:* **hesitant**, in doubt, unsure, uncertain, in two minds, in a quandary/dilemma. **2** *it is doubtful whether he will come:* **in doubt**, uncertain, open to question, unsure, debatable, up in the air. **3** *the whole trip is looking rather doubtful:* **unlikely**, improbable, dubious. **4** *they are doubtful of the methods used:* **distrustful**, mistrustful, suspicious, wary, chary, leery, apprehensive; sceptical, unsure, ambivalent, dubious. **5** *this decision is of doubtful validity:* **questionable**, arguable, debatable, controversial, contentious; informal iffy; Brit. informal dodgy.
– OPPOSITES confident, certain, probable, trusting.

doubtless adverb **undoubtedly**, indubitably, no doubt; unquestionably, indisputably, undeniably, incontrovertibly, irrefutably; certainly, surely, of course.

dour adjective **stern**, unsmiling, unfriendly, severe, forbidding, gruff, surly, grim, sullen, solemn, austere, stony.
– OPPOSITES cheerful, friendly.

douse verb **1** *a mob doused the thieves with petrol:* **drench**, soak, saturate, wet, slosh. **2** *a guard doused the flames:* **extinguish**, put out, quench, smother, dampen down.

dovetail verb **fit in**, go together, be consistent, match, conform, harmonize, be in tune, correspond; informal square; N. Amer. informal jibe.

dowdy adjective **unfashionable**, frumpy, old-fashioned, inelegant, shabby, frowzy; Brit. informal mumsy; Austral./NZ informal daggy.
– OPPOSITES fashionable.

down[1] adjective **1** *I'm feeling a bit down:* **depressed**, sad, unhappy, melancholy, miserable, wretched, sorrowful, gloomy, dejected, downhearted, despondent, dispirited, low; informal blue, down in the dumps/mouth, fed up. **2** *the computer is down:* **not working**, inoperative, malfunctioning, out of order, broken; not in service, out of action, out of commission; informal conked out, bust, kaput; N. Amer. informal on the fritz.
– OPPOSITES elated, up.
• verb (informal) **1** *he struck Slater, downing him:* **knock down/over**, knock to the ground, bring down, topple; informal deck, floor, flatten. **2** *he downed his beer:* **drink**, gulp down, guzzle, quaff, drain, toss off, slug, finish off; informal sink, knock back, put away; N. Amer. informal scarf, snarf.

down[2] noun **feathers**, hair; fluff, fuzz.

down and out adjective **destitute**, poverty-stricken, impoverished, indigent, impecunious, penniless, insolvent; needy, in straitened circumstances, badly off; homeless, on the streets, vagrant, sleeping rough; informal hard up, broke, strapped for cash; Brit. informal skint; N. Amer. informal on skid row.
– OPPOSITES wealthy.
• noun **(down-and-out)** beggar, homeless person, vagrant, tramp, derelict, vagabond; N. Amer. hobo; Austral. bagman; informal bag lady; Brit. informal dosser; N. Amer. informal bum.

down at heel adjective **shabby**, unkempt, run down, dilapidated, neglected, uncared-for, in disrepair; seedy, insalubrious, squalid, wretched; informal tatty, scruffy, scuzzy; Brit. informal grotty.
– OPPOSITES smart.

downbeat adjective **pessimistic**, gloomy, negative, defeatist, cynical, bleak, fatalistic, dark, black; despairing, despondent, depressing, demoralizing, hopeless, melancholy, glum.

downcast adjective **despondent**, disheartened, discouraged, dispirited, downhearted, crestfallen, down, low, disconsolate, despairing; sad, melancholy, gloomy, glum, morose, doleful, dismal, woebegone, miserable, depressed, dejected; informal blue, down in the mouth/dumps.
– OPPOSITES elated.

downfall noun **undoing**, ruin, ruination; defeat, conquest, overthrow; nemesis, destruction, annihilation,

elimination; end, collapse, fall, crash, failure; Waterloo.
– OPPOSITES rise.

downgrade verb **demote**, reduce, relegate, reclassify; sideline, marginalize.
– OPPOSITES upgrade, promote.

downhearted adjective **despondent**, disheartened, discouraged, dispirited, downcast, crestfallen, down, low, disconsolate, wretched; melancholy, gloomy, glum, doleful, dismal, woebegone, miserable, depressed, dejected, sorrowful, sad; informal blue, down in the mouth/dumps.
– OPPOSITES elated.

downmarket adjective (Brit.) **cheap**, inferior, low-rent; lowbrow, unsophisticated, rough; informal tacky, naff, dumbed down.

downpour noun **rainstorm**, cloudburst, deluge; thunderstorm; torrential/pouring rain.

downright adjective *downright lies:* **complete**, total, absolute, utter, thorough, out-and-out, outright, sheer, arrant, pure, real, veritable, categorical, unmitigated, unadulterated, unalloyed, unequivocal; Brit. informal proper.
• adverb *that's downright dangerous:* **thoroughly**, utterly, positively, profoundly, really, completely, totally, entirely; in every respect, through and through; informal plain, just.

downside noun **drawback**, disadvantage, snag, stumbling block, catch, pitfall, fly in the ointment; handicap, limitation, trouble, difficulty, problem, complication, nuisance; hindrance; weak spot/point; informal minus, flip side.
– OPPOSITES advantage.

down-to-earth adjective **practical**, sensible, realistic, matter-of-fact, rational, logical, balanced, sober, pragmatic, level-headed, commonsensical, sane.
– OPPOSITES idealistic.

downtrodden adjective **oppressed**, persecuted, repressed, tyrannized, crushed, enslaved, exploited, victimized, bullied; disadvantaged, underprivileged, powerless, helpless; abused, maltreated.

downy adjective **soft**, velvety, smooth, fleecy, fluffy, fuzzy, feathery, furry, woolly, silky.

doze verb **catnap**, nap, drowse, sleep lightly, rest; informal snooze, snatch forty winks, get some shut-eye; Brit. informal kip; N. Amer. informal catch some Zs.
• noun **catnap**, nap, siesta, rest; informal snooze, forty winks; Brit. informal kip, zizz.
■ **doze off** fall asleep, go to sleep, drop off; informal nod off, drift off; N. Amer. informal sack out, zone out.

dozy adjective **1** *she felt really dozy:* **drowsy**, sleepy, half asleep, heavy-eyed, somnolent; weary, tired, fatigued; informal dopey. **2** *the dozy woman at reception:* **slow-witted**, stupid, incompetent; informal dopey.

drab adjective **1** *a drab interior:* **colourless**, grey, dull, washed out, muted; dingy, dreary, dismal, cheerless, gloomy, sombre. **2** *a drab existence:* **uninteresting**, dull, boring, tedious, monotonous, dry, dreary; unexciting, uninspiring, insipid, flat, stale, wishy-washy, colourless; lame, tired, sterile, anaemic, barren, tame; run-of-the-mill, mediocre, nondescript, characterless, mundane, unremarkable, humdrum.
– OPPOSITES bright, cheerful, interesting.

draconian adjective **harsh**, severe, strict, extreme, drastic, stringent, tough; cruel, oppressive, ruthless, relentless, punitive; authoritarian, despotic, tyrannical, repressive; Brit. swingeing.
– OPPOSITES lenient.

draft noun **1** *the first draft of his speech:* **version**, attempt, effort. **2** *a draft of the building:* **plan**, blueprint, design, diagram, drawing, sketch, map, layout, representation. **3** *a banker's draft:* **cheque**, order, money order, bill of exchange.

> Don't confuse **draft** with **draught**. In British English **draught** chiefly means 'a current of air'.

drag verb **1** *she dragged the chair backwards:* **haul**, pull, tug, heave, lug, draw; trail. **2** *the day dragged:* **wear on**, pass slowly, hang heavy, creep by.
• noun **1** *the drag from the parachute:* **pull**, resistance, tug. **2** (informal)

work can be a drag: **bore**, nuisance, bother, trouble, pest, annoyance, trial; informal pain, bind, headache, hassle.

■ **drag on** *the dispute dragged on for years:* continue, go on, carry on, run on, endure, persist. **drag something out** prolong, protract, draw out, spin out, string out, extend, lengthen, carry on, continue.

drain verb **1** *a valve for draining the tank:* **empty**, void, clear out, evacuate, unload. **2** *drain off any surplus liquid:* **draw off**, extract, withdraw, remove, siphon off, pour out, pour off; bleed, tap, void, filter, discharge. **3** *the water drained away to the sea:* **flow**, pour, trickle, stream, run, rush, gush, flood, surge; leak, ooze, seep, dribble, issue, filter, bleed, leach. **4** *more people would just drain our resources:* **use up**, exhaust, deplete, consume, expend, get through, sap, strain, tax; milk, bleed. **5** *he drained his beer:* **drink**, gulp down, guzzle, quaff, swallow, finish off, toss off, slug; informal sink, down, swig, swill down, polish off, knock back, put away.

– OPPOSITES fill.

• noun **1** *the drain filled with water:* **sewer**, channel, conduit, ditch, culvert, duct, pipe, gutter. **2** *a drain on the battery:* **strain**, pressure, burden, load, tax, demand.

drama noun **1** *a television drama:* **play**, show, piece, dramatization. **2** *he is studying drama:* **acting**, the theatre, the stage, the performing arts, stagecraft. **3** *she liked to create a drama:* **incident**, scene, spectacle, crisis; excitement, thrill, sensation; disturbance, commotion, turmoil; dramatics, theatrics, histrionics.

dramatic adjective **1** *dramatic art:* **theatrical**, theatric, thespian, stage, dramaturgical. **2** *a dramatic increase:* **considerable**, substantial; significant, remarkable, extraordinary, exceptional, phenomenal; informal tidy. **3** *there were dramatic scenes in the city:* **exciting**, stirring, action-packed, sensational, spectacular; startling, unexpected, tense, gripping, riveting, thrilling, hair-raising; rousing, lively, electrifying, impassioned, moving. **4** *dramatic headlands:* **striking**, impressive, imposing, spectacular, breathtaking, dazzling, sensational, awesome, awe-inspiring, remarkable, outstanding, incredible, phenomenal. **5** *a dramatic gesture:* **exaggerated**, theatrical, ostentatious, actressy, stagy, showy, melodramatic, overdone, histrionic, affected, mannered, artificial; informal hammy, ham.

– OPPOSITES insignificant, boring, restrained.

dramatist noun **playwright**, scriptwriter, screenwriter.

dramatize verb **1** *the novel was dramatized for television:* **adapt**, recast. **2** *the tabloids dramatized the event:* **exaggerate**, overdo, overstate, hyperbolize, magnify, amplify, inflate; sensationalize, embroider, colour, aggrandize, embellish, elaborate; informal blow up out of all proportion.

drape verb **1** *she draped a shawl round her:* **wrap**, wind, swathe, sling, hang. **2** *the chair was draped with blankets:* **cover**, envelop, swathe, shroud, deck, festoon, overlay, cloak, wind, enfold.

drastic adjective **extreme**, serious, desperate, radical, far-reaching, momentous, substantial; heavy, severe, harsh, rigorous; oppressive, draconian.

– OPPOSITES moderate.

draught noun **1** *the draught made Robin shiver:* **current of air**, rush of air; waft, wind, breeze, gust, puff, blast. **2** *a deep draught of beer:* **gulp**, drink, swallow, mouthful, slug; informal swig, swill.

> ! Don't confuse **draught** and **draft**, which means 'a first version of a piece of writing' (*the first draft of his speech*), or 'prepare the first version of a piece of writing' (*he drafted a letter of resignation*). American English uses the same spelling for both words.

draw verb **1** **sketch**, outline, rough out, trace; illustrate, represent, portray, depict, delineate. **2** *she drew her chair in to the table:* **pull**, haul, drag, tug, heave, lug, trail, tow; informal yank. **3** *the train drew into the station:* **move**, go, come, proceed, progress, travel, advance, pass, drive; inch, roll, glide, cruise; sweep. **4** *he drew some fluid off the*

d

knee joint: **drain**, extract, withdraw, remove, suck, pump, siphon, bleed, tap. **5** *he drew his gun:* **pull out**, take out, produce, fish out, extract, withdraw; unsheathe. **6** *she was drawing huge audiences:* **attract**, win, capture, catch, engage, lure, entice, bring in. **7** *what conclusion can we draw?* **deduce**, infer, conclude, derive, gather, glean.
• **noun 1** *she won the Christmas draw:* **raffle**, lottery, sweepstake, sweep, tombola, ballot; N. Amer. lotto. **2** *the match ended in a draw:* **tie**, dead heat, stalemate. **3** *the draw of central London:* **attraction**, lure, allure, pull, appeal, glamour, enticement, temptation, charm, seduction, fascination, magnetism.
■ **draw on** call on, have recourse to, avail yourself of, turn to, look to, fall back on, rely on, exploit, use, employ, utilize, bring into play. **draw something out 1** *he drew out a gun.* See **DRAW** verb sense 5. **2** *they always drew their parting out:* prolong, protract, drag out, spin out, string out, extend, lengthen; Brit. informal make a meal of. **draw up** stop, pull up, halt, come to a standstill, brake, park; arrive. **draw something up** compose, formulate, frame, write down, draft, prepare, think up, devise, work out; create, invent, design.

drawback **noun** **disadvantage**, snag, downside, stumbling block, catch, hitch, pitfall, fly in the ointment; weak spot/point, weakness, imperfection; handicap, limitation, trouble, difficulty, problem, complication; hindrance, obstacle, impediment, obstruction, inconvenience, discouragement; Brit. spanner in the works; informal minus, hiccup.
– OPPOSITES benefit.

drawing **noun** **sketch**, picture, illustration, representation, portrayal, depiction, composition, study; diagram, outline, design, plan.

> **WORD LINKS**
> **graphic** relating to drawing

drawn **adjective** *she looked pale and drawn:* **pinched**, haggard, drained, wan, hollow-cheeked; fatigued, tired, exhausted; tense, stressed, strained, worried, anxious, harassed; informal hassled.

dread **verb** **fear**, be afraid of, be terrified by, shudder at the prospect of, shrink from, worry about.
• **noun** **fear**, apprehension, trepidation, anxiety, worry, concern, foreboding, disquiet, misgiving, unease, angst; fright, panic, alarm; terror, horror; informal the jitters, the heebie-jeebies.
– OPPOSITES confidence.

dreadful **adjective 1** *a dreadful accident:* **terrible**, frightful, horrible, grim, awful, dire; horrifying, shocking, distressing, appalling, harrowing; ghastly, fearful, horrendous; tragic, calamitous; formal grievous. **2** *a dreadful meal:* **frightful**; shocking, awful, abysmal, atrocious, disgraceful, deplorable; informal pathetic, woeful, crummy, rotten, sorry, third-rate, lousy, ropy, God-awful; Brit. informal duff, chronic, rubbish. **3** *you're a dreadful flirt:* **outrageous**, shocking; inordinate, immoderate, unrestrained; incorrigible.
– OPPOSITES pleasant, excellent.

dreadfully **adverb 1** *I'm dreadfully hungry:* **extremely**, very, really, exceedingly, tremendously, exceptionally, extraordinarily; decidedly; N. English right; informal terrifically, terribly, desperately, awfully, devilishly, mega, seriously, majorly; Brit. informal jolly, dead, well; N. Amer. informal real, mighty, awful; informal, dated frightfully. **2** *she missed James dreadfully:* **very much**, lots, a lot, a great deal, intensely, desperately. **3** *the company performed dreadfully:* **terribly**, awfully, atrociously, appallingly, abominably; informal abysmally, pitifully, diabolically.

dream **noun 1** *she went around in a dream:* **daydream**, reverie, trance, daze, stupor, haze; Scottish dwam. **2** *he realized his childhood dream:* **ambition**, aspiration, hope; goal, aim, objective, holy grail, intention, intent, target; desire, wish, yearning; daydream, fantasy. **3** *he's an absolute dream:* **delight**, joy, marvel, wonder, gem, treasure; beauty, vision.
• **verb 1** *I dreamed of making the Olympic team:* **fantasize about**, daydream about; wish for, hope for, long for, yearn for, hanker after,

set your heart on; aspire to, aim for, set your sights on. **2** *I wouldn't dream of being late:* **think**, consider, contemplate, conceive.
• **adjective** *his dream home:* **ideal**, perfect, ultimate, fantasy.
■ **dream something up** think up, invent, concoct, devise, hatch, contrive, create, work out, come up with; informal cook up.

> **WORD LINKS**
> **oneiric** relating to dreams

dreamer noun fantasist, daydreamer; romantic, sentimentalist, idealist, wishful thinker, Don Quixote; utopian, visionary.
– OPPOSITES realist.

dreamlike adjective ethereal, phantasmagorical, trance-like; surreal; nightmarish, Kafkaesque; hazy, shadowy, faint, indistinct, unclear.

dreamy adjective *a dreamy expression:* **daydreaming**, dreaming; pensive, thoughtful, reflective, meditative, ruminative; preoccupied, distracted, inattentive, vague, absorbed, absent-minded, with your head in the clouds, in a world of your own; informal miles away.
– OPPOSITES alert.

dreary adjective dull, uninteresting, flat, tedious, wearisome, boring, unexciting, unstimulating, uninspiring, soul-destroying; humdrum, monotonous, uneventful, unremarkable, featureless.
– OPPOSITES exciting.

dregs plural noun *the dregs from a bottle of wine:* **sediment**, deposit, residue, sludge, lees, grounds, settlings; remains.

drench verb soak, saturate, wet through, permeate, douse, souse; steep, bathe.

dress verb 1 *she dressed in her warmest clothes:* **wear**, put on. **2** *she was dressed in a navy blue suit:* **clothe**, attire, garb, deck out, trick out/up, costume, array, robe; informal get up, doll up. **3** *she enjoyed dressing the tree:* **decorate**, trim, deck, adorn, ornament, embellish, beautify, prettify; festoon, garland. **4** *they dressed his wounds:* **bandage**, cover, bind, wrap.
• **noun 1** *a long blue dress:* **frock**, gown, robe, shift. **2** *full evening dress:* **clothes**, clothing, garments, attire; costume, outfit, ensemble, garb, turnout; informal gear, get-up, togs, duds, glad rags; Brit. informal clobber; N. Amer. informal threads; formal apparel; old use raiment.

> **WORD LINKS**
> **sartorial** to do with a person's style of dress

dressmaker noun tailor, seamstress, needlewoman; outfitter, costumier, clothier; couturier, designer; dated modiste.

dressy adjective smart, formal; elaborate, ornate; stylish, elegant, chic, fashionable; informal snazzy, trendy.
– OPPOSITES casual.

dribble verb 1 *the baby started to dribble:* **drool**, slaver, slobber, salivate, drivel, water at the mouth; Scottish & Irish slabber. **2** *rainwater dribbled down her face:* **trickle**, drip, fall, run, drizzle; ooze, seep.

dried adjective dehydrated, desiccated, dry, dried up.

drift verb 1 *his raft drifted down the river:* **be carried**, be borne; float, bob, waft, meander. **2** *the guests drifted away:* **wander**, meander, stray, potter, dawdle, float; Brit. informal mooch. **3** *don't allow your attention to drift:* **stray**, digress, wander, deviate, diverge, veer. **4** *snow drifted over the path:* **pile up**, bank up, heap up, accumulate, gather, amass.
• **noun 1** *a drift from the country to urban areas:* **movement**, shift, flow, transfer, gravitation. **2** *he caught the drift of her thoughts:* **gist**, essence, meaning, sense, substance, significance; thrust, import, tenor; implication, intention; direction. **3** *a drift of deep snow:* **pile**, heap, bank, mound, mass, accumulation.

drifter noun wanderer, traveller, transient, roamer, rolling stone; tramp, vagabond, vagrant; N. Amer. hobo.

drill noun 1 *military drill:* **training**, instruction, coaching, teaching; exercises, workout; informal square-bashing. **2** *Estelle knew the drill:*

procedure, routine, practice, programme, schedule; method, system.
• verb **1** *drill a hole in the wood:* **bore**, pierce, puncture, perforate. **2** *a sergeant drilling new recruits:* **train**, instruct, coach, teach, discipline; exercise, put someone through their paces. **3** *his mother had drilled politeness into him:* **instil**, hammer, drive, drum, din, implant, ingrain; teach, indoctrinate, brainwash.

d

drink verb **1** *she drank her coffee:* **swallow**, gulp down, quaff, guzzle, sup; imbibe, sip, consume; drain, toss off, slug; informal swig, down, knock back, put away, neck, sink, swill. **2** *she doesn't drink or smoke:* **drink alcohol**, tipple, indulge; carouse; informal hit the bottle, booze.
• noun **1** *he took a sip of his drink:* **beverage**; dram, nightcap, nip, tot; pint; Brit. informal bevvy; humorous libation. **2** *she turned to drink:* **alcohol**, liquor; informal booze, hooch, the hard stuff, firewater, rotgut, moonshine, the bottle, the sauce, grog, Dutch courage. **3** *she took a drink of her wine:* **swallow**, gulp, sip, mouthful, draught, slug; informal swig, swill. **4** *a drink of orange juice:* **glass**, cup, mug.
■ **drink something in** absorb, assimilate, digest, ingest, take in; be rapt in, be lost in, be fascinated by, pay close attention to.

drinker noun **drunkard**, drunk, inebriate, tippler; alcoholic, dipsomaniac; informal boozer, soak, lush, wino, alky, sponge, barfly; Austral./NZ informal hophead.
– OPPOSITES teetotaller.

drip verb **1** *a tap was dripping:* **dribble**, leak. **2** *sweat dripped from his chin:* **drop**, dribble, trickle, run, splash, plop; leak, emanate, issue.
• noun **1** *a bucket to catch the drips:* **drop**, dribble, spot, trickle, splash. **2** (informal) *he's such a drip:* **weakling**, ninny, milksop, namby-pamby, crybaby, softie, doormat; informal wimp, weed, sissy; Brit. informal wet, big girl's blouse; N. Amer. informal panty-waist, pussy, wuss.

drive verb **1** *a police officer was driving the vehicle:* **operate**, handle, manage; pilot, steer; sail, fly. **2** *I'll drive you to the airport:* **take**, give someone a lift, run, ferry, transport, convey, carry, chauffeur. **3** *the engine drives the front wheels:* **power**, propel, move, push. **4** *he drove a nail into the wood:* **hammer**, screw, ram, sink, plunge, thrust, propel, knock. **5** *his addiction drove him to commit crime:* **compel**, force, prompt. **6** *you are driving yourself too hard:* **work**, push, tax, exert.
• noun **1** *an afternoon drive:* **excursion**, outing, trip, jaunt, tour; ride, run, journey; informal spin. **2** *sexual drives:* **urge**, appetite, desire, need; impulse, instinct. **3** *she lacked the drive to succeed:* **motivation**, ambition, single-mindedness, will power, dedication, doggedness, tenacity; enthusiasm, zeal, commitment, aggression, spirit; energy, vigour, verve, vitality, pep; informal get-up-and-go. **4** *an anti-corruption drive:* **campaign**, crusade, movement, effort, push, appeal, initiative.
■ **drive at** suggest, imply, hint at, allude to, intimate, insinuate, indicate; refer to, mean, intend; informal get at.

drivel noun *he was talking complete drivel:* **nonsense**, twaddle, claptrap, balderdash, gibberish, rubbish, mumbo-jumbo; N. Amer. garbage; informal rot, poppycock, phooey, piffle, tripe, bosh, bull, hogwash, baloney; Brit. informal cobblers, codswallop, waffle, tosh, double Dutch; N. Amer. informal flapdoodle; informal, dated bunkum.
• verb *you always drivel on:* **talk nonsense**, talk rubbish, babble, ramble, gibber, blather, prattle, gabble; Brit. informal waffle, witter.

driver noun **motorist**, chauffeur; pilot, operator.

drizzle noun *a drizzle of olive oil:* **trickle**, dribble, drip, stream, rivulet; sprinkle, sprinkling.
• verb *drizzle the cream over the fruit:* **trickle**, drip, dribble, pour, splash, sprinkle.

droll adjective **funny**, humorous, amusing, comic, comical, mirthful, hilarious; zany, quirky; jocular, light-hearted, witty, whimsical, wry, tongue-in-cheek; informal waggish, wacky, side-splitting, rib-tickling.
– OPPOSITES serious.

drone verb **1** *a plane droned overhead:* **hum**, buzz, whirr, vibrate,

murmur, rumble, purr. **2** *he droned on about right and wrong:* **go on and on**, talk at length; pontificate, hold forth; informal spout, sound off.
• noun *the drone of aircraft taking off:* **hum**, buzz, whirr, vibration, murmur, purr.

drool verb *his mouth was drooling:* **salivate**, dribble, slaver, slobber; Scottish & Irish slabber.
• noun *a fine trickle of drool:* **saliva**, spit, spittle, dribble, slaver, slobber.

droop verb **hang down**, dangle, sag, flop; wilt, sink, slump, drop.

droopy adjective **pendulous**, dangling, drooping, hanging down; sagging, floppy.

drop verb **1** *he dropped the box:* **let fall**, let go of, lose your grip on; release, relinquish; old use unhand. **2** *water drops from the cave roof:* **drip**, fall, dribble, trickle, run, leak. **3** *a plane dropped out of the sky:* **fall**, descend, plunge, plummet, dive, nosedive, tumble. **4** *pre-tax profits dropped 38%:* **decrease**, fall, dip, sink, slump, plunge, plummet, tumble diminish, depreciate; decline, dwindle. **5** *he was dropped from the team:* **exclude**, expel, throw out, leave out; dismiss, let go; informal boot out, kick out, turf out. **6** *pupils can drop history if they wish:* **give up**, discontinue, stop, abandon, have done with; informal pack in, quit. **7** *he dropped his unsuitable friends:* **abandon**, desert; renounce, disown, turn your back on, wash your hands of; reject, give up, cast off; neglect, shun; literary forsake.
– OPPOSITES lift, rise, increase.
• noun **1** *a drop of water:* **droplet**, blob, globule, bead. **2** *it needs a drop of oil:* **bit**, dash, spot; dribble, sprinkle, trickle, splash, soupçon; dab, speck, smattering, sprinkling, modicum; informal smidgen, tad. **3** *a small drop in profits:* **decrease**, reduction, decline, fall-off, downturn, slump; cut, cutback, curtailment; depreciation. **4** *I walked to the edge of the drop:* **cliff**, abyss, chasm, gorge, gully, precipice; slope, descent, incline.
– OPPOSITES increase.
■ **drop off 1** *trade dropped off sharply.* See DROP verb sense 4. **2** *I must have dropped off:* fall asleep, doze off, nap, catnap, drowse; informal nod off, drift off, snooze. **drop out of** *he dropped out of university:* leave; informal quit, pack in, jack in.

dropout noun **nonconformist**, hippy, beatnik, bohemian, free spirit, rebel; idler, layabout, loafer; informal oddball, deadbeat, waster.

droppings plural noun **excrement**, excreta, faeces, stools, dung, ordure, manure; informal poo.

dross noun **rubbish**, junk; debris, chaff, detritus, flotsam and jetsam; N. Amer. garbage, trash; informal dreck.

drowsy adjective **sleepy**, dozy, heavy-eyed, groggy, somnolent; tired, weary, fatigued, exhausted, yawning, nodding; lethargic, sluggish, torpid, listless, languid; informal snoozy, dopey, yawny, dead beat, all in, dog-tired; Brit. informal knackered.
– OPPOSITES alert.

drudgery noun **hard work**, menial work, donkey work, toil, labour; chores; informal skivvying; Brit. informal graft.

drug noun **1** *drugs prescribed by doctors:* **medicine**, medication; remedy, cure, antidote. **2** *she was under the influence of drugs:* **narcotic**, stimulant, hallucinogen; informal dope, gear.
• verb **1** *he was drugged:* **anaesthetize**; poison; knock out; informal dope. **2** *she drugged his coffee:* **tamper with**, lace, poison; informal dope, spike, doctor.

> **WORD LINKS**
> **pharmaceutical** relating to medicinal drugs
> **pharmacology** the branch of science concerned with the uses and effects of drugs
> **pharmacy** (Brit. **chemist**; N. Amer. **drugstore**) a shop selling medicinal drugs

drum noun *a drum of radioactive waste:* **canister**, barrel, cylinder, tank, bin, can; container.
• verb **1** *she drummed her fingers on the desk:* **tap**, beat, rap, thud, thump; tattoo; thrum. **2** *the rules were drummed into us at school:* **instil**, drive, din, hammer, drill, implant, ingrain, inculcate.
■ **drum someone out** expel, dismiss, throw out, oust; drive out, get rid of;

d

d

exclude, banish; informal give someone the boot, boot out, kick out, give someone their marching orders, give someone the push, show someone the door, send packing; Military cashier. **drum something up** round up, gather, collect; summon, attract; canvass, solicit, petition.

drunk adjective **intoxicated**, inebriated, drunken, incapable, tipsy, the worse for drink, under the influence; informal tight, merry, three sheets to the wind, pie-eyed, plastered, smashed, wrecked, wasted, sloshed, sozzled, blotto, tanked up, in your cups; Brit. informal legless, ratted, bevvied, paralytic, Brahms and Liszt, half cut, bladdered, trolleyed, squiffy, tiddly; N. Amer. informal loaded, trashed; euphemistic tired and emotional.
–OPPOSITES sober.
•noun **drunkard**, inebriate, drinker, tippler, sot; alcoholic, dipsomaniac; informal boozer, soak, lush, wino, sponge, barfly.

drunken adjective **1** *a drunken driver.* See DRUNK adjective. **2** *a drunken all-night party:* **debauched**, dissipated, unrestrained, uninhibited, abandoned; bacchanalian; informal boozy.

drunkenness noun **intoxication**, inebriation, tipsiness; intemperance, overindulgence, debauchery; heavy drinking, alcoholism, alcohol abuse, dipsomania.

dry adjective **1** *the land is dry and barren:* **arid**, parched, scorched, baked; waterless; dehydrated, desiccated, thirsty. **2** *dry leaves:* **withered**, dried, shrivelled, wizened; crisp, crispy, brittle. **3** *a dry debate:* **dull**, uninteresting, boring, tedious, tiresome, wearisome, dreary, monotonous; unimaginative, sterile, flat, bland, lacklustre, prosaic, humdrum, mundane; informal deadly. **4** *a dry sense of humour:* **wry**, subtle, laconic, sharp; ironic, sardonic, sarcastic, cynical; satirical.
–OPPOSITES wet, moist, fresh, lively.
•verb **parch**, scorch, bake; dehydrate, desiccate, wither, shrivel; drain.
■ **dry up** *currency reserves began to dry up:* dwindle, subside, peter out, taper off, ebb, come to a halt/end, run out, give out, disappear, vanish.

dual adjective **double**, twofold, binary; twin, matching, paired, coupled.
–OPPOSITES single.

dub verb *he was dubbed 'the world's sexiest man':* **nickname**, call, name, label, christen, term, tag, entitle, style; designate, characterize, nominate.

dubious adjective **1** *I was rather dubious about the idea:* **doubtful**, uncertain, unsure, hesitant; sceptical, suspicious; informal iffy. **2** *a dubious businessman:* **suspicious**, suspect, untrustworthy, unreliable, questionable; informal shady, fishy; Brit. informal dodgy.
–OPPOSITES certain, trustworthy.

duck verb **1** *he ducked behind the wall:* **bob down**, bend down, stoop down; crouch, squat, hunch down, hunker down. **2** *she was ducked in the river:* **dip**, dunk, plunge, immerse, submerge, lower, sink. **3** (informal) *they cannot duck the issue forever:* **shirk**, dodge, evade, avoid, elude, escape, back out of, shun, sidestep, bypass, circumvent; informal cop out of, get out of, wriggle out of, funk; Austral./NZ informal duck-shove.

duct noun **tube**, channel, canal, vessel; conduit; pipe, outlet, inlet, flue, shaft, vent.

dud (informal) noun *their new product is a dud:* **failure**, flop, let-down, disappointment; Brit. damp squib; informal washout, lemon, no-hoper, non-starter, dead loss, lead balloon; N. Amer. informal clinker.
–OPPOSITES success.
•adjective **1** *a dud computer:* **defective**, faulty, unsound, inoperative, broken, malfunctioning; informal bust, busted, kaput, conked out; Brit. informal duff, knackered. **2** *a dud £50 note:* **counterfeit**, fraudulent, forged, fake, false, bogus; invalid, worthless; informal phoney.
–OPPOSITES sound, genuine.

due adjective **1** *their fees were due:* **owing**, owed, payable; outstanding, overdue, unpaid, unsettled, undischarged; N. Amer. delinquent. **2** *the chancellor's statement is due today:* **expected**, anticipated, scheduled for, awaited; required. **3** *the respect due to a great artist:* **deserved by**, merited by, warranted by; appropriate to, fit for, fitting for, right for, proper to. **4** *he drove without due care:* **proper**, correct, rightful, suitable, appropriate, apt; adequate, sufficient, enough, satisfactory, requisite.

• **noun** *members have paid their dues:* **fee**, subscription, charge; payment, contribution.

• **adverb** *he hiked due north:* **directly**, straight, exactly, precisely, dead.

■ **due to 1** *her death was due to an infection:* caused by, the result of, the consequence of. **2** *the train was cancelled due to staff shortages:* because of, owing to, on account of, as a consequence of, as a result of, thanks to, in view of; formal by reason of.

duel **noun 1** *he was killed in a duel:* **single combat**; fight, confrontation, head-to-head; informal face-off, shoot-out. **2** *a snooker duel:* **contest**, match, game, meet, encounter, clash.

dulcet **adjective** **sweet**, soothing, mellow, honeyed, mellifluous, pleasant, agreeable; melodious, melodic, lilting, lyrical, silvery, golden.

– OPPOSITES harsh.

dull **adjective 1** *a very dull film:* **uninteresting**, boring, tedious, monotonous, unimaginative, uneventful; characterless, featureless, colourless, lifeless, insipid, unexciting, uninspiring, flat, bland, dry, stale, tired, banal, lacklustre, stodgy, dreary, humdrum, mundane; mind-numbing, soul-destroying, wearisome, tiring, tiresome, irksome; informal deadly; Brit. informal samey; N. Amer. informal dullsville. **2** *a dull morning:* **overcast**, cloudy, gloomy, dark, dismal, dreary, sombre, grey, murky, sunless. **3** *dull colours:* **drab**, sombre, dark, subdued, muted, faded, washed out, muddy. **4** *a dull sound:* **muffled**, muted, quiet, soft, faint, indistinct; stifled. **5** *a rather dull child:* **unintelligent**, stupid, slow, foolish; informal dense, dim, thick, dozy, slow on the uptake.

– OPPOSITES interesting, bright, loud.

• **verb 1** *the pain was dulled by drugs:* **lessen**, decrease, diminish, reduce, dampen, blunt, deaden, allay, ease, soothe, assuage, alleviate. **2** *sleep dulled her mind:* **numb**, benumb, deaden, desensitize, stupefy, daze.

– OPPOSITES intensify, brighten.

duly **adverb 1** *the document was duly signed:* **properly**, correctly, appropriately, suitably, fittingly. **2** *he duly arrived to collect Alice:* **on time**, punctually.

dumb **adjective 1** *she stood dumb while he shouted:* **mute**, speechless, tongue-tied, silent, at a loss for words; taciturn, uncommunicative, untalkative, tight-lipped, close-mouthed. **2** (informal) *he is not as dumb as you'd think:* **stupid**, unintelligent, ignorant, dense, brainless, mindless, foolish, slow, dull, simple, empty-headed, vacuous, vapid, idiotic, half-baked; informal thick, dim, moronic, cretinous, dopey, dozy, thickheaded, wooden-headed, fat-headed, birdbrained, pea-brained; Brit. informal daft.

– OPPOSITES clever.

dumbfound **verb** **astonish**, astound, amaze, stagger, surprise, startle, stun, confound, stupefy, daze, nonplus, take aback, stop someone in their tracks, strike dumb, leave open-mouthed, leave aghast; informal flabbergast, floor, knock sideways, bowl over; Brit. informal knock for six.

dumbfounded **adjective** **astonished**, astounded, amazed, staggered, startled, stunned, confounded, nonplussed, stupefied, dazed, dumbstruck, open-mouthed, speechless, thunderstruck; taken aback, disconcerted; informal flabbergasted, flummoxed; Brit. informal gobsmacked.

dummy **noun** *a shop-window dummy:* **mannequin**, model, figure.

• **adjective** *a dummy attack:* **simulated**, practice, trial, mock, make-believe; informal pretend, phoney.

– OPPOSITES real.

dump **noun 1** *take the rubbish to the dump:* **tip**, rubbish dump, rubbish heap, dumping ground; dustheap, slag heap. **2** (informal) *the house is a dump:* **hovel**, shack, slum; mess; informal hole, pigsty.

d

• verb **1** *he dumped his bag on the table:* **put down**, set down, deposit, place, shove, unload; drop, throw down; informal stick, park, plonk; Brit. informal bung; N. Amer. informal plunk. **2** *they will dump asbestos at the site:* **dispose of**, get rid of, throw away/out, discard, bin, jettison; informal ditch, junk. **3** (informal) *he's dumped her:* **abandon**, desert, leave, jilt, break up with, finish with, throw over; informal walk out on, drop, ditch, chuck, give someone the elbow; Brit. informal give someone the big E.

dumpy adjective **short**, squat, stubby; plump, stout, chubby, chunky, portly, fat, bulky; informal tubby, roly-poly, pudgy, porky; Brit. informal podgy.
– OPPOSITES tall, slender.

dune noun **bank**, mound, hillock, hummock, knoll, ridge, heap, drift.

dupe verb *they were duped by a con man:* **deceive**, trick, hoodwink, hoax, swindle, defraud, cheat, double-cross; gull, mislead, take in, fool, inveigle; informal con, do, rip off, diddle, shaft, pull the wool over someone's eyes, pull a fast one on, sell a pup to; N. Amer. informal sucker, snooker; Austral. informal pull a swifty on.
• noun *an innocent dupe in her game:* **victim**, pawn, puppet, instrument; fool, innocent; informal sucker, stooge, sitting duck, muggins, fall guy; Brit. informal mug; N. Amer. informal pigeon, patsy, sap.

duplicate noun *a duplicate of the invoice:* **copy**, photocopy, facsimile, reprint; replica, reproduction, clone; trademark Xerox, photostat.
• adjective *duplicate keys:* **matching**, identical, twin, corresponding, equivalent.
• verb **1** *she will duplicate the newsletter:* **copy**, photocopy, photostat, xerox, reproduce, replicate, reprint, run off. **2** *a feat difficult to duplicate:* **repeat**, do again, redo, replicate.

duplicity noun **deceitfulness**, deceit, deception, double-dealing, underhandedness, dishonesty, fraud, fraudulence, sharp practice, chicanery, trickery, subterfuge, skulduggery, treachery; informal crookedness, shadiness, dirty tricks, shenanigans, monkey business.
– OPPOSITES honesty.

durability noun **imperishability**, longevity; resilience, strength, sturdiness, toughness, robustness.
– OPPOSITES fragility.

durable adjective **1** *durable carpets:* **hard-wearing**, long-lasting, heavy-duty, tough, resistant, imperishable, indestructible, strong, sturdy, robust. **2** *a durable peace:* **lasting**, long-lasting, long-term, enduring, persistent, abiding; stable, secure, firm, deep-rooted, permanent, undying, everlasting.
– OPPOSITES delicate, short-lived.

duration noun **full length**, time, time span, time scale, period, term, span, fullness, length, extent.

duress noun **coercion**, compulsion, force, pressure, intimidation, constraint; threats; informal arm-twisting.

during preposition **throughout**, through, in, in the course of.

dusk noun **twilight**, nightfall, sunset, sundown, evening, close of day; semi-darkness, gloom, murkiness; literary gloaming, eventide.
– OPPOSITES dawn.

dust noun **1** *the desk was covered in dust:* **dirt**, grime, filth, smut, soot. **2** *they fought in the dust:* **earth**, soil, dirt.
• verb **1** *she dusted her mantelpiece:* **wipe**, clean, brush, sweep. **2** *dust the cake with icing sugar:* **sprinkle**, scatter, powder, dredge, sift, cover, strew.

dusty adjective **1** *the floor was dusty:* **dirty**, grimy, grubby, mucky, sooty. **2** *dusty sandstone:* **powdery**, crumbly, chalky, friable; granular, gritty, sandy.
– OPPOSITES clean.

dutiful adjective **conscientious**, responsible, dedicated, devoted, attentive; obedient, compliant; deferential, reverent, reverential, respectful.
– OPPOSITES remiss.

duty noun **1** *a misguided sense of duty:* **responsibility**, obligation, commitment; allegiance, loyalty, faithfulness, fidelity, homage. **2** *it was his duty to attend the king:* **job**, task, assignment, mission, function, charge, place, role, responsibility, obligation; dated office. **3** *the duty was raised on alcohol:* **tax**, levy,

tariff, excise, toll, fee, payment, rate; dues.
■ **off duty** not working, at leisure, on holiday, on leave, off work, free. **on duty** working, at work, busy, occupied, engaged; informal on the job, tied up.

dwarf noun *stories about dwarfs, elves, and giants:* **gnome**, goblin, hobgoblin, troll; imp, elf, brownie, leprechaun.
• adjective *dwarf conifers:* **miniature**, small, little, tiny, toy, pocket, diminutive, baby, pygmy; Scottish wee; informal mini, teeny, teeny-weeny, itsy-bitsy, tiddly, pint-sized; Brit. informal titchy; N. Amer. informal little-bitty.
– OPPOSITES giant.
• verb **1** *the buildings dwarf the trees:* **dominate**, tower over, loom over, overshadow. **2** *her progress was dwarfed by her sister's success:* **overshadow**, outshine, surpass, exceed, outclass, outstrip, outdo, top, trump, transcend; diminish.

dwell verb (formal) *thousands now dwell in these monasteries:* **reside**, live, be settled, be housed, lodge, stay; formal abide.
■ **dwell on** linger over, mull over, muse on, brood about/over, think about; be preoccupied by, obsess about, eat your heart out over; harp on about, discuss at length.

dwelling noun (formal) **residence**, home, house, accommodation; lodgings, quarters, rooms; informal place, pad, digs; formal abode, domicile, habitation.

dwindle verb **diminish**, decrease, reduce, lessen, shrink, wane; fall off, tail off, drop, fall, slump, plummet; informal nosedive.
– OPPOSITES increase.

dye noun *a blue dye:* **colourant**, colouring, colour, dyestuff, pigment, tint, stain, wash.
• verb *the gloves were dyed:* **colour**, tint, pigment, stain, wash.

dyed-in-the-wool adjective **inveterate**, confirmed, entrenched, established, long-standing, deep-rooted, diehard; complete, absolute, thorough, thoroughgoing, out-and-out, true blue; firm, unshakeable, staunch, steadfast, committed, devoted, dedicated, loyal, unswerving; N. Amer. full-bore; informal card-carrying.

dying adjective **1** *his dying aunt:* **terminally ill**, at death's door, on your deathbed, near death, fading fast, expiring, moribund, not long for this world; informal on your last legs, with one foot in the grave. **2** *a dying art form:* **declining**, vanishing, fading, waning; informal on the way out. **3** *her dying words:* **final**, last.
– OPPOSITES thriving.

dynamic adjective **energetic**, spirited, active, lively, zestful, vital, vigorous, forceful, powerful, positive; high-powered, aggressive, bold, enterprising; magnetic, passionate, fiery, high-octane; informal go-getting, gutsy, spunky, feisty, go-ahead.
– OPPOSITES half-hearted.

dynamism noun **energy**, spirit, liveliness, zestfulness, vitality, vigour, forcefulness, power, potency, positivity; aggression, drive, ambition, enterprise; magnetism, passion, fire; informal pep, get-up-and-go, vim and vigour, guts, feistiness.

dynasty noun **bloodline**, line, lineage, house, family; regime, empire.

dyspeptic adjective **bad-tempered**, short-tempered, irritable, snappish, testy, tetchy, touchy, crabby, crotchety, grouchy, cantankerous, peevish, cross, disagreeable, waspish, prickly; informal snappy, on a short fuse; Brit. informal stroppy, ratty; N. Amer. informal cranky, ornery.

Ee

each pronoun *there are 5000 books and each must be cleaned:* **every one**, each one, each and every one, all, the whole lot.
•determiner *he visited each month:* **every**, each and every, every single.
•adverb *they gave a tenner each:* **apiece**, per person, per capita.

eager adjective **1** *an eager bird-watcher:* **keen**, enthusiastic, avid, fervent, ardent; highly motivated, committed, earnest; informal as keen as mustard. **2** *she's eager to get involved:* **anxious**, impatient, longing, yearning, wishing, hoping; desirous of, hankering after; informal itching, gagging, dying.
–OPPOSITES apathetic.

eagerness noun **keenness**, enthusiasm, fervour, zeal, earnestness, commitment, dedication; impatience, desire, longing, yearning, hunger, appetite, yen.

eagle noun

> **WORD LINKS**
> **aquiline** like an eagle
> **eyrie** an eagle's nest

ear noun **1** *he had the ear of the president:* **attention**, notice. **2** *he has an ear for a good song:* **appreciation**, feel, instinct, intuition, sense.
■ **play it by ear**. See **PLAY**.

> **WORD LINKS**
> **aural**, **auricular**, **otic** relating to the ear or hearing
> **auditory** relating to hearing
> **binaural** relating to both ears
> **audiology** the branch of medicine concerned with hearing
> **otology** the study of the anatomy and diseases of the ear

early adjective **1** *early copies of the book:* **advance**, forward; initial, preliminary, first; pilot, trial. **2** *an early death:* **untimely**, premature, unseasonable. **3** *early man:* **primitive**, ancient, prehistoric, primeval. **4** *an early response:* **prompt**, timely, quick, speedy, rapid, fast.
–OPPOSITES late, modern, overdue.
•adverb **1** *she has to get up early:* **at dawn**, at daybreak, at cockcrow, with the lark. **2** *they hoped to leave school early:* **prematurely**, ahead of time, too soon.
–OPPOSITES late.

earmark verb **set aside**, keep, reserve; designate, assign, mark; allocate, allot, devote, pledge, give over.

earn verb **1** *they earned £20,000:* **be paid**, take home, gross; receive, get, make, obtain, collect, bring in; informal pocket, bank, rake in, net, bag. **2** *he has earned their trust:* **deserve**, merit, warrant, justify; gain, win, secure, establish, obtain, procure, get, acquire.
–OPPOSITES lose.

earnest adjective **1** *he is dreadfully earnest:* **serious**, solemn, grave, sober, humourless, staid, intense; committed, dedicated, keen, diligent, zealous. **2** *earnest prayer:* **devout**, heartfelt, wholehearted, sincere, impassioned, fervent, ardent, intense, urgent.
–OPPOSITES frivolous, half-hearted.
■ **in earnest 1** *we are in earnest about stopping burglaries:* serious, sincere, wholehearted, genuine; committed, firm, resolute, determined. **2** *he started writing in earnest:* zealously, purposefully, determinedly, resolutely; passionately, wholeheartedly.

earnestly adverb **seriously**, solemnly, gravely, intently; sincerely, resolutely, firmly, ardently, fervently, eagerly.

earnings plural noun **income**, wages, salary, stipend, pay, payment, fees; revenue, yield, profit, takings, proceeds, dividends, return, remuneration.

earth noun **1** *the moon orbits the earth:* **world**, globe, planet. **2** *he brought the plane back to earth:* **land**, ground, terra firma; floor. **3** *he ploughed the earth:* **soil**, clay, loam; dirt, sod, turf; ground.

> **WORD LINKS**
> **terrestrial**, **telluric** relating to the earth

earthly adjective **worldly**, temporal, mortal, human; material; carnal, fleshly, bodily, physical, corporeal, sensual.
– OPPOSITES extraterrestrial, heavenly.

earthquake noun **earth tremor**, shock, convulsion; informal quake.

> **WORD LINKS**
> **seismic** relating to earthquakes
> **seismology** the branch of science concerned with earthquakes
> **Richter scale** a scale for measuring the magnitude of an earthquake

earthy adjective **1** *earthy peasant food:* **down-to-earth**, unsophisticated, unrefined, simple, plain, unpretentious, natural; honest. **2** *earthy language:* **bawdy**, ribald, off colour, racy, rude, vulgar, lewd, crude, foul, coarse, uncouth, unseemly, indelicate, indecent, obscene; informal blue, locker-room, X-rated; Brit. informal fruity, near the knuckle.

ease noun **1** *he defeated them all with ease:* **effortlessness**, no trouble, simplicity. **2** *his ease of manner:* **naturalness**, casualness, informality, amiability, affability; unconcern, composure, nonchalance, insouciance. **3** *a life of ease:* **affluence**, wealth, prosperity, luxury, plenty; comfort, contentment, enjoyment, well-being.
– OPPOSITES difficulty, formality, trouble, hardship.
• verb **1** *the alcohol eased his pain:* **relieve**, alleviate, mitigate, soothe, palliate, moderate, dull, deaden, numb; reduce, lighten, diminish. **2** *the rain eased off:* **abate**, subside, die down, let up, slacken off, diminish, lessen, peter out, relent. **3** *work helped to ease her mind:* **calm**, quieten, pacify, soothe, comfort, console; hearten, gladden, uplift, encourage. **4** *he eased out the cork:* **slide**, slip, squeeze; guide, manoeuvre, inch, edge.
– OPPOSITES aggravate, worsen, hinder.

easily adverb **1** *I overcame this problem easily:* **effortlessly**, comfortably, simply; with ease, without difficulty, without a hitch; informal no problem/sweat. **2** *he's easily the best:* **undoubtedly**, without doubt, without question, indisputably, undeniably, definitely, certainly, clearly, obviously, patently; by far, far and away, by a mile.

eastern adjective **east**, easterly; oriental.

easy adjective **1** *the task was very easy:* **uncomplicated**, undemanding, unchallenging, effortless, painless, trouble-free, simple, straightforward, elementary, plain sailing; informal a piece of cake, child's play, kids' stuff, a cinch, no sweat, a doddle, a breeze; Brit. informal easy-peasy; N. Amer. informal duck soup, a snap. **2** *an easy baby:* **docile**, manageable, placid, compliant, acquiescent, obliging, cooperative, easy-going. **3** *an easy target:* **vulnerable**, susceptible, defenceless; naive, gullible, trusting. **4** *Vic's easy manner:* **natural**, casual, informal, unceremonious, unreserved, unaffected, easy-going, amiable, affable, genial, good-humoured; carefree, nonchalant, unconcerned; informal laid-back. **5** *an easy life:* **quiet**, tranquil, serene, peaceful, untroubled, contented, relaxed, comfortable, secure, safe; informal cushy. **6** *an easy pace:* **leisurely**, unhurried, comfortable, undemanding, easy-going, gentle, sedate, moderate, steady.
– OPPOSITES difficult, demanding, formal.

easy-going adjective **relaxed**, even-tempered, placid, mellow, mild, happy-go-lucky, carefree, free and easy, nonchalant, insouciant, imperturbable; amiable, considerate, undemanding, patient,

tolerant, lenient, broad-minded, understanding; good-natured, pleasant, agreeable; informal laid-back, unflappable.
– OPPOSITES intolerant.

eat verb **1** *we ate a hearty breakfast:* **consume**, devour, ingest, partake of; gobble down, guzzle, bolt, wolf down; munch, chomp; informal put away, demolish, dispose of, polish off, pig out on; Brit. informal scoff; N. Amer. informal scarf, snarf. **2** *acidic water can eat away at pipes:* **erode**, corrode, burn through, consume, dissolve, decay, rot; damage, destroy.

e

eavesdrop verb **listen in**, spy; overhear; informal snoop, earwig.

ebb verb **1** *the tide ebbed:* **recede**, go out, retreat. **2** *his courage began to ebb:* **diminish**, dwindle, wane, fade away, peter out, decline, flag.
– OPPOSITES increase.

ebony adjective **black**, jet black, pitch black, coal black, sable, inky, sooty, raven.

ebullience noun **exuberance**, buoyancy, cheerfulness, cheeriness, merriment, jollity, sunniness, jauntiness, high spirits; animation, sparkle, vivacity, enthusiasm, perkiness; informal bubbliness, chirpiness, bounciness.

ebullient adjective **exuberant**, buoyant, cheerful, joyful, cheery, merry, jolly, sunny, jaunty; animated, sparkling, vivacious, irrepressible; informal bubbly, bouncy, upbeat, chirpy, full of beans.
– OPPOSITES depressed.

eccentric adjective *eccentric behaviour:* **unconventional**, abnormal, irregular, aberrant, anomalous, queer, strange, peculiar, weird, bizarre, odd, outlandish; idiosyncratic, quirky, nonconformist; informal way out, offbeat, freaky, oddball, wacky, cranky; Brit. informal rum; N. Amer. informal kooky, wacko.
– OPPOSITES conventional.
• noun *he was something of an eccentric:* **oddity**, free spirit; misfit; informal oddball, weirdo, freak, nut, crank; Brit. informal one-off, odd bod, nutter; N. Amer. informal wacko, screwball.

eccentricity noun **peculiarity**, oddity, singularity, oddness, strangeness, weirdness, quirkiness; foible, idiosyncrasy, quirk; N. Amer. informal kookiness.

ecclesiastical adjective **priestly**, ministerial, clerical, canonical, sacerdotal; church, churchly, religious, spiritual, holy, divine; informal churchy.

echelon noun **level**, rank, grade, step, rung, tier, position, order.

echo noun *a faint echo of my shout:* **reverberation**, reflection, ringing, repetition, repeat.
• verb **1** *his laughter echoed round the room:* **reverberate**, resonate, resound, reflect, ring, vibrate. **2** *Bill echoed Rex's words:* **repeat**, restate, reiterate; copy, imitate, parrot, mimic; reproduce, recite, quote, regurgitate; informal recap. **3** *the garden echoes the relaxed style of the interior:* **repeat**, reflect, continue, complement.

eclectic adjective **wide-ranging**, broad-based, extensive, comprehensive, encyclopedic; varied, diverse, catholic, all-embracing, multifaceted, multifarious, heterogeneous, miscellaneous, assorted.

eclipse verb *she was eclipsed by her brother:* **outshine**, overshadow, surpass, exceed, outclass, outstrip, outdo, top, trump, transcend, upstage.

economic adjective **1** *economic reform:* **financial**, monetary, budgetary, fiscal; commercial. **2** *the firm cannot remain economic:* **profitable**, moneymaking, lucrative, remunerative, fruitful, productive; solvent, viable, cost-effective. **3** *an economic alternative to carpeting:* **cheap**, inexpensive, low-cost, budget, economy, economical, cut-price, discount, bargain.
– OPPOSITES unprofitable, expensive.

economical adjective **1** *an economical car:* **cheap**, inexpensive, low-cost, budget, economy, economic; cut-price, discount, bargain. **2** *a very economical shopper:* **thrifty**, provident, prudent, sensible, frugal, sparing, abstemious; mean, parsimonious, penny-pinching, miserly; N. Amer. forehanded; informal stingy.
– OPPOSITES expensive, spendthrift.

economize verb **save money**, cut costs; cut back, make cutbacks, retrench, budget, make economies, be thrifty, be frugal, scrimp, cut corners, tighten your belt, draw in your horns, watch the pennies.

economy noun **1** *the nation's economy:* **wealth**, financial resources. **2** *one can combine good living with economy:* **thrift**, thriftiness, prudence, careful budgeting, economizing, saving, restraint, frugality, abstemiousness; N. Amer. forehandedness.
– OPPOSITES extravagance.

ecstasy noun **rapture**, bliss, elation, euphoria, transports, rhapsodies; joy, jubilation, exultation.
– OPPOSITES misery.

ecstatic adjective **enraptured**, elated, euphoric, rapturous, joyful, overjoyed, blissful; on cloud nine, in seventh heaven, beside yourself with joy, jumping for joy, delighted, thrilled, exultant; informal over the moon, on top of the world, blissed out.

ecumenical adjective **non-denominational**, universal, all-embracing, all-inclusive.
– OPPOSITES denominational.

eddy noun *the current formed eddies in the river:* **swirl**, whirlpool, vortex. • verb *snow eddied around her:* **swirl**, whirl, spiral, wind, circulate, twist; flow, ripple, stream, surge.

edge noun **1** *the edge of the lake:* **border**, boundary, extremity, fringe, margin, side; lip, rim, brim, brink, verge; perimeter, circumference, periphery, limits, bounds. **2** *she had an edge in her voice:* **sharpness**, severity, bite, sting, acerbity, acidity, trenchancy; sarcasm, malice, spite, venom. **3** *they have an edge over their rivals:* **advantage**, lead, head start, the whip hand, the upper hand; superiority, dominance, ascendancy, supremacy, primacy.
– OPPOSITES middle, disadvantage.
• verb **1** *poplars edged the orchard:* **border**, fringe, skirt; surround, enclose, encircle, circle, encompass, bound. **2** *a frock edged with lace:* **trim**, decorate, finish; border, fringe; hem. **3** *he edged closer to the fire:* **creep**, inch, work your way, ease yourself; sidle, steal, slink.
■ **on edge**. See EDGY.

edgy adjective **1** *she seemed edgy and paced to and fro:* **tense**, nervous, on edge, anxious, apprehensive, uneasy, unsettled; twitchy, jumpy, nervy, keyed up, restive, skittish, neurotic, insecure; informal uptight, wired; Brit. informal strung up. **2** (informal) *the band has lost none of its edgy style:* **unconventional**, original, innovative, cutting-edge, contemporary, sharp; avant-garde, experimental.
– OPPOSITES calm.

edible adjective **safe/fit to eat**, fit for human consumption; digestible, palatable.

edict noun **decree**, order, command, commandment, mandate, proclamation, pronouncement, dictate; law, statute, act, bill, ruling, injunction; formal ordinance.

edifice noun **building**, structure, construction, complex; property, development, premises.

edify verb (formal) **educate**, instruct, teach, school, tutor, train, guide; enlighten, inform, cultivate, develop, improve, better.

edit verb **1** *she edited the text:* **correct**, check, copy-edit, improve, emend, polish; modify, adapt, revise, rewrite, reword, rework, redraft; shorten, condense, cut, abridge; informal clean up. **2** *he's editing a collection of the poet's essays:* **select**, choose, assemble, organize, put together, compile.

edition noun **issue**, number, volume, impression, publication; version.

educate verb **teach**, school, tutor, instruct, coach, train, drill; guide, inform, enlighten; inculcate, indoctrinate; formal edify.

educated adjective **informed**, literate, schooled, tutored, well read, learned, knowledgeable, enlightened; intellectual, academic, erudite, scholarly, cultivated, cultured.

education noun **1** *the education of young children:* **teaching**, schooling, tuition, tutoring, instruction, coaching, training, tutelage, guidance; formal edification. **2** *a woman of some education:* **learning**, knowledge, scholarship, enlightenment.

WORD LINKS

pedagogic relating to education

e

educational adjective **1** *an educational establishment:* **academic**, scholastic, learning, teaching, pedagogic. **2** *an educational experience:* **instructive**, instructional, educative, informative, illuminating, enlightening; formal edifying.

educative adjective. See **EDUCATIONAL** sense 2.

e

educator noun **teacher**, tutor, instructor, schoolteacher, schoolmaster, schoolmistress; educationalist; lecturer, professor; guide, mentor, guru; N. Amer. informal schoolmarm; formal pedagogue.

eerie adjective **uncanny**, sinister, ghostly, unnatural, unearthly, supernatural, other-worldly; strange, abnormal, odd, weird, freakish; informal creepy, scary, spooky, freaky.

efface verb **erase**, eradicate, expunge, blot out, rub out, wipe out, remove, eliminate; delete, cancel, obliterate, blank out.

effect noun **1** *the effect of rapid social change:* **result**, consequence, upshot, outcome, repercussions, ramifications; end result, conclusion, culmination, corollary, concomitant, aftermath; fruits, product, by-product; informal pay-off. **2** *the experience had a profound effect on him:* **impact**, influence; impression. **3** *the dead man's effects:* **belongings**, possessions, worldly goods, chattels; property.
– OPPOSITES cause.
• verb *they effected many changes:* **achieve**, accomplish, carry out, realize, bring off, bring about, execute, engineer, perform, do, complete; formal effectuate.
■ **in effect** really, in reality, in truth, in fact, effectively, essentially, in essence, practically, to all intents and purposes, all but, as good as, more or less, almost, nearly; literary well-nigh, nigh on. **take effect 1** *these measures will take effect in May:* come into force, come into operation, begin, become valid, become law, apply, be applied. **2** *the drug started to take effect:* work, act, be effective.

> ! Don't confuse **effect** with **affect**, which chiefly means 'make a difference to' (*the experience affected her personality*).

effective adjective **1** *an effective treatment:* **successful**, effectual, potent, powerful; helpful, beneficial, advantageous, valuable, useful; formal efficacious. **2** *an effective argument:* **convincing**, compelling, strong, forceful, sound, valid; impressive, persuasive, plausible, credible, authoritative; logical, reasonable, lucid, coherent, cogent, eloquent. **3** *the new law will be effective from next week:* **operative**, in force, in effect; valid, official, lawful, legal, binding; Law effectual. **4** *the country was under effective Japanese control:* **virtual**, practical, essential, actual, implicit, tacit.
– OPPOSITES weak, invalid, theoretical.

effectiveness noun **success**, productiveness, potency, power; formal efficacy.

effectual adjective **effective**, successful, productive, constructive; worthwhile, helpful, beneficial, advantageous, valuable, useful; formal efficacious.

effeminate adjective **womanish**, effete, foppish, mincing; informal camp, limp-wristed.
– OPPOSITES manly.

effervesce verb **fizz**, sparkle, bubble; froth, foam.

effervescence noun **1** *wines full of effervescence:* **fizz**, fizziness, sparkle, bubbliness. **2** *his cheeky effervescence:* **vivacity**, liveliness, high spirits, ebullience, exuberance, buoyancy, sparkle, gaiety, jollity, cheerfulness, perkiness, breeziness, enthusiasm, irrepressibility, vitality, zest, energy, dynamism; informal pep, bounce.

effervescent adjective **1** *an effervescent drink:* **fizzy**, sparkling, carbonated, aerated, gassy, bubbly. **2** *effervescent young people:* **vivacious**, lively, animated, high-spirited, bubbly, ebullient, buoyant, sparkling, scintillating, light-hearted, jaunty, happy, jolly, cheery, cheerful, perky, sunny, enthusiastic, irrepressible, vital, zestful, energetic, dynamic; informal peppy, bouncy, upbeat, chirpy, full of beans.
– OPPOSITES still, depressed.

effete adjective **1** *effete trendies from art college:* **affected**, pretentious,

precious, mannered, over-refined; Brit. informal **poncey**. **2** *an effete young man:* **effeminate**, girlish, feminine; soft, timid, cowardly, lily-livered, spineless, pusillanimous; informal sissy, wimpish, wimpy.
– OPPOSITES manly, powerful.

efficacious adjective (formal) **effective**, effectual, successful, productive, constructive; helpful, beneficial, advantageous, valuable, useful.

efficacy noun (formal) **effectiveness**, success, productiveness, power; benefit, advantage, value, virtue, usefulness.

efficiency noun **1** *we need reforms to bring efficiency:* **organization**, order, orderliness, regulation, coherence; productivity, effectiveness. **2** *I compliment you on your efficiency:* **competence**, capability, ability, proficiency, adeptness, expertise, professionalism, skill, effectiveness.

efficient adjective **1** *efficient techniques:* **organized**, methodical, systematic, logical, orderly, businesslike, streamlined, productive, effective, cost-effective. **2** *an efficient secretary:* **competent**, capable, able, proficient, adept, skilful, skilled, effective, productive, organized, businesslike.
– OPPOSITES disorganized, incompetent.

effigy noun **statue**, statuette, sculpture, model, dummy; guy; likeness, image; bust.

effluent noun **waste**, sewage, effluvium, outflow, discharge, emission.

effort noun **1** *an effort to work together:* **attempt**, try, endeavour; informal crack, shot, stab, bash. **2** *a fine effort:* **achievement**, accomplishment, feat; undertaking, enterprise, work; result, outcome. **3** *the job requires little effort:* **exertion**, energy, work, application, labour, muscle, toil, strain; informal sweat, elbow grease; Brit. informal graft.

effortless adjective **easy**, undemanding, unchallenging, painless, simple, uncomplicated, straightforward, elementary; fluent, natural; informal as easy as pie, child's play, kids' stuff, a cinch, no sweat, a doddle, a breeze; Brit. informal easy-peasy; N. Amer. informal duck soup, a snap.
– OPPOSITES difficult.

effrontery noun **impudence**, impertinence, cheek, insolence, audacity, temerity, presumption, nerve, gall, shamelessness, impoliteness, disrespect, bad manners; informal brass neck, face, chutzpah; Brit. informal sauce.

effusive adjective **gushing**, unrestrained, extravagant, fulsome, demonstrative, lavish, enthusiastic, lyrical; expansive, wordy, verbose.
– OPPOSITES restrained.

egg noun **ovum**; gamete, germ cell; (**eggs**) roe, spawn.
■ **egg someone on** urge, goad, incite, provoke, push, drive, prod, prompt, induce, impel, spur on; encourage, exhort, motivate, galvanize.

> **WORD LINKS**
> **oval**, **ovate**, **ovoid** egg-shaped
> **oviparous** egg-laying

ego noun **self-esteem**, self-importance, self-worth, self-respect, self-image, self-confidence.

egocentric adjective **self-centred**, egomaniacal, self-interested, selfish, self-seeking, self-absorbed, self-obsessed; narcissistic, vain, self-important.
– OPPOSITES altruistic.

egotism, **egoism** noun **self-centredness**, egomania, egocentricity, self-interest, selfishness, self-seeking, self-serving, self-regard, self-obsession; narcissism, vanity, conceit, self-importance; boastfulness.

egotist, **egoist** noun **self-seeker**, egocentric, egomaniac, narcissist; boaster, braggart; informal swank, show-off, big-head; N. Amer. informal showboat.

egotistic, **egoistic** adjective **self-centred**, selfish, egocentric, egomaniacal, self-interested, self-seeking, self-absorbed, self-obsessed; narcissistic, vain, conceited, self-important; boastful.

egress noun (formal) **departure**, exit, withdrawal, retreat; way out, escape route.
– OPPOSITES entrance.

eight cardinal number **octet**, eightsome, octuplets.

> WORD LINKS
> **octagon** a plane figure with eight sides

eject verb **1** *the volcano ejected ash:* **emit**, spew out, discharge, give off, send out, belch, vent; expel, release, disgorge, spout, vomit, throw up. **2** *the pilot had time to eject:* **bail out**, escape, get out. **3** *they were ejected from the hall:* **expel**, throw out, turn out, remove, oust; evict, banish; informal chuck out, kick out, turf out, boot out; N. Amer. informal give someone the bum's rush.
– OPPOSITES admit, appoint.

ejection noun **1** *the ejection of electrons:* **emission**, discharge, expulsion, release; elimination. **2** *their ejection from the ground:* **expulsion**, removal; eviction.

eke verb *I had to eke out my remaining funds:* **husband**, stretch, use sparingly, be thrifty with, be frugal with, be sparing with, use economically; informal go easy on.
– OPPOSITES squander.

elaborate adjective **1** *an elaborate plan:* **complicated**, complex, intricate, involved; detailed, painstaking, careful; tortuous, convoluted, Byzantine. **2** *an elaborate plasterwork ceiling:* **ornate**, decorated, embellished, adorned, ornamented, fancy, fussy, busy, ostentatious, extravagant, showy, baroque, rococo.
– OPPOSITES simple, plain.
• verb *both sides refused to elaborate on their reasons:* **expand on**, enlarge on, add to, flesh out; develop, fill out, amplify.

elan noun **flair**, style, panache, confidence, dash, éclat; energy, vigour, vitality, liveliness, brio, esprit, animation, vivacity, zest, verve, spirit, pep, sparkle, enthusiasm, gusto, eagerness, feeling, fire; informal pizzazz, zing, zip, vim, oomph.

elapse verb **pass**, go by/past, wear on, slip by/away/past, roll by/past, slide by/past, steal by/past, tick by/past.

elastic adjective **1** *elastic material:* **stretchy**, elasticated, springy, flexible, pliant, pliable, supple. **2** *an elastic concept of nationality:* **adaptable**, flexible, adjustable, accommodating, variable, fluid, versatile.
– OPPOSITES rigid.

elasticity noun **1** *the skin's natural elasticity:* **stretchiness**, flexibility, pliancy, suppleness, springiness; informal give. **2** *the elasticity of the term:* **adaptability**, flexibility, adjustability, fluidity, versatility.

elated adjective **thrilled**, delighted, overjoyed, ecstatic, euphoric, jubilant, beside yourself, exultant, rapturous, in raptures, walking on air, on cloud nine, in seventh heaven, jumping for joy, in transports of delight; informal on top of the world, over the moon, on a high, tickled pink; Austral. informal wrapped.
– OPPOSITES miserable.

elation noun **euphoria**, ecstasy, happiness, delight, joy, jubilation, exultation, bliss, rapture.

elbow verb **push**, shove, force, shoulder, jostle, barge, muscle, bulldoze.

elder adjective *his elder brother:* **older**, senior, big.
• noun *the church elders:* **leader**, patriarch, father.

elderly adjective **aged**, old, advanced in years, ageing, long in the tooth, past your prime; grey-haired, grey-bearded, grizzled, hoary; in your dotage, decrepit, doddering, senescent; informal getting on, past it, over the hill.
– OPPOSITES young, youthful.
• noun (**the elderly**) **old people**, senior citizens, old-age pensioners, OAPs; geriatrics; N. Amer. seniors, retirees, golden agers; informal wrinklies; N. Amer. informal oldsters, woopies.

elect verb **1** *a new president was elected:* **vote for**, **vote in**, return; choose, pick, select, appoint. **2** *she elected to stay behind:* **choose**, decide, opt, vote.

election noun **ballot**, vote, popular vote; poll; Brit. by-election; US primary.

> WORD LINKS
> **psephology** the study of elections and voting trends

electioneer verb **campaign**, canvass, go on the hustings, doorstep.

elector noun **voter**, constituent.

electric adjective *the atmosphere was electric:* **exciting**, charged, electrifying, thrilling, dramatic, intoxicating, dynamic, stimulating, galvanizing, rousing, stirring, moving; tense.

electricity noun **power**, energy, current, voltage, static; Brit. mains; Canadian hydro; Brit. informal leccy.

electrify verb *his masterpiece electrified cinema audiences around the world:* **excite**, thrill, stimulate, arouse, rouse, inspire, stir, exhilarate, intoxicate, galvanize, move, fire with enthusiasm, fire someone's imagination, invigorate, animate; startle, jolt, shock; N. Amer. light a fire under; informal give someone a buzz.

elegance noun **1** *he was attracted by her elegance:* **style**, stylishness, grace, gracefulness, taste, tastefulness, sophistication; refinement, dignity, beauty, poise; suaveness, urbanity. **2** *the elegance of the idea:* **neatness**, simplicity.

elegant adjective **1** *an elegant black outfit:* **stylish**, graceful, tasteful, sophisticated, classic, chic, smart; refined, poised; cultivated, polished, cultured; dashing, debonair, suave, urbane. **2** *an elegant solution:* **neat**, simple.
–OPPOSITES gauche.

elegiac adjective **mournful**, melancholic, melancholy, plaintive, sorrowful, sad, lamenting; funereal; nostalgic, poignant.
–OPPOSITES cheerful.

elegy noun **lament**, requiem, funeral poem/song; Irish keen; Irish & Scottish coronach.

element noun **component**, constituent, part, section, portion, piece, segment, bit; aspect, factor, feature, facet, ingredient, strand, detail, point; member, unit, module, item.

elemental adjective **natural**; primal, mythic, fundamental, essential, basic; rudimentary, profound, deep-rooted.

elementary adjective **1** *an elementary astronomy course:* **basic**, rudimentary; preparatory, introductory. **2** *a lot of the work is elementary:* **easy**, simple, straightforward, uncomplicated, undemanding, painless, child's play, plain sailing; informal as easy as falling off a log, as easy as pie, as easy as ABC, a piece of cake, no sweat, kids' stuff; Brit. informal easy-peasy.
–OPPOSITES advanced, difficult.

elevate verb **1** *we need a breeze to elevate the kite:* **raise**, lift, upraise; hoist, hike up, haul up. **2** *he was elevated to Secretary of State:* **promote**, upgrade, move up, raise; exalt; informal kick upstairs, move up the ladder.
–OPPOSITES lower, demote.

elevated adjective **1** *an elevated section of motorway:* **raised**, upraised, high up; overhead. **2** *elevated language:* **lofty**, grand, exalted, fine, sublime; inflated, pompous, bombastic. **3** *his elevated status:* **high**, high-ranking, lofty, exalted; grand, noble.
–OPPOSITES lowly.

elevation noun **1** *his elevation to the peerage:* **promotion**, upgrading, advancement, advance. **2** *1500 to 3000 metres in elevation:* **altitude**, height.

elf noun **pixie**, fairy, sprite, imp, brownie; dwarf, gnome, goblin, hobgoblin; leprechaun, puck, troll.

elfin adjective **elf-like**, elfish, pixie-like; puckish, impish, playful, mischievous; dainty, delicate, small, petite, slight, little, tiny, diminutive.

elicit verb **obtain**, draw out, extract, bring out, evoke, call forth, bring forth, induce, prompt, generate, engender, trigger, provoke.

eligible adjective **1** *those people eligible to vote:* **entitled**, permitted, allowed, qualified, able. **2** *an eligible bachelor:* **desirable**, suitable; available, single, unmarried, unattached.

eliminate verb **1** *a policy that would eliminate inflation:* **remove**, get rid of, put an end to, do away with, end, stop, eradicate, destroy, annihilate, stamp out, wipe out, extinguish; informal knock something on the head. **2** *he was eliminated from the title race:* **knock out**, beat; exclude, rule out, disqualify. **3** *his critics were eliminated:* **kill**, assassinate, murder, execute, do away with, liquidate.

elite noun **best**, pick, cream, crème de la crème, flower; high society, jet set, beautiful people.
–OPPOSITES dregs.

elixir noun **potion**, concoction, brew, mixture; medicine, tincture; extract, essence, concentrate, distillation; literary draught.

elliptical adjective **1** *elliptical comments:* **cryptic**, abstruse, ambiguous, obscure, oblique. **2** *an elliptical shape:* **oval**, egg-shaped, ovoid.

elongate verb **lengthen**, extend, stretch, draw out.
–OPPOSITES shorten.

eloquence noun **fluency**, articulacy, articulateness, expressiveness, silver tongue, persuasiveness, effectiveness; oratory, rhetoric; informal gift of the gab, way with words, blarney.

eloquent adjective **fluent**, articulate, expressive, silver-tongued; persuasive, well expressed, effective, lucid, vivid; smooth-tongued.
–OPPOSITES inarticulate.

elsewhere adverb **somewhere else**, in/at/to another place, in/at/to a different place, hence; not here, not present, absent, away, abroad, out.
–OPPOSITES here.

elucidate verb **explain**, make clear, illuminate, throw/shed light on, clarify, clear up, sort out, unravel, spell out; interpret.
–OPPOSITES confuse.

elude verb **evade**, avoid, get away from, dodge, escape from, run away from; lose, shake off, give someone the slip, slip away from, throw someone off the scent; informal slip through someone's fingers, slip through the net.

elusive adjective **1** *her elusive husband:* **difficult to find/locate/track down**; evasive, slippery. **2** *an elusive quality:* **indefinable**, intangible, impalpable; fugitive; ambiguous.

emaciated adjective **thin**, skeletal, bony, gaunt, wasted, thin as a rake; scrawny, skinny, scraggy, skin and bone, raw-boned, sticklike; starved, underfed, undernourished, underweight, half-starved; cadaverous, shrivelled, shrunken, withered; informal anorexic, like a bag of bones.
–OPPOSITES fat.

emanate verb **1** *warmth emanated from the fireplace:* **issue**, spread, radiate. **2** *the proposals emanated from a committee:* **originate**, stem, derive, proceed, spring, issue, emerge, flow, come. **3** *he emanated an air of power:* **exude**, emit, radiate, give off/out, send out/forth.

emancipated adjective **liberated**, independent, unconstrained, uninhibited; free.

embankment noun **bank**, mound, ridge, earthwork, causeway, barrier, levee, dam, dyke.

embargo noun *an embargo on oil sales:* **ban**, bar, prohibition, stoppage, interdict, veto, moratorium; restriction, restraint, block, barrier; boycott.
•verb *arms sales were embargoed:* **ban**, bar, prohibit, stop, outlaw; restrict, restrain, block; boycott.
–OPPOSITES allow.

embark verb **1** *he embarked at Dover:* **board ship**, go on board, go aboard. **2** *he embarked on a new career:* **begin**, start, commence, undertake, set out on, take up, get down to; enter into, venture into, launch into, plunge into, engage in, settle down to; informal get cracking on, get going on.

embarrass verb **mortify**, shame, put someone to shame, humiliate, abash, make uncomfortable; discomfit; informal show up.

embarrassed adjective **mortified**, red-faced, blushing, abashed, shamed, ashamed, shamefaced, humiliated, chagrined, self-conscious, uncomfortable, not knowing where to look, sheepish; discomfited, disconcerted; flustered, agitated; tongue-tied; informal with egg on your face, wishing the earth would swallow you up.

embarrassing adjective **humiliating**, shameful, mortifying, ignominious; awkward, uncomfortable, compromising; discomfiting; informal cringeworthy, cringe-making, toe-curling.

embarrassment noun **1** *he was scarlet with embarrassment:* **mortification**, humiliation, shame, shamefacedness, awkwardness, self-consciousness, sheepishness, discomfort, discomfiture; ignominy. **2** *his current financial embarrassment:* **difficulty**, predicament, plight, problem, mess; informal bind, jam, pickle, fix, scrape. **3** *an embarrassment of riches:* **surplus**, excess, over-abundance, superabundance, glut, surfeit, superfluity.

embed, **imbed** verb **implant**, plant, set, fix, lodge, root, insert, place; sink, drive in, hammer in, ram in.

embellish verb **1** *weapons embellished with precious metal:* **decorate**, adorn, ornament; beautify, enhance, grace; trim, garnish, gild; deck, bedeck, festoon, emblazon. **2** *the legend was embellished by an American academic:* **elaborate**, embroider, expand on, exaggerate.

embellishment noun **1** *architectural embellishments:* **decoration**, ornamentation, adornment; enhancement. **2** *we wanted the truth, not romantic embellishments:* **elaboration**, addition, exaggeration.

embezzle verb *she had embezzled £50,000 of company funds:* **misappropriate**, steal, thieve, pilfer, purloin, appropriate, defraud someone of, siphon off, pocket, help yourself to; put your hand in the till; informal rob, rip off, skim, line your pockets; Brit. informal pinch, nick, half-inch.

embezzlement noun **misappropriation**, theft, stealing, robbery, thieving, pilfering, purloining, pilferage, appropriation, swindling; fraud, larceny.

embittered adjective **bitter**, resentful, rancorous, jaundiced, aggrieved, sour, frustrated, dissatisfied, alienated, disaffected.

emblazon verb **1** *shirts emblazoned with the company name:* **adorn**, decorate, ornament, embellish; inscribe. **2** *a flag with a hammer and sickle emblazoned on it:* **display**, depict, show.

emblem noun **symbol**, representation, token, image, figure, mark, sign; crest, badge, device, insignia, stamp, seal, coat of arms, shield; logo, trademark.

emblematic adjective **symbolic**, representative, demonstrative, suggestive, indicative.

embodiment noun **personification**, incarnation, realization, manifestation, expression, representation, actualization, symbol; paradigm, epitome, paragon, soul, model; type, essence, quintessence, exemplification, exemplar, ideal; formal reification.

embody verb **1** *Gradgrind embodies the spirit of industrial capitalism:* **personify**, realize, manifest, symbolize, represent, express, incarnate, epitomize, stand for, typify, exemplify. **2** *the changes embodied in the Act:* **incorporate**, include, contain, encompass.

embolden verb **fortify**, make brave/braver, encourage, hearten, strengthen, brace, stiffen the resolve of, lift the morale of; rouse, stir, stimulate, cheer, rally, fire, animate, invigorate; informal buck up.
– OPPOSITES dishearten.

embrace verb **1** *he embraced her warmly:* **hug**, take/hold in your arms, hold, cuddle, clasp to your bosom, squeeze, clutch; caress; enfold; informal canoodle, smooch. **2** *most western European countries have embraced the concept:* **welcome**, welcome with open arms, accept, take up, take to your heart, adopt; espouse. **3** *the faculty embraces a wide range of disciplines:* **include**, take in, comprise, contain, incorporate, encompass, cover, involve, subsume.
• noun *a fond embrace:* **hug**, cuddle, squeeze, clinch, caress; bear hug.

embroider verb **1** *a cushion embroidered with a pattern of golden keys:* **sew**, stitch; decorate, adorn, ornament, embellish. **2** *she embroidered her stories with colourful detail:* **elaborate**, embellish, enlarge on, exaggerate, dress up, gild, colour; informal jazz up.

embroidery noun **1** **needlework**, needlepoint, needlecraft, sewing. **2** *fanciful embroidery of the facts:* **elaboration**, embellishment, adornment, ornamentation, colouring,

e

enhancement; exaggeration, overstatement.

embroil verb **involve**, entangle, ensnare, enmesh, catch up, mix up, bog down, mire.

embryonic adjective **rudimentary**, undeveloped, unformed, immature, incomplete, incipient; fledgling, budding, nascent, emerging, developing.
–OPPOSITES mature.

e

emerge verb **1** *a policeman emerged from the alley:* **come out**, appear, come into view, become visible, surface, materialize, issue, come forth. **2** *several unexpected facts emerged:* **become known**, become apparent, be revealed, come to light, come out, turn up, transpire, unfold, turn out, prove to be the case.

emergence noun **appearance**, arrival, coming, materialization; advent, inception, dawn, birth, origination, start, development.

emergency noun *a military emergency:* **crisis**; extremity; disaster, catastrophe, calamity; informal panic stations.
• adjective **1** *an emergency meeting:* **urgent**, crisis; extraordinary. **2** *emergency supplies:* **reserve**, standby, backup, fallback.

emergent adjective **emerging**, developing, rising, dawning, budding, embryonic, infant, fledgling, nascent, incipient.

emigrate verb **move abroad**, move overseas, leave your country, migrate; relocate, resettle.
–OPPOSITES immigrate.

emigration noun **migration**; exodus, diaspora; relocation, resettling.

eminence noun **fame**, celebrity, illustriousness, distinction, renown, pre-eminence, greatness, prestige, importance, reputation, note; prominence, superiority, stature, standing.

eminent adjective **1** *an eminent man of letters:* **illustrious**, distinguished, renowned, esteemed, pre-eminent, notable, noteworthy, great, prestigious, important, influential, outstanding, noted, of note; famous, celebrated, prominent, well known, acclaimed, exalted, revered, venerable. **2** *the eminent reasonableness of their claims:* **obvious**, clear, conspicuous, marked, singular, signal; total, complete, utter, absolute, thorough, perfect, downright, sheer.
–OPPOSITES unknown.

eminently adverb **very**, greatly, highly, exceedingly, extremely, particularly, exceptionally, supremely, uniquely; conspicuously, singularly; totally, completely, utterly, absolutely, thoroughly, perfectly, downright.

emissary noun **envoy**, ambassador, delegate, attaché, consul; agent, representative.

emission noun **discharge**, release, outpouring, outflow, outrush, leak, excretion, secretion, ejection.

emit verb **1** *hydrocarbons emitted from vehicle exhausts:* **discharge**, release, give out/off, pour out, send forth, throw out, issue; leak, ooze, excrete, disgorge, secrete, eject; spout, belch, spew out; emanate, radiate, exude. **2** *he emitted a loud cry:* **utter**, voice, let out, produce, give vent to, come out with.
–OPPOSITES absorb.

emotion noun **1** *she was good at hiding her emotions:* **feeling**, sentiment; reaction, response. **2** *overcome by emotion, she turned away:* **passion**, strength of feeling. **3** *responses based purely on emotion:* **instinct**, intuition, gut feeling; sentiment, the heart.

emotional adjective **1** *an emotional young man:* **passionate**, hot-blooded, ardent, fervent, excitable, temperamental, melodramatic, tempestuous; demonstrative, responsive, sentimental, sensitive. **2** *he paid an emotional tribute to his wife:* **poignant**, moving, touching, affecting, powerful, stirring, emotive, heart-rending, heart-warming, impassioned, dramatic; informal tear-jerking.
–OPPOSITES unfeeling.

emotionless adjective **unemotional**, unfeeling, dispassionate, passionless, unexpressive, cool, cold, cold-blooded, impassive, indifferent, detached, remote, aloof; toneless, flat, dead, expressionless, blank, wooden, stony, deadpan.

emotive adjective **controversial**, contentious, inflammatory; sensitive, delicate, difficult, problematic, touchy, awkward, prickly, ticklish.

empathize verb **identify**, sympathize, understand, share someone's feelings, be in tune; relate to, feel for, have insight into; informal put yourself in someone else's shoes.

emperor noun **ruler**, sovereign, king, monarch, potentate.

> **WORD LINKS**
> **imperial** relating to an emperor or empire

emphasis noun **1** *the curriculum gave more emphasis to reading and writing:* **prominence**, importance, significance, value; stress, weight, accent, attention, priority, pre-eminence, urgency, force. **2** *the emphasis is on the word 'little':* **stress**, accent, weight, prominence; beat.

emphasize verb **stress**, underline, highlight, focus attention on, point up, lay stress on, draw attention to, spotlight, foreground; bring to the fore, belabour; accentuate, underscore; informal press home, rub it in.
– OPPOSITES understate.

emphatic adjective **vehement**, firm, wholehearted, forceful, energetic, vigorous, direct, insistent; certain, definite, out-and-out, one hundred per cent; decided, determined, categorical, unqualified, unconditional, unequivocal, unambiguous, absolute, explicit, downright, outright, clear.
– OPPOSITES hesitant.

empire noun **1** *the Ottoman Empire:* **kingdom**, realm, domain, territory; commonwealth; power, world power, superpower. **2** *a worldwide shipping empire:* **organization**, corporation, multinational, conglomerate, consortium, company, business, firm, operation.

empirical adjective **experiential**, practical, first-hand, hands-on; observed, seen.
– OPPOSITES theoretical.

employ verb **1** *she employed a chauffeur:* **hire**, engage, recruit, take on, sign up, put on the payroll, enrol, appoint; retain. **2** *Sam was employed in carving a stone figure:* **occupy**, engage, involve, keep busy, tie up; absorb, engross, immerse. **3** *the team employed subtle psychological tactics:* **use**, utilize, make use of, avail yourself of; apply, exercise, practise, put into practice, exert, bring into play, bring to bear; draw on, resort to, turn to, have recourse to.
– OPPOSITES dismiss.

employed adjective **working**, in work, in employment, holding down a job; earning, waged.

employee noun **worker**, member of staff; blue-collar worker, white-collar worker, workman, labourer, hand; (**employees**) personnel, staff, workforce, human resources, liveware.

employment noun **work**, labour, service; job, post, position, situation, occupation, profession, trade, métier, business, line, line of work, calling, vocation, craft.

emporium noun **shop**, store, outlet, retail outlet; department store, chain store, supermarket, hypermarket, superstore, megastore; establishment.

empower verb **1** *the act empowered Henry to punish heretics:* **authorize**, entitle, permit, allow, license, enable. **2** *movements to empower the poor:* **emancipate**, unshackle, set free, liberate.
– OPPOSITES forbid.

empress noun **ruler**, sovereign, queen, monarch, potentate.

emptiness noun **void**, vacuum, empty space, gap, hole.

empty adjective **1** *an empty house:* **vacant**, unoccupied, uninhabited, untenanted, bare, desolate, deserted, abandoned; clear, free. **2** *an empty threat:* **meaningless**, hollow, idle, vain, futile, worthless, useless, ineffectual. **3** *without her my life is empty:* **futile**, pointless, purposeless, worthless, meaningless, valueless, of no value, useless, of no use, aimless, senseless, inconsequential. **4** *his eyes were empty:* **blank**, expressionless, vacant, wooden, stony, impassive, absent, glazed, fixed, lifeless, emotionless, unresponsive.
– OPPOSITES full, serious, worthwhile.

• verb **1** *I emptied the dishwasher:* **unload**, unpack; clear, evacuate. **2** *he emptied out the contents of the case:* **remove**, take out, extract, tip out, pour out.
– OPPOSITES fill.

emulate verb **imitate**, copy, mirror, echo, follow, model yourself on, take a leaf out of someone's book; match, equal, parallel, be on a par with, be in the same league as, come close to; compete with, contend with, rival, surpass.

e

enable verb **allow**, permit, let, equip, empower, make able, fit; authorize, entitle, qualify.
– OPPOSITES prevent.

enact verb **act out**, act, perform, appear in, stage, mount, put on, present.

enactment noun **acting**, performing, performance, staging, presentation.

enamoured adjective **in love**, love-struck, infatuated, besotted, smitten, captivated, enchanted, fascinated, bewitched, beguiled; keen on, taken with; informal mad about, crazy about, wild about, bowled over by, struck on, sweet on, carrying a torch for.

encampment noun **camp**, military camp, bivouac; campsite; tents.

encapsulate verb **summarize**, sum up, put in a nutshell; capture, express.

enchant verb **captivate**, charm, delight, enrapture, entrance, enthral, beguile, bewitch, spellbind, fascinate, hypnotize, mesmerize, rivet, grip, transfix; informal bowl someone over.
– OPPOSITES bore.

enchanting adjective **captivating**, charming, delightful, bewitching, beguiling, adorable, lovely, attractive, appealing, engaging, winning, fetching, winsome, alluring, disarming, irresistible, fascinating.

enchantment noun **allure**, delight, charm, beauty, attractiveness, appeal, fascination, irresistibility, magnetism, pull, draw, lure.

encircle verb **surround**, enclose, circle, girdle, ring, encompass; close in, shut in, fence in, wall in, hem in, confine; literary gird.

enclose verb **1** *tall trees enclosed the garden:* **surround**, circle, ring, girdle, encompass, encircle; close in, shut in, fence in, wall in, hedge in, hem in. **2** *please enclose a stamped addressed envelope:* **include**, insert, put in; send.

> **WORD LINKS**
> **claustrophobia** fear of enclosed spaces

enclosure noun **paddock**, fold, pen, compound, stockade, ring, yard; sty, coop; N. Amer. corral.

encompass verb **cover**, embrace, include, incorporate, take in, contain, comprise, involve, deal with.

encounter verb **1** *I encountered a girl I used to know:* **meet**, run into, come across/upon, stumble across/on, chance on, happen on; informal bump into. **2** *we encountered a slight problem:* **experience**, run into, come up against, face, be faced with, confront.
• noun **1** *an unexpected encounter:* **meeting**, chance meeting. **2** *a violent encounter between police and demonstrators:* **battle**, fight, clash, confrontation, struggle, skirmish, engagement; informal run-in, set-to, dust-up, scrap.

encourage verb **1** *the players were encouraged by the crowd's response:* **hearten**, cheer, buoy up, uplift, inspire, motivate, spur on, stir, stir up, fire up, stimulate, invigorate, vitalize, revitalize, embolden, fortify; informal buck up, pep up, give a shot in the arm to. **2** *she had encouraged him to go:* **persuade**, coax, urge, press, push, pressure, pressurize, prod, goad, egg on, prompt, influence, sway. **3** *the Government was keen to encourage local businesses:* **support**, back, champion, promote, further, foster, nurture, cultivate, strengthen, stimulate; help, assist, aid, boost, fuel.
– OPPOSITES discourage, dissuade, hinder.

encouragement noun **1** *she needed a bit of encouragement:* **support**, cheering up, inspiration, motivation, stimulation; morale-boosting; informal a shot in the arm. **2** *they* *required no encouragement to get back to work:* **persuasion**, coaxing, urging, prodding, prompting, inducement, incentive, carrot. **3** *the encouragement of foreign investment:* **support**, backing, championship, championing, sponsoring, promotion, furtherance, furthering, fostering, nurture, cultivation; help, assistance; N. Amer. boosterism.

encouraging adjective **1** *an encouraging start:* **promising**, hopeful, auspicious, favourable; heartening, reassuring, cheering, comforting, welcome, pleasing, gratifying. **2** *my parents were very encouraging:* **supportive**, understanding, helpful; positive, responsive, enthusiastic.

encroach verb **intrude**, trespass, impinge, invade, infiltrate, interrupt, infringe, violate, interfere with, disturb; tread/step on someone's toes; informal horn in on, muscle in on.

encroachment noun **intrusion**, trespass, invasion, infiltration, incursion, obtrusion, infringement, impingement.

encumber verb **1** *her movements were encumbered by her heavy skirts:* **hamper**, hinder, obstruct, impede, cramp, inhibit, restrict, limit, constrain, restrain, bog down, retard, slow; inconvenience, disadvantage, handicap. **2** *they are encumbered with debt:* **burden**, load, weigh down, saddle; overwhelm, tax, overload; Brit. informal lumber.

encumbrance noun **burden**, responsibility, obligation, liability, weight, load, pressure, trouble, worry; millstone, albatross.

encyclopedic adjective **comprehensive**, complete, thorough, thorough-going, full, exhaustive, in-depth, wide-ranging, all-inclusive, all-embracing, all-encompassing, universal, vast; formal compendious.

end noun **1** *the end of the road:* **extremity**, furthermost part, limit; margin, edge, border, boundary, periphery; point, tip, tail end; N. Amer. tag end. **2** *the end of the novel:* **conclusion**, termination, ending, finish, close, resolution, climax, finale, culmination, denouement. **3** *a cigarette end:* **butt**, stub, stump. **4** *wealth is a means and not an end in itself:* **aim**, goal, purpose, objective, object, holy grail, target; intention, intent; aspiration, wish, desire, ambition. **5** *the commercial end of the business:* **aspect**, side, section, area, field, part, share, portion, segment, province. **6** *his end might come at any time:* **death**, dying, demise, passing, expiry; doom, extinction, annihilation, extermination, destruction; downfall, ruin, ruination, Waterloo; formal decease.

– OPPOSITES beginning.

• verb **1** *the show ended with a wedding scene:* **finish**, conclude, terminate, come to an end, draw to a close, close, stop, cease; culminate, climax. **2** *she ended their relationship:* **break off**, call off, bring to an end, put an end to, stop, finish, terminate, discontinue; dissolve, cancel.

– OPPOSITES begin.

endanger verb **imperil**, jeopardize, risk, put at risk, put in danger; threaten, pose a threat to, be a danger to.

endearing adjective **lovable**, adorable, cute, sweet, dear, delightful, lovely, charming, appealing, attractive, engaging, winning, captivating, enchanting, beguiling, winsome.

endeavour verb *the company endeavoured to expand its activities:* **try**, attempt, seek, undertake, aspire, aim, set out; strive, struggle, labour, toil, work.

• noun **1** *an endeavour to build a more buoyant economy:* **attempt**, try, bid, effort, venture; informal go, crack, shot, stab, bash. **2** *an extremely unwise endeavour:* **undertaking**, enterprise, venture, exercise, activity, exploit, deed, act, action, move; scheme, plan, project; informal caper.

ending noun **end**, finish, close, closing, conclusion, resolution, summing-up, denouement, finale; cessation, stopping, termination, discontinuation.

– OPPOSITES beginning.

endless adjective **1** *a woman with endless energy:* **unlimited**, limitless, infinite, inexhaustible, boundless,

unbounded, untold, immeasurable, measureless, incalculable; abundant, abounding, great; ceaseless, unceasing, unending, without end, everlasting, constant, continuous, continual, interminable, unfading, unfailing, perpetual, eternal, enduring, lasting. **2** *as children we played endless games:* **countless**, innumerable, untold, legion, numberless, unnumbered, numerous, very many, manifold, multitudinous, multifarious; a great number of, infinite numbers of, a multitude of; informal umpteen, no end of, loads of, stacks of, heaps of, masses of, oodles of, zillions of; N. Amer. informal gazillions of; literary myriad, divers.
–OPPOSITES limited, few.

e

endorse verb **support**, back, agree with, approve, favour, subscribe to, recommend, champion, stick up for, uphold, affirm, sanction; informal throw your weight behind.
–OPPOSITES oppose.

endorsement noun **support**, backing, approval, seal of approval, agreement, recommendation, championship, patronage, affirmation, sanction.

endow verb **provide**, supply, furnish, equip, invest, favour, bless, grace, gift; give, bestow.

endowment noun **1** *a generous endowment:* **bequest**, legacy, inheritance; gift, present, grant, award, donation, contribution, subsidy, settlement. **2** *his natural endowments:* **quality**, characteristic, feature, attribute, faculty, ability, talent, gift, strength, aptitude, capability, capacity.

endurable adjective **bearable**, tolerable, supportable, manageable, sustainable.

endurance noun **1** *she pushed him beyond the limit of his endurance:* **toleration**, tolerance, sufferance, forbearance, patience, acceptance, resignation, stoicism. **2** *the race is a test of endurance:* **stamina**, staying power, fortitude, perseverance, persistence, tenacity, doggedness, grit, indefatigability, resolution, determination; informal stickability.

endure verb **1** *he endured years of pain:* **undergo**, go through, live through, experience; cope with, deal with, face, suffer, tolerate, put up with, brave, bear, withstand, sustain, weather. **2** *our love will endure for ever:* **last**, live, live on, go on, survive, abide, continue, persist, remain.
–OPPOSITES fade.

enduring adjective **lasting**, long-lasting, abiding, durable, continuing, persisting, eternal, perennial, permanent, unending, everlasting; constant, stable, steady, steadfast, fixed, firm, unwavering, unfaltering, unchanging.
–OPPOSITES short-lived.

enemy noun **opponent**, adversary, rival, antagonist, combatant, challenger, competitor, opposition, competition, other side; literary foe.
–OPPOSITES ally.

energetic adjective **1** *an energetic woman:* **active**, lively, dynamic, spirited, animated, vital, vibrant, bouncy, bubbly, exuberant, sprightly, tireless, indefatigable, enthusiastic; informal peppy, sparky, feisty, full of beans, full of the joys of spring, bright-eyed and bushy-tailed. **2** *energetic exercises:* **vigorous**, strenuous, brisk; hard, arduous, demanding, taxing, tough, rigorous. **3** *an energetic advertising campaign:* **forceful**, vigorous, high-powered, all-out, determined, bold, powerful, potent; intensive, hard-hitting, pulling no punches, aggressive, high-octane; informal punchy, in-your-face.
–OPPOSITES lethargic, gentle, half-hearted.

energize verb **enliven**, liven up, animate, vitalize, invigorate, perk up, excite, electrify, stimulate, stir up, fire up, rouse, motivate, move, drive, spur on, encourage, galvanize; informal pep up, buck up, give a shot in the arm to.

energy noun **vitality**, vigour, life, liveliness, animation, vivacity, spirit, verve, enthusiasm, zest, vibrancy, spark, sparkle, effervescence, exuberance, buoyancy, sprightliness; dynamism, drive; fire, passion; informal zip, zing, pep, pizzazz, punch, bounce, oomph, go, get-up-and-go; N. Amer. informal feistiness.

enfeeble verb **weaken**, debilitate, incapacitate, lay low; drain, sap, exhaust, tire.
– OPPOSITES strengthen.

enfold verb **envelop**, engulf, sheathe, swathe, swaddle, cocoon, shroud, veil, cloak, drape, cover; surround, enclose, encase, encircle.

enforce verb **1** *the sheriff enforced the law:* **impose**, apply, administer, implement, bring to bear, discharge, execute. **2** *they cannot enforce cooperation between the parties:* **force**, compel, coerce, exact.

enforced adjective **compulsory**, obligatory, mandatory, involuntary, forced, imposed, required, prescribed, contractual, binding.
– OPPOSITES voluntary.

engage verb **1** *tasks which engage children's interest:* **capture**, catch, arrest, grab, draw, attract, gain, win, hold, grip, absorb, occupy. **2** *he engaged a secretary:* **employ**, hire, recruit, take on, enrol, appoint. **3** *the chance to engage in a wide range of pursuits:* **participate in**, take part in, partake in/of, enter into. **4** *infantry units engaged the enemy:* **fight**, do battle with, attack, take on, clash with; encounter, meet.
– OPPOSITES lose, dismiss.

engagement noun **1** *a business engagement:* **appointment**, meeting, arrangement, commitment; date, assignation, rendezvous. **2** *Britain's continued engagement in open trading:* **participation**, involvement, association. **3** *the first engagement of the war:* **battle**, fight, clash, confrontation, encounter, conflict, skirmish; action, combat, hostilities.

engaging adjective **charming**, appealing, attractive, pleasing, pleasant, agreeable, likeable, lovable, sweet, winning, winsome, fetching; Scottish & N. English bonny.
– OPPOSITES unappealing.

engender verb **cause**, be the cause of, give rise to, bring about, occasion, lead to, result in, produce, create, generate, arouse, rouse, inspire, provoke, kindle, trigger, spark, stir up, whip up.

engine noun **1** *a car engine:* **motor**; turbine. **2** *the main engine of change:* **cause**, agent, instrument, originator, initiator, generator.

engineer noun **1** *a structural engineer:* designer, planner, builder. **2** *a ship's engineer:* **operator**, driver, controller.
• verb *he engineered a takeover deal:* **bring about**, arrange, pull off, bring off, contrive, manoeuvre, manipulate, negotiate, organize, orchestrate, choreograph, mount, stage, mastermind, originate, manage, stage-manage, coordinate, direct.

England noun Brit. informal Blighty; Austral./NZ informal Old Dart; literary Albion.

engrave verb **1** *my name was engraved on the trophy:* **carve**, inscribe, cut, incise, chisel, score. **2** *the image was engraved in his memory:* **fix**, set, imprint, stamp, brand, impress, embed, etch.

engraving noun **etching**, print; plate, picture, illustration.

engross verb **absorb**, engage, rivet, grip, hold, interest, involve, occupy, preoccupy; fascinate, captivate, enthral, intrigue.

engrossed adjective **absorbed**, involved, interested, occupied, preoccupied, immersed, caught up, riveted, gripped, rapt, fascinated, intent, captivated, enthralled.

engrossing adjective **absorbing**, interesting, riveting, gripping, captivating, compelling, compulsive, fascinating, enthralling; informal unputdownable.

engulf verb **inundate**, flood, deluge, immerse, swamp, swallow up, submerge; bury, envelop, overwhelm.

enhance verb **increase**, add to, intensify, heighten, magnify, amplify, inflate, strengthen, build up, supplement, augment, boost, raise, lift, elevate, exalt; improve, enrich, complement.
– OPPOSITES diminish.

enigma noun **mystery**, puzzle, riddle, conundrum, paradox.

enigmatic adjective **mysterious**, inscrutable, puzzling, mystifying, baffling; cryptic, elliptical, paradoxical, obscure, oblique.

enjoin verb **urge**, encourage, admonish, press; instruct, direct, require, order, command, tell, call on, demand, charge; literary bid.

e

enjoy verb **1** *he enjoys playing the piano:* **like**, be fond of, delight in, appreciate, relish, revel in, adore, lap up, savour, luxuriate in, bask in; informal get a kick out of, get a thrill out of, get a buzz out of. **2** *she had always enjoyed good health:* **benefit from**, have the benefit of; be blessed with, be favoured with, be endowed with, possess, own, boast.
–OPPOSITES dislike, lack.
■ **enjoy yourself** have fun, have a good time, have the time of your life; make merry, celebrate, revel; informal party, have a ball, have a whale of a time, let your hair down.

enjoyable adjective **entertaining**, amusing, delightful, pleasant, congenial, convivial, fine, good, agreeable, pleasurable, satisfying, gratifying.

enjoyment noun **pleasure**, fun, entertainment, amusement, recreation, relaxation; happiness, merriment, joy, jollity; satisfaction, gratification, liking; humorous delectation.

enlarge verb **1** *they enlarged the scope of their research:* **extend**, expand, grow, add to, amplify, augment, magnify, build up, supplement; widen, broaden, stretch, lengthen; elongate, deepen, thicken. **2** *the lymph glands had enlarged:* **swell**, distend, bloat, bulge, dilate, blow up, puff up, balloon. **3** *he enlarged on this subject:* **elaborate on**, expand on, add to, build on, flesh out; develop, fill out, embellish, embroider.
–OPPOSITES reduce, shrink.

enlargement noun **expansion**, extension, growth, amplification, augmentation, addition, magnification, widening, broadening, lengthening; elongation, deepening, thickening; swelling, dilation.

enlighten verb **inform**, tell, make aware, open someone's eyes, illuminate, apprise, brief, update, bring up to date; informal put in the picture, clue in, fill in, put wise, bring up to speed.

enlightened adjective **informed**, well informed, aware, sophisticated, advanced, developed, liberal, open-minded, broad-minded, educated, knowledgeable, wise; civilized, refined, cultured, cultivated.
–OPPOSITES benighted.

enlightenment noun **insight**, understanding, awareness, wisdom, education, learning, knowledge; illumination, awakening, instruction, teaching; open-mindedness, broad-mindedness; culture, refinement, cultivation, civilization.

enlist verb **1** *he enlisted in the Royal Engineers:* **join up**, join, enrol in, sign up for, volunteer for. **2** *he was enlisted in the army:* **recruit**, call up, enrol, sign up; conscript; US draft. **3** *he enlisted the help of a friend:* **obtain**, engage, secure, win, get, procure.

enliven verb **1** *a meeting enlivened by her wit:* **liven up**, spice up, ginger up, leaven; informal perk up, pep up. **2** *the visit had enlivened my mother:* **cheer up**, brighten up, liven up, perk up, raise someone's spirits, uplift, gladden, buoy up, animate, vivify, vitalize, invigorate, restore, revive, refresh, stimulate, rouse, boost; informal buck up, pep up.

en masse adverb **all together**, as a group, as one, en bloc, as a whole, wholesale.

enmesh verb **embroil**, entangle, ensnare, snare, trap, entrap, ensnarl, involve, catch up, mix up, bog down, mire.

enmity noun **hostility**, animosity, antagonism, friction, antipathy, animus, acrimony, bitterness, rancour, resentment, ill feeling, bad feeling, ill will, bad blood, hatred, loathing, odium.
–OPPOSITES friendship.

ennoble verb **dignify**, honour, exalt, elevate, raise, enhance, distinguish.
–OPPOSITES demean.

enormity noun **1** *the enormity of the task:* **immensity**, hugeness; size, extent, magnitude, greatness. **2** *the enormity of his crimes:* **wickedness**, vileness, baseness, depravity; outrageousness, monstrousness, hideousness, heinousness, brutality, savagery, viciousness.

enormous adjective **huge**, vast, immense, gigantic, great, giant, massive, colossal, mammoth, tremendous, mighty, monumental, epic, prodigious, mountainous,

king-size, titanic, towering, gargantuan; informal mega, monster, whopping, humongous, jumbo, astronomical; Brit. informal whacking great, ginormous.
– OPPOSITES tiny.

enormously adverb **1** *an enormously important factor:* **very**, extremely, really, exceedingly, exceptionally, tremendously, immensely, hugely; informal terrifically, awfully, terribly, seriously, desperately, ultra; Brit. informal dead, jolly; N. Amer. informal real, mighty; informal, dated frightfully. **2** *prices vary enormously:* **considerably**, greatly, a great deal, a lot.
– OPPOSITES slightly.

enough determiner *they had enough food:* **sufficient**, adequate, ample, the necessary, plenty of.
– OPPOSITES insufficient.
• pronoun *there's enough for everyone:* **sufficient**, plenty, a sufficient amount, an adequate amount, as much as necessary; a sufficiency, an ample supply; your fill.

enquire verb **1** *I enquired about part-time training courses:* **ask**, make enquiries. **2** *the commission is to enquire into alleged illegal payments:* **investigate**, probe, look into; research, examine, explore, delve into; informal check out.

enquiring adjective **inquisitive**, curious, interested, questioning, probing, searching; investigative.

enquiry noun **1** *telephone enquiries:* **question**, query. **2** *an enquiry into alleged security leaks:* **investigation**, probe, examination, exploration; inquest, hearing.

enrage verb **anger**, infuriate, incense, madden, inflame; antagonize, provoke, exasperate; informal drive mad/crazy, drive up the wall, make someone see red, make someone's blood boil, make someone's hackles rise, get someone's back up; N. Amer. informal burn up.
– OPPOSITES placate.

enraged adjective **furious**, infuriated, irate, incensed, raging, incandescent, fuming, ranting, raving, seething, beside yourself; informal mad, hopping mad, wild, livid, boiling, apoplectic, hot under the collar, foaming at the mouth, steamed up, in a paddy, fit to be tied.
– OPPOSITES calm.

enrich verb **enhance**, improve, better, add to, augment; supplement, complement; boost, elevate, raise, lift, refine.
– OPPOSITES spoil.

enrol verb **1** *they both enrolled for the course:* **register**, sign on/up, put your name down, apply, volunteer; enter, join. **2** *280 new members were enrolled:* **accept**, admit, take on, register, sign on/up, recruit, engage.

en route adverb **along/on the way**, in transit, during the journey, along/on the road, on the move; coming, going, proceeding, travelling.

ensemble noun **1** *a Bulgarian folk ensemble:* **group**, band; company, troupe, cast, chorus, corps; informal combo. **2** *the buildings present a charming provincial ensemble:* **whole**, entity, unit, body, set, combination, composite, package; sum, total, totality, entirety, aggregate. **3** *a pink and black ensemble:* **outfit**, costume, suit; informal get-up.

enshrine verb **set down**, set out, express, lay down, embody, realize, manifest, incorporate, represent, contain, include, preserve, treasure, immortalize.

ensign noun **flag**, standard, colours, banner.

enslavement noun **slavery**, servitude; exploitation, oppression.
– OPPOSITES liberation.

ensnare verb **capture**, catch, trap, entrap, snare, net; entangle, embroil, enmesh.

ensue verb **result**, follow, develop, proceed, succeed, emerge, arise, derive, issue.

ensure verb **1** *ensure that the surface is completely clean:* **make sure**, make certain, see to it; check, confirm, establish, verify. **2** *legislation to ensure equal opportunities for all:* **secure**, guarantee, assure, certify.

entail verb **involve**, necessitate, require, need, demand, call for; mean, imply; cause, produce, result in, lead to, give rise to, occasion.

e

e

entangle verb **1** *their parachutes became entangled:* **twist**, intertwine, entwine, tangle, snarl, knot, coil. **2** *he was entangled in a lawsuit:* **involve**, embroil, mix up, catch up, bog down, mire.

enter verb **1** *police entered the house:* **go into**, come into, set foot in, gain access to. **2** *a bullet entered his chest:* **penetrate**, pierce, puncture, perforate. **3** *he entered politics in 1997:* **get involved in**, join, throw yourself into, engage in, embark on, take up. **4** *the planning entered a new phase:* **reach**, move into, get to, begin, start, commence. **5** *they entered the Army at eighteen:* **join**, enrol in/for, enlist in, volunteer for, sign up for. **6** *she entered a cookery competition:* **go in for**, register for, enrol for, sign on/up for; compete in, take part in, participate in. **7** *the cashier entered the details in a ledger:* **record**, write, put down, take down, note, jot down; register, log; key, type. **8** (Law) *he entered a plea of guilty:* **submit**, register, lodge, record, file, put forward, present.
– OPPOSITES leave.

enterprise noun **1** *a joint enterprise:* **undertaking**, endeavour, venture, exercise, activity, operation, task, business; project, scheme, plan, programme, campaign. **2** *a woman with enterprise:* **initiative**, resourcefulness, entrepreneurialism, imagination, ingenuity, inventiveness, originality, creativity; dynamism, drive, ambition, energy; informal get-up-and-go, oomph. **3** *a profit-making enterprise:* **business**, company, firm, venture, organization, operation, concern, corporation, establishment, partnership; informal outfit, set-up.

enterprising adjective **resourceful**, entrepreneurial, imaginative, ingenious, inventive, creative; dynamic, ambitious, energetic, adventurous; informal go-ahead.
– OPPOSITES unimaginative.

entertain verb **1** *he wrote stories to entertain them:* **amuse**, please, charm, cheer, interest; engage, occupy. **2** *he often entertains foreign visitors:* **receive**, play host/hostess to, throw a party for; wine and dine, cater for, feed, fete. **3** *I would never entertain such an idea:* **consider**, give consideration to, contemplate, think of; countenance; formal brook.
– OPPOSITES bore.

entertainer noun **performer**, artiste, artist.

entertaining adjective **delightful**, enjoyable, amusing, pleasing, agreeable, appealing, engaging, interesting, fascinating, absorbing, compelling; humorous, funny, comical; informal fun.

entertainment noun **amusement**, pleasure, leisure, recreation, relaxation, fun, enjoyment, interest; N. Amer. informal rec.

enthral verb **captivate**, charm, enchant, bewitch, fascinate, beguile, entrance, delight; absorb, engross, rivet, grip, transfix, hypnotize, mesmerize, spellbind.
– OPPOSITES bore.

enthralling adjective **fascinating**, entrancing, enchanting, bewitching, captivating, delightful; absorbing, engrossing, compelling, riveting, gripping, exciting, spellbinding; informal unputdownable.

enthuse verb **1** *I enthused about the idea:* **rave**, wax lyrical, praise something to the skies; N. Amer. informal ballyhoo. **2** *he enthuses people:* **motivate**, inspire, stimulate, encourage, galvanize, rouse, excite, stir, fire with enthusiasm.

enthusiasm noun **eagerness**, keenness, ardour, fervour, passion, zeal, zest, gusto, energy, verve, vigour, vehemence, fire, spirit; wholeheartedness, commitment, devotion, earnestness; informal get-up-and-go.
– OPPOSITES apathy.

enthusiast noun **fan**, devotee, aficionado, lover, admirer, follower; expert, connoisseur, authority, pundit; informal buff, freak, fanatic, nut, fiend, addict, maniac.

enthusiastic adjective **eager**, keen, avid, ardent, fervent, passionate, zealous, vehement; excited, wholehearted, committed, devoted, fanatical, earnest.

entice verb **tempt**, lure, attract, appeal to; invite, persuade, convince, beguile, coax, woo; seduce; informal sweet-talk.

enticement noun **lure**, temptation, attraction, appeal, draw, pull; charm, seduction.

enticing adjective **tempting**, alluring, attractive, appealing, inviting, seductive, beguiling, charming.

entire adjective **whole**, complete, total, full.

entirely adverb **1** *that's entirely out of the question:* **absolutely**, completely, totally, wholly, utterly, quite; altogether, in every respect, thoroughly. **2** *a gift entirely for charitable purposes:* **solely**, only, exclusively, purely, merely, just, alone.

entirety noun
■ **in its entirety** completely, as a whole, fully, wholly, entirely, totally, from start to finish.

entitle verb **1** *this pass entitles you to visit the museum:* **qualify**, make eligible, authorize, allow, permit; enable, empower. **2** *a chapter entitled 'Comedy and Tragedy':* **name**, title, call, label, designate, dub.

entitlement noun **1** *their entitlement to benefits:* **right**, claim. **2** *your holiday entitlement:* **allowance**, allocation, quota, ration, limit.

entity noun **being**, creature, individual, organism, life form; body, object, article, thing.

entourage noun **retinue**, staff, bodyguards; attendants, minders; informal people, posse.

entrails plural noun **intestines**, bowels, guts, viscera, internal organs, vital organs; offal; informal insides, innards.

entrance[1] noun **1** *the main entrance:* **entry**, way in, access, approach; door, portal, gate; opening, mouth; entrance hall, foyer, lobby, porch; N. Amer. entryway. **2** *the entrance of Mrs Knight:* **appearance**, arrival, entry, coming. **3** *he was refused entrance:* **admission**, admittance, entry, access.
– OPPOSITES exit, departure.

entrance[2] verb *I was entranced by her beauty:* **enchant**, bewitch, beguile, captivate, mesmerize, hypnotize, spellbind, transfix; enthral, engross, absorb, fascinate; stun, electrify; charm, delight; informal bowl over, knock out.

entrant noun **competitor**, contestant, contender, participant; candidate, applicant.

entreat verb **implore**, beg, plead with, pray, ask, request; bid, enjoin, appeal to, call on; literary beseech.

entreaty noun **plea**, appeal, request, petition, suit, supplication; prayer.

entrenched, **intrenched** adjective **ingrained**, established, fixed, firm, deep-seated, deep-rooted; unshakeable, ineradicable.

entrepreneur noun **businessman/woman**; dealer, trader; promoter, impresario; informal wheeler-dealer, whizz-kid, mover and shaker, go-getter.

entrust verb **1** *he was entrusted with the task:* **charge**, invest, endow. **2** *the powers entrusted to the Home Secretary:* **assign**, confer on, bestow on, vest in, consign; delegate; give, grant, vouchsafe.

entry noun **1** *both men stood up at Becca's entry:* **appearance**, arrival, entrance, coming. **2** *the entry to the flats:* **entrance**, way in, access, approach; door, portal, gate; entrance hall, foyer, lobby; N. Amer. entryway. **3** *he was refused entry:* **admission**, admittance, entrance, access. **4** *entries in the cash book:* **item**, record, note; memo, memorandum. **5** *data entry:* **recording**, archiving, logging, documentation, capture. **6** *we must pick a winner from the entries:* submission, entry form, application.
– OPPOSITES departure, exit.

entwine verb **wind round**, twist round, coil round; weave, intertwine, interlace; entangle, tangle; twine.

enumerate verb **list**, itemize, set out, give; cite, name, specify, identify, spell out, detail, particularize.

enunciate verb **pronounce**, articulate; say, speak, utter, voice, vocalize, sound, mouth.

envelop verb **surround**, cover, enfold, engulf, encircle, encompass, cocoon, sheathe, swathe, enclose; cloak, screen, shield, veil, shroud.

enviable adjective **desirable**, desired, favoured, sought-after, attractive; fortunate, lucky; informal to die for.

envious adjective **jealous**, covetous, desirous; grudging, begrudging, resentful.

environment noun **1** *the hospital environment:* **situation**, **setting**, milieu, background, backdrop, scene, location; context, framework; sphere, world, realm; ambience, atmosphere. **2** *the impact of pesticides on the environment:* **the natural world**, nature, the earth, the ecosystem, the biosphere, Mother Nature; wildlife, flora and fauna, the countryside.

e

WORD LINKS

ecology the study of the relationships of living things to their environment

environmentalist noun **conservationist**, ecologist, nature-lover; informal eco-warrior, tree-hugger.

environs plural noun **surroundings**, surrounding area, vicinity; locality, neighbourhood, district, region; precincts; N. Amer. vicinage.

envisage verb **1** *it was envisaged that the hospital would open soon:* **foresee**, predict, forecast, anticipate, expect, think likely. **2** *I cannot envisage what the future holds:* **imagine**, contemplate, picture; conceive of, think of.

envoy noun **ambassador**, emissary, diplomat, consul, attaché, chargé d'affaires; representative, delegate, spokesperson; agent, intermediary, mediator; informal go-between.

envy noun *she felt a pang of envy:* **jealousy**, covetousness; resentment, bitterness, discontent.
• verb **1** *I admired and envied her:* **be envious of**, be jealous of, resent, be resentful of. **2** *we envied her lifestyle:* **covet**, desire, aspire to, wish for, want, long for, yearn for, hanker after, crave.

ephemeral adjective **transitory**, transient, fleeting, passing, short-lived, momentary, brief, short; temporary, impermanent, short-term.
– OPPOSITES permanent.

epic adjective *their epic journey:* **ambitious**, heroic, grand, great; monumental.

epidemic noun **1** *an epidemic of typhoid:* **outbreak**, plague, pandemic. **2** *a joyriding epidemic:* **spate**, rash, wave, eruption, outbreak, craze; flood, torrent; upsurge, upturn, increase, growth, rise.
• adjective *the craze is now epidemic:* **rife**, rampant, widespread, wide-ranging, extensive, pervasive; global, universal, ubiquitous; endemic, pandemic.

epilogue noun **afterword**, postscript, PS, coda, codicil, appendix, tailpiece, supplement, addendum, rider.
– OPPOSITES prologue.

episode noun **1** *the best episode of his career:* **incident**, event, occurrence, happening; occasion, interlude, chapter, experience, adventure, exploit; matter, affair, thing. **2** *the final episode of the series:* **instalment**, chapter, passage; part, portion, section; programme, show. **3** *an episode of illness:* **period**, spell, bout, attack, phase; informal dose.

episodic adjective **in episodes**, in instalments, in sections, in parts.
– OPPOSITES continuous.

epitaph noun **elegy**, commemoration, obituary; inscription.

epithet noun **sobriquet**, nickname, byname, title, name, label, tag; description, designation; informal moniker, handle.

epitome noun **personification**, embodiment, incarnation, paragon; essence, quintessence, archetype, paradigm, typification; exemplar, model, soul, example; height.

epitomize verb **embody**, encapsulate, typify, exemplify, represent, manifest, symbolize, illustrate, sum up; personify.

epoch noun **era**, age, period, time, span, stage; aeon.

equable adjective **1** *an equable man:* **even-tempered**, calm, composed, collected, self-possessed, relaxed, easy-going; mellow, mild, tranquil, placid, stable, level-headed; imperturbable, unexcitable, untroubled, well balanced; informal unflappable, together, laid-back. **2** *an equable climate:* **stable**, constant, uniform, unvarying, consistent, unchanging, changeless; moderate, temperate.
– OPPOSITES temperamental, extreme.

equal adjective **1** *lines of equal length:* **identical**, uniform, alike, like, the same; matching, corresponding. **2** *fares equal to a fortnight's wages:* **equivalent**, identical, amounting; on a par with. **3** *equal treatment before the law:* **impartial**, non-partisan, fair, just, equitable; unprejudiced, non-discriminatory. **4** *an equal contest:* **evenly matched**, even, balanced, level, on an equal footing; informal fifty-fifty, level pegging, neck and neck.
– OPPOSITES different, discriminatory.
• noun *they did not treat him as their equal:* **equivalent**, peer, fellow, like; counterpart, match, parallel.
• verb **1** *two plus two equals four:* **be equal to**, be equivalent to, be the same as; come to, amount to, make, total, add up to. **2** *he equalled the world record:* **match**, reach, parallel, be level with.
■ **equal to** capable of, fit for, up to, good/strong enough for; suitable for, suited to, appropriate for; informal having what it takes.

equality noun **fairness**, equal rights, equal opportunities, equitability; impartiality, even-handedness; justice.

equalize verb **1** *attempts were made to equalize their earnings:* **even out/up**, make even, level, regularize, standardize, balance, square, match; bring into line. **2** *Villa equalized in the second half:* **level the score**, draw.

equanimity noun **composure**, calm, level-headedness, self-possession, cool-headedness, presence of mind; serenity, tranquillity, imperturbability, equilibrium; poise, assurance, self-confidence, aplomb, sangfroid, nerve; informal cool.
– OPPOSITES anxiety.

equate verb **1** *he equates criticism with treachery:* **identify**, compare, bracket, class, associate, connect, link, relate, ally. **2** *moves to equate supply and demand:* **equalize**, balance, even out/up, level, square, tally, match; make equal, make even, make equivalent.

equation noun **1** *the equation of success with riches:* **identification**, association, connection. **2** *other factors came into the equation:* **situation**, problem, case, question, issue.

equestrian adjective **on horseback**, mounted, riding.

equilibrium noun **1** *the equilibrium of the economy:* **balance**, symmetry; harmony, stability. **2** *his equilibrium was never shaken:* **composure**, calm, equanimity, sangfroid; poise, presence of mind; self-possession, self-command; tranquillity, serenity; informal cool.
– OPPOSITES imbalance, agitation.

equip verb **1** *the boat was equipped with a flare gun:* **provide**, furnish, supply, issue, kit out, stock, provision, arm, endow. **2** *the course will equip them for the workplace:* **prepare**, qualify, ready, suit; train.

equipment noun **apparatus**, paraphernalia; tools, utensils, implements, instruments, hardware, gadgets, gadgetry; stuff, things; kit, tackle; resources, supplies; trappings, appurtenances, accoutrements; informal gear; Military materiel, baggage.

equitable adjective **fair**, just, impartial, even-handed, unbiased, unprejudiced, egalitarian; informal fair and square.
– OPPOSITES unfair.

equity noun **1** *the equity of Finnish society:* **fairness**, justness, impartiality, egalitarianism. **2** *he owns 25% of the equity in the property:* **value**, worth; ownership, rights, proprietorship.

equivalence noun **equality**, sameness, interchangeability, comparability, correspondence; uniformity, similarity, likeness, nearness.

equivalent adjective *a degree or equivalent qualification:* **equal**, identical; similar, parallel, analogous, comparable, corresponding, commensurate.
• noun *the French equivalent of the Bank of England:* **counterpart**, parallel, alternative, analogue, twin, opposite number; equal, peer.

equivocal adjective **ambiguous**, indefinite, non-committal, vague, imprecise, inexact, inexplicit, hazy; unclear; ambivalent, uncertain, unsure, indecisive.
– OPPOSITES definite.

equivocate verb **prevaricate**, be

evasive, be non-committal, be vague, be ambiguous, dodge the issue, beat about the bush, hedge your bets, pussyfoot around; vacillate, shilly-shally, waver, hesitate, stall; Brit. hum and haw; informal sit on the fence, duck the issue.

era noun **epoch**, age, period, time, span, aeon; generation.

eradicate verb **eliminate**, get rid of, remove, obliterate; exterminate, destroy, annihilate, kill, wipe out; abolish, stamp out, extinguish, quash; erase, efface, excise, expunge.

erase verb **delete**, rub out, wipe off, blank out; expunge, excise, remove, obliterate.

erect adjective **upright**, straight, vertical, perpendicular, standing on end.
• verb **build**, construct, put up; assemble, put together, fabricate.
– OPPOSITES demolish.

erection noun **1** *the erection of a house:* **construction**, building, assembly, fabrication, elevation. **2** *a bleak concrete erection:* **building**, structure, edifice, construction, pile.

erode verb **wear away/down**, abrade, grind down, crumble; weather; undermine, weaken, deteriorate, destroy.

erosion noun **wearing away**, abrasion, attrition; weathering; dissolution; deterioration, disintegration, destruction.

erotic adjective **sexually arousing**, titillating, suggestive, risqué, pornographic, explicit; sexual, sexy, seductive, alluring, tantalizing; informal blue, X-rated, steamy, raunchy; euphemistic adult.

err verb **make a mistake**, be wrong, be in error, be mistaken, blunder, be incorrect, miscalculate, get it wrong; informal slip up, screw up, foul up, goof, make a boo-boo.

errand noun **task**, job, chore, assignment.

erratic adjective **unpredictable**, inconsistent, changeable, variable, inconstant, irregular, fitful, unstable, turbulent, unsettled, changing, varying, fluctuating, mutable; unreliable, undependable, volatile, mercurial, capricious, fickle, temperamental.
– OPPOSITES consistent.

erroneous adjective **wrong**, incorrect, mistaken, in error, inaccurate, untrue, false, fallacious; unsound, specious, faulty, flawed; informal off beam, way out.
– OPPOSITES correct.

error noun **mistake**, inaccuracy, miscalculation, blunder, oversight; fallacy, misconception, delusion; misprint; informal slip-up, bloomer, boo-boo; Brit. informal boob.
■ **in error** wrongly, by mistake, mistakenly, incorrectly; accidentally, by accident, inadvertently, unintentionally, by chance.

ersatz adjective **artificial**, substitute, imitation, synthetic, fake, false, mock, simulated; pseudo, sham, bogus, spurious, counterfeit; manufactured, man-made; informal phoney.
– OPPOSITES genuine.

erudite adjective **learned**, scholarly, educated, knowledgeable, well read, well informed, intellectual; intelligent, clever, academic, literary; highbrow, cerebral; informal brainy.
– OPPOSITES ignorant.

erupt verb **1** *the volcano erupted:* **give out lava**, become active, explode. **2** *fighting erupted:* **break out**, flare up; start.

eruption noun **1** *a volcanic eruption:* **discharge**, explosion, lava flow, pyroclastic flow. **2** *an eruption of violence:* **outbreak**, flare-up, upsurge, outburst, explosion; wave, spate.

escalate verb **1** *prices have escalated:* **increase rapidly**, soar, rocket, shoot up, mount, spiral, climb, go up; informal go through the roof, skyrocket. **2** *the dispute escalated:* **grow**, develop, mushroom, increase, heighten, intensify, accelerate.
– OPPOSITES plunge, shrink.

escalation noun **1** *an escalation in oil prices:* **increase**, rise, hike, growth, leap, upsurge, upturn. **2** *an escalation of the conflict:* **intensification**, aggravation, exacerbation; expansion, build-up, increase; deterioration.

escapade noun **exploit**, stunt, caper, antics; adventure, venture; deed, feat, experience; incident, occurrence, event.

escape verb **1** *two prisoners escaped yesterday:* **run away**, get out, break out, break free, bolt, make your getaway; disappear, vanish, slip away, sneak away; informal do a vanishing act, fly the coop, leg it; Brit. informal do a bunk, do a runner; N. Amer. informal go on the lam. **2** *he escaped his pursuers:* **get away from**, elude, avoid, dodge, shake off; informal give someone the slip. **3** *they escaped injury:* **avoid**, evade, elude, cheat, sidestep, circumvent, steer clear of; shirk; informal duck. **4** *water was escaping from the pipes:* **leak**, seep, issue, discharge, flow, pour.
• noun **1** *his escape from prison:* **getaway**, breakout, flight; Brit. informal flit. **2** *a gas escape:* **leak**, leakage, spill, seepage, discharge, outflow, outpouring.

escapee noun **runaway**, escaper, absconder; jailbreaker, fugitive; truant; deserter, defector.

escapism noun **fantasy**, fantasizing, daydreaming, daydreams, reverie; imagination, flights of fancy, pipe dreams, wishful thinking; informal pie in the sky.
– OPPOSITES realism.

escort noun *a police escort:* **guard**, bodyguard, protector, minder, custodian; attendant, chaperone; entourage, retinue; protection, convoy.
• verb *he was escorted home by the police:* **conduct**, accompany, guide, usher, shepherd, take.

esoteric adjective **abstruse**, obscure, arcane, rarefied, recondite, abstract; enigmatic, inscrutable, cryptic; complex, complicated, incomprehensible, impenetrable, mysterious.

especially adverb **1** *work poured in, especially from Kent:* **mainly**, mostly, chiefly, principally, largely; substantially, particularly, primarily. **2** *a committee especially for the purpose:* **expressly**, specially, specifically, exclusively, just, particularly, explicitly. **3** *he is especially talented:* **exceptionally**, particularly, specially, extremely, singularly, distinctly, unusually, extraordinarily, uncommonly, uniquely, remarkably, outstandingly; informal seriously, majorly; Brit. informal jolly, dead, well.

espionage noun **spying**, infiltration; surveillance, reconnaissance.

espousal noun **adoption**, embracing, acceptance; support, championship, encouragement, defence; sponsorship, promotion, endorsement, advocacy, approval.

espouse verb **adopt**, embrace, take up, accept; support, back, champion.
– OPPOSITES reject.

essay noun **article**, composition, paper, dissertation, thesis, discourse, treatise; commentary, critique, polemic; piece, feature; N. Amer. theme.

essence noun **1** *the very essence of economics:* **quintessence**, soul, spirit, nature; core, heart, substance; basis, principle, reality; informal nitty-gritty. **2** *essence of ginger:* **extract**, concentrate, elixir, juice; oil.
■ **in essence** essentially, basically, fundamentally, primarily, principally, chiefly, predominantly, substantially; above all, first and foremost; effectively, virtually, to all intents and purposes. **of the essence.** See ESSENTIAL adjective sense 1.

essential adjective **1** *it is essential to remove the paint:* **crucial**, key, vital, indispensable, all-important, of the essence, critical, imperative; urgent, pressing, high-priority. **2** *the essential simplicity of his style:* **basic**, inherent, fundamental, quintessential, intrinsic, underlying, characteristic, innate, primary.
– OPPOSITES unimportant, secondary.
• noun **1** *an essential for broadcasters:* **necessity**, prerequisite, requisite; informal must, must have. **2** *the essentials of the job:* **fundamentals**, basics, rudiments, first principles, foundations; essence, basis, core, kernel, crux; informal nitty-gritty, nuts and bolts.

establish verb **1** *they established an office in Moscow:* **set up**, start, initiate, institute, form, found, create, inaugurate; build, construct, install. **2** *evidence to establish his guilt:* **prove**, demonstrate, show, indicate, determine, confirm.

established adjective **1** *established practice:* **accepted**, traditional, orthodox, habitual, set, fixed, official; usual, customary, common, normal, general, prevailing, accustomed, familiar, expected, conventional, standard. **2** *an established composer:* **well known**, recognized, esteemed, respected, famous, prominent, noted, renowned.

e

establishment noun **1** *the establishment of a democracy:* **foundation**, institution, formation, inception, creation, installation; inauguration, start, initiation. **2** *a dressmaking establishment:* **business**, firm, company, concern, enterprise, venture, organization, operation; factory, plant, shop; informal outfit, set-up. **3** *educational establishments:* **institution**, place, premises, institute. **4** *they dare to poke fun at the Establishment:* **the authorities**, the powers that be, the system, the ruling class; informal Big Brother.

estate noun **1** *the Balmoral estate:* **property**, grounds, gardens, park, parkland, land; territory. **2** *a housing estate:* **area**, development, complex; Scottish scheme. **3** *a coffee estate:* **plantation**, farm, holding; forest, vineyard; N. Amer. ranch. **4** *he left an estate worth £610,000:* **assets**, capital, wealth, riches, holdings, fortune; property, effects, possessions, belongings.

esteem noun *she was held in high esteem:* **respect**, admiration, acclaim, approbation, appreciation, favour, recognition, honour, reverence; estimation, regard. • verb *such ceramics are highly esteemed:* **respect**, **admire**, value, regard, appreciate, like, prize, treasure, favour, revere.

estimate verb *I estimated the property to be worth £150,000:* **calculate**, assess, evaluate, judge, gauge, reckon, determine; consider, believe, deem; informal guesstimate. • noun *an estimate of the cost:* **rough calculation**, approximation, estimation, rough guess; costing, quotation, valuation, evaluation; informal guesstimate.

estimation noun **1** *an estimation of economic growth:* **estimate**, approximation, rough calculation, rough guess, evaluation; informal guesstimate. **2** *he rated highly in Carl's estimation:* **assessment**, judgement; esteem, opinion, view.

estrange verb **alienate**, antagonize, turn away, drive away, distance; drive a wedge between.

estrangement noun **alienation**, disaffection, unfriendliness; difference; parting, separation, divorce, break-up, split, breach, schism.

estuary noun **river mouth**, firth; delta.

etch verb **1** *intricate designs were etched into the stone:* **engrave**, cut, carve, inscribe, incise, chase, score, print, mark. **2** *the incident was etched indelibly in her mind:* **fix**, imprint, stamp, impress.

etching noun **engraving**, print, plate.

eternal adjective **1** *eternal happiness:* **everlasting**, never-ending, endless, perpetual, undying, immortal, abiding, permanent, enduring, timeless. **2** *eternal vigilance:* **constant**, continual, continuous, perpetual, persistent, sustained, unremitting, unrelieved, uninterrupted, unbroken, never-ending, non-stop, round-the-clock, endless, ceaseless.
– OPPOSITES transient, intermittent.

eternity noun **1** *the memory will remain for eternity:* **ever**, all time, perpetuity. **2** (informal) *I waited an eternity for you:* **a long time**, an age, ages, a lifetime, aeons; forever; informal donkey's years, a month of Sundays; Brit. informal yonks.

ethereal adjective **1** *her ethereal beauty:* **delicate**, exquisite; fragile, airy, fine, subtle. **2** *ethereal beings:* **celestial**, heavenly, spiritual, otherworldly.
– OPPOSITES substantial, earthly.

ethical adjective **1** *an ethical dilemma:* **moral**. **2** *an ethical investment policy:* **morally correct**, right-minded, principled, good, moral; just, honourable, fair.

ethics plural noun **morals**, morality, values, principles, ideals, standards of behaviour.

ethnic adjective **racial**, race-related, ethnological; national, tribal.

ethos noun **spirit**, character, atmosphere, climate, mood, feeling, essence; disposition, rationale, morality, moral code.

etiquette noun **protocol**, manners, accepted behaviour, the rules, decorum, good form; courtesy, propriety, formalities, niceties; custom, convention; informal the done thing.

eulogize verb **extol**, acclaim, sing the praises of, praise to the skies, wax lyrical about, rave about, enthuse about; N. Amer. informal ballyhoo.
– OPPOSITES criticize.

eulogy noun **accolade**, tribute, compliment, commendation; praise, acclaim.
– OPPOSITES attack.

euphemism noun **polite term**, substitute, alternative.

euphemistic adjective **polite**, substitute, understated, indirect, neutral, evasive; diplomatic, alternative, nice.

euphoria noun **elation**, happiness, joy, delight, glee; excitement, exhilaration, jubilation, exultation; ecstasy, bliss, rapture.
– OPPOSITES misery.

euphoric adjective **elated**, happy, joyful, delighted, gleeful; excited, exhilarated, jubilant, exultant; ecstatic, blissful, rapturous, on cloud nine, in seventh heaven; informal on top of the world, over the moon, on a high.

euthanasia noun **mercy killing**, assisted suicide.

evacuate verb **1** *local residents were evacuated:* **remove**, move out, take away. **2** *they evacuated the building:* **leave**, vacate, abandon, move out of, quit, withdraw from, retreat from, decamp from, flee, depart from. **3** *police evacuated the area:* **clear**, empty.

evacuation noun **1** *the evacuation of civilians:* **removal**, clearance, movement; deportation. **2** *the evacuation of military bases:* **clearance**; abandonment, vacation, desertion.

evade verb **1** *they evaded the guards:* **elude**, avoid, dodge, escape, steer clear of, sidestep; lose, leave behind, shake off; informal give someone the slip. **2** *he evaded the question:* **avoid**, dodge, sidestep, bypass, skirt round, fudge, be evasive about; informal duck, cop out of.
– OPPOSITES confront.

evaluate verb **assess**, judge, gauge, rate, estimate, appraise, analyse, weigh up, get the measure of; informal size up, check out.

evaluation noun **assessment**, appraisal, judgement, consideration, analysis.

evangelical adjective **1** *evangelical Christianity:* **scriptural**, biblical; fundamentalist. **2** *an evangelical socialist:* **evangelistic**, evangelizing, passionate, crusading, proselytizing; fanatical, ardent, zealous.

evangelist noun **preacher**, missionary, proselytizer, crusader, propagandist.

evangelistic adjective. See **EVANGELICAL** sense 2.

evaporate verb **1** *the water evaporated:* **vaporize**; dry up. **2** *enthusiasm for the idea has evaporated:* **melt away**, disappear, vanish, wear off, fade, peter out, pass, end, cease to exist.
– OPPOSITES condense.

evasion noun **1** *the evasion of immigration control:* **avoidance**, circumvention, dodging, sidestepping. **2** *she grew tired of all the evasion:* **prevarication**, evasiveness, beating about the bush, hedging, pussyfooting, equivocation, vagueness; Brit. humming and hawing.

evasive adjective **equivocal**, prevaricating, elusive, ambiguous, non-committal, vague, inexplicit, unclear; roundabout, indirect; informal cagey.

eve noun *the eve of the election:* **day before**, evening before, night before; the run-up to.
– OPPOSITES morning.

even adjective **1** *an even surface:* **flat**, smooth, uniform; level, plane. **2** *an even temperature:* **uniform**, constant, steady, stable, consistent, unvarying, unchanging, regular. **3** *the score was even:* **level**, drawn, tied, all square, balanced; neck and neck; Brit. level pegging; informal even-steven. **4** *an even disposition:* **even-tempered**, balanced, stable, equable, placid, calm, composed, poised, cool, relaxed, easy, imperturbable, unexcitable,

unruffled, untroubled; informal together, laid-back, unflappable.
–OPPOSITES uneven, irregular, unequal.
• verb **1** *the canal bottom was evened out:* **flatten**, level off/out, smooth out. **2** *the union wants to even up our wages:* **equalize**, make equal, level up, balance, square; standardize, regularize.

• adverb *it got even colder:* **still**, yet, more, all the more.
■ **get even** have your revenge, avenge yourself, even the score, settle the score, pay someone back, reciprocate, retaliate; informal get your own back, give someone a taste of their own medicine; literary be revenged.

even-handed adjective **fair**, just, equitable, impartial, unbiased, unprejudiced, non-partisan, non-discriminatory.
–OPPOSITES biased.

evening noun night; twilight, dusk, nightfall, sunset, sundown.

event noun **1** *an annual event:* **occurrence**, happening, incident, affair, occasion, phenomenon; function, gathering; informal bash, do. **2** *a team event:* **competition**, contest, tournament, match, fixture; race, game.
■ **in any event/at all events** regardless, whatever happens, come what may, no matter what, at any rate, in any case, anyhow, anyway, even so, still, nevertheless, nonetheless; N. Amer. informal anyways. **in the event** as it turned out, as it happened, in the end; as a result, as a consequence.

even-tempered adjective **serene**, calm, composed, tranquil, relaxed, easy-going, unworried, untroubled, unruffled, imperturbable, placid, stable, level-headed; informal unflappable, laid-back.
–OPPOSITES excitable.

eventful adjective **busy**, action-packed, full, lively, active, hectic.
–OPPOSITES dull.

eventual adjective **final**, ultimate, resulting, ensuing, consequent, subsequent.

eventuality noun **event**, situation, circumstance, case, contingency, chance; outcome, result.

eventually adverb **in the end**, in due course, by and by, in time, after some time, after a bit, finally, at last; ultimately, in the long run, at the end of the day, one day, some day, sometime, sooner or later.

ever adverb **1** *the best I've ever done:* **at any time**, at any point, on any occasion, under any circumstances, on any account; up till now, until now. **2** *he was ever the optimist:* **always**, forever, eternally. **3** *an ever increasing rate of crime:* **continually**, constantly, always, endlessly, perpetually, incessantly, unremittingly. **4** *will she ever learn?* **at all**, in any way.
■ **ever so** (Brit. informal) very, extremely, exceedingly, especially, immensely, particularly, really, truly; N. English right; informal awfully, terribly, desperately, mega, ultra; Brit. informal well, dead, jolly; N. Amer. informal real, mighty, awful.

everlasting adjective **eternal**, endless, never-ending, perpetual, undying, abiding, enduring, infinite.
–OPPOSITES transient, occasional.

evermore adverb **always**, forever, ever, for always, for all time, eternally, in perpetuity; ever after, henceforth; Brit. for evermore, forever more; N. Amer. forevermore; informal until the cows come home, until hell freezes over.

every determiner **1** *he exercised every day:* **each**, each and every, every single. **2** *we make every effort to satisfy our clients:* **all possible**, the utmost.

everybody pronoun **everyone**, every person, each person, all, one and all, all and sundry, the whole world, the public; informal {every Tom, Dick, and Harry}, every man jack, every mother's son.

everyday adjective **1** *the everyday demands of a baby:* **daily**, day-to-day, quotidian; ongoing. **2** *everyday drugs like aspirin:* **commonplace**, ordinary, common, usual, regular, familiar, conventional, run-of-the-mill, standard, stock; household, domestic; Brit. common or garden; informal bog-standard.
–OPPOSITES unusual.

everyone pronoun **everybody**, every person, each person, all, one and all, all and sundry, the whole world, the public; informal {every Tom, Dick, and Harry}, every man jack, every mother's son.

everything pronoun the lot; informal the whole caboodle, the whole shebang, the works; Brit. informal the full monty; N. Amer. informal the whole ball of wax.
– OPPOSITES nothing.

everywhere adverb **all over**, all around, in every nook and cranny, far and wide, near and far, high and low, {here, there, and everywhere}; throughout the land, the world over, worldwide; informal all over the place; Brit. informal all over the shop; N. Amer. informal all over the map.
– OPPOSITES nowhere.

evict verb **expel**, eject, remove, dislodge, turn out, throw out, drive out; dispossess; informal chuck out, kick out, boot out, give someone the heave-ho, throw someone out on their ear; Brit. informal turf out; N. Amer. informal give someone the bum's rush.

eviction noun **expulsion**, ejection, removal, dislodgement, displacement.

evidence noun **1** *evidence of his infidelity:* **proof**, confirmation, verification, substantiation, corroboration. **2** *the court accepted her evidence:* **testimony**, statement, declaration, submission; Law deposition, representation, affidavit. **3** *evidence of a struggle:* **signs**, indications, pointers, marks, traces, suggestions, hints; manifestation.
■ **in evidence** noticeable, conspicuous, obvious, perceptible, visible, on view, plain to see.

evident adjective **obvious**, apparent, noticeable, conspicuous, perceptible, visible, discernible, clear, plain, manifest, patent; palpable, tangible, distinct; informal as plain as the nose on your face, sticking out like a sore thumb, sticking out a mile, as clear as day.

evidently adverb **1** *he was evidently upset:* **obviously**, clearly, plainly; unmistakably, undeniably, undoubtedly. **2** *evidently, she believed him:* **seemingly**, apparently, from/by all appearances, on the face of it; it seems, it appears.

evil adjective **1** *an evil deed:* **wicked**, bad, wrong, immoral, sinful, foul, vile, iniquitous, depraved, villainous, vicious, malicious; malevolent, sinister, demonic, devilish, diabolical, fiendish, dark; monstrous, shocking, despicable, atrocious, heinous, odious, contemptible, horrible. **2** *an evil spirit:* **harmful**, bad, malign; unclean. **3** *evil weather:* **unpleasant**, disagreeable, nasty, horrible, foul, filthy, vile.
– OPPOSITES good, beneficial, pleasant.
• noun **1** *the evil in our midst:* **wickedness**, badness, wrongdoing, sin, sinfulness, immorality, vice, iniquity, degeneracy, corruption, depravity, villainy; formal turpitude. **2** *nothing but evil will result:* **harm**, pain, misery, sorrow, suffering, trouble, disaster, misfortune, catastrophe, affliction, woe. **3** *the evil of war:* **abomination**, atrocity, obscenity, outrage, monstrosity, barbarity.

evocative adjective **reminiscent**, suggestive, redolent; expressive, vivid, powerful, haunting, moving, poignant.

evoke verb **bring to mind**, conjure up, summon up, invoke, elicit, stimulate, stir up, awaken, arouse.

evolution noun **1** *the evolution of Bolshevism:* **development**, growth, rise, progress, expansion. **2** *his interest in evolution:* **Darwinism**, natural selection.

evolve verb **develop**, progress, advance; mature, grow, expand, spread; change, transform, adapt, metamorphose; humorous transmogrify.

exacerbate verb **aggravate**, worsen, inflame, compound; intensify, increase, heighten, magnify, add to.
– OPPOSITES reduce.

exact adjective **1** *an exact description:* **precise**, accurate, correct, faithful, close, true; literal, strict, perfect; detailed, minute, meticulous, thorough; informal on the nail, on the mark; Brit. informal spot on, bang on; N. Amer. informal on the money, on the button. **2** *an exact record keeper:* **careful**, meticulous, painstaking, punctilious, conscientious, scrupulous, exacting.
– OPPOSITES inaccurate, careless.
• verb *they exacted a terrible*

vengeance on him: **inflict**, impose, administer, apply, wreak.

exacting adjective *an exacting training routine:* **demanding**, stringent, testing, challenging, arduous, laborious, taxing, gruelling, punishing, hard, tough.
– OPPOSITES easy, easy-going.

exactly adverb *it's exactly as I expected:* **precisely**, entirely, absolutely, completely, totally, just, quite, in every way, in every respect, one hundred per cent, every inch, to the hilt; informal to a T.

exaggerate verb **overstate**, overemphasize, overestimate, inflate; embellish, embroider, elaborate, overplay, dramatize, stretch the truth; Brit. informal make a mountain out of a molehill, blow out of all proportion, make a big thing of.
– OPPOSITES understate.

exaggerated adjective **overstated**, inflated, magnified, excessive; overelaborate, overdone, overplayed, overdramatized, highly coloured, melodramatic; informal over the top, OTT.

exaggeration noun **overstatement**, overemphasis; dramatization, elaboration, embellishment, embroidery, hyperbole, overkill, gilding the lily.

exalted adjective **1** *his exalted office:* **high**, high-ranking, elevated, superior, lofty, eminent, prestigious, illustrious, distinguished, esteemed. **2** *his exalted aims:* **noble**, lofty, high-minded, elevated, ambitious.

exam noun **test**, examination; assessment; paper; N. Amer. quiz.

examination noun **1** *artefacts were spread out for examination:* **scrutiny**, inspection, perusal, study, investigation, consideration, analysis, appraisal, evaluation. **2** *a medical examination:* **inspection**, check-up, assessment, appraisal; probe, test, scan; informal once-over, overhaul. **3** *a school examination:* **test**, exam, assessment; N. Amer. quiz.

examine verb **1** *they examined the bank records:* **inspect**, scrutinize, investigate, look at, study, sift through, appraise, analyse, review, survey; informal check out. **2** *students were examined after a year:* **test**, question; assess, appraise.

examiner noun **assessor**, marker, questioner, interviewer, inspector, adjudicator, scrutineer.

example noun **1** *a fine example of Chinese porcelain:* **specimen**, sample, exemplar, instance, case, illustration. **2** *we must follow their example:* **precedent**, lead, model, pattern, exemplar, ideal. **3** *he was hanged as an example to others:* **warning**, lesson, deterrent; moral; disincentive.
■ **for example** for instance, e.g., such as, like.

exasperate verb **infuriate**, anger, annoy, irritate, madden, provoke, irk, vex, get on someone's nerves, ruffle someone's feathers; Brit. rub up the wrong way; informal aggravate, rile, bug, needle, hack off, get up someone's nose, get someone's back up, get someone's goat, give someone the hump; Brit. informal nark, wind up, get on someone's wick; N. Amer. informal tee off, tick off.
– OPPOSITES please.

exasperating adjective **infuriating**, annoying, irritating, maddening, trying; informal aggravating.

exasperation noun **irritation**, annoyance, vexation, anger, fury; informal aggravation.

excavate verb **unearth**, dig up, uncover, reveal; disinter, exhume.

excavation noun **hole**, pit, trench, trough; archaeological site; dig.

exceed verb **be more than**, be greater than, be over, go beyond, top; surpass.

exceeding (old use) adjective *his exceeding kindness:* **great**, considerable, exceptional, tremendous, immense, extreme, supreme, outstanding.
• adverb *the Lord has been exceeding gracious.* See EXCEEDINGLY.

exceedingly adverb **extremely**, exceptionally, especially, tremendously, very, really, truly, most; informal terribly, awfully, seriously, mega, ultra; Brit. informal well, dead, jolly; N. Amer. informal real, mighty; old use exceeding.

excel verb **1** *he excelled at football:* **shine**, be excellent, be outstanding, be skilful, be talented; stand out, be second to none. **2** *she excelled* *him in her work:* **surpass**, outdo, outshine, outclass, outstrip, beat, top, transcend, better, pass, eclipse, overshadow.

excellence noun **distinction**, quality, superiority, brilliance, greatness, calibre, eminence; skill, talent, virtuosity, accomplishment, mastery.

excellent adjective **very good**, superb, outstanding, exceptional, marvellous, wonderful; perfect, matchless, peerless, supreme, first-rate, first-class, superlative, splendid, fine; informal A1, ace, great, terrific, tremendous, fantastic, fabulous, fab, top-notch, class, awesome, magic, wicked, cool, out of this world; Brit. informal brilliant, brill, smashing; Austral. informal bonzer.
– OPPOSITES inferior.

except preposition *they work every day except Sunday:* **excluding**, not including, excepting, omitting, not counting, but, besides, apart from, aside from, barring, bar, other than, saving; with the exception of; formal save.
– OPPOSITES including.

> ! Don't confuse **except** and **accept**. **Except** means 'apart from', while **accept** means 'agree to receive or do something' (*she accepted the job*).

exception noun *this case is an exception:* **anomaly**, irregularity, deviation, special case, peculiarity, abnormality, oddity; misfit; informal freak.
■ **take exception** object, take offence, take umbrage, demur, disagree; resent; informal kick up a fuss, kick up a stink. **with the exception of**. See EXCEPT preposition.

exceptional adjective **1** *the drought was exceptional:* **unusual**, uncommon, abnormal, atypical, out of the ordinary, rare, unprecedented, unexpected, surprising; strange, odd, freakish, anomalous, peculiar. **2** *her exceptional ability:* **outstanding**, extraordinary, remarkable, special, phenomenal, prodigious; unequalled, unparalleled, unsurpassed, peerless, matchless.
– OPPOSITES normal, average.

exceptionally adverb **exceedingly**, outstandingly, extraordinarily, remarkably, especially, phenomenally, prodigiously.

excerpt noun **extract**, part, section, piece, portion, snippet, clip, bit; reading, citation, quotation, quote, line, passage; N. Amer. cite.

excess noun **1** *an excess of calcium:* **surplus**, surfeit, over-abundance, superabundance, superfluity, glut; too much. **2** *the excess is turned into fat:* **remainder**, rest, residue; leftovers, remnants; surplus, extra, difference. **3** *a life of excess:* **overindulgence**, intemperance, immoderation, profligacy, extravagance, decadence, self-indulgence.
– OPPOSITES lack, restraint.
• adjective *excess oil:* **surplus**, superfluous, redundant, unwanted, unneeded, excessive; extra.
■ **in excess of** more than, over, above, upwards of, beyond.

excessive adjective **1** *excessive alcohol consumption:* **immoderate**, intemperate, overindulgent, unrestrained, uncontrolled; lavish, extravagant. **2** *the cost is excessive:* **exorbitant**, extortionate, unreasonable, outrageous, uncalled for, extreme, unwarranted, disproportionate, too much; informal over the top, OTT.

excessively adverb **inordinately**, unduly, unnecessarily, unreasonably, ridiculously, overly; very, extremely, exceedingly, exceptionally, impossibly; immoderately, too much.

exchange noun **1** *the exchange of ideas:* **interchange**, trade, trading, swapping, traffic, trafficking. **2** *a heated exchange:* **conversation**, dialogue, chat, talk, discussion; debate, argument.
• verb *we exchanged shirts:* **trade**, swap, switch, change.

excise[1] noun *the excise on spirits:* **duty**, tax, levy, tariff.

excise[2] verb **1** *the tumours were excised:* **cut out/off/away**, take out, extract, remove. **2** *all unnecessary detail was excised:* **delete**, cross out/through, strike out, score out, cancel, put a line through; erase.

excitable adjective **temperamental**, mercurial, volatile, emotional, sensitive, highly strung, unstable,

nervous, tense, edgy, jumpy, twitchy, neurotic; informal uptight, wired.
– OPPOSITES placid.

excite verb **1** *the prospect of a holiday excited me:* **thrill**, exhilarate, animate, enliven, rouse, stir, stimulate, galvanize, electrify; informal buck up, pep up, ginger up, give someone a buzz/kick. **2** *the decision excited controversy:* **provoke**, stir up, rouse, arouse, kindle, trigger, spark off, incite, cause.
– OPPOSITES bore, depress.

excited adjective **thrilled**, exhilarated, animated, enlivened, electrified, enraptured, intoxicated, enthusiastic, beside yourself; informal fired up, on a high.

excitement noun **1** *the excitement of seeing a leopard in the wild:* **thrill**, pleasure, delight, joy; informal kick, buzz; N. Amer. informal charge. **2** *her eyes sparkled with excitement:* **exhilaration**, elation, animation, enthusiasm, eagerness, anticipation.

exciting adjective **thrilling**, exhilarating, stirring, rousing, stimulating, intoxicating, electrifying, invigorating; gripping, compelling, powerful, dramatic.

exclaim verb **cry**, call, shout, yell, sing out; blurt out.

exclamation noun **cry**, call, shout, yell.

exclude verb **1** *women were excluded from the club:* **keep out**, deny access to, shut out, bar, ban, prohibit. **2** *the clause excluded any judicial review:* **rule out**, preclude. **3** *the price excludes postage:* **be exclusive of**, not include.
– OPPOSITES admit, include.

exclusion noun **1** *the exclusion of women from the society:* **barring**, banning, prohibition. **2** *the exclusion of other factors:* **elimination**, ruling out, precluding. **3** *the exclusion of pupils:* **expulsion**, ejection; suspension.
– OPPOSITES acceptance, inclusion.

exclusive adjective **1** *an exclusive club:* **select**, chic, high-class, elite, fashionable, stylish, elegant, premier; expensive; Brit. upmarket; N. Amer. high-toned; informal posh, ritzy, classy; Brit. informal swish; N. Amer. informal tony. **2** *a room for your exclusive use:* **sole**, unshared, unique, individual, personal, private. **3** *prices exclusive of VAT:* **not including**, excluding, leaving out, omitting, excepting.
– OPPOSITES inclusive.
• noun *a six-page exclusive:* **scoop**, exposé, special.

excrement noun **faeces**, excreta, droppings; ordure, dung, manure, guano.

excrescence noun *the new buildings were an excrescence:* **eyesore**, blot on the landscape, monstrosity.

excrete verb **expel**, pass, void, discharge, eject, evacuate.
– OPPOSITES ingest.

excruciating adjective **agonizing**, severe, acute, intense, violent, racking, searing, piercing, stabbing, raging; unbearable, unendurable; informal splitting, killing.

excursion noun **trip**, outing, jaunt, expedition, journey, tour; day trip/out, drive, run, ride; informal junket, spin.

excusable adjective **forgivable**, pardonable, defensible, justifiable.
– OPPOSITES unforgivable.

excuse verb **1** *please excuse me:* **forgive**, pardon. **2** *such conduct cannot be excused:* **justify**, defend, condone; forgive, overlook, disregard, ignore, tolerate. **3** *she was excused from her duties:* **let off**, release, relieve, exempt, absolve, free.
– OPPOSITES punish, blame, condemn.
• noun **1** *that's no excuse for stealing:* **justification**, defence, reason, explanation, mitigating circumstances, mitigation. **2** *an excuse to get away:* **pretext**, pretence; Brit. get-out; informal story, alibi. **3** (informal) *that pathetic excuse for a man!* **travesty of**; informal apology for.

execute verb **1** *he was finally executed:* **put to death**, kill. **2** *he executed a series of financial deals:* **carry out**, accomplish, bring off/about, achieve, complete, engineer; informal pull off.

execution noun **1** *the execution of the plan:* **implementation**, carrying out, accomplishment, bringing off/about, attainment, realization. **2** *the execution of the play:* **perform-**

ance, presentation, rendition, rendering, staging, delivery. **3** *a public execution | he was sentenced to execution:* **killing**; capital punishment, the death penalty.

executive adjective *executive powers:* **administrative**, decision-making, managerial; law-making.
• noun **1** *top-level executives:* **chief**, head, director, senior official, senior manager; informal boss, exec, suit. **2** *the future role of the executive:* **administration**, management, directorate; government.

exemplary adjective **1** *her exemplary behaviour:* **perfect**, ideal, model, faultless, flawless, impeccable, irreproachable; excellent, outstanding, above/beyond reproach. **2** *exemplary jail sentences:* **deterrent**, cautionary, warning.
– OPPOSITES deplorable.

exemplify verb **1** *this story exemplifies current trends:* **typify**, epitomize, be an example of, be representative of, symbolize. **2** *he exemplified his point with an anecdote:* **illustrate**, give an example of, demonstrate.

exempt adjective **free**, not liable/subject, exempted, excepted, excused, absolved.
– OPPOSITES subject to.
• verb **excuse**, free, release, exclude, give/grant immunity, spare, absolve; informal let off; N. Amer. informal grandfather.

exemption noun **immunity**, exception, dispensation, indemnity, exclusion, freedom, release, relief, absolution; informal let-off.

exercise noun **1** *exercise improves your heart:* **physical activity**, a workout, working out. **2** *translation exercises:* **task**, piece of work, problem, assignment. **3** *military exercises:* **manoeuvres**, operations.
• verb **1** *she exercised every day:* **work out**, do exercises, train. **2** *he must learn to exercise patience:* **use**, employ, make use of, utilize; practise, apply. **3** *the problem continued to exercise him:* **worry**, trouble, concern, bother, disturb, perturb, distress, preoccupy, prey on someone's mind, make uneasy; informal bug, do someone's head in.

exert verb **1** *he exerted considerable pressure on me:* **bring to bear**, apply, use, utilize, deploy. **2** *he had clearly been exerting himself:* **push yourself**, work hard.

exertion noun **1** *she was panting with the exertion:* **effort**, strain. **2** *the exertion of pressure:* **use**, application, exercise, employment, utilization.

exhale verb **breathe out**, blow out, puff out; sigh.
– OPPOSITES inhale.

exhaust verb **1** *the effort had exhausted him:* **tire out**, wear out, overtire, fatigue, weary, drain, run someone into the ground; informal do in, take it out of someone, wipe out, knock out, shatter; Brit. informal knacker; N. Amer. informal poop, tucker out. **2** *the country has exhausted its reserves:* **use up**, run through, go through, consume, finish, deplete, spend, empty, drain; informal blow.
– OPPOSITES invigorate, replenish.

exhausted adjective *I'm completely exhausted:* **tired out**, worn out, weary, dog-tired, ready to drop, drained, fatigued; informal done in, all in, dead beat, shattered, bushed, frazzled; Brit. informal knackered, whacked, jiggered; N. Amer. informal pooped, tuckered out; Austral./NZ informal stonkered.

exhausting adjective **tiring**, wearying, taxing, wearing, draining; arduous, strenuous, onerous, demanding, gruelling; informal killing, murderous; Brit. informal knackering.

exhaustion noun **1** *sheer exhaustion forced Paul to give up:* **tiredness**, overtiredness, fatigue, weariness. **2** *the exhaustion of fuel reserves:* **consumption**, depletion, using up; draining, emptying.

exhaustive adjective **comprehensive**, all-inclusive, complete, full, encyclopedic, thorough, in-depth; detailed, meticulous, painstaking.
– OPPOSITES perfunctory.

exhibit verb **1** *the paintings were exhibited in Glasgow:* **put on display**, put on show, display, show, showcase. **2** *Luke exhibited signs of jealousy:* **show**, reveal, display, manifest; indicate, demonstrate, present; formal evince.
• noun **1** *an exhibit at the British*

e

Museum: **item**, piece, artefact. **2** (N. Amer.) *people flocked to the exhibit.* See EXHIBITION sense 1.

exhibition noun **1** *a photography exhibition:* **display**, show, showing, presentation, demonstration, exposition; N. Amer. exhibit. **2** *a convincing exhibition of concern:* **display**, show, demonstration, manifestation, expression.

e

exhibitionist noun poser, self-publicist; extrovert; informal show-off; N. Amer. informal showboat.

exhilarate verb **thrill**, excite, intoxicate, elate, delight, enliven, animate, invigorate, energize, stimulate; informal give someone a thrill/buzz.

exhilarating adjective **thrilling**, exciting, invigorating, stimulating; electrifying.

exhilaration noun **elation**, euphoria, exultation, exaltation, joy, happiness, delight, jubilation, rapture, ecstasy; literary joyousness.

exhort verb **urge**, encourage, call on, enjoin, charge, press; bid, appeal to, entreat, implore; literary beseech.

exhortation noun **entreaty**, appeal, call, charge.

exhume verb **disinter**, dig up, disentomb.
– OPPOSITES bury.

exile noun **1** *his exile from his homeland:* **banishment**, isolation. **2** *political exiles:* **émigré**, expatriate; displaced person, DP, refugee, deportee; informal expat.

exist verb **1** *animals that existed long ago:* **live**, be alive, be living. **2** *the liberal climate that now exists:* **prevail**, occur, be found, be in existence; be the case. **3** *she had to exist on a low income:* **survive**, subsist, live, support yourself; manage, make do, get by, scrape by, make ends meet.

existence noun **1** *the industry's continued existence:* **survival**, continuation; actuality, being, reality. **2** *her suburban existence:* **way of life/living**, life, lifestyle.
■ **in existence 1** *there are many species in existence:* alive, existing, extant, existent. **2** *the only copy still in existence:* surviving, remaining, in circulation.

existing adjective **present**, current; in existence, surviving, remaining, extant.

exit noun **1** *the fire exit:* **way out**, door, escape route; formal egress. **2** *take the second exit:* **turning**, turn-off, turn; N. Amer. turnout. **3** *his sudden exit:* **departure**, leaving, withdrawal, going, decamping, retreat; flight, exodus, escape.
– OPPOSITES entrance, arrival.
• verb *the doctor had just exited:* **leave**, go out, depart, withdraw, retreat.
– OPPOSITES enter.

exodus noun **mass departure**, withdrawal, evacuation; migration, emigration; flight, escape.

exonerate verb **absolve**, clear, acquit, find innocent, discharge; formal exculpate.
– OPPOSITES convict.

exorbitant adjective **extortionate**, excessive, prohibitive, outrageous, unreasonable, inflated, huge, enormous; Brit. over the odds; informal steep, stiff, over the top, a rip-off; Brit. informal daylight robbery.
– OPPOSITES reasonable.

exotic adjective **1** *exotic birds:* **foreign**, non-native, tropical. **2** *exotic places:* **foreign**, faraway, far-off, far-flung, distant. **3** *Linda's exotic appearance:* **striking**, colourful, eye-catching; unusual, unconventional, extravagant, outlandish.
– OPPOSITES native, nearby, conventional.

expand verb **1** *metals expand when heated:* **increase in size**, become larger, enlarge; swell; lengthen, stretch, thicken, fill out. **2** *the company is expanding:* **grow**, become/make larger, become/make bigger, increase in size/scope; extend, augment, broaden, widen, develop, diversify, build up; branch out, spread, proliferate. **3** *the minister expanded on the proposals:* **elaborate on**, enlarge on, go into detail about, flesh out, develop.
– OPPOSITES shrink, contract.

expanse noun **area**, stretch, sweep, tract, swathe, belt, region; sea, carpet, blanket, sheet.

expansion noun **1** *expansion and contraction:* **enlargement**, increase,

swelling; lengthening, elongation, stretching, thickening. **2** *the expansion of the company:* **growth**, increase, enlargement, extension, development; spread, diversification.
–OPPOSITES contraction.

expansive adjective **1** *expansive moorland:* **extensive**, sweeping, rolling. **2** *expansive coverage:* **wide-ranging**, extensive, broad, wide, comprehensive, thorough. **3** *Cara grew more expansive:* **communicative**, forthcoming, sociable, friendly, outgoing, affable, chatty, talkative.

expatriate noun **emigrant**, émigré, migrant; informal expat.
–OPPOSITES national.

expect verb **1** *I expect she'll be late:* **suppose**, presume, imagine, assume, surmise; informal guess, reckon; N. Amer. informal figure. **2** *a 10 per cent rise was expected:* **anticipate**, await, look for, hope for, look forward to; contemplate, bargain for/on, bank on; predict, forecast, envisage. **3** *we expect total loyalty:* **require**, ask for, call for, want, insist on, demand.

expectancy noun **anticipation**, expectation, eagerness, excitement.

expectant adjective **1** *expectant fans:* **eager**, excited, waiting with bated breath, hopeful. **2** *an expectant mother:* **pregnant**; informal expecting, in the family way, preggers.

expectation noun **1** *her expectations were unrealistic:* **supposition**, assumption, presumption, conjecture, calculation, prediction. **2** *he grew tense with expectation:* **anticipation**, expectancy, eagerness, excitement, suspense.

expecting adjective (informal). See EXPECTANT sense 2.

expedient adjective **convenient**, advantageous, useful, of use, beneficial, of benefit, helpful; practical, pragmatic, politic, prudent, judicious.
• noun **measure**, means, method, stratagem, scheme, plan, move, tactic, manoeuvre, device, contrivance, ploy, dodge; Austral. informal lurk.

expedite verb **speed up**, accelerate, hurry, hasten, step up, quicken, precipitate, dispatch; advance, facilitate, ease, make easier, further, promote, aid, push through, urge on, boost, stimulate, spur on, help along.
–OPPOSITES delay.

expedition noun **1** *an expedition to the South Pole:* **journey**, voyage, tour, odyssey; safari, trek, hike. **2** (informal) *a shopping expedition:* **trip**, excursion, outing. **3** *all members of the expedition:* **group**, team, party, crew, squad.

expel verb **throw out**, bar, ban, debar, drum out, get rid of, dismiss; Military **cashier**; informal **chuck out**, **sling out**, **kick/boot out**; Brit. informal **turf out**; N. Amer. informal **give someone the bum's rush**.
–OPPOSITES admit.

expend verb **use**, utilize, consume, eat up, deplete, get through.
–OPPOSITES save, conserve.

expendable adjective **dispensable**, replaceable, non-essential, inessential, unnecessary, not required, superfluous.
–OPPOSITES indispensable.

expenditure noun **outgoings**, costs, payments, expenses, overheads, spending.
–OPPOSITES income.

expense noun **cost**, price, charge, outlay; outgoings, payments, expenditure, bills, overheads.

expensive adjective **costly**, dear, high-priced, overpriced, exorbitant, extortionate; informal steep, pricey, costing an arm and a leg, costing the earth, costing a bomb.
–OPPOSITES cheap, economical.

experience noun **1** *her business experience was invaluable:* **skill**, practical knowledge, understanding; background, record, history; maturity, worldliness, sophistication; informal know-how. **2** *his first experience of war:* **involvement in**, participation in, contact with, acquaintance with, exposure to. **3** *an unforgettable experience:* **incident**, occurrence, event, happening, episode; adventure, exploit, escapade.
• verb *we have experienced some difficulties:* **encounter**, undergo, meet, come into contact with, come across, come up against, face, be faced with.

WORD LINKS
empirical based on experience rather than theory

experienced adjective **1** *an experienced broadcaster:* **skilled**, skilful, expert, knowledgeable; proficient, trained, competent, capable, well trained, well versed; seasoned, practised, mature, veteran. **2** *she deluded herself that she was experienced:* **worldly**, sophisticated, mature, knowing worldly-wise; informal streetwise.
– OPPOSITES novice, naive.

experiment noun **1** *he carried out an experiment:* **test**, investigation, trial, examination, observation; assessment, evaluation, appraisal, analysis, study. **2** *these results have been established by experiment:* **research**, experimentation, observation, analysis, testing.
• verb *they experimented with various techniques:* **carry out trials/tests**, conduct experiments, conduct research; test, trial, try out, investigate, examine, assess, appraise, evaluate.

experimental adjective **1** *the experimental stage:* **exploratory**, investigational, trial, test, pilot; speculative, conjectural, hypothetical, tentative, preliminary. **2** *experimental music:* **new**, radical, avant-garde, alternative; unorthodox, unconventional, left-field; informal way-out.

expert noun **specialist**, authority, pundit; adept, maestro, virtuoso, master, wizard; connoisseur, aficionado; informal ace, buff, pro, whizz, hotshot; Brit. informal dab hand; N. Amer. informal maven, crackerjack.
• adjective **skilful**, skilled, adept, accomplished, talented, fine; masterly, virtuoso, great, excellent, first-class, first-rate, superb; proficient, good, able, capable, experienced, practised, knowledgeable; informal wizard, ace, crack, mean.
– OPPOSITES incompetent.

expertise noun **skill**, skilfulness, prowess, proficiency, competence; knowledge, ability, aptitude, capability; informal know-how.

expire verb **1** *my contract has expired:* **run out**, become invalid, become void, lapse; end, finish, stop, come to an end, terminate. **2** *the spot where he expired:* **die**, pass away/on, breathe your last; informal kick the bucket, bite the dust, croak, buy it; Brit. informal snuff it, peg out, pop your clogs.

expiry noun **end**, finish, termination, conclusion; lapse.

explain verb **1** *he explained the procedure:* **describe**, give an explanation of, make clear/intelligible, spell out, put into words; elucidate, expound, clarify, throw light on. **2** *that could explain his behaviour:* **account for**, give an explanation for, give a reason for.

explanation noun **1** *an explanation of his theory :* **clarification**; description, statement; interpretation, commentary. **2** *I owe you an explanation:* **account**, reason; justification, excuse, defence, vindication.

explanatory adjective **explaining**, descriptive, describing, illustrative, elucidatory.

expletive noun **swear word**, oath, curse, obscenity, profanity, four-letter word, dirty word; informal cuss word, cuss; formal imprecation; (**expletives**) bad language, foul language, strong language, swearing.

explicable adjective **explainable**, understandable, comprehensible, accountable, intelligible, interpretable.

explicit adjective **1** *explicit instructions:* **clear**, plain, straightforward, crystal clear, easily understandable; precise, exact, specific, unequivocal, unambiguous; detailed, comprehensive, exhaustive. **2** *sexually explicit material:* **uncensored**, graphic, candid, full-frontal.
– OPPOSITES vague.

explode verb **1** *a bomb has exploded:* **blow up**, detonate, go off, burst apart, shatter. **2** *he just exploded:* **lose your temper**, blow up; informal fly off the handle, hit the roof, blow your top, see red, go off the deep end; N. Amer. informal blow your lid/stack. **3** *the county's population exploded:* **increase suddenly/rapidly**, mushroom, snowball, escalate, burgeon, rocket. **4** *new*

research has exploded the myths: **disprove**, refute, rebut, repudiate, debunk, give the lie to; informal shoot full of holes, blow out of the water.
– OPPOSITES defuse.

exploit verb **1** *we should exploit this opportunity:* **utilize**, use, make use of, turn/put to good use, make the most of, capitalize on, benefit from; informal cash in on. **2** *a ruling class which exploited the workers:* **take advantage of**, abuse, impose on, treat unfairly, misuse, ill-treat; informal walk all over, take for a ride, rip off.
• noun *his exploits brought him notoriety:* **feat**, deed, act, adventure, stunt, escapade; achievement.

exploitation noun **1** *the exploitation of mineral resources:* **utilization**, use, making use of, making the most of, capitalization on; informal cashing in on. **2** *the exploitation of the poor:* **taking advantage**, abuse, misuse, ill-treatment, unfair treatment, oppression.

exploration noun **investigation**, study, survey, research, inspection, examination, scrutiny, observation.

exploratory adjective **investigative**, explorative, probing, fact-finding; trial, test, preliminary, provisional.

explore verb **1** *they explored the possibilities:* **investigate**, look into, consider; examine, evaluate, assess, research, survey, scrutinize, study, review; informal check out. **2** *an opportunity to explore the countryside:* **travel through**, tour; survey, take a look at, reconnoitre.

explorer noun **traveller**, discoverer, voyager, adventurer; surveyor, scout, prospector.

explosion noun **1** *Ed heard the explosion:* **detonation**, eruption; bang, blast, boom. **2** *an explosion of anger:* **outburst**, flare-up, outbreak, eruption, storm, rush, surge; fit, paroxysm, attack. **3** *a population explosion:* **sudden/rapid increase**, mushrooming, snowballing, escalation, multiplication, burgeoning, rocketing.

explosive adjective **1** *explosive gases:* **volatile**, inflammable, flammable, combustible, incendiary. **2** *Marco's explosive temper:* **fiery**, stormy, violent, volatile, passionate, tempestuous, turbulent, touchy, irascible, hot-headed, short-tempered. **3** *an explosive situation:* **tense**, highly charged, overwrought; dangerous, perilous, hazardous, sensitive, delicate, unstable, volatile.
• noun *stocks of explosives:* **bomb**, incendiary device.

exponent noun **1** *an exponent of free trade:* **advocate**, supporter, proponent, upholder, backer, defender, champion; promoter, propagandist, campaigner, fighter, crusader, enthusiast, apologist. **2** *a karate exponent:* **practitioner**, performer, player.
– OPPOSITES critic, opponent.

export verb **1** *they export oil to the US:* **sell overseas/abroad**, send overseas/abroad, trade internationally. **2** *he is trying to export his ideas to America:* **transmit**, spread, disseminate, circulate, communicate, pass on.
– OPPOSITES import.

expose verb **1** *he has exposed the truth about the conflict:* **uncover**, reveal, unveil, unmask, lay bare; discover, bring to light, make known; informal spill the beans on, blow the whistle on. **2** *he was exposed to radiation:* **subject**. **3** *they were exposed to new ideas:* **introduce to**, bring into contact with, make aware of, familiarize with, acquaint with.
– OPPOSITES cover, hide.

exposé noun **revelation**, disclosure, exposure; report, feature, piece, column; informal scoop.
– OPPOSITES cover-up.

exposed adjective **unprotected**, unsheltered, open to the elements; vulnerable, defenceless, undefended.
– OPPOSITES sheltered.

exposition noun **explanation**, description, elucidation, explication, interpretation; account, commentary, appraisal, assessment, discussion.

expostulate verb **remonstrate**, disagree, argue, take issue, protest, reason, express disagreement, raise objections.

exposure noun **1** *the exposure of a banking fraud:* **uncovering**,

e

e

revelation, disclosure, unveiling, unmasking, discovery, detection. **2** *we're getting a lot of exposure:* **publicity**, advertising, public interest/attention, media interest/attention; informal hype. **3** *his exposure to English literature:* **introduction to**, experience of, contact with, acquaintance with, awareness of. **4** *they were suffering from exposure:* **frostbite**, cold, hypothermia.

expound verb **present**, put forward, set forth, propose, propound; explain, give an explanation of, detail, spell out, describe.

express[1] verb **communicate**, convey, indicate, show, demonstrate, reveal, put across/over, get across/over; articulate, put into words, voice, give voice to; state, assert, air, make public, give vent to.
■ **express yourself** communicate your thoughts/opinions/views, put thoughts into words, speak your mind, say what's on your mind.

express[2] adjective *an express train:* **rapid**, swift, fast, high-speed; non-stop, direct.
– OPPOSITES slow.

expression noun **1** *the free expression of their views:* **utterance**, communication, uttering, voicing, declaration, articulation. **2** *his expression was troubled:* **look**, appearance, air, manner, countenance, mien. **3** *a well-known expression:* **idiom**, phrase; proverb, saying, adage, maxim, axiom, aphorism; platitude, cliché. **4** *try adding a bit more expression:* **emotion**, feeling, spirit, passion, intensity.

expressionless adjective **1** *his face was expressionless:* **inscrutable**, deadpan, poker-faced; blank, vacant, emotionless, unemotional, inexpressive; glazed, stony, wooden, impassive. **2** *a flat, expressionless tone:* **dull**, dry, toneless, monotonous, flat, wooden, unmodulated, unvarying, emotionless.
– OPPOSITES expressive, lively.

expressive adjective **1** *an expressive shrug:* **eloquent**, meaningful, demonstrative, suggestive. **2** *an expressive song:* **emotional**, passionate, poignant, moving, stirring, emotionally charged.
– OPPOSITES expressionless, unemotional.

expressly adverb **1** *he was expressly forbidden to see her:* **explicitly**, clearly, directly, plainly, distinctly; absolutely; specifically, categorically, pointedly, emphatically. **2** *a machine expressly built for speed:* **solely**, specifically, particularly, specially, exclusively, just, only, explicitly.

expropriate verb **seize**, take, appropriate, take possession of, requisition, commandeer, claim, acquire, sequestrate, confiscate.

expulsion noun **1** *expulsion from the party:* **removal**, debarment, dismissal, exclusion, discharge, ejection, drumming out. **2** *the expulsion of bodily waste:* **discharge**, ejection, excretion, voiding, evacuation, elimination, passing.
– OPPOSITES admission.

expunge verb **erase**, remove, delete, rub out, wipe out, efface; cross out, strike out, blot out, blank out; destroy, obliterate, eradicate, eliminate.

expurgate verb **censor**, bowdlerize, cut, edit; clean up, sanitize.

exquisite adjective **1** *exquisite antiques:* **beautiful**, lovely, elegant, fine; magnificent, superb, wonderful; delicate, fragile, dainty, subtle. **2** *exquisite taste:* **discriminating**, discerning, sensitive, fastidious; refined.

extant adjective **existing**, in existence, existent, surviving, remaining.

extemporary, extemporaneous adjective *an extemporary prayer.* See **EXTEMPORE**.

extempore adjective **impromptu**, spontaneous, unscripted, ad lib, extemporary, extemporaneous; improvised, unrehearsed, unplanned, unprepared, off the top of your head; informal off-the-cuff.
– OPPOSITES rehearsed.
• **adverb spontaneously**, extemporaneously, ad lib, without preparation, without rehearsal, off the top of your head; informal off the cuff.

extemporize verb **improvise**, ad lib, play it by ear, think on your feet, do something off the top of your head; informal busk it, wing it, do something off the cuff.

extend verb **1** *we've extended the kitchen:* **expand**, enlarge, increase; lengthen, widen, broaden. **2** *the garden extends as far as the road:* **continue**, carry on, run on, stretch, reach, spread. **3** *we have extended our range of services:* **widen**, expand, broaden; augment, supplement, increase, add to, enhance, develop. **4** *she decided to extend her holiday:* **prolong**, lengthen, increase; protract, spin out, string out. **5** *he extended a hand in greeting:* **hold out**, reach out, stretch out; offer, give, outstretch, proffer.
– OPPOSITES reduce, narrow, shorten.
■ **extend to** include, take in, incorporate, encompass.

extended adjective **prolonged**, protracted, long-lasting, long-drawn-out, long.

extension noun **1** *they are planning a new extension:* **addition**, add-on, adjunct, annex, wing; N. Amer. ell. **2** *an extension of our knowledge:* **expansion**, increase, enlargement, widening, broadening, deepening; augmentation, enhancement, development, growth, continuation. **3** *an extension of opening hours:* **prolongation**, lengthening, increase.

extensive adjective **1** *a mansion with extensive grounds:* **large**, sizeable, substantial, considerable, ample, great, vast. **2** *extensive knowledge:* **comprehensive**, thorough, exhaustive; broad, wide, wide-ranging, catholic.

extent noun **1** *two acres in extent:* **area**, size, expanse, length; proportions, dimensions. **2** *the full extent of her illness:* **degree**, scale, level, magnitude, scope; size, breadth, width, reach, range.

extenuating adjective **mitigating**, excusing, justifying, vindicating.

exterior adjective **outer**, outside, outermost, outward, external.
– OPPOSITES interior.
• noun **outside**, external surface, outward appearance, facade.

exterminate verb **kill**, put to death, dispatch; slaughter, butcher, massacre, wipe out, eliminate, eradicate, annihilate; murder, assassinate, execute; informal do away with, bump off, do in, top, take out, blow away; N. Amer. informal ice, rub out, waste; literary slay.

extermination noun **killing**, murder, assassination, putting to death, execution, dispatch, slaughter, massacre, liquidation, elimination, eradication, annihilation; literary slaying.

external adjective **1** *an external wall:* **outer**, outside, outermost, outward, exterior. **2** *an external examiner:* **outside**, independent.
– OPPOSITES internal, in-house.

extinct adjective **1** *an extinct species:* **vanished**, lost, died out, wiped out, destroyed, gone. **2** *an extinct volcano:* **inactive**.
– OPPOSITES extant, dormant.

extinction noun **dying out**, disappearance, vanishing; extermination, destruction, elimination, eradication, annihilation.

extinguish verb **douse**, put out, stamp out, smother.
– OPPOSITES light.

extirpate verb **weed out**, destroy, eradicate, stamp out, root out, wipe out, eliminate, suppress, crush, put down, put an end to, get rid of.

extol verb **praise**, go into raptures about/over, wax lyrical about, sing the praises of, praise to the skies, acclaim, eulogize, rave about, enthuse about/over; informal go wild about, go on about; N. Amer. informal ballyhoo; formal laud; old use panegyrize.
– OPPOSITES criticize.

extort verb **obtain by force**, extract, exact, wring, wrest, screw, squeeze; N. Amer. & Austral. informal put the bite on someone for.

extortion noun **demanding money with menaces**, blackmail; N. Amer. informal shakedown.

extortionate adjective **exorbitant**, excessively high, excessive, outrageous, unreasonable, inordinate, inflated, prohibitive, punitive; informal over the top, OTT.

extra adjective **additional**, more, added, supplementary, further, auxiliary, ancillary, subsidiary, secondary.

• adverb **exceptionally**, particularly, specially, especially, very, extremely; unusually, extraordinarily, uncommonly, remarkably, outstandingly, amazingly, incredibly, really; informal seriously, mucho, awfully, terribly; Brit. jolly, dead, well; informal, dated frightfully.
• noun **addition**, supplement, adjunct, addendum, add-on.

e

extract verb **1** *he extracted the cassette:* **take out**, draw out, pull out, remove, withdraw; release, extricate. **2** *they extracted a confession:* **wrest**, exact, wring, screw, squeeze, obtain by force, extort. **3** *the roots are crushed to extract the juice:* **squeeze out**, press out, obtain, get. **4** *data extracted from the report:* **excerpt**, select, reproduce, copy, take.
– OPPOSITES insert.
• noun **1** *an extract from his article:* **excerpt**, passage, citation, quotation. **2** *an extract of ginseng:* **distillation**, distillate, concentrate, essence, juice, derivative.

extraction noun **1** *the extraction of gall stones:* **removal**, taking out, drawing out, pulling out, withdrawal; extrication. **2** *the extraction of grape juice:* **squeezing**, pressing, obtaining. **3** *a man of Irish extraction:* **descent**, ancestry, parentage, ancestors, family, antecedents; lineage, line, origin, birth; genealogy, heredity, stock, pedigree, blood; roots, origins.
– OPPOSITES insertion.

extradite verb *he was extradited to Germany:* **deport**, send back, repatriate.

extradition noun **deportation**, repatriation, expulsion.

extraneous adjective **irrelevant**, immaterial, beside the point, unrelated, unconnected, inapposite, inapplicable.

extraordinary adjective **1** *an extraordinary coincidence:* **remarkable**, exceptional, amazing, astonishing, astounding, sensational, stunning, incredible, unbelievable, phenomenal; striking, outstanding, momentous, impressive, singular, memorable, unforgettable, unique, noteworthy; out of the ordinary, unusual, uncommon, rare, surprising; informal fantastic, terrific, tremendous, stupendous; literary wondrous. **2** *extraordinary speed:* **very great**, tremendous, enormous, immense, prodigious, stupendous, monumental; informal almighty.

extravagance noun **1** *a fit of extravagance:* **profligacy**, improvidence, wastefulness, prodigality, lavishness. **2** *the wine was an extravagance:* **luxury**, indulgence, self-indulgence, treat, extra, non-essential. **3** *the extravagance of the decor:* **ornateness**, elaborateness; ostentation. **4** *the extravagance of his compliments:* **excessiveness**, exaggeration, outrageousness, immoderation.

extravagant adjective **1** *an extravagant lifestyle:* **lavish**, indulgent, expensive, costly; spendthrift, profligate, wasteful, improvident, prodigal. **2** *extravagant praise:* **excessive**, immoderate, exaggerated, gushing, unrestrained, effusive, fulsome. **3** *an extravagant style:* **ornate**, elaborate, fancy; over-elaborate, ostentatious, exaggerated, baroque, rococo; informal flash, flashy.
– OPPOSITES thrifty, cheap, plain.

extravaganza noun **spectacular**, display, spectacle, show, pageant.

extreme adjective **1** *extreme danger:* **utmost**, very great, maximum, great, acute, enormous, severe, high, exceptional, extraordinary, serious. **2** *extreme measures:* **drastic**, serious, desperate, dire, radical, far-reaching; heavy, sharp, severe, austere, harsh, tough, strict, rigorous, oppressive, draconian; Brit. swingeing. **3** *extreme views:* **radical**, extremist, immoderate, fanatical, revolutionary, subversive, militant. **4** *the extreme north-west:* **furthest**, farthest, furthermost, farthermost, very, utmost, ultra-.
– OPPOSITES slight, moderate.
• noun *the two extremes | extremes of temperature:* **opposite**, antithesis, polar opposite, extremity; contrast.
■ **in the extreme.** See EXTREMELY.

extremely adverb **very**, exceedingly, exceptionally, especially, extraordinarily, in the extreme, tremendously, immensely, hugely,

supremely, highly, really, mightily; informal terrifically, awfully, fearfully, terribly, majorly, seriously, mega, ultra; Brit. informal well, dead, jolly; N. Amer. informal real, mighty, awful; informal, dated frightfully; old use exceeding.
– OPPOSITES slightly.

extremist noun **fanatic**, radical, zealot, fundamentalist, hardliner, militant, activist.
– OPPOSITES moderate.

extremity noun **1** *the eastern extremity:* **limit**, end, edge, side, boundary, border, frontier; perimeter, periphery, margin, tip. **2** *she lost feeling in her extremities:* **hands and feet**, fingers and toes, limbs. **3** *the extremity of the violence:* **intensity**, magnitude, acuteness, ferocity, vehemence, fierceness, violence, severity, seriousness, strength, power, powerfulness, vigour, force, forcefulness.

extricate verb **extract**, free, release, disentangle, get out, remove, withdraw, disengage; informal get someone/yourself off the hook.

extrovert noun *like most extroverts he was a good dancer:* **outgoing person**, sociable person, socializer, life and soul of the party.
– OPPOSITES introvert.
• adjective *his extrovert personality:* **outgoing**, extroverted, sociable, gregarious, genial, affable, friendly, unreserved.
– OPPOSITES introverted.

extrude verb **force out**, thrust out, squeeze out, express, eject, expel, release, emit.

exuberant adjective **ebullient**, buoyant, cheerful, high-spirited, exhilarated, excited, elated, exultant, euphoric, joyful, cheery, merry, jubilant, vivacious, enthusiastic, irrepressible, energetic, animated, full of life, lively, vigorous; informal bubbly, bouncy, full of beans; literary blithe.
– OPPOSITES gloomy.

exude verb **1** *milkweed exudes a milky sap:* **give off/out**, discharge, release, emit, issue; ooze, secrete. **2** *he exuded self-confidence:* **emanate**, radiate, ooze, emit; display, show, exhibit, manifest.

exult verb **rejoice**, be joyful, be happy, be delighted, be elated, be ecstatic, be overjoyed, be cock-a-hoop, be jubilant, be rapturous, be in raptures, be thrilled, jump for joy, be on cloud nine, be in seventh heaven; celebrate, cheer; informal be over the moon, be on top of the world; Austral. informal be wrapped; literary joy; old use jubilate.
■ **exult in** rejoice at/in, revel in, glory in, delight in, relish, savour, enjoy, take pleasure in; be proud of, congratulate yourself on.
– OPPOSITES sorrow.

exultant adjective **jubilant**, thrilled, triumphant, delighted, exhilarated, happy, overjoyed, joyful, gleeful, cock-a-hoop, excited, rejoicing, ecstatic, euphoric, elated, rapturous, in raptures, enraptured, on cloud nine, in seventh heaven; informal over the moon; N. Amer. informal wigged out; literary joyous.

exultation noun **jubilation**, rejoicing, happiness, pleasure, joy, gladness, delight, glee, elation, cheer, euphoria, exhilaration, delirium, ecstasy, rapture, exuberance.

eye noun **1** *he rubbed his eyes:* **eyeball**; informal peeper. **2** *his sharp eyes missed nothing:* **eyesight**, vision, sight, powers of observation, visual perception. **3** *to European eyes, the city may seem overcrowded:* **opinion**, way of thinking, mind, view, viewpoint, attitude, standpoint, perspective, belief, judgement, assessment, analysis, estimation.
• verb **1** *he eyed me suspiciously:* **look at**, observe, view, gaze at, stare at, regard, contemplate, survey, scrutinize, consider, glance at; watch; informal check out, size up; N. Amer. informal eyeball. **2** *he's eyeing young women in the street:* **ogle**, leer at, stare at, make eyes at; informal eye up; Austral./NZ informal perv on.
■ **see eye to eye** agree, concur, be in agreement, be of the same mind/opinion, be in accord, think as one; be on the same wavelength, get on/along. **up to your eyes** (informal) busy, overloaded, overburdened, overworked, under pressure, hard-pressed, rushed/run off your feet; informal pushed, up against it.

WORD LINKS

ocular, **ophthalmic** relating to the eye
ophthalmology the branch of medicine concerned with the eye

eye-catching adjective **striking**, arresting, conspicuous, dramatic, impressive, spectacular, breathtaking, dazzling, amazing, stunning, sensational, remarkable, distinctive, unusual, out of the ordinary.

eyelash noun **lash**; Anatomy cilium.

eyesight noun **sight**, vision, faculty of sight, ability to see, visual perception.

WORD LINKS

optometry the measurement of eyesight

eyesore noun **blot on the landscape**, monstrosity, excrescence, blight, scar, blemish.

eyewitness noun **observer**, onlooker, witness, bystander, passer-by.

Ff

fable noun **parable**, allegory.

fabled adjective **1** *a fabled musician:* **celebrated**, renowned, famed, famous, well known, prized, noted, notable, acclaimed, esteemed. **2** *a fabled giant of Irish myth:* **legendary**, mythical, fabulous, fairy-tale.

fabric noun **1** *the finest fabrics:* **cloth**, material, textile. **2** *the fabric of the building:* **structure**, material, infrastructure.

> **WORD LINKS**
>
> **clothier**, **draper** a person who sells fabrics

fabricate verb *they fabricated the evidence:* **make up**, invent, trump up; fake, falsify, counterfeit.

fabrication noun **invention**, piece of fiction, falsification, lie, untruth, falsehood, fib, myth, fairy story/tale; informal cock and bull story; Brit. informal porky pie.

fabulous adjective **1** *his fabulous wealth:* **stupendous**, prodigious, phenomenal, remarkable, exceptional; astounding, amazing, fantastic, breathtaking, staggering, unthinkable, unimaginable, incredible, unbelievable, unheard of, untold, undreamed of, beyond your wildest dreams; informal mind-boggling, mind-blowing. **2** (informal) *we had a fabulous time.* See **EXCELLENT**.

facade noun **1** *a house with a half-timbered facade:* **front**, frontage, face, exterior, outside; technical elevation. **2** *a facade of bonhomie:* **show**, front, appearance, pretence, simulation, affectation, semblance, illusion, act, masquerade, charade, mask, veneer.

face noun **1** *her beautiful face:* **countenance**, physiognomy, features; informal mug; Brit. informal mush, phiz, phizog; rhyming slang boat race; literary visage. **2** *her face grew sad:* **expression**, look, appearance, countenance. **3** *a cube has six faces:* **side**, surface, facet, aspect, plane, wall; elevation. **4** *he put on a brave face:* **front**, show, display, act, appearance, facade, exterior, mask. • verb **1** *the hotel faces the sea:* **look out on**, front on to, look over/across, overlook, be opposite. **2** *you'll just have to face the truth:* **accept**, become reconciled to, get used to, become accustomed to, adjust to, acclimatize yourself to; learn to live with, cope with, deal with, come to terms with, become resigned to. **3** *he faced the challenge boldly:* **confront**, face up to, encounter, meet, brave. **4** *the problems facing our police force:* **beset**, worry, trouble, confront; torment, plague, bedevil, curse. ■ **make a face** grimace, scowl, wince, frown, pout. **on the face of it** ostensibly, to all appearances, to all intents and purposes, at first glance, on the surface, superficially; apparently, seemingly, outwardly, as far as you can see/tell, by all accounts.

facelift noun **1** *she's planning to have a facelift:* **cosmetic surgery**, plastic surgery. **2** (informal) *the theatre is reopening after a facelift:* **makeover**, redecoration, refurbishment, revamp, renovation, overhaul, modernization, restoration, repairs, redevelopment, rebuilding, reconstruction, refit.

facet noun **1** *different facets of his character:* **aspect**, feature, side, dimension; strand, component, constituent, element. **2** *the facets of the gem:* **surface**, face, side, plane.

facetious adjective **flippant**, flip, glib, frivolous, tongue-in-cheek, playful, mischievous, jokey, jocular.
–OPPOSITES serious.

facile adjective **simplistic**, superficial, oversimplified; shallow, glib, naive.

facilitate verb **make easy/easier**, promote, ease, make possible, smooth the way for; enable, assist, help, aid, oil the wheels of, expedite, speed up.
–OPPOSITES impede.

f

facility noun **1** *cooking facilities | a wealth of local facilities:* **amenity**, service, resource; provision, means, equipment. **2** *the camera has a zoom facility:* **feature**, setting, mode, option. **3** *a medical facility:* **establishment**, centre, station, premises, site, post, base; informal outfit. **4** *he had a facility for languages:* **aptitude**, ability, gift, talent, flair.

facing noun **cladding**, veneer, skin, surface, facade, front, coating, covering, dressing, overlay.

facsimile noun **copy**, reproduction, duplicate, photocopy, replica, likeness, carbon copy, print, reprint; trademark Xerox.
–OPPOSITES original.

fact noun **1** *a fact that we cannot ignore:* **reality**, actuality, certainty; truth, verity, gospel. **2** *every fact was double-checked:* **detail**, piece of information, particular, item, element, point, feature, circumstance, aspect, facet; (**facts**) information, findings, data.
–OPPOSITES lie, fiction.
■ **in fact** actually, in actual fact, really, in reality, in point of fact, as a matter of fact, in truth, to tell the truth.

faction noun **1** *a faction of the Liberal Party:* **group**, grouping, set, section, camp, caucus, wing, arm, branch; clique, coterie, cabal; pressure group, splinter group; Brit. ginger group. **2** *the council was split by faction:* **infighting**, dissension, dissent, dispute, discord, strife, conflict, friction, argument, disagreement, controversy, quarrelling, wrangling, bickering, squabbling, disharmony, disunity, schism.

factor noun **element**, part, component, ingredient, strand, constituent, point, detail, item, feature, facet, aspect, characteristic, consideration, influence, circumstance.

factory noun **works**, plant, yard, mill; workshop.

factual adjective **truthful**, true, accurate, authentic, historical, genuine, fact-based; true-to-life, correct, exact, honest, faithful, literal, verbatim, word for word, unbiased, objective.
–OPPOSITES fictitious.

faculty noun **1** *the faculty of speech:* **power**, capability, capacity, facility, means; (**faculties**) senses, wits, reason, intelligence. **2** *the arts faculty:* **department**, school, division, section.

fad noun **craze**, vogue, trend, fashion, mode, enthusiasm, passion, obsession, mania, rage, compulsion, fixation, fetish, fancy; informal thing.

fade verb **1** *sunlight had faded the picture:* **bleach**, wash out, make pale, blanch; discolour. **2** *the afternoon light began to fade:* **grow dim**, grow faint, fail, dwindle, die away, wane, disappear, vanish, decline, melt away, evaporate.
–OPPOSITES brighten.

fail verb **1** *the scheme had failed:* **be unsuccessful**, not succeed, fall through, fall flat, collapse, founder, backfire, meet with disaster, come to nothing, misfire; informal flop, bomb. **2** *he failed his exams:* **be unsuccessful in**, not pass; not make the grade; informal flunk. **3** *his friends had failed him:* **let down**, disappoint; desert, abandon, betray, be disloyal to; literary forsake. **4** *the ventilation system has failed:* **break down**, stop working, cut out, crash; malfunction, go wrong, develop a fault; informal conk out, go on the blink; Brit. informal pack up. **5** *900 businesses are failing each week:* **collapse**, crash, go under, go bankrupt, go into receivership, go into liquidation, cease trading, be wound up; informal fold, flop, go bust, go broke, go to the wall.
–OPPOSITES succeed, pass.
■ **without fail** without exception, unfailingly, regularly, invariably, predictably, conscientiously, religiously, come what may.

failing noun *she accepted him despite*

his failings: **fault**, shortcoming, weakness, imperfection, defect, flaw, frailty, vice.
– OPPOSITES strength.

failure noun **1** *the failure of the escape attempt:* **lack of success**, defeat, collapse, foundering. **2** *the scheme had been a complete failure:* **fiasco**, debacle, catastrophe, disaster; informal flop, washout, dead loss. **3** *it was a failure on my part:* **negligence**, dereliction of duty; omission, oversight. **4** *everyone regarded him as a failure:* **underachiever**, disappointment; informal loser, no-hoper, dead loss. **5** *the failure of the heating system:* **breaking down**, breakdown, malfunction; crash. **6** *company failures:* **collapse**, crash, bankruptcy, insolvency, liquidation, closure.
– OPPOSITES success.

faint adjective **1** *a faint mark | a faint image:* **indistinct**, vague, unclear, indefinite, ill-defined, unobtrusive; pale, light, faded, dim. **2** *a faint cry:* **quiet**, muted, muffled, stifled; feeble, weak, whispered, murmured, indistinct, subdued, low, soft, gentle. **3** *a faint possibility:* **slight**, slender, slim, small, tiny, negligible, remote, vague. **4** *I suddenly felt faint:* **dizzy**, giddy, light-headed, unsteady; informal woozy.
– OPPOSITES clear, loud.
• verb *he nearly fainted:* **pass out**, lose consciousness, black out, keel over; informal conk out; literary swoon.
• noun *a dead faint:* **blackout**, fainting fit, loss of consciousness; literary swoon.

> Don't confuse **faint** with **feint**, which means 'a deceptive movement intended to make someone think that you are going to do something'.

faint-hearted adjective **timid**, timorous, nervous, fearful, afraid; cowardly, craven, spineless, pusillanimous, lily-livered; informal yellow, yellow-bellied, chicken, chicken-hearted, gutless.
– OPPOSITES brave.

faintly adverb **1** *she called his name faintly:* **indistinctly**, softly, gently, weakly; in a whisper, in a murmur, in a low voice, sotto voce. **2** *he looked faintly bewildered:* **slightly**, vaguely, somewhat, quite, fairly, rather, a little, a bit, a touch, a shade.

fair[1] adjective **1** *the courts were generally fair:* **just**, equitable, honest; impartial, unbiased, unprejudiced, non-partisan, neutral, even-handed. **2** *the weather was fair:* **fine**, dry, bright, clear, sunny, cloudless; warm, balmy, clement, benign, pleasant. **3** *her fair hair:* **blonde**, yellow, golden, flaxen, light. **4** *fair skin:* **pale**, light, light-complexioned, white, creamy. **5** *a fair achievement:* **reasonable**, passable, tolerable, satisfactory, acceptable, respectable, decent, all right, good enough, pretty good, not bad, average, middling; informal OK, so-so.
– OPPOSITES unfair, inclement, dark.
■ **fair and square** honestly, fairly, by the book; lawfully, legally, legitimately; informal on the level.

fair[2] noun **1** *a country fair:* **fete**, gala, festival, carnival. **2** *an antiques fair:* **market**, bazaar, mart, sale. **3** *a new art fair:* **exhibition**, display, show, exposition; N. Amer. exhibit.

fairly adverb **1** *we were treated fairly:* **justly**, equitably, impartially, without bias, without prejudice, even-handedly; equally, the same. **2** *the boat's in fairly good condition:* **reasonably**, passably, tolerably, adequately, moderately, quite, relatively, comparatively; informal pretty.

fairy noun **sprite**, pixie, elf, imp, puck, leprechaun, brownie; literary faerie, fay.

faith noun **1** *I have complete faith in him:* **trust**, belief, confidence, conviction. **2** *she died for her faith | people of other faiths:* **religion**, belief; church, denomination, religious persuasion, ideology, creed.
– OPPOSITES mistrust.

faithful adjective **1** *his faithful assistant:* **loyal**, steadfast, staunch, constant, true, devoted, unswerving, dedicated, committed; dependable, reliable; humorous trusty. **2** *a faithful copy:* **accurate**, exact, faultless, precise, true, close, strict; realistic, authentic.
– OPPOSITES unfaithful, disloyal, inaccurate.

faithless adjective **unfaithful**, disloyal, inconstant, untrue, adulterous, traitorous; deceitful, two-faced, double-crossing; informal cheating, two-timing, back-stabbing; literary perfidious, false-hearted.
– OPPOSITES faithful, loyal.

fake adjective **1** *fake banknotes:* **counterfeit**, forged, fraudulent, imitation, false, bogus; informal phoney, dud. **2** *fake diamonds:* **imitation**, artificial, synthetic, simulated, mock, faux; ersatz, false, bogus; informal pretend, phoney, pseudo. **3** *a fake Cockney accent:* **feigned**, faked, put-on, assumed, invented, affected; artificial, mock; informal phoney, pseud; Brit. informal cod.
– OPPOSITES genuine, authentic.
• noun **1** *the painting was a fake:* **forgery**, counterfeit, copy; imitation, reproduction; informal phoney. **2** *that doctor is a fake:* **charlatan**, quack, sham, fraud, impostor, confidence trickster; informal phoney, con man, con artist.
• verb **1** *the certificate was faked:* **forge**, counterfeit, falsify, copy, reproduce, replicate. **2** *he faked a yawn:* **feign**, pretend, simulate, put on, affect.

fall verb **1** *bombs began to fall from the plane:* **drop**, descend, come down, go down; plummet, plunge, sink, dive, tumble; cascade. **2** *he tripped and fell:* **topple over**, tumble over, keel over, fall down/over, go head over heels, go headlong, collapse, take a spill, pitch forward; trip, stumble, slip; informal come a cropper. **3** *the water level began to fall:* **subside**, recede, drop, retreat, fall away, go down, sink. **4** *profits fell by 12 per cent:* **decrease**, decline, diminish, fall off, drop off, lessen, dwindle; plummet, plunge, slump, sink; depreciate, devalue; informal go through the floor, nosedive, crash. **5** *those who fell in the war:* **die**, perish, lose your life, be killed, be slain, be lost, meet your death; informal bite the dust; Brit. informal snuff it. **6** *the town fell to the barbarians:* **surrender**, yield, submit, give in, capitulate, succumb; be taken by, be defeated by, be conquered by, be overwhelmed by. **7** *she fell ill:* **become**, grow, get, turn.
– OPPOSITES rise, increase.
• noun **1** *he had a fall and broke his hip:* **tumble**, trip, spill, topple, slip. **2** *a fall in sales:* **decline**, fall-off, drop, decrease, cut, dip, reduction, downswing; slump; informal nosedive, crash. **3** *the fall of the Roman Empire:* **downfall**, collapse, failure, decline; destruction, overthrow, demise. **4** *the fall of Berlin:* **surrender**, capitulation, yielding, submission; defeat.
– OPPOSITES increase, rise.
■ **fall back** retreat, withdraw, back off, draw back, pull back, move away. **fall back on** resort to, turn to, look to, call on, have recourse to; rely on, depend on, lean on. **fall for** (informal) **1** *she really fell for him:* fall in love with, become infatuated with, lose your heart to, take a fancy to, be smitten by. **2** *she won't fall for that trick:* be deceived by, be duped by, be fooled by, be taken in by, believe, trust, be convinced by; informal go for, buy, swallow. **fall out** quarrel, argue, fight, squabble, bicker, have words, disagree, be at odds, clash, wrangle, cross swords, lock horns, be at loggerheads, be at each other's throats; Brit. row; informal scrap, argufy. **fall through** *the deal fell through at the last minute:* collapse, come to nothing, be unsuccessful, miscarry, go awry, founder, come to grief; informal come a cropper.

fallacious adjective **erroneous**, false, untrue, wrong, incorrect, flawed, inaccurate, mistaken, misinformed, misguided; specious, spurious, bogus; groundless, unfounded, unproven, unsupported, uncorroborated.
– OPPOSITES correct.

fallacy noun **misconception**, misbelief, delusion, misapprehension, misinterpretation, misconstruction, error, mistake; untruth, myth.

fallible adjective **imperfect**, flawed, errant, liable to err, prone to error, weak.

false adjective **1** *a false report:* **incorrect**, untrue, wrong, erroneous, fallacious, flawed, distorted, inaccurate, imprecise; untruthful, fictitious, fabricated,

invented, made up, trumped up, unfounded, spurious; counterfeit, forged, fraudulent. **2** *false pearls:* **fake**, artificial, imitation, synthetic, simulated, ersatz, man-made, mock; informal phoney, pseudo. **3** (literary) *a false friend:* **faithless**, unfaithful, disloyal, untrue, inconstant, treacherous, traitorous, two-faced, double-crossing, deceitful, dishonest, duplicitous, untrustworthy; untruthful; informal cheating, two-timing, back-stabbing.
–OPPOSITES correct, genuine.

falsehood noun **1** *a downright falsehood:* **lie**, untruth, fib, falsification, fabrication, invention, story, flight of fancy; informal cock and bull story, whopper; Brit. informal porky pie; humorous terminological inexactitude. **2** *he accused me of falsehood:* **lying**, untruthfulness, mendacity, perjury; deceit, deception, double-crossing, treachery.
–OPPOSITES truth, honesty.

falsify verb *someone has falsified the records:* **alter**, change, tamper with, manipulate, misrepresent, misreport, distort, embellish, embroider; forge, fake, counterfeit, fabricate.

falter verb **hesitate**, delay, drag your feet, stall; waver, vacillate, be indecisive, be irresolute, blow hot and cold; Brit. haver, hum and haw; informal sit on the fence, dilly-dally, shilly-shally.

fame noun **renown**, celebrity, stardom, popularity, prominence; distinction, importance, eminence, prestige, stature, esteem, repute; notoriety, infamy.
–OPPOSITES obscurity.

famed adjective **famous**, celebrated, well known, prominent, renowned, noted, notable, respected, esteemed, acclaimed; notorious, infamous.
–OPPOSITES unknown, obscure.

familiar adjective **1** *a familiar situation:* **well known**, recognized, accustomed; common, commonplace, everyday, day-to-day, ordinary, habitual, usual, customary, routine, standard, stock, mundane, run-of-the-mill. **2** *are you familiar with the subject?* **acquainted with**, conversant with, versed in, knowledgeable about, well informed about; at home with, no stranger to, au fait with; informal well up on, genned up on, clued up on, up to speed with. **3** *he is too familiar with the teachers:* **overfamiliar**, presumptuous, disrespectful, forward, bold, impudent, impertinent.
–OPPOSITES unfamiliar, formal.

familiarity noun **1** *a familiarity with politics:* **acquaintance with**, awareness of, experience of, insight into; knowledge of, understanding of, comprehension of, grasp of, skill in, proficiency in. **2** *she was affronted by his familiarity:* **overfamiliarity**, presumption, presumptuousness, forwardness, boldness, audacity, cheek, impudence, impertinence, disrespect.

familiarize verb **acquaint**, make familiar, make conversant; accustom to, habituate to, instruct in, teach in, educate in, school in, prime in, introduce to.

family noun **1** *I haven't met his family:* **relatives**, relations, next of kin, kith and kin, kinsfolk, kindred, your flesh and blood, your nearest and dearest; informal folks; dated people. **2** *her family have all grown up:* **children**, youngsters; offspring, progeny; brood; descendants, heirs; Law issue; informal kids.

family tree noun **ancestry**, genealogy, descent, lineage, line, bloodline, pedigree, background, extraction; family, dynasty, house; forebears, forefathers, antecedents, roots, origins.

famine noun **1** *a nation threatened by famine:* **food shortages**. **2** *the cotton famine of the 1860s:* **shortage**, scarcity, lack, dearth, deficiency, insufficiency, shortfall.
–OPPOSITES plenty.

famished adjective **ravenous**, hungry, starving, starved, empty; informal peckish.
–OPPOSITES full, replete.

famous adjective **well known**, prominent, popular; renowned, illustrious, celebrated, acclaimed, great, legendary, noted, eminent, distinguished, esteemed, respected; notorious, infamous.
–OPPOSITES unknown.

f

fan[1] verb **1** *his article fanned public fears:* **intensify**, increase, inflame, exacerbate; stimulate, stir up, whip up, fuel, kindle, arouse. **2** *the police squad fanned out:* **spread**, branch; split up, divide up.

fan[2] noun *a basketball fan:* **enthusiast**, devotee, admirer, lover; supporter, follower, disciple, adherent, zealot; expert, connoisseur, aficionado; informal buff, fiend, freak, nut, addict, fanatic, groupie; N. Amer. informal jock.

fanatic noun **1** *a religious fanatic:* **zealot**, extremist, militant, dogmatist, devotee; sectarian, partisan, radical, diehard. **2** (informal) *a keep-fit fanatic.* See FAN[2].

fanatical adjective **1** *a fanatical religious fundamentalist:* **extremist**, extreme, zealous, rabid, militant, dogmatic, uncompromising, radical, diehard; intolerant, single-minded, blinkered, inflexible. **2** *a fanatical supporter of the team | he's fanatical about baseball:* **enthusiastic**, eager, keen, fervent, passionate; obsessive, obsessed, fixated, compulsive; informal wild, nuts, crazy.

fanciful adjective **1** *a fanciful story:* **far-fetched**, fantastic, implausible, unbelievable; ridiculous, ludicrous, absurd, preposterous; imaginary, made-up; informal hard to swallow. **2** *a fanciful girl:* **imaginative**, inventive; whimsical, impractical, dreamy, quixotic; out of touch with reality, in a world of your own.
– OPPOSITES literal, practical.

fancy verb **1** (Brit. informal) *I fancied a change of scene:* **want**, feel like, wish to have, have a yen for; desire, long for, yearn for, crave, thirst for, hanker after, dream of, covet; old use be desirous of. **2** (Brit. informal) *I'm sure she fancies him:* **be attracted to**, find attractive, be taken with; desire, lust after; informal have a crush on, have the hots for, carry a torch for. **3** *I fancied I could see lights:* **think**, imagine, believe, be under the impression, be of the opinion; informal reckon.
• adjective *the fancy decor:* **elaborate**, ornate, ornamental, decorative, embellished; ostentatious, showy, flamboyant; luxurious, lavish, extravagant, expensive; informal flash, flashy, bling-bling, jazzy, ritzy, snazzy; Brit. informal swish.
– OPPOSITES plain.
• noun *he had a fancy to own a farm:* **desire**, wish, yen, urge; inclination, whim, impulse, notion; yearning, longing, hankering, craving; informal itch.

fantasize verb **daydream**, dream, muse, make-believe, pretend, imagine, be living in a dream world.

fantastic adjective **1** *a fantastic notion:* **fanciful**, extravagant, extraordinary, far-fetched, wild, absurd, nonsensical, incredible, unbelievable, unthinkable, implausible, improbable, unlikely, doubtful, dubious; strange, peculiar, odd, weird, eccentric, bizarre, whimsical; informal crazy, off the wall. **2** (informal) *a fantastic performance:* **marvellous**, wonderful, sensational, superb, outstanding, excellent, first-rate, first-class, dazzling, out of this world, breathtaking, spectacular; informal great, terrific, fabulous, fab, mega, super, ace, magic, cracking, cool, wicked, awesome; Brit. informal brilliant, smashing; Austral./NZ informal bonzer.
– OPPOSITES reasonable, ordinary.

fantasy noun **1** *a mix of fantasy and realism:* **imagination**, fancy, make-believe; daydreaming. **2** *he had a fantasy about appearing on TV:* **dream**, daydream, pipe dream, fanciful notion, wish; fond hope, delusion, illusion; informal pie in the sky.
– OPPOSITES realism.

far adverb **1** *we're not far from the beach:* **a long way**, a great distance, a good way; afar. **2** *her charm far outweighs any flaws:* **considerably**, greatly, significantly, substantially, appreciably; much, to a great extent, by a long way, by far, by a mile, easily.
– OPPOSITES near.
• adjective **1** *the far reaches of the empire:* **distant**, faraway, far-off, remote, far-flung. **2** *the far side of the campus:* **further**, more distant; opposite.
– OPPOSITES near.
■ **by far** *this is by far the best film of the three:* easily, by a long way, far and away, undoubtedly, without doubt, without question;

significantly, substantially, appreciably, much; Brit. by a long chalk. **far and away**. See **BY FAR**. **go far** be successful, succeed, prosper, flourish, thrive, get on, make good; informal make a name for yourself, make your mark, go places. **so far** **1** *nobody has noticed so far:* until now, up to now, up to this point, as yet, thus far, hitherto, up to the present, to date. **2** *his liberalism only extends so far:* to a certain extent, up to a point, to a degree, within reason, within limits.

faraway adjective **1** *faraway places:* **distant**, far-off, far, remote, far-flung, outlying. **2** *the faraway look in her eyes:* **dreamy**, daydreaming, abstracted, absent-minded, distracted, preoccupied, vague; lost in thought, in a world of your own; informal miles away.
– OPPOSITES nearby.

farce noun *this farce of a justice system lets criminals go unpunished:* **charade**, pantomime, travesty, mockery, masquerade, joke; informal shambles.

farcical adjective **ridiculous**, preposterous, ludicrous, absurd, laughable, risible, nonsensical; senseless, pointless, useless; silly, foolish, idiotic, stupid; informal crazy; Brit. informal barmy, daft.

fare noun **1** *I can't afford the fare:* **ticket price**, cost, charge, fee, tariff. **2** *the taxi picked up a fare:* **passenger**, traveller, customer; Brit. informal punter. **3** *a range of traditional Scottish fare:* **food**, meals, foodstuffs, provender, provisions; cooking, cuisine; diet; informal grub, nosh, eats, chow; dated victuals.
• verb *how are you faring at the moment?* **get on**, get along, cope, manage, do; informal make out.

farewell exclamation *farewell, my dear:* **goodbye**, adieu; au revoir, ciao; informal bye, so long, cheerio; Brit. informal ta-ta; informal, dated toodle-pip.
• noun *an emotional farewell:* **goodbye**, valediction, adieu; leave-taking, parting, departure; send-off.

far-fetched adjective **improbable**, unlikely, implausible, unconvincing, dubious, doubtful, incredible, unbelievable, unthinkable; contrived, fanciful, unrealistic, ridiculous, absurd, preposterous; informal hard to swallow.
– OPPOSITES likely.

farm noun **smallholding**, farmstead, plantation, estate; farmland; Brit. grange, croft; Scottish steading; N. Amer. ranch; Austral./NZ station.
• verb **breed**, rear, keep, raise, tend.
■ **farm something out** contract out, outsource, subcontract, delegate.

farmer noun **agriculturalist**, agronomist, smallholder, breeder; Brit. crofter; N. Amer. rancher.

farming noun **agriculture**, cultivation, land management; husbandry; agronomy, agribusiness; Brit. crofting.

WORD LINKS
agrarian relating to agriculture

far-reaching adjective **extensive**, wide-ranging, sweeping, comprehensive, widespread, all-embracing, overarching, blanket, wholesale; important, significant, radical, major, drastic, substantial.
– OPPOSITES limited.

far-sighted adjective **prescient**, visionary, forward-thinking, shrewd, discerning, judicious, canny, prudent.

farther adverb & adjective. See **FURTHER**.

farthest adjective. See **FURTHEST**.

fascinate verb **captivate**, enthral, enchant, entrance, intrigue, engross, absorb, transfix, rivet, mesmerize, charm, attract, interest, draw.
– OPPOSITES bore.

fascinating adjective **captivating**, enthralling, intriguing, engrossing, absorbing, spellbinding, riveting, compelling, compulsive, gripping, thrilling; alluring, tempting, irresistible, charming, attractive, entertaining, interesting.

fascination noun **1** *her fascination with all things Russian:* **interest in**, preoccupation with, passion for, obsession with. **2** *the fascination of Morocco:* **allure**, lure, charm, attraction, intrigue, appeal, pull, draw.

fascism noun **authoritarianism**, totalitarianism, dictatorship, despotism; Nazism.

fascist adjective **authoritarian**, totalitarian, dictatorial, despotic, autocratic, undemocratic, illiberal.
– OPPOSITES democratic, liberal.

fashion noun **1** *the current fashion for tight clothes:* **vogue**, trend, craze, rage, mania, fad; style, look; tendency, convention, custom, practice; informal thing. **2** *the world of fashion:* **clothes**, couture; informal the rag trade. **3** *the work was carried out in a sensible fashion:* **manner**, way, method, mode, style; system, approach.
• verb *the objects were fashioned from scrap metal:* **make**, construct, build, manufacture; cast, shape, form, mould, sculpt; forge, hew, carve.
■ **in fashion** fashionable, stylish, in vogue, up to date, up to the minute, all the rage, chic, à la mode; informal trendy, on-trend, fashion-forward, cool, in, hot, big, hip, happening, groovy, with it; N. Amer. informal tony, fly. **out of fashion** unfashionable, dated, old-fashioned, out of date, outdated, outmoded, behind the times; unstylish, unpopular, passé, démodé; informal old hat, out, square, out of the ark.

fashionable adjective **in vogue**, in fashion, stylish, chic, elegant; popular, trendsetting, modern, all the rage, modish, voguish, à la mode, up to date, up to the minute; informal trendy, on-trend, fashion-forward, cool, in, hot, big, hip, funky, happening, groovy, with it; N. Amer. informal tony, fly.

fast[1] adjective **1** *a fast pace:* **swift**, rapid, quick, speedy; high-speed, express, blistering, breakneck; hasty, hurried; informal nippy, zippy, scorching, supersonic; Brit. informal cracking; literary fleet. **2** *he held the door fast:* **secure**, fastened, tight, firm, closed, shut; immovable. **3** *the dyes are boiled to produce a fast colour:* **indelible**, lasting, permanent, stable.
– OPPOSITES slow, loose.
• adverb **1** *she drove fast | let's get out of here fast:* **quickly**, rapidly, swiftly, speedily, briskly, at speed, at full tilt; hastily, hurriedly, in a hurry, post-haste, pell-mell; like a shot, like a flash, on the double; informal double quick, pdq (pretty damn quick), like lightning, hell for leather, like mad, like the wind, like a bat out of hell; Brit. informal like the clappers, at a rate of knots, like billy-o; N. Amer. informal lickety-split; literary apace. **2** *his wheels were stuck fast:* **securely**, firmly; tight. **3** *he's fast asleep:* **deeply**, sound, completely.
– OPPOSITES slowly.

fast[2] verb *we must fast and pray:* **eat nothing**, go without food, go hungry, starve yourself, abstain.
– OPPOSITES eat.

fasten verb **1** *he fastened the door:* **bolt**, lock, secure, make fast, chain, seal. **2** *they fastened splints to his leg:* **attach**, fix, affix, clip, pin, tack; stick, bond, join. **3** *he fastened his horse to a tree:* **tie**, tether, hitch, lash, anchor, strap, rope; truss, fetter, bind. **4** *his gaze fastened on me:* **focus**, fix, be riveted, concentrate, zero in, zoom in, be directed at.
– OPPOSITES unfasten, remove.

fastidious adjective **scrupulous**, meticulous, punctilious, pains-taking, particular; perfectionist, fussy, finicky; critical, overcritical, hard to please, exacting, demanding; informal pernickety, nit-picking, choosy, picky; N. Amer. informal persnickety.
– OPPOSITES lax.

fat adjective **1** *a fat man:* **plump**, stout, overweight, large, chubby, portly, flabby, paunchy, pot-bellied, meaty, of ample proportions, rotund; obese, corpulent, gross, fleshy; informal tubby, roly-poly, beefy, porky, blubbery, chunky; Brit. informal podgy. **2** *fat bacon:* **fatty**, greasy, oily. **3** *a fat book:* **thick**, big, chunky, substantial; long.
– OPPOSITES thin, lean, small.
• noun *you need to lose some of that fat:* **blubber**, adipose tissue; informal flab.

fatal adjective **1** *a fatal disease:* **deadly**, lethal, mortal, death-dealing; terminal, incurable, untreatable, inoperable; literary deathly. **2** *a fatal mistake:* **disastrous**, catastrophic, calamitous, dire; costly, devastating, ruinous; formal grievous.
– OPPOSITES harmless, beneficial.

fatalism noun **acceptance**, resignation, stoicism; passivity.

fatality noun **death**, casualty, mortality, victim.

fate noun **1** *what has fate in store for me?* **destiny**, providence, the stars, chance, luck, serendipity, fortune, kismet, karma. **2** *my fate was in their hands:* **future**, destiny, outcome, end, lot.
• verb *it was as if they were fated to meet again:* **predestine**, preordain, destine, be meant, be doomed.

fateful adjective **1** *that fateful day:* **decisive**, critical, crucial, pivotal, life-changing; momentous, portentous, important, significant, historic. **2** *the fateful defeat of 1402:* **disastrous**, ruinous, calamitous, devastating, tragic, terrible.
– OPPOSITES unimportant.

father noun **1** *their father was Scottish:* **male parent**; patriarch, paterfamilias; informal dad, daddy, pa, pop; Brit. informal, dated pater. **2** (literary) *the religion of my fathers:* **ancestors**, forefathers, forebears, predecessors, antecedents, progenitors. **3** *one of the fathers of psychoanalysis:* **founder**, originator, prime mover, architect, pioneer.
• verb **sire**; literary beget.

WORD LINKS

paternal relating to a person's father
patricide the killing of a father by his child

fathom verb **understand**, comprehend, work out, make sense of, grasp, divine, puzzle out, get to the bottom of; interpret, decipher, decode; informal make head or tail of, tumble to, crack; Brit. informal **twig**, suss out.

fatigue noun **tiredness**, weariness, exhaustion.
– OPPOSITES energy.
• verb **tire**, exhaust, wear out, drain, weary, overtire, prostrate; informal take it out of; Brit. informal knacker.
– OPPOSITES invigorate.

fatty adjective **greasy**, oily; technical adipose.
– OPPOSITES lean.

fatuous adjective **silly**, foolish, stupid, inane, idiotic, vacuous, asinine; pointless, senseless, ridiculous, ludicrous, absurd; informal dumb, gormless; Brit. informal daft.
– OPPOSITES sensible.

fault noun **1** *he has his faults | I can find no faults in his work:* **defect**, failing, imperfection, flaw, blemish, shortcoming, weakness, frailty, foible, vice; error, mistake. **2** *a computer fault put the line out of action:* **defect**, bug; informal glitch, gremlin. **3** *the fault lies with the director:* **responsibility**, liability, culpability.
– OPPOSITES merit, strength.
• verb *you can't fault their commitment:* **find fault with**, criticize, attack, condemn, reproach; complain about, moan about; informal knock, gripe about, beef about, pick holes in; Brit. informal slag off, have a go at.
■ **at fault** *the driver of the car was at fault:* to blame, blameworthy, culpable; responsible, guilty, in the wrong. **to a fault** *he's generous to a fault:* excessively, unduly, overly, immoderately, needlessly.

faultless adjective **perfect**, flawless, without fault, error-free, exact, impeccable, accurate, precise, correct, exemplary.
– OPPOSITES flawed.

faulty adjective **1** *a faulty electric blanket:* **defective**, malfunctioning, broken, damaged, not working, out of order; informal on the blink, kaput, bust; Brit. informal knackered, duff; N. Amer. informal on the fritz. **2** *her logic is faulty:* **flawed**, unsound, inaccurate, incorrect, erroneous, fallacious, wrong.
– OPPOSITES working, sound.

faux pas noun **gaffe**, blunder, mistake, indiscretion, impropriety; informal boo-boo; Brit. informal boob; N. Amer. informal blooper.

favour noun **1** *she looked on him with favour:* **approval**, approbation, liking, goodwill, kindness, benevolence. **2** *will you do me a favour?* **good turn**, service, good deed, act of kindness, courtesy.
– OPPOSITES disservice, disapproval.
• verb **1** *the party favours electoral reform:* **advocate**, recommend, approve of, be in favour of, support, back, champion; campaign for, stand up for, press for, lobby for, promote; informal plug, push for. **2** *Robyn favours loose clothes:* **prefer**, like more/better, go for, choose, opt for, select, pick, plump for, be partial to.

f

3 *the conditions favoured the other team:* **benefit**, be to the advantage of, help, assist, aid, be of service to.
– OPPOSITES oppose, dislike, hinder.
■ **in favour of** *the union was in favour of the proposal:* on the side of, pro, all for, sympathetic to.

favourable adjective **1** *a favourable review:* **approving**, complimentary, flattering, glowing, enthusiastic; good, encouraging, positive. **2** *favourable conditions for economic growth:* **advantageous**, beneficial, in your favour, good, right, suitable, fitting, appropriate; propitious, auspicious, promising, encouraging. **3** *a favourable reply:* **positive**, affirmative; encouraging, reassuring.
– OPPOSITES critical, disadvantageous, unfavourable.

favourably adverb **positively**, approvingly, sympathetically, enthusiastically, appreciatively.

favoured adjective **preferred**, favourite, recommended, chosen.

favourite adjective **best-loved**, most-liked, favoured, dearest; preferred, chosen.
• noun **first choice**, pick, preference, pet, darling, the apple of your eye; informal golden boy; Brit. informal blue-eyed boy/girl; N. Amer. informal fair-haired boy/girl.

favouritism noun **partiality**, partisanship, preferential treatment, favour, nepotism, prejudice, bias, inequality, unfairness, discrimination.

fawn[1] adjective *a fawn carpet:* **beige**, buff, sand, oatmeal, café au lait, camel, taupe, stone, mushroom, greige.

fawn[2] verb *they were fawning over the President:* **be obsequious to**, ingratiate yourself with, curry favour with, pay court to, dance attendance on, play up to, crawl to; informal suck up to, grovel to, make up to, be all over.

fawning adjective **obsequious**, servile, sycophantic, flattering, ingratiating, unctuous, grovelling; informal bootlicking, smarmy.

fear noun **1** *she felt fear at entering the house:* **terror**, fright, fearfulness, horror, alarm, panic, agitation, trepidation, dread, dismay, distress, consternation; anxiety, worry, unease, uneasiness, apprehension, apprehensiveness, nervousness, nerves, foreboding; informal the creeps, the willies, the heebie-jeebies, the jitters. **2** *a fear of heights:* **phobia**, aversion, antipathy, dread; nightmare, horror, terror; anxiety, neurosis; informal hang-up.
• verb **1** *she feared her husband:* **be afraid of**, be fearful of, be scared of, be apprehensive of, dread, live in fear of, be terrified of; worry about, feel apprehensive about. **2** *he feared to tell them what had happened:* **be too afraid**, be too scared, hesitate, dare not. **3** *they feared for his health:* **worry about**, feel anxious about, feel concerned about, have anxieties about. **4** *they feared for his health:* **worry about**, be anxious about, be concerned about. **5** *I fear you may be right:* **suspect**, have a sneaking suspicion, be inclined to think, be afraid, have a hunch, think it likely.

fearful adjective **1** *they are fearful of becoming victims themselves:* **afraid**, frightened, scared, terrified, petrified; alarmed, panicky, nervy, nervous, tense, apprehensive, uneasy, worried, anxious; informal jittery, jumpy. **2** (informal) *there's been a fearful accident:* **terrible**, dreadful, awful, appalling, frightful, ghastly, horrific, horrible, horrifying, horrendous, terribly bad, shocking, atrocious, abominable, hideous, gruesome.

fearfully adverb *she opened the door fearfully:* **apprehensively**, uneasily, nervously, timidly, timorously, hesitantly, with your heart in your mouth.

fearless adjective **courageous**, brave, bold, intrepid, valiant, valorous, gallant, plucky, heroic, daring, indomitable, doughty; unafraid, undaunted, unflinching; informal gutsy, spunky, ballsy, feisty.
– OPPOSITES timid, cowardly.

fearsome adjective **frightening**, horrifying, terrifying, menacing, chilling, spine-chilling, hair-raising, alarming, unnerving, daunting, formidable, forbidding, disturbing; informal scary.

feasible adjective **practicable**, practical, workable, achievable, attain-

able, realizable, viable, realistic, sensible, reasonable, within reason; suitable, possible; informal doable.
– OPPOSITES impractical.

feast noun **1** *a wedding feast:* **banquet**, meal, dinner; revels, festivities; informal blowout, spread; Brit. informal nosh-up, beanfeast, bunfight, beano, slap-up meal. **2** *a feast for the eyes:* **treat**, delight, joy, pleasure. • verb *they feasted on lobster:* **gorge on**, dine on, eat your fill of; eat, devour, consume, partake of; informal stuff yourself with, pig yourself on, pig out on.

feat noun **achievement**, accomplishment, attainment, coup, triumph; undertaking, enterprise, venture, operation, exercise, endeavour, effort, performance, exploit, stunt.

feather noun **plume**, quill; (**feathers**) plumage, down.

feature noun **1** *a typical feature of his music:* **characteristic**, attribute, quality, property, trait, hallmark, trademark; aspect, facet, factor, ingredient, component, element, theme; peculiarity, idiosyncrasy, quirk. **2** *her delicate features:* **face**, countenance, physiognomy; informal mug; Brit. informal mush, phiz, phizog; literary visage. **3** *her sculptures are a real feature of the garden:* **centrepiece**, special attraction, highlight, focal point, focus of attention, conversation piece. **4** *he's writing a feature about the local team:* **article**, piece, item, report, story, column, review, commentary, write-up. • verb **1** *Radio 3 is featuring a week of live concerts:* **present**, promote, spotlight, highlight, showcase, focus on. **2** *she is to feature in a new movie:* **appear**, star, participate.

feckless adjective **irresponsible**, unreliable, good-for-nothing, useless, worthless, incompetent, inept, ne'er-do-well; lazy, idle, slothful, indolent, shiftless; informal no-good.

fecund adjective **1** *the fecund land:* **fertile**, fruitful, productive, high-yielding; rich, lush, flourishing, thriving. **2** *her fecund imagination:* **prolific**, fertile, inventive, creative.
– OPPOSITES barren.

federal adjective **confederate**, federated; combined, allied, united, amalgamated, integrated.

federation noun **confederation**, confederacy, league; combination, alliance, coalition, union, syndicate, guild, consortium, partnership, cooperative, association.

fee noun **payment**, price, cost, charge, tariff, rate, amount, sum, figure; (**fees**) dues; formal emolument.

feeble adjective **1** *she's old and feeble:* **weak**, weakened, frail, infirm, delicate, sickly, ailing, unwell, poorly, enfeebled, debilitated, incapacitated, decrepit. **2** *a feeble argument:* **ineffective**, ineffectual, inadequate, unconvincing, implausible, unsatisfactory, poor, flimsy. **3** *he's too feeble to stand up to her:* **cowardly**, faint-hearted, spineless, lily-livered; timid, timorous, fearful, unassertive, weak, ineffectual; informal wimpy, sissy, gutless, chicken; Brit. informal wet. **4** *the lamp shed a feeble light:* **faint**, dim, weak, pale, soft, subdued, muted.
– OPPOSITES strong, brave.

feed verb **1** *she has a large family to feed:* **provide for**, cater for, cook for; suckle. **2** *the birds feed on nuts:* **live on/off**, exist on, subsist on, eat, consume. **3** *she fed secrets to the Russians for years:* **supply**, provide, give, deliver, furnish. **4** *the incident fed his suspicion:* **increase**, fuel, encourage, strengthen, reinforce. • noun *animal feed:* **fodder**, food, provender.

feel verb **1** *she felt the fabric:* **touch**, stroke, caress, fondle, finger, handle. **2** *she felt a breeze on her back:* **perceive**, sense, detect, discern, notice, be aware of, be conscious of. **3** *he won't feel any pain:* **experience**, undergo, go through, bear, endure, suffer. **4** *he felt his way towards the door:* **grope**, fumble, scrabble. **5** *feel the temperature of the water first:* **test**, try, gauge, assess. **6** *he still feels that he should go:* **believe**, think, consider, be of the opinion, hold, maintain, judge; informal reckon, figure. **7** *the air feels damp:* **seem**, appear, strike someone as. • noun **1** *the feel of the paper:* **texture**, finish; weight, thickness, consistency. **2** *the feel of the house:* **atmosphere**, ambience, aura, mood, feeling, air, impression, character, spirit, flavour; informal vibrations, vibes. **3** *she has a feel for languages:* **aptitude**, knack, flair, bent, talent, gift, faculty, ability.

■ **feel for** *poor man—I feel for him:* sympathize with, be sorry for, pity, feel sympathy for, feel compassion for, be moved by; commiserate with, condole with. **feel like** *I really feel like an ice cream:* want, would like, wish for, desire, fancy, have a yen for, feel in need of, long for; informal be dying for.

f

feeler noun **antenna**, tentacle.

feeling noun **1** *he laughed to conceal his true feelings:* **emotion**, sentiment. **2** *she was overcome by a feeling of nausea:* **sensation**, sense. **3** *I had a feeling that I would win:* **sneaking suspicion**, notion, inkling, hunch, intuition, fancy, idea; presentiment, premonition; informal gut feeling. **4** *they are out of touch with public feeling:* **sentiment**, emotion; opinion, attitude, belief, ideas, views, consensus. **5** *he had hurt her feelings:* **sensibilities**, sensitivities, self-esteem, pride. **6** *the strength of her feeling for him:* **love**, affection, fondness, tenderness, warmth, warmness, emotion, sentiment; passion, ardour, desire. **7** *a feeling of peace:* **atmosphere**, ambience, aura, air, feel, mood, impression, spirit, quality, flavour; informal vibrations, vibes. **8** *he had a remarkable feeling for language:* **aptitude**, knack, flair, bent, talent, feel, gift, faculty, ability.

feign verb **simulate**, fake, sham, affect, pretend.

feigned adjective **pretended**, simulated, affected, artificial, insincere, put-on, fake, false, sham; informal pretend, phoney.
– OPPOSITES sincere.

feint noun **bluff**, blind, ruse, deception, subterfuge, hoax, trick, ploy, dodge, sham, pretence, cover, smokescreen, distraction, contrivance; informal red herring.

> ! Don't confuse **feint** with **faint**, which means 'not clearly seen, heard, or smelt' or 'lose consciousness'.

feisty adjective **spirited**, lively, energetic, dynamic; brave, plucky, bold, confident, fearless; informal spunky, gutsy, go-getting.

felicitations plural noun **congratulations**, good/best wishes, regards, blessings, compliments, respects.

felicitous adjective **apt**, well chosen, fitting, suitable, appropriate, apposite, pertinent, germane, relevant.
– OPPOSITES inappropriate, infelicitous.

feline adjective **catlike**, graceful, sinuous, sleek.
• noun **cat**, kitten; informal puss, pussy; Brit. informal moggie, mog; old use grimalkin.

fell verb **1** *the dead trees had to be felled:* **cut down**, chop down, hack down, saw down, clear. **2** *she felled him with one punch:* **knock down/over**, knock to the ground, floor, prostrate; knock out, knock unconscious; informal deck, flatten, down, lay out, KO; Brit. informal knock for six.

fellow noun **1** *he's a decent sort of fellow:* **man**, boy; person, individual, soul; informal guy, geezer, lad, character, customer; Brit. informal chap, bloke; N. Amer. informal dude, hombre; Austral./NZ informal digger; informal, dated body, dog, cove. **2** *he exchanged glances with his fellows:* **companion**, friend, comrade, partner, associate, co-worker, colleague; informal chum, pal, buddy; Brit. informal mate. **3** *some workers were wealthier than their fellows:* **peer**, equal, contemporary.

■ **fellow feeling** sympathy, empathy, feeling, compassion, care, concern, solicitude, solicitousness, warmth, tenderness, brotherly love; pity, sorrow, commiseration.

fellowship noun **1** *a community bound together in fellowship:* **companionship**, camaraderie, friendship, comradeship, mutual support; togetherness, solidarity. **2** *the church fellowship:* **association**, society, club, league, union, guild, alliance, fraternity, brotherhood, sorority, sodality.

female adjective **feminine**, womanly, ladylike.
– OPPOSITES male.
• noun. See **WOMAN** sense 1.

feminine adjective **1** *feminine tact and sensitivity:* **womanly**, female.

2 *he seemed slightly feminine:* **effeminate**, womanish, effete.
–OPPOSITES masculine, manly.

femme fatale noun **seductress**, temptress, siren; Mata Hari; informal vamp.

fen noun **marsh**, marshland, salt marsh, fenland, wetland; bog, swamp, swampland; N. Amer. moor.

fence noun **barrier**, paling, railing, enclosure, barricade, stockade, palisade.
•verb **1** *they fenced off the meadow:* **enclose**, surround, encircle; separate off, isolate. **2** *he fenced in the chickens:* **confine**, pen in, coop up, shut in/up; N. Amer. corral.

fend verb *they were unable to fend off the invasion:* **ward off**, head off, stave off, hold off, repel, repulse, resist, fight off, defend yourself against, prevent, stop, block.
■ **fend for yourself** take care of yourself, look after yourself, provide for yourself, shift for yourself, manage by yourself, cope alone, stand on your own two feet.

feral adjective **1** *feral dogs:* **wild**, untamed, undomesticated. **2** *a feral snarl:* **fierce**, ferocious, vicious, savage; predatory, menacing; atavistic.
–OPPOSITES tame, pet.

ferment verb *an environment that ferments disorder:* **cause**, bring about, give rise to, generate, engender, spawn, instigate, provoke, incite, excite, stir up, whip up, foment.

ferocious adjective **1** *ferocious animals:* **fierce**, savage, wild, predatory, aggressive, dangerous. **2** *a ferocious attack:* **brutal**, vicious, violent, bloody, barbaric, savage, sadistic, ruthless, cruel, merciless, heartless, bloodthirsty, murderous, frenzied.
–OPPOSITES gentle, mild.

ferocity noun **savagery**, brutality, barbarity, fierceness, violence, bloodthirstiness, murderousness; ruthlessness, cruelty, mercilessness, heartlessness.

ferret verb **1** *she ferreted around in her handbag:* **rummage**, feel, grope, forage, fish, poke; search through, hunt through, rifle through; Austral./NZ informal fossick through. **2** *a journalist who is trying to ferret out the facts:* **unearth**, uncover, discover, detect, search out, bring to light, track down, dig up, root out, nose out.

ferry verb **transport**, convey, carry, ship, run, take, bring, shuttle.

fertile adjective **1** *the soil is moist and fertile:* **fecund**, fruitful, productive, rich, lush. **2** *a fertile imagination:* **creative**, inventive, innovative, visionary, original, ingenious; productive, prolific.
–OPPOSITES barren.

fertilization noun **conception**; impregnation, insemination; pollination.

fertilize verb **1** *the field was fertilized:* mulch, feed, compost, manure, dress, top-dress. **2** *these orchids are fertilized by insects:* **pollinate**.

fervent adjective **passionate**, impassioned, intense, vehement, ardent, sincere, heartfelt; enthusiastic, zealous, fanatical, wholehearted, avid, eager, keen, committed, dedicated, devout.
–OPPOSITES apathetic.

fervour noun **passion**, ardour, intensity, zeal, vehemence, emotion, warmth, earnestness, avidity, eagerness, keenness, enthusiasm, excitement, animation, vigour, energy, fire, spirit, zest.
–OPPOSITES apathy.

fester verb **1** *the wound festered:* **suppurate**, become septic, weep; Medicine maturate, be purulent. **2** *rubbish festered in the streets:* **rot**, moulder, decay, decompose, putrefy. **3** *below the surface, the old antagonisms festered:* **smoulder**, simmer; deepen, grow, increase, intensify.

festival noun **celebration**, gala, festivities, jamboree; fair, fete, carnival, fiesta.

festive adjective **jolly**, merry, joyful, happy, jovial, light-hearted, cheerful, jubilant, convivial, high-spirited, uproarious; celebratory; literary joyous.

festivity noun **celebration**, festival, entertainment, party; merrymaking, feasting, revelry, jollification; revels, fun and games; informal bash,

f

shindig; Brit. informal rave-up, knees-up, beanfeast, bunfight, beano.

festoon verb **decorate**, adorn, ornament, trim, deck, hang, loop, drape, swathe, garland, wreathe, bedeck; informal do up/out, get up, trick out.

fetch verb **1** *he went to fetch a doctor:* **get**, go for, call for, summon, pick up, collect, bring, carry, convey, transport. **2** *the land could fetch millions:* **sell for**, bring in, raise, realize, yield, make, command, cost, be priced at; informal go for.

f

fetching adjective **attractive**, appealing, sweet, pretty, lovely, delightful, charming, prepossessing, captivating, enchanting, irresistible; Scottish & N. English bonny; old use comely, fair.

fete noun (Brit.) **gala**, bazaar, fair, festival, fiesta, jubilee, carnival; fund-raiser.

fetid adjective **stinking**, smelly, foul-smelling, malodorous, reeking, pungent, acrid, high, rank, foul, noxious; Brit. informal niffy, pongy, whiffy, humming; N. Amer. informal funky; literary noisome.
– OPPOSITES fragrant.

fetish noun **1** *a rubber fetish:* **fixation**, obsession, compulsion, mania; weakness, fancy, fascination; informal thing, hang-up. **2** *an African fetish:* totem, talisman, charm, amulet; idol, image, effigy.

fetter verb *we are fettered by the new legislation:* **restrict**, restrain, constrain, limit; hinder, hamper, impede, obstruct, hamstring, inhibit, check, curb, trammel.

fettle noun *his players were in fine fettle:* **shape**, trim, physical fitness, health; condition, form, repair, order; Brit. informal nick.

fetus noun embryo, unborn baby.

> **WORD LINKS**
> **feticide** the killing of a fetus

feud noun **vendetta**, conflict; rivalry, hostility, enmity, strife, discord; quarrel, argument.
• verb **quarrel**, fight, argue, bicker, squabble, fall out, dispute, clash, differ, be at odds; informal scrap.

fever noun **1** *during the second stage of the illness, the fever worsens:* **feverishness**, high temperature; Medicine pyrexia. **2** *the nation has been gripped by World Cup fever:* **excitement**, mania, frenzy, furore, ferment; ecstasy, rapture, passion.

> **WORD LINKS**
> **febrile** relating to fever
> **febrifuge** a medicine used to reduce fever

fevered adjective **1** *her fevered brow:* **feverish**, febrile, hot, burning. **2** *a fevered imagination:* **excited**, agitated, frenzied, overwrought.
– OPPOSITES cool, calm.

feverish adjective **1** *her hands were cool against his feverish forehead:* **febrile**, fevered, hot, burning. **2** *a state of feverish excitement:* **frenzied**, frenetic, hectic, agitated, excited, restless, nervous, worked up, overwrought, frantic, furious, hysterical, wild, uncontrolled, unrestrained.

few determiner *police are revealing few details:* **not many**, hardly any, scarcely any; a small number of, a small amount of, one or two, a handful of.
– OPPOSITES many.
• adjective *comforts here are few:* **scarce**, scant, meagre, in short supply; thin on the ground, few and far between, infrequent, uncommon, rare.
– OPPOSITES plentiful.
■ **a few** a small number, a handful, one or two, a couple, two or three; not many, hardly any.

fiancé, **fiancée** noun **betrothed**, husband-to-be, wife-to-be, bride-to-be; informal intended.

fiasco noun **failure**, disaster, catastrophe, debacle, farce, mess, wreck; informal shambles, flop, washout; Brit. informal cock-up; N. Amer. informal snafu; Austral./NZ informal fizzer.
– OPPOSITES success.

fib noun **lie**, untruth, falsehood, fabri cation, made-up story, invention, deception, piece of fiction; white lie, half-truth; informal tall story/tale, whopper; Brit. informal porky pie.
– OPPOSITES truth.
• verb **lie**, tell a fib, tell a lie.

fibre noun **1** *fibres from his coat were found on the body:* **thread**, strand, filament. **2** *clothing made from natural fibres:* **material**, cloth, fabric. **3** *a man with no fibre:*

strength of character, moral fibre, fortitude, resolve, backbone, spine. **4** *you need fibre in your diet:* **roughage**, bulk.

fickle adjective **capricious**, disloyal, changeable, unreliable, inconstant, volatile, mercurial; undependable, unpredictable, unfaithful, faithless, treacherous; flighty, giddy, skittish; literary mutable.
– OPPOSITES loyal, constant.

fiction noun **1** *the traditions of British fiction:* **novels**, stories, writing, literature. **2** *she dismissed the allegations as absolute fiction:* **lies**, untruths, falsehoods, fibs, nonsense, invention, fabrication, fantasy.
– OPPOSITES fact.

fictional adjective **fictitious**, invented, imaginary, made up, make-believe, unreal, fabricated; mythical.
– OPPOSITES real.

fictitious adjective **1** *he used a fictitious name:* **false**, fake, assumed, fabricated, sham; bogus, spurious, invented, made up; informal pretend, phoney. **2** *a fictitious character.* See FICTIONAL.
– OPPOSITES genuine.

fiddle noun (Brit. informal) *a VAT fiddle:* **fraud**, swindle, confidence trick; informal racket, con trick.
• verb **1** *he fiddled with a beer mat:* **fidget**, play, toy, fuss; twiddle, finger, handle; informal mess about; Brit. informal muck about. **2** *someone's fiddled with the dials:* **adjust**, tinker, meddle, interfere; informal tweak. **3** (Brit. informal) *managers had been fiddling the figures:* **falsify**, manipulate, massage, rig, distort, misrepresent, doctor, alter, tamper with, interfere with; informal fix, cook the books.

fidelity noun **1** *marital fidelity:* **faithfulness**, loyalty, constancy; trustworthiness, dependability, reliability; formal troth. **2** *the fidelity of the reproduction:* **accuracy**, exactness, precision, preciseness; faithfulness, authenticity.
– OPPOSITES disloyalty, infidelity, inaccuracy.

fidget verb **1** *the audience began to fidget:* **be/get restless**, wriggle, squirm, twitch, jiggle, shuffle. **2** *she fidgeted with her scarf:* **play**, fuss, toy, twiddle; informal fiddle, mess about/around.

fidgety adjective **restless**, restive, on edge, uneasy, nervous, nervy, keyed up, anxious, agitated; informal jittery, twitchy.

field noun **1** *a large field full of cows:* **meadow**, pasture, paddock, grassland, pastureland; literary lea, mead, sward. **2** *a football field:* **pitch**, ground, sports field, playing field, recreation ground. **3** *the field of biotechnology:* **area**, sphere, discipline, province, department, domain, sector, branch, subject. **4** *your field of vision:* **scope**, range, sweep, reach, extent. **5** *she is well ahead of the rest of the field:* **competitors**, entrants, competition; applicants, candidates, possibles.
• verb **1** *she fielded the ball:* **catch**, stop, retrieve; return, throw back. **2** *he fielded some awkward questions:* **deal with**, handle, cope with, answer, reply to, respond to.

fiend noun *a heartless fiend:* **brute**, beast, villain, barbarian, monster, ogre, sadist.

fiendish adjective **1** *a fiendish act:* **wicked**, cruel, vicious, villainous, evil, malevolent; brutal, savage, barbaric, barbarous, inhuman, murderous, ruthless, merciless. **2** (informal) *a fiendish plot:* **cunning**, clever, ingenious, crafty, canny, wily, devious, shrewd; informal sneaky. **3** (informal) *a fiendish puzzle:* **difficult**, complex, challenging, complicated, intricate, involved, knotty, thorny.

fierce adjective **1** *a large, fierce dog:* **ferocious**, savage, vicious, aggressive. **2** *fierce loyalty | fierce opposition:* **intense**, vehement, passionate, impassioned, heartfelt, fervent, ardent, keen, strong, forceful, vigorous. **3** *a fierce wind:* **powerful**, strong, violent, vigorous, forceful; stormy, blustery, gusty, tempestuous.
– OPPOSITES gentle, mild.

fiery adjective **1** *a fiery blast:* **burning**, blazing, flaming; on fire, ablaze. **2** *a fiery red:* **bright**, brilliant, vivid, intense, rich. **3** *her fiery spirit:* **passionate**, impassioned, ardent, fervent, spirited; quick-tempered, volatile, explosive.

fight verb **1** *men were fighting in the street:* **brawl**, exchange blows, come to blows, attack each other, hit each other; clash, skirmish; struggle, grapple, wrestle; N. Amer. informal rough-house. **2** *men who had fought for King and country:* **do battle**, go to war, take up arms. **3** *a war fought for freedom:* **engage in**, wage, conduct, prosecute, pursue, undertake. **4** *she and her sister are always fighting:* **quarrel**, argue, bicker, squabble, fall out, wrangle, be at odds, disagree, differ, have words, be at each other's throats, be at loggerheads; Brit. row; informal scrap. **5** *they are fighting for better working conditions:* **campaign**, strive, battle, struggle, contend, crusade, agitate, lobby, push, press. **6** *we will fight the decision:* **oppose**, contest, challenge, appeal against, combat, dispute, make a stand against. **7** *I fought the urge to cry:* **repress**, restrain, suppress, stifle, smother, hold back, keep in check, curb, control, rein in, choke back.
•noun **1** *a fight outside a club:* **brawl**, fracas, melee, rumpus, skirmish, sparring match, struggle, scuffle, altercation, scrum, clash, disturbance; fisticuffs; informal scrap, dust-up, set-to, shindig; Brit. informal punch-up, bust-up, ruck; N. Amer. informal rough house; Austral./NZ informal stoush; Law, dated affray. **2** *a heavyweight fight:* **boxing match**, bout, match, contest, encounter. **3** *the fight against terrorism:* **battle**, struggle, war, campaign, crusade; action, hostilities. **4** *I'd had a fight with my girlfriend:* **argument**, quarrel, squabble, wrangle, disagreement, falling-out, contretemps; Brit. row; altercation, dispute; informal tiff, spat, slanging match; Brit. informal barney, ding-dong, bust-up. **5** *their fight for control of the company:* **struggle**, battle, campaign, push, effort. **6** *she had no fight left in her:* **will**, resistance, spirit, courage, pluck, pluckiness, grit, strength, backbone, determination, resolution, resolve.
■ **fight back 1** *don't fight back—turn the other cheek:* retaliate, counter-attack, strike back, hit back, respond, reciprocate, return fire. **2** *she fought back tears.* See FIGHT verb sense 7. **fight someone/something off** *she fought off her attackers who then fled:* fend off, drive away/back, force back, beat off/back, repulse, repel, ward off, keep/hold at bay.

fighter noun **soldier**, warrior, combatant, serviceman/woman; troops, personnel, militia; Brit. informal squaddie; old use man-at-arms.

fighting noun **violence**, hostilities, conflict, action, combat; warfare, war, battle, skirmish; Law, dated affray.
–OPPOSITES peace.

figment noun *it really was Ross and not just a figment of her imagination:* **invention**, creation; hallucination, illusion, delusion, fancy; vision.

figurative adjective **metaphorical**, non-literal, symbolic, allegorical, representative, emblematic.
–OPPOSITES literal.

figure noun **1** *the second figure is 9:* **digit**, numeral, character, symbol. **2** *the production figures are down this month:* **statistic**, number, quantity, amount, level, total, sum; (**figures**) data. **3** *a figure of £2000 was mentioned:* **price**, cost, amount, value, valuation. **4** *her petite figure:* **physique**, build, frame, body, proportions, shape, form. **5** *a dark figure emerged from the shadows:* **silhouette**, outline, shape, form. **6** *a figure of authority:* **person**, individual, man, woman, character, personality; representative, embodiment, personification, epitome. **7** *life-size clay figures:* **model**, effigy, representation, carving, image. **8** *geometrical figures:* **shape**, pattern, design, motif. **9** *see figure 4:* **diagram**, illustration, drawing, picture, plate.
•verb **1** *he figures in many myths:* **feature**, appear, be featured, be mentioned. **2** (informal) *I figured that Ed had won:* **assume**, conclude, take it as read, presume, deduce, infer, gather, dare say; suppose, think, believe, consider, expect, take it, suspect, sense; N. Amer. guess.
■ **figure on** (N. Amer. informal) *I figured on paying about $10:* plan on, anticipate, expect to, bargain on. **figure something out** (informal) *he tried to*

figure out what she meant: work out, fathom, puzzle out, decipher, ascertain, make sense of, think through, get to the bottom of; understand, comprehend, see, grasp, get the hang of, get the drift of; informal twig, crack; Brit. informal suss out.

filament noun **fibre**, thread, strand.

file[1] noun **1** *he opened the file:* **folder**, portfolio, binder. **2** *we have files on all of you:* **dossier**, document, record, report; data, information, documentation, annals, archives. **3** *the files had been deleted:* **document**; data, information, material; text.
• verb **1** *file the documents correctly:* **categorize**, classify, organize, put in place/order, order, arrange, catalogue, store, archive. **2** *Debbie has filed for divorce:* **apply**, register, ask petition. **3** *two women have filed a civil suit:* **bring**, press, lodge, place; formal prefer.

file[2] noun *a file of schoolboys:* **line**, column, row, string, chain, procession; Brit. informal crocodile.
• verb *we filed out into the park:* **walk**, march, parade, troop, process.

file[3] verb *they filed down the rough edges:* **smooth**, shape, buff, rub, polish; scrape, abrade.

filigree noun **tracery**, fretwork, latticework, scrollwork, lacework.

fill verb **1** *let me fill your glass:* **make/become full**, fill up, top up, charge. **2** *guests filled the kitchen:* **crowd into**, throng, pack into, occupy, squeeze into, cram into; overcrowd. **3** *he began filling his shelves:* **stock**, pack, load, supply, replenish, restock, refill. **4** *fill all the holes with putty:* **block up**, stop up, plug, seal. **5** *her perfume filled the room:* **pervade**, permeate, suffuse, be diffused through, penetrate, infuse. **6** *he filled the post of Foreign Minister for many years:* **occupy**, hold, take up; informal hold down.
– OPPOSITES empty.
■ **fill in** deputize, stand in, cover, substitute, take over, act as stand-in, take the place of; informal step into someone's shoes/boots; N. Amer. informal pinch-hit. **fill someone in** inform, advise, tell, acquaint with, apprise, brief, update; informal put in the picture, bring up to speed. **fill something in** *have you filled in the form?* (Brit.) complete, answer; N. Amer. fill out. **fill something out** **1** *this account needs to be filled out:* expand, enlarge, add to, elaborate on, flesh out; supplement, extend, develop, amplify. **2** (N. Amer.) *he filled out the forms.* See **FILL SOMETHING IN**.

filling noun *filling for cushions:* **stuffing**, padding, wadding.
• adjective *a cheap but filling meal:* **substantial**, hearty, ample, satisfying, square; heavy, stodgy.

fillip noun **stimulus**, boost, incentive, impetus; tonic, spur, push, aid, help; informal shot in the arm.

film noun **1** *a film of sweat:* **layer**, coat, coating, covering, cover, sheet, patina, overlay. **2** *I haven't seen his latest film:* **movie**, picture, motion picture; video, DVD; informal flick. **3** *she'd like to work in film:* **cinema**, movies, the pictures; the silver screen, the big screen.
• verb **1** *they're filming the next scene:* **record**, shoot, capture, video. **2** *his eyes had filmed over:* **cloud**, mist, haze; blur.

WORD LINKS

cinematographic relating to film-making

filmy adjective **sheer**, diaphanous, transparent, see-through, translucent, gossamer; delicate, fine, light, thin, silky.
– OPPOSITES thick, opaque.

filter noun **strainer**, sieve; gauze, net.
• verb **1** *the farmers filter the water:* **strain**, filtrate, sieve, sift; clarify, purify, refine, treat. **2** *the rain had filtered through her jacket:* **seep**, percolate, leak, trickle, ooze, leach.

filth noun **dirt**, muck, grime, mud, mire, sludge, slime, ooze; excrement, excreta, dung, manure, ordure, sewage; pollution, contamination; squalor; Brit. informal gunge.

filthy adjective **1** *the room was filthy | a pile of filthy clothes:* **dirty**, grubby, mucky, grimy, muddy, slimy; foul, squalid, sordid, stained, soiled, unwashed, smeared, black, blackened; polluted, contaminated, unhygienic, unsanitary; informal scuzzy; literary besmirched, sullied. **2** *a string of filthy jokes:* **obscene**,

indecent, dirty, smutty, rude, improper, coarse, bawdy, vulgar, lewd, racy, off colour, ribald, risqué, pornographic, explicit; informal blue, X-rated; euphemistic adult. **3** (informal) *he's in a filthy mood:* **bad**, foul, bad-tempered, irritable, grumpy, grouchy, cross, fractious, peevish; informal snappish, snappy; Brit. informal shirty, stroppy, narky, ratty; N. Amer. informal cranky, ornery.
–OPPOSITES clean.

f

final adjective **1** *the final moments of the game:* **last**, closing, concluding, finishing, end, terminal; ultimate, eventual. **2** *their decisions are final:* **irrevocable**, binding, definitive, set in stone, unalterable, absolute, conclusive, irrefutable, incontrovertible, indisputable.
–OPPOSITES first, provisional.

finale noun **climax**, culmination; end, ending, finish, close, conclusion, termination; denouement.
–OPPOSITES beginning.

finality noun **conclusiveness**, decisiveness, definiteness, definitiveness, certainty, certitude; irrevocability, irrefutability, incontrovertibility.

finalize verb *the two countries have yet to finalize a deal:* **conclude**, complete, clinch, settle, work out, secure, wrap up, wind up, put the finishing touches to; reach agreement on, agree on, come to terms on; informal sew up.

finally adverb **1** *she finally got married:* **eventually**, ultimately, in the end, after a long time, at last; in the long run, in the fullness of time. **2** *finally, attach the ribbon:* **lastly**, last, in conclusion. **3** *this should finally dispel that myth:* **conclusively**, irrevocably, decisively, definitively, for ever, for good, once and for all.

finance noun **1** *he knows all about finance:* **financial affairs**, money, economics, commerce, business, investment. **2** *they need short-term finance:* **funds**, assets, money, capital, resources, cash, reserves, revenue, income; funding, backing, sponsorship.
•verb *a project financed by the Arts Council:* **fund**, pay for, back, capitalize, subsidize, invest in; underwrite, guarantee, sponsor, support, endow; N. Amer. informal bankroll.

financial adjective **monetary**, money, economic, pecuniary, fiscal, commercial, business.

financier noun **investor**, speculator, banker, capitalist, industrialist, businessman, businesswoman, stockbroker; informal money man.

find verb **1** *I found the book I wanted | a group of kids found her in the street:* **discover**, locate, track down, unearth, pinpoint; search out, nose out, root out, retrieve; come across, chance on, light on, happen on, stumble on, encounter; spot, notice. **2** *he's struggling to find enough money:* **obtain**, get, come up with, raise, secure, earn, achieve, gain. **3** *I found the courage to speak:* **summon up**, gather, muster, screw up, call up. **4** *caffeine is found in both tea and coffee:* **be present**, occur, exist, appear. **5** *we soon found that it was a lively area:* **discover**, become aware, realize, observe, notice, note, learn. **6** *I find their decision strange:* **consider**, think, believe to be, feel to be, look on as, view as, see as, judge, deem, regard as. **7** *he was found guilty:* **judge**, deem, rule, declare, pronounce. **8** *the arrow found its mark:* **arrive at**, reach; hit, strike.
–OPPOSITES lose.
•noun **1** *an archaeological find:* **discovery**, acquisition. **2** *this table is a real find:* **bargain**; godsend, boon; informal good buy.
■ **find out** discover, become aware, learn, detect, discern, observe, notice, note, get/come to know, realize; bring to light, reveal, expose, unearth, disclose; informal figure out, cotton on, catch on, tumble to, get wise; Brit. informal twig, suss.

finding noun **1** *the finding of the leak:* **discovery**, location, locating, detection, detecting, uncovering. **2** *the tribunal's findings:* **conclusion**, decision, verdict, pronouncement, judgement, ruling, rule, decree, recommendation; Law determination; N. Amer. resolve.

fine[1] adjective **1** *a really fine piece of*

work: **excellent**, first-class, first-rate, great, exceptional, outstanding, splendid, magnificent, exquisite, supreme, superb, wonderful, superlative, second to none; informal A1, top-notch. **2** *fine wines:* **good**, choice, select, prime, quality, superior, of distinction, premium, premier, classic, vintage. **3** *the food was fine, but the service was terrible:* **all right**, acceptable, suitable, good enough, passable, satisfactory, adequate, reasonable, tolerable; informal OK. **4** *I feel fine:* **good**, well, healthy, all right, fit, blooming, thriving, in good shape/condition, in fine fettle; informal OK, great, in the pink. **5** *a fine day:* **fair**, dry, bright, clear, cloudless, sunny, warm, balmy, summery. **6** *fine clothes:* **elegant**, stylish, expensive, smart, chic, fashionable; fancy, sumptuous, opulent; informal flashy, swanky, ritzy, plush. **7** *he has a fine mind:* **keen**, quick, alert, sharp, razor-sharp, bright, brilliant, astute, clever, intelligent. **8** *fine china:* **delicate**, fragile, dainty; thin, light. **9** *the fine material of her dress:* **sheer**, light, lightweight, thin, flimsy; diaphanous, filmy, gossamer, silky, transparent, translucent, see-through; wispy, flyaway. **10** *a beach of fine golden sand:* **fine-grained**, powdery; dusty, ground, crushed. **11** *for fine work you need a smaller brush:* **intricate**, delicate, detailed, elaborate, dainty. **12** *a fine distinction:* **subtle**, nice, hair-splitting.
– OPPOSITES poor, unsatisfactory, ill, inclement, thick, coarse.
• **adverb** (informal) *you're doing fine:* **well**, all right, satisfactorily, adequately; informal OK.
– OPPOSITES badly.

fine[2] **noun** *they can expect heavy fines:* **financial penalty**, sanction, fee, charge.
• **verb** *he was fined for late payment:* **penalize**, charge.

finery **noun** **regalia**, best clothes, Sunday best; informal glad rags, best bib and tucker.

finesse **noun** **1** *their routine is performed with great finesse:* **skill**, skilfulness, expertise, subtlety, flair, panache, elan, polish, artistry, virtuosity, mastery. **2** *these situations call for a modicum of finesse:* **tact**, tactfulness, discretion, diplomacy, delicacy, sensitivity.

finger **noun** **digit**.
• **verb** **1** *he fingered his moustache:* **touch**, feel, stroke, rub, caress, fondle, toy with, play with, fiddle with. **2** (N. Amer. informal) *no one fingered the culprit:* **identify**, recognize, pick out; inform on, point the finger at; informal rat on, squeal on, tell on, blow the whistle on, snitch on, peach on; Brit. informal grass on.

finicky **adjective** **fussy**, fastidious, punctilious, over-particular, difficult, exacting, demanding; informal picky, choosy, pernickety; N. Amer. informal persnickety.

finish **verb** **1** *they'd finished the job by 6.30:* **complete**, end, conclude, terminate, bring to a conclusion/end, wind up; crown, cap, round off, put the finishing touches to; accomplish, discharge, carry out, do, fulfil; informal wrap up, sew up. **2** *he finished off the last of his soup:* **consume**, eat, devour, drink, finish off, gulp down; use, exhaust, empty, drain, get through; informal down, polish off. **3** *the programme has finished:* **end**, come to an end, stop, conclude, come to a conclusion/close, cease. **4** *some items were finished in black lacquer:* **varnish**, lacquer, veneer, coat, stain, wax, enamel, glaze, paint.
– OPPOSITES start, begin, continue.
• **noun** **1** *the finish of the war:* **end**, ending, completion, conclusion, close, closing, termination; finale, denouement. **2** *a shiny finish:* **veneer**, lacquer, lamination, glaze, coating, covering; gloss, patina, sheen, lustre; surface, texture.
– OPPOSITES start, beginning.
■ **finish someone/something off** **1** *they took some of the hostages outside and finished them off:* kill, destroy, massacre; informal wipe out, do in, take out, dispose of; N. Amer. informal ice, waste. **2** *two late goals finished them off:* overwhelm, overcome, defeat, get the better of, bring down.

finished **adjective** **1** *a very finished performance:* **accomplished**, polished, flawless, faultless, perfect; expert, proficient, masterly, impeccable, virtuoso, skilful, skilled, professional. **2** *he knew he was finished:* **ruined**, defeated, beaten, doomed, bankrupt, broken; informal washed up, through.

finite adjective **limited**, restricted, determinate, fixed, measurable.
– OPPOSITES infinite.

fire noun **1** *the fire destroyed most of the factory:* **blaze**, conflagration, inferno; flames, burning, combustion. **2** *she switched the fire on:* **heater**, radiator, convector; boiler, furnace. **3** *he lacked fire:* **dynamism**, energy, vigour, animation, vitality, vibrancy, exuberance, zest, elan; passion, ardour, zeal, spirit, verve, vivacity, vivaciousness; enthusiasm, eagerness, gusto, fervour; informal pep, vim, go, get-up-and-go, oomph. **4** *the sound of rapid machine-gun fire:* **gunfire**, firing, bombardment; volley, salvo.
• verb **1** *he fired off a few rounds | someone fired a gun:* **discharge**, shoot, launch, let fly with; let off, set off. **2** (informal) *he was fired last week:* **dismiss**, discharge, give someone their notice, lay off, let go, get rid of, axe; Military cashier; informal sack, give someone the sack, boot out, give someone the boot, give someone the push, give someone their marching orders; Brit. informal give someone their cards. **3** *the stories fired my imagination:* **stimulate**, stir up, excite, awaken, arouse, rouse, inflame, animate, inspire, motivate.
■ **catch fire** ignite, catch light, burst into flames, go up in flames. **on fire** burning, alight, ablaze, blazing, aflame, in flames.

WORD LINKS
pyromania an obsessive desire to set things on fire

firearm noun **gun**, weapon; informal shooter; N. Amer. informal piece, shooting iron.

firebrand noun **radical**, revolutionary, agitator, rabble-rouser, incendiary, subversive, troublemaker.

fireproof adjective **non-flammable**, incombustible, fire resistant, flame resistant, heatproof.
– OPPOSITES inflammable.

fireworks plural noun **pyrotechnics**.

firm[1] adjective **1** *the ground is fairly firm:* **hard**, solid, unyielding, resistant; solidified, hardened, compacted, compressed, dense, stiff, rigid, set. **2** *firm foundations:* **secure**, stable, steady, strong, fixed, fast, taut, tight; immovable, stationary, motionless. **3** *a firm handshake:* **strong**, vigorous, sturdy, forceful. **4** *he was very firm:* **resolute**, determined, decided, resolved, steadfast; adamant, emphatic, insistent, single-minded, in earnest. **5** *a firm Labour supporter:* **committed**, dedicated, wholehearted, faithful, long-standing, steady, steadfast, constant, unfaltering, unwavering, unswerving **6** *they became firm friends:* **close**, good, boon, intimate, inseparable, dear, special, fast, devoted. **7** *she had no firm plans:* **definite**, fixed, settled, decided, established, confirmed, agreed; unalterable, unchangeable, irreversible.
– OPPOSITES soft, unstable, indefinite.

firm[2] noun *an accountancy firm:* **company**, business, concern, enterprise, organization, corporation, conglomerate, office, bureau, agency, consortium; informal outfit, set-up, operation.

first adjective **1** *the first chapter:* **earliest**, initial, opening, introductory. **2** *first principles:* **fundamental**, basic, rudimentary, primary; key, cardinal, central, chief, vital, essential. **3** *our first priority:* **foremost**, principal, highest, greatest, paramount, top, uppermost, prime, chief, leading, main, major; overriding, predominant, prevailing, central, core, dominant; informal number-one. **4** *first prize:* **top**, best, prime, premier, winning.
– OPPOSITES last, closing.
• adverb **1** *the room they had first entered:* **at first**, to begin with, first of all, at the outset, initially. **2** *she wouldn't go—she'd die first!* **in preference**, sooner, rather.

first-class adjective *a first-class hotel:* **superior**, first-rate, top-quality, five-star, high-grade, high-quality, second to none; prime, premier, premium, grade A, best, select,

exclusive, excellent, superb, outstanding, marvellous, magnificent, splendid; informal A1, top-notch, top-tier, super, great, tremendous, terrific, fantastic; Brit. informal smashing; informal, dated capital.
– OPPOSITES poor.

first-hand adjective **direct**, immediate, personal, hands-on.
– OPPOSITES vicarious, indirect.

first-rate adjective **superior**, first-class, top-quality, five-star, high-grade, high-quality, second to none; prime, premier, premium, grade A, best, select, exclusive, excellent, superb, outstanding, marvellous, magnificent, splendid; informal A1, top-notch, top-tier, super, great, tremendous, terrific, fantastic; Brit. informal smashing; informal, dated capital.

fiscal adjective *the government's fiscal policy:* **tax**, budgetary; financial, economic, monetary, money.

fish verb **1** *some people were fishing in the lake:* **go fishing**, angle, trawl. **2** *she fished for her purse:* **search**, delve, look, hunt; grope, fumble, ferret about/around, root about/around, rummage.
■ **fish someone/something out** *they fished him out of the water:* pull out, haul out, remove, extricate, extract, retrieve; rescue from, save from.

WORD LINKS
ichthyology the study of fish
pisciculture the breeding and rearing of fish

fisherman noun **angler**.

fishing noun **angling**, trawling.

fishy adjective (informal) *there's something fishy here:* **suspicious**, questionable, dubious, doubtful, suspect; odd, queer, peculiar, strange; informal funny, shady, crooked, bent; Brit. informal dodgy, iffy; Austral./NZ informal shonky.

fission noun **splitting**, division, dividing, rupture, breaking, severance.
– OPPOSITES fusion.

fissure noun **opening**, crevice, crack, cleft, breach, crevasse, chasm; break, fracture, fault, rift, rupture, split.

fit[1] adjective **1** *the house is not fit to live in | a fit subject for a book:* **suitable**, good enough, -worthy; relevant, pertinent, apt, appropriate, suited, apposite, fitting. **2** *she's not fit to look after children:* **competent**, able, capable; ready, prepared, equipped. **3** *he looked tanned and fit:* **healthy**, well, in good health, in good shape, in trim, in good condition, fighting fit, as fit as a fiddle/flea; athletic, muscular, strong, robust, hale and hearty.
– OPPOSITES unsuitable, unfit, unwell.
• verb **1** *they're having new carpets fitted:* **lay**, install, put in; position, place, fix, arrange. **2** *cameras fitted with autofocus:* **equip**, provide, supply, fit out, furnish. **3** *they fitted the slabs together:* **join**, connect, put together, piece together, attach, unite, link. **4** *a sentence that fits his crime:* **be appropriate to**, suit, match, correspond to, tally with, go with, accord with, correlate to, be congruous with, be congruent with, be consonant with. **5** *an MSc fits you for a scientific career:* **qualify**, prepare, make ready, train.
• noun *the fit between philosophy and practice:* **correlation**, correspondence, agreement, consistency, equivalence, match, similarity, compatibility, concurrence.
■ **fit in** conform, be in harmony, blend in, be in line, be assimilated into. **fit someone/something out/up** equip, provide, supply, furnish, kit out, rig out.

fit[2] noun **1** *an epileptic fit:* **convulsion**, spasm, paroxysm, seizure, attack. **2** *a fit of the giggles:* **outbreak**, outburst, attack, bout, spell. **3** *my mother would have a fit:* **tantrum**, frenzy; informal paddy; heart attack; N. Amer. informal blowout.
■ **in/by fits and starts** spasmodically, intermittently, sporadically, erratically, irregularly, fitfully, haphazardly.

fitful adjective **intermittent**, sporadic, spasmodic, broken, disturbed, disrupted, patchy, irregular, uneven, unsettled.

fitness noun **1** *polo requires tremendous fitness:* **good health**, strength, robustness, vigour, athleticism, toughness, physical fitness, stamina. **2** *his fitness for active service:* **suitability**, capability, competence, ability, aptitude; readiness, preparedness.

fitted adjective **1** *a fitted wardrobe:* **built-in**, integral, integrated, fixed, custom-made, shaped, made to measure. **2** *he wasn't fitted for the job:* **well suited**, right, suitable; equipped, fit; informal cut out.

fitting noun **1** *a light fitting:* **attachment**, connection, part, piece, component, accessory. **2** *bathroom fittings:* **furnishings**, furniture, fixtures, fitments, equipment. **3** *the fitting of catalytic converters:* **installation**, installing.
• adjective *a fitting conclusion:* **apt**, appropriate, suitable, apposite; fit, proper, right, seemly, correct; old use meet.
–OPPOSITES unsuitable.

five cardinal number **quintet**, fivesome; quintuplets.

> **WORD LINKS**
> **pentagon** a five-sided figure
> **pentagram**, **pentangle** a five-pointed star drawn using a continuous line

fix verb **1** *signs were fixed to lamp posts:* **fasten**, attach, affix, secure; join, connect, couple, link; install, implant, embed; stick, glue, pin, nail, screw, bolt, clamp, clip. **2** *his words are fixed in my memory:* **stick**, lodge, embed. **3** *his eyes were fixed on the ground:* **focus**, direct, level, point, train. **4** *he's fixed my car:* **repair**, mend, put right, get working, restore; overhaul, service, renovate, recondition. **5** *let's fix a date:* **decide on**, select, choose, resolve on; determine, settle, set, arrange, establish, allot; designate, name, appoint, specify. **6** (informal) *she's fixing her hair:* **arrange**, put in order, adjust; style, groom, comb, brush; informal do. **7** (informal) *I'll fix supper:* **prepare**, cook, make, get; informal rustle up; Brit. informal knock up. **8** *chemicals that fix the dye:* **make permanent**, make fast, set. **9** (informal) *the fight was fixed:* **rig**; tamper with, skew, influence; informal fiddle.
–OPPOSITES remove.
• noun (informal) **1** *they are in a bit of a fix:* **predicament**, plight, difficulty, awkward situation, corner, tight spot; mess, dire straits; informal pickle, jam, hole, scrape, bind, sticky situation. **2** *a quick fix for the industry's problems:* **solution**, answer, resolution, way out, remedy, cure; informal magic bullet. **3** *the result was a fix:* **fraud**, swindle, trick, charade, sham; informal set-up, fiddle.
■ **fix someone up with** (informal) *they've fixed us up with a room:* provide with, supply with, furnish with. **fix something up** *I've fixed up a meeting:* organize, arrange, make arrangements for, fix, sort out; engineer; informal wangle, swing.

fixated adjective *the media were fixated on the wedding:* **obsessed**, preoccupied, obsessive; focused, keen, gripped, engrossed, immersed, wrapped up, enthusiastic, fanatical; informal hooked.

fixation noun **obsession**, preoccupation, mania, addiction, compulsion; informal thing, bug, craze, fad.

fixed adjective **predetermined**, set, established, arranged, specified, decided, agreed, determined, confirmed, prescribed, definite, defined, explicit, precise.

fixture noun **1** *fixtures and fittings:* **fixed appliance**, installation, unit; Brit. fitment. **2** (Brit.) *their first fixture of the season:* **match**, race, game, competition, contest, event.

fizz verb *the mixture fizzed like mad:* **effervesce**, sparkle, bubble, froth.
• noun *the process that puts the fizz in champagne:* **effervescence**, sparkle, fizziness, bubbles, bubbliness, gassiness, carbonation, froth.

fizzle verb
■ **fizzle out** *their romance just fizzled out:* peter out, die off, ease off, cool off; tail off, wither away.

fizzy adjective **effervescent**, sparkling, carbonated, gassy, bubbly, frothy.
–OPPOSITES still, flat.

flab noun (informal) **fat**, excess weight, plumpness; paunch, pot belly, beer gut.

flabbergasted adjective (informal). See **ASTONISHED**.

flabbiness noun **fat**, fleshiness, plumpness, chubbiness, corpulence; softness, looseness, flaccidity; informal flab.

flabby adjective **1** *his flabby stomach:*

soft, loose, flaccid, slack, untoned, drooping, sagging. **2** *a flabby woman:* **fat**, fleshy, overweight, plump, chubby, portly, rotund, broad in the beam, of ample proportions, corpulent; informal tubby, roly-poly, well covered, well upholstered; Brit. informal podgy.
– OPPOSITES firm, thin.

flaccid adjective **1** *flaccid muscles:* **soft**, loose, flabby, slack, lax; drooping, sagging. **2** *a flaccid performance:* **lacklustre**, lifeless, listless, uninspiring, unanimated, tame.
– OPPOSITES firm, spirited.

flag[1] noun *the Irish flag:* **banner**, standard, ensign, pennant, streamer; colours; Brit. pendant.
• verb *flag the misspelt words:* **indicate**, identify, point out, mark, label, tag, highlight.
■ **flag someone/something down** *she flagged down a taxi:* hail, wave down, stop, halt.

> **WORD LINKS**
> **vexillary** relating to flags
> **vexillology** the study of flags

flag[2] verb **1** *they were flagging towards the finish:* **tire**, grow tired/weary, weaken, grow weak, wilt, droop. **2** *my energy flags in the afternoon:* **fade**, decline, wane, ebb, diminish, decrease, lessen, dwindle; wither, melt away, die away/down.
– OPPOSITES revive.

flagrant adjective **blatant**, glaring, obvious, overt, conspicuous, barefaced, shameless, brazen, undisguised, unconcealed.
– OPPOSITES secret, hidden.

flail verb **1** *he fell headlong, his arms flailing:* **wave**, swing, thrash about, flap about. **2** *I was flailing about in the water:* **flounder**, struggle, thrash, writhe, splash.

flair noun **1** *a flair for publicity:* **aptitude**, talent, gift, instinct, natural ability, facility, skill, bent, feel. **2** *she dressed with flair:* **style**, stylishness, panache, dash, elan, poise; informal class.

> ! Don't confuse **flair** with **flare**, which means 'burn or shine with sudden intensity' (***lightning flared***) or 'become wider' (***her dress flared out from the hips***).

flak noun (informal) *he's come in for a lot of flak:* **criticism**, censure, disapproval, hostility, complaints; vilification, abuse, brickbats; Brit. informal stick, verbal; formal castigation, excoriation.

flake[1] noun **sliver**, wafer, shaving, paring; chip; fragment, scrap, shred.
• verb **peel off**, chip, blister, come off.

flake[2] verb
■ **flake out** (informal) *she flaked out in her chair:* fall asleep, go to sleep, drop off; collapse, faint, pass out, lose consciousness, black out; informal conk out, nod off; N. Amer. informal sack out, zone out; literary swoon.

flaky adjective **flaking**, peeling, scaly, blistering, scabrous.

flamboyant adjective **1** *her flamboyant personality:* **ostentatious**, exuberant, confident, lively, animated, vibrant, vivacious, larger than life. **2** *a flamboyant cravat:* **colourful**, brightly coloured, bright, vibrant, vivid; dazzling, eye-catching, bold; showy, gaudy, garish, lurid, loud; informal jazzy, flashy.
– OPPOSITES restrained.

flame noun **1** *a sheet of flames:* **fire**; blaze, conflagration, inferno. **2** (informal) *an old flame:* **sweetheart**, boyfriend, girlfriend, lover, partner.
• verb **1** *logs crackled and flamed:* **burn**, blaze, flare, be on fire, be alight; flicker. **2** *Erica's cheeks flamed:* **go red**, blush, flush, redden, go pink/crimson/scarlet, colour, glow.
■ **in flames** on fire, burning, alight, flaming, blazing, ignited, aflame; literary afire.

flameproof adjective **non-flammable**, non-inflammable, flame-resistant, fire-resistant, flame-retardant.
– OPPOSITES flammable.

flaming adjective **1** *a flaming bonfire:* **blazing**, burning, ablaze, on fire. **2** *a flaming row:* **furious**, violent, vehement, frenzied, angry, passionate.

flammable adjective **inflammable**, combustible.

flank noun **1** *the horse's flanks:* **side**, haunch, quarter, thigh. **2** *the southern flank of the Eighth Army:* **side**, wing; face, aspect.
• verb *the garden is flanked by two*

f

rivers: **edge**, bound, line, border, fringe.

flap verb **1** *the mallards flapped their wings:* **beat**, flutter, agitate, wave, wag, swing. **2** *the flag flapped in the breeze:* **flutter**, fly, blow, swing, sway, ripple, stir.
• noun **1** *pockets with buttoned flaps:* **fold**, covering, top. **2** *the bird gave a last flap of its wing:* **flutter**, stroke, beat, movement. **3** (Brit. informal) *she's in a bit of a flap:* **panic**, fluster; informal state, dither, stew, tizzy; N. Amer. informal twit.

f

flare noun **1** *the flare of the match:* **blaze**, flash, burst, flicker. **2** *a flare set off by the crew:* **distress signal**, rocket, beacon, light, signal, maroon.
• verb **1** *the match flared:* **blaze**, flash, flare up, flame, burn; flicker. **2** *her nostrils flared:* **spread**, widen; dilate.
■ **flare up 1** *his injury has flared up again:* recur, reoccur, reappear; break out, erupt. **2** *I flared up at him:* lose your temper, become enraged, fly into a temper, go berserk; informal blow your top, fly off the handle, go mad, go bananas, hit the roof, go up the wall, go off the deep end, lose your rag, flip your lid, explode, have a fit; Brit. informal go spare, go crackers, do your nut; N. Amer. informal flip your wig, blow your lid/stack.

> ! Don't confuse **flare** with **flair**, which means 'a natural ability or talent' (*he had a real flair for design*).

flash verb **1** *a torch flashed:* **shine**, flare, blaze, gleam, glint, sparkle, burn; blink, wink, flicker, shimmer, twinkle, glimmer, glisten, scintillate; literary glister. **2** (informal) *he's always flashing his money about:* **show off**, flaunt, flourish, display, parade. **3** *racing cars flashed past:* **zoom**, streak, tear, shoot, dash, dart, fly, whistle, hurtle, rush, bolt, race, speed, career, whizz, whoosh, buzz; informal belt, zap; Brit. informal bomb, bucket; N. Amer. informal barrel.
• noun **1** *a flash of light:* **flare**, blaze, burst; gleam, glint, sparkle, flicker, shimmer, twinkle, glimmer. **2** *a sudden flash of inspiration:* **burst**, outburst, wave, rush, surge, flush.
• adjective (informal) *a flash sports car.* See FLASHY.
■ **in/like a flash** instantly, suddenly, abruptly, immediately, all of a sudden; quickly, rapidly, swiftly, speedily; in an instant/moment, in a split second, in a trice, in the blink of an eye; informal in a jiffy, before you can say Jack Robinson.

flashy adjective (informal) **ostentatious**, flamboyant, showy, conspicuous, extravagant, expensive; vulgar, tasteless, brash, lurid, garish, loud, gaudy; informal snazzy, fancy, swanky, flash, jazzy, glitzy, bling.
– OPPOSITES understated.

flask noun **bottle**, container; hip flask, vacuum flask; trademark Thermos.

flat[1] adjective **1** *a flat surface:* **level**, horizontal; smooth, even, uniform, regular, plane. **2** *the sea was flat:* **calm**, still, glassy, smooth, placid, like a millpond. **3** *a flat box:* **shallow**, low. **4** *his voice was flat:* **monotonous**, toneless, droning, boring, dull, tedious, soporific; bland, dreary, colourless, featureless, emotionless, expressionless, lifeless, spiritless, lacklustre. **5** *he felt flat and weary:* **depressed**, dejected, dispirited, despondent, downhearted, disheartened, low, low-spirited, down, unhappy, blue; without energy, weary, tired out, worn out, exhausted, drained; informal down in the mouth/dumps. **6** *the market was flat:* **slow**, inactive, sluggish, slack, quiet, depressed. **7** (Brit.) *a flat battery:* **expired**, dead, finished, used up, run out. **8** *a flat tyre:* **deflated**, punctured, burst; blown. **9** *a flat fee:* **fixed**, set, regular, unchanging, unvarying, invariable. **10** *a flat denial:* **outright**, direct, absolute, definite, positive, straight, plain, explicit; firm, resolute, adamant, assertive, emphatic, categorical, unconditional, unqualified, unequivocal.
– OPPOSITES vertical, uneven.
• adverb *she lay flat on the floor:* **stretched out**, outstretched, spreadeagled, sprawling, prone, supine, prostrate, recumbent.
■ **flat out** hard, as hard as possible, for all your worth, to the full/limit, all out; at full speed, as fast as possible, at full tilt; informal like crazy, like mad, like the wind, like

a bomb; Brit. informal like billy-o, like the clappers.

flat² noun *a two-bedroom flat:* **apartment**, penthouse; rooms; Austral. home unit; N. Amer. informal crib.

flatten verb **1** *Tom flattened the crumpled paper:* **smooth**, press, even out, level out. **2** *the cows flattened the grass:* **compress**, press down, crush, squash, compact, trample. **3** *tornadoes can flatten buildings in seconds:* **demolish**, raze to the ground, tear down, knock down, destroy, wreck, devastate, obliterate; N. Amer. informal total.
– OPPOSITES crumple, raise, build.

flatter verb **1** *it amused him to flatter her:* **compliment**, praise, curry favour with, pay court to, fawn on; humour, flannel, blarney; informal sweet-talk, soft-soap, butter up, play up to. **2** *I was flattered to be asked:* **honour**, gratify, please, delight; informal tickle pink. **3** *a hairstyle that flattered her:* **suit**, become, look good on, go well with; informal do something/a lot for.
– OPPOSITES insult, offend.

flatterer noun **sycophant**, toady, lickspittle, lackey; informal bootlicker, yes man.

flattering adjective **1** *flattering remarks:* **complimentary**, favourable, admiring, appreciative, good; honeyed, sugary, silver-tongued, honey-tongued; fawning, oily, obsequious, ingratiating, servile, sycophantic; informal sweet-talking, soft-soaping, crawling, bootlicking. **2** *it was very flattering to be nominated:* **pleasing**, gratifying, honouring. **3** *her most flattering dress:* **becoming**, enhancing.
– OPPOSITES unflattering.

flattery noun **praise**, adulation, compliments, blandishments, honeyed words; fawning, blarney; informal sweet talk, soft soap; Brit. informal flannel.

flaunt verb *they openly flaunted their wealth:* **show off**, display, make a show of, put on show/display, parade; brag about, crow about, vaunt; informal flash.

> Don't confuse **flaunt** with **flout**, which means 'openly fail to follow a rule or convention' (*retailers have been flouting the law for years*).

flavour noun **1** *salami can add extra flavour:* **taste**, savour, tang, flavouring, seasoning, tastiness, relish, bite, piquancy, pungency, spice, spiciness, zest; informal zing, zip. **2** *a strong international flavour:* **character**, quality, feel, feeling, ambience, atmosphere, aura, air, mood, tone; spirit, essence, nature; informal vibe. **3** *this excerpt will give you a flavour of the report:* **impression**, suggestion, hint, taste.
• verb *use spices to flavour the food:* **season**, spice up, add piquancy to, ginger up, enrich; informal pep up.

flavouring noun **1** *only natural flavourings are permitted:* **seasoning**, spice, herb. **2** *vanilla flavouring:* **essence**, extract, concentrate, distillate.

flaw noun **defect**, blemish, fault, imperfection, deficiency, weakness, weak spot/point, Achilles heel, inadequacy, shortcoming, limitation, failing, foible; Computing bug; informal glitch.
– OPPOSITES strength.

flawed adjective *the findings of the report were flawed:* **unsound**, defective, faulty, distorted, inaccurate, incorrect, erroneous, fallacious.
– OPPOSITES sound.

flawless adjective **perfect**, unblemished, unmarked, unimpaired; whole, intact, sound, unbroken, undamaged, mint, pristine; impeccable, immaculate, consummate, accurate, correct, faultless, error-free, unerring; exemplary, model, ideal, copybook.
– OPPOSITES imperfect.

fleck noun *flecks of pale blue:* **spot**, mark, dot, speck, speckle, freckle, patch, smudge, streak, blotch, dab; informal splosh, splodge.
• verb *the deer's flanks were flecked with white:* **spot**, mark, dot, speckle, bespeckle, freckle, stipple, stud, bestud, blotch, mottle, streak, splash, spatter, bespatter, scatter, sprinkle, dust, pepper; informal splosh, splodge.

fledgling adjective *fledgling industries in the developing world:* **emerging**, emergent, sunrise, dawning, embryonic, infant,

nascent; developing, in the making, budding, up-and-coming, rising.
– OPPOSITES declining, mature.

flee verb **run**, run away, make a run for it, take flight, make off, take off, take to your heels, make a break for it, bolt, beat a retreat, make a quick exit, make your getaway, escape, decamp, abscond; informal beat it, clear off/out, vamoose, skedaddle, split, leg it, turn tail, scram; Brit. informal scarper; N. Amer. informal light out, bug out, cut out, peel out; old use fly.

fleece noun **wool**, coat.
• verb (informal). See SWINDLE verb.

fleecy adjective **fluffy**, woolly, downy, soft, fuzzy, furry, shaggy.
– OPPOSITES coarse.

fleet[1] noun *the fleet set sail:* **navy**, naval force, naval task force, armada, flotilla, squadron, convoy.

fleet[2] adjective (literary) *as fleet as a greyhound:* **nimble**, agile, lithe, lissom, acrobatic, supple, light-footed, light on your feet, spry, sprightly; quick, fast, swift, rapid, speedy, brisk, smart; informal nippy, zippy, twinkle-toed.

fleeting adjective **brief**, short, short-lived, quick, momentary, cursory, transient, ephemeral, fugitive, passing, transitory.
– OPPOSITES lasting.

flesh noun **1** *his smooth, white flesh:* **tissue**, skin, body; muscle, fat; informal blubber, flab. **2** *strip the flesh away from the bone:* **meat**, muscle. **3** *a fruit with juicy flesh:* **pulp**, marrow, meat. **4** *the pleasures of the flesh:* **the body**, human nature, physicality, carnality, animality; sensuality, sexuality.
■ **your flesh and blood** family, relatives, relations, kin, kinsfolk, kinsman, kinsmen, kinswoman, kinswomen, kindred, nearest and dearest, people; informal folks. **flesh out** put on weight, gain weight, get heavier, fatten up, get fat/fatter, fill out. **flesh something out** expand on, elaborate on, add to, build on, add flesh to, put flesh on the bones of, expatiate on, supplement, reinforce, augment, fill out, enlarge on. **in the flesh** in person, before your very eyes; in real life, live; physically, bodily, in bodily/human form, incarnate.

fleshy adjective **plump**, chubby, portly, fat, obese, overweight, stout, corpulent, paunchy, well padded, well covered, well upholstered, rotund; informal tubby, pudgy, beefy, porky, roly-poly, blubbery; Brit. informal podgy; N. Amer. informal corn-fed.
– OPPOSITES thin.

flex[1] verb **1** *you must flex your elbow:* **bend**, crook, hook, cock, angle, double up. **2** *she flexed her cramped muscles:* **tighten**, tauten, tense, tension, contract.
– OPPOSITES straighten, relax.

flex[2] noun (Brit.) *an electric flex:* **cable**, wire, lead; N. Amer. cord.

flexibility noun **1** *the flexibility of wood:* **pliability**, suppleness, pliancy, plasticity; elasticity, stretchiness, springiness, spring, resilience, bounce; informal give. **2** *the flexibility of an endowment loan:* **adaptability**, adjustability, variability, versatility, open-endedness, freedom, latitude. **3** *the flexibility shown by the local authority:* **willingness to compromise**, accommodation, amenability, cooperation, tolerance.
– OPPOSITES rigidity, inflexibility, intransigence.

flexible adjective **1** *flexible tubing:* **pliable**, supple, bendable, pliant, plastic; elastic, stretchy, springy, resilient, bouncy; informal bendy. **2** *a flexible arrangement:* **adaptable**, adjustable, variable, versatile, open-ended, open, free. **3** *the need to be flexible towards tenants:* **accommodating**, amenable, willing to compromise, cooperative, tolerant.
– OPPOSITES rigid, inflexible, intransigent.

flick verb **1** *he flicked the switch:* **click**, snap, flip, jerk; throw, pull, push. **2** *the horse flicked its tail:* **swish**, twitch, wave, wag, waggle, jiggle, shake.
• noun *a flick of the wrist:* **jerk**, snap, flip, whisk.
■ **flick through** *she flicked through her diary:* thumb through, leaf through, flip through, skim through, scan, look through, browse through, dip into, glance at/through, run your eye over.

flicker verb **1** *the lights flickered:*

glimmer, flare, dance, gutter; twinkle, sparkle, blink, wink, flash. **2** *his eyelids flickered:* **flutter**, quiver, tremble, shiver, shudder, jerk, twitch.

flier noun. See FLYER.

flight noun **1** *the history of flight:* **aviation**, flying, air transport, aeronautics. **2** *the flight of a cricket ball:* **trajectory**, flight path, track, orbit. **3** *his headlong flight from home:* **escape**, getaway, hasty departure, exit, exodus, breakout, bolt, disappearance; Brit. informal flit. **4** *a flight of birds:* **flock**, swarm, cloud, throng.

■ **take flight** flee, run away/off, run for it, make a run for it, be gone, make off, take off, take to your heels, make a break for it, bolt, beat a retreat, make a quick exit, make your getaway, escape; informal beat it, clear off/out, vamoose, skedaddle, split, leg it, turn tail, scram; Brit. informal scarper; N. Amer. informal light out, bug out, cut out, peel out; old use fly.

flighty adjective **fickle**, inconstant, mercurial, whimsical, capricious, skittish, volatile, impulsive; irresponsible, giddy, wild, careless, thoughtless.

–OPPOSITES steady, responsible.

flimsy adjective **1** *a flimsy building:* **insubstantial**, fragile, frail, shaky, unstable, wobbly, tottery, rickety, ramshackle, makeshift; jerry-built, badly built, shoddy, gimcrack. **2** *a flimsy dress:* **thin**, light, fine, filmy, floaty, diaphanous, sheer, delicate, gossamer, gauzy. **3** *flimsy evidence:* **weak**, feeble, poor, inadequate, insufficient, thin, unsubstantial, unconvincing, implausible, unsatisfactory.

–OPPOSITES sturdy, thick, sound.

flinch verb **1** *he flinched at the noise:* **wince**, start, shudder, shy away, quiver, jerk. **2** *he never flinched from his duty:* **shrink from**, recoil from, shy away from, swerve from, demur from; dodge, evade, avoid, duck, baulk at, fight shy of.

fling verb *he flung the axe into the river:* **throw**, toss, sling, hurl, cast, pitch, lob; informal chuck, heave, bung.

• noun *she had a brief fling with him years ago:* **affair**, love affair, relationship, romance, liaison, entanglement, involvement, attachment.

flip verb **1** *the wave flipped the dinghy over | the plane flipped on to its back:* **overturn**, turn over, tip over, roll over, upturn, capsize; upend, invert, knock over; keel over, topple over, turn turtle. **2** *he flipped the key through the air:* **throw**, flick, toss, fling, sling, pitch, cast, spin, lob; informal chuck, bung. **3** *I flipped the transmitter switch:* **flick**, click; throw, push, pull.

■ **flip through** *she flipped through a magazine:* thumb through, leaf through, flick through, skim through, scan, look through, browse through, dip into, glance at/through, run your eye over.

flippancy noun **frivolity**, levity, facetiousness; disrespect, irreverence, cheek, impudence, impertinence; Brit. informal sauce; N. Amer. informal sassiness.

–OPPOSITES seriousness, respect.

flippant adjective **frivolous**, facetious, tongue-in-cheek; disrespectful, irreverent, cheeky, impudent, impertinent; informal flip, saucy, waggish; N. Amer. informal sassy.

–OPPOSITES serious, respectful.

flirt verb **1** *he liked to flirt with her:* **tease**, lead on; informal chat up. **2** *those who flirt with fascism:* **dabble in**, toy with, trifle with, play with, tinker with, dip into, scratch the surface of.

• noun *Anna was quite a flirt:* **tease**, philanderer, coquette, heartbreaker.

flirtation noun **coquetry**, teasing.

flirtatious adjective **coquettish**, flirty, kittenish, teasing.

flit verb **dart**, dance, skip, play, dash, trip, flutter, bob, bounce.

float verb **1** *the balloon floated in the air:* **hover**, be suspended, hang, levitate, defy gravity. **2** *a cloud floated across the moon:* **drift**, glide, sail, slip, slide, waft. **3** *they have floated an idea or two:* **suggest**, put forward, come up with, submit, propose, advance, test; informal run something up the flagpole. **4** *the company was floated on the Stock Exchange:* **launch**, offer, sell, introduce.

–OPPOSITES sink.

floating adjective **1** *floating seaweed:*

buoyant, afloat, drifting. **2** *floating gas balloons:* **hovering**, hanging, suspended. **3** *floating voters:* **uncommitted**, undecided, uncertain, unsure, undeclared. **4** *a floating population:* **unsettled**, transient, temporary, variable, fluctuating; migrant, wandering, nomadic, on the move, migratory, travelling, drifting, roving, roaming, itinerant. **5** *a floating exchange rate:* **variable**, changeable, changing, fluid, fluctuating.

f

flock noun **1** *a flock of sheep:* **herd**, drove. **2** *a flock of birds:* **flight**, swarm, cloud. **3** *flocks of people:* **crowd**, throng, horde, mob, rabble, mass, multitude, host, army, pack, swarm, sea; informal gaggle.
•verb **1** *people flocked around her:* **gather**, collect, congregate, assemble, converge, mass, crowd, throng, cluster, swarm. **2** *tourists flock to the tiny village:* **stream**, swarm, crowd, troop.

flog verb **1** *he was publicly flogged:* **whip**, scourge, birch, cane, beat. **2** (Brit. informal) *he's flogging his car:* **sell**, put on sale, put up for sale, offer for sale, trade in, deal in, peddle; informal push.

flood noun **1** *villages were cut off by the flood:* **inundation**, deluge; torrent, overflow, flash flood; Brit. spate. **2** *a flood of complaints:* **succession**, series, string, chain; barrage, volley, battery; avalanche, torrent, stream, tide, spate, storm, shower, cascade.
–OPPOSITES trickle.
•verb **1** *the whole town was flooded:* **inundate**, swamp, deluge, immerse, submerge, drown, engulf. **2** *the river could flood:* **overflow**, burst its banks, brim over, run over. **3** *cheap goods are flooding the market:* **glut**, swamp, saturate. **4** *refugees flooded in:* **pour**, stream, flow, surge, swarm, pile, crowd.
–OPPOSITES trickle.

floor noun *the second floor:* **storey**, level, deck, tier.
•verb **1** *he floored his attacker:* **knock down**, knock over, bring down, fell, prostrate; informal lay out. **2** (informal) *the question floored him:* **baffle**, defeat, confound, perplex, puzzle, nonplus, mystify; informal beat, flummox, stump, fox, make someone scratch their head.

flop verb **1** *he flopped into a chair:* **collapse**, slump, crumple, sink, drop. **2** *his hair flopped over his eyes:* **hang**, dangle, droop, sag, loll. **3** (informal) *the play flopped:* **be unsuccessful**, fail, not work, fall flat, founder, misfire, backfire, be a disappointment, do badly, lose money, be a disaster; informal bomb, go to the wall, come a cropper, bite the dust; N. Amer. informal tank.
–OPPOSITES succeed.
•noun (informal) *the play was a flop:* **failure**, disaster, debacle, catastrophe; Brit. damp squib; informal washout, also-ran, dog, lemon, non-starter; N. Amer. informal clinker.
–OPPOSITES success.

floppy adjective **limp**, flaccid, slack, relaxed; drooping, droopy; loose, flowing.
–OPPOSITES erect, stiff.

florid adjective **1** *a florid complexion:* **ruddy**, red, red-faced, rosy, rosy-cheeked, pink; flushed, blushing, high-coloured; literary rubicund. **2** *florid language:* **flowery**, flamboyant, high-flown, high-sounding, grandiloquent, ornate, fancy, bombastic, elaborate; informal highfalutin, purple.
–OPPOSITES pale, plain.

flotsam noun **wreckage**; rubbish, debris, detritus, waste, dross, refuse, scrap; N. Amer. trash, garbage; informal junk.

flounce[1] verb *she flounced off to her room:* **storm**, stride, sweep, stomp, stamp, march, strut, stalk.

flounce[2] noun *a lace flounce:* **frill**, ruffle, ruff, ruche.

flounder verb **1** *she floundered, not knowing what to say:* **struggle**, be out of your depth, have difficulty, be confused; informal scratch your head, be flummoxed, be clueless, be foxed, be fazed, be floored. **2** *people were floundering about in the water:* **struggle**, thrash, flail, twist and turn, splash, stagger, stumble, reel, wallow, lurch, blunder, squirm, writhe.

> Don't confuse **flounder** with **founder**, which means 'fail' (*a proposed merger between the two airlines foundered*).

flourish verb **1** *ferns flourish in the shade:* **grow**, thrive, prosper, do well, burgeon, increase, multiply, proliferate; spring up, shoot up, bloom, blossom, bear fruit, run riot. **2** *the arts flourished:* **thrive**, prosper, bloom, be in good health, be vigorous, be in its heyday; progress, make progress, advance, make headway, develop, improve; evolve, make strides, move forward in leaps and bounds, expand; informal be in the pink, go places, go great guns, get somewhere. **3** *he flourished a sword:* **brandish**, wave, shake, wield; swing, twirl; display, show off.
– OPPOSITES die, wither, decline.

flout verb *retailers have been flouting the law for years:* **defy**, refuse to obey, disobey, break, violate, fail to comply with, fail to observe, contravene, infringe, breach, commit a breach of, transgress against; ignore, disregard; informal cock a snook at.
– OPPOSITES observe.

> ! Don't confuse **flout** with **flaunt**, which means 'display something in a way intended to attract attention' (*they openly flaunted their wealth*).

flow verb **1** *the water flowed down the channel:* **run**, course, glide, drift, circulate; trickle, seep, ooze, dribble, drip, drizzle, spill; stream, swirl, surge, sweep, gush, cascade, pour, roll, rush. **2** *many questions flow from today's announcement:* **result**, proceed, arise, follow, ensue, derive, stem, accrue; originate, emanate, spring, emerge; be consequent on.
• noun *a good flow of water:* **movement**, motion, current, circulation; trickle, ooze; stream, swirl, surge, gush, rush, spate, tide.

flower noun **1** *blue flowers:* **bloom**, blossom. **2** *the flower of the nation's youth:* **best**, finest, pick, choice, cream, the crème de la crème, elite.

> **WORD LINKS**
> **floral** relating to flowers
> **florist** a person who sells cut flowers

flowery adjective **1** *flowery fabrics:* **floral**. **2** *flowery language:* **florid**, flamboyant, ornate, fancy, convoluted; high-flown, high-sounding, grandiloquent, overblown; informal highfalutin, purple.
– OPPOSITES plain.

flowing adjective **1** *long flowing hair:* **loose**, free. **2** *soft, flowing lines:* **sleek**, streamlined, aerodynamic, smooth, clean; elegant, graceful. **3** *he writes in an easy, flowing style:* **fluent**, fluid, free-flowing, effortless, easy, natural, smooth.
– OPPOSITES stiff, awkward.

fluctuate verb **vary**, change, differ, shift, alter, waver, swing, oscillate, alternate, rise and fall, go up and down, see-saw, yo-yo, be unstable.

fluctuation noun **variation**, change, shift, alteration, swing, movement, oscillation, alternation, rise and fall, see-sawing, yo-yoing, instability, unsteadiness.
– OPPOSITES stability.

flue noun **duct**, tube, shaft, vent, pipe, passage, channel, conduit; funnel, chimney, smokestack.

fluent adjective *a fluent speech:* **articulate**, eloquent, expressive, silver-tongued; lucid, coherent, cogent.
– OPPOSITES inarticulate.

fluff noun *she brushed fluff off the costumes:* **fuzz**, lint, dust; N. Amer. dustballs, dust bunnies.
• verb (informal) *he fluffed his only line:* **bungle**, make a mess of, fumble, miss, deliver badly, muddle up, forget; informal mess up, botch, make a hash of, muck up, foul up, screw up; Brit. informal make a pig's ear of, cock up; N. Amer. informal flub, goof up.

fluffy adjective **fleecy**, woolly, fuzzy, hairy, feathery, downy, furry; soft.
– OPPOSITES rough.

fluid noun *the fluid seeps up the tube:* **liquid**, solution; **gas**, vapour.
– OPPOSITES solid.
• adjective **1** *a fluid substance:* **free-flowing**; liquid, liquefied, melted, molten, runny, running; gaseous, gassy. **2** *his plans were still fluid:* **adaptable**, flexible, adjustable, open-ended, open, open to change, changeable, variable. **3** *this fluid state of affairs:* **fluctuating**, changeable, subject/likely to change, shifting, inconstant; unstable, unsettled, turbulent, volatile. **4** *he stood up in one fluid movement:*

f

smooth, fluent, flowing, effortless, easy, continuous; graceful, elegant.
–OPPOSITES solid, firm, static, jerky.

fluke noun **chance**, coincidence, accident, twist of fate; piece of luck, stroke of good luck/fortune.

flummox verb (informal) **baffle**, perplex, puzzle, bewilder, mystify, bemuse, confuse, confound, nonplus; informal faze, stump, beat, fox, floor; N. Amer. informal discombobulate.

f

flurry noun **1** *a flurry of snow:* **swirl**, whirl, eddy, shower, gust. **2** *a flurry of activity:* **burst**, outbreak, spurt, fit, spell, bout, rash, eruption. **3** *a flurry of phone calls and emails:* **spate**, wave, flood, deluge, torrent, stream, tide, avalanche; series, succession, string, outbreak, rash, explosion, run, rush.

flush[1] verb **1** *she flushed in embarrassment:* **blush**, redden, go pink, go red, go crimson, go scarlet, colour. **2** *fruit helps to flush toxins from the body:* **rinse**, wash, sluice, swill, cleanse, clean; Brit. informal sloosh. **3** *they flushed out the snipers:* **drive**, chase, force, dislodge, expel.
–OPPOSITES pale.
•noun **1** *a flush crept over her face:* **blush**, colour, rosiness, pinkness, ruddiness, bloom. **2** *the first flush of manhood:* **bloom**, glow, freshness, radiance, vigour, rush.
–OPPOSITES paleness.

flush[2] adjective (informal) **1** *the company was flush with cash:* **well supplied**, well provided, well stocked, overflowing; informal awash. **2** *soaring housing markets left consumers feeling flush:* **well off**, rich, prosperous, wealthy; informal loaded, made of money. **3** *the years when cash was flush:* **plentiful**, abundant, in abundance.

flushed adjective **1** *their flushed faces:* **red**, pink, ruddy, glowing, rosy, florid, high-coloured, healthy-looking, aglow, burning, feverish; blushing, red-faced, embarrassed, shamefaced. **2** *the Olympics left them flushed with success:* **elated**, excited, thrilled, exhilarated, happy, delighted, overjoyed, gleeful, jubilant, exultant, ecstatic, euphoric, rapturous; informal blissed out, over the moon, high, on a high; N. Amer. informal wigged out; literary joyous.
–OPPOSITES pale, dismayed.

fluster verb *she was flustered by his presence:* **unsettle**, unnerve, agitate, ruffle, upset, bother, put on edge, disquiet, disturb, worry, perturb, disconcert, confuse, throw off balance, confound, nonplus; informal rattle, faze; N. Amer. informal discombobulate.
–OPPOSITES calm.
•noun *try not to get into a fluster:* **panic**, frenzy, fret; informal dither, tizz, tizzy, state, sweat; Brit. informal flap; N. Amer. informal twit.

fluted adjective **grooved**, channelled, furrowed, ribbed, corrugated, ridged.
–OPPOSITES smooth, plain.

flutter verb **1** *butterflies fluttered around:* **flit**, hover, dance. **2** *a tern was fluttering its wings:* **flap**, beat, vibrate; bat. **3** *flags fluttered in the breeze:* **wave**, flap, ripple, undulate, quiver, tremble; fly.
•noun **1** *the flutter of wings:* **beating**, flapping, quivering. **2** *a flutter of nervousness:* **tremor**, wave, rush, surge, flash, stab, flush, tremble, quiver, shiver, frisson, chill, thrill, tingle, shudder, ripple, flicker.

flux noun **change**, variability, fluidity, instability, fluctuation, changeability, inconstancy, unsteadiness, variation, shift, movement, oscillation, alternation, rise and fall, see-sawing, yo-yoing.
–OPPOSITES stability.

fly[1] verb **1** *a bird flew overhead:* **glide**, wing its way, soar, wheel; hover, hang; take wing, take to the air. **2** *military planes flew in supplies:* **transport**, airlift, lift, drop, parachute. **3** *who's flying the plane?* **pilot**, operate, control, manoeuvre, steer. **4** *the ship was flying a French flag:* **display**, show, exhibit. **5** *flags flew in the town:* **flutter**, flap, wave, ripple, quiver.
■ **fly at** attack, assault, pounce on, set upon, set about, weigh into, let fly at, turn on, round on, lash out at, hit out at, belabour, fall on; informal lay into, tear into, sail into, pitch into, wade into, jump; Brit. informal have a go at; N. Amer. informal light into.

fly[2] adjective (Brit. informal) **shrewd**, sharp, astute, acute, canny, worldly-

wise, knowing, clever; informal street-wise, not born yesterday, smart, no fool, nobody's fool; Brit. informal suss; Scottish & N. English informal pawky.
–OPPOSITES naive.

fly-by-night adjective **unreliable**, undependable, untrustworthy, disreputable; dishonest, deceitful, dubious, unscrupulous; informal iffy, shady, shifty, slippery, crooked; Brit. informal dodgy, bent; Austral./NZ informal shonky.
–OPPOSITES reliable, honest.

flyer, flier noun *flyers promoting a new bar:* **handbill**, bill, handout, leaflet, circular, advertisement; N. Amer. dodger.

flying adjective **1** *a flying beetle:* **airborne**, in the air, in flight; winged. **2** *a flying visit:* **brief**, short, lightning, fleeting, hasty, rushed, hurried, quick, whistle-stop, cursory, perfunctory; informal quickie.
–OPPOSITES long.

foam noun *the foam on the waves:* **froth**, spume, surf; fizz, effervescence, bubbles, head; lather, suds.
•verb *the water foamed:* **froth**; fizz, effervesce, bubble; lather; ferment, rise; boil, seethe.

foamy adjective **frothy**, foaming, bubbly, aerated, bubbling; sudsy; whipped, whisked.

fob verb
■ **fob someone off** *I'm not going to be fobbed off:* put off, stall, give someone the runaround, deceive; placate, appease. **fob something off on** *he fobbed off the kids on Cliff:* impose, palm off, unload, dump, get rid of, foist, offload; saddle someone with something, land someone with something, lumber someone with something.

focus noun **1** *a focus of community life:* **centre**, focal point, central point, centre of attention, hub, pivot, nucleus, heart, cornerstone, linchpin. **2** *the focus is on helping people:* **emphasis**, accent, priority, attention, concentration. **3** *the main focus of this chapter:* **subject**, theme, concern, subject matter, topic, issue, thesis, point, thread; substance, essence, gist, matter.
•verb **1** *he focused his binoculars on the tower:* **aim**, point, turn. **2** *the investigation will focus on areas of need:* **concentrate**, centre, zero in, zoom in; address itself to, pay attention to, pinpoint, revolve around, have as its starting point.
■ **in focus** sharp, crisp, distinct, clear, well defined, well focused. **out of focus** blurred, unfocused, indistinct, blurry, fuzzy, hazy, misty, cloudy, lacking definition, nebulous.

foe noun (literary) **enemy**, adversary, opponent, rival, antagonist, combatant, challenger, competitor, opposer, opposition, competition, other side.
–OPPOSITES friend.

fog noun **mist**, smog, murk, haze, haar; N. English sea fret; informal pea-souper.
•verb *the windscreen fogged up | his breath fogged the glass:* **steam up**, mist over, cloud over, film over.
–OPPOSITES demist, clear.

foggy adjective **1** *the weather was foggy:* **misty**, smoggy, hazy, murky. **2** *a foggy memory:* **muddled**, confused, dim, hazy, shadowy, cloudy, blurred, obscure, vague, indistinct, unclear.
–OPPOSITES clear.

foible noun **weakness**, failing, shortcoming, flaw, imperfection, blemish, fault, defect, limitation; quirk, kink, idiosyncrasy, eccentricity, peculiarity.
–OPPOSITES strength.

foil[1] verb *the escape attempt was foiled:* **thwart**, frustrate, obstruct, hamper, hinder, snooker, scotch, derail; stop, block, prevent, defeat; informal do for, put paid to, stymie; Brit. informal scupper, nobble, put the mockers on.
–OPPOSITES assist.

foil[2] noun *the wine was a perfect foil to pasta:* **contrast**, complement; antithesis.

foist verb **impose**, force, thrust, offload, unload, dump, palm off, fob off; pass off, get rid of; saddle someone with, land someone with, lumber someone with.

fold[1] verb **1** *I folded the cloth:* **double over/up**, turn under/up/over, bend; tuck, gather, pleat. **2** *fold the cream into the mixture:* **mix**, blend, stir gently. **3** *he folded her in his arms:* **enfold**, wrap, envelop; take, gather, clasp, squeeze, clutch; embrace,

hug, cuddle, cradle. **4** *the firm folded last year:* **fail**, collapse, founder; go bankrupt, become insolvent, cease trading, go into receivership, go into liquidation, be wound up, be closed down, be shut down; informal crash, go bust, go broke, go under, go to the wall, go belly up.
• **noun** *there was a fold in the paper:* **crease**, knife-edge; wrinkle, crinkle, pucker, furrow; pleat, gather.

f

fold[2] **noun enclosure**, pen, paddock, pound, compound, ring; N. Amer. corral.

folder noun file, binder, ring binder, portfolio, document case, envelope, sleeve, wallet.

foliage noun leaves, leafage; greenery, vegetation; literary verdure.

folk noun (informal) **1** *the local folk:* **people**, individuals, {men, women, and children}, living souls, mortals; citizenry, inhabitants, residents, populace, population; informal peeps; formal denizens. **2** *my folks live in Hull:* **relatives**, relations, family, nearest and dearest, people, kinsfolk, kinsmen, kinswomen, kin, kith and kin, kindred, flesh and blood.

folklore noun mythology, lore, tradition; legends, fables, myths, folk tales, folk stories, old wives' tales.

follow verb 1 *we'll let the others follow:* **come behind**, come after, go behind, go after, walk behind. **2** *loads of people followed the band around:* **accompany**, go along with, go around with, travel with, escort, attend, trail around with, string along with; informal tag along with. **3** *the police followed her everywhere:* **shadow**, trail, stalk, track; informal tail. **4** *follow the instructions:* **obey**, comply with, conform to, adhere to, stick to, keep to, act in accordance with, abide by, observe, heed, pay attention to. **5** *I couldn't follow what he said:* **understand**, comprehend, apprehend, take in, grasp, fathom, appreciate, see; informal make head or tail of, get, figure out, savvy, get your head around, get your mind around, get the drift of; Brit. informal suss out. **6** *he follows Manchester United:* **be a fan of**, be a supporter of, support, watch.
– OPPOSITES lead, flout, misunderstand.
■ **follow something through** complete, bring to completion, see through; stay/continue with, carry on with, keep on/going with; informal stick something out. **follow something up** investigate, research, look into, dig into, delve into, make enquiries into, enquire about, ask questions about, pursue, chase up; informal check out; N. Amer. informal scope out.

follower noun 1 *a follower of Christ:* **disciple**, apostle, supporter, defender, champion; believer, worshipper. **2** *followers of Scottish football:* **fan**, enthusiast, admirer, devotee, lover, supporter, adherent; N. Amer. informal rooter. **3** *the president's followers:* **entourage**, attendants, staff.
– OPPOSITES opponent, leader.

following noun *his devoted following:* **admirers**, supporters, backers, fans, adherents, devotees, public, audience; entourage, retinue, train.
– OPPOSITES opposition.
• **adjective 1** *the following day:* **next**, ensuing, succeeding, subsequent. **2** *the following questions:* **below**, underneath; these.
– OPPOSITES preceding, aforementioned.

folly noun foolishness, foolhardiness, stupidity, idiocy, lunacy, madness, rashness, recklessness, imprudence, injudiciousness, irresponsibility, thoughtlessness, indiscretion; informal craziness; Brit. informal daftness.
– OPPOSITES wisdom.

foment verb *they were accused of fomenting civil unrest:* **instigate**, incite, provoke, agitate, excite, stir up, whip up, encourage, urge, fan the flames of.

fond adjective 1 *she was fond of dancing | I'm very fond of her:* **keen on**, partial to, addicted to, enthusiastic about, passionate about; attached to, attracted to, enamoured of, in love with, having a soft spot for; informal into, hooked on, gone on, sweet on, struck on. **2** *his fond father:* **adoring**, devoted, doting, loving, caring, affectionate, kind, attentive. **3** *a fond hope:* **unrealistic**, naive, foolish, over-

optimistic, deluded, delusory, absurd, vain.
– OPPOSITES indifferent, uncaring, realistic.

fondle verb **caress**, stroke, pat, pet, finger, tickle, play with; maul, molest; informal paw, grope, feel up, touch up, cop a feel of.

fondness noun **1** *they look at each other with fondness:* **affection**, love, liking, warmth, tenderness, kindness, devotion, endearment, attachment, friendliness. **2** *a fondness for spicy food:* **liking**, love, taste, partiality, keenness, inclination, penchant, predilection, passion, appetite; weakness, soft spot, yen; informal thing.
– OPPOSITES hatred.

food noun **1** *I need some food | they love Italian food:* **nourishment**, sustenance, nutriment, fare; cooking, cuisine; foodstuffs, provender, refreshments, meals, provisions, rations; informal eats, eatables, nosh, grub, chow, nibbles; Brit. informal scoff, tuck; N. Amer. informal chuck; formal comestibles; dated victuals. **2** *food for the cattle:* **fodder**, feed, provender, forage.

> **WORD LINKS**
> **alimentary** relating to food or nutrition

fool noun **1** *stop acting like a fool:* **idiot**, halfwit, blockhead, dunce, simpleton, clod; informal dope, ninny, nincompoop, ass, chump, dimwit, dumbo, dummy, fathead, numbskull, dunderhead, airhead, lamebrain, cretin, moron, nerd, imbecile, pea-brain, birdbrain, jerk, dipstick, donkey, noodle; Brit. informal nit, nitwit, twit, clot, goat, plonker, berk, prat, pillock, wally, dork, twerp, charlie, mug; Scottish informal nyaff; N. Amer. informal schmuck, bozo, turkey, chowderhead, dumbhead, goofball, goof, goofus, galoot, lummox, klutz, putz, schlemiel, sap; Austral./NZ informal drongo. **2** *she made a fool of me:* **laughing stock**, dupe, gull; informal stooge, sucker, mug, fall guy; N. Amer. informal sap.
• verb **1** *he'd been fooled:* **deceive**, trick, hoax, dupe, take in, mislead, delude, hoodwink, bluff, gull; swindle, defraud, cheat, double-cross; informal con, bamboozle, pull a fast one on, take for a ride, pull the wool over someone's eyes, put one over on, diddle, fiddle, rip off, do, sting, shaft; Brit. informal sell a pup to; N. Amer. informal sucker, snooker, stiff; Austral. informal pull a swifty on; literary cozen. **2** *I'm not fooling, I promise:* **pretend**, make believe, put on an act, act, sham, fake; joke, jest; informal kid; Brit. informal have someone on.
■ **fool around** fiddle, play about/around, toy, trifle, meddle, tamper, interfere, monkey about/around; informal mess about/around; Brit. informal muck about/around.

foolhardy adjective **reckless**, rash, irresponsible, impulsive, hotheaded, impetuous, daredevil, devil-may-care, death-or-glory, madcap, hare-brained, precipitate, hasty, overhasty.
– OPPOSITES prudent.

foolish adjective **stupid**, silly, idiotic, witless, brainless, mindless, unintelligent, thoughtless, half-baked, imprudent, incautious, injudicious, unwise; ill-advised, ill-considered, impolitic, rash, reckless, foolhardy; informal dumb, dim, dim-witted, half-witted, thick, gormless, hare-brained, crackbrained, pea-brained, wooden-headed; Brit. informal barmy, daft; Scottish & N. English informal glaikit; N. Amer. informal dumb-ass, chowderheaded.
– OPPOSITES sensible, wise.

foolishness noun **folly**, stupidity, idiocy, imbecility, silliness, inanity, thoughtlessness, imprudence, injudiciousness, irresponsibility, indiscretion, foolhardiness, rashness, recklessness; Brit. informal daftness.
– OPPOSITES sense, wisdom.

foolproof adjective **infallible**, dependable, reliable, trustworthy, certain, sure, guaranteed, safe, sound, tried and tested; watertight, airtight, flawless, perfect; informal sure-fire.
– OPPOSITES flawed.

foot noun **1** *the animal's foot:* paw, hoof, trotter, pad; informal tootsie. **2** *the foot of the hill:* **bottom**, base, lowest part; end; foundation.
■ **foot the bill** (informal) pay, settle up; informal pick up the tab, cough up, fork out, shell out, come across; N. Amer. informal pick up the check.

WORD LINKS
chiropody, **podiatry** the medical treatment of the feet

football noun (Brit.) **soccer**, Association Football; informal footy.

footing noun **1** *Jenny lost her footing:* **foothold**, toehold, grip, purchase. **2** *a solid financial footing:* **basis**, base, foundation. **3** *on an equal footing:* **standing**, status, position; condition, arrangement, basis; relationship, terms.

f

footnote noun **note**, annotation, comment, gloss; aside, incidental remark, digression.

footprint noun **footmark**, mark, impression; (**footprints**) track, spoor.

footstep noun **footfall**, step, tread, stomp, stamp.

foppish adjective **dandyish**, dandified, dapper, dressy; affected, preening, vain; informal natty; Brit. informal poncey.

forage verb *I rummaged in the kitchen for something to eat:* **hunt**, search, look, rummage, ferret about/around, root about/around, scratch about/around, nose around/about/round, scavenge.
•noun **hunt**, search, look, quest, rummage, scavenge.

foray noun **1** *my first foray into journalism:* **venture**; experience of, encounter with, brush with. **2** *a brief foray into town:* **trip**, visit, outing, expedition, sortie, sally. **3** *the garrison made a foray against Richard's camp:* **raid**, attack, assault, incursion, swoop, strike, onslaught, sortie, sally, push, thrust.

forbear verb **refrain**, abstain, resist, desist, keep, restrain yourself, stop yourself, hold back, withhold; eschew, avoid, decline to.

forbearance noun **tolerance**, patience, resignation, endurance, fortitude, stoicism; leniency, clemency, indulgence; restraint, self-restraint, self-control.

forbearing adjective **patient**, tolerant, easy-going, lenient, clement, forgiving, understanding, accommodating, indulgent; long-suffering, resigned, stoic; restrained, self-controlled.
–OPPOSITES impatient, intolerant.

forbid verb **prohibit**, ban, outlaw, make illegal, veto, proscribe, disallow, embargo, bar, debar, interdict.
–OPPOSITES permit.

forbidden adjective **prohibited**, verboten, taboo; illegal, illicit, against the law.
–OPPOSITES permitted.

forbidding adjective **1** *a forbidding manner:* **hostile**, unwelcoming, unfriendly, off-putting, unsympathetic, unapproachable, grim, stern, hard, tough, frosty. **2** *the castle looked forbidding:* **threatening**, ominous, menacing, sinister, brooding, daunting, fearsome, frightening, chilling, disturbing, disquieting.
–OPPOSITES friendly, inviting.

force noun **1** *he pushed with all his force:* **strength**, power, energy, might, effort, exertion; impact, pressure, weight, impetus. **2** *they used force to achieve their aims:* **coercion**, compulsion, constraint, duress, oppression, harassment, intimidation, violence; informal arm-twisting. **3** *the force of the argument:* **cogency**, weight, effectiveness, soundness, validity, strength, power, significance, influence, authority; informal punch; formal efficacy. **4** *a force for good:* **agency**, power, influence, instrument, vehicle, means. **5** *a peacekeeping force:* **body**, group, outfit, party, team; detachment, unit, squad.
–OPPOSITES weakness.
•verb **1** *he was forced to pay:* **compel**, coerce, make, constrain, oblige, impel, drive, pressurize, pressure, press, push, press-gang, bully, dragoon, bludgeon; informal put the screws on, lean on, twist someone's arm. **2** *the door had to be forced:* **break open**, knock/smash/break down, kick in. **3** *I forced my way through the crowd:* **push**, thrust, shove, drive, press; propel, pump. **4** *they forced a confession out of the kids:* **extract**, exact, extort, wrest, wring, drag, screw, squeeze, beat. **5** *the new arrangements were forced on us:* **impose**, inflict, thrust.
■ **in force 1** *the law is now in force:* effective, in operation, operative, operational, in action, valid. **2** *her fans were out in force:* in great numbers, in hordes/droves, in their

hundreds/thousands; Brit. informal mob-handed.

forced adjective **1** *forced entry:* **violent**, forcible. **2** *forced repatriation:* **enforced**, compulsory, obligatory, mandatory, involuntary, imposed, required. **3** *a forced smile:* **strained**, unnatural, artificial, false, feigned, simulated, contrived, laboured, stilted, studied, mannered, affected, unconvincing, insincere, hollow; informal phoney, pretend, put on.
– OPPOSITES voluntary, natural.

forceful adjective **1** *a forceful personality:* **dynamic**, energetic, assertive, authoritative, vigorous, powerful, strong, pushy, driving, determined, insistent, commanding, dominant, domineering; informal bossy, in-your-face, go-ahead, feisty. **2** *a forceful argument:* **cogent**, convincing, compelling, strong, powerful, potent, weighty, effective, well founded, telling, persuasive, irresistible, eloquent, coherent.
– OPPOSITES weak, submissive, unconvincing.

forcible adjective **1** *forcible entry:* **forced**, violent. **2** *forcible repatriation.* See FORCED sense 2.

forebear noun **ancestor**, forefather, antecedent, progenitor.
– OPPOSITES descendant.

foreboding noun **1** *a feeling of foreboding:* **apprehension**, anxiety, trepidation, disquiet, unease, uneasiness, misgiving, suspicion, worry, fear, fearfulness, dread, alarm; informal the willies, the heebie-jeebies, the jitters. **2** *their forebodings proved justified:* **premonition**, presentiment, bad feeling, sneaking suspicion, funny feeling, intuition.

forecast verb *they forecast record profits:* **predict**, prophesy, foretell, foresee; estimate, project.
• noun *a gloomy forecast:* **prediction**, prophecy, prognostication, prognosis; projection, outlook, estimate.

forefather noun **forebear**, ancestor, antecedent, progenitor.
– OPPOSITES descendant.

forefront noun **vanguard**, spearhead, head, lead, front, fore, front line, cutting edge, leading edge.
– OPPOSITES rear, background.

forego verb. See FORGO.

foregone adjective
■ **a foregone conclusion** certainty, inevitability, matter of course, predictable result; informal sure thing; Brit. informal cert, dead cert.

foreground noun **1** *the foreground of the picture:* **front**, fore. **2** *he likes to keep himself in the foreground:* **front**, limelight, spotlight, fore, front line, vanguard.

forehead noun **brow**, temple.

foreign adjective **1** *foreign investors:* **overseas**, external. **2** *foreign lands | foreign species:* **distant**, far-off, exotic, alien; non-native, non-indigenous. **3** *the concept is foreign to us:* **unfamiliar**, unknown, unheard of, strange, alien; novel, new.
– OPPOSITES domestic, native, familiar.

foreigner noun **foreign national**, alien, non-native, stranger, outsider; immigrant, settler, newcomer, incomer.
– OPPOSITES native.

WORD LINKS
xenophobia intense or irrational dislike or fear of foreigners

foreman, forewoman noun **supervisor**, overseer, superintendent, team leader; foreperson; Brit. chargehand, captain, ganger; Scottish grieve; Mining overman.

foremost adjective **leading**, principal, premier, prime, top, greatest, best, supreme, pre-eminent, outstanding, most important, most notable; N. Amer. ranking; informal number-one.
– OPPOSITES minor.

forerunner noun **1** *the forerunners of the dinosaurs:* **predecessor**, precursor, antecedent, ancestor, forebear. **2** *headaches may be the forerunner of other complaints:* **prelude**, herald, harbinger, precursor.
– OPPOSITES descendant.

foresee verb **anticipate**, predict, forecast, expect, envisage, envision, see; foretell, prophesy; Scottish spae.

foreshadow verb **signal**, indicate, signify, mean, be a sign of, suggest, herald, be a harbinger of, warn of,

f

portend, prefigure, presage, promise, point to, anticipate; informal spell; literary betoken.

foresight noun **forethought**, planning, far-sightedness, vision, anticipation, prudence, care, caution; N. Amer. forehandedness.
– OPPOSITES hindsight.

forest noun **wood**, woods, woodland, trees, plantation; jungle, rainforest.

> **WORD LINKS**
> **sylvan** relating to forests
> **silviculture** the growing and cultivation of trees

forestall verb **pre-empt**, steal a march on; anticipate, second-guess; nip in the bud, thwart, frustrate, foil, stave off, ward off, fend off, avert, preclude, obviate, prevent; informal beat someone to it.

foretaste noun **sample**, taster, taste, preview, specimen, example; indication, suggestion, hint, whiff; warning, forewarning, omen.

foretell verb **predict**, forecast, prophesy, prognosticate; foresee, anticipate, envisage, envision, see; warn of, point to, signal; Scottish spae.

forethought noun **anticipation**, planning, forward planning, provision, precaution, prudence, care, caution; foresight, far-sightedness, vision.
– OPPOSITES impulse, recklessness.

forever adverb **1** *their love would last forever:* **for always**, evermore, for ever and ever, for good, for all time, until the end of time, until hell freezes over, eternally; N. Amer. forevermore; informal until the cows come home, until doomsday, until kingdom come. **2** *he was forever banging into things:* **always**, continually, constantly, perpetually, incessantly, endlessly, persistently, repeatedly, regularly; non-stop, day and night, {morning, noon, and night}; all the time, the whole time; Scottish aye; informal 24-7.
– OPPOSITES never, occasionally.

forewarn verb **warn**, warn in advance, give advance warning, give notice, apprise, inform; alert, caution, put someone on their guard; informal tip off; Brit. informal tip someone the wink.

foreword noun **preface**, introduction, prologue, preamble; informal intro.
– OPPOSITES conclusion.

forfeit verb **lose**, be deprived of, surrender, relinquish, sacrifice, give up, yield, renounce, forgo; informal pass up, lose out on.
– OPPOSITES retain.
• noun **penalty**, sanction, punishment, penance; fine; confiscation, loss, relinquishment, forfeiture, surrender.

forge[1] verb **1** *he forged a huge sword:* **hammer out**, beat out, fashion. **2** *they forged a partnership:* **build**, construct, form, create, establish, set up. **3** *he forged her signature:* **fake**, falsify, counterfeit, copy, imitate, reproduce, replicate, simulate; informal pirate.

forge[2] verb *they forged on through swamps:* **advance**, press on, push on, soldier on, march on, push forward, make progress, make headway.
■ **forge ahead** advance, progress, make progress, put a spurt on.

forged adjective **fake**, faked, false, counterfeit, imitation, copied, pirate; sham, bogus; informal phoney, dud.
– OPPOSITES genuine.

forgery noun *the painting was a forgery:* **fake**, counterfeit, fraud, imitation, replica, copy, pirate copy; informal phoney.

forget verb **1** *he forgot where he'd parked the car:* **fail to remember**, fail to recall. **2** *I never forget my briefcase:* **leave behind**, fail to take/bring, travel/leave home without. **3** *I forgot to close the door:* **neglect**, fail, omit. **4** *you can forget that idea:* **stop thinking about**, put out of your mind; shut out, blank out, pay no heed to, not worry about, ignore, overlook, take no notice of.
– OPPOSITES remember.
■ **forget yourself** misbehave, behave badly, get up to mischief, get up to no good; be rude; informal carry on, act up.

forgetful adjective **1** *I'm so forgetful these days:* **absent-minded**, vague, scatterbrained, disorganized, dreamy, abstracted; Medicine amnesic, amnesiac; informal scatty, having a mind/memory like a sieve. **2** *they were momentarily forgetful of his*

presence: **heedless**, careless; inattentive to, negligent about, oblivious to, unconcerned about, indifferent to.
– OPPOSITES reliable, heedful.

forgetfulness noun **absent-mindedness**, poor memory, vagueness, abstraction; amnesia; informal scattiness.

forgivable adjective **pardonable**, excusable, understandable, tolerable, permissible, allowable, justifiable.

forgive verb **1** *she would not forgive him:* **pardon**, excuse, exonerate, absolve; formal exculpate. **2** *you must forgive his rude conduct:* **excuse**, overlook, disregard, ignore, pass over, make allowances for, allow; turn a blind eye to, turn a deaf ear to, indulge, tolerate.
– OPPOSITES blame, resent, punish.

forgiveness noun **pardon**, absolution, exoneration, dispensation, indulgence, clemency, mercy; reprieve, amnesty; informal let-off.
– OPPOSITES mercilessness, punishment.

forgiving adjective *she is very forgiving:* **merciful**, lenient, compassionate, magnanimous, humane, soft-hearted, forbearing, tolerant, indulgent, understanding.
– OPPOSITES merciless, vindictive.

forgo, **forego** verb **do without**, go without, give up, waive, renounce, surrender, relinquish, part with, drop, sacrifice, abstain from, refrain from, eschew, cut out; informal swear off; formal forswear, abjure.
– OPPOSITES keep.

forgotten adjective **unremembered**, out of mind, consigned to oblivion; left behind; neglected, overlooked, ignored, disregarded, unrecognized.
– OPPOSITES remembered.

fork verb **split**, branch off, divide, subdivide, separate, part, diverge, bifurcate.

forked adjective **split**, branching, branched, bifurcated, Y-shaped, V-shaped, divided.
– OPPOSITES straight.

forlorn adjective **1** *he sounded forlorn:* **unhappy**, sad, miserable, sorrowful, dejected, despondent, disconsolate, wretched, down, downcast, dispirited, downhearted, crestfallen, depressed, melancholy, gloomy, glum, mournful, despairing, doleful; informal blue, down in the mouth, down in the dumps, fed up. **2** *a forlorn attempt:* **hopeless**; useless, futile, pointless, purposeless, vain, unavailing.
– OPPOSITES happy.

form noun **1** *the form of the landscape | form is less important than content:* **shape**, configuration, formation, structure, construction, arrangement, appearance, exterior, outline, format, layout, design. **2** *the human form:* **body**, shape, figure, frame, physique, anatomy; informal vital statistics. **3** *the infection takes different forms:* **manifestation**, appearance, embodiment, incarnation, semblance, shape, guise. **4** *sponsorship is a form of advertising:* **kind**, sort, type, class, category, variety, genre, brand, style; species, genus, family. **5** *you have to fill in a form:* **questionnaire**, document, coupon, slip. **6** *what form is your daughter in?* **class**, year; N. Amer. grade. **7** *he's in good form:* **condition**, fettle, shape, health; Brit. informal nick. **8** (Brit.) *a wooden form:* **bench**, pew, stall.
– OPPOSITES content.
• verb **1** *the pads are formed from mild steel:* **make**, construct, build, manufacture, fabricate, assemble, put together; create, produce, concoct, devise, contrive, fashion, shape. **2** *he formed a plan:* **formulate**, devise, conceive, work out, think up, lay, draw up, put together, produce, fashion, concoct, forge, hatch, develop; informal dream up. **3** *they formed a company:* **set up**, establish, found, launch, create, bring into being, institute, start, get going, initiate, bring about, inaugurate. **4** *a mist was forming:* **materialize**, come into being/existence, emerge, develop; take shape, gather, accumulate, collect, amass; crystallize, precipitate, condense. **5** *his men formed themselves into a line:* **arrange**, assemble, organize, order, range, array, dispose, marshal, deploy. **6** *these parts form an integrated whole:* **comprise**, make, make up, constitute, compose, add up to. **7** *the city formed a natural meeting*

f

f

point: **constitute**, serve as, act as, function as, make.
–OPPOSITES dissolve, disappear.
■ **good form** good manners, manners, convention, etiquette, protocol; informal the done thing.

formal adjective **1** *a formal dinner:* **ceremonial**, ritualistic, ritual, conventional, traditional; stately, courtly, solemn, dignified; elaborate, ornate, dressy. **2** *a very formal manner:* **aloof**, reserved, remote, detached, unapproachable; stiff, prim, stuffy, staid, ceremonious, correct, proper, decorous, conventional, precise, exact, punctilious, unbending, inflexible, strait-laced; informal stand-offish. **3** *you will need to get formal permission:* **official**, legal, authorized, approved, validated, certified, endorsed, documented, sanctioned, licensed, recognized, authoritative.
–OPPOSITES informal, casual, unofficial.

formality noun **1** *the formality of the occasion:* **ceremony**, ritual, red tape, protocol, decorum; stateliness, courtliness, solemnity. **2** *his formality was off-putting:* **aloofness**, reserve, remoteness, detachment, unapproachability; stiffness, primness, stuffiness, staidness, correctness, decorum, punctiliousness, inflexibility; informal stand-offishness. **3** *we keep the formalities to a minimum:* **official procedure**, bureaucracy, red tape, paperwork. **4** *the interview is just a formality:* **routine**, routine practice, normal procedure.
–OPPOSITES informality.

format noun **design**, style, presentation, appearance, look; form, shape, size; arrangement, plan, structure, scheme, composition, configuration.

formation noun **1** *the formation of the island:* **emergence**, genesis, development, evolution, origin. **2** *the formation of a new government:* **establishment**, setting up, institution, foundation, inception, creation, inauguration. **3** *fighters flying in a V formation:* **configuration**, arrangement, pattern, array, alignment; order.
–OPPOSITES destruction, disappearance, dissolution.

formative adjective **1** *a formative stage:* **developmental**, early, fluid, experimental, trial; malleable, impressionable. **2** *a formative influence:* **determining**, controlling, influential, guiding.

former adjective **1** *the former bishop:* **one-time**, erstwhile, sometime, ex-; previous, foregoing, preceding, earlier, prior, last; formal quondam. **2** *former times:* **earlier**, old, past, bygone, olden, long-ago, gone by, long past, of old; literary of yore. **3** *I support the former theory:* **first-mentioned**, first.
–OPPOSITES future, next, latter.

formerly adverb **previously**, earlier, before, until now/then, hitherto, née, once, once upon a time, at one time, in the past.

formidable adjective **1** *they face a formidable task:* **onerous**, arduous, taxing, difficult, hard, heavy, laborious, burdensome, strenuous, back-breaking, uphill, Herculean, monumental, colossal; demanding, tough, challenging, exacting. **2** *he is a formidable opponent:* **intimidating**, forbidding, daunting, awesome, fearsome, awe-inspiring; strong, powerful, redoubtable, indomitable. **3** *a formidable pianist:* **impressive**, skilled, proficient, adept, accomplished, skilful, gifted, talented, masterly, virtuoso, expert.
–OPPOSITES easy, weak.

formless adjective **shapeless**, amorphous, indeterminate; structureless, unstructured.

formula noun **1** *a legal formula:* **form of words**, set expression, phrase, saying. **2** *a peace formula:* **recipe**, prescription, blueprint, plan; method, procedure, technique, system. **3** *a formula for removing grease:* **preparation**, concoction, mixture, compound, creation, substance.

formulate verb **1** *the miners formulated a plan:* **devise**, conceive, work out, think up, lay, draw up, put together, form, produce, fashion, concoct, contrive, forge, hatch, prepare, develop; informal dream up. **2** *this is how Marx formulated his question:* **express**, phrase, word, put into words, frame, couch, put, articulate, say, state, utter.

forsake verb (literary) **1** *he forsook his wife:* **abandon**, desert, leave, turn your back on, cast aside. **2** *I won't forsake my principles:* **renounce**, abandon, relinquish, give up, drop; formal forswear.

forte noun **strength**, strong point, speciality, strong suit, talent, skill, bent, gift, métier; informal thing.
– OPPOSITES weakness.

forth adverb **1** *smoke billowed forth:* **out**, into view; into existence. **2** *from that day forth:* **onwards**, onward, on, forward.

forthcoming adjective **1** *forthcoming events:* **imminent**, impending, coming, upcoming, approaching, future; close, in store, in the wind, in the air, in the offing, in the pipeline, on the horizon, on the way, about to happen. **2** *no reply was forthcoming:* **available**, on offer; offered. **3** *he was not very forthcoming about himself:* **communicative**, talkative, chatty; expansive, expressive, frank, open, candid.
– OPPOSITES past, current, unforthcoming.

forthright adjective **frank**, direct, straightforward, honest, candid, open, sincere, outspoken, straight, blunt, plain-spoken, no-nonsense, bluff, matter-of-fact, to the point; informal upfront.
– OPPOSITES secretive, evasive.

forthwith adverb **immediately**, at once, instantly, directly, right away, straight away, post-haste, without delay, without hesitation; quickly, speedily, promptly; informal pronto.
– OPPOSITES sometime.

fortification noun **rampart**, wall, defence, palisade, stockade, earthwork, parapet, barricade.

fortify verb **1** *measures were taken to fortify the building:* **strengthen**, secure, barricade, protect, defend. **2** *I'll have a drink to fortify me:* **invigorate**, strengthen, energize, enliven, liven up, animate, vitalize, rejuvenate, restore, revive, refresh; informal pep up, buck up.
– OPPOSITES weaken, subdue.

fortitude noun **courage**, bravery, endurance, resilience, mettle, moral fibre, strength of mind, strength of character, backbone, spirit, grit, steadfastness; informal guts; Brit. informal bottle.
– OPPOSITES faint-heartedness.

fortress noun **fort**, castle, citadel, bunker, stronghold, fortification.

fortuitous adjective **lucky**, fortunate, providential, chance, advantageous, timely, opportune, adventitious, serendipitous; inadvertent, unintentional, unintended, unplanned, unexpected, unanticipated, unforeseen.
– OPPOSITES predictable, unlucky.

fortunate adjective **1** *he was fortunate enough to survive:* **lucky**, favoured, blessed, leading a charmed life, in luck. **2** *we are in a fortunate position:* **favourable**, advantageous, happy.
– OPPOSITES unfortunate, unfavourable.

fortunately adverb **luckily**, by good luck, by good fortune, as luck would have it; mercifully, thankfully.

fortune noun **1** *fortune favoured him:* **chance**, accident, coincidence, serendipity, destiny, providence; N. Amer. happenstance. **2** *a change of fortune:* **luck**, fate, destiny, predestination, the stars, karma, kismet, lot. **3** *an upswing in Sheffield's fortunes:* **circumstances**, state of affairs, condition, position, situation; plight, predicament. **4** *he made his fortune in steel:* **wealth**, money, riches, assets, resources, means, possessions, estate. **5** *this dress cost a fortune:* **huge amount**, king's ransom, millions, billions; informal small fortune, packet, mint, bundle, pile, wad, arm and a leg, pretty penny, tidy sum, big money; Brit. informal bomb, shedloads; N. Amer. informal big bucks, gazillions.
– OPPOSITES pittance.

forum noun **1** *forums were held for staff:* **meeting**, assembly, gathering, rally, conference, seminar, convention, symposium, colloquium; N. Amer. & NZ caucus; informal get-together. **2** *a forum for discussion:* **setting**, place, context, stage, framework, backdrop.

forward adverb **ahead**, forwards, onwards, onward, on, further; forth.
– OPPOSITES backwards.
• adjective **1** *a forward movement:*

f

onward, advancing. **2** *you need to do some forward planning:* **forward-looking**, for the future, anticipatory. **3** *the girls seemed very forward:* **bold, brazen**, brazen-faced, shameless, familiar, overfamiliar; informal fresh.
–OPPOSITES backward, retrospective, shy.
•**verb 1** *my mother forwarded your letter:* **send on**, post on, redirect, readdress, pass on. **2** *the goods were forwarded by sea:* **send**, dispatch, transmit, carry, convey, deliver, ship.

f

forward-looking adjective **progressive**, enlightened, dynamic, bold, enterprising, ambitious, pioneering, cutting-edge, innovative, modern, positive, reforming, radical; informal go-ahead.
–OPPOSITES backward-looking.

forwards adverb. See FORWARD adverb.

fossilized adjective *a fossilized idea:* **archaic**, antiquated, antediluvian, old-fashioned, outdated, outmoded, behind the times, anachronistic, stuck in time; informal prehistoric.

foster verb **1** *he fostered the arts:* **encourage**, promote, further, stimulate, cultivate, nurture, strengthen, enrich; help, aid, assist, support, back. **2** *they fostered two children:* **bring up**, rear, raise, care for, take care of, look after, provide for.
–OPPOSITES neglect.

foul adjective **1** *a foul smell:* **disgusting**, revolting, horrible, awful, dreadful, ghastly, terrible, repulsive, repugnant, abhorrent, hideous, loathsome, offensive, sickening, nauseating, nauseous, stomach-churning, stomach-turning, distasteful, obnoxious, objectionable, odious, noxious; N. Amer. vomitous; informal ghastly, gruesome, gross, putrid, sick-making; Brit. informal beastly; literary noisome. **2** *he had been foul to her:* **unkind**, malicious, mean, nasty, unpleasant, unfriendly, spiteful, cruel, vicious, malevolent, despicable, contemptible; informal horrible, horrid, rotten; Brit. informal beastly. **3** *foul weather:* **terrible**, dreadful, awful, unpleasant, disagreeable, bad; rough, stormy, squally, gusty, windy, blustery, wild, blowy, rainy, wet; Brit. informal filthy. **4** *foul drinking water:* **contaminated**, polluted, infected, tainted, impure, filthy, dirty, unclean. **5** *foul language:* **vulgar**, crude, coarse, filthy, dirty, obscene, indecent, naughty, lewd, suggestive, smutty, ribald, salacious, scatological, offensive, abusive; informal blue.
–OPPOSITES pleasant, kind, clean.
•**verb 1** *the river had been fouled:* **dirty**, infect, pollute, contaminate, poison, taint, sully, soil, stain, muddy, splash, spatter, smear, blight, defile, make filthy. **2** *the trawler had fouled its nets:* **tangle up**, entangle, snarl, catch, entwine, enmesh, twist.

foul-mouthed adjective **vulgar**, crude, coarse; obscene, rude, smutty, dirty, filthy, indecent, indelicate, offensive, lewd, X-rated, scatological, abusive; informal blue.

found verb **1** *he founded his company in 1989:* **establish**, set up, start, begin, get going, institute, inaugurate, launch, form, create, bring into being, originate, develop. **2** *they founded a new city:* **build**, establish; construct, erect, put up. **3** *their relationship was founded on trust:* **base**, build, construct; ground in, root in; rest, hinge, depend.
–OPPOSITES dissolve, liquidate, abandon.

foundation noun **1** *the foundations of the wall:* **footing**, foot, base, substructure, underpinning; bottom. **2** *there was no foundation for the claim:* **justification**, grounds, evidence, basis. **3** *an educational foundation:* **institution**, agency, charity.

founder[1] noun *the founder of modern physics:* **originator**, creator, father, architect, engineer, designer, developer, pioneer, author, planner, inventor, mastermind.

founder[2] verb **1** *the scheme foundered:* **fail**, be unsuccessful, not succeed, fall flat, fall through, collapse, backfire, meet with disaster, come to nothing/naught; informal flop, bomb. **2** *the ship foundered:* **sink**, go to the bottom, go down, be lost at sea; informal go to Davy Jones's locker.
–OPPOSITES succeed.

> ! Don't confuse **founder** with **flounder**, which means 'have trouble doing or understanding something' (*the school was floundering in confusion about its role in the world*).

fountain noun **1** *a fountain of water:* **jet**, spray, spout, spurt, well, cascade. **2** *a fountain of knowledge:* **source**, fount, well; reservoir, fund, mass, mine.

four cardinal number **quartet**, foursome, quadruplets.

> **WORD LINKS**
> **quadrilateral** a four-sided plane figure
> **tetrahedron** a four-sided solid figure

fox noun

> **WORD LINKS**
> **vulpine** relating to foxes

foyer noun **entrance hall**, hall, hallway, entrance, entry, porch, reception area, atrium, concourse, lobby; N. Amer. entryway.

fracas noun **disturbance**, brawl, melee, rumpus, skirmish, struggle, scuffle, scrum, clash, fisticuffs, altercation; informal scrap, dust-up, set-to, shindy, shindig; Brit. informal punch-up, bust-up, ruck; N. Amer. informal rough house, brannigan; Austral./NZ informal stoush; Law, dated affray.

fraction noun **1** *a fraction of the population:* **part**, portion, segment, slice, section, sector; proportion, percentage, ratio, measure; selection, fragment, snippet, snatch. **2** *he moved a fraction closer:* **tiny amount**, little, bit, touch, soupçon, trifle, mite, shade, jot; informal smidgen, smidge, tad.
– OPPOSITES whole.

fractious adjective **1** *fractious children:* **grumpy**, bad-tempered, irascible, irritable, crotchety, grouchy, cantankerous, tetchy, testy, ill-tempered, ill-humoured, peevish, cross, pettish, waspish, crabby, crusty, prickly; Brit. informal shirty, stroppy, narky, ratty; N. Amer. informal cranky, ornery; Austral./NZ informal snaky. **2** *the fractious parliamentary party:* **unruly**, uncontrollable, unmanageable, out of hand, obstreperous, difficult, headstrong, recalcitrant, intractable; disobedient, insubordinate, disruptive, disorderly, undisciplined, wilful, wayward.
– OPPOSITES contented, affable.

fracture noun **break**, crack.
• verb **break**, crack, snap, shatter, splinter; informal bust.

fragile adjective **1** *fragile vases:* **breakable**, easily broken; delicate, dainty, fine, brittle, flimsy. **2** *a fragile political alliance:* **precarious**, insecure, shaky, unreliable, vulnerable, weak. **3** *she is still very fragile:* **weak**, delicate, frail, debilitated; ill, unwell, ailing, poorly, sickly, infirm.
– OPPOSITES strong, durable, robust.

fragment noun **1** *small fragments of pottery:* **piece**, bit, particle, speck; chip, shard, sliver, splinter; shaving, paring, snippet, scrap, offcut, flake, shred, wisp, morsel; Scottish skelf. **2** *a fragment of conversation:* **snatch**, snippet, scrap, bit.
• verb *explosions caused the chalk to fragment:* **break up**, break into pieces, crack open/apart, shatter, splinter, fracture; disintegrate, fall to pieces, fall apart.

fragmentary adjective **incomplete**, fragmented, disconnected, disjointed, broken, discontinuous, piecemeal, scrappy, bitty, sketchy, uneven.

fragrance noun **1** *the fragrance of spring flowers:* **sweet smell**, scent, perfume, bouquet; aroma, nose. **2** *a daring new fragrance:* **perfume**, scent, eau de toilette, toilet water; eau de cologne, cologne.

fragrant adjective **sweet-scented**, sweet-smelling, scented, perfumed, aromatic.
– OPPOSITES smelly.

frail adjective **1** *a frail old lady:* **weak**, delicate, feeble, enfeebled, debilitated; infirm, ill, ailing, unwell, sickly, poorly, in poor health. **2** *a frail structure:* **fragile**, easily damaged, delicate, flimsy, insubstantial, unsteady, unstable, rickety.
– OPPOSITES strong, robust.

frailty noun **1** *the frailty of old age:* **infirmity**, weakness, enfeeblement, debility; fragility, delicacy; ill health, sickliness. **2** *his many frailties:* **weakness**, fallibility; weak point, flaw, imperfection,

defect, failing, fault, shortcoming, deficiency, inadequacy, limitation.
–OPPOSITES strength.

frame noun **1** *a tubular metal frame:* **framework**, structure, substructure, skeleton, chassis, shell; support, scaffolding, foundation. **2** *his tall, slender frame:* **body**, figure, form; shape, physique, build, proportions.
•verb **1** *he had the picture framed:* **mount**, set, encase. **2** *the legislators who frame the regulations:* **formulate**, draw up, draft, plan, shape, compose, put together, form, devise, create.
■ **frame of mind** mood, state of mind, humour, temper, disposition.

framework noun **frame**, substructure, structure, skeleton, chassis; support, scaffolding, foundation.

franchise noun **1** *the extension of the franchise to women:* **suffrage**, the vote, voting rights, enfranchisement. **2** *the company lost its TV franchise:* **warrant**, charter, licence, permit, authorization, permission, sanction.

frank[1] adjective **1** *he was quite frank with me:* **candid**, direct, forthright, plain, plain-spoken, straight, straightforward, straight from the shoulder, explicit, to the point, matter-of-fact; open, honest, truthful, sincere; bluff, blunt, unsparing, not afraid to call a spade a spade; informal upfront. **2** *she looked at Sam with frank admiration:* **open**, undisguised, unconcealed, naked, unmistakable, clear, obvious, transparent, patent, manifest, evident, perceptible, palpable.
–OPPOSITES evasive.

frank[2] verb *the envelope had not been franked:* **stamp**, postmark.

frankly adverb **1** *frankly, I'm not interested:* **to be frank**, to be honest, to tell you the truth, to be truthful, in all honesty. **2** *he stated the case quite frankly:* **candidly**, directly, plainly, straightforwardly, straight from the shoulder, forthrightly, openly, honestly, without beating about the bush, without mincing your words; bluntly, with no holds barred.

frantic adjective **panic-stricken**, panicky, beside yourself, at your wits' end, distraught, overwrought, worked up, agitated, distressed; frenzied, wild, frenetic, fraught, feverish, hysterical, desperate; informal in a state, in a tizzy/tizz, wound up, het up, in a flap, tearing your hair out; Brit. informal having kittens, in a flat spin.
–OPPOSITES calm.

fraternity noun **1** *a spirit of fraternity:* **brotherhood**, fellowship, kinship, friendship, mutual support, solidarity, community, union, togetherness; sisterhood. **2** *the teaching fraternity:* **profession**, community, trade, set, circle. **3** (N. Amer.) *a college fraternity:* **society**, club, association; group, set.

fraternize verb **associate**, mix, consort, socialize, keep company, rub shoulders; N. Amer. rub elbows; informal hobnob, hang around/round, hang out, run around, knock about/around.

fraud noun **1** *he was arrested for fraud:* **fraudulence**, sharp practice, cheating, swindling, embezzlement, deceit, deception, double-dealing, chicanery. **2** *social security frauds:* **swindle**, racket, deception, trick, cheat, hoax; informal scam, con, con trick, rip-off, sting, diddle, fiddle; N. Amer. informal bunco, hustle, grift. **3** *they exposed him as a fraud:* **impostor**, fake, sham, charlatan, quack; swindler, fraudster, racketeer, cheat, confidence trickster; informal phoney, con man, con artist.

fraudulent adjective **dishonest**, cheating, corrupt, criminal, illegal, unlawful, illicit; deceitful, double-dealing, duplicitous, dishonourable, unscrupulous, unprincipled; informal crooked, shady, dirty; Brit. informal bent, dodgy; Austral./NZ informal shonky.
–OPPOSITES honest.

fraught adjective **1** *their world is fraught with danger:* **full of**, filled with, rife with; attended by. **2** *she sounded a bit fraught:* **anxious**, worried, stressed, upset, distraught, overwrought, worked up, agitated, distressed, distracted, desperate, frantic, panic-stricken, panicky; beside yourself, at your wits' end, at the end of your tether; informal wound up, in a state, in a flap, tearing your hair out; Brit. informal having kittens, in a flat spin.

frayed adjective **1** *a frayed shirt collar:* **worn**, threadbare, tattered, ragged, holey, moth-eaten, in holes, the worse for wear; informal tatty; N. Amer. informal raggedy. **2** *his frayed nerves:* **strained**, fraught, tense, edgy, stressed.

freak noun **1** (informal) *a fitness freak:* **enthusiast**, fan, devotee, lover, aficionado; informal fiend, nut, fanatic, addict, maniac. **2** *the accident was a freak:* **anomaly**, aberration, rarity, oddity, one-off; fluke, twist of fate. **3** (informal) *a bunch of freaks:* **oddity**, eccentric, misfit; crank, lunatic; informal oddball, weirdo, nutcase, nut; Brit. informal nutter; N. Amer. informal wacko, kook.

• **adjective** *a freak storm | a freak result:* **unusual**, anomalous, aberrant, atypical, unrepresentative, irregular, exceptional, unaccountable; unpredictable, unforeseeable, unexpected, unanticipated, surprising; isolated.

– OPPOSITES normal.

freakish adjective *freakish weather.* See **FREAK** adjective.

free adjective **1** *admission is free:* **without charge**, free of charge, for nothing; complimentary, gratis; informal for free, on the house. **2** *she was free of any pressures:* **unencumbered by**, unaffected by, clear of, without, rid of; exempt from, not liable to, safe from, immune to, excused of; informal sans, minus. **3** *I'm free this afternoon:* **unoccupied**, not busy, available; off duty, off work, off, on holiday, on leave; at leisure, with time on your hands, with time to spare. **4** *the bathroom's free:* **vacant**, empty, available, unoccupied, not taken, not in use. **5** *a proud, free nation:* **independent**, self-governing, self-governed, self-ruling, self-determining, sovereign, autonomous; democratic. **6** *the killer is still free:* **on the loose**, at liberty, at large, loose; unconfined, unbound, untied, unchained, unrestrained. **7** *the free flow of water:* **unimpeded**, unobstructed, unrestricted, unhampered, clear, open. **8** *she was free with her money:* **generous**, liberal, open-handed, unstinting, bountiful; lavish, extravagant, prodigal. **9** *his free and open manner:* **frank**, open, candid, direct, plain-spoken; unrestrained, unconstrained, free and easy, uninhibited.

– OPPOSITES busy, occupied, captive, mean.

• **verb 1** *the hostages were freed:* **release**, set free, let go, liberate, discharge, deliver; set loose, let loose, turn loose, untie, unchain, unfetter, unshackle, unleash. **2** *victims were freed by firefighters:* **extricate**, release, get out, pull out, pull free; rescue. **3** *they wish to be freed from all legal ties:* **exempt**, except, excuse, relieve, unburden.

– OPPOSITES confine, trap.

■ **free and easy** easy-going, relaxed, casual, informal, unceremonious, unforced, natural, open, spontaneous, uninhibited, friendly; tolerant, liberal; informal laid-back.

freedom noun **1** *a desperate bid for freedom:* **liberty**, liberation, release, deliverance, delivery. **2** *the fight for freedom:* **independence**, self-government, self-determination, self-rule, home rule, sovereignty, autonomy; democracy. **3** *freedom from political accountability:* **exemption**, immunity, dispensation; impunity. **4** *patients have more freedom to choose who treats them:* **right**, entitlement, privilege, prerogative; scope, latitude, leeway, flexibility, space, breathing space, room, elbow room; licence, leave, free rein, a free hand, carte blanche.

– OPPOSITES captivity, subjection, liability.

free-for-all noun **brawl**, fight, scuffle, tussle, struggle, confrontation, clash, altercation, fray, fracas, melee, rumpus, disturbance; breach of the peace; informal dust-up, scrap, set-to, shindy; Brit. informal punch-up, bust-up, barney; Scottish informal rammy.

freely adverb **1** *may I speak freely?* **openly**, candidly, frankly, directly, without constraint, without inhibition; truthfully, honestly, without beating about the bush, without mincing your words, without prevarication. **2** *they gave their time and labour freely:* **voluntarily**, willingly, readily; of your own volition, of your own accord, of your own free will, without compulsion.

free will noun **self-determination**, freedom of choice, autonomy, liberty, independence.
■ **of your own free will** voluntarily, willingly, readily, freely, without reluctance, without compulsion, of your own accord, of your own volition, of your own choosing.

f

freeze verb **1** *the stream had frozen:* **ice over**, ice up, solidify. **2** *we froze in winter:* **be very cold**, be numb with cold, turn blue with cold, shiver, be chilled to the bone/ marrow. **3** *she froze in horror:* **stop dead**, stop in your tracks, stop, stand stock still, go rigid, become motionless, become paralysed. **4** *the prices of basic foodstuffs were frozen:* **fix**, hold, peg, set; limit, restrict, cap, confine, regulate; hold/ keep down.
– OPPOSITES thaw.
■ **freeze someone out** (informal) exclude, leave out, shut out, cut out, ignore, ostracize, spurn, snub, shun, cut, cut dead, turn your back on, cold-shoulder, leave out in the cold; Brit. send to Coventry; Brit. informal blank.

freezing adjective **1** *a freezing wind:* **bitter**, bitterly cold, icy, chill, frosty, glacial, wintry, arctic, sub-zero; raw, biting, piercing, penetrating, cutting, numbing. **2** *you must be freezing:* **frozen**, numb with cold, chilled to the bone/marrow, frozen stiff.
– OPPOSITES balmy, hot.

freight noun **goods**, cargo, merchandise.

frenetic adjective **frantic**, wild, frenzied, hectic, fraught, feverish, fevered, mad, manic, hyperactive, energetic, intense, fast and furious, turbulent, tumultuous.
– OPPOSITES calm.

frenzied adjective **frantic**, wild, frenetic, hectic, fraught, feverish, fevered, mad, crazed, manic, intense, furious, uncontrolled, out of control.
– OPPOSITES calm.

frenzy noun **1** *the crowd worked themselves into a state of frenzy:* **hysteria**, madness, mania, delirium, fever, agitation, turmoil, tumult; wild excitement, euphoria, elation, ecstasy. **2** *a frenzy of anger:* **fit**, paroxysm, spasm, bout.

frequency noun **rate of occurrence**, incidence, amount, commonness, prevalence; Statistics distribution.

frequent adjective **1** *frequent bouts of infection:* **recurrent**, recurring, repeated, periodic, continual, successive; many, numerous, lots of, several. **2** *a frequent traveller:* **habitual**, regular; experienced.
– OPPOSITES occasional, infrequent.
• verb *he frequented many of the local pubs:* **visit**, patronize, haunt; informal hang out in.

frequently adverb **regularly**, often, very often, all the time, habitually, customarily, routinely; many times, many a time, lots of times, again and again, time and again, over and over again, repeatedly, recurrently, continually; N. Amer. oftentimes.

fresh adjective **1** *fresh fruit:* **newly picked**, raw, natural, unprocessed. **2** *a fresh sheet of paper:* **clean**, blank, empty, clear, white; unused, new, pristine, unmarked, untouched. **3** *a fresh approach:* **new**, modern; original, novel, different, innovative, unusual, unconventional, unorthodox; radical, revolutionary; informal offbeat. **4** *fresh recruits:* **young**, youthful; new, inexperienced, naive, untrained, unqualified, untried, raw. **5** *her fresh complexion:* **healthy**, healthy-looking, clear, bright, youthful, blooming, glowing, unblemished; fair, rosy, rosy-cheeked, pink, ruddy. **6** *the night air was fresh:* **cool**, crisp, refreshing, invigorating; pure, clean, clear, uncontaminated, untainted. **7** *a fresh wind:* **chilly**, chill, cool, cold, brisk, bracing, invigorating; strong; informal nippy; Brit. informal parky. **8** (informal) *he's getting a little too fresh:* **impudent**, impertinent, insolent, presumptuous, forward, cheeky, disrespectful, rude, lippy, mouthy, saucy; N. Amer. informal sassy.
– OPPOSITES stale, old, tired.

freshen verb **1** *the cold water freshened him:* **refresh**, revitalize, restore, revive, wake up, rouse, enliven, liven up, energize, brace, invigorate; informal buck up, pep up. **2** *he opened a window to freshen the room:* **ventilate**, air, aerate; purify, cleanse; refresh, cool. **3** (N. Amer.) *the waitress freshened their coffee:* **refill**, top up, fill up, replenish.

freshman, freshwoman noun **first year student**, undergraduate; newcomer, new recruit, starter, probationer; beginner, learner, novice; informal undergrad, rookie; Brit. informal fresher.

fret verb **worry**, be anxious, feel uneasy, be distressed, be upset, upset yourself, concern yourself; agonize, sigh, pine, brood, eat your heart out.

fretful adjective **distressed**, upset, miserable, unsettled, uneasy, ill at ease, uncomfortable, edgy, agitated, worked up, tense, stressed, restive, fidgety; informal het up, uptight, twitchy.

friable adjective **crumbly**, easily crumbled, powdery, dusty, chalky, soft; dry.

friction noun **1** *the lubrication reduces friction:* **abrasion**, rubbing, chafing, grating, rasping, scraping; resistance, drag. **2** *there was friction between father and son:* **discord**, strife, conflict, disagreement, dissension, dissent, opposition, contention, dispute, disputation, arguing, argument, quarrelling, bickering, squabbling, wrangling, fighting, feuding, rivalry; hostility, animosity, antipathy, enmity, antagonism, resentment, acrimony, bitterness, bad feeling, ill feeling, ill will, bad blood.
– OPPOSITES harmony.

friend noun **1** *a close friend:* **companion**, best friend, intimate, confidante, confidant, familiar, soul mate, playmate, playfellow, classmate, schoolmate, workmate; ally, associate; sister, brother; informal pal, chum, sidekick, crony; Brit. informal mate, mucker; N. Amer. informal buddy, amigo. **2** *the friends of the Opera:* **patron**, backer, supporter, benefactor, benefactress, sponsor; well-wisher, defender, champion.
– OPPOSITES enemy.

friendless adjective **alone**, by yourself, solitary, lonely, with no one to turn to, unwanted, unloved, abandoned, rejected, forsaken, shunned, spurned, forlorn; N. Amer. lonesome.
– OPPOSITES popular.

friendliness noun **affability**, amiability, geniality, congeniality, bonhomie, cordiality, good nature, good humour, warmth, affection, conviviality, joviality, companionability, sociability, gregariousness, camaraderie, neighbourliness, hospitableness, approachability, accessibility, openness, kindness, kindliness, sympathy, amenability, benevolence.

friendly adjective **1** *a friendly woman:* **affable**, amiable, genial, congenial, cordial, warm, affectionate, demonstrative, convivial, companionable, sociable, gregarious, outgoing, clubbable, comradely, neighbourly, hospitable, approachable, engaging, accessible, communicative, open, unreserved, easy-going, good-natured, kind, kindly, amenable, agreeable; Scottish couthy; Brit. informal matey; N. Amer. informal buddy-buddy. **2** *friendly conversation:* **amicable**, congenial, cordial, pleasant, easy, relaxed, casual, informal, unceremonious; close, intimate, familiar.
– OPPOSITES hostile, unfriendly.

friendship noun **1** *lasting friendships:* **relationship**, attachment, association, bond, tie, link, union. **2** *ties of love and friendship:* **camaraderie**, friendliness, amity, comradeship, companionship, fellowship, closeness, affinity, rapport, understanding, harmony, unity; intimacy, affection.
– OPPOSITES enmity.

fright noun **1** *she was paralysed with fright:* **fear**, terror, horror, alarm, panic, dread, trepidation, dismay, nervousness, apprehension, disquiet; the shivers, the shakes; informal the jitters, the heebie-jeebies, the willies, the creeps, a cold sweat. **2** *the experience gave everyone a fright:* **scare**, shock, surprise, turn, jolt, start.

frighten verb **scare**, startle, alarm, terrify, petrify, shock, chill, panic, shake, disturb, dismay, unnerve, unman, intimidate, terrorize, cow, daunt; strike terror into, put the fear of God into, chill someone to the bone/marrow, make someone's blood run cold; informal scare the living daylights out of, scare stiff, scare someone out of their wits, scare witless, scare to death, scare the pants off, spook, make someone's hair stand on end, make someone jump out of their skin; Brit. informal put the wind up, give someone the heebie-jeebies; Irish informal scare the bejesus out of; old use affright.

frightening adjective **terrifying**, horrifying, alarming, startling, chilling, spine-chilling, hair-raising, blood-curdling, disturbing, unnerving, intimidating, daunting, upsetting, traumatic; eerie, sinister, fearsome, nightmarish, macabre, menacing; Scottish eldritch; informal scary, spooky, creepy, hairy.

frightful adjective **1** *a frightful accident:* **horrible**, horrific, ghastly, horrendous, serious, awful, dreadful, terrible, nasty, grim, dire, unspeakable; alarming, shocking, terrifying, appalling, fearful; hideous, gruesome, grisly; informal horrid. **2** (informal) *they're making a frightful racket:* **awful**, terrible, dreadful, appalling, ghastly, abominable; insufferable, unbearable; informal God-awful.

frigid adjective **1** *a frigid January night:* **very cold**, bitterly cold, bitter, freezing, frozen, frosty, icy, chilly, chill, wintry, bleak, sub-zero, arctic, glacial. **2** *frigid politeness:* **stiff**, formal, stony, wooden, unemotional, passionless, unfeeling, distant, aloof, remote, reserved, unapproachable; frosty, cold, icy, cool, unsmiling, forbidding, unfriendly, unwelcoming; informal offish, stand-offish.
– OPPOSITES hot, friendly.

frill noun **ruffle**, flounce, ruff, ruche, fringe.
■ **no-frills** plain, simple, basic, straightforward, unpretentious, down to earth; practical, serviceable; economical, cheap; workaday, modest, utilitarian, minimalist, functional.

frilly adjective **ruffled**, flounced, frilled, crimped, ruched, trimmed, lacy, frothy; fancy, ornate.

fringe noun **1** *the city's northern fringe:* **perimeter**, periphery, border, margin, rim, outer edge, edge, extremity, limit; outer limits, limits, borders, bounds, outskirts. **2** *blue curtains with a yellow fringe:* **edging**, edge, border, trimming, frill, flounce, ruffle.
– OPPOSITES middle.
• adjective *fringe theatre:* **alternative**, avant-garde, experimental, left-field, radical, extreme.
– OPPOSITES mainstream.
• verb **1** *a robe of gold, fringed with black:* **trim**, edge, hem, border, braid; decorate, adorn, ornament, embellish, finish. **2** *the lake is fringed by trees:* **border**, edge, bound, skirt, line, surround, enclose, encircle, circle, ring.

fringe benefit noun **extra**, added extra, additional benefit, privilege; informal perk; formal perquisite.

frisk verb **1** *the spaniels frisked around my ankles:* **frolic**, gambol, cavort, caper, scamper, skip, dance, romp, prance, leap, spring, hop, jump, bounce. **2** *the officer frisked him:* **search**, body-search, check.

frisky adjective **lively**, bouncy, bubbly, perky, active, energetic, animated, zestful; playful, coltish, skittish, spirited, high-spirited, in high spirits, exuberant; informal full of beans, sparky; literary frolicsome.

fritter verb **squander**, waste, misuse, misspend, dissipate; overspend, spend like water, be prodigal with, run through, get through; informal blow, splurge, pour/chuck something down the drain.
– OPPOSITES save.

frivolity noun **light-heartedness**, levity, joking, jocularity, gaiety, fun, frivolousness, silliness, foolishness, flightiness, skittishness; superficiality, shallowness, vacuity, empty-headedness.

frivolous adjective **1** *a frivolous girl:* **skittish**, flighty, giddy, silly, foolish, superficial, shallow, feather-brained, empty-headed, pea-brained, birdbrained, vacuous, vapid; informal dizzy, dippy; N. Amer. informal ditzy. **2** *frivolous remarks:* **flippant**, glib, facetious, joking, jokey, light-hearted; fatuous, inane,

senseless, thoughtless; informal flip. **3** *new rules to stop frivolous lawsuits:* **time-wasting**, pointless, trivial, trifling, minor.
– OPPOSITES sensible, serious.

frizzy adjective **curly**, curled, corkscrew, ringlety, crimped, crinkly, kinky, frizzed; permed.
– OPPOSITES straight.

frock noun **dress**, gown, robe, shift; garment, costume.

frog noun

> **WORD LINKS**
> **anuran**, **batrachian** relating to frogs

frolic verb **play**, amuse yourself, romp, disport yourself, frisk, gambol, cavort, caper, scamper, skip, dance, prance, leap about, jump about; dated sport.

front noun **1** *the front of the boat:* **fore**, foremost part, forepart, anterior, nose, head; bow, prow; foreground. **2** *a shop front:* **frontage**, face, facing, facade; window. **3** *the front of the queue:* **head**, beginning, start, top, lead. **4** *she kept up a brave front:* **appearance**, air, face, manner, demeanour, bearing, pose, exterior, veneer, outward show, act, pretence. **5** *the shop was a front for his real business:* **cover**, blind, disguise, facade, mask, cloak, screen, smokescreen, camouflage.
– OPPOSITES rear, back.
• adjective **leading**, lead, first, foremost.
– OPPOSITES last.
• verb *the houses fronted on a reservoir:* **overlook**, look out on/over, face, lie opposite; have a view of, command a view of.
■ **in front** ahead, to/at the fore, at the head, up ahead, in the vanguard, in the van, in the lead, leading, coming first; at the head of the queue; informal up front.

frontier noun **border**, boundary, borderline, dividing line; perimeter, limit, edge, rim; marches, bounds.

frost noun **ice**, rime, verglas; informal Jack Frost; old use hoar.

frosty adjective **1** *a frosty morning:* **freezing**, cold, bitter, bitterly cold, chill, wintry, frigid, glacial, arctic; frozen, icy; informal nippy; Brit. informal parky; literary rimy. **2** *a frosty look:* **cold**, frigid, icy, glacial, unfriendly, inhospitable, unwelcoming, forbidding, hostile, stony, stern, hard.

froth noun **foam**, head; bubbles, fizz, effervescence; lather, suds; scum.
• verb **bubble**, fizz, effervesce, foam, lather; churn, seethe.

frothy adjective **1** *a frothy liquid:* **foaming**, foamy, bubbling, bubbly, fizzy, sparkling, effervescent, gassy, carbonated; sudsy. **2** *a frothy pink evening dress:* **frilly**, flouncy, lacy.

frown verb **1** *she frowned at him:* **scowl**, glower, glare, lour, make a face, look daggers, give someone a black look; knit/furrow your brows; informal give someone a dirty look. **2** *public displays of affection were frowned on:* **disapprove of**, discourage, dislike, look askance at, not take kindly to, take a dim view of, take exception to, object to, have a low opinion of.
– OPPOSITES smile.

frozen adjective **1** *the frozen ground:* **icy**, ice-covered, ice-bound, frosty, frosted; frozen solid, hard, as hard as iron. **2** *they were frozen:* **freezing**, icy, cold, chilled to the bone/marrow, numb, numbed, frozen stiff.
– OPPOSITES boiling.

frugal adjective **1** *a hard-working, frugal man:* **thrifty**, economical, careful, cautious, prudent, provident, unwasteful, sparing; abstemious, austere, self-denying, ascetic, monkish, spartan; parsimonious, miserly, niggardly, cheese-paring, penny-pinching, close-fisted; N. Amer. forehanded; informal tight-fisted, tight, stingy. **2** *their frugal breakfast:* **meagre**, scanty, scant, paltry, skimpy; plain, simple, spartan, inexpensive, cheap, economical.
– OPPOSITES extravagant, lavish.

fruit noun *the fruits of their labours:* **reward**, benefit, profit, product, return, yield, legacy, issue; result, outcome, upshot, consequence, effect.

> **WORD LINKS**
> **frugivorous** fruit-eating
> **pomiculture** fruit-growing

fruitful adjective **1** *a fruitful tree:* **fertile**, fecund, prolific, high-yielding. **2** *fruitful discussions:*

f

productive, constructive, useful, of use, worthwhile, helpful, beneficial, valuable, rewarding, profitable, advantageous, successful.
– OPPOSITES barren, futile, fruitless.

fruition noun **fulfilment**, realization, actualization, materialization, achievement, attainment, accomplishment, resolution; success, completion, consummation, conclusion, close, finish, perfection, maturity.

f

fruitless adjective **futile**, vain, in vain, to no avail, to no effect, idle; pointless, useless, worthless, wasted, hollow; ineffectual, ineffective; unproductive, unrewarding, profitless, unsuccessful, unavailing, barren, for naught; abortive.
– OPPOSITES productive.

fruity adjective *his fruity voice:* **deep**, rich, resonant, full, mellow, clear, strong, vibrant.

frumpy adjective **dowdy**, frumpish, unfashionable, old-fashioned; drab, dull, shabby; Brit. informal mumsy.
– OPPOSITES fashionable.

frustrate verb **1** *his plans were frustrated:* **thwart**, defeat, foil, block, stop, put a stop to, counter, spoil, check, disappoint, forestall, dash, scotch, quash, crush, derail, snooker; obstruct, impede, hamper, hinder, hamstring, stand in the way of; informal stymie, foul up, screw up, put the kibosh on, banjax, do for; Brit. informal scupper. **2** *the delays frustrated him:* **exasperate**, infuriate, annoy, anger, vex, irritate, irk, try someone's patience; informal aggravate, bug, miff, hack off.
– OPPOSITES help, facilitate.

frustration noun **1** *he clenched his fists in frustration:* **exasperation**, annoyance, anger, vexation, irritation; disappointment, dissatisfaction, discontentment, discontent; informal aggravation. **2** *the frustration of his plans:* **thwarting**, defeat, prevention, foiling, blocking, spoiling, forestalling, derailment; obstruction, hampering, hindering; failure, collapse.

fuddled adjective **stupefied**, addled, befuddled, confused, muddled, bewildered, dazed, stunned, muzzy, groggy, foggy, fuzzy, vague, disorientated, disoriented, all at sea; informal dopey, woozy, fazed, not with it; N. Amer. informal discombobulated.

fuddy-duddy noun (informal) **old fogey**, conservative, traditionalist, conformist; fossil, dinosaur, troglodyte; Brit. museum piece; informal stick-in-the-mud, square, stuffed shirt, dodo.

fudge verb *the minister tried to fudge the issue:* **evade**, avoid, dodge, skirt, duck, gloss over; hedge, prevaricate, be non-committal, beat about the bush, equivocate; Brit. hum and haw; informal cop out, sit on the fence.
• noun **compromise**, cover-up; spin; informal cop-out.

fuel noun **1** *the car ran out of fuel:* **petrol**, diesel; power; N. Amer. gasoline, gas. **2** *she added more fuel to the fire:* **firewood**, wood, kindling, logs; coal, coke, anthracite; paraffin, kerosene.
• verb **1** *power stations fuelled by coal:* **power**, fire; drive, run. **2** *the rumours fuelled anxiety among MPs:* **fan**, feed, stoke up, inflame, intensify, stimulate, encourage, provoke, incite, whip up; sustain, keep alive.

fugitive noun **escapee**, runaway, deserter, absconder; refugee.
• adjective **escaped**, runaway, on the run, on the loose, at large; wanted; informal AWOL; N. Amer. informal on the lam.

fulfil verb **1** *he fulfilled a lifelong ambition:* **achieve**, attain, realize, actualize, make happen, succeed in, bring to completion, bring to fruition, satisfy. **2** *she failed to fulfil her duties:* **carry out**, perform, accomplish, execute, do, discharge, conduct; complete, finish, conclude. **3** *they fulfilled the criteria:* **meet**, satisfy, comply with, conform to, fill, answer.

fulfilled adjective **satisfied**, content, contented, happy, pleased; serene, placid, untroubled, at ease, at peace.
– OPPOSITES discontented.

full adjective **1** *her glass was full:* **filled**, filled to capacity, brimming, brimful. **2** *streets full of people:* **crowded**, packed, crammed, congested; teeming, swarming, thronged, overrun; abounding, bursting, overflowing; informal jam-

packed, wall-to-wall, stuffed, chock-a-block, chock-full, bursting at the seams, packed to the gunwales, awash. **3** *all the seats were full:* **occupied**, taken, in use. **4** *I can't eat any more—I'm full:* **replete**, full up, satisfied, sated, satiated; gorged, glutted; informal stuffed. **5** *she'd had a full life:* **eventful**, interesting, exciting, lively, action-packed, busy, active. **6** *a full list of facilities:* **comprehensive**, thorough, exhaustive, all-inclusive, all-encompassing, all-embracing, in-depth; complete, entire, whole, unabridged, uncut. **7** *we were travelling at full speed:* **maximum**, top. **8** *a full figure:* **plump**, rounded, buxom, shapely, ample, curvaceous, voluptuous, womanly, Junoesque; informal curvy, well upholstered, well endowed; N. Amer. informal zaftig. **9** *a full skirt:* **loose-fitting**, loose, baggy, voluminous, roomy, capacious, billowing.
– OPPOSITES empty, hungry, selective, thin.
• **adverb** *she looked full into his face:* **directly**, right, straight, squarely, square, dead, point-blank; informal bang, slap bang, plumb.
■ **in full** in its entirety, in toto, in total, unabridged, uncut.

full-blooded **adjective** **uncompromising**, all-out, out and out, committed, vigorous, strenuous, intense; unrestrained, uncontrolled, unbridled, hard-hitting, no-holds-barred.
– OPPOSITES half-hearted.

full-blown **adjective** **fully developed**, full-scale, full-blooded, fully fledged, complete, total, thorough, entire; advanced.

full-grown **adjective** **adult**, mature, grown-up, of age; fully grown, fully developed, fully fledged, ripe.
– OPPOSITES infant.

fullness **noun** **1** *the fullness of the information they provide:* **comprehensiveness**, completeness, thoroughness, exhaustiveness. **2** *the fullness of her body:* **plumpness**, roundedness, roundness, shapeliness, curvaceousness, voluptuousness, womanliness; informal curviness. **3** *the recording has a fullness and warmth:* **resonance**, richness, intensity, depth, vibrancy, strength, clarity.
■ **in the fullness of time** in due course, eventually, in time, one day, some day, sooner or later; ultimately, finally, in the end.

full-scale **adjective** **1** *a full-scale model:* **full-size**, life-size. **2** *a full-scale public inquiry:* **thorough**, comprehensive, extensive, exhaustive, complete, all-out, all-encompassing, all-inclusive, all-embracing, thoroughgoing, wide-ranging, sweeping, in-depth.
– OPPOSITES small-scale.

fully **adverb** **completely**, entirely, wholly, totally, quite, thoroughly, in all respects, in every respect, without reservation, without exception, to the hilt.
– OPPOSITES partly, nearly.

fully fledged **adjective** **trained**, qualified, proficient, experienced; mature, fully developed, full grown; Brit. time-served.
– OPPOSITES novice.

fulminate **verb** **protest**, rail, rage, rant, thunder, storm, declaim, inveigh, speak out, make/take a stand; denounce, decry, condemn, criticize, censure, disparage, attack, arraign; informal mouth off about, kick up a stink about.

fulsome **adjective** **excessive**, extravagant, immoderate, over-appreciative, flattering, adulatory, fawning, unctuous, ingratiating, cloying, saccharine; enthusiastic, effusive, rapturous, glowing, gushing, profuse, generous, lavish; informal over the top, OTT.

fumble **verb** **1** *he fumbled for his keys:* **grope**, fish, search, feel, scrabble. **2** *the keeper fumbled the ball:* **miss**, drop, mishandle; misfield.

fume **noun** *toxic fumes:* **smoke**, vapour, gas; pollution.
• **verb** *Ella was fuming at his arrogance:* **be furious**, be enraged, seethe, be livid, be incensed, boil, be beside yourself, spit; rage, rant and rave; informal be hot under the collar, foam at the mouth, see red.

fumigate **verb** **disinfect**, purify, sterilize, sanitize, decontaminate, cleanse.
– OPPOSITES pollute.

fun **noun** **1** *I joined in with the fun:*

enjoyment, entertainment, amusement, pleasure; jollification, merrymaking; recreation, leisure, relaxation; informal R & R, beer and skittles. **2** *she's full of fun:* **merriment**, cheerfulness, cheeriness, jollity, joviality, jocularity, high spirits, gaiety, mirth, laughter, hilarity, glee, gladness, light-heartedness, levity. **3** *he became a figure of fun:* **ridicule**, derision, mockery, laughter, scorn, contempt.
– OPPOSITES boredom, misery.
• **adjective** (informal) *a fun evening:* **enjoyable**, entertaining, amusing, pleasurable, pleasing, agreeable, interesting.
■ **in fun** playfully, in jest, as a joke, tongue in cheek, light-heartedly, for a laugh, teasingly. **make fun of** tease, poke fun at; ridicule, mock, laugh at, taunt, jeer at, scoff at, deride; parody, lampoon, caricature, satirize; informal take the mickey out of, rib, kid, have on, pull someone's leg, send up; Brit. informal wind up; N. Amer. informal goof on, rag on, razz.

function noun **1** *the main function of the machine:* **purpose**, task, use, role. **2** *my function was to train the recruits:* **responsibility**, duty, role, concern, province, activity, assignment, obligation, charge; task, job, mission, undertaking, commission. **3** *a function attended by local dignitaries:* **social event**, party, social occasion, affair, gathering, reception, soirée, jamboree, gala; N. Amer. levee; informal do, bash, shindig; Brit. informal beanfeast.
• **verb 1** *the system had ceased to function:* **work**, go, run, be in working/running order, operate, be operative. **2** *the museum functions as an education centre:* **act**, serve, operate; perform, work.

functional adjective **1** *a small functional kitchen:* **practical**, useful, utilitarian, workaday, serviceable; minimalist, plain, simple, basic, modest, unadorned, unpretentious, no-frills; impersonal, characterless, soulless, institutional, clinical, austere, spartan. **2** *the machine is now fully functional:* **working**, in working order, functioning, in service, in use, up and running; going, running, operative, operating, in operation, in commission, in action, active.

functionary noun **official**, public servant, civil servant, bureaucrat, administrator, apparatchik.

fund noun **1** *an emergency fund:* **collection**, kitty, reserve, pool, purse; endowment, foundation, trust, grant, investment; savings, nest egg; informal stash. **2** *I was very short of funds:* **money**, cash; wealth, means, assets, resources, savings, capital, reserves, the wherewithal; informal dough, bread, loot, dosh; Brit. informal lolly, spondulicks, readies. **3** *his fund of stories:* **stock**, store, supply, accumulation, collection, bank, pool; mine, reservoir, storehouse, treasury, treasure house, hoard, repository.
• **verb** *we were funded by the Treasury:* **finance**, pay for, back, capitalize, sponsor, put up the money for, subsidize, underwrite, endow, support, maintain; informal foot the bill for, pick up the tab for; N. Amer. informal bankroll, stake.

fundamental adjective **basic**, underlying, core, rudimentary, elemental, elementary, root; primary, prime, cardinal, first, principal, chief, key, central, vital, essential, important, indispensable, necessary, crucial, pivotal, critical.
– OPPOSITES secondary, unimportant.

fundamentally adverb **essentially**, in essence, basically, at heart, at bottom, deep down; primarily, above all, first and foremost, first of all; informal at the end of the day, when all is said and done.

fundamentals plural noun **basics**, essentials, rudiments, foundations, basic principles, first principles, preliminaries; crux, heart of the matter, essence, core, heart, base, bedrock; informal nuts and bolts, nitty-gritty, brass tacks, ABC.

funeral noun **burial**, interment, entombment, committal, inhumation, laying to rest; cremation.

funereal adjective **sombre**, gloomy, mournful, melancholy, lugubrious, sepulchral, miserable, doleful, woeful, sad, sorrowful, cheerless, joyless, bleak, dismal, depressing, dreary.
– OPPOSITES cheerful.

fungus noun **mushroom**, toadstool; mould, mildew.

> **WORD LINKS**
> **mycology** the scientific study of fungi
> **fungicide** a chemical that destroys fungi

funnel verb *money was funnelled back into Europe:* **channel**, feed, direct, convey, move, pass; pour, filter.
• noun *smoke poured from the ship's funnels:* **chimney**, flue.

funny adjective **1** *a very funny film:* **amusing**, humorous, witty, comic, comical, droll, facetious, jocular, jokey; hilarious, hysterical, riotous, uproarious; entertaining, diverting, sparkling, scintillating; silly, farcical, slapstick; informal side-splitting, rib-tickling, laugh-a-minute, wacky, zany, waggish, off the wall, a scream, rich, priceless. **2** *a funny coincidence:* **strange**, peculiar, odd, queer, weird, bizarre, curious, freakish, freak, quirky; mysterious, mystifying, puzzling, perplexing; unusual, uncommon, anomalous, irregular, abnormal, exceptional, singular, out of the ordinary, extraordinary; Brit. informal, dated rum. **3** *there's something funny about him:* **suspicious**, suspect, dubious, untrustworthy, questionable; informal shady, fishy; Brit. informal dodgy.
– OPPOSITES serious, unsurprising, trustworthy.

fur noun **hair**, wool; coat, fleece, pelt.

furious adjective **1** *he was furious when we told him:* **enraged**, infuriated, irate, incensed, raging, incandescent, fuming, ranting, raving, seething, beside yourself, outraged; informal mad, hopping mad, wild, livid, boiling, apoplectic, on the warpath, foaming at the mouth, steamed up, in a paddy, fit to be tied; literary wrathful. **2** *a furious debate:* **heated**, hot, passionate, fiery; fierce, vehement, violent, wild, tumultuous, turbulent, tempestuous, stormy, acrimonious.
– OPPOSITES calm.

furnish verb **1** *the bedrooms are elegantly furnished:* **fit out**, appoint, outfit; Brit. informal do out. **2** *they furnished us with waterproofs:* **supply**, provide, equip, issue, kit out, present, give; informal fix up.

furniture noun **furnishings**, effects; Law chattels; informal stuff, things.

furore noun **commotion**, uproar, outcry, fuss, upset, brouhaha, palaver, pother, agitation, pandemonium, disturbance, hubbub, rumpus, tumult, turmoil; stir, excitement; informal song and dance, to-do, hoo-ha, hullabaloo, ballyhoo, kerfuffle, stink; Brit. informal flap, carry-on.

furrow noun **1** *furrows in a ploughed field:* **groove**, trench, rut, trough, channel. **2** *the furrows on either side of her mouth:* **wrinkle**, line, crease, crinkle, crow's foot.
• verb *his brow furrowed:* **wrinkle**, crease, line, crinkle, pucker, screw up, scrunch up.

furry adjective **hairy**, downy, fleecy, soft, fluffy, fuzzy, woolly.

further adverb *further, this gave him an alibi:* **furthermore**, moreover, what's more, also, additionally, in addition, besides, as well, too, to boot, on top of that, over and above that, into the bargain, by the same token.
• adjective **1** *the further side of the field:* **more distant**, remoter, outer, farther; far, other, opposite. **2** *I need further information:* **additional**, more, extra, supplementary; new, fresh.
• verb *an attempt to further his career:* **promote**, advance, forward, develop, facilitate, aid, assist, help, help along, boost, encourage.
– OPPOSITES impede.

furthermore adverb **moreover**, further, what's more, also, additionally, in addition, besides, as well, too, on top of that, over and above that, into the bargain, by the same token.

furthest adjective **most distant**, most remote, remotest, farthest, furthermost, farthermost; outlying, outer, outermost, extreme, uttermost.
– OPPOSITES nearest.

furtive adjective **secretive**, secret, surreptitious, clandestine, hidden, covert, conspiratorial, cloak-and-dagger, backstairs; sly, sneaky, under-the-table; informal hush-hush, shifty.
– OPPOSITES open.

f

fury noun **1** *she exploded with fury:* **rage**, anger, wrath, outrage, temper; indignation, umbrage, annoyance, exasperation; literary ire. **2** *the fury of the storm:* **ferocity**, fierceness, violence, turbulence, tempestuousness, savagery; severity, intensity, vehemence, force, forcefulness, power, strength.

fuse verb **1** *a band which fuses rap with rock:* **combine**, amalgamate, put together, join, unite, marry, blend, merge, meld, mingle, integrate, intermix, intermingle, synthesize; coalesce, compound, alloy. **2** *metal fused to coloured glass:* **bond**, stick, bind, weld, solder. **3** (Brit.) *a light had fused:* **short-circuit**, stop working, trip; informal go, blow.
–OPPOSITES separate.

fusion noun **blend**, combination, amalgamation, union, marrying, bonding, merging, melding, mingling, integration, intermingling, synthesis.

fuss noun **1** *what's all the fuss about?* **excitement**, agitation, stir, commotion, confusion, disturbance, brouhaha, uproar, furore, palaver, storm in a teacup; bother; informal hoo-ha, to-do, ballyhoo, song and dance, performance, pantomime, kerfuffle; Brit. informal carry-on. **2** *they settled in with very little fuss:* **bother**, trouble, inconvenience, effort, exertion, labour; informal hassle. **3** *he didn't put up a fuss:* **protest**, complaint, objection.
• verb *he was still fussing about his clothes:* **worry**, fret, be anxious, be agitated, make a big thing out of; make a mountain out of a molehill; informal be in a tizzy, be in a stew, make a meal of; Brit. informal flap.

fussy adjective **1** *he's very fussy about what he eats:* **finicky**, particular, fastidious, discriminating, selective; hard to please, difficult, exacting, demanding; faddish; informal pernickety, choosy, picky; Brit. informal faddy; N. Amer. informal persnickety. **2** *a fussy bridal gown:* **over-elaborate**, ornate, fancy, overdone; busy, cluttered.

fusty adjective **1** *the room smelt fusty:* **stale**, musty, dusty; stuffy, airless, unventilated; damp, mildewed. **2** *a fusty conservative:* **old-fashioned**, out of date, outdated, behind the times, antediluvian, backward-looking; fogeyish; informal square, out of the ark.
–OPPOSITES fresh.

futile adjective **fruitless**, vain, pointless, useless, ineffectual, ineffective, to no effect, of no use, in vain, to no avail, unavailing; unsuccessful, failed, thwarted; unproductive, unprofitable, abortive; impotent, hollow, empty, forlorn, idle, hopeless.
–OPPOSITES useful.

futility noun **fruitlessness**, pointlessness, uselessness, ineffectiveness, inefficacy; failure, unprofitability; hollowness, emptiness, forlornness, hopelessness.

future noun **1** *we made plans for the future:* **time to come**, time ahead; what lies ahead. **2** *her future lay in acting:* **destiny**, fate, fortune; prospects, chances.
–OPPOSITES past.
• adjective **1** *a future date:* **later**, to come, following, ensuing, succeeding, subsequent, coming. **2** *his future wife:* **to be**, destined; intended, planned, prospective.
■ **in future** from now on, after this, from this day forward, hence, henceforward, subsequently, in time to come; formal hereafter.

fuzz noun *the soft fuzz on his cheeks:* **hair**, down; fur, fluff.

fuzzy adjective **1** *her fuzzy hair:* **frizzy**, fluffy, woolly; downy, soft. **2** *a fuzzy picture:* **blurry**, blurred, indistinct, unclear, out of focus, misty. **3** *a fuzzy concept:* **imprecise**, unfocused, nebulous; ill-defined, indefinite, vague, hazy, loose, woolly. **4** *my mind was fuzzy:* **confused**, muddled, addled, fuddled, befuddled, groggy, disoriented, disorientated, mixed up; foggy, bleary.

Gg

gabble verb **jabber**, babble, prattle, rattle, drivel, twitter; Brit. informal waffle, rabbit, chunter, witter.

gadget noun **appliance**, device, machine, apparatus, instrument, implement, tool, utensil, contrivance, contraption, mechanism, invention, gimmick; informal gizmo, widget.

gaffe noun **blunder**, mistake, error, slip, faux pas, indiscretion, impropriety, miscalculation, solecism; informal slip-up, howler, boo-boo; Brit. informal boob, bloomer, clanger; N. Amer. informal blooper, goof.

gag[1] verb **1** *the government tried to gag its critics:* **silence**, muzzle, mute, suppress, stifle; censor, curb, check, restrain, restrict. **2** *the stench made her gag:* **retch**, heave.

gag[2] noun (informal) *he told a few gags:* **joke**, jest, witticism, quip, pun, double entendre; informal crack, wisecrack, one-liner, funny.

gain verb **1** *he gained a scholarship:* **obtain**, get, secure, acquire, come by, procure, attain, achieve, earn, win, capture, clinch, pick up, carry off; informal land, net, bag, scoop, wangle, swing, walk away/off with. **2** *they stood to gain from the deal:* **profit**, make money, benefit, do well out of; informal make a killing. **3** *she gained weight:* **put on**, increase in. **4** *they were gaining on us:* **catch up with**, catch someone up, catch, close in on, near, approach.
– OPPOSITES lose.

gainful adjective **profitable**, paid, well paid, remunerative, lucrative, moneymaking; rewarding, fruitful, worthwhile, useful, productive, constructive, beneficial, advantageous, valuable.

gait noun **walk**, step, stride, pace, tread, way of walking; bearing, carriage; Brit. deportment.

gala noun **fete**, fair, festival, carnival, pageant, jubilee, jamboree, party, celebration.

galaxy noun **1** *a distant galaxy:* **star system**; constellation. **2** *a galaxy of TV's biggest stars:* **host**, multitude, array, gathering, assemblage, assembly, company, group.

gale noun **1** *a howling gale:* **wind**, high wind, hurricane, tornado, cyclone, whirlwind; storm, squall, tempest, typhoon; N. Amer. windstorm; informal burster, buster. **2** *gales of laughter:* **peal**, howl, hoot, shriek, scream, roar; outburst, burst, fit, paroxysm.

gall[1] noun *she had the gall to ask for money:* **effrontery**, impudence, impertinence, cheek, cheekiness, insolence, audacity, temerity, presumption, cockiness, nerve, shamelessness, disrespect, bad manners; informal brass neck, face, chutzpah; Brit. informal sauce; N. Amer. informal sass.

gall[2] verb *it galled him to have to sit in silence:* **irritate**, annoy, vex, anger, infuriate, exasperate, irk, pique, nettle, put out, displease, rankle, antagonize; informal aggravate, peeve, miff, rile, needle, bug, hack off, get up someone's nose, get someone's goat, get someone's back up, get someone's dander up, drive mad/crazy, drive round the bend/twist, drive up the wall; Brit. informal wind up, nark, get on someone's wick, give someone the hump; N. Amer. informal tee off, tick off.

gallant adjective **1** *his gallant comrades:* **brave**, courageous, valiant, bold, plucky, daring, fearless, intrepid, heroic, stout-hearted;

informal gutsy, spunky. **2** *her gallant companion:* **chivalrous**, gentlemanly, courteous, polite, attentive, respectful, gracious, considerate, thoughtful.
– OPPOSITES cowardly, discourteous.

gallantry noun **bravery**, courage, courageousness, valour, pluck, nerve, daring, boldness, fearlessness, heroism, stout-heartedness, mettle, grit; informal guts, spunk; Brit. informal bottle; N. Amer. informal moxie.

gallery noun **1** *the National Gallery:* **art gallery**, museum. **2** *they sat up in the gallery:* **balcony**, circle, upper circle; informal gods. **3** *a long gallery with doors along each side:* **passage**, passageway, corridor, walkway, arcade.

g

galling adjective **annoying**, irritating, vexing, vexatious, infuriating, maddening, irksome, provoking, exasperating, trying, tiresome, troublesome, bothersome, displeasing, disagreeable; informal aggravating.

gallop verb **rush**, race, run, sprint, bolt, dart, dash, career, charge, shoot, hurtle, hare, fly, speed, zoom, streak; informal tear, belt, pelt, scoot, zip, whip, hotfoot it, leg it; Brit. informal bomb, go like the clappers; N. Amer. informal barrel.
– OPPOSITES amble.

galvanize verb **jolt**, shock, startle, impel, stir, spur, prod, urge, motivate, stimulate, electrify, excite, rouse, arouse, awaken; invigorate, fire, animate, vitalize, energize, exhilarate, thrill, dynamize, inspire; N. Amer. light a fire under; informal give someone a shot in the arm.

gambit noun **stratagem**, scheme, plan, tactic, manoeuvre, move, course of action, device; machination, ruse, trick, ploy; Brit. informal wheeze, wangle.

gamble verb **1** *he started to gamble:* **bet**; Brit. informal punt, have a flutter. **2** *investors are gambling that the pound will fall:* **take a chance**, take a risk; N. Amer. take a flyer; informal stick your neck out, go out on a limb; Brit. informal chance your arm.
• noun *I took a gamble and it paid off:* **risk**, chance, leap in the dark; pot luck.

gambol verb **frolic**, frisk, cavort, caper, skip, dance, romp, prance, leap, hop, jump, spring, bound, bounce; play.

game noun **1** *the children invented a new game:* **pastime**, diversion, entertainment, amusement, distraction, recreation, sport, activity. **2** *we haven't lost a game all season:* **match**, contest, fixture, meeting; tie, play-off. **3** *he's in the banking game:* **business**, profession, occupation, trade, industry, line of work; informal racket.
• adjective *I need a bit of help—are you game?* **willing**, prepared, ready, disposed; eager, keen, enthusiastic.

gamut noun **range**, spectrum, span, scope, sweep, compass, area, breadth, reach, extent, catalogue, scale; variety.

gang noun **1** *a gang of teenagers:* **band**, group, crowd, pack, horde, throng, mob, herd, swarm, troop; company, gathering; informal posse, bunch, gaggle, load. **2** (informal) *John's one of our gang:* **circle**, set, group, clique, in-crowd, coterie, lot, ring; informal crew. **3** *a gang of workmen:* **crew**, team, group, squad, shift, detachment, unit.
■ **gang up** conspire, cooperate, work together, act together, combine, join forces, team up, get together, unite, ally.

gangling, **gangly** adjective **lanky**, rangy, tall, thin, skinny, spindly, stringy, bony, angular, scrawny, spare; awkward, uncoordinated, ungainly, gawky, inelegant, graceless, ungraceful.
– OPPOSITES squat.

gangster noun **hoodlum**, racketeer, thug, villain, criminal; Mafioso; informal mobster, crook; N. Amer. informal hood.

gaol noun (Brit. dated). See **JAIL**.

gaoler noun (Brit. dated). See **JAILER**.

gap noun **1** *a gap in the shutters:* **opening**, aperture, space, breach, chink, slit, crack, crevice, cranny, cavity, hole, orifice, perforation, break, fracture, rift, rent, fissure, cleft, divide. **2** *a gap between meetings:* **pause**, intermission, interval, interlude, break, breathing space, breather, respite, hiatus; N. Amer. recess. **3** *a gap in our records:*

omission, blank, lacuna. **4** *the gap between rich and poor:* **chasm**, gulf, rift, split, separation, breach; contrast, difference, disparity, divergence, imbalance.

gape verb **1** *he gaped at her in disbelief:* **stare**, stare open-mouthed, goggle, gaze, ogle; informal gawk, rubberneck; Brit. informal gawp. **2** *a jacket which gaped at every seam:* **open**, yawn; part, split.

gaping adjective **cavernous**, yawning, wide, broad; vast, huge, enormous, immense.

garbage (N. Amer.) noun **1** *the garbage was taken away:* **rubbish**, refuse, waste, detritus, litter, junk, scrap; scraps, scourings, leftovers, remains; N. Amer. trash. **2** *what he says is garbage:* **rubbish**, nonsense, balderdash, claptrap, twaddle; dross; informal hogwash, baloney, tripe, bilge, bull, bunk, poppycock, rot, piffle, dreck; Brit. informal tosh, codswallop, cobblers, stuff and nonsense.

garble verb **mix up**, muddle, jumble, confuse, obscure, distort.

garden noun park, estate, grounds.
■ **lead someone up the garden path** (informal) deceive, mislead, delude, hoodwink, dupe, trick, beguile, take in, fool, pull the wool over someone's eyes, gull; informal con, pull a fast one on, string along, take for a ride, put one over on.

WORD LINKS
horticultural relating to gardens and gardening

gargantuan adjective **huge**, enormous, vast, gigantic, giant, massive, colossal, mammoth, immense, mighty, monumental, mountainous, titanic, towering, tremendous, king-size, prodigious; informal mega, monster, whopping, humongous, jumbo; Brit. informal ginormous.
– OPPOSITES tiny.

garish adjective **gaudy**, lurid, loud, harsh, glaring, showy, glittering, brassy, brash; tasteless, vulgar; informal flash, flashy, tacky.
– OPPOSITES drab.

garland noun **wreath**, ring, circle, crown.
• verb **festoon**, wreathe, swathe, hang; adorn, deck, bedeck, array.

garment noun **item of clothing**; (**garments**) clothes, clothing, dress, garb, outfit, costume, attire; informal get-up, rig-out, gear, togs, duds; N. Amer. informal threads; formal apparel.

garner verb **gather**, collect, accumulate, amass, get together, assemble.

garnish verb **decorate**, adorn, ornament, trim, dress, embellish.
• noun **decoration**, adornment, ornament, embellishment, enhancement, finishing touch.

garrison noun *the English garrison had left:* **troops**, militia, soldiers, forces; force, detachment, unit.
• verb *troops were garrisoned in York:* **station**, post, deploy, assign; base, site, place, position; billet.

g

garrulous adjective **talkative**, loquacious, voluble, verbose, chatty, gossipy; effusive, expansive, forthcoming, conversational, communicative; informal mouthy, gabby, having the gift of the gab; Brit. informal able to talk the hind legs off a donkey.
– OPPOSITES taciturn.

gash noun **laceration**, cut, wound, injury, slash, tear; slit, split, rip, rent; scratch; Medicine lesion.
• verb **lacerate**, cut, wound, injure, hurt, slash, tear, gouge, puncture, slit, split, rend; scratch.

gasp verb **1** *I gasped in surprise:* **catch your breath**, gulp. **2** *he fell on the ground, gasping:* **pant**, puff, puff and blow, wheeze, breathe hard/heavily, choke, fight for breath.
• noun *a gasp of dismay:* **gulp**; exclamation, cry.

gate noun **1** *wooden gates:* **barrier**, turnstile. **2** *she went through the gate:* **gateway**, doorway, entrance, exit; door, portal; N. Amer. entryway.

gather verb **1** *we gathered in the hotel lobby:* **congregate**, assemble, meet, collect, come/get together, convene, muster, rally, converge.
2 *he gathered his family together:* **summon**, call together, bring together, assemble, convene, rally, round up, muster, marshal. **3** *knick-knacks she had gathered over the years:* **collect**, accumulate, amass, garner, accrue. **4** *I gather he's a footballer:* **understand**, believe, be led to believe, conclude, deduce, infer, assume, take it, surmise; hear, learn, discover. **5** *her dress was*

gathered at the waist: **pleat**, pucker, tuck, fold, ruffle.
–OPPOSITES disperse.

gathering noun **1** *she addressed the gathering:* **assembly**, meeting, convention, rally, council, congress; congregation, audience, crowd, group, throng, mass, multitude; informal get-together. **2** *the gathering of information:* **collecting**, collection, garnering, amassing, accumulation, accrual.

gauche adjective **awkward**, gawky, inelegant, graceless, ungraceful, ungainly, maladroit, inept; unsophisticated, uncultured, uncultivated, unrefined.
–OPPOSITES elegant, sophisticated.

g

gaudy adjective **garish**, lurid, loud, glaring, harsh, showy, glittering, brassy, ostentatious; tasteless, vulgar, unattractive; informal flash, flashy, tacky.
–OPPOSITES drab, tasteful.

gauge noun **1** *the temperature gauge:* **meter**, measure; indicator, dial, scale, display. **2** *an important gauge of economic activity:* **measure**, indicator, barometer, point of reference, guide, guideline, touchstone, yardstick, benchmark, criterion, test. **3** *guitar strings of different gauges:* **size**, diameter, thickness; bore, calibre.
• verb **1** *astronomers can gauge the star's brightness:* **measure**, calculate, compute, work out, determine, ascertain; count, weigh, quantify, put a figure on. **2** *it is hard to gauge how effective the ban was:* **assess**, evaluate, determine, estimate, appraise, weigh up, get the measure of, judge, guess; informal size up.

gaunt adjective **haggard**, drawn, thin, lean, skinny, spindly, spare, bony, angular, raw-boned, pinched, hollow-cheeked, scrawny, scraggy, as thin as a rake, cadaverous, skeletal, emaciated, skin and bone; wasted, withered; informal like a bag of bones.
–OPPOSITES plump.

gauzy adjective **translucent**, transparent, sheer, see-through, fine, delicate, flimsy, filmy, gossamer, diaphanous, wispy, thin, light, floaty, insubstantial.
–OPPOSITES opaque, thick.

gawky adjective **awkward**, ungainly, gangling, gauche, maladroit, clumsy, inelegant, uncoordinated, graceless, ungraceful; unsophisticated, unconfident.
–OPPOSITES graceful.

gay adjective **1** *gay men and women:* **homosexual**, lesbian. **2** (dated) *she had a gay disposition and a pretty face:* **cheerful**, cheery, merry, jolly, carefree, jovial, glad, happy, joyful, exuberant, animated, lively, vivacious, buoyant, bouncy, bubbly, perky, effervescent, playful; informal chirpy. **3** (dated) *gay checked curtains:* **bright**, brightly coloured, vivid, vibrant; multicoloured; flamboyant, showy, gaudy.

gaze verb **stare**, gape, goggle, eye, look, study, scrutinize, take a good look; ogle, leer; informal gawk, rubberneck; Brit. informal gawp; N. Amer. informal eyeball.
• noun **stare**, fixed look, gape; regard, inspection, scrutiny.

gazebo noun **summer house**, pavilion, belvedere.

gear noun (informal) **1** *his fishing gear:* **equipment**, apparatus, paraphernalia, articles, appliances; tools, utensils, implements, instruments; stuff, things; kit, rig, tackle; trappings, appurtenances, accoutrements, regalia; Brit. informal clobber, gubbins. **2** *I'll go back to my hotel and pick up my gear:* **belongings**, possessions, effects, paraphernalia, bits and pieces, bits and bobs, bags, baggage. **3** *the best designer gear:* **clothes**, clothing, garments, outfits, attire, garb; dress, wear; informal togs, duds, get-up; Brit. informal clobber, kit; N. Amer. informal threads; formal apparel.

gel, jell verb **1** *leave the mixture to gel:* **set**, stiffen, solidify, thicken, harden. **2** *things started to gel very quickly:* **take shape**, fall into place, come together, work out; crystallize.

gelatinous adjective **glutinous**, viscous; sticky, gluey, slimy; informal gooey.

gem noun **1** *rubies and other gems:* **jewel**, gemstone, precious stone. **2** *this recording contains some real gems:* **masterpiece**, tour de force, pièce de résistance; pearl, treasure, wonder.

genealogy noun **lineage**, line of descent, family tree, bloodline; pedigree, ancestry, heritage, parentage, family, stock, blood, roots.

general adjective **1** *the general opinion was that prices would fall:* **widespread**, common, prevailing, popular, public, mainstream, extensive, universal, wide. **2** *a general pay increase:* **comprehensive**, overall, across the board, blanket, umbrella, mass, wholesale, sweeping, broad-ranging, inclusive; universal, global, worldwide, nationwide. **3** *this is not the general practice:* **usual**, customary, habitual, traditional, normal, conventional, typical, standard, regular; familiar, accepted, prevailing, routine, run-of-the-mill, established, everyday, ordinary, common. **4** *a general description:* **broad**, imprecise, inexact, rough, loose, approximate, unspecific, vague, woolly, indefinite; N. Amer. informal ballpark.
– OPPOSITES restricted, localized, exceptional, specific.

generality noun **generalization**, general statement, general principle, sweeping statement; abstraction.

generally adverb **1** *summers were generally hot:* **normally**, in general, as a rule, by and large, more often than not, almost always, mainly, mostly, for the most part, predominantly, on the whole; usually, habitually, customarily, typically, ordinarily, commonly. **2** *the idea was generally accepted:* **widely**, commonly, extensively, universally, popularly.

generate verb **cause**, give rise to, lead to, result in, bring about, create, make, produce, engender, spawn, precipitate, prompt, provoke, trigger, spark off, stir up, induce, promote, foster.

generation noun **1** *people of the same generation:* **age**, age group, peer group; demographic. **2** *the generation of new ideas:* **creation**, production, initiation, origination, inception. **3** *the next generation of computers:* **crop**, batch, wave, range.

generic adjective **1** *a generic term:* **general**, common, collective, non-specific, inclusive, all-encompassing, broad, comprehensive, blanket, umbrella. **2** *generic drugs:* **unbranded**, non-proprietary.
– OPPOSITES specific.

generosity noun **1** *the generosity of our host:* **liberality**, lavishness, magnanimity, munificence, open-handedness, unselfishness; kindness, benevolence, altruism, charity, big-heartedness, goodness. **2** *the generosity of the portions:* **abundance**, plentifulness, lavishness, liberality, largeness, size.

generous adjective **1** *she is generous with money:* **liberal**, lavish, magnanimous, giving, open-handed, bountiful, unselfish, ungrudging, free, indulgent. **2** *a generous amount of food and drink:* **lavish**, plentiful, copious, ample, liberal, large, great, abundant, profuse, bumper, prolific; informal a gogo, galore.
– OPPOSITES mean, selfish, meagre.

genesis noun **origin**, source, root, beginning, start.

genial adjective **friendly**, affable, cordial, amiable, warm, easy-going, approachable, sympathetic; good-natured, good-humoured, cheerful; neighbourly, hospitable, companionable, sociable, convivial, outgoing, gregarious; informal chummy, pally; Brit. informal matey.
– OPPOSITES unfriendly.

genius noun **1** *the world knew of his genius:* **brilliance**, intelligence, intellect, ability, cleverness, brains. **2** *he has a genius for organization:* **talent**, gift, flair, aptitude, facility, knack, bent, ability, expertise, capacity, faculty; strength, forte, brilliance. **3** *he is a genius:* **brilliant person**, gifted person, mastermind, Einstein, intellectual, brain; prodigy; informal egghead, bright spark; Brit. informal brainbox, clever clogs; N. Amer. informal brainiac.
– OPPOSITES stupidity, dunce.

genocide noun **mass murder**, massacre; annihilation, extermination, elimination, liquidation, eradication, butchery; ethnic cleansing, holocaust.

genre noun **category**, class, classification, group, set, list; type, sort, kind, variety, style, model, school, ilk.

genteel adjective **refined**, respectable, well mannered, courteous,

polite, proper, correct, seemly; well bred, cultured, sophisticated, ladylike, gentlemanly, dignified, gracious; affected; Brit. informal posh.
– OPPOSITES uncouth.

gentle adjective **1** *his manner was gentle:* **kind**, tender, sympathetic, considerate, understanding, compassionate, benevolent; humane, lenient, merciful, clement; mild, placid, serene, sweet-tempered. **2** *a gentle breeze:* **light**, soft. **3** *a gentle slope:* **gradual**, slight, easy.
– OPPOSITES brutal, strong, steep.

g

gentleman noun **man**; nobleman; informal gent.

gentlemanly adjective **chivalrous**, gallant, honourable, noble, courteous, polite, gracious, considerate, thoughtful; well bred.
– OPPOSITES rude.

genuine adjective **1** *a genuine Picasso:* **authentic**, real, actual, original, bona fide, true, veritable; attested, undisputed; informal pukka, the real McCoy, the real thing, kosher; Austral./NZ informal dinkum. **2** *a very genuine person:* **sincere**, honest, truthful, straightforward, direct, frank, candid, open; artless, natural, unaffected; informal straight, upfront, on the level; N. Amer. informal on the up and up.
– OPPOSITES bogus, insincere.

genus noun **type**, sort, kind, genre, style, variety, category, class; breed, family.

germ noun **1** *this detergent kills germs:* **microbe**, microorganism, bacillus, bacterium, virus; informal bug. **2** *the germ of an idea:* **start**, beginning, seed, embryo, bud, root, rudiments; origin, source, potential; core, nucleus, kernel, essence.

WORD LINKS

germicide a substance that destroys germs

germane adjective **relevant**, pertinent, applicable, apposite; connected, related.
– OPPOSITES irrelevant.

germinate verb **1** *the grain is allowed to germinate:* **sprout**, shoot, bud, spring up; develop, grow. **2** *the idea began to germinate:* **develop**, take root, grow, emerge, evolve, mature, expand, advance, progress.

gestation noun **pregnancy**, incubation; development, maturation.

gesticulate verb **gesture**, signal, motion, wave, sign.

gesticulation noun **gesturing**, gesture, hand movement, signals, signs; wave, indication; body language.

gesture noun **1** *a gesture of surrender:* **signal**, sign, motion, indication, gesticulation. **2** *a symbolic gesture:* **action**, act, deed, move.
• verb *he gestured to her:* **signal**, motion, gesticulate, wave, indicate, sign; beckon.

get verb **1** *he managed to get tickets for the game:* **acquire**, obtain, come by, receive, gain, earn, win, come into, be given; buy, purchase, procure, secure; gather, collect, pick up, hook, net, land; achieve, attain; informal get your hands on, get your mitts on, get hold of, grab, bag, score. **2** *your tea's getting cold:* **become**, grow, turn, go. **3** *she's gone to get the children:* **fetch**, collect, call for, pick up; bring, deliver, convey, ferry, transport. **4** *the chairman gets £650,000 a year:* **earn**, be paid, take home, bring in, make, receive, collect, gross; informal pocket, bank, rake in, net, bag. **5** *did the police get him?* **apprehend**, catch, arrest, capture, seize; informal collar, grab, nab, nail, run in, bust, pick up, pull in; Brit. informal nick. **6** *she got flu:* **catch**, contract, develop, fall ill with; succumb to, go/come down with, fall victim to, be struck down with, be afflicted by/with; Brit. go down with; informal take ill with; N. Amer. informal take sick with. **7** *I didn't get what he said:* **hear**, catch, make out; understand follow, take in, comprehend, grasp; informal get the drift of, figure out. **8** *they got to the restaurant at 9.00:* **arrive**, reach, come, make it, turn up, appear, enter, present yourself, come along, show your face; informal show up, roll in/up. **9** *we got her to agree:* **persuade**, induce, prevail on, influence; talk into, cajole into. **10** *I'll get supper:* **prepare**, cook, make; informal fix, rustle up; Brit. informal knock up.
– OPPOSITES give, send, take, leave.
■ **get something across** communicate, get over, impart, convey, transmit, make clear, express. **get**

ahead prosper, flourish, thrive, do well; succeed, make it, advance, make good; informal go places, make the big time. **get away** escape, run away/off, break out, break free, break loose, bolt, flee, take flight, make off, take off, decamp, abscond, make a run for it; informal skedaddle, do a disappearing act, scarper, leg it; Brit. informal do a bunk, do a runner. **get someone down** depress, sadden, dishearten, demoralize, discourage, crush, weigh down, oppress; upset, distress. **get by** manage, cope, survive, exist, subsist, muddle through/along, scrape by, make ends meet, make do, keep the wolf from the door; informal make out. **get off** alight, step off, dismount, descend, disembark, leave, exit. **get on 1** *we got on the train:* board, enter, step aboard, climb on, mount, ascend, catch. **2** *how are you getting on?* fare, manage, progress, get along, do, cope, survive; informal make out. **3** *they don't really get on:* be friendly, be compatible, get along; agree, see eye to eye, be on the same wavelength; informal hit it off. **get out of** evade, dodge, shirk, avoid, escape, sidestep; informal duck out of, wriggle out of, cop out of; Austral./NZ informal duck-shove. **get something over**. See **GET SOMETHING ACROSS**. **get round someone** cajole, persuade, wheedle, coax, prevail on, win over, bring round, sway, beguile, charm, inveigle, influence; informal sweet-talk, soft-soap, butter up, twist someone's arm.

getaway noun **escape**, breakout, bolt for freedom, flight; disappearance, vanishing act; Brit. informal flit.

get-together noun **party**, meeting, gathering; informal do, bash; Brit. informal rave-up, knees-up, jolly, bunfight, beano.

ghastly adjective **1** *a ghastly murder:* **terrible**, frightful, horrible, grim, awful; horrifying, shocking, appalling; dreadful, horrendous, monstrous, gruesome, grisly. **2** (informal) *a ghastly building:* **unpleasant**, objectionable, disagreeable, distasteful, awful, terrible, dreadful, frightful, detestable, insufferable, vile, hideous; informal horrible, horrid.
–OPPOSITES pleasant, charming.

ghost noun **spectre**, phantom, wraith, spirit, presence; apparition; informal spook.

ghostly adjective **spectral**, ghostlike, phantom, wraithlike; unearthly, unnatural, supernatural; insubstantial, shadowy; eerie, weird, uncanny; frightening, spine-chilling, hair-raising, blood-curdling, terrifying, chilling, sinister; informal creepy, scary, spooky.

ghoulish adjective **macabre**, grisly, gruesome, grotesque, ghastly; unhealthy, unwholesome.

giant noun **colossus**, titan, behemoth, man mountain.
• adjective **huge**, colossal, massive, enormous, gigantic, mammoth, vast, immense, monumental, mountainous, titanic, towering, king-size, gargantuan; informal mega, monster, whopping, humongous, jumbo, hulking, bumper; Brit. informal ginormous.
–OPPOSITES miniature.

gibber verb **prattle**, babble, ramble, drivel, jabber, gabble, burble, twitter, mutter, mumble; informal blabber, blather; Brit. informal witter, chunter.

gibberish noun **nonsense**, rubbish, balderdash, blather; informal drivel, gobbledegook, mumbo-jumbo, tripe, hogwash, baloney, bilge, bull, bunk, guff, eyewash, piffle, twaddle, poppycock; Brit. informal cobblers, codswallop, double Dutch, tosh; N. Amer. informal garbage, blathers.

gibe noun & verb. See **JIBE**.

giddiness noun **dizziness**, light-headedness; faintness, unsteadiness, shakiness, wobbliness; informal wooziness.

giddy adjective **1** *she felt giddy:* **dizzy**, light-headed, faint, weak, vertiginous; unsteady, shaky, wobbly, reeling; informal woozy. **2** *she was young and giddy:* **flighty**, silly, frivolous, skittish, irresponsible, flippant; feather-brained, scatty, thoughtless, heedless, carefree; informal dippy; N. Amer. informal ditzy.
–OPPOSITES steady, sensible.

gift noun **1** *a generous gift:* **present**, handout, donation, offering, bonus, award, endowment; tip, gratuity; informal prezzie, freebie, perk. **2** *a gift* *for music:* **talent**, flair, aptitude, facility, knack, bent, ability, expertise, capacity, capability, faculty; endowment, strength, genius, brilliance, skill.

gifted adjective **talented**, skilful, skilled, accomplished, expert, consummate, masterly, first-rate, able, apt, adept, proficient; intelligent, clever, bright, brilliant; precocious; informal crack, top-notch, ace.
–OPPOSITES inept.

gigantic adjective **huge**, enormous, vast, giant, massive, colossal, mammoth, immense, monumental, mountainous, titanic, towering, king-size, gargantuan; informal mega, monster, whopping, humongous, jumbo, hulking, bumper; Brit. informal ginormous.
–OPPOSITES tiny.

giggle verb & noun **titter**, snigger, snicker, chuckle, chortle, laugh.

gimmick noun **publicity device**, stunt, contrivance, scheme, stratagem, ploy; informal shtick.

gingerly adverb **cautiously**, carefully, with care, warily, charily, delicately; hesitantly, timidly.
–OPPOSITES recklessly.

girl noun **1** *a five-year-old girl:* schoolgirl; Scottish & N. English lass, lassie. See also CHILD. **2** *he's talking to some girls at the bar:* **young woman**, young lady, miss; Scottish lass, lassie; Irish colleen; informal chick; Brit. informal bird; N. Amer. informal gal, broad, dame; Austral./NZ informal sheila; literary maid, damsel; old use wench.

girlfriend noun **sweetheart**, lover, partner, significant other, girl, woman; fiancée; informal steady; Brit. informal bird; N. Amer. informal squeeze; dated lady, lady-love, betrothed.

girlish adjective **youthful**, childish, immature; feminine.

gist noun **essence**, substance, central theme, heart of the matter, nub, kernel, marrow, meat, crux; thrust, drift, sense, meaning, significance, import; informal nitty-gritty.

give verb **1** *he gave them £2000:* **present with**, provide with, supply with, furnish with; hand, offer, proffer; award, grant, bestow, accord, confer, make over; donate, contribute, put up. **2** *can I give him a message?* **convey**, pass on, impart, communicate, transmit; send, deliver, relay; tell. **3** *a baby given into their care:* **entrust**, commit, consign, assign; formal commend. **4** *he gave his life for them:* **sacrifice**, give up, relinquish; devote, dedicate. **5** *he gave her time to think:* **allow**, permit, grant, accord; offer. **6** *this leaflet gives our opening times:* **show**, display, set out, indicate, detail, list. **7** *garlic gives flavour:* **produce**, yield, afford, impart, lend. **8** *he gave a party:* **organize**, arrange, lay on, throw, host, hold, have, provide. **9** *Dominic gave a bow:* **perform**, execute, make, do. **10** *she gave a shout:* **utter**, let out, emit, produce, make. **11** *he gave Harry a black eye:* **administer**, deliver, deal, inflict, impose. **12** *the door gave:* **give way**, cave in, collapse, break, fall apart; bend, buckle.
–OPPOSITES receive, take.
•noun *there isn't enough give in the jacket:* **elasticity**, flexibility, stretch; slack, play.
■ **give someone away** betray, inform on; informal split on, rat on, peach on, do the dirty on, blow the whistle on, sell down the river; Brit. informal grass on, shop; N. Amer. informal rat out, finger. **give in** capitulate, concede defeat, admit defeat, give up, surrender, yield, submit, back down, give way, defer, relent, throw in the towel/sponge. **give something off** emit, produce, send out, throw out; discharge, release, exude, vent. **give something out** distribute, issue, hand out, pass round, dispense; dole out, dish out, mete out; allocate, allot, share out. **give up**. See GIVE IN. **give something up** stop, cease, discontinue, desist from, abstain from, cut out, renounce, forgo; resign from, stand down from; informal quit, kick, swear off, leave off, pack in, lay off; Brit. informal jack in.

give and take noun **compromise**, concession; cooperation, reciprocity, teamwork, interplay.

given adjective *a given number of years:* **specified**, stated, designated, set, particular, specific; prescribed, agreed, appointed, prearranged, predetermined.
–OPPOSITES unspecified.

• preposition *given the issue's complexity, a summary is difficult:* **considering**, in view of, bearing in mind, in the light of; assuming.
■ **given to** prone, liable, inclined, disposed, predisposed.

glad adjective **1** *I'm really glad you're coming:* **pleased**, happy, delighted, thrilled, overjoyed, cock-a-hoop, elated; gratified, grateful, thankful; informal tickled pink, over the moon; Brit. informal chuffed; N. English informal made up; Austral. informal wrapped. **2** *I'd be glad to help:* **willing**, eager, happy, pleased, delighted; ready, prepared.
– OPPOSITES dismayed, reluctant.

gladden verb **delight**, please, make happy, elate; cheer up, hearten, buoy up, give someone a lift, uplift; gratify; informal tickle someone pink, buck up.
– OPPOSITES sadden.

gladly adverb **with pleasure**, happily, cheerfully; willingly, readily, eagerly, freely, ungrudgingly.

glamorous adjective **1** *a glamorous woman:* **beautiful**, elegant, chic, stylish, fashionable; informal classy, glam. **2** *a glamorous lifestyle:* **exciting**, glittering, glossy, colourful, exotic; informal ritzy, glitzy, jet-setting.
– OPPOSITES dowdy, dull.

glamour noun **1** *she had undeniable glamour:* **beauty**, allure, elegance, chic, style; charisma, charm, magnetism. **2** *the glamour of TV:* **allure**, attraction, fascination, charm, magic, romance, mystique, spell; excitement, thrill; glitter, the bright lights; informal glitz, glam.

glance verb **1** *Rachel glanced at him:* **look**, peek, peep; glimpse; informal have a gander; Brit. informal take a dekko, have a shufti, have a butcher's. **2** *I glanced through the report:* **read quickly**, scan, skim, leaf, flick, flip, thumb, browse; dip into. **3** *a bullet glanced off the wall:* **ricochet**, rebound, be deflected, bounce.
• noun *he took a glance at his watch:* **peek**, peep, look, glimpse; informal gander; Brit. informal dekko, shufti, butcher's.

glare verb *she glared at him:* **scowl**, glower, look daggers, frown, lour, give someone a black look; informal give someone a dirty look.
• noun **1** *a cold glare:* **scowl**, glower, stare, frown, black look; informal dirty look. **2** *the glare of the lights:* **blaze**, dazzle, shine, beam; brilliance.

glaring adjective **1** *glaring lights:* **dazzling**, blinding, blazing, strong, harsh. **2** *a glaring omission:* **obvious**, conspicuous, unmistakable, inescapable, unmissable, striking; flagrant, blatant, outrageous, gross; overt, patent, transparent, manifest; informal standing/sticking out like a sore thumb.
– OPPOSITES soft, minor.

glass noun **1** *a glass of water:* **tumbler**. **2** *we sell china and glass:* **glassware**, crystal, crystalware.

> **WORD LINKS**
> **vitreous** relating to glass
> **glazier** a glass-fitter

glasses plural noun **spectacles**; N. Amer. eyeglasses; informal specs.

glasshouse noun **greenhouse**, hothouse, conservatory.

glassy adjective **1** *the glassy surface of the lake:* **smooth**, mirror-like, gleaming, shiny, glossy, vitreous; slippery, icy; calm, still, flat. **2** *a glassy stare:* **expressionless**, glazed, blank, vacant, fixed, motionless; emotionless, impassive, lifeless, wooden.
– OPPOSITES rough, expressive.

glaze verb **1** *pastry glazed with caramel:* **cover**, coat, brush; ice, frost. **2** *his eyes glazed over:* **become glassy**, go blank; mist over, film over.
• noun *a cake with an apricot glaze:* **coating**, topping; icing, frosting.

gleam verb **shine**, glimmer, glint, glitter, shimmer, sparkle, twinkle, flicker, wink, glisten, flash; literary glister.
• noun **1** *a gleam of light:* **glimmer**, glint, shimmer, twinkle, sparkle, flicker, flash; beam, ray, shaft. **2** *the gleam of brass:* **shine**, lustre, gloss, sheen; glint, glitter, glimmer, sparkle; brilliance, radiance, glow.

glean verb **obtain**, get, take, draw, derive, extract, cull, garner, gather; learn, find out.

glee noun **delight**, pleasure, happiness, joy, gladness; amusement,

g

mirth, merriment; excitement; triumph, jubilation, relish, satisfaction, gratification.
– OPPOSITES disappointment.

gleeful adjective **delighted**, pleased, joyful, happy, glad, overjoyed; amused, mirthful, merry, exuberant; cock-a-hoop, jubilant; informal over the moon.

glib adjective **slick**, pat, plausible; smooth-talking, fast-talking, silver-tongued, smooth; disingenuous, insincere, facile, shallow, superficial, flippant; informal flip, sweet-talking.
– OPPOSITES sincere.

glide verb **1** *a gondola glided past:* **slide**, slip, sail, float, drift, flow; coast, freewheel, roll; skim, skate. **2** *seagulls glide over the waves:* **soar**, wheel, plane; fly.

glimmer verb *moonlight glimmered on the lawn:* **gleam**, shine, glint, flicker, shimmer, glisten, glow, twinkle, sparkle, glitter, wink, flash; literary glister.
• noun **1** *a glimmer of light:* **gleam**, glint, flicker, shimmer, glow, twinkle, sparkle, flash, ray. **2** *a glimmer of hope:* **gleam**, ray, trace, sign, suggestion, hint.

glimmer noun **1** *a glimmer of light:* **gleam**, glint, flicker, shimmer, glow, twinkle, ray. **2** *a glimmer of hope:* **gleam**, flicker, ray, trace, sign, suggestion, hint.

glimpse noun *a glimpse of her face:* **brief look**; glance, peek, peep.
• verb *he glimpsed a figure:* **catch sight of**, notice, discern, spot, spy, sight, pick out, make out; Brit. informal clock.

glint verb **shine**, catch the light, glitter, sparkle, twinkle, shimmer, flash; literary glister.
• noun **glitter**, gleam, sparkle, twinkle, glimmer, flash.

glisten verb **shine**, sparkle, twinkle, glitter, glimmer, shimmer, wink, flash; literary glister.

glitter verb *crystal glittered in the candlelight:* **shine**, sparkle, twinkle, glint, shimmer, glimmer, wink, flash, catch the light; literary glister.
• noun *the glitter of light on the water:* **sparkle**, twinkle, glint, shimmer, glimmer, flicker, flash.

gloat verb *she gloated over his humiliation:* **delight in**, relish, revel in, rejoice in, glory in, exult in, triumph over, crow over.

global adjective **1** *the global economy:* **worldwide**, international, world, intercontinental. **2** *a global view of the problem:* **comprehensive**, overall, general, all-inclusive, all-encompassing, universal, blanket; broad.

globe noun **1** *every corner of the globe:* **world**, earth, planet. **2** *the sun is a globe:* **sphere**, orb, ball.

gloom noun **1** *she peered into the gloom:* **darkness**, dark, dimness, blackness, shadows, shade. **2** *his gloom deepened:* **despondency**, depression, dejection, melancholy, unhappiness, sadness, glumness, gloominess, misery, sorrow, woe, wretchedness; despair, pessimism, hopelessness.
– OPPOSITES light, happiness.

gloomy adjective **1** *a gloomy room:* **dark**, shadowy, sunless, dim, sombre, dingy, dismal, dreary, murky, unwelcoming, cheerless, comfortless, funereal. **2** *Joanna looked gloomy:* **despondent**, downcast, downhearted, dejected, dispirited, disheartened, discouraged, demoralized, crestfallen; depressed, desolate, low, sad, unhappy, glum, melancholy, miserable, fed up, mournful, forlorn, morose; informal blue, down in the mouth, down in the dumps. **3** *gloomy forecasts about the economy:* **pessimistic**, depressing, downbeat, disheartening, disappointing; unfavourable, bleak, bad, black, sombre, grim, cheerless, hopeless.
– OPPOSITES bright, cheerful, optimistic.

glorify verb **1** *the film does not glorify war:* **celebrate**, glamorize, romanticize, idealize, ennoble, dignify; promote, elevate, applaud. **2** *they gather to glorify God:* **praise**, worship, pay homage to, honour, give thanks to, extol, exalt, revere, venerate.

glorious adjective **wonderful**, marvellous, magnificent, superb, sublime, spectacular, lovely, fine, delightful; informal super, great,

stunning, fantastic, terrific, tremendous, sensational, heavenly, divine, gorgeous, fabulous, fab, awesome, ace; Brit. informal smashing; literary wondrous.
– OPPOSITES undistinguished.

glory noun **1** *a sport that won him glory:* **renown**, fame, prestige, honour, distinction, kudos, eminence, acclaim, praise; celebrity, recognition, reputation. **2** *a house restored to its former glory:* **magnificence**, splendour, grandeur, majesty, greatness, nobility; opulence, beauty, elegance. **3** *the glories of Vermont:* **wonder**, beauty, delight, marvel.
– OPPOSITES shame, obscurity, modesty.
• verb *we gloried in our independence:* **take pleasure in**, revel in, rejoice in, delight in; relish, savour; be proud of; informal get a kick out of, get a thrill out of.

gloss noun *hair with a healthy gloss:* **shine**, sheen, lustre, gleam, patina, brilliance, shimmer.
• verb *he tried to gloss over his problems:* **conceal**, cover up, hide, disguise, mask, veil; shrug off, brush aside, play down, minimize, understate, make light of; informal brush under the carpet.

glossy adjective **1** *a glossy wooden floor:* **shiny**, gleaming, lustrous, brilliant, glistening, satiny, smooth; polished, lacquered, glazed. **2** *a glossy magazine:* **expensive**, high-quality; stylish, fashionable, glamorous; Brit. upmarket, coffee-table; informal classy, glitzy.

glove noun **mitten**, mitt, gauntlet.

glow verb **1** *lights glowed from the windows:* **shine**, gleam, glimmer, flicker, flare. **2** *a fire glowed in the hearth:* **smoulder**, burn. **3** *she glowed with pride:* **tingle**, thrill; beam.
• noun *the glow of the fire:* **radiance**, light, gleam, glimmer, incandescence; warmth, heat.

glower verb **scowl**, glare, look daggers, frown, lour, give someone a black look; informal give someone a dirty look.

glowing adjective **1** *glowing coals:* **bright**, shining, radiant, incandescent, luminous; smouldering. **2** *his glowing cheeks:* **rosy**, pink, red, flushed, blushing; radiant, blooming, ruddy, burning. **3** *glowing colours:* **vivid**, vibrant, bright, brilliant, rich, intense, strong, radiant, warm. **4** *a glowing report:* **complimentary**, favourable, enthusiastic, admiring, rapturous; fulsome.

glue noun *a tube of glue:* **adhesive**, gum, paste.
• verb **1** *the planks were glued together:* **stick**, gum, paste; fix. **2** (informal) *she was glued to the television:* **be riveted to**, be gripped by, be hypnotized by, be mesmerized by.

glum adjective **gloomy**, downcast, downhearted, dejected, despondent, crestfallen, disheartened; depressed, desolate, unhappy, doleful, melancholy, miserable, mournful, forlorn, in the doldrums, morose; informal fed up, blue, down in the mouth, down in the dumps.
– OPPOSITES cheerful.

glut noun **surplus**, excess, surfeit, superfluity, over-abundance, superabundance.
– OPPOSITES dearth.
• verb **cram**, overfill, overload, over-supply, saturate, flood, inundate, deluge, swamp; informal stuff.

glutinous adjective **sticky**, viscous; thick, treacly; informal gooey.

glutton noun **gourmand**; informal pig, greedy guts; Brit. informal gannet.

gluttonous adjective **greedy**, voracious, insatiable, wolfish; informal piggish.

gluttony noun **greed**, greediness, overeating, gourmandizing; informal piggishness.

gnarled adjective **1** *a gnarled tree trunk:* **knobbly**, knotty, knotted, gnarly, lumpy, bumpy; twisted, bent, crooked, distorted, contorted. **2** *gnarled hands:* **twisted**, bent, misshapen; arthritic; rough, wrinkled, wizened.

gnash verb **grind**, grate, rasp, grit.

gnaw verb **1** *the dog gnawed at a bone:* **chew**, champ, chomp, bite, munch, crunch; nibble, worry. **2** *the doubts gnawed at her:* **nag**, plague, torment, torture, trouble, distress, worry, haunt, oppress, burden, hang over, bother, fret; niggle.

go verb **1** *go to the main entrance:* **move**, proceed, make your way, advance, progress, pass; travel, journey. **2** *it's time to go:* **leave**, depart, take yourself off, go away, withdraw, absent yourself, make an exit, exit; set off, start out, get under way, be on your way; decamp, retreat, retire, make off, clear out, run off/away, flee; Brit. make a move; informal make tracks, push off, beat it, take off, skedaddle, scram, split, scoot; Brit. informal sling your hook. **3** *the road goes to London:* **extend**, stretch, reach; lead. **4** *the money will go to charity:* **be given**, be donated, be granted, be presented, be awarded; be devoted. **5** *all our money had gone:* **be used up**, be spent, be exhausted, be consumed, be drained, be depleted. **6** *everything went well:* **turn out**, work out, develop, come out; result, end up; informal pan out. **7** *his hair had gone grey:* **become**, get, turn, grow. **8** *those colours don't go:* **match**, harmonize, blend, be suited, be complementary, coordinate, be compatible. **9** *my car won't go:* **function**, work, run, operate. **10** *the ceiling's gone:* **collapse**, give way, fall down, cave in, crumble, disintegrate.

– OPPOSITES arrive, come, return.

• **noun** (informal) **attempt**, try, effort, bid; informal shot, stab, crack, bash, whirl, whack.

■ **go about** set about, begin, embark on, start, commence, address yourself to, get down to, get to work on, get going on, undertake; approach, tackle, attack; informal get cracking on. **go along with** agree to, fall in with, comply with, cooperate with, acquiesce in, assent to, follow; submit to, yield to, defer to. **go away**. See **GO** verb sense 2. **go back on** renege on, break, fail to honour, default on, repudiate, retract; do a U-turn; Brit. do an about-turn; informal cop out of. **go down 1** *the ship went down:* sink, founder. **2** *interest rates are going down:* decrease, get lower, fall, drop, decline; plummet, plunge, slump. **3** *his name will go down in history:* be remembered, be recorded, be commemorated. **go for 1** *I went for the tuna:* choose, pick, opt for, select, plump for, decide on. **2** *the man went for her:* attack, assault, hit, strike, beat up, assail, set upon, rush at, lash out at; informal lay into; Brit. informal have a go at, duff up; N. Amer. informal beat up on. **3** *he goes for older women:* be attracted to, like, fancy; prefer, favour, choose; informal have a thing about. **go in for** take part in, participate in, engage in, get involved in, join in, enter into, undertake; practise, pursue; espouse, adopt, embrace. **go into** investigate, examine, enquire into, look into, research, probe, explore, delve into; consider, review, analyse. **go off 1** *the bomb went off:* explode, detonate, blow up. **2** (Brit.) *the milk's gone off:* go bad, go stale, go sour, turn, spoil, go rancid. **go on 1** *the lecture went on for hours:* last, continue, carry on, run on, proceed; endure, persist; take. **2** *she went on about her plans for the future:* ramble, rattle, chatter, prattle, gabble, blather, twitter; informal yak; Brit. informal witter, rabbit, natter, waffle, chunter; N. Amer. informal run off at the mouth. **3** *I'm not sure what went on:* happen, take place, occur, transpire; N. Amer. informal go down. **go over 1** *go over the figures carefully:* examine, study, scrutinize, inspect, look at, scan, check; analyse, appraise, review. **2** *we are going over our lines:* rehearse, practise, read through, run through. **go round 1** *the wheels were going round:* spin, revolve, turn, rotate, whirl. **2** *a nasty rumour's going round:* be spread, be circulated, be put about, circulate. **go through 1** *the terrible things she has gone through:* undergo, experience, face, suffer, be subjected to, live through, endure, brave, bear, tolerate, withstand, put up with, cope with, weather. **2** *he went through hundreds of pounds:* spend, use up, run through, get through; waste, squander, fritter away. **3** *he went through her bag:* search, look, hunt, rummage, rifle. **4** *I went through the report:* examine, study, scrutinize, inspect, look over, scan, check. **go under** go bankrupt, cease trading, go into receivership, go into liquidation, be wound up, be shut down; fail; informal go broke, go to the wall, go belly up, fold.

goad verb **provoke**, spur, prod, egg on, hound, badger, rouse, stir, move, stimulate, motivate, prompt, induce, encourage, urge, inspire; impel, pressure.

go-ahead (informal) noun **permission**, consent, leave, licence, clearance; authorization, assent, agreement, approval, endorsement, sanction, blessing, the nod; informal the thumbs up, the OK, the green light.
• adjective **enterprising**, resourceful; progressive, pioneering, forward-looking, enlightened; enthusiastic, ambitious, entrepreneurial; adventurous, dynamic; informal go-getting.

goal noun **objective**, aim, end, target, design, intention, intent, plan, purpose; holy grail; ambition, aspiration, wish, dream, desire, hope.

goat noun

> **WORD LINKS**
> **caprine** relating to goats

gobble verb **guzzle**, bolt, gulp, devour, wolf, cram, gorge yourself on; informal tuck into, put away, demolish, polish off, shovel down, pig out on; Brit. informal scoff, shift; N. Amer. informal scarf, snarf.

gobbledegook noun (informal) **gibberish**, nonsense, rubbish, mumbo-jumbo; N. Amer. garbage; Brit. informal double Dutch.

go-between noun **intermediary**, middleman, agent, broker, liaison, linkman, contact; negotiator, interceder, intercessor, mediator.

goblet noun **wine glass**, chalice; glass, beaker, tumbler, cup.

goblin noun **hobgoblin**, gnome, dwarf, troll, imp, elf, brownie, fairy, pixie, leprechaun.

god noun **1** *a gift from God:* **the Lord**, the Almighty, the Creator; Allah, Jehovah, Yahweh. **2** *the gods and goddesses of Greek mythology:* **deity**, divine being, divinity, immortal.

> **WORD LINKS**
> **divine** relating to God or a god
> **theology** the study of God and religious belief

godforsaken adjective **wretched**, miserable, dreary, dismal, depressing, grim, cheerless, bleak, desolate, gloomy; deserted, neglected, isolated, remote.

godless adjective *a godless society:* **atheistic**, unbelieving, agnostic, sceptical, heretical, faithless, irreligious, ungodly, impious, profane; heathen, idolatrous, pagan; old use infidel.

godly adjective **religious**, devout, pious, reverent, believing, God-fearing, saintly, holy, prayerful, churchgoing.
– OPPOSITES irreligious.

godsend noun **boon**, blessing, bonus, plus, benefit, advantage, help, aid, asset; stroke of luck; informal perk; formal perquisite.
– OPPOSITES curse.

g

goggle verb **stare**, gape, gaze, ogle; informal gawk, rubberneck; Brit. informal gawp.

goings-on plural noun **events**, happenings, affairs, business; mischief, misbehaviour, misconduct, funny business; informal monkey business, hanky-panky, shenanigans; Brit. informal jiggery-pokery, carry-on; N. Amer. informal monkeyshines.

golden adjective **1** *long golden hair:* **blonde**, blond, yellow, fair, flaxen. **2** *a golden opportunity:* **excellent**, fine, superb, splendid; special, unique; favourable, opportune, promising, bright, full of promise; advantageous, profitable, valuable, providential.
– OPPOSITES dark.

gone adjective **1** *he wasn't gone long:* **away**, absent, off, out; missing, unavailable. **2** *those days are gone:* **past**, over, done with, finished, ended; forgotten, dead and buried. **3** *the milk's all gone:* **used up**, consumed, finished, spent.
– OPPOSITES present, here.

good adjective **1** *a good product:* **fine**, superior, quality; excellent, superb, outstanding, magnificent, exceptional, marvellous, wonderful, first-rate, first-class, sterling; informal great, A1, ace, terrific, fantastic, fabulous, fab, top-notch, class, awesome, wicked; informal, dated capital; Brit. informal smashing, brilliant, brill; Austral. informal beaut, bonzer; Brit. informal, dated spiffing, top hole. **2** *a good driver:* **capable**, able, proficient, adept, adroit, accomplished, skilful, skilled, talented, masterly, expert; informal great, mean, wicked, nifty, ace; N. Amer. informal crackerjack. **3** *the play had good reviews:* **favourable**, complimentary, approving, positive, enthusiastic; rapturous, glowing. **4** *we've had some good news:* **pleasing**, pleasant, welcome, gratifying, encouraging. **5** *a good person:* **virtuous**, righteous, upright, upstanding, moral, ethical, principled; exemplary, law-abiding, blameless, guiltless, honourable, reputable, decent, respectable, noble, trustworthy; whiter than white, saintly, saintlike, angelic; informal squeaky clean. **6** *the children are good at school:* **well behaved**, obedient, dutiful, polite, courteous, respectful. **7** *it was good of you to come:* **kind**, kind-hearted, generous, charitable, magnanimous, gracious; altruistic, unselfish, selfless. **8** *a good friend:* **close**, intimate, dear, bosom, special, best, firm, valued, treasured; loving, devoted, loyal, faithful, constant, reliable, dependable, trustworthy, trusty, true, unfailing, staunch. **9** *we had a good time:* **enjoyable**, pleasant, agreeable, pleasurable, delightful, great, nice, lovely; amusing; informal super, fantastic, fabulous, fab, terrific, grand; Brit. informal brilliant, brill, smashing; N. Amer. informal peachy; Austral./NZ informal beaut, bonzer. **10** *a good time to call:* **convenient**, suitable, appropriate, fitting, fit; opportune, timely, favourable, advantageous, expedient. **11** *milk is good for you:* **wholesome**, healthy, healthful, nourishing, nutritious, nutritional, beneficial, salubrious. **12** *a good reason:* **valid**, genuine, authentic, legitimate, sound, bona fide; convincing, persuasive, telling, potent, cogent, compelling. **13** *good weather:* **fine**, fair, dry; bright, clear, sunny, cloudless; calm, windless; warm, mild, balmy, clement, pleasant, nice. **14** *a good number of them:* **considerable**, sizeable, substantial, significant; goodly, fair, reasonable; plentiful, abundant, great, large, generous; informal tidy.

– OPPOSITES bad, poor, wicked.

• **noun 1** *issues of good and evil:* **virtue**, righteousness, goodness, morality, integrity, rectitude; honesty, truth, honour, probity. **2** *it's all for your good:* **benefit**, advantage, profit, gain, interest, welfare, well-being.

– OPPOSITES wickedness, disadvantage.

■ **for good** *those days are gone for good:* forever, permanently, for always, for evermore, for ever and ever, for eternity; informal for keeps.

goodbye exclamation **farewell**, adieu, au revoir, ciao, auf Wiedersehen, adios; informal bye; Brit. informal cheers, cheerio, ta-ta; informal, dated toodle-oo, toodle-pip.

good-for-nothing adjective *a good-for-nothing layabout:* **feckless**, lazy, idle, shiftless, indolent, slothful; useless, worthless, incompetent, ne'er-do-well.

good-humoured adjective **genial**, affable, cordial, friendly, amiable, easy-going, approachable, good-natured, cheerful, cheery.

– OPPOSITES grumpy.

good-looking adjective **attractive**, beautiful, pretty, handsome, lovely, stunning, striking, arresting, gorgeous, prepossessing, fetching, captivating, bewitching, beguiling, charming, enchanting, appealing, delightful; sexy, seductive, alluring, tantalizing, irresistible, ravishing, desirable; Scottish & N. English bonny; informal fanciable, tasty, hot, easy on the eye, drop-dead gorgeous; Brit. informal fit; N. Amer. informal cute, foxy; Austral./NZ informal spunky; literary beauteous; old use comely, fair.

– OPPOSITES ugly.

good-natured adjective **amiable**, affable, friendly, warm-hearted, kind, considerate; understanding, sympathetic, easy-going, accommodating, obliging, helpful; Brit. informal decent.

– OPPOSITES malicious.

goodness noun *a belief in the basic goodness of mankind:* **virtue**, good, righteousness, morality, integrity, rectitude; honesty, truth, truthfulness, honour, nobility, decency; kindness, humanity, benevolence, goodwill; sympathy, compassion, care, concern, understanding, tolerance, generosity, charity, leniency, clemency, magnanimity.

goods plural noun **1** *he dispatched the goods:* **merchandise**, wares, stock,

g

commodities, produce, products, articles. **2** (Brit.) *most goods went by train:* **freight**, cargo.

good-tempered adjective **equable**, even-tempered, easy-going, mellow, mild, mild-mannered, calm, relaxed; amiable, affable, good-natured, pleasant, agreeable, likeable; well balanced, stable, level-headed, imperturbable, unruffled, unflustered, untroubled, cheerful, upbeat; informal laid-back.
– OPPOSITES grumpy.

goodwill noun **benevolence**, compassion, goodness, kindness, consideration, charity, thoughtfulness, decency, sympathy, understanding, neighbourliness.
– OPPOSITES hostility.

goose noun

> **WORD LINKS**
> **anserine** relating to geese

gore[1] noun **blood**; bloodshed, slaughter, carnage, butchery; violence.

gore[2] verb **pierce**, stab, stick, impale, spear.

gorge noun **ravine**, canyon, gully, defile, couloir; chasm, gulf; N. English clough, gill; N. Amer. gulch, coulee. ■ **gorge yourself on** feast on, devour, wolf down, guzzle, gobble; informal scoff, stuff yourself with, pig out on.

gorgeous adjective **1** *a gorgeous girl:* **good-looking**, attractive, beautiful, pretty, handsome, lovely, stunning, striking, arresting, fetching, captivating, charming, enchanting, appealing, delightful; sexy, seductive, alluring, irresistible, ravishing, desirable; Scottish & N. English bonny; informal fanciable, tasty, hot; Brit. informal fit; N. Amer. informal cute, foxy; Austral./NZ informal spunky; literary beauteous; old use comely, fair. **2** *a gorgeous view:* **spectacular**, splendid, superb, wonderful, grand, impressive, awe-inspiring, awesome, amazing, stunning, breathtaking, incredible; informal sensational, fabulous, fantastic. **3** *gorgeous decorations and costumes:* **resplendent**, magnificent, sumptuous, luxurious, elegant, opulent. **4** (informal) *gorgeous weather:* **excellent**, marvellous, superb, very good, first-rate, first-class, wonderful, magnificent, splendid; informal great, glorious, terrific, fantastic, fabulous, fab, ace; Brit. informal smashing, brilliant, brill; Austral./NZ informal bonzer.
– OPPOSITES ugly, drab, terrible.

gory adjective **grisly**, gruesome, violent, bloody, brutal, savage; ghastly, frightful, horrid, fearful, hideous, macabre, horrible, horrific.

gospel noun **1** *they preached the Gospel:* **Christianity**; the word of God, the New Testament. **2** *don't treat this as gospel:* **the truth**; fact, actual fact, a certainty.

gossamer adjective **gauzy**, fine, diaphanous, delicate, filmy, floaty, wispy, thin, light, insubstantial, flimsy; translucent, transparent, see-through, sheer.

gossip noun **1** *tell me all the gossip:* **news**, rumours; scandal, hearsay; informal dirt, buzz; Brit. informal goss; N. Amer. informal scuttlebutt. **2** *they went for a gossip:* **chat**, talk, conversation, chatter, heart-to-heart, tête-à-tête; informal jaw; Brit. informal natter, chinwag; N. Amer. informal gabfest; Austral./NZ informal yarn. **3** *she's such a gossip:* busybody, muckraker.
• verb *everyone was gossiping about their relationship:* **spread rumours**, tittle-tattle, tattle, talk, whisper, tell tales; informal dish the dirt.

gouge verb **scoop out**, hollow out, excavate; cut, dig, scrape, scratch.

gourmet noun **gastronome**, epicure, epicurean; connoisseur; informal foodie.

govern verb **1** *he governs the province:* **rule**, preside over, control, be in charge of; run, head, administer, manage, regulate, oversee, supervise. **2** *the rules governing social behaviour:* **determine**, decide, control, regulate, direct, rule, dictate, shape; affect.

government noun **administration**, executive, regime, authority, council; powers that be; cabinet, ministry.

governor noun **leader**, ruler, chief, head; premier, president, chancellor; administrator, principal, director, chairman/woman, chair, superintendent, commissioner, controller; informal boss.

gown noun **dress**, frock, robe.

grab verb **seize**, grasp, snatch, take hold of, grip, clasp, clutch; take; dive for, lunge for.
•noun **lunge**, snatch, dive.

grace noun **1** *the grace of a ballerina:* **elegance**, poise, gracefulness, finesse. **2** *he had the grace to apologize:* **courtesy**, decency, good manners, politeness, respect, tact. **3** *he fell from grace:* **favour**, approval, approbation, acceptance, esteem, regard, respect.
–OPPOSITES inelegance, effrontery, disfavour.
•verb **1** *the proceedings were graced by her presence:* **dignify**, distinguish, honour, ennoble. **2** *magnificent oil paintings graced the walls:* **adorn**, decorate, ornament, embellish; enhance, beautify, enrich, bedeck.

graceful adjective **elegant**, fluid, fluent, natural; agile, supple, nimble, light-footed.

graceless adjective **gauche**, maladroit, inept, awkward, unsure, unpolished, unsophisticated, uncultured, unrefined; clumsy, ungainly, ungraceful, inelegant, uncoordinated, gawky, gangling, bumbling; tactless, thoughtless, inconsiderate; informal cack-handed.

gracious adjective **1** *a gracious hostess:* **courteous**, polite, civil, well mannered; tactful, diplomatic; kind, considerate, thoughtful, obliging, accommodating, indulgent; hospitable. **2** *gracious buildings:* **elegant**, stylish, tasteful, graceful; comfortable, luxurious, sumptuous, opulent, grand, high-class; informal swanky, plush.
–OPPOSITES rude, crude.

gradation noun **1** *a gradation of ability:* **range**, scale, spectrum, compass, span; progression, hierarchy, ladder, pecking order. **2** *each pay band has a number of gradations:* **level**, grade, rank, position, stage, standard, rung, step, notch; class, stratum, group, grouping, set.

grade noun **1** *hotels within the same grade:* **category**, set, class, classification, grouping, group, bracket. **2** *his job is of the lowest grade:* **rank**, level, standing, position, class, status, order; step, rung, stratum, tier. **3** *the best grades in the school:* **mark**, score; assessment, evaluation, appraisal. **4** (N. Amer.) *the fifth grade:* **year**, form, class.
•verb **1** *eggs are graded by size:* **classify**, class, categorize, bracket, sort, group, arrange, pigeonhole; rank, evaluate, rate, value. **2** (N. Amer.) *the essays have been graded:* **assess**, mark, score, judge, evaluate, appraise.
■ **make the grade** (informal) come up to standard, come up to scratch, qualify, pass, pass muster, measure up; succeed, win through; informal be up to snuff, cut it, cut the mustard.

gradient noun **slope**, incline, hill, rise, ramp, bank; N. Amer. grade.

gradual adjective **1** *a gradual transition:* **slow**, measured, unhurried, cautious; piecemeal, step-by-step, little-by-little, bit-by-bit; progressive, continuous, steady. **2** *a gradual slope:* **gentle**, moderate, slight, easy.
–OPPOSITES abrupt, steep.

gradually adverb **slowly**, slowly but surely, cautiously, gently, gingerly; piecemeal, little by little, bit by bit, inch by inch, by degrees; progressively, systematically; regularly, steadily.

graduate verb **1** *he graduated last summer:* **qualify**, complete your degree. **2** *she graduated to serious drama:* **progress**, advance, move up. **3** *a thermometer graduated in Fahrenheit:* **calibrate**, mark off, measure out, grade.

graft noun *a skin graft:* **transplant**, implant.
•verb **1** *graft a bud on to the stem:* **affix**, join, insert, splice. **2** *tissue is grafted on to the cornea:* **transplant**, implant.

grain noun **1** *fields of grain:* **cereal**. **2** *a grain of corn:* **kernel**, seed. **3** *grains of sand:* **granule**, particle, speck; bit, piece. **4** *a grain of truth:* **trace**, hint, tinge, suggestion, shadow; bit, soupçon; ounce, iota, jot, whit, scrap, shred, crumb, fragment, morsel; informal smidgen, smidge, tad. **5** *the grain of the timber:* **texture**; weave, pattern.

grammatical adjective **1** *the grammatical structure of a sentence:*

syntactic, morphological; linguistic. **2** *a grammatical sentence:* **well formed**, correct, idiomatic; proper.

grand adjective **1** *a grand hotel:* **magnificent**, imposing, impressive, awe-inspiring, splendid, resplendent, majestic, monumental; palatial, stately, large; luxurious, sumptuous, lavish, opulent; Brit. upmarket; N. Amer. upscale; informal fancy, posh, plush, classy, swanky; Brit. informal swish. **2** *a grand scheme:* **ambitious**, bold, epic, big, extravagant. **3** *a grand old lady:* **august**, distinguished, illustrious, eminent, esteemed, honoured, venerable, dignified, respectable; pre-eminent, prominent, notable, renowned, celebrated, famous. **4** *the grand staircase:* **main**, principal, central, prime. **5** (informal) *you're doing a grand job:* **excellent**, very good, marvellous, splendid, first-class, first-rate, wonderful, outstanding, sterling, fine; informal superb, terrific, great, super, ace; Brit. informal smashing, brilliant, brill.
– OPPOSITES inferior, humble.

grandeur noun **splendour**, magnificence, impressiveness, glory, resplendence, majesty, greatness; stateliness, pomp, ceremony.

grandiose adjective **1** *the court's grandiose facade:* **magnificent**, impressive, grand, imposing, splendid, majestic, glorious, elaborate; palatial, stately, luxurious, opulent; informal plush, swanky, flash. **2** *a grandiose plan:* **ambitious**, bold, overambitious, extravagant, high-flown, flamboyant; informal over the top, OTT.
– OPPOSITES humble, modest.

grant verb **1** *he granted them leave of absence:* **allow**, accord, permit, afford, vouchsafe. **2** *he granted them £20,000:* **give**, award, bestow on, confer on, present with, provide with, endow with, supply with. **3** *I grant that the difference is slight:* **admit**, accept, concede, allow, appreciate, recognize, acknowledge, confess; agree.
– OPPOSITES refuse, deny.
• noun *a grant from the council:* **award**, allowance, subsidy, donation, contribution, handout, allocation, gift; scholarship, bursary, endowment.

granular adjective **powder**, powdered, powdery, grainy, granulated, gritty.

granule noun **grain**, particle, fragment, bit, crumb, morsel, speck.

grape noun

> **WORD LINKS**
> **viticulture**, **viniculture** the cultivation of grapevines

graph noun **chart**, diagram.

graphic adjective **1** *a graphic representation:* **visual**, pictorial, illustrative, diagrammatic; drawn. **2** *a graphic account:* **vivid**, explicit, detailed; powerful, colourful, lurid, shocking; realistic, descriptive, illustrative.
– OPPOSITES vague.
• noun (Computing) *add some graphics to your file:* **picture**, illustration, image; diagram, graph, chart.

grapple verb **1** *the police grappled with him:* **wrestle**, struggle, tussle; scuffle, battle. **2** *IT consultants are grappling with the problem:* **tackle**, confront, face, deal with, cope with, get to grips with.

grasp verb **1** *she grasped his hand:* **grip**, clutch, clasp, hold, clench; catch, seize, grab, snatch. **2** *he grasped the important points:* **understand**, comprehend, take in, perceive, see, apprehend, assimilate, absorb; informal get, catch on to, figure out, get your head around, take on board; Brit. informal twig, suss out. **3** *he grasped the opportunity:* **take advantage of**, act on; seize, leap at, snatch, jump at.
– OPPOSITES release, overlook.
• noun **1** *his grasp on her hand:* **grip**, hold; clutch, clasp. **2** *a prize lay within their grasp:* **reach**, scope, power, range; sights. **3** *a grasp of history:* **understanding**, comprehension, apprehension, awareness, grip, knowledge; mastery, command.

grasping adjective **avaricious**, acquisitive, greedy, rapacious, mercenary, materialistic; mean, miserly, parsimonious; informal tight-fisted, tight, stingy, money-grubbing; N. Amer. informal cheap.

grass noun **turf**; lawn, green; literary sward.
• verb (Brit. informal) *he grassed on them:* **inform**, tell; give away, betray, sell

out; informal split, blow the whistle, rat, squeal, do the dirty, stitch up, sell down the river; Brit. informal shop; N. Amer. informal finger.

grate verb **1** *grate the cheese into the sauce:* **shred**, grind, crumble, granulate. **2** *a sound of metal grating against metal:* **grind**, rub, rasp, scrape, jar, creak. **3** *the tune grates slightly:* **irritate**, set someone's teeth on edge, jar; annoy, nettle, chafe.

grateful adjective **thankful**, appreciative; indebted, obliged, obligated, in someone's debt, beholden.

gratification noun **satisfaction**, fulfilment, indulgence, relief, appeasement; pleasure, enjoyment.

gratify verb **1** *it gratified him to be seen with her:* **please**, gladden, make happy, delight, satisfy, thrill; informal tickle pink, give someone a buzz. **2** *he gratified his desires:* **satisfy**, fulfil, indulge, give in to, satiate, feed.
–OPPOSITES displease, frustrate.

grating[1] adjective **1** *a grating noise:* **scraping**, scratching, grinding, rasping. **2** *a grating voice:* **harsh**, raucous, strident, piercing, shrill, screechy; discordant, jarring.
–OPPOSITES harmonious, pleasing.

grating[2] noun *an iron grating:* **grid**, grate, grille, lattice, trellis.

gratis adverb **free**, without charge, for nothing, at no cost; informal on the house, for free.

gratitude noun **gratefulness**, thankfulness, thanks, appreciation, indebtedness; recognition, acknowledgement, credit.

gratuitous adjective **unjustified**, uncalled for, unwarranted, unprovoked, undue; indefensible, unjustifiable; needless, unnecessary, inessential, unmerited, groundless, senseless, wanton, indiscriminate; excessive, immoderate, inordinate, inappropriate.
–OPPOSITES necessary, paid.

grave[1] noun *she left flowers at the grave:* **burial place**, last resting place; tomb, sepulchre, vault, mausoleum, crypt.

grave[2] adjective **1** *a grave matter:* **serious**, important, weighty, profound, significant, momentous; critical, urgent, pressing; dire, terrible, awful, dreadful. **2** *the doctor looked grave:* **solemn**, serious, sober, unsmiling, grim, sombre; severe, stern, dour.
–OPPOSITES trivial, cheerful.

gravel noun **shingle**, grit, pebbles, stones.

gravelly adjective **1** *a gravelly beach:* **shingly**, pebbly, stony, gritty. **2** *his gravelly voice:* **husky**, gruff, throaty, deep, croaky, rasping, grating, harsh, rough.

gravestone noun **headstone**, tombstone, stone, monument, memorial.

graveyard noun **cemetery**, churchyard, burial ground, necropolis.

gravitate verb **move**, head, drift, be drawn, be attracted; tend, lean, incline.

gravity noun **1** *the gravity of the situation:* **seriousness**, importance, significance, weight, consequence, magnitude; acuteness, urgency; awfulness, dreadfulness. **2** *the gravity of his demeanour:* **solemnity**, seriousness, sombreness, sobriety, soberness, severity, grimness, dourness.

graze[1] verb *sheep grazed in the field:* **feed**, eat, crop, nibble, browse.

graze[2] verb **1** *he grazed his arm:* **scrape**, skin, scratch, chafe, scuff, rasp; cut, nick. **2** *his shot grazed the bar:* **touch**, brush, shave, skim, kiss, scrape, clip, glance off.
• noun **scratch**, scrape, abrasion, cut.

grease noun **oil**, fat; lubricant, lubrication.
• verb **lubricate**, oil.

greasy adjective **1** *greasy food:* **fatty**, oily, buttery. **2** *the pitch was very greasy:* **slippery**, slick, slimy, slithery, oily; informal slippy. **3** *a greasy little man:* **ingratiating**, obsequious, sycophantic, fawning, toadying, grovelling; effusive, gushing; unctuous, oily; informal smarmy, slimy.

great adjective **1** *a man of great courage:* **considerable**, substantial, significant; exceptional, extraordinary. **2** *a great expanse of water:* **large**, big, extensive, expansive, broad, wide, ample; vast, immense, huge, enormous, massive; informal humongous, whopping; Brit. informal ginormous. **3** *great writers:* **prominent**, eminent, distinguished,

illustrious, celebrated, acclaimed, admired, esteemed, renowned, notable, famous, well known; leading, top, major, principal. **4** *a great castle:* **magnificent**, imposing, impressive, awe-inspiring, grand, splendid, majestic. **5** *a great sportsman:* **expert**, skilful, skilled, adept, accomplished, talented, fine, masterly, master, brilliant, virtuoso, marvellous, outstanding, first class, superb; informal crack, ace, A1, class. **6** *a great fan of rugby:* **enthusiastic**, eager, keen, zealous, devoted, ardent, fanatical, passionate, dedicated, committed. **7** *we had a great time:* **enjoyable**, delightful, lovely; excellent, marvellous, wonderful, fine, splendid; informal terrific, fantastic, fabulous, fab, super, grand, cool; Brit. informal smashing, brilliant, brill; Austral./NZ informal bonzer, beaut.
– OPPOSITES little, small, minor, poor.

greatly adverb **very much**, considerably, substantially, appreciably, significantly, markedly, sizeably, seriously, materially, profoundly; enormously, vastly, immensely, tremendously, mightily, extremely, exceedingly.
– OPPOSITES slightly.

greatness noun **1** *a woman destined for greatness:* **eminence**, distinction; importance, significance; celebrity, fame, prominence, renown. **2** *his greatness as a writer:* **brilliance**, genius, prowess, talent, expertise, mastery, artistry, virtuosity, skill, proficiency; flair, finesse; calibre, distinction.

greed, **greediness** noun **1** *they are motivated by greed:* **avarice**, acquisitiveness, covetousness, rapacity; materialism, mercenariness. **2** *their greed for power:* **desire**, appetite, hunger, thirst, craving, longing, yearning, hankering; informal itch. **3** *her mouth watered with greed:* **gluttony**, hunger, voracity, self-indulgence.

greedy adjective **1** *a greedy eater:* **gluttonous**, ravenous, voracious, insatiable; informal piggish, piggy. **2** *a greedy property developer:* **avaricious**, acquisitive, covetous, grasping, materialistic, mercenary; informal money-grubbing, money-grabbing.

green adjective **1** *a green scarf:* olive green, pea green, emerald green, lime green, bottle green, Lincoln green, sea green. **2** *a green island:* **verdant**, grassy, leafy. **3** *Green issues:* **environmental**, ecological, conservation, eco-. **4** *a green alternative to diesel:* **environmentally friendly**, eco-friendly, carbon-neutral. **5** *green bananas:* **unripe**, immature. **6** *green recruits, fresh from college:* **inexperienced**, callow, raw, unseasoned, untried; ignorant; unsophisticated, unpolished; naive, innocent, unworldly; informal wet behind the ears.
– OPPOSITES barren, ripe, experienced.
• noun **1** *a canopy of green over the road:* **foliage**, greenery, plants, leaves, vegetation. **2** *the village green:* **lawn**, common; literary sward. **3** *Greens are against the bypass:* **environmentalist**, conservationist; informal eco-warrior, tree-hugger.

greenery noun **foliage**, vegetation, plants, green, leaves, undergrowth, plant life, flora; literary verdure.

greenhouse noun **hothouse**, glasshouse, conservatory.

greet verb **1** *she greeted him cheerily:* **address**, salute, hail; welcome, meet, receive. **2** *the decision was greeted with outrage:* **receive**, respond to, react to, take.

greeting noun **1** *he shouted a greeting:* **hello**, salutation, address; welcome; acknowledgement. **2** *birthday greetings:* **best wishes**, good wishes, congratulations, felicitations; compliments, regards, respects.
– OPPOSITES farewell.

gregarious adjective **sociable**, convivial, companionable, outgoing, clubbable.
– OPPOSITES unsociable.

grey adjective **1** *a grey suit:* silvery, gunmetal, slate, charcoal, smoky. **2** *his grey hair:* **white**, silver, hoary, grizzled. **3** *a grey day:* **cloudy**, overcast, dull, sunless, gloomy, dreary, dismal, sombre, bleak, murky. **4** *her face looked grey:* **ashen**, wan, pale, pasty, pallid, colourless, bloodless, white, waxen; sickly, peaky, drained, drawn, deathly. **5** *his grey existence:* **characterless**, colourless,

g

nondescript, flat, bland; dull, boring, tedious, monotonous; soulless. **6** *a grey area:* **ambiguous**, doubtful, unclear, uncertain, indefinite, open to question, debatable.

grid noun **1** *a metal grid:* **grating**, mesh, grille, gauze, lattice. **2** *the grid of streets:* **network**, matrix.

grief noun **sorrow**, misery, sadness, anguish, pain, distress, heartache, heartbreak, agony, woe, desolation; mourning, mournfulness, bereavement.
–OPPOSITES joy.
■ **come to grief** fail, meet with disaster, fall through, fall flat, founder; informal come unstuck, come a cropper, flop.

g

grief-stricken adjective **sorrowful**, sorrowing, heartbroken, broken-hearted, anguished, distressed, despairing, devastated, upset, inconsolable; mourning, grieving, mournful, bereaved.
–OPPOSITES joyful.

grievance noun **complaint**, criticism, objection, grumble, grouse; ill feeling, bad feeling, resentment, bitterness; informal gripe, beef.

grieve verb **1** *she grieved for her father:* **mourn**, sorrow; cry, sob, weep. **2** *it grieved me to leave her:* **sadden**, upset, distress, pain, hurt, wound, break someone's heart.
–OPPOSITES rejoice, please.

grievous (formal) adjective **serious**, severe, grave, bad, critical, dreadful, terrible, awful, crushing.
–OPPOSITES slight, trivial.

grim adjective **1** *his grim expression:* **stern**, forbidding, uninviting, unsmiling, dour, formidable, harsh, steely, flinty, stony. **2** *grim humour:* **black**, dark, bleak, cynical. **3** *grim secrets:* **dreadful**, ghastly, horrible, terrible, awful, appalling, frightful, shocking, grisly, gruesome, hideous, macabre; depressing, distressing, upsetting, worrying, unpleasant. **4** *a grim little hovel:* **bleak**, dismal, dingy, wretched, miserable, depressing, cheerless, joyless, gloomy, uninviting;. **5** *grim determination:* **resolute**, firm, determined, steadfast; obstinate, stubborn, unyielding, intractable, uncompromising, unshakeable, unrelenting, relentless, dogged, tenacious.
–OPPOSITES amiable, pleasant.

grimace noun *his mouth twisted into a grimace:* **scowl**, frown, rictus, sneer; wince.
• verb *Nina grimaced at him:* **scowl**, frown, sneer, glower; wince, pull a face.
–OPPOSITES smile.

grime noun **dirt**, smut, soot, dust, mud, filth, mire; informal **muck**; Brit. informal **gunge**.

grimy adjective **dirty**, grubby, mucky, soiled, stained, filthy, smutty, sooty, dusty, muddy; Brit. informal manky, grotty; Austral./NZ scungy.
–OPPOSITES clean.

grin verb **smile**, beam; smirk.
• noun **smile**, beam; smirk.
–OPPOSITES frown, scowl.

grind verb **1** *the ore is ground into powder:* **crush**, pound, pulverize, mill, crumble. **2** *one stone grinds against another:* **rub**, grate, scrape.
• noun *the daily grind:* **drudgery**, toil, labour, donkey work, exertion, chores, slog.
■ **grind someone down** oppress, crush, break someone's spirit.

grip verb **1** *she gripped the edge of the table:* **grasp**, clutch, hold, clasp, take hold of, clench, grab, seize, cling to; squeeze, press. **2** *a country gripped by civil war:* **afflict**, affect, take over, beset, rack, convulse. **3** *we were gripped by the drama:* **engross**, enthral, absorb, rivet, spellbind, hold spellbound, bewitch, fascinate, mesmerize.
–OPPOSITES release.
• noun **1** *a tight grip:* **grasp**, hold. **2** *the wheels lost their grip on the road:* **traction**, purchase, friction, adhesion. **3** *he was in the grip of an obsession:* **control**, power, hold, stranglehold, clutches, influence.
■ **come/get to grips with** deal with, cope with, handle, grasp, tackle, take on, grapple with, face, face up to, confront.

gripping adjective **engrossing**, enthralling, absorbing, riveting, captivating, spellbinding, bewitching, fascinating, compelling, mesmerizing; thrilling, exciting, action-packed, dramatic,

stimulating; informal unputdownable, page-turning.
– OPPOSITES boring.

grisly adjective **gruesome**, ghastly, frightful, horrid, horrifying, fearful, hideous, macabre, horrible, grim, awful, dreadful, terrible, horrific, shocking, appalling, abominable, loathsome, abhorrent, odious, monstrous.

gristly adjective **stringy**, sinewy, fibrous; tough, leathery, chewy.

grit noun **gravel**, pebbles, stones, shingle, sand; dust, dirt.

gritty adjective **sandy**, gravelly, pebbly, stony; powdery, dusty.

grizzled adjective **grey**, greying, silver, silvery, snowy, white, salt-and-pepper; grey-haired.

groan verb **1** *she groaned and rubbed her stomach:* **moan**, cry, wail, whimper. **2** *the wheels groaned under the strain:* **creak**; grate.
• noun **1** *a groan of anguish:* **moan**, cry, wail, whimper. **2** *the groan of the timbers:* **creaking**, creak, grating, grinding.

groggy adjective **dazed**, disoriented, disorientated, stupefied, befuddled, dizzy, muzzy, punch-drunk, unsteady, wobbly, weak, faint; informal dopey, woozy, not with it.

groom verb **1** *his hair was carefully groomed:* **brush**, comb, arrange, do; informal fix. **2** *they were groomed for stardom:* **prepare**, prime, condition, tailor; coach, train, drill, teach, school.
• noun *the bride and groom:* **bridegroom**.

groove noun **furrow**, channel, trench, trough, canal, hollow, indentation, rut, gutter, fissure.

grooved adjective **furrowed**, fluted, corrugated, ribbed, ridged.

grope verb **1** *she groped for her glasses:* **fumble**, scrabble, fish, ferret, rummage, feel, search, hunt. **2** (informal) *one of the men groped her:* **fondle**, touch; informal paw, maul, feel up, touch up.

gross adjective **1** (informal) *the place smelled gross:* **disgusting**, revolting, repulsive, foul, nasty, obnoxious, sickening, nauseating, stomach-churning; N. Amer. vomitous. **2** *a gross distortion of the truth:* **flagrant**, blatant, glaring, obvious, overt, naked, barefaced, shameless, brazen, patent, transparent, manifest, palpable; out and out, utter, complete. **3** *gross income:* **total**, full, overall, combined, aggregate; before tax.
– OPPOSITES pleasant, net.
• verb *he grosses over a million a year:* **earn**, make, bring in, take, get, receive, collect; informal rake in.

grotesque adjective **1** *a grotesque creature:* **malformed**, deformed, misshapen, distorted, twisted; ugly, monstrous, hideous, freakish, unnatural, abnormal, strange, odd, peculiar. **2** *grotesque mismanagement of funds:* **outrageous**, monstrous, shocking, appalling, preposterous; ridiculous, ludicrous, farcical, unbelievable, incredible.
– OPPOSITES normal.

grotto noun **cave**, cavern, hollow.

grouchy adjective **grumpy**, cross, irritable, bad-tempered, crotchety, crabby, cantankerous, tetchy, curmudgeonly, testy, waspish, prickly; informal snappy; Brit. informal narky, ratty; N. Amer. informal cranky.

ground noun **1** *she collapsed on the ground:* **floor**, earth, terra firma; informal deck. **2** *soggy ground:* **earth**, soil, turf; land, terrain. **3** *the team's home ground:* **stadium**, pitch, field, arena, track. **4** *the mansion's grounds:* **estate**, gardens, park, parkland, land, property, surroundings, territory. **5** *grounds for dismissal:* **reason**, cause, basis, foundation, justification, rationale, argument, premise, occasion, excuse, pretext, motive, motivation.
• verb *an assertion grounded on results of several studies:* **base**, found, establish, root, build, construct, form.

groundless adjective **baseless**, without basis, without foundation, ill-founded, unfounded, unsupported, uncorroborated, unproven, empty, idle, unsubstantiated, unwarranted, unjustified, unjustifiable.

groundwork noun **preliminary work**, preliminaries, preparations, spadework, legwork, donkey work; planning, arrangements, organization, homework; basics, essentials, fundamentals.

g

g

group noun **1** *the exhibits were divided into three groups:* **category**, class, classification, grouping, set, batch, type, sort, kind, variety, family, species, genus; grade, grading, rank. **2** *a group of tourists:* **crowd**, party, body, band, company, gathering, congregation, assembly, collection, cluster, flock, pack, troop, gang; informal bunch. **3** *a group within the party:* **faction**, division, section, clique, coterie, circle, set, ring, camp, bloc, caucus, fringe movement, splinter group. **4** *the women's group:* **association**, club, society, league, guild, circle, union. **5** *a small group of trees:* **cluster**, knot, collection, mass, clump. **6** *a folk group:* **band**, ensemble, act; informal line-up, combo, outfit.
• verb **1** *patients were grouped according to age:* **categorize**, classify, class, catalogue, sort, bracket, pigeonhole, grade, rate, rank. **2** *chairs were grouped round the table:* **place**, arrange, assemble, organize, range, line up, lay out. **3** *the two parties grouped together:* **unite**, join together, team up, join forces, get together, affiliate, combine; collaborate, work together, pull together, cooperate.

grouse verb *she groused about the food.* See COMPLAIN.
• noun *our biggest grouse was about the noise.* See COMPLAINT.

grove noun **copse**, wood, thicket, coppice; orchard, plantation; Brit. spinney.

grovel verb **1** *George grovelled at her feet:* **prostrate yourself**, lie, kneel, cringe. **2** *she was not going to grovel to him:* **be obsequious**, fawn on, kowtow, bow and scrape, toady, dance attendance on, ingratiate yourself with; informal crawl, creep, suck up to, lick someone's boots.

grow verb **1** *the boys had grown:* **get bigger**, get taller, increase in size, fill out. **2** *profits continue to grow:* **increase**, swell, multiply, snowball, mushroom, balloon, build up, mount up, pile up; informal skyrocket. **3** *the family business grew:* **expand**, extend, develop, progress; flourish, thrive, burgeon, prosper, succeed, boom. **4** *flowers grew among the rocks:* **sprout**, germinate, spring up, develop, bud, burst forth, bloom, flourish, thrive, run riot. **5** *he grew vegetables:* **cultivate**, produce, propagate, raise, rear; farm. **6** *Leonora grew bored:* **become**, get, turn, begin to feel.
– OPPOSITES shrink, decline.

growl verb **snarl**, bark, yap, bay.

grown-up adjective *she has two grown-up daughters:* **adult**, mature, of age; fully grown, full-grown.

growth noun **1** *population growth:* **increase**, expansion, proliferation, multiplication, enlargement, mushrooming, snowballing, rise, escalation, build-up. **2** *the growth of local enterprises:* **expansion**, extension, development, progress, advance, advancement, spread; rise, success, boom, upturn, upswing. **3** *the growth of plants:* **development**, growing, sprouting; blooming. **4** *a growth on his jaw:* **tumour**, malignancy, cancer; lump, swelling, nodule; cyst, polyp.
– OPPOSITES decrease, decline.

grub noun **larva**; maggot; caterpillar.

grubby adjective **dirty**, grimy, filthy, mucky, unwashed, stained, soiled, smeared, spotted; informal cruddy; Brit. informal manky, grotty.
– OPPOSITES clean.

grudge noun **grievance**, resentment, bitterness, rancour, dissatisfaction, ill will, animosity, antipathy, antagonism; informal a chip on your shoulder.

grudging adjective **reluctant**, unwilling, forced, half-hearted, unenthusiastic, hesitant; begrudging, resentful.
– OPPOSITES eager.

gruelling adjective **exhausting**, tiring, wearying, taxing, draining; demanding, exacting, difficult, hard, arduous, strenuous, laborious, back-breaking, harsh, severe, stiff, punishing, crippling; informal murderous, hellish; Brit. informal knackering.

gruesome adjective **grisly**, ghastly, frightful, horrid, horrifying, hideous, horrible, grim, awful, dreadful, terrible, horrific, shocking, appalling, disgusting, revolting, sickening, unspeakable; informal sick, gross.
– OPPOSITES pleasant.

gruff adjective **1** *a gruff reply | his*

gruff exterior: **abrupt**, brusque, curt, short, blunt; taciturn; surly, grumpy, crusty, ungracious; informal grouchy. **2** *a gruff voice:* **rough**, guttural, throaty, gravelly, husky, croaking, rasping, hoarse, harsh; low.
– OPPOSITES friendly, soft.

grumble verb **complain**, grouse, whine, mutter, bleat, carp, protest, make a fuss; informal moan, bellyache, beef, bitch, grouch, gripe, whinge; Brit. informal chunter, create; N. English informal mither; N. Amer. informal kvetch.
• noun **complaint**, grouse, grievance, protest, cavil, criticism; informal grouch, moan, whinge, beef, gripe.

grumpy adjective **bad-tempered**, crabby, short-tempered, crotchety, tetchy, crabbed, touchy, irascible, crusty, cross, cantankerous, curmudgeonly, surly, ill-humoured, fractious, disagreeable; informal grouchy; Brit. informal narky, ratty, like a bear with a sore head; N. Amer. informal cranky, ornery, soreheaded.
– OPPOSITES good-humoured.

guarantee noun **1** *a one-year guarantee:* **warranty**. **2** *he gave a guarantee that the hospital would stay open:* **promise**, assurance, word of honour, pledge, vow, oath, commitment, covenant. **3** *a guarantee for loans:* **collateral**, security, surety.
• verb **1** *I guarantee he will accept the offer:* **promise**, swear, pledge, vow, give your word, give an assurance, give an undertaking. **2** *he agreed to guarantee the loan:* **underwrite**.

guard verb **1** *troops guarded the bridge:* **protect**, stand guard over, watch over, keep an eye on; cover, patrol, police, defend. **2** *the men were guarded by armed officers:* **watch**, mind; protect. **3** *we must guard against poachers:* **beware of**, keep watch for, be alert to, keep an eye out for, be on the alert for, be on the lookout for.
• noun **1** *border guards:* **sentry**, sentinel, nightwatchman; protector, defender, guardian; lookout, watch. **2** *a prison guard:* **warder**, warden, keeper; jailer; informal screw. **3** *a metal guard:* **cover**, shield, screen, fender; bumper, buffer.
■ **off guard** *they were caught off guard by the announcement:* unprepared, inattentive, unwary, unsuspecting; informal napping, asleep at the wheel, on the hop. **on guard** *computer users must remain on guard:* vigilant, alert, on the alert, wary, watchful, cautious, careful, heedful, chary, circumspect, on the lookout, on your toes, prepared, ready, wideawake, attentive, observant.

guarded adjective **cautious**, careful, circumspect, wary, chary, reluctant, non-committal; informal cagey.

guardian noun **protector**, defender, preserver, custodian, warden, guard, keeper; curator, caretaker, steward, trustee.

WORD LINKS
tutelary relating to a guardian

guerrilla noun freedom fighter, irregular, partisan; rebel, revolutionary; terrorist.

guess verb **1** *he guessed that she was about 40:* **estimate**, reckon, judge; postulate, speculate, conjecture, surmise. **2** (informal) *I guess I owe you an apology:* **suppose**, think, imagine, expect, suspect, dare say; informal reckon, figure.
• noun *my guess was right:* **hypothesis**, theory, postulation, conjecture, surmise, estimate, belief, opinion, supposition, speculation, suspicion, impression, feeling.

guesswork noun **guessing**, conjecture, surmise, supposition, assumptions, presumptions, speculation, hypothesizing, theorizing; approximation.

guest noun **1** *we have guests:* **visitor**, caller; company. **2** *hotel guests:* **resident**, boarder, lodger; patron, client; N. Amer. roomer.
– OPPOSITES host.

guffaw verb **roar with laughter**, laugh heartily/loudly, bellow, cackle.

guidance noun **1** *she looked to him for guidance:* **advice**, counsel, direction, instruction; suggestions, tips, hints, pointers, guidelines. **2** *work continued under the guidance of an expert:* **direction**, control, leadership, management, supervision, charge.

guide noun **1** *our guide took us back to the hotel:* **escort**, attendant, courier; usher; chaperone. **2** *he is my inspiration and my guide:*

adviser, mentor, counsellor; guru. **3** *the techniques given serve as a guide:* **outline**, template, example, exemplar; introduction, overview. **4** *a guide to Paris:* **guidebook**, travelogue, vade mecum; companion, handbook, directory, A to Z; informal bible.
• verb **1** *he guided her to her seat:* **lead**, conduct, show, show someone the way, usher, shepherd, direct, steer, pilot, escort; see, take, help, assist. **2** *the chairman guides the meeting:* **direct**, steer, manage, conduct, run, be in charge of, govern, preside over, supervise, oversee; handle, regulate. **3** *he was always there to guide me:* **advise**, counsel, direct.

g

guidebook noun **guide**, travel guide, travelogue, vade mecum; companion, handbook, directory, A to Z; informal bible.

guideline noun **recommendation**, instruction, direction, suggestion, advice; regulation, rule, principle; standard, criterion.

guild noun **association**, society, union, league, organization, company, cooperative, fellowship, club.

guile noun **cunning**, craftiness, craft, artfulness, artifice, wiliness, slyness, deviousness; deception, deceit, duplicity, underhandedness, double-dealing, trickery.
– OPPOSITES honesty.

guileless adjective **artless**, naive, open, simple, childlike, innocent, unsophisticated, unworldly, trusting.
– OPPOSITES scheming.

guilt noun **1** *the proof of his guilt:* **culpability**, guiltiness. **2** *a terrible feeling of guilt:* **self-reproach**, shame, a guilty conscience, pangs of conscience; remorse, regret, contrition.
– OPPOSITES innocence.

guiltless adjective **innocent**, blameless, not to blame, without fault; informal squeaky clean, whiter than white, as pure as the driven snow.
– OPPOSITES guilty.

guilty adjective **1** *the guilty party:* **culpable**, to blame, at fault, in the wrong. **2** *I still feel guilty about the way I behaved:* **ashamed**, guilt-ridden, conscience-stricken, remorseful, sorry, contrite, repentant, penitent, regretful, rueful, abashed, shamefaced, sheepish, hangdog.
– OPPOSITES innocent, unrepentant.

guise noun **1** *Zeus appeared in the guise of a swan:* **likeness**, appearance, semblance, form, shape, image; disguise. **2** *sums paid under the guise of consultancy fees:* **pretence**, disguise, front, facade, cover, blind, screen, smokescreen.

gulf noun **1** *the ice gave way and the gulf widened:* **hole**, crevasse, fissure, cleft, split, rift, pit, chasm, abyss, void; ravine, gorge, canyon, gully. **2** *a gulf between rich and poor:* **divide**, division, separation, gap; difference, contrast, polarity.

gullet noun **oesophagus**, throat, pharynx; crop, craw.

gullible adjective **credulous**, naive, easily deceived, impressionable, unsuspecting, ingenuous, innocent, inexperienced, green; informal wet behind the ears.
– OPPOSITES suspicious.

gully noun **1** *a steep icy gully:* **ravine**, canyon, gorge, pass, defile, couloir; N. Amer. gulch, coulee. **2** *water runs from the drainpipe into a gully:* **channel**, conduit, trench, ditch, drain, culvert, gutter.

gulp verb **1** *she gulped her juice:* **swallow**, quaff, swill down; informal swig, down, knock back. **2** *he gulped down the rest of his meal:* **gobble**, guzzle, devour, bolt, wolf; informal put away, demolish, polish off, shovel down; Brit. informal scoff. **3** *Jenny gulped back her tears:* **choke back**, fight back, suppress, stifle, smother.
– OPPOSITES sip.
• noun *a gulp of cold beer:* **mouthful**, swallow, draught; informal swig.

gum[1] noun *photographs stuck down with gum:* **glue**, adhesive, paste.
• verb *the receipts were gummed into a book:* **stick**, glue, paste; fix, affix, attach, fasten.
■ **gum something up** clog up, choke up, stop up, plug; obstruct; informal bung up.

gum[2] (Anatomy) noun

WORD LINKS
gingival relating to the gums
gingivitis inflammation of the gums

gumption noun (informal) **initiative**, resourcefulness, enterprise, imagination; sense, common sense, wit; informal get-up-and-go, spunk, nous, savvy, horse sense; N. Amer. informal smarts.

gun noun **firearm**; pistol, revolver, handgun, rifle, shotgun, machine gun; weapon; informal shooter; N. Amer. informal piece, shooting iron.

gunfire noun **gunshots**, shots, shooting, firing, shelling.

gunman noun robber, gangster, terrorist; sniper, gunfighter; assassin, murderer, killer; informal hit man, gunslinger, mobster; N. Amer. informal shootist, hood.

gurgle verb *the water swirled and gurgled:* **babble**, burble, tinkle, bubble, ripple, murmur, purl, splash.
• noun *the gurgle of a small brook:* **babbling**, tinkling, bubbling, murmur, purling, splashing.

guru noun **1** *a Hindu guru and mystic:* **teacher**, tutor, sage, mentor, spiritual leader, master; Hinduism swami, Maharishi. **2** *a management guru:* **expert**, authority, pundit, leading light, master, specialist.
– OPPOSITES disciple.

gush verb **surge**, burst, spout, spurt, jet, stream, rush, pour, spill, cascade, flood; flow, run, issue; Brit. informal sloosh.
• noun **surge**, stream, spurt, jet, spout, outpouring, outflow, burst, rush, cascade, flood, torrent; technical efflux.

gushing adjective **effusive**, enthusiastic, overenthusiastic, unrestrained, extravagant, fulsome, lavish; informal over the top, OTT, laid on with a trowel.
– OPPOSITES restrained.

gust noun **flurry**, blast, puff, blow, rush; squall.
• verb **blow**, bluster, roar.

gusto noun **enthusiasm**, relish, appetite, enjoyment, delight, glee, pleasure; zest, zeal, fervour, verve, keenness.
– OPPOSITES apathy, distaste.

gusty adjective **blustery**, windy, breezy; squally, stormy, tempestuous, wild, turbulent; informal blowy.
– OPPOSITES calm.

gut noun **1** *an ache in his gut:* **stomach**, belly, abdomen; intestines, bowels; informal tummy, insides, innards. **2** *fish guts:* **entrails**; intestines, viscera; offal; informal insides, innards. **3** (informal) *she has a lot of guts:* **courage**, bravery, backbone, nerve, pluck, spirit, boldness, daring, grit, fearlessness, toughness, determination; informal spunk; Brit. informal bottle; N. Amer. informal moxie.
• adjective (informal) *a gut feeling:* **instinctive**, intuitive, deep-seated; knee-jerk, automatic, involuntary, spontaneous, unthinking.
• verb **1** *first gut the sardines:* **clean**, disembowel, draw; formal eviscerate. **2** *the church was gutted by fire:* **devastate**, destroy, lay waste, ravage, ruin, wreck.

> **WORD LINKS**
> **visceral** relating to the gut

gutless adjective (informal). See **COWARDLY**.

gutsy adjective (informal). See **BRAVE**.

gutter noun **drain**, sluice, culvert, sewer; channel, conduit, pipe; trough, trench, ditch.

guttural adjective **throaty**, husky, gruff, gravelly, growly, growling, croaky, croaking, harsh, rough, rasping; deep, low, thick.

guy noun (informal) **man**, fellow; youth, boy; informal lad, fella, geezer, gent; Brit. informal chap, bloke; N. Amer. informal dude, hombre.

guzzle verb **1** *he guzzled his burger:* **gobble**, bolt, wolf, devour; informal tuck into, demolish, polish off, pig yourself on, shovel down; Brit. informal scoff, shift; N. Amer. informal snarf, scarf. **2** *she guzzled down the orange juice:* **gulp down**, swallow, quaff, swill; informal knock back, swig, down, slug down.

Gypsy, **Gipsy** noun **Romany**.

gyrate verb **rotate**, revolve, wheel, turn, whirl, circle, pirouette, twirl, swirl, spin, swivel.

Hh

habit noun **1** *it was his habit to go for a run every morning:* **custom**, practice, routine, way; formal wont. **2** *she had many irritating habits:* **mannerism**, way, quirk, foible, trick, trait, idiosyncrasy, peculiarity, oddity, eccentricity. **3** (informal) *his cocaine habit:* **addiction**, dependence, craving, fixation. **4** *a monk's habit:* **garments**, dress, garb, clothing, attire, outfit, costume; formal apparel.
■ **in the habit of** accustomed to, used to, given to, inclined to; literary wont to.

habitable adjective **fit to live in**, inhabitable, in good repair, liveable-in.
–OPPOSITES uninhabitable.

habitat noun **natural environment**, home, domain, haunt.

habitation noun **1** *the house isn't fit for human habitation:* **occupancy**, occupation, tenancy. **2** (formal) *his principal habitation:* **residence**, house, home, seat; formal dwelling, dwelling place, abode, domicile.

habitual adjective **1** *habitual criminals:* **inveterate**, confirmed, compulsive, incorrigible, hardened, ingrained, chronic, regular. **2** *his habitual secretiveness:* **customary**, accustomed, regular, usual, normal, characteristic; literary wonted.
–OPPOSITES occasional, unaccustomed.

habituate verb **accustom**, make used, familiarize, adapt, adjust, attune, acclimatize, condition; N. Amer. acclimate.

habitué noun **frequent visitor**, regular customer, familiar face, regular, patron.

hack[1] verb **cut**, chop, hew, lop, saw, slash.
■ **hack it** (informal) cope, manage; stand it, tolerate it, bear it, put up with it; informal handle it, abide it, stick it.

hack[2] noun **journalist**, reporter, newspaperman, newspaperwoman, writer; informal scribbler.

hackneyed adjective **overused**, overdone, overworked, worn out, time-worn, stale, tired, threadbare; trite, banal, clichéd.
–OPPOSITES original.

Hades noun. See HELL sense 1.

haft noun **handle**, grip, hilt, shaft, butt, stock.

haggard adjective **drawn**, tired, exhausted, drained, careworn; gaunt, pinched, hollow-cheeked, hollow-eyed.
–OPPOSITES healthy.

haggle verb **barter**, bargain, negotiate, wrangle.

hail[1] verb **1** *a friend hailed him:* **call**, shout to, address; greet, salute. **2** *he hailed a cab:* **flag down**, wave down, signal to. **3** *critics hailed the film as a masterpiece:* **acclaim**, praise, applaud. **4** *Rick hails from Australia:* **come from**, be from, be a native of.

hail[2] noun *a hail of bullets:* **barrage**, volley, shower, stream, salvo.
• verb **beat**, shower, rain, fall, pour.

hair noun **1 tresses**, locks, curls, ringlets. **2 hairstyle**, haircut; informal hairdo. **3 fur**, wool; coat, fleece, mane.

WORD LINKS
trichology the branch of medicine concerned with the hair and scalp

hairdresser noun **hairstylist**, stylist, coiffeur, coiffeuse; barber; informal crimper.

hairless adjective **bald**; shaven, shorn, clean-shaven, smooth-faced.
–OPPOSITES hairy.

hairpiece noun wig, toupee; informal rug.

hair-raising adjective **terrifying**, frightening, petrifying, chilling, horrifying, spine-chilling, blood-curdling; informal hairy, spooky, scary, creepy.

hair-splitting adjective **pedantic**; quibbling, niggling; informal nit-picking; Brit. informal pernickety, picky; N. Amer. informal persnickety.

hairstyle noun **haircut**, cut, style, hair, coiffure; informal hairdo.

hairy adjective **1** *animals with hairy coats:* **shaggy**, bushy, long-haired; woolly, furry, fleecy. **2** *his hairy face:* **bearded**, bewhiskered, stubbly, bristly; formal hirsute. **3** (informal) *a hairy situation:* **risky**, dangerous, perilous, hazardous; tricky; informal dicey, sticky; Brit. informal dodgy.

hale adjective **healthy**, fit, fighting fit, well, in good health, in fine fettle, as fit as a fiddle/flea; strong, robust, vigorous, hardy, sturdy, hearty, lusty, able-bodied; informal in the pink, as right as rain.

half adverb **partially**, partly, incompletely, to a certain extent/degree, up to a point.
– OPPOSITES fully, completely.

half-baked adjective **ill-conceived**, hare-brained, ill-judged, impractical, unrealistic, unworkable, ridiculous; informal crackpot.

half-hearted adjective **unenthusiastic**, cool, lukewarm, tepid, apathetic.
– OPPOSITES enthusiastic.

halfway adjective *the halfway point:* **midway**, middle, mid, central, centre, intermediate.
■ **meet someone halfway** compromise, reach an agreement, make a deal, find the middle ground, strike a balance.

hall noun **1 entrance hall**, hallway, entry, entrance, lobby, foyer, vestibule. **2** *the village hall:* **assembly room**, meeting room, chamber; auditorium, theatre, house.

hallmark noun *the tiny bubbles are the hallmark of fine champagnes:* **mark**, distinctive feature, characteristic, sign, sure sign, telltale sign, badge, stamp, trademark, indication, indicator.

hallucination noun **delusion**, illusion, figment of the imagination, mirage, chimera, fantasy; informal trip.

halo noun **aura**, nimbus, corona, aureole.

halt verb **1 stop**, come to a halt, come to a standstill; pull up, draw up. **2** *a strike has halted production:* **stop**, bring to a stop, put a stop to; suspend, arrest; check, curb, stem, staunch, block, stall; informal pull the plug on, put the kibosh on.
– OPPOSITES start, continue.
• noun **1 stop**, standstill. **2** *a halt in production:* **stoppage**, break, pause, interval, interruption, hiatus.

halting adjective *a halting conversation | halting English:* **hesitant**, faltering, hesitating, stumbling, stammering, stuttering; broken, imperfect.
– OPPOSITES fluent.

ham-fisted adjective **clumsy**, bungling, incompetent, amateurish, inept, inexpert, maladroit, gauche, bumbling; informal cack-handed; Brit. informal all fingers and thumbs.
– OPPOSITES skilful.

hammer noun **mallet**, gavel, sledgehammer.
• verb **1 beat**, forge, shape, form, mould, fashion. **2** *she hammered at the door:* **batter**, pummel, beat, strike, bang, pound; knock, thump; informal bash, wallop, clobber.

hamper[1] noun **basket**, pannier.

hamper[2] verb **hinder**, obstruct, impede, inhibit, curb, delay, slow down, hold up, interfere with; restrict, constrain, block, check, curtail, handicap, hamstring; informal stymie.
– OPPOSITES help.

hamstring verb **handicap**, hamper, hinder, obstruct, impede, inhibit, constrain, restrict, shackle, fetter, encumber, block, frustrate; informal stymie.
– OPPOSITES help.

hand noun **1** palm, fist; informal paw, mitt. **2** *the clock's second hand:* **pointer**, indicator, needle. **3** *they're in the hands of the government:* **control**, power; command, management, care, supervision, jurisdiction; possession, custody. **4** *a manuscript written in his own*

hand: **handwriting**, writing, script. **5** *a factory hand:* **worker**, manual worker, unskilled worker, blue-collar worker, workman, labourer, operative, roustabout.
• verb **pass**, give, throw, toss; present to; informal chuck, bung.
■ **at hand 1** *close at hand:* readily available, handy, within reach, accessible, close, nearby, at the ready, at your fingertips, at your disposal. **2** *the time for action is at hand:* imminent, approaching, coming, on the horizon. **hand something down** pass on, pass down; bequeath, leave, make over, give, transfer. **hand in glove** in collaboration, in close association, in partnership, in league, in collusion; informal in cahoots. **hand something on** give, pass, hand, transfer, grant. **hand something out** distribute, hand round, give out/round, pass out/round, share out, dole out, dish out, deal out, issue, dispense. **hand something over** yield, give, give up, pass, grant, entrust, surrender, relinquish, turn over, deliver up, forfeit, sacrifice. **to hand** readily available, handy, within reach, accessible, ready, close, nearby, at the ready, at your fingertips, convenient.

WORD LINKS
manual relating to the hands

handbag noun **bag**, shoulder bag, clutch bag; N. Amer. purse, pocketbook.

handbill noun **notice**, advertisement, flyer, leaflet, circular, handout, brochure; N. Amer. dodger; informal ad; Brit. informal advert.

handbook noun **manual**, instructions, ABC, A to Z; almanac, companion, guide, guidebook, vade mecum.

handcuff verb **manacle**, shackle; restrain, clap someone in irons; informal cuff.

handcuffs plural noun **manacles**, shackles, irons, restraints; informal cuffs, bracelets; old use darbies.

handful noun **a few**, a small number, a small amount, a small quantity, one or two, some, not many.

handgun noun **pistol**, revolver, side arm, six-shooter; N. Amer. informal piece, Saturday night special.

handicap noun *a handicap to industrial competitiveness:* **impediment**, hindrance, obstacle, barrier, encumbrance, constraint; disadvantage, stumbling block.
– OPPOSITES benefit, advantage.
• verb *lack of funding handicapped the research:* **hamper**, impede, hinder, impair, hamstring; restrict, constrain; informal stymie.
– OPPOSITES help.

handicapped adjective **disabled**; euphemistic physically challenged, differently abled.

handicraft noun **craft**, handiwork, craftwork.

handiwork noun **creation**, product, work, achievement.

handkerchief noun tissue; trademark Kleenex; informal hanky; literary kerchief.

handle verb **1 hold**, pick up, grasp, grip, lift. **2** *a car which is easy to handle:* **control**, drive, steer, operate, manoeuvre. **3** *she handled the job well:* **deal with**, manage, tackle, take care of, attend to, see to, sort out. **4** *the company handling the account:* **administer**, manage, control, conduct, direct, supervise, oversee, be in charge of, take care of, look after. **5** *the traders handled imported goods:* **trade in**, deal in, buy, sell, supply; peddle, traffic in.
• noun *the knife's handle:* **haft**, grip, hilt, stock, shaft, butt.

handout noun **1** *she existed on handouts:* **charity**, benefits, donations, subsidies; historical alms. **2** *a photocopied handout:* **leaflet**, pamphlet, brochure; handbill, flyer, circular, mailshot.

handsome adjective **1** *a handsome man:* **good-looking**, attractive, personable, striking, gorgeous; informal hunky, tasty, fanciable, dishy; Brit. informal fit; Austral./NZ informal spunky. **2** *a handsome profit:* **substantial**, considerable, sizeable, princely, large, big, ample, bumper; informal tidy, whopping; Brit. informal whacking great.
– OPPOSITES ugly, meagre.

handwriting noun **writing**, script, hand; calligraphy; informal scrawl, scribble.

WORD LINKS
graphology the study of handwriting

handy adjective **1 useful**, convenient, practical, easy-to-use, user-friendly, helpful. **2** *keep your credit card handy:* **readily available**, to hand, within reach, accessible, ready, close, nearby, at the ready, at your fingertips. **3** *he's handy with a needle:* **skilful**, skilled, dexterous, deft, able, adept, proficient; good with your hands.
– OPPOSITES inconvenient, inept.

handyman noun **odd-job man**, odd-jobber, jack of all trades; informal Mr Fixit.

hang verb **1** *lights hung from the trees:* **be suspended**, dangle, swing, sway. **2** *hang the picture at eye level:* **put up**, pin up, display. **3** *the room was hung with streamers:* **decorate**, adorn, drape, festoon, deck out. **4** *he was hanged for murder:* **send to the gallows**, execute; informal string up. **5** *a pall of smoke hung over the city:* **hover**, float, be suspended.
■ **hang about/around** (informal) **1** *I've seen him hanging around outside her house:* loiter, skulk. **2** *they spent their time hanging around in bars:* kill time, kick your heels, twiddle your thumbs; informal hang out. **3** *she's hanging around with a bunch of hippies:* associate, mix, socialize, fraternize, rub shoulders; N. Amer. rub elbows; informal hang out, run around, knock about/around, hobnob. **hang fire** delay, hold back, stall, pause; informal sit tight. **hang on 1** *he hung on to her coat:* hold on, grip, clutch, grasp, hold tightly, cling. **2** *her future hung on his decision:* depend on, turn on, hinge on, rest on. **3** *I'll hang on as long as I can:* persevere, hold on, keep going, keep at it, continue; informal soldier on, stick at it, stick it out. **hang out.** See HANG AROUND senses 2, 3.

hangdog adjective **shamefaced**, sheepish, guilty-looking, cowed, dejected, downcast.
– OPPOSITES defiant.

hanger-on noun **follower**, camp follower, cohort, toady; parasite, leech, dependant; informal groupie, sponger, freeloader, passenger.

hanging noun *silk wall hangings:* **drape**, tapestry; drapery.
• adjective *hanging fronds of honeysuckle:* **dangling**, trailing, drooping, pendent, pendulous.

hang-out noun **haunt**, stamping ground, meeting place, watering hole; N. Amer. stomping ground.

hang-up noun **neurosis**, phobia, preoccupation, fixation, obsession; inhibition, mental block; informal complex, thing, issue, bee in your bonnet.

hank noun **coil**, length, loop, twist, skein.

hanker verb **yearn**, long, wish, have a yen, hunger, thirst, lust, ache; informal itch.

hankering noun **longing**, yearning, craving, yen, hunger, thirst, ache, lust; informal itch.
– OPPOSITES aversion.

hanky-panky noun (informal) **goings-on**, funny business, mischief, chicanery, skulduggery; informal monkey business, shenanigans, carryings-on; Brit. informal jiggery-pokery.

haphazard adjective **random**, indiscriminate, chaotic, hit-and-miss, aimless; chance; informal higgledy-piggledy.
– OPPOSITES methodical.

hapless adjective **unfortunate**, unlucky, unhappy, wretched, miserable.
– OPPOSITES lucky.

happen verb **1** *remember what happened last time:* **occur**, take place, come about; N. Amer. informal go down; literary come to pass. **2** *I wonder what happened to her:* **become of**; literary befall, betide.

happening noun *bizarre happenings:* **occurrence**, event, incident, episode.
• adjective (informal) *a happening nightclub:* **fashionable**, popular; informal trendy, funky, hot, cool, with it, hip, in, now, groovy; N. Amer. informal tony.
– OPPOSITES unfashionable.

happiness noun **pleasure**, contentment, satisfaction, cheerfulness, merriment, joy, well-being.

happy adjective **1 cheerful**, cheery, merry, joyful, jovial, jolly, carefree, smiling, beaming, grinning, in good spirits, in a good mood, pleased, contented, content, satisfied, sunny, radiant; elated, ecstatic, blissful, euphoric, overjoyed, in seventh

heaven, on cloud nine; informal chirpy, over the moon, on top of the world; N. English informal made up. **2** *we will be happy to advise you:* **glad**, pleased, delighted, more than willing. **3** *a happy coincidence:* **fortunate**, lucky, timely, convenient.
–OPPOSITES sad, unhappy, unfortunate.

happy-go-lucky adjective **easy-going**, carefree, casual, free and easy, blithe, nonchalant; informal laid-back.
–OPPOSITES anxious.

harangue verb **rant at**, lecture, shout at; berate, criticize, attack.
•noun **tirade**, diatribe, lecture, rant, polemic.

h

harass verb **persecute**, intimidate, hound, victimize; pester, bother; informal hassle, bug, give someone a hard time, pick on; N. Amer. informal ride.

harassed adjective **stressed**, hard-pressed, careworn, worried, troubled, beleaguered; informal hassled.
–OPPOSITES carefree.

harassment noun **persecution**, intimidation, victimization; informal hassle.

harbour noun **port**, dock, marina; mooring, waterfront.
•verb **1** *he is harbouring a dangerous criminal:* **shelter**, conceal, hide, shield, protect. **2** *Rose harboured a grudge against him:* **bear**, hold, nurse.

hard adjective **1** *hard ground:* **firm**, solid, rigid, stiff, unbreakable, inflexible, impenetrable, unyielding, compacted; tough, strong. **2** *hard physical work:* **arduous**, strenuous, tiring, exhausting, back-breaking, gruelling, heavy, laborious; difficult, taxing, exacting, challenging, demanding, punishing, tough, formidable; Brit. informal knackering. **3** *hard workers:* **industrious**, diligent, assiduous, conscientious, energetic, keen, enthusiastic, indefatigable; studious. **4** *a hard problem:* **difficult**, puzzling, perplexing, baffling, bewildering, mystifying, thorny, problematic. **5** *times are hard:* **harsh**, grim, difficult, bad, bleak, tough, austere, dark. **6** *a hard taskmaster:* **strict**, harsh, severe, stern, tough, demanding, exacting; uncompromising, implacable, unrelenting; ruling with a rod of iron. **7** *a hard winter:* **cold**, bitter, harsh, severe, bleak, freezing, icy. **8** *a hard blow:* **forceful**, heavy, strong, sharp, violent, powerful. **9** *hard facts:* **reliable**, definite, undeniable, indisputable, verifiable.
–OPPOSITES soft, easy, lazy, gentle.
■ **hard and fast** definite, fixed, set, strict, rigid, clear-cut, cast-iron. **hard up** (informal) poor, short of money, badly off, impoverished; formal impecunious, in reduced circumstances; informal broke, strapped for cash; Brit. informal skint.

hardbitten adjective **hardened**, tough, cynical, unsentimental, hard-headed; informal hard-nosed, hard-boiled.
–OPPOSITES sentimental.

hard-boiled adjective (informal). See HARDBITTEN.

hard-core adjective **diehard**, staunch, dedicated, committed, dyed-in-the-wool; hard-line.

harden verb **1** *this glue hardens in four hours:* **solidify**, set, stiffen, thicken. **2** *their suffering had hardened them:* **toughen**, desensitize, inure, harden someone's heart; numb.
–OPPOSITES liquefy, soften.

hardened adjective **1** *a hardened criminal:* **inveterate**, seasoned, habitual, chronic, compulsive, confirmed, dyed-in-the-wool; incorrigible. **2** *he was hardened to violence:* **inured**, desensitized, deadened; accustomed, habituated, acclimatized, used.

hard-headed adjective **unsentimental**, practical, businesslike, realistic, down-to-earth, matter-of-fact, no-nonsense; informal hard-nosed.
–OPPOSITES idealistic.

hard-hearted adjective **unfeeling**, heartless, cold, hard, callous, unsympathetic, uncaring, having a heart of stone, as hard as nails.
–OPPOSITES compassionate.

hard-hitting adjective **uncompromising**, forthright, frank, direct, tough; unsparing, pulling no punches, not mincing your words.

hardiness **noun robustness**, strength, toughness, ruggedness, sturdiness, resilience.
– OPPOSITES frailty.

hard-line **adjective uncompromising**, strict, extreme, diehard.
– OPPOSITES moderate.

hardly **adverb** *we hardly know each other:* **scarcely**, barely, only just.

hard-nosed **adjective** (informal) **tough-minded**, unsentimental, no-nonsense, hard-headed, hardbitten, down-to-earth.
– OPPOSITES sentimental.

hard-pressed **adjective troubled**, beleaguered, ailing, harassed; overburdened.

hardship **noun difficulty**, privation, destitution, poverty, austerity, penury, need; distress, suffering, adversity, trials and tribulations, dire straits.
– OPPOSITES prosperity, ease.

hardware **noun equipment**, apparatus, gear, paraphernalia, tackle, kit, machinery.

hard-wearing **adjective durable**, strong, tough, resilient, stout, rugged.
– OPPOSITES flimsy.

hard-working **adjective diligent**, industrious, conscientious, assiduous, persevering, studious.
– OPPOSITES lazy.

hardy **adjective robust**, healthy, fit, strong, sturdy, tough, rugged; dated stalwart.
– OPPOSITES delicate.

hare-brained **adjective** *a hare-brained scheme:* **foolish**, madcap, stupid, ridiculous, idiotic, half-baked; informal crackpot, crazy; Brit. informal daft, barmy.
– OPPOSITES sensible, intelligent.

harm **noun** *it won't do you any harm:* **injury**, damage, mischief.
– OPPOSITES benefit.
• **verb 1** *he's never harmed anybody in his life:* **hurt**, lay a finger on, mistreat, ill-treat. **2** *this could harm his World Cup prospects:* **damage**, spoil, affect, undermine, compromise.

harmful **adjective damaging**, injurious, detrimental, dangerous, negative, unhealthy, unwholesome, hurtful, destructive; noxious, hazardous; formal deleterious.
– OPPOSITES beneficial.

harmless **adjective safe**, innocuous; inoffensive.
– OPPOSITES dangerous, harmful.

harmonious **adjective 1** *a harmonious relationship:* **friendly**, amicable, cordial, amiable, congenial, easy. **2** *a harmonious blend of traditional and modern:* **balanced**, coordinated, pleasing, tasteful.
– OPPOSITES discordant, hostile, incongruous.

harmonize **verb 1** *colours which harmonize:* **coordinate**, go together, match, blend, mix, balance, tone in; be compatible, be harmonious, suit each other, set each other off. **2** *the need to harmonize tax laws across Europe:* **standardize**, coordinate, integrate, synchronize, make consistent, bring into line, systematize.
– OPPOSITES clash.

harmony **noun 1** *musical harmony:* **tunefulness**, euphony, melodiousness. **2** *the harmony of the whole design:* **balance**, symmetry, congruity, coordination. **3** *the villagers live together in harmony:* **accord**, agreement, peace, amity, friendship, fellowship, cooperation, understanding, unity, like-mindedness; formal concord.
– OPPOSITES dissonance, disagreement.

harness **noun tack**, tackle, equipment; yoke; old use equipage.
• **verb** *attempts to harness solar energy:* **exploit**, utilize, use, make use of, put to use, channel.

harp **verb**
▪ **harp on about** keep on about, go on about, dwell on, make an issue of.

harridan **noun harpy**, termagant, shrew, nag, virago, martinet; hag, crone, gorgon; informal battleaxe, witch; old use scold.

harrowing **adjective distressing**, traumatic, upsetting; shocking, disturbing.

harry **verb harass**, hound, torment, pester, worry, badger, nag, plague; informal hassle, bug, lean on, give someone a hard time.

harsh **adjective 1** *a harsh voice:*

grating, rasping, strident, raucous, discordant; screeching, shrill; rough. **2** *harsh colours:* **glaring**; loud, garish, gaudy, lurid. **3** *his harsh treatment of captives:* **cruel**, savage, barbarous, merciless, inhumane; ruthless, pitiless; severe, hard-hearted. **4** *they took harsh measures to end the crisis:* **severe**, stringent, firm, stiff, hard, stern, rigorous, draconian. **5** *harsh words:* **rude**, discourteous, impolite; unfriendly, sharp, bitter, unkind, disparaging. **6** *harsh conditions:* **austere**, grim, spartan, hard, inhospitable. **7** *a harsh winter:* **hard**, severe, cold, bitter, bleak, freezing, icy. **8** *harsh cream cleaners:* **abrasive**, coarse, rough.
– OPPOSITES soft, kind, mild.

harvest noun *a poor harvest:* **yield**, crop, vintage.
• verb *they harvested the wheat:* **gather in**, bring in, reap, pick, collect.

hassle (informal) noun *parking is such a hassle:* **inconvenience**, bother, nuisance, trouble, annoyance, irritation, fuss; informal aggravation, stress, headache, pain.
• verb *don't hassle me!* **harass**, pester, badger, hound, bother, torment; informal bug, give someone a hard time, be on someone's back; N. English informal mither.

hassled adjective (informal) **harassed**, agitated, stressed, flustered; beleaguered; under pressure, hot and bothered; informal up against it.
– OPPOSITES calm.

haste noun **speed**, hurriedness, swiftness, rapidity, quickness, briskness.
– OPPOSITES delay.
■ **in haste** quickly, rapidly, fast, speedily, in a rush, in a hurry.

hasten verb **1** *we hastened back:* **hurry**, rush, dash, race; go quickly; informal scoot, zip, hotfoot it, leg it; N. Amer. informal hightail; dated make haste. **2** *chemicals can hasten ageing:* **bring on**, precipitate, advance.
– OPPOSITES dawdle, delay.

hastily adverb *Meg retreated hastily:* **hurriedly**, quickly, swiftly, rapidly, speedily, briskly, without delay, post-haste; on the double; informal double quick; Brit. informal at a rate of knots; N. Amer. informal lickety-split.

hasty adjective **1** *a hasty departure:* **hurried**, quick, swift, rapid, speedy, brisk. **2** *a hasty decision:* **rash**, impetuous, impulsive, reckless, precipitate, spur-of-the-moment.
– OPPOSITES slow, considered.

hat noun **cap**, bonnet; headgear.

> **WORD LINKS**
> **milliner** a person who makes or sells women's hats

hate verb **1** *they hate each other:* **loathe**, detest, despise, dislike, abhor, be unable to bear/stand. **2** *I hate to bother you:* **be sorry**, be reluctant, be loath.
– OPPOSITES love.
• noun **1** *feelings of hate:* **hatred**, loathing, detestation, abhorrence, abomination, execration, revulsion; disgust. **2** *her pet hate was pushy parents:* **bugbear**, bane, bête noire, thorn in your flesh/side; N. Amer. bugaboo.
– OPPOSITES love.

hateful adjective **detestable**, horrible, despicable, objectionable, revolting, loathsome, abhorrent, abominable, odious, disgusting, obnoxious, vile.
– OPPOSITES delightful.

hatred noun **loathing**, hate, detestation, abhorrence, execration; formal odium.

haughtiness noun **arrogance**, pride, hauteur, condescension; superciliousness; informal snootiness.
– OPPOSITES modesty.

haughty adjective **arrogant**, proud, superior, supercilious, condescending; above yourself; informal stuck-up, snooty, high and mighty, la-di-da; Brit. informal toffee-nosed.
– OPPOSITES humble.

haul verb *she hauled the basket upstairs:* **drag**, pull, heave, lug; informal hump.

haunches plural noun **hindquarters**, rump, rear.

haunt verb *the sight haunted me for years:* **torment**, disturb, trouble, worry, plague; prey on someone's mind, weigh on, nag at, obsess; informal bug.
• noun *a favourite haunt of artists:* **hang-out**, stamping ground, meeting place; spot, venue; N. Amer. stomping ground.

haunted adjective **1** *a haunted house:* **possessed**; cursed, jinxed. **2** *his haunted eyes:* **tormented**, anguished, tortured, troubled, worried.

haunting adjective **evocative**, affecting, stirring, powerful; poignant; memorable.

hauteur noun **haughtiness**, superciliousness, arrogance, pride, superiority; condescension; airs and graces; informal snootiness.

have verb **1** *he had a new car:* **own**, possess, be in possession of; be blessed with, boast, enjoy. **2** *the flat has five rooms:* **comprise**, consist of, contain, include, incorporate, be composed of, be made up of. **3** *they had tea together:* **eat**, partake of; drink, imbibe, quaff. **4** *she's having a party:* **organize**, hold, give, throw, put on, lay on. **5** *he had trouble finding the restaurant:* **experience**, encounter, meet with, run into. **6** *many of them still have doubts:* **harbour**, entertain, feel, nurse. **7** *I have to get up at six:* **must**, be obliged to, be required to, be compelled to, be forced to, be bound to. **8** (informal) *you've been had:* **trick**, fool, deceive, cheat, dupe, take in; informal do, con; N. Amer. informal sucker.
■ **have someone on** (Brit. informal) play a trick on, play a joke on, pull someone's leg; Brit. informal wind up; N. Amer. informal put on.

haven noun *a safe haven:* **refuge**, retreat, shelter, sanctuary; oasis.

haversack noun **knapsack**, rucksack, backpack.

havoc noun **chaos**, disorder, disruption, mayhem, bedlam, pandemonium.

hawk verb **peddle**, sell, trade in, deal in, traffic in; Brit. informal flog.

hazard noun *the hazards of radiation:* **danger**, risk, peril, threat.

hazardous adjective **risky**, dangerous, unsafe, perilous, fraught with danger; high-risk; informal dicey; Brit. informal dodgy.
– OPPOSITES safe, certain.

haze noun **mist**, fog, haar, cloud.

hazy adjective **1** *a hazy day:* **misty**, foggy; smoggy, murky. **2** *hazy memories:* **vague**, dim, nebulous, blurred, fuzzy.

head noun **1** *her head hit the wall:* skull, cranium; informal nut, noggin; informal, dated noddle. **2** *he had to use his head:* **brain**, brainpower, intellect, intelligence; grey matter; Brit. informal loaf; N. Amer. informal smarts. **3** *she had a head for business:* **aptitude**, talent, gift, capacity. **4** *the head of an international organization:* **leader**, chief, controller, governor, superintendent; commander, captain; director, manager; principal, president; informal boss, head honcho; Brit. informal gaffer, guv'nor; N. Amer. informal big kahuna. **5** *the head of the queue:* **front**, beginning, start; top.
– OPPOSITES back.
• adjective *the head waiter:* **chief**, principal, leading, main, first, top, highest; N. Amer. ranking.
• verb *he heads a company making £150 million profits:* **command**, control, lead, manage, direct, supervise, superintend, oversee, preside over.
■ **at the head of** in charge of, controlling, leading, managing, running, directing; at the wheel of, at the helm of. **head someone/something off 1** *he went to head off the visitors:* intercept, divert, redirect, re-route, turn away. **2** *they headed off an argument:* forestall, avert, stave off, nip in the bud; prevent, avoid, stop.

WORD LINKS
cephalic relating to the head

heading noun **1** *chapter headings:* **title**, caption, legend, rubric, headline. **2** *this topic falls under four main headings:* **category**, division, class, section, group, topic, area.

headland noun **cape**, promontory, point, foreland, peninsula, ness, spit, horn, bill, bluff; Scottish mull.

headlong adverb **1** *he fell headlong into the water:* **head first**. **2** *she rushed headlong into marriage:* **without thinking**, precipitously, impetuously, rashly, recklessly, hastily.
– OPPOSITES cautiously.

head-on adjective *a head-on confrontation:* **direct**, face to face, eyeball to eyeball, personal.

headquarters plural noun **head**

h

office, HQ, base, nerve centre, mission control.

headstone noun **gravestone**, tombstone, memorial.

headstrong adjective **wilful**, strong-willed, stubborn, obstinate, obdurate; contrary, perverse, wayward.

head teacher noun **head**, headmaster, headmistress, principal, director.

heady adjective **1** *the heady days of my youth:* **exhilarating**, exciting, thrilling, intoxicating. **2** *a heady local brew:* **potent**, intoxicating, strong.
– OPPOSITES boring.

h

heal verb **1** *he sought to heal the sick:* **cure**, treat, restore to health. **2** *his knee had healed:* **get better**, recover, mend. **3** *time will heal the pain:* **alleviate**, ease, assuage, lessen, allay. **4** *we tried to heal the rift:* **put right**, repair, resolve, settle; informal patch up.
– OPPOSITES aggravate, worsen.

healing adjective **curative**, therapeutic, medicinal, restorative.
– OPPOSITES harmful.

health noun **1** *he was restored to health:* **well-being**, fitness, good condition; strength, vigour. **2** *her poor health is cause for concern:* **condition**, physical shape, constitution.
– OPPOSITES illness.

> **WORD LINKS**
> **salubrious** good for the health

healthful adjective **healthy**, beneficial, wholesome, nourishing, nutritious.
– OPPOSITES unhealthy.

healthy adjective **1** *a healthy baby:* **well**, fit, in good shape, in fine fettle, in tip-top condition; strong, robust, fighting fit. **2** *a healthy diet:* **health-giving**, good for you; wholesome, nutritious, nourishing, healthful.
– OPPOSITES ill, unhealthy.

heap noun **1** *a heap of boxes:* **pile**, stack, mound, mountain. **2** (informal) *we have heaps of books:* **a lot**, lots, plenty, an abundance; many, numerous; informal hundreds, thousands, millions, loads, piles, umpteen, oodles, stacks, masses, reams, wads, tons, zillions; Brit. informal lashings.
• verb **1** *she heaped logs on the fire:* **pile**, stack, load. **2** *they heaped praise on her:* **shower**, lavish, pour.

hear verb **1** *she could hear voices:* **make out**, catch, get, perceive; overhear. **2** *they heard that I had moved:* **learn**, find out, discover, gather, understand. **3** *a jury heard the case:* **try**, judge; adjudicate.

hearing noun **1** *she moved out of hearing:* **earshot**, hearing distance. **2** *he gave evidence at the hearing:* **trial**, court case, inquiry, inquest, tribunal.

> **WORD LINKS**
> **auditory**, **aural** relating to hearing

hearsay noun **rumour**, gossip, tittle-tattle, idle talk; stories, tales.

heart noun **1** *he poured out his heart:* **emotions**, feelings, sentiments; soul, mind. **2** *he has no heart:* **compassion**, sympathy, humanity, feeling, empathy, understanding; soul, goodwill. **3** *they lost heart:* **enthusiasm**, spirit, determination, resolve, nerve; Brit. informal **bottle**. **4** *the heart of the city:* **centre**, middle, hub, core. **5** *the heart of the matter:* **essence**, crux, core, nub, root, meat, substance, kernel; informal nitty-gritty.
– OPPOSITES edge.
▪ **at heart** deep down, basically, fundamentally, essentially, in essence, intrinsically; informal when you get right down to it. **by heart** from memory, off pat, word for word, verbatim, parrot-fashion, word-perfect.

> **WORD LINKS**
> **cardiac** relating to the heart
> **coronary** relating to the arteries of the heart
> **cardiology** the branch of medicine concerning the heart

heartache noun **anguish**, suffering, distress, unhappiness, misery, sorrow, sadness, heartbreak, pain, hurt, woe.
– OPPOSITES happiness.

heartbreak noun. See **HEARTACHE**.

heartbreaking adjective **heart-rending**, upsetting, disturbing, distressing, tragic, painful, sad, agonizing, harrowing.

heartbroken adjective **anguished**, devastated, broken-hearted, heavy-hearted, grieving, grief-stricken, inconsolable, crushed, shattered, desolate, despairing; miserable, sorrowful, sad, despondent; informal choked.

heartburn noun **indigestion**, dyspepsia, pyrosis.

hearten verb **cheer**, cheer up, encourage, raise someone's spirits, boost, buoy up, perk up; informal buck up, pep up.

heartfelt adjective **sincere**, genuine, from the heart; earnest, profound, deep, wholehearted; honest.
– OPPOSITES insincere.

heartily adverb **1** *we heartily welcome the changes:* **wholeheartedly**, warmly, profoundly, with all your heart; eagerly, enthusiastically. **2** *they were heartily sick of her:* **thoroughly**, completely, absolutely, utterly, downright, really; informal seriously; Brit. informal well; N. Amer. informal real, mighty.

heartless adjective **unfeeling**, unsympathetic, unkind, uncaring, hard-hearted; cold, callous, cruel, merciless, pitiless, inhuman.
– OPPOSITES compassionate.

heart-rending adjective **heartbreaking**, upsetting, disturbing, distressing, tragic, painful, sad, agonizing, harrowing.

heart-to-heart adjective *a heart-to-heart chat:* **intimate**, one-to-one, one-on-one; man-to-man, woman-to-woman, candid, honest.
• noun *they had a long heart-to-heart:* **private conversation**, tête-à-tête, talk.

heart-warming adjective **touching**, heartening, stirring, uplifting, life-affirming, cheering, gratifying.
– OPPOSITES distressing.

hearty adjective **1** *there was hearty cheering from the home fans:* **exuberant**, high-spirited, lively, enthusiastic, jovial, ebullient, cheerful, uninhibited, animated, vivacious, energetic, eager, effusive, loud, noisy. **2** *hearty congratulations:* **wholehearted**, heartfelt, sincere, genuine, real, true. **3** *a hearty woman of sixty-five:* **robust**, healthy, hardy, fit; vigorous, sturdy, strong. **4** *a hearty meal:* **substantial**, large, ample, satisfying, filling, generous.
– OPPOSITES half-hearted, frail, light.

heat noun **1** *a plant sensitive to heat:* **warmth**, high temperature. **2** *the summer heat:* **hot weather**, sultriness, mugginess, humidity; heatwave, hot spell. **3** *he took the heat out of the dispute:* **passion**, intensity, vehemence, warmth, fervour, excitement, agitation; anger.
– OPPOSITES cold, apathy.
• verb *heat the soup in a microwave:* **warm up**; reheat, cook.
– OPPOSITES cool.

WORD LINKS
thermal relating to heat

heated adjective **1** *a heated swimming pool:* **warm**, hot. **2** *a heated argument:* **vehement**, passionate, impassioned, animated, 'lively', acrimonious; angry, bitter, furious, fierce. **3** *Robert grew heated as he spoke of the risks:* **excited**, animated, worked up, wound up, keyed up; informal het up.

heater noun **radiator**, convector, fire, brazier.

heathen adjective *a heathen practice:* **pagan**, heretical, idolatrous; unbelieving, non-believing, irreligious.

heave verb **1** *she heaved the sofa backwards:* **haul**, pull, drag, tug; informal yank. **2** (informal) *she heaved a brick at him:* **throw**, fling, cast, hurl, lob, pitch; informal chuck, sling. **3** *he heaved a sigh of relief:* **let out**, breathe, give; emit, utter. **4** *the sea heaved:* **rise and fall**, roll, swell, surge, churn, seethe.

heaven noun **1** *the good will have a place in heaven:* **paradise**, Zion; the hereafter, the next world, the afterworld; Elysium, Valhalla; literary the empyrean. **2** *a good book is my idea of heaven:* **bliss**, ecstasy, rapture, contentment, happiness, delight, joy; paradise, nirvana.
3 (literary) *he observed the heavens:* **the sky**, the skies; literary the firmament, the wide blue yonder.
– OPPOSITES hell, misery.
■ **in seventh heaven** ecstatic, euphoric, thrilled, elated, delighted,

overjoyed, on cloud nine, walking on air, jumping for joy, transported, delirious, blissful; informal over the moon, on top of the world, on a high, tickled pink, as pleased as Punch, cock-a-hoop.

WORD LINKS

celestial belonging or relating to heaven

heavenly adjective **1** *heavenly choirs:* **divine**, holy, celestial; angelic. **2** *heavenly constellations:* **celestial**, cosmic, stellar; sidereal. **3** (informal) *a heavenly morning:* **delightful**, wonderful, glorious, sublime; exquisite, beautiful, lovely, gorgeous, enchanting; informal divine, super, great, fantastic, fabulous, terrific.
–OPPOSITES mortal, infernal, terrestrial.

heaven-sent adjective **auspicious**, providential, propitious, felicitous, opportune, golden, favourable, serendipitous, lucky, fortunate.
–OPPOSITES inopportune.

heavy adjective **1** *a heavy box:* **weighty**, hefty, substantial, ponderous; solid, dense, leaden. **2** *a heavy man:* **big**, fat, obese, corpulent, large, bulky, stout, overweight, portly, plump, fleshy; informal tubby. **3** *a heavy blow to the head:* **forceful**, hard, strong, violent, powerful, mighty, sharp, severe. **4** *a gardener did the heavy work for me:* **strenuous**, hard, physical, difficult, arduous, demanding, back-breaking, gruelling; old use toilsome. **5** *a heavy burden of responsibility:* **onerous**, burdensome, demanding, difficult, weighty; oppressive. **6** *heavy fog:* **dense**, thick, soupy, murky, impenetrable. **7** *a heavy sky:* **overcast**, cloudy, grey, murky, dark, black, stormy, leaden, louring. **8** *heavy rain:* **torrential**, relentless, teeming, severe. **9** *heavy soil:* **clay**, muddy, sticky, wet; Brit. claggy. **10** *a heavy fine:* **sizeable**, hefty, substantial, colossal, big; stiff; whopping. **11** *heavy seas:* **tempestuous**, turbulent, rough, wild, stormy, choppy. **12** *heavy fighting:* **intense**, fierce, relentless, severe, serious. **13** *a heavy drinker:* **immoderate**, excessive, intemperate, chronic. **14** *a heavy meal:* **substantial**, filling, stodgy, rich, big.
–OPPOSITES light, gentle.

heavy-handed adjective **1** *they are heavy-handed with the equipment:* **clumsy**, awkward, maladroit; informal ham-fisted, cack-handed; Brit. informal all fingers and thumbs. **2** *heavy-handed policing:* **insensitive**, oppressive, overbearing, harsh, severe; tactless, undiplomatic, inept.
–OPPOSITES dexterous, sensitive.

heavy-hearted adjective **melancholy**, sad, sorrowful, mournful, gloomy, depressed, despondent, dejected, downhearted, downcast, disconsolate, miserable, wretched, woebegone, doleful, unhappy; literary dolorous.
–OPPOSITES cheerful.

heckle verb **jeer**, shout down, boo, hiss; Brit. barrack; informal give someone a hard time.
–OPPOSITES cheer.

hectic adjective **frantic**, frenetic, frenzied, feverish, manic, busy, active, fast and furious.
–OPPOSITES leisurely.

hector verb **bully**, intimidate, browbeat, harass, torment, plague; coerce, pressurize, strong-arm.

hedge noun *the fund is an excellent hedge against a fall in sterling:* **safeguard**, protection, shield, screen, guard, buffer, cushion.
•verb **1** *fields hedged with hawthorn:* **surround**, enclose, border, edge, bound. **2** *he hedged at every new question:* **prevaricate**, equivocate, dodge the issue, be non-committal, be evasive, be vague; Brit. hum and haw; informal sit on the fence, duck the question. **3** *the company hedged its position on the market:* **safeguard**, protect, shield, guard, cushion.

hedonism noun **self-indulgence**, pleasure-seeking, self-gratification, sybaritism, lotus-eating; decadence, intemperance, extravagance, high living.
–OPPOSITES self-restraint.

hedonist noun **sybarite**, sensualist, voluptuary, pleasure-seeker, lotus-eater, bon viveur.
–OPPOSITES ascetic.

hedonistic adjective **self-indulgent**, pleasure-seeking, sybaritic; unrestrained, intemperate, immoderate, decadent.

heed verb *he should have heeded the warnings:* **pay attention to**, take notice of, take note of, pay heed to, attend to, listen to; be mindful of, consider, take into account, obey, adhere to, abide by, observe, take to heart, be alert to.
– OPPOSITES disregard.
• noun *he paid no heed:* **attention**, notice, note, regard.

heedful adjective **attentive**, careful, mindful, cautious, prudent, circumspect; alert, aware, wary, chary.

heedless adjective **unmindful**, taking no notice, neglectful, oblivious, inattentive, blind, deaf; incautious, imprudent, rash, reckless, foolhardy.

heft verb **lift**, raise, heave, hoist, haul; carry, lug; informal cart, tote, hump.

hefty adjective **1** *a hefty young man:* **burly**, heavy, sturdy, strapping, bulky, strong, muscular, large, big, solid, well built; informal hulking, beefy. **2** *a hefty kick:* **powerful**, violent, hard, forceful. **3** *a hefty fine:* **substantial**, sizeable, considerable, stiff, large, heavy; informal astronomical, whopping.
– OPPOSITES slight, light.

hegemony noun **leadership**, dominance, supremacy, authority, mastery, control, power, rule.

height noun **1** *the height of the wall:* **elevation**, altitude; stature, tallness. **2** *the mountain heights:* **summit**, top, peak, crest, crown, tip, cap, pinnacle. **3** *the height of their fame:* **highest point**, peak, acme, zenith, apogee, pinnacle, climax. **4** *the height of bad manners:* **epitome**, acme, quintessence; ultimate, utmost.
– OPPOSITES width, nadir.

WORD LINKS
altimetry the measurement of height
acrophobia an extreme fear of heights

heighten verb **1** *the roof had to be heightened:* **raise**, lift, elevate. **2** *her pleasure was heightened by guilt:* **intensify**, increase, enhance, add to, augment, boost, strengthen, deepen, magnify, reinforce.
– OPPOSITES lower, reduce.

heinous adjective **odious**, wicked, evil, atrocious, monstrous, abominable, detestable, despicable, horrific, terrible, awful, abhorrent, loathsome, hideous, unspeakable, execrable.
– OPPOSITES admirable.

heir, **heiress** noun **successor**, next in line, inheritor, beneficiary, legatee.

WORD LINKS
hereditary relating to an heir

helix noun **spiral**, coil, corkscrew, twist, gyre.

hell noun **1** *they feared hell:* **the netherworld**, the Inferno; eternal damnation, perdition; hellfire, fire and brimstone; Hades; literary the pit. **2** *he made her life hell:* **a misery**, torture, agony, a torment, a nightmare, an ordeal.
– OPPOSITES heaven, paradise.
■ **hell for leather** at top speed, rapidly, speedily, swiftly, full pelt, headlong, hotfoot, post-haste, helter-skelter, at the speed of light; informal like a bat out of hell, like the wind, like greased lightning, like a bomb; Brit. informal like the clappers, at a rate of knots; N. Amer. informal lickety-split.

WORD LINKS
infernal relating to hell

hell-bent adjective **intent**, determined, dead set, insistent, fixed, resolved.

hellish adjective **1** *the hellish face of Death:* **infernal**; diabolical, fiendish, satanic, demonic. **2** (informal) *a hellish week:* **horrible**, rotten, awful, terrible, dreadful, ghastly, vile, foul, appalling, atrocious, horrendous, frightful, nasty, disagreeable; tough, hard, traumatic, gruelling; informal murderous, lousy; Brit. informal beastly; N. Amer. informal hellacious.
– OPPOSITES angelic, wonderful.

help verb **1** **assist**, aid, lend a hand, give assistance, come to someone's aid; be of service, be of use; do someone a favour, do someone a service, do someone a good turn, give someone a leg up; rally round, pitch in. **2** *sore throats are helped by lozenges:* **relieve**, soothe, ease, alleviate, improve, assuage, lessen. **3** *he could not not help laughing:*

h

resist, refrain from, forbear from, stop yourself.
–OPPOSITES hinder, worsen.
•noun **1** *this could be of help to you:* **assistance**, aid, support, succour; benefit, use, advantage, service, comfort. **2** *he sought help for his eczema:* **relief**, alleviation, improvement, assuagement, healing.
■ **help yourself to** steal, take, appropriate, pocket, purloin; informal swipe, nab, filch, snaffle, walk off with; Brit. informal nick, pinch, whip, knock off.

helper noun **assistant**, aide, deputy, auxiliary, second, right-hand man/woman, attendant.

h

helpful adjective **1** *the staff are very helpful:* **obliging**, eager to please, kind, accommodating, supportive; sympathetic, neighbourly. **2** *we found your comments helpful:* **useful**, beneficial, valuable, constructive; informative, instructive. **3** *a helpful new tool:* **handy**, useful, convenient, practical, easy-to-use, serviceable; informal neat, nifty.
–OPPOSITES unsympathetic, useless, unhelpful.

helping noun **portion**, serving, piece, slice, share; informal dollop.

helpless adjective **dependent**, incapable, powerless, weak; defenceless, vulnerable, exposed, unprotected.
–OPPOSITES independent.

helter-skelter adverb *they ran helter-skelter down the hill:* **headlong**, pell-mell, hotfoot, post-haste, at full pelt, at full tilt, hell for leather; informal like a bat out of hell, like the wind, like greased lightning, like a bomb; Brit. informal like the clappers, at a rate of knots; N. Amer. informal lickety-split.

hence adverb **consequently**, as a consequence, for this reason, therefore, ergo, so, accordingly, as a result.

henceforth, **henceforward** adverb **from now on**, as of now, in future, subsequently, from this day on; formal hereafter.

henchman noun **right-hand man**, assistant, aide, helper, cohort; bodyguard, minder; informal sidekick, crony, heavy.

henpecked adjective **browbeaten**, downtrodden, bullied, dominated, subjugated, oppressed, intimidated.
–OPPOSITES domineering.

herald noun **1** (historical) *a herald announced the armistice:* **messenger**, courier. **2** *the first herald of spring:* **harbinger**, sign, indicator, signal, portent, omen; literary foretoken.
•verb **1** *shouts heralded their approach:* **proclaim**, announce, broadcast, publicize, declare, advertise. **2** *the speech heralded a policy change:* **signal**, indicate, announce; usher in, pave the way for, be a harbinger of; literary foretoken, betoken.

Herculean adjective *a Herculean task:* **superhuman**, heroic, formidable, tough, huge, massive.
–OPPOSITES easy.

herd noun **1** *a herd of cows:* **drove**, flock, pack. **2** *a herd of tourists:* **crowd**, group, bunch, horde, mob, pack, swarm, company. **3** *they consider themselves above the herd:* **the common people**, the masses, the crowd; the hoi polloi, the mob, the proletariat, the rabble, the riff-raff, the great unwashed; informal the proles, the plebs.
•verb **1** *we herded the sheep into the pen:* **drive**, shepherd, guide; round up, gather, collect. **2** *we all herded into the room:* **crowd**, pack, flock; cluster, huddle.

hereafter adverb (formal) *nothing I say hereafter is intended to offend:* **from now on**, after this, from this moment forth, subsequently, hence, henceforth, henceforward; formal hereinafter.
•noun *our preparation for the hereafter:* **life after death**, the afterlife, the afterworld, the next world; eternity, heaven, paradise.

hereditary adjective **1** *a hereditary right:* **inherited**; bequeathed, willed, handed down, passed down, passed on. **2** *a hereditary disease:* **genetic**, inborn, inherited, innate; in the family, in the blood, in the genes.

heresy noun **dissension**, dissent, nonconformity, heterodoxy, unorthodoxy, apostasy, blasphemy.

heretic noun **dissenter**, nonconformist, apostate, iconoclast.
–OPPOSITES conformist, believer.

heritage noun **1** *Europe's cultural heritage:* **tradition**, history, past, background; culture, customs. **2** *his Greek heritage:* **ancestry**, lineage, descent, extraction, parentage, roots, heredity.

hermetic adjective **airtight**, sealed; watertight, waterproof.

hermit noun **recluse**, loner, ascetic; historical anchorite, anchoress; old use eremite.

hero, **heroine** noun **1** *a sporting hero:* **star**, superstar, megastar, idol, celebrity, luminary; favourite. **2** *the hero of the film:* **protagonist**, main character/role, starring role; lead, leading man.
– OPPOSITES coward, villain.

heroic adjective **1** *heroic rescuers:* **brave**, courageous, valiant, intrepid, bold, fearless, daring; doughty, plucky, stout-hearted, mettlesome; gallant, chivalrous; informal gutsy, spunky. **2** *the building's heroic scale:* **prodigious**, grand, enormous, huge, massive, titanic, colossal, monumental; epic; informal mega.

heroism noun **bravery**, courage, valour, daring, fearlessness, pluck; backbone, spine, grit, mettle; gallantry, chivalry; informal guts, spunk; Brit. informal bottle; N. Amer. informal moxie.

hero-worship noun **idolization**, adulation, admiration, idealization, worship, adoration, veneration, lionization.

hesitancy noun. See HESITATION.

hesitant adjective **1** *she is hesitant about buying:* **uncertain**, undecided, unsure, doubtful, dubious, nervous, reluctant; ambivalent, in two minds; Brit. havering, humming and hawing; informal iffy. **2** *a hesitant child:* **timid**, diffident, shy, bashful, insecure.
– OPPOSITES certain, decisive, confident.

hesitate verb **1** *she hesitated, unsure of what to say:* **pause**, delay, wait, stall; be uncertain, be unsure, be doubtful, be indecisive, equivocate, vacillate, waver; Brit. haver, hum and haw; informal dilly-dally. **2** *don't hesitate to contact me:* **be reluctant**, be unwilling, be disinclined, scruple; have misgivings about, have qualms about, shrink from, think twice about.

hesitation noun **uncertainty**, doubt, dubiousness; irresolution, indecision; equivocation, vacillation; dithering, stalling, delay; reluctance, disinclination unease, ambivalence.

heterodox adjective **unorthodox**, nonconformist, dissenting, dissident, rebellious, renegade.
– OPPOSITES orthodox.

heterogeneous adjective **diverse**, varied, varying, miscellaneous, assorted, mixed, sundry, disparate, different, differing, unrelated.
– OPPOSITES homogeneous.

hew verb **chop**, hack, cut, lop; carve, shape, fashion, sculpt, model.

heyday noun **prime**, peak, height, pinnacle, acme, zenith.

hiatus noun **pause**, break, gap, lacuna, interval, intermission, interlude, interruption.

hidden adjective **1** *a hidden camera:* **concealed**, secret, invisible, unseen; camouflaged. **2** *a hidden meaning:* **obscure**, unclear, concealed; cryptic, mysterious, secret, covert, abstruse, arcane; ulterior, deep, subliminal, coded.
– OPPOSITES visible, obvious.

hide[1] verb **1** *he hid the money:* **conceal**, secrete, cache; informal stash. **2** *they hid in an air vent:* **conceal yourself**, secrete yourself, take cover; lie low, go to ground; informal hole up; Brit. informal, dated lie doggo. **3** *clouds hid the moon:* **obscure**, block out, blot out, obstruct, cloud, shroud, veil, eclipse. **4** *he could not hide his dislike:* **conceal**, keep secret, cover up, keep quiet about, bottle up, suppress; disguise, mask; informal keep a/the lid on.
– OPPOSITES flaunt, reveal.

hide[2] noun *the hide of an ox:* **skin**, pelt, coat.

hideaway noun **retreat**, refuge, hiding place, hideout, den, bolt-hole; informal hidey-hole.

hidebound adjective **conservative**, reactionary, conventional, orthodox; set in your ways, rigid.
– OPPOSITES liberal.

hideous adjective **1** *a hideous face:* **ugly**, repulsive, repellent, unsightly, revolting, gruesome, grotesque, monstrous. **2** *hideous cases of*

h

torture: **horrific**, terrible, appalling, awful, dreadful, frightful, horrible, horrendous, horrifying, shocking, sickening, gruesome, ghastly.
– OPPOSITES beautiful, pleasant.

hideout noun **hiding place**, hideaway, retreat, shelter, bolt-hole, safe house; informal hidey-hole.

hiding place noun **hideaway**, hideout, retreat, refuge, shelter, sanctuary, sanctum, bolt-hole, safe house; informal hidey-hole.

hierarchy noun **pecking order**, ranking, grading, ladder, scale.

hieroglyphic noun **1** *hieroglyphics on a stone monument:* **symbols**, signs, ciphers, sigils. **2** *notebooks filled with hieroglyphics:* **scribble**, scrawl, code; shorthand.

h

higgledy-piggledy (informal) adjective *a higgledy-piggledy pile of papers:* **disorderly**, disorganized, untidy, messy, chaotic, jumbled, muddled, confused, unsystematic, irregular; Brit. informal shambolic.
– OPPOSITES tidy.
• adverb *the cars were parked higgledy-piggledy:* **untidily**, haphazardly, in a muddle, in disarray; informal topsy-turvy.

high adjective **1** *a high building:* **tall**, lofty, towering, giant, big; multistorey, high-rise. **2** *a high position in the government:* **high-ranking**, leading, top, prominent, senior; influential, powerful, important, prime, premier, exalted; N. Amer. ranking; informal top-notch. **3** *high principles:* **noble**, lofty, moral, ethical, honourable, admirable, upright. **4** *high prices:* **inflated**, excessive, unreasonable, expensive, exorbitant, extortionate; informal steep, stiff. **5** *work of high quality:* **excellent**, outstanding, exemplary, exceptional, admirable, fine, first-class, superior, superlative, superb; impeccable, unimpeachable; informal A1, top-notch. **6** *high winds:* **strong**, powerful, violent, intense, stiff; blustery, gusty, tempestuous, turbulent. **7** *the high life:* **luxurious**, lavish, extravagant, grand, opulent; Brit. upmarket; N. Amer. upscale. **8** *I have a high opinion of her:* **favourable**, good, positive, approving, admiring, complimentary. **9** *a high note:* **high-pitched**; soprano, treble, falsetto, shrill, sharp, piercing, penetrating.
– OPPOSITES short, lowly, cheap, low.
• noun *prices were at a rare high:* **high point**, peak; zenith, acme, height.
– OPPOSITES low.
■ **high and dry** destitute, bereft, helpless, in the lurch, stranded, marooned. **high and mighty** (informal) self-important, disdainful, supercilious, superior, snobbish, conceited, above yourself; informal stuck-up, snooty, hoity-toity, la-di-da; Brit. informal toffee-nosed. **on a high** (informal) ecstatic, euphoric, delirious, elated, thrilled, overjoyed, walking on air, on cloud nine, in seventh heaven, jumping for joy, in raptures; informal blissed out, over the moon, on top of the world; Austral./NZ informal wrapped.

WORD LINKS
acrophobia a fear of high places

highbrow adjective **intellectual**, scholarly, bookish, academic, educated, donnish, bluestocking; erudite, learned; informal brainy.
– OPPOSITES lowbrow.

high-class adjective **superior**, first-rate; excellent, select, choice, premier, top, top-flight; deluxe, top-quality; Brit. upmarket; informal top-notch, top-drawer, A1, classy, posh.

highfalutin adjective (informal). See PRETENTIOUS.

high-flown adjective **grand**, extravagant, elaborate, flowery, ornate, overblown, overdone, overwrought, grandiloquent, grandiose, inflated; informal purple.
– OPPOSITES plain.

high-handed adjective **imperious**, peremptory, arrogant, haughty, domineering, overbearing; autocratic, authoritarian, dictatorial; informal bossy, high and mighty.
– OPPOSITES liberal.

high jinks plural noun **antics**, pranks, stunts, tricks; skylarking, mischief, horseplay, tomfoolery, clowning; informal shenanigans, monkey business.

highland noun **uplands**, mountains, hills, heights, moors; plateau; Brit. wolds.

highlight noun *the highlight of his*

career: **high point**, climax, peak, pinnacle, height, acme, zenith, summit.
– OPPOSITES nadir.
• verb *he has highlighted shortcomings in the plan:* **spotlight**, call attention to, focus on, underline, show up, bring out, accentuate, accent, stress, emphasize.

highly adverb **1** *a highly dangerous substance:* **very**, extremely, exceedingly, particularly, most, really, thoroughly, decidedly, distinctly, exceptionally, immensely, inordinately, singularly, extraordinarily; informal awfully, terribly, seriously, mega, ultra; Brit. informal well, dead, jolly; N. Amer. informal real, mighty, awful; dated frightfully. **2** *he spoke highly of her abilities:* **favourably**, well, approvingly, admiringly, enthusiastically.
– OPPOSITES slightly, unfavourably.

highly strung adjective **nervous**, nervy, excitable, temperamental, sensitive, unstable; brittle, edgy, jumpy, anxious, overwrought, neurotic; informal uptight.
– OPPOSITES easy-going.

high-minded adjective **principled**, honourable, moral, upright, noble, righteous, virtuous, worthy.
– OPPOSITES unprincipled.

high-pitched adjective **high**, shrill, sharp, piercing; soprano, treble, falsetto.
– OPPOSITES deep.

high-powered adjective **dynamic**, demanding, challenging, high-level, fast-moving, high-pressure.

high-pressure adjective. See HIGH-POWERED.

high-sounding adjective **grand**, high-flown, extravagant, elaborate, grandiose, inflated.
– OPPOSITES plain.

high-speed adjective **fast**, quick, rapid, speedy, swift, breakneck, lightning; express, whistle-stop; supersonic; literary fleet.
– OPPOSITES slow.

high-spirited adjective **lively**, full of fun, fun-loving, animated, bouncy, bubbly, sparkling, vivacious, buoyant, exuberant, ebullient, irrepressible; informal chirpy, sparky, bright and breezy, full of beans; literary frolicsome.

high spirits plural noun **liveliness**, vitality, spirit, energy, bounce, sparkle, vivacity, cheerfulness, exuberance, ebullience, joie de vivre.

hijack verb **commandeer**, seize, take over; appropriate, expropriate.

hike noun **walk**, trek, tramp, trudge, slog, footslog, march; ramble; Brit. informal yomp.
• verb **walk**, trek, tramp, trudge, slog, march; ramble; Brit. informal yomp.
■ **hike something up 1** *he hiked up his trousers:* hitch up, pull up, hoist; informal yank up. **2** *they hiked up the price:* increase, raise, up, put up, push up; informal jack up, bump up.

hilarious adjective **1** *a hilarious story:* **very funny**, hysterical, uproarious, rib-tickling; informal side-splitting, priceless, a scream, a hoot. **2** *a hilarious evening:* **amusing**, entertaining, animated, high-spirited, lively, funny, merry, jolly, mirthful, uproarious.
– OPPOSITES sad, serious.

hilarity noun **amusement**, mirth, laughter, merriment, light-heartedness, fun, humour, jollity, gaiety, exuberance, high spirits.

hill noun **high ground**, prominence, hillock, hillside, rise, mound, knoll, hummock, tor, fell, pike, mesa; ridge, slope, incline, gradient; Scottish & Irish drum; Scottish brae; Geology drumlin; formal eminence.

hillock noun **mound**, prominence, rise, knoll, hummock, hump; bank, ridge; formal eminence.

hilt noun **handle**, haft, grip, shaft, shank, stock.
■ **to the hilt** completely, fully, wholly, totally, entirely, utterly, unreservedly, unconditionally, in every respect, one hundred per cent, every inch, to the full, all the way.

hind adjective **back**, rear, hinder, hindmost, posterior.
– OPPOSITES fore, front.

hinder verb **hamper**, impede, inhibit, retard, thwart, foil, curb, delay, interfere with, set back, slow down, hold back, hold up; restrict, restrain, constrain, curtail, frustrate, cramp, handicap, hamstring; Brit. throw a spanner in the works; informal stymie.
– OPPOSITES facilitate.

h

hindrance noun **impediment**, obstacle, barrier, obstruction, handicap, hurdle, restraint, restriction, encumbrance; complication, delay, drawback, setback, difficulty, inconvenience, hitch, stumbling block, fly in the ointment, hiccup; Brit. spanner in the works.
– OPPOSITES help.

hinge verb *our future hinges on the election:* **depend**, hang, rest, turn, centre, be contingent, be dependent; be determined by.

hint noun **1** *a hint that he would leave:* **clue**, inkling, suggestion, indication, sign, signal, pointer, intimation, insinuation, mention. **2** *handy hints about painting:* **tip**, suggestion, pointer, clue, guideline, recommendation. **3** *a hint of garlic:* **trace**, touch, suspicion, suggestion, dash, soupçon, modicum; informal smidgen, tad.
• verb *what are you hinting at?* **imply**, insinuate, intimate, suggest; refer to, drive at, mean; informal get at.

h

hinterland noun **the backwoods**, the back of beyond; Austral./NZ the outback, the backblocks; informal the sticks, the middle of nowhere; N. Amer. informal the boondocks.

hip[1] noun

> **WORD LINKS**
> **sciatic** relating to the hips

hip[2] adjective (informal). See **FASHIONABLE**.

hire verb **1** *we hired a car:* **rent**, lease, charter. **2** *they hire labour in line with demand:* **employ**, engage, recruit, appoint, take on, sign up, commission.
– OPPOSITES dismiss.
• noun *the hire of the machine:* **rental**, rent, hiring, lease.

hirsute adjective (formal) **hairy**, shaggy, bushy; woolly, furry, fleecy; bearded, unshaven.

hiss verb **1** *the escaping gas hissed:* **fizz**, whistle, wheeze. **2** *the audience hissed:* **jeer**, boo, catcall, whistle, hoot; informal blow a raspberry.

historian noun **chronicler**, annalist, archivist, recorder; antiquarian.

historic adjective **significant**, notable, important, momentous, memorable, remarkable; ground-breaking, epoch-making, red-letter; informal earth-shattering.
– OPPOSITES insignificant.

> **!** Don't confuse **historic** and **historical**. **Historic** means 'famous or important in history', while **historical** chiefly means 'relating to history'.

historical adjective **1** *historical evidence:* **documented**, recorded, chronicled; authentic, factual, actual. **2** *historical figures:* **past**, bygone, ancient, old, former; literary of yore.
– OPPOSITES contemporary.

history noun **1** *my interest in history:* **the past**, former times, the olden days, yesterday, antiquity; literary days of yore, yesteryear. **2** *a history of the Civil War:* **chronicle**, archive, record, report, narrative, account, study. **3** *she related the details of her history:* **background**, past, life story, experiences, record.

histrionic adjective **melodramatic**, theatrical, dramatic, exaggerated, stagy, showy, affected, overacted; informal hammy.

histrionics plural noun **dramatics**, theatrics, tantrums; affectation.

hit verb **1** **strike**, slap, smack, cuff, punch, thump, swat; beat, thrash, batter, belabour, pound, pummel, box someone's ears; informal whack, wallop, bash, biff, bop, clout, clip, sock, swipe, beat the living daylights out of, give someone a hiding, belt, tan, lay into, deck; Brit. informal stick one on, slosh; N. Amer. informal slug, boff; literary smite. **2** *a car hit the barrier:* **crash into**, run into, smash into, knock into, bump into, plough into, collide with, meet head-on. **3** *the tragedy hit her hard:* **devastate**, affect badly; upset, shatter, crush, shock, traumatize; informal knock sideways, knock the stuffing out of; Brit. informal knock for six. **4** (informal) *spending will hit £1,800 million:* **reach**, arrive at, rise to, climb to. **5** *it hit me that I had forgotten:* **occur to**, strike, dawn on, come to; enter your head, cross your mind.
• noun **1** **blow**, thump, punch, knock, bang, cuff, slap, smack, tap, crack; informal whack, wallop, bash, belt, biff, clout, swipe; N. Amer. informal boff,

slug. **2** *he directed many big hits:* **success**, sell-out, winner, triumph, sensation; best-seller; informal smash hit, knockout, crowd-puller.
– OPPOSITES failure.
■ **hit back** retaliate, respond, reply, react, counter, defend yourself. **hit home** strike home, hit the mark, register, be understood, get through, sink in. **hit it off** (informal) get on, get along, be compatible, be on the same wavelength, see eye to eye, take to each other, warm to each other; informal click. **hit on** discover, come up with, think of, conceive of, dream up, invent, create, devise. **hit out at** criticize, attack, censure, denounce, condemn, lambaste, rail against, inveigh against, arraign; informal pan, slam, hammer, lay into; Brit. informal slate, rubbish; N. Amer. informal trash; formal excoriate.

hitch verb **1** *she hitched the blanket around her:* **pull**, hike, lift, raise; informal yank. **2** *Tom hitched the pony to his cart:* **harness**, yoke, couple, fasten, connect, attach.
• noun *it went without a hitch:* **problem**, difficulty, snag, setback, obstacle, obstruction, complication; informal glitch, hiccup.

hit-or-miss, hit-and-miss adjective **erratic**, haphazard, disorganized, sloppy, unmethodical, uneven, inconsistent, random; informal slap-happy.
– OPPOSITES meticulous.

hoard noun *a hoard of weapons:* **cache**, stockpile, stock, store, collection, supply, reserve, fund; informal stash.
• verb *they hoarded their rations:* **stockpile**, store, put aside, put by, lay by, set aside, stow away; amass, collect, save, accumulate, squirrel away; informal stash away, salt away.
– OPPOSITES squander.

> Don't confuse **hoard** with **horde**, which means 'a large group of people' (*hordes of tourists flock to the city each summer*).

hoarse adjective **rough**, harsh, croaky, throaty, gruff, husky, grating, rasping.
– OPPOSITES mellow, clear.

hoax noun *the call was a hoax:* **practical joke**, prank, trick; deception, fraud; informal con, spoof, wind-up, scam.
• verb *gullible viewers had been hoaxed:* **play a practical joke on**, trick, fool; deceive, hoodwink, dupe, take in, lead on, gull; informal con, kid, have on, pull a fast one on, put one over on, wind up; N. Amer. informal sucker, snooker.

hobble verb **limp**, shamble, totter, dodder, stagger, stumble; Scottish hirple.

hobby noun **pastime**, leisure activity; sideline, diversion; recreation, amusement.

hobgoblin noun **goblin**, imp, gremlin, demon, bogey.

hobnob verb (informal) **associate**, mix, fraternize, socialize, spend time, go around, mingle, consort, rub shoulders; N. Amer. rub elbows; informal hang around/out, knock about/around.

hocus-pocus noun **jargon**, mumbo-jumbo, gibberish, balderdash, claptrap, nonsense, rubbish, twaddle, garbage; informal gobbledegook, double Dutch; N. Amer. informal flapdoodle; informal, dated bunkum.

hodgepodge noun (N. Amer.). See HOTCHPOTCH.

hog verb (informal) *he hogged the limelight:* **monopolize**, dominate, corner, control, take over.

hoist verb *we hoisted the mainsail:* **raise**, lift, haul up, heave up, winch up, pull up, upraise, uplift, elevate, erect.
– OPPOSITES lower.
• noun *a mechanical hoist:* **crane**, winch, block and tackle, pulley, windlass.

hold verb **1** *she held a small suitcase:* **clasp**, clutch, grasp, grip, clench, cling to, hold on to; carry, bear. **2** *I wanted to hold her:* **embrace**, hug, clasp, cradle, enfold, squeeze, cuddle. **3** *do you hold a driving licence?* **possess**, have, own, bear, carry. **4** *the branch held my weight:* **support**, bear, carry, take, keep up, sustain. **5** *the police were holding him:* **detain**, imprison, lock up, keep behind bars, put in prison, put in jail, incarcerate, confine, intern; informal put away, put inside. **6** *he held a senior post:* **occupy**, have, fill; informal hold down. **7** *the tank held*

h

250 gallons: **take**, contain, accommodate, fit; have room for, house. **8** *the court held that there was no evidence:* **maintain**, consider, take the view, believe, think, feel, deem, be of the opinion; judge, rule, decide; informal reckon; formal opine. **9** *the offer still holds:* **stand**, be valid, apply, remain, exist, be in force, be in effect. **10** *they held a meeting:* **convene**, call, summon; conduct, have, organize, run; formal convoke.

– OPPOSITES release, lose, end.

• **noun 1** *she kept a hold on my hand:* **grip**, grasp, clasp, clutch. **2** *Tom had a hold over his father:* **influence**, power, control, dominance, authority. **3** *the military tightened their hold on the capital:* **control**, grip, power, stranglehold, dominion.

h

■ **hold back** hesitate, pause, stop yourself, desist, forbear. **hold someone back** hinder, hamper, impede, obstruct, check, curb, block, thwart, frustrate, stand in someone's way. **hold something back 1** *she held back her tears:* suppress, fight back, choke back, stifle, smother, subdue, rein in, repress, curb, control. **2** *don't hold anything back from me:* withhold, hide, conceal; informal sit on, keep under your hat. **hold forth** speak at length, talk at length, go on, sound off; declaim, spout, pontificate, orate, preach, sermonize; informal speechify, preachify, drone on. **hold something off** resist, repel, repulse, rebuff, parry, deflect, fend off, stave off, ward off, keep at bay. **hold on** *if only they could hold on a while:* keep going, persevere, survive, last, continue, struggle on, carry on, hold out, see it through, stay the course; informal soldier on, stick at it, hang in there. **hold something out** extend, proffer, offer, present; outstretch, reach out, stretch out, put out. **hold something up 1** *they held up the trophy:* display, hold aloft, show off, flourish, brandish; informal flash. **2** *concrete pillars hold up the bridge:* support, hold, bear, carry, take, keep up, prop up, shore up, buttress. **3** *our flight was held up:* delay, detain, make late, set back. **4** *a lack of cash has held up progress:* obstruct, impede, hinder, hamper, inhibit, thwart, curb; informal stymie. **hold with** approve of, agree with, be in favour of, endorse, accept, countenance, support, subscribe to, give your blessing to, take kindly to; informal stand for.

holder **noun container**, receptacle, case, cover, housing, sheath.

holdings **plural noun assets**, funds, capital, resources, savings, investments, securities, equities, bonds, stocks and shares, reserves.

hold-up **noun delay**, setback, hitch, snag, difficulty, problem, glitch, hiccup; traffic jam, tailback; informal snarl-up.

hole **noun 1** *a hole in the roof:* **opening**, aperture, gap, space, vent, chink; breach, crack, rupture; puncture, perforation, split, gash, slit, crevice, fissure. **2** *a hole in the ground:* **pit**, crater, depression, hollow; well, borehole, excavation, dugout; pothole. **3** *the badger's hole:* **burrow**, lair, den, earth, sett; retreat, shelter. **4** (informal) *I was living in a real hole:* **hovel**, slum; informal dump, dive, pigsty.

• **verb** *a fuel tank was holed:* **puncture**, perforate, pierce, penetrate, rupture, split.

holiday **noun break**, rest; time off, time out, leave, furlough, sabbatical; trip, tour, journey, voyage; N. Amer. vacation.

holier-than-thou **adjective sanctimonious**, self-righteous, smug, self-satisfied; priggish, pious; informal goody-goody, preachy.

– OPPOSITES humble.

hollow **adjective 1** *hollow cheeks:* **sunken**, deep-set, concave, depressed, recessed. **2** *a hollow voice:* **dull**, low, flat, toneless, expressionless.

• **noun 1** *a hollow under the tree:* **hole**, pit, cavity, crater, trough; depression, indentation, dip; niche, nook, cranny, recess. **2** *the village lay in a hollow:* **valley**, vale, dale; Brit. dene, combe; N. English clough; Scottish glen, strath; literary dell.

• **verb** *a tunnel hollowed out of a mountain:* **gouge**, scoop, dig, cut; excavate, channel.

holocaust **noun slaughter**, mass murder, genocide; massacre, carnage.

holy adjective **1** *holy men:* **saintly**, godly, pious, religious, devout, God-fearing, spiritual; righteous, good, virtuous, pure; canonized, beatified; ordained. **2** *a Jewish holy place:* **sacred**, consecrated, hallowed, sanctified, venerated, revered, religious, dedicated.
– OPPOSITES sinful, irreligious.

homage noun **respect**, honour, reverence, worship, admiration, esteem, adulation, acclaim; tribute, acknowledgement, recognition.
■ **pay homage to** honour, acclaim, applaud, salute, praise, commend, pay tribute to, take your hat off to; formal laud.

home noun **1** *low-cost homes for first-time buyers:* **residence**, place of residence, house; flat, apartment, bungalow, cottage; accommodation, property, quarters, lodgings, rooms; address, place; informal pad, digs; formal domicile, abode, dwelling, habitation. **2** *I am far from my home:* **homeland**, native land, home town, birthplace, roots, fatherland, mother country, motherland, country of origin, the old country. **3** *a home for the elderly:* **institution**; nursing home, retirement home, rest home; children's home; hospice, shelter, refuge, retreat, asylum, hostel.
• adjective *the UK home market:* **domestic**, internal, local, national.
– OPPOSITES foreign, international.
■ **hit home**. See HIT. **home in on** focus on, concentrate on, zero in on, centre on, fix on; highlight, spotlight, underline, pinpoint; informal zoom in on.

homeland noun **native land**, country of origin, home, fatherland, motherland, mother country, the old country.

homeless adjective **of no fixed abode**, without a roof over your head, on the streets, vagrant, sleeping rough; destitute, down and out.

homely adjective **1** *a homely atmosphere:* **cosy**, comfortable, snug, welcoming, friendly, congenial, intimate, warm, hospitable, informal, relaxed, pleasant, cheerful; informal comfy. **2** (N. Amer.) *she's rather homely:* **unattractive**, plain, unprepossessing, ugly; informal not much to look at; Brit. informal no oil painting.

homespun adjective **unsophisticated**, plain, simple, unpolished, unrefined, rustic, folksy; coarse, rough, crude, rudimentary.
– OPPOSITES sophisticated.

homicidal adjective **murderous**, violent, brutal, savage, ferocious, vicious, bloody, bloodthirsty, barbarous, barbaric, psychopathic.

homicide noun **killing**; murder, assassination, execution; patricide, matricide, infanticide.

homily noun **sermon**, lecture, discourse, address, lesson, talk, speech, oration.

homogeneous adjective *a homogeneous group:* **uniform**, alike, similar, much the same, all of a piece; informal much of a muchness.

hone verb **sharpen**, whet, strop, grind, file.

honest adjective **1** *an honest man:* **upright**, honourable, principled, righteous, right-minded, respectable; virtuous, good, decent, law-abiding, upstanding, incorruptible, truthful, trustworthy, reliable, conscientious, scrupulous. **2** *I haven't been honest with you:* **truthful**, sincere, candid, frank, open, forthright, straight; straightforward; informal upfront. **3** *an honest mistake:* **genuine**, real, actual, true, bona fide, legitimate, fair and square; informal legit, kosher, on the level, honest-to-goodness.
– OPPOSITES dishonest, insincere.

honesty noun **1** *I can attest to his honesty:* **integrity**, uprightness, honourableness, honour, righteousness; virtue, goodness, probity, high-mindedness, fairness, incorruptibility, truthfulness, trustworthiness, reliability, dependability. **2** *they spoke with honesty about their fears:* **sincerity**, candour, frankness, directness, truthfulness, truth, openness, straightforwardness.

honeyed adjective **sweet**, sugary, saccharine, pleasant, flattering, unctuous; dulcet, soothing, soft, mellow, mellifluous.
– OPPOSITES harsh.

h

honorary adjective **1** *an honorary doctorate:* **titular**, nominal, in name only, unofficial, token. **2** (Brit.) *an honorary treasurer:* **unpaid**, unsalaried, voluntary, volunteer; N. Amer. pro bono.

honour noun **1** *a man of honour:* **integrity**, honesty, uprightness, morals, morality, principles, righteousness, high-mindedness; virtue, goodness, decency, probity, scrupulousness, fairness, justness, trustworthiness. **2** *a mark of honour:* **distinction**, privilege, glory, kudos, cachet, prestige. **3** *our honour is at stake:* **reputation**, good name, character, repute, image, standing, status. **4** *the honour of meeting the Queen:* **privilege**, pleasure; compliment.
– OPPOSITES unscrupulousness, dishonour, shame.
• verb **1** *we should honour our parents:* **esteem**, respect, admire, defer to, look up to; appreciate, value, cherish; revere, venerate. **2** *they were honoured at a special ceremony:* **applaud**, acclaim, praise, salute, recognize, celebrate, commemorate, commend, hail, eulogize, pay homage to, pay tribute to; formal laud. **3** *he honoured the contract:* **fulfil**, observe, keep, obey, heed, follow, carry out; keep to, abide by, adhere to, comply with, conform to, be true to. **4** *the cheque was not honoured:* **accept**, take, clear, pass, cash; Brit. encash.
– OPPOSITES disgrace, dishonour, disobey.

honourable adjective **1** *an honourable man:* **honest**, moral, principled, righteous, right-minded; decent, respectable, virtuous, good, upstanding, upright, noble, fair, just, truthful, trustworthy, law-abiding, reputable, dependable. **2** *an honourable career:* **illustrious**, distinguished, eminent, great, glorious, prestigious.
– OPPOSITES dishonourable.

hoodlum noun **gangster**, mobster, Mafioso, heavy, hit man, thug, criminal; N. Amer. informal hood.

hoodwink verb **deceive**, trick, dupe, fool, delude, cheat, take in, hoax, mislead, defraud, double-cross, swindle, gull; informal con, bamboozle, do, have, sting, diddle, shaft, rip off, pull a fast one on, put one over on, take for a ride; N. Amer. informal sucker, snooker; Austral. informal pull a swifty on; literary cozen.

hook noun **peg**, nail; fastener, clasp, hasp, clip.
• verb **1** *they hooked baskets on to the ladder:* **attach**, hitch, fasten, fix, secure, hang, clasp. **2** *he hooked a 24 lb pike:* **catch**, land, net, take, bag.
■ **off the hook** (informal) out of trouble, in the clear, free, scot-free; informal let off.

hooked adjective **1** *a hooked nose:* **curved**, aquiline, angular, bent. **2** (informal) *they're hooked on cocaine:* **addicted to**, dependent on; informal using; N. Amer. informal having a jones for. **3** (informal) *he's hooked on crosswords:* **keen on**, enthusiastic about, addicted to, obsessed with, fanatical about; informal mad about.
– OPPOSITES straight.

hooligan noun **lout**, thug, tearaway, vandal, ruffian, troublemaker; Austral. larrikin; informal tough, rough, bruiser, roughneck; Brit. informal yob, yobbo, bovver boy, lager lout; Scottish informal ned.

hoop noun **ring**, band, circle, circlet, loop; technical annulus.

hoot noun **1** *the hoot of an owl:* **screech**, shriek, call, cry; tu-whit tu-whoo. **2** *the hoot of a horn:* **beep**, honk, toot, blast, blare. **3** *hoots of derision:* **shout**, yell, cry, howl, shriek, whoop, whistle; boo, jeer, catcall.
• verb **1** *an owl hooted:* **screech**, shriek, cry, call. **2** *a car horn hooted:* **beep**, honk, toot, blare, blast, sound. **3** *they hooted in disgust:* **shout**, yell, cry, howl, shriek, whistle; boo, jeer, catcall.

hop verb **jump**, bound, spring, bounce, skip, leap; prance, dance, frolic, gambol.
■ **on the hop** (Brit. informal) *he was caught on the hop:* unprepared, unready, off guard, unawares, by surprise, with your defences down; informal napping; Brit. informal with your trousers down.

hope noun **1** *I had high hopes:* **aspiration**, desire, wish, expectation, ambition, aim, plan; dream. **2** *a life filled with hope:* **hopefulness**,

optimism, expectation, expectancy; confidence, faith, belief.
–OPPOSITES pessimism.
•verb **1** *he's hoping for a medal:* **expect**, anticipate, look for, want, aspire to, dream of, long for. **2** *we're hoping to address this issue next week:* **aim**, intend, have in mind, plan.

hopeful adjective **1** *he remained hopeful:* **optimistic**, full of hope, confident, positive, buoyant, sanguine, bullish, cheerful. **2** *hopeful signs:* **promising**, encouraging, heartening, reassuring, favourable, optimistic.

hopefully adverb **1** *he rode on hopefully:* **optimistically**, full of hope, confidently. **2** *hopefully, the work should be finished soon:* **all being well**, God willing, with luck; most likely, probably; touch wood, fingers crossed.

hopeless adjective **1** *a hopeless case:* **irremediable**, beyond hope, lost, irreparable, irreversible; incurable; impossible, futile, forlorn, unworkable, impracticable; old use bootless. **2** *he was hopeless at maths:* **bad**, poor, awful, terrible, dreadful, appalling, atrocious; inferior, incompetent, unskilled; informal pathetic, useless, lousy, rotten; Brit. informal rubbish.

horde noun *hordes of tourists flock to the city each summer:* **crowd**, mob, pack, gang, troop, army, swarm, mass; throng, multitude, host, flock; informal load.

> ! Don't confuse **horde** with **hoard**, which means 'a secret store' (*a hoard of gold and silver coins*).

horizontal adjective **1** *a horizontal surface:* **level**, flat, plane, smooth, even; straight, parallel. **2** *she was stretched horizontal on a sunbed:* **flat**, supine, prone, prostrate.
–OPPOSITES vertical.

horrendous adjective. See **HORRIBLE**.

horrible adjective **1** *a horrible murder:* **dreadful**, awful, terrible, shocking, appalling, horrifying, horrific, horrendous, grisly, ghastly, gruesome, harrowing, unspeakable; macabre, spine-chilling; loathsome, monstrous, abominable, atrocious, sickening. **2** (informal) *a horrible little man:* **nasty**, horrid, disagreeable, awful, dreadful, terrible, appalling, repulsive, ghastly; obnoxious, hateful, odious, objectionable, insufferable, vile, loathsome; informal frightful, God-awful; Brit. informal beastly.
–OPPOSITES pleasant, agreeable.

horrid adjective. See **HORRIBLE**.

horrific adjective **dreadful**, horrendous, horrible, frightful, awful, terrible, atrocious; horrifying, shocking, appalling, harrowing; hideous, grisly, ghastly, unspeakable, sickening.

horrify verb *he was horrified by her remarks:* **shock**, appal, outrage, scandalize, offend; disgust, revolt, nauseate, sicken.

horror noun **1** *children screamed in horror:* **terror**, fear, fright, alarm, panic; dread. **2** *to her horror she found herself alone:* **dismay**, consternation, alarm, distress; disgust, shock. **3** (informal) *he's a little horror:* **rascal**, devil, imp, monkey, monster; informal terror, scamp, scallywag, tyke; Brit. informal perisher; N. Amer. informal varmint.
–OPPOSITES delight, satisfaction.
■ **have a horror of** hate, detest, loathe, abhor; formal abominate.

horse noun **mount**, charger, cob, nag, hack; pony, foal, yearling, colt, stallion, gelding, mare, filly; N. Amer. bronco; Austral./NZ moke; informal gee-gee; literary steed.
■ **horse about** (informal) fool about, play the fool, clown about, monkey about; informal mess about, lark about; Brit. informal muck about.

> **WORD LINKS**
> **equine** relating to horses
> **equestrian** relating to horse riding
> **equitation** horse riding

horseman, **horsewoman** noun **rider**, jockey; cavalryman, trooper; historical hussar, dragoon, knight; old use cavalier.

horseplay noun **tomfoolery**, fooling around, clowning, buffoonery; antics, high jinks; informal shenanigans, monkey business.

horticulture noun **gardening**, floriculture, arboriculture.

hose noun **pipe**, tube, duct, outlet, pipeline, siphon.

h

hospitable adjective **welcoming**, friendly, congenial, sociable, convivial, cordial; gracious, helpful, obliging, accommodating, warm, kind, generous, bountiful.

hospital noun **infirmary**, clinic, sanatorium, hospice; Brit. cottage hospital; Military field hospital.

hospitality noun **1** *he is renowned for his hospitality:* **friendliness**, helpfulness, warmth, kindness, congeniality, cordiality, generosity. **2** *corporate hospitality:* **entertainment**; catering, food and drink.

host[1] noun *the host of a TV series:* **presenter**, compère, anchor, anchorman, anchorwoman, announcer.
– OPPOSITES guest.
• verb *she hosts a weekly radio show:* **present**, introduce, compère, front, anchor.

h

host[2] noun **1** *a host of memories:* **multitude**, abundance, wealth, profusion; informal load, heap, mass, pile, ton; Brit. informal shedload; literary myriad. **2** *a host of well-wishers:* **crowd**, throng, flock, swarm, horde, mob, army, legion.

hostage noun **captive**, prisoner, detainee, internee.

hostile adjective **1** *a hostile attitude:* **unfriendly**, unkind, unsympathetic, rancorous; antagonistic, aggressive, confrontational, belligerent, truculent. **2** *hostile climatic conditions:* **unfavourable**, adverse, bad, harsh, grim, inhospitable, forbidding. **3** *they are hostile to the idea:* **opposed**, averse, antagonistic, ill-disposed, unsympathetic, antipathetic, against; informal anti, down on.
– OPPOSITES friendly, favourable.

hostility noun **1** *he glared at her with hostility:* **antagonism**, unfriendliness, malevolence, unkindness, rancour, venom, hatred; aggression, belligerence. **2** *their hostility to the present regime:* **opposition**, antagonism, animosity, antipathy, ill feeling, resentment, enmity. **3** *a cessation of hostilities:* **fighting**, conflict, combat, warfare, war, bloodshed, violence.

hot adjective **1** *a jug of hot water:* **heated**, piping hot, steaming, boiling, scalding. **2** *a hot day:* **very warm**, balmy, summery; tropical, scorching, searing, blistering; sweltering; informal boiling, baking, roasting. **3** *she felt very hot:* **feverish**, febrile; burning, flushed. **4** *a hot chilli:* **spicy**, peppery, fiery, strong; piquant, powerful. **5** *the competition was hot:* **fierce**, intense, keen, competitive, cut-throat, ruthless, aggressive, strong. **6** (informal) *hot news:* **breaking**, recent, late, up to date, up to the minute; just out. **7** (informal) *a hot new act:* **popular**, in demand, sought-after; fashionable, in vogue, all the rage; informal big, in, now, hip, trendy, cool. **8** (informal) *she is hot on local history:* **knowledgeable about**, well informed about, au fait with, up on, well versed in; informal clued up about, genned up about.
– OPPOSITES cold, mild.

hotbed noun *a hotbed of crime:* **breeding ground**, den, cradle, nest.

hot-blooded adjective **passionate**, amorous, lustful, libidinous; informal horny, randy.
– OPPOSITES cold.

hotchpotch noun **mixture**, mixed bag, assortment, miscellany, medley, potpourri, melange; jumble, ragbag, mishmash; N. Amer. hodgepodge.

hotel noun **inn**, motel, boarding house, guest house, bed and breakfast, B & B, hostel.

hotfoot adverb **hastily**, hurriedly, speedily, quickly, fast, rapidly, swiftly, without delay, post-haste, helter-skelter; N. Amer. informal lickety-split.
– OPPOSITES slowly.
■ **hotfoot it** (informal) hurry, dash, run, race, sprint, bolt, dart, charge, shoot, hare, fly, speed, zoom, streak; informal tear, belt, pelt, scoot, clip, leg it; Brit. informal bomb; N. Amer. informal hightail it.

hot-headed adjective **impetuous**, impulsive, rash, irresponsible, foolhardy; excitable, volatile, fiery, hot-tempered.

hothouse noun **greenhouse**, glasshouse, conservatory, orangery, vinery, winter garden.

hotly adverb **1** *the rumours were hotly denied:* **vehemently**, vigorously, strenuously, fiercely, heatedly; angrily, indignantly. **2** *they were hotly pursued by angry fans:* **closely**, swiftly, quickly.

hot-tempered adjective **irascible**, quick-tempered, short-tempered, irritable, fiery, bad-tempered; touchy, volatile, testy, tetchy; informal on a short fuse.
–OPPOSITES placid.

hound noun **dog**, canine, mongrel, cur; informal pooch, mutt.
•verb **1** *she was hounded by the press:* **pursue**, chase, follow, shadow, stalk, track, trail; harass, persecute, pester, badger, torment. **2** *they hounded him out of office:* **force**, drive, push, urge, coerce, dragoon, strong-arm; informal bulldoze, railroad; Brit. informal bounce; N. Amer. informal hustle.

house noun **1** *an estate of 200 houses:* **residence**, home; homestead; formal habitation, dwelling, abode, domicile. **2** *the house of Stewart:* **family**, clan, tribe; dynasty, line, bloodline, lineage. **3** *a printing house:* **firm**, business, company, corporation, enterprise, establishment, institution, concern, organization, operation; informal outfit, set-up. **4** *the country's upper house:* assembly, legislative body, chamber, council, parliament, congress, senate, diet.
•verb **1** *we can house twelve adults:* **accommodate**, lodge, quarter, board, billet, take in, sleep, put up. **2** *this panel houses the main switch:* **contain**, hold, store; cover, protect, enclose.

householder noun **homeowner**, owner, occupant, resident; leaseholder; proprietor, freeholder; Brit. occupier, owner-occupier.

housing noun **1 houses**, homes, residences; accommodation, living quarters; formal dwellings. **2 casing**, covering, case, cover, holder, fairing, sleeve.

hovel noun **shack**, slum, shanty, hut; informal dump, hole.

hover verb **1** *helicopters hovered overhead:* **hang**, be poised, be suspended, float; fly. **2** *a servant hovered nearby:* **wait**, linger.

however adverb *however, this is not inevitable:* **nevertheless**, nonetheless, even so, for all that, despite that, in spite of that; be that as it may.

howl noun **1** *the howl of a wolf:* **baying**, cry, bark, yelp. **2** *a howl of anguish:* **wail**, cry, yell, yelp; bellow, roar, shout, shriek, scream, screech.
•verb **1** *dogs howled in the distance:* **bay**, cry, bark, yelp. **2** *a baby started to howl:* **wail**, cry, yell, bawl, bellow, shriek, scream, screech, caterwaul; informal holler. **3** *we howled with laughter:* **laugh**, guffaw, roar; be doubled up, split your sides; informal fall about, crack up, be in stitches.

howler noun (informal) **mistake**, error, blunder, gaffe, slip; informal **slip-up**, boo-boo, clanger; Brit. informal boob; N. Amer. informal blooper.

hub noun *the hub of family life:* **centre**, core, heart, focus, focal point, nucleus, kernel, nerve centre.
–OPPOSITES periphery.

hubbub noun **1** *her voice was lost in the hubbub:* **noise**, din, racket, commotion, clamour, cacophony, babel, rumpus; Brit. row. **2** *she fought through the hubbub:* **confusion**, chaos, pandemonium, bedlam, mayhem, tumult, fracas, hurly-burly.

huckster noun **trader**, dealer, vendor, salesman, pedlar, hawker; informal pusher.

huddle verb **1** *they huddled together:* **crowd**, cluster, gather, bunch, throng, flock, collect, group, congregate; press, pack, squeeze. **2** *he huddled beneath the sheets:* **curl up**, snuggle, nestle, hunch up.
–OPPOSITES disperse.
•noun *a huddle of passengers:* **group**, cluster, bunch; collection; informal gaggle.

hue noun **1** *paints in a variety of hues:* **colour**, shade, tone, tint. **2** *men of all political hues:* **complexion**, type, kind, sort, cast, stamp, character, persuasion, nature.

hue and cry noun **commotion**, outcry, uproar, fuss, clamour, furore, ruckus, rumpus; Brit. row; informal hoo-ha, hullabaloo, ballyhoo, kerfuffle, to-do, song and dance.

huff noun **bad mood**, sulk, pet; temper; informal grump; Brit. informal strop; N. Amer. informal snit.

huffy adjective **irritable**, irritated, annoyed, cross, grumpy, bad-tempered, crotchety, crabby, cantankerous, moody; Brit. informal narky, miffed, shirty.

hug verb *they hugged each other:* **embrace**, cuddle, squeeze, clasp, clutch, hold tight.
• noun *there were hugs and kisses as we left:* **embrace**, cuddle, squeeze, bear hug.

huge adjective **enormous**, vast, immense, great, massive, colossal, prodigious, gigantic, gargantuan, mammoth, monumental; giant, towering, mountainous, titanic; epic, Herculean; informal jumbo, mega, monster, whopping, humongous, hulking, bumper, astronomical; Brit. informal ginormous.
– OPPOSITES tiny.

h

hulk noun **1** *the rusting hulks of ships:* **wreck**, ruin; shell, skeleton, hull. **2** *a great hulk of a man:* **giant**; informal clodhopper, ape, gorilla; N. Amer. informal lummox.

hull[1] noun *the ship's hull:* **framework**, body, shell, frame, skeleton, structure.

hull[2] noun *separate the nut from its hull:* **shell**, husk, pod, case, covering, integument; Botany pericarp.
• verb **shell**, husk, peel, pare, skin; technical decorticate.

hullabaloo noun (informal) **fuss**, commotion, hue and cry, uproar, outcry, clamour, storm, furore, hubbub, ruckus, brouhaha; pandemonium, mayhem, tumult, turmoil; informal hoo-ha, to-do, kerfuffle, song and dance.

hum verb **1** *the engine was humming:* **purr**, drone, murmur, buzz, thrum, whirr, throb, vibrate. **2** *she hummed a tune:* sing, croon, murmur. **3** *the workshops are humming:* **be busy**, be active, be lively, buzz, bustle, be a hive of activity, throb.
• noun *a low hum of conversation:* **murmur**, drone, purr, buzz.
■ **hum and haw** (Brit.) hesitate, dither, vacillate, be indecisive, equivocate, prevaricate, waver, blow hot and cold; Brit. haver; Scottish swither; informal shilly-shally.

human adjective **1** *they're only human:* **mortal**, flesh and blood; fallible, weak, frail, imperfect, vulnerable; physical, bodily, fleshly. **2** *his human side:* **compassionate**, humane, kind, considerate, understanding, sympathetic; approachable, accessible.
– OPPOSITES immortal, infallible.
• noun *the link between humans and animals:* **person**, human being, Homo sapiens, man, woman, individual, mortal, living soul; earthling; (**humans**) the human race, humanity, humankind, mankind, man, people.

> **WORD LINKS**
> **anthropology** the study of humankind

humane adjective **compassionate**, kind, considerate, understanding, sympathetic, tolerant; lenient, forbearing, forgiving, merciful, humanitarian, charitable.
– OPPOSITES cruel.

humanitarian adjective **compassionate**, humane; unselfish, altruistic, generous, charitable, philanthropic, public-spirited.
– OPPOSITES selfish.
• noun **philanthropist**, altruist, benefactor, social reformer, good Samaritan.

humanity noun **1** *appalling crimes against humanity:* **humankind**, mankind, man, people, the human race. **2** *he praised them for their humanity:* **compassion**, brotherly love, fellow feeling, kindness, consideration, understanding, sympathy, tolerance; leniency, mercy, pity, tenderness; benevolence, charity.

humanize verb **civilize**, improve, better; educate, enlighten; socialize; formal edify.

humble adjective **1** *she was very humble:* **meek**, deferential, respectful, submissive, self-effacing, unassertive; unpresuming, modest, unassuming, self-deprecating. **2** *a humble background:* **lowly**, poor, undistinguished, mean; common, ordinary, simple, unremarkable, insignificant. **3** *my humble abode:* **modest**, plain, simple, ordinary, little.
– OPPOSITES proud, noble, grand.
• verb **1** *he was humbled by the events of the last few weeks:* **chasten**, take down a peg or two, put someone in their place; informal cut down to size.

2 *in today's match, Australia were humbled by Somerset:* **defeat**, beat, trounce, rout, overwhelm, get the better of; informal walk all over.

humbug noun **1** *that is sheer humbug:* **hypocrisy**, posturing, cant, empty talk. **2** *you see what a humbug I am?* **hypocrite**, fraud, fake, plaster saint; charlatan, cheat, deceiver; informal phoney.

humdrum adjective **mundane**, dull, dreary, boring, tedious, monotonous, prosaic; routine, ordinary, everyday, run-of-the-mill, workaday, pedestrian.
– OPPOSITES remarkable, exciting.

humid adjective **muggy**, hot, sultry, sticky, steamy, oppressive, airless, close, stifling, suffocating, stuffy, clammy, heavy.
– OPPOSITES cold, fresh.

humiliate verb **embarrass**, mortify, shame, put to shame, disgrace; discomfit, chasten, deflate, crush, squash; demean, degrade; take down a peg or two; informal show up, put down, cut down to size; N. Amer. informal make someone eat crow.

humiliating adjective **embarrassing**, mortifying, ignominious, inglorious, shameful; discreditable, undignified, chastening, demeaning, degrading, deflating.

humiliation noun **embarrassment**, mortification, shame, indignity, ignominy, disgrace, dishonour, degradation, discredit, obloquy, opprobrium; loss of pride, loss of face; blow to your pride, slap in the face, kick in the teeth.
– OPPOSITES honour.

humility noun **modesty**, humbleness, meekness, diffidence, unassertiveness; lack of pride, lack of vanity.
– OPPOSITES pride.

hummock noun **hillock**, hump, mound, knoll, prominence, elevation, rise, dune; formal eminence.

humorist noun **wit**, comic, funny man/woman, comedian, comedienne, joker; informal wag.

humorous adjective **amusing**, funny, comic, comical, entertaining, diverting, witty, jocular, light-hearted, tongue-in-cheek, wry; hilarious, uproarious, riotous, zany, farcical, droll.
– OPPOSITES serious.

humour noun **1** *the humour of the situation:* **comedy**, funny side, hilarity; absurdity, ludicrousness, drollness; satire, irony. **2** *the stories are spiced up with humour:* **jokes**, jests, quips, witticisms, funny remarks, puns; wit, comedy, drollery; informal gags, wisecracks, waggishness, one-liners. **3** *his good humour was infectious:* **mood**, temper, disposition, temperament, state of mind; spirits.
• verb *she was always humouring him:* **indulge**, accommodate, pander to, cater to, yield to, give way to, give in to, go along with; mollify, placate.

humourless adjective **serious**, solemn, sober, sombre, grave, grim, dour, unsmiling, stony-faced; gloomy, glum, sad, melancholy, dismal, joyless, cheerless, lugubrious; dry.
– OPPOSITES jovial.

hump noun *a hump at the base of the spine:* **protuberance**, prominence, lump, bump, knob, protrusion, projection, bulge, swelling; growth, outgrowth.
• verb (informal) *he humped boxes up the stairs:* **heave**, carry, lug, lift, hoist, heft; informal schlep, tote.

hunch noun *my hunch is that he'll be back:* **feeling**, guess, suspicion, impression, inkling, idea, notion, fancy, intuition; informal gut feeling.

hundred cardinal number century; informal ton.

> **WORD LINKS**
> **centenary**, **centennial** the hundredth anniversary of an event

hunger noun **1** *she was faint with hunger:* **lack of food**; starvation, malnutrition, malnourishment, undernourishment. **2** *a hunger for news:* **desire**, craving, longing, yearning, hankering, yen, appetite, thirst; informal itch.
■ **hunger after/for** desire, crave; long for, yearn for, pine for, ache for, hanker after, thirst for, lust for; want, need, have a yen for; informal itch for, be dying for, be gagging for.

hungry adjective **1** *I was really hungry:* **ravenous**, starving, starved, famished; malnourished, undernourished, underfed; informal peckish. **2** *they are hungry for success:* **eager**, keen, longing, yearning, aching, greedy; craving, desirous of, hankering after; informal itching, dying, gagging.
– OPPOSITES sated.

hunk noun **1** *a hunk of bread:* **chunk**, wedge, block, slab, lump; Brit. informal wodge. **2** (informal) *he's a real hunk:* **muscleman**, strongman, macho man, Adonis; informal he-man, stud.
– OPPOSITES wimp.

h

hunt verb **1** *they hunted deer:* **chase**, stalk, pursue, course; track, trail. **2** *police are still hunting for her:* **search**, look, scour the area; seek, try to find.
• noun **chase**, pursuit; search, quest.

hunted adjective *his eyes had a hunted look:* **harassed**, persecuted, harried, hounded, beleaguered, troubled, tormented; informal hassled.
– OPPOSITES carefree.

hunting noun **blood sports**, field sports, shooting, coursing; the chase; old use venery.

hurdle noun **1** *his leg hit a hurdle:* **fence**, jump, barrier, barricade, bar, railing, rail. **2** *the final hurdle to overcome:* **obstacle**, difficulty, problem, barrier, bar, snag, stumbling block, impediment, obstruction, complication, hindrance.

hurl verb. See THROW.

hurly-burly noun **bustle**, hustle and bustle, hubbub, confusion, disorder, uproar, tumult, pandemonium, mayhem; informal hoo-ha, hullabaloo.

hurricane noun **cyclone**, typhoon, tornado, storm, windstorm, whirlwind, gale; Austral. willy-willy; N. Amer. informal twister.

hurried adjective **quick**, fast, swift, rapid, speedy, brisk, hasty, rushed; cursory, perfunctory, brief, short, fleeting; precipitate, spur-of-the-moment, impetuous.
– OPPOSITES slow, considered.

hurriedly adverb **hastily**, speedily, quickly, rapidly, swiftly, briskly; without delay.

hurry verb **1** *hurry or you'll be late:* **be quick**, hurry up, hasten, speed up; run, dash, rush, race, fly; scurry, scramble, scuttle, sprint; informal get a move on, step on it, get cracking, get moving, shake a leg; Brit. informal shift, get your skates on, get a wiggle on; dated make haste. **2** *she hurried him out:* **hustle**, hasten, push, urge, usher.
– OPPOSITES dawdle, delay.
• noun *in all the hurry, we forgot:* **rush**, haste, hustle and bustle, confusion, commotion, hubbub.

hurt verb **1** *my back hurts:* **be painful**, be sore, be tender; ache, smart, sting, burn, throb; informal be killing; Brit. informal be playing up. **2** *he hurt his leg:* **injure**, wound, damage; bruise, cut, gash, graze, scrape, scratch, lacerate. **3** *his words hurt her:* **distress**, pain, wound, sting, upset, sadden, devastate, grieve, mortify. **4** *high interest rates are hurting the economy:* **harm**, damage, weaken, blight, impede, jeopardize, undermine, ruin, wreck, sabotage, cripple.
– OPPOSITES heal, comfort, benefit.
• noun *all the hurt he had caused:* **distress**, pain, suffering, grief, misery, anguish, trauma, woe, upset, sadness, sorrow; harm, damage, trouble.
– OPPOSITES joy.
• adjective *a hurt expression:* **pained**, distressed, anguished, upset, sad, mortified, offended; informal miffed, peeved.
– OPPOSITES pleased.

hurtful adjective *hurtful words:* **upsetting**, distressing, wounding, painful; unkind, cruel, nasty, mean, malicious, spiteful.

hurtle verb **speed**, rush, run, race, career, whizz, zoom, charge, shoot, streak, gallop, hare, fly, go like the wind; informal belt, pelt, tear, go like a bat out of hell; Brit. informal bomb, bucket, go like the clappers; N. Amer. informal barrel.

husband noun **spouse**, partner, mate, consort, man; informal hubby, old man, your better half; Brit. informal other half.

hush verb **1** *he tried to hush her:* **silence**, quieten, shush; gag, muzzle; informal shut up. **2** *they hushed up the dangers:* **keep secret**,

conceal, hide, suppress, cover up, keep quiet about; obscure, veil, sweep under the carpet.
– OPPOSITES disclose.
• noun *a hush descended:* **silence**, quiet; stillness, peace, calm, tranquillity.
– OPPOSITES noise.

husk noun **shell**, hull, pod, case, covering, integument; Botany pericarp.

husky adjective *a husky voice:* **throaty**, gruff, gravelly, hoarse, croaky, rough, guttural, harsh, rasping, raspy.
– OPPOSITES shrill, soft.

hustle verb *I was hustled away:* **manhandle**, push, shove, thrust, frogmarch; rush, hurry, whisk, usher, show; informal bundle.
▪ **hustle and bustle** confusion, bustle, tumult, hubbub, activity, action, liveliness, excitement, whirl; informal toing and froing, comings and goings, hoo-ha, hullabaloo.

hut noun **shack**, shanty, cabin, shelter, shed, lean-to; hovel; Scottish bothy; N. Amer. cabana.

hybrid noun **cross**, cross-breed; mixture, blend, amalgamation, combination, composite, fusion.
• adjective *hybrid roses:* **composite**, cross-bred, interbred; mixed, blended, compound.

hybridize verb **cross-breed**, cross, interbreed, cross-fertilize, cross-pollinate; mix, blend, combine, amalgamate.

hygiene noun **cleanliness**, sanitation, sterility, purity, disinfection; public health, environmental health.

hygienic adjective **sanitary**, clean, germ-free, disinfected, sterilized, sterile, antiseptic, aseptic, unpolluted, uncontaminated.
– OPPOSITES unhygienic, insanitary.

hyperbole noun **exaggeration**, overstatement, magnification, embroidery, embellishment, excess, overkill.
– OPPOSITES understatement.

hypercritical adjective. See **OVERCRITICAL**.

hypnosis noun **mesmerism**, hypnotism, hypnotic suggestion, auto-suggestion.

hypnotic adjective **mesmerizing**, mesmeric, spellbinding, entrancing, bewitching, irresistible, compelling; soporific, sedative, numbing.

hypnotize verb *they were hypnotized by the dancers:* **entrance**, spellbind, enthral, transfix, captivate, bewitch, enrapture, grip, rivet, absorb.

hypocrisy noun **sanctimoniousness**, piousness, cant, posturing, humbug, pretence; insincerity, falseness; informal phoneyness.
– OPPOSITES sincerity.

hypocrite noun **pretender**, humbug, deceiver, dissembler, plaster saint; informal phoney; literary whited sepulchre.

hypocritical adjective **sanctimonious**, pious, self-righteous, holier-than-thou, superior; insincere, false; two-faced; informal phoney.

hypothesis noun **theory**, theorem, thesis, conjecture, supposition, postulate, proposition, premise, assumption; notion, concept, idea.

hypothetical adjective **theoretical**, speculative, conjectured, notional, supposed, assumed; academic, imaginary.
– OPPOSITES actual.

hysteria noun **frenzy**, feverishness, hysterics, derangement, mania; panic, alarm, distress.
– OPPOSITES calm.

hysterical adjective **1** *she was hysterical and began to scream:* **overwrought**, overemotional, out of control, frenzied, frantic, wild; beside yourself, driven to distraction, manic, unhinged; informal in a state. **2** (informal). See **HILARIOUS**.

Ii

ice noun **1** *a lake covered with ice:* icicles; black ice, verglas, frost, rime, permafrost, hoar frost; N. Amer. glaze. **2** *assorted ices:* **ice cream**, water ice, sorbet; N. Amer. sherbet.
■ **on ice** (informal) pending, deferred, postponed, put off, put to one side, up in the air; informal in cold storage, on the back burner.

> **WORD LINKS**
> **glacial** relating to ice

ice-cold adjective **icy**, freezing, glacial, sub-zero, frozen, wintry; arctic, polar, Siberian; bitter, biting, raw.
–OPPOSITES hot.

icon noun **image**, idol, portrait, representation, symbol.

iconoclast noun **dissenter**, sceptic; heretic, dissident; rebel, renegade, mutineer.

icy adjective **1** *icy roads:* **frosty**, frozen, iced over, ice-bound, ice-covered; slippery; literary rimy. **2** *an icy wind:* **freezing**, chill, biting, bitter, raw, arctic, glacial, Siberian, polar. **3** *an icy voice:* **unfriendly**, hostile, forbidding; cold, chilly, frosty, glacial; haughty, stern, hard.

idea noun **1** *the idea of death scares her:* **concept**, notion, conception, thought. **2** *our idea is to open a new shop:* **plan**, scheme, design, proposal, proposition, suggestion; aim, intention, objective, object, goal, target, concept. **3** *Liz had various ideas on the subject:* **thought**, theory, view, opinion, feeling, belief, conclusion. **4** *I had an idea that it might happen:* **sense**, feeling, suspicion, fancy, inkling, hunch, notion, impression. **5** *an idea of the cost:* **estimate**, approximation, guess, conjecture; informal guesstimate.

ideal adjective **1** *ideal flying weather:* **perfect**, optimum, faultless, exemplary, classic, model, ultimate, quintessential. **2** *an ideal world:* **unattainable**, unachievable, impracticable; unreal, hypothetical, theoretical, utopian.
–OPPOSITES bad, real.
• noun **1** *an ideal to aim at:* **model**, pattern, exemplar, example, paradigm. **2** *liberal ideals:* **principle**, standard, value, belief, conviction; (**ideals**) morals, ethics, ideology, creed.

idealist noun **utopian**, visionary, romantic, dreamer.
–OPPOSITES realist.

idealistic adjective **utopian**, visionary, romantic, unrealistic, impractical.

idealize verb **romanticize**, glamorize, sentimentalize.

identical adjective **exactly the same**, indistinguishable, twin, interchangeable; alike, matching.
–OPPOSITES different.

identifiable adjective **distinguishable**, recognizable; noticeable, perceptible, discernible, detectable, observable, perceivable, visible.
–OPPOSITES unrecognizable.

identification noun **1** *the identification of the suspect:* **recognition**, singling out, pinpointing, naming. **2** *early identification of problems:* **determination**, establishment, ascertainment, discovery, diagnosis. **3** *may I see your identification?* **ID**, papers, documents, credentials; card, pass, badge. **4** *the identification of the party with high taxes:* **association**, linking, connection. **5** *his identification with the music:* **empathy**, rapport, sympathy, understanding.

identify verb **1** *she identified her attacker:* **recognize**, pick out, spot, point out, pinpoint, put your finger on, name. **2** *I identified four problem areas:* **determine**, establish, ascertain, make out, discern, distinguish. **3** *we identify sport with glamour:* **associate**, link, connect, relate. **4** *Peter identifies with the team captain:* **empathize**, sympathize; understand, relate to, feel for.

identity noun *she was afraid of losing her identity:* **individuality**, self; personality, character, originality, distinctiveness, uniqueness.

ideology noun **belief**; doctrine, creed, theory.

idiocy noun **stupidity**, folly, foolishness, foolhardiness; madness, insanity, lunacy; thoughtlessness, senselessness, irresponsibility, absurdity, ludicrousness, fatuousness.
– OPPOSITES sense.

idiom noun **expression**, phrase, turn of phrase.

idiomatic adjective **colloquial**, everyday, conversational, vernacular; natural.

idiosyncrasy noun **peculiarity**, oddity, eccentricity, mannerism, quirk, characteristic.

idiosyncratic adjective **distinctive**, individual, individualistic, characteristic, peculiar, typical, special, specific, unique, personal; eccentric, unconventional, quirky.

idiot noun. See FOOL.

idiotic adjective. See STUPID.

idle adjective **1** *an idle fellow:* **lazy**, indolent, slothful, work-shy, shiftless. **2** *I was bored with being idle:* **unemployed**, jobless, out of work, redundant, unoccupied; Brit. informal on the dole, resting. **3** *their idle hours:* **unoccupied**, spare, empty, unfilled. **4** *idle remarks:* **frivolous**, trivial, trifling, minor, insignificant, unimportant. **5** *idle threats:* **empty**, meaningless, worthless, vain.
– OPPOSITES industrious, working, busy.

idler noun **loafer**, layabout, good-for-nothing, ne'er-do-well; informal skiver, waster, slacker, slob, lazybones; N. Amer. informal slowpoke; literary wastrel.
– OPPOSITES workaholic.

idol noun **1** *an idol in a shrine:* **icon**, effigy, statue, figure, figurine, totem. **2** *the pop world's latest idol:* **hero**, heroine, star, superstar, icon, celebrity; darling; informal pin-up, heart throb.

idolize verb **hero-worship**, worship, revere, venerate, look up to, exalt; informal put on a pedestal.

idyllic adjective **perfect**, wonderful, blissful, halcyon, happy; literary Arcadian.

if conjunction **1** *if the weather is fine, we can walk:* **on condition that**, provided, presuming, supposing, assuming, as long as, in the event that. **2** *I wonder if he noticed:* **whether**, whether or not.

ignite verb **1** *the petrol ignited:* **catch fire**, burst into flames, explode. **2** *a cigarette ignited the fumes:* **light**, set fire to, set alight. **3** *the campaign failed to ignite voter interest:* **arouse**, kindle, trigger, spark, excite, provoke, stimulate, stir up, incite.
– OPPOSITES extinguish.

ignoble adjective **dishonourable**, unworthy, base, shameful, contemptible, despicable, shabby.

ignominious adjective **humiliating**, undignified, embarrassing, inglorious.
– OPPOSITES glorious.

ignominy noun **shame**, humiliation, embarrassment; disgrace, dishonour, indignity.

ignorance noun **1** *his ignorance of economics:* **incomprehension**, unfamiliarity, inexperience, innocence, lack of knowledge. **2** *their attitudes are based on ignorance:* **lack of knowledge**; unenlightenment, benightedness.
– OPPOSITES knowledge, education.

ignorant adjective **1** *an ignorant country girl:* **uneducated**, unschooled, untutored, illiterate, uninformed, unenlightened, benighted; inexperienced, unsophisticated. **2** *he is ignorant of working-class life:* **unaware**, unconscious, unfamiliar, unacquainted, uninformed.
– OPPOSITES educated, aware.

ignore verb **1** *he ignored her:* **take no notice of**, pay no attention to; snub, look right through, cold-shoulder; Brit. informal blank. **2** *doctors ignored her husband's instructions:*

disregard, take no account of; fail to observe, disobey, defy.
– OPPOSITES acknowledge, obey.

ill adjective **1** *she was feeling rather ill:* **unwell**, sick, poorly; bad; informal under the weather, lousy, rough; Brit. informal ropy, grotty; Austral./NZ informal crook. **2** *the ill effects of smoking:* **harmful**, damaging, detrimental, deleterious, adverse, injurious, pernicious, dangerous; old use baneful.
– OPPOSITES well, healthy, beneficial, auspicious.
• noun **1** *the ills of society:* **problems**, troubles, difficulties, misfortunes, trials, tribulations; informal headaches, hassles. **2** *he wished them no ill:* **harm**, hurt, injury, pain, trouble, misfortune, distress.
• adverb **1** *he can ill afford the loss of income:* **barely**, scarcely, hardly, only just. **2** *we are ill prepared:* **inadequately**, insufficiently, poorly, badly.
– OPPOSITES well.
■ **ill at ease** awkward, uneasy, uncomfortable, embarrassed, self-conscious, out of place; restless, restive, fidgety, worried, anxious, on edge, edgy, nervous, tense; informal twitchy, jittery; N. Amer. informal discombobulated, antsy.

ill-advised adjective **unwise**, misguided, imprudent, ill-considered, ill-judged; foolhardy, hare-brained, rash, reckless.
– OPPOSITES judicious.

ill-considered adjective **rash**, ill-advised, ill-judged, injudicious, imprudent, unwise, hasty, ill-conceived, foolish, misguided.
– OPPOSITES judicious.

ill-defined adjective **vague**, indistinct, unclear, imprecise; blurred, fuzzy, hazy, woolly, nebulous.

ill-disposed adjective **hostile**, antagonistic, unfriendly, unsympathetic, antipathetic, inimical, unfavourable.
– OPPOSITES friendly.

illegal adjective **unlawful**, illicit, criminal, felonious; unlicensed, unauthorized; outlawed, banned, forbidden, prohibited, proscribed.
– OPPOSITES lawful, legitimate.

illegible adjective **unreadable**, indecipherable, unintelligible.

illegitimate adjective **illegal**, unlawful, illicit, criminal, felonious; fraudulent, corrupt, dishonest; informal crooked, shady; Brit. informal bent, dodgy.
– OPPOSITES legal, lawful.

ill-fated adjective **doomed**, blighted, damned, cursed, ill-starred, jinxed; literary star-crossed.

ill-founded adjective **baseless**, groundless, without foundation, unjustified; misinformed, misguided.

ill-humoured adjective **bad-tempered**, ill-tempered, cross; irritable, irascible, tetchy, crotchety, touchy, cantankerous, curmudgeonly, peevish, fractious, waspish, prickly; grumpy, grouchy, crabby, splenetic; N. Amer. informal cranky, ornery; Austral./NZ informal snaky.
– OPPOSITES amiable.

illiberal adjective **intolerant**, conservative, reactionary, undemocratic, authoritarian, repressive, oppressive.

illicit adjective **illegal**, unlawful, criminal; outlawed, banned, forbidden, prohibited, proscribed; unlicensed, unauthorized; contraband, black-market, bootleg.
– OPPOSITES lawful, legal.

illiterate adjective *many of them are politically illiterate:* **ignorant**, unaware, uneducated, uninformed.

ill-judged adjective **ill-considered**, unwise, ill-thought-out; imprudent, incautious, injudicious, misguided, ill-advised, impolitic.
– OPPOSITES judicious.

ill-mannered adjective **bad-mannered**, discourteous, rude, impolite, abusive; insolent, impertinent, impudent, cheeky, loutish, uncouth; informal ignorant.
– OPPOSITES polite.

illness noun **sickness**, disease, ailment, complaint, malady, affliction, infection; informal bug, virus; dated contagion.

illogical adjective **irrational**, unreasonable, unsound, unreasoned; erroneous, invalid, spurious, fallacious.

ill-tempered noun. See ILL-HUMOURED.

ill-timed adjective **untimely**, mistimed, badly timed.
– OPPOSITES timely.

ill-treat verb **abuse**, mistreat, maltreat, ill-use, misuse.
– OPPOSITES pamper.

ill-treatment noun **abuse**, mistreatment, maltreatment, misuse.

illuminate verb **1** *a flash of lightning illuminated the house:* **light**, throw light on, brighten, shine on; literary illumine. **2** *documents often illuminate people's thought processes:* **clarify**, elucidate, explain, reveal, shed light on.
– OPPOSITES obscure.

illuminating adjective **informative**, enlightening, revealing, explanatory, instructive, helpful, educational.

illumination noun **light**, lighting, radiance, gleam, glow, glare.

illusion noun **1** *the lighting increases the illusion of depth:* **appearance**, impression, semblance. **2** *it's just an illusion:* **mirage**, hallucination, apparition, figment of the imagination, trick of the light, chimera.

illusory adjective **false**, imagined, imaginary, fanciful, unreal; sham, fallacious.
– OPPOSITES genuine.

illustrate verb **1** *the photographs that illustrate the text:* **decorate**, adorn, ornament, accompany, support. **2** *this can be illustrated through a brief example:* **explain**, elucidate, clarify, demonstrate, show; informal get across/over.

illustration noun **1** *the illustrations in children's books:* **picture**, drawing, sketch, figure, plate, print. **2** *by way of illustration:* **exemplification**, demonstration; example, analogy.

illustrious adjective **eminent**, distinguished, acclaimed, notable, noteworthy, prominent, pre-eminent, foremost, leading, important; renowned, famous, well known, celebrated.
– OPPOSITES unknown.

ill will noun **animosity**, hostility, enmity, antipathy; ill feeling, bad blood, antagonism, resentment, bitterness.
– OPPOSITES goodwill.

image noun **1** *images of the Queen:* **likeness**; depiction, portrayal, representation; painting, picture, portrait, drawing, photograph. **2** *the image of this country as a democracy:* **conception**, impression, idea, perception, notion. **3** *his public image:* **persona**, profile, face.

> **WORD LINKS**
> **iconography**, **iconology** the use or study of images

imaginable adjective **thinkable**, conceivable.

imaginary adjective **unreal**, non-existent, fictional, pretend, make-believe, illusory; made-up.
– OPPOSITES real.

imagination noun **creativity**, vision, inventiveness, resourcefulness, ingenuity; originality.

imaginative adjective **creative**, visionary, inventive, resourceful, ingenious; original, innovative.

imagine verb **1** *you can imagine the scene:* **visualize**, envisage, picture, see in your mind's eye; dream up, think up/of, conceive. **2** *I imagine he was at home:* **assume**, presume, expect, take it, suppose.

imbalance noun **disparity**, variation, contrast, lack of harmony; gap.

imbed verb. See **EMBED**.

imbue verb **permeate**, saturate, suffuse; inject, inculcate; fill.

imitate verb **1** *other artists have imitated his style:* **emulate**, copy, follow, echo, parrot; informal rip off. **2** *he could imitate Winston Churchill:* **mimic**, do an impression of, impersonate; informal take off, send up; N. Amer. informal make like.

imitation noun **1** *an imitation of a sailor's hat:* **copy**, simulation, reproduction, replica. **2** *learning by imitation:* **emulation**, copying. **3** *a perfect imitation of Francis:* **impersonation**, impression, parody, caricature; informal send-up, take-off, spoof.
• adjective *imitation ivory:* **artificial**, synthetic, simulated, man-made, manufactured, ersatz, substitute; mock, fake.
– OPPOSITES real, genuine.

immaculate adjective **1** *an immaculate white shirt:* **clean**, spotless, pristine; shining, shiny, gleaming. **2** *immaculate condition:* **perfect**, pristine, mint; flawless, faultless, unblemished; informal tip-top, A1. **3** *his immaculate record:* **unblemished**, spotless, impeccable,

unsullied, untarnished; informal squeaky clean.
– OPPOSITES dirty, damaged.

immaterial adjective **irrelevant**, unimportant, inconsequential, insignificant, of no matter, of little account, beside the point, neither here nor there.
– OPPOSITES significant.

immature adjective *an extremely immature girl:* **childish**, babyish, infantile, juvenile, puerile, callow, unsophisticated, naive, jejune; informal wet behind the ears.

immeasurable adjective **incalculable**, inestimable, innumerable; limitless, boundless, unbounded; vast, immense.

i

immediate adjective **1** *the UN called for immediate action:* **instant**, instantaneous, prompt, swift, speedy, rapid, quick. **2** *their immediate concerns:* **current**, present; urgent, pressing. **3** *our immediate neighbours:* **nearest**, close, next-door; adjacent, adjoining.
– OPPOSITES delayed, distant.

immediately adverb **1** *it was necessary to make a decision immediately:* **straight away**, at once, right away, instantly, now, directly, forthwith, this/that minute, this/that instant, there and then, without delay, post-haste. **2** *I sat immediately behind him:* **directly**, right, exactly, precisely, squarely, just, dead; informal slap bang; N. Amer. informal smack dab.

immense adjective **huge**, vast, massive, enormous, gigantic, colossal, great, monumental, towering, tremendous; giant, monstrous, mammoth, titanic, king-sized; informal mega, monster, whopping, humongous, jumbo; Brit. informal whacking great, ginormous.
– OPPOSITES tiny.

immensely adverb **extremely**, very, exceedingly, exceptionally, extraordinarily, tremendously, hugely, outstandingly, uncommonly, supremely, highly, really, truly, mightily, thoroughly, in the extreme; informal terrifically, awfully, fearfully, terribly, devilishly, seriously, mega; Brit. informal dead, jolly; N. Amer. informal mighty, awful; informal, dated frightfully; old use exceeding.
– OPPOSITES slightly.

immerse verb **1** *the metal was immersed in acid:* **submerge**, dip, dunk, duck, sink. **2** *Elliot was immersed in his work:* **absorb**, engross, occupy, engage, involve, bury; preoccupy; informal lose yourself in.

immigrant noun **newcomer**, settler, incomer, migrant; non-native, foreigner, alien.
– OPPOSITES native.

imminent adjective **impending**, close at hand, near, fast approaching, coming, forthcoming, on the way, expected, looming; informal on the cards.

immobile adjective **motionless**, without moving, still, stock-still, static, stationary; rooted to the spot, rigid, frozen, transfixed, like a statue, not moving a muscle.

immobilize verb **put out of action**, disable, deactivate, paralyse; bring to a standstill, halt, stop; clamp, wheel-clamp.

immoderate adjective **excessive**, heavy, intemperate, unrestrained, unrestricted, uncontrolled, unbridled, overindulgent; undue, inordinate; extravagant, lavish, prodigal, profligate.

immodest adjective **indecorous**, improper, indecent, indelicate, immoral; forward, bold, brazen, shameless, loose, wanton; informal fresh, cheeky, saucy.

immoral adjective **unethical**, bad, wrong, wicked, unprincipled, unscrupulous, dishonourable, dishonest, corrupt; sinful, impure, unchaste, promiscuous.
– OPPOSITES ethical, chaste.

immorality noun **wickedness**, badness, corruption, dishonesty, sin, vice, debauchery, dissolution, perversion, promiscuity.

immortal adjective **1** *our immortal souls:* **undying**, deathless, eternal, everlasting; imperishable, indestructible. **2** *an immortal classic:* **timeless**, perennial, classic, time-honoured, enduring, evergreen.
• noun *one of the immortals of soccer:* **great**, hero, myth, legend, demigod, superstar.

immortality noun **1** *the dream of*

immortality: **eternal life**, everlasting life; indestructibility, imperishability. **2** *the book has achieved immortality:* **timelessness**, legendary status, classic status, lasting fame/renown.

immortalize verb **commemorate**; celebrate, eulogize, pay tribute to, honour, salute, exalt, glorify.

immovable adjective **1** *lock your bike to something immovable:* **fixed**, secure, set firm, set fast; stuck, jammed, stiff. **2** *he sat, stiff and immovable, in the hard chair:* **motionless**, unmoving, stationary, still, stock-still, not moving a muscle, rooted to the spot; transfixed, paralysed, frozen. **3** *she was immovable in her loyalty:* **steadfast**, unwavering, unswerving, resolute, determined, firm, unshakeable, unfailing, dogged, tenacious, inflexible, unyielding, unbending, uncompromising.
– OPPOSITES mobile, moving.

immune adjective **resistant**, not subject, not liable, not vulnerable; protected from, safe from, secure against.
– OPPOSITES susceptible.

immunity noun **1** *their immunity to malaria:* **resistance**; protection against, defence against. **2** *his immunity from prosecution:* **exemption**, exception, freedom. **3** *he claimed diplomatic immunity:* **indemnity**, privilege, prerogative, licence; exemption, impunity, protection.

immunize verb **vaccinate**, inoculate, inject.

immutable adjective **fixed**, set, rigid, inflexible, permanent, established; unchanging, unvarying, constant.
– OPPOSITES variable.

imp noun **1** **demon**, devil; hobgoblin, goblin. **2** *a cheeky young imp:* **rascal**, monkey, devil, wretch; informal scamp, brat, horror, tyke; Brit. informal perisher; N. Amer. informal hellion, varmint; old use scapegrace, rapscallion.

impact noun **1** *the force of the impact:* **collision**, crash, smash, bump, knock. **2** *the job losses will have a major impact:* **effect**, influence; consequences, repercussions, ramifications.
• verb **1** (N. Amer.) **crash into**, smash into, collide with, hit, strike, smack into, bang into. **2** *interest rates have impacted on spending:* **affect**, influence, have an effect, make an impression; hit.

impair verb **harm**, damage, hurt, mar, spoil, weaken, undermine, compromise; diminish, reduce, lessen, decrease, limit, restrict, impede, hinder, hamper.
– OPPOSITES improve, enhance.

impale verb **stick**, skewer, spear, spike, transfix; pierce, run through.

impalpable adjective **intangible**, insubstantial, incorporeal; indefinable.

impart verb **1** *she had news to impart:* **communicate**, pass on, convey, transmit, relay, relate, recount, tell, make known, make public, report, announce; disclose, reveal, divulge. **2** *the brush imparts a good sheen:* **give**, bestow, confer, grant, lend, afford, provide, supply.

impartial adjective **unbiased**, unprejudiced, neutral, non-partisan, disinterested, detached, dispassionate, objective, open-minded.
– OPPOSITES biased, partisan.

impassable adjective *heavy snow means many roads are impassable:* **closed**, blocked, unusable; treacherous.

impasse noun **deadlock**, dead end, stalemate, checkmate, stand-off; standstill.

impassioned adjective **emotional**, heartfelt, earnest, sincere, fervent, passionate.

impassive adjective **expressionless**, inexpressive, inscrutable, blank, poker-faced, straight-faced; stony.
– OPPOSITES expressive.

impatience noun **1** *he was shifting in his seat with impatience:* **restlessness**, agitation, nervousness; eagerness, keenness. **2** *a burst of impatience:* **irritability**, tetchiness, irascibility, peevishness, frustration, exasperation, annoyance.

impatient adjective **1** *Melissa grew impatient:* **restless**, agitated, nervous, anxious, ill at ease, edgy, jumpy; informal twitchy, jittery, uptight. **2** *they are impatient to get*

back home: **anxious**, eager, keen; informal itching, dying. **3** *an impatient gesture:* **irritated**, annoyed, angry, tetchy, snappy, cross; abrupt, curt, brusque, terse, short.
– OPPOSITES calm, reluctant.

impeach verb (N. Amer.) **indict**, charge, accuse, arraign, prosecute.

impeccable adjective **flawless**, faultless, unblemished, spotless, stainless, perfect, exemplary; irreproachable; informal squeaky clean.
– OPPOSITES imperfect, sinful.

impede verb **hinder**, obstruct, hamper, hold back/up, delay, interfere with, disrupt, retard, slow down.
– OPPOSITES facilitate.

i

impediment noun **1** *an impediment to economic improvement:* **hindrance**, obstruction, obstacle, barrier, bar, block, check, curb, restriction. **2** *a speech impediment:* **defect**, impairment; stammer, stutter, lisp.

impel verb *financial difficulties impelled her to seek work:* **force**, compel, oblige, require, make, urge, drive, push, prompt.

impending adjective **imminent**, close at hand, near, approaching, coming, brewing, looming, threatening.

impenetrable adjective **1** *impenetrable armour:* **unbreakable**, indestructible, solid, thick, unyielding. **2** *impenetrable forest:* **impassable**; dense, thick, overgrown. **3** *impenetrable statistics:* **incomprehensible**, unfathomable, unintelligible, baffling, bewildering, confusing, opaque.

imperative adjective **vital**, crucial, critical, essential, urgent, of the utmost necessity.
– OPPOSITES unimportant.

imperceptible adjective **unnoticeable**, undetectable, indiscernible, invisible, inaudible, impalpable; slight, small, subtle, faint.
– OPPOSITES noticeable.

imperfect adjective **faulty**, flawed, defective, shoddy, unsound, inferior, second-rate, substandard; damaged, blemished, torn, broken, cracked, scratched; Brit. informal **duff**.

imperfection noun **1** *the glass is free from imperfections:* **defect**, fault, flaw, deformity, discoloration; crack, scratch, chip, dent, blemish, stain, spot, mark. **2** *he was aware of her imperfections:* **flaw**, fault, failing, deficiency, weakness, weak point, shortcoming, inadequacy, limitation.
– OPPOSITES strength.

imperial adjective **royal**, regal, monarchic, sovereign, kingly, queenly, princely.

imperil verb **endanger**, jeopardize, risk; threaten.

imperious adjective **peremptory**, high-handed, overbearing, domineering, authoritarian, dictatorial, authoritative, bossy, arrogant; informal pushy, high and mighty.

imperishable adjective **enduring**, everlasting, undying, immortal, perennial, long-lasting; indestructible, inextinguishable, unfading.

impermanent adjective **temporary**, transient, transitory, passing, fleeting, momentary, ephemeral; short-lived, brief, here today, gone tomorrow; literary evanescent.

impermeable adjective **watertight**, waterproof, damp-proof, airtight, hermetically sealed.

impersonal adjective **aloof**, distant, remote, detached, anonymous; unemotional, unsentimental, cold, cool, indifferent, unconcerned; formal, stiff, businesslike; informal starchy, stand-offish.
– OPPOSITES warm.

impersonate verb **imitate**, mimic, do an impression of, ape; parody, caricature, satirize, lampoon; masquerade as, pose as, pass yourself off as; informal take off, send up; N. Amer. informal make like.

impersonation noun **impression**, imitation; parody, caricature, pastiche; informal take-off, send-up.

impertinence noun **rudeness**, insolence, impoliteness, bad manners, disrespect; impudence, cheek; informal brass neck, chutzpah.

impertinent adjective **rude**, insolent, impolite, ill-mannered, bad-mannered, disrespectful; impudent, cheeky, presumptuous, forward; informal brass-necked, saucy; N. Amer. informal sassy.
– OPPOSITES polite.

imperturbable adjective **self-**

possessed, composed, {cool, calm, and collected}, serene, phlegmatic; informal unflappable, laid-back.
– OPPOSITES excitable.

impervious adjective **1** *he seemed impervious to criticism:* **unaffected**, untouched, immune, indifferent. **2** *an impervious damp-proof course:* **impermeable**, impenetrable, waterproof, watertight.
– OPPOSITES susceptible, permeable.

impetuous adjective **impulsive**, rash, hasty, reckless, foolhardy, imprudent, injudicious, ill-considered; spontaneous, impromptu, spur-of-the-moment.
– OPPOSITES considered.

impetus noun **1** *the flywheel lost its impetus:* **momentum**, drive, thrust; energy, force, power, push. **2** *the sales force were given fresh impetus:* **motivation**, stimulus, incentive, inspiration.

impinge verb **affect**, have an effect, touch, impact on.

impious adjective **godless**, ungodly, irreligious, sinful, immoral, sacrilegious, profane, blasphemous, irreverent.

impish adjective **mischievous**, roguish, wicked, rascally, naughty, playful, puckish.

implacable adjective **unforgiving**; intransigent, inflexible, unyielding, unbending, uncompromising, unrelenting, ruthless, remorseless, merciless.

implant verb **1** *the collagen is implanted under the skin:* **insert**, embed, bury, lodge, place. **2** *he implanted the idea in my mind:* **instil**, inculcate, introduce, inject, plant, sow.
• noun *a silicone implant:* **transplant**, graft, implantation, insert.

implausible adjective **unlikely**, improbable, questionable, doubtful, debatable; unconvincing, far-fetched.
– OPPOSITES convincing.

implement noun *garden implements:* **tool**, utensil, instrument, device, apparatus, gadget, contraption, appliance, contrivance; informal gizmo.
• verb *the cost of implementing the new law:* **execute**, apply, put into effect/action, put into practice, carry out/through, perform, enact; fulfil, discharge, bring about.

implicate verb **1** *he had been implicated in a financial scandal:* **incriminate**; involve, connect, embroil, enmesh. **2** *viruses are implicated in the development of cancer:* **involve in**, concern with, associate with, connect with.

implication noun **1** *he was smarting at their implication:* **suggestion**, inference, insinuation, innuendo, intimation, imputation. **2** *important political implications:* **consequence**, result, ramification, repercussion, reverberation, effect. **3** *his implication in the murder:* **incrimination**, involvement, connection, entanglement, association.

implicit adjective **1** *implicit assumptions:* **implied**, inferred, understood, hinted at, suggested; unspoken, unstated, tacit, taken for granted. **2** *assumptions implicit in the way questions are asked:* **inherent**, latent, underlying, inbuilt, incorporated. **3** *an implicit trust in human nature:* **absolute**, complete, total, wholehearted, utter; unqualified, unconditional; unshakeable, unquestioning, firm.
– OPPOSITES explicit.

implicitly adverb **completely**, absolutely, totally, wholeheartedly, utterly, unconditionally, unreservedly, without reservation.

implied adjective. See IMPLICIT sense 1.

implore verb *his mother implored him to continue studying:* **plead with**, beg, entreat, appeal to, ask, request, call on; exhort, urge; literary beseech.

imply verb **1** *the article implied that he was guilty:* **insinuate**, suggest, hint, intimate, give someone to understand, indicate, make out. **2** *the forecast traffic increase implies more roads:* **involve**, entail; mean, point to, signify, indicate, signal.

> Don't confuse **imply** with **infer**. If you **imply** something, you are suggesting it but not stating it directly. If you **infer** something, you come to the conclusion that this is what is meant (e.g. *we inferred from his words that the General was a traitor*).

impolite adjective **rude**,

bad-mannered, ill-mannered, discourteous, uncivil, disrespectful, inconsiderate, boorish, ungentlemanly, unladylike; insolent, impudent, impertinent, cheeky; informal ignorant, lippy.

impolitic adjective **imprudent**, unwise, injudicious, incautious, irresponsible; ill-judged, ill-advised; undiplomatic, tactless.
– OPPOSITES prudent.

import verb *the UK imports iron ore:* **bring in**, buy in, ship in.
– OPPOSITES export.
• noun **1** *a matter of great import:* **importance**, significance, consequence, momentousness, magnitude, substance, weight, note, gravity, seriousness. **2** *the full import of her words:* **meaning**, sense, essence, gist, drift, message, thrust, substance, implication.
– OPPOSITES insignificance.

i

importance noun **1** *an event of immense importance:* **significance**, momentousness, import, consequence, note; seriousness, gravity. **2** *she had an exaggerated sense of her own importance:* **power**, influence, authority; prominence, eminence, pre-eminence, notability, worth.
– OPPOSITES insignificance.

important adjective **1** *an important meeting:* **significant**, consequential, momentous, of great import, major; critical, crucial, vital, pivotal, decisive, urgent, historic. **2** *the important thing is that you do your best:* **main**, chief, principal, key, major, salient, prime, foremost, paramount, overriding, crucial, vital, critical, essential, significant; central, fundamental; informal number-one. **3** *the school was important to the community:* **valuable**, necessary, essential, indispensable, vital. **4** *he was an important man:* **powerful**, influential, well-connected, high-ranking; prominent, eminent, pre-eminent, notable; distinguished, esteemed, respected, prestigious, great; informal major league.
– OPPOSITES trivial, insignificant.

impose verb **1** *he imposed his ideas on everyone:* **foist**, force, inflict, press, urge. **2** *new taxes will be imposed:* **levy**, charge, apply, enforce; set, establish, institute, introduce, bring into effect. **3** *how dare you impose on me like this!* **take advantage of**, exploit, take liberties with; bother, trouble, disturb, inconvenience, put out, put to trouble.

imposing adjective **impressive**, striking, arresting, eye-catching, dramatic, spectacular, stunning, awesome, formidable, splendid, grand, majestic.
– OPPOSITES modest.

imposition noun **1** *the imposition of an alien culture:* **imposing**, foisting, forcing, inflicting. **2** *the imposition of VAT:* **levying**, charging, application, enforcement, enforcing; setting, establishment, introduction, institution. **3** *it would be no imposition:* **burden**, encumbrance, bother, worry; informal hassle.

impossible adjective **1** *the winds made fishing impossible:* **out of the question**, impracticable, non-viable, unworkable. **2** *an impossible dream:* **unattainable**, unachievable, unobtainable, hopeless, impracticable, unworkable. **3** *food shortages made life impossible:* **unbearable**, intolerable, unendurable. **4** (informal) *an impossible woman:* **unreasonable**, difficult, awkward; intolerable, unbearable; exasperating, maddening, infuriating.
– OPPOSITES attainable, bearable.

impostor noun **impersonator**, deceiver, hoaxer, fraudster; fake, fraud; informal phoney.

impotent adjective **powerless**, ineffective, ineffectual; useless, feeble; emasculated.
– OPPOSITES powerful, effective.

impound verb **confiscate**, appropriate, take possession of, seize, commandeer, expropriate, requisition, take over, sequester, sequestrate; Law distrain.

impoverish verb **1** *the widow had been impoverished by debt:* **make poor**, make penniless, reduce to penury, bankrupt, ruin. **2** *the trees were impoverishing the soil:* **weaken**, exhaust, deplete.

impoverished adjective **1** *an impoverished peasant farmer:* **poor**, poverty-stricken, penniless, destitute, indigent, needy, on the

breadline; bankrupt, ruined, insolvent; informal on your uppers, on skid row; formal penurious. **2** *the soil is impoverished:* **weakened**, exhausted, drained, sapped, depleted, spent; barren, unproductive, infertile.
– OPPOSITES rich.

impracticable adjective **unworkable**, unfeasible, non-viable, unachievable, unattainable, unrealizable; impractical.
– OPPOSITES workable, feasible.

impractical adjective **1** *an impractical suggestion:* **unrealistic**, unworkable, unfeasible, non-viable; ill-thought-out, absurd; idealistic, fanciful, romantic; informal cockeyed, crackpot, crazy. **2** *impractical white ankle boots:* **unsuitable**, not sensible, inappropriate, unserviceable.
– OPPOSITES practical, sensible.

imprecise adjective **1** *a rather imprecise definition:* **vague**, loose, indistinct, inaccurate, non-specific, sweeping, broad, general; hazy, fuzzy, woolly, nebulous, ambiguous, equivocal, uncertain. **2** *an imprecise estimate:* **inexact**, approximate, rough; N. Amer. informal ballpark.
– OPPOSITES exact.

impregnable adjective **1** *an impregnable castle:* **invulnerable**, impenetrable, unassailable, inviolable, secure, strong, well fortified, well defended; invincible, unconquerable. **2** *an impregnable parliamentary majority:* **unassailable**, unbeatable, undefeatable, unshakeable, invincible, invulnerable.
– OPPOSITES vulnerable.

impregnate verb **infuse**, soak, steep, saturate, drench; marinate.

impresario noun **organizer**, manager, producer; promoter, publicist, showman; director, conductor, maestro.

impress verb **1** *their performance impressed him:* **make an impression on**, have an impact on, influence, affect, move, stir, rouse, excite, inspire; dazzle, awe; informal grab. **2** *goldsmiths impressed his likeness on the medallions:* **imprint**, print, stamp, mark, emboss, punch. **3** *impress upon her the need to save:* **emphasize to**, stress to, bring home to, instil in, inculcate into, drum into, knock into.
– OPPOSITES disappoint.

impression noun **1** *he got the impression she was hiding something:* **feeling**, sense, fancy, sneaking suspicion, inkling, intuition, hunch; notion, idea, funny feeling; informal gut feeling. **2** *a favourable impression:* **opinion**, view, image, picture, perception, judgement, verdict, estimation. **3** *school made a profound impression on me:* **impact**, effect, influence. **4** *the lid had left a circular impression:* **indentation**, dent, mark, outline, imprint. **5** *he did a good impression of their science teacher:* **impersonation**, imitation; parody, caricature; informal take-off, send-up, spoof. **6** *an artist's impression of the gardens:* **representation**, portrayal, depiction, rendition, interpretation, picture. **7** *a revised impression of the 1981 edition:* **print run**, imprint, reprint, issue, edition.

impressionable adjective **easily influenced**, suggestible, susceptible, persuadable, pliable, malleable, pliant, ingenuous, trusting, naive, gullible.

impressive adjective **1** *an impressive building:* **magnificent**, majestic, imposing, splendid, spectacular, grand, awe-inspiring, stunning, breathtaking. **2** *they played some impressive football:* **admirable**, masterly, accomplished, expert, skilled, skilful, consummate; excellent, outstanding, first-class, first-rate, fine; informal great, mean, nifty, cracking, ace, wizard; N. Amer. informal crackerjack.
– OPPOSITES ordinary, mediocre.

imprint verb **1** *patterns can be imprinted in the clay:* **stamp**, print, impress, mark. **2** *the image was imprinted on his mind:* **fix**, establish, stick, lodge, implant, embed.
• noun **1** *her feet left imprints on the floor:* **impression**, print, mark, indentation. **2** *colonialism has left its imprint:* **impact**, effect, influence, impression.

imprison verb **incarcerate**, send to prison, jail, lock up, put away, intern, detain, hold prisoner, hold captive; informal send down, put

behind bars, put inside; Brit. informal bang up.
– OPPOSITES free, release.

imprisoned adjective **incarcerated**, in prison, in jail, jailed, locked up, interned, detained, held prisoner, held captive; informal sent down, behind bars, doing time, inside; Brit. informal doing porridge, banged up.

imprisonment noun **incarceration**, internment, confinement, detention, captivity; informal time; Brit. informal porridge.

improbability noun **unlikelihood**, implausibility; doubtfulness, uncertainty, dubiousness.

improbable adjective **1** *it seemed improbable that the hot weather would continue:* **unlikely**, doubtful, dubious, debatable, questionable, uncertain. **2** *an improbable exaggeration:* **unconvincing**, unbelievable, implausible, unlikely.
– OPPOSITES certain, believable.

impromptu adjective *an impromptu lecture:* **unrehearsed**, unprepared, unscripted, extempore, extemporized, improvised, spontaneous, unplanned; informal off-the-cuff.
– OPPOSITES prepared, rehearsed.

improper adjective **1** *it is improper for policemen to accept gifts:* **inappropriate**, unacceptable, unsuitable, unprofessional, irregular; unethical, dishonest, dishonourable; informal not cricket. **2** *it was improper for young ladies to drive a young man home:* **unseemly**, unfitting, unladylike, ungentlemanly, inappropriate, immodest, indecorous. **3** *an extremely improper remark:* **indecent**, indelicate, risqué, off colour, suggestive, naughty, ribald, vulgar, crude, rude.
– OPPOSITES acceptable, proper, decent.

impropriety noun **1** *a suggestion of impropriety:* **wrongdoing**, misconduct, dishonesty, corruption, unscrupulousness, unprofessionalism, irregularity; unseemliness, indelicacy, indecency, immorality. **2** *fiscal improprieties:* **transgression**, misdemeanour, offence, misdeed, crime; indiscretion, mistake, peccadillo.

improve verb **1** *ways to improve the service:* **make better**, ameliorate, upgrade, refine, enhance, boost, build on, raise; informal tweak, fine-tune. **2** *communications improved during the 18th century:* **get better**, advance, progress, develop; make headway, make progress, pick up, look up, move forward. **3** *the patient is improving:* **recover**, get better, recuperate, gain strength, rally, revive, get back on your feet, be on the mend. **4** *they need to improve their offer:* **increase**, make larger, raise, augment, supplement, top up; reconsider; informal up, bump up.
– OPPOSITES worsen, deteriorate.
■ **improve on** surpass, better, do better than, outdo, exceed, beat, top, cap.

improvement noun **advance**, development, upgrade, refinement, enhancement, amelioration; boost, augmentation; rally, recovery, upswing; step forward.

improvident adjective **spendthrift**, wasteful, prodigal, profligate, extravagant, lavish, immoderate; imprudent, irresponsible, careless, reckless.
– OPPOSITES thrifty.

improvise verb **1** *she was improvising in front of the cameras:* **extemporize**, ad-lib; informal speak off the cuff, speak off the top of your head, wing it. **2** *she improvised a sandpit:* **contrive**, devise, throw together, cobble together, rig up; informal whip up, rustle up; Brit. informal knock up.

improvised adjective **1** *an improvised speech:* **impromptu**, unrehearsed, unprepared, unscripted, extempore, spontaneous, unplanned; informal off-the-cuff. **2** *an improvised shelter:* **makeshift**, cobbled-together, rough and ready, make-do.
– OPPOSITES prepared, rehearsed.

imprudent adjective **unwise**, injudicious, incautious, misguided, ill-advised, improvident, irresponsible, short-sighted, foolish.
– OPPOSITES sensible.

impudence noun **impertinence**, insolence, effrontery, cheek, cockiness, brazenness; presumption, disrespect, flippancy; rudeness, impoliteness, ill manners, discourteousness, gall; informal brass neck, chutzpah, nerve; N. Amer. informal sassiness.

impudent adjective **impertinent**, insolent, cheeky, cocky, brazen; presumptuous, forward, disrespectful, insubordinate; rude, impolite, ill-mannered, discourteous; informal brass-necked, saucy, lippy; N. Amer. informal sassy.
– OPPOSITES polite.

impulse noun **1** *she had an impulse to run and hide:* **urge**, instinct, drive, compulsion, itch; whim, desire, fancy, notion. **2** *a man of impulse:* **spontaneity**, impetuosity, recklessness, rashness. **3** *passions provide the main impulse of poetry:* **inspiration**, stimulation, stimulus, incitement, motivation, encouragement, spur, catalyst. **4** *impulses from the spinal cord to the muscles:* **pulse**, current, wave, signal.
■ **on (an) impulse** impulsively, spontaneously, on the spur of the moment, without thinking.

impulsive adjective **1** *he had an impulsive nature:* **impetuous**, spontaneous, hasty, passionate, emotional. **2** *an impulsive decision:* **impromptu**, snap, spontaneous, unpremeditated, spur-of-the-moment, extemporaneous.
– OPPOSITES cautious, premeditated.

impunity noun *the impunity enjoyed by military officers:* **immunity**, indemnity, exemption from punishment, licence; privilege, liberty.
– OPPOSITES liability.
■ **with impunity** without punishment, scot-free, unpunished.

impure adjective **1** *impure gold:* **unrefined**, crude, raw; adulterated, blended, diluted, alloyed. **2** *the water was impure:* **contaminated**, polluted, tainted, unwholesome, poisoned; dirty; unhygienic, unsanitary. **3** *impure thoughts:* **immoral**, sinful, wrongful, wicked; unchaste, lustful, lecherous, lewd, lascivious, obscene, indecent, ribald, risqué, improper, crude, coarse.
– OPPOSITES clean, chaste.

impurity noun **1** *the impurity of the air:* **contamination**, pollution; dirtiness, filthiness, foulness, unwholesomeness. **2** *the impurities in beer:* **contaminant**, pollutant, foreign body; dross, dirt, filth. **3** *sin and impurity:* **immorality**, sin, sinfulness, wickedness; lustfulness, lechery, lewdness, lasciviousness, obscenity, crudeness, indecency, impropriety, vulgarity, coarseness.

impute verb **attribute**, ascribe, assign, credit; connect with, associate with.

in adverb & adjective **1** *no one's in:* **present**, home; inside, indoors. **2** (informal) *miniskirts are in:* **fashionable**, in fashion, in vogue, popular, chic, à la mode, de rigueur; informal trendy, all the rage, cool, the in thing, hip.
– OPPOSITES out, unfashionable.
■ **ins and outs** (informal) details, particulars, facts, features, characteristics, nuts and bolts; informal nitty gritty.

inability noun **lack of ability**, incapability, incapacity, powerlessness, impotence, helplessness.

inaccessible adjective **1** *an inaccessible woodland site:* **unreachable**; cut-off, isolated, remote, in the back of beyond, out of the way. **2** *the book was elitist and inaccessible:* **esoteric**, obscure, abstruse, recondite, arcane; elitist, exclusive, difficult.

inaccuracy noun **1** *the inaccuracy of recent opinion polls:* **incorrectness**, inexactness, imprecision, erroneousness, fallaciousness, faultiness. **2** *the article contained a number of inaccuracies:* **error**, mistake, fault; erratum; Brit. literal; informal howler, boo-boo, typo; N. Amer. informal blooper, goof.
– OPPOSITES correctness.

inaccurate adjective **inexact**, imprecise, incorrect, wrong, erroneous, faulty, imperfect, flawed, defective, unsound, unreliable; false, mistaken, untrue; informal off beam; Brit. informal adrift.

inaction noun **inactivity**, non-intervention; apathy, inertia, indolence.

inactive adjective **1** *over the next few days I remained inactive:* **idle**, indolent, lazy, slothful, lethargic, inert, sluggish, unenergetic, listless, torpid. **2** *the device remains inactive until the computer starts up:* **inoperative**, idle; not working, out of service, unused, not in use.

inactivity noun **1** *years of inactivity:*

idleness, indolence, laziness, slothfulness, lethargy, inertia, sluggishness, listlessness. **2** *government inactivity:* **inaction**, non-intervention; neglect, negligence, apathy, inertia.
– OPPOSITES action, activity.

inadequacy noun **1** *the inadequacy of available resources:* **insufficiency**, deficiency, scarcity, scarceness, sparseness, dearth, paucity, shortage, want, lack; paltriness, meagreness. **2** *her feelings of personal inadequacy:* **incompetence**, incapability, unfitness, ineffectiveness, inefficiency, inefficacy, ineptness, uselessness, impotence, powerlessness. **3** *the inadequacies of the present system:* **shortcoming**, defect, fault, failing, weakness, limitation, flaw, imperfection.
– OPPOSITES abundance, competence.

i

inadequate adjective **1** *inadequate water supplies:* **insufficient**, deficient, poor, scant, scarce, sparse, in short supply; paltry, meagre, limited. **2** *he's a bit inadequate:* **incapable**; immature, juvenile; informal sad.
– OPPOSITES sufficient.

inadmissible adjective **unallowable**, invalid, unacceptable, impermissible, disallowed, forbidden, prohibited, precluded.

inadvertent adjective **unintentional**, unintended, accidental, unplanned.
– OPPOSITES deliberate.

inadvertently adverb **accidentally**, by accident, unintentionally, unwittingly.

inadvisable adjective **unwise**, ill-advised, imprudent, ill-judged, ill-considered, injudicious, impolitic.
– OPPOSITES shrewd.

inalienable adjective **inviolable**, absolute, sacrosanct; non-negotiable.

inane adjective **silly**, foolish, stupid, fatuous, idiotic, asinine, frivolous, vapid; informal dumb, moronic; Brit. informal daft.
– OPPOSITES sensible.

inanimate adjective **lifeless**, inert, insentient.
– OPPOSITES living.

inapplicable adjective **irrelevant**, immaterial, not germane, unrelated, extraneous, beside the point.
– OPPOSITES relevant, applicable.

inapposite adjective **inappropriate**, unsuitable, inapt, out of place, infelicitous, misplaced, ill-judged, ill-advised.
– OPPOSITES appropriate.

inappreciable adjective **imperceptible**, minute, tiny, slight, small; insignificant, inconsequential, unimportant, negligible; informal piddling, piffling.
– OPPOSITES considerable.

inappropriate adjective **unsuitable**, unfitting, unseemly, unbecoming, improper; out of place/keeping, inapposite, inapt; informal out of order.
– OPPOSITES suitable.

inapt adjective. See INAPPROPRIATE.

inarticulate adjective **1** *an inarticulate young man:* **tongue-tied**, lost for words. **2** *an inarticulate reply:* **unintelligible**, incomprehensible, incoherent, unclear, indistinct, mumbled, muffled. **3** *inarticulate rage:* **unspoken**, silent, unexpressed, wordless, unvoiced.
– OPPOSITES fluent.

inattention noun **distraction**, inattentiveness, preoccupation, absent-mindedness, daydreaming, abstraction.
– OPPOSITES concentration.

inattentive adjective **1** *an inattentive pupil:* **distracted**, preoccupied, absent-minded, daydreaming, dreamy, abstracted; informal miles away. **2** *inattentive service:* **negligent**, neglectful, slack, sloppy, slapdash, lax.
– OPPOSITES alert.

inaudible adjective **unclear**, indistinct; faint, muted, soft, low, muffled, whispered, muttered, murmured, mumbled.

inaugural adjective **first**, opening, initial, introductory.
– OPPOSITES final.

inaugurate verb **1** *he inaugurated a new policy:* **initiate**, begin, start, institute, launch, get going, get under way, establish, lay the foundations of; bring in, usher in; informal kick off. **2** *the new President will be inaugurated:* **admit to office**, install, instate, swear in; invest, ordain, crown.

inauspicious adjective **unpromising**, unpropitious, unfavourable, unfortunate, infelicitous, ominous.
– OPPOSITES promising.

inborn adjective **innate**, congenital; inherent, natural, inbred, inherited, hereditary, in your genes.

inbuilt adjective **1** *an inbuilt CD-ROM drive:* **built-in**, integral, incorporated, inboard, on-board, hard-wired. **2** *our inbuilt survival instinct:* **inherent**, intrinsic, innate, congenital, natural.

incalculable adjective **inestimable**, indeterminable, untold, immeasurable, incomputable; enormous, immense, huge, vast, innumerable.

incandescent adjective **1** *incandescent fragments of lava:* **white-hot**, red-hot, burning, fiery, blazing; glowing, aglow, radiant, bright, brilliant. **2** *the minister was incandescent:* **furious**, incensed, seething, infuriated, enraged, raging, fuming, irate, beside yourself; informal livid, foaming at the mouth, hopping mad, wild, apoplectic.

incantation noun **1** *he muttered some weird incantations:* **chant**, invocation, spell, formula; NZ makutu; informal mumbo-jumbo, hocus-pocus. **2** *ritual incantation:* **chanting**, intonation, recitation.

incapable adjective **1** *an incapable government:* **incompetent**, inept, inadequate, ineffective, ineffectual, unfit, unqualified, unequal to the task; informal not up to it, not up to snuff, a dead loss. **2** *he was mentally incapable:* **incapacitated**, helpless, powerless, incompetent.
– OPPOSITES competent.

incapacitated adjective *he was temporarily incapacitated:* **indisposed**, unfit, out of action, out of commission; informal laid up.
– OPPOSITES fit.

incapacity noun **disability**, incapability, debility, impairment, indisposition; incompetence, inadequacy, ineffectiveness.
– OPPOSITES capability.

incarcerate verb **imprison**, put in prison, send to prison, jail, lock up, put under lock and key, put away, intern, confine, detain, hold, put in chains, clap in irons, hold prisoner, hold captive; Brit. detain at Her Majesty's pleasure; informal send down, put behind bars, put inside; Brit. informal bang up.
– OPPOSITES release.

incarceration noun **imprisonment**, internment, confinement, detention, custody, captivity, restraint; informal time; Brit. informal porridge.

incarnate adjective **made flesh**, personified, in bodily form; corporeal, embodied, made manifest.

incarnation noun **1** *the incarnation of artistic genius:* **embodiment**, personification, exemplification, epitome; manifestation; archetype, exemplar. **2** *a previous incarnation:* **lifetime**, life, existence.

incautious adjective **rash**, unwise, careless, thoughtless, reckless, unthinking, imprudent, ill-advised, ill-judged, injudicious.
– OPPOSITES circumspect.

incendiary adjective **1** *an incendiary device:* **combustible**, flammable, inflammable. **2** *an incendiary speech:* **inflammatory**, rabble-rousing, provocative; contentious, controversial.

incense verb *his taunts incensed me:* **enrage**, infuriate, anger, madden, outrage, exasperate, antagonize, provoke; informal make someone see red, make someone's blood boil, make someone's hackles rise, drive mad/crazy; N. Amer. informal burn up.
– OPPOSITES placate, please.

incensed adjective **enraged**, furious, infuriated, irate, raging, incandescent, fuming, seething, beside yourself, outraged; informal mad, hopping mad, wild, livid, apoplectic, foaming at the mouth.

incentive noun **inducement**, motivation, motive, reason, stimulus, spur, impetus, encouragement, impulse, carrot; incitement; informal sweetener.
– OPPOSITES deterrent.

inception noun **establishment**, institution, foundation, founding, formation, initiation, setting up, start-up, origination, constitution, inauguration, opening, day one; beginning, commencement, start, birth; informal kick-off.
– OPPOSITES end.

incessant adjective **ceaseless**, unceasing, constant, continual, unabating, interminable, endless, unending, never-ending, perpetual, continuous, non-stop, uninterrupted, unbroken, unremitting, unrelenting, sustained.
– OPPOSITES intermittent.

incessantly adverb **constantly**, continually, all the time, non-stop, without stopping, without a break, round the clock, {morning, noon, and night}, interminably, unremittingly, ceaselessly, endlessly; informal 24-7.
– OPPOSITES occasionally.

incidence noun **occurrence**, prevalence; rate, frequency; amount, degree, extent.

i

incident noun **1** *incidents in his youth:* **event**, occurrence, episode, experience, happening, occasion, affair, business; adventure, exploit, escapade; matter, development. **2** *police are investigating another incident:* **disturbance**, clash, confrontation, accident, shooting, explosion; situation; Law, dated affray. **3** *the journey was not without incident:* **excitement**, adventure, drama; danger, peril.

incidental adjective **1** *incidental details:* **secondary**, subsidiary; minor, peripheral, background, by-the-by, unimportant, insignificant, inconsequential, tangential, extraneous. **2** *an incidental discovery:* **chance**, accidental, random; fluky, fortuitous, serendipitous, coincidental, unlooked for.
– OPPOSITES essential, deliberate.

incidentally adverb **1** *incidentally, I haven't had a reply yet:* **by the way**, by the by, in passing, en passant, speaking of which; informal as it happens. **2** *the infection was discovered incidentally:* **by chance**, by accident, accidentally, fortuitously, by a fluke, by happenstance.

incinerate verb **burn**, reduce to ashes, carbonize; cremate.

incipient adjective **developing**, growing, emerging, emergent, dawning, initial; nascent, embryonic, fledgling, in its infancy.
– OPPOSITES full-blown.

incision noun **1** *a surgical incision:* **cut**, opening, slit. **2** *incisions on the marble:* **notch**, nick, scratch, carving; scarification.

incisive adjective **penetrating**, acute, sharp, razor-sharp, keen, astute, trenchant, shrewd, piercing, perceptive, insightful, perspicacious; concise, succinct, pithy, to the point, crisp, clear; informal punchy.
– OPPOSITES rambling, vague.

incite verb **1** *he was arrested for inciting racial hatred:* **stir up**, whip up, encourage, stoke up, fuel, kindle, ignite, inflame, stimulate, instigate, provoke, excite, arouse, awaken, inspire, trigger, spark off. **2** *she incited him to commit murder:* **egg on**, encourage, urge, goad, provoke, spur on, drive, push, prod, prompt, induce, impel; informal put up to.
– OPPOSITES discourage, deter.

incivility noun **rudeness**, discourtesy, impoliteness, bad manners, disrespect, boorishness, ungraciousness.
– OPPOSITES politeness.

inclement adjective **cold**, chilly, bleak, wintry, freezing, snowy, icy; wet, rainy, drizzly, damp; stormy, blustery, wild, rough, squally, windy; unpleasant, bad, foul, nasty, filthy, severe, extreme, harsh.
– OPPOSITES fine.

inclination noun **1** *his political inclinations:* **tendency**, propensity, proclivity, leaning, predisposition, predilection, impulse, bent; penchant, preference, appetite, affinity; taste. **2** *an inclination of his head:* **nod**, bow, bending, lowering, movement.
– OPPOSITES aversion.

incline verb **1** *his prejudice inclines him to overlook obvious facts:* **predispose**, lead, make, dispose, prejudice; prompt, induce. **2** *I incline to the opposite view:* **prefer**, favour, go for; tend, lean, swing, veer, gravitate, be drawn. **3** *he inclined his head:* **bend**, bow, nod, bob, lower, dip. **4** *the columns incline away from the vertical:* **lean**, tilt, angle, tip, slope, slant, bend, curve; list.
• noun *a steep incline:* **slope**, gradient, pitch, ramp, bank, ascent, rise, dip, descent; hill; N. Amer. grade, downgrade, upgrade.

inclined adjective **1** *I'm inclined to believe her:* **disposed**, minded, of a mind. **2** *she's inclined to gossip:* **prone**, given, in the habit of, liable, apt; literary wont.

include verb **1** *activities include drama and music:* **incorporate**, comprise, encompass, cover, embrace, take in, number, contain. **2** *don't forget to include the cost of repairs:* **allow for**, count, take into account, take into consideration.
– OPPOSITES exclude.

including preposition **inclusive of**, counting; as well as, plus, together with.

inclusive adjective **1** *an inclusive price | an inclusive definition:* **all-in**, comprehensive, overall, full, all-round, umbrella, catch-all, all-encompassing. **2** *prices are inclusive of VAT:* **including**, incorporating, taking in, counting, covering.

incoherent adjective **1** *a long, incoherent speech:* **unclear**, confused, muddled, incomprehensible, hard to follow, disjointed, disconnected, disordered, garbled, jumbled, scrambled; rambling, wandering, discursive, disorganized, illogical; inarticulate; mumbling, slurred. **2** *she was incoherent and shivering violently:* **delirious**, raving, babbling, hysterical, irrational.
– OPPOSITES lucid.

income noun **earnings**, salary, pay, remuneration, wages, stipend; revenue, receipts, takings, profits, proceeds, turnover, yield, dividend; N. Amer. take; formal emolument.
– OPPOSITES expenditure, outgoings.

incoming adjective *the incoming president:* **new**, next, future; -to-be; elect, designate.
– OPPOSITES outgoing.

incomparable adjective **without equal**, beyond compare, unparalleled, matchless, peerless, unmatched, without parallel, beyond comparison, second to none, in a class of its own, unequalled, unrivalled, inimitable.

incomparably adverb **far and away**, by far, infinitely, immeasurably, easily.

incompatible adjective **1** *they are totally incompatible:* **unsuited**, mismatched, ill-matched, poles apart, worlds apart, like day and night; Brit. like chalk and cheese. **2** *incompatible economic objectives:* **irreconcilable**, conflicting, opposed, opposite, contradictory, antagonistic, antipathetic; clashing, inharmonious, discordant; mutually exclusive. **3** *a theory incompatible with that of his predecessor:* **inconsistent with**, at odds with, out of keeping with, at variance with, contrary to, in conflict with, in opposition to, diametrically opposed to, counter to, irreconcilable with.
– OPPOSITES compatible, harmonious, consistent.

incompetent adjective **inept**, unskilled, inexpert, amateurish, unprofessional, bungling, blundering, clumsy, inadequate, ineffective, inefficient, ineffectual; informal useless, pathetic, cack-handed, ham-fisted, not up to it.

incomplete adjective **1** *the manuscript is still incomplete:* **unfinished**, uncompleted, partial, half-finished. **2** *inaccurate or incomplete information:* **deficient**, insufficient, partial, sketchy, fragmentary, scrappy, bitty; expurgated, bowdlerized, censored.

incomprehensible adjective **unintelligible**, impossible to understand, impenetrable, unclear, indecipherable; baffling, bewildering; abstruse, esoteric, recondite, arcane; Brit. informal double Dutch.
– OPPOSITES intelligible, clear.

inconceivable adjective **unbelievable**, beyond belief, incredible, unthinkable, unimaginable, out of the question; informal hard to swallow.
– OPPOSITES likely.

inconclusive adjective **indecisive**; indefinite, indeterminate, unresolved, unproven, unsettled, open to question/doubt; informal up in the air, left hanging.

incongruous adjective **1** *the women looked somewhat incongruous in their fur coats:* **out of place**; wrong, strange, odd, absurd, bizarre. **2** *an incongruous collection of objects:* **ill-matched**, ill-assorted, mismatched, disparate.
– OPPOSITES appropriate, harmonious.

i

inconsequential adjective **insignificant**, unimportant, of little/no consequence, neither here nor there, incidental, immaterial, irrelevant; negligible, slight, minor, trivial, trifling, petty; informal piddling, piffling.
– OPPOSITES important.

inconsiderate adjective **thoughtless**, unthinking, insensitive, selfish, self-centred, impolite, discourteous, rude; tactless, undiplomatic; informal ignorant.
– OPPOSITES thoughtful.

inconsistent adjective **1** *his inconsistent behaviour:* **erratic**, changeable, unpredictable, variable, unstable, unsettled, uneven; capricious, fickle, unreliable, mercurial, volatile; informal up and down; technical labile. **2** *he had done nothing inconsistent with his morality:* **incompatible with**, conflicting with, at odds with, at variance with, contrary to, irreconcilable with, out of keeping with; antithetical to.

inconsolable adjective **heartbroken**, broken-hearted, grief-stricken, beside yourself, devastated, distraught; informal gutted.

inconspicuous adjective **unobtrusive**, unnoticeable, unremarkable, unexceptional, modest, unassuming, discreet, low-profile.
– OPPOSITES noticeable.

incontestable adjective **incontrovertible**, indisputable, undeniable, irrefutable, unassailable, beyond dispute, unquestionable, beyond question, indubitable, beyond doubt.
– OPPOSITES questionable.

incontinent adjective **unrestrained**, uncontrolled, unbridled, unchecked.

incontrovertible adjective **indisputable**, incontestable, undeniable, irrefutable, unassailable, beyond dispute, unquestionable, beyond question, indubitable, beyond doubt, unarguable; conclusive, categorical.
– OPPOSITES questionable.

inconvenience noun **1** *we apologize for any inconvenience caused:* **trouble**, bother, problems, disruption, difficulty, disturbance; informal aggravation, hassle. **2** *his early arrival was clearly an inconvenience:* **nuisance**, trouble, bother, problem; informal headache, pain, pain in the neck, pain in the backside, drag, hassle; N. Amer. informal pain in the butt.
• verb *I don't want to inconvenience you:* **trouble**, bother, put out, put to any trouble, disturb, impose on.

inconvenient adjective **awkward**, difficult, inopportune, untimely, ill-timed, unsuitable, inappropriate, unfortunate.

incorporate verb **1** *the region was incorporated into Moldavian territory:* **absorb**, include, subsume, assimilate, integrate, take in, swallow up. **2** *the model incorporates some advanced features:* **include**, contain, embrace, build in; offer, boast. **3** *a small amount of salt is incorporated with the butter:* **blend**, mix, combine; fold in, stir in.

incorporeal adjective **intangible**, impalpable; disembodied; spiritual, ethereal; insubstantial, transcendental; ghostly, spectral, supernatural.
– OPPOSITES tangible.

incorrect adjective **1** *an incorrect answer:* **wrong**, erroneous, in error, mistaken; untrue, false; informal off beam, out, way out. **2** *incorrect behaviour:* **inappropriate**, wrong, unsuitable, inapt, inapposite; ill-advised, ill-considered, ill-judged, unacceptable, improper, unseemly; informal out of order.

incorrigible adjective **inveterate**, habitual, confirmed, hardened, incurable, irredeemable, hopeless; unrepentant, unapologetic, unashamed.

incorruptible adjective **honest**, honourable, trustworthy, principled, good, upright, virtuous.
– OPPOSITES venal.

increase verb **1** *demand is likely to increase:* **grow**, get bigger, get larger, enlarge, expand, swell; rise, climb; intensify, strengthen, extend, spread, widen; mount, accumulate; literary wax. **2** *higher expectations will increase user demand:* **add to**, make larger, make bigger, augment, supplement, top up, build up, extend, raise, swell, inflate; magnify, intensify, strengthen,

heighten; informal up, jack up, bump up, crank up.
– OPPOSITES decrease, reduce.
• noun *the increase in size | an increase in demand:* **growth**, rise, enlargement, expansion, extension, elevation; increment, addition, augmentation; magnification, intensification, amplification, escalation, surge; informal hike.

incredible adjective **1** *I find his story incredible:* **unbelievable**, hard to believe, unconvincing, far-fetched, implausible, improbable, highly unlikely, dubious, doubtful; inconceivable, unthinkable, unimaginable. **2** *an incredible feat of engineering:* **magnificent**, wonderful, marvellous, spectacular, remarkable, phenomenal, prodigious, breathtaking, extraordinary, unbelievable, amazing, stunning, astounding, astonishing, awe-inspiring, staggering, formidable, awesome, superhuman; informal fantastic, terrific, tremendous, stupendous, mind-boggling, mind-blowing, out of this world; literary wondrous.

incredulity noun **disbelief**, scepticism, mistrust, suspicion, doubt; cynicism.

incredulous adjective **disbelieving**, sceptical, distrustful, suspicious, doubtful, dubious, unconvinced; cynical.

increment noun **increase**, addition, supplement, gain, augmentation.
– OPPOSITES reduction.

incriminate verb **implicate**, involve, enmesh; point the finger at.

inculcate verb **instil**, implant, fix, impress, imprint; hammer into, drum into, drill into.

incumbent adjective **1** *it is incumbent on the government to give a clear lead:* **necessary**, essential, imperative. **2** *the incumbent president:* **current**, present, in office; reigning.
• noun *the first incumbent of the post:* **holder**, bearer, occupant.

incur verb **bring on yourself**, expose yourself to, lay yourself open to; run up; sustain, experience.

incurable adjective **1** *an incurable illness:* **untreatable**, inoperable, irremediable; terminal, fatal; chronic. **2** *an incurable romantic:* **inveterate**, dyed-in-the-wool, confirmed, established, absolute, complete, utter, thoroughgoing, out-and-out; incorrigible, hopeless.

incursion noun **attack**, assault, raid, invasion, foray, blitz, sortie, sally, advance, push, thrust.
– OPPOSITES retreat.

indebted adjective **beholden**, obliged, grateful, in someone's debt.

indecent adjective **1** *indecent photographs:* **obscene**, dirty, filthy, rude, naughty, vulgar, crude, lewd, smutty, off colour; pornographic, offensive; ribald, risqué, racy; informal blue, porn, X-rated, raunchy, skin; Brit. informal saucy; euphemistic adult. **2** *indecent clothes:* **revealing**, skimpy, scanty, low cut; erotic, arousing, sexy, provocative, titillating. **3** *indecent haste:* **unseemly**, improper, unbecoming, inappropriate.

indecipherable adjective **illegible**, unreadable, unintelligible, unclear.

indecision noun **indecisiveness**, hesitation, tentativeness; ambivalence, doubt, uncertainty; vacillation, equivocation; shilly-shallying, dithering; Brit. humming and hawing; Scottish swithering; informal dilly-dallying, sitting on the fence.

indecisive adjective **1** *an indecisive result:* **inconclusive**, proving nothing, open, indeterminate, unclear, ambiguous. **2** *an indecisive leader:* **irresolute**, hesitant, tentative, weak; vacillating, dithering, wavering; blowing hot and cold, unsure, uncertain; undecided.

indeed adverb *there was, indeed, quite a furore:* **as expected**, to be sure; in truth, in fact, as a matter of fact, actually.

indefatigable adjective **tireless**, untiring, unwearying, unflagging, dogged, unshakeable, indomitable.

indefensible adjective **1** *an indefensible system of dual justice:* **unjustifiable**, unacceptable, unwarrantable, unsustainable, untenable, unjustified, inexcusable; wrong, flawed, misguided. **2** *the towns were indefensible:* **defenceless**, vulnerable, exposed, open to attack.

indefinable adjective **hard to**

define, hard to describe, indescribable; vague, elusive.

indefinite adjective **1** *an indefinite period:* **indeterminate**, unspecified, undefined, unlimited; limitless, infinite, endless. **2** *an indefinite meaning:* **vague**, ill-defined, unclear, loose, imprecise, nebulous, blurred, fuzzy.
– OPPOSITES fixed, clear.

indelible adjective **ineradicable**, permanent, lasting, enduring, unfading, unforgettable.

indelicate adjective **insensitive**, tactless, undiplomatic, impolitic, indiscreet, improper, indecent, rude.

indemnity noun **1** *no indemnity will be given for loss of cash:* **insurance**, assurance, protection, security, indemnification, surety. **2** *the company was paid $100,000 in indemnity:* **compensation**, reimbursement, recompense, repayment, restitution, redress, reparation, damages.

indentation noun **hollow**, depression, dip, dent, cavity, concavity, pit; dimple; recess, bay, inlet, cove.

independence noun **1** *the struggle for American independence:* **self-government**, self-rule, home rule, self-determination, sovereignty, autonomy. **2** *the adviser's independence:* **impartiality**, neutrality, disinterestedness, detachment, objectivity. **3** *independence of spirit:* **freedom**, individualism, unconventionality, unorthodoxy.

independent adjective **1** *an independent country:* **self-governing**, self-ruling, self-determining, sovereign, autonomous, non-aligned. **2** *two independent groups verified the results:* **separate**, different, unconnected, unrelated, discrete. **3** *an independent school:* **private**, non-state-run, private-sector, fee-paying; privatized, deregulated, denationalized. **4** *independent advice:* **impartial**, unbiased, unprejudiced, neutral, disinterested, uninvolved, detached, dispassionate, objective, non-partisan, with no axe to grind. **5** *an independent spirit:* **freethinking**, free, individualistic, unconventional, maverick, bold, unconstrained, uninhibited.
– OPPOSITES subservient, related, public, biased.

independently adverb **alone**, on your own, separately, unaccompanied, solo; unaided, unassisted, without help, by your own efforts, under your own steam, single-handed, off your own bat, on your own initiative.

indescribable adjective **inexpressible**, indefinable, beyond words/description, incommunicable; unutterable, unspeakable; intense, extreme, acute, strong, powerful, profound; incredible, extraordinary, remarkable.

indestructible adjective **unbreakable**, shatterproof, vandal-proof, durable; lasting, enduring, everlasting, undying, immortal, imperishable; literary adamantine.
– OPPOSITES fragile.

indeterminate adjective **1** *an indeterminate period of time:* **undetermined**, uncertain, unknown, unspecified, unstipulated, indefinite, unfixed. **2** *some indeterminate background noise:* **vague**, indefinite, unclear, nebulous, indistinct.

index noun **list**, listing, inventory, catalogue, register, directory, database.

indicate verb **1** *sales indicate a growing market for such art:* **point to**, be a sign of, be evidence of, demonstrate, show, testify to, be symptomatic of, denote, mark, signal, reflect, signify, suggest, imply; literary betoken. **2** *the president indicated his willingness to use force:* **state**, declare, make known, communicate, announce, mention; put it on record. **3** *please indicate your choice of prize on the form:* **specify**, designate, stipulate; show.

indication noun **sign**, signal, indicator, symptom, mark, demonstration; pointer, guide, hint, clue, intimation, omen, warning.

indicative adjective **symptomatic**, expressive, suggestive, representative, emblematic, symbolic.

indicator noun **1** *these tests are a reliable indicator of performance:* **measure**, gauge, barometer, guide, index, mark, sign, signal. **2** *the* *depth indicator:* **meter**, measuring device, measure, gauge, dial.

indict verb **charge**, accuse, arraign, take to court, put on trial, prosecute; summons, cite, prefer charges against; N. Amer. impeach.
– OPPOSITES acquit.

indictment noun **charge**, accusation, arraignment; citation, summons; N. Amer. impeachment.

indifference noun **lack of concern**, disinterest, lack of interest, nonchalance; boredom, unresponsiveness, impassivity, detachment, coolness.

indifferent adjective **1** *an indifferent shrug:* **unconcerned**, uninterested, uncaring, casual, nonchalant, offhand, unenthusiastic; unimpressed, bored, unmoved, impassive, detached, cool. **2** *an indifferent performance:* **mediocre**, ordinary, average, middle-of-the-road, uninspired, undistinguished, unexceptional, unexciting, unremarkable, run-of-the-mill, pedestrian, prosaic, lacklustre, forgettable, amateurish; informal OK, so-so, fair-to-middling, no great shakes; Brit. informal not much cop; N. Amer. informal bush-league; NZ informal half-pie.
– OPPOSITES enthusiastic, brilliant.

indigenous adjective **native**, original, aboriginal.

indigestion noun **dyspepsia**, heartburn, pyrosis, acidity.

indignant adjective **aggrieved**, affronted, displeased, cross, angry, annoyed, offended, exasperated, piqued, in high dudgeon; informal peeved, irked, put out, miffed, riled, in a huff; Brit. informal narked; N. Amer. informal sore.

indignation noun **resentment**, umbrage, affront, displeasure, anger, annoyance, exasperation, offence, pique.

indignity noun **shame**, humiliation, loss of self-respect, embarrassment, mortification; disgrace, dishonour; abuse, offence, injustice, slight, snub, discourtesy, disrespect; informal slap in the face, kick in the teeth.

indirect adjective **1** *an indirect effect:* **incidental**, secondary, subordinate, ancillary, collateral, concomitant, contingent. **2** *an indirect route:* **roundabout**, circuitous, meandering, serpentine, winding, tortuous. **3** *an indirect attack:* **oblique**, implicit, implied.

indirectly adverb **1** *I heard of the damage indirectly:* **second-hand**; informal on the grapevine, on the bush/jungle telegraph. **2** *he referred to the subject indirectly:* **obliquely**, by implication, tangentially.

indiscernible adjective **1** *an almost indiscernible change:* **unnoticeable**, imperceptible, undetectable, indistinguishable; tiny, minute, minuscule, microscopic, infinitesimal, negligible. **2** *an indiscernible shape:* **indistinct**, nebulous, unclear, fuzzy, vague, indefinite, amorphous, shadowy, dim.
– OPPOSITES distinct.

indiscreet adjective **imprudent**, unwise, impolitic, injudicious, incautious, irresponsible, ill-judged, careless, rash; undiplomatic, indelicate, tactless.

indiscretion noun **1** *he was prone to indiscretion:* **imprudence**, injudiciousness, irresponsibility; tactlessness, insensitivity. **2** *his past indiscretions:* **blunder**, lapse, gaffe, mistake, faux pas, error, slip, impropriety; misdemeanour, transgression, peccadillo, misdeed.

indiscriminate adjective **non-selective**, undiscriminating, uncritical, aimless, hit-or-miss, haphazard, random, arbitrary, unsystematic; wholesale, general, sweeping, blanket; casual, careless.
– OPPOSITES selective.

indispensable adjective **essential**, necessary, all-important, of the utmost importance, vital, crucial, key; invaluable.
– OPPOSITES superfluous.

indisposed adjective **ill**, unwell, sick, poorly, ailing; out of action.
– OPPOSITES well.

indisposition noun **illness**, malady, ailment, disorder, sickness; condition, complaint, problem.

indisputable adjective **incontrovertible**, incontestable, undeniable, irrefutable, beyond dispute, unquestionable, beyond question, indubitable, beyond doubt, unarguable; demonstrable, self-evident, clear, clear-cut.
– OPPOSITES questionable.

i

indistinct adjective **1** *the shoreline was indistinct:* **blurred**, fuzzy, hazy, misty, foggy, cloudy, shadowy, dim; unclear, obscure, faint. **2** *indistinct sounds:* **muffled**, muted, low, quiet, soft, faint; muttered, mumbled, whispered.
–OPPOSITES distinct, clear.

indistinguishable adjective **1** *the two girls were indistinguishable:* **identical**, impossible to tell apart, like two peas in a pod; informal dead ringers. **2** *his words were indistinguishable:* **unintelligible**, incomprehensible; unclear.
–OPPOSITES unalike, clear.

individual adjective **1** *exhibitions devoted to individual artists:* **single**, separate, discrete, independent; sole, lone. **2** *he had his own individual style of music:* **unique**, characteristic, distinctive, distinct, particular, idiosyncratic, peculiar, personal, special. **3** *a highly individual apartment:* **original**, unique, exclusive, singular, different, unusual, novel, unorthodox, out of the ordinary.
• noun **1** *he was a rather stuffy individual:* **person**, human being, soul, creature; man, woman, boy, girl; character; informal type, sort, beggar, cookie, customer, guy, geezer, devil; Brit. informal bod, gent. **2** *she was a real individual:* **individualist**, free spirit, nonconformist, original, eccentric, character, maverick; Brit. informal one-off.

individualism noun **independence**, freedom of thought, originality; unconventionality, eccentricity.

individualist noun **free spirit**, individual, nonconformist, original, eccentric, maverick; Brit. informal one-off.
–OPPOSITES conformist.

individualistic adjective **unconventional**, unorthodox, atypical, singular, unique, original, nonconformist, independent, free-thinking; eccentric, maverick, idiosyncratic.

individuality noun **distinctiveness**, uniqueness, originality, singularity, particularity, peculiarity; personality, character, identity, self.

individually adverb **one at a time**, one by one, singly, separately, independently.
–OPPOSITES together.

indoctrinate verb **brainwash**, propagandize, proselytize, inculcate, re-educate, condition, mould; instruct, teach, school, drill.

indolence noun **laziness**, idleness, slothfulness, shiftlessness, inactivity, lethargy, languor, torpor.

indolent adjective **lazy**, idle, slothful, work-shy, sluggardly, shiftless, lackadaisical, languid, inactive, lethargic; slack, good-for-nothing, feckless; informal bone idle.
–OPPOSITES industrious, energetic.

indomitable adjective **invincible**, unconquerable, unbeatable, unassailable, invulnerable, unshakeable; indefatigable, unyielding, unbending, steadfast, staunch, resolute, firm; unflinching, intrepid.
–OPPOSITES submissive.

indubitable adjective **unquestionable**, undoubtable, indisputable, unarguable, incontestable, undeniable, irrefutable, incontrovertible, unequivocal, absolute, conclusive; beyond doubt, beyond dispute, not in doubt.
–OPPOSITES doubtful.

induce verb **1** *the pickets induced many workers to stay away:* **persuade**, convince, prevail on, get, make, prompt, encourage, cajole into, talk into. **2** *these activities induce a feeling of togetherness:* **bring about**, cause, produce, effect, create, give rise to, generate, instigate, engender, set in motion, trigger off, arouse, foster, promote, encourage; literary beget.
–OPPOSITES dissuade, prevent.

inducement noun **incentive**, encouragement, attraction, stimulus, carrot, motivation; bribe; informal sweetener.
–OPPOSITES deterrent.

induct verb **admit to**, introduce to, initiate into, install in, instate in, swear into; appoint to.

indulge verb **1** *she was able to indulge her passion for literature:* **satisfy**, gratify, fulfil, feed; yield to, give in to. **2** *they indulged in dreams of stardom:* **wallow in**, give way to, abandon yourself to, luxuriate in, revel in. **3** *she did not like her chil-*

dren to be indulged: **pamper**, spoil, overindulge, coddle, mollycoddle, cosset; pander to, wait on hand and foot.
– OPPOSITES frustrate.
■ **indulge yourself** treat yourself, splash out; informal go to town, splurge.

indulgence noun **1** *the indulgence of all his desires:* **satisfaction**, gratification, fulfilment. **2** *indulgence contributed to his ill health:* **self-gratification**, self-indulgence, overindulgence, intemperance, excess, lack of restraint, extravagance, hedonism. **3** *they viewed holidays as an indulgence:* **extravagance**, luxury, treat, non-essential, extra, frill. **4** *his parents view his lapses with indulgence:* **tolerance**, forbearance, understanding, compassion, sympathy, leniency.

indulgent adjective **generous**, permissive, easy-going, liberal, tolerant, forgiving, forbearing, lenient, kind, kindly, soft-hearted.
– OPPOSITES strict.

industrialist noun **manufacturer**, factory owner; captain of industry, magnate, tycoon.

industrious adjective **hard-working**, diligent, assiduous, dedicated, conscientious, studious; busy, active, bustling, energetic, productive; with your shoulder to the wheel, with your nose to the grindstone.
– OPPOSITES indolent.

industry noun **1** *British industry:* **manufacturing**, production; construction. **2** *the publishing industry:* **business**, trade, field, line of business; informal racket. **3** *the kitchen was a hive of industry:* **activity**, energy, productiveness; hard work, industriousness, diligence, application, dedication.

inebriated adjective. See DRUNK.

inedible adjective **uneatable**, indigestible, unsavoury, unpalatable; stale, rotten, off, bad.

ineffable adjective **indescribable**, inexpressible, beyond words; undefinable, unutterable; overwhelming, breathtaking, awesome, staggering, amazing.

ineffective adjective **1** *an ineffective scheme:* **unsuccessful**, unproductive, unprofitable, inefficacious. **2** *an ineffective president:* **ineffectual**, inefficient, inadequate, incompetent, incapable, unfit, inept, weak, poor; informal useless, hopeless.

ineffectual adjective. See INEFFECTIVE.

inefficacious adjective. See INEFFECTIVE sense 1.

inefficient adjective **1** *an inefficient worker:* **ineffective**, ineffectual, incompetent, inept; disorganized, unprepared. **2** *inefficient processes:* **uneconomical**, wasteful, unproductive, time-wasting, slow; deficient, disorganized, unsystematic.

inelegant adjective **1** *an inelegant bellow of laughter:* **unrefined**, uncouth, unsophisticated, coarse, vulgar. **2** *inelegant dancing:* **graceless**, ungraceful, ungainly, uncoordinated, awkward, clumsy, lumbering.
– OPPOSITES refined, graceful.

inept adjective **incompetent**, unskilful, unskilled, inexpert, amateurish; clumsy, awkward, maladroit, bungling, blundering.
– OPPOSITES competent.

inequality noun **imbalance**, inequity, inconsistency, variation, variability; divergence, disparity, discrepancy, dissimilarity, difference; bias, prejudice, discrimination, unfairness.

inequitable adjective **unfair**, unjust, unequal, uneven, discriminatory, preferential, biased, partisan, prejudiced.
– OPPOSITES fair.

inequity noun **unfairness**, injustice, discrimination, partisanship, favouritism, bias, prejudice.

inert adjective **unmoving**, motionless, immobile, inanimate, still, stationary, static; dormant, sleeping; unconscious, comatose, lifeless, insensible.
– OPPOSITES active.

inertia noun **inactivity**, inaction, inertness; apathy, lethargy, listlessness; motionlessness, immobility, lifelessness; formal stasis.

inescapable adjective **unavoidable**, inevitable, ineluctable, inexorable; assured, sure, certain.
– OPPOSITES avoidable.

inessential adjective **unnecessary**, non-essential, unwanted, uncalled for, needless, redundant, superfluous, expendable; unimportant, peripheral, minor.

inestimable adjective **immeasurable**, incalculable, innumerable; limitless, boundless.

inevitable adjective **unavoidable**, inescapable, inexorable, ineluctable; assured, certain, sure.
– OPPOSITES uncertain.

inevitably adverb **naturally**, necessarily, automatically, as a matter of course, of necessity, inescapably, unavoidably, certainly, surely; informal like it or not; formal perforce.

i

inexact adjective **imprecise**, approximate, rough, crude, general, vague; N. Amer. informal ballpark.

inexcusable adjective **indefensible**, unjustifiable, unwarranted, unpardonable, unforgivable; unacceptable, unreasonable; uncalled for.

inexhaustible adjective **1** *her patience is inexhaustible:* **unlimited**, limitless, infinite, boundless, endless, never-ending, unfailing, everlasting. **2** *the dancers were inexhaustible:* **tireless**, indefatigable, untiring, unfaltering, unflagging.
– OPPOSITES limited, weary.

inexorable adjective **relentless**, unstoppable, inescapable, inevitable, unavoidable; persistent, continuous, non-stop, steady, unceasing, unremitting, unrelenting.

inexpensive adjective **cheap**, low-priced, low-cost, economical, competitive, affordable, reasonable, budget, economy, bargain, cut-price, reduced, discounted, discount.

inexperience noun **ignorance**, naivety, innocence, immaturity.

inexperienced adjective **inexpert**, unpractised, untrained, unschooled, unqualified, unskilled; ignorant, unseasoned; naive, unsophisticated, callow, immature; informal wet behind the ears, wide-eyed.

inexpert adjective **unskilled**, unskilful, amateurish, unprofessional, inexperienced; inept, incompetent, maladroit, clumsy, bungling, blundering; informal cack-handed, ham-fisted, butterfingered.

inexplicable adjective **unaccountable**, unexplainable, incomprehensible; baffling, puzzling, perplexing, mystifying, bewildering; mysterious.
– OPPOSITES understandable.

inexpressible adjective **indescribable**, undefinable, unutterable, unspeakable, beyond words; unimaginable, inconceivable, unthinkable.

inexpressive adjective **expressionless**, impassive, emotionless; inscrutable, blank, vacant, glazed, lifeless, deadpan, wooden, stony; poker-faced.

inextinguishable adjective **irrepressible**, unquenchable, indestructible, undying, unfailing, enduring, everlasting, eternal.

infallible adjective **1** *an infallible sense of timing:* **unerring**, unfailing, faultless, flawless, impeccable, perfect, precise, accurate, meticulous, scrupulous; Brit. informal spot on. **2** *infallible cures:* **unfailing**, guaranteed, dependable, trustworthy, reliable, sure, certain, safe, foolproof, effective; informal sure-fire; formal efficacious.

infamous adjective **notorious**, disreputable, of ill repute; legendary, fabled.
– OPPOSITES reputable.

infamy noun **notoriety**, disrepute, ill fame, ill repute.

infancy noun **1** *she died in infancy:* **babyhood**, early childhood. **2** *the infancy of broadcasting:* **beginnings**, early days, early stages; seeds, roots; start, emergence, dawn, birth, inception.
– OPPOSITES end.

infant noun **baby**, newborn, child, tiny tot; Medicine neonate; Scottish & N. English bairn, wean; literary babe.
• adjective *infant industries:* **developing**, emergent, emerging, embryonic, nascent, new, fledgling, budding, up-and-coming.

infantile adjective **childish**, babyish, immature, puerile, juvenile, adolescent; silly, inane, fatuous.

infatuated adjective **besotted**, in love, obsessed; captivated, enchanted, bewitched, under someone's spell; informal smitten, sweet on, stuck on, mad about, crazy about.

infatuation noun **passion**, adoration, desire, devotion; obsession, fixation; informal crush, thing, hang-up, pash.

infect verb **1** *nitrates were infecting the rivers:* **contaminate**, pollute, taint, foul, dirty, blight, damage, ruin; poison. **2** *his high spirits infected everyone:* **affect**, influence, touch; excite, inspire, stimulate, animate.

infection noun **1** *a kidney infection:* **disease**, virus; illness, ailment, sickness, infirmity; informal bug. **2** *the infection in his wounds:* **contamination**, poison; septicaemia, suppuration, inflammation; germs; Medicine sepsis.

infectious adjective **1** *infectious diseases:* **contagious**, communicable, transmittable, transmissible, transferable, spreadable; epidemic; informal catching. **2** *her laughter is infectious:* **irresistible**, compelling, contagious, catching.

infelicitous adjective **unfortunate**, unsuitable, inappropriate, inapposite, inapt; untimely, inopportune.
– OPPOSITES appropriate.

infer verb *we inferred from his words that the General was a traitor:* **deduce**, conclude, surmise, reason; gather, understand, presume, assume, take it; read between the lines; N. Amer. figure; Brit. informal suss out.

> Don't confuse **infer** with **imply**. If you **infer** something, you come to the conclusion that this is what is meant. If you **imply** something you are suggesting it but not stating it directly (e.g. *the article implied that he was guilty*).

inference noun **deduction**, conclusion, reasoning, presumption, assumption, supposition, reckoning, extrapolation; guesswork.

inferior adjective **1** *she regards him as inferior:* **second-class**, lower-ranking, subordinate, junior, minor, lowly, humble, menial, beneath one. **2** *inferior accommodation:* **second-rate**, substandard, low-quality, low-grade, unsatisfactory, shoddy, deficient; poor, bad, awful, dreadful, wretched; informal crummy, dire, rotten, lousy, third-rate.
– OPPOSITES superior, luxury.
• noun *how dare she treat him as an inferior?* **subordinate**, junior, underling, minion.

infernal adjective *the infernal regions:* **hellish**, lower, nether, subterranean, underworld.

infertile adjective **1** *infertile soil:* **barren**, unproductive; sterile, impoverished, arid. **2** *she was infertile:* **sterile**, barren; childless; Medicine infecund.

infest verb **overrun**, spread through, invade, infiltrate, pervade, permeate, inundate, overwhelm; beset, plague.

infested adjective **overrun**, swarming, teeming, crawling, alive, ridden; plagued, beset.

infidel noun (old use) **unbeliever**, non-believer; heathen, pagan, idolater, heretic.

infidelity noun **unfaithfulness**, adultery; disloyalty, treachery, double-dealing, duplicity, deceit; affair; informal playing around, fooling around, cheating, two-timing; formal fornication.

infiltrate verb *American agents infiltrated the organization:* **insinuate yourself into**, gain access to, penetrate; invade.

infiltrator noun **spy**, agent, plant, intruder, interloper, subversive, informer, mole, entryist, fifth columnist; N. Amer. informal spook.

infinite adjective **1** *the universe is infinite:* **boundless**, unbounded, unlimited, limitless, never-ending; immeasurable, fathomless. **2** *an infinite number of birds:* **countless**, uncountable, innumerable, numberless, immeasurable, incalculable, untold; great, huge, enormous. **3** *she bathed him with infinite care:* **great**, immense, extreme, supreme, absolute.
– OPPOSITES limited, small.

infinitesimal adjective **minute**, tiny, minuscule, very small; microscopic, imperceptible, indiscernible; Scottish wee; informal teeny, teeny-weeny, itsy-bitsy, tiddly; Brit. informal titchy; N. Amer. informal little-bitty.
– OPPOSITES huge.

i

infinity noun **1** *the infinity of space:* **endlessness**, infiniteness, boundlessness, limitlessness; vastness, immensity. **2** *an infinity of different molecules:* **infinite number**; abundance, profusion, host, multitude, mass, wealth; informal heap, load.

infirm adjective **frail**, weak, debilitated, disabled; ill, unwell, sick, sickly, poorly, ailing.
– OPPOSITES healthy.

infirmity noun **1** *they were excused due to infirmity:* **frailty**, weakness, delicacy, debility; disability, impairment; illness, sickness, poor health. **2** *the infirmities of old age:* **ailment**, malady, illness, disorder, sickness, affliction, complaint.

inflame verb **1** *he inflamed a sensitive situation:* **aggravate**, exacerbate, intensify, worsen, compound. **2** *his opinions inflamed his rival:* **enrage**, incense, anger, madden, infuriate, exasperate, provoke, antagonize, rile; informal make someone see red, make someone's blood boil.
– OPPOSITES calm, soothe, placate.

inflamed adjective **swollen**, puffed up; red, hot, burning, itchy; raw, sore, painful, tender; infected.

inflammable adjective **flammable**, combustible, incendiary, ignitable; volatile, unstable.
– OPPOSITES fireproof.

inflammation noun **swelling**, puffiness; redness, heat, burning; rawness, soreness, tenderness; infection.

inflammatory adjective **provocative**, incendiary, stirring, rousing, rabble-rousing, seditious, mutinous; like a red rag to a bull; fiery, passionate; controversial, contentious.

inflate verb **1** *to inflate the life jacket, pull the red tag:* **blow up**, pump up, fill up, puff up/out; dilate, distend, swell. **2** *the demand inflated prices:* **increase**, raise, boost, escalate, put up; informal hike up, jack up, bump up. **3** *the figures were inflated by the press:* **exaggerate**, overplay, overstate, enhance, embellish; increase, augment.
– OPPOSITES decrease, understate.

inflated adjective **1** *an inflated balloon:* **blown up**, filled, puffed up/out, pumped up; distended, expanded, engorged, swollen. **2** *inflated prices:* **high**, sky-high, excessive, unreasonable, prohibitive, outrageous, exorbitant, extortionate; Brit. over the odds; informal steep. **3** *an inflated opinion of himself:* **exaggerated**, immoderate, overblown, overstated. **4** *inflated language:* **high-flown**, extravagant, exaggerated, elaborate, overblown, overwrought, grandiose.

inflection noun **stress**, cadence, rhythm, accentuation, intonation, emphasis, modulation, lilt.

inflexible adjective **1** *his inflexible attitude:* **stubborn**, obstinate, intransigent, unbending, immovable, unyielding; pig-headed, uncompromising. **2** *inflexible rules:* **unalterable**, unchangeable, immutable; fixed, set, strict. **3** *an inflexible structure:* **rigid**, stiff, unyielding, unbending; hard, firm.
– OPPOSITES accommodating, pliable.

inflict verb **1** *severe penalties will be inflicted on drug suppliers:* **impose**, exact, wreak, deal out, mete out. **2** *I won't inflict my views on my children:* **impose**, force, thrust, foist.

influence noun **1** *the influence of parents on their children:* **effect**, impact; control, sway, hold, power. **2** *a good influence on younger players:* **example to**, role model for, inspiration to. **3** *his political influence:* **power**, authority, sway, leverage, weight, pull; informal clout, muscle, teeth; N. Amer. informal drag.
• verb **1** *they can influence public opinion:* **affect**, have an impact on, determine, guide, control, shape, govern, decide; change, alter. **2** *an attempt to influence the jury:* **sway**, bias, prejudice, suborn; pressurize, coerce; intimidate, browbeat; informal lean on; Brit. informal nobble.

influential adjective **powerful**, controlling; important.

influx noun **1** *an influx of tourists:* **inundation**, rush, stream, flood, incursion; invasion. **2** *an influx of river water:* **inflow**, inrush, flood, inundation.

inform verb **1** *she informed him that she was ill:* **tell**, notify, apprise, advise, impart to, communicate to, let someone know; brief, enlighten, send word to. **2** *he informed on two colleagues:* **denounce**, give away, betray, incriminate, report; sell out, stab in the back; informal rat, squeal, split, tell, blow the whistle, snitch, stitch up; Brit. informal grass, shop; Scottish informal clype; N. Amer. informal rat out, finger; Austral./NZ informal dob. **3** *the articles were informed by feminism:* **suffuse**, pervade, permeate, infuse, imbue.

informal adjective **1** *an informal discussion:* **unofficial**, casual, relaxed, easy-going; low key. **2** *informal language:* **colloquial**, vernacular, idiomatic, demotic, popular; familiar, everyday; simple, natural, unpretentious; informal slangy, chatty, folksy. **3** *informal clothes:* **casual**, relaxed, comfortable, everyday, sloppy, leisure; informal comfy.
– OPPOSITES formal, official, literary, smart.

informality noun **lack of ceremony**, casualness, unpretentiousness; homeliness; ease, naturalness, approachability.

information noun **details**, particulars, facts, figures, statistics, data; knowledge, intelligence; advice, guidance, direction, counsel, enlightenment; news; informal info, gen, the low-down, the dope, the inside story.

informative adjective **instructive**, illuminating, enlightening, revealing, explanatory; factual, educational, edifying, didactic; informal newsy.

informed adjective **knowledgeable**, enlightened, educated; briefed, up to date, up to speed, in the picture, in the know, au fait; informal clued-up, genned-up, plugged-in; Brit. informal switched-on, sussed.
– OPPOSITES ignorant.

informer noun **informant**, betrayer, traitor, Judas, collaborator, stool pigeon, fifth columnist, spy, double agent, infiltrator, plant; telltale; N. Amer. tattletale; informal rat, squealer, whistle-blower, snitch; Brit. informal grass, supergrass, nark, snout; Scottish informal clype; N. Amer. informal fink, stoolie.

infraction noun **infringement**, contravention, breach, violation, transgression.

infrequent adjective **rare**, uncommon, unusual, exceptional, few and far between, like gold dust, as scarce as hens' teeth; unaccustomed, unwonted; isolated, scarce, scattered; sporadic, intermittent; informal once in a blue moon.
– OPPOSITES common, frequent.

infringe verb **1** *the bid infringed EU rules:* **contravene**, violate, transgress, break, breach. **2** *surveillance could infringe personal liberties:* **undermine**, erode, diminish, weaken, impair, damage, compromise, encroach on.
– OPPOSITES obey, preserve.

infuriate verb **enrage**, incense, anger, madden, inflame; exasperate; informal make someone see red, get someone's back up, make someone's blood boil, get up someone's nose; Brit. informal wind up, get to.
– OPPOSITES please.

infuriating adjective **exasperating**, maddening.

infuse verb **1** *she was infused with a sense of hope:* **fill**, suffuse, imbue, inspire, charge, pervade, permeate. **2** *he infused new life into the group:* **instil**, breathe, inject, impart, introduce. **3** *infuse the dried leaves:* **steep**, brew, stew, soak, immerse, souse; Brit. informal mash.

ingenious adjective **inventive**, creative, imaginative, original, innovative, pioneering, resourceful, enterprising, inspired; clever.
– OPPOSITES unimaginative.

ingenuous adjective **naive**, innocent, simple, childlike, trusting, trustful; wide-eyed, inexperienced; open, artless, guileless.
– OPPOSITES artful.

inglorious adjective **shameful**, dishonourable, ignominious, discreditable, disgraceful, scandalous; ignoble, undignified, wretched.

ingrained adjective **1** *ingrained attitudes:* **entrenched**, established, deep-rooted, deep-seated, fixed, firm, unshakeable, abiding, enduring, stubborn. **2** *ingrained dirt:* **ground-in**, fixed, deep; permanent, indelible.
– OPPOSITES transient, superficial.

ingratiate verb
■ **ingratiate yourself** curry favour, cultivate, win over, get in someone's good books; toady to, crawl to, grovel to, kowtow to, play up to, flatter, court; informal suck up to.

ingratiating adjective **sycophantic**, toadying, fawning, unctuous, obsequious; flattering; informal smarmy, slimy, creepy.

ingratitude noun **ungratefulness**, thanklessness, unthankfulness.

ingredient noun **constituent**, component, element; part, piece, bit, strand, portion, unit, feature, aspect, attribute.

inhabit verb **live in**, occupy; settle in, people, populate, colonize; dwell in, reside in.

i

inhabitant noun **resident**, occupant, occupier, dweller, settler; local, native; (**inhabitants**) population, populace, people, public, community, citizenry, townsfolk, townspeople; formal denizen.

inhale verb **breathe in**, draw in, suck in, sniff in, drink in.

inherent adjective **intrinsic**, innate, immanent, built-in, inborn, ingrained, deep-rooted; essential, fundamental, basic, structural, organic; natural, instinctive, instinctual.
– OPPOSITES acquired.

inherit verb **1** *she inherited the farm:* **come into/by**, be bequeathed, be left, be willed. **2** *Richard inherited the title:* **succeed to**, assume, take over, come into; formal accede to.

inheritance noun **1** *a comfortable inheritance:* **legacy**, bequest, endowment; birthright, heritage, patrimony. **2** *his inheritance of the title:* **succession to**, accession to, assumption of, elevation to.

> **WORD LINKS**
> **hereditary** relating to inheritance

inhibit verb **impede**, hinder, hamper, hold back, discourage, interfere with, obstruct, slow down, retard.
– OPPOSITES assist, encourage.

inhibited adjective **shy**, reticent, reserved, self-conscious, diffident, bashful, coy; hesitant, insecure, unconfident, unassertive, timid; withdrawn, repressed, undemonstrative; informal uptight.

inhibition noun **shyness**, reticence, self-consciousness, reserve, diffidence; wariness, hesitance, hesitancy, insecurity; unassertiveness, timidity; repression, reservation; informal problem, phobia, hang-up.

inhospitable adjective **1** *the inhospitable climate:* **hostile**, bleak, forbidding, cheerless, harsh, desolate, stark. **2** *forgive me if I seem inhospitable:* **unwelcoming**, unfriendly, unsociable, unsocial, unneighbourly, uncongenial; cold, frosty, aloof, distant, remote, offhand; uncivil, discourteous, ungracious.
– OPPOSITES welcoming.

inhuman adjective **1** *inhuman treatment:* **cruel**, harsh, inhumane, brutal, callous, sadistic, savage, vicious, barbaric, barbarous. **2** *hellish and inhuman shapes:* **monstrous**, devilish, ghostly, demonic, animal, bestial; unearthly.
– OPPOSITES humane.

inhumane adjective *it's inhumane to separate a mother from her children:* **cruel**, inhuman, callous, harsh, brutal, barbaric, barbarous; abhorrent, shameful, despicable, deplorable.
– OPPOSITES humane, compassionate.

inimical adjective **harmful**, injurious, detrimental, deleterious, prejudicial, damaging; antagonistic, hostile, contrary.
– OPPOSITES advantageous.

inimitable adjective **unique**, exclusive, distinctive, individual, special, idiosyncratic; incomparable, in a class of its own.

iniquity noun **1** *the iniquity of his conduct:* **wickedness**, sinfulness, immorality. **2** *I will forgive their iniquities:* **sin**, crime, transgression, wrongdoing, wrong, offence.
– OPPOSITES goodness, virtue.

initial adjective **beginning**, opening, commencing, starting, embryonic; first, early, primary, preliminary, preparatory; introductory, inaugural.
– OPPOSITES final.

initially adverb **at first**, at the start, at the outset, in/at the beginning, to begin with, to start with, originally.

initiate verb **1** *the government*

initiated the scheme: **begin**, start, commence; institute, inaugurate, launch, instigate, establish, set up. **2** *he was initiated into a religious cult:* **introduce**, admit, induct, install, incorporate, swear in; ordain, invest.
– OPPOSITES finish, expel.

initiative noun **1** *employers are looking for initiative:* **enterprise**, resourcefulness, inventiveness, imagination, ingenuity, originality, creativity. **2** *he has lost the initiative:* **advantage**, upper hand, edge, lead. **3** *a recent initiative on recycling:* **plan**, scheme, strategy, measure, proposal, step, action, approach.

inject verb **1** *he injected the codeine:* **administer**; take; informal shoot up, mainline, fix. **2** *a pump injects air into the valve:* **insert**, introduce, feed, push, force, shoot. **3** *he injected new life into the team:* **introduce**, instil, infuse, imbue, breathe.

injection noun **inoculation**, vaccination, immunization, booster; dose; informal jab, shot.

injudicious adjective **imprudent**, unwise, inadvisable, ill-advised, misguided; ill-considered, ill-judged, foolish.
– OPPOSITES prudent.

injunction noun **order**, ruling, direction, directive, command, instruction; decree, edict, dictum, dictate, fiat, mandate.

injure verb **1** *he injured his leg:* **hurt**, wound, damage, harm; break; Brit. informal knacker. **2** *a libel injured her reputation:* **damage**, mar, spoil, ruin, blight, blemish, tarnish, blacken.

injured adjective **1** *his injured arm:* **hurt**, wounded, damaged, sore, bruised; broken, fractured; Brit. informal gammy. **2** *an injured tone:* **upset**, hurt, wounded, offended, reproachful, pained, aggrieved.
– OPPOSITES healthy.

injurious adjective **harmful**, damaging, deleterious, detrimental, hurtful; disadvantageous, unfavourable, undesirable, adverse, inimical.

injury noun **1** *she sustained minor injuries:* **wound**, bruise, cut, gash, scratch, graze, abrasion, contusion, lesion; Medicine trauma. **2** *they escaped without injury:* **harm**, hurt, damage, pain, suffering.

injustice noun **1** *the injustice of the world:* **unfairness**, unjustness, inequity; cruelty, tyranny, repression, exploitation, corruption; bias, prejudice, discrimination, intolerance. **2** *his sacking was an injustice:* **wrong**, offence, crime, sin, outrage, atrocity, scandal, disgrace, affront.

inkling noun **idea**, notion, sense, impression, suggestion, indication; clue, intimation.

inlaid adjective **inset**, set, studded, lined, panelled; ornamented, decorated.

inland adjective **interior**, inshore, central, internal, upcountry.
– OPPOSITES coastal.
• adverb **upcountry**, inshore, ashore.

inlet noun **1 cove**, bay, bight, creek, estuary, fjord, sound; Scottish firth. **2** *an air inlet:* **vent**, flue, shaft, duct, channel, pipe.

inmate noun **1** *the inmates of the hospital:* **patient**, inpatient; resident, occupant. **2** *the prison's inmates:* **prisoner**, convict, captive, detainee, internee, occupant.

inmost adjective. See INNERMOST.

inn noun **tavern**, bar, hostelry; Brit. pub, public house; Canadian beer parlour; informal watering hole; dated alehouse.

innards plural noun (informal) **entrails**, internal organs, viscera, intestines, bowels, guts; informal insides.

innate adjective **inborn**, inbred, inherent, natural, intrinsic, instinctive, intuitive; hereditary, inherited, in the blood, in the family; inbuilt, deep-rooted, deep-seated.
– OPPOSITES acquired.

inner adjective **1** *inner London:* **central**, downtown, innermost. **2** *the inner gates:* **internal**, interior, inside, innermost. **3** *the Queen's inner circle:* **private**, restricted, exclusive, intimate. **4** *the inner meaning:* **hidden**, secret, deep, underlying; veiled, esoteric. **5** *one's inner life:* **mental**, intellectual, psychological, spiritual, emotional.
– OPPOSITES external, apparent.

innermost adjective **1** *the innermost shrine:* **central**, internal, interior. **2** *her innermost feelings:* **deepest**, deep-seated, underlying, intimate, private, personal, secret, hidden, concealed; true, real, honest.

innocence noun **1** *he protested his innocence:* **guiltlessness**, blamelessness. **2** *she took advantage of his innocence:* **naivety**, credulity, inexperience, gullibility, guilelessness, ingenuousness.

innocent adjective **1** *he was entirely innocent:* **guiltless**, blameless, faultless; honest, upright, law-abiding. **2** *innocent fun:* **harmless**, innocuous, safe, inoffensive. **3** *innocent foreign students:* **naive**, ingenuous, trusting, credulous; impressionable, easily led; inexperienced, unsophisticated; artless, guileless.
–OPPOSITES guilty, sinful, worldly.

i

innocuous adjective **1** *an innocuous fungus:* **harmless**, safe, non-toxic; edible. **2** *an innocuous comment:* **inoffensive**, unobjectionable, unexceptionable, harmless; anodyne.
–OPPOSITES harmful, offensive.

innovation noun **change**, alteration, upheaval; reorganization, restructuring; novelty.

innovative adjective **original**, new, novel, fresh, unusual, experimental, inventive, ingenious; pioneering, groundbreaking, revolutionary, radical.

innovator noun **pioneer**, trailblazer, pathfinder, groundbreaker; modernizer, progressive; experimenter, inventor.

innuendo noun **insinuation**, suggestion, intimation, implication; aspersion, slur.

innumerable adjective **countless**, numerous, untold, legion, numberless, limitless; informal umpteen, no end of, loads of, masses of, oodles of, zillions of; N. Amer. informal gazillions of; literary myriad.
–OPPOSITES few.

inoculate verb **immunize**, vaccinate, inject; protect against.

inoculation noun **immunization**, vaccination, vaccine; injection, booster; informal jab, shot.

inoffensive adjective **harmless**, innocuous, unobjectionable, unexceptionable; mild, peaceful, peaceable, gentle; tame, innocent.

inoperable adjective **1** *the airfield was left inoperable:* **unusable**, out of action, out of service. **2** *the agreement is now inoperable:* **impractical**, unworkable, unfeasible, non-viable, impracticable.

inoperative adjective **1** *the fan is inoperative:* **out of order**, out of service, broken, out of commission, unserviceable, faulty, defective; down; informal bust, kaput, on the blink, shot; Brit. informal knackered. **2** *the contract is inoperative:* **void**, null and void, invalid, ineffective, non-viable; cancelled, revoked, terminated.
–OPPOSITES working, valid.

inopportune adjective **inconvenient**, unsuitable, inappropriate, unfavourable, unfortunate; untimely, ill-timed.
–OPPOSITES convenient.

inordinate adjective **excessive**, undue; massive, huge; disproportionate, extreme; immoderate, extravagant.
–OPPOSITES moderate.

inorganic adjective **inanimate**, inert; mineral.

input noun **contribution**, feedback, comments, response, participation, say, effort.
• verb **enter**, put in, load, insert; key in, type in.

inquest noun **inquiry**, investigation, probe, examination, review; hearing.

inquire verb **1** *the commission is to inquire into alleged illegal payments:* **investigate**, probe, look into; research, examine, explore; informal check out. **2** *I inquired about part-time courses:* **ask**, make inquiries.

inquiring adjective *an inquiring mind:* **inquisitive**, curious, interested, questioning, probing, searching.

inquiry noun **1** *a formal inquiry into the cause of the accident:* **investigation**, probe, examination, exploration; inquest, hearing. **2** *telephone inquiries:* **question**, query.

inquisition noun **interrogation**, cross-examination; investigation, inquiry, inquest; informal grilling.

inquisitive adjective **curious**, interested; prying; informal nosy.
–OPPOSITES indifferent.

insane adjective **1** *she was declared insane:* **of unsound mind**, certifiable; psychotic, schizophrenic; mad, deranged, demented, out of your mind, non compos mentis, sick in the head, unhinged, crazed; informal crazy, bonkers, cracked, batty, loony, loopy, nuts, screwy, bananas, wacko, off your rocker, off your head, round the bend; Brit. informal crackers, barmy, barking, off your trolley, round the twist; N. Amer. informal nutso, out of your tree; Austral./NZ informal bushed. **2** *an insane suggestion:* **stupid**, idiotic, nonsensical, absurd, ridiculous, ludicrous, preposterous; informal crazy, mad; Brit. informal daft, barmy.
– OPPOSITES sensible, sane.

insanitary adjective **unhygienic**, unsanitary, unhealthy, dirty, filthy, contaminated; infected, germ-ridden.
– OPPOSITES hygienic.

insanity noun **1** *insanity runs in her family:* **mental illness**; dementia; mania, psychosis. **2** *it would be insanity to take this loan:* **folly**, madness, idiocy, stupidity, lunacy.

insatiable adjective **unquenchable**, uncontrollable; voracious, ravenous, wolfish; avid, eager, keen.

inscribe verb **carve**, write, engrave, incise, cut; imprint, stamp.

inscription noun **1** *the inscription on the sarcophagus:* **lettering**; wording, writing, legend; epitaph. **2** *the book had an inscription:* **dedication**, message; signature, autograph.

inscrutable adjective **enigmatic**, unreadable, mysterious; inexpressive, expressionless, impassive, blank, deadpan, poker-faced, dispassionate.
– OPPOSITES expressive.

insect noun bug; informal creepy-crawly; Brit. informal minibeast.

WORD LINKS
entomology the study of insects

insecure adjective **1** *an insecure young man:* **unconfident**, uncertain, unsure, doubtful, hesitant, self-conscious, inhibited; anxious, fearful. **2** *insecure windows:* **unprotected**, unguarded, vulnerable, unsecured. **3** *an insecure footbridge:* **unstable**, rickety, wobbly, shaky, unsteady, precarious.
– OPPOSITES confident, stable.

insecurity noun **1** *he hid his insecurity:* **lack of confidence**, self-doubt, diffidence, timidity, uncertainty, nervousness, inhibition; anxiety, worry, unease. **2** *the insecurity of our situation:* **vulnerability**; instability, fragility, frailty, shakiness.

insensible adjective **unconscious**, inert, comatose, passed out, blacked out; informal out cold, out for the count; Brit. informal spark out.
– OPPOSITES conscious.

insensitive adjective **1** *an insensitive bully:* **heartless**, unfeeling, inconsiderate, thoughtless, thick-skinned; hard-hearted, uncaring, unsympathetic, unkind. **2** *he was insensitive to her feelings:* **impervious to**, oblivious to, unaware of, unresponsive to, indifferent to.
– OPPOSITES compassionate.

insentient adjective **inanimate**, lifeless, inorganic, inert; unconscious, unaware, unfeeling.

insert verb **1** *he inserted a tape in the machine:* **put**, place, push, thrust, slide, slip, load, fit, slot, install; informal pop, stick, bung. **2** *she inserted an extra clause:* **enter**, introduce, incorporate, interpose, interject; add.
– OPPOSITES extract, remove.
• noun *the newspaper carried an insert:* **enclosure**, supplement; circular, advertisement, pamphlet, leaflet; informal ad, flyer.

inside noun **1** *the inside of the volcano:* **interior**; centre, core, middle, heart, bowels. **2** (informal) *my insides are out of order:* **stomach**, gut, bowels, intestines; informal belly, tummy, guts.
– OPPOSITES exterior.
• adjective **1** *his inside pocket:* **inner**, interior, internal, innermost. **2** *inside information:* **confidential**, classified, restricted, privileged, private, secret, exclusive; informal hush-hush.
– OPPOSITES outer, public.
• adverb **1** *she ushered me inside:* **indoors**, within, in. **2** *how do you feel inside?* **inwardly**, within, privately, deep down, at heart, emotionally, mentally, psychologically, spiritually. **3** (informal) *he's back*

i

inside: **in prison**, in jail, in custody; locked up, imprisoned, incarcerated; informal behind bars, doing time; Brit. informal banged up.
–OPPOSITES outside.

insider noun **member**, worker, employee, representative; person in the know; mole.

insidious adjective **stealthy**, subtle, cunning, crafty, artful, sly, wily, underhand, indirect; informal sneaky.

insight noun **1** *your insight has been invaluable:* **intuition**, perception, understanding, comprehension, appreciation, penetration, acumen, perspicacity, judgement, acuity; vision, imagination; informal nous, savvy. **2** *an insight into the government:* **understanding of**, appreciation of; introduction to; informal eye-opener.

i

insignia noun **badge**, crest, emblem, symbol, sign, mark, seal, coat of arms, logo.

insignificant adjective **unimportant**, trivial, trifling, negligible, inconsequential, of no account, paltry, petty, insubstantial, worthless, irrelevant, immaterial, peripheral; informal piddling.

insincere adjective **false**, fake, hollow, artificial, feigned, pretended, put-on; disingenuous, hypocritical, cynical, deceitful, duplicitous, double-dealing, two-faced, untruthful; informal phoney, pretend, pseud.

insinuate verb **imply**, suggest, hint, intimate; informal make out.
■ **insinuate yourself into** worm your way into, ingratiate yourself with, curry favour with; infiltrate, impinge on; informal muscle in on.

insinuation noun **implication**, inference, suggestion, hint, intimation, innuendo; undertone; aspersion.

insipid adjective **1** *insipid coffee:* **tasteless**, flavourless, bland, weak, wishy-washy; unappetizing. **2** *insipid pictures:* **unimaginative**, uninspired, uninspiring, characterless, flat, uninteresting, bland, run-of-the-mill, pedestrian, tired, lame, tame, anaemic.
–OPPOSITES tasty, interesting.

insist verb **1** *be prepared to insist:* **stand firm**, stand your ground, be resolute, be determined, hold out, be emphatic, not take no for an answer; persevere, persist; informal stick to your guns. **2** *she insisted that they pay up:* **demand**, command; urge, exhort. **3** *he insisted that he knew nothing:* **maintain**, assert, protest, swear, declare, repeat, reiterate; formal aver.

insistence noun **1** *she sat down at Anne's insistence:* **demand**, bidding, command, dictate, instruction, requirement, request, entreaty, exhortation; informal say-so; literary behest. **2** *his insistence that he loved her:* **assertion**, contention, assurance, affirmation, avowal.

insistent adjective **1** *Tony's insistent questioning:* **persistent**, determined, tenacious, unyielding, dogged, unrelenting, inexorable. **2** *an insistent buzzing:* **incessant**, constant, unremitting.

insolent adjective **impertinent**, impudent, cheeky, ill-mannered, bad mannered, rude, impolite, discourteous, disrespectful, insubordinate; cocky; informal fresh, lippy, saucy; N. Amer. informal sassy.
–OPPOSITES polite.

insoluble adjective *some problems are insoluble:* **unsolvable**, unanswerable, unresolvable; unworkable.

insolvency noun **bankruptcy**, liquidation, failure, collapse, financial ruin; pennilessness, penury; Brit. administration, receivership.

insolvent adjective **bankrupt**, ruined, liquidated; penniless; Brit. in receivership; informal bust, broke, belly up, gone to the wall, on the rocks, in the red, hard up, strapped for cash.

insomnia noun **sleeplessness**, wakefulness, restlessness.

insouciance noun **nonchalance**, unconcern, indifference; informal cool.
–OPPOSITES anxiety.

insouciant adjective **nonchalant**, untroubled, unworried, unruffled, unconcerned, indifferent, blasé, carefree, free and easy; informal laid-back.

inspect verb **examine**, check, scrutinize, investigate, vet, test, monitor, survey, study, look over, probe; informal check out, give something a/the once-over.

inspection noun **examination**, check-up, survey, scrutiny, probe, exploration, investigation; informal once-over, going-over, look-see.

inspector noun **examiner**, scrutineer, investigator, surveyor, assessor, reviewer, analyst; observer, overseer, supervisor, monitor, watchdog, ombudsman; auditor.

inspiration noun **1** *she's an inspiration to others:* **stimulus**, motivation, encouragement, influence, spur; example, model; exemplar. **2** *his work lacks inspiration:* **creativity**, inventiveness, innovation, ingenuity, imagination, originality; insight, vision. **3** *she had a sudden inspiration:* **bright idea**, revelation; informal brainwave; N. Amer. informal brainstorm.

inspire verb **1** *the landscape inspired him to write:* **stimulate**, motivate, encourage, influence, rouse, move, stir, energize, galvanize, incite. **2** *the film inspired a musical:* **give rise to**, lead to, bring about, cause, prompt, spawn, engender; literary beget. **3** *Charles inspired awe in her:* **arouse**, awaken, prompt, induce, ignite, trigger, kindle, produce, bring out.

inspired adjective **outstanding**, wonderful, marvellous, excellent, magnificent, exceptional, first-class, first-rate, virtuoso, superlative; informal tremendous, superb, ace, wicked, awesome, out of this world; Brit. informal brilliant.
–OPPOSITES poor.

inspiring adjective **inspirational**, encouraging, heartening, uplifting, stirring, rousing, electrifying; moving.

instability noun **1** *the instability of political life:* **unreliability**, uncertainty, unpredictability, insecurity, volatility, capriciousness; changeability, mutability. **2** *emotional instability:* **volatility**, unpredictability, variability, inconsistency; frailty, weakness. **3** *the instability of the foundations:* **unsteadiness**, unsoundness, shakiness, weakness, fragility.
–OPPOSITES steadiness.

install verb **1** *a photocopier was installed in the office:* **put**, place, station, site; connect, fit. **2** *they installed a new president:* **swear in**, induct, instate, inaugurate, invest; appoint; ordain, consecrate, anoint; enthrone, crown. **3** *she installed herself behind the table:* **ensconce**, position, settle, seat, plant; sit down; informal plonk, park.
–OPPOSITES remove.

installation noun **1** *the installation of radiators:* **installing**, fitting, putting in. **2** *the installation of the chancellor:* **swearing in**, induction, inauguration, investiture; ordination, consecration; enthronement, coronation. **3** *a new computer installation:* **unit**, system, set-up. **4** *an army installation:* **base**, camp, post, depot, centre, facility.

instalment noun **part**, episode, chapter, issue, programme, section, volume.

instance noun **example**, occasion, occurrence, case; illustration.
■ **in the first instance** initially, at first, at the start, at the outset, in/at the beginning, to begin with, to start with, originally.

instant adjective **immediate**, instantaneous, on-the-spot, prompt, swift, speedy, rapid, quick; informal snappy.
• noun **moment**, minute, second, split second, twinkling of an eye, flash, trice; informal jiffy, the blink of an eye.

instantaneous adjective **immediate**, instant, on-the-spot, prompt, swift, speedy, quick.
–OPPOSITES delayed.

instantly adverb **immediately**, at once, straight away, right away, instantaneously; forthwith, there and then, here and now, this/that minute, this/that instant.

instead adverb
■ **instead of** as an alternative to, as a substitute for, as a replacement for, in place of, in lieu of, in preference to; rather than.

instigate verb **set in motion**, get under way, get off the ground, start, commence, begin, initiate, launch, institute, set up, inaugurate, establish, organize; informal kick off.
–OPPOSITES halt.

instigation noun **prompting**, suggestion; request, entreaty, demand, insistence.

instigator noun **initiator**, prime mover, architect, designer, planner, inventor, mastermind, originator, author, creator, agent; founder, founding father; ringleader.

instil verb **inculcate**, implant, ingrain, impress; engender, produce, induce, foster; drum into.

instinct noun **1** *some instinct told me to be careful:* **inclination**, urge, drive, compulsion; intuition, feeling, sixth sense; nose. **2** *a good instinct for acting:* **talent**, gift, ability, aptitude, skill, flair, feel, knack.

instinctive adjective **intuitive**, natural, instinctual, innate, inborn, inherent; unconscious, subconscious; automatic, reflex, knee-jerk; informal gut.
– OPPOSITES learned.

institute noun **organization**, establishment, institution, foundation, centre; academy, school, college, university; society, association, federation, body, guild.
• verb **initiate**, set in motion, get under way, get off the ground, start, commence, begin, launch; set up, inaugurate, found, establish, organize.
– OPPOSITES end.

institution noun **1** *an academic institution:* **establishment**, organization, institute, foundation, centre; academy, school, college, university; society, association, body, guild. **2** *they spent their lives in institutions:* **home**, hospital; asylum; prison. **3** *traditional values and institutions:* **practice**, custom, convention, tradition. **4** *the institution of legal proceedings:* **initiation**, instigation, launch, start, commencement.

institutional adjective **organized**, established, bureaucratic, conventional, procedural, set, formal, formalized, systematic, systematized, structured, regulated.

instruct verb **1** *the union instructed them to strike:* **order**, direct, command, tell, enjoin, call on, mandate, charge. **2** *nobody instructed him in how to operate it:* **teach**, school, coach, train, educate, tutor, guide, show. **3** *the bank was instructed that money would be withdrawn:* **inform**, tell, notify, apprise, advise.

instruction noun **1** *do not disobey my instructions:* **order**, command, directive, direction, decree, edict, injunction, mandate, dictate, commandment. **2** *read the instructions:* **directions**, key, specification; handbook, manual, guide; informal spec. **3** *he gave instruction in self defence:* **tuition**, teaching, coaching, schooling, tutelage; lessons, classes, lectures; training, drill, guidance.

instructive adjective **informative**, instructional, illuminating, enlightening, explanatory; educational, educative, edifying; useful, helpful.

instructor noun **trainer**, coach, teacher, tutor; adviser, counsellor, guide.

instrument noun **1** *a wound made with a sharp instrument:* **implement**, tool, utensil; device, apparatus, contrivance, gadget. **2** *check all the cockpit instruments:* **gauge**, meter; indicator, dial, display. **3** *an instrument of learning:* **agent**, agency, cause, channel, medium, means, vehicle. **4** *a mere instrument acting under coercion:* **pawn**, puppet, creature, dupe, cog; tool; informal stooge.

instrumental adjective
■ **be instrumental in** play a part in, contribute to, be a factor in, have a hand in; add to, promote, advance, further.

insubordinate adjective **disobedient**, unruly, wayward, errant, badly behaved, disorderly, undisciplined, delinquent, troublesome, rebellious, defiant; Brit. informal bolshie.
– OPPOSITES obedient.

insubordination noun **disobedience**, unruliness, indiscipline, bad behaviour, misbehaviour, misconduct; rebellion, defiance, mutiny, revolt.

insubstantial adjective **1** *an insubstantial structure:* **flimsy**, slight, fragile, breakable, weak, frail, unstable, shaky, wobbly, rickety, ramshackle, jerry-built. **2** *insubstantial evidence:* **weak**, flimsy, feeble, poor, inadequate, insufficient, tenuous, inconse-

quential, unconvincing, implausible, unsatisfactory.
– OPPOSITES sturdy, sound, tangible.

insufferable adjective **1** *the heat was insufferable:* **intolerable**, unbearable, unendurable, oppressive, overwhelming, overpowering; more than flesh and blood can stand; informal too much. **2** *his win made him insufferable:* **conceited**, arrogant, boastful, cocky, cocksure, full of yourself, swollen-headed, self-important; vain, self-satisfied, self-congratulatory, smug; informal big-headed, too big for your boots.
– OPPOSITES bearable, modest.

insufficient adjective **inadequate**, deficient, poor, scant, scanty; not enough, too little, too few, too small; limited.

insular adjective **1** *insular people:* **narrow-minded**, blinkered, inward-looking, parochial. **2** *an insular existence:* **isolated**, cut off, segregated, detached, solitary, lonely.
– OPPOSITES broad-minded, cosmopolitan.

insulate verb **1** *pipes must be insulated:* **wrap**, sheathe, cover, encase, enclose; lag, heatproof, soundproof. **2** *they were insulated from the impact of the war:* **protect**, save, shield, shelter, screen, cushion, cocoon.

insulation noun **1** *a layer of insulation:* **lagging**; protection, padding. **2** *insulation from the rigours of city life:* **protection**, defence, shelter; separation.

insult verb **abuse**, revile, call someone names, slight, disparage, discredit, libel, slander, malign, defame, denigrate, cast aspersions on; offend, hurt, humiliate; Brit. barrack; informal bad-mouth; Brit. informal slag off.
– OPPOSITES compliment.
• noun **jibe**, affront, slight, slur, indignity; abuse, aspersions; informal dig, put-down.

insulting adjective **abusive**, rude, offensive, disparaging, belittling, derogatory, deprecating, disrespectful, uncomplimentary, pejorative; defamatory, slanderous, libellous, scurrilous, blasphemous; informal bitchy, catty.

insuperable adjective **insurmountable**, invincible, unassailable; overwhelming.

insurance noun **indemnity**, assurance, financial protection, security, cover.

insure verb **cover**, indemnify, protect, underwrite; Brit. assure.

insurgent adjective **rebellious**, rebel, mutinous, insurrectionist; renegade, seditious, subversive.
– OPPOSITES loyal.
• noun **rebel**, revolutionary, mutineer, insurrectionist, agitator, subversive, renegade; guerrilla, terrorist.
– OPPOSITES loyalist.

insurmountable adjective **insuperable**, unconquerable, invincible, unassailable; overwhelming, hopeless, impossible.

insurrection noun **rebellion**, revolt, uprising, mutiny, revolution, insurgence, sedition; civil disorder, unrest, anarchy.

intact adjective **whole**, entire, complete, unbroken, undamaged, unscathed, untouched, unspoiled, unblemished, unmarked; undefiled, unsullied; in one piece.
– OPPOSITES damaged.

intangible adjective **indefinable**, indescribable, inexpressible, nameless; vague, obscure, unclear, indefinite, subtle, elusive.

integral adjective **1** *an integral part of human behaviour:* **essential**, fundamental, basic, intrinsic, inherent; vital, necessary. **2** *the dryer has an integral heat sensor:* **built-in**, inbuilt, integrated, inboard, fitted. **3** *an integral approach to learning:* **unified**, integrated, comprehensive, holistic, all-embracing.
– OPPOSITES peripheral, fragmented.

integrate verb **combine**, amalgamate, merge, unite, fuse, blend, consolidate, meld, mix; incorporate, unify, assimilate, homogenize; desegregate.
– OPPOSITES separate.

integrated adjective **1** *an integrated package of services:* **unified**, united, consolidated, amalgamated, combined, homogeneous, assimilated, cohesive. **2** *an integrated school:* **desegregated**, unsegregated, mixed; multi-faith, multiracial.

i

i

integrity noun **1** *I never doubted his integrity:* **honesty**, probity, rectitude, honour, sincerity, truthfulness, trustworthiness. **2** *the integrity of the federation:* **unity**, coherence, cohesion; solidity. **3** *the structural integrity of the aircraft:* **soundness**, strength, sturdiness, solidity, durability, stability, rigidity.
– OPPOSITES dishonesty, division, fragility.

intellect noun **1** *a film that appeals to the intellect:* **mind**, brain, intelligence, reason, judgement; grey matter, brain cells. **2** *one of the finest intellects:* **thinker**, intellectual; mind, brain.

intellectual adjective **1** *his intellectual capacity:* **mental**; rational, conceptual, theoretical, analytical, logical. **2** *an intellectual man:* **cerebral**, academic, erudite, bookish, highbrow, scholarly.
– OPPOSITES physical.

intelligence noun **1** *a man of great intelligence:* **cleverness**, intellect, brainpower, judgement, reasoning; acumen, wit, insight, perception, smartness. **2** *intelligence from our agents:* **information**, facts, details, particulars, data, knowledge, material; informal info, gen, dope.

intelligent adjective **1** *an intelligent woman:* **clever**, bright, quick-witted, smart, astute, insightful, perceptive; informal brainy. **2** *intelligent life:* **rational**, reasoning, thinking. **3** *intelligent machines:* **self-regulating**, capable of learning, smart.

intelligible adjective **comprehensible**, understandable; accessible, digestible, user-friendly; lucid, clear, coherent, plain, unambiguous.

intemperance noun **over-indulgence**, immoderation, excess, extravagance; overindulgence, self-gratification, hedonism, lotus-eating.

intemperate adjective **immoderate**, excessive, uncontrolled; overindulgent, extravagant, unrestrained, prodigal, profligate.
– OPPOSITES moderate.

intend verb **plan**, mean, have in mind, aim, propose; hope, expect, envisage.

intended adjective **deliberate**, intentional, calculated, conscious, planned, knowing, wilful, wanton, done on purpose, premeditated, pre-planned; Law aforethought.
– OPPOSITES accidental.

intense adjective **1** *intense heat:* **extreme**, great, acute, fierce, severe, high; exceptional, extraordinary; harsh, strong, powerful; informal serious. **2** *a very intense young man:* **passionate**, impassioned, zealous, vehement; earnest, eager, committed.
– OPPOSITES mild, apathetic.

intensify verb **escalate**, increase, step up, raise, strengthen, reinforce; pick up, build up, heighten, deepen, extend, expand, amplify, magnify; aggravate, exacerbate, worsen, inflame, compound.
– OPPOSITES abate.

intensity noun **1** *the intensity of the sun:* **strength**, power, force; severity, ferocity, vehemence, fierceness, harshness. **2** *his eyes had a glowing intensity:* **passion**, ardour, fervour, vehemence, fire, emotion; eagerness, animation.

intensive adjective **thorough**, thoroughgoing, in-depth, rigorous, exhaustive; vigorous, detailed, minute, close, meticulous, scrupulous, painstaking, methodical; extensive.
– OPPOSITES cursory.

intent noun *he tried to divine his father's intent:* **aim**, intention, purpose, objective, object, goal, target.
• adjective **1** *he was intent on proving his point:* **bent**, set, determined, insistent, resolved, hell-bent, keen; committed to; determined to. **2** *an intent expression:* **attentive**, absorbed, engrossed, fascinated, enthralled, rapt; focused, studious, preoccupied.
■ **to all intents and purposes** in effect, effectively, in essence, essentially, virtually, practically; more or less, just about, all but, as good as, in all but name; almost, nearly; informal pretty well; literary nigh on.

intention noun **aim**, purpose, intent, objective, object, goal, target.

intentional adjective **deliberate**, calculated, conscious, intended, planned, meant, knowing, wilful, purposeful, done on purpose, premeditated, pre-planned, preconceived; Law aforethought.

intently adverb **attentively**, closely, keenly, earnestly, hard, carefully, fixedly.

inter verb **bury**, lay to rest, entomb; literary inhume.
– OPPOSITES exhume.

intercede verb **mediate**, arbitrate, conciliate, negotiate, moderate.

intercept verb **stop**, head off, cut off; catch, seize, grab, snatch; block.

intercession noun **mediation**, arbitration, conciliation, negotiation.

interchange verb **1** *they interchange ideas:* **exchange**, trade, swap, barter, bandy. **2** *the terms are often interchanged:* **substitute**, transpose, exchange, switch, swap round, change round.
• noun **1** *the interchange of ideas:* **exchange**, trade, swapping, give and take, traffic. **2** *a motorway interchange:* **junction**, intersection; N. Amer. cloverleaf.

interchangeable adjective **identical**, indistinguishable, the same; informal much of a muchness.

intercourse noun **1** *social intercourse:* **dealings**, relations, relationships, association, contact; interchange, communication, communion. **2** *she did not consent to intercourse:* **sexual intercourse**, sex, sexual relations, copulation; technical coitus; formal fornication; dated carnal knowledge.

interdict noun **prohibition**, ban, bar, veto, embargo, moratorium, injunction.
– OPPOSITES permission.

interest noun **1** *we listened with interest:* **attentiveness**, attention; regard, notice; curiosity; enjoyment, delight. **2** *places of interest:* **attraction**, appeal, fascination, charm, beauty, allure. **3** *this will be of interest to those involved:* **concern**, consequence, importance, import, significance, note, relevance, value. **4** *her interests include reading:* **hobby**, pastime, leisure pursuit, recreation, diversion; passion, love, obsession; informal thing, bag, cup of tea. **5** *a financial interest in the firm:* **stake**, share, claim, investment; involvement, concern. **6** *his attorney guarded his interests:* **concern**, business, affair. **7** *her savings earned interest:* **dividends**, profits, returns; a percentage.
– OPPOSITES boredom.
• verb *a topic that interests you:* **appeal to**, attract, intrigue, engage your imagination; amuse, divert, entertain; arouse your curiosity, whet your appetite; informal tickle someone's fancy.
– OPPOSITES bore.

interested adjective **1** *an interested crowd:* **attentive**, fascinated, riveted, gripped, captivated, agog; intrigued, curious; keen, eager; informal all ears. **2** *the government consulted with interested bodies:* **concerned**, involved, affected.

interesting adjective **absorbing**, engrossing, fascinating, riveting, gripping, compelling, captivating, engaging, enthralling; appealing; amusing, entertaining, stimulating, thought-provoking, diverting, intriguing.

interfere verb **1** *don't let emotion interfere with duty:* **impede**, obstruct, stand in the way of, hinder, inhibit, restrict, constrain, hamper, handicap; disturb, disrupt, influence, affect, confuse. **2** *she tried not to interfere:* **butt in**, barge in, intrude, encroach; informal poke your nose in, stick your oar in.

interference noun **1** *they resent state interference:* **intrusion**, intervention, involvement; meddling, prying. **2** *radio interference:* **disruption**, disturbance, static, noise.

interfering adjective **meddlesome**, meddling, intrusive, prying; informal nosy-parker.

interim adjective **provisional**, temporary, pro tem, stopgap, short-term, caretaker, acting, intervening, transitional.
– OPPOSITES permanent.

interior adjective **1** *the house has interior panelling:* **inside**, inner, internal. **2** *the interior deserts of the US:* **inland**, upcountry, inner, innermost, central. **3** *the country's interior affairs:* **internal**, home, domestic, national, state, civil, local.

4 *an interior monologue:* **inner**, mental, spiritual, psychological; private, personal, secret.
–OPPOSITES exterior, outer, foreign.
•noun **1** *the interior of the castle:* **inside**, depths, recesses, bowels, belly; heart. **2** *the country's interior:* **centre**, heartland.
–OPPOSITES exterior, outside.

interject verb **1** *she interjected a comment:* **interpose**, introduce, throw in, add. **2** *he interjected before anyone could say anything:* **interrupt**, intervene, cut in, butt in, chime in; Brit. informal chip in; N. Amer. informal put your two cents in.

interjection noun **exclamation**; cry, shout, vociferation, utterance; dated ejaculation.

i

interlock verb **interconnect**, interlink, engage, mesh, join, unite, connect, couple.

interloper noun **intruder**, trespasser, invader, infiltrator; uninvited guest; outsider; informal gatecrasher.

interlude noun **interval**, intermission, break, recess, pause, rest, breathing space, gap, hiatus, lull; informal breather, let-up, time out.

intermediary noun **mediator**, go-between, negotiator, arbitrator, peacemaker; middleman, broker.

intermediate adjective **halfway**, in-between, middle, mid, midway, intervening, transitional.

interment noun **burial**, burying, committal, entombment, inhumation; funeral.

interminable adjective **endless**, never-ending, unending, ceaseless, unceasing, incessant, constant, continual.

intermingle verb **mix**, intermix, mingle, blend, fuse, merge, combine, amalgamate; associate, fraternize; literary commingle.

intermission noun **interval**, interlude, break, recess, time out.

intermittent adjective **sporadic**, irregular, fitful, spasmodic, discontinuous, isolated, random, patchy, scattered; occasional, periodic.
–OPPOSITES continuous.

intern verb *they were interned without trial:* **imprison**, incarcerate, impound, jail, put behind bars, detain, hold captive, lock up, confine; Brit. informal bang up.
•noun *an intern at a local firm:* **trainee**, apprentice, probationer, student.

internal adjective **1** *an internal courtyard:* **inner**, interior, inside; central. **2** *the state's internal affairs:* **domestic**, home, interior, civil, local; national, state. **3** *an internal struggle:* **mental**, psychological, emotional; personal, private, inner.
–OPPOSITES external, foreign.

international adjective **global**, worldwide, intercontinental, universal; cosmopolitan, multiracial, multinational.
–OPPOSITES national, local.

interplay noun **interaction**, interchange; reciprocity, give and take.

interpolate verb **insert**, interpose, enter, add, incorporate, introduce.

interpret verb **1** *rabbis interpret the Jewish law:* **explain**, elucidate, expound, clarify. **2** *the remark was interpreted as an invitation:* **understand**, construe, take, see, regard. **3** *the symbols are difficult to interpret:* **decipher**, decode, translate; understand.

interpretation noun **1** *the interpretation of the Bible's teachings:* **explanation**, elucidation, exposition, exegesis, clarification. **2** *she did not care what interpretation he put on her haste:* **meaning**, understanding, explanation, inference. **3** *the interpretation of experimental findings:* **analysis**, evaluation. **4** *his interpretation of Mozart:* **rendition**, execution, presentation, performance, reading, playing, singing.

interrogate verb **question**, cross-examine, quiz; interview, examine, debrief, give someone the third degree; informal pump, grill.

interrupt verb **1** *she opened her mouth to interrupt:* **cut in**, break in, interject; N. Amer. put your two cents in; informal butt in, chime in; Brit. informal chip in. **2** *the band had to interrupt their tour:* **suspend**, adjourn, break off; stop, halt; informal put on ice. **3** *their view was interrupted by houses:* **obstruct**, impede, block, restrict.

interruption noun **1** *he was not*

pleased at her interruption: **cutting in**, barging in, intervention, intrusion; informal butting in. **2** *an interruption of the power supply:* **suspension**, breaking off, cutting.

intersection noun **1** *the intersection of the two curves:* **crossing**, meeting. **2** *the driver stopped at an intersection:* **junction**, T-junction, interchange, crossroads; Brit. roundabout.

intersperse verb **1** *alpine plants were interspersed among the rocks:* **scatter**, spread, arrange, dot. **2** *the beech trees are interspersed with conifers:* **mix**, alternate, punctuate.

intertwine verb **entwine**, interweave, interlace, twist, coil.

interval noun **intermission**, interlude, break, recess, time out.

intervene verb **intercede**, involve yourself, get involved, step in; interfere, intrude.

intervention noun **involvement**, intercession; interference, intrusion.

interview noun *all applicants will be called for an interview:* **meeting**, discussion; interrogation, cross-examination, debriefing; audience, talk, chat; informal grilling.
• verb *we interviewed seventy subjects for the survey:* **talk to**, question, interrogate, cross-examine, debrief; poll, canvass, sound out; informal grill, pump; Law examine.

interviewer noun **questioner**, interrogator, examiner, assessor; journalist, reporter; inquisitor.

interweave verb **1** *the threads are interwoven:* **intertwine**, interlace, splice, braid, plait; twist together, weave together, wind together. **2** *their fates were interwoven:* **interlink**, link, connect; intertwine.

intestines plural noun **gut**, guts, entrails, viscera; small intestine, large intestine; informal insides, innards.

> **WORD LINKS**
> **visceral** relating to the intestines
> **enteritis** inflammation of the intestine

intimacy noun **closeness**, togetherness, rapport, attachment, familiarity, friendliness, affection, warmth.

intimate[1] adjective **1** *they are on intimate terms:* **close**, loving, affectionate, friendly, familiar. **2** *an intimate atmosphere:* **friendly**, warm, welcoming, hospitable, relaxed, informal; cosy, comfortable. **3** *an intimate knowledge:* **detailed**, thorough, exhaustive, deep, in-depth, profound. **4** *intimate thoughts:* **personal**, private, confidential, secret; innermost, inward, unspoken. **5** *intimate relations:* **sexual**, carnal.
– OPPOSITES distant, formal.

intimate[2] verb **1** *he intimated his decision:* **announce**, state, proclaim, make known, make public, disclose, reveal, divulge. **2** *her feelings were subtly intimated:* **imply**, suggest, hint at, indicate.

intimation noun **suggestion**, hint, indication, sign, signal, inkling, suspicion, impression.

intimidate verb **frighten**, menace, scare, terrorize; threaten, browbeat, bully, harass, harry, hound; informal lean on.

intolerable adjective **unbearable**, insufferable, insupportable, unendurable, more than flesh and blood can stand, too much to bear.
– OPPOSITES bearable.

intolerant adjective **1** *he was extremely intolerant:* **bigoted**, narrow-minded, illiberal; prejudiced. **2** *her son was intolerant to several foods:* **allergic**, sensitive, hypersensitive.

intonation noun **1** *she read the sentence with the wrong intonation:* **inflection**, pitch, tone, cadence, lilt, modulation. **2** *the intonation of hymns:* **chanting**, recitation, singing.

intone verb **chant**, sing, recite.

intoxicate verb *he was intoxicated by cinema:* **exhilarate**, thrill, elate, delight, captivate, enthral, entrance, enrapture, excite, inspire.

intoxicated adjective. See DRUNK.

intoxicating adjective **1** *intoxicating drink:* **alcoholic**, strong, hard. **2** *an intoxicating sense of freedom:* **heady**, exhilarating, thrilling, stirring, stimulating, invigorating, electrifying; powerful, potent; informal mind-blowing.
– OPPOSITES non-alcoholic.

intoxication noun. See DRUNKENNESS.

intractable adjective **1** *intractable*

problems: **unmanageable**, uncontrollable, insurmountable. **2** *an intractable man:* **stubborn**, obstinate, obdurate, inflexible, unbending, unyielding, uncompromising, unaccommodating, difficult, awkward, pig-headed.
– OPPOSITES manageable, compliant.

intransigent adjective **uncompromising**, inflexible, unbending, unyielding, unwavering, stubborn, obstinate, pig-headed.
– OPPOSITES compliant.

intrenched adjective. See **ENTRENCHED**.

intrepid adjective **fearless**, unflinching, bold, daring, heroic, dynamic, indomitable; brave, valiant, doughty.
– OPPOSITES fearful.

i

intricate adjective **complex**, complicated, convoluted, tangled; elaborate, ornate, detailed.

intrigue verb *her answer intrigued him:* **interest**, fascinate, arouse someone's curiosity, attract; engage. • noun *the intrigue that accompanied the selection of a new leader:* **plotting**, conniving, scheming, machination, double-dealing, subterfuge.

intriguing adjective **interesting**, fascinating, absorbing, engaging.

intrinsic adjective **inherent**, innate, inborn, inbred, congenital, natural; integral, basic, fundamental, essential.

introduce verb **1** *he has introduced a new system:* **institute**, initiate, launch, inaugurate, establish, found; bring in, set in motion, start, begin, get going. **2** *she introduced Lindsey to the young man:* **present**, make known, acquaint with. **3** *introducing nitrogen into canned beer:* **insert**, inject, put, force, shoot, feed. **4** *she introduced a note of seriousness:* **instil**, infuse, inject, add. **5** *the same presenter introduces the programme each week:* **announce**, present; host; open.

introduction noun **1** *the introduction of democratic reforms:* **institution**, establishment, initiation, launch, inauguration, foundation; pioneering. **2** *an introduction to the king:* **presentation**; meeting, audience. **3** *the introduction to the catalogue:* **foreword**, preface, preamble, prologue, prelude. **4** *an introduction to the history of the period:* **basic explanation**, way in, overview; the basics, the rudiments, the fundamentals.
– OPPOSITES afterword.

introductory adjective **1** *the introductory chapter:* **opening**, initial, starting, initiatory, first, preliminary. **2** *an introductory course:* **elementary**, basic, rudimentary, entry-level.
– OPPOSITES final, advanced.

introspection noun **self-analysis**, soul-searching, introversion; contemplation, reflection; informal navel-gazing.

introspective adjective **inward-looking**, self-analysing, introverted, introvert; contemplative, thoughtful, reflective; informal navel-gazing.

introverted adjective **shy**, reserved, withdrawn, reticent, diffident, retiring, quiet; introspective, introvert, inward-looking; pensive.
– OPPOSITES extroverted.

intrude verb **encroach**, impinge, trespass, infringe; invade, violate, disturb, disrupt.

intruder noun **trespasser**, interloper, invader, infiltrator; burglar, housebreaker.

intrusion noun **encroachment**; invasion, incursion, intervention, disruption, impingement.

intrusive adjective **1** *an intrusive journalist:* **intruding**, invasive, inquisitive, prying; informal nosy. **2** *intrusive questions:* **personal**, prying, impertinent.

intuition noun **1** *he works by intuition:* **instinct**, feeling; spirit, soul. **2** *this confirms an intuition I had:* **hunch**, feeling, inkling, sneaking suspicion; premonition; informal gut feeling.

intuitive adjective **instinctive**; innate, inborn, inherent, natural; unconscious, subconscious; informal gut.

inundate verb **1** *many buildings were inundated:* **flood**, deluge, swamp, submerge, engulf. **2** *we have been inundated by complaints:* **overwhelm**, overrun, overload, swamp, besiege, snow under.

inure verb **harden**, toughen, desensi-

tize, condition; accustom, habituate.
– OPPOSITES sensitize.

invade verb **1** *the island was invaded:* **occupy**, conquer, capture, seize, take over, annex, overrun, storm. **2** *someone had invaded our privacy:* **intrude on**, violate, encroach on, infringe on, trespass on, disturb, disrupt.
– OPPOSITES withdraw.

invader noun **attacker**, raider, marauder; occupier, conqueror; intruder.

invalid[1] adjective *her invalid husband:* **ill**, sick, ailing, unwell, infirm; incapacitated, bedridden, frail, sickly, poorly.
– OPPOSITES healthy.
• verb *an officer invalided by a chest wound:* **disable**, incapacitate, hospitalize, put out of action, lay up.

invalid[2] adjective **1** *the law was invalid:* **void**, null and void, illegitimate, inapplicable. **2** *the whole theory is invalid:* **false**, fallacious, spurious, unsound, wrong; untenable.
– OPPOSITES valid, true.

invalidate verb **1** *a low turnout invalidated the ballot:* **render invalid**, void, nullify, annul, negate, cancel, overturn, overrule. **2** *this invalidates your argument:* **disprove**, refute, explode, negate; undermine.

invaluable adjective **indispensable**, crucial, key, vital, irreplaceable, all-important.
– OPPOSITES dispensable.

invariable adjective **unvarying**, unchanging, unvaried; constant, stable, set, steady; unchangeable, unalterable.
– OPPOSITES varied.

invariably adverb **always**, at all times, without fail, without exception; consistently, habitually, unfailingly.
– OPPOSITES sometimes, never.

invasion noun **1** *the invasion of the islands:* **occupation**, conquering, capture, seizure, annexation, takeover. **2** *an invasion of my privacy:* **violation**, infringement, interruption, encroachment, disturbance, disruption, breach.
– OPPOSITES withdrawal.

invective noun **abuse**, insults, expletives, swear words, swearing, curses, bad/foul language.
– OPPOSITES praise.

inveigle verb **cajole**, wheedle, coax, persuade, talk; informal sweet-talk, soft-soap, con; N. Amer. informal sucker.

invent verb **1** *Louis Braille invented an alphabet to help blind people:* **originate**, create, design, devise, contrive, develop. **2** *they invented the story for a laugh:* **make up**, fabricate, concoct, hatch, dream up; informal cook up.

invention noun **1** *the invention of the telescope:* **origination**, creation, development, design. **2** *medieval inventions:* **innovation**, creation, contraption, contrivance, device, gadget. **3** *a journalistic invention:* **fabrication**, concoction, piece of fiction, story, tale; lie, untruth, falsehood, fib.

inventive adjective **1** *the most inventive composer of his time:* **creative**, original, innovative, imaginative, resourceful. **2** *a fresh, inventive comedy:* **original**, innovative, unusual, fresh, novel, new; groundbreaking, unorthodox, unconventional.
– OPPOSITES unimaginative, hackneyed.

inventor noun **originator**, creator; designer, deviser, developer, maker, producer; author, architect; father.

inventory noun **list**, listing, catalogue, record, register, checklist, log, archive.

inverse adjective **reverse**, reversed, inverted, opposite, converse, contrary, counter, antithetical.

inversion noun **reversal**, transposition; reverse, antithesis, converse.

invert verb **turn upside down**, upturn, upend, flip over, turn over.

invest verb **1** *he invested in a steel mill:* **put/plough money into**, fund, back, finance, underwrite. **2** *they invested £18 million:* **spend**, expend, put in, plough in; informal lay out. **3** *the powers invested in the bishop:* **vest in**, confer on, bestow on, grant to. **4** *bishops whom the king had invested:* **instate**, install, induct, swear in; ordain, crown.

investigate verb **enquire into**,

look into, go into, probe, explore, scrutinize; analyse, study, examine; informal check out, suss out; N. Amer. informal scope out.

investigation noun **examination**, inquiry, study, inspection, exploration, analysis; research, scrutiny; probe, review.

investigator noun **inspector**, examiner, analyst; researcher, factfinder, scrutineer; detective.

investiture noun **inauguration**, appointment, installation, initiation, swearing in; ordination, consecration, crowning.

investment noun **1** *it's a good investment:* **venture**, proposition. **2** *an investment of £305,000:* **stake**, payment, outlay. **3** *a substantial investment of time:* **sacrifice**, commitment, input.

i

inveterate adjective **1** *an inveterate gambler:* **confirmed**, hardened, incorrigible, addicted, compulsive, obsessive; informal pathological, chronic. **2** *an inveterate Democrat:* **staunch**, steadfast, committed, devoted, dedicated, dyed-in-the-wool, diehard.

invidious adjective **1** *that put her in an invidious position:* **unpleasant**, awkward, difficult; undesirable, unenviable. **2** *an invidious comparison:* **unfair**, unjust, unwarranted.
– OPPOSITES pleasant, fair.

invigorate verb **revitalize**, energize, refresh, revive, enliven, liven up, perk up, wake up, animate, galvanize, fortify, rouse, exhilarate; informal buck up, pep up.
– OPPOSITES tire.

invigorating adjective *a brisk, invigorating walk:* **refreshing**, bracing, stimulating, energizing, exhilarating, revitalizing, restorative.
– OPPOSITES tiring.

invincible adjective **invulnerable**, indestructible, unconquerable, unbeatable, indomitable, unassailable; impregnable.
– OPPOSITES vulnerable.

inviolable adjective **inalienable**, absolute, unalterable, unchallengeable; sacrosanct, sacred.

inviolate adjective **untouched**, undamaged, unharmed, unscathed; unspoiled, unsullied, unstained, undefiled; intact.

invisible adjective **not visible**; undetectable; inconspicuous, imperceptible; unseen, unnoticed, unobserved, hidden, out of sight.

invitation noun **1** *an invitation to dinner:* **call**, summons; informal invite. **2** *an open door is an invitation to a thief:* **encouragement**, magnet, enticement; informal come-on.

invite verb **1** *they invited us to lunch:* **ask**; summon. **2** *applications are invited for the post:* **ask for**, request, call for, appeal for, solicit, seek. **3** *airing such views invites trouble:* **cause**, induce, provoke, ask for, encourage, lead to; bring on yourself, arouse.

inviting adjective **tempting**, enticing, alluring, beguiling; attractive, appealing; appetizing, mouth-watering; intriguing, seductive.
– OPPOSITES repellent.

invoice noun *an invoice for the goods:* **bill**, account, statement; N. Amer. check; informal tab.
• verb *we'll invoice you for the damage:* **bill**, charge.

invoke verb **1** *he invoked his statutory rights:* **cite**, refer to; resort to, have recourse to, turn to. **2** *they invoked the Holy Spirit:* **pray to**, call on, appeal to. **3** *no one dared speak, for fear of invoking his wrath:* **cause**, give rise to, elicit, evoke.

involuntary adjective **1** *an involuntary shudder:* **reflex**, automatic; instinctive, unintentional, uncontrollable. **2** *involuntary repatriation:* **compulsory**, obligatory, mandatory, forced, prescribed.
– OPPOSITES deliberate, optional.

involve verb **1** *the inspection involved a lot of work:* **require**, necessitate, demand, call for; entail. **2** *I try to involve everyone in key decisions:* **include**, bring in, consult.
– OPPOSITES preclude, exclude.

involved adjective **1** *social workers involved in the case:* **associated**, connected, concerned. **2** *he had been involved in burglaries:* **implicated**, caught up, mixed up. **3** *a long and involved story:* **complicated**, intricate, complex; convoluted. **4** *they were totally involved in their work:*

engrossed, absorbed, immersed, caught up, preoccupied, intent.
– OPPOSITES unconnected, straightforward.

involvement noun **1** *his involvement in the plot:* **participation**; collaboration, collusion, complicity; association, connection, entanglement. **2** *emotional involvement:* **attachment**, friendship, intimacy; commitment.

invulnerable adjective **impervious**, immune; indestructible, impregnable, unassailable, invincible, secure.

inward adverb *the door opened inward.* See INWARDS.

inwards adverb **inside**, into the interior, inward, within.

iota noun **bit**, mite, speck, scrap, shred, ounce, jot.

irascible adjective **irritable**, quick-tempered, short-tempered, snappy, tetchy, touchy, crabby, waspish; grouchy, cantankerous, curmudgeonly, peevish, querulous, fractious; informal prickly, ratty.

irate adjective **angry**, furious, infuriated, enraged, fuming, seething; raging, outraged, up in arms; indignant, irritated; literary wrathful.

Ireland noun Eire; Hibernia, the Emerald Isle; literary Erin.

iridescent adjective **shimmering**, shining, gleaming, glowing, lustrous, opalescent.

irk verb **irritate**, annoy, pique, nettle, vex; anger; peeve, miff, needle, bug, hack off; Brit. informal get on someone's wick; N. Amer. informal tee off.
– OPPOSITES please.

irksome adjective **irritating**, annoying, vexing, galling; tiresome, trying, difficult.

iron noun *leg irons:* **manacles**, shackles, fetters, chains, handcuffs; informal cuffs.
• adjective *he had an iron will:* **uncompromising**, unrelenting, unyielding, unbending, rigid, unwavering; steely.
■ **iron something out** *we've ironed out all the minor snags:* resolve, straighten out, sort out, clear up, put right, solve, rectify; eliminate, eradicate; informal fix.

> WORD LINKS
> **ferric**, **ferrous** relating to or containing iron

ironic adjective **1** *Edward's tone was ironic:* **sarcastic**, sardonic, dry, caustic, scathing, acerbic, bitter, trenchant; mocking, derisive, scornful; Brit. informal sarky. **2** *it's ironic that I've ended up writing:* **paradoxical**, funny, strange; typical.
– OPPOSITES sincere.

irony noun **1** *that note of irony in her voice:* **sarcasm**, bitterness; mockery, ridicule, derision, scorn. **2** *the irony of the situation:* **paradox**.
– OPPOSITES sincerity.

irrational adjective **unreasonable**, illogical; groundless, baseless, unfounded, unjustifiable.
– OPPOSITES logical.

irreconcilable adjective **incompatible**, at odds, at variance, conflicting, antagonistic, mutually exclusive, diametrically opposed; poles apart.
– OPPOSITES compatible.

irrecoverable adjective **unrecoverable**, irretrievable, irredeemable, unsalvageable, gone for ever.

irrefutable adjective **indisputable**, undeniable, unquestionable, incontrovertible, incontestable, beyond question, beyond doubt; conclusive, definite, definitive, decisive.

irregular adjective **1** *irregular features:* **asymmetrical**, uneven, crooked, misshapen, lopsided, twisted. **2** *irregular surfaces:* **rough**, bumpy, uneven, pitted, rutted; lumpy, knobbly, gnarled. **3** *an irregular heartbeat:* **inconsistent**, unsteady, uneven, fitful, patchy, variable, varying, changeable, inconstant, erratic, unstable, unsettled, spasmodic, intermittent. **4** *irregular financial dealings:* **improper**, illegitimate, unethical, unprofessional; informal shady, dodgy. **5** *an irregular army:* **guerrilla**, underground; paramilitary; mercenary.
– OPPOSITES straight, smooth.

irregularity noun **1** *the irregularity of the coastline:* **asymmetry**, non-uniformity, unevenness, crookedness, lopsidedness. **2** *the irregularity of the surface:* **roughness**, bumpiness, unevenness. **3** *irregularities in*

i

the concrete: **bump**, lump, bulge, hump, protuberance, kink; hole, hollow, pit, crater; crack, chink, fissure. **4** *the irregularity of the bus service:* **inconsistency**, unevenness, fitfulness, patchiness, inconstancy, variability, changeableness, unpredictability, unreliability. **5** *financial irregularities:* **impropriety**, wrongdoing, misconduct, dishonesty.

irregularly adverb **erratically**, intermittently, in/by fits and starts, fitfully, haphazardly, inconsistently, unsteadily, unevenly, variably, spasmodically.

irrelevance noun **inapplicability**; unimportance, inconsequentiality, insignificance.

i

irrelevant adjective **beside the point**, immaterial, unconnected, unrelated, peripheral, extraneous; unimportant, inconsequential, insignificant, trivial.

irreligious adjective **atheistic**, non-believing, agnostic, faithless, godless, ungodly, impious, profane.
– OPPOSITES pious.

irreparable adjective **irreversible**, irrevocable, irrecoverable, unrepairable, beyond repair.
– OPPOSITES repairable.

irreplaceable adjective **unique**, unrepeatable, incomparable.

irrepressible adjective **ebullient**, exuberant, buoyant, breezy, jaunty, high-spirited, vivacious, animated, full of life, lively; informal bubbly, bouncy, peppy, chipper, chirpy, full of beans.

irreproachable adjective **impeccable**, exemplary, immaculate, outstanding, exceptional, admirable, perfect; above/beyond reproach, blameless; informal squeaky clean, whiter than white.
– OPPOSITES reprehensible.

irresistible adjective **1** *her irresistible smile:* **captivating**, enticing, alluring; enchanting. **2** *an irresistible impulse:* **uncontrollable**, overwhelming, overpowering, ungovernable.

irrespective adjective **regardless of**, without regard to/for, notwithstanding, whatever, no matter what.

irresponsible adjective **1** *irresponsible behaviour:* **reckless**, rash, careless, unwise, imprudent, ill-advised, injudicious, hasty, foolhardy, impetuous. **2** *an irresponsible teenager:* **immature**, foolish; unreliable, undependable, untrustworthy.
– OPPOSITES sensible.

irretrievable adjective **irreversible**, unrectifiable, irrecoverable, irreparable.
– OPPOSITES reversible.

irreverent adjective **disrespectful**; impertinent, cheeky, flippant, rude, discourteous.
– OPPOSITES respectful.

irreversible adjective **irreparable**, unrepairable, unrectifiable, irrevocable, permanent; unalterable.

irrevocable adjective **irreversible**, unalterable, unchangeable, immutable, final, binding, permanent.

irritability noun **irascibility**, tetchiness, testiness, cantankerousness, short temper, ill humour, peevishness, fractiousness, crabbiness, waspishness, prickliness; N. Amer. informal crankiness.

irritable adjective **bad-tempered**, short-tempered, irascible, tetchy, testy, grumpy, grouchy, crotchety, cantankerous, peevish, fractious, pettish, crabby, waspish, prickly, splenetic, dyspeptic; informal on a short fuse; Brit. informal shirty, ratty; N. Amer. informal cranky, ornery; Austral./NZ informal snaky.
– OPPOSITES good-humoured.

irritant noun **annoyance**, irritation, thorn in someone's side/flesh, nuisance; informal pain in the neck, headache; N. Amer. informal nudnik, burr under someone's saddle; Austral./NZ informal nark.

irritate verb **1** *his tone irritated her:* **annoy**, exasperate, irk, gall, pique, anger, vex, get on someone's nerves, ruffle someone's feathers, make someone's hackles rise, nettle, rankle; Brit. rub up the wrong way; informal aggravate, hassle, rile, needle, bug, hack off, get up someone's nose, get someone's goat, get someone's back up; Brit. informal wind up, nark, get on someone's wick; N. Amer. informal tee off, tick off; informal, dated give someone the pip. **2** *some sand irritated my eyes:* **inflame**, hurt, chafe, scratch, scrape, rub.

irritated adjective **annoyed**, cross, angry, vexed, exasperated, irked, piqued, displeased, put out, disgruntled, nettled; informal aggravated, peeved, miffed, riled, hacked off; Brit. informal narked, shirty; N. Amer. informal teed off, ticked off, sore, bent out of shape; Austral./NZ informal crook.

irritating adjective **annoying**, infuriating, exasperating, maddening, trying, tiresome, troublesome, bothersome, irksome, vexing, galling; informal aggravating.

irritation noun. See **ANNOYANCE**.

island noun **isle**, islet; atoll; Brit. holm; (**islands**) archipelago.

> **WORD LINKS**
> **insular** relating to an island

isolate verb **1** *she isolated herself from her family | the contaminated area was isolated:* **separate**, segregate, detach, cut off, shut away, alienate, distance; cloister, seclude; cordon off, seal off, close off, fence off. **2** *the computer can isolate the offending vehicles:* **identify**, single out, pick out, point out, pinpoint.
–OPPOSITES integrate.

isolated adjective **1** *isolated communities:* **remote**, out of the way, outlying, off the beaten track, in the back of beyond, godforsaken, inaccessible, cut-off; informal in the middle of nowhere, in the sticks; N. Amer. informal jerkwater, in the tall timbers; Austral./NZ informal Barcoo, beyond the black stump. **2** *he lived a very isolated existence:* **solitary**, lonely; secluded, reclusive, hermit-like; N. Amer. lonesome. **3** *an isolated incident:* **unique**, lone, solitary; unusual, exceptional, untypical, freak; informal one-off.
–OPPOSITES accessible, sociable, common.

isolation noun **1** *their feeling of isolation:* **solitariness**, loneliness, friendlessness. **2** *the isolation of some mental hospitals:* **remoteness**, inaccessibility.
–OPPOSITES contact.

issue noun **1** *the committee discussed the issue:* **matter**, question, point, affair, case, subject, topic; problem, situation. **2** *the latest issue of our magazine:* **edition**, number, instalment, copy. **3** *the issue of a special stamp:* **issuing**, release, publication. •verb **1** *the minister issued a statement:* **release**, put out, deliver, publish, broadcast, circulate, distribute. **2** *the captain issued the crew with guns:* **supply**, provide, furnish, arm, equip, fit out, rig out, kit out; informal fix up. **3** *delicious smells issued from the kitchen:* **emanate**, emerge, drift, waft: flow, pour, drip, seep, be exuded.
–OPPOSITES withdraw.
■ **at issue** in question, in dispute, under discussion, under consideration, up for debate. **take issue** disagree; challenge, dispute, question, call into question.

item noun **1** *an item of farm equipment | the main item in a badger's diet:* **thing**, article, object, artefact, piece, product; element, constituent, component, ingredient. **2** *the meeting discussed the item:* **issue**, matter, affair, case, situation, subject, topic, question, point. **3** *a news item:* **report**, story, article, piece, write-up, bulletin, feature, review. **4** *items in the profit and loss account:* **entry**, record, statement.

itemize verb *Steinburg itemized thirty-two design faults:* **list**, catalogue, record, document, register, detail, specify, identify.

iterate verb **repeat**, recapitulate; restate, reiterate; informal recap.

itinerant adjective **travelling**, peripatetic, wandering, roving, roaming, touring, nomadic, migrant, homeless, vagrant; of no fixed address/abode.

itinerary noun **route**, plan, schedule, timetable, programme.

Jj

jab verb *he jabbed the Englishman with his finger:* **poke**, prod, dig, nudge; thrust, stab, push.
• noun *a jab in the ribs:* **poke**, prod, dig, nudge; thrust, stab, push.

jabber verb **prattle**, babble, chatter, gabble, rattle on/away, blather; informal yak, yap, blabber; Brit. informal witter, rabbit, natter.

jacket noun **wrapping**, wrapper, sleeve, cover, covering, sheath.

jaded adjective **bored**, tired, weary, wearied, fatigued; satiated, sated, dulled, blunted, unenthusiastic; informal fed up.
– OPPOSITES fresh.

jagged adjective **spiky**, barbed, ragged, rough, uneven, irregular, broken; serrated, spiny, sawtooth.
– OPPOSITES smooth.

jail noun *he was thrown into jail:* **prison**, lock-up, detention centre; N. Amer. penitentiary, jailhouse, correctional facility; informal clink, cooler, the slammer, inside, jug; Brit. informal nick; N. Amer. informal can, pen, slam, pokey.
• verb *she was jailed for killing her husband:* **send to prison/jail**, put in prison/jail, imprison, incarcerate, lock up, put away, detain; informal send down, put behind bars, put inside; Brit. informal bang up.
– OPPOSITES acquit, release.

jailer noun **prison officer**, warder, warden, guard; informal screw; old use turnkey.

jam[1] verb **1** *he jammed a finger in each ear:* **stuff**, shove, force, ram, thrust, press, push, stick. **2** *hundreds of people jammed into the hall:* **crowd**, pack, pile, press, squeeze, cram; throng, mob, fill, block. **3** *the rudder had jammed:* **stick**, get stuck, catch, seize up. **4** *dust can jam the mechanism:* **immobilize**, paralyse, disable; clog up; informal bung up.
• noun *a traffic jam:* **tailback**, hold-up, queue, congestion, bottleneck; N. Amer. gridlock; informal snarl-up.

jam[2] noun *raspberry jam:* **preserve**, conserve, jelly, marmalade.

jamb noun **post**, doorpost, upright, frame.

jamboree noun **rally**, gathering, convention, conference; festival, fete, fiesta, gala, carnival; informal bash, shindig, do.

jangle verb **1** *keys jangled at his waist:* **clank**, clink, jingle, tinkle. **2** *the noise jangled her nerves:* **grate on**, jar on, irritate, disturb, fray, put/set on edge.

janitor noun **caretaker**, custodian, porter, concierge, doorkeeper, doorman, warden; cleaner; N. Amer. superintendent.

jar[1] noun *a jar of honey:* **pot**, container, crock.

jar[2] verb **1** *each step jarred my whole body:* **jolt**, jerk, shake, vibrate. **2** *her shrill voice jarred on him:* **grate**, set someone's teeth on edge, irritate, annoy, get on someone's nerves. **3** *the verse jars with the words that follow:* **clash**, conflict, contrast, be incompatible, be at variance, be at odds, be inconsistent.

jargon noun **slang**, cant, argot, patter; gobbledegook; informal lingo, -speak, -ese.

jarring adjective **clashing**, conflicting, contrasting, incompatible, incongruous; discordant, dissonant, harsh, grating, strident, shrill.
– OPPOSITES harmonious.

jaundiced adjective **bitter**, resentful, cynical, soured, disenchanted, disillusioned, pessimistic, sceptical, distrustful, suspicious.

jaunt noun **trip**, outing, excursion, day trip, day out; tour, drive, ride, run; informal spin, junket.

jaunty adjective **cheerful**, cheery, happy, merry, jolly, joyful; lively, perky, bright, buoyant, bubbly, bouncy, breezy, exuberant, ebullient; carefree, light-hearted; informal full of beans, chirpy; literary blithe.
– OPPOSITES depressed, serious.

javelin noun **spear**, harpoon, dart.

jaw noun **1** *a broken jaw:* **jawbone**; Anatomy mandible, maxilla. **2** *the whale seized a seal in its jaws:* **mouth**, maw, muzzle; informal chops.

WORD LINKS
mandibular, **maxillary** relating to the jaw

jazzy adjective **bright**, colourful, eye-catching, vivid, lively, vibrant, bold, flamboyant, showy; informal flashy.
– OPPOSITES dull.

jealous adjective **1** *he's jealous of her success:* **envious**, resentful, grudging, green with envy; covetous. **2** *a jealous lover:* **suspicious**, distrustful, mistrustful, insecure; possessive, proprietorial, overprotective. **3** *they are jealous of their rights:* **protective**, vigilant, watchful, mindful, careful.

jealousy noun **1** *he was consumed with jealousy:* **envy**; resentment, bitterness. **2** *her life was ruined by his jealousy:* **suspicion**, suspiciousness, distrust, mistrust, insecurity; possessiveness, overprotectiveness.

jeer verb *the demonstrators jeered the police:* **taunt**, mock, ridicule, sneer at, deride, insult, abuse, jibe at, scoff at; heckle, boo, whistle at; Brit. barrack.
– OPPOSITES applaud, cheer.
• noun *the jeers of the crowd:* **taunt**, sneer, insult, shout, jibe, boo, catcall; derision; abuse, scorn, heckling; Brit. barracking.
– OPPOSITES applause, cheer.

jell verb. See **GEL**.

jeopardize verb **threaten**, endanger, imperil, risk, put in danger/jeopardy; compromise, prejudice.
– OPPOSITES safeguard.

jeopardy noun
■ **in jeopardy** *the peace talks are in jeopardy:* in danger, at risk, under threat, vulnerable, in peril.

jerk noun **1** *she gave the reins a jerk:* **yank**, tug, pull, wrench. **2** *he let the clutch in with a jerk:* **jolt**, lurch, bump, judder, jump; bounce, shake.
• verb **1** *she jerked her arm free:* **yank**, tug, pull, wrench, wrest, drag, snatch. **2** *the car jerked along:* **jolt**, lurch, bump, judder, bounce.

jerky adjective **convulsive**, spasmodic, fitful, twitchy, shaky.
– OPPOSITES smooth.

jerry-built adjective **shoddy**, gimcrack, rickety, ramshackle, flimsy; second-rate, third-rate.
– OPPOSITES sturdy.

jersey noun **pullover**, sweater; Brit. jumper; informal woolly.

jet[1] noun **1** *a jet of water:* **stream**, spurt, spray, spout; gush, surge, burst. **2** *carburettor jets:* **nozzle**, head, spout.

jet[2] adjective *her glossy jet hair:* **black**, pitch-black, coal-black, ebony, raven, sable, sooty.

jettison verb **1** *six aircraft jettisoned their loads:* **dump**, drop, ditch, discharge, throw out, tip out, unload. **2** *he jettisoned his unwanted papers | the scheme was jettisoned:* **discard**, dispose of, throw away/out, get rid of; reject, scrap, axe, abandon, drop; informal chuck away/out, dump, ditch, bin, junk.
– OPPOSITES retain.

jetty noun **pier**, landing stage, quay, wharf, dock; N. Amer. dockominium, levee.

jewel noun **1** *priceless jewels:* **gem**, gemstone, precious stone; informal sparkler, rock. **2** *the jewel of his collection:* **showpiece**, pride and joy, cream, crème de la crème, jewel in the crown, prize, pick. **3** *the girl is a jewel:* **treasure**, angel, gem, marvel, find, godsend; informal one in a million, a star.

jewellery noun **jewels**, gems, gemstones, precious stones, costume jewellery.

jibe noun *cruel jibes:* **snide remark**, taunt, sneer, jeer, insult, barb; informal dig, put-down.

jig verb **bob**, jump, spring, skip, hop, prance, bounce.

jiggle verb **shake**, waggle, wiggle.

j

jilt verb **leave**, walk out on, throw over, finish with, break up with; informal chuck, ditch, dump, drop, run out on, give someone the push/elbow, give someone the big E; literary forsake.

jingle noun **1** *the jingle of money in the till:* **clink**, chink, tinkle, jangle. **2** *advertising jingles:* **slogan**, catchphrase; song, rhyme, tune; N. Amer. informal tag line.
•verb **1** *her bracelets jingled noisily:* **clink**, chink, tinkle, jangle. **2** *the bell jingled:* **tinkle**, ring, ding, ping, chime.

jingoism noun **chauvinism**, ultranationalism, xenophobia.

jinx noun *the jinx struck six days later:* **curse**, spell, hoodoo, malediction; the evil eye, black magic, bad luck; N. Amer. hex; old use malison.
•verb *the family is jinxed:* **curse**, cast a spell on, put the evil eye on; Austral. point the bone at; N. Amer. hex.

job noun **1** *my job involves a lot of travelling:* **position**, post, situation, appointment; occupation, profession, trade, career, work, métier, craft; vocation, calling; vacancy, opening; Austral. informal grip. **2** *this job will take three months:* **task**, piece of work, assignment, project; chore, errand; undertaking, venture, operation. **3** *it's your job to protect her:* **responsibility**, duty, charge, task; role, function, mission; informal department.

jobless adjective **unemployed**, out of work, out of a job, unwaged, redundant, laid off; Brit. informal signing on, on the dole, resting; Austral./NZ informal on the wallaby track.
– OPPOSITES employed.

jockey verb *ministers began jockeying for position:* **compete**, contend, vie; struggle, fight, scramble, jostle.

jocular adjective **humorous**, funny, witty, comic, comical, amusing, droll, jokey, facetious, tongue-in-cheek, teasing, playful; light-hearted, jovial, cheerful, cheery, merry.
– OPPOSITES solemn.

jog verb **1** *he jogged along the road:* **run**, trot, lope. **2** *a hand jogged his elbow:* **nudge**, prod, poke, push, bump, jar.

joie de vivre noun **gaiety**, cheerfulness, cheeriness, light-heartedness, happiness, joy, joyfulness, high spirits, jollity, exuberance, ebullience, liveliness, vivacity, verve, effervescence, buoyancy, zest, zestfulness; informal pep, zing.
– OPPOSITES sobriety.

join verb **1** *the two parts of the mould are joined with clay:* **connect**, unite, couple, fix, affix, attach, fasten, stick, glue, fuse, weld, amalgamate, bond, link, merge, secure, make fast, tie, bind. **2** *here the path joins a major road:* **meet**, touch, reach, abut, adjoin. **3** *I'm off to join the search party:* **help in**, participate in, get involved in, contribute to; enlist in, join up, sign up; band together, get together, team up.
– OPPOSITES separate, leave.
•noun. See **JOINT** sense 1.

joint noun **1** *a leaky joint:* **join**, junction, intersection, link, connection; weld, seam. **2** (informal) *a classy joint:* **place**, establishment; restaurant, bar, club, nightclub, venue.
•adjective *matters of joint interest | a joint effort:* **common**, shared, communal, collective; mutual, cooperative, collaborative, concerted, combined, united.
– OPPOSITES separate.

jointly adverb **together**, in partnership, in cooperation, cooperatively, in conjunction, in combination, mutually.

joke noun **1** *tell me a joke:* **funny story**, jest, witticism, quip; pun; informal gag, wisecrack, crack, funny, one-liner; N. Amer. informal boffola. **2** *they played a joke on her:* **trick**, prank, stunt, hoax, jape; informal leg-pull, spoof, wind-up. **3** (informal) *he soon became a joke:* **laughing stock**, figure of fun, object of ridicule. **4** (informal) *the present system is a joke:* **farce**, travesty, waste of time; shambles; N. Amer. informal shuck.
•verb *she joked with the guests:* **tell jokes**, jest, banter, quip; informal wisecrack, josh.

joker noun **humorist**, comedian, comedienne, comic, wit, jester; prankster, practical joker, hoaxer, trickster, clown; informal card, wag.

jolly adjective **cheerful**, happy, cheery, good-humoured, jovial,

j

merry, sunny, joyful, light-hearted, in high spirits, bubbly, exuberant, ebullient, genial, fun-loving; informal chipper, chirpy, perky, bright-eyed and bushy-tailed; formal jocund; literary joyous, blithe.
– OPPOSITES miserable.
• **adverb** (Brit. informal) *a jolly good idea.* See **VERY** adverb.

jolt **verb 1** *the train jolted the passengers to one side:* **push**, thrust, jar, bump, knock, bang; shake, jog. **2** *the car jolted along:* **bump**, bounce, jerk, rattle, lurch, shudder, judder. **3** *she was jolted out of her reverie:* **startle**, surprise, shock, stun, shake, take aback; informal rock, floor, knock sideways; Brit. informal knock for six.
• **noun 1** *a series of sickening jolts:* **bump**, bounce, shake, jerk, lurch. **2** *he woke up with a jolt:* **start**, jerk, jump. **3** *the sight of the dagger gave him a jolt:* **fright**, shock, scare, surprise; informal turn.

jostle **verb 1** *she was jostled by noisy students:* **push**, shove, elbow; barge. **2** *people jostled for the best position:* **struggle**, vie, jockey, scramble, fight.

jot **verb** *I've jotted down a few details:* **write**, note, take down; scribble, sketch.

journal **noun 1** *a medical journal:* **periodical**, magazine, gazette, digest, review, newsletter, newssheet, bulletin; newspaper, paper; daily, weekly, monthly, quarterly. **2** *he keeps a journal:* **diary**, log, logbook, chronicle; N. Amer. daybook.

journalism **noun 1** *a career in journalism:* **newspapers**, magazines, the press; Brit. Fleet Street. **2** *his incisive style of journalism:* **reporting**, writing, reportage, coverage; articles, reports, features, pieces, stories, reviews.

journalist **noun** **reporter**, correspondent, newspaperman, newspaperwoman, newsman, newswoman, columnist, writer, commentator, reviewer; informal news hound, hack, hackette, stringer, journo; N. Amer. informal newsy.

journey **noun** *his journey round the world:* **trip**, expedition, tour, trek, voyage, cruise, ride, drive; crossing, passage, flight; odyssey, pilgrimage; old use peregrination.
• **verb** *they journeyed south:* **travel**, go, voyage, sail, cruise, fly, hike, trek, ride, drive, make your way.

jovial **adjective** **cheerful**, jolly, happy, cheery, good-humoured, convivial, genial, good-natured, affable, outgoing; smiling, merry, sunny, joyful, high-spirited, exuberant; formal jocund; literary joyous, blithe.
– OPPOSITES miserable.

joy **noun 1** *whoops of joy:* **delight**, pleasure, joyfulness, jubilation, triumph, exultation, rejoicing, happiness, gladness, elation, euphoria, bliss, ecstasy, rapture. **2** *it was a joy to be with her:* **pleasure**, delight, treat, thrill; informal **buzz**, kick.
– OPPOSITES misery, trial.

joyful **adjective 1** *his joyful mood:* **cheerful**, happy, jolly, merry, sunny, light-hearted, bubbly, exuberant, ebullient, cheery, smiling, mirthful; jubilant, gleeful; jovial, genial, good-humoured, full of the joys of spring; formal jocund; literary joyous, blithe. **2** *joyful news:* **pleasing**, happy, good, cheering, gladdening, welcome, heart-warming. **3** *a joyful occasion:* **happy**, cheerful, merry, jolly, festive; literary joyous.
– OPPOSITES sad, distressing.

joyless **adjective 1** *a joyless man:* **gloomy**, melancholy, morose, lugubrious, glum, sombre, saturnine, sullen, dour, humourless. **2** *a joyless place:* **depressing**, cheerless, gloomy, dreary, bleak, drab, dismal, desolate, austere, sombre; literary drear.
– OPPOSITES cheerful, welcoming.

joyous **adjective**. See **JOYFUL** senses 1, 3.

jubilant **adjective** **overjoyed**, exultant, triumphant, joyful, cock-a-hoop, exuberant, elated, thrilled, gleeful, euphoric, ecstatic, enraptured, in raptures, walking on air, in seventh heaven, on cloud nine; informal over the moon, on top of the world; N. Amer. informal wigged out; Austral. informal wrapped.
– OPPOSITES despondent.

jubilation **noun** **exultation**, joy, elation, euphoria, ecstasy, rapture, glee, exuberance; literary joyousness.

jubilee **noun** **anniversary**, commemoration; celebration, festival.

judge noun **1** *the judge sentenced him to five years:* **justice**, magistrate, recorder, sheriff; N. Amer. jurist; Brit. informal beak. **2** *a panel of judges will select the winner:* **adjudicator**, arbiter, assessor, examiner, moderator, scrutineer.
•verb **1** *I judged that she was simply exhausted:* **conclude**, decide; consider, believe, think, deem; deduce, gather, infer, gauge, estimate, guess, surmise, conjecture; regard as, look on as, take to be, rate as, class as; informal reckon, figure. **2** *the case was judged by a tribunal:* **try**, hear, adjudicate, decide; arbitrate. **3** *she was judged innocent of murder:* **pronounce**, decree, rule, find. **4** *entries were judged by a panel of experts:* **assess**, appraise, evaluate; examine, review, moderate.

j

judgement noun **1** *his temper could affect his judgement:* **discernment**, perception, discrimination, powers of reasoning, reason, logic; mind. **2** *I am relying on your judgement:* **acumen**, shrewdness, astuteness, common sense, perspicacity, acuity, discrimination, wisdom, wit, judiciousness, prudence, sharpness; informal nous, savvy, horse sense, gumption; N. Amer. informal smarts. **3** *a court judgement:* **verdict**, decision, adjudication, ruling, pronouncement, decree, finding; sentence.

judgemental adjective **critical**, censorious, disapproving, disparaging, deprecating, negative, overcritical.

judicial adjective **legal**, juridical; official.

judicious adjective **wise**, sensible, prudent, shrewd, astute, canny, discerning.
–OPPOSITES ill-advised.

jug noun **pitcher**, ewer, crock, jar, urn; carafe, flask, flagon, decanter; N. Amer. creamer.

juice noun *the juice from two lemons:* **liquid**, fluid, sap, milk, gum; extract; concentrate, essence.

juicy adjective **succulent**, tender, moist; ripe.
–OPPOSITES dry.

jumble noun **1** *the books were in a jumble:* **heap**, muddle, mess, tangle; confusion, disarray, chaos; hotchpotch, mishmash, miscellany, mixed bag, medley; N. Amer. hodgepodge. **2** (Brit.) *bags of jumble:* **junk**, bric-a-brac; Brit. lumber.
•verb *the photographs are all jumbled up:* **mix up**, muddle up, disorganize, disorder.

jumbo adjective (informal). See HUGE.

jump verb **1** *the cat jumped off his lap | Flora began to jump about:* **leap**, spring, bound, hop; skip, caper, dance, prance, frolic, cavort. **2** *he jumped the fence:* **vault over**, leap over, clear, sail over, hop over, hurdle. **3** *pre-tax profits jumped:* **rise**, go up, shoot up, soar, surge, climb, increase; informal skyrocket. **4** *the noise made her jump:* **start**, jolt, flinch, recoil, shudder.
•noun **1** *the short jump across the gully:* **leap**; gap, distance. **2** *the horse cleared the last jump:* **obstacle**, barrier; fence, hurdle. **3** *a jump in profits:* **rise**, leap, increase, upsurge, upswing; informal hike. **4** *I woke up with a jump:* **start**, jerk, spasm, shudder.

jumper noun (Brit.) **sweater**, pullover, jersey; informal woolly.

jumpy adjective (informal) **nervous**, on edge, edgy, tense, nervy, anxious, ill at ease, uneasy, restless, fidgety, keyed up, overwrought; informal a bundle of nerves, jittery, like a cat on a hot tin roof, uptight, het up, in a tizz/tizzy; Brit. informal like a cat on hot bricks; N. Amer. informal spooky, squirrelly, antsy; Austral./NZ informal toey.
–OPPOSITES calm.

junction noun **crossroads**, intersection, interchange, T-junction; turn, turn-off, exit; Brit. roundabout; N. Amer. turnout, cloverleaf.

jungle noun **rainforest**, forest.

junior adjective **1** *the junior members of the family:* **younger**, youngest. **2** *a junior minister:* **low-ranking**, subordinate, lesser, lower, minor, secondary.
–OPPOSITES older, senior.

junk (informal) noun *an attic full of junk:* **rubbish**, clutter, odds and ends, bits and pieces, bric-a-brac; refuse, litter, scrap, waste, debris, detritus, dross; Brit. lumber; N. Amer. trash.

jurisdiction noun **1** *an area under*

French jurisdiction: **authority**, control, power, dominion, rule, administration, command, sway, leadership, sovereignty. **2 territory**, region, province, district, area, domain, realm.

just adjective *a just and democratic society:* **fair**, fair-minded, equitable, even-handed, impartial, unbiased, objective, neutral, disinterested, unprejudiced, open-minded, non-partisan; honourable, upright, decent, honest, righteous, moral, virtuous, principled.
– OPPOSITES unjust, unfair.
• adverb **1** *she's just right for him:* **exactly**, precisely, absolutely, completely, totally, entirely, perfectly, utterly, wholly, thoroughly, in all respects; informal down to the ground, to a T, dead. **2** *we just made it:* **narrowly**, by a hair's breadth, by the skin of your teeth; barely, scarcely, hardly; informal by a whisker. **3** *she's just a child:* **only**, merely, simply, but, no more than. **4** *the colour's just fantastic:* **really**, absolutely, completely, entirely, totally, quite; indeed, truly, utterly.

justice noun **1** *I appealed to his sense of justice:* **fairness**, justness, fair play, fair-mindedness, equity, even-handedness, impartiality, objectivity, neutrality, disinterestedness, honesty, righteousness, morality. **2** *the justice of his case:* **validity**, justification, soundness, well-foundedness, legitimacy. **3 judge**, magistrate, recorder, sheriff; N. Amer. jurist; Brit. informal beak.

WORD LINKS
judicial relating to a system of justice

justifiable adjective **valid**, legitimate, warranted, well founded, justified, just, reasonable; defensible, tenable, supportable, acceptable.
– OPPOSITES indefensible.

justification noun **grounds**, reason, basis, rationale, premise, vindication, explanation; defence, argument; case.

justify verb **1** *directors must justify the expenditure:* **explain**, give grounds for, account for, rationalize; defend, vindicate, back up, support. **2** *the situation justified further investigation:* **warrant**, be good reason for, be a justification for.

justly adverb **1** *he is justly proud of his achievement:* **justifiably**, with reason, legitimately, rightly, rightfully, deservedly. **2** *they were treated justly:* **fairly**, with fairness, equitably, even-handedly, impartially, without bias, objectively, without prejudice.

jut verb **stick out**, project, protrude, bulge out, overhang.

juvenile adjective **1** *juvenile offenders:* **young**, teenage, adolescent, junior, pubescent, prepubescent. **2** *juvenile behaviour:* **childish**, immature, puerile, infantile, babyish; foolish, silly.
– OPPOSITES adult, mature.
• noun *many victims are juveniles:* **young person**, youngster, child, teenager, adolescent, minor, junior; informal kid.
– OPPOSITES adult.

juxtapose verb **put together**; compare, contrast.

Kk

kaleidoscopic adjective **multi-coloured**, many-hued, variegated, psychedelic, rainbow; ever-changing.
– OPPOSITES monochrome, constant.

keel noun *the upturned keel of the boat:* **base**, bottom, underside.
■ **keel over 1** *the boat keeled over:* capsize, turn turtle, turn upside down, founder; overturn, turn over, tip over. **2** *the slightest activity made him keel over:* collapse, faint, pass out, black out, lose consciousness; literary swoon.

k

keen adjective **1** *his publishers were keen to capitalize on his success:* **eager**, anxious, intent, impatient, determined; informal raring, itching, dying. **2** *a keen birdwatcher:* **enthusiastic**, avid, eager, ardent, fervent; conscientious, committed, dedicated, zealous, obsessive. **3** *they are keen on horses | a girl he was keen on:* **enthusiastic**, interested, passionate; attracted to, fond of, taken with, smitten with, enamoured of, infatuated with; informal struck on, gone on, mad about, crazy about, nuts about. **4** *a keen cutting edge:* **sharp**, well-honed, razor-sharp. **5** *keen eyesight:* **acute**, sharp, discerning, sensitive, perceptive, clear. **6** *a keen mind:* **acute**, penetrating, astute, incisive, sharp, perceptive, piercing, razor-sharp, shrewd, discerning, clever, intelligent, brilliant, bright, smart, wise, insightful. **7** *a keen wind:* **cold**, icy, freezing, harsh, raw, bitter; penetrating, piercing, biting. **8** *a keen sense of duty:* **intense**, acute, fierce, passionate, burning, fervent, ardent, strong, powerful.
– OPPOSITES reluctant, unenthusiastic.

keenness noun **1** *the company's keenness to sign a deal:* **eagerness**, willingness, readiness, impatience; enthusiasm, fervour, wholeheartedness, zest, zeal, ardour, passion. **2** *keenness of hearing:* **acuteness**, sharpness, sensitivity, perceptiveness, clarity. **3** *the keenness of his mind:* **acuity**, sharpness, incisiveness, astuteness, perceptiveness, shrewdness, insight, cleverness, discernment, intelligence, brightness, brilliance. **4** *the keenness of his sense of loss:* **intensity**, acuteness, strength, power; depth.

keep[1] verb **1** *you should keep all the old forms:* **retain**, hold on to; save, store, put by/aside, set aside; N. Amer. set by; informal hang on to. **2** *I tried to keep calm:* **remain**, stay, carry on being. **3** *he keeps going on about the murder:* **persist in**, keep on, carry on, continue, insist on. **4** *I shan't keep you long:* **detain**, keep waiting, delay, hold up, slow down. **5** *most people kept the rules | he had to keep his promise:* **comply with**, obey, observe, conform to, abide by, adhere to, stick to, heed, follow; carry out, act on, make good, honour, keep to, stand by. **6** *they're keeping the old traditions:* **preserve**, keep alive/up, keep going, carry on, perpetuate, maintain, uphold, sustain. **7** *the shop keeps a good stock of Californian wines:* **stock**, carry, have, hold; offer, boast. **8** *he stole to keep his family:* **provide for**, support, feed, maintain, sustain; take care of, look after. **9** *she keeps cattle and sheep:* **breed**, rear, raise, farm. **10** *his parents kept a small shop:* **manage**, run, own, operate.
– OPPOSITES discard, break, abandon.
• noun *who is paying for their keep?* **maintenance**, sustenance, board and lodging, food, livelihood.
■ **keep off** avoid, steer clear of, stay

away from. **keep on at** nag, go on at, badger, chivvy, harass, hound, pester; informal hassle. **keep to 1** *I've got to keep to the rules:* obey, abide by, observe, follow, comply with, adhere to, respect, stick to, be bound by. **2** *please keep to the point:* stick to, restrict yourself to, confine yourself to.

keep² noun *the enemy stormed the keep:* **fortress**, fort, stronghold, tower, donjon, castle, citadel, bastion.

keeper noun **curator**, custodian, guardian, administrator, overseer, steward, caretaker.

keeping noun *the document is in the keeping of the county archivist:* **care**, custody, charge, possession, trust, protection.
■ **in keeping with** consistent with, in harmony with, in accord with, in agreement with, in line with, in character with, compatible with; appropriate to, befitting, suitable for.

keepsake noun **memento**, souvenir, reminder, remembrance, token.

keg noun **barrel**, cask, vat, butt, hogshead; historical firkin.

kernel noun **1** *the kernel of a nut:* **seed**, grain, core, centre. **2** *the kernel of the argument:* **essence**, core, heart, essentials, quintessence, fundamentals, basics, nub, gist, substance; informal nitty-gritty. **3** *a kernel of truth:* **nucleus**, germ, grain, nugget.

key noun *the key to the mystery | the key to success:* **answer**, clue, solution, explanation; basis, foundation, requisite, precondition, means, way, route, path, passport, secret, formula.
• adjective *a key figure:* **crucial**, central, essential, indispensable, pivotal, critical, dominant, vital, principal, prime, chief, major, leading, main, important, significant.
– OPPOSITES peripheral.

keynote noun **theme**, gist, substance, burden, tenor, pith, marrow, essence, heart, core, basis.

keystone noun **foundation**, basis, linchpin, cornerstone, base, guiding principle, core, heart, centre, crux.

kick verb **1** *he kicked the ball into the net:* **boot**; Football punt. **2** (informal) *he's struggled to kick his drug habit:* **give up**, break, abandon, end, stop, cease, desist from, renounce; informal quit.
• noun **1** *a kick on the knee:* **blow**; Football punt; informal boot. **2** (informal) *I get a kick out of driving:* **thrill**, excitement, stimulation, tingle, frisson; informal buzz, high; N. Amer. informal charge. **3** (informal) *a drink with a powerful kick to it:* **effect**, strength, power; tang, zest, bite, edge; informal punch, hit. **4** (informal) *a health kick:* **craze**, obsession, mania; informal fad, trip, thing.
■ **kick off** (informal) start, commence, begin, get going, get off the ground, get under way; open, start off, set in motion, launch, initiate, introduce, inaugurate, usher in. **kick someone out** (informal) expel, eject, throw out, oust, evict, get rid of, axe; dismiss, discharge; informal chuck out, send packing, boot out, give someone their marching orders, sack, fire; Brit. informal turf out; N. Amer. informal give someone the bum's rush.

kickback noun (informal) **bribe**, inducement; N. Amer. payola; informal pay-off, sweetener, backhander.

kick-off noun (informal) **beginning**, start, commencement, outset, opening.

kid noun (informal) **child**, youngster, baby, toddler, tot, infant, boy, girl, minor, juvenile, adolescent, teenager, youth; offspring, son/daughter; Scottish bairn; informal kiddie, nipper, kiddiewink, shaver; Brit. informal sprog; N. Amer. informal rug rat; Austral./NZ ankle-biter; derogatory brat; literary babe.

kidnap verb **abduct**, carry off, capture, seize, snatch, take hostage.

kidney noun

> **WORD LINKS**
> **renal** relating to the kidneys

kill verb **1** *gangs killed twenty-seven people:* **murder**, put to death, execute, assassinate, eliminate, terminate, dispatch, finish off; slaughter, butcher, massacre, wipe out, annihilate, exterminate, liquidate, mow down; informal bump off, polish off, do away with, do in, knock off, top, take out, blow away, dispose of; N. Amer. informal rub out, waste; literary slay. **2** *this would kill all hopes of progress:* **destroy**, put an end to, end, extinguish, dash, quash, ruin, wreck, shatter, smash, crush, scotch, thwart; informal put paid to, put the kibosh on, stymie; Brit. informal scupper. **3** *we had a few hours to kill at the airport:* **while away**, fill, occupy, beguile, pass, spend, waste. **4** *a shot of morphine to kill the pain:* **alleviate**, assuage, soothe, allay, dull, blunt, deaden, stifle, suppress, subdue.

killer noun **murderer**, assassin, butcher, serial killer, gunman; executioner; informal hit man; literary slayer.

killing noun **murder**, assassination, homicide, manslaughter, execution; slaughter, massacre, butchery, carnage, bloodshed, extermination, annihilation; literary slaying.

k

killjoy noun **spoilsport**, prophet of doom; informal wet blanket, party-pooper, misery; Austral./NZ informal wowser.

kin noun **relatives**, relations, family, kindred; kinsfolk, kinsmen, kinswomen, people; informal folks.

kind[1] noun **1** *all kinds of gifts | the kinds of bird that could be seen:* **sort**, type, variety, style, form, class, category, genre; genus, species, race, breed. **2** *they were different in kind | the first of its kind:* **character**, nature, essence, quality, disposition, make-up; type, style, manner, description, temperament, ilk; N. Amer. stripe.

■ **kind of** (informal) rather, quite, fairly, somewhat, a little, slightly, a shade; informal sort of, a bit, kinda, pretty, a touch, a tad.

kind[2] adjective *a kind and caring person:* **kindly**, good-natured, kind-hearted, warm-hearted, caring, affectionate, loving, warm; considerate, helpful, thoughtful, obliging, unselfish, selfless, altruistic, good, attentive; compassionate, sympathetic, understanding, big-hearted, benevolent, benign, friendly, neighbourly, hospitable, well meaning, public-spirited; generous, liberal, open-handed, bountiful, munificent; Brit. informal decent.

– OPPOSITES inconsiderate, mean.

kind-hearted adjective **kind**, caring, warm-hearted, kindly, benevolent, good-natured, tender, warm, compassionate, sympathetic, understanding; indulgent, altruistic, benign.

kindle verb **1** *he kindled a fire:* **light**, ignite, set light to, set fire to, put a match to. **2** *his early recordings kindled my interest in music:* **rouse**, arouse, wake, awaken; stimulate, inspire, stir up, excite, evoke, provoke, fire, inflame, trigger, activate, spark off.

– OPPOSITES extinguish.

kindliness noun **kindness**, benevolence, warmth, gentleness, tenderness, care, humanity, sympathy, compassion, understanding; generosity, charity, kind-heartedness, warm-heartedness, thoughtfulness.

kindly adjective *a kindly old lady:* **benevolent**, kind, kind-hearted, warm-hearted, generous, good-natured; gentle, warm, compassionate, caring, loving, benign, well meaning; helpful, thoughtful, considerate, good-hearted, nice, friendly, neighbourly.

– OPPOSITES unkind, cruel.

• adverb **nicely**, warmly, affectionately, tenderly, lovingly, compassionately; considerately, thoughtfully, helpfully, obligingly, generously, selflessly, unselfishly.

– OPPOSITES unkindly, harshly.

kindness noun **kindliness**, kind-heartedness, warm-heartedness, affection, warmth, gentleness, concern, care; consideration, helpfulness, thoughtfulness, unselfishness, selflessness, altruism, compassion, sympathy, understanding, big-heartedness, benevolence, friendliness, neighbourliness, hospitality; generosity, magnanimity.

king noun **1** *the king of France:* **ruler**, sovereign, monarch, Crown, emperor, prince, potentate. **2** (informal) *the king of world football:* **number one**, leading light, master, leader; informal supremo, maestro, top dog.

WORD LINKS

regal, royal relating to a king or queen

regicide the killing of a king

kingdom noun **realm**, domain, dominion, country, empire, land, territory; nation, sovereign state, state, province.

kink noun **curl**, twist, twirl, loop; knot, tangle, entanglement, bend.

kinky adjective **1** (informal) *a kinky relationship:* **perverted**, abnormal, deviant, unnatural, depraved, degenerate, perverse; informal pervy. **2** (informal) *kinky underwear:* **sexy**, provocative, arousing, erotic, titillating, naughty, rude; Brit. informal saucy.

kinship noun **1** *ties of kinship:* **relationship**, family, blood, ancestry, kindred. **2** *she felt kinship with the others:* **affinity**, sympathy, rapport, harmony, understanding, empathy, closeness, bond, compatibility; similarity, likeness, correspondence.

kiosk noun **booth**, stand, stall, counter, news-stand.

kiss verb informal peck someone on the cheek, give someone a smacker; smooch, canoodle, neck, pet; Brit. informal snog; N. Amer. informal buss; informal, dated spoon; rare osculate. • **noun** informal peck on the cheek, smacker; Brit. informal snog; N. Amer. informal buss.

kit noun **1** *his tool kit:* **equipment**, tools, implements, instruments, gadgets, utensils, appliances, tools of the trade, gear, tackle, hardware, paraphernalia; Military accoutrements. **2** (Brit. informal) *their football kit:* **clothes**, clothing, rig, outfit, dress, costume, garments, attire, garb, gear, get-up, rig-out. **3** *a model aircraft kit:* **set**, pack, flat-pack.
■ **kit someone/something out** equip, fit out/up, furnish, supply, provide, issue; dress, clothe, array, attire, rig out, deck out; informal fix up.

kitchen noun kitchenette, kitchen-diner, cooking area, galley, cookhouse; N. Amer. cookery.

kittenish adjective **playful**, light-hearted, skittish, lively; coquettish, flirtatious, frivolous, flippant, superficial, trivial, shallow, silly; informal flirty, dizzy; literary frolicsome.
– OPPOSITES serious.

knack noun **1** *a knack for making money | it takes practice to acquire the knack:* **gift**, talent, flair, genius, instinct, faculty, ability, capability, capacity, aptitude, bent, forte, facility; technique, method, trick, skill, art, expertise; informal the hang of something. **2** *he has a knack of getting injured at the wrong time:* **tendency**, propensity, habit, proneness, liability, predisposition.

knapsack noun **rucksack**, backpack, haversack, pack, kitbag.

knead verb **1** *kneading the dough:* **pummel**, work, pound, squeeze, shape, mould. **2** *she kneaded the base of his neck:* **massage**, press, manipulate, rub.

kneel verb **fall to your knees**, get down on your knees, genuflect; historical kowtow.

knick-knack noun **ornament**, novelty, trinket, trifle, bauble, curio; memento, souvenir; N. Amer. kickshaw; N. Amer. informal tchotchke; old use bijou.

k

knife verb *he was knifed in the back:* **stab**, hack, gash, slash, lacerate, cut, bayonet.

knight noun **cavalier**, cavalryman, horseman; lord, noble, nobleman; historical chevalier, paladin.

knit verb **1** *disparate regions began to knit together:* **unite**, unify, come together, bond, fuse, coalesce, merge, meld, blend. **2** *we expect broken bones to knit:* **heal**, mend, join, fuse. **3** *Marcus knitted his brows:* **furrow**, contract, gather, wrinkle.

knob noun **1** *a black rod with a knob at the base:* **lump**, bump, protuberance, protrusion, bulge, swelling, knot, node, nodule, ball, boss. **2** *the knobs on the radio:* **dial**, button. **3** *a knob of butter:* **lump**, nugget, pat, ball, dollop, piece; N. Amer. informal gob.

knock verb **1** *he knocked on the door:* **bang**, tap, rap, thump, pound, hammer; strike, beat. **2** *she knocked her knee on the table:* **bump**, bang, hit, strike, crack; injure, hurt; informal bash, whack. **3** *he knocked into an elderly man:* **collide with**, bump into, bang into, run into, crash into, smash into, plough into; N. Amer. impact. **4** (informal) *I'm not knocking the company.* See CRITICIZE.

• noun **1** *a knock at the door:* **tap**, rap, rat-tat, knocking, bang, banging, pounding, hammering, thump, thud. **2** *the casing is tough enough to withstand knocks:* **bump**, blow, bang, jolt, jar, shock; collision, crash, smash, impact. **3** *life's hard knocks:* **setback**, reversal, defeat, failure, difficulty, misfortune, mishap, blow, disaster, calamity, disappointment; informal kick in the teeth.

■ **knock someone down** fell, floor, flatten, bring down; knock over, run over/down. **knock something down** demolish, pull down, tear down, destroy; raze to the ground, level, flatten, bulldoze. **knock someone out 1** *I hit him and knocked him out:* fell, floor, prostrate; informal lay out, KO. **2** *they were knocked out by Portugal in the second round:* eliminate, beat, defeat, overwhelm, trounce; literary vanquish. **knock something up** (Brit. informal) improvise, contrive; informal whip up, rig up, throw together, cobble together, rustle up.

knoll noun **hillock**, mound, rise, hummock, hill, hump, tor, bank, ridge, elevation; Scottish brae; literary eminence.

knot noun **1** *a knot in the wood:* **nodule**, gnarl, node; lump, knob, swelling, protuberance, bump. **2** *a small knot of people:* **cluster**, group, band, huddle, bunch, circle, ring, gathering.

• verb *a scarf knotted round her throat:* **tie**, fasten, secure, bind, do up.

knotted adjective **tangled**, knotty, matted, snarled, unkempt, uncombed, tousled; informal mussed up.

knotty adjective *a knotty problem:* **complex**, complicated, involved, intricate, convoluted; difficult, hard, thorny, taxing, awkward, tricky, problematic, troublesome.

– OPPOSITES straightforward.

know verb **1** *she doesn't know I'm here:* **be aware**, realize, be conscious; notice, perceive, see, sense, recognize. **2** *I don't know his address:* **have**, be apprised of; formal be cognizant of. **3** *do you know the rules?* **be familiar with**, be conversant with, be acquainted with, be versed in, have a good grasp of, understand, comprehend; have learned; informal be clued up on. **4** *I don't know many people here:* **be acquainted with**, be familiar with; Scottish ken.

know-all noun (informal) **wiseacre**; informal smart alec, wise guy, smarty-pants; Brit. informal clever clogs, clever Dick; N. Amer. informal know-it-all.

know-how noun (informal) **knowledge**, expertise, skill, proficiency, understanding, mastery, technique; ability, capability, competence, capacity, adeptness, dexterity, deftness, adroitness; informal savvy.

knowing adjective **1** *a knowing smile:* **significant**, meaningful, expressive, suggestive; arch, sly, mischievous, impish, superior. **2** *she's a very knowing child:* **sophisticated**, worldly, worldly-wise, urbane, experienced; knowledgeable, well informed, enlightened; shrewd, astute, canny, sharp, wily, perceptive; informal streetwise. **3** *a knowing infringement of the rules:* **deliberate**, intentional, conscious, calculated, wilful, done on purpose, premeditated, planned; cynical.

knowingly adverb **deliberately**, intentionally, consciously, wittingly, on purpose, by design, premeditatedly, wilfully; cynically.

knowledge noun **1** *his knowledge of history | technical knowledge:* **understanding**, comprehension, grasp, command, mastery; expertise, skill, proficiency, expertness, accomplishment, adeptness, capacity, capability; informal know-how. **2** *people anxious to display their knowledge:* **learning**, erudition, education, scholarship, schooling, wisdom. **3** *he slipped away without my knowledge:* **awareness**, consciousness, realization, cognition, apprehension, perception, appreciation; formal cognizance. **4** *an intimate knowledge of the countryside:* **familiarity**, acquaintance, conversance, intimacy.

– OPPOSITES ignorance.

WORD LINKS
gnostic relating to knowledge

knowledgeable adjective **1** *a knowledgeable old man:* **well informed**, learned, well read, educated, erudite, scholarly,

cultured, cultivated, enlightened. **2** *he is knowledgeable about modern art:* **conversant**, familiar, well acquainted, au fait; up on, up to date with, abreast of; informal clued-up, genned up; Brit. informal switched-on.
– OPPOSITES ill-informed.

known adjective *a known criminal:* **recognized**, well known, widely known, noted, celebrated, notable, notorious; acknowledged, self-confessed, declared, overt.

kowtow verb **grovel**, be obsequious, be servile, be sycophantic, fawn on, bow and scrape, toady, abase yourself; curry favour with, dance attendance on, ingratiate yourself with; informal crawl, creep, suck up, lick someone's boots; Austral./NZ informal smoodge to.

kudos noun **prestige**, cachet, glory, honour, status, standing, distinction, fame, celebrity; admiration, respect, esteem, acclaim, praise, credit.

label noun **1** *the price is clearly stated on the label:* **tag**, ticket, tab, sticker, marker, docket. **2** *a designer label:* **brand**, name, trademark, make, logo. **3** *I resented the label the media came up with for me:* **designation**, description, tag; name, epithet, nickname, title, sobriquet, pet name; formal appellation.
•verb **1** *label each jar with the date:* **tag**, ticket, mark. **2** *tests labelled him as an underachiever:* **categorize**, classify, class, describe, designate, identify; mark, stamp, brand, condemn, pigeonhole, stereotype, typecast; call, name, term, dub, nickname.

laborious adjective **1** *a laborious job:* **arduous**, hard, heavy, difficult, strenuous, gruelling, punishing, exacting, tough, onerous, burdensome, back-breaking, trying, challenging; wearing; tedious, boring. **2** *his slow, laborious style:* **laboured**, strained, forced, stiff, stilted, unnatural, artificial, overwrought, heavy, ponderous.
–OPPOSITES easy, effortless.

labour noun **1** *manual labour:* **work**, toil, exertion, industry, drudgery, effort, donkey work; informal slog, grind, sweat, elbow grease; Brit. informal graft; literary travail. **2** *the conflict between capital and labour:* **workers**, employees, the workforce, staff, labourers, the proletariat. **3** *a difficult labour:* **childbirth**, birth, delivery; contractions; literary travail; dated confinement.
–OPPOSITES rest.
•verb **1** *a project on which he had laboured for many years:* **work**, toil, slave away, grind away, exert yourself, work your fingers to the bone, work like a Trojan, work like a dog; informal slog away, plug away; Brit. informal graft. **2** *Newcastle laboured to break down their defence:* **strive**, struggle, endeavour, work, try hard, make every effort, do your best, do your utmost, give your all, go all out, fight, exert yourself; informal bend over backwards, pull out all the stops.

laboured adjective **1** *his laboured breathing:* **strained**, difficult, forced, laborious. **2** *a rather laboured joke:* **contrived**, forced, strained, unnatural, artificial, overdone, ponderous, unconvincing.

labourer noun **workman**, worker, working man, manual worker, blue-collar worker, hand, roustabout; Brit. dated navvy.

labyrinth noun **1** *a labyrinth of little streets:* **maze**, warren, network, complex, web. **2** *the labyrinth of conflicting laws and regulations:* **tangle**, web, maze, morass, jungle.

labyrinthine adjective **1** *labyrinthine corridors:* **maze-like**, winding, twisting, serpentine, meandering. **2** *a labyrinthine criminal justice system:* **complicated**, intricate, complex, involved, tortuous, convoluted, tangled, elaborate; confusing, puzzling, mystifying, bewildering, baffling.

lace verb **1** *he laced up his running shoes:* **fasten**, do up, tie up, secure, knot. **2** *tea laced with rum:* **flavour**, mix, fortify, strengthen, season, spice, liven up; doctor, adulterate; informal spike.

lacerate verb **cut**, gash, slash, tear, rip, shred, score, scratch; wound, hurt; literary rend.

laceration noun **gash**, cut, wound, injury, tear, slash, scratch, scrape, abrasion, graze.

lack noun *a lack of cash:* **absence**,

shortage, deficiency, dearth, shortfall, scarcity, paucity, scarceness, deficit; want, need.
– OPPOSITES abundance.
• verb *she's immature and lacks judgement:* **be without**, be in need of, need, be lacking, require, want, be short of, be deficient in, be low on, have insufficient; informal be strapped for.
– OPPOSITES have, possess.

lackadaisical adjective **careless**, lazy, lax, slapdash, sloppy, haphazard, casual, desultory, unenthusiastic, half-hearted, unconcerned, blasé; apathetic, lethargic, listless; informal laid back, couldn't-care-less.
– OPPOSITES enthusiastic.

lacking adjective **1** *proof was lacking:* **absent**, missing, non-existent, unavailable. **2** *the advocate general found the government lacking:* **deficient**, defective, inadequate, wanting; flawed, faulty, unacceptable. **3** *the game was lacking in atmosphere:* **without**, devoid of, bereft of; deficient in, low on, short on, in need of.
– OPPOSITES present, plentiful.

lacklustre adjective **uninspired**, uninspiring, unimaginative, dull, humdrum, colourless, characterless, bland, insipid, flat, dry, lifeless, tame, prosaic; dreary, tedious.
– OPPOSITES inspired.

laconic adjective **brief**, concise, terse, brusque, short, monosyllabic, succinct, pithy.
– OPPOSITES verbose.

lad noun (informal) **1** *a twelve-year-old lad:* **boy**, schoolboy, youth, youngster, juvenile; informal kid, nipper, whippersnapper; Scottish informal laddie; derogatory brat; humorous stripling. **2** *a hard-working lad:* **young man**, man, fellow; informal guy, geezer; Brit. informal chap, bloke; N. Amer. informal dude, hombre; Austral./NZ informal digger.

ladder noun *the academic ladder:* **hierarchy**, scale, ranking, pecking order.

laden adjective **loaded**, burdened, weighed down, overloaded, piled high; full, filled, packed, stuffed, crammed; informal chock-full, chock-a-block.

ladle verb **spoon out**, scoop out, dish up/out, serve, distribute.

lady noun **1** *several ladies were present:* **woman**, female; N. Amer. informal dame, broad; Austral./NZ informal sheila; literary maid, damsel; old use wench. **2** *lords and ladies:* **noblewoman**, duchess, countess, peeress, viscountess, baroness; old use gentlewoman.

ladylike adjective **genteel**, polite, refined, well bred, cultivated, polished, decorous, proper, respectable, seemly, well mannered, cultured, sophisticated, elegant; Brit. informal posh.
– OPPOSITES coarse.

lag verb **fall behind**, straggle, fall back, trail, hang back, bring up the rear.

laid-back adjective (informal) **relaxed**, easy-going, equable, free and easy, casual, nonchalant, insouciant, unexcitable, blasé, cool, calm, unconcerned; leisurely, unhurried; informal unflappable.
– OPPOSITES uptight.

laid up adjective (informal) **bedridden**, housebound, incapacitated, injured; ill, sick, unwell, poorly, ailing, indisposed.
– OPPOSITES healthy, active.

lair noun **1** *the lair of a large animal:* **den**, burrow, hole, tunnel, cave. **2** *a villain's lair:* **hideaway**, hiding place, hideout, den, base; informal hidey-hole.

lake noun pond, pool, tarn, reservoir, lagoon, waterhole, inland sea; Scottish loch; Anglo-Irish lough; N. Amer. bayou; literary mere.

WORD LINKS
lacustrine relating to lakes

lambaste verb **criticize**, chastise, censure, take to task, harangue; upbraid, scold, reprimand, rebuke, chide, reprove, admonish, berate; informal lay into, give someone a dressing-down, carpet, tell off, bawl out; Brit. informal tick off, slam; N. Amer. informal chew out; formal castigate, excoriate.

lame adjective **1** *the mare was lame:* **limping**, hobbling; incapacitated; informal gammy. **2** *a lame excuse:* **feeble**, weak, thin, flimsy, poor; unconvincing, implausible, unlikely.
– OPPOSITES convincing.

lament verb **bemoan**, bewail, complain about, deplore; protest against, object to, oppose, fulminate against, inveigh against, denounce.
– OPPOSITES celebrate.

lamentable adjective *the industry is in a lamentable state:* **deplorable**, regrettable, terrible, awful, wretched, woeful, dire, disastrous, desperate, grave, appalling, dreadful; pitiful, shameful, unfortunate; formal egregious.
– OPPOSITES commendable.

lamentation noun **weeping**, wailing, crying, sobbing, moaning, grieving, mourning.

lamp noun **light**, lantern; torch.

lampoon verb *he was mercilessly lampooned in the press:* **satirize**, mock, ridicule, make fun of, caricature, parody, tease; informal send up.
• noun *a lampoon of student life in the 1970s:* **satire**, burlesque, parody, skit, caricature, mockery; informal send-up, take-off, spoof.

l

lance noun *a knight with a lance:* **spear**, pike, javelin.

land noun **1** *Lyme Park has 1323 acres of land | publicly owned land:* **grounds**, fields, open space; property, territory, acres, acreage, estate, lands, real estate; countryside, rural area, green belt; historical demesne. **2** *Tunisia is a land of variety:* **country**, nation, nation state, realm, kingdom, province; region, area, place, domain. **3** *the lookout sighted land to the east:* **terra firma**, dry land; coast, coastline, shore.
• verb **1** *Allied troops landed in France:* **disembark**, go ashore, debark, alight, get off. **2** *the ship landed at Le Havre:* **berth**, dock, moor, anchor, drop anchor, tie up, put in. **3** *their plane landed at Chicago:* **touch down**, come in to land, come down. **4** *a bird landed on the branch:* **perch**, settle, come to rest, alight. **5** (informal) *Nick landed the job of editor:* **get**, obtain, acquire, secure, gain, net, win, achieve, attain, bag, carry off; informal swing. **6** (informal) *that habit landed her in trouble:* **get**, bring, lead. **7** (informal) *they landed her with the bill:* **burden**, leave, saddle, encumber; informal dump; Brit. informal lumber.
– OPPOSITES sail, take off.
■ **land up** finish up, find yourself, end up; informal wind up, fetch up.

WORD LINKS
terrestrial relating to land

landlord, **landlady** noun **1** *the landlord of the pub:* **publican**, licensee, innkeeper, owner, hotelier, restaurateur; manager, manageress. **2** *the landlady had objected to the noise:* **owner**, proprietor, proprietress, lessor, householder, landowner.
– OPPOSITES tenant.

landmark noun **1** *one of London's most famous landmarks:* **monument**, feature; building. **2** *the ruling was hailed as a landmark:* **turning point**, milestone, watershed, critical point.

landscape noun **scenery**, countryside, topography, country, terrain, land.

landslide noun **1** *floods and landslides:* **landslip**, mudslide; avalanche. **2** *the Labour landslide:* **victory**, overwhelming majority, triumph.

lane noun **1** *country lanes:* **byroad**, byway, track, road; alley, alleyway. **2** *cycle lanes:* **track**, way, course.

language noun **1** *the grammatical structure of language:* **speech**, writing, communication, discourse; conversation, speaking, talking, talk; words, vocabulary, text. **2** *the English language:* **tongue**, mother tongue, native tongue, dialect; informal lingo; lingua franca. **3** *the booklet is written in simple, everyday language:* **wording**, phrasing, phraseology, style, vocabulary, terminology, expressions, turn of phrase, parlance, form of expression, usage, idiolect; speech, dialect, patois, slang, idiom, jargon, argot, cant.

WORD LINKS
linguistic relating to language
linguistics the scientific study of language

languid adjective **1** *a languid wave of the hand:* **relaxed**, unhurried, languorous, slow; lazy, idle, indolent, lethargic, listless, apathetic; informal laid-back. **2** *a pale, languid individual:* **sickly**, weak,

faint, feeble, frail, delicate; tired, weary, fatigued.
–OPPOSITES energetic.

languish verb **1** *all the plants languished and died:* **weaken**, deteriorate, decline, go downhill; wither, droop, wilt, fade, waste away. **2** *the general is now languishing in prison:* **waste away**, rot, be abandoned, be neglected, be forgotten, suffer; lie.
–OPPOSITES thrive.

languor noun **lassitude**, sleepiness, drowsiness, lethargy, listlessness, torpor, fatigue, weariness, tiredness; laziness, idleness, indolence, inertia.
–OPPOSITES vigour.

lank adjective *lank, greasy hair:* **limp**, lifeless, lustreless, dull; straggling; straight, long.

lanky adjective **tall**, **thin**, lean, skinny, spindly, spare, gangling, gangly, gawky; slender, slim, rangy.
–OPPOSITES stocky.

lap[1] noun *a book lay open on her lap:* **knee**, knees, thighs.

lap[2] noun *a race of eight laps:* **circuit**.
•verb *she lapped the other runners:* **overtake**, outstrip, leave behind, pass, go past; catch up with.

lap[3] verb **1** *waves lapped against the sea wall:* **splash**, wash, swish, slosh, break; literary plash. **2** *the dog lapped water out of a puddle:* **drink**, lick up, swallow, slurp, gulp.
■ **lap something up** *she lapped up all the attention:* relish, revel in, savour, delight in, wallow in, glory in, enjoy.

lapse noun **1** *a lapse of concentration:* **failure**, slip, error, mistake, blunder, fault, omission; informal slip-up. **2** *his lapse into petty crime:* **decline**, fall, descent, slide, drop, deterioration, degeneration, backsliding, regression. **3** *a lapse of time:* **interval**, gap, pause, interlude, lull, hiatus, break.
•verb **1** *the planning permission has lapsed:* **expire**, become void, become invalid, run out. **2** *the country has lapsed into chaos:* **degenerate**, deteriorate, sink, slide, slip, decline, backslide, fall, drop, regress; revert, relapse.

lapsed adjective **1** *a lapsed Catholic:* **non-practising**, backsliding, apostate. **2** *a lapsed season ticket:* **expired**, void, invalid, out of date.
–OPPOSITES practising, valid.

larceny noun. See **THEFT**.

larder noun **pantry**, food store; cooler; Brit. buttery.

large adjective **1** *a large house | large numbers of people:* **big**, sizeable, substantial, considerable, immense, enormous, massive, gigantic, colossal, vast, prodigious; tall, high; voluminous. **2** *a large red-faced man:* **big**, burly, heavy, tall, bulky, thickset, chunky, hefty, muscular, brawny, solid, powerful, sturdy, strong; fat, plump, overweight, chubby, stout, meaty, fleshy, portly, rotund, flabby, paunchy, obese, corpulent; informal beefy, tubby, pudgy; Brit. informal podgy; N. Amer. informal zaftig, corn-fed. **3** *a large supply of wool:* **abundant**, copious, plentiful, ample, liberal, generous, lavish, bountiful, good, considerable, superabundant; literary plenteous.
–OPPOSITES small, meagre.

largely adverb **mostly**, mainly, to a large/great extent, chiefly, predominantly, primarily, principally, for the most part, in the main; typically, commonly.

largesse noun **generosity**, liberality, munificence, bountifulness, beneficence, altruism, charity, philanthropy, magnanimity, benevolence, charitableness, open-handedness, kindness.
–OPPOSITES meanness.

lark (informal) noun **1** *we were just having a bit of a lark:* **laugh**, giggle, joke; prank, trick, jape. **2** *I've got this snowboarding lark sussed:* informal **thing**, business, racket, caper, trip.
•verb *he's always larking about:* **fool about/around**, play tricks, make mischief, monkey about/around, clown about/around, have fun, skylark; informal mess about/around; Brit. informal muck about/around.

lascivious adjective **lecherous**, lewd, lustful, licentious, libidinous, salacious, lubricious, prurient, dirty, smutty, naughty, suggestive, indecent; informal horny; Brit. informal randy; formal concupiscent.

lash verb **1** *rain lashed the window panes:* **beat against**, dash against,

l

pound, batter, strike, hit, drum against. **2** *the tiger began to lash its tail:* **swish**, flick, twitch, whip. **3** *two boats were lashed together:* **fasten**, tie, bind, tether, hitch, knot, rope, make fast.

■ **lash out 1** *the president lashed out at the opposition:* criticize, attack, condemn, denounce, lambaste, harangue, pillory; berate, upbraid, rebuke, reproach; informal lay into; formal castigate. **2** *he lashed out at her with a knife:* hit out, strike, let fly, take a swing; set upon/about, turn on, round on, attack; informal lay into, pitch into.

lass noun (Scottish & N. English) **girl**, young woman, young lady; Scottish lassie; Irish colleen; N. Amer. informal dame, babe, gal, broad; Austral./NZ informal sheila; literary maid, maiden, damsel; old use wench.

lassitude noun **lethargy**, listlessness, weariness, languor, sluggishness, tiredness, fatigue, torpor, apathy.
– OPPOSITES vigour.

last[1] adjective **1** *the last woman in the queue:* **rearmost**, hindmost, endmost, furthest back, final, ultimate. **2** *Rembrandt spent his last years in Amsterdam:* **closing**, concluding, final, end, terminal; later, latter. **3** *we met last year:* **previous**, preceding; prior, former. **4** *this was his last chance:* **final**, only remaining.
– OPPOSITES first, early, next.
• noun *the most important business was left to the last:* **end**, ending, finish, close, conclusion, finale.
– OPPOSITES beginning.

■ **at last** finally, in the end, eventually, ultimately, at long last, after a long time, in time. **the last word** *the last word in luxury:* the best, the peak, the acme, the epitome, the latest; the pinnacle, the apex, the apogee, the ultimate, the height, the zenith, the crème de la crème.

last[2] verb **1** *the storm lasted for six hours:* **continue**, go on, carry on, keep on/going, proceed, take; stay, remain, persist. **2** *how long will he last as manager?* **survive**, endure, hold on/out, keep going, persevere; informal stick it out, hang on, hack it. **3** *the car is built to last:* **endure**, wear well, stand up, bear up; informal go the distance.

last-ditch adjective *a last-ditch attempt to save the plan from collapse:* **last-minute**, last-chance, eleventh-hour, last-resort, desperate, final; informal last-gasp.

lasting adjective **enduring**, long-lasting, long-lived, abiding, continuing, long-term, permanent; durable, stable, secure, long-standing; eternal, undying, ever-lasting, unending, never-ending.
– OPPOSITES ephemeral.

lastly adverb **finally**, in conclusion, to conclude, to sum up, to end, last, ultimately.
– OPPOSITES firstly.

late adjective **1** *the train was late:* **behind time**, behind schedule; tardy, overdue, delayed. **2** *her late husband:* **dead**, departed, lamented, passed on/away; formal deceased.
– OPPOSITES punctual, early.
• adverb *she had arrived late:* **behind schedule**, behind time, belatedly, tardily, at the last minute.

lately adverb **recently**, of late, latterly.

lateness noun **unpunctuality**, tardiness, delay.

latent adjective **dormant**, untapped, unused, undiscovered, hidden, concealed, unseen, undeveloped, unrealized, unfulfilled, potential.

later adjective *a later chapter:* **subsequent**, following, succeeding, future, upcoming, to come, ensuing, next.
– OPPOSITES earlier.
• adverb **1** *later, the film rights were sold:* **subsequently**, eventually, then, next, later on, after this/that, afterwards, at a later date, in the future, in due course, by and by, in a while, in time. **2** *two days later a letter arrived:* **afterwards**, later on, after this/that, subsequently, following; formal thereafter.

lateral adjective **1** *lateral movements:* **sideways**, sideward, to the side, edgeways, oblique. **2** *lateral thinking:* **unorthodox**, creative, imaginative, original, innovative; new, novel, different.

latest adjective **most recent**, newest, just out, just released, fresh, up to date, up to the minute, state-of-the-art, cutting-edge, leading-edge, current, modern, contemporary,

fashionable, in fashion, in vogue; informal in, with it, trendy, hip, hot, happening, cool.
– OPPOSITES old.

lather noun *a rich, soapy lather:* **foam**, froth, suds, bubbles; literary spume.

latitude noun **freedom**, scope, leeway, space, flexibility, liberty, independence, free rein, licence, room to manoeuvre, slack.
– OPPOSITES restriction.

latter adjective **1** *the latter half of the season:* **later**, closing, end, concluding, final. **2** *Russia chose the latter option:* **last-mentioned**, second, last, final.
– OPPOSITES former.

latter-day adjective **modern**, present-day, current, contemporary.

latterly adverb **1** *latterly, she has been in more pain:* **recently**, lately, of late. **2** *latterly he worked as a political editor:* **ultimately**, finally, towards the end.

lattice noun **grid**, framework, trellis, network, mesh; matrix.

laudable adjective **praiseworthy**, commendable, admirable, worthy, deserving, creditable, estimable, exemplary.
– OPPOSITES shameful.

laugh verb **1** *he started to laugh:* **chuckle**, chortle, guffaw, giggle, titter, snigger, snicker, burst out laughing, roar, hoot, dissolve into laughter, split your sides, be doubled up; informal be in stitches, be rolling in the aisles, crease up, fall about, crack up. **2** *people laughed at his theories:* **ridicule**, mock, deride, scoff at, jeer at, sneer at, jibe at, make fun of, poke fun at, scorn; lampoon, satirize; informal take the mickey out of, pooh-pooh.
• noun **1** *she gave a short laugh:* **chuckle**, chortle, guffaw, giggle, titter, snigger, snicker, roar, hoot, shriek, belly laugh. **2** (informal) *he was a right laugh:* **joker**, wit, clown, jester, prankster, character; informal card, case, hoot, scream, riot, barrel of laughs; informal wag; Austral./NZ informal hard case. **3** (informal) *I entered the contest for a laugh:* **joke**, prank, bit of fun, jest; informal lark.
■ **laugh something off** dismiss, make a joke of, make light of, shrug off, brush aside, scoff at; informal pooh-pooh.

laughable adjective **ridiculous**, ludicrous, absurd, risible, preposterous; foolish, silly, idiotic, stupid, nonsensical, crazy, insane, outrageous; Brit. informal daft.

laughing stock noun **figure of fun**, dupe, butt, stooge.

laughter noun **1** *the laughter subsided:* **laughing**, chuckling, chortling, guffawing, giggling, tittering, sniggering. **2** *a source of laughter:* **amusement**, entertainment, humour, mirth, merriment, gaiety, hilarity, jollity, fun.

launch verb **1** *the government launched a new campaign:* **initiate**, get going, get under way, start, commence, begin, present, inaugurate, set up, introduce; informal kick off. **2** *a chair was launched at him:* **throw**, hurl, fling, pitch, lob, let fly; fire, shoot; informal chuck, heave, sling.

lavatory noun **toilet**, WC, public convenience, cloakroom, powder room, urinal, privy, latrine; N. Amer. washroom, bathroom, rest room, men's/ladies' room, comfort station; Nautical head; Brit. informal loo, bog, the Ladies, the Gents, khazi; N. Amer. informal can, john; Austral./NZ informal dunny; old use closet, jakes.

lavish adjective **1** *a lavish apartment:* **sumptuous**, luxurious, gorgeous, costly, expensive, opulent, grand, splendid, rich, fancy; informal posh. **2** *he was lavish with his hospitality:* **generous**, liberal, bountiful, unstinting, unsparing, free, munificent, extravagant, prodigal. **3** *lavish amounts of champagne:* **abundant**, copious, plentiful, liberal, prolific, generous; literary plenteous.
– OPPOSITES meagre, frugal.
• verb *she lavished money on her children:* **shower**, heap, throw at.

law noun **1** *the law of the land:* **rules and regulations**, constitution, legislation, legal code. **2** *a new law:* **regulation**, statute, act, bill, decree, edict, rule, ruling, resolution, dictum, command, order, directive, dictate, diktat, fiat, by-law; N. Amer. formal ordinance. **3** *the laws of the game:* **rule**, regulation, principle, convention, instruction; guidelines.

4 *a moral law:* **principle**, rule, precept, commandment, belief, creed, credo, maxim, tenet, doctrine, canon.

> **WORD LINKS**
> **legal**, **judicial**, **juridical** relating to laws

law-abiding adjective **honest**, lawful, upright, upstanding, good, decent, dutiful, obedient, virtuous, moral, righteous.
– OPPOSITES criminal.

lawbreaker noun **criminal**, felon, wrongdoer, evildoer, offender, transgressor, miscreant; villain, rogue; informal crook; formal malefactor.

lawful adjective **legitimate**, legal, licit, just, permissible, permitted, allowable, allowed, rightful, sanctioned, authorized, warranted, within the law; informal legit.
– OPPOSITES illegal, unlawful.

lawless adjective **anarchic**, disorderly, wild, ungovernable, unruly, rebellious, insubordinate, riotous, mutinous.
– OPPOSITES orderly.

l

lawlessness noun **anarchy**, disorder, chaos, unruliness, mob rule; criminality, crime.

lawyer noun **solicitor**, barrister, advocate, counsel, Queen's Counsel, QC; N. Amer. attorney, counselor; informal brief.

lax adjective **slack**, slipshod, negligent, remiss, careless, sloppy, slapdash, offhand, casual; easy-going, permissive, overindulgent.
– OPPOSITES strict.

lay[1] verb **1** *Curtis laid the newspaper on the table:* **put**, place, set, deposit, rest, position; informal stick, dump, park, plonk; Brit. informal bung. **2** *they are going to lay charges:* **bring**, press, prefer, lodge, register, place, file. **3** *we laid plans for the next voyage:* **devise**, arrange, make, prepare, work out, hatch, design, plan, scheme, plot, conceive, put together, draw up, produce, develop, formulate; informal cook up.
■ **lay something down 1** *they were forced to lay down their weapons:* relinquish, surrender, give up, abandon. **2** *the ground rules have been laid down:* formulate, set down, draw up, frame; prescribe, ordain, dictate, decree; enact, pass, decide, determine. **lay something in** stock up with/on, stockpile, store, amass, hoard, put aside/away/by, garner, collect, squirrel away; informal salt away, stash away. **lay into** (informal) **1** *police officers laid into protestors.* See ASSAULT verb. **2** *he laid into her with a string of insults.* See CRITICIZE. **lay off** (informal) give up, stop, refrain from, abstain from, desist from, cut out; informal pack in, leave off, quit. **lay someone off** make redundant, dismiss, let go, discharge, give notice to; informal sack, fire, give someone their cards, give someone their marching orders, give someone the boot/push. **lay something on** provide, supply, furnish, line up, organize, prepare, produce, make available; informal fix up. **lay something out 1** *Robyn laid the plans out on the desk:* spread out, set out, display; unfold, unroll, open. **2** *a paper laying out our priorities:* outline, sketch out, detail, draw up, formulate, work out, frame, draft. **3** (informal) *he had to lay out £70.* See PAY verb sense 2. **lay waste to** devastate, wipe out, destroy, demolish, annihilate, raze, ruin, wreck, level, flatten, ravage, pillage, sack, despoil.

lay[2] adjective *a lay audience:* **non-professional**, non-specialist, non-technical, untrained, unqualified.

layabout noun **idler**, good-for-nothing, loafer, lounger, shirker, sluggard, laggard, malingerer; informal skiver, waster, slacker, lazybones; Austral./NZ informal bludger; literary wastrel.

layer noun **coating**, sheet, coat, film, covering, blanket, skin.

layman noun. See LAYPERSON senses 1, 2.

layout noun **1** *the layout of the house:* **arrangement**, geography, design, organization; plan. **2** *the magazine's layout:* **design**, format, arrangement, presentation, style; structure, organization, composition, configuration.

layperson noun **1** *a prayer book for laypeople:* **member of the congregation**, layman, laywoman; (**laypeople**) the laity. **2** *engineering sounds highly specialized to the* *layperson:* **non-expert**, layman, non-professional, non-specialist.

laze verb **relax**, unwind, idle, do nothing, loaf around/about, lounge around/about, loll around/about, lie around/about, take it easy; informal chill, chill out, hang around/round, veg out.

lazy adjective **idle**, indolent, slothful, work-shy, shiftless, inactive, sluggish, lethargic; slack, lax.
– OPPOSITES industrious.

lazybones noun (informal) **idler**, loafer, layabout, good-for-nothing, shirker, sluggard, laggard; informal skiver, waster, slacker; Austral./NZ informal bludger; literary wastrel.

leach verb **drain**, filter, percolate, strain.

lead verb **1** *Michelle led them into the house:* **guide**, conduct, show, usher, escort, steer, shepherd; accompany, see, take. **2** *fascination with art led him to start a collection of paintings:* **prompt**, induce, move, persuade, influence, drive, make, cause; incline, dispose, predispose, condition. **3** *this reform might lead to job losses:* **result in**, cause, give rise to, create, produce, bring on/about, effect, generate, contribute to, promote; provoke, stir up, spark off, arouse, instigate; involve, necessitate, entail. **4** *she led a coalition of radicals:* **preside over**, head, command, govern, rule, be in charge of, be in command of, be in control of, run, control, be at the helm of; administer, organize, manage; reign over; informal head up. **5** *the champion was leading the field:* **be ahead of**, head; outrun, outstrip, outpace, leave behind; outdo, outclass, beat. **6** *I just want to lead a normal life:* **live**, have, spend, pass, enjoy.
– OPPOSITES follow.
• noun **1** *I was in the lead early on:* **first place**, van, vanguard; ahead, in front, winning. **2** *they took the lead in the personal computer market:* **first position**, forefront, primacy, dominance, superiority, ascendancy; pre-eminence, supremacy, advantage. **3** *he's not used to playing the lead:* **leading role**, star/starring role, title role, principal role. **4** *detectives were following up a new lead:* **clue**, pointer, hint, tip, tip-off, suggestion, indication, sign. **5** Brit. *the dog was not on a lead:* **leash**, tether, cord, rope, chain.
• adjective *the lead position:* **leading**, first, top, foremost, front, head; chief, principal, premier; pole.
■ **lead someone on** deceive, mislead, delude, hoodwink, dupe, trick, fool; tease, flirt with; informal string along, lead up the garden path, take for a ride.

leaden adjective **1** *he shuffled towards us with leaden steps:* **sluggish**, heavy, lumbering, slow. **2** *leaden prose:* **boring**, dull, unimaginative, uninspired, heavy, laboured, wooden. **3** *a leaden sky:* **grey**, black, dark; cloudy, gloomy, overcast, dull, sunless, louring, oppressive, threatening.

leader noun **1** *he's a natural leader:* **chief**, head, principal; commander, captain; controller, superior; chairman, chairwoman, chairperson, chair; director, managing director, MD, manager, superintendent, supervisor, overseer, master, mistress; president, premier, governor; ruler, monarch, king, queen, sovereign, emperor; informal boss, skipper, gaffer, number one, head honcho. **2** *a world leader in the use of video conferencing:* **pioneer**, front runner, innovator, trailblazer, groundbreaker, trendsetter.
– OPPOSITES follower, supporter.

leadership noun **1** *the leadership of the Conservative Party:* **control**, rule, command, dominion; directorship, premiership, governorship, captaincy. **2** *we need firm leadership:* **guidance**, direction, control, management, supervision; organization, government.

leading adjective **1** *he played the leading role in his team's victory:* **main**, chief, major, prime, principal, foremost, key, central, focal, paramount, dominant, essential. **2** *the leading industrialized countries:* **most powerful**, most important, greatest, chief, pre-eminent, principal, dominant. **3** *last season's leading scorer:* **top**, highest, best, first; front, lead; star.
– OPPOSITES subordinate, minor.

leaf noun *a leaf of paper:* **page**, sheet, folio.
• verb *he leafed through the documents:* **flick**, flip, thumb, skim, browse, glance, riffle; scan, run your eye over.

WORD LINKS
foliar relating to the leaves of trees

leaflet noun **pamphlet**, booklet, brochure, handbill, circular, flyer, handout, bulletin; N. Amer. folder, dodger.

league noun **1** *a league of nations:* **alliance**, confederation, confederacy, federation, union, association, coalition, consortium, affiliation, cooperative, guild, partnership, fellowship, syndicate. **2** *the store is not in the same league:* **class**, group, category, level.
■ **in league with** collaborating with, cooperating with, in alliance with, allied with, conspiring with, hand in glove with; informal in cahoots with.

leak verb **1** *oil was leaking from the tanker:* **seep**, escape, ooze, issue, drip, dribble, drain, bleed. **2** *the tanks are leaking gasoline:* **discharge**, exude, emit, release, drip, dribble, ooze, secrete. **3** *civil servants leaked information:* **disclose**, divulge, reveal, make public, tell, impart, pass on, relate, communicate, expose, release, bring into the open.
• noun **1** *check that there are no leaks in the bag:* **hole**, opening, puncture, perforation, gash, slit, rupture, tear, nick; break, crack, fissure. **2** *a gas leak:* **discharge**, leakage, seepage, escape. **3** *a series of leaks to the media:* **disclosure**, revelation, exposé.

leaky adjective **leaking**, dripping; cracked, split, punctured, perforated.
– OPPOSITES watertight.

lean[1] verb **1** *Polly leaned against the door:* **rest**, recline. **2** *trees leaning in the wind:* **slant**, incline, bend, tilt, slope, tip, list. **3** *he leans towards existentialist philosophy:* **tend**, incline, gravitate, have a preference for, have an affinity with; be partial to, have a liking for. **4** *she needs someone she can lean on:* **depend**, rely, count, bank, trust in.

lean[2] adjective **1** *a tall, lean man:* **slim**, thin, slender, spare, wiry, lanky. **2** *a lean harvest:* **meagre**, sparse, poor, mean, inadequate, insufficient, paltry. **3** *lean times:* **unproductive**, barren; hard, bad, difficult, tough; austere.
– OPPOSITES fat, abundant, prosperous.

leaning noun **inclination**, tendency, bent, proclivity, propensity, penchant, predisposition, predilection, partiality, preference, bias, attraction, liking, fondness, taste.

leap verb **1** *he leapt over the gate:* **jump over**, vault over, spring over, bound over, hop over, hurdle, clear. **2** *Claudia leapt to her feet:* **spring**, jump, bound. **3** *profits leapt by 55%:* **jump**, soar, rocket, skyrocket, shoot up; rise.
• noun *a leap of 33%:* **sudden rise**, surge, upsurge, upswing, upturn.
■ **in/by leaps and bounds** rapidly, swiftly, quickly, speedily, at a rate of knots.

learn verb **1** *he learned the ins and outs of the retail business:* **acquire**, grasp, master, take in, absorb, assimilate, digest, familiarize yourself with; study, read up on, be taught; informal get the hang of. **2** *she learnt the poem by heart:* **memorize**, commit to memory, learn parrot-fashion, get off pat, learn by rote. **3** *he learned that the school would be closing:* **discover**, find out, become aware, be informed, hear; informal get wind of the fact.

learned adjective **scholarly**, erudite, knowledgeable, widely read, cultured, intellectual, academic, literary, bookish, highbrow; informal brainy.
– OPPOSITES ignorant.

learner noun **beginner**, trainee, apprentice, pupil, student, novice, newcomer, starter, probationer, tyro, fledgling, neophyte; N. Amer. informal greenhorn, tenderfoot.
– OPPOSITES veteran.

learning noun **1** *a centre of learning:* **study**, education, schooling, tuition, teaching; research, investigation. **2** *the astonishing range of his learning:* **scholarship**, knowledge, education, erudition; understanding, wisdom.
– OPPOSITES ignorance.

lease noun *a 15-year lease:* **tenancy**, tenure, period of occupancy.
•verb **rent**, hire, charter; let, sublet.

leash noun *keep your dog on a leash:* **lead**, tether, rope, chain; restraint.

leathery adjective *leathery skin:* **rough**, wrinkled, wrinkly, furrowed, lined, wizened, weather-beaten, calloused, gnarled.

leave[1] verb **1** *they were the last to leave:* **depart**, go, withdraw, retire, take yourself off, absent yourself, take your leave, pull out; quit, abandon, desert, decamp from, vacate; say your farewells/goodbyes, make yourself scarce; informal push off, shove off, clear out/off, split, vamoose, scoot, make tracks, up sticks; Brit. informal sling your hook. **2** *the next morning we left for Liverpool:* **set off**, head, make; set sail. **3** *he's left his wife:* **abandon**, desert, jilt, leave in the lurch, leave high and dry, throw over; informal dump, ditch, chuck, drop, walk/run out on; literary forsake. **4** *he left his job in November:* **resign from**, retire from, step down from, withdraw from, pull out of, give up; informal quit, jack in. **5** *she left her handbag on a bus:* **leave behind**, forget, lose, mislay. **6** *I thought I'd leave it to the experts:* **entrust**, hand over, pass on, refer; delegate; defer. **7** *he left her £100,000:* **bequeath**, will, endow, hand down.
– OPPOSITES arrive.
▪ **leave someone in the lurch** leave stranded, leave high and dry, abandon, desert, let down. **leave off** (informal) stop, cease, finish, desist from, break off, give up, refrain from, eschew; informal quit, lay off, knock off, jack in, swear off; formal forswear. **leave someone/something out 1** *Adam left out the address:* miss out, omit, overlook, forget; skip, miss. **2** *he was left out of the England squad:* exclude, omit, drop, pass over.

leave[2] noun **1** *he was on leave:* **holiday**, break, furlough, sabbatical, leave of absence; N. Amer. vacation; informal hols, vac. **2** *the judge granted leave to appeal:* **permission**, consent, authorization, sanction, dispensation, approval, clearance, blessing, agreement, backing, assent, acceptance, licence; informal the go-ahead, the green light, the OK, the thumbs up.

leaven verb *formal proceedings leavened by humour:* **enliven**, liven up, season, spice up, energize, ginger up, perk up, brighten up; permeate, infuse, pervade, imbue, suffuse; informal pep up.

lecher noun **womanizer**, libertine, debauchee, rake, roué.

lecherous adjective **lustful**, licentious, lascivious, libidinous, lewd, salacious, debauched, dissolute, wanton, dirty, filthy; informal randy, horny; formal concupiscent.
– OPPOSITES chaste.

lecture noun **1** *a lecture on contemporary art:* **speech**, talk, address, discourse, presentation, oration, disquisition. **2** *he got a severe lecture:* **scolding**, reprimand, rebuke, reproof, reproach, upbraiding, admonishment; informal dressing-down, telling-off, talking-to, tongue-lashing; formal castigation.
•verb **1** *he lectured on the dangers of drugs:* talk, speak, discourse, hold forth, declaim; informal spout, sound off. **2** *she lectures at Dublin university:* **teach**, tutor; work. **3** *his family lectured him about his drinking:* **scold**, reprimand, rebuke, reproach, upbraid, berate, chastise, admonish, lambaste, haul over the coals, take to task; informal give someone a dressing-down, give someone a talking-to, tell off, bawl out; Brit. informal tick off, carpet; formal castigate.

lecturer noun **university/college teacher**, tutor, scholar, don, professor, fellow; academic; formal pedagogue.

ledge noun **shelf**, sill, mantel, mantelpiece; projection, protrusion, overhang, ridge, prominence.

ledger noun **account book**, record book, register, log; records, books; balance sheet, financial statement.

leer verb *Henry leered at her:* **ogle**, eye; informal give someone a/the once-over, lech.

leery adjective (informal) **wary**, cautious, careful, guarded, chary, suspicious, distrustful; worried, anxious, apprehensive.

leeway noun **freedom**, scope, latitude, space, room, liberty, flexibility, licence, free hand, free rein.

left adjective **left-hand**, sinistral; Nautical port; Nautical, old use larboard; Heraldry sinister.
– OPPOSITES right, starboard.

leftover noun **1** *a leftover from the 60s:* **residue**, survivor, vestige, legacy. **2** *put the leftovers in the fridge:* **remainder**, scraps, remnants, remains; excess, surplus.
• adjective *leftover food:* **remaining**, left, uneaten; excess, surplus, superfluous, unused, unwanted, spare.

left-wing adjective **socialist**, communist, leftist, Labour, Marxist–Leninist, Bolshevik, Trotskyite, Maoist; informal Commie, lefty, red, pinko.
– OPPOSITES right-wing, conservative.

leg noun **1** *he broke his leg:* **lower limb**, shank; technical femur, tibia, fibula; informal peg, pin. **2** *a table leg:* **upright**, support. **3** *the first leg of a European tour:* **part**, stage, section, segment, portion, phase, stretch, lap.
■ **leg it** (Brit. informal) **1** *if the dog starts barking, leg it!* run away, flee, make off, make a break for it, escape; informal hightail it, hotfoot it, run for it, skedaddle, vamoose, split, scoot, scram; Brit. informal scarper. **2** *he's part of a team legging it around London:* walk, march, tramp, trek, trudge, plod, wander.

legacy noun **1** *a legacy from a great aunt:* **bequest**, inheritance, endowment, gift, birthright; formal benefaction. **2** *the legacy of the war:* **consequences**, effects, repercussions, results, aftermath; by-product.

legal adjective **lawful**, legitimate, within the law, legalized, valid; permissible, permitted, allowable, allowed, above board, admissible, acceptable; constitutional; informal legit, kosher.
– OPPOSITES illegal, criminal.

legality noun **lawfulness**, legitimacy, validity, admissibility, permissibility, constitutionality; justice.

legalize verb **make legal**, decriminalize, legitimize, permit, allow, authorize, sanction, license; regularize, normalize.
– OPPOSITES prohibit.

legend noun **1** *the Arthurian legends:* **myth**, saga, epic, folk tale, folk story, fable; folklore, lore, mythology, folk tradition. **2** *pop legends:* **celebrity**, star, superstar, icon, phenomenon, luminary, giant, hero; informal celeb, megastar. **3** *the wording of the legend:* **caption**, heading, title, explanation, key, guide.

legendary adjective **1** *legendary kings:* **fabled**, heroic, traditional, fairy-tale, storybook, mythical, mythological. **2** *a legendary figure in the trade-union movement:* **famous**, celebrated, famed, renowned, acclaimed, illustrious, esteemed, honoured, exalted, venerable, distinguished, great, eminent, pre-eminent.
– OPPOSITES historical.

legibility noun **readability**, clarity, clearness, neatness.

legible adjective **readable**, easy to read, clear, plain, neat, intelligible.

legion noun *the legions of TV cameras:* **horde**, throng, multitude, crowd, mass, mob, gang, swarm, flock, herd, army.
• adjective *her fans are legion:* **numerous**, countless, innumerable, incalculable, many, abundant, plentiful; literary myriad.

legislation noun **law**, rules, rulings, regulations, acts, bills, statutes; N. Amer. formal ordinances.

legislative adjective **law-making**, judicial, parliamentary, governmental, policymaking.

legislator noun **lawmaker**, lawgiver, parliamentarian, Member of Parliament, MP, congressman, congresswoman, senator.

legitimate adjective **1** *the only form of legitimate gambling:* **legal**, lawful, authorized, permitted, permissible, allowable, allowed, sanctioned, approved, licensed, statutory, constitutional; informal legit. **2** *the legitimate heir:* **rightful**, lawful, genuine, authentic, real, true, proper. **3** *legitimate grounds for unease:* **valid**, sound, admissible, acceptable, well founded, justifiable, reasonable, sensible, just, fair, bona fide.
– OPPOSITES illegal, invalid.

legitimize verb **validate**, legitimate, permit, authorize, sanction, license,

condone, justify, endorse, support; legalize.
–OPPOSITES outlaw.

leisure noun *the balance between leisure and work:* **free time**, spare time, time off; recreation, relaxation; informal R & R.
–OPPOSITES work.

leisurely adjective **unhurried**, relaxed, easy, gentle, sedate, comfortable, restful, undemanding, slow.
–OPPOSITES hurried.

lend verb **1** *I'll lend you the money:* **loan**, advance; Brit. informal sub. **2** *these examples lend weight to his assertions:* **add**, impart, give, bestow, confer, provide, supply, furnish, contribute.
–OPPOSITES borrow.

length noun **1** *a length of three or four metres | the whole length of the valley:* **extent**, distance, span, reach; area, expanse, stretch, range. **2** *a considerable length of time:* **period**, duration, stretch, span. **3** *MPs criticized the length of the speech:* **protractedness**, lengthiness, extent, extensiveness; prolixity, wordiness, verboseness, long-windedness.
■ **at length 1** *he spoke at length:* for a long time, for ages, for hours, interminably, endlessly, unendingly. **2** *he was questioned at length:* thoroughly, fully, in detail, in depth, comprehensively, exhaustively, extensively. **3** *his search led him, at length, to Seattle:* eventually, in time, finally, at last, in the end, ultimately.

lengthen verb **1** *he lengthened his stride:* **elongate**, extend; expand, enlarge. **2** *the diversion will lengthen journey times:* **prolong**, increase, extend, protract, stretch out.
–OPPOSITES shorten.

lengthy adjective **long**, long-lasting, prolonged, protracted, long-drawn-out, time-consuming; interminable, endless.
–OPPOSITES short.

leniency noun **mercifulness**, mercy, clemency, forgiveness; tolerance, forbearance, charity, indulgence, mildness.

lenient adjective **merciful**, forgiving, forbearing, tolerant, charitable, humane, indulgent, magnanimous.
–OPPOSITES severe.

lesion noun **wound**, injury, bruise, abrasion, contusion; ulcer, sore, abscess.

lessen verb **1** *deep tissue massage lessens the pain:* **reduce**, minimize, decrease; allay, assuage, alleviate, attenuate, ease, dull, deaden, blunt, moderate, mitigate, dampen, soften, tone down, dilute, weaken. **2** *the pain began to lessen:* **decrease**, diminish, decline, subside, abate; fade, die down/off, let up, ease off, tail off, dwindle, ebb, wane, recede. **3** *his behaviour lessened him in their eyes:* **diminish**, degrade, discredit, devalue, belittle.
–OPPOSITES increase.

lesser adjective **1** *a lesser offence:* **less important**, minor, secondary, subsidiary, marginal, ancillary, auxiliary, supplementary, peripheral. **2** *you look down at us lesser mortals:* **subordinate**, minor, inferior, second-class, subservient, lowly, humble.
–OPPOSITES greater, superior.

lesson noun **1** *a maths lesson:* **class**, session, seminar, tutorial, lecture, period. **2** *these developments should be a lesson for all investors:* **warning**, deterrent, caution; example, message; moral.

let verb **1** *let him come in:* **allow**, permit, give permission to, give leave to, authorize, license, empower, enable, entitle; assent to, consent to, agree to; informal give the green light to, give the go-ahead to, give the thumbs up to, OK; formal accede to; old use suffer. **2** *they've let their flat:* **rent out**, let out, lease, hire out, sublet.
–OPPOSITES prevent, prohibit.
■ **let someone down** fail, disappoint, disillusion; abandon, desert, leave stranded, leave in the lurch. **let go** release, loosen your grip on, relinquish; old use unhand. **let someone go** make redundant, dismiss, discharge, lay off, give notice to, axe; informal sack, fire, give someone their cards, give someone their marching orders, send packing, give someone the boot/push. **let something off** detonate, discharge, explode, set off, fire. **let someone off 1** (informal) *I'll let you off this time:* pardon, forgive; acquit, absolve, exonerate, clear, vindicate;

informal let someone off the hook; formal exculpate. **2** *he let me off work:* excuse from, exempt from, spare from. **let on** (informal) *I never let on that I knew:* reveal, make known, tell, disclose, mention, divulge, let slip, give away, make public; blab; informal let the cat out of the bag, give the game away. **let something out 1** *I let out a cry of triumph:* utter, emit, give, produce, issue, express, voice, release. **2** *she let out that he'd given her a lift home:* reveal, make known, tell, disclose, mention, divulge, let slip, give away, let it be known, blurt out. **let someone out** release, liberate, free, set free, let go, discharge; set/turn loose. **let up** (informal) **1** *the rain has let up:* abate, lessen, decrease, diminish, subside, relent, slacken, die down, ease off, tail off; ebb, wane, dwindle, fade; stop. **2** *you never let up, do you?* relax, ease up/off, slow down; pause, take a break, rest, stop.

l

let-down noun **disappointment**, anticlimax, comedown, non-event, fiasco, setback, blow; informal washout, downer, damp squib.

lethal adjective **fatal**, deadly, mortal, life-threatening; poisonous, toxic, noxious, venomous; dangerous, destructive, harmful; literary deathly, nocuous; old use baneful.
– OPPOSITES harmless, safe.

lethargic adjective **sluggish**, inert, inactive, slow, lifeless; languid, listless, apathetic, weary, tired, fatigued.

lethargy noun **sluggishness**, inertia, inactivity, inaction, slowness, torpor, lifelessness, listlessness, languor, languidness, apathy, passivity, weariness, tiredness.
– OPPOSITES vigour, energy.

letter noun **1** *capital letters:* **character**, sign, symbol, mark, figure, rune. **2** *she's received a letter from him:* **message**, communication, note, line, missive, dispatch; correspondence; post, mail; formal epistle. **3** *a man of letters:* **learning**, scholarship, erudition, education.
■ **to the letter** strictly, precisely, exactly, accurately, closely, faithfully, religiously, punctiliously, literally, in every detail.

> **WORD LINKS**
> **epistolary** relating to the writing of letters

let-up noun (informal) **abatement**, lessening, decrease, decline, relenting, remission, slackening, weakening, relaxation, dying down, easing off, tailing off, dropping away/off; respite, break, interval, hiatus, stop, pause.

level adjective **1** *a level surface:* **flat**, smooth, even, uniform, plane, flush. **2** *he kept his voice level:* **steady**, even, uniform, regular, constant; calm. **3** *the scores were level:* **equal**, even, drawn, tied, all square, neck and neck, level pegging, on a par, evenly matched; informal even-steven.
– OPPOSITES uneven, unsteady, unequal.
• noun **1** *the post is at research-officer level:* **rank**, position; degree, grade, stage, standard; class, group, set, classification. **2** *a high level of employment:* **quantity**, amount, extent, measure, degree, volume. **3** *the sixth level:* **floor**, storey, deck.
• verb **1** *tilt the tin to level the mixture:* **even off/out**, flatten, smooth out. **2** *bulldozers levelled the building:* **raze to the ground**, demolish, flatten, bulldoze; destroy. **3** *he levelled his opponent with a single blow:* **knock down/out**, lay out, prostrate, flatten, floor, fell; informal KO. **4** *we levelled the score in the second half:* **equalize**, equal, even up, make level. **5** *he levelled his pistol at me:* **aim**, point, direct, train, focus, turn.
■ **on the level** (informal) genuine, straight, honest, above board, fair, true, sincere, straightforward; informal upfront; N. Amer. informal on the up and up.

level-headed adjective **sensible**, practical, realistic, prudent, pragmatic, reasonable, rational, mature, sound, sober, businesslike, no-nonsense, {cool, calm, and collected}, having your feet on the ground, grounded; informal together, unflappable.
– OPPOSITES excitable.

lever noun **1** *you can insert a lever and prise the rail off:* **crowbar**, bar, jemmy. **2** *he pulled the lever:* **handle**, arm, switch.

• verb *he levered the door open:* **prise**, force, wrench, pull, wrest; N. Amer. pry; informal jemmy.

leverage noun **1** *the long handles provide increased leverage:* **grip**, purchase, hold; support, anchorage. **2** *they have significant leverage in negotiations:* **influence**, power, authority, weight, sway, pull, control, say, advantage, pressure; informal clout, muscle, teeth.

levity noun **light-heartedness**, high spirits, cheerfulness, humour, gaiety, hilarity, frivolity, amusement, mirth, laughter, merriment, glee, jollity.
– OPPOSITES seriousness.

levy verb **impose**, charge, exact, raise, collect.
• noun **tax**, tariff, toll, excise, duty.

lewd adjective **1** *a lewd old man:* **lecherous**, lustful, licentious, lascivious, dirty, prurient, salacious, lubricious, libidinous; debauched, depraved, degenerate, perverted; informal horny; Brit. informal randy; formal concupiscent. **2** *a lewd song:* **vulgar**, crude, smutty, dirty, filthy, obscene, coarse, off colour, indecent, salacious; rude, racy, risqué, naughty, earthy, spicy, bawdy, ribald; informal blue, raunchy, X-rated; N. Amer. informal raw.
– OPPOSITES chaste, clean.

liability noun **1** *they have big liabilities:* **financial obligations**, debts, arrears, dues, financial commitments. **2** *he's become a bit of a liability:* **hindrance**, encumbrance, burden, handicap, nuisance, inconvenience, embarrassment; impediment, disadvantage; millstone round someone's neck.
– OPPOSITES asset.

liable adjective **1** *they are liable for negligence:* **responsible**, accountable, answerable; blameworthy, at fault, culpable, guilty. **2** *my income is liable to fluctuate wildly:* **likely**, inclined, tending, disposed, apt, predisposed, prone, given. **3** *areas liable to flooding:* **exposed**, prone, subject, susceptible, vulnerable, in danger of, at risk of.

liaise verb **cooperate**, collaborate; communicate, network, interface, link up.

liaison noun **1** *the branches work in close liaison:* **cooperation**, contact, association, connection, collaboration, communication, alliance, partnership. **2** *my White House liaison:* **intermediary**, mediator, middleman, contact, link, go-between, representative, agent. **3** *a secret liaison:* **affair**, relationship, romance, attachment, fling, tryst.

liar noun **fibber**, deceiver, perjurer, fabricator; informal storyteller.

libel noun *she sued two newspapers for libel:* **defamation of character**, character assassination, calumny, misrepresentation; denigration, vilification, disparagement, malicious gossip, scandalmongering; lie, slur, smear, untruth, insult; informal mud-slinging.
• verb *she claimed the magazine had libelled her:* **defame**, malign, blacken someone's name, sully someone's reputation, smear, cast aspersions on, drag someone's name through the mud/mire, besmirch, tarnish, taint, stain, vilify, denigrate, disparage; N. Amer. slur.

libellous adjective **defamatory**, denigratory, disparaging, derogatory, false, untrue, insulting, scurrilous.

liberal adjective **1** *the values of a liberal society:* **tolerant**, unprejudiced, broad-minded, open-minded, enlightened; permissive, free and easy, easy-going, libertarian, indulgent, lenient. **2** *a liberal social agenda:* **progressive**, advanced, modern, forward-looking, forward-thinking, enlightened, reformist, radical; informal go-ahead. **3** *a liberal interpretation of divorce laws:* **flexible**, broad, loose, rough, free, non-literal, imprecise, vague, indefinite. **4** *liberal coatings of paint:* **abundant**, copious, ample, plentiful, generous, lavish. **5** *they were liberal with their cash:* **generous**, open-handed, unsparing, unstinting, lavish, free, munificent, bountiful, benevolent, big-hearted, philanthropic, charitable.
– OPPOSITES reactionary, strict, miserly.

liberate verb **free**, set free, release, let out/go, set/let loose, save, rescue; emancipate, enfranchise.
– OPPOSITES imprison, enslave.

liberation noun **1** *the liberation of prisoners:* **freeing**, release, rescue; emancipation. **2** *women's liberation:* **freedom**, equality, equal rights, emancipation, enfranchisement.
– OPPOSITES confinement, oppression.

liberator noun **rescuer**, saviour, deliverer, emancipator.

libertine noun **philanderer**, playboy, rake, roué, Don Juan, Lothario, Casanova, Romeo; lecher, seducer, womanizer, adulterer, debauchee, profligate, wanton; informal ladykiller, lech.

liberty noun **1** *the essence of British liberty:* **independence**, freedom, autonomy, sovereignty, self-government, self-rule, self-determination; civil liberties, human rights. **2** *the liberty to go where one pleases:* **right**, prerogative, entitlement, privilege, permission, sanction, authorization, authority, licence.
■ **at liberty 1** *he was at liberty for three months:* free, on the loose, at large, on the run, unconfined. **2** *I am not at liberty to say:* free, able, entitled, eligible.

libidinous adjective **lustful**, lecherous, lascivious, lewd, salacious, prurient, licentious, lubricious, dissolute, debauched, depraved, degenerate, dissipated, wanton, promiscuous; informal horny; Brit. informal randy; formal concupiscent.

libido noun **sex drive**, sexual appetite; sexual desire.

licence noun **1** *a driving licence:* **permit**, certificate, document, documentation, authorization, warrant; credentials; pass, papers. **2** *the army was given too much licence:* **freedom**, liberty, free rein, latitude, independence, scope, impunity, a free hand, carte blanche. **3** *products made under licence from US companies:* **permission**, consent, sanction, warrant, warranty, charter; franchise. **4** *poetic licence:* **disregard**, inventiveness, invention, creativity, imagination, fancy, freedom, looseness.

license verb **permit**, allow, authorize, grant/give authority to, grant/give permission to; certify, empower, entitle, enable, let, qualify, sanction.
– OPPOSITES ban.

licentious adjective **dissolute**, dissipated, debauched, degenerate, immoral, wanton, decadent, depraved, corrupt; lustful, lecherous, lascivious, libidinous, prurient, lubricious, lewd, promiscuous; formal concupiscent.
– OPPOSITES moral.

lick verb **1** *the spaniel licked his face:* tongue, wash; lap, slurp; slobber over. **2** *flames licking round the coal:* **flicker**, play, dance.

lid noun *the lid of a saucepan:* **cover**, top, cap, covering.
■ **put a/the lid on** (informal) stop, control, end, put an end/stop to, put paid to. **lift the lid off/on** (informal) expose, reveal, make known, go public on/with, bring into the open, disclose, divulge; informal spill the beans, blow the gaff.

lie[1] noun *I'm sick of all the lies:* **untruth**, falsehood, fib, fabrication, deception, invention, piece of fiction, falsification, white lie; informal tall story, whopper; Brit. informal porky pie; humorous terminological inexactitude.
– OPPOSITES truth.
• verb *he had lied to the police:* **tell a lie**, fib, dissemble, dissimulate, perjure yourself, commit perjury; formal forswear yourself.

WORD LINKS
mendacious telling lies

lie[2] verb **1** *he was lying on the bed:* **recline**, lie down/back, be recumbent, be prostrate, be supine, be prone, be stretched out, sprawl, rest, repose, lounge, loll. **2** *her handbag lay on the chair:* **rest**, be situated, be positioned, be arranged, be displayed. **3** *Liechtenstein lies on the border of Switzerland and Austria:* **be situated**, be located, be placed, be found, be sited. **4** *his body lies in a crypt:* **be buried**, be interred, be laid to rest, rest, be entombed.
– OPPOSITES stand.
■ **lie low** hide, go into hiding, conceal yourself, keep out of sight, go to ground; informal hole up; Brit. informal, dated lie doggo.

lieutenant noun **deputy**, second in command, right-hand man/woman, number two, assistant, aide; informal sidekick.

life noun **1** *the joy of giving life to a child:* **existence**, being, living, animation; sentience, creation. **2** *the numerous threats to life on this planet:* **living creatures**; fauna, flora, the ecosystem, the biosphere, the ecosphere; human beings, humanity, humankind, mankind, man. **3** *an easy life:* **way of life**, lifestyle, situation, fate, lot. **4** *the last nine months of his life:* **lifetime**, life span, days, time on earth, existence. **5** *he's always full of life:* **vivacity**, animation, liveliness, vitality, verve, high spirits, exuberance, zest, buoyancy, enthusiasm, energy, vigour, dynamism, elan, gusto, bounce, spirit, fire; hustle and bustle, movement; informal oomph, pizzazz, pep, zing, zip. **6** *more than 1,500 lives were lost in the accident:* **person**, human being, individual, soul. **7** *a life of Chopin:* **biography**, autobiography, profile, chronicle, account, portrait.
– OPPOSITES death.

WORD LINKS
animate, **vital** having life

life-and-death adjective **vital**, of vital importance, crucial, critical, urgent, pivotal, momentous, key, serious, grave, significant; informal earth-shattering.
– OPPOSITES trivial.

lifeblood noun *new ideas are the lifeblood of any company:* **life force**, driving force, inspiration, vital spark, stimulus, essence, crux, heart, soul, core.

life-giving adjective **sustaining**, revitalizing, animating, energizing, invigorating, stimulating.

lifeless adjective **1** *a lifeless body:* **dead**, stiff, cold, inert; formal deceased. **2** *a lifeless landscape:* **barren**, sterile, bare, desolate, stark, arid, infertile, uninhabited; bleak, colourless, characterless, soulless. **3** *a lifeless performance:* **lacklustre**, apathetic, lethargic; expressionless, emotionless, colourless, characterless, wooden, blank.
– OPPOSITES alive, lively.

lifelike adjective **realistic**, true to life, faithful, detailed, vivid, graphic, natural, naturalistic; representational.
– OPPOSITES unrealistic.

lifelong adjective **lasting**, long-lasting, long-term, constant, enduring, permanent.
– OPPOSITES ephemeral.

lifestyle noun **way of life**, life, situation; conduct, behaviour, habits, mores.

lift verb **1** *lift the pack on to your back:* **raise**, hoist, heave, haul up, heft, raise up/aloft, elevate, hold high; pick up, grab, take up; winch up, jack up; informal hump. **2** *the news lifted his spirits:* **boost**, raise, buoy up, cheer up, perk up, brighten up, gladden, encourage, stimulate, revive; informal buck up. **3** *the fog had lifted:* **clear**, rise, disperse, dissipate, disappear, vanish, dissolve. **4** *the ban has been lifted:* **cancel**, remove, withdraw, revoke, rescind, end, stop, terminate. **5** *the RAF lifted them to safety:* **airlift**, transport, fly; winch; whisk. **6** (informal) *he lifted sections from a 1986 article:* **copy**, plagiarize, reproduce, borrow, steal; informal nick, crib, rip off.
– OPPOSITES drop, put down.
• noun **1** *give me a lift up:* **push**, hand, heave, thrust, shove. **2** *he gave me a lift to the airport:* **ride**; run, drive. **3** *that goal will give his confidence a real lift:* **boost**, fillip, impetus, encouragement, spur, push; improvement, enhancement; informal shot in the arm.
■ **lift off** take off, become airborne, take to the air, blast off.

light[1] noun **1** *the light of the candles:* **illumination**, brightness, shining, gleam, brilliance, radiance, glow, blaze, glare; sunlight, moonlight, starlight, lamplight, firelight; literary effulgence. **2** *switch the lights off:* **lamp**; headlight, sidelight; street light, floodlight; lantern; torch, flashlight, bulb. **3** *we'll be driving in the light:* **daylight**, daytime, day; sunlight. **4** *he saw the problem in a different light:* **aspect**, angle, slant, approach, viewpoint, standpoint, context, hue, complexion.
– OPPOSITES darkness.
• adjective **1** *a light bedroom:* **bright**, well lit, sunny. **2** *light blue:* **pale**, pastel; faded, washed out, insipid.
– OPPOSITES dark, gloomy.
■ **come to light** be discovered, be uncovered, be unearthed, come out, become known, become apparent,

appear, emerge. **light something up** brighten, illuminate, throw/cast light on, shine on; floodlight; literary illumine. **throw/cast/shed light on** explain, elucidate, clarify, clear up.

WORD LINKS
optics the study of light
photometry the measurement of light

light[2] adjective **1** *the camera is light and compact:* **lightweight**; portable. **2** *a light cotton dress:* **flimsy**, lightweight, thin; floaty, gauzy, diaphanous. **3** *she is light on her feet:* **nimble**, agile, lithe, graceful; quick; sprightly; informal twinkle-toed; literary fleet. **4** *a light soil:* **crumbly**, friable, loose, workable, sandy. **5** *a light dinner:* **small**, modest, simple; quick. **6** *light duties:* **easy**, simple, undemanding, untaxing; informal cushy. **7** *light reading:* **entertaining**, lightweight, diverting, undemanding; middle-of-the-road, mainstream; frivolous, superficial, trivial. **8** *light footsteps | a light touch:* **gentle**, delicate, dainty, soft, faint; careful, sensitive, subtle.
–OPPOSITES heavy.

light[3] verb
■ **light on** come across, chance on, hit on, happen on, stumble on/across, find, discover, uncover, come up with.

lighten[1] verb **1** *the sky was beginning to lighten:* **become/grow/get lighter**, brighten. **2** *the first touch of dawn lightened the sky:* **brighten**, make brighter, light up, illuminate; literary illumine. **3** *he used lemon juice to lighten his hair:* **make lighter**, whiten, bleach, blanch; fade.
–OPPOSITES darken.

lighten[2] verb **1** *measures designed to lighten the burden of medical costs:* **reduce**, lessen, decrease, diminish, ease; alleviate, relieve. **2** *an attempt to lighten her mood:* **cheer up**, brighten, gladden, lift, boost, buoy up, revive, restore, revitalize.
–OPPOSITES increase, depress.

light-headed adjective **dizzy**, giddy, faint; muzzy, feverish; informal woozy.

light-hearted adjective **carefree**, cheerful, cheery, happy, merry, glad, playful, blithe, bright, vivacious, bubbly, jaunty, bouncy, breezy; entertaining, amusing, diverting; informal chirpy, upbeat; dated gay.
–OPPOSITES miserable.

lightly adverb **1** *Maisie kissed him lightly on the cheek:* **softly**, gently, faintly, delicately. **2** *season very lightly:* **sparingly**, sparsely, moderately, delicately; subtly.
–OPPOSITES hard, heavily.

lightweight adjective **1** *a lightweight jacket:* **thin**, light, flimsy, insubstantial; summery. **2** *lightweight entertainment:* **trivial**, insubstantial, superficial, shallow, undemanding, frivolous.
–OPPOSITES heavy.

like[1] verb **1** *I've always liked him:* **be fond of**, have a soft spot for, think highly of, admire, respect; be attracted to, fancy, be taken with; informal rate. **2** *he likes French cuisine:* **enjoy**, have a taste for, have a liking for, be partial to, be keen on, have a penchant for; appreciate, love, adore, relish; informal have a thing about. **3** *feel free to say what you like:* **choose**, please, wish, want, see/think fit, care to, will.
–OPPOSITES hate.

like[2] preposition **1** *you're just like a teacher:* **similar to**, the same as, identical to, analogous to, akin to, resembling. **2** *the figure landed like a cat:* **in the same way as**, in a similar way to. **3** *cities like Birmingham:* **such as**, for example, for instance; in particular, namely, viz. **4** *Richard sounded mean, which isn't like him:* **characteristic of**, typical of, in character with.
• noun *we shan't see his like again:* **equal**, match, equivalent, counterpart, twin, parallel.
• adjective *a like situation:* **similar**, comparable, corresponding, analogous, parallel, equivalent; related, kindred; matching.
–OPPOSITES dissimilar.

likeable adjective **pleasant**, nice, friendly, agreeable, affable, amiable, genial, personable, good-natured, engaging, appealing, endearing, convivial, congenial.
–OPPOSITES unpleasant.

likelihood noun **probability**, chance, prospect, possibility, odds; risk, threat, danger; hope, promise.

likely adjective **1** *it seemed likely that*

a scandal would break: **probable**, very possible, odds-on; predictable, foreseeable; informal on the cards. **2** *a likely explanation:* **plausible**, reasonable, feasible, acceptable, believable, credible, tenable.
– OPPOSITES unlikely, improbable.

liken verb **compare**, equate.
– OPPOSITES contrast.

likeness noun **1** *her likeness to Anne is quite uncanny:* **resemblance**, similarity, correspondence. **2** *a likeness of the president:* **representation**, image, depiction, portrayal; picture, drawing, sketch, painting, portrait, photograph, study.
– OPPOSITES dissimilarity.

likewise adverb **1** *an ambush was out of the question, likewise poison:* **also**, equally, in addition, too, as well, to boot; besides, moreover, furthermore. **2** *encourage your family and friends to do likewise:* **the same**, similarly, correspondingly.

liking noun **fondness**, love, affection, penchant, attachment; enjoyment, taste, passion; preference, partiality, predilection.
– OPPOSITES dislike.

lilt noun **cadence**, inflection, intonation, rhythm, swing, beat, pulse, tempo.

limb noun **arm**, **leg**, appendage; old use member.

limber verb
■ **limber up** warm up, loosen up, prepare, practise, train, stretch.

limbo noun
■ **in limbo** in abeyance, unattended to, unfinished; suspended, deferred, postponed, put off, pending, on ice, in cold storage; unresolved, undetermined, up in the air; informal on the back burner, on hold.

limelight noun **attention**, interest, scrutiny, the public eye/gaze, the glare of publicity, prominence, the spotlight; fame, celebrity.
– OPPOSITES obscurity.

limit noun **1** *the city limits:* **boundary**, border, frontier, edge; perimeter, margin. **2** *a limit of 4,500 supporters:* **maximum**, ceiling, upper limit.
• verb *the pressure to limit costs:* **restrict**, curb, cap, hold in check, restrain; regulate, control, govern.

limitation noun **1** *a limitation on the number of newcomers:* **restriction**, curb, restraint, control, check. **2** *he is aware of his own limitations:* **imperfection**, flaw, defect, failing, shortcoming, weak point, deficiency, failure, frailty, weakness, inconsistency.
– OPPOSITES increase, strength.

limited adjective **restricted**, finite, small, tight, slight, in short supply, short; meagre, scanty, sparse, inadequate, insufficient, paltry, poor, minimal.
– OPPOSITES limitless, ample.

limitless adjective **boundless**, unbounded, unlimited; infinite, endless, never-ending, unending, everlasting, untold, immeasurable, bottomless, interminable, perpetual.
– OPPOSITES limited.

limp[1] verb *she limped out of the house:* **hobble**; lurch, stagger.

limp[2] adjective **1** *a limp handshake:* **soft**, flaccid, loose, slack, lax; floppy, drooping, droopy, sagging. **2** *he felt too limp to argue:* **weak**, drained, exhausted, tired, worn out, weary, debilitated, enervated, spent.
– OPPOSITES firm.

limpid adjective **1** *a limpid pool:* **clear**, transparent, glassy, crystal clear, translucent, unclouded. **2** *his limpid prose style:* **lucid**, clear, transparent, plain, unambiguous, simple; accessible.
– OPPOSITES opaque.

line[1] noun **1** *a thick black line:* **stroke**, dash, underline, underscore; slash, solidus; stripe, strip, band, belt; technical striation; Brit. oblique. **2** *there were lines round her eyes:* **wrinkle**, furrow, crease, crinkle, crow's foot. **3** *the classic lines of the Bentley:* **contour**, outline, configuration, shape, design, profile. **4** *the county line:* **boundary line**, limit, border, borderline, frontier, margin, perimeter. **5** *a line of soldiers:* **file**, rank, column, string, train, procession; row, queue; Brit. informal crocodile. **6** *her own line of thought | another line of enquiry:* **course**, direction, drift, tack, tendency, trend; avenue, route, channel. **7** *they took a very tough line with the industry | the party line:* **course of action**, procedure; policy, practice,

approach, programme, position, stance, philosophy, way. **8** *a new line of convenience food:* **brand**, kind, sort, type, variety.
• verb **1** *her face was lined with age:* **furrow**, wrinkle, crease. **2** *the driveway was lined by poplars:* **border**, edge, fringe, bound.
■ **draw the line at** stop short of, refuse to accept, baulk at, jibe at. **in line** *the adverts are in line with our editorial style:* in agreement, in accord, in accordance, in harmony, in step, in compliance. **line someone/something up** *we've lined up an all-star cast:* assemble, get together, organize, prepare, arrange, fix up, lay on; book, schedule, timetable.

line² verb *a cardboard box lined with a blanket:* cover, back, pad; insulate, lag, seal.

lineage noun **ancestry**, family, parentage, birth, descent, line, extraction, genealogy, roots, origin, background; stock, bloodline, breeding, pedigree.

l

lined adjective **1** *lined paper:* **ruled**, feint, striped, banded. **2** *his lined face:* **wrinkled**, wrinkly, furrowed, wizened.
– OPPOSITES plain, smooth.

liner noun **ship**, ocean liner, passenger vessel, boat.

line-up noun **1** *a star-studded line-up:* **cast**, bill, programme. **2** *United's line-up:* **team**, squad, side; configuration.

linger verb **1** *the crowd still lingered:* **wait**, stand around, remain, stay put; loiter; informal stick around, hang around; old use tarry. **2** *the infection can linger for years:* **persist**, continue, remain, stay, endure, carry on, last.
– OPPOSITES vanish.

lingerie noun **underwear**, underclothes, underclothing, undergarments; informal undies; Brit. informal smalls.

lingering adjective **1** *lingering doubts:* **remaining**, surviving, persisting, abiding, nagging, niggling. **2** *a slow, lingering death:* **protracted**, prolonged, long-drawn-out; agonizing.

linguistic adjective semantic, rhetorical, verbal, phonetic; grammatical.

lining noun **backing**, facing, padding, insulation.

link noun **1** *a chain of steel links:* **loop**, ring. **2** *the links between transport and the environment:* **connection**, relationship, association, linkage, tie-up. **3** *their links with the labour movement:* **bond**, tie, attachment, connection, association, affiliation.
• verb **1** *four boxes were linked together:* **join**, connect, fasten, attach, bind; secure, fix, tie, couple, yoke. **2** *the evidence linking him with the body:* **associate**, connect, relate; bracket.

lion noun

> **WORD LINKS**
> **leonine** relating to lions

lionize verb **celebrate**, fete, glorify, honour, exalt, admire, praise, extol, venerate, eulogize; formal laud.
– OPPOSITES vilify.

lip noun *the lip of the crater:* **edge**, rim, brim, border, verge, brink.

liquefy verb **liquidize**, purée; pulp; condense; melt.

liquid adjective *liquid fuels:* **fluid**, liquefied; melted, molten, thawed, dissolved; Chemistry hydrous.
– OPPOSITES solid.
• noun *drain off the excess liquid:* **fluid**; moisture; liquor, solution, juice, sap.

liquidate verb *the company was liquidated:* **close down**, wind up, dissolve, sell off.

liquidize verb **purée**, cream, liquefy, blend.

liquor noun **alcohol**, spirits, drink; informal booze, the hard stuff, hooch; moonshine.

list¹ noun *a list of the world's wealthiest people:* **catalogue**, inventory, record, register, roll, file, index, directory, checklist.
• verb *the accounts are listed below:* **record**, register, enter; itemize, enumerate, catalogue, file, log, minute, categorize, inventory; classify, group, sort, rank, index.

list² verb *the boat listed to one side:* **lean**, tilt, tip, heel, careen, pitch, incline, slant, slope, bank.

listen verb **1** *are you listening?* **pay attention**, be attentive, attend, concentrate; keep your ears open, prick up your ears; informal be all ears; literary hark. **2** *policymakers should listen to popular opinion:* heed, take heed of, take notice/note of, take into consideration/account, bear in mind.

■ **listen in** eavesdrop, spy, overhear, tap, bug, monitor.

listless adjective **lethargic**, lifeless; languid, inactive, inert, sluggish.
– OPPOSITES energetic.

literal adjective *the literal sense of the word 'dreadful':* **strict**, technical, concrete, original, true.
– OPPOSITES figurative.

literary adjective **1** *literary works:* **artistic**, poetic, dramatic. **2** *her literary friends:* **scholarly**, intellectual, academic.

literate adjective *people who are economically and politically literate:* **educated**, well read, widely read, scholarly, learned, knowledgeable, cultured, cultivated, well informed.
– OPPOSITES ignorant.

literature noun **1** *English literature:* **writing**; poetry, drama, prose. **2** *the literature on prototype theory:* **publications**, reports, studies; material. **3** *election literature:* **documentation**, material, publicity, blurb, propaganda, advertising; informal bumf.

lithe adjective **agile**, graceful, supple, loose-limbed, nimble, deft, flexible.
– OPPOSITES clumsy.

litigation noun **legal/judicial proceedings**, legal action, lawsuit, legal dispute, case, prosecution, indictment.

litter noun **1** *never drop litter:* **rubbish**, refuse, junk, waste, debris, detritus; N. Amer. trash, garbage. **2** *the litter of glasses around her:* **clutter**, jumble, muddle, mess, heap; informal shambles.
• verb *clothes littered the floor:* **cover**, clutter up; pepper.

little adjective **1** *a little house:* **small**, small-scale, compact; miniature, tiny, bijou; toy, baby, undersized; Scottish wee; informal teeny-weeny, teensy-weensy, itsy-bitsy, tiddly; Brit. informal titchy, dinky; N. Amer. informal vest-pocket. **2** *a little woman:* **short**, small, slight, petite, diminutive, tiny; Scottish wee; informal pint-sized. **3** *my little sister:* **young**, younger, baby. **4** *a few little problems:* **minor**, unimportant, insignificant, trivial, trifling, petty, paltry, inconsequential.
– OPPOSITES big, large, important.
• determiner *they have little political influence:* **limited**, restricted, modest, minimal, negligible, scant.
– OPPOSITES considerable.
• adverb **1** *he is little known as a teacher:* **hardly**, barely, scarcely. **2** *this disease is little seen nowadays:* **rarely**, seldom, infrequently, hardly, scarcely.
– OPPOSITES well, often.

■ **a little 1** *add a little salt:* some, a bit of, a touch of, a soupçon of, a dash of, a taste of, a spot of; a hint of; a dribble of, a splash of, a pinch of, a sprinkling of, a speck of; informal a smidgen of, a tad of. **2** *this reminds me a little of the Adriatic:* slightly; somewhat, quite, to some degree. **little by little** gradually, slowly, slowly but surely, by degrees, by stages, step by step, bit by bit, inch by inch, progressively; imperceptibly.

live[1] verb **1** *the greatest mathematician who ever lived:* **exist**, be alive; breathe, draw breath, walk the earth. **2** *I live in London:* **reside**, have your home, lodge; inhabit, occupy, populate; Scottish stay; formal dwell. **3** *she had lived a difficult life:* **experience**, spend, pass, lead, have, go through, undergo. **4** *they live by hunting and fishing:* **survive**, make a living, eke out a living; subsist, support yourself, sustain yourself, make ends meet, keep body and soul together.
– OPPOSITES die.

■ **live it up** (informal) enjoy yourself, live in the lap of luxury, have a good time; informal party, push the boat out, have a ball; N. Amer. informal live high on/off the hog. **live off/on** subsist on, feed on/off, eat, consume.

live[2] adjective *a live issue:* **topical**, current; important, relevant, burning, pressing, controversial.

livelihood noun **income**, means of support, living, subsistence, daily bread, bread and butter; job, work, employment, occupation.

lively adjective **1** *a lively young woman:* **energetic**, active, animated,

dynamic, full of life, outgoing, spirited, high-spirited, vivacious, enthusiastic, vibrant, buoyant, exuberant, effervescent, cheerful; bouncy, bubbly, sparkling; informal full of beans, chirpy, chipper. **2** *a lively bar:* **busy**, crowded, bustling, buzzing; vibrant, boisterous, jolly. **3** *a lively debate:* **heated**, vigorous, animated, spirited, enthusiastic, forceful; exciting, interesting, memorable. **4** *a lively portrait of the local community:* **vivid**, colourful, striking, graphic. **5** *he bowled at a lively pace:* **brisk**, quick, fast, rapid, swift, speedy, smart.
–OPPOSITES quiet, dull.

liven verb
■ **liven up** brighten up, cheer up, perk up, revive, rally, pick up, bounce back; informal buck up. **liven someone/something up** enliven, animate, raise someone's spirits, perk up, spice up, wake up, invigorate, revive, refresh, galvanize, stimulate, stir up, get going; informal buck up, pep up.

liver noun

> **WORD LINKS**
> **hepatic** relating to the liver
> **hepatitis** inflammation of the liver

livery noun **uniform**, regalia, costume, dress, attire, garb, clothing, outfit, ensemble; informal get-up, gear, kit; formal apparel; old use raiment, vestments.

livid adjective **1** (informal) *Mum was absolutely livid.* See FURIOUS sense 1. **2** *a livid bruise:* **purplish**, bluish, dark, purple; angry.

living noun **1** *she cleaned floors for a living:* **livelihood**, income, means of support, subsistence, keep, daily bread, bread and butter; job, work, employment, occupation. **2** *healthy living:* **way of life**, lifestyle, life; conduct, behaviour, activities, habits.
• adjective **1** *living organisms:* **alive**, live, animate, sentient; breathing, existing. **2** *a living language:* **current**, contemporary; active.
–OPPOSITES dead, extinct.

living room noun **sitting room**, lounge, front room.

load noun **1** *a lorry has shed its load on the A40:* **cargo**, freight, consignment, delivery, shipment, goods, merchandise; pack, bundle, parcel; lorryload, truckload, shipload, boatload, vanload. **2** (informal) *I bought a load of clothes:* **a lot**, a great deal, a large amount/number; many, plenty; informal a heap, a mass, a pile, a stack, a ton, lots, heaps, masses, piles, stacks, tons. **3** *a heavy teaching load:* **commitment**, responsibility, duty, obligation, burden.
• verb **1** *we quickly loaded the van:* **fill**, pack, charge, stock, stack; old use lade. **2** *they loaded boxes into the jeep:* **pack**, stow, store, stack, bundle; place, deposit, put away. **3** *he was loaded with responsibilities:* **burden**, weigh down, saddle, charge; overburden, overwhelm, encumber, tax, strain. **4** *he loaded the gun:* **prime**, charge; set up, prepare. **5** *load the cassette into the camcorder:* **insert**, put, place, slot, slide.

loaded adjective **1** *a loaded freight train:* **full**, filled, laden, packed, stuffed, crammed, brimming, stacked; informal chock-full, chock-a-block. **2** *a politically loaded word:* **charged**, emotive, sensitive, delicate.

loaf verb *he was just loafing around:* **laze**, lounge, loll, idle; informal hang around/round; Brit. informal hang about, mooch about/around; N. Amer. informal bum around.

loan noun *a loan of £7,000:* **credit**, advance; mortgage, overdraft; Brit. informal sub.

loath adjective **reluctant**, unwilling, disinclined; averse, opposed, resistant.
–OPPOSITES willing.

> ! Don't confuse with **loathe**, which means 'to feel hatred or disgust for'.

loathe verb **hate**, detest, abhor, despise; formal abominate.
–OPPOSITES love.

loathing noun **hatred**, hate, abhorrence, odium; antipathy, dislike, hostility, animosity, ill feeling, bad feeling, malice, enmity; repugnance.

loathsome adjective **hateful**, detestable, abhorrent, repulsive, odious, repugnant, repellent, disgusting, revolting, sickening, abominable, despicable, contemptible, reprehensible; vile, horrible, nasty, obnoxious, gross, foul; informal horrid; literary noisome.

lob verb **throw**, toss, fling, pitch, hurl, sling, launch, propel; informal chuck, bung, heave.

lobby noun **1** *the hotel lobby:* **entrance**, hallway, hall, vestibule, foyer, reception area. **2** *the anti-hunt lobby:* **pressure group**, interest group, movement, campaign, crusade; faction, camp, contingent.
• verb **1** *readers are urged to lobby their MPs:* **approach**, contact; petition, appeal to, pressurize. **2** *a group lobbying for better rail services:* **campaign**, crusade, press, push, ask, call, demand; promote, advocate, champion.

local adjective **1** *the local council:* **community**, district, neighbourhood, regional, town, municipal, provincial, village, parish. **2** *a local restaurant:* **neighbourhood**, nearby, near, at hand, close by; handy, convenient. **3** *a local infection:* confined, restricted, contained, localized; limited.
– OPPOSITES national.
• noun *complaints from the locals:* **local person**, native, inhabitant, resident, parishioner.
– OPPOSITES outsider.

locale noun **place**, site, spot, area; position, location, setting, scene, venue, background, backdrop, environment; neighbourhood, district, region, locality.

locality noun *other schools in the locality:* **vicinity**, neighbourhood, area, district, region; informal neck of the woods.

localize verb **limit**, restrict, confine, contain, circumscribe, concentrate.
– OPPOSITES generalize, globalize.

locate verb **1** *spotter planes located the submarines:* **find**, pinpoint, track down, unearth, sniff out, smoke out, search out, uncover. **2** *a company located near Pittsburgh:* **situate**, site, position, place, base; put, build, establish, found, station, install.

location noun **position**, place, situation, site, locality, locale, spot, whereabouts; scene, setting, area, environment; venue, address; technical locus.

lock¹ noun *the lock on the door:* **bolt**, catch, fastener, clasp, hasp, latch.
• verb **1** *he locked the door:* **bolt**, fasten, secure; padlock, latch, chain. **2** *she locked her legs:* **join**, interlock, link, engage, combine, connect; couple. **3** *the wheels locked:* **become stuck**, stick, jam, seize. **4** *he locked her in an embrace:* **clasp**, clench, grasp, embrace, hug, squeeze.
– OPPOSITES unlock, open, separate, divide.
■ **lock someone up** imprison, jail, incarcerate, intern, send to prison, put behind bars, put under lock and key, put in chains, clap in irons, cage, pen, coop up; informal send down, put away, put inside.

lock² noun *a lock of hair:* **tress**, tuft, curl, ringlet, hank, strand, wisp, coil.

locker noun **cupboard**, cabinet, chest, safe, box, case, coffer; storeroom.

lock-up noun *they stored spare furniture in a lock-up:* **storeroom**, store, warehouse, depository; garage.

locomotion noun **movement**, motion; travel; mobility, motility; walking, running; progress, passage, transport; formal perambulation.

lodge noun **1** *the porter's lodge:* **gatehouse**, cottage. **2** *a hunting lodge:* **house**, cottage, cabin, chalet; Brit. shooting box. **3** *a Masonic lodge:* **section**, branch, wing; hall, clubhouse, meeting room; N. Amer. chapter.
• verb **1** *William lodged at our house:* **reside**, board, stay, live, stop; N. Amer. room; informal have digs; formal dwell; old use abide. **2** *the government lodged a protest:* **submit**, register, enter, put forward, advance, lay, present, tender, proffer, put on record, record, table, file. **3** *the money was lodged in a bank:* **deposit**, put, bank; stash, store, stow, put away. **4** *the bullet lodged in his back:* **become embedded**, get/become stuck, stick, catch, become caught, wedge.

lodger noun **boarder**, paying guest, tenant; N. Amer. roomer.

lodging noun **accommodation**, rooms, chambers, living quarters, place to stay, a roof over your head, housing, shelter; informal digs; formal abode, residence, dwelling, dwelling place, habitation.

lofty adjective **1** *a lofty tower:* **tall**, high. **2** *lofty ideals:* **noble**, exalted, high, high-minded, worthy, grand, fine, elevated. **3** *lofty disdain:* **haughty**, arrogant, disdainful, supercilious, condescending, scornful, contemptuous, self-important, conceited, snobbish; informal stuck-up, snooty; Brit. informal toffee-nosed.
–OPPOSITES low, short, base, lowly, modest.

log noun *a log of phone calls:* **record**, register, logbook, journal, diary, minutes, chronicle, record book, ledger, account, tally.
• verb **1** *all complaints are logged:* **register**, record, note down, write down, jot down, put in writing, enter, file, minute. **2** *the pilot had logged 95 hours:* **attain**, achieve, chalk up, make, do, go, cover, clock up.

logic noun **1** *this case appears to defy all logic:* **reason**, judgement, rationality, wisdom, sense, good sense, common sense, sanity. **2** *the logic of their argument:* **reasoning**, line, rationale, argument.

logical adjective **1** *information displayed in a logical fashion:* **reasoned**, rational, sound, cogent, valid; coherent, clear, systematic, orderly, methodical, analytical, consistent, objective. **2** *the logical outcome:* **natural**, reasonable, sensible, understandable; predictable, unsurprising, only to be expected, likely.
–OPPOSITES illogical, irrational, unlikely, surprising.

logistics plural noun **organization**, planning, plans, management, arrangement, administration, orchestration, coordination, execution, handling, running.

logo noun **emblem**, trademark, device, symbol, design, sign, mark; insignia, crest, seal, coat of arms, shield, badge, motif, monogram.

loiter verb **linger**, wait, skulk; loaf, lounge, idle, laze; informal hang around/round; Brit. informal hang about, mooch about/around.

loll verb **1** *he lolled in an armchair:* **lounge**, sprawl; slouch, slump; recline, relax. **2** *her head lolled to one side:* **hang**, droop, sag, drop, flop.

lone adjective **1** *a lone police officer:* **solitary**, single, unaccompanied, solo, sole; isolated. **2** *a lone parent:* **single**, unmarried; separated, divorced, widowed.

loneliness noun **1** *his loneliness was unbearable:* **isolation**, friendlessness, abandonment, rejection; N. Amer. lonesomeness. **2** *the enforced loneliness of a prison cell:* **solitariness**, solitude, aloneness, separation. **3** *the loneliness of the village:* **isolation**, remoteness, seclusion.

lonely adjective **1** *she felt very lonely:* **isolated**, alone, friendless, with no one to turn to, abandoned, rejected, unloved, unwanted; N. Amer. lonesome. **2** *the lonely life of a writer:* **solitary**, isolated. **3** *a lonely road:* **deserted**, uninhabited, desolate, isolated, remote, out of the way, secluded, in the back of beyond, godforsaken; informal in the middle of nowhere.
–OPPOSITES popular, sociable, crowded.

loner noun **recluse**, introvert, lone wolf, hermit, misanthrope, outsider; historical anchorite.

long[1] adjective *a long silence:* **lengthy**, extended, prolonged, protracted, long-lasting, drawn-out, endless, lingering, interminable.
–OPPOSITES short, brief.

long[2] verb *I longed for the holidays:* **yearn**, pine, ache, hanker for/after, hunger, thirst, have a yen, be eager, be desperate; crave, dream of; informal itch, be dying.

longing noun *a longing for the countryside:* **yearning**, craving, ache, burning, hunger, thirst, hankering, yen; informal itch.
• adjective *a longing look:* **yearning**, hungry, thirsty, wistful, covetous, desperate.

long-lasting adjective **enduring**, lasting, abiding, long-lived, long-term, permanent.
–OPPOSITES short-lived, ephemeral.

long-lived adjective. See LONG-LASTING.

long-standing adjective **well established**, long-established; time-honoured, traditional; abiding, enduring.
–OPPOSITES new, recent.

long-suffering adjective **patient**, forbearing, tolerant, uncomplaining, stoical; accommodating, forgiving.
– OPPOSITES impatient, complaining.

long-winded adjective **verbose**, wordy, lengthy, long, overlong, prolix, interminable; discursive, rambling, tortuous, meandering, repetitious; Brit. informal waffly.
– OPPOSITES concise, succinct, laconic.

look verb **1** *I looked at the house across the street:* **glance**, gaze, stare, gape, peer; peep, peek, take a look; watch, observe, view, regard, examine, inspect, eye, scan, scrutinize, survey, study, contemplate, take in, ogle; informal take a gander, rubberneck, get a load of; Brit. informal take a dekko, take a butcher's, take a shufti, gawp; N. Amer. informal eyeball. **2** *her room looked out on Broadway:* **overlook**, face, front. **3** *they looked shocked:* **seem**, appear; come across/over as.
– OPPOSITES ignore.
• noun **1** *I've had a look at the website:* **glance**, examination, study, inspection, scrutiny, peep, peek, glimpse; informal eyeful, gander, look-see, once-over, squint, recce; Brit. informal shufti, dekko, butcher's. **2** *the look on her face:* **expression**, mien. **3** *that rustic look:* **appearance**, air, aspect, manner, demeanour, impression, effect, ambience. **4** *this season's look:* **fashion**, style; informal thing, groove.
■ **look after** take care of, care for, attend to, minister to, tend, mind, keep an eye on, keep safe, be responsible for, protect; nurse, babysit, childmind. **look back on** reflect on, think back to, remember, recall, reminisce about. **look down on** disdain, scorn, look down your nose at, sneer at, despise. **look for** search for, hunt for, try to find, seek, cast about for, forage for. **look into** investigate, enquire into, go into, probe, explore, follow up, research, study, examine; informal check out; N. Amer. informal scope out. **look like** resemble, bear a resemblance to, take after, have the look of, remind you of; informal be the spitting image of, be a dead ringer for. **look on** regard, consider, think of, deem, judge, see, view, count, reckon. **look out** beware, watch out, mind out, be on your guard, be alert, be wary, be vigilant, be careful, take care, be cautious, pay attention, take heed, keep your eyes open/peeled, keep an eye out; watch your step. **look something over** inspect, examine, scrutinize, cast an eye over, take stock of, vet, view, peruse, read through; informal take a dekko at, give something a/the once-over; N. Amer. check out. **look to 1** *we must look to the future:* consider, think about, turn your thoughts to, focus on, take heed of, pay attention to, attend to, address. **2** *they look to the government for help:* turn to, resort to, have recourse to, fall back on, rely on. **look up** improve, get better, pick up, come along/on, progress, make progress, make headway, perk up, rally, take a turn for the better. **look up to** admire, have a high opinion of, think highly of, hold in high regard, respect, esteem, venerate, idolize.

lookalike noun **double**, twin, clone, duplicate, exact likeness, replica, copy, facsimile, Doppelgänger; informal spitting image, dead ringer.

lookout noun **1** *the lookout sighted sails:* **watchman**, watch, guard, sentry, sentinel; observer. **2** (Brit. informal) *that's your lookout:* **problem**, concern, business, affair, responsibility, worry; informal pigeon.
■ **be on the lookout/keep a lookout** keep watch, keep an eye out, keep your eyes peeled, be alert.

loom verb **1** *ghostly shapes loomed out of the fog:* **emerge**, appear, materialize, reveal itself. **2** *the church loomed above him:* **soar**, tower, rise, rear up; hang, overshadow. **3** *without reforms, disaster looms:* **be imminent**, be on the horizon, impend, threaten, brew, be just around the corner.

loop noun **coil**, ring, circle, noose, spiral, curl, bend, curve, arc, twirl, whorl, twist, helix.
• verb **coil**, wind, twist, snake, spiral, curve, bend, turn.

loophole noun **flaw**, discrepancy, inconsistency, ambiguity, omission; Brit. get-out.

loose adjective **1** *a loose floorboard:* **not secure**, unsecured, unattached;

wobbly, unsteady. **2** *she wore her hair loose:* **untied**, free, down. **3** *there's a wolf loose:* **free**, at large, at liberty, on the loose, on the rampage. **4** *a loose interpretation:* **vague**, imprecise, approximate; broad, general, rough; liberal. **5** *a loose jacket:* **baggy**, generously cut, slack, roomy; oversized, shapeless, sagging, sloppy, big.
– OPPOSITES secure, literal, narrow, tight.
• **verb 1** *the hounds had been loosed:* **free**, let loose, release; untie, unchain, unfasten, unleash. **2** *her fingers loosed their hold:* **relax**, slacken, loosen; lessen.
– OPPOSITES confine, tighten.
■ **on the loose** free, at liberty, at large, escaped; on the run, on the rampage; N. Amer. informal on the lam.

> Don't confuse **loose** with **lose**, which means 'no longer have' or 'become unable to find' (*he might lose his job*).

l

loose-limbed **adjective supple**, limber, lithe, willowy; agile, nimble.

loosen **verb 1** *you simply loosen two screws:* **undo**, slacken; unfasten, detach, release, disconnect. **2** *her fingers loosened:* **slacken**, become loose, let go, ease. **3** *Philip loosened his grip:* **weaken**, relax, slacken, loose, lessen, reduce.
■ **loosen up** relax, unwind, ease up/off; informal let up, hang loose, lighten up, go easy.
– OPPOSITES tighten.

loot **noun** *a bag full of loot:* **booty**, spoils, plunder, stolen goods, contraband; informal swag, ill-gotten gains.
• **verb** *troops looted the cathedral:* **plunder**, pillage, ransack, sack, rifle, rob; strip, clear out, gut.

lop **verb cut**, chop, hack, saw, hew; prune, clip, trim, snip.

lope **verb stride**, run, bound; lollop.

lopsided **adjective crooked**, askew, awry, off-centre, uneven, out of true, out of line, asymmetrical, tilted, at an angle, slanting, squint; Scottish agley; informal cockeyed; Brit. informal skew-whiff, wonky.
– OPPOSITES even, level, balanced.

loquacious **adjective talkative**, voluble, garrulous, chatty, gossipy; informal gabby, gassy; Brit. informal able to talk the hind legs off a donkey.
– OPPOSITES reticent, taciturn.

lord **noun 1** *lords and ladies:* **noble**, nobleman, peer, aristocrat. **2** *it is my duty to obey my lord's wishes:* **master**, ruler, leader, chief, superior, monarch, sovereign, king, emperor, prince, governor, commander.
– OPPOSITES commoner, servant, inferior.

lore **noun 1** *Arthurian lore:* **mythology**, myths, legends, stories, traditions, folklore. **2** *cricket lore:* **knowledge**, learning, wisdom; tradition; informal know-how.

lorry **noun truck**, wagon, van, juggernaut, trailer; articulated lorry, heavy goods vehicle, HGV; dated pantechnicon.

lose **verb 1** *I've lost my watch:* **mislay**, misplace. **2** *you've lost your opportunity:* **waste**, squander, fail to take advantage of, let pass, miss; informal pass up, lose out on, blow. **3** *he lost his pursuers:* **escape from**, evade, elude, dodge, avoid, give someone the slip, shake off, throw off; leave behind, outdistance, outstrip, outrun. **4** *they lost 4–0:* **be defeated**, be beaten; informal come a cropper, go down.
– OPPOSITES find, win.

> Don't confuse **lose** with **loose**, which means 'not fixed in place or tied up' (*she wore her hair loose*).

loser **noun 1** *the loser still gets a medal:* **runner-up**, also-ran. **2** (informal) *he's a complete loser:* **failure**, underachiever, ne'er-do-well, dead loss; write-off, has-been; informal flop, non-starter, no-hoper, washout.
– OPPOSITES winner, success.

loss **noun 1** *the loss of the papers:* mislaying, misplacement; destruction, theft, selling. **2** *loss of earnings:* **forfeiture**, diminution, erosion, reduction, depletion. **3** *the loss of her husband:* **death**, demise, passing away, end; formal decease. **4** *British losses in the war:* **casualty**, fatality, victim; dead. **5** *a loss of £15,000:* **deficit**, debit, debt.
– OPPOSITES recovery, profit.
■ **at a loss** baffled, nonplussed, mystified, puzzled, perplexed,

bewildered, bemused, confused, dumbfounded, stumped, stuck; informal flummoxed, beaten.

lost adjective **1** *her lost keys:* **missing**, mislaid, misplaced; stolen. **2** *I think we're lost:* **off course**, going round in circles, adrift, at sea. **3** *a lost opportunity:* **missed**, wasted, squandered, gone by the board; informal down the drain. **4** *lost traditions:* **bygone**, past, former, old, vanished, forgotten, consigned to oblivion, extinct, dead, gone. **5** *lost species and habitats:* **extinct**, died out, defunct, vanished, gone; destroyed, wiped out, exterminated. **6** *a lost cause:* **hopeless**, futile, forlorn, failed, beyond recovery. **7** *lost souls:* **damned**, fallen, condemned, cursed, doomed; literary accursed. **8** *she was lost in thought:* **engrossed**, absorbed, rapt, immersed, deep, intent, engaged, wrapped up.

lot pronoun *a lot of money | lots of friends:* **a large amount**, a good/great deal, an abundance, a wealth, a profusion, plenty, scores; many, numerous, copious; informal hundreds, thousands, millions, billions, loads, masses, heaps, piles, umpteen, oodles, stacks, reams, wads, pots, oceans, mountains, miles, tons, zillions; Brit. informal a shedload, lashings.
• adverb *I work in pastels a lot:* **a great deal**, a good deal, much; often, frequently, regularly.
• noun **1** (informal) *what do your lot think?* **group**, crowd, circle, crew; informal bunch, gang, mob, posse; Brit. informal shower. **2** *the books were auctioned in lots | lot 69:* **item**, article; batch, group, bundle, parcel. **3** *his lot in life:* **fate**, destiny, fortune; situation, circumstances, state, condition, position, plight, predicament. **4** (N. Amer.) *a trailer was parked in the vacant lot:* **piece/patch of ground**, plot; N. Amer. plat.

lotion noun **ointment**, cream, salve, balm, rub, moisturizer, lubricant, unguent, liniment, embrocation.

lottery noun **raffle**, prize draw, sweepstake, sweep, tombola, pools.

loud adjective **1** *loud music:* **noisy**, blaring, booming, deafening, roaring, thunderous, ear-splitting, piercing; powerful, stentorian; Music forte, fortissimo. **2** *loud complaints:* **vociferous**, clamorous, insistent, vehement, emphatic. **3** *a loud T-shirt:* **garish**, gaudy, lurid, showy, ostentatious; vulgar, tasteless; informal flashy, naff, tacky.
– OPPOSITES quiet, soft, gentle, sober, tasteful.

loudly adverb **at the top of your voice**, noisily, stridently, vociferously, shrilly; Music forte, fortissimo.
– OPPOSITES quietly, softly.

loudspeaker noun **speaker**, monitor; loudhailer, megaphone; public address system, PA; Brit. trademark tannoy; N. Amer. bullhorn.

lounge verb **laze**, lie, loll, lie back, lean back, recline, relax, rest, repose, take it easy; sprawl, slump, slouch; loaf, idle, do nothing.
• noun **living room**, sitting room, front room, drawing room, morning room; dated parlour.

lour verb **scowl**, frown, glower, glare, look daggers; informal give someone a dirty look.
– OPPOSITES smile.

louring, lowering adjective **overcast**, dark, leaden, grey, cloudy, clouded, gloomy, threatening, menacing.
– OPPOSITES sunny, bright.

lout noun **hooligan**, ruffian, thug, boor, oaf, rowdy; informal tough, roughneck, bruiser; Brit. informal yob, yobbo.
– OPPOSITES smoothie, gentleman.

loutish adjective **uncouth**, rude, ill-mannered, coarse; thuggish, boorish, uncivilized, rough; informal slobbish; Brit. informal yobbish.
– OPPOSITES polite, well behaved.

lovable adjective **adorable**, dear, sweet, cute, charming, lovely, likeable, engaging, endearing.
– OPPOSITES hateful, loathsome.

love noun **1** *his love for her grew stronger:* **infatuation**, adoration, attachment, devotion, fondness, tenderness, warmth, intimacy, passion, desire, lust, yearning, besottedness. **2** *her love of fashion:* **liking**, enjoyment, appreciation, relish, passion, zeal, zest, enthusiasm, keenness, fondness, weakness, partiality, taste, predilection, penchant. **3** *their love for their fellow human beings:*

compassion, care, regard, solicitude, concern, altruism, unselfishness, philanthropy, benevolence, humanity. **4** *he was her one true love:* **beloved**, loved one; dearest, darling, sweetheart.
–OPPOSITES hatred.
•verb **1** *she loves him dearly:* **be in love with**, be infatuated with, be smitten with, be besotted with, adore, idolize, worship, think the world of, be devoted to, dote on, care for, hold dear; informal be mad/crazy about, carry a torch for. **2** *Laura loved painting:* **like**, delight in, enjoy, take great pleasure in; have a weakness for, be partial to, be taken with; informal have a thing about, be mad/crazy about, be hooked on, get a buzz out of.
–OPPOSITES hate.
■ **in love with** infatuated with, besotted with, enamoured of, smitten with; captivated by, bewitched by, enthralled by, entranced by; devoted to; informal mad/crazy about.

l

WORD LINKS
amatory relating to sexual love

love affair noun **1** *he had a love affair with a teacher:* **relationship**, affair, romance, liaison, fling; Brit. informal carry-on. **2** *a love affair with the motor car:* **enthusiasm**, mania, devotion, passion, obsession.

loveless adjective **passionless**, unloving, sterile, empty, barren, hollow.

lovely adjective **1** *a lovely young woman:* **beautiful**, pretty, attractive, good-looking, handsome, adorable; enchanting, gorgeous, alluring, ravishing, glamorous; Scottish & N. English bonny; informal tasty, stunning, drop-dead gorgeous; Brit. informal fit; N. Amer. informal cute, foxy; old use comely. **2** *a lovely view:* **scenic**, picturesque, pleasing; magnificent, stunning, splendid. **3** (informal) *we had a lovely day:* **delightful**, very pleasant, very nice, marvellous, wonderful, sublime, superb; informal terrific, fabulous, heavenly, divine, amazing, glorious.
–OPPOSITES ugly, horrible.

lover noun **1** *she had a secret lover:* **boyfriend**, **girlfriend**, sweetheart; mistress; partner; informal bit on the side, toy boy, fancy man, fancy woman; dated beau; old use paramour. **2** *a dog lover:* **devotee**, admirer, fan, enthusiast, aficionado; informal buff, freak, nut.

lovesick adjective **lovelorn**, pining, languishing, longing, yearning, infatuated.

loving adjective **affectionate**, fond, devoted, adoring, doting, solicitous; caring, tender, warm, close; amorous, passionate.

low[1] adjective **1** *a low fence:* **short**, small, little; squat, stubby, stunted. **2** *a dress with a low neckline:* **low cut**, skimpy, revealing, plunging. **3** *low prices:* **cheap**, economical, moderate, reasonable, modest, bargain, bargain-basement, rock-bottom. **4** *fuel supplies were low:* **scarce**, scant, meagre, sparse, few, little; reduced, depleted, diminished. **5** *cheap goods of low quality:* **inferior**, substandard, poor, bad, low-grade, second-rate, unsatisfactory. **6** *they had very low expectations:* **unambitious**, unaspiring, modest, humble, lowly. **7** *a low opinion:* **unfavourable**, poor, bad, adverse, negative. **8** *a low voice:* **quiet**, soft, faint, gentle, muted, subdued, muffled, hushed. **9** *a low note:* **bass**, low-pitched, deep, rumbling, booming, sonorous. **10** *she was feeling very low:* **depressed**, dejected, despondent, downhearted, downcast, down, miserable, dispirited; flat, weary; informal fed up, down in the mouth, down in the dumps, blue.
–OPPOSITES high, expensive, plentiful, superior, loud, cheerful.
•noun *the dollar fell to an all-time low:* **nadir**, low point, lowest level; rock bottom.
–OPPOSITES high.

low[2] verb *cattle were lowing:* **moo**, bellow.

lowbrow adjective **mass-market**, tabloid, popular, lightweight, unsophisticated, trashy, simplistic; Brit. downmarket; informal dumbed down, rubbishy.
–OPPOSITES highbrow, intellectual.

lower[1] adjective **1** *the lower house of parliament:* **subordinate**, inferior,

lesser, junior, minor, secondary, subsidiary, subservient. **2** *her lower lip:* **bottom**, bottommost, nether, under. **3** *a lower price:* **cheaper**, reduced, cut.
– OPPOSITES upper, higher, increased.

lower[2] verb **1** *lower your voice:* **drop**, soften, quieten, hush, tone down, muffle, turn down, modulate. **2** *they are lowering their prices:* **reduce**, decrease, drop, bring down, cut, slash.
– OPPOSITES raise, increase.

low-key adjective **restrained**, modest, understated, muted, subtle, quiet, low-profile, inconspicuous, unostentatious, unobtrusive, discreet.
– OPPOSITES ostentatious, obtrusive.

lowly adjective **humble**, low, low-ranking; common, ordinary, plain, modest, simple; obscure.
– OPPOSITES aristocratic, exalted.

loyal adjective **faithful**, true, devoted; constant, steadfast, staunch, dependable, reliable, trustworthy, trusty; patriotic.
– OPPOSITES treacherous.

loyalty noun **allegiance**, faithfulness, obedience, adherence, devotion; steadfastness, staunchness, dedication, commitment; patriotism.
– OPPOSITES treachery.

lozenge noun **1** *the pattern consists of overlapping lozenges:* **diamond**, rhombus. **2** *a throat lozenge:* **pastille**, drop; cough sweet; dated cachou.

lubricant noun **grease**, oil, lubrication, lotion, unguent; informal lube.

lubricate verb **grease**, oil.

lucid adjective **1** *a lucid description:* **intelligible**, comprehensible, understandable, cogent, coherent, articulate; clear, transparent; plain, straightforward. **2** *he was not lucid enough to explain:* **rational**, sane, in possession of your faculties, compos mentis, clear-headed, sober; informal all there.
– OPPOSITES confusing, confused.

luck noun **1** *with luck you'll make it:* **good fortune**, good luck; stroke of luck; informal lucky break. **2** *I wish you luck:* **success**, prosperity, good fortune, good luck. **3** *it is a matter of luck whether it hits or misses:* **fortune**, fate, serendipity; chance, accident, a twist of fate; Austral./NZ informal mozzle.
– OPPOSITES bad luck, misfortune.

luckily adverb **fortunately**, happily, providentially, by good fortune, as luck would have it; mercifully, thankfully.
– OPPOSITES unfortunately.

luckless adjective **unlucky**, unfortunate, unsuccessful, hapless, doomed, ill-fated; literary star-crossed.
– OPPOSITES lucky.

lucky adjective **1** *the lucky winner:* **fortunate**, in luck, favoured, charmed; successful; Brit. informal jammy. **2** *a lucky escape:* **providential**, fortunate, timely, opportune, serendipitous; chance, fortuitous, accidental.
– OPPOSITES unfortunate.

lucrative adjective **profitable**, gainful, remunerative, money-making, paying, well paid; rewarding, worthwhile; thriving, flourishing, successful, booming.
– OPPOSITES unprofitable.

ludicrous adjective **absurd**, ridiculous, farcical, laughable, risible, preposterous, mad, insane, idiotic, stupid, asinine, nonsensical; informal crazy.
– OPPOSITES sensible.

lug verb **carry**, lift, heave, hoist, manhandle; haul, drag, tug, tow; informal hump, tote; N. Amer. informal schlep.

luggage noun **baggage**; bags, suitcases, cases. See also **BAG** noun.

lugubrious adjective **mournful**, gloomy, sad, unhappy, melancholy, doleful, woeful, miserable, forlorn, sombre, solemn, sorrowful, morose, dour, cheerless, joyless, dismal; funereal; literary dolorous.
– OPPOSITES cheerful.

lukewarm adjective **1** *lukewarm coffee:* **tepid**, warmish, at room temperature. **2** *a lukewarm response:* **indifferent**, cool, half-hearted, apathetic, unenthusiastic, tepid, offhand, perfunctory, non-committal.
– OPPOSITES hot, cold, enthusiastic.

lull verb **1** *the sound of the bells lulled us to sleep:* **soothe**, calm, hush; rock to sleep. **2** *his suspicions were soon*

l

lulled: **allay**, ease, alleviate, quiet, quieten; reduce, diminish; quell, banish, dispel. **3** *the noise had lulled:* **abate**, die down, subside, let up, moderate, lessen, dwindle, decrease, diminish.
– OPPOSITES waken, agitate, arouse, intensify.
• **noun 1** *a lull in the fighting:* **pause**, respite, interval, break, suspension, breathing space; informal let-up, breather. **2** *the lull before the storm:* **calm**, stillness, quiet, tranquillity, peace, silence, hush.
– OPPOSITES agitation, activity.

lumber[1] **verb** *elephants lumbered past:* **lurch**, stumble, trundle, shamble, shuffle; trudge, clump.

lumber[2] **noun 1** *a spare room packed with lumber:* **jumble**, clutter, odds and ends, bits and pieces; rubbish; informal junk, odds and sods. **2** *the lumber trade:* **timber**, wood.
• **verb** (Brit. informal) *she was lumbered with a husband and child:* **burden**, saddle, encumber.
– OPPOSITES free.

l

lumbering **adjective** **clumsy**, awkward, slow, bumbling, inept; ponderous; informal clodhopping.
– OPPOSITES nimble, agile.

luminary **noun** **leading light**, inspiration, hero, heroine, leader, expert, master; legend, great, giant.
– OPPOSITES nobody.

luminous **adjective** **shining**, bright, brilliant, radiant, dazzling, glowing, scintillating; luminescent, phosphorescent, fluorescent, incandescent.
– OPPOSITES dark.

lump **noun 1** *a lump of coal:* **chunk**, hunk, piece, block, wedge, slab, ball, knob, clod, gobbet, dollop; informal glob, gob. **2** *a lump on his head:* **swelling**, bump, bulge, protuberance, protrusion, growth, nodule.
• **verb** *it is convenient to lump them together:* **combine**, put, group, bunch.

lumpy **adjective** **bumpy**, knobbly, uneven, rough, gnarled.

lunacy **noun** **folly**, foolishness, madness, stupidity, silliness, idiocy, recklessness, irresponsibility; informal craziness; Brit. informal daftness.
– OPPOSITES sense, prudence.

lunatic **noun** *he drives like a lunatic:* **maniac**, madman, madwoman; fool, idiot; informal loony, nutcase, head case, psycho; Brit. informal nutter; N. Amer. informal screwball.
• **adjective** *a lunatic idea.* See MAD sense 3.

lunch **noun** **midday meal**, luncheon; Brit. dinner.

lung **noun**

WORD LINKS
pulmonary relating to the lungs

lunge **noun** *he made a lunge at his attacker:* **thrust**, dive, rush, charge, grab.
• **verb** *he lunged at Finn with a knife:* **thrust**, dive, spring, launch yourself, rush.

lurch **verb 1** *he lurched into the kitchen:* **stagger**, stumble, sway, reel, roll, totter. **2** *the car lurched to the left:* **swing**, list, roll, pitch, veer, swerve.

lure **verb** *consumers are frequently lured into debt:* **tempt**, entice, attract, induce, coax, persuade, inveigle, seduce, beguile.
– OPPOSITES deter, put off.
• **noun** *the lure of the stage:* **temptation**, attraction, pull, draw, appeal; inducement, allure, fascination, interest, glamour.

lurid **adjective 1** *lurid colours:* **bright**, vivid, glaring, fluorescent, intense, gaudy, loud. **2** *lurid details of the murder:* **sensational**, extravagant, colourful; salacious, graphic, explicit, prurient, shocking; gruesome, gory, grisly; informal juicy.
– OPPOSITES muted, restrained.

lurk **verb** **skulk**, loiter, lie in wait, hide.

luscious **adjective 1** *luscious fruit:* **delicious**, succulent, juicy, mouth-watering, sweet, tasty, appetizing; informal scrumptious, yummy; N. Amer. informal nummy. **2** *a luscious Swedish starlet:* **gorgeous**, nubile, ravishing, alluring, sultry, beautiful, stunning; informal fanciable, tasty, curvy; Brit. informal fit; N. Amer. informal foxy, cute; Austral./NZ informal spunky.
– OPPOSITES unappetizing, plain, scrawny.

lush **adjective 1** *lush vegetation:* **luxuriant**, rich, abundant, profuse, riotous, vigorous; dense, thick,

rampant. **2** *a lush apartment:* **luxurious**, sumptuous, palatial, opulent, lavish, elaborate, extravagant, fancy; informal plush, ritzy, posh, swanky; Brit. informal swish; N. Amer. informal swank.
– OPPOSITES barren, sparse, austere.

lust noun **1** *his lust for her:* **desire**, longing, passion; libido, sex drive, sexuality; lechery, lecherousness, lasciviousness. **2** *a lust for power:* **greed**, desire, craving, eagerness, longing, yearning, hunger, thirst, appetite, hankering.
– OPPOSITES dread, aversion.
• verb **1** *he lusted after his employer's wife:* **desire**, be consumed with desire for; informal have the hots for, fancy, have a thing about/for. **2** *she lusted after adventure:* **crave**, desire, want, long for, yearn for, dream of, hanker for/after, hunger for, thirst for, ache for.
– OPPOSITES dread, avoid.

lustful adjective **lecherous**, lascivious, libidinous, licentious, salacious; wanton, immodest, indecent, dirty, prurient; passionate, sensual; informal horny, randy, raunchy; formal concupiscent.
– OPPOSITES chaste, pure.

lustily adverb **heartily**, vigorously, loudly, at the top of your voice, powerfully, forcefully, strongly.
– OPPOSITES feebly, quietly.

lustre noun **sheen**, gloss, shine, gleam, patina.
– OPPOSITES dullness.

lustreless adjective **dull**, lacklustre, matt, unpolished, tarnished, dingy, flat.
– OPPOSITES lustrous, bright.

lustrous adjective **shiny**, shining, satiny, silky, glossy, gleaming, burnished, polished; bright, brilliant, luminous.
– OPPOSITES dull, dark.

lusty adjective **1** *lusty young men:* **healthy**, strong, fit, vigorous, robust, energetic; rugged, sturdy, muscular, muscly, strapping, hefty, burly; informal beefy; dated stalwart. **2** *lusty singing:* **loud**, vigorous, hearty; enthusiastic.
– OPPOSITES feeble, quiet.

luxuriant adjective **lush**, rich, abundant, profuse, riotous, prolific, vigorous; dense, thick, rampant.
– OPPOSITES barren, sparse.

luxuriate verb **revel**, bask, delight, wallow; (**luxuriate in**) enjoy, relish, savour.
– OPPOSITES dislike.

luxurious adjective **opulent**, sumptuous, grand, palatial, magnificent, extravagant, fancy; Brit. upmarket; informal plush, posh, classy, ritzy, swanky; Brit. informal swish; N. Amer. informal swank.
– OPPOSITES plain, basic.

luxury noun **1** *we'll live in luxury:* **opulence**, sumptuousness, grandeur, magnificence, splendour, lavishness. **2** *a TV is his only luxury:* **indulgence**, extravagance, treat, extra, frill.
– OPPOSITES simplicity, necessity.

lying noun *she was no good at lying:* **untruthfulness**, fabrication, fibbing, perjury; dishonesty, mendacity, telling lies, misrepresentation, deceit, duplicity; literary perfidy.
– OPPOSITES honesty.
• adjective *he was a lying womanizer:* **untruthful**, false, dishonest, mendacious, deceitful, deceiving, duplicitous, double-dealing, two-faced; literary perfidious.
– OPPOSITES truthful.

lyrical adjective **1** *a subtle, lyrical film:* **expressive**, emotional, deeply felt, personal, passionate. **2** *she was lyrical about her success:* **enthusiastic**, effusive, rapturous, ecstatic, euphoric.
– OPPOSITES unenthusiastic.

lyrics plural noun **words**; libretto, text, lines.

Wordfinder

Contents

Animals
Birds
Cat breeds
Dinosaurs
Dog breeds
Fish
Horse and pony breeds
Insects and arachnids
Mammals
Reptiles and amphibians
Shellfish and other crustaceans and molluscs
Male and female animals
Young animals
Collective names for animals and birds

Clothing and fabrics
Clothes
Footwear
Headgear
Fabrics and fibres

Food and drink
Bread
Cakes, biscuits, and desserts
Cheeses
Fruit and nuts
Herbs and spices
Meat cuts and joints
Meat types and products
Pasta
Vegetables
Alcoholic drinks
Wine and grape varieties
Types of sherry and dessert wine
Wine bottles
Cocktails and other mixed drinks
Non-alcoholic drinks

Music
Musical instruments
Dances and types of dancing

Plants
Flowering plants
Trees and shrubs
Mushrooms, toadstools, and other fungi

Science
Chemical elements and symbols
Alloys
Rocks and minerals

Transport
Motor vehicles
Carriages and carts
Ships and boats
Aircraft
Trains and rolling stock

Animals

Birds

albatross
auk
avocet
barnacle goose
barn owl
bird of paradise
bittern
blackbird
blackcap
bluebird
blue tit
booby
bowerbird
brambling
budgerigar
bullfinch
bunting
bustard
butcher-bird
buzzard
Canada goose
canary
capercaillie
caracara
cassowary
chaffinch
chicken
chiffchaff
chough
coal tit
cockatiel
cockatoo
condor
coot
cormorant
corncrake
crane
crossbill
crow
cuckoo
curlew
dabchick
dodo
dotterel
dove
duck
dunlin
dunnock
eagle
egret
eider duck
emu
falcon
fantail
fieldfare
finch
flamingo
flycatcher
fulmar
gannet
goldcrest
golden eagle
goldfinch
goose
goshawk
great tit
grebe
greenfinch
grouse
guillemot
guineafowl
gull
gyrfalcon
harrier
hawfinch
hawk
hen
heron
hobby
hoopoe
hornbill
house martin
hummingbird
ibis
jackdaw
jay
kestrel
kingfisher
kite
kittiwake
kiwi
kookaburra
lammergeier
lapwing
lark
linnet
lovebird
lyrebird
macaw
magpie
mallard
martin
merlin
mistle thrush
moa
mockingbird
moorhen
mynah bird
nightingale
nightjar
nuthatch
ortolan
osprey
ostrich
ouzel
owl
oystercatcher
parakeet
parrot
partridge
peacock
peewit
pelican
penguin
peregrine falcon
petrel
pheasant
pigeon
pintail
pipit
plover
ptarmigan
puffin
quail
rail
raven
red kite
redpoll
redstart
redwing
rhea
ringdove
roadrunner
robin
rook
sandpiper
seagull
shag
shearwater
shelduck
shrike
siskin
skua
skylark
snipe
song thrush
sparrow
sparrowhawk
spoonbill
starling
stonechat
stork
sunbird
swallow
swan
swift
tawny owl
tern
thrush
tit
toucan
treecreeper
turkey
turtle dove
vulture
wagtail
warbler
waxwing
weaver bird
wigeon
whinchat
whippoorwill
woodcock
woodlark
woodpecker
wren
yellowhammer

Cat breeds

Abyssinian
Angora
Balinese
Bengal
Birman
British shorthair
Burmese
Burmilla
Cornish Rex
Devon Rex
Japanese Bobtail
Maine Coon
Manx
Ocicat
Persian
Ragdoll
Russian Blue
Siamese
Somali
Sphynx
Tiffanie
Tonkinese
Turkish Van

Dinosaurs

allosaurus
ankylosaur
apatosaurus
brachiosaurus
brontosaurus
carnosaur
coelurosaur
deinonychus
diplodocus
dromaeosaur
duck-billed dinosaur
hadrosaur
iguanodon
megalosaurus
pliosaur
protoceratops
pteranodon
pterodactyl
raptor
saurischian
sauropod
seismosaurus
stegosaurus
thecodont

theropod
triceratops
tyrannosaurus
ultrasaurus
velociraptor

Dog breeds

Aberdeen terrier
affenpinscher
Afghan hound
Airedale terrier
Akita
Alsatian
basenji
basset hound
beagle
bearded collie
Bedlington terrier
Belgian sheepdog
Bernese mountain dog
bichon frise
black and tan
Blenheim spaniel
bloodhound
Border collie
Border terrier
borzoi
Boston terrier
bouvier
boxer
bulldog
bull mastiff
bull terrier
cairn terrier
Cape hunting dog
Cavalier King Charles
chihuahua
chow
Clumber spaniel
Clydesdale
cocker spaniel
collie
coonhound
corgi
dachshund
Dalmatian
Dandie Dinmont
deerhound
Dobermann pinscher
elk hound
English setter
English springer
foxhound
fox terrier
German Shepherd
golden retriever
Gordon setter
Great Dane
greyhound
griffon
harrier
husky
Ibizan hound
Irish setter
Irish terrier
Irish wolfhound
Jack Russell terrier
keeshond
kelpie
Kerry blue
King Charles spaniel
Komondor
Labradoodle
Labrador retriever
laika
Lakeland terrier
Leonberg
Lhasa apso
malamute/ malemute
Maltese dog/ terrier
Manchester terrier
mastiff
Mexican hairless
Newfoundland
Norfolk terrier
Norwich terrier
Old English sheepdog
papillon
peke
Pekinese/ Pekingese
Pharaoh hound
pit bull terrier
pointer
Pomeranian
poodle
pug dog
puli
Pyrenean mountain dog
Pyrenean sheepdog
Pyrenean wolfhound
Queensland blue heeler
redbone
red setter
retriever
Rhodesian ridgeback
Rottweiler
rough collie
St Bernard
saluki
Samoyed
schipperke
schnauzer
Scottie dog
Scottish terrier
Sealyham terrier
setter
Shar Pei
sheepdog
sheltie
Shetland sheepdog
shih-tzu
Skye terrier
spaniel
Spinone
spitz
springer spaniel
Staffordshire bull terrier
staghound
terrier
Tibetan mastiff
Tibetan spaniel
Tibetan terrier
tosa
vizsla
Weimaraner
Welsh corgi
Welsh hound
Welsh springer
Welsh terrier
West Highland terrier
wheaten terrier
whippet
wolfhound
Yorkshire terrier

Fish

anchovy
angelfish
anglerfish
archerfish
barbel
barracouta
barracuda
bass
beluga
blenny
bluefin
bonito
boxfish
bream
brill
brisling
bullhead
carp
catfish
charr
chub
clownfish
cod
coelacanth
coley
conger eel
dab
dace
damselfish
dogfish
dorado
dory
Dover sole
eel
filefish
flatfish
flathead
flounder
flying fish
garfish
goby
goldfish
gourami
grayling
great white shark
grouper
gudgeon
guppy
gurnard
haddock
hake
halfbeak
halibut
hammerhead
herring
hoki
huss
John Dory
koi
lamprey
lanternfish
lemon sole
ling
loach
lumpsucker
lungfish
mackerel
mako
manta
marlin
megamouth
minnow
monkfish
moray eel
mudskipper
mullet
needlefish
nurse shark
oarfish
orfe
parrotfish
perch
pike
pilchard
pilotfish
pipefish
piranha
plaice
pollack

porbeagle
puffer fish
rabbitfish
rainbow trout
ray
remora
roach
sailfish
saithe
salmon
sardine
sawfish
scorpionfish
sea horse
shad
shark
skate
skipjack
skipper
smelt
snapper
sockeye
sole
sprat
stargazer
stickleback
stingray
stonefish
sturgeon
sunfish
surgeonfish
swordfish
swordtail
tarpon
tench
tetra
thresher
tope
triggerfish
trout
tuna
turbot
weever
whaler shark
whitebait
whitefish
whiting
wobbegong
wrasse
yellowfin
zander

Horse and pony breeds

American Saddle Horse
Andalusian
Anglo-Arab
Appaloosa
Arab
Barb
brumby
Camargue
Cleveland Bay
Clydesdale
Conestoga
Connemara pony
criollo
Dales pony
Dartmoor pony
Dutch draught
Dutch warmblood
Exmoor pony
Falabella
Fell pony
hackney
Haflinger
Hanoverian
Highland pony
Holstein
hunter
hyracotherium *or* eohippus (extinct)
Lipizzaner/ Lippizaner
miohippus (extinct)
Morgan
mustang
New Forest pony
Percheron
Pinto
pliohippus (extinct)
polo pony
pony of the Americas
Przewalski's horse
Quarter Horse
Saddlebred
Shetland pony
shire horse
Standardbred
Suffolk Punch
tarpan (extinct)
Tartar pony
Tennessee Walking Horse
thoroughbred
Timor pony
Trakehner
trotter
Waler
warmblood
Welsh mountain pony

Insects and arachnids

ant
aphid
bedbug
bee
beetle
blackfly
black widow
blowfly
bluebottle
bombardier beetle
borer
botfly
bumblebee
butterfly
cabbage white
caddis fly
caterpillar
chafer
chigger
cicada
cockchafer
cockroach
crane fly
cricket
daddy-long-legs
damselfly
death-watch beetle
dragonfly
earwig
firefly
flea
fly
fritillary
froghopper
gadfly
glow-worm
gnat
grasshopper
greenfly
harvestman
hawkmoth
honeybee
hornet
horsefly
housefly
hoverfly
ichneumon
lacewing
ladybird
leafcutter ant
leafhopper
leatherjacket
locust
louse
mantis
May bug
mayfly
mealy bug
midge
mite
mosquito
moth
pond skater
praying mantis
red admiral
sandfly
sawfly
scarab
scorpion
silverfish
spider
springtail
stag beetle
stick insect
swallowtail
tarantula
termite
thrips
thunderbug
thunderfly
tick
tortoiseshell
tsetse fly
warble fly
wasp
water boatman
weevil
whirligig
whitefly
witchetty grub

Mammals

aardvark
alpaca
angora
anteater
antelope
ape
armadillo
ass
aurochs
baboon
badger
bandicoot
bat
bear
beaver
beluga
bison
blue whale
boar
bobcat
bottlenose dolphin
buffalo
bushbaby
camel
capuchin monkey
capybara
caribou
cat
chamois
cheetah
chimpanzee
chinchilla

chipmunk
civet
coati
colobus
cougar
cow
coyote
coypu
deer
dingo
dog
dolphin
donkey
dormouse
dromedary
duck-billed platypus
dugong
duiker
echidna
eland
elephant
elk
ermine
fallow deer
fennec
ferret
flying fox
fox
gazelle
gemsbok
gerbil
gibbon
giraffe
gnu
goat
gopher
gorilla
grampus
grizzly bear
groundhog
guinea pig
hamster
hare
hartebeest
hedgehog
hippopotamus
hog
horse
howler monkey
humpback whale
hyena
hyrax
ibex
impala
jackal
jaguar
jerboa
kangaroo
killer whale
kinkajou
koala
kudu
langur
lemming
lemur
leopard
lion
llama
loris
lynx
macaque
manatee
mandrill
margay
marmot
marmoset
marten
meerkat
mink
minke whale
mole
mongoose
monkey
moose
mouse
mule
muntjac
musk ox
narwhal
ocelot
okapi
onager
opossum
orang-utan
orca
oryx
otter
ox
panda
pangolin
panther
peccary
phalanger
pig
pine marten
pipistrelle
platypus
polar bear
polecat
porcupine
porpoise
possum
potto
prairie dog
proboscis monkey
puma
rabbit
raccoon
rat
reindeer
rhesus monkey
rhinoceros
roe deer
rorqual
sea cow
seal
sea lion
serval
sheep
shrew
skunk
sloth
sperm whale
spider monkey
springbok
squirrel
stoat
tamarin
tapir
tarsier
Tasmanian devil
tiger
vampire bat
vervet monkey
vole
wallaby
walrus
wapiti
warthog
waterbuck
water buffalo
weasel
whale
wildcat
wildebeest
wolf
wolverine
wombat
woodchuck
yak
zebra

Reptiles and amphibians

adder
alligator
anaconda
asp
axolotl
basilisk
boa constrictor
bullfrog
caiman
cane toad
chameleon
cobra
constrictor
crocodile
frog
galliwasp
gecko
gharial
Gila monster
grass snake
iguana
Komodo dragon
leatherback
lizard
loggerhead turtle
mamba
moloch
monitor lizard
natterjack toad
newt
puff adder
python
rattlesnake
rinkhals
salamander
sidewinder
skink
slow-worm
snake
taipan
terrapin
toad
tortoise
turtle
viper

Shellfish and other crustaceans and molluscs

abalone
argonaut
auger shell
barnacle
clam
cockle
conch
cowrie
crab
crawfish
crayfish
cuttlefish
hermit crab
krill
langoustine
limpet
lobster
mitre
murex
mussel
nautilus
nerite
octopus
ormer
oyster
paua
periwinkle
piddock
prawn
quahog
razor shell
sandhopper
scallop
sea slug
slug
shrimp
snail
spider crab
squid
teredo
triton
wentletrap
whelk
winkle
woodlouse

Male and female animals

antelope: *buck*, *doe*
badger: *boar*, *sow*
bear: *boar*, *sow*
bird: *cock*, *hen*
buffalo: *bull*, *cow*
cat: *tom*, *queen*
cattle: *bull*, *cow*
chicken: *cock*, *hen*
deer: *stag*, *doe*
dog: *dog*, *bitch*
donkey: *jackass*, *jenny*
duck: *drake*, *duck*
elephant: *bull*, *cow*
ferret: *hob*, *gill*
fish: *cock*, *hen*
fox: *dog*, *vixen*
goat: *billy goat*, *nanny goat*
goose: *gander*, *goose*
hare: *buck*, *doe*
horse: *stallion*, *mare*
kangaroo: *buck*, *doe*
leopard: *leopard*, *leopardess*
lion: *lion*, *lioness*
otter: *dog*, *bitch*
pheasant: *cock*, *hen*
pig: *boar*, *sow*
rabbit: *buck*, *doe*
seal: *bull*, *cow*
sheep: *ram*, *ewe*
swan: *cob*, *pen*
tiger: *tiger*, *tigress*
whale: *bull*, *cow*
wolf: *dog*, *bitch*
zebra: *stallion*, *mare*

Young animals

calf (*antelope*, *buffalo*, *camel*, *cattle*, *elephant*, *elk*, *giraffe*, *rhinoceros*, *seal*, *whale*)
chick (*chicken*, *hawk*, *pheasant*)
colt (*male horse*)
cub (*badger*, *bear*, *fox*, *leopard*, *lion*, *tiger*, *walrus*, *wolf*)
cygnet (*swan*)
duckling (*duck*)
eaglet (*eagle*)
elver (*eel*)
eyas (*hawk*)
fawn (*caribou*, *deer*)
filly (*female horse*)
foal (*horse*, *zebra*)
fry (*fish*)
gosling (*goose*)
joey (*kangaroo*, *wallaby*, *possum*)
kid (*goat*, *roe deer*)
kit (*beaver*, *ferret*, *fox*, *mink*, *weasel*)
kitten (*cat*, *cougar*, *rabbit*, *skunk*)
lamb (*sheep*)
leveret (*hare*)
owlet (*owl*)
parr (*salmon*)
piglet (*pig*)
pup (*dog*, *rat*, *seal*, *wolf*)
puppy (*coyote*, *dog*)
smolt (*salmon*)
squab (*pigeon*)
tadpole (*frog*, *toad*)
whelp (*dog*, *wolf*)

Collective names for animals

a shrewdness of **apes**
a herd/pace of **asses**
a troop of **baboons**
a cete of **badgers**
a sloth of **bears**
a swarm/drift/hive/erst of **bees**
a flock/flight/pod of **birds**
a herd/gang/obstinacy of **buffalo**
a bellowing of **bullfinches**
a drove of **bullocks**
an army of **caterpillars**
a clowder/glaring of **cats**
a herd/drove of **cattle**
a brood/clutch/peep of **chickens**
a chattering of **choughs**
a rag/rake of **colts**
a covert of **coots**
a herd of **cranes**
a bask of **crocodiles**
a murder of **crows**
a litter of **cubs**
a herd of **curlew**
a herd/mob of **deer**
a pack/kennel of **dogs**
a school of **dolphins**
a trip of **dotterel** (type of plover)
a flight/dole/piteousness of **doves**
a paddling of **ducks** (on water)
a safe of **ducks** (on land)
a fling of **dunlins**
a herd/parade of **elephants**
a herd/gang of **elk**
a busyness of **ferrets**
a charm of **finches**
a shoal/run of **fish**
a swarm/cloud of **flies**
a skulk of **foxes**
a gaggle of **geese** (on land)
a skein/team/wedge of **geese** (in flight)
a herd of **giraffes**
a cloud of **gnats**
a flock/herd/trip of **goats**
a band of **gorillas**
a pack/covey of **grouse**
a down/mute/husk of **hares**
a cast of **hawks**
a siege of **herons**
a bloat of **hippopotami**
a drove/string/stud/team of **horses**
a pack/cry/kennel of **hounds**
a flight/swarm of **insects**
a fluther/smack of **jellyfish**
a mob/troop of **kangaroos**
a kindle/litter of **kittens**
a desert of **lapwings**
a bevy/exaltation of **larks**
a leap/lepe of **leopards**
a pride/sawt of **lions**
a tiding of **magpies**
a sord/suit of **mallard**
a stud of **mares**
a richesse of **martens**
a labour of **moles**
a troop of **monkeys**
a span/barren of **mules**
a watch of **nightingales**
a parliament/stare of **owls**
a yoke of **oxen**

a pandemonium of **parrots**
a covey of **partridges**
a muster of **peacocks**
a muster/parcel/rookery of **penguins**
a bevy/head of **pheasants**
a kit of **pigeons** (in flight)
a litter/herd of **pigs**
a congregation/stand/wing of **plovers**
a rush/flight of **pochards**
a pod/school/herd/turmoil of **porpoises**
a covey of **ptarmigan**
a litter of **pups**
a bevy/drift of **quail**
a bury of **rabbits**
a string of **racehorses**
an unkindness of **ravens**
a crash of **rhinoceros**
a bevy of **roe deer**
a parliament/building/rookery of **rooks**
a hill of **ruffs**
a pod/herd/rookery of **seals**
a flock/herd/trip/mob of **sheep**
a dopping of **sheldrake**
a wisp/walk of **snipe**
a host of **sparrows**
a murmuration of **starlings**
a flight of **swallows**
a game/herd of **swans** (on land)
a wedge of **swans** (in flight)
a drift/herd/sounder of **swine**
a spring of **teal**
a knot of **toads**
a hover of **trout**
a rafter of **turkeys**
a bale/turn of **turtles**
a bunch/knob of **waterfowl**
a school/herd/pod/gam of **whales**
a company/trip of **wigeon**
a sounder of **wild boar**
a dout/destruction of **wild cats**
a team of **wild ducks** (in flight)
a bunch/trip/plump/knob of **wildfowl**
a pack/rout of **wolves**
a fall of **woodcock**
a descent of **woodpeckers**
a herd of **wrens**
a zeal of **zebras**

Many of these are fanciful or humorous terms which probably never had any real currency in English but have been popularized in books such as *Sports and Pastimes of England* (1801) by Joseph Strutt.

Clothing and fabrics

Clothes

anorak
apron
ballgown
bandanna
bandeau
basque
bell-bottoms
belt
Bermuda shorts
bib
bikini
blazer
bloomers
blouse
blouson
boa
bodice
body
body stocking
bolero
bolo tie
bomber jacket
bow tie
boxer shorts
bra
braces
breeches
burka/burkha/burqa
burnous
bustier
cagoule
camisole
camiknickers
cape
capri pants
cardigan
cargo pants
carpenter trousers
catsuit
chador
chemise
cheongsam
chinos
churidars
coat
combat trousers
corset
cravat
crew neck
crinoline
crop top
culottes
cummerbund
dhoti
dinner jacket
dirndl
djellaba
dolman
donkey jacket
doublet
drainpipes
dress
dressing gown
dress shirt
duffel coat
dungarees
fichu
flares
fleece
flying jacket
foulard
frock coat
gilet
glove
gown
greatcoat
guernsey
gymslip
hipsters
hoody/hoodie
hose
hot pants
housecoat
hula skirt
jacket
jeans
jerkin
jersey
jilbab
jodhpurs
jumper
jumpsuit
kaftan
kagoul
kameez
kilt
kimono
knickers
knickerbockers
lederhosen
leggings
leg warmers
leotard
loincloth
lumberjacket
mac
mackintosh/macintosh
maillot
mantilla
mantle
maxi
mini
miniskirt
mitten
morning coat
muff
muffler
muumuu
neckerchief
nightdress
nightshirt
oilskins
overalls
overcoat
Oxford bags

palazzo pants
pantaloons
panties
pants
pantyhose
parka
pashmina
pedal pushers
peignoir
pencil skirt
peplum
petticoat
pinafore
pinafore dress
plus fours
polo neck
polo shirt
poncho
pullover
pyjamas
raincoat
redingote
reefer jacket
robe
ruff
safari jacket
sailor suit
salopettes
sari
sarong
sash
scarf
serape/sarape
shalwar
shawl
sheepskin
shell suit
shift
shirt
shirtwaister
shorts
shrug
skinny-rib
ski pants
skirt
slacks
slip
smock
smoking jacket
sock
stirrup pants
stock
stocking
stole
suit
sundress
suspenders
sweater
sweatpants
sweatshirt
swimsuit
T-shirt
tabard
tailcoat
tails
tank top
tee
thong
tie
tights
tippet
toga
top
topcoat
tracksuit
trench coat
trews
trousers
trouser suit
trunks
tunic
turtleneck
tutu
tux/tuxedo
twinset
ulster
underpants
underskirt
veil
vest
V-neck
waistcoat
windcheater
wrap
yashmak

Footwear

beetle-crusher
boot
bootee
brogue
Chelsea boot
clog
court shoe
cowboy boot
Cuban heel
deck shoe
desert boot
Dr Martens (trademark)
espadrille
flip-flop
galosh
gumboot
high top
hobnail boot
jackboot
jelly shoe
kitten heel
lace-up
loafer
moccasin
moon boot
mukluk
mule
overshoe
Oxford
patten
peep-toe
platform
plimsoll
pump
sabot
sandal
shoe
slingback
slip-on
slipper
sneaker
stiletto
trainer
wader
wedge
wellington boot
winkle-picker

Headgear

balaclava
balmoral
bandeau
baseball cap
beanie
bearskin
beret
biretta
boater
bonnet
bowler
busby
cap
chaplet
circlet
cloche
coif
coronet
cowl
crown
deerstalker
derby
diadem
Dolly Varden
fedora
fez
garland
glengarry
headband
headscarf
helmet
hijab
homburg
hood
Juliet cap
keffiyeh
kepi
mantilla
mitre
mob cap
mortar board
panama
pillbox hat
pork-pie hat
skullcap
slouch hat
snood
sola topi
sombrero
sou'wester
Stetson (trademark)
stovepipe hat
tam-o'-shanter
tarboosh
ten-gallon hat
tiara
top hat
topi
topper
toque
tricorne
trilby
turban
veil
wimple

Fabrics and fibres

acetate
acrylic
alpaca
angora
astrakhan
bafta
baize
barathea
barkcloth
batiste
blanketing
bobbinet
bobbin lace
bombazine
Botany wool
bouclé
broadcloth
brocade
buckram
burlap
butter muslin
calico
cambric
camel hair
candlewick
canvas
cashmere
cavalry twill
challis
chambray
Chantilly lace
cheesecloth
chenille
cheviot
chiffon
chinchilla
chino
chintz
ciré
cloqué

coconut matting
coir
cord
corduroy
cotton
crêpe
crêpe de Chine
crépon
cretonne
crewel
Crimplene (trademark)
crinoline
crushed velvet
cupro
Dacron (trademark)
damask
denim
devoré
dimity
doeskin
drab
Dralon (trademark)
drill
duchesse lace
duchesse satin
duffel
dungaree
dupion
elastane
faille
felt
fishnet
flannel
flannelette
flax
fleece
flock
foulard
frieze
fustian
gaberdine/ gabardine
gauze
georgette
gimp
gingham
Gore-tex (trademark)
gossamer
grasscloth
grogram
grosgrain
gros point
guipure
haircloth
Harris tweed (trademark)
hemp
herringbone
hessian
holland
Honiton lace
hopsack
horsehair
huckaback
ikat
jaconet
jacquard
jersey
jute
kapok
kemp
Kendal Green
kersey
kerseymere
khadi
khaki
kikoi
lace
lambswool
lamé
lawn
leathercloth
leatherette (trademark)
leno
Lincoln green
linen
linsey-woolsey
lint
lisle
loden
Lurex (trademark)
Lycra (trademark)
madras
marocain
marquisette
matting
melton
merino
microfibre
micromesh
mohair
moiré
moleskin
moquette
moreen
mousseline
mungo
muslin
nainsook
nankeen
needlecord
net
Nottingham lace
nylon
oakum
oilcloth
oilskin
organdie
organza
organzine
Orlon (trademark)
ottoman
paisley
panne velvet
pashmina
peau-de-soie
percale
petersham
pillow lace
pilot cloth
piqué
plaid
plush
plush velvet
point lace
polycotton
polyester
pongee
poplin
raffia
ramie
rayon
rep
ripstop
sackcloth
sacking
sailcloth
sarsenet
sateen
satin
satinette
saxony
sea-island cotton
seersucker
serge
shahtoosh
sharkskin
Shetland wool
shoddy
silk
sisal
slub
Spandex (trademark)
spun silk
stockinet
suede
surah
swansdown
tabaret
taffeta
tapestry
tarlatan
tarpaulin
tattersall
tatting
terry
Terylene (trademark)
ticking
tiffany
toile
toile de Jouy
torchon
towelling
tricot
tulle
tussore
tweed
twill
Valenciennes
Velcro (trademark)
velour
velvet
velveteen
vicuña
viscose
Viyella (trademark)
voile
waxcloth
webbing
whipcord
wild silk
wincey
winceyette
wool
worsted

Food and drink

Bread

bagel
baguette
bannock
bap
bloomer
bridge roll
brioche
bun
challah
chapatti
ciabatta
cob
cornbread
cottage loaf
croissant
crumpet
farl
flatbread
focaccia
French stick
fruit loaf
granary bread (trademark)
hoagie
malt loaf
matzo
muffin
nan/naan
paratha
pikelet

pitta
pone
poppadom
pumpernickel
puri
rye
soda bread
sourdough

Cakes, biscuits, and desserts

angel cake
apfelstrudel
baba
baked Alaska
Bakewell tart
baklava
banana split
banoffi/banoffee pie
Bath bun
Battenberg
beignet
biscotti
Black Forest gateau
blancmange
bombe
bourbon
brack
brandy snap
bread pudding
bread-and-butter pudding
Brown Betty
brownie
bun
butterfly cake
cabinet pudding
cassata
charlotte
charlotte russe
cheesecake
clafoutis
cobbler
compote
cookie
cream cracker
cream puff
crème brûlée
crème caramel
crêpe
crêpe Suzette
crispbread
crumble
crumpet
cupcake
custard cream
custard pie
custard tart
Danish pastry
devil's food cake
digestive
doughnut
drop scone
dumpling
Dundee cake
Eccles cake
eclair
egg custard
Eve's pudding
fairy cake
fancy
flapjack
Florentine
flummery
fool
fortune cookie
frangipane
garibaldi
gateau
Genoa cake
gingerbread
ginger nut
ginger snap
granita
halwa
hot cross bun
ice cream
jelly
junket
Knickerbocker Glory
kulfi
lady's finger
langue de chat
lardy cake
macaroon
Madeira cake
madeleine
marble cake
meringue
milk pudding
millefeuille
mince pie
Mississippi mud pie
mousse
muffin
oatcake
pancake
panettone
panforte
panna cotta
parfait
parkin
pavlova
peach Melba
petit four
plum duff
plum pudding
popover
pound cake
profiterole
queen of puddings
ratafia
rice pudding
rock cake
roly-poly
rusk
Sachertorte
sago pudding
Sally Lunn
sandwich
savarin
scone
seed cake
shortbread
shortcake
simnel cake
sorbet
soufflé
sponge
spotted dick
stollen
strudel
summer pudding
sundae
Swiss roll
syllabub
tart
tarte Tatin
tartlet
tartufo
tipsy cake
tiramisu
torte
treacle tart
trifle
turnover
tutti-frutti
upside-down cake
Victoria sponge
waffle
water biscuit
water ice
whip
yogurt
yule log
zabaglione

Cheeses

asiago
Bel Paese (trademark)
blue vinny
Boursin (trademark)
Brie
Caerphilly
Camembert
Chaumes
Cheddar
Cheshire
chèvre
cottage cheese
cream cheese
Danish blue
Derby
Dolcelatte (trademark))
Double Gloucester
Edam
Emmental
feta
fontina
Gloucester
Gorgonzola
Gouda
Gruyère
halloumi
havarti
Jarlsberg (trademark)
Lancashire
Leicester
Limburger
Manchego
mascarpone
Monterey Jack
mozzarella
paneer/panir
Parmesan
Parmigiano Reggiano
pecorino
Port Salut
provolone
Red Leicester
ricotta
Romano
Roquefort (trademark)
sage Derby
scamorza
Stilton (trademark)
taleggio
Tilsit
Wensleydale

Fruit and nuts

almond
apple
apricot
avocado
banana
betel nut
bilberry
blackberry
blackcurrant
blueberry
boysenberry
Brazil nut
breadfruit
butternut
cantaloupe
Cape gooseberry
carambola
cashew

cherimoya
cherry
chestnut
Chinese gooseberry
citron
clementine
cloudberry
cobnut
coconut
cola nut
cowberry
crab apple
cranberry
currant
damson
date
elderberry
fig
filbert
galia melon
gooseberry
gourd
grape
grapefruit
greengage
groundnut
guava
hazelnut
honeydew melon
huckleberry
jackfruit
jujube
kiwi fruit
kumquat
lemon
lime
loganberry
loquat
lychee
macadamia
mandarin
mango
medlar
melon
monkey nut
mulberry
nectarine
olive
orange
ortanique
papaya
passion fruit
pawpaw
peach
peanut
pear
pecan
persimmon
pineapple
pine nut
pistachio
plum
pomegranate
pomelo
prickly pear
pumpkin
quince
rambutan
raspberry
redcurrant
salmonberry
sapodilla
satsuma
serviceberry
sharon fruit
sloe
star anise
starfruit
strawberry
tamarillo
tangerine
tayberry
tiger nut
Ugli fruit (trademark)
walnut
watermelon
whortleberry

Herbs and spices

allspice
angelica
anise
aniseed
asafoetida
basil
bay leaf
bergamot
black pepper
borage
camomile
caper
caraway
cardamom
cassia
cayenne pepper
chervil
chilli
chives
cilantro
cinnamon
clary
clove
coriander
cumin
curry powder
damiana
dill
dittany
dong quai
echinacea
fenugreek
feverfew
galangal
garam masala
garlic
ginger
ginseng
grains of Paradise
hyssop
juniper berry
lavender
lemon balm
lemon grass
lemon mint
lovage
mace
marjoram
milk thistle
mint
mustard
nutmeg
oregano
paprika
parsley
pepper
peppermint
rosemary
rue
saffron
sage
savory
sorrel
spearmint
St John's wort
sumac
sweet balm
sweet cicely
tarragon
thyme
turmeric
vanilla

Meat cuts and joints

baron of beef
belly
best end
breast
brisket
chateaubriand
chine
chop
chuck
collar
cutlet
entrecôte
escalope
fillet
fricandeau
gigot
hock
knuckle
leg
loin
neck
noisette
porterhouse steak
rack
rib
rump
saddle
scrag
shank
shin
shoulder
side
silverside
sirloin
skirt
spare rib
T-bone
tenderloin
topside
tournedos
undercut
wing

Meat types and products

bacon
beef
beefburger
black pudding
bologna
bratwurst
brawn
bresaola
burger
cervelat
chicken
chipolata
chitterlings
chorizo
corned beef
duck
faggot
frankfurter
game
gammon
goose
grouse
haggis
ham
hamburger
haslet
heart
kidney
knackwurst
lamb
lamb's fry
lights
liver
luncheon meat
merguez
mince
mortadella
mutton
offal
oxtail
tongue
Parma ham
partridge
pâté
pepperoni

pheasant
pig's trotters
pork
poultry
prosciutto
quail
rabbit
rissole
salami
sausage
saveloy
sidemeat
spam (trademark)
steak
sweetbread
tongue
tripe
turkey
veal
venison
wiener
wurst

Pasta

agnolotti
angel hair
cannelloni
capellini
conchiglie
ditalini
farfalle
fettuccine
fusilli
lasagne
linguine
macaroni
noodles
orecchiette
orzo
pappardelle
penne
radiatori
ravioli
rigatoni
spaghetti
spaghettini
tagliatelle
tagliolini
tortelli
tortellini
tortelloni
vermicelli
ziti

Vegetables

aduki/adzuki bean
alfalfa
artichoke
asparagus
aubergine
bamboo shoots
bean
beet
beetroot
black bean
black-eyed bean
borlotti bean
breadfruit
broad bean
broccoli
Brussels sprout
butter bean
butternut squash
cabbage
calabrese
cannellini bean
capsicum
carrot
cassava
cauliflower
celeriac
celery
chard
chervil
chickpea
chicory
Chinese leaves
corn on the cob
cos lettuce
courgette
cress
cucumber
eggplant
endive
fennel
flageolet
French bean
garlic
gherkin
globe artichoke
gourd
haricot bean
iceberg lettuce
Jerusalem artichoke
kale
kidney bean
kohlrabi
lamb's lettuce
leek
lentil
lettuce
lima bean
lollo rosso
mache
mangetout
marrow
marrowfat pea
mooli
mung bean
mushroom
okra
onion
pak choi
parsnip
pea
pepper
petits pois
pimiento
pinto bean
plantain
potato
pumpkin
radicchio
radish
rocket
romaine
runner bean
salsify
samphire
savoy cabbage
shallot
snow pea
soybean
spinach
spring greens
spring onion
squash
string bean
sugar snap
swede
sweetcorn
sweet pepper
sweet potato
tomato
turnip
vegetable spaghetti
water chestnut
watercress
waxpod
yam
zucchini

Alcoholic drinks

absinthe
advocaat
alcopop
ale
amaretto
aquavit
Armagnac
barley wine
beer
bitter
bock
bourbon
brandy
burgundy
Calvados
cassis
champagne
chartreuse
cherry brandy
cider
cocktail
cognac
crème de menthe
curaçao
genever
gin
ginger wine
grappa
hock
ice beer
Irish whiskey
kirsch
kümmel
kvass
lager
liqueur
malt whisky
maraschino
mead
mescal
mild
milk stout
ouzo
pale ale
perry
Pils
Pilsner/Pilsener
port
porter
poteen
raki
ratafia
retsina
rum
rye
sack
sake
sambuca
sangria
schnapps
Scotch whisky
scrumpy
shandy
sherry
single malt
slivovitz
sloe gin
stout
tequila
triple sec
vermouth
vodka
whiskey/whisky
wine

Wines and grape varieties

White wines and grapes

Aligoté
Asti
Auslese
Barsac
Blanc de blancs
Blanc Fumé
Bourgogne Blanc
Burgundy
Cava
Chablis
Champagne
Chardonnay
Chenin Blanc
Eiswein
Entre-Deux-Mers
Frascati
Gavi
Gewürztraminer
Grenache
Graves
Hock
Kabinett
Liebfraumilch
Lutomer Riesling
Mâcon
Mâcon Villages
Malvasia Bianca
Meursault
Minervois
Montrachet
Moselle
Muscadelle
Muscadet
Niersteiner
Orvieto
Piesporter
Pinot Blanc
Pinot Grigio
Pouilly-Fuissé
Pouilly-Fumé
Prosecco
Retsina
Riesling
Rioja
sack
Sancerre
Saumur
Sauvignon
Sekt
Sémillon
Soave
Spätlese
Spumante
Tokay
Traminer
Trebbiano
Verdicchio
Vernaccia
Vinho Verde
Viognier
Vouvray

Red wines and grapes

Bandol
Bardolino
Barolo
Beaujolais
Beaune
Bourgogne Rouge
Brouilly
Brunello de Montalcino
Bull's Blood
Burgundy
Cabernet Franc
Cabernet Sauvignon
Cahors
Chianti
Cinsault
claret
Côtes du Rhône
Crozes-Hermitage
Dão
Fitou
Fleurie
Gamay
Gevrey-Chambertin
Gigondas
Graves
Grenache
Lambrusco
Malbec
Malvasia
Margaux
Médoc
Merlot
Montepulciano
Nebbiolo
Nuits St George
Pauillac
Pinot Noir
Pinotage
Pomerol
Rioja
Saint-Émilion
Saint-Estèphe
Sangiovese
Shiraz/Syrah
Tempranillo
Valdepeñas
Valpolicella
Vino Nobile di Montepulciano
Zinfandel

Types of sherry and dessert wines

Sherry

amontillado
fino
manzanilla
oloroso

Dessert wine

Bual
Madeira
malmsey
Marsala
Monbazillac
moscato
Muscat
Muscat de Beaumes de Venise
muscatel
Sauternes
Sercial
Verhdelho
vin de paille
vin santo

Wine bottles

Bottle	Normal bottles	Bottle	Normal bottles	Bottle	Normal bottles
magnum	2	methuselah	8	nebuchadnezzar	20
jeroboam	4	salmanazar	12		
rehoboam	6	balthazar	16		

Cocktails and other mixed drinks

Bellini
B52
Black Russian
black velvet
Bloody Mary
blue lagoon
brandy Alexander
Bronx
Buck's Fizz
caipirinha
champagne cocktail
cobbler
cosmopolitan
Cuba libre
daiquiri
egg flip
eggnog
gimlet
gin sling
grog
Harvey Wallbanger
highball
Irish coffee
John Collins
Kir
Kir Royale
Long Island iced tea
mai tai
manhattan
margarita
Martini (trademark)
mint julep
mojito
negroni
old-fashioned
pina colada
pink gin
planter's punch
prairie oyster
punch
rattlesnake
rum and black
sangria
screwdriver
sea breeze
sex on the beach
sidecar
Singapore sling
slammer

snakebite
snowball
sour
spritzer
tequila slammer
tequila sunrise
toddy
Tom Collins
whisky mac
whisky sour
White Lady
White Russian
zombie

Non-alcoholic drinks

barley water
bitter lemon
buttermilk
cafe au lait
caffè latte
caffè macchiato
camomile tea
cappuccino
chai
cherryade
citron pressé
club soda (trademark)
cocoa
coffee
cola
cordial
cream soda
dandelion and burdock
espresso
filter coffee
ginger ale
ginger beer
green tea
horchata
hot chocolate
lassi
latte
lemonade
limeade
malted milk
maté
milkshake
mineral water
mint tea
mocha
mochaccino
orangeade
prairie oyster
pressé
root beer
sarsaparilla
seltzer
sherbet
smoothie
soda water
squash
St Clements
tea
tisane
tonic water
yerba maté

Music

Musical instruments

accordion
acoustic guitar
aeolian harp
alpenhorn
althorn
American organ
autoharp
bagpipes
balalaika
banjo
barrel organ
basset horn
bassoon
bell
bombarde
bombardon
bongos
bouzouki
bugle
castanet
celesta
cello
Celtic harp
chamber organ
chitarrone
cimbalom
citole
cittern
clarinet
clarion
clarsach
claves
clavichord
clavier
conga drum
contrabass
contrabassoon
cor anglais
cornet
cornetto
cymbal
didgeridoo
double bass
drum
dulcimer
electric guitar
electric organ
euphonium
fiddle
fife
fipple flute
flageolet
flugelhorn
flute
fortepiano
French horn
gamba
glockenspiel
gong
grand piano
guitar
Hammond organ (trademark)
handbell
harmonica
harmonium
harp
harpsichord
heckelphone
helicon
hi-hat
horn
hurdy-gurdy
Jew's harp
kazoo
kettledrum
krummhorn
lute
lyre
mandola
mandolin
maraca
melodeon
melodica
mouth organ
oboe
oboe d'amore
ocarina
ondes martenot
organ
oud
piano
piano accordion
pianoforte
pianola
piano organ
piccolo
pipe
pipe organ
player piano
portative organ
psaltery
rebec
recorder
reed organ
sackbut
samisen
santoor
sarod
sarrusophone
saxhorn
saxophone
shawm
side drum
sitar
snare drum
sousaphone
Spanish guitar
spinet
steel drum
string bass
synthesizer
tabla
tabor
tambour
tamboura
tambourine
tamburitza
tam-tam
temple block
theorbo
thumb piano
timpani
tin whistle
tom-tom
triangle
triple harp
trombone
trumpet
tuba
tubular bells
ukulele/ukelele
upright piano
vibraphone
vihuela
viol
viola
viola da gamba
viola d'amore
violin
violoncello

violone
virginals
Wagner tuba
Welsh harp
wobbleboard
Wurlitzer (trademark)
xylophone
zither

Dances and types of dancing

ballet
ballroom
barn dance
beguine
belly dance
body popping
bolero
boogaloo
bossa nova
Boston
break-dancing
cakewalk
cancan
carioca
ceroc
cha-cha
charleston
conga
cotillion
country dance
cumbia
disco
do-si-do
ecossaise
eightsome reel
fandango
farruca
flamenco
fling
foxtrot
galop
gavotte
Gay Gordons
Highland fling
hoedown
hokey-cokey
hornpipe
hula-hula
jig
jitterbug
jive
jota
lambada
Lambeth Walk
limbo
line dancing
mambo
mazurka
minuet
moonstomp
moonwalk
morris dance
mosh
one-step
pas de deux
paso doble
pas seul
Paul Jones
pogo
polka
polonaise
quadrille
quickstep
reel
rock and roll
ronde
rumba
salsa
samba
shake
shimmy
shuffle
skank
square dance
stomp
tango
tap dance
turkey trot
twist
two-step
vogueing
waltz

Plants

Flowering plants

acacia
acanthus
aconite
African violet
agapanthus
aloe
alstroemeria
alyssum
amaranth
amaryllis
anemone
aquilegia
arrowgrass
arum lily
asphodel
aspidistra
aster
astilbe
aubretia
avens
azalea
balsam
banksia
bedstraw
begonia
belladonna
bellflower
bergamot
betony
bilberry
bindweed
bird's-foot trefoil
blackthorn
bluebell
boneset
borage
bougainvillea
bramble
broom
bryony
buddleia
bugloss
bulrush
burdock
burnet
busy Lizzie
buttercup
cactus
calceolaria
calendula
camellia
camomile
campanula
campion
candytuft
Canterbury bell
carnation
catmint
ceanothus
celandine
chickweed
chicory
Chinese lantern
chives
choisya
chokeberry
Christmas cactus
Christmas rose
chrysanthemum
cicely
cinquefoil
clematis
clove pink
clover
cockscomb
coltsfoot
columbine
comfrey
convolvulus
coreopsis
cornflower
corydalis
cotoneaster
cottonweed
cow parsley
cowslip
cranesbill
crocus
cuckoo pint
cyclamen
daffodil
dahlia
daisy
damask rose
dandelion
daphne
deadly nightshade
delphinium
dianthus
dill
dittany
dock
dog rose
duckweed
echinacea
edelweiss
eglantine
elder
evening primrose
eyebright
feverfew
figwort
firethorn
flax
forget-me-not
forsythia
foxglove
frangipani
freesia
fritillary
fuchsia
furze
gardenia
gentian
geranium
gerbera
gladiolus
gloxinia
golden rod
gorse
grape hyacinth
groundsel
guelder rose
gypsophila

harebell
hawkweed
hawthorn
heartsease
heather
hebe
helianthemum
helianthus
heliotrope
hellebore
hemlock
heuchera
hibiscus
hogweed
holly
hollyhock
honesty
honeysuckle
hosta
hyacinth
hydrangea
iris
jacaranda
japonica
jasmine
jonquil
kingcup
knapweed
knotgrass
laburnum
lady's mantle
lady's tresses
larkspur
lavatera
lavender
lemon balm
lilac
lily
lily of the valley
lobelia
London pride
loosestrife
lords and ladies
lotus
lovage
love-in-a-mist
love-lies-bleeding
lungwort
lupin
madonna lily
magnolia
mahonia
mallow
mandrake
marguerite
marigold
marshwort
may
mayflower
meadow rue
meadow saffron
meadowsweet
Michaelmas daisy
milfoil
mimosa
mint
mistletoe
mock orange
montbretia
morning glory
musk rose
myrtle
narcissus
nasturtium
nettle
nicotiana
nigella
night-scented stock
nightshade
old man's beard
oleander
orchid
ox-eye daisy
oxlip
pansy
Parma violet
parsley
pasque flower
passion flower
pelargonium
pennyroyal
penstemon
peony
peppermint
periwinkle
petunia
phlox
pimpernel
pink
pitcher plant
plantain
plumbago
poinsettia
polyanthus
poppy
potentilla
prickly pear
primrose
primula
privet
pulsatilla
pyracantha
pyrethrum
ragwort
ramsons
red-hot poker
rhododendron
rock rose
rose
rosebay willowherb
rose of Sharon
safflower
St John's wort
salvia
samphire
saxifrage
scabious
scarlet pimpernel
scilla
sedum
shamrock
skimmia
snapdragon
snowdrop
soapwort
sorrel
speedwell
spikenard
spiraea
spurge
spurrey
squill
starwort
stock
stonecrop
streptocarpus
sunflower
sweet pea
sweet william
tansy
teasel
thistle
thrift
toadflax
tradescantia
trefoil
tulip
valerian
Venus flytrap
verbena
veronica
vervain
vetch
viburnum
violet
viper's bugloss
wallflower
water lily
willowherb
wintergreen
wisteria
witch hazel
wolfsbane
woodruff
wormwood
yarrow
yucca
zinnia

Trees and shrubs

acacia
acer
alder
almond
apple
apricot
araucaria
ash
aspen
azalea
balsa
bamboo
banksia
banyan
baobab
basswood
bay tree
beech
beefwood
bergamot
birch
blackthorn
bottlebrush
bottle tree
bo tree
box
box elder
bristlecone pine
broom
buckeye
buckthorn
butternut
cacao
calabash
camellia
candleberry
candlenut
carambola
carob
cassava
cassia
casuarina
cedar
cherimoya
cherry
chestnut
cinnamon
citron
coco de mer
coconut palm
cola
coolibah
copper beech
cork oak
coromandel
cottonwood
crab apple
cypress
dogwood
dragon tree
ebony
elder
elm
eucalyptus
euonymus
ficus
fig
filbert
fir
firethorn
flame tree
frangipani
gean
ginkgo
gorse
grapefruit
greengage
guava
gum tree
hawthorn
hazel
hickory
holly
holm oak
honeysuckle
hornbeam
horse chestnut
hydrangea
ilex
iroko
ironbark
ironwood
jacaranda
jackfruit
jack pine
japonica
jasmine
juniper
kalmia

kapok
kermes oak
laburnum
larch
laurel
lemon
Leyland cypress
leylandii
lilac
lime
linden
lodgepole pine
logwood
macadamia
magnolia
mahogany
maidenhair tree
mango
mangosteen
mangrove
maple
mastic
may
mimosa
mirabelle
monkey puzzle
mountain ash
mulberry
mulga
myrtle
nutmeg
nux vomica
oak
oleaster
olive
osier
pagoda tree
palm
papaya
paperbark
pawpaw
pear
persimmon
pine
pistachio
pitch pine
plane
plum
pomegranate
pomelo
poplar
privet
pussy willow
quassia
quince
rambutan
red cedar
redwood
rhododendron
robinia
rosewood
rowan
rubber plant
rubber tree
sallow
sandalwood
sapele
sapodilla
sassafras
satinwood
senna
sequoia
service tree
silver birch
Sitka cypress
slippery elm
smoke tree
soapberry
spindle
spruce
star anise
stinkwood
storax
sumac
sycamore
tamarind
tamarisk
tea
teak
tea tree
thuja
tulip tree
tulipwood
umbrella tree
viburnum
walnut
weeping willow
wellingtonia
whitebeam
willow
witch hazel
wych elm
yew

Mushrooms, toadstools, and other fungi

agaric
amethyst deceiver
armillaria
beefsteak fungus
bird's-nest
black bulgar
blewit
blusher
boletus
bracket fungus
button mushroom
cep
champignon
chanterelle
death cap
destroying angel
earthstar
fairies' bonnets
field mushroom
fly agaric
grisette
honey fungus
horn of plenty
horse mushroom
ink cap
Jew's ear
liberty cap
morel
mousseron
oyster mushroom
parasol mushroom
penny bun
polypore
porcini
portobello
puffball
reishi
russula
shiitake
sickener
stinkhorn
straw mushroom
tartufo
truffle

Science

Chemical elements and symbols

Element	Symbol	Element	Symbol	Element	Symbol
actinium	Ac	cadmium	Cd	einsteinium	Es
aluminium	Al	caesium	Cs	erbium	Er
americium	Am	calcium	Ca	europium	Eu
antimony	Sb	californium	Cf	fermium	Fm
argon	Ar	carbon	C	fluorine	F
arsenic	As	cerium	Ce	francium	Fr
astatine	At	chlorine	Cl	gadolinium	Gd
barium	Ba	chromium	Cr	gallium	Ga
berkelium	Bk	cobalt	Co	germanium	Ge
beryllium	Be	copper	Cu	gold	Au
bismuth	Bi	curium	Cm	hafnium	Hf
bohrium	Bh	darmstadtium	Ds	hassium	Hs
boron	B	dubnium	Db	helium	He
bromine	Br	dysprosium	Dy	holmium	Ho

Element	Symbol	Element	Symbol	Element	Symbol
hydrogen	H	nobelium	Nb	selenium	Se
indium	In	osmium	Os	silicon	Si
iodine	I	oxygen	O	silver	Ag
iridium	Ir	palladium	Pd	sodium	Na
iron	Fe	phosphorus	P	strontium	Sr
krypton	Kr	platinum	Pt	sulphur	S
lanthanum	La	plutonium	Pu	tantalum	Ta
lawrencium	Lr	polonium	Po	technetium	Tc
lead	Pb	potassium	K	tellurium	Te
lithium	Li	praseodymium	Pr	terbium	Tb
lutetium	Lu	promethium	Pm	thallium	Tl
magnesium	Mg	protactinium	Pa	thorium	Th
manganese	Mn	radium	Ra	thulium	Tm
meitnerium	Mt	radon	Rn	tin	Sn
mendelevium	Md	rhenium	Re	titanium	Ti
mercury	Hg	rhodium	Rh	tungsten	W
molybdenum	Mo	roentgenium	Rg	uranium	U
neodymium	Nd	rubidium	Rb	vanadium	V
neon	Ne	ruthenium	Ru	xenon	Xe
neptunium	Np	rutherfordium	Rf	ytterbium	Yb
nickel	Ni	samarium	Sm	yttrium	Y
niobium	Nb	scandium	Sc	zinc	Zn
nitrogen	N	seaborgium	Sg	zirconium	Zr

Alloys

babbitt metal
bell metal
billon
brass
Britannia metal
bronze
constantan
cupro-nickel
Dutch metal
electrum
eureka
German silver
gunmetal
magnox
misch metal
nitinol
ormolu
permalloy
pewter
pinchbeck
platinoid
red gold
solder
speculum metal
spiegeleisen
steel
terne
type metal
white gold
white metal

Rocks and minerals

agate
alabaster
alexandrite
almandine
amber
amethyst
aquamarine
asbestos
baryte
basalt
beryl
bloodstone
Blue John
borax
breccia
cairngorm
calcite
carbuncle
carnelian
cat's-eye
chalcedony
chalk
chert
chromite
chrysolite
chrysoprase
cinnabar
cipolin
citrine
coal
conglomerate
cornelian
corundum
cryolite
diamond
diorite
dolerite
dolomite
emerald
emery
feldspar
flint
fluorite
fluorspar
fool's gold
gabbro
galena
garnet
girasol
gneiss
granite
graphite
greenstone
gypsum
haematite
hornblende
hornfels
ironstone
jacinth
jade
jadeite
jasper
lapis lazuli
lava
limestone
magnetite
malachite
manganite
marble
marcasite
marl
mica
moonstone
moss agate
mudstone
muscovite
natron
nephrite
obsidian
olivine
onyx
oolite
opal
orpiment
pegmatite
peridot
peridotite
phosphorite
pitchblende
porphyry
pumice
pyrites
pyrope
quartz
quartzite
rhyolite
ruby
sandstone
sapphire
sardonyx
schist
serpentine
shale
slate
spinel
steatite
sunstone
talc
topaz
tourmaline

tuff
turquoise
vermiculite
zeolite
zircon

Transport

Motor vehicles

all-terrain vehicle
ambulance
articulated lorry
automobile
Black Maria
bowser (trademark)
buggy
bulldozer
bus
cab
cabriolet
camper
car
caravan
charabanc
coach
convertible
coupé
dirt bike
double-decker bus
dragster
drophead
DUKW
dumper truck
dustcart
estate
fastback
fire engine
flatbed
forklift truck
four-by-four
four-wheel drive (4WD)
go-kart
hackney cab
half-track
hardtop
hatchback
hearse
heavy goods vehicle (HGV)
horsebox
hot rod
juggernaut
kart
limousine
lorry
low-loader
milk float
minelayer
minicab
moped
motorbike
motorcycle
motorhome
multi-purpose vehicle (MPV)
notchback
off-roader
omnibus
pantechnicon
people carrier
pickup
public service vehicle (PSV)
quad bike
recreational vehicle (RV)
roadster
saloon
scooter
scrambler
sedan
shooting brake
snowcat
snowmobile
snowplough
soft top
sports car
sportster
sport utility vehicle (SUV)
station wagon
stock car
stretch limo
superbike
supercar
supermini
tank
tanker
taxi
taxicab
tourer
touring car
tracklayer
tractor
trail bike
trailer
tram
transporter
trolleybus
truck
van
wagon/waggon

Carriages and carts

barouche
brake
brougham
buggy
cab
cabriolet
carriole
chaise
chariot
clarence
coach
coach-and-four
coupé
curricle
dog cart
dray
droshky
fiacre
fly
gig
hackney
hansom
landau
phaeton
postchaise
rickshaw
stagecoach
tilbury
trailer
trap
trishaw
tumbril
Victoria
wagon/waggon
wagonette

Ships and boats

airboat
aircraft carrier
barge
barque
barquentine
bateau mouche
bathyscaphe
battlecruiser
battleship
bireme
brig
brigantine
bulk carrier
cabin cruiser
caique
canoe
capital ship
caravel
carrack
catamaran
catboat
clipper
coaster
collier
container ship
coracle
corvette
cruiser
cutter
destroyer
dhow
dinghy
dory
dragon boat
dreadnought
dredger
drifter
dugout
E-boat
East Indiaman
factory ship
felucca
ferry
flag boat
flagship
flatboat
freighter
frigate
full-rigger
galleon
galley
galliot
gig
gondola
gulet
gunboat
houseboat
hovercraft
hydrofoil
hydroplane
iceboat
icebreaker
Indiaman
ironclad
jetboat
jetfoil
jet ski (trademark)
jolly
junk

kayak
keelboat
ketch
landing craft
launch
liberty boat
lifeboat
life raft
lighter
lightship
liner
longboat
longship
lugger
mailboat
man-of-war
merchantman
merchant ship
minesweeper
monitor
monohull
motor boat
multihull
narrowboat
outrigger
paddle steamer
pedalo
pink
pinnace
pirogue
pocket battleship
pontoon
powerboat
privateer
proa
punt
Q-ship
quinquereme
raft
rigger
riverboat
roll-on roll-off
rowing boat
sampan
schooner
scow
scull
shallop
shell
ship of the line
showboat
side-wheeler
single-hander
skiff
skipjack
sloop
smack
speedboat
square-rigger
stake boat
steamboat
steamer
steamship
sternwheeler
submarine
submersible
supertanker
tall ship
tanker
tender
torpedo boat
trader
tramp steamer
trawler
trimaran
trireme
troopship
tub
tugboat
U-boat
vaporetto
warship
weekender
whaleboat
whaler
wherry
windjammer
xebec
yacht
yawl

Aircraft

airliner
airship
autogiro
biplane
blimp
bomber
delta-wing
dirigible
drone
fighter
floatplane
flying boat
freighter
glider
gunship
gyrocopter
gyroplane
hang-glider
helicopter
hot-air balloon
hydroplane
jet
jetliner
jumbo jet
jump jet
microlight
monoplane
sailplane
seaplane
spaceplane
swept-wing
tanker
towplane
triplane
troop carrier
turbofan
turbojet
turboprop
warplane
whirlybird
widebody
Zeppelin

Trains and rolling stock

bogie
boxcar
brake van
buffet car
bullet train
caboose
car
carriage
coach
couchette
dining car
double-header
engine
express
flatcar
guard's van
handcar
hopper
locomotive
maglev
metro
milk train
monorail
motor coach
multiple unit
observation car
pannier tank
passenger train
Pullman
railcar
restaurant car
saddle tank
shunter
sleeper
sleeping car
smokebox
smoker
steam locomotive
steam train
stopping train
tank engine
tender
TGV
wagon-lit

Mm

macabre adjective **gruesome**, grisly, grim, gory, ghastly, grotesque.

macerate verb **pulp**, soften, liquefy, soak.

Machiavellian adjective **devious**, cunning, crafty, wily, sly, scheming, treacherous, unscrupulous, deceitful, dishonest; literary perfidious.
– OPPOSITES straightforward, ingenuous.

machinations plural noun **scheming**, plotting, intrigue, conspiracies, tricks, stratagems, manoeuvring.

machine noun **1** *a machine that is cheap to run:* **device**, appliance, apparatus, engine, gadget, mechanism. **2** *an efficient publicity machine:* **organization**, system, structure; informal set-up.

machinery noun **1** *road-making machinery:* **equipment**, apparatus, plant, hardware, gear; gadgetry, technology. **2** *the machinery of local government:* **workings**, organization, system, structure, institution; informal set-up.

machinist noun **operator**, operative.

machismo noun **masculinity**, virility, manliness; male chauvinism, sexism; informal laddishness.

macho adjective **male**, masculine, manly, tough; virile, red-blooded; chauvinist, sexist; informal laddish.
– OPPOSITES wimpish.

mackintosh noun **raincoat**, gaberdine, trench coat, waterproof; Brit. pakamac; N. Amer. slicker; Brit. informal mac.

mad adjective **1** *he was killed by his mad brother:* **insane**, mentally ill, certifiable, deranged, demented, of unsound mind, out of your mind, sick in the head, crazy, crazed, lunatic, non compos mentis, unhinged, disturbed, raving, psychotic, mad as a hatter, mad as a March hare, away with the fairies; informal mental, off your head, off your nut, nuts, off your rocker, not right in the head, round the bend, batty, bonkers, dotty, cuckoo, cracked, loopy, loony, doolally, bananas, loco, screwy, schizoid, touched, gaga, not all there; Brit. informal barmy, crackers, barking, round the twist, off your trolley, not the full shilling; N. Amer. informal nutso, out of your tree, wacko, gonzo; Austral./NZ informal bushed; NZ informal porangi; (**go mad**) lose your mind, take leave of your senses; informal lose your marbles, crack up. **2** (informal) *I'm still mad at him:* **angry**, furious, infuriated, enraged, fuming, incensed, beside yourself; informal livid, spare; N. Amer. informal sore; literary wrathful; (**go mad**) lose your temper, rant and rave; informal explode, go off the deep end, go ape, flip, flip your lid; Brit. informal do your nut; N. Amer. informal flip your wig. **3** *some mad scheme:* **foolish**, insane, stupid, lunatic, idiotic, absurd, silly, inane, asinine, wild; informal crazy, crackpot; Brit. informal daft. **4** (informal) *they're all mad Derby supporters* | *he's mad about her:* **passionate**, fanatical; ardent, fervent, avid; devoted to, infatuated with, in love with; informal crazy, dotty, nuts, wild, hooked on; Brit. informal potty; N. Amer. informal nutso. **5** *it was a mad dash to get ready:* **frenzied**, frantic, frenetic, feverish, hysterical, wild, hectic, manic.
– OPPOSITES sane, sensible.

madcap adjective **1** *a madcap scheme:* **reckless**, rash, foolhardy, foolish, hare-brained, wild; informal crazy, crackpot. **2** *a madcap comedy:* **zany**,

m

eccentric, unconventional; informal wacky.

madden verb **1** *what maddens people most is his vagueness:* **infuriate**, exasperate, irritate; incense, anger, enrage, provoke, upset, agitate, vex, irk, make someone's hackles rise, make someone see red; informal aggravate, make someone's blood boil, get up someone's nose, get someone's goat, get someone's back up; Brit. informal nark; N. Amer. informal tee off, tick off. **2** *they were maddened with pain:* **drive mad**, derange, unhinge, unbalance; informal drive round the bend.

made-up adjective **invented**, fabricated, trumped up, concocted, fictitious, fictional, false, untrue, specious, spurious, bogus, apocryphal.

madhouse noun (informal) **bedlam**, mayhem, chaos, pandemonium, uproar, turmoil, madness; N. Amer. three-ring circus.

madman, madwoman noun **lunatic**, maniac, psychotic, psychopath; informal loony, nut, nutcase, head case, psycho; Brit. informal nutter; N. Amer. informal screwball.

m

madness noun **1** *today madness is called mental illness:* **insanity**, mental illness, dementia, derangement; lunacy; mania, psychosis; informal craziness. **2** *it would be madness to do otherwise:* **folly**, foolishness, idiocy, stupidity, insanity, lunacy. **3** *it's absolute madness in here:* **bedlam**, mayhem, chaos, pandemonium, uproar, turmoil, all hell broken loose; N. Amer. three-ring circus.
– OPPOSITES sanity, common sense, good sense, calm.

maelstrom noun *the maelstrom of war:* **turbulence**, tumult, turmoil, chaos, confusion, upheaval, pandemonium, bedlam, whirlwind.

maestro noun **virtuoso**, master, expert, genius, wizard; informal ace, whizz, hotshot.
– OPPOSITES tyro, beginner.

magazine noun **journal**, periodical, supplement, colour supplement; informal glossy, mag, 'zine.

maggot noun **grub**, larva.

magic noun **1** *do you believe in magic?* **sorcery**, witchcraft, necromancy, enchantment, the supernatural, occultism, the occult, black magic, the black arts; voodoo. **2** *he does magic at children's parties:* **conjuring tricks**, legerdemain, sleight of hand; formal prestidigitation. **3** *the magic of the stage:* **allure**, excitement, fascination, charm, glamour.
• adjective **supernatural**, magical, miraculous.

magical adjective **1** *magical powers:* **supernatural**, magic, mystical, other-worldly. **2** *the news had a magical effect:* **extraordinary**, remarkable, incredible, amazing, astonishing, astounding, staggering, miraculous; literary wondrous. **3** *this magical island:* **enchanting**, entrancing, spellbinding, bewitching, beguiling, fascinating, captivating, alluring, enthralling, charming, lovely, delightful, beautiful; informal heavenly, divine, gorgeous.

magician noun **1** **sorcerer**, sorceress, witch, wizard, warlock, enchanter, enchantress, necromancer. **2** **conjuror**, illusionist; formal prestidigitator.

magisterial adjective **1** *a magisterial performance:* **authoritative**, masterful, assured, commanding. **2** *his magisterial style of questioning:* **domineering**, dictatorial, autocratic, imperious, overbearing; informal bossy.
– OPPOSITES untrustworthy, humble, hesitant, tentative.

magnanimity noun **generosity**, charity, benevolence, beneficence, big-heartedness, altruism, philanthropy, humanity, chivalry, nobility.
– OPPOSITES meanness, selfishness.

magnanimous adjective **generous**, charitable, benevolent, beneficent, big-hearted, handsome, philanthropic, chivalrous, noble.
– OPPOSITES mean-spirited, selfish.

magnate noun **tycoon**, mogul, captain of industry; baron, lord, king; informal big shot; derogatory fat cat.

magnet noun *a magnet for tourists:* **attraction**, focus, draw, lure.

magnetic adjective *a magnetic personality:* **alluring**, attractive, fascinating, captivating, enchanting, enthralling, entrancing, seductive, irresistible, charismatic.

magnetism noun *his personal magnetism drew people in:* **charisma**, charm, attraction, fascination, appeal, draw, magic, spell, allure.

magnification noun **enlargement**, enhancement, increase, augmentation, extension, expansion, amplification, intensification.
– OPPOSITES reduction, understatement.

magnificence noun **splendour**, resplendence, grandeur, impressiveness, glory, majesty, nobility, pomp, stateliness, elegance, sumptuousness, opulence, luxury, lavishness, richness, brilliance.
– OPPOSITES modesty, tawdriness, weakness.

magnificent adjective **1** *a magnificent view of the mountains:* **splendid**, spectacular, impressive, striking, glorious, superb, majestic, awesome, awe-inspiring, breathtaking. **2** *a magnificent apartment overlooking the lake:* **sumptuous**, grand, impressive, imposing, monumental, palatial, opulent, luxurious, lavish, rich, dazzling, beautiful; informal splendiferous, ritzy, posh. **3** *a magnificent performance:* **masterly**, skilful, virtuoso, brilliant; outstanding.
– OPPOSITES uninspiring, modest, tawdry, poor, weak.

magnify verb **enlarge**, boost, enhance, maximize, increase, augment, extend, expand, amplify, intensify; informal blow up.
– OPPOSITES reduce, minimize, understate.

magnitude noun **1** *the magnitude of the task:* **immensity**, vastness, hugeness, enormity; size, extent. **2** *events of such magnitude:* **importance**, import, significance, consequence.
– OPPOSITES smallness, triviality.

maid noun (literary) **girl**, young woman, young lady, lass, miss; Scottish lassie; literary maiden, damsel; old use wench.

maiden noun (literary). See MAID.
• adjective **1** *a maiden aunt:* **unmarried**, spinster, unwed, single. **2** *a maiden voyage:* **first**, inaugural, introductory.

mail noun *the mail arrived:* **post**, letters, correspondence; postal system, postal service, post office; email; informal snail mail; N. Amer. the mails.
• verb *we mailed the parcels:* **send**, post, dispatch, forward, redirect, ship; email.

maim verb **injure**, wound, incapacitate, mutilate, lacerate, disfigure, deform, mangle.

main adjective *the main item:* **principal**, chief, leading, foremost, most important, major, ruling, dominant, central, focal, key, prime, primary, first, fundamental, predominant, pre-eminent.
– OPPOSITES subsidiary, minor.

mainly adverb **mostly**, for the most part, in the main, on the whole, largely, by and large, to a large extent, predominantly, chiefly, principally, primarily.

mainspring noun **motive**, motivation, impetus, driving force, incentive, impulse, reason, root.

mainstay noun **foundation**, base, prop, linchpin, cornerstone, pillar, bulwark, buttress, backbone, anchor.

mainstream adjective **normal**, conventional, ordinary, orthodox, accepted, established, common, prevailing, popular.
– OPPOSITES fringe.

maintain verb **1** *they wanted to maintain peace:* **preserve**, conserve, keep, retain, keep going, prolong, perpetuate, sustain, carry on, continue. **2** *the council maintains the roads:* **look after**, service, care for, take care of. **3** *the costs of maintaining a family:* **support**, provide for, keep, sustain. **4** *he maintained that he was innocent:* **insist**, declare, assert, protest, affirm, avow, profess, claim, allege, contend, argue; formal aver.
– OPPOSITES break, discontinue, neglect, deny.

maintenance noun **1** *the maintenance of peace:* **preservation**, conservation, keeping, perpetuation, carrying on, continuation. **2** *car maintenance:* **upkeep**, service, servicing, repair, care, aftercare. **3** *the maintenance of his children:* **support**, keeping, upkeep, sustenance. **4** *absent fathers are forced to*

pay maintenance: **financial support**, child support, alimony; upkeep.
–OPPOSITES breakdown, neglect.

majestic adjective **stately**, dignified, distinguished, solemn, magnificent, grand, splendid, glorious, impressive, noble, awe-inspiring, monumental, palatial; imposing, heroic.
–OPPOSITES modest, wretched.

majesty noun **stateliness**, dignity, solemnity, magnificence, pomp, grandeur, grandness, splendour, glory, impressiveness, nobility.
–OPPOSITES modesty, wretchedness.

major adjective **1** *the major English poets:* **greatest**, best, finest, most important, chief, main, prime, principal, leading, foremost, outstanding, pre-eminent. **2** *an issue of major importance:* **crucial**, vital, great, considerable, paramount, utmost, prime. **3** *a major factor:* **important**, big, significant, weighty, crucial, key. **4** *major surgery:* **serious**, radical, complicated, difficult.
–OPPOSITES minor, little, trivial.

m

majority noun **1** *the majority of cases:* **larger part/number**, greater part/number, best/better part, most; bulk, mass, main body, preponderance, lion's share. **2** *a majority in the election:* **winning margin**; landslide, whitewash.
–OPPOSITES minority.

make verb **1** *he used to make model aeroplanes:* **construct**, build, assemble, put together, manufacture, produce, fabricate, create, form, fashion, model; improvise. **2** *she made me do it:* **force**, compel, coerce, press, drive, pressurize, oblige, require; prevail on, bludgeon, strong-arm, impel, constrain; informal railroad, bulldoze, steamroller. **3** *they made a terrible noise:* **cause**, create, produce, generate. **4** *she made a little bow:* **perform**, execute, give, do. **5** *they made him chairman:* **appoint**, designate, name, nominate, select, elect, vote in, install; induct, institute, invest, ordain. **6** *he's made a lot of money:* **acquire**, obtain, gain, get, secure, win, earn; bring in. **7** *I've made some lunch:* **prepare**, get ready, put together, concoct, cook, dish up, throw together, whip up; informal fix. **8** *she made a short announcement:* **utter**, give, deliver, recite, pronounce. **9** *we've made a decision:* **reach**, come to, settle on, conclude. **10** *the sofa makes a good bed:* **be**, act as, serve as, function as, constitute.
–OPPOSITES destroy, lose, miss.
• noun **brand**, marque, label.
■ **make believe** pretend, fantasize, daydream, dream, imagine, play. **make do** scrape by, get by/along, manage, cope, survive, muddle through/along, improvise, make ends meet, keep the wolf from the door, keep your head above water; informal make out. **make for** *constant arguing doesn't make for a happy marriage:* contribute to, be conducive to, produce, promote, facilitate, foster. **make off** run away/off, take to your heels, beat a hasty retreat, flee, make a run for it, take off, take flight, bolt, make yourself scarce, do a disappearing act; informal clear off/out, beat it, leg it, skedaddle, vamoose, hightail it, hotfoot it, split, scoot, scram; Brit. informal scarper, do a runner; N. Amer. informal take a powder. **make off with** take, steal, purloin, pilfer, abscond with, run away/off with, carry off, snatch; informal walk away/off with, swipe, filch, snaffle, nab, lift; Brit. informal pinch, half-inch, nick, whip, knock off. **make something out 1** *I could just make out a figure in the distance:* see, discern, distinguish, detect, observe, recognize; literary espy. **2** *he couldn't make out what she was saying:* understand, grasp, follow, work out, make sense of, interpret, decipher, make head or tail of, get, catch. **3** *she made out that he was violent:* allege, claim, suggest, imply, hint, insinuate, indicate, intimate; formal aver. **make something up 1** *exports make up 42% of earnings:* comprise, form, compose, constitute, account for. **2** *he made up an excuse:* invent, fabricate, concoct, think up; devise, manufacture, formulate; informal cook up. **make up for 1** *she tried to make up for what she'd said:* atone for, make amends for, compensate for; expiate. **2** *job satisfaction can make up for low pay:* offset, counterbalance, counteract, compensate for; cancel out.

make-believe **noun** **fantasy**, pretence, daydreaming, invention, fancy, fabrication, play-acting, charade, masquerade.
– OPPOSITES reality.
• **adjective** **imaginary**, imagined, made-up, fantasy, dreamed-up, fanciful, fictitious, fake, mock, sham, simulated; informal pretend, phoney.
– OPPOSITES real, actual.

maker **noun** **creator**, manufacturer, constructor, builder, producer.

makeshift **adjective** **temporary**, provisional, stopgap, standby, rough and ready, improvised, ad hoc, extempore, thrown together.
– OPPOSITES permanent.

make-up **noun** **1** *she used too much make-up:* **cosmetics**; informal warpaint, slap. **2** *the cellular make-up of plants:* **composition**, constitution, structure, configuration, arrangement. **3** *jealousy isn't part of his make-up:* **character**, nature, temperament, personality, disposition, mentality, persona, psyche.

making **noun** **1** *the making of cars:* **manufacture**, mass production, building, construction, assembly, production, creation, putting together, fabrication. **2** *she has the makings of a champion:* **qualities**, characteristics, ingredients; potential, capacity, capability; stuff.
– OPPOSITES destruction.

maladjusted **adjective** **disturbed**, unstable, neurotic, dysfunctional; informal mixed up, screwed up, hung up, messed up.
– OPPOSITES normal, stable.

maladministration **noun** (formal) **mismanagement**, mishandling, incompetence; malpractice, misconduct; Law malfeasance.
– OPPOSITES probity, efficiency.

maladroit **adjective** **bungling**, awkward, inept, clumsy, bumbling, incompetent, heavy-handed, gauche; informal ham-fisted, cack-handed.
– OPPOSITES adroit, skilful.

malady **noun** **illness**, sickness, disease, infection, ailment, disorder, complaint, affliction, infirmity; informal bug, virus.

malaise **noun** **unhappiness**, discomfort, melancholy, depression, despondency, dejection, angst, ennui; lassitude, listlessness, weariness; infirmity, illness, sickness, disease.
– OPPOSITES comfort, well-being.

malapropism **noun** wrong word, solecism, misuse; slip of the tongue.

malcontent **noun** **troublemaker**, mischief-maker, agitator, dissident, rebel; moaner; informal stirrer, whinger; N. Amer. informal kvetch.

male **adjective** **masculine**; virile, manly, macho.
– OPPOSITES female.
• **noun** *an elderly male.* See **MAN** noun sense 1.

malefactor **noun** (formal) **wrongdoer**, miscreant, offender, criminal, culprit, villain, lawbreaker, felon, evildoer, delinquent; Law malfeasant.

malevolence **noun** **malice**, hostility, hate, hatred, ill will, enmity, ill feeling, venom, rancour, vindictiveness, vengefulness; literary maleficence.
– OPPOSITES benevolence.

malevolent **adjective** **malicious**, hostile, baleful, venomous, evil, malign, malignant, rancorous, vicious, vindictive, vengeful; literary maleficent.
– OPPOSITES benevolent.

malformation **noun** **deformity**, distortion, crookedness, disfigurement, abnormality.

malformed **adjective** **deformed**, misshapen, ill-proportioned, disfigured, distorted, crooked, contorted, twisted, warped; abnormal; Scottish thrawn.
– OPPOSITES perfect, normal, healthy.

malfunction **verb** *the computer has malfunctioned:* **crash**, go wrong, break down, fail, stop working; informal conk out, go kaput, fall over, act up; Brit. informal play up, pack up.
• **noun** *a computer malfunction:* **crash**, breakdown, fault, failure, bug; informal glitch.

malice **noun** **spite**, malevolence, ill will, vindictiveness, vengefulness, malignity, animus, enmity, rancour; literary maleficence.
– OPPOSITES benevolence.

malicious **adjective** **spiteful**,

malevolent, vindictive, vengeful, malign, nasty, hurtful, mischievous, cruel; literary maleficent.
– OPPOSITES benevolent.

malign adjective *a malign influence:* **harmful**, evil, bad, baleful, destructive, malignant, injurious.
– OPPOSITES beneficial.
• verb *he maligned an innocent man:* **defame**, slander, libel, blacken someone's name, smear, vilify, cast aspersions on, run down, denigrate, disparage, slur, abuse; informal bad-mouth, knock; Brit. informal rubbish, slag off.
– OPPOSITES praise.

malignant adjective **1** *a malignant disease:* **virulent**, invasive, uncontrollable, dangerous, deadly, fatal, life-threatening. **2** *a malignant growth:* **cancerous**; technical metastatic. **3** *a malignant thought:* **spiteful**, malicious, malevolent, vindictive, vengeful, malign, nasty, hurtful, mischievous, cruel.
– OPPOSITES benign, benevolent.

malinger verb **sham**, feign, fake, pretend; shirk; informal put it on, fake it; Brit. informal skive, swing the lead; N. Amer. informal goldbrick.

malingerer noun **shirker**, idler, layabout; informal slacker; Brit. informal skiver; N. Amer. informal gold brick.

mall noun **shopping precinct**, shopping centre, arcade, galleria; N. Amer. plaza.

malleable adjective **1** *a malleable substance:* **pliable**, ductile, plastic, pliant, soft, workable. **2** *a malleable young woman:* **easily influenced**, suggestible, susceptible, impressionable, easily led; vulnerable.
– OPPOSITES hard, intractable.

malnutrition noun **undernourishment**, malnourishment, poor diet.

malodorous adjective **foul-smelling**, evil-smelling, fetid, smelly, stinking, reeking, rank, high, putrid, noxious; informal stinky; Brit. informal niffy, pongy, whiffy, humming; N. Amer. informal funky; literary noisome, mephitic.
– OPPOSITES fragrant.

malpractice noun **wrongdoing**, professional misconduct, unprofessionalism; negligence, carelessness, incompetence, corruption.

maltreat verb **ill-treat**, mistreat, abuse, ill-use, mishandle; knock about/around, hit, beat, manhandle, persecute; informal beat up, rough up, do over.

maltreatment noun **ill-treatment**, mistreatment, abuse; violence, harm, persecution.

mammoth adjective. See **huge**.

man noun **1** *a handsome man:* **gentleman**, male, fellow; youth; informal guy, geezer, gent; Brit. informal bloke, chap, lad, cove; Scottish & Irish informal bodach; N. Amer. informal dude, hombre; Austral./NZ informal digger. **2** *all men are mortal:* **human being**, human, person, mortal, individual, personage, soul. **3** *the evolution of man:* **the human race**, the human species, Homo sapiens, humankind, humanity, human beings, humans, people, mankind. **4** *the men voted to strike:* **workers**, workforce, employees, staff, personnel, human resources, manpower, labour force; troops; informal liveware. **5** *have you met her new man?* **boyfriend**, partner, husband, spouse, lover, fiancé; live-in lover, significant other, cohabitee; informal fancy man, toy boy, sugar daddy, intended; N. Amer. informal squeeze; dated beau, steady, young man. **6** *his man brought him a cocktail:* **manservant**, valet, attendant, retainer; page, footman, flunkey; N. Amer. houseman; Military, dated batman.
• verb **1** *the office is manned from 9 a.m. to 5 p.m.* **staff**, crew, occupy, people. **2** *firemen manned the pumps:* **operate**, work, use.
■ **man to man** frankly, openly, honestly, directly, candidly, plainly, without beating about the bush; woman to woman. **to a man** without exception, bar none, one and all, everyone, unanimously, as one.

> **WORD LINKS**
> **male, masculine, virile** relating to men
> **misandry** hatred of men (i.e. the male sex)

manacle verb **shackle**, fetter, chain, put/clap in irons, handcuff, restrain; secure; informal cuff.

manacles plural noun **handcuffs**, shackles, chains, irons, fetters, restraints, bonds; informal cuffs, bracelets.

manage verb **1** *she manages a staff of 80:* **be in charge of**, run, head, direct, control, preside over, lead, govern, rule, command, supervise, oversee, administer, organize, conduct, handle, be at the helm of; informal head up. **2** *how much work can you manage this week?* **accomplish**, achieve, do, carry out, perform, undertake, bring about, finish, deal with, get through. **3** *will you be able to manage without him?* **cope**, get along/on, make do, be all right, carry on, survive, get by, muddle through/along, fend for yourself, shift for yourself, make ends meet; informal make out, hack it. **4** *she can't manage that horse:* **control**, handle, master; cope with, deal with.

manageable adjective **1** *a manageable amount of work:* **achievable**, doable, practicable, feasible, reasonable, attainable, viable. **2** *a manageable child:* **compliant**, tractable, pliant, biddable, docile, amenable, accommodating, acquiescent. **3** *a manageable tool:* **user-friendly**, easy to use, handy.
–OPPOSITES difficult, impossible.

management noun **1** *he's responsible for the management of the firm:* **administration**, running, managing, organization; direction, leadership, control, governance, rule, command, supervision, handling, guidance, operation. **2** *workers are in dispute with the management:* **managers**, employers, directors, board of directors, board, directorate, executive, administration, leadership; owners, proprietors; informal bosses, top brass.

manager noun **executive**, head of department, line manager, supervisor, principal, administrator, head, director, managing director, superintendent, foreman, forewoman, overseer; informal boss, chief, governor; Brit. informal gaffer, guv'nor.

mandate noun **1** *he called an election to seek a mandate for his policies:* **authority**, approval, ratification, endorsement, sanction, authorization. **2** *a mandate from the UN:* **instruction**, directive, decree, command, order, injunction, edict, ruling, fiat; formal ordinance.

mandatory adjective **obligatory**, compulsory, binding, required, requisite, necessary, essential, imperative.
–OPPOSITES optional.

manfully adverb **bravely**, courageously, gallantly, heroically, valiantly; determinedly, hard, strongly, vigorously; with all your strength, to the best of your abilities, desperately.

mangle verb **mutilate**, disfigure, damage, injure, crush; cut up, tear apart, butcher, maul.

mangy adjective **scruffy**, moth-eaten, shabby, worn; dirty, squalid, sleazy, seedy; informal tatty, the worse for wear, ratty, scuzzy; Brit. informal grotty.

manhandle verb **1** *he was manhandled by a gang of youths:* **push**, shove, jostle, hustle; maul; informal paw, rough up; N. Amer. informal roust. **2** *we manhandled the piano down the stairs:* **heave**, haul, push, shove; pull, tug, drag, lug, manoeuvre; informal hump.

manhood noun **1** *the transition from boyhood to manhood:* **maturity**, sexual maturity, adulthood. **2** *an insult to his manhood:* **virility**, manliness, machismo, masculinity, maleness.

mania noun **1** *fits of mania:* **madness**, derangement, dementia, insanity, lunacy, psychosis, mental illness; delirium, frenzy, hysteria, raving, wildness. **2** *his mania for gadgets:* **obsession**, compulsion, fixation, fetish, fascination, preoccupation, passion, enthusiasm, desire, urge, craving; craze, fad, rage; informal thing.

maniac noun **1** *a homicidal maniac:* **lunatic**, madman, madwoman, psychopath; informal loony, nutcase, nut, psycho, head case, headbanger, sicko; Brit. informal nutter; N. Amer. informal crazy, meshuggener. **2** (informal) *a football maniac:* **enthusiast**, fan, devotee, aficionado; informal freak, fiend, fanatic, nut, buff, addict.

manic adjective **1** *a manic grin:* **mad**, insane, deranged, demented, maniacal, wild, crazed, demonic, hysterical, raving, unhinged; informal crazy. **2** *manic activity:* **frenzied**, feverish, frenetic, hectic, intense; informal mad.
–OPPOSITES sane, calm.

manifest verb **display**, show, exhibit, demonstrate, betray, present, reveal; formal evince.
–OPPOSITES hide.
•adjective **obvious**, clear, plain, apparent, evident, patent, palpable, distinct, definite, blatant, overt, transparent, conspicuous, undisguised.
–OPPOSITES secret.

manifestation noun **1** *the manifestation of anxiety:* **display**, demonstration, show, exhibition, presentation. **2** *manifestations of global warming:* **sign**, indication, evidence, symptom, testimony, proof, mark, reflection, example, instance.

manifesto noun **policy statement**, mission statement, platform, programme, declaration, proclamation, pronouncement.

manifold adjective **many**, numerous, multiple, multifarious, legion, diverse, various, several, varied, different, miscellaneous, assorted, sundry; literary myriad, divers.

m

manipulate verb **1** *he manipulated some knobs and levers:* **operate**, work; turn, pull, push, twist, slide. **2** *she manipulated the muscles of his back:* **massage**, rub, knead, press, squeeze; palpate. **3** *the government tried to manipulate the situation:* **control**, influence, exploit, manoeuvre, engineer, steer, direct; twist. **4** *they accused him of manipulating the data:* **falsify**, rig, distort, alter, change, doctor, massage, juggle, tamper with, tinker with, interfere with, misrepresent; informal cook, fiddle.

manipulative adjective **scheming**, calculating, cunning, crafty, wily, shrewd, devious, designing, conniving, Machiavellian, artful, slippery, sly, unscrupulous, disingenuous.

manipulator noun **opportunist**, strategist, player, wheeler-dealer; exploiter, user; informal operator.

mankind noun **the human race**, man, humanity, human beings, humans, Homo sapiens, humankind, people, men and women.

manly adjective **1** *his manly physique:* **virile**, masculine, strong, all-male, muscular, muscly, strapping, well built, sturdy, robust, rugged, tough, powerful, brawny; informal hunky. **2** *their manly deeds:* **brave**, courageous, bold, valiant, valorous, fearless, plucky, macho, intrepid, daring, heroic, gallant, chivalrous, swashbuckling.
–OPPOSITES effeminate, cowardly.

man-made adjective **artificial**, synthetic, manufactured; imitation, ersatz, simulated, mock, fake.
–OPPOSITES natural, real.

manner noun **1** *it was dealt with in a very efficient manner:* **way**, fashion, mode, means, method, system, style, approach, technique, procedure, process. **2** (old use) *what manner of person is he?* **kind**, sort, type, variety, breed, brand, class, category, order. **3** *her rather unfriendly manner:* **demeanour**, air, aspect, attitude, bearing, cast, behaviour, conduct; mien. **4** *the life and manners of Victorian society:* **customs**, habits, ways, practices, conventions, usages. **5** *you ought to teach him some manners:* **etiquette**, social graces, protocol, politeness, decorum, propriety, civility, Ps and Qs.

mannered adjective **affected**, pretentious, unnatural, artificial, contrived, stilted, stiff, forced, put-on, theatrical, precious, stagy, camp.
–OPPOSITES natural.

mannerism noun **idiosyncrasy**, quirk, oddity, foible, trait, peculiarity, habit, characteristic.

mannish adjective **unfeminine**, masculine, unladylike; informal butch.
–OPPOSITES feminine, girlish.

manoeuvre verb **1** *I manoeuvred the car into the space:* **steer**, guide, drive, negotiate, navigate, pilot, direct, manipulate, move, work. **2** *he manoeuvred things to suit himself:* **manipulate**, contrive, manage, engineer, devise, plan, fix, organize, arrange, set up, orchestrate, choreograph, stage-manage; informal wangle. **3** *he began manoeuvring for the party leadership:* **intrigue**, plot, scheme, plan, conspire, pull strings.
•noun **1** *a tricky parking manoeuvre:* **operation**, exercise, move, movement, action. **2** *diplomatic manoeuvres:* **stratagem**, tactic,

gambit, ploy, trick, dodge, ruse, scheme, device, plot, machination, artifice, subterfuge, intrigue.

manservant noun **valet**, attendant, retainer, equerry, gentleman's gentleman, man; steward, butler, footman, flunkey, page, houseboy, lackey; N. Amer. houseman; Military, dated batman.

mansion noun **country house**, stately home, hall, manor house; informal palace, pile.
– OPPOSITES hovel.

mantle noun **1** *a dark green velvet mantle:* **cloak**, cape, shawl, wrap, stole. **2** *a thick mantle of snow:* **covering**, layer, blanket, sheet, veil, canopy, cover, cloak, pall, shroud. **3** *the mantle of leadership:* **role**, burden, onus, duty, responsibility.

manual adjective **1** *manual work:* **physical**, labouring, blue-collar. **2** *a manual typewriter:* **hand-operated**, hand.
• noun *a training manual:* **handbook**, instruction book, instructions, guide, companion, ABC, guidebook; informal bible.

manufacture verb **1** *the company manufactures laser printers:* **make**, produce, mass-produce, build, construct, assemble, put together, create, turn out. **2** *a story manufactured by the press:* **make up**, invent, fabricate, concoct, hatch, dream up, think up, trump up, devise, formulate, contrive; informal cook up.
• noun *the manufacture of aircraft engines:* **production**, making, manufacturing, mass production, construction, building, assembly.

manufacturer noun **maker**, producer; industrialist, captain of industry.

manure noun **dung**, muck, excrement, droppings, ordure, guano, cowpats; fertilizer; N. Amer. informal cow chips, horse apples.

manuscript noun **document**, text, script, paper, typescript; holograph.

many determiner & adjective **1** *many animals were killed:* **numerous**, a lot of, plenty of, countless, innumerable, scores of, crowds of, droves of, an army of, a horde of, a multitude of, a multiplicity of, untold; diverse, multifarious; copious, abundant, profuse, an abundance of, a profusion of; frequent; informal lots of, umpteen, loads of, masses of, stacks of, heaps of, piles of, bags of, tons of, oodles of, dozens of, hundreds of, thousands of, millions of, billions of, zillions of, a slew of; Brit. informal a shedload of; N. Amer. informal gazillions of; Austral./NZ informal a swag of; literary myriad, divers.
2 *sacrificing the individual for the sake of the many:* **the people**, the common people, the masses, the multitude, the populace, the public, the rank and file; derogatory the hoi polloi, the common herd, the mob, the proletariat, the riff-raff, the great unwashed, the proles, the plebs.
– OPPOSITES few.

map noun **plan**, chart; A to Z, street plan, guide; atlas.
• verb *the region was mapped from the air:* **chart**, plot, delineate, draw, record.
■ **map something out** outline, set out, lay out, sketch out, trace out, delineate, detail, draw up, formulate, work out, frame, draft, plan, plot out.

> **WORD LINKS**
> **cartography** the science of drawing maps

mar verb **1** *an ugly bruise marred his features:* **spoil**, impair, disfigure, blemish, scar. **2** *the celebrations were marred by violence:* **spoil**, ruin, damage, wreck; taint, tarnish.
– OPPOSITES enhance.

marauder noun **raider**, plunderer, looter, robber, pirate, freebooter, bandit, rustler; literary brigand; old use buccaneer, corsair.

marauding adjective **predatory**, rapacious, thieving, plundering, looting.

march verb **1** *the men marched past:* **stride**, walk, troop, step, pace, tread; slog, tramp, hike, trudge; parade, file. **2** *she marched in without even knocking:* **stride**, stalk, strut, flounce, storm, stomp, sweep, sail, steam.
• noun **1** *a 20-mile march:* **hike**, trek, slog, walk. **2** *police sought to ban the march:* **parade**, procession, cortège; demonstration; informal demo. **3** *the march of technology:* **progress**,

advance; development, evolution; passage.

margin noun **1** *the margin of the lake:* **edge**, side, verge, border, perimeter, brink, brim, rim, fringe, boundary, periphery, bound, extremity. **2** *there's no margin for error:* **leeway**, latitude, scope, room, space; slack, excess, allowance. **3** *they won by a narrow margin:* **gap**, majority, amount.

marginal adjective **1** *the difference is marginal:* **slight**, small, tiny, minute, insignificant, minimal, negligible. **2** *a very marginal case:* **borderline**, disputable, questionable, doubtful.

marijuana noun **cannabis**, hashish, ganja, bhang, hemp; informal dope, hash, grass, pot, blow, draw, the weed, skunk; Brit. informal wacky baccy; N. Amer. informal locoweed.

marinate verb **souse**, soak, steep, immerse, marinade.

marine adjective **1** *marine plants:* **seawater**, sea, saltwater; aquatic; technical pelagic, thalassic. **2** *a marine insurance company:* **maritime**, nautical, naval; seafaring, seagoing, ocean-going.

m

mariner noun **sailor**, seaman, seafarer.

marital adjective **matrimonial**, married, wedded, conjugal, nuptial, marriage, wedding; literary connubial.

maritime adjective **naval**, marine, nautical; seafaring, seagoing, sea, ocean-going.

mark noun **1** *a dirty mark:* **blemish**, streak, spot, fleck, dot, blot, stain, smear, speck, speckle, blotch, smudge, smut, fingermark, fingerprint; bruise, discoloration; informal splotch, splodge. **2** *a punctuation mark:* **symbol**, sign, character; diacritic. **3** *books bearing the mark of a well-known bookseller:* **logo**, seal, stamp, symbol, emblem, device, insignia, badge, brand, trademark, monogram, hallmark, logotype, watermark, coat of arms. **4** *unemployment passed the three million mark:* **point**, level, stage. **5** *a mark of respect:* **sign**, token, symbol, indication, badge, emblem; symptom, proof. **6** *the war left its mark on him:* **impression**, imprint; effect, impact, influence. **7** *the mark of a civilized society:* **characteristic**, feature, trait, attribute, quality, hallmark, indicator. **8** *he got a good mark for maths:* **grade**, grading, rating, score, percentage.
• verb **1** *be careful not to mark the paintwork:* **discolour**, stain, smear, smudge, streak; dirty, bruise; informal splotch, splodge; literary smirch. **2** *her possessions were clearly marked:* **name**, initial, label. **3** *I've marked the relevant passages:* **indicate**, label, tick; show, identify, highlight. **4** *a festival to mark the town's 200th anniversary:* **celebrate**, observe, recognize, acknowledge, keep, honour, commemorate, remember. **5** *the incidents marked a new phase in their campaign:* **represent**, signify, indicate, herald. **6** *his style is marked by simplicity and concision:* **characterize**, distinguish, identify, typify. **7** *I have a pile of essays to mark:* **assess**, evaluate, appraise, correct; N. Amer. grade.

marked adjective **noticeable**, pronounced, decided, distinct, striking, clear, glaring, blatant, unmistakable, obvious, plain, manifest, patent, palpable, prominent, significant, conspicuous, notable, recognizable, identifiable, distinguishable, discernible.
– OPPOSITES imperceptible.

market noun **1** **shopping centre**, marketplace, mart, flea market, bazaar, souk, fair; old use emporium. **2** *there's no market for such goods:* **demand**, call, want, desire, need, requirement. **3** *the market is sluggish:* **trade**, trading, business, things.
• verb *the product was marketed worldwide:* **sell**, retail, merchandise, trade, peddle, hawk; advertise, promote.

marksman, markswoman noun **sniper**, sharpshooter; good shot; informal crack shot; N. Amer. informal deadeye, shootist.

maroon verb **strand**, cast away, cast ashore; abandon, leave behind, leave.

marriage noun **1** *a proposal of marriage:* **matrimony**, wedlock. **2** *the marriage took place at St Margaret's:* **wedding**, ceremony, nuptials, union. **3** *a marriage of jazz, pop, and gospel:* **union**, fusion,

mixture, mix, blend, amalgamation, combination, hybrid.
– OPPOSITES divorce, separation.

> **WORD LINKS**
> **marital**, **matrimonial**, **nuptial**, **conjugal** relating to marriage

married adjective **1** *a married couple:* **wedded**, wed; informal spliced, hitched. **2** *married life:* **marital**, matrimonial, conjugal, nuptial; literary connubial.
– OPPOSITES single.

marry verb **1** *the couple married last year:* **get married**, wed, be wed, plight/pledge your troth; informal tie the knot, walk down the aisle, take the plunge, get spliced, get hitched, say 'I do'. **2** *the show marries poetry with art:* **join**, unite, combine, fuse, mix, blend, merge, amalgamate, link, connect, couple, knit, yoke.
– OPPOSITES divorce, separate.

marsh noun **swamp**, marshland, bog, swampland, morass, mire, quagmire, slough, fen, fenland; Scottish & N. English moss.

> **WORD LINKS**
> **paludal** relating to marshes

marshal verb **assemble**, gather, collect, muster, call together, draw up, line up, array, organize, group, arrange, deploy, position; mobilize, summon, round up.

marshy adjective **boggy**, swampy, muddy, squelchy, soggy, waterlogged; Scottish & N. English mossy.
– OPPOSITES dry, firm.

martial adjective **military**, soldierly, army; warlike, fighting, militaristic; informal gung-ho.

martinet noun **disciplinarian**, slave-driver, hard taskmaster, authoritarian, tyrant.

marvel verb *she marvelled at their courage:* **be amazed**, be astonished, be awed, wonder; informal be gobsmacked.
• noun *a marvel of technology:* **wonder**, miracle, sensation, spectacle, phenomenon.

marvellous adjective **excellent**, splendid, wonderful, magnificent, superb, glorious, sublime, lovely, delightful; informal super, great, amazing, fantastic, terrific, tremendous, sensational, heavenly, divine, gorgeous, grand, fabulous, fab, awesome, magic, ace, wicked, mind-blowing, far out, out of this world; Brit. informal smashing, brilliant, brill; N. Amer. informal boss; Austral./NZ informal beaut, bonzer; Brit. informal, dated champion, wizard, ripping, spiffing, top-hole; N. Amer. informal, dated swell.
– OPPOSITES commonplace, awful.

masculine adjective **1** *a masculine trait:* **male**, man's, men's; male-oriented. **2** *a powerfully masculine man:* **virile**, macho, manly, all-male; muscular, muscly, strong, strapping, well built, rugged, robust, brawny, powerful, red-blooded, vigorous; informal hunky. **3** *a rather masculine woman:* **mannish**, unfeminine, unladylike; informal butch.
– OPPOSITES feminine, effeminate.

masculinity noun **virility**, manliness, maleness, machismo.

mash verb **pulp**, crush, purée, cream, pound, beat.

mask noun **1** *she wore a mask to conceal her face:* **disguise**; historical visor; old use vizard. **2** *he dropped his mask of good humour:* **pretence**, semblance, veil, screen, front, facade, veneer, disguise, cover, cloak, camouflage.
• verb *poplar trees masked the factory:* **hide**, conceal, disguise, cover up, obscure, screen, cloak, camouflage.

masquerade noun *he couldn't keep up the masquerade much longer:* **pretence**, deception, pose, act, front, facade, disguise, cover-up, play-acting, make-believe; informal put-on.
• verb **pretend**, disguise, impersonate, pass yourself off, pose, play, profess, dissimulate.

mass noun **1** *a soggy mass of fallen leaves:* **pile**, heap; accumulation. **2** *a mass of cyclists:* **crowd**, horde, throng, host, troop, army, herd, flock, swarm, mob, pack, flood, multitude. **3** *the mass of the population:* **majority**, greater part/number, best/better part, major part, bulk, main body, lion's share. **4** *the masses:* **the common people**, the populace, the public, the people, the rank and file, the crowd; derogatory the hoi polloi, the mob, the proletariat, the common herd, the great unwashed, the plebs.

• adjective *mass hysteria:* **widespread**, general, wholesale, universal.
• verb *they began massing troops in the region:* **assemble**, gather together.

massacre noun *a cold-blooded massacre:* **slaughter**, killing, murder, execution, annihilation, liquidation, extermination; carnage, butchery, bloodbath, bloodletting.
• verb *thousands were massacred:* **slaughter**, butcher, murder, kill, annihilate, exterminate, execute, liquidate, eliminate, mow down, cut down.

massage noun **rub**, rub-down; shiatsu, reflexology, acupressure, osteopathy.
• verb **1** *he massaged her tired muscles:* **rub**, knead, manipulate, pummel, work. **2** *the statistics have been massaged:* **alter**, tamper with, manipulate, doctor, falsify, juggle, fiddle with, tinker with, distort, change, rig, interfere with; informal fix, cook, fiddle.

massive adjective **huge**, enormous, vast, immense, mighty, great, colossal, tremendous, prodigious, gigantic, gargantuan, mammoth, monstrous, monumental, giant, mountainous, titanic; epic, Herculean; informal monster, jumbo, mega, whopping, humongous, astronomical; Brit. informal whacking great, ginormous.
– OPPOSITES tiny.

master noun **1** (historical) *he acceded to his master's wishes:* **lord**, ruler, sovereign, monarch. **2** *the dog's master:* **owner**, keeper, handler. **3** *a chess master:* **expert**, adept, genius, maestro, virtuoso, authority; informal ace, wizard, whizz, hotshot; Brit. informal dab hand; N. Amer. informal maven, crackerjack. **4** *the master of the ship:* **captain**, commander; informal skipper. **5** *the geography master:* **teacher**, schoolteacher, schoolmaster, tutor, instructor. **6** *their spiritual master:* **guru**, teacher, leader, guide, mentor.
– OPPOSITES servant, amateur, pupil.
• verb **1** *I managed to master my fears:* **overcome**, conquer, beat, quell, suppress, control, triumph over, subdue, subjugate, curb, check, defeat, get the better of, get a grip on, get over; informal lick; literary vanquish. **2** *it took ages to master the technique:* **learn**, pick up, grasp, understand, acquire, manage; informal get the hang of.
• adjective *a master craftsman:* **expert**, adept, proficient, skilled, skilful, deft, dexterous, adroit, practised, experienced, masterly, accomplished; informal crack, ace; N. Amer. informal crackerjack.

masterful adjective **1** *a masterful man:* **commanding**, powerful, imposing, authoritative. **2** *their masterful handling of the situation:* **expert**, adept, masterly, skilful, skilled, adroit, proficient, deft, dexterous, accomplished, polished, consummate.
– OPPOSITES weak, inept.

masterly adjective. See MASTERFUL sense 2.

mastermind verb *he masterminded the whole campaign:* **plan**, control, direct, be in charge of, run, conduct, organize, arrange, preside over, orchestrate, stage-manage, engineer, manage, coordinate.
• noun *the mastermind behind the project:* **genius**, intellect; informal brain, brains.

masterpiece noun **chef-d'œuvre**, pièce de résistance, masterwork, magnum opus, tour de force.

master stroke noun **stroke of genius**, coup, triumph, tour de force.

mastery noun **1** *her mastery of the language:* **proficiency**, ability, capability; knowledge, understanding, comprehension, familiarity, command, grasp, grip. **2** *man's mastery over nature:* **control**, domination, command, supremacy, pre-eminence, superiority; power, authority, jurisdiction, dominion, sovereignty.

masticate verb **chew**, munch, champ, chomp; ruminate.

mat noun **1** *the hall mat:* **rug**, carpet; doormat. **2** *he placed his glass on the mat:* **coaster**, beer mat, doily; Brit. drip mat. **3** *a thick mat of hair:* **mass**, tangle, mop, thatch, shock, mane.
• verb *his hair was matted with blood:* **tangle**, entangle, knot, snarl up.

match noun **1** *a football match | a boxing match:* **contest**, competition,

game, tournament, tie, fixture, trial, test, meet, bout, fight; friendly, derby; play-off, replay, rematch. **2** *the vase was an exact match of the one she already owned:* **lookalike**, double, twin, duplicate, mate, companion, counterpart, pair; replica, copy; informal spitting image, dead ringer. **3** *a love match:* **marriage**, betrothal, relationship, partnership, union.
• verb **1** *the curtains matched the duvet cover:* **go with**, coordinate with, complement, suit. **2** *did their statements match?* **correspond**, be in agreement, tally, agree, match up, coincide, square. **3** *no one can match him at chess:* **equal**, compare with, be in the same league as, touch, keep up with, rival, compete with; informal hold a candle to.

matching adjective **corresponding**, equivalent, parallel, analogous; coordinating, complementary; paired, twin, identical, like, alike.
– OPPOSITES different, clashing.

matchless adjective **incomparable**, unrivalled, beyond compare/comparison, unparalleled, unequalled, peerless, second to none, unsurpassed, unsurpassable.

mate noun **1** (Brit. informal) *he's gone out with his mates:* **friend**, companion, schoolmate, classmate, work-mate; informal pal, chum; Brit. informal mucker; N. Amer. informal buddy, amigo, compadre. **2** *she's finally found her ideal mate:* **partner**, husband, wife, spouse, lover, significant other, companion; informal better half; Brit. informal other half. **3** *a plumber's mate:* **assistant**, helper, apprentice.
• verb *pandas rarely mate in captivity:* **breed**, couple, copulate.

material noun **1** *the decomposition of organic material:* **matter**, substance, stuff. **2** *the materials for a new building:* **constituent**, raw material, component. **3** *cleaning materials:* **things**, items, articles, stuff; Brit. informal gubbins. **4** *curtain material:* **fabric**, cloth, textiles. **5** *material for a magazine article:* **information**, data, facts, facts and figures, statistics, evidence, details, particulars, background, notes; informal info, gen, dope.
• adjective **1** *the material world:* **physical**, corporeal, tangible, mundane, worldly, earthly, secular, temporal, concrete, real. **2** *she was too fond of material pleasures:* **sensual**, physical, carnal, corporal, fleshly, bodily. **3** *information that could be material to the inquiry:* **relevant**, pertinent, applicable, germane; vital, essential, key.
– OPPOSITES spiritual, aesthetic, irrelevant.

materialistic adjective **consumerist**, acquisitive, greedy; worldly, capitalistic, bourgeois.

materialize verb **1** *the forecast investment boom did not materialize:* **happen**, occur, come about, take place, transpire; informal come off; literary come to pass. **2** *Harry materialized at the door:* **appear**, turn up, arrive, emerge, surface, pop up; informal show up, fetch up.

maternal adjective **1** *her maternal instincts:* **motherly**, protective, caring, nurturing. **2** *his maternal grandparents:* **on your mother's side**, on the distaff side; Anthropology matrilineal.

mathematical adjective **1** *mathematical symbols:* **arithmetical**, numerical; statistical, algebraic, geometric, trigonometric. **2** *with mathematical precision:* **rigorous**, meticulous, scrupulous, strict, pinpoint, unerring.

matrimonial adjective **marital**, conjugal, married, wedded; nuptial; literary connubial.

matrimony noun **marriage**, wedlock, union; nuptials.
– OPPOSITES divorce.

matted adjective **tangled**, knotted, tousled, dishevelled, uncombed, unkempt, ratty; black English natty.

matter noun **1** *decaying vegetable matter:* **material**, stuff. **2** *the heart of the matter:* **affair**, business, proceedings, situation, events, incident, episode, experience; subject, topic, issue, question, point, point at issue, case.
• verb *it doesn't matter what you wear:* **be important**, make any difference, be of consequence, be relevant, count.

matter-of-fact adjective **unemotional**, practical, down-to-earth, sensible, realistic, unsentimental, pragmatic, businesslike, commonsensical, level-headed, hard-headed, no-nonsense, straightforward.

mature adjective **1** *a mature woman:* **adult**, grown, fully grown, full-grown, in your prime. **2** *he's very mature for his age:* **grown-up**, sensible, responsible, adult, level-headed, reliable, dependable; wise, sophisticated. **3** *mature cheese:* **ripe**, mellow; rich, strong, flavoursome, full-bodied.
– OPPOSITES adolescent, childish.
• verb **1** *kittens mature when they are about a year old:* **be fully grown**; come of age, reach adulthood, reach maturity. **2** *he's matured since he left home:* **grow up**; blossom. **3** *leave the cheese to mature:* **ripen**, mellow; age. **4** *their friendship didn't have time to mature:* **develop**, grow, evolve, bloom, blossom, flourish, thrive.

maturity noun **1** *her progress from childhood to maturity:* **adulthood**, coming of age, manhood/womanhood. **2** *he displayed a maturity beyond his years:* **responsibility**, sense, level-headedness; wisdom, sophistication.

m

maudlin adjective **mawkish**, sentimental, mushy, slushy, sloppy; Brit. twee; informal schmaltzy, cheesy, corny, toe-curling; Brit. informal soppy; N. Amer. informal cornball.

maul verb **savage**, attack, lacerate, claw, scratch.

mausoleum noun **tomb**, sepulchre, crypt, vault, burial chamber, catacomb, undercroft.

maverick noun **individualist**, nonconformist, free spirit, original, eccentric; rebel, dissenter, dissident.
– OPPOSITES conformist.

mawkish adjective **sentimental**, maudlin, mushy, slushy, sloppy, cloying, saccharine, sugary, syrupy, nauseating; Brit. twee; informal schmaltzy, weepy, cutesy, lovey-dovey, cheesy, corny, sick-making, toe-curling; Brit. informal soppy; N. Amer. informal cornball, hokey.

maxim noun **saying**, adage, aphorism, proverb, motto, saw, axiom, dictum, precept, epigram.

maximum adjective *the maximum amount:* **greatest**, highest, biggest, largest, top, most, utmost.
– OPPOSITES minimum.
• noun *production levels are near their maximum:* **upper limit**, limit, utmost, greatest, most, peak, height, ceiling, top.
– OPPOSITES minimum.

maybe adverb **perhaps**, possibly; for all you know; N. English **happen**; literary peradventure, perchance.

mayhem noun **chaos**, havoc, bedlam, pandemonium, uproar, turmoil, a riot, anarchy; informal a madhouse.

maze noun **labyrinth**, network, warren; web, tangle, jungle.

meadow noun **field**, paddock; pasture; literary lea, mead.

meagre adjective **inadequate**, scant, paltry, limited, restricted, modest, sparse, negligible, skimpy, slender, miserable, pitiful, puny, miserly, niggardly; informal measly, stingy, pathetic, piddling.
– OPPOSITES abundant.

meal noun snack; feast, banquet; informal bite to eat, spread, blowout, feed; Brit. informal nosh-up; formal repast.

WORD LINKS
prandial relating to meals

mean[1] verb **1** *flashing lights mean the road is blocked:* **signify**, denote, indicate, connote, show, express, spell out; stand for, represent, symbolize; imply, suggest, intimate, refer to, allude to; literary betoken. **2** *she didn't mean to break it:* **intend**, aim, plan, have in mind, set out, aspire, desire, want, wish, expect. **3** *the closures will mean a rise in unemployment:* **entail**, involve, necessitate, lead to, result in, give rise to, bring about, cause, engender, produce. **4** *a red sky in the morning usually means rain:* **presage**, portend, foretell, augur, promise, foreshadow, herald, signal, bode; literary betoken.

mean[2] adjective **1** *he's too mean to leave a tip:* **miserly**, niggardly, parsimonious, penny-pinching, cheeseparing; informal tight-fisted, stingy, tight, mingy; N. Amer. informal cheap. **2** *a mean trick:* **unkind**, nasty, unpleasant, spiteful, malicious, unfair, cruel, shabby, despicable, contemptible, obnoxious, vile, odious, loathsome, base, low; informal horrible, horrid, hateful, rotten, low-down; Brit. informal beastly.
– OPPOSITES generous, kind.

mean³ noun *a mean between saving and splashing out:* **middle course**, middle way, midpoint, happy medium, golden mean, compromise, balance; median, norm, average. • adjective *the mean temperature:* **average**, median, normal, standard.

meander verb **1** *the river meandered gently:* **zigzag**, wind, twist, turn, curve, bend, snake. **2** *we meandered along the path:* **stroll**, saunter, amble, wander, drift; Scottish stravaig; informal mosey, tootle.

meandering adjective **1** *a meandering stream:* **winding**, windy, zigzag, twisting, turning, serpentine, sinuous, twisty. **2** *a meandering letter:* **rambling**, circuitous, roundabout, digressive, discursive, convoluted.
– OPPOSITES straight, succinct.

meaning noun **1** *the meaning of his remark:* **significance**, sense, signification, import, gist, thrust, drift, implication, tenor, message. **2** *the word has several different meanings:* **definition**, sense, explanation, denotation, connotation, interpretation. **3** *my life has no meaning:* **value**, validity, worth, significance, point.

> **WORD LINKS**
> **semantic** relating to meaning

meaningful adjective **1** *a meaningful remark:* **significant**, relevant, important, telling. **2** *a meaningful relationship:* **sincere**, deep, serious, earnest, significant, important. **3** *a meaningful glance:* **expressive**, eloquent, pointed; pregnant, revealing, suggestive.
– OPPOSITES inconsequential.

meaningless adjective **1** *a jumble of meaningless words:* **unintelligible**, incomprehensible, incoherent. **2** *she felt her life was meaningless:* **futile**, pointless, aimless, empty, hollow, vain, purposeless, valueless, useless, worthless, senseless, unimportant, insignificant, inconsequential.
– OPPOSITES worthwhile.

means plural noun **1** *the best means to achieve your goal:* **method**, way, manner, course, procedure. **2** *she doesn't have the means to support herself:* **money**, resources, capital, income, finance, funds, cash, the wherewithal, assets; informal dough, bread; Brit. informal dosh, brass, lolly, spondulicks, ackers. **3** *a man of means:* **wealth**, riches, affluence, substance, fortune, property.

meantime adverb. See MEANWHILE.

meanwhile adverb **1** *meanwhile, I'll stay here:* **for now**, for the moment, for the present, for the time being, meantime, in the meantime, in the interim, in the interval. **2** *cook for a further half hour; meanwhile, make the stuffing:* **at the same time**, simultaneously, concurrently.

measurable adjective **1** *a measurable amount:* **quantifiable**, assessable. **2** *a measurable improvement:* **appreciable**, noticeable, significant, visible, perceptible, definite, obvious.

measure verb **calculate**, compute, count, quantify, weigh, size, evaluate, assess, gauge, determine. • noun **1** *cost-cutting measures:* **action**, act, course of action, deed, procedure, step, expedient; manoeuvre, initiative, programme, operation. **2** *the Senate passed the measure:* **statute**, act, bill, law. **3** *sales are the measure of the company's success:* **yardstick**, test, standard, barometer, touchstone, benchmark.
■ **get the measure of** evaluate, assess, gauge, judge, weigh up; understand, fathom, read, be wise to, see through; informal suss out, have someone's number. **measure up** pass muster, match up, come up to standard, fit/fill the bill, be acceptable; informal come up to scratch, make the grade, cut the mustard, be up to snuff. **measure up to** meet, come up to, equal, match, bear comparison with, be on a level with; achieve, satisfy, fulfil.

measured adjective **1** *his measured tread:* **regular**, steady, even, rhythmic, unfaltering; slow, dignified, stately, sedate, leisurely, unhurried. **2** *his measured tones:* **thoughtful**, careful, considered, deliberate, restrained.

measureless adjective **boundless**, limitless, unlimited, unbounded, immense, vast, endless, infinite, immeasurable, incalculable.
– OPPOSITES limited.

measurement noun **1** *measurement of the effect is difficult:* **quantification**, computation, calculation; evaluation, assessment. **2** *all measurements are in metric units:* **size**, dimension, proportions; value, amount, quantity.

meat noun **flesh**.

WORD LINKS
carnivorous meat-eating

meaty adjective **1** *a tall, meaty young man:* **beefy**, brawny, burly, muscular, muscly. **2** *a good, meaty story:* **solid**, substantial, satisfying, thought-provoking.

mechanical adjective **1** *a mechanical device:* **mechanized**; machine-driven, automated, automatic. **2** *a mechanical response:* **automatic**, unthinking, habitual, routine; unemotional, unfeeling, lifeless.
– OPPOSITES manual.

mechanism noun **1** *an electrical mechanism:* **machine**, appliance, apparatus, device, instrument, contraption, gadget; informal gizmo. **2** *the train's safety mechanism:* **machinery**, gear, system, equipment. **3** *a formal mechanism for citizens to lodge complaints:* **procedure**, process, system, method, means, medium, channel.

mechanize verb **automate**, industrialize, motorize, computerize.

medal noun **decoration**, ribbon, star, badge, award; honour; Brit. informal gong.

meddle verb **1** *don't meddle in my affairs:* **interfere**, intrude, intervene, pry; informal poke your nose in; N. Amer. informal kibitz. **2** *someone had been meddling with her things:* **fiddle**, interfere, tamper, mess; Brit. informal muck about/around.

meddlesome adjective **interfering**, meddling, prying; informal nosy, nosy-parker.

mediate verb **1** *Austria tried to mediate between the two sides:* **arbitrate**, conciliate, moderate, make peace; intervene, intercede, liaise, step in. **2** *a tribunal was set up to mediate disputes:* **resolve**, settle, arbitrate in, umpire, reconcile, referee; mend, clear up; informal patch up.

mediation noun **arbitration**, conciliation, reconciliation, intervention, intercession; negotiation, shuttle diplomacy.

mediator noun **arbitrator**, arbiter, negotiator, conciliator, peacemaker, go-between, middleman, intermediary, moderator, broker, liaison officer; umpire, referee, adjudicator, judge.

medicinal adjective **curative**, healing, remedial, therapeutic, restorative, health-giving.

medicine noun **medication**, drug, prescription, treatment, remedy, cure; nostrum, panacea, cure-all.

WORD LINKS
pharmaceutical relating to medicines
pharmacy (Brit. **chemist**; N. Amer. **drugstore**) a shop selling medicines

medieval adjective **1** *medieval times:* **Middle Age**; Dark Age; Gothic. **2** (informal) *the plumbing's a bit medieval:* **primitive**, antiquated, archaic, antique, antediluvian, old-fashioned, outdated, outmoded; informal out of the ark; N. Amer. informal horse-and-buggy, clunky.
– OPPOSITES modern.

mediocre adjective **ordinary**, average, uninspired, undistinguished, indifferent, unexceptional, unexciting, unremarkable, run-of-the-mill, pedestrian, prosaic, lacklustre, forgettable, amateurish; informal OK, so-so.
– OPPOSITES excellent.

meditate verb **contemplate**, think, consider, ponder, muse, reflect, deliberate, ruminate, brood, mull over; formal cogitate.

meditation noun **contemplation**, thought, musing, consideration, reflection, deliberation, rumination, brooding, reverie, concentration; formal cogitation.

meditative adjective **pensive**, contemplative, reflective, ruminative, introspective, brooding.

medium noun **means**, method, avenue, channel, vehicle, organ, instrument, mechanism.
• adjective **average**, middling, medium-sized, middle-sized, moderate, normal, standard.

medley noun **assortment**, miscellany, mixture, melange, variety, mixed bag, mix, collection, selection, potpourri, patchwork.

meek adjective **submissive**, obedient, compliant, tame, biddable, acquiescent, timid, unprotesting; quiet, mild, gentle, docile, shy, diffident, unassuming, self-effacing.
–OPPOSITES assertive.

meet verb **1** *I met an old friend on the train:* **encounter**, come face to face with, run into, run across, come across/upon, chance on, happen on, stumble across; informal bump into. **2** *she first met Paul at a party:* **get to know**, be introduced to, make the acquaintance of. **3** *the committee met on Saturday:* **assemble**, gather, come together, get together, congregate, convene. **4** *the place where three roads meet:* **converge**, connect, touch, link up, intersect, cross, join. **5** *the announcement was met with widespread hostility:* **greet**, receive, treat. **6** *he does not meet our requirements:* **fulfil**, satisfy, measure up to, match up to, conform to, come up to, comply with, answer.
• noun *an athletics meet.* See **MEETING** sense 5.

meeting noun **1** *he stood up to address the meeting:* **gathering**, assembly, conference, congregation, convention, summit, rally; N. Amer. caucus; informal get-together. **2** *she demanded a meeting with the minister:* **consultation**, audience, interview. **3** *he intrigued her on their first meeting:* **encounter**, contact; appointment, assignation, rendezvous. **4** *the meeting of land and sea:* **convergence**, coming together, confluence, conjunction, union; intersection, crossing. **5** *an athletics meeting:* **event**, tournament, meet, rally, competition, match, game, contest.

melancholy adjective **sad**, sorrowful, unhappy, mournful, lugubrious, gloomy, despondent, downhearted, downcast, disconsolate, glum, miserable, morose, woeful, doleful, joyless; informal down in the dumps, down in the mouth, blue.
–OPPOSITES cheerful.
• noun *a feeling of melancholy:* **sadness**, sorrow, unhappiness, melancholia, dejection, depression, despondency, gloom, misery; informal the blues.

melange noun **mixture**, medley, assortment, blend, variety, mixed bag, mix, miscellany, selection, potpourri, patchwork.

melee, **mêlée** noun **fracas**, disturbance, rumpus, tumult, commotion, disorder, fray; brawl, fight, scuffle, struggle, skirmish, free-for-all, tussle; informal scrap, set-to; N. Amer. informal rough house.

mellifluous adjective **sweet-sounding**, dulcet, honeyed, mellow, soft, liquid, silvery, soothing, rich, smooth, euphonious, harmonious, tuneful.
–OPPOSITES cacophonous.

mellow adjective **1** *the mellow tone of his voice:* **dulcet**, sweet-sounding, tuneful, melodious, mellifluous; soft, smooth, warm, full, rich. **2** *a mellow wine:* **full-bodied**, mature, full-flavoured, rich, smooth. **3** *a mellow mood:* **genial**, affable, amiable, good-humoured, good-natured, pleasant, relaxed, easy-going.

melodious adjective **tuneful**, melodic, musical, mellifluous, dulcet, sweet-sounding, silvery, harmonious, euphonious, lyrical; informal easy on the ear.
–OPPOSITES discordant.

melodramatic adjective **exaggerated**, histrionic, extravagant, overdramatic, overdone, sensationalized, overemotional; theatrical, stagy, actressy; informal hammy.

melody noun **1** *familiar melodies:* **tune**, air, strain, theme, song, refrain. **2** *his unique gift for melody:* **melodiousness**, tunefulness, musicality.

melt verb **1** *the snow was beginning to melt:* **liquefy**, thaw, defrost, soften, dissolve. **2** *his anger melted away:* **vanish**, disappear, fade, dissolve, evaporate.

member noun **subscriber**, associate, fellow.

membrane noun **layer**, sheet, skin, film, tissue.

memento noun **souvenir**, keepsake, reminder, remembrance, token, memorial; trophy, relic.

memoir noun **1** *a touching memoir of her childhood:* **account**, history, record, chronicle, narrative, story, portrayal, depiction, portrait,

m

profile. **2** *he published his memoirs in 1955:* **autobiography**, life story; journal, diary.

memorable adjective **unforgettable**, indelible, catchy, haunting; momentous, significant, historic, notable, noteworthy, important, special, outstanding, arresting, impressive, distinctive, distinguished.

memorandum noun **message**, communication, note, email, letter, missive; informal memo.

memorial noun **1** *the war memorial:* **monument**, cenotaph, mausoleum; statue, plaque, cairn; shrine. **2** *the festival is a memorial to his life's work:* **tribute**, testimonial; remembrance, memento.
• adjective *a memorial service:* **commemorative**, remembrance.

memorize verb **commit to memory**, remember, learn by heart, become word-perfect in, get off pat.

memory noun **1** *happy memories of her childhood:* **recollection**, remembrance, reminiscence; impression. **2** *the town built a statue in memory of him:* **commemoration**, remembrance; honour, tribute, recognition, respect.

m

WORD LINKS
mnemonic helping the memory

menace noun **1** *an atmosphere full of menace:* **threat**, intimidation; malevolence, oppression. **2** *a menace to society:* **danger**, peril, risk, hazard, threat. **3** *that child is a menace:* **nuisance**, pest, troublemaker, mischief-maker.
• verb **1** *the elephants are still menaced by poaching:* **threaten**, endanger, put at risk, jeopardize, imperil. **2** *a gang of skinheads menaced local residents:* **intimidate**, threaten, terrorize, frighten, scare, terrify.

menacing adjective **threatening**, ominous, intimidating, frightening, forbidding, hostile, sinister, baleful.
– OPPOSITES friendly.

mend verb **repair**, fix, restore; sew, stitch, darn, patch; renew, renovate, fill in; informal patch up.
– OPPOSITES break.

menial adjective **unskilled**, lowly, humble, low-grade, low-status, degrading.

mental adjective **1** *mental faculties:* **intellectual**, cerebral, rational, cognitive. **2** *a mental disorder:* **psychiatric**, psychological; behavioural.
– OPPOSITES physical.

mentality noun **way of thinking**, mindset, mind, psychology, attitude, outlook, make-up.

mentally adverb **intellectually**, cognitively, inwardly, internally, in your head.

mention verb **1** *don't mention what happened last week:* **allude to**, refer to, touch on; bring up, raise, broach. **2** *he mentioned that he'd met them before:* **state**, say, indicate, let someone know, disclose, divulge, reveal. **3** *I'll gladly mention your work to my friends:* **recommend**, commend, put in a good word for; informal plug.
• noun **reference**, allusion, comment; citation; informal namecheck, plug.

mentor noun **1** *his political mentors:* **adviser**, guide, guru, consultant; confidant, confidante. **2** *regular meetings between mentor and trainee:* **trainer**, teacher, tutor, instructor, counsellor.

menu noun **bill of fare**, carte du jour, set menu, table d'hôte.

mercantile adjective **commercial**, trade, trading, business, merchant, sales.

mercenary adjective **grasping**, greedy, acquisitive, avaricious, venal, materialistic; informal money-grubbing.

merchandise noun **goods**, wares, stock, commodities, produce, products.
• verb **promote**, market, sell, retail; advertise, publicize, push; informal hype, plug.

merchant noun **trader**, dealer, wholesaler, broker, agent, seller, buyer, vendor, distributor.

merciful adjective **forgiving**, compassionate, pitying, forbearing, lenient, humane, mild, kind, soft-hearted, tender-hearted, gracious, sympathetic, humanitarian, liberal, tolerant, indulgent, generous, magnanimous, benign, benevolent.
– OPPOSITES cruel.

mercifully adverb **luckily**, fortunately, happily, thankfully, thank goodness/God/heavens.

merciless adjective **ruthless**, remorseless, pitiless, unforgiving, implacable, inexorable, relentless, inhumane, inhuman, unfeeling, intolerant, severe, cold-blooded, hard-hearted, stony-hearted, heartless, harsh, callous, cruel, brutal, barbarous, cut-throat.
– OPPOSITES compassionate.

mercurial adjective **volatile**, capricious, temperamental, excitable, fickle, changeable, unpredictable, variable, mutable, erratic, inconstant, inconsistent, unstable, unsteady, fluctuating, ever-changing, moody, flighty, wayward, impulsive; technical labile.
– OPPOSITES stable.

mercy noun *he showed no mercy to the others:* **leniency**, clemency, compassion, pity, charity, forgiveness, forbearance, quarter, humanity; soft-heartedness, tender-heartedness, kindness, sympathy, indulgence, tolerance, generosity, magnanimity, beneficence.
– OPPOSITES ruthlessness, cruelty.
■ **at the mercy of** in the power of, under the control of, in the clutches of, under the heel of, subject to; defenceless against, prey to.

merely adverb **only**, purely, solely, simply, just, but.

merge verb **1** *the company merged with a European firm:* **join together**, join forces, amalgamate, unite, affiliate, team up, link up. **2** *the two organizations were merged:* **amalgamate**, bring together, join, consolidate, conflate, unite, unify, combine, incorporate, integrate, link, yoke. **3** *the two colours merged:* **mingle**, blend, fuse, mix, intermix, intermingle, coalesce; literary commingle.
– OPPOSITES separate.

merger noun **amalgamation**, combination, union, fusion, coalition, affiliation, unification, incorporation, consolidation, link-up, alliance.
– OPPOSITES split.

merit noun **1** *composers of outstanding merit:* **excellence**, quality, calibre, worth, worthiness, value, distinction, eminence. **2** *the merits of the scheme:* **good point**, strong point, advantage, benefit, value, asset, plus.
– OPPOSITES inferiority, fault, disadvantage.
• verb *the accusation did not merit a response:* **deserve**, earn, warrant, rate, justify, be entitled to, have a right to, have a claim to/on.

meritorious adjective **praiseworthy**, laudable, commendable, admirable, estimable, creditable, worthy, deserving, excellent, exemplary, good.
– OPPOSITES discreditable.

merriment noun **high spirits**, exuberance, cheerfulness, gaiety, fun, buoyancy, levity, liveliness, cheer, joy, joyfulness, jollity, happiness, gladness, jocularity, conviviality, festivity, merrymaking, revelry, mirth, glee, laughter, hilarity, light-heartedness, amusement, pleasure; literary joyousness.
– OPPOSITES misery.

merry adjective **1** *merry throngs of students:* **cheerful**, cheery, in high spirits, bright, sunny, smiling, light-hearted, buoyant, lively, carefree, joyful, joyous, jolly, convivial, festive, mirthful, gleeful, happy, glad, laughing; informal chirpy; formal jocund; literary joyous, blithe. **2** (Brit. informal) *after three beers he began to feel quite merry:* **tipsy**, mellow; Brit. informal tiddly, squiffy.
– OPPOSITES miserable.

mesh noun *wire mesh:* **netting**, net; grille, screen, lattice, gauze.
• verb **1** *one gear meshes with the input gear:* **engage**, connect, lock, interlock. **2** *our ideas just do not mesh:* **harmonize**, fit together, match, dovetail, connect, interconnect.

mesmerize verb **enthral**, spellbind, entrance, dazzle, bewitch, charm, captivate, enchant, fascinate, transfix, grip, hypnotize.

mesmerizing adjective **enthralling**, spellbinding, entrancing, dazzling, captivating, enchanting, fascinating, gripping, hypnotic, compelling, bewitching.

mess noun **1** *they've left the place in a mess | clean up this mess:* **disarray**, disorder, untidiness, clutter, shambles, muddle, chaos; Brit. informal

tip. **2** *I've got to get out of this mess:* **plight**, predicament, trouble, quandary, dilemma, problem, muddle, mix-up; morass, quagmire.
■ **make a mess of** mismanage, mishandle, bungle, fluff, spoil, ruin, wreck; informal mess up, botch, make a hash of, muck up, foul up; Brit. informal make a pig's ear of, cock up. **mess about/around** potter about, fool about/around, play about/around, footle about/around; fidget, toy, trifle, tamper, tinker, interfere, meddle, monkey about/around; Brit. informal muck about/around. **mess something up** dirty; clutter up, jumble; rumple; N. Amer. informal muss up.

message noun **1** *she's left him a message:* **note**, letter, memo, email, missive, report, bulletin, communiqué, dispatch; communication, news, information. **2** *the message of his teaching:* **meaning**, sense, import, idea; point, thrust, gist, essence, content, subject, substance, implication, drift, lesson.
■ **get the message** (informal) understand, get the point, realize, comprehend; informal twig, catch on, latch on, get the picture.

m

messenger noun **courier**, postman, runner, dispatch rider, envoy, emissary, agent, go-between; historical herald; old use legate.

messy adjective **1** *messy clothes:* **dirty**, filthy, grubby, soiled, grimy; mucky, muddy, slimy, sticky, stained, smeared, smudged; dishevelled, scruffy, unkempt, rumpled, matted, tousled, bedraggled, tangled; Brit. informal manky. **2** *a messy kitchen:* **untidy**, disordered, in a muddle, chaotic, confused, disorganized, in disarray; cluttered, jumbled; informal like a bomb's hit it; Brit. informal shambolic. **3** *a messy legal battle:* **complex**, tangled, confused, convoluted; unpleasant, nasty, bitter, acrimonious.
– OPPOSITES clean, tidy.

metallic adjective **1** *a metallic sound:* **tinny**, jangling, jingling; grating, screeching, grinding; harsh, jarring. **2** *metallic paint:* sparkly, glittery; lustrous, shiny, glossy.

metamorphose verb **transform**, change, mutate, transmute, convert, alter, modify; morph; humorous transmogrify.

metamorphosis noun **transformation**, mutation, transmutation, change, alteration; humorous transmogrification.

metaphor noun **figure of speech**, image, trope, analogy, comparison, symbol.

metaphorical adjective **figurative**, allegorical, symbolic; imaginative, extended.
– OPPOSITES literal.

metaphysical adjective **1** *metaphysical questions:* **abstract**, theoretical, conceptual, philosophical; speculative, intellectual, academic. **2** *a metaphysical battle between Good and Evil:* **transcendental**, spiritual, supernatural.

mete verb
■ **mete something out** dispense, hand out, allocate, allot, apportion, issue, deal out, dole out, dish out, assign, administer.

meteoric adjective **rapid**, lightning, swift, fast, speedy, instant, sudden, spectacular, dramatic, overnight.
– OPPOSITES gradual.

method noun **1** *they use very old-fashioned methods:* **procedure**, technique, system, practice, routine, modus operandi, process; strategy, tactic, approach. **2** *there's no method in his approach:* **order**, organization, structure, form, system, logic, planning, design, consistency.
– OPPOSITES disorder.

methodical adjective **orderly**, well ordered, well organized, well planned, efficient, businesslike, systematic, structured, logical, analytical, disciplined; consistent, scientific.

meticulous adjective **careful**, conscientious, diligent, scrupulous, punctilious, painstaking; thorough, studious, rigorous, detailed, perfectionist, fastidious, methodical, particular.
– OPPOSITES careless.

métier noun **1** *he had another métier besides the priesthood:* **occupation**, job, profession, business, employment, career, vocation, trade, craft, line of work; N. Amer. specialty. **2** *television is more my métier:* **forte**, strong point, strength, speciality, talent, bent; informal thing, cup of tea.

metropolis noun **capital city**, conurbation, megalopolis.

mettle noun **spirit**, fortitude, strength of character, moral fibre, steel, determination, resolve, resolution, backbone, grit, courage, courageousness, bravery, valour, fearlessness, daring; informal guts, spunk; Brit. informal bottle.

miasma noun (literary) **stink**, reek, stench, smell, odour, effluvium; Brit. informal pong, niff, whiff.

microscopic adjective **tiny**, minute, infinitesimal, minuscule, nanoscopic; Scottish wee; informal teeny; Brit. informal titchy.
– OPPOSITES huge.

midday noun **noon**, twelve noon, high noon, noonday.
– OPPOSITES midnight.

middle noun **1** *a shallow dish with a spike in the middle:* **centre**, midpoint, halfway point, dead centre, focus, hub; eye, heart, core, kernel. **2** *he had a towel round his middle:* **midriff**, waist, belly, stomach; informal tummy.
– OPPOSITES edge.
• adjective **1** *the middle point:* **central**, mid, mean, medium, median, midway, halfway. **2** *the middle level:* **intermediate**, intermediary.

middleman noun **intermediary**, go-between; dealer, broker, agent, factor, wholesaler, distributor.

middling adjective **average**, standard, normal, middle-of-the-road; moderate, ordinary, commonplace, everyday, workaday, tolerable, passable; run-of-the-mill, fair; informal OK, so-so, bog-standard, fair-to-middling; NZ informal half-pie.

midnight noun **twelve midnight**, twenty-four hundred hours, the witching hour.
– OPPOSITES midday.

mien noun **appearance**, look, expression, countenance, aura, demeanour, attitude, air, manner, bearing; formal comportment.

might noun **strength**, force, power, vigour, energy, brawn, powerfulness, forcefulness.

mighty adjective **1** *a mighty blow:* **powerful**, forceful, vigorous, hefty, thunderous, violent. **2** *a mighty warrior:* **strong**, powerful, tough, formidable, doughty, fierce, fearsome; brave, courageous, heroic, valiant; renowned, legendary. **3** *mighty oak trees:* **huge**, enormous, massive, gigantic, giant, colossal, mammoth, immense, titanic; informal monster, whopping great, humongous; Brit. informal whacking great, ginormous.
– OPPOSITES feeble, puny, tiny.
• adverb (N. Amer. informal) *I'm mighty pleased to see you:* **extremely**, very, exceedingly, enormously, immensely, tremendously, hugely; informal awfully, dreadfully; Brit. informal jolly; informal, dated frightfully.

migrant noun **immigrant**, **emigrant**; nomad, itinerant, traveller, transient, wanderer, drifter.
• adjective **travelling**, mobile, wandering, drifting, nomadic, itinerant, transient.

migrate verb *rural populations migrated to urban areas:* **relocate**, resettle, move, travel; emigrate.

mild adjective **1** *a mild tone of voice:* **gentle**, tender, soft, sympathetic, peaceable, quiet; reasonable. **2** *a mild punishment:* **lenient**, light. **3** *he was eyeing her with mild interest:* **slight**, faint, vague. **4** *mild weather:* **warm**, balmy, temperate, clement. **5** *a mild curry:* **bland**, light; insipid.
– OPPOSITES harsh, strong, severe.

milieu noun **environment**, sphere, background, backdrop, setting, context, atmosphere, ambience; location, conditions, surroundings, environs.

militant adjective **hard-line**, extreme, active, extremist, committed, zealous, fanatical, radical.
• noun **activist**, extremist, radical, zealot.

militaristic adjective **warmongering**, warlike, martial, hawkish, pugnacious, combative, aggressive, belligerent, bellicose; informal gung-ho.
– OPPOSITES peaceable.

military adjective *an increase in military forces:* fighting; army, armed, defence, martial.
– OPPOSITES civilian.
• noun *the military took power:* **armed forces**, services, militia; army, navy, air force, marines, generals.

militate verb
■ **militate against** *the situation militates against economic success:* work against, hinder, discourage, prejudice.

> Don't confuse **militate** with **mitigate**, which means 'make something less severe' (*drugs mitigate the symptoms of the disease*).

milk verb *he milked his unsuspecting clients:* **exploit**, drain, suck dry; informal bleed, squeeze, fleece.

> **WORD LINKS**
> **dairy**, **lactic** relating to milk

milky adjective **pale**, white, milk-white, chalky, pearly, ivory, alabaster.
–OPPOSITES swarthy.

mill noun *a steel mill:* **factory**, plant, works, workshop, shop, foundry.
• verb *the wheat is milled into flour:* **grind**, pulverize, powder, granulate, pound, crush, press; technical comminute.
■ **mill around/about** *dozens of spectators milled around the site:* wander, drift, swarm, stream; crowd, pack, fill.

m

mime noun *a mime of someone fencing:* **dumb show**, pantomime, action.
• verb *she mimed picking up a phone:* **act out**, gesture, simulate, pretend, represent.

mimic verb **imitate**, copy, impersonate, ape, caricature, parody; informal send up, take off, spoof.
• noun **impersonator**, impressionist, imitator; informal copycat.

mimicry noun **imitation**, impersonation, copying.

mince verb **grind**, chop up, cut up; N. Amer. hash.

mind noun **1** *a good teacher must stretch pupils' minds:* **brain**, intelligence, intellect, brains, brainpower, wits, understanding, reasoning, judgement, sense, head; informal grey matter, brainbox, brain cells; Brit. informal loaf; N. Amer. informal smarts. **2** *he kept his mind on the job:* **attention**, thoughts, concentration. **3** *the tragedy affected her mind:* **sanity**, mental faculties, senses, wits, reason, reasoning, judgement. **4** *one of the great minds of his day:* **intellect**, thinker, brain, scholar.
• verb **1** *do you mind if I smoke?* **object**, care, be bothered, be annoyed, be upset, take offence, disapprove, look askance; informal give/care a damn, give/care a toss, give/care a hoot. **2** *mind the step!* **watch out for**, look out for, beware of. **3** *her husband was minding the baby:* **look after**, take care of, keep an eye on, attend to, care for.
■ **be in two minds** be undecided, be uncertain, be unsure, hesitate, waver, vacillate, dither; Brit. haver, hum and haw; informal dilly-dally, shilly-shally. **mind out** take care, be careful, watch out, look out, beware.

> **WORD LINKS**
> **cognitive**, **mental**, **psychological** relating to the mind
> **psychology** the study of the mind
> **psychiatry** the branch of medicine dealing with the mind

mindful adjective **aware**, conscious, sensible, alive, alert, acquainted; informal wise, hip; formal cognizant.
–OPPOSITES heedless.

mindless adjective **1** *a mindless idiot:* **stupid**, idiotic, brainless, asinine, witless, empty-headed, slow-witted, feather-brained; informal dumb, pig-ignorant, brain-dead, cretinous, moronic, thick, birdbrained, pea-brained, dopey, dim, half-witted, dippy, fat-headed, boneheaded; N. Amer. informal chowderheaded. **2** *mindless acts of vandalism:* **unthinking**, thoughtless, senseless, gratuitous, wanton, indiscriminate. **3** *a mindless task:* **mechanical**, routine; tedious, boring, monotonous, brainless, mind-numbing.

mine noun **1** *a coal mine:* **pit**, excavation, quarry, workings, diggings; strip mine; Brit. opencast mine; N. Amer. open-pit mine. **2** *a mine of information:* **store**, storehouse, reservoir, repository, gold mine, treasure house, treasury.
• verb *the iron ore was mined from shallow pits:* **quarry**, excavate, dig up, extract, remove.

mingle verb **1** *fact and fiction are skilfully mingled in his novels:* **mix**, blend, intermingle, intermix, interweave, interlace, combine, merge,

fuse, unite, join, amalgamate, meld, mesh; literary commingle. **2** *wedding guests mingled in the marquee:* **socialize**, circulate, fraternize, get together; informal hobnob.
–OPPOSITES separate.

miniature adjective *a miniature railway:* **small-scale**, mini; little, small, baby, toy, pocket, dwarf, pygmy, diminutive; Scottish wee; N. Amer. vest-pocket.
–OPPOSITES giant.

minimal adjective *access can be arranged at minimal expense:* **negligible**, minimum, the least possible, very little/small; nominal, token.
–OPPOSITES maximum.

minimize verb **1** *the aim is to minimize costs:* **keep down**, reduce, decrease, cut, lessen, curtail, diminish, prune; informal slash. **2** *we should not minimize his contribution:* **belittle**, make light of, play down, underestimate, underrate, downplay, undervalue, understate.
–OPPOSITES maximize, exaggerate.

minimum noun *costs will be kept to the minimum:* **lowest level**, lower limit, rock bottom; least, lowest, slightest.
–OPPOSITES maximum.
• adjective *the minimum amount of effort:* **minimal**, least, smallest, least possible, slightest, lowest, minutest.

minion noun **underling**, flunkey, lackey, hanger-on, follower, servant, stooge.

minister noun **1** *a government minister:* **official**, politician, cabinet minister, secretary of state. **2** *a minister of religion:* **clergyman**, clergywoman, cleric, pastor, vicar, rector, priest, parson, father, man/woman of the cloth, man/woman of God, churchman, churchwoman; curate, chaplain; informal reverend, padre. **3** *the British minister in Egypt:* **ambassador**, chargé d'affaires, envoy, emissary, consul, representative; old use legate.
• verb *doctors were ministering to the injured:* **tend**, care for, look after, nurse, treat, attend to, see to, help, assist.

ministry noun **1** *the ministry for foreign affairs:* **department**, bureau, agency, office. **2** *he's training for the ministry:* **holy orders**, the priesthood, the cloth, the church.

minor adjective **1** *a minor problem:* **slight**, small; unimportant, insignificant, inconsequential, subsidiary, negligible, trivial, trifling, paltry, petty; N. Amer. nickel-and-dime; informal piffling, piddling. **2** *a minor poet:* **little known**, unknown, lesser, unimportant, insignificant, obscure; N. Amer. minor-league; informal small-time; N. Amer. informal two-bit.
–OPPOSITES major, important.
• noun *the accused was a minor:* **child**, infant, youth, adolescent, teenager, boy, girl; informal kid.
–OPPOSITES adult.

mint noun (informal) *they made a mint out of the deal:* **a fortune**, millions, billions, a king's ransom; informal a packet, a pile; Brit. informal a bomb, big money; N. Amer. informal big bucks; Austral. informal big bickies.
• verb *the shilling was minted in 1742:* **coin**, stamp, strike, cast, forge, manufacture.
■ **in mint condition** brand new, pristine, perfect, immaculate, unblemished, undamaged, unmarked, unused, first-class, excellent.

minuscule adjective **tiny**, minute, microscopic, nanoscopic, micro, baby; Scottish wee; informal teeny, teensy, itsy-bitsy, tiddly; Brit. informal titchy.
–OPPOSITES huge.

minute[1] noun **1** *at that minute, Tony walked in:* **point**, moment, instant, second, juncture. **2** *their objection was noted in the minutes:* **records**, proceedings, log, notes; transcript, summary.
■ **in a minute** very soon, in a moment, in a trice, shortly, any minute, in less than no time, before long; N. Amer. momentarily; informal anon, in a jiffy, in two shakes, before you can say Jack Robinson; Brit. informal in two ticks. **this minute** at once, immediately, directly, this second, instantly, straight away, right away/now, forthwith; informal pronto. **up to the minute** latest, newest, up to date, modern, fashionable, chic, stylish, all the rage, in vogue; informal trendy, in, fashion-forward.

minute² adjective **1** *minute particles:* **tiny**, minuscule, microscopic, nanoscopic, micro, diminutive, miniature; Scottish wee; informal teeny, teensy, itsy-bitsy; Brit. informal titchy, tiddly. **2** *a minute chance of success:* **negligible**, slight, infinitesimal, minimal. **3** *minute detail:* **exhaustive**, painstaking, meticulous, rigorous, scrupulous, punctilious.
– OPPOSITES huge.

minutely adverb **exhaustively**, painstakingly, meticulously, rigorously, scrupulously, punctiliously.

minutiae plural noun **details**, niceties, finer points, particulars, trivia.

miracle noun *Germany's economic miracle:* **wonder**, marvel, sensation, phenomenon.

miraculous adjective *a miraculous escape:* **amazing**, astounding, remarkable, extraordinary, incredible, unbelievable, sensational.

mirage noun **optical illusion**, hallucination, apparition, fantasy, chimera, figment of the imagination, vision; literary phantasm.

m

mire noun *the land has been reduced to a mire:* **swamp**, bog, morass, quagmire.
• verb *he has become mired in lawsuits:* **entangle**, tangle up, embroil, bog down, catch up, mix up, involve.

mirror noun **1** *take a quick look in the mirror:* **looking glass**; Brit. glass. **2** *the Frenchman's life was a mirror of his own:* **reflection**, parallel; replica, copy, match.
• verb *pop music mirrored the mood of desperation:* **reflect**, match, reproduce, imitate, copy, mimic, echo, parallel.

mirth noun **merriment**, high spirits, cheerfulness, hilarity, glee, laughter, gaiety, euphoria, exhilaration, light-heartedness, joviality, joy.
– OPPOSITES misery.

mirthless adjective **humourless**, grim, sour, surly, dour, sullen, sulky, gloomy, mournful, doleful, miserable.
– OPPOSITES cheerful.

misadventure noun **accident**, difficulty, misfortune, mishap; setback, reversal, stroke of bad luck; failure, disaster, tragedy, calamity, woe, tribulation, catastrophe.

misanthropic adjective **unsociable**, antisocial, unfriendly, reclusive, uncongenial, cynical, jaundiced.

misapply verb **misuse**, misemploy, abuse; distort, warp, misinterpret, misconstrue, misrepresent.

misapprehension noun **misunderstanding**, misinterpretation, misreading, misjudgement, misconception, misbelief, false impression, delusion.

misappropriate verb **embezzle**, expropriate, steal, thieve, pilfer, pocket; informal swipe, filch, rip off; Brit. informal pinch, nick, whip, knock off.

misappropriation noun **embezzlement**, expropriation, stealing, theft, thieving, pilfering.

misbehave verb **behave badly**, be naughty, be disobedient, get up to mischief, get up to no good; be rude; informal carry on, act up.

misbehaviour noun **bad behaviour**, misconduct, naughtiness, disobedience, mischief; bad manners, rudeness.

miscalculate verb **misjudge**, make a mistake, overestimate, underestimate, overvalue, undervalue; go wrong, err, be wide of the mark.

miscalculation noun **error of judgement**, misjudgement, mistake, overestimate, underestimate.

miscarry verb *our plan miscarried:* **go wrong**, go awry, go amiss, be unsuccessful, fail, misfire, abort, founder, come to nothing, fall through, fall flat; informal flop.
– OPPOSITES succeed.

miscellaneous adjective **various**, varied, different, assorted, mixed, sundry, diverse, disparate; diversified, motley, multifarious, heterogeneous; literary divers.

miscellany noun **assortment**, mixture, melange, blend, variety, mixed bag, mix, medley, diversity, collection, selection, assemblage, potpourri, mishmash, hotchpotch, ragbag; N. Amer. hodgepodge.

mischance noun **accident**, misfortune, mishap, misadventure, disaster, tragedy, calamity, catastrophe, upset, blow; bad luck, ill fortune.

mischief noun **1** *the boys are always getting up to mischief:* **naughtiness**, bad behaviour, misbehaviour, mischievousness, misconduct, disobedience; pranks, tricks, capers, nonsense, devilry, funny business; informal monkey business, shenanigans, hanky-panky; Brit. informal carryings-on, jiggery-pokery. **2** *the mischief in her eyes:* **impishness**, roguishness, devilment; glint, twinkle.

mischievous adjective **1** *a mischievous child:* **naughty**, badly behaved, troublesome; rascally, roguish. **2** *a mischievous smile:* **playful**, wicked, impish, roguish. **3** *a mischievous allegation:* **malicious**, malevolent, spiteful, vindictive, vengeful, malign, pernicious, mean, nasty, harmful, hurtful, cruel, unkind.
– OPPOSITES well behaved.

misconceive verb **misunderstand**, misinterpret, misconstrue, misapprehend, mistake, misread; miscalculate, be mistaken, get the wrong idea.

misconception noun **misapprehension**, misunderstanding, mistake, error, misinterpretation, misconstruction, misreading, misjudgement, misbelief, miscalculation, false impression, illusion, fallacy, delusion.

misconduct noun **1** *allegations of misconduct:* **wrongdoing**, unlawfulness, criminality; unprofessionalism, malpractice, negligence, impropriety; formal maladministration. **2** *misconduct in the classroom:* **misbehaviour**, bad behaviour, mischief, naughtiness, rudeness.

misconstrue verb **misunderstand**, misinterpret, misconceive, misapprehend, mistake, misread.

miscreant noun **criminal**, culprit, wrongdoer, offender, villain, lawbreaker, evildoer, delinquent, reprobate; formal malefactor.

misdeed noun **wrong**, crime, felony, misdemeanour, misconduct, offence, error, transgression, sin; old use trespass.

misdemeanour noun **wrongdoing**, crime, felony; misdeed, misconduct, offence, error, peccadillo, transgression, sin; old use trespass.

miser noun **penny-pincher**, niggard, cheese-parer, Scrooge; informal skinflint, meanie, money-grubber, cheapskate; N. Amer. informal tightwad.
– OPPOSITES spendthrift.

miserable adjective **1** *I'm too miserable to eat:* **unhappy**, sad, sorrowful, dejected, depressed, downcast, downhearted, down, despondent, disconsolate, wretched, glum, gloomy, dismal, melancholy, woebegone, doleful, forlorn, heartbroken; informal blue, down in the mouth/dumps. **2** *their miserable surroundings:* **dreary**, dismal, gloomy, drab, wretched, depressing, grim, cheerless, bleak, desolate; poor, shabby, squalid, seedy, dilapidated. **3** *a miserable old man:* **grumpy**, sullen, bad-tempered, dour, surly, sour, glum, moody, unsociable, lugubrious, irritable, churlish, cantankerous, crotchety, cross, crabby, grouchy, testy, peevish, crusty, waspish. **4** *they work long hours for miserable wages:* **inadequate**, meagre, scanty, paltry, small, poor, pitiful, niggardly; informal measly, stingy, pathetic.
– OPPOSITES cheerful, lovely.

miserliness noun **meanness**, niggardliness, closeness, parsimoniousness; informal stinginess, tight-fistedness; N. Amer. cheapness.

miserly adjective **1** *his miserly great-uncle:* **mean**, niggardly, parsimonious, close-fisted, penny-pinching, cheese-paring, grasping, Scrooge-like; informal stingy, tight, tight-fisted; N. Amer. informal cheap. **2** *the prize is a miserly £300:* **meagre**, paltry, negligible, miserable, pitiful, niggardly; informal measly, stingy, pathetic.
– OPPOSITES generous.

misery noun **1** *periods of intense misery:* **unhappiness**, distress, wretchedness, suffering, anguish, anxiety, angst, torment, pain, grief, heartache, heartbreak, despair, despondency, dejection, depression, desolation, gloom, melancholy, woe, sadness, sorrow; informal the blues. **2** *the miseries of war:* **affliction**, misfortune, difficulty, problem, ordeal, trouble, hardship; sorrow,

trial, tribulation, woe. **3** (Brit. informal) *he's a real old misery:* **killjoy**, dog in the manger, spoilsport; informal sourpuss, grouch, grump, party-pooper.
– OPPOSITES contentment, pleasure.

misfire verb **go wrong**, go awry, fail, founder, fall through/flat; backfire; informal flop, go up in smoke.

misfit noun **nonconformist**, eccentric, maverick, individualist, square peg in a round hole; informal oddball, weirdo, freak; N. Amer. informal screwball.

misfortune noun **problem**, difficulty, setback, trouble, adversity, bad luck, misadventure, mishap, blow, failure, accident, disaster; sorrow, misery, woe, trial, tribulation.

misgiving noun **qualm**, doubt, reservation; suspicion, second thoughts; trepidation, scepticism, unease, anxiety, apprehension, disquiet.

misguided adjective **erroneous**, fallacious, unsound, misplaced, misconceived, ill-advised, ill-considered, ill-judged, inappropriate, unwise, injudicious, imprudent.

m

mishandle verb **mismanage**, make a mess of; informal botch, muck up; Brit. informal make a pig's ear of.

mishap noun **accident**, trouble, problem, difficulty, setback, adversity, misfortune, blow; disaster, tragedy, catastrophe, calamity.

mishmash noun **jumble**, confusion, hotchpotch, ragbag, patchwork, assortment, medley, miscellany, mixture, melange, blend, mix, potpourri, conglomeration; N. Amer. hodgepodge.

misinform verb **mislead**, misguide, delude, deceive, lie to, hoodwink; informal lead up the garden path, take for a ride; N. Amer. informal give someone a bum steer.

misinformation noun **disinformation**; propaganda, spin; lies, fibs, half-truths.

misinterpret verb **misunderstand**, misconceive, misconstrue, misapprehend, mistake, misread.

misjudge verb **get wrong**, miscalculate, misread; overestimate, underestimate, overvalue, undervalue, underrate.

mislay verb **lose**, misplace.
– OPPOSITES find.

mislead verb **deceive**, delude, take in, lie to, fool, lead astray, hoodwink, throw off the scent, pull the wool over someone's eyes, misinform, misdirect; informal lead up the garden path, take for a ride; N. Amer. informal give someone a bum steer.

misleading adjective **deceptive**, confusing, deceiving, equivocal, ambiguous.

mismanage verb **bungle**, fluff, make a mess of, mishandle, spoil, ruin, wreck; informal botch, make a hash of, mess up, muck up; Brit. informal make a pig's ear of.

mismatch noun **discrepancy**, inconsistency, contradiction, incongruity, conflict, discord, clash.

mismatched adjective **unsuited**, incongruous, incompatible, inconsistent, at odds; out of keeping, clashing, dissimilar, different, at variance, disparate, unrelated, divergent, contrasting.
– OPPOSITES matching.

misplace verb **lose**, mislay.
– OPPOSITES find.

misplaced adjective **1** *his comments were misplaced:* **misguided**, unwise, ill-advised, ill-considered, ill-judged, inappropriate. **2** *misplaced keys:* **lost**, mislaid, missing.

misprint noun **mistake**, error, erratum; Brit. literal; informal typo.

misquote verb **misreport**, misrepresent, misstate, distort, twist, slant, bias, put a spin on, falsify.

misrepresent verb **misreport**, misquote, misstate, misinterpret, distort, slant, twist, bias, put a spin on, falsify.

miss[1] verb **1** *the shot missed her by inches:* **be/go wide of**, fall short of, pass, overshoot. **2** *I left early to miss the traffic:* **avoid**, beat, evade, escape, dodge, sidestep, elude, circumvent, bypass. **3** *she missed him so much:* **pine for**, yearn for, ache for, long for.
– OPPOSITES hit, catch.

■ **miss someone/something out** leave out, exclude, fail to mention, pass over, skip, omit, ignore.

miss² noun *a headstrong young miss:* **young woman**, young lady, girl, schoolgirl; Scottish lass, lassie; Irish colleen; informal girlie, chick, bit, doll; Brit. informal bird; N. Amer. informal broad, dame; Austral./NZ informal sheila; literary maiden, maid, damsel; old use wench.

misshapen adjective **deformed**, malformed, distorted, crooked, twisted, warped, out of shape, bent, disfigured, grotesque.

missing adjective **1** *his wallet is missing:* **lost**, mislaid, misplaced, absent, gone astray, unaccounted for. **2** *passion was missing from her life:* **absent**, lacking, gone, wanting.
– OPPOSITES present.

mission noun **1** *a two-week fact-finding mission:* **assignment**, commission, expedition, journey, trip, undertaking, operation, project. **2** *her mission in life:* **vocation**, calling, goal, aim, quest, purpose, function; task, job, labour, work, duty. **3** *a trade mission:* **delegation**, deputation, commission. **4** *a bombing mission:* **sortie**, operation, raid.

missionary noun **evangelist**, apostle, proselytizer, preacher; zealot.

missive noun **message**, communication, letter, word, note, memorandum, line, communiqué, dispatch, news; informal memo; formal epistle; literary tidings.

misspent adjective **wasted**, dissipated, squandered, thrown away, frittered away, misused, misapplied.

misstate verb **misreport**, misrepresent, misquote, distort, twist, slant, bias, put a spin on, falsify.

mist noun **haze**, fog, smog, murk, cloud; Scottish haar.
■ **mist over/up** steam up, become misty, cloud over.

mistake noun **1** *the mistake landed us with a massive bill:* **error**, fault, inaccuracy, omission, slip, blunder, miscalculation, misunderstanding, oversight, misinterpretation, gaffe, faux pas, solecism; informal slip-up, boo-boo, howler; Brit. informal boob, clanger, bloomer; N. Amer. informal goof. **2** *spelling mistakes:* **misprint**, error, erratum; Brit. literal; informal typo.
• verb **1** *men are apt to mistake their own feelings:* **misunderstand**, misinterpret, get wrong, misconstrue, misread. **2** *children often mistake pills for sweets:* **confuse with**, mix up with, take for.
■ **make a mistake** go wrong, err, make an error, blunder, miscalculate; informal slip up, screw up, make a boo-boo, make a howler; Brit. informal boob; N. Amer. informal drop the ball, goof up.

mistaken adjective **wrong**, erroneous, inaccurate, incorrect, off beam, false, fallacious, unfounded, misguided, misinformed.
■ **be mistaken** be wrong, be in error, be misinformed, be misguided; informal be barking up the wrong tree, get the wrong end of the stick.
– OPPOSITES correct.

mistakenly adverb **wrongly**, in error, erroneously, incorrectly, falsely, fallaciously, inaccurately.
– OPPOSITES correctly.

mistimed adjective **ill-timed**, badly timed, inopportune, inappropriate, untimely.
– OPPOSITES opportune.

mistreat verb **ill-treat**, maltreat, abuse, knock about/around, hit, beat, strike, injure, harm, hurt; misuse, mishandle; informal beat up, rough up.

mistreatment noun **ill-treatment**, maltreatment, abuse, beating, injury, harm; mishandling, manhandling.

mistress noun **lover**, girlfriend, kept woman; informal fancy woman; old use paramour.

mistrust verb **be suspicious of**, be mistrustful of, be distrustful of, be sceptical of, be wary of, be chary of, distrust, have doubts about, have misgivings about, have reservations about, suspect.
• noun **suspicion**, distrust, doubt, misgivings, wariness, reservations.

mistrustful adjective **suspicious**, chary, wary, distrustful, doubtful, dubious, uneasy, sceptical, leery.

misty adjective **hazy**, foggy, cloudy.
– OPPOSITES clear.

misunderstand verb **misapprehend**, misinterpret, misconstrue, misconceive, mistake, misread; be mistaken, get the wrong idea; informal be barking up the wrong tree, get the wrong end of the stick.

misunderstanding noun **1** *a fundamental misunderstanding of juvenile crime:* **misinterpretation**, misreading, misapprehension, misconception, false impression. **2** *we have had our misunderstandings:* **disagreement**, difference of opinion, dispute, falling-out, quarrel, argument, altercation, wrangle, clash; Brit. row; informal spat, scrap, tiff.

misuse verb **1** *he has been misusing public funds:* **embezzle**, misappropriate, abuse; waste, squander. **2** *she had been misused by her husband:* **ill-treat**, maltreat, mistreat, abuse, knock about/around, hit, beat, injure, harm, hurt; manhandle; informal beat up, rough up.
• noun *a misuse of company assets:* **embezzlement**, fraud; squandering, waste.

mitigate verb *drugs mitigate the symptoms of the disease:* **alleviate**, reduce, diminish, lessen, weaken, lighten, attenuate, take the edge off, allay, ease, assuage, palliate, relieve, tone down.
– OPPOSITES aggravate.

> Don't confuse **mitigate** with **militate**: **militate against** means 'be a powerful factor in preventing' (*the situation militates against economic success*).

m

mitigating adjective **extenuating**, justifying, vindicating, qualifying; formal exculpatory.

mitigation noun **1** *the mitigation of the problems:* **alleviation**, reduction, diminution, lessening, easing, weakening, assuagement, relief. **2** *what did she say in mitigation?* **extenuation**, explanation, excuse; justification.

mix verb **1** *mix all the ingredients together:* **blend**, mingle, combine, put together, jumble; beat, fold, whisk, stir, toss; fuse, unite, join, amalgamate, incorporate, meld, marry, coalesce, homogenize, intermingle, intermix; technical admix; literary commingle. **2** *she mixes with all sorts:* **associate**, socialize, fraternize, keep company, consort; mingle, circulate; Brit. rub shoulders; N. Amer. rub elbows; informal hang out/around, knock about/around, hobnob; Brit. informal hang about.
– OPPOSITES separate.
• noun *a mix of ancient and modern:* **mixture**, blend, combination, compound, fusion, alloy, union, amalgamation, hybrid; medley, melange, collection, selection, assortment, variety, mixed bag, miscellany, potpourri, jumble, hotchpotch, ragbag, patchwork; N. Amer. hodgepodge.
▪ **mixed up in** involved in, embroiled in, caught up in, entangled in.

mixed adjective **1** *a mixed collection:* **assorted**, varied, variegated, miscellaneous, disparate, diverse, diversified, motley, sundry, jumbled, heterogeneous. **2** *mixed reactions:* **ambivalent**, equivocal, contradictory, conflicting, confused, muddled.
– OPPOSITES homogeneous.

mixed up adjective (informal) **confused**, befuddled, bemused, bewildered, muddled; maladjusted, disturbed, neurotic, unbalanced; informal hung up, messed up.

mixture noun **1** *the pudding mixture:* **blend**, mix, brew, combination, concoction; composition, compound, alloy, amalgam. **2** *a strange mixture of people:* **assortment**, miscellany, medley, melange, blend, variety, mixed bag, mix, diversity, collection, selection, potpourri, mishmash, hotchpotch, ragbag, patchwork; N. Amer. hodgepodge. **3** *the animal was a mixture of breeds:* **cross**, cross-breed, mongrel, hybrid.

mix-up noun **confusion**, muddle, misunderstanding, mistake, error.

moan noun **1** *moans of pain:* **groan**, wail, whimper, sob, cry. **2** (informal) *there were moans about the delay:* **complaint**, grouse, grumble, whine, carping; informal gripe, bellyache, bitch, whingeing, beef.
• verb **1** *he moaned in agony:* **groan**, wail, whimper, sob, cry. **2** (informal) *you're always moaning about the weather:* **complain**, grouse, grumble, whine, carp; informal gripe, grouch, bellyache, bitch, beef, whinge; N. English informal mither.

mob noun **1** *troops dispersed the mob:*

crowd, horde, multitude, rabble, mass, throng, gathering, assembly. **2** *the mob were excluded from political life:* **the common people**, the masses, the rank and file, the proletariat; the hoi polloi, the lower classes, the rabble, the riff-raff, the great unwashed; informal the proles, the plebs.
•**verb 1** *the Chancellor was mobbed when he visited Berlin:* **surround**, besiege, jostle; heckle. **2** *reporters mobbed her hotel:* **crowd into**, fill, pack, throng; invade, occupy, besiege.

mobile adjective **1** *both patients are mobile:* **able to move**, able to walk, walking; informal up and about; Medicine ambulant. **2** *her mobile face:* **expressive**, animated. **3** *a mobile library:* **travelling**, portable, movable; itinerant, peripatetic. **4** *an increasingly mobile society:* **adaptable**, flexible, independent.
– OPPOSITES immobile, motionless, static.

mobilize verb **1** *the government mobilized the troops:* **marshal**, deploy, muster, rally, call up, assemble, mass, organize, prepare. **2** *he began to mobilize support for the party:* **generate**, arouse, awaken, excite, incite, provoke, foment, prompt, stimulate, stir up, galvanize, encourage, inspire, whip up.

mock verb **1** *the local children mocked them:* **ridicule**, jeer at, sneer at, deride, scorn, make fun of, laugh at, scoff at, tease, taunt; informal take the mickey out of; N. Amer. informal goof on, rag on, pull someone's chain. **2** *they mocked the way he speaks:* **parody**, ape, take off, imitate, mimic; informal send up.
•**adjective** *mock leather:* **imitation**, artificial, man-made, simulated, synthetic, ersatz, fake, faux, reproduction, false, counterfeit; informal pretend, phoney.
– OPPOSITES genuine.

mockery noun **1** *the mockery in his voice:* **ridicule**, derision, jeering, sneering, contempt, scorn, scoffing, teasing, taunting, sarcasm. **2** *the trial was a mockery:* **travesty**, charade, farce, parody; joke.

mocking adjective **sneering**, derisive, contemptuous, scornful, sardonic, ironic, sarcastic.

mode noun **1** *an informal mode of policing:* **manner**, way, fashion, means, method, system, style, approach. **2** *the camera is in manual mode:* **function**, position, operation, setting; option. **3** *the mode for active wear:* **fashion**, vogue, style, look, trend; craze, rage, fad.

model noun **1** *a working model:* **replica**, copy, representation, mock-up, dummy, imitation, duplicate, reproduction, facsimile. **2** *the American model of airline deregulation:* **prototype**, archetype, type, version; mould, template, framework, pattern, design, blueprint. **3** *she was a model as a teacher:* **ideal**, paragon, perfect example/specimen, exemplar; perfection, acme, epitome. **4** *a top model:* **fashion model**, supermodel, mannequin; informal clothes horse. **5** *the latest model of car:* **version**, type, design, variety, kind, sort.
•**adjective 1** *model trains:* **replica**, **toy**, miniature, dummy, imitation, duplicate, reproduction, facsimile. **2** *a model teacher:* **ideal**, perfect, exemplary, classic; flawless, faultless.

moderate adjective **1** *moderate success:* **average**, modest, medium, middling, tolerable, passable, adequate, fair; indifferent, unexceptional, unremarkable; informal OK, so-so, bog-standard, fair-to-middling. **2** *moderate prices:* **reasonable**, acceptable; inexpensive, fair, modest. **3** *moderate views:* **middle-of-the-road**, non-extremist; liberal, pragmatic.
– OPPOSITES great, unreasonable, extreme.
•**verb 1** *the wind has moderated:* **die down**, abate, let up, calm down, lessen, decrease, diminish; recede, weaken, subside. **2** *you can help her moderate her temper:* **curb**, control, check, temper, restrain, subdue; repress, tame, lessen, decrease, lower, reduce, diminish, alleviate, allay, appease, assuage, ease, soothe, calm, tone down.
– OPPOSITES increase.

moderately adverb **somewhat**, quite, fairly, reasonably, comparatively, relatively, to some extent; tolerably, passably, adequately; informal pretty.

m

moderation noun **1** *he urged them to show moderation:* **self-restraint**, restraint, self-control, self-discipline; temperance, leniency. **2** *a moderation of their confrontational style:* **relaxation**, easing, reduction, abatement, weakening, slackening, tempering, softening, diminution, lessening; modulation, modification; informal let-up.

modern adjective **1** *modern times:* **present-day**, contemporary, present, current, twenty-first-century, latter-day, recent. **2** *her clothes are very modern:* **fashionable**, up to date, trendsetting, stylish, voguish, modish, chic, à la mode; the latest, new, newest, newfangled, modernistic, advanced; informal trendy, on-trend, fashion-forward, cool, in, with it, now, hip, happening.
–OPPOSITES past, old-fashioned.

modernize verb *they are modernizing their manufacturing facilities:* **update**, bring up to date, streamline, rationalize, overhaul; renovate, remodel, refashion, revamp.

m

modest adjective **1** *she was modest about her poetry:* **self-effacing**, self-deprecating, humble, unassuming; shy, diffident, reserved, reticent, coy. **2** *modest success:* **moderate**, fair, limited, tolerable, passable, adequate, satisfactory, acceptable, unexceptional. **3** *a modest house:* **small**, ordinary, simple, plain, humble, inexpensive, unostentatious, unpretentious. **4** *her modest dress:* **decorous**, decent, seemly, demure, proper; appropriate, sensitive, sensible.
–OPPOSITES conceited, great, grand.

modesty noun **1** *Hannah's modesty cloaks many talents:* **self-effacement**, humility; shyness, bashfulness, self-consciousness, reserve, reticence, timidity. **2** *the modesty of his home:* **unpretentiousness**, simplicity, plainness, ordinariness.

modicum noun **small amount**, particle, speck, fragment, scrap, crumb, grain, morsel, shred, dash, drop, pinch, jot, iota, whit, atom, smattering, scintilla, hint; informal smidgen, tad.

modification noun **1** *the design is undergoing modification:* **alteration**, adjustment, change, adaptation, refinement, revision. **2** *some minor modifications were made:* **revision**, refinement, improvement, amendment, adaptation, adjustment, change, alteration.

modify verb **1** *their economic policy has been modified:* **alter**, change, adjust, adapt, amend, revise, reshape, refashion, restyle, revamp, rework, remodel, refine; informal tweak. **2** *he modified his more extreme views:* **moderate**, revise, temper, soften, tone down, qualify.

modish adjective **fashionable**, stylish, chic, modern, contemporary, voguish, up to the minute, à la mode; informal trendy, cool, with it, in, now, hip, happening;.

modulate verb **1** *the cells modulate the body's response:* **regulate**, control, adjust, set, modify, moderate. **2** *she modulated her voice:* **adjust**, alter, soften, lower.

modus operandi noun **method**, way, manner, technique, style, approach, methodology, strategy, plan, formula; formal praxis.

mogul noun **magnate**, tycoon, VIP, notable, personage, baron, captain, king, lord, grandee; informal bigwig, big shot, big noise, top dog; N. Amer. informal top banana, big enchilada.

moist adjective **1** *the air was moist:* **damp**, steamy, humid, muggy, clammy, dank, wet, soggy, sweaty, sticky. **2** *a moist fruitcake:* **succulent**, juicy; soft, tender.
–OPPOSITES dry.

moisten verb **dampen**, wet, damp, water, humidify.

moisture noun **wetness**, wet, water, liquid, condensation, steam, vapour, dampness, damp, humidity, clamminess, mugginess, dankness.

moisturizer noun **lotion**, cream, balm, emollient, salve, unguent, lubricant; technical humectant.

molest verb **abuse**, assault, interfere with; rape, violate.

mollify verb **appease**, placate, pacify, soothe, calm down, propitiate, assuage.
–OPPOSITES enrage.

mollycoddle verb *his parents mollycoddle him:* **pamper**, cosset, coddle, spoil, indulge, overindulge, pet, baby, nanny, wait on hand and foot, wrap in cotton wool.

molten adjective **liquefied**, liquid, fluid, melted, flowing.

moment noun **point**, time, hour; instant, second, minute.
■ **in a moment** very soon, in a minute, in a second, in a trice, shortly, any minute, in the twinkling of an eye; N. Amer. momentarily; informal in a jiffy, before you can say Jack Robinson.

momentarily adverb **1** *he paused momentarily:* **briefly**, fleetingly, for a moment, for a second, for an instant. **2** (N. Amer.) *my husband will be here momentarily.* See **IN A MOMENT**.

momentary adjective **brief**, short, short-lived, fleeting, passing, transient, ephemeral; literary evanescent.
– OPPOSITES lengthy.

momentous adjective **important**, significant, historic, portentous, critical, crucial, life-and-death, decisive, pivotal, consequential, of consequence, far-reaching; informal earth-shattering.
– OPPOSITES insignificant.

momentum noun **impetus**, energy, force, power, strength, thrust, speed, velocity.

monarch noun **sovereign**, ruler, Crown, crowned head, potentate; king, queen, emperor, empress.

monastery noun friary, abbey, priory.

monastic adjective *a monastic existence:* **austere**, ascetic, simple, solitary, monkish, celibate, quiet, cloistered, sequestered, secluded, reclusive, hermit-like.

monetary adjective **financial**, fiscal, pecuniary, money, cash, economic, budgetary.

money noun **1** *I haven't got enough money:* **cash**, ready money; the means, the wherewithal, funds, capital, finances, filthy lucre; banknotes, notes, coins, change, currency; Brit. sterling; N. Amer. bills; informal dough, bread, loot, shekels, moolah, the necessary; Brit. informal dosh, brass, lolly, readies, spondulicks; N. Amer. informal dinero, bucks; US informal greenbacks. **2** *she married him for his money:* **wealth**, riches, fortune, affluence, liquid assets, resources, means. **3** *the money here is better:* **pay**, salary, wages, remuneration; formal emolument.
■ **in the money** (informal) rich, wealthy, affluent, well-to-do, well off, prosperous, moneyed, in clover, opulent; informal rolling in it, loaded, stinking rich, well heeled, made of money.

WORD LINKS

monetary, **pecuniary** relating to money

numismatics the study or collection of coins and banknotes

moneyed adjective **rich**, wealthy, affluent, well-to-do, well off, prosperous, opulent, of means, of substance; informal rolling in it, loaded, stinking/filthy rich, well heeled, made of money.
– OPPOSITES poor.

money-grubbing adjective (informal) **acquisitive**, avaricious, grasping, money-grabbing, rapacious, mercenary, materialistic.

moneymaking adjective **profitable**, profit-making, remunerative, lucrative, successful, financially rewarding.
– OPPOSITES loss-making.

mongrel noun **cross-breed**, cross, mixed breed, half-breed; tyke, cur, mutt.

monitor noun **1** *monitors covered all entrances:* **camera**, CCTV, scanner, recorder; sensor. **2** *UN monitors:* **observer**, watchdog, overseer, supervisor; scrutineer. **3** *a computer monitor:* **screen**, display, VDU.
• verb *his movements were closely monitored:* **observe**, watch, track, keep an eye on, keep under surveillance, record, note, oversee; informal keep tabs on.

monkey noun **primate**, ape.
■ **monkey with** tamper with, fiddle with, interfere with, meddle with, tinker with, play with; informal mess with; Brit. informal muck about/around with.

WORD LINKS

simian relating to or resembling monkeys or apes

primatology the study of monkeys or apes

monolith noun **standing stone**, menhir, megalith.

monolithic adjective **1** *a monolithic building:* **massive**, huge, vast, colossal, gigantic, immense, giant, enormous; featureless, characterless. **2** *the old monolithic Communist party:* **inflexible**, rigid, unbending, unchanging, fossilized; faceless, impersonal.

monologue noun **soliloquy**; speech, address, lecture, sermon; formal oration.

monopolize verb **1** *the company has monopolized the market:* **corner**, control, take over, dominate, gain a stranglehold over, gain control/dominance over. **2** *he monopolized the conversation:* **dominate**, take over; informal hog.

monotonous adjective **1** *a monotonous job:* **tedious**, boring, dull, uninteresting, unexciting, repetitive, repetitious, unvarying, unchanging, humdrum, routine, mechanical, mind-numbing, soul-destroying; colourless, featureless, dreary; informal deadly; Brit. informal samey; N. Amer. informal dullsville. **2** *a monotonous voice:* **toneless**, flat, featureless, soporific; robotic, mechanical.
–OPPOSITES interesting.

monotony noun **1** *the monotony of everyday life:* **tedium**, tediousness, dullness, boredom, repetitiveness, uniformity, routineness; uneventfulness, dreariness, colourlessness, featurelessness. **2** *the monotony of her voice:* **tonelessness**, flatness.

monster noun **1** *legendary sea monsters:* **creature**, beast, being; giant, demon, dragon. **2** *her husband is a monster:* **animal**, fiend, beast, devil, demon, barbarian, savage, brute; informal swine, pig, psycho. **3** *the boy's a little monster:* **horror**, imp, monkey, wretch, devil, rascal; informal scamp, scallywag, tyke; Brit. informal perisher; N. Amer. informal varmint, hellion; old use rapscallion. **4** *he's a monster of a man:* **giant**, mammoth, colossus, leviathan, titan.

monstrosity noun **eyesore**, blot on the landscape, carbuncle, excrescence.

monstrous adjective **1** *a monstrous creature:* **grotesque**, hideous, ugly, ghastly, gruesome, horrible, horrific, horrifying, grisly, disgusting, repulsive, dreadful, frightening, terrible, terrifying. **2** *a monstrous tidal wave.* See HUGE. **3** *monstrous acts of violence:* **appalling**, wicked, abominable, terrible, horrible, dreadful, vile, outrageous, shocking, disgraceful; unspeakable, despicable, vicious, savage, barbaric, barbarous, inhuman; Brit. informal beastly.
–OPPOSITES lovely, small.

monument noun **1** *a stone monument:* **memorial**, statue, pillar, column, obelisk, cross; cenotaph, tomb, mausoleum, shrine. **2** *a monument was placed over the grave:* **gravestone**, headstone, tombstone. **3** *a monument to a past era:* **testament**, record, reminder, remembrance, memorial, commemoration.

monumental adjective **1** *a monumental task:* **huge**, enormous, gigantic, massive, colossal, mammoth, immense, tremendous, mighty, stupendous. **2** *a monumental error of judgement:* **terrible**, dreadful, awful, colossal, staggering, huge, enormous, unforgivable. **3** *monumental works of art:* **vast**, huge, majestic, grand, awe-inspiring, heroic, epic.

mood noun **1** *all in all, her mood was good:* **frame of mind**, state of mind, humour, temper; disposition, spirit. **2** *he's obviously in a mood:* **bad mood**, bad temper, sulk; low spirits, the doldrums, the blues; Brit. informal paddy. **3** *the mood of the film:* **atmosphere**, feeling, spirit, ambience, aura, character, tenor, flavour, feel, tone.
■ **in the mood** in the right frame of mind, wanting to, inclined to, disposed to, minded to, eager to, willing to.

moody adjective **temperamental**, emotional, volatile, capricious, changeable, mercurial; sullen, sulky, morose, glum, depressed, dejected, despondent, doleful.
–OPPOSITES cheerful.

moon noun **satellite**.
•verb **1** *stop mooning about:* **waste time**, loaf, idle; Brit. informal mooch; N. Amer. informal lollygag. **2** *he's*

m

mooning over her photograph: **mope**, pine, brood, daydream.

WORD LINKS
lunar relating to the moon

moor[1] verb *a boat was moored to the quay:* **tie**, secure, make fast, fix, berth, dock.

moor[2] noun *a walk on the moor:* **upland**, heath, moorland; Brit. fell, wold.

moot adjective *a moot point:* **debatable**, arguable, questionable, open to doubt, disputable, controversial, contentious, disputed, unresolved, unsettled, up in the air.
• verb *the idea was first mooted in the 1930s:* **raise**, bring up, broach, mention, put forward, introduce, advance, propose, suggest.

mop noun *her tousled mop of hair:* **shock**, mane, tangle, mass.
• verb *a man was mopping the floor:* **wash**, clean, wipe.
■ **mop something up 1** *I mopped up the spilt coffee:* wipe up, clean up, sponge up. **2** *troops mopped up the last pockets of resistance:* finish off, deal with, dispose of, take care of, clear up, eliminate.

mope verb **1** *it's no use moping:* **brood**, sulk, be miserable, be despondent, pine, eat your heart out, fret, grieve; informal be down in the dumps/mouth. **2** *she was moping about the house:* **languish**, moon, loaf; Brit. informal mooch; N. Amer. informal lollygag.

moral adjective **1** *moral issues:* **ethical. 2** *a very moral man:* **virtuous**, good, righteous, upright, upstanding, high-minded, principled, honourable, honest, just, noble, respectable, decent, clean-living, law-abiding. **3** *moral support:* **psychological**, emotional, mental.
– OPPOSITES immoral, dishonourable.
• noun **1** *the moral of the story:* **lesson**, message, meaning, significance, import, point, teaching. **2** *he has no morals:* **moral code**, code of ethics, values, principles, standards, morality, scruples.

morale noun **confidence**, self-confidence, self-esteem, spirit, team spirit, esprit de corps; motivation.

moral fibre noun **strength of character**, fibre, fortitude, resolve, backbone, spine, mettle.

morality noun **1** *the morality of nuclear weapons:* **ethics**, rights and wrongs; whys and wherefores; informal ins and outs. **2** *a sharp decline in morality:* **virtue**, goodness, good behaviour, righteousness, uprightness; morals, principles, honesty, integrity, propriety, honour, justice, decency. **3** *Christian morality:* **morals**, standards, ethics, principles; mores.

moralize verb **pontificate**, sermonize, lecture, preach.

morass noun **confusion**, chaos, muddle, tangle, entanglement; quagmire.

moratorium noun **embargo**, ban, prohibition, suspension, postponement, stay, halt, freeze, respite; hiatus.

morbid adjective *a morbid fascination with contemporary warfare:* **ghoulish**, macabre, unhealthy, gruesome, unwholesome; informal sick.
– OPPOSITES wholesome.

mordant adjective **caustic**, trenchant, biting, cutting, acerbic, sardonic, sarcastic, scathing, acid, sharp, keen; critical, bitter, virulent, vitriolic.

more determiner *I could do with some more clothes:* **additional**, further, added, extra, increased, new, other, supplementary.
– OPPOSITES less, fewer.
■ **more or less** approximately, roughly, nearly, almost, close to, about, of the order of, in the region of.

moreover adverb **besides**, furthermore, what's more, in addition, also, as well, too, to boot, additionally, on top of that, into the bargain; old use withal.

mores plural noun **customs**, conventions, ways, traditions, practices, habits.

moribund adjective **1** *the patient was moribund:* **dying**, expiring, on your deathbed, near death, at death's door, not long for this world. **2** *the moribund shipbuilding industry:* **declining**, in decline, waning, dying, stagnating, stagnant, crumbling, on its last legs.
– OPPOSITES thriving.

morning noun dawn, daybreak,

sunrise, first light; N. Amer. sunup; literary cockcrow, morn.

WORD LINKS
matutinal relating to the morning

morose adjective **sullen**, sulky, gloomy, bad-tempered, ill-tempered, surly, sour, glum, moody, ill-humoured, grumpy, irritable, cantankerous, crotchety, crabby, grouchy, testy, snappish, peevish, crusty.
– OPPOSITES cheerful.

morsel noun **mouthful**, bite, nibble, bit, taste, spoonful, forkful, sliver, drop, dollop, spot, gobbet; titbit; informal smidgen.

mortal adjective **1** *mortal remains | all men are mortal:* **perishable**, physical, bodily, corporeal, fleshly, earthly; human, impermanent, transient, ephemeral. **2** *a mortal blow:* **deadly**, fatal, lethal, death-dealing, murderous, terminal. **3** *mortal enemies:* **irreconcilable**, deadly, sworn, bitter, out-and-out, implacable. **4** *they are living in mortal fear:* **extreme**, great, terrible, awful, dreadful, intense, severe, dire, unbearable.
• noun *we are mere mortals:* **human being**, person, man/woman; earthling.

m

mortality noun **1** *a sense of his own mortality:* **impermanence**, transience, ephemerality, perishability; humanity; corporeality. **2** *the causes of mortality:* **death**, loss of life, dying.

mortification noun **embarrassment**, humiliation, chagrin, discomfiture, discomposure, shame.

mortify verb **1** *I'd be mortified if my friends found out:* **embarrass**, humiliate, chagrin, discomfit, shame, abash, horrify, appal. **2** *he was mortified at being excluded:* **hurt**, wound, affront, offend, put out, pique, irk, annoy, vex; informal rile.

mortuary noun **morgue**, funeral parlour; Brit. chapel of rest.

most pronoun *most of the guests brought flowers:* **nearly all**, almost all, the greatest part/number, the majority, the bulk, the preponderance.
– OPPOSITES little, few.

■ **for the most part** mostly, mainly, in the main, on the whole, largely, by and large, to a large extent, predominantly, chiefly, principally, generally, usually, typically, commonly, as a rule.

mostly adverb **1** *the other passengers were mostly businessmen:* **mainly**, for the most part, on the whole, in the main, largely, chiefly, predominantly, principally, primarily. **2** *I mostly wear jeans:* **usually**, generally, in general, as a rule, ordinarily, normally, customarily, typically, most of the time, almost always.

moth-eaten adjective **threadbare**, worn, old, ancient, shabby, scruffy, tattered, ragged; informal tatty; N. Amer. informal raggedy.

mother noun **female parent**, matriarch; informal ma; Brit. informal mum; N. Amer. informal mom; Brit. informal, dated mater.
• verb *she mothered him like a baby:* **look after**, care for, take care of, nurse, protect, tend; pamper, coddle, cosset, fuss over.
– OPPOSITES neglect.

WORD LINKS
maternal relating to a mother
matricide the killing of a mother by her child

motherly adjective **maternal**, maternalistic, protective, caring, loving, nurturing.

motif noun **1** *a colourful tulip motif:* **design**, pattern, decoration, figure, shape, device, emblem. **2** *a recurring motif in Pinter's work:* **theme**, idea, concept, subject, topic, leitmotif.

motion noun **1** *the rocking motion of the boat | a planet's motion around the sun:* **movement**, moving, locomotion, rise and fall, shifting; progress, passage, transit, course, travel; orbit. **2** *a motion of the hand:* **gesture**, movement, signal, sign, indication; wave, nod, gesticulation. **3** *the motion failed to obtain a majority:* **proposal**, proposition, recommendation.
• verb *he motioned her to sit down:* **gesture**, signal, direct, indicate; wave, beckon, nod.
■ **in motion** moving, on the move, going, running, functioning,

operational. **set in motion** start, commence, begin, activate, initiate, launch, get under way, get going, get off the ground; trigger off, set off, spark off, generate, cause.

WORD LINKS
kinetic relating to motion

motionless adjective **unmoving**, still, stationary, stock-still, immobile, static, not moving a muscle, rooted to the spot, transfixed, paralysed, frozen, petrified.
– OPPOSITES moving.

motivate verb **1** *he was motivated by greed:* **prompt**, drive, move, inspire, influence, activate, impel, propel, spur on. **2** *it's the teacher's job to motivate the child:* **inspire**, stimulate, encourage, excite, fire with enthusiasm; incentivize.

motivation noun **1** *his motivation was financial:* **motive**, motivating force, incentive, stimulus, stimulation, inspiration, inducement, incitement, spur. **2** *staff motivation:* **enthusiasm**, drive, determination, commitment, enterprise; informal get-up-and-go.

motive noun **reason**, motivation, motivating force, rationale, grounds, cause, basis.
• adjective *motive force:* **kinetic**, driving, propulsive, dynamic.

motley adjective **miscellaneous**, disparate, diverse, assorted, varied, heterogeneous.
– OPPOSITES homogeneous.

mottled adjective **blotchy**, blotched, streaked, streaky, marbled, dappled; informal splotchy.

motto noun **maxim**, saying, proverb, aphorism, adage, saw, axiom, formula, expression, phrase, dictum, precept; slogan, catchphrase.

mould noun **1** *the molten metal is poured into a mould:* **cast**, die, form, matrix, shape, template, pattern, frame. **2** *an actress in the traditional Hollywood mould:* **pattern**, form, type, style, tradition, school.
• verb **1** *a figure moulded from clay:* **shape**, form, fashion, model, work, construct, make, create, sculpt, cast. **2** *the ideas that are moulding US policy:* **determine**, direct, control, guide, influence, shape, form, fashion, make.

moulder verb **decay**, decompose, rot, go mouldy, go off, go bad, spoil, putrefy.

mouldy adjective **mildewed**, mildewy, musty, mouldering, fusty; decaying, decayed, rotting, rotten, bad, spoiled, decomposing.

mound noun **1** *a grassy mound:* **hillock**, hill, knoll, rise, hummock, hump; Scottish brae; Geology drumlin. **2** *a mound of dirty crockery:* **heap**, pile, stack, mountain.

mount verb **1** *he mounted the stairs:* **go up**, ascend, climb, scale. **2** *the museum is mounting an exhibition:* **put on**, present, produce; organize, stage, set up. **3** *the company mounted a takeover bid:* **organize**, stage, prepare, arrange; launch, set in motion, initiate. **4** *their losses mounted rapidly:* **increase**, grow, rise, escalate, soar, spiral, shoot up, rocket, climb, accumulate, build up, multiply. **5** *cameras were mounted above the door:* **install**, place, fix, set, put, position.
– OPPOSITES descend.
• noun **setting**, backing, support, mounting, frame, stand.

mountain noun **1** *one of the world's highest mountains:* **peak**, summit; (**mountains**) range, massif, sierra; Scottish ben, Munro. **2** *a mountain of paperwork:* **a lot**; informal heap, pile, stack, slew, lots, loads, tons, masses. **3** *the EC's butter mountain:* **surplus**, surfeit, glut.

mountainous adjective **1** *a mountainous region:* **hilly**, craggy, rocky, alpine. **2** *mountainous waves:* **huge**, enormous, gigantic, massive, giant, colossal, immense, tremendous, mighty; informal whopping, humongous; Brit. informal whacking great, ginormous.
– OPPOSITES flat, tiny.

mourn verb **1** *Isobel mourned her husband:* **grieve for**, sorrow over, lament for, weep for. **2** *he mourned the loss of the beautiful buildings:* **deplore**, bewail, bemoan, rue, regret.

mournful adjective **sad**, sorrowful, doleful, melancholy, woeful, grief-stricken, miserable, heartbroken, broken-hearted, gloomy, dismal, desolate, dejected, despondent,

depressed, downcast, disconsolate, woebegone, forlorn, rueful.
– OPPOSITES cheerful.

mourning noun **grief**, grieving, sorrowing, lamentation.

mouse noun

> WORD LINKS
> **murine** relating to mice

mousy adjective *a small, mousy woman:* **timid**, quiet, timorous, shy, self-effacing, diffident.

mouth noun **1** *open your mouth:* lips, jaws; muzzle; informal trap, chops, kisser; Brit. informal gob, cakehole; N. Amer. informal puss. **2** *the mouth of the cave:* **entrance**, opening. **3** *the mouth of the river:* outlet; estuary, delta, firth. **4** (informal) *he's all mouth:* **talk**, threats, promises, bluster; informal hot air.
• verb *he mouthed platitudes:* **utter**, speak; pronounce, enunciate, articulate, voice, express; churn out.

> WORD LINKS
> **oral** relating to the mouth

m

mouthful noun **1** *a mouthful of pizza:* **bite**, nibble, taste, bit, piece; spoonful, forkful. **2** *a mouthful of beer:* **draught**, sip, swallow, drop, gulp, slug; informal swig.

mouthpiece noun **spokesperson**, spokesman, spokeswoman, agent, representative, propagandist, voice; informal spin doctor.

movable adjective **portable**, transportable, transferable; mobile.
– OPPOSITES fixed.

move verb **1** *she moved to the door | don't move!* **go**, walk, step, proceed, progress, advance; budge, stir, shift. **2** *he moved the chair closer to the fire:* **carry**, transfer, shift, push, pull, lift, slide. **3** *things were moving too fast:* **go**, progress, advance, develop, evolve, change, happen. **4** *he urged the council to move quickly:* **act**, take action, take steps; react, respond; informal get moving. **5** *she's moved to Cambridge:* **relocate**, move house, change address, leave, go, decamp; Brit. informal up sticks; N. Amer. informal pull up stakes. **6** *I was moved by the story:* **affect**, touch, impress, shake, upset, disturb. **7** *she was moved to find out more about the subject:* **inspire**, prompt, stimulate, motivate, provoke, influence, rouse, induce. **8** *they are not prepared to move on this issue:* **change**, budge, shift your ground, change your mind, have second thoughts; do a U-turn, do an about-face; Brit. do an about-turn. **9** *she moves in rarefied circles:* **circulate**, mix, socialize, keep company, associate; informal hang out/around. **10** *I move that we adjourn:* **propose**, submit, suggest, advocate, recommend, urge.
• noun **1** *his eyes followed her every move:* **movement**, motion, action; gesture. **2** *his recent move to London:* **relocation**, change of address, transfer, posting. **3** *the latest move in the war against drugs:* **initiative**, step, action, measure, manoeuvre, tactic, stratagem. **4** *it's your move:* **turn**, go; Scottish shot.

movement noun **1** *Rachel made a sudden movement | there was almost no movement:* **motion**, move; gesture, sign, signal; action, activity. **2** *the movement of supplies:* **transportation**, conveyance, transfer. **3** *a political movement:* **group**, party, faction, wing, lobby, camp; division, sect, cult. **4** *a movement to declare war on poverty:* **campaign**, crusade, drive, push, initiative. **5** *there have been movements in the financial markets:* **development**, change, fluctuation, variation. **6** *the movement towards equality:* **trend**, tendency, drift, swing, shift; march. **7** *a symphony in three movements:* **part**, section, division; act.

> WORD LINKS
> **kinetic** relating to movement

movie noun **1** **film**, picture, motion picture; informal flick. **2** (**the movies**) **the cinema**, the pictures, the silver screen; informal the flicks, the big screen.

moving adjective **1** *moving parts | a moving train:* **in motion**, operating, operational, working, on the move, active; movable, mobile. **2** *a moving book:* **affecting**, touching, poignant, heart-warming, heart-rending, emotional; inspiring, inspirational, stimulating, stirring.
– OPPOSITES fixed, stationary.

mow verb *she had mown the grass:* **cut**, trim.

■ mow someone/something down kill, gun down, shoot, cut down, butcher, slaughter, massacre, annihilate, wipe out; informal blow away.

much determiner *is there much food?* **a lot of**, a great/good deal of, a great/large amount of, plenty of, ample, abundant, plentiful; informal lots of, loads of, heaps of, masses of, tons of, stacks of.
– OPPOSITES little.
• adverb **1** *it didn't hurt much:* **greatly**, a great deal, a lot, considerably, appreciably. **2** *does he come here much?* **often**, frequently, many times, regularly, habitually, routinely, usually, normally, commonly; informal a lot.
• pronoun *he did much for our team:* **a lot**, a great/good deal, plenty; informal lots, loads, heaps, masses, tons.

muck noun **dirt**, grime, filth, mud, slime, mess; informal crud, gunk; Brit. informal gunge.
■ muck something up (informal) make a mess of, mess up, bungle, spoil, ruin, wreck; informal botch, make a hash of, muff, fluff, foul up; Brit. informal make a pig's ear of; N. Amer. informal goof up. **muck about/around** (Brit. informal) **1** *he was mucking about with his mates:* fool about/around, play about/around, clown about/around; informal mess about/around, horse about/around, lark about/around. **2** *someone's been mucking about with the video:* interfere, fiddle, tamper, meddle, tinker; informal mess about/around.

mucky adjective **dirty**, filthy, grimy, muddy, grubby, messy, soiled, stained, smeared, slimy, sticky; informal cruddy; Brit. informal grotty; Austral./NZ informal scungy; literary besmirched, begrimed, befouled.
– OPPOSITES clean.

mud noun mire, sludge, ooze, silt, clay, dirt, soil.

muddle verb **1** *the papers have got muddled up:* **confuse**, mix up, jumble up, disarrange, disorganize, disorder, mess up. **2** *it would only muddle you:* **bewilder**, confuse, bemuse, perplex, puzzle, baffle, nonplus, mystify.
• noun **1** *the files are in a muddle:* **mess**, confusion, jumble, tangle, hotchpotch, mishmash, chaos, disorder, disarray, disorganization; N. Amer. hodgepodge. **2** *a bureaucratic muddle:* **bungle**, mix-up, misunderstanding, mess; informal foul-up; N. Amer. informal snafu.
■ muddle along/through cope, manage, get by/along, scrape by/along, make do.

muddled adjective **1** *a muddled pile of photographs:* **jumbled**, in a muddle, in a mess, chaotic, in disarray, topsy-turvy, disorganized, disordered, disorderly, mixed up, at sixes and sevens; informal higgledy-piggledy. **2** *she felt muddled:* **confused**, bewildered, bemused, perplexed, disoriented, in a muddle; N. Amer. informal discombobulated. **3** *muddled thinking:* **incoherent**, confused, muddle-headed, woolly, vague.
– OPPOSITES orderly, clear.

muddy adjective **1** *muddy ground:* **waterlogged**, boggy, marshy, swampy, squelchy, squishy, mucky, slimy, spongy, wet, soft. **2** *muddy boots:* **dirty**, filthy, mucky, grimy, soiled. **3** *muddy water:* **murky**, cloudy, turbid; N. Amer. riled, roily. **4** *a muddy pink:* **dingy**, dirty, drab, dull, sludgy.
– OPPOSITES clean, clear.
• verb **dirty**, soil, spatter, bespatter; literary besmirch.

muff verb (informal) **mishandle**, mismanage, mess up, make a mess of, bungle; informal botch, muck up, make a hash of, fluff; Brit. informal make a pig's ear of; N. Amer. informal goof up.

muffle verb **1** *everyone was muffled up in coats:* **wrap up**, swathe, enfold, envelop, cloak. **2** *the sound of their footsteps was muffled:* **deaden**, dull, dampen, mute, soften, quieten, mask, stifle, smother.

muffled adjective **indistinct**, faint, muted, dull, soft, stifled, smothered.
– OPPOSITES loud.

mug[1] noun *a china mug:* **beaker**, cup; tankard, glass, stein, flagon.
• verb (informal) *he was mugged by three youths:* **assault**, attack, set upon, beat up, rob; informal jump, rough up, lay into; Brit. informal duff up, do over.

mug[2] verb
■ mug something up (informal) study,

read up on, cram; informal bone up on; Brit. informal swot.

muggy adjective **humid**, close, sultry, sticky, oppressive, airless, stifling, suffocating, stuffy, clammy, damp, heavy, fuggy.
– OPPOSITES fresh.

mull verb
■ **mull something over** ponder, consider, think over/about, reflect on, contemplate, turn over in your mind, chew over, cogitate on, give some thought to; old use pore on.

multicoloured adjective **kaleidoscopic**, psychedelic, colourful, multicolour, many-coloured, many-hued, rainbow, jazzy, variegated.
– OPPOSITES monochrome.

multifarious adjective **diverse**, many, numerous, various, varied, multiple, multitudinous, multiplex, manifold, multifaceted, different, heterogeneous, miscellaneous, assorted; literary myriad, divers.
– OPPOSITES homogeneous.

multiple adjective **numerous**, many, various, different, diverse, several, manifold, multifarious, multitudinous; literary myriad, divers.
– OPPOSITES single.

m

multiplicity noun **abundance**, mass, host, array, variety; range, diversity, heterogeneity, plurality, profusion; informal load, stack, heap, ton; literary myriad.

multiply verb **increase**, grow, accumulate, proliferate, mount up, mushroom, snowball.
– OPPOSITES decrease.

multitude noun **1** *a multitude of birds:* **host**, horde, mass, swarm, abundance, profusion; scores, droves; informal loads, masses, stacks, heaps, tons, hundreds, thousands, millions; N. Amer. informal gazillions. **2** *Father Peter addressed the multitude:* **crowd**, gathering, assembly, congregation, throng, horde, mob.

multitudinous adjective **numerous**, many, abundant, profuse, prolific, copious, multifarious; literary divers, myriad.

mumble verb **mutter**, murmur, whisper.

mumbo-jumbo noun **nonsense**, gibberish, claptrap, rubbish, balderdash, hocus-pocus; informal gobbledegook, double Dutch.

munch verb **chew**, champ, chomp, masticate, crunch, eat.

mundane adjective **1** *her mundane life:* **humdrum**, dull, boring, tedious, monotonous, tiresome, unexciting, uninteresting, uneventful, unremarkable, routine, ordinary, everyday, day-to-day, run-of-the-mill, commonplace, workaday. **2** *the mundane world:* **earthly**, worldly, terrestrial, material, temporal, secular; literary sublunary.
– OPPOSITES extraordinary, spiritual.

municipal adjective **civic**, civil, metropolitan, urban, city, town, borough.
– OPPOSITES rural.

municipality noun **borough**, town, city, district; N. Amer. precinct, township; Scottish burgh.

munificence noun **generosity**, bountifulness, open-handedness, magnanimity, lavishness, liberality, philanthropy, largesse, big-heartedness, beneficence; literary bounty.

munificent adjective **generous**, bountiful, open-handed, magnanimous, philanthropic, princely, handsome, lavish, liberal, charitable, big-hearted, beneficent; literary bounteous.
– OPPOSITES mean.

murder noun **1** *a brutal murder:* **killing**, assassination, execution, slaughter, butchery, massacre; homicide, manslaughter; informal liquidation; literary slaying. **2** (informal) *driving there was murder:* **hell**, a nightmare, misery, torture, agony; informal the pits.
• verb *someone tried to murder him:* **kill**, put to death, assassinate, execute, eliminate, dispatch, butcher, slaughter, massacre, wipe out; informal bump off, do in, do away with, knock off, take out, dispose of, liquidate; N. Amer. informal ice, rub out, waste; literary slay.

murderer, **murderess** noun **killer**, assassin, serial killer, butcher; informal hit man, hired gun; dated homicide; literary slayer.

murderous adjective *a murderous attack:* **homicidal**, brutal, violent, savage, ferocious, fierce, vicious, bloodthirsty, barbarous, barbaric;

fatal, lethal, deadly, mortal, death-dealing; old use sanguinary.

murky adjective **1** *a murky winter afternoon:* **dark**, gloomy, grey, leaden, dull, dim, overcast, cloudy, clouded, sunless, dismal, dreary, bleak. **2** *murky water:* **dirty**, muddy, cloudy, turbid; N. Amer. riled, roily. **3** *her murky past:* **questionable**, suspicious, suspect, dubious, dark, mysterious, secret; informal shady.
– OPPOSITES bright, clear.

murmur noun **1** *his voice was a murmur:* **whisper**, mutter, mumble. **2** *there were murmurs in Tory ranks:* **complaint**, grumble, grouse; informal gripe, moan. **3** *the murmur of bees:* **hum**, buzz, drone; sigh, rustle; literary susurration.
• verb **1** *he heard them murmuring in the hall:* **mutter**, mumble, whisper. **2** *no one murmured at the delay:* **complain**, mutter, grumble, grouse; informal gripe, moan. **3** *the wind was murmuring through the trees:* **rustle**, sigh; burble; literary whisper, purl.

muscle noun **1** *he had muscle but no brains:* **strength**, power, muscularity, brawn; informal beef, beefiness. **2** *financial muscle:* **influence**, power, strength, might, force, forcefulness, weight; informal clout.
■ **muscle in** (informal) interfere, butt in, push in, force your way in, impose yourself, encroach; informal horn in.

muscular adjective **1** *he's very muscular:* **strong**, brawny, muscly, well built, burly, strapping, sturdy, powerful, athletic; Physiology mesomorphic; informal hunky, beefy. **2** *a muscular economy:* **vigorous**, robust, strong, powerful, dynamic, potent, active.

muse[1] noun *the poet's muse:* **inspiration**, creativity, stimulus.

muse[2] verb *I mused on Toby's story:* **ponder**, consider, think over/about, mull over, reflect on, contemplate, turn over in your mind, chew over, cogitate on; think, daydream; old use pore on.

mush noun **1** *a sodden pink mush:* **pulp**, slop, paste, purée, mash; informal gloop, goo; N. Amer. informal glop. **2** *romantic mush:* **rubbish**, garbage; informal schmaltz, corn, slush; N. Amer. informal slop.

mushroom verb *ecotourism mushroomed in the 1980s:* **proliferate**, burgeon, spread, increase, expand, boom, explode, snowball, rocket, skyrocket; thrive, flourish, prosper.
– OPPOSITES contract.

mushy adjective **1** *cook until the fruit is mushy:* **soft**, pulpy, sloppy, spongy, squashy, squelchy, squishy; informal gooey, gloopy; Brit. informal squidgy. **2** *a mushy film:* **sentimental**, mawkish, slushy, emotional, saccharine; informal schmaltzy, weepy, corny; Brit. informal soppy; N. Amer. informal cornball, sappy, hokey.
– OPPOSITES firm.

musical adjective **tuneful**, melodic, melodious, harmonious, sweet-sounding, sweet, mellifluous, euphonious.
– OPPOSITES discordant.

musician noun **player**, performer, instrumentalist, accompanist, soloist, virtuoso, maestro; historical minstrel.

musing noun **meditation**, thinking, contemplation, deliberation, pondering, reflection, rumination, introspection, daydreaming, reverie, dreaming, preoccupation, brooding; formal cogitation.

must verb *I must go:* **ought to**, should, have to, need to, be obliged to, be required to, be compelled to.

muster verb **1** *they mustered 50,000 troops:* **assemble**, mobilize, rally, raise, summon, gather, collect, convene, call up, call to arms, recruit, conscript; US draft. **2** *reporters mustered outside her house:* **congregate**, assemble, gather, come together, collect, mass, convene, rally. **3** *she mustered her courage:* **summon up**, screw up, call up, rally.
■ **pass muster** be good enough, come up to standard, come up to scratch, measure up, be acceptable, fill/fit the bill; informal make the grade, be up to snuff, cut the mustard.

musty adjective **mouldy**, stale, fusty, damp, dank, mildewy, smelly, stuffy, airless, unventilated; N. Amer. informal funky.
– OPPOSITES fresh.

mutable adjective **changeable**,

variable, varying, fluctuating, shifting, inconsistent, unpredictable, inconstant, uneven, unstable, protean.
–OPPOSITES invariable.

mutant noun **freak**, monstrosity, monster, mutation.

mutate verb **change**, metamorphose, evolve; transmute, transform; humorous transmogrify.

mutation noun **1 alteration**, change, transformation, metamorphosis, transmutation; humorous transmogrification. **2** *a genetic mutation:* **mutant**, freak, monstrosity, monster.

mute adjective **1** *Yasmin remained mute:* **silent**, speechless, dumb, unspeaking, tight-lipped, taciturn; informal mum. **2** *a mute appeal:* **wordless**, silent, dumb, unspoken. **3** *the church was mute:* **quiet**, silent, hushed.
–OPPOSITES voluble, spoken.
•verb **1** *the noise was muted by the heavy curtains:* **deaden**, muffle, dampen, soften; stifle, smother, suppress. **2** *Bruce muted his criticisms:* **restrain**, soften, tone down, moderate, temper.
–OPPOSITES intensify.

muted adjective **1** *the muted hum of traffic:* **muffled**, faint, indistinct, quiet, soft, low; distant, faraway. **2** *muted tones:* **subdued**, pastel, delicate, subtle, understated, restrained.

mutilate verb **1** *the bodies had been mutilated:* **mangle**, maim, disfigure, dismember; slash, hack. **2** *the carved screen had been mutilated:* **vandalize**, damage, deface, violate, desecrate; slash, hack.

mutinous adjective **rebellious**, insubordinate, subversive, seditious, insurgent, insurrectionary.

mutiny noun **insurrection**, rebellion, revolt, riot, uprising, insurgence, insubordination.
•verb **rise up**, rebel, revolt, riot; strike.

mutt noun (informal) *a long-haired mutt:* **dog**, hound, mongrel, cur.

mutter verb **1** *a group of men stood muttering:* **murmur**, mumble, whisper. **2** *backbenchers muttered about the reshuffle:* **grumble**, complain, grouse, carp, whine; informal moan, gripe, beef, whinge; Brit. informal chunter; N. Amer. informal kvetch.

mutual adjective **reciprocal**, reciprocated, requited, returned; common, joint, shared.

muzzle noun *the dog's velvety muzzle:* **snout**, nose, mouth, maw.
•verb *the government attempted to muzzle the media:* **gag**, silence, censor, stifle, restrain, check, curb, fetter.

muzzy adjective **1** *she felt muzzy:* **groggy**, light-headed, faint, dizzy, befuddled; informal dopey, woozy. **2** *a slightly muzzy picture:* **blurred**, blurry, fuzzy, unfocused, unclear, ill-defined, foggy.
–OPPOSITES clear.

myopic adjective **1** *a myopic patient:* **short-sighted**; N. Amer. nearsighted. **2** *the government's myopic attitude:* **unimaginative**, short-sighted, narrow-minded, small-minded, short-term.
–OPPOSITES long-sighted, far-sighted.

myriad (literary) noun *myriads of insects:* **multitude**, scores, mass, host, droves, hordes; informal lots, loads, masses, stacks, tons, hundreds, thousands, millions; N. Amer. informal gazillions.
•adjective *the myriad lights of the city:* **innumerable**, countless, infinite, numberless, untold, unnumbered, immeasurable, multitudinous.

mysterious adjective **1** *he vanished in mysterious circumstances:* **puzzling**, strange, peculiar, curious, funny, queer, odd, weird, bizarre, mystifying, inexplicable, baffling, perplexing. **2** *he was being very mysterious:* **enigmatic**, inscrutable, secretive, reticent, evasive, furtive, surreptitious.
–OPPOSITES straightforward.

mystery noun **1** *his death remains a mystery:* **puzzle**, enigma, conundrum, riddle, secret; paradox. **2** *her past is shrouded in mystery:* **secrecy**, obscurity, uncertainty, mystique.

mystic, **mystical** adjective **spiritual**, religious, transcendental, paranormal, other-worldly, supernatural, occult, metaphysical.

mystify verb **bewilder**, puzzle, perplex, baffle, confuse, confound, bemuse, nonplus, throw; informal flummox, stump, bamboozle, faze, fox.

mystique noun **charisma**, glamour, romance, mystery, magic, charm, appeal, allure.

myth noun **1** *ancient Greek myths:* **folk tale**, folk story, legend, fable, saga; lore, folklore. **2** *the myths surrounding childbirth:* **misconception**, fallacy, old wives' tale, fairy story/tale, fiction; informal cock and bull story.

mythical adjective **1** *mythical beasts:* **legendary**, mythological, fabled, fabulous, fairy-tale, storybook; fantastical, imaginary, imagined, fictitious. **2** *her mythical child:* **imaginary**, fictitious, make-believe, fantasy, invented, made-up, non-existent; informal pretend.

mythological adjective **fabled**, fabulous, fairy-tale, legendary, mythical, mythic, traditional; fictitious, imaginary.

mythology noun **myths**, legends, folklore, folk tales/stories, lore, tradition.

Nn

nadir noun **low point**, all-time low, bottom, rock bottom; informal the pits.
–OPPOSITES zenith.

nag verb **1** *she's constantly nagging me:* **harass**, keep on at, go on at, badger, give someone a hard time, chivvy, hound, criticize, find fault with, moan at, grumble at; henpeck; informal hassle; N. Amer. informal ride; Austral. informal heavy. **2** *this has been nagging me for weeks:* **trouble**, worry, bother, plague, torment, niggle, prey on someone's mind; informal bug, aggravate.
• noun *she can be such a nag:* **bully**; shrew, harpy, harridan; old use scold.

n

nagging adjective **1** *his nagging wife:* **bullying**, shrewish, complaining, grumbling, fault-finding, scolding, carping, bossy. **2** *a nagging pain:* **persistent**, continuous, niggling, unrelenting, unremitting; chronic.

nail noun **1** **tack**, pin, staple. **2** **fingernail**, thumbnail, toenail.
• verb **fasten**, attach, fix, affix, secure, tack, hammer, pin.
■ **on the nail** immediately, at once, without delay, straight away, right away, promptly, directly, now, this minute; N. Amer. on the barrelhead.

naive adjective **innocent**, unsophisticated, artless, ingenuous, inexperienced, guileless, unworldly, trusting; gullible, credulous, immature, callow, raw, green; informal wet behind the ears.
–OPPOSITES worldly.

naivety noun **innocence**, ingenuousness, guilelessness, unworldliness, trustfulness; gullibility, credulousness, credulity, immaturity, callowness.

naked adjective **1** *a naked woman:* **nude**, bare, in the nude, stark naked, stripped, unclothed, undressed, in a state of nature; informal without a stitch on, in your birthday suit, in the raw/buff, in the altogether, in the nuddy, mother naked; Brit. informal starkers; Scottish informal in the scud, N. Amer. informal buck naked. **2** *a naked flame:* **unprotected**, uncovered, exposed, unguarded. **3** *the naked branches of the trees:* **bare**, barren, denuded, stripped, uncovered. **4** *I felt naked and exposed:* **vulnerable**, helpless, weak, powerless, defenceless, exposed, open to attack. **5** *the naked truth | naked hostility:* **undisguised**, plain, unadorned, unvarnished, unqualified, stark, bald; overt, obvious, open, patent, evident, manifest, unmistakable, blatant.
–OPPOSITES clothed, covered.

nakedness noun **nudity**, state of undress, déshabillé, bareness.

name noun **1** *I've forgotten his name:* designation, honorific, title, tag, epithet, label; informal moniker, handle; formal appellation. **2** *the top names in the fashion industry:* **celebrity**, star, superstar, VIP, leading light, luminary; expert, authority; informal celeb, somebody, megastar, big noise, big shot, bigwig, big gun. **3** *the good name of the firm:* **reputation**, character, repute, standing, stature, esteem, prestige, cachet, kudos; renown, popularity, distinction.
• verb **1** *they named the child Pamela:* **call**, dub; label, style, term, title; baptize, christen; formal denominate. **2** *fear of assault was named as the main reason:* **identify**, specify, single out, give, cite, mention. **3** *he has named his successor:* **choose**, select, pick, decide on, nominate, designate.

WORD LINKS
onomastic relating to names

named adjective **1** *a girl named Anne:* **called**, known as, by the name of, baptized, christened; dubbed, entitled, styled, termed, labelled. **2** *named individuals:* **specified**, designated, identified, cited, mentioned, singled out; specific, particular.

nameless adjective **1** *a nameless photographer:* **unnamed**, unidentified, anonymous, unspecified, unacknowledged, uncredited; unknown, unsung. **2** *nameless fears:* **unspeakable**, unutterable, inexpressible, indescribable; indefinable, vague, unspecified.

namely adverb **that is**, to be specific, specifically, viz., to wit; in other words.

nanny noun *the children's nanny:* **nursemaid**, au pair, childminder, carer; dated nurse.
• verb *stop nannying me:* **mollycoddle**, cosset, coddle, wrap in cotton wool, baby, feather-bed; spoil, pamper, indulge, overindulge.

nap noun *she's taking a nap:* **sleep**, catnap, siesta, doze, lie-down, rest; informal snooze, forty winks, shut-eye; Brit. informal kip.

narcissism noun **vanity**, self-love, self-admiration, self-absorption, self-obsession, conceit, self-centredness, self-regard, egotism.
– OPPOSITES modesty.

narcissistic adjective **vain**, self-absorbed, self-obsessed, conceited, self-centred, self-regarding, egotistic, egotistical.

narcotic noun **drug**, opiate; painkiller, analgesic, anodyne, palliative.
• adjective **soporific**, sleep-inducing; painkilling, pain-relieving, analgesic, anodyne.

narrate verb **tell**, relate, recount, describe, chronicle, report; voice-over, commentate, present, deliver.

narration noun **1** *a narration of past events:* **account**, narrative, chronicle, description, report, relation. **2** *his narration of the story:* **voice-over**, commentary; delivery, presentation.

narrative noun **account**, chronicle, history, description, record, report; story, tale.

narrator noun **1** *the narrator of 'the Arabian Nights':* **storyteller**, relater, chronicler, presenter, author. **2** *the film's narrator:* **voice-over**, commentator; presenter.
– OPPOSITES listener, audience.

narrow adjective **1** *the path became narrower:* **small**, tapered, tapering; old use strait. **2** *her narrow waist:* **slender**, slim, small, slight, spare, attenuated, thin, tiny. **3** *a narrow space:* **confined**, cramped, tight, restricted, limited, constricted, small, tiny. **4** *a narrow range of products:* **limited**, restricted, small, inadequate, insufficient, deficient. **5** *a narrow view of the world.* See NARROW-MINDED. **6** *nationalism in the narrowest sense of the word:* **strict**, literal, exact, precise. **7** *a narrow escape:* **close**, near, by a hair's breadth; informal by a whisker.
– OPPOSITES wide, broad.
• verb *the path narrowed | narrowing the gap between rich and poor:* **get/become/make narrower**, get/become/make smaller, taper, diminish, decrease, reduce, contract, shrink, constrict; old use straiten.

narrowly adverb **1** *one bullet narrowly missed him:* **just**, barely, scarcely, hardly, by a hair's breadth; informal by a whisker. **2** *she looked at me narrowly:* **closely**, carefully, searchingly, attentively.

narrow-minded adjective **intolerant**, illiberal, reactionary, conservative, parochial, provincial, insular, small-minded, petty, blinkered, inward-looking, narrow, hidebound, prejudiced, bigoted; N. Amer. informal jerkwater.
– OPPOSITES tolerant.

nastiness noun **unkindness**, unpleasantness, unfriendliness, disagreeableness, rudeness, spitefulness, maliciousness, meanness, ill temper, offensiveness, viciousness, malevolence, vileness; informal bitchiness, cattiness.

nasty adjective **1** *a nasty smell:* **unpleasant**, disagreeable, disgusting, distasteful, awful, dreadful, horrible, terrible, vile, foul, abominable, frightful, loathsome, revolting, repulsive, odious, sickening, nauseating, repellent, repugnant, horrendous, appalling,

n

atrocious, obnoxious, unsavoury, unappetizing, off-putting; noxious, foul-smelling, smelly, stinking, rank, fetid, malodorous; informal ghastly, horrid, diabolical, God-awful; Brit. informal whiffy, pongy; literary noisome, mephitic. **2** *the weather turned nasty:* **unpleasant**, disagreeable, foul, filthy, inclement; wet, stormy, cold. **3** *she can be really nasty:* **unkind**, unpleasant, unfriendly, disagreeable, rude, spiteful, malicious, mean, ill-tempered, vicious, malevolent, obnoxious, hateful, hurtful; informal bitchy, catty. **4** *a nasty accident | a nasty cut:* **serious**, dangerous, bad, awful, dreadful, terrible, severe; painful, ugly.
–OPPOSITES nice, pleasant.

nation noun **country**, state, land, realm, kingdom, republic; fatherland, motherland; people, race, tribe, clan.

national adjective **1** *national politics:* **state**, public, federal, governmental; civic, civil, domestic, internal. **2** *a national strike:* **nationwide**, countrywide, state, general, widespread.
–OPPOSITES local, international.
•noun *a French national:* **citizen**, subject, native; voter, passport-holder.

nationalism noun **patriotism**, xenophobia, chauvinism, jingoism.

nationalistic adjective **patriotic**, nationalist, xenophobic, chauvinistic, jingoistic.

nationality noun **1** *British nationality:* **citizenship**. **2** *people of different nationalities:* **country**, ethnic group, ethnic minority, race, nation.

nationwide adjective **national**, countrywide, state, general, widespread, extensive.
–OPPOSITES local.

native noun *a native of Sweden:* **inhabitant**, resident, local; citizen, national; formal dweller.
–OPPOSITES foreigner.
•adjective **1** *the native population:* **indigenous**, original. **2** *native produce | native plants:* **domestic**, home-grown, home-made, local; indigenous. **3** *a native instinct for politics:* **innate**, inherent, inborn, instinctive, intuitive, natural. **4** *her native tongue:* **mother**; home, local.
–OPPOSITES immigrant.

natter (Brit. informal) **verb & noun**. See CHAT.

natty adjective (informal) **smart**, stylish, fashionable, dapper, debonair, dashing, spruce, well dressed, chic, elegant, trim; N. Amer. trig; informal snazzy, trendy, snappy, nifty; N. Amer. informal sassy, spiffy, fly, kicky.
–OPPOSITES scruffy.

natural adjective **1** *a natural occurrence:* **normal**, ordinary, everyday, usual, regular, common, commonplace, typical, routine, standard. **2** *natural products:* **unprocessed**, organic, pure, unrefined, high-fibre, additive-free; green, GM-free, ecologically sound. **3** *his natural instincts:* **innate**, inborn, inherent, native; hereditary, inherited, inbred, congenital. **4** *she seemed very natural:* **unaffected**, spontaneous, uninhibited, relaxed, unselfconscious, genuine, open, artless, guileless, unpretentious. **5** *it was quite natural to think she admired him:* **reasonable**, logical, understandable, to be expected, predictable.
–OPPOSITES abnormal, unnatural, artificial.

naturalist noun **natural historian**, scientist; biologist, botanist, zoologist, ornithologist, entomologist; ecologist, conservationist.

naturalistic adjective **realistic**, real-life, true-to-life, lifelike, representational, photographic; graphic, down-to-earth, gritty, unsentimental, unflinching, unsparing.
–OPPOSITES abstract.

naturally adverb **1** *he's naturally shy:* **by nature**, by character, inherently, innately, congenitally, pathologically. **2** *try to act naturally:* **normally**, spontaneously, genuinely, instinctively, unpretentiously; informal natural. **3** *naturally, they wanted everything kept quiet:* **of course**, as might be expected, needless to say; obviously, clearly, it goes without saying.
–OPPOSITES self-consciously.

naturalness noun **unselfconsciousness**, spontaneity, straightforwardness, genuineness, openness, unpretentiousness.

nature noun **1** *the beauty of nature:* **the natural world**, Mother Nature, Mother Earth, the environment; the universe, the cosmos; wildlife, flora and fauna, the countryside, the land, the landscape. **2** *such crimes are, by their very nature, difficult to hide:* **essence**, inherent/basic/essential features, character, complexion. **3** *it was not in Daisy's nature to be negative:* **character**, personality, disposition, temperament, make-up, psyche, constitution. **4** *experiments of a similar nature:* **kind**, sort, type, variety, category, ilk, class, species, genre, style, cast, order, mould, stamp; N. Amer. stripe.

naughty adjective **1** *a naughty boy:* **badly behaved**, disobedient, bad, wayward, defiant, unruly, insubordinate, wilful, delinquent, undisciplined, disorderly, disruptive, fractious, recalcitrant, wild, obstreperous, difficult, troublesome, awkward, contrary, perverse; mischievous, impish, roguish, rascally; informal brattish; formal refractory. **2** *naughty jokes:* **indecent**, risqué, rude, racy, ribald, bawdy, suggestive, improper, indelicate, indecorous; vulgar, dirty, filthy, smutty, crude, coarse, obscene, lewd, pornographic; informal raunchy; Brit. informal fruity, saucy; N. Amer. informal gamy; euphemistic adult.
– OPPOSITES well behaved, decent.

nausea noun **1** *symptoms include nausea:* **sickness**, biliousness, queasiness; vomiting, retching; travel-sickness, seasickness, carsickness, airsickness. **2** *it induces a feeling of nausea:* **disgust**, revulsion, repugnance, repulsion, distaste, aversion, loathing, abhorrence.

nauseate verb **make someone sick**, sicken, turn someone's stomach; disgust, revolt; N. Amer. informal gross out.

nauseating adjective **sickening**, stomach-churning, nauseous, emetic; disgusting, revolting, loathsome, foul; N. Amer. vomitous; informal sick-making, gross.

nauseous adjective *the food made her feel nauseous:* **sick**, nauseated, queasy, bilious, green about/at the gills, ill, unwell; seasick, carsick, airsick, travel-sick; N. Amer. informal barfy.

nautical adjective **maritime**, marine, naval, seafaring; boating, sailing.

navel noun informal **belly button**, tummy button; Anatomy umbilicus.

navigable adjective **passable**, negotiable, traversable; clear, open, unobstructed, unblocked.

navigate verb **steer**, pilot, guide, direct, captain; sail, cross, traverse, negotiate; Nautical con; informal skipper.

navigation noun **1** *the navigation of the ship:* **steering**, piloting, sailing, guiding, directing, guidance. **2** *the skills of navigation:* **helmsmanship**, steersmanship, seamanship, map-reading.

navy noun **1** *a 600-ship navy:* **fleet**, flotilla, armada. **2** *a navy suit:* **navy blue**, dark blue, indigo.

near adverb **1** *her children all live near:* **close by**, nearby, close at hand, in the neighbourhood, in the vicinity, within reach, on the doorstep, a stone's throw away; informal within spitting distance. **2** *near perfect conditions:* **almost**, just about, nearly, practically, virtually; literary well-nigh.

• adjective **1** *the final judgement is near:* **imminent**, in the offing, on its way, coming, impending, looming. **2** *a near escape:* **narrow**, close; by a hair's breadth; informal by a whisker.
– OPPOSITES distant.

• verb **1** *by dawn we were nearing Moscow:* **approach**, draw near to, get closer to, advance towards, close in on. **2** *the death toll is nearing 3,000:* **verge on**, border on, approach; informal be getting on for.

nearby adjective & adverb **close by**, close at hand, near, neighbouring, within reach, on the doorstep; accessible, handy, convenient.
– OPPOSITES faraway.

nearly adverb **almost**, just about, more or less, practically, virtually, all but, as good as, not far off, to all intents and purposes; not quite; informal pretty much, pretty well; literary well-nigh.

near miss noun **close thing**, near thing, narrow escape; informal close shave.

nearness noun **1** *the town's nearness*

to Rome: **closeness**, proximity; accessibility, handiness. **2** *the nearness of death:* **imminence**, closeness, immediacy.

nearsighted adjective (N. Amer.) **short-sighted**, myopic.
–OPPOSITES long-sighted

neat adjective **1** *the bedroom was neat and clean:* **tidy**, orderly, well ordered, in order, shipshape, in apple-pie order, spick and span, uncluttered, straight, trim. **2** *he's very neat:* **smart**, spruce, dapper, trim, well groomed, well turned out; N. Amer. trig. **3** *his neat footwork:* **skilful**, deft, dexterous, adroit, adept, expert; informal nifty. **4** *a neat solution:* **clever**, ingenious, inventive; imaginative. **5** *neat gin:* **undiluted**, straight; N. Amer. informal straight up.
–OPPOSITES untidy.

neaten verb **tidy up**, straighten up, smarten up, spruce up, put in order; N. Amer. informal fix up.

neatly adverb **1** *neatly arranged papers:* **tidily**, methodically, systematically; smartly; in order. **2** *the point was neatly put:* **cleverly**, aptly, elegantly, well, effectively. **3** *a neatly executed header:* **skilfully**, deftly, adroitly, adeptly, expertly.

n

neatness noun **tidiness**, orderliness, trimness; smartness.

nebulous adjective **1** *a nebulous figure:* **indistinct**, indefinite, unclear, vague, hazy, fuzzy, blurred, blurry, foggy; faint, shadowy, obscure. **2** *nebulous ideas:* **vague**, ill-defined, unclear, hazy, uncertain, imprecise, muddled, confused, ambiguous; woolly, fuzzy.
–OPPOSITES clear.

necessarily adverb **as a consequence**, as a result, automatically, as a matter of course, certainly, incontrovertibly, inevitably, unavoidably, inescapably, of necessity; formal perforce.

necessary adjective **1** *planning permission is necessary:* **obligatory**, requisite, required, compulsory, mandatory, imperative, needed, de rigueur; essential, vital. **2** *a necessary consequence:* **inevitable**, unavoidable, inescapable, inexorable.

necessitate verb **make necessary**, entail, involve, mean, require, demand, call for, be grounds for, force.

necessity noun **1** *email is now regarded as a necessity:* **essential**, requisite, prerequisite, necessary, basic, sine qua non; informal must-have. **2** *political necessity forced him to resign:* **force of circumstance**, obligation, need, call, exigency. **3** *the necessity of growing old:* **inevitability**, certainty, inescapability, inexorability. **4** *necessity made them steal:* **poverty**, need, neediness, deprivation, privation, destitution; desperation.
■ **of necessity** necessarily, inevitably, unavoidably, inescapably; as a matter of course, naturally, automatically, certainly, surely, definitely, incontrovertibly, undoubtedly; formal perforce.

neck noun technical cervix; old use scrag.
• verb (informal) **kiss**, caress, pet; informal smooch, canoodle; Brit. informal snog; N. Amer. informal make out; informal, dated spoon.
■ **neck and neck** level, equal, tied, side by side; Brit. level pegging; informal even-steven.

WORD LINKS
jugular relating to the neck or throat

necklace noun **chain**, choker, necklet; beads, pearls; pendant, locket; historical torc.

necromancy noun **sorcery**, black magic, witchcraft, witchery, wizardry, the occult, occultism, voodoo, hoodoo.

née adjective *Jill Wyatt, née Peters:* **born**, formerly, previously.

need verb **1** *do you need any money?* **require**, be in need of, have need of, want; be crying out for, be desperate for; demand, call for, necessitate, entail, involve; lack, be without, be short of. **2** *you need to bring sheets:* **have to**, be obliged to, be compelled to, must. **3** *she needed him so much:* **yearn for**, pine for, long for, desire, miss.
• noun **1** *there's no need to apologize:* **necessity**, requirement, call, demand. **2** *basic human needs:* **requirement**, necessity, want, requisite, prerequisite. **3** *your need is greater than mine:* **neediness**,

want, poverty, deprivation, privation, hardship, destitution. **4** *my hour of need:* **difficulty**, trouble, distress; crisis, emergency, urgency, extremity.

■ **in need** needy, deprived, disadvantaged, underprivileged, poor, impoverished, poverty-stricken, destitute, impecunious, indigent; Brit. on the breadline.

needed adjective **necessary**, required, wanted, desired, lacking.
– OPPOSITES optional.

needle noun **1** *the virus is transmitted via needles:* hypodermic needle; informal spike; syringe. **2** *the needle on the meter:* **indicator**, pointer, marker, arrow, hand.
• **verb** (informal) *he's always enjoyed needling people:* **annoy**, irritate, nettle, provoke, antagonize, get on someone's nerves; Brit. rub up the wrong way; informal aggravate, bug, hack off, get someone's goat; Brit. informal wind up, nark.

needless adjective **unnecessary**, unneeded, uncalled for; gratuitous, pointless; dispensable, superfluous, redundant, excessive.
– OPPOSITES necessary.

needy adjective **poor**, deprived, disadvantaged, underprivileged, in need, hard up, poverty-stricken, indigent, impoverished, destitute, impecunious, penniless; Brit. on the breadline; informal on your uppers, broke, strapped for cash; Brit. informal skint, in Queer Street; formal penurious.
– OPPOSITES wealthy.

negate verb **1** *alcohol negates the effect of the drug:* **neutralize**, cancel out, nullify, undo, reverse. **2** *the supreme court attempted to negate the decision:* **invalidate**, annul, nullify, void, revoke, rescind, repeal, retract, countermand, overrule, overturn. **3** *negating the political nature of education:* **deny**, dispute, contradict, refute, rebut, reject, repudiate; formal controvert.
– OPPOSITES validate, confirm.

negation noun **denial**, contradiction, repudiation, refutation, rebuttal; nullification, cancellation, revocation, repeal, retraction; formal abrogation.

negative adjective **1** *a negative reply:* **opposing**, opposed, contrary, anti-, dissenting. **2** *stop being so negative:* **pessimistic**, defeatist, gloomy, cynical, fatalistic, dismissive; unenthusiastic, apathetic, unresponsive. **3** *a negative effect on the economy:* **harmful**, bad, adverse, damaging, detrimental, unfavourable, disadvantageous.
– OPPOSITES positive, optimistic, favourable.

negativity noun **pessimism**, defeatism, gloom, cynicism, hopelessness, despair, despondency; apathy, indifference.

neglect verb **1** *she neglected the children:* **fail to look after**, leave alone, abandon; literary forsake. **2** *he's neglecting his work:* **pay no attention to**, let slide/slip, be remiss about, be lax about, leave undone. **3** *I neglected to inform her:* **fail**, omit, forget.
– OPPOSITES cherish, heed, remember.
• **noun 1** *the place had an air of neglect:* **disrepair**, dilapidation, shabbiness, disuse, abandonment. **2** *her doctor was guilty of neglect:* **negligence**, dereliction of duty, carelessness, laxity, slackness, irresponsibility. **3** *the neglect of women:* **disregard**, ignoring, overlooking; inattention to; exclusion.
– OPPOSITES care, attention.

neglected adjective **1** *neglected animals:* **uncared for**, abandoned; mistreated, maltreated; literary forsaken. **2** *a neglected cottage:* **derelict**, dilapidated, tumble-down, ramshackle, untended. **3** *a neglected masterpiece:* **disregarded**, forgotten, overlooked, ignored, unrecognized, unnoticed, unsung, underrated.

neglectful adjective. See **NEGLIGENT**.

negligent adjective **neglectful**, remiss, careless, lax, irresponsible, inattentive, thoughtless, unmindful, forgetful; slack, sloppy; N. Amer. derelict.
– OPPOSITES dutiful.

negligible adjective **trivial**, trifling, insignificant, unimportant, minor, inconsequential; minimal, small, slight, inappreciable, infinitesimal; informal minuscule, piddling.
– OPPOSITES significant.

n

negotiable adjective **1** *the salary will be negotiable:* **open to discussion**, flexible. **2** *the path was negotiable:* **passable**, navigable, crossable, usable, traversable; clear, unblocked, unobstructed; open.

negotiate verb **1** *she refused to negotiate:* **discuss terms**, talk, consult, parley, confer, debate; compromise; mediate, intercede, arbitrate, moderate, conciliate; bargain, haggle. **2** *he negotiated a new contract:* **arrange**, broker, work out, thrash out, agree on; settle, clinch, conclude, pull off, bring off, transact; informal sort out, swing. **3** *I negotiated the obstacles:* **get round**, get past, get over, clear, cross; surmount, overcome, deal with, cope with.

negotiation noun **1** *the negotiations resume next week:* **discussions**, talks; conference, debate, dialogue, consultation. **2** *the negotiation of a deal:* **arrangement**, brokering; settlement, conclusion, completion, transaction.

negotiator noun **mediator**, arbitrator, go-between, middleman, intermediary; representative, spokesperson, broker.

n

neigh verb **whinny**, bray, snicker.

neighbourhood noun **1** *a quiet neighbourhood:* **district**, area, locality, locale, quarter, community; part, region, zone; informal neck of the woods; Brit. informal manor; N. Amer. informal hood, nabe. **2** *in the neighbourhood of Canterbury:* **vicinity**, environs; purlieus.

neighbouring adjective **adjacent**, adjoining, bordering, connecting, next-door, nearby.
–OPPOSITES remote.

neighbourly adjective **obliging**, helpful, friendly, kind, amiable, amicable, affable, genial, agreeable, hospitable, companionable, civil, cordial, good-natured, nice, pleasant, generous; considerate, thoughtful, unselfish; Brit. informal decent.
–OPPOSITES unfriendly.

nemesis noun *this could be the bank's nemesis:* **downfall**, undoing; ruin, ruination, destruction, Waterloo.

nepotism noun **favouritism**, preferential treatment, the old boy network, looking after your own, bias, partiality, partisanship; Brit. jobs for the boys, the old school tie.
–OPPOSITES impartiality.

nerve noun **1** *the nerves that transmit pain:* neuron, axon; Physiology dendrite. **2** *the match will be a test of nerve:* **confidence**, assurance, cool-headedness, self-possession; courage, bravery, pluck; determination, will power, spirit, backbone, fortitude, mettle, grit; informal guts, spunk; Brit. informal bottle; N. Amer. informal moxie. **3** *pre-wedding nerves:* **anxiety**, tension, nervousness, stress, worry, cold feet, apprehension; informal butterflies, collywobbles, jitters, shakes; Brit. informal the screaming abdabs. **4** *he had the nerve to chat her up:* **audacity**, cheek, effrontery, gall, temerity, presumption, impudence, impertinence, arrogance; informal face, front, brass neck, chutzpah; Brit. informal sauce.

■ **get on someone's nerves** irritate, annoy, irk, anger, bother, vex, provoke, displease, exasperate, infuriate, gall, pique, needle, ruffle someone's feathers, try someone's patience; jar on, grate on, rankle; Brit. rub up the wrong way; informal aggravate, get to, bug, miff, peeve, rile, nettle, get up someone's nose, hack off, get someone's goat; Brit. informal nark, get on someone's wick, wind up.

WORD LINKS

neural relating to nerves in the body
neuritis inflammation of a nerve
neurology, **neuropathology**, **neurosurgery** branches of medicine concerned with the nerves

nerve-racking adjective **stressful**, anxious, worrying, fraught, nail-biting, tense, difficult, trying, worrisome, daunting, frightening; informal scary, hairy.

nervous adjective **1** *a nervous woman:* **highly strung**, anxious, edgy, nervy, tense, excitable, jumpy, skittish, brittle, neurotic; timid. **2** *he was so nervous he couldn't eat:* **anxious**, worried, apprehensive, on edge, edgy, tense, stressed, agitated, uneasy, restless, worked up, keyed up, overwrought, jumpy; fearful, frightened, scared, shaky, in a cold

sweat; informal with butterflies in your stomach, jittery, twitchy, in a state, uptight, wired, in a flap, het up; Brit. informal strung up/out, having kittens; N. Amer. informal spooky, squirrelly. **3** *a nervous disorder:* **neurological**, neural; mental.
–OPPOSITES relaxed, calm.

nervousness noun **anxiety**, edginess, tension, agitation, stress, worry, apprehension, uneasiness, disquiet, fear, trepidation, alarm; Brit. nerviness; informal butterflies (in your stomach), collywobbles, the jitters, the willies, the heebie-jeebies, the shakes.

nervy adjective. See **NERVOUS** senses 1, 2.

nestle verb **snuggle**, cuddle, huddle, nuzzle, settle, burrow.

net[1] noun *a dress of green net:* **netting**, meshwork, tulle, fishnet, lace.
•verb *they netted some big criminals:* **catch**, capture, trap, snare, bag, get; informal nab, collar, bust; British informal nick.

net[2] adjective **1** *net earnings:* **after tax**, after deductions, take-home, final; informal bottom line. **2** *the net result:* **final**, end, ultimate, closing; overall, actual, effective.
–OPPOSITES gross.
•verb *she netted £50,000:* **earn**, make, get, take home, bring in, pocket, realize, be paid; informal walk away with.

nether adjective **lower**, low, bottom, under; underground.
–OPPOSITES upper.

nettle verb **irritate**, annoy, irk, gall, vex, anger, exasperate, infuriate, provoke; upset, displease, offend, pique, rankle, get on someone's nerves, try someone's patience, ruffle someone's feathers; Brit. rub up the wrong way; informal aggravate, rile, needle, get to, bug, get up someone's nose, hack off, get someone's goat; Brit. informal nark, get on someone's wick, wind up; N. Amer. informal tick off.

network noun **1** *a network of arteries:* **web**, lattice, net, matrix, mesh, criss-cross, grid, reticulation; Anatomy plexus. **2** *a network of lanes:* **maze**, labyrinth, warren, tangle.

neurosis noun **obsession**, phobia, fixation, mania; fetish.

neurotic adjective **overanxious**, oversensitive, nervous, nervy, tense, highly strung, paranoid; obsessive, fixated, hysterical, overwrought, irrational; informal twitchy.
–OPPOSITES stable, calm.

neuter adjective **asexual**, sexless; androgynous.
•verb *have your pets neutered:* **sterilize**, castrate, spay, geld, cut, fix; N. Amer. & Austral. alter; Brit. informal doctor.

neutral adjective **1** *she's neutral on this issue:* **impartial**, unbiased, unprejudiced, objective, open-minded, non-partisan, disinterested, dispassionate, detached, impersonal, indifferent, uncommitted. **2** *Switzerland remained neutral:* **unaligned**, non-aligned, unaffiliated; uninvolved. **3** *a neutral topic of conversation:* **inoffensive**, bland, unobjectionable, unexceptionable, anodyne, uncontroversial; safe, harmless, innocuous. **4** *a neutral background:* **pale**, light, colourless, nondescript, indeterminate, drab, insipid, dull.
–OPPOSITES biased, partisan, provocative, colourful.

neutralize verb **counteract**, offset, counterbalance, balance, counterpoise, countervail, compensate for, make up for; cancel out, nullify, negate.

never-ending adjective **1** *never-ending noise:* **incessant**, continuous, unceasing, ceaseless, constant, continual, perpetual, uninterrupted, unbroken, steady, unremitting, relentless, persistent, interminable, non-stop, endless, unending, everlasting, eternal. **2** *never-ending tasks:* **endless**, countless, innumerable, limitless, boundless; literary myriad.

nevertheless adverb **nonetheless**, even so, however, still, yet, though; in spite of that, despite that, be that as it may, for all that, that said, just the same, all the same; notwithstanding, regardless, anyway, anyhow.

new adjective **1** *new technology:* **recent**, up to date, the latest, current, state-of-the-art,

n

contemporary, advanced, cutting-edge, modern. **2** *new ideas:* **novel**, original, fresh; imaginative, creative, experimental; newfangled, ultra-modern, avant-garde, futuristic; informal edgy, way out, far out. **3** *a new car:* **unused**, brand new, pristine, in mint condition. **4** *new neighbours moved in:* **different**, another, alternative; unfamiliar, unknown, strange; unaccustomed, untried. **5** *they had a new classroom built:* **additional**, extra, supplementary, further, another, fresh. **6** *I came back a new woman:* **reinvigorated**, restored, revived, improved, refreshed, regenerated, reborn.
– OPPOSITES old, second-hand.

newcomer noun **1** *a newcomer to the village:* **new arrival**, immigrant, incomer, settler; stranger, outsider, foreigner, alien; N. English offcomer; informal johnny-come-lately, new kid on the block; Austral. informal blow-in. **2** *photography tips for the newcomer:* **beginner**, novice, learner; trainee, apprentice, probationer, tyro, initiate, neophyte; informal rookie, newbie; N. Amer. informal tenderfoot, greenhorn.

n

newfangled adjective **new**, the latest, modern, ultra-modern, up to the minute, state-of-the-art, advanced, contemporary; informal trendy, flash.
– OPPOSITES dated.

newly adverb **recently**, just, lately, freshly.

news noun **report**, announcement, story, account; article, newsflash, newscast, headlines, press release, communication, communiqué, bulletin; message, dispatch, statement, intelligence; disclosure, revelation, word, talk, gossip; informal scoop; literary tidings.

newspaper noun **paper**, journal, gazette, news-sheet; tabloid, broadsheet; Brit. red top; informal rag; N. Amer. informal tab.

newsworthy adjective **interesting**, topical, notable, noteworthy, important, significant, momentous, historic, remarkable, sensational.
– OPPOSITES unremarkable.

next adjective **1** *the next chapter:* **following**, succeeding, upcoming, to come. **2** *the next house in the street:* **neighbouring**, adjacent, adjoining, next-door, bordering on, connected to, attached to; closest, nearest.
– OPPOSITES previous.
• adverb *where shall we go next?* **then**, after, afterwards, after this/that, following that/this, later, subsequently; formal thereafter.
– OPPOSITES before.
▪ **next to** beside, by, alongside, by the side of, next door to, adjacent to, side by side with; close to, near, neighbouring, adjoining.

nibble verb **bite**, gnaw at, snack on; toy with; taste, sample; informal graze on.
• noun *drinks and nibbles available from 6 p.m.* **snack**, titbit, canapé, hors d'oeuvre.

nice adjective **1** *have a nice time:* **enjoyable**, pleasant, agreeable, good, satisfying, gratifying; entertaining, amusing, diverting; informal lovely, great; N. Amer. informal neat. **2** *nice people:* **pleasant**, likeable, agreeable, personable, congenial, amiable, affable, genial, friendly, charming, delightful, engaging; sympathetic, compassionate, good. **3** *nice manners:* **polite**, courteous, civil, refined, polished, genteel, elegant. **4** *that's a rather nice distinction:* **subtle**, fine, delicate, precise, strict, close; careful, meticulous, scrupulous. **5** *it's a nice day:* **fine**, pleasant, agreeable; dry, sunny, warm, mild.
– OPPOSITES unpleasant, nasty, rough.

nicety noun *legal niceties:* **subtlety**, fine point, nuance, refinement, detail.

niche noun **1** *a niche in the wall:* **recess**, alcove, nook, cranny, hollow, bay, cavity, cubbyhole, pigeonhole. **2** *he found his niche in life:* **ideal position**, vocation, calling, métier.

nick noun **1** *a slight nick in the blade:* **cut**, scratch, incision, snick, notch, chip; dent, indentation. **2** (Brit. informal) *she's in the nick.* See **PRISON**. **3** (Brit. informal) *he's at the nick:* **police station**, station; N. Amer. precinct, station house; informal cop shop. **4** (Brit. informal) *the car's in good nick:* **condition**, repair, shape, state, order, form, fettle, trim.

• verb **1** *I nicked my toe:* **cut**, scratch, snick, graze. **2** (Brit. informal) *she nicked his wallet.* See **STEAL** verb sense 1. **3** (Brit. informal) *Steve's been nicked.* See **ARREST** verb sense 1.

nickname noun **sobriquet**, byname, tag, label, epithet, cognomen; pet name, diminutive, endearment; informal moniker; formal appellation.

nifty adjective (informal) **1** *nifty camerawork:* **skilful**, deft, agile, adroit, nice; informal fancy, classy. **2** *a nifty little gadget:* **useful**, handy, practical, neat; compact. **3** *a nifty suit:* **fashionable**, stylish, smart, nice; informal classy.
– OPPOSITES clumsy.

niggle verb **irritate**, annoy, bother, provoke, exasperate, upset, gall, irk, rankle with; informal rile, get to, bug.
• noun **quibble**, complaint, criticism, grumble, grouse, cavil; informal gripe, moan, beef, grouch.

niggling adjective *niggling doubts:* **persistent**, nagging, lingering, irritating, annoying.

night noun night-time; darkness, dark.
– OPPOSITES day.
■ **night and day** all the time, around the clock, {morning, noon, and night}, {day in, day out}, ceaselessly, endlessly, incessantly, unceasingly, interminably, constantly, perpetually, continually, relentlessly; informal 24-7.

WORD LINKS
nocturnal relating to night
nyctophobia fear of the night

nightclub noun **discotheque**, night spot, club, bar; N. Amer. cafe; informal disco, niterie.

nightfall noun **sunset**, sundown, dusk, twilight, evening, dark; literary eventide.
– OPPOSITES dawn.

nightmare noun *the journey was a nightmare:* **hell**, misery, agony, torture, murder, purgatory, disaster; informal the pits.

nightmarish adjective **unearthly**, spine-chilling, hair-raising, horrific, macabre, hideous, unspeakable, gruesome, grisly, ghastly, harrowing, disturbing; informal scary, creepy.

nihilism noun **scepticism**, disbelief, unbelief; negativity, cynicism, pessimism; rejection, denial; despair.

nihilist noun sceptic, disbeliever, unbeliever; cynic, pessimist.

nihilistic adjective **negative**, pessimistic, bleak, hopeless, cynical, despairing.

nil noun **nothing**, none; nought, zero, o; Tennis love; Cricket a duck; N. English nowt; informal zilch, nix; Brit. informal sweet Fanny Adams, sweet FA; N. Amer. informal zip, nada; old use naught.

nimble adjective **1** *he was nimble on his feet:* **agile**, sprightly, light, spry, quick, lithe, limber; skilful, deft, dexterous, adroit; informal nippy, twinkle-toed. **2** *a nimble mind:* **quick**, alert, lively, wide awake, observant, astute, perceptive, penetrating, discerning, shrewd, sharp; intelligent, bright, smart, clever, brilliant; informal quick on the uptake.
– OPPOSITES clumsy, dull.

nine cardinal number **nonet**.

WORD LINKS
nonagon a nine-sided figure

nip verb & noun **bite**, nibble, peck; pinch, tweak, squeeze.

nippy adjective (informal) **1** *a nippy little hatchback:* **fast**, quick, lively, speedy; informal zippy. **2** *it's a bit nippy in here:* **chilly**, cold, frosty.
– OPPOSITES lumbering, slow, warm.

nit-picking adjective (informal). See **PEDANTIC**.

nitty-gritty noun (informal) **basics**, essentials, fundamentals, substance, quintessence, heart of the matter; nub, crux, gist, meat, kernel; informal brass tacks, nuts and bolts.

no adverb absolutely not, definitely not, most certainly not, of course not, under no circumstances, by no means, not at all, negative, never, not really; informal nope, nah, not on your life, no way, not a chance; Brit. informal no fear, not on your nelly; old use nay.
– OPPOSITES yes.

nobility noun **1** *a member of the nobility:* **aristocracy**, peerage, peers (of the realm), lords, nobles, noblemen, noblewomen; informal aristos; Brit. informal nobs. **2** *the* *nobility of his deed:* **virtue**, goodness, honour, decency, integrity; magnanimity, generosity, selflessness.

noble adjective **1** *a noble family:* **aristocratic**, blue-blooded, high-born, titled; old use gentle. **2** *a noble cause:* **righteous**, virtuous, good, honourable, worthwhile; upright, decent, worthy, moral, ethical, reputable. **3** *a noble pine forest:* **magnificent**, splendid, grand, stately, imposing, dignified, proud, striking, majestic, glorious, awesome, monumental, regal.
– OPPOSITES humble, dishonourable, base.
• noun *Scottish nobles:* **aristocrat**, nobleman, noblewoman, lord, lady, peer (of the realm), peeress; informal aristo; Brit. informal nob.

nod verb **1** *she nodded her head:* **incline**, bob, bow, dip. **2** *he nodded to me to start:* **signal**, gesture, gesticulate, motion, sign, indicate.
• noun **1** *she gave a nod to the manager:* **signal**, indication, sign, cue; gesture. **2** *a quick nod of his head:* **inclination**, bob, bow, dip.
■ **nod off** fall asleep, go to sleep, doze off, drop off; informal drift off, flake out, go out like a light; N. Amer. informal sack out.

node noun **junction**, intersection, interchange, fork, confluence, convergence, meeting.

noise noun **sound**, din, hubbub, clamour, racket, uproar, tumult, commotion, pandemonium, babel; Brit. row; informal hullabaloo.
– OPPOSITES silence.

noisy adjective **1** *a noisy crowd:* **rowdy**, raucous, clamorous, boisterous; chattering, talkative, vociferous, shouting, screaming. **2** *noisy music:* **loud**, blaring, booming, deafening, thunderous, ear-splitting, piercing, strident, cacophonous.
– OPPOSITES quiet, soft.

nomad noun **itinerant**, migrant, wanderer; Gypsy, Romany; Traveller.

nomadic adjective *nomadic tribes | a nomadic lifestyle:* **itinerant**, travelling, wandering, migrant, migratory, roaming, roving, peripatetic; vagrant.

nominal adjective **1** *the nominal head of the campaign:* **in name only**, titular, formal, official; theoretical, supposed, ostensible, so-called. **2** *a nominal rent:* **token**, symbolic; minimal, small; Brit. peppercorn; N. Amer. informal nickel-and-dime.
– OPPOSITES real, considerable.

nominate verb **propose**, recommend, suggest, name, put forward, present, submit.

nonchalant adjective **calm**, composed, unconcerned, cool; indifferent, blasé, dispassionate, casual, insouciant; informal laid-back.
– OPPOSITES anxious.

non-committal adjective **evasive**, equivocal, guarded, circumspect, reserved; vague; informal cagey.

nonconformist noun **dissenter**, protester, rebel, renegade, schismatic; freethinker, apostate, heretic; individualist, free spirit, maverick, eccentric, original, deviant, misfit, dropout, outsider; informal freak, oddball; N. Amer. informal screwball, kook.

nondescript adjective **undistinguished**, unremarkable, unexceptional, featureless, characterless, unmemorable; ordinary, commonplace, average, run-of-the-mill, mundane; uninteresting, uninspiring, colourless, bland.
– OPPOSITES distinctive.

nonentity noun **nobody**, cipher, nothing, small fry, lightweight; informal no-hoper, non-starter, no-mark.
– OPPOSITES celebrity.

non-essential adjective **unnecessary**, inessential, unneeded, superfluous, uncalled for, redundant, dispensable, expendable, unimportant, extraneous.

nonetheless adverb **nevertheless**, even so, however, still, yet, though; in spite of that, despite that, be that as it may, for all that, that said, just the same, all the same; notwithstanding, regardless, anyway, anyhow.

non-existent adjective **imaginary**, imagined, unreal, fictional, fictitious, made up, invented, fanciful; fantastic, mythical; illusory.
– OPPOSITES real.

non-observance noun **infringement**, breach, violation, contravention, transgression, non-compliance, infraction.

nonplussed adjective **surprised**, taken aback, disconcerted, confused, thrown, at a loss, puzzled, bemused, perplexed, baffled, bewildered; informal fazed, flummoxed; N. Amer. informal discombobulated.

nonsense noun **1** *he was talking nonsense:* **rubbish**, balderdash, gibberish, claptrap, blarney, garbage; informal hogwash, rot, guff, baloney, tripe, drivel, gobbledegook, bilge, bosh, bunk, hot air, piffle, poppycock, phooey, twaddle; Brit. informal cobblers, codswallop, tosh, double Dutch; Scottish & N. English informal havers; N. Amer. informal flapdoodle; informal, dated bunkum, tommyrot. **2** *she stands no nonsense:* **mischief**, messing about, misbehaviour, funny business; informal tomfoolery, monkey business, shenanigans, hanky-panky; Brit. informal monkey tricks, jiggery-pokery. **3** *the whole thing is a nonsense:* **joke**, farce, travesty, sham; insanity, madness.
– OPPOSITES sense, wisdom.

nonsensical adjective **1** *nonsensical psychobabble:* **meaningless**, senseless, illogical. **2** *a nonsensical idea:* **foolish**, stupid, idiotic, absurd, silly, inane, hare-brained, ridiculous, ludicrous, preposterous; informal crazy, crackpot, nutty; Brit. informal daft.
– OPPOSITES logical, sensible.

non-stop adjective *non-stop entertainment:* **continuous**, constant, continual, perpetual, incessant, unceasing, ceaseless, uninterrupted, round-the-clock; unremitting, relentless, persistent.
– OPPOSITES occasional.
• adverb *we worked non-stop:* **continuously**, continually, incessantly, unceasingly, ceaselessly, all the time, constantly, perpetually, round the clock, steadily, relentlessly, persistently; informal 24-7.
– OPPOSITES occasionally.

noon noun **midday**, twelve o'clock, twelve hundred hours, twelve noon, high noon, noonday; literary noontide, noontime.

norm noun **1** (**the norm**) *long tailbacks on this road are now the norm:* **standard**, usual, the rule; normal, typical, average, unexceptional, par for the course, expected. **2** *norms of diplomatic behaviour:* **convention**, standard; criterion, yardstick, benchmark, touchstone, rule, formula, pattern, guide, guideline, model, exemplar.

normal adjective **1** *they issue books in the normal way:* **usual**, standard, ordinary, customary, conventional, habitual, accustomed, expected; typical, common, everyday, regular, routine, traditional; literary wonted. **2** *a normal couple:* **ordinary**, average, typical, run-of-the-mill, middle-of-the-road, common, conventional, mainstream, unremarkable, unexceptional; N. Amer. garden-variety; Brit. informal common or garden, bog-standard; N. Amer. informal a dime a dozen. **3** *the man was not normal:* **sane**, in your right mind, right in the head, of sound mind, compos mentis; informal all there.
– OPPOSITES unusual, insane.

normality noun **normalcy**, business as usual, the daily round; routine, order, regularity.

normally adverb **1** *normally we'd keep quiet about this:* **usually**, ordinarily, as a rule, generally, in general, mostly, for the most part, by and large, mainly, most of the time, on the whole; typically, traditionally. **2** *she was behaving normally:* **naturally**, conventionally, characteristically.

northern adjective *the northern coasts of Europe:* **north**, northerly; polar, Arctic; technical boreal.

nose noun **1** *a punch on the nose:* snout, muzzle, proboscis, trunk; informal beak, conk, schnozzle, hooter. **2** *a journalist with a nose for a good story:* **instinct**, feeling, sixth sense, intuition, insight, feel. **3** *a dry wine with a fruity nose:* **smell**, bouquet, aroma, fragrance, perfume, scent, odour.
• verb **1** *the dog nosed the ball:* **nuzzle**, nudge, push. **2** *she's always nosing into my business:* **pry**, inquire, poke about/around, interfere in, meddle in, stick/poke your nose in; informal snoop; Austral./NZ informal stickybeak. **3** *he nosed the*

car into the traffic: **ease**, inch, edge, move, manoeuvre, steer, guide.
■ **nose around/about** investigate, explore, ferret, rummage, search; delve into; prowl around/about; informal snoop around/about.

WORD LINKS
nasal, **rhinal** relating to the nose
rhinitis inflammation of the nose
rhinoplasty plastic surgery performed on the nose

nosedive (informal) **noun** *sterling took a nosedive:* **tumble**, drop, plunge, decline, slump; informal crash.
– OPPOSITES climb, rise.
• **verb** *profits have nosedived:* **fall**, drop, sink, plunge, plummet, tumble, slump, go down, decline; informal crash.
– OPPOSITES soar.

nostalgia **noun** **reminiscence**, remembrance, recollection; wistfulness, regret, sentimentality.

nostalgic **adjective** **wistful**, romantic, sentimental; regretful, dewy-eyed, maudlin.

nosy **adjective** (informal) **prying**, inquisitive, curious, busybody, spying, eavesdropping, intrusive; informal snooping.

n

notable **adjective 1** *notable examples of workmanship:* **noteworthy**, remarkable, outstanding, important, significant, memorable; marked, striking, impressive. **2** *a notable author:* **prominent**, important, well known, famous, famed, noted, distinguished, eminent, illustrious, respected, esteemed, renowned, celebrated, acclaimed, influential, prestigious, of note.
– OPPOSITES unremarkable, unknown.
• **noun** *movie stars and other notables:* **celebrity**, public figure, VIP, dignitary, worthy, luminary; star, superstar; informal celeb, bigwig, megastar; Brit. informal nob.
– OPPOSITES nonentity.

notably **adverb 1** *other countries, notably the USA:* **in particular**, particularly, especially; primarily, principally. **2** *these are notably short-lived birds:* **remarkably**, especially, exceptionally, singularly, particularly, peculiarly, distinctly, significantly, unusually, uncommonly, decidedly, conspicuously.

notation **noun 1** *algebraic notation:* **symbols**, characters; alphabet, script; code. **2** *notations in the margin:* **annotation**, jotting, comment, footnote, entry, memo, gloss.

notch **noun** **nick**, cut, incision, score, scratch, slit, snick, slot, groove, cleft, indentation.
■ **notch something up** score, achieve, attain, gain, earn, make; rack up, chalk up; register, record.

note **noun 1** *a note in her diary:* **record**, entry, reminder; informal memo. **2** *he will take notes of the meeting:* **minutes**, record, details; report, account, transcript; synopsis, summary, outline. **3** *see note iv below:* **annotation**, footnote, comment. **4** *he wrote me a note:* **message**, letter, line; formal epistle, missive. **5** (Brit.) *a £20 note:* **banknote**; N. Amer. bill; US informal greenback; (**notes**) paper money. **6** *this is worthy of note:* **attention**, consideration, notice; comment. **7** *a composer of note:* **distinction**, importance, renown, repute, stature, standing, consequence, account. **8** *a note of hopelessness in her voice:* **tone**, intonation, inflection, sound; hint, indication, sign, element, suggestion, sense.
• **verb 1** *we will note your suggestion:* **bear in mind**, be mindful of, consider, take notice of; register, record, enter. **2** *the letter noted the ministers' concern:* **mention**, refer to, touch on, indicate, point out, make known, state. **3** *note the date in your diary:* **write down**, put down, jot down, take down, enter, mark, record, register, pencil.

notebook **noun** **notepad**, exercise book; register, logbook, log, diary, journal, record; Brit. jotter, pocketbook; N. Amer. scratch pad.

noted **adjective** **renowned**, well known, famous, famed, prominent, celebrated; notable, of note, important, eminent, distinguished, illustrious, acclaimed, esteemed; of distinction, of repute.
– OPPOSITES unknown.

noteworthy **adjective** **notable**, interesting, significant, important;

remarkable, striking, outstanding, memorable, unique, special; unusual, extraordinary, singular.
– OPPOSITES unexceptional.

nothing pronoun **1** *there's nothing you can do:* **not a thing**, zero; N. English nowt; informal zilch, sweet Fanny Adams, sweet FA, nix, not a dicky bird; N. Amer. informal zip, nada, diddly-squat; old use naught. **2** *the share value fell to nothing:* **zero**, nought, nil, o; Tennis love; Cricket a duck.
– OPPOSITES something.
■ **nothing but** *he's nothing but a nuisance:* merely, only, just, solely, simply, purely, no more than.

nothingness noun **oblivion**, blankness, darkness, blackness, emptiness; void, vacuum, abyss.

notice noun **1** *nothing escaped his notice:* **attention**, observation, awareness, consciousness, perception; regard, consideration, scrutiny; watchfulness, vigilance, attentiveness. **2** *a notice on the wall:* **poster**, bill, handbill, advertisement, announcement, bulletin; flyer, leaflet, pamphlet; sign, card; informal ad; Brit. informal advert. **3** *we will give you notice of any changes:* **notification**, advance warning; news, word. **4** *the film got bad notices:* **review**, write-up, report.
• verb *I noticed that the door was open:* **observe**, note, see, discern, detect, spot, distinguish; Brit. informal clock.
– OPPOSITES overlook.

noticeable adjective **distinct**, evident, obvious, apparent, manifest, plain, clear, marked, conspicuous, unmistakable, pronounced, prominent, striking; perceptible, discernible, detectable, observable, visible, appreciable.

notification noun **information**, word, advice, news, intelligence; communication, message; literary tidings.

notify verb **inform**, tell, advise, apprise, let someone know; alert, warn.

notion noun **1** *he had a notion that something was wrong:* **idea**, belief, conviction, opinion, view, thought, impression, perception; hypothesis, theory; feeling, sneaking suspicion, intuition, hunch. **2** *Claire had no notion of what he meant:* **understanding**, idea, clue, inkling. **3** *he got a notion to return:* **impulse**, inclination, whim, desire, wish, fancy.

notional adjective **hypothetical**, theoretical, conjectural, putative, conceptual; academic, imaginary, supposed.
– OPPOSITES actual.

notoriety noun **infamy**, disrepute, bad name, dishonour, discredit.

notorious adjective **infamous**, scandalous; well known, famous, famed, legendary.

nought noun **nil**, zero, o, nothing; Tennis love; Cricket a duck; informal zilch; Brit. informal not a sausage; N. Amer. informal zip, nada.

nourish verb **1** *patients must be well nourished:* **feed**, provide for, sustain, maintain. **2** *we nourish the talents of children:* **encourage**, promote, foster, nurture, cultivate, boost, strengthen, enrich. **3** *the hopes Ursula nourished:* **cherish**, nurture, foster, harbour, nurse, entertain, maintain, hold, have, keep.

nourishing adjective **nutritious**, wholesome, good for you, healthy, health-giving, healthful, beneficial.
– OPPOSITES unhealthy.

nourishment noun **food**, sustenance, nutriment, nutrition, provisions, provender; informal grub, nosh, chow, eats; Brit. informal scoff; N. Amer. informal chuck; formal comestibles; dated victuals.

novel[1] noun *his latest novel:* **book**, paperback, hardback; story, tale, narrative, romance; best-seller; informal blockbuster.

novel[2] adjective *a novel way of making money:* **new**, original, unusual, unfamiliar, unconventional, unorthodox; different, fresh, imaginative, innovative, inventive, modern; avant-garde, pioneering, groundbreaking, revolutionary; unprecedented; experimental, untested, untried; strange, exotic, newfangled.
– OPPOSITES traditional.

novelist noun **writer**, author; informal scribbler.

novelty noun **1** *the novelty of our approach:* **originality**, newness,

n

freshness, unconventionality, unfamiliarity; imaginativeness, creativity; uniqueness. **2** *we sell seasonal novelties:* **knick-knack**, trinket, bauble, toy, trifle, ornament; N. Amer. kickshaw.

novice noun **beginner**, learner, newcomer, fledgling; apprentice, trainee, probationer, student, pupil; informal rookie; N. Amer. informal tenderfoot, greenhorn.
–OPPOSITES expert, veteran.

now adverb **1** *I'm extremely busy now:* **at the moment**, at present, currently; N. Amer. presently; Brit. informal at the minute. **2** *television is now the main source of news:* **nowadays**, today, these days, in this day and age. **3** *you must leave now:* **at once**, straight away, right away, this minute, this instant, immediately, instantly, directly, without further ado, promptly, without delay, as soon as possible, asap; informal pronto.
■ **now and again** occasionally, every now and then, from time to time, sometimes, every so often, every now and again, at times, on occasions, every once in a while; periodically.

n

nowadays adverb **these days**, today, at the present time, in these times, in this day and age, now, currently, at the moment, at present; N. Amer. presently.

noxious adjective **poisonous**, toxic, deadly, harmful, dangerous, damaging, destructive; unpleasant, nasty, disgusting, awful, dreadful, horrible, terrible; vile, revolting, foul, nauseating, appalling, offensive; malodorous, fetid, putrid; informal ghastly, horrid; literary noisome.
–OPPOSITES innocuous.

nuance noun **fine distinction**, subtle difference; shade, gradation, variation, degree; subtlety, nicety.

nub noun **crux**, main point, core, heart of the matter, nucleus, essence, quintessence, kernel, meat, pith; gist, substance; informal nitty-gritty.

nucleus noun *the nucleus of the banking world:* **core**, centre, heart, hub, middle, focal point, pivot, crux.

nude adjective **naked**, stark naked, bare, unclothed, undressed, uncovered, stripped, as nature intended, au naturel; informal without a stitch on, in your birthday suit, in the raw/buff, in the altogether, in the nuddy; Brit. informal starkers; Scottish informal in the scud; N. Amer. informal buck naked.
–OPPOSITES clothed.

nudge verb **1** *he nudged her in the ribs:* **poke** prod, elbow, dig, jab, push. **2** *unemployment was nudging 3,000,000:* **approach**, near, come close to, touch, be verging on, border on.

nugget noun **lump**, chunk, piece, hunk, gobbet; N. Amer. informal gob.

nuisance noun **annoyance**, inconvenience, bore, bother, irritation, trial, burden; pest, thorn in your side/flesh; informal pain, hassle, bind, drag, aggravation, headache; Scottish informal nyaff.
–OPPOSITES blessing.

nullify verb **annul**, render null and void, void, invalidate; repeal, reverse, rescind, revoke, cancel, abolish; do away with, terminate, quash.
–OPPOSITES ratify.

numb adjective *his fingers were numb:* **without sensation**, dead, without feeling, numbed, desensitized, unfeeling, frozen; anaesthetized; dazed, stunned, stupefied, paralysed, immobilized.
–OPPOSITES sensitive.
•verb *the cold numbed her senses:* **deaden**, desensitize, dull; anaesthetize; daze, stupefy, paralyse, immobilize, freeze.
–OPPOSITES sensitize.

number noun **1** *a whole number:* **numeral**, integer, figure, digit; character, symbol; decimal, unit; cardinal number, ordinal number. **2** *a large number of complaints:* **amount**, quantity; total, aggregate, tally; quota, average. **3** *the wedding of one of their number:* **group**, company, crowd, circle, party, band, crew, set; informal gang. **4** *the band performed another number:* **song**, piece of music, tune, track; routine, sketch, dance, act.
•verb **1** *visitors numbered more than two million:* **add up to**, amount to, total, come to. **2** *he numbers*

the fleet at a thousand: **calculate**, count, total, compute, reckon, estimate, tally; assess; Brit. tot up; formal enumerate. **3** *he numbers her among his friends:* **include**, count, reckon, deem.

■ **a number of** several, various, quite a few, sundry, some. **without number** countless, innumerable, unlimited, limitless, untold, numberless, uncountable, uncounted; numerous, many, legion; informal more——than you can shake a stick at; literary myriad.

WORD LINKS

numerical relating to numbers

numberless adjective **innumerable**, countless, unlimited, endless, limitless, untold, uncountable, uncounted; numerous, legion; informal more——than you can shake a stick at; literary myriad.

numbing adjective **1** *menthol has a numbing action:* **desensitizing**, deadening, benumbing, anaesthetic, anaesthetizing; paralysing. **2** *numbing cold:* **freezing**, raw, bitter, biting, arctic.

numeral noun **number**, integer, figure, digit; character, symbol, unit.

numerous adjective **many**, a number of, a lot of; several; plenty of, copious, an abundance of; frequent; informal umpteen.
–OPPOSITES few.

nunnery noun **convent**, priory, abbey.

nuptial adjective **matrimonial**, marital, marriage, wedding, conjugal, bridal; married, wedded; Law spousal; literary connubial.

nuptials plural noun **wedding**, marriage, union; old use espousal.

nurse noun **1** *skilled nurses:* **carer**; informal Florence Nightingale; N. Amer. informal candy-striper. **2** (dated) *she had been his nurse in childhood:* **nanny**, nursemaid, childminder, au pair, ayah.
• verb **1** *they nursed smallpox patients:* **care for**, take care of, look after, tend, minister to. **2** *they nursed old grievances:* **harbour**, foster, bear, have, hold on to, retain.

nursemaid noun. See **NURSE** noun sense 2.

nurture verb **1** *she nurtured her children into adulthood:* **bring up**, care for, take care of, look after, tend, rear, raise, support. **2** *we nurtured these plants:* **cultivate**, grow, keep, tend. **3** *he nurtured my love of art:* **encourage**, promote, stimulate, develop, foster, cultivate, boost, strengthen, fuel.
–OPPOSITES neglect, hinder.

nut noun **1** (informal) *he smacked her on the nut:* **head**, skull, cranium, crown; informal noodle, noggin; Brit. informal bonce; informal, dated conk, noddle. **2** (informal) *some nut arrived at the office:* **maniac**, lunatic, madman, madwoman; eccentric; informal loony, nutcase, fruitcake, head case, crank, crackpot, weirdo; Brit. informal nutter; N. Amer. informal screwball. **3** (informal) *a movie nut:* **enthusiast**, fan, devotee, aficionado; informal freak, fiend, fanatic, addict, buff; N. Amer. informal jock.

■ **do your nut** (informal) be furious, lose your temper; informal go mad, go crazy, go wild, go bananas, have a fit, blow your top, hit the roof, go off the deep end, go ape, freak out, flip, lose your rag; Brit. informal go spare.

nutrition noun **nourishment**, nutriment, nutrients, sustenance, food; informal grub, chow, nosh; Brit. informal scoff; literary viands; dated victuals.

nutritious adjective **nourishing**, good for you, full of goodness; wholesome, healthy, healthful, beneficial, sustaining.

nuts adjective (informal) **1** *they thought we were nuts.* See **MAD** sense 1. **2** *he's nuts about her:* **infatuated with**, devoted to, in love with, smitten with, enamoured of, hot for; informal mad, crazy, nutty, wild, hooked on, gone on, dead keen on; Brit. informal potty.

nuts and bolts plural noun **basics**, fundamentals, practicalities, essentials, mechanics; informal nitty-gritty, ins and outs, brass tacks.

Oo

oaf noun **lout**, boor, barbarian, Neanderthal; fool, idiot, imbecile; informal cretin, ass, goon, yahoo, ape, meathead, bonehead, lamebrain; Brit. informal clot, plonker, berk, pillock, yob, yobbo; Scottish informal nyaff; N. Amer. informal bozo, dumbhead, lummox, klutz, goofus; Austral. informal drongo.

oafish adjective **stupid**, foolish, idiotic; loutish, awkward, gawkish, clumsy, lumbering, ape-like, Neanderthal, uncouth, boorish, rough, brutish, ill-mannered, unrefined; informal clodhopping, blockheaded, boneheaded, thick-headed; Brit. informal yobbish.

oasis noun **refuge**, haven, retreat, sanctuary.

O

oath noun **1** *an oath of allegiance:* **vow**, pledge, promise, affirmation, guarantee. **2** *a stream of oaths:* **swear word**, profanity, expletive, four-letter word, dirty word, obscenity, curse; formal imprecation.

obdurate adjective **stubborn**, obstinate, intransigent, inflexible, unyielding, unbending, pig-headed, stiff-necked; headstrong; Brit. informal bloody-minded.
–OPPOSITES malleable.

obedient adjective **compliant**, biddable, acquiescent, tractable, amenable, pliant; dutiful, good, law-abiding, deferential, respectful, manageable, governable, docile, tame, meek, passive, submissive.
–OPPOSITES rebellious.

obelisk noun **column**, pillar, needle, shaft, monolith, monument.

obese adjective **fat**, overweight, corpulent, gross, stout, fleshy, heavy, portly, pot-bellied, bloated, flabby; informal porky, roly-poly, blubbery.
–OPPOSITES thin.

obey verb **1** *I obeyed him:* **submit to**, defer to, bow to, yield to. **2** *he refused to obey the order:* **carry out**, perform, act on, execute, discharge, implement. **3** *the rules have to be obeyed:* **comply with**, adhere to, observe, abide by, act in accordance with, conform to, respect, follow, keep to, stick to.
–OPPOSITES defy, ignore.

object noun **1** *wooden objects:* **thing**, article, item; informal doodah, thing-amajig, thingummy, whatsit, whatchamacallit; Brit. informal gubbins; N. Amer. informal doodad. **2** *he became the object of criticism:* **target**, butt, focus, recipient, victim. **3** *his object was to resolve the crisis:* **objective**, aim, goal, target, purpose, end, plan, point; ambition, design, intention, idea.
•verb *teachers objected to the scheme:* **protest about**, oppose, take exception to, take issue with, take a stand against, argue against, quarrel with, condemn, draw the line at, demur at, mind, complain about; beg to differ; informal kick up a fuss/stink about.
–OPPOSITES approve, accept.

objection noun **protest**, protestation, demurral, complaint, cavil; opposition, counter-argument, disagreement, disapproval, dissent.

objectionable adjective **unpleasant**, disagreeable, distasteful, undesirable, obnoxious, offensive, nasty, horrible, horrid, disgusting, awful, dreadful, appalling, insufferable, odious, vile, foul, unsavoury, repulsive, repellent, repugnant, revolting, abhorrent, loathsome, detestable; informal ghastly; Brit. informal beastly.
–OPPOSITES pleasant.

objective adjective **1** *try to be*

objective: **impartial**, unbiased, unprejudiced, non-partisan, disinterested, neutral, uninvolved, even-handed, equitable, fair, open-minded, dispassionate, detached. **2** *objective knowledge:* **factual**, actual, real, empirical, verifiable.
– OPPOSITES biased, subjective.
• noun *our objective is to make a profit:* **aim**, intention, purpose, target, goal, intent, object, point; idea, plan.

objectively adverb **impartially**, without bias/prejudice, even-handedly, dispassionately, with an open mind, without fear or favour.

objectivity noun **impartiality**, fairness, fair-mindedness, neutrality, even-handedness, open-mindedness, disinterest, detachment.

obligation noun **1** *his professional obligations:* **duty**, commitment, responsibility; function, task, job, burden, charge, onus, liability, requirement, debt. **2** *a sense of obligation:* **duty**, compulsion, indebtedness; duress, necessity, pressure, constraint.

obligatory adjective **compulsory**, mandatory, prescribed, required, demanded, statutory, enforced, binding, incumbent; requisite, necessary, imperative, unavoidable, inescapable, essential.
– OPPOSITES optional.

oblige verb **1** *we are obliged to accept the decision:* **require**, compel, bind, constrain, leave someone no option, force. **2** *I'll be happy to oblige you:* **do someone a favour**, accommodate, help, assist; indulge, humour.

obliged adjective **thankful**, grateful, appreciative; beholden, indebted, in someone's debt.

obliging adjective **helpful**, accommodating, cooperative, agreeable, amenable, generous, kind, hospitable, amiable, gracious, unselfish; Brit. informal decent.
– OPPOSITES unhelpful.

oblique adjective **1** *an oblique line:* **slanting**, slanted, sloping, at an angle, angled, diagonal, askew, squint; N. Amer. cater-cornered. **2** *an oblique reference:* **indirect**, roundabout, circuitous, implicit, implied, elliptical, evasive.
– OPPOSITES straight, direct.
• noun **slash**, solidus, backslash.

obliquely adverb **1** *the sun shone obliquely across the tower:* **diagonally**, at an angle, slantwise, sideways, sidelong. **2** *he referred obliquely to the war:* **indirectly**, in a roundabout way, circuitously, evasively.

obliterate verb **1** *he tried to obliterate the memory:* **erase**, eradicate, expunge, wipe out, blot out, delete. **2** *a bomb that would obliterate a city:* **destroy**, wipe out, annihilate, demolish, wipe off the face of the earth; informal zap. **3** *clouds obliterated the sun:* **hide**, obscure, blot out, block, cover, screen.

oblivion noun **1** *I drank myself into oblivion:* **unconsciousness**, insensibility, stupor; coma, blackout. **2** *they rescued him from artistic oblivion:* **obscurity**, limbo, anonymity.
– OPPOSITES consciousness, fame.

oblivious adjective **unaware**, unconscious, heedless, unmindful, insensible, ignorant, blind, deaf; unconcerned, impervious.
– OPPOSITES conscious.

obnoxious adjective **unpleasant**, disagreeable, nasty, offensive, objectionable, unsavoury, revolting, repulsive, repellent, repugnant, disgusting, odious, vile, foul, loathsome, nauseating, sickening, hateful, insufferable, intolerable; informal horrible, horrid, ghastly, gross, sick-making, God-awful; Brit. informal beastly.
– OPPOSITES delightful.

obscene adjective **1** *obscene literature:* **pornographic**, indecent, smutty, dirty, filthy, X-rated, explicit, lewd, rude, vulgar, coarse, immoral, improper, off colour; scatological; informal blue, porn; euphemistic adult. **2** *an obscene amount:* **scandalous**, shocking, outrageous, immoral.

obscenity noun **1** *they were prosecuted for obscenity:* **indecency**, immorality, impropriety, lewdness. **2** *the men muttered obscenities:* **expletive**, swear word, oath, profanity, curse, four-letter word, dirty word, blasphemy; informal cuss; formal imprecation. **3** *the obscenity of* *the arms trade:* **scandal**, outrage, immorality.

obscure adjective **1** *his origins remain obscure:* **unclear**, uncertain, unknown, mysterious, hazy, vague, indeterminate. **2** *obscure references to Proust:* **cryptic**, oblique, opaque, elliptical, unintelligible, incomprehensible, impenetrable, unfathomable; recondite, arcane, esoteric. **3** *an obscure Peruvian painter:* **little known**, unknown, unheard of; unsung, unrecognized, forgotten.
– OPPOSITES clear, plain, famous.
• verb **1** *clouds obscured the sun:* **hide**, conceal, cover, veil, shroud, screen, mask, cloak, block, obliterate, eclipse. **2** *recent events have obscured the issue:* **confuse**, complicate, obfuscate, cloud, blur, muddy.
– OPPOSITES reveal, clarify.

obscurity noun **insignificance**, inconspicuousness, unimportance, anonymity; limbo, twilight, oblivion.
– OPPOSITES fame.

obsequious adjective **servile**, ingratiating, sycophantic, fawning, unctuous, oily, grovelling, cringing, subservient, submissive, slavish; informal slimy, bootlicking, smarmy.
– OPPOSITES rebellious.

observable adjective **noticeable**, visible, perceptible, perceivable, detectable, distinguishable, discernible, recognizable.

observance noun **compliance**, adherence, accordance, respect, observation, fulfilment, obedience; keeping, obeying.

observant adjective **alert**, sharp-eyed, sharp, eagle-eyed, keen-eyed, watchful; informal beady-eyed, not missing a trick, on the ball.
– OPPOSITES inattentive.

observation noun **1** *detailed observation of their behaviour:* **monitoring**, watching, scrutiny, survey, surveillance, attention, study. **2** *his observations were correct:* **remark**, comment; opinion, impression, thought, reflection.

observe verb **1** *she observed that he was drunk:* **notice**, see, note, perceive, discern, spot. **2** *he had been observing her:* **watch**, look at, contemplate, view, survey, regard, keep an eye on, scrutinize, keep under observation/surveillance, keep watch on, monitor; informal keep tabs on, keep a beady eye on. **3** *'You look tired,' she observed:* **remark**, comment, say, mention, declare, announce, state, pronounce. **4** *they agreed to observe the ceasefire:* **comply with**, abide by, keep, obey, adhere to, heed, honour, fulfil, respect, follow, consent to, accept.

observer noun **1** *the casual observer:* **spectator**, onlooker, watcher, fly on the wall, viewer, witness. **2** *industry observers are worried:* **commentator**, reporter; monitor.

obsess verb **1** *it obsessed him for years:* **preoccupy**, prey on someone's mind, possess, haunt, consume, plague, torment, hound, bedevil, take over, eat up, grip. **2** *stop obsessing about it:* **worry**, go on, dwell, brood.

obsessed adjective **fixated**, possessed, consumed; infatuated, besotted; informal smitten, hung up; N. Amer. informal hipped.

obsession noun **fixation**, passion, mania, compulsion, preoccupation, infatuation, addiction, fetish, craze; hobby horse; phobia, complex, neurosis; informal bee in your bonnet, hang-up, thing.

obsessive adjective **consuming**, compulsive, controlling, fanatical, neurotic, excessive; informal pathological.

obsolescent adjective **dying out**, on the decline/wane, disappearing, moribund, out of date, outdated, old-fashioned, outmoded; informal on the way out.

obsolete adjective **out of date**, outdated, outmoded, old-fashioned, passé; superannuated, outworn, antiquated, antediluvian, anachronistic, discontinued, old, dated, archaic, ancient, fossilized, extinct, defunct, dead, bygone; informal out of the ark, prehistoric; Brit. informal past its sell-by date.
– OPPOSITES current, modern.

obstacle noun **barrier**, hurdle, stumbling block, obstruction, bar, block, impediment, hindrance, snag, catch, drawback, hitch, fly in the ointment, handicap, difficulty, problem, disadvantage; Brit. spanner in the works.
– OPPOSITES advantage, aid.

obstinacy noun **stubbornness**, inflexibility, intransigence, pig-headedness, wilfulness, recalcitrance, implacability; persistence, tenacity, doggedness.

obstinate adjective **stubborn**, unyielding, inflexible, unbending, intransigent, intractable, obdurate, stubborn as a mule, pig-headed, self-willed, headstrong, stiff-necked, uncompromising, implacable, immovable, unshakeable; persistent, tenacious, dogged.
– OPPOSITES compliant.

obstreperous adjective **unruly**, disorderly, rowdy, disruptive, difficult, riotous, wild, turbulent, boisterous; noisy, loud; informal rumbustious; Brit. informal stroppy, bolshie; N. Amer. informal rambunctious.
– OPPOSITES quiet, restrained.

obstruct verb **1** *ensure that vents are not obstructed:* **block**, clog up, cut off, bung up, choke, dam up; technical occlude. **2** *he was obstructing the traffic:* **hold up**, bring to a standstill, stop, halt, block. **3** *they may obstruct aid distribution:* **impede**, hinder, interfere with, hamper, block, interrupt, hold up, stand in the way of, frustrate, sabotage; slow down, delay, stonewall, stop, halt, restrict, limit, curb.
– OPPOSITES clear, facilitate.

obstruction noun **obstacle**, barrier, stumbling block, impediment, hindrance, difficulty, check, restriction; blockage, stoppage, congestion, bottleneck, hold-up; Medicine occlusion.

obstructive adjective **unhelpful**, uncooperative, awkward, difficult, perverse, contrary; Brit. informal bloody-minded, bolshie; N. Amer. informal balky.
– OPPOSITES helpful.

obtain verb **get**, acquire, come by, secure, procure, pick up, be given; gain, earn, achieve, attain; informal get hold of, get/lay your hands on, land.
– OPPOSITES lose.

obtainable adjective **available**, to be had, in circulation, on the market, on offer, in season, at your disposal, at hand, accessible; informal up for grabs, on tap, get-at-able.

obtrusive adjective **conspicuous**, prominent, noticeable, obvious, unmistakable, out of place; informal sticking out a mile, sticking out like a sore thumb.
– OPPOSITES inconspicuous.

obtuse adjective **stupid**, foolish, slow-witted, slow, unintelligent, simple-minded; informal dim, dim-witted, dense, dumb, slow on the uptake, half-witted, brain-dead, moronic, cretinous, thick, dopey, dozy; Brit. informal divvy; Scottish & N. English informal glaikit; N. Amer. informal dumb-ass, chowderheaded.
– OPPOSITES clever.

obviate verb **preclude**, prevent, remove, get rid of, do away with, get round, rule out, eliminate.

obvious adjective **clear**, crystal clear, plain, evident, apparent, manifest, patent, conspicuous, pronounced, transparent, palpable, prominent, marked, decided, distinct, noticeable, perceptible, visible, discernible; informal as plain as the nose on your face, sticking out like a sore thumb, sticking out a mile.
– OPPOSITES imperceptible.

obviously adverb **clearly**, evidently, plainly, patently, visibly, discernibly, manifestly, noticeably; of course, naturally, needless to say, it goes without saying.
– OPPOSITES perhaps.

O

occasion noun **1** *a previous occasion:* **time**, instance, juncture, point, episode, experience; situation, case, circumstance. **2** *a special occasion:* **event**, affair, function, celebration, party, get-together, gathering; informal do, bash.
■ **on occasion**. See OCCASIONALLY.

occasional adjective **infrequent**, intermittent, irregular, periodic, sporadic, odd; N. Amer. sometime.
– OPPOSITES regular, frequent.

occasionally adverb **sometimes**, from time to time, now and then, now and again, at times, every so often, once in a while, on occasion, periodically, at intervals, intermittently, on and off, off and on.
– OPPOSITES often.

occult adjective **supernatural**, magic, magical, satanic, mystical; psychic.
■ **the occult** the supernatural, magic, black magic, witchcraft, necromancy, the black arts,

occultism, devil worship, satanism, Wicca, voodoo, white magic; NZ makutu.

occupancy noun **occupation**, tenancy, residence, residency, inhabitation, habitation, living, owner-occupancy; formal dwelling.

occupant noun **resident**, inhabitant, owner, householder, tenant, leaseholder, lessee; Brit. occupier, owner-occupier.

occupation noun **1** *his father's occupation:* **job**, profession, work, line of work, trade, employment, business, career, métier, vocation, calling, craft; Austral. informal grip. **2** *a property suitable for immediate occupation:* **residence**, residency, habitation, inhabitation, occupancy, tenancy, living in. **3** *the Roman occupation of Britain:* **conquest**, capture, invasion, seizure; colonization, rule, control.

occupational adjective **job-related**, work, professional, vocational, employment, business, career.

occupied adjective **1** *tasks which kept her occupied:* **busy**, working, at work, active; informal tied up, hard at it, on the go. **2** *the table was occupied:* **in use**, full, engaged, taken. **3** *only two flats are occupied:* **inhabited**, lived-in.
– OPPOSITES free, vacant.

O

occupy verb **1** *Carol occupied the basement flat:* **live in**, inhabit, lodge in; move into; people, populate, settle; Scottish stay in. **2** *he occupies a post at the Treasury:* **hold**, fill, have; informal hold down. **3** *something to occupy my mind:* **engage**, busy, distract, absorb, engross, preoccupy, hold, interest, involve, entertain. **4** *the region was occupied by Japan:* **capture**, seize, conquer, invade, take over, overrun, colonize, annex, subjugate.

occur verb **1** *an accident occurred at 3.30:* **happen**, take place, come about; N. Amer. informal go down. **2** *the disease occurs in the tropics:* **be found**, be present, exist, appear. **3** *an idea occurred to her:* **enter your head/mind**, cross your mind, come/spring to mind, strike one, hit one, come to one, dawn on one, suggest itself.

occurrence noun **1** *a rare occurrence:* **event**, incident, happening, phenomenon. **2** *the occurrence of cancer:* **existence**, instance, appearance; frequency, incidence, rate, prevalence; Statistics distribution.

ocean noun **the sea**; informal the drink; Brit. informal the briny; literary the deep, the waves.

> **WORD LINKS**
> **marine**, **maritime**, **oceanic**, **pelagic**, **thalassic** relating to the ocean

odd adjective **1** *an odd man:* **strange**, peculiar, queer, funny, bizarre, eccentric, unusual, weird, unconventional, quirky, zany; informal wacky, kooky, screwy, offbeat, off the wall. **2** *some odd things had happened:* **strange**, unusual, peculiar, funny, curious, weird, bizarre, uncanny, queer, unexpected, abnormal, atypical, anomalous, different, puzzling, mystifying, baffling, unaccountable. **3** *we have the odd drink together | he does odd jobs for friends:* **occasional**, casual, irregular, isolated, sporadic, periodic; miscellaneous, various, varied, sundry. **4** *odd shoes:* **mismatched**, unmatched, unpaired; single, lone, solitary, extra, leftover.
– OPPOSITES normal, ordinary, regular.

oddity noun **1** *she was a bit of an oddity:* **eccentric**, crank, misfit, maverick, nonconformist, individualist; informal character, oddball, weirdo; N. Amer. informal kook. **2** *the oddities of human nature:* **peculiarity**, idiosyncrasy, eccentricity, quirk, twist.

oddments plural noun **1** *oddments of material:* **scraps**, remnants, odds and ends, bits, pieces, bits and bobs, leftovers, fragments, snippets, offcuts. **2** *a cellar full of oddments.* See **ODDS AND ENDS** at **ODDS**.

odds plural noun *the odds are that he is still alive:* **likelihood**, probability, chances.
■ **at odds 1** *he was at odds with his colleagues:* in conflict, in disagreement, at loggerheads, quarrelling, arguing; N. Amer. on the outs. **2** *behaviour at odds with the interests of the company:* at variance, conflicting, contrary,

incompatible, inconsistent, irreconcilable. **odds and ends** bits and pieces, bits and bobs, bits, pieces, stuff, paraphernalia, things, sundries, bric-a-brac, knick-knacks, oddments; informal junk; Brit. informal odds and sods, clobber, gubbins.

odious adjective **revolting**, repulsive, repellent, repugnant, disgusting, offensive, objectionable, vile, foul, abhorrent, loathsome, nauseating, sickening, hateful, detestable, abominable, monstrous, appalling, insufferable, intolerable, despicable, contemptible, unspeakable, atrocious, awful, terrible, dreadful, frightful, obnoxious, unpleasant, disagreeable, nasty; informal ghastly, horrible, horrid, God-awful; Brit. informal beastly.
– OPPOSITES delightful.

odour noun **smell**, stench, stink, reek, effluvium; Brit. informal pong, whiff, niff, hum; N. Amer. informal funk; literary miasma.

odyssey noun **journey**, voyage, trek, travels, quest, crusade, pilgrimage.

off adjective **1** *Kate's off today:* **away**, absent, off duty, on holiday, on leave; free; N. Amer. on vacation. **2** *the game's off:* **cancelled**, postponed, called off. **3** *the fish was off:* **rotten**, bad, stale, mouldy, sour, rancid, turned, spoiled.
■ **off and on** periodically, at intervals, on and off, once in a while, every so often, now and then, now and again, from time to time, occasionally, sometimes, intermittently, irregularly.

offbeat adjective (informal) **unconventional**, unorthodox, unusual, eccentric, idiosyncratic, strange, bizarre, weird, peculiar, odd, freakish, outlandish, out of the ordinary, Bohemian, alternative, left-field, zany, quirky; informal wacky, freaky, way-out, off the wall, kooky, oddball.
– OPPOSITES conventional.

off colour adjective **1** (Brit.) *I'm feeling a bit off colour:* **unwell**, ill, poorly, out of sorts, not yourself, sick, queasy, nauseous, peaky, run down, washed out, below par; informal under the weather, rough; Brit. informal ropy, off; Scottish informal wabbit, peely-wally; Austral./NZ informal crook. **2** *off-colour jokes:* **smutty**, dirty, rude, crude, suggestive, indecent, indelicate, risqué, racy, bawdy, naughty, blue, vulgar, ribald, coarse; informal raunchy; Brit. informal fruity, saucy; euphemistic adult.
– OPPOSITES well.

offence noun **1** *he has committed an offence:* **crime**, illegal/unlawful act, misdemeanour, breach of the law, felony, infringement. **2** *an offence to natural justice:* **affront**, slap in the face, insult, outrage, violation. **3** *I do not want to cause offence:* **annoyance**, resentment, indignation, displeasure, hard/bad/ill feelings, animosity.
■ **take offence** be offended, take exception, take something personally, take something amiss, get upset/annoyed/angry; Brit. informal get the hump.

offend verb **1** *I'm sorry if I offended him:* **upset**, annoy, insult, affront, displease, outrage, distress, injure, hurt, wound; Brit. rub up the wrong way. **2** *criminals who offend repeatedly:* **break the law**, commit a crime, do wrong.

offended adjective **affronted**, insulted, aggrieved, displeased, upset, hurt, wounded, put out, indignant.
– OPPOSITES pleased.

offender noun **wrongdoer**, criminal, lawbreaker, miscreant, felon, delinquent, culprit, guilty party; formal malefactor.

offensive adjective **1** *offensive remarks:* **insulting**, rude, derogatory, disrespectful, personal, hurtful, wounding, abusive; formal exceptionable. **2** *an offensive smell:* **unpleasant**, disagreeable, nasty, distasteful, objectionable, off-putting, awful, terrible, dreadful, frightful, obnoxious, abominable, disgusting, repulsive, repellent, vile, foul, sickening, nauseating; informal ghastly, horrible, horrid, gross, God-awful; Brit. informal beastly.
– OPPOSITES complimentary, pleasant.
• noun *a military offensive:* **attack**, assault, onslaught, drive, invasion, push, thrust, charge, sortie, sally, foray, raid, incursion, blitz, campaign.

offer verb **1** *he offered a suggestion:* **put forward**, proffer, give, present, come up with, suggest, propose, advance, submit, tender. **2** *she offered to help:* **volunteer**, step/come forward, show willing. **3** *he offered $200:* **bid**, tender, put in a bid/offer of. **4** *a job offering good prospects:* **provide**, afford, supply, give, furnish, present, hold out. **5** *she offered no resistance:* **attempt**, try, give, show, express.
– OPPOSITES withdraw, refuse.
• noun **1** *offers of help:* **proposal**, proposition, suggestion, submission, approach, overture. **2** *the highest offer:* **bid**, tender.

offering noun **contribution**, donation.

offhand adjective **casual**, careless, uninterested, unconcerned, indifferent, cool, nonchalant, blasé, insouciant, cavalier, glib, perfunctory, cursory, dismissive; informal couldn't-care-less, take-it-or-leave-it.
• adverb **on the spur of the moment**, without consideration, spontaneously; informal off the cuff, off the top of your head, just like that.

office noun **1** *we met at her office:* **place of work**, place of business, workplace, workroom. **2** *the company's Paris office:* **branch**, division, section, bureau, department. **3** *the office of President:* **post**, position, appointment, job, occupation, role, situation, function, capacity.

O

officer noun **1** *officers and men:* **army officer**. **2** *all officers carry warrant cards.* See POLICE OFFICER. **3** *the officers of the society:* **official**, office-holder, committee member, board member.

official adjective **1** *an official inquiry:* **authorized**, approved, validated, authenticated, certified, accredited, endorsed, sanctioned, licensed, recognized, legitimate, legal, lawful, valid, bona fide, proper; informal kosher. **2** *an official function:* **ceremonial**, formal, solemn; bureaucratic.
– OPPOSITES unauthorized, informal.
• noun *a union official:* **officer**, administrator, executive, functionary; bureaucrat, mandarin; representative, agent; derogatory apparatchik.

officiate verb **be in charge of**, take charge of, preside over; oversee, superintend, supervise, conduct, run.

officious adjective **self-important**, bumptious, self-assertive, overbearing, interfering, intrusive, meddlesome, meddling; informal bossy.
– OPPOSITES self-effacing.

off-key adjective **out of tune**, flat, tuneless, discordant.
– OPPOSITES harmonious.

offload verb **1** *the cargo was being offloaded:* **unload**, remove, empty out, tip out. **2** *he offloaded 5,000 of the shares:* **dispose of**, dump, jettison, get rid of, transfer, shift; palm off, foist, fob off.

off-putting adjective **1** *an off-putting aroma:* **unpleasant**, unattractive, disagreeable, offensive, distasteful, unappetizing, objectionable, nasty, disgusting, repellent; informal horrid, horrible. **2** *her manner was most off-putting:* **discouraging**, disheartening, daunting, disconcerting, unnerving, unsettling.

offset verb **counterbalance**, balance out, cancel out, even out/up, counteract, countervail, neutralize, compensate for, make up for.

offshoot noun **outcome**, result, effect, consequence, upshot, product, by-product, spin-off, development, ramification.

offspring noun **children**, sons and daughters, progeny, youngsters, babies, infants, brood; descendants, heirs, successors; Law issue; informal kids; Brit. informal sprogs, brats; derogatory spawn.

often adverb **frequently**, many times, on many/numerous occasions, a lot, as often as not, repeatedly, again and again; regularly, routinely, usually, habitually, commonly, generally, in many cases/instances, ordinarily; N. Amer. oftentimes.
– OPPOSITES seldom.

ogle verb **leer at**, stare at, eye, make eyes at; informal eye up; Austral./NZ informal perv on.

ogre noun **monster**, **brute**, fiend,

beast, barbarian, savage, animal, tyrant, bogeyman.

oily adjective **1** *oily substances:* **greasy**, oleaginous; technical sebaceous; formal pinguid. **2** *oily food:* **greasy**, fatty, buttery. **3** *an oily man:* **unctuous**, ingratiating, smooth-talking, fulsome, flattering; obsequious, sycophantic; informal smarmy, slimy.

ointment noun **lotion**, cream, salve, liniment, embrocation, rub, gel, balm, emollient, unguent.

OK, okay (informal) exclamation *OK, I'll go with him:* **all right**, right, right then, right you are, very well, very good, fine; informal okey-doke(y); Brit. informal righto, righty-ho.
• adjective **1** *the film was OK:* **satisfactory**, all right, acceptable, competent; adequate, tolerable, passable, reasonable, fair, decent, not bad, average, middling, moderate, unremarkable, unexceptional; informal so-so, fair-to-middling. **2** *she's feeling OK now:* **fine**, all right, well, better. **3** *is it OK for me to come?* **permissible**, allowable, acceptable, all right, in order, permitted, fitting, suitable, appropriate.
– OPPOSITES unsatisfactory, ill.
• noun *he's given me the OK:* **authorization**, approval, seal of approval, agreement, consent, assent, permission, endorsement, ratification, sanction, confirmation, blessing, leave; informal the go-ahead, the green light, the thumbs up, say-so.
– OPPOSITES refusal.
• verb *the move must be OK'd by the president:* **authorize**, approve, agree to, consent to, sanction, pass, ratify, endorse, allow, give something the nod; informal give the go-ahead, give the green light, give the thumbs up; formal accede to.
– OPPOSITES refuse, veto.

old adjective **1** *old people:* **elderly**, aged, older, senior, advanced in years, venerable; in your dotage, long in the tooth, grey-haired, grizzled, past your prime, ancient, decrepit, doddery, senescent, senile, superannuated; informal getting on, past it, over the hill. **2** *old farm buildings:* **dilapidated**, broken-down, run down, tumbledown, ramshackle, decaying, crumbling, disintegrating. **3** *old clothes:* **worn**, worn out, shabby, threadbare, frayed, patched, tattered, moth-eaten, ragged; old-fashioned, out of date, outmoded; cast-off, hand-me-down; informal tatty. **4** *old cars:* **antique**, veteran, vintage, classic. **5** *she's old for her years:* **mature**, wise, sensible, experienced, worldly-wise. **6** *the old days:* **bygone**, past, former, olden, of old, previous, early, earlier, earliest. **7** *the same old phrases:* **hackneyed**, banal, trite, overused, overworked, tired, worn out, stale, clichéd, stock; informal corny. **8** *an old girlfriend:* **former**, previous, ex-, one-time, sometime, erstwhile.
– OPPOSITES young, new, modern.
■ **old age** age, declining years, advanced years, senescence, senility, dotage. **old person** senior citizen, senior, pensioner, OAP, elder; crone; N. Amer. golden ager; informal old stager, old-timer, oldie, wrinkly, crumbly, greybeard, old biddy; N. Amer. informal oldster, woopie; old use beldam.

WORD LINKS
geriatric relating to old people or old age
geriatrics the branch of medicine concerning old people
gerontology the scientific study of old age

old-fashioned adjective **out of date**, outdated, dated, outmoded, unfashionable, passé, frumpy; outworn, old, behind the times, archaic, obsolescent, obsolete, ancient, antiquated, superannuated, defunct; medieval, prehistoric, antediluvian, old-fogeyish, backward-looking, quaint, anachronistic, fusty, moth-eaten, olde worlde; informal old hat, square, out of the ark; N. Amer. informal horse-and-buggy, clunky.
– OPPOSITES modern.

old-time adjective **former**, bygone, past, old-fashioned; traditional, folk, old-world, quaint.
– OPPOSITES modern.

omen noun **portent**, sign, signal, token, forewarning, warning, harbinger, auspice, presage, indication; literary foretoken.

O

ominous adjective **threatening**, menacing, baleful, forbidding, sinister; black, dark, gloomy.
– OPPOSITES promising.

omission noun **1** *the omission of certain news items:* **exclusion**, leaving out. **2** *I regret any omission on my part:* **negligence**, neglect, dereliction, oversight, lapse, failure.

omit verb **1** *they omitted his name from the list:* **leave out**, exclude, leave off, miss out, miss, cut. **2** *I omitted to mention this:* **forget**, neglect, fail.
– OPPOSITES add, include, remember.

omnipotence noun **supremacy**, all-powerfulness, pre-eminence, supreme power; invincibility.

omnipotent adjective **all-powerful**, almighty, supreme, pre-eminent; invincible.

omnipresent adjective **ubiquitous**, all-pervasive, everywhere; rife, pervasive, prevalent.

omniscient adjective **all-knowing**, all-seeing.

on adjective *the computer's on:* **functioning**, working, in use, operating, online, up, running.
– OPPOSITES off.
■ **on and off** periodically, at intervals, off and on, once in a while, every so often, now and then, now and again, from time to time, occasionally, sometimes, intermittently, irregularly.

O

once adverb *they were friends once:* **formerly**, previously, in the past, at one time, at one point, once upon a time, in days/times gone by, in the old days, long ago; literary in days/times of yore.
■ **at once 1** *we must leave at once:* immediately, right away, right now, this moment/second/minute, now, straight away, instantly, directly, forthwith, without delay/hesitation, without further ado; quickly, as fast as possible, as soon as possible, asap. **2** *they all spoke at once:* at the same time, together, simultaneously; as a group, in unison. **once and for all** conclusively, decisively, finally, positively, definitely, definitively, irrevocably; for good, for always, forever, permanently. **once in a while** occasionally, from time to time, every now and then/again, every so often, on occasion, at times, sometimes, off and on, at intervals, periodically, sporadically, intermittently.

oncoming adjective **approaching**, advancing.

one cardinal number **1 unit**, item; technical monad. **2** *only one person came:* **a single**, a solitary, a sole, a lone. **3** *her one concern:* **only**, single, solitary, sole. **4** *they have become one:* **united**, a unit, amalgamated, consolidated, integrated, combined, incorporated, allied, affiliated, linked, joined, unified, in league, in partnership; wedded, married.

onerous adjective **burdensome**, arduous, strenuous, difficult, hard, severe, heavy, back-breaking, oppressive, weighty, exhausting, tiring, taxing, demanding, punishing, gruelling.
– OPPOSITES easy.

one-sided adjective **1** *a one-sided account:* **biased**, prejudiced, partisan, partial, slanted, unfair. **2** *a one-sided game:* **unequal**, uneven, unbalanced.
– OPPOSITES impartial.

one-time adjective **former**, ex-, old, previous, sometime, erstwhile.

ongoing adjective **1** *negotiations are ongoing:* **in progress**, under way, going on, continuing, proceeding. **2** *an ongoing struggle:* **continuous**, continuing, non-stop, constant, ceaseless, unceasing, unending, endless, never-ending, unremitting.

onlooker noun **eyewitness**, witness, observer, spectator, bystander; sightseer; informal rubberneck.

only adverb **1** *there's only enough for two:* **at most**, at best, just, no/not more than. **2** *this is for your eyes only:* **exclusively**, solely. **3** *you're only saying that:* **merely**, simply, just.
• adjective *their only son:* **sole**, single, one, solitary, lone, unique; exclusive.

onset noun **start**, beginning, commencement, arrival, appearance, inception, day one; outbreak.
– OPPOSITES end.

onslaught noun **assault**, attack, offensive, advance, charge, rush, foray, push, thrust, drive, blitz, bombardment, barrage.

onus noun **burden**, responsibility, obligation, duty, weight, load, charge.

ooze verb **1** *blood oozed from the wound:* **seep**, discharge, flow, exude, trickle, drip, dribble, issue, leak, drain, bleed. **2** *she was positively oozing charm:* **exude**, gush, drip, emanate, radiate.

opaque adjective **1** *opaque glass:* **non-transparent**, cloudy, filmy, blurred, smeared, misty. **2** *opaque language:* **obscure**, unclear, unfathomable, incomprehensible, unintelligible, impenetrable; informal as clear as mud.
–OPPOSITES transparent, clear.

open adjective **1** *the door's open:* **unlocked**, off the latch, ajar. **2** *a silk shirt, open at the neck:* **unfastened**, undone, unbuttoned, unzipped; gaping, yawning. **3** *the roads are open:* **clear**, passable, navigable. **4** *open countryside | open spaces:* **unenclosed**, rolling, sweeping, exposed; spacious, uncluttered; undeveloped. **5** *the bank isn't open:* **trading**, working, in operation. **6** *the position is still open:* **available**, vacant, free, unfilled; informal up for grabs. **7** *she was very open about her feelings:* **frank**, candid, honest, forthcoming, communicative, forthright, direct, unreserved, plain-spoken, outspoken; informal upfront. **8** *open hostility:* **overt**, manifest, palpable, conspicuous, plain, undisguised, unconcealed, clear, naked; blatant, flagrant, barefaced, brazen. **9** *I'm always open to suggestions:* **receptive**, amenable, responsive. **10** *what other options are open to us?* **available**, accessible, on hand, on offer. **11** *the system is open to abuse:* **vulnerable**, subject, susceptible, liable, exposed.
–OPPOSITES shut.
• verb **1** *she opened the front door:* **unfasten**, unlock; throw wide. **2** *Katherine opened the parcel:* **unwrap**, undo, untie. **3** *he opened the map:* **spread out**, unfold, unfurl, unroll, straighten out. **4** *the prime minister opened the meeting:* **begin**, start, commence, initiate, set in motion, get going, get under way, get off the ground; informal kick off.
–OPPOSITES close, shut.

WORD LINKS
agoraphobia fear of open spaces

open air adjective **outdoor**, out-of-doors, outside, alfresco.
–OPPOSITES indoor.

opening noun **1** *an opening in the roof:* **hole**, gap, aperture, orifice, vent, crack, slit, chink; spyhole, peephole. **2** *United created openings but were unable to score:* **opportunity**, chance, window, possibility. **3** *the opening of the session:* **beginning**, start, commencement, outset; informal kick-off. **4** *a gallery opening:* **launch**, inauguration; opening/first night, premiere.

openly adverb **1** *drugs were openly on sale:* **publicly**, blatantly, flagrantly, overtly. **2** *he spoke openly of his problems:* **frankly**, candidly, explicitly, honestly, sincerely, forthrightly, freely.
–OPPOSITES secretly.

open-minded adjective **unbiased**, unprejudiced, neutral, objective, disinterested; tolerant, liberal, permissive, broad-minded.
–OPPOSITES prejudiced, narrow-minded.

open-mouthed adjective **astounded**, amazed, stunned, staggered, thunderstruck, aghast, stupefied, shocked, speechless, dumbstruck; informal flabbergasted; Brit. informal gobsmacked.

operate verb **1** *he can operate the crane:* **work**, run, use, handle, control, manage; drive, steer, manoeuvre. **2** *the machine ceased to operate:* **function**, work, go, run. **3** *the way the law operates:* **take effect**, act, apply, work, function. **4** *we operated the mines until 1979:* **direct**, control, manage, run, be in control/charge of.

operation noun **1** *the sliders ensure smooth operation:* **functioning**, working, running, performance, action. **2** *the operation of the factory:* **management**, running, administration, supervision. **3** *a heart bypass operation:* **surgery**, surgical intervention. **4** *a military operation:* **action**, exercise, undertaking, enterprise, manoeuvre, campaign. **5** *their mining operation:*

business, enterprise, company, firm; informal outfit.
■ **in operation**. See OPERATIONAL.

operational adjective **up and running**, working, functioning, operative, in operation, in use, in action; in working order, serviceable, functional, usable.

operative adjective **1** *the steam railway is operative.* See OPERATIONAL. **2** *the operative word:* **key**, significant, relevant, crucial, critical.
• noun **1** *the operatives clean the machines:* **machinist**, operator, mechanic, engineer, worker, workman, hand. **2** *a CIA operative:* **agent**, spy, mole, plant; N. Amer. informal spook.

opiate noun **drug**, narcotic, sedative, anaesthetic, painkiller, analgesic; morphine, heroin, opium; informal dope.

opinion noun **belief**, judgement, thoughts, thinking, mind, view, viewpoint, point of view, position, standpoint.

opinionated adjective **dogmatic**, pushy.

opponent noun **rival**, adversary, competitor, enemy, antagonist, combatant, contender, challenger; literary foe.
– OPPOSITES ally, supporter.

opportune adjective **auspicious**, propitious, favourable, advantageous, felicitous; timely, convenient, suitable, appropriate, apt, fitting.
– OPPOSITES disadvantageous.

opportunism noun **expediency**, pragmatism; striking while the iron is hot, making hay while the sun shines.

opportunity noun **chance**; time, occasion, moment, opening, option, window, possibility, scope, freedom; informal shot, break, look-in.

oppose verb **be against**, object to, be hostile to, disagree with, dislike, disapprove of; resist, take a stand against, put up a fight against, fight, challenge; argue with/against; informal be anti.
– OPPOSITES support.

opposed adjective **1** *they are opposed to the nuclear power plants:* **against**, dead set against; averse, hostile, antagonistic, antipathetic, resistant; informal anti. **2** *their interests were opposed:* **conflicting**, contrasting, incompatible, irreconcilable, antithetical, contradictory, clashing, at variance, at odds, divergent, poles apart.

opposing adjective **1** *opposing points of view:* **conflicting**, contrasting, opposite, incompatible, irreconcilable, contradictory, antithetical, clashing, at variance, at odds, divergent, opposed. **2** *opposing sides:* **rival**, opposite, enemy. **3** *the opposing page:* **opposite**, facing.

opposite adjective **1** *they sat opposite each other:* **facing**, face to face with, across from. **2** *the opposite page:* **facing**, opposing. **3** *opposite views:* **conflicting**, contrasting, incompatible, irreconcilable, antithetical, contradictory, at variance, at odds, different, differing, divergent, opposing. **4** *opposite sides:* **rival**, opposing, enemy.
– OPPOSITES same.
• noun *the opposite was true:* **reverse**, converse, antithesis, contrary, inverse, obverse.

opposition noun **1** *the proposal met with opposition:* **resistance**, hostility, antagonism, antipathy, objection, dissent, disapproval. **2** *they beat the opposition:* **opponents**, opposing side, other side/team, competition, rivals, adversaries. **3** *the opposition between the public and the private :* **conflict**, clash, disparity, antithesis, polarity.

oppress verb **persecute**, tyrannize, crush, repress, subjugate, subdue, keep down.

oppressed adjective **persecuted**, downtrodden, abused, ill-treated, subjugated, tyrannized, repressed, subdued; disadvantaged, underprivileged.

oppression noun **persecution**, abuse, ill-treatment, tyranny, repression, suppression, subjection, subjugation; cruelty, brutality, injustice.

oppressive adjective **1** *an oppressive dictatorship:* **harsh**, cruel, brutal, repressive, tyrannical, despotic; ruthless, merciless, pitiless. **2** *an oppressive silence:* **overwhelming**, overpowering, unbearable,

unendurable, intolerable. **3** *it was overcast and oppressive:* **muggy**, close, heavy, hot, humid, sticky, airless, stuffy, stifling, sultry.
– OPPOSITES lenient.

oppressor noun **persecutor**, ruler.

opt verb **choose**, select, pick, decide on, go for, settle on, plump for.

optimism noun **hopefulness**, hope, confidence, buoyancy, positivity, positive attitude.
– OPPOSITES pessimism.

optimistic adjective **1** *she felt optimistic about the future:* **positive**, confident, hopeful, sanguine, bullish, buoyant; informal upbeat. **2** *the forecast is optimistic:* **encouraging**, promising, hopeful, reassuring, favourable.
– OPPOSITES pessimistic.

optimum adjective **best**, most favourable, most advantageous, ideal, perfect, prime, optimal.

option noun **choice**, alternative, possibility, course of action.

optional adjective **voluntary**, discretionary, non-compulsory.
– OPPOSITES compulsory.

opulence noun **luxuriousness**, sumptuousness, lavishness, richness, luxury, luxuriance, splendour, magnificence, grandeur, splendidness; informal plushness.
– OPPOSITES poverty.

opulent adjective **luxurious**, sumptuous, palatial, lavishly appointed, rich, splendid, magnificent, grand, grandiose, fancy; informal plush, swanky; Brit. informal swish; N. Amer. informal swank.
– OPPOSITES spartan.

opus noun **composition**, work, work of art, piece.

oral adjective **spoken**, verbal, unwritten, vocal, uttered, said.
– OPPOSITES written.
• noun **oral examination**; Brit. viva.

orator noun **speaker**, speech-maker, rhetorician.

orb noun **sphere**, globe, ball, circle.

orbit noun **course**, path, circuit, track, trajectory, rotation, revolution, circle.
• verb **revolve round**, circle round, go round, travel round.

orchestra noun **ensemble**; informal band.

orchestrate verb **1** *the piece was orchestrated by Mozart:* **arrange**, adapt, score. **2** *he orchestrated a campaign of civil disobedience:* **organize**, arrange, plan, set up, bring about, mobilize, mount, stage, mastermind, coordinate, direct, engineer.

ordain verb **1** *the decision to ordain women:* **consecrate**, appoint, anoint, invest, elect. **2** *the path ordained by God:* **predetermine**, predestine, preordain, determine, prescribe, designate.

ordeal noun **nightmare**, trial, trauma, hell, torture, torment, agony.

order noun **1** *alphabetical order:* **sequence**, arrangement, organization, system, series. **2** *order was eventually restored:* **peace**, control, orderliness, law and order, lawfulness, calm, peace and quiet; routine. **3** *I had to obey his orders:* **command**, instruction, directive, direction, decree, edict, injunction, dictate. **4** *the company has won the order:* **commission**, request, requisition. **5** *the established order:* **system**, hierarchy, pecking order. **6** *the lower orders of society:* **class**, level, rank, grade, caste. **7** *a religious order:* **community**, brotherhood. **8** *the Orange Order:* **organization**, association, society, fellowship, fraternity, lodge, guild, league, union, club. **9** *skills of a very high order:* **type**, kind, sort, nature, variety; quality, calibre, standard.
– OPPOSITES chaos.
• verb **1** *he ordered me to return:* **instruct**, command, direct, enjoin, tell; old use bid. **2** *he ordered that their assets be confiscated:* **decree**, ordain, rule. **3** *order your tickets by phone:* **request**, apply for; book, reserve. **4** *the messages are ordered chronologically:* **organize**, arrange, sort out, lay out; group, classify, categorize, catalogue.
■ **in order 1** *list the dates in order:* in sequence, in alphabetical order, in numerical order, in order of priority. **2** *everything is in order:* tidy, neat, orderly, straight, trim, shipshape, in apple-pie order; in position, in place. **3** *I think a drink would be in order:* appropriate, fitting, suitable, acceptable,

permissible, permitted, allowable; informal okay. **out of order 1** *the lift's out of order:* not working, broken, out of service, out of commission, inoperative; down; informal conked out, bust, kaput; N. Amer. informal on the fritz. **2** (Brit. informal) *that's really out of order:* unacceptable, unfair, unjust, unjustified, uncalled for, below the belt, unreasonable, unwarranted, beyond the pale.

orderly adjective **1** *an orderly room:* **neat**, tidy, well ordered, in order, trim, in apple-pie order, spick and span. **2** *the orderly presentation of information:* **well organized**, efficient, methodical, systematic, meticulous; coherent, structured, logical. **3** *the crowd was orderly:* **well behaved**, law-abiding, disciplined, peaceful, peaceable, non-violent.
– OPPOSITES untidy, disorganized, disorderly.

ordinarily adverb **usually**, normally, as a rule, generally, in general, for the most part, mainly, mostly, typically, commonly, routinely.

ordinary adjective **1** *the ordinary course of events:* **usual**, normal, standard, typical, common, customary, habitual, everyday, regular, routine, day-to-day. **2** *my life seemed very ordinary:* **average**, normal, run-of-the-mill, standard, typical, middle-of-the-road, conventional, unremarkable, unexceptional, workaday, undistinguished, nondescript, colourless, commonplace, humdrum, mundane, unmemorable, pedestrian, prosaic, uninteresting, uneventful, dull, boring, bland; informal bog-standard, nothing to write home about, no great shakes; Brit. informal common or garden; N. Amer. informal ornery.
– OPPOSITES unusual.

ordnance noun **guns**, cannon, artillery, weapons, arms; munitions.

organ noun *the official organ of the Communist Party:* **newspaper**, paper, journal, periodical, magazine, newsletter, mouthpiece.

organic adjective **1** *organic matter:* **living**, live, animate, biological. **2** *organic vegetables:* **pesticide-free**, additive-free, natural. **3** *an organic part of the drama:* **essential**, fundamental, integral, intrinsic, vital, indispensable, inherent. **4** *a society is an organic whole:* **structured**, organized, coherent, integrated, coordinated, ordered, harmonious.

organism noun **1** *fish and other organisms:* **living thing**, being, creature, animal, plant, life form. **2** *a complex political organism:* **structure**, system, organization, entity.

organization noun **1** *the organization of conferences:* **planning**, arrangement, coordination, organizing, running, management. **2** *the overall organization of the book:* **structure**, arrangement, plan, pattern, order, form, format, framework, composition, constitution. **3** *his lack of organization:* **efficiency**, order, orderliness, planning. **4** *a large organization:* **company**, firm, corporation, institution, group, consortium, conglomerate, agency, association, society; informal outfit.

organize verb **1** *you need to organize the information carefully:* **structure**, order, arrange, sort out, assemble, marshal, group, classify, collate, categorize, catalogue. **2** *they organized a search party:* **arrange**, coordinate, put together, fix up, set up, lay on, orchestrate, mobilize; take care of, deal with.

organized adjective **well ordered**, well run, well regulated, structured; orderly, efficient, neat, tidy, methodical; informal together.
– OPPOSITES inefficient, disorganized.

orgiastic adjective **debauched**, wild, riotous, wanton, dissolute, depraved.

orgy noun **1** *a drunken orgy:* **wild party**; informal binge, booze-up, bender; Brit. informal rave-up; N. Amer. informal toot. **2** *an orgy of violence:* **bout**, spree; informal binge.

orient, orientate verb **1** *she found it hard to orient herself:* **get/find your bearings**. **2** *you need to orientate yourself to your new life:* **adapt**, adjust, familiarize, acclimatize, accustom, attune. **3** *magazines oriented to the business community:* **aim**, direct, pitch, design, intend. **4** *the stones are oriented from north* *to south:* **align**, place, position, arrange.

orientation noun **1** *the orientation of the radar station:* **positioning**, location, position, situation, placement, alignment. **2** *the movement was broadly Marxist in orientation:* **attitude**, inclination; belief, view, outlook. **3** *orientation courses:* **induction**, training, initiation, briefing.

orifice noun **opening**, hole, aperture, slot, slit, cleft.

origin noun **1** *the origins of life:* **beginning**, start, genesis, birth, dawning, dawn, emergence, creation; source, basis, cause, roots. **2** *the origin of the word:* **source**, derivation, root, provenance, etymology; N. Amer. provenience. **3** *his Scottish origins:* **descent**, ancestry, parentage, pedigree, lineage, line, heritage, birth, extraction, family; roots.

original adjective **1** *the original inhabitants:* **indigenous**, native; first, earliest, early. **2** *an original Rembrandt:* **authentic**, genuine, actual, true, bona fide. **3** *a highly original film:* **innovative**, creative, imaginative, inventive; new, novel, fresh; unusual, unconventional, unorthodox, groundbreaking, pioneering, unique, distinctive. • noun **1** *a copy of the original:* **prototype**, source, master. **2** *he really is an original:* **individual**, eccentric, nonconformist, free spirit, maverick; informal character; Brit. informal one-off.

originality noun **inventiveness**, ingenuity, creativeness, creativity, innovation, novelty, freshness, imagination, individuality, unconventionality, uniqueness, distinctiveness.

originally adverb **at first**, in/at the beginning, to begin with, initially, in the first place, at the outset.

originate verb **1** *the disease originates from Africa:* **arise**, have its origin, begin, start, stem, spring, emerge, emanate. **2** *Bill originated the idea:* **invent**, create, initiate, devise, think up, dream up, conceive, formulate, form, develop, generate, engender, produce, mastermind, pioneer.

originator noun **inventor**, creator, architect, author, father, mother, initiator, innovator, founder, pioneer, mastermind.

ornament noun **knick-knack**, trinket, bauble; informal whatnot, doodah; N. Amer. informal tchotchke, kickshaw, bijou.

ornamental adjective **decorative**, fancy; ornate, ornamented.

ornamentation noun **decoration**, adornment, embellishment, ornament, trimming, accessories.

ornate adjective **1** *an ornate mirror:* **elaborate**, decorated, embellished, adorned, ornamented, fancy, fussy, ostentatious, showy; informal flash, flashy. **2** *ornate language:* **elaborate**, flowery, florid; grandiose, pompous, pretentious, high-flown, bombastic, overwrought, overblown; informal highfalutin.
– OPPOSITES plain.

orthodox adjective **conventional**, mainstream, conformist, established, traditional, traditionalist, prevalent, popular, conservative, unoriginal.
– OPPOSITES unconventional, unorthodox.

orthodoxy noun **conventionality**, conventionalism, conformism, conservatism, traditionalism, conformity.

oscillate verb **1** *the pendulum started to oscillate:* **swing**, sway. **2** *they oscillated between fear and bravery:* **waver**, swing, fluctuate, alternate, see-saw, yo-yo, sway, vacillate, hover; informal wobble.

ostensible adjective **apparent**, outward, superficial, professed, supposed, alleged, purported.
– OPPOSITES genuine.

ostensibly adverb **apparently**, seemingly, on the face of it, to all intents and purposes, outwardly, superficially, allegedly, supposedly, purportedly.

ostentation noun **showiness**, show, ostentatiousness, pretentiousness, vulgarity, conspicuousness, display, flamboyance, gaudiness, brashness, extravagance, ornateness, exhibitionism; informal flashiness, glitz, glitziness, ritziness.

ostentatious adjective **showy**,

pretentious, conspicuous, flamboyant, gaudy, brash, vulgar, loud, extravagant, fancy, ornate, overelaborate; informal flash, flashy, over the top, OTT, bling, glitzy, ritzy; N. Amer. informal superfly.
– OPPOSITES restrained.

ostracize verb **exclude**, shun, spurn, cold-shoulder, reject, shut out, ignore, snub, cut dead; blackball, blacklist; Brit. send to Coventry; informal freeze out; Brit. informal blank.
– OPPOSITES welcome.

other adjective **1** *these homes use other fuels:* **alternative**, different; various. **2** *are there any other questions?* **more**, further, additional, extra, added, supplementary.

other-worldly adjective **ethereal**, dreamy, dreamlike, spiritual, mystic, mystical; unearthly.

ounce noun **particle**, scrap, bit, speck, iota, jot, trace, atom, shred, crumb, fragment, grain, drop, spot; informal smidgen.

oust verb **drive out**, expel, force out, remove, eject, get rid of, depose, topple, unseat, overthrow, bring down, overturn, dismiss, dislodge, displace.

O

out adjective & adverb **1** *she's out at the moment:* **away**, elsewhere. **2** *the secret was out:* **revealed**, in the open, common knowledge. **3** *the roses are out:* **in flower**, flowering, in bloom, blooming, in blossom, blossoming. **4** *the book should be out soon:* **available**, obtainable, in the shops, published, in print. **5** (informal) *grunge is out:* **unfashionable**, out of fashion, dated, outdated, passé; informal old hat. **6** *smoking is out:* **forbidden**, not permitted, not allowed, unacceptable; informal not on. **7** *he was slightly out in his calculations:* **mistaken**, inaccurate, incorrect, wrong, in error.
– OPPOSITES in.
• verb (informal) *it was not our intention to out him:* **expose**, unmask.

out-and-out adjective **utter**, downright, thoroughgoing, absolute, complete, thorough, total, unmitigated, outright, real, perfect; N. Amer. full-bore; informal deep-dyed; Brit. informal right; Austral./NZ informal fair.
– OPPOSITES partial.

outbreak noun **1** *outbreaks of violence:* **eruption**, flare-up, upsurge, rash, wave, spate, burst, flurry. **2** *the outbreak of war:* **start**, beginning, commencement, onset.

outburst noun **eruption**, explosion, flare-up, flood, storm, outpouring, surge, fit.

outcast noun **pariah**, persona non grata, reject, outsider.

outclass verb **surpass**, be superior to, be better than, outshine, overshadow, eclipse, outdo, outplay, outstrip, get the better of, upstage; beat, defeat; informal be a cut above, be head and shoulders above, run rings round.

outcome noun **result**, consequence, net result, upshot, conclusion, issue.

outcry noun **protests**, protestations, complaints, objections, furore, fuss, commotion, uproar, outbursts, opposition, dissent; informal hullabaloo, ballyhoo, ructions, stink.

outdated adjective **old-fashioned**, out of date, outmoded, out of fashion, unfashionable, dated, passé, old, behind the times, obsolete, antiquated; informal out, old hat, square, out of the ark; N. Amer. informal horse-and-buggy, clunky.
– OPPOSITES modern.

outdistance verb **outrun**, outstrip, outpace, leave behind; overtake, pass.

outdo verb **surpass**, outshine, overshadow, eclipse, outclass, outmanoeuvre, get the better of, put in the shade, upstage; exceed, transcend, top, cap, beat, better, leave behind, get ahead of; informal be a cut above, be head and shoulders above, run rings round.

outdoor adjective **open air**, out-of-doors, outside, al fresco.
– OPPOSITES indoor.

outer adjective **outside**, outermost, outward, exterior, external, surface.
– OPPOSITES inner.

outface verb **stand up to**, face down.

outfit noun **1** *a new outfit:* **costume**, suit, uniform, ensemble, attire, clothes, clothing, dress, garb; informal get-up, gear, togs; Brit. informal kit, rig-out; formal apparel. **2** (informal) *a local manufacturing outfit:* **organization**, enterprise, company, firm, business; group, body, team; informal set-up. •verb *enough swords to outfit an army:* **equip**, kit out, fit out/up, rig out, supply, arm; dress, clothe, deck out.

outflow noun **discharge**, outflowing, outpouring, rush, flood, deluge, spurt, jet, cascade, stream, torrent, gush, outburst; flow.

outgoing adjective **1** *outgoing children:* **extrovert**, uninhibited, unreserved, demonstrative, affectionate, warm, sociable, convivial, lively, gregarious; communicative, responsive, open, forthcoming, frank. **2** *the outgoing president:* **departing**, retiring, leaving.
–OPPOSITES introverted, incoming.

outgoings plural noun **expenses**, expenditure, spending, outlay, payments, costs, overheads.

outgrowth noun **protuberance**, swelling, excrescence, growth, lump, bump, bulge.

outing noun **trip**, excursion, jaunt, expedition, day out, tour, drive, ride, run; informal junket, spin.

outlandish adjective **weird**, queer, far out, eccentric, unconventional, unorthodox, funny, bizarre, unusual, strange, peculiar, odd, curious; informal offbeat, off the wall, way-out, wacky, freaky, kinky, oddball.
–OPPOSITES ordinary.

outlast verb *the buildings outlasted generations of occupants:* **outlive**, survive; ride out, weather, withstand.

outlaw noun **fugitive**, wanted criminal; bandit, robber; dated desperado. •verb **ban**, bar, prohibit, forbid, veto, make illegal, proscribe.
–OPPOSITES permit.

outlay noun **expenditure**, expenses, spending, outgoings, payment, investment.
–OPPOSITES profit.

outlet noun **1** *a central-heating outlet:* **vent**, way out; outfall, opening, channel, conduit, duct. **2** *an outlet for farm produce:* **market**, retail outlet, shop, store. **3** *an outlet for their energies:* **means of expression**, means of release, vent, avenue, channel.

outline noun **1** *the outline of the building:* **silhouette**, profile, shape, contours, form, lines. **2** *an outline of our proposal:* **rough idea**, thumbnail sketch, rundown, summary, synopsis, résumé, precis; essence, main points, gist, bare bones. •verb *she outlined the plan briefly:* **rough out**, sketch out, map out, draft, give a rough idea of, summarize, precis.

outlive verb **outlast**, survive.

outlook noun **1** *a positive outlook:* **point of view**, viewpoint, way of thinking, perspective, attitude, standpoint, stance, frame of mind. **2** *a lovely open outlook:* **view**, vista, prospect, panorama. **3** *the outlook for the economy:* **prospects**, future.

outlying adjective **distant**, remote, out of the way, faraway, far-flung, inaccessible, off the beaten track.

outmanoeuvre verb **outwit**, outsmart, out-think, steal a march on, trick, get the better of.

outmoded adjective **out of date**, old-fashioned, outdated, dated, behind the times, antiquated, obsolete, passé, anachronistic; informal old hat.

out of date adjective **1** *the design is so out of date:* **old-fashioned**, outmoded, outdated, dated, old, passé, behind the times, obsolete, antiquated, anachronistic; informal old hat, out of the ark; N. Amer. informal horse-and-buggy, clunky. **2** *your ticket is out of date:* **expired**, lapsed, invalid, void.
–OPPOSITES fashionable, up to date, current.

out of the way adjective **outlying**, distant, remote, faraway, far-flung, isolated, lonely, godforsaken, inaccessible, off the beaten track.
–OPPOSITES accessible.

out of work adjective **unemployed**, jobless; redundant, laid off; Brit. informal on the dole; Austral. informal on the wallaby track.

outpouring noun **outflow**, outrush, rush, flood, deluge, jet, cascade, stream, torrent, gush, outburst, flow.

output noun **production**, yield, gross domestic product; work.

outrage noun **1** *public outrage:*

indignation, fury, anger, rage, wrath. **2** *it is an outrage:* **scandal**, offence, insult, affront, disgrace.
• verb *his remarks outraged everyone:* **enrage**, infuriate, incense, anger, scandalize, offend, affront, shock, horrify, disgust, appal.

outrageous adjective **1** *outrageous behaviour:* **shocking**, disgraceful, scandalous, atrocious, appalling, dreadful; attention-seeking, controversial. **2** *outrageous clothes:* **eye-catching**, flamboyant, showy, gaudy, ostentatious; informal saucy, flashy.

outright adverb **1** *he rejected the proposal outright:* **completely**, entirely, wholly, totally, categorically, absolutely, utterly, flatly, unreservedly, out of hand. **2** *I told her outright:* **explicitly**, directly, frankly, candidly, bluntly, plainly, in plain language, to someone's face, straight from the shoulder; Brit. informal straight up. **3** *they were killed outright:* **instantly**, instantaneously, immediately, at once, straight away, then and there, on the spot.
• adjective **1** *an outright lie:* **out-and-out**, absolute, complete, downright, utter, sheer, categorical. **2** *the outright winner:* **undisputed**, definite, unequivocal, clear, unmistakable.

outrun verb **outstrip**, outdistance, outpace, leave behind, lose; informal leave standing.

outset noun **start**, starting point, beginning; informal the word go.
– OPPOSITES end.

outshine verb **surpass**, overshadow, eclipse, outclass, put in the shade, beat, better; informal be a cut above, be head and shoulders above, run rings round.

outside noun *the outside of the building:* **outer/external surface**, exterior, case, skin, shell, covering, facade.
• adjective **1** *outside lights:* **exterior**, external, outer, outdoor, out-of-doors. **2** *outside contractors:* **independent**, freelance, casual, external.
• adverb *they went outside | shall we eat outside?* **outdoors**, out of doors, alfresco.
– OPPOSITES inside.

outsider noun **stranger**, visitor, non-member; foreigner, alien, immigrant, emigrant, émigré; incomer, newcomer.

outsize adjective **huge**, oversized, enormous, gigantic, great, giant, colossal, massive, mammoth, vast, immense, tremendous, monumental, prodigious, king-sized; informal mega, monster, whopping, humongous, jumbo, bumper; Brit. informal whacking great, ginormous.

outskirts plural noun **edges**, fringes, suburbs, suburbia.

outsmart verb **outwit**, outmanoeuvre, steal a march on, trick, get the better of; informal pull a fast one on, put one over on.

outspoken adjective **forthright**, direct, candid, frank, straightforward, open, straight from the shoulder, plain-spoken; blunt.

outspread adjective **outstretched**, spread out, unfolded, unfurled, wide open.

outstanding adjective **1** *an outstanding painter:* **excellent**, marvellous, magnificent, superb, fine, wonderful, superlative, exceptional, first-class, first-rate; informal great, terrific, tremendous, super, amazing, fantastic, sensational, fabulous, ace, cracking, A1, mean, awesome, out of this world; Brit. informal smashing, brilliant; N. Amer. informal neat; Austral. informal bonzer. **2** *how much work is still outstanding?* **to be done**, undone, unfinished, incomplete, remaining, pending. **3** *outstanding debts:* **unpaid**, unsettled, owing, owed, to be paid, payable, due, overdue; N. Amer. delinquent.

outstrip verb **1** *he outstripped the police cars:* **outrun**, outdistance, outpace, leave behind, lose; informal leave standing. **2** *demand far outstrips supply:* **surpass**, exceed, top, eclipse.

outward adjective **external**, outer, outside, exterior; surface, superficial, seeming, apparent, ostensible.
– OPPOSITES inward.

outwardly adverb **externally**, on the surface, superficially, on the face of it, to all intents and purposes, apparently, ostensibly, seemingly.

outweigh verb **be greater than**,

exceed, be superior to, prevail over, have the edge on/over, override, supersede, offset, cancel out, more than make up for, compensate for.

outwit verb **outsmart**, outmanoeuvre, steal a march on, trick, get the better of; informal pull a fast one on, put one over on.

outworn adjective **out of date**, outdated, old-fashioned, outmoded, dated, antiquated, obsolete, defunct.
– OPPOSITES up to date.

oval adjective **egg-shaped**, ovoid, elliptical.

ovation noun **round of applause**, cheers, bravos, acclaim, standing ovation; informal a big hand.

oven noun **stove**, cooker, microwave; rotisserie.

over preposition **1** *there was cloud over the hills:* **above**, on top of, atop, covering. **2** *over 2,000 people wrote in:* **more than**, above, in excess of, upwards of. **3** *he has three people over him:* **superior to**, above, higher up than, in charge of, responsible for. **4** *an argument over money:* **on the subject of**, about, concerning, regarding.
– OPPOSITES under.
• adverb *the relationship is over:* **at an end**, finished, concluded, terminated, ended, no more, a thing of the past.
■ **over and above** in addition to, on top of, plus, as well as, besides, along with. **over and over** repeatedly, again and again, time and time again, many times, frequently, constantly, continually, persistently, ad nauseam.

overact verb **exaggerate**, overdo it, overplay it; informal ham it up, camp it up.

overall adjective *the overall cost:* **total**, all-inclusive, gross, final, inclusive.
• adverb *overall, things are better:* **generally**, in general, altogether, all in all, on balance, on average, for the most part, in the main, on the whole, by and large, to a large extent.

overawe verb **intimidate**, daunt, cow, disconcert, unnerve, subdue, dismay, frighten, alarm, scare; informal psych out.

overbalance verb **fall over**, topple over, lose your balance, tip over.

overbearing adjective **domineering**, dominating, autocratic, tyrannical, despotic, oppressive, high-handed, bullying; informal bossy.

overblown adjective **florid**, grandiose, pompous, flowery, overwrought, pretentious, high-flown; informal highfalutin.

overcast adjective **cloudy**, dull, grey, leaden, dark, black, heavy, murky.
– OPPOSITES sunny, bright.

overcharge verb **swindle**, charge too much, cheat, defraud, fleece, short-change; informal rip off, sting, screw, rob, diddle, do; N. Amer. informal gouge.

overcome verb *an experienced England side overcame the home team:* **defeat**, beat, get the better of, triumph over, conquer, overwhelm, overpower, prevail over, outclass; control, master, subdue; informal lick, best; literary vanquish.
• adjective **overwhelmed**, moved, affected, speechless.
■ **overcome by** overwhelm, overpower, asphyxiate, render unconscious, suffocate, poison.

overconfident adjective **cocksure**, cocky, smug, conceited, self-assured, brash, blustering, overbearing; informal too big for your boots.

O

overcritical adjective **fault-finding**, hypercritical, hair-splitting, overparticular; fussy, finicky, fastidious, pedantic, overscrupulous; informal nit-picking, pernickety.

overcrowded adjective **overfull**, overflowing, full to overflowing/bursting, crammed full, congested, overpopulated, crowded, swarming, teeming; informal bursting/bulging at the seams, full to the gunwales, jam-packed.
– OPPOSITES empty.

overdo verb *she overdoes the love scenes:* **exaggerate**, overplay, overact, overdramatize, overstate, overemphasize; informal go overboard with.
– OPPOSITES understate.
■ **overdo it** work too hard, overwork, burn the candle at both ends, run yourself into the ground, wear yourself to a shadow, wear yourself out, strain yourself; informal kill yourself, knock yourself out.

overdue adjective **1** *the ship is overdue:* **late**, behind schedule, behind time, delayed. **2** *overdue payments:* **unpaid**, unsettled, owing, owed, payable, due, outstanding, undischarged; N. Amer. delinquent.
– OPPOSITES early, punctual.

overeat verb **eat too much**, gorge yourself, overindulge, feast, gourmandize; informal binge, make a pig of yourself, pig out; N. Amer. informal scarf out.

overemphasize verb **overstress**, exaggerate, make too much of, overplay, overdo; informal make a big thing about/of, blow up out of all proportion.
– OPPOSITES understate, play down.

overflow verb **spill over**, flow over, brim over, well over, flood.
• noun **surplus**, excess, additional people/things, extra people/things, remainder, overspill.

overflowing adjective **overfull**, full to overflowing/bursting, spilling over, running over, crammed full, overcrowded, overloaded; informal bursting/bulging at the seams, jam-packed.
– OPPOSITES empty.

overhaul verb **1** *the government planned to overhaul the tax system:* **improve**, reorganize, reform; modernize, upgrade, update; reshape, remodel, revamp, rebuild. **2** *the engine had been overhauled:* **service**, repair, mend, fix up, recondition.
• noun *a complete overhaul of the banking system:* **reorganization**, modernization, revamp, improvement, upgrade, makeover, facelift.

overheads plural noun **running costs**, operating costs, fixed costs, expenses.
– OPPOSITES profit.

overindulge verb **1** *we all overindulge at Christmas:* **eat too much**, overeat, overindulge, overdo it, gorge, gourmandize; informal binge, stuff yourself, make a pig of yourself, pig out; N. Amer. informal scarf out. **2** *his mother had overindulged him:* **spoil**, give in to, indulge, humour, pander to, pamper, mollycoddle, baby.
– OPPOSITES abstain.

overindulgence noun **intemperance**, immoderation, excess, extravagance, self-gratification; decadence.
– OPPOSITES abstinence.

overjoyed adjective **ecstatic**, euphoric, thrilled, elated, delighted, on cloud nine, in seventh heaven, jubilant, rapturous, jumping for joy, delirious, blissful, in raptures, as pleased as Punch, cock-a-hoop, as happy as a sandboy, as happy as Larry; informal over the moon, on top of the world, tickled pink; N. Amer. informal as happy as a clam; Austral. informal wrapped.
– OPPOSITES unhappy.

overload verb **strain**, overtax, overwork, overuse, swamp, overwhelm.

overlook verb **1** *he overlooked the mistake:* **fail to notice**, fail to spot, miss. **2** *his work has been overlooked:* **disregard**, neglect, ignore, pass over, forget. **3** *she was willing to overlook his faults:* **ignore**, disregard, take no notice of, make allowances for, turn a blind eye to, excuse, pardon, forgive. **4** *the lounge overlooks the garden:* **have a view of**, look over/across, look on to, look out on/over.

overly adverb **unduly**, excessively, inordinately, too.

overpower verb **overwhelm**, get the better of, overthrow, subdue, suppress, subjugate, repress, bring someone to their knees.

overpowering adjective **1** *overpowering grief:* **overwhelming**, oppressive, unbearable, unendurable, intolerable, shattering. **2** *an overpowering smell:* **stifling**, suffocating, strong, pungent, powerful; nauseating, offensive, acrid, fetid.

overrate verb **overestimate**, overvalue, overpraise, exaggerate, glorify.
– OPPOSITES underestimate.

overreact verb **react disproportionately**, blow something up out of all proportion; Brit. informal go over the top.

override verb **disallow**, overrule, countermand, veto, quash, overturn, overthrow; cancel, reverse, rescind, revoke, repeal, annul, nullify, invalidate, negate, void.

overriding adjective **most important**, uppermost, top, first, foremost, highest, pre-eminent, predominant, principal, primary, paramount, chief, main, major, foremost, central, key; informal number-one.

overrule verb **countermand**, cancel, reverse, rescind, repeal, revoke, retract, disallow, override, veto, quash, overturn, overthrow, annul, nullify, invalidate, negate, void.

overrun verb **invade**, storm, occupy, swarm into, surge into, inundate, overwhelm, descend on.

oversee verb **supervise**, superintend, be in charge/control of, be responsible for, look after, keep an eye on, inspect, administer, organize, manage, direct, preside over.

overseer noun **supervisor**, foreman, forewoman, team leader, controller, manager, head of department, superintendent, captain; informal boss, chief, governor; Brit. informal gaffer, guv'nor.

overshadow verb **1** *the trees that overshadow the square:* **tower over**, dominate, overlook. **2** *a childhood overshadowed by illness:* **blight**, take the edge off, mar, spoil, ruin. **3** *he was overshadowed by his brother:* **outshine**, eclipse, surpass, exceed, outclass, outstrip, outdo, upstage; informal be head and shoulders above.

oversight noun **1** *a stupid oversight:* **mistake**, error, omission, lapse, slip, blunder; informal slip-up, boo-boo; Brit. informal boob; N. Amer. informal goof. **2** *the omission was due to oversight:* **carelessness**, inattention, negligence, forgetfulness.

overstate verb **exaggerate**, overdo, overemphasize, overplay, dramatize; informal blow up out of all proportion.

– OPPOSITES understate.

overstatement noun **exaggeration**, overemphasis, dramatization, hyperbole.

overt adjective **undisguised**, unconcealed, plain, clear, conspicuous, obvious, noticeable, manifest, patent, open, blatant, flagrant.

– OPPOSITES covert.

overtake verb **1** *a green car overtook us:* **pass**, leave behind, outdistance, outstrip; Brit. overhaul. **2** *Goa overtook Ibiza as their favourite destination:* **outstrip**, surpass, overshadow, eclipse, outshine, outclass; exceed, top, cap. **3** *the calamity which overtook us:* **befall**, happen to, come upon, hit, strike, overwhelm, overcome.

overthrow verb **1** *the President was overthrown:* **depose**, bring down, topple, oust, displace, supplant, unseat. **2** *an attempt to overthrow Soviet rule:* **defeat**, conquer, overcome, abolish.

• noun **1** *the overthrow of the Shah:* **removal**, downfall, fall, toppling, deposition, ousting, displacement, supplanting, unseating. **2** *the overthrow of capitalism:* **ending**, defeat, displacement, fall, collapse, downfall, demise.

overtone noun **connotation**, hidden meaning, implication, association, undercurrent, undertone, echo, vibrations, hint, suggestion, insinuation, intimation, suspicion, feeling, nuance.

overture noun **1 prelude**, introduction, opening, start, beginning, lead-in. **2** *peace overtures:* **opening move**, approach, advances, feeler, signal.

overturn verb **1** *the boat overturned:* **capsize**, turn turtle, keel over, tip over, topple over, turn over. **2** *I overturned the stool:* **upset**, tip over, topple over, turn over, knock over, upend. **3** *the Senate may overturn this ruling:* **cancel**, reverse, rescind, repeal, revoke, retract, countermand, disallow, override, overrule, veto, quash, overthrow, annul, nullify, invalidate, negate, void.

overused adjective **hackneyed**, overworked, worn out, time-worn, tired, played out, clichéd, stale, trite, banal, stock, unoriginal.

overweight adjective **fat**, obese, stout, corpulent, gross, fleshy, plump, portly, chubby, pot-bellied, flabby, well padded, broad in the beam; informal tubby, blubbery; Brit. informal podgy.

– OPPOSITES skinny.

overwhelm verb **1** *she was overwhelmed by a sense of tragedy:* **overcome**, move, stir, affect, touch, strike, dumbfound, shake, devastate, leave speechless; informal bowl over, knock sideways, floor; Brit. informal knock/hit for six. **2** *Spain overwhelmed Russia in the hockey:* **trounce**, beat hollow, rout, defeat, conquer, triumph over, overcome, overthrow, crush; informal thrash, wipe the floor with; literary vanquish. **3** *huge waves overwhelmed the ship:* **swamp**, submerge, engulf, deluge, flood, inundate.

overwhelming adjective **1** *an overwhelming number of people:* **very large**, enormous, immense, inordinate, massive, huge. **2** *an overwhelming desire to laugh:* **very strong**, powerful, uncontrollable, irrepressible, irresistible, overpowering, compelling.

overwork verb **work too hard**, run yourself into the ground, work your fingers to the bone, burn the candle at both ends, overtax yourself, burn yourself out, overdo it, strain yourself, overload yourself; informal kill yourself, knock yourself out.

overworked adjective **1** *overworked staff:* **stressed**, overburdened, overloaded, exhausted, worn out. **2** *an overworked phrase:* **hackneyed**, overused, worn out, tired, played out, clichéd, threadbare, stale, trite, banal, stock, unoriginal.

O

overwrought adjective **tense**, agitated, nervous, on edge, edgy, keyed up, worked up, highly strung, neurotic, overexcited, beside yourself, distracted, distraught, frantic, hysterical; informal in a state, in a tizzy, uptight, wound up, het up.
–OPPOSITES calm.

owe verb **be in debt**, be in arrears; be indebted to, be under an obligation to.

owing adjective *the rent was owing:* **unpaid**, to be paid, payable, due, overdue, undischarged, owed, outstanding, in arrears; N. Amer. delinquent.
–OPPOSITES paid.
■ **owing to** because of, as a result of, on account of, due to, as a consequence of, thanks to, in view of.

own adjective *each user has their own security code:* **personal**, individual, particular, private, personalized, unique.
• verb **1** *I don't own anything valuable:* **possess**, have. **2** (formal) *she had to own that she agreed:* **admit**, concede, grant, accept, acknowledge, agree, confess.
■ **on your own 1** *I am on my own:* alone, by yourself, solitary, unaccompanied; informal by your lonesome; Brit. informal on your tod. **2** *she works well on her own:* unaided, unassisted, without help, without assistance, by yourself, independently. **own up** confess, tell the truth, admit responsibility, plead guilty, make a clean breast of it; informal come clean.

owner noun **possessor**, holder, proprietor/proprietress, homeowner, freeholder, landlord, landlady.

ownership noun **possession**, proprietorship, proprietary rights, freehold, title.

Pp

pace noun **1** *ten paces forward:* **step**, stride. **2** *his slow, steady pace:* **gait**, stride, walk, march. **3** *he set off at a furious pace:* **speed**, rate, velocity.
• verb *she paced up and down:* **walk**, stride, march, pound.

pacifism noun **non-violence**; peace-making.

pacifist noun **peace-lover**, conscientious objector, dove.
– OPPOSITES warmonger.

pacify verb **placate**, appease, calm down, conciliate, propitiate, assuage, mollify, soothe.
– OPPOSITES enrage.

pack noun **1** *a pack of cigarettes:* **packet**, container, package, box, carton, parcel. **2** *a pack of wolves:* **group**, herd, troop. **3** *a pack of hooligans:* **crowd**, mob, group, band, party, set, gang, rabble, horde, throng, huddle, mass, assembly, gathering, host; informal crew, bunch.
• verb **1** *she packed the car with supplies:* **fill**, load. **2** *they packed their belongings:* **stow**, put away, store, box up. **3** *the glasses were packed in straw:* **wrap**, package, parcel, swathe, swaddle, encase, envelop, bundle. **4** *shoppers packed the store:* **throng**, crowd into, fill, cram into, jam, squash into, squeeze into.

package noun **1** *the delivery of a package:* **parcel**, packet, box. **2** *a package of services:* **collection**, bundle, combination, range, complement, raft, platform.
• verb *goods packaged in recyclable materials:* **wrap**, gift-wrap; pack, box.

packaging noun **wrapping**, packing, covering.

packed adjective **crowded**, full, filled to capacity, crammed, jammed, solid, teeming, seething, swarming; informal jam-packed, chock-full, chock-a-block, full to the gunwales, bursting at the seams.

packet noun **1** *a packet of cigarettes:* **pack**, carton, container, case, package. **2** (informal) *the trip cost a packet:* **a fortune**, a king's ransom, millions, billions; informal a mint, a bundle, a pile, a tidy sum, a pretty penny, big money; Brit. informal a bomb; N. Amer. informal big bucks, gazillions; Austral. informal big bickies.

pact noun **agreement**, treaty, entente, protocol, deal, settlement; armistice, truce; formal concord.

pad[1] noun **1** *a pad covered one eye:* **dressing**, pack, wad. **2** *he jotted some notes in a pad:* **notebook**, notepad, writing pad, jotter; N. Amer. scratch pad.
■ **pad something out** expand, fill out, amplify, increase, flesh out, lengthen, spin out.

pad[2] verb *he padded along the landing:* **walk**, lope, trot; creep, tiptoe, steal, pussyfoot.

padded adjective **quilted**, insulated, lined, cushioned, stuffed; thick; lagged.

padding noun **1** *the thick padding of his jacket:* **wadding**, cushioning, stuffing, filling, lining. **2** *a concise style with no padding:* **verbiage**, wordiness, prolixity; Brit. informal waffle.

paddle[1] noun **oar**, scull.
• verb **row**, scull, pull; propel, steer.

paddle[2] verb **wade**, splash, dabble.

paddock noun **field**, meadow, pasture; pen, pound; N. Amer. corral.

padre noun **priest**, chaplain, minister, pastor, father, parson, clergyman, cleric, man of the cloth, vicar, rector, curate; informal reverend, Holy Joe.

pagan noun **heathen**; old use infidel.
• adjective **heathen**, ungodly, irreligious, infidel; non-Christian, pre-Christian.

page[1] noun **folio**, sheet, side, leaf.

page[2] noun **errand boy**, messenger boy; N. Amer. bellboy, bellhop.
• verb **call**, message, summon, send for, buzz.

pageant noun **parade**, procession, cavalcade, tableau; spectacle, extravaganza, show.

pageantry noun **spectacle**, display, ceremony, magnificence, pomp, splendour, grandeur, show; informal razzle-dazzle, razzmatazz.

pain noun **1** *she endured great pain:* **suffering**, agony, torture, torment, discomfort. **2** *a pain in the stomach:* **ache**, aching, soreness, throbbing, sting, twinge, shooting pain, stab, pang; discomfort, irritation. **3** *the pain of losing a loved one:* **sorrow**, grief, heartache, heartbreak, sadness, unhappiness, distress, misery, wretchedness, despair; agony, torment, torture. **4** (informal) *that child is a pain.* See **NUISANCE**. **5** *he took great pains to hide his feelings:* **care**, effort, bother, trouble.
• verb **sadden**, grieve, distress, trouble, oppress.
▪ **be at pains** try hard, put yourself out; strive, endeavour, try, do your best, do your utmost, go all out; informal bend over backwards.

p

WORD LINKS
analgesic a drug for reducing pain
anaesthetic a drug that makes someone unable to feel pain

pained adjective **upset**, hurt, wounded, injured, insulted, offended, aggrieved, displeased, disgruntled, annoyed, indignant, irritated, resentful; informal riled, miffed, aggravated, peeved, hacked off, browned off; Brit. informal narked, cheesed off; N. Amer. informal teed off, ticked off, sore.

painful adjective **1** *a painful arm:* **sore**, hurting, tender, aching, throbbing. **2** *a painful experience:* **disagreeable**, unpleasant, nasty, distressing, upsetting, traumatic, miserable, sad, heartbreaking, agonizing, harrowing.

painkiller noun **analgesic**, anaesthetic, narcotic; palliative.

painless adjective **1** *a simple, painless operation:* **pain-free**. **2** *getting rid of him proved painless:* **easy**, trouble-free, straightforward, simple, uncomplicated.
– OPPOSITES painful, difficult.

painstaking adjective **careful**, meticulous, thorough, assiduous, attentive, diligent, industrious, conscientious, punctilious, scrupulous, rigorous, particular; pedantic, fussy.
– OPPOSITES slapdash.

paint noun **colouring**, colourant, tint, dye, stain, pigment, colour.
• verb **1** *slogans had been painted on the wall:* **daub**, smear, spray-paint, airbrush. **2** *he painted his mother many times:* **portray**, depict, represent, picture.

painting noun **picture**, illustration, portrayal, depiction, representation, image, artwork; oil, watercolour, canvas, fresco.

pair noun **1** *a pair of gloves:* **set**, matching set, brace. **2** *the pair were arrested:* **two**, couple, duo.
• verb *a cardigan paired with a matching skirt:* **match**, put together, couple, combine.

palace noun **royal residence**, castle, chateau, mansion, stately home.

WORD LINKS
palatial like a palace

palatable adjective **1** *a palatable meal:* **edible**; tasty, appetizing, delicious, mouth-watering, toothsome, succulent; informal scrumptious, yummy, scrummy, moreish. **2** *the truth is not always palatable:* **pleasant**, acceptable, agreeable, attractive.
– OPPOSITES disagreeable.

palate noun **taste**, appetite, stomach.

palatial adjective **luxurious**, magnificent, sumptuous, splendid, grand, opulent, lavish, stately; fancy; Brit. upmarket; informal plush, swanky, posh, ritzy; Brit. informal swish.
– OPPOSITES modest.

palaver noun (informal) **fuss**, bother, commotion, trouble, rigmarole; informal song and dance, performance, to-do, carry-on, kerfuffle, hoo-ha, hullabaloo, ballyhoo.

pale adjective **1** *she looked pale:*

white, pallid, pasty, wan, colourless, anaemic, bloodless, washed out, peaky, ashen, grey, whey-faced, drained, sickly, sallow, as white as a sheet; milky, ivory, milk-white, alabaster; informal like death warmed up. **2** *pale colours:* **light**, light-coloured, pastel, muted, subtle, soft; faded, bleached, washed out. **3** *the pale light of morning:* **dim**, faint, weak, feeble. **4** *a pale imitation:* **feeble**, weak, insipid, poor, inadequate; informal pathetic.
–OPPOSITES dark.
•verb **go/turn white**, grow/turn pale, blanch, lose colour.

pall[1] noun *a pall of smoke:* **cloud**, covering, cloak, shroud, layer, blanket.
■ **cast a pall over** spoil, cast a shadow over, overshadow, cloud, put a damper on.

pall[2] verb *the high life was beginning to pall:* **become/grow tedious**, become/grow boring, wear off, weary, tire, cloy.

pallid adjective **1** *her pallid skin:* **pale**, white, pasty, wan, colourless, anaemic, washed out, peaky, whey-faced, ashen, grey, drained, sickly, sallow; informal like death warmed up. **2** *pallid watercolours:* **insipid**, uninspired, colourless, uninteresting, unexciting, unimaginative, lifeless, bland.

pallor noun **paleness**, lack of colour, wanness, ashen hue, greyness, sickliness, sallowness.

palpable adjective **1** *a palpable bump:* **tangible**, touchable, noticeable, detectable. **2** *his reluctance was palpable:* **perceptible**, visible, noticeable, discernible, detectable, observable, tangible, unmistakable, transparent; obvious, clear, plain, evident, apparent, manifest, written all over someone.
–OPPOSITES imperceptible.

palpitate verb **beat**, pound, throb, thud, thump, hammer, race; tremble, quiver, quake, shake.

paltry adjective **small**, meagre, trifling, insignificant, negligible, inadequate, insufficient, derisory, pitiful, pathetic, miserable, niggardly, beggarly; informal measly, piddling, poxy; formal exiguous.
–OPPOSITES considerable.

pamper verb **spoil**, indulge, over-indulge, cosset, mollycoddle, coddle, baby, wait on someone hand and foot.

pamphlet noun **brochure**, leaflet, booklet, circular, flyer, handbill; N. Amer. mailer, folder, dodger.

pan noun **saucepan**, frying pan, skillet.
•verb (informal). See CRITICIZE.
■ **pan out** turn out, work out, end, come out, develop.

panacea noun **universal cure**, cure-all, elixir, wonder drug; informal magic bullet.

panache noun **flamboyance**, confidence, self-assurance, style, flair, elan, dash, verve, zest, spirit, brio, éclat, vivacity, gusto, liveliness, vitality, energy; informal pizzazz, oomph, zip, zing.

pancake noun **crêpe**, tortilla, blini, tostada, latke; N. Amer. flapjack.

pandemic adjective **widespread**, prevalent, pervasive, rife, rampant.

pandemonium noun **bedlam**, chaos, mayhem, uproar, turmoil, tumult, commotion, confusion, anarchy, furore, hubbub, rumpus; informal hullabaloo.
–OPPOSITES peace.

pander verb
■ **pander to** indulge, gratify, satisfy, cater to, accommodate, give in to, comply with.

panel noun **1** *a control panel:* **console**, instrument panel, dashboard; instruments, controls, dials; array. **2** *a panel of judges:* **group**, team, body, committee, board.

pang noun **pain**, shooting pain, twinge, stab, prick, spasm.

panic noun *a wave of panic | she's in a panic:* **alarm**, anxiety, nervousness, fear, fright, trepidation, dread, terror, agitation, hysteria, consternation, dismay, apprehension; informal fluster, cold sweat, funk, tizzy; Brit. informal flap.
–OPPOSITES calm.
•verb **1** *there's no need to panic:* **be alarmed**, be scared, be nervous, be afraid, take fright, be agitated, be hysterical, lose your nerve, get worked up; informal get in a flap, lose your cool, get into a tizzy, run around like a headless chicken, freak out, get in a stew; Brit. informal

get the wind up, go into a flat spin, have kittens. **2** *talk of love panicked her:* **frighten**, alarm, scare, unnerve; informal throw into a tizzy, freak out; Brit. informal put the wind up.

panic-stricken adjective **alarmed**, frightened, scared, terrified, terror-stricken, petrified, horrified, horror-stricken, panicky, frantic, frenzied, nervous, agitated, hysterical, beside yourself, worked up, overwrought; informal in a cold sweat, in a flap; Brit. informal in a flat spin.

panorama noun **view**, vista, prospect, scene, scenery, landscape, seascape, cityscape, skyline.

panoramic adjective **sweeping**, wide, extensive, scenic, commanding.

pant verb **breathe heavily**, breathe hard, puff and blow, huff and puff, gasp, wheeze.

panting adjective **out of breath**, breathless, short of breath, puffed out, puffing and blowing, huffing and puffing, gasping for breath, wheezing, wheezy.

pap noun **rubbish**, nonsense, froth; Brit. candyfloss; informal drivel, trash, twaddle.

paper noun **1** *a sheet of paper:* writing paper, notepaper, foolscap. **2** *the local paper:* **newspaper**, journal, gazette, periodical; tabloid, broadsheet, daily, weekly; informal rag; N. Amer. informal tab. **3** *the paper was peeling off the walls:* **wallpaper**, wallcovering; Brit. woodchip; trademark Anaglypta. **4** *toffee papers:* **wrapper**, wrapping. **5** *a three-hour paper:* **exam**, examination, test. **6** *he's published a paper on the subject:* **essay**, article, monograph, thesis, work, dissertation, treatise, study, report, analysis, tract, critique, review; N. Amer. theme. **7** *personal papers:* **documents**, certificates, letters, files, deeds, records, archives, paperwork, documentation. **8** *they asked us for our papers:* **identification papers/documents**, identity card, ID, credentials.
• verb *we papered the hall:* **wallpaper**, decorate.
■ **paper something over** cover up, hide, conceal, disguise, camouflage, gloss over. **on paper 1** *he put his thoughts down on paper:* in writing, in black and white, in print. **2** *the teams were evenly matched on paper:* in theory, theoretically, supposedly.

P

par noun
■ **below par 1** *their performances have been below par:* substandard, inferior, below average, second-rate, mediocre, poor, undistinguished; N. Amer. informal bush-league. **2** *I'm feeling below par:* unwell, out of sorts; ill, poorly, washed out, run down, peaky; Brit. off colour; informal under the weather, lousy, rough; Brit. informal ropy, grotty; Austral./NZ informal crook. **on a par with** as good as, comparable with, in the same class/league as, equivalent to, equal to, on a level with, of the same standard as. **par for the course** normal, typical, standard, usual, expected.

parable noun **allegory**, moral story/tale, fable.

parade noun **1** *a victory parade:* **procession**, march, cavalcade, motorcade, spectacle, display, pageant; review, tattoo; Brit. march past. **2** *she walked along the parade:* **promenade**, walkway, esplanade, mall; N. Amer. **boardwalk**; Brit. informal prom.
• verb **1** *the teams paraded through the city:* **march**, process, file, troop. **2** *she paraded up and down:* **strut**, swagger, stride. **3** *he was keen to parade his knowledge:* **display**, exhibit, make a show of, flaunt, show off, demonstrate.

paradigm noun **model**, pattern, example, exemplar, standard, prototype, archetype.

paradise noun **1** *souls in paradise:* **heaven**, Elysium, Valhalla. **2** *a tropical paradise:* **Utopia**, Shangri-La, heaven on earth, idyll. **3** *this is sheer paradise!* **bliss**, ecstasy, delight, joy, happiness.
– OPPOSITES hell.

paradox noun **contradiction in terms**, self-contradiction, inconsistency, incongruity, conflict; enigma, puzzle, mystery, conundrum.

paradoxical adjective **contradictory**, self-contradictory, inconsistent, incongruous; illogical, puzzling, baffling, incomprehensible, inexplicable.

paragon noun **perfect/shining**

example, model, epitome, archetype, ideal, exemplar, embodiment, personification, quintessence, acme.

paragraph noun **section**, subdivision, part, subsection, division, portion, segment, passage.

parallel adjective **1** *parallel lines:* **side by side**, aligned, collateral, equidistant. **2** *parallel careers:* **similar**, analogous, comparable, corresponding, like, of a kind, akin, related, equivalent, matching. **3** *a parallel universe:* **coexisting**, concurrent; contemporaneous, simultaneous.
– OPPOSITES divergent.
• noun **1** *an exact parallel:* **counterpart**, analogue, equivalent, likeness, match, twin, duplicate, mirror. **2** *there is an interesting parallel between these figures:* **similarity**, likeness, resemblance, analogy, correspondence, equivalence, correlation, relation, symmetry.
• verb **1** *his experiences parallel mine:* **resemble**, be similar to, be like, bear a resemblance to; correspond to, be analogous to, be comparable/equivalent to, equate with/to, correlate with, echo, duplicate, mirror, follow, match. **2** *her performance has never been paralleled:* **equal**, match, rival, emulate.

paralysed adjective **immobilized**; Medicine paraplegic, quadriplegic, tetraplegic.

parameter noun **framework**, variable, limit, boundary, limitation, restriction, criterion, guideline.

paramount adjective **most important**; uppermost, supreme, chief, overriding, predominant, foremost, prime, primary, principal, highest, main, key, central, leading, major, top, greatest; informal number-one.

paranoia noun **persecution complex**, delusions, obsession, psychosis.

paranoid adjective **over-suspicious**, paranoiac, suspicious, mistrustful, fearful, insecure.

parapet noun **balustrade**, barrier, wall.

paraphernalia plural noun **equipment**, stuff, things, apparatus, kit, implements, tools, utensils, materials, appliances, accoutrements, appurtenances, odds and ends, bits and pieces; informal gear; Brit. informal clobber.

paraphrase verb **reword**, rephrase, put/express differently, rewrite, gloss.
• noun **rewording**, rephrasing, rewriting, rewrite, gloss.

parasite noun **hanger-on**, cadger, leech, passenger; informal bloodsucker, sponger, scrounger, freeloader; Austral./NZ informal bludger.

parcel noun **1** *a parcel of clothes:* **package**, packet; pack, bundle, box, case, bale. **2** *a parcel of land:* **plot**, piece, patch, tract; Brit. allotment; N. Amer. lot, plat.
• verb *she parcelled up the papers:* **pack**, package, wrap, gift-wrap, tie up, bundle up.

parched adjective **1** *the parched earth:* **dry**, bone dry, dried up/out, arid, desiccated, dehydrated, baked, burned, scorched; withered, shrivelled. **2** (informal) *I'm parched.* See THIRSTY sense 1.
– OPPOSITES waterlogged.

pardon noun **forgiveness**, absolution; reprieve, amnesty, release, discharge.
• verb **forgive**, absolve, excuse; reprieve, spare; informal let off.
– OPPOSITES punish.

pare verb **cut**, trim, peel, strip, skin; technical decorticate.
■ **pare something down** reduce, diminish, decrease, cut, trim, slim down, prune, curtail.

parent noun **mother**, **father**, guardian, progenitor.
• verb **bring up**, look after, take care of, rear, raise.

> **WORD LINKS**
> **parricide** the killing of a parent or other close relative

parentage noun **origins**, extraction, birth, family, ancestry, lineage, heritage, pedigree, descent, blood, stock, roots.

parenthood noun **childcare**, child-rearing, motherhood, fatherhood, parenting, guardianship.

pariah noun **outcast**, persona non grata, leper, undesirable, unperson.

parish noun **1** *a large rural parish:* **district**, community. **2** *the vicar scandalized the parish:* **parishioners**, churchgoers, congregation, fold, flock, community.

> WORD LINKS
> **parochial** relating to a parish

parity noun **equality**, equivalence, uniformity, consistency, correspondence, congruity, levelness, unity.

park noun **1** *a public park:* **garden**, recreation ground, playground. **2** *fifty acres of park:* **parkland**, grassland, woodland, gardens, lawns, grounds, estate.
• verb **1** *he parked his car:* **leave**, position; stop, pull up. **2** (informal) *park your bag by the door:* **put**, place, deposit, leave, stick, shove, dump; informal plonk; Brit. informal bung.

parlance noun **jargon**, language, phraseology, talk, speech, argot, patois, cant; informal lingo, -ese, -speak.

parliament noun *the Russian parliament:* **legislature**, congress, senate, upper/lower house, upper/lower chamber, council, convocation, diet, assembly.

parliamentary adjective **legislative**, law-making, governmental, congressional, senatorial, democratic, elected, representative.

parochial adjective **narrow-minded**, small-minded, provincial, narrow, small-town, conservative, illiberal, intolerant; N. Amer. informal jerkwater.
– OPPOSITES broad-minded.

P

parochialism noun **narrow-mindedness**, provincialism, small-mindedness.

parody noun **1** *a parody of the news:* **satire**, burlesque, lampoon, pastiche, caricature, imitation; informal spoof, take-off, send-up. **2** *a parody of the truth:* **distortion**, travesty, caricature, misrepresentation, perversion, corruption, debasement.
• verb *parodying science fiction:* **satirize**, lampoon, caricature, mimic, imitate, ape, copy, make fun of, take off; informal send up.

paroxysm noun **spasm**, attack, fit, burst, bout, convulsion, seizure, outburst, eruption, explosion.

parrot verb **repeat**, echo; chant, intone.

> WORD LINKS
> **psittacine** relating to parrots

parrot-fashion adverb **mechanically**, mindlessly, automatically, by rote.

parry verb **1** *Sharpe parried the blow:* **ward off**, fend off; deflect, block. **2** *I parried her questions:* **evade**, sidestep, avoid, dodge, field.

parsimonious adjective **mean**, miserly, niggardly, close, penny-pinching, Scrooge-like; informal tight-fisted, tight, stingy, mingy; N. Amer. informal cheap.
– OPPOSITES generous.

parson noun **vicar**, rector, clergyman, cleric, chaplain, pastor, curate, man of the cloth, minister, priest; informal reverend, padre.

part noun **1** *the last part of the cake | a large part of their life:* **bit**, slice, chunk, lump, hunk, wedge, piece; portion, proportion, percentage, fraction. **2** *car parts:* **component**, bit, constituent, element, module. **3** *body parts:* organ, limb, member. **4** *the third part of the book:* **section**, division, volume, chapter, act, scene, instalment. **5** *another part of the country:* **district**, neighbourhood, quarter, section, area, region. **6** *the part of Juliet:* **role**, character. **7** *he's learning his part:* **lines**, words, script, speech; libretto, lyrics, score. **8** *he was jailed for his part in the affair:* **involvement**, role, function, hand, work, responsibility, capacity, position, participation, contribution; informal bit.
– OPPOSITES whole.
• verb **1** *the curtains parted slowly:* **separate**, divide, split. **2** *we parted at the station:* **split up**, go your separate ways, separate, say goodbye/farewell, say your goodbyes.
– OPPOSITES join, meet.
• adjective *a part payment:* **incomplete**, partial, half, semi-, limited.
– OPPOSITES complete.
• adverb *the west wing is part completed:* **partly**, partially, in part, half, up to a point.
– OPPOSITES completely.
■ **for the most part**. See MOST. **part with** give up/away, relinquish, forgo, surrender, hand over, deliver up. **take part in** participate in, engage in, join in, get involved in, enter, share in, contribute, assist, help, lend a hand; informal get in

on the act. **take someone's part** support, take the side of, side with, stand by, stick up for, back, be loyal to, defend, come to the defence of, champion.

partake verb **1** (formal) *visitors can partake in golf:* **participate in**, take part in, engage in, join in, get involved in. **2** *she had partaken of lunch:* **consume**, have, eat, drink, devour.

partial adjective **1** *a partial recovery:* **incomplete**, limited, qualified, imperfect, fragmentary, unfinished. **2** *a very partial view of the situation:* **biased**, prejudiced, partisan, one-sided, slanted, skewed, coloured, unbalanced.
– OPPOSITES complete, unbiased, impartial.
▪ **be partial to** like, love, enjoy, have a liking for, be fond of, be keen on, have a soft spot for, have a taste for, have a penchant for; informal adore, have a thing about; N. Amer. informal cotton to.

partiality noun **1** *his perceived partiality towards their cause:* **bias**, prejudice, favouritism, favour, partisanship. **2** *her partiality for brandy:* **liking**, love, fondness, taste, soft spot, predilection, penchant, passion.

partially adverb **to a limited extent/degree**, to a certain extent/degree, partly, in part, up to a point, somewhat, comparatively, slightly.

participant noun **participator**, contributor, party, member; entrant, competitor, player, contestant, candidate.

participate verb **take part**, join, engage, get involved, share, partake, contribute, help, assist, have a hand in.

participation noun **involvement**, part, contribution, association.

particle noun **bit**, piece, speck, spot; fragment, sliver, splinter, shred.

particular adjective **1** *a particular group of companies:* **specific**, certain, distinct, separate, discrete, definite, precise; single, individual. **2** *an issue of particular importance:* **especial**, exceptional, notable, noteworthy, remarkable, unique. **3** *he was particular about what he ate:* **fussy**, fastidious, finicky, meticulous, discriminating, selective, painstaking, exacting, demanding; informal pernickety, choosy, picky; Brit. informal faddy.
– OPPOSITES general, careless.
• noun *the same in every particular:* **detail**, item, point, element, fact, feature.
▪ **in particular 1** *nothing in particular:* specific, special. **2** *the poor, in particular, were hit by rising prices:* particularly, specifically, especially, specially.

particularly adverb **1** *the acoustics are particularly good:* **especially**, specially, extremely, exceptionally, singularly, unusually, remarkably, outstandingly, amazingly, incredibly, really. **2** *he particularly asked that I should help you:* **specifically**, explicitly, expressly, in particular, especially, specially.

parting noun *an emotional parting:* **farewell**, leave-taking, goodbye, adieu, departure.
• adjective *a parting kiss:* **farewell**, goodbye, last, final.

partisan noun **guerrilla**, freedom fighter, resistance fighter, irregular.
• adjective **biased**, prejudiced, one-sided, discriminatory, partial, sectarian, factional.
– OPPOSITES unbiased.

partition noun **1** *the partition of their land:* **division**, separation, break-up. **2** *room partitions:* **screen**, divider, dividing wall, barrier, panel.
• verb **divide**, separate, split, break up; subdivide; section off, screen off.

partly adverb **to a certain extent/degree**, to some extent/degree, in part, partially, a little, somewhat, relatively, moderately, up to a point, slightly.
– OPPOSITES completely.

partner noun **1** *business partners:* **colleague**, associate, co-worker, fellow worker, collaborator, comrade, teammate; Brit. informal oppo; Austral./NZ informal offsider. **2** *his partner in crime:* **accomplice**, confederate, accessory, collaborator, fellow conspirator, helper; informal sidekick. **3** *your relationship with your partner:* **spouse**, husband, wife; lover, girlfriend, boyfriend, fiancé, fiancée, significant other, live-in lover, common-law husband/wife, man, woman, mate; informal hubby, missus, old man, old lady/woman, better half; Brit. informal other half.

partnership noun **1** *close partnership:* **cooperation**, association, collaboration, coalition, alliance, union, affiliation, connection. **2** *thriving partnerships:* **company**, firm, business, corporation, organization, association, consortium, syndicate.

party noun **1** *150 people attended the party:* **gathering**, function, get-together, celebration, reunion, festivity, reception, soirée, social; N. Amer. hoedown; informal bash, shindig; Brit. informal rave-up, knees-up, beanfeast, beano, bunfight. **2** *a party of visitors:* **group**, company, body, gang, band, crowd, pack, contingent; informal bunch, crew, posse. **3** *a left-wing party:* **faction**, group, bloc, camp, caucus; alliance. **4** *don't mention a certain party:* **person**, individual.
• verb (informal) *let's party!* **celebrate**, have fun, enjoy yourself, make merry; informal go out on the town, paint the town red, whoop it up, let your hair down, live it up, have a ball.

pass[1] verb **1** *so much traffic passes through the village:* **go**, proceed, move, progress, make your way, travel. **2** *a car passed him:* **overtake**, pull ahead of; Brit. overhaul. **3** *time passed:* **elapse**, go by/past, advance, wear on, roll by, tick by. **4** *he passed the time reading:* **occupy**, spend, fill, use, employ, while away. **5** *pass me the salt:* **hand**, give, reach. **6** *he passed the ball:* **kick**, hit, throw, lob. **7** *her estate passed to her grandson:* **be transferred**, go, be left, be bequeathed, be handed down/on; Law devolve. **8** *his death passed unnoticed:* **happen**, occur, take place. **9** *the storm passed:* **end**, , finish, cease, fade away, blow over, run its course, die down. **10** *he passed the exam:* **succeed in**, get through, qualify; informal sail through, scrape through. **11** *the Senate passed the bill:* **approve**, vote for, accept, ratify, adopt, agree to, authorize, endorse, legalize, enact; informal OK.
– OPPOSITES stop, fail, reject.
• noun **1** *you must show your pass:* **permit**, warrant, authorization, licence. **2** *a cross-field pass:* **kick**, hit, throw, shot.
■ **make a pass at** make advances to, proposition; informal come on to, make a play for; N. Amer. informal hit on, make time with, put the make on. **pass away/on**. See DIE sense 1. **pass out** faint, lose consciousness, black out. **pass something up** turn down, reject, refuse, decline, give up, forgo, let pass, miss out on; informal give something a miss.

pass[2] noun *a mountain pass:* **route**, way, road, passage; N. Amer. notch.

passable adjective **1** *the beer was passable:* **adequate**, all right, acceptable, satisfactory, average, tolerable, fair; mediocre, middling, ordinary, indifferent, unremarkable, unexceptional; informal OK, so-so; NZ informal half-pie. **2** *the road is still passable:* **navigable**, traversable, negotiable, open, clear.

passably adverb **quite**, rather, somewhat, fairly, reasonably, moderately, comparatively, relatively, tolerably; informal pretty.

passage noun **1 passing**, advance, progress; course, march. **2 way**, route, path, passageway. **3 journey**, crossing, voyage, transit. **4** *a passage from 'Macbeth':* **extract**, excerpt, quotation, quote, reading.

passageway noun **1** *secret passageways:* **corridor**, hall, passage, hallway. **2** *a narrow passageway off the main street:* **alley**, alleyway, passage, lane, path, pathway, footpath, track, thoroughfare; N. Amer. areaway.

passé adjective. See OLD-FASHIONED.

passenger noun **traveller**, commuter, fare payer; consumer.

passing adjective **1** *the story was only of passing interest:* **fleeting**, transient, transitory, ephemeral, brief, short-lived, temporary, momentary. **2** *a passing glance:* **hasty**, rapid, hurried, brief, quick; cursory, superficial, casual, perfunctory.
• noun **1** *the passing of time:* **passage**, course, progress, advance. **2** *we all mourned his passing:* **death**, demise, passing away/on, end, loss, quietus; formal decease. **3** *the passing of the*

new bill: **enactment**, ratification, approval, adoption, authorization, legalization, endorsement.

passion noun **1** *the passion of activists:* **fervour**, ardour, enthusiasm, eagerness, zeal, zealousness, vigour, fire, energy, animation, spirit, fanaticism. **2** *he worked himself up into a passion:* **rage**, temper, tantrum, fury, frenzy; Brit. informal paddy. **3** *their all-consuming passion for each other:* **desire**, lust, ardour, lustfulness. **4** *his passion for football:* **enthusiasm**, love, mania, fascination, obsession, fanaticism, fixation, compulsion, appetite, addiction; informal thing. **5** *wine is a passion with me:* **obsession**, preoccupation, craze, mania, hobby horse.
– OPPOSITES apathy.

passionate adjective **1** *a passionate entreaty:* **intense**, impassioned, ardent, fervent, vehement, fiery, heated, emotional, heartfelt, excited, animated, spirited. **2** *McGregor is passionate about sport:* **very keen**, very enthusiastic, addicted; informal mad, crazy, hooked, nuts; N. Amer. informal nutso; Austral./NZ informal shook. **3** *a passionate kiss:* **amorous**, ardent, hot-blooded, loving, sexy, sensual, erotic, lustful; informal steamy, hot, turned on. **4** *a passionate woman:* **excitable**, emotional, fiery, volatile, mercurial, quick-tempered, highly strung, impulsive, temperamental.
– OPPOSITES apathetic.

passionless adjective **unemotional**, cold, cold-blooded, emotionless, frigid, cool, unfeeling, unloving, unresponsive, undemonstrative, impassive.

passive adjective **1** *a passive role:* **inactive**, non-active, uninvolved. **2** *passive victims:* **submissive**, acquiescent, unresisting, compliant, pliant, obedient, docile, malleable, pliable.
– OPPOSITES proactive, active.

past adjective **1** *those days are past:* **gone by**, bygone, former, of old, olden, long-ago. **2** *the past few months:* **last**, recent, preceding. **3** *a past chairman:* **previous**, former, foregoing, erstwhile, one-time, sometime, ex-; formal quondam.
– OPPOSITES present, future.
• noun *details of her past:* **history**, background, life story.
■ **in the past** formerly, previously, in days/years/times gone by, in former times, in the old days, in days of old, in olden times, once upon a time.

paste noun **1** *blend the ingredients to a paste:* **purée**, pulp, mush. **2** *wallpaper paste:* **adhesive**, glue, gum; N. Amer. mucilage. **3** *fish paste:* **spread**, pâté.
• verb *a notice was pasted on the door:* **glue**, stick, gum, fix, affix.

pastel adjective **pale**, soft, light.
– OPPOSITES dark, bright.

pastiche noun **imitation**, parody; informal take-off.

pastille noun **lozenge**, sweet, drop; tablet, pill.

pastime noun **hobby**, leisure activity/pursuit, sport, game, recreation, amusement, diversion, entertainment, interest, sideline.

past master noun **expert**, master, wizard, genius, old hand, veteran, maestro, authority; Brit. informal dab hand; N. Amer. informal maven, crackerjack.

pastor noun **priest**, minister, parson, clergyman, cleric, chaplain, padre, man of the cloth, vicar, rector, curate; informal reverend.

pastoral adjective **rural**, country, countryside, rustic, agricultural, bucolic; literary sylvan, Arcadian.
– OPPOSITES urban.

pasture noun **grassland**, grass; meadow, field; literary lea, mead.

pasty adjective **pale**, pallid, wan, colourless, anaemic, ashen, white, grey, washed out, sallow.

pat[1] verb *Brian patted her on the shoulder:* **tap**, clap, touch.
• noun **1** *a pat on the cheek:* **tap**, clap, touch. **2** *a pat of butter:* **piece**, lump, portion, knob, mass, ball, curl.
■ **pat someone on the back** congratulate, praise, take your hat off to; commend, compliment, applaud, acclaim.

pat[2] adjective *his answers sounded too pat:* **glib**, simplistic, facile, unconvincing.
■ **off pat** word-perfect, by heart, by rote, by memory, parrot-fashion. **get something off pat** memorize, commit to memory, remember, learn by heart.

patch noun **1** *a patch over one eye:* **cover**, eyepatch, covering, pad. **2** *a reddish patch on her wrist:* **blotch**, mark, spot, smudge, smear, stain, streak, blemish; informal splodge, splotch. **3** *a patch of ground:* **plot**, area, piece, strip, tract, parcel; bed; Brit. allotment; N. Amer. lot. **4** (Brit. informal) *they're going through a difficult patch:* **period**, time, spell, phase, stretch; Brit. informal spot.
• verb *her jeans were neatly patched:* **mend**, repair, sew, stitch.
▪ **patch something up** (informal) repair, mend, fix, rectify, put to rights; reconcile, make up, settle, clear up, resolve.

patchwork noun **assortment**, miscellany, mixture, melange, medley, blend, mixed bag, mix, collection, selection, combination, potpourri, jumble, mishmash, ragbag, hotchpotch; N. Amer. hodgepodge.

patchy adjective **1** *their teaching has been patchy:* **uneven**, bitty, varying, variable, intermittent, fitful, sporadic, erratic, irregular. **2** *patchy evidence:* **fragmentary**, inadequate, insufficient, rudimentary, limited, sketchy.
– OPPOSITES uniform, comprehensive.

patent adjective **1** *patent nonsense:* **obvious**, clear, plain, evident, manifest, transparent, overt, conspicuous, blatant, downright, barefaced, flagrant, undisguised, unconcealed, unmistakable. **2** *patent medicines:* **proprietary**, patented, licensed, branded.

paternal adjective **1** *his face showed paternal concern:* **fatherly**; protective. **2** *his paternal grandfather:* **on your father's side**, on the spear side; Anthropology patrilineal.

path noun **1** *the path to the beach:* **footpath**, pathway, track, trail, bridle path, lane; cycle path/track; N. Amer. bikeway. **2** *journalists blocked his path:* **route**, way, course. **3** *the best path to follow:* **course of action**, route, road, avenue, line, approach, tack.

pathetic adjective **1** *a pathetic sight:* **pitiful**, moving, touching, poignant, plaintive, wretched, forlorn. **2** (informal) *a pathetic excuse:* **feeble**, woeful, sorry, poor, pitiful, lamentable, deplorable, contemptible.

pathological adjective **1** *a pathological condition:* **morbid**, diseased. **2** (informal) *a pathological liar:* **compulsive**, obsessive, inveterate, habitual, persistent, chronic, hardened, confirmed.

pathos noun **poignancy**, tragedy, sadness, pitifulness.

patience noun **1** *she tried everyone's patience:* **forbearance**, tolerance, restraint, stoicism; composure, equanimity, understanding, indulgence. **2** *a task requiring patience:* **perseverance**, persistence, endurance, tenacity, application, staying power, doggedness.

patient adjective **1** *I must ask you to be patient:* **forbearing**, uncomplaining, tolerant; calm, composed, even-tempered, accommodating, understanding, indulgent. **2** *patient research:* **persevering**, persistent, tenacious, dogged, determined.
• noun *a doctor's patient:* **sick person**, case.

patio noun **terrace**; courtyard, quadrangle, quad; N. Amer. sun deck.

patriot noun **nationalist**, loyalist; chauvinist, jingoist, flag-waver.

patriotic adjective **nationalist**, nationalistic, loyalist, loyal; chauvinistic, jingoistic, flag-waving.
– OPPOSITES traitorous.

patriotism noun **nationalism**; chauvinism, jingoism, flag-waving.

patrol noun **1** *a night patrol:* **vigil**, guard, watch; surveillance. **2** *the patrol stopped a woman:* **squad**, detachment, party, force.
• verb *a guard was patrolling the estate:* **keep guard on**, guard, keep watch on; police, make the rounds of; stand guard over, defend, safeguard.

patron noun **1** *a patron of the arts:* **sponsor**, backer, benefactor, benefactress, contributor, subscriber, donor; philanthropist, promoter, friend, supporter. **2** *club patrons:* **customer**, client, consumer, user, visitor, guest; informal regular.

patronage noun **1** *patronage of the arts:* **sponsorship**, backing, funding, financing, assistance, support. **2** *political patronage:* **power**

of appointment, favouritism, nepotism. **3** *thank you for your patronage:* **custom**, trade, business.

patronize verb **1** *don't patronize me!* **condescend to**, talk down to, put down. **2** *they patronized local tradesmen:* **use**, buy from, shop at, deal with, frequent, support.

patronizing adjective **condescending**, supercilious, superior, imperious, scornful; informal uppity, high and mighty.

patter[1] verb **1** *raindrops pattered against the window:* **go pitter-patter**, tap, drum, beat, pound, go pit-a-pat. **2** *she pattered across the floor:* **scurry**, scuttle, skip, trip.
• noun *the patter of rain:* **pitter-patter**, tapping, pattering, drumming, beating, pounding, rat-a-tat, pit-a-pat.

patter[2] noun *the salesmen's patter:* **sales pitch**; informal line, spiel.

pattern noun **1** *the pattern on the wallpaper:* **design**, decoration, motif, marking. **2** *a change in working patterns:* **system**, order, arrangement, form, method, structure, scheme, plan, format. **3** *this set the pattern for a generation:* **model**, example, criterion, standard, basis, point of reference, norm, yardstick, touchstone, benchmark; blueprint.

patterned adjective **decorated**, ornamented, fancy, adorned, embellished.
– OPPOSITES plain.

paunch noun **pot belly**, beer belly; informal beer gut, pot.

pauper noun **poor person**, down-and-out; informal have-not.

pause verb *she paused for a moment:* **stop**, halt, break off; rest, wait, hesitate, hang back, falter.
• noun *there was a brief pause in the rain:* **break**, interruption, lull, respite, breathing space, hiatus, gap, interlude; rest, wait, hesitation; informal let-up.

pavement noun **footpath**, walkway; N. Amer. sidewalk.

pawn noun *she was just a pawn in their battle for the throne:* **puppet**, dupe, hostage, tool, cat's paw, instrument.

pay verb **1** *I must pay him for his work:* **reward**, reimburse, recompense, remunerate. **2** *I paid £7 for a ticket:* **spend**, pay out; informal lay/shell/fork out, cough up; N. Amer. informal ante up, pony up. **3** *he's paid his debts:* **discharge**, settle, pay off, clear. **4** *it may pay you to be early:* **benefit**, be advantageous to, be of advantage to, be beneficial to. **5** *he will pay for his mistakes:* **suffer**, be punished, atone, answer, make amends.
• noun *the campaign for equal pay:* **salary**, wages, payment, stipend, fee; earnings, remuneration, reimbursement, income, revenue; formal emolument.
■ **pay something back** repay, pay off, return, reimburse, refund. **pay for** finance, fund; sponsor, subsidize; informal foot the bill for, pick up the tab for; N. Amer. informal bankroll. **pay something off** discharge, settle, clear, liquidate.

payable adjective **due**, owed, owing, outstanding, unpaid, overdue; N. Amer. delinquent.

payment noun **1 remittance**, instalment, premium; settlement. **2 salary**, wages, pay, earnings, fees, remuneration.

pay-off noun (informal) **outcome**, denouement, culmination, conclusion, development, result.

peace noun **1** *peace of mind:* **serenity**, peacefulness, tranquillity, calm, calmness, composure, ease, contentment. **2** *we pray for peace:* **order**, harmony; formal concord. **3** *a lasting peace:* **treaty**, truce, ceasefire, armistice.
– OPPOSITES anxiety, war.

peaceable adjective **peace-loving**, non-violent, non-aggressive, easy-going, placid, gentle, good-natured, even-tempered, amiable, affable, genial.
– OPPOSITES aggressive.

peaceful adjective **1** *everything was quiet and peaceful:* **tranquil**, calm, restful, quiet, still, relaxing, soothing, undisturbed, untroubled, private, secluded. **2** *his peaceful mood:* **serene**, calm, tranquil, composed, placid, at ease, untroubled, unworried, content. **3** *peaceful relations:* **harmonious**, on good terms, amicable, friendly, cordial, non-violent.
– OPPOSITES noisy, agitated, hostile.

P

peacemaker noun **arbitrator**, arbiter, mediator, negotiator, conciliator, go-between, intermediary.

peak noun **1** *the peaks of the mountains:* **summit**, top, crest, pinnacle, cap. **2** *the highest peak:* **mountain**, hill, height. **3** *the peak of a cap:* **brim**, visor. **4** *the peak of his career:* **height**, high point/spot, pinnacle, summit, top, climax, culmination, apex, zenith, crowning point, acme, apogee, prime, heyday.
• verb *inflation had finally peaked:* **reach its height**, come to a head; spike.
• adjective *peak condition | a peak speed of 163 mph:* **optimum**, optimal, best; maximum greatest, highest.

> Don't confuse **peak** with **peek**, which means 'look quickly or secretly' (*she peeked through the curtains*) or 'a quick or secret look' (*she sneaked a peek at the map*).

peaky adjective **pale**, pasty, wan, drained, washed out, drawn, pallid, anaemic, ashen, grey, sickly, sallow; ill, unwell, poorly, run down; Brit. off colour; informal under the weather, rough; Brit. informal grotty, ropy.

peal noun **1** *a peal of bells:* **chime**, ring. **2** *peals of laughter:* **shriek**, shout, scream, howl, gale, fit, roar, hoot. **3** *a peal of thunder:* **rumble**, roar, boom, crash, clap, crack.

p

peasant noun **agricultural worker**, rustic; historical villein, serf.

peculiar adjective **1** *his increasingly peculiar behaviour:* **strange**, unusual, odd, funny, curious, bizarre, weird, queer; eccentric, quirky, unconventional, outlandish, extraordinary, abnormal; suspicious, unnatural; informal wacky, freaky, oddball, offbeat, off the wall; N. Amer. informal wacko. **2** (informal) *I feel a bit peculiar.* See UNWELL. **3** *customs peculiar to this area:* **characteristic of**, typical of, exclusive to. **4** *their own peculiar contribution:* **distinctive**, characteristic, distinct, individual, special, unique, personal.
– OPPOSITES ordinary.

peculiarity noun **1** *a legal peculiarity:* **oddity**, anomaly, abnormality. **2** *a physical peculiarity:* **idiosyncrasy**, mannerism, quirk, foible. **3** *the peculiarity of this notion:* **strangeness**, oddness, bizarreness, weirdness, queerness, unexpectedness, incongruity. **4** *the peculiarity of her appearance:* **outlandishness**, bizarreness, unconventionality, weirdness, oddness, eccentricity, strangeness, quirkiness.

pedant noun **dogmatist**, purist, literalist, formalist; quibbler, hair-splitter; informal nit-picker.

pedantic adjective **overscrupulous**, precise, exact, punctilious, fussy, fastidious, finicky; dogmatic, purist; hair-splitting, quibbling; informal nit-picking, pernickety.

pedantry noun **dogmatism**, purism; overscrupulousness, perfectionism, fastidiousness, punctiliousness, hair-splitting, casuistry, sophistry; informal nit-picking.

peddle verb **1** *they are peddling water filters:* **sell**, hawk, tout; trade in, deal in, traffic in. **2** *the book peddles the same old views:* **advocate**, preach, put forward, proclaim, propound, promote.

pedestal noun *a bust on a pedestal:* **plinth**, base, support, mount, stand, pillar, column.
■ **put someone on a pedestal** idealize, look up to, hold in high regard, think highly of, admire, esteem, revere, worship.

pedestrian adjective **dull**, boring, tedious, monotonous, uneventful, unremarkable, uninspired, unimaginative, unexciting, routine; commonplace, workaday; ordinary, everyday, run-of-the-mill, mundane, humdrum; informal bog-standard.
– OPPOSITES exciting.

pedigree noun **ancestry**, lineage, line of descent, genealogy, extraction, derivation, origins, heritage, parentage, bloodline, background, roots.
• adjective **pure-bred**, thoroughbred.

pedlar noun **1** *an old pedlar:* **travelling salesman**, door-to-door salesman, huckster; street trader, hawker. **2** *a drug pedlar:* **trafficker**, dealer; informal pusher.

peek verb *they peeked from behind the curtains:* **peep**, sneak a look; informal take a gander, have a squint; Brit. informal have a dekko, have/take a butcher's, take a shufti.

•**noun** *a peek at the map:* **peep**, glance, glimpse, quick look; informal gander, squint; Brit. informal dekko, butcher's, shufti.

> Don't confuse **peek** with **peak**, which means 'the pointed top of a mountain' or 'the point of highest achievement or intensity' (*the peak of his career*).

peel verb *peel and core the fruit:* **pare**, skin; hull, shell.
•**noun** *orange peel:* **rind**, skin, covering, zest.

peep verb **1** *I peeped through the keyhole:* **look**, sneak a look, peek, glance; informal take a gander, have a squint; Brit. informal have a dekko, have a butcher's, take a shufti. **2** *the moon peeped through the clouds:* **appear**, show, emerge, peek, peer out.
•**noun** *I'll just take a peep:* **look**, peek, glance; informal gander, squint; Brit. informal dekko, butcher's, shufti.

peer[1] verb *he peered at the manuscript:* **look closely**, squint.

peer[2] noun **1** *hereditary peers:* **aristocrat**, lord, lady, noble, nobleman, noblewoman. **2** *his academic peers:* **equal**, fellow; contemporary.

peerage noun **aristocracy**, nobility; the House of Lords, the Lords.

peerless adjective **incomparable**, matchless, unrivalled, beyond compare/comparison, unparalleled, without equal, second to none, unsurpassed; unique, consummate.

peeve verb (informal) **irritate**, annoy, vex, anger, irk, gall, pique, nettle, put out; informal aggravate, rile, needle, get to, bug, hack off, get someone's goat, get/put someone's back up; N. Amer. informal tee off, tick off.

peeved adjective (informal) **irritated**, annoyed, cross, angry, vexed, displeased, disgruntled, indignant, galled, irked, put out, aggrieved, offended, affronted, piqued, nettled, in high dudgeon; informal aggravated, miffed, riled; Brit. informal narked, cheesed off, brassed off; N. Amer. informal teed off, ticked off, sore.

peg noun **pin**, nail, dowel; Mountaineering piton.
•**verb** **1** *the flysheet is pegged to the ground:* **fix**, pin, attach, fasten, secure. **2** *we decided to peg our prices:* **hold down**, keep down, fix, set, hold, freeze.

pejorative adjective **disparaging**, derogatory, defamatory, slanderous, libellous, abusive, insulting.
–OPPOSITES complimentary.

pellet noun **1** *a pellet of mud:* **ball**, piece. **2** *pellet wounds:* **bullet**, shot, lead shot, buckshot.

pelt[1] verb **1** *they pelted him with snowballs:* **bombard**, shower, attack, assail, pepper. **2** *rain was pelting down:* **pour down**, teem down, stream down, tip down, rain cats and dogs; Brit. informal bucket down. **3** (informal) *they pelted into the factory:* **dash**, run, race, rush, sprint, bolt, dart, career, charge, shoot, hurtle, hare, fly, speed, zoom, streak; hurry; informal tear, belt, hotfoot it, scoot, leg it; Brit. informal bomb; N. Amer. informal hightail it.

pelt[2] noun *an animal's pelt:* **skin**, hide, fleece, coat, fur.

pen[1] verb *he penned a number of articles:* **write**, compose, draft, dash off.

pen[2] noun *a sheep pen:* **enclosure**, fold, pound, compound, stockade; sty, coop; N. Amer. corral.
•**verb** *the hostages were penned up in a basement:* **confine**, coop up, shut in, box up/in, lock up/in, trap, imprison, incarcerate, cage.

penal adjective **1** *a penal institution:* **disciplinary**, punitive, correctional. **2** *penal rates of interest:* **exorbitant**, extortionate, excessive, outrageous, preposterous, unreasonable, inflated, sky-high.

penalize verb **1** *if you break the rules you will be penalized:* **punish**, discipline. **2** *genuine claimants may be penalized by the proposed amendment:* **handicap**, disadvantage, discriminate against.
–OPPOSITES reward.

penalty noun **1** *increased penalties for speeding:* **punishment**, sanction; fine, forfeit, sentence. **2** *the penalties of old age:* **disadvantage**, difficulty, drawback, handicap, downside, minus; burden, trouble.
–OPPOSITES reward.

penance noun **atonement**, expiation, amends; punishment, penalty.

penchant noun **liking**, fondness, preference, taste, appetite, partiality, love, passion, weakness, inclination, bent, proclivity, predilection, predisposition.

pencil verb **write**, note, jot down, scribble.

pendant noun **necklace**, locket, medallion.

pending adjective **1** *nine cases were still pending:* **unresolved**, undecided, unsettled, up in the air, ongoing, outstanding, not done, unfinished, incomplete; informal on the back burner. **2** *he will preside at the pending trial:* **imminent**, impending, forthcoming, on the way, coming, approaching, looming, near, close, in the offing.
• preposition *they were released on bail pending an appeal:* **awaiting**, until, till.

pendulous adjective **drooping**, dangling, droopy, sagging, floppy; hanging.

penetrate verb **1** *the knife penetrated his lungs:* **pierce**, puncture, enter, perforate. **2** *they penetrated enemy lines:* **infiltrate**, slip/get into, enter. **3** *his words finally penetrated:* **register**, sink in, become clear, fall into place; informal click.

penetrating adjective **1** *a penetrating wind:* **piercing**, cutting, biting, stinging, keen, sharp, harsh, raw, freezing, chill, bitter, cold. **2** *a penetrating voice:* **shrill**, strident, piercing, ear-splitting. **3** *her penetrating gaze:* **piercing**, searching, intent, probing, sharp, keen. **4** *a penetrating analysis:* **perceptive**, insightful, keen, sharp, intelligent, clever, smart, incisive, trenchant, astute, shrewd, clear, acute.
– OPPOSITES mild, soft.

penetration noun **perforation**, piercing, puncturing, entry.

peninsula noun **cape**, promontory, point, head, headland, ness, horn, bluff, mull.

penitence noun **repentance**, contrition, regret, remorse, sorrow, pangs of conscience, shame, sackcloth and ashes.

penitent adjective **repentant**, contrite, remorseful, sorry, apologetic, regretful, conscience-stricken, shamefaced, abject, in sackcloth and ashes.
– OPPOSITES unrepentant.

pen name noun **pseudonym**, nom de plume; assumed name, alias.

pennant noun **flag**, standard, ensign, colours, banner.

penniless adjective **destitute**, poverty-stricken, impoverished, poor, impecunious, needy, indigent; bankrupt, insolvent; Brit. on the breadline, without a penny to your name; informal broke, cleaned out, on your uppers, without a brass farthing, bust; Brit. informal skint; N. Amer. informal on skid row.
– OPPOSITES wealthy.

penny-pinching adjective **mean**, miserly, niggardly, parsimonious, cheese-paring, grasping, Scrooge-like; informal stingy, mingy, tight, tight-fisted, money-grubbing.
– OPPOSITES generous.

pension noun **old-age pension**, superannuation; allowance, benefit, support, welfare.

pensioner noun **retired person**, old-age pensioner, OAP, senior citizen; N. Amer. senior, retiree.

pensive adjective **thoughtful**, reflective, contemplative, meditative, introspective, ruminative, absorbed, preoccupied, deep/lost in thought, brooding.

pent-up adjective **repressed**, suppressed, stifled, smothered, restrained, confined, bottled up.

people plural noun **1** *crowds of people:* **human beings**, persons, individuals, humans, mortals, living souls, personages, {men, women, and children}; informal folk. **2** *the British people:* **citizens**, subjects, electors, voters, taxpayers, residents, inhabitants, public, citizenry, nation, population, populace. **3** *a man of the people:* **the common people**, the proletariat, the masses, the populace, the rank and file; derogatory the hoi polloi, the common herd, the great unwashed; informal, derogatory the proles, the plebs. **4** (dated) *her people don't live far away:* **family**, parents, relatives, relations, folk, kinsfolk, flesh and blood, nearest and dearest; informal folks. **5** (singular) *an ancient African people:* **ethnic group**, race, tribe.
• verb *those who once peopled*

Newfoundland: **populate**, settle in, colonize, inhabit, live in, occupy; formal reside in, dwell in.

WORD LINKS
anthropology the study of people and human origins
ethnic relating to a people with a common national or cultural tradition
demotic relating to language used by ordinary people

pep verb
■ **pep something up** (informal) enliven, animate, liven up, put new life into, invigorate, vitalize, revitalize, vivify, ginger up, energize, galvanize, put some spark into, stimulate, perk up; brighten up, cheer up; informal buck up.

pepper verb **1** *stars peppered the desert skies:* **sprinkle**, fleck, dot, spot, stipple. **2** *gunfire peppered the area:* **bombard**, pelt, shower, rain down on, strafe, rake, blitz.

peppery adjective **spicy**, hot, fiery, piquant, pungent, sharp.
– OPPOSITES mild, bland.

perceive verb **1** *he perceived a tear in her eye:* **see**, discern, detect, catch sight of, spot, observe, notice. **2** *he was perceived as too negative:* **regard**, look on, view, consider, think of, judge, deem.

perceptible adjective **noticeable**, detectable, discernible, visible, observable, recognizable, appreciable; obvious, apparent, clear, distinct.

perception noun **1** *popular perceptions about old age:* **impression**, idea, conception, notion, thought, belief. **2** *he talks with great perception:* **insight**, perceptiveness, understanding, intelligence, intuition, incisiveness, trenchancy, astuteness, shrewdness, acuteness, acuity, penetration, thoughtfulness.

perceptive adjective **insightful**, discerning, sensitive, intuitive, observant; piercing, penetrating, clear-sighted, far-sighted, intelligent, clever, canny, keen, sharp, astute, shrewd, quick, smart, acute; informal on the ball; N. Amer. informal heads-up.
– OPPOSITES obtuse.

perch verb **1** *a swallow perched on the telegraph wire:* **sit**, rest; alight, settle, land. **2** *she perched her glasses on her nose:* **put**, place, set, rest, balance.

percolate verb **1** *chemicals percolated through the soil:* **filter**, drain, drip, ooze, seep, trickle, dribble, leak, leach. **2** *these views began to percolate through society:* **spread**, be disseminated, filter, pass; permeate.

peremptory adjective **brusque**, imperious, high-handed, abrupt, summary.

perennial adjective **abiding**, enduring, lasting, everlasting, perpetual, eternal, continuing, unending, unceasing, never-ending, endless, ceaseless, constant, continual.

perfect adjective **1** *a perfect wife:* **ideal**, model, faultless, flawless, consummate, exemplary, best, ultimate, copybook. **2** *an E-type Jaguar in perfect condition:* **flawless**, mint, as good as new, pristine, immaculate; superb, optimum, prime, peak, excellent; informal tip-top, A1. **3** *a perfect copy:* **exact**, precise, accurate, faithful, true; Brit. informal spot on; N. Amer. informal on the money. **4** *the perfect Christmas present:* **ideal**, just right, appropriate, fitting, fit, suitable, apt, tailor-made; very; Brit. informal spot on, just the job. **5** *she felt a perfect idiot:* **absolute**, complete, total, real, out-and-out, thorough, downright, utter, in every respect, unalloyed; Brit. informal right; Austral./NZ informal fair.
• verb *he's perfecting his style:* **improve**, polish up, hone, refine, brush up, fine-tune.

perfection noun **1** *the perfection of his technique:* **improvement**, refining, honing. **2** *for her, he was perfection:* **the ideal**, a paragon, the last word, the ultimate; informal the tops, the bee's knees.

perfectionist noun **purist**, stickler for perfection, idealist.

perfectly adverb **1** *a perfectly cooked meal:* **superbly**, superlatively, excellently, flawlessly, faultlessly, to perfection, impeccably, immaculately, exquisitely, consummately; informal like a dream, to a T. **2** *we understand each other perfectly:*

p

absolutely, completely, altogether, entirely, wholly, totally, fully, utterly. **3** *you know perfectly well what I mean:* **very**, quite, full; informal damn.

perforate verb **pierce**, penetrate, enter, puncture, prick, bore through, riddle.

perform verb **1** *he has performed his duties admirably:* **carry out**, do, execute, discharge, conduct, implement; informal pull off; formal effectuate. **2** *the car performs well:* **function**, work, operate, run, go, respond, behave, act. **3** *the play was performed in Britain:* **stage**, put on, present, mount, act, produce. **4** *the band performed live:* **play**, sing.
– OPPOSITES neglect.

performance noun **1** *the evening performance:* **show**, production, showing, presentation, staging; concert, recital; informal gig. **2** *their performance was excellent:* **rendition**, interpretation, playing, acting. **3** *the performance of his duty:* **carrying out**, execution, discharge, completion, fulfilment; formal effectuation. **4** *the performance of the processor:* **functioning**, working, operation, running, behaviour; response, economy. **5** (informal) *he made a great performance about it:* **fuss**, palaver, scene, issue; NZ bobsy-die; informal song and dance, to-do, hoo-ha, business, pantomime.

performer noun **actor, actress**, artiste, artist, entertainer, trouper, player, musician, singer, dancer, comic, comedian, comedienne.

perfume noun **1** *a bottle of perfume:* **scent**, fragrance, eau de toilette, toilet water. **2** *the heady perfume of lilacs:* **smell**, scent, fragrance, aroma, bouquet.

perfumed adjective **sweet-smelling**, scented, fragrant, fragranced, perfumy, aromatic.

perfunctory adjective **cursory**, desultory, quick, brief, hasty, hurried, rapid, fleeting, token, casual, superficial, offhand.
– OPPOSITES careful, thorough.

perhaps adverb **maybe**, for all you know, it could be, possibly, conceivably; N. English happen; literary perchance.

peril noun **danger**, jeopardy, risk, hazard, menace, threat.

perilous adjective **dangerous**, hazardous, risky, unsafe, treacherous.
– OPPOSITES safe.

perimeter noun **1** *the perimeter of a circle:* **circumference**, outside, outer edge. **2** *the perimeter of the camp:* **boundary**, border, limits, bounds, edge, margin, fringes, periphery.

period noun **1** *a six-week period:* **time**, spell, interval, stretch, term, span, phase, bout, chapter, stage; while; Brit. informal patch. **2** *the post-war period:* **era**, age, epoch, time, days, years; Geology aeon. **3** *a double Maths period:* **lesson**, class, session. **4** (N. Amer.) *a comma instead of a period:* **full stop**, full point, stop.

periodic adjective **regular**, periodical, at fixed intervals, recurrent, recurring, repeated, cyclical, seasonal; occasional, infrequent, intermittent, sporadic, spasmodic, odd.

periodical noun **journal**, publication, magazine, newspaper, paper, review, digest, gazette, newsletter, organ, quarterly; informal mag, book, glossy.

peripatetic adjective **nomadic**, itinerant, travelling, wandering, roving, roaming, migrant, migratory, unsettled.

peripheral adjective **1** *the city's peripheral housing estates:* **outlying**, outer. **2** *peripheral issues:* **secondary**, subsidiary, incidental, tangential, marginal, minor, unimportant, lesser, ancillary.
– OPPOSITES central.

periphery noun **edge**, margin, fringe, boundary, border, perimeter, rim; outskirts, outer limits/reaches.
– OPPOSITES centre.

perish verb **1** *millions of soldiers perished:* **die**, lose your life, be killed, fall, expire, meet your death, be lost; informal buy it. **2** *the rubber had perished:* **go bad**, spoil, rot, decay, decompose.

perk[1] verb
■ **perk up** cheer up, brighten up, liven up, revive, bounce back, rally; informal buck up. **perk someone/something up** cheer up, liven up,

brighten up, raise someone's spirits, give someone a boost/lift, revitalize, reinvigorate, put new life/heart into, rejuvenate, refresh; informal buck up, pep up.

perk[2] noun *a job with a lot of perks:* **fringe benefit**, advantage, bonus, extra, plus; informal freebie; formal perquisite.

perky adjective **cheerful**, lively, vivacious, bubbly, effervescent, bouncy, spirited, cheery, merry, buoyant, exuberant, jaunty, frisky, sprightly, spry, bright, sunny, jolly, full of the joys of spring; informal full of beans, bright-eyed and bushy-tailed, chirpy, chipper; N. Amer. informal peppy; dated gay.

permanence noun **stability**, durability, fixity, changelessness, immutability, endurance, constancy, continuity, immortality, indestructibility.

permanent adjective **1** *permanent brain damage:* **lasting**, enduring, indefinite, continuing, constant, irreparable, irreversible, lifelong, indelible, standing. **2** *a permanent job:* **long-term**, stable, secure.
– OPPOSITES temporary.

permanently adverb **1** *the attack left her permanently scarred:* **for all time**, forever, for good, for always, for ever and ever, for evermore, indelibly; informal for keeps. **2** *I was permanently hungry:* **continually**, constantly, perpetually, always.

permeable adjective **porous**, absorbent.

permeate verb **1** *the smell permeated the entire flat:* **pervade**, spread through, fill; filter through, penetrate, pass through, percolate through, suffuse, steep, impregnate. **2** *these resins permeate the timber:* **soak through**, penetrate, seep through, saturate, percolate through, leach through.

permissible adjective **permitted**, allowable, allowed, acceptable, legal, lawful, legitimate, admissible, licit, authorized; informal legit, OK.
– OPPOSITES forbidden.

permission noun **authorization**, consent, leave, authority, sanction, licence, dispensation, assent, acquiescence, agreement, approval, seal of approval, approbation, endorsement, blessing, clearance; informal the go-ahead, the thumbs up, the OK, the green light, say-so.

permissive adjective **liberal**, broad-minded, open-minded, free and easy, easy-going, live-and-let-live, libertarian, tolerant, indulgent, lenient; overindulgent, lax, soft.
– OPPOSITES intolerant, strict.

permit verb **allow**, let, authorize, sanction, grant, license, empower, enable, entitle; consent to, assent to, give your blessing to, agree to, tolerate; legalize, legitimatize; informal give the go-ahead to, give the thumbs up to, OK, give the OK to, give the green light to; formal accede to; old use suffer.
– OPPOSITES ban, forbid.
• noun **authorization**, licence, pass, ticket, warrant, documentation, certification; passport, visa.

permutation noun **arrangement**, order, grouping, disposition, organization, combination.

pernicious adjective **harmful**, damaging, destructive, injurious, hurtful, detrimental, deleterious, dangerous, adverse, unhealthy, unfavourable, bad, malign, malignant, noxious, corrupting.
– OPPOSITES beneficial.

pernickety adjective (informal) **fussy**, difficult to please, finicky, fastidious, particular, punctilious, hair-splitting; informal nit-picking, picky; N. Amer. informal persnickety.
– OPPOSITES easy-going.

perpendicular adjective **1** *the perpendicular stones:* **upright**, vertical, erect, straight, standing, upended. **2** *lines perpendicular to each other:* **at right angles**, at 90 degrees.
– OPPOSITES horizontal.

perpetrate verb *they perpetrated a series of attacks and assaults:* **commit**, carry out, perform, execute, do, effect; inflict, wreak; informal pull off.

perpetual adjective **1** *deep caves in perpetual darkness:* **everlasting**, eternal, permanent, unending, without end, lasting, abiding, unchanging, continuous, unremitting, unending. **2** *her mother's perpetual nagging:*

interminable, incessant, ceaseless, unceasing, endless, relentless, unrelenting, persistent, continual, continuous, non-stop, never-ending, repeated, unremitting, round-the-clock, unabating; informal eternal.
– OPPOSITES temporary, intermittent.

perpetuate verb *a monument to perpetuate the memory of those killed in war:* **keep alive**, keep going, preserve, conserve, sustain, maintain, continue, extend.

Don't confuse **perpetuate** with **perpetrate**, which means 'carry out a bad or illegal act'.

perplex verb **puzzle**, baffle, mystify, bemuse, bewilder, confound, confuse, nonplus, disconcert.

perplexing adjective **puzzling**, baffling, mystifying, mysterious, bewildering, confusing, disconcerting, worrying.

perplexity noun **confusion**, bewilderment, puzzlement, bafflement, incomprehension, mystification, bemusement.

per se adverb **in itself**, of itself, by itself, as such, intrinsically; by its very nature, in essence, by definition, essentially.

persecute verb **1** *they were persecuted for their beliefs:* **oppress**, abuse, victimize, ill-treat, mistreat, maltreat, torment, torture. **2** *she was persecuted by the press:* **harass**, hound, plague, badger, harry, intimidate, pick on, pester, bother, bedevil; informal hassle, give someone a hard time, get on someone's back; Austral. informal heavy.

persecution noun **1** *religious persecution:* **oppression**, victimization, ill-treatment, mistreatment, abuse, discrimination. **2** *the persecution I endured at school:* **harassment**, hounding, intimidation, bullying.

perseverance noun **persistence**, tenacity, determination, staying power; patience, endurance, application, dedication, commitment, doggedness, stamina; informal stickability; N. Amer. informal stick-to-it-iveness.

persevere verb **persist**, continue, carry on, go on, keep on, keep going, struggle on, hammer away, be persistent, keep at it, not take no for an answer, be tenacious, plod on, plough on; informal soldier on, hang on, plug away, stick to your guns, stick it out, hang in there.
– OPPOSITES give up.

persist verb **1** *Corbett persisted with his questioning.* See PERSEVERE. **2** *if dry weather persists, water the lawn thoroughly:* **continue**, hold, carry on, last, keep on, remain, linger, stay, endure.

persistence noun. See PERSEVERANCE.

persistent adjective **1** *a very persistent man:* **tenacious**, determined, resolute, dogged, tireless, indefatigable, patient, untiring, insistent, unrelenting. **2** *persistent rain:* **constant**, continuous, continuing, continual, non-stop, never-ending, steady, uninterrupted, unbroken, interminable, incessant, endless, unending, unrelenting. **3** *a persistent cough:* **chronic**, nagging, frequent; repeated, habitual.
– OPPOSITES irresolute, intermittent.

person noun **human being**, individual, man/woman, human, being, living soul, mortal, creature; personage, character, customer; informal type, sort; informal, dated body.
■ **in person** physically, in the flesh, personally; yourself.

persona noun **image**, face, public face, character, identity; front, facade, exterior.

personable adjective **pleasant**, agreeable, likeable, nice, amiable, affable, congenial, pleasing; attractive, presentable, good-looking, nice-looking, pretty, appealing; Scottish couthy; Scottish & N. English bonny.
– OPPOSITES disagreeable, unattractive.

personage noun **important person**, VIP, luminary, celebrity, personality, famous name, household name, public figure, star, dignitary, notable, worthy; informal celeb, somebody, big shot.

personal adjective **1** *a highly personal style:* **distinctive**, characteristic, unique, individual, idiosyncratic. **2** *a personal appearance:* **in person**, in the flesh, actual, live, physical. **3** *his personal life:* **private**, intimate. **4** *a personal*

friend: **intimate**, close, dear, bosom. **5** *personal knowledge:* **direct**, empirical, first-hand, immediate. **6** *personal remarks:* **derogatory**, disparaging, belittling, insulting, rude, disrespectful, offensive, pejorative.
–OPPOSITES public, general.

personality noun **1** *her cheerful personality:* **character**, nature, disposition, temperament, make-up, psyche. **2** *she had loads of personality:* **charisma**, magnetism, character, charm, presence. **3** *a famous personality:* **celebrity**, VIP, star, superstar, big/famous name, somebody, leading light, luminary, notable, personage; informal celeb.

personalize verb **customize**, individualize.

personally adverb **1** *I'd like to thank him personally:* **in person**, yourself. **2** *personally, I like it:* **for my part**, for myself, to my way of thinking, to my mind, in my estimation, as far as I am concerned, in my view/opinion, from my point of view, from where I stand, as I see it, if you ask me, for my money, in my book.

personification noun **embodiment**, incarnation, epitome, quintessence, essence, type, symbol, soul, model, exemplification, exemplar, image, representation.

personify verb **epitomize**, embody, typify, exemplify, represent, symbolize, stand for.

personnel noun **staff**, employees, workforce, workers, labour force, manpower, human resources.

perspective noun **outlook**, view, viewpoint, point of view, standpoint, position, stand, stance, angle, slant, attitude, frame of mind, frame of reference.

perspiration noun **sweat**, moisture; Medicine hidrosis.

perspire verb **sweat**.

persuadable adjective **malleable**, tractable, pliable, compliant, amenable, adaptable, accommodating, cooperative, flexible, acquiescent, biddable, complaisant, like putty in your hands, suggestible.

persuade verb **1** *he persuaded her to go with him:* **prevail on**, talk into, coax, convince, get, induce, win over, bring round, influence, sway; informal sweet-talk. **2** *lack of money persuaded them to abandon the scheme:* **cause**, lead, move, dispose, incline.
–OPPOSITES dissuade, deter.

persuasion noun **1** *Monica needed a lot of persuasion:* **coaxing**, persuading, inducement, convincing, encouragement, urging, enticement; informal sweet-talking. **2** *various religious persuasions:* **group**, grouping, sect, denomination, party, camp, side, faction, affiliation, school of thought, belief, creed, faith.

persuasive adjective **convincing**, cogent, compelling, forceful, powerful, eloquent, impressive, sound, valid, strong, effective, telling; plausible, credible.
–OPPOSITES unconvincing.

pert adjective **jaunty**, neat, trim, stylish, smart, perky, rakish; informal natty; N. Amer. informal saucy.

pertain verb **1** *developments pertaining to the economy:* **concern**, relate to, be connected with, be relevant to, apply to, refer to, have a bearing on, affect, involve, touch on; old use regard. **2** *the economic situation that pertained in Britain:* **exist**, be the order of the day, be the case, prevail; formal obtain.

pertinent adjective **relevant**, to the point, apposite, appropriate, suitable, fitting, fit, apt, applicable, material, germane.
–OPPOSITES irrelevant.

perturb verb **worry**, upset, unsettle, disturb, concern, trouble, disquiet; disconcert, discomfit, unnerve, alarm, bother; informal rattle.
–OPPOSITES reassure.

perturbed adjective **upset**, worried, unsettled, disturbed, concerned, troubled, anxious, ill at ease, uneasy, disquieted, fretful; disconcerted, discomposed, agitated, flustered, ruffled; informal twitchy, rattled, fazed; N. Amer. informal discombobulated.
–OPPOSITES calm.

peruse verb **read**, study, scrutinize, inspect, examine, wade through, look through; browse through, leaf through, scan, run your eye over, glance through, flick through, skim through, thumb through.

pervade verb **permeate**, spread through, fill, suffuse, imbue, penetrate, filter through, infuse, inform.

pervasive adjective **prevalent**, pervading, extensive, ubiquitous, omnipresent, universal, widespread, general.

perverse adjective **1** *he is being deliberately perverse:* **awkward**, contrary, difficult, unreasonable, uncooperative, unhelpful, obstructive, stubborn, obstinate, obdurate; informal cussed; Brit. informal bloody-minded; formal refractory. **2** *a verdict that is manifestly perverse:* **illogical**, irrational, wrong-headed. **3** *perverse forms of pleasure:* **perverted**, depraved, unnatural, abnormal, deviant, warped, twisted; informal kinky, sick, pervy.
–OPPOSITES accommodating, reasonable.

perversion noun **1** *a perversion of the truth:* **distortion**, misrepresentation, travesty, twisting, corruption, misuse. **2** *sexual perversion:* **deviance**, abnormality; depravity.

perversity noun **1** *out of sheer perversity, he refused:* **contrariness**, awkwardness, recalcitrance, stubbornness, obstinacy, obduracy; informal cussedness; Brit. informal bloody-mindedness. **2** *the perversity of the decision:* **unreasonableness**, irrationality, illogicality, wrongheadedness.

p

pervert verb **corrupt**, lead astray, debase, warp, pollute, poison, deprave, debauch.
•noun **deviant**, degenerate; informal perv, dirty old man, sicko.

perverted adjective **unnatural**, deviant, warped, twisted, abnormal, unhealthy, depraved, perverse, aberrant, debased, degenerate, wrong, bad; informal sick, kinky, pervy.

pessimism noun **defeatism**, negativity, doom and gloom, gloominess, cynicism, fatalism; hopelessness, depression, despair, despondency.
–OPPOSITES optimism.

pessimist noun **defeatist**, fatalist, prophet of doom, cynic; sceptic, doubter; misery, killjoy; informal doom and gloom merchant, wet blanket; N. Amer. informal gloomy Gus.
–OPPOSITES optimist.

pessimistic adjective **gloomy**, negative, defeatist, downbeat, cynical, bleak, fatalistic, dark, black, despairing, despondent, depressed, hopeless.
–OPPOSITES optimistic.

pest noun **nuisance**, annoyance, irritant, thorn in your flesh/side, trial, the bane of your life, menace, trouble, problem, worry, bother; informal pain in the neck, headache; Scottish informal skelf.

pester verb **badger**, hound, harass, plague, annoy, bother, trouble, persecute, torment, bedevil, harry, worry; informal hassle, bug, get on someone's back; N. English informal mither; N. Amer. informal devil.

pet adjective **1** *a pet lamb:* **tame**, domesticated, domestic; Brit. house-trained; N. Amer. housebroken. **2** *his pet theory:* **favourite**, favoured, cherished; particular, special, personal.
•verb **1** *the cats came to be petted:* **stroke**, caress, fondle, pat. **2** *couples petting in their cars:* **kiss and cuddle**, kiss, cuddle, embrace, caress; informal canoodle, neck, smooch; Brit. informal snog; N. Amer. informal make out, get it on; informal, dated spoon.

peter verb
■ **peter out** fizzle out, fade away, die away/out, dwindle, diminish, taper off, tail off, trail away/off, wane, ebb, melt away, evaporate, disappear.

petite adjective **small**, dainty, diminutive, slight, little, elfin, delicate, small-boned; Scottish wee.

petition noun **appeal**, round robin.
•verb **appeal to**, request, ask, call on, entreat, beg, implore, plead with, apply to, press, urge; literary beseech.

petrified adjective **1** *she looked petrified:* **terrified**, horrified, scared/frightened out of your wits, scared/frightened to death. **2** *petrified remains of prehistoric animals:* **ossified**, fossilized, calcified.

petrify verb **terrify**, horrify, scare/frighten to death, scare/frighten the living daylights out of; paralyse, transfix; informal scare the pants off; Irish informal scare the bejesus out of.

petrol noun **fuel**; N. Amer. gasoline, gas; informal juice.

petticoat noun **slip**, underskirt, half slip, underslip.

petty adjective **1** *petty regulations:* **trivial**, trifling, minor, insignificant, inconsequential, paltry, footling, pettifogging; informal piffling, piddling. **2** *a petty form of revenge:* **small-minded**, mean, shabby, spiteful.
– OPPOSITES important, magnanimous.

petulant adjective **peevish**, bad-tempered, querulous, pettish, fretful, irritable, sulky, crotchety, touchy, tetchy, testy, fractious; informal grouchy; Brit. informal ratty; N. English informal mardy; N. Amer. informal cranky.
– OPPOSITES good-humoured.

phantasmagorical adjective **dreamlike**, psychedelic, kaleidoscopic, surreal, unreal, hallucinatory, fantastic.

phantom noun **ghost**, apparition, spirit, spectre, wraith; informal spook; literary phantasm, shade.

phase noun **1** *the final phase of the campaign:* **stage**, period, chapter, episode, part, step, leg. **2** *he's going through a difficult phase:* **period**, stage, time, spell; Brit. informal patch.

phenomenal adjective **remarkable**, exceptional, extraordinary, amazing, astonishing, astounding, stunning, incredible, unbelievable; marvellous, magnificent, wonderful, outstanding, unprecedented; informal fantastic, terrific, tremendous, stupendous, awesome, out of this world; literary wondrous.
– OPPOSITES ordinary.

phenomenon noun **1** *a rare phenomenon:* **occurrence**, event, happening, fact, situation, circumstance, experience, case, incident, episode. **2** *a pop phenomenon:* **marvel**, sensation, wonder, prodigy.

philander verb **womanize**, have affairs, flirt; informal play around, carry on, play the field, play away, sleep around; N. Amer. informal fool around.

philanderer noun **womanizer**, Casanova, Don Juan, Lothario, flirt, ladies' man, playboy; informal stud, ladykiller.

philanthropic adjective **charitable**, generous, benevolent, humanitarian, public-spirited, altruistic, magnanimous; unselfish, kind.
– OPPOSITES selfish, mean.

philanthropist noun **benefactor**, good Samaritan; do-gooder.

philanthropy noun **benevolence**, generosity, humanitarianism, public-spiritedness, altruism, social conscience, charity, fellow feeling, magnanimity, unselfishness, humanity, kindness, kind-heartedness, compassion.

philistine adjective **uncultured**, lowbrow, uncultivated, uncivilized, uneducated, unenlightened, commercial, materialist, bourgeois; ignorant, crass, boorish, barbarian. • noun **barbarian**, boor, yahoo, materialist.

philosopher noun **thinker**, theorist, theoretician; scholar, intellectual, sage.

philosophical adjective **1** *a philosophical question:* **theoretical**, metaphysical. **2** *a philosophical mood:* **thoughtful**, reflective, pensive, meditative, contemplative, introspective. **3** *he was very philosophical about it:* **stoical**, self-possessed, serene, dispassionate, phlegmatic, forbearing, long-suffering, resigned.

philosophize verb **theorize**, speculate; pontificate, preach, sermonize, moralize.

philosophy noun **1** *the philosophy of Aristotle:* **thinking**, thought, reasoning. **2** *her political philosophy:* **beliefs**, credo, ideology, ideas, thinking, notions, theories, doctrine, tenets, principles, views.

phlegm noun **1 mucus**, catarrh. **2 calmness**, coolness, composure, equanimity, placidity, impassivity, imperturbability, impassiveness; informal cool, unflappability.

phlegmatic adjective **calm**, cool, composed, controlled, serene, tranquil, placid, impassive, imperturbable, unruffled, philosophical; informal unflappable.
– OPPOSITES excitable.

phobia noun **fear**, dread, horror, terror, aversion, antipathy, revulsion; complex, neurosis; informal thing, hang-up.

phone **noun** **telephone**, mobile; N. Amer. cell, cellphone; Brit. informal blower; Brit. rhyming slang dog and bone.
• **verb** *I'll phone you later:* **telephone**, call; Brit. ring, give someone a ring; informal give someone a buzz; Brit. informal give someone a bell/tinkle, get on the blower to.

phoney (informal) **adjective** *a phoney address:* **bogus**, false, fake, fraudulent, spurious; counterfeit, forged, imitation; pretended, contrived, affected, insincere; informal pretend, put-on; Brit. informal cod.
– OPPOSITES authentic.
• **noun 1** *he's nothing but a phoney:* **impostor**, sham, fake, fraud, charlatan; informal con artist. **2** *the diamond's a phoney:* **fake**, imitation, counterfeit, forgery.

photocopy **noun** *a photocopy of the letter:* **copy**, duplicate, reproduction, facsimile; trademark Xerox, photostat.
• **verb** *I photocopied the form:* **copy**, duplicate, xerox, photostat, reproduce.

photograph **noun** **picture**, photo, snap, snapshot, shot, likeness, print, still.
• **verb** **snap**, take, shoot, film.

photographer **noun** **lensman**, paparazzo; cameraman; informal pap; N. Amer. informal shutterbug.

photographic **adjective 1** *a photographic record:* **pictorial**, in photographs. **2** *a photographic memory:* **detailed**, exact, precise, accurate, vivid; Psychology eidetic.

phrase **noun** **expression**, construction, term, turn of phrase; idiom; saying.
• **verb** **express**, put into words, put, word, formulate, couch, frame, articulate, verbalize.

phraseology **noun** **wording**, phrasing, choice of words, usage, idiom, diction, parlance, words, language, vocabulary, terminology, style; jargon; informal lingo, -speak, -ese.

physical **adjective 1** *physical pleasure:* **bodily**, corporeal, corporal; carnal, fleshly, non-spiritual. **2** *physical work:* **manual**, labouring, blue-collar. **3** *the physical universe:* **material**, concrete, tangible, palpable, solid, substantial, real, actual, visible.
– OPPOSITES mental, spiritual.

physician **noun** **doctor**, medical practitioner, general practitioner, GP, clinician; specialist, consultant; informal doc, medic.

physiognomy **noun** **face**, features, countenance, expression, look, mien; informal mug; Brit. informal phizog, phiz; Brit. rhyming slang boat race; N. Amer. informal puss; literary visage.

physique **noun** **body**, build, figure, frame, anatomy, shape, form, proportions; muscles, musculature; informal vital statistics, bod.

pick **verb 1** *pick a time that suits you:* **choose**, select, single out, take, opt for, plump for, elect, decide on, settle on, fix on, sort out; name, nominate. **2** *he got a job picking apples:* **harvest**, gather, collect, pluck. **3** *he tried to pick a fight:* **provoke**, start, cause, incite, instigate, prompt, bring about.
• **noun** *the pick of the crop:* **best**, finest, choice, choicest, prime, cream, jewel, crème de la crème, elite.
■ **pick on** bully, victimize, torment, persecute, criticize, taunt, tease; informal get at, needle. **pick something out 1** *one painting was picked out for special mention:* choose, select, single out, elect, settle on; name, nominate. **2** *she picked out Jessica in the crowd:* see, make out, distinguish, discern, spot, perceive, detect, notice, recognize, identify, catch sight of, glimpse; literary espy. **pick up** improve, recover, rally, make a comeback, bounce back, perk up, look up, take a turn for the better, turn the corner, be on the mend, make headway, make progress. **pick someone/something up** lift, take up, raise, hoist, scoop up, gather up, snatch up. **pick someone up** *I'll pick you up after lunch:* fetch, collect, call for. **pick something up 1** *we picked it up at a flea market:* find, discover, come across, stumble across, happen on, chance on; acquire, obtain, come by, get; purchase, buy; informal get hold of, bag, land. **2** *he picked up the story in the 1950s:* resume, take up, start again, recommence, continue, carry/go on with. **3** *she picked up a virus:* catch, contract, get, go/come down

with. **4** *we're picking up a distress signal:* receive, detect, get, hear.

picket noun **1** *forty pickets were arrested:* **striker**, demonstrator, protester. **2** *fences made of cedar pickets:* **stake**, post, paling; upright. •verb *workers picketed the factory:* **demonstrate at**; blockade.

pickle noun **1** *a jar of pickle:* **relish**, chutney. **2** (informal) *they got into an awful pickle:* **plight**, predicament, mess, difficulty, trouble, dire/desperate straits, problem; informal tight corner, tight spot, jam, fix, scrape, bind, hole, hot water. •verb *fish pickled in brine:* **preserve**, souse, marinate.

pickup noun **improvement**, recovery, revival, upturn, upswing, rally, comeback, resurgence, renewal, turnaround.
–OPPOSITES slump.

pictorial adjective **illustrated**, in pictures, photographic, graphic.

picture noun **1** *pictures in an art gallery:* **painting**, **drawing**, sketch, watercolour, print, canvas, portrait, portrayal, illustration, artwork, depiction, likeness, representation, image; fresco, mural. **2** *we were told not to take pictures:* **photograph**, photo, snap, snapshot, shot, exposure, still, enlargement. **3** *my picture of the ideal woman:* **concept**, idea, impression, image, vision, visualization, notion. **4** *the picture of health:* **personification**, embodiment, epitome, essence, quintessence, soul, model. **5** *a picture starring Robert De Niro:* **film**, movie, motion picture; informal flick. •verb **1** *they were pictured playing in the snow:* **paint**, **draw**, sketch, photograph, depict, portray, show. **2** *Anne still pictured Richard as he had been:* **visualize**, see in your mind's eye, imagine, remember.

picturesque adjective **attractive**, pretty, beautiful, lovely, scenic, charming, quaint, pleasing, delightful.
–OPPOSITES ugly.

piddling adjective (informal) **trivial**, trifling, petty, tiny, insignificant, unimportant, inconsequential; meagre, inadequate, insufficient, paltry, derisory, pitiful, miserable, puny, niggardly, mere; informal measly, pathetic, piffling, mingy, poxy; N. Amer. informal nickel-and-dime.

piece noun **1** *a piece of cheese | a piece of wood:* **bit**, slice, chunk, segment, section, lump, hunk, wedge, slab, block, cake, bar, cube, stick, length; fragment, sliver, splinter, wafer, chip, crumb, scrap, remnant, shred, shard, snippet; mouthful, morsel; Brit. informal wodge. **2** *the pieces of a clock:* **component**, part, bit, section, constituent, element; unit, module. **3** *a piece of furniture:* **item**, article, specimen. **4** *a piece of the profit:* **share**, portion, slice, quota, part, bit, percentage, amount, quantity, ration, fraction; informal cut, rake-off; Brit. informal whack. **5** *pieces from his collection:* **work**, work of art, artwork, artefact; composition, opus. **6** *the reporter who wrote the piece:* **article**, item, story, report, essay, feature, review, column. **7** *the pieces on a chess board:* **token**, counter, man, disc, chip, tile.
■ **in one piece** unbroken, entire, whole, intact, undamaged, unharmed, unhurt, unscathed, safe and sound. **go to pieces** have a breakdown, break down, go out of your mind, lose control, lose your head, fall apart; informal crack up, lose it, fall apart at the seams, freak.

pièce de résistance noun **masterpiece**, magnum opus, chef-d'œuvre, masterwork, tour de force, showpiece, prize, jewel in the crown.

piecemeal adverb **a little at a time**, bit by bit, gradually, slowly, in stages/steps, step by step, little by little, by degrees, in fits and starts.

pier noun **jetty**, quay, wharf, dock, landing stage.

pierce verb **penetrate**, puncture, perforate, prick.

piercing adjective **1** *his piercing gaze:* **searching**, probing, penetrating, sharp, keen. **2** *a piercing shriek:* **shrill**, ear-splitting, high-pitched, penetrating, strident. **3** *the piercing wind:* **bitter**, biting, cutting, penetrating, sharp, keen, stinging, raw; freezing, frigid, glacial, arctic, chill.

piety noun **devoutness**, devotion, piousness, holiness, godliness; reverence, faith, spirituality.

piffle noun (informal). See **NONSENSE** sense 1.

P

piffling adjective (informal) **inadequate**, tiny, minimal, trifling, paltry, pitiful, negligible; miserly, miserable; informal measly, stingy, lousy, pathetic, piddling, mingy, poxy.

pig noun **1** *a herd of pigs:* **hog**, boar, sow, porker, swine; piglet; children's word piggy. **2** (informal) *he's such a pig:* **glutton**; informal hog, greedy guts; Brit. informal gannet.

> **WORD LINKS**
> **porcine** relating to pigs

pigeonhole noun *the film didn't fit the costume-drama pigeonholes:* **category**, class, group, designation. •verb *they were pigeonholed as an indie guitar band:* **categorize**, compartmentalize, classify, characterize, label, brand, tag, designate.

pig-headed adjective **obstinate**, stubborn, obdurate, headstrong, self-willed, wilful, perverse, contrary, recalcitrant, stiff-necked, intransigent, unyielding; Brit. informal bloody-minded; formal refractory.

pigment noun **colouring**, colour, tint, dye.

pile[1] noun **1** *a pile of stones:* **heap**, stack, mound, pyramid, mass; collection, accumulation, assemblage, stockpile, hoard. **2** (informal) *I've a pile of work to do:* **lot**, reams, mountain; abundance, cornucopia, plethora; informal load, heap, mass, slew, ocean, stack, ton; Brit. informal shedload; Austral./NZ informal swag. •verb **1** *he piled his plate with salad:* **load**, heap, fill, stack, charge. **2** *we piled into the car:* **crowd**, climb, pack, squeeze.

■ **pile up** *his debts are piling up:* accumulate, grow, mount up, escalate, soar, spiral, rocket, increase, accrue, build up, multiply.

pile[2] noun *a carpet with a short pile:* **nap**, fibres, threads.

pile-up noun **crash**, collision, smash, accident; Brit. RTA (road traffic accident); N. Amer. wreck; Brit. informal shunt.

pilfer verb **steal**, thieve, take, snatch, purloin, loot; informal swipe, rob, nab, rip off, lift, filch, snaffle; Brit. informal pinch, half-inch, nick, whip, knock off, nobble; N. Amer. informal heist.

pilgrimage noun **journey**, expedition, visit, trek; odyssey.

pill noun **tablet**, capsule, pellet, lozenge, pastille.

pillage verb **1** *the abbey was pillaged:* **ransack**, rob, plunder, raid, loot; sack, devastate, lay waste, ravage. **2** *columns pillaged from an ancient tomb:* **steal**, take, purloin, loot; informal rob, nab, lift; Brit. informal pinch, nick.

pillar noun **1** *stone pillars:* **column**, post, support, upright, pier, pile, pilaster, stanchion, prop; obelisk, monolith. **2** *a pillar of the community:* **stalwart**, mainstay, bastion, rock; leading light, worthy, backbone, support, upholder, champion.

pillory verb **attack**, criticize, censure, condemn, lambaste, savage, denounce; informal knock, slam, pan, bash, crucify, hammer; Brit. informal slate, rubbish, slag off; formal excoriate.

pillow noun **cushion**, bolster, pad; headrest.

pilot noun **1** *a fighter pilot:* **airman**, **airwoman**, flyer; captain; informal skipper; N. Amer. informal jock; dated aviator, aeronaut. **2** *a harbour pilot:* **navigator**, helmsman, steersman, coxswain. **3** *a pilot for a TV series:* **trial**; sample, experiment. •adjective *a pilot project:* **experimental**, exploratory, trial, test, sample, speculative; preliminary. •verb *he piloted the jet to safety:* **navigate**, guide, manoeuvre, steer, control, direct, captain; fly, aviate; drive; sail; informal skipper.

pimple noun **spot**, pustule, boil, swelling, eruption, blackhead, carbuncle; (**pimples**) acne; informal whitehead, zit; Scottish informal plook.

pin noun **1** *fasten the hem with a pin:* **tack**, safety pin, nail, staple, fastener. **2** *a broken pin in the machine:* **bolt**, peg, rivet, dowel. •verb **1** *she pinned the brooch to her dress:* **attach**, fasten, affix, fix, clip; join, secure. **2** *she was pinned against the door:* **hold**, press; pinion.

pinch verb **1** *he pinched my arm:* **nip**, tweak, squeeze, grasp; hurt. **2** (Brit. informal) *someone pinched her phone:* **steal**, take, snatch, pilfer, purloin; informal swipe, rob, nab, lift, filch; Brit. informal nick, half-inch, whip.

• **noun** *a pinch of salt:* **bit**, touch, dash, spot, trace, soupçon, speck, taste; informal smidgen, tad.

pinched adjective **strained**; tired, worn; thin, drawn, haggard, gaunt.
– OPPOSITES healthy.

pine verb **yearn**, long, ache, sigh, hunger, languish; miss, mourn.

pinion verb **hold down**, pin down, restrain, hold fast, immobilize; tie, bind, truss, shackle, fetter, hobble, manacle, handcuff; informal cuff.

pink adjective **rose**, rosy, rosé, pale red, salmon, coral; flushed, blushing.
■ **in the pink** (informal) in good health, healthy, well, hale and hearty; blooming, flourishing, thriving, vigorous, strong, lusty, robust, in fine fettle, in excellent shape.

pinnacle noun **1** *pinnacles of rock:* **peak**, needle, crag, tor; summit, crest, apex, tip. **2** *the pinnacle of the sport:* **highest level**, peak, height, high point, top, apex, zenith, apogee, acme.
– OPPOSITES nadir.

pinpoint noun **point**, spot, speck, dot.
• **adjective** **precise**, strict, exact, meticulous, scrupulous.
• **verb** **identify**, determine, distinguish, discover, find, locate, detect, track down, spot, diagnose, recognize, pin down, home in on, put your finger on.

pioneer noun **1** *the pioneers of the Wild West:* **settler**, colonist, colonizer, frontiersman/woman, explorer. **2** *a pioneer of motoring:* **developer**, innovator, trailblazer, groundbreaker; founding father, architect, creator.
• **verb** *he pioneered the sale of insurance:* **introduce**, develop, launch, instigate, initiate, spearhead, institute, establish, found, be the father/mother of, originate, set in motion, create; lay the groundwork, prepare the way, blaze a trail, break new ground.

pious adjective **1** *a pious family:* **religious**, devout, God-fearing, churchgoing, holy, godly, saintly, reverent, righteous. **2** *a pious platitude:* **sanctimonious**, hypocritical, insincere, self-righteous, holier-than-thou, churchy; informal goody-goody. **3** *a pious hope:* **forlorn**, vain, doomed, hopeless, desperate; unlikely, unrealistic.
– OPPOSITES irreligious.

pip noun **seed**, stone, pit.

pipe noun **1** *a central-heating pipe:* **tube**, conduit, hose, main, duct, line, channel, pipeline, drain; tubing, piping. **2** *she was playing a pipe:* **whistle**, penny whistle, flute, recorder, fife; chanter. **3** *the sound of the pipes:* **bagpipes**, uillean pipes, Northumberland pipes.
• **verb** **1** *the beer is piped into barrels:* **siphon**, feed, channel, run, convey. **2** *programmes piped in from London:* **transmit**, feed, patch.
■ **pipe down** (informal) be quiet, be silent, hush, hold your tongue; informal shut up, shut your mouth, button it, button your lip, belt up, put a sock in it.

pipe dream noun **fantasy**, false hope, illusion, delusion, daydream, chimera; castle in the air; informal pie in the sky.

pipeline noun *a gas pipeline:* **pipe**, conduit, main, line, duct, tube.
■ **in the pipeline** on the way, coming, forthcoming, upcoming, imminent, about to happen, near, close, brewing, in the offing, in the wind.

piquant adjective **1** *a piquant sauce:* **spicy**, tangy, peppery, hot; tasty, flavoursome, savoury; pungent, sharp, tart, zesty, strong, salty. **2** *a piquant story:* **intriguing**, stimulating, interesting, fascinating, colourful, exciting, lively; spicy, provocative, racy; informal juicy.
– OPPOSITES bland, dull.

pique noun *a fit of pique:* **irritation**, annoyance, resentment, anger, displeasure, indignation, petulance, ill humour, vexation, exasperation, disgruntlement, discontent.
• **verb** **1** *his curiosity was piqued:* **stimulate**, arouse, rouse, provoke, whet, awaken, excite, kindle, stir, galvanize. **2** *she was piqued by his neglect:* **irritate**, annoy, bother, vex, displease, upset, offend, affront, anger, gall, irk, nettle; informal peeve, aggravate, miff, rile, bug, needle, get someone's back up, hack off, get someone's goat; Brit. informal nark; N. Amer. informal tick off, tee off.

piracy noun **1** *piracy on the high seas:* **robbery**, freebooting, hijacking; old use buccaneering. **2** *software piracy:* **copying**, plagiarism, copyright infringement, bootlegging.

pirate noun *pirates boarded the ship:* **freebooter**, hijacker, marauder, raider; historical privateer; old use buccaneer, corsair.
•verb *designers may pirate good ideas:* **steal**, copy, plagiarize, poach, appropriate, bootleg; informal crib, lift, rip off; Brit. informal nick, pinch.

pirouette noun **spin**, twirl, whirl, turn.
•verb **spin round**, twirl, whirl, turn round, revolve.

pistol noun **handgun**, gun, revolver, side arm; six-shooter; informal gat; N. Amer. informal piece, shooting iron.

pit[1] noun **1 hole**, trough, hollow, excavation, cavity, crater, pothole; shaft. **2 coal mine**, colliery, quarry.
•verb *his skin had been pitted by acne:* **mark**, pockmark, pock, scar.

pit[2] noun *cherry pits:* **stone**, pip, seed.

pitch[1] noun **1** *the pitch was unfit for cricket:* **playing field**, ground; Brit. park. **2** *her voice rose in pitch:* **tone**, key, modulation, frequency. **3** *the pitch of the roof:* **gradient**, slope, slant, angle, steepness, tilt, incline. **4** *her anger reached such a pitch that she screamed:* **level**, intensity, point, degree, height, extent. **5** *his sales pitch:* **patter**, talk; informal spiel, line. **6** *street traders reserved their pitches:* **site**, place, spot, station; Brit. informal patch.
•verb **1** *he pitched the note into the fire:* **throw**, toss, fling, hurl, cast, lob, flip; informal chuck, sling, heave, bung. **2** *he pitched overboard:* **fall**, tumble, topple, plunge, plummet. **3** *they pitched their tents:* **put up**, set up, erect, raise. **4** *the boat pitched:* **lurch**, toss, plunge, roll, reel, sway, rock, list.
■ **pitch in** help, assist, lend a hand, join in, participate, contribute, do your bit, chip in, cooperate, collaborate; Brit. informal muck in.

pitch[2] noun *cement coated with pitch:* **bitumen**, asphalt, tar.

pitch-black adjective **black**, dark, inky, jet-black, coal-black, ebony; starless.

pitcher noun **jug**, ewer, jar; N. Amer. creamer.

pitfall noun **hazard**, danger, risk, peril, difficulty, catch, snag, stumbling block, drawback.

pith noun **essence**, main point, fundamentals, heart, substance, nub, core, quintessence, crux, gist, meat, kernel, marrow, burden; informal nitty-gritty.

pithy adjective **succinct**, terse, concise, compact, short, short and sweet, brief, condensed, to the point, epigrammatic, crisp; significant, meaningful, telling.
–OPPOSITES verbose.

pitiful adjective **1** *the child was in a pitiful state:* **distressing**, sad, piteous, pitiable, pathetic, heartrending, moving, touching, tear-jerking; plaintive, poignant, forlorn; poor, sorry, wretched, abject, miserable. **2** *a pitiful £50 a month:* **paltry**, miserable, meagre, trifling, negligible, pitiable, derisory; informal pathetic, measly, piddling, mingy; Brit. informal poxy. **3** *his performance was pitiful:* **dreadful**, awful, terrible, lamentable, hopeless, feeble, pitiable, woeful, inadequate, deplorable, laughable; informal pathetic, useless, appalling, lousy, abysmal, dire.

pitiless adjective **merciless**, unmerciful, ruthless, cruel, heartless, remorseless, hard-hearted, cold-hearted, harsh, callous, severe, unsparing, unforgiving, unfeeling, uncaring, unsympathetic, uncharitable.
–OPPOSITES merciful.

pittance noun **a tiny amount**, next to nothing; informal peanuts, chicken feed; N. Amer. informal chump change.

pitted adjective **1** *his skin was pitted:* **pockmarked**, pocked, scarred, marked, blemished. **2** *the pitted lane:* **potholed**, rutted, bumpy, rough, uneven.
–OPPOSITES smooth.

pity noun **compassion**, commiseration, condolence, sympathy, fellow feeling, understanding; mercy, clemency.
–OPPOSITES indifference, cruelty.
•verb **feel sorry for**, feel for, sympathize with, empathize with, commiserate with, condole with, grieve for.

p

pivot noun **fulcrum**, axis, axle, swivel; pin, shaft, hub, spindle, hinge, kingpin.
• verb **1** *the panel pivots inwards:* **rotate**, turn, swivel, revolve, spin. **2** *it all pivoted on his response:* **depend**, hinge, turn, centre, hang, rely, rest; revolve around.

pivotal adjective **central**, crucial, vital, critical, focal, essential, key, decisive.

pixie noun **elf**, fairy, sprite, imp, brownie, puck, leprechaun.

placard noun **notice**, poster, sign, bill, advertisement; banner; informal ad; Brit. informal advert.

placate verb **pacify**, calm, appease, mollify, soothe, win over, conciliate, propitiate, make peace with, humour; Austral./NZ square someone off.
– OPPOSITES provoke.

place noun **1** *an ideal place for dinner:* **location**, site, spot, setting, position, situation, area, region, locale; venue; technical locus. **2** *foreign places:* **country**, state, area, region, town, city; district; literary clime. **3** *a place of her own:* **home**, house, flat, apartment; accommodation, property, pied-à-terre; rooms, quarters; informal pad, digs; Brit. informal gaff; formal residence, abode, dwelling, domicile, habitation. **4** *I offered him a place in the company:* **job**, position, post, appointment, situation; employment. **5** *I know my place:* **status**, position, standing, rank, niche. **6** *it was not her place to sort it out:* **responsibility**, duty, job, task, role, function, concern, affair, charge.
• verb **1** *books were placed on the table:* **put**, set, lay, deposit, position, plant, rest, stand, station, situate, leave; informal stick, dump, bung, park, plonk, pop; N. Amer. informal plunk. **2** *the trust you placed in me:* **put**, lay, set, invest. **3** *a survey placed the company sixth:* **rank**, order, grade, class, classify; put, set, assign. **4** *Joe couldn't quite place her:* **identify**, recognize, remember, put a name to, pin down; locate, pinpoint. **5** *we were placed with foster parents:* **accommodate**, house; allocate, assign.
■ **in place 1** *the veil was held in place by pearls:* in position, in situ. **2** *the plans are in place:* ready, set up, all set, established, arranged, in order.**out of place 1** *he said something out of place:* inappropriate, unsuitable, unseemly, improper, untoward, out of keeping, unbecoming, wrong. **2** *she seemed out of place in her country clothes:* incongruous, out of your element, like a fish out of water; uncomfortable, uneasy. **put someone in their place** humiliate, take down a peg or two, deflate, crush, squash, humble; informal cut down to size. **take place** happen, occur, come about, transpire, crop up, materialize, arise; N. Amer. informal go down; literary come to pass. **take the place of** replace, stand in for, substitute for, act for, fill in for, cover for, relieve.

placement noun **1** *the placement of the chairs:* **positioning**, placing, arrangement, position, deployment, location. **2** *teaching placements:* **job**, post, assignment, posting, position, appointment, engagement.

placid adjective **1** *she's normally very placid:* **even-tempered**, calm, tranquil, equable, unexcitable, serene, mild, composed, self-possessed, poised, easy-going, level-headed, steady, unruffled, unperturbed, phlegmatic; informal unflappable. **2** *a placid village:* **quiet**, calm, tranquil, still, peaceful, undisturbed, restful, sleepy.
– OPPOSITES excitable, bustling.

plagiarism noun **copying**, infringement of copyright, piracy, theft, stealing; informal cribbing.

plagiarize verb **copy**, pirate, steal, poach, appropriate; informal rip off, crib, 'borrow'; Brit. informal pinch, nick.

plague noun **1** *they died of the plague:* **bubonic plague**, the Black Death; dated contagion; old use pestilence. **2** *a plague of cat fleas:* **infestation**, epidemic, invasion, swarm, multitude, host. **3** *staff theft is often the plague of restaurants:* **bane**, curse, scourge; affliction, blight.
• verb **1** *he was plagued by poor health:* **afflict**, bedevil, torment, trouble, beset, dog, curse. **2** *he plagued her with questions:* **pester**, harass, badger, bother, torment, persecute, bedevil, harry, hound, trouble, nag; informal hassle, bug, aggravate; N. English informal mither.

p

plain adjective **1** *it was plain that something was wrong:* **obvious**, clear, evident, apparent; unmistakable, transparent, crystal clear; pronounced, marked, manifest, striking, conspicuous, self-evident, indisputable; as plain as a pikestaff, writ large; informal standing/sticking out like a sore thumb, standing/sticking out a mile. **2** *plain English:* **intelligible**, comprehensible, understandable, clear, lucid, simple, straightforward, user-friendly. **3** *plain speaking:* **candid**, frank, outspoken, forthright, direct, honest, truthful, blunt, bald, unequivocal; informal upfront. **4** *a plain dress:* **simple**, ordinary, unadorned, homely, basic, modest, unsophisticated; restrained, muted; everyday, workaday. **5** *a plain girl:* **unattractive**, unprepossessing, ugly, ordinary; N. Amer. homely; informal not much to look at; Brit. informal no oil painting. **6** *it was plain bad luck:* **sheer**, pure, downright, out-and-out.
– OPPOSITES obscure, complicated, attractive, pretentious.
• adverb *that's just plain stupid:* **downright**, utterly, absolutely, completely, totally, really, thoroughly, unquestionably, positively; informal plumb.
• noun *the plains of North America:* **grassland**, flatland, prairie, savannah, steppe; tundra, pampas, veld.

p

plain-spoken adjective **candid**, frank, outspoken, forthright, direct, honest, truthful, open, blunt, straightforward, explicit, unequivocal, unambiguous, not afraid to call a spade a spade; informal upfront.
– OPPOSITES evasive.

plaintive adjective **mournful**, sad, pathetic, pitiful, melancholy, sorrowful, unhappy, wretched, woeful, forlorn.

plan noun **1** *a plan for raising money:* **scheme**, idea, proposal, proposition; project, programme, system, method, strategy, stratagem, formula, recipe. **2** *her plan was to break even:* **intention**, aim, idea, intent, objective, object, goal, target, ambition. **3** *plans for the clubhouse:* **blueprint**, drawing, diagram, sketch; N. Amer. plat.
• verb **1** *plan your route in advance:* **organize**, arrange, work out, design, outline, map out, prepare, formulate, frame, develop, devise, concoct. **2** *he plans to buy a house:* **intend**, aim, propose, mean, hope. **3** *I'm planning a new garden:* **design**, draw up, sketch out, map out; N. Amer. plat.

plane[1] noun *a higher plane of achievement:* **level**, degree, standard, stratum; dimension.
• adjective *a plane surface:* **flat**, level, horizontal, even; smooth, regular, uniform.
• verb *boats planed across the water:* **skim**, glide.

plane[2] noun *the plane took off:* **aircraft**, airliner; jet; Brit. aeroplane; N. Amer. airplane, ship.

> **WORD LINKS**
> **aeronautics** the science of flight

planet noun **celestial body**, heavenly body, satellite, asteroid; literary orb, sphere.

plank noun **board**, floorboard, timber.

planning noun **preparation**, organization, arrangement, design; forethought, groundwork.

plant noun **1** *garden plants:* flower, vegetable, herb, shrub, weed; (**plants**) vegetation, greenery, flora. **2** *a CIA plant:* **spy**, informant, informer, secret agent, mole, infiltrator, operative; N. Amer. informal spook. **3** *a chemical plant:* **factory**, works; refinery, mill.
• verb **1** *plant the seeds:* **sow**, scatter; transplant. **2** *he planted his feet on the ground:* **place**, put, set, position, situate, settle; informal plonk. **3** *she planted the idea in his mind:* **instil**, implant, put, place, introduce, fix, establish, lodge.

> **WORD LINKS**
> **botany** the scientific study of plants
> **herbivorous** plant-eating
> **herbicide** a substance used to kill plants

plaque noun **plate**, tablet, panel, sign.

plaster noun **1** *the plaster covering the bricks:* **plasterwork**, stucco. **2** *a statuette made of plaster:* **plaster**

of Paris, gypsum. **3** *waterproof plasters:* **sticking plaster**, dressing; trademark Elastoplast, Band-Aid.
• verb **1** *bread plastered with butter:* **spread**, smother, smear, cake, coat. **2** *his hair was plastered down with sweat:* **flatten down**, smooth down, slick down.

plastic adjective **1** *at high temperatures the rocks become plastic:* **malleable**, mouldable, pliable, ductile, flexible, soft, workable, bendable; informal bendy. **2** *the plastic minds of children:* **impressionable**, malleable, receptive, pliable, pliant, flexible; persuadable, susceptible, manipulable. **3** *a plastic smile:* **artificial**, false, fake, superficial, bogus, unnatural, insincere; informal phoney, pretend.
– OPPOSITES rigid, intractable, genuine.

plate noun **1** *a dinner plate:* **dish**, platter, salver; historical trencher; old use charger. **2** *a plate of spaghetti:* **plateful**, helping, portion, serving. **3** *steel plates:* **panel**, sheet, slab. **4** *a brass plate on the door:* **plaque**, sign, tablet. **5** *the book has colour plates:* **picture**, print, illustration, photograph, photo.
• verb *the roof was plated with steel:* **cover**, coat, overlay, laminate, veneer, armour.

plateau noun **upland**, mesa, highland.

platform noun **1** *he made a speech from the platform:* **stage**, dais, rostrum, podium. **2** *the Democratic Party's platform:* **policy**, programme, party line, manifesto.

platitude noun **cliché**, truism, commonplace, old chestnut.

platonic adjective **non-sexual**, non-physical, chaste; intellectual.
– OPPOSITES sexual, physical.

platoon noun **unit**, patrol, troop, squad, squadron, team, company, corps, outfit, detachment, contingent.

platter noun **plate**, dish, salver, tray; historical trencher; old use charger.

plaudits plural noun **praise**, acclaim, commendation, congratulations, accolades, compliments, cheers, applause, tributes.
– OPPOSITES criticism.

plausible adjective **credible**, reasonable, believable, likely, feasible, tenable, possible, conceivable, imaginable; convincing.
– OPPOSITES unlikely.

play verb **1** *the children played with toys:* **amuse yourself**, entertain yourself, enjoy yourself, have fun; relax, occupy yourself, divert yourself; frolic, romp; informal mess about/around, lark about/around. **2** *I used to play football:* **take part in**, participate in, be involved in, compete in, do. **3** *Liverpool play Oxford on Sunday:* **compete against**, take on, meet. **4** *he was to play Macbeth:* **portray**, perform, depict, represent, impersonate, act, appear as. **5** *the sunlight played on the water:* **dance**, glitter; sparkle, glint.
• noun **1** *work and play:* **amusement**, relaxation, recreation, diversion, leisure; enjoyment, pleasure, fun; informal R & R. **2** *a Shakespeare play:* **drama**, theatrical work; comedy, tragedy; production, performance. **3** *there was no play in the rope:* **movement**, slack, give.
■ **play ball** (informal) cooperate, collaborate, play the game, show willing, help, lend a hand, assist. **play something down** make light of, make little of, gloss over, downplay, understate; soft-pedal, diminish, trivialize, underrate, underestimate, undervalue. **play for time** stall, temporize, delay, hold back, hang fire, procrastinate, drag your feet. **play it by ear** improvise, extemporize, ad lib, make it up as you go along, think on your feet; informal busk it, wing it. **play on** exploit, take advantage of, use, turn to account, profit by, capitalize on, trade on, milk, abuse. **play up** (Brit. informal) **1** *the boys really did play up:* misbehave, be bad, be naughty. **2** *the boiler's playing up:* malfunction, not work, be defective, be faulty; informal go on the blink, act up. **play up to** ingratiate yourself with, curry favour with, court, fawn over, make up to, toady to, crawl to, pander to, flatter; informal soft-soap, suck up to, butter up.

playboy noun **socialite**, pleasure-seeker; ladies' man, womanizer, philanderer, rake, roué; informal ladykiller.

player noun **1 participant**, contestant, competitor, contender. **2 musician**, performer, instrumentalist. **3 actor**, **actress**, performer, thespian, entertainer, artist, artiste, trouper.

playful adjective **1** *a playful mood:* **frisky**, lively, full of fun, frolicsome, high-spirited, exuberant; mischievous, impish, rascally, tricksy; informal full of beans. **2** *a playful remark:* **light-hearted**, jokey, teasing, humorous, jocular, facetious, frivolous, flippant; informal waggish.
– OPPOSITES serious.

playmate noun **friend**, playfellow, companion; informal chum, pal; Brit. informal mate; N. Amer. informal buddy.

playwright noun **dramatist**; scriptwriter, screenwriter, writer.

plea noun **appeal**, entreaty, supplication, petition, request, call, suit, solicitation.

plead verb **1** *he pleaded with her to stay:* **beg**, implore, entreat, appeal to, ask, importune, supplicate; literary beseech. **2** *she pleaded ignorance:* **claim**, assert, allege, argue, state, maintain.

pleasant adjective **1** *a pleasant evening:* **enjoyable**, pleasurable, nice, agreeable; entertaining, amusing, delightful, charming; fine, balmy; informal lovely, great. **2** *the staff are pleasant:* **friendly**, agreeable, amiable, nice, genial, cordial, likeable, good-natured, personable; hospitable, approachable, gracious, courteous, polite, obliging, helpful, considerate; charming, lovely, delightful, sweet.
– OPPOSITES disagreeable.

pleasantry noun **banter**, badinage; polite/casual remark.

please verb **1** *it pleased him to be seen with her:* **make happy**, delight, charm, amuse, cheer; satisfy, gratify, humour, oblige, content, suit; informal tickle someone pink. **2** *do as you please:* **like**, want, wish, desire, see fit, think fit, choose, will, prefer.
– OPPOSITES annoy.

pleased adjective **happy**, glad, delighted, gratified, grateful, thankful, content, contented, satisfied; thrilled; informal over the moon, tickled pink, on cloud nine; Brit. informal chuffed; N. English informal made up; Austral. informal wrapped.
– OPPOSITES unhappy.

pleasing adjective **1** *a pleasing result:* **good**, agreeable, pleasant, pleasurable, satisfying, gratifying, great. **2** *her pleasing manner:* **friendly**, amiable, pleasant, agreeable, affable, nice, genial, likeable, charming, engaging, delightful.

pleasurable adjective **pleasant**, enjoyable, nice, pleasing, agreeable, gratifying; fun, entertaining, amusing, diverting.

pleasure noun **1** *she smiled with pleasure:* **happiness**, delight, joy, gladness, glee, satisfaction, gratification, contentment, enjoyment, amusement. **2** *his greatest pleasure in life:* **joy**, amusement, diversion, recreation, pastime; treat, thrill. **3** *don't mix business and pleasure:* **enjoyment**, fun, entertainment; recreation, leisure, relaxation. **4** *a life of pleasure:* **hedonism**, indulgence, self-indulgence, gratification, lotus-eating.
■ **take pleasure in** enjoy, delight in, love, like, appreciate, relish, savour, revel in, glory in; informal get a kick out of, get a thrill out of.

pleat noun **fold**, crease, gather, tuck.
• verb **fold**, crease, gather, tuck, crimp.

plebeian noun *plebeians and gentry lived together:* **proletarian**, commoner, working-class person, worker; peasant; derogatory pleb, prole.
– OPPOSITES aristocrat.
• adjective **1** *people of plebeian descent:* **lower-class**, working-class, proletarian, common, peasant; mean, humble, lowly. **2** *plebeian tastes:* **uncultured**, uncultivated, unrefined, lowbrow, philistine, uneducated; coarse, uncouth, common, vulgar; Brit. informal non-U.
– OPPOSITES noble, refined.

plebiscite noun **vote**, referendum, ballot, poll.

pledge noun *his election pledge:* **promise**, undertaking, vow, word of honour, commitment, assurance, oath, guarantee.
• verb **1** *he pledged to root out corruption:* **promise**, vow, swear, undertake, commit yourself,

declare, affirm. **2** *they pledged £100 million:* **promise**, donate, contribute, give, put up.

plenary adjective **full**, complete, entire.

plentiful adjective **abundant**, copious, ample, profuse, rich, lavish, generous, bountiful, large, great, bumper, prolific; informal a gogo, galore; literary plenteous.
– OPPOSITES scarce.

plenty noun *times of plenty:* **prosperity**, affluence, wealth, opulence, comfort, luxury; plentifulness, abundance.
• pronoun *there are plenty of books:* **a lot of**, many, a great deal of, a plethora of, enough, no lack of, sufficient, a wealth of; informal loads of, lots of, heaps of, stacks of, masses of, tons of, oodles of.

plethora noun **excess**, abundance, superabundance, surplus, glut, surfeit, profusion, too many, too much, enough and to spare.
– OPPOSITES dearth.

pliable adjective **1** *leather is pliable:* **flexible**, pliant, bendable, supple, workable, plastic; informal bendy. **2** *pliable teenage minds:* **malleable**, impressionable, flexible, adaptable, pliant, biddable, tractable, suggestible, persuadable, manipulable.
– OPPOSITES rigid, obdurate.

pliant adjective. See PLIABLE senses 1, 2.

plight noun **predicament**, difficult situation, dire straits, trouble, difficulty, extremity, bind; informal dilemma, tight corner, tight spot, hole, pickle, jam, fix.

plod verb **trudge**, walk heavily, clump, stomp, tramp, lumber, slog; Brit. informal trog.

plot noun **1** *a plot to overthrow him:* **conspiracy**, intrigue, plan. **2** *the plot of her novel:* **storyline**, story, scenario, action, thread. **3** *a three-acre plot:* **piece of ground**, patch, area, tract, acreage; Brit. allotment; N. Amer. lot, plat; N. Amer. & Austral./NZ homesite.
• verb **1** *he plotted their downfall:* **plan**, scheme, arrange, organize, hatch, concoct, devise, dream up; informal cook up. **2** *his brother was plotting against him:* **conspire**, scheme, intrigue, connive. **3** *the points were plotted on a graph:* **mark**, chart, map.

plotter noun **conspirator**, schemer, intriguer.

plough verb **1** *the fields were ploughed:* **till**, furrow, harrow, cultivate, work. **2** *the car ploughed into a wall:* **crash**, smash, career, plunge, bulldoze, hurtle, cannon, run, drive; N. Amer. informal barrel.

ploy noun **ruse**, tactic, move, device, stratagem, scheme, trick, gambit, plan, manoeuvre, dodge, subterfuge; Brit. informal wheeze.

pluck verb **1** *he plucked a thread from his lapel:* **remove**, pick, pull, extract, take. **2** *she plucked at his T-shirt:* **pull**, tug, clutch, snatch, grab, tweak; informal yank. **3** *she plucked the guitar strings:* **strum**, pick, thrum, twang.
• noun *he showed a lot of pluck:* **courage**, bravery, nerve, backbone, spine, daring, spirit, grit; informal guts, spunk; Brit. informal bottle; N. Amer. informal moxie.

plucky adjective **brave**, courageous, spirited, game; informal gutsy, spunky.
– OPPOSITES timid.

plug noun **1** *she pulled out the plug:* **stopper**, bung, cork, seal; N. Amer. stopple. **2** (informal) *a plug for his new book:* **advertisement**, promotion, commercial, recommendation, mention, good word; informal hype, push, puff, ad, boost; Brit. informal advert.
• verb **1** *plug the holes:* **stop up**, seal, close, block, fill. **2** (informal) *she plugged her new film:* **publicize**, promote, advertise, mention, bang the drum for; informal hype up, push.
■ **plug away** (informal) toil, labour, slave away, soldier on, persevere, persist, keep on, plough on; informal slog away, beaver away, peg away.

plumb[1] verb *an attempt to plumb the depths of the human psyche:* **explore**, probe, delve into, search, examine, investigate, fathom, penetrate, understand.
• adverb **1** (informal) *it went plumb through the screen:* **right**, exactly, precisely, directly, dead, straight; informal slap bang. **2** (N. Amer. informal) *he's plumb crazy:* **utterly**, absolutely, completely, downright, totally, quite, thoroughly.

plumb[2] verb *he plumbed in the washing machine:* **install**, put in, fit.

plume noun **feather**, quill.

plummet verb **plunge**, fall, drop, tumble, hurtle, dive, nosedive.

plump[1] adjective *a plump child:* **chubby**, fat, rotund, well padded, ample, round, chunky, portly, overweight, fleshy, paunchy, bulky, corpulent; informal tubby, roly-poly, pudgy; Brit. informal podgy; N. Amer. informal zaftig, corn-fed.
– OPPOSITES thin.

plump[2] verb *he plumped down on to a chair:* **flop**, collapse, sink, fall, drop, slump; informal plonk yourself.
■ **plump for** choose, decide on, go for, opt for, pick, settle on, select, take, elect.

plunder verb **1** *they plundered the countryside:* **pillage**, loot, rob, raid, ransack, despoil, strip, ravage, lay waste, sack, devastate. **2** *money plundered from pension funds:* **steal**, purloin, seize, pillage; embezzle.
• noun *huge quantities of plunder:* **booty**, loot, stolen goods, spoils, ill-gotten gains; informal swag.

plunge verb **1** *Joy plunged into the sea:* **dive**, jump, throw yourself. **2** *the aircraft plunged to the ground:* **plummet**, nosedive, drop, fall, tumble, descend. **3** *the car plunged down an alley:* **charge**, hurtle, career, plough, tear; N. Amer. informal barrel. **4** *oil prices plunged:* **fall sharply**, plummet, drop, go down, tumble, slump; informal crash, nosedive. **5** *he plunged the dagger into her back:* **thrust**, stab, sink, stick, ram, drive, push, shove, force. **6** *plunge the pears into water:* **immerse**, submerge, dip, dunk. **7** *the room was plunged into darkness:* **throw**, cast.
• noun **1** *a plunge in the pool:* **dive**, jump, dip. **2** *a plunge in profits:* **fall**, drop, slump; informal nosedive, crash.
■ **take the plunge** commit yourself, go for it; informal go for broke.

plurality noun **variety**, diversity, range, multitude, multiplicity, wealth, profusion, abundance, plethora, host; informal load, stack, heap, mass.

plus preposition *he wrote four novels plus various poems:* **as well as**, together with, along with, in addition to, and.
• noun *one of the pluses of the job:* **advantage**, good point, asset, pro, benefit, bonus, extra, attraction; informal perk.
– OPPOSITES disadvantage, minus.

plush adjective (informal) **luxurious**, luxury, deluxe, sumptuous, palatial, lavish, opulent, magnificent, rich, expensive, fancy, grand; Brit. upmarket; informal posh, ritzy, swanky, classy; Brit. informal swish; N. Amer. informal swank.
– OPPOSITES austere.

ply[1] verb **1** *he plied a profitable trade:* **engage in**, carry on, pursue, conduct, practise. **2** *ferries ply between all lake resorts:* **travel**, shuttle, go back and forth. **3** *she plied me with food and drink:* **provide**, supply, regale, present. **4** *he plied her with questions:* **bombard**, assail, pester, plague.

ply[2] noun *a three-ply tissue:* **layer**, thickness, strand, sheet, leaf.

poach verb **1** *he's been poaching deer:* **hunt**, catch; steal. **2** *workers were poached by other firms:* **steal**, appropriate, take; headhunt.

pocket noun **1** *a bag with two pockets:* **pouch**, compartment. **2** *isolated pockets of resistance remain:* **area**, patch, region, island; group cluster.
• adjective *a pocket dictionary:* **small**, miniature, mini, compact, concise, abridged, potted, portable; N. Amer. vest-pocket.
• verb *he was found to have pocketed the proceeds:* **steal**, take, appropriate, purloin, misappropriate, embezzle; informal filch, swipe, snaffle; Brit. informal pinch, nick, whip.

pockmark noun **scar**, pit, pock, mark, blemish.

pod noun **shell**, husk, hull, case; N. Amer. shuck; Botany pericarp, capsule.

podgy adjective (Brit. informal) **chubby**, plump, fat, well padded, ample, round, chunky, portly, overweight, fleshy, paunchy, bulky, corpulent; informal tubby, roly-poly, pudgy, beefy, porky, blubbery; N. Amer. informal zaftig, corn-fed.
– OPPOSITES thin.

podium noun **platform**, stage, dais, rostrum, stand.

poem noun **verse**, rhyme, ditty; ode, sonnet, ballad, lyric, lay.

P

poet **noun** literary bard; derogatory poetaster.

poetic **adjective** **1** *poetic compositions:* **poetical**, verse, metrical. **2** *poetic language:* **expressive**, figurative, symbolic, flowery, artistic, imaginative, creative.

poetry **noun** **poems**, verse, versification, rhyme.

poignancy **noun** **pathos**, pitifulness, sadness, sorrow, mournfulness, wretchedness, misery, tragedy.

poignant **adjective** **touching**, moving, sad, affecting, pitiful, pathetic, sorrowful, mournful, wretched, miserable, distressing, heart-rending, tear-jerking, plaintive, tragic.

point[1] **noun** **1** *the point of a needle:* **tip**, end, extremity; prong, spike, tine, nib, barb. **2** *points of light:* **pinpoint**, dot, spot, speck. **3** *a meeting point:* **place**, position, location, site, spot. **4** *this point in her life:* **time**, stage, juncture, period, phase. **5** *the tension had reached a very high point:* **level**, degree, stage, pitch, extent. **6** *an important point:* **detail**, item, fact, thing, argument, consideration, factor, element; subject, issue, topic, question, matter. **7** *get to the point:* **heart of the matter**, essence, nub, core, crux; informal brass tacks, nitty-gritty. **8** *what's the point of this?* **purpose**, aim, object, objective, goal, intention; use, sense, value, advantage. **9** *he had his good points:* **attribute**, characteristic, feature, trait, quality, property, aspect, side.
• **verb** **1** *she pointed the gun at him:* **aim**, direct, level, train. **2** *the evidence pointed to his guilt:* **indicate**, suggest, evidence, signal, signify, denote.
■ **beside the point** irrelevant, immaterial, unimportant, neither here nor there, inconsequential, incidental, unconnected, peripheral, tangential. **on the point of** on the verge of, on the brink of, ready to, preparing to, all set to. **point of view** opinion, view, belief, attitude, feeling, sentiment, thoughts; position, perspective, viewpoint, standpoint, outlook. **point something out** identify, show, draw attention to, indicate, specify, detail, mention. **point something up** emphasize, highlight, draw attention to, accentuate, underline, spotlight, foreground, bring to the fore. **to the point** relevant, pertinent, apposite, germane, applicable, apropos, appropriate, apt. **up to a point** partly, to some extent, to a certain degree, in part, partially.

point[2] **noun** *the ship rounded the point:* **promontory**, headland, foreland, cape, peninsula, bluff, ness, horn.

point-blank **adverb** **1** *he fired the pistol point-blank:* **at close range**, close up/to. **2** *she couldn't say it point-blank:* **bluntly**, directly, straight, frankly, candidly, openly, explicitly, unequivocally, unambiguously, plainly, flatly, categorically, outright.
• **adjective** *a point-blank refusal:* **blunt**, direct, straight, straightforward, frank, candid, forthright, explicit, unequivocal, plain, clear, flat, decisive, unqualified, categorical, outright.

pointed **adjective** **1** *a pointed stick:* **sharp**, tapering, tapered, spiked, barbed; informal pointy. **2** *a pointed remark:* **cutting**, trenchant, biting, incisive, acerbic, caustic, scathing, venomous, sarcastic; informal sarky; N. Amer. informal snarky.

pointer **noun** **1** *the pointer moved to 100 rpm:* **indicator**, needle, arrow, hand. **2** *a pointer to the outcome of the election:* **indication**, indicator, clue, hint, sign, signal, evidence, intimation, inkling, suggestion. **3** *I can give you a few pointers:* **tip**, hint, suggestion, guideline, recommendation.

pointless **adjective** **senseless**, futile, hopeless, unavailing, aimless, idle, worthless, valueless; absurd, insane, stupid, silly, foolish.
– OPPOSITES valuable.

poise **noun** **1** *poise and good deportment:* **grace**, gracefulness, elegance, balance, control. **2** *in spite of the setback she retained her poise:* **composure**, equanimity, self-possession, aplomb, self-assurance, self-control, sangfroid, dignity; informal cool.
• **verb** **1** *the coach hung, poised over the 90 ft drop:* **balance**, be suspended, hang, hover. **2** *he was poised for action:* **prepare yourself**,

ready yourself, brace yourself, gear yourself up, stand by.

poison noun **toxin**, venom.
•verb **1** *he poisoned her drink with mercury from a thermometer:* **contaminate**, adulterate, lace, doctor; informal spike. **2** *the Amazon basin is being poisoned:* **pollute**, contaminate, taint, spoil. **3** *they poisoned his mind:* **twist**, warp, corrupt.

> WORD LINKS
> **toxicology** the branch of science concerned with poisons

poisonous adjective **1** *a poisonous snake:* **venomous**, deadly. **2** *a poisonous chemical:* **toxic**, noxious, deadly, fatal, lethal, mortal, death-dealing. **3** *a poisonous glance:* **malicious**, malevolent, hostile, spiteful, bitter, venomous, vindictive, vitriolic, rancorous, malign.
–OPPOSITES harmless, non-toxic, benevolent.

poke verb **1** *she poked him in the ribs:* **prod**, jab, dig, nudge, shove, elbow, stab, stick. **2** *leave the cable poking out:* **stick out**, jut out, protrude, project, extend.
■ **poke about/around** search, hunt, rummage, forage, grub, root, scavenge, nose around, ferret; sift through, rifle through, scour, comb. **poke fun at** mock, make fun of, ridicule, laugh at, jeer at, sneer at, deride, scorn, scoff at, pillory, lampoon; informal send up, take the mickey out of. **poke your nose into** pry into, interfere in, intrude on, butt into, meddle with; informal snoop into.

poky adjective **small**, little, tiny, cramped, confined, restricted, boxy; euphemistic compact, bijou.
–OPPOSITES spacious.

polar adjective **opposite**, opposed, dichotomous, extreme, contrary, contradictory, antithetical.

polarity noun **difference**, dichotomy, separation, opposition, contradiction, antithesis, antagonism.

pole[1] noun **post**, pillar, stanchion, stake, stick, support, prop, batten, bar, rail, rod, beam; staff, stave, cane, baton.

pole[2] noun **extremity**, extreme, limit.
■ **poles apart** completely different, antithetical, incompatible, irreconcilable, worlds apart, at opposite extremes; Brit. like chalk and cheese.

polemic noun **diatribe**, invective, rant, tirade, broadside, attack, harangue.

police noun **police force/service**, police officers, policemen, policewomen, the forces of law and order; Brit. constabulary; informal the cops, the fuzz, the law, the boys in blue; Brit. informal the Old Bill, coppers, bobbies, busies, the force; N. Amer. informal the heat; informal, derogatory pigs.
•verb **1** *we must police the area:* **guard**, watch over, protect, defend, patrol; control, regulate. **2** *the regulations will be policed by the ministry:* **enforce**, regulate, oversee, supervise, monitor, check.

police officer noun **policeman**, **policewoman**, officer; Brit. constable; N. Amer. patrolman, trooper, roundsman; informal cop; Brit. informal copper, bobby, rozzer, busy, plod; N. Amer. informal uniform; informal, derogatory pig.

policy noun **plans**, approach, code, system, guidelines, theory; line, position, stance.

polish verb **1** *polish the surface with a clean cloth:* **shine**, wax, buff, rub up/down; gloss, burnish. **2** *I need to polish up my essay:* **perfect**, refine, improve, hone, enhance; brush up, revise, edit, correct, touch up.
•noun **sophistication**, refinement, urbanity, suaveness, elegance, style, grace, finesse; informal class.
■ **polish something off** (informal) *he polished off an apple pie:* eat, finish, consume, devour, guzzle, wolf down, down, bolt; drink, drain, quaff, gulp down; informal put away, scoff, shovel down, sink, swill, knock back; Brit. informal shift; N. Amer. informal scarf, snarf.

polished adjective **1** *a polished table:* **shiny**, glossy, gleaming, lustrous, glassy; waxed, buffed, burnished. **2** *a polished performance:* **expert**, accomplished, masterly, masterful, skilful, adept, adroit, dexterous; consummate, superb, superlative, first-rate, fine.
–OPPOSITES dull, inexpert.

polite adjective **1** *a very polite girl:* **well mannered**, civil, courteous, respectful, well behaved, well bred, gentlemanly, ladylike, genteel, gracious; tactful, diplomatic. **2** *polite society:* **civilized**, refined, cultured, sophisticated.
– OPPOSITES rude, uncivilized.

politic adjective **wise**, prudent, sensible, judicious; advantageous, beneficial, profitable; appropriate, suitable, fitting, apt.
– OPPOSITES unwise.

political adjective **governmental**, government, constitutional, ministerial, parliamentary; diplomatic, legislative, administrative.

politician noun **legislator**, Member of Parliament, MP, minister, statesman, stateswoman; senator, congressman/woman; informal politico.

politics noun **1** *a career in politics:* **government**, affairs of state, public affairs; diplomacy. **2** *office politics:* **power struggles**, machinations, manoeuvring, realpolitik.

poll noun **1** *a second-round poll:* **vote**, ballot, show of hands, referendum, plebiscite; election. **2** *the poll was unduly low:* **voting figures**, vote, returns, count, turnout. **3** *a poll to investigate holiday choices:* **survey**, opinion poll; market research, census.
• verb **1** *most of those polled supported him:* **canvass**, survey, ask, question, interview, ballot. **2** *she polled 119 votes:* **get**, gain, register, record, return.

pollute verb **contaminate**, taint, poison, foul, dirty, soil, infect.
– OPPOSITES purify.

pollution noun **contamination**, impurity; dirt, filth, infection.

pomp noun **ceremony**, solemnity, ritual, display, spectacle, pageantry; show, ostentation, splendour, grandeur, magnificence, majesty, stateliness, glory; informal razzmatazz.

pompous adjective **self-important**, imperious, overbearing, sententious, grandiose, affected, pretentious, puffed up, haughty, proud, conceited, supercilious, condescending, patronizing; informal snooty, uppity.
– OPPOSITES modest.

pond noun **pool**, waterhole; tarn; literary mere.

ponder verb **think about**, contemplate, consider, review, reflect on, mull over, meditate on, muse on, deliberate about, cogitate on, dwell on, brood on, ruminate on, chew over, turn over in your mind.

ponderous adjective **1** *a ponderous procession:* **slow**, awkward, lumbering, cumbersome, ungainly, graceless. **2** *a ponderous speech:* **laboured**, laborious, lifeless, plodding, pedestrian, boring, dull, tedious, monotonous.
– OPPOSITES light, lively.

pontificate verb **hold forth**, expound, declaim, preach, lay down the law, sound off, lecture; informal mouth off.

pooh-pooh verb (informal) **dismiss**, reject, wave aside, disregard, discount; play down, make light of, belittle, deride, sneer at; Austral./NZ informal wipe.

pool noun **1** *pools of water:* **puddle**, pond. **2** *a pool of skilled labour:* **supply**, reserve, reservoir, fund; store, bank, stock, cache. **3** *a pool of money for emergencies:* **fund**, reserve, kitty, pot, bank, purse.
• verb *they pooled their skills:* **combine**, group, join, unite, merge; share.

poor adjective **1** *a poor family:* **poverty-stricken**, penniless, impoverished, impecunious, needy, destitute, unable to make ends meet, indigent; insolvent; Brit. on the breadline; informal broke, hard up, cleaned out, strapped for cash, on your uppers; Brit. informal skint; formal penurious. **2** *poor workmanship:* **substandard**, bad, deficient, defective, faulty, imperfect, inferior; unsatisfactory, second-rate, third-rate, shoddy, crude, inadequate, unacceptable; informal crummy, rotten, tenth-rate; Brit. informal ropy, duff, rubbish, dodgy. **3** *a poor crop:* **meagre**, scanty, scant, paltry, disappointing, limited, reduced, modest, sparse, spare, deficient, insubstantial, skimpy, small, lean, slender; informal measly, stingy, pathetic, piddling. **4** *the poor girl:* **unfortunate**, unlucky, hapless, pitiful, wretched.
– OPPOSITES rich, superior, good.

poorly adverb *the text is poorly written:* **badly**, imperfectly, incompetently; crudely, shoddily, inadequately.
• adjective *she's still rather poorly:* **ill**, unwell, ailing, indisposed, out of sorts, under/below par, peaky; sick, queasy, nauseous; Brit. off colour; informal under the weather, funny, peculiar, rough; Brit. informal ropy, grotty; Scottish informal wabbit; Austral./NZ informal crook.

pop verb **burst**, explode, go off, crack, snap.
• noun **bang**, crack, snap; explosion.
■ **pop up** appear, occur, arrive, materialize, happen, emerge, arise, crop up, turn up, present itself, come to light; informal show up.

pope noun **pontiff**, Bishop of Rome, Holy Father, Vicar of Christ, His Holiness.

WORD LINKS
papal, **pontifical** relating to the pope
papacy the position or period of office of a pope

populace noun **population**, inhabitants, residents; community, country, general public, people, nation; common people, man/woman in the street, masses, multitude, rank and file; Brit. informal Joe Public; derogatory the hoi polloi, common herd, rabble, riff-raff.

p

popular adjective **1** *the restaurant is very popular:* **well liked**, sought-after, in demand; commercial, marketable, fashionable, in vogue, all the rage, hot; informal in, cool, big. **2** *popular science:* **non-specialist**, non-technical, amateur, lay person's, general, middle-of-the-road; accessible, simplified, plain, simple, easy, straightforward, understandable; mass-market, middlebrow, lowbrow. **3** *popular opinion:* **widespread**, general, common, current, prevailing, standard; ordinary, conventional. **4** *a popular movement for independence:* **mass**, general, communal, collective, social, group, civil, public.
– OPPOSITES highbrow.

popularize verb **1** *his books helped to popularize the sport:* **make popular**, make fashionable; market, publicize; informal hype. **2** *they are skilled at popularizing genetics:* **simplify**, make accessible, demystify.

popularly adverb **1** *old age is popularly associated with illness:* **widely**, generally, commonly, usually, habitually, conventionally, traditionally. **2** *the rock was popularly known as 'Arthur's Seat':* **informally**, unofficially.

populate verb **1** *the island is populated by goats:* **inhabit**, occupy, people; live in/on. **2** *an attempt to populate the island:* **settle**, colonize, people, occupy.

population noun **inhabitants**, residents, people, citizens, citizenry, public, community, populace, society, occupants; formal denizens.

populous adjective **densely populated**, congested, crowded, packed, teeming.
– OPPOSITES deserted.

porch noun **vestibule**, foyer, entrance, entry, lobby; N. Amer. stoop.

pore verb *I spent hours poring over the books:* **study**, read intently, peruse, scrutinize, scan, examine, go over.

! Don't confuse **pore** with **pour**, which means 'flow in a steady stream' (*water poured off the roof*).

pornographic adjective **obscene**, indecent, lewd, dirty, smutty, filthy; erotic, titillating, arousing, suggestive, sexy, risqué; off colour, X-rated, hard-core, soft-core; informal blue; euphemistic adult.

pornography noun **erotica**, blue movies; obscenity, indecency; informal sexploitation; dated facetiae.

porous adjective **permeable**, penetrable; absorbent, spongy.
– OPPOSITES impermeable.

port noun **1 harbour**, dock, marina. **2 aperture**, opening, outlet, inlet, vent, duct.

portable adjective **transportable**, movable, mobile; lightweight, compact, handy, convenient.

portal noun **doorway**, gateway, entrance, exit, opening; door, gate; N. Amer. entryway.

portend verb **presage**, augur, foreshadow, foretell, prophesy; be a sign, warn, be an omen, indicate, herald, signal, bode, promise, threaten, signify, spell, denote; literary betoken.

portent noun **omen**, sign, signal, token, warning, foreshadowing, prediction, prophecy, harbinger, augury, auspice, presage; writing on the wall, indication, hint; literary foretoken.

portentous adjective **pompous**, bombastic, self-important, solemn, sonorous, grandiloquent.

porter[1] noun *a porter helped with the bags:* **carrier**, bearer; N. Amer. redcap, skycap.

porter[2] noun (Brit.) *the college porter:* **doorman**, doorkeeper, commissionaire, gatekeeper.

portion noun **1** *the upper portion of the chimney:* **part**, piece, bit, section, segment. **2** *her portion of the allowance:* **share**, slice, quota, part, percentage, amount, quantity, fraction, division, allocation, tranche, measure; informal cut, rake-off; Brit. informal whack. **3** *a portion of cake:* **helping**, serving; slice, piece, chunk, wedge, slab, hunk; Brit. informal wodge.
• verb *she portioned out the food:* **share out**; distribute, hand out, deal out, dole out, give out, dispense.

portly adjective **stout**, plump, fat, overweight, heavy, corpulent, fleshy, pot-bellied, well padded, rotund, stocky, bulky; informal tubby, roly-poly, beefy, porky; Brit. informal podgy; N. Amer. informal corn-fed.
– OPPOSITES slim.

portrait noun **1** *a portrait of the King:* **picture**, likeness; painting, drawing, photograph; image. **2** *a vivid portrait of Italy:* **description**, portrayal, representation, depiction, impression, account.

portray verb **1** *he always portrays Windermere in sunny weather:* **paint**, draw, sketch, picture, depict, represent, illustrate, render, show. **2** *the media portrayed him as a courageous reformer:* **describe**, depict, characterize, represent delineate, present. **3** *the actor portrays a spy:* **play**, depict, represent, impersonate, appear as.

portrayal noun **1** *her portrayal of adolescence:* **description**, representation, characterization, depiction, evocation. **2** *Brando's portrayal of Corleone:* **performance as**, representation, interpretation, rendering.

pose verb **1** *pollution poses a threat to health:* **constitute**, present, offer, be. **2** *the question posed earlier:* **raise**, ask, put, submit, advance, propose, suggest, moot. **3** *the guys posing at the bar:* **posture**, attitudinize, put on airs; informal show off, ponce about/up and down.
• noun **1** *a sexy pose:* **posture**, position, stance, attitude. **2** *her pose of aggrieved innocence:* **act**, affectation, show, display, posture, expression.
■ **pose as** pretend to be, impersonate, pass yourself off as, masquerade as.

poser[1] noun *this situation's a bit of a poser:* **difficult question**, problem, puzzle, mystery, riddle, conundrum; informal facer.

poser[2] noun *he's such a poser:* **exhibitionist**, poseur, poseuse; informal show-off, pseud.

poseur noun. See POSER[2].

posh adjective **1** (informal) *a posh hotel:* **smart**, stylish, fancy, high-class, fashionable, chic, luxurious, luxury, deluxe, exclusive; Brit. upmarket; informal classy, swanky, snazzy, plush, ritzy, flash; Brit. informal swish; N. Amer. informal swank, tony. **2** (Brit. informal) *a posh accent:* **upper-class**, aristocratic; Brit. informal plummy, Sloaney.

posit verb **postulate**, put forward, advance, propound, submit, propose, assert.

position noun **1** *the aircraft's position:* **location**, place, situation, spot, site, locality, setting, area; whereabouts, bearings, orientation. **2** *a standing position:* **posture**, stance, attitude, pose. **3** *our financial position:* **situation**, state, condition, circumstances; predicament, plight. **4** *their position in society:* **status**, place, level, rank, standing; stature, prestige, reputation, importance. **5** *a secretarial position:* **job**, post, situation, appointment; opening, vacancy, placement. **6** *the government's position on the matter:* **viewpoint**, opinion, outlook, attitude, stand, standpoint, stance, perspective, thinking, policy, feelings.
• verb *he positioned a chair between them:* **put**, place, locate, situate,

set, site, stand, station; plant, stick, install; arrange; informal plonk, park.

positive adjective **1** *a positive response:* **affirmative**, favourable, good, enthusiastic, supportive, encouraging. **2** *say something positive:* **constructive**, useful, productive, helpful, worthwhile, beneficial. **3** *she seems a lot more positive:* **optimistic**, hopeful, confident, cheerful, sanguine, buoyant; informal upbeat. **4** *positive economic signs:* **favourable**, good, promising, encouraging, heartening, propitious, auspicious. **5** *positive proof:* **definite**, certain, reliable, concrete, tangible, clear-cut, explicit, firm, decisive, real, actual. **6** *I'm positive he's coming back:* **certain**, sure, convinced, confident, satisfied.
– OPPOSITES negative, pessimistic, doubtful, unsure.

positively adverb **1** *I could not positively identify the voice:* **confidently**, definitely, with certainty, conclusively. **2** *he was positively livid:* **absolutely**, downright; virtually; informal plain.

possess verb **1** *the only hat she possessed:* **own**, have. **2** *he did not possess a sense of humour:* **have**, be blessed with, be endowed with; enjoy, boast. **3** *an evil force possessed him:* **seize**, take over, control, dominate; bewitch, enchant, enslave.

p

possessed adjective **mad**, demented, insane, crazed, berserk; bewitched, enchanted, under a spell.

possession noun **1** *the estate came into their possession:* **ownership**, control, hands, keeping, care, custody, charge. **2** *she packed her possessions:* **belongings**, things, property, worldly goods, personal effects, assets, valuables; stuff, bits and pieces; luggage, baggage; informal gear, junk; Brit. informal clobber.

possessive adjective **proprietorial**, overprotective, controlling, dominating, jealous, clingy.
– OPPOSITES generous.

possibility noun **1** *there's a possibility that he might be alive:* **chance**, likelihood, probability, hope; risk, hazard, danger, fear. **2** *buying a smaller house is one possibility:* **option**, alternative, choice, course of action, solution. **3** *the idea has distinct possibilities:* **potential**, promise, prospects.

possible adjective **1** *it's not possible to check the figures:* **feasible**, practicable, viable, attainable, achievable, workable; informal on, doable. **2** *a possible reason for his disappearance:* **conceivable**, plausible, potential, imaginable, believable, credible, likely, probable, prospective.
– OPPOSITES impossible, unlikely.

possibly adverb **1** *possibly he took her with him:* **perhaps**, maybe, it is possible. **2** *you can't possibly refuse:* **conceivably**, under any circumstances, by any means. **3** *could you possibly help me?* **please**, kindly, be so good as to.

post[1] noun *wooden posts:* **pole**, stake, upright, shaft, prop, support, picket, strut, pillar, baluster, stanchion.
• verb **1** *the notice posted on the wall:* **affix**, attach, fasten, display, pin, put up, stick. **2** *the group posted a net profit:* **announce**, report, make known, publish, publicize, advertise.

post[2] (Brit.) noun **letters**, correspondence, mail.
• verb **send**, mail, dispatch.

post[3] noun **1** *there were seventy candidates for the post:* **job**, position, appointment, situation, place; vacancy, opening; Austral. informal grip. **2** *back to your posts:* **position**, station.
• verb **1** *he'd been posted to Berlin:* **send**, assign, dispatch; transfer, second. **2** *armed guards were posted at the gates:* **put on duty**, station, place, position, locate, situate.

poster noun **notice**, placard, bill, sign, advertisement, playbill; Brit. fly-poster.

posterior adjective *the posterior part of the skull:* **rear**, hind, back.
– OPPOSITES anterior.

posterity noun **future generations**, the future.

post-haste adverb **as quickly as possible**, without delay, without further/more ado, with all speed, promptly, immediately, at once, straight away, right away, asap; informal pronto.

post-mortem noun **1** *the hospital carried out a post-mortem:* **autopsy**, PM, necropsy. **2** *a post-mortem of the interview:* **analysis**, evaluation, assessment, examination, review; debriefing.

postpone verb **put off/back**, delay, defer, reschedule, adjourn, shelve; N. Amer. put over, take a rain check on; informal put on ice, put on the back burner.
– OPPOSITES bring forward.

postponement noun **deferral**, deferment, delay, putting off/back, rescheduling, adjournment, shelving.

postulate verb **put forward**, suggest, advance, posit, hypothesize, propose.

posture noun **1** *a kneeling posture:* **position**, pose, attitude, stance. **2** *good posture:* **bearing**, carriage, stance, comportment; Brit. deportment. **3** *trade unions adopted a militant posture:* **attitude**, stance, standpoint, point of view, opinion, position.
• verb *Keith postured, flexing his biceps:* **pose**, strike an attitude, strut.

posy noun **bouquet**, bunch of flowers, spray, nosegay, corsage; buttonhole.

pot noun **container**, receptacle, vessel; pan, saucepan, casserole, cauldron; bowl, basin.
■ **go to pot** (informal) deteriorate, decline, degenerate, go to rack and ruin, go downhill, go to seed; informal go to the dogs, go down the tubes; Austral./NZ informal go to the pack.

pot-bellied adjective **portly**, rotund; informal tubby, roly-poly.

potency noun **1** *the potency of his words:* **forcefulness**, force, effectiveness, persuasiveness, cogency, authoritativeness, authority, power, powerfulness. **2** *the potency of the drugs:* **strength**, powerfulness, power, effectiveness; formal efficacy.

potent adjective **1** *a potent political force:* **powerful**, strong, mighty, formidable, influential, dominant. **2** *a potent argument:* **forceful**, convincing, cogent, compelling, persuasive, powerful, strong. **3** *a potent drug:* **strong**, powerful, effective; formal efficacious.
– OPPOSITES weak.

potential adjective **possible**, likely, prospective, future, probable.
• noun **possibilities**, potentiality, prospects; promise, capability, capacity.

potion noun **concoction**, mixture, brew, elixir, drink; medicine, tonic; literary draught.

potpourri noun **mixture**, assortment, collection, selection, assemblage, medley, miscellany, mix, variety, mixed bag, patchwork; ragbag, hotchpotch, mishmash, jumble; N. Amer. hodgepodge.

potter verb **amble**, wander, meander, stroll, saunter; informal mosey, tootle, toddle; N. Amer. informal putter.

pottery noun **ceramics**, crockery, earthenware, terracotta, stoneware, china.

pouch noun **bag**, purse, sack, sac, pocket; Scottish sporran.

pounce verb **jump**, spring, leap, dive, lunge, attack.

pound[1] verb **1** *the two men pounded him with their fists:* **beat**, strike, hit, batter, thump, pummel, punch, rain blows on, belabour, hammer, set upon; informal bash, clobber, wallop, beat the living daylights out of, whack, thwack, lay into; N. Amer. informal light into. **2** *waves pounded the seafront:* **beat against**, crash against, batter, dash against, lash, buffet. **3** *gunships pounded the capital:* **bombard**, bomb, shell. **4** *pound the garlic to a paste:* **crush**, grind, pulverize, mash, pulp. **5** *I heard him pounding along the gangway:* **stomp**, lumber, clomp, clump, tramp. **6** *her heart was pounding:* **throb**, thump, thud, hammer, pulse, race, go pit-a-pat.

pound[2] noun *he owes me ten pounds:* pound sterling, £; Brit. informal quid, smacker, nicker.

pound[3] noun *a dog pound:* **enclosure**, compound, pen, yard.

pour verb **1** *water poured off the roof:* **stream**, flow, run, gush, course, jet, spurt, surge, spill. **2** *Amy poured wine into his glass:* **tip**, splash, spill, decant; informal slosh, slop. **3** *it was pouring:* **rain heavily/hard**, teem down, pelt down, tip down, rain cats and dogs; informal be chucking it down; Brit. informal bucket down, come down in stair rods; N. Amer. informal

P

rain pitchforks. **4** *customers poured into the shop:* **crowd**, surge, swarm, stream, flood.

> Don't confuse **pour** with **pore**, which means 'study or read closely' (*I spent hours poring over the books*).

poverty noun **1** *abject poverty:* **penury**, destitution, indigence, pennilessness, impoverishment, neediness, hardship, impecuniousness. **2** *the poverty of choice:* **scarcity**, deficiency, dearth, shortage, paucity, absence, lack. **3** *the poverty of her imagination:* **inferiority**, mediocrity, poorness, sterility.
–OPPOSITES wealth, abundance.

poverty-stricken adjective **destitute**, impoverished, penniless, in penury, impecunious, indigent, poor, needy; Brit. on the breadline; informal on your uppers, on your beam ends; informal penurious.
–OPPOSITES wealthy.

powder noun **dust**; historical pounce.
•verb *the grains are powdered:* **crush**, grind, pulverize, pound, mill.

powdery adjective **fine**, dry, fine-grained, powder-like, dusty, chalky, floury, sandy, crumbly, friable.

power noun **1** *the power of speech:* **ability**, capacity, capability, potential, faculty. **2** *these companies have enormous power over our lives:* **control**, authority, influence, dominance, mastery, domination, dominion, sway, weight, leverage; informal clout, teeth. **3** *the power to stop and search:* **authority**, right, authorization. **4** *a major European power:* **state**, country, nation. **5** *he hit the ball with as much power as he could:* **strength**, might, force, forcefulness, vigour, energy; Brit. informal welly. **6** *the power of his arguments:* **forcefulness**, powerfulness, potency, strength, force, cogency, persuasiveness. **7** *the new engine has more power:* **driving force**, horsepower, hp, acceleration, torque; informal poke.
–OPPOSITES impotence, weakness.

> **WORD LINKS**
> **megalomania** an obsession with power

powerful adjective **1** *powerful shoulders:* **strong**, muscular, muscly, sturdy, strapping, robust, brawny, burly, athletic, manly, well built, solid; informal beefy, hunky; dated stalwart. **2** *a powerful blow:* **violent**, forceful, hard, mighty. **3** *he felt a powerful urge to kiss her:* **intense**, keen, fierce, strong, irresistible, overpowering, overwhelming. **4** *a powerful nation:* **influential**, strong, important, dominant, commanding, formidable. **5** *a powerful critique:* **cogent**, compelling, convincing, persuasive, forceful, effective.
–OPPOSITES weak, gentle.

powerless adjective **impotent**, helpless, ineffectual, ineffective, useless, defenceless, vulnerable.

practicable adjective **realistic**, feasible, possible, within the bounds/realms of possibility, viable, reasonable, sensible, workable, achievable; informal doable.

practical adjective **1** *practical experience:* **empirical**, hands-on, actual, experiential. **2** *there are no practical alternatives:* **feasible**, practicable, realistic, viable, workable, possible, reasonable, sensible; informal doable. **3** *make sure you wear practical clothes:* **functional**, serviceable, sensible, utilitarian. **4** *try to be more practical:* **realistic**, sensible, down-to-earth, businesslike, commonsensical, hard-headed, no-nonsense; informal hard-nosed. **5** *a practical certainty:* **virtual**, effective, near.
–OPPOSITES theoretical, impractical.

practicality noun **1** *the practicality of the proposal:* **feasibility**, practicability, viability, workability. **2** *practicality of design:* **functionalism**, functionality, serviceability, utility. **3** *his calm practicality:* **common sense**, realism, pragmatism. **4** *the practicalities of army life:* **practical details**; informal nitty gritty, nuts and bolts.

practical joke noun **trick**, joke, prank, jape, hoax; informal leg-pull.

practically adverb **1** *the cinema was practically empty:* **almost**, nearly, virtually, just about, all but, more or less, as good as, to all intents and purposes, verging on, bordering on; informal pretty well; literary well-nigh. **2** *'You can't afford it,' he pointed out practically:* **realistically**, sensibly, reasonably.

practice noun **1** *the practice of radiotherapy:* **application**, exercise, use, operation, implementation, execution. **2** *common practice:* **custom**, procedure, policy, convention, tradition; formal praxis. **3** *it takes lots of practice | the team's final practice:* **training**, rehearsal, repetition, preparation, dummy run, run-through; informal dry run. **4** *the practice of medicine:* **profession**, career, business, work. **5** *a small legal practice:* **business**, firm, office, company; informal outfit.
■ **in practice** in reality, realistically, practically. **out of practice** rusty, unpractised. **put something into practice** use, make use of, put to use, utilize, apply.

practise verb **1** *he practised the songs every day:* **rehearse**, run through, go over/through, work on/at; polish, perfect. **2** *the performers were practising:* **train**, rehearse, prepare, go through your paces. **3** *we still practise these rituals today:* **carry out**, perform, observe.

practised adjective **expert**, experienced, seasoned, skilled, skilful, accomplished, proficient, talented, able, adept.

pragmatic adjective **practical**, matter of fact, sensible, down-to-earth, commonsensical, business-like, having both/your feet on the ground, hard-headed, no-nonsense; informal hard-nosed.
– OPPOSITES impractical.

praise verb **commend**, applaud, pay tribute to, speak highly of, compliment, congratulate, sing the praises of, rave about, go into raptures about, heap praise on, wax lyrical about, make much of, pat on the back, take your hat off to, hail, eulogize; N. Amer. informal ballyhoo.
– OPPOSITES criticize.
• noun **approval**, acclaim, admiration, approbation, plaudits, congratulations, commendation, eulogy; tribute, accolade, compliment, a pat on the back.

WORD LINKS
laudatory expressing praise

praiseworthy adjective **commendable**, admirable, laudable, worthy (of admiration), meritorious, estimable.

prance verb **cavort**, dance, jig, trip, caper, jump, leap, spring, bound, skip, hop, frisk, romp, frolic.

prank noun **practical joke**, trick, escapade, stunt, caper, jape, game, hoax; informal lark, leg-pull.

prattle verb & noun. See CHATTER.

preach verb **1** *he preached to a large congregation:* **give a sermon**, address, speak. **2** *a Church that preaches the the good news of Jesus:* **proclaim**, teach, spread, expound. **3** *they preach toleration and moderation:* **advocate**, recommend, advise, urge, teach, counsel. **4** *who are you to preach?* **moralize**, sermonize, pontificate, lecture, harangue; informal preachify.

WORD LINKS
homiletics the art of preaching or writing sermons

preamble noun **introduction**, preface, prologue; foreword, prelude; informal intro.

prearranged adjective **arranged beforehand**, agreed in advance, predetermined, pre-established, pre-planned.

precarious adjective **uncertain**, insecure, unpredictable, risky, parlous, hazardous, dangerous, unsafe; unsettled, unstable, unsteady, shaky; informal dicey, chancy, iffy; Brit. informal dodgy.
– OPPOSITES safe.

precaution noun **safeguard**, preventative/preventive measure, safety measure, insurance; informal backstop.

precautionary adjective **preventative**, preventive, safety.

precede verb **go/come before**, go/come first, lead up to, pave/prepare the way for, herald, introduce, usher in.
– OPPOSITES follow, succeed.

precedent noun **model**, exemplar, example, pattern; paradigm, criterion, yardstick, standard.

preceding adjective **foregoing**, previous, prior, former, earlier, above, aforementioned; formal anterior.

precept noun **principle**, rule, tenet, canon, doctrine, command, order, decree, dictate, dictum, injunction, commandment.

precinct noun **1** *a pedestrian precinct:* **area**, zone, sector. **2** *within the precincts of the City:* **bounds**, boundaries, limits, confines. **3** *the cathedral precinct:* **enclosure**, close, court.

precious adjective **1** *precious works of art:* **valuable**, costly, expensive; invaluable, priceless. **2** *her most precious possession:* **valued**, cherished, treasured, prized, favourite, dear, dearest, beloved, special. **3** *his precious manners:* **affected**, pretentious; informal la-di-da; Brit. informal poncey.

precipice noun **cliff**, crag, escarpment, bluff.

precipitate verb **1** *the incident precipitated a crisis:* **bring about/on**, cause, lead to, give rise to, instigate, trigger, spark, touch off, provoke. **2** *they were precipitated down the mountain:* **hurl**, catapult, throw, plunge, launch, fling, propel.
• adjective **1** *their actions were precipitate:* **hasty**, overhasty, rash, hurried, rushed; impetuous, impulsive, precipitous, incautious, imprudent, injudicious, ill-advised, reckless. **2** *a precipitate decline.* See PRECIPITOUS sense 2.

precipitous adjective **1** *a precipitous drop:* **steep**, sheer, perpendicular, abrupt, sharp, vertical. **2** *his precipitous fall from power:* **sudden**, rapid, swift, abrupt, headlong, speedy, quick, fast. **3** *he was too precipitous.* See PRECIPITATE adjective sense 1.

precis noun **summary**, synopsis, résumé, abstract, outline, summarization, summation; abridgement, digest, overview, epitome; N. Amer. wrap-up.
• verb **summarize**, sum up; abridge, condense, shorten, abstract, outline, abbreviate.

precise adjective **1** *precise measurements:* **exact**, accurate, correct, specific, detailed, explicit. **2** *at that precise moment:* **exact**, particular, very, specific. **3** *precise attention to detail:* **meticulous**, careful, exact, scrupulous, punctilious, conscientious, particular, methodical, strict, rigorous.
– OPPOSITES inaccurate.

precisely adverb **1** *at 2 o'clock precisely:* **exactly**, sharp, on the dot; promptly, prompt, dead on; informal bang on; Brit. informal spot on; N. Amer. informal on the button/nose. **2** *he's precisely the man I am looking for:* **exactly**, just, in all respects; informal to a T. **3** *fertilization can be timed precisely:* **accurately**, exactly.

precision noun **exactness**, exactitude, accuracy, correctness, preciseness; care, carefulness, meticulousness, scrupulousness, punctiliousness, rigour, rigorousness.

preclude verb **prevent**, stop, prohibit, debar, bar, hinder, impede, inhibit, exclude, rule out, debar.

preconceived adjective **predetermined**, prejudged; prejudiced, biased.

preconception noun **preconceived idea/notion**, presupposition, assumption, presumption, prejudgement; prejudice.

precondition noun **prerequisite**, condition, requirement, stipulation, necessity, essential, imperative, sine qua non; informal must.

precursor noun *a precursor of the guitar:* **forerunner**, predecessor, forefather, father, antecedent, ancestor, forebear.

precursory adjective **preliminary**, prior, previous, introductory, preparatory, prefatory.

predatory adjective **1** *predatory birds:* **predacious**, carnivorous, hunting; of prey. **2** *his predatory appetites:* **exploitative**, wolfish, rapacious, manipulative.

predecessor noun **1** *the Prime Minister's predecessor:* **forerunner**, precursor, antecedent. **2** *our Victorian predecessors:* **ancestor**, forefather, forebear, antecedent.
– OPPOSITES successor, descendant.

predestined adjective **preordained**, ordained, predetermined, destined, fated.

predetermined adjective **1** *they met at a predetermined location:* **prearranged**, established in advance, preset, agreed. **2** *our predetermined fate:* **predestined**, preordained.

predicament noun **difficult situation**, mess, difficulty, plight, quandary, muddle; informal hole, fix, jam, pickle, scrape, bind, tight spot/corner, dilemma.

predicate verb **base**, be dependent, found, establish, rest, ground, premise.

predict verb **forecast**, foretell, foresee, prophesy, anticipate, tell in advance, envision, envisage.

predictable adjective **foreseeable**, to be expected, anticipated, foreseen, unsurprising, inevitable.

prediction noun **forecast**, prophecy, prognosis, prognostication; projection, conjecture, guess.

predilection noun **liking**, fondness, preference, partiality, taste, penchant, weakness, soft spot, fancy, inclination, leaning, bias, propensity, bent, proclivity, predisposition, appetite.
–OPPOSITES dislike.

predispose verb **1** *lack of exercise may predispose you to obesity:* **make susceptible**, make liable, make prone, make vulnerable, put at risk of. **2** *attitudes that predispose people to behave badly:* **lead**, influence, induce, prompt, dispose.

predisposed adjective **inclined**, prepared, ready, of a mind, disposed, minded, willing.

predisposition noun **1** *a predisposition to heart disease:* **susceptibility**, proneness, tendency, liability, inclination, vulnerability. **2** *their political predispositions:* **preference**, predilection, inclination, leaning.

predominance noun **1** *the predominance of women carers:* **prevalence**, dominance, preponderance. **2** *military predominance:* **supremacy**, mastery, control, power, ascendancy, dominance, pre-eminence, superiority.

predominant adjective **1** *our predominant objectives:* **main**, chief, principal, most important, primary, prime, central, leading, foremost, key, paramount; informal number-one. **2** *the predominant political forces:* **controlling**, dominant, predominating, more/most powerful, pre-eminent.
–OPPOSITES subsidiary.

predominantly adverb **mainly**, mostly, for the most part, chiefly, principally, primarily, in the main, on the whole, largely, by and large, typically, generally, usually.

predominate verb **1** *small-scale producers predominate:* **be in the majority**, preponderate, prevail. **2** *private interest predominates over the public good:* **prevail**, dominate; override, outweigh.

pre-eminence noun **superiority**, supremacy, greatness, excellence, distinction, prominence, predominance, eminence, importance, prestige, stature, fame, renown.

pre-eminent adjective **greatest**, leading, foremost, best, finest, chief, outstanding, excellent, distinguished, prominent, eminent, important, top, famous, renowned, celebrated, illustrious; N. Amer. marquee.
–OPPOSITES undistinguished.

pre-empt verb **forestall**, prevent, beat, anticipate.

preen verb **1** *the robin preened its feathers:* **clean**, tidy, groom, smooth, arrange. **2** *she preened before the mirror:* **admire yourself**, primp yourself, groom yourself, spruce yourself up; informal titivate yourself, doll yourself up; Brit. informal tart yourself up; N. Amer. informal gussy yourself up.

preface noun **introduction**, foreword, preamble, prologue, prelude; front matter; informal prelims, intro.
• verb **precede**, introduce, begin, open, start.

prefer verb **1** *I'd prefer white wine:* **like better**, favour, rather; choose, select, pick, opt for, go for, plump for; informal fancy. **2** (formal) *do you want to prefer charges?* **bring**, press, file, lodge, lay.

preferable adjective **better**, best, more desirable, more suitable, advantageous, superior, preferred, recommended.

preferably adverb **ideally**, if possible.

preference noun **1** *her preference for gin:* **liking**, partiality, fondness, taste, inclination, leaning, bent, penchant, predisposition. **2** *preference was given to female applicants:* **priority**, favour, precedence, preferential treatment.
■ **in preference to** rather than, instead of, in place of, sooner than.

preferential adjective **special**, better, privileged, superior,

P

favourable; partial, discriminatory, partisan, biased.

prefigure verb **foreshadow**, presage, be a harbinger of, herald; literary foretoken.

pregnancy noun gestation.

pregnant adjective **1** *a pregnant woman:* **expecting a baby**, expectant; informal expecting, in the family way; Brit. informal up the duff, in the club, up the spout; N. Amer. informal knocked up; old use with child. **2** *a pregnant pause:* **meaningful**, significant, suggestive, expressive, charged.

prehistoric adjective **1** *prehistoric times:* **primitive**, primeval, primordial, primal, ancient, early. **2** *the special effects look prehistoric:* **out of date**, outdated, outmoded, old-fashioned, passé, antiquated, archaic, behind the times, primitive, antediluvian; informal out of the ark; N. Amer. informal clunky.
– OPPOSITES modern.

prejudice noun **1** *male prejudices about women:* **preconceived idea**, preconception. **2** *they are motivated by prejudice:* **bigotry**, bias, partisanship, partiality, intolerance, discrimination, unfairness, inequality.
• verb **1** *the article could prejudice the jury:* **bias**, influence, sway, predispose, make biased, make partial, colour. **2** *this could prejudice his chances:* **damage**, be detrimental to, be prejudicial to, injure, harm, hurt, spoil, impair, undermine, hinder, compromise.

prejudiced adjective **biased**, bigoted, discriminatory, partisan, intolerant, narrow-minded, unfair, unjust, inequitable, coloured.
– OPPOSITES impartial.

prejudicial adjective **detrimental**, damaging, injurious, harmful, disadvantageous, hurtful, deleterious.
– OPPOSITES beneficial.

preliminary adjective *the discussions are still at a preliminary stage:* **preparatory**, introductory, initial, opening; early, exploratory.
– OPPOSITES final.
• noun *he began without any preliminaries:* **introduction**, preamble, opening remarks, formalities.

prelude noun **preliminary**, overture, opening, preparation, introduction, start, commencement, beginning, lead-in, precursor.

premature adjective **1** *his premature death:* **untimely**, early, unseasonable. **2** *such a step would be premature:* **rash**, overhasty, hasty, precipitate, precipitous, impulsive, impetuous; informal previous.
– OPPOSITES overdue.

prematurely adverb *don't act prematurely:* **rashly**, overhastily, hastily, precipitately, precipitously.

premeditated adjective **planned**, intentional, deliberate, pre-planned, calculated, cold-blooded, conscious, prearranged.
– OPPOSITES spontaneous.

premeditation noun **planning**, forethought, pre-planning; Law malice aforethought, criminal intent.

premier adjective **leading**, foremost, chief, principal, head, top-ranking, top, prime, primary, first, highest, pre-eminent, senior, outstanding, master; N. Amer. ranking.
• noun **head of government**, prime minister, PM, president, chancellor.

premiere noun **first performance**, first night, opening night.

premise noun **proposition**, assumption, hypothesis, thesis, presupposition, postulate, supposition, presumption, surmise, conjecture, speculation, assertion, belief.

premises plural noun **building**, property, establishment, site, office.

premium noun **1** *monthly premiums of £30:* **payment**, instalment. **2** *you must pay a premium for organic fruit:* **surcharge**, additional payment, extra.
■ **at a premium** scarce, in great demand, hard to come by, in short supply, thin on the ground, few and far between. **put a premium on** value greatly, attach great importance to, set great store by, put a high value on.

premonition noun **foreboding**, presentiment, intuition, feeling, hunch, suspicion, feeling in your bones.

preoccupation noun **1** *an air of preoccupation:* **pensiveness**, concentration, engrossment, absorption, self-absorption, thinking, deep thought, brooding; abstraction. **2** *their main preoccupation was* *food:* **obsession**, concern; passion, enthusiasm, hobby horse.

preoccupied adjective **1** *he's preoccupied with work:* **obsessed**, concerned, absorbed, engrossed, intent, involved, wrapped up. **2** *she looked preoccupied:* **lost/deep in thought**, pensive, distracted.

preoccupy verb **engross**, concern, absorb, distract, obsess, occupy, prey on someone's mind.

preordain verb **predestine**, destine, ordain, fate, predetermine.

preparation noun **1** *the preparation of a plan:* **devising**, putting together, drawing up, construction, composition, production, getting ready, development. **2** *preparations for the party:* **arrangements**, planning, plans. **3** *a preparation to kill mites:* **mixture**, compound, concoction, solution, medicine, potion, cream, ointment, lotion.

preparatory adjective **preliminary**, initial, introductory, opening, precursory.

prepare verb **1** *I'll prepare a report:* **draw up**, draft, put together, produce, compose, formulate, organize, arrange, assemble, construct. **2** *the meal is easy to prepare:* **cook**, make, put together, concoct; informal fix, rustle up; Brit. informal knock up. **3** *he was preparing for a dangerous mission:* **get ready**, ready yourself, make preparations, make arrangements, make plans; count down to; informal psych yourself up for. **4** *prepare yourself for a shock:* **brace**, steel, steady, nerve.

prepared adjective **1** *we're prepared for action:* **ready**, all set, equipped, primed; waiting, poised. **2** *I'm prepared to negotiate:* **willing**, ready, disposed, inclined, of a mind, minded.

preponderance noun **1** *the preponderance of women among older people:* **prevalence**, predominance, dominance. **2** *the preponderance of the evidence:* **bulk**, majority, greater quantity, larger part, best/better part, most.

prepossessing adjective **attractive**, beautiful, pretty, handsome, good-looking, fetching, charming.
– OPPOSITES ugly.

preposterous adjective **absurd**, ridiculous, foolish, stupid, ludicrous, farcical, laughable, comical, risible, nonsensical, senseless, insane; outrageous, monstrous; informal crazy.
– OPPOSITES sensible.

prerequisite noun **condition**, precondition, essential, requirement, requisite, necessity, stipulation, sine qua non; informal must.
• adjective **necessary**, required, essential, requisite, obligatory, compulsory.
– OPPOSITES unnecessary.

prerogative noun **entitlement**, right, privilege, advantage, due, birthright.

prescience noun **far-sightedness**, foresight, foreknowledge; insight, intuition, perception.

prescient adjective **prophetic**, predictive, visionary; far-sighted; insightful, intuitive, perceptive.

prescribe verb **1** *marriage is often prescribed as a universal remedy:* **advise**, recommend, advocate, suggest, endorse, champion, promote. **2** *rules prescribing the grounds on which an appeal may be made:* **stipulate**, lay down, dictate, specify, determine.

> ! Don't confuse **prescribe** with **proscribe**, which means 'condemn or forbid' (*gambling was strictly proscribed by the authorities*).

p

prescriptive adjective **dictatorial**, narrow, rigid, authoritarian, arbitrary, repressive, dogmatic.

presence noun **1** **attendance**, appearance; existence. **2** *a woman of great presence:* **aura**, charisma, personality.
– OPPOSITES absence.
■ **presence of mind** composure, equanimity, self-possession, level-headedness, self-assurance, calmness, sangfroid, imperturbability; alertness, quick-wittedness; informal cool, unflappability.

present[1] adjective **1** *a doctor must be present:* **in attendance**, here, there, near, nearby, close at hand, available. **2** *the present economic climate:* **current**, present-day, existing.
– OPPOSITES absent.
• noun *think about the present:* **now**, today, the here and now.
– OPPOSITES past, future.

■ **at present** at the moment, just now, right now, currently.

present[2] verb **1** *he presented a cheque to the winner:* **hand**, give, confer, bestow, award, grant, accord. **2** *I presented my driving licence:* **submit**, offer, tender; show, display, exhibit. **3** *she presented a special TV show:* **host**, introduce, compère; put on, produce, mount, stage; N. Amer. informal emcee. **4** *they present him as a criminal:* **represent**, describe, portray, depict.
■ **present itself** *an opportunity presented itself:* occur, arise, happen, come about/up, appear, crop up, turn up.

present[3] noun *a birthday present:* **gift**, donation, offering, contribution; informal prezzie.

presentable adjective **tidy**, neat, straight, clean, spick and span, in good order, shipshape, smart.

presentation noun **1** *the presentation of his certificate:* **awarding**, presenting, giving, handing over/out, bestowal, granting. **2** *the presentation of food:* **appearance**, arrangement, packaging, layout. **3** *the presentation of new proposals:* **submission**, proffering, offering, tendering, advancing, proposal, suggestion, mooting, tabling. **4** *a sales presentation:* **demonstration**, talk, lecture, address, speech, show, exhibition, display, introduction, launch, launching, unveiling. **5** *a presentation of his latest play:* **staging**, production, performance, mounting, showing.

present-day adjective **current**, present, contemporary, latter-day, present-time, modern, twenty-first-century.

presentiment noun **premonition**, foreboding, intuition, feeling, hunch, feeling in your bones, sixth sense.

presently adverb **1** *I shall see you presently:* **soon**, shortly, quite soon, in a short time, in a little while, at any moment/minute/second, before long; N. Amer. momentarily; informal pretty soon; Brit. informal in a mo. **2** *he is presently abroad:* **at present**, currently, at the/this moment.

preservation noun **1** *the preservation of old buildings:* **conservation**, protection, care, repair. **2** *the preservation of the status quo:* **continuation**, conservation, maintenance, upholding, sustaining, perpetuation.

preserve verb **1** *oil preserves the wood:* **conserve**, protect, care for, look after. **2** *they wish to preserve the status quo:* **continue with**, conserve, keep going, maintain, uphold, sustain, perpetuate. **3** *a place for preserving endangered species:* **guard**, protect, keep, defend, safeguard, shelter, shield.
• noun **1** *strawberry preserve:* **jam**, marmalade, conserve; US jelly. **2** *the preserve of the rich:* **domain**, area, field, sphere, orbit, realm, province, territory; informal turf, bailiwick. **3** (N. Amer.) *a game preserve:* **sanctuary**, reserve, reservation.

preside verb *the chairman presides at the meeting:* **chair**, officiate at, conduct, lead.
■ **preside over** be in charge of, be responsible for, be at the head/helm of, head, be head of, manage, administer, be in control of, control, direct, lead, govern, rule, command, supervise, oversee; informal head up.

president noun **head**, chief, director, leader, governor, principal; chairman, chairwoman; managing director, MD, chief executive officer, CEO.

press verb **1** *press the paper down firmly:* **push**, depress, hold down, force, thrust; flatten, squeeze, compress. **2** *his shirt was pressed:* **iron**. **3** *she pressed the child to her bosom:* **clasp**, hold close, hug, cuddle, squeeze, clutch, grasp, embrace. **4** *the crowd pressed round:* **cluster**, gather, converge, congregate, flock, swarm, throng, crowd. **5** *the government pressed its claim:* **plead**, urge, advance, present, submit, put forward. **6** *they pressed him to agree:* **urge**, put pressure on, pressure, pressurize, push; informal lean on, put the screws on, twist someone's arm. **7** *they pressed for a ban:* **call**, ask, clamour, push, campaign, demand, insist on.
• noun *the freedom of the press:* **the media**, the papers, the fourth estate; journalism, reporters; Brit. dated Fleet Street.
■ **press on** proceed, keep going,

continue, carry on, make progress, make headway, press ahead, push on, keep on, persevere, keep at it, plod on, plough on; informal soldier on, plug away, stick at it.

pressing adjective **1** *a pressing problem:* **urgent**, critical, crucial, acute, desperate, serious, grave, life-and-death. **2** *a pressing engagement:* **important**, high-priority, critical, crucial, unavoidable.

pressure noun **1** *the gates were buckling under the pressure of the crowd:* **force**, load, stress, thrust; compression, weight. **2** *they put pressure on us to repay the money:* **coercion**, force, compulsion, constraint, duress; pestering, harassment, intimidation, arm-twisting, persuasion. **3** *she had a lot of pressure from work:* **strain**, stress, tension, trouble, difficulty; informal hassle.
• verb *they pressured him into resigning.* See PRESSURIZE.

pressurize verb *he pressurized us into selling:* **coerce**, pressure, push, persuade, force, bulldoze, hound, nag, badger, browbeat, bully, bludgeon, intimidate, dragoon, twist someone's arm; informal railroad, lean on; N. Amer. informal hustle.

prestige noun **status**, standing, stature, prestigiousness, reputation, repute, note, renown, honour, esteem, importance, prominence, influence, eminence; kudos, cachet.

prestigious adjective **1** *prestigious journals:* **reputable**, distinguished, respected, esteemed, eminent, august, highly regarded, illustrious, leading, renowned. **2** *a prestigious job:* **impressive**, important, prominent, high-ranking, influential, powerful.
– OPPOSITES obscure, minor.

presumably adverb **I presume**, I expect, I assume, I take it, I imagine, I dare say, I guess, doubtless, no doubt.

presume verb *I presume it was once an attic:* **assume**, suppose, imagine, take it, expect.

presumption noun **1** *this presumption may be easily rebutted:* **assumption**, supposition, presupposition, belief, judgement, hypothesis, inference, deduction, conclusion. **2** *he apologized for his presumption:* **brazenness**, audacity, boldness, temerity, arrogance, presumptuousness, forwardness; impudence, impertinence, effrontery.

presumptuous adjective **brazen**, audacious, forward, familiar, impertinent, insolent, impudent, rude.

presuppose verb **presume**, assume, take it for granted, take it as read, suppose, surmise, think, accept, consider.

presupposition noun **presumption**, assumption, supposition.

pretence noun **1** *they've finally ended all the pretence:* **make-believe**, acting, dissembling, play-acting, posturing; deception, deceit, trickery, dishonesty, hypocrisy. **2** *he made a pretence of being concerned:* **show**, semblance, affectation, simulation, appearance, outward appearance, impression, front, guise, facade, display.
– OPPOSITES honesty.

pretend verb **1** *they pretend to listen:* **make as if**, act like, affect; go through the motions, fake it. **2** *I'll pretend to be the dragon:* **make believe**, play at, act, impersonate.
• adjective (informal) **mock**, fake, sham, simulated, artificial, ersatz, false, pseudo; informal phoney.

pretended adjective **fake**, faked, affected, professed, spurious, mock, simulated, make-believe, pseudo, sham, false, bogus; informal pretend, phoney.

pretender noun **claimant**, aspirant.

pretension noun **pretentiousness**, affectation, artificiality, airs, posing, posturing, show, flashiness; pomposity.

pretentious adjective **affected**, ostentatious, showy; pompous, overblown, high-sounding, flowery, grandiose; informal pseudo; Brit. informal poncey.

preternatural adjective **extraordinary**, exceptional, unusual, uncommon, singular, unprecedented, remarkable, phenomenal, abnormal, inexplicable, unaccountable.

pretext noun **(false) excuse**; guise, ploy, pretence, ruse.

prettify verb **beautify**, adorn,

ornament, decorate, titivate, smarten up; informal doll up, do up; Brit. informal tart up.

pretty adjective **attractive**, good-looking, nice-looking, personable, fetching, prepossessing, appealing, charming, delightful, cute; Scottish & N. English bonny; old use fair.
–OPPOSITES plain, ugly.
• **adverb** (informal) **quite**, rather, somewhat, fairly.

prevail verb **1** *common sense will prevail:* **win**, triumph, be victorious, carry the day, come out on top, succeed; rule, reign. **2** *the conditions that prevailed in the 1950s:* **exist**, be present, be the case, occur, be prevalent, be in force/effect; formal obtain.
■ **prevail on** persuade, induce, talk someone into, coax, convince, make, get, urge, coerce; informal sweet-talk, soft-soap.

prevailing adjective **current**, existing, prevalent, usual, common, general, widespread.

prevalence noun **commonness**, currency, widespread presence, popularity, pervasiveness, extensiveness.

prevalent adjective **widespread**, frequent, usual, common, current, popular, general.
–OPPOSITES rare.

prevaricate verb **beat about the bush**, hedge, shilly-shally, equivocate; temporize, stall for time; Brit. hum and haw.

P

prevent verb **stop**, avert, nip in the bud; foil, thwart; prohibit, forbid.
–OPPOSITES allow.

preventive adjective **1** *preventive measures:* **pre-emptive**, precautionary, protective. **2** *preventive medicine:* **prophylactic**; proactive.
• **noun** *a preventive against crime:* **precautionary measure**, deterrent, safeguard, security, protection, defence.

previous adjective **1** *the previous five years | her previous boyfriend:* **foregoing**, preceding; old, earlier, prior, former, ex-, past, last, sometime, one-time, erstwhile; formal quondam. **2** (informal) *I was a bit previous:* **overhasty**, hasty, premature; informal ahead of yourself.
–OPPOSITES next.
■ **previous to** before, prior to, until.

previously adverb **formerly**, earlier, before, hitherto, at one time, in the past, in days/times gone by, in bygone days, in times past, in former times.

prey noun **quarry**, victim, target.
–OPPOSITES predator.
■ **prey on 1** *few animals prey on grey wolves:* hunt, kill; eat, feed on, live on/off. **2** *they prey on the elderly:* exploit, victimize, pick on, take advantage of. **3** *the problem preyed on his mind:* oppress, weigh on, gnaw at; trouble, worry, disturb, distress, haunt, nag, torment, plague, obsess.

price noun **1** *the purchase price:* **cost**, charge, fee, fare, amount, sum. **2** *the price of success:* **consequence**, result, cost, penalty, sacrifice; downside, drawback, disadvantage, minus.

priceless adjective *priceless works of art:* **of incalculable value/worth**, invaluable, beyond price; irreplaceable.
–OPPOSITES worthless, cheap.

pricey adjective (informal). See **EXPENSIVE**.

prick verb **1** *prick the potatoes with a fork:* **pierce**, puncture, stab, perforate, nick, jab. **2** *his conscience pricked him:* **trouble**, worry, distress, perturb, disturb. **3** *the horse pricked its ears:* **raise**, erect.
• **noun jab**, sting, pinprick, stab.
■ **prick up your ears** listen carefully, pay attention, become attentive, attend; informal be all ears.

prickle noun **1** *the cactus is covered with prickles:* **thorn**, needle, barb, spike, point, spine. **2** *a cold prickle of fear:* **tingle**, chill, thrill, rush.

prickly adjective **1** *a prickly cactus:* **spiky**, spiked, thorny, barbed, spiny. **2** *my skin feels prickly:* **tingly**, tingling, prickling. **3** *a prickly character.* See **IRRITABLE**. **4** *a prickly question:* **problematic**, awkward, ticklish, tricky, delicate, sensitive, difficult, knotty, thorny, troublesome.

pride noun **1** *a source of pride:* **self-esteem**, dignity, honour, self-respect. **2** *pride in a job well done:* **pleasure**, joy, delight, gratification, fulfilment, satisfaction, sense of achievement. **3** *he refused out of pride:* **arrogance**,

vanity, self-importance, hubris, conceitedness, egotism, snobbery.
– OPPOSITES shame, humility.
■ **the pride of** best, finest, top, cream, pick, choice, prize, the jewel in the crown. **pride yourself on** be proud of, take pride in, take satisfaction in.

priest noun **clergyman, clergywoman**, minister, cleric, pastor, vicar, rector, parson, churchman, churchwoman, man/woman of the cloth, man/woman of God, father, curate, chaplain; Scottish kirkman; N. Amer. dominie; informal reverend, padre.

> WORD LINKS
> **clerical, hieratic, sacerdotal** relating to priests

prig noun **prude**, puritan, killjoy; informal goody-goody, Holy Joe; N. Amer. informal bluenose.

priggish adjective **self-righteous**, holier-than-thou, sanctimonious, moralistic, prudish, puritanical, prim, strait-laced, stuffy, prissy, narrow-minded; informal goody-goody, starchy.
– OPPOSITES broad-minded.

prim adjective **demure**, formal, stuffy, strait-laced, prudish; prissy, mimsy, priggish, puritanical; Brit. po-faced; informal starchy.

primacy noun **priority**, precedence, pre-eminence, superiority, supremacy, ascendancy, dominance.

primal adjective **basic**, fundamental, essential, elemental, atavistic.

primarily adverb **mostly**, for the most part, chiefly, mainly, in the main, on the whole, largely, principally, predominantly, especially, generally, usually, typically.

primary adjective **main**, chief, key, prime, central, principal, foremost, first, most important, predominant, paramount; informal number-one.
– OPPOSITES secondary.

prime[1] adjective **1** *their prime concern is his well-being:* **main**, chief, key, primary, central, principal, foremost, first, most important, paramount, major; informal number-one. **2** *prime agricultural land:* **top-quality**, top, best, first-class, first-rate, grade A, superior, choice, select, finest; informal tip-top, A1, top-notch. **3** *a prime example:* **archetypal**, typical, classic, characteristic, quintessential.
– OPPOSITES secondary, inferior.
• noun *he is in his prime:* **heyday**; peak, pinnacle, high point/spot, zenith.

prime[2] verb **1** *he primed the gun:* **prepare**, load. **2** *Lucy had primed him carefully:* **brief**, fill in, prepare, advise, instruct, coach, drill.

prime minister noun **premier**, first minister.

primeval adjective **1** *primeval forest:* **ancient**, earliest, first, prehistoric, primordial; pristine, virgin. **2** *primeval fears:* **instinctive**, primitive, basic, primal, primordial, intuitive, inborn, innate, inherent.

primitive adjective **1** *primitive times:* **ancient**, earliest, first, prehistoric, primordial, primeval; uncivilized, preliterate. **2** *primitive tools:* **crude**, simple, rough, basic, unsophisticated, rudimentary, rude, makeshift.
– OPPOSITES modern, sophisticated.

primordial adjective **1** *the primordial oceans:* **ancient**, earliest, first, prehistoric, primeval. **2** *their primordial desires:* **instinctive**, primitive, basic, primal, primeval, intuitive, inborn.

primp verb **groom**, tidy, arrange, brush, comb; smarten up, spruce up; informal titivate, doll up; Brit. informal tart up; N. Amer. informal gussy up.

prince noun **ruler**, sovereign, monarch.

princely adjective *a princely sum.* See HANDSOME sense 3.

principal adjective *their principal concern was survival:* **main**, chief, primary, leading, foremost, first, most important, predominant, dominant, pre-eminent, highest, top, topmost; informal number-one.
– OPPOSITES minor.
• noun **head teacher**, headmaster, headmistress; dean, rector, chancellor, vice chancellor, president, provost; N. Amer. informal prexy.

> ! Don't confuse **principal** with **principle**, which is a noun meaning 'a truth or general law used as the basis for something' (*the basic principles of algebra*).

principally adverb **mainly**, mostly, chiefly, for the most part, in the main, on the whole, largely, predominantly, primarily.

principle noun **1** *the basic principles of their faith:* **doctrine**, belief, creed, credo, code, precept, tenet, dictum, dogma, canon, law, truth; concept, idea, theory, fundamental, essential. **2** *a woman of principle | sticking to one's principles:* **morals**, morality, code of ethics, beliefs, ideals, standards; integrity, righteousness, virtue, probity, honour, decency, conscience, scruples.
■ **in principle 1** *there is no reason, in principle, why not:* in theory, theoretically, on paper. **2** *he accepted the idea in principle:* in general, in essence, on the whole, in the main.

principled adjective **moral**, ethical, virtuous, righteous, upright, upstanding, honourable, honest.

print verb **1** *patterns were printed on the cloth:* **imprint**, impress, stamp, mark. **2** *they printed 30,000 copies:* **publish**, issue, release, circulate. **3** *the incident is printed on her memory:* **register**, record, impress, imprint, engrave, etch, stamp, mark.
• noun **1** *small print:* **type**, printing, letters, lettering, characters, type size, typeface, font. **2** *prints of his left hand:* **impression**, fingerprint, footprint. **3** *sporting prints:* **picture**; engraving, etching, lithograph, linocut, woodcut. **4** *prints and negatives:* **photograph**, photo, snap, snapshot, picture, still; Brit. enprint. **5** *soft floral prints:* **printed cloth/ fabric**, patterned cloth/fabric.
■ **in print** published, printed, available, obtainable. **out of print** no longer available, unavailable, unobtainable.

prior adjective **earlier**, previous, preceding, advance.
– OPPOSITES subsequent.
■ **prior to** before, until, till, up to, previous to, earlier than.

priority noun **1** *safety is our priority:* **prime concern**, main consideration. **2** *giving priority to education:* **precedence**, preference, pre-eminence, predominance, primacy. **3** *oncoming traffic has priority:* **right of way**.

prise verb **1** *I prised the lid off:* **lever**, jemmy; wrench, wrest, twist; N. Amer. pry, jimmy. **2** *he had to prise information from them:* **wring**, wrest, winkle out, screw, squeeze, force.

prison noun **jail**, lock-up, penal institution; N. Amer. jailhouse, penitentiary, correctional facility; informal clink, slammer, stir, jug, brig; Brit. informal nick; N. Amer. informal can, pen, cooler, pokey, slam; Brit. Military glasshouse.
■ **be in prison** be behind bars; informal be inside, do time; Brit. informal do bird, do porridge.

WORD LINKS
custodial relating to prison

prisoner noun **1** *a prisoner serving a life sentence:* **convict**, detainee, inmate; informal jailbird, con; N. Amer. informal yardbird. **2** *the army took many prisoners:* **prisoner of war**, POW, internee, captive.

prissy adjective **prudish**, priggish, prim, prim and proper, strait-laced, Victorian, schoolmarmish; Brit. po-faced; informal starchy.
– OPPOSITES broad-minded.

pristine adjective **immaculate**, perfect, in mint condition, as new, unspoilt, spotless, flawless, clean, fresh, new, virgin, pure.
– OPPOSITES dirty, spoilt.

privacy noun **seclusion**, solitude, isolation.

private adjective **1** *his private plane:* **personal**, own, special, exclusive. **2** *private talks:* **confidential**, secret, classified. **3** *private thoughts:* **intimate**, personal, secret; innermost, undisclosed, unspoken, unvoiced. **4** *a very private man:* **reserved**, introverted, self-contained, reticent, retiring, unsociable, withdrawn, solitary, reclusive. **5** *somewhere private to talk:* **secluded**, undisturbed, remote, isolated. **6** *he's acting in a private capacity:* **unofficial**, personal. **7** *private industry:* **independent**, non-state; privatized; commercial, private-enterprise.
– OPPOSITES public, open, extrovert, busy, crowded, official, state, nationalized.
• noun *a private in the army:* **private soldier**; trooper; Brit. sapper, gunner; US GI; Brit. informal Tommy, squaddie.

■ **in private** in secret, secretly, privately, behind closed doors, in camera.

private detective noun **private investigator**; informal private eye, PI, sleuth, snoop; N. Amer. informal shamus, gumshoe; informal, dated private dick.

privately adverb **1** *we must talk privately:* **in private**, behind closed doors, in camera. **2** *privately, I was glad:* **secretly**, inwardly, deep down. **3** *he lived very privately:* **out of the public eye**, out of public view.
–OPPOSITES publicly.

privation noun **deprivation**, hardship, destitution, impoverishment, need.
–OPPOSITES plenty, luxury.

privilege noun **1** *senior pupils have certain privileges:* **advantage**, benefit; prerogative, entitlement, right; concession, freedom, liberty. **2** *it was a privilege to meet her:* **honour**, pleasure.

privileged adjective **1** *a privileged background:* **wealthy**, rich, affluent, prosperous. **2** *privileged information:* **confidential**, private, secret, restricted, classified, not for publication, off the record, inside; informal hush-hush.
–OPPOSITES underprivileged, disadvantaged, public.

prize noun **1** *an art prize:* **award**, reward, purse; trophy, medal. **2** *the prizes of war:* **spoils**, booty, plunder, loot, pickings, trophy.
•adjective **1** *a prize bull:* **champion**, award-winning, top, best. **2** *a prize idiot:* **utter**, complete, total, absolute, real, perfect; Brit. informal right; Austral./NZ informal fair.

prized adjective **treasured**, precious, cherished, much loved, beloved, valued, esteemed, highly regarded.

prizewinner noun **champion**, winner, gold medallist, victor.

probability noun **1** *the probability of winning:* **likelihood**, prospect, expectation, chance, odds. **2** *relegation is a distinct probability:* **prospect**, possibility.

probable adjective **likely**, odds-on, expected, anticipated; informal on the cards, a safe bet.
–OPPOSITES unlikely.

probably adverb **in all likelihood**, in all probability, as likely as not, ten to one, the chances are.

probation noun **trial**, test period; apprenticeship.

probe noun **investigation**, enquiry, examination, inquest, study.
•verb **examine**, feel, explore, prod, poke.

probity noun **integrity**, honesty, uprightness, decency, morality, rectitude, goodness, virtue.
–OPPOSITES untrustworthiness.

problem noun **1** *there's been a problem:* **difficulty**, complication; snag, hitch, drawback, stumbling block, obstacle, hiccup, setback, catch; misfortune, mishap, misadventure; informal dilemma, headache. **2** *I don't want to be a problem:* **nuisance**, bother; informal drag, pain. **3** *arithmetical problems:* **puzzle**, question, poser, riddle, conundrum; informal brain-teaser.
•adjective *a problem child:* **troublesome**, difficult, unmanageable, unruly, disobedient, uncontrollable, recalcitrant, delinquent.
–OPPOSITES well behaved, manageable.

problematic adjective **difficult**, troublesome, tricky, awkward, controversial, ticklish, complicated, complex, knotty, thorny, prickly, vexed; informal sticky; Brit. informal dodgy.
–OPPOSITES easy, simple, straightforward.

procedure noun **course/line of action**, policy, method, system, strategy, way, approach, formula, mechanism, methodology, technique; routine, drill, practice.

proceed verb **1** *she was uncertain how to proceed:* **begin**, make a start, get going, move. **2** *he proceeded down the road:* **go**, make your way, advance, move, progress, carry on, press on, push on. **3** *we should proceed with the talks:* **go ahead**, carry on, go on, continue, keep on, get on; pursue, prosecute.
–OPPOSITES stop.

proceedings plural noun **1** *the evening's proceedings:* **events**, activities, happenings, goings-on. **2** *the proceedings of the meeting:* **report**, transactions, minutes, account, record; annals, archives. **3** *legal* *proceedings:* **litigation**; lawsuit, case, prosecution.

proceeds plural noun **profits**, earnings, receipts, returns, takings, income, revenue; Sport gate; N. Amer. take.

process noun **1** *investigation is a long process:* **procedure**, operation, action, activity, exercise, affair, business, job, task, undertaking. **2** *a new canning process:* **method**, system, technique, means, practice, way, approach, methodology.
• verb *applications are processed rapidly:* **deal with**, attend to, see to, sort out, handle, take care of.
■ **in the process of** in the middle of, in the course of, in the midst of, in the throes of, busy with, occupied in/with, taken up with/by, involved in.

procession noun **1** *a procession through the town:* **parade**, march, march past, motorcade, cortège; column, file. **2** *a procession of dance routines:* **series**, succession, stream, string, sequence.

proclaim verb **1** *messengers proclaimed the good news:* **declare**, announce, pronounce, state, make known, give out, advertise, publish, broadcast, trumpet. **2** *the men proclaimed their innocence:* **assert**, declare, profess, maintain, protest. **3** *he proclaimed himself president:* **declare**, pronounce, announce.

proclamation noun **declaration**, announcement, pronouncement, statement, notification, broadcast; assertion, profession, protestation; decree, order, edict, ruling.

proclivity noun **inclination**, tendency, leaning, disposition, proneness, propensity, bent, bias, penchant, predisposition; predilection, partiality, liking, preference, taste, fondness.

procrastinate verb **delay**, put off, postpone action, defer action, stall, play for time.

procreate verb **produce offspring**, reproduce, multiply, propagate, breed.

procure verb **obtain**, acquire, get, find, come by, secure, pick up; buy, purchase; informal get hold of, get your hands on.

prod verb **poke**, jab, dig, elbow, stab.
• noun **poke**, jab, dig, elbow, thrust.

prodigal adjective **wasteful**, extravagant, spendthrift, profligate.
– OPPOSITES thrifty.

prodigious adjective **enormous**, huge, colossal, immense, vast, great, massive, gigantic, mammoth, tremendous, inordinate, monumental; amazing, astonishing, astounding, staggering, stunning, remarkable, phenomenal, spectacular, extraordinary, exceptional, breathtaking, incredible; informal humongous, stupendous, fantastic, fabulous, mega, awesome; Brit. informal ginormous.
– OPPOSITES small, unexceptional.

prodigy noun **genius**, mastermind, virtuoso, wunderkind; informal whizz-kid, whizz, wizard.

produce verb **1** *the company produces furniture:* **manufacture**, make, construct, build, fabricate, put together, assemble, turn out, create; mass-produce; informal churn out. **2** *the vineyards produce excellent wines:* **yield**, grow, give, supply, provide, furnish, bear. **3** *she produced an ID card:* **present**, offer, proffer, show, display, bring out, pull out, extract; supply, provide, furnish. **4** *the decision produced a fierce reaction:* **give rise to**, bring about, cause, occasion, generate, engender, lead to, result in, effect, induce, set off; provoke, precipitate, breed, spark off, trigger. **5** *he produced and directed the play:* **stage**, put on, mount, present.
• noun *local produce:* **food**, foodstuffs, products; fruit, vegetables.

producer noun **1** *a car producer:* **manufacturer**, maker, builder, constructor. **2** *coffee producers:* **grower**, farmer. **3** *the producer of the show:* **impresario**, manager, administrator, promoter.

product noun **1** *household products:* **artefact**, commodity; (**products**) goods, wares, merchandise, produce. **2** *a product of experience:* **result**, consequence, outcome, effect, upshot.

production noun **1** *the production of cars:* **manufacture**, making, construction, building, fabrication, assembly, creation; mass production. **2** *the production of literary works:* **creation**, origination, fashioning; composition, writing. **3** *agricultural production:* **output**, yield; productivity. **4** *admission only on production of a ticket:* **presentation**, showing. **5** *a theatre production:* **performance**, staging, presentation, show, piece, play.

productive adjective **1** *a productive artist:* **prolific**, inventive, creative. **2** *productive talks:* **useful**, constructive, profitable, fruitful, gainful, valuable, effective, worthwhile, helpful. **3** *productive land:* **fertile**, fruitful, rich, fecund.
– OPPOSITES sterile, barren.

productivity noun **1** *workers have boosted productivity:* **efficiency**, work rate; output, yield, production. **2** *the productivity of the soil:* **fruitfulness**, fertility, richness, fecundity.
– OPPOSITES sterility, barrenness.

profane adjective **1** *subjects both sacred and profane:* **secular**, lay, non-religious. **2** *profane language:* **obscene**, blasphemous, indecent, foul, vulgar, crude, filthy, dirty, coarse, rude, offensive.
– OPPOSITES religious, reverent, decorous.
• verb *invaders profaned our temples:* **desecrate**, violate, defile.

profanity noun **1** *he hissed a profanity | an outburst of profanity:* **oath**, swear word, expletive, curse, obscenity, four-letter word, dirty word; blasphemy, swearing, foul language, bad language, cursing. **2** *acts of profanity:* **sacrilege**, blasphemy, ungodliness, impiety, irreverence, disrespect.

profess verb **1** *he professed his love:* **declare**, announce, proclaim, assert, state, affirm, avow, maintain, protest. **2** *she professed to loathe publicity:* **claim**, pretend, purport, affect; make out.

professed adjective **claimed**, supposed, ostensible, self-styled, apparent, pretended, purported.

profession noun **1** *his chosen profession:* **career**, occupation, calling, vocation, métier, work, line of work, job, business, trade, craft; informal racket. **2** *a profession of allegiance:* **declaration**, affirmation, statement, announcement, proclamation, assertion, avowal, vow, claim, protestation.

professional adjective **1** *professional occupations:* **white-collar**, non-manual. **2** *a professional cricketer:* **paid**, salaried. **3** *a very professional job:* **expert**, accomplished, skilful, masterly, masterful, fine, polished, skilled, proficient, competent, able, businesslike, deft. **4** *he has not behaved in a professional way:* **appropriate**, fitting, proper, honourable, ethical.
– OPPOSITES manual, amateur, unprofessional.

proffer verb **offer**, tender, submit, extend, volunteer, suggest, propose, put forward.
– OPPOSITES refuse, withdraw.

proficiency noun **skill**, expertise, accomplishment, competence, mastery, prowess, professionalism, ability; informal know-how.
– OPPOSITES incompetence.

proficient adjective **skilled**, skilful, expert, accomplished, competent, masterly, adept, adroit, deft, dexterous, able, professional; informal crack, ace, mean.
– OPPOSITES incompetent.

profile noun **1** *his handsome profile:* **side view**, outline, silhouette, contour, shape, form, lines. **2** *a profile of the organization:* **description**, account, study, portrait, rundown, sketch, outline.
• verb *he was profiled in the Times:* **describe**, write about, portray, depict, outline.

profit noun **1** *profits of £50,000:* **gain**, return, yield, proceeds, earnings, winnings, surplus, excess; informal pay dirt, bottom line. **2** *there was little profit in going on:* **advantage**, benefit, value, use, good, avail; informal mileage.
– OPPOSITES loss, disadvantage.
• verb **1** *she profited from the experience:* **benefit from**, take advantage of, capitalize on, make the most of, turn to your advantage, put to good use, exploit; informal cash in on. **2** *how will that profit us?* **benefit**, be advantageous to, be of use/value to, help, be of service to, serve, assist, aid.
– OPPOSITES lose, disadvantage.

profitable adjective **1** *a profitable company:* **moneymaking**, profit-making, commercial, successful, money-spinning, solvent, in the black, gainful, remunerative, financially rewarding, paying, lucrative, bankable. **2** *profitable study:* **beneficial**, useful, advantageous, valuable, productive, worthwhile; rewarding, fruitful, illuminating, informative, well spent.
– OPPOSITES loss-making, fruitless, useless.

profligate adjective **1** *profligate local authorities:* **wasteful**, extravagant, spendthrift, improvident, prodigal. **2** *a profligate lifestyle:* **dissolute**, degenerate, debauched; promiscuous, loose, wanton, licentious, decadent, abandoned.
– OPPOSITES thrifty, frugal, moral, upright.

profound adjective **1** *profound relief:* **heartfelt**, intense, keen, great, extreme, acute, severe, sincere, earnest, deep, deep-seated, overpowering, overwhelming. **2** *a profound change:* **far-reaching**, radical, extensive, sweeping, exhaustive, thoroughgoing. **3** *a profound analysis:* **wise**, learned, intelligent, scholarly, discerning, penetrating, perceptive, astute, thoughtful, insightful. **4** *profound truths:* **complex**, abstract, deep, weighty, difficult.
– OPPOSITES superficial, mild, slight, simple.

profuse adjective **1** *profuse apologies:* **copious**, prolific, abundant, liberal, unstinting, fulsome, effusive, extravagant, lavish, gushing. **2** *profuse blooms:* **luxuriant**, plentiful, copious, abundant, lush, rich, exuberant, riotous, teeming, rank, rampant.
– OPPOSITES meagre, sparse.

profusion noun **abundance**, mass, host, cornucopia, riot, plethora, superabundance; informal sea, wealth.

progeny noun **offspring**, young, babies, children, sons and daughters, family, brood; descendants, heirs; Law issue.

prognosis noun **forecast**, prediction, prognostication.

prognosticate verb **forecast**, predict, prophesy.

prognostication noun **prediction**, forecast, prophecy, prognosis.

programme noun **1** *our programme for the day:* **schedule**, agenda, calendar, timetable; order of events, line-up. **2** *the government's reform programme:* **scheme**, plan, package, strategy. **3** *a television programme:* **broadcast**, production, show, presentation, transmission, performance; informal prog. **4** *a programme of study:* **course**, syllabus, curriculum. **5** *a theatre programme:* **guide**; N. Amer. playbill.
• verb *demolition of the properties is programmed for next year:* **arrange**, organize, schedule, plan, map out, timetable, line up; N. Amer. slate.

progress noun **1** *snow made their progress difficult:* **movement**, advance, passage. **2** *scientific progress:* **development**, advance, advancement, headway, step forward; improvement, growth.
– OPPOSITES relapse.
• verb **1** *they progressed slowly down the road:* **go**, make your way, move, proceed, advance, continue, work your way. **2** *the school has progressed rapidly:* **develop**, make progress, advance, make headway, move on, get on, gain ground; improve, get better, come on, come along, make strides; thrive, prosper, blossom, flourish.
– OPPOSITES relapse.
■ **in progress** under way, going on, ongoing, happening, occurring, taking place, proceeding, continuing; N. Amer. in the works.

progression noun **1** *progression to the next stage:* **progress**, advancement, movement, passage; development, evolution, growth. **2** *a progression of peaks on the graph:* **succession**, series, sequence, string, stream, chain, train, row, cycle.

progressive adjective **1** *progressive deterioration:* **continuing**, continuous, ongoing; gradual, step-by-step, cumulative. **2** *progressive views:* **modern**, liberal, advanced, forward-thinking, enlightened, enterprising, innovative, pioneering, dynamic, bold, reforming, reformist, radical; informal go-ahead.
– OPPOSITES conservative, reactionary.

•noun *he is very much a progressive:* **innovator**, reformer, reformist, liberal.

prohibit verb **1** *state law prohibits gambling:* **forbid**, ban, bar, interdict, proscribe, make illegal, embargo, outlaw, disallow; Law enjoin. **2** *a cash shortage prohibited the visit:* **prevent**, stop, rule out, preclude, make impossible.
–OPPOSITES allow.

prohibited adjective **illegal**, illicit, against the law; Islam haram; informal not on, out, no go.
–OPPOSITES permitted.

prohibition noun **1** *the prohibition of cannabis:* **banning**, forbidding, prohibiting, barring, proscription, outlawing. **2** *a prohibition was imposed:* **ban**, bar, interdict, veto, embargo, injunction, moratorium.

prohibitive adjective **1** *prohibitive costs:* **excessively high**, sky-high, overinflated; out of the question, beyond your means; extortionate, unreasonable, exorbitant; informal steep, criminal. **2** *prohibitive regulations:* **proscriptive**, restrictive, repressive.

project noun **1** *an engineering project:* **scheme**, plan, programme, enterprise, undertaking, venture; proposal, idea, concept. **2** *a history project:* **assignment**, piece of work, task.
•verb **1** *profits are projected to rise:* **forecast**, predict, expect, estimate, calculate, reckon, extrapolate. **2** *balconies projected over the lake:* **stick out**, jut out, protrude, extend, stand out, bulge out, poke out; overhang. **3** *the sun projected his shadow on the wall:* **cast**, throw, send, shed, shine. **4** *she tried to project a calm image:* **convey**, put across, put over, communicate, present, promote.

projectile noun **missile.**

projecting adjective **sticking out**, protuberant, protruding, prominent, jutting out, overhanging, proud, bulging.
–OPPOSITES sunken, flush.

projection noun **1** *a sales projection:* **forecast**, prediction, prognosis, expectation, estimate. **2** *tiny projections on the cliff face:* **protuberance**, protrusion, prominence, eminence, outcrop, outgrowth; overhang, ledge, shelf.

proletarian adjective *a proletarian background:* **working-class**, plebeian, cloth-cap, common.
–OPPOSITES aristocratic.

proletariat noun **the workers**, working-class people, wage-earners, the labouring classes, the common people, the lower classes, the masses, the commonalty, the rank and file; derogatory the hoi polloi, the great unwashed, the mob, the rabble; informal, derogatory the plebs, the proles.
–OPPOSITES aristocracy.

proliferate verb **increase rapidly**, grow rapidly, multiply, rocket, mushroom, snowball, burgeon, run riot.
–OPPOSITES decrease, dwindle.

prolific adjective **1** *a prolific crop of tomatoes:* **plentiful**, abundant, bountiful, profuse, copious, luxuriant, rich, lush; fruitful; literary plenteous. **2** *a prolific composer:* **productive**, fertile.

prologue noun **introduction**, foreword, preface, preamble, prelude; informal intro.
–OPPOSITES epilogue.

prolong verb **lengthen**, extend, draw/drag out, protract, spin/stretch out; carry on, continue, keep up, perpetuate.
–OPPOSITES shorten.

promenade noun **1** *the tree-lined promenade:* **esplanade**, front, seafront, parade, walk, boulevard, avenue; N. Amer. boardwalk; Brit. informal prom. **2** *our nightly promenade:* **walk**, stroll, turn, amble, airing; dated constitutional.
•verb *we promenaded in the park:* **walk**, stroll, saunter, wander, amble, stretch your legs, take a turn.

prominence noun **1** *his rise to prominence:* **fame**, celebrity, eminence, pre-eminence, importance, distinction, greatness, note, notability, prestige, stature, standing. **2** *a rocky prominence:* **hillock**, hill, hummock, mound; outcrop, crag, spur, rise; ridge; peak, pinnacle; promontory, cliff, headland.

prominent adjective **1** *a prominent surgeon:* **important**, well known, leading, eminent, distinguished, notable, noteworthy, noted, illustrious, celebrated, famous,

renowned; N. Amer. major-league. **2** *prominent cheekbones:* **protuberant**, protruding, projecting, jutting out, standing out, sticking out, proud, bulging. **3** *a prominent feature of the landscape:* **conspicuous**, noticeable, easily seen, obvious, unmistakable, eye-catching, pronounced, salient, striking, dominant; obtrusive.
– OPPOSITES unimportant, unknown, inconspicuous.

promiscuity noun **licentiousness**, wantonness, immorality.
– OPPOSITES chastity, virtue.

promiscuous adjective **licentious**, indiscriminate, wanton, immoral, of easy virtue; dated loose.
– OPPOSITES chaste, virtuous.

promise noun **1** *you broke your promise:* **word of honour**, assurance, pledge, vow, guarantee, oath, bond, undertaking, agreement, commitment, contract, covenant. **2** *he shows promise:* **potential**, possibility. **3** *a promise of fine weather:* **indication**, hint, suggestion, sign. • verb **1** *she promised to go:* **give your word**, swear, pledge, vow, undertake, guarantee, contract, engage, give an assurance, commit yourself, bind yourself, swear/take an oath, covenant. **2** *the skies promised sunshine:* **indicate**, point to, be a sign of, be evidence of, give hope of, bespeak, presage, augur, herald, bode, portend.

promising adjective **1** *a promising start:* **good**, encouraging, favourable, hopeful, full of promise, auspicious, propitious, bright, rosy, heartening, reassuring. **2** *a promising actor:* **with potential**, budding, up-and-coming, rising, coming, in the making.
– OPPOSITES unfavourable, hopeless.

promontory noun **headland**, point, cape, head, horn, bill, ness, peninsula; Scottish mull.

promote verb **1** *she's been promoted:* **upgrade**, elevate, raise, advance, move up. **2** *an organization promoting justice:* **encourage**, further, advance, foster, develop, boost, stimulate, forward, work for. **3** *she is promoting her new film:* **advertise**, publicize, beat/bang the drum for, market, merchandise; informal push, plug, hype; N. Amer. informal ballyhoo, flack.
– OPPOSITES demote, obstruct, play down.

promoter noun **advocate**, champion, supporter, backer, proponent, protagonist, campaigner; N. Amer. booster.

promotion noun **1** *her promotion at work:* **upgrading**, preferment, elevation, advancement, step up the ladder. **2** *the promotion of justice:* **encouragement**, furtherance, furthering, advancement, contribution to, fostering, boosting, stimulation; N. Amer. boosterism. **3** *the promotion for her new film:* **advertising**, marketing, publicity, campaign, propaganda; informal hard sell, plug, hype, puff; N. Amer. informal ballyhoo.

prompt verb **1** *curiosity prompted him to look:* **induce**, make, move, motivate, lead, dispose, persuade, incline, encourage, stimulate, prod, impel, spur on, inspire. **2** *the statement prompted a hostile reaction:* **give rise to**, bring about, cause, occasion, result in, lead to, elicit, produce, engender, induce, precipitate, trigger, spark off, provoke. **3** *the actors needed prompting:* **remind**, cue, feed, help out; jog someone's memory.
– OPPOSITES deter.
• adjective *a prompt reply:* **quick**, swift, rapid, speedy, fast, direct, immediate, instant, early, punctual, in good time, on time.
– OPPOSITES slow, late.
• adverb *at 3.30 prompt:* **exactly**, precisely, sharp, on the dot, dead, punctually, on the nail; informal bang on; N. Amer. informal on the button/nose.

promptly adverb **1** *William arrived promptly at 7.30:* **punctually**, on time; informal on the dot, bang on; Brit. informal spot on; N. Amer. informal on the button/nose. **2** *I expect the matter to be dealt with promptly:* **without delay**, straight/right away, at once, immediately, now, asap; quickly, swiftly, rapidly, speedily, fast; informal pronto, pdq (pretty damn quick).
– OPPOSITES late, slowly.

promulgate verb **make known**, make public, publicize, spread, communicate, propagate, disseminate, broadcast, promote, preach.

prone adjective **1** *softwood is prone to rotting | prone to rot:* **susceptible**, vulnerable, subject, open, liable, given, predisposed, likely, disposed, inclined, apt. **2** *his prone body:* **face down**, flat, horizontal, prostrate.
–OPPOSITES resistant, immune, upright.

prong noun **tine**, spike, point, tip, projection.

pronounce verb **1** *his name is difficult to pronounce:* **say**, enunciate, utter, voice, sound, vocalize, get your tongue round. **2** *the doctor pronounced her fit for work:* **declare**, proclaim; judge, rule, decree.

pronounced adjective **noticeable**, marked, strong, conspicuous, striking, distinct, prominent, unmistakable, obvious.
–OPPOSITES slight.

pronouncement noun **announcement**, proclamation, declaration, assertion; judgement, ruling.

pronunciation noun **accent**, diction, delivery, intonation; articulation, enunciation, vocalization.

proof noun **evidence**, verification, corroboration, authentication, confirmation, certification, documentation.
• adjective **resistant**, immune, unaffected, impervious.

prop noun **1** *the roof is held up by props:* **pole**, post, support, upright, brace, buttress, stay, strut. **2** *a prop for the economy:* **mainstay**, pillar, anchor, support.
• verb *he propped his bike against the wall:* **lean**, rest, stand, balance.
■ **prop something up 1** *this post is propping the wall up:* hold up, shore up, buttress, support, brace, underpin. **2** *they prop up loss-making industries:* subsidize, underwrite, fund, finance.

propaganda noun **information**, promotion, advertising, publicity; disinformation; informal hype.

propagate verb **1** *an easy plant to propagate:* **breed**, grow, cultivate. **2** *these shrubs propagate easily:* **reproduce**, multiply, proliferate, increase, spread. **3** *they propagated socialist ideas:* **spread**, disseminate, communicate, make known, promulgate, circulate, broadcast, publicize, proclaim, preach, promote.

propel verb **1** *a boat propelled by oars:* **move**, power, push, drive. **2** *the impact propelled him into the street:* **throw**, thrust, toss, fling, hurl, pitch, send, shoot.

propeller noun **rotor**, screw; informal prop.

propensity noun **tendency**, inclination, predisposition, proneness, proclivity, readiness, liability, disposition, leaning, weakness.

proper adjective **1** *he's not a proper scientist:* **real**, genuine, actual, true, bona fide; informal kosher. **2** *the proper channels:* **right**, correct, accepted, conventional, established, official, regular, acceptable, appropriate. **3** *they were terribly proper:* **formal**, conventional, correct, orthodox, polite, punctilious, respectable. **4** (Brit. informal) *a proper mess:* **complete**, absolute, real, perfect, total, thorough, utter, out-and-out; Brit. informal right; Austral./NZ informal fair.
–OPPOSITES fake, inappropriate, wrong, unconventional.

property noun **1** *lost property:* **possessions**, belongings, things, effects, stuff, goods; informal gear. **2** *private property:* **building(s)**, premises, house(s), land; Law realty; N. Amer. real estate. **3** *garlic is known for its healing properties:* **quality**, attribute, characteristic, feature, power, trait, mark, hallmark.

prophecy noun **prediction**, forecast, prognostication, prognosis, divination.

prophesy verb **predict**, foretell, forecast, foresee, prognosticate.

prophet, prophetess noun **seer**, soothsayer, fortune-teller, clairvoyant; oracle.

prophetic adjective **prescient**, predictive, far-seeing.

propitiate verb **appease**, placate, mollify, pacify, make peace with, conciliate, soothe, calm.
–OPPOSITES provoke.

propitious adjective **favourable**, auspicious, promising, providential, advantageous, optimistic, bright, rosy, heaven-sent, hopeful; opportune, timely.
–OPPOSITES inauspicious, unfortunate.

proponent noun **advocate**, champion, supporter, promoter, protagonist, campaigner; N. Amer. booster.

proportion noun **1** *a proportion of the land:* **part**, portion, amount, quantity, bit, piece, percentage, fraction, section, segment, share. **2** *the proportion of water to alcohol:* **ratio**, distribution, relative amount/number. **3** *a sense of proportion:* **balance**, symmetry, harmony, correspondence, correlation, agreement. **4** *men of huge proportions:* **size**, dimensions, magnitude, measurements; mass, volume, bulk; expanse, extent, width, breadth.

proportional adjective **corresponding**, proportionate, comparable, in proportion, pro rata, commensurate, equivalent.
– OPPOSITES disproportionate.

proposal noun **1** *the proposal was rejected:* **scheme**, plan, idea, project, programme, motion, proposition, suggestion, submission. **2** *the proposal of a new constitution:* **putting forward**, proposing, submission.
– OPPOSITES withdrawal.

propose verb **1** *he proposed a solution:* **put forward**, suggest, submit, advance, offer, present, move, come up with. **2** *do you propose to go?* **intend**, mean, plan, have in mind/view, aim.
– OPPOSITES withdraw.

proposition noun **1** *a business proposition:* **proposal**, scheme, plan, project, idea, programme. **2** *they face Arsenal, a different proposition for any team:* **task**, job, undertaking, venture, activity, affair.

propound verb **put forward**, advance, offer, proffer, present, set forth, submit, tender, suggest, postulate, propose, posit.

proprietor, **proprietress** noun **owner**, possessor, holder, master, mistress; landowner, landlord, landlady; innkeeper, shopkeeper; Brit. publican.

propriety noun **decorum**, respectability, decency, correctness, good manners, courtesy, politeness, rectitude.
– OPPOSITES indecorum.

propulsion noun **thrust**, motive force, impetus, impulse, drive, driving force, actuation, push, pressure, power.

prosaic adjective **ordinary**, everyday, commonplace, conventional, straightforward, routine, run-of-the-mill; unimaginative, uninspired, uninspiring, matter-of-fact, dull, dreary, humdrum, mundane, pedestrian, tame, plodding.
– OPPOSITES interesting, imaginative, inspired.

proscribe verb **forbid**, prohibit, ban, bar, make illegal, embargo, outlaw, disallow, veto.
– OPPOSITES allow, authorize, accept.

> ! Don't confuse **proscribe** with **prescribe**, which means 'recommend' or 'officially state what should be done' (*an offence for which the maximum penalty is prescribed by statute*).

prosecute verb **1** *they prosecute offenders:* **take to court**, press charges, sue, try, bring to trial, put on trial, put in the dock, indict, arraign; N. Amer. impeach. **2** *they helped him prosecute the war:* **pursue**, fight, wage, carry on, conduct, direct, engage in, proceed with.
– OPPOSITES defend, let off, give up.

proselytize verb **evangelize**, convert, win over, preach to, recruit.

prospect noun **1** *there is little prospect of success:* **likelihood**, hope, expectation, chance, odds, probability, possibility, promise, lookout; fear, danger. **2** *her job prospects:* **possibilities**, potential, expectations, outlook. **3** *a daunting prospect:* **vision**, thought, idea; task, undertaking.
• verb *they are prospecting for oil:* **search**, look, explore, survey, scout, hunt.

prospective adjective **potential**, possible, probable, likely, future, eventual, -to-be, soon-to-be, in the making; intending, aspiring, would-be.

prospectus noun **brochure**, pamphlet, description; syllabus, curriculum, catalogue, programme, list, schedule.

prosper verb **flourish**, thrive, do well, bloom, blossom, burgeon,

progress, do all right for yourself, get ahead, get on, be successful; informal go places.
– OPPOSITES fail.

prosperity noun **success**, affluence, wealth, ease, plenty.
– OPPOSITES hardship, failure.

prosperous adjective **thriving**, flourishing, successful, strong, vigorous, profitable, lucrative, expanding, booming, burgeoning; affluent, wealthy, rich, moneyed, well off, well-to-do; informal in the money.
– OPPOSITES ailing, poor.

prostitute noun **call girl**, sex worker, whore; informal working girl; N. Amer. informal hooker.
• verb *he has prostituted his talent for cash:* **betray**, sell out, debase, degrade, demean, devalue, cheapen, lower, shame, misuse.

prostrate adjective **1** *the prostrate figure on the ground:* **prone**, lying flat, lying down, stretched out, spreadeagled, sprawling, horizontal, recumbent. **2** *his wife was prostrate with grief:* **overwhelmed**, overcome, overpowered, stunned, dazed; speechless, helpless; informal knocked/hit for six.
– OPPOSITES upright.
▪ **prostrate yourself** bow down, kneel, submit, grovel, cringe.

protagonist noun **1** *the protagonist in the plot:* **chief/central/principal/main/leading character**, hero/heroine, leading man/lady, title role, lead. **2** *a protagonist of deregulation:* **champion**, advocate, upholder, supporter, backer, promoter, proponent, exponent, campaigner, fighter, crusader; apostle, apologist; N. Amer. booster.
– OPPOSITES opponent.

protean adjective **ever-changing**, variable, changeable, mutable, kaleidoscopic, unstable, shifting, fluctuating, fluid.
– OPPOSITES constant, consistent.

protect verb **keep safe**, keep from harm, save, safeguard, preserve, defend, shield, cushion, insulate, shelter, screen, guard, watch over, look after, take care of, keep.
– OPPOSITES expose, neglect, attack, harm.

protection noun **1** *protection against frost:* **defence**, security, safe keeping, safety, sanctuary, shelter, refuge, immunity, insurance, indemnity. **2** *the protection of the Church:* **safe keeping**, care, charge, keeping, aegis, auspices, umbrella, guardianship, support, patronage. **3** *a good protection against noise:* **barrier**, buffer, shield, screen, cushion, bulwark.

protective adjective **1** *protective clothing:* **special**, safety; thick, heavy, insulated; -proof, -resistant. **2** *he felt protective towards her:* **solicitous**, caring, paternal/maternal; overprotective, possessive, jealous.

protector noun **1** *a protector of the environment:* **defender**, preserver, guardian, champion, patron, custodian. **2** *ear protectors:* **guard**, shield, buffer, cushion, pad, screen.

protégé, protégée noun **pupil**, student, trainee, apprentice; disciple, follower; ward.

protest noun **1** *a storm of protest:* **objection**, complaint, challenge, dissent, demurral, remonstration, fuss, outcry. **2** *the women staged a protest:* **demonstration**, rally, vigil; sit-in, occupation; work-to-rule, stoppage, strike, walkout, mutiny, picket, boycott; informal demo.
– OPPOSITES support, approval.
• verb **1** *residents protested at the plans:* **express opposition**, object, dissent, take issue, make/take a stand, put up a fight, take exception, complain, express disapproval, disagree, demur, make a fuss; cry out, speak out, rail, inveigh, fulminate; informal kick up a fuss/stink. **2** *people protested outside the cathedral:* **demonstrate**, march, rally. **3** *he protested his innocence:* **insist on**, maintain, assert, affirm, announce, proclaim, declare, profess.
– OPPOSITES acquiesce, support, deny.

protestation noun **1** *his protestations of innocence:* **declaration**, announcement, profession, assertion, insistence, claim, affirmation, assurance. **2** *we helped him despite his protestations:* **objection**, protest, exception, complaint, disapproval, opposition, dissent, demurral.
– OPPOSITES denial, acquiescence, support.

protester noun **demonstrator**, marcher; striker, picket.

protocol noun **1** *a stickler for protocol:* **etiquette**, convention, formalities, custom, the rules, procedure, ritual, decorum, the done thing. **2** *the two countries signed a protocol:* **agreement**, treaty, entente, concordat, convention, deal, pact, contract, compact.

prototype noun **1** *a prototype of the weapon:* **original**, master, template, pattern, sample. **2** *the prototype of an ideal wife:* **typical example**, paradigm, archetype, exemplar.

protract verb **prolong**, lengthen, extend, draw out, drag out, spin out, stretch out, string out.
– OPPOSITES curtail, shorten.

protracted adjective **prolonged**, extended, long-drawn-out, lengthy, long.
– OPPOSITES short.

protrude verb **stick out**, jut out, project, extend, stand out, bulge out, poke out.

protruding adjective **sticking out**, protuberant, projecting, prominent, overhanging, proud, bulging.
– OPPOSITES sunken, flush.

protrusion noun **bump**, lump, knob; protuberance, projection, swelling, outcrop, outgrowth.

protuberance noun **bump**, lump, knob, projection, protrusion, prominence, swelling, outcrop, outgrowth.

proud adjective **1** *the proud parents:* **pleased**, glad, happy, delighted, thrilled, satisfied, gratified. **2** *a proud day:* **pleasing**, gratifying, satisfying, cheering, heart-warming; happy, good, glorious, memorable, notable. **3** *they were poor but proud:* **dignified**, noble; self-respecting, independent. **4** *a proud, arrogant man:* **immodest**, self-important, full of yourself, conceited, boastful, cocky, haughty, overbearing, overweening; smug, self-satisfied, complacent; informal big-headed,
– OPPOSITES ashamed, shameful, humble, modest.

prove verb **1** *that proves I'm right:* **show**, demonstrate; substantiate, verify, validate, authenticate. **2** *the rumour proved to be correct:* **turn out**, be found.
– OPPOSITES disprove.

provenance noun **origin**, source; pedigree, derivation; N. Amer. provenience.

proverb noun **saying**, adage, saw, maxim, axiom, motto, aphorism, epigram, dictum, precept.

proverbial adjective **well known**, famous, famed, renowned, traditional, time-honoured, legendary.

provide verb **1** *we will provide funds:* **supply**, give, issue, furnish, come up with, dispense, bestow, impart, produce, yield, deliver, donate, contribute, allocate, distribute, allot, put up; informal fork out, lay out; N. Amer. informal ante up, pony up. **2** *he was provided with tools:* **equip**, furnish, issue, supply, outfit; fit out, rig out, kit out, arm, provision; informal fix up. **3** *he had to provide for his family:* **feed**, nurture, nourish; support, maintain, keep, sustain. **4** *the test may provide the answer:* **offer**, present, afford, give, add, bring, yield, impart, reveal. **5** *we have provided for further restructuring:* **prepare**, allow, make provision, arrange, plan, cater. **6** *the banks have to provide against bad debts:* **take precautions**, take steps/measures, guard; make provision for.
– OPPOSITES refuse, withhold, deprive, neglect.

provided conjunction **if**, on condition that, providing that, provided that, presuming that, assuming that, on the assumption that, as long as, given that, with/on the understanding that.

providence noun **fate**, destiny, predestination, predetermination, the stars.

provident adjective **prudent**, far-sighted, judicious, circumspect, wise, sensible; thrifty, economical.
– OPPOSITES improvident.

providential adjective **opportune**, advantageous, favourable, auspicious, propitious, welcome, lucky, happy, fortunate, felicitous, timely, well timed, seasonable, convenient.
– OPPOSITES inopportune.

provider noun **supplier**, donor, giver, contributor, source.

providing conjunction. See **PROVIDED**.

province noun **1** *a province of the Roman Empire:* **territory**, region,

p

state, department, canton, area, district, sector, zone, division. **2** *people in the provinces:* **the regions**, the rest of the country, rural areas/districts, the countryside, the backwoods, the wilds; informal the sticks, the middle of nowhere; N. Amer. informal the boondocks.

provincial adjective **1** *the provincial government:* **regional**, state, territorial, district, local, county. **2** *provincial areas:* **non-metropolitan**, small-town, non-urban, outlying, rural, country, rustic, backwoods, backwater; informal one-horse; N. Amer. informal hick, freshwater. **3** *they're so dull and provincial:* **unsophisticated**, narrow-minded, parochial, small-town, suburban, insular, inward-looking, conservative; small-minded, blinkered; N. Amer. informal jerkwater.
– OPPOSITES national, metropolitan, cosmopolitan.

provision noun **1** *the provision of weapons to guerrillas:* **supply**, providing, giving, donation. **2** *there's limited provision for young children:* **facilities**, services, amenities, resources, arrangements; means, funds, assistance. **3** *provisions for the trip:* **supplies**, food and drink, stores, groceries, foodstuffs, rations; formal comestibles; dated victuals. **4** *he made no provision for the future:* **preparations**, plans, arrangements, precautions, contingency. **5** *the provisions of the Act:* **term**; requirement, specification, stipulation.

provisional adjective **interim**, temporary; transitional, changeover, stopgap, short-term, fill-in, acting, caretaker; working, tentative.
– OPPOSITES permanent, definite.

provisionally adverb **temporarily**, short-term, for the interim, for the present, for the time being, for now, subject to confirmation, conditionally, tentatively.

proviso noun **condition**, stipulation, provision, clause, rider, qualification, restriction, caveat.

provocation noun **goading**, prodding, incitement, pressure; harassment; teasing, taunting, torment; informal hassle, aggravation.

provocative adjective **1** *provocative remarks:* **annoying**, irritating, exasperating, infuriating, maddening, vexing, galling; insulting, offensive, inflammatory, incendiary, controversial; informal aggravating. **2** *a provocative pose:* **sexy**, sexually arousing/exciting, alluring, seductive, suggestive, inviting, tantalizing, titillating; indecent, pornographic, indelicate, immodest, shameless; erotic, sensuous, slinky, coquettish, amorous, flirtatious; informal tarty, come-hither.
– OPPOSITES soothing, calming, modest, decorous.

provoke verb **1** *the plan has provoked outrage:* **arouse**, produce, evoke, cause, give rise to, occasion, call forth, elicit, induce, excite, spark off, touch off, kindle, generate, engender, instigate, result in, lead to, bring on, precipitate, prompt, trigger. **2** *he was provoked into replying:* **goad**, spur, prick, sting, prod, incite, rouse, stir, move, stimulate, inflame, impel. **3** *he's dangerous if provoked:* **annoy**, anger, enrage, irritate, antagonize; Brit. rub up the wrong way; informal aggravate, rile; Brit. informal wind up.
– OPPOSITES allay, deter, pacify.

prow noun **bow**, stem, front, nose, head; Brit. humorous sharp end.

prowess noun **skill**, expertise, mastery, ability, capability, capacity, talent, aptitude, dexterity, competence, proficiency, finesse; informal know-how.
– OPPOSITES inability, ineptitude.

prowl verb **steal**, slink, skulk, sneak, stalk, creep; informal snoop.

proximity noun **closeness**, nearness; accessibility, handiness.

proxy noun **deputy**, representative, substitute, delegate, agent, surrogate, stand-in, go-between.

prude noun **puritan**, prig, killjoy, moralist; informal goody-goody; N. Amer. informal bluenose.

prudence noun **1** *beyond the bounds of prudence:* **wisdom**, good judgement, common sense. **2** *financial prudence:* **caution**, care, providence, foresight, circumspection; thrift, economy.
– OPPOSITES folly, recklessness, extravagance.

prudent adjective **1** *it is prudent to obtain consent:* **wise**, sensible, politic, judicious, shrewd, advisable, well advised. **2** *a prudent approach to borrowing:* **cautious**, careful, provident, far-sighted, judicious, shrewd, circumspect; thrifty, economical.
– OPPOSITES unwise, reckless, extravagant.

prudish adjective **puritanical**, priggish, prim, prim and proper, moralistic, sententious, censorious, strait-laced, Victorian, stuffy; informal goody-goody.
– OPPOSITES permissive.

prune verb *staff numbers have been pruned:* **cut**, trim, reduce, pare down, slim down, downsize, axe, shrink; informal slash.
– OPPOSITES increase.

prurient adjective **salacious**, licentious, voyeuristic, lascivious, lecherous, lustful, lewd, libidinous.

pry verb **intrude**, spy, ferret about, interfere, meddle; informal poke your nose in, snoop; Austral./NZ informal stickybeak.

pseud noun **poser**, poseur, fraud; informal show-off, phoney.

pseudo adjective **bogus**, sham, phoney, mock, ersatz, quasi-, fake, false, spurious, contrived, affected, insincere; informal pretend, put-on; Brit. informal cod.
– OPPOSITES genuine.

pseudonym noun **pen name**, nom de plume, assumed name, alias, sobriquet, stage name, nom de guerre.

psyche noun **soul**, spirit, inner self, ego, persona, subconscious, mind, intellect.

psychiatrist noun **psychotherapist**, psychoanalyst; informal shrink.

psychic adjective **1** *psychic powers:* **supernatural**, paranormal, other-worldly, preternatural, metaphysical, extrasensory, magic, mystical, occult. **2** *I'm not psychic:* **clairvoyant**, telepathic. **3** *psychic development:* **emotional**, spiritual, inner; mental.
• noun **clairvoyant**, fortune-teller; medium, spiritualist; telepath, mind-reader.

psychological adjective **1** *his psychological state:* **mental**, cognitive; emotional, inner, subconscious. **2** *her pain was psychological:* **psychosomatic**, all in the mind, subjective.
– OPPOSITES physical.

psychology noun *the psychology of the road user:* **mindset**, mind, mental processes, thought processes, way of thinking, mentality, psyche, attitude, make-up, character.

psychopath noun **madman**, **madwoman**, maniac, lunatic, sociopath; informal nut, psycho; Brit. informal nutter.

pub noun (Brit.) **bar**, inn, tavern, hostelry, taproom, roadhouse; Brit. public house; Austral./NZ hotel; informal watering hole; Brit. informal local, boozer; dated alehouse; N. Amer. historical saloon.

puberty noun **adolescence**, pubescence, growing up; youth, young adulthood, teenage years, teens; formal juvenescence.

public adjective **1** *public affairs | public services:* **state**, national; constitutional, civic, civil, official, social, municipal, local; nationalized. **2** *we are simply responding to public demand:* **popular**, general, common, collective, shared, joint, universal, widespread. **3** *a public figure:* **prominent**, well known, important, leading, eminent, distinguished, celebrated, household, famous; N. Amer. major-league. **4** *a public library | public amenities:* communal, accessible, open, available, free, unrestricted, community. **5** *the news became public:* **known**, published, publicized, in circulation.
– OPPOSITES private, restricted.
• noun **1** *the British public:* **people**, citizens, subjects, general public, electors, electorate, voters, taxpayers, residents, inhabitants, citizenry, population, populace, community, society, country, nation. **2** *his adoring public:* **audience**, spectators, followers, following, fans, devotees, admirers; patrons, clientele, market, consumers, buyers, customers, readers.
■ **in public** publicly, in full view, openly, in the open, for all to see, blatantly, flagrantly, brazenly, overtly.

p

WORD LINKS
agoraphobia fear of public places

publication noun **1** *the author of this publication:* **book**, volume, title, work, tome, opus; newspaper, paper, magazine, periodical, newsletter, bulletin, journal, report; informal rag, mag, 'zine. **2** *the publication of her new book:* **issuing**, publishing, printing, distribution, spreading, dissemination, promulgation, appearance.

publicity noun **1** *the case attracted wide publicity:* **public attention**, media attention, the limelight, media exposure. **2** *advance publicity for her new movie:* **promotion**, advertising, propaganda; boost, push; informal hype, ballyhoo, build-up, razzmatazz; plug.

publicize verb **1** *I never publicize this fact:* **make known**, make public, announce, broadcast, spread, promulgate, disseminate, circulate, air. **2** *he just wants to publicize his book:* **advertise**, promote, build up, talk up, push, beat the drum for, boost; informal hype, plug.
–OPPOSITES conceal, suppress.

public-spirited adjective **philanthropic**, charitable, altruistic, humanitarian, generous, unselfish, community-minded.

publish verb **1** *we publish novels:* **issue**, bring out, produce, print. **2** *he ought to publish his views:* **make known**, make public, publicize, announce, broadcast, issue, put out, distribute, spread, promulgate, disseminate, circulate, air.

pucker verb **wrinkle**, crinkle, crease, furrow, crumple, rumple, ruck up, scrunch up, ruffle, screw up, shrivel.

puckish adjective **mischievous**, naughty, impish, roguish, playful; informal waggish.

pudding noun **dessert**, sweet, last course; Brit. informal afters, pud.

puddle noun **pool**, spill.

puerile adjective **childish**, immature, infantile, juvenile, babyish; silly, inane, fatuous, foolish.
–OPPOSITES mature, sensible.

puff noun **1** *a puff of wind:* **gust**, blast, flurry, rush, draught, waft, breeze, breath. **2** *he took a puff at his cigar:* **pull**; informal drag, toke.
•verb **1** *he walked fast, puffing a little:* **breathe heavily**, pant, blow; gasp. **2** *she puffed at her cigarette:* **smoke**, draw on, drag on, suck at/on.
■ **puff out/up** bulge, swell, stick out, become distended, balloon out, expand. **puff something out/up** distend, expand, dilate, inflate, blow up, pump up, enlarge, bloat.

puffed adjective **out of breath**, breathless, short of breath; panting, puffing, gasping, wheezing, wheezy, winded.

puffed-up adjective **self-important**, conceited, arrogant, bumptious, pompous, overbearing; affected, vain; informal snooty, uppity, uppish.

puffy adjective **swollen**, puffed up, distended, enlarged, inflated, dilated, bloated, engorged, bulging.

pugnacious adjective **combative**, aggressive, antagonistic, belligerent, quarrelsome, argumentative, hostile, truculent.
–OPPOSITES peaceable.

puke verb (informal). See **VOMIT**.

pull verb **1** *he pulled the box towards him:* **tug**, haul, drag, draw, tow, heave, jerk, wrench; informal yank. **2** *she pulled a muscle:* **strain**, sprain, wrench, tear. **3** *race day pulled big crowds:* **attract**, draw, bring in, lure, seduce, entice, tempt, beckon, interest, fascinate.
–OPPOSITES push, repel.
•noun **1** *give the chain a pull:* **tug**, jerk, heave; informal yank. **2** *she took a pull on her beer:* **gulp**, draught, drink, swallow, mouthful, slug; informal swig. **3** *the pull of the theatre:* **attraction**, draw, lure, magnetism, fascination, appeal, allure.
■ **pull back** withdraw, retreat, fall back, back off; pull out, retire, disengage. **pull something down** demolish, knock down, tear down, dismantle, raze to the ground, level, flatten, bulldoze, destroy. **pull in** stop, halt, come to a halt, pull over, pull up, draw up, brake, park. **pull something off** achieve, fulfil, succeed in, accomplish, bring off, carry off, clinch, fix, effect, engineer. **pull out** withdraw, resign, leave, retire, step down, bow out, back out, give up; informal quit. **pull through** get better, improve, recover, rally, come through,

p

recuperate. **pull yourself together** regain your composure, recover, get a grip; informal snap out of it, get your act together, buck up. **pull someone up** reprimand, rebuke, scold, chide, chastise, upbraid, berate, reprove, reproach, censure, take to task, admonish, lecture; informal tell off; Brit. informal tick off.

pulp noun **1** *crush the fruit into a pulp:* **mush**, mash, paste, purée. **2** *the sweet pulp on cocoa seeds:* **flesh**, marrow, meat.
• verb *pulp the gooseberries:* **mash**, purée, cream, crush, press, liquidize, liquefy.
• adjective *pulp fiction:* **trashy**, cheap, sensational, lurid, tasteless.

pulpit noun **stand**, lectern, platform, podium, dais, rostrum.

pulsate verb **palpitate**, pulse, throb, pump, undulate, surge, heave, rise and fall; beat, thump.

pulse[1] noun **1** *the pulse in her neck:* **heartbeat**, heart rate. **2** *the pulse of the engine:* **rhythm**, beat, tempo, pounding, throbbing, thudding, drumming. **3** *pulses of ultrasound:* **burst**, blast, surge.
• verb *music pulsed through the building:* **throb**, pulsate, vibrate, beat, pound, thud, thump, drum, reverberate, echo.

pulse[2] noun *eat plenty of pulses:* **legume**, bean.

p

pulverize verb **1** *the seeds are pulverized:* **grind**, crush, pound, powder, mill, press, pulp, mash; technical comminute. **2** (informal) *he pulverized the opposition.* See TROUNCE.

pummel verb **batter**, pound, belabour, beat; punch, strike, hit, thump; informal clobber, wallop, bash, whack, give someone a hiding, belt, biff, lay into.

pump verb **1** *they pumped air down the tube:* **force**, drive, push; suck, draw. **2** *she pumped up the tyre:* **inflate**, blow up, fill up; swell, enlarge, distend, expand, dilate, puff up. **3** *blood was pumping from his leg:* **spurt**, spout, squirt, jet, surge, spew, gush, stream, flow, pour, spill, well, cascade, run, course.

pun noun **play on words**, wordplay, double entendre, innuendo, witticism.

punch[1] verb *Jim punched him in the face:* **hit**, strike, thump, jab, smash; batter, buffet, pound, pummel; informal sock, slug, biff, bop, wallop, clobber, bash, whack, thwack, clout; Brit. informal stick one on, dot, slosh; N. Amer. informal boff, bust.
• noun *a punch on the nose:* **blow**, hit, knock, thump, box, jab, clip, welt; uppercut, hook; informal sock, slug, biff, bop, wallop, bash, whack, clout, belt; N. Amer. informal boff, bust.

punch[2] verb *he punched her ticket:* **perforate**, puncture, pierce, stamp, cut.

punch-up noun (Brit. informal). See FIGHT noun sense 1.

punchy adjective **forceful**, incisive, strong, powerful, vigorous, dynamic, effective; dramatic, passionate, vivid.
–OPPOSITES languid.

punctilious adjective **meticulous**, conscientious, diligent, scrupulous, careful, painstaking, rigorous, perfectionist; fussy, fastidious, finicky, pedantic; informal nit-picking, pernickety; N. Amer. informal persnickety.
–OPPOSITES careless.

punctual adjective **on time**, prompt, on schedule, in time; informal on the dot.
–OPPOSITES late.

punctuate verb *his talk was punctuated by slides:* **break up**, interrupt, intersperse, pepper, sprinkle, scatter.

puncture noun **1** *the tyre developed a puncture:* **hole**, perforation, rupture; cut, gash, slit; leak. **2** *my car has a puncture:* **flat tyre**; informal flat.
• verb *he punctured the balloon:* **make a hole in**, pierce, rupture, perforate, stab, cut, slit, prick; deflate.

pundit noun **expert**, authority, specialist, doyen/doyenne, master, guru, sage, savant; informal buff, whizz.

pungent adjective **strong**, powerful, pervasive, penetrating; sharp, acid, sour, biting, bitter, tart, vinegary, tangy; aromatic, spicy, piquant, peppery, hot, garlicky.
–OPPOSITES bland, mild.

punish verb **1** *they punished their children:* **discipline**, teach someone a lesson; tan someone's hide; informal murder, wallop, have someone's guts for garters; Brit. informal give someone what for; dated chastise. **2** *higher charges would punish the poor:* **penalize**, disadvantage, handicap, hurt.

punishing adjective **arduous**, demanding, taxing, strenuous, rigorous, stressful, trying; hard, heavy, difficult, tough, exhausting, tiring, gruelling, relentless.
–OPPOSITES easy.

punishment noun *the punishment should fit the crime:* **penalty**, sanction, forfeit; sentence, judgement; discipline.

> **WORD LINKS**
> **penal**, **punitive** relating to punishment

punitive adjective **1** *punitive measures:* **penal**, disciplinary, corrective, retributive. **2** *punitive taxes:* **harsh**, severe, stiff, stringent, crushing, crippling; high, sky-high, inflated, exorbitant, extortionate, excessive; Brit. swingeing.

punter noun (Brit. informal) **customer**, client, patron; buyer, purchaser, shopper, consumer; (**punters**) clientele, audience, trade, business; Brit. informal bums on seats.

puny adjective **1** *a puny boy:* **undersized**, stunted, slight, small, little; weak, feeble, sickly, delicate, frail, fragile; informal weedy. **2** *their puny efforts:* **pitiful**, pitiable, miserable, sorry, meagre, paltry, trifling, inconsequential; informal pathetic, measly, piddling.
–OPPOSITES sturdy, substantial.

pupil noun **1** *former pupils of the school:* **student**, scholar; schoolchild, schoolboy, schoolgirl. **2** *the guru's pupils:* **disciple**, follower, student, protégé, apprentice, trainee, novice.

puppet noun **1** *a show with puppets:* **marionette**; glove puppet, finger puppet. **2** *a puppet of the government:* **pawn**, tool, instrument, cat's paw, poodle; mouthpiece, minion, stooge.

purchase verb *we purchased new software:* **buy**, acquire, obtain, pick up, procure; invest in; informal get hold of, score.
–OPPOSITES sell.
•noun **1** *he's happy with his purchase:* **acquisition**, buy, investment, order, bargain; shopping, goods. **2** *he could get no purchase on the wall:* **grip**, grasp, hold, foothold, toehold, anchorage, support; traction, leverage.
–OPPOSITES sale.

purchaser noun **buyer**, shopper, customer, consumer, patron.

pure adjective **1** *pure gold:* **unadulterated**, undiluted; sterling, solid, 100%; flawless, perfect, genuine, real. **2** *the air is so pure:* **clean**, clear, fresh, sparkling, unpolluted, uncontaminated, untainted; wholesome, natural, healthy; uninfected, disinfected, germ-free, sterile, sterilized, aseptic. **3** *pure in body and mind:* **virtuous**, moral, good, righteous, saintly, honourable, reputable, wholesome, clean, honest, upright, upstanding, exemplary; chaste; decent, worthy, noble, blameless, guiltless, spotless, unsullied, uncorrupted, undefiled; informal squeaky clean. **4** *pure maths:* **theoretical**, abstract, conceptual, academic. **5** *three hours of pure magic:* **sheer**, utter, absolute, out-and-out, complete, total, perfect.
–OPPOSITES adulterated, polluted, immoral, practical.

purely adverb **entirely**, wholly, exclusively, solely, only, just, merely.

purgatory noun **torment**, torture, misery, suffering, affliction, anguish, agony, woe, hell; an ordeal, a nightmare.
–OPPOSITES paradise.

purge verb **cleanse**, clear, purify.
•noun **removal**, expulsion, ejection, exclusion, eviction, dismissal, sacking, ousting, eradication.

purify verb **clean**, cleanse, refine, decontaminate; filter, clear, freshen, deodorize; sanitize, disinfect, sterilize.

purist noun **pedant**, perfectionist, formalist, literalist, stickler, traditionalist, dogmatist; informal nit-picker.

puritan noun **moralist**, prude, prig,

killjoy; ascetic; informal goody-goody, Holy Joe; N. Amer. informal bluenose.

puritanical adjective **moralistic**, puritan, strait-laced, stuffy, prudish, prim, priggish; narrow-minded, sententious, censorious; austere, severe, ascetic, abstemious; informal goody-goody, starchy.
– OPPOSITES permissive.

purity noun **1** *the purity of our tap water:* **cleanness**, freshness. **2** *they sought purity in a foul world:* **virtue**, morality, goodness, righteousness, piety, honour, honesty, integrity, decency; innocence, chastity.

purloin verb (formal) **steal**, thieve, rob, take, snatch, pilfer, loot, appropriate; informal swipe, nab, rip off, lift, filch, snaffle; Brit. informal pinch, half-inch, nick, whip, knock off, nobble; N. Amer. informal heist.

purport verb *this work purports to be objective:* **claim**, profess, pretend.

purpose noun **1** *the purpose of his visit:* **motive**, motivation, grounds, cause, occasion, reason, point, basis, justification. **2** *their purpose was to subvert the economy:* **intention**, aim, object, objective, goal, end, plan, scheme, target; ambition, aspiration. **3** *I cannot see any purpose in it:* **advantage**, benefit, good, use, value, merit, worth, profit; informal mileage. **4** *the original purpose of the porch:* **function**, role, use. **5** *they started with some purpose:* **determination**, resolution, resolve, enthusiasm, ambition, motivation, commitment, conviction, dedication; informal get-up-and-go.
■ **on purpose** deliberately, intentionally, purposely, by design, wilfully, knowingly, consciously; expressly, specifically, especially, specially.

purposeful adjective **determined**, resolute, steadfast, single-minded, committed.
– OPPOSITES aimless.

purse noun **1 wallet**; N. Amer. billfold, pocketbook. **2** (N. Amer.) See **HANDBAG**.
• verb *he pursed his lips:* **press together**, compress, tighten, pucker, pout.

pursue verb **1** *I pursued him down the garden:* **follow**, run after, chase; hunt, stalk, track, trail, hound. **2** *the determination with which he pursues his goals:* **strive for**, work towards, seek, search for, aim at/for, aspire to. **3** *she pursued a political career:* **engage in**, be occupied in, practise, follow, conduct, ply, take up, undertake, carry on. **4** *we will not pursue the matter:* **investigate**, research, inquire into, look into, examine, scrutinize, analyse, delve into, probe.
– OPPOSITES avoid, shun.

pursuit noun **1** *the pursuit of profit:* **striving for**, quest after/for, search for. **2** *a worthwhile pursuit:* **activity**, hobby, pastime, diversion, recreation, amusement; occupation, trade, vocation, business, work, job, employment.

purvey verb **sell**, supply, provide, furnish, cater, retail, deal in, trade, stock, offer; peddle, tout, traffic in; informal flog.

purveyor noun **seller**, vendor, retailer, supplier, stockist, trader, pedlar.

pus noun **suppuration**; discharge, secretion.

push verb **1** *he pushed her through the door:* **shove**, thrust, propel; send, drive, force, ram, squeeze; prod, poke, nudge; elbow, shoulder, manhandle, hustle. **2** *he pushed the panic button:* **press**, depress, hold down, squeeze; operate, activate. **3** *his father pushed him to accept:* **urge**, press, pressure, pressurize, force, coerce, nag; browbeat into; informal lean on, twist someone's arm, bulldoze. **4** *they push their own products:* **advertise**, publicize, promote, bang the drum for; sell, market, merchandise; informal plug, hype, flog; N. Amer. informal ballyhoo.
– OPPOSITES pull.
• noun **1** *I felt a push in the back:* **shove**, thrust, prod, poke, nudge; bump, jolt. **2** *the army's eastward push:* **advance**, drive, thrust, charge, attack, assault, onslaught, onrush, offensive, sortie, sally, incursion.
■ **push someone around** bully, domineer, trample on, bulldoze, browbeat, tyrannize, intimidate, threaten, victimize, pick on; informal lean on, boss about/around. **push for** demand, call for, request, press for, campaign for, lobby for, speak up for; urge, promote, advocate, champion. **push off** (informal) go away, go, depart, leave, get out; informal

skedaddle, scram, beat it, get lost, shove off, buzz off, clear off, on your bike; Brit. informal sling your hook, hop it; N. Amer. informal bug off, take a hike; Austral./NZ informal rack off. **push on** press on, continue, carry on, advance, proceed, go on, forge ahead.

pushover noun **1** *the teacher was a pushover:* **weakling**, man of straw; informal soft touch, easy meat. **2** *this course is a pushover:* gift, five-finger exercise; child's play; informal doddle, piece of cake, money for old rope, cinch, breeze; Brit. informal doss; N. Amer. informal duck soup, snap; Austral./NZ informal bludge.

pushy adjective **assertive**, overbearing, domineering, aggressive, forceful, forward; thrusting, ambitious, over-confident, cocky; informal bossy.
–OPPOSITES submissive.

pusillanimous adjective **timid**, timorous, cowardly, fearful, faint-hearted, lily-livered, spineless, craven; informal chicken, gutless, wimpy, wimpish, sissy, yellow, yellow-bellied.
–OPPOSITES brave.

pussyfoot verb **equivocate**, be evasive, be non-committal, sidestep the issue, prevaricate, quibble, hedge, beat about the bush; Brit. hum and haw; informal duck the question, sit on the fence, shilly-shally.

pustule noun **pimple**, spot, boil, swelling, eruption, carbuncle, blister, abscess; informal zit; Scottish informal plook.

put verb **1** *she put the parcel on a chair:* **place**, set, lay, deposit, position; leave, plant; informal stick, dump, bung, park, plonk, pop; N. Amer. informal plunk. **2** *he didn't want to be put in a category:* **assign to**, consign to, allocate to, place in. **3** *don't put the blame on me:* **lay**, pin, place, fix; attribute to, impute to, assign to, allocate to, ascribe to. **4** *the proposals were put to the committee:* **submit**, present, tender, offer, advance, suggest, propose. **5** *she put it bluntly:* **express**, word, phrase, frame, formulate, render, convey, couch; state, say, utter. **6** *he put the cost at £8,000:* **estimate**, calculate, reckon, gauge, assess, evaluate, value, judge, measure, compute, fix, set.

■ **put something about** *the rumour had been put about:* spread, circulate, make public, disseminate, broadcast, publicize, pass on, propagate, bandy about. **put something across/over** communicate, convey, get across/over, explain, make clear, spell out. **put something aside 1** *we've got a bit put aside in the bank:* save, put by, set aside, deposit, reserve, store, stockpile, hoard, stow, cache; informal salt away, squirrel away, stash away. **2** *they put aside their differences:* disregard, set aside, ignore, forget, discount, bury. **put someone away** (informal) jail, imprison, put in prison, put behind bars, lock up, incarcerate; Brit. informal bang up, send down. **put someone down** (informal) criticize, belittle, disparage, deprecate, denigrate, slight, humiliate; informal show up, cut down to size. **put something down 1** *he put his ideas down on paper:* write down, note down, jot down, take down, set down; list, record, register, log. **2** *they put down the rebellion:* suppress, check, crush, quash, squash, quell, overthrow, stamp out, repress, subdue. **3** *the horse had to be put down:* destroy, put to sleep, put out of its misery, put to death, kill. **4** *put it down to the heat:* attribute, ascribe, impute; blame on. **put something forward**. See PUT sense 4. **put someone off** deter, discourage, dissuade, daunt, unnerve, intimidate, scare off; distract, disturb, divert, sidetrack; informal turn off. **put something off** postpone, defer, delay, put back, adjourn, hold over, reschedule, shelve, table; informal put on ice, put on the back burner. **put something on 1** *she put on a pair of jeans:* dress in, don, pull on, throw on, slip into, change into. **2** *put the heating on:* switch on, turn on, activate. **3** *they put on an extra train:* provide, lay on, supply, make available. **4** *the museum put on an exhibition:* organize, stage, mount, present, produce. **5** *she put on an American accent:* feign, fake, simulate, affect, assume. **6** *he put a fiver on Oxford United:* bet, gamble, stake, wager; place, lay. **put someone out 1** *Maria was put out by the remark:* annoy, anger, irritate, offend, affront, displease, irk, vex, pique, nettle, gall, upset; informal rile, miff, peeve; Brit. informal nark. **2** *I don't want to put you out:* inconvenience, trouble, bother, impose on. **put something out 1** *firefighters put out the blaze:* extinguish, quench, douse, smother; blow out, snuff out. **2** *he put out a press release:* issue, publish, release, bring out, circulate, publicize, post. **put someone up 1** *we can put him up for a few days:* accommodate, house, take in; give someone a roof over their head. **2** *they put up a candidate:* nominate, propose, put forward, recommend. **put something up 1** *the building was put up 100 years ago:* build, construct, erect, raise. **2** *she put up a poster:* display, pin up, stick up, hang up, post. **3** *the Chancellor put up taxes:* increase, raise; informal jack up, hike, bump up. **4** *he put up most of the funding:* provide, supply, furnish, give, contribute, donate, pledge, pay; informal fork out, cough up, shell out; N. Amer. informal ante up, pony up. **put someone up to something** (informal) persuade to, encourage to, urge to, egg on to, incite to, goad into. **put up with** tolerate, take, stand for, accept, stomach, swallow, endure, bear, support, take something lying down; informal abide, lump it; Brit. informal stick; formal brook; old use suffer.

putative adjective **supposed**, assumed, presumed; accepted, recognized; alleged, reputed, reported, rumoured.

put-down noun (informal) **snub**, slight, affront, rebuff, sneer, rejoinder, barb, jibe, criticism; informal dig.

putrefy verb **decay**, rot, decompose, go bad, go off, spoil, fester, perish, deteriorate; moulder.

putrid adjective **decomposing**, decaying, rotting, rotten, bad, off, putrefied, putrescent, rancid, mouldy; foul, fetid, rank.

puzzle verb **1** *her decision puzzled me:* **perplex**, confuse, bewilder, bemuse, baffle, mystify, confound, nonplus; informal flummox, faze, stump, beat; N. Amer. informal discombobulate. **2** *she puzzled over the problem:* **mull over**, muse over, ponder, contemplate, meditate on, consider, deliberate on, chew over, wonder about, think about.
• noun *the poem has always been a puzzle:* **enigma**, mystery, paradox, conundrum, poser, riddle, problem.

puzzled adjective **perplexed**, confused, bewildered, bemused, baffled, mystified, confounded, nonplussed, at a loss; informal flummoxed, stumped, fazed; N. Amer. informal discombobulated.

puzzling adjective **baffling**, perplexing, bewildering, confusing, complicated, unclear, mysterious, enigmatic, ambiguous, obscure, abstruse, unfathomable, incomprehensible, impenetrable, cryptic.
– OPPOSITES clear.

pyromaniac noun **arsonist**, incendiary; Brit. fire-raiser; informal firebug; N. Amer. informal torch.

Qq

quack noun *a quack selling fake medicines:* **swindler**, charlatan, mountebank, trickster, fraudster, impostor, hoaxer, sharper; informal con man, shark.

quadrangle noun **courtyard**, quad, court, cloister, precinct; square, plaza, piazza.

quaff verb **drink**, swallow, gulp down, guzzle, slurp, down, drain, empty; imbibe, partake of, consume, sup, sip; informal sink, kill, glug, swig, swill, slug, knock back.

quagmire noun **1** *the field became a quagmire:* **swamp**, morass, bog, marsh, mire, slough. **2** *a judicial quagmire:* **muddle**, mix-up, mess, predicament, mare's nest, quandary, tangle, imbroglio; informal sticky situation, pickle, stew, dilemma, fix, bind.

quail verb **cower**, cringe, flinch, shrink, recoil, shy away, pull back; shiver, tremble, shake, quake, blench.

quaint adjective **1** *a quaint town:* **picturesque**, charming, sweet, attractive, old-fashioned, old-world; Brit. twee; N. Amer. cunning; mock old-fashioned olde worlde. **2** *quaint customs:* **unusual**, different, out of the ordinary, curious, eccentric, quirky, bizarre, whimsical, unconventional; informal offbeat.
– OPPOSITES ugly, ordinary.

quake verb **1** *the ground quaked:* **shake**, tremble, quiver, shudder, sway, rock, wobble, move, heave, convulse. **2** *we quaked when we saw the soldiers:* **tremble**, shake, quiver, shiver; blench, blanch, flinch, shrink, recoil, cower, cringe.

qualification noun **1** *a teaching qualification:* **certificate**, diploma, degree, licence, document, warrant; eligibility, acceptability, adequacy; proficiency, skill, ability, capability, aptitude. **2** *I can't accept it without qualification:* **modification**, limitation, reservation, stipulation; alteration, amendment, revision, moderation, mitigation; condition, proviso, caveat.

qualified adjective **certified**, certificated, chartered, licensed, professional; trained, fit, competent, accomplished, proficient, skilled, experienced, expert.

qualify verb **1** *I qualify for free travel:* **be eligible**, meet the requirements; be entitled to, be permitted. **2** *they qualify as refugees:* **count**, be considered, be designated, be eligible. **3** *she qualified as a solicitor:* **be certified**, be licensed; pass, graduate, succeed. **4** *the course qualified them to teach:* **authorize**, empower, allow, permit, license; equip, prepare, train, educate, teach. **5** *they qualified their findings:* **modify**, limit, restrict, make conditional; moderate, temper, modulate, mitigate.

quality noun **1** *a poor quality of signal:* **standard**, grade, class, calibre, condition, character, nature, form, rank, value, level; sort, type, kind, variety. **2** *work of such quality:* **excellence**, superiority, merit, worth, value, virtue, calibre, eminence, distinction, incomparability; talent, skill, virtuosity, craftsmanship. **3** *her good qualities:* **feature**, trait, attribute, characteristic, point, aspect, facet, side, property.

qualm noun **misgiving**, doubt, reservation, second thought, worry, concern, anxiety; (**qualms**) hesitation, demur, reluctance, disinclination, apprehension, trepidation, unease; scruples, remorse, compunction.

quandary noun **predicament**, plight, difficult situation; trouble, muddle, mess, confusion, difficulty, mare's nest; informal dilemma, sticky situation, pickle, hole, stew, fix, bind, jam.

quantify verb *the extent of the problem is impossible to quantify:* **measure**, put a figure on, determine, gauge, assess

quantity noun **1** *the quantity of food collected:* **amount**, total, aggregate, sum, quota, mass, weight, volume, bulk; quantum, proportion, portion, part. **2** *a quantity of ammunition:* **amount**, lot, great deal, an abundance, a wealth, a profusion, plenty; informal piles, oodles, tons, lots, loads, heaps, masses, stacks; Brit. informal shedloads.

quarrel noun *they had a quarrel about money:* **argument**, disagreement, squabble, fight, dispute, wrangle, clash, altercation, feud, contretemps, disputation, falling-out, war of words, shouting match; Brit. row; informal tiff, slanging match, run-in; Brit. informal barney, bust-up.
• verb *they rowed over who should pay:* **argue**, fight, disagree, fall out; differ, be at odds; bicker, squabble, cross swords, lock horns, be at each other's throats; Brit. row.
■ **quarrel with** *you can't quarrel with the decision:* fault, criticize, object to, oppose, take exception to; attack, take issue with, impugn, contradict, dispute, controvert; informal knock; formal gainsay.

q

quarrelsome adjective **argumentative**, disputatious, confrontational, captious, pugnacious, combative, antagonistic, bellicose, belligerent, cantankerous, choleric; Brit. informal stroppy; N. Amer. informal scrappy.
– OPPOSITES peaceable.

quarry noun **prey**, victim; object, goal, target; kill, game.

quarter noun **1** *the Latin quarter:* **district**, area, region, part, side, neighbourhood, precinct, locality, sector, zone; ghetto, community, enclave. **2** *help arrived from an unexpected quarter:* **source**, direction, place, location; person. **3** *the servants' quarters:* **accommodation**, lodgings, rooms, chambers; home; informal pad, digs; formal abode, residence, domicile. **4** *the riot squads gave no quarter:* **mercy**, leniency, clemency, compassion, pity, charity, sympathy, tolerance.
• verb *they were quartered in a huge villa:* **accommodate**, house, board, lodge, put up, take in, install, shelter; Military billet.

quash verb **1** *he may quash the sentence:* **cancel**, reverse, rescind, repeal, revoke, retract, countermand, withdraw, overturn, overrule, veto, annul, nullify, invalidate, negate, void; formal abrogate. **2** *we want to quash these rumours:* **put an end to**, put a stop to, stamp out, crush, put down, check, curb, nip in the bud, squash, quell, subdue, suppress, extinguish, stifle.
– OPPOSITES validate.

quasi- combining form **1** *quasi-scientific:* **supposedly**, seemingly, apparently, allegedly, ostensibly, on the face of it, on the surface, to all intents and purposes, outwardly, superficially, purportedly, nominally; pseudo-. **2** *a quasi-autonomous organization:* **partly**, partially, half, relatively, comparatively, up to a point; almost, nearly, just about, all but.

quaver verb **tremble**, waver, quiver, shake, vibrate, oscillate, fluctuate, falter, warble.

quay noun **wharf**, pier, jetty, landing stage, berth; marina, dock, harbour.

queasy adjective **nauseous**, bilious, sick; ill, unwell, poorly, green about the gills; Brit. off colour.

queen noun **1** *the Queen was crowned:* **monarch**, sovereign, ruler, head of state; Her Majesty; king's consort, queen consort. **2** (informal) *the queen of soul music:* **doyenne**, star, leading light, big name, prima donna, idol, heroine, favourite, darling, goddess.

queer adjective *it seemed queer to see him here:* **odd**, strange, unusual, funny, peculiar, curious, bizarre, weird, uncanny, freakish, eerie, unnatural; unconventional, unorthodox, unexpected, unfamiliar,

abnormal, anomalous, atypical, out of the ordinary, incongruous, irregular; informal fishy, creepy, spooky, freaky; Brit. informal rum.
– OPPOSITES normal.

quell verb **1** *troops quelled the unrest:* **put an end to**, put a stop to, end, crush, put down, check, crack down on, curb, nip in the bud, squash, quash, subdue, suppress, overcome; informal squelch. **2** *he quelled his misgivings:* **calm**, soothe, pacify, settle, quieten, silence, allay, assuage, mitigate, moderate; literary stay.

quench verb **1** *they quenched their thirst:* **satisfy**, slake, sate, satiate, gratify, relieve, assuage, take the edge off, indulge; lessen, reduce, diminish, check, suppress, extinguish, overcome. **2** *the flames were quenched:* **extinguish**, put out, snuff out, smother, douse.

querulous adjective **petulant**, peevish, pettish, complaining, fractious, fretful, irritable, testy, tetchy, cross, snappish, crabby, crotchety, cantankerous, miserable, moody, grumpy, bad-tempered, sullen, sulky, sour, churlish; informal snappy, grouchy, whingy; Brit. informal ratty, cranky; N. English informal mardy; N. Amer. informal soreheaded.

query noun **1** *we are happy to answer any queries:* **question**, enquiry; Brit. informal quiz. **2** *there was a query as to who owned the hotel:* **doubt**, uncertainty, question mark.
• verb **1** *'Why do that?' queried Isobel:* **ask**, enquire, question; Brit. informal quiz. **2** *folk may query his credentials:* **question**, challenge, dispute, cast aspersions on, doubt, have suspicions about.

quest noun **1** *their quest for her killer:* **search**, hunt; pursuance of. **2** *Sir Galahad's quest:* **expedition**, journey, voyage, trek, travels, odyssey, adventure, exploration, search; crusade, mission, pilgrimage.
■ **in quest of** in search of, in pursuit of, seeking, looking for, on the lookout for, after.

question noun **1** *please answer my question:* **enquiry**, query; interrogation. **2** *there is no question that he is ill:* **doubt**, dispute, argument, debate, uncertainty, reservation. **3** *the political questions of the day:* **issue**, matter, business, problem, concern, topic, theme, case; debate, argument, dispute, controversy.
– OPPOSITES answer, certainty.
• verb **1** *the magistrate questions the suspect:* **interrogate**, cross-examine, cross-question, quiz, catechize; interview, debrief, examine; informal grill, pump. **2** *she questioned his motives:* **query**, challenge, dispute, cast aspersions on, doubt, suspect.
■ **beyond question** *her loyalty is beyond question:* undoubted, certain, indubitable, indisputable, incontrovertible, unquestionable, beyond doubt, undeniable, clear, patent, manifest. **in question** at issue, under discussion, under consideration, on the agenda, to be decided. **out of the question** impossible, impracticable, unfeasible, unworkable, inconceivable, unimaginable, unrealizable, unsuitable; informal not on.

> **WORD LINKS**
> **interrogative** expressing a question

questionable adjective **1** *jokes of questionable taste:* **controversial**, contentious, doubtful, dubious, uncertain, debatable, arguable; unverified, unprovable, unresolved, unconvincing, implausible, improbable; borderline, marginal, moot; informal iffy; Brit. informal dodgy. **2** *questionable financial dealings:* **suspicious**, suspect, dubious, irregular, odd, strange, murky, dark, unsavoury, disreputable; informal funny, fishy, shady, iffy; Brit. informal dodgy.
– OPPOSITES indisputable, honest.

questionnaire noun **question sheet**, survey form, opinion poll; test, quiz.

queue noun **1** *a queue of people:* **line**, row, column, file, chain, string; procession, train, cavalcade; waiting list; N. Amer. wait list; Brit. informal crocodile. **2** *a queue of traffic:* **tailback**, gridlock; N. Amer. backup; informal snarl-up.
• verb *we queued for ice creams:* **line up**, wait in line, fall in.

quibble noun *I have just one quibble:* **criticism**, objection, complaint, protest, argument, exception,

q

grumble, grouse, cavil; informal niggle, moan, gripe, beef, grouch. •verb *no one quibbled with the title:* **object to**, find fault with, complain about, cavil at; split hairs, chop logic; criticize, query, fault, pick holes in; informal nit-pick.

quick adjective **1** *a quick worker:* **fast**, swift, rapid, speedy, expeditious, brisk, smart; lightning, whirlwind, fast-track, whistle-stop, breakneck; informal nippy, zippy. **2** *a quick look:* **hasty**, hurried, cursory, perfunctory, desultory, superficial, summary; brief, short, fleeting, transient, transitory, short-lived, lightning, momentary. **3** *a quick end to the recession:* **sudden**, instantaneous, immediate, abrupt, precipitate. **4** *she isn't as quick as the others:* **intelligent**, bright, clever, gifted, able, astute, sharp-witted, smart; observant, alert, sharp, perceptive; informal brainy, on the ball.
–OPPOSITES slow, long.

quicken verb **1** *she quickened her pace:* **speed up**, accelerate, step up, hasten, hurry (up); informal gee up. **2** *the film quickened his interest in nature:* **stimulate**, excite, arouse, rouse, stir up, activate, galvanize, whet, inspire, kindle; invigorate, revive, revitalize.

quickly adverb **1** *he moved very quickly:* **fast**, swiftly, briskly, rapidly, speedily, at full tilt, at the double, post-haste, hotfoot; informal double quick, like lightning, hell for leather, like blazes, like the wind; Brit. informal like the clappers, like billy-o; N. Amer. informal lickety-split; literary apace. **2** *you'd better leave quickly:* **immediately**, directly, at once, now, straight away, right away, asap, instantly, forthwith, without delay, without further ado; soon, promptly, early; N. Amer. momentarily; informal like a shot, pdq (pretty damn quick), pronto. **3** *she checked her reflection quickly:* **briefly**, hastily, hurriedly, cursorily, perfunctorily.

quick-tempered adjective **irritable**, irascible, hot-tempered, short-tempered, snappish, fiery, touchy, volatile; cross, crabby, crotchety, cantankerous, grumpy, ill-tempered, bad-tempered, testy, tetchy, prickly, choleric; informal snappy, grouchy, cranky, on a short fuse; Brit. informal narky, ratty, eggy; N. Amer. informal soreheaded.
–OPPOSITES placid.

quick-witted adjective **intelligent**, bright, clever, gifted, able, astute, quick, smart, sharp-witted; observant, alert, sharp, perceptive; informal brainy, on the ball, quick on the uptake.
–OPPOSITES slow.

quid pro quo noun **exchange**, trade, swap, switch, barter, substitute, reciprocation, return; amends, compensation, recompense, restitution, reparation.

quiescent adjective **inactive**, inert, idle, dormant, at rest, inoperative, deactivated, quiet; still, motionless, immobile, passive.
–OPPOSITES active.

quiet adjective **1** *the whole pub went quiet:* **silent**, still, hushed, noiseless, soundless; mute, dumb, speechless. **2** *a quiet voice:* **soft**, low, muted, muffled, faint, indistinct, inaudible, hushed, whispered, suppressed. **3** *a quiet village:* **peaceful**, sleepy, tranquil, calm, still, restful, undisturbed, untroubled; unfrequented. **4** *can I have a quiet word?* **private**, confidential, secret, discreet, unofficial, off the record, between ourselves. **5** *you can't keep it quiet for long:* **secret**, confidential, classified, unrevealed, undisclosed, unknown, under wraps; informal hush-hush, mum. **6** *business is quiet:* **slow**, stagnant, slack, sluggish, inactive, idle.
–OPPOSITES loud, busy, public.
•noun *the quiet of the countryside:* **peace**, restfulness, calm, tranquillity, serenity; silence, still, hush.

quieten verb **1** *her mother tried to quieten her:* **silence**, hush, shush; informal shut up. **2** *her companions quietened:* **fall silent**, stop talking, break off, shush, hold your tongue; informal shut up, clam up, pipe down.

quietly adverb **1** *she entered the room quietly:* **silently**, noiselessly, soundlessly, inaudibly. **2** *he spoke quietly:* **softly**, in a low voice, in a whisper, in a murmur, under your breath, in an undertone, sotto voce, gently, faintly, weakly, feebly. **3** *some bonds were sold quietly:*

q

discreetly, privately, confidentially, secretly, unofficially, off the record.

quilt noun **duvet**, cover; Brit. eiderdown; N. Amer. comforter.

quintessence noun **1** *it's the quintessence of the modern home:* **perfect example**, exemplar, prototype, stereotype, picture, epitome, embodiment, ideal. **2** *the quintessence of intelligence:* **essence**, soul, spirit, nature, core, heart, crux, kernel, marrow, substance; informal nitty-gritty.

quintessential adjective **typical**, prototypical, stereotypical, archetypal, classic, model, standard, stock, representative, conventional; ideal, consummate, exemplary, best, ultimate.

quip noun **joke**, witticism, jest, pun, sally, pleasantry, bon mot; informal one-liner, gag, wisecrack, funny.

quirk noun **1** *they all know his quirks:* **idiosyncrasy**, peculiarity, oddity, eccentricity, foible, whim, vagary, caprice, fancy, crotchet, habit, characteristic, trait, fad. **2** *a quirk of fate:* **chance**, fluke, freak, anomaly, twist.

quirky adjective **eccentric**, idiosyncratic, unconventional, unorthodox, unusual, strange, bizarre, peculiar, odd, outlandish, zany; informal wacky, freaky, way-out, far out, offbeat.
–OPPOSITES conventional.

quit verb **1** *he quit the office at 12.30:* **leave**, vacate, exit, depart from. **2** (informal) *he quit his job:* **resign from**, leave, give up, hand in your notice; informal chuck, pack in. **3** (informal) *quit living in the past:* **give up**, stop, discontinue, drop, abandon, abstain from; informal pack in, leave off.

quite adverb **1** *two quite different types:* **completely**, entirely, totally, wholly, absolutely, utterly, thoroughly, altogether. **2** *it's quite warm outside:* **fairly**, rather, somewhat, slightly, relatively, comparatively, moderately, reasonably, to a certain extent; informal pretty.

quiver verb **1** *I quivered with terror:* **tremble**, shake, shiver, quaver, quake, shudder. **2** *the bird quivers its wings:* **flutter**, flap, beat, agitate, vibrate.

quixotic adjective **idealistic**, romantic, visionary, utopian, extravagant, starry-eyed, unrealistic, unworldly; impracticable, unworkable, impossible.

quiz noun **competition**, test.
• verb *a man was being quizzed by police:* **question**, interrogate, cross-examine, cross-question, interview, sound out, give someone the third degree; informal grill, pump.

quizzical adjective **enquiring**, questioning, curious; puzzled, perplexed, baffled, mystified; amused, mocking, teasing.

quota noun **allocation**, share, allowance, limit, ration, portion, slice; percentage, commission; proportion, fraction, bit, amount, quantity; informal cut, rake-off; Brit. informal whack.

quotation noun **1** *a quotation from Dryden:* **citation**, quote, excerpt, extract, passage, line, paragraph, verse, phrase; reference, allusion; N. Amer. cite. **2** *a quotation for the building work:* **estimate**, quote, price, tender, bid, costing, charge, figure.

quote verb **1** *he quoted from the book:* **recite**, repeat, reproduce, retell, echo, iterate; take, extract. **2** *she quoted one case in which a girl died:* **cite**, mention, refer to, name, instance, specify, identify; relate, recount; allude to, point out, present, offer, advance.
• noun **1** *a Shakespeare quote.* See QUOTATION sense 1. **2** *ask the contractor for a quote.* See QUOTATION sense 2.

quotidian adjective **1** *the quotidian routine:* **daily**, everyday, day-to-day, diurnal. **2** *her dreadfully quotidian car:* **ordinary**, average, run-of-the-mill, everyday, standard, typical, middle-of-the-road, common, conventional, mainstream, unremarkable, unexceptional, workaday, commonplace, mundane, uninteresting; informal bog-standard, a dime a dozen; Brit. informal common or garden.
–OPPOSITES unusual.

Rr

rabbit noun Brit. coney; informal bunny.

rabble noun **1** *a rabble of youths:* **mob**, crowd, throng, gang, swarm, horde, pack, mass, group. **2** *rule by the rabble:* **the common people**, the masses, the populace, the multitude, the rank and file, the commonality, the plebeians, the proletariat, the peasantry, the lower classes; derogatory the hoi polloi, the riff-raff; informal, derogatory the proles, the plebs.
– OPPOSITES nobility.

rabble-rouser noun **agitator**, troublemaker, instigator, firebrand, revolutionary, demagogue.

rabid adjective *a rabid anti-royalist:* **extreme**, fanatical, overzealous, extremist, maniacal, passionate, fervent, diehard, uncompromising, illiberal; informal gung-ho.
– OPPOSITES moderate.

race[1] noun **1 contest**, competition, event, fixture, heat, trial. **2** *the race for naval domination:* **competition**, rivalry, contention, scramble; quest.
• verb **1 run**, dash, rush, sprint, bolt, dart, hurry, career, charge, shoot, hurtle, hare, fly, speed, scurry; informal tear, belt, pelt, scoot, hotfoot it, leg it; Brit. informal bomb. **2** *her heart was racing:* **pound**, throb, pulsate, thud, thump, hammer, palpitate, flutter, pitter-patter, quiver, pump.

race[2] noun **1** *pupils of different races:* **ethnic group**, racial type, origin. **2** *a bloodthirsty race:* **people**, nation.

racial adjective **ethnic**, ethnological, race-related; cultural, national, tribal.

racism noun **racial discrimination**, racialism, xenophobia, chauvinism, bigotry.

racist adjective *a racist society:* **discriminatory**, racialist, prejudiced, bigoted, xenophobic.

rack noun **frame**, framework, stand, holder, trestle, support, shelf.
• verb **torment**, afflict, torture, agonize, harrow; plague, bedevil, persecute, trouble, worry.

racket noun **noise**, din, hubbub, clamour, uproar, tumult, commotion, rumpus, pandemonium, babel; Brit. row; informal hullabaloo.

raconteur noun **storyteller**, narrator, anecdotalist.

racy adjective **risqué**, suggestive, naughty, sexy, spicy, ribald; indecorous, indecent, immodest, off colour, dirty, rude, smutty, crude, salacious; informal raunchy, blue; Brit. informal saucy; euphemistic adult.
– OPPOSITES prim.

raddled adjective **haggard**, gaunt, drawn, tired, fatigued, drained, exhausted, worn out, washed out; unwell, unhealthy; informal the worse for wear.

radiance noun **1** *the radiance of the sun:* **light**, brightness, brilliance, luminosity, beams, rays, illumination, blaze, glow, gleam, lustre, glare; luminescence, incandescence. **2** *her face flooded with radiance:* **joy**, elation, jubilance, ecstasy, rapture, euphoria, delirium, happiness, delight, pleasure.

radiant adjective **1** *the radiant moon:* **shining**, bright, illuminated, brilliant, gleaming, glowing, ablaze, luminous, lustrous, incandescent, dazzling, shimmering. **2** *she looked radiant:* **joyful**, elated, thrilled, overjoyed, jubilant, rapturous, ecstatic, euphoric, in seventh heaven, on cloud nine, delighted, very happy; informal on top of the world, over the moon.
– OPPOSITES dark, gloomy.

radiate verb **1** *stars radiate energy:* **emit**, give off, discharge, diffuse; shed, cast. **2** *light radiated from the hall:* **shine**, beam, emanate. **3** *their faces radiate hope:* **display**, show, exhibit. **4** *four spokes radiate from the hub:* **fan out**, spread out, branch out/off, extend, issue.

radical adjective **1** *radical reform:* **thorough**, complete, total, comprehensive, exhaustive, sweeping, far-reaching, wide-ranging, extensive, profound, major, stringent, rigorous. **2** *radical differences between the two theories:* **fundamental**, basic, essential, quintessential; structural, deep-seated, intrinsic, organic, constitutive. **3** *a radical political movement:* **revolutionary**, progressive, reformist, revisionist, progressivist; extreme, fanatical, militant, diehard.
– OPPOSITES superficial, minor, conservative.

raffish adjective **rakish**, unconventional, bohemian; devil-may-care, casual, careless.

raffle noun **lottery**, prize draw, sweepstake, sweep, tombola; N. Amer. lotto.

ragamuffin noun **urchin**, waif, guttersnipe; informal scarecrow.

ragbag noun **jumble**, hotchpotch, mishmash, mess, hash; assortment, mixture, miscellany, medley, melange, variety, diversity, potpourri.

rage noun **fury**, anger, wrath, outrage, indignation, temper, spleen, resentment, pique, annoyance, vexation, displeasure; informal grump, strop; literary ire, choler.
• verb **seethe**, fume; rave, storm, rant, fulminate, rail; thunder, rampage.
■ **all the rage** popular, fashionable, in vogue, in great demand; informal in, cool, big, trendy, hot, hip.

ragged adjective **1** *a pair of ragged jeans:* **tattered**, torn, ripped, moth-eaten, frayed, worn, threadbare, scruffy, shabby, down at heel, unkempt; informal tatty. **2** *a ragged coastline:* **jagged**, craggy, rugged, uneven, rough, irregular; serrated, sawtooth, indented.
– OPPOSITES smart.

raging adjective **1** *a raging mob:* **angry**, furious, enraged, incensed, infuriated, irate, fuming, seething, ranting; informal livid, wild; literary wrathful. **2** *raging seas:* **stormy**, violent, wild, turbulent, tempestuous. **3** *a raging headache:* **excruciating**, agonizing, painful, throbbing, acute, bad. **4** *her raging thirst:* **severe**, extreme, great, excessive.

raid noun **1** *the raid on Dieppe:* **attack**, assault, descent, blitz, incursion, sortie; onslaught, storming, charge, offensive, invasion, blitzkrieg. **2** *a raid on a shop:* **robbery**, burglary, hold-up, break-in, ram raid; looting, plunder; informal smash-and-grab, stick-up; Brit. informal blag; N. Amer. informal heist. **3** *a police raid on the flat:* **swoop**, search; N. Amer. informal bust, takedown.
• verb **1** *they raided shipping in the harbour:* **attack**, assault, set upon, descend on, swoop on, blitz, assail, storm, rush. **2** *armed men raided the store:* **rob**, hold up, break into; plunder, steal from, pillage, loot, ransack, sack; informal stick up. **3** *homes were raided by police:* **search**, swoop on; N. Amer. informal bust.

raider noun **robber**, burglar, thief, housebreaker, plunderer, pillager, looter, marauder; attacker, assailant, invader.

rail verb **protest**, fulminate, inveigh, rage, speak out, make a stand; expostulate about, criticize, denounce, condemn; informal kick up a fuss about.

railing noun **fence**, fencing, rails, paling, palisade, balustrade, banister, hurdle.

raillery noun **teasing**, mockery, chaff, ragging, joshing; banter, badinage; informal leg-pulling, ribbing, kidding.

rain noun **1** *another day of wind and rain:* **rainfall**, precipitation, raindrops; drizzle, mizzle, shower, rainstorm, cloudburst, torrent, downpour, deluge, storm. **2** *a rain of hot ash:* **shower**, deluge, flood, torrent, avalanche, flurry; storm, hail.
• verb **1** *it rained heavily during the night:* **pour**, pelt down, tip down, teem down, beat down, lash down,

sheet down; fall, drizzle, spit; informal be chucking it down; Brit. informal bucket down. **2** *bombs rained on the city:* **fall**, hail, drop, shower.

WORD LINKS
pluvial relating to rain

rainy adjective **wet**, showery, drizzly, damp, inclement.

raise verb **1** *they raised a giant flag outside the house:* **lift**, hoist, haul up, elevate, uplift, upraise, hold aloft; hitch up; Brit. informal hoick up. **2** *they raised their prices:* **increase**, put up, push up, up, mark up, escalate, inflate; informal hike up, jack up, bump up. **3** *he raised his voice:* **amplify**, magnify, intensify, boost, lift, increase, heighten, augment. **4** *we raised over £50,000:* **get**, obtain, acquire; accumulate, amass, collect, fetch, net, make. **5** *he raised several objections:* **bring up**, air, ventilate; present, table, propose, submit, advance, suggest, moot, put forward. **6** *the disaster raised doubts about safety:* **give rise to**, occasion, cause, produce, engender, elicit, create, result in, lead to, prompt, awaken, arouse, stir up, trigger, spark off, provoke. **7** *most parents raise their children well:* **bring up**, rear, nurture, look after, care for, provide for, mother, parent, tend, cherish; educate, train. **8** *he raised cattle:* **breed**, rear, keep, tend; grow, farm, cultivate, produce.
– OPPOSITES lower, reduce.

raised adjective **embossed**, relief, relievo, die-stamped.

rake[1] verb **1** *he raked the leaves into a pile:* **scrape up**, collect, gather. **2** *she raked the gravel:* **smooth out**, level, even out, flatten, comb. **3** *the cat raked his arm with its claws:* **scratch**, lacerate, scrape, rasp, graze, grate.

rake[2] noun **playboy**, libertine, profligate; degenerate, roué, debauchee; lecher, seducer, womanizer, philanderer, adulterer, Don Juan, Lothario, Casanova; informal ladykiller, ladies' man, lech.

rakish adjective **dashing**, debonair, stylish, jaunty, devil-may-care; raffish, disreputable, louche; informal sharp.

rally verb **1** *the troops rallied and held their ground:* **regroup**, reassemble, re-form, reunite. **2** *he rallied an army:* **muster**, marshal, mobilize, raise, call up, recruit, enlist, conscript; assemble, gather, round up; US draft; formal convoke. **3** *ministers rallied to denounce the rumours:* **get together**, band together, assemble, join forces, unite, ally, collaborate, cooperate, pull together. **4** *share prices rallied:* **recover**, improve, get better, pick up, revive, bounce back, perk up, look up, turn a corner.
– OPPOSITES disperse, disband, slump.
• noun **1** *a rally in support of the strike:* **meeting**, gathering, assembly; demonstration, march; informal demo. **2** *a rally in oil prices:* **recovery**, upturn, improvement, comeback, resurgence.
– OPPOSITES slump.

ram verb **1** *he rammed his sword into its sheath:* **force**, thrust, plunge, stab, push, sink, dig, stick, cram, jam, stuff, pack. **2** *a van rammed the car:* **hit**, strike, crash into, collide with, impact, run into, smash into, bump into, butt.

ramble verb **1** *we rambled around the lanes:* **walk**, hike, tramp, trek, backpack; wander, stroll, saunter, amble, roam, range, rove, traipse; Scottish & Irish stravaig; informal mosey, tootle; formal perambulate. **2** *she does ramble on:* **chatter**, babble, prattle, prate, blather, gabble, jabber, twitter, rattle, maunder; informal jaw, gas, gab, yak, yabber; Brit. informal witter, chunter, natter, waffle, rabbit.

rambler noun **walker**, hiker, backpacker, wanderer, rover; literary wayfarer.

rambling adjective **1** *a rambling speech:* **long-winded**, verbose, wordy, prolix; digressive, maundering, roundabout, circuitous, circumlocutory; disconnected, disjointed, incoherent. **2** *rambling streets:* **winding**, twisting, labyrinthine; sprawling. **3** *a rambling rose:* **trailing**, creeping, climbing, vining.
– OPPOSITES concise.

ramification noun **consequence**, result, aftermath, outcome, effect, upshot; development, implication.

ramp noun **slope**, bank, incline, gradient, tilt; rise, ascent, acclivity; drop, descent, declivity.

rampage verb **riot**, run amok, go berserk; storm, charge, tear.
■ **go on the rampage** riot, go berserk, get out of control, run amok; N. Amer. informal go postal.

rampant adjective **1** *rampant inflation:* **uncontrolled**, unrestrained, unchecked, unbridled, widespread; out of control, out of hand, rife. **2** *rampant vegetation:* **luxuriant**, exuberant, lush, rich, riotous, rank, profuse, vigorous; informal jungly.

rampart noun **defensive wall**, embankment, earthwork, parapet, breastwork, battlement, bulwark, outwork.

ramshackle adjective **tumbledown**, dilapidated, derelict, decrepit, neglected, run down, gone to rack and ruin, crumbling, decaying; rickety, shaky, unsound.
– OPPOSITES sound.

rancid adjective **sour**, stale, turned, rank, putrid, foul, rotten, bad, off; gamy, high, fetid.
– OPPOSITES fresh.

rancorous adjective **bitter**, spiteful, hateful, resentful, acrimonious, malicious, malevolent, hostile, venomous, vindictive, baleful, vitriolic, vengeful, pernicious, mean, nasty; informal bitchy, catty.
– OPPOSITES amicable.

rancour noun **bitterness**, spite, hate, hatred, resentment, malice, ill will, malevolence, animosity, antipathy, enmity, hostility, acrimony, venom, vitriol.

random adjective *random checks:* **unsystematic**, unmethodical, arbitrary, unplanned, undirected, casual, indiscriminate, non-specific, haphazard, stray, erratic.
– OPPOSITES systematic.
■ **at random** unsystematically, arbitrarily, randomly, unmethodically, haphazardly.

range noun **1** *his range of vision:* **span**, scope, compass, sweep, extent, area, field, orbit, ambit, horizon, latitude; limits, bounds, confines, parameters. **2** *a range of foods:* **assortment**, variety, diversity, mixture, collection, array, selection, choice. **3** *a range of mountains:* **row**, chain, sierra, ridge, massif; line, string, series.
• verb **1** *charges range from 1% to 5%:* **vary**, differ, fluctuate; extend, stretch, reach, cover, go, run. **2** *all sorts of fresh foods are ranged on the stalls:* **arrange**, line up, order, position, dispose, set out, array. **3** *the herdsmen ranged over the steppes:* **roam**, rove, traverse, travel, journey, wander, drift, ramble, meander, stroll, traipse, walk, hike, trek.

rangy adjective **long-legged**, long-limbed, leggy, tall; slender, slim, lean, thin, gangly, lanky, spindly, skinny, spare.
– OPPOSITES squat.

rank[1] noun **1** *he was elevated to ministerial rank:* **position**, level, grade, echelon; class, status, standing, station. **2** *a family of rank:* **high standing**, blue blood, high birth, nobility, aristocracy; eminence, distinction, prestige; prominence, influence, consequence, power. **3** *a rank of riflemen:* **row**, line, file, column, string, train, procession.
• verb **classify**, class, categorize, rate, grade, bracket, group, pigeonhole, designate; catalogue, file, list.
■ **the rank and file 1** *the officers and the rank and file:* other ranks, soldiers, NCOs, lower ranks; men, troops. **2** *a speech appealing to the rank and file:* the people, the proletariat, the masses, the populace, the rabble, the commonality, the third estate, the plebeians, the great unwashed; derogatory the hoi polloi, the riff-raff, the proles, the plebs.

rank[2] adjective **1** *rank vegetation:* **abundant**, lush, luxuriant, dense, profuse, vigorous, overgrown; informal jungly. **2** *a rank smell:* **offensive**, unpleasant, nasty, revolting, sickening, obnoxious, noxious; foul, fetid, smelly, stinking, reeking, high, off, rancid, putrid, malodorous; Brit. informal niffy, pongy, whiffy, humming; literary noisome. **3** *rank stupidity:* **downright**, utter, outright, out-and-out, absolute, complete, sheer, arrant, thoroughgoing, unqualified, unmitigated, positive.
– OPPOSITES sparse, pleasant.

rankle verb **annoy**, upset, anger,

irritate, offend, affront, displease, provoke, irk, vex, pique, nettle, gall; informal rile, miff, peeve, aggravate, hack off; Brit. informal nark; N. Amer. informal tick off.

ransack verb **plunder**, pillage, raid, rob, loot, sack, strip, despoil; ravage, devastate, turn upside down; scour, rifle, comb, search.

ransom noun **pay-off**, payment, sum, price.
• verb **release**, free, deliver, liberate, rescue.

rant verb *she ranted on about the unfairness:* **hold forth**, go on, fulminate, vociferate, sound off, spout, pontificate, bluster, declaim; shout, yell, bellow; informal mouth off.
• noun *he went into a rant about them:* **tirade**, diatribe, broadside.

rap[1] verb **1** *she rapped his fingers with a ruler:* **hit**, strike; informal whack, thwack, bash, wallop; literary smite. **2** *I rapped on the door:* **knock**, tap, bang, hammer, pound.

rap[2] noun *they didn't care a rap:* **whit**, iota, jot, hoot, scrap, bit, fig; informal damn, monkey's.

rapacious adjective **grasping**, greedy, avaricious, acquisitive, covetous; mercenary, materialistic; informal money-grubbing.
– OPPOSITES generous.

rape noun **1** *he was charged with rape:* **sexual assault**. **2** *the rape of rainforests:* **destruction**, violation, ravaging, pillaging, plundering, desecration, defilement, sacking, sack.
• verb **1 sexually assault**, violate, abuse; dated ravish; old use defile. **2** *they raped our country:* **ravage**, violate, desecrate, defile, plunder, pillage, despoil; lay waste, ransack, sack.

rapid adjective **quick**, fast, swift, speedy, expeditious, express, brisk; lightning, meteoric, whirlwind; sudden, instantaneous, instant, immediate; hurried, hasty, precipitate.
– OPPOSITES slow

rapidly adverb **quickly**, fast, swiftly, speedily, post-haste, hotfoot, at full tilt, briskly; hurriedly, hastily, in haste, precipitately; informal like a shot, double quick, pdq (pretty damn quick), in a flash, hell for leather, at the double, like lightning; Brit. informal like the clappers, at a rate of knots, like billy-o; N. Amer. informal lickety-split; literary apace.
– OPPOSITES slowly.

rapport noun **affinity**, close relationship, mutual understanding, bond, empathy, sympathy, accord.

rapt adjective **fascinated**, enthralled, spellbound, captivated, riveted, gripped, mesmerized, enchanted, entranced, bewitched; transported, enraptured, thrilled, ecstatic.
– OPPOSITES inattentive.

rapture noun **ecstasy**, bliss, exaltation, euphoria, elation, joy, enchantment, delight, happiness, pleasure.
■ **go into raptures** enthuse, rhapsodize, rave, gush, wax lyrical.

rapturous adjective **ecstatic**, joyful, elated, euphoric, enraptured, on cloud nine, in seventh heaven, transported, enchanted, blissful, happy; enthusiastic, delighted, thrilled, overjoyed, rapt; informal over the moon, on top of the world, blissed out; Austral. informal wrapped.

rare adjective **1** *rare moments of privacy:* **infrequent**, scarce, sparse, few and far between, thin on the ground, like gold dust; occasional, limited, odd, isolated, unaccustomed, unwonted; Brit. out of the common. **2** *rare stamps:* **unusual**, recherché, uncommon. **3** *a man of rare talent:* **exceptional**, outstanding, unparalleled, peerless, matchless, unique, unrivalled, inimitable, singular, beyond compare, without equal, second to none, unsurpassed; consummate, superior, superlative, first-class; informal A1, top-notch.
– OPPOSITES common, commonplace.

rarefied adjective **esoteric**, exclusive, select; elevated, lofty.

rarely adverb **seldom**, infrequently, hardly ever, scarcely ever, not often; once in a while, now and then, occasionally; informal once in a blue moon.
– OPPOSITES often.

raring adjective **eager**, keen, enthusiastic; impatient, longing, desperate; ready; informal dying, itching, gagging.

rarity noun **1** *the rarity of*

earthquakes in the UK: **infrequency**, unusualness, scarcity. **2** *this book is a rarity:* **collector's item**, rare thing, rare bird, rara avis; wonder, nonpareil, one of a kind; curiosity, oddity; Brit. informal one-off.

rascal noun **scallywag**, imp, monkey, mischief-maker, wretch; informal scamp, tyke, horror, monster.

rash[1] noun **1** *he broke out in a rash:* **spots**, breakout, eruption; hives. **2** *a rash of articles in the press:* **series**, succession, spate, wave, flood, deluge, torrent; outbreak, epidemic, flurry.

rash[2] adjective **reckless**, impulsive, impetuous, hasty, foolhardy, incautious, precipitate; careless, heedless, thoughtless, imprudent, foolish; ill-advised, injudicious, ill-judged, misguided, hare-brained.
– OPPOSITES prudent.

rasping adjective **harsh**, grating, jarring; scratchy, hoarse, rough, gravelly, croaky, gruff, husky, throaty, guttural.

rate noun **1** *a fixed rate of interest:* **percentage**, ratio, proportion; scale, standard. **2** *an hourly rate of £30:* **charge**, price, cost, tariff, fare, levy, toll; fee, remuneration, payment, wage, allowance. **3** *the rate of change:* **speed**, pace, tempo, velocity, momentum.
• verb **1** *they rated their ability at driving:* **assess**, evaluate, appraise, judge, weigh up, estimate, calculate, gauge, measure, adjudge; grade, rank, classify, categorize. **2** *the scheme was rated effective:* **consider**, judge, reckon, think, hold, deem, find; regard as, look on as, count as. **3** *he rated only a brief mention:* **merit**, deserve, warrant. **4** (informal) *Ben doesn't rate him:* **think highly of**, set much store by; admire, esteem, value.
■ **at any rate** in any case, anyhow, anyway, in any event, nevertheless; whatever happens, come what may, regardless, notwithstanding.

rather adverb **1** *I'd rather you went:* **sooner**, by preference, by choice. **2** *it's rather complicated:* **quite**, a bit, a little, fairly, slightly, somewhat, relatively, to some degree, comparatively; informal pretty, sort of, kind of. **3** *her true feelings—or rather, lack of feelings:* **more precisely**, to be exact, strictly speaking. **4** *she seemed sad rather than angry:* **more**; as opposed to, instead of. **5** *it was not impulsive, but rather a considered decision:* **on the contrary**, instead.

ratify verb **confirm**, approve, sanction, endorse, agree to, accept, uphold, authorize, formalize, validate, recognize; sign.
– OPPOSITES reject.

rating noun **grade**, classification, ranking, category, designation; assessment, evaluation, appraisal; mark, score.

ratio noun **proportion**, comparative number, correlation, relationship, correspondence; percentage, fraction, quotient.

ration noun **1** *a daily ration of chocolate:* **allowance**, allocation, quota, quantum, share, portion, helping; amount, quantity, measure, proportion, percentage. **2** *the garrison ran out of rations:* **supplies**, provisions, food, foodstuffs, eatables, edibles, provender; stores; informal grub, eats; N. Amer. informal chuck; formal comestibles.
• verb *fuel supplies were rationed:* **control**, limit, restrict; conserve.

rational adjective **1** *a rational approach:* **logical**, reasoned, sensible, reasonable, cogent, intelligent, judicious, shrewd, common-sense, sound, prudent; down-to-earth, practical, pragmatic. **2** *she was not rational at the time of signing:* **sane**, compos mentis, of sound mind; normal, balanced, lucid, coherent; informal all there. **3** *man is a rational being:* **intelligent**, thinking, reasoning; cerebral, logical, analytical.
– OPPOSITES irrational, illogical, insane.

rationale noun **reason**, thinking, logic, grounds, sense; principle, theory, argument, case; motive, explanation, justification, excuse; the whys and wherefores.

rationalize verb **1** *he tried to rationalize his behaviour:* **justify**, explain, account for, defend, vindicate, excuse. **2** *an attempt to rationalize the industry:* **streamline**, reorganize, modernize, update; trim, hone, simplify, downsize, prune.

rattle verb **1** *hailstones rattled against the window:* **clatter**, patter; clink, clunk. **2** *he rattled the coins in his pocket:* **jingle**, jangle, clink, tinkle. **3** *the bus rattled along:* **jolt**, bump, bounce, jounce, shake, judder. **4** *the government was rattled by the strike:* **unnerve**, disconcert, disturb, fluster, shake, perturb, discompose, discomfit, ruffle, throw; informal faze.

raucous adjective **1** *raucous laughter:* **harsh**, strident, screeching, piercing, shrill, grating, discordant, dissonant; noisy, loud, cacophonous. **2** *a raucous hen night:* **rowdy**, noisy, boisterous, roisterous, wild.
–OPPOSITES soft, quiet.

raunchy adjective (informal). See **SEXY** sense 2.

ravage verb **lay waste**, devastate, ruin, destroy, wreak havoc on; pillage, plunder, despoil, ransack, sack, loot; literary rape.

ravages plural noun **destruction**, damage, devastation, ruin, havoc, depredations.

rave verb **1** *he was raving about the fires of hell:* **talk wildly**, babble, jabber. **2** *I raved and swore at them:* **rant (and rave)**, rage, lose your temper, storm, fulminate, fume; shout, roar, thunder, bellow; informal fly off the handle, blow your top, go up the wall, hit the roof; Brit. informal go spare; N. Amer. informal flip your wig. **3** *he raved about her talent:* **praise enthusiastically**, go into raptures about/over, wax lyrical about, sing the praises of, rhapsodize over, enthuse about/over, acclaim, eulogize, extol; N. Amer. informal ballyhoo; formal laud.
–OPPOSITES criticize.

raven adjective *her raven hair:* **black**, jet-black, ebony; literary sable.

WORD LINKS
corvine relating to ravens

ravenous adjective **1** *I'm absolutely ravenous:* **very hungry**, starving, famished. **2** *her ravenous appetite:* **voracious**, insatiable; greedy, gluttonous.

ravine noun **gorge**, canyon, gully, defile, couloir; chasm, abyss, gulf; N. Amer. gulch, coulee.

ravings plural noun **gibberish**, rambling, babbling, wild/incoherent talk.

ravishing adjective **very beautiful**, gorgeous, stunning, wonderful, lovely, striking, magnificent, dazzling, radiant, delightful, charming, enchanting; informal amazing, sensational, fantastic, fabulous, terrific; Brit. informal smashing.
–OPPOSITES hideous.

raw adjective **1** *a piece of raw carrot:* **uncooked**, fresh. **2** *raw materials:* **unprocessed**, untreated, unrefined, crude, natural. **3** *raw recruits:* **inexperienced**, new, untrained, untried, untested; callow, immature, green, naive. **4** *his skin is raw in places:* **sore**, red, painful, tender; abraded, chafed. **5** *a raw morning:* **bleak**, cold, chilly, freezing, icy, wintry, bitter; informal nippy; Brit. informal parky. **6** *raw emotions:* **strong**, intense, passionate, fervent, powerful, violent.
–OPPOSITES cooked, processed.

ray noun **1** *rays of light:* **beam**, shaft, streak, stream. **2** *a ray of hope:* **glimmer**, flicker, spark, hint, suggestion, sign.

raze verb **destroy**, demolish, tear down, pull down, knock down, level, flatten, bulldoze, wipe out, lay waste.

re preposition **about**, concerning, regarding, relating to, apropos, on the subject of, in respect of, with reference to, in connection with.

reach verb **1** *he reached out a hand:* **stretch out**, hold out, extend, outstretch, thrust out, stick out. **2** *inflation reached the bank's 2% target:* **attain**, rise to, climb to; make, arrive at, touch; informal hit. **3** *the leaders reached an agreement:* **achieve**, work out, draw up, put together, negotiate, thrash out, hammer out.
• noun **1** *set small goals within your reach:* **grasp**, range, capabilities, capacity. **2** *beyond the reach of the law:* **jurisdiction**, authority, influence; scope, range, compass, ambit.

react verb *how would he react if she told him?* **behave**, act, take it, conduct yourself; respond, reply, answer.

reaction noun **1** *his reaction*

bewildered her: **response**, answer, reply, rejoinder, retort, riposte; informal comeback. **2** *a reaction against modernism:* **backlash**, counteraction.

reactionary adjective *a reactionary policy:* **right-wing**, conservative, rightist, traditionalist, conventional.
– OPPOSITES progressive.
• noun *an extreme reactionary:* **right-winger**, conservative, rightist, traditionalist, conventionalist.
– OPPOSITES radical.

read verb **1** *he was reading the newspaper:* **peruse**, study, scrutinize, look through; pore over, be absorbed in; run your eye over, cast an eye over, leaf through, scan. **2** *he read a passage of the letter:* **read out/aloud**, recite, declaim. **3** *I can't read my own writing:* **decipher**, make out, make sense of, interpret, understand. **4** *his remark could be read as a criticism:* **interpret**, take, construe, see, understand. **5** *he read history:* **study**, take; N. Amer. & Austral./NZ major in.
■ **read something into something** infer from, interpolate from, assume from, attribute to. **read up on** study; informal bone up on; Brit. informal mug up on, swot.

> **WORD LINKS**
> **legible** readable
> **illegible** unreadable
> **literacy** the ability to read and write
> **illiteracy** the inability to read and write

readable adjective **1** *the inscription is readable:* **legible**, decipherable, clear, intelligible, comprehensible. **2** *her novels are immensely readable:* **enjoyable**, entertaining, interesting, absorbing, gripping, enthralling, engrossing; informal unputdownable.
– OPPOSITES illegible.

readily adverb **1** *Durkin readily offered to drive:* **willingly**, unhesitatingly, ungrudgingly, gladly, happily, eagerly, promptly. **2** *the island is readily accessible:* **easily**, without difficulty.
– OPPOSITES reluctantly.

readiness noun **1** *their readiness to accept change:* **willingness**, preparedness, enthusiasm, eagerness, keenness; promptness, quickness, alacrity. **2** *the readiness of his reply:* **promptness**, quickness, rapidity, swiftness, speed.
■ **in readiness** at the ready, ready, available, on hand, accessible, handy.

reading noun **1** *a cursory reading of the page:* **perusal**, study, browse through, look through, glance through. **2** *a man of wide reading:* **learning**, scholarship, education, erudition. **3** *readings from the Bible:* **passage**, lesson; section, piece. **4** *my reading of the situation:* **interpretation**, construal, understanding, explanation, analysis. **5** *a meter reading:* **record**, figure, indication, measurement.

ready adjective **1** *are you ready?* **prepared**, all set, organized, primed; informal fit, psyched up, geared up. **2** *everything is ready:* **completed**, finished, prepared, organized, done, arranged, fixed. **3** *he's always ready to help:* **willing**, prepared, pleased, inclined, disposed; eager, keen, happy, glad; informal game. **4** *a ready supply of food:* **available**, accessible; handy, close at hand, to/on hand, convenient, within reach, near, at your fingertips. **5** *a ready answer:* **prompt**, quick, swift, speedy, fast, immediate, unhesitating; clever, sharp, astute, shrewd, keen, perceptive, discerning.
• verb **prepare**, organize; gear yourself up; informal psych yourself up.
■ **at the ready** in position, poised, waiting.

ready-made adjective **pre-assembled**, pre-cooked, oven-ready, convenience, ready-to-wear, off-the-peg.

real adjective **1** *is she a fictional character or a real person?* **actual**, non-fictional, factual; historical; material, physical, tangible, concrete, palpable. **2** *it's real gold:* **genuine**, authentic, bona fide, actual; informal pukka, kosher. **3** *tears of real grief:* **sincere**, genuine, true, unfeigned, heartfelt, unaffected. **4** *a real man:* **proper**, true; informal regular. **5** *you're a real idiot:* **complete**, utter, thorough, absolute, total, prize, perfect; Brit. informal right, proper.
– OPPOSITES imaginary, imitation.

realism noun **1** *optimism tinged with realism:* **pragmatism**, practicality, common sense, level-headedness. **2** *a degree of realism:* **authenticity**, fidelity, verisimilitude, truthfulness.

realistic adjective **1** *you've got to be realistic:* **practical**, pragmatic, matter-of-fact, down-to-earth, sensible, commonsensical; rational, reasonable, level-headed, clear-sighted; informal no-nonsense. **2** *a realistic aim:* **achievable**, attainable, feasible, practicable, viable, reasonable, sensible, workable; informal doable. **3** *a realistic portrayal of war:* **true to life**, lifelike, truthful, faithful, graphic.
–OPPOSITES unrealistic, idealistic, impracticable.

reality noun **1** *you need to distinguish fantasy from reality:* **the real world**, real life, actuality; truth. **2** *the harsh realities of life:* **fact**, actuality, truth. **3** *the reality of the detail:* **verisimilitude**, authenticity, fidelity.
–OPPOSITES fantasy.
■ **in reality** in fact, actually, really, in truth; in practice.

realization noun **1** *a growing realization of the danger:* **awareness**, understanding, comprehension, consciousness, appreciation, recognition, discernment; formal cognizance. **2** *the realization of our dreams:* **fulfilment**, achievement, accomplishment, attainment; formal effectuation.

realize verb **1** *he suddenly realized what she meant:* **register**, understand, grasp, comprehend, see, recognize, work out, fathom out, apprehend; perceive, discern, notice; informal latch on to, cotton on to, tumble to, savvy, figure out, get the message; Brit. informal twig, suss. **2** *they realized their dream:* **fulfil**, achieve, accomplish, make a reality, bring to fruition, bring about/off, carry out/through; formal effectuate. **3** *the company realized significant profits:* **make**, clear, gain, earn, return, produce; gross, net. **4** *he realized his assets:* **cash in**, liquidate, capitalize.

really adverb **1** *he is really very wealthy:* **in fact**, actually, in reality, in truth. **2** *he really likes her:* **genuinely**, truly, honestly; undoubtedly, certainly, assuredly, unquestionably. **3** *they were really kind:* **very**, extremely, thoroughly, decidedly, dreadfully, exceptionally, exceedingly, immensely, tremendously, uncommonly, remarkably, eminently, extraordinarily, most; N. Amer. quite; informal awfully, terribly, terrifically, ultra; Brit. informal jolly, dead; N. Amer. informal real, mighty, awful.

realm noun **1** *peace in the realm:* **kingdom**, country, land, dominion, nation. **2** *the realm of academia:* **domain**, sphere, area, field, world, province, territory.

reap verb **1** *the corn was reaped:* **harvest**, garner, gather in, bring in. **2** *we are reaping the benefits of these investments:* **receive**, obtain, get, acquire, secure, realize.

rear[1] verb **1** *I was reared in Newcastle:* **bring up**, raise, care for, look after, nurture, parent. **2** *he reared cattle:* **breed**, raise, keep. **3** *laboratory-reared plants:* **grow**, cultivate.

rear[2] noun **back**, end, hind part; Nautical stern.
–OPPOSITES front.
• adjective *the rear bumper:* **back**, end, rearmost; hind; technical posterior.

rearrange verb **1** *the furniture has been rearranged:* **reposition**, move round, change round. **2** *he's rearranged his schedule:* **reorganize**, alter, adjust, change, reschedule; Brit. rejig.

reason noun **1** *the main reason for his decision:* **cause**, ground, basis, rationale; motive, purpose, point, aim, intention, objective, goal; explanation, justification, argument, defence, vindication, excuse. **2** *postmodern voices railing against reason and science:* **rationality**, logic, cognition. **3** *he was losing his reason:* **sanity**, mind, mental faculties; senses, wits; informal marbles.
• verb **1** *a young child is unable to reason:* **think rationally**, think logically; formal cogitate. **2** *Scott reasoned that Annabel might be ill:* **conclude**, come to the conclusion, reckon, think, judge, deduce, infer, surmise; informal figure.
■ **reason something out** work out, think through, make sense of, get to the bottom of, puzzle out; informal figure out. **reason with someone**

talk round, bring round, persuade, prevail on, convince; make someone see the light. **with reason** justifiably, justly, legitimately, rightly.

WORD LINKS

rational relating to reason

reasonable adjective **1** *a reasonable man | a reasonable explanation:* **sensible**, rational, logical, fair, just, equitable; intelligent, wise, level-headed, practical, realistic; sound, valid, commonsensical; tenable, plausible, credible, believable. **2** *take reasonable precautions:* **practicable**, sensible; appropriate, suitable. **3** *the cars are in reasonable condition:* **fairly good**, acceptable, satisfactory, average, adequate, fair, all right, tolerable, passable; informal OK. **4** *reasonable prices:* **inexpensive**, moderate, low, cheap, budget, bargain.

reasoned adjective **logical**, rational, well thought out, clear, lucid, coherent, cogent, considered, sensible.

reasoning noun **thinking**, train of thought, logic, analysis, interpretation, explanation, rationalization.

reassure verb **put someone's mind at rest**, encourage, hearten, buoy up, cheer up; comfort, soothe.
– OPPOSITES alarm.

rebate noun **refund**, repayment; discount, deduction, reduction, decrease.

rebel noun **1** *the rebels took control of the capital:* **revolutionary**, insurgent, mutineer, insurrectionist, guerrilla, terrorist, freedom fighter. **2** *the concept of the artist as a rebel:* **nonconformist**, dissenter, dissident, iconoclast, maverick.
• verb **1** *the citizens rebelled:* **revolt**, mutiny, riot, rise up, take up arms. **2** *most teenagers rebel against their parents:* **defy**, disobey, kick against, challenge, oppose, resist.
– OPPOSITES obey.
• adjective **1** *rebel troops:* **insurgent**, revolutionary, mutinous, insurrectionary. **2** *rebel MPs:* **rebellious**, defiant, disobedient, insubordinate, subversive, resistant, recalcitrant; nonconformist, maverick, iconoclastic.
– OPPOSITES compliant.

rebellion noun **1** *troops suppressed the rebellion:* **uprising**, revolt, insurrection, mutiny, revolution, insurgence; riot, disorder, unrest. **2** *an act of rebellion:* **defiance**, disobedience, insubordination, subversion, resistance.

rebellious adjective **1** *rebellious troops:* **rebel**, insurgent, mutinous, riotous, insurrectionary, revolutionary. **2** *a rebellious adolescent:* **defiant**, disobedient, insubordinate, unruly, mutinous, wayward, obstreperous, recalcitrant, intractable; Brit. informal bolshie.

rebirth noun **revival**, renaissance, resurrection, reawakening, renewal, regeneration; revitalization, rejuvenation.

rebound verb **bounce back**, spring back, ricochet, boomerang; backfire; N. Amer. carom.

rebuff verb *his offer was rebuffed:* **reject**, turn down, spurn, refuse, decline, repudiate; snub, slight, dismiss, brush off.
– OPPOSITES accept.
• noun *the rebuff did little to dampen his ardour:* **rejection**, snub, slight; refusal, spurning; informal brush-off, kick in the teeth, slap in the face.

rebuild verb **reconstruct**, renovate, restore, remodel, remake, reassemble.
– OPPOSITES demolish.

rebuke verb *she never rebuked him:* **reprimand**, reproach, scold, admonish, reprove, upbraid, berate, take to task, criticize, censure; informal tell off, give someone a talking-to, give someone a dressing-down; Brit. informal give someone a rocket, tick off; N. Amer. informal chew out; formal castigate.
– OPPOSITES praise.
• noun *a severe rebuke:* **reprimand**, reproach, scolding, admonition, reproof, criticism, recrimination, censure; informal telling-off, dressing-down, talking-to; Brit. informal rocket, ticking-off; formal castigation.
– OPPOSITES praise.

rebut verb **refute**, deny, disprove; invalidate, negate, contradict, controvert, counter, discredit, give the lie to, explode; informal shoot full of holes; formal confute.
– OPPOSITES confirm.

rebuttal noun **refutation**, denial, countering, invalidation, negation, contradiction.

recalcitrant adjective **uncooperative**, intractable, insubordinate, defiant, rebellious, wilful, wayward, headstrong, self-willed, contrary, perverse, difficult, awkward; Brit. informal bloody-minded, bolshie, stroppy; formal refractory.
–OPPOSITES amenable.

recall verb **1** *he recalled his student days:* **remember**, recollect, call to mind; think back on/to, reminisce about. **2** *their exploits recall the days of chivalry:* **bring to mind**, call up, conjure up, evoke.
–OPPOSITES forget.
• noun *people can improve their recall of dreams:* **recollection**, remembrance, memory.

recant verb **1** *he was forced to recant his beliefs:* **renounce**, disavow, deny, repudiate, renege on; formal forswear, abjure. **2** *he refused to recant:* **change your mind**, be apostate. **3** *he recanted his testimony:* **retract**, take back, withdraw.

recantation noun **renunciation**, renouncement, disavowal, denial, repudiation, retraction, withdrawal.

recapitulate verb **summarize**, sum up; restate, repeat, reiterate, go over, review; informal recap.

recede verb **1** *the waters receded:* **retreat**, go back/down, move back/away, withdraw, ebb, subside, abate. **2** *the lights receded into the distance:* **disappear from view**, be lost to view. **3** *fears of violence have receded:* **diminish**, lessen, decrease, dwindle, fade, abate, subside, ebb, wane.
–OPPOSITES advance, grow.

receipt noun **1** *the receipt of a letter:* **receiving**, obtaining; arrival, delivery. **2** *make sure you get a receipt:* **proof of purchase**, sales ticket. **3** *receipts from house sales:* **proceeds**, takings, income, revenue, earnings; profits, returns; N. Amer. take.

receive verb **1** *he received an award | they received £650 in damages:* **be given**, be presented with, be awarded, collect; get, obtain, gain, acquire; win, be paid, earn, gross, net. **2** *Alex received the news on Monday:* **hear**, be told, be informed of, be notified of, discover, find out, learn; informal get wind of. **3** *she received a serious injury:* **experience**, sustain, undergo, meet with; suffer, bear.
–OPPOSITES give, send.

recent adjective *recent research:* **new**, the latest, current, fresh, modern, contemporary, up to date, up to the minute.
–OPPOSITES old, out of date.

recently adverb **not long ago**, a little while back; lately, latterly, just now.

receptacle noun **container**, holder, repository.

reception noun **1** *a chilly reception:* **response**, reaction, treatment. **2** *a wedding reception:* **party**, function, social occasion, soirée; N. Amer. levee; informal do, bash; Brit. informal knees-up, beanfeast, bunfight.

receptive adjective **open-minded**, responsive, amenable, well disposed, flexible, approachable, accessible.
–OPPOSITES unresponsive.

recess noun **1** *two recesses fitted with bookshelves:* **alcove**, bay, niche, nook, corner, hollow, oriel. **2** *the deepest recesses of Broadcasting House:* **innermost parts**, remote/secret places, heart, depths, bowels. **3** *the Christmas recess:* **adjournment**, break, interlude, interval, rest; holiday; N. Amer. vacation.

recession noun **downturn**, depression, slump, slowdown.
–OPPOSITES boom.

recherché adjective **obscure**, rare, esoteric, abstruse, arcane, recondite, exotic, strange, unusual, unfamiliar.

recipe noun *a recipe for success:* **formula**, prescription, blueprint; guarantee, key, passport, answer, solution.

recipient noun **receiver**, beneficiary, legatee, donee.
–OPPOSITES donor.

reciprocal adjective **mutual**, common, shared, joint, corresponding, complementary.

reciprocate verb **1** *I was happy to reciprocate:* **respond**, do the same, return the favour. **2** *a love that was not reciprocated:* **requite**, return, give back.

recital noun **1** *a piano recital:* **concert**, performance, rendition.

2 *her recital of Adam's failures:* **enumeration**, list, litany, catalogue, detailing; account, report, description, recitation, recapitulation, recounting.

recitation noun **1** *the recitation of his poem:* **recital**, reading, declamation, rendering, rendition, delivery, performance. **2** *a recitation of her life story:* **account**, description, narration, story.

recite verb **1** *he began to recite the Koran:* **quote**, say aloud, declaim, deliver, render. **2** *Sir John recited the facts they knew:* **enumerate**, list, detail, reel off; recount, relate, describe, narrate, recapitulate, repeat.

reckless adjective **rash**, careless, thoughtless, heedless, precipitate, impetuous, impulsive, daredevil, devil-may-care; irresponsible, foolhardy, audacious.
– OPPOSITES careful.

reckon verb **1** *the cost was reckoned at £60:* **calculate**, compute, work out, figure; count, add up, total; Brit. tot up. **2** *Anselm reckoned Hugh among his friends:* **include**, count, regard as, look on as. **3** *it was reckoned a failure:* **regard as**, consider, judge, hold to be, think of as; deem, rate, gauge, count. **4** *they had reckoned on a day or two more of privacy:* **expect**, anticipate, hope for, plan for; count on, rely on, depend on, bank on; N. Amer. informal figure on.
■ **to be reckoned with** important, significant; influential, powerful, strong, potent, formidable, redoubtable. **reckon with 1** *it's her mother you'll have to reckon with:* deal with, contend with, face. **2** *they hadn't reckoned with her burning ambition:* anticipate, foresee, be prepared for, bargain for/on, consider; formal take cognizance of. **reckon without** overlook, disregard, forget.

reckoning noun **1** *by my reckoning, this comes to £2 million:* **calculation**, estimation, computation, working out, summation, addition. **2** *by her reckoning, the train was late:* **opinion**, view, judgement, evaluation, estimate. **3** *the terrible reckoning that he deserved:* **retribution**, fate, doom, nemesis, punishment.
■ **day of reckoning** judgement day, day of retribution, doomsday.

reclaim verb **1** *expenses can be reclaimed:* **get back**, claim back, recover, regain, retrieve, recoup. **2** *Henrietta had reclaimed him from a life of vice:* **save**, rescue, redeem; reform.

recline verb **lie down**, lean back, be recumbent; relax, repose, loll, lounge, sprawl, stretch out.

recluse noun **1** *a religious recluse:* **hermit**, ascetic, eremite; historical anchorite. **2** *a natural recluse:* **loner**, solitary, lone wolf.

reclusive adjective **solitary**, secluded, isolated, hermitic, eremitic, cloistered.
– OPPOSITES gregarious.

recognition noun **1** *there was no sign of recognition on his face:* **identification**, recollection, remembrance. **2** *his recognition of his lack of experience:* **acknowledgement**, acceptance, admission; realization, awareness, consciousness, knowledge, appreciation; formal cognizance. **3** *official recognition:* **official approval**, certification, accreditation, endorsement, validation. **4** *you deserve recognition for the great job you are doing:* **appreciation**, gratitude, thanks, congratulations, credit, commendation, acclaim, acknowledgement.

recognizable adjective **identifiable**, noticeable, perceptible, discernible, detectable, distinguishable, observable, perceivable; distinct, unmistakable, clear.
– OPPOSITES imperceptible.

recognize verb **1** *she recognized him at once:* **identify**, place, know, put a name to; remember, recall, recollect; Scottish & N. English ken. **2** *they recognized Alan's ability:* **acknowledge**, accept, admit; realize, be aware of, be conscious of, perceive, discern, appreciate; formal be cognizant of. **3** *therapists who are recognized by the BPS:* **officially approve**, certify, accredit, endorse, sanction, validate. **4** *the Trust recognized their hard work:* **pay tribute to**, appreciate, be grateful for, acclaim, commend.

recoil verb **1** *she instinctively recoiled:* **draw back**, jump back, pull back; flinch, shy away, shrink, blench. **2** *he recoiled from the idea:*

shudder at, shrink from, baulk at; abhor, loathe, hate, despise.

recollect verb **remember**, recall, call to mind, think of; think back to, reminisce about.
– OPPOSITES forget.

recollection noun **memory**, remembrance, impression, reminiscence.

recommend verb **1** *his former employer recommended him for the post:* **advocate**, endorse, commend, suggest, put forward, propose, nominate, put up; speak favourably of, put in a good word for, vouch for; informal plug. **2** *the committee recommended a cautious approach:* **advise**, counsel, urge, exhort, enjoin, prescribe, argue for, back, support; suggest, advocate, propose.

recommendation noun **1** *the adviser's recommendations:* **advice**, counsel, guidance, direction, enjoinder; suggestion, proposal. **2** *a personal recommendation:* **commendation**, endorsement, good word, testimonial; suggestion, tip; informal plug. **3** *the pillow's only recommendation was that it matched the upholstery:* **advantage**, good point/feature, benefit, asset, boon, attraction, appeal.

recompense verb *offenders should recompense their victims:* **compensate**, indemnify, repay, reimburse, make reparation to, make restitution to, make amends to.
• noun *damages were paid in recompense:* **compensation**, reparation, restitution, indemnification; reimbursement, repayment, redress.

reconcilable adjective **compatible**, consistent, congruous.

reconcile verb **1** *the news reconciled us:* **reunite**, bring back together; pacify, appease, placate, mollify; formal conciliate. **2** *he tried to reconcile his religious beliefs with his career:* **make compatible**, harmonize, square, balance. **3** *they had to reconcile themselves to drastic losses:* **accept**, resign yourself to, come to terms with, learn to live with, get used to, make the best of.
– OPPOSITES estrange.

reconciliation noun **reunion**, bringing together, conciliation; pacification, appeasement, mollification; agreement, compromise, understanding, peace.

recondite adjective **obscure**, abstruse, arcane, esoteric, recherché, profound, difficult, complex, complicated, involved.

recondition verb **overhaul**, rebuild, renovate, restore, repair, reconstruct, remodel, refurbish; informal do up, revamp.

reconnaissance noun **survey**, exploration, observation, investigation, examination, inspection; patrol, search; informal recce.

reconnoitre verb **survey**, explore, scout out, find out the lie of the land; investigate, examine, scrutinize, inspect, observe, take a look at; patrol; informal recce, check out.

reconsider verb **rethink**, review, revisit, revise, re-examine, re-evaluate, reassess, reappraise; have second thoughts, change your mind.

reconsideration noun **review**, rethink, re-examination, reassessment, re-evaluation, reappraisal.

reconstruct verb **1** *the building had to be reconstructed:* **rebuild**, restore, renovate, recreate, remake, reassemble, remodel, refashion, revamp, recondition, refurbish. **2** *reconstructing the events of that day proved hard:* **recreate**, piece together, re-enact.

record noun **1** *police records show that accidents have almost doubled:* **account**, document, file, dossier, report, evidence, data; annals, archives, chronicles; minutes, transactions, proceedings, transcripts; register, log. **2** *he enjoyed listening to records:* album, CD, LP, single. **3** *his previous good record:* **previous conduct**, history, reputation. **4** *a lasting record of what they have achieved:* **reminder**, memorial, souvenir, memento, remembrance, testament.
• adjective *the company announced record profits:* **record-breaking**, unsurpassed, unparalleled, unequalled, second to none.
• verb **1** *the doctor recorded her blood pressure:* **write down**, take down, note, jot down, put down on paper; document, enter, minute, register, log. **2** *the thermometer recorded a*

r

high temperature: **indicate**, register, show, display. **3** *the team recorded their fourth win:* **achieve**, accomplish, chalk up, notch up; informal clock up.

■ **off the record 1** *his comments were off the record:* unofficial, confidential. **2** *they admitted, off the record, that they had made a mistake:* unofficially, privately, confidentially, between ourselves.

recount verb **tell**, relate, narrate, describe, report, outline, delineate, relay, convey, communicate, impart.

recoup verb **get back**, regain, recover, win back, retrieve, redeem, recuperate.

recourse noun **option**, possibility, alternative, resort, way out, hope, remedy, choice, expedient.

■ **have recourse to** resort to, make use of, avail yourself of, turn to, call on, look to, fall back on.

recover verb **1** *he's recovering from a heart attack:* **recuperate**, get better, convalesce, regain your strength; be on the mend, pick up, rally, respond to treatment, improve, heal, pull through, bounce back. **2** *the stolen material has been recovered:* **retrieve**, regain, get back, recoup, reclaim, repossess, redeem, recuperate, find, track down; salvage, save, rescue.
– OPPOSITES deteriorate.

■ **recover yourself** pull yourself together, regain your composure, regain your self-control; informal get a grip on yourself.

recovery noun **1** *her recovery may be slow:* **recuperation**, convalescence. **2** *the economy was showing signs of recovery:* **improvement**, rallying, picking up, upturn, upswing. **3** *the recovery of stolen goods:* **retrieval**, repossession, reclamation, recouping, redemption.
– OPPOSITES relapse, deterioration.

recreation noun **1** *cycling is a popular form of recreation:* **pleasure**, leisure, relaxation, fun, enjoyment, entertainment, amusement; informal R & R. **2** *his favourite recreations:* **pastime**, hobby, leisure activity.
– OPPOSITES work.

recrimination noun **accusation**, countercharge, counter-attack, retaliation.

recruit verb **1** *more soldiers were recruited:* **enlist**, call up, conscript; US draft, muster in. **2** *the king recruited an army:* **muster**, form, raise, mobilize. **3** *the company is recruiting staff:* **hire**, employ, take on; enrol, sign up, engage.
– OPPOSITES disband, dismiss.
• noun **1** *new recruits were enlisted:* **conscript**; US draftee; N. Amer. informal yardbird. **2** *graduate recruits:* **newcomer**, initiate, beginner, novice; informal rookie, newbie; N. Amer. informal tenderfoot, greenhorn.

rectify verb **correct**, put right, sort out, deal with, amend, remedy, repair, fix, make good, resolve, settle; informal patch up.

rectitude noun **righteousness**, goodness, virtue, morality, honour, integrity, principle, probity, honesty, trustworthiness, decency, good character.

recumbent adjective **lying**, flat, horizontal, stretched out, sprawled, reclining, prone, prostrate, supine.
– OPPOSITES upright.

recuperate verb **1** *he went to France to recuperate:* **get better**, recover, convalesce, get well, regain your strength/health. **2** *he recuperated the money:* **get back**, regain, recover, recoup, retrieve, reclaim, repossess, redeem.

recur verb **happen again**, reoccur, repeat itself; come back, return, reappear; formal recrudesce.

recurrent adjective **repeated**, repetitive, periodic, cyclical, seasonal, perennial, regular, frequent; intermittent, sporadic, spasmodic.

recycle verb **reuse**, reprocess, reclaim, recover.

red adjective **1** *a red dress:* scarlet, vermilion, ruby, cherry, cerise, cardinal, carmine, wine; literary damask. **2** *he was red in the face:* **flushed**, pink, florid, rubicund; ruddy, rosy. **3** *her long red hair:* auburn, Titian, chestnut, ginger.

red-blooded adjective **manly**, masculine, virile, macho.

redden verb **blush**, flush, colour, go red, crimson, burn.

redeem verb **1** *one feature alone redeems the book:* **save**, vindicate.

2 *he redeemed his earlier mistake with a tremendous goal:* **compensate for**, make up for, cancel out. **3** *owners were unable to redeem their mortgages:* **repay**, clear, discharge, pay off. **4** *this voucher can be redeemed at any branch:* **exchange**, cash in, convert, trade in. **5** *he redeemed the items from the pawnbrokers:* **retrieve**, regain, recover, get back, reclaim, repossess; buy back.

redeeming adjective *the film's only redeeming feature:* **compensating**, compensatory, extenuating, mitigating.

redemption noun **1** *the redemption of their possessions:* **retrieval**, recovery, reclamation, repossession, return. **2** *the redemption of credit vouchers:* **exchange**, cashing in, conversion. **3** *the redemption of the mortgage:* **paying off/back**, discharge, clearing.

red-handed adjective **in the act**, in flagrante delicto; Brit. informal with your trousers down.

redolent adjective **evocative**, suggestive, reminiscent.

redoubtable adjective **formidable**, awe-inspiring, fearsome, daunting; impressive, commanding, indomitable, invincible, doughty, mighty.

redress verb *the need to redress social wrongs:* **rectify**, correct, right, put right, amend, remedy, make good, resolve, settle.
• noun *your best hope of redress:* **compensation**, reparation, restitution, recompense, repayment, indemnity, retribution, satisfaction.

r

reduce verb **1** *the aim is to reduce pollution:* **lessen**, lower, bring down, decrease, diminish, minimize; shrink, narrow, contract, shorten. **2** *the workforce has been reduced to some 6,000:* **cut**, trim, prune, shrink, scale back, streamline, downsize; Brit. rationalize. **3** *he reduced her to tears:* **bring**, drive.
– OPPOSITES increase.

reduction noun **1** *a reduction in carbon emissions:* **decrease**, lessening, lowering, diminution, moderation. **2** *a reduction in staff numbers:* **cut**, cutback, scaling down, pruning, streamlining, downsizing; Brit. rationalization. **3** *substantial price reductions:* **discount**, markdown, deduction, cut, concession.
– OPPOSITES increase.

redundancy noun **1** *redundancy in language:* **superfluity**, unnecessariness, excess. **2** *redundancies are in the offing:* **sacking**, dismissal, layoff, discharge; unemployment.

redundant adjective **1** *many churches are redundant:* **unnecessary**, not required, unneeded, uncalled for, surplus to requirements, superfluous. **2** *2,000 workers were made redundant:* **sacked**, dismissed, laid off, discharged; unemployed, jobless, out of work.
– OPPOSITES employed.

reef noun **barrier reef**, coral reef, atoll, key.

reek verb **stink**, smell.
• noun **stink**, smell, stench, malodour; Brit. informal niff, pong, whiff.

reel verb **stagger**, lurch, sway, rock, stumble, totter, wobble; whirl, spin, revolve, swirl, twirl, turn.

refer verb **1** *he referred to errors in the article:* **mention**, allude to, touch on, speak of/about, talk of/about, write about, comment on, deal with, point out, call attention to. **2** *the matter has been referred to my insurers:* **pass**, hand on/over, send on, transfer, remit, entrust, assign. **3** *these figures refer only to 2001:* **apply to**, be relevant to, concern, relate to, be connected with, pertain to, be pertinent to, have a bearing on, cover; formal appertain to. **4** *the name refers to a Saxon village:* **denote**, describe, indicate, mean, signify, designate. **5** *the constable referred to his notes:* **consult**, turn to, look at, have recourse to.

referee noun **1** *the referee blew his whistle:* **umpire**, judge, adjudicator; informal ref. **2** *include the names of two referees:* **supporter**, character witness, advocate.
• verb **umpire**, judge, adjudicate.

reference noun **1** *previous references to the subject:* **mention**, allusion, comment, remark.

2 *references are given in the bibliography:* **source**, citation, authority, credit. **3** *a glowing reference:* **testimonial**, recommendation; credentials.

■ **with reference to** apropos, with regard to, with respect to, on the subject of, re; in relation to, in connection with.

referendum noun **vote**, ballot, poll, plebiscite.

refine verb **1** *crude oil is refined to make petroleum products:* **purify**, process, treat. **2** *we aim to help students refine their skills:* **improve**, perfect, polish up, hone, fine-tune.

refined adjective **1** *refined sugar:* **purified**, processed, treated. **2** *a refined lady:* **cultivated**, cultured, polished, stylish, elegant, sophisticated, urbane; polite, gracious, well mannered, well bred. **3** *a person of refined taste:* **discriminating**, discerning, fastidious, exquisite, impeccable, fine.

–OPPOSITES crude, coarse.

refinement noun **1** *writing needs endless refinement:* **improvement**, polishing, honing, fine-tuning, touching up, finishing off, revision, editing. **2** *a woman of refinement:* **style**, elegance, finesse, polish, sophistication, urbanity; politeness, grace, good manners, good breeding, gentility.

reflect verb **1** *the snow reflects light:* **send back**, throw back, cast back. **2** *their expressions reflected their feelings:* **indicate**, show, display, demonstrate, be evidence of, register, reveal, betray, disclose; express, communicate; formal evince. **3** *he reflected on his responsibilities:* **think about**, consider, review, mull over, contemplate, cogitate about/on, meditate on, muse on, brood on/over.

■ **reflect badly on** discredit, disgrace, shame, damage, bring into disrepute.

reflection noun **1** *her reflection in the mirror:* **image**, likeness. **2** *healthy skin is a reflection of good health in general:* **indication**, display, demonstration, manifestation; expression, evidence. **3** *after some reflection, he turned the offer down:* **thought**, consideration, contemplation, deliberation, pondering, meditation, musing, rumination; formal cogitation. **4** *write down your reflections:* **opinion**, thought, view, belief, feeling, idea, impression, conclusion, assessment; comment, observation, remark.

reflex adjective **instinctive**, automatic, involuntary, impulsive, intuitive, spontaneous, unconscious, unconditioned, untaught, unlearned.

–OPPOSITES conscious.

reform verb **1** *a plan to reform the system:* **improve**, make better, ameliorate, refine; alter, change, adjust, adapt, amend, revise, reshape, redesign, revamp, rebuild, reconstruct, remodel, reorganize. **2** *after his marriage he reformed:* **mend your ways**, change for the better, turn over a new leaf, improve.

• noun *the reform of the prison system:* **improvement**, amelioration, refinement; alteration, change, adaptation, amendment, revision, reshaping, refashioning, redesign, revamp, renovation, rebuilding, reconstruction, remodelling, reorganization.

refractory adjective (formal) **obstinate**, stubborn, mulish, pig-headed, obdurate, headstrong, self-willed, wayward, wilful, perverse, contrary, recalcitrant, obstreperous, disobedient; Brit. informal bloody-minded, bolshie, stroppy.

–OPPOSITES obedient.

refrain verb **abstain**, desist, hold back, stop yourself, forbear, avoid, eschew, shun, renounce; informal swear off; formal forswear, abjure.

refresh verb **1** *the cool air will refresh me:* **reinvigorate**, revitalize, revive, restore, fortify, enliven, perk up, stimulate, freshen, energize, exhilarate, reanimate, wake up, revivify, blow away the cobwebs; informal buck up, pep up. **2** *let me refresh your memory:* **jog**, stimulate, prompt, prod. **3** (N. Amer.) *I refreshed his glass:* **refill**, top up, replenish, recharge.

–OPPOSITES weary.

refreshing adjective **1** *a refreshing drink:* **invigorating**, revitalizing, reviving, restoring, bracing, fortifying, enlivening, stimulating, energizing, exhilarating. **2** *a refreshing change of direction:* **welcome**, stimulating, fresh, imaginative, innovative.

refreshment noun **1** *refreshments were available:* **food and drink**, sustenance, provender; snacks, titbits; informal nibbles, eats, grub, nosh; formal comestibles. **2** *spiritual refreshment:* **invigoration**, revival, stimulation, reanimation, revivification, rejuvenation, regeneration, renewal.

refuge noun **shelter**, protection, safety, security, asylum, sanctuary, haven; retreat, bolt-hole, hiding place, hideaway, hideout.

refugee noun **displaced person**, DP, fugitive, asylum seeker, exile, émigré.

refund verb **1** *we will refund your money if you're not satisfied:* **repay**, give back, return, pay back. **2** *they refunded the subscribers:* **reimburse**, compensate, recompense, remunerate, indemnify.
• noun *a full refund:* **repayment**, reimbursement, rebate.

refurbish verb **renovate**, recondition, rehabilitate, revamp, overhaul, restore, renew, redevelop, rebuild, reconstruct; redecorate, spruce up, upgrade, refit; informal do up.

refusal noun **1** *we had one refusal to our invitation:* **rejection**, non-acceptance, no, demurral, turn-down. **2** *the refusal of planning permission:* **withholding**, denial.

r

refuse[1] verb **1** *he refused the invitation:* **decline**, turn down; reject, spurn, rebuff, dismiss; informal pass up. **2** *the Council refused planning permission:* **withhold**, deny.
– OPPOSITES accept, grant.

refuse[2] noun *piles of refuse:* **rubbish**, waste, debris, litter, detritus, dross; N. Amer. garbage, trash; informal dreck, junk.

refute verb **1** *attempts to refute Einstein's theory:* **disprove**, prove wrong/false, controvert, rebut, give the lie to, explode, debunk, discredit, invalidate; informal shoot full of holes; formal confute. **2** *she refuted the allegation:* **deny**, reject, repudiate, rebut; contradict; formal gainsay.

regain verb **1** *government troops regained the capital:* **recover**, get back, win back, recoup, retrieve, reclaim, repossess; take back, retake, recapture, reconquer. **2** *they regained dry land:* **return to**, get back to, reach again, rejoin.

regal adjective *his regal forebears:* **royal**, kingly, queenly, princely.

regale verb **1** *they were lavishly regaled:* **entertain**, wine and dine, fete, feast, serve, feed. **2** *he regaled her with stories:* **entertain**, amuse, divert, delight, fascinate, captivate.

regard verb **1** *we regard the results as encouraging:* **consider**, look on, view, see, think of, judge, deem, estimate, assess, reckon, adjudge, rate, gauge. **2** *he regarded her coldly:* **look at**, contemplate, eye, gaze at, stare at; watch, observe, view, study, scrutinize; literary behold.
• noun **1** *he has no regard for life:* **consideration**, care, concern, thought, notice, heed, attention. **2** *doctors are held in high regard:* **esteem**, respect, acclaim, admiration, approval, approbation, estimation. **3** *in this regard I disagree:* **respect**, aspect, point, item, particular, detail, specific; matter, issue, topic, question. **4** *send her my regards:* **best wishes**, greetings, felicitations, salutations, respects, compliments.
■ **with regard to**. See REGARDING.

regarding preposition **concerning**, as regards, with/in regard to, with respect to, with reference to, relating to, respecting, re, about, apropos, on the subject of, in connection with, vis-à-vis.

regardless adverb *he decided to go, regardless:* **anyway**, anyhow, in any case, nevertheless, nonetheless, despite everything, even so, all the same, in any event, come what may; informal irregardless.
■ **regardless of** *the allowance is paid regardless of age or income:* irrespective of, notwithstanding, without reference to, without regard to; informal irregardless of.

regenerate verb **revive**, revitalize, renew, restore, breathe new life into, revivify, rejuvenate, reanimate, resuscitate; informal give a shot in the arm to.

regime noun **1** *the Communist regime:* **government**, rule, authority, control, command, administration, leadership. **2** *a health regime:* **system**, arrangement, scheme; order, pattern, method, procedure, routine, course, plan, programme.

regiment noun **unit**, outfit, force, corps, division, brigade, battalion, squadron, company, platoon.
•verb **organize**, order, systematize, control, regulate, manage, discipline.

regimented adjective **strictly regulated**, organized, disciplined, controlled, ordered, systematic.

region noun **district**, province, territory, division, area, section, sector, zone, belt, part, quarter; informal parts.
■ **in the region of**. See APPROXIMATELY.

regional adjective **1** *regional variation:* **geographical**, territorial. **2** *a regional parliament:* **local**, provincial, district, parochial.
–OPPOSITES national.

register noun **1** *the register of electors:* **official list**, roll, roster, index, directory, catalogue, inventory. **2** *the parish register:* **record**, chronicle, log, ledger, archive; annals, files. **3** *the lower register of the piano:* **range**, reaches; notes, octaves.
•verb **1** *I wish to register a complaint:* **record**, enter, file, lodge, write down, submit, report, note, minute, log. **2** *it is not too late to register:* **enrol**, put your name down, enlist, sign on/up, apply. **3** *the dial registered 100 mph:* **indicate**, read, record, show, display. **4** *her face registered anger:* **display**, show, express, exhibit, betray, evidence, reveal, manifest, demonstrate, bespeak; formal evince. **5** *the content of her statement did not register:* **make an impression**, get through, sink in, penetrate, have an effect, strike home.

regress verb **revert**, retrogress, relapse, lapse, backslide, slip back; deteriorate, decline, worsen, degenerate; informal go downhill.
–OPPOSITES progress.

regret verb **1** *they came to regret their decision:* **rue**, repent of, be sorry about. **2** *a poem which regrets the passing of youth:* **mourn**, grieve for/over, weep over, sigh over, lament, sorrow for, deplore.
•noun **1** *both players expressed regret:* **remorse**, sorrow, contrition, repentance, penitence, guilt, compunction, remorsefulness, ruefulness. **2** *they left with genuine regret:* **sadness**, sorrow, disappointment, unhappiness, grief.
–OPPOSITES satisfaction.

regretful adjective **sorry**, remorseful, contrite, repentant, rueful, penitent, conscience-stricken, apologetic, guilt-ridden, ashamed, shamefaced.
–OPPOSITES unrepentant.

regrettable adjective **undesirable**, unfortunate, unwelcome, sorry, woeful, disappointing.

regular adjective **1** *plant the seeds at regular intervals:* **uniform**, even, consistent, fixed; symmetrical. **2** *a regular beat:* **rhythmic**, steady, constant, unchanging, unvarying. **3** *the proposal is the subject of regular protests:* **frequent**, repeated, continual, recurrent, periodic, constant, perpetual, numerous. **4** *regular methods of business:* **established**, conventional, orthodox, proper, official, approved, bona fide, standard, usual, traditional, tried and tested. **5** *his regular route to work:* **usual**, normal, customary, habitual, routine, typical, accustomed, established.
–OPPOSITES irregular, erratic, occasional.

regulate verb **1** *the flow has been regulated:* **control**, adjust, set. **2** *a new act to regulate these businesses:* **supervise**, police, monitor, check up on, be responsible for; control, manage, direct, guide, govern.

regulation noun **1** *EC regulations:* **rule**, order, directive, act, law, bylaw, statute, edict, canon, pronouncement, dictate, decree. **2** *the regulation of financial services:* **supervision**, policing, superintendence, monitoring, inspection; control, management, responsibility for.
•adjective *regulation uniform:* **official**, prescribed, set, statutory, standard; compulsory, obligatory, mandatory.

r

regurgitate verb *he simply regurgitates the old clichés:* **repeat**, restate, reiterate, recite, parrot; informal trot out.

rehabilitate verb **1** *efforts to rehabilitate patients:* **reintegrate**, readapt; N. Amer. informal rehab. **2** *former dissidents were rehabilitated:* **reinstate**, restore, bring back; pardon, absolve, exonerate, forgive; formal exculpate. **3** *we're committed to rehabilitating vacant housing:* **recondition**, restore, renovate, refurbish, revamp, overhaul, redevelop, rebuild, reconstruct; N. Amer. informal rehab.

rehearsal noun **practice**, trial performance, read-through, run-through; informal dry run.

rehearse verb **1** *the children are rehearsing their roles:* **prepare**, practise, read through, run through/over, go over. **2** *the document rehearsed all the arguments:* **enumerate**, list, itemize, detail, spell out, catalogue, recite, rattle off; restate, repeat, reiterate, recapitulate, go over, run through; informal recap.

reign verb **1** *Robert II reigned for nineteen years:* **be king/queen**, be monarch, be sovereign, wear the crown, rule, govern, command. **2** *chaos reigned:* **prevail**, exist, be present, occur, be prevalent, be current, be rife, be rampant, be the order of the day; formal obtain.
• noun *Henry VIII's reign:* **rule**, sovereignty, monarchy.

r

reigning adjective **1** *the reigning monarch:* **ruling**, regnant; on the throne. **2** *the reigning champion:* **incumbent**, current.

reimburse verb **1** *they will reimburse your costs:* **repay**, refund, return, pay back. **2** *we'll reimburse you:* **compensate**, recompense, repay.

rein noun *there is no rein on his behaviour:* **restraint**, check, curb, constraint, restriction, limitation, control, brake.
• verb *they reined back costs:* **restrain**, check, curb, constrain, hold back/in, regulate, restrict, control, curtail, limit.
■ **free rein** freedom, a free hand, leeway, latitude, flexibility, liberty, independence, free play, licence, room to manoeuvre, carte blanche. **keep a tight rein on** regulate, discipline, regiment, keep in line.

reinforce verb **1** *troops reinforced the dam:* **strengthen**, fortify, bolster up, shore up, buttress, prop up, underpin, brace, support. **2** *the initiative aimed to reinforce these cultural links:* **strengthen**, fortify, support; cement, boost, promote, encourage, deepen, enrich, enhance, intensify, improve. **3** *the need to reinforce NATO troops:* **augment**, increase, add to, supplement, boost, top up.

reinforcement noun **1** *the reinforcement of our defences:* **strengthening**, fortification, bolstering, shoring up, buttressing, bracing. **2** *they returned with reinforcements:* **additional troops**, auxiliaries, reserves; support, backup, help.

reinstate verb **restore**, put back, bring back, reinstitute, reinstall.

reiterate verb **repeat**, restate, recapitulate, go over, rehearse.

reject verb **1** *the miners rejected the offer:* **turn down**, refuse, decline, spurn; informal give the thumbs down to. **2** *her family rejected her:* **rebuff**, spurn, shun, snub, repudiate, cast off/aside, discard, abandon, desert, turn your back on, have nothing more to do with, wash your hands of; literary forsake.
– OPPOSITES accept.

rejection noun **1** *a rejection of the offer:* **refusal**, declining, turning down, dismissal, spurning. **2** *Madeleine's rejection of him:* **repudiation**, rebuff, spurning, abandonment, desertion; informal brush-off; literary forsaking.

rejoice verb **1** *they rejoiced when she returned:* **be delighted**, be thrilled, be elated, be ecstatic, be euphoric, be overjoyed, be as pleased as Punch, be cock-a-hoop, be jubilant, be thrilled, be on cloud nine; celebrate, make merry; informal be over the moon. **2** *he rejoiced in their success:* **revel in**, glory in, delight in, relish, savour.
– OPPOSITES mourn.

rejoicing noun **happiness**, pleasure, joy, gladness, delight, elation, jubilation, exuberance, exultation, celebration, revelry, merrymaking.

rejoinder noun **answer**, reply, response, retort, riposte, counter; informal comeback.

rejuvenate verb **revive**, revitalize, regenerate, breathe new life into, revivify, reanimate, resuscitate, refresh, reawaken; informal give a shot in the arm to, pep up, buck up.

relapse verb **1** *a few patients relapse:* **deteriorate**, degenerate, worsen. **2** *she relapsed into silence:* **revert**, lapse; regress, retrogress, slip back, slide back, degenerate.
– OPPOSITES improve.

relate verb **1** *high unemployment is related to high crime rates:* **connect**, associate, link, correlate; ally, couple. **2** *many versions of the story have been related:* **tell**, recount, narrate, report, chronicle, outline, retail, recite, repeat.
■ **relate to 1** *the legislation relating to pensions:* apply to, be relevant to, concern, pertain to, have a bearing on, involve; formal appertain to. **2** *kids relate to him because he's rebellious:* get on with, identify with, empathize with, understand, feel sympathy with, feel for; informal hit it off with.

related adjective **1** *related ideas:* **connected**, interconnected, associated, linked, coupled, allied, affiliated, concomitant, corresponding, analogous, kindred, parallel, comparable, homologous, equivalent. **2** *are you two related?* **kin**, kindred, family; formal consanguineous.
– OPPOSITES unrelated.

relation noun **1** *the relation between church and state:* **connection**, relationship, association, link, correlation, correspondence, parallel, alliance, bond, interrelation, interconnection. **2** *this had no relation to national security:* **relevance**, applicability, reference, pertinence, bearing. **3** *are you a relation of his?* **relative**, member of the family, kinsman, kinswoman; (**relations**) kin, family, kith and kin, kindred. **4** *he sought to improve relations with India:* **dealings**, communication, relationship, connections, contact, interaction.

relationship noun **1** *the relationship between diet and diabetes:* **connection**, relation, association, link, correlation, correspondence, parallel, alliance, bond, interrelation, interconnection. **2** *evidence of their relationship to a common ancestor:* **family ties/ connections**, blood relationship, kinship, affinity, common ancestry; formal consanguinity. **3** *the end of their relationship:* **romance**, affair, liaison, amour.

relative adjective **1** *the relative importance of each factor:* **comparative**, respective, comparable, correlative, parallel, corresponding. **2** *the food required is relative to body weight:* **proportionate**, commensurate, corresponding.
• noun **relation**, next of kin, kinsman, kinswoman; (**relatives**) family, kin, kith and kin, kindred, kinsfolk.

relatively adverb **comparatively**; quite, fairly, reasonably, rather, somewhat, to a certain extent/ degree, to an extent, to a degree, tolerably, passably; informal pretty, kind of, sort of.

relax verb **1** *yoga is helpful in learning to relax:* **unwind**, loosen up, ease up/off, slow down, calm down, destress, unbend, rest, put your feet up, take it easy; informal unbutton; N. Amer. informal hang loose, chill out. **2** *he relaxed his grip:* **loosen**, slacken, unclench, weaken, lessen. **3** *they relaxed the restrictions:* **moderate**, modify, temper, ease, loosen, lighten, weaken, reduce, decrease; informal let up on.
– OPPOSITES tense, tighten.

relaxation noun **1** *a state of relaxation:* **repose**, calm, tranquillity, peacefulness, peace. **2** *I just play for relaxation:* **recreation**, enjoyment, amusement, entertainment, fun, pleasure, leisure; informal R & R. **3** *relaxation of censorship rules:* **moderation**, easing, loosening, lightening; alleviation, mitigation, weakening, reduction.

relay noun *a live relay of the performance:* **broadcast**, transmission, showing.
• verb *I'd relayed the messages:* **pass on**, hand on, transfer, repeat,

communicate, send, transmit, disseminate, spread, circulate.

release verb **1** *all prisoners were released:* **free**, set free, let go/out, liberate, set at liberty. **2** *he released the chains:* **untie**, undo, loose. **3** *she released Stephen from his promise:* **excuse**, exempt, discharge, deliver, absolve; informal let off. **4** *police released the news yesterday:* **make public**, make known, issue, break, announce, declare, report, reveal, divulge, disclose, publish, broadcast, circulate, communicate, disseminate. **5** *the film was released this weekend:* **launch**, premier, bring out.
– OPPOSITES imprison, tie up.
• noun **1** *the release of political prisoners:* **freeing**, liberation, deliverance; freedom, liberty. **2** *the release of the news:* **issuing**, announcement, declaration, reporting, revealing, divulging, disclosure, publication, communication, dissemination. **3** *a press release:* **announcement**, bulletin, newsflash, dispatch, proclamation.

relegate verb **downgrade**, demote, move down, lower, marginalize, sideline.
– OPPOSITES upgrade.

relent verb **1** *the government relented:* **change your mind**, do a U-turn, back-pedal, back down, give way/in, capitulate; Brit. do an about-turn; formal accede. **2** *the rain relented:* **ease off/up**, slacken, let up, abate, drop, die down, lessen, decrease, subside, weaken, tail off.

relentless adjective **1** *their relentless pursuit of quality:* **persistent**, constant, continual, non-stop, never-ending, unabating, interminable, incessant, unceasing, endless, unremitting; unfaltering, unflagging, untiring, unwavering, dogged, single-minded, tireless, indefatigable; formal pertinacious. **2** *a relentless taskmaster:* **harsh**, grim, cruel, severe, strict, remorseless, merciless, pitiless, ruthless, unmerciful, heartless, hard-hearted, unforgiving.

relevant adjective **pertinent**, applicable, apposite, material, apropos, to the point, germane; connected, related, linked.

reliable adjective **1** *reliable evidence:* **dependable**, good, well founded, authentic, valid, genuine, sound, true. **2** *a reliable friend:* **trustworthy**, dependable, good, true, faithful, devoted, steadfast, staunch, constant, loyal, trusty, dedicated, unfailing. **3** *a reliable firm:* **reputable**, dependable, trustworthy, honest, responsible, established, proven, safe, fail-safe.
– OPPOSITES untrustworthy, unreliable.

reliance noun **1** *reliance on the state:* **dependence**. **2** *reliance on his judgement:* **trust**, confidence, faith, belief, conviction.

relic noun **1** *a Viking relic:* **artefact**, historical object, antiquity. **2** *a saint's relics:* **remains**, corpse, bones, reliquiae.

relief noun **1** *it was a relief to talk to someone:* **reassurance**, consolation, comfort, solace. **2** *pain relief:* **alleviation**, assuagement, palliation, allaying, soothing, easing, lessening, reduction, remission. **3** *a little light relief:* **respite**, amusement, diversion, entertainment, jollity, recreation. **4** *they bring relief to the starving:* **help**, aid, assistance, succour, sustenance; charity, gifts, donations. **5** *his relief arrived to take over:* **replacement**, substitute, deputy, reserve, cover, stand-in, supply, locum, understudy.
– OPPOSITES intensification.

relieve verb **1** *this will help to relieve the pain:* **alleviate**, mitigate, assuage, ease, dull, reduce, lessen, diminish. **2** *the helpers relieved us:* **replace**, take over from, stand in for, fill in for, substitute for, deputize for, cover for. **3** *this relieves the teacher of a heavy load:* **free**, release, discharge; save, spare.
– OPPOSITES aggravate.

relieved adjective **glad**, thankful, grateful, pleased, happy, reassured, consoled, comforted.
– OPPOSITES worried.

religion noun **faith**, belief, worship, creed; sect, cult, church, denomination.

WORD LINKS
divinity, **theology** the study of religion

religious adjective **1** *a religious person:* **devout**, pious, reverent, godly, God-fearing, churchgoing, practising, faithful, devoted, committed. **2** *religious beliefs:* **spiritual**, theological, scriptural, doctrinal, ecclesiastical, church, holy, divine, sacred. **3** *religious attention to detail:* **scrupulous**, conscientious, meticulous, sedulous, punctilious, strict, rigorous, close.
– OPPOSITES atheistic, secular.

relinquish verb **1** *he relinquished control of the company:* **renounce**, give up/away, hand over, let go of. **2** *he relinquished his post:* **leave**, resign from, stand down from, bow out of, give up; informal quit.
– OPPOSITES retain.

relish noun **1** *he dug into his food with relish:* **enjoyment**, gusto, delight, pleasure, glee, rapture, satisfaction, contentment, appreciation, enthusiasm, appetite; humorous delectation. **2** *a hot relish:* **condiment**, sauce, dressing.
– OPPOSITES dislike.
• verb **1** *he was relishing his moment of glory:* **enjoy**, delight in, love, adore, take pleasure in, rejoice in, appreciate, savour, revel in, luxuriate in, glory in. **2** *I don't relish the drive:* **look forward to**, fancy.

reluctance noun **unwillingness**, disinclination; hesitation, wavering, vacillation; doubts, second thoughts, misgivings.

reluctant adjective *they seemed reluctant to let her go:* **unwilling**, disinclined, loath, indisposed, opposed; unenthusiastic, resistant, hesitant.
– OPPOSITES willing, eager.

rely verb **1** *we can rely on his discretion:* **depend**, count, bank, place reliance, reckon; be confident of, be sure of, believe in, have faith in, trust in; informal swear by; N. Amer. informal figure on. **2** *we rely on government funding:* **be dependent**, depend.

remain verb **1** *the problem will remain:* **continue to exist**, endure, last, abide, carry on, persist, prevail, survive, live on. **2** *he remained at home:* **stay**, wait, be left, hang on; informal hang around/round. **3** *union leaders remain sceptical:* **continue to be**, stay.

remainder noun **residue**, balance, rest, remnant, remains, surplus, extra, excess, leftovers.

remaining adjective **1** *the remaining supplies:* **residual**, surviving, left over. **2** *his remaining jobs:* **unsettled**, outstanding, unfinished, incomplete, to be done, unattended to. **3** *my only remaining memories:* **surviving**, lasting, enduring, continuing, persisting, abiding, existing.

remains plural noun **1** *the remains of her drink:* **remainder**, residue, rest, remnants, leftovers. **2** *Roman remains:* **antiquities**, relics, reliquiae. **3** *the saint's remains:* **corpse**, body, carcass; bones, skeleton.

remark verb **1** *'You're quiet,' he remarked:* **comment**, say, observe, mention, reflect, state, declare, announce, pronounce, assert; formal opine. **2** *many critics remarked on their rapport:* **comment**, mention, refer to, speak of, pass comment on.
• noun **1** *his remarks have been misinterpreted:* **comment**, statement, utterance, observation, declaration, pronouncement. **2** *worthy of remark:* **attention**, notice, comment, mention, observation, acknowledgement.

remarkable adjective **extraordinary**, exceptional, amazing, astonishing, astounding, marvellous, wonderful, sensational, stunning, incredible, unbelievable, phenomenal, outstanding, momentous; informal fantastic, terrific, tremendous, stupendous, awesome; literary wondrous.
– OPPOSITES ordinary.

remediable adjective **curable**, treatable, operable; solvable, reparable, rectifiable, resolvable.
– OPPOSITES incurable.

remedy noun **1** *herbal remedies:* **treatment**, cure, medicine, medication, medicament, drug. **2** *a remedy for all kinds of problems:* **solution**, answer, cure, antidote, curative, nostrum, panacea, cure-all.
• verb *little has been done to remedy the situation:* **put/set right**, rectify, solve, sort out, straighten out,

resolve, correct, redress, repair, mend, make good.

remember verb **1** *they remembered happier times:* **recall**, call to mind, recollect, think of; reminisce about, look back on. **2** *can you remember all that?* **memorize**, retain; learn off by heart. **3** *you must remember she's only five:* **bear/keep in mind**, be mindful of the fact; take into account, take into consideration. **4** *the nation remembered those who gave their lives:* **commemorate**, pay tribute to, honour, salute, pay homage to.
–OPPOSITES forget.

remembrance noun **1** *an expression of remembrance:* **recollection**, reminiscence; recalling, recollecting, reminiscing. **2** *she smiled at the remembrance:* **memory**, recollection, reminiscence, thought. **3** *we sold poppies in remembrance:* **commemoration**, memory, recognition. **4** *a remembrance of my father:* **memento**, reminder, keepsake, souvenir, memorial, token.

remind verb **1** *I left a note to remind him:* **jog someone's memory**, prompt. **2** *the song reminded me of my sister:* **make you think of**, make you remember, put you in mind of, bring/call to mind, evoke.

reminder noun **prompt**, aide-memoire.

reminisce verb **remember**, cast your mind back to, look back on, recall, recollect, reflect on, call to mind.

r

reminiscences plural noun **memories**, recollections, reflections.

reminiscent adjective **similar to**, comparable with, evocative of, suggestive of, redolent of.

remiss adjective **negligent**, neglectful, irresponsible, careless, thoughtless, heedless, lax, slack, slipshod, lackadaisical; N. Amer. derelict; informal sloppy.
–OPPOSITES careful.

remission noun **1** *the remission of tuition fees:* **cancellation**, waiving; deferral, suspension. **2** *the cancer is in remission:* **respite**, abeyance. **3** *the remission of sins:* **forgiveness**, pardoning, absolution, exoneration; formal exculpation.

remit noun *that decision is outside his remit:* **area of responsibility**, sphere, orbit, scope, ambit, province; brief, instructions, orders; informal bailiwick.
•verb **1** *they refused to remit the customs duties to the authorities:* **send**, dispatch, forward, hand over; pay. **2** *the fines imposed on him were remitted:* **cancel**, waive, set aside, suspend.

remittance noun *send the form with your remittance:* **payment**, money, fee; cheque; formal monies.

remnant noun **1** *the remnants of the picnic:* **remains**, remainder, leftovers, residue, rest. **2** *remnants of cloth:* **scrap**, piece, bit, fragment, shred, offcut, oddment.

remonstrate verb *they remonstrated with the referee:* **protest to**, complain to, argue with, challenge, take issue with.

remorse noun **contrition**, deep regret, repentance, penitence, guilt, compunction, remorsefulness, ruefulness, contriteness.

remorseful adjective **sorry**, regretful, contrite, repentant, penitent, guilt-ridden, conscience-stricken, chastened, self-reproachful.
–OPPOSITES unrepentant.

remorseless adjective **1** *the remorseless military build-up continued:* **relentless**, unremitting, unabating, inexorable, unstoppable. **2** *a remorseless killer:* **heartless**, pitiless, merciless, ruthless, callous, cruel, hard-hearted, inhumane, unmerciful, unforgiving, unfeeling.

remote adjective **1** *areas remote from hospitals:* **far**, distant. **2** *a remote village:* **isolated**, out of the way, off the beaten track, secluded, lonely, in the back of beyond, godforsaken, inaccessible; N. Amer. in the backwoods; informal in the sticks, in the middle of nowhere. **3** *events remote from everyday experience:* **irrelevant to**, unrelated to, unconnected to, not pertinent to, immaterial to; foreign to, alien to. **4** *a remote possibility:* **unlikely**, improbable, implausible, doubtful, dubious; faint, slight, slim, small, slender. **5** *she seems very remote:* **aloof**, distant, detached,

withdrawn, reserved, uncommunicative, unforthcoming, unapproachable, unresponsive, unfriendly, unsociable, introspective, introverted; informal stand-offish.
– OPPOSITES close, central.

removal noun **1** *the removal of church treasures:* **taking away**, moving, carrying away, transporting. **2** *his removal from office:* **dismissal**, ejection, expulsion, ousting, displacement, deposition, unseating; N. Amer. ouster; informal sacking, firing. **3** *the removal of customs barriers:* **withdrawal**, elimination, abolition.
– OPPOSITES installation.

remove verb **1** *remove the plug:* **detach**, unfasten; pull out, take out, disconnect. **2** *she removed the lid:* **take off**, undo, unfasten. **3** *he removed a note from his wallet:* **take out**, produce, bring out, get out, pull out, withdraw. **4** *police removed boxes of documents:* **take away**, carry away, move, transport; confiscate; informal cart off. **5** *Henry removed his coat:* **take off**, pull off, slip out of; Brit. informal peel off. **6** *he was removed from his post:* **dismiss**, discharge, get rid of, dislodge, displace, expel, oust, depose; informal sack, fire, kick out; Brit. informal turf out. **7** *tax relief was removed:* **withdraw**, abolish, eliminate, get rid of, do away with, stop, cut, axe. **8** *Gabriel removed two words:* **delete**, erase, rub out, cross out, strike out, score out.
– OPPOSITES attach, insert, replace.

removed adjective **distant**, remote, disconnected; unrelated, unconnected, alien, foreign.

remunerate verb **pay**, reward, reimburse, recompense.

remuneration noun **payment**, pay, salary, wages; earnings, fee, reward, recompense, reimbursement; formal emolument.

remunerative adjective **lucrative**, well paid, financially rewarding; profitable.

renaissance noun **revival**, renewal, resurrection, reawakening, re-emergence, rebirth, reappearance, resurgence, regeneration; formal renascence.

rend verb **tear/rip apart**, split, rupture, sever.

render verb **1** *her fury rendered her speechless:* **make**, turn, leave. **2** *we are not in a position to render assistance:* **give**, provide, supply, furnish, contribute; offer, proffer. **3** *paintings rendered in vivid colours:* **paint**, draw, depict, portray, represent, execute. **4** *the characters are vividly rendered:* **act**, perform, play, depict, interpret. **5** *the phrase was rendered into English:* **translate**, put, express, rephrase, reword.

rendezvous noun *Edward was late for their rendezvous:* **meeting**, appointment, assignation; informal date; literary tryst.
• verb *the bar where they had agreed to rendezvous:* **meet**, come together, gather, assemble.

rendition noun **1** *our rendition of Beethoven's Fifth:* **performance**, interpretation, presentation, execution, delivery. **2** *the artist's rendition of Adam and Eve:* **depiction**, portrayal, representation. **3** *an interpreter's rendition of the message:* **translation**, interpretation, version.

renegade noun *he was denounced as a renegade:* **traitor**, defector, deserter, turncoat, rebel, mutineer.
• adjective **1** *renegade troops:* **treacherous**, traitorous, disloyal, treasonous, rebel, mutinous. **2** *a renegade monk:* **apostate**, heretic, heretical, dissident.
– OPPOSITES loyal.

renege verb **default on**, fail to honour, go back on, break, back out of, withdraw from, retreat from, backtrack on; break your word/promise.
– OPPOSITES honour.

renew verb **1** *I renewed my search:* **resume**, return to, restart, recommence; continue, carry on. **2** *they renewed their vows:* **reaffirm**, reassert; repeat, reiterate, restate. **3** *something to renew her interest in life:* **revive**, regenerate, revitalize, reinvigorate, restore, resuscitate, breathe new life into. **4** *they renewed her contract:* **extend**, prolong.

renewal noun **1** *the renewal of our friendship:* **resumption**, recommencement, re-establishment; continuation.

r

2 *spiritual renewal:* **regeneration**, revival, reinvigoration, revitalization. **3** *the renewal of older urban areas:* **renovation**, restoration, modernization, reconditioning, overhauling, redevelopment, rebuilding, reconstruction.

renounce verb **1** *Edward renounced his claim to the throne:* **give up**, relinquish, abandon, abdicate, surrender, waive, forgo; formal abnegate. **2** *Hungary renounced the agreement:* **reject**, refuse to abide by, repudiate. **3** *she renounced her family:* **repudiate**, deny, reject, abandon, wash your hands of, turn your back on, disown, spurn, shun; literary forsake. **4** *he renounced alcohol:* **abstain from**, give up, desist from, refrain from, keep off, eschew; informal quit, pack in, lay off; formal forswear.
– OPPOSITES assert, accept.
■ **renounce the world** become a recluse, cloister yourself, hide yourself away.

renovate verb **modernize**, restore, refurbish, revamp, recondition, rehabilitate, overhaul, redevelop; update, upgrade, refit; informal do up; N. Amer. informal rehab.

renown noun **fame**, distinction, eminence, prominence, repute, reputation, prestige, acclaim, celebrity, notability.

renowned adjective **famous**, celebrated, famed, eminent, distinguished, acclaimed, illustrious, prominent, great, esteemed, of note, of repute, well known.
– OPPOSITES unknown.

r

rent[1] verb **hire**, lease, charter; let, sublet.

rent[2] noun **rip**, tear, split, hole, slash, slit.

renunciation noun **1** *Henry's renunciation of his throne:* **relinquishment**, giving up, abandonment, abdication, surrender, waiving, forgoing. **2** *their renunciation of violence:* **repudiation**, rejection, abandonment, eschewal; formal forswearing.

reorganize verb **restructure**, change, alter, adjust, transform, shake up, rationalize, rearrange, reshape, overhaul.

repair[1] verb **1** *the car was repaired:* **mend**, fix, put/set right, restore, overhaul, service; informal patch up. **2** *she sought to repair the wrong she had done:* **rectify**, make good, right, put right, correct, make up for, make amends for, make reparation for.
• noun **1** *the building was in need of repair:* **restoration**, renovation, refurbishment. **2** *the machine's in good repair:* **condition**, working order, state, shape, fettle; Brit. informal nick.
■ **beyond repair** irreparable, irreversible, irretrievable, irremediable, irrecoverable, past hope.

repair[2] verb (formal) *we repaired to the sitting room:* **go to**, head for, adjourn, wend your way; formal remove.

reparable adjective **rectifiable**, remediable, curable, restorable, recoverable, retrievable, salvageable.

reparation noun **amends**, restitution, redress, compensation, recompense, repayment, atonement.

repartee noun **banter**, badinage, bantering, raillery, witticisms, ripostes, sallies, quips, joking, jesting, chaff; formal persiflage.

repay verb **1** *the bank was forced to repay its customers:* **reimburse**, refund, pay back, recompense, compensate, indemnify. **2** *the grants have to be repaid:* **pay back**, return, refund, reimburse; settle, clear, discharge, pay off. **3** *I'd like to repay her generosity:* **reciprocate**, return, requite, recompense, reward.

repayment noun **1** *the repayment of tax:* **refund**, reimbursement, paying back. **2** *repayment for all they have done:* **recompense**, reward, compensation.

repeal verb *the Act was repealed:* **revoke**, rescind, cancel, reverse, annul, nullify, quash, abolish; formal abrogate.
– OPPOSITES enact.
• noun *the repeal of the law:* **revocation**, rescinding, cancellation, reversal, annulment, nullification, quashing, abolition; formal abrogation.

repeat verb **1** *she repeated her story:* **say again**, restate, reiterate, go/run through again, recapitulate; informal recap. **2** *children can repeat chunks* *of text:* **recite**, quote, parrot, regurgitate; informal trot out. **3** *Steele was invited to repeat his work in a laboratory:* **do again**, redo, replicate, duplicate. **4** *the episodes were repeated:* **rebroadcast**, rerun, reshow.

•noun **1** *a repeat of the previous year's final:* **repetition**, replication, duplicate. **2** *repeats of his TV show:* **rerun**, rebroadcast, reshowing.

■ **repeat itself** reoccur, recur, happen again.

repeated adjective **recurrent**, frequent, successive, persistent, continual, incessant, constant; regular, periodic, numerous, many.
–OPPOSITES occasional.

repeatedly adverb **frequently**, often, again and again, over and over again, time and time again, many times; persistently, recurrently, constantly, continually, regularly; N. Amer. oftentimes; informal 24-7; literary oft.

repel verb **1** *the rebels were repelled:* **fight off**, repulse, drive back/away, force back, beat back, push back; hold off, ward off, keep at bay; Brit. see off. **2** *the coating will repel water:* **be impervious to**, be impermeable to, keep out, resist. **3** *the thought of kissing him repelled me:* **revolt**, disgust, repulse, sicken, nauseate, turn someone's stomach, be distasteful, be repugnant; informal turn off; N. Amer. informal gross out.

repellent adjective **1** *a repellent stench:* **revolting**, repulsive, disgusting, repugnant, sickening, nauseating, stomach-turning, vile, nasty, foul, horrible, awful, dreadful, terrible, obnoxious, loathsome, offensive, objectionable; abhorrent, despicable, reprehensible, contemptible, odious, hateful, execrable; N. Amer. vomitous; informal ghastly, horrid, gross; literary noisome. **2** *a repellent coating:* **impermeable**, impervious, resistant; -proof.
–OPPOSITES delightful.

repent verb **feel remorse**, regret, be sorry, rue, reproach yourself, be ashamed, feel contrite; be penitent, be remorseful.

repentance noun **remorse**, contrition, penitence, regret, ruefulness, shame, guilt.

repentant adjective **penitent**, contrite, regretful, rueful, remorseful, apologetic, chastened, ashamed, shamefaced.
–OPPOSITES unrepentant, impenitent.

repercussion noun **consequence**, result, effect, outcome; reverberation, backlash, aftermath, fallout.

repertoire noun **collection**, stock, range, repertory, reserve, store, repository, supply.

repetition noun **1** *the statistics bear repetition:* **reiteration**, restatement, retelling. **2** *the repetition of the words:* **repeating**, echoing, parroting. **3** *a repetition of the scene in the kitchen:* **recurrence**, reoccurrence, rerun, repeat. **4** *there is some repetition:* **repetitiousness**, repetitiveness, redundancy, tautology.

repetitious adjective. See **REPETITIVE**.

repetitive adjective **monotonous**, tedious, boring, humdrum, mundane, dreary, tiresome; unvaried, unchanging, recurrent, repeated, repetitious, routine, mechanical, automatic.

rephrase verb **reword**, paraphrase.

replace verb **1** *Adam replaced the receiver:* **put back**, return, restore. **2** *a new chairman came in to replace him:* **take the place of**, succeed, take over from, supersede; stand in for, substitute for, deputize for, cover for, relieve; informal step into someone's shoes/boots. **3** *she replaced the spoon with a fork:* **substitute**, exchange, change, swap.
–OPPOSITES remove.

replacement noun **1** *we have to find a replacement:* **successor**; **substitute**, stand-in, locum, relief, cover. **2** *the wiring was in need of replacement:* **renewal**.

replenish verb **1** *she replenished their glasses:* **refill**, top up, fill up, recharge; N. Amer. freshen. **2** *their supplies were replenished:* **stock up**, restock, restore, replace.
–OPPOSITES empty, exhaust.

replete adjective **1** *the guests were replete:* **well fed**, sated, satiated, full; informal stuffed. **2** *a sumptuous environment replete with antiques:* **filled**, full, well stocked, well supplied, crammed, packed, jammed, teeming, overflowing,

r

bursting; informal jam-packed, chock-a-block.

replica noun **copy**, model, duplicate, reproduction, replication, clone; dummy, imitation, facsimile.

replicate verb **copy**, reproduce, duplicate, recreate, repeat, perform again; clone.

reply verb **1** *Rachel didn't reply:* **answer**, respond, come back, write back. **2** *he replied defensively:* **respond**, answer, rejoin, retort, riposte, counter, come back.
• noun *he waited for a reply:* **answer**, response, rejoinder, retort, riposte; informal comeback.

report verb **1** *the company reported a loss:* **announce**, describe, detail, outline, communicate, divulge, disclose, reveal, make public, publish, broadcast, proclaim, publicize. **2** *the newspapers reported on the scandal:* **investigate**, look into, inquire into; write about, cover, describe, give details of, commentate on. **3** *I reported him to the police:* **inform on**, tattle on; informal shop, tell on, squeal on, rat on; Brit. informal grass on. **4** *Juliet reported for duty:* **present yourself**, arrive, turn up, clock in, sign in; Brit. clock on; N. Amer. punch in; informal show up.
• noun **1** *a full report on the meeting:* **account**, review, record, description, statement; transactions, proceedings, transcripts, minutes. **2** *reports of drug dealing:* **news**, information, word, intelligence; literary tidings. **3** *newspaper reports:* **story**, account, article, piece, item, column, feature, bulletin, dispatch. **4** (Brit.) *a school report:* **assessment**, evaluation, appraisal; N. Amer. report card. **5** *reports of his imminent resignation:* **rumour**, whisper; informal buzz. **6** *the report of a gun:* **bang**, blast, crack, shot, gunshot, explosion, boom.

reporter noun **journalist**, correspondent, newsman, newswoman, columnist; Brit. pressman; N. Amer. legman, wireman; Austral. roundsman; informal news hound, hack, stringer, journo; N. Amer. informal newsy.

repose noun **rest**, relaxation, inactivity, sleep, slumber; peace, quiet, calm, tranquillity.
• verb **lie**, recline, rest; sleep; literary slumber.

repository noun **store**, storehouse, depository; reservoir, bank, cache, treasury, fund, mine.

reprehensible adjective **deplorable**, disgraceful, discreditable, despicable, blameworthy, culpable, wrong, bad, shameful, dishonourable, objectionable, opprobrious, repugnant, inexcusable, unforgivable, indefensible, unjustifiable.
– OPPOSITES praiseworthy.

represent verb **1** *a character representing a single quality:* **symbolize**, stand for, personify, epitomize, typify, embody, illustrate. **2** *the initials which represent her qualification:* **stand for**, designate, denote. **3** *Hathor is represented as a woman with cow's horns:* **depict**, portray, render, picture, delineate, show, illustrate. **4** *ageing represents a threat to one's independence:* **constitute**, be, amount to, be regarded as. **5** *a panel representing a cross section of the public:* **be a typical sample of**, be representative of, typify. **6** *his solicitor represented him in court:* **appear for**, act for, speak on behalf of. **7** *the Queen was represented by Lord Lewin:* **deputize for**, substitute for, stand in for.

representation noun **1** *Rossetti's representation of women:* **portrayal**, depiction, delineation, presentation, rendition. **2** *representations of the human form:* **likeness**, painting, drawing, picture, illustration, sketch, image, model, figure, statue. **3** (formal) *they made representations to the council:* **statement**, deposition, allegation, declaration, exposition, report, protestation.

representative adjective **1** *a representative sample:* **typical**, characteristic, illustrative; prototypical, archetypal. **2** *a female figure representative of Britain:* **symbolic**, emblematic. **3** *representative government:* **elective**, democratic, popular.
– OPPOSITES unrepresentative, totalitarian.
• noun **1** *a representative of the Royal Society:* **spokesperson**, spokesman, spokeswoman, agent, official, mouthpiece. **2** *a sales representative:* **salesman**, saleswoman, agent; informal rep. **3** *the Cambodian*

representative at the UN: **delegate**, commissioner, ambassador, attaché, envoy, emissary, chargé d'affaires, deputy. **4** *he acted as his father's representative:* **deputy**, substitute, stand-in, proxy.

repress verb **1** *the rebellion was repressed:* **suppress**, quell, quash, subdue, put down, crush, extinguish, stamp out, defeat, conquer, rout, overwhelm, contain. **2** *the peasants were repressed:* **oppress**, subjugate, keep down, tyrannize, crush. **3** *these emotions may well be repressed:* **restrain**, hold back/in, keep back, suppress, keep in check, control, curb, stifle, bottle up; informal button up, keep the lid on.

repressed adjective **1** *a repressed country:* **oppressed**, subjugated, subdued, tyrannized. **2** *repressed emotions:* **restrained**, suppressed, held back/in, kept in check, stifled, pent up, bottled up. **3** *an emotionally repressed woman:* **inhibited**, frustrated, restrained; informal uptight, hung up.
–OPPOSITES democratic, uninhibited.

repression noun **1** *the repression of the protests:* **suppression**, quashing, subduing, crushing, stamping out. **2** *political repression:* **oppression**, subjugation, suppression, tyranny, despotism, authoritarianism. **3** *the repression of sexual urges:* **restraint**, holding back, keeping back, suppression, keeping in check, control, stifling, bottling up.

repressive adjective **oppressive**, authoritarian, despotic, tyrannical, dictatorial, fascist, autocratic, totalitarian, undemocratic.

reprieve verb **1** *she was reprieved:* **pardon**, spare, amnesty; informal let off. **2** *the project has been reprieved:* **save**, rescue.

reprimand verb *he was publicly reprimanded:* **rebuke**, admonish, chastise, chide, upbraid, reprove, reproach, scold, berate, take to task, haul over the coals, lecture, criticize, censure; informal tell off, give someone a talking-to, dress down, give someone a roasting, rap over the knuckles, slap someone's wrist, bawl out; Brit. informal tick off, carpet, tear off a strip, give someone what for, give someone a rollicking; N. Amer. informal chew out; formal castigate.
–OPPOSITES praise.
• noun *a severe reprimand:* **rebuke**, reproach, scolding, admonition, reproof, criticism, censure; informal telling-off, dressing-down, talking-to; Brit. informal rocket, ticking-off; formal castigation.
–OPPOSITES praise.

reprisal noun **retaliation**, counter-attack, comeback; revenge, vengeance, retribution, requital; informal a taste of your own medicine.

reproach verb & noun See **REPRIMAND**.
■ **beyond/above reproach** perfect, blameless, above suspicion, without fault, flawless, irreproachable, exemplary, impeccable, immaculate, unblemished, spotless, untarnished, stainless, unsullied, whiter than white; informal squeaky clean.

reproachful adjective **disapproving**, reproving, critical, censorious, disparaging, withering, accusatory, admonitory; formal castigatory.
–OPPOSITES approving.

reprobate noun *a hardened reprobate:* **rogue**, rascal, scoundrel, miscreant, good-for-nothing, villain, wretch, rake, degenerate, libertine, debauchee.
• adjective *reprobate behaviour:* **unprincipled**, bad, roguish, wicked, rakish, shameless, immoral, degenerate, dissipated, debauched, depraved.

reproduce verb **1** *each artwork is reproduced in colour:* **copy**, duplicate, replicate; photocopy, xerox, photostat, print. **2** *this work has not been reproduced in other laboratories:* **repeat**, replicate, recreate, redo; simulate, imitate, emulate, mirror, mimic. **3** *some animals reproduce prolifically:* **breed**, procreate, propagate, multiply.

reproduction noun **1** *colour reproduction:* **copying**, duplication; photocopying, xeroxing, photostatting, printing. **2** *a reproduction of the original:* **print**, copy, reprint, duplicate, facsimile, photocopy; trademark Xerox. **3** *the process of reproduction:* **breeding**, procreation, multiplying, propagation.

reproductive adjective **generative**,

procreative, propagative; sexual, genital.

reproof noun **rebuke**, reprimand, reproach, admonishment, admonition; disapproval, censure, criticism, condemnation; informal telling-off, dressing down; Brit. informal ticking-off; dated rating.

reprove verb **reprimand**, rebuke, reproach, scold, admonish, chastise, chide, upbraid, berate, take to task, haul over the coals, criticize, censure; informal tell off, give someone a talking-to, dress down, give someone a roasting, rap over the knuckles, slap someone's wrist; Brit. informal tick off, carpet, tear off a strip; formal castigate.

reptile noun

> **WORD LINKS**
> **herpetology** the study of reptiles and amphibians

reptilian adjective *a grovelling, reptilian character:* **unpleasant**, distasteful, nasty, disagreeable, unattractive, off-putting, horrible; unctuous, ingratiating, oily, oleaginous; informal smarmy, slimy.

repudiate verb **1** *she repudiated communism:* **reject**, renounce, abandon, give up, turn your back on, disown, cast off, lay aside; formal forswear, abjure; literary forsake. **2** *Cranham repudiated the allegations:* **deny**, refute, contradict, controvert, rebut, dispute, dismiss, brush aside; formal gainsay. **3** *Egypt repudiated the treaty:* **cancel**, revoke, rescind, reverse, overrule, overturn, invalidate, nullify; disregard, flout, renege on; Law disaffirm; formal abrogate.
– OPPOSITES embrace, confirm.

repudiation noun **1** *the repudiation of one's religion:* **rejection**, renunciation, abandonment, forswearing, giving up. **2** *his repudiation of the allegations:* **denial**, refutation, rebuttal, rejection. **3** *a repudiation of the contract:* **cancellation**, revocation, rescindment, reversal, invalidation, nullification; formal abrogation.

repugnance noun **revulsion**, disgust, abhorrence, repulsion, loathing, hatred, detestation, aversion, distaste, antipathy, contempt.

repugnant adjective **abhorrent**, revolting, repulsive, repellent, disgusting, offensive, objectionable, vile, foul, nasty, loathsome, sickening, nauseating, hateful, detestable, execrable, abominable, monstrous, appalling, insufferable, intolerable, unacceptable, contemptible, unsavoury, unpalatable; informal ghastly, gross, horrible; literary noisome.
– OPPOSITES pleasant.

repulse verb **1** *the rebels were repulsed:* **repel**, drive back/away, fight back/off, put to flight, force back, beat off/back; ward off, hold off; Brit. see off. **2** *her advances were repulsed:* **rebuff**, reject, spurn, snub, cold-shoulder; informal give someone the brush-off, freeze out; Brit. informal knock back; N. Amer. informal give someone the bum's rush. **3** *his bid for the company was repulsed:* **reject**, turn down, refuse, decline. **4** *the brutality repulsed her:* **revolt**, disgust, repel, sicken, nauseate, turn someone's stomach; informal turn off; N. Amer. informal gross out.
• noun **rebuff**, rejection, snub, slight; informal brush-off, knock-back.

repulsion noun **disgust**, revulsion, abhorrence, repugnance, nausea, horror, aversion, distaste.

repulsive adjective **revolting**, disgusting, abhorrent, repellent, repugnant, offensive, objectionable, vile, foul, nasty, loathsome, sickening, nauseating, hateful, detestable, execrable, abominable, monstrous, noxious, horrendous, awful, terrible, dreadful, frightful, obnoxious, unsavoury, unpleasant, disagreeable, distasteful; ugly, hideous, grotesque; informal ghastly, horrible, gross; literary noisome.
– OPPOSITES attractive.

reputable adjective **well thought of**, highly regarded, respected, respectable, of good repute, prestigious, established; reliable, dependable, trustworthy.
– OPPOSITES disreputable, untrustworthy.

reputation noun **good name**, character, repute, standing, stature, status, position, renown, esteem, prestige.

repute noun **1** *a woman of ill repute:* **reputation**, name, character. **2** *a* *firm of international repute:* **fame**, renown, celebrity, distinction, high standing, stature, prestige.

reputed adjective **1** *they are reputed to be very rich:* **thought**, said, reported, rumoured, believed, held, considered, regarded, deemed, alleged. **2** *his reputed father:* **supposed**, putative.

reputedly adverb **supposedly**, by all accounts, so I'm told, so people say, allegedly.

request noun **1** *requests for assistance:* **appeal**, entreaty, plea, petition, application, demand, call. **2** *Charlotte spoke, at Ursula's request:* **bidding**, entreaty, demand, insistence. **3** *indicate your requests on the form:* **requirement**, wish, desire; choice.
• verb **1** *the government requested aid:* **ask for**, appeal for, call for, seek, solicit, plead for, apply for, demand. **2** *the girls requested him to stay:* **call on**, beg, entreat, implore; literary beseech.

require verb **1** *the child required hospital treatment:* **need**. **2** *a situation requiring patience:* **necessitate**, demand, call for, involve, entail. **3** *unquestioning obedience is required:* **demand**, insist on, call for, ask for, expect. **4** *she was required to pay costs:* **order**, instruct, command, enjoin, oblige, compel, force. **5** *do you require anything else?* **want**, desire; lack, be short of.

required adjective **1** *this book is required reading:* **essential**, vital, indispensable, necessary, compulsory, obligatory, mandatory, prescribed. **2** *cut the cloth to the required length:* **desired**, preferred, chosen; correct, proper, right.
– OPPOSITES optional.

requirement noun **need**, wish, demand, want, necessity, essential, prerequisite, stipulation.

requisite adjective **necessary**, required, prerequisite, essential, indispensable, vital.
– OPPOSITES optional.
• noun **requirement**, need, necessity, essential, prerequisite, precondition, sine qua non; informal must.

requisition noun **1** *requisitions for staff:* **order**, request, call, application, claim, demand; Brit. indent. **2** *the requisition of cultural treasures:* **appropriation**, commandeering, seizure, confiscation, expropriation.
• verb *the house was requisitioned by the army:* **commandeer**, appropriate, take over, take possession of, occupy, seize, confiscate, expropriate.

requite verb **1** *they are quick to requite a kindness:* **return**, reciprocate, repay. **2** *Drake had requited the wrongs inflicted on them:* **avenge**, revenge, pay someone back for; take reprisals, settle the score, get even.

rescind verb **revoke**, repeal, cancel, reverse, overturn, overrule, annul, nullify, void, invalidate, quash, abolish; formal abrogate.
– OPPOSITES enforce.

rescue verb **1** *an attempt to rescue the hostages:* **save**, come to the aid of; free, set free, release, liberate. **2** *Boyd rescued his papers:* **retrieve**, recover, salvage, get back.
• noun *the rescue of 10 crewmen:* **saving**, rescuing; release, freeing, liberation, deliverance, redemption.
▪ **come to someone's rescue** help, assist, lend a hand to, bail out; informal save someone's neck/skin.

research noun **1** *medical research:* **investigation**, experimentation, testing, analysis, fact-finding, examination, scrutiny. **2** *he continued his researches:* **experiments**, tests, inquiries, studies.
• verb **1** *the phenomenon has been widely researched:* **investigate**, study, inquire into, look into, probe, explore, analyse, examine, scrutinize, review. **2** *I researched all the available material:* **study**, read, sift through; informal check out.

resemblance noun **similarity**, likeness, similitude, correspondence, congruence, coincidence, conformity, agreement, equivalence, comparability, parallelism, uniformity, sameness.

resemble verb **look like**, be similar to, remind someone of, take after, favour, have the look of; smack of, have the hallmarks of; correspond to, echo, mirror, parallel.

resent verb **begrudge**, feel aggrieved about, grudge, be resentful of, dislike, take exception to, object to,

take amiss, take offence at, take umbrage at.
–OPPOSITES welcome.

resentful adjective **aggrieved**, indignant, irritated, piqued, put out, in high dudgeon, dissatisfied, disgruntled, discontented, offended, bitter, jaundiced; envious, jealous; informal miffed, peeved; Brit. informal narked; N. Amer. informal sore.

resentment noun **bitterness**, indignation, irritation, pique, dissatisfaction, disgruntlement, discontentment, bad/feelings, ill will, acrimony, rancour, animosity, jaundice.

reservation noun **1** *grave reservations:* **doubt**, qualm, scruple; misgivings, scepticism, unease, hesitation, objection. **2** *the reservation of the room:* **booking**, ordering, securing. **3** *an Indian reservation:* **reserve**, enclave, sanctuary, territory, homeland.
■ **without reservation** wholeheartedly, unreservedly, without qualification, fully, completely, totally, entirely, wholly, unconditionally.

reserve verb **1** *ask your newsagent to reserve a copy for you:* **put aside**, set aside, keep, save, hold back, keep in reserve, earmark. **2** *he reserved a table:* **book**, order, arrange for, secure. **3** *reserve your judgement until you know him better:* **defer**, postpone, put off, delay, withhold.
•noun **1** *reserves of petrol:* **stock**, store, supply, stockpile, pool, hoard, cache. **2** *the army are calling up reserves:* **reinforcements**, extras, auxiliaries. **3** *a nature reserve:* **national park**, sanctuary, conservation area; N. Amer. preserve. **4** *his habitual reserve:* **reticence**, detachment, distance, remoteness, coolness, aloofness, constraint, formality; shyness, diffidence, timidity, taciturnity, inhibition; informal stand-offishness. **5** *she trusted him without reserve:* **reservation**, qualification, condition, limitation, hesitation, doubt.
•adjective *a reserve goalkeeper:* **substitute**, stand-in, relief, replacement, fallback, spare, extra.
■ **in reserve** available, to/on hand, ready, in readiness, set aside, at your disposal.

r

reserved adjective **1** *he's rather reserved:* **reticent**, quiet, private, uncommunicative, unforthcoming, undemonstrative, unsociable, formal, constrained, cool, aloof, detached, distant, remote, unapproachable, unfriendly, withdrawn, secretive, silent, taciturn; shy, retiring, diffident, timid, self-effacing, inhibited, introverted; informal stand-offish. **2** *that table is reserved:* **booked**, taken, spoken for, prearranged.
–OPPOSITES outgoing.

reservoir noun **1** **lake**, pool. **2** *an ink reservoir:* **receptacle**, container, holder, repository, tank. **3** *a vast reservoir of knowledge and experience:* **supply**, stock, repository, store, reserve, bank, pool, fund, source.

reshuffle verb **reorganize**, restructure, rearrange, change, shake up, shuffle.
•noun *a management reshuffle:* **reorganization**, restructuring, change, rearrangement; informal shake-up.

reside verb **1** *most students reside in flats:* **live in**, occupy, inhabit, stay in, lodge in; formal dwell in, be domiciled in. **2** *the paintings reside in a vault:* **be situated**, be found, be located, lie. **3** *executive power resides in the president:* **be vested in**, be bestowed on, be conferred on, be in the hands of. **4** *the qualities that reside within each individual:* **be inherent**, be present, exist.

residence noun **1** (formal) *her private residence:* **home**, house, address; quarters, lodgings; informal pad; formal dwelling, domicile, abode. **2** *his place of residence:* **occupancy**, habitation; formal abode.

resident noun **1** *the residents of New York City:* **inhabitant**, local, citizen, native; householder, homeowner, occupier, tenant; formal denizen. **2** (Brit.) *the bar is open to residents only:* **guest**, lodger.
•adjective **1** *he is resident in the UK:* **living**, residing; formal dwelling. **2** *a resident nanny:* **live-in**. **3** *the resident registrar in obstetrics:* **permanent**, incumbent.

residual adjective **1** *residual heat:* **remaining**, leftover, unused, unconsumed. **2** *residual affection:*

lingering, enduring, abiding, surviving, vestigial.

residue noun **remainder**, rest, remains, remnant; surplus, extra, excess; leftovers.

resign verb **1** *the manager resigned:* **leave**, give notice, stand down, step down; informal quit. **2** *19 MPs resigned their seats:* **give up**, leave, vacate, stand down from; informal quit, pack in. **3** *we resigned ourselves to a wait:* **reconcile yourself to**, come to terms with.

resignation noun **1** *his resignation from his post:* **departure**, leaving, standing down, stepping down; abdication. **2** *she handed in her resignation:* **notice**. **3** *he accepted his fate with resignation:* **patience**, forbearance, stoicism, fortitude, fatalism, acceptance, acquiescence, compliance, passivity.

resigned adjective **patient**, long-suffering, uncomplaining, forbearing, stoical, philosophical, fatalistic, acquiescent, compliant.

resilient adjective **1** *resilient materials:* **flexible**, pliable, supple; durable, hard-wearing, stout, strong, sturdy, tough. **2** *young and resilient:* **strong**, tough, hardy; quick to recover, buoyant, irrepressible.

resist verb **1** *the plant will resist cold weather:* **withstand**, be proof against, combat, weather, endure, keep out, stand up to; hold off, fend off, ward off. **2** *they resisted his attempts to change things:* **oppose**, fight against, object to, defy, set your face against, kick against; obstruct, impede, hinder, block, thwart, frustrate. **3** *I resisted the urge to retort:* **refrain from**, forbear from, desist from, restrain yourself from, stop yourself from.

resistance noun **1** *his resistance to change:* **opposition**, hostility. **2** *a spirited resistance:* **opposition**, fight, stand, struggle. **3** *the French resistance:* **freedom fighters**, underground, partisans.

resistant adjective **1** *resistant to water:* **impervious**, unsusceptible, immune, invulnerable, proof against, unaffected by. **2** *resistant to change:* **opposed**, averse, hostile, inimical, against; informal anti.

resolute adjective **determined**, purposeful, resolved, adamant, single-minded, firm, unswerving, unwavering, steadfast, staunch, stalwart, unfaltering, unhesitating, persistent, indefatigable, tenacious, strong-willed, unshakeable; informal gutsy, spunky; formal pertinacious.
–OPPOSITES half-hearted.

resolution noun **1** *her resolution not to smoke:* **intention**, resolve, decision, intent, aim, plan; commitment, pledge, promise. **2** *the committee passed the resolution:* **motion**, proposal, proposition; N. Amer. resolve. **3** *she handled the work with resolution:* **determination**, purpose, resolve, single-mindedness, firmness of purpose; formal pertinacity. **4** *a satisfactory resolution of the problem:* **solution**, answer, end, settlement, conclusion.

resolve verb **1** *this matter cannot be resolved overnight:* **settle**, sort out, solve, fix, straighten out, deal with, put right, rectify; informal hammer out, thrash out, figure out.
2 *Charity resolved not to wait any longer:* **determine**, decide, make up your mind, take a decision. **3** *the committee resolved that the project should proceed:* **vote**, rule, decide formally, agree. **4** *the compounds were resolved into their active constituents:* **break down/up**, separate, reduce, divide.
• noun **1** *their intimidation merely strengthened his resolve.* See RESOLUTION sense 3. **2** (N. Amer.) *he made a resolve not to go again:* **decision**, resolution, commitment.

r

resolved adjective **determined**, hell bent, intent, set.

resonant adjective **1** *a resonant voice:* **deep**, low, sonorous, full, full-bodied, vibrant, rich, clear, ringing; loud, booming, thunderous.
2 *valleys resonant with the sound of church bells:* **reverberant**, resounding, echoing, filled.
3 *resonant words:* **evocative**, suggestive, expressive, redolent.

resort noun **1** *settle the matter without resort to legal proceedings:* **recourse to**, turning to, the use of, utilizing. **2** *strike action is our last resort:* **expedient**, measure, step, recourse, alternative, option, choice, possibility, hope.
■ **in the last resort** ultimately, in the

end, in the long run, when all is said and done. **resort to** have recourse to, fall back on, turn to, make use of, use, employ, avail yourself of.

resound verb **1** *the explosion resounded round the street:* **echo**, reverberate, ring out, boom, thunder, rumble. **2** *a large building resounding with the clang of hammers:* **reverberate**, echo, resonate, ring. **3** *nothing will resound like their earlier achievements:* **be acclaimed**, be celebrated, be renowned, be famed, be glorified, be trumpeted.

resounding adjective **1** *a resounding voice:* **reverberating**, resonating, echoing, ringing, sonorous, deep, rich, clear; loud, booming. **2** *a resounding success:* **enormous**, huge, very great, tremendous, terrific, colossal; emphatic, decisive, conclusive, outstanding, remarkable, phenomenal.

resource noun **1** *use your resources efficiently:* **assets**, funds, wealth, money, capital; staff; supplies, materials, stores, stocks, reserves. **2** *your tutor is there as a resource:* **facility**, amenity, aid, help, support. **3** *tears were her only resource:* **expedient**, resort, course, scheme, stratagem; trick, ruse, device. **4** *a person of resource:* **initiative**, resourcefulness, enterprise, ingenuity, inventiveness; talent, ability, capability; informal gumption.

resourceful adjective **ingenious**, enterprising, inventive, creative; clever, talented, able, capable.

r

respect noun **1** *the respect due to a great artist:* **esteem**, regard, high opinion, admiration, appreciation, honour, reverence, deference, veneration. **2** *his lack of respect for other people:* **consideration**, thought, thoughtfulness, regard; politeness, courtesy. **3** *the report was accurate in every respect:* **aspect**, regard, facet, feature, way, sense, particular, point, detail.
–OPPOSITES contempt, disrespect.
• verb **1** *he was highly respected by his colleagues:* **esteem**, admire, think highly of, have a high opinion of, look up to, revere, honour. **2** *they respected our privacy:* **show consideration for**, have regard for, observe, be mindful of. **3** *I respected her wishes:* **abide by**, comply with, follow, adhere to, conform to, act in accordance with, defer to, obey, observe, keep.
–OPPOSITES despise, disobey.
▪ **with respect to/in respect of** concerning, regarding, in/with regard to, with reference to, re, about, apropos, on the subject of, in connection with, vis-à-vis.

respectable adjective **1** *a respectable middle-class background:* **reputable**, upright, honest, honourable, trustworthy, decent, good, well bred, clean-living. **2** *a respectable salary:* **fairly good**, decent, fair, reasonable, moderately good.
–OPPOSITES disreputable, paltry.

respectful adjective **deferential**, reverent, dutiful; polite, well mannered, civil, courteous, gracious.
–OPPOSITES rude.

respective adjective **separate**, personal, own, particular, individual, specific, special, appropriate, different, various.

respite noun **rest**, break, breathing space, interval, intermission, interlude, recess, lull, pause, time out; relief, relaxation, repose; informal breather, let-up.

resplendent adjective **splendid**, magnificent, brilliant, dazzling, glittering, gorgeous, impressive, imposing, spectacular, striking, stunning, majestic; informal splendiferous.

respond verb **1** *they do not respond to questions:* **answer**, reply; acknowledge. **2** *'No,' she responded:* **answer**, reply, rejoin, retort, riposte, counter. **3** *they were slow to respond:* **react**, reciprocate, retaliate.

response noun **1** *his response to the question:* **answer**, reply, rejoinder, retort, riposte; informal comeback. **2** *an angry response:* **reaction**, reply, retaliation; informal comeback.
–OPPOSITES question.

responsibility noun **1** *it was his responsibility to find witnesses:* **duty**, task, function, job, role, business; Brit. informal pigeon. **2** *they denied responsibility for the attack:* **blame**, fault, guilt, culpability, liability. **3** *a sense of responsibility:*

trustworthiness, common sense, maturity, reliability, dependability. **4** *managerial responsibility:* **authority**, control, power, leadership.

responsible adjective **1** *who is responsible for prisons?* **in charge of**, in control of, at the helm of, accountable for, liable for. **2** *I am responsible for the mistake:* **accountable**, answerable, to blame, guilty, culpable, blameworthy, at fault, in the wrong. **3** *a responsible job:* **important**, powerful, executive. **4** *a responsible tenant:* **trustworthy**, sensible, mature, reliable, dependable.

responsive adjective **reactive**, receptive, open to suggestions, amenable, flexible, forthcoming.

rest[1] verb **1** *he needed to rest:* **relax**, ease up/off, let up, slow down, have/take a break, unwind, recharge your batteries, take it easy, put your feet up; lie down; informal take five, have/take a breather; N. Amer. informal chill out. **2** *his hands rested on the rail:* **lie**, be laid, repose, be placed. **3** *she rested her basket on the ground:* **support**, prop, lean, lay, set, stand, position, place, put. **4** *the film script rests on an improbable premise:* **be based**, depend, rely, hinge, turn on, be contingent, revolve around.
• noun **1** *try to get some rest:* **repose**, relaxation, leisure, respite, time off, breathing space; informal lie-down. **2** *a short rest from work:* **holiday**, break, breathing space, interval, interlude, intermission, time off/out; N. Amer. vacation; informal breather. **3** *she took the poker from its rest:* **stand**, base, holder, support, rack, frame, shelf. **4** *we came to rest 100 metres lower:* **a standstill**, a halt, a stop.

rest[2] noun *the rest of the food was thrown away:* **remainder**, remains, residue, balance, remnant, surplus, excess, leftovers.

restful adjective **relaxing**, quiet, calm, tranquil, soothing, peaceful, placid, reposeful, leisurely, undisturbed, untroubled.
– OPPOSITES exciting.

restitution noun **1** *restitution of the land seized:* **return**, restoration, handing back, surrender. **2** *restitution for the damage caused:* **compensation**, recompense, reparation, damages, indemnification, reimbursement, repayment, remuneration, redress.

restive adjective **1** *Edward is getting restive.* See RESTLESS sense 1. **2** *the militants are increasingly restive:* **unruly**, disorderly, uncontrollable, unmanageable, wilful, recalcitrant, insubordinate; Brit. informal bolshie; formal refractory.

restless adjective **1** *Maria was restless:* **uneasy**, ill at ease, restive, fidgety, edgy, tense, worked up, nervous, nervy, agitated, anxious, on tenterhooks, keyed up; informal jumpy, jittery, twitchy, uptight; Brit. informal like a cat on hot bricks. **2** *a restless night:* **sleepless**, wakeful; fitful, broken, disturbed, troubled, unsettled.

restlessness noun **unease**, restiveness, edginess, tenseness, nervousness, agitation, anxiety, fretfulness, apprehension, disquiet; informal jitteriness.

restoration noun **1** *the restoration of democracy:* **reinstatement**, reinstitution, re-establishment, reimposition, return. **2** *the restoration of derelict housing:* **repair**, fixing, mending, refurbishment, reconditioning, rehabilitation, rebuilding, reconstruction, overhaul, redevelopment, renovation; N. Amer. informal rehab.

restore verb **1** *the aim to restore democracy:* **reinstate**, bring back, reinstitute, reimpose, reinstall, re-establish. **2** *he restored the bike to its rightful owner:* **return**, give back, hand back. **3** *the building has been restored:* **repair**, fix, mend, refurbish, recondition, rehabilitate, rebuild, reconstruct, remodel, overhaul, redevelop, renovate; informal do up; N. Amer. informal rehab. **4** *a good sleep can restore you:* **reinvigorate**, revitalize, revive, refresh, energize, fortify, revivify, regenerate, stimulate, freshen.
– OPPOSITES abolish.

restrain verb **1** *he restrained his anger:* **control**, check, curb, suppress, repress, contain, dampen, subdue, rein back/in; informal keep the lid on. **2** *she could barely restrain herself from swearing:*

prevent, stop, keep, hold back. **3** *some inmates were physically restrained:* **tie up**, bind, chain, fetter, shackle, manacle.

restrained adjective **1** *Julie was quite restrained:* **self-controlled**, not given to excesses, sober, steady, unemotional, undemonstrative. **2** *restrained elegance:* **muted**, soft, discreet, subtle, quiet, unobtrusive, unostentatious, understated, tasteful.

restraint noun **1** *a restraint on their impulsiveness:* **constraint**, check, control, restriction, limitation, curtailment; rein, bridle, brake, damper, impediment, obstacle. **2** *the customary restraint of the police:* **self-control**, self-discipline, control, moderation, prudence, judiciousness. **3** *the room has been decorated with restraint:* **subtlety**, understatedness, taste, tastefulness, discretion, discrimination.

restrict verb **1** *a busy working life restricted his leisure activities:* **limit**, keep within bounds, regulate, control, moderate, cut down. **2** *the cuff supports the ankle without restricting movement:* **hinder**, interfere with, impede, hamper, obstruct, block, check, curb. **3** *he restricted himself to a 15-minute speech:* **confine**, limit.

restricted adjective **1** *restricted space:* **cramped**, confined, constricted, small, narrow, tight. **2** *a restricted calorie intake:* **limited**, controlled, regulated, reduced. **3** *restricted information:* **secret**, classified, private; informal hush-hush.
– OPPOSITES unlimited.

restriction noun **1** *there is no restriction on the number of places:* **limitation**, constraint, control, check, curb; condition, proviso, qualification. **2** *the restriction of personal freedom:* **reduction**, limitation, diminution, curtailment. **3** *restriction of movement:* **hindrance**, impediment, slowing, reduction, limitation.

result noun **1** *stress is the result of overwork:* **consequence**, outcome, upshot, sequel, effect, reaction, repercussion, ramification, conclusion, culmination. **2** *what is your result?* **answer**, solution; sum, total, product. **3** *exam results:* **mark**, score, grade. **4** *the result of the trial:* **verdict**, decision, outcome, conclusion, judgement, findings, ruling.
– OPPOSITES cause.
• verb **1** *differences between species could result from their habitat:* **follow**, ensue, develop, stem, spring, arise, derive, evolve, proceed; occur, happen, take place, come about; be caused by, be produced by, originate in, be consequent on. **2** *the shooting resulted in five deaths:* **end in**, culminate in, finish in, terminate in, lead to, prompt, precipitate, trigger; cause, bring about, occasion, effect, give rise to, produce, engender, generate; literary beget.

resume verb **1** *the government resumed negotiations:* **restart**, recommence, begin again, start again, reopen; renew, return to, continue with, carry on with. **2** *the priest resumed his kneeling posture:* **return to**, come back to, take up again, reoccupy.
– OPPOSITES suspend, abandon.

résumé noun **summary**, precis, synopsis, abstract, outline, summarization, summation, epitome; abridgement, digest, condensation, abbreviation, overview, review.

resumption noun **restart**, recommencement, reopening; continuation, carrying on, renewal, return to.

resurgence noun **renewal**, revival, recovery, comeback, reawakening, resurrection, reappearance, re-emergence, regeneration; resumption, recommencement, continuation; formal renascence.

resurrect verb *an attempt to resurrect his career:* **revive**, restore, regenerate, revitalize, breathe new life into, reinvigorate, resuscitate, rejuvenate, stimulate, re-establish, relaunch.

resuscitate verb **1** *medics resuscitated him:* **bring round**, revive; give artificial respiration to, give the kiss of life to. **2** *measures to resuscitate the economy:* **revive**, resurrect, restore, regenerate, revitalize, breathe new life into, reinvigorate, rejuvenate, stimulate.

retain verb **1** *drain the beans and retain the water:* **keep**, hold on to, hang on to, conserve, save; maintain, preserve. **2** *some students retain facts easily:* **remember**, memorize, absorb.
– OPPOSITES lose, forget.

retainer noun *a faithful retainer.* See **SERVANT**.

retaliate verb **fight back**, hit back, respond, react, reply, reciprocate, counter-attack, get back at someone, give tit for tat; have/get/ take your revenge, avenge yourself, take reprisals, get even, pay someone back; informal get your own back.

retaliation noun **revenge**, vengeance, reprisal, retribution, requital, recrimination, repayment; response, reaction, reply, counter-attack.

retard verb **delay**, slow down/up, hold back/up, set back, postpone, put back, detain, decelerate; hinder, hamper, obstruct, inhibit, impede, check, restrain, restrict, trammel.
– OPPOSITES accelerate.

retch verb *the taste made her retch:* gag, heave.

reticence noun **reserve**, restraint, inhibition, diffidence, shyness; unresponsiveness, quietness, taciturnity.

reticent adjective **reserved**, withdrawn, introverted, inhibited, diffident, shy; uncommunicative, unforthcoming, unresponsive, tight-lipped, quiet, taciturn, silent.
– OPPOSITES expansive.

retinue noun **entourage**, escort, company, court, staff, personnel, household, train, suite, following, bodyguard.

retire verb **1** *he has retired:* **give up work**, stop work. **2** *we've retired him on full pension:* **pension off**, force to retire. **3** *Gillian retired to her office:* **withdraw**, go away, take yourself off, decamp, shut yourself away; formal repair. **4** *everyone retired early:* **go to bed**, call it a day; informal turn in, hit the hay/sack.

retirement noun **1** *they are nearing retirement:* **giving up work**, stopping work. **2** *retirement in an English village:* **seclusion**, retreat, solitude, isolation, obscurity.

retiring adjective **1** *the retiring president:* **departing**, outgoing. **2** *a retiring man:* **shy**, diffident, self-effacing, unassuming, unassertive, reserved, reticent, quiet, timid, modest.
– OPPOSITES incoming, outgoing.

retort verb *'Oh, sure,' she retorted:* **answer**, reply, respond, return, counter, rejoin, riposte, retaliate.

retract verb **1** *the sea otter can retract its claws:* **pull in/back**, draw in. **2** *he retracted his allegation:* **take back**, withdraw, recant, disavow, disclaim, repudiate, renounce, reverse, revoke, rescind, go back on, backtrack on; formal abjure.

retreat verb **1** *the army retreated:* **withdraw**, retire, draw back, pull back/out, fall back, give way, give ground. **2** *the tide was retreating:* **go out**, ebb, recede, fall, go down. **3** *the government had to retreat:* **change your mind**; back down, climb down, do a U-turn, backtrack, back-pedal, give in, concede defeat; Brit. do an about-turn.
– OPPOSITES advance.
• noun **1** *the retreat of the army:* **withdrawal**, pulling back. **2** *the President's retreat:* **climbdown**, backdown, about-face; Brit. about-turn. **3** *her rural retreat:* **refuge**, haven, sanctuary; hideaway, hideout, hiding place; informal hidey-hole. **4** *a period of retreat from the world:* **seclusion**, withdrawal, retirement, solitude, isolation, sanctuary.

retrench verb **economize**, cut back, make savings, make economies, be frugal, tighten your belt.

retribution noun **punishment**, penalty, your just deserts; revenge, reprisal, requital, retaliation, vengeance, an eye for an eye (and a tooth for a tooth), tit for tat; redress, reparation, restitution, recompense, repayment, indemnification, atonement, amends.

retrieve verb **1** *I retrieved my property:* **get back**, recover, regain, recoup, reclaim, repossess, redeem; find, locate. **2** *one last attempt to retrieve the situation:* **put right**, rectify, remedy, restore, sort out, straighten out, resolve.

retrograde adjective **1** *a retrograde step:* **for the worse**, regressive,

negative, downhill, unwelcome. **2** *retrograde motion:* **backward**, reverse, rearward.
– OPPOSITES positive.

retrospective adjective **backdated**, retroactive, ex post facto.

return verb **1** *he returned to London:* **go back**, come back, arrive back, come home, retrace your steps. **2** *the symptoms returned:* **recur**, reoccur, repeat itself; reappear, re-emerge. **3** *Peter returned the book to the shelf:* **restore**, put back, replace, reinstall. **4** *she returned his love:* **reciprocate**, requite, repay, give back. **5** *the jury returned a unanimous verdict:* **deliver**, bring in, hand down.
– OPPOSITES leave, depart.
• noun **1** *the return of hard times:* **recurrence**, reoccurrence, repeat, repetition, reappearance, revival, resurrection, re-emergence, resurgence. **2** *the return of democracy:* replacement, restoration, reinstatement, restitution. **3** *a quick return on investments:* **yield**, profit, gain, revenue, interest, dividend. **4** *a census return:* **statement**, report, submission, record, dossier; document, form.
– OPPOSITES departure.

revamp verb **renovate**, redecorate, refurbish, recondition, rehabilitate, overhaul, make over; upgrade, refit, re-equip; remodel, refashion, redesign, restyle; informal do up, give something a facelift, vamp up; Brit. informal tart up; N. Amer. informal rehab.

r

reveal verb **1** *she revealed his whereabouts to the press:* **divulge**, disclose, tell, let slip/drop, give away/out, blurt out, release, leak; make known, make public, broadcast, publicize, circulate, disseminate; informal let on. **2** *the company has revealed its new fashion ranges:* **show**, display, exhibit, unveil.
– OPPOSITES hide.

revel verb **1** *they revelled all night:* **celebrate**, make merry, carouse, roister; informal party, live it up, whoop it up, make whoopee, rave, paint the town red. **2** *he revelled in the applause:* **enjoy**, delight in, love, like, adore, take pleasure in, appreciate, relish, lap up, savour; informal get a kick out of.
• noun *late-night revels:* **celebration**, festivity, jollification, merrymaking, carousal, carouse, spree; party, jamboree; informal rave, shindig, bash; Brit. informal rave-up, knees-up; N. Amer. informal wingding, blast.

revelation noun **1** *revelations about his personal life:* **disclosure**, announcement, report; admission, confession. **2** *the revelation of a secret:* **divulgence**, disclosure, letting slip/drop, giving away/out, leak, betrayal, unveiling, making known, making public, broadcasting, publicizing, dissemination, report, declaration.

reveller noun **merrymaker**, partygoer, carouser, roisterer.

revelry noun **celebration**, festivity, jollification, merrymaking, carousal, roistering; informal partying.

revenge noun **1** *she is seeking revenge:* **vengeance**, retribution, retaliation, reprisal, requital, recrimination, an eye for an eye (and a tooth for a tooth), redress, satisfaction. **2** *they were filled with revenge:* **vengefulness**, vindictiveness, vitriol, spite, malice, malevolence, ill will, animosity, hate, rancour, bitterness.
• verb **1** *he revenged his brother's murder:* **avenge**, exact retribution for, take reprisals for, get redress for. **2** *I'll be revenged on the whole pack of you:* **avenge yourself on**, take vengeance on, get even with, settle a/the score with, pay back, take reprisals against; informal get your own back on.

revenue noun **income**, takings, receipts, proceeds, earnings, profits.
– OPPOSITES expenditure.

reverberate verb **resound**, echo, resonate, ring, boom, rumble.

reverberation noun **1** *natural reverberation:* **resonance**, echo, resounding, ringing, booming, rumbling. **2** *political reverberations:* **repercussions**, ramifications, consequences, shock waves; aftermath, fallout, backlash.

revere verb **respect**, admire, think highly of, esteem, look up to.
– OPPOSITES despise.

reverence noun **high esteem**, high regard, great respect, acclaim,

admiration, appreciation, estimation, favour.
– OPPOSITES scorn.

reverent adjective **respectful**, admiring, devoted, devout, dutiful, awed, deferential.

reverie noun **daydream**, trance, musing; inattention, inattentiveness, wool-gathering, preoccupation, absorption, abstraction.

reversal noun **1** *there was no reversal on this issue:* **turnaround**, turnabout, about-face, volte-face, change of heart, U-turn, backtracking; Brit. about-turn. **2** *a reversal of roles:* **swap**, exchange, change, interchange. **3** *the reversal of the decision:* **alteration**, changing; countermanding, undoing, overturning, overthrow, disallowing, overriding, overruling, veto, revocation, repeal, rescinding, annulment, nullification, voiding, invalidation; formal rescission, abrogation. **4** *they suffered a reversal:* **setback**, upset, failure, misfortune, mishap, disaster, blow, disappointment, adversity, hardship, affliction, vicissitude, defeat.

reverse verb **1** *the car reversed:* **back**, move back/backwards. **2** *they have reversed their roles:* **swap**, change round, exchange, interchange, switch. **3** *the decision was reversed by the Court of Appeal:* **overturn**, overthrow, override, overrule, retract, revoke, rescind, annul, nullify, void, invalidate; change; Brit. do an about-turn on; formal abrogate.
• noun **1** *the reverse is the case:* **opposite**, contrary, converse, inverse, obverse, antithesis. **2** *successes and reverses.* See REVERSAL sense 4. **3** *the reverse of the page:* **other side**, back, underside, verso, obverse.

revert verb **1** *life will soon revert to normal:* **return**, go back, change back, default; fall back, regress, relapse. **2** *the property reverted to the landlord:* **be returned**.

review noun **1** *the Council undertook a review:* **analysis**, evaluation, assessment, appraisal, examination, investigation, inquiry, probe, inspection, study. **2** *the rent is due for review:* **reconsideration**, reassessment, re-evaluation, reappraisal; change, alteration, modification, revision. **3** *book reviews:* **criticism**, critique, assessment, evaluation, commentary; Brit. informal crit. **4** *a scientific review:* **journal**, periodical, magazine, publication. **5** *their review of the economy:* **survey**, report, study, account, description, statement, overview.
• verb **1** *I reviewed the evidence:* **survey**, study, research, consider, analyse, examine, scrutinize, explore, look into, probe, investigate, inspect, assess, appraise; informal size up. **2** *the referee reviewed his decision:* **reconsider**, re-examine, reassess, re-evaluate, reappraise, rethink; change, alter, modify, revise. **3** *he reviewed the day:* **remember**, recall, reflect on, think through, go over in your mind, look back on. **4** *she reviewed the play:* **comment on**, evaluate, assess, appraise, judge, critique, criticize.

reviewer noun **critic**, **commentator**, judge, observer, pundit, analyst.

revile verb **criticize**, censure, condemn, attack, inveigh against, rail against, lambaste, denounce; slander, libel, malign, vilify, besmirch, abuse; informal knock, slam, pan, crucify, roast, bad-mouth; Brit. informal slate, rubbish, slag off; N. Amer. informal pummel; formal excoriate.
– OPPOSITES praise.

revise verb **1** *she revised her opinion:* **reconsider**, review, re-examine, reassess, re-evaluate, reappraise, rethink; change, alter, modify. **2** *the editor revised the text:* **amend**, emend, correct, alter, change, edit, rewrite, redraft, rephrase, rework. **3** (Brit.) *revise your lecture notes carefully:* **go over**, reread, memorize; cram; informal bone up on; Brit. informal swot up on, mug up on.

revision noun **1** *a major revision of the system:* **reconsideration**, review, re-examination, reassessment, re-evaluation, reappraisal, rethink; change, amendment, alteration, modification, recasting. **2** (Brit.) *he was doing some revision:* **studying**, cramming; Brit. informal swotting.

revitalize verb **reinvigorate**,

re-energize, boost, regenerate, revive, revivify, rejuvenate, reanimate, resuscitate, refresh, stimulate, breathe new life into; informal give a shot in the arm to, pep up, buck up.

revival noun **1** *a revival in the economy:* **improvement**, rallying, picking up, amelioration, turn for the better, upturn, upswing, resurgence. **2** *the revival of traditional crafts:* **comeback**, re-establishment, reintroduction, restoration, reappearance, resurrection, regeneration, rejuvenation.
– OPPOSITES downturn, disappearance.

revive verb **1** *attempts to revive her failed:* **resuscitate**, bring round, wake up. **2** *a cup of tea revived her:* **reinvigorate**, revitalize, refresh, energize, reanimate, resuscitate, revivify, rejuvenate, regenerate, enliven, stimulate. **3** *we are reviving many of the old traditions:* **reintroduce**, re-establish, restore, resurrect, bring back, regenerate, resuscitate.

revoke verb **cancel**, repeal, rescind, reverse, annul, nullify, void, invalidate, countermand, retract, withdraw, overrule, override; formal abrogate.

revolt verb **1** *the people revolted:* **rebel**, rise up, take to the streets, riot, mutiny. **2** *the smell revolted him:* **disgust**, sicken, nauseate, repel, turn someone's stomach, put off, be offensive to; informal turn off; N. Amer. informal gross out.
• noun *an armed revolt:* **rebellion**, revolution, insurrection, mutiny, uprising, riot, insurgence, seizure of power, coup, coup d'état.

revolting adjective **disgusting**, sickening, nauseating, stomach-turning, repulsive, repellent, repugnant, appalling, abominable, hideous, horrible, awful, dreadful, terrible, obnoxious, vile, nasty, foul, loathsome, offensive, objectionable; N. Amer. vomitous; informal ghastly, putrid, horrid, gross; literary noisome.
– OPPOSITES attractive, pleasant.

revolution noun **1** *the French Revolution:* **rebellion**, revolt, insurrection, mutiny, uprising, riot, insurgence, coup, coup d'état. **2** *a revolution in printing techniques:* **transformation**, sea change, metamorphosis, change, innovation, reorganization, restructuring; informal shake-up; N. Amer. informal shakedown. **3** *one revolution of a wheel:* **turn**, rotation, circle, spin; circuit, lap; orbit.

revolutionary adjective **1** *revolutionary troops:* **rebellious**, insurgent, rioting, mutinous, renegade, insurrectionary, seditious, subversive, extremist. **2** *revolutionary change:* **thoroughgoing**, complete, total, absolute, utter, comprehensive, sweeping, far-reaching, extensive, profound. **3** *a revolutionary kind of wheelchair:* **new**, novel, original, unusual, unconventional, unorthodox, newfangled, innovatory, modern, state-of-the-art, futuristic, pioneering.
• noun *political revolutionaries:* **rebel**, insurgent, mutineer, insurrectionist, agitator, subversive.

revolutionize verb **transform**, shake up, turn upside down, restructure, reorganize, transmute, metamorphose; humorous transmogrify.

revolve verb **1** *a fan revolved slowly:* **go round**, turn round, rotate, spin. **2** *the moon revolves around the earth:* **circle**, travel, orbit. **3** *his life revolves around cars:* **be concerned with**, be preoccupied with, focus on, centre around.

revulsion noun **disgust**, repulsion, abhorrence, repugnance, nausea, horror, aversion, abomination, distaste.
– OPPOSITES delight.

reward noun *a reward for its safe return:* **recompense**, prize, award, honour, decoration, bonus, premium, bounty, present, gift, payment; informal pay-off, perk; formal perquisite.
• verb *they were well rewarded:* **recompense**, pay, remunerate.
– OPPOSITES punish.

rewarding adjective **satisfying**, gratifying, pleasing, fulfilling, enriching, edifying, beneficial, illuminating, worthwhile, productive, fruitful.

reword verb **rewrite**, rephrase, recast, redraft, revise; paraphrase.

r

rewrite verb **revise**, recast, reword, rephrase, redraft.

rhetoric noun **1** *a form of rhetoric:* **oratory**, eloquence, command of language, way with words. **2** *empty rhetoric:* **bombast**, turgidity, grandiloquence, magniloquence, pomposity, extravagant language, purple prose; wordiness, verbosity, prolixity; informal hot air.

rhetorical adjective **1** *rhetorical devices:* **stylistic**, oratorical, linguistic, verbal. **2** *rhetorical hyperbole:* **extravagant**, grandiloquent, magniloquent, high-flown, orotund, bombastic, grandiose, pompous, pretentious, overblown, oratorical, turgid, flowery, florid; informal highfalutin.

rhyme noun **poem**, verse; (**rhymes**) poetry, doggerel.

rhythm noun **1** *the rhythm of the music:* **beat**, cadence, tempo, time, pulse, throb, swing. **2** *poetic features such as rhythm:* **metre**, measure, stress, accent, cadence. **3** *the rhythm of daily life:* **pattern**, flow, tempo.

rhythmic adjective **rhythmical**, measured, throbbing, beating, pulsating, regular, steady, even.

ribald adjective. See CRUDE sense 3.

rich adjective **1** *rich people:* **wealthy**, affluent, moneyed, well off, well-to-do, prosperous, opulent; N. Amer. silk-stocking; informal rolling in money, loaded, well heeled, made of money. **2** *rich furnishings:* **sumptuous**, opulent, luxurious, deluxe, lavish, gorgeous, splendid, magnificent, costly, expensive, fancy; informal posh, plush, ritzy, swanky, classy; Brit. informal swish; N. Amer. informal swank. **3** *a garden rich in flowers:* **abounding**, well provided, well stocked, crammed, packed, teeming, bursting; informal jam-packed, chock-a-block; Austral./NZ informal chocker. **4** *a rich supply of restaurants:* **plentiful**, abundant, copious, ample, profuse, lavish, liberal, generous, bountiful; literary plenteous, bounteous. **5** *rich soil:* **fertile**, productive, fecund, fruitful. **6** *a rich sauce:* **creamy**, fatty, heavy, full-flavoured. **7** *a rich wine:* **full-bodied**, heavy, fruity. **8** *rich colours:* **strong**, deep, full, intense, vivid, brilliant. **9** *her rich voice:* **sonorous**, full, resonant, deep, clear, mellow, mellifluous.
–OPPOSITES poor, light.

riches plural noun **1** *his new-found riches:* **money**, wealth, funds, cash, filthy lucre, wherewithal, means, assets, capital, resources, reserves; opulence, affluence, prosperity; informal dough, bread, loot, readies; Brit. informal dosh, brass, lolly, spondulicks; N. Amer. informal bucks; US informal greenbacks. **2** *underwater riches:* **resources**, treasure, bounty, jewels, gems.

richly adverb **1** *the richly furnished chamber:* **sumptuously**, opulently, luxuriously, lavishly, gorgeously, splendidly, magnificently. **2** *the joy she richly deserves:* **fully**, thoroughly, well, completely, wholly, totally, entirely, absolutely, amply, utterly.
–OPPOSITES meanly.

rickety adjective **shaky**, unsteady, unsound, unsafe, tumbledown, broken-down, dilapidated, ramshackle.

rid verb **clear**, free, purge, empty, strip.
■ **get rid of 1** *we must get rid of some stuff:* dispose of, throw away/out, clear out, discard, scrap, dump, bin, jettison; informal chuck away, ditch, junk; Brit. informal get shot of; N. Amer. informal trash. **2** *the cats got rid of the rats:* destroy, eliminate, annihilate, obliterate, wipe out, kill.

riddle[1] noun **puzzle**, conundrum, brain-teaser, problem, question, poser, enigma, mystery.

riddle[2] verb **1** *his car was riddled by gunfire:* **perforate**, hole, pierce, puncture, pepper. **2** *he was riddled with cancer:* **permeate**, suffuse, fill, pervade, spread through, imbue, saturate, overrun, beset.

ride verb **1** *he taught me to ride a bike when I was six:* **manage**, handle, control; use, operate, work. **2** *they ride round the town on motor bikes:* **travel**, drive, cycle, pedal; roar, speed, hurtle.
• noun *he took us out for a ride:* **trip**, journey, drive, run, excursion, outing, jaunt; lift; informal spin.

ridicule noun *he was subjected to ridicule:* **mockery**, derision, laughter, scorn, scoffing, contempt,

jeering, sneering, jibes, teasing, taunts, ragging, chaffing; informal kidding, ribbing, joshing.
– OPPOSITES respect.
• verb *his theory was ridiculed:* **deride**, mock, laugh at, heap scorn on, jeer at, jibe at, sneer at, scorn, make fun of, scoff at, satirize, lampoon, burlesque, caricature, parody, tease, taunt, rag, chaff; informal kid, rib, josh, take the mickey out of.

ridiculous adjective **1** *that looks ridiculous:* **laughable**, absurd, comical, funny, hilarious, risible, droll, amusing, farcical, silly, ludicrous. **2** *a ridiculous suggestion:* **senseless**, silly, foolish, foolhardy, stupid, inane, fatuous, half-baked, hare-brained, ill-thought-out, crackpot, idiotic. **3** *a ridiculous exaggeration:* **absurd**, preposterous, ludicrous, laughable, risible, nonsensical, senseless, outrageous.
– OPPOSITES sensible.

rife adjective **1** *violence is rife:* **widespread**, general, common, universal, extensive, ubiquitous, omnipresent, endemic, inescapable, insidious, prevalent. **2** *the village was rife with gossip:* **overflowing**, bursting, alive, teeming, abounding.
– OPPOSITES unknown.

rifle verb **1** *she rifled through her wardrobe:* **rummage**, search, hunt, forage. **2** *a thief rifled her home:* **burgle**, rob, steal from, loot, raid, plunder, ransack.

rift noun **1** *a deep rift in the ice:* **crack**, fault, flaw, split, break, breach, fissure, fracture, cleft, crevice, cavity, opening. **2** *the rift between them:* **breach**, division, split; quarrel, squabble, disagreement, falling-out, argument, dispute, conflict, feud; Brit. row; informal spat, scrap; Brit. informal bust-up.

rig[1] verb **1** *the boats were rigged with a single sail:* **equip**, kit out, fit out, supply, furnish, provide, arm. **2** *I rigged myself out in black:* **dress**, clothe, attire, robe, garb, array, deck out, drape, accoutre, outfit, get up; informal doll up. **3** *he will rig up a shelter:* **set up**, erect, assemble; throw together, cobble together, put together, whip up, improvise, contrive; Brit. informal knock up.
• noun **1** *a CB radio rig:* **apparatus**, appliance, machine, device, instrument, contraption, system. **2** *the rig of the American Army Air Corps:* **uniform**, costume, ensemble, outfit, livery, attire, clothes, garments, dress, garb, regimentals, regalia, trappings; Brit. strip; informal get-up, gear, togs; Brit. informal kit; formal apparel.

rig[2] verb *they rigged the election:* **manipulate**, engineer, distort, misrepresent, pervert, tamper with, doctor; falsify, fake, trump up; informal fix; Brit. informal fiddle.

right adjective **1** *you've done the right thing:* **just**, fair, proper, good, moral, ethical, honourable, honest; lawful, legal. **2** *the right answer:* **correct**, accurate, exact, precise; Brit. informal spot on. **3** *the right person for the job:* **suitable**, appropriate, fitting, correct, proper, desirable, preferable, ideal. **4** *I was waiting for the right moment:* **opportune**, advantageous, favourable, propitious, good, lucky, happy, fortunate, providential, felicitous. **5** *he's not right in the head:* **sane**, lucid, rational, balanced, compos mentis; informal all there. **6** *on my right side:* Nautical starboard; Heraldry dexter.
– OPPOSITES wrong, left.
• adverb **1** *I'm right out of ideas:* **completely**, fully, totally, absolutely, utterly, thoroughly, quite. **2** *the hotel's right in the middle of the village:* **exactly**, precisely, directly, immediately, just, squarely, dead; informal slap bang, smack, plumb. **3** *keep going right on:* **straight**, directly, as the crow flies. **4** *I think I heard right:* **correctly**, accurately, properly.
• noun **1** *the difference between right and wrong:* **justice**, fairness, equity, virtue, integrity, rectitude, propriety, morality, honesty, honour. **2** *you have the right to say no:* **entitlement**, prerogative, privilege, birthright, liberty, authority, power, licence, permission, dispensation, leave, sanction.
– OPPOSITES wrong.
• verb *we must do what we can to right the situation:* **remedy**, rectify, retrieve, fix, resolve, sort out, settle, square; straighten out, correct, repair, mend, redress, make good, ameliorate, better.

r

■ **put something to rights**. See RIGHT verb. **right away** at once, straight away, now, this minute, this instant, immediately, instantly, directly, forthwith, without further ado, promptly, quickly, without delay, asap, as soon as possible; N. Amer. in short order; informal pdq (pretty damn quick), pronto. **within your rights** entitled, permitted, allowed, at liberty, justified.

righteous adjective **1** *righteous living:* **good**, virtuous, upright, upstanding, decent; ethical, principled, moral, high-minded, law-abiding, honest, honourable, blameless, irreproachable, noble. **2** *righteous anger:* **justifiable**, legitimate, defensible, supportable, rightful.
– OPPOSITES sinful, unjustifiable.

rightful adjective **1** *the car's rightful owner:* **legal**, lawful, real, true, proper, correct, recognized, genuine, authentic, acknowledged, approved, licensed, valid, bona fide; informal legit, kosher. **2** *their rightful place in society:* **deserved**, merited, due, just, right, fair, proper, fitting, appropriate, suitable.
– OPPOSITES wrongful.

right-wing adjective **conservative**, rightist, blimpish, diehard; reactionary, traditionalist, conventional, unprogressive.
– OPPOSITES left-wing.

rigid adjective **1** *a rigid container:* **stiff**, hard, firm, inflexible, unbending, unyielding, inelastic. **2** *a rigid routine:* **fixed**, set, firm, inflexible, unalterable, unchangeable, immutable, unvarying, invariable, hard and fast, cast-iron. **3** *a rigid approach to funding:* **strict**, severe, stern, stringent, rigorous, inflexible, uncompromising, intransigent.
– OPPOSITES flexible, lenient.

rigmarole noun **1** *the rigmarole of dressing up:* **fuss**, bother, trouble, folderol, ado; informal palaver, song and dance, performance, to-do, pantomime, hassle; Brit. informal carry-on. **2** *that rigmarole about the house being haunted:* **tale**, saga, yarn, shaggy-dog story; informal spiel.

rigorous adjective **1** *rigorous attention to detail:* **meticulous**, conscientious, punctilious, careful, diligent, attentive, scrupulous, painstaking, exact, precise, accurate, thorough, particular, strict, demanding, exacting; informal pernickety. **2** *the rigorous enforcement of rules:* **strict**, severe, stern, stringent, tough, harsh, rigid, relentless, unsparing, inflexible, draconian, intransigent, uncompromising, exacting. **3** *rigorous conditions:* **harsh**, severe, bad, bleak, extreme, inclement; unpleasant, disagreeable, foul, nasty, filthy.
– OPPOSITES slapdash, lax, mild.

rigour noun **1** *a mine operated under conditions of rigour:* **strictness**, severity, stringency, toughness, harshness, rigidity, inflexibility, intransigence. **2** *intellectual rigour:* **meticulousness**, thoroughness, carefulness, diligence, scrupulousness, exactness, exactitude, precision, accuracy, correctness, strictness. **3** *the rigours of the journey:* **hardship**, harshness, severity, adversity; ordeal, misery, trial.

rim noun **1** *the rim of her cup:* **brim**, edge, lip. **2** *the rim of the crater:* **edge**, border, side, margin, brink, fringe, boundary, perimeter, circumference, limits, periphery.

rind noun **skin**, peel, zest, integument.

ring[1] noun **1** *a ring round the moon:* **circle**, band, halo, disc; technical annulus. **2** *a circus ring:* **arena**, enclosure, field, ground. **3** *a spy ring:* **gang**, syndicate, cartel, mob, band, circle, organization, association, society, alliance, league, coterie, cabal.
• verb *police ringed the building:* **surround**, circle, encircle, encompass, girdle, enclose, hem in, confine, seal off.

ring[2] verb **1** *church bells rang:* **toll**, sound, peal, chime, clang, bong; literary knell. **2** *the room rang with laughter:* **resound**, reverberate, resonate, echo. **3** *I'll ring you tomorrow:* **telephone**, phone, call; informal give someone a buzz; Brit. informal give someone a bell, give someone a tinkle, get on the blower to.

rinse verb **wash**, clean, cleanse, bathe; dip, drench, splash, swill, sluice, hose down.

riot noun **uproar**, disturbance,

disorder, commotion, upheaval, furore, tumult, melee, turmoil, fracas, fray, brawl, free-for-all; uprising, insurrection, revolt, violence, fighting, anarchy, lawlessness.
• verb **go on the rampage**, run riot, run amok, go berserk; rise up, revolt; informal raise hell.

riotous adjective **1** *a riotous demonstration:* **unruly**, rowdy, disorderly, uncontrollable, unmanageable, undisciplined, uproarious, tumultuous; violent, wild, ugly, lawless, anarchic. **2** *a riotous party:* **boisterous**, lively, loud, noisy, unrestrained, uninhibited, uproarious; Brit. informal rumbustious.
– OPPOSITES peaceable.

rip verb **1** *he ripped the posters down:* **tear**, wrench, wrest, pull, snatch, tug, prise, heave, drag, peel, pluck; informal yank. **2** *she ripped Leo's note into pieces:* **tear**, claw, hack, slit, cut; literary rend.

ripe adjective **1** *a ripe tomato:* **mature**, full grown. **2** *the dock is ripe for development:* **ready**, fit, suitable, right. **3** *the ripe old age of ninety:* **advanced**, hoary, venerable, old. **4** *the time is ripe for his return:* **opportune**, advantageous, favourable, auspicious, propitious, promising, good, right, fortunate, benign, providential, felicitous, seasonable.
– OPPOSITES unsuitable, young.

ripen verb **mature**, mellow.

riposte noun **retort**, counter, rejoinder, sally, return, answer, reply, response; informal comeback.

ripple noun **wavelet**, wave, undulation, ridge.

rise verb **1** *clouds of smoke rose into the air:* **go up**, ascend, climb, mount, soar. **2** *he rose from his chair:* **stand up**, get up, jump up, leap up, spring up; formal arise. **3** *prices rose:* **increase**, go up, soar, shoot up, surge, leap, jump, rocket, escalate. **4** *living standards have risen:* **improve**, get better, advance, go up, soar. **5** *the noise rose to a crescendo:* **grow**, increase, swell, intensify. **6** *he rose at dawn:* **get up**, rouse yourself, stir, bestir yourself; informal surface; formal arise. **7** *the Rhine rises in the Alps:* **originate**, begin, start, emerge; issue from, spring from, flow from, emanate from. **8** *the nation rose against its oppressors:* **rebel**, revolt, mutiny, riot, take up arms. **9** *the ground rose gently:* **slope**, incline, climb. **10** *mountains rose above us:* **tower**, rear up, soar, loom.
– OPPOSITES fall, descend, drop.
• noun **1** *a price rise:* **increase**, hike, leap, upsurge, upswing, climb, escalation. **2** *he got a rise of 11%:* **raise**, pay increase; hike, increment. **3** *a rise in standards:* **improvement**, amelioration, upturn, leap. **4** *his rise to power:* **progress**, climb, promotion, elevation, aggrandizement. **5** *we walked up the rise:* **slope**, incline, acclivity, hillock, hill.

risible adjective **laughable**, ridiculous, absurd, comical, amusing, funny, hilarious, humorous, droll, farcical, silly, ludicrous, hysterical; informal rib-tickling, priceless.

risk noun **1** *there is a certain amount of risk:* **chance**, uncertainty, unpredictability, precariousness, instability, insecurity, perilousness. **2** *the risk of fire:* **possibility**, chance, probability, likelihood, danger, peril, threat, menace, fear, prospect.
– OPPOSITES safety.
• verb *he risked his life to save them:* **endanger**, imperil, jeopardize, hazard, gamble with, chance; put on the line, put in jeopardy.
■ **at risk** in danger, in peril, in jeopardy, under threat.

risky adjective **dangerous**, hazardous, perilous, unsafe, insecure, precarious, parlous, touch-and-go, treacherous; uncertain, unpredictable; informal chancy, dicey, hairy; N. Amer. informal gnarly.

risqué adjective **ribald**, rude, bawdy, racy, earthy, indecent, suggestive, improper, naughty, locker-room; vulgar, dirty, smutty, crude, coarse, obscene, lewd, X-rated; informal blue, raunchy; Brit. informal fruity, off colour, saucy; euphemistic adult.

rite noun **ceremony**, ritual, ceremonial; service, sacrament, liturgy, worship, office; act, practice, custom, tradition, convention.

ritual noun *an elaborate civic ritual:* **ceremony**, rite, observance; service, sacrament, liturgy; act, practice,

custom, tradition, convention, formality, procedure, protocol.
• **adjective** *a ritual burial:* **ceremonial**, prescribed, set, formal; sacramental, liturgical; traditional, conventional.

rival **noun 1** *his rival for the nomination:* **opponent**, challenger, competitor, contender; adversary, antagonist, enemy; literary foe. **2** *the tool has no rival:* **equal**, match, peer, equivalent, counterpart, like.
– OPPOSITES ally.
• **verb** *few countries can rival it for scenery:* **match**, compare with, compete with, vie with, equal, measure up to, be in the same league as, be on a par with, touch, challenge; informal hold a candle to.
• **adjective** *rival candidates:* **competing**, opposing, contending.

rivalry **noun** **competitiveness**, competition, contention, vying; opposition, conflict, feuding, antagonism, friction, enmity; informal keeping up with the Joneses.

river **noun 1** **watercourse**, waterway, tributary, stream, rivulet, brook, inlet; Scottish & N. English burn; N. English beck; S. English bourn; N. Amer. & Austral./NZ creek; Austral. billabong. **2** *a river of molten lava:* **stream**, torrent, flood, deluge, cascade.

> **WORD LINKS**
> **fluvial** relating to rivers
> **riparian**, **riverine** relating to or situated on the banks of a river

riveted **adjective 1** *she stood riveted to the spot:* **fixed**, rooted, frozen, unable to move. **2** *he was riveted by the newsreels:* **fascinated**, engrossed, gripped, captivated, enthralled, spellbound, mesmerized, transfixed. **3** *their eyes were riveted on the teacher:* **fixed**, fastened, focused, concentrated, locked.
– OPPOSITES bored.

riveting **adjective** **fascinating**, gripping, engrossing, interesting, intriguing, absorbing, captivating, enthralling, compelling, spellbinding, mesmerizing; informal unputdownable.
– OPPOSITES boring.

road **noun 1** *the roads were crowded:* **street**, thoroughfare, roadway, avenue, broadway, bypass, ring road, trunk road, byroad; Brit. dual carriageway, clearway, motorway; N. Amer. highway, freeway, parkway, throughway, expressway; US turnpike, interstate. **2** *a step on the road to recovery:* **way**, path, route, course.
■ **on the road** on tour, travelling.

roam **verb** **wander**, rove, ramble, drift, walk, traipse; range, travel, tramp, traverse, trek; Scottish & Irish stravaig; informal cruise, mosey; formal perambulate.

roar **noun 1** *the roars of the crowd:* **shout**, bellow, yell, cry, howl; clamour; informal holler. **2** *the roar of the sea:* **boom**, crash, rumble, roll, thundering. **3** *roars of laughter:* **guffaw**, howl, hoot, shriek, gale, peal.
• **verb 1** *'Get out!' roared Angus:* **bellow**, yell, shout, bawl, howl; informal holler. **2** *thunder roared:* **boom**, rumble, crash, roll, thunder. **3** *the movie left them roaring:* **guffaw**, laugh, hoot; informal split your sides, be rolling in the aisles, be doubled up, crack up, be in stitches; Brit. informal crease up, fall about.

roast **verb** **cook**, bake, grill; N. Amer. broil.

rob **verb 1** *the gang robbed a bank:* **burgle**, steal from, hold up, break into; raid, loot, plunder, pillage; N. Amer. burglarize; informal do, turn over, knock off, stick up. **2** *he robbed an old woman:* **steal from**; informal mug, jump; N. Amer. informal clip. **3** *he was robbed of his savings:* **cheat**, swindle, defraud; informal do out of, con out of, fleece. **4** *defeat robbed him of his title:* **deprive**, strip, divest; deny.

robber **noun** **burglar**, thief, housebreaker, mugger, shoplifter; stealer, pilferer, raider, looter, plunderer, pillager; bandit, highwayman; Brit. informal tea leaf.

robbery **noun** *they were arrested for the robbery:* **burglary**, theft, stealing, breaking and entering, housebreaking, larceny, shoplifting; embezzlement, fraud; hold-up, break-in, raid; informal mugging, smash-and-grab, stick-up; Brit. informal blag; N. Amer. informal heist.

robe **noun 1** *the women wore black robes:* **cloak**, gown, kaftan, djellaba;

wrap. **2** *the queen's robes of state:* **garb**, regalia, costume, finery; garments, clothes; formal apparel; old use raiment, vestments. **3** *a towelling robe:* **dressing gown**, bathrobe, housecoat; peignoir, negligee; N. Amer. wrapper.

• verb *he robed for Mass:* **dress**, get dressed, clothe yourself; formal enrobe.

robot noun **automaton**, android, golem; informal bot, droid.

robust adjective **1** *a robust man:* **strong**, vigorous, sturdy, tough, powerful, solid, muscular, sinewy, rugged, hardy, strapping, brawny, burly, husky; healthy, fit, fighting fit, hale and hearty; informal beefy, hunky. **2** *these knives are robust:* **durable**, resilient, tough, hard-wearing, long-lasting, sturdy, strong. **3** *her usual robust view of things:* **down-to-earth**, practical, realistic, pragmatic, common-sense, matter-of-fact, businesslike, sensible, unromantic, unsentimental; informal no-nonsense.

– OPPOSITES frail, fragile.

rock[1] verb **1** *the ship rocked on the water:* **move to and fro**, sway, see-saw; roll, pitch, plunge, toss, lurch, reel, list. **2** *the building began to rock:* **shake**, vibrate, quake, tremble. **3** *Wall Street was rocked by the news:* **stun**, shock, stagger, astonish, startle, surprise, shake, take aback, throw, unnerve, disconcert.

rock[2] noun **1** *a gully strewn with rocks:* **boulder**, stone, pebble. **2** *a castle built on a rock:* **crag**, cliff, outcrop. **3** *he was the rock on which they relied:* **foundation**, cornerstone, support, prop, mainstay; tower of strength, bulwark, anchor.

> **WORD LINKS**
> **petrography**, **petrology** the study of rocks

rocket verb *prices have rocketed:* **shoot up**, soar, increase, rise, escalate, spiral; informal go through the roof.

– OPPOSITES plummet.

rocky[1] adjective *a rocky path:* **stony**, pebbly, shingly; rough, bumpy; craggy, mountainous.

rocky[2] adjective **1** *that table's rocky:* **unsteady**, shaky, unstable, wobbly, tottery, rickety. **2** *a rocky marriage:* **difficult**, problematic, precarious, unstable, unreliable; informal iffy, up and down.

– OPPOSITES steady, stable.

rococo adjective **ornate**, fancy, elaborate, extravagant, baroque; fussy, busy, ostentatious, showy.

– OPPOSITES plain.

rod noun **1** *an iron rod:* **bar**, stick, pole, baton, staff; shaft, strut, rail, spoke. **2** *the ceremonial rod:* **staff**, mace, sceptre. **3** *instruction was accompanied by the rod:* **corporal punishment**, the cane, the lash, the birch; beating, flogging.

rogue noun **scoundrel**, villain, miscreant, reprobate, rascal, good-for-nothing, ne'er-do-well, wretch.

roguish adjective **1** *a roguish character:* **unprincipled**, dishonest, deceitful, unscrupulous, untrustworthy, shameless; wicked, villainous; informal shady. **2** *a roguish grin:* **mischievous**, playful, teasing, cheeky, naughty, wicked, impish, devilish; informal waggish.

role noun **1** *a small role in the film:* **part**; character. **2** *his role as President:* **capacity**, position, job, post, office, duty, responsibility, mantle, place.

roll verb **1** *the ball rolled into the net | the wheels began to roll:* **bowl**, spin; rotate, revolve, turn round. **2** *waiters rolled in the trolleys:* **wheel**, push, trundle. **3** *tears rolled down her cheeks:* **flow**, run, course, stream, pour, spill, trickle. **4** *the months rolled by:* **pass**, go by, slip by, fly by, elapse, wear on, march on. **5** *he rolled his handkerchief into a ball:* **wind**, coil, fold, curl; twist. **6** *they rolled about with laughter:* **stagger**, lurch, reel, totter, teeter. **7** *the ship began to roll:* **lurch**, toss, rock, pitch, plunge, sway, reel, list, keel. **8** *thunder rolled:* **rumble**, reverberate, echo, resound, boom, roar.

• noun **1** **cylinder**, tube; reel, spool. **2** *bread rolls:* **bun**, bagel; Brit. bap, muffin; N. Amer. hoagie. **3** *the electoral roll:* **list**, register, directory, record, file, index, catalogue, inventory. **4** *a roll of thunder:* **rumble**, reverberation, echo, boom, clap, crack, roar, grumble.

■ **roll something out** unroll, spread out, unfurl, unfold, open out, unwind, uncoil. **roll something up** fold, furl, wind up, coil, bundle up.

rollicking adjective **lively**, boisterous, exuberant, spirited; riotous, noisy, wild, rowdy; Brit. informal rumbustious.

romance noun **1** *their romance blossomed:* **love**, passion, ardour, adoration, devotion. **2** *he's had many romances:* **love affair**, relationship, liaison, courtship, attachment. **3** *an author of historical romances:* **love story**; informal tear jerker. **4** *the romance of the East:* **mystery**, glamour, excite- ment, exoticism, mystique; appeal, allure, charm.
• verb **1** (dated) *he was romancing Meg:* **woo**, chase, pursue; go out with, pay court to; informal see, go steady with, date. **2** *I am romancing the past:* **romanticize**, idealize, paint a rosy picture of.

romantic adjective **1** *he's so romantic:* **loving**, amorous, passionate, tender, affectionate; informal lovey-dovey. **2** *romantic songs:* **sentimental**, hearts-and-flowers; mawkish, sickly, saccharine, syrupy; informal slushy, mushy, sloppy, schmaltzy, gooey; Brit. informal soppy. **3** *a romantic setting:* **idyllic**, picturesque, fairy-tale; beautiful, lovely, charming, pretty. **4** *romantic notions of rural communities:* **idealistic**, unrealistic, fanciful, impractical; head-in-the-clouds, starry-eyed, optimistic, hopeful, visionary, utopian, fairy-tale.
– OPPOSITES unsentimental, realistic.
• noun *an incurable romantic:* **idealist**, sentimentalist, romanticist; dreamer, visionary, utopian, Don Quixote, fantasist.
– OPPOSITES realist.

Romeo noun **ladies' man**, Don Juan, Casanova, Lothario, womanizer, playboy, seducer, philanderer, flirt; gigolo; informal ladykiller, stud.

romp verb **1** *two fox cubs romped playfully:* **play**, frolic, frisk, gambol, skip, prance, caper, cavort, rollick. **2** *South Africa romped to a win:* **sail**, coast, sweep; win hands down, run away with it; informal walk it.

room noun **1** *there isn't much room:* **space**; headroom, legroom; area, expanse, extent. **2** *there's always room for improvement:* **scope**, capacity, leeway, latitude, freedom. **3** *he had rooms in the Pepys building:* **lodgings**, quarters; accommodation; informal a pad, digs.

roomy adjective **spacious**, capacious, sizeable, generous, big, large, extensive; voluminous, ample; formal commodious.
– OPPOSITES cramped.

root noun **1** *the root of the problem:* **source**, origin, germ, beginnings, genesis; cause, reason, basis, foundation, bottom, seat; core, heart, nub, essence. **2** *he rejected his roots:* **origins**, beginnings, family, ancestors, predecessors, heritage.
• verb *he rooted around in the cupboard:* **rummage**, hunt, search, rifle, delve, forage, dig, nose, poke; Brit. informal rootle.
■ **put down roots** settle, establish yourself, set up home. **root and branch** *a root-and-branch reform of the service:* complete, total, thorough, radical. **root something out** *we are determined to root out corruption:* eradicate, eliminate, weed out, destroy, wipe out, stamp out, extirpate, abolish, end, put a stop to. **take root 1** *leave the plants to take root:* germinate, sprout, establish, strike, take. **2** *Christianity took root in Persia:* become established, take hold, develop.

rooted adjective **1** *views rooted in Indian culture:* **embedded**, fixed, established, entrenched, ingrained. **2** *Neil was rooted to the spot:* **frozen**, riveted, paralysed, glued, fixed.

rootless adjective **itinerant**, unsettled, drifting, roving, footloose; homeless, of no fixed abode.

rope noun **cord**, cable, line, hawser; string.
• verb **tie**, bind, lash, truss; secure, moor, fasten, attach; hitch, tether, lasso.

ropy adjective **stringy**, thready, fibrous, filamentous; viscous, sticky.

roster noun **schedule**, list, register, agenda, calendar; Brit. rota.

rostrum noun **dais**, platform, podium, stage; soapbox.

rosy adjective **1** *a rosy complexion:* **pink**, roseate, reddish; glowing, healthy, fresh, radiant, blooming;

blushing, flushed; ruddy, high-coloured, florid. **2** *his future looks rosy:* **promising**, optimistic, auspicious, hopeful, encouraging, favourable, bright, golden; informal upbeat.
– OPPOSITES pale, bleak.

rot verb **1** *the floorboards rotted:* **decay**, decompose; disintegrate, crumble, perish. **2** *the meat began to rot:* **go bad**, go off, spoil; moulder, putrefy, fester. **3** *poor neighbourhoods have been left to rot:* **deteriorate**, degenerate, decline, decay, go to seed, go downhill; informal go to pot, go to the dogs.
– OPPOSITES improve.
• noun **1** *the leaves turned black with rot:* **decay**, decomposition, mould, mildew, blight, canker.
2 *traditionalists said the rot had set in:* **deterioration**, decline; corruption, cancer.

rota noun (Brit.). See **ROSTER**.

rotary adjective **rotating**, revolving, turning, spinning, gyratory.

rotate verb **1** *the wheels rotate continually:* **revolve**, go round, turn, spin, gyrate, whirl, twirl, swivel, circle, pivot. **2** *many nurses rotate jobs:* **alternate**, take turns, change, switch, interchange, exchange, swap.

rotation noun **1** *the rotation of the wheels:* **revolving**, turning, spinning, gyration, circling. **2** *a rotation of the Earth:* **turn**, revolution, orbit, spin. **3** *each member is chair for six months in rotation:* **sequence**, succession; alternation, cycle.

rotten adjective **1** *rotten meat:* **decaying**, decayed, bad, off, decomposing, putrid, putrescent, perished, mouldy, rancid, festering, fetid; addled. **2** *he's rotten to the core:* **corrupt**, unprincipled, dishonest, dishonourable, unscrupulous, untrustworthy, immoral; villainous, bad, wicked, evil, iniquitous, venal; informal crooked, warped; Brit. informal bent.
3 (informal) *it was a rotten thing to do:* **nasty**, unkind, unpleasant, spiteful, mean, malicious, hateful, hurtful; unfair, uncalled for, shabby; informal low-down; Brit. informal out of order.
– OPPOSITES fresh, honourable.

rotund adjective **1** *a small, rotund man:* **plump**, chubby, fat, stout, portly, dumpy, round, chunky, overweight, heavy, paunchy, ample; flabby, fleshy, bulky, corpulent, obese; informal tubby, roly-poly, pudgy, beefy, porky; Brit. informal podgy. **2** *rotund cauldrons:* **round**, bulbous, spherical.
– OPPOSITES thin.

roué noun **libertine**, rake, debauchee, degenerate, profligate; lecher, seducer, womanizer, philanderer, adulterer, Don Juan, Lothario; informal ladykiller, lech, dirty old man.

rough adjective **1** *rough ground:* **uneven**, irregular, bumpy, stony, rocky, rugged, rutted, pitted. **2** *the terrier's rough coat:* **coarse**, bristly, scratchy, prickly; shaggy, hairy, bushy. **3** *rough skin:* **dry**, leathery, weather-beaten; chapped, calloused, scaly, scabrous. **4** *his voice was rough:* **gruff**, hoarse, harsh, rasping, husky, throaty, gravelly, guttural.
5 *he gets rough when he's drunk:* **violent**, brutal, vicious; aggressive, belligerent, pugnacious, thuggish; boisterous, rowdy, disorderly, unruly, riotous. **6** *a machine that can take rough handling:* **careless**, clumsy, inept, unskilful. **7** *rough manners:* **boorish**, loutish, oafish, brutish, coarse, crude, uncouth, vulgar, unrefined, unladylike, ungentlemanly, uncultured. **8** *rough seas:* **turbulent**, stormy, tempestuous, violent, heavy, heaving, choppy. **9** *a rough draft:* **preliminary**, hasty, quick, sketchy, cursory, basic, crude, rudimentary, raw, unpolished; incomplete, unfinished. **10** *a rough estimate:* **approximate**, inexact, imprecise, vague, estimated, hazy; N. Amer. informal ballpark.
– OPPOSITES smooth, sleek, soft, dulcet, sweet, gentle, careful, refined, calm, exact.
• noun **1** *the artist's initial roughs:* **sketch**, draft, outline, mock-up.
2 (Brit.) *a bunch of roughs attacked him:* **ruffian**, thug, lout, hooligan, hoodlum, rowdy; informal tough, roughneck, bruiser; Brit. informal yob.
■ **rough something out** draft, sketch out, outline, block out, mock up.

rough and ready adjective **basic**, simple, crude, unrefined, unsophisticated; makeshift, provisional, stopgap, improvised, extemporary, ad hoc.

roughly adverb **1** *he shoved her roughly:* **violently**, forcefully, forcibly, abruptly, unceremoniously. **2** *they treated him roughly:* **harshly**, unkindly, unsympathetically; brutally, savagely, mercilessly, cruelly, heartlessly. **3** *roughly £2.4 million:* **approximately**, about, around, circa, in the region of, of the order of, or thereabouts, more or less, give or take; nearly, close to, approaching.

round adjective **1** *a round window:* **circular**, disc-shaped, ring-shaped, hoop-shaped; spherical, globular; cylindrical; bulbous, rounded, rotund. **2** *a short, round man:* **plump**, chubby, fat, stout, rotund, portly, dumpy, chunky, overweight, pot-bellied, paunchy; flabby, corpulent, fleshy, bulky, obese; informal tubby, roly-poly, pudgy, beefy, porky; Brit. informal podgy. **3** *his deep, round voice:* **sonorous**, resonant, rich, full, mellow, mellifluous, orotund. **4** *a round dozen:* **complete**, entire, whole, full.
– OPPOSITES thin.
• **noun 1** *mould the dough into rounds:* **ball**, sphere, globe, orb, circle, disc, ring, hoop. **2** *a policeman on his rounds:* **circuit**, beat, route, tour. **3** *the first round of the contest:* **stage**, level; heat, game, bout, contest. **4** *an endless round of parties:* **succession**, sequence, series, cycle. **5** *the gun fires thirty rounds a second:* **bullet**, cartridge, shell, shot.
• **preposition & adverb** *the alleys round the station:* **around**, about, encircling; near, in the vicinity of; orbiting.
• **verb** *the ship rounded the point:* **go round**, travel round, skirt, circumnavigate, orbit.
■ **round about** approximately, around, circa, roughly, of the order of, more or less, close to, near to, practically; or so, or thereabouts, give or take; nearly, almost, approaching. **round the clock 1** *we're working round the clock:* day and night, {morning, noon, and night}, continuously, non-stop, steadily, unremittingly; informal 24-7. **2** *round-the-clock supervision:* continuous, constant, non-stop, uninterrupted. **round something off** *the party rounded off a successful year:* complete, finish off, crown, cap, top; conclude, close, end. **round someone/something up** gather together, herd together, muster, marshal, rally, assemble, collect, group; N. Amer. corral.

roundabout adjective **1** *a roundabout route:* **circuitous**, indirect, meandering, serpentine, tortuous. **2** *I asked in a roundabout sort of way:* **indirect**, oblique, circuitous, circumlocutory, periphrastic, digressive, long-winded.
– OPPOSITES direct.
• **noun** (Brit.) **1** *go straight on at the roundabout:* N. Amer. rotary, traffic circle. **2** *a roundabout with wooden horses:* **merry-go-round**, carousel.

roundly adverb **1** *he was roundly condemned:* **vehemently**, emphatically, fiercely, forcefully, severely; plainly, frankly, candidly. **2** *she was roundly defeated:* **utterly**, completely, thoroughly, decisively, conclusively, heavily, soundly.

round-up noun **1** *a cattle round-up:* **assembly**, muster, rally; N. Amer. rodeo. **2** *the sports round-up:* **summary**, synopsis, overview, review, outline, digest, precis; N. Amer. wrap-up; informal recap.

rouse verb **1** *he roused Ralph at dawn:* **wake**, wake up, awaken, arouse; Brit. informal knock up; formal waken. **2** *he roused the crowd:* **stir up**, excite, galvanize, electrify, stimulate, inspire, move, inflame, agitate, goad, provoke; N. Amer. light a fire under. **3** *he's got a temper when he's roused:* **provoke**, annoy, anger, infuriate, madden, incense, vex, irk; informal aggravate. **4** *her disappearance roused my suspicions:* **arouse**, awaken, prompt, provoke, stimulate, pique, trigger, spark off, touch off, kindle, elicit.
– OPPOSITES calm, pacify, allay.

rousing adjective **stirring**, inspiring, exciting, stimulating, moving, electrifying, invigorating, energizing, exhilarating; enthusiastic, vigorous, spirited.

rout noun **1** *the army's ignominious rout:* **retreat**, flight. **2** *Newcastle scored 13 tries in the rout:* **trouncing**,

annihilation, decisive defeat; informal licking, hammering, thrashing, pasting, drubbing, massacre.
–OPPOSITES victory.
•**verb 1** *his army was routed:* **put to flight**, drive off, scatter; defeat, beat, conquer, crush, overpower; literary vanquish. **2** *he routed the defending champion:* **trounce**, defeat decisively, get the better of; informal lick, hammer, clobber, thrash, paste, demolish, annihilate, drub, cane, wipe the floor with, walk all over, make mincemeat of, massacre, slaughter; Brit. informal stuff.
–OPPOSITES lose.

route noun way, course, road, path, direction.
•**verb direct**, send, convey, dispatch, forward.

routine noun 1 *his morning routine:* **procedure**, practice, pattern, drill, regime, regimen; programme, schedule, plan. **2** *a stand-up routine:* **act**, performance, number, turn, piece; informal spiel, patter.
•**adjective 1** *a routine health check:* **standard**, regular, customary, normal, usual, ordinary, typical; everyday, common, conventional, habitual. **2** *a routine action movie:* **boring**, tedious, tiresome, wearisome, monotonous, humdrum, run-of-the-mill, prosaic, dreary, pedestrian; predictable, hackneyed, stock, unimaginative, unoriginal, banal, trite.
–OPPOSITES unusual.

rove verb wander, roam, ramble, drift, meander; range, travel; Scottish stravaig.

rover noun wanderer, traveller, globetrotter, drifter, itinerant; nomad; tramp, vagrant, vagabond; N. Amer. hobo.

row[1] noun 1 *rows of children:* **line**, column, file, queue; procession, chain, string, succession; informal crocodile. **2** *the middle row of seats:* **tier**, line, rank, bank.
■ **in a row** *three days in a row:* consecutively, in succession; running, straight; informal on the trot.

row[2] (Brit. informal) **noun 1** *have you two had a row?* **argument**, quarrel, squabble, fight, contretemps, dispute, clash, shouting match; informal tiff, set-to, run-in, slanging match, spat; Brit. informal barney, bust-up. **2** *I couldn't hear for the row:* **din**, noise, racket, uproar, hubbub, rumpus, babel; informal hullabaloo.
•**verb** *they rowed about money:* **argue**, quarrel, squabble, bicker, fight, fall out, disagree, have words; informal scrap.

rowdy adjective unruly, disorderly, obstreperous, riotous, undisciplined, uncontrollable, ungovernable, disruptive, out of control, rough, wild, lawless; boisterous, uproarious, noisy, loud, clamorous; Brit. informal rumbustious.
–OPPOSITES peaceful.

royal adjective 1 *the royal prerogative:* **regal**, kingly, queenly, princely; sovereign, monarchical. **2** *a royal welcome:* **excellent**, fine, magnificent, splendid, superb, wonderful, first-rate; informal fantastic, great, tremendous.

rub verb 1 *Polly rubbed her arm:* **massage**, knead; stroke, pat. **2** *he rubbed sun lotion on her back:* **apply**, smear, spread, work in. **3** *my shoes rub painfully:* **chafe**, pinch.
•**noun 1** *she gave his back a rub:* **massage**, rub-down. **2** *I gave my shoes a rub:* **polish**, wipe, clean. **3** *it's too complicated—that's the rub:* **problem**, difficulty, trouble, drawback, hindrance, impediment; snag, hitch, catch.
■ **rub something down** clean, sponge, wash. **rub off on** be transferred to, be passed on to, be transmitted to, be communicated to; affect, influence. **rub something out** erase, delete, remove, efface, obliterate, expunge. **rub something up** polish, buff up, burnish, shine, wax; clean, wipe.

rubbish noun 1 *28 million tonnes of household rubbish goes to landfill:* **refuse**, waste, litter, debris, detritus, scrap, dross; N. Amer. garbage, trash; informal junk. **2** *she's talking rubbish:* **nonsense**, balderdash, gibberish, claptrap, blarney, moonshine, garbage; informal hogwash, baloney, tripe, drivel, bilge, bunk, piffle, poppycock, phooey, twaddle, gobbledegook; Brit. informal codswallop, cobblers, tosh.

rubble noun debris, remains, ruins, wreckage.

ruddy adjective *a ruddy complexion:* **rosy**, red, pink, roseate, rubicund; healthy, glowing, fresh; flushed, blushing; florid, high-coloured.
– OPPOSITES pale.

rude adjective **1** *a rude man:* **ill-mannered**, bad-mannered, impolite, discourteous, uncivil, mannerless; impertinent, insolent, impudent, disrespectful, cheeky; churlish, curt, brusque, brash, offhand, short, sharp; offensive, insulting, derogatory, disparaging, abusive. **2** *rude jokes:* **vulgar**, coarse, smutty, dirty, filthy, crude, lewd, obscene, off colour, offensive, indelicate, tasteless; risqué, naughty, ribald, bawdy, racy; informal blue; Brit. informal near the knuckle; euphemistic adult. **3** *a rude awakening:* **abrupt**, sudden, sharp, startling; unpleasant, nasty, harsh.
– OPPOSITES polite, clean.

rudimentary adjective **1** *rudimentary skills:* **basic**, elementary, essential, fundamental. **2** *the equipment was rudimentary:* **primitive**, crude, simple, unsophisticated, rough and ready, makeshift. **3** *a rudimentary thumb:* **vestigial**, undeveloped, incomplete.
– OPPOSITES advanced, sophisticated, developed.

rudiments plural noun **basics**, fundamentals, essentials, first principles, foundation; informal nuts and bolts, ABC.

rue verb **regret**, be sorry about, feel remorseful about, repent of, reproach yourself for; deplore, lament, bemoan, bewail.

rueful adjective **regretful**, apologetic, sorry, remorseful, shamefaced, sheepish, hangdog, contrite, repentant, penitent, conscience-stricken, self-reproachful; sorrowful, sad.

ruffian noun **thug**, lout, hooligan, hoodlum, vandal, delinquent, rowdy, scoundrel, villain, rogue, bully boy, brute; informal tough, bruiser; Brit. informal rough, yob.

ruffle verb **1** *he ruffled her hair:* **disarrange**, tousle, rumple, mess up; N. Amer. informal muss up. **2** *don't let him ruffle you:* **annoy**, irritate, vex, nettle, anger, exasperate; disconcert, unnerve, fluster, agitate, harass, upset, disturb, discomfit, put off, perturb, unsettle, bother, worry, trouble; informal rattle, faze, throw, get to, rile, needle, aggravate, bug, peeve; Brit. informal wind up, nark.
– OPPOSITES smooth, soothe.
• noun *a shirt with ruffles:* **frill**, flounce, ruff, ruche.

rug noun **1** *they sat on the rug:* **mat**, carpet, drugget, runner; N. Amer. floorcloth. **2** *he was wrapped in a tartan rug:* **blanket**, coverlet, throw, wrap; N. Amer. lap robe.

rugged adjective **1** *the rugged path:* **rough**, uneven, bumpy, rocky, stony, pitted, jagged, craggy. **2** *a rugged vehicle:* **robust**, durable, sturdy, strong, tough, resilient. **3** *rugged manly types:* **well built**, burly, strong, muscular, muscly, brawny, strapping, husky, hulking; tough, hardy, robust, sturdy, solid; informal hunky, beefy. **4** *his rugged features:* **strong**, craggy, rough-hewn; manly, masculine.
– OPPOSITES smooth, flimsy, weedy, delicate.

ruin noun **1** *the buildings were saved from ruin:* **disintegration**, decay, disrepair, dilapidation; destruction, demolition, wreckage. **2** *the ruins of a church:* **remains**, remnants, fragments, relics; rubble, debris, wreckage. **3** *a single misstep could spell political ruin:* **downfall**, collapse, defeat, undoing, failure, breakdown; Waterloo. **4** *shopkeepers are facing ruin:* **bankruptcy**, insolvency, penury, poverty, destitution, impoverishment, indigence.
– OPPOSITES preservation, triumph, wealth.
• verb **1** *don't ruin my plans:* **wreck**, destroy, spoil, mar, blight, shatter, dash, torpedo, scotch, mess up; sabotage; informal screw up, foul up, put the kibosh on, do for; Brit. informal scupper. **2** *the bank's collapse ruined them:* **bankrupt**, make insolvent, impoverish, pauperize, wipe out, break, cripple; bring someone to their knees. **3** *a country ruined by civil war:* **destroy**, devastate, lay waste, ravage; raze, demolish, wreck, wipe out, flatten.
– OPPOSITES save, rebuild.
■ **in ruins 1** *the abbey is in ruins:* derelict, in disrepair, falling to pieces, dilapidated, tumbledown,

ramshackle, decrepit, decaying. **2** *his career is in ruins:* destroyed, in pieces, in ashes; over, finished; informal in tatters, on the rocks, done for.

ruined adjective **derelict**, dilapidated, tumbledown, ramshackle, decrepit, falling to pieces, crumbling, decaying, disintegrating.

ruinous adjective **1** *a ruinous trade war:* **disastrous**, devastating, catastrophic, calamitous, crippling, crushing, damaging, destructive, harmful; costly. **2** *ruinous interest rates:* **extortionate**, exorbitant, excessive, sky-high, outrageous, inflated; Brit. over the odds; informal criminal, steep.

rule noun **1** *health and safety rules:* **regulation**, directive, order, act, law, statute, edict, canon, mandate, command, dictate, decree, fiat, injunction, commandment, stipulation, requirement, guideline, direction; formal ordinance. **2** *church attendance on Sunday was the general rule:* **procedure**, practice, protocol, convention, norm, routine, custom, habit, wont; formal praxis. **3** *moderation is the golden rule:* **precept**, principle, standard, axiom, truth, maxim. **4** *the territory was under British rule:* **control**, jurisdiction, command, power, dominion; government, administration, sovereignty, leadership, supremacy, authority.
• verb **1** *El Salvador was ruled by Spain:* **govern**, preside over, control, lead, dominate, run, head, administer, manage. **2** *Mary ruled for six years:* **be in power**, be in control, be in command, be in charge, govern; reign, be monarch, be sovereign. **3** *the judge ruled that they be set free:* **decree**, order, pronounce, judge, adjudge, ordain; decide, find, determine, resolve, settle. **4** *subversion ruled:* **prevail**, predominate, be the order of the day, reign supreme; formal obtain.
■ **as a rule** usually, in general, normally, ordinarily, customarily, for the most part, on the whole, by and large, in the main, mostly, commonly, typically. **rule something out** exclude, eliminate, disregard; preclude, prohibit, prevent, disallow.

r

ruler noun **leader**, sovereign, monarch, potentate, king, queen, emperor, empress, prince, princess; crowned head, head of state, president, premier, governor.
– OPPOSITES subject.

ruling noun *the judge's ruling:* **judgement**, decision, adjudication, finding, verdict; pronouncement, resolution, decree, injunction.
• adjective **1** *the ruling monarch:* **reigning**, sovereign, regnant. **2** *Japan's ruling party:* **governing**, controlling, commanding, supreme, leading, dominant, ascendant. **3** *football was their ruling passion:* **main**, chief, principal, major, prime, dominating, foremost; predominant, central, focal; informal number-one.

rumble verb **boom**, thunder, roll, roar, resound, reverberate, echo, grumble.

ruminate verb *we ruminated on life:* **think about**, contemplate, consider, meditate on, muse on, mull over, ponder on/over, deliberate about/on, chew over, puzzle over; formal cogitate about.

rummage verb **search**, hunt, root about, ferret about, fish about, poke around, dig, delve, go through, explore, sift through, rifle through.

rumour noun **gossip**, hearsay, talk, tittle-tattle, speculation, word; (**rumours**) reports, stories, whispers, canards; informal the grapevine, the word on the street, the buzz.

rump noun **1** *a smack on the rump:* **rear end**, backside, seat; buttocks; Brit. bottom; informal behind, derrière; Brit. informal bum; N. Amer. informal butt, fanny; humorous fundament, posterior. **2** *the rump of the army:* **remainder**, rest, remnant, remains.

rumple verb **crumple**, crease, wrinkle, crinkle, ruck up, scrunch up; ruffle, disarrange, tousle, mess up; N. Amer. informal muss up.
– OPPOSITES smooth.

rumpus noun **disturbance**, commotion, uproar, furore, brouhaha, hue and cry, ruckus; fracas, melee, tumult, noise, racket, din; Brit. row; informal to-do, hullabaloo, hoo-ha, kerfuffle.

run verb **1** *she ran across the road:* **sprint**, race, dart, rush, dash,

hasten, hurry, scurry, scamper, hare, bolt, fly, gallop, career, charge, shoot, hurtle, speed, zoom, go like lightning, go hell for leather, go like the wind; jog, trot; informal tear, pelt, scoot, hotfoot it, leg it, belt, zip, whip; Brit. informal bomb. **2** *the robbers turned and ran:* **flee**, take flight, make off, take off, take to your heels, make a break for it, bolt, make your getaway, escape; informal beat it, clear off/out, vamoose, skedaddle, split, leg it, scram; Brit. informal do a runner, scarper, do a bunk. **3** *he ran in the marathon:* **compete**, take part, participate. **4** *a shiver ran down my spine:* **go**, pass, slide, move, travel. **5** *the road runs the length of the valley:* **extend**, stretch, reach, continue. **6** *water ran from the eaves:* **flow**, pour, stream, gush, flood, cascade, roll, course, spill, trickle, drip, dribble, leak. **7** *he runs a transport company:* **be in charge of**, manage, direct, control, head, govern, supervise, superintend, oversee. **8** *it's expensive to run a car:* **maintain**, keep, own, possess, have. **9** *I'll run you home:* **drive**, take, bring, ferry, chauffeur, give someone a lift. **10** *they ran some tests:* **carry out**, do, perform, execute. **11** *he left the engine running:* **operate**, function, work, go; tick over, idle. **12** *the lease runs for twenty years:* **be valid**, last, be in effect, be operative, continue.
•**noun 1** *his morning run along the river:* **sprint**, jog, trot. **2** *she did the school run:* **route**, journey; circuit, round, beat. **3** *a run in the car:* **drive**, ride, turn; trip, excursion, outing, jaunt, airing; informal spin, tootle. **4** *an unbeaten run of victories:* **series**, succession, sequence, string, chain, streak, spell, stretch, spate. **5** *a run on sterling:* **demand for**, rush on. **6** *the usual run of cafes:* **type**, kind, sort, variety, class. **7** *against the run of play, he scored again:* **trend**, tendency, course, direction, movement, drift, tide. **8** *a chicken run:* **enclosure**, pen, coop. **9** *a ski run:* **slope**, track, piste; N. Amer. trail. **10** *a run in her tights:* **ladder**, rip, tear, snag, hole.
■ **in the long run** eventually, in the end, ultimately, when all is said and done, in the fullness of time; Brit. informal at the end of the day. **on the run** on the loose, at large; running away, fleeing, fugitive; informal AWOL. **run across** meet, come across, run into, chance on, stumble on, happen on; informal bump into. **run away 1** *her attacker ran away.* See **RUN** verb sense 2. **2** *she ran away with the championship:* win easily; informal win by a mile, walk it, romp home. **run down** decline, degenerate, go downhill, go to seed, decay, go to rack and ruin; informal go to pot, go to the dogs. **run someone down 1** *he was run down by joyriders:* run over, knock down/over; hit, strike. **2** *she ran him down in front of other people:* criticize, denigrate, belittle, disparage, deprecate, find fault with; informal put down, knock, bad-mouth; Brit. informal rubbish, slag off; formal derogate. **run into 1** *a car ran into his van:* collide with, hit, strike, crash into, smash into, plough into, ram, impact. **2** *I ran into Hugo the other day:* meet, run across, chance on, stumble on, happen on; informal bump into. **3** *we ran into a problem:* experience, encounter, meet with, be faced with, be confronted with. **4** *his debts run into six figures:* amount to, add up to, total, come to, equal, reach. **run low** *supplies were running low:* dwindle, diminish, become depleted, be used up, be in short supply, be tight. **run off** *the youths ran off.* See **RUN** verb sense 2. **run on** *the call ran on for hours:* continue, go on, carry on, last, keep going, stretch. **run out 1** *food supplies ran out:* be used up, dry up, be exhausted, be finished, peter out. **2** *they ran out of cash:* be out of; use up, consume, expend, be cleaned out of. **3** *her contract ran out:* expire, end, terminate, finish; lapse. **run over 1** *the bathwater ran over:* overflow, spill over, brim over. **2** *the project ran over budget:* exceed, go over, overshoot, overreach. **3** *he quickly ran over the story:* recapitulate, repeat, run through, go over, reiterate, review; look over, read through; informal recap on. **run someone over**. See **RUN SOMEONE DOWN** sense 1. **run through 1** *they quickly ran through their money:* squander, spend, fritter away,

dissipate, waste, go through, consume, use up; informal blow. **2** *this attitude runs through all his writing:* pervade, permeate, suffuse, imbue, inform. **3** *he ran through his notes.* See **RUN OVER** sense 3. **4** *let's run through scene three:* rehearse, practise, go over, repeat; N. Amer. run down; informal recap on. **run to** *we can't run to champagne:* afford, stretch to, manage.

runaway noun *a teenage runaway:* **fugitive**, escaper; refugee; truant; absconder, deserter.
• adjective **1** *a runaway horse:* **out of control**, escaped, loose. **2** *a runaway victory:* **easy**, effortless. **3** *runaway inflation:* **rampant**, out of control, unchecked, unbridled.

rundown noun **summary**, synopsis, precis, run-through, summarization, review, overview, briefing, sketch, outline; informal low-down, recap.

run down adjective **1** *a run-down area of London:* **dilapidated**, tumble-down, ramshackle, derelict, ruinous, crumbling; neglected, uncared-for, seedy, shabby, squalid; depressed, disadvantaged; Brit. informal grotty. **2** *she was feeling rather run down:* **unwell**, ill, poorly, unhealthy, peaky; tired, drained, exhausted, fatigued, worn out, below par, washed out; Brit. off colour; informal under the weather; Brit. informal off, ropy, knackered; Austral./NZ informal crook.

runner noun **1** *runners were limbering up:* **athlete**, sprinter, hurdler, racer, jogger. **2** *a runner from the strawberry plant:* **shoot**, offshoot, sprout, tendril.

r

running noun **1** *the day-to-day running of the school:* **administration**, management, organization, coordination, orchestration, handling, direction, control, regulation, supervision. **2** *the smooth running of her department:* **operation**, working, function, performance.
• adjective **1** *the sound of running water:* **flowing**, gushing, rushing, moving. **2** *a running argument:* **ongoing**, sustained, continuous; recurrent, recurring. **3** *she was late two days running:* **in succession**, in a row, in sequence, consecutively; straight, together; informal on the trot.

runny adjective **liquefied**, liquid, fluid, melted, molten; watery, thin.
– OPPOSITES solid.

run-of-the-mill adjective **ordinary**, average, middle-of-the-road, commonplace, humdrum, mundane, standard, nondescript, characterless, conventional; unremarkable, unexceptional, uninteresting, dull, boring, routine, bland, lacklustre; N. Amer. garden-variety; informal bog-standard, nothing special, a dime a dozen; Brit. informal common or garden.
– OPPOSITES exceptional.

rupture noun **1** *pipeline ruptures:* **break**, fracture, crack, burst, split, fissure. **2** *a rupture due to personal differences:* **rift**, estrangement, falling-out, break-up, breach, split, separation, parting, division, schism; informal bust-up.
• verb **1** *the reactor core might rupture:* **break**, fracture, crack, breach, burst, split; informal bust. **2** *the problem ruptured their relationships:* **sever**, break off, breach, disrupt; literary sunder.

rural adjective **country**, bucolic, rustic, pastoral; agricultural, agrarian; literary sylvan.
– OPPOSITES urban.

ruse noun **ploy**, stratagem, tactic, scheme, trick, gambit, dodge, subterfuge, machination, wile; Brit. informal wheeze.

rush verb **1** *she rushed after him:* **hurry**, dash, run, race, sprint, bolt, dart, career, charge, shoot, hurtle, hare, fly, speed, zoom, scurry, scuttle, scamper, hasten; informal tear, belt, pelt, scoot, zip, whip, hotfoot it, leg it; Brit. informal bomb. **2** *water rushed along gutters:* **flow**, pour, gush, surge, stream, cascade, run, course. **3** *the new tax was rushed through parliament:* **push**, hurry, hasten, speed, hustle, press, force. **4** *demonstrators rushed the cordon of troops:* **attack**, charge, run at, assail, storm.
• noun **1** *spectators made a rush for the exit:* **dash**, run, sprint, dart, bolt, charge, scramble, break. **2** *why all the rush?* **hurry**, haste, urgency; commotion. **3** *a last-minute rush for flights:* **demand**, clamour, call, request; run on. **4** *a*

rush of adrenalin: **surge**, flow, flood, spurt, stream; dart, thrill, flash. **5** *a rush of cold air:* **gust**, draught, flurry. **6** *I made a sudden rush at him:* **charge**, onslaught, attack, assault, onrush.
• adjective *a rush job:* **urgent**, high-priority, emergency; hurried, hasty, fast, quick, swift.

rushed adjective **1** *a rushed divorce:* **hasty**, fast, speedy, quick, swift, rapid, hurried. **2** *he was too rushed to enjoy his stay:* **pushed for time**, busy, in a hurry, run off your feet.

rust verb **corrode**, oxidize, tarnish.

rustic adjective **1** *a rustic setting:* **rural**, country, pastoral, bucolic; agricultural, agrarian; literary sylvan. **2** *rustic wooden tables:* **plain**, simple, homely, unsophisticated; rough, rude, crude. **3** *rustic peasants:* **unsophisticated**, uncultured, unrefined, simple; artless, unassuming, guileless, naive, ingenuous; coarse, rough, uncouth, boorish; N. Amer. informal hillbilly, hick.
– OPPOSITES urban, ornate, sophisticated.
• noun **peasant**, countryman, countrywoman, bumpkin, yokel, country cousin; N. Amer. informal hillbilly, hayseed, hick; Austral./NZ informal bushy.

rustle verb **1** *a wind rustled through the trees:* **swish**, whoosh, whisper, sigh. **2** *he was rustling cattle:* **steal**, thieve, take.

rusty adjective **1** *rusty wire:* **rusted**, rust-covered, corroded, oxidized; tarnished, discoloured. **2** *a rusty colour:* **reddish-brown**, chestnut, auburn, tawny, russet, coppery, Titian, red. **3** *my French is a little rusty:* **out of practice**, below par.

rut noun **1** *the car bumped across the ruts:* **furrow**, groove, trough, ditch, hollow, pothole, crater. **2** *he was stuck in a rut:* **boring routine**, humdrum existence, groove, dead end.

ruthless adjective **merciless**, pitiless, cruel, heartless, hard-hearted, cold-hearted, cold-blooded, harsh, callous, unmerciful, unforgiving, uncaring, unsympathetic, uncharitable; remorseless, unbending, inflexible, implacable.
– OPPOSITES merciful.

Ss

sabotage verb **damage**, wreck, destroy, incapacitate, vandalize; obstruct, hinder, disrupt, spoil, ruin, undermine, threaten, subvert. •noun **damage**, destruction, vandalism; obstruction, disruption, subversion.

saccharine adjective *the soundtrack is full of saccharine ballads:* **sentimental**, sickly, mawkish, cloying, sugary, sickening; informal schmaltzy, cheesy, corny, toe-curling; Brit. informal soppy, twee; N. Amer. informal cornball.

sack noun **bag**, pouch, pocket, pack. •verb (informal) **dismiss**, discharge, lay off, make redundant, let go, throw out; Military cashier; informal fire, give someone the sack, give someone their marching orders; Brit. informal give someone their cards.
■ **the sack** (informal) dismissal, discharge, redundancy; informal the boot, the axe, the heave-ho, your marching orders, the elbow, the push.

sacred adjective **1** *a sacred place:* **holy**, hallowed, blessed, consecrated, sanctified. **2** *sacred music:* **religious**, spiritual, devotional, church, ecclesiastical.
–OPPOSITES secular, profane.

sacrifice noun **1** *the sacrifice of animals:* **ritual slaughter**, votive offering. **2** *the sacrifice of privileges:* **surrender**, giving up, abandonment, renunciation, forfeiture, relinquishment.
•verb **1** *two goats were sacrificed:* **offer up**, slaughter. **2** *he sacrificed his principles:* **give up**, abandon, renounce, relinquish; betray. **3** *he sacrificed his life:* **give**, lay down; surrender, forfeit.

sacrilege noun **desecration**, profanity, blasphemy, irreverence, disrespect.
–OPPOSITES piety.

sacrilegious adjective **profane**, blasphemous, impious, sinful, irreverent, unholy, disrespectful.

sacrosanct adjective **sacred**, hallowed, inviolable, inalienable; off limits, protected.

sad adjective **1** *we felt sad:* **unhappy**, sorrowful, depressed, downcast, miserable, down, despondent, wretched, glum, gloomy, doleful, melancholy, mournful, forlorn, heartbroken; informal blue, down in the mouth, down in the dumps. **2** *a sad story:* **tragic**, unhappy, miserable, wretched, sorry, pitiful, pathetic, heartbreaking, heart-rending. **3** *a sad state of affairs:* **unfortunate**, regrettable, sorry, deplorable, lamentable, pitiful, shameful, disgraceful.
–OPPOSITES happy, cheerful, fortunate.

sadden verb **depress**, dispirit, deject, dishearten, grieve, discourage, upset, get down, break someone's heart.

saddle verb **burden**, encumber, lumber; land, charge.

sadism noun **cruelty**, viciousness, cold-bloodedness, brutality.

sadistic adjective **cruel**, vicious, brutal, callous; unnatural, perverted.

sadness noun **unhappiness**, sorrow, dejection, depression, misery, despondency, wretchedness, gloom, gloominess, melancholy, mournfulness, woe, heartache, grief.

safe adjective **1** *the jewels are safe in the bank:* **secure**, protected, out of harm's way. **2** *the children are all safe:* **unharmed**, unhurt, uninjured, unscathed, all right, fine, well, in one piece, out of danger; informal OK.

3 *a safe place:* **secure**, sound, impregnable, invulnerable; secret. **4** *a safe driver:* **cautious**, circumspect, prudent, careful; unadventurous, conservative. **5** *the drug is safe:* **harmless**, innocuous, benign, non-toxic, non-poisonous.
– OPPOSITES insecure, dangerous, reckless, harmful.

safeguard noun **protection**, defence, buffer, provision, security; surety, cover, insurance.
• verb **protect**, preserve, conserve, save, secure, shield, guard, keep safe.
– OPPOSITES jeopardize.

safety noun **1** *the safety of the residents:* **welfare**, well-being, protection, security. **2** *the safety of ferries:* **security**, soundness, dependability, reliability. **3** *the safety of the shore:* **shelter**, sanctuary, refuge.

sag verb **1** *he sagged back in his chair:* **sink**, slump, loll, flop, crumple. **2** *the floors all sag:* **dip**, droop; bulge, bag.

saga noun **story**, tale, narrative; epic, legend, myth; informal yarn.

sage noun **wise man/woman**, philosopher, scholar, guru; prophet, mystic.

sail verb **1** *we sailed across the Atlantic:* **voyage**, travel, navigate, cruise. **2** *we sail tonight:* **set sail**, put to sea, leave, weigh anchor. **3** *who is sailing the ship?* **steer**, pilot, captain; informal skipper. **4** *clouds were sailing past:* **glide**, drift, float, flow, sweep, skim, coast, flit, scud. **5** *a pencil sailed past his ear:* **whizz**, speed, streak, shoot, whip, zoom, flash; fly; informal zip.

sailor noun **seaman**, seafarer, mariner; yachtsman, yachtswoman; hand; Brit. informal matelot; merchant seaman.

saint noun

> **WORD LINKS**
> **hagiography** writings about the lives of saints

saintly adjective **holy**, godly, pious; religious, devout, spiritual, prayerful; virtuous, righteous, good, pure.
– OPPOSITES ungodly.

sake noun **1** *for the sake of clarity:* **purpose**, reason. **2** *for her son's sake:* **benefit**, advantage, good, well-being, welfare.

salacious adjective **pornographic**, obscene, indecent, crude, lewd, vulgar, dirty, filthy; erotic, titillating, arousing, suggestive, sexy, risqué, ribald, smutty; X-rated; informal **blue**; euphemistic **adult**.

salary noun **pay**, wages, earnings, payment, remuneration, fees, stipend, income; formal emolument.

sale noun **1** *the sale of firearms:* **selling**; dealing, trading. **2** *they make a sale every minute:* **deal**, transaction, bargain.
– OPPOSITES purchase.
■ **for/on sale** on the market, on offer, available, obtainable.

salesperson noun **sales assistant**, salesman, saleswoman, agent; shopkeeper, trader, merchant, dealer; N. Amer. clerk; informal rep.

salient adjective **important**, main, principal, major, chief, primary; noteworthy, outstanding, conspicuous, striking, noticeable, obvious, prominent, dominant; key, crucial, vital, essential.
– OPPOSITES minor.

saliva noun **spit**, spittle, dribble, drool, slaver, slobber, sputum.

sallow adjective **yellowish**, jaundiced; unhealthy, sickly, washed out, peaky.

salon noun **shop**, establishment, premises; boutique, store.

salty adjective **salt**, salted, saline, briny, brackish.

salubrious adjective **pleasant**, agreeable, nice, select, high-class; Brit. upmarket; informal posh, swanky, classy; Brit. informal swish; N. Amer. informal swank.

salutary adjective **beneficial**, advantageous, good, profitable, productive, helpful, useful, valuable, worthwhile; timely.
– OPPOSITES unwelcome.

salutation noun **greeting**, salute, address, welcome.

salute noun **tribute**, testimonial, homage, honour; celebration, acknowledgement, recognition.
• verb **pay tribute to**, pay homage to, honour, celebrate, acknowledge, recognize, take your hat off to.

salvage verb **rescue**, save, recover, retrieve, reclaim.

salvation noun **1** *pray for their salvation:* **redemption**, deliverance. **2** *that man was her salvation:* **lifeline**; means of escape; saviour.
– OPPOSITES damnation.

salve noun **ointment**, cream, balm, unguent; embrocation, liniment.

salver noun **platter**, plate, dish, tray.

same adjective **1** *we both stayed at the same hotel:* **identical**, selfsame, very same. **2** *they had the same symptoms:* **matching**, identical, alike, carbon-copy, twin; indistinguishable, interchangeable, corresponding, equivalent, parallel, like, comparable, similar.
– OPPOSITES another, different.
■ **the same** *their menu is the same worldwide:* unchanging, unvarying, unvaried, consistent, uniform.

WORD LINKS
homogeneous consisting of parts which are of the same kind.

sample noun **1** *a sample of the fabric:* **specimen**, example, bit, snippet, swatch; taste, taster. **2** *a representative sample:* **cross section**, selection.
• verb *we sampled the food:* **try**, taste, test, put to the test; appraise, evaluate; informal check out.
• adjective *a sample copy:* **specimen**, test, trial, pilot, dummy.

sanctimonious adjective **self-righteous**, holier-than-thou, pious, churchy, moralizing, smug, superior, priggish, hypocritical, insincere; informal goody-goody.

sanction noun **1** *trade sanctions:* **penalty**, punishment, deterrent; restriction; embargo, ban, prohibition, boycott. **2** *the scheme has the sanction of the court:* **authorization**, consent, leave, permission, authority, dispensation, assent, acquiescence, agreement, approval, approbation, endorsement, blessing; informal the go-ahead, the thumbs up, the OK, the green light.
– OPPOSITES reward, prohibition.
• verb *the rally was sanctioned by the government:* **authorize**, permit, allow, endorse, approve, accept, back, support; informal OK.
– OPPOSITES prohibit.

sanctity noun **importance**, primacy; centrality.

S

sanctuary noun **1** *he was given sanctuary in the embassy:* **refuge**, safety, protection, shelter, immunity, asylum. **2** *the flat is my sanctuary:* **haven**, refuge, sanctum, shelter, retreat, bolt-hole, hideaway. **3** *a bird sanctuary:* **reserve**, park, reservation; N. Amer. preserve. **4** *the sanctuary at Delphi:* **holy place**, temple; shrine, altar; sanctum, holy of holies.

sand noun **beach**, sands, shore; dunes.

sane adjective **1** *he is presumed to be sane:* **of sound mind**, in your right mind, compos mentis, lucid, rational, balanced, stable, normal; informal all there. **2** *a sane suggestion:* **sensible**, practical, realistic, prudent, reasonable, rational, level-headed.
– OPPOSITES mad, foolish.

sanguine adjective **optimistic**, bullish, hopeful, buoyant, positive, confident, cheerful, cheery; informal upbeat.
– OPPOSITES gloomy.

sanitary adjective **hygienic**, clean, antiseptic, aseptic, sterile.

sanitized adjective **censored**, doctored, expurgated, airbrushed, revised, edited.

sanity noun **1** *she was losing her sanity:* **mental health**, reason, rationality, stability, lucidity; sense, wits, mind. **2** *sanity has prevailed:* **common sense**, wisdom, prudence, rationality.

sap noun **juice**, secretion, fluid, liquid.
• verb **erode**, wear away/down, deplete, reduce, lessen, undermine, drain, bleed.

sarcasm noun **irony**; derision, mockery, ridicule, scorn.

sarcastic adjective **ironic**; sardonic, derisive, scornful, contemptuous, mocking; caustic, scathing, trenchant, acerbic; Brit. informal sarky; N. Amer. informal snarky.

sardonic adjective **mocking** cynical, scornful, derisive, sneering, jeering; scathing, caustic, trenchant, cutting, acerbic.

sash noun **belt**, cummerbund, waistband, girdle.

satanic adjective **diabolical**, fiendish, devilish, demonic, ungodly, hellish, infernal, wicked, evil, sinful.

sate verb. See SATIATE.

satiate verb **fill**, satisfy, sate; slake, quench; gorge, stuff, surfeit, glut, sicken, nauseate.

satire noun **parody**, burlesque, caricature, irony; lampoon, skit; informal spoof, take-off, send-up.

satirical adjective **mocking**, ironic, sardonic; acerbic; critical, irreverent, disparaging, disrespectful.

satirize verb **mock**, ridicule, deride, make fun of, parody, lampoon, caricature, take off; criticize; informal send up, take the mickey out of.

satisfaction noun **1** *he derived great satisfaction from his work:* **contentment**, content, pleasure, gratification, fulfilment, enjoyment, happiness, pride. **2** *investors turned to the courts for satisfaction:* **compensation**, recompense, redress, reparation, restitution, repayment, reimbursement.

satisfactory adjective **adequate**, all right, acceptable, good enough, sufficient, reasonable, competent, fair, decent, average, passable; fine, in order, up to scratch, up to the mark.
–OPPOSITES inadequate, poor.

satisfied adjective **1** *a satisfied smile:* **pleased**, contented, happy, proud, triumphant; smug, self-satisfied. **2** *I am satisfied that this is true:* **convinced**, certain, sure, positive, persuaded.
–OPPOSITES dissatisfied, unhappy.

satisfy verb **1** *her job no longer satisfied her:* **content**, please, fulfil. **2** *a chance to satisfy his hunger for romance:* **fulfil**, gratify, meet, fill; indulge, cater to, pander to; appease, assuage; quench, slake, satiate, sate, take the edge off. **3** *products which satisfy EC law:* **comply with**, meet, fulfil, answer, conform to; measure up to, come up to. **4** *she satisfied herself that it had been an accident:* **convince**, persuade, assure; reassure, put someone's mind at rest.
–OPPOSITES dissatisfy, frustrate.

satisfying adjective **fulfilling**, rewarding, gratifying, pleasing, enjoyable, pleasurable.

saturate verb **1** *rain had saturated the ground:* **soak**, drench, waterlog. **2** *the company has saturated the market:* **flood**, glut, oversupply, overfill, overload.

saturated adjective **soaked**, soaking, wet through, sopping, sodden, waterlogged, dripping, wringing wet, drenched; waterlogged, flooded.
–OPPOSITES dry.

sauce noun **relish**, condiment, ketchup; dip, dressing; jus, coulis, gravy.

saucepan noun **pan**, pot, casserole, skillet; billy, billycan.

saunter verb **stroll**, amble, wander, meander, walk; informal mosey, tootle; formal promenade.

savage adjective **1** *packs of savage dogs:* **ferocious**, fierce, vicious; wild, feral. **2** *a savage assault:* **vicious**, brutal, cruel, sadistic, ferocious, fierce, violent. **3** *a savage attack on free trade:* **fierce**, blistering, scathing, searing, stinging, devastating, withering, virulent, vitriolic.
–OPPOSITES tame, mild.
• noun *she described her assailants as savages:* **brute**, beast, monster, barbarian, sadist, animal.
• verb **1** *the child was savaged by a dog:* **maul**, attack, lacerate, claw, bite. **2** *critics savaged the film:* **criticize**, attack, lambaste, condemn, denounce, pillory, revile; informal pan, tear to pieces, hammer, slam; Brit. informal slate, rubbish; N. Amer. informal trash; Austral./NZ informal monster.

save verb **1** *the captain was saved by his crew:* **rescue**; set free, free, liberate, deliver, extricate; bail out; informal save someone's bacon/neck/skin. **2** *the house was saved from demolition:* **preserve**, keep, protect, safeguard; salvage, retrieve, reclaim, rescue. **3** *start saving old newspapers:* **put/set aside**, put by/to one side, keep, retain, reserve, conserve, stockpile, store, hoard; informal squirrel/stash away, hang on to. **4** *asking her saved a lot of trouble:* **prevent**, obviate, forestall, spare; stop; avoid, avert.
• preposition & conjunction (formal) *no one save herself:* **except**, apart from, but, other than, besides, aside from, bar.

saving noun **1** *a considerable saving in development costs:* **reduction**, cut, decrease, economy. **2** *I'll have to use my savings:* **nest egg**; capital, assets, funds, resources, reserves.

saviour noun *the country's saviour:* **rescuer**, liberator, deliverer, emancipator; champion, knight in shining armour, good Samaritan.

savoir faire noun **social skills**, social graces, urbanity, suavity, finesse, sophistication, poise, aplomb, polish, style, smoothness; informal savvy.
–OPPOSITES gaucheness.

savour verb *she savoured every moment:* **relish**, enjoy, appreciate, delight in, revel in, luxuriate in.
•noun *the subtle savour of wood smoke:* **smell**, aroma, fragrance, scent, perfume, bouquet; taste, flavour, tang, smack.

savoury adjective **1** *sweet or savoury dishes:* **salty**; spicy, tangy, meaty. **2** *one of the less savoury aspects of the affair:* **acceptable**, pleasant, appealing, palatable, seemly.
–OPPOSITES sweet, unsavoury.
•noun *cocktail savouries:* **canapé**, hors d'oeuvre, appetizer, titbit.

say verb **1** *he said her name:* **speak**, utter, voice, pronounce, vocalize, enunciate. **2** *'I must go,' she said:* **declare**, state, announce, remark, observe, mention, comment, note, add; reply, respond, answer. **3** *he says he's innocent:* **claim**, maintain, assert, hold, insist, contend; allege. **4** *I'll miss you more than I can say:* **express**, put into words, articulate, communicate, make known, put/get across, convey, verbalize; reveal, divulge, impart, disclose; imply, suggest. **5** *they said a prayer:* **recite**, repeat, utter, deliver, perform. **6** *her watch said one twenty:* **indicate**, show, read. **7** *I'd say it's about five miles:* **estimate**, judge, guess, hazard a guess, predict, speculate, surmise, conjecture, venture; informal reckon. **8** *let's say you'd won a million pounds:* **suppose**, assume, imagine, presume.
•noun **1** *everyone had their say:* **chance to speak**; informal twopenn'orth. **2** *don't I have any say in the matter?* **influence**, sway, weight, voice, input.

saying noun **proverb**, maxim, aphorism, axiom, adage, saw, tag, motto, epigram, dictum; expression, phrase, formula; slogan, catchphrase; platitude, cliché, commonplace, truism.

S

scalding adjective **hot**, burning, blistering, searing, red-hot; piping hot; informal boiling, sizzling.

scale noun **1** *the Celsius scale:* **system**. **2** *opposite ends of the social scale:* **hierarchy**, ladder, ranking, pecking order, order, spectrum. **3** *the scale of the map:* **ratio**, proportion. **4** *the scale of the disaster:* **extent**, size, scope, magnitude, dimensions, range, breadth, degree, reach.
•verb *thieves scaled an 8 ft high fence:* **climb**, ascend, clamber/scramble up, shin up, mount; N. Amer. shinny up.
■ **scale something down** reduce, cut, decrease, lessen, lower, trim, slim down, prune. **scale something up** increase, expand, augment, build up; step up, boost, escalate.

scaly adjective **dry**, flaky, flaking, rough, scabrous, mangy.

scamper verb **scurry**, scuttle, dart, run, rush, race, dash, hurry; informal scoot.

scan verb **1** *Adam scanned the horizon:* **scrutinize**, examine, study, inspect, survey, search, scour, sweep; look/stare/gaze at, eye, watch; informal check out; N. Amer. informal scope. **2** *I scanned the papers:* **glance/look through**, have a look at, run/cast your eye over, skim/flick/flip/leaf through.
•noun **1** *a quick scan through the report:* **glance**, look, flick, browse. **2** *a brain scan:* **examination**, screening.

scandal noun **1** *the scandal led him to resign:* **affair**, issue, incident, skeleton in the closet; crisis, fiasco, debacle, furore, controversy. **2** *divorce was then a cause for scandal:* **outrage**, anger; gossip, rumours, calumny, aspersions, muckraking. **3** *their treatment is a scandal:* **disgrace**, outrage; crying shame, sin.

scandalize verb **shock**, appal, outrage, horrify, disgust; offend, affront, cause raised eyebrows.
–OPPOSITES impress.

scandalous adjective **1** *a scandalous waste of money:* **disgraceful**, shocking, outrageous, monstrous, criminal, wicked, shameful, appalling, deplorable, inexcusable, intolerable, unforgivable, unpardonable. **2** *a series of scandalous affairs:* **discreditable**, disreputable, dishonourable, improper, unseemly, sordid. **3** *scandalous rumours:* **scurrilous**, malicious, slanderous, libellous, defamatory.

scant adjective **little**, little or no, minimal, limited, negligible, meagre; insufficient, inadequate.
– OPPOSITES abundant, ample.

scanty adjective **1** *their scanty wages:* **meagre**, scant, minimal, limited, modest, restricted, sparse; tiny, small, paltry, negligible; scarce, in short supply, thin on the ground, few and far between; informal measly, piddling, mingy, pathetic. **2** *her scanty nightdress:* **skimpy**, revealing; short, brief; low, low cut.
– OPPOSITES ample, plentiful.

scapegoat noun **whipping boy**, Aunt Sally; informal fall guy; N. Amer. informal patsy.

scar noun **1** *the scar on his arm:* **mark**, blemish, disfigurement, discoloration; pockmark, pit; lesion; stitches. **2** *psychological scars:* **trauma**, damage, injury.
• verb **1** *he's likely to be scarred for life:* **disfigure**, mark, blemish. **2** *a landscape scarred by mining:* **damage**, spoil, mar, deface, injure. **3** *she was deeply scarred by the incident:* **traumatize**, damage, injure; distress, disturb, upset.

scarce adjective **1** *food was scarce:* **in short supply**, scant, meagre, sparse, hard to find, hard to come by, insufficient, deficient, inadequate. **2** *wading birds are now scarce:* **rare**, few and far between, thin on the ground.
– OPPOSITES plentiful.

scarcely adverb **1** *she could scarcely hear him:* **hardly**, barely, only just. **2** *I scarcely see her:* **rarely**, seldom, infrequently, not often, hardly ever; informal once in a blue moon.

scarcity noun **shortage**, dearth, lack, undersupply, insufficiency, paucity, poverty; deficiency, inadequacy; unavailability, absence.

scare verb *stop it, you're scaring me:* **frighten**, startle, alarm, terrify, unnerve, worry, intimidate, terrorize, cow; put the fear of God into, make someone's blood run cold; informal freak out, make someone's hair stand on end, make someone jump out of their skin; Brit. informal put the wind up; N. Amer. informal spook.
• noun *you gave me a scare:* **fright**, shock, start, turn, jump.

scared adjective **frightened**, afraid, fearful, nervous, panicky; terrified, petrified, panic-stricken, scared stiff; Scottish feart; informal in a cold sweat, in a funk; N. Amer. informal spooked.

scaremonger noun **alarmist**, prophet of doom, doom-monger; informal doom and gloom merchant.

scarf noun **muffler**, headscarf; mantilla, stole, tippet; N. Amer. babushka.

scarper verb (Brit. informal). See **RUN** verb sense 2.

scary adjective (informal) **frightening**, alarming, terrifying, hair-raising, spine-chilling, blood-curdling, horrifying, nerve-racking, unnerving; eerie, sinister; informal creepy, spine-tingling, spooky, hairy.

scathing adjective **withering**, blistering, searing, devastating, fierce, ferocious, savage, severe, stinging, biting, cutting, virulent, vitriolic, scornful, bitter, harsh.
– OPPOSITES mild.

scatter verb **1** *scatter the seeds evenly:* **throw**, strew, toss, fling; sprinkle, spread, distribute, sow. **2** *the crowd scattered | onlookers were scattered in all directions:* **disperse**, break up, disband, separate, dissolve; drive, send, chase. **3** *the floor was scattered with books:* **cover**, dot, sprinkle, stipple, spot, pepper, litter.
– OPPOSITES gather, assemble.

scatterbrained adjective **absent-minded**, forgetful, disorganized; dreamy, feather-brained, giddy; informal scatty, having a mind/memory like a sieve, dizzy, dippy.

scavenge verb **search**, hunt, look, forage, rummage, root about/around, grub about/around.

scenario noun **1** *every possible scenario must be explored:* **sequence of events**, course of events, chain of events. **2** *he wrote scenarios for a major Hollywood studio:* **plot**, outline, storyline; screenplay, script.

scene noun **1** *the scene of the*

accident: **location**, site, place, position, point, spot. **2** *the scene is London in the 1890s:* **background**, setting, context, milieu, backdrop. **3** *scenes of violence:* **incident**, event, episode, happening. **4** *an impressive mountain scene:* **view**, vista, outlook, panorama; landscape, scenery. **5** *she made a scene:* **fuss**, exhibition of yourself, performance, tantrum, commotion, disturbance, upset, furore; informal to-do; Brit. informal carry-on. **6** *the political scene:* **arena**, stage, sphere, world, milieu, realm, domain; field. **7** *a scene from a movie:* **clip**, section, segment, part, sequence, extract.

scenery noun **1** *Ireland's beautiful scenery:* **landscape**, countryside, country, terrain, setting, surroundings, environment; view, vista, panorama. **2** *scenery and costumes:* **stage set**, backdrop; technical mise en scène.

scenic adjective **picturesque**, pretty, pleasing, attractive, lovely, beautiful, charming; impressive, striking, spectacular, breathtaking; panoramic.

scent noun **1** *the scent of freshly cut hay:* **smell**, fragrance, aroma, perfume, savour, odour; bouquet, nose. **2** *a bottle of scent:* **perfume**, fragrance, eau de toilette, cologne, eau de cologne. **3** *the hounds picked up the scent:* **spoor**, trail, track.
• verb *a shark can scent blood from far away:* **smell**, detect, pick up, register, sense, discern, recognize.

scented adjective **perfumed**, fragranced, perfumy; sweet-smelling, fragrant, aromatic.

S

sceptic noun **cynic**, doubter; pessimist, prophet of doom; unbeliever, doubting Thomas.

sceptical adjective **dubious**, doubtful, taking something with a pinch of salt, doubting; cynical, distrustful, suspicious, disbelieving, unconvinced; pessimistic, defeatist, negative.
– OPPOSITES certain, convinced.

scepticism noun **doubt**, a pinch of salt; disbelief, cynicism, distrust, suspicion, incredulity; pessimism, defeatism.

schedule noun **1** *our production schedule:* **plan**, programme, timetable, scheme. **2** *I have a busy schedule:* **timetable**, agenda, diary, calendar; itinerary.
• verb *a meeting has been scheduled:* **arrange**, organize, plan, set up, programme, timetable, line up; N. Amer. slate.
■ **ahead of schedule** early, ahead of time; prematurely. **behind schedule** late, overdue, behind time.

scheme noun **1** *fund-raising schemes:* **plan**, project, programme, strategy, stratagem, tactic; system, procedure, design, formula, recipe; Brit. informal wheeze. **2** *his schemes and plots:* **plot**, intrigue, conspiracy; ruse, ploy, stratagem, manoeuvre, subterfuge; machinations; informal game, racket, scam. **3** *the poem's rhyme scheme:* **arrangement**, system, organization, configuration, pattern, format.
• verb *he schemed endlessly:* **plot**, conspire, intrigue, connive, manoeuvre, plan.

scheming adjective **cunning**, crafty, calculating, devious, conniving, wily, sly, tricky, artful, slippery, manipulative, Machiavellian, unscrupulous; duplicitous, deceitful, underhand, treacherous.
– OPPOSITES ingenuous, honest.

schism noun **division**, split, rift, breach, rupture, break, separation; chasm, gulf; discord, disagreement, dissension.

schismatic adjective **separatist**, heterodox, dissident, dissenting, heretical; breakaway, splinter.
– OPPOSITES orthodox.

scholar noun **academic**, intellectual, learned person, man/woman of letters; authority, expert; informal egghead; N. Amer. informal pointy head.

scholarly adjective **learned**, erudite, academic, well read, widely read, intellectual; literary, lettered, educated, highbrow; studious, bookish, donnish, cerebral; N. Amer. informal pointy-headed.
– OPPOSITES uneducated, illiterate.

scholarship noun **1** *a centre of scholarship:* **learning**, knowledge, erudition, education, letters, culture, academic study/achievement. **2** *a scholarship of £2000:* **grant**, award, endowment, payment; Brit. bursary.

scholastic adjective **academic**, educational, school, scholarly.

school noun **1** *the village school:* **educational institution**; academy, college; alma mater. **2** *the university's School of English:* **department**, faculty, division. **3** *the great school of Dutch painters:* **group**, set, circle; followers, disciples, apostles, students, pupils, admirers, devotees, votaries. **4** *the school of linguistics associated with him:* **way of thinking**, school of thought, approach, method, style, brand, persuasion, creed, credo, doctrine.
• verb **1** *he was schooled in Paris:* **educate**, teach, instruct. **2** *he schooled her in horsemanship:* **train**, teach, tutor, coach, instruct, drill, discipline; prepare, groom; prime, verse.

WORD LINKS
scholastic relating to schools

schooling noun **education**, teaching, tuition, instruction, tutoring, tutelage; lessons.

schoolteacher noun **teacher**, schoolmaster, schoolmistress, tutor; Brit. master, mistress; N. Amer. informal schoolmarm; Austral./NZ informal chalkie, schoolie; formal pedagogue.

science noun *the science of criminology:* **branch of knowledge**, body of knowledge/information, area of study, discipline, field.

scientific adjective **1** *scientific research:* technological, technical; evidence-based, empirical. **2** *a more scientific approach:* **systematic**, methodical, organized, ordered, orderly, meticulous, rigorous; exact, precise, accurate, mathematical; analytical, rational.

scintillating adjective **brilliant**, dazzling, exciting, exhilarating, stimulating; sparkling, lively, vivacious, vibrant, animated, effervescent; witty, clever.
– OPPOSITES dull, boring.

scoff[1] verb **mock**, deride, ridicule, sneer, jeer, laugh at, dismiss, belittle; informal pooh-pooh.

scoff[2] verb (Brit. informal) **eat**, devour, consume, guzzle, gobble, wolf down, bolt; informal put away, nosh, polish off, demolish, shovel down, pig yourself on; N. Amer. informal scarf, snarf.

scold verb **rebuke**, reprimand, reproach, reprove, admonish, chastise, chide, upbraid, berate, haul over the coals; informal tell off, dress down, give someone an earful, give someone a roasting, bawl out, give someone hell; Brit. informal tick off, have a go at, carpet, tear someone off a strip, give someone what for, give someone a rollicking; N. Amer. informal chew out; formal castigate.
– OPPOSITES praise.

scoop noun **1** *a measuring scoop:* **spoon**, ladle, dipper. **2** *a scoop of ice cream:* **spoonful**, ladleful, portion, lump, ball; informal dollop.
• verb **1** *a hole was scooped out in the ground:* **hollow out**, gouge out, dig, excavate. **2** *cut the tomatoes in half and scoop out the flesh:* **remove**, take out, spoon out, scrape out. **3** *she scooped up armfuls of clothes:* **pick up**, gather up, lift, take up; snatch up, grab.

scope noun **1** *the scope of the investigation:* **extent**, range, breadth, width, reach, sweep, span; area, sphere, realm, compass, orbit, ambit, terms/field of reference, remit; limit. **2** *the scope for change is limited:* **opportunity**, freedom, latitude, leeway, capacity, room to manoeuvre; possibility, chance.

scorch verb **1** *trees were scorched by the fire:* **burn**, sear, singe, char, blacken, discolour. **2** *grass scorched by the sun:* **dry up**, parch, wither, shrivel.

scorching adjective **hot**, red-hot, blazing, flaming, fiery, burning, blistering, searing, sweltering, torrid; N. Amer. broiling; informal boiling, baking, sizzling.
– OPPOSITES freezing, mild.

score noun **1** *the final score was 4–3:* **result**, outcome; total, sum total, tally, count. **2** *an IQ score of 161:* **rating**, grade, mark, percentage.
• verb **1** *he's scored 13 goals this season:* **get**, gain, chalk up, achieve, make; record, rack up, notch up; informal bag, knock up. **2** *the piece was scored for flute:* **orchestrate**, arrange, set, adapt; write, compose. **3** *score the wood in criss-cross patterns:* **scratch**, cut, notch, incise, scrape, nick, gouge; mark.
■ **score points off** get the better of, gain the advantage over, outdo, have the edge over; make a fool of,

humiliate; informal get/be one up on, get one over on. **score something out/through** cross out, strike out, put a line through; delete, obliterate, expunge.

scorn noun *the scorn in his voice:* **contempt**, derision, disdain, mockery, sneering.
– OPPOSITES admiration, respect.
• verb **1** *critics scorned the paintings:* **deride**, pour scorn on, mock, scoff at, sneer at, jeer at, laugh at; disparage, slight; dismiss. **2** *they scorned my offers of help:* **spurn**, rebuff, reject, ignore, shun, snub.
– OPPOSITES admire, respect.

scornful adjective **contemptuous**, derisive, withering, mocking, sneering, jeering, scathing, snide, disparaging, supercilious, disdainful.
– OPPOSITES admiring, respectful.

scotch verb **put an end to**, put a stop to, nip in the bud, put the lid on; ruin, wreck, destroy, smash, shatter, demolish; frustrate, thwart; informal put paid to, put the kibosh on; Brit. informal scupper.

scot-free adverb **unpunished**, without punishment.

Scotland noun Caledonia; Brit. north of the border.

scoundrel noun **rogue**, rascal, miscreant, villain, good-for-nothing, reprobate; cheat, swindler, fraudster, trickster, charlatan; informal rat, louse, swine, wretch; informal, dated rotter; dated cad; old use blackguard, knave.

scour[1] verb *use mild abrasives to scour pots and pans:* **scrub**, rub, clean, wash; polish, buff, shine, burnish; abrade.

S

scour[2] verb *Christine scoured the shops:* **search**, comb, hunt through, rummage through, go through with a fine-tooth comb, look high and low in; ransack, turn upside-down; Austral./NZ informal fossick through.

scourge noun **affliction**, bane, curse, plague, menace, evil, misfortune, burden; blight, cancer, canker.
– OPPOSITES blessing, godsend.

scout noun **1** *scouts reported that the Romans were advancing:* **lookout**, outrider; spy. **2** *a scout round the area:* **reconnaissance**, reconnoitre; exploration, search, expedition; informal recce; Brit. informal shufti; N. Amer. informal recon. **3** *a record company scout:* **talent spotter**, talent scout; N. Amer. informal bird dog.
• verb **1** *I scouted around for some logs:* **search**, look, hunt, ferret about/around, root about/around. **2** *a patrol was sent to scout out the area:* **reconnoitre**, explore, inspect, investigate, spy out, survey; examine, scan, study, observe; informal check out, case; Brit. informal take a shufti round.

scowl verb **glower**, frown, glare, grimace, lour, look daggers at; informal give someone a dirty look.
– OPPOSITES smile, grin.

scraggy adjective **scrawny**, thin, skinny, skin-and-bones, gaunt, bony, angular, gawky, raw-boned.
– OPPOSITES fat.

scramble verb **1** *we scrambled over the boulders:* **clamber**, climb, crawl, claw your way, scrabble, struggle; N. Amer. shinny. **2** *the alcohol has scrambled his brains:* **muddle**, confuse, mix up, jumble up, disturb, mess up.
• noun **1** *a short scramble over the rocks:* **clamber**, climb. **2** *the scramble for a seat:* **tussle**, jostle, scrimmage, scuffle, struggle, free-for-all, competition, jockeying; muddle, confusion, melee.

scrap noun **1** *a scrap of paper:* **fragment**, piece, bit, snippet, shred; offcut, oddment, remnant. **2** *there wasn't a scrap of evidence:* **bit**, speck, iota, particle, ounce, whit, jot, shred, scintilla. **3** *the foxes ate all the scraps:* **leftovers**, crumbs, remains, remnants, residue, odds and ends, bits and pieces.
• verb **1** *old computers have been scrapped:* **throw away**, throw out, dispose of, get rid of, discard, dispense with, bin; decommission, break up, demolish; informal chuck away/out, ditch, dump, junk; Brit. informal get shot of; N. Amer. informal trash. **2** *MPs called for the plans to be scrapped:* **abandon**, drop, abolish, withdraw, do away with, put an end to, cancel, axe; informal ditch, dump, junk.
– OPPOSITES keep, preserve.

scrape verb **1** *we scraped all the paint off the windows:* **abrade**, sand, sandpaper, scour, scratch, rub, file. **2** *their boots scraped along the floor:*

grate, creak, rasp, grind, scratch. **3** *she scraped her shins on the wall:* **graze**, scratch, scuff, rasp, skin, cut, lacerate, bark, chafe.
• noun **1** *he heard the scrape of her key in the lock:* **grating**, creaking, grinding, rasp, scratch. **2** *there was a long scrape on his shin:* **graze**, scratch, abrasion, cut, laceration, wound. **3** (informal) *he's always getting into scrapes:* **predicament**, plight, tight corner/spot, problem, crisis, mess, muddle; informal jam, fix, stew, bind, hole, hot water; Brit. informal spot of bother.
■ **scrape by** manage, cope, survive, muddle through/along, make ends meet, get by/along, make do, keep the wolf from the door, keep your head above water, eke out a living; informal make out.

scrappy adjective **disorganized**, untidy, disjointed, unsystematic, uneven, bitty, sketchy; piecemeal; fragmentary, incomplete, unfinished.

scratch verb **1** *the paintwork was scratched:* **score**, abrade, scrape, scuff. **2** *thorns scratched her skin:* **graze**, scrape, abrade, skin, cut, lacerate, bark, chafe; wound. **3** *many names had been scratched out:* **cross out**, strike out, score out, delete, erase, remove, expunge, obliterate. **4** *she was forced to scratch from the race:* **withdraw**, pull out of, back out of, bow out of, stand down.
• noun **1** *he had scratches on his cheek:* **graze**, scrape, abrasion, cut, laceration, wound. **2** *a scratch on the paintwork:* **score**, mark, line, scrape.
■ **up to scratch** good enough, up to the mark, up to standard, up to par, satisfactory, acceptable, adequate, passable, sufficient, all right; informal OK, up to snuff.

scrawl verb **scribble**, write quickly, dash off; daub, emblazon.
• noun **scribble**, squiggles, hieroglyphics.

scrawny adjective **skinny**, thin, as thin as a rake, skin-and-bones, gaunt, bony, angular, gawky, scraggy.
– OPPOSITES fat.

scream verb **shriek**, screech, yell, howl, shout, bellow, bawl, cry out, call out, yelp, squeal, wail, squawk; informal holler.
• noun **shriek**, screech, yell, howl, shout, bellow, bawl, cry, yelp, squeal, wail, squawk; informal holler.

screech verb & noun. See SCREAM.

screen noun **1** *he dressed behind the screen:* **partition**, divider. **2** *a computer with a 15-inch screen:* **display**, monitor, visual display unit, VDU. **3** *the hedge acts as a screen against the wind:* **buffer**, protection, shield, shelter, guard; windbreak.
• verb **1** *the end of the hall had been screened off:* **partition off**, divide off, separate off, curtain off. **2** *the cottage was screened by the trees:* **conceal**, hide, veil; shield, shelter, shade, protect. **3** *the prospective candidates will have to be screened:* **vet**, check, investigate, examine, test; informal check out. **4** *the programme is screened on Thursday:* **show**, broadcast, transmit, televise, put out, air.

screw noun **1** *four steel screws:* bolt, fastener. **2** *the ship's twin screws:* **propeller**, rotor.
• verb **1** *he screwed the lid back on the jar:* **tighten**, turn, twist, wind; fasten, secure, fix, attach. **2** (informal) *she intended to screw more money out of them:* **extort**, force, extract, wrest, wring, squeeze; informal bleed.
■ **screw something up 1** *Christina screwed up her face in disgust:* wrinkle, pucker, crumple, crease, furrow, contort, distort, twist. **2** (informal) *they've screwed up the deal:* wreck, ruin, spoil, mess up, mishandle, botch; informal foul up, make a hash of; Brit. informal cock up.

scribble verb **scrawl**, write hurriedly, dash off, jot down; doodle, sketch.
• noun **scrawl**, squiggles, jottings; doodle, doodlings.

scrimp verb
■ **scrimp and save** economize, skimp, save; be thrifty, be frugal, tighten your belt, cut back, draw in your horns, watch your pennies; N. Amer. pinch the pennies.

script noun **1** *her neat, tidy script:* **handwriting**, writing, hand. **2** *the script of the play:* **text**, screenplay; libretto, score; lines, dialogue, words.

Scrooge noun **miser**, penny-pincher,

S

niggard; informal skinflint, meanie, money-grubber, cheapskate; N. Amer. informal tightwad.
– OPPOSITES spendthrift.

scrounge verb **beg**, borrow; informal cadge, sponge, bum, touch someone for; N. Amer. informal mooch; Austral./NZ informal bludge.

scrounger noun **beggar**, parasite, cadger; informal sponger, freeloader; N. Amer. informal mooch, moocher, schnorrer; Austral./NZ informal bludger.

scrub[1] verb **1** *he scrubbed the kitchen floor:* **scour**, rub; clean, cleanse, wash, wipe. **2** (informal) *the plans were scrubbed:* **abandon**, scrap, drop, cancel, call off, axe, jettison, discard, discontinue, abort; informal ditch, dump, junk.

scrub[2] noun *there the buildings ended and the scrub began:* **brush**, brushwood, scrubland, undergrowth.

scruffy adjective **shabby**, worn, down at heel, ragged, tattered, mangy, dirty; untidy, unkempt, bedraggled, messy, dishevelled, ill-groomed; informal tatty, the worse for wear; N. Amer. informal raggedy.
– OPPOSITES smart, tidy.

scrumptious adjective (informal) **delicious**, delectable, mouthwatering, tasty, appetizing, toothsome; succulent, luscious; informal scrummy, yummy; Brit. informal moreish; N. Amer. informal finger-licking, nummy.
– OPPOSITES unpalatable.

scrunch verb **crumple**, crunch, crush, rumple, screw up, squash, squeeze, compress; informal squidge.

S

scruples plural noun **qualms**, compunction, hesitation, doubt, reservations, second thoughts, misgivings, uneasiness, reluctance.

scrupulous adjective **careful**, meticulous, painstaking, thorough, assiduous, sedulous, attentive, conscientious, punctilious, searching, close, minute, rigorous, particular, strict.
– OPPOSITES careless.

scrutinize verb **examine**, inspect, survey, study, look at, peruse; investigate, explore, probe, inquire into, go into, check.

scrutiny noun **examination**, inspection, survey, study, perusal; investigation, exploration, probe, inquiry; informal going-over.

scud verb **speed**, race, rush, sail, shoot, sweep, skim, whip, whizz, flash, fly, scurry, flit.

scuff verb **scrape**, scratch, rub, abrade; mark.

scuffle noun **fight**, struggle, tussle, fracas, rough and tumble, scrimmage; informal scrap, dust-up, set-to, shindy; N. Amer. informal rough house; Law, dated affray.
• verb **fight**, struggle, tussle, clash; informal scrap.

sculpt verb **carve**, model, chisel, sculpture, fashion, form, shape, cut, hew.

sculpture noun **model**, carving, statue, statuette, figure, figurine, effigy, bust, head, likeness; construction, form.

scum noun **film**, layer, covering, froth; filth, dross, dirt.

scupper verb (Brit. informal) **ruin**, wreck, destroy, sabotage, torpedo, spoil.

scurrilous adjective **defamatory**, slanderous, libellous, scandalous, insulting, offensive; abusive, malicious; informal bitchy.

scurry verb **hurry**, hasten, run, rush, dash; scamper, scuttle, scramble; informal scoot, beetle.
– OPPOSITES amble.

scuttle verb. See **SCURRY**.

sea noun **1** *the sea sparkled in the sun:* **the ocean**, the waves; informal the drink; Brit. informal the briny; literary the deep. **2** *the boat overturned in the heavy seas:* **waves**, swell, breakers. **3** *a sea of roofs and turrets:* **expanse**, stretch, area, tract, sweep, carpet, mass; multitude, host, profusion, abundance, plethora.
– OPPOSITES land.
• adjective *sea creatures:* **marine**, ocean, oceanic; saltwater, seawater; ocean-going, seagoing, seafaring; maritime, naval, nautical; technical pelagic.
■ **at sea** confused, perplexed, puzzled, baffled, mystified, bemused, bewildered, nonplussed, disconcerted, disoriented, dumbfounded, at a loss, at sixes and sevens; informal flummoxed, bamboozled, fazed; N. Amer. informal discombobulated.

WORD LINKS
marine, **maritime**, **nautical** relating to the sea
submarine existing, happening, or used under the sea
oceanography the branch of science concerned with the sea

seafaring adjective **maritime**, nautical, naval, seagoing, sea.

seal noun **1** *the seal round the bath:* **sealant**, adhesive, mastic. **2** *the royal seal:* **emblem**, symbol, insignia, device, badge, crest, coat of arms, monogram, stamp.
• verb **1** *seal each bottle while it is hot:* **stop up**, cork, stopper, plug. **2** *he held out his hand to seal the bargain:* **clinch**, secure, settle, conclude, complete, establish, confirm, guarantee.
■ **seal of approval** ratification, approval, blessing, consent, agreement, permission, sanction, endorsement, clearance. **seal something off** *police sealed off the High Street:* close off, shut off, cordon off, fence off, isolate.

seam noun **1** *the seam was coming undone:* **join**, stitching. **2** *a seam of coal:* **layer**, stratum, vein, lode.

seaman noun **sailor**, seafarer, mariner, boatman, hand; Brit. informal matelot.
– OPPOSITES landlubber.

seamy adjective **sordid**, disreputable, seedy, sleazy, squalid, insalubrious, unwholesome, unsavoury, rough, unpleasant.
– OPPOSITES salubrious.

sear verb **1** *the heat of the blast seared his face:* **scorch**, burn, singe, char. **2** *sear the meat before adding the other ingredients:* **flash-fry**, seal, brown.

search verb **1** *I searched for the key:* **hunt**, look, seek, forage, look high and low, rummage, ferret about, root about. **2** *he searched the house:* **look through**, scour, go through, sift through, comb, go through with a fine-tooth comb; turn upside down, turn inside out; Austral./NZ informal fossick through. **3** *the guards searched him:* **examine**, inspect, check, frisk.
• noun *we continued our search:* **hunt**, look, quest.
■ **in search of** searching for, hunting for, seeking, looking for, on the lookout for, in pursuit of.

searching adjective **penetrating**, piercing, probing, keen, shrewd, sharp, intent.

searing adjective **1** *the searing heat:* **scorching**, blistering, sweltering, blazing, burning, fiery; informal boiling, baking, sizzling, roasting. **2** *searing pain:* **intense**, excruciating, agonizing, sharp, severe, extreme, racking. **3** *a searing attack:* **fierce**, savage, scathing, stinging, mordant, trenchant, caustic, cutting, withering.

seaside noun **coast**, shore, seashore; beach, sand, sands; technical littoral.

season noun **period**, time, time of year, spell, term.
• verb **flavour**, spice, salt, pepper.
■ **in season** available, obtainable, to be had, on offer, on the market; plentiful, abundant.

seasonable adjective **usual**, expected, predictable, normal.

seasoned adjective **experienced**, practised, well versed, knowledgeable, established, habituated, veteran, hardened, battle-scarred.
– OPPOSITES inexperienced.

seasoning noun **flavouring**, salt and pepper; herbs, spices, condiments.

seat noun **1** *a wooden seat:* **chair**, bench, stool; Brit. informal pew. **2** *the seat of government:* **headquarters**, base, centre, nerve centre, hub, heart; location, site, whereabouts, place. **3** *the family's country seat:* **residence**, ancestral home, mansion; formal abode, dwelling.
• verb **1** *they seated themselves round the table:* **position**, ensconce, install, settle; put, place; informal plonk, park. **2** *the hall can seat 500 people:* **accommodate**, take, sit, hold, contain.

seating noun **seats**, room, places, chairs, accommodation.

secede verb **withdraw from**, break with, separate from, break away, leave, split off from, disaffiliate from, resign from, pull out of; informal quit.
– OPPOSITES join.

secluded adjective **sheltered**, private, concealed, hidden, unfrequented, sequestered, tucked away.
– OPPOSITES busy.

seclusion noun **isolation**, solitude, retreat, privacy, retirement, withdrawal, purdah, concealment, hiding, secrecy.

second[1] adjective **1** *the second day of the trial:* **next**, following, subsequent, succeeding. **2** *a second pair of glasses:* **additional**, extra, alternative, another, spare, backup; N. Amer. alternate. **3** *second prize:* **secondary**, subordinate, subsidiary, lesser, inferior.
– OPPOSITES first.
• noun *Eva had been working as his second:* **assistant**, attendant, helper, aide, supporter, auxiliary, right-hand man/woman, girl/man Friday, second in command, number two, deputy, understudy, subordinate; informal sidekick.
• verb *George seconded the motion:* **support**, vote for, back, approve, endorse.
■ **second to none** incomparable, matchless, unrivalled, inimitable, beyond compare, unparalleled, without equal, in a class of its own, peerless, unsurpassable; unique; perfect, consummate, transcendent, superlative, supreme.

second[2] noun *I'll only be gone for a second:* **moment**, bit, little while; informal sec, jiffy; Brit. informal mo, tick.
■ **in a second** very soon, in a minute, in a moment, in a trice, shortly, any minute, in the twinkling of an eye; N. Amer. momentarily; informal in a jiffy, in two shakes of a lamb's tail, before you can say Jack Robinson.

S

second[3] verb *he was seconded to the Welsh office:* **assign**, transfer, move, shift, relocate, send.

secondary adjective **1** *a secondary issue:* **less important**, subordinate, lesser, minor, peripheral, incidental, ancillary, subsidiary. **2** *secondary infections:* **accompanying**, attendant, concomitant, consequential, resulting, resultant.
– OPPOSITES primary, main.

second-class adjective **second-rate**, second-best, inferior, lesser, unimportant.

second-hand adjective **1** *second-hand clothes:* **used**, old, worn, pre-owned, handed-down, hand-me-down, cast-off. **2** *second-hand information:* **indirect**; vicarious, mediated.
– OPPOSITES new, direct.
• adverb *I heard this second-hand:* **indirectly**; informal on the grapevine.
– OPPOSITES directly.

second in command noun **deputy**, number two, subordinate, right-hand man/woman; understudy.

secondly adverb **furthermore**, also, moreover; second, secondarily, next.

second-rate adjective **inferior**, substandard, low-quality, below par, bad, poor, deficient, defective, faulty, shoddy, inadequate, insufficient, unacceptable; Brit. informal ropy, duff, rubbish.
– OPPOSITES first-rate, excellent.

secrecy noun **1** *the secrecy of the material:* **confidentiality**. **2** *a government which thrived on secrecy:* **secretiveness**, covertness, furtiveness, stealth.

secret adjective **1** *a secret plan:* **confidential**, top secret, classified, undisclosed, private, under wraps; informal hush-hush. **2** *a secret drawer in the table:* **hidden**, concealed, disguised. **3** *a secret campaign:* **clandestine**, covert, undercover, underground, surreptitious, cloak-and-dagger, hole-and-corner. **4** *a secret message | a secret code:* **cryptic**, encoded, coded; mysterious, abstruse, recondite, arcane, esoteric. **5** *a secret place:* **secluded**, private, concealed, hidden, out of the way, tucked away.
– OPPOSITES public, open.
• noun **1** *he just can't keep a secret:* **confidential matter**; confidence; skeleton in the cupboard. **2** *the secrets of the universe:* **mystery**, enigma. **3** *the secret of their success:* **recipe**, magic formula, blueprint, key, answer, solution.
■ **in secret** secretly, in private, privately, behind closed doors, behind the scenes, in camera, under cover, under the counter, discreetly, behind someone's back, furtively, stealthily, on the sly, on the quiet, conspiratorially, covertly, clandestinely, on the side; informal on the q.t.

secretary noun **assistant**, personal assistant, PA, administrator, girl/man Friday.

secrete[1] verb *a substance secreted by the liver:* **produce**, discharge, emit, excrete, release, send out.
– OPPOSITES absorb.

secrete[2] verb *we secreted ourselves in the bushes:* **conceal**, hide, stow away; bury, cache; informal stash away.
– OPPOSITES reveal.

secretive adjective **uncommunicative**, secret, unforthcoming, playing your cards close to your chest, reticent, reserved, silent, tight-lipped.
– OPPOSITES open, communicative.

secretly adverb **1** *they met secretly:* **in secret**, in private, privately, behind closed doors, in camera, behind the scenes, under cover, under the counter, behind someone's back, furtively, stealthily, on the sly, on the quiet, covertly, clandestinely, on the side; informal on the q.t. **2** *he was secretly jealous of her:* **privately**, in your heart of hearts, deep down, inwardly.

sect noun **group**, grouping, cult, denomination, order; splinter group, faction.

sectarian adjective **factional**, separatist, partisan; doctrinaire, dogmatic, illiberal, intolerant, bigoted, narrow-minded.
– OPPOSITES tolerant, liberal.

section noun **1** *the separate sections of the box:* **part**, bit, segment, compartment, module, area. **2** *the last section of the questionnaire:* **subdivision**, part, subsection, portion, bit, chapter, passage, clause. **3** *the reference section of the library:* **department**, area, part, division.

sector noun **1** *every sector of the industry is affected:* **part**, branch, arm, division, area, department, field, sphere. **2** *the north-eastern sector of the town:* **district**, quarter, part, section, zone, region, area, belt.

secular adjective **non-religious**, lay, temporal, worldly, earthly, profane.
– OPPOSITES holy, religious.

secure adjective **1** *check that all bolts are secure:* **fastened**, fixed, secured, done up; closed, shut, locked. **2** *a place where children feel secure:* **safe**, protected, safe and sound, out of harm's way, in a safe place, in safe hands, invulnerable; at ease, unworried, relaxed, happy, confident. **3** *a secure future:* **certain**, assured, reliable, dependable, settled, fixed.
– OPPOSITES loose, vulnerable, uncertain.
• verb **1** *pins secure the handle to the main body:* **fix**, attach, fasten, affix, connect, couple. **2** *the doors had not been properly secured:* **fasten**, close, shut, lock, bolt, chain, seal. **3** *they sought to secure the country against attack:* **protect**, make safe, fortify, strengthen. **4** *a written constitution would secure our rights:* **assure**, ensure, guarantee, protect, confirm, establish; enshrine. **5** *the division secured a major contract:* **obtain**, acquire, gain, get; informal land.

security noun **1** *the security of our citizens:* **safety**, protection. **2** *he could give her the security she needed:* **peace of mind**, stability, certainty. **3** *security at the court was tight:* **safety measures**, safeguards, surveillance, defence, protection, policing. **4** *additional security for your loan:* **guarantee**, collateral, surety, pledge, bond.
– OPPOSITES vulnerability, insecurity.

sedate[1] verb *the patient had to be sedated:* **tranquillize**, put under, drug.

sedate[2] adjective **1** *a sedate pace:* **slow**, steady, dignified, unhurried, relaxed, measured, leisurely, slow-moving, easy, easy-going, gentle. **2** *he had lived a sedate life:* **calm**, placid, tranquil, quiet, uneventful; boring, dull.
– OPPOSITES exciting, fast.

sedative adjective **tranquillizing**, calming, calmative, relaxing, soporific.
• noun **tranquillizer**, sleeping pill; narcotic, opiate.

sedentary adjective **sitting**, seated, desk-bound; inactive.
– OPPOSITES active.

sediment noun **dregs**, lees, precipitate, deposit, grounds, residue, remains; silt; technical residuum.

sedition noun **rabble-rousing**, subversion, troublemaking, provocation; rebellion, insurrection, mutiny, insurgence, civil disorder.

seditious adjective **rabble-rousing**, provocative, inflammatory, subversive, troublemaking; rebellious, mutinous, insurgent.

seduce verb *customers are seduced by the advertising:* **attract**, lure, tempt, entice, ensnare, beguile, inveigle, manipulate.

seductive adjective **alluring**, tempting, beguiling, attractive; manipulative.

sedulous adjective **diligent**, careful, meticulous, thorough, assiduous, attentive, industrious, conscientious, punctilious, scrupulous, painstaking, rigorous, particular.

see verb **1** *he saw her in the street:* **spot**, notice, catch sight of, glimpse, make out, pick out, spy, distinguish, discern, detect, perceive, note; informal clap/lay/set eyes on, clock; literary behold, espy. **2** *would you like to see the house?* **inspect**, view, look round, tour, survey, examine, scrutinize; informal give something a once-over. **3** *I finally saw what she meant:* **understand**, grasp, comprehend, follow, realize, appreciate, recognize, work out, get the drift of, perceive, fathom out; informal get, latch on to, cotton on to, catch on to, tumble to, savvy, figure out, get a fix on; Brit. informal twig, suss out. **4** *I must see what she's up to:* **find out**, discover, learn, ascertain, determine, establish. **5** *I see trouble ahead:* **foresee**, predict, forecast, prophesy, anticipate, envisage, picture, visualize. **6** *you'd better see a doctor:* **consult**, confer with, talk to, speak to, have recourse to, call on, call in, turn to, ask. **7** *he saw her to her car:* **escort**, accompany, show, walk, conduct, lead, take, usher. **8** *he's seeing someone else now:* **go out with**, date, take out, be involved with; informal go steady with; N. Amer. informal, dated step out with; dated court. **9** *they still see each other from time to time:* **meet**, meet up, get together, socialize.
■ **see someone through** sustain, encourage, buoy up, keep going, support, comfort, help out, stand by, stick by. **see something through** persevere with, persist with, continue, carry on with, keep at, follow through, stay with; informal stick at, stick it out. **see to** attend to, deal with, see about, take care of, look after, sort out, fix, organize, arrange.

S

seed noun pip, stone, kernel.
■ **go/run to seed** deteriorate, degenerate, decline, decay, fall into decay, go to rack and ruin, go downhill, moulder, rot; informal go to pot, go to the dogs.

WORD LINKS
seminal relating to the seed of a plant

seedy adjective **1** *the seedy world of prostitution:* **sordid**, disreputable, tawdry, seamy, sleazy, squalid, unsavoury. **2** *a seedy part of town:* **dilapidated**, tumbledown, ramshackle, decrepit, gone to rack and ruin, run down, down at heel, shabby, dingy, insalubrious, squalid; informal crummy; Brit. informal grotty.
–OPPOSITES high-class.

seek verb **1** *he is seeking work:* **search for**, try to find, look for, be after, hunt for. **2** *the company is seeking a judicial review:* **try to obtain**, work towards, be intent on, aim at/for. **3** *he sought help from a motorist:* **ask for**, request, solicit, call for, appeal for, apply for, put in for. **4** *we constantly seek to improve the service:* **try**, attempt, endeavour, strive, work, do your best.

seem verb **appear**, look, have the air of, give the impression of; come across as, strike someone as, sound.

seeming adjective **apparent**, ostensible, supposed, outward, surface, superficial.
–OPPOSITES actual, genuine.

seemingly adverb **apparently**, on the face of it, to all appearances, on the surface, to all intents and purposes, outwardly, superficially, supposedly.

seemly adjective **decorous**, proper, decent, becoming, fitting, suitable, appropriate, in good taste, the done thing, right, correct, acceptable.
–OPPOSITES unseemly, unbecoming.

seep verb **ooze**, trickle, exude, drip, dribble, flow, issue, escape, leak, drain, bleed, filter, percolate, soak.

seer noun **soothsayer**, oracle, prophet, prophetess, diviner; literary sibyl.

see-saw verb **fluctuate**, swing, go up and down, rise and fall, oscillate, alternate, yo-yo, vary.

seethe verb **1** *I seethed at the injustice of it all:* **be angry**, be furious, be enraged, be incensed, be beside yourself, simmer, fume, smoulder; informal be hot under the collar. **2** *the cellar was seething with spiders:* **teem**, swarm; be full of, be crowded with, be alive with.

see-through adjective **transparent**, translucent, clear; thin, lightweight, flimsy, sheer, diaphanous, filmy, gauzy.
–OPPOSITES opaque.

segment noun **piece**, bit, section, part, chunk, portion, division, slice; fragment, wedge, lump, tranche.
• verb **divide**, subdivide, separate, split, cut up, carve up, slice up, break up.
–OPPOSITES amalgamate.

segregate verb **separate**, set apart, keep apart, isolate, quarantine, closet; partition, divide.
–OPPOSITES amalgamate.

seize verb **1** *she seized the microphone:* **grab**, grasp, snatch, take hold of. **2** *rebels seized the air base:* **capture**, take, overrun, occupy, conquer, take over. **3** *the drugs were seized by customs:* **confiscate**, impound, commandeer, requisition, appropriate, expropriate. **4** *terrorists seized his wife:* **kidnap**, abduct, take captive, take prisoner, take hostage; informal snatch.
–OPPOSITES relinquish, release.
■ **seize on** *they seized on the opportunity:* take advantage of, exploit, grasp with both hands, leap at, jump at, pounce on.

seizure noun **1** *Napoleon's seizure of Spain:* **capture**, takeover, annexation, invasion, occupation, colonization. **2** *the seizure of defaulters' property:* **confiscation**, appropriation, expropriation, sequestration. **3** *the seizure of UN staff:* **kidnapping**, kidnap, abduction. **4** *the baby suffered a seizure:* **convulsion**, fit, spasm, paroxysm; Medicine ictus.

seldom adverb **rarely**, infrequently, hardly ever, scarcely ever; informal once in a blue moon.
–OPPOSITES often.

select verb **choose**, pick, single out, sort out, take.
• adjective **1** *a small, select group:* choice, hand-picked, elite; informal top-flight. **2** *a very select area:* **exclusive**, privileged; wealthy; informal posh.
–OPPOSITES inferior.

selection noun **1** *Jim made his selection:* **choice**, pick; option, preference. **2** *a wide selection of dishes:* **range**, array, diversity, variety, assortment, mixture. **3** *a selection of his poems:* **anthology**, assortment, collection, assemblage; miscellany, medley.

selective adjective **discerning**, discriminating, exacting, demanding, particular; fussy, fastidious, faddish; informal choosy, pernickety, picky.

self noun **ego**, I, yourself, persona, person, identity, character, personality, psyche, soul, spirit, mind, inner self.
–OPPOSITES other.

WORD LINKS
autobiography an account of a person's life written by that person
egomania obsessive self-centredness
suicide the action of killing yourself deliberately

self-assembly adjective **flat-pack**, kit, self-build, do-it-yourself, DIY.

self-assurance noun **self-confidence**, confidence, assertiveness, self-reliance, self-possession, composure.
–OPPOSITES diffidence.

self-assured adjective **self-confident**, confident, assertive, assured, authoritative, self-possessed, poised.

self-centred adjective **egocentric**, egotistic, self-absorbed, self-obsessed, self-seeking, self-interested, self-serving; narcissistic, vain; inconsiderate, thoughtless; informal looking after number one.

self-confidence noun **morale**, confidence, self-assurance, assurance, composure.

self-conscious adjective **embarrassed**, uncomfortable, uneasy, nervous.
–OPPOSITES confident.

self-contained adjective **1** *a self-contained unit:* **complete**, independent, separate, free-standing, stand-alone, autonomous. **2** *a very self-contained child:*

independent, self-sufficient, self-reliant.

self-control noun **self-discipline**, restraint, self-possession, will power, composure; moderation, temperance, abstemiousness; informal cool.

self-denial noun **self-sacrifice**, selflessness, unselfishness; asceticism, abstemiousness, abstinence, abstention.
– OPPOSITES self-indulgence.

self-discipline noun **self-control**; restraint, self-restraint; will power, strong-mindedness, moral fibre.

self-employed adjective **freelance**, independent, casual; consultant.

self-esteem noun **self-respect**, pride, dignity, self-regard, faith in yourself; morale, self-confidence, confidence, self-assurance.

self-evident adjective **obvious**, clear, plain, evident, apparent, manifest, patent.
– OPPOSITES unclear.

self-explanatory adjective **easily understood**, comprehensible, intelligible, straightforward, unambiguous, accessible, crystal clear, self-evident, obvious.
– OPPOSITES impenetrable.

self-governing adjective **independent**, sovereign, autonomous, free; self-determining.
– OPPOSITES dependent.

self-important adjective **conceited**, arrogant, bumptious, full of yourself, puffed up, pompous, overbearing; presumptuous, sententious.
– OPPOSITES humble.

S

self-indulgent adjective **hedonistic**, pleasure-seeking, sybaritic, indulgent, luxurious, epicurean; intemperate, immoderate, overindulgent, excessive, extravagant, licentious, dissolute, decadent.
– OPPOSITES abstemious.

self-interest noun **self-seeking**, self-regard; selfishness; informal looking after number one.
– OPPOSITES altruism.

self-interested adjective **self-seeking**, self-serving, selfish.

selfish adjective **egocentric**, egotistic, self-centred, self-absorbed, self-obsessed, self-seeking, self-serving, wrapped up in yourself; inconsiderate, thoughtless, unthinking, uncaring; mean, miserly, grasping, greedy, mercenary, acquisitive, opportunistic; informal looking after number one.
– OPPOSITES altruistic.

selfless adjective **unselfish**, altruistic; considerate, compassionate, kind, noble, generous, magnanimous, ungrudging.
– OPPOSITES inconsiderate.

self-possessed adjective **assured**, self-assured, calm, cool, composed, at ease, unperturbed, unruffled, confident, self-confident, poised; informal together, unfazed, unflappable.
– OPPOSITES unsure.

self-reliant adjective **self-sufficient**, self-contained, able to stand on your own two feet; independent.

self-respect noun **self-esteem**, self-regard, pride, dignity, morale, self-confidence.

self-restraint noun **self-control**, restraint, self-discipline, will power, moderation, temperance, abstemiousness.
– OPPOSITES self-indulgence.

self-righteous adjective **sanctimonious**, holier-than-thou, self-satisfied, smug, priggish, complacent, pious, moralizing, superior, hypocritical; informal goody-goody.
– OPPOSITES humble.

self-sacrifice noun **self-denial**, selflessness, unselfishness.

self-satisfied adjective **complacent**, self-congratulatory, smug, superior, pleased with yourself.

self-seeking adjective **self-interested**, self-serving, selfish; informal looking after number one.
– OPPOSITES altruistic.

self-styled adjective **would-be**, so-called, self-appointed, professed; supposed, alleged.

self-sufficient adjective **self-supporting**, self-reliant, self-sustaining, able to stand on your own two feet; independent.

self-willed adjective **wilful**, contrary, perverse, uncooperative, wayward, headstrong, stubborn, obstinate, obdurate, pig-headed,

intransigent, recalcitrant, intractable; Brit. informal bloody-minded; formal refractory.
– OPPOSITES biddable.

sell verb **1** *they're selling their car:* **put up for sale**, put on the market, auction; trade in. **2** *we sell a variety of electrical goods:* **trade in**, deal in, traffic in, stock, carry, offer for sale, peddle, retail, market. **3** *the product sells for £70:* **cost**, retail at, go for.
– OPPOSITES buy.
■ **sell someone out** betray, inform on; double-cross, stab in the back; informal tell on, sell down the river, stitch up, do the dirty on; Brit. informal grass on, shop; N. Amer. informal finger.

seller noun **vendor**, retailer, purveyor, supplier, stockist, trader, merchant, dealer; salesperson, salesman, saleswoman, pedlar; auctioneer.

semblance noun **appearance**, air, show, facade, front, veneer, guise, pretence.

seminal adjective **influential**, formative, groundbreaking, pioneering, original, innovative; major, important.

seminar noun **1** *a seminar for education officials:* **conference**, symposium, meeting, convention, forum, summit. **2** *a history seminar:* **study group**, workshop, tutorial, class.

send verb **1** *they sent a message to HQ:* **dispatch**, post, mail, consign, direct, forward; transmit, convey, communicate, broadcast; email, fax, text. **2** *we sent for a doctor:* **call**, summon; ask for, request, order. **3** *the pump sent out a jet of petrol:* **propel**, project, eject, deliver, discharge, spout, fire, shoot, release; throw, let fly, spew. **4** *it's enough to send one mad:* **make**, drive, turn.
– OPPOSITES receive.
■ **send someone down** (informal) send to prison, imprison, jail, incarcerate, lock up, confine, detain, intern; informal put away; Brit. informal bang up. **send someone off** (Sport) order off, dismiss; show the red card; informal red-card, send for an early bath. **send someone/something up** (informal) satirize, ridicule, make fun of, parody, lampoon, mock, caricature, imitate, ape; informal take off, spoof, take the mickey out of.

send-off noun **farewell**, goodbye, adieu, leave-taking, valediction; funeral.
– OPPOSITES welcome.

send-up noun (informal) **satire**, lampoon, pastiche, caricature, imitation, impression, impersonation; informal spoof, take-off.

senile adjective **doddering**, decrepit, senescent, infirm, feeble; confused; informal gaga.

senior adjective **1** *senior school pupils:* **older**, elder. **2** *a senior officer:* **superior**, higher-ranking, more important; N. Amer. ranking.
– OPPOSITES junior, subordinate.

senior citizen noun **pensioner**, old-age pensioner, OAP; geriatric; N. Amer. senior, retiree, golden ager; informal old-timer, oldie, wrinkly.

seniority noun **rank**, superiority, standing, primacy, precedence, priority; age.

sensation noun **1** *a sensation of heaviness:* **feeling**, sense, perception, impression. **2** *she caused a sensation:* **commotion**, stir, uproar, furore, scandal, impact; informal splash, to-do, hullabaloo.

sensational adjective **1** *a sensational murder trial:* **shocking**, scandalous, appalling; amazing, startling, astonishing; fascinating, interesting, noteworthy, significant, remarkable, momentous, historic, newsworthy. **2** *sensational stories:* **overdramatized**, melodramatic, exaggerated, sensationalist; graphic, explicit, lurid; informal shock-horror, juicy. **3** (informal) *she looked sensational:* **gorgeous**, stunning, wonderful, exquisite, lovely, radiant, delightful, charming, enchanting, captivating; superb, excellent, first-class; informal great, terrific, tremendous, fantastic, fabulous, fab, heavenly, divine, knockout, awesome, magic, wicked, out of this world; Brit. informal smashing, brilliant, brill.
– OPPOSITES dull, understated, unremarkable.

sense noun **1** *the sense of touch:* **faculty**, sensation, perception; sight, hearing, touch, taste, smell. **2** *a sense of guilt:* **feeling**, awareness, sensation, recognition.

3 *a fine sense of comic timing:* **appreciation**, awareness, understanding, sensibility; discernment. **4** *she had the sense to leave:* **wisdom**, common sense; wit, intelligence, cleverness, shrewdness, judgement, reason, logic, brains; informal gumption, nous, horse sense, savvy; Brit. informal loaf; N. Amer. informal smarts. **5** *I can't see the sense in this:* **purpose**, point, reason, object, motive; use, value, advantage, benefit. **6** *different senses of the word 'dark':* **meaning**, definition; nuance; drift, gist, thrust, tenor, message.
–OPPOSITES stupidity.
•verb *she sensed their hostility:* **discern**, feel, recognize, pick up, be aware of, distinguish, identify, observe, notice; suspect, have a hunch, divine, intuit.

senseless adjective **1** *a senseless waste of time and money:* **pointless**, futile, useless, needless, unavailing, in vain, purposeless, meaningless, unprofitable; absurd, foolish, insane, stupid, idiotic, ridiculous, ludicrous. **2** *they found him senseless on the floor:* **unconscious**, stunned, insensible, comatose, knocked out, out cold, out for the count; Brit. informal spark out.
–OPPOSITES prudent, conscious.

sensibility noun **feelings**, emotions, sensitivities, susceptibilities.

sensible adjective **practical**, realistic, responsible, reasonable, common-sensical, rational, logical, sound, balanced, sober, no-nonsense, level-headed, thoughtful, down-to-earth, wise, grounded.
–OPPOSITES foolish.

S

sensitive adjective **1** *she's sensitive to changes in temperature:* **responsive to**, reactive to, sensitized to; aware of, conscious of; susceptible to, affected by, vulnerable to; attuned to. **2** *sensitive skin:* **delicate**, fragile; tender, sore. **3** *the matter needs sensitive handling:* **tactful**, careful, thoughtful, diplomatic, delicate, subtle, kid-glove. **4** *he's sensitive about his bald patch:* **touchy**, oversensitive, hypersensitive, easily offended, thin-skinned, defensive; paranoid, neurotic; informal uptight. **5** *a sensitive issue:* **difficult**, delicate, tricky, awkward, problematic, ticklish, precarious; controversial, emotive.
–OPPOSITES impervious, resilient, insensitive, thick-skinned.

sensitivity noun **1** *the sensitivity of the skin:* **responsiveness**, sensitiveness, reactivity. **2** *the job calls for sensitivity:* **tact**, diplomacy, delicacy, subtlety; understanding, empathy; insight. **3** *her sensitivity on the subject:* **touchiness**, oversensitivity, hypersensitivity, defensiveness. **4** *the sensitivity of the issue:* **delicacy**, awkwardness, ticklishness.

sensual adjective **1** *sensual pleasure:* **physical**, carnal, bodily, fleshly, animal. **2** *a very sensual woman:* **passionate**, sexual, physical, tactile; hedonistic.
–OPPOSITES spiritual, passionless.

sensualist noun **hedonist**, pleasure-seeker; epicure, gastronome; bon vivant, bon viveur.

sensuality noun **sexuality**, eroticism; physicality, carnality, pleasure.

sensuous adjective **1** *big sensuous canvases:* **rich**, sumptuous, luxurious. **2** *sensuous lips:* **voluptuous**, sexy, seductive, luscious, lush, ripe.

sentence noun **prison term**; punishment; informal time, stretch, stint.
•verb *they were sentenced to death:* **condemn**, doom; punish, convict.

sententious adjective **moralistic**, moralizing, sanctimonious, self-righteous, pious, priggish, judgemental; pompous, self-important.

sentient adjective **feeling**, living, live; conscious, aware, responsive, reactive.

sentiment noun **1** *the comments echo my own sentiments:* **view**, feeling, attitude, thought, opinion, belief. **2** *there's no room for sentiment:* **sentimentality**; emotion, softness; informal schmaltz, mush, slushiness, cheese; Brit. informal soppiness; N. Amer. informal sappiness.

sentimental adjective **1** *she kept the vase for sentimental reasons:* **nostalgic**, tender, emotional. **2** *the film is too sentimental:* **mawkish**,

overemotional, cloying, sickly, saccharine, sugary; romantic; Brit. twee; informal slushy, mushy, tear-jerking, schmaltzy, gooey, drippy, cheesy, corny; Brit. informal soppy; N. Amer. informal cornball, sappy, hokey. **3** *she is very sentimental:* **soft-hearted**, soft; informal soppy.
– OPPOSITES practical.

sentry noun **guard**, sentinel, lookout, watch, watchman.

separate adjective **1** *his personal life was separate from his job:* **unconnected**, unrelated, different, distinct, discrete; detached, divorced, disconnected, independent, autonomous. **2** *the infirmary was separate from the school:* **set apart**, detached; fenced off, cut off, segregated, isolated; free-standing, self-contained.
– OPPOSITES linked, attached.
• verb **1** *they separated the two youths:* **split up**, break up, part, pull apart. **2** *the connectors can be separated:* **disconnect**, detach, disengage, uncouple; split, divide, sever; disentangle. **3** *the wall that separated the two estates:* **partition**, divide, keep apart; bisect, intersect. **4** *the south aisle was separated off:* **isolate**, partition off, section off, set apart; close off, shut off, cordon off, fence off. **5** *they separated at the airport:* **part**, part company, go their separate ways, split up; say goodbye; disperse, scatter. **6** *the road separated:* **fork**, divide, branch, bifurcate, diverge. **7** *her parents separated:* **split up**, break up, part, divorce.
– OPPOSITES unite, join, link, merge.

separately adverb **individually**, one by one, one at a time, singly, severally; apart, independently, alone, by yourself, on your own.

separation noun **1** *the separation of the two companies:* **disconnection**, splitting, dividing up, disaffiliation, breaking up. **2** *her parents' separation:* **break-up**, split, estrangement; divorce; Brit. informal bust-up. **3** *the separation between art and life:* **distinction**, difference, division, dividing line; gulf, gap, chasm.

septic adjective **infected**, festering, suppurating, putrid, putrefying, poisoned; Medicine purulent.

sepulchral adjective **gloomy**, lugubrious, sombre, melancholy, mournful, dismal.
– OPPOSITES cheerful.

sepulchre noun **tomb**, vault, burial chamber, crypt; grave.

sequel noun *a sequel to the riots:* **consequence**, result, upshot, postscript; after-effect; informal follow-on.

sequence noun **1** *the sequence of events:* **succession**, order, course, series, chain, train, progression, chronology; pattern, flow. **2** *a sequence from his film:* **excerpt**, clip, extract, section.

sequester verb **1** *he sequestered himself from the world:* **isolate yourself**, hide away, shut yourself away, seclude yourself, cut yourself off, segregate yourself; closet yourself, withdraw, retire. **2** *the government sequestered his property.* See **SEQUESTRATE**.

sequestrate verb **confiscate**, seize, take, sequester, appropriate, expropriate, impound, commandeer.

serendipitous adjective **chance**, accidental, coincidental; lucky, fortuitous; unexpected.

serendipity noun **chance**, happy accident, happy coincidence; luck, good luck, good fortune, providence.

serene adjective **1** *on the surface she seemed serene:* **calm**, composed, tranquil, peaceful, untroubled, relaxed, at ease, unperturbed, unruffled, unworried; placid; N. Amer. centered; informal together, unflappable. **2** *serene valleys:* **peaceful**, tranquil, quiet, still.
– OPPOSITES agitated, turbulent.

series noun **succession**, sequence, string, chain, run, round; spate, wave, rash; set, course, cycle; row, line.

serious adjective **1** *a serious expression:* **solemn**, earnest, grave, sombre, sober, unsmiling, poker-faced, stern, grim, dour, humourless, stony-faced. **2** *serious decisions:* **important**, significant, consequential, momentous, weighty, far-reaching, major, grave, urgent, crucial, critical. **3** *give serious consideration to this suggestion:* **careful**, detailed, in-depth. **4** *a*

serious play: **intellectual**, highbrow, heavyweight, deep, profound, literary, learned, scholarly; informal heavy. **5** *serious injuries:* **severe**, grave, bad, critical, acute, terrible, dire, dangerous; formal grievous. **6** *we're serious about equality:* **in earnest**, sincere, wholehearted, genuine; committed, resolute, determined.
– OPPOSITES light-hearted, trivial, minor.

sermon noun **1** *he delivered a sermon:* **homily**, address, speech, talk, discourse, oration; lesson. **2** *a lengthy sermon about drugs:* **lecture**, speech, monologue.

serpentine adjective **winding**, zigzag, twisty, twisting and turning, meandering, sinuous, snaky, tortuous.
– OPPOSITES straight.

serrated adjective **jagged**, sawtoothed, zigzag, notched, toothed; technical crenulated.
– OPPOSITES smooth.

servant noun **attendant**, retainer; lackey, flunkey, minion; maid, housemaid, footman, page boy, valet, butler, manservant; housekeeper, steward; drudge, slave.

serve verb **1** *they served their masters faithfully:* **work for**, attend, assist; obey; do the bidding of. **2** *this job serves the community:* **help**, assist, aid, do your bit for, do something for, benefit. **3** *she served on the committee:* **sit on**, be on, work on. **4** *he served his apprenticeship in Scotland:* **carry out**, perform, do, fulfil, complete, discharge; spend. **5** *serve the soup hot:* **dish up/out**, give out, distribute; present, provide, supply; offer. **6** *she served another customer:* **attend to**, deal with, see to; **assist**, help, look after. **7** *they served him with a writ:* **present**, deliver, give, hand over. **8** *official forms will serve in most cases:* **suffice**, be adequate, fit/fill the bill, do, meet requirements, suit.

service noun **1** *their conditions of service:* **work**, employment, labour. **2** *he has done us a service:* **favour**, kindness, good turn, helping hand; (**services**) assistance, help, aid. **3** *a marriage service:* **ceremony**, ritual, rite; liturgy. **4** *a range of local services:* **amenity**, facility, resource, utility. **5** *many soldiers are leaving the services:* **armed forces**, military; army, navy, air force.
• verb *the appliances are serviced regularly:* **overhaul**, check, go over, maintain.
■ **be of service** help, assist, be of assistance, be useful, be of use; do someone a good turn. **out of service** out of order, broken, out of commission, unserviceable, faulty, defective, inoperative; down; informal conked out, bust, kaput, on the blink, acting up; Brit. informal knackered.

serviceable adjective **1** *a serviceable heating system:* **in working order**, working, functioning, operational; usable, workable, viable. **2** *serviceable lace-up shoes:* **functional**, utilitarian, sensible, practical; hard-wearing, durable, tough, robust.

servile adjective **obsequious**, sycophantic, deferential, subservient, fawning, ingratiating, unctuous, grovelling, toadyish; informal slimy, bootlicking, smarmy; N. Amer. informal apple-polishing.
– OPPOSITES assertive.

serving noun **portion**, helping, plateful, plate, bowlful.

servitude noun **slavery**, enslavement, bondage, subjugation, domination.
– OPPOSITES liberty.

session noun **1** *a session of the committee:* **meeting**, sitting, assembly, conclave, plenary; hearing; N. Amer. & NZ caucus. **2** *training sessions:* **period**, time; class, lesson, meeting. **3** *the next college session begins in August:* **academic year**, school year; term, semester; N. Amer. trimester.

set[1] verb **1** *she set the bag on the table:* **put**, place, lay, deposit, position, settle, leave, stand, plant; informal stick, dump, bung, park, plonk, pop. **2** *the cottage is set on a hill:* **be situated**, be located, lie, stand, be sited. **3** *the fence is set in concrete:* **fix**, embed, insert; mount. **4** *a ring set with precious stones:* **adorn**, ornament, decorate, embellish. **5** *I'll go and set the table:* **lay**, prepare, arrange, fix. **6** *we set them some work:* **assign**, allocate, give, allot.

S

7 *they set a date for the election:* **decide on**, select, choose, arrange, schedule; fix, settle on, determine, designate, name, appoint, specify, stipulate. **8** *his jump set a new record:* **establish**, create, institute. **9** *he set his watch:* **adjust**, regulate, synchronize; calibrate; put right, correct. **10** *the adhesive will set in an hour:* **solidify**, harden, stiffen, thicken, gel; cake, congeal, coagulate, clot.

■ **set about 1** *they set about raising the £5000:* begin, start, commence, go about, get to work on, get down to, embark on, tackle, address yourself to, undertake. **2** *the youths set about him:* attack, assault, hit, strike, beat, thrash, pummel, wallop, set upon, fall on; informal lay into, let someone have it, do/work over, rough up, knock about/around; Brit. informal duff up, have a go at; N. Amer. informal beat up on. **set someone/something apart** distinguish, differentiate, mark out, single out, separate, demarcate. **set something aside 1** *set aside some money each month:* save, put by/aside/away, keep, reserve; store, stockpile, hoard; informal squirrel/stash away. **2** *he set aside his cup:* put down, put aside, discard, abandon. **3** *set aside your differences:* disregard, put aside, ignore, forget, bury. **4** *the Appeal Court set aside the decision:* overrule, overturn, reverse, revoke, nullify, quash, dismiss, reject. **set someone/something back** delay, hold up/back, slow down/up, retard; hinder, impede, obstruct, hamper, inhibit. **set someone free** release, free, let go, turn loose, let out, liberate, deliver. **set off** set out, start out, sally forth, leave, depart, embark, set sail; informal hit the road. **set something off 1** *a bomb was set off:* detonate, explode, blow up, touch off, trigger; ignite. **2** *the announcement set off a wave of protest:* give rise to, cause, lead to, set in motion, occasion, bring about, initiate, precipitate, prompt, trigger, spark off, provoke, incite. **3** *the blue dress set off her hair:* enhance, bring out, emphasize, show off; complement. **set on/upon** attack, assault, hit, set about, fall on; informal lay into, let someone have it, work over, rough up, knock about/around; Brit. informal duff up; N. Amer. informal beat up on. **set out 1** *he set out early.* See SET OFF. **2** *you've done what you set out to achieve:* aim, intend, mean, seek; hope, aspire, want. **set something out 1** *the gifts were set out on tables:* arrange, lay out, put out, array, dispose, display, exhibit. **2** *they set out some guidelines:* present, set forth, detail; state, declare, announce; submit, put forward, advance, propose, propound. **set someone up** establish; finance, fund, back, subsidize. **set something up 1** *a monument was set up:* erect, put up, construct, build. **2** *she set up her own business:* establish, start, begin, institute, found, create. **3** *let's set up a meeting:* arrange, organize, fix, schedule, timetable, line up.

set² noun **1** *a set of postcards:* **group**, collection, series; assortment, selection, batch, number; arrangement, array. **2** *the literary set:* **clique**, coterie, circle, crowd, group, crew, band, company, ring, camp, fraternity, school, faction; informal gang, bunch. **3** *a chemistry set:* **kit**, pack, outfit. **4** *a set of cutlery:* **canteen**, box, case. **5** *he's in the bottom set at school:* **class**, form, group; stream, band.

set³ adjective **1** *a set routine:* **fixed**, established, predetermined, hard and fast, prearranged, prescribed, specified, defined; unvarying, unchanging, invariable, rigid, inflexible, strict, settled; routine, standard, customary, regular, usual, habitual, accustomed, wonted. **2** *she had very set ideas:* **inflexible**, rigid, fixed; entrenched. **3** *he had a set way of doing things:* **stock**, standard, routine, rehearsed, well worn, formulaic. **4** *I was all set for the evening:* **ready**, prepared, organized, equipped, primed; informal geared up, psyched up.

– OPPOSITES variable, flexible, original, unprepared.

setback noun **problem**, difficulty, hitch, complication, upset; blow, stumbling block, hindrance, impediment, obstruction, hold-up; informal glitch, hiccup.

– OPPOSITES breakthrough.

settee noun **sofa**, couch, divan, chaise longue, chesterfield; Brit. put-you-up; N. Amer. davenport, day bed.

setting noun **surroundings**, position, situation, environment, background, backdrop, milieu; spot, place, location, locale, site, scene.

settle verb **1** *they settled the dispute:* **resolve**, sort out, clear up, end, fix, work out, iron out, set right, reconcile; informal patch up. **2** *she settled her affairs:* **put in order**, sort out, tidy up, arrange, organize, order, clear up. **3** *they settled on a date for the wedding:* **decide on**, set, fix, agree on, name, establish, arrange, appoint, designate, assign; choose, pick. **4** *she went to settle her bill:* **pay**, square, clear. **5** *they settled for a 4.2% pay rise:* **accept**, agree to, assent to; formal accede to. **6** *he settled in London:* **make your home**, set up home, take up residence, put down roots, establish yourself; live. **7** *immigrants settled much of Australia:* **colonize**, occupy, populate. **8** *Catherine settled down to her work:* **apply yourself to**, get on with, set about, attack; concentrate on, focus on, devote yourself to, immerse yourself in. **9** *the class wouldn't settle down:* **calm down**, quieten down, be quiet, be still; informal shut up. **10** *a brandy will settle your nerves:* **calm**, quieten, quiet, soothe, pacify, quell. **11** *he settled into an armchair:* **sit down**, seat yourself, install yourself, ensconce yourself, plant yourself; informal park yourself. **12** *a butterfly settled on the flower:* **land**, come to rest, alight, perch; old use light. **13** *sediment settles at the bottom:* **sink**, fall, gravitate; accumulate, concentrate, gather.
– OPPOSITES agitate, rise.

settlement noun **1** *a pay settlement:* **agreement**, deal, arrangement, resolution, understanding, pact. **2** *the settlement of the dispute:* **resolution**, settling, solution, reconciliation. **3** *a frontier settlement:* **community**, colony, outpost, encampment, post; village. **4** *the settlement of the area:* **colonization**, settling, populating.

settler noun **colonist**, colonizer, frontiersman, frontierswoman, pioneer; immigrant, newcomer, incomer.
– OPPOSITES native.

set-up noun (informal) **1** *the telecommunications set-up:* **system**, structure, organization, arrangement, framework. **2** *a set-up called Film International:* **organization**, group, body, agency, association, operation; company, firm; informal outfit. **3** *the whole thing was a set-up:* **trick**, trap; informal put-up job.

seven cardinal number **septet**, septuplets.

> **WORD LINKS**
> **heptagon** a seven-sided plane figure
> **heptahedron** a seven-sided solid figure

sever verb **1** *the head was severed from the body:* **cut**, chop, detach, separate, amputate; rupture, split. **2** *they severed diplomatic relations:* **break off**, discontinue, suspend, end, cease, dissolve.
– OPPOSITES join, maintain.

several adjective **some**, a number of, a few; various, assorted.

severe adjective **1** *severe injuries:* **acute**, very bad, serious, grave, critical, dreadful, terrible, awful; dangerous, life-threatening; formal grievous. **2** *severe storms:* **fierce**, violent, strong, powerful. **3** *a severe winter:* **harsh**, bitter, cold, freezing, icy, arctic. **4** *a severe headache:* **excruciating**, agonizing, intense, dreadful, awful, terrible, unbearable; informal splitting, pounding. **5** *a severe test of their stamina:* **difficult**, demanding, tough, arduous, formidable, exacting, rigorous, punishing, gruelling. **6** *severe criticism:* **harsh**, scathing, sharp, strong, fierce, savage, devastating, withering. **7** *a severe training programme:* **harsh**, stern, hard, uncompromising, unrelenting; brutal, cruel, savage. **8** *his severe expression:* **stern**, dour, grim, forbidding, disapproving, unsmiling, unfriendly, sombre, grave, serious, stony, steely; cold, frosty. **9** *a severe style of architecture:* **plain**, simple, austere, unadorned, stark, spartan, ascetic; clinical, uncluttered.
– OPPOSITES minor, gentle, mild.

severely adverb **1** *he was severely injured:* **badly**, seriously, critically,

2 *she was severely criticized:* **sharply**, roundly, soundly, fiercely, savagely. **3** *murderers should be treated more severely:* **harshly**, strictly, sternly, rigorously. **4** *she looked severely at Harriet:* **sternly**, grimly, dourly, disapprovingly. **5** *she dressed severely in black:* **plainly**, simply, austerely.

sew verb *she sewed the seams of the tunic:* **stitch**, tack; seam, hem; embroider.

sewing noun **stitching**, needlework, needlecraft.

sex noun **1** **sexual intercourse**, lovemaking, making love, sexual relations; mating, copulation; formal fornication; technical coitus; dated carnal knowledge. **2** *adults of both sexes:* **gender**.
■ **have sex** make love, sleep with, go to bed with; mate, copulate; formal fornicate.

WORD LINKS
carnal relating to sexual urges and activities

sexism noun **sexual discrimination**, chauvinism, prejudice, bias.

sexless adjective **asexual**, non-sexual, neuter; androgynous, epicene.

sexual adjective **1** *the sexual organs:* **reproductive**, genital, sex, procreative. **2** *sexual activity:* **carnal**, erotic; formal venereal; technical coital.

sexual intercourse noun. See **sex** sense 1.

sexuality noun **1** *she oozed sexuality:* **sensuality**, sexiness, seductiveness, desirability, eroticism, physicality; sexual appetite, passion, desire, lust. **2** *I'm open about my sexuality:* **sexual orientation**, sexual preference, leaning, persuasion.

sexy adjective **1** *she's very sexy:* **sexually attractive**, seductive, desirable, alluring, sensual, sultry, provocative, tempting, tantalizing; nubile, voluptuous, luscious; informal fanciable, beddable; Brit. informal fit; N. Amer. informal foxy, cute; Austral. informal spunky. **2** *sexy videos:* **erotic**, sexually explicit, arousing, exciting, stimulating, hot, titillating, racy, naughty, risqué, X-rated, pornographic; informal raunchy, steamy, blue; euphemistic adult.

shabby adjective **1** *a shabby little bar:* **run down**, scruffy, dilapidated; seedy, insalubrious, squalid, sordid; informal crummy, scuzzy; Brit. informal grotty. **2** *a shabby grey coat:* **scruffy**, old, worn out, threadbare, ragged, frayed, tattered, battered, faded, moth-eaten, mangy; informal tatty, ratty; N. Amer. informal raggedy. **3** *her shabby treatment of Ben:* **contemptible**, despicable, dishonourable, discreditable, mean, low, dirty, hateful, shameful, ignoble, unfair, unworthy, unkind, shoddy, nasty; informal rotten, low-down.
–OPPOSITES smart, honourable.

shack noun **hut**, shanty, cabin, lean-to, shed; hovel; Scottish bothy.
■ **shack up with** (informal) cohabit, move in with, live with; informal, dated live in sin.

shackle verb **1** *he was shackled to the wall:* **chain**, fetter, manacle; secure, tie, bind, tether, hobble; put in chains, clap in irons, handcuff. **2** *journalists were shackled by the new law:* **restrain**, restrict, limit, constrain, handicap, hamstring, hamper, hinder, impede, obstruct, inhibit.

shackles plural noun **chains**, fetters, irons, leg irons, manacles, handcuffs.

shade noun **1** *they sat in the shade of a nearby tree:* **shadow**, shelter, cover; cool. **2** *shades of blue:* **colour**, hue, tone, tint, tinge. **3** *shades of meaning:* **nuance**, gradation, degree, difference, variation; nicety, subtlety; undertone, overtone. **4** *the window shade:* **blind**, curtain, screen, cover, covering; awning, canopy.
–OPPOSITES light.
• verb *vines shaded the garden:* **cast a shadow over**, shadow, shelter, cover, screen.
■ **put someone/something in the shade** surpass, outshine, outclass, overshadow, eclipse, cap, top, outstrip, outdo, put to shame, beat hollow, upstage; informal run rings around, be a cut above, leave standing.

shadow noun **1** *he saw her shadow in the doorway:* **silhouette**, outline, shape, contour, profile. **2** *he emerged from the shadows:* **shade**, darkness, twilight; gloom. **3** *the shadow of war:* **cloud**, pall; spectre;

threat. **4** *a shadow of a smile:* **trace**, hint, suggestion, suspicion, ghost, glimmer.
• verb *he is shadowing a suspect:* **follow**, trail, track, stalk, pursue; informal tail, keep tabs on.

shadowy adjective **1** *a shadowy corridor:* **dark**, dim, gloomy, murky, shady, shaded. **2** *a shadowy outline:* **indistinct**, hazy, indefinite, vague, ill-defined, faint, blurred, blurry, unclear; ghostly, spectral, wraithlike. **3** *a shadowy figure:* **mysterious**, enigmatic.
– OPPOSITES bright, clear, high-profile.

shady adjective **1** *a shady garden:* **shaded**, shadowy, dim, dark; sheltered; leafy. **2** (informal) *shady deals:* **suspicious**, suspect, questionable, dubious, doubtful, irregular; N. Amer. snide; informal fishy, murky; Brit. informal dodgy; Austral./NZ informal shonky.
– OPPOSITES bright, honest.

shaft noun **1** *the shaft of a golf club:* **pole**, shank, stick, rod, staff; handle, hilt, stem. **2** *shafts of sunlight:* **ray**, beam, gleam, streak. **3** *a ventilation shaft:* **tunnel**, passage; borehole, bore; duct, well, flue, vent.

shaggy adjective **hairy**, bushy, thick, woolly; tangled, tousled, unkempt, dishevelled, untidy; formal hirsute.
– OPPOSITES sleek.

shake verb **1** *the whole building shook:* **vibrate**, tremble, quiver, quake, shiver, shudder, judder, jiggle, wobble, rock, sway; convulse. **2** *she shook the bottle:* **jiggle**, agitate; informal wiggle, waggle. **3** *he shook his stick at them:* **brandish**, wave, flourish, swing, wield; informal waggle. **4** *the look in his eyes shook her:* **upset**, distress, disturb, unsettle, disconcert, discompose, unnerve, trouble, throw off balance, agitate, fluster; shock, alarm, frighten, scare, worry; informal rattle. **5** *this will shake their confidence:* **weaken**, undermine, damage, impair, harm.
• noun **1** *he gave his coat a shake:* **jiggle**, joggle; informal waggle. **2** *a shake of his fist:* **flourish**, wave.
■ **shake someone off** get away from, escape, elude, dodge, lose, leave behind, get rid of, give someone the slip, throw off the scent; Brit. informal get shot of. **shake something off** recover from, get over; get rid of, free yourself from; Brit. informal get shot of; N. Amer. informal shuck off. **shake someone/something up 1** *the accident shook him up.* See **SHAKE** verb sense 4. **2** *plans to shake up the legal profession:* reorganize, restructure, revolutionize, alter, change, transform, reform, overhaul.

shake-up noun (informal) **reorganization**, restructuring, reshuffle, change, overhaul, makeover; N. Amer. informal shakedown.

shaky adjective **1** *shaky legs:* **trembling**, shaking, tremulous, quivering, unsteady, wobbly, weak; doddery; informal trembly. **2** *I feel a bit shaky:* **faint**, dizzy, light-headed, giddy; weak, wobbly; in shock, upset. **3** *a shaky table:* **unsteady**, unstable, wobbly, rickety; Brit. informal wonky. **4** *the evidence is shaky:* **unreliable**, untrustworthy, questionable, dubious, doubtful, tenuous, suspect, flimsy, weak; informal iffy; Brit. informal dodgy.
– OPPOSITES steady, stable, sound.

shallow adjective **superficial**, facile, insubstantial, lightweight, empty, trivial, trifling; surface, skin-deep; frivolous, foolish, silly.
– OPPOSITES profound.

sham noun **pretence**, fake, act, fiction, simulation, fraud, feint, lie, counterfeit; humbug.
• adjective *sham concern:* **fake**, pretended, feigned, simulated, false, artificial, bogus, insincere, affected, make-believe; informal pretend, put-on, phoney.
– OPPOSITES genuine.
• verb **pretend**, fake, dissemble; malinger; informal put it on; Brit. informal swing the lead.

shaman noun witch doctor, medicine man/woman, healer.

shamble verb **shuffle**; lumber, totter; hobble, limp.

shambles plural noun **1** *we have to sort out this shambles:* **chaos**, mess, muddle, confusion, disorder, havoc; Brit. informal dog's dinner/breakfast. **2** *the room was a shambles:* **mess**, pigsty; informal disaster area; Brit. informal tip.

shambolic adjective (Brit. informal). See **CHAOTIC**.

S

shame noun **1** *her face was scarlet with shame:* **humiliation**, mortification, chagrin, ignominy, embarrassment, indignity, discomfort. **2** *a sense of shame:* **guilt**; remorse, contrition. **3** *he brought shame on the family:* **disgrace**, dishonour, discredit, ignominy, disrepute, infamy, scandal, opprobrium. **4** *it's a shame she never married:* **pity**, sad thing; bad luck; informal bummer, crime, sin.
– OPPOSITES pride, honour.
• verb **1** *you shamed your family:* **disgrace**, dishonour, discredit, taint, sully, tarnish, besmirch, blacken, drag through the mud. **2** *he was shamed in public:* **humiliate**, embarrass, humble, take down a peg or two, cut down to size; informal show up; N. Amer. informal make someone eat crow.
– OPPOSITES honour.
■ **put someone/something to shame** outshine, outclass, eclipse, surpass, excel, outstrip, outdo, put in the shade; informal run rings around, leave standing; Brit. informal knock spots off.

shamefaced adjective **ashamed**, abashed, sheepish, guilty, contrite, sorry, remorseful, repentant, penitent, regretful, rueful, apologetic; informal with your tail between your legs.
– OPPOSITES unrepentant.

shameful adjective **1** *shameful behaviour:* **disgraceful**, deplorable, despicable, contemptible, dishonourable, discreditable, reprehensible, low, unworthy, ignoble, shabby; shocking, scandalous, outrageous, abominable, atrocious, appalling; inexcusable, unforgivable. **2** *a shameful secret:* **embarrassing**, mortifying, humiliating, ignominious.
– OPPOSITES admirable.

shameless adjective **flagrant**, blatant, barefaced, overt, brazen, undisguised, unconcealed; unabashed, unashamed, unblushing, unrepentant.
– OPPOSITES modest.

shanty noun **shack**, hut, cabin, lean-to, shed; hovel; Scottish bothy.

shape noun **1** *the shape of the dining table:* **form**, appearance, configuration, structure; figure, build, physique, body; contours, lines, outline, silhouette, profile. **2** *a spirit in the shape of a fox:* **guise**, likeness, semblance, form, appearance, image. **3** *the animal's in good shape:* **condition**, health, trim, fettle, order; Brit. informal nick.
• verb **1** *the metal is shaped into tools:* **form**, fashion, make, mould, model; sculpt, carve, cut, whittle, bend. **2** *attitudes were shaped by his report:* **determine**, form, fashion, mould, develop; influence, affect.
■ **take shape** become clear, become definite, become tangible, crystallize, come together, fall into place.

shapeless adjective **1** *shapeless lumps:* **formless**, amorphous, unformed, indefinite. **2** *a shapeless dress:* **baggy**, saggy, ill-fitting, oversized, unshapely, formless.

shapely adjective **well proportioned**, clean-limbed, curvaceous, voluptuous, full-figured, Junoesque; attractive, sexy; informal curvy.

shard noun **fragment**, sliver, splinter, chip, piece, bit.

share noun *her share of the profits:* **portion**, part, division, quota, allowance, ration, allocation, measure, due; percentage, commission, dividend; helping, serving; informal cut, slice, rake-off; Brit. informal whack.
• verb **1** *we share the bills:* **split**, divide, go halves on; informal go fifty-fifty. **2** *they shared out the money:* **apportion**, divide, allocate, portion out, measure out; carve up; Brit. informal divvy up. **3** *we all share in the learning process:* **participate in**, take part in, play a part in, be involved in, contribute to, have a hand in, partake in.

sharp adjective **1** *a sharp knife:* **keen**, razor-edged; sharpened, well-honed; pointed. **2** *a sharp pain:* **excruciating**, agonizing, intense, stabbing, shooting, severe, acute, keen, fierce, searing. **3** *a sharp taste:* **tangy**, piquant; acidic, acid, sour, tart, pungent, acrid. **4** *a sharp cry:* **loud**, piercing, shrill, high-pitched, penetrating, harsh, strident, ear-splitting, deafening. **5** *a sharp wind:* **cold**, chilly, chill, brisk, keen, penetrating, biting, icy, bitter,

S

freezing, raw. **6** *sharp words:* **harsh**, bitter, cutting, spiteful, hurtful, nasty, cruel. **7** *a sharp sense of loss:* **intense**, acute, keen, strong, bitter, fierce, heartfelt, overwhelming. **8** *the lens brings images into sharp focus:* **distinct**, clear, crisp; stark, obvious, marked, definite, pronounced. **9** *a sharp increase:* **sudden**, abrupt, rapid; steep, precipitous. **10** *his sharp eyes missed nothing:* **keen**, perceptive, observant, acute, beady. **11** *she was sharp and witty:* **perceptive**, incisive, keen, acute, quick-witted, shrewd, canny, astute, intelligent, intuitive, bright, alert, smart, quick off the mark; informal on the ball, quick on the uptake, savvy; N. Amer. informal heads-up.
– OPPOSITES blunt, mild, sweet, soft, kind, gradual.
• **adverb** **precisely**, exactly, on the dot; promptly, prompt, punctually, dead on; informal on the nose; N. Amer. informal on the button.
– OPPOSITES roughly.

sharpen **verb** **hone**, whet, strop, grind, file.

shatter **verb** **1** *the glasses shattered:* **smash**, break, splinter, crack, fracture, fragment, disintegrate. **2** *the announcement shattered their hopes:* **destroy**, wreck, ruin, dash, crush, devastate, demolish, torpedo, scotch; informal put the kibosh on, do for, put paid to; Brit. informal scupper. **3** *we were shattered by the news:* **devastate**, shock, stun, daze, traumatize; informal knock sideways; Brit. informal knock for six.

S

shattered **adjective** **1** *he was shattered by the reviews:* **devastated**, shocked, stunned, dazed, traumatized. **2** (informal) *I feel too shattered to move.* See EXHAUSTED.
– OPPOSITES thrilled.

shave **verb** **1** *he shaved his beard:* **cut off**; crop, trim, barber. **2** *shave off excess wood:* **plane**, pare, whittle, scrape.

sheaf **noun** **bundle**, bunch, stack, pile, heap, mass; Brit. informal wodge.

sheath **noun** **1** *put the sword in its sheath:* **scabbard**, case. **2** *the wire has a plastic sheath:* **covering**, cover, case, casing, sleeve.

shed[1] **noun** *the rabbit lives in the shed:* **hut**, lean-to, outhouse, outbuilding; shack; Brit. lock-up.

shed[2] **verb** **1** *the trees shed their leaves:* **drop**, spill. **2** *the caterpillar shed its skin:* **slough off**, cast off, moult. **3** *we shed our clothes:* **take off**, remove, discard, climb out of, slip out of; Brit. informal peel off. **4** *much blood has been shed:* **spill**, discharge. **5** *the firm is to shed ten workers:* **make redundant**, dismiss, let go, discharge, get rid of, discard; informal sack, fire. **6** *the moon shed a watery light:* **cast**, radiate, diffuse, disperse, give out.

sheen **noun** **shine**, lustre, gloss, patina, shininess, burnish, polish, shimmer, brilliance, radiance.

sheep **noun**

> **WORD LINKS**
> **ovine** relating to sheep

sheepish **adjective** **embarrassed**, uncomfortable, hangdog, self-conscious; shamefaced, ashamed, abashed, mortified, chastened, remorseful, contrite, apologetic, penitent, repentant.

sheer[1] **adjective** **1** *the sheer audacity of the plan:* **utter**, complete, absolute, total, pure, downright, out-and-out; Austral./NZ informal fair. **2** *a sheer drop:* **precipitous**, steep, vertical, perpendicular, abrupt, sharp. **3** *a sheer dress:* **diaphanous**, gauzy, thin, translucent, transparent, see-through, insubstantial.
– OPPOSITES gradual, thick.

> ! Don't confuse **sheer** with **shear**, which means 'cut the wool off a sheep'.

sheer[2] **verb** *the boat sheered off along the coast:* **swerve**, veer, slew, skew, swing.

sheet **noun** **1** *a sheet of ice:* **layer**, stratum, covering, blanket, coat, film, skin; expanse, area, stretch, sweep. **2** *a sheet of glass:* **pane**, panel, piece, plate. **3** *a fresh sheet of paper:* **piece**, leaf, page.

shelf **noun** **ledge**, sill.

shell **noun** **1** *a crab shell:* **carapace**, exterior; armour; Zoology exoskeleton. **2** *peanut shells:* **pod**, husk, hull, casing, case, covering; N. Amer. shuck. **3** *shells passed overhead:* **projectile**, bomb, missile;

bullet. **4** *the metal shell of the car:* **hull**, body.
• verb **1** *they were shelling peas:* **hull**, pod, husk; N. Amer. shuck. **2** *rebel artillery shelled the city:* **bombard**, fire on, attack, bomb, blitz, strafe.

> **WORD LINKS**
> **conchology** the scientific study of shells

shellfish noun **crustacean**, bivalve, mollusc.

shelter noun **1** *the trees provide shelter for animals:* **protection**, cover, shade; safety, security, refuge. **2** *a shelter for abandoned cats:* **sanctuary**, refuge, home, haven, safe house.
– OPPOSITES exposure.
• verb **1** *the hut sheltered him from the sun:* **protect**, shield, screen, cover, shade, defend, cushion, guard, insulate. **2** *where the convoy sheltered:* **take shelter**, take refuge, take cover; informal hole up.
– OPPOSITES expose.

sheltered adjective **1** *a sheltered stretch of water:* **protected**, tranquil, still; shady. **2** *a sheltered life:* **protected**, cloistered; privileged, secure, safe, quiet.

shelve verb **postpone**, put off, delay, defer, put back, reschedule, hold over/off, put to one side, suspend, stay, mothball; N. Amer. put over, table, take a rain check on; informal put on ice, put on the back burner.
– OPPOSITES execute.

shepherd verb *we shepherded them away:* **usher**, steer, herd, lead, take, escort, guide, conduct, marshal, walk; show, see.

shield noun *a shield against radiation | a gum shield:* **protection**, guard, defence, cover, screen.
• verb *he shielded his eyes:* **protect**, cover, screen, shade.
– OPPOSITES expose.

shift verb **1** *he shifted some chairs:* **move**, transfer, transport, switch, relocate, reposition, rearrange. **2** *MPs are unlikely to shift their stance:* **change**, alter, adjust; modify, revise, reverse. **3** *the cargo has shifted:* **move**, slide, slip, be displaced, subside. **4** *the wind shifted:* **veer**, alter, change, turn. **5** (Brit.) *this brush really shifts the dirt:* **get rid of**, remove, get off, budge, lift.
• noun **1** *a shift in public opinion:* **change**, alteration, adjustment, variation, modification, revision, reversal, U-turn; Brit. about-turn. **2** *they worked three shifts:* **stint**, stretch, spell. **3** *the night shift went home:* **workers**, crew, gang, team, squad, patrol.

shiftless adjective **lazy**, idle, indolent, slothful, lethargic, feckless, good-for-nothing, worthless.

shifty adjective (informal) **devious**, evasive, slippery, duplicitous, deceitful, untrustworthy; N. Amer. snide; Brit. informal dodgy; Austral./NZ informal shonky.
– OPPOSITES honest.

shimmer verb **glint**, glisten, twinkle, sparkle, flash, gleam, glow, glimmer, glitter, wink; literary glister.
• noun **glint**, twinkle, sparkle, flash, gleam, glow, glimmer, lustre, glitter.

shin verb **climb**, clamber, scramble, swarm; mount, ascend, scale; descend; N. Amer. shinny.

shine verb **1** *the sun shone:* beam, radiate, gleam, glow, glint, glimmer, sparkle, twinkle, glitter, glisten, shimmer, flash, glare; literary glister. **2** *she shone her shoes:* **polish**, burnish, buff, rub up. **3** *they shone at university:* **excel**, stand out.
• noun *linseed oil restores the shine:* **polish**, gleam, gloss, lustre, sheen, patina.

shining adjective **1** *a shining expanse of water:* **gleaming**, bright, brilliant, lustrous, glowing, glinting, sparkling, twinkling, glittering, glistening, shimmering, dazzling, luminous, incandescent. **2** *their shining faces:* **glowing**, beaming, radiant, happy. **3** *shining chromium tubes:* **shiny**, bright, polished, gleaming, glossy, lustrous.
■ **a shining example** paragon, model, epitome, archetype, ideal, exemplar, paradigm.

shiny adjective **glossy**, glassy, bright, polished, gleaming, satiny, sheeny, lustrous.
– OPPOSITES matt.

ship noun **boat**, vessel, craft.

> **WORD LINKS**
> **marine**, **maritime**, **nautical**, **naval** relating to ships

S

shirk verb **evade**, dodge, avoid, get out of, sidestep, shrink from, shun, skip; neglect; informal duck out of, cop out of; Brit. informal skive off; N. Amer. informal cut; Austral./NZ informal duck-shove.

shirker noun **dodger**, truant, absentee, layabout, loafer, idler; informal slacker; Brit. informal skiver.

shiver verb *she was shivering with fear:* **tremble**, quiver, shake, shudder, quake.
• noun *she gave a shiver as the door opened:* **shudder**, twitch, start.

shock[1] noun **1** *the news came as a shock:* **blow**, upset; surprise, revelation, a bolt from the blue, rude awakening, eye-opener. **2** *you gave me a shock:* **fright**, scare, start; informal turn. **3** *the first shock of the earthquake:* **vibration**, reverberation, shake, jolt; impact, blow.
• verb *the revelations shocked the nation:* **appal**, horrify, outrage, revolt, disgust; traumatize, distress, upset, disturb, disquiet, unsettle; stun, rock, shake, take aback, throw, unnerve.

shock[2] noun *a shock of red hair:* **mass**, mane, mop, thatch, head, bush, tangle, cascade, halo.

shocking adjective **appalling**, horrifying, horrific, dreadful, awful, frightful, terrible; scandalous, outrageous, disgraceful, abominable, atrocious, disgusting; distressing, upsetting, disturbing, startling, surprising.

shoddy adjective **1** *shoddy goods:* **poor-quality**, inferior, second-rate, third-rate, jerry-built; Brit. informal rubbish. **2** *shoddy workmanship:* **careless**, slapdash, sloppy, slipshod; negligent.
– OPPOSITES quality, careful.

shoot verb **1** *they shot him in the street:* **gun down**, mow down, hit, wound, injure; kill; informal blast, pump full of lead, plug. **2** *they shot at the police:* **fire**, open fire, snipe, let fly; bombard, shell. **3** *it can shoot bullets or grenades:* **discharge**, fire, launch, release. **4** *a car shot past:* **race**, speed, flash, dash, dart, rush, hurtle, streak, whizz, go like lightning, go hell for leather, zoom; career, fly; informal belt, tear, zip, whip; Brit. informal bomb, bucket; N. Amer. informal clip, hightail it, barrel. **5** *the film was shot in Tunisia:* **film**, photograph, take, make, record.
• noun *new shoots:* **sprout**, bud, runner, tendril.

shop noun **1** *a shop selling gloves:* **store**, boutique, retail outlet, emporium, supermarket, hypermarket, superstore; N. Amer. mart. **2** *he works in the machine shop:* **workshop**, plant, factory, works.

shopkeeper noun **shop-owner**, vendor, retailer, dealer, trader, salesperson; N. Amer. storekeeper.

shopper noun **buyer**, purchaser, customer, consumer, client, patron.

shore[1] noun *he swam to the shore:* **seashore**, beach, sand, shoreline, coast.

> **WORD LINKS**
> **littoral** relating to a shore

shore[2] verb *we had to shore up the building:* **prop up**, hold up, bolster, support, brace, buttress, strengthen, reinforce, underpin.

short adjective **1** *a short red-haired woman:* **small**, little, petite, tiny, diminutive, elfin; Scottish wee; informal pint-sized. **2** *a short report:* **concise**, brief, succinct, compact, pithy; abridged, abbreviated, condensed. **3** *a short visit:* **brief**, fleeting, lightning, quick. **4** *money is a bit short:* **scarce**, scant, meagre, sparse, insufficient, deficient, inadequate, lacking, wanting. **5** *he was rather short with her:* **curt**, sharp, abrupt, blunt, brusque, terse, offhand, gruff, surly, rude.
– OPPOSITES tall, long, plentiful, courteous.
• adverb *she stopped short:* **abruptly**, suddenly, sharply, all of a sudden, unexpectedly, without warning.
■ **in short** briefly, in a word, in a nutshell, in essence. **short of** deficient in, lacking, wanting, in need of, low on, short on, missing; informal strapped for, pushed for, minus.

shortage noun **scarcity**, dearth, poverty, insufficiency, deficiency, inadequacy, famine, lack, want, deficit, shortfall.
– OPPOSITES abundance.

shortcoming noun **defect**, fault,

S

flaw, imperfection, deficiency, limitation, failing, drawback, weakness, weak point.
– OPPOSITES strength.

shorten verb **cut**, abbreviate, abridge, condense, contract, compress, reduce, shrink, diminish; trim, pare down, prune; curtail, truncate.
– OPPOSITES extend.

short-lived adjective **brief**, short, temporary, impermanent, fleeting, fugitive, transitory, transient, ephemeral.

shortly adverb **1** *she will be with you shortly:* **soon**, presently, in a little while, at any moment, in a minute, in next to no time, before long, by and by; N. Amer. momentarily; informal anon, any time now, in a jiffy; Brit. informal in a mo. **2** *'I know,' he replied shortly:* **curtly**, sharply, abruptly, bluntly, brusquely, tersely.

short-sighted adjective **1** *I'm a little short-sighted:* **myopic**, nearsighted; informal as blind as a bat. **2** *short-sighted critics:* **narrow-minded**, unimaginative, small-minded.
– OPPOSITES long-sighted, imaginative.

short-staffed adjective **understaffed**, short-handed, undermanned, below strength.

short-tempered adjective **irritable**, irascible, hot-tempered, quick-tempered, touchy, volatile, on a short fuse; Brit. informal narky, ratty.
– OPPOSITES placid.

shot noun **1** *a shot rang out:* report, crack, bang, blast; (**shots**) gunfire, firing. **2** *a winning shot:* **stroke**, hit, strike; kick, throw. **3** *he's an excellent shot:* **marksman**, markswoman, shooter. **4** *a shot of us on holiday:* **photograph**, photo, snap, snapshot, picture, print, slide, still. **5** (informal) *it's nice to get a shot at driving:* **attempt**, try; turn, chance, opportunity; informal go, stab, crack, bash. **6** *tetanus shots:* **injection**, inoculation, immunization, vaccination, booster; informal jab.
■ **like a shot** (informal) without hesitation, unhesitatingly, eagerly; immediately, at once, right away/now, straight away, instantly, instantaneously, without delay; informal in/like a flash, before you can say Jack Robinson.

shoulder verb **1** *I shouldered the responsibility:* **take on**, undertake, accept, assume; bear, carry. **2** *another lad shouldered him aside:* **push**, shove, thrust, jostle, force, bulldoze, bundle.

shout verb **yell**, cry, call, roar, howl, bellow, bawl, clamour, shriek, scream, trumpet; raise your voice; informal holler.
– OPPOSITES whisper.

shove verb **push**, thrust, propel, drive, force, barge, ram, knock, elbow, shoulder; jostle, bundle, hustle, manhandle.

shovel verb **dig**, scoop, heap, clear, shift, move.

show verb **1** *he showed his ID card:* **display**, produce, present, offer; exhibit, put on display. **2** *Frank showed his frustration:* **manifest**, exhibit, reveal, convey, communicate, make known; express, make plain, make obvious, disclose, betray. **3** *I'll show you how to make it:* **demonstrate**, explain, describe, illustrate; teach, instruct. **4** *events showed this to be true:* **prove**, demonstrate, confirm; substantiate, corroborate, verify, establish, attest, bear out. **5** *she showed them to their seats:* **escort**, accompany, take, conduct, lead, usher, guide, direct, steer, shepherd.
– OPPOSITES conceal.
• noun **1** *a spectacular show of bluebells:* **display**, array. **2** *the motor show:* **exhibition**, fair, festival, exposition; parade; N. Amer. exhibit. **3** *a Broadway show:* musical, play. **4** *she made a show of looking busy:* **pretence**, outward appearance, false front, guise, semblance, pose.
■ **show off** (informal) put on airs, put on an act, swank, strut, grandstand, posture; draw attention to yourself; N. Amer. informal cop an attitude. **show something off** display, exhibit, demonstrate, parade, draw attention to, flaunt. **show up** (informal) *only two members of staff showed up:* turn up, appear, arrive, come, put in an appearance, materialize. **show someone/something up 1** *the sun showed up the shabbiness of the room:* expose, reveal, make visible, highlight, emphasize, draw attention to.

S

2 (informal) *they showed him up in front of his friends.* See **HUMILIATE**.

showdown noun **confrontation**, clash, face-off.

shower noun **1** *a shower of rain:* **fall**, drizzle, sprinkling. **2** *a shower of missiles:* **volley**, hail, salvo, barrage. •verb **1** *confetti showered down on us:* **rain**, fall, hail. **2** *she showered them with gifts:* **deluge**, flood, inundate, swamp, engulf; overwhelm, overload, snow under.

showing noun **1** *another showing of the series:* **presentation**, broadcast, airing. **2** *the party's present showing:* **performance**, track record, results, success, achievements.

showman noun **1** *a travelling showman:* **impresario**; ringmaster, host, compère, master of ceremonies, MC; presenter; N. Amer. informal emcee. **2** *he is a great showman:* **entertainer**, performer, virtuoso; informal show-off.

show-off noun (informal) **exhibitionist**, extrovert, poser, poseur, swaggerer, self-publicist; informal pseud.

showy adjective **ostentatious**, conspicuous, flamboyant, gaudy, garish, brash, vulgar, loud, extravagant, fancy, ornate; informal flash, flashy, glitzy, bling, ritzy, swanky; N. Amer. informal superfly.
–OPPOSITES restrained.

shred noun **1** *her dress was torn to shreds:* **tatters**, ribbons, rags. **2** *there's not a shred of evidence:* **scrap**, bit, speck, iota, particle, ounce, whit, jot, crumb, fragment, grain, drop, trace, scintilla, spot. •verb **chop**, cut up, grate, mince, grind.

shrewd adjective **astute**, sharp, smart, acute, intelligent, clever, canny, perceptive, wise; informal on the ball, savvy; N. Amer. informal heads-up.
–OPPOSITES stupid.

shrewdness noun **astuteness**, acuteness, acumen, intelligence, cleverness, smartness, wit, insight, understanding, perception, perceptiveness; informal savvy.

shriek verb & noun **scream**, screech, squeal, squawk, roar, howl, shout, yelp.

shrill adjective **high-pitched**, piercing, high, sharp, ear-piercing, ear-splitting, penetrating.

shrine noun **tomb**, sanctuary, memorial, monument.

shrink verb **1** *the number of competitors shrank:* **get/grow smaller**, contract, diminish, lessen, reduce, decrease, dwindle, decline, fall/drop off. **2** *he shrank back against the wall:* **draw back**, recoil, back away, retreat, withdraw, cringe, cower. **3** *he doesn't shrink from naming names:* **recoil**, shy away, flinch, be averse, be afraid, hesitate.
–OPPOSITES expand, increase.

shrivel verb **wither**, shrink; wilt; dry up, dehydrate, parch, frazzle.

shroud noun **covering**, cover, cloak, mantle, blanket, layer, cloud, veil. •verb **cover**, envelop, veil, cloak, blanket, screen, conceal, hide, mask, obscure.

shrug verb
■ **shrug something off** disregard, dismiss, take no notice of, ignore, play down, make light of.

shudder verb **shake**, shiver, tremble, quiver; judder. •noun **shake**, shiver, tremor, trembling, quivering, vibration; judder.

shuffle verb **1** *they shuffled along the passage:* **shamble**, drag your feet, totter, stumble, dodder, hobble. **2** *he shuffled the cards:* **mix up**, rearrange, jumble up.

shun verb **avoid**, evade, eschew, steer clear of, shy away from, give a wide berth to, have nothing to do with; snub, give someone the cold shoulder, cold-shoulder, ignore, cut dead, look right through; reject, rebuff, spurn, ostracize; informal give someone the brush-off, freeze out; Brit. informal send to Coventry.
–OPPOSITES welcome.

shut verb **close**, pull/push to, slam, fasten; put the lid on, lock, secure.
–OPPOSITES open.
■ **shut down** cease trading, close, close down; informal fold. **shut someone/something in** confine, enclose, shut up, pen in/up, fence in, lock up/in, cage, imprison; N. Amer. corral. **shut up** (informal) be quiet, keep quiet, hold your tongue; informal cut the cackle, belt up, put a sock in it. **shut someone up** (informal) silence, quieten, hush, gag, muzzle.

shuttle verb **ply**, run, commute, go to and fro; ferry.

shy adjective *I was painfully shy:* **bashful**, diffident, timid, reserved, reticent, introverted, retiring, self-effacing, withdrawn.
– OPPOSITES confident.
■ **shy away from** flinch, recoil, hang back; be loath, be reluctant, be unwilling, be disinclined, be hesitant, hesitate, baulk at; informal boggle at.

shyness noun **bashfulness**, diffidence, reserve, introversion, reticence, timidity, coyness.

sibling noun brother, sister.

sick adjective **1** *the children are sick:* **ill**, unwell, poorly, ailing, indisposed; Brit. off colour; informal laid up, under the weather; Austral./NZ informal crook. **2** *he was feeling sick:* **nauseous**, queasy, bilious, green about the gills; seasick, carsick, travel-sick. **3** *I'm sick of this music:* **fed up**, bored, tired, weary. **4** (informal) *a sick joke | sick humour:* **macabre**, tasteless, ghoulish, black, perverted, gruesome, gallows, cruel.
– OPPOSITES well.
■ **be sick** (Brit.) vomit, heave; informal throw up, puke, chuck up, hurl, spew; N. Amer. informal spit up, barf, upchuck; Austral./NZ informal chunder.

sicken verb *the stench sickened him:* **nauseate**, revolt, disgust, repel, turn someone's stomach; N. Amer. informal gross out.
– OPPOSITES recover.

sickening adjective **nauseating**, stomach-turning, stomach-churning; repulsive, revolting, disgusting, repellent, vile, nasty, foul, loathsome, offensive, objectionable, off-putting, distasteful, obscene, gruesome, grisly; N. Amer. vomitous; informal gross.

sickly adjective **1** *a sickly child:* **unhealthy**, in poor health, delicate, frail, weak. **2** *sickly faces:* **pale**, wan, pasty, sallow, pallid, ashen, anaemic. **3** *sickly love songs:* **sentimental**, mawkish, cloying, sugary, syrupy, saccharine; informal mushy, slushy, schmaltzy, cheesy, corny; Brit. informal soppy; N. Amer. informal cornball, sappy, hokey.
– OPPOSITES healthy.

sickness noun **1** *she was absent through sickness:* **illness**, disease, ailment, infection, malady, infirmity; informal bug, virus; Brit. informal lurgy; Austral. informal wog. **2** *a wave of sickness:* **nausea**, biliousness, queasiness. **3** *symptoms include sickness and diarrhoea:* **vomiting**, retching; travel-sickness, seasickness, carsickness, airsickness, motion sickness; informal throwing up, puking.

side noun **1** *the side of the garden:* **edge**, border, verge, boundary, margin, fringes, flank, bank, perimeter, extremity, periphery, outer limit, limits. **2** *the wrong side of the road:* **half**, part; carriageway, lane. **3** *the east side of the city:* **district**, quarter, area, region, part, neighbourhood, sector, section, zone, ward. **4** *one side of the paper:* **surface**, face. **5** *his side of the argument:* **point of view**, viewpoint, perspective, opinion, way of thinking, standpoint, position, outlook, slant, angle. **6** *the losing side:* **faction**, camp, bloc, party. **7** *the players in their side:* **team**, squad, line-up.
– OPPOSITES centre, end.
• adjective *a side issue:* **subordinate**, lesser, lower-level, secondary, minor, peripheral, incidental, ancillary, subsidiary, extraneous.
– OPPOSITES central.
• verb *they're siding with the underdog.* See TAKE SOMEONE'S SIDE.
■ **take someone's side** support, take someone's part, side with, stand by, back, give someone your backing, be loyal to, defend, champion, ally yourself with, sympathize with, favour.

S

WORD LINKS

lateral relating to the side or sides of something

sideline verb **overlook**, marginalize, bypass, ignore, disregard, exclude, overshadow; demote, downgrade.

sidelong adjective *a sidelong glance:* **indirect**, oblique, sideways, sideward; surreptitious, furtive, covert, sly.
– OPPOSITES overt.

sidestep verb **avoid**, evade, dodge, circumvent, skirt round, bypass; informal duck.

sidetrack verb **distract**, divert, deflect, draw away.

sideways adverb **1** *I slid sideways:* **to the side**, laterally. **2** *the expansion slots are mounted sideways:* **edgeways**, sidewards, side first, end on; US edgewise.
• adjective **1** *sideways force:* **lateral**, sideward, on the side, side to side. **2** *a sideways look.* See **SIDELONG**.

sidle verb **creep**, sneak, slink, slip, slide, steal, edge, inch.

siege noun **blockade**, encirclement; stand-off.
– OPPOSITES relief.

siesta noun **nap**, catnap, doze, rest; informal snooze, lie-down, forty winks, shut-eye; Brit. informal kip.

sieve noun **strainer**, sifter, filter, screen.
• verb **strain**, sift, screen, filter, riddle; old use bolt.

sift verb **1** *sift the flour into a large bowl:* **sieve**, strain, screen, filter. **2** *we sift out unsuitable applications:* **separate out**, filter out, sort out, weed out, get rid of, remove. **3** *officers were sifting through every scrap of information:* **search through**, look through, examine, inspect, scrutinize, pore over, investigate, analyse, dissect.

sigh verb *she sighed in exasperation:* **breathe out**, exhale; groan, moan.

sight noun **1** *she has excellent sight:* **eyesight**, vision, eyes. **2** *her first sight of the city:* **view**, glimpse, glance, look. **3** *they were within sight of the enemy:* **range**, view, field of vision. **4** *the city's historic sights:* **landmark**, place of interest, monument, spectacle, view, marvel, wonder.
• verb *one of the helicopters sighted wreckage:* **glimpse**, catch a glimpse of, catch sight of, see, spot, spy, make out, pick out, notice, observe; literary espy.
■ **catch sight of** *when she caught sight of him she smiled:* glimpse, catch/get a glimpse of, see, spot, spy, make out, pick out; notice, observe, perceive, discern, sight; literary behold, espy.

> **WORD LINKS**
> **optical**, **visual** relating to sight

> ! Don't confuse **sight** with **site**, which means 'a place where something is located or happens' (*the site of a famous temple*).

sightseer noun **tourist**, visitor, tripper, holidaymaker.

sign noun **1** *a sign of affection:* **indication**, signal, symptom, pointer, suggestion, intimation, mark, manifestation, demonstration, token. **2** *a sign of things to come:* **portent**, omen, warning; promise, threat. **3** *at his sign they attacked:* **gesture**, signal, wave, cue, nod. **4** *signs saying 'danger':* **notice**, signpost. **5** *the dancers were daubed with signs:* **symbol**, cipher, letter, character, figure, hieroglyph, ideogram, rune, emblem, device, logo.
• verb **1** *they signed the treaty:* **authorize**, endorse, agree to, approve, ratify; autograph, initial, countersign. **2** *he signed his name:* **write**, inscribe, pen. **3** *we have signed a new player:* **recruit**, engage, employ, take on, appoint, sign on/up, enlist. **4** *she signed to Susan to leave:* **gesture**, signal, motion; wave, beckon, nod.
■ **sign on/up** enlist, join, enrol, register, volunteer. **sign someone on/up**. See **SIGN** verb sense 3.

signal[1] noun **1** *a signal to stop:* **gesture**, sign, wave, cue, indication, warning. **2** *a clear signal that we're in trouble:* **indication**, sign, symptom, hint, pointer, intimation, clue, demonstration, evidence, proof. **3** *at his signal, they attacked:* **cue**, prompt.
• verb **1** *the driver signalled to her:* **gesture**, sign, indicate, motion; wave, beckon, nod. **2** *they signalled their displeasure:* **indicate**, show, express, communicate. **3** *his death signals the end of an era:* **mark**, signify, mean, be a sign of, be evidence of.

signal[2] adjective *the campaign was a signal failure:* **notable**, striking, glaring, significant, momentous, obvious, conspicuous.

significance noun **1** *a matter of significance:* **importance**, import, consequence, seriousness, gravity, weight, magnitude; formal moment. **2** *the significance of his remarks:*

S

meaning, sense, signification, import, thrust, drift, gist, implication, message, essence, substance, point.

significant adjective **1** *a significant fact:* **notable**, noteworthy, remarkable, important, of consequence; formal of moment. **2** *a significant increase:* **sizeable**, considerable, appreciable, conspicuous, striking; meaningful, obvious; large, sudden. **3** *a significant look:* **meaningful**, expressive, eloquent, suggestive, knowing, telling.

significantly adverb **1** *the results are significantly better:* **notably**, remarkably, materially, appreciably; markedly, considerably, obviously, conspicuously, strikingly. **2** *he paused significantly:* **meaningfully**, expressively, eloquently, revealingly, suggestively, knowingly.

signify verb **1** *this signified a change:* **be evidence of**, be a sign of, mark, signal, be symptomatic of, herald, indicate. **2** *the egg signifies life:* **mean**, denote, designate, represent, symbolize, stand for. **3** *signify your agreement by signing below:* **express**, indicate, show, declare.

silence noun **1** *the silence of the night:* **quietness**, quiet, still, stillness, hush, tranquillity, noiselessness, peacefulness, peace. **2** *she was reduced to silence:* **speechlessness**, wordlessness, dumbness, muteness.
–OPPOSITES noise.
•verb **quieten**, quiet, hush, mute, muffle, deaden, dampen, subdue.

silent adjective **1** *the night was silent:* **quiet**, still, hushed, noiseless, soundless; inaudible. **2** *she remained silent:* **speechless**, unspeaking, tongue-tied, dumb, mute; taciturn, uncommunicative, tight-lipped. **3** *silent thanks:* **unspoken**, wordless; tacit.
–OPPOSITES audible, noisy.

silently adverb **1** *Nancy crept silently up the stairs:* **quietly**, inaudibly, noiselessly, soundlessly, in silence. **2** *they drove on silently:* **without a word**, saying nothing, in silence.
–OPPOSITES audibly, out loud.

silhouette noun **outline**, contour, profile, form, shape.
•verb **outline**, delineate, define.

silky adjective **smooth**, soft, sleek, fine, glossy, silken.

silly adjective **1** *don't be so silly:* **foolish**, stupid; scatterbrained; frivolous, giddy, inane, immature, childish, puerile, empty-headed; informal dotty, scatty. **2** *that was a silly thing to do:* **unwise**, imprudent, thoughtless, foolish, stupid, unintelligent, idiotic, brainless, senseless, mindless; rash, reckless, foolhardy, irresponsible, injudicious; informal crazy, mad; Brit. informal daft. **3** *he would worry about silly things:* **trivial**, trifling, frivolous, petty, small, insignificant, unimportant; informal piffling, piddling; N. Amer. informal small-bore.
–OPPOSITES sensible.

silt noun **sediment**, deposit, alluvium, mud.

similar adjective **1** *you two are very similar:* **alike**, much the same, homogeneous; informal much of a muchness. **2** *northern India and similar areas:* **comparable**, like, corresponding, equivalent, analogous. **3** *other parts were similar to Wales:* **like**, much the same as, comparable to.
–OPPOSITES different, unlike.

similarity noun **resemblance**, likeness, sameness, comparability, correspondence, parallel, equivalence, homogeneity, uniformity.

similarly adverb **likewise**, in similar fashion, comparably, correspondingly, in the same way.

simmer verb **1** *the soup was simmering on the stove:* **boil**, bubble, cook. **2** *she was simmering with resentment:* **seethe**, fume, smoulder.

simple adjective **1** *it's really pretty simple:* **straightforward**, easy, uncomplicated, uninvolved, undemanding, elementary, child's play, effortless; informal as easy as falling off a log, as easy as pie, as easy as ABC, a piece of cake, a cinch, no sweat, a doddle, a pushover, money for old rope, kids' stuff, a breeze; Brit. informal easy-peasy; N. Amer. informal duck soup, a snap; Austral./NZ informal a bludge. **2** *simple language:* **clear**, plain, lucid, straightforward,

S

accessible; informal user-friendly. **3** *a simple white blouse:* **plain**, unadorned, basic, unsophisticated, no-frills; classic, understated, uncluttered, restrained. **4** *the simple truth:* **candid**, frank, honest, sincere, plain, absolute, bald, stark, unadorned, unvarnished. **5** *simple country people:* **unpretentious**, unsophisticated, ordinary, unaffected, unassuming, natural, straightforward; N. Amer. cracker-barrel.
– OPPOSITES difficult, complex, fancy.

simplicity noun **1** *the simplicity of the recipes:* **straightforwardness**, ease, easiness, simpleness. **2** *the simplicity of the language:* **clarity**, clearness, plainness, simpleness, intelligibility, comprehensibility, straightforwardness, accessibility. **3** *the building's simplicity:* **plainness**, austerity, spareness, clean lines. **4** *the simplicity of their lifestyle:* **plainness**, modesty, naturalness.

simplify verb **make simple/simpler**, make plainer, clarify; paraphrase, put in words of one syllable.
– OPPOSITES complicate.

simplistic adjective **facile**, superficial, oversimplified.

simply adverb **1** *he spoke simply and forcefully:* **straightforwardly**, directly, clearly, plainly, lucidly, unambiguously. **2** *she was dressed simply:* **plainly**, soberly, unfussily, classically. **3** *they lived simply:* **modestly**, plainly, quietly. **4** *they are welcomed simply because they are rich:* **merely**, just, purely, solely, only. **5** *she was simply delighted:* **utterly**, absolutely, completely, positively, just; informal plain.

simulate verb **1** *they simulated pleasure:* **feign**, pretend, fake, affect, put on. **2** *a test that simulates conditions at higher altitudes:* **imitate**, reproduce, replicate, duplicate, mimic.

simulated adjective **1** *simulated fear:* **feigned**, fake, mock, affected, sham; informal pretend, put-on, phoney. **2** *simulated leather:* **artificial**, imitation, fake, mock, synthetic, man-made, ersatz.
– OPPOSITES real.

simultaneous adjective **concurrent**, happening at the same time, contemporaneous, concomitant, coinciding, coincident, synchronous, synchronized.

simultaneously adverb **at the same time**, at the same instant/moment, at once, concurrently, concomitantly; together, in unison, in concert, in chorus.

sin noun **1** *a sin in the eyes of God:* **immoral act**, wrong, wrongdoing, act of evil/wickedness, transgression, crime, offence, misdeed, misdemeanour; old use trespass. **2** *the human capacity for sin:* **wickedness**, wrongdoing, evil, evildoing, sinfulness, immorality, iniquity, vice, crime.
– OPPOSITES virtue.
• verb *I know that I have sinned:* **transgress**, do wrong, misbehave, go astray.

sincere adjective **1** *our sincere gratitude:* **heartfelt**, wholehearted, profound, deep; true, honest. **2** *a sincere person:* **honest**, genuine, truthful, direct, frank, candid; informal straight, upfront, on the level; N. Amer. informal on the up and up.

sincerely adverb **genuinely**, honestly, really, truly, truthfully, wholeheartedly, earnestly.

sincerity noun **honesty**, genuineness, truthfulness, integrity, openness, candour.

sinewy adjective **muscular**, muscly, strong, powerful, athletic.
– OPPOSITES puny.

sinful adjective **immoral**, wicked, wrong, evil, bad, iniquitous, corrupt, depraved.
– OPPOSITES virtuous.

sinfulness noun **immorality**, wickedness, sin, wrongdoing, evil, evildoing, iniquitousness, corruption, depravity, degeneracy, vice; formal turpitude.
– OPPOSITES virtue.

sing verb **1** *he began to sing:* croon, trill, chant, intone, chorus. **2** *the birds were singing:* **warble**, trill, chirp, chirrup, cheep.

singe verb **scorch**, burn, sear, char.

singer noun **vocalist**, soloist, songster, songstress, cantor.

single adjective **1** *a single red rose:* **one only**, sole, lone, solitary,

unaccompanied, alone. **2** *every single word:* **individual**, separate, distinct. **3** *is she single?* **unmarried**, unwed, unattached, free, a bachelor, a spinster.
– OPPOSITES double, multiple, married.
■ **single someone/something out** select, pick out, choose, decide on; target, earmark, mark out, separate out, set apart/aside.

single-handed adverb **by yourself**, alone, on your own, solo, unaided, unassisted, without help.

single-minded adjective **determined**, committed, unswerving, unwavering, resolute, purposeful, devoted, dedicated, uncompromising, tireless, tenacious, persistent, dogged.
– OPPOSITES half-hearted.

singly adverb **one by one**, one at a time, one after the other, individually, separately.
– OPPOSITES together.

singular adjective **remarkable**, extraordinary, exceptional, outstanding, signal, notable, noteworthy.

sinister adjective **1** *there was a sinister undertone in his words:* **menacing**, threatening, ominous, forbidding, frightening, alarming, disturbing, disquieting, dark. **2** *a sinister motive:* **evil**, wicked, criminal, nefarious, villainous, base, malicious; informal shady.
– OPPOSITES innocent.

sink verb **1** *the sun sank towards the horizon:* **descend**, fall, drop, go down/downwards, set. **2** *the cruise liner sank yesterday:* **founder**, go down. **3** *they sank their ships:* **scuttle**; Brit. scupper. **4** *Loretta sank into an armchair:* **lower yourself**, flop, collapse, drop down, slump; informal plonk yourself. **5** *she would never sink to your level:* **stoop**, lower yourself, descend. **6** *sink the pots into the ground:* **embed**, insert, drive, plant. **7** *they sank their life savings in the company:* **invest**, venture, risk.
– OPPOSITES rise, float.
■ **sink in** register, be understood, be comprehended, be grasped, get through.

sinner noun **wrongdoer**, evildoer, transgressor, miscreant, offender, criminal.

sinuous adjective **1** *a sinuous river:* **winding**, windy, serpentine, curving, twisting, meandering, snaking, zigzag, curling, coiling. **2** *sinuous grace:* **lithe**, supple, graceful, loose-limbed, lissom.
– OPPOSITES straight, awkward

sip noun **mouthful**, taste, swallow, drink, sup, drop, dram, nip.

siren noun **alarm**, warning, danger signal, horn, hooter; trademark klaxon.

sister noun **1** *I have two sisters:* **sibling**. **2** *our European sisters:* **comrade**, partner, colleague; counterpart. **3** *the sisters in the convent:* **nun**, novice; abbess, prioress.

> **WORD LINKS**
> **sororal** relating to a sister

sit verb **1** *you'd better sit down:* **take a seat**, seat yourself, be seated, perch, ensconce yourself, plump yourself, flop; informal take the weight off your feet, plonk yourself; Brit. informal take a pew. **2** *she sat the package on the table:* **put**, place, set, lay, deposit, rest, stand; informal stick, park. **3** *she sat for Picasso:* **pose**, model. **4** *a hotel sitting on the bank of the River Dee:* **be situated**, be located, be sited, stand. **5** *the committee sits on Saturday:* **be in session**, meet, be convened. **6** *she sits on the tribunal:* **serve on**, have a seat on, be a member of.
– OPPOSITES stand.
■ **sit in for** stand in for, fill in for, cover for, substitute for, deputize for. **sit in on** attend, be present at, observe; N. Amer. audit.

site noun *the site of a famous temple:* **location**, place, position, situation, locality, whereabouts; technical locus.
• verb **place**, put, position, situate, locate.

> ! Don't confuse **site** with **sight**, which means 'the ability to see' (*she has excellent sight*).

sitting noun **session**, meeting, assembly; hearing.
• adjective **sedentary**, seated.
– OPPOSITES standing.

sitting room noun **living room**, lounge, front room, drawing room, reception room; dated parlour.

S

situate verb **locate**, site, position, place, station.

situation noun **1** *their financial situation:* **circumstances**, affairs, state, condition, position; context, environment, background. **2** *the hotel's pleasant situation:* **location**, position, spot, site, setting, environment. **3** *he was offered a situation in America:* **job**, post, position, appointment; employment.

six cardinal number **sextet**, sextuplets.

> **WORD LINKS**
> **hexagon** a six-sided plane figure
> **hexahedron** a six-sided solid figure

size noun **dimensions**, measurements, proportions, magnitude, largeness, area, expanse; breadth, width, length, height, depth; immensity, hugeness, vastness.
•verb **sort**, categorize, classify.
■ **size someone/something up** (informal) assess, appraise, get the measure of, judge, take stock of, evaluate; Brit. informal suss out.

sizeable adjective **fairly/pretty large**, substantial, considerable, respectable, significant, largish, biggish, goodly.
–OPPOSITES small.

sizzle verb **crackle**, frizzle, sputter, spit.

sizzling adjective (informal) **1** *sizzling temperatures:* **scorching**, blazing, burning, sweltering; N. Amer. broiling; informal boiling, baking. **2** *a sizzling affair:* **passionate**, torrid, ardent, lustful, erotic; informal steamy, hot.
–OPPOSITES freezing.

S

skeletal adjective **emaciated**, painfully thin, as thin as a rake, cadaverous, skin-and-bones, skinny, bony, gaunt; informal anorexic.
–OPPOSITES fat.

skeleton noun **1** *the human skeleton:* **bones**; technical endoskeleton, exoskeleton. **2** *the concrete skeleton of a building:* **framework**, frame, structure; chassis.
•adjective *a skeleton staff:* **minimum**, minimal, basic; essential.

sketch noun **1** *a sketch of the proposed design:* **drawing**, outline; diagram, design, plan; informal rough. **2** *she gave a brief sketch of what had happened:* **outline**, brief description, rundown, main points, thumbnail sketch, bare bones; summary, synopsis, summarization, precis, résumé; N. Amer. wrap-up. **3** *a hilarious sketch:* **skit**, scene, piece, act, item, routine.
•verb *the company sketched out its plans:* **describe**, outline, explain, set out, rough out, map out; summarize, precis.

sketchily adverb **perfunctorily**, cursorily, incompletely, patchily, vaguely, imprecisely; hastily, hurriedly.

sketchy adjective **incomplete**, patchy, fragmentary, cursory, perfunctory, scanty, vague, imprecise; hurried, hasty.
–OPPOSITES detailed.

skilful adjective **expert**, skilled, accomplished, masterly, master, virtuoso, consummate, proficient, talented, adept, adroit, deft, dexterous, able, good, competent, capable, handy; informal mean, wicked, crack, ace, wizard; N. Amer. informal crackerjack.

skill noun **1** *his skill as a politician:* **expertise**, skilfulness, expertness, adeptness, adroitness, deftness, dexterity, ability, prowess, mastery, competence, capability, aptitude, artistry, virtuosity, talent. **2** *bringing up a family demands many skills:* **accomplishment**, strength, ability.
–OPPOSITES incompetence.

skilled adjective **experienced**, trained, qualified, proficient, practised, accomplished, expert, skilful, adept, adroit, deft, dexterous, able, good, competent; informal crack; N. Amer. informal crackerjack.
–OPPOSITES inexperienced, unskilled.

skim verb **1** *skim off the fat:* **remove**, scoop off. **2** *the boat skimmed over the water:* **glide**, move lightly, slide, sail, skate. **3** *he skimmed the pebble across the water:* **throw**, toss, cast, pitch. **4** *she skimmed through the newspaper:* **glance**, flick, flip, leaf, thumb, read quickly, scan, run your eye over. **5** *Hannah skimmed over this part of the story:* **mention briefly**, pass over quickly, skate over, gloss over.

skimp verb **stint on**, scrimp on, economize on, cut back on, be sparing, be frugal, be mean, cut corners; informal be stingy, be mingy, be tight.

skimpy adjective **revealing**, short, low, low cut.

skin noun **1** *these chemicals could damage the skin:* **epidermis**, dermis, derma. **2** *Mary's fair skin:* **complexion**, colouring, pigmentation. **3** *leopard skins:* **hide**, pelt, fleece. **4** *a banana skin:* **peel**, rind. **5** *milk with a skin on it:* **film**, layer, membrane. **6** *the plane's skin was damaged:* **casing**, exterior, membrane.
• verb **1** *first skin the tomatoes:* **peel**, pare, hull. **2** *he skinned his knee:* **graze**, scrape, abrade, bark, rub something raw, chafe.

WORD LINKS
cutaneous relating to the skin
subcutaneous beneath the skin
dermatology the branch of medicine concerned with skin disorders

skin-deep adjective **superficial**, surface, external, outward, shallow.

skinflint noun (informal). See **MISER**.

skinny adjective. See **THIN** adjective sense 1.

skip verb **1** *the girls skipped down the path:* **caper**, prance, trip, dance, bound, bounce, gambol. **2** *we skipped the boring stuff:* **omit**, leave out, miss out, dispense with, pass over, skim over, disregard; informal give something a miss. **3** *I skipped school:* **play truant from**, miss; N. Amer. cut; Brit. informal skive off; N. Amer. informal play hookey from; Austral./NZ informal play the wag from.

skirmish noun **1** *the unit was caught up in a skirmish:* **fight**, battle, clash, conflict, encounter, engagement. **2** *a skirmish over the budget:* **argument**, quarrel, squabble, contretemps, disagreement, difference of opinion, falling-out, dispute, clash, altercation, tussle; Brit. row; informal tiff, spat; Brit. informal barney.
• verb *they skirmished with enemy soldiers:* **fight**, do battle with, engage with, close with, combat, clash with.

skirt verb **1** *he skirted the city:* **go round**, walk round, circle. **2** *the fields that skirt the park:* **border**, edge, flank, line, lie alongside/next to. **3** *he carefully skirted round the subject:* **avoid**, evade, sidestep, dodge, pass over, gloss over; informal duck; Austral./NZ informal duck-shove.

skit noun **sketch**, parody, pastiche, satire; informal spoof, take-off, send-up.

skittish adjective **1** *she grew increasingly skittish:* **playful**, lively, high-spirited, frisky; literary frolicsome. **2** *his horse was skittish:* **restive**, excitable, nervous, jumpy, highly strung.

skive verb (Brit. informal) **malinger**, play truant, truant, shirk, idle; Brit. informal bunk off, swing the lead; N. Amer. informal goldbrick, play hookey, goof off; Austral./NZ informal play the wag.

skulduggery noun **trickery**, sharp practice, underhandedness, chicanery; informal shenanigans, funny business, monkey business; Brit. informal jiggery-pokery; N. Amer. informal monkeyshines.

skulk verb **lurk**, loiter, hide; creep, sneak, slink, prowl.

skull noun

WORD LINKS
cranial relating to the skull

sky noun *the sun was shining in the sky:* literary the heavens, the firmament, the blue, the wide blue yonder.

WORD LINKS
celestial relating to the sky

slab noun **piece**, block, hunk, chunk, lump; cake, tablet, brick.

slack adjective **1** *the rope went slack:* **loose**, limp. **2** *slack skin:* **flaccid**, flabby, loose, sagging, saggy. **3** *business is slack:* **sluggish**, slow, quiet, slow-moving, flat, depressed, stagnant. **4** *slack accounting procedures:* **lax**, negligent, careless, slapdash, slipshod; informal sloppy, slap-happy.
– OPPOSITES tight, taut.
• noun **1** *the rope had some slack in it:* **looseness**, play, give. **2** *foreign demand will help pick up the slack:* **surplus**, excess, spare capacity.
• verb (Brit. informal) **idle**, shirk, be lazy, be indolent, waste time, lounge about; Brit. informal skive; N. Amer. informal goof off.

slacken verb **1** *he slackened his grip:* **loosen**, release, relax, loose, lessen, weaken. **2** *he slackened his pace:* **slow**, decelerate. **3** *the rain is slackening:* **decrease**, lessen, subside, ease up/off, let up, abate, diminish, die down, fall off.
– OPPOSITES tighten.

slake verb **quench**, satisfy, sate, satiate, relieve, assuage.

slam verb **1** *he slammed the door behind him:* **bang**, throw shut, crash. **2** *the car slammed into a lamp post:* **crash into**, smash into, collide with, hit, strike, ram, plough into, run into, bump into; N. Amer. impact.

slander noun **defamation of character**, character assassination, calumny, libel; malicious gossip, disparagement, denigration, vilification; lie, slur, smear, insult; informal mud-slinging.
• verb **defame**, blacken someone's name, speak ill of, libel, smear, cast aspersions on, besmirch, tarnish; malign, vilify, disparage, denigrate, run down; N. Amer. slur.

slanderous adjective **defamatory**, denigratory, disparaging, libellous, pejorative, false, misrepresentative, scurrilous, scandalous, malicious.
– OPPOSITES complimentary.

slang noun **informal language**, colloquialisms, patois, argot, cant.

slant verb **1** *the floor was slanting:* **slope**, tilt, incline, angle, tip, lean, dip, pitch, shelve, list, bank. **2** *their findings were slanted in our favour:* **bias**, distort, twist, skew, weight.
• noun **1** *the slant of the roof:* **slope**, incline, tilt, gradient, pitch, angle, camber, inclination. **2** *a feminist slant:* **point of view**, viewpoint, standpoint, stance, angle, perspective, approach, view, attitude, position; bias, leaning.

S

slanting adjective **oblique**, sloping, at an angle, inclined, tilting, tilted, slanted, diagonal.

slap verb **1** *he slapped her hard:* **hit**, strike, smack, clout, cuff, spank; informal whack, wallop, biff, bash; Brit. informal slosh. **2** *he slapped down a £10 note:* **fling**, throw, slam, bang; informal plonk. **3** *slap on a coat of paint:* **daub**, plaster, throw. **4** (informal) *they slapped a huge tax on imports:* **impose**, levy, put on.
• noun *a slap across the face:* **smack**, blow, cuff, clout; informal whack, thwack, wallop, clip.
■ **a slap in the face** rebuff, rejection, snub, insult, put-down, humiliation. **a slap on the back** congratulations, commendation, approbation, approval, accolades, compliments, tributes, a pat on the back, praise, acclaim. **a slap on the wrist** reprimand, rebuke, reproof, scolding, admonishment; informal telling-off, rap over the knuckles, dressing-down; Brit. informal ticking-off.

slapdash adjective **careless**, slipshod, hurried, haphazard, unsystematic, untidy, messy, hit-or-miss, negligent, neglectful, lax; informal sloppy, slap-happy; Brit. informal shambolic.
– OPPOSITES meticulous.

slash verb **1** *her tyres had been slashed:* **cut**, gash, slit, split open, lacerate, knife. **2** (informal) *the company slashed prices:* **reduce**, cut, lower, bring down, mark down. **3** (informal) *they have slashed 10,000 jobs:* **get rid of**, axe, cut, shed.
• noun **1** *a slash across his temple:* **cut**, gash, laceration, slit, incision; wound. **2** *sentence breaks are indicated by slashes:* **solidus**, oblique; forward slash, backslash.

slate verb (Brit. informal). See CRITICIZE.

slaughter verb **1** *the cattle were slaughtered:* **kill**, butcher; cull, put down. **2** *innocent civilians were slaughtered:* **massacre**, murder, butcher, kill, annihilate, wipe out, put to death; literary slay.
• noun **1** *the slaughter of 20 demonstrators:* **massacre**, murdering, murder, killing, execution, annihilation; literary slaying. **2** *a scene of slaughter:* **carnage**, bloodshed, bloodletting, bloodbath.

slaughterhouse noun **abattoir**; old use shambles.

slave noun **1** *the work was done by slaves:* historical serf, vassal; old use bondsman, bondswoman. **2** *he treats her like a slave:* **servant**, lackey; informal gofer; Brit. informal skivvy, dogsbody.
– OPPOSITES freeman, master.
• verb *I'm slaving away for a pittance:* **toil**, labour, grind, sweat, work your fingers to the bone, work like a

Trojan, work like a dog; informal kill yourself, sweat blood, slog away; Brit. informal graft.

> **WORD LINKS**
> **servile** relating to a slave or slaves

slaver verb **drool**, slobber, dribble, salivate.

slavery noun **bondage**, enslavement, servitude, serfdom.
– OPPOSITES freedom.

slavish adjective **unoriginal**, uninspired, unimaginative, uninventive, imitative, mindless.

slay verb (literary) **kill**, murder, put to death, butcher, cut down, slaughter, massacre, shoot down, gun down, mow down, eliminate, annihilate, exterminate, liquidate; informal wipe out, bump off.

slaying noun (literary) **murder**, killing, butchery, slaughter, massacre, extermination, liquidation.

sleazy adjective **1** *sleazy politicians:* **corrupt**, immoral. **2** *a sleazy bar:* **squalid**, seedy, seamy, sordid, insalubrious, mean, cheap, low-class, run down; informal scruffy, scuzzy, crummy; Brit. informal grotty.
– OPPOSITES reputable, upmarket.

sledge noun **toboggan**, bobsleigh, sleigh; N. Amer. sled.

sleek adjective **1** *his sleek dark hair:* **smooth**, glossy, shiny, shining, lustrous, silken, silky. **2** *the car's sleek lines:* **streamlined**, elegant, graceful. **3** *sleek young men in city suits:* **well groomed**, stylish.

sleep noun **nap**, doze, siesta, catnap, beauty sleep; informal snooze, forty winks; Brit. informal kip; literary slumber.
• verb **be asleep**, doze, take a siesta, take a nap, catnap; informal snooze, snatch forty winks, get some shut-eye; Brit. informal kip, get your head down; N. Amer. informal catch some Zs; humorous be in the land of Nod; literary slumber.
– OPPOSITES wake up.
■ **go to sleep** fall asleep; informal drop off, nod off, drift off, crash out, flake out; N. Amer. informal sack out, zone out.
put something to sleep put down, destroy, slaughter; N. Amer. euthanize.

> **WORD LINKS**
> **sedative**, **soporific** causing drowsiness or sleep

sleepiness noun **drowsiness**, tiredness, somnolence, languor, doziness; lethargy, sluggishness, lassitude, enervation.

sleepless adjective **wakeful**, restless, insomniac; wide awake, tossing and turning.

sleeplessness noun **insomnia**, wakefulness.

sleepwalker noun **somnambulist**.

sleepy adjective **1** *she felt very sleepy:* **drowsy**, tired, somnolent, heavy-eyed, asleep on your feet; lethargic, enervated, torpid; informal dopey. **2** *a sleepy little village:* **quiet**, peaceful, tranquil, placid, slow-moving; dull, boring.
– OPPOSITES awake, alert.

sleight of hand noun **1** *impressive sleight of hand:* **dexterity**, adroitness, deftness, skill. **2** *financial sleight of hand:* **deception**, deceit, chicanery, trickery, sharp practice.

slender adjective **1** *her tall slender figure:* **slim**, lean, willowy, sylphlike, svelte, lissom, graceful; slight, thin, skinny. **2** *slender evidence:* **meagre**, limited, slight, scanty, scant, sparse, paltry, insubstantial. **3** *the chances seemed slender:* **faint**, remote, flimsy, tenuous, fragile, slim; unlikely, improbable.
– OPPOSITES plump.

slice noun **1** *a slice of fruitcake:* **piece**, portion, slab, sliver, wafer, rasher. **2** *a huge slice of public spending:* **share**, part, portion, tranche, piece, proportion, allocation, percentage.
• verb *slice the meat thinly:* **cut**, carve.

slick adjective **1** *a slick advertising campaign:* **efficient**, smooth, smooth-running, polished, well organized, well run, streamlined. **2** *his slick use of words:* **glib**, smooth, fluent, plausible. **3** *a slick salesman:* **suave**, urbane, polished, assured, self-assured, smooth-talking, glib; informal smarmy. **4** *her slick brown hair:* **shiny**, glossy, shining, sleek, smooth.
• verb *his hair was slicked down:* **smooth**, sleek, grease, oil, gel.

slide verb **1** *the glass slid across the table:* **glide**, slip, slither, skim, skate; skid, slew. **2** *tears slid down her*

cheeks: **trickle**, run, flow, pour, stream. **3** *four men slid out of the shadows:* **creep**, steal, slink, slip, tiptoe, sidle. **4** *the country is sliding into recession:* **sink**, fall, drop, descend; decline, degenerate.
• **noun 1** *the current slide in house prices:* **fall**, decline, drop, slump, downturn, downswing. **2** *black and white slides:* **transparency**; photograph.
– OPPOSITES rise.

slight adjective **1** *the chance of success is slight:* **small**, modest, tiny, minute, negligible, insignificant, minimal, remote, slim, faint; informal minuscule. **2** *the book is a slight work:* **minor**, inconsequential, trivial, unimportant, lightweight. **3** *her slight figure:* **slim**, slender, petite, diminutive, small, delicate, dainty.
– OPPOSITES considerable.
• **verb** *he had been slighted:* **insult**, snub, rebuff, ignore, disregard, give someone the cold shoulder, cut dead.
– OPPOSITES respect.
• **noun** *an unintended slight:* **insult**, affront, snub, rebuff; informal put-down.
– OPPOSITES compliment.

slightly adverb **a little**, a bit, somewhat, rather, moderately, to a certain extent, faintly, vaguely, a shade.
– OPPOSITES very.

slim adjective **1** *she's tall and slim:* **slender**, lean, willowy, sylphlike, svelte, lissom, trim; skinny, thin. **2** *a slim silver bracelet:* **narrow**, slender. **3** *a slim chance:* **slight**, small, slender, faint, poor, remote.
– OPPOSITES plump.
• **verb 1** *I'm trying to slim:* **lose weight**; N. Amer. slenderize. **2** *the number of staff had been slimmed down:* **reduce**, cut down/back, scale down, decrease, diminish, pare down.

slime noun **ooze**; informal goo, gunk, gloop; Brit. informal gunge; N. Amer. informal glop.

slimy adjective **1** *the floor was slimy:* **slippery**, slithery, greasy; informal slippy, gooey, gloopy. **2** (informal) *her slimy press agent.* See **OBSEQUIOUS**.

sling verb **1** *a hammock was slung between two trees:* **hang**, suspend, string, swing. **2** (informal) *she slung her jacket on the sofa:* **throw**, toss, hurl, fling, cast, lob; informal chuck; Brit. informal bung.

slink verb **creep**, sneak, steal, slip, slide, sidle, tiptoe.

slinky adjective (informal) **1** *a slinky black dress:* **tight-fitting**, close-fitting, figure-hugging, sexy. **2** *her slinky elegance:* **sinuous**, feline, willowy, sleek.

slip[1] verb **1** *she slipped on the ice:* **slide**, skid, slither; fall, lose your balance, tumble. **2** *we slipped out by a back door:* **creep**, steal, sneak, slide, sidle, slope, slink, tiptoe. **3** *standards have slipped:* **decline**, deteriorate, degenerate, worsen, get worse, fall, drop; informal go downhill, go to the dogs, go to pot. **4** *the bank's shares slipped 1.5p:* **drop**, go down, sink, slump, decrease, depreciate. **5** *she slipped the map into her pocket:* **put**, tuck, shove; informal pop, stick.
• **noun 1** *a single slip could send them plummeting down:* **false step**, slide, skid, fall, tumble. **2** *a careless slip:* **mistake**, error, blunder, gaffe; oversight, omission, lapse; informal slip-up, boo-boo, howler; Brit. informal boob, clanger, bloomer; N. Amer. informal goof, blooper. **3** *a silk slip:* **underskirt**, petticoat.
■ **give someone the slip** (informal) escape from, get away from, evade, dodge, elude, lose, shake off, throw off the scent. **let something slip** reveal, disclose, divulge, let out, give away, blurt out; informal let on, blab. **slip up** (informal) make a mistake, blunder, make an error, err; informal make a boo-boo; Brit. informal boob, drop a clanger; N. Amer. informal goof up.

slip[2] noun *a slip of paper:* **piece of paper**, scrap of paper, sheet, note; chit.

slippery adjective **1** *the roads are slippery:* **slithery**, greasy, oily, icy, glassy, smooth, slimy, wet; informal slippy. **2** *a slippery customer:* **evasive**, unreliable; devious, crafty, cunning, wily, tricky, artful, slick, sneaky, scheming, untrustworthy, deceitful, duplicitous, dishonest, treacherous, two-faced; N. Amer. snide; informal shady, shifty; Brit. informal dodgy; Austral./NZ informal shonky.

slipshod adjective **careless**, lackadaisical, slapdash, disorganized, haphazard, hit-or-miss, untidy, messy, unsystematic, casual, negligent, neglectful, lax, slack; informal sloppy, slap-happy.
– OPPOSITES meticulous.

slip-up noun (informal) **mistake**, slip, error, blunder, oversight, omission, gaffe, inaccuracy; informal boo-boo, howler; Brit. informal boob, clanger, bloomer; N. Amer. informal goof, blooper, bloop.

slit noun **1** *three diagonal slits:* **cut**, incision, split, slash, gash, laceration. **2** *a slit in the curtains:* **opening**, gap, chink, crack, aperture, slot.
• verb *he threatened to slit her throat:* **cut**, slash, split open, slice open.

slither verb **slide**, slip, glide, wriggle, crawl; skid.

sliver noun **splinter**, shard, chip, flake, shred, scrap, shaving, paring, piece, fragment.

slob noun (informal) **layabout**, good-for-nothing, sluggard, laggard; informal slacker, couch potato.

slobber verb **drool**, slaver, dribble, salivate.

slog verb **1** *they were all slogging away:* **work hard**, toil, labour, work your fingers to the bone, work like a Trojan, work like a dog, exert yourself, grind, slave, plough, plod, peg; informal beaver, plug, work your socks off, sweat blood; Brit. informal graft. **2** *they slogged around the streets:* **trudge**, tramp, traipse, toil, plod, trek; N. Amer. informal schlep.
– OPPOSITES relax.
• noun **1** *10 months' slog:* **hard work**, toil, labour, effort, exertion, grind; informal sweat; Brit. informal graft. **2** *a steady uphill slog:* **trudge**, tramp, traipse, plod, trek; N. Amer. informal schlep.

slogan noun **catchphrase**, catchline, jingle; N. Amer. informal tag line.

slop verb **spill**, flow, overflow, run, slosh, splash.

slope noun **1** *the slope of the roof:* **gradient**, incline, angle, slant, inclination, pitch, decline, fall, tilt, tip, downslope, upslope; N. Amer. grade, downgrade, upgrade. **2** *a grassy slope:* **hill**, hillside, hillock, bank, escarpment, scarp. **3** *the ski slopes:* **piste**, run; N. Amer. trail.
• verb *the garden sloped down to a stream:* **slant**, incline, tilt; drop/fall away, descend, shelve, lean; rise, ascend, climb.
■ **slope off** (informal) leave, go away, slip away, steal away, slink off, creep off, sneak off; informal push off.

sloping adjective **slanting**, angled, inclining, inclined, tilting, tilted, slanted, aslant, leaning, oblique, cambered, dipping.
– OPPOSITES level.

sloppy adjective **1** *sloppy chicken curry:* **runny**, watery, thin, liquid, semi-liquid, mushy; informal gloopy. **2** *their defending was sloppy:* **careless**, slapdash, slipshod, lackadaisical, haphazard, lax, slack, slovenly; informal slap-happy; Brit. informal shambolic. **3** *sloppy letters:* **sentimental**, mawkish, cloying, sugary, syrupy; romantic; informal slushy, schmaltzy, lovey-dovey; Brit. informal soppy; N. Amer. informal cornball, sappy, hokey.

slosh verb **1** *beer sloshed over the side of the glass:* **spill**, slop, splash, flow, overflow. **2** *workers sloshed round in boots:* **splash**, squelch, wade; informal splosh. **3** *she sloshed more wine into her glass:* **pour**, slop, splash.

slot noun **1** *he slid a coin into the slot:* **aperture**, slit, crack, hole, opening. **2** *a mid-morning slot:* **spot**, time, period, niche, space; informal window.
• verb *he slotted a cassette into the machine:* **insert**, put, place, slide, slip.

sloth noun **laziness**, idleness, indolence, slothfulness, inactivity, inertia, sluggishness, shiftlessness, apathy, listlessness, lassitude, lethargy, languor.
– OPPOSITES industriousness.

slothful adjective **lazy**, idle, indolent, work-shy, inactive, sluggish, apathetic, lethargic, listless, languid, torpid; informal bone idle.

slouch verb **slump**, hunch; loll, droop.

slovenly adjective **1** *his slovenly appearance:* **scruffy**, untidy, messy, unkempt, ill-groomed, dishevelled, bedraggled, tousled, rumpled, frowzy; informal slobbish, slobby; N. Amer. informal raggedy, raunchy. **2** *his work is slovenly:* **careless**, slapdash,

slipshod, haphazard, hit-or-miss, untidy, messy, negligent, lax, lackadaisical, slack; informal sloppy, slap-happy.
– OPPOSITES tidy, careful.

slow adjective **1** *their slow pace:* **unhurried**, leisurely, steady, sedate, plodding, dawdling. **2** *a slow process:* **long-drawn-out**, time-consuming, lengthy, protracted, prolonged, gradual. **3** *he can be a bit slow:* **obtuse**, stupid, insensitive, unintelligent; informal dense, dim, dim-witted, thick, slow on the uptake, dumb, dopey; Brit. informal dozy. **4** *they were slow to voice their opinions:* **reluctant**, unwilling, disinclined, loath, hesitant, afraid. **5** *trade was slow over the summer:* **sluggish**, quiet, inactive, flat, depressed, stagnant, dead. **6** *the first half was pretty slow:* **dull**, boring, uninteresting, unexciting, uneventful, tedious, tiresome, wearisome, monotonous, dreary.
– OPPOSITES fast.
• verb **1** *the traffic forced him to slow down:* **reduce speed**, go slower, decelerate, brake. **2** *you need to slow down:* **take it easy**, relax, ease up/off, take a break, let up; N. Amer. informal chill out, hang loose. **3** *this would slow down economic growth:* **hold back/up**, delay, retard, set back; restrict, check, curb, inhibit, impede, obstruct, hinder, hamper.
– OPPOSITES accelerate.

slowly adverb **1** *Rose walked off slowly:* **without hurrying**, unhurriedly, steadily, at a leisurely pace, at a snail's pace; Music adagio, lento, largo. **2** *her health is improving slowly:* **gradually**, bit by bit, little by little, slowly but surely, step by step.
– OPPOSITES quickly.

sludge noun **mud**, muck, mire, ooze, silt, alluvium; informal gunk, crud, gloop, goo; Brit. informal gunge; N. Amer. informal glop.

sluggish adjective **1** *Alex felt tired and sluggish:* **lethargic**, listless, lacking in energy, lifeless, inactive, slow, torpid, languid, apathetic, weary, tired, fatigued, sleepy, drowsy; lazy, idle, indolent, slothful, sluggardly; informal dozy, dopey. **2** *the economy is sluggish:* **inactive**, quiet, slow, slack, flat, depressed, stagnant.
– OPPOSITES vigorous.

sluice verb **wash**, rinse, clean, swill.

slum noun **hovel**; (**slums**) ghetto, shanty town.

slump verb **1** *he slumped into a chair:* **sit heavily**, flop, collapse, sink, fall; informal plonk yourself. **2** *houses prices slumped:* **fall steeply**, plummet, tumble, drop, go down; informal crash, nosedive. **3** *reading standards have slumped:* **decline**, deteriorate, degenerate, worsen, slip; informal go downhill.
• noun **1** *a slump in profits:* **steep fall**, drop, tumble, downturn, downswing, slide, decline, decrease; informal nosedive. **2** *an economic slump:* **recession**, economic decline, depression, slowdown.
– OPPOSITES rise, boom.

slur verb **mumble**, speak unclearly, garble.
• noun **insult**, slight, slander, smear, allegation.

sly adjective **1** *she's very sly:* **cunning**, crafty, clever, wily, artful, guileful, tricky, scheming, devious, deceitful, duplicitous, dishonest, underhand, sneaky. **2** *a sly grin:* **roguish**, mischievous, impish, playful, wicked, arch, knowing. **3** *she took a sly sip of water:* **surreptitious**, furtive, stealthy, covert.

smack[1] noun **1** *she gave him a smack:* **slap**, clout, cuff, blow, rap, swat, crack, thump, punch; informal whack, thwack, clip, biff, wallop, belt, bash. **2** (informal) *a smack on the lips:* **kiss**, peck; informal smacker.
• verb **1** *he tried to smack her:* **slap**, hit, strike, spank, cuff, clout, thump, punch, swat; box someone's ears; informal whack, clip, wallop, belt, bash; Scottish & N. English informal skelp. **2** *the waiter smacked a plate down:* **bang**, slam, crash, thump; sling, fling; informal plonk; N. Amer. informal plunk.
• adverb (informal) *smack in the middle:* **exactly**, precisely, straight, right, directly, squarely, dead, plumb, point-blank; informal slap, bang; N. Amer. informal smack dab.

smack[2] verb
■ **smack of 1** *the tea smacked of tannin:* taste of, have the flavour of. **2** *the plan smacked of self-promotion:*

suggest, hint at, have overtones of, give the impression of, have the stamp of, seem like; smell of, reek of.

small adjective **1** *a small flat:* **little**, compact, tiny, miniature, mini; minute, microscopic, minuscule; toy, baby; poky, cramped, boxy; Scottish wee; informal tiddly, teeny, pocket-sized, dinky; Brit. informal titchy; N. Amer. informal little-bitty. **2** *a very small woman:* **short**, little, petite, diminutive, elfin, tiny; puny, undersized; Scottish wee; informal teeny, pint-sized. **3** *a few small changes:* **slight**, minor, unimportant, trifling, trivial, insignificant, inconsequential, negligible, infinitesimal; informal minuscule, piffling, piddling. **4** *small helpings:* **inadequate**, meagre, insufficient, ungenerous; informal measly, stingy, mingy, pathetic. **5** *they made him feel small:* **foolish**, stupid, insignificant, unimportant; embarrassed, humiliated, uncomfortable, mortified, ashamed; crushed.
– OPPOSITES big, tall, major, ample.

small change noun **coins**, change, coppers, silver, cash.

small-minded adjective **narrow-minded**, petty, mean-spirited, uncharitable.
– OPPOSITES tolerant.

small-time adjective **minor**, small-scale; petty, unimportant, insignificant, inconsequential; N. Amer. minor-league; informal penny-ante, piddling; N. Amer. informal two-bit, bush-league, picayune.
– OPPOSITES major.

smarmy adjective (informal) **unctuous**, ingratiating, slick, oily, greasy, obsequious, sycophantic, fawning; informal slimy.

smart adjective **1** *you look very smart:* **well dressed**, stylish, chic, fashionable, modish, elegant, neat, spruce, trim, dapper; N. Amer. trig; informal snazzy, natty, snappy, sharp, cool; N. Amer. informal sassy, spiffy, fly, kicky. **2** *a smart restaurant:* **fashionable**, stylish, high-class, exclusive, chic, fancy; Brit. upmarket; N. Amer. high-toned; informal trendy, posh, ritzy, plush, classy, swanky, glitzy; Brit. informal swish; N. Amer. informal swank. **3** (informal) *he's very smart:* **clever**, bright, intelligent, sharp-witted, quick-witted, shrewd, astute; perceptive; informal brainy, savvy, quick on the uptake. **4** *a smart pace:* **brisk**, quick, fast, rapid, swift, lively, energetic, vigorous; informal cracking. **5** *a smart blow on the snout:* **sharp**, severe, forceful, violent.
– OPPOSITES untidy, downmarket, stupid, slow, gentle.
• verb **1** *her eyes were smarting:* **sting**, burn, tingle, prickle; hurt. **2** *she smarted at the accusations:* **feel annoyed**, feel upset, take offence, feel aggrieved, feel indignant, be put out, feel hurt.

smarten verb **spruce up**, clean up, tidy up, neaten; groom, freshen, preen, primp, beautify; redecorate, refurbish, modernize; informal do up, titivate, doll up; Brit. informal tart up; N. Amer. informal gussy up.

smash verb **1** *he smashed a window:* **break**, shatter, splinter, crack; informal bust. **2** *she's smashed the car:* **crash**, wreck; Brit. write off; Brit. informal prang; N. Amer. informal total. **3** *they smashed into a wall:* **crash into**, collide with, hit, strike, ram, smack into, slam into, plough into, run into, bump into; N. Amer. impact. **4** *Don smashed him over the head:* **hit**, strike, thump, punch, smack; informal whack, bash, bop, clout, wallop, crown; Brit. informal slosh; N. Amer. informal slug.
• noun **1** *he heard the smash of glass:* **breaking**, shattering, crash. **2** *a motorway smash:* **crash**, collision, accident, road traffic accident, bump; Brit. RTA; N. Amer. wreck; informal pile-up; Brit. informal prang, shunt. **3** (informal) *a box-office smash:* **success**, sensation, sell-out, triumph; informal hit, winner, crowd-puller.

smattering noun **bit**, little, modicum, touch, soupçon; nodding acquaintance; rudiments, basics; informal smidgen, smidge, tad.

smear verb **1** *the table was smeared with grease:* **streak**, smudge, mark; cover, coat. **2** *she smeared sunblock on her skin:* **spread**, rub, daub, slap, smother, plaster, slick. **3** *they are trying to smear our reputation:* **sully**, tarnish, blacken, drag through the mud, taint, damage, defame, discredit, malign, slander,

libel; N. Amer. slur; informal do a hatchet job on; literary besmirch.
• **noun 1** *smears of blood:* **streak**, smudge, daub, dab, spot, patch, blotch, mark; informal splotch, splodge. **2** *press smears about his closest aides:* **false accusation**, lie, untruth, slur, slander, libel, defamation of character.

smell noun **odour**, aroma, fragrance, scent, perfume, redolence; bouquet, nose; stench, stink, reek, effluvium; Brit. informal pong, niff, whiff, hum; Scottish informal guff; N. Amer. informal funk.
• **verb 1** *he smelled her perfume:* **scent**, detect, sniff. **2** *the cellar smells:* **stink**, reek; Brit. informal pong, hum, niff, whiff.

WORD LINKS
olfactory relating to the sense of smell

smelly adjective **foul-smelling**, stinking, reeking, fetid, malodorous, pungent, rank, noxious; off; musty, fusty; informal stinky; Brit. informal pongy, whiffy, humming; N. Amer. informal funky; literary noisome.

smile verb & noun **beam**, grin; smirk, simper; leer.
– OPPOSITES frown.

smirk verb **smile smugly**, simper, snigger; leer.

smitten adjective **1** *he was smitten with cholera:* **struck down**, laid low, suffering, affected, afflicted. **2** *Jane's smitten with you:* **infatuated**, besotted, in love, obsessed, head over heels; enamoured of, attracted to, taken with; captivated, enchanted, under someone's spell; informal bowled over, swept off your feet, crazy about, mad about, keen on; Brit. informal potty about.

S

smog noun **fog**, haze; fumes, smoke, pollution; Brit. informal pea-souper.

smoke verb **1** *the fire was smoking:* **smoulder**. **2** *he smoked his cigarette:* **puff on**, draw on, pull on; inhale; informal drag on.
• **noun** *the smoke from the bonfire:* **fumes**, exhaust, gas, vapour; smog.

smoky adjective **smoke-filled**, sooty, smoggy, hazy, murky, thick; Brit. informal fuggy.

smooth adjective **1** *a smooth surface:* **flat**, level, even, plane; featureless; glassy, glossy, silky, polished. **2** *a smooth sauce:* **creamy**, velvety. **3** *a smooth sea:* **calm**, still, tranquil, undisturbed, unruffled, even, flat, like a millpond. **4** *the smooth running of the equipment:* **steady**, regular, uninterrupted, unbroken; straightforward, easy, effortless, trouble-free. **5** *a smooth, confident man:* **suave**, urbane, sophisticated, polished, debonair; courteous, gracious; glib, slick, ingratiating, unctuous; informal smarmy.
– OPPOSITES uneven, rough.
• **verb 1** *she smoothed the fabric:* **flatten**, level out/off, even out/off; press, iron, plane. **2** *a plan to smooth the way for the agreement:* **ease**, facilitate, clear the way for, pave the way for, expedite, assist, aid, help, oil the wheels of, lubricate.

smoothly adverb **1** *her hair was combed smoothly back:* **evenly**, level, flat, flush. **2** *the door closed smoothly:* **fluidly**, fluently, steadily, easily; quietly. **3** *the plan had gone smoothly:* **without a hitch**, like clockwork, without difficulty, easily, according to plan, swimmingly, satisfactorily, very well; informal like a dream.

smooth-talking adjective (informal) **persuasive**, glib, plausible, silver-tongued, slick, eloquent, fast-talking; ingratiating, flattering, unctuous, obsequious, sycophantic; informal smarmy.
– OPPOSITES blunt.

smother verb **1** *she tried to smother her baby:* **suffocate**, asphyxiate, stifle, choke. **2** *we smothered the flames:* **extinguish**, put out, snuff out, dampen, douse, stamp out. **3** *we smothered ourselves with suncream:* **smear**, daub, spread, cover. **4** *she smothered a sigh:* **stifle**, muffle, strangle, repress, suppress, hold back, fight back, bite back, swallow, conceal, hide; bite your lip; informal keep a/the lid on.

smoulder verb **1** *the bonfire still smouldered:* **smoke**, glow, burn. **2** *she was smouldering with resentment:* **seethe**, boil, fume, burn, simmer, be beside yourself; informal be livid.

smudge noun *a smudge of blood:*

streak, smear, mark, stain, blotch, blob, dab; informal splotch, splodge.
• verb *her face was smudged with dust:* **streak**, mark, dirty, soil, blotch, blacken, smear, blot, daub, stain; informal splotch, splodge.

smug adjective **self-satisfied**, self-congratulatory, complacent, pleased with yourself.

smuggle verb **import/export illegally**, traffic in, run.

smuggler noun **runner**, courier, bootlegger; informal mule.

smutty adjective **vulgar**, rude, crude, dirty, filthy, salacious, coarse, obscene, lewd, pornographic, X-rated; risqué, racy, earthy, bawdy, suggestive, naughty; informal blue, raunchy; Brit. informal near the knuckle, saucy; N. Amer. informal gamy; euphemistic adult.

snack noun refreshments; nibbles, titbit; informal bite to eat; Brit. informal elevenses; dated tiffin.

snag noun **complication**, difficulty, catch, hitch, obstacle, stumbling block, pitfall, problem, impediment, hindrance, inconvenience, setback, hurdle, disadvantage, downside, drawback.

snake noun literary serpent; Austral./NZ rhyming slang Joe Blake.
• verb *the road snakes inland:* **twist**, wind, meander, zigzag, curve.

> **WORD LINKS**
> **colubrine**, **ophidian**, **serpentine** relating to or resembling a snake

snap verb **1** *the branch snapped:* **break**, fracture, splinter, split, crack; informal bust. **2** *'Shut up!' she snapped:* **snarl**, bark, growl; retort; shout, cry, exclaim, scream, shriek, yell; informal jump down someone's throat. **3** *a dog was snapping at his heels:* **bite**, nip.
• noun **1** *a cold snap:* **period**, spell, time, interval, stretch; Brit. informal patch. **2** (informal) *holiday snaps:* **photograph**, picture, photo, shot, snapshot, print.
■ **snap something up** buy eagerly, jump at, take advantage of, grab, seize, pounce on.

snappy adjective (informal) **1** *a snappy mood:* **irritable**, irascible, short-tempered, touchy; cross, crabby, crotchety, cantankerous, grumpy, bad-tempered, testy, tetchy; informal grouchy, cranky; Brit. informal narky, ratty. **2** *a snappy catchphrase:* **concise**, succinct, memorable, catchy, neat, clever, crisp, pithy, witty, incisive, brief, short. **3** *a snappy dresser:* **smart**, fashionable, stylish, chic, modish, elegant, neat, spruce, dapper; informal snazzy, natty, sharp, nifty, cool; N. Amer. informal sassy, spiffy, fly.
– OPPOSITES peaceable, long-winded, slovenly.

snare noun *a fox caught in a snare:* **trap**; gin, net, noose.
• verb **1** *game birds were snared:* **trap**, catch, net, bag. **2** *five blackmailers were snared in a police sting:* **ensnare**, entrap, catch, get hold of, bag, hook, land.

snarl[1] verb *'Shut up!' he snarled:* **growl**, bark, snap; informal jump down someone's throat.

snarl[2] verb **1** *the rope got snarled up in a bush:* **tangle**, entangle, entwine, enmesh, ravel, knot, foul. **2** *this case has snarled up the court process:* **complicate**, confuse, muddle, jumble; informal mess up.

snarl-up noun (informal) **traffic jam**, tailback, gridlock.

snatch verb **1** *she snatched the microphone:* **grab**, seize, take hold of, take, pluck; grasp at, clutch at. **2** (informal) *someone snatched my bag.* See **STEAL** verb sense 1. **3** (informal) *she snatched the baby from the hospital.* See **ABDUCT**.
• noun **1** *brief snatches of sleep:* **period**, spell, time, fit, bout, interval, stretch. **2** *a snatch of conversation:* **fragment**, snippet, bit, scrap, part, extract, excerpt, portion.

sneak verb **1** *I sneaked out:* **creep**, slink, steal, slip, slide, sidle, edge, tiptoe, pad, prowl, skulk, lurk. **2** *she sneaked a camera in:* **smuggle**, spirit, slip.
• adjective *I managed to get a sneak peek:* **furtive**, secret, stealthy, sly, surreptitious, clandestine, covert; unofficial, private, quick, exclusive.

sneaking adjective **1** *she had a sneaking admiration for him:* **secret**, private, hidden, concealed, unvoiced, undisclosed. **2** *a sneaking feeling:* **niggling**, nagging, lurking,

S

insidious, lingering, gnawing, persistent.

sneaky adjective **sly**, crafty, cunning, wily, artful, scheming, devious, deceitful, duplicitous, underhand; furtive, secretive, secret, stealthy, surreptitious, clandestine, covert.
–OPPOSITES honest.

sneer noun **1** *a sneer on her face:* **smirk**, curled lip. **2** *the sneers of others:* **jibe**, jeer, taunt, insult; informal dig.
•verb **1** *he looked at me and sneered:* **smirk**, curl your lip. **2** *it is easy to sneer at them:* **scoff at**, scorn, disdain, mock, laugh at, ridicule, deride; N. Amer. slur.

snicker verb *they all snickered at her:* **snigger**, titter, giggle, chortle, simper.
•noun *he could not suppress a snicker:* **snigger**, titter, giggle, chortle, simper.

snide adjective **disparaging**, derogatory, deprecating, insulting, contemptuous; mocking, taunting, sneering, scornful, derisive, sarcastic, spiteful, nasty, mean.

sniff verb **1** *she sniffed and blew her nose:* **inhale**; snuffle. **2** *Tom sniffed the fruit:* **smell**, scent, get a whiff of.
•noun **1** *she gave a loud sniff:* **snuffle**, snort. **2** *a sniff of fresh air:* **smell**, scent, whiff; lungful. **3** (informal) *the first sniff of trouble:* **indication**, hint, whiff, inkling, suggestion, whisper, trace, sign, suspicion.
■ **sniff at** scorn, disdain, look down on, sneer at, scoff at; informal turn your nose up at. **sniff something out** (informal) detect, find, discover, bring to light, track down, dig up, hunt/root out, uncover, unearth.

snigger verb *they snigger at him behind his back:* **snicker**, titter, giggle, chortle, laugh; sneer, smirk.
•noun *the joke got a snigger:* **snicker**, titter, giggle, chortle, laugh; sneer, smirk.

snip verb *snip off the faded flowers:* **cut off**, trim off, clip off, prune, chop off, sever, detach, remove, take off.
•noun **1** *make snips along the edge:* **cut**, slit, snick, nick, notch, incision. **2** *a collage made from snips of wallpaper:* **scrap**, cutting, shred, remnant, fragment, sliver, bit, piece. **3** (Brit. informal) *the book was a snip.* See **BARGAIN** noun sense 2.

snippet noun **piece**, bit, scrap, fragment, particle, shred; excerpt, extract.

snivel verb **sniffle**, snuffle, whimper, whine, weep, cry; Scottish greet; informal blubber; Brit. informal grizzle.

snobbery noun **affectation**, pretension, pretentiousness, arrogance, haughtiness, airs and graces, elitism; disdain, condescension; informal snootiness, uppitiness.

snobbish adjective **elitist**, snobby, superior, supercilious; arrogant, condescending; pretentious, affected; informal snooty, uppity, high and mighty, la-di-da, stuck-up, snotty; Brit. informal toffee-nosed.

snoop (informal) verb **pry**, inquire, poke about/around, be a busybody, poke your nose into; root about/around; informal be nosy; Austral./NZ informal stickybeak.
•noun **search**, nose, look, prowl, ferret, root, poke.

snooper noun **meddler**, busybody, eavesdropper; informal nosy parker, snoop; Austral./NZ informal stickybeak.

snooty adjective (informal) **arrogant**, proud, haughty, conceited, aloof, superior, self-important, disdainful, supercilious, snobbish, snobby; informal uppity, high and mighty, la-di-da, stuck-up; Brit. informal toffee-nosed.
–OPPOSITES modest.

snooze (informal) noun **nap**, doze, sleep, rest, siesta, catnap; informal forty winks; Brit. informal kip.
•verb **nap**, doze, sleep, rest, take a siesta, catnap; informal snatch forty winks, get some shut-eye; Brit. informal kip, get your head down; N. Amer. informal catch some Zs.

snout noun **muzzle**, nose, proboscis, trunk; Scottish & N. English neb.

snow noun **snowflakes**, flakes, snowfall, snowstorm, blizzard, sleet; snowdrift.

snub verb **rebuff**, spurn, cold-shoulder, give the cold shoulder to, keep at arm's length; cut dead, ignore, disregard; insult, slight; informal freeze out, knock back; N. Amer. informal stiff.
•noun **rebuff**, slap in the face; informal brush-off, put-down.

S

snuff verb **extinguish**, put out, douse, smother, choke, blow out, quench, stub out.

snug adjective **1** *our tents were snug:* **cosy**, comfortable, warm, homely, sheltered, secure; informal comfy. **2** *a snug dress:* **tight**, skintight, close-fitting, figure-hugging, slinky.
– OPPOSITES bleak, loose.

snuggle verb **nestle**, curl up, cuddle up, nuzzle, settle, huddle; N. Amer. snug down.

soak verb **1** *soak the beans in water:* **immerse**, steep, submerge, bathe, douse, marinate, souse, dip, dunk. **2** *rain soaked the soil:* **drench**, wet through, saturate, waterlog, deluge, inundate, submerge, drown, swamp. **3** *the sweat soaked through his clothes:* **permeate**, penetrate, seep, spread through, infuse, impregnate. **4** *use towels to soak up the water:* **absorb**, suck up, blot up, mop up, sponge up.

soaking adjective **drenched**, wet through, soaked, sodden, soggy, waterlogged, saturated, sopping wet, dripping wet, wringing wet.
– OPPOSITES parched.

soar verb **1** *the bird soared into the air:* **fly**, wing, ascend, climb, rise; take off, take flight. **2** *the gulls soared on the winds:* **glide**, plane, float, drift, wheel, hover. **3** *the cost of living soared:* **increase**, escalate, shoot up, rise, spiral; informal go through the roof, skyrocket.
– OPPOSITES plummet.

sob verb **weep**, cry, shed tears, snivel, whimper; howl, bawl; Scottish greet; informal blubber; Brit. informal grizzle.

sober adjective **1** *the driver was clearly sober:* **not drunk**, clear-headed; teetotal, abstinent; informal on the wagon. **2** *a sober view of life:* **serious**, solemn, sensible, grave, sombre, staid, level-headed, businesslike, down-to-earth. **3** *a sober suit:* **sombre**, subdued, severe; conventional, traditional, quiet, drab, plain.
– OPPOSITES drunk, frivolous, flamboyant.
• verb *his expression sobered her:* **make serious**, subdue, calm down, quieten, steady; bring down to earth, give someone pause for thought.

sobriety noun **seriousness**, solemnity, gravity, dignity, level-headedness, self-control, self-restraint, conservatism.

so-called adjective **inappropriately named**, supposed, alleged, presumed, ostensible, reputed, self-styled, professed, self-appointed.

sociable adjective **friendly**, affable, companionable, gregarious, convivial, clubbable, amicable, cordial, warm, genial.
– OPPOSITES unsociable, unfriendly.

social adjective **1** *a major social problem:* **communal**, community, collective, group, general, popular, civil, public. **2** *a social club:* **recreational**, leisure, entertainment, amusement. **3** *a social animal:* **gregarious**, collective; pack, herd.
– OPPOSITES individual.
• noun *the club has a social once a month:* **party**, gathering, function, get-together; celebration; informal bash, shindig, do; Brit. informal rave-up, knees-up, beano, bunfight, jolly.

socialist adjective *the socialist movement:* **left-wing**, leftist, Labour; communist, Marxist, Leninist; informal, derogatory lefty, Commie.

socialize verb **interact**, converse, be sociable, mix, mingle, get together, meet, fraternize, consort; entertain, go out; informal hobnob.

society noun **1** *a danger to society:* **the community**, the general public, the people, the population; civilization, humankind, mankind, humanity. **2** *an industrial society:* **culture**, community, civilization, nation, population. **3** *a local history society:* **association**, club, group, circle; fellowship, guild, lodge, fraternity, brotherhood, sisterhood, sorority, league, union, alliance. **4** *the society of others:* **company**, companionship, fellowship, friendship. **5** *Lady Angela will help you enter society:* **high society**, polite society, the upper classes, the elite, the smart set, the beautiful people; informal the upper crust, the top drawer.

WORD LINKS
sociology the study of human society

sodden adjective **1** *his clothes were*

S

sodden: **soaking**, soaked, wet through, saturated, drenched, sopping wet, wringing wet. **2** *sodden fields:* **waterlogged**, soggy, saturated, boggy, swampy, miry, marshy; squelchy.
– OPPOSITES arid.

sofa noun **settee**, couch, divan, chaise longue, chesterfield; Brit. put-you-up; N. Amer. davenport, day bed.

soft adjective **1** *cook until the fruit is soft:* **mushy**, squashy, pulpy, slushy, squelchy, squishy, doughy; informal gooey; Brit. informal squidgy. **2** *soft ground:* **swampy**, spongy, marshy, boggy, miry, oozy; heavy, squelchy. **3** *a soft surface:* **springy**, pliable, pliant, resilient, malleable. **4** *soft fabric:* **velvety**, smooth, fleecy, downy, furry, silky, silken, satiny. **5** *a soft wind:* **gentle**, light, mild, moderate. **6** *soft light:* **dim**, low, faint, subdued, muted, mellow. **7** *soft colours:* **pale**, pastel, muted, restrained, subdued, subtle. **8** *soft voices:* **quiet**, low, gentle; faint, muted, subdued, muffled, hushed, whispered, murmured, dulcet. **9** *soft words:* **kind**, gentle, sympathetic, soothing, tender, sensitive, affectionate, loving, warm, sweet, sentimental. **10** *she's too soft with her pupils:* **lenient**, easy-going, tolerant, forgiving, forbearing, indulgent, clement, permissive, liberal, lax.
– OPPOSITES hard, firm, rough, harsh.

soften verb **alleviate**, ease, relieve, soothe, take the edge off, assuage, cushion, moderate, mitigate, palliate, diminish, blunt, deaden.
■ **soften someone up** charm, win over, persuade, influence, weaken, disarm, sweeten, butter up, soft-soap.

softly-softly adjective **cautious**, circumspect, discreet, gentle, patient, tactful, diplomatic.

soggy adjective **mushy**, squashy, pulpy, slushy, squelchy, squishy; swampy, marshy, boggy; soaking, soaked through, wet, saturated, drenched; Brit. informal squidgy.

soil[1] noun **1** *acid soil:* **earth**, loam, dirt, clay, sod, turf; ground. **2** *British soil:* **territory**, land, domain, dominion, region, country.

soil[2] verb *he soiled his tie:* **dirty**, stain, spot, spatter, splatter, smear, smudge, sully, spoil, foul.

sojourn noun (formal) **stay**, visit, stop, stopover; holiday, vacation.

solace noun **comfort**, consolation, cheer, support, relief.

soldier noun **fighter**, trooper, serviceman, servicewoman; warrior; US GI; Brit. informal **squaddie**; old use man-at-arms.
■ **soldier on** (informal). See **PERSEVERE**.

WORD LINKS
military relating to soldiers

sole adjective **only**, one and only, single, solitary, lone, unique, exclusive.

solecism noun **mistake**, error, blunder; informal howler, blooper; Brit. informal boob.

solely adverb **only**, simply, just, merely, uniquely, exclusively, entirely, wholly; alone.

solemn adjective **1** *a solemn occasion:* **dignified**, ceremonial, stately, formal, courtly, majestic; imposing, splendid, magnificent, grand. **2** *he looked very solemn:* **serious**, grave, sober, sombre, unsmiling, stern, grim, dour, humourless. **3** *a solemn promise:* **sincere**, earnest, honest, genuine, firm, heartfelt, whole-hearted, sworn.
– OPPOSITES frivolous, light-hearted, insincere.

solemnize verb **perform**, celebrate; formalize, officiate at.

solicit verb **1** *he began to solicit funds for his campaign:* **ask for**, request, seek, apply for, put in for, call for, beg for, plead for. **2** *historians are solicited for their opinions:* **ask**, approach, appeal to, lobby, petition, importune, call on, press.

solicitor noun (Brit.) **lawyer**; legal representative, advocate, attorney; Brit. articled clerk; Scottish law agent; informal brief.

solicitous adjective **concerned**, caring, considerate, attentive, mindful, thoughtful, interested; anxious, worried.

solid adjective **1** *the plaster was solid:* **hard**, rock-hard, rigid, firm, solidified, set; frozen. **2** *24-carat solid gold:* **pure**, unadulterated, genuine. **3** *a solid line:* **continuous**, uninterrupted, unbroken,

undivided. **4** *solid houses:* **well built**, sound, substantial, strong, sturdy, durable. **5** *a solid argument:* **well founded**, valid, sound, logical, authoritative, convincing, cogent. **6** *a solid friendship:* **firm**, unshakeable, stable, steadfast. **7** *solid citizens:* **sensible**, dependable, trustworthy, decent, law-abiding, upright, upstanding, worthy. **8** *solid support from their colleagues:* **unanimous**, united, consistent, undivided.
– OPPOSITES liquid, broken, flimsy.

solidarity noun **unanimity**, unity, agreement, accord, harmony, consensus, concurrence; formal concord.

solidify verb **harden**, set, thicken, stiffen, congeal, cake; freeze, ossify, fossilize, petrify.
– OPPOSITES liquefy.

solitary adjective **1** *a solitary man:* **lonely**, unaccompanied, by yourself, on your own, alone, friendless; unsociable, withdrawn, reclusive; N. Amer. lonesome. **2** *solitary farmsteads:* **isolated**, remote, lonely, out of the way, in the back of beyond, outlying, off the beaten track, godforsaken, obscure, inaccessible, cut-off; secluded, private, sequestered; N. Amer. in the backwoods; literary lone. **3** *a solitary piece of evidence:* **single**, lone, sole; only, one, individual.
– OPPOSITES sociable, accessible.

solitude noun **loneliness**, solitariness, isolation, seclusion, privacy, peace.

solo adjective **unaccompanied**, single-handed, unescorted, unattended, independent, solitary; alone, on your own, by yourself, unaided.

solution noun **1** *a solution to the problem:* **answer**, result, resolution, way out; key, formula, explanation, interpretation. **2** *a solution of salt and water:* **mixture**, blend, compound; tincture, infusion.

solve verb **resolve**, answer, work out, find a solution to, find the key to, puzzle out, fathom, decipher, decode, clear up, straighten out, get to the bottom of, unravel, explain; informal figure out, crack; Brit. informal suss out.

solvent adjective **financially sound**, in the black, in credit, creditworthy, solid, secure.

sombre adjective **1** *sombre clothes:* **dark**, drab, dull, dingy; restrained, subdued, sober, funereal. **2** *a sombre expression:* **solemn**, earnest, serious, grave, sober, unsmiling, stern, grim, dour, humourless; gloomy, sad, melancholy, dismal, doleful, mournful, lugubrious.
– OPPOSITES bright, cheerful.

somebody noun *she wanted to be a somebody:* **important person**, VIP, public figure, notable, dignitary, worthy; someone, (big/household) name, celebrity, star, superstar, luminary; informal celeb, bigwig, big shot, big cheese, hotshot, megastar.
– OPPOSITES nonentity.

somehow adverb **one way or another**, by fair means or foul, by hook or by crook, come what may, come hell or high water.

sometime adverb **1** *you must come and visit sometime:* **some day**, one day, one of these days, at a future date, sooner or later, by and by, in due course, in the fullness of time, in the long run. **2** *sometime on Sunday:* **at some time/stage**; during, in the course of.
• adjective *my sometime editor:* **former**, past, previous, erstwhile, one-time, ex-; formal quondam.

sometimes adverb **occasionally**, from time to time, now and then, every so often, once in a while, on occasion, at times, off and on, at intervals, periodically, sporadically, spasmodically, intermittently.

somewhat adverb **1** *matters have improved somewhat:* **a little**, a bit, to some extent, up to a point. **2** *a somewhat longer book:* **slightly**, relatively, comparatively, moderately, fairly, rather, quite, marginally.
– OPPOSITES greatly.

son noun **male child**, boy, heir; descendant, offspring; informal lad.

> **WORD LINKS**
> **filial** relating to a son or daughter
> **filicide** the killing of a son or daughter by one of their parents

song noun **1** *a beautiful song:* **air**, strain, ditty, melody, tune, number, track; ballad, madrigal, lyric, carol, anthem, hymn. **2** *the song of the birds:* **call**, chirping, cheeping, chirruping, warbling, trilling, twitter.

sonorous adjective **resonant**, rich, full, round, booming, deep, clear, mellow, strong, resounding, reverberant.

soon adverb **1** *we'll be there soon:* **shortly**, presently, in the near future, before long, in a little while, in a minute, in a moment, before you know it, any minute, by and by; informal anon; Brit. informal in two ticks. **2** *how soon can you get here?* **early**, quickly, fast.

sooner adverb **1** *he should have done it sooner:* **earlier**, before. **2** *I would sooner stay:* **rather**, preferably, given the choice.

soothe verb **1** *Rachel tried to soothe him:* **calm**, calm down, pacify, comfort, hush, quiet, settle; appease, mollify; Brit. quieten. **2** *an anaesthetic to soothe the pain:* **alleviate**, ease, relieve, take the edge off, assuage, allay, lessen, reduce.
–OPPOSITES agitate, aggravate.

soothing adjective **1** *soothing music:* **relaxing**, restful, calm, calming, tranquil, peaceful. **2** *soothing ointment:* **palliative**, gentle.

sophisticated adjective **1** *sophisticated technology:* **advanced**, modern, state of the art, the latest, new, up to the minute; cutting-edge, trailblazing; complex, complicated, intricate. **2** *a sophisticated woman:* **worldly**, worldly-wise, experienced, cosmopolitan; urbane, cultured, cultivated, polished, refined; elegant, stylish.
–OPPOSITES crude, naive, unsophisticated.

S

sophistication noun **worldliness**, experience; urbanity, culture, polish, refinement; elegance, style, poise, finesse, savoir faire.

soporific adjective **sleep-inducing**, sedative, somnolent; narcotic; drowsy, sleepy.
–OPPOSITES invigorating.

soppy adjective (Brit. informal) See SENTIMENTAL sense 2.

sorcerer, **sorceress** noun **wizard**, witch, magician, warlock, enchanter, enchantress, magus; shaman, witch doctor; old use mage.

sorcery noun **magic**, witchcraft, wizardry, enchantment, spells, necromancy, black magic, the black arts; voodoo; shamanism.

sordid adjective **1** *his sordid past:* **sleazy**, seamy, unsavoury, tawdry, disreputable, discreditable, ignominious, shameful, wretched. **2** *a sordid little street:* **squalid**, dirty, filthy, shabby, sleazy, seedy; informal crummy, scuzzy; Brit. informal grotty.
–OPPOSITES respectable.

sore adjective **1** *a sore leg:* **painful**, hurting, hurt, aching, throbbing, smarting, stinging, agonizing, excruciating; inflamed, sensitive, tender, raw, bruised, injured. **2** (N. Amer. informal) *they were sore at us:* **upset**, angry, annoyed, cross, vexed, displeased, disgruntled, dissatisfied, irritated, galled, irked, put out, aggrieved, offended, affronted, piqued, nettled; informal aggravated, miffed, peeved, hacked off, riled; Brit. informal narked, cheesed off, brassed off; N. Amer. informal teed off, ticked off.
•noun **inflammation**, swelling, lesion; ulcer, boil, abscess.

sorrow noun **1** *he felt sorrow at her death:* **sadness**, unhappiness, misery, despondency, regret, despair, desolation, dejection, wretchedness, gloom, woe, heartache, grief. **2** *the sorrows of life:* **trouble**, difficulty, problem, adversity, misery, woe, affliction, trial, tribulation, misfortune, setback, reverse, blow, failure, tragedy.
–OPPOSITES joy.

sorrowful adjective **sad**, unhappy, dejected, regretful, downcast, miserable, downhearted, despondent, despairing, disconsolate, desolate, glum, gloomy, doleful, dismal, mournful, woeful, forlorn, heartbroken.
–OPPOSITES joyful.

sorry adjective **1** *I was sorry to hear about his accident:* **sad**, moved, sorrowful, distressed; regretful. **2** *he felt sorry for her:* **full of pity**, sympathetic, compassionate, moved, empathetic, concerned. **3** *I'm sorry I was rude:* **regretful**, remorseful, contrite, repentant,

rueful, penitent, apologetic, guilty, ashamed. **4** *a sorry sight:* **pitiful**, pathetic, wretched.
– OPPOSITES glad, unsympathetic, unrepentant.

sort noun *what sort of book is it?* **type**, kind, manner, variety, class, category, style; quality, form, genre, species, make, model, brand, ilk; N. Amer. stripe.
• verb *they sorted the books alphabetically:* **classify**, class, group; organize, arrange, order.
■ **out of sorts** *I'm feeling out of sorts:* unwell, ill, poorly, sick, peaky, run down, below par; Brit. off colour; informal under the weather, funny, rough; Brit. informal off, ropy; Scottish informal wabbit, peely-wally; Austral./NZ informal crook. **sort of** (informal) *you look sort of familiar:* slightly, faintly, vaguely; somewhat, quite, rather, fairly, reasonably, relatively; informal pretty. **sort something out 1** *we need to sort out the travelling arrangements:* arrange, organize, plan, coordinate, fix up, set up. **2** *they must sort out their problems:* resolve, settle, solve, fix, work out, straighten out, deal with, put right, set right, rectify, iron out.

sortie noun **1** *a sortie against their besiegers:* **foray**, charge, offensive, attack, assault, onslaught, thrust, drive. **2** *a bombing sortie:* **raid**, flight, mission, operation.

so-so adjective (informal) **mediocre**, indifferent, average, middle-of-the-road, middling, moderate, ordinary, adequate, fair; uninspired, undistinguished, unexceptional, unremarkable, run-of-the-mill, lacklustre; informal bog-standard, no great shakes; NZ informal half-pie.

soul noun **1 spirit**, psyche, inner self. **2** *she's the soul of discretion:* **embodiment**, personification, incarnation, epitome, essence; model.

soulful adjective **emotional**, heartfelt, sincere, passionate; moving, stirring; sad, mournful, doleful.

soulless adjective **characterless**, featureless, bland, dull, colourless, dreary, drab, impersonal.
– OPPOSITES exciting.

sound¹ noun **1** *the sound of a car engine:* **noise**; din, racket, hubbub; resonance, reverberation; Brit. row. **2** *she did not make a sound:* **utterance**, cry, word, noise, peep. **3** *the sound of the flute:* **music**, tone, timbre; call, song, voice. **4** *I don't like the sound of that:* **idea**, thought, prospect.
– OPPOSITES silence.
• verb **1** *the buzzer sounded:* ring, chime, ping, peal, buzz; resonate, resound, reverberate, go off. **2** *drivers must sound their horns:* **blow**, blast, toot, ring; use, operate, activate, set off. **3** *do you sound the 'h'?* **pronounce**, verbalize, voice, enunciate, articulate, vocalize, say. **4** *she sounded a warning:* **utter**, voice, deliver. **5** *it sounds a crazy idea:* **appear**, seem.

> **WORD LINKS**
> **acoustic**, **sonic** relating to sound

sound² adjective **1** *his heart is still sound:* **healthy**, in good condition, fit, hale and hearty, in fine fettle; undamaged, unimpaired. **2** *a sound building:* **well built**, solid, substantial, strong, sturdy, durable, stable, intact, unimpaired. **3** *this is sound advice:* **well founded**, valid, reasonable, logical, weighty, authoritative, reliable. **4** *a sound judge of character:* **reliable**, dependable, trustworthy, fair; good. **5** *the company is financially sound:* **solvent**, debt-free, in the black, in credit, creditworthy, secure. **6** *a sound sleep:* **deep**, undisturbed, uninterrupted, untroubled, peaceful. **7** *a sound thrashing:* **thorough**, proper, real, complete, unqualified, out-and-out, thoroughgoing, severe; informal right.
– OPPOSITES unhealthy, unsafe, unreliable, insolvent.

sound³ verb
■ **sound someone/something out** investigate, test, check, examine, probe, research, look into; canvass, survey, poll, question, interview; informal pump.

soup noun **broth**; potage, consommé, bouillon, chowder, bisque.

sour adjective **1** *sour wine:* **acid**, acidic, tart, bitter, sharp, vinegary, pungent; N. Amer. acerb; technical acerbic. **2** *sour milk:* **bad**, off, turned, curdled, rancid, high, fetid.

3 *a sour old man:* **embittered**, resentful, jaundiced, bitter; irritable, peevish, fractious, cross, crabby, crotchety, cantankerous, disagreeable, ill-humoured; informal grouchy.
– OPPOSITES sweet, fresh, amiable.
• **verb** *the dispute soured relations between the two towns:* **spoil**, mar, damage, harm, impair, wreck, upset, poison, blight.
– OPPOSITES improve.

source **noun 1** *the source of the river:* **spring**, origin. **2** *the source of the rumour:* **origin**, starting point; derivation, root; author, originator, initiator, inventor. **3** *historical sources:* **reference**, authority, informant; document.

souse **verb** **drench**, douse, soak, steep, saturate, plunge, immerse, submerge, dip, sink, dunk.

southern **adjective** *the southern coast of England:* **south**, southerly, meridional; technical austral.

souvenir **noun** **memento**, keepsake, reminder, remembrance, token, memorial; trophy, relic.

sovereign **noun** **ruler**, monarch, potentate, overlord; king, queen, emperor, empress, prince, princess.
• **adjective** *a sovereign state:* **independent**, autonomous, self-governing, self-determining; non-aligned, free.

sovereignty **noun 1** *their sovereignty over the islands:* **jurisdiction**, rule, supremacy, dominion, power, ascendancy, hegemony, domination, authority, control. **2** *full sovereignty was achieved in 1955:* **autonomy**, independence, self-government, self-rule, home rule, self-determination, freedom.

S

sow **verb 1** *sow the seeds in April:* **plant**, broadcast, disperse, strew, distribute; seed. **2** *the new policy has sown confusion:* **cause**, bring about, create, lead to, produce, engender, generate, prompt, precipitate, trigger, provoke; foster, foment; literary beget.

space **noun 1** *there was not enough space:* **room**, capacity, latitude, margin, leeway, play, clearance. **2** *green spaces in London:* **area**, expanse, stretch, sweep, tract. **3** *a space between the timbers:* **gap**, interval, opening, aperture, cavity, cranny, fissure, crack. **4** *write your name in the appropriate space:* **blank**, gap, box. **5** *a space of seven years:* **period**, span, time, duration, stretch, course, interval, gap. **6** *the first woman in space:* **outer space**, deep space; the universe, the galaxy, the solar system; infinity.
• **verb** *the chairs were spaced widely:* **position**, arrange, range, array, spread, lay out, set, stand.

spacious **adjective** **roomy**, capacious, sizeable, generous, large, big, vast, immense.
– OPPOSITES cramped.

span **noun 1** *a six-foot wing span:* **extent**, length, width, reach, stretch, spread, distance, range. **2** *the span of one week:* **period**, space, time, duration, course, interval.
• **verb 1** *an arch spanned the stream:* **bridge**, cross, traverse, pass over. **2** *his career spanned twenty years:* **last**, cover, extend, spread over.

spank **verb** **smack**, slap, hit; informal wallop, belt, whack, give someone a hiding; Scottish & N. English skelp.

spar **verb** **quarrel**, argue, fight, disagree, differ, be at odds, be at variance, dispute, squabble, wrangle, cross swords, lock horns; informal scrap.

spare **adjective 1** *a spare set of keys:* **extra**, supplementary, additional, second, other, alternative; emergency, reserve, backup, relief, substitute; N. Amer. alternate. **2** *they sold off the spare land:* **surplus**, superfluous; excess, leftover; redundant, unnecessary, unneeded, unwanted. **3** *your spare time:* **free**, leisure, own. **4** *her spare, elegant form:* **slender**, lean, willowy, svelte, lissom, rangy; thin, skinny, gaunt, lanky, spindly.
• **verb 1** *he couldn't spare any money:* **afford**, manage; part with, give, provide. **2** *they were spared by their captors:* **pardon**, let off, forgive, reprieve, release, free.
■ **to spare** left over, remaining, unused, unneeded, not required, surplus to requirements, superfluous, extra; informal going begging.

sparing **adjective** **thrifty**, economical,

frugal, canny, careful, prudent, cautious; mean, miserly, niggardly, parsimonious, ungenerous.
– OPPOSITES lavish.

spark noun **flash**, glint, twinkle, flicker, flare.
• verb *the trial sparked a furious row:* **cause**, give rise to, lead to, occasion, bring about, start, initiate, trigger, precipitate, prompt, provoke, stimulate, stir up.

sparkle verb **glitter**, glint, glisten, twinkle, flash, blink, wink, shimmer.
• noun **glitter**, glint, twinkle, flicker, shimmer, flash.

sparkling adjective **1** *sparkling wine:* **effervescent**, fizzy, carbonated, aerated. **2** *a sparkling performance:* **brilliant**, dazzling, scintillating, exciting, exhilarating, stimulating, invigorating; vivacious, lively, vibrant.
– OPPOSITES still, dull.

sparse adjective **scant**, scanty, scattered, scarce, infrequent, few and far between; meagre, paltry, limited, in short supply.
– OPPOSITES abundant.

spartan adjective **austere**, harsh, hard, frugal, rigorous, strict, stern, severe; ascetic; bleak, joyless, grim, bare, stark, plain.
– OPPOSITES luxurious.

spasm noun **1** *a muscle spasm:* **contraction**, convulsion, cramp; twitch, jerk, tic, shudder, shiver, tremor. **2** *a spasm of coughing:* **fit**, paroxysm, attack, burst, bout, seizure, outburst.

spasmodic adjective **intermittent**, fitful, irregular, sporadic, erratic, occasional, infrequent, scattered, patchy, isolated, periodic.

spate noun **series**, succession, run, cluster, string, rash, epidemic, outbreak, wave, flurry.

spatter verb **splash**, splatter, spray, sprinkle, shower, speckle, fleck, mark; informal splotch; Brit. informal splodge.

spawn verb **give rise to**, bring about, occasion, generate, engender; lead to, result in, effect, initiate, start, set off, precipitate, trigger; breed, bear.

speak verb **1** *she refused to speak about it | he spoke the truth:* **talk**; utter, state, declare, tell, voice, express, pronounce, articulate, enunciate, vocalize, verbalize. **2** *we spoke the other day:* **converse**, talk, communicate, chat, have a word, gossip; informal have a confab, chew the fat; Brit. informal natter. **3** *the Minister spoke to a large audience:* **give a speech**, talk, lecture, hold forth, discourse, expound, expatiate, pontificate, orate, sermonize; informal spout, spiel, sound off. **4** *he was spoken of as a promising student:* **mention**, talk about, discuss, refer to, remark on, allude to. **5** *you must speak to him about his rudeness:* **reprimand**, rebuke, admonish, chastise, chide, upbraid, reprove, reproach, scold, remonstrate with, take to task, pull up; informal tell off, dress down; Brit. informal tick off, have a go at, tear someone off a strip, give someone what for; formal castigate.
■ **speak against** oppose, condemn, attack, criticize. **speak for 1** *she speaks for the Liberal Democrats:* represent, act for, be spokesperson for. **2** *I spoke for the motion:* advocate, champion, uphold, defend, support, promote, recommend, back, endorse, sponsor. **speak out** speak publicly, speak openly, speak your mind, sound off, stand up and be counted. **speak up** speak loudly, speak clearly, raise your voice.

speaker noun **speech-maker**, lecturer, talker, orator; spokesperson, spokesman/woman, mouthpiece; reader, commentator, broadcaster, narrator; historical demagogue.

spear noun **javelin**, lance, harpoon; historical pike.

spearhead verb *we're spearheading a campaign:* **lead**, head, front.

special adjective **1** *a very special person:* **exceptional**, unusual, singular, remarkable, outstanding, unique. **2** *our town's special character:* **distinctive**, distinct, individual, particular, specific, peculiar. **3** *a special occasion:* **momentous**, significant, memorable, important, historic. **4** *a special tool for cutting tiles:* **specific**, particular, purpose-built, tailor-made, custom-built.
– OPPOSITES ordinary, general.

specialist **noun** **expert**, authority, pundit, professional; connoisseur; master, maestro, adept, virtuoso; informal buff.
– OPPOSITES amateur.

speciality **noun** **1** *his speciality was watercolours:* **forte**, strong point, strength, métier, strong suit, talent, skill, bent, gift; informal bag, thing, cup of tea. **2** *a speciality of the region:* **delicacy**, specialty.

species **noun** **type**, kind, sort; genus, family, order; breed, strain, variety, class, classification, category, set, bracket; style, manner, form, genre.

specific **adjective** **1** *a specific purpose:* **particular**, specified, fixed, set, determined, distinct, definite. **2** *I gave him specific instructions:* **detailed**, explicit, express, clear-cut, unequivocal, precise, exact.
– OPPOSITES general, vague.

specification **noun** **1** *clear specification of objectives:* **statement**, identification, definition, description, setting out, framing, enumeration; stipulation. **2** *a shelter built to their specifications:* **instructions**, guidelines, parameters, stipulations, requirements, conditions, order; description, details.

specify **verb** **state**, name, identify, define, describe, set out, frame, itemize, detail, list, spell out, enumerate, cite, instance; stipulate.

specimen **noun** **sample**, example, instance, illustration, demonstration.

S

specious **adjective** **misleading**, deceptive, false, fallacious, unsound.

speck **noun** **1** *a mere speck in the distance:* **dot**, pinprick, spot. **2** *a speck of dust:* **particle**, grain, molecule; bit, trace.

speckled **adjective** **flecked**, speckly, freckled, freckly, spotted, spotty, dotted, mottled, dappled.

spectacle **noun** **1** *visitors were treated to a magnificent spectacle:* **display**, show, performance, extravaganza, spectacular, pageant, exhibition; pomp and circumstance. **2** *the spectacle of the city below:* **sight**, vision, scene, prospect, vista, picture.

spectacles **plural noun** **glasses**, eyewear; N. Amer. eyeglasses; informal specs.

spectacular **adjective** **impressive**, striking, magnificent, glorious, splendid, dazzling, sensational, dramatic, picturesque, breathtaking, arresting, eye-catching, remarkable, outstanding, memorable, unforgettable; informal out of this world.
– OPPOSITES unimpressive, dull.
• **noun** *a medieval spectacular.* See SPECTACLE sense 1.

spectator **noun** **watcher**, viewer, observer, onlooker, bystander, witness; commentator, reporter; literary beholder.
– OPPOSITES participant.

spectral **adjective** **ghostly**, phantom, wraithlike, shadowy, incorporeal, insubstantial, disembodied, unearthly, other-worldly; informal spooky.

spectre **noun** **1** *the spectres in the crypt:* **ghost**, phantom, apparition, spirit, wraith, presence; informal spook; literary phantasm, shade. **2** *the spectre of war:* **threat**, menace, shadow, cloud; prospect; danger, peril, fear, dread.

spectrum **noun** **range**, gamut, sweep, scope, span; compass, ambit.

speculate **verb** **1** *they speculated about my private life:* **conjecture**, theorize, hypothesize, guess, surmise, wonder, muse. **2** *investors speculate on the stock market:* **gamble**, venture, wager; invest, play the market; Brit. informal punt.

speculative **adjective** **1** *any discussion is largely speculative:* **conjectural**, suppositional, theoretical, hypothetical; tentative, unproven, unfounded, groundless, unsubstantiated. **2** *a speculative investment:* **risky**, hazardous, unsafe, uncertain, unpredictable; informal chancy, dicey, iffy; Brit. informal dodgy.

speech **noun** **1** *the power of speech:* **speaking**, talking, verbal communication. **2** *her speech was slurred:* **diction**, elocution, articulation, enunciation, pronunciation, delivery; words. **3** *an after-dinner speech:* **talk**, address, lecture, discourse, oration, presentation;

sermon, homily; monologue; informal spiel. **4** *the speech of ordinary people:* **language**, parlance, idiom; dialect, vernacular, patois.

WORD LINKS

oral, **lingual**, **phonic** relating to speech or speech sounds

speechless adjective **lost for words**, dumbstruck, tongue-tied, inarticulate, mute, dumb, voiceless, silent.
– OPPOSITES verbose.

speed noun **1** *the speed of their progress:* **rate**, pace, tempo, momentum. **2** *the speed with which they responded:* **rapidity**, swiftness, quickness, promptness, immediacy, briskness, sharpness; haste, hurry, precipitateness; acceleration, velocity; informal lick; literary celerity. • verb **1** *I sped home:* **hurry**, rush, dash, run, race, sprint, gallop, career, shoot, hurtle, hare, fly, zoom, hasten; informal tear, belt, pelt, scoot, zip, whip, hotfoot it, leg it; Brit. informal bomb; N. Amer. informal hightail it. **2** *a holiday will speed his recovery:* **hasten**, speed up, accelerate, advance, further, promote, boost, stimulate, aid, assist, facilitate.
– OPPOSITES slow, hinder.
■ **speed up** hurry up, accelerate, go faster, get a move on, put a spurt on, gather speed; informal get cracking/moving, step on it, shake a leg; Brit. informal get your skates on; N. Amer. informal get a wiggle on.

WORD LINKS

tachometer an instrument used for measuring the speed of an engine

speedily adverb **rapidly**, swiftly, quickly, fast, post-haste; promptly, immediately, briskly; hastily, hurriedly, precipitately; informal pdq (pretty damn quick), double quick, hell for leather, at the double; literary apace.

speedy adjective **rapid**, swift, quick, fast; prompt, immediate, expeditious, brisk, sharp; hasty, hurried, precipitate, rushed, snappy.
– OPPOSITES slow.

spell[1] verb *the drought spelled disaster:* **signal**, signify, mean, amount to, add up to, constitute.
■ **spell something out** explain, make clear, make plain, elucidate, clarify; specify, itemize, detail, enumerate, list, expound, catalogue.

WORD LINKS

orthography the conventional spelling system of a language

spell[2] noun **1** *the witch muttered a spell:* **incantation**, charm, formula; (**spells**) magic, sorcery, witchcraft; N. Amer. hex. **2** *she surrendered to his spell:* **influence**, animal magnetism, charisma, charm; magic.
■ **put a spell on** bewitch, enchant, entrance; curse, jinx, witch; N. Amer. hex.

spell[3] noun **1** *a spell of dry weather:* **period**, time, interval, season, stretch, run, course, streak; Brit. informal patch. **2** *a spell of dizziness:* **bout**, fit, attack.

spellbinding adjective **fascinating**, enthralling, entrancing, bewitching, captivating, riveting, engrossing, gripping, absorbing, compelling, compulsive, mesmerizing, hypnotic; informal unputdownable.
– OPPOSITES boring.

spellbound adjective **enthralled**, fascinated, rapt, riveted, transfixed, gripped, captivated, bewitched, enchanted, mesmerized, hypnotized.

spend verb **1** *she spent £185 on a pair of shoes:* **pay out**; squander, waste, fritter away; informal blow, splurge, fork out, lay out, shell out. **2** *the morning was spent gardening:* **pass**, occupy, fill, take up, while away. **3** *I've spent hours on this essay:* **put in**, devote; waste.

spendthrift noun **profligate**, prodigal, squanderer, waster; informal big spender.
– OPPOSITES miser.
• adjective **profligate**, improvident, wasteful, extravagant, prodigal.
– OPPOSITES frugal.

spent adjective **used up**, consumed, exhausted, finished, depleted, drained; informal burnt out.

spew verb **1** *factories spewed out smoke:* **emit**, discharge, eject, expel, belch/pour out. **2** (informal). See **VOMIT**.

sphere noun **1** *a glass sphere:* **globe**, ball, orb; bubble. **2** *sphere of influence:* **area**, field, compass, orbit; range, scope, extent. **3** *the*

S

sphere of foreign affairs: **domain**, realm, province, field, area, territory, arena, department.

spherical adjective **round**, globular.

spice noun **1** *the spices in curry powder:* **seasoning**, flavouring, condiment. **2** *the risk added spice to their affair:* **excitement**, interest, colour, piquancy, zest; an edge.
■ **spice something up** enliven, liven up, perk up, vitalize, put some life into, galvanize, electrify, boost; informal pep up, perk up, jazz up.

spicy adjective **piquant**, tangy, peppery, hot; spiced, highly seasoned; pungent.
– OPPOSITES bland.

spider noun

WORD LINKS
arachnophobia fear of spiders

spiel noun (informal) **speech**, patter, sales pitch, talk; monologue; rigmarole, story, saga.

spike noun **prong**, barb, point; skewer, stake, spit; tine, pin; spur; Mountaineering piton.
• verb (informal) **adulterate**, contaminate, drug, lace; informal dope, doctor, cut.

spill verb **1** *he spilled his drink:* **knock over**, tip over, upset, overturn. **2** *the bath water spilled on to the floor:* **overflow**, flow, pour, run, slop, slosh, splash; leak. **3** *students spilled out of the building:* **stream**, pour, surge, swarm, flood, throng, crowd.
• noun *an oil spill:* **spillage**, leak, leakage, overflow, flood.
■ **spill the beans** (informal) reveal all, tell all, give the game away, talk; informal let the cat out of the bag, blab, come clean.

S

spin verb **1** *the wheels are spinning:* **revolve**, rotate, turn, go round, whirl. **2** *she spun round to face him:* **whirl**, wheel, twirl, turn, swing, twist, swivel, pivot. **3** *her head was spinning:* **reel**, whirl, go round, swim. **4** *she spun me a yarn:* **tell**, recount, relate, narrate; weave, concoct, invent, fabricate, make up.
• noun **1** *a spin of the wheel:* **rotation**, revolution, turn, whirl, twirl. **2** *a positive spin:* **slant**, angle, twist, bias. **3** *a spin in the car:* **trip**, jaunt, outing, excursion, journey; drive, ride, run, turn; informal tootle.
■ **spin something out** prolong, protract, draw out, drag out, string out, extend, carry on, continue; fill out, pad out.

spindle noun **pivot**, pin, rod, axle, capstan; axis.

spindly adjective **1** *he was pale and spindly:* **lanky**, thin, skinny, lean, spare, gangling, gangly, scrawny, bony, rangy, angular. **2** *spindly chairs:* **rickety**, flimsy, wobbly, shaky.
– OPPOSITES stocky.

spine noun **1** *he injured his spine:* **backbone**, spinal column, vertebrae; back. **2** *cactus spines:* **needle**, quill, bristle, barb, spike, prickle; thorn.

spine-chilling adjective *a spine-chilling ghost story:* **terrifying**, blood-curdling, petrifying, hair-raising, frightening, chilling, horrifying; informal scary, creepy, spooky.

spineless adjective **weak**, weak-willed, feeble, soft, ineffectual; cowardly, timid, faint-hearted, pusillanimous, craven, lily-livered, chicken-hearted; informal wimpish, wimpy, gutless.
– OPPOSITES bold, brave, strong-willed.

spiny adjective **prickly**, spiky, thorny, bristly, bristled, spiked, barbed, scratchy, sharp.

spiral adjective *a spiral column:* **coiled**, helical, curling, winding, twisting.
• noun *a spiral of smoke:* **coil**, helix, corkscrew, curl, twist, whorl, scroll.
• verb **1** *smoke spiralled up:* **coil**, wind, swirl, twist, snake. **2** *prices spiralled:* **soar**, shoot up, rocket, escalate, climb; informal skyrocket, go through the roof. **3** *the economy is spiralling out of control:* **veer**, shoot, lurch, swing, hurtle.
– OPPOSITES fall.

spirit noun **1** *body and spirit:* **soul**, psyche, inner self, mind. **2** *a spirit haunts the island:* **ghost**, phantom, spectre, apparition, presence. **3** *they're in good spirits:* **mood**, frame of mind, state of mind, humour, temper, attitude. **4** *team spirit is high:* **morale**, esprit de corps, confidence, self-confidence. **5** *the spirit of the age:* **ethos**, essence, quintessence; atmosphere,

mood, feeling, climate. **6** *they played with spirit:* **enthusiasm**, liveliness, vivacity, animation, energy, verve, vigour, dynamism, zest, dash, elan, panache, sparkle, exuberance, gusto, fervour, zeal, fire, passion; informal get-up-and-go. **7** *the spirit of the law:* **real/true meaning**, essence, substance; idea. **8** *he never drinks spirits:* **strong liquor/drink**; informal the hard stuff, firewater, hooch; Brit. informal shorts.
– OPPOSITES body, flesh.
■ **spirit someone/something away** whisk away/off, run away with, carry off, steal, abduct, kidnap, snatch, seize.

spirited adjective **lively**, vivacious, vibrant, full of life, vital, animated, sparkling, sprightly, energetic, active, vigorous, dynamic, enthusiastic, passionate; informal feisty, spunky, have-a-go, gutsy; N. Amer. informal peppy.
– OPPOSITES timid, apathetic, lifeless.

spiritual adjective **1** *your spiritual self:* **non-material**, incorporeal; inner, mental, psychological; transcendent, ethereal, mystic, metaphysical. **2** *spiritual writings:* **religious**, sacred, divine, holy, church, ecclesiastical, devotional.
– OPPOSITES physical, secular.

spit[1] verb **1** *he coughed and spat:* **expectorate**, hawk; Brit. informal gob. **2** *the fire began to crackle and spit:* **sizzle**, hiss; crackle, sputter. **3** (Brit.) *it's spitting:* **rain lightly**, drizzle, spot; N. English mizzle.
• noun *spit dribbled from his mouth:* **spittle**, saliva, sputum, slobber, dribble; Brit. informal gob.

spit[2] noun *chicken cooked on a spit:* **skewer**, brochette, rotisserie.

spite noun *he said it out of spite:* **malice**, malevolence, ill will, vindictiveness, vengefulness, malignity; informal bitchiness, cattiness.
– OPPOSITES benevolence.
• verb *he did it to spite me:* **upset**, hurt, wound.
– OPPOSITES please.
■ **in spite of** despite, notwithstanding, regardless of, for all; in defiance of, in the face of; even though, although.

spiteful adjective **malicious**, malevolent, vindictive, vengeful, mean, nasty, hurtful, mischievous, cruel, unkind; informal bitchy, catty.
– OPPOSITES kind, charitable.

splash verb **1** *splash cool water over your face:* **sprinkle**, spray, shower, squirt; daub; wash, wet. **2** *his boots were splashed with mud:* **spatter**, splatter, speck, smear, stain, mark. **3** *waves splashed on the beach:* **wash**, break, lap; pound. **4** *children splashed in the water:* **paddle**, wade; wallow. **5** *the story was splashed across the front pages:* **blazon**, display, spread, plaster, trumpet.
• noun **1** *a splash of rain:* **spot**, blob, smear, speck. **2** *a splash of lemonade:* **drop**, dash, bit, spot, soupçon, dribble; Scottish informal scoosh.
■ **splash out** (Brit. informal) be extravagant; informal lash out, splurge; Brit. informal push the boat out.

spleen noun **bad temper**, ill humour, anger, wrath, vexation, annoyance, irritation, displeasure, dissatisfaction, resentment; spite, malice, bitterness, animosity, venom, bile.
– OPPOSITES good humour.

splendid adjective **1** *splendid costumes:* **magnificent**, sumptuous, grand, imposing, superb, spectacular, opulent, luxurious, deluxe, rich, fine, costly, expensive, lavish, ornate, gorgeous, glorious, dazzling, handsome, beautiful; informal plush, posh, swanky, ritzy, splendiferous; Brit. informal swish; N. Amer. informal swank. **2** (informal) *a splendid holiday:* **excellent**, wonderful, marvellous, superb, glorious, sublime, lovely, delightful, first-class, first-rate; informal super, great, amazing, fantastic, terrific, tremendous, phenomenal, sensational, heavenly, gorgeous, grand, fabulous, fab, awesome, magic, ace, cool, mean, out of this world; Brit. informal smashing, brilliant, brill; dated divine, capital; Brit. informal, dated champion, wizard, ripping, cracking, spiffing, top-hole; N. Amer. informal, dated swell.
– OPPOSITES modest, awful.

splendour noun **magnificence**, sumptuousness, grandeur, opulence, luxury, richness, fineness, lavishness, ornateness, glory; majesty, stateliness; informal ritziness.
– OPPOSITES ordinariness, simplicity, modesty.

splenetic adjective **bad-tempered**, ill-tempered, peevish, petulant, irritable, irascible, dyspeptic, testy, tetchy, waspish, crotchety, crabby, querulous, resentful, bilious.
–OPPOSITES good-humoured.

splice verb **interweave**, braid, plait, intertwine, interlace.

splinter noun **sliver**, chip, shard; fragment, piece, bit, shred; Scottish skelf.
•verb **shatter**, smash, break into smithereens, fracture, split, crack, disintegrate.

split verb **1** *the ice cracked and split:* **break**, fracture, rupture, snap, come apart, splinter, fragment. **2** *her dress was split:* **tear**, rip, slash, slit. **3** *the issue could split the Party:* **divide**, separate, sever; literary tear asunder. **4** *they split the profit:* **share**, divide, distribute, dole out, parcel out, measure out; carve up, slice up. **5** *the path split:* **fork**, divide, bifurcate, diverge, branch. **6** *the band split up last year:* **break up**, separate, part, part company, go their separate ways.
–OPPOSITES join, unite, converge.
•noun **1** *a split in the rock face:* **crack**, fissure, cleft, crevice, break, fracture, breach. **2** *a split in the curtain:* **rip**, tear, cut, rent, slash, slit. **3** *a split in the Party:* **division**, rift, breach, schism, rupture, partition. **4** *the acrimonious split with his wife:* **break-up**, separation, parting, estrangement, rift.
–OPPOSITES join, merger.

WORD LINKS
fissile easily split

S

spoil verb **1** *smoking spoils your complexion:* **damage**, impair, blemish, disfigure, blight, deface, harm. **2** *rain spoiled my plans:* **ruin**, wreck, destroy, upset, undo, mess up, sabotage, scotch, torpedo; informal foul up, muck up, put the kibosh on, do for; Brit. informal scupper. **3** *his sisters spoil him:* **overindulge**, pamper, indulge, mollycoddle, cosset, wait on hand and foot. **4** *stockpiled food may spoil:* **go bad**, go off, go rancid, turn, go sour, rot, perish.
–OPPOSITES improve, enhance, help, neglect.
■ **spoiling for** eager for, itching for, looking for, after, bent on, longing for.

spoils plural noun **booty**, loot, plunder, haul, pickings, ill-gotten gains.

spoilsport noun **killjoy**, dog in the manger, misery; informal wet blanket, party-pooper.

spoken adjective *spoken communication:* **verbal**, oral, vocal; unwritten; by word of mouth.
–OPPOSITES non-verbal, written.
■ **spoken for** reserved, set aside, claimed, booked.

spokesman, spokeswoman noun **spokesperson**, representative, agent, mouthpiece, voice, official; informal spin doctor.

sponge verb **1** *I'll sponge your face:* **wash**, clean, wipe, swab; mop, rinse, sluice, swill. **2** (informal) *he lived by sponging off others:* **scrounge**, beg; live off; informal freeload, cadge, bum; N. Amer. informal mooch; Austral./NZ bludge.

sponger noun (informal) **parasite**, hanger-on, leech, scrounger; informal freeloader; N. Amer. informal mooch, moocher, schnorrer; Austral./NZ informal bludger.

spongy adjective **soft**, squashy, cushioned, yielding; springy; porous, absorbent, permeable; Brit. informal squidgy.
–OPPOSITES hard, solid.

sponsor noun **backer**, patron, promoter, benefactor, supporter, contributor, subscriber, friend, guarantor, underwriter.
•verb **finance**, fund, subsidize, back, promote, support, contribute to, underwrite; N. Amer. informal bankroll.

sponsorship noun **backing**, support, promotion, patronage, subsidy, funding, financing, aid, assistance.

spontaneous adjective **1** *a spontaneous display of affection:* **unplanned**, unpremeditated, unrehearsed, impulsive, impromptu, spur-of-the-moment, extempore; unprompted, unbidden, unsolicited; informal off-the-cuff. **2** *a spontaneous reaction to danger:* **reflex**, automatic, knee-jerk, involuntary, unthinking, unconscious, instinctive. **3** *a spontaneous kind of person:* **natural**,

uninhibited, relaxed, unself-conscious, unaffected, open, genuine; impulsive, impetuous.
– OPPOSITES planned, calculated, conscious, voluntary, inhibited.

spontaneously adverb **1** *they applauded spontaneously:* **of your own accord**, voluntarily, on impulse, impulsively, on the spur of the moment, extemporaneously; informal off the cuff. **2** *he reacted spontaneously:* **without thinking**, automatically, instinctively.

spooky adjective (informal) **eerie**, sinister, ghostly, uncanny, weird, unearthly, mysterious; informal creepy, scary.

sporadic adjective **occasional**, infrequent, irregular, periodic, scattered, patchy, isolated, odd; intermittent, spasmodic, fitful, desultory, erratic, unpredictable.
– OPPOSITES frequent, steady, continuous.

sport noun **games**, physical recreation, exercise; activity, pursuit, pastime.
• verb **wear**, have on, dress in; display, exhibit, show off, flourish, parade, flaunt.

sporting adjective **sportsmanlike**, generous, considerate; fair, just, honourable; Brit. informal decent.
– OPPOSITES dirty, unfair.

sporty adjective (informal) **1** *he's quite a sporty type:* **athletic**, fit, active, energetic. **2** *a sporty outfit:* **stylish**, casual; informal trendy, cool, snazzy; N. Amer. informal sassy.
– OPPOSITES lazy.

spot noun **1** *a grease spot:* **mark**, patch, dot, fleck, smudge, smear, stain, blotch, splash; informal splotch, splodge. **2** *a spot on his nose:* **pimple**, pustule, blackhead, boil, swelling; (**spots**) acne; informal zit; Scottish informal plook. **3** *a secluded spot:* **place**, location, site, position, situation, setting, locale; venue.
• verb **1** *she spotted him near the entrance:* **notice**, see, observe, detect, make out, recognize, identify, locate; catch sight of, glimpse; Brit. informal clock; literary behold, espy. **2** *her clothes were spotted with grease:* **stain**, mark, fleck, speckle, smudge, streak, splash, spatter; informal splotch, splodge.
■ **spot on** (Brit. informal) accurate, correct, right, perfect, exact, unerring; Brit. informal bang on; N. Amer. informal on the money, on the nose.

spotless adjective **clean**, pristine, immaculate, shining, shiny, gleaming, spick and span.
– OPPOSITES filthy.

spotlight noun **public eye**, glare of publicity, limelight.
• verb **focus attention on**, highlight, point up, draw/call attention to, give prominence to, throw into relief, bring to the fore.

spotted adjective **polka-dot**, spotty, dotted.
– OPPOSITES plain.

spotty adjective **1** *a spotty dress:* **polka-dot**, spotted, dotted. **2** (Brit.) *his spotty face:* **pimply**, pimpled, acned; Scottish informal plooky.

spouse noun **partner**, husband, wife; mate, consort; informal better half; Brit. informal other half.

spout verb **1** *lava spouting from the crater:* **spurt**, gush, spew, erupt, shoot, squirt, spray; discharge, emit, belch. **2** *he spouted about morality:* **hold forth**, sound off, go on; informal mouth off.
• noun *a can with a spout:* **nozzle**, lip.

sprawl verb **1** *he sprawled on the sofa:* **stretch out**, lounge, loll, lie, recline, drape yourself, slump, flop, slouch. **2** *the town sprawled ahead of them:* **spread**, stretch, extend, spill.

spray[1] noun **1** *a spray of water:* **shower**, sprinkle, jet, mist, drizzle; spume; foam, froth. **2** *a perfume spray:* **atomizer**, vaporizer, aerosol.
• verb **1** *we sprayed water on the soil:* **sprinkle**, dribble, drizzle. **2** *spray the plants with weedkiller:* **water**, mist; coat, soak, douse. **3** *water sprayed into the air:* **spout**, jet, gush, spurt, shoot, squirt.

spray[2] noun **1** *a spray of holly:* **sprig**, twig. **2** *a spray of flowers:* **bouquet**, bunch, posy, nosegay; corsage, buttonhole.

spread verb **1** *he spread the map out:* **lay out**, open out, unfurl, unroll, roll out; straighten out, fan out; stretch out, extend. **2** *the landscape spread out below:* **extend**, stretch, open out, be displayed; sprawl. **3** *papers were spread all over his* *desk:* **scatter**, strew, disperse, distribute. **4** *he's spreading rumours:* **disseminate**, circulate, put about, communicate, purvey, broadcast, publicize, propagate, promulgate; repeat. **5** *the disease spread rapidly:* **travel**, move, be borne, sweep; develop, diffuse; reproduce, thrive, be passed on, be transmitted. **6** *she spread sun cream on her arms:* **smear**, daub, plaster, slather, lather, apply, put; rub. **7** *he spread his toast with jam:* **cover**, coat, smear, smother.

•noun **1** *the spread of learning:* **expansion**, proliferation, extension, growth; dissemination, diffusion, transmission, propagation. **2** *a spread of six feet:* **span**, width, extent, stretch, reach. **3** *a wide spread of subjects:* **range**, span, spectrum, sweep; variety. **4** (informal) *his mother laid on a huge spread:* **meal**, feast, banquet; informal blowout; Brit. informal nosh-up.

spree noun **1** *a shopping spree:* **bout**, orgy; informal binge, splurge. **2** *a drinking spree:* **bout**; informal binge, bender, session.

sprig noun **stem**, spray, twig.

sprightly adjective **spry**, lively, agile, nimble, energetic, active, vigorous, spirited, animated, vivacious, frisky.
–OPPOSITES doddery, lethargic.

spring verb **1** *the cat sprang off her lap:* **leap**, jump, bound, vault. **2** *the branch sprang back:* **fly**, whip, flick, whisk, kick, bounce. **3** *all art springs from feelings:* **originate**, derive, arise, stem, emanate, proceed, issue, evolve, come. **4** *houses are springing up all over the area:* **appear**, materialize, pop up, sprout; proliferate, mushroom.

•noun **1** *with a sudden spring he leapt up:* **leap**, jump, bound. **2** *the mattress has lost its spring:* **springiness**, bounciness, bounce, resilience, elasticity, flexibility, stretch, stretchiness, give. **3** *there was a spring in his step:* **buoyancy**, bounce, energy, liveliness, jauntiness, sprightliness, confidence. **4** *a mineral spring:* **well**, well head; spa, geyser.

WORD LINKS
vernal relating to the season of spring

springy adjective **elastic**, stretchy, tensile; flexible, pliable; bouncy, resilient.
–OPPOSITES rigid, squashy.

sprinkle verb **1** *he sprinkled water on the cloth:* **splash**, trickle, spray, shower; drip. **2** *sprinkle sesame seeds over the top:* **scatter**, strew. **3** *sprinkle the cake with icing sugar:* **dredge**, dust.

sprinkling noun **1** *a sprinkling of nutmeg:* **scattering**, sprinkle, dusting; pinch, dash. **2** *there's also a a sprinkling of overseas visitors:* **few**, one or two, couple, handful, small number, trickle, scattering.

sprint verb **run**, race, rush, dash, hurry, bolt, fly, gallop, charge, shoot, speed, zoom, go hell for leather, go like the wind; informal tear, pelt, scoot, hotfoot it, leg it, belt, zip, whip; Brit. informal bomb; N. Amer. informal hightail it.
–OPPOSITES walk.

sprite noun **fairy**, elf, pixie, imp.

sprout verb **grow**, germinate; spring up, shoot up, develop, appear.

spruce adjective **neat**, well groomed, well turned out, well dressed, smart, trim, dapper; informal natty, snazzy; N. Amer. informal spiffy, trig.
–OPPOSITES untidy.

■ **spruce up 1** *the flat had been spruced up:* smarten up, tidy up, clean; informal do up; Brit. informal tart up; N. Amer. informal gussy up. **2** *Sarah had spruced herself up:* groom, tidy, smarten, preen, primp; N. Amer. trig; informal titivate, doll up; Brit. informal tart up.

spry adjective **sprightly**, lively, agile, nimble, active; spirited, animated, vivacious, frisky.
–OPPOSITES doddery, lethargic.

spume noun **foam**, froth, surf, spindrift, bubbles.

spur noun **1** *the spur of competition:* **stimulus**, incentive, encouragement, inducement, impetus. **2** *a spur of bone:* **projection**, spike, point; technical process.
–OPPOSITES disincentive.

•verb *the thought spurred him into action:* **stimulate**, encourage, prompt, propel, prod, induce, impel, motivate, move, galvanize, inspire, drive, stir; incite, goad, provoke, sting.
–OPPOSITES discourage.

S

spurious adjective **bogus**, fake, false, fraudulent, sham, artificial, imitation, simulated, feigned; informal phoney.
–OPPOSITES genuine.

spurn verb **reject**, rebuff, scorn, turn down, treat with contempt, disdain, look down your nose at; snub, slight, jilt, brush off, turn your back on; give someone the cold shoulder; informal turn your nose up at, give someone the brush-off; Brit. informal knock back.
–OPPOSITES welcome, accept.

spurt verb *water spurted from the tap:* **squirt**, shoot, jet, erupt, gush, pour, stream, pump, surge, spew, course, well, spring, burst; discharge, emit, expel, eject.
• noun **1** *a spurt of water:* **squirt**, jet, spout, gush, stream, rush, surge; flood, cascade, torrent. **2** *a spurt of energy:* **burst**, fit, bout, rush, spate, surge.

spy noun *a foreign spy:* **agent**, mole, plant; N. Amer. informal spook.
• verb **1** *he spied for the West:* **be a spy**, gather intelligence. **2** *officials spied on them:* **observe**, keep under surveillance/observation, watch. **3** *she spied a coffee shop:* **notice**, observe, see, spot, sight, catch sight of, glimpse, make out, discern, detect; literary espy, behold.

spying noun **espionage**, intelligence gathering, surveillance, infiltration.

squabble noun **quarrel**, disagreement, argument, contretemps, falling-out, dispute, clash, altercation, shouting match, exchange, war of words; Brit. row; informal tiff, set-to, run-in, slanging match, shindig, spat, scrap, dust-up; Brit. informal barney, ding-dong.
• verb **quarrel**, argue, bicker, fall out, disagree, have words; Brit. row; informal scrap.

squad noun **1** *a maintenance squad:* **team**, crew, gang, force. **2** *a squad of marines:* **detachment**, detail, unit, platoon, battery, troop, patrol, squadron, cadre, commando.

squalid adjective **1** *a squalid flat:* **dirty**, filthy, grubby, grimy, foul, poor, sorry, wretched, miserable, mean, seedy, shabby, sordid, insalubrious; neglected, run down, down at heel, dilapidated, ramshackle, tumbledown, crumbling, decaying; informal scruffy, crummy; Brit. informal grotty. **2** *a squalid deal:* **improper**, sordid, unseemly, unsavoury, sleazy, shoddy, cheap, base, low, corrupt, dishonest, dishonourable, disreputable, discreditable, contemptible, shameful.
–OPPOSITES smart, upmarket.

squall noun **gust**, storm, blast, flurry, shower, gale.

squally adjective **stormy**, gusty, blustery, windy, blowy; wild, tempestuous, rough.

squalor noun **dirt**, filth, grubbiness, grime, muck, foulness, poverty, wretchedness, shabbiness, sordidness; neglect, decay, dilapidation; informal scruffiness, crumminess, grunge; Brit. informal grottiness.
–OPPOSITES cleanliness, pleasantness, smartness.

squander verb **waste**, misspend, misuse, throw away, fritter away, spend like water; informal blow, go through, splurge, pour down the drain.
–OPPOSITES save.

square noun *a shop in the market square:* marketplace, plaza, piazza.
• adjective **1** *a square frame:* **quadrilateral**, right-angled. **2** *the two sides were all square at half-time:* **level**, even, drawing, equal, tied; neck and neck, level pegging, nip and tuck, side by side, evenly matched; informal even-steven.
• verb **1** *this does not square with the data:* **agree**, tally, be in agreement, be consistent, match up, correspond, fit, coincide, accord, conform, be compatible. **2** *his goal squared the match 1–1:* **level**, even up.

squash verb **1** *the fruit got squashed:* **crush**, squeeze, flatten, compress, distort, pound, trample, stamp on; pulverize. **2** *she squashed her clothes inside the bag:* **force**, ram, thrust, push, cram, jam, stuff, pack, squeeze, wedge, press.

squashy adjective **mushy**, pulpy, slushy, squelchy, squishy, oozy, doughy, soft; Brit. informal squidgy.
–OPPOSITES firm, hard.

squat verb **crouch**, hunker down, sit on your haunches, sit on your heels.

• adjective **stocky**, thickset, dumpy, stubby, stumpy, short, small.

squawk verb & noun **screech**, squeal, shriek, scream, croak, crow, caw, cluck, cackle, hoot, cry, call.

squeak noun & verb **1** *the vole's squeak | the rat squeaked:* **peep**, cheep, squeal, tweet, yelp, whimper. **2** *the squeak of the hinge | the hinges squeaked:* **squeal**, creak, scrape, grate, rasp, groan.

squeal noun & verb **screech**, scream, shriek, squawk.

squeeze verb **1** *I squeezed the bottle:* **compress**, press, crush, squash, pinch, nip, grasp, grip, clutch. **2** *squeeze the juice from both oranges:* **extract**, press, force, express. **3** *she squeezed her feet into the sandals:* **force**, thrust, cram, ram, jam, stuff, pack, wedge, press, squash. **4** *we all squeezed into the van:* **crowd**, crush, cram, pack, jam, squash, wedge yourself, shove, push, force your way.
• noun **1** *he gave her hand a squeeze:* **press**, pinch, nip; grasp, grip, clutch, hug. **2** *it was quite a squeeze:* **crush**, jam, squash; congestion. **3** *a squeeze of lemon:* **few drops**, dash, splash, dribble, trickle, spot, hint, touch.

squint verb *the sun made them squint:* **screw up your eyes**, narrow your eyes, peer, blink.
• noun *he was born with a squint:* **cross-eyes**, strabismus.

squirm verb **1** *I tried to squirm away:* **wriggle**, wiggle, writhe, twist, slither, fidget, twitch, toss and turn. **2** *he squirmed as everyone laughed:* **wince**, shudder.

S

squirrel verb
■ **squirrel something away** save, put aside, put by, lay by, set aside, lay aside, keep in reserve, stockpile, accumulate, stock up with/on, hoard; informal salt away, stash away.

squirt verb **1** *a jet of ink squirted out of the tube:* **spurt**, shoot, spray, jet, erupt; gush, rush, pump, surge, stream, spew, well, issue, emanate; emit, belch. **2** *she squirted me with scent:* **splash**, spray, shower, sprinkle.
• noun *a squirt of water:* **spurt**, jet, spray, fountain, gush, stream, surge.

stab verb **1** *he stabbed him in the stomach:* **knife**, run through, skewer, spear, gore, spike, impale, transfix, pierce, prick, puncture. **2** *she stabbed at the earth with a fork:* **lunge**, thrust, jab, poke, prod, dig.
• noun **1** *a stab in the leg:* **wound**, puncture, cut, perforation. **2** *a stab of pain:* **twinge**, pang, throb, spasm, cramp, prick, flash, thrill. **3** (informal) *a stab at writing:* **attempt**, try, endeavour; informal go, shot, crack, bash.
■ **stab someone in the back** betray, desert, double-cross, sell out.

stability noun **firmness**, solidity, steadiness, security, strength, sturdiness, strength, durability, permanence.
– OPPOSITES instability, weakness.

stable adjective **1** *a stable vehicle:* **firm**, solid, steady, secure. **2** *a stable person:* **well balanced**, of sound mind, compos mentis, sane, normal, grounded. **3** *a stable relationship:* **secure**, solid, strong, steady, firm, sure, steadfast; established, enduring, lasting.
– OPPOSITES wobbly, unstable, insecure.

stack noun **1** *a stack of boxes:* **heap**, pile, mound, mountain, pyramid, tower. **2** (informal) *a stack of money.* See LOT pronoun.
– OPPOSITES few, little.
• verb **1** *Leo was stacking the empty plates:* **heap up**, pile up; collect. **2** *they stacked the shelves:* **load**, fill, pack, charge; stock.
– OPPOSITES clear.

stadium noun **arena**, field, ground, pitch; track, course, racetrack, racecourse, speedway, velodrome.

staff noun **1** *we'll take on new staff:* **employees**, workers, workforce, personnel, human resources, manpower, labour. **2** *a wooden staff:* **stick**, stave, pole, crook. **3** *a staff of office:* **rod**, mace, wand, sceptre, crozier.
• verb *the centre is staffed by teachers:* **man**, people, crew, work, operate, occupy.

stage noun **1** *this stage of the development:* **phase**, period, juncture, step, point, time, moment, instant, level. **2** *the last stage of the race:* **part**, section, portion, stretch, leg, lap, circuit. **3** *a raised stage:* **platform**, dais, stand, rostrum,

podium. **4** *she has written for the stage:* **theatre**, drama, dramatics, thespianism; informal the boards.
• verb **1** *they staged two plays:* **put on**, present, produce, mount, direct; perform, act, give. **2** *workers staged a protest:* **organize**, arrange, set up; orchestrate, engineer; take part in, participate in, join in.

stagger verb **1** *he staggered to the door:* **lurch**, reel, sway, teeter, totter, stumble. **2** *I was absolutely staggered:* **amaze**, astound, astonish, surprise, stun, confound, stupefy, daze, take aback, leave open-mouthed; informal flabbergast; Brit. informal knock for six. **3** *the meetings are staggered:* **spread out**, space out.

stagnant adjective **1** *stagnant water:* **still**, standing, dead; foul, stale, putrid. **2** *a stagnant economy:* **inactive**, sluggish, slow-moving, lethargic, static, flat, depressed, moribund, dead, dormant.
– OPPOSITES flowing, fresh, active, vibrant.

stagnate verb **languish**, decline, deteriorate, fall, become stagnant, do nothing, stand still, be sluggish.
– OPPOSITES boom.

staid adjective **sedate**, respectable, serious, steady, conventional, traditional, unadventurous, set in your ways, sober, formal, stuffy, stiff; informal starchy, stick-in-the-mud.
– OPPOSITES frivolous, daring, informal.

stain verb **1** *her clothing was stained with blood:* **discolour**, soil, mark, muddy, spot, spatter, splatter, smear, splash, smudge, blotch. **2** *the wood was stained:* **colour**, tint, dye, pigment.
• noun **1** *a mud stain:* **mark**, spot, blotch, smudge, smear. **2** *a stain on his character:* **blemish**, taint, blot, smear, dishonour; damage.

stake[1] noun *a stake in the ground:* **post**, pole, stick, spike, upright, support, prop, strut, pale, cane.
• verb *the plants have to be staked:* **prop up**, tie up, support, hold up, brace, truss.
■ **stake something out 1** *builders staked out the plot:* mark off/out, demarcate, measure out. **2** (informal) *the police staked out his flat:* observe, watch, keep an eye on, keep under observation, keep under surveillance, keep watch on, monitor.

stake[2] noun **1** *playing dice for high stakes:* **bet**, wager, ante. **2** *they are racing for record stakes:* **prize money**, purse, pot, winnings. **3** *we'll keep you one step ahead in the fashion stakes:* **competition**, contest, battle, challenge, race, running, struggle, scramble. **4** *a 40% stake in the business:* **share**, interest, ownership, involvement.
• verb *he staked his week's pay:* **bet**, wager, lay, put on, gamble.

stale adjective **1** *stale food:* **old**, past its best; off, dry, hard, musty, rancid. **2** *stale air:* **stuffy**, close, musty, fusty, stagnant; Brit. fuggy. **3** *stale beer:* **flat**, spoiled, off, insipid, tasteless. **4** *stale jokes:* **hackneyed**, tired, worn out, overworked, threadbare, banal, clichéd; out of date, outdated, outmoded, passé, archaic, obsolete; N. Amer. played out.
– OPPOSITES fresh, original.

stalemate noun **deadlock**, impasse, stand-off, gridlock; draw, tie, dead heat.

stalk[1] noun *the stalk of a plant:* **stem**, shoot; trunk.

stalk[2] verb **1** *he was stalking a deer:* **trail**, follow, shadow, track, go after, hunt; informal tail. **2** *she stalked out:* **strut**, stride, march, flounce, storm, stomp, sweep.

stall noun **1** *a market stall:* **stand**, table, counter, booth, kiosk. **2** *stalls for larger animals:* **pen**, coop, sty, corral, enclosure, compartment.
• verb **1** *the Government has stalled the project:* **block**, impede, hinder, hamper, interrupt, hold up, hold back, thwart, delay, stonewall, check, stop, halt; informal stymie. **2** *quit stalling:* **delay**, play for time, procrastinate, hedge, drag your feet, filibuster, stonewall. **3** *stall him for a bit:* **delay**, divert, distract, hold off.

stalwart adjective **staunch**, loyal, faithful, committed, devoted, dedicated, dependable, reliable, steady, constant, trusty, steadfast, unwavering.
– OPPOSITES disloyal, unfaithful, unreliable.

stamina noun **endurance**, staying power, tirelessness, fortitude, strength, energy, toughness, determination, tenacity, perseverance, grit.

stammer verb **stutter**, stumble over your words, hesitate, falter, pause.

stamp verb **1** *he stamped on my toe:* **trample**, step, stomp, tread, tramp; crush, squash, flatten. **2** *the name is stamped on the cover:* **imprint**, print, impress, punch, inscribe, emboss. **3** *his face was stamped on Martha's memory:* **fix**, inscribe, etch, carve, imprint, impress. **4** *his style stamps him as a player to watch:* **identify**, characterize, brand, distinguish, classify, mark out, set apart, single out.
•noun *the stamp of authority:* **mark**, hallmark, sign, seal, smack, savour, air.
■ **stamp something out** put an end/stop to, end, stop, crush, put down, crack down on, curb, nip in the bud, scotch, quash, quell, suppress, extinguish, stifle, abolish, get rid of, eliminate, eradicate, destroy, wipe out.

stampede noun **charge**, panic, rush, flight, rout.
•verb **bolt**, charge, flee, take flight; race, rush, career, run.

stance noun **1** *a natural golfer's stance:* **posture**, position, pose, attitude. **2** *a liberal stance:* **attitude**, stand, point of view, viewpoint, standpoint, position, angle, perspective, approach, line, policy.

stand verb **1** *the men stood up:* **rise**, get up, straighten up, pick yourself up, be upstanding; formal arise. **2** *today a house stands on the site:* **be situated**, be located, be positioned, be sited, lie. **3** *he stood the vase on the shelf:* **put**, set, place, position, prop, lean, install, arrange; informal stick, park. **4** *my decision stands:* **remain in force**, hold, hold good, apply, be the case, exist. **5** *his heart could not stand the strain:* **withstand**, endure, bear, put up with, take, cope with, handle, sustain, resist, stand up to. **6** (informal) *I can't stand any more of this:* **tolerate**, endure, bear, take, put up with, abide; informal hack.
–OPPOSITES sit, lie.
•noun **1** *the party's stand on immigration:* **attitude**, stance, point of view, viewpoint, opinion, way of thinking, outlook, standpoint, position, approach, thinking, policy, line. **2** *a stand against tyranny:* **opposition**, resistance. **3** *a mirror on a stand:* **base**, support, platform, rest, plinth; tripod, rack, trivet. **4** *a newspaper stand:* **stall**, counter, booth, kiosk.
■ **stand by someone/something** **1** *she stood by her husband:* support, stick by, stand up for, stick up for, defend, back up. **2** *the government must stand by its pledges:* abide by, keep, adhere to, hold to, stick to, observe, comply with. **stand for 1** *V stands for volts:* mean, be short for, represent, signify, denote, indicate, symbolize. **2** (informal) *I won't stand for any nonsense:* put up with, tolerate, accept, allow, permit; formal brook. **3** *we stand for animal welfare:* advocate, champion, uphold, defend, stand up for, support, back, endorse, be in favour of, promote. **stand in** deputize, substitute, fill in, sit in, take over, cover, hold the fort, step into the breach; replace, relieve, take over from; informal sub, step into someone's shoes; N. Amer. pinch-hit. **stand out 1** *his veins stood out:* project, stick out, bulge out, be proud, jut out. **2** *she certainly stood out:* be noticeable, be conspicuous, stick out, attract attention, catch the eye, leap out; informal stick/stand out a mile, stick/stand out like a sore thumb. **stand up for** support, defend, back, stick up for, champion, promote, uphold, take someone's part, take someone's side, side with. **stand up to** defy, confront, challenge, resist, take on, argue with, take a stand against.

standard noun **1** *the standard of her work:* **quality**, level, calibre, merit, excellence. **2** *a safety standard:* **guideline**, norm, yardstick, benchmark, measure, criterion, guide, touchstone, model, pattern. **3** *a standard to live by:* **principle**, ideal; (**standards**) code of behaviour, morals, ethics. **4** *the regiment's standard:* **flag**, banner, ensign, colours.
•adjective **1** *the standard way of doing it:* **normal**, usual, typical, stock,

common, ordinary, customary, conventional, wonted, established, settled, set, fixed, traditional, prevailing. **2** *the standard work on the subject:* **definitive**, established, classic, recognized, accepted.
– OPPOSITES unusual, special.

standardize verb **systematize**, make consistent, make uniform, regulate, normalize, bring into line, equalize, homogenize.

stand-in noun **substitute**, replacement, deputy, surrogate, proxy, understudy, locum, cover, relief, stopgap; informal temp; N. Amer. informal pinch-hitter.
• adjective **substitute**, replacement, deputy, fill-in, stopgap, surrogate, relief, acting, temporary, provisional, caretaker; N. Amer. informal pinch-hitting.

standing noun **1** *his standing in the community:* **status**, ranking, position; reputation, stature. **2** *a person of some standing:* **seniority**, rank, eminence, prominence, prestige, repute, stature, esteem, importance, account, consequence, influence, distinction; informal clout.

stand-off noun **deadlock**, stalemate, impasse.

stand-offish adjective (informal) **aloof**, distant, remote, cold, detached, withdrawn, reserved, uncommunicative, unforthcoming, unapproachable, unresponsive, unfriendly, unsociable.
– OPPOSITES friendly, approachable.

standpoint noun **point of view**, viewpoint, vantage point, attitude, stance, view, opinion, position, way of thinking, outlook, perspective.

standstill noun **halt**, stop, dead stop; gridlock.

staple adjective **main**, principal, chief, major, primary, leading, foremost, first, most important, predominant, dominant, basic, standard, prime, premier; informal number-one.

star noun **1** *the sky was full of stars:* **celestial/heavenly body**; sun; planet. **2** *the stars of the film:* **principal**, leading lady/man, lead, hero, heroine. **3** *a star of the world of chess:* **celebrity**, superstar, big/famous name, household name, someone, somebody, leading light, VIP, personality, luminary; informal celeb, big shot, big noise, megastar.
– OPPOSITES nobody.
• adjective **1** *she was a star pupil:* **outstanding**, exceptional. **2** *the star attraction:* **top**, leading, best, greatest, foremost, major, pre-eminent.
– OPPOSITES poor, minor.

> **WORD LINKS**
> **astral**, **sidereal**, **stellar** relating to stars
> **astronomy** the science of stars, planets, and the universe

starchy adjective (informal) *the starchy but soft-hearted ward sister:* **stiff**, formal, reserved, serious, stuffy, set in your ways; informal uptight, stand-offish.

stare verb **gaze**, gape, goggle, glare, ogle, peer; informal gawk; Brit. informal gawp.

stark adjective **1** *a stark silhouette:* **sharp**, crisp, distinct, clear, clear-cut. **2** *a stark landscape:* **desolate**, bare, barren, empty, godforsaken, bleak, arid. **3** *a stark room:* **austere**, severe, plain, simple, bare, unadorned. **4** *stark terror:* **sheer**, utter, absolute, total, pure, downright, out-and-out, outright. **5** *the stark facts speak for themselves:* **blunt**, bald, bare, simple, basic, plain, unvarnished, harsh, grim.
– OPPOSITES fuzzy, indistinct, pleasant, ornate, disguised.
• adverb *stark naked:* **completely**, totally, utterly, absolutely, entirely, wholly, fully, quite, altogether, thoroughly, truly.

start verb **1** *the meeting starts at 7.45:* **begin**, commence, get under way, go ahead, get going; informal kick off. **2** *this was how her illness started:* **come into being**, begin, commence, be born, arise, originate, develop. **3** *she started her own charity:* **establish**, set up, found, create, bring into being, institute, initiate, inaugurate, introduce, open, launch. **4** *we had better start on the work:* **make a start**, begin, commence, get going, set things moving, start/get/set the ball rolling, buckle to/down; informal get moving/cracking, get stuck in, get down to business. **5** *he started*

across the field: **set off/out**, depart, leave, get under way, make a start, embark; informal hit the road. **6** *you can start the machine:* **activate**, switch/turn on, start up, fire up; boot up. **7** *the machine started:* **begin working**, start up, get going, spring into life. **8** *'Oh my!' she said, starting:* **flinch**, jerk, jump, twitch, recoil, shrink, wince.
– OPPOSITES finish, stop, clear up, wind up, hang about, give up, arrive, stay, close down.
• **noun 1** *the start of the event:* **beginning**, commencement, inception. **2** *the start of her illness:* **onset**, commencement, emergence. **3** *a quarter of an hour's start:* **lead**, head start, advantage. **4** *she awoke with a start:* **jerk**, twitch, spasm, jump.
– OPPOSITES end, finish.

startle verb **surprise**, frighten, scare, alarm, give someone a shock/fright/jolt, make someone jump.
– OPPOSITES put at ease.

startling adjective **surprising**, astonishing, amazing, unexpected, unforeseen, shocking, stunning; frightening, alarming, scary.
– OPPOSITES predictable, ordinary.

starvation noun **hunger**, lack of food, famine, undernourishment, malnourishment, fasting.

starving adjective **hungry**, undernourished, malnourished, starved, half-starved; ravenous, famished.
– OPPOSITES full.

stash (informal) verb **store**, stow, pack, load, cache, hide, conceal, secrete; hoard, save, stockpile.
• **noun cache**, hoard, stock, stockpile, store, supply, reserve.

S

state[1] noun **1** *the state of the economy:* **condition**, shape, position; predicament, plight. **2** (informal) *don't get into a state:* **fluster**, frenzy, fret, panic; informal tizzy, stew; Brit. informal flap; N. Amer. informal twit. **3** (informal) *your room is in a state:* **mess**, chaos, disarray, muddle, shambles. **4** *an autonomous state:* **country**, nation, land, sovereign state, nation state, kingdom, realm, power, republic. **5** *the country is divided into thirty-two states:* **province**, region, territory, canton, department, county, district; Brit. shire. **6** *the power of the state:* **government**, parliament, administration, regime, authorities.
• **adjective** *a state visit to China:* **ceremonial**, official, formal, public.
– OPPOSITES unofficial, private, informal.

state[2] verb **express**, voice, utter, put into words, declare, announce, make known, put across/over, communicate, air, reveal, disclose, divulge, proclaim, present, expound.

stated adjective **specified**, agreed, declared, designated.
– OPPOSITES tacit, unstated.

stately adjective **dignified**, majestic, ceremonious, courtly, imposing, solemn, regal, grand; slow-moving, measured, deliberate.

statement noun **declaration**, expression, affirmation, assertion, announcement, utterance, communication, proclamation, presentation, account, testimony, evidence, report, bulletin, communiqué.

state-of-the-art adjective **modern**, the latest, new, up to the minute; advanced; sophisticated.

static adjective **1** *prices remained static:* **unchanged**, fixed, stable, steady, unchanging, constant. **2** *a static display:* **stationary**, motionless, immobile, unmoving, still, fixed.
– OPPOSITES variable, mobile, dynamic.

station noun **1** *a railway station:* **stop**; terminus, terminal, depot. **2** *a research station:* **establishment**, base, camp; post, depot; mission; site, facility, installation, yard. **3** *a police station:* **office**, depot, base, headquarters; N. Amer. precinct, station house. **4** *a radio station:* **channel**; wavelength.
• **verb** *the regiment was stationed at Woolwich:* **base**, post; establish, install; deploy, garrison.

stationary adjective **static**, parked, motionless, immobile, unmoving, still, stock-still, at a standstill, at rest; not moving a muscle, like a statue, rooted to the spot, inactive, inert, lifeless, inanimate.
– OPPOSITES moving, shifting.

Don't confuse **stationary** with **stationery**, which means 'paper and other writing materials'.

statue noun **sculpture**, figure, effigy, statuette, figurine, idol; carving, bronze, graven image, model; bust.

statuesque adjective **imposing**, striking, stately, majestic, noble, magnificent, regal.

stature noun **1** *small in stature:* **height**, tallness; size, build. **2** *an architect of international stature:* **reputation**, repute, standing, status, position, prestige, distinction, eminence, pre-eminence, prominence, importance, influence, fame, renown, acclaim.

status noun **1** *the status of women:* **standing**, rank, position, level, place; dated station. **2** *wealth and status:* **prestige**, kudos, cachet, standing, stature, regard, fame, note, renown, honour, esteem, image, importance.

statute noun **law**, regulation, act, bill, decree, edict, rule, ruling, resolution, dictum, command, order, directive, by-law; N. Amer. formal ordinance.

staunch[1] adjective **stalwart**, loyal, faithful, committed, devoted, dedicated, steadfast, redoubtable, unwavering.
– OPPOSITES disloyal, unfaithful, unreliable.

staunch[2] verb **stem**, stop, halt, check; block, dam; N. Amer. stanch; old use stay.

stave verb
■ **stave something off** avert, prevent, avoid, counter, preclude, forestall, nip in the bud; ward off, fend off, head off, keep off, keep at bay.

stay[1] verb **1** *he stayed where he was:* **remain**; wait, linger, stick, be left, hold on, hang on; informal hang around; Brit. informal hang about. **2** *they won't stay hidden:* **continue to be**, remain, keep, carry on being, go on being, persist in being. **3** *some friends are staying with us:* **visit**, stop off/over; holiday; lodge, be housed, be accommodated, be billeted; live, reside; N. Amer. vacation; formal sojourn.
– OPPOSITES leave.
• noun *a stay at a hotel:* **visit**, stop, stop-off, stopover, break, holiday; N. Amer. vacation; formal sojourn.

stay[2] noun **strut**, **wire**, brace, tether, guy, prop, rod, support, truss.

steadfast adjective **1** *a steadfast friend:* **loyal**, faithful, devoted, dedicated, dependable, reliable, steady, true, constant, staunch, trusty. **2** *steadfast commitment:* **firm**, determined, resolute, relentless, implacable, single-minded.
– OPPOSITES disloyal, irresolute.

steady adjective **1** *the ladder must be steady:* **stable**, firm, fixed, secure, fast, safe; anchored, moored. **2** *keep the camera steady:* **motionless**, still, static, stationary, unmoving. **3** *a steady gaze:* **fixed**, intent, unwavering, unfaltering. **4** *a steady income:* **constant**, regular, consistent, reliable. **5** *steady rain:* **continuous**, continual, unceasing, ceaseless, perpetual, unremitting, unwavering, unfaltering, unending, endless, round-the-clock. **6** *a steady boyfriend:* **regular**, settled, firm; committed, long-term.
– OPPOSITES unsteady, unstable, loose, shaky, fluctuating, sporadic.
• verb **1** *he steadied the rifle:* **stabilize**, hold steady; brace, support; balance, rest. **2** *she needed to steady her nerves:* **calm**, soothe, quieten, compose, settle; subdue, quell.

steal verb **1** *burglars stole the TV:* **purloin**, thieve, take, help yourself to, pilfer, run off with, carry off, shoplift; embezzle; have your fingers/hand in the till; informal walk off with, swipe, nab, rip off, lift, filch, snaffle; Brit. informal nick, pinch, whip, knock off; N. Amer. informal heist. **2** *copyright law protects you from having your ideas stolen:* **plagiarize**, copy, pirate; informal rip off, lift, crib. **3** *he stole out of the room:* **creep**, sneak, slink, slip, slide, glide, tiptoe, slope.

WORD LINKS
kleptomania a recurrent urge to steal things

stealing noun **theft**, thieving, robbery, larceny, burglary, shoplifting, pilfering; embezzlement.

stealth noun **furtiveness**, secretiveness, secrecy, surreptitiousness.
– OPPOSITES openness.

stealthy adjective **furtive**, secretive, secret, surreptitious.
– OPPOSITES open.

steam noun **water vapour**, condensation, mist, haze, fog, moisture.

steamy adjective **1** *the steamy jungle:* **humid**, muggy, sticky, moist, damp, clammy, sultry, sweaty, steaming. **2** (informal) *a steamy love scene.* See **EROTIC**.

steel verb
■ **steel yourself** brace yourself, summon up your courage, screw up your courage, gear yourself up, prepare yourself; fortify yourself, harden yourself; informal psych yourself up; literary gird up your loins.

steely adjective **1** *his steely gaze:* **piercing**, penetrating; merciless, ruthless, pitiless, severe, unrelenting, unpitying, unforgiving. **2** *steely determination:* **resolute**, firm, steadfast, single-minded; ruthless, iron, grim, gritty; unflinching, unswerving, unfaltering, untiring, unwavering; literary adamantine.

steep adjective **1** *steep cliffs:* **precipitous**, sheer, abrupt, sharp, perpendicular, vertical, vertiginous. **2** *a steep increase:* **sharp**, sudden, dramatic, precipitous.
– OPPOSITES gentle, gradual, reasonable.

steeped adjective *a city steeped in history:* **imbued with**, filled with, permeated with, suffused with, soaked in.

steeple noun **spire**, tower; bell tower, belfry, campanile.

steer verb **1** *he steered the boat:* **guide**, direct, manoeuvre, drive, pilot, navigate. **2** *Luke steered her down the path:* **guide**, conduct, direct, lead, take, usher, shepherd, marshal, herd.
■ **steer clear of** keep away from, keep your distance from, keep at arm's length, give a wide berth to, avoid, have nothing to do with; shun, eschew.

S

stem[1] noun *a plant stem:* **stalk**, shoot, trunk.
■ **stem from** have its origins in, arise from, originate from, spring from, derive from, come from, emanate from, flow from, proceed from.

stem[2] verb **staunch**, stop, halt, check, hold back, restrict, control, contain, curb; N. Amer. stanch; old use stay.

stench noun **stink**, reek, effluvium; Brit. informal niff, pong, whiff; N. Amer. informal funk; literary miasma.

step noun **1** *he took a step forward:* **pace**, stride. **2** *she heard a step on the stairs:* **footstep**, footfall, tread. **3** *the top step:* **stair**, tread; (**steps**) **stairs**, staircase. **4** *resigning is a very serious step:* **course of action**, measure, move, act, action. **5** *a significant step towards a ceasefire:* **advance**, development, move, movement; breakthrough.
• verb *she stepped forward:* **walk**, move, tread, pace, stride.
■ **in step with** in accord with, in harmony with, in agreement with, in tune with, in line with, in keeping with, in conformity with. **out of step with** at odds with, at variance with, in disagreement with, out of tune with. **step by step** one step at a time, bit by bit, gradually, in stages, by degrees, slowly, steadily. **step down** resign, stand down, bow out, abdicate; informal quit. **step in** intervene, intercede. **step something up** increase, intensify, strengthen, escalate; speed up, accelerate; informal up, crank up.

stereotype noun **standard/conventional image**, received idea, cliché, formula.
• verb **typecast**, pigeonhole, conventionalize, categorize, label, tag.

stereotyped adjective **stock**, conventional, stereotypical, standard, formulaic, predictable; hackneyed, clichéd, cliché-ridden; typecast.
– OPPOSITES unconventional, original.

sterile adjective **1** *sterile desert:* **unproductive**, infertile, unfruitful, barren. **2** *a sterile debate:* **pointless**, unproductive, useless, futile, vain, idle. **3** *sterile conditions:* **aseptic**, sterilized, germ-free, antiseptic, disinfected; uncontaminated, unpolluted, pure, clean; sanitary, hygienic.
– OPPOSITES fertile, productive, septic.

sterilize verb **1** *the scalpel was first sterilized:* **disinfect**, fumigate, decontaminate, sanitize; pasteurize; clean, cleanse, purify. **2** *stray dogs are usually sterilized:* **neuter**, castrate, spay, geld; N. Amer. & Austral. alter; Brit. informal doctor.
–OPPOSITES contaminate.

sterling adjective (Brit.) **excellent**, first-rate, first-class, exceptional, outstanding, splendid, superlative, laudable, commendable, admirable.
–OPPOSITES poor, unexceptional.

stern[1] adjective **1** *a stern expression:* **serious**, unsmiling, frowning, severe, forbidding, grim, unfriendly, austere, dour, stony, flinty, steely, unrelenting, unforgiving, unsympathetic, disapproving. **2** *stern measures:* **strict**, severe, stringent, harsh, drastic, hard, tough, extreme, ruthless, rigorous, uncompromising, unsparing, draconian.
–OPPOSITES genial, friendly, lenient, lax.

stern[2] noun *the stern of the ship:* **rear**, back, poop, transom, tail.
–OPPOSITES bow.

stew noun **1** *a beef stew:* **casserole**, hotpot, ragout, goulash; N. Amer. burgoo. **2** (informal) *she's in a right old stew:* **panic**, fluster; informal sweat, lather, tizzy, state; Brit. informal flap; N. Amer. informal twit.
•verb **1** *stew the meat for an hour:* **braise**, casserole, simmer. **2** (informal) *there's no point stewing over it.* See WORRY verb sense 1.

steward noun **1** *an air steward:* **flight attendant**; stewardess, air hostess. **2** *the race stewards:* **official**, marshal. **3** *the steward of the estate:* **manager**, agent, overseer, custodian, caretaker.

stick[1] noun **1** *a fire made of sticks:* **piece of wood**, twig, branch. **2** *he walks with a stick:* **walking stick**, cane, staff, crook, crutch. **3** *the plants need supporting on sticks:* **cane**, pole, post, stake. **4** *he beat me with a stick:* **club**, cudgel; truncheon, baton; cane, switch, rod; Brit. cosh.
■ **the sticks** (informal) the country, the countryside, the provinces; the backwoods, the back of beyond, the wilds, the hinterland, a backwater; N. Amer. the backcountry; Austral./NZ the backblocks; S. African the backveld; informal the middle of nowhere; N. Amer. informal the boondocks.

stick[2] verb **1** *he stuck his fork into the sausage:* **thrust**, push, insert, jab, poke, dig, plunge. **2** *the bristles stuck into his skin:* **pierce**, penetrate, puncture, prick, stab. **3** *the mug stuck to the mat:* **adhere**, cling. **4** *stick the stamp there:* **affix**, attach, fasten, fix; paste, glue, gum, tape. **5** *the wheels stuck fast:* **jam**, catch, get caught. **6** *that image stuck in his mind:* **remain**, stay, linger, persist, continue, endure. **7** (informal) *just stick the file on my desk:* **put**, place, set, lay, deposit; leave, stow; informal dump, bung, park, plonk, pop; N. Amer. informal **plunk**. **8** (Brit. informal) *I can't stick this any longer:* **tolerate**, put up with, take, stand, stomach, endure, bear; informal abide.
■ **stick at** persevere with, persist with, work at, continue with, carry on with, stay with; go the distance, stay the course; informal soldier on with, hang in there. **stick by** be loyal to, be faithful to, be true to, stand by. **stick out 1** *his front teeth stuck out:* protrude, jut out, project, stand out, extend, poke out; bulge. **2** *they stuck out in their new clothes:* be conspicuous, be obvious, stand out, attract attention, leap out; informal stick/stand out a mile, stick/stand out like a sore thumb. **stick to** abide by, keep, adhere to, hold to, comply with, fulfil, make good, stand by. **stick up for** support, take someone's side/part, side with, stand by, stand up for, defend.

sticky adjective **1** *sticky tape:* **adhesive**, gummed. **2** *sticky clay:* **glutinous**, viscous, gluey, tacky, treacly; Brit. claggy; informal gooey. **3** *sticky weather:* **humid**, hot, muggy, oppressive, close, sultry, steamy, sweaty. **4** *a sticky situation:* **awkward**, difficult, tricky, ticklish, delicate, embarrassing, sensitive, uncomfortable; informal hairy.
–OPPOSITES dry, cool.

stiff adjective **1** *stiff cardboard:* **rigid**, hard, firm. **2** *a stiff paste:* **semi-solid**, viscous, thick, firm. **3** *I'm stiff all over:* **aching**, achy, painful; arthritic. **4** *a rather stiff manner:* **formal**, reserved, wooden, forced, strained, stilted; informal starchy, uptight, stand-offish. **5** *a stiff fine:*

harsh, severe, heavy, stringent, drastic, draconian; Brit. swingeing. **6** *stiff resistance:* **vigorous**, determined, strong, spirited, resolute, tenacious, steely, dogged, stubborn. **7** *a stiff climb:* **difficult**, hard, arduous, tough, strenuous, laborious, uphill, exacting, tiring, demanding, formidable, challenging, punishing, gruelling; Brit. informal knackering. **8** *a stiff breeze:* **strong**, fresh, brisk. **9** *a stiff drink:* **strong**, potent, alcoholic.
– OPPOSITES flexible, plastic, limp, runny, supple, relaxed, informal, lenient, mild, half-hearted, easy, gentle, weak.

stiffen verb **1** *stir until the mixture stiffens:* **thicken**, set, solidify, harden, gel, congeal, coagulate, clot. **2** *she stiffened her muscles:* **tense**, tighten, tauten. **3** *intimidation stiffened their resolve:* **strengthen**, harden, toughen, fortify, reinforce.
– OPPOSITES soften, relax, weaken.

stifle verb **1** *Eleanor stifled a yawn:* **suppress**, smother, restrain, fight back, check, swallow, curb, silence. **2** *cartels stifle competition:* **constrain**, hinder, hamper, impede, hold back, curb, prevent, inhibit, suppress.
– OPPOSITES let out, encourage.

stifling adjective **airless**, suffocating, oppressive; sweltering; humid, close, muggy; informal boiling.
– OPPOSITES fresh, airy, cold.

stigma noun **shame**, disgrace, dishonour, ignominy, humiliation.
– OPPOSITES honour, credit.

stigmatize verb **condemn**, denounce; brand, label, mark out.

S

still adjective **1** *she lay completely still:* **motionless**, unmoving, stock-still, immobile, rooted to the spot, transfixed, static, stationary. **2** *a still night:* **quiet**, silent; calm, peaceful, serene, windless. **3** *the lake was still:* **calm**, flat, even, smooth, placid, waveless, glassy, like a millpond, unruffled.
– OPPOSITES active, noisy, rough.
• noun *the still of the night:* **quiet**, silence, stillness, hush; calm, tranquillity, peace.
– OPPOSITES noise.
• adverb **1** *he's still here:* **even now**, yet. **2** *He's crazy. Still, he's harmless:* **nevertheless**, nonetheless, all the same, even so, but, however, despite that, in spite of that, for all that, be that as it may.
• verb *he stilled the crowd:* **quieten**, quiet, silence, hush; calm, settle, pacify, subdue.
– OPPOSITES stir up.

stilted adjective **strained**, forced, contrived, laboured, stiff, self-conscious, awkward, unnatural, wooden.
– OPPOSITES natural, effortless, spontaneous.

stimulant noun **1** *caffeine is a stimulant:* **tonic**, restorative; informal pick-me-up. **2** *a stimulant to industrial development:* **stimulus**, incentive, encouragement, impetus, fillip, boost, spur; informal shot in the arm.
– OPPOSITES deterrent.

stimulate verb **encourage**, act as an incentive, act as an impetus, act as a spur to, prompt, prod, motivate, trigger, spark, spur on, galvanize, activate, fire, fuel; inspire, incentivize, rouse, excite, animate, electrify; N. Amer. light a fire under.
– OPPOSITES discourage.

stimulating adjective **thought-provoking**, interesting, inspiring, inspirational, lively, exciting, stirring, rousing, refreshing, invigorating; provocative, challenging.
– OPPOSITES sedative, uninspiring, uninteresting, boring.

stimulus noun **spur**, stimulant, encouragement, impetus, boost, prompt, prod, incentive, inducement, inspiration; motivation, impulse.
– OPPOSITES deterrent, discouragement.

sting noun **1** *a bee sting:* **prick**, wound, injury. **2** *this cream will take the sting away:* **smart**, pricking; pain, soreness, hurt, irritation.
• verb **1** *she was stung by a scorpion:* **prick**, wound; poison. **2** *the smoke made her eyes sting:* **smart**, burn, hurt, be irritated, be sore. **3** *the criticism stung her:* **upset**, wound, cut to the quick, hurt, pain, mortify. **4** *he was stung into action:* **provoke**, goad, incite, spur, prick, prod, rouse, drive, galvanize.
– OPPOSITES deter.

stingy adjective (informal) **mean**,

miserly, niggardly, close-fisted, parsimonious, penny-pinching, cheese-paring, Scrooge-like; informal tight-fisted, tight, mingy; N. Amer. informal cheap.
– OPPOSITES generous, liberal.

stink verb **reek**, smell.
• noun **1** *the stink of sweat:* **stench**, reek, effluvium; Brit. informal pong, niff; N. Amer. informal funk; literary miasma. **2** (informal) *she kicked up a stink:* **fuss**, commotion, trouble, outcry, uproar, furore; informal song and dance, to-do, kerfuffle, hoo-ha.

stinking adjective **foul-smelling**, smelly, reeking, fetid, malodorous, rank, noxious; informal stinky, reeky; Brit. informal niffy, pongy, whiffy; N. Amer. informal funky; literary noisome.
– OPPOSITES sweet-smelling, fragrant.

stint noun **spell**, stretch, turn, session, term, shift, tour of duty.

stipulate verb **specify**, set down/out, lay down; demand, require, insist on.

stipulation noun **condition**, precondition, proviso, provision, prerequisite, specification; demand, requirement.

stir verb **1** *stir the mixture well:* **mix**, blend; beat, whip, whisk, fold in; N. Amer. muddle. **2** *a breeze stirred the leaves:* **disturb**, rustle, shake, move, agitate, shift. **3** *he finally stirred at ten o'clock:* **get up**, rouse yourself, rise; wake, wake up; informal surface; formal arise; literary waken. **4** *a film that really stirs the imagination:* **arouse**, rouse, fire, kindle, inspire, stimulate, excite, awaken, quicken. **5** *the war stirred him to action:* **spur**, drive, rouse, prompt, propel, prod, motivate, encourage; urge, impel; provoke, goad, sting, incite; N. Amer. light a fire under.
• noun *the news caused a stir:* **commotion**, disturbance, fuss, excitement, turmoil, sensation; informal to-do, hoo-ha, hullabaloo, splash; Brit. informal flap.
■ **stir something up** whip up, work up, foment, fan the flames of, trigger, spark off, precipitate, excite, provoke, incite.

stirring adjective **exciting**, thrilling, rousing, stimulating, moving, inspiring, heady.
– OPPOSITES boring, pedestrian.

stitch verb **sew**, tack; seam, hem; darn.

stock noun **1** *the shop doesn't carry much stock:* **merchandise**, goods, wares; range, choice, variety. **2** *a stock of fuel:* **store**, supply, stockpile, reserve, hoard, cache, bank. **3** *farm stock:* **animals**, livestock, beasts; flocks, herds. **4** *his mother was of French stock:* **descent**, ancestry, origin, parentage, pedigree, lineage, heritage, birth, extraction, family, blood. **5** *chicken stock:* **bouillon**, broth. **6** *the stock of a weapon:* **handle**, butt, haft, grip, shaft, shank.
• adjective *the stock response:* **usual**, routine, predictable, set, standard, staple, customary, familiar, conventional, traditional, stereotyped, clichéd, hackneyed, unoriginal, formulaic.
– OPPOSITES non-standard, original, unusual.
• verb **1** *we do not stock GM food:* **sell**, carry, keep, offer, have, supply. **2** *the fridge was well stocked with milk:* **supply**, provide, furnish, provision, equip, fill.
■ **stock up on/with** amass, stockpile, hoard, cache, lay in, buy up/in, put away/by, put/set aside, collect, accumulate, save; informal squirrel away, salt away, stash away. **take stock of** review, assess, weigh up, appraise, evaluate; informal size up.

stockpile noun **stock**, store, supply, collection, reserve, hoard, cache; informal stash.
• verb **store**, amass, accumulate, stock up on, hoard, cache, collect, lay in, put away, put/set aside, put by, stow away, save; informal salt away, stash away.

stocky adjective **thickset**, sturdy, heavily built, chunky, burly, strapping, brawny, solid, heavy, hefty, beefy.
– OPPOSITES slender, skinny.

stodgy adjective **1** *a stodgy pudding:* **solid**, substantial, filling, hearty, heavy, indigestible. **2** *stodgy prose:* **boring**, dull, uninteresting, dreary, turgid, tedious, heavy going, unimaginative, uninspired, unexciting.
– OPPOSITES light, interesting, lively.

stoical adjective **long-suffering**, uncomplaining, patient, forbearing,

accepting, tolerant, resigned, phlegmatic, philosophical.
– OPPOSITES complaining, intolerant.

stoicism noun **patience**, forbearance, resignation, fortitude, endurance, acceptance, tolerance, philosophicalness, phlegm.
– OPPOSITES intolerance.

stolid adjective **impassive**, phlegmatic, unemotional, cool, calm, placid, unexcitable; dependable; unimaginative, dull.
– OPPOSITES emotional, lively, imaginative.

stomach noun **1 abdomen**, belly, gut, middle; informal tummy, insides. **2 paunch**, pot belly, beer belly/gut; informal spare tyre, middle-aged spread; N. Amer. informal bay window. **3** *he had no stomach for a fight:* **appetite**, taste; inclination, desire, wish.
• verb *they couldn't stomach her attitude:* **tolerate**, put up with, take, stand, endure, bear; informal hack, abide; Brit. informal stick.

> **WORD LINKS**
> **gastric** relating to the stomach
> **gastroenterology** the branch of medicine that deals with the stomach and intestines

stomach ache noun **indigestion**, dyspepsia; colic; informal bellyache, tummy ache, gut ache, collywobbles.

stone noun **1** *someone threw a stone:* **rock**, pebble, boulder. **2** *a commemorative stone:* **tablet**, monument, monolith, obelisk; gravestone, headstone, tombstone. **3** *paving stones:* **slab**, flagstone, flag. **4** *a precious stone:* **gem**, gemstone, jewel; informal rock, sparkler. **5** *a peach stone:* **kernel**, seed, pip, pit.

> **WORD LINKS**
> **lapidary** relating to the cutting and polishing of stones and gems

stony adjective **1** *a stony path:* **rocky**, pebbly, gravelly, shingly; rough. **2** *a stony stare:* **unfriendly**, hostile; hard, flinty, steely, stern, severe; expressionless, blank, poker-faced; unfeeling, uncaring, unsympathetic, indifferent.
– OPPOSITES smooth, friendly, sympathetic.

stooge noun **underling**, minion, lackey, subordinate; henchman; puppet, pawn, cat's paw; informal sidekick; Brit. informal dogsbody, poodle.

stoop verb **bend down**, lean over/down, crouch down, hunch over.
■ **stoop to** lower yourself, sink, descend, resort; go as far as, sink as low as.

stop verb **1** *the music stopped:* **come to an end**, cease, end, finish, draw to a close, be over, conclude; pause, break off. **2** *he stopped smoking:* **cease**, discontinue, desist from, break off; give up, abandon, cut out; informal quit, leave off, pack in, lay off; Brit. informal jack in. **3** *the car stopped:* **pull up**, draw up, come to a halt, come to a standstill, come to rest, pull in/over. **4** *the strike has stopped production:* **put an end to**, bring to an end, end, halt; finish, terminate, discontinue, cut short, interrupt, nip in the bud; deactivate, shut down. **5** *the police stopped her leaving:* **prevent**, obstruct, impede, block, bar, preclude; dissuade from. **6** *protesters have stopped the developers' plans:* **thwart**, foil, frustrate, stand in the way of; scotch, derail; informal put paid to, put the kibosh on, do for, stymie; Brit. informal scupper. **7** *divers stopped the flow of oil:* **stem**, staunch, check, curb, block, dam; N. Amer. stanch. **8** *he tried to stop the hole:* **block**, plug, close,; seal, bung up; technical occlude.
– OPPOSITES start, begin, continue.
• noun **1** *all business came to a stop:* **halt**, end, finish, close, standstill. **2** *a brief stop in the town:* **break**, stopover, stop-off, stay, visit. **3** *the next stop is Oxford Street:* **station**.
– OPPOSITES start, beginning, continuation.
■ **stop off/over** break your journey, take a break, pause; stay, remain, put up, lodge, rest; formal sojourn.

stopgap noun *the system is just a stopgap:* **temporary solution**, expedient, makeshift.
• adjective *a stopgap measure:* **temporary**, provisional, interim, short-term, working, makeshift, emergency.
– OPPOSITES permanent.

stopover noun **break**, stop, stop-off, visit, stay; formal sojourn.

S

stoppage noun **1** *a stoppage over pay:* **strike**, walkout; industrial action. **2** (Brit.) *she got £10.00 an hour before stoppages:* **deduction**, subtraction.

stopper noun **bung**, plug, cork, spigot, seal; N. Amer. stopple.

store noun **1** *a store of food:* **stock**, supply, stockpile, hoard, cache, reserve, bank, pool. **2** *a grain store:* **storeroom**, storehouse, repository, depository, stockroom, depot, warehouse; informal lock-up. **3** *ship's stores:* **supplies**, provisions, stocks; food, rations, provender; materials, equipment, hardware; Military materiel, accoutrements. **4** *a DIY store:* **shop**, retail outlet, boutique, emporium; supermarket, hypermarket, superstore, megastore; N. Amer. mart.
• verb *they've stored enough food to last the winter:* **keep**, stockpile, lay in, put/set aside, put away/by, save, collect, accumulate, hoard; informal squirrel away, salt away, stash away.
– OPPOSITES use, discard.

storehouse noun **warehouse**, depository, repository, store, storeroom, depot.

storey noun **floor**, level, deck.

storm noun **1** *the coast was battered by storms:* **tempest**, squall; gale, hurricane, tornado, cyclone, typhoon; thunderstorm, rainstorm, monsoon, hailstorm, snowstorm, blizzard; N. Amer. windstorm. **2** *there was a storm over his remarks:* **uproar**, outcry, fuss, furore, rumpus, trouble, hue and cry, controversy; Brit. row; informal to-do, hoo-ha, hullabaloo, ballyhoo, ructions, stink. **3** *a storm of protest:* **outburst**, outbreak, explosion, outpouring, surge, blaze; wave, flood.
• verb **1** *she stormed out:* **stride**, stomp, march, stalk, flounce, stamp, fling. **2** *police stormed the building:* **attack**, charge, rush; descend on, swoop on.

stormy adjective **1** *stormy weather:* **blustery**, squally, windy, gusty, blowy; rainy, thundery; wild, tempestuous, turbulent, violent, rough, foul. **2** *a stormy debate:* **angry**, heated, fiery, fierce, furious, passionate, 'lively', acrimonious.
– OPPOSITES calm, fine, peaceful.

story noun **1** *an adventure story:* **tale**, narrative; account, anecdote; saga, chronicle, legend, myth; informal yarn, spiel. **2** *the novel has a good story:* **plot**, storyline, scenario; formal diegesis. **3** *the story appeared in all the papers:* **item**, report, article, feature, piece. **4** *there have been a lot of stories going round:* **rumour**, whisper, allegation; speculation, gossip. **5** *Harper changed his story:* **testimony**, statement, report, account, version. **6** *she never told stories:* **lie**, falsehood, untruth, fib.

> ! Don't confuse **story** and **storey**. In British English **storey** means 'a floor of a building' (*a flat on the second storey*).

stout adjective **1** *a short stout man:* **fat**, plump, portly, rotund, dumpy, chunky, corpulent; informal tubby, pudgy; Brit. informal podgy; N. Amer. informal zaftig, corn-fed. **2** *stout leather shoes:* **strong**, sturdy, solid, substantial, robust, tough, durable, hard-wearing. **3** *stout resistance:* **determined**, vigorous, forceful, spirited, committed; informal gutsy, spunky.
– OPPOSITES thin, flimsy, feeble.

stout-hearted adjective **brave**, determined, courageous, bold, plucky, spirited, valiant, valorous, fearless, intrepid, stalwart; informal gutsy, spunky.

stove noun **oven**, range, cooker, hob.

stow verb **pack**, load, store, place, put, deposit, stash.
– OPPOSITES unload.

straddle verb **1** *she straddled the motorbike:* **sit/stand astride**, bestride, mount, get on. **2** *a mountain range straddling the border:* **lie on both sides of**, lie/extend across, span.

strafe verb **bomb**, shell, bombard, fire on, machine-gun, rake with gunfire.

straggle verb **trail**, lag, dawdle; fall behind, bring up the rear.

straggly adjective **untidy**, messy, unkempt, straggling, dishevelled.

straight adjective **1** *he kept a straight course:* **unswerving**, undeviating, linear. **2** *that picture isn't straight:* **level**, even, in line, aligned, square; vertical, upright, perpendicular;

horizontal. **3** *we must get the place straight:* **in order**, tidy, neat, shipshape, orderly, organized, arranged, sorted out, straightened out. **4** *a straight answer:* **honest**, direct, frank, candid, truthful, sincere, forthright, straightforward, plain-spoken, blunt, unequivocal, unambiguous; informal upfront. **5** *three straight wins:* **successive**, in succession, consecutive, in a row, running; informal on the trot. **6** *straight brandy:* **undiluted**, neat, pure; N. Amer. informal straight up.
– OPPOSITES winding, crooked, evasive.
• **adverb 1** *he looked me straight in the eyes:* **right**, directly, squarely, full; informal smack, slap bang; N. Amer. informal smack dab. **2** *she drove straight home:* **directly**, right. **3** *I'll call you straight back:* **right/straight away**, immediately, directly, at once. **4** *I told her straight:* **frankly**, directly, candidly, honestly, forthrightly, plainly, point-blank, bluntly, flatly, straight from the shoulder, without beating about the bush, without mincing your words, unequivocally, unambiguously, in plain English, to someone's face; Brit. informal straight up. **5** *he can't think straight:* **logically**, rationally, clearly, lucidly, coherently, cogently.
■ **straight away** at once, right away, right now, this minute, this instant, immediately, instantly, directly, forthwith, without further ado, promptly, quickly, without delay, then and there, asap; N. Amer. in short order; informal in double quick time, pronto, before you can say Jack Robinson; N. Amer. informal lickety-split.

S

straighten verb **1** *he straightened the papers on his desk:* **adjust**, arrange, rearrange, tidy. **2** *we must straighten things out with her:* **put/set right**, sort out, clear up, settle, resolve, put in order, rectify, remedy; informal patch up.

straightforward adjective **1** *the process was remarkably straightforward:* **uncomplicated**, simple, easy, effortless, painless, plain sailing, child's play; informal a piece of cake, a cinch, a snip, a doddle, a breeze; Brit. informal easy-peasy; N. Amer. informal duck soup, a snap; Austral./NZ informal a bludge. **2** *a straightforward man:* **honest**, frank, candid, open, truthful, sincere, on the level; forthright, plain-speaking, direct; informal upfront; N. Amer. informal on the up and up.
– OPPOSITES complicated.

strain[1] verb **1** *take care that you don't strain yourself:* **overtax**, overwork, overextend, overreach, overdo it; exhaust, wear out; informal knock yourself out. **2** *he's strained a muscle:* **injure**, damage, pull, wrench, twist, sprain. **3** *we strained to haul the guns up the slope:* **struggle**, labour, toil, make every effort, break your back; informal pull out all the stops, go all out, bust a gut. **4** *the bear strained at the chain:* **pull**, tug, heave, haul; informal yank. **5** *strain the mixture into a bowl:* **sieve**, sift, filter, screen.
• **noun 1** *the rope snapped under the strain:* **tension**, tightness, tautness. **2** *muscle strain:* **injury**, sprain, wrench, twist. **3** *the strain of her job:* **pressure**, demands, burdens; stress; informal hassle. **4** *Melissa was showing signs of strain:* **stress**, nervous tension; exhaustion, fatigue, pressure, overwork. **5** *the strains of Brahms's lullaby:* **sound**, music; melody, tune.

strain[2] noun *a different strain of flu:* **variety**, kind, type, sort; breed, genus.

strained adjective **1** *relations were strained:* **awkward**, tense, uneasy, uncomfortable, edgy, difficult, troubled. **2** *Jean's strained face:* **drawn**, careworn, worn, pinched, tired, exhausted, drained, haggard. **3** *a strained smile:* **forced**, unnatural; artificial, insincere, false, affected, put-on.
– OPPOSITES friendly.

strait noun **1** *a strait about six miles wide:* **channel**, sound, inlet, stretch of water. **2** *the company was in desperate straits:* **a difficult situation**, difficulty, trouble, crisis, a mess, a predicament, a plight; informal , a hole.

straitened adjective **impoverished**, poverty-stricken, poor, destitute, penniless, in penury, impecunious, unable to make ends meet, in reduced circumstances; Brit. on the breadline; informal on your uppers.

strait-laced adjective **prim**, prim and proper, prudish, puritanical, prissy; conservative, old-fashioned, stuffy, staid; informal starchy, square, fuddy-duddy.
– OPPOSITES broad-minded.

strand noun **1** *strands of wool:* **thread**, filament, fibre; length. **2** *the various strands of the ecological movement:* **element**, component, factor, ingredient, aspect, feature, strain.

stranded adjective **1** *a stranded ship:* **beached**, grounded, run aground, high and dry; shipwrecked, wrecked, marooned. **2** *she was stranded in a strange city:* **helpless**, abandoned, lost.

strange adjective **1** *strange things have been happening:* **unusual**, odd, curious, peculiar, funny, bizarre, weird, uncanny, queer, unexpected, unfamiliar, atypical, anomalous, out of the ordinary, puzzling, mystifying, mysterious, perplexing, baffling, unaccountable, inexplicable, singular, freakish; suspicious; eerie, unnatural; informal fishy, creepy, spooky. **2** *strange clothes:* **weird**, eccentric, odd, peculiar, funny, bizarre, unusual; unconventional, outlandish, quirky, zany; informal wacky, way out, freaky, kooky, offbeat, off the wall; N. Amer. informal screwy. **3** *visiting a strange house:* **unfamiliar**, unknown, new. **4** *Jean was feeling strange:* **ill**, unwell, poorly; Brit. off colour; informal under the weather, funny, peculiar; Brit. informal off, ropy, grotty; Austral./NZ informal crook.
– OPPOSITES ordinary, familiar.

strangeness noun **oddity**, eccentricity, peculiarity, curiousness, bizarreness, weirdness, unusualness, abnormality, unaccountability, inexplicability, incongruousness, outlandishness, singularity.

stranger noun **newcomer**, new arrival, visitor, outsider; Austral. informal blow-in.
■ **a stranger to** unaccustomed to, unfamiliar with, unused to, new to, fresh to, inexperienced in.

strangle verb **throttle**, choke, garrotte.

strap noun *thick leather straps:* **thong**, tie, band, belt.
• verb **1** *a bag was strapped to the bicycle:* **fasten**, secure, tie, bind, make fast, lash, truss. **2** *his knee was strapped up:* **bandage**, bind.

strapping adjective **big**, strong, well-built, brawny, burly, muscular; informal hunky, beefy.
– OPPOSITES weedy.

stratagem noun **plan**, scheme, tactic, manoeuvre, ploy, device, trick, ruse, plot, machination, dodge; subterfuge, artifice; Brit. informal wheeze; Austral. informal lurk.

strategic adjective **planned**, calculated, tactical, judicious, prudent, shrewd.

strategy noun **master plan**, grand design, game plan, plan of action, policy, programme.

stratum noun **1** *a stratum of flint:* **layer**, vein, seam, bed. **2** *this stratum of society:* **level**, class, echelon, rank, grade, group, set; caste.

stray verb **1** *the gazelle had strayed from the herd:* **wander off**, get separated, get lost. **2** *we strayed from our original topic:* **digress**, deviate, wander, get sidetracked, go off at a tangent; get off the subject.
• adjective **1** *a stray dog:* **homeless**, lost, abandoned. **2** *a stray bullet:* **random**, chance, freak, unexpected.

streak noun **1** *a streak of light:* **band**, line, strip, stripe, vein, slash, ray. **2** *streaks of paint:* **mark**, smear, smudge, stain, blotch; informal splotch. **3** *a streak of self-destructiveness:* **element**, vein, strain. **4** *a winning streak:* **period**, spell, stretch, run; Brit. informal patch.
• verb **1** *the sky was streaked with red:* **stripe**, band, fleck. **2** *overalls streaked with paint:* **mark**, daub, smear; informal splotch. **3** *the cat streaked across the road.* See RUN verb sense 1.

streaky adjective **striped**, stripy, streaked, banded, veined, brindled.

stream noun **1** *a mountain stream:* **brook**, rivulet; tributary; Scottish & N. English burn; N. English beck; S. English bourn; N. Amer. & Austral./NZ creek; Austral. billabong. **2** *a stream of boiling water:* **jet**, flow, rush, gush, surge, torrent, flood, cascade, outpouring, outflow; technical efflux.

3 *a steady stream of visitors:* **succession**, series, string.
• **verb 1** *tears were streaming down her face:* **flow**, pour, course, run, gush, surge, flood, cascade, spill. **2** *children streamed out of the classrooms:* **pour**, surge, flood, swarm, pile, crowd. **3** *a flag streamed from the mast:* **flutter**, float, flap, fly, blow, waft, wave.

streamer **noun** **pennant**, pennon, flag, banner.

streamlined **adjective 1** *streamlined cars:* **aerodynamic**, smooth, sleek. **2** *a streamlined organization:* **efficient**, smooth-running, well run.

street **noun** **road**, thoroughfare, avenue, drive, boulevard, parade; side street/road, lane; N. Amer. highway.
■ **the man/woman in the street** the ordinary person, Mr/Mrs Average; Brit. informal Joe Bloggs, Joe Public; N. Amer. informal John Doe, Joe Sixpack. **on the streets** homeless, sleeping rough, down and out.

strength **noun 1** *enormous physical strength:* **power**, muscle, sturdiness, robustness, toughness, hardiness; vigour, force, might. **2** *Oliver began to regain his strength:* **health**, fitness, vigour, stamina. **3** *her great inner strength:* **fortitude**, resilience, spirit, backbone; courage, bravery, pluck, courageousness, grit; informal guts, spunk. **4** *the strength of the retaining wall:* **robustness**, sturdiness, firmness, toughness, soundness, solidity, durability. **5** *Europe's military strength:* **power**; influence; informal clout. **6** *strength of feeling:* **intensity**, vehemence, force, depth. **7** *the strength of their argument:* **cogency**, forcefulness, force, weight, power, persuasiveness, soundness, validity. **8** *what are your strengths?* **strong point**, advantage, asset, forte, aptitude, talent, skill; speciality. **9** *the strength of the army:* **size**, extent, magnitude.
– OPPOSITES weakness.

strengthen **verb 1** *calcium strengthens growing bones:* **make strong/stronger**, build up, give strength to. **2** *engineers strengthened the walls:* **reinforce**, make stronger, buttress, shore up, underpin. **3** *heat strengthens the glass:* **toughen**, temper, harden. **4** *the wind had strengthened:* **become strong/stronger**, gain strength, intensify, pick up. **5** *his insistence strengthened her determination:* **fortify**, bolster, make stronger, boost, reinforce, harden, stiffen, toughen, fuel. **6** *the argument is strengthened by this evidence:* **reinforce**, lend more weight to; support, back up, confirm, bear out, corroborate.
– OPPOSITES weaken.

strenuous **adjective 1** *a strenuous climb:* **arduous**, difficult, hard, tough, taxing, demanding, exacting, exhausting, tiring, gruelling, back-breaking; Brit. informal knackering. **2** *strenuous efforts:* **vigorous**, energetic, forceful, strong, spirited, intense, determined, resolute, dogged.
– OPPOSITES easy, half-hearted.

stress **noun 1** *he's under a lot of stress:* **strain**, pressure, tension, worry, anxiety, trouble, difficulty; informal hassle. **2** *we are laying greater stress on education:* **emphasis**, importance, weight. **3** *the stress falls on the first syllable:* **emphasis**, accent, accentuation; beat.
• **verb** *they stress the need for reform:* **emphasize**, draw attention to, press home, underline, underscore, point up, highlight, foreground, accentuate, accent.
– OPPOSITES play down.

stressed **adjective** **harassed**, under pressure, hard-pressed, strained, careworn, tense, worried, anxious, beleaguered, overworked, overburdened, overloaded; informal hassled.
– OPPOSITES carefree.

stressful **adjective** **demanding**, trying, taxing, difficult, hard, tough; fraught, traumatic, tense, frustrating.
– OPPOSITES relaxing.

stretch **verb 1** *he stretched the elastic:* **pull**, draw out, extend, lengthen, elongate, expand. **2** *she stretched out on the sofa:* **lie down**, recline, lean back, sprawl, lounge, loll. **3** *she stretched out her hand:* **reach out**, hold out, proffer, extend, straighten out. **4** *the desert stretches for miles:* **extend**, spread, continue, go on. **5** *the court case stretched*

their finances: **put a strain on**, overtax, overextend, drain, sap, tax.
– OPPOSITES shorten.
• noun **1** *magnificent stretches of forest:* **expanse**, area, tract, belt, sweep, extent. **2** *a four-hour stretch:* **period**, time, spell, run, stint, session, shift.

strew verb **scatter**, spread, disperse, litter, toss.

stricken adjective **troubled**, affected, afflicted; injured, wounded.

strict adjective **1** *a strict interpretation of the law:* **precise**, exact, literal, faithful, accurate, careful, meticulous, rigorous. **2** *strict controls on spending:* **stringent**, rigorous, severe, harsh, hard, rigid, tough. **3** *strict parents:* **stern**, severe, harsh, uncompromising, authoritarian, firm. **4** *in strict confidence:* **absolute**, utter, complete, total. **5** *a strict Roman Catholic:* **orthodox**, devout, conscientious.
– OPPOSITES loose, liberal.

stricture noun **constraint**, restriction, limitation, restraint, curb, impediment, barrier, obstacle.
– OPPOSITES freedom.

stride verb **march**, pace, step, sweep; strut, stalk, stomp.
• noun **step**, pace; walk, gait.

strident adjective **harsh**, raucous, rough, grating, jarring, loud, shrill, screeching, piercing, ear-piercing.
– OPPOSITES soft.

strife noun **conflict**, friction, discord, disagreement, dissension, dispute, argument, quarrelling, wrangling, bickering, controversy; ill/bad feeling, falling-out, bad blood, hostility, animosity.
– OPPOSITES peace.

strike verb **1** *the man struck her on the head:* **hit**, slap, smack, thump, punch, cuff, beat; informal clout, wallop, belt, whack, thwack, bash, clobber, bop, biff, swipe; literary smite. **2** *the car struck a tree:* **crash into**, collide with, hit, run into, bump into, smash into, bang into; N. Amer. impact. **3** *we have struck a deal:* **agree on**, come to, settle on; achieve, reach, arrive at, establish; informal clinch. **4** *he struck a heroic pose:* **assume**, adopt, take on/up, affect; N. Amer. informal cop. **5** *a thought struck her:* **occur to**, come to mind, dawn on someone, hit, spring to mind, enter your head. **6** *you strike me as intelligent:* **seem**, appear; come across as. **7** *train drivers are to strike:* **take industrial action**, go on strike, down tools, walk out.
• noun **1** *a 48-hour strike:* **industrial action**, walkout, stoppage; Brit. go-slow. **2** *a military strike:* **attack**, assault, bombing.
■ **strike something out** delete, cross out, erase, rub out. **strike something up** *we struck up a conversation:* begin, start, commence, embark on, establish.

striking adjective **1** *a striking resemblance:* **noticeable**, obvious, conspicuous, evident, marked, notable, unmistakable, strong; remarkable, extraordinary, incredible, amazing, astounding, astonishing, staggering. **2** *Kenya's striking landscape:* **impressive**, imposing, grand, splendid, magnificent, spectacular, breathtaking, superb, marvellous, wonderful, stunning, staggering, sensational, dramatic.
– OPPOSITES unremarkable.

string noun **1** *a ball of string:* **twine**, cord, yarn, thread, strand. **2** *a string of brewers:* **chain**, group, firm, company. **3** *a string of convictions:* **series**, succession, chain, sequence, run, streak. **4** *a string of wagons:* **queue**, procession, line, file, column, convoy, train, cavalcade. **5** *a string of pearls:* **strand**, rope, necklace. **6** *a guaranteed loan with no strings:* **conditions**, qualifications, provisions, provisos, caveats, stipulations, riders, prerequisites, limitations, limits, constraints, restrictions; informal catches.
• verb **1** *lights were strung across the promenade:* **hang**, suspend, sling, stretch, run; thread, loop, festoon. **2** *beads strung on a silver chain:* **thread**, loop, link.
■ **string someone along** (informal) mislead, deceive, take advantage of, dupe, hoax, fool, make a fool of. **string something out** spin out, drag out, lengthen.

stringent adjective **strict**, firm, rigid, rigorous, severe, harsh, tough, tight, exacting, demanding.

stringy adjective **1** *stringy hair:* **straggly**, lank, thin. **2** *stringy meat:* **fibrous**, gristly, sinewy, chewy, tough.

strip[1] verb **1** *he stripped and got into bed:* **undress**, strip off, strip naked, unclothe, disrobe. **2** *first strip the paint off the door:* **peel**, remove, take off, scrape, clean. **3** *they stripped him of his doctorate:* **deprive**, dispossess, divest, relieve; confiscate. **4** *I stripped down the engine:* **dismantle**, disassemble, take to bits/pieces, take apart. **5** *the house had been stripped:* **empty**, clear, clean out; plunder, rob, burgle, loot, pillage, ransack, despoil, sack.
– OPPOSITES dress.
• noun *the team's new strip:* **outfit**, dress, garb; Brit. kit; informal gear, get-up; Brit. informal rig-out.

strip[2] noun *a strip of paper:* **piece**, bit, band, belt, ribbon, slip, shred.

stripe noun **line**, band, strip, belt, bar, streak, vein, flash; technical stria, striation.

striped adjective. See STRIPY.

stripling noun (humorous) **youth**, youngster, boy, schoolboy, lad; informal kid, young 'un, nipper, whippersnapper, shaver.

stripy adjective **striped**, barred, lined, banded; streaky, variegated; technical striated.

strive verb **1** *I shall strive to be fair:* **try**, endeavour, attempt, aim, venture, make every effort, exert yourself, do your best, do your utmost, labour, work; informal go all out. **2** *scholars must strive against bias:* **struggle**, fight, battle, combat.

stroke noun **1** *five strokes of the cane:* **blow**, hit, thump, punch, slap, smack. **2** *light upward strokes:* **movement**, action, motion. **3** *broad brush strokes:* **mark**, line. **4** *he suffered a stroke:* **thrombosis**, seizure; Medicine ictus.
• verb *she stroked the cat:* **caress**, fondle, pat, pet, touch, rub, massage.

stroll verb *they strolled along the river:* **saunter**, amble, wander, meander, ramble, promenade, walk, stretch your legs, get some air; informal mosey; formal perambulate.
• noun *a stroll in the park:* **saunter**, amble, wander, walk, turn, promenade; informal mosey; dated constitutional; formal perambulation.

strong adjective **1** *a strong lad:* **powerful**, sturdy, robust, athletic, tough, rugged, lusty. **2** *she isn't very strong:* **well**, healthy, fit. **3** *a strong character:* **forceful**, determined, spirited, self-assertive, tough, tenacious, formidable, redoubtable, strong-minded; informal gutsy, feisty. **4** *a strong fortress:* **secure**, well built, well fortified, well protected, solid. **5** *strong cotton bags:* **durable**, hard-wearing, heavy-duty, tough, sturdy, well made, long-lasting. **6** *the current is very strong:* **forceful**, powerful, vigorous, fierce, intense. **7** *a strong interest in literature:* **keen**, passionate, fervent. **8** *strong feelings:* **intense**, forceful, passionate, ardent, fervent, deep-seated. **9** *a strong supporter:* **keen**, eager, enthusiastic, dedicated. **10** *strong arguments:* **compelling**, cogent, forceful, powerful, convincing, sound, valid, well founded, persuasive. **11** *a need for strong action:* **firm**, forceful, drastic, extreme. **12** *she bore a very strong resemblance to Vera:* **marked**, noticeable, pronounced, distinct, definite, unmistakable, notable. **13** *a strong voice:* **loud**, powerful, forceful, resonant, sonorous, rich, deep, booming. **14** *strong language:* **bad**, foul, obscene, profane. **15** *a strong blue colour:* **intense**, deep, rich, bright, brilliant, vivid, vibrant. **16** *strong lights:* **bright**, brilliant, dazzling, glaring. **17** *strong coffee:* **concentrated**, undiluted. **18** *strong cheese:* **highly flavoured**, flavourful, flavoursome; mature, ripe; piquant, tangy, spicy. **19** *strong drink:* **alcoholic**, intoxicating, hard, stiff.
– OPPOSITES weak, gentle, mild.

stronghold noun **1** *the enemy stronghold:* **fortress**, fort, castle, citadel, garrison. **2** *a Tory stronghold:* **bastion**, centre, hotbed.

strong-minded adjective **determined**, firm, resolute, purposeful, strong-willed, uncompromising, unbending, forceful, persistent, tenacious, dogged.

strong point noun **strength**, strong suit, forte, speciality.
– OPPOSITES weakness.

strong-willed adjective **determined**, resolute, stubborn, obstinate, wilful, headstrong, strong-minded, self-willed, unbending, unyielding.

structure noun **1** *a vast Gothic structure:* **building**, edifice, construction, erection. **2** *the structure of local government:* **construction**, form, formation, shape, composition, anatomy, make-up, constitution; organization, system, arrangement, design, framework, configuration, pattern.
• verb *the programme is structured around periods of study:* **arrange**, organize, design, shape, construct, build.

struggle verb **1** *they struggled to do better:* **strive**, try hard, endeavour, make every effort. **2** *James struggled with the raiders:* **fight**, grapple, wrestle, scuffle, brawl, spar; informal scrap. **3** *the teams struggled to be first:* **compete**, contend, vie, fight, battle, jockey. **4** *she struggled over the dunes:* **scramble**, flounder, stumble, fight/battle your way, labour.
• noun **1** *the struggle for justice:* **endeavour**, striving; campaign, battle, crusade, drive, push. **2** *there were no signs of a struggle:* **fight**, scuffle, brawl, tussle, skirmish, fracas; informal bust-up, ding-dong. **3** *many perished in the struggle:* **conflict**, fight, battle, confrontation, clash, skirmish; hostilities, fighting, war, warfare, campaign. **4** *a struggle within the leadership:* **contest**, competition, fight, clash; rivalry, friction, feuding, conflict. **5** *life has been a struggle for me:* **effort**, trial, trouble, stress, strain, battle; informal grind, hassle.

strut verb **swagger**, swank, parade, stride, sweep; informal sashay.

stub noun **1** *a cigarette stub:* **butt**, end; informal dog-end. **2** *a ticket stub:* **counterfoil**, slip, tab, remnant, stump.

stubble noun **1** *a field of stubble:* **stalks**, straw. **2** *grey stubble:* **bristles**, whiskers, facial hair; informal five o'clock shadow.

stubbly adjective **bristly**, unshaven, whiskered; prickly, rough, coarse, scratchy.

stubborn adjective **1** *you're too stubborn to admit it:* **obstinate**, headstrong, wilful, strong-willed, pig-headed, obdurate, recalcitrant, inflexible, uncompromising, unbending; informal stiff-necked. **2** *stubborn stains:* **indelible**, permanent, persistent, tenacious, resistant.
– OPPOSITES compliant.

stubby adjective **dumpy**, stocky, chunky, chubby, squat; short, stumpy.
– OPPOSITES slender, tall.

stuck adjective **1** *a message was stuck to his screen:* **fixed**, fastened, attached, glued, pinned. **2** *the gate was stuck:* **immovable**, jammed. **3** *if you get stuck, leave a blank:* **baffled**, beaten, at a loss, at your wits' end; informal stumped, bogged down, flummoxed, fazed, bamboozled.
■ **stuck with** lumbered with, left with; informal landed with.

studded adjective *the sky was studded with stars:* **dotted**, scattered, sprinkled, covered, spangled; peppered.

student noun **1** *a university student:* **undergraduate**, postgraduate; N. Amer. sophomore; Brit. informal fresher. **2** *a former student:* **pupil**, schoolchild, schoolboy, schoolgirl, scholar. **3** *a nursing student:* **trainee**, apprentice, probationer, novice.

studied adjective **deliberate**, careful, considered, conscious, calculated, intentional; affected.

studio noun **workshop**, workroom.

studious adjective **1** *a studious nature:* **scholarly**, academic, bookish, intellectual. **2** *studious attention:* **diligent**, careful, attentive, assiduous, painstaking, thorough, meticulous.

study noun **1** *two years of study:* **learning**, education, schooling, scholarship, tuition, research; informal swotting, cramming. **2** *a study of global warming:* **investigation**, enquiry, research, examination, analysis, review, survey. **3** *he's in the study:* **office**, workroom, studio.
• verb **1** *she studied hard:* **work**, revise; informal swot, cram. **2** *they are studying the effects of climate change:* **investigate**, research, look at,

examine, analyse. **3** *she studied him thoughtfully:* **scrutinize**, examine, inspect, consider, regard, look at, observe, watch, survey; informal check out; N. Amer. informal eyeball.

stuff noun **1** *suede is tough stuff:* **material**, fabric, cloth; substance. **2** *first-aid stuff:* **items**, articles, objects, goods, paraphernalia, kit; belongings, possessions, effects; informal things, gear, bits and pieces, odds and ends.
• verb **1** *she stuffed her clothes into a bag:* **shove**, thrust, push, ram, cram, squeeze, force, jam, pack, pile, stick. **2** (informal) *they stuffed themselves with chocolate:* **fill**, gorge, overindulge, sate, satiate.

stuffing noun **padding**, wadding, filling, packing.

stuffy adjective **1** *a stuffy atmosphere:* **airless**, close, musty, stale; Brit. informal fuggy. **2** *a stuffy young man:* **staid**, sedate, sober, prim, priggish, strait-laced, conformist, conservative, old-fashioned; informal straight, starchy, fuddy-duddy. **3** *a stuffy nose:* **blocked**, stuffed up, bunged up.
– OPPOSITES airy, clear.

stultifying adjective *a stultifying existence:* **restrictive**, stifling, oppressive, constrained; tedious, dull, dreary, soul-destroying.
– OPPOSITES stimulating.

stumble verb **1** *he stumbled and fell:* **trip**, lose your balance, lose/miss your footing, slip; lurch, stagger, totter. **2** *he stumbled during his speech:* **stammer**, stutter, hesitate, falter.
▪ **stumble across/on** come across/upon, chance on, happen on, light on; discover, find, unearth, uncover; informal dig up.

stumbling block noun **obstacle**, hurdle, barrier, bar, hindrance, impediment, handicap, disadvantage; snag, hitch, catch, drawback, difficulty, problem; informal fly in the ointment.

stump verb (informal) **baffle**, perplex, puzzle, confuse, confound, nonplus, defeat, put at a loss; informal flummox, fox, throw, floor; N. Amer. informal discombobulate.

stun verb **1** *the force of the blow stunned him:* **daze**, stupefy, knock out, lay out. **2** *she was stunned by the news:* **astound**, amaze, astonish, dumbfound, stupefy, stagger, shock, take aback; informal flabbergast, knock sideways.

stunning adjective **1** *a stunning win:* **remarkable**, extraordinary, staggering, incredible, outstanding, amazing, astonishing, marvellous, phenomenal; informal fabulous, fantastic, tremendous. **2** *she looked stunning.* See BEAUTIFUL.
– OPPOSITES ordinary.

stunt[1] verb **inhibit**, impede, hamper, hinder, restrict, retard, slow, curb, check.
– OPPOSITES encourage.

stunt[2] noun **feat**, exploit, trick.

stunted adjective **small**, undersized, diminutive.

stupefaction noun **bewilderment**, confusion, perplexity, wonder, amazement, astonishment.

stupefy verb **1** *the blow had stupefied her:* **stun**, daze, knock unconscious, knock out. **2** *his reply stupefied us:* **shock**, stun, astound, dumbfound, overwhelm, stagger, amaze, astonish, take someone's breath away; informal flabbergast, knock sideways, bowl over, floor; Brit. informal knock for six.

stupendous adjective **amazing**, astounding, astonishing, extraordinary, remarkable, phenomenal, staggering, breathtaking; informal fantastic, mind-boggling, awesome, tremendous; literary wondrous.
– OPPOSITES unremarkable.

stupid adjective **1** *a stupid boy:* **unintelligent**, obtuse, dense, ignorant, foolish, slow, vacuous, vapid; informal thick, dim, dumb, dopey, dozy, moronic, cretinous, pea-brained, half-witted, soft in the head; Brit. informal daft. **2** *a stupid mistake:* **foolish**, silly, idiotic, ill-advised, ill-considered, unwise, injudicious; mad; informal crazy, half-baked, cockeyed, hare-brained, nutty, dotty, batty, loony, loopy; Brit. informal potty. **3** *he drank himself stupid:* **senseless**, into a stupor; unconscious.
– OPPOSITES intelligent, sensible.

stupidity noun **foolishness**, folly, silliness, idiocy, senselessness, ineptitude, inanity, absurdity, ludicrousness, ridiculousness, fatuousness, madness, insanity, lunacy; informal craziness; Brit. informal daftness.

stupor noun **daze**, torpor, insensibility, oblivion.

sturdy adjective **1** *a sturdy lad:* **strapping**, well built, muscular, strong, hefty, brawny, powerful, solid, burly; informal beefy. **2** *sturdy boots:* **robust**, strong, well built, solid, stout, tough, durable, long-lasting, hard-wearing.
–OPPOSITES feeble.

stutter verb **stammer**, stumble, falter.

style noun **1** *differing styles of management:* **manner**, way, technique, method, approach, system, form. **2** *a non-directive style of counselling:* **type**, kind, variety, sort, school, brand, pattern, model. **3** *she always dresses with style and taste:* **flair**, stylishness, elegance, grace, poise, polish, suaveness, sophistication, panache, elan; informal class. **4** *Laura travelled in style:* **comfort**, luxury. **5** *modern styles:* **fashion**, trend, vogue.
• verb *sportswear styled by Karl:* **design**, fashion, tailor.

stylish adjective **fashionable**, modish, modern, up to date; smart, sophisticated, elegant, chic, dapper, dashing; informal trendy, natty, classy, nifty, snazzy; N. Amer. informal fly, kicky, tony, spiffy.
–OPPOSITES unfashionable.

suave adjective **charming**, sophisticated, debonair, urbane, polished, refined, poised, self-possessed, gallant; smooth.
–OPPOSITES unsophisticated.

subconscious adjective **unconscious**, latent, suppressed, repressed, subliminal, dormant, underlying, innermost.
• noun **mind**, psyche, inner self, imagination.

subdue verb **conquer**, defeat, overcome, overwhelm, crush, quash, beat, trounce, subjugate, suppress, bring someone to their knees; literary vanquish.

subdued adjective **1** *Lewis's subdued air:* **sombre**, downcast, sad, dejected, depressed, gloomy, despondent, dispirited, disheartened, forlorn, woebegone; withdrawn. **2** *subdued voices:* **hushed**, muted, quiet, low, soft, faint, muffled, indistinct. **3** *subdued lighting:* **dim**, muted, soft, low.
–OPPOSITES cheerful, loud, bright.

subject noun **1** *the subject of this chapter:* **theme**, subject matter, topic, issue, question, concern. **2** *popular university subjects:* **branch of study**, discipline, field. **3** *six subjects did the trials:* **participant**, volunteer; informal guinea pig. **4** *British subjects:* **citizen**, national; taxpayer, voter.
• verb *he subjected her to a terrifying ordeal:* **put through**, cause to undergo, expose to.
■ **subject to** conditional on, contingent on, dependent on.

subjection noun **subjugation**, domination, oppression, repression, suppression.

subjective adjective **personal**, individual, emotional; intuitive.
–OPPOSITES objective.

subjugate verb **conquer**, defeat, crush, quash, bring someone to their knees, enslave, subdue, suppress; literary vanquish.
–OPPOSITES liberate.

sublime adjective **1** *sublime music:* **exalted**, elevated, noble, lofty, awe-inspiring, majestic, magnificent, glorious, superb, wonderful, marvellous, splendid; informal fantastic, fabulous, terrific, heavenly, divine, out of this world. **2** *the sublime confidence of youth:* **supreme**, total, complete, utter, consummate.

subliminal adjective **subconscious**; hidden, concealed.
–OPPOSITES explicit.

submerge verb **1** *the U-boat submerged:* **go under**, dive, sink. **2** *submerge the bowl in water:* **immerse**, plunge, sink. **3** *the farmland was submerged:* **flood**, deluge, swamp, inundate.
–OPPOSITES surface.

submission noun **1** *submission to authority:* **yielding**, capitulation, acceptance, consent, compliance. **2** *Tim raised his hands in submission:* **surrender**, capitulation, resignation, defeat. **3** *he wanted her total submission:* **compliance**,

submissiveness, acquiescence, obedience, docility, subservience, servility, subjection. **4** *a report for submission to the Board:* **presentation**, presenting, proffering, tendering, proposing. **5** *his original submission:* **proposal**, suggestion, proposition, recommendation. **6** *the judge rejected his submission:* **argument**, assertion, contention, statement, claim, allegation.
– OPPOSITES defiance, resistance.

submissive adjective **compliant**, yielding, acquiescent, passive, obedient, dutiful, docile, pliant; informal under someone's thumb.

submit verb **1** *she was forced to submit:* **give in/way**, yield, back down, cave in, capitulate; surrender. **2** *he refused to submit to their authority:* **be governed by**, abide by, comply with, accept, adhere to, be subject to, agree to, consent to, conform to. **3** *we submitted an application:* **put forward**, present, offer, tender, propose, suggest; put in, send in, register. **4** *they submitted that the judgement was incorrect:* **contend**, assert, argue, state, claim, posit.
– OPPOSITES resist, withdraw.

subordinate adjective **lower-ranking**, junior, lower, supporting.
– OPPOSITES senior.
• noun **junior**, assistant, second in command, number two, deputy, aide, underling, minion.
– OPPOSITES superior.

subscribe verb *I can't subscribe to that theory:* **agree with**, accept, go along with, endorse, support; formal accede to.

S

subscriber noun **reader**, member, patron; customer, consumer, client, user.

subscription noun **1** *the club's subscription:* **membership fee**, dues, annual payment, charge. **2** *their subscription to capitalism:* **agreement**, belief, endorsement, backing, support.

subsequent adjective **following**, ensuing, succeeding, later, future, coming, to come, next.
– OPPOSITES previous.

subsequently adverb **later**, at a later date, afterwards, in due course, following this/that, eventually; formal thereafter.

subservient adjective **1** *subservient women:* **submissive**, deferential, compliant, obedient, dutiful, docile, passive, subdued, downtrodden; informal under someone's thumb. **2** *individual rights are subservient to the interests of the state:* **subordinate**, secondary, subsidiary.
– OPPOSITES independent.

subside verb **1** *wait until the storm subsides:* **abate**, let up, quieten down, calm, slacken off, ease, relent, die down, diminish, decline, dwindle, fade, wane, ebb. **2** *the flood waters have subsided:* **recede**, ebb, fall, go down, abate. **3** *the house is gradually subsiding:* **sink**, settle, cave in, collapse, give way.
– OPPOSITES intensify, rise.

subsidiary adjective **subordinate**, secondary, ancillary, auxiliary, subservient, supplementary, peripheral.
– OPPOSITES principal.
• noun **branch**, division, subdivision, derivative, offshoot.

subsidize verb **give money to**, contribute to, invest in, sponsor, support, fund, finance, underwrite; informal shell out for, fork out for, cough up for; N. Amer. informal bankroll.

subsidy noun **grant**, allowance, contribution, handout; backing, support, sponsorship, finance, funding.

subsist verb **survive**, live, stay alive, exist, eke out an existence/living; support yourself, manage, get by, make ends meet.

subsistence noun **survival**, existence, living, life, sustenance, nourishment.

substance noun **1** *organic substances:* **material**, compound; matter, stuff. **2** *ghostly figures with no substance:* **solidity**, body; density, mass, weight. **3** *none of the objections have any substance:* **meaningfulness**, significance, importance, import, validity, foundation. **4** *the substance of the tale is very thin:* **content**, subject matter, theme, message, essence. **5** *men of substance:* **wealth**, fortune, riches, affluence, prosperity, money, means.

substandard adjective **inferior**, second-rate, poor, below par, imperfect, faulty, defective, shoddy, shabby, unsound, unsatisfactory; informal tenth-rate, crummy, lousy; Brit. informal duff.

substantial adjective **1** *substantial progress had been made:* **considerable**, real, significant, important, major, valuable, useful. **2** *substantial damages:* **sizeable**, considerable, significant, large, ample, appreciable. **3** *substantial Victorian villas:* **sturdy**, solid, stout, strong, well built, durable, long-lasting, hard-wearing. **4** *substantial agreement:* **fundamental**, essential, basic.

substantially adverb **1** *the cost has fallen substantially:* **considerably**, significantly, to a great/large extent, greatly, markedly, appreciably. **2** *the draft was substantially accepted:* **largely**, for the most part, by and large, on the whole, in the main, mainly, in essence, basically, fundamentally, to all intents and purposes.
–OPPOSITES slightly.

substantiate verb **prove**, show to be true, support, justify, vindicate, validate, corroborate, verify, authenticate, confirm.
–OPPOSITES disprove.

substitute noun *substitutes for permanent employees:* **replacement**, deputy, relief, proxy, reserve, surrogate, cover, stand-in, understudy; informal sub.
•adjective *a substitute teacher:* **acting**, replacement, deputy, relief, reserve, surrogate, stand-in.
–OPPOSITES permanent.
•verb **1** *curd cheese can be substituted for yogurt:* **exchange**, replace, switch, swap, change, interchange. **2** *the Senate was empowered to substitute for the President:* **deputize**, stand in, cover.

substitution noun **exchange**, change; replacement, replacing.

subterfuge noun **1** *the use of subterfuge by journalists:* **trickery**, intrigue, deviousness, deceit, deception, dishonesty, cheating, duplicity, guile, cunning, craftiness, chicanery, pretence, fraud, fraudulence. **2** *a disreputable subterfuge:* **trick**, hoax, ruse, wile, ploy, stratagem, artifice, dodge, bluff, pretence, deception; informal con, scam.

subtle adjective **1** *a subtle distinction:* **fine**, fine-drawn, precise, nice; nuanced. **2** *subtle colours | subtle lighting:* **understated**, muted, unobtrusive, discreet, subdued, restrained, low-key; delicate, faint, pale, soft. **3** *he tried a more subtle approach:* **indirect**, oblique, discreet, delicate, tactful, sensitive, low-key, softly-softly.

subtlety noun **delicacy**; understatedness, mutedness, softness.

subtract verb **take away/off**, deduct, debit, dock; informal knock off, minus.
–OPPOSITES add.

suburb noun **residential area**, commuter belt; suburbia.

suburban adjective **1** *a suburban area:* **residential**, commuter. **2** *her drab suburban existence:* **dull**, boring, uninteresting, conventional, ordinary, commonplace, unremarkable, unexceptional; bourgeois, middle-class.

subversive adjective **disruptive**, troublemaking, insurrectionary; seditious, dissident.

subvert verb **1** *a plot to subvert the state:* **destabilize**, unsettle, overthrow, overturn; bring down, topple; disrupt, wreak havoc on, sabotage, ruin, undermine, weaken, damage. **2** *attempts to subvert Soviet youth:* **corrupt**, pervert, deprave, contaminate, poison.

subway noun **1** *he walked through the subway:* **underpass**. **2** *Tokyo's subway:* **underground**, metro; Brit. trademark tube.

succeed verb **1** *their plan succeeded:* **be successful**, work; informal come off, pay off. **2** *the skills you need to succeed:* **triumph**, do well, thrive, prosper; informal make it, make the grade, make a name for yourself. **3** *he succeeded Gladstone as Prime Minister:* **replace**, take over from, follow, supersede.
–OPPOSITES fail, precede.

succeeding adjective **subsequent**, successive, following, ensuing, later, future, coming.

success noun **1** *the success of the scheme:* **favourable outcome**, successfulness, triumph. **2** *the trappings of success:* **prosperity**,

affluence, wealth, riches, opulence. **3** *a box-office success:* **triumph**, best-seller, sell-out; informal hit, smash, winner.
–OPPOSITES failure.

successful adjective **1** *a successful designer:* **prosperous**, affluent, wealthy, rich; famous, eminent, top; respected. **2** *successful companies:* **flourishing**, thriving, booming, buoyant, doing well, profitable, moneymaking, lucrative.

succession noun **1** *a succession of exciting events:* **sequence**, series, progression, chain, string, train, line, run. **2** *his succession to the throne:* **accession**.
■ **in succession** one after the other, in a row, consecutively, successively, in sequence; running; informal on the trot.

successive adjective **consecutive**, in a row, sequential, in succession, running; informal on the trot.

successor noun **heir**, inheritor, next-in-line.
–OPPOSITES predecessor.

succinct adjective **concise**, short, short and sweet, brief, compact, condensed, crisp, laconic, terse, to the point, pithy.
–OPPOSITES verbose.

succour noun **aid**, help, a helping hand, assistance; comfort, ease, relief, support.

succulent adjective **juicy**, moist, luscious, soft, tender; choice, mouth-watering, appetizing, flavour-some, tasty, delicious; informal scrumptious, scrummy.
–OPPOSITES dry.

S

succumb verb **1** *she finally succumbed to temptation:* **yield**, give in/way, submit, surrender, capitulate, cave in. **2** *he succumbed to the disease:* **die from/of**.
–OPPOSITES resist.

suck verb **1** *they sucked orange juice through straws:* **sip**, sup, siphon, slurp, draw, drink. **2** *Fran sucked in a deep breath:* **draw**, pull, breathe, gasp. **3** *they got sucked into crime:* **involve in**, draw into; informal mix up in.
■ **suck up to** (informal) grovel, creep, kowtow, bow and scrape; fawn on; informal lick someone's boots.

suckle verb **breastfeed**, feed, nurse.

sudden adjective **unexpected**, unforeseen; immediate, instantaneous, instant, precipitous, abrupt, rapid, swift, quick.

suddenly adverb **all of a sudden**, all at once, abruptly, swiftly; unexpectedly, without warning, out of the blue.
–OPPOSITES gradually.

suds plural noun **lather**, foam, froth, bubbles, soap.

sue verb **1** *he sued for negligence:* **take legal action**, take to court. **2** *the rebels were forced to sue for peace:* **appeal**, petition, ask; solicit, request, seek.

suffer verb **1** *I hate to see him suffer:* **hurt**, ache, be in pain; be in distress, be upset, be miserable. **2** *he suffers from asthma:* **be afflicted by**, be affected by, be troubled with, have. **3** *England suffered a humiliating defeat:* **undergo**, experience, be subjected to, receive, endure, face. **4** *our reputation has suffered:* **be impaired**, be damaged, decline.

suffering noun **hardship**, distress, misery, wretchedness, adversity; pain, agony, anguish, trauma, torment, torture, hurt, affliction, sadness, unhappiness, sorrow, grief, woe, angst, heartache, heartbreak, stress.
–OPPOSITES pleasure, joy.

suffice verb **be enough**, be sufficient, be adequate, do.

sufficient adjective & determiner **enough**, adequate, plenty of, ample.
–OPPOSITES insufficient, inadequate.

suffocate verb **1** *she suffocated her baby:* **smother**, asphyxiate, stifle; choke. **2** *she was suffocating in the heat:* **be breathless**, be short of air, struggle for air; be too hot, swelter; informal roast, bake, boil.

suffrage noun **franchise**, the vote, enfranchisement, ballot.

suffuse verb **permeate**, spread over, cover, bathe, pervade, wash, saturate, imbue.

suggest verb **1** *they suggested Mumbai as a possible venue:* **propose**, put forward, recommend, advocate; advise. **2** *evidence suggests that voters are unhappy:* **indicate**, lead to the belief, demonstrate, show; argue. **3** *what exactly are you suggesting?* **hint**, insinuate, imply, intimate.

suggestion noun **1** *some suggestions for tackling this problem:* **proposal**, proposition, recommendation; advice, counsel, hint, tip, clue, idea. **2** *the suggestion of a smirk:* **hint**, trace, touch, suspicion; ghost, semblance, shadow, glimmer. **3** *a suggestion that he knew about the plot:* **insinuation**, hint, implication.

suggestive adjective **1** *suggestive remarks:* **indecent**, indelicate, improper, unseemly, sexual, sexy, smutty, dirty. **2** *an odour suggestive of a brewery:* **redolent**, evocative, reminiscent; characteristic, indicative, typical.

suit noun **1** *a pinstriped suit:* **outfit**, ensemble, costume. **2** *a medical malpractice suit:* **legal action**, lawsuit, court case, action, legal/judicial proceedings, litigation.
• verb **1** *blue really suits you:* **look attractive on**, look good on, become, flatter. **2** *savings schemes to suit all pockets:* **be convenient for**, be suitable for, meet the requirements of; informal fit.

suitable adjective **1** *suitable employment:* **acceptable**, satisfactory, fitting; informal right up someone's street. **2** *a drama suitable for all ages:* **appropriate**, fitting, fit, acceptable, right. **3** *music suitable for a dinner party:* **appropriate**, suited, befitting, in keeping with. **4** *they treated him with suitable respect:* **proper**, seemly, decent, appropriate, fitting, correct, due.
– OPPOSITES unsuitable, inappropriate.

suitcase noun **bag**, case, valise, portmanteau; (**suitcases**) luggage, baggage.

suite noun **apartment**, flat, rooms.

suited adjective *a course suited to anyone interested in interior design:* **appropriate**, suitable, right; tailored, adapted, designed, geared, oriented.

suitor noun **admirer**, boyfriend, sweetheart, lover; dated beau; literary swain.

sulk verb **mope**, brood, be in a bad mood, be in a huff.
• noun **mood**, fit of pique, pet, huff.

sulky adjective **sullen**, surly, moody; petulant, disgruntled, put out; bad-tempered, grumpy.
– OPPOSITES cheerful.

sullen adjective **surly**, sulky, morose, resentful, moody, grumpy, bad-tempered; uncommunicative.
– OPPOSITES cheerful.

sully verb **taint**, defile, soil, tarnish, stain, blemish, pollute, spoil, mar; literary besmirch.

sultry adjective **1** *a sultry day:* **humid**, close, airless, stifling, oppressive, muggy, sticky, sweltering, tropical, heavy; hot; informal boiling, roasting. **2** *a sultry film star:* **passionate**, sensual, sexy, seductive.

sum noun **1** *a large sum of money:* **amount**, quantity. **2** *the sum of two numbers:* **total**, sum total, grand total, aggregate, tally, reckoning. **3** *the sum of his wisdom:* **entirety**, totality, total, whole, beginning and end.
■ **sum something up** summarize, give a summary of, precis, outline, recapitulate, review, put in a nutshell, encapsulate; informal recap.

summarily adverb **immediately**, instantly, right away, straight away, at once, on the spot, promptly; speedily, swiftly, rapidly, without delay; arbitrarily, without formality, peremptorily.

summarize verb **sum up**, abridge, condense, encapsulate, outline, put in a nutshell, recapitulate, give a synopsis of, precis, give a résumé of; informal recap.

summary noun *a summary of the findings:* **synopsis**, precis, résumé, abstract; outline, rundown, summing-up, overview, recapitulation; informal recap.
• adjective **1** *a summary financial statement:* **abridged**, abbreviated, shortened, condensed, concise, short. **2** *summary execution:* **immediate**, instant, instantaneous, on-the-spot; arbitrary, peremptory.

summer noun

> **WORD LINKS**
> **aestival** relating to summer

summer house noun **gazebo**, pavilion, belvedere; literary bower.

summit noun **1** *the summit of Mont Blanc:* **top**, peak, crest, crown, pinnacle, apex, tip, cap, hilltop. **2** *the next superpower summit:* **meeting**, conference, talks.
– OPPOSITES foot, base.

S

summon verb **1** *he was summoned to the Embassy:* **send for**, call for, request the presence of; ask, invite. **2** *they were summoned as witnesses:* **summons**, subpoena. **3** *he summoned the courage to move closer:* **muster**, gather, collect, rally, screw up. **4** *they summoned an evil spirit:* **conjure up**, call up, invoke.

summons noun **writ**, subpoena, warrant, court order.
• verb **serve with a summons**, summon, subpoena.

sumptuous adjective **lavish**, luxurious, opulent, magnificent, resplendent, gorgeous, splendid, grand, palatial, rich; informal plush, ritzy; Brit. informal swish.
– OPPOSITES plain.

sun noun **sunshine**, sunlight, daylight, light, warmth; beams, rays.

WORD LINKS
solar relating to the sun

sunbathe verb **sun yourself**, bask, get a tan, tan yourself; informal catch some rays.

sunburnt adjective **1** *his sunburnt shoulders:* **burnt**, sunburned, red, pink. **2** *a handsome sunburnt face:* **tanned**, suntanned, brown, bronzed.
– OPPOSITES pale.

Sunday noun **the Sabbath**.

sundry adjective **various**, varied, miscellaneous, assorted, mixed, diverse, diversified; several, numerous, many, manifold, multifarious, multitudinous; literary divers.

sunken adjective **hollowed**, hollow, depressed, deep-set, concave, indented, inset.

S

sunless adjective **dark**, overcast, cloudy, grey, gloomy, dismal, murky, dull; shady, shadowy.

sunny adjective **1** *a sunny day:* **bright**, sunlit, clear, fine, cloudless. **2** *a sunny disposition:* **cheerful**, cheery, happy, bright, merry, joyful, bubbly, jolly, jovial, animated, buoyant, ebullient, upbeat, vivacious.
– OPPOSITES dull, miserable.

sunrise noun **dawn**, daybreak, break of day, first light, cockcrow; N. Amer. sunup.

sunset noun **nightfall**, twilight, dusk, evening; N. Amer. sundown; literary gloaming.

super adjective (informal) **excellent**, superb, superlative, first-class, outstanding, marvellous, magnificent, wonderful, splendid, glorious; informal great, fantastic, fabulous, terrific, ace, divine, wicked, cool; Brit. informal smashing, brilliant, brill.
– OPPOSITES rotten.

superannuated adjective **1** *a superannuated civil servant:* **pensioned off**, retired; elderly, old. **2** *superannuated computing equipment:* **old**, old-fashioned, antiquated, out of date, outmoded, broken-down, obsolete, disused, defunct; informal clapped out.

superb adjective **1** *a superb goal:* **excellent**, superlative, first-rate, first-class, outstanding, marvellous, magnificent, wonderful, splendid, admirable, fine, exquisite, exceptional, glorious; informal great, fantastic, fabulous, terrific, super, awesome, ace, A1; Brit. informal brilliant, brill, smashing. **2** *a superb house:* **magnificent**, splendid, grand, impressive, imposing, awe-inspiring, breathtaking; gorgeous, beautiful.
– OPPOSITES poor, inferior.

supercilious adjective **arrogant**, haughty, conceited, disdainful, overbearing, pompous, condescending, superior, patronizing, imperious, proud, snobbish, smug, scornful, sneering; informal high and mighty, snooty, stuck-up, snotty.

superficial adjective **1** *superficial burns:* **surface**, exterior, external, outer; slight. **2** *a superficial relationship:* **shallow**, artificial; empty, hollow, meaningless. **3** *a superficial investigation:* **cursory**, perfunctory, casual, sketchy, desultory, token, slapdash, offhand, rushed, hasty, hurried. **4** *a superficial resemblance:* **apparent**, seeming, outward, ostensible, cosmetic, slight. **5** *a superficial biography:* **trivial**, lightweight. **6** *a superficial person:* **facile**, shallow, flippant, empty-headed, trivial, frivolous, silly, inane.
– OPPOSITES deep, thorough.

superficially adverb **apparently**, seemingly, ostensibly, outwardly, on the surface, on the face of it, to all intents and purposes, at first glance, to the casual observer.

superfluity noun **surplus**, excess, over-abundance, glut, surfeit, profusion, plethora.
– OPPOSITES shortage.

superfluous adjective **surplus**, redundant, unneeded, excess, extra, spare, remaining, unused, left over, in excess, waste.
– OPPOSITES essential, necessary.

superhuman adjective **1** *a superhuman effort:* **extraordinary**, phenomenal, prodigious, stupendous, exceptional, immense, heroic. **2** *superhuman powers:* **supernatural**, preternatural, paranormal, other-worldly, unearthly.
– OPPOSITES mundane.

superintend verb **supervise**, oversee, be in charge of, be in control of, preside over, direct, administer, manage, run, be responsible for.

superintendent noun **manager**, director, administrator, supervisor, overseer, controller, chief, head, governor; informal boss.

superior adjective **1** *a superior officer:* **higher-ranking**, higher-level, senior, higher. **2** *the superior candidate:* **better**; worthier, fitter, preferred. **3** *superior workmanship:* **finer**, better, higher-grade; accomplished, expert. **4** *superior chocolate:* **top-quality**; choice, select, exclusive, prime, prize, fine, excellent, best, choicest, finest. **5** *a superior smile:* **condescending**, supercilious, patronizing, haughty, disdainful; informal high and mighty.
– OPPOSITES junior, inferior.
• noun *my immediate superior:* **manager**, chief, supervisor, senior, controller, foreman; informal boss.
– OPPOSITES subordinate.

superiority noun **supremacy**, advantage, lead, dominance, primacy, ascendancy, eminence.

superlative adjective **excellent**, magnificent, wonderful, marvellous, supreme, consummate, outstanding, remarkable, first-rate, first-class, premier, prime, unsurpassed, unequalled, unparalleled, unrivalled, pre-eminent; informal crack, ace, wicked; Brit. informal brilliant.
– OPPOSITES mediocre.

supernatural adjective **1** *supernatural powers:* **paranormal**, psychic, magic, magical, occult, mystic, mystical, superhuman. **2** *a supernatural being:* **ghostly**, phantom, spectral, other-worldly, unearthly.

supersede verb **replace**, take the place of, take over from, succeed; supplant, displace, oust, overthrow, remove, unseat.

superstition noun **myth**, belief, old wives' tale.

supervise verb **1** *he had to supervise the work of two committees:* **superintend**, oversee, be in charge of, preside over, direct, manage, run, look after, be responsible for, govern, organize, handle. **2** *you may need to supervise her:* **watch**, oversee, keep an eye on, observe, monitor, mind.

supervision noun **1** *the supervision of the banking system:* **administration**, management, control, charge; regulation, government, governance. **2** *keep your children under supervision:* **observation**, guidance, custody, charge, safe keeping, care, guardianship; control.

supervisor noun **manager**, director, overseer, controller, superintendent, governor, chief, head; steward, foreman; informal boss; Brit. informal gaffer.

supine adjective **1** *she lay supine on the sand:* **flat on your back**, face up, flat, stretched out. **2** *a supine media:* **weak**, spineless; docile, acquiescent, submissive, passive.
– OPPOSITES prostrate, strong.

supper noun **dinner**, evening meal; snack, bite to eat.

supplant verb **1** *the technology was not intended to supplant human labour:* **replace**, supersede, displace, take over from. **2** *the man he supplanted as Prime Minister:* **oust**, usurp, overthrow, remove, topple, unseat, depose, dethrone; succeed.

supple adjective **1** *her supple body:* **lithe**, limber, lissom, willowy, flexible, loose-limbed, agile, acrobatic, nimble, double-jointed. **2** *supple leather:* **pliant**, pliable, flexible, soft, bendy, workable, stretchy, springy.
– OPPOSITES stiff, rigid.

supplement noun **1** *a dietary supplement:* **extra**, add-on, accessory, adjunct. **2** *a single room supplement:* **surcharge**, addition, increase. **3** *a supplement to the essay:* **appendix**, addendum, postscript, addition, coda. **4** *a special supplement with today's paper:* **pull-out**, insert.
• verb *he supplemented his income by teaching:* **augment**, increase, add to, boost, swell, amplify, enlarge, top up.

supplementary adjective **additional**, supplemental, extra, more, further; add-on, subsidiary, auxiliary, ancillary.

supply verb **1** *they supplied money to the rebels:* **give**, contribute, provide, furnish, donate, bestow, grant, endow, impart; dispense, disburse, allocate, assign; informal fork out, shell out. **2** *the lake supplies the city with water:* **provide**, furnish, endow, serve, confer; equip, arm. **3** *windmills supply their power needs:* **satisfy**, meet, fulfil, cater for.
• noun **1** *a limited supply of food:* **stock**, store, reserve, reservoir, stockpile, hoard, cache; fund, bank. **2** *the supply of alcoholic liquor:* **provision**, dissemination, distribution, serving. **3** *go to the supermarket for supplies:* **provisions**, stores, rations, food, necessities; informal eats; formal comestibles.
• adjective *a supply teacher:* **substitute**, stand-in, fill-in, locum, temporary, stopgap.

support verb **1** *a roof supported by pillars:* **hold up**, bear, carry, prop up, keep up, brace, shore up, underpin, buttress, reinforce. **2** *he struggled to support his family:* **provide for**, maintain, sustain, keep, take care of, look after. **3** *she supported him to the end:* **stand by**, defend, back, stand/stick up for. **4** *a proposal supported by most of the delegates:* **back**, champion, advocate, recommend, promote, favour, subscribe to, espouse; vote for, stand behind, sponsor, second, endorse, sanction; informal throw your weight behind. **5** *these studies support our findings:* **substantiate**, back up, bolster, bear out, corroborate, confirm, attest to, verify, prove, validate, authenticate, endorse, ratify. **6** *the money supports charitable projects:* **help**, aid, assist; contribute to, back, subsidize, fund, finance; N. Amer. informal bankroll.
– OPPOSITES contradict, oppose.
• noun **1** *bridge supports:* **pillar**, post, prop, upright, brace, buttress; substructure, foundation, underpinning. **2** *I was lucky to have their support:* **encouragement**, friendship, backing, help, assistance, protection, patronage; approval, endorsement. **3** *he was a great support for me:* **tower of strength**, rock, prop, mainstay, bulwark. **4** *thank you for your generous support:* **contributions**, backing, donations, money, subsidy, funding, funds.

S

supporter noun **1** *supporters of gun control:* **advocate**, backer, adherent, promoter, champion, defender, upholder, proponent, campaigner, apologist. **2** *Labour supporters:* **backer**, helper, adherent, follower, voter, disciple; member. **3** *the charity relies on its supporters:* **contributor**, donor, benefactor, sponsor, backer, patron, subscriber, well-wisher. **4** *the team's supporters:* **fan**, follower, enthusiast, devotee, admirer; informal buff, addict.

supportive adjective **encouraging**, caring, sympathetic, reassuring, understanding, concerned, helpful.

suppose verb **1** *I suppose he's used to it by now:* **assume**, presume, expect, dare say, take it; guess. **2** *suppose you had a spacecraft:* **assume**, imagine, say; hypothesize, theorize, speculate.

supposed adjective **1** *the supposed phenomena:* **alleged**, putative, reputed, rumoured, claimed, purported. **2** *I'm supposed to meet him at 8.30:* **meant**, intended, expected; required, obliged.

supposition noun **belief**, surmise, idea, notion, conjecture, speculation, inference, theory, hypothesis, guess work, feeling, assumption, presumption.

suppress verb **1** *they will suppress any criticism:* **subdue**, repress, crush, quell, quash, squash, stamp out; put down, crack down on. **2** *she suppressed her irritation:* **conceal**, restrain, stifle, smother, check,

curb, contain, keep a rein on, put a lid on. **3** *the report was suppressed:* **censor**, keep secret, conceal, hide, hush up, gag, withhold, cover up, stifle; sweep under the carpet.
– OPPOSITES incite, reveal.

suppurate verb **fester**, discharge, run, weep.

supremacy noun **ascendancy**, predominance, primacy, dominion, hegemony, authority, mastery, control, power, rule, sovereignty; dominance, superiority, the upper hand, the whip hand, the edge.

supreme adjective **1** *the supreme commander:* **highest**, chief, head, top, foremost, principal, superior, premier, first, prime. **2** *a supreme achievement:* **extraordinary**, remarkable, incredible, phenomenal, exceptional, outstanding, great, incomparable, unparalleled, peerless. **3** *the supreme sacrifice:* **ultimate**, final, last; utmost, extreme, greatest, highest.
– OPPOSITES subordinate, insignificant.

sure adjective **1** *I'm sure they knew:* **certain**, positive, convinced, confident, definite, satisfied, persuaded. **2** *someone was sure to find out:* **bound**; likely, destined, fated. **3** *a sure sign of spring:* **reliable**, definite, dependable, unfailing, infallible, certain, true, foolproof, established, guaranteed, unerring, proven; informal sure-fire. **4** *the sure hand of the surgeon:* **firm**, steady, steadfast, unfaltering, unwavering.
– OPPOSITES uncertain, unsure, unlikely.
■ **for sure** (informal) definitely, surely, certainly, without doubt, without question, undoubtedly, indubitably, absolutely, undeniably, unmistakably. **make sure** check, confirm, make certain, ensure, assure; verify, corroborate, substantiate.

surety noun **1** *she's a surety for his debts:* **guarantor**, sponsor. **2** *bail of £10,000 with a further £10,000 surety:* **pledge**, collateral, guarantee, bond, assurance, insurance, deposit; security, indemnity.

surface noun *the surface of the wall:* **outside**, exterior; top, side; finish, veneer.
– OPPOSITES inside, interior.
• adjective *surface appearances can be deceptive:* **superficial**, external, exterior, outward, ostensible, apparent, cosmetic.
– OPPOSITES underlying.
• verb *problems began to surface two years ago:* **emerge**, arise, appear, come to light, crop up, materialize, spring up.
■ **on the surface** at first glance, to the casual eye, outwardly, to all appearances, apparently, ostensibly, superficially, externally.

surfeit noun **excess**, surplus, abundance, oversupply, superabundance, superfluity, glut; overdose; too much; informal **bellyful**.
– OPPOSITES lack.

surge noun **1** *a surge of water:* **gush**, rush, outpouring, stream, flow. **2** *a surge in demand:* **increase**, rise, growth, upswing, upsurge, escalation, leap. **3** *a sudden surge of anger:* **rush**, storm, torrent, blaze, outburst, eruption.
• verb **1** *the water surged into people's homes:* **gush**, rush, stream, flow, burst, pour, cascade, spill, sweep, roll. **2** *the Dow Jones index surged 47.63 points:* **increase**, rise, grow, leap.

surly adjective **sullen**, sulky, moody, unfriendly, unpleasant, scowling, unsmiling; bad-tempered, grumpy; gruff, churlish, ill-humoured.
– OPPOSITES pleasant.

surmise verb **guess**, conjecture, suspect, deduce, infer, conclude, theorize, speculate, divine; assume, presume, suppose, understand, gather.

surmount verb **1** *he has surmounted many obstacles:* **overcome**, prevail over, triumph over, beat; clear, cross; literary vanquish. **2** *they surmounted the ridge:* **climb over**, top, ascend, scale, mount. **3** *the dome is surmounted by a statue:* **cap**, top, crown, finish.
– OPPOSITES descend.

surname noun **family name**, last name, second name.

surpass verb **excel**, exceed, transcend; outdo, outshine, outstrip, outclass, eclipse; improve on, top, trump, cap, beat, better, outperform.

surplus noun **excess**, surfeit,

superabundance, superfluity, oversupply, glut; remainder, residue, remains, leftovers.
–OPPOSITES dearth.
•adjective **excess**, leftover, unused, remaining, extra, additional, spare; superfluous, redundant, unwanted, unneeded, dispensable, expendable.
–OPPOSITES insufficient.

surprise noun **1** *Kate looked at me in surprise:* **astonishment**, amazement, wonder, bewilderment, disbelief. **2** *the test came as a big surprise:* **shock**, bolt from the blue, bombshell, revelation, rude awakening, eye-opener; informal turn up for the books.
•verb **1** *I was surprised by his statement:* **astonish**, amaze, startle, astound, stun, stagger, shock; leave open-mouthed, take aback, shake; informal bowl over, floor, flabbergast; Brit. informal knock for six. **2** *she surprised a burglar:* **take by surprise**, catch unawares, catch off guard, catch red-handed.

surprised adjective **astonished**, amazed, astounded, startled, stunned, staggered, nonplussed, shocked, taken aback, dumbfounded, speechless, thunderstruck; informal bowled over, flabbergasted, floored, flummoxed.

surprising adjective **unexpected**, unforeseen; astonishing, amazing, startling, astounding, staggering, incredible, extraordinary, breathtaking, remarkable; informal mind-blowing.

surrender verb **1** *the gunmen surrendered:* **capitulate**, give in, give yourself up, concede defeat, submit, back down, crumble; lay down your arms. **2** *they surrendered power to the government:* **give up**, relinquish, renounce, forswear; cede, abdicate, waive, forfeit, sacrifice; hand over, turn over, yield, transfer, grant.
–OPPOSITES resist, seize.
•noun **1** *the surrender of the hijackers:* **capitulation**, submission, yielding, succumbing, acquiescence. **2** *a surrender of power to the shop floor:* **relinquishment**, renunciation, cession, abdication, resignation, transfer.

surreptitious adjective **secret**, secretive, stealthy, clandestine, sneaky, sly, furtive.
–OPPOSITES blatant.

surrogate noun **substitute**, proxy, replacement; deputy, representative, stand-in.

surround verb **encircle**, enclose, encompass, ring; fence in, hem in, confine, bound, circumscribe, cut off; besiege, trap.
•noun **border**, edging, edge, perimeter, boundary.

surrounding adjective **neighbouring**, nearby, near, local; adjoining, adjacent.

surroundings plural noun **environment**, setting, milieu, background, backdrop; vicinity, locality, habitat.

surveillance noun **observation**, scrutiny, watch, view, inspection, supervision; spying, espionage; informal bugging.

survey verb **1** *he surveyed his work:* **look at**, look over, view, contemplate, regard, gaze at, stare at, eye; scrutinize, examine, inspect, scan, study, consider, review, take stock of; informal size up. **2** *they surveyed 4000 drug users:* **interview**, question, canvass, poll, cross-examine, investigate, research, study. **3** *he was asked to survey the house:* **appraise**, assess, prospect; value.
•noun **1** *a survey of the current literature:* **study**, review, overview; examination, inspection, appraisal. **2** *a survey of sexual behaviour:* **poll**, review, investigation, inquiry, study, probe, questionnaire, census, research. **3** *a thorough survey of the property:* **appraisal**, assessment, valuation.

survive verb **1** *he survived by escaping through a hole:* **remain alive**, live, sustain yourself, pull through, hold out, make it. **2** *the theatre must survive:* **continue**, remain, persist, endure, live on, persevere, abide, go on, carry on. **3** *he was survived by his sons:* **outlive**, outlast.

susceptible adjective **1** *susceptible children:* **impressionable**, credulous, gullible, innocent, ingenuous, naive, easily led; defenceless, vulnerable. **2** *people susceptible to blackmail:* **open to**, vulnerable to; an easy target for.

3 *he is susceptible to ulcers:* **liable to**, prone to, subject to, inclined to, predisposed to, disposed to, given to.
– OPPOSITES sceptical, immune, resistant.

suspect verb **1** *I suspect she's made a mistake:* **think**, believe, have a feeling, feel, fancy, reckon, guess, surmise, conjecture, conclude, infer; fear. **2** *he had no reason to suspect me:* **doubt**, distrust, mistrust, have misgivings about, have qualms about, be suspicious of.
• adjective *a suspect package:* **suspicious**, dubious, doubtful, untrustworthy; informal fishy, funny; Brit. informal dodgy.

suspend verb **1** *the court case was suspended:* **adjourn**, interrupt, break off; cut short, discontinue; N. Amer. table. **2** *he was suspended from college:* **exclude**, debar, remove; expel, eject. **3** *lights were suspended from the ceiling:* **hang**, sling, string; swing, dangle.

suspense noun *I can't bear the suspense:* **tension**, uncertainty, doubt, anticipation, excitement, anxiety, strain.

suspension noun **1** *the suspension of army operations:* **adjournment**, interruption, postponement, deferral, deferment, stay; cessation, halt, stoppage. **2** *his suspension from school:* **exclusion**, debarment, removal; expulsion, ejection.

suspicion noun **1** *she had a suspicion that he didn't like her:* **intuition**, feeling, impression, inkling, hunch, fancy, notion, idea, theory; presentiment, premonition; informal gut feeling, sixth sense. **2** *I confronted him with my suspicions:* **misgiving**, doubt, qualm, reservation, hesitation, question.

suspicious adjective **1** *she gave him a suspicious look:* **doubtful**, sceptical, distrustful, mistrustful, dubious, disbelieving, unconvinced, cynical, unsure, wary, chary. **2** *a suspicious character:* **disreputable**, unsavoury, dubious, suspect; informal shifty, shady; Brit. informal dodgy. **3** *she disappeared in suspicious circumstances:* **questionable**, odd, strange, dubious, irregular, funny, doubtful, mysterious, murky; informal fishy; Brit. informal dodgy.
– OPPOSITES trusting, honest, innocent.

sustain verb **1** *her memories sustained her:* **comfort**, help, assist, encourage, support, give strength to, buoy up. **2** *they were unable to sustain a coalition:* **continue**, carry on, keep up, keep alive, maintain, preserve, perpetuate, retain. **3** *she had bread and cheese to sustain her:* **nourish**, feed, nurture; maintain, preserve, keep alive, keep going. **4** *she sustained slight injuries:* **undergo**, experience, suffer, endure. **5** *the allegation was not sustained:* **uphold**, validate, ratify, vindicate, confirm, endorse; verify, corroborate, substantiate, bear out, prove, authenticate, back up.

sustained adjective **continuous**, ongoing, steady, continual, constant, prolonged, persistent, non-stop, perpetual, relentless, incessant, unceasing, ceaseless, round the clock.
– OPPOSITES sporadic.

sustenance noun **nourishment**, food, nutrition, provisions, rations; informal grub, chow; Brit. informal scoff; literary viands; dated victuals.

swagger verb **strut**, parade, stride, breeze, waltz; walk confidently; informal sashay.

swallow verb **eat**, gulp down, consume, devour, put away; drink, guzzle, quaff, imbibe, sup, slug; informal polish off, swig, swill, down; Brit. informal scoff.
■ **swallow someone/something up** **1** *the darkness swallowed them up:* engulf, swamp, devour, overwhelm, overcome. **2** *the colleges were swallowed up by universities:* take over, engulf, absorb, assimilate, incorporate.

swamp noun *he got stuck in the swamp:* **marsh**, bog, quagmire; quicksand; N. Amer. bayou.
• verb **1** *the rain was swamping the boat:* **flood**, inundate, deluge, immerse. **2** *he was swamped by media attention:* **overwhelm**, inundate, flood, deluge, engulf, snow under, overload, overpower, weigh down, besiege, beset.

swampy adjective **marshy**, boggy; soft, soggy, muddy, spongy, heavy, squelchy, waterlogged, sodden, wet.

swap verb **1** *she swapped her house*

for a motorhome: **exchange**, switch, change, replace, substitute; trade, barter, interchange. **2** *we swapped jokes:* **bandy**, exchange, trade.
• noun *a job swap:* **exchange**, trade, switch, trade-off, substitution.

swarm noun **1** *a swarm of bees:* **hive**, flock, collection. **2** *swarms of screaming teenage fans:* **crowd**, multitude, horde, host, mob, throng, mass, army, troop, herd, pack.
• verb *protesters were swarming into the building:* **flock**, crowd, throng, surge, stream.
■ **be swarming with** be crowded with, be thronged with, be overrun with, be full of, be teeming with, bristle with, be alive with, be crawling with, be infested with, overflow with.

swarthy adjective **dark-skinned**, olive-skinned, dusky, tanned.
– OPPOSITES pale.

swashbuckling adjective **daring**, heroic, daredevil, dashing, adventurous, bold, valiant, fearless, devil-may-care.
– OPPOSITES timid.

swathe verb **wrap**, envelop, bind, swaddle, bandage, cover, shroud, drape, wind, enfold.

sway verb **1** *the curtains swayed in the breeze:* **swing**, shake, undulate, move to and fro, move back and forth. **2** *she swayed on her feet:* **stagger**, wobble, rock, lurch, reel, roll, list, stumble. **3** *we are swayed by the media:* **influence**, affect; manipulate, bend, mould.
• noun **1** *the sway of her hips:* **swing**, roll, shake, undulation. **2** *a province under the sway of the Franks:* **jurisdiction**, rule, government, sovereignty, dominion, control, command, power, authority.
■ **hold sway** hold/wield power, rule, be in control, predominate.

S

swear verb **1** *they swore to protect each other:* **promise**, vow, pledge, give your word, undertake, guarantee. **2** *she swore she would never go back:* **insist**, avow, pronounce, declare, proclaim, assert, profess, maintain, contend, emphasize, stress. **3** *Kate spilled her wine and swore:* **curse**, blaspheme, use bad language; informal cuss, eff and blind.
■ **swear by** (informal) believe in, have faith in, trust; set store by, value; informal rate.

swearing noun **bad language**, strong language, cursing, blaspheming; profanities, obscenities, curses, oaths, expletives, swear words; informal effing and blinding, four-letter words.

sweat noun *beads of sweat broke out on his forehead:* **perspiration**, moisture.
• verb **1** *she was sweating heavily:* **perspire**. **2** *I've sweated over this for six months:* **work**, labour, toil, slog, slave, work your fingers to the bone; informal graft.

> **WORD LINKS**
> **sudorific** relating to or causing sweating

sweaty adjective **perspiring**, sweating, clammy, sticky; moist, damp.

sweep verb **1** *I swept the crumbs off the table:* **brush**, clean, wipe, clear; dust. **2** *he was swept out to sea:* **carry**, pull, drag, tow. **3** *a limousine swept past:* **glide**, sail, breeze, speed, fly, zoom, whizz. **4** *riots swept the country:* **engulf**, overwhelm, overrun.
• noun **1** *an expansive sweep of his hand:* **gesture**, stroke, wave, movement. **2** *a long sweep of golden sand:* **expanse**, tract, stretch, extent. **3** *the whole sweep of human history:* **range**, span, scope, compass, reach, spread, ambit, extent.
■ **sweep something aside** disregard, ignore, take no notice of, dismiss, shrug off, brush aside.

sweeping adjective **1** *sweeping changes:* **extensive**, wide-ranging, global, broad, comprehensive, wholesale, thoroughgoing, thorough, far-reaching, across the board; radical, root-and-branch; informal wall-to-wall. **2** *sweeping statements:* **generalized**, general, broad; oversimplified, simplistic. **3** *sweeping, desolate moorlands:* **broad**, extensive, expansive, vast.
– OPPOSITES limited, specific.

sweet adjective **1** *sweet biscuits:* **sugary**, sweetened; sugared, honeyed, candied, glacé. **2** *the sweet scent of roses:* **fragrant**, aromatic, perfumed. **3** *her sweet voice:*

melodious, mellifluous, musical, tuneful, soft, dulcet, harmonious, silvery, honeyed, mellow, golden. **4** *life was still sweet:* **pleasant**, pleasing, agreeable, delightful, nice, satisfying, gratifying, good; informal lovely, great. **5** *she has a sweet nature:* **likeable**, appealing, engaging, amiable, pleasant, agreeable, nice, kind, thoughtful, considerate; charming, enchanting, captivating, delightful, lovely. **6** *a sweet little kitten:* **cute**, lovable, adorable, endearing, charming.

– OPPOSITES sour, savoury, disagreeable.

• **noun 1** *a bag of sweets:* **confectionery**, chocolate, bonbon, toffee; N. Amer. candy; informal sweetie. **2** *a delicious sweet for the guests:* **dessert**, pudding; Brit. informal afters, pud. **3** *happy birthday my sweet!* **dear**, darling, dearest, love, sweetheart, beloved, honey, pet, treasure, angel.

sweeten verb 1 *he chewed gum to sweeten his breath:* **freshen**, refresh, purify, deodorize. **2** (informal) *a bigger dividend to sweeten shareholders:* **mollify**, placate, soothe, soften up, pacify, appease, win over.

sweetheart noun 1 *you look lovely, sweetheart:* **darling**, dear, dearest, love, beloved, sweet; informal honey, sweetie, sugar, baby, babe, poppet. **2** *my high-school sweetheart:* **lover**, love, girlfriend, boyfriend; dated beau.

swell verb 1 *her ankle swelled up:* **puff up**, become swollen, become bloated, balloon, bulge, become distended. **2** *the population swelled:* **grow**, enlarge, increase, expand, rise, escalate, multiply, proliferate, snowball, mushroom. **3** *she swelled with pride:* **be filled**, be bursting, brim, overflow. **4** *the graduate scheme swelled entry numbers:* **increase**, enlarge, augment, boost, top up, step up, multiply. **5** *the low murmur swelled to a roar:* **intensify**, heighten, rise, escalate.

– OPPOSITES shrink, decrease.

• **noun 1** *a brief swell in demand:* **increase**, rise, surge, boost. **2** *a heavy swell on the sea:* **surge**, wave, roll.

– OPPOSITES decrease, dip.

swelling noun bump, lump, bulge, protuberance, protrusion, nodule, tumescence; boil, blister, bunion, carbuncle.

sweltering adjective hot, stifling, humid, sultry, sticky, muggy, close, stuffy; tropical, torrid, searing, blistering; informal boiling, baking, roasting, sizzling.

– OPPOSITES freezing.

swerve verb veer, deviate, diverge, weave, zigzag, change direction; Sailing tack.

swift adjective 1 *a swift response:* **rapid**, quick, fast, speedy, prompt, immediate, instant, instantaneous, sudden; abrupt, hasty, hurried, precipitate. **2** *a swift pace:* **fast**, rapid, quick, speedy, brisk, lively; informal nippy, supersonic.

– OPPOSITES slow, leisurely.

swill verb 1 (informal) *he was swilling pints:* **drink**, quaff, swallow, down, gulp, drain, sup, slurp, consume, slug; informal swig, knock back, put away; N. Amer. informal chug. **2** *he swilled out a glass:* **wash**, rinse, sluice, clean, flush.

• **noun** *swill for the pigs:* **pigswill**, mash, slops, scraps, refuse, scourings, leftovers.

swim verb 1 *they swam in the pool:* **bathe**, take a dip, splash around; float. **2** *his food was swimming in gravy:* **be saturated in**, be drenched in, be soaked in, be steeped in, be immersed in, be covered in, be full of.

swimmingly adverb (informal) **well**, smoothly, easily, effortlessly, like clockwork, without a hitch, as planned, to plan; informal like a dream.

swimsuit noun bathing suit, swimming trunks, bikini, tankini; Brit. bathing costume, swimming costume; informal cossie; Austral./NZ informal bathers.

swindle verb defraud, cheat, trick, dupe, deceive, fool, hoax, hoodwink, bamboozle; informal fleece, do, con, diddle, swizzle, rip off, take for a ride, pull a fast one on, put one over on; N. Amer. informal stiff, euchre; literary cozen.

• **noun fraud**, trick, deception, deceit, cheat, sham, artifice, ruse, dodge, racket; sharp practice; informal con, fiddle, diddle, rip-off, flimflam; N. Amer. informal bunco.

swindler noun **fraudster**, fraud, confidence trickster, cheat, rogue, charlatan, impostor, hoaxer; informal con man, con artist, shark, hustler, phoney, crook.

swing verb **1** *the sign swung in the wind:* **sway**, move back and forth, move to and fro, wave, rock. **2** *Helen swung the bottle:* **brandish**, wave, flourish, wield, shake, twirl. **3** *the road swings to the left:* **curve**, bend, veer, turn, bear, wind, twist, deviate, slew, head. **4** *the balance swung from one party to the other:* **change**, fluctuate, shift, alter, alternate, see-saw, yo-yo, vary.
•noun **1** *a swing of the pendulum:* **oscillation**, sway, wave. **2** *the swing to the Conservatives:* **change**, move; turnaround, turnabout, reversal. **3** *mood swings:* **fluctuation**, change, shift, variation, oscillation.

swingeing adjective (Brit.) **severe**, extreme, serious, substantial, drastic, harsh, punishing, excessive, heavy.
– OPPOSITES minor.

swipe verb (informal) **steal**, thieve, take, pilfer, purloin, snatch; informal filch, lift, snaffle, rob, nab; Brit. informal nick, pinch, whip.

swirl verb **whirl**, eddy, billow, spiral, circulate, revolve, spin, twist; flow, stream, surge, seethe.

switch noun **1** *the switch on top of the telephone:* **button**, lever, control. **2** *a switch from direct to indirect taxation:* **change**, move, shift, transition, transformation; reversal, turnaround, U-turn, changeover, transfer, conversion.
•verb **1** *he switched sides:* **change**, shift; informal chop and change. **2** *he managed to switch the envelopes:* **exchange**, swap, interchange, change round, rotate.
■ **switch something on** turn on, put on, activate, start, set going, set in motion, operate, initiate, actuate, initialize, energize. **switch something off** turn off, shut off, stop, cut, halt, deactivate.

swivel verb **turn**, rotate, revolve, pivot, swing; spin, twirl, whirl, wheel.

swollen adjective **distended**, enlarged, bulging, inflated, dilated, bloated, puffed up, puffy, tumescent; inflamed.

swoop verb **1** *pigeons swooped down after the grain:* **dive**, descend, pounce, plunge, pitch, nosedive; rush, dart, speed, zoom. **2** *police swooped on the flat:* **raid**, descend on; pounce on, attack; N. Amer. informal bust.

sword noun **blade**, foil, épée, cutlass, rapier, sabre, scimitar.
■ **cross swords** quarrel, disagree, dispute, wrangle, bicker, be at odds, be at loggerheads, lock horns; fight, contend; informal scrap.

sycophant noun **toady**, lickspittle, flatterer; informal bootlicker, yes-man, creep.

sycophantic adjective **obsequious**, servile, subservient, grovelling, toadying, fawning, ingratiating, unctuous; informal smarmy, bootlicking.

syllabus noun **curriculum**, course, programme of study; timetable, schedule.

symbol noun **1** *the lotus is the symbol of purity:* **emblem**, token, sign, representation, figure, image; metaphor, allegory. **2** *the chemical symbol for helium:* **sign**, character, mark, letter, ideogram. **3** *the Red Cross symbol:* **logo**, emblem, badge, stamp, trademark, crest, insignia, coat of arms, seal, device, monogram, hallmark, flag, motif.

symbolic adjective **1** *the Colosseum is symbolic of the Roman Empire:* **emblematic**, representative, typical, characteristic, symptomatic. **2** *symbolic poetry:* **figurative**, emblematic, metaphorical, allegorical, allusive, suggestive.
– OPPOSITES literal.

symbolize verb **represent**, stand for, be a sign of, exemplify; denote, signify, mean, indicate, convey, express, imply, suggest; embody, epitomize, encapsulate, personify.

symmetrical adjective **regular**, uniform, consistent; even, equal; balanced, proportional.

symmetry noun **regularity**, evenness, uniformity, consistency, conformity, correspondence, equality; balance, proportion.

sympathetic adjective **1** *talking to a sympathetic listener can help:* **compassionate**, caring, concerned, solicitous, understanding, sensitive, supportive, encouraging. **2** *the most sympathetic character in the book:*

likeable, pleasant, agreeable, congenial. **3** *I was sympathetic to his cause:* **in favour of**, in sympathy with, pro, on the side of, supportive of, encouraging of; favourably disposed to, receptive to.
–OPPOSITES unsympathetic, unfeeling, opposed.

sympathize verb **1** *I sympathized with her:* **pity**, feel sorry for, commiserate, offer condolences to, feel for, show concern; identify with, understand, relate to. **2** *they sympathize with the rebels:* **agree with**, support, be in favour of, favour, approve of, back, side with.

sympathizer noun **supporter**, backer, well-wisher, advocate, ally, partisan; collaborator.

sympathy noun **1** *her sympathy for the unemployed:* **compassion**, care, concern, solicitude; commiseration, pity. **2** *their sympathy with the Republicans:* **agreement**, favour, approval, approbation, support, encouragement, partiality; association, alignment, affiliation.
–OPPOSITES indifference, hostility.

symptom noun **1** *the symptoms of the disease:* **manifestation**, indication, indicator, mark, feature, trait. **2** *a symptom of the country's present turmoil:* **expression**, sign, indication, mark, token, manifestation; portent, warning, clue, hint; testimony, evidence, proof.

symptomatic adjective **indicative**, characteristic, suggestive, typical, representative, symbolic.

synopsis noun **summary**, precis, abstract, outline, rundown, round-up, abridgement.

synthesis noun **combination**, union, amalgam, blend, mixture, compound, fusion, composite, alloy.

synthetic adjective **artificial**, fake, imitation, mock, simulated, ersatz, substitute; pseudo, so-called; man-made, manufactured, fabricated; informal phoney, pretend.
–OPPOSITES natural.

system noun **1** *a system of canals:* **structure**, organization, arrangement, complex, network; informal set-up. **2** *a system for regulating sales:* **method**, methodology, technique, process, procedure, approach, practice; means, way, mode, framework; scheme, plan, policy, programme, regimen, formula, routine. **3** *there was no system in his work:* **order**, method, orderliness, planning, logic, routine. **4** *youngsters have no faith in the system:* **the establishment**, the administration, the authorities, the powers that be; bureaucracy, officialdom; the status quo.

systematic adjective **structured**, methodical, organized, orderly, planned, systematized, regular, routine, standardized, standard; logical, coherent, consistent; efficient, businesslike, practical.
–OPPOSITES disorganized.

Tt

tab noun **tag**, label, flap.

table noun **1** *he provides an excellent table:* **meal**, food, fare, menu, nourishment; informal spread, grub, chow, eats, nosh. **2** *the report has numerous tables:* **chart**, diagram, figure, graphic, graph, plan; list, tabulation.
• verb *she tabled a question in parliament:* **submit**, put forward, propose, suggest, move, lodge, file, introduce, air, moot.

tableau noun *she fixed her eyes on the central figure in the tableau:* **scene**, arrangement, grouping, group; picture, spectacle, image, vignette.

tablet noun **1** *a carved tablet:* **slab**, stone, panel, plaque, plate, sign. **2** *a headache tablet:* **pill**, capsule, lozenge, pastille, drop; informal tab. **3** *a tablet of soap:* **bar**, cake, slab, brick, block.

taboo noun *the taboo against healing on the sabbath:* **prohibition**, proscription, veto, interdict, ban.
• adjective *taboo language:* **forbidden**, prohibited, banned, proscribed, interdicted, outlawed, illegal, unlawful, off limits; unmentionable, unspeakable, unutterable; informal no go.
– OPPOSITES acceptable.

t

tabulate verb **chart**, arrange, order, organize, systematize, catalogue, list, index, classify, class, codify.

tacit adjective **implicit**, understood, implied, inferred, hinted, suggested; unspoken, unstated, unsaid, unexpressed, unvoiced; taken for granted, taken as read.
– OPPOSITES explicit.

taciturn adjective **untalkative**, uncommunicative, reticent, unforthcoming, quiet, secretive, tight-lipped, close-mouthed; silent, mute, dumb, inarticulate.
– OPPOSITES talkative.

tack noun **1** *tacks held the carpet down:* **pin**, nail, staple, rivet, stud. **2** *the brig bowled past on the opposite tack:* **heading**, bearing, course, track, path. **3** *the defender changed his tack:* **approach**, way, method; policy, procedure, technique, tactic, plan, strategy.
• verb **1** *a photo tacked to the wall:* **pin**, nail, staple, fix, fasten, attach, secure, affix. **2** *the dress was roughly tacked together:* **stitch**, baste, sew, bind. **3** *the yachts tacked back and forth:* **change course**, change direction, swerve, zigzag, veer. **4** *poems tacked on at the end of the book:* **add**, append, join, tag.

tackle noun **1** *fishing tackle:* **gear**, equipment, apparatus, kit, hardware; implements, instruments, accoutrements, paraphernalia, trappings; informal things, stuff, clobber. **2** *lifting tackle:* **pulleys**, gear, hoist, crane, winch. **3** *a tackle by the scrum half:* **interception**, challenge, block, attack.
• verb **1** *we must tackle the problems now:* **get to grips with**, address, get to work on, approach, take on, attend to, see to; deal with, take care of, handle, manage. **2** *I tackled Nina about it:* **confront**, speak to, interview, question, cross-examine. **3** *he tackled an intruder:* **confront**, face up to, take on, contend with, challenge; seize, grab, intercept, block, stop; bring down, floor, fell; informal have a go at. **4** *the winger was tackled:* **intercept**, challenge, block, stop, attack.

tacky[1] adjective *the paint was still tacky:* **sticky**, wet, gluey, viscous; informal gooey.

tacky[2] adjective *a tacky game show:*

tawdry, tasteless, kitsch, vulgar, crude, garish, gaudy, trashy, cheap; informal cheesy; Brit. informal naff.
– OPPOSITES tasteful.

tact noun **diplomacy**, sensitivity, understanding, thoughtfulness, consideration, delicacy, discretion, prudence, judiciousness, subtlety; informal savvy.

tactful adjective **diplomatic**, discreet, considerate, sensitive, understanding, thoughtful, delicate, judicious, subtle; informal savvy.

tactic noun **1** *a tax-saving tactic:* **strategy**, scheme, plan, manoeuvre; method, expedient, gambit, tack; device, trick, ploy, dodge, ruse, machination; informal wangle. **2** *our fleet's superior tactics:* **strategy**, policy, campaign, game plans, manoeuvres, logistics.

tactical adjective **calculated**, planned, strategic; prudent, politic, diplomatic, judicious, shrewd, cunning, artful.

tactless adjective **insensitive**, inconsiderate, thoughtless, indelicate, undiplomatic, impolitic, indiscreet, unsubtle, inept, gauche; blunt, frank, outspoken, abrupt, crude.

tag noun **1** *a price tag:* **label**, ticket, badge, mark, tab, sticker, docket. **2** *he gained a 'bad boy' tag:* **designation**, label, description, characterization, identity; nickname, name, epithet, title, sobriquet; informal handle, moniker; formal denomination, appellation.
• verb **1** *bottles tagged with coloured stickers:* **label**, mark, ticket, identify, flag, indicate. **2** *he is tagged as a 'thinking' actor:* **label**, class, categorize, characterize, designate, describe, identify, classify; mark, stamp, brand, pigeonhole, stereotype, typecast, compartmentalize, typify. **3** *a poem tagged on as an afterthought:* **add**, tack, join; attach, append. **4** *he was tagging along behind:* **follow**, trail; come after, shadow, dog; accompany, attend, escort; informal tail.

tail noun **1** *the tail of the queue:* **rear**, end, back, extremity; bottom. **2** *the tail of the hunting season:* **close**, end, conclusion.
– OPPOSITES head, front, start.
■ **turn tail** run away, flee, bolt, make off, take to your heels, cut and run, beat a retreat; informal scram, scarper.

WORD LINKS
caudal relating to an animal's tail

Don't confuse **tail** with **tale**, which means 'a story' (*a fairy tale*).

tailback noun **traffic jam**, queue, line; congestion.

tailor verb *services can be tailored to requirements:* **customize**, adapt, adjust, modify, change, convert, alter, attune, mould, gear, fit, cut, shape, tune.

taint noun *the taint of corruption:* **trace**, touch, suggestion, hint, tinge; stain, blot, stigma.
• verb **1** *the wilderness is tainted by pollution:* **contaminate**, pollute, adulterate, infect, blight, spoil, soil, ruin. **2** *fraudulent firms taint our firm's reputation:* **tarnish**, sully, blacken, stain, blot, stigmatize, mar, corrupt, defile, soil, damage, hurt.
– OPPOSITES clean, improve.

take verb **1** *she took his hand:* **get hold of**, lay hold of, grasp, grip, clasp, clutch, grab. **2** *he took an envelope from his pocket:* **remove**, pull, draw, withdraw, extract, fish. **3** *the passage is taken from my book:* **extract**, quote, cite, excerpt, derive, abstract, copy, cull. **4** *the priest took her home:* **escort**, accompany, help, assist, show, lead, guide, see, usher, convey. **5** *I'll take it back to London:* **bring**, carry, bear, transport, convey, move, transfer, shift, ferry; informal cart, tote. **6** *all the seats were taken:* **occupy**, use, utilize, fill, hold; reserve, engage; informal bag. **7** *someone's taken my car:* **steal**, remove, appropriate, make off with, pilfer, purloin; informal filch, swipe, snaffle; Brit. informal pinch, nick. **8** *the journey took six hours:* **last**, continue for, go on for, carry on for; require, call for, need, necessitate, entail, involve. **9** *I'll take the minutes:* **write**, note down, jot down, scribble, scrawl, record, register, document, minute. **10** *he decided to take the job:* **accept**, undertake. **11** *she took first prize:* **receive**, obtain, gain, get, acquire, collect, accept, be awarded; secure, come by, win, earn, pick up, carry

t

off; informal land, bag, net, scoop. **12** *I took the chance to postpone the trip:* **act on**, take advantage of, capitalize on, use, exploit, make the most of, leap at, jump at, pounce on, seize, grasp, grab, accept. **13** *he took great pleasure in painting:* **derive**, draw, acquire, obtain, get, gain, extract. **14** *she took his temperature:* **ascertain**, determine, establish, measure, find out, discover. **15** *Liz took the news badly:* **receive**, respond to, react to, meet, greet; deal with, cope with. **16** *I take it that you are hungry:* **assume**, presume, suppose, imagine, expect, reckon, gather, dare say, trust, surmise, deduce, guess, conjecture, fancy, suspect. **17** *do you take me for a fool?* **regard as**, consider to be, view as, see as, believe to be, reckon to be, imagine to be, deem to be. **18** *take four from the total:* **subtract**, deduct, remove; discount; informal knock off, minus. **19** *I can't take much more:* **endure**, bear, tolerate, stand, put up with, abide, stomach, accept, allow, countenance, support, shoulder; formal brook. **20** *many prisoners were taken:* **capture**, seize, catch, arrest, apprehend, take into custody; carry off, abduct. **21** *applicants must take an aptitude test:* **carry out**, do, complete, conduct, perform, execute, discharge, accomplish, fulfil. **22** *I take your point:* **understand**, grasp, get, comprehend, apprehend, see, follow; accept, appreciate, acknowledge. **23** *take, for instance, the English:* **consider**, contemplate, ponder, think about, weigh up, mull over, examine, study, meditate over, ruminate about. **24** *I'd take this over the other option:* **pick**, choose, select; prefer, favour, opt for, plump for, vote for.

–OPPOSITES give, add.

•**noun 1** *the whalers' take:* **catch**, haul, bag, yield, net. **2** *the state's tax take:* **revenue**, income, gain, profit; takings, proceeds, returns, receipts, winnings, pickings, earnings, spoils; purse. **3** *a wry take on gender issues:* **view of**, reading of, version of, interpretation of, understanding of, account of, analysis of, approach to.

■ **take after** resemble, look like; remind someone of, recall, conjure up, suggest, evoke; informal favour, be a chip off the old block, be the spitting image of. **take something apart** dismantle, pull to pieces, pull apart, disassemble, break up; tear down, demolish, destroy, wreck. **take something back 1** *I take back every word:* retract, withdraw, renounce, disclaim, unsay, disavow, recant, repudiate; formal abjure. **2** *I must take the keys back:* return, bring back, give back, restore. **take something down** write down, note down, jot down, set down, record, register, draft, document, minute, pen. **take someone in 1** *she took in paying guests:* accommodate, board, house, feed, put up. **2** *you were taken in by a hoax:* deceive, delude, hoodwink, mislead, trick, dupe, fool, cheat, defraud, swindle, outwit, gull, hoax, bamboozle; informal con, put one over on. **take something in 1** *she could hardly take in the news:* comprehend, understand, grasp, follow, absorb; informal get. **2** *this route takes in some great scenery:* include, encompass, embrace, contain, comprise, cover, incorporate, comprehend, hold. **take it out of someone** exhaust, drain, enervate, tire, fatigue, wear out, weary, debilitate; informal knacker, poop. **take off 1** *the officer took off after his men:* rush, hurry, hasten, race, run, sprint, charge, fly, speed; Brit. hare; informal tear, belt, pelt, scoot, hotfoot it. **2** *the plane took off:* become airborne, take to the air, take wing; lift off, blast off. **3** *the idea really took off:* succeed, do well, become popular, catch on, prosper, flourish, thrive, boom. **take someone on 1** *there was no challenger to take him on:* compete against, oppose, challenge, confront, face, fight, vie with, contend with, stand up to. **2** *we took on extra staff:* engage, hire, employ, enrol, enlist, sign up. **take something on 1** *he took on more responsibility:* undertake, accept, assume, shoulder, acquire, carry, bear. **2** *the study took on political meaning:* acquire, assume, come to have. **take something over** assume control of, take charge of, take command of, seize, hijack, commandeer. **take your time** go slowly, dally, dawdle, delay, linger, drag your feet; informal dilly-dally. **take to 1** *he took to carrying his money in his sock:* make a habit of, resort to, turn to; start, begin. **2** *Ruth took to him instantly:* like, get on with; informal take a shine to. **take something up 1** *he took up abstract painting:* engage in, get involved in; begin, start, commence. **2** *the meetings took up all her time:* consume, fill, absorb, use, occupy. **3** *her cousin took up the story:* resume, recommence, restart, carry on, continue, pick up, return to. **4** *he took up their suggestion:* accept, agree to, adopt; formal accede to.

take-off noun **departure**, lift-off, launch, blast-off; ascent, flight.
– OPPOSITES touchdown.

takeover noun **buyout**, merger, amalgamation; purchase, acquisition.

takings plural noun **proceeds**, returns, receipts, earnings, winnings, pickings, spoils; profit, gain, income, revenue.

tale noun **1** *a tale of witches:* **story**, narrative, anecdote, report, account, history; legend, fable, myth, parable, allegory, saga; informal yarn. **2** *she told tales to her mother:* **lie**, fib, falsehood, story, untruth, fabrication, fiction; informal tall story, fairy story/tale, cock and bull story.

> ! Don't confuse **tale** with **tail**, which means 'the rear or end part of an animal or thing'.

talent noun **flair**, aptitude, facility, gift, knack, technique, touch, bent, ability, expertise, capacity, faculty; strength, forte, genius, brilliance.

talented adjective **gifted**, skilful, accomplished, brilliant, expert, consummate, masterly, adroit, dexterous, able, deft, adept, proficient; informal ace.
– OPPOSITES inept.

talisman noun **lucky charm**, fetish, amulet, mascot, totem, juju.

talk verb **1** *we talked for over an hour:* **speak**, converse, chat, chatter, gossip, prattle, rattle on; communicate, confer, consult; negotiate, parley; informal yak, chew the fat; Brit. informal natter, rabbit on, witter on. **2** *he talked her into going with him:* **persuade**, argue, cajole, coax, bring round, inveigle, wheedle, sweet-talk, prevail on; informal hustle, fast-talk.
• noun **1** *he was bored with all this talk:* **chatter**, gossip, prattle, jabbering; informal yakking; Brit. informal nattering. **2** *we had a long talk:* **conversation**, chat, discussion, tête-à-tête, heart-to-heart, dialogue, parley, powwow; informal confab, chit-chat, gossip. **3** *peace talks:* **negotiations**, discussions; conference, summit, meeting, consultation, symposium, seminar; mediation, arbitration. **4** *she gave a talk on her travels:* **lecture**, speech, address, discourse, oration, presentation, report, sermon; informal spiel.
■ **talk down to** condescend to, patronize, look down your nose at, put down.

talkative adjective **chatty**, loquacious, garrulous, voluble, conversational, communicative; long-winded, wordy, verbose; informal mouthy.
– OPPOSITES taciturn.

tall adjective **1** *a tall man:* **big**, large, huge, towering, colossal, gigantic, giant, monstrous; leggy; informal long. **2** *tall buildings:* **high**, big, lofty, towering, elevated, sky-high. **3** *she's five feet tall:* **in height**, high, from head to toe; from top to bottom. **4** *a tall tale:* **unlikely**, improbable, exaggerated, far-fetched, implausible, dubious, unbelievable, incredible, absurd, untrue; informal cock and bull.
– OPPOSITES short, low.

tally noun **total**, running total, count, sum, score, record, reckoning.
• verb **1** *these statistics tally with government figures:* **correspond**, agree, accord, concur, coincide, match, fit, be consistent, conform, equate, harmonize, dovetail, correlate, parallel; informal square. **2** *votes were tallied with abacuses:* **count**, calculate, add up, total, compute; figure out, work out, reckon, measure, quantify; Brit. tot up; formal enumerate.
– OPPOSITES disagree.

tame adjective **1** *a tame elephant:* **domesticated**, docile, broken, trained; gentle, mild; pet. **2** *a tame affair:* **unexciting**, uninteresting, uninspiring, dull, bland, flat, insipid, spiritless, pedestrian, colourless, humdrum, boring.
– OPPOSITES wild, exciting.
• verb **1** *wild rabbits can be tamed:*

domesticate, break, train, master, subdue. **2** *she learned to tame her emotions:* **subdue**, curb, control, calm, master, moderate, discipline, suppress, temper, soften, bridle; informal lick.

tamper verb **1** *she saw them tampering with her car:* **interfere**, monkey around, meddle, tinker, fiddle, fool around, play around; informal mess about/around; Brit. informal muck about/around. **2** *the defendant tampered with the jury:* **influence**, get at, rig, manipulate, bribe, corrupt, bias; informal fix; Brit. informal nobble.

tan adjective **yellowish-brown**, light brown, tawny.

tang noun **flavour**, taste, savour; sharpness, zest, bite, edge, smack, piquancy, spice; smell, odour, aroma, fragrance; informal kick.

tangible adjective **touchable**, palpable, material, physical, real, substantial, corporeal, solid, concrete; visible, noticeable; actual, definite, clear, distinct, perceptible, discernible.
– OPPOSITES abstract.

tangle verb **1** *the wool got tangled up:* **entangle**, snarl, catch, entwine, twist, enmesh, knot, mat. **2** *he tangled with his old rival:* **come into conflict**, dispute, argue, quarrel, fight, wrangle, squabble, contend, cross swords, lock horns.
• noun *a tangle of branches:* **snarl**, mass, knot, mesh, mishmash.

tangled adjective **1** *tangled hair:* **knotted**, snarled up, twisted, matted, messy; tousled, unkempt; informal mussed up. **2** *a tangled bureaucratic mess:* **confused**, jumbled, mixed up, messy, chaotic, complicated, involved, complex, intricate, knotty, tortuous.
– OPPOSITES simple.

t

tangy adjective **zesty**, sharp, acid, tart, sour, bitter, piquant, spicy, tasty, flavoursome, pungent.
– OPPOSITES bland.

tank noun *a water tank:* **container**, receptacle, vat, cistern, repository, reservoir, basin.

tantalize verb **tease**, torment, torture, bait; tempt, entice, lure, allure, beguile; excite, fascinate, titillate, intrigue.

tantamount adjective *this is tantamount to mutiny:* **equivalent to**, equal to, as good as, more or less, comparable to, on a par with, commensurate with.

tantrum noun **fit of temper**, fit of rage, outburst, pet, paroxysm, frenzy; informal paddy, wobbly; N. Amer. informal hissy fit.

tap[1] noun **1** *she turned the tap on:* **valve**, stopcock; N. Amer. faucet, spigot. **2** *a phone tap:* **bug**, wiretap, microphone, receiver.
• verb **1** *their telephones were tapped:* **bug**, wiretap; monitor, overhear, eavesdrop on. **2** *the resources were to be tapped for our benefit:* **draw on**, exploit, milk, mine, use, utilize, turn to account.

tap[2] verb **1** *she tapped on the door:* **knock**, rap, strike, beat, drum. **2** *Dad tapped me on the knee:* **pat**, hit, strike, slap, jab, poke, dig.

tape noun **1** *a package tied with tape:* **binding**, ribbon, string, braid. **2** *a collection of old tapes:* **cassette**, tape recording; video.
• verb **1** *a card was taped to the box:* **stick**, fix, fasten, secure, attach. **2** *they taped off the area:* **cordon**, seal, close, shut, mark, fence; isolate, segregate. **3** *police taped his confession:* **record**, tape-record; video.

taper verb **1** *the leaves taper:* **narrow**, come to a point, attenuate. **2** *the rainfall tapered off:* **decrease**, lessen, dwindle, diminish, reduce, decline, die down, peter out, slacken off, ease, wane, ebb, let up, thin out.
– OPPOSITES thicken, increase.
• noun **candle**, spill, sconce.

target noun **1** *targets positioned at a range of 200 yards:* **mark**, bullseye, goal. **2** *eagles can spot their targets from half a mile:* **prey**, quarry, game, kill. **3** *their profit target:* **objective**, goal, aim, end; plan, intention, design, aspiration, ambition, ideal, desire, wish. **4** *she was the target for abuse:* **victim**, butt, recipient, focus, object, subject.
• verb **1** *he was targeted by a gunman:* **pick out**, single out, earmark, fix on; attack, aim at, fire at. **2** *the product is targeted at a specific market:* **aim**, direct, level, intend, focus.

■ **on target 1** *the striker was bang on target:* accurate, precise, unerring, sure, on the mark; Brit. informal spot on. **2** *the project was on target:* on schedule, on track, on course, on time.

tariff noun **tax**, duty, toll, excise, levy, charge, rate, fee; price list.

tarnish verb **1** *gold does not tarnish easily:* **discolour**, rust, oxidize, corrode, stain, dull, blacken. **2** *this behaviour tarnished his reputation:* **sully**, blacken, stain, blemish, blot, taint, soil, ruin, disgrace, mar, damage, harm, hurt, undermine, dishonour, stigmatize.
– OPPOSITES polish, enhance.
• noun **1** *the tarnish on the candlesticks:* **discoloration**, oxidation, rust, verdigris; film. **2** *the tarnish on his reputation:* **smear**, stain, blemish, blot, taint, stigma.

tart[1] noun *a jam tart:* **pastry**, flan, quiche, pie.

tart[2] (informal) verb **1** *she tarted herself up:* **dress up**, make up, smarten up, preen yourself, beautify yourself, groom yourself; informal doll yourself up, titivate yourself. **2** *we must tart this place up a bit:* **decorate**, renovate, refurbish, redecorate; smarten up; informal do up, fix up.

tart[3] adjective **1** *a tart apple:* **sour**, sharp, acidic, zesty, tangy, piquant; lemony. **2** *a tart reply:* **acerbic**, sharp, biting, cutting, astringent, caustic, trenchant, incisive, barbed, scathing, sarcastic, acrimonious, nasty, rude, vicious, spiteful, venomous.
– OPPOSITES sweet, kind.

task noun **job**, duty, chore, charge, assignment, detail, mission, engagement, occupation, undertaking, exercise, business, responsibility, burden, endeavour, enterprise, venture.

taste noun **1** *a distinctive sharp taste:* **flavour**, savour, relish, tang, smack. **2** *a taste of brandy:* **mouthful**, drop, bit, sip, nip, swallow, touch, soupçon, dash, modicum. **3** *it's too sweet for my taste:* **palate**, appetite, stomach. **4** *a taste for adventure:* **liking**, love, fondness, fancy, desire, preference, penchant, predilection, inclination, partiality. **5** *my first taste of prison:* **experience**, impression; exposure to, contact with, involvement with. **6** *the house was furnished with taste:* **judgement**, discrimination, discernment, refinement, finesse, elegance, grace, style. **7** *the photo was rejected on grounds of taste:* **decorum**, propriety, etiquette, politeness, delicacy, sensitivity, discretion.
• verb **1** *Adam tasted the wine:* **sample**, test, try, savour; sip, sup. **2** *he could taste blood:* **perceive**, discern, make out, distinguish.

WORD LINKS

gustatory relating to the sense of taste

tasteful adjective **1** *the decor is tasteful:* **aesthetically pleasing**, refined, cultured, elegant, stylish, smart, chic, attractive, exquisite. **2** *this video is erotic but tasteful:* **decorous**, proper, seemly, respectable, appropriate, modest.
– OPPOSITES tasteless, improper.

tasteless adjective **1** *the vegetables are tasteless:* **flavourless**, bland, insipid, unappetizing, savourless, watery. **2** *tasteless leather panelling:* **vulgar**, crude, tawdry, garish, gaudy, loud, trashy, showy, ostentatious, cheap, inelegant; informal flash, tacky, kitsch; Brit. informal naff. **3** *a tasteless remark:* **crude**, vulgar, indelicate, uncouth, crass, tactless, undiplomatic, indiscreet, inappropriate, offensive.
– OPPOSITES tasty, tasteful, seemly.

tasty adjective **delicious**, palatable, luscious, mouth-watering, delectable, flavoursome; appetizing, tempting; informal yummy, scrumptious, scrummy, finger-licking, moreish.
– OPPOSITES bland.

tatters plural noun *the satin had frayed to tatters:* **rags**, scraps, shreds, bits, pieces, ribbons.
■ **in tatters 1** *his clothes were in tatters:* ragged, torn, ripped, frayed, in pieces, worn out, moth-eaten, falling to pieces, threadbare. **2** *her marriage is in tatters:* in ruins, on the rocks, destroyed, finished, devastated.

taunt noun *the taunts of his classmates:* **jeer**, jibe, sneer, insult, barb, catcall; (**taunts**) teasing, provocation, goading, derision, mockery; informal dig, put-down.
• verb *she taunted him about his job:*

jeer at, sneer at, scoff at, poke fun at, make fun of, get at, insult, tease, chaff, torment, goad, ridicule, deride, mock, heckle; N. Amer. ride; informal rib, needle.

taut adjective **1** *the rope was pulled taut:* **tight**, stretched, rigid. **2** *his muscles remained taut:* **flexed**, tense, hard, solid, firm, rigid, stiff. **3** *a taut expression:* **fraught**, strained, stressed, tense; informal uptight. **4** *a taut tale of gang life:* **concise**, controlled, crisp, pithy, sharp, succinct, compact, terse. **5** *he ran a taut ship:* **orderly**, tight, trim, neat, disciplined, tidy, spruce, smart.
– OPPOSITES slack, relaxed.

tavern noun **bar**, inn, hostelry, taphouse; Brit. pub; informal watering hole; Brit. informal local; dated alehouse; N. Amer. historical saloon.

tawdry adjective **gaudy**, flashy, showy, garish, loud; tasteless, vulgar, trashy, cheap, shoddy, shabby, gimcrack; informal rubbishy, tacky, kitsch.
– OPPOSITES tasteful.

tax noun *they have to pay tax:* **duty**, excise, customs, dues; levy, tariff, toll, tithe, charge, fee.
– OPPOSITES rebate.
• verb *the ordeal has sorely taxed her strength:* **strain**, stretch, overburden, overload, encumber, push too far; overwhelm, try, wear out, exhaust, sap, drain, weary, weaken.

> WORD LINKS
> **fiscal** relating to the income received by a government through taxes

taxing adjective **demanding**, exacting, challenging, burdensome, arduous, onerous, difficult, hard, tough, laborious, back-breaking, strenuous, rigorous, punishing; tiring, exhausting, enervating, wearing, stressful; informal murderous.
– OPPOSITES easy.

teach verb **1** *she teaches small children:* **educate**, instruct, school, tutor, coach, train. **2** *teach your teenager how to negotiate:* **train**, show, guide, instruct, demonstrate.

> WORD LINKS
> **didactic**, **pedagogic** relating to teaching

teacher noun **educator**, tutor, instructor, schoolteacher, master, mistress, schoolmarm, governess, educationist, preceptor; coach, trainer; lecturer, professor, don; guide, mentor, guru; formal pedagogue.

team noun **1** *the sales team:* **group**, squad, company, party, crew, troupe, band, side, line-up; informal bunch, gang, posse. **2** *a team of horses:* **pair**, yoke, duo, set, tandem.
• verb **1** *team a T-shirt with matching shorts:* **match**, coordinate, complement, pair up. **2** *you could team up with another artist:* **join forces**, collaborate, work together; unite, combine, cooperate, link, ally, associate, club together.

> ! Don't confuse **team** with **teem**, which means 'be full of' or 'rain heavily'.

tear[1] verb **1** *I tore up the letter:* **rip up**, pull to pieces, shred. **2** *his flesh was torn:* **lacerate**, cut, gash, slash, scratch, hack, pierce, stab. **3** *the trauma tore her family apart:* **divide**, split, sever, break up, disunite, rupture; literary rend. **4** *Gina tore the book from his hands:* **snatch**, grab, seize, rip, wrench, wrest, pull, pluck; informal yank.
• noun *a tear in her dress:* **rip**, hole, split, slash, slit; ladder, snag.
■ **tear something down** demolish, knock down, raze to the ground, flatten, level, bulldoze.

tear[2] noun
■ **in tears** crying, weeping, sobbing, wailing, howling, bawling, whimpering; informal weepy, blubbing.

> WORD LINKS
> **lachrymal** relating to tears
> **lachrymose** tending to cry easily or causing tears

tearaway noun **hooligan**, hoodlum, ruffian, lout, rowdy, roughneck; informal yahoo; Brit. informal yob; Austral./NZ informal roughie.

tearful adjective **1** *she sounded tearful:* **close to tears**, emotional, upset, distressed, sad, unhappy; in tears, crying, weeping, sobbing; informal weepy; formal lachrymose. **2** *a tearful farewell:* **emotional**, upsetting, distressing, sad, heart-

breaking, sorrowful; poignant, moving, touching, tear-jerking.
– OPPOSITES cheerful.

tease verb **make fun of**, chaff, laugh at, guy; taunt, bait, goad, pick on; deride, mock, ridicule; informal take the mickey out of, rag, send up, rib, josh, have on, pull someone's leg; Brit. informal wind up.

technical adjective **1** *an important technical achievement:* **practical**, scientific, technological, high-tech. **2** *this might seem very technical:* **specialist**, specialized, scientific; complex, complicated, esoteric. **3** *a technical fault:* **mechanical**.

technique noun **1** *different techniques for solving the problem:* **method**, approach, procedure, system, modus operandi, way; means, strategy, tack, tactic, line; routine, practice. **2** *I was impressed with his technique:* **skill**, ability, proficiency, expertise, mastery, talent, genius, artistry, craftsmanship; aptitude, adroitness, deftness, dexterity, facility, competence; performance, delivery; informal know-how.

tedious adjective **boring**, dull, monotonous, repetitive, unrelieved, unvaried, uneventful; characterless, colourless, lifeless, insipid, uninteresting, unexciting, uninspiring, lacklustre, dreary, humdrum, mundane; mind-numbing, soul-destroying, wearisome; informal deadly; Brit. informal samey; N. Amer. informal dullsville.
– OPPOSITES interesting, exciting, gripping.

tedium noun **monotony**, boredom, ennui, uniformity, routine, dreariness, dryness, banality, vapidity, insipidity.
– OPPOSITES variety.

teem[1] verb *the pond was teeming with fish:* **be full of**, be alive with, be brimming with, abound in, be swarming with; be packed with, be crawling with, be overrun by, bristle with, seethe with, be thick with; informal be jam-packed with, be chock-a-block with.

> ! Don't confuse **teem** with **team**, which means 'a group of people playing or working together'.

teem[2] verb *the rain was teeming down:* **pour**, pelt, tip, beat, lash, sheet, rain cats and dogs; informal be chucking it down; Brit. informal bucket down, come down in stair rods.

teenage adjective **adolescent**, juvenile; informal teen.

teenager noun **adolescent**, youth, young person, minor, juvenile; informal teen, teeny-bopper.

teeter verb **1** *Daisy teetered towards them:* **totter**, wobble, toddle, sway, stagger, stumble, reel, lurch, pitch. **2** *the situation teetered between tragedy and farce:* **see-saw**, veer, fluctuate, oscillate, swing, alternate, waver.

teetotal adjective **abstinent**, abstemious; sober, dry; informal on the wagon.
– OPPOSITES alcoholic.

telepathic adjective **psychic**, clairvoyant.

telepathy noun **mind-reading**, thought transference; extrasensory perception, ESP; clairvoyance, sixth sense; psychometry.

telephone noun **phone**, handset, receiver; mobile, cellphone; informal blower.
• verb **phone**, call, dial; Brit. ring; informal give someone a buzz; Brit. informal give someone a bell, give someone a tinkle.

telescope verb **1** *the front of the car was telescoped:* **concertina**, compact, compress, crush, squash. **2** *his experience can be telescoped into a paragraph:* **condense**, shorten, reduce, abbreviate, abridge, summarize, precis, abstract, shrink, consolidate; truncate, curtail.

televise verb **broadcast**, screen, air, telecast; transmit, relay.

television noun **TV**; informal the small screen; Brit. informal telly, the box; N. Amer. informal the tube.

tell verb **1** *why didn't you tell me?* **inform**, notify, apprise, let know, make aware, acquaint with, advise, put in the picture, brief, fill in; alert, warn; informal clue in/up. **2** *she told the story slowly:* **relate**, recount, narrate, report, recite, describe, sketch, weave, spin; utter, voice, state, declare, communicate, impart, divulge. **3** *she told him to* *leave:* **instruct**, order, command, direct, charge, enjoin, call on, require; literary bid. **4** *I tell you, I did nothing wrong:* **assure**, promise, give your word, swear, guarantee. **5** *the figures tell a different story:* **reveal**, show, indicate, be evidence of, disclose, convey, signify. **6** *promise you won't tell?* **give the game away**, talk, tell tales, tattle; informal spill the beans, let the cat out of the bag, blab; Brit. informal blow the gaff. **7** *she was bound to tell on him:* **inform on**, tell tales on, give away, denounce, sell out; informal split on, blow the whistle on, rat on, peach on, squeal on; Brit. informal grass on, sneak on, shop; N. Amer. informal finger; Austral./NZ informal dob on. **8** *it was hard to tell what he meant:* **ascertain**, determine, work out, make out, deduce, discern, perceive, see, identify, recognize, understand, comprehend; informal figure out; Brit. informal suss out. **9** *he couldn't tell one from the other:* **distinguish**, differentiate, discriminate. **10** *the strain began to tell on him:* **take its toll**, leave its mark; affect.

teller noun **1** *a bank teller:* **cashier**, clerk. **2** *a teller of tales:* **narrator**, raconteur; storyteller, anecdotalist.

telling adjective **revealing**, significant, weighty, important, meaningful, influential, striking, potent, powerful, compelling.
– OPPOSITES insignificant.

telltale adjective **revealing**, revelatory, suggestive, meaningful, significant; informal giveaway.
• noun **informer**, whistle-blower; N. Amer. tattletale; informal snitch, squealer; Brit. informal sneak.

temerity noun **audacity**, nerve, effrontery, impudence, impertinence, cheek, gall, presumption; daring; informal face, front, brass neck, chutzpah.

temper noun **1** *he walked out in a temper:* **fit of rage**, fury, fit of pique, tantrum, mood, pet, sulk, huff; informal grump, snit; Brit. informal strop, paddy; N. Amer. informal hissy fit. **2** *a display of temper:* **anger**, fury, rage, annoyance, vexation, irritation, irritability, ill humour, spleen, pique, petulance, testiness, tetchiness, crabbiness; Brit. informal stroppiness; literary ire, choler. **3** *she struggled to keep her temper:* **composure**, equanimity, self-control, self-possession, sangfroid, calm, good humour; informal cool.
• verb **1** *the steel is tempered by heat:* **harden**, strengthen, toughen, fortify, anneal. **2** *their idealism is tempered with realism:* **moderate**, modify, modulate, mitigate, alleviate, reduce, weaken, lighten, soften.
■ **lose your temper** fly into a rage, erupt, lose control, go berserk, flare up; informal go mad, go crazy, go bananas, have a fit, see red, fly off the handle, blow your top, do your nut, hit the roof, go off the deep end, go ape, flip, lose your rag; Brit. informal go spare, throw a wobbly.

temperament noun **disposition**, nature, character, personality, make-up, constitution, mind, spirit; stamp, mettle, mould; mood, frame of mind, attitude, outlook, humour.

temperamental adjective **1** *a temperamental chef:* **volatile**, excitable, emotional, mercurial, capricious, erratic, unpredictable, changeable, inconsistent; hot-headed, fiery, quick-tempered, irritable, irascible, impatient; touchy, moody, sensitive, highly strung. **2** *a temperamental dislike of conflict:* **inherent**, innate, natural, inborn, constitutional, deep-rooted, ingrained, congenital.
– OPPOSITES placid.

temperance noun **teetotalism**, abstinence, abstention, sobriety, self-restraint; prohibition.

temperate adjective **1** *temperate climates:* **mild**, clement, benign, gentle, balmy. **2** *he was temperate in his consumption:* **self-restrained**, moderate, self-controlled, disciplined; abstemious, self-denying; teetotal, abstinent.
– OPPOSITES extreme.

tempestuous adjective **1** *the tempestuous political environment:* **turbulent**, stormy, tumultuous, wild, lively, explosive, feverish, frenetic, frenzied. **2** *a tempestuous woman:* **emotional**, passionate, impassioned, fiery, intense; temperamental, volatile, excitable, mercurial, capricious, unpredictable, quick-tempered. **3** *the day was tempestuous:* **stormy**, blustery,

squally, wild, turbulent, windy, gusty, blowy, rainy.
– OPPOSITES peaceful, placid, calm.

temple noun house of God, shrine, sanctuary; church, cathedral, mosque, synagogue, shul.

tempo noun **1** *the tempo of the music:* **cadence**, speed, rhythm, beat, time, pulse; measure, metre. **2** *the tempo of life in Western society:* **pace**, rate, speed, velocity.

temporal adjective **secular**, non-spiritual, worldly, profane, material, mundane, earthly, terrestrial; non-religious, lay.
– OPPOSITES spiritual.

temporarily adverb **1** *the girl was temporarily placed with a foster family:* **for the time being**, for the moment, for now, for the present, in the interim, for the nonce, in/for the meantime; provisionally, pro tem; informal for the minute. **2** *he was temporarily blinded by the light:* **briefly**, momentarily, fleetingly.
– OPPOSITES permanently.

temporary adjective **1** *temporary accommodation | the temporary captain:* **non-permanent**, short-term, interim; provisional, pro tem, makeshift, stopgap; acting, fill-in, stand-in, caretaker. **2** *a temporary loss of self-control:* **brief**, short-lived, momentary, fleeting, passing.
– OPPOSITES permanent, lasting.

temporize verb **equivocate**, procrastinate, play for time, stall, delay, hang back, prevaricate; Brit. hum and haw.

tempt verb **1** *the manager tried to tempt him to stay:* **entice**, persuade, convince, inveigle, induce, cajole, coax, woo; informal sweet-talk. **2** *more customers are being tempted by credit:* **allure**, attract, appeal to, whet the appetite of; lure, seduce, beguile, tantalize, draw.
– OPPOSITES discourage, deter.

temptation noun **1** *Mary resisted the temptation to answer back:* **desire**, urge, itch, impulse, inclination. **2** *the temptations of London:* **lure**, allurement, enticement, seduction, attraction, draw, pull. **3** *the temptation of travel to exotic locations:* **allure**, appeal, attraction, fascination.

tempting adjective **1** *tempting shops:* **enticing**, alluring, attractive, appealing, inviting, captivating, seductive, beguiling, fascinating, tantalizing. **2** *a plate of tempting cakes:* **appetizing**, mouth-watering, delicious, toothsome; informal scrumptious, yummy.
– OPPOSITES off-putting, uninviting.

temptress noun **seductress**, siren, femme fatale, Mata Hari; informal vamp.

ten cardinal number **decade.**

WORD LINKS

decimal relating to a system of numbers based on the number ten
decagon a ten-sided plane figure
decahedron a ten-sided solid figure

tenable adjective **defensible**, justifiable, supportable, sustainable, arguable, able to hold water, reasonable, rational, sound, viable, plausible, credible, believable, conceivable.
– OPPOSITES indefensible, untenable.

tenacious adjective **1** *his tenacious grip:* **firm**, tight, fast, clinging; strong, forceful, powerful, unshakeable, immovable, iron. **2** *a tenacious man:* **persevering**, persistent, determined, dogged, strong-willed, tireless, indefatigable, resolute, patient, purposeful, unflagging, staunch, steadfast, untiring, unwavering, unswerving, unshakeable, unyielding, insistent; formal pertinacious.
– OPPOSITES weak, irresolute.

tenacity noun **persistence**, determination, perseverance, doggedness, strength of purpose, bulldog spirit, tirelessness, indefatigability, resolution, resoluteness, resolve, firmness, patience, purposefulness, staunchness, steadfastness, staying power, application; formal pertinacity.

tenancy noun **occupancy**, occupation, residence, habitation, holding, possession; tenure, lease, rental; leasehold.

tenant noun **occupant**, resident, inhabitant; leaseholder, lessee, renter; Brit. occupier.
– OPPOSITES owner, freeholder.

tend[1] verb **1** *I tend to get very involved in my work:* **be inclined**, be apt, be disposed, be prone, be liable, have a propensity. **2** *younger* *voters tended towards the tabloid press:* **incline**, lean, gravitate, move; prefer, favour; N. Amer. trend.

tend[2] verb *ambulance crews were tending to the injured:* **look after**, take care of, minister to, attend to, see to, wait on; watch over, keep an eye on, mind, protect, watch, guard.
– OPPOSITES neglect.

tendency noun **1** *his tendency to take the law into his own hands:* **propensity**, proclivity, proneness, aptness, likelihood, inclination, disposition, predisposition, bent, leaning, penchant, predilection, susceptibility, liability. **2** *this tendency towards cohabitation:* **trend**, movement, drift, swing, gravitation, direction, course; orientation, bias.

tender[1] adjective **1** *a gentle, tender man:* **caring**, kind, kind-hearted, soft-hearted, compassionate, sympathetic, warm, fatherly, motherly, maternal, gentle, mild, benevolent, generous. **2** *a tender kiss:* **affectionate**, fond, loving, emotional, warm, gentle, soft; informal lovey-dovey. **3** *tender love songs:* **romantic**, sentimental, emotional, emotive, touching, moving, poignant; Brit. informal soppy. **4** *simmer until the meat is tender:* **soft**, easy to chew, succulent, juicy; tenderized. **5** *her ankle was swollen and tender:* **sore**, painful, sensitive, inflamed, raw; hurting, aching, throbbing, smarting. **6** *the tender age of fifteen:* **young**, youthful; impressionable, inexperienced, immature, unsophisticated, unseasoned, juvenile, callow, green, raw; informal wet behind the ears.
– OPPOSITES hard-hearted, callous, tough.

t

tender[2] verb **1** *she tendered her resignation:* **offer**, proffer, present, put forward, propose, suggest, advance, submit, extend, give, render; hand in. **2** *firms tendered for the work:* **put in a bid**, quote, give an estimate.
• noun *contractors were invited to submit tenders:* **bid**, offer, quotation, quote, estimate, price; proposal, submission.

tenderness noun **1** *I felt an enormous tenderness for her:* **affection**, fondness, love, devotion, emotion, sentiment. **2** *with unexpected tenderness, he told her what had happened:* **kindness**, kind-heartedness, tender-heartedness, compassion, care, concern, sympathy, warmth, fatherliness, motherliness, gentleness, benevolence, generosity. **3** *abdominal tenderness:* **soreness**, pain, inflammation; ache, smarting, throbbing.

tenet noun *the basic tenets of their religion:* **principle**, belief, doctrine, precept, creed, credo, article of faith, dogma, canon; theory, thesis, conviction, idea, view, opinion, position, hypothesis, postulation; ideology, code of belief, teaching.

tenor noun **1** *the general tenor of his speech:* **sense**, meaning, theme, drift, thread, import, purport, intent, intention, burden, thrust, significance, message; gist, essence, substance, spirit. **2** *the even tenor of life in the village:* **course**, direction, movement, drift, current, trend.

tense adjective **1** *tense muscles:* **taut**, tight, rigid, stretched, strained, stiff. **2** *Loretta was feeling tense:* **anxious**, nervous, on edge, edgy, strained, stressed, under pressure, agitated, ill at ease, uneasy, restless, worked up, keyed up, overwrought, jumpy, nervy, on tenterhooks, worried, apprehensive, panicky; informal a bundle of nerves, jittery, twitchy, uptight; N. Amer. informal spooky, squirrelly. **3** *a tense moment:* **nerve-racking**, stressful, anxious, worrying, fraught, charged, strained, nail-biting, difficult, uneasy, uncomfortable; exciting.
– OPPOSITES slack, calm.
• verb *Hebden tensed his muscles:* **tighten**, tauten, flex, contract, brace, stiffen; screw up, knot, strain, stretch.
– OPPOSITES relax.

tension noun **1** *the tension of the rope:* **tightness**, tautness, rigidity; pull, traction. **2** *the tension was unbearable:* **strain**, stress, anxiety, pressure; worry, apprehensiveness, agitation, nervousness, jumpiness, edginess, restlessness; suspense, uncertainty, anticipation, excitement; informal butterflies (in your stomach), collywobbles. **3** *months of tension between the military and* *the government:* **strained relations**, strain; ill feeling, friction, antagonism, antipathy, hostility, enmity.

tentative adjective **1** *tentative arrangements | a tentative conclusion:* **provisional**, unconfirmed, pencilled in, preliminary, to be confirmed, TBC; speculative, conjectural, untried, unproven, exploratory, experimental, trial, test, pilot. **2** *he took a few tentative steps:* **hesitant**, uncertain, cautious, timid, hesitating, faltering, shaky, unsteady, halting; wavering, unsure.
–OPPOSITES definite, confident.

tenterhooks plural noun
■ **on tenterhooks** in suspense, waiting with bated breath; anxious, nervous, nervy, apprehensive, worried, on edge, edgy, tense, strained, stressed, agitated, restless, worked up, keyed up, jumpy; informal with butterflies in your stomach, jittery, twitchy, in a state, uptight; N. Amer. informal squirrelly.

tenuous adjective **1** *a tenuous connection:* **slight**, insubstantial, flimsy, weak, doubtful, dubious, questionable, suspect; vague, nebulous, hazy. **2** *a tenuous thread:* **fine**, thin, slender, delicate, gossamer, fragile.
–OPPOSITES convincing, strong.

tenure noun **1** *residents should have security of tenure:* **tenancy**, occupancy, holding, occupation, residence; possession, title, ownership. **2** *his tenure as Secretary of State:* **incumbency**, term (of office), period (of/in office), time (in office).

tepid adjective **1** *tepid water:* **lukewarm**, warmish. **2** *a tepid response:* **unenthusiastic**, apathetic, half-hearted, indifferent, cool, lukewarm, uninterested.
–OPPOSITES hot, cold, enthusiastic.

term noun **1** *scientific terms:* **word**, expression, phrase, idiom, locution; name, title, designation, label; formal appellation, denomination. **2** *a protest in the strongest terms:* **language**, mode of expression, manner of speaking, phraseology, terminology; words, phrases, expressions. **3** *the terms of the contract:* **conditions**, stipulations, specifications, provisions, provisos; restrictions, qualifications. **4** *a policy offering favourable terms:* **rates**, prices, charges, costs, fees; tariff. **5** *the President is elected for a four-year term:* **period**, length of time, spell, stint, duration; stretch, run; period of office, incumbency. **6** *the summer term:* **session**; N. Amer. semester, trimester, quarter.
•verb *he has been termed the father of modern theology:* **call**, name, entitle, title, style, designate, describe as, dub, label, tag; nickname; formal denominate.
■ **come to terms 1** *the two sides came to terms:* reach an agreement/understanding, make a deal, reach a compromise, meet each other halfway. **2** *she eventually came to terms with her situation:* accept, reconcile yourself to, learn to live with, become resigned to, make the best of; face up to.

terminal adjective **1** *a terminal illness:* **incurable**, untreatable, inoperable; fatal, mortal, deadly. **2** *a terminal bonus may be payable:* **final**, last, concluding, closing, end.
•noun **1** *a railway terminal:* **station**, last stop, end of the line; depot; Brit. terminus. **2** *a computer terminal:* **workstation**, VDU, visual display unit.

terminate verb **1** *treatment was terminated:* **bring to an end**, bring to a close, close, conclude, finish, stop, wind up, discontinue, cease, cut short, abort, axe; informal pull the plug on. **2** *the train will terminate in Stratford:* **end its journey**, finish up, stop.
–OPPOSITES begin, start, continue.

termination noun *the termination of a contract:* **ending**, end, closing, conclusion, finish, stopping, winding up, discontinuance, discontinuation; cancellation, dissolution.
–OPPOSITES start, beginning.

terminology noun **phraseology**, terms, expressions, words, language, parlance, vocabulary, nomenclature; usage, idiom; jargon, cant, argot; informal lingo, -speak, -ese.

terminus noun (Brit.) *the bus terminus:* **station**, last stop, end of the line, terminal; depot, garage.

terrain noun **land**, ground, territory; topography, landscape, countryside, country.

terrestrial adjective **earthly**, worldly, mundane, earthbound.

terrible adjective **1** *a terrible crime | terrible injuries:* **dreadful**, awful, appalling, horrific, horrifying, horrible, horrendous, atrocious, abominable, abhorrent, frightful, shocking, hideous, ghastly, grim, dire, unspeakable, gruesome, monstrous, sickening, heinous, vile; serious, grave, acute; formal grievous. **2** *a terrible smell:* **nasty**, disgusting, awful, dreadful, ghastly, horrid, horrible, vile, foul, abominable, frightful, loathsome, revolting, repulsive, odious, nauseating, repellent, horrendous, hideous, appalling, offensive, objectionable, obnoxious; informal gruesome, putrid, diabolical, sick-making, God-awful, gross; Brit. informal beastly. **3** *he was in terrible pain:* **severe**, extreme, intense, excruciating, agonizing, unbearable, intolerable, unendurable. **4** *the film was terrible:* **very bad**, dreadful, awful, frightful, atrocious, hopeless, poor; informal pathetic, pitiful, useless, lousy, appalling, abysmal, dire; Brit. informal duff, chronic, poxy, rubbish. **5** *I feel terrible:* **ill**, poorly, sick, nauseous; guilty, conscience-stricken, remorseful, ashamed, chastened, contrite, sorry; informal rotten.
– OPPOSITES minor, slight, pleasant, wonderful.

terribly adverb **1** *he played terribly:* **very badly**, atrociously, awfully, dreadfully, appallingly, execrably; informal abysmally, pitifully, diabolically. **2** (informal) *I shall miss you terribly:* **very much**, greatly, a great deal, a lot; informal loads.

terrific adjective **1** *a terrific bang:* **tremendous**, huge, massive, gigantic, colossal, mighty, great, prodigious, formidable, sizeable, considerable; intense, extreme, extraordinary; informal mega, whopping, humongous; Brit. informal whacking great, ginormous. **2** (informal) *a terrific game of top-quality football:* **marvellous**, wonderful, sensational, outstanding, superb, excellent, first-rate, first-class, dazzling, out of this world, breathtaking; informal great, fantastic, fabulous, fab, mega, super, ace, magic, cracking, cool, wicked, awesome; Brit. informal brilliant, smashing.

terrified adjective **petrified**, frightened, scared, horrified, shaking in your shoes.

terrify verb **petrify**, horrify, frighten, scare, strike terror into, put the fear of God into; paralyse, transfix.

territory noun **1** *British overseas territories:* **area of land**, area, region, enclave; country, state, land, dependency, colony, dominion, protectorate, fief. **2** *mountainous territory:* **terrain**, land, ground, countryside. **3** *the territory of biblical scholarship:* **domain**, area of interest/knowledge, province, department, field, preserve, sphere, arena, realm, world. **4** *Sheffield was his territory:* **sphere of operations**, area, section; informal turf; Brit. informal patch, manor.

terror noun **1** *she screamed in terror:* **extreme fear**, dread, horror, fright, alarm, panic, shock. **2** *the terrors of her own mind:* **demon**, fiend, devil, monster; horror, nightmare.

terrorist noun bomber, arsonist; gunman, assassin; hijacker; revolutionary, anarchist, radical, guerrilla, freedom fighter.

terrorize verb **persecute**, victimize, torment, tyrannize, intimidate, menace, threaten, bully, browbeat; scare, frighten, terrify, petrify; Brit. informal put the frighteners on.

terse adjective **brief**, short, to the point, concise, succinct, crisp, pithy, incisive, laconic, elliptical; brusque, abrupt, curt, clipped, blunt.
– OPPOSITES long-winded, polite.

test noun **1** *a series of scientific tests:* **trial**, experiment, pilot study, tryout; check, examination, assessment, evaluation, appraisal, investigation, inspection, analysis, scrutiny, study, probe, exploration; screening. **2** *candidates may be required to take a test:* **exam**, examination; N. Amer. quiz. **3** *the test of a good wine:* **criterion**, proof, indication, yardstick, touchstone, standard, measure, litmus test, acid test.
• verb **1** *a small-scale prototype was tested:* **try out**, trial, put through

its paces, experiment with, pilot; check, examine, assess, evaluate, appraise, investigate, analyse, scrutinize, study, probe, explore; sample; screen. **2** *such behaviour would test any marriage:* **put a strain on**, tax, try; make demands on, stretch, challenge.

testament noun *an achievement which is a testament to his professionalism:* **testimony**, witness, evidence, proof, attestation; demonstration, indication, exemplification.

testify verb **1** *you may be required to testify in court:* **give evidence**, bear witness, give your testimony, attest. **2** *he testified that he had been threatened by a fellow officer:* **attest**, swear, state on oath, declare, assert, affirm; allege, submit, claim. **3** *the exhibits testify to the talents of the sculptors:* **be evidence/proof of**, attest to, confirm, prove, corroborate, substantiate, bear out; show, demonstrate, bear witness to, indicate.

testimonial noun **reference**, letter of recommendation, commendation.

testimony noun **1** *Smith was in court to hear her testimony:* **evidence**, sworn statement, attestation, affidavit; statement, declaration, assertion, affirmation; allegation, submission, claim. **2** *the work is a testimony to his professional commitment:* **testament**, proof, evidence, attestation, witness; confirmation, corroboration; demonstration, indication.

testing adjective **difficult**, challenging, tough, hard, demanding, taxing, stressful.
– OPPOSITES easy.

tetchy adjective **irritable**, cantankerous, irascible, bad-tempered, grumpy, grouchy, crotchety, crabby, testy, crusty, curmudgeonly, ill-tempered, ill-humoured, peevish, cross, fractious, pettish, crabbed, prickly, waspish; Brit. informal shirty, stroppy, narky, ratty; N. Amer. informal cranky, ornery.
– OPPOSITES good-humoured.

tether verb *the horse was tethered to a post:* **tie**, hitch, rope, chain; fasten, secure.
– OPPOSITES unleash.

text noun **1** *a text which explores pain and grief:* **book**, work; textbook. **2** *the pictures relate well to the text:* **words**; content, body. **3** *a text from the First Book of Samuel:* **passage**, extract, quotation, verse, line; reading. **4** *he took as his text the fact that Australia is a paradise:* **theme**, subject, topic, motif; thesis, argument.

textiles plural noun **fabrics**, cloths, materials.

texture noun **feel**, touch; appearance, finish, surface, grain.

thank verb **express your gratitude**, show your appreciation; recognize, acknowledge.

thankful adjective **grateful**, relieved, pleased, glad.

thankless adjective **1** *a thankless task:* **unenviable**, difficult, unpleasant, unrewarding; unappreciated, unrecognized, unacknowledged. **2** *her thankless children:* **ungrateful**, unappreciative.
– OPPOSITES rewarding, grateful.

thanks plural noun *they expressed their thanks:* **gratitude**, appreciation; acknowledgement, recognition, credit.
■ **thanks to** as a result of, owing to, due to, because of, through, as a consequence of, on account of, by virtue of.

thaw verb **melt**, unfreeze, soften, liquefy; defrost.
– OPPOSITES freeze.

theatre noun **1** **playhouse**, auditorium, amphitheatre. **2** *what made you want to go into the theatre?* **acting**, performing, the stage; drama, dramaturgy; show business; informal the boards, showbiz. **3** *a lecture theatre:* **hall**, room, auditorium. **4** *the theatre of war:* **scene**, arena, field/sphere of action.

theatrical adjective **1** *a theatrical career:* **stage**, dramatic, thespian, dramaturgical; show-business; informal showbiz. **2** *Henry looked over his shoulder with theatrical caution:* **exaggerated**, ostentatious, stagy, showy, melodramatic, overacted, overdone, histrionic, affected, mannered.

theft noun **robbery**, stealing, larceny, shoplifting, burglary, embezzlement; raid, hold-up; informal smash and grab; N. Amer. informal heist, stick-up.

WORD LINKS
kleptomania compulsive theft

theme noun **1** *the theme of her speech:* **subject**, topic, thesis, argument, text, burden, thrust; thread, motif, keynote. **2** *the first violin takes up the theme:* **melody**, tune, air; motif, leitmotif.

then adverb **1** *I was living in Cairo then:* **at that time**, in those days; at that point, on that occasion. **2** *she won the first and then the second game:* **next**, afterwards, subsequently. **3** *and then there's another problem:* **in addition**, also, besides, as well, on top of that, moreover, furthermore, what's more, to boot; too.

theological adjective **religious**, scriptural, ecclesiastical, doctrinal; divine, holy.

theoretical adjective **hypothetical**, conjectural, academic, suppositional, speculative, notional, postulatory, assumed, presumed, untested, unproven, unsubstantiated.
– OPPOSITES actual, real.

theorize verb **speculate**, conjecture, hypothesize, postulate, propose, posit, suppose.

theory noun **1** *I reckon that confirms my theory:* **hypothesis**, thesis, conjecture, supposition, speculation, postulation, proposition, premise, surmise, assumption, presupposition; opinion, view, belief, contention. **2** *modern economic theory:* **principles**, ideas, concepts; philosophy, ideology, thinking.
■ **in theory** in principle, on paper, in the abstract, in an ideal world; hypothetically.

t

therapeutic adjective **healing**, curative, remedial, medicinal, restorative, health-giving, tonic.
– OPPOSITES harmful.

therapist noun **psychologist**, psychotherapist, analyst, psychoanalyst, psychiatrist; counsellor; informal shrink; Brit. humorous trick cyclist.

therapy noun **1** *complementary therapies:* **treatment**, remedy, cure. **2** *he's currently in therapy:* **psychotherapy**, psychoanalysis; counselling.

thereafter adverb **after that**, following that, afterwards, subsequently, then, next.

therefore adverb **consequently**, so, as a result, hence, thus, accordingly, for that reason, ergo, that being the case.

thesis noun **1** *the central thesis of his lecture:* **theory**, contention, argument, proposal, proposition, premise, assumption, hypothesis, postulation, surmise, supposition. **2** *a doctoral thesis:* **dissertation**, essay, paper, treatise, disquisition, composition, study; N. Amer. theme.

thick adjective **1** *the walls are five feet thick:* **in extent/diameter**, across, wide, broad, deep. **2** *his short, thick legs:* **stocky**, sturdy, chunky, hefty, thickset, beefy, meaty, big, solid; fat, stout, plump. **3** *a thick sweater:* **chunky**, bulky, heavy; woolly. **4** *the station was thick with people:* **crowded**, full, filled, packed, teeming, seething, swarming, crawling, crammed, thronged, bursting at the seams, solid, overflowing, choked, jammed, congested; informal jam-packed, chock-a-block, stuffed; Austral./NZ informal chocker. **5** *the thick vegetation:* **plentiful**, abundant, profuse, luxuriant, bushy, rich, riotous, exuberant; rank, rampant; dense, close-packed; informal jungly. **6** *a thick paste:* **semi-solid**, firm, stiff, heavy; clotted, coagulated, viscous, gelatinous. **7** *thick fog:* **dense**, heavy, opaque, impenetrable, soupy, murky.
– OPPOSITES thin, slender, sparse.
• noun *he found himself in the thick of the crisis:* **midst**, centre, hub, middle, core, heart.

thicken verb **become thick/thicker**, stiffen, condense; solidify, set, gel, congeal, clot, coagulate.

thicket noun **copse**, coppice, grove, brake, covert, clump; wood; Brit. spinney.

thickness noun **1** *the gateway is several feet in thickness:* **width**, breadth, depth, diameter. **2** *several thicknesses of limestone:* **layer**, stratum, stratification, seam, vein.

thickset adjective **stocky**, sturdy, heavily built, well built, chunky,

burly, strapping, brawny, solid, beefy.
– OPPOSITES slight.

thick-skinned adjective **insensitive**, unfeeling, tough, impervious, hardened.
– OPPOSITES sensitive.

thief noun **robber**, burglar, housebreaker, shoplifter, pickpocket, mugger; kleptomaniac; informal crook; Brit. rhyming slang tea leaf.

thieve verb **steal**, take, purloin, help yourself to, snatch, pilfer; embezzle, misappropriate; informal rob, swipe, nab, lift, filch, snaffle; Brit. informal nick, pinch, knock off; N. Amer. informal heist.

thin adjective **1** *a tall, thin woman:* **slim**, lean, slender, rangy, willowy, svelte, sylphlike, spare, slight; skinny, underweight, scrawny, scraggy, bony, gaunt, sticklike, emaciated, skeletal, wasted, pinched; lanky, spindly, gangly; informal anorexic. **2** *a thin cotton nightdress:* **lightweight**, light, fine, delicate, floaty, flimsy, diaphanous, gossamer, insubstantial; sheer, gauzy, filmy, chiffony, transparent, see-through. **3** *a thin white line:* **narrow**, fine, attenuated. **4** *thin soup:* **watery**, weak, dilute; runny, sloppy.
– OPPOSITES fat, thick, broad.
• verb **1** *some paint must be thinned down:* **dilute**, water down, weaken. **2** *the crowds were beginning to thin out:* **disperse**, dissipate, scatter; decrease, diminish, dwindle.

thing noun **1** *the room was full of strange things:* **object**, article, item, artefact, commodity; device, gadget, instrument, utensil, tool, implement; informal widget; Brit. informal gubbins. **2** *I'll collect my things:* **belongings**, possessions, stuff, property, worldly goods, personal effects, paraphernalia, bits and pieces; luggage, baggage; informal gear, junk; Brit. informal clobber. **3** *his gardening things:* **equipment**, apparatus, gear, kit, tackle, stuff; implements, tools, utensils; accoutrements. **4** *I've got several things to do:* **task**, job, chore; activity, act, action, deed, undertaking, exploit, feat. **5** *I've got other things on my mind:* **thought**, idea; concern, matter, worry, preoccupation. **6** *a few odd things happened:* **incident**, episode, event, happening, occurrence, phenomenon. **7** *one of the things I like about you:* **characteristic**, quality, attribute, property, trait, feature, point, aspect, facet. **8** *there's another thing you should know:* **fact**, piece of information, point, detail, particular, factor. **9** *she had a thing about men who wore glasses:* **penchant**, preference, taste, inclination, partiality, predilection, soft spot, weakness, fancy, fondness, liking, love, fetish.

think verb **1** *I think he's gone home:* **believe**, be of the opinion, be of the view, be under the impression; expect, imagine, anticipate; surmise, suppose, conjecture, guess, fancy; informal reckon, figure. **2** *his family was thought to be enormously rich:* **deem**, judge, hold, reckon, consider, presume, estimate; regard as, view as. **3** *Jack thought for a moment:* **ponder**, reflect, deliberate, consider, meditate, contemplate, muse, ruminate, brood; concentrate, rack your brains; informal put on your thinking cap, sleep on it; formal cogitate. **4** *she thought of all the visits she had made:* **recall**, remember, recollect, call to mind. **5** *she forced herself to think of how he must be feeling:* **imagine**, picture, visualize, envisage.
▪ **think better of** have second thoughts about, think twice about, change your mind about; reconsider, decide against; informal get cold feet about. **think something over** consider, contemplate, deliberate about, weigh up, consider the pros and cons of, mull over, ponder, reflect on, muse on, ruminate on. **think something up** devise, dream up, come up with, invent, create, concoct, make up; hit on.

t

thinker noun **theorist**, ideologist, philosopher, scholar, savant, sage, intellectual, intellect, mind; informal brain.

thinking noun *the thinking behind the campaign:* **reasoning**, ideas, theory, thoughts, philosophy, beliefs; opinions, views, position, judgement, assessment, evaluation.
• adjective *a thinking man:* **intelligent**, sensible, reasonable, rational;

logical, analytical; thoughtful, reflective, meditative, contemplative, pensive, philosophical.
– OPPOSITES stupid, irrational.

third-rate adjective **substandard**, bad, inferior, poor, low-grade, inadequate, unsatisfactory, unacceptable.
– OPPOSITES excellent.

thirst noun *his thirst for knowledge:* **craving**, desire, longing, yearning, hunger, hankering, yen, keenness, eagerness, lust, appetite; informal itch. • verb *she thirsted for power:* **crave**, want, covet, desire, hunger for, lust after, hanker after; wish for, long for.

thirsty adjective **1** *the boys were hot and thirsty:* **dehydrated**, dry; informal parched, gasping; Brit. informal spitting feathers. **2** *the thirsty soil:* **dry**, arid, parched, baked, desiccated. **3** *they are thirsty for information:* **eager**, hungry, longing, yearning, hankering; impatient, desperate; informal itching, dying.

thorn noun **prickle**, spike, barb, spine.

thorny adjective **1** *thorny undergrowth:* **prickly**, spiky, barbed, spiny, sharp. **2** *a thorny subject:* **problematic**, tricky, ticklish, delicate, controversial, awkward, difficult, knotty, tough; complicated, complex, involved, intricate; vexed; informal sticky.

thorough adjective **1** *a thorough investigation:* **rigorous**, in-depth, exhaustive, minute, detailed, close, meticulous, methodical, careful, complete, comprehensive, full, extensive, widespread, sweeping, all-embracing, all-inclusive. **2** *he is slow but thorough:* **meticulous**, scrupulous, assiduous, conscientious, painstaking, punctilious, methodical, careful, diligent, industrious, hard-working. **3** *the child is being a thorough nuisance:* **utter**, downright, absolute, complete, total, out-and-out, arrant, real, perfect, proper; Brit. informal right; Austral./NZ informal fair.
– OPPOSITES superficial, cursory, careless.

thoroughbred adjective **pure-bred**, pedigree, pure-blooded.

thoroughfare noun **1** *the park is used as a thoroughfare:* **through route**, access route; Brit. informal rat run. **2** *the teeming thoroughfares of central London:* **street**, road, roadway, avenue, boulevard; N. Amer. highway, freeway, throughway.

thoroughly adverb **1** *we will investigate all complaints thoroughly:* **rigorously**, in depth, exhaustively, from top to bottom, minutely, closely, in detail, meticulously, scrupulously, assiduously, conscientiously, painstakingly, methodically, carefully, comprehensively, fully. **2** *she is thoroughly spoilt:* **utterly**, downright, absolutely, completely, totally, entirely, really, perfectly, positively, in every respect; informal plain, clean.

though conjunction *though she smiled bravely, she looked tired:* **although**, even though/if, despite the fact that, notwithstanding that, for all that. • adverb *You can't always succeed. You can try, though:* **nevertheless**, nonetheless, even so, however, be that as it may, for all that, despite that, having said that.

thought noun **1** *what are your thoughts on the matter?* **idea**, notion, opinion, view, impression, feeling, theory. **2** *he gave up any thought of taking a degree:* **hope**, aspiration, ambition, dream; intention, idea, plan, design, aim. **3** *it only took a moment's thought:* **thinking**, contemplation, musing, pondering, consideration, reflection, introspection, deliberation, rumination, meditation, brooding; formal cogitation. **4** *have you no thought for others?* **compassion**, sympathy, care, concern, regard, solicitude, empathy; consideration, understanding, sensitivity, thoughtfulness, charity.

thoughtful adjective **1** *a thoughtful expression:* **pensive**, reflective, contemplative, musing, meditative, introspective, philosophical, ruminative, preoccupied; formal cogitative. **2** *how very thoughtful of you!* **considerate**, caring, attentive, understanding, sympathetic, solicitous, concerned, helpful, obliging, accommodating, kind, compassionate, charitable.
– OPPOSITES vacant, inconsiderate.

t

thoughtless adjective **1** *I'm so sorry—how thoughtless of me:* **inconsiderate**, uncaring, insensitive, uncharitable, unkind, tactless, undiplomatic, indiscreet, careless. **2** *thoughtless pleasure:* **unthinking**, heedless, careless, unmindful, absent-minded, injudicious, ill-advised, ill-considered, imprudent, unwise, foolish, silly, stupid, reckless, rash, precipitate, negligent, neglectful, remiss.
– OPPOSITES considerate, careful.

thousand cardinal number informal k, thou.

> **WORD LINKS**
> **millennium**, **millenary** a period of a thousand years

thrash verb **1 hit**, beat, strike, batter, thump, hammer, pound; assault, attack; informal wallop, belt, bash, whack, clout, clobber, slug, tan, biff, bop, sock. **2** *he was thrashing around in pain:* **flail**, writhe, thresh, jerk, toss, twist, twitch.

thread noun **1** *a needle and thread:* **cotton**, yarn, filament, fibre. **2** *she lost the thread of the conversation:* **train of thought**, drift, direction, theme, motif, tenor.
• verb **1** *he threaded the rope through a pulley:* **pass**, string, work, ease, push, poke. **2** *she threaded her way through the tables:* **weave**, inch, squeeze, navigate, negotiate.

threadbare adjective **worn**, old, holey, moth-eaten, mangy, ragged, frayed, tattered, battered; decrepit, shabby, scruffy; informal tatty, the worse for wear.

threat noun **1** *Maggie ignored his threats:* **threatening remark**, warning, ultimatum. **2** *a possible threat to aircraft:* **danger**, peril, hazard, menace, risk. **3** *the company faces the threat of liquidation:* **possibility**, chance, probability, likelihood, risk.

threaten verb **1** *how dare you threaten me?* **menace**, intimidate, browbeat, bully, terrorize. **2** *these events could threaten the stability of Europe:* **endanger**, jeopardize, imperil, put at risk. **3** *the grey skies threatened snow:* **herald**, bode, warn of, presage, augur, portend, foreshadow, be a harbinger of, indicate, point to, be a sign of, signal, spell.

threatening adjective **1** *a threatening letter:* **menacing**, intimidating, bullying, frightening; formal minatory. **2** *threatening black clouds:* **ominous**, sinister, menacing, dark, black.

three cardinal number **trio**, threesome, triple, triad, trinity, troika, triumvirate, trilogy, triptych, trefoil.

> **WORD LINKS**
> **triangle** a three-sided figure
> **tercentenary** a three-hundredth anniversary

threesome noun **trio**, triumvirate, triad, trinity, troika.

threshold noun **1** *the threshold of the church:* **doorstep**, entrance, entry, gate, portal. **2** *the threshold of a new era:* **start**, beginning, commencement, brink, verge, dawn, inception, day one, opening, debut; informal kick-off. **3** *the human threshold of pain:* **lower limit**, minimum.

thrift noun **frugality**, economy, providence, prudence, saving, abstemiousness, parsimony, penny-pinching.
– OPPOSITES extravagance.

thriftless adjective **extravagant**, profligate, spendthrift, wasteful, improvident, imprudent, prodigal, lavish.

thrifty adjective **frugal**, economical, sparing, careful with money, provident, prudent, abstemious, parsimonious, penny-pinching.
– OPPOSITES extravagant.

thrill noun **1** *experience the thrill of white-water rafting:* **excitement**, pleasure; fun, enjoyment, amusement, delight, joy; informal buzz, kick. **2** *a thrill of excitement ran through her:* **wave**, rush, surge, flash, blaze, stab, dart, throb, tremor, quiver, flutter, shudder.
• verb *his words thrilled her:* **excite**, stimulate, arouse, rouse, delight, exhilarate, intoxicate, stir, electrify, galvanize, move, fire with enthusiasm; informal give someone a buzz; N. Amer. informal give someone a charge.
– OPPOSITES bore.

thrilling adjective **exciting**, stirring, action-packed, rip-roaring, gripping, riveting, fascinating, dramatic,

hair-raising; rousing, stimulating, electrifying.
–OPPOSITES boring.

thrive verb **flourish**, prosper, burgeon, bloom, blossom, do well, advance, succeed, boom.
–OPPOSITES decline, wither.

thriving adjective **flourishing**, prospering, growing, developing, burgeoning, blooming, healthy, successful, booming, profitable, expanding; informal going strong.
–OPPOSITES moribund.

throat noun **gullet**, oesophagus; windpipe, trachea.

> **WORD LINKS**
> **jugular** relating to the neck or throat

throaty adjective **gravelly**, husky, rough, guttural, deep, thick, gruff, growly, hoarse, croaky; raspy.
–OPPOSITES high-pitched.

throb verb *a vein throbbed in his neck:* **pulsate**, beat, pulse, palpitate, pound, thud, thump, drum, vibrate, quiver.
•noun *the throb of the ship's engines:* **pulsation**, beat, pulse, palpitation, pounding, thudding, thumping, drumming.

throes plural noun *the throes of childbirth:* **agony**, pain, pangs, suffering, torture.
■ **in the throes of** in the middle of, in the process of, in the midst of, busy with, occupied with, taken up with/by, involved in; struggling with, wrestling with, grappling with.

thrombosis noun **blood clot**, embolism, thrombus, infarction.

throne noun **sovereign power**, sovereignty, rule, dominion.

t

throng noun *throngs of people blocked her way:* **crowd**, horde, mass, multitude, host, army, herd, flock, drove, swarm, sea, troupe, pack, press, crush; informal gaggle, bunch, gang.
•verb **1** *the pavements were thronged with tourists:* **fill**, crowd, pack, cram, jam. **2** *people thronged to see the play:* **flock**, stream, swarm, troop. **3** *visitors thronged round him:* **crowd**, cluster, mill, swarm, congregate, gather.

throttle verb **1** *he tried to throttle her:* **choke**, strangle, garrotte. **2** *attempts to throttle the supply of drugs:* **suppress**, inhibit, stifle, control, restrain, check.

through preposition **1** *he worked through the night:* **throughout**, for the duration of. **2** *he got the job through an advertisement:* **by means of**, by way of, by dint of, via, using, thanks to, by virtue of, as a result of, as a consequence of, on account of, owing to.
•adjective *a through train:* **direct**, non-stop.
■ **through and through** in every respect, to the core; thoroughly, utterly, absolutely, completely, totally, wholly, fully, entirely, unconditionally, out-and-out.

throughout preposition **1** *the dispute had repercussions throughout Europe:* **all over**, in every part of, everywhere in. **2** *Rose had been very fit throughout her life:* **all through**, for the duration of, for the whole of, until the end of.

throw verb **1** *she threw the ball back:* **hurl**, toss, fling, pitch, cast, lob, launch; bowl; informal chuck, heave, sling, bung; dated shy. **2** *he threw the door open:* **push**, thrust, fling. **3** *a chandelier threw its light over the walls:* **cast**, send, give off, emit, radiate, project, direct. **4** *he threw another punch:* **deliver**, give, land. **5** *his question threw me:* **disconcert**, unnerve, fluster, ruffle, put off, throw off balance, unsettle, confuse; informal rattle, faze; N. Amer. informal discombobulate.
■ **throw something away** discard, throw out, dispose of, get rid of, scrap, dump, jettison; informal chuck away/out, ditch, bin, junk; Brit. informal get shot of. **throw someone out** expel, eject, evict, drive out, force out, oust, remove; get rid of, depose, topple, unseat, overthrow; informal boot out, kick out, give someone the boot; Brit. informal turf out. **throw something out 1** See THROW SOMETHING AWAY. **2** *his case was thrown out by the magistrate:* reject, dismiss, turn down, refuse, disallow. **3** *a thermal light bulb throws out a lot of heat:* radiate, emit, give out/off, send out.

thrust verb **1** **shove**, push, force, plunge, stick, drive, ram. **2** *fame had been thrust on him:* **force**, foist, impose, inflict. **3** *he thrust his way*

past her: **push**, shove, force, elbow, shoulder, barge.
• noun **1** *a hard thrust:* **shove**, push, lunge, poke. **2** *a thrust by the Third Army:* **advance**, push, drive, attack, assault, onslaught, offensive, charge. **3** *only one engine is producing thrust:* **force**, propulsion, power, impetus. **4** *the thrust of the speech:* **gist**, substance, drift, burden, message, import, tenor.

thrusting adjective **ambitious**, pushy, forceful, aggressive, assertive, self-assertive, full of yourself, determined, power-hungry.
– OPPOSITES meek.

thud noun & verb **thump**, clunk, clonk, crash, smack, bang; informal wham.

thug noun **ruffian**, hooligan, bully boy, hoodlum, gangster, villain; informal tough, bruiser, heavy; Brit. informal rough, bovver boy; N. Amer. informal hood, goon.

thumb verb **1** *he thumbed through his notebook:* **leaf**, flick, flip, riffle. **2** (**thumbed**) *his dictionaries were thumbed and ink-stained:* **soiled**, marked, dog-eared. **3** *he was thumbing his way across France:* **hitch-hike**; informal hitch, hitch/ thumb a lift.
■ **thumbs down** (informal) rejection, refusal, veto, no, rebuff; informal red light. **thumbs up** (informal) approval, seal of approval, endorsement; permission, authorization, consent, yes, leave, authority, nod, assent, blessing, rubber stamp, clearance; informal go-ahead, OK, green light, say-so.

thump verb **1** **hit**, strike, smack, cuff, punch; informal whack, wallop, bash, biff, bop, lam, clout, clobber, sock, swipe, crown, belt; Brit. informal stick one on, slosh; N. Amer. informal slug, boff; literary smite. **2** *her heart thumped with fright:* **throb**, pound, thud, hammer, pulsate, pulse, pump, palpitate.
• noun **1** **blow**, punch, box, cuff, smack; informal whack, thwack, wallop, bash, belt, biff, clout; Brit. informal slosh; N. Amer. informal boff, slug. **2** *she put the box down with a thump:* **thud**, clunk, clonk, crash, smack, bang.

thunder noun **rumble**, boom, roar, pounding, thud, crash, reverberation.
• verb **1** *below me the surf thundered:* **rumble**, boom, roar, pound, thud, thump, bang. **2** *'Answer me!' he thundered:* **roar**, bellow, bark, bawl; informal holler.

thunderous adjective **very loud**, tumultuous, booming, roaring, resounding, reverberating, ringing, deafening, ear-splitting.

thunderstruck adjective **astonished**, amazed, astounded, staggered, stunned, shocked, aghast, dumbfounded, dumbstruck; informal flabbergasted; Brit. informal gobsmacked, knocked for six.

thus adverb **1** *the studio handled production, thus cutting its costs:* **consequently**, so, therefore, ergo, accordingly, hence, as a result. **2** *legislation forbids such data being held thus:* **like that**, in that way, so, like so.
■ **thus far** so far, until now, up to now, up to this point, hitherto.

thwart verb **foil**, frustrate, baulk, forestall, derail, dash; stop, check, block, prevent, defeat, impede, obstruct; informal put paid to, put the kibosh on, do for, stymie; Brit. informal scupper.
– OPPOSITES facilitate.

tic noun **twitch**, spasm, jerk, tremor.

ticket noun **1** *a bus ticket:* **pass**, authorization, permit; token, coupon, voucher. **2** *a price ticket:* **label**, tag, sticker, tab.

tickle verb **1** **stroke**, pet, chuck. **2** *something tickled his imagination:* **stimulate**, interest, appeal to, arouse, excite. **3** *the idea tickled Lewis:* **amuse**, entertain, divert, please, delight.

ticklish adjective **difficult**, problematic, tricky, delicate, sensitive, awkward, prickly, thorny, tough; vexed; informal sticky.

tide noun **1** **tidal flow**, ebb and flow, ebb, current. **2** *the tide of history:* **course**, movement, direction, trend, current, drift, run.

tidy adjective **1** *a tidy room:* **neat**, orderly, well ordered, well kept, shipshape, in apple-pie order, uncluttered, straight. **2** *a very tidy person:* **neat**, trim, spruce, dapper, well groomed, well turned out; organized, methodical, meticulous.
– OPPOSITES messy, untidy.

• **verb** **clear up**, sort out, straighten up, clean up, spruce up, smarten up, declutter.

tie **verb** **1** *we tied the rope to the truck:* **bind**, tie up, tether, hitch, strap, truss, fetter, rope, make fast, moor, lash. **2** *women can feel tied by childcare responsibilities:* **restrict**, restrain, limit, tie down, constrain, trammel, confine, cramp, hamper, handicap, hamstring, encumber, shackle. **3** *a pay deal tied to a productivity agreement:* **link**, connect, couple, relate, join, marry. **4** *they tied for second place:* **draw**, be equal, be even.
• **noun** **1** *he tightened the ties of his robe:* **lace**, string, cord, fastening. **2** *family ties:* **bond**, connection, link, relationship, attachment, affiliation. **3** *pets can be a tremendous tie:* **restriction**, constraint, curb, limitation, restraint, hindrance, encumbrance, handicap; obligation, commitment. **4** *a tie for first place:* **draw**, dead heat. **5** (Brit.) *Turkey's World Cup tie against Holland:* **match**, game, contest, fixture.
■ **tie in** be consistent, tally, agree, be in agreement, accord, concur, fit in, harmonize, be in tune, dovetail; informal square. **tie someone/something up 1** *the attacker tied up his arms and legs:* bind, fasten together, truss up. **2** *he is tied up in meetings all morning:* occupy, engage, keep busy. **3** *they were anxious to tie up the contract:* finalize, conclude, complete, finish off, seal, settle, secure, clinch; informal wrap up.

tie-in **noun** **connection**, link, association, correlation, tie-up, relationship.

t

tier **noun** **1** *six tiers of seats:* **row**, rank, bank, line; layer, level. **2** *a tier of management:* **grade**, gradation, echelon, rung on the ladder.

tight **adjective** **1** *a tight grip:* **firm**, fast, secure. **2** *the rope was pulled tight:* **taut**, rigid, stiff, tense, stretched, strained. **3** *tight jeans:* **close-fitting**, narrow, figure-hugging, skintight; informal sprayed on. **4** *a tight mass of fibres:* **compact**, compressed, dense, solid. **5** *a tight space:* **small**, tiny, narrow, limited, restricted, confined, cramped, constricted. **6** *a tight joint:* **impervious**, impenetrable, sealed, sound, hermetic. **7** *tight limits:* **strict**, rigorous, stringent, tough, rigid, firm. **8** *he's in a tight spot:* **difficult**, tricky, delicate, awkward, problematic; informal sticky; Brit. informal dodgy. **9** *a tight piece of writing:* **succinct**, concise, pithy, incisive, crisp, to the point. **10** *money is a bit tight just now:* **limited**, restricted, in short supply, scarce, depleted, diminished, low.
– OPPOSITES slack, loose.

tighten **verb** **1** **make tighter**, make fast, screw up. **2** *he tightened his grip:* **strengthen**, harden. **3** *she tightened the rope:* **tauten**, stretch, strain, stiffen, tense. **4** *he tightened his lips:* **narrow**, constrict, contract, compress, screw up, pucker, purse; N. Amer. squinch. **5** *security has been tightened up:* **increase**, make stricter, toughen up, heighten, scale up.
– OPPOSITES loosen, slacken, relax.

tight-lipped **adjective** **reticent**, uncommunicative, unforthcoming, close-mouthed, silent, taciturn; informal mum.
– OPPOSITES forthcoming.

till[1] **preposition & conjunction** See **UNTIL**.

till[2] **noun** *the money in the till:* **cash register**, cash box, cash drawer; checkout, cash desk.

till[3] **verb** *he went back to tilling the land:* **cultivate**, work, farm, plough, dig.

tilt **verb** *the ground seemed to tilt:* **slope**, tip, lean, list, bank, slant, incline, pitch, cant, angle.
• **noun** *a tilt of some 45°:* **slope**, list, camber, gradient, bank, slant, incline, pitch, cant, bevel, angle.

timber **noun** **1** *houses built of timber:* **wood**; N. Amer. lumber. **2** *the timbers of wrecked ships:* **beam**, spar, plank, batten, lath, board, joist, rafter.

timbre **noun** **tone**, sound, voice, colour, tonality.

time **noun** **1** *now might be a good time to tell her:* **moment**, point, occasion, juncture. **2** *he worked there for a time:* **while**, spell, stretch, stint, season, interval, period, length of time, duration, phase, stage. **3** *the time of the dinosaurs:* **era**, age, epoch, period, years, days. **4** *tunes in waltz time:* **rhythm**, tempo, beat; metre, measure, cadence, pattern.
• **verb** **schedule**, set, arrange,

organize, fix, book, line up, timetable, plan; N. Amer. slate.
■ **all the time** constantly, around the clock, day and night, night and day, {morning, noon, and night}, {day in, day out}, always, without a break, ceaselessly, endlessly, incessantly, perpetually, permanently, continuously, continually, eternally; informal 24-7. **at one time** formerly, previously, once, in the past, at one point, once upon a time, in days/times gone by, in times past, in the old days; literary in days of yore. **at the same time 1** *they arrived at the same time:* simultaneously, at the same moment, together. **2** *I can't really explain it, but at the same time I'm not convinced:* nonetheless, even so, however, but, still, yet, though; in spite of that, despite that, be that as it may, for all that, that said; anyhow. **at times** occasionally, sometimes, from time to time, now and then, every so often, once in a while, on occasion, off and on, at intervals, periodically. **for the time being** for now, for the moment, for the present, in the interim, in the meantime; temporarily, provisionally, pro tem. **from time to time**. See **AT TIMES** above. **in good time** punctually, on time, early, with time to spare, ahead of schedule. **in time 1** *I came back in time for the party:* early enough, in good time, punctually, on time, with time to spare, on schedule. **2** *in time, she forgot about it:* eventually, in the end, in due course, by and by, finally; one day, some day, sometime, sooner or later. **on time** punctually, in good time, to/on schedule; informal on the dot. **time after time** repeatedly, frequently, often, again and again, over and over again, time and again; persistently, recurrently, constantly, continually; N. Amer. oftentimes; literary oft, oft-times.

> **WORD LINKS**
> **chronological**, **temporal** relating to time
> **horology** the study and measurement of time

timeless adjective **lasting**, enduring, classic, ageless, permanent, perennial, abiding, unfailing, unchanging, unvarying, never-changing, changeless, unfading, eternal, everlasting.
–OPPOSITES ephemeral.

timely adjective **opportune**, well timed, convenient, appropriate, expedient, seasonable.
–OPPOSITES ill-timed.

timetable noun **schedule**, programme, agenda, calendar.
• verb **schedule**, arrange, programme, organize, fix, time, line up; N. Amer. slate.

timid adjective **easily frightened**, fearful, afraid, faint-hearted, timorous, nervous, scared, frightened; shy, diffident, self-effacing.
–OPPOSITES bold.

tinge verb **1** *white blossom tinged with pink:* **tint**, colour, stain, shade, wash. **2** *his optimism is tinged with realism:* **touch**, colour, qualify, temper; imbue, permeate.
• noun **1** *a blue tinge:* **tint**, colour, shade, tone, hue. **2** *a tinge of cynicism:* **trace**, note, touch, suggestion, hint, flavour, element, streak, suspicion, soupçon.

tingle verb **prickle**, sting.
• noun **prickle**, pricking, sting.

tinker verb **fiddle with**, adjust, try to mend, play about with, mess about with; Brit. informal muck about with.

tinkle verb **1** *the bell tinkled:* **ring**, jingle, jangle, chime, ding, ping. **2** *cool water tinkled in the stone fountain:* **splash**, purl, babble; literary plash.
• noun **1** *the tinkle of the doorbell:* **ring**, chime, ding, ping, jingle, jangle. **2** *the faint tinkle of water:* **splash**, purl, babble, burble; literary plash.

tinny adjective **1** *tinny music:* **jangly**, jingly. **2** *a tinny little car:* **cheap**, poor-quality, inferior, low-grade, gimcrack, shoddy, jerry-built; informal tacky, rubbishy.

tint noun **1** *an apricot tint:* **shade**, colour, tone, hue, tinge, cast, flush, blush. **2** *a hair tint:* **dye**, colourant, colouring, wash.

tiny adjective **minute**, minuscule, microscopic, nanoscopic, mini, diminutive, miniature, baby, toy; Scottish wee; informal teeny, teensy, itsy-bitsy; Brit. informal titchy, tiddly.
–OPPOSITES huge.

tip[1] noun **1** *the tip of the spear:* **point**, end, extremity, head, spike, prong. **2** *the tips of the mountains:* **peak**, top, summit, apex, crown, crest, pinnacle. **3** *the sticks have tips fitted to protect them:* **cap**, cover, ferrule. •verb *mountains tipped with snow:* **cap**, top, crown.

tip[2] verb **1** *the boat tipped over:* **overturn**, turn over, topple over, fall over; keel over, capsize, turn turtle. **2** *a whale could tip over a small boat:* **upset**, overturn, topple over, turn over, push over, upend, capsize; informal roll; old use overset. **3** *the car tipped to one side:* **lean**, tilt, list, slope, bank, slant, incline, pitch, cant. **4** *she tipped the water into the trough:* **pour**, empty, drain, dump, discharge; decant.

tip[3] noun **1** *a generous tip:* **gratuity**, baksheesh; present, gift, reward. **2** *useful tips:* **piece of advice**, suggestion, word of advice, pointer; clue, hint; informal wrinkle.

tip-off noun (informal) **piece of information**, warning, lead; hint, clue; advice.

tippler noun **drinker**, imbiber; alcoholic, drunk, drunkard, dipsomaniac; informal boozer, alky, barfly, sponge, dipso, wino, soak; Austral./NZ informal hophead; old use toper.
–OPPOSITES teetotaller.

tipsy adjective **merry**, mellow, slightly drunk; Brit. informal tiddly, squiffy.
–OPPOSITES sober.

tirade noun **diatribe**, harangue, rant, attack, polemic, broadside, fulmination, tongue-lashing; informal blast; literary philippic.

tire verb **1** *he began to tire:* **get tired**, weaken, flag, droop. **2** *the journey had tired him:* **fatigue**, tire out, exhaust, wear out, drain, weary, wash out, enervate; informal knock out, take it out of, do in, fag out; Brit. informal knacker. **3** *they tired of his difficult behaviour:* **weary**, get tired, get fed up, get sick, get bored.

tired adjective **1** *she was tired and irritable:* **exhausted**, worn out, weary, fatigued, dog-tired, bone-tired, ready to drop, drained, enervated; drowsy, sleepy; informal done in, all in, dead beat, shattered, bushed, frazzled; Brit. informal knackered, whacked, jiggered; N. Amer. informal pooped, tuckered out; Austral./NZ informal stonkered. **2** *I'm tired of all the travelling:* **fed up with**, weary of, bored with, sick of; informal up to here with. **3** *tired jokes:* **hackneyed**, overused, overworked, worn out, stale, clichéd, predictable, unimaginative, unoriginal, dull, boring; informal corny, played out.
–OPPOSITES energetic, lively, fresh.

tiredness noun **fatigue**, weariness, exhaustion, enervation; sleepiness, drowsiness, somnolence.
–OPPOSITES energy.

tireless adjective **vigorous**, energetic, industrious, determined, enthusiastic, keen, zealous, spirited, dynamic, stout, untiring, unwearying, indefatigable, unflagging.
–OPPOSITES lazy.

tiresome adjective **boring**, dull, tedious, wearisome, wearing; annoying, irritating, trying; informal aggravating, pesky.
–OPPOSITES interesting, enjoyable.

tiring adjective **exhausting**, wearying, taxing, fatiguing, wearing, enervating, draining; hard, heavy, arduous, strenuous, onerous, demanding, gruelling; informal killing; Brit. informal knackering.

tissue noun **1** *living tissue:* **matter**, material, substance; flesh. **2** *a box of tissues:* **paper handkerchief**, paper towel; trademark Kleenex. **3** *a tissue of lies:* **web**, complex, mass, set, series, chain.

titbit noun **1** *tasty titbits:* **delicacy**, tasty morsel, bonne bouche, treat; nibble, savoury, appetizer; informal goody; N. Amer. tidbit. **2** *a fascinating titbit:* **piece of gossip**, bit of scandal, piece of information.

titillate verb **arouse**, excite, tantalize, stimulate, stir, thrill, interest, attract, fascinate; informal turn on.
–OPPOSITES bore.

titillating adjective **arousing**, exciting, stimulating, sexy, thrilling, provocative, tantalizing, interesting, fascinating; suggestive, salacious, lurid; Brit. informal saucy.
–OPPOSITES boring.

title noun **1** *the title of the book:* **name**. **2** *the cartoon title:* **caption**, legend, inscription, label, heading, subheading. **3** *the company publishes*

40 titles a year: **publication**, work, book, newspaper, paper, magazine, periodical. **4** *the title of Duke of Marlborough:* **designation**, name, form of address; epithet, style; rank, office, position; informal moniker, handle; formal appellation, denomination. **5** *an Olympic title:* **championship**, crown, first place; laurels. **6** *the vendor is obliged to prove his title to the land:* **ownership**, proprietorship, possession, holding, freehold, entitlement, right, claim.
•**verb** *a policy paper titled 'Law and Order':* **call**, entitle, name, dub, designate, style, term; formal denominate.

titter **verb & noun** **giggle**, snigger, snicker, tee-hee, chuckle, laugh; informal chortle.

tittle-tattle **noun** *she would never listen to tittle-tattle:* **gossip**, rumours, idle talk, hearsay, whispers, titbits; scandal.

titular **adjective** **1** *the titular head of a university:* **nominal**, in title/name only, ceremonial; token, puppet. **2** *the work's titular song:* **eponymous**, identifying.

toady **noun** *she surrounded herself with toadies:* **sycophant**, flatterer, lickspittle; informal bootlicker, yes-man.
•**verb** *people were toadying up to the prime minister:* **ingratiate yourself with**, grovel to, be obsequious to, kowtow to, pander to, crawl to, truckle to, bow and scrape to, make up to, fawn on/over; informal suck up to, lick someone's boots, butter up.

toast **noun** **1** *he raised his glass in a toast:* **tribute**, salutation. **2** *he was the toast of the West End:* **darling**, favourite, pet, heroine, hero; talk; Brit. informal blue-eyed boy/girl.
•**verb** **1** *she toasted her hands in front of the fire:* **warm**, take the chill off. **2** *we toasted the couple with champagne:* **drink to the health of**, raise your glass to, salute, honour, pay tribute to.

today **adverb** *the complex tasks demanded of computers today:* **nowadays**, these days, at the present time, in these times, in this day and age, now, currently, at the moment; in the present climate; N. Amer. presently.

toddle **verb** **totter**, teeter, wobble, falter, waddle, stumble.

together **adverb** **1** *they worked together:* **in partnership**, in conjunction, jointly, in cooperation, in collaboration, in combination, in league, side by side, hand in hand, shoulder to shoulder, cheek by jowl; in collusion, hand in glove; informal in cahoots. **2** *they both spoke together:* **simultaneously**, at the same time, at once, all together, as a group, in unison, in chorus. **3** *I was not able to get up for days together:* **in succession**, in a row, at a time, successively, consecutively, running, straight, on end, one after the other; informal on the trot.
–OPPOSITES separately.
•**adjective** (informal) *a very together young woman.* See LEVEL-HEADED.

toil **verb** **1** *she toiled all night:* **work**, labour, exert yourself, slave, grind away, strive, work your fingers to the bone, work like a Trojan, work like a dog, keep your nose to the grindstone; informal slog away, plug away, peg away, beaver away; Brit. informal graft. **2** *she began to toil up the path:* **struggle**, trudge, tramp, traipse, slog, plod, trek, footslog, drag yourself; N. Amer. informal schlep.
–OPPOSITES rest, relax.
•**noun** *a life of toil:* **hard work**, labour, exertion, drudgery, effort, industry, {blood, sweat, and tears}; informal slog, elbow grease; Brit. informal graft.

toilet **noun** **1** **lavatory**, WC, public convenience, cloakroom, powder room, urinal, privy, latrine; N. Amer. washroom, bathroom, rest room, men's/ladies' room, comfort station; Brit. informal loo, bog, the Ladies, the Gents, khazi; N. Amer. informal can, john; Austral./NZ informal dunny; old use closet, jakes. **2** *she always took a long time over her toilet:* **washing**, bathing, showering; grooming; humorous ablutions.

token **noun** **1** *a token of our appreciation:* **symbol**, sign, emblem, badge, representation, indication, mark, manifestation, expression, pledge, demonstration. **2** *he kept the menu as a token of the wedding:* **memento**, souvenir, keepsake, reminder. **3** *a book token:* **voucher**, coupon. **4** *a telephone token:* **counter**, disc, jetton, chip.

• adjective **1** *a one-day token strike:* **symbolic**, emblematic, indicative; peppercorn. **2** *the practice now meets only token resistance:* **perfunctory**, slight, nominal, minimal, minor, mild, superficial.

tolerable adjective **1** *a tolerable noise level:* **bearable**, endurable, supportable, acceptable. **2** *he had a tolerable voice:* **fairly good**, passable, adequate, all right, acceptable, satisfactory, average, fair; mediocre, middling, ordinary, unexceptional; informal OK, so-so, no great shakes.
– OPPOSITES intolerable, outstanding.

tolerance noun **1** *an attitude of tolerance towards people:* **acceptance**; open-mindedness, broad-mindedness, forbearance; patience, charity, understanding. **2** *the plant's tolerance of pollution:* **endurance**, resilience, resistance, immunity. **3** *a 1% maximum tolerance in measurement:* **deviation**, variation, play; inaccuracy, imprecision.

tolerant adjective **open-minded**, forbearing, broad-minded, liberal, unprejudiced, unbiased; patient, long-suffering, understanding, charitable, lenient, easy-going.
– OPPOSITES intolerant.

tolerate verb **1** *a regime unwilling to tolerate dissent:* **allow**, permit, condone, accept, swallow, countenance; formal brook. **2** *he couldn't tolerate her moods any longer:* **endure**, put up with, bear, take, stand, support, stomach; informal hack, abide; Brit. informal stick, wear; formal brook; old use suffer.

toleration noun **acceptance**, endurance; forbearance, open-mindedness, broad-mindedness; patience, charity, understanding.

t

toll[1] noun **1** *a motorway toll:* **charge**, fee, payment, levy, tariff, tax. **2** *the toll of dead and injured:* **number**, count, tally, total, sum. **3** *the toll on the environment has been high:* **adverse effect**, detriment, harm, damage, injury, hurt; cost, price, loss, disadvantage.

toll[2] verb *I heard the bell toll:* **ring**, chime, strike, peal; sound, clang, resound, reverberate; literary knell.

tomb noun **burial chamber**, sepulchre, mausoleum, vault, crypt, undercroft, catacomb; grave.

> **WORD LINKS**
> **sepulchral** relating to a tomb

tombstone noun **gravestone**, headstone; memorial, monument.

tome noun **volume**, book, work, opus, publication, title.

tomfoolery noun **antics**, pranks, clowning, capers, tricks, buffoonery, nonsense, horseplay, mischief; informal larks, shenanigans.

tone noun **1** *the tone of the tuba:* **timbre**, sound, voice, colour, tonality. **2** *his friendly tone:* **intonation**, modulation, accentuation. **3** *the impatient tone of his letter:* **mood**, air, feel, flavour, note, attitude, character, temper; tenor, vein, drift, gist. **4** *a dialling tone:* **note**, signal, bleep. **5** *tones of lavender and rose:* **shade**, colour, hue, tint, tinge.
• verb *the shirt toned well with her cream skirt:* **harmonize**, go, blend, coordinate, team; match, suit, complement.
▪ **tone something down 1** *the colour needs to be toned down a bit:* soften, lighten, mute, subdue. **2** *the papers refused to tone down their criticism:* moderate, modify, modulate, mitigate, temper, dampen, soften.

tongue noun **1** *a foreign tongue:* **language**; informal lingo. **2** *her sharp tongue:* **way of speaking**, speech, parlance.

> **WORD LINKS**
> **lingual** relating to the tongue

tongue-tied adjective **lost for words**, speechless, dumbstruck; mute, silent; informal mum.
– OPPOSITES loquacious.

tonic noun **1** *ginseng can be used as a tonic:* **stimulant**, restorative, refresher; informal pick-me-up, bracer. **2** *the change of scene was a tonic:* **stimulant**, boost, fillip; informal shot in the arm, pick-me-up.

too adverb **1** *invasion would be too risky:* **excessively**, overly, unduly, immoderately, inordinately, unreasonably, extremely, very. **2** *he was unhappy, too, you know:* **also**, as well, in addition, into the bargain, besides, furthermore, moreover.

tool noun **1** *garden tools:* **implement**, utensil, instrument, device, appar-

atus, gadget, appliance, machine, contrivance, contraption; informal gizmo. **2** *the beautiful Estella is Miss Havisham's tool:* **puppet**, pawn, creature; minion, lackey; informal stooge.
• **verb** *red leather, tooled in gold:* **ornament**, embellish, decorate, work.

tooth **noun** **fang**, tusk; informal gnasher; Brit. informal pearly white.

> **WORD LINKS**
> **dental** relating to teeth
> **odontology** the scientific study of teeth

top **noun 1** *the top of the cliff:* **summit**, peak, pinnacle, crest, crown, brow, head, tip, apex, vertex. **2** *the top of the table:* **upper part**, upper surface. **3** *the top of the coffee jar:* **lid**, cap, cover, stopper. **4** *a short-sleeved top:* **sweater**, jumper, jersey, sweat shirt; T-shirt, shirt, blouse. **5** *he was at the top of his profession:* **high point**, height, peak, pinnacle, zenith, acme, culmination, climax, crowning point; prime.
– OPPOSITES bottom, base.
• **adjective 1** *the top floor:* **highest**, topmost, uppermost. **2** *top scientists:* **foremost**, leading, principal, pre-eminent, greatest, best, finest, elite; informal top-notch. **3** *the organization's top management:* **chief**, principal, main, leading, highest, ruling, commanding, most powerful, most important. **4** *a top hotel:* **prime**, excellent, superb, superior, choice, select, first-rate, grade A, best, finest, premier; informal A1, top-notch. **5** *they are travelling at top speed:* **maximum**, greatest, utmost.
– OPPOSITES bottom, lowest, minimum.
• **verb 1** *sales are expected to top £1 billion:* **exceed**, surpass, go beyond, better, beat, outstrip, outdo, outshine, eclipse. **2** *their CD is currently topping the charts:* **lead**, head. **3** *mousse topped with cream:* **cover**, cap, coat; finish, garnish.
■ **top something up** fill, refill, refresh, freshen, replenish, recharge, resupply.

topic **noun** **subject**, theme, issue, matter, point, question, concern, argument, thesis, text, keynote.

topical **adjective** **current**, up to date, up to the minute, contemporary, recent, relevant; in the news.
– OPPOSITES out of date.

topmost **adjective 1** *the tree's topmost branches:* **highest**, top, uppermost. **2** *the topmost authority on the subject:* **foremost**, leading, principal, premier, prime, top, greatest, best, supreme, pre-eminent, outstanding, main, chief; N. Amer. ranking; informal number-one.

topple **verb 1** *she toppled over:* **fall**, tumble, overbalance, overturn, tip, keel; lose your balance. **2** *protesters toppled a statue:* **knock over**, upset, push over, tip over, upend. **3** *a plot to topple the government:* **overthrow**, oust, unseat, overturn, bring down, defeat, get rid of, dislodge, eject.

torch **noun 1** *an electric torch:* **flashlight**. **2** (historical) *a flaming torch:* **firebrand**, brand.

torment **noun 1** *emotional torment:* **agony**, suffering, torture, pain, anguish, misery, distress, affliction, trauma, wretchedness. **2** *it was a torment to see him like that:* **ordeal**, affliction, scourge, curse, plague, bane; sorrow, tribulation.
• **verb 1** *she was tormented by shame:* **torture**, afflict, rack, harrow, plague, haunt, distress, agonize. **2** *she began to torment the boys:* **tease**, taunt, bait, harass, provoke, goad, plague, bother, trouble, persecute; informal needle.

torn **adjective 1** *a torn shirt:* **ripped**, rent, cut, slit; ragged, tattered. **2** *she was torn between the two options:* **wavering**, vacillating, irresolute, dithering, uncertain, unsure, undecided, in two minds.

tornado **noun** **whirlwind**, cyclone, typhoon, storm, hurricane, windstorm; N. Amer. informal twister.

torpor **noun** **lethargy**, sluggishness, inertia, inactivity, lifelessness, listlessness, languor, lassitude, laziness, idleness, indolence, sloth, passivity; tiredness, weariness, exhaustion.

torrent **noun 1** *a torrent of water:* **flood**, deluge, inundation, spate, cascade, rush, stream, current, flow, overflow, tide. **2** *a torrent of abuse:* **outburst**, outpouring, stream, flood, volley, barrage, tide, spate.
– OPPOSITES trickle.

torrential adjective **copious**, heavy, teeming, severe, relentless.

torrid adjective **1** *a torrid summer:* **hot**, dry, scorching, searing, blazing, blistering, sweltering, burning; informal boiling, baking. **2** *a torrid affair:* **passionate**, ardent, lustful, amorous; informal steamy, sizzling.
– OPPOSITES cold.

tortuous adjective **1** *a tortuous route:* **twisting**, winding, zigzag, sinuous, snaky, meandering, serpentine. **2** *a tortuous argument:* **convoluted**, complicated, complex, labyrinthine, involved, Byzantine, lengthy.
– OPPOSITES straight, straightforward.

torture noun **1** *the torture of political prisoners:* **abuse**, ill-treatment, maltreatment. **2** *the torture of losing a loved one:* **torment**, agony, suffering, pain, anguish, misery, distress, heartbreak, trauma, wretchedness.
• verb **1** *the forces routinely tortured suspects:* **abuse**, ill-treat, mistreat, maltreat, persecute; informal work over. **2** *he was tortured by grief:* **torment**, rack, afflict, harrow, plague, agonize.

toss verb **1** *he tossed his tools into the boot:* **throw**, hurl, fling, sling, cast, pitch, lob, propel, project, launch; informal heave, chuck, bung. **2** *he tossed a coin:* **flip**, flick, spin. **3** *the ship tossed about on the waves:* **pitch**, lurch, rock, roll, plunge, reel, list, keel, sway. **4** *toss the ingredients together:* **shake**, stir, turn, mix, combine.

tot[1] noun **1** **infant**, baby, toddler, child, mite; Scottish bairn. **2** *a tot of rum:* **dram**, drink, nip, drop, slug; informal shot, finger, snifter.

tot[2] verb **1** *he totted up some figures:* **add**, total, count, calculate, compute, reckon, tally. **2** *we've totted up 8 victories:* **accumulate**, build up, amass, accrue.

total adjective **1** *the total cost:* **entire**, complete, whole, full, comprehensive, combined, aggregate, gross, overall. **2** *a total disaster:* **complete**, utter, absolute, thorough, perfect, downright, out-and-out, outright, sheer, unmitigated; Brit. informal right.
– OPPOSITES partial.
• noun *a total of £16:* **sum**, aggregate; whole, entirety, totality.
• verb **1** *the prize money totalled £33,050:* **add up to**, amount to, come to, run to, make, work out as. **2** *he totalled up his score:* **add up**, count, reckon, tot up, compute, work out.

totalitarian adjective **autocratic**, undemocratic, one-party, dictatorial, tyrannical, despotic, fascist, oppressive; authoritarian, absolutist.
– OPPOSITES democratic.

totality noun **entirety**, whole, total, aggregate, sum.

totally adverb **completely**, entirely, wholly, thoroughly, fully, utterly, absolutely, perfectly, unreservedly, unconditionally, downright; in every way, one hundred per cent, every inch, to the hilt, all the way; informal dead.
– OPPOSITES partly.

totter verb **1** *he tottered off down the road:* **teeter**, stagger, wobble, stumble, shuffle, shamble, toddle; reel. **2** *the foundations began to heave and totter:* **shake**, sway, tremble, quiver, teeter, shudder, judder, rock, quake.

touch verb **1** *his shoes were touching the bed:* **be in contact with**, meet, join, connect with, converge with, be contiguous with, be against. **2** *he touched her cheek:* **press lightly**, tap, pat; feel, stroke, fondle, caress, pet; brush, graze. **3** *sales touched twenty grand:* **reach**, attain, come to, make; rise to, soar to; sink to, plummet to; informal hit. **4** *nobody can touch him when he's on form:* **compare with**, be on a par with, equal, match, be in the same class/league as, parallel, rival, come/get close to, measure up to; better, beat; informal hold a candle to. **5** *you're not supposed to touch the computer:* **handle**, hold, pick up, move, use; meddle with, play with, fiddle with, interfere with, tamper with, disturb, lay a finger on. **6** *I was touched by her kindness:* **affect**, move.
• noun **1** *her touch on his shoulder:* **tap**, pat; stroke, caress; brush, graze. **2** *his political touch:* **skill**, expertise, dexterity, deftness, adroitness, adeptness, ability, talent, flair, facility, proficiency, knack. **3** *there was a touch of bitterness in her voice | add a touch of vinegar:*

trace, bit, suggestion, suspicion, hint, scintilla, tinge, overtone, undertone; dash, taste, spot, drop, dab, soupçon. **4** *the gas lights are a nice touch:* **detail**, feature, point; addition, accessory. **5** *have you been in touch with him?* **contact**, communication, correspondence.
■ **touch down** land, alight, come down, put down, arrive. **touch on 1** *many television programmes have touched on the subject:* refer to, mention, comment on, remark on, bring up, raise, broach, allude to; cover, deal with. **2** *a self-confident manner touching on the arrogant:* come close to, verge on, border on, approach. **touch something up 1** *these paints are handy for touching up small areas:* repaint, retouch, patch up, fix up; renovate, refurbish, revamp; informal do up. **2** *touch up your CV and improve your interview skills:* improve, enhance, refine; informal tweak.

WORD LINKS
tactile relating to the sense of touch

touch-and-go adjective **uncertain**, precarious, risky, hazardous, dangerous, critical, suspenseful, cliffhanging.
– OPPOSITES certain.

touched adjective **affected**, moved.

touching adjective **moving**, affecting, heart-warming, emotional, emotive, tender, sentimental; poignant, sad, tear-jerking.

touchstone noun **criterion**, standard, yardstick, benchmark, barometer, litmus test; measure, point of reference, norm, gauge, test, guide, exemplar, model, pattern.

touchy adjective **1** *she can be touchy:* **sensitive**, oversensitive, hypersensitive, easily offended, thin-skinned, highly strung, tense; irritable, tetchy, testy, crotchety, peevish, querulous, bad-tempered, petulant; informal snappy, ratty; N. Amer. informal cranky. **2** *a touchy subject:* **delicate**, sensitive, tricky, ticklish, embarrassing, awkward, difficult; contentious, controversial.
– OPPOSITES affable.

tough adjective **1** *tough leather:* **durable**, strong, resilient, sturdy, rugged, solid, stout, robust, hard-wearing, long-lasting, heavy-duty, well built, made to last. **2** *the steak was tough:* **chewy**, leathery, gristly, stringy, fibrous. **3** *he'll survive—he's pretty tough:* **robust**, resilient, strong, hardy, rugged, fit; informal hard; dated stalwart. **4** *tough sentencing for offenders:* **strict**, stern, severe, stringent, rigorous, hard, firm, hard-hitting, uncompromising. **5** *the training was pretty tough:* **arduous**, onerous, strenuous, gruelling, exacting, difficult, demanding, hard, heavy, taxing, tiring, exhausting, punishing, laborious. **6** *tough questions:* **difficult**, hard, knotty, thorny, tricky.
– OPPOSITES soft, weak, easy.
• **noun** *a gang of toughs:* **ruffian**, thug, hoodlum, hooligan, bully boy; Brit. rough; informal roughneck, heavy, bruiser; Brit. informal yob.

toughen verb **1** *the process toughens the wood fibres:* **strengthen**, fortify, reinforce, harden, temper, anneal. **2** *the government could toughen the penalties for libel:* **increase**, make stricter, stiffen, tighten up.

tour noun **1** *a three-day walking tour:* **trip**, excursion, journey, expedition, jaunt, outing; trek, safari. **2** *a tour of the factory:* **visit**, inspection, walkabout. **3** *his tour of duty in Ulster:* **stint**, stretch, spell, turn, assignment, period of service.
• **verb 1** *this hotel is well placed for touring Devon:* **travel round**, explore, holiday in; informal do. **2** *the prince toured a local factory:* **visit**, go round, walk round, inspect.

tourist noun **holidaymaker**, traveller, sightseer, visitor, backpacker, globetrotter, tripper; N. Amer. vacationer, out-of-towner.
– OPPOSITES local.

tournament noun **competition**, contest, championship, meeting, meet, event, match, fixture.

tousled adjective **untidy**, dishevelled, wind-blown, messy, disordered, disarranged, messed up, rumpled, uncombed, ungroomed, tangled, wild, unkempt; informal mussed up.
– OPPOSITES neat, tidy.

tout verb **1** *street merchants were*

touting their wares: **peddle**, sell, hawk, offer for sale; informal flog. **2** *minicab drivers were touting for business:* **solicit**, seek, drum up; ask, petition, appeal, canvas. **3** *he's being touted as the next Scotland manager:* **recommend**, speak of, talk of; predict; Brit. tip.

tow verb **pull**, haul, drag, draw, tug, lug.

towards preposition **1** *towards evening dark clouds gathered:* **just before**, near, around, approaching, close to. **2** *her attitude towards politics:* **with regard to**, respecting, in relation to, concerning, about, apropos.

tower noun *a church tower:* **steeple**, spire; minaret; turret; bell tower, belfry, campanile.
• verb **1** *snow-capped peaks towered over the valley:* **soar**, rise, rear; overshadow, overhang, hang over, dominate. **2** *he towered over most other theologians:* **dominate**, overshadow, outshine, outclass, eclipse, be head and shoulders above.

towering adjective **1** *a towering skyscraper:* **high**, tall, lofty, soaring, sky-high, sky-scraping, multi-storey; giant, gigantic, enormous, huge, massive; informal ginormous. **2** *a towering intellect:* **outstanding**, pre-eminent, leading, foremost, finest, top, surpassing, supreme, great, incomparable, unrivalled, unsurpassed, peerless. **3** *a towering rage:* **extreme**, fierce, terrible, intense, overpowering, mighty, violent, vehement, passionate.

town noun **urban area**, conurbation, municipality; city, metropolis; Brit. borough; Scottish burgh.
– OPPOSITES country.

WORD LINKS
civic, municipal, urban relating to a town or city

toxic adjective **poisonous**, virulent, noxious, dangerous, harmful, injurious, pernicious.
– OPPOSITES harmless.

toy noun **1** *children's toys:* **plaything**, game. **2** *an executive toy:* **gadget**, device; trinket, knick-knack; informal gizmo.
• adjective **1** *a toy gun:* **model**, imitation, replica; miniature. **2** *a toy poodle:* **miniature**, small, tiny, diminutive.
■ **toy with 1** *I was toying with the idea of writing a book:* think about, consider, flirt with, entertain the possibility of; informal kick around. **2** *Adam toyed with his glasses:* fiddle with, play with, fidget with, twiddle; finger. **3** *she toyed with her food:* nibble, pick at, peck at.

trace verb **1** *police hope to trace the owner:* **track down**, find, discover, detect, unearth, turn up, hunt down, ferret out, run to ground. **2** *she traced a pattern in the sand:* **draw**, outline, mark. **3** *the analysis traces out the consequences of such beliefs:* **outline**, map out, sketch out, delineate, depict, show, indicate.
• noun **1** *no trace had been found of the missing plane:* **vestige**, sign, mark, indication, evidence, clue; remains, remnant. **2** *a trace of bitterness crept into her voice:* **bit**, touch, hint, suggestion, suspicion, shadow, whiff; drop, dash, tinge; informal smidgen, tad. **3** *the ground was hard and they left no traces:* **trail**, tracks, marks, prints, footprints; spoor.

track noun **1** *a gravel track:* **path**, pathway, footpath, lane, trail, route, way, course. **2** *the final lap of the track:* **course**, racecourse, racetrack; velodrome; Brit. circuit. **3** *he found the tracks of a fox:* **traces**, marks, prints, footprints, trail, spoor. **4** *commuters had to walk along the tracks:* **rail**, line. **5** *the album's title track:* **song**, recording, number, piece.
• verb *he tracked the bear for 40 km:* **follow**, trail, trace, pursue, shadow, stalk; informal tail.
■ **keep track of** monitor, follow, keep up with, keep an eye on; keep in touch with, keep up to date with; informal keep tabs on. **track someone/something down** discover, find, detect, hunt down/out, unearth, uncover, turn up, dig up, ferret out, bring to light, run to ground.

tract[1] noun *large tracts of land:* **area**, region, expanse, sweep, stretch, extent, belt, swathe, zone.

tract[2] noun *a political tract:* **treatise**, essay, article, paper, work, monograph, disquisition, dissertation, thesis; pamphlet, booklet, leaflet.

tractable adjective **malleable**,

manageable, amenable, pliable, governable, yielding, complaisant, compliant, persuadable, accommodating, docile, biddable, obedient, submissive, meek.
–OPPOSITES recalcitrant.

traction noun **grip**, purchase, friction, adhesion.

trade noun **1** *a move to ban all trade in ivory:* **commerce**, buying and selling, dealing, business, marketing, merchandising; dealings, transactions; traffic, trafficking. **2** *the glazier's trade:* **craft**, occupation, job, career, profession, business, line of work, métier, walk of life, field; work, employment.
•verb **1** *he made his fortune trading in diamonds:* **deal**, buy and sell, market, merchandise; traffic, peddle; informal hawk, flog. **2** *the business is trading at a loss:* **operate**, run, do business. **3** *I traded the old machine for a newer model:* **swap**, exchange, switch; barter.
■ **trade on** exploit, take advantage of, capitalize on, profit from, use; milk; informal cash in on.

WORD LINKS
mercantile relating to trade

trademark noun **1** *the company's trademark:* **logo**, emblem, sign, mark, stamp, symbol, device, badge, crest, monogram, colophon; trade name, brand name, proprietary name. **2** *it had all the trademarks of a Mafia hit:* **characteristic**, hallmark, sign, trait, quality, attribute, feature.

trader noun **dealer**, merchant, buyer, seller, marketeer, merchandiser, broker, agent; distributor, vendor, purveyor, supplier; trafficker; shopkeeper, retailer, wholesaler.

tradesman, **tradeswoman** noun **1** *tradesmen standing outside their stores:* **shopkeeper**, retailer, vendor, wholesaler; N. Amer. storekeeper. **2** *a qualified tradesman:* **craftsman**, workman, artisan.

tradition noun **1** *during a maiden speech, by tradition, everyone keeps absolutely silent:* **historical convention**, unwritten law; oral history, lore, folklore. **2** *an age-old tradition:* **custom**, practice, convention, ritual, observance, way, usage, habit, institution; formal praxis.

traditional adjective **1** *traditional Christmas fare:* **long-established**, customary, time-honoured, established, classic, wonted, accustomed, standard, regular, normal, conventional, usual, orthodox, habitual, ritual; age-old. **2** *traditional beliefs:* **handed-down**, folk, unwritten, oral.

traffic noun **1** *they might be stuck in traffic:* **traffic jam**, congestion, gridlock, tailback, hold-up, queue; informal snarl-up. **2** *the increased use of railways for goods traffic:* **transport**, freight, conveyancing, shipping. **3** *the illegal traffic in stolen art:* **trade**, dealing, commerce, business, buying and selling; smuggling, bootlegging, black market; dealings, transactions.
•verb *he confessed to trafficking in ivory:* **trade**, deal, do business, buy and sell; smuggle, bootleg; informal run.

tragedy noun **disaster**, calamity, catastrophe, cataclysm, misfortune, reverse, vicissitude, adversity.

tragic adjective **1** *a tragic accident:* **disastrous**, calamitous, catastrophic, cataclysmic, devastating, terrible, dreadful, awful, appalling, horrendous; fatal. **2** *a tragic tale:* **sad**, unhappy, pathetic, moving, distressing, painful, harrowing, heart-rending, piteous, wretched, sorry. **3** *a tragic waste of talent:* **dreadful**, terrible, awful, deplorable, lamentable, regrettable; formal grievous.
–OPPOSITES fortunate, happy.

trail noun **1** *a trail of clues | a trail of devastation:* **series**, string, chain, succession, sequence; aftermath. **2** *wolves on the trail of their prey:* **track**, spoor, path, scent; traces, marks, signs, prints, footprints. **3** *the plane's vapour trail:* **wake**, tail, stream. **4** *a trail of ants:* **line**, column, train, file, procession, string, chain, convoy; queue. **5** *country parks with nature trails:* **path**, pathway, way, footpath, track, course, route.
•verb **1** *her robe trailed along the ground:* **drag**, sweep; dangle, hang, droop. **2** *Sharpe suspected they were trailing him:* **follow**, pursue,

track, shadow, stalk, hunt; informal tail. **3** *I hate trailing round the shops:* **trudge**, plod, drag yourself, traipse, trek; N. Amer. informal schlep. **4** *her voice trailed off:* **fade**, tail off/away, grow faint, die away, dwindle, subside, peter out.

train verb **1** *the bank trained its staff to use the software:* **instruct**, teach, coach, tutor, school, educate, prime, drill, ground. **2** *she's training to be a hairdresser:* **study**, learn, prepare. **3** *with the Olympics in mind, athletes are training hard:* **exercise**, work out, get in shape, practise. **4** *she trained the gun on him:* **aim**, point, direct, level, focus.
•noun **1** *a minister and his train of attendants:* **retinue**, entourage, cortège, following, staff, household, court, suite, retainers. **2** *a train of elephants:* **procession**, line, file, column, convoy, cavalcade, caravan, succession. **3** *a bizarre train of events:* **chain**, string, series, sequence, succession, set, course.

trainer noun **coach**, instructor, teacher, tutor; handler.

training noun **1** *in-house training for staff:* **instruction**, teaching, coaching, tuition, tutoring, schooling, education. **2** *four months' hard training before the match:* **exercise**, working out; practice, preparation.

traipse verb **trudge**, trek, tramp, trail, plod, drag yourself, slog; N. Amer. informal schlep.

trait noun **characteristic**, attribute, feature, quality, property; habit, custom, mannerism, idiosyncrasy, peculiarity, quirk, oddity, foible.

traitor noun **betrayer**, back-stabber, double-crosser, renegade, Judas, quisling, fifth columnist; turncoat, defector; informal snake in the grass.

traitorous adjective **treacherous**, disloyal, treasonous, back-stabbing; double-crossing, unfaithful, two-faced, duplicitous, false.
–OPPOSITES loyal.

trajectory noun **course**, path, route, track, line, orbit.

tramp verb **1** *men were tramping through the shrubbery:* **trudge**, plod, stamp, trample, lumber, clomp, stomp; informal traipse. **2** *he spent ten days tramping through the jungle:* **trek**, slog, footslog, trudge, drag yourself, walk, hike, march; informal traipse; Brit. informal yomp; N. Amer. informal schlep.
•noun **1** *a dirty old tramp:* **vagrant**, vagabond, homeless person, down-and-out; beggar, mendicant; N. Amer. hobo; N. Amer. informal bum. **2** *the tramp of boots:* **footstep**, step, footfall, tread, stomp. **3** *a tramp round York:* **trek**, slog, trudge, hike, march, walk; Brit. informal yomp; N. Amer. informal schlep.

trample verb **1** *someone had trampled on the tulips:* **tread**, stamp, walk over; squash, crush, flatten. **2** *he trampled over their feelings:* **treat with contempt**, ride roughshod over, disregard, set at naught, show no consideration for.

trance noun **daze**, stupor, hypnotic state, dream.

tranquil adjective **1** *a tranquil village:* **peaceful**, calm, restful, quiet, still, relaxing, undisturbed. **2** *Martha smiled, perfectly tranquil:* **calm**, serene, relaxed, unruffled, unperturbed, unflustered, untroubled, composed; equable, placid; informal unflappable.
–OPPOSITES busy, excitable.

tranquillity noun *the tranquillity of the countryside:* **peace**, restfulness, repose, calm, calmness, quiet, stillness, serenity.

tranquillize verb **sedate**, narcotize, drug.

tranquillizer noun **sedative**, barbiturate, calmative, narcotic, opiate; informal trank, downer.
–OPPOSITES stimulant.

transact verb **conduct**, carry out, negotiate, do, perform, execute.

transaction noun **1** *property transactions:* **deal**, arrangement, bargain, negotiation, agreement, settlement; proceedings. **2** *the transactions of the Historical Society:* **proceedings**, report, records, minutes, account. **3** *the transaction of government business:* **conduct**, carrying out, negotiation, performance, execution.

transcend verb **1** *an issue that transcended party politics:* **go beyond**, rise above, cut across. **2** *his military exploits far transcended those of his predecessors:* **surpass**, exceed, beat, top, cap, outdo, outclass, outstrip, leave behind, outshine, eclipse, overshadow.

transcendence noun **excellence**, supremacy, incomparability, matchlessness, peerlessness, magnificence.

transcendent adjective **1** *a transcendent level of knowledge:* **mystical**, spiritual; metaphysical. **2** *a transcendent genius:* **incomparable**, matchless, peerless, unrivalled, inimitable, unparalleled, unequalled, second to none, unsurpassed, nonpareil; formal unexampled.

transcribe verb **1** *each interview was taped and transcribed:* **write out**, copy out, put on paper. **2** *a person who can take and transcribe shorthand:* **transliterate**, interpret, translate.

transcript noun **written version**, printed version, text, transliteration, record.

transfer verb **1** *the hostages were transferred to a safe house:* **move**, convey, take, bring, shift, remove, carry, transport. **2** *the property was transferred to his wife:* **hand over**, pass on, make over, turn over, sign over, consign, devolve, assign. • noun *his transfer to hospital:* **move**, conveyance, relocation, removal.

transfigure verb **transform**, transmute, change, alter, metamorphose; humorous transmogrify.

transfix verb **1** *he was transfixed by the images:* **mesmerize**, hypnotize, spellbind, bewitch, captivate, entrance, enthral, fascinate, enrapture, grip, rivet. **2** *a mouse is transfixed by the owl's talons:* **impale**, stab, spear, pierce, spike, skewer, gore, stick, run through.

transform verb **change**, alter, convert, metamorphose, transfigure, transmute; revolutionize, overhaul; remodel, reshape, remould, redo, reconstruct, rebuild, reorganize, rearrange, rework, revamp; humorous transmogrify.

transformation noun **change**, alteration, conversion, metamorphosis, transfiguration, transmutation; revolution, overhaul; remodelling, reshaping, remoulding, redoing, reconstruction, rebuilding, reorganization, rearrangement, reworking, revamp; humorous transmogrification.

transgress verb **1** *if they transgress the punishment is harsh:* **misbehave**, break the law, err, fall from grace, sin, do wrong, go astray; old use trespass. **2** *she had transgressed an unwritten law:* **infringe**, breach, contravene, disobey, defy, violate, break, flout.

transgression noun **1** *a punishment for past transgressions:* **offence**, crime, sin, wrong, wrongdoing, misdemeanour, misdeed, lawbreaking; error, lapse; old use trespass. **2** *Adam's transgression of God's law:* **infringement**, breach, contravention, violation, defiance, disobedience, non-observance.

transgressor noun **wrongdoer**, offender, miscreant, lawbreaker, criminal, villain, felon, culprit; sinner; formal malefactor; old use trespasser.

transient adjective **transitory**, temporary, short-lived, short-term, ephemeral, impermanent, brief, short, momentary, fleeting, passing.
– OPPOSITES permanent.

transit noun **transport**, movement, conveyance, shipment, haulage, freightage, carriage.
■ **in transit** en route, on the journey, on the way, along/on the road.

transition noun **change**, passage, move, transformation, conversion, metamorphosis, alteration, changeover, shift, switch.

transitional adjective **1** *a transitional period:* **intermediate**, interim, changeover; changing, fluid, unsettled. **2** *the transitional government:* **interim**, temporary, provisional, pro tem, acting, caretaker.

transitory adjective **transient**, temporary, brief, short, short-lived, short-term, impermanent, ephemeral, momentary, fleeting, passing.
– OPPOSITES permanent.

translate verb **1** *the German original had been translated into English:* **render**, put, express, convert, change; transcribe, transliterate. **2** *translate the jargon into normal English:* **render**, paraphrase, reword, rephrase, convert, decipher, decode, gloss, explain. **3** *ideas cannot always be translated into movies:* **change**, convert, transform, alter, adapt, turn, transmute; humorous transmogrify.

translation noun **1** *the translation of the Bible into English:* **rendition**, conversion; transcription, transliteration. **2** *the translation of these policies into practice:* **conversion**, change, transformation, alteration, adaptation, transmutation; humorous transmogrification.

translucent adjective **semi-transparent**, pellucid, limpid, clear; diaphanous, gossamer, sheer.
– OPPOSITES opaque.

transmission noun **1** *the transmission of knowledge:* **transference**, communication, conveyance; dissemination, spreading, circulation. **2** *the transmission of the film:* **broadcasting**, relaying, airing, televising. **3** *a live transmission:* **broadcast**, programme, show.

transmit verb **1** *the use of computers to transmit information:* **transfer**, pass on, hand on, communicate, convey, impart, channel, carry, relay, dispatch; disseminate, spread, circulate. **2** *the programme will be transmitted on Sunday:* **broadcast**, relay, send out, air, televise.

transmute verb **change**, alter, adapt, transform, convert, metamorphose, translate; humorous transmogrify.

transparency noun **1** *the transparency of the glass:* **translucency**, limpidity, glassiness, clearness, clarity. **2** *colour transparencies:* **slide**, diapositive.

transparent adjective **1** *transparent blue water:* **clear**, see-through, translucent, pellucid, limpid, glassy. **2** *fine transparent fabrics:* **see-through**, sheer, filmy, gauzy, diaphanous. **3** *the symbolism of this myth is transparent:* **obvious**, unambiguous, unequivocal, clear, plain, apparent, unmistakable, manifest, conspicuous, patent, indisputable, evident, undisguised.
– OPPOSITES opaque, obscure.

transpire verb **1** *it transpired that her family had moved:* **become known**, emerge, come to light, be revealed, turn out, come out, be discovered. **2** *I'm going to find out exactly what transpired:* **happen**, occur, take place, arise, come about, turn up, befall; literary come to pass.

transplant verb **1** *it was proposed to transplant the club to the vacant site:* **transfer**, move, remove, shift, relocate, take. **2** *the seedlings should be transplanted in pots:* **replant**, repot, relocate. **3** *kidneys must be transplanted within 48 hours of removal:* **transfer**, implant.

transport verb **1** *the blocks were transported by lorry:* **convey**, carry, take, transfer, move, shift, send, deliver, bear, ship, ferry; informal cart. **2** *he was convicted of theft and transported:* **banish**, exile, deport, expatriate, extradite. **3** *she was completely transported by the excitement:* **thrill**, delight, carry away, enrapture, entrance, enchant, enthral, electrify, captivate, bewitch, fascinate, spellbind, charm.
• noun **1** *alternative forms of transport:* **conveyance**; vehicle. **2** *the transport of crude oil:* **conveyance**, carriage, freight, shipment, haulage; transit. **3** *transports of delight:* **rapture**, ecstasy, elation, exaltation, exhilaration, euphoria, bliss, seventh heaven, paradise, high; informal cloud nine.

transpose verb **1** *the blue and black plates were transposed:* **interchange**, exchange, switch, swap round, reverse. **2** *the themes are transposed from the sphere of love to that of work:* **transfer**, shift, relocate, transplant, move, displace.

transverse adjective **crosswise**, horizontal, diagonal, oblique.

trap noun **1** *an animal caught in a trap:* **snare**, net, mesh, gin; N. Amer. deadfall. **2** *the question was set as a trap:* **trick**, ploy, ruse, deception, subterfuge; informal set-up.
• verb **1** *police trapped the men:* **snare**, ensnare, entrap; capture, catch, corner, ambush. **2** *a rat trapped in a barn:* **confine**, cut off, corner, shut in, pen in, hem in; imprison, hold captive. **3** *I hoped to trap him into an admission:* **trick**, dupe, deceive, lure, inveigle, beguile, fool, hoodwink.

trappings plural noun *the spectacular ritual and trappings of the monarchy:* **regalia**, panoply, finery, paraphernalia, apparatus, equipment, effects, features, accessories, accoutrements, ornamentation, adornment, decoration; formal appurtenances.

trash noun **1** (N. Amer.) *the entrance was blocked with trash:* **rubbish**, refuse, waste, litter, junk, detritus; N. Amer. garbage. **2** (informal) *they read trash:* **rubbish**, nonsense, trivia, pulp fiction, pap; N. Amer. garbage; informal drivel, dreck.
• verb (informal) *the apartment had been trashed:* **wreck**, ruin, destroy, wreak havoc on, devastate; vandalize; informal total.

trauma noun **1** *the trauma of divorce:* **shock**, upheaval, distress, stress, strain, pain, anguish, suffering, upset, agony, misery, sorrow, grief, heartache; ordeal, trial, tribulation. **2** *severe trauma to the liver:* **injury**, damage, wound.

traumatic adjective **disturbing**, shocking, distressing, upsetting, heartbreaking, painful, agonizing, hurtful, stressful, awful, terrible, devastating, harrowing.

travel verb **1** *he spent much of his time travelling:* **journey**, tour, voyage, go sightseeing, globetrot, backpack; informal gallivant. **2** *we travelled the length and breadth of the island:* **journey through**, cross, traverse, cover; roam, rove, range, trek. **3** *light travels faster than sound:* **move**, be transmitted.
• noun (**travels**) **journeys**, expeditions, trips, tours, excursions, voyages, treks, explorations, wanderings, odysseys, pilgrimages, jaunts; informal gallivanting.

traveller noun *thousands of travellers were left stranded:* **tourist**, tripper, holidaymaker, sightseer, visitor, globetrotter, backpacker; passenger, commuter; N. Amer. vacationer.

travelling adjective **1** *a travelling population:* **nomadic**, itinerant, peripatetic, wandering, roaming, roving, wayfaring, migrant. **2** *a travelling clock:* **portable**, lightweight, compact.

traverse verb **1** *he traversed the deserts:* **travel over/across**, cross, journey over/across, pass over; cover; ply; wander, roam, range. **2** *a ditch traversed by a bridge:* **cross**, bridge, span; extend across, lie across, stretch across.

travesty noun *a travesty of justice:* **misrepresentation**, distortion, perversion, corruption, mockery, parody; farce, charade, pantomime, sham; informal apology for.

treacherous adjective **1** *her treacherous brother:* **traitorous**, disloyal, unfaithful, duplicitous, deceitful, false, back-stabbing, double-crossing, two-faced, untrustworthy, unreliable; apostate, renegade. **2** *treacherous driving conditions:* **dangerous**, hazardous, perilous, unsafe, precarious, risky; informal dicey, hairy.
– OPPOSITES loyal, faithful, reliable.

treachery noun **betrayal**, disloyalty, unfaithfulness, infidelity, breach of trust, duplicity, deceit, back-stabbing, double-dealing, untrustworthiness; treason.

tread verb **1** *he trod purposefully down the hall:* **walk**, step, stride, pace, go; march, tramp, plod, stomp, trudge. **2** *the snow had been trodden down by the horses:* **crush**, flatten, press down, squash; trample on, stamp on.
• noun *we heard his heavy tread on the stairs:* **step**, footstep, footfall, tramp.

treason noun **treachery**, lese-majesty; disloyalty, betrayal, faithlessness; sedition, subversion, mutiny, rebellion.
– OPPOSITES allegiance, loyalty.

treasonable adjective **traitorous**, treacherous, disloyal; seditious, subversive, mutinous, rebellious.
– OPPOSITES loyal.

treasure noun **1** *a casket of treasure:* **riches**, valuables, jewels, gems, gold, silver, precious metals, money, cash; wealth, fortune. **2** *art treasures:* **valuable object**, work of art, object of virtu, masterpiece. **3** (informal) *she's a real treasure:* **paragon**, gem, angel, nonpareil; find, prize; informal star, one of a kind, one in a million.
• verb *I treasure the photographs:* **cherish**, hold dear, prize, set great store by, value greatly.

treasury noun **1** *the national treasury:* **exchequer**, purse; bank, coffers. **2** *the area is a treasury of fossils:* **rich source**, repository, storehouse, treasure house; fund, mine, bank. **3** *a treasury of stories:* **anthology**, collection, miscellany, compilation, compendium.

treat verb **1** *she treated him badly:* **behave towards**, act towards, use; deal with, handle. **2** *police are treating the fires as arson:* **regard**, consider, view, look on; put down as. **3** *the issue is treated more fully in Chapter 5:* **deal with**, tackle, handle, discuss, explore, investigate; consider, study, analyse. **4** *she was treated at the local hospital:* **care for**, minister to, nurse, tend, attend to. **5** *the plants may prove useful in treating cancer:* **cure**, heal; cope with, deal with, manage. **6** *he treated her to lunch:* **buy**, take out for, stand, give; pay for; entertain, wine and dine; informal foot the bill for. **7** *the fans were treated to quite a spectacle:* **regale with**, entertain with/by, fete with, amuse with, divert with.

• noun **1** *a birthday treat:* **celebration**, entertainment, amusement; surprise. **2** *I bought you some chocolate as a treat:* **present**, gift; titbit, delicacy, luxury, indulgence, extravagance; informal goody. **3** *it was a real treat to see them:* **pleasure**, delight, thrill, joy.

treatise noun **disquisition**, essay, paper, work, exposition, discourse, dissertation, thesis, monograph, study, critique.

treatment noun **1** *the company's treatment of its workers:* **behaviour towards**, conduct towards; handling of, dealings with. **2** *she's responding well to treatment:* **medical care**, therapy, nursing; medication, drugs, medicaments. **3** *her treatment of the topic:* **discussion**, handling, investigation, exploration, consideration, study, analysis, critique.

treaty noun **agreement**, settlement, pact, deal, entente, concordat, accord, protocol, compact, convention, contract, covenant, bargain, pledge; formal concord.

tree noun

> **WORD LINKS**
>
> **arboreal** living in trees or relating to trees
>
> **arboriculture, silviculture** the cultivation of trees

trek noun **journey**, trip, expedition, safari, odyssey; hike, march, slog, tramp, walk; Brit. informal yomp.

trellis noun **lattice**, framework, espalier; network, mesh, tracery.

tremble verb **1** *Joe's hands were trembling:* **shake**, quiver, twitch. **2** *the entire building trembled:* **shake**, shudder, judder, wobble, rock, vibrate, move, sway. **3** *she trembled at the thought of what he had in store for her:* **be afraid**, be frightened, be apprehensive, worry; quail, shrink, blench, shudder.

tremendous adjective **1** *tremendous sums of money:* **huge**, enormous, immense, colossal, massive, prodigious, stupendous, monumental, mammoth, vast, gigantic, giant, mighty, epic, titanic, towering, king-size, gargantuan, Herculean; substantial, considerable; informal whopping, astronomical, humongous; Brit. informal whacking great, ginormous. **2** *a tremendous explosion:* **very loud**, deafening, ear-splitting, booming, thunderous, resounding.
– OPPOSITES tiny, small.

tremor noun **1** *the sudden tremor of her hands:* **tremble**, shake, quiver, twitch, tic. **2** *a tremor of fear ran through her:* **frisson**, shiver, spasm, thrill, tingle, stab, dart, shaft; wave, surge, rush, ripple. **3** *the epicentre of the tremor:* **earthquake**, shock; informal quake.

tremulous adjective **1** *a tremulous voice:* **shaky**, trembling, unsteady, quavering, wavering, quivering, quaking, weak. **2** *a tremulous smile:* **timid**, diffident, shy, hesitant, uncertain, nervous, timorous, fearful, frightened, scared.
– OPPOSITES steady, confident.

trench noun **ditch**, channel, trough, excavation, furrow, rut, conduit, cut, drain, watercourse; earthwork, moat.

trenchant adjective **incisive**, penetrating, sharp, keen, acute, shrewd, razor-sharp, rapier-like, piercing.
– OPPOSITES vague.

trend noun **1** *an upward trend in unemployment:* **tendency**, movement, drift, swing, shift, course, current, direction, inclination, leaning. **2** *the latest trend in music:*

fashion, vogue, style, mode, craze, mania, rage; informal fad, thing.
• verb *interest rates are trending up:* **move**, go, head, drift, gravitate, swing, shift, turn, incline, tend, lean, veer.

trendy adjective (informal). See **FASHIONABLE.**

trepidation noun **fear**, apprehension, dread, agitation, anxiety, worry, nervousness, tension, misgivings, unease, foreboding, disquiet, dismay, consternation, alarm, panic; informal butterflies (in your stomach), the jitters, a cold sweat, the collywobbles.
– OPPOSITES equanimity, composure.

trespass verb **1** *he was trespassing on railway property:* **intrude on**, encroach on, enter without permission, invade. **2** *I must not trespass on your good nature:* **take advantage of**, impose on, play on, exploit, abuse; encroach on, infringe. **3** (old use) *he would be the last among us to trespass:* **sin**, transgress, offend, do wrong, err, go astray, fall from grace.
• noun **1** *his alleged trespass on council land:* **unlawful entry**, intrusion, encroachment, invasion. **2** (old use) *he asked forgiveness for his trespasses:* **sin**, wrong, wrongdoing, transgression, crime, offence, misdeed, misdemeanour, error, lapse.

trespasser noun *a high wall discouraged trespassers:* **intruder**, interloper, unwelcome visitor, encroacher.

tresses plural noun **hair**, mane; locks, curls, ringlets.

trial noun **1** *the trial is expected to last several weeks:* **court case**, lawsuit, suit, hearing, inquiry, tribunal, litigation, proceedings, legal action; court martial. **2** *the drug is undergoing clinical trials:* **test**, try-out, experiment, pilot study; examination, check, assessment, evaluation, appraisal; informal dry run. **3** *she could be a bit of a trial at times:* **nuisance**, pest, bother, irritant, problem, inconvenience, plague, thorn in your flesh; informal pain, headache, drag, nightmare. **4** *an account of her trials and tribulations:* **trouble**, anxiety, worry, burden, affliction, ordeal, tribulation, adversity, hardship, tragedy, trauma, difficulty, problem, misfortune, bad luck, mishap, misadventure; informal hassle.
• adjective *a three-month trial period:* **test**, experimental, pilot, exploratory, probationary, provisional.
• verb *the cash card has been trialled by several banks:* **test**, try out, put through its paces; pilot.

tribe noun **1** *the nomadic tribes of the Sahara:* **ethnic group**, people; family, dynasty, house; nation, clan. **2** *a tribe of children trailed after her:* **group**, crowd, gang, company, body, band, host, bevy, party, pack, army, herd, flock, drove, horde; informal bunch, crew, gaggle, posse.

tribulation noun **1** *the tribulations of her life:* **trouble**, difficulty, problem, worry, anxiety, burden, cross to bear, ordeal, trial, adversity, hardship, tragedy, trauma; informal hassle. **2** *his time of tribulation was just beginning:* **suffering**, distress, trouble, misery, wretchedness, unhappiness, sadness, heartache, woe, grief, pain, anguish, agony.

tribunal noun **1** *a rent tribunal:* **arbitration board/panel**, board, panel, committee. **2** *an international war-crimes tribunal:* **court**; court of inquiry; N. Amer. forum.

tributary noun **headwater**, branch, feeder, side stream, influent; N. Amer. & Austral./NZ creek.

tribute noun **1** *tributes flooded in from colleagues:* **accolade**, praise, commendation, salute, testimonial, homage, eulogy, paean; congratulations, compliments, plaudits; gift, present, offering; informal bouquet; formal laudation. **2** *it is a tribute to his determination that he ever played again:* **testimony**, indication, manifestation, evidence, proof, attestation. **3** *the Vikings demanded tributes in silver:* **payment**, contribution, dues, levy, tax, duty, impost.
– OPPOSITES criticism, condemnation.
■ **pay tribute to** praise, speak highly of, commend, acclaim, take your hat off to, applaud, salute, honour, recognize, acknowledge, pay homage to, extol; formal laud.

trick noun **1** *he's capable of any mean*

t

trick: **stratagem**, ploy, ruse, scheme, device, manoeuvre, contrivance, machination, artifice, wile, dodge; deceit, subterfuge, chicanery, sharp practice; swindle, hoax, fraud; informal con, set-up, game, scam, sting; Brit. informal wheeze. **2** *I think he's playing a trick on us:* **practical joke**, prank, jape; informal leg-pull, spoof, put-on. **3** *conjuring tricks:* **feat**, stunt; (**tricks**) **sleight of hand**, legerdemain, prestidigitation; magic. **4** *it was probably a trick of the light:* **illusion**, figment of the imagination; mirage. **5** *the tricks of the trade:* **knack**, art, skill, technique; secret.

• **verb** *many people have been tricked by villains with false identity cards:* **deceive**, delude, hoodwink, mislead, take in, dupe, fool, double-cross, cheat, defraud, swindle, catch out, hoax; informal con, diddle, rook, pull a fast one on, take for a ride, shaft, do; N. Amer. informal sucker.

trickery **noun** **deception**, dishonesty, cheating, duplicity, double-dealing, legerdemain, sleight of hand, guile, craftiness, deviousness, subterfuge, skulduggery, chicanery, fraud, swindling, sharp practice; informal jiggery-pokery.
– OPPOSITES honesty.

trickle **verb** *blood was trickling from two cuts:* **drip**, dribble, ooze, leak, seep, spill.
– OPPOSITES pour, gush.
• **noun** *trickles of water:* **dribble**, drip, thin stream, rivulet.

trickster **noun** **swindler**, cheat, fraud; charlatan, mountebank, quack, impostor, sham, hoaxer; rogue, villain, scoundrel; informal con man, sharp; Brit. informal twister; dated confidence man.

tricky **adjective** **1** *a tricky situation:* **difficult**, awkward, problematic, delicate, ticklish, sensitive, embarrassing, touchy; risky, uncertain, precarious, touch-and-go; informal sticky, dicey; N. Amer. informal gnarly. **2** *a tricky and unscrupulous politician:* **cunning**, crafty, wily, guileful, artful, devious, sly, scheming, calculating, designing, sharp, shrewd, astute, canny; duplicitous, dishonest, deceitful; informal foxy.
– OPPOSITES straightforward, honest.

trifle **noun** *we needn't bother the headmaster over such trifles:* **triviality**, thing of no consequence, bagatelle, inessential, nothing; technicality; (**trifles**) trivia, minutiae.
■ **a trifle** a little, a bit, somewhat, a touch, a spot, a mite; informal a tad.
trifle with play with, amuse yourself with, toy with, dally with, flirt with; informal mess about with.

trifling **adjective** **trivial**, unimportant, insignificant, inconsequential, petty, minor, of little/no account, footling, incidental; silly, idle, superficial, small, tiny, inconsiderable, nominal, negligible; informal piffling, piddling; formal exiguous.
– OPPOSITES important.

trigger **verb** **1** *the incident triggered an acrimonious debate:* **precipitate**, prompt, set off, spark, touch off, provoke, stir up; cause, give rise to, lead to, set in motion, occasion, bring about, generate, engender, begin, start, initiate. **2** *burglars triggered the alarm:* **activate**, set off, trip.

trill **verb** **warble**, sing, chirp, chirrup, tweet, twitter, cheep.

trim **verb** **1** *his hair had been trimmed:* **cut**, barber, crop, bob, shorten, clip, snip, shear. **2** *trim off the lower leaves:* **cut off**, remove, take off, chop off, lop off; prune. **3** *costs need to be trimmed:* **reduce**, decrease, cut down, scale down, prune, slim down, pare down, dock. **4** *the story was trimmed for the film version:* **shorten**, abridge, condense, abbreviate, telescope, truncate. **5** *a pair of gloves trimmed with fake fur:* **decorate**, adorn, ornament, embellish; edge, pipe, border, fringe.
• **noun** **1** *white curtains with a blue trim:* **decoration**, ornamentation, adornment, embellishment; border, edging, piping, fringe, frill. **2** *an unruly mop in need of a trim:* **haircut**, cut, barbering, clip, snip; pruning.
• **adjective** **1** *a fitted jacket looks trim with a long-line skirt:* **smart**, stylish, chic, spruce, dapper, elegant, crisp; informal natty, sharp. **2** *a trim little villa:* **neat**, tidy, orderly, uncluttered, well kept, well maintained, immaculate, spick and span. **3** *her trim figure:* **slim**,

slender, lean, sleek, willowy, lissom, sylphlike, svelte; streamlined.
– OPPOSITES untidy, messy.
■ **in trim** fit, in good health, in fine fettle; slim, in shape.

trimming noun **1** *a black dress with lace trimming:* **decoration**, ornamentation, adornment, embroidery; border, edging, piping, fringing, frills. **2** *roast turkey with all the trimmings:* **accompaniments**, extras, frills, accessories, accoutrements, trappings, paraphernalia; garnishing. **3** *hedge trimmings:* **cuttings**, clippings, parings, shavings.

trinket noun **knick-knack**, bauble, ornament, bibelot, curio, trifle, toy, novelty, gimcrack, gewgaw.

trio noun **threesome**, three, triumvirate, triad, troika, trinity; trilogy, triptych.

trip verb **1** *he tripped on the stones:* **stumble**, lose your footing, catch your foot, slip, lose your balance, fall, tumble, topple, take a spill. **2** *taxpayers often trip up by not declaring taxable income:* **make a mistake**, miscalculate, blunder, go wrong, make an error, err; informal slip up, screw up; Brit. informal boob; N. Amer. informal goof up. **3** *the question was intended to trip him up:* **catch out**, trick, outwit, outsmart; throw off balance, disconcert, unsettle, discountenance, discomfit; informal throw, wrong-foot; Brit. informal catch on the hop. **4** *they tripped up the steps:* **skip**, run, dance, prance, bound, spring, scamper. **5** *Hoffman tripped the alarm:* **set off**, activate, trigger; turn on, switch on, throw.
• noun **1** *a trip to Paris:* **excursion**, outing, jaunt; holiday, visit, tour, journey, expedition, voyage; drive, run, day out; informal junket, spin. **2** *trips and falls cause nearly half such accidents:* **stumble**, slip, misstep.

triple adjective **1** *a triple alliance:* **three-way**, tripartite; threefold. **2** *they paid him triple the going rate:* **three times**, treble.

trite adjective **banal**, hackneyed, clichéd, platitudinous, vapid, commonplace, stock, conventional, stereotyped, overused, overdone, overworked, time-worn, tired, hoary, hack, unimaginative, unoriginal; informal old hat, corny, played out.
– OPPOSITES original, imaginative.

triumph noun **1** *Napoleon's triumphs:* **victory**, win, conquest, success; achievement. **2** *his eyes shone with triumph:* **jubilation**, exultation, elation, delight, joy, happiness, glee, pride, satisfaction. **3** *a triumph of Victorian engineering:* **tour de force**, masterpiece, crowning example, coup, wonder, master stroke.
– OPPOSITES defeat, disappointment.
• verb **1** *he triumphed in the Grand Prix:* **win**, succeed, come first, be victorious, carry the day, prevail, take the honours. **2** *they had no chance of triumphing over the Nationalists:* **defeat**, beat, conquer, trounce, worst, overcome, overpower, overwhelm, get the better of; informal lick, best; literary vanquish. **3** *'You can't touch me,' she triumphed:* **crow**, gloat; rejoice, exult.
– OPPOSITES lose.

triumphant adjective **1** *the triumphant team:* **victorious**, successful, winning, conquering. **2** *a triumphant expression:* **jubilant**, exultant, elated, rejoicing, joyful, delighted, gleeful, proud, cock-a-hoop; gloating.
– OPPOSITES unsuccessful, despondent.

trivia plural noun **minor details**, minutiae, niceties, technicalities, trifles, non-essentials.

trivial adjective **1** *trivial problems:* **unimportant**, insignificant, inconsequential, minor, of no account, of no importance; incidental, inessential, petty, trifling, footling, small, slight, little, negligible, paltry; informal piddling, piffling. **2** *a trivial person:* **frivolous**, superficial, shallow, unthinking, empty-headed, feather-brained, lightweight.
– OPPOSITES important, significant, serious.

triviality noun **1** *the triviality of the subject matter:* **unimportance**, insignificance, inconsequence, pettiness. **2** *he need not concern himself with such trivialities:* **minor detail**, petty detail, thing of no importance/consequence, trifle, non-essential; technicality; (**trivialities**) trivia, minutiae.

trivialize verb **treat as unimportant**, minimize, play down, underestimate, underplay, make light of, treat lightly, dismiss; informal pooh-pooh.

troop noun **1** *a troop of tourists:* **group**, party, band, gang, bevy, body, company, crowd, throng, horde, pack, drove, flock, swarm, multitude, host, army; informal bunch, gaggle, crew, posse. **2** *British troops were stationed here:* **soldiers**, armed forces, service men/women.
• verb **1** *we trooped out of the hall:* **walk**, march, file; flock, crowd, throng, stream, swarm, surge, spill. **2** *Caroline trooped wearily home:* **trudge**, plod, traipse, trail, drag yourself, tramp; N. Amer. informal schlep.

trophy noun **1** *a swimming trophy:* **cup**, medal; prize, award. **2** *trophies from his travels:* **souvenir**, memento, keepsake; spoils, booty.

tropical adjective *tropical weather:* **very hot**, sweltering, humid, sultry, steamy, sticky, oppressive, stifling; informal boiling.
– OPPOSITES cold, arctic.

trot verb **run**, jog; scuttle, scurry, bustle, scamper.

trouble noun **1** *you've caused enough trouble:* **problems**, difficulty, bother, inconvenience, worry, anxiety, distress, stress, agitation, harassment, unpleasantness; informal hassle. **2** *she poured out all her troubles:* **problem**, misfortune, difficulty, trial, tribulation, trauma, burden, pain, woe, grief, heartache, misery, affliction, suffering. **3** *he's gone to a lot of trouble:* **bother**, inconvenience, fuss, effort, exertion, work, labour; pains, care. **4** *I wouldn't want to be a trouble to her:* **nuisance**, bother, inconvenience, irritation, problem, trial, pest; informal headache, pain, drag. **5** *you're too gullible, that's your trouble:* **shortcoming**, weakness, failing, fault, imperfection, defect, blemish; problem, difficulty. **6** *he had heart trouble:* **disease**, illness, sickness, ailments, complaints, problems; disorder, disability. **7** *the crash was due to engine trouble:* **malfunction**, dysfunction, failure, breakdown. **8** *a match marred by crowd trouble:* **disturbance**, disorder, unrest, fighting, ructions, fracas, breach of the peace.
• verb **1** *this matter had been troubling her for some time:* **worry**, bother, concern, disturb, upset, agitate, distress, perturb, annoy, irritate, vex, irk, nag, niggle, prey on someone's mind, weigh down, burden; informal bug. **2** *he was troubled by ill health:* **afflict**, burden; suffer from, be cursed with. **3** *there is nothing you need trouble about:* **worry**, upset yourself, fret, be anxious, be concerned. **4** *don't trouble to see me out:* **bother**, exert yourself, go out of your way. **5** *I'm sorry to trouble you:* **inconvenience**, bother, impose on, disturb, put out, disoblige; informal hassle; formal discommode.
■ **in trouble** in difficulty, in a mess, in a bad way, in a predicament; informal in a tight corner/spot, in a fix, in a hole, in hot water, in a pickle, up against it.

troubled adjective **1** *Joanna looked troubled:* **anxious**, worried, concerned, perturbed, disturbed, bothered, uneasy, unsettled, agitated; distressed, upset, dismayed. **2** *we live in troubled times:* **difficult**, problematic, unsettled, hard, tough, stressful, dark.

troublemaker noun **mischief-maker**, rabble-rouser, firebrand, agitator, agent provocateur, ringleader, incendiary; scandalmonger, gossipmonger, meddler; informal stirrer.

troublesome adjective **1** *a troublesome problem:* **annoying**, irritating, exasperating, maddening, infuriating, irksome, vexatious, bothersome, tiresome, worrying, disturbing, upsetting, niggling, nagging; difficult, awkward, problematic, taxing; informal aggravating; N. Amer. informal pesky. **2** *a troublesome child:* **difficult**, awkward, trying, demanding, uncooperative, rebellious, unmanageable, unruly, obstreperous, disruptive, disobedient, naughty, recalcitrant; formal refractory.
– OPPOSITES simple, cooperative.

trough noun **1** *a large feeding trough:* **manger**, feedbox, feeder, fodder rack, crib. **2** *a thirty-yard trough:*

channel, conduit, trench, ditch, gully, drain, culvert, cut, flume, gutter.

trounce verb **defeat utterly**, beat hollow, rout, crush, overwhelm; informal hammer, clobber, thrash, drub, demolish, destroy, annihilate; Brit. informal stuff.

troupe noun **group**, company, band, ensemble, set; cast.

trousers plural noun **slacks**; N. Amer. pants; Brit. informal trews, strides, kecks, breeches; Austral. informal daks.

truant noun **absentee**; Brit. informal skiver.
■ **play truant** Brit. informal skive off, bunk off; N. Amer. informal play hookey; Austral./NZ informal play the wag.

truce noun **ceasefire**, armistice, peace; respite, lull; informal let-up.

truck[1] noun *a heavily laden truck:* **lorry**, heavy goods vehicle, juggernaut; van, pickup; Brit. HGV; dated pantechnicon.

truck[2] noun *we are to have no truck with him:* **dealings**, association, contact, communication, connection, relations; business, trade.

truculent adjective **defiant**, aggressive, antagonistic, belligerent, pugnacious, confrontational, obstreperous, argumentative, quarrelsome, uncooperative; bad-tempered, short-tempered, cross, snappish; informal feisty; Brit. informal stroppy, bolshie.
– OPPOSITES cooperative, amiable.

trudge verb **plod**, tramp, drag yourself, walk heavily, plough, slog, toil, trek; informal traipse; N. Amer. informal schlep.

true adjective **1** *you'll see that what I say is true:* **correct**, accurate, right, verifiable, in accordance with the facts, the case, so; faithful, literal, factual, unelaborated. **2** *true craftsmanship:* **genuine**, authentic, real, actual, bona fide, proper; informal honest-to-goodness, kosher, pukka, legit. **3** *the true owner:* **rightful**, legitimate, legal, lawful, authorized, bona fide. **4** *the necessity for true repentance:* **sincere**, genuine, real, unfeigned, heartfelt. **5** *a true friend:* **loyal**, faithful, constant, devoted, staunch, steadfast, unswerving, unwavering; trustworthy, reliable, dependable. **6** *a true reflection of life in the 1950s:* **accurate**, faithful, telling it like it is, fact-based, realistic, close, lifelike.
– OPPOSITES untrue, false, disloyal, inaccurate.

truism noun **platitude**, commonplace, cliché, stock phrase, banality, old chestnut, bromide.

truly adverb **1** *tell me truly what you want:* **truthfully**, honestly, frankly, candidly, openly; informal pulling no punches. **2** *I'm truly grateful:* **sincerely**, genuinely, really, indeed, heartily, profoundly; very, extremely, dreadfully, immensely, tremendously, most; informal awfully, terribly; Brit. informal jolly. **3** *a truly dreadful song:* **really**, absolutely, simply, utterly, totally, perfectly, thoroughly, completely. **4** *the programme truly reflected jazz at the sharp end:* **accurately**, correctly, exactly, precisely, faithfully.

trump verb *by wearing the simplest of dresses, she had trumped them all:* **outshine**, outclass, upstage, put in the shade, eclipse, surpass, outdo, outperform; beat; informal be a cut above, leave standing; Brit. informal knock spots off.

trumped-up adjective **bogus**, spurious, specious, false, fabricated, invented, manufactured, contrived, made-up, fake, factitious; informal phoney.
– OPPOSITES genuine.

trumpet verb **1** *'Come on!' he trumpeted:* **shout**, bellow, roar, yell, cry out, call out; informal holler. **2** *companies trumpeted their enthusiasm for the multimedia revolution:* **proclaim**, announce, declare, noise abroad, shout something from the rooftops.
■ **blow your own trumpet** boast, brag, sing your own praises, show off, swank, congratulate yourself.

truncate verb **shorten**, cut, curtail, bring to an untimely end; abbreviate, condense, reduce.
– OPPOSITES lengthen, extend.

truncheon noun (Brit.) **club**, baton, cudgel, bludgeon; stick, staff; Brit. life preserver, cosh; N. Amer. billy, blackjack, nightstick.

trunk noun **1** *the trunk of a tree:*

main stem, bole, stock. **2** *his powerful trunk:* **torso**, body. **3** *an elephant's trunk:* **proboscis**, nose, snout. **4** *an enormous tin trunk:* **chest**, box, crate, coffer; case, portmanteau. **5** (N. Amer.) *the trunk of his car:* **luggage compartment**; Brit. boot.

truss noun **1** *the bridge is supported by three steel trusses:* **support**, buttress, joist, brace, prop, strut, stay, stanchion, pier. **2** *a hernia truss:* **surgical appliance**, support.
• verb *they trussed us up with ropes:* **tie up**, bind, chain up; pinion, fetter, tether, secure.

trust noun **1** *Cate's trust in him paid off:* **confidence**, belief, faith, certainty, assurance, conviction, credence; reliance. **2** *a position of trust:* **responsibility**, duty, obligation. **3** *the money is to be held in trust:* **safe keeping**, protection, charge, care, custody; trusteeship, guardianship.
– OPPOSITES distrust, mistrust, doubt.
• verb **1** *I should never have trusted her:* **have faith in**, have confidence in, believe in, pin your hopes/faith on. **2** *he can be trusted to carry out an impartial investigation:* **rely on**, depend on, bank on, count on, be sure of. **3** *I trust we shall meet again:* **hope**, expect, take it, assume, presume. **4** *they don't like to trust their money to anyone outside the family:* **entrust**, consign, commit, give, hand over, turn over, assign; formal commend.
– OPPOSITES distrust, mistrust, doubt.

WORD LINKS
fiduciary relating to or involving trust

trustee noun **administrator**, agent; custodian, keeper, steward, depositary; executor.

trusting adjective **trustful**, unsuspecting, unquestioning, unguarded, unwary; naive, innocent, childlike, ingenuous, wide-eyed, credulous, gullible, easily taken in.
– OPPOSITES distrustful, suspicious.

trustworthy adjective **reliable**, dependable, honest, honourable, upright, principled, true, truthful, as good as your word, ethical, virtuous, incorruptible, unimpeachable, above suspicion; responsible, sensible, level-headed; loyal, faithful, staunch, steadfast; safe, sound, reputable; informal on the level; N. Amer. informal straight-up.
– OPPOSITES unreliable.

trusty adjective **reliable**, dependable, trustworthy, unfailing; loyal, faithful, true, staunch, steadfast, constant.
– OPPOSITES untrustworthy, unreliable.

truth noun **1** *he doubted the truth of her statement:* **veracity**, verity, sincerity, candour, honesty; accuracy, correctness, validity, factuality, authenticity. **2** *truth is stranger than fiction:* **fact**, reality, real life, actuality. **3** *scientific truths:* **fact**, verity, certainty, certitude; law, principle.
– OPPOSITES lies, fiction, falsehood.
■ **in truth** in fact, in reality, really, actually.

truthful adjective **1** *a truthful answer:* **honest**, sincere, trustworthy, genuine; candid, frank, open, forthright, straight; informal upfront, on the level. **2** *a truthful account:* **true**, accurate, correct, factual, faithful, reliable; unvarnished, unembellished; formal veracious.
– OPPOSITES deceitful, untrue.

try verb **1** *try to help him:* **attempt**, endeavour, make an effort, exert yourself, strive, do your best, do your utmost, move heaven and earth; undertake, aim, take it on yourself; informal have a go, give it your best shot, go all out; formal essay. **2** *try it and see what you think:* **test**, sample, taste, inspect, investigate, examine, appraise, evaluate, assess; informal check out, give something a whirl. **3** *Mary tried everyone's patience:* **tax**, strain, test, stretch, sap, drain, exhaust, wear out. **4** *the case is to be tried by a jury:* **adjudicate**, consider, hear, examine.
• noun *I'll have one last try:* **attempt**, effort, endeavour; informal go, shot, crack, stab, bash, whack; formal essay.
■ **try something out** test, trial, experiment with, pilot; put through its paces; assess, evaluate.

trying adjective **1** *a trying day:*

stressful, taxing, demanding, difficult, tough, challenging, hard, pressured, frustrating, fraught; arduous, gruelling, tiring, exhausting; informal hellish. **2** *her sister was very trying:* **annoying**, irritating, exasperating, maddening, infuriating; tiresome, irksome, troublesome, bothersome; informal aggravating.

tub noun **1** *a wooden tub:* **container**, butt, barrel, cask, drum, keg. **2** *a tub of yogurt:* **pot**, carton.

tuck verb **1** *he tucked his shirt into his trousers:* **push**, insert, slip; thrust, stuff, stick, cram; informal pop. **2** *the dress was tucked all over:* **pleat**, gather, fold, ruffle. **3** *he tucked the knife behind his seat:* **hide**, conceal, secrete; store, stow; informal stash.
■ **tuck someone in/up** make comfortable, settle down, cover up; put to bed.

tuft noun **clump**, bunch, knot, cluster, tussock, tuffet; lock, wisp; crest, topknot; tassel.

tug verb **1** *Ben tugged at her sleeve:* **pull**, pluck, tweak, twitch, jerk, wrench; catch hold of; informal yank. **2** *she tugged him towards the door:* **drag**, pull, lug, draw, haul, heave, tow, trail.

tuition noun **instruction**, teaching, coaching, tutoring, tutelage, lessons, education, schooling; training, drill, preparation, guidance.

tumble verb **1** *he tumbled over:* **fall over**, topple over, lose your balance, keel over, take a spill, go headlong, go head over heels, trip, stumble; informal come a cropper. **2** *they all tumbled from the room:* **hurry**, rush, scramble, scurry, bound, pile, bundle. **3** *a brook tumbled over the rocks:* **cascade**, fall, flow, pour, spill, stream. **4** *oil prices tumbled:* **plummet**, plunge, fall, dive, nosedive, drop, slump, slide, decrease, decline; informal crash.
– OPPOSITES rise.

tumbledown adjective **dilapidated**, ramshackle, decrepit, neglected, run down, decaying, derelict, crumbling; rickety, shaky.

tumour noun **cancerous growth**, cancer, malignancy; lump, swelling; Medicine carcinoma, sarcoma.

tumult noun **1** *she added her voice to the tumult:* **clamour**, din, noise, racket, uproar, commotion, ruckus, pandemonium, babel, melee, frenzy; Brit. row; informal hullabaloo. **2** *years of political tumult:* **turmoil**, confusion, disorder, disarray, unrest, chaos, turbulence, mayhem, havoc, upheaval.
– OPPOSITES tranquillity.

tumultuous adjective **1** *tumultuous applause:* **loud**, deafening, thunderous, uproarious, noisy, clamorous, vociferous. **2** *a tumultuous crowd:* **disorderly**, unruly, rowdy, turbulent, boisterous, excited, agitated, restless, wild, riotous.
– OPPOSITES soft, orderly.

tune noun *she hummed a tune:* **melody**, air, strain, theme; song, jingle, ditty.
• verb *a body clock tuned to the tides:* **attune**, adapt, adjust; regulate, modulate.
■ **in tune** in accord, in keeping, in agreement, in harmony, in step, in line, in sympathy.

tuneful adjective **melodious**, musical, mellifluous, dulcet, euphonious, harmonious, lyrical, lilting, sweet.
– OPPOSITES discordant.

tuneless adjective **discordant**, unmelodious, dissonant, harsh, cacophonous.
– OPPOSITES melodious.

tunnel noun **underground passage**, underpass, subway; shaft; burrow, hole.
• verb **dig**, burrow, mine, bore, drill.

turbid adjective **murky**, opaque, cloudy, muddy, thick.
– OPPOSITES clear.

turbulent adjective **1** *the country's turbulent past:* **tempestuous**, stormy, unstable, unsettled, tumultuous, chaotic; violent, anarchic, lawless. **2** *turbulent seas:* **rough**, stormy, tempestuous, heavy, violent, wild, seething, choppy, agitated, boisterous.
– OPPOSITES peaceful, calm.

turf noun **1** *they walked across the turf:* **grass**, lawn, sod; literary sward. **2** *devotees of the turf:* **horse racing**; racecourses.

turgid adjective *turgid prose:*

bombastic, pompous, overblown, inflated, tumid, high-flown, affected, pretentious, grandiose, florid, ornate, magniloquent, grandiloquent, orotund; informal highfalutin.
– OPPOSITES simple.

turmoil noun **confusion**, upheaval, turbulence, tumult, disorder, disturbance, agitation, ferment, unrest, trouble, disruption, chaos, mayhem; uncertainty.
– OPPOSITES peace.
■ **in turmoil** confused, in a whirl, at sixes and sevens; reeling, disorientated; informal all over the place.

turn verb **1** *the wheels were still turning:* **go round**, revolve, rotate, spin, roll, circle, wheel, whirl, gyrate, swivel, pivot. **2** *I turned and headed back:* **change direction**, change course, make a U-turn, wheel round. **3** *the car turned the corner:* **go round**, negotiate, take. **4** *the path turned to right and left:* **bend**, curve, wind, twist, meander, snake, zigzag. **5** *he turned his pistol on them:* **aim at**, point at, level at, direct at, train on. **6** *he turned his ankle:* **sprain**, twist, wrench. **7** *their honeymoon turned into a nightmare:* **become**, develop into, change into, metamorphose into. **8** *his hair had turned white:* **become**, go, grow, get. **9** *he turned the house into flats:* **convert**, change, transform, make; adapt, modify, rebuild, reconstruct. **10** *the milk had turned:* **go sour**, go off, curdle, become rancid, go bad, spoil.
• noun **1** *a turn of the wheel:* **rotation**, revolution, spin, whirl, gyration, swivel. **2** *a sharp left turn:* **bend**, corner, dog-leg, junction, crossroads; N. Amer. turnout; Brit. hairpin bend. **3** *you'll get your turn in a minute:* **opportunity**, chance, say; stint, time; try; informal go, shot, stab, crack. **4** *a comic turn:* **act**, routine, performance, number, piece. **5** *a turn around the garden:* **stroll**, walk, saunter, amble, wander, airing, promenade; outing, excursion, jaunt; informal mosey, tootle, spin; Brit. informal pootle. **6** *you gave me quite a turn!* **shock**, start, surprise, jolt; fright, scare. **7** *she did me some good turns:* **service**, deed, act; favour, kindness; disservice, wrong.
■ **in turn** one after the other, one by one, one at a time, in succession, sequentially. **turn someone/something down 1** *she turned down his proposal:* reject, spurn, rebuff, refuse, decline; Brit. informal knock back. **2** *turn the sound down:* reduce, lower, decrease, lessen; muffle, mute. **turn someone in** betray, inform on, denounce, sell out, stab someone in the back; informal split on, blow the whistle on, rat on; Brit. informal grass on, shop. **turn something off** switch off, shut off, put off, extinguish, deactivate, power down; informal kill, cut. **turn something on** switch on, put on, start up, activate, trip. **turn on someone** attack, set on, fall on, let fly at, lash out at, hit out at, round on; informal lay into, tear into; Brit. informal have a go at; N. Amer. informal light into. **turn out 1** *a huge crowd turned out:* come, be present, attend, appear, turn up, arrive; assemble, gather; informal show up. **2** *it turned out that she had been abroad:* transpire, emerge, come to light, become apparent. **3** *things didn't turn out as I'd intended:* happen, occur, come about; develop, work out, come out, end up; informal pan out; formal eventuate. **turn someone out** throw out, eject, evict, expel, oust, drum out, banish; informal kick out, send packing, boot out, show someone the door, turf out. **turn something out 1** *turn out the light.* See TURN SOMETHING OFF. **2** *they turn out a million engines a year:* produce, make, manufacture, fabricate, put out, churn out. **3** *she turned out the cupboards:* clear out, clean out, empty. **turn over** overturn, upturn, capsize, keel over, turn turtle, be upended. **turn something over 1** *I turned over a few pages:* flip over, flick through, leaf through. **2** *she turned the proposal over in her mind:* think about/over, consider, weigh up, ponder, contemplate, reflect on, chew over, mull over, muse on, ruminate on. **3** *he turned over the business to his brother:* transfer, hand over, pass on, consign. **turn someone's stomach** nauseate, sicken, make someone's gorge rise. **turn to someone/some-**

thing seek help from, have recourse to, approach, apply to, appeal to; take to, resort to. **turn up 1** *the documents turned up:* be found, be discovered, be located, reappear. **2** *eventually the police turned up:* arrive, appear, present yourself; informal show up. **3** *something better will turn up:* present itself, occur, happen, crop up. **turn something up** increase, raise, amplify, intensify.

turncoat noun **traitor**, renegade, defector, deserter, betrayer, Judas.

turning noun **turn-off**, side road, exit; N. Amer. turnout.

turning point noun **watershed**, critical moment, decisive moment, moment of truth, crossroads, crisis.

turnout noun **1** *the lecture attracted a good turnout:* **attendance**, audience, house; crowd, gathering, throng, assembly. **2** *his turnout was very elegant:* **outfit**, clothing, dress, garb, attire, ensemble; informal get-up, gear, togs; Brit. informal clobber, kit; formal apparel.

turnover noun **1** *an annual turnover of £2 million:* **revenue**, income, yield; sales. **2** *the high turnover of staff:* **replacement**, change, movement, churn rate.

tussle noun *his glasses were smashed in the tussle:* **scuffle**, fight, struggle, skirmish, brawl, scrum, rough and tumble, free-for-all, fracas, fray, rumpus, melee; informal scrap, dust-up, spat; Brit. informal ding-dong, bust-up.
• verb *demonstrators tussled with police:* **scuffle**, fight, struggle, brawl, grapple, wrestle, clash; informal scrap.

tutor noun *a history tutor:* **teacher**, instructor, educator, lecturer, trainer, mentor; formal pedagogue.
• verb *he was tutored at home:* **teach**, instruct, educate, school, coach, train, drill.

tutorial noun **lesson**, class, seminar.

tweak verb **pull**, jerk, tug, twist, pinch, squeeze.

twee adjective (Brit.) **1** *twee little shops:* **quaint**, sweet, dainty, pretty; informal cute. **2** *the lyrics are too twee in places:* **sentimental**, mawkish, sickly; Brit. informal soppy.

twelve cardinal number **dozen**.

WORD LINKS

duodecimal relating to a counting system with twelve as a base
dodecagon a twelve-sided plane figure
dodecahedron a twelve-sided solid figure

twenty cardinal number **score**.

twiddle verb **turn**, twist, swivel, twirl; adjust, move, jiggle; fiddle with, play with.
■ **twiddle your thumbs** be idle, kick your heels, kill time; informal hang around/round.

twig noun *leafy twigs:* **stick**, sprig, withy, shoot, stem, branchlet.

twilight noun **1** *we arrived at twilight:* **dusk**, sunset, sundown, nightfall, evening, close of day; literary eventide, gloaming. **2** *the twilight of his career:* **decline**, waning, ebb; autumn, final years.
– OPPOSITES dawn.
• adjective *a twilight world:* **shadowy**, dark, shady, dim, gloomy, obscure.

WORD LINKS

crepuscular resembling or relating to twilight

twin noun *a sitting room that was the twin of her own:* **duplicate**, double, carbon-copy, exact likeness, mirror image, replica, lookalike, clone; counterpart, match, pair; informal spitting image, dead ringer.
• adjective **1** *the twin towers of the stadium:* **matching**, identical, paired. **2** *the twin aims of conservation and recreation:* **twofold**, double, dual; related, linked, connected; corresponding, parallel, complementary, equivalent.
• verb *the company twinned its brewing with distilling:* **combine**, join, link, couple, pair.

twine noun **string**, cord, thread, yarn.
• verb **1** *she twined her arms around him:* **wind**, entwine, wrap, wreathe. **2** *convolvulus twined around the tree:* **entwine itself**, coil, loop, twist, spiral, curl. **3** *a bloom was twined in her hair:* **weave**, interlace, intertwine, braid, twist.

twinge noun **1** *twinges in her stomach:* **pain**, spasm, ache, throb; cramp, stitch. **2** *a twinge of guilt:* **pang**, prick, dart.

twinkle verb **1** *lights twinkled:* **glitter**, sparkle, shine, glimmer, shimmer, glint, gleam, glisten, flicker, flash, wink; literary coruscate, glister. **2** *his feet twinkled over the ground:* **dart**, dance, skip, flit, glide.

twinkling adjective **sparkling**, glistening, glittering, glimmering, glinting, gleaming, flickering, winking, shining, scintillating; literary coruscating.

twirl verb **1** *she twirled her parasol:* **spin**, whirl, turn, gyrate, pivot, swivel, twist, revolve, rotate. **2** *she twirled her hair round her fingers:* **wind**, twist, coil, curl, wrap.
• noun *she did a quick twirl:* **pirouette**, spin, whirl, turn, twist, rotation, revolution, gyration.

twist verb **1** *the impact twisted the chassis:* **crumple**, crush, buckle, mangle, warp, deform, distort, contort, screw up. **2** *he twisted round in his seat:* **turn**, swivel, spin round, pivot; wriggle, squirm, writhe. **3** *I twisted my ankle:* **sprain**, wrench, turn, rick, crick. **4** *you are twisting my words:* **distort**, misrepresent, change, alter, pervert, falsify, warp, skew, misinterpret, misconstrue, misstate, misquote. **5** *he twisted the knob:* **twiddle**, adjust, turn, rotate, swivel. **6** *the wires were twisted together:* **twine**, intertwine, interlace, weave, plait, braid, coil, wind, twirl, curl, wrap. **7** *the road twisted and turned:* **wind**, bend, curve, turn, meander, weave, zigzag, swerve, snake, loop.
• noun **1** *the twists of the road:* **bend**, curve, turn, loop, zigzag, kink, dogleg. **2** *long twists of black hair:* **ringlet**, curl, corkscrew, coil, spiral. **3** *the twists and turns of the plot:* **convolution**, complication, complexity, intricacy. **4** *a new twist on an old theme:* **interpretation**, slant, outlook, angle, approach, treatment; variation.

t

twisted adjective **1** *twisted metal:* **crumpled**, bent, crushed, buckled, warped, misshapen, distorted, deformed. **2** *a twisted smile:* **crooked**, lopsided; contorted, wry. **3** *his twisted mind:* **perverted**, warped, deviant, depraved, corrupt, abnormal, unhealthy, aberrant, distorted, debauched, debased; informal sick, kinky, pervy.

twisty adjective **windy**, bendy, zigzag, meandering, curving, sinuous, snaky, serpentine.
– OPPOSITES straight.

twitch verb *he twitched and then lay still:* **jerk**, convulse, quiver, tremble, shiver, shudder.
• noun **1** *a twitch of her lips:* **spasm**, convulsion, quiver, tremor, shiver, shudder; tic. **2** *he felt a twitch of pain:* **pang**, twinge, dart, stab, prick.

twitter verb **1** *sparrows twittered:* **chirp**, chirrup, cheep, tweet, peep, chatter, trill, warble. **2** *she twittered on about her plans:* **prattle**, babble, chatter, go on, ramble; informal yak; Brit. informal witter, rabbit, chunter, waffle.

two cardinal number **pair**, duo, duet, double, dyad, duplet, tandem.

> **WORD LINKS**
> **binary**, **dual** composed of or involving two parts or things
> **biannual** taking place twice a year
> **biennial** taking place every two years
> **bicentenary** a two-hundredth anniversary

two-faced adjective **deceitful**, insincere, double-dealing, hypocritical, back-stabbing, false, untrustworthy, duplicitous, deceiving; disloyal, treacherous, faithless.
– OPPOSITES sincere.

twosome noun **couple**, pair, duo.

tycoon noun **magnate**, mogul, businessman, captain of industry, industrialist, financier, entrepreneur; millionaire; informal big shot, honcho; Brit. informal supremo; N. Amer. informal big wheel; derogatory fat cat.

type noun **1** *a curate of the old-fashioned type:* **kind**, sort, variety, class, category, set, genre, species, order, breed, race; style, nature, manner, rank. **2** (informal) *sporty types:* **person**, individual, character, sort; Brit. informal bod. **3** *his sayings are the type of modern wisdom:* **epitome**, quintessence, essence, archetype, paradigm, model, embodiment. **4** *italic type:* **print**, typeface, characters, lettering; font; Brit. fount.

typhoon noun **cyclone**, tropical storm, tornado, hurricane, whirlwind; N. Amer. informal twister.

typical adjective **1** *a typical example*

of Art Deco: **representative**, classic, quintessential, archetypal, prototypical, stereotypical. **2** *a fairly typical day:* **normal**, average, ordinary, standard, regular, routine, run-of-the-mill, conventional, unremarkable; informal bog-standard. **3** *it's typical of him to forget:* **characteristic**, in keeping, usual, normal, par for the course, predictable, true to form.
– OPPOSITES unusual, exceptional, atypical.

typify verb **1** *he typified the civil servant:* **epitomize**, exemplify, characterize, be representative of; personify, embody. **2** *the sun typified the Greeks:* **symbolize**, represent, stand for, be emblematic of.

tyrannical adjective **dictatorial**, despotic, autocratic, oppressive, repressive, totalitarian, undemocratic, illiberal; authoritarian, high-handed, imperious, iron-handed, severe, cruel, brutal, ruthless.
– OPPOSITES liberal.

tyrannize verb **dominate**, dictate to, browbeat, intimidate, bully; persecute, victimize, torment; oppress, repress, crush, subjugate; informal push around.

tyranny noun **despotism**, absolute power, autocracy, dictatorship, totalitarianism, fascism; oppression, repression, subjugation, enslavement.

tyrant noun **dictator**, despot, autocrat, authoritarian, oppressor; slave-driver, martinet, bully.

WORD LINKS

tyrannicide the killing of a tyrant

t

Uu

ubiquitous adjective **omnipresent**, everywhere, all over the place, all-pervasive; universal, worldwide, global.
– OPPOSITES rare.

UFO noun flying saucer, foo fighter.

> **WORD LINKS**
> **ufology** the study of UFOs

ugly adjective **1 unattractive**, ill-favoured, hideous, plain, unprepossessing, unsightly, horrible, ghastly, repellent, repugnant; grotesque, monstrous; N. Amer. homely; informal not much to look at; Brit. informal no oil painting. **2** *things got pretty ugly:* **unpleasant**, nasty, disagreeable, alarming, charged; dangerous, perilous, threatening, menacing, hostile, ominous, sinister. **3** *an ugly rumour:* **horrible**, despicable, reprehensible, nasty, appalling, offensive, obnoxious, vile, vicious, spiteful.
– OPPOSITES beautiful, pleasant.

ulcer noun **sore**, abscess, boil, carbuncle, wen.

ulterior adjective **underlying**, undisclosed, undivulged, concealed, hidden, covert, secret.
– OPPOSITES overt.

ultimate adjective **1** *the ultimate collapse of the Empire:* **eventual**, final, concluding, terminal, end; resulting, ensuing, consequent, subsequent. **2** *ultimate truths:* **fundamental**, basic, primary, elementary, absolute, central, key, crucial, essential, pivotal. **3** *the ultimate gift for cat lovers:* **best**, ideal, greatest, supreme, paramount, superlative, optimum, quintessential.
• noun *the ultimate in luxury living:* **utmost**, optimum, last word, height, epitome, peak, pinnacle, acme, zenith.

ultimately adverb **1** *the cost will ultimately fall on us:* **eventually**, in the end, in the long run, at length, finally, in time, one day; informal when push comes to shove; Brit. informal at the end of the day. **2** *two ultimately contradictory reasons:* **fundamentally**, basically, primarily, essentially, at heart, deep down.

ultra- combining form *an ultra-conservative view:* **extremely**, exceedingly, immensely, exceptionally; N. English right; informal mega, majorly; Brit. informal dead, well.
• noun *ultras in the animal rights movement:* **extremist**, radical, fanatic, zealot, diehard, militant.

umbrage noun
■ **take umbrage** take offence, take exception, be aggrieved, be affronted, be annoyed, be indignant, be put out, be insulted, be piqued; informal be miffed; Brit. informal get the hump.

umpire noun *the umpire reversed his decision:* **referee**, linesman, adjudicator, arbitrator, judge, moderator; informal ref.
• verb *he umpired a boat race:* **referee**, adjudicate, arbitrate, judge, moderate, oversee; informal ref.

unabashed adjective **unashamed**, shameless, unembarrassed, brazen, audacious, barefaced, blatant, flagrant, bold.
– OPPOSITES sheepish.

unable adjective **powerless**, impotent, inadequate, incompetent, unfit, incapable.

unabridged adjective **complete**, entire, whole, intact, uncut, unshortened, unexpurgated.

unacceptable adjective **intolerable**, insufferable, unsatisfactory,

inadmissible, inappropriate, unsuitable, undesirable, unreasonable, insupportable; informal not on, a bit much, out of order; Brit. informal a bit thick, a bit off; formal exceptionable.
– OPPOSITES satisfactory.

unaccompanied adjective **alone**, on your own, by yourself, solo, lone, solitary, single-handed; unescorted, unchaperoned; Brit. informal on your tod.

unaccountable adjective **1** *for some unaccountable reason, no figures are available:* **inexplicable**, incomprehensible, unfathomable, impenetrable, puzzling, perplexing, baffling, bewildering, mystifying, peculiar, strange, odd, obscure; informal weird. **2** *the Council is unaccountable to anyone:* **unanswerable**, not liable; unsupervised.

unaccustomed adjective **1** *she was unaccustomed to being bossed about:* **unused**, new, fresh; unfamiliar with, inexperienced in. **2** *he showed unaccustomed emotion:* **unusual**, unfamiliar, uncommon, unwonted, rare, surprising, atypical.
– OPPOSITES accustomed, habitual.

unadorned adjective **unembellished**, unornamented, undecorated, unfussy, no-nonsense, no-frills; plain, basic; bare, stark.
– OPPOSITES ornate.

unadventurous adjective **cautious**, careful, circumspect, wary, hesitant, timid; conservative, conventional, unenterprising; informal square, straight, stick-in-the-mud.
– OPPOSITES adventurous, enterprising.

unaffected adjective **1** *they are unaffected by the reshuffle:* **unchanged**, uninfluenced; untouched, unmoved, unresponsive to. **2** *his manner was unaffected:* **unassuming**, unpretentious, down-to-earth, natural, easy, uninhibited, open, artless, guileless.
– OPPOSITES affected, pretentious.

unafraid adjective **undaunted**, fearless, brave, courageous, plucky, intrepid, stout-hearted, bold, daring, confident, audacious; informal gutsy, spunky.
– OPPOSITES timid, afraid.

unanimous adjective **1** *doctors were unanimous about the effects:* **united**, in agreement, in accord, of one mind, in harmony, concordant, undivided. **2** *a unanimous vote:* **uniform**, consistent, united, congruent.
– OPPOSITES divided.

unanswerable adjective **1** *an unanswerable case:* **irrefutable**, indisputable, undeniable, incontestable, incontrovertible; conclusive, absolute, positive. **2** *unanswerable questions:* **insoluble**, unsolvable, inexplicable.

unanswered adjective **unresolved**, undecided, unsettled, undetermined; pending, up in the air.

unappetizing adjective **unpalatable**, uninviting, unappealing, unpleasant, off-putting, distasteful, unsavoury, insipid, flavourless; informal gross.
– OPPOSITES tempting.

unapproachable adjective *her boss appeared unapproachable:* **aloof**, distant, remote, detached, reserved, withdrawn, uncommunicative, unforthcoming, unfriendly, unsympathetic; cool, frosty, stiff; informal stand-offish.
– OPPOSITES friendly, approachable.

unarmed adjective **defenceless**; unprotected, unguarded, exposed, unshielded.

unassailable adjective **1** *an unassailable fortress:* **impregnable**, invulnerable, impenetrable, invincible; secure, safe, strong, indestructible. **2** *his logic was unassailable:* **indisputable**, undeniable, unquestionable, incontestable, incontrovertible, irrefutable, indubitable, watertight.
– OPPOSITES defenceless.

unassertive adjective **passive**, retiring, unforthcoming, submissive, humble, meek, unconfident, shy, timid; informal mousy.
– OPPOSITES bold, assertive.

unassuming adjective **modest**, self-effacing, humble, meek, reserved, diffident; unobtrusive, unostentatious, unpretentious, unaffected, natural.

unattached adjective **1** *they were both unattached:* **single**, unmarried, unwed, partnerless, footloose and fancy free. **2** *we are unattached to any organization:* **unaffiliated**,

unallied; autonomous, independent, non-aligned, separate, unconnected.
– OPPOSITES married.

unattended adjective **1** *his cries went unattended:* **ignored**, disregarded, neglected, passed over. **2** *an unattended vehicle:* **unguarded**, unwatched; abandoned. **3** *she had to walk there unattended:* **unaccompanied**, unescorted, partnerless, unchaperoned, alone, on your own, by yourself, solo; Brit. informal on your tod.

unattractive adjective **plain**, ugly, ill-favoured, unappealing, unsightly, unlovely, unprepossessing, displeasing; N. Amer. homely; informal not much to look at; Brit. informal no oil painting.
– OPPOSITES beautiful.

unauthorized adjective **unofficial**, unsanctioned, unaccredited, unlicensed, unwarranted, unapproved; disallowed, prohibited, banned, forbidden, outlawed, illegal, illicit, proscribed.
– OPPOSITES official, authorized.

unavoidable adjective **inescapable**, inevitable, inexorable, assured, certain, predestined, predetermined, ineluctable; necessary, compulsory, required.

unaware adjective **ignorant**, unknowing, unconscious, heedless, unmindful, oblivious, unsuspecting, uninformed, unenlightened, unwitting, innocent; informal in the dark.
– OPPOSITES aware, conscious.

unawares adverb **1** *brigands caught them unawares:* **by surprise**, unexpectedly, without warning, suddenly, abruptly, unprepared, off guard; informal with your trousers down, napping; Brit. informal on the hop. **2** *the roach approached the pike unawares:* **unknowingly**, unwittingly, unconsciously; unintentionally, inadvertently, accidentally, by mistake.
– OPPOSITES prepared, knowingly.

unbalanced adjective **1** *he is unbalanced and dangerous:* **unstable**, mentally ill, deranged, demented, disturbed, unhinged, insane, mad; informal crazy, loopy, nuts, batty, dotty, bonkers, round the bend/twist; Brit. informal barmy, potty, crackers, barking. **2** *an unbalanced article:* **biased**, prejudiced, one-sided, partisan, inequitable, unfair.
– OPPOSITES sane, unbiased.

unbearable adjective **intolerable**, insufferable, insupportable, unendurable, unacceptable, unmanageable, overpowering; informal too much.
– OPPOSITES tolerable.

unbeatable adjective **invincible**, unstoppable, unassailable, indomitable, unconquerable, unsurpassable, matchless, peerless.

unbeaten adjective **undefeated**, unconquered, unsurpassed, unequalled, unrivalled; triumphant, victorious, supreme, matchless, second to none.

unbecoming adjective **1** *an unbecoming dress:* **unflattering**, unattractive, unsightly. **2** *conduct unbecoming to the Senate:* **inappropriate**, unfitting, unsuitable, inapt, out of keeping, incorrect, unacceptable; unworthy, improper, unseemly, undignified.
– OPPOSITES flattering, appropriate.

unbelievable adjective **incredible**, inconceivable, unthinkable, unimaginable; unconvincing, far-fetched, implausible, improbable; informal hard to swallow.
– OPPOSITES credible.

unbend verb **straighten**, extend, flex, uncurl.

unbending adjective *unbending attitudes:* **uncompromising**, inflexible, unyielding, hard-line, tough, strict, firm, resolute, determined, unrelenting, inexorable, intransigent, immovable.

unbiased adjective **impartial**, unprejudiced, neutral, non-partisan, disinterested, detached, objective, dispassionate, equitable, even-handed, fair.
– OPPOSITES prejudiced.

unblemished adjective **impeccable**, flawless, faultless, perfect, pure, clean, spotless, unsullied, unspoilt, undefiled, untarnished; incorrupt, innocent; informal squeaky clean.
– OPPOSITES flawed.

unborn adjective **embryonic**, fetal, in the womb, in utero.

unbreakable adjective **shatterproof**,

indestructible, imperishable, durable; toughened, sturdy, stout, resistant, hard-wearing, heavy-duty.
–OPPOSITES fragile.

unbridled adjective **unrestrained**, unconstrained, uncontrolled, uninhibited, unrestricted, unchecked, uncurbed, rampant, irrepressible, unstoppable.
–OPPOSITES restrained.

unbroken adjective **1** *the last unbroken window:* **undamaged**, unharmed, unscathed, untouched, sound, intact, whole. **2** *an unbroken horse:* **untamed**, undomesticated, wild, feral. **3** *an unbroken chain of victories:* **uninterrupted**, continuous, endless, constant, unremitting, ongoing. **4** *his record is still unbroken:* **unbeaten**, undefeated, unsurpassed, unrivalled, unmatched, supreme.

unburden verb *she had a sudden wish to unburden herself:* **open your heart**, confess, tell all; informal come clean.

uncalled for adjective **gratuitous**, unnecessary, needless; undeserved, unmerited, unwarranted, unjustified, unreasonable, unfair, inappropriate; unsolicited, unprompted, unprovoked.

uncanny adjective **1** *the silence was uncanny:* **eerie**, unnatural, unearthly, other-worldly, ghostly, strange, abnormal, weird, bizarre; informal creepy, spooky. **2** *an uncanny resemblance:* **striking**, remarkable, extraordinary, exceptional, incredible, arresting.

unceasing adjective **incessant**, constant, continual, unabating, interminable, endless, never-ending, everlasting, eternal, perpetual, continuous, non-stop, uninterrupted, unbroken, unremitting, persistent, unrelenting, unrelieved, sustained.
–OPPOSITES intermittent.

unceremonious adjective *an unceremonious dismissal:* **abrupt**, sudden, hasty, hurried, summary, perfunctory, undignified; rude, impolite, discourteous, offhand.

uncertain adjective **1** *the effects are uncertain:* **unknown**, debatable, open to question, in doubt, undetermined, unsure, in the balance, up in the air; unpredictable, unforeseeable, incalculable; informal iffy. **2** *Ed was uncertain about the decision:* **unsure**, doubtful, dubious, undecided, irresolute, hesitant, vacillating, vague, unclear, ambivalent, in two minds. **3** *an uncertain smile:* **hesitant**, tentative, faltering, unsure, unconfident.
–OPPOSITES predictable, sure, certain.

unchangeable adjective **unalterable**, immutable, invariable, changeless, fixed, hard and fast, cast-iron, set in stone, established, permanent, enduring, abiding, lasting, indestructible, ineradicable, irreversible.
–OPPOSITES variable.

unchanging adjective **consistent**, constant, regular, unvarying, predictable, stable, steady, fixed, permanent, perpetual, eternal.

uncharitable adjective **mean**, unkind, selfish, self-centred, inconsiderate, thoughtless, insensitive, unfriendly, unsympathetic, uncaring, ungenerous, ungracious, unfair.

uncharted adjective **unexplored**, undiscovered, unmapped, untravelled, unfamiliar, unplumbed, unknown, new.

uncivilized adjective **uncouth**, coarse, rough, boorish, vulgar, philistine, uneducated, uncultured, benighted, unsophisticated; ill-bred; barbarian, primitive, savage.

unclear adjective **uncertain**, unsure, unsettled, up in the air, debatable, in doubt; ambiguous, equivocal, indefinite, vague, mysterious, obscure, hazy, foggy, nebulous; informal iffy.
–OPPOSITES clear, definite.

uncomfortable adjective **1** *an uncomfortable chair:* **painful**, confining, cramped. **2** *I felt uncomfortable in her presence:* **uneasy**, awkward, nervous, tense, strained, edgy, restless, embarrassed, anxious; informal rattled, twitchy.
–OPPOSITES relaxed.

uncommitted adjective *a focus group of uncommitted voters:* **floating**, undecided, non-partisan, unaffiliated, neutral, impartial, independent, undeclared, uncertain; informal sitting on the fence.

uncommon adjective **1** *an uncommon plant:* **unusual**, abnormal, rare, atypical, unconventional, unfamiliar, strange, odd, curious, extraordinary, singular, peculiar, bizarre; informal weird, oddball, offbeat. **2** *abductions are uncommon:* **rare**, scarce, few and far between, exceptional, abnormal, isolated, infrequent.

uncommonly adverb **unusually**, remarkably, extraordinarily, exceptionally, singularly, particularly, especially, decidedly, notably, eminently, extremely, very; N. English right; informal awfully, terribly, seriously; Brit. informal jolly, dead.

uncommunicative adjective **taciturn**, quiet, unforthcoming, reserved, reticent, laconic, tongue-tied, silent, tight-lipped; guarded, secretive, close, private; distant, remote, aloof, withdrawn; informal mum, stand-offish.
–OPPOSITES talkative.

uncomplicated adjective **simple**, straightforward, clear, accessible, undemanding, unchallenging, unsophisticated, trouble-free, painless, effortless, easy, elementary, idiot-proof, plain sailing; informal a piece of cake, child's play, a cinch, a doddle, a breeze; Brit. informal easy-peasy.
–OPPOSITES complex, complicated.

uncompromising adjective **inflexible**, unbending, unyielding, unshakeable, resolute, rigid, hard-line, immovable, intractable, firm, determined, iron-willed, obstinate, stubborn, adamant, obdurate, intransigent, headstrong, pig-headed; Brit. informal bloody-minded.
–OPPOSITES flexible.

unconcerned adjective **1** *he is unconcerned about their responses:* **indifferent**, unmoved, apathetic, uninterested, incurious, dispassionate, heedless, unmindful. **2** *she tried to look unconcerned:* **untroubled**, unworried, unruffled, insouciant, nonchalant, blasé, carefree; informal laid-back.
–OPPOSITES concerned, interested, anxious.

unconditional adjective **unquestioning**, unqualified, unreserved, unlimited, unrestricted, wholehearted; complete, total, entire, full, absolute, out-and-out, unequivocal.

unconnected adjective **1** *the earth wire was unconnected:* **detached**, disconnected, loose. **2** *unconnected tasks:* **unrelated**, dissociated, separate, independent, distinct, different, disparate, discrete. **3** *unconnected chains of thought:* **disjointed**, incoherent, rambling, wandering, diffuse, disorderly, garbled, mixed, muddled.
–OPPOSITES attached, related, coherent.

unconscious adjective **1** *she made sure he was unconscious:* **insensible**, senseless, insentient, comatose, inert, knocked out; informal out cold, out for the count. **2** *she was unconscious of the pain:* **heedless**, unmindful, disregarding, oblivious to, insensible to, impervious to, unaffected by; unaware, unknowing. **3** *an unconscious desire:* **subconscious**, latent, suppressed, subliminal, inherent, instinctive, involuntary, uncontrolled; informal gut.
–OPPOSITES conscious, aware.
• noun *fantasies raging in the unconscious:* **subconscious**, psyche, ego, id, inner self.

uncontrollable adjective **1** *the crowds were uncontrollable:* **unmanageable**, ungovernable, wild, unruly, disorderly, recalcitrant, undisciplined; formal refractory. **2** *an uncontrollable rage:* **ungovernable**, irrepressible, unstoppable, unquenchable; wild, violent, frenzied, furious, mad, hysterical, passionate.
–OPPOSITES compliant.

unconventional adjective **unusual**, irregular, unorthodox, unfamiliar, uncommon, unwonted, out of the ordinary, atypical, singular, alternative, different; new, novel, innovative, groundbreaking, pioneering, original, unprecedented; eccentric, idiosyncratic, quirky, odd, strange, bizarre, weird, outlandish, curious; extraordinary; nonconformist, bohemian, avant-garde; informal edgy, way out, far out, offbeat, wacky,

madcap, zany; N. Amer. informal kooky.
– OPPOSITES conventional, orthodox.

unconvincing adjective **improbable**, unlikely, implausible, incredible, unbelievable, questionable, dubious, doubtful; strained, laboured, far-fetched, unrealistic, fanciful, fantastic; informal hard to swallow.
– OPPOSITES persuasive.

uncooperative adjective **unhelpful**, awkward, disobliging, recalcitrant, perverse, contrary, stubborn, wilful, unyielding, unbending, inflexible, immovable, obstructive; Brit. informal bloody-minded.
– OPPOSITES obliging.

uncoordinated adjective **clumsy**, awkward, blundering, bumbling, lumbering, graceless, gawky, ungainly, ungraceful; informal butter-fingered, cack-handed, ham-fisted; Brit. informal all fingers and thumbs; N. Amer. informal klutzy.
– OPPOSITES dexterous.

uncouth adjective **uncivilized**, uncultured, unrefined, unpolished, unsophisticated, rough, coarse, crude, loutish, boorish, uncivil, rude, impolite, discourteous, disrespectful, bad-mannered, ill-bred, vulgar, crass.
– OPPOSITES refined.

uncover verb **1** *she uncovered her face:* **expose**, reveal, lay bare; unwrap, unveil. **2** *they uncovered a plot:* **detect**, discover, come across, stumble on, chance on, find, turn up, unearth, dig up; expose, bring to light, unmask, unveil, reveal, lay bare, betray, give away; informal blow the whistle on.

unctuous adjective **sycophantic**, ingratiating, obsequious, fawning, servile, grovelling, subservient, insincere, gushing, effusive; glib, smooth, slick, oily, greasy; informal smarmy, slimy.

undaunted adjective **unafraid**, undismayed, unflinching, unshrinking, unabashed, fearless, intrepid, bold, valiant, brave, courageous, plucky, mettlesome, gritty; informal gutsy, spunky.
– OPPOSITES fearful.

undecided adjective **unresolved**, uncertain, unsure, unclear, unsettled, indefinite, undetermined, unknown, in the balance, up in the air, moot, open to question, doubtful, vague; indecisive, irresolute, hesitant, wavering, vacillating, uncommitted, ambivalent, in two minds; informal iffy.
– OPPOSITES certain.

undefined adjective **unspecified**, unexplained, unspecific, indeterminate, unsettled; unclear, vague, woolly, imprecise, inexact, indefinite, indistinct, nebulous, hazy, shadowy.
– OPPOSITES definite, distinct.

undemonstrative adjective **unemotional**, unaffectionate, impassive, dispassionate, restrained, reserved, unresponsive, stiff, guarded, aloof, distant, detached, remote, withdrawn; cool, frosty, frigid; informal stand-offish.
– OPPOSITES emotional, unrestrained.

undeniable adjective **indisputable**, indubitable, unquestionable, beyond doubt, undebatable, incontrovertible, irrefutable, unassailable; certain, sure, definite, positive, conclusive, self-evident, patent, unequivocal.
– OPPOSITES questionable.

under preposition **1** *they hid under a bush:* **beneath**, below, underneath. **2** *the rent is under £250:* **less than**, lower than, below. **3** *branch managers are under the retail director:* **subordinate to**, junior to, inferior to, subservient to, answerable to, responsible to, subject to, controlled by. **4** *forty homes are under construction:* **undergoing**, in the process of. **5** *the town was under water:* **flooded by**, immersed in, submerged by, sunk in, engulfed by, inundated by.
– OPPOSITES above, over.

undercover adjective **covert**, secret, clandestine, underground, surreptitious, furtive, cloak-and-dagger, stealthy; informal hush-hush.
– OPPOSITES overt.

undercurrent noun **1** *the undercurrent of despair in his words:* **undertone**, overtone, suggestion, intimation, hint, nuance, undertow; feeling, quality, flavour, atmosphere. **2** *the undercurrents* *in French society:* **movement**, tendency, trend, drift.

undercut verb **1** *the firm undercut their rivals:* **charge less than**, undersell, underbid. **2** *his authority was being undercut:* **undermine**, weaken, impair, sap, threaten, subvert, destabilize.

underdog noun **outsider**, amateur; loser; informal no-hoper.

underestimate verb **underrate**, undervalue, do an injustice to, sell short, play down, understate; minimize, underemphasize, diminish, downgrade, gloss over, trivialize; miscalculate, misjudge.
–OPPOSITES exaggerate, overestimate.

undergo verb **go through**, experience, undertake, face, submit to, be subjected to, come in for, receive, sustain, endure, brave, bear, tolerate, stand, withstand, weather; Brit. informal wear.

underground adjective **1** *an underground car park:* **subterranean**, buried, sunken, basement. **2** *underground organizations:* **clandestine**, secret, surreptitious, covert, undercover, closet, cloak-and-dagger, furtive; resistance, subversive; informal hush-hush. **3** *the underground art scene:* **alternative**, radical, revolutionary, unconventional, unorthodox, avant-garde, experimental, innovative.
• adverb **1** *the insects live underground:* **below ground**, in the earth. **2** *the rebels went underground:* **into hiding**, into seclusion, undercover.
• noun **1** *he took the underground:* **metro**; N. Amer. subway; Brit. trademark tube. **2** *information from the French underground:* **resistance**; partisans, guerrillas, freedom fighters.

u

undergrowth noun **shrubbery**, vegetation, greenery, ground cover, brush, scrub, covert, thicket, copse; bushes, plants, brambles.

underhand adjective **deceitful**, dishonest, dishonourable, disreputable, unethical, unprincipled, immoral, unscrupulous, fraudulent; treacherous, duplicitous, double-dealing; devious, artful, crafty, conniving, scheming, sly, wily; clandestine, sneaky, furtive, covert, cloak-and-dagger; informal crooked, shady, bent; Brit. informal dodgy.
–OPPOSITES honest.

underline verb **1** *she underlined a phrase:* **underscore**, mark, pick out, emphasize, highlight. **2** *the programme underlines the benefits of exercise:* **emphasize**, stress, highlight, accentuate, accent, focus on, spotlight.

underling noun **subordinate**, inferior, junior, minion, lackey, flunkey, menial, retainer, vassal, servant, henchman, factotum; informal dogsbody, gofer; Brit. informal skivvy.
–OPPOSITES boss.

underlying adjective **1** *the underlying aims:* **fundamental**, basic, primary, central, principal, chief, key, elementary. **2** *an underlying feeling of irritation:* **latent**, repressed, suppressed, undisclosed, unexpressed, concealed, hidden.

undermine verb **1** *their integrity is being undermined:* **subvert**, sabotage, threaten, weaken, compromise, diminish, reduce, impair, mar, spoil, ruin, damage, sap, shake. **2** *the damp had so undermined the wall that it collapsed:* **erode**, wear away, eat away at.
–OPPOSITES strengthen, support.

underprivileged adjective **needy**, deprived, disadvantaged, poor, impoverished.
–OPPOSITES wealthy, privileged.

underrate verb **undervalue**, underestimate, do an injustice to, sell short, play down, understate, trivialize.
–OPPOSITES exaggerate.

understand verb **1** *he couldn't understand anything we said:* **comprehend**, grasp, take in, see, apprehend, follow, make sense of, fathom; informal work out, figure out, make head or tail of, take on board, get the drift of, get, cotton on; Brit. informal twig, suss. **2** *she understood how hard he'd worked:* **appreciate**, recognize, realize, acknowledge, know, be aware of, be conscious of; formal be cognizant of. **3** *I understand that you wish to go:* **believe**, gather, take it, hear, learn.

understandable adjective **1** *make it understandable to the* *layman:* **comprehensible**, intelligible, coherent, clear, explicit, unambiguous, transparent, plain, straightforward. **2** *an understandable desire:* **unsurprising**, expected, predictable, inevitable; reasonable, acceptable, logical, rational, normal, natural; justifiable, excusable, pardonable, forgivable.

understanding noun **1** *test your understanding of the language:* **comprehension**, apprehension, grasp, mastery, appreciation, assimilation, absorption; knowledge, awareness, insight, skill, expertise, proficiency; informal know-how; formal cognizance. **2** *a young man of brilliant understanding:* **intellect**, intelligence, brainpower, judgement, reasoning, mentality; insight, intuition, acumen, sagacity, wisdom; informal nous, savvy. **3** *it was my understanding that this was free:* **belief**, perception, view, conviction, feeling, opinion, intuition, impression, assumption, supposition. **4** *he treated me with understanding:* **compassion**, sympathy, pity, feeling, concern, consideration, kindness, sensitivity, decency, humanity, charity, goodwill. **5** *we had a tacit understanding:* **agreement**, arrangement, deal, bargain, settlement, pledge, pact.
–OPPOSITES ignorance, indifference.
• adjective *an understanding friend:* **compassionate**, sympathetic, sensitive, considerate, tender, kind, thoughtful, tolerant, patient, forbearing, lenient, forgiving, humane.

understate verb **play down**, underrate, underplay, trivialize, minimize, diminish, downgrade, brush aside, gloss over; informal sell short.
–OPPOSITES exaggerate.

understudy noun **stand-in**, substitute, replacement, reserve, fill-in, locum, proxy, backup, relief, standby; informal sub; N. Amer. informal pinch-hitter.

undertake verb **1** *the team are to undertake a further project:* **take on**, handle, manage, deal with, tackle, be responsible for, commit yourself to; embark on, begin, engage in, set about, get down to, get to grips with. **2** *they undertook to keep prices to a minimum:* **promise**, pledge, guarantee; agree.

undertaker noun **funeral director**; N. Amer. mortician.

undertaking noun **1** *a risky undertaking:* **enterprise**, venture, project, campaign, scheme, plan, operation, endeavour, effort, task, activity, pursuit, exploit, business, affair, procedure; mission, quest. **2** *sign this undertaking to comply with the rules:* **pledge**, agreement, promise, oath, covenant, vow, commitment, guarantee, assurance.

undertone noun **1** *he said something in an undertone:* **low voice**, murmur, whisper, mutter. **2** *the story's dark undertones:* **undercurrent**, overtone, suggestion, nuance, vein, atmosphere, aura, tenor, flavour.

undervalue verb **underrate**, underestimate, play down, understate, diminish, minimize, downgrade, reduce, brush aside, gloss over, trivialize; informal sell short.

underwater adjective **submerged**, immersed, sunken, subaqueous; undersea, submarine.

underwear noun **underclothes**, undergarments, underthings, lingerie; Brit. informal smalls.

underworld noun **1** *Osiris, god of the underworld:* **the netherworld**, hell, the abyss; eternal damnation; Gehenna, Tophet, Sheol, Hades. **2** *the city's violent underworld:* **criminal world**, gangland; criminals, gangsters; informal mobsters.
–OPPOSITES heaven.

underwrite verb **sponsor**, support, back, insure, indemnify, subsidize, pay for, finance, fund; N. Amer. informal bankroll.

undesirable adjective **1** *undesirable effects:* **unpleasant**, disagreeable, nasty, unwelcome, unwanted, unfortunate, infelicitous. **2** *undesirable people:* **unpleasant**, disagreeable, obnoxious, nasty, awful, terrible, dreadful, abhorrent, loathsome, hateful, detestable, deplorable, appalling, contemptible, odious, vile, unsavoury; informal ghastly, horrible.
–OPPOSITES pleasant, agreeable.

undignified adjective **unseemly**,

demeaning, unbecoming, unworthy, unbefitting, degrading, dishonourable, ignominious, discreditable, ignoble, untoward, unsuitable; scandalous, disgraceful, indecent, low, base; informal infra dig.

undisciplined adjective **unruly**, disorderly, disobedient, recalcitrant, wilful, wayward, delinquent, naughty, rebellious, insubordinate, disruptive, errant, out of control, wild; disorganized, unsystematic, unmethodical, lax, slapdash, sloppy; Brit. informal stroppy, bolshie; formal refractory.

undisguised adjective **obvious**, evident, patent, manifest, transparent, overt, unconcealed, unhidden, unmistakable, undeniable, plain, clear, clear-cut, explicit, naked, visible; blatant, flagrant, glaring, bold; informal standing/sticking out a mile.

undisputed adjective **undoubted**, indubitable, uncontested, unchallenged, incontrovertible, unequivocal, undeniable, irrefutable, unmistakable, certain, definite, accepted, acknowledged, recognized.
–OPPOSITES doubtful.

undistinguished adjective **unexceptional**, indifferent, run-of-the-mill, middle-of-the-road, ordinary, average, commonplace, mediocre, humdrum, lacklustre, uninspired, unremarkable, featureless, nondescript; N. Amer. garden-variety; informal nothing special, no great shakes, OK, so-so, bog standard; Brit. informal common or garden.
–OPPOSITES extraordinary.

undivided adjective **complete**, full, total, whole, entire, absolute, unqualified, unreserved, unmitigated, unbroken, consistent, thorough, exclusive, dedicated; focused, engrossed, absorbed, attentive, committed.

u

undo verb **1** *he undid a button:* **unfasten**, unbutton, unhook, untie, unlace; unlock, unbolt; loosen, detach, free, open. **2** *they will undo a decision by the law lords:* **revoke**, overrule, overturn, repeal, rescind, reverse, countermand, cancel, annul, nullify, invalidate, void, negate. **3** *she undid much of their good work:* **ruin**, undermine, subvert, overturn, scotch, sabotage, spoil, impair, mar, destroy, wreck; cancel out, neutralize, thwart; informal blow, muck up; Brit. informal scupper.
–OPPOSITES fasten, ratify, enhance.

undoing noun **1** *she plotted the king's undoing:* **downfall**, defeat, conquest, deposition, overthrow, ruin, failure; Waterloo. **2** *their complacency was their undoing:* **fatal flaw**, Achilles heel, weak point, failing, misfortune.

undoubted adjective **undisputed**, unchallenged, unquestioned, indubitable, incontrovertible, irrefutable, incontestable, certain, unmistakable; definite, accepted, acknowledged, recognized.

undoubtedly adverb **doubtless**, indubitably; unquestionably, indisputably, undeniably, incontrovertibly, clearly, obviously, patently, certainly, definitely, of course, indeed.

undress verb **strip**, disrobe; Brit. informal peel off.

undue adjective **excessive**, immoderate, intemperate, inordinate, disproportionate; uncalled for, unnecessary, unwarranted, unreasonable unjustified; inappropriate, unmerited, unsuitable, improper.
–OPPOSITES appropriate.

undulate verb **rise and fall**, surge, swell, heave, ripple, flow; wind, wobble, oscillate.

undying adjective **abiding**, lasting, enduring, permanent, constant, infinite; unceasing, perpetual, incessant, unending; immortal, eternal.

unearth verb **1** *workmen unearthed an artillery shell:* **dig up**, excavate, exhume, disinter, root out, uncover. **2** *I unearthed an interesting fact:* **discover**, uncover, find, come across, hit on, bring to light, expose, turn up.

unearthly adjective **1** *an unearthly chill in the air:* **other-worldly**, supernatural, preternatural, alien; ghostly, spectral, phantom, mysterious, spine-chilling, hair-raising; uncanny, eerie, strange,

weird, unnatural, bizarre; informal spooky, creepy, scary. **2** (informal) *they rose at some unearthly hour:* **unreasonable**, preposterous, abnormal, extraordinary, absurd, ridiculous; informal ungodly, unholy.
– OPPOSITES normal, reasonable.

uneasy adjective **1** *the doctor made him feel uneasy:* **worried**, anxious, troubled, disturbed, nervous, nervy, tense, overwrought, edgy, apprehensive, restless, discomfited, perturbed, fearful, uncomfortable, unsettled; informal jittery. **2** *he had an uneasy feeling:* **worrying**, disturbing, troubling, alarming, dismaying, disquieting, unsettling, disconcerting, upsetting. **3** *the victory ensured an uneasy peace:* **tense**, awkward, strained, fraught; precarious, unstable, insecure.
– OPPOSITES calm, stable.

uneconomic, uneconomical adjective **unprofitable**, loss-making, uncommercial, non-viable, worthless; wasteful, inefficient, improvident.

uneducated adjective **untaught**, unschooled, untutored, untrained, unread, unscholarly, illiterate, ignorant, ill-informed; uncouth, unsophisticated, uncultured, unaccomplished, unenlightened, philistine.
– OPPOSITES educated.

unemotional adjective **reserved**, undemonstrative, sober, restrained, passionless, emotionless, unsentimental, unexcitable, impassive, phlegmatic, stoical, equable.

unemployed adjective **jobless**, out of work, unwaged, redundant, laid off; on benefit; Brit. signing on; N. Amer. on welfare; Brit. informal on the dole, 'resting'.

unending adjective **endless**, interminable, perpetual, eternal, incessant, unceasing, non-stop, uninterrupted, continuous, constant, persistent, unbroken, unabating, unremitting, relentless.

unenthusiastic adjective **indifferent**, apathetic, half-hearted, lukewarm, casual, cool, lacklustre, offhand, unmoved.
– OPPOSITES keen, enthusiastic.

unenviable adjective **disagreeable**, nasty, unpleasant, undesirable, horrible, thankless; unwanted, unwished for.

unequal adjective **1** *they are unequal in length:* **different**, dissimilar, unlike, disparate, unmatched, variable. **2** *the unequal distribution of wealth:* **unfair**, unjust, disproportionate, inequitable, biased. **3** *an unequal contest:* **one-sided**, uneven, unfair, ill-matched, unbalanced. **4** *she felt unequal to the task:* **inadequate for**, incapable of, unqualified for, unsuited to, incompetent at, not up to; informal not cut out for.
– OPPOSITES equal, identical, fair.

unequalled adjective **unbeaten**, unmatched, unrivalled, second to none, unsurpassed, unparalleled, peerless, incomparable, inimitable, unique.

unequivocal adjective **unambiguous**, unmistakable, indisputable, incontrovertible, indubitable, undeniable; clear, plain, explicit, specific, categorical, straightforward, blunt, candid, emphatic.
– OPPOSITES ambiguous.

unerring adjective **unfailing**, infallible, perfect, flawless, faultless, impeccable, unimpeachable; sure, true, assured, deadly; informal sure-fire.

unethical adjective **immoral**, amoral, unprincipled, unscrupulous, dishonourable, dishonest, wrong, deceitful, unconscionable, fraudulent, underhand; unprofessional, improper.

uneven adjective **1** *uneven ground:* **bumpy**, rough, lumpy, stony, rocky, potholed, rutted. **2** *uneven teeth:* **irregular**, unequal, unbalanced, lopsided, askew, crooked, asymmetrical. **3** *uneven quality:* **inconsistent**, variable, fluctuating, irregular, erratic, patchy. **4** *an uneven contest:* **one-sided**, unequal, unfair, unjust, inequitable, ill-matched, unbalanced.
– OPPOSITES even, regular, equal.

uneventful adjective **unexciting**, uninteresting, monotonous, boring, dull, tedious, humdrum, routine, unvaried, ordinary, run-of-the-mill.
– OPPOSITES exciting.

unexceptional adjective **ordinary**,

average, typical, everyday, mediocre, run-of-the-mill, middle-of-the-road, indifferent; informal OK, so-so, nothing special, no great shakes, no big deal, nothing to write home about, forgettable; Brit. informal common or garden.

unexpected adjective **unforeseen**, unanticipated, unpredicted, without warning; sudden, abrupt, surprising, out of the blue.

unfailing adjective *his unfailing good humour:* **constant**, reliable, dependable, steadfast, steady; endless, undying, unfading, inexhaustible, boundless, ceaseless.

unfair adjective **1** *the trial was unfair:* **unjust**, inequitable, prejudiced, biased, discriminatory; one-sided, unequal, uneven, unbalanced, partisan. **2** *his comments were unfair:* **undeserved**, unmerited, uncalled for, unreasonable, unjustified; Brit. informal out of order. **3** *unfair play:* **unsporting**, dirty, below the belt, underhand, dishonourable. **4** *you're being very unfair:* **inconsiderate**, thoughtless, insensitive, selfish, mean, unkind, unreasonable.
– OPPOSITES fair, just, justified.

unfaithful adjective *her husband had been unfaithful:* **adulterous**, faithless, fickle, untrue, inconstant; informal cheating, two-timing.
– OPPOSITES faithful, loyal.

unfaltering adjective **steady**, resolute, firm, steadfast, fixed, decided, unswerving, unwavering, tireless, indefatigable, persistent, unyielding, relentless, unremitting.
– OPPOSITES unsteady.

unfamiliar adjective **1** *an unfamiliar part of the city:* **unknown**, new, strange, foreign, alien. **2** *unfamiliar sounds:* **unusual**, uncommon, unconventional, novel, exotic, unorthodox, odd, peculiar, curious, uncharacteristic, out of the ordinary. **3** *investors unfamiliar with the market:* **unacquainted**, unused, unaccustomed, unconversant, inexperienced, uninformed, new to, a stranger to.

unfashionable adjective **out of fashion**, outdated, old-fashioned, outmoded, dated, unstylish, passé; informal out, square, out of the ark, uncool, unhip, untrendy.

unfasten verb **undo**, open, disconnect, remove, untie, unbutton, unzip, loosen, free, unlock, unbolt.

unfathomable adjective **1** *unfathomable eyes:* **inscrutable**, incomprehensible, enigmatic, indecipherable, obscure, esoteric, mysterious, deep, profound. **2** *unfathomable water:* **deep**, immeasurable, unplumbed, bottomless.
– OPPOSITES revealing.

unfavourable adjective **1** *unfavourable comment:* **adverse**, critical, hostile, inimical, unfriendly, unsympathetic, negative; discouraging, disapproving, uncomplimentary, unflattering. **2** *the unfavourable economic climate:* **disadvantageous**, adverse, inauspicious, unpropitious, gloomy; unsuitable, inappropriate, inopportune.
– OPPOSITES positive, favourable.

unfeeling adjective **uncaring**, unsympathetic, unemotional, uncharitable; heartless, hard-hearted, harsh, austere, cold.
– OPPOSITES compassionate, sympathetic.

unfettered adjective **unrestrained**, unrestricted, unconstrained, free, unbridled, unchecked, uncontrolled.
– OPPOSITES restricted.

unfinished adjective **1** *an unfinished essay:* **incomplete**, uncompleted; partial, half-done; unpolished, unrefined, sketchy, fragmentary, rough. **2** *the door can be supplied unfinished:* **unpainted**, untreated, unvarnished.
– OPPOSITES complete.

unfit adjective **1** *the film is unfit for children:* **unsuitable**, unsuited, inappropriate, unsafe. **2** *an unfit parent:* **incompetent**, inadequate, unsatisfactory, unqualified, ill-equipped.
– OPPOSITES fit, suitable.

unflagging adjective **tireless**, persistent, dogged, tenacious, determined, resolute, staunch, single-minded, unrelenting, unfaltering, unfailing.

unflattering adjective **1** *an unflattering review:* **unfavourable**,

uncomplimentary, harsh, unsympathetic, critical, hostile, scathing. **2** *an unflattering dress:* **unattractive**, unbecoming, unsightly.
– OPPOSITES complimentary, becoming.

unflinching adjective **resolute**, determined, single-minded, dogged, resolved, firm, committed, steady, unwavering, unflagging, unswerving, unfaltering, untiring, undaunted, fearless.

unfold verb **1** *he unfolded the map:* **open out**, spread out, flatten, straighten out, unroll. **2** *I watched the events unfold:* **develop**, evolve, happen, take place, occur, transpire, progress.

unforeseen adjective **unpredicted**, unexpected, unanticipated, unplanned, unlooked for, not bargained for.
– OPPOSITES expected.

unforgettable adjective **memorable**, haunting, catchy; striking, impressive, outstanding, extraordinary, exceptional.
– OPPOSITES unexceptional.

unforgivable adjective **inexcusable**, unpardonable, unjustifiable, indefensible, inexpiable, irremissible.
– OPPOSITES venial.

unfortunate adjective **1** *unfortunate people:* **unlucky**, hapless, wretched, forlorn, poor, pitiful; informal down on your luck. **2** *an unfortunate start to our holiday:* **adverse**, disadvantageous, unfavourable, unlucky, unwelcome, unpromising, inauspicious, unpropitious; formal grievous. **3** *an unfortunate remark:* **regrettable**, inappropriate, unsuitable, infelicitous, tactless, injudicious.
– OPPOSITES fortunate, lucky, auspicious.

unfortunately adverb **unluckily**, sadly, regrettably, unhappily, alas, sad to say; informal worse luck.

unfounded adjective **groundless**, baseless, unsubstantiated, unproven, unsupported, uncorroborated, unconfirmed, unverified, unattested, without basis, speculative, conjectural.
– OPPOSITES proven.

unfriendly adjective **hostile**, disagreeable, antagonistic, aggressive, confrontational, threatening, intimidating; bad-tempered, ill-natured, unpleasant, surly, grumpy, uncongenial, unsympathetic, uncooperative; inhospitable, unwelcoming, aloof, cold, chilly, frosty; informal stand-offish.
– OPPOSITES amiable, friendly.

ungainly adjective **awkward**, clumsy, ungraceful, inelegant, gawky, maladroit, gauche, uncoordinated.
– OPPOSITES graceful.

ungovernable adjective **uncontrollable**, unmanageable, anarchic, intractable; unruly, disorderly, rebellious, riotous, wild, mutinous, undisciplined.

ungracious adjective **rude**, impolite, uncivil, discourteous, ill-mannered, uncouth, disrespectful, insolent.
– OPPOSITES polite.

ungrateful adjective **unappreciative**, unthankful, ungracious; inconsiderate, thoughtless, disrespectful.

unguarded adjective **1** *an unguarded frontier:* **undefended**, unprotected, unfortified; vulnerable, insecure. **2** *an unguarded remark:* **careless**, ill-considered, thoughtless, rash, foolhardy, indiscreet, imprudent, injudicious, ill-judged, insensitive; literary temerarious. **3** *an unguarded moment:* **unwary**, inattentive, off guard, distracted, absent-minded.

unhappiness noun **sadness**, sorrow, dejection, depression, misery, downheartedness, despondency, despair, desolation, wretchedness, glumness, gloom, dolefulness; melancholy, low spirits, mournfulness, woe, heartache, distress, chagrin, grief; informal the blues.

unhappy adjective **1** *an unhappy childhood:* **sad**, miserable, sorrowful, dejected, despondent, disconsolate, morose, heartbroken, down, dispirited, downhearted, depressed, melancholy, mournful, gloomy, glum, doleful, forlorn, woeful, long-faced; informal down in the mouth/dumps, fed up, blue. **2** *in the unhappy event of litigation:* **unfortunate**, unlucky; ill-starred, ill-fated, doomed; informal

jinxed. **3** *I was unhappy with the service:* **dissatisfied**, displeased, discontented, disappointed, disgruntled.
– OPPOSITES cheerful.

unharmed adjective **1** *they released the hostage unharmed:* **uninjured**, unhurt, unscathed, safe, alive and well, in one piece, without a scratch. **2** *the tomb was unharmed:* **undamaged**, unbroken, unmarred, unspoiled, unsullied, unmarked; sound, intact, unblemished.
– OPPOSITES injured, damaged.

unhealthy adjective **1** *an unhealthy lifestyle:* **harmful**, detrimental, destructive, injurious, damaging, deleterious; noxious, poisonous, insalubrious. **2** *an unhealthy pallor:* **ill-looking**, unwell, ailing, sick, poorly, weak, frail, infirm, washed out, run down, peaky. **3** *an unhealthy obsession:* **unwholesome**, morbid, macabre, twisted, abnormal, warped, depraved, unnatural; informal sick.

unheard of adjective **1** *a game unheard of in the UK:* **unknown**, unfamiliar, new. **2** *such behaviour was unheard of:* **unprecedented**, exceptional, extraordinary, unthought of, undreamed of, unbelievable, inconceivable, unimaginable, unthinkable.

unheeded adjective **disregarded**, ignored, neglected, overlooked, unnoted, unrecognized.

unholy adjective **1** *an unholy act:* **ungodly**, irreligious, impious, blasphemous, sacrilegious, profane, irreverent; wicked, evil, immoral, sinful. **2** (informal) *an unholy row:* **shocking**, dreadful, outrageous, appalling, terrible, horrendous, frightful. **3** *an unholy alliance:* **unnatural**, unusual, improbable, made in Hell.

u

unhurried adjective **leisurely**, easy, relaxed, slow, deliberate, measured, calm.
– OPPOSITES hasty, hurried.

unhygienic adjective **insanitary**, dirty, filthy, contaminated, unhealthy, unwholesome, insalubrious.
– OPPOSITES hygienic, sanitary.

unidentified adjective **unknown**, unnamed, anonymous, incognito, nameless, unfamiliar, strange.
– OPPOSITES known, familiar.

unification noun **union**, merger, fusion, amalgamation, coalition, combination, confederation.

uniform adjective **1** *a uniform temperature:* **constant**, consistent, steady, invariable, unfluctuating, unchanging, stable, static, regular, fixed, even. **2** *pieces of uniform size:* **identical**, matching, similar, equal; same, like, homogeneous, consistent.
– OPPOSITES variable.
• noun *a soldier in uniform:* **costume**, livery, regalia, suit, ensemble, outfit; regimentals, colours; informal get-up, rig, gear.

uniformity noun **1** *uniformity in tax law:* **constancy**, consistency, conformity, invariability, stability, regularity, evenness, homogeneity. **2** *a dull uniformity:* **monotony**, tedium, dullness, dreariness, flatness, sameness.
– OPPOSITES variation, variety.

unify verb **unite**, bring together, join together, merge, fuse, amalgamate, coalesce, combine, consolidate.
– OPPOSITES separate.

unimaginable adjective **unthinkable**, inconceivable, incredible, unbelievable, untold, beyond your wildest dreams.

unimaginative adjective **uninspired**, uninventive, unoriginal, uncreative, commonplace, pedestrian, mundane, ordinary, routine, humdrum, workaday, run-of-the-mill, hackneyed, trite.

unimpeded adjective **unrestricted**, unhindered, unblocked, clear, unhampered, free.

unimportant adjective **insignificant**, inconsequential, trivial, minor, trifling, of no account, irrelevant, peripheral, extraneous, petty, paltry; informal piddling.

uninhabited adjective **1** *much of this land was uninhabited:* **unpopulated**, unpeopled, unsettled. **2** *an uninhabited hut:* **vacant**, empty, unoccupied, untenanted.

uninhibited adjective **1** *uninhibited dancing:* **unrestrained**, wild, unrepressed, abandoned, reckless; unrestricted, uncontrolled, unchecked, intemperate, wanton.

2 *I'm pretty uninhibited:* **unreserved**, unrepressed, liberated, unselfconscious, free and easy, relaxed, informal, open, outgoing, extrovert, outspoken; informal upfront.
– OPPOSITES repressed.

uninspired adjective **unimaginative**, uninventive, pedestrian, mundane, unoriginal, commonplace, ordinary, routine, humdrum, run-of-the-mill, hackneyed, trite.

uninspiring adjective **boring**, dull, dreary, unexciting, unstimulating; dry, colourless, bland, lacklustre, tedious, humdrum, run-of-the-mill.

unintelligent adjective **stupid**, ignorant, dense, brainless, dull-witted, slow, simple-minded, idiotic; informal thick, dim, dumb, dopey, half-witted, dozy.

unintelligible adjective **1** *unintelligible sounds:* **incomprehensible**, indiscernible, mumbled, indistinct, unclear, slurred, inarticulate, incoherent, garbled. **2** *unintelligible graffiti:* **illegible**, indecipherable, unreadable.

unintentional adjective **accidental**, inadvertent, involuntary, unwitting, unthinking, unpremeditated, unconscious.
– OPPOSITES deliberate.

uninterested adjective **indifferent**, unconcerned, uninvolved, apathetic, lukewarm, unenthusiastic.

uninteresting adjective **unexciting**, boring, dull, tiresome, wearisome, tedious, dreary, lifeless, humdrum, colourless, bland, insipid, banal, dry, pedestrian; informal samey.
– OPPOSITES exciting.

uninterrupted adjective *10 hours of uninterrupted sleep:* **unbroken**, continuous, undisturbed, untroubled.
– OPPOSITES intermittent.

uninvited adjective **1** *an uninvited guest:* **unasked**, unexpected; unwelcome, unwanted. **2** *uninvited suggestions:* **unsolicited**, unsought, unrequested.

uninviting adjective **unappealing**, unattractive, unappetizing, off-putting; bleak, cheerless, dreary, dismal, depressing, grim, inhospitable.
– OPPOSITES tempting.

union noun **1** *the union of art and nature:* **unification**, joining, merger, fusion, amalgamation, coalition, combination, synthesis, blend. **2** *they live in perfect union:* **unity**, accord, harmony, agreement, concurrence; formal concord. **3** *the National Farmers' Union:* **association**, league, guild, confederation, federation.
– OPPOSITES separation, division.

unique adjective **1** *each site is unique:* **distinctive**, individual, special, idiosyncratic; single, sole, lone, unrepeated, solitary, exclusive, rare, uncommon; informal one-off. **2** *a unique insight into history:* **remarkable**, special, singular, noteworthy, notable, extraordinary; unequalled, unparalleled, unmatched, unsurpassed, incomparable; formal unexampled. **3** *species unique to the island:* **peculiar**, specific.

unison noun
■ **in unison 1** *they lifted their arms in unison:* simultaneously, at the same time, at once, together. **2** *we are in complete unison:* in agreement, in accord, in harmony, as one; formal in concord.

unit noun **1** *the family is the fundamental unit of society:* **component**, element, constituent, subdivision. **2** *a unit of currency:* **quantity**, measure, denomination. **3** *a guerrilla unit:* **detachment**, contingent, division, company, squadron, corps, regiment, brigade, platoon, battalion; cell, faction.

unite verb **1** *uniting the nation:* **unify**, join, link, connect, combine, amalgamate, fuse, weld, bond, bring together. **2** *environmentalists and activists united:* **join together**, join forces, combine, band together, ally, cooperate, collaborate, work together, pull together, team up. **3** *he sought to unite comfort with elegance:* **merge**, mix, blend, mingle, combine.
– OPPOSITES divide.

united adjective **1** *a united Germany:* **unified**, integrated, amalgamated, joined, merged; federal, confederate. **2** *a united response:* **common**, shared, joint, combined, communal, cooperative, collective, collaborative. **3** *they were united in their views:* **in agreement**, in unison, of the same opinion, like-minded, as one, in accord, in harmony.

United States of America noun America; informal the States, the US of A, Uncle Sam; literary Columbia.

unity noun **1** *European unity:* **union**, unification, integration, amalgamation; coalition, federation, confederation. **2** *unity between opposing factions:* **harmony**, accord, cooperation, collaboration, agreement, consensus, solidarity; formal concord. **3** *the organic unity of the universe:* **oneness**, singleness, wholeness, uniformity, homogeneity.
–OPPOSITES division, discord.

universal adjective **general**, ubiquitous, comprehensive, common, omnipresent, all-inclusive; global, worldwide, international, widespread.

universally adverb **invariably**, always, without exception, in all cases; everywhere, worldwide, globally, internationally; widely, commonly, generally.

universe noun **1** *the physical universe:* **cosmos**, macrocosm, totality; infinity, all existence. **2** *the universe of computer hardware:* **province**, world, sphere, preserve, domain, field.

> WORD LINKS
> **cosmic** relating to the universe
> **cosmology** the science of the origin and development of the universe
> **astronomy** the study of stars, planets, and the universe

university noun **college**, academy, institute; N. Amer. school; historical polytechnic.

unjust adjective **1** *an unjust society:* **biased**, prejudiced, unfair, inequitable, discriminatory, partisan, one-sided. **2** *an unjust law:* **wrongful**, unfair, undeserved, unmerited, unwarranted, unreasonable, unjustifiable, indefensible.
–OPPOSITES fair, just.

unjustifiable adjective **1** *an unjustifiable extravagance:* **indefensible**, inexcusable, unforgivable, unpardonable, uncalled for; excessive, immoderate. **2** *an unjustifiable slur on his character:* **groundless**, unfounded, baseless, unsubstantiated, uncorroborated.
–OPPOSITES reasonable.

unkempt adjective **untidy**, messy, scruffy, disordered, wild, dishevelled, disarranged, rumpled, windblown, ungroomed, bedraggled, messed up; tousled, uncombed.
–OPPOSITES tidy.

unkind adjective **uncharitable**, unpleasant, disagreeable, nasty, mean, cruel, vicious, spiteful, malicious, callous, unsympathetic, hard-hearted; unfriendly, uncivil, inconsiderate, insensitive, hostile; informal bitchy, catty.
–OPPOSITES kind, considerate.

unkindness noun **nastiness**, unpleasantness, disagreeableness, cruelty, malice, meanness, viciousness, callousness, hard-heartedness; unfriendliness, hostility; informal bitchiness, cattiness.

unknown adjective **1** *the outcome was unknown:* **undisclosed**, unrevealed, secret; undetermined, undecided, unresolved, unsettled, unascertained. **2** *unknown country:* **unexplored**, uncharted, unmapped, untravelled, undiscovered. **3** *persons unknown:* **unidentified**, unnamed, anonymous. **4** *firearms were unknown to the Indians:* **unfamiliar**, unheard of, new, novel, strange. **5** *unknown artists:* **obscure**, unheard of, unsung, minor, undistinguished.
–OPPOSITES familiar.

unlawful adjective **illegal**, illicit, illegitimate, against the law; criminal, felonious; prohibited, banned, outlawed, proscribed, forbidden.
–OPPOSITES legal, lawful.

unleash verb **let loose**, release, free, set free, untie, untether, unchain.

unlike preposition **1** *he's totally unlike his screen persona:* **different from**, dissimilar to. **2** *unlike Elena, he wasn't superstitious:* **in contrast to**, as opposed to.
–**unlikely** adjective **1** *it is unlikely they will recover:* **improbable**, doubtful, dubious. **2** *an unlikely story:* **implausible**, improbable, questionable, unconvincing, far-fetched, unrealistic, incredible, unbelievable, inconceivable; informal tall, cock and bull.
–OPPOSITES probable, likely.

unlimited adjective **1** *unlimited supplies of water:* **inexhaustible**,

limitless, boundless, immeasurable, incalculable, untold, infinite, endless. **2** *unlimited travel:* **unrestricted**, unconstrained, unrestrained, unchecked, unbridled, uncurbed. **3** *unlimited power:* **total**, unqualified, unconditional, unrestricted, absolute, supreme.
– OPPOSITES finite, restricted.

unload verb **1** *we unloaded the van:* **unpack**, empty. **2** *they unloaded the cases from the lorry:* **remove**, offload, discharge. **3** *the state unloaded its 25 per cent stake:* **sell**, discard, jettison, offload, get rid of, dispose of; informal dump, get shot/shut of.

unlock verb **unbolt**, unlatch, unbar, unfasten, open.

unlooked for adjective **unexpected**, unforeseen, unanticipated, unsought, unpredicted, undreamed of, fortuitous, serendipitous, chance.

unloved adjective **uncared-for**, unwanted, friendless, unvalued; rejected, unwelcome, shunned, spurned, neglected, abandoned.

unlucky adjective **1** *the unlucky passengers have to wait until Friday:* **unfortunate**, hapless, ill-fated, ill-starred. **2** *an unlucky number:* **unfavourable**, inauspicious, unpropitious, ominous, cursed, ill-fated, ill-omened.
– OPPOSITES lucky, fortunate, favourable.

unmanageable adjective **1** *households burdened with unmanageable debts:* **enormous**, huge, massive; cumbersome, unwieldy. **2** *his son's behaviour was becoming unmanageable:* **uncontrollable**, ungovernable, unruly, disorderly, out of hand/control, troublesome, difficult, disruptive, undisciplined, wayward.

unmanly adjective **effeminate**, effete, unmasculine; weak, soft, timid, limp-wristed; informal sissy, wimpy.
– OPPOSITES virile.

unmarried adjective **single**, unwed; unattached, available, eligible, free.

unmatched adjective **1** *a talent for publicity unmatched by any other politician:* **unequalled**, unrivalled, unparalleled, unsurpassed. **2** *unmatched clarity and balance:* **peerless**, without equal, incomparable, inimitable, superlative, second to none, in a class of its own.

unmentionable adjective **taboo**, censored, forbidden, banned, proscribed, prohibited, ineffable, unspeakable, unutterable, unprintable, off limits; informal no go.

unmerciful adjective **ruthless**, cruel, harsh, merciless, pitiless, cold-blooded, hard-hearted, callous, brutal, severe, unforgiving, inhumane, inhuman, heartless, unsympathetic, unfeeling.

unmistakable adjective **distinctive**, distinct, telltale, indisputable, indubitable, undoubted; plain, clear, definite, obvious, evident, manifest, patent, unequivocal, pronounced.

unmitigated adjective **absolute**, unqualified, categorical, complete, total, downright, outright, utter, out-and-out, unequivocal, veritable, consummate, pure, sheer.

unmoved adjective **1** *he was totally unmoved by her outburst:* **unaffected**, untouched, unimpressed, undismayed, unworried; aloof, cool, unconcerned, uncaring, indifferent, impassive, unresponsive, dry-eyed; impervious, oblivious. **2** *he remained unmoved on the crucial issues:* **steadfast**, firm, unwavering, unswerving, resolute, decided, resolved, inflexible, unbending, implacable, adamant.

unnatural adjective **1** *wanting to help other people is not unnatural:* **abnormal**, unusual, uncommon, extraordinary, strange, unorthodox, exceptional, irregular, untypical. **2** *an unnatural colour:* **artificial**, man-made, synthetic, manufactured. **3** *her voice sounded unnatural:* **affected**, artificial, stilted, forced, laboured, strained, false, fake, insincere; informal put on, phoney.
– OPPOSITES normal, natural, genuine.

unnecessary adjective **unneeded**, inessential, not required, uncalled for, useless, unwarranted, unwanted, undesired, dispensable,

optional, extraneous, expendable, redundant, pointless, purposeless.
– OPPOSITES essential.

unnerve verb **demoralize**, discourage, dishearten, dispirit, alarm, frighten, disconcert, perturb, upset, discomfit, take aback, unsettle, disquiet, fluster, shake, ruffle, throw off balance; informal rattle, faze; Brit. informal put the wind up; N. Amer. informal discombobulate.
– OPPOSITES hearten.

unobtrusive adjective **discreet**, inconspicuous, unnoticeable, low-key, understated, self-effacing, unostentatious.
– OPPOSITES obtrusive, conspicuous.

unoccupied adjective **1** *an unoccupied house:* **vacant**, empty, uninhabited; free, available, to let. **2** *many young people were unoccupied:* **at leisure**, idle, free, at a loose end, with time on your hands.
– OPPOSITES inhabited, occupied, busy.

unofficial adjective **1** *unofficial figures:* **unauthenticated**, unconfirmed, uncorroborated, unsubstantiated, off the record. **2** *an unofficial committee:* **informal**, casual; unauthorized, unsanctioned, unaccredited.
– OPPOSITES official, formal.

unorthodox adjective **1** *they had unorthodox views on management:* **unconventional**, unusual, radical, nonconformist, avant-garde, eccentric; informal off the wall, way out, offbeat. **2** *unorthodox religious views:* **heterodox**, heretical, nonconformist, dissenting.
– OPPOSITES conventional.

unpaid adjective **1** *unpaid bills:* **unsettled**, outstanding, owed, payable, undischarged. **2** *unpaid work:* **voluntary**, volunteer, honorary, unremunerative, unsalaried.

unpalatable adjective **1** *unpalatable food:* **unappetizing**, unappealing, unsavoury, inedible; disgusting, revolting, nauseating, tasteless, flavourless. **2** *the unpalatable truth:* **disagreeable**, unpleasant, regrettable, unwelcome, upsetting, distressing, dreadful.
– OPPOSITES palatable, pleasant.

unparalleled adjective **exceptional**, unique, singular, rare, unequalled, unprecedented; matchless, peerless, unrivalled, unsurpassed, incomparable, second to none.

unperturbed adjective **untroubled**, undisturbed, unworried, unconcerned, unmoved, unflustered, unruffled; calm, composed, cool, collected, unemotional, self-possessed, self-assured; informal unfazed, laid-back.

unpleasant adjective **1** *the side effects can be unpleasant:* **disagreeable**, distressing, nasty, horrible, distasteful, invidious; irksome, troublesome. **2** *when drunk, he became very unpleasant:* **objectionable**, obnoxious, disagreeable, nasty, rude, offensive, insufferable, unbearable; annoying, irritating. **3** *an unpleasant smell:* **distasteful**, unpalatable, unsavoury, unappetizing, uninviting, unappealing; offensive, obnoxious, disgusting, revolting, nauseating, sickening, repugnant, repulsive, repellent.
– OPPOSITES pleasant, agreeable.

unpolished adjective **1** *unpolished wood:* **unvarnished**, unfinished, untreated, natural. **2** *an awkward, unpolished performance:* **amateurish**, sloppy, slipshod, incompetent, inept, inexpert, clumsy, gauche, maladroit, awkward, unsophisticated, unrefined, crude, rough.

unpopular adjective **disliked**, friendless, unloved; unwelcome, avoided, ignored, rejected, shunned, spurned, cold-shouldered.

unprecedented adjective **unparalleled**, unequalled, unmatched, unrivalled, out of the ordinary, unusual, exceptional, singular, remarkable, unique; unheard of, unknown, new, groundbreaking, revolutionary, pioneering.

unpredictable adjective **1** *unpredictable results:* **unforeseeable**, uncertain, doubtful, in the balance, up in the air. **2** *unpredictable behaviour:* **erratic**, moody, volatile, unstable, capricious, temperamental, mercurial, changeable, variable.

unprejudiced adjective **1** *unprejudiced observation:* **objective**, impartial, unbiased, neutral, non-partisan, detached, disinterested. **2** *unprejudiced attitudes:* **unbiased**, tolerant, non-discriminatory, liberal, broad-minded, unbigoted.
– OPPOSITES partisan, prejudiced.

unpremeditated adjective *this was not an unpremeditated attack:* **unplanned**, spontaneous, impulsive, impromptu, spur-of-the-moment.

unprepared adjective **1** *we were unprepared for the new regime:* **unready**, off guard, surprised, taken aback; informal caught napping, caught on the hop. **2** *they are unprepared to support the reforms:* **unwilling**, disinclined, loath, reluctant, resistant, opposed.
– OPPOSITES prepared, ready, willing.

unpretentious adjective **1** *he was unpretentious:* **unaffected**, modest, unassuming, without airs, natural, straightforward, open, honest, sincere, frank. **2** *an unpretentious hotel:* **simple**, plain, modest, humble, unostentatious, homely, unsophisticated.

unprincipled adjective **immoral**, unethical, unscrupulous, dishonourable, dishonest, deceitful, devious, corrupt, crooked, wicked, evil, villainous, shameless, base, low.

unproductive adjective **1** *unproductive soil:* **sterile**, barren, infertile, unfruitful, poor. **2** *unproductive activities:* **fruitless**, futile, vain, idle, useless, worthless, valueless, pointless, ineffective, unprofitable, unrewarding.
– OPPOSITES productive, fruitful.

unprofessional adjective **1** *unprofessional conduct:* **improper**, unethical, unprincipled, unscrupulous, dishonourable, disreputable; informal shady, crooked. **2** *he accused the detectives of being unprofessional:* **amateurish**, unskilful, inexpert, unqualified, inexperienced, incompetent, second-rate, inefficient.

unpromising adjective **inauspicious**, unfavourable, unpropitious, discouraging, disheartening, gloomy, bleak, black, portentous, ominous, ill-omened.
– OPPOSITES auspicious.

unqualified adjective **1** *an unqualified accountant:* **uncertificated**, unlicensed, untrained. **2** *those unqualified to look after children:* **unsuitable**, unfit, ineligible, incompetent, incapable. **3** *unqualified support:* **unconditional**, unreserved, unlimited, categorical, unequivocal, unambiguous, wholehearted; complete, absolute, downright, undivided, total, utter.

unquestionable adjective **indubitable**, undoubted, indisputable, undeniable, irrefutable, incontestable, incontrovertible, unequivocal; certain, definite, evident, manifest, obvious, apparent, patent.

unravel verb **1** *he unravelled the strands:* **untangle**, disentangle, separate out, unwind, untwist. **2** *detectives are trying to unravel the mystery:* **solve**, resolve, clear up, puzzle out, get to the bottom of, explain, clarify; informal figure out, suss.
– OPPOSITES entangle.

unreadable adjective **1** *unreadable writing:* **illegible**, indecipherable, unintelligible, scrawled. **2** *heavy, unreadable novels:* **dull**, tedious, boring, uninteresting, dry, wearisome, difficult, heavy. **3** *Nathan's expression was unreadable:* **inscrutable**, enigmatic, impenetrable, cryptic, mysterious, deadpan; informal poker-faced.
– OPPOSITES legible, accessible.

unreal adjective **imaginary**, fictitious, pretend, make-believe, made-up, dreamed-up, mock, false, illusory, mythical, fanciful; hypothetical, theoretical; informal phoney.

unrealistic adjective **1** *it is unrealistic to expect changes overnight:* **impractical**, unfeasible; unreasonable, irrational, illogical, senseless, silly, foolish, fanciful, idealistic, romantic, starry-eyed. **2** *unrealistic images:* **unlifelike**, unnatural, abstract.
– OPPOSITES pragmatic, realistic.

unreasonable adjective **1** *an unreasonable woman:* **uncooperative**, unhelpful, disobliging, unaccommodating, awkward, contrary, difficult; obstinate, obdurate, wilful, headstrong, pig-headed, intractable, intransigent, inflexible. **2** *unreasonable demands:* **unacceptable**, preposterous, outrageous; excessive, immoderate, disproportionate, undue, inordinate, intolerable, unjustified, unwarranted.

unrecognizable adjective **unidentifiable**; disguised.

unrefined adjective **1** *unrefined clay:* **unprocessed**, untreated, crude, raw, natural, unprepared, unfinished. **2** *unrefined men:* **uncultured**, uncultivated, uncivilized, uneducated, unsophisticated; boorish, oafish, loutish, coarse, vulgar, rude, uncouth.
–OPPOSITES processed.

unrelated adjective **1** *unrelated incidents:* **separate**, unconnected, independent, unassociated, distinct, discrete, disparate. **2** *a reason unrelated to my work:* **irrelevant**, immaterial, inapplicable, unconcerned, off the subject, not pertinent.

unrelenting adjective **1** *the unrelenting heat:* **continual**, constant, unremitting, unabating, unrelieved, incessant, unceasing, endless, persistent. **2** *an unrelenting opponent:* **implacable**, inflexible, uncompromising, unyielding, unbending, determined, dogged, tireless, unswerving, unwavering.
–OPPOSITES intermittent.

unreliable adjective **1** *unreliable volunteers:* **undependable**, untrustworthy, irresponsible, fickle, capricious, erratic, unpredictable, inconstant, faithless. **2** *an unreliable indicator:* **questionable**, doubtful, dubious, suspect, unsound, tenuous, fallible; risky, chancy, inaccurate; informal iffy, dicey.

unremitting adjective **relentless**, continual, constant, unabating, unrelieved, sustained, unceasing, unending, persistent, perpetual, interminable.

unrepentant adjective **impenitent**, unashamed, unapologetic, unabashed.

unreserved adjective **1** *unreserved support:* **unconditional**, unqualified, unlimited, categorical, unequivocal, unambiguous; absolute, complete, thorough, whole-hearted, total, utter, undivided. **2** *an unreserved man:* **uninhibited**, extrovert, outgoing, unrestrained, open, unselfconscious, frank, candid. **3** *unreserved seats:* **unbooked**, unallocated, free, unoccupied, empty, vacant.
–OPPOSITES qualified, reticent, booked.

unresolved adjective **undecided**, unsettled, undetermined, uncertain, open, pending, open to debate/question, in doubt, up in the air.
–OPPOSITES decided.

unrest noun **disruption**, disturbance, trouble, turmoil, disorder, chaos, anarchy; discord, dissent, strife, protest, rebellion, uprising, rioting.
–OPPOSITES peace.

unrestrained adjective **uncontrolled**, unrestricted, unchecked, unbridled, unlimited, unfettered, uninhibited, unbounded, undisciplined.

unrestricted adjective **unlimited**, open, free, clear, unhindered, unimpeded, unhampered, unchecked, unrestrained, unblocked, unbounded, unconfined, unqualified.
–OPPOSITES restricted, limited.

unripe adjective **immature**, unready, green, sour.

unrivalled adjective **unequalled**, unparalleled, unmatched, unsurpassed, unexcelled, incomparable, inimitable, second to none.

unruffled adjective **calm**, composed, self-controlled, self-possessed, untroubled, unperturbed, at ease, relaxed, serene, cool, unemotional, stoical; informal unfazed.

unruly adjective **disorderly**, rowdy, wild, unmanageable, uncontrollable, disobedient, disruptive, undisciplined, wayward, wilful, headstrong, obstreperous, difficult, intractable, out of hand, recalcitrant; formal refractory.
–OPPOSITES disciplined.

unsafe adjective **1** *the building was unsafe:* **dangerous**, risky, perilous, hazardous, high-risk, treacherous, insecure, unsound; harmful, injurious, toxic. **2** *the verdict was*

u

unsafe: **unreliable**, insecure, unsound, questionable, doubtful, dubious, suspect; informal iffy; Brit. informal dodgy.
– OPPOSITES safe, harmless, secure.

unsaid adjective **unspoken**, unuttered, unstated, unexpressed, unvoiced, suppressed; tacit, implicit, understood, not spelt out, taken as read, implied.

unsanitary adjective **unhygienic**, dirty, filthy, unclean, contaminated, unhealthy, germ-ridden, disease-ridden, infested.
– OPPOSITES hygienic.

unsatisfactory adjective **disappointing**, undesirable, disagreeable, displeasing; inadequate, unacceptable, poor, bad, substandard, weak, mediocre, not up to par, defective, deficient, imperfect, inferior; informal leaving a lot to be desired.

unsavoury adjective **unpalatable**, distasteful, disagreeable, unappealing, unpleasant, off-putting; disreputable, dishonourable, dishonest, unprincipled, unscrupulous, immoral; informal shady.

unscathed adjective **unharmed**, unhurt, uninjured, undamaged, in one piece, intact, safe, unmarked, untouched, unscratched.

unscrupulous adjective **unprincipled**, unethical, immoral, shameless, reprobate, exploitative, corrupt, dishonest, dishonourable, deceitful, devious, underhand, unsavoury, disreputable, evil, wicked, villainous; informal crooked, shady.

unseat verb *an attempt to unseat the party leader:* **depose**, oust, topple, overthrow, bring down, dislodge, supplant, usurp, overturn, eject.

unseemly adjective **indecorous**, improper, unbecoming, unfitting, unbefitting, unworthy, undignified, indiscreet, indelicate, ungentlemanly, unladylike.
– OPPOSITES decorous.

unseen adjective **hidden**, concealed, obscured, camouflaged, out of sight, imperceptible, undetectable, unnoticed, unobserved.

unselfish adjective **altruistic**, disinterested, selfless, self-denying, self-sacrificing; generous, philanthropic, public-spirited, charitable, benevolent, noble.

unsettle verb **discompose**, unnerve, upset, disturb, disquiet, perturb, discomfit, disconcert, alarm, dismay, trouble, bother, agitate, fluster, ruffle, shake, throw; informal rattle, faze.

unsettled adjective **1** *an unsettled life:* **aimless**, directionless, purposeless; rootless, nomadic. **2** *an unsettled child:* **restless**, restive, fidgety, anxious, worried, troubled, fretful; agitated, ruffled, uneasy, disconcerted, discomposed, unnerved, ill at ease, edgy, tense, nervous, apprehensive, disturbed, perturbed; informal rattled, fazed. **3** *unsettled weather:* **changeable**, variable, inconstant, inconsistent, erratic, unstable, undependable, unreliable, uncertain, unpredictable. **4** *unsettled areas:* **uninhabited**, unpopulated, unpeopled, desolate, lonely.

unshakeable adjective **steadfast**, resolute, staunch, firm, decided, determined, unswerving, unwavering; unyielding, inflexible, dogged, obstinate, persistent, indefatigable, tireless, unflagging, unremitting, unrelenting.

unsightly adjective **ugly**, unattractive, unprepossessing, unlovely, disagreeable, displeasing, hideous, horrible, repulsive, revolting, offensive, grotesque.
– OPPOSITES attractive.

unskilful adjective **inexpert**, incompetent, inept, amateurish, unprofessional, inexperienced, untrained, unpractised; informal ham-fisted, cack-handed.

unskilled adjective **untrained**, unqualified; manual, blue-collar, menial; inexpert, inexperienced, amateurish, unprofessional.

unsociable adjective **unfriendly**, uncongenial, unneighbourly, unapproachable, introverted, reticent, reserved, withdrawn, retiring, aloof, distant, remote, detached; informal stand-offish.
– OPPOSITES friendly, sociable.

unsolicited adjective **uninvited**, unasked for, unrequested.

unsophisticated adjective **1** *she*

seemed unsophisticated: **unworldly**, naive, simple, innocent, green, immature, callow, inexperienced, childlike, artless, guileless, ingenuous, natural, unaffected, unassuming, unpretentious. **2** *unsophisticated software:* **simple**, crude, basic, rudimentary, primitive, rough and ready.

unsound adjective **1** *the building is structurally unsound:* **unsafe**, unstable, dangerous, in poor condition; weak, rickety. **2** *this submission appears unsound:* **untenable**, flawed, defective, faulty, ill-founded, flimsy, unreliable, questionable, dubious, tenuous, suspect, fallacious; informal iffy. **3** *she was mentally unsound:* **disordered**, deranged, disturbed, demented, unstable, unbalanced, unhinged, insane; informal touched.
– OPPOSITES sound, strong.

unsparing adjective **1** *he is unsparing in his criticism:* **merciless**, pitiless, ruthless, relentless, remorseless, unmerciful, unforgiving, implacable, uncompromising; stern, strict, severe, harsh. **2** *unsparing approval:* **ungrudging**, unstinting, free, ready; lavish, liberal, generous, magnanimous, open-handed.

unspeakable adjective **1** *unspeakable delights:* **indescribable**, inexpressible, unutterable, indefinable, unimaginable, inconceivable, marvellous, wonderful. **2** *an unspeakable crime:* **dreadful**, awful, appalling, horrific, horrendous, abominable, frightful, shocking, ghastly, monstrous, heinous, deplorable, despicable, execrable, vile.

unspecified adjective **unnamed**, unstated, unidentified, undesignated, undefined, undecided, undetermined, uncertain; unknown, indefinite, indeterminate, vague.

unspoilt adjective **unimpaired**, perfect, pristine, immaculate, unblemished, unharmed, undamaged, untouched, unmarked, untainted.

unspoken adjective **unstated**, unexpressed, unuttered, unsaid, unvoiced, unarticulated, undeclared, not spelt out; tacit, implicit, implied, understood, taken as read.
– OPPOSITES explicit.

unstable adjective **1** *icebergs are notoriously unstable:* **unsteady**, rocky, wobbly, rickety, shaky, unsafe, insecure, precarious. **2** *unstable coffee prices:* **changeable**, volatile, variable, fluctuating, irregular, unpredictable, erratic. **3** *he was mentally unstable:* **unbalanced**, of unsound mind, mentally ill, deranged, demented, disturbed, unhinged.
– OPPOSITES steady, firm, stable.

unsteady adjective **1** *she was unsteady on her feet:* **unstable**, rocky, wobbly, rickety, shaky, doddery. **2** *an unsteady flow:* **irregular**, uneven, variable, erratic, spasmodic, changeable, fluctuating, inconstant, intermittent, fitful.
– OPPOSITES stable, steady, regular.

unstinted, **unstinting** adjective **lavish**, liberal, generous, open-handed, ungrudging, unsparing, ready, profuse, abundant.

unsubstantiated adjective **unconfirmed**, unsupported, uncorroborated, unverified, unattested, unproven; unfounded, groundless, baseless.

unsuccessful adjective **1** *an unsuccessful attempt:* **failed**, abortive, ineffective, fruitless, profitless, unproductive; vain, futile, useless, pointless, worthless. **2** *an unsuccessful business:* **unprofitable**, loss-making. **3** *an unsuccessful candidate:* **failed**, losing, beaten; unlucky.

unsuitable adjective **1** *an unsuitable product:* **inappropriate**, ill-suited, inapt, inapposite, unacceptable, unfitting, incompatible, out of place/keeping. **2** *an unsuitable moment:* **inopportune**, infelicitous; formal malapropos.
– OPPOSITES appropriate, suitable.

unsullied adjective **spotless**, untarnished, unblemished, unspoilt, untainted, impeccable, undamaged, unimpaired, immaculate, pristine.
– OPPOSITES tarnished.

unsung adjective **unacknowledged**, uncelebrated, unacclaimed,

unapplauded, unhailed; neglected, unrecognized, overlooked, forgotten.
– OPPOSITES celebrated.

unsure adjective **1** *she felt very nervous and unsure of herself:* **unconfident**, insecure, hesitant, diffident, anxious, apprehensive. **2** *he was unsure about accepting the offer:* **undecided**, in two minds, in a quandary; dubious, doubtful, sceptical, uncertain, unconvinced.
– OPPOSITES sure, confident.

unsurpassed adjective **unmatched**, unrivalled, unparalleled, unique, unequalled, matchless, peerless, inimitable, incomparable, unsurpassable.

unsurprising adjective **predictable**, foreseeable, to be expected, foreseen, anticipated, par for the course; informal inevitable, on the cards.

unsuspecting adjective **unsuspicious**, unwary, unconscious, ignorant, unwitting; trusting, gullible, naive.
– OPPOSITES wary.

unswerving adjective **unwavering**, unfaltering, steadfast, unshakeable, staunch, firm, resolute, stalwart, dedicated, committed, constant, single-minded, dogged, indefatigable, unyielding, unbending, indomitable.

unsympathetic adjective **1** *unsympathetic staff:* **uncaring**, unconcerned, unfeeling, insensitive, unkind, pitiless, heartless, hard-hearted. **2** *the government was unsympathetic to these views:* **opposed**, against, set against, antagonistic, ill-disposed; informal anti. **3** *an unsympathetic character:* **unlikeable**, disagreeable, unpleasant, objectionable, unsavoury.
– OPPOSITES caring, sympathetic.

unsystematic adjective **unmethodical**, uncoordinated, disorganized, unplanned, indiscriminate; random, inconsistent, irregular, erratic, casual, haphazard, chaotic.

untangle verb **1** *I untangled the fishing tackle:* **disentangle**, unravel, straighten out, untwist, unknot. **2** *an attempt to untangle the mysteries of his past:* **solve**, find the answer to, resolve, puzzle out, fathom, clear up, clarify, get to the bottom of; informal figure out.

untarnished adjective **unsullied**, unblemished, untainted, impeccable, undamaged, unspoilt, spotless.

untenable adjective **indefensible**, undefendable, insupportable, unsustainable, unjustifiable, flimsy, weak, shaky.

unthinkable adjective **unimaginable**, inconceivable, unbelievable, incredible, implausible.

unthinking adjective **thoughtless**, inconsiderate, careless, casual, injudicious, imprudent, unwise, foolish, reckless, rash, precipitate; automatic, unquestioning, uncritical, unconsidered, knee-jerk, reflexive.

untidy adjective **1** *untidy hair:* **scruffy**, tousled, dishevelled, unkempt, messy, disordered, disarranged, rumpled, bedraggled, uncombed, ungroomed, straggly, ruffled, tangled, matted. **2** *the room was untidy:* **disordered**, messy, disorganized, cluttered, in chaos, haywire, in disarray; informal higgledy-piggledy.
– OPPOSITES neat, orderly.

untie verb **undo**, unknot, unbind, unfasten, unlace, untether, unhitch; loose, free.

until preposition & conjunction **1** *I was working until midnight:* **till**, up to, as late as; N. Amer. through. **2** *this did not happen until 1998:* **before**, prior to, previous to, up to, earlier than.

untimely adjective **1** *an untimely interruption:* **ill-timed**, mistimed; inopportune, inappropriate; inconvenient, unwelcome, infelicitous; formal malapropos. **2** *his untimely death:* **premature**, early, too soon.
– OPPOSITES timely, opportune.

untiring adjective **vigorous**, energetic, determined, resolute, enthusiastic, keen, zealous, spirited, dogged, tenacious, persistent, persevering, staunch; tireless, unflagging, unfailing, unfaltering, unwavering, indefatigable, unrelenting, unswerving.

untold adjective **1** *untold damage:*

boundless, measureless, limitless, infinite, immeasurable, incalculable. **2** *untold billions:* **countless**, innumerable, endless, limitless, numberless, uncountable; numerous, many, multiple; literary multitudinous, myriad. **3** *the untold story:* **unreported**, unrecounted, unrevealed, undisclosed, undivulged, unpublished.
– OPPOSITES limited.

untouched adjective **1** *the food was untouched:* **uneaten**, unconsumed. **2** *one of the few untouched areas:* **unspoilt**, unmarked, unblemished, unsullied, undefiled, undamaged, unharmed; pristine, natural, immaculate, in perfect condition, unaffected, unchanged, unaltered.

untoward adjective **unexpected**, unanticipated, unforeseen, unpredictable, unpredicted, surprising, unusual; unwelcome, unfavourable, adverse, unfortunate, infelicitous; formal malapropos.

untrained adjective **unskilled**, untaught, unschooled, untutored, unpractised, inexperienced; unqualified, unlicensed, amateur, non-professional.

untried adjective **untested**, new, experimental, unattempted, trial, test, pilot, unproven.
– OPPOSITES established.

untroubled adjective **unworried**, unperturbed, unconcerned, unruffled, undismayed, unbothered, unflustered; insouciant, nonchalant, blasé, carefree, serene; informal laid-back.

untrue adjective *these suggestions are totally untrue:* **false**, fabricated, made up, invented, concocted, trumped up; erroneous, wrong, incorrect, inaccurate; fallacious, unfounded.
– OPPOSITES correct, true.

untrustworthy adjective **dishonest**, deceitful, double-dealing, treacherous, two-faced, duplicitous, dishonourable, unprincipled, unscrupulous, corrupt; unreliable, undependable.
– OPPOSITES reliable.

untruth noun *the emails contained many untruths:* **lie**, falsehood, fib, fabrication, invention, falsification, exaggeration; informal tall story, cock and bull story, whopper; Brit. informal porky pie.

untruthful adjective **1** *the answers may be untruthful:* **false**, untrue, fabricated, made up, invented, trumped up; erroneous, wrong, incorrect, inaccurate, fallacious, fictitious. **2** *an untruthful person:* **lying**, mendacious, dishonest, deceitful, duplicitous, false, two-faced; informal crooked, bent.
– OPPOSITES truthful, honest.

untwist verb **unravel**, disentangle, unwind, unroll, uncoil, unfurl, straighten out.

unused adjective **1** *unused food stocks:* **superfluous**, surplus, to spare, left over, remaining, unnecessary, unneeded, not required. **2** *he was unused to such directness:* **unaccustomed**, new, a stranger, unfamiliar, unconversant, unacquainted.
– OPPOSITES used, accustomed.

unusual adjective **1** *an unusual sight:* **uncommon**, abnormal, atypical, unexpected, surprising, unfamiliar, different; strange, odd, curious, extraordinary, unorthodox, unconventional, singular, peculiar, bizarre; rare, scarce, exceptional, isolated, occasional, infrequent; informal weird, offbeat, way out, freaky. **2** *a man of unusual talent:* **remarkable**, extraordinary, exceptional, singular, particular, outstanding, notable, noteworthy, distinctive, striking, significant, special, unique, unparalleled, prodigious.
– OPPOSITES common, ordinary, usual.

unutterable adjective *an existence of unutterable boredom:* **indescribable**, inexpressible, unspeakable, undefinable, inconceivable, unimaginable; extreme, great, overwhelming, profound; dreadful, awful, appalling, terrible.

unvarnished adjective **1** *unvarnished wood:* **bare**, unpainted, unpolished, unfinished, untreated. **2** *the unvarnished truth:* **straightforward**, plain, simple, stark; truthful, candid, honest, frank, forthright, direct, blunt.

unveil verb **reveal**, present, disclose,

divulge, make known, make public, communicate, publish, broadcast; display, show, exhibit; release, bring out.

unwanted adjective **1** *an unwanted development:* **unwelcome**, undesirable, unpopular, unfortunate, unlucky, unfavourable, untoward; unpleasant, disagreeable, displeasing, distasteful, objectionable; regrettable, deplorable; unacceptable, intolerable, awful, terrible, wretched, appalling. **2** *tins of unwanted food:* **unused**, left over, surplus, superfluous; uneaten, unconsumed, untouched. **3** *an unwanted guest:* **uninvited**, unbidden, unasked, unrequested, unsolicited. **4** *many ageing people feel unwanted:* **friendless**, unloved, forsaken, rejected, shunned; superfluous, useless, unnecessary.
– OPPOSITES welcome.

unwarranted adjective *the criticism is unwarranted:* **unjustified**, indefensible, inexcusable, unforgivable, unpardonable, uncalled for, unnecessary, unjust, groundless.
– OPPOSITES justified.

unwary adjective **incautious**, careless, thoughtless, heedless, inattentive, off your guard.

unwavering adjective **steady**, fixed, resolute, resolved, firm, steadfast, unswerving, unfaltering, untiring, tireless, indefatigable, unyielding, relentless, unremitting, sustained.
– OPPOSITES unsteady.

unwelcome adjective **1** *I was made to feel unwelcome:* **unwanted**, uninvited. **2** *even a small increase is unwelcome:* **undesirable**, unpopular, unfortunate, upsetting, unlucky; disappointing, distressing, disagreeable, displeasing; regrettable, deplorable, lamentable.

unwell adjective **ill**, sick, poorly, indisposed, ailing, not yourself, under/below par, peaky; Brit. off colour; informal under the weather, funny, lousy, rough; Brit. informal grotty; Austral./NZ informal crook.

unwieldy adjective **cumbersome**, unmanageable, unmanoeuvrable; awkward, clumsy, massive, heavy, hefty, bulky.

unwilling adjective **1** *unwilling conscripts:* **reluctant**, unenthusiastic, hesitant, resistant, grudging, involuntary, forced. **2** *he was unwilling to take on that responsibility:* **disinclined**, reluctant, averse, loath.
▪ **be unwilling to do something** baulk at, demur at, shy away from, flinch from, shrink from, have qualms about, have misgivings about, have reservations about, not have the heart to.
– OPPOSITES keen, willing.

unwillingness adjective **disinclination**, reluctance, hesitation, diffidence, wavering, vacillation, resistance, objection, opposition, doubts, second thoughts, scruples, qualms, misgivings.

unwind verb **1** *Ella unwound the scarf:* **unroll**, uncoil, unravel, untwist, disentangle, open out, straighten out. **2** *you need to unwind:* **relax**, loosen up, ease up/off, slow down, de-stress, put your feet up, take it easy; informal wind down; N. Amer. informal hang loose, chill out, kick back.

unwise adjective **injudicious**, ill-advised, imprudent, foolish, silly, inadvisable, impolitic, misguided, foolhardy, irresponsible, rash, reckless.
– OPPOSITES sensible, wise.

unwitting adjective **1** *an unwitting accomplice:* **unknowing**, unconscious, unsuspecting, oblivious, unaware, innocent. **2** *an unwitting mistake:* **unintentional**, inadvertent, involuntary, unconscious, accidental.
– OPPOSITES conscious.

unworldly adjective **1** *a gauche, unworldly girl:* **naive**, simple, inexperienced, innocent, green, raw, callow, immature, unsophisticated, gullible, ingenuous, artless, guileless. **2** *unworldly beauty:* **unearthly**, other-worldly, ethereal, ghostly, preternatural, supernatural, paranormal, mystical. **3** *an unworldly religious order:* **non-materialistic**, spiritualistic.

unworthy adjective **1** *he was unworthy of trust:* **undeserving**, ineligible, unqualified, unfit. **2** *unworthy behaviour:* **unbecoming**, unsuitable,

inappropriate, unbefitting, unfitting, unseemly, improper; discreditable, shameful, dishonourable, despicable, ignoble, contemptible, reprehensible.
– OPPOSITES deserving, becoming.

unwritten adjective **tacit**, implicit, unvoiced, taken for granted, accepted, recognized, understood; traditional, customary, conventional.

unyielding adjective *his unyielding defence of traditional doctrines:* **resolute**, steadfast, staunch, unwavering, unshakeable, immovable, firm, determined, adamant, uncompromising, unbending, dogged, tenacious; intractable, intransigent, inflexible, rigid, obstinate, stubborn, obdurate, implacable, single-minded.

up-and-coming adjective **promising**, budding, rising, on the up and up, with potential; talented, gifted, able.

upbeat adjective **optimistic**, cheerful, cheery, positive, confident, hopeful, sanguine, bullish, buoyant.
– OPPOSITES pessimistic, negative.

upbraid verb **reprimand**, rebuke, admonish, chastise, chide, reprove, reproach, scold, berate, take to task, haul over the coals; informal tell off, rap over the knuckles, bawl out; Brit. informal tick off, tear off a strip; N. Amer. informal chew out, ream out; formal castigate.

upbringing noun **childhood**, early life, formative years, teaching, instruction, rearing.

update verb **1** *security measures are continually updated:* **modernize**, upgrade, improve, overhaul. **2** *I'll update him on developments:* **brief**, bring up to date, inform, fill in, tell, notify, apprise, keep posted; informal clue in, put in the picture, bring/keep up to speed.

u

upgrade verb **1** *there are plans to upgrade the system:* **improve**, modernize, update, make better, ameliorate, reform. **2** *he was upgraded to a seat in the cabinet:* **promote**, elevate, move up, raise.
– OPPOSITES downgrade, demote.

upheaval noun **disruption**, disturbance, trouble, turbulence, disorder, confusion, turmoil, pandemonium, chaos, mayhem, cataclysm.

uphill adjective *an uphill task:* **arduous**, difficult, hard, tough, taxing, demanding, exacting, stiff, formidable, laborious, gruelling, onerous, Herculean; informal no picnic, killing.

uphold verb **1** *the court upheld his claim:* **confirm**, endorse, sustain, approve, support, back, stand by, defend. **2** *they've a tradition to uphold:* **maintain**, sustain, continue, preserve, protect, keep, hold to, keep alive, keep going.
– OPPOSITES overturn, oppose.

upkeep noun **1** *the upkeep of the road:* **maintenance**, repair, service, care, preservation, conservation; running. **2** *the child's upkeep:* **financial support**, maintenance, keep, subsistence, care.

uplift verb *she needs something to uplift her spirits:* **boost**, raise, buoy up, cheer up, perk up, enliven, brighten up, lighten, stimulate, inspire, revive, restore; informal buck up.

uplifting adjective **inspiring**, stirring, inspirational, rousing, moving, touching, affecting, cheering, heartening, encouraging.

upper adjective **1** *the upper floor:* **higher**, superior; top. **2** *the upper echelons of the party:* **senior**, superior, higher-level, higher-ranking, top.
– OPPOSITES lower.
■ **the upper hand** an advantage, the edge, a lead, a head start, ascendancy, superiority, supremacy, sway, control, power, mastery, dominance, command.

upper-class adjective **aristocratic**, noble, patrician, titled, blue-blooded, high-born, elite, landed, born with a silver spoon in your mouth; Brit. county; informal upper-crust, top-drawer; Brit. informal posh.

uppermost adjective **1** *the uppermost branches:* **highest**, top, topmost. **2** *their own problems remained uppermost in their minds:* **predominant**, of greatest importance, to the fore, foremost, dominant, principal, chief, main, paramount, major.

upright adjective **1** *an upright position:* **vertical**, perpendicular, plumb, straight, erect, on end; on

your feet. **2** *an upright member of the community:* **honest**, honourable, upstanding, respectable, high-minded, law-abiding, worthy, righteous, decent, good, virtuous, principled.
– OPPOSITES horizontal, dishonourable.

uprising noun **rebellion**, revolt, insurrection, revolution, mutiny, insurgence, rioting; civil disobedience, unrest, anarchy; coup.

uproar noun **1** *the uproar in the kitchen continued:* **turmoil**, disorder, confusion, chaos, commotion, disturbance, rumpus, tumult, turbulence, mayhem, pandemonium, bedlam, noise, din, clamour, hubbub, racket; Brit. row; informal hullabaloo. **2** *there was an uproar when he was dismissed:* **outcry**, furore; fuss, commotion, hue and cry, rumpus; Brit. row; informal stink, ructions.
– OPPOSITES calm.

uproarious adjective **1** *an uproarious party:* **riotous**, rowdy, noisy, loud, wild, unruly, rip-roaring, rollicking, boisterous. **2** *an uproarious joke:* **hilarious**, rib-tickling; informal priceless, side-splitting, a scream, a hoot.
– OPPOSITES quiet.

uproot verb **1** *don't uproot wild flowers:* **pull up**, root out, deracinate, grub out/up. **2** *a revolution is necessary to uproot the social order:* **eradicate**, get rid of, eliminate, root out, destroy, put an end to, do away with, wipe out, stamp out.
– OPPOSITES plant.

upset verb **1** *the accusation upset her:* **distress**, trouble, perturb, dismay, disturb, discompose, unsettle, disconcert, disquiet, worry, bother, agitate, fluster, throw, ruffle, unnerve, shake; hurt, sadden, grieve. **2** *he upset a tureen of soup:* **knock over**, overturn, upend, tip over, topple; spill. **3** *the dam will upset the ecological balance:* **disrupt**, interfere with, disturb, throw into confusion, mess up.
• noun **1** *a legal dispute will cause worry and upset:* **distress**, trouble, perturbation, dismay, disquiet, worry, bother, agitation; hurt, grief. **2** *a stomach upset:* **disorder**, complaint, ailment, illness, sickness, malady; informal bug; Brit. informal lurgy.
• adjective **1** *I was upset by the news:* **distressed**, troubled, perturbed, dismayed, disturbed, unsettled, disconcerted, worried, bothered, anxious, agitated, flustered, ruffled, unnerved, shaken; hurt, saddened, grieved; informal cut up, choked; Brit. informal gutted. **2** *an upset stomach:* **disturbed**, unsettled, queasy, bad, poorly; informal gippy.
– OPPOSITES unperturbed, calm.

upshot noun **result**, consequence, outcome, conclusion; effect, repercussion, reverberations, ramification.
– OPPOSITES cause.

upside down adjective **1** *an upside-down canoe:* **upturned**, upended, wrong side up, overturned, inverted; capsized. **2** *they left the flat upside down:* **in disarray**, in disorder, jumbled up, in a muddle, untidy, disorganized, in chaos, in confusion; informal higgledy-piggledy.

upstanding adjective *an upstanding member of the community:* **honest**, honourable, upright, respectable, high-minded, law-abiding, worthy, righteous, decent, good, virtuous, principled, noble, incorruptible.
– OPPOSITES dishonourable.

upstart noun **parvenu**, arriviste, nouveau riche; status seeker, social climber; informal johnny-come-lately.

up to date adjective **1** *up-to-date equipment:* **modern**, contemporary, the latest, state-of-the-art, new, up to the minute; advanced. **2** *the newsletter will keep you up to date:* **informed**, up to speed, in the picture, in touch, au fait, conversant, familiar, knowledgeable, acquainted.
– OPPOSITES out of date, old-fashioned.

upturn noun **improvement**, upswing; recovery, revival, rally, resurgence, increase, rise, jump, leap, upsurge, boost, escalation.
– OPPOSITES fall, slump.

upward adjective *an upward trend:* **rising**, ascending, climbing, mounting; uphill.
– OPPOSITES downward.

upwards adverb *he inched his way upwards:* **up**, upward, uphill; to

the top.
–OPPOSITES downward.
■ **upward(s) of** more than, above, over, in excess of, exceeding, beyond.

urban adjective **town**, city, municipal, metropolitan, built-up, inner-city, suburban.
–OPPOSITES rural.

urbane adjective **suave**, sophisticated, debonair, worldly, cultivated, cultured, civilized; smooth, polished, refined, self-possessed; courteous, polite, civil, well mannered, mannerly, charming, gentlemanly, gallant.
–OPPOSITES uncouth, unsophisticated.

urchin noun **ragamuffin**, waif, stray; imp, rascal; derogatory guttersnipe.

urge verb **1** *she urged him to try:* **encourage**, exhort, enjoin, press, entreat, implore, call on, appeal to, beg, plead with; egg on, spur; formal adjure; literary beseech. **2** *I urge caution in interpreting these results:* **advise**, counsel, advocate, recommend.
•noun *his urge to travel:* **desire**, wish, need, compulsion, longing, yearning, hankering, yen, craving, appetite, hunger, thirst; informal itch.

urgent adjective **1** *the urgent need for more funding:* **acute**, pressing, dire, desperate, critical, serious, grave, intense, crying, burning, compelling, extreme, high-priority; life-and-death. **2** *an urgent whisper:* **insistent**, persistent, importunate, earnest, pleading, begging.

usable adjective **ready/fit for use**, disposable; working, functional, serviceable, operational, up and running.

usage noun **1** *energy usage:* **use**, consumption, utilization. **2** *the usage of equipment:* **use**, utilization, operation, manipulation, running, handling. **3** *the intricacies of English usage:* **phraseology**, parlance, idiom, way of speaking/writing, mode of expression; idiolect.

use verb **1** *she used her key to open the door:* **utilize**, avail yourself of, employ, work, operate, wield, ply, apply, manoeuvre, put into service. **2** *the court will use its discretion:* **exercise**, employ, bring into play, practise, apply. **3** *use your troops well and they will not let you down:* **manage**, handle, treat, deal with, behave/act towards, conduct yourself towards. **4** *I couldn't help feeling that she was using me:* **take advantage of**, exploit, manipulate, take liberties with, impose on, abuse; capitalize on, profit from, trade on, milk; informal cash in on, walk all over. **5** *we have used all the available funds:* **consume**, get/go through, exhaust, deplete, expend, spend.
•noun **1** *the use of such weapons:* **utilization**, application, employment, operation, manipulation. **2** *his use of other people for his own ends:* **exploitation**, manipulation; abuse. **3** *what is the use of that?* **advantage**, benefit, service, utility, help, good, gain, avail, profit, value, worth, point, object, purpose, sense, reason. **4** *composers have not found much use for the device:* **need**, necessity, call, demand, requirement.

used adjective *a used car:* **second-hand**, pre-owned, nearly new, old; worn, hand-me-down, cast-off.
–OPPOSITES new.
■ **used to** accustomed to, no stranger to, familiar with, at home with, in the habit of, experienced in, versed in, conversant with, acquainted with.

useful adjective **1** *a useful tool:* **functional**, practical, handy, convenient, utilitarian, serviceable, of service; informal nifty. **2** *a useful experience:* **beneficial**, advantageous, helpful, worthwhile, profitable, rewarding, productive, constructive, valuable, fruitful. **3** (informal) *they had some very useful players:* **competent**, capable, able, skilful, talented, proficient, accomplished, good, handy; informal nifty.
–OPPOSITES useless, disadvantageous, incompetent.

useless adjective **1** *it was useless to try | useless knowledge:* **futile**, to no avail, vain, pointless, to no purpose, unavailing, hopeless, ineffectual, fruitless, unprofitable, unproductive; broken, kaput. **2** (informal) *he was useless at his job:* **incompetent**, inept, ineffective, incapable, inadequate, hopeless, bad; informal pathetic, a dead loss.
–OPPOSITES useful, beneficial, competent.

usher verb *she ushered him to a seat:* **escort**, accompany, take, show, see, lead, conduct, guide, steer, shepherd.

■ **usher something in** *the railways ushered in an era of cheap mass travel:* herald, mark the start of, signal, set the scene for, pave the way for; start, begin, introduce, open the door to, get going, set in motion, get under way, kick off, launch.

usual adjective **habitual**, customary, accustomed, wonted, normal, routine, regular, standard, typical, established, set, settled, stock, conventional, traditional, expected, predictable, familiar; average, general, ordinary, everyday.
– OPPOSITES exceptional.

usually adverb **normally**, generally, habitually, customarily, routinely, typically, ordinarily, commonly, conventionally, traditionally; as a rule, in general, more often than not, mainly, mostly.

usurp verb **1** *Richard usurped the throne:* **seize**, take over, take possession of, take, commandeer, assume. **2** *the Hanoverian dynasty had usurped the Stuarts:* **oust**, overthrow, remove, topple, unseat, depose, dethrone; supplant, replace.

utensil noun **implement**, tool, instrument, device, apparatus, gadget, appliance, contrivance, contraption, aid; informal gizmo.

utilitarian adjective **practical**, functional, serviceable, useful, sensible, efficient, utility, workaday; plain, unadorned.
– OPPOSITES decorative.

utility noun **usefulness**, use, benefit, value, advantage, help, profitability, practicality, effectiveness, avail, service; formal efficacy.

utilize verb **use**, employ, avail yourself of, bring/press into service, bring into play, deploy, draw on, exploit.

utmost adjective **1** *a matter of the utmost importance:* **greatest**, highest, maximum, most; extreme, supreme, paramount. **2** *the utmost tip of Shetland:* **furthest**, farthest, extreme, very, outermost.

Utopia noun **paradise**, heaven, Eden, Shangri-La, Elysium; idyll, nirvana; literary Arcadia.

utopian adjective **idealistic**, visionary, romantic, starry-eyed, fanciful, unrealistic; ideal, perfect, paradisal, heavenly, idyllic, blissful, Elysian; literary Arcadian.

utter[1] adjective *that's utter nonsense:* **complete**, total, absolute, thorough, perfect, downright, out-and-out, outright, sheer, arrant, positive, prize, rank, pure, real, veritable, consummate, categorical, unmitigated.

utter[2] verb **1** *he uttered an exasperated snort:* **emit**, let out, give, produce. **2** *he hardly uttered a word:* **say**, speak, voice, express, articulate, pronounce, enunciate, verbalize, vocalize.

utterance noun **remark**, comment, word, statement, observation, declaration, pronouncement.

utterly adverb **completely**, totally, absolutely, entirely, wholly, fully, thoroughly, quite, altogether, one hundred per cent, downright, really, to the hilt, to the core; informal dead.

U-turn noun *a complete U-turn in economic policy:* **volte-face**, turnaround, about-face, reversal, shift, change of heart, change of mind, backtracking, change of plan; Brit. about-turn.

Vv

vacancy noun **1** *there are vacancies for technicians:* **opening**, position, post, job, opportunity. **2** *Cathy stared into vacancy, seeing nothing:* **empty space**, emptiness, nothingness, void. **3** *a vacancy of mind:* **empty-headedness**, lack of intelligence, brainlessness, vacuity.

vacant adjective **1** *a vacant house:* **empty**, unoccupied, available, not in use, free, unfilled; uninhabited, untenanted. **2** *a vacant look:* **blank**, expressionless, unresponsive, emotionless, impassive, vacuous, empty, glazed.
– OPPOSITES full, occupied, expressive.

vacate verb **1** *he was forced to vacate the premises:* **leave**, move out of, evacuate, quit, depart from. **2** *he will be vacating his post next year:* **resign from**, leave, stand down from, give up, bow out of, retire from, relinquish; informal quit.
– OPPOSITES occupy, take up.

vacation noun **1** **holiday**, trip, tour, break; leave, time off, recess; formal sojourn. **2** *the squatters' vacation of the land:* **departure**, evacuation, abandonment, desertion.

vacillate verb **dither**, be indecisive, waver, hesitate, be in two minds, blow hot and cold; Brit. haver, hum and haw; informal dilly-dally.

vacillating adjective **irresolute**, indecisive, dithering, hesitant, wavering, ambivalent, divided, uncertain, in two minds, blowing hot and cold; informal dilly-dallying.
– OPPOSITES resolute.

vacuous adjective **silly**, inane, unintelligent, foolish, stupid, brainless, vapid, vacant, empty-headed; informal gormless, moronic, brain-dead.
– OPPOSITES intelligent.

vacuum noun **1** *people longing to fill the spiritual vacuum in their lives:* **emptiness**, void, nothingness, vacancy. **2** *the political vacuum left by the Emperor's death:* **gap**, space, lacuna, void.

vagary noun **change**, fluctuation, variation, quirk, peculiarity, oddity, eccentricity, unpredictability, caprice, whim, fancy.

vagrant noun **tramp**, drifter, down-and-out, beggar, itinerant, wanderer, nomad, traveller, vagabond, transient, homeless person; N. Amer. hobo; N. Amer. informal **bum**.
• adjective *vagrant beggars:* **homeless**, drifting, transient, roaming, itinerant, wandering, nomadic, travelling, vagabond.

vague adjective **1** *a vague shape:* **indistinct**, indefinite, indeterminate, unclear, ill-defined; hazy, fuzzy, misty, blurry, out of focus, faint, shadowy, dim, obscure. **2** *a vague description:* **imprecise**, rough, approximate, inexact, non-specific, generalized, ambiguous, equivocal, hazy, woolly. **3** *vague plans:* **hazy**, uncertain, undecided, unsure, unclear, unsettled, indefinite, indeterminate, unconfirmed, up in the air, speculative. **4** *she's a bit vague:* **absent-minded**, forgetful, dreamy, abstracted; informal scatty.
– OPPOSITES clear, precise, certain.

vaguely adverb **1** *she looks vaguely familiar:* **slightly**, a little, a bit, somewhat, rather, in a way; faintly, obscurely. **2** *he fired his rifle vaguely in our direction:* **roughly**, more or less, approximately. **3** *he smiled vaguely:* **absent-mindedly**, abstractedly, vacantly.
– OPPOSITES very, exactly.

vain adjective **1** *their flattery made*

him vain: **conceited**, narcissistic, self-loving, egotistic; proud, arrogant, boastful, cocky, immodest; informal big-headed. **2** *a vain attempt:* **futile**, useless, pointless; ineffective, fruitless, unproductive, unsuccessful, failed, abortive; thwarted, frustrated, foiled.
– OPPOSITES modest, successful.
■ **in vain** unsuccessfully, to no avail, to no purpose, fruitlessly.

> Don't confuse **vain** with **vein**, which means 'a tube that carries blood around the body'.

valedictory adjective **farewell**, goodbye, leaving, parting; last, final.

valet noun **manservant**, gentleman's gentleman, Jeeves.

valiant adjective **brave**, courageous, plucky, intrepid, heroic, gallant, lion-hearted, bold, fearless, daring, audacious; unflinching, unafraid, undaunted, doughty, indomitable, mettlesome, stout-hearted; informal game, gutsy.
– OPPOSITES cowardly.

valid adjective **1** *a valid criticism:* **well founded**, sound, reasonable, rational, logical, justifiable, defensible, viable, bona fide; cogent, credible, forceful, strong, weighty. **2** *a valid contract:* **legally binding**, lawful, official; in force, in effect.

validate verb **1** *clinical trials exist to validate this claim:* **prove**, substantiate, corroborate, verify, support, back up, bear out, confirm, authenticate. **2** *250 course proposals were validated:* **ratify**, endorse, approve, agree to, accept, authorize, legalize, legitimize, warrant, license, certify, recognize.
– OPPOSITES disprove.

valley noun **dale**, vale; hollow, gully, gorge, ravine, canyon, rift; Brit. combe, dene; N. English **clough**; Scottish glen, strath; literary dell, dingle.

valour noun **bravery**, courage, pluck, nerve, daring, fearlessness, boldness, audacity, stout-heartedness, heroism; informal guts; Brit. informal bottle.
– OPPOSITES cowardice.

valuable adjective **1** *a valuable watch:* **precious**, costly, high-priced, expensive, dear; worth its weight in gold, priceless. **2** *a valuable contribution:* **useful**, helpful, beneficial, invaluable, productive, worthwhile, worthy, important.
– OPPOSITES cheap, worthless, useless.

valuables plural noun **precious items**, costly items, prized possessions, treasures.

value noun **1** *houses exceeding £250,000 in value:* **price**, cost, worth; market price. **2** *the value of adequate preparation:* **worth**, usefulness, advantage, benefit, gain, profit, good, help; importance, significance. **3** *society's values:* **principles**, ethics, morals, standards, code of behaviour.
• verb **1** *his estate was valued at £45,000:* **evaluate**, assess, estimate, appraise, price. **2** *she valued his opinion:* **think highly of**, have a high opinion of, rate highly, esteem, set great store by, respect.

valued adjective *a valued friend:* **cherished**, treasured, dear, prized; esteemed, respected.

vanguard noun **forefront**, van, advance guard, spearhead, front, fore, lead, cutting edge; leaders, founders, pioneers, trailblazers, groundbreakers.
– OPPOSITES rear.

vanish verb **1** *he vanished into the darkness:* **disappear**, be lost to sight/view, become invisible. **2** *all hope vanished:* **fade**, evaporate, melt away, dissolve, end, cease to exist, die.
– OPPOSITES appear, materialize.

vanity noun **1** *she had none of the vanity often associated with beautiful women:* **conceit**, narcissism, self-love, self-admiration, egotism; pride, arrogance, boastfulness, cockiness, swagger; informal big-headedness. **2** *the vanity of all desires of the will:* **futility**, uselessness, pointlessness, worthlessness, fruitlessness.
– OPPOSITES modesty.

vanquish verb **conquer**, defeat, beat, trounce, rout, triumph over, be victorious over, get the better of, worst; overcome, overwhelm, overpower, overthrow, subdue, subjugate, quell, quash, crush, bring someone to their knees.

vapid adjective **insipid**, uninspired,

colourless, uninteresting, feeble, dull, boring, tedious, unexciting, unimaginative, lifeless, tame, bland.
– OPPOSITES lively, colourful.

vapour noun **haze**, mist, steam, condensation; fumes, exhalation, fog, smog, smoke.

variable adjective **changeable**, shifting, fluctuating, irregular, inconstant, inconsistent, fluid, unstable, unsettled, protean, wavering, vacillating, capricious, fickle; informal up and down.
– OPPOSITES constant.

variance noun **difference**, variation, discrepancy, dissimilarity, disagreement, conflict, divergence, deviation, contrast, contradiction.
■ **at variance 1** *his recollections were at variance with evidence:* inconsistent, at odds, not in keeping, out of line, out of step, in conflict, in disagreement, different, discrepant, dissimilar, contrary, incompatible, contradictory. **2** *they were at variance with their former allies:* in disagreement, at odds, at cross purposes, at loggerheads, in conflict, in dispute.

variant noun *there are a number of variants of the same idea:* **variation**, form, alternative, adaptation, alteration, modification, permutation.
• adjective *a variant spelling of the word:* **alternative**, other, different, divergent.

variation noun **1** *regional variations in farming:* **difference**, dissimilarity; disparity, contrast, discrepancy, imbalance. **2** *opening times are subject to variation:* **change**, alteration, modification. **3** *there was very little variation from the pattern:* **deviation**, variance, divergence, departure, fluctuation. **4** *hurling is an Irish variation of hockey:* **variant**, form; development, adaptation, alteration, modification.

varied adjective *a varied selection of produce | a long and varied career:* **diverse**, assorted, miscellaneous, mixed, sundry, heterogeneous, wide-ranging, multifarious; eclectic, multifaceted; disparate, motley.

variegated adjective **multicoloured**, particoloured, polychromatic, prismatic, kaleidoscopic; mottled, marbled, streaked, speckled, flecked, dappled.
– OPPOSITES plain, monochrome.

variety noun **1** *the lack of variety in the curriculum:* **diversity**, variation, diversification, multifariousness, heterogeneity; change, difference. **2** *a wide variety of flowers:* **assortment**, miscellany, range, array, collection, selection, mixture, medley; mixed bag, motley collection, potpourri. **3** *fifty varieties of pasta:* **sort**, kind, type, class, category, style, form; make, model, brand; strain, breed, genus.
– OPPOSITES uniformity.

various adjective **diverse**, different, differing, varied, a variety of, assorted, mixed, sundry, miscellaneous, heterogeneous, disparate, motley.
– OPPOSITES uniform.

varnish noun & verb **lacquer**, shellac, japan, enamel, glaze; polish.

vary verb **1** *estimates of the cost vary:* **differ**, be dissimilar. **2** *rates of interest vary over time:* **fluctuate**, rise and fall, go up and down, change, alter, shift, swing, deviate. **3** *the diaphragm is used for varying the aperture:* **modify**, change, alter, adjust, regulate, control, set; diversify.

vast adjective **huge**, extensive, expansive, broad, wide, boundless, immeasurable, limitless, infinite; enormous, immense, great, massive, colossal, gigantic, gargantuan, mammoth; giant, towering, mountainous, titanic; informal jumbo, mega, whopping, humongous; Brit. informal ginormous.
– OPPOSITES tiny.

vat noun **tub**, tank, cistern, barrel, butt, cask, tun, drum; vessel, receptacle, container, holder, reservoir.

vault[1] noun **1** *the highest Gothic vault in Europe:* **arched roof**, dome, arch. **2** *the vault under the church:* **cellar**, basement, underground chamber; crypt, undercroft, catacomb, burial chamber. **3** *valuables stored in the vault:* **strongroom**, safe deposit.

vault[2] verb *he vaulted over the gate:*

jump over, leap over, spring over, bound over; hurdle, clear.

vaunt verb **boast about**, brag about, crow about, parade, acclaim, extol, celebrate; formal laud.

veer verb **turn**, swerve, swing, career, weave, wheel; change direction/course, deviate.

vegetate verb **do nothing**, idle, languish, laze, lounge, loll; informal veg out, slob out.

vegetation noun **plants**, flora; greenery, foliage, herbage; literary verdure.

vehemence noun **passion**, force, ardour, fervour, violence, urgency, strength, vigour, intensity, keenness, enthusiasm, zeal.

vehement adjective **passionate**, forceful, ardent, impassioned, heated, spirited, urgent, fervent, violent, fierce, strong, forcible, powerful, emphatic, vigorous, intense, earnest, keen, enthusiastic, zealous.
– OPPOSITES mild, apathetic.

vehicle noun **1** *a stolen vehicle:* **means of transport**, conveyance. **2** *a vehicle for the communication of ideas:* **channel**, medium, means, agent, instrument, mechanism, organ, apparatus.

WORD LINKS
automotive relating to motor vehicles

veil noun *a thin veil of cloud:* **covering**, screen, curtain, mantle, cloak, mask, blanket, shroud, canopy, cloud, pall.
• verb *the peak was veiled in mist:* **envelop**, surround, swathe, enfold, cover, conceal, hide, screen, shield, cloak, blanket, shroud; obscure.

veiled adjective *veiled threats:* **disguised**, camouflaged, masked, covert, hidden, concealed, suppressed, underlying, implicit, indirect.
– OPPOSITES overt.

vein noun **1 blood vessel**. **2** *the veins in the rock:* **layer**, lode, seam, stratum, stratification, deposit. **3** *white marble with grey veins:* **streak**, mark, line, stripe, strip, band, thread, strand. **4** *he closes the article in a humorous vein:* **mood**, humour, disposition, attitude, tenor, tone, key, spirit, character, feel, flavour, quality, atmosphere; manner, way, style.

WORD LINKS
vascular, **venous** relating to veins
phlebotomy surgical incision into a vein

! Don't confuse **vein** with **vain**, which means 'having too high an opinion of yourself' or 'unsuccessful' (*a vain attempt to find a solution*).

velocity noun **speed**, pace, rate, tempo, momentum, impetus; swiftness, rapidity; literary fleetness, celerity.

vendetta noun **feud**, quarrel, argument, falling-out, dispute, fight, war; bad blood, enmity.

vendor noun **seller**, retailer, purveyor, dealer, trader, merchant, supplier, stockist.

veneer noun **1** *cherry wood with a maple veneer:* **surface**, lamination, layer, overlay, facing, covering, finish, exterior. **2** *a veneer of sophistication:* **facade**, front, show, outward display, appearance, impression, semblance, guise, mask, pretence, camouflage, cover.

venerable adjective **respected**, revered, honoured, esteemed, hallowed, august, distinguished, eminent, great.

venerate verb **revere**, worship, hallow, hold sacred, exalt, adore, honour, respect, esteem.

veneration noun **reverence**, worship, adoration, exaltation, devotion, honour, respect, esteem.

vengeance noun **revenge**, retribution, retaliation, requital, reprisal, an eye for an eye.

vengeful adjective **vindictive**, revengeful, unforgiving.
– OPPOSITES forgiving.

venom noun **1** *snake venom:* **poison**, toxin. **2** *his voice was full of venom:* **rancour**, malevolence, vitriol, spite, vindictiveness, malice, animosity, antagonism, hostility, bile, hate; informal bitchiness, cattiness.

venomous adjective **1** *a venomous snake | a venomous bite:* **poisonous**, toxic; dangerous, deadly, lethal, fatal. **2** *venomous remarks:* **vicious**, spiteful, rancorous, malevolent, vitriolic, vindictive, malicious,

poisonous, virulent, hostile, cruel; informal bitchy, catty.
– OPPOSITES harmless, benevolent.

vent noun *an air vent:* **outlet, inlet,** opening, aperture, hole, gap, orifice, space; duct, flue, shaft, well, airway, passage.
• verb *the crowd vented their fury:* **let out,** release, pour out, express, air, voice.

ventilate verb **1** *the greenhouse must be ventilated:* **air,** aerate, oxygenate; freshen, cool. **2** *the workers ventilated their discontent:* **express,** air, communicate, voice, verbalize, discuss, debate.

venture noun *a business venture:* **enterprise,** undertaking, project, scheme, operation, endeavour, speculation.
• verb **1** *we ventured across the moor:* **set out,** go, travel, journey. **2** *may I venture an opinion?* **put forward,** advance, proffer, offer, air, suggest, submit, propose, moot.

verbal adjective **oral,** spoken, stated, said; unwritten.

verbatim adverb **word for word,** letter for letter, literally, exactly, precisely, closely, faithfully.

verbose adjective **wordy,** loquacious, garrulous, talkative, voluble; long-winded, lengthy, prolix, circumlocutory, circuitous, discursive, digressive, rambling; Brit. informal waffly.
– OPPOSITES succinct, laconic.

verbosity noun **wordiness,** loquacity, garrulity, talkativeness, volubility; long-windedness, verbiage, prolixity, circumlocution; Brit. informal waffle.

verdant adjective **green,** leafy, grassy; lush, rich.

verdict noun **judgement,** adjudication, decision, finding, ruling, resolution, pronouncement.

V

verge noun **1** *the verge of the lake:* **edge,** border, margin, side, brink, rim, lip; fringe, boundary, perimeter. **2** *Spain was on the verge of an economic crisis:* **brink,** threshold, edge, point.
• verb *a degree of caution that verged on the obsessive:* **approach,** border on, be close/near to, be tantamount to; tend towards, approximate to.

verification noun **confirmation,** substantiation, proof, corroboration, support, attestation, validation, authentication, endorsement.

verify verb **substantiate,** confirm, prove, corroborate, back up, bear out, justify, support, uphold, attest to, testify to, validate, authenticate, endorse.
– OPPOSITES refute.

vernacular noun **everyday language,** colloquial language, conversational language, common parlance; dialect, regional language, patois; informal lingo.

versatile adjective **adaptable,** flexible, all-round, multitalented, resourceful; adjustable, multi-purpose, all-purpose.

verse noun **1** *Elizabethan verse:* **poetry,** versification; balladry, lyrics. **2** *a verse he'd composed to mark my anniversary:* **poem,** lyric, ballad, sonnet, ode, limerick, rhyme, ditty, lay. **3** *a poem with sixty verses:* **stanza,** canto, couplet.
– OPPOSITES prose.

version noun **1** *his version of events:* **account,** report, statement, description, record, story, rendering, interpretation, explanation, understanding, reading, impression, side. **2** *the English version will be published next year:* **edition,** translation, impression. **3** *they have replaced coal-burning fires with gas versions:* **form,** sort, kind, type, variety.

vertical adjective **upright,** erect, perpendicular, plumb, on end, standing.
– OPPOSITES horizontal.

vertigo noun **dizziness,** giddiness, light-headedness, loss of balance.

verve noun **enthusiasm,** vigour, energy, pep, dynamism, go, elan, vitality, vivacity, buoyancy, liveliness, animation, zest, sparkle, spirit, ebullience, brio, gusto, keenness, passion, zeal, relish, ardour; informal zing, zip, vim, pizzazz, oomph.

very adverb *that's very kind of you:* **extremely,** exceedingly, exceptionally, extraordinarily, tremendously, immensely, hugely, intensely, acutely, abundantly, singularly, unusually, decidedly, highly, remarkably, really; informal awfully,

terrifically, terribly, majorly, seriously, mega, ultra; Brit. informal well, dead, jolly; N. Amer. informal real, mighty, awful.
– OPPOSITES slightly.
• adjective **1** *those were his very words:* **exact**, actual, precise. **2** *the very thought of food made her feel ill:* **mere**, simple, pure; sheer.

vessel noun **1** *a fishing vessel:* **boat**, ship, craft; literary barque. **2** *pour the mixture into a heatproof vessel:* **container**, receptacle; basin, bowl, pan, pot.

vest verb *executive power is vested in the President:* **confer on**, entrust to, invest in, bestow on, grant to, give to; endow, lodge, lay, place.

vestibule noun **entrance hall**, porch, portico, foyer, lobby, anteroom, antechamber, waiting room.

vestige noun **1** *the last vestiges of colonialism:* **remnant**, fragment, relic, echo, indication, sign, trace, mark, legacy, reminder. **2** *she showed no vestige of emotion:* **bit**, touch, hint, suggestion, suspicion, shadow, scrap, tinge, speck, shred, jot, iota, whit; informal smidgen, tad.

vestigial adjective **1** *vestigial limbs:* **rudimentary**, undeveloped; non-functional; Biology primitive. **2** *he felt a vestigial flicker of anger from last night:* **remaining**, surviving, residual, leftover, lingering.

vet verb **check**, examine, scrutinize, investigate, inspect, look over, screen, assess, evaluate, appraise; informal check out.

veteran noun *a veteran of 16 political campaigns:* **old hand**, past master; informal old-timer.
– OPPOSITES novice.
• adjective *a veteran diplomat:* **long-serving**, seasoned, old, hardened; adept, expert, practised, experienced; informal battle-scarred.

veto noun *parliament's right of veto:* **rejection**, dismissal; prohibition, proscription, embargo, ban, interdict; informal thumbs down, red light.
– OPPOSITES approval.
• verb *the president vetoed the bill:* **reject**, turn down, throw out, dismiss; prohibit, forbid, interdict, proscribe, disallow, embargo, ban; informal kill, put the kibosh on, give the thumbs down to, give the red light to.
– OPPOSITES approve.

vex verb **annoy**, irritate, irk, pique, rankle; informal aggravate, peeve, miff, rile, nettle, needle, bug, hack off, get up someone's nose; Brit. informal wind up, nark; N. Amer. informal tee off, tick off.

vexed adjective **1** *a vexed expression:* **annoyed**, irritated, cross, angry, infuriated, exasperated, irked, piqued, displeased, put out, disgruntled; informal aggravated, peeved, nettled, miffed, riled, hacked off; Brit. informal narked, shirty; N. Amer. informal teed off. **2** *the vexed issue of immigration:* **disputed**, contested, contentious, debated, at issue, controversial, moot; problematic, difficult, knotty, thorny.

viable adjective **feasible**, workable, practicable, practical, usable, possible, realistic, achievable, attainable; informal doable.
– OPPOSITES impracticable.

vibrant adjective **1** *a vibrant woman:* **spirited**, lively, energetic, vigorous, vital, animated, sparkling, effervescent, vivacious, dynamic, passionate, fiery; informal peppy, feisty. **2** *vibrant colours:* **vivid**, bright, striking, brilliant, strong, rich. **3** *his vibrant voice:* **resonant**, sonorous, reverberant, resounding, ringing, echoing; strong, rich.
– OPPOSITES lifeless, pale.

vibrate verb **1** *the floor vibrated:* **quiver**, shake, tremble, shiver, shudder, throb, pulsate. **2** *a low rumbling sound began to vibrate through the car:* **reverberate**, resonate, resound, ring, echo.

vibration noun **tremor**, shaking, quivering, quaking, shuddering, throb, pulsation.

vicar noun **minister**, rector, priest, parson, clergyman, clergywoman, cleric, churchman, churchwoman, ecclesiastic, pastor, man/woman of the cloth, curate, chaplain, preacher; informal reverend, padre, Holy Joe.

vicarious adjective **indirect**, secondary, second-hand, derived, substitute.

vice noun **1** *youngsters may be driven*

to vice: **immorality**, wrongdoing, wickedness, badness, evil, iniquity, villainy, corruption, misconduct; sin, ungodliness; depravity, degeneracy, dissolution, dissipation, debauchery, decadence; formal turpitude. **2** *smoking is my only vice:* **shortcoming**, failing, flaw, fault, defect, weakness, deficiency, foible, frailty.
–OPPOSITES virtue.

vice versa adverb **conversely**, inversely; reciprocally.

vicinity noun **neighbourhood**, surrounding area, locality, area, district, region, quarter, zone; environs, surroundings, precincts; informal neck of the woods.
■ **in the vicinity of** around, about, nearly, circa, approaching, roughly, more or less; in the region of, near to, close to; Brit. getting on for.

vicious adjective **1** *a vicious killer:* **brutal**, ferocious, savage, violent, dangerous, ruthless, merciless, heartless, callous, cruel, harsh, cold-blooded, inhuman, barbaric, bloodthirsty, sadistic. **2** *a vicious hate campaign:* **malicious**, malevolent, malign, spiteful, vindictive, venomous, rancorous, cruel, bitter, acrimonious, hostile, nasty.
–OPPOSITES gentle, kindly.

victim noun **1** *a victim of crime:* **sufferer**, injured party, casualty; fatality, loss; survivor. **2** *the victim of a confidence trick:* **dupe**, stooge, gull; target, prey, quarry, object, subject, focus, recipient; informal sucker, fall guy; N. Amer. informal patsy, pigeon, sap.
■ **fall victim to** fall ill with, be stricken with, catch, develop, contract, pick up; succumb to; informal go down with.

victimize verb **persecute**, pick on, bully, abuse, discriminate against, ill-treat, terrorize, harass; exploit, prey on, take advantage of, dupe, cheat, double-cross; informal get at, have it in for, lean on.

victorious adjective **triumphant**, conquering, winning, champion, successful; literary vanquishing.

victory noun **success**, triumph, conquest, win, landslide, coup; mastery, superiority, supremacy; informal walkover, thrashing, trouncing.
–OPPOSITES defeat.

vie verb **compete**, contend, contest, struggle, fight, battle, cross swords, lock horns, jockey; war, feud.

view noun **1** *the view from her flat:* **outlook**, prospect, panorama, vista, scene, aspect; scenery, landscape. **2** *we agree with this view:* **opinion**, viewpoint, belief, judgement, thinking, notion, idea, conviction, persuasion, attitude, feeling, sentiment; stance, standpoint, approach. **3** *the church came into view:* **sight**, perspective, vision, visibility.
•verb **1** *they viewed the landscape:* **look at**, eye, observe, gaze at, contemplate, regard, scan, survey, inspect, scrutinize; informal check out, gawp at; Brit. informal clock; N. Amer. informal eyeball; literary espy, behold. **2** *the law was viewed as a last resort:* **consider**, regard, look on, see, perceive, judge, deem, reckon.
■ **in view of** considering, bearing in mind, on account of, in the light of, owing to, because of, as a result of. **on view** on display, on exhibition, on show.

viewer noun **watcher**, spectator, onlooker, observer; (**viewers**) audience, crowd; literary beholder.

vigilant adjective **watchful**, observant, attentive, alert, eagle-eyed, on the lookout; on your guard, cautious, wary, heedful, mindful; informal beady-eyed.
–OPPOSITES inattentive.

vigorous adjective **1** *a tall, vigorous man:* **robust**, healthy, hale and hearty, strong, sturdy, fit; hardy, tough; bouncing, thriving, flourishing; energetic, lively, active, perky, spirited, vibrant, vital; informal peppy. **2** *a vigorous defence:* **strenuous**, powerful, forceful, spirited, mettlesome, determined, aggressive, zealous, ardent, fervent, vehement, passionate; tough, hard-hitting; informal punchy.
–OPPOSITES weak, feeble.

vigorously adverb **strenuously**, strongly, powerfully, forcefully, energetically, heartily, all out, fiercely, hard; Brit. informal like billy-o.

vigour noun **robustness**, health,

hardiness, strength, sturdiness, toughness; bloom, radiance, energy, life, vitality, verve, spirit; zeal, passion, determination, dynamism, zest, pep, drive; informal **oomph**, get-up-and-go.
– OPPOSITES lethargy.

vile adjective **foul**, nasty, unpleasant, bad, horrid, dreadful, abominable, atrocious, offensive, obnoxious, odious, repulsive, disgusting, hateful, nauseating; disgraceful, appalling, shocking, shameful, dishonourable, execrable, heinous, abhorrent, deplorable, monstrous, wicked, evil, iniquitous, depraved, debased; contemptible, despicable, reprehensible; informal gross, low-down.
– OPPOSITES pleasant.

vilify verb **disparage**, denigrate, defame, run down, revile, abuse, speak ill of, criticize, condemn; malign, slander, libel; N. Amer. slur; informal pull apart, bad-mouth; Brit. informal rubbish, slate; formal derogate.
– OPPOSITES praise.

villain noun **criminal**, lawbreaker, offender, felon, convict, miscreant, wrongdoer; rogue, scoundrel, reprobate, hoodlum; informal crook, con, baddy.

villainous adjective **wicked**, evil, iniquitous, sinful, nefarious, heinous, egregious, fiendish, vicious, murderous; criminal, illicit, unlawful, illegal, lawless; immoral, corrupt, degenerate, sordid, depraved, dishonest, unscrupulous, unprincipled; informal crooked, bent, low-down, dirty, shady; dated dastardly.
– OPPOSITES virtuous.

villainy noun **wickedness**, badness, evil, iniquity, wrongdoing, dishonesty, roguery, delinquency; crime, vice, criminality, lawlessness, corruption; formal turpitude.

vindicate verb **1** *he was vindicated by the jury:* **acquit**, clear, absolve, exonerate; discharge, free; informal let off; formal exculpate. **2** *I had fully vindicated my request:* **justify**, warrant, substantiate, ratify, authenticate, verify, confirm, corroborate, prove, defend, support, back, endorse.

vindictive adjective **vengeful**, unforgiving, resentful, acrimonious, bitter; spiteful, mean, rancorous, venomous, malicious, malevolent, nasty, cruel; informal catty.
– OPPOSITES forgiving.

vintage noun **1** *the best vintage for years:* **harvest**, crop, yield. **2** *furniture of Louis XV vintage:* **period**, era, epoch, time, origin; genre, style, kind, sort, type.
• adjective **1** *vintage French wine:* **high-quality**, quality, choice, select, superior, best. **2** *vintage motor vehicles:* **classic**, ageless, timeless; old, antique, heritage, historic.

violate verb **1** *this practice violates basic human rights:* **contravene**, breach, infringe, break, transgress, overstep, disobey, defy, flout; disregard, ignore. **2** *the tomb was violated:* **desecrate**, profane, defile, degrade, debase; damage, vandalize, deface, destroy.
– OPPOSITES respect.

violation noun **1** *a violation of human rights:* **contravention**, breach, infringement, infraction, transgression, defiance. **2** *a violation of their private lives:* **invasion**, breach, infraction; trespass, intrusion, encroachment.

violence noun **1** *police violence:* **brutality**, ferocity, savagery, cruelty, barbarity. **2** *the violence of the blow:* **force**, power, strength, might, savagery, ferocity, brutality. **3** *the violence of his passion:* **intensity**, severity, strength, force, vehemence, power, potency, ferocity, fury.

violent adjective **1** *a violent criminal:* **brutal**, vicious, savage, rough, aggressive, threatening, fierce, ferocious; barbaric, thuggish, cut-throat, homicidal, murderous, cruel. **2** *a violent blow:* **powerful**, forceful, hard, sharp, smart, strong, vigorous, mighty, hefty; savage, ferocious, brutal, vicious. **3** *violent jealousy:* **intense**, extreme, strong, powerful, intemperate, unbridled, uncontrollable, ungovernable, consuming, passionate.
– OPPOSITES gentle, weak, mild, moderate.

VIP noun **celebrity**, famous person, very important person, personality, big name, star; dignitary, luminary, worthy, grandee, notable; informal heavyweight, celeb, bigwig, big shot, big cheese, honcho, top dog.

virago noun **harridan**, shrew, dragon, vixen; fishwife, witch, she-devil, martinet, spitfire, ogress; informal battleaxe.

virgin adjective *acres of virgin forest:* **untouched**, unspoilt, untainted, pristine, flawless; spotless, unsullied, unpolluted, undefiled, perfect; unchanged, intact; unexplored, uncharted.

virginity noun **chastity**, maidenhood; purity, innocence, honour.

virile adjective **manly**, masculine, male; strong, tough, vigorous, robust, muscly, brawny; red-blooded, fertile; informal macho, laddish, butch, beefy, hunky.
– OPPOSITES effeminate.

virtual adjective **effective**, near, essential, practical, to all intents and purposes; indirect, implied, unacknowledged, tacit.

virtually adverb **effectively**, all but, more or less, practically, almost, nearly, close to, verging on, just about, as good as, essentially, to all intents and purposes; roughly, approximately; informal pretty much/well; literary well nigh.

virtue noun **1** *the simple virtue of peasant life:* **goodness**, righteousness, morality, integrity, dignity, rectitude, honour, decency, respectability; principles, ethics. **2** *promptness was not one of his virtues:* **good point**, good quality, strong point, asset, forte, attribute, strength, talent. **3** *I can see no virtue in this:* **merit**, advantage, benefit, usefulness, strength.
– OPPOSITES vice, failing, disadvantage.

V

■ **by virtue of** because of, on account of, by dint of, by means of, by way of, via, through, as a result of, as a consequence of, on the strength of, owing to, thanks to, due to, by reason of.

virtuosity noun **skill**, mastery, expertise, prowess, proficiency, ability, aptitude; excellence, brilliance, talent, genius, artistry, flair, panache, finesse, wizardry; informal know-how.

virtuoso noun *the pianist is a virtuoso:* **genius**, expert, past master, maestro, artist, prodigy, marvel, adept, professional, doyen/doyenne, veteran; star, champion; informal hotshot, wizard, pro, ace; Brit. informal dab hand.
• adjective *a virtuoso violinist:* **skilful**, expert, accomplished, master, consummate, proficient, talented, gifted, adept, good, masterly; impressive, outstanding, exceptional, magnificent, supreme, first-rate, brilliant, excellent; informal superb, mean, ace.
– OPPOSITES incompetent.

virtuous adjective **righteous**, good, moral, ethical, upright, upstanding, high-minded, principled, exemplary; irreproachable, honest, honourable, reputable, decent, respectable, worthy; pure, whiter than white, saintly, angelic; informal squeaky clean.

virulent adjective **1** *virulent herbicides:* **poisonous**, toxic, venomous, noxious, deadly, lethal, fatal, mortal, pernicious, damaging, destructive; literary deathly. **2** *a virulent epidemic:* **infectious**, contagious, communicable, transmittable, spreading, pestilential; informal catching. **3** *a virulent attack on morals:* **vitriolic**, malicious, malevolent, hostile, spiteful, venomous, vicious, vindictive, bitter, rancorous, acrimonious, scathing, caustic, withering, nasty, savage, harsh.
– OPPOSITES harmless.

viscous adjective **sticky**, gummy, gluey, adhesive, tacky, treacly, syrupy; glutinous, gelatinous, thick, mucous; informal gooey, gloopy.

visible adjective **perceptible**, seeable, observable, noticeable, detectable, discernible; in sight, in/on view, on display; evident, apparent, manifest, transparent, plain, clear, conspicuous, obvious, patent, unmistakable, prominent.

vision noun **1** *her vision was blurred:* **eyesight**, sight, observation, visual perception; eyes; view, perspective. **2** *his speech lacked vision:*

imagination, creativity, inventiveness, innovation, inspiration, intuition, perception, insight, foresight, prescience. **3** *nightmarish visions of the dead:* **apparition**, spectre, phantom, ghost, wraith, manifestation; hallucination, illusion, mirage; informal spook.

WORD LINKS
visual, **optical** relating to vision

visionary adjective **inspired**, imaginative, creative, inventive, ingenious, enterprising, innovative; insightful, perceptive, intuitive, prescient, discerning; idealistic, romantic, quixotic, dreamy; informal starry-eyed.
• noun **1** *a visionary pictured him in hell:* **seer**, mystic, oracle, prophet, soothsayer, augur, diviner, clairvoyant. **2** *a visionary can't run a business effectively:* **dreamer**, idealist, romantic, fantasist, utopian.

visit verb **1** *she's gone to visit her parents:* **call on**, look in on; stay with, holiday with; stop by, drop by; informal pop in on, drop in on, look up. **2** *Alex was visiting America:* **stay in**, holiday in; tour, explore; N. Amer. vacation in.
• noun **trip**, tour; stopover, stay, call; holiday, break; N. Amer. vacation; formal sojourn.

visitation noun *a visitation from God:* **apparition**, vision, appearance, manifestation, materialization.

visitor noun **1** *I am expecting a visitor:* **guest**, caller; company. **2** *the monument attracts many visitors:* **tourist**, traveller, holidaymaker, tripper, sightseer; pilgrim; N. Amer. vacationer.

vista noun **view**, prospect, panorama, aspect, sight; scenery, landscape.

visual adjective *visual defects:* **optical**, ocular, eye.

visualize verb **envisage**, conjure up, picture, call to mind, see, imagine, evoke, dream up, conceptualize.

vital adjective **1** *it is vital that action is taken:* **essential**, critical, crucial, indispensable, all-important, imperative, mandatory, high-priority; informal earth-shattering, world-shaking. **2** *the vital organs:* **major**, main, chief; essential, necessary. **3** *he is young and vital:* **lively**, energetic, active, sprightly, spirited, vivacious, exuberant, bouncy, zestful, dynamic, vigorous, lusty; informal peppy, full of beans.
– OPPOSITES unimportant, minor, listless.

vitality noun **liveliness**, life, energy, spirit, vivacity, exuberance, buoyancy, bounce, verve, vim, pep, brio, zest, sparkle, dynamism, vigour, drive; informal get-up-and-go.

vitriolic adjective **acrimonious**, rancorous, bitter, caustic, acerbic, trenchant, spiteful, savage, venomous, malicious; nasty, cruel, unkind, harsh, vindictive, scathing, cutting, withering; informal bitchy, catty.

vivacious adjective **lively**, spirited, bubbly, ebullient, buoyant, merry, happy, jolly, full of fun, cheery, perky, sunny, breezy, enthusiastic, vibrant, dynamic; informal peppy, bouncy, upbeat, chirpy.
– OPPOSITES listless.

vivid adjective **1** *vivid descriptions of life in the 1950s:* **graphic**, clear, detailed, striking, arresting, impressive, colourful, rich, dramatic, lively, stimulating, interesting, fascinating; memorable, powerful, evocative, stirring, moving, haunting; realistic, lifelike. **2** *a vivid red:* **bright**, colourful, brilliant, radiant, vibrant, strong, bold, deep, intense, rich, warm.
– OPPOSITES vague, dull.

viz. adverb **namely**, that is to say, in other words, to wit, specifically; such as, like, for instance, for example; formal videlicet.

vocal adjective **1** *vocal sounds:* **vocalized**, voiced, uttered, articulated, oral; spoken, said. **2** *a vocal critic of the justice system:* **vociferous**, outspoken, forthright, plain-spoken, blunt, frank, candid, open; vehement, vigorous, emphatic, insistent.

vocation noun **calling**, life's work, mission, purpose; profession, occupation, career, job, employment, trade, craft, business, line of work, métier.

vociferous adjective. See **VOCAL** sense 2.

vogue noun *the skirt is enjoying a*

V

new vogue: **fashion**, trend, fad, fancy, craze, rage, enthusiasm, passion; fashionableness, popularity, currency, favour.
■ **in vogue** fashionable, stylish, modish, up to date, modern, current; prevalent, popular, in favour, in demand, sought-after, all the rage; chic, smart, le dernier cri; informal trendy, on-trend, hip, cool, happening, now, in.

voice noun **1** *he gave voice to his anger:* **expression**, utterance, verbalization, vocalization. **2** *the voice of the people:* **opinion**, view, feeling, wish, desire; vote. **3** *a powerful voice for conservation:* **mouthpiece**, representative, spokesperson, intermediary; forum, vehicle, instrument, channel, organ, agent.
• verb *they voiced their opposition:* **express**, vocalize, communicate, declare, state, assert, reveal, proclaim, announce, air, vent; utter, say, speak, articulate; informal come out with.

WORD LINKS
vocal relating to the human voice

void adjective **1** *the contract was void:* **invalid**, null and void, not legally binding; worthless, useless. **2** *the tundra is seemingly void of life:* **devoid of**, empty of, bereft of, free from; lacking, wanting, without. **3** *vast void spaces:* **empty**, blank, unfilled.
– OPPOSITES valid, full.
• noun *the black void of space:* **vacuum**, emptiness, nothingness, blankness; empty space, chasm, abyss.
• verb *the contract was voided:* **invalidate**, annul, nullify; negate, quash, cancel, countermand, repeal, revoke, rescind, retract, withdraw, reverse, undo, abolish; formal abrogate.

V

volatile adjective **1** *the political situation was volatile:* **unpredictable**, unstable, changeable, fluctuating; tense, strained, fraught, uneasy, uncomfortable; highly charged, explosive, turbulent. **2** *an extremely volatile personality:* **temperamental**, highly strung, excitable, emotional, fiery, moody, tempestuous, changeable, inconstant, inconsistent, unpredictable, erratic, unstable, blowing hot and cold, mutable; mercurial, capricious, fickle. **3** *a volatile organic compound:* **evaporative**, vaporous; explosive, inflammable; unstable, labile.
– OPPOSITES stable, calm.

volition noun
■ **of your own volition** of your own free will, of your own accord, by choice, by preference; voluntarily, willingly, readily, freely, intentionally, consciously, deliberately, on purpose.

volley noun **barrage**, cannonade, battery, bombardment, salvo; storm, hail, shower, deluge, torrent.

voluble adjective **talkative**, loquacious, garrulous, verbose, wordy, chatty, effusive, gushing, forthcoming, communicative, expansive; articulate, fluent.
– OPPOSITES taciturn.

volume noun **1** *a volume from the library:* **book**, publication, tome, hardback, paperback, title. **2** *a syringe of known volume:* **capacity**, size, magnitude, mass, bulk, extent; dimensions, proportions, measurements. **3** *a huge volume of water:* **quantity**, amount, proportion, measure, mass, bulk. **4** *she turned the volume down:* **loudness**, sound, amplification.

voluminous adjective **capacious**, roomy, spacious, ample, full, big, large, generous; billowing, baggy, loose-fitting; formal commodious.

voluntarily adverb **of your own free will**, of your own accord, of your own volition, by choice, by preference; willingly, readily, freely, purposely, spontaneously.

voluntary adjective **1** *attendance is voluntary:* **optional**, discretionary, elective, non-compulsory, volitional. **2** *she does voluntary work:* **unpaid**, unsalaried, for free, without charge, for nothing; honorary.
– OPPOSITES compulsory, paid.

volunteer verb **1** *I volunteered my services:* **offer**, tender, proffer, put forward, put up, venture. **2** *he volunteered as a driver:* **offer your services**, present yourself, make yourself available.

• noun *each volunteer was tested three times:* **subject**, participant, case, client, patient; informal guinea pig.

voluptuous adjective **1** *a voluptuous model:* **curvaceous**, shapely, ample, buxom, full-figured, Junoesque, Rubenesque; sexually attractive, seductive, sexy; informal curvy. **2** *voluptuous crimson velvet:* **sensual**, luxurious, rich, sensuous; hedonistic, sybaritic.

vomit verb **be sick**, spew; heave, retch, gag; informal throw up, puke, chuck up; N. Amer. informal barf, upchuck; Austral./NZ informal chunder.

voracious adjective **insatiable**, unquenchable, unappeasable, prodigious, uncontrollable, compulsive, gluttonous, greedy, rapacious; enthusiastic, eager, keen, avid, desirous; informal piggish.

vortex noun **whirlwind**, whirlpool, gyre, maelstrom, eddy.

vote noun **1** *a rigged vote:* **ballot**, poll, election, referendum, plebiscite; show of hands. **2** *in 1918 women got the vote:* **suffrage**, franchise; voice, say.
• verb *I vote we have one more game:* **suggest**, propose, recommend, advocate, move, table, submit.
■ **vote someone in** elect, return, select, choose, pick, adopt, appoint, designate, opt for.

WORD LINKS
psephology the study of elections and voting

vouch verb
■ **vouch for** attest to, confirm, verify, swear to, testify to, bear out, back up, support, stick up for, corroborate, substantiate, prove, uphold, endorse, certify, validate.

voucher noun **coupon**, token, ticket; chit, slip, stub, docket; Brit. informal chitty.

vow noun *a vow of silence:* **oath**, pledge, promise, bond, covenant, commitment, profession, affirmation, attestation; word of honour.
• verb *I vowed to do better:* **swear**, pledge, promise, undertake, make a commitment, give your word, guarantee.

voyage noun *the voyage lasted 12 days:* **journey**, trip, expedition, excursion, tour; hike, trek; pilgrimage; cruise, passage.
• verb *he voyaged through Peru:* **travel**, journey, tour; sail, steam, cruise.

vulgar adjective **1** *a vulgar joke:* **rude**, indecent, indelicate, offensive, distasteful, coarse, crude, ribald, risqué, racy, earthy, off colour, bawdy, obscene, lewd, salacious, smutty, dirty, filthy; informal sleazy, raunchy, blue, locker-room; Brit. informal saucy. **2** *the decor was lavish but vulgar:* **tasteless**, crass, tawdry, ostentatious, flamboyant, showy, gaudy, garish, brassy, kitsch; informal flash, tacky. **3** *it was considered vulgar for a woman to whistle:* **impolite**, ill-mannered, indecorous, unseemly, boorish, uncouth, crude; unsophisticated, unrefined.
– OPPOSITES tasteful, decorous.

vulnerable adjective **1** *a vulnerable city:* **in danger**, in peril, in jeopardy, at risk, unprotected, unguarded; open to attack, assailable, exposed; undefended, unfortified, unarmed, pregnable. **2** *he is vulnerable to criticism:* **exposed to**, open to, liable to, prone to, prey to, susceptible to, subject to.
– OPPOSITES resilient.

Ww

wad noun **1** *a wad of cotton wool:* **lump**, clump, mass, plug, pad, ball; Brit. informal wodge. **2** *a wad of dollar bills:* **bundle**, roll, pile, stack, sheaf. **3** *a wad of tobacco:* **quid**, twist, plug, chew.

wadding noun **stuffing**, filling, packing, padding, cushioning, quilting.

waddle verb **toddle**, totter, wobble, shuffle; duckwalk.

wade verb **1** *they waded across the stream:* **paddle**; informal splosh. **2** *I had to wade through some hefty documents:* **plough**, plod, trawl, labour, toil.

waffle (Brit. informal) verb *they waffled on about the baby:* **prattle**, chatter, babble, ramble, jabber, gabble; informal blather; Brit. informal rabbit, witter, natter.
• noun *my panic reduced the interview to waffle:* **prattle**, drivel, nonsense, twaddle, gibberish, mumbo-jumbo; informal hot air, gobbledegook.

waft verb **1** *smoke wafted through the air:* **drift**, float, glide, whirl, travel. **2** *a breeze wafted the smell:* **convey**, carry, transport, bear; blow.

wag[1] verb **1** *the dog's tail wagged frantically:* **swing**, swish, switch, sway, shake; informal waggle. **2** *he wagged his stick at them:* **shake**, wave, wiggle, flourish, brandish.

wag[2] noun (informal) *he's a bit of a wag.* See JOKER.

W

wage noun **1** *the workers' wages:* **pay**, remuneration, salary, stipend, fee, honorarium; income; earnings; formal emolument. **2** *the wages of sin is death:* **reward**, recompense, retribution; returns, deserts.
• verb *they waged war on the guerrillas:* **engage in**, carry on, conduct, execute, pursue, prosecute, proceed with.

wager noun *a wager of £10:* **bet**, gamble, speculation; stake, pledge, ante; Brit. informal flutter.
• verb *I'll wager a fiver on the home team:* **bet**, gamble, lay odds; stake, pledge, risk, venture, hazard, chance; informal punt.

waif noun **ragamuffin**, urchin; foundling, orphan, stray.

wail noun *a wail of anguish:* **howl**, bawl, cry, moan, groan; shriek, scream, yelp.
• verb *the children began to wail:* **howl**, weep, cry, sob, lament, yowl, snivel, whimper, whine, bawl, shriek, scream, yelp, caterwaul; Scottish greet.

wait verb **1** *we waited in the airport:* **stay**, remain, stop, halt, pause; linger, loiter; bide your time, hang fire, mark time, kill time, waste time, kick your heels, twiddle your thumbs; informal hold on, stick around, hang around, sit tight. **2** *they were waiting for the post:* **await**; anticipate, expect.
• noun *there may be a long wait:* **delay**, hold-up, interval, interlude, pause, break, suspension, stoppage, halt, interruption, lull, respite, recess, moratorium, hiatus, gap.

waiter, waitress noun **server**, stewardess, steward, attendant, garçon; butler, servant; N. Amer. waitperson.

waive verb **1** *he waived his right to a hearing:* **relinquish**, renounce, give up, abandon, surrender, yield, dispense with, sacrifice, turn down. **2** *the manager waived the rules:* **disregard**, ignore, overlook, set aside, forgo.

> Don't confuse **waive** with **wave**. As a verb **wave** means 'move to and fro' (*thousands of fans waved flags and banners*).

wake[1] **verb 1** *he woke early:* **awake**, waken, rouse yourself, stir, come to, come round; formal arise. **2** *the shock woke him up a bit:* **galvanize**, stir up, spur on, stimulate, enliven, invigorate, revitalize; informal perk up.
–OPPOSITES sleep.
•**noun vigil**, watch; funeral.

wake[2] **noun** *the cruiser's wake:* **backwash**, slipstream; trail, path.
■ **in the wake of** in the aftermath of, after, subsequent to, following, as a result of, as a consequence of, on account of, because of.

Wales noun Cambria; Brit. the Principality.

walk verb 1 *they walked along the road:* **stroll**, saunter, amble, trudge, plod, hike, tramp, trek, march, stride, troop, wander, ramble, promenade, traipse; informal mosey, hoof it; formal perambulate. **2** *he walked her home:* **accompany**, escort, guide, show, see, take, chaperone.
•**noun 1** *her elegant walk:* **gait**, step, stride, tread. **2** *the riverside walk:* **pathway**, footpath, track, walkway, promenade, footway, pavement, trail, towpath.
■ **walk out 1** *he walked out in a temper:* leave, depart, storm off/out, flounce out, absent yourself; informal take off. **2** *teachers walked out in protest:* go on strike, stop work, take industrial action; protest, mutiny, revolt; Brit. informal down tools. **walk out on** desert, abandon, leave, betray, jilt, run out on; informal chuck, dump, ditch; literary forsake.

walker noun hiker, rambler, stroller; pedestrian; literary wayfarer.

walkout noun strike, stoppage, industrial action.

walkover noun easy victory, rout, landslide; informal piece of cake, doddle, pushover, cinch, breeze, picnic, whitewash, massacre.

wall noun fortification, rampart, barricade, bulwark, stockade.
•**verb 1** *tenements walled in the courtyard:* **enclose**, bound, encircle, confine, hem, close in, fence in. **2** *the doorway had been walled up:* **block**, seal, close, brick up.

wallet noun purse; N. Amer. billfold, pocketbook.

wallow verb 1 *buffalo wallowed in the lake:* **loll about**, lie around, splash about; slosh, wade, paddle. **2** *she seems to wallow in self-pity:* **luxuriate**, bask, take pleasure, take satisfaction, indulge (yourself), delight, revel, glory; informal get a kick out of.

wan adjective 1 *she looked wan and frail:* **pale**, ashen, white, grey; anaemic, colourless, waxen, pasty, peaky, sickly, washed out, ghostly. **2** *the wan light of the moon:* **dim**, faint, weak, feeble, pale, watery.
–OPPOSITES flushed, bright.

wand noun baton, stick, staff, dowel, rod.

wander verb 1 *I wandered around the estate:* **stroll**, amble, saunter, walk, potter, ramble, meander; roam, rove, range, drift; Scottish & Irish stravaig; informal traipse, mosey. **2** *we are wandering from the point:* **stray**, depart, diverge, veer, swerve, deviate, digress, drift, get side-tracked. **3** *the child wandered off:* **get lost**, go astray.

wanderer noun traveller, rambler, hiker, migrant, roamer, rover; itinerant, rolling stone, nomad; tramp, drifter, vagabond, vagrant; N. Amer. informal hobo; literary wayfarer.

wane verb 1 *the moon is waning:* **decrease**, diminish, dwindle. **2** *their support was waning:* **decline**, diminish, decrease, dwindle, shrink, tail off, ebb, fade, lessen, peter out, fall off, recede, slump, weaken, wither, evaporate, die out.
–OPPOSITES wax, grow.
■ **on the wane** declining, decreasing, diminishing, dwindling, shrinking, contracting, tapering off, subsiding, ebbing, fading away, dissolving, petering out, falling off, on the way out, receding, flagging, melting away, crumbling, withering, disintegrating, evaporating, dying out.

want verb desire, wish for, hope for, fancy, care for, like; have a yen for, long for, yearn for, crave, hanker after, hunger for, thirst for, cry out for, covet; informal be dying for.
•**noun 1** *his want of vigilance:* **lack**,

absence, non-existence; dearth, deficiency, inadequacy, insufficiency, paucity, shortage, scarcity, deficit. **2** *a time of want:* **need**, austerity, privation, deprivation, poverty, penury, destitution. **3** *her wants would be taken care of:* **wish**, desire, demand, longing, yearning, fancy, craving, hankering; need, requirement.

wanting adjective **1** *the defences were found wanting:* **deficient**, inadequate, lacking, insufficient, imperfect, unacceptable, flawed, unsound, substandard, inferior, second-rate. **2** *millions were left wanting for food:* **without**, lacking, deprived of, devoid of, bereft of, in need of; deficient in, short on; informal minus.

wanton adjective **1** *wanton destruction:* **deliberate**, wilful, malicious, spiteful, wicked, cruel; gratuitous, unprovoked, motiveless, arbitrary, groundless, unjustifiable, needless, unnecessary, uncalled for, senseless, pointless, purposeless. **2** *a wanton seductress:* **promiscuous**, immoral, immodest, indecent, shameless, unchaste, fast, impure, abandoned, lustful, lecherous, lascivious, libidinous, licentious, dissolute, debauched, degenerate, disreputable; dated loose.
– OPPOSITES justifiable, chaste.

war noun **1** *the Napoleonic Wars:* **conflict**, warfare, combat, fighting, action, bloodshed, struggle; battle, skirmish, fight, clash, engagement, encounter; offensive, attack, campaign; hostilities; crusade. **2** *the war against drugs:* **campaign**, crusade, battle, fight, struggle.
– OPPOSITES peace.
• verb *rival Emperors warred against each other:* **fight**, battle, combat, wage war, take up arms; feud, quarrel, struggle, contend, wrangle, cross swords; attack, engage, take on, skirmish with.

W

WORD LINKS
martial relating to war
belligerent engaged in a war

warble verb **trill**, sing, chirp, chirrup, cheep, twitter, tweet, chatter, peep.

ward noun **1** *the surgical ward:* **room**, department, unit, area. **2** *the most marginal ward in Westminster:* **district**, constituency, division, quarter, zone, parish. **3** *the boy is my ward:* **dependant**, charge, protégé.

warden noun **1** *the flats have a resident warden:* **superintendent**, caretaker, janitor, porter, custodian, watchman, concierge, doorman. **2** *a game warden:* **ranger**, custodian, keeper, guardian, protector. **3** *he was handcuffed to a warden:* **prison officer**, guard, jailer, warder, keeper, sentry; informal screw. **4** (Brit.) *the college warden:* **principal**, head, governor, master, mistress, rector, provost, president, director, chancellor.

wardrobe noun **1** **cupboard**; N. Amer. closet. **2** *her wardrobe has an outfit for every mood:* **collection of clothes**; garments, attire, outfits.

warehouse noun **storeroom**, depot, depository, stockroom; magazine; granary; informal lock-up.

wares plural noun **merchandise**, goods, products, produce, stock, commodities; lines, range.

warfare noun **fighting**, war, combat, conflict, action, hostilities; bloodshed, battles, skirmishes.

warlike adjective **aggressive**, belligerent, warring, bellicose, pugnacious, combative; hostile, threatening; militaristic; informal gung-ho.

warlock noun **sorcerer**, wizard, magician, enchanter.

warm adjective **1** *a warm day:* **balmy**, summery, hot, sultry, close; mild, temperate. **2** *warm water:* **heated**, tepid, lukewarm. **3** *a warm kitchen:* **cosy**, snug, hot. **4** *a warm welcome:* **friendly**, cordial, amiable, genial, kind, pleasant, fond; welcoming, hospitable, benevolent, benign, charitable; sincere, genuine, heartfelt, enthusiastic, eager, hearty.
– OPPOSITES cold, chilly, hostile.
• verb **heat**, reheat, cook; thaw.
– OPPOSITES chill.
■ **warm to/towards** like, take to, get on with, hit it off with. **warm up** *the players were warming up:* limber up, loosen up, stretch; prepare, rehearse.

warmonger noun **militarist**, hawk, jingoist, sabre-rattler, aggressor, belligerent.

warmth noun **1** *the warmth of the fire:* **heat**; cosiness. **2** *the warmth of* *their welcome:* **friendliness**, amiability, geniality, cordiality, kindness, tenderness, fondness; benevolence, charity; enthusiasm, eagerness.

warn verb **1** *David warned her that it was too late:* **notify**, alert, apprise, inform, tell, remind; informal tip off, put wise. **2** *police are warning galleries to be alert:* **advise**, exhort, urge, counsel, caution.

warning noun **1** *the earthquake came without warning:* **advance notice**; hint, signal, sign, alarm bells; informal a tip-off. **2** *a health warning:* **caution**, alert, notification, information; advice. **3** *a warning of things to come:* **omen**, premonition, foreboding, prophecy, prediction, forecast, token, portent, signal, sign. **4** *his sentence is a warning to other drunk drivers:* **example**, deterrent, lesson, caution, exemplar, message, moral.

warp verb **1** *timber which is too dry will warp:* **buckle**, twist, bend, become distorted, deform, curve, bow, contort. **2** *he warped the mind of her child:* **corrupt**, twist, pervert, deprave.

warrant noun **1** *a warrant for his arrest:* **authorization**, order, licence, permit, document; writ, summons, subpoena; mandate, decree, edict. **2** *a travel warrant:* **voucher**, chit, slip, ticket, coupon, pass. **3** *there's no warrant for this assumption:* **justification**, grounds, cause, rationale, basis, authority, licence, sanction, vindication.
• verb **1** *industrial action is warranted | this warrants further investigation:* **justify**, call for, need, necessitate; deserve, merit, qualify for. **2** *the vendor warrants the accuracy of the report:* **guarantee**, affirm, swear to, attest to; vouch for, testify to, bear witness to.

warranty noun **guarantee**, assurance, promise, commitment, undertaking, agreement.

warring adjective **opposing**, conflicting, fighting, battling, quarrelling; competing, hostile, rival.

warrior noun **fighter**, soldier, serviceman, combatant; old use man-at-arms.

wary adjective **1** *he was trained to be wary:* **cautious**, careful, circumspect, on your guard, chary, alert, on the lookout; attentive, heedful, watchful, vigilant, observant. **2** *we are wary of strangers:* **suspicious**, chary, leery, careful, distrustful.
– OPPOSITES inattentive, trustful.

wash verb **1** *she washed down all the kitchen surfaces:* **clean**, cleanse, rinse, sponge, scrub, wipe, scour, mop; swab, disinfect, sluice down, hose down. **2** *she washed off the blood:* **remove**, sponge off, scrub off, wipe off, rinse off. **3** *her clothes had been washed and ironed:* **launder**, clean. **4** *waves washed against the hull:* **splash**, lap, dash, break, beat, surge, ripple, roll. **5** *the wreckage was washed downstream:* **sweep**, carry, convey, transport; deposit. **6** *a feeling of sadness washed over her:* **course through**, rush through, surge through, flood over, flow over.
– OPPOSITES dirty, soil.
• noun **1** *that shirt should go in the wash:* **laundry**, washing. **2** *antiseptic skin wash:* **lotion**, salve, preparation, rinse, liquid; liniment, embrocation. **3** *the wash of a motor boat:* **backwash**, wake, trail, path.
▪ **wash something away** erode, abrade, wear away, eat away, undermine.

waste verb **1** *he doesn't like to waste money:* **squander**, misspend, misuse, fritter away, throw away, lavish, dissipate; informal blow, splurge. **2** *kids are wasting away in the streets:* **grow weak**, grow thin, shrink, wilt, fade, flag, deteriorate. **3** *the disease wasted his legs:* **emaciate**, atrophy, wither, shrivel, shrink, weaken.
– OPPOSITES conserve, thrive.
• adjective **1** *waste material:* **unwanted**, excess, superfluous, left over, scrap; unusable, unprofitable. **2** *waste ground:* **uncultivated**, barren, desert, arid, bare; desolate, uninhabited, unpopulated; wild.
• noun **1** *a waste of money:* **misuse**, misapplication, misemployment, abuse; extravagance, lavishness. **2** *household waste:* **rubbish**, refuse, litter, debris, dross, junk, detritus, scrap; sewage, effluent; N. Amer. garbage, trash. **3** *the frozen wastes of the South Pole:* **desert**, wasteland, wilderness, emptiness, wilds.

wasted adjective **1** *a wasted effort:*

squandered, misspent, misdirected, dissipated; pointless, useless, unnecessary, needless. **2** *a wasted opportunity:* **missed**, lost, forfeited, neglected, squandered; informal down the drain. **3** *his wasted legs:* **emaciated**, atrophied, withered, shrunken, skeletal, scrawny, wizened.

wasteful adjective **prodigal**, profligate, uneconomical, extravagant, lavish, excessive, imprudent, improvident; thriftless, spendthrift; needless, useless.
– OPPOSITES frugal.

wasteland noun **wilderness**, desert; wilds, wastes, badlands.

watch verb **1** *she watched him as he spoke:* **observe**, view, look at, eye, gaze at, peer at; contemplate, survey, keep an eye on; inspect, scrutinize, scan, examine, study, regard, mark; informal check out, get a load of, recce, eyeball; Brit. informal have a butcher's at; literary behold. **2** *he was being watched by the police:* **spy on**, keep in sight, track, monitor, survey, follow; informal keep tabs on, stake out. **3** *will you watch the kids?* **look after**, mind, keep an eye on, take care of, supervise, tend; guard, protect. **4** *we stayed to watch the boat:* **guard**, protect, shield, defend; cover, patrol, police. **5** *watch what you say:* **be careful**, mind, be aware of, pay attention to, consider.
– OPPOSITES ignore, neglect.
• noun **1** *Bill looked at his watch:* **timepiece**, chronometer. **2** *we kept watch on the yacht:* **guard**, vigil, lookout, an eye; observation, surveillance.
■ **watch out/it/yourself** be careful, be on your guard, beware, be wary, be cautious, mind out, look out, pay attention, take care, keep an eye open/out, keep your eyes peeled, be vigilant.

watchdog noun **ombudsman**, monitor, scrutineer, inspector, supervisor.

W

watcher noun **onlooker**, spectator, observer, viewer, fly on the wall; witness, bystander; spy; voyeur; informal rubberneck; literary beholder.

watchful adjective **observant**, alert, vigilant, attentive, aware, sharp-eyed, eagle-eyed; on the lookout, wary, cautious, careful.

watchman noun **security guard**, custodian, warden; sentry, guard, patrolman, lookout, sentinel, scout.

watchword noun **guiding principle**, motto, slogan, maxim, mantra, catchword, byword; informal buzzword.

water noun *a house down by the water:* **sea**, ocean; lake, loch, river.
• verb **1** *water the plants:* **sprinkle**, moisten, dampen, wet, spray, splash. **2** *my mouth watered:* **moisten**, salivate.
■ **water something down 1** *staff had watered down the drinks:* dilute, thin out, weaken. **2** *the proposals were watered down:* moderate, temper, mitigate, tone down, soften, tame; understate, play down, soft-pedal.

WORD LINKS
aquatic, **aqueous** relating to water

waterfall noun **cascade**, cataract, rapids.

waterproof adjective **watertight**, water-repellent, water-resistant, damp-proof; impermeable, impervious.

watertight adjective **1** *a watertight container:* **impermeable**, impervious, hermetically sealed; waterproof, water-repellent, water-resistant, damp-proof. **2** *a watertight alibi:* **indisputable**, unquestionable, incontrovertible, irrefutable, unassailable; foolproof, sound, flawless, airtight, conclusive.
– OPPOSITES leaky, flawed.

watery adjective **1** *a watery discharge:* **liquid**, fluid, aqueous. **2** *watery porridge:* **thin**, runny, weak, sloppy, dilute; tasteless, insipid, bland. **3** *watery light:* **pale**, wan, faint, weak, feeble; informal wishy-washy. **4** *watery eyes:* **tearful**, weepy, moist; formal lachrymose.
– OPPOSITES thick, bright.

wave verb **1** *he waved his flag:* **move up and down**, move to and fro, wag, shake, swish, swing, brandish, flourish, wield. **2** *the grass waved in the breeze:* **ripple**, flutter, undulate, stir, flap, sway, shake, quiver, move. **3** *the waiter waved them closer:* **gesture**, gesticulate, signal, beckon, motion.
• noun **1** *she gave him a friendly wave:*

gesticulation; signal, sign, motion. **2** *he surfs the big waves:* **breaker**, roller, comber, boomer, ripple; (**waves**) swell, surf, froth. **3** *a wave of emigration:* **flow**, rush, surge, flood, stream, tide, deluge, spate. **4** *a wave of self-pity:* **surge**, rush, stab, dart, upsurge; feeling. **5** *his hair grew in thick waves:* **curl**, kink, twist, ringlet. **6** *electromagnetic waves:* ripple, vibration, oscillation.
■ **wave something aside** dismiss, reject, brush aside, shrug off, disregard, ignore, discount, play down; informal pooh-pooh. **wave someone/something down** flag down, hail, stop, summon, call, accost.

> ! **Wave** is sometimes confused with **waive**, which means 'choose not to insist on or demand a right or claim' (*he waived all rights to the money*).

waver verb **1** *the candlelight wavered in the draught:* **flicker**, quiver. **2** *his voice wavered:* **falter**, wobble, tremble, quaver. **3** *he wavered between the choices:* **be undecided**, be irresolute, hesitate, dither, equivocate, vacillate; think twice, change your mind, blow hot and cold; Brit. haver, hum and haw; informal shilly-shally, sit on the fence.

wavy adjective **curly**, curvy, undulating, squiggly, rippled, crinkly, zigzag.

wax verb **get bigger**, increase, enlarge.
– OPPOSITES wane.

way noun **1** *a way of reducing the damage:* **method**, means, procedure, technique, system, process; plan, strategy, scheme; mechanism, approach, tack, avenue; modus operandi, MO. **2** *she kissed him in her brisk way:* **manner**, style, fashion, mode. **3** *I've changed my ways:* **practice**, wont, habit, custom, convention, routine; trait, attribute, peculiarity, idiosyncrasy; conduct, behaviour, manner, style. **4** *which way leads home?* **route**, course, direction; road, street, track, path. **5** *they still had a long way ahead of them:* **distance**, length, stretch, journey; space, interval, span. **6** *in some ways, he may be better off:* **respect**, regard, aspect, facet, sense; detail, point, particular. **7** *the country is in a bad way:* **state**, condition, situation, circumstances, position; predicament, plight; informal shape.
■ **give way 1** *the government gave way and passed the bill:* yield, back down, surrender, concede defeat, give in, submit, succumb; acquiesce, agree, assent; informal throw in the towel, cave in. **2** *the door gave way:* collapse, give, cave in, fall in, come apart, crumple. **on the way** coming, imminent, forthcoming, close, near, approaching, impending; en route, in transit.

waylay verb **1** *we were waylaid and robbed:* **ambush**, hold up, attack, assail, rob; informal mug, stick up. **2** *several people waylaid her to chat:* **accost**, detain, intercept, take aside, pounce on, importune; informal buttonhole.

wayward adjective **wilful**, headstrong, stubborn, obstinate, obdurate, perverse, contrary, disobedient, undisciplined; rebellious, defiant, recalcitrant, unruly, wild; formal refractory.
– OPPOSITES docile.

weak adjective **1** *they are too weak to be moved:* **frail**, feeble, delicate, fragile; infirm, sick, debilitated, incapacitated, ailing, indisposed, decrepit; tired, fatigued, exhausted; informal weedy. **2** *bats have weak eyes:* **inadequate**, poor, feeble; defective, faulty, deficient, imperfect, substandard. **3** *a weak excuse:* **unconvincing**, tenuous, implausible, unsatisfactory, poor, inadequate, feeble, flimsy, lame, hollow; informal pathetic. **4** *I was too weak to be a rebel:* **spineless**, craven, cowardly, timid; irresolute, indecisive, ineffectual, meek, tame, soft, faint-hearted; informal yellow, gutless. **5** *a weak light:* **dim**, pale, wan, faint, feeble, muted. **6** *a weak voice:* **indistinct**, muffled, muted, hushed, faint, low. **7** *weak coffee:* **watery**, dilute, watered down, thin. **8** *a weak smile:* **unenthusiastic**, feeble, half-hearted, lame.
– OPPOSITES strong, powerful, bright, loud.

weaken verb **1** *the virus weakened him:* **enfeeble**, debilitate, incapacitate, sap, tire, exhaust. **2** *our morale weakened:* **decrease**, dwindle, diminish, wane, ebb, subside, peter out, fizzle out, tail off, decline, falter. **3** *the move weakened her authority:* **impair**, undermine, compromise; invalidate, negate.

weakling noun **milksop**, namby-pamby, coward, pushover; informal wimp, weed, sissy, drip, softie, doormat, chicken, yellow-belly; N. Amer. informal wuss.

weakness noun **1** *with old age came weakness:* **frailty**, feebleness, fragility, delicacy; infirmity, debility, incapacity, indisposition, decrepitude; informal weediness. **2** *he has worked on his weaknesses:* **fault**, flaw, defect, deficiency, failing, shortcoming, imperfection, Achilles heel. **3** *a weakness for champagne:* **fondness**, liking, partiality, love, penchant, predilection, inclination, taste; enthusiasm, appetite. **4** *the President was accused of weakness:* **timidity**, cravenness, cowardliness; indecision, irresolution, ineffectuality, ineptitude, meekness, ineffectiveness, impotence. **5** *the basic weakness of this argument:* **untenability**, implausibility, poverty, inadequacy, transparency; flimsiness, hollowness.

weak-willed adjective **spineless**, irresolute, indecisive; impressionable, submissive, unassertive, compliant; informal wimpish.

weal noun **welt**, wound, lesion, swelling; scar.

wealth noun **1** *a gentleman of wealth:* **affluence**, prosperity, riches, means, fortune; money, cash, lucre, capital, treasure, finance; informal wherewithal, dough, bread. **2** *a wealth of information:* **abundance**, profusion, plethora, mine, store, treasury, bounty, cornucopia; informal lot, load, mountain, stack, ton; Brit. informal shedload; formal plenitude.
– OPPOSITES poverty, dearth.

W

wealthy adjective **rich**, affluent, moneyed, well off, well-to-do, prosperous; of substance; informal well heeled, rolling in it, made of money, loaded, flush, quids in.
– OPPOSITES poor.

wear verb **1** *he wore a linen suit:* **be dressed in**, be clothed in, have on, sport. **2** *Barbara wore a broad smile:* **bear**, have, show, display, exhibit; put on, assume. **3** *the bricks have been worn down:* **erode**, abrade, rub away, grind away, wash away; corrode, eat away at, dissolve. **4** *the tyres are wearing well:* **last**, endure, hold up, bear up.
• noun **1** *you won't get much wear out of that:* **use**, service, utility, value; informal mileage. **2** *evening wear:* **clothes**, garments, dress, attire, garb, wardrobe; informal get-up, gear, togs; Brit. informal kit, clobber; formal apparel. **3** *the varnish will withstand a lot of wear:* **damage**, friction, erosion, attrition, abrasion.
■ **wear off** *the novelty soon wore off:* fade, diminish, lessen, dwindle, decrease, wane, ebb, peter out, fizzle out, pall, disappear, vanish. **wear someone out** fatigue, tire out, weary, exhaust, drain, sap, overtax, enervate; informal whack, poop, shatter, do in; Brit. informal knacker.

wearing adjective **tiring**, exhausting, wearying, fatiguing, enervating, draining, sapping; demanding, exacting, taxing, arduous, gruelling, punishing, laborious, strenuous, rigorous.

weary adjective **1** *he was weary after the long journey:* **tired**, worn out, exhausted, fatigued, sapped, spent, drained; informal done in, dead beat, ready to drop, bushed, shattered, frazzled; Brit. informal knackered, whacked; N. Amer. informal pooped, tuckered out. **2** *she was weary of the arguments:* **tired of**, fed up with, bored with, sick of. **3** *a weary journey:* **tiring**, exhausting, fatiguing, enervating, draining, sapping, wearing, trying, demanding, taxing, arduous, gruelling.
– OPPOSITES fresh, keen, refreshing.

weather noun *what's the weather like?* **forecast**, outlook; meteorological conditions, climate, atmospheric pressure, temperature; elements.
• verb *we weathered the recession:* **survive**, come through, ride out, pull through; withstand, endure, rise above, surmount, overcome, resist; informal stick out.

weathered adjective **weather-beaten**, worn; tanned, bronzed; lined, creased, wrinkled.

weave[1] verb **1** *flowers were woven into their hair:* **entwine**, lace, twist, knit, braid, plait. **2** *he weaves colourful plots:* **invent**, make up, fabricate, construct, create, contrive, spin.

weave[2] verb *he had to weave his way through the crowds:* **thread**, wind, wend; dodge, zigzag.

web noun **1** *a spider's web:* **mesh**, net, lattice, lacework; gauze, gossamer. **2** *a web of friendships:* **network**, nexus, complex, set, chain.

wedded adjective **1** *wedded bliss:* **married**, matrimonial, marital, conjugal, nuptial. **2** *he is wedded to his work:* **dedicated to**, devoted to, attached to, fixated on, single-minded about.

wedding noun **marriage**, nuptials, union.

> **WORD LINKS**
> **nuptial** relating to a wedding

wedge noun *a wedge of cheese:* **triangle**, segment, slice, section; chunk, lump, slab, hunk, block, piece.
• verb *she wedged her case between two bags:* **squeeze**, cram, jam, ram, force, push, shove; informal stuff, bung.

weed verb
■ **weed something/someone out** isolate, separate out, sort out, sift out, winnow out, filter out, set apart, segregate; eliminate, get rid of, remove; informal lose.

weep verb **cry**, shed tears, sob, snivel, whimper, wail, bawl; keen; Scottish greet; informal blub.

weepy adjective **tearful**; in tears, crying, snivelling; formal lachrymose.
– OPPOSITES cheerful.

weigh verb **1** *he weighed 118 kg:* tip the scales at. **2** *the situation weighed heavily on him.* See **WEIGH SOMEONE DOWN** sense 2. **3** *he has to weigh up all the possibilities:* **consider**, contemplate, think about, mull over, chew over, reflect on, ruminate about, muse on; assess, appraise, analyse, examine, review, explore, take stock of. **4** *they need to weigh benefit against risk:* **balance**, evaluate, compare, juxtapose, contrast.
■ **weigh someone down 1** *my fishing gear weighed me down:* burden, saddle, overload, overburden, encumber. **2** *the silence weighed me down:* oppress, depress, lie heavy on, burden, cast down, hang over; trouble, worry, bother, disturb, upset, haunt, torment, afflict, plague.

weight noun **1** *the weight of the oak panels:* **heaviness**, mass, load. **2** *his recommendation will carry great weight:* **influence**, force, leverage, sway, pull, importance, significance, value, substance, power, authority; informal clout. **3** *a weight off her mind:* **burden**, load, millstone, albatross, encumbrance; trouble, worry, strain. **4** *the weight of the evidence is against him:* **preponderance**, majority, bulk, body, lion's share, predominance; most.

weighty adjective **1** *a weighty tome:* **heavy**, thick, bulky, hefty, cumbersome, ponderous. **2** *a weighty subject:* **important**, significant, momentous, consequential, far-reaching, key, major, vital, critical, crucial; serious, grave, solemn. **3** *a weighty responsibility:* **burdensome**, onerous, heavy, oppressive, taxing, troublesome. **4** *weighty arguments:* **compelling**, cogent, strong, forceful, powerful, potent, effective, sound, valid, persuasive, convincing.
– OPPOSITES light, trivial, weak.

weird adjective *weird apparitions:* **uncanny**, eerie, unnatural, supernatural, unearthly, otherworldly, ghostly, mysterious, strange, abnormal, unusual; informal creepy, spooky, freaky.
– OPPOSITES normal, conventional.

welcome noun *a welcome from the vicar:* **greeting**, salutation; reception, hospitality; the red carpet.
• verb **1** *welcome your guests in their own language:* **greet**, salute, receive, meet, usher in. **2** *we welcomed their decision:* **be pleased by**, be glad about, approve of, appreciate, embrace; informal give the thumbs up to.
• adjective *welcome news:* **pleasing**, agreeable, encouraging, gratifying, heartening, promising, favourable, pleasant.

weld verb **fuse**, bond, stick, join, attach, seal, splice, melt, solder.

welfare noun **1** *the welfare of children:* **well-being**, health, comfort, security, safety, protection, success; interest, good. **2** *we cannot claim welfare:* **social security**, benefit, public assistance; pension, credit, support; sick pay, unemployment benefit; Brit. informal the dole.

well[1] adverb **1** *he behaved well:* **satisfactorily**, correctly, properly, appropriately, suitably, fittingly. **2** *they get on well together:* **harmoniously**, happily, amicably, amiably; informal famously. **3** *he plays the piano well:* **skilfully**, ably, competently, proficiently, adeptly, deftly, expertly, excellently. **4** *treat your employees well:* **decently**, fairly, kindly, generously. **5** *mix the ingredients well:* **thoroughly**, completely; rigorously, carefully. **6** *I know her very well:* **intimately**, deeply, profoundly, personally. **7** *they studied the car market well:* **carefully**, closely, attentively, rigorously, in depth, exhaustively, in detail, meticulously, scrupulously, methodically, comprehensively, fully, extensively. **8** *they speak well of him:* **admiringly**, highly, approvingly, favourably, appreciatively, warmly, enthusiastically, glowingly. **9** *she makes enough money to live well:* **comfortably**, in the lap of luxury, prosperously.
–OPPOSITES badly, poorly.
•adjective **1** *she was completely well again:* **healthy**, fine, fit, robust, strong, vigorous, blooming, thriving, in fine fettle; informal in the pink. **2** *all is not well:* **satisfactory**, all right, fine, in order, acceptable; informal OK, hunky-dory.
–OPPOSITES poorly, unsatisfactory.
■ **as well** too, also, in addition, into the bargain, besides, furthermore, moreover, to boot. **as well as** together with, along with, besides, plus, and, with, on top of, not to mention, to say nothing of, let alone.

well[2] noun **1** *she drew water from the well:* **borehole**, spring, waterhole. **2** *an apparently bottomless well of information:* **source**, supply, fount, reservoir, mine, fund, treasury.
•verb *tears welled from her eyes:* **flow**, spill, stream, run, rush, gush, roll, cascade, flood, spout; burst, issue.

well behaved adjective **orderly**, obedient, disciplined, peaceable, docile, controlled, restrained, cooperative, compliant; mannerly, polite, civil, courteous, respectful, proper, decorous, refined.
–OPPOSITES naughty.

well-being noun. See **WELFARE** sense 1.

well bred adjective **well brought up**, polite, civil, mannerly, courteous, respectful; ladylike, gentlemanly, genteel, cultivated, urbane, proper, refined.

well built adjective **sturdy**, strapping, brawny, burly, hefty, muscular, strong, rugged, Herculean; informal hunky, beefy.
–OPPOSITES puny.

well dressed adjective **smart**, fashionable, stylish, chic, modish, elegant, neat, spruce, trim, dapper; informal snazzy, natty, snappy, sharp.
–OPPOSITES scruffy.

well founded adjective **justifiable**, warranted, legitimate, defensible, valid, understandable, excusable, acceptable, reasonable, sensible, sound.
–OPPOSITES groundless.

well known adjective **1** *well-known principles:* **familiar**, popular, common, everyday, established. **2** *a well-known family of architects:* **famous**, famed, prominent, notable, renowned, distinguished, eminent, illustrious, acclaimed.
–OPPOSITES obscure.

well off adjective **1** *her family's very well off.* See **WEALTHY**. **2** *the prisoners were relatively well off:* **fortunate**, lucky, comfortable.

well read adjective **knowledgeable**, erudite, scholarly, literate, well informed, educated, cultured, bookish, studious.
–OPPOSITES ignorant.

well spoken adjective **articulate**; refined, polite; Brit. informal posh.

welter noun **confusion**, jumble, tangle, mess, hotchpotch, mishmash, mass.

wend verb **meander**, wind your way, wander, amble, stroll, saunter, drift, roam, traipse, walk; informal mosey, tootle.

western adjective *the western coast*

of Scotland: **west**, westerly; literary occidental.

wet adjective **1** *wet clothes | a patch of wet ground:* **damp**, moist, soaked, drenched, saturated, sodden, sopping, dripping, soggy; waterlogged, squelchy; dank, clammy. **2** *it was cold and wet:* **rainy**, pouring, teeming, showery, drizzly; damp. **3** *the paint is still wet:* **sticky**, tacky. **4** *a wet mortar mix:* **aqueous**, watery, sloppy.
– OPPOSITES dry, fine.
• verb *wet the clothes before ironing them:* **dampen**, moisten; sprinkle, spray, splash; soak, saturate, douse, drench.
– OPPOSITES dry.

wharf noun **quay**, pier, dock, berth, landing, jetty; harbour, dockyard, marina.

wheedle verb **coax**, cajole, inveigle, induce, entice, charm, tempt, beguile, flatter, persuade, influence, win someone over, bring someone round, convince, prevail on, get round; informal sweet-talk, soft-soap.

wheel noun disc, hoop, ring, circle.
• verb **1** *she wheeled the trolley away:* **push**, trundle, roll. **2** *the flock of doves wheeled round:* **turn**, go round, circle, orbit.
■ **at/behind the wheel** driving, steering, in control.

wheeze verb **gasp**, rasp, croak, pant, cough, whistle, hiss.

whereabouts noun **location**, position, site, place, situation, spot, point; home, address, locale, neighbourhood; bearings, orientation.

wherewithal noun **money**, cash, capital, finances, funds; resources, means, ability, capability; informal dough, bread, loot, readies, the necessary; Brit. informal dosh, brass, lolly; N. Amer. informal bucks.

whet verb **1** *he whetted his knife on a stone:* **sharpen**, hone, strop, grind, file. **2** *something to whet your appetite:* **stimulate**, excite, arouse, rouse, kindle, trigger, spark, quicken, stir, inspire, animate, fuel, fire, activate, tempt, galvanize.
– OPPOSITES blunt.

whiff noun **1** *I caught a whiff of perfume:* **faint smell**, trace, sniff, scent, odour, aroma. **2** *the faintest whiff of irony:* **trace**, hint, suggestion, impression, suspicion, soupçon, nuance, intimation, tinge, vein, shred, whisper, overtone.

while noun *we chatted for a while:* **time**, spell, stretch, stint, span, interval, period; duration, phase; Brit. informal patch.
• verb *tennis helped to while away the time:* **pass**, spend, occupy, use up, kill.

whim noun **1** *she bought it on a whim:* **impulse**, urge, notion, fancy, foible, caprice, conceit, vagary, inclination. **2** *human whim:* **capriciousness**, caprice, volatility, fickleness, idiosyncrasy.

whimper verb **whine**, cry, sob, moan, snivel, wail, groan; Brit. informal grizzle.

whimsical adjective **1** *a whimsical sense of humour:* **fanciful**, playful, mischievous, waggish, quaint, curious, droll; eccentric, quirky, idiosyncratic, unconventional, outlandish; informal offbeat. **2** *whimsical likes and dislikes:* **volatile**, capricious, fickle, changeable, unpredictable, variable, erratic, mercurial, mutable, inconstant, inconsistent, unstable, protean.

whine verb **1** *a child was whining:* **wail**, whimper, cry, mewl, moan, howl, yowl. **2** *he's always whining about something:* **complain**, grouse, grouch, grumble, moan, carp; informal gripe, bellyache, whinge.

whip noun **lash**, strap, belt; historical scourge, cat-o'-nine-tails.
• verb **1** *they whipped him until he was unconscious:* **flog**, lash, thrash, beat, flagellate, tan someone's hide, horsewhip. **2** *whip the cream into soft peaks:* **whisk**, beat. **3** *he whipped his listeners into a frenzy:* **rouse**, stir up, excite, fire up, inflame, agitate, goad, provoke; galvanize, electrify, stimulate, inspire.

whippersnapper noun (informal) **upstart**; informal pipsqueak, squirt; humorous stripling.

whirl verb **1** *leaves whirled in the wind:* **rotate**, circle, wheel, turn, revolve, orbit, spin, twirl. **2** *his mind was whirling:* **spin**, reel, swim.
• noun **1** *a whirl of dust:* **swirl**, flurry,

eddy. **2** *the mad social whirl:* **hurly-burly**, activity, bustle, rush, flurry, merry-go-round; informal to-do. **3** *Laura's mind was in a whirl:* **spin**, daze, stupor, muddle, jumble; confusion; informal dither.

whirlpool noun **eddy**, vortex, maelstrom.

whirlwind noun **1** *the building was hit by a whirlwind:* **tornado**, hurricane, typhoon, cyclone, vortex; N. Amer. informal twister. **2** *a whirlwind of activity:* **maelstrom**, welter, bedlam, mayhem, babel, swirl, tumult, hurly-burly, commotion, confusion; N. Amer. three-ring circus.
• adjective *a whirlwind romance:* **rapid**, lightning, headlong, impulsive, breakneck, meteoric, sudden, swift, fast, quick, speedy.

whisk verb **1** *the cable car will whisk you to the top:* **speed**, hurry, rush, sweep, hurtle, shoot. **2** *she whisked the cloth away:* **pull**, snatch, pluck, tug, jerk; informal whip, yank. **3** *whisk the egg yolks:* **whip**, beat, mix.
• noun **beater**, mixer, blender.

whisper verb *Alison whispered in his ear:* **murmur**, mutter, mumble, speak softly, breathe, speak sotto voce.
– OPPOSITES shout.
• noun **1** *she spoke in a whisper:* **murmur**, mutter, mumble, low voice, undertone. **2** *I heard a whisper that he's left town:* **rumour**, story, report, speculation, hint, suggestion, insinuation; informal buzz.
– OPPOSITES shout.

whit noun **scrap**, bit, speck, iota, jot, atom, crumb, shred, grain, mite, touch, trace, shadow, suggestion, whisper, suspicion, scintilla; informal smidgen.

white adjective **1** *white cotton:* **colourless**, bleached; snow-white, milky, chalky, ivory. **2** *her face was white with fear:* **pale**, pallid, wan, ashen, bloodless, waxen, chalky, pasty, peaky, washed out, ghostly, deathly. **3** *an old man with white hair:* **snowy**, grey, silver, hoary, grizzled. **4** *his whiter than white image:* **virtuous**, moral, ethical, good, righteous, honourable, reputable, wholesome, honest, upright, upstanding, irreproachable; decent, worthy, noble; blameless, spotless, impeccable, unsullied, unblemished, uncorrupted, untainted; informal squeaky clean.
– OPPOSITES black, florid, immoral.

white-collar adjective **clerical**, professional, executive, office.
– OPPOSITES blue-collar.

whiten verb **bleach**, blanch, lighten, fade.

whitewash noun **1** *the report was a whitewash:* **cover-up**, camouflage, deception, facade, veneer, pretext. **2** *a four-match whitewash:* **walkover**, rout, landslide; informal pushover, cinch, breeze.
– OPPOSITES exposé.
• verb *don't try to whitewash what happened:* **cover up**, sweep under the carpet, hush up, suppress, draw a veil over, conceal, veil, obscure, keep secret; gloss over, downplay, soft-pedal.
– OPPOSITES expose.

whittle verb **1** *he sat whittling a piece of wood:* **pare**, shave, trim, carve, shape, model. **2** *his powers were whittled away:* **erode**, wear away, eat away, reduce, diminish, undermine, weaken, subvert, impair, impede, hinder, sap. **3** *the ten teams have been whittled down to six:* **reduce**, cut down, prune, trim, slim down, pare down, decrease, diminish.

whole adjective **1** *the whole report:* **entire**, complete, full, unabridged, uncut. **2** *a whole marble mantelpiece:* **intact**, in one piece, unbroken; undamaged, flawless, unmarked, perfect.
– OPPOSITES incomplete.
• noun **1** *a single whole:* **entity**, unit, body, ensemble. **2** *the whole of the year:* **all**, every part, the lot, the sum.
■ **on the whole** overall, all in all, all things considered, for the most part, in the main, in general, by and large; normally, usually, more often than not, almost always, typically, ordinarily.

wholehearted adjective **committed**, positive, emphatic, devoted, dedicated, enthusiastic, unshakeable, unswerving; unqualified, unreserved, unconditional, unequivocal, unmitigated; complete, full, total, absolute.
– OPPOSITES half-hearted.

wholesale adverb *the images were removed wholesale:* **extensively**, on a large scale, comprehensively; indiscriminately, without exception.
– OPPOSITES selectively.
• adjective *wholesale destruction:* **extensive**, widespread, large-scale, wide-ranging, comprehensive, total, mass; indiscriminate.
– OPPOSITES partial.

wholesome adjective **1** *wholesome food:* **healthy**, health-giving, good, nutritious, nourishing; natural, uncontaminated, organic. **2** *wholesome fun:* **moral**, ethical, good, clean, virtuous, pure, innocent, chaste; uplifting, edifying; informal squeaky clean.

wholly adverb **1** *the measures were wholly inadequate:* **completely**, totally, absolutely, entirely, fully, thoroughly, utterly, downright, in every respect; informal one hundred per cent. **2** *they rely wholly on me:* **exclusively**, only, solely, purely, alone.

wicked adjective **1** *wicked deeds:* **evil**, sinful, immoral, wrong, bad, iniquitous, corrupt, base, mean, vile; villainous, nefarious, erring, foul, monstrous, shocking, outrageous, atrocious, abominable, reprehensible, detestable, despicable, odious, contemptible, heinous, execrable, fiendish, barbarous; criminal, dishonest, unscrupulous; informal crooked. **2** *a wicked sense of humour:* **mischievous**, playful, naughty, impish, roguish, arch, puckish, cheeky.
– OPPOSITES virtuous.

wickedness noun **evil**, sin, iniquity, vileness, baseness, badness, wrongdoing, dishonesty, unscrupulousness, roguery, villainy, degeneracy, depravity, immorality, vice, corruption, devilry, fiendishness; formal turpitude.

wide adjective **1** *a wide river:* **broad**, extensive, spacious, vast. **2** *a wide knowledge of music:* **comprehensive**, broad, extensive, large, wide-ranging, all-inclusive, all-embracing; encyclopedic, catholic. **3** *his shot was wide:* **off target**, off the mark, inaccurate.
– OPPOSITES narrow.

wide-eyed adjective **1** *the whole class was wide-eyed:* goggle-eyed, open-mouthed, dumbstruck, amazed, astonished, astounded, stunned, staggered; informal flabbergasted; Brit. informal gobsmacked. **2** *wide-eyed visitors:* **innocent**, naive, impressionable, ingenuous, childlike, credulous, trusting.

widen verb **1** *a proposal to widen the motorway:* **broaden**, open up/out, expand, extend, enlarge. **2** *the Party must widen its support:* **increase**, augment, boost, swell, enlarge.

wide open adjective **1** *their mouths were wide open:* **agape**. **2** *the championship is wide open:* **unpredictable**, uncertain, in the balance, up in the air; informal anyone's guess. **3** *they were wide open to attacks:* **vulnerable**, exposed, unprotected, defenceless, undefended, at risk, in danger.

widespread adjective **general**, extensive, universal, common, global, worldwide, omnipresent, ubiquitous, across the board, predominant, prevalent, rife, broad.
– OPPOSITES limited.

width noun **1** *the width of the river:* **breadth**, thickness, span, diameter, girth. **2** *the width of experience required:* **range**, breadth, compass, scope, span, scale, extent, extensiveness, comprehensiveness.
– OPPOSITES length, narrowness.

wield verb **1** *he was wielding a sword:* **brandish**, flourish, wave, swing; use, employ, handle. **2** *he has wielded power since 1972:* **exercise**, exert, hold, maintain, command, control.

wife noun **spouse**, partner, mate, consort, woman, helpmate, bride; informal old lady, better half, missus; Brit. informal other half, her indoors, trouble and strife.

> **WORD LINKS**
> **uxorial** relating to a wife
> **uxorious** very fond of your wife
> **uxoricide** the killing of a wife by her husband

wiggle verb **jiggle**, wriggle, twitch, shimmy, wag, squirm, writhe; informal waggle.

wild adjective **1** *wild animals:* **untamed**, undomesticated, feral; fierce, ferocious, savage. **2** *wild*

flowers: **uncultivated**, native, indigenous. **3** *wild hill country:* **uninhabited**, unpopulated, uncultivated; rugged, rough, inhospitable, desolate, barren. **4** *a wild night:* **stormy**, blustery, squally, tempestuous, turbulent. **5** *her wild black hair:* **dishevelled**, tousled, tangled, windswept, untidy, unkempt. **6** *wild parties weren't my scene:* **disorderly**, riotous, unrestrained, out of control, undisciplined, unruly, uncontrolled, rowdy. **7** *the fans were wild with excitement:* **in a frenzy**, frenzied, delirious, hysterical, beside yourself, berserk; informal mad, crazy **8** *his wild schemes:* **impractical**, impracticable, unworkable, ill-considered, extravagant; madcap, ridiculous, ludicrous, foolish, stupid, foolhardy, idiotic, absurd, silly; informal crazy. **9** *a wild guess:* **random**, arbitrary, haphazard, uninformed.
– OPPOSITES tame, cultivated, calm, disciplined.
■ **run wild** run amok, run riot, get out of control.

wilderness noun **1** *the Siberian wilderness:* **wilds**, wastes; desert. **2** *a litter-strewn wilderness:* **wasteland**.

wildlife noun **wild animals**, creatures, fauna.

wilds plural noun **remote areas**, wilderness; backwoods; N. Amer. backcountry; Austral./NZ outback, bush; N. Amer. informal boondocks.

wiles plural noun **tricks**, ruses, ploys, schemes, dodges, manoeuvres, subterfuges, artifices; guile, artfulness, cunning, craftiness.

wilful adjective **1** *wilful destruction:* **deliberate**, intentional, premeditated, planned, conscious. **2** *a wilful child:* **headstrong**, strong-willed, obstinate, stubborn, pig-headed, recalcitrant, uncooperative, obstreperous; Brit. informal bloody-minded, bolshie; formal refractory.
– OPPOSITES accidental, amenable.

W

will noun **1** *the will to succeed:* **determination**, strength of character, resolve, single-mindedness, drive, commitment, dedication, doggedness, tenacity, staying power. **2** *they stayed against their will:* **desire**, wish, preference, inclination, intention, choice.
• verb **1** *do what you will:* **want**, wish, please, see/think fit, think best, like, choose, prefer. **2** *God willed it:* **decree**, order, ordain, command. **3** *she willed the money to her husband:* **bequeath**, leave, hand down, pass on.

willing adjective **1** *I'm willing to give it a try:* **ready**, prepared, disposed, inclined, minded; happy, glad, pleased, agreeable, amenable; informal game. **2** *willing help:* **readily given**, ungrudging.
– OPPOSITES reluctant.

willingly adverb **voluntarily**, of your own free will, of your own accord; readily, without reluctance, ungrudgingly, cheerfully, happily, gladly, with pleasure.
– OPPOSITES reluctantly.

willingness noun **readiness**, inclination, will, wish, desire.
– OPPOSITES reluctance.

willowy adjective **tall**, **slim**, slender, svelte, lissom, sylphlike, long-limbed, graceful, lithe.

willy-nilly adverb **1** *cars were parked willy-nilly:* **haphazardly**, at random, all over the place. **2** *we are, willy-nilly, in a new situation:* **whether you like it or not**, of necessity; informal like it or lump it; formal perforce.

wilt verb **1** *the roses had begun to wilt:* **droop**, sag, become limp, flop; wither, shrivel. **2** *the crowds were wilting in the heat:* **languish**, flag, droop, become listless. **3** *Shelley's happy mood wilted:* **fade**, ebb, wane, evaporate, melt away.
– OPPOSITES flourish.

wily adjective **shrewd**, clever, sharp, astute, canny, smart; crafty, cunning, artful, sly, scheming, calculating, devious; informal tricky, foxy.
– OPPOSITES naive.

win verb **1** *she was determined to win:* **come first**, be victorious, carry the day, succeed, triumph, prevail. **2** *he won a cash prize:* **secure**, gain, collect, pick up, walk away/off with, carry off; informal land, net, bag, scoop.
– OPPOSITES lose.
• noun *a 3–0 win:* **victory**, triumph, conquest, success.
– OPPOSITES defeat.

■ **win someone round/over** persuade, talk round, convince, sway.

wince verb *he winced at the pain:* **grimace**, pull a face, flinch, blench, start.

wind[1] noun **1** *trees were swaying in the wind:* **breeze**, current of air; gale, hurricane; informal blow; literary zephyr. **2** *he's got his wind back:* **breath**; informal puff.
■ **in the wind** *changes are in the wind:* on the way, coming, about to happen, in the offing, in the air, on the horizon, approaching, looming, brewing, afoot; informal on the cards.

WORD LINKS
anemometer an instrument for measuring wind speed

wind[2] verb **1** *the road winds up the mountain:* **twist and turn**, bend, curve, loop, zigzag, weave, snake. **2** *he wound a towel around his waist:* **wrap**, furl, entwine, lace. **3** *Anne wound the wool into a ball:* **coil**, roll, twist, twine.
■ **wind down** *the campaign was winding down:* draw to a close, come to an end, tail off, slack off, slow down.

winded adjective **out of breath**, breathless, panting, puffing.

windfall noun **bonanza**, jackpot, pennies from heaven.

winding noun *the windings of the stream:* **twist**, turn, turning, bend, loop, curve, zigzag, meander.
• adjective *the winding country roads:* **twisting and turning**, meandering, twisty, bending, curving, zigzag, serpentine, sinuous, snaking.
– OPPOSITES straight.

windswept adjective **1** *the windswept moors:* **exposed**, bleak, bare, desolate. **2** *his windswept hair:* **dishevelled**, tousled, unkempt, wind-blown, untidy.

windy adjective **1** *a windy day:* **breezy**, blowy, fresh, blustery, gusty; wild, stormy, squally, tempestuous. **2** *a windy hillside:* **windswept**, exposed, open to the elements, bare, bleak.
– OPPOSITES still, sheltered.

wine noun informal plonk, vino, the grape; literary vintage.

WORD LINKS
vinous relating to wine
oenology the study of wines
viticulture the cultivation of grape vines

wing noun **1** *the east wing of the house:* **part**, section, side; annexe, extension. **2** *the radical wing of the party:* **faction**, camp, caucus, arm, branch, group, section, set, coterie, cabal.
• verb **1** *a gull winged its way over the sea:* **fly**, glide, soar. **2** *she was shot at and winged:* **wound**, graze, hit.

wink verb **1** *he winked an eye at her:* **blink**, flutter, bat. **2** *the diamond winked in the moonlight:* **sparkle**, twinkle, flash, glitter, gleam, shine, scintillate.
■ **wink at** turn a blind eye to, close your eyes to, ignore, overlook, disregard; connive at, condone, tolerate.

winner noun **victor**, champion, conqueror, hero; medallist; informal champ, top dog; literary vanquisher.
– OPPOSITES loser.

winning adjective **1** *the winning team:* **victorious**, successful, triumphant, conquering; first, top; literary vanquishing. **2** *a winning smile:* **engaging**, charming, appealing, endearing, sweet, cute, winsome, attractive, prepossessing, fetching, disarming, captivating.

winnings plural noun **prize money**, gains, booty, spoils; proceeds, profits, takings, purse.

winsome adjective. See **WINNING** sense 2.

wintry adjective **1** *wintry weather:* **bleak**, cold, chilly, frosty, freezing, icy, snowy, arctic, glacial, bitter, raw; informal nippy; Brit. informal parky. **2** *a wintry smile:* **unfriendly**, unwelcoming, cool, cold, frosty, frigid.
– OPPOSITES summery, warm.

WORD LINKS
hibernal relating to winter

wipe verb **1** *Beth wiped the table:* **rub**, mop, sponge, swab; clean, dry, polish. **2** *he wiped the marks off the window:* **rub off**, clean off, clear up, remove, get rid of, take off, erase,

efface. **3** *she wiped the memory from her mind:* **obliterate**, expunge, erase, blot out, blank out.
■ **wipe someone/something out** destroy, annihilate, eradicate, eliminate; slaughter, massacre, kill, exterminate; demolish, raze to the ground; informal take out, zap; N. Amer. informal waste; literary slay.

wire noun **cable**, lead; Brit. flex.

wiry adjective **1** *a wiry man:* **sinewy**, tough, athletic, strong; lean, spare, thin, stringy, skinny. **2** *wiry hair:* **coarse**, rough, strong.
– OPPOSITES flabby, smooth.

wisdom noun **1** *we questioned the wisdom of the decision:* **sagacity**, intelligence, sense, common sense, shrewdness, astuteness, smartness, judiciousness, judgement, prudence, circumspection; logic, rationale, soundness, advisability. **2** *the wisdom of the East:* **knowledge**, learning, erudition, scholarship, philosophy; lore.
– OPPOSITES folly.

wise adjective *a wise old man:* **sage**, sagacious, intelligent, clever, learned, knowledgeable, enlightened; astute, smart, shrewd, sharp-witted, canny, knowing; sensible, prudent, discerning, judicious, perceptive, insightful; rational, logical, sound, sane; Brit. informal fly; formal sapient.
– OPPOSITES foolish.
■ **wise to** (informal) aware of, familiar with, acquainted with; formal cognizant of.

wish verb **1** *I wished for power:* **desire**, want, hope for, covet, dream of, long for, yearn for, crave, hunger for, lust after; aspire to, set your heart on, seek, fancy, hanker after, have a yen for. **2** *they can do as they wish:* **want**, desire, feel inclined, feel like, care; choose, please, think fit. **3** *I wish you to send them a message:* **want**, desire, require.
• noun **1** *he fulfilled his wish to travel the world:* **desire**, longing, yearning, inclination, urge, whim, craving, hunger, hankering, yen; hope, aspiration, aim, ambition, dream. **2** *her parents' wishes:* **request**, requirement, bidding, instruction, direction, demand, order, command; want, desire; will; literary behest.

wisp noun **strand**, tendril, lock; scrap, shred, thread.

wispy adjective **thin**, fine, feathery, flyaway.

wistful adjective **nostalgic**, yearning, longing; plaintive, regretful, rueful, melancholy, mournful; pensive, reflective, contemplative.

wit noun **1** *he needed all his wits to escape:* **intelligence**, shrewdness, astuteness, cleverness, sense, wisdom, sagacity, judgement, acumen, insight; brains, mind; informal nous, gumption, savvy. **2** *my sparkling wit:* **wittiness**, humour, drollery; repartee, badinage, banter, wordplay; jokes, witticisms, quips, puns. **3** *she's such a wit:* **comedian**, humorist, comic, joker; informal wag; informal, dated card.

witch noun **1** *the witch cast a spell:* **sorceress**, enchantress, hex; Wiccan. **2** (informal) *she's a right old witch:* **hag**, crone, harpy, harridan, she-devil; informal battleaxe.

witchcraft noun **sorcery**, black magic, wizardry, spells, incantations, necromancy; Wicca.

witch doctor noun **medicine man**, shaman, healer.

with preposition **accompanied by**, escorted by; alongside, in addition to, as well as.

withdraw verb **1** *she withdrew her hand from his:* **remove**, extract, pull out, take out; take back. **2** *the ban on advertising was withdrawn:* **abolish**, cancel, lift, set aside, end, stop, remove, reverse, revoke, rescind, repeal, annul, void. **3** *she withdrew the allegation:* **retract**, take back, go back on, recant, disavow, disclaim, repudiate, renounce; back down, climb down, backtrack, back-pedal, do a U-turn, eat your words. **4** *the troops withdrew from the city:* **leave**, pull out of, evacuate, quit, retreat from. **5** *his partner withdrew from the project:* **pull out of**, back out of, bow out of; get cold feet. **6** *they withdrew to their rooms:* **retire**, retreat, adjourn, decamp; leave, depart, absent yourself; formal repair; dated remove; literary betake yourself.
– OPPOSITES insert, introduce, deposit, enter.

withdrawal noun **1** *the withdrawal*

W

of subsidies: **removal**, abolition, cancellation, discontinuation, termination, elimination. **2** *the withdrawal of the troops:* **departure**, pull-out, exit, exodus, evacuation, retreat.

withdrawn adjective **introverted**, unsociable, inhibited, uncommunicative, unforthcoming, quiet, reticent, reserved, retiring, private, reclusive; shy, timid; aloof; informal stand-offish.
– OPPOSITES outgoing.

wither verb **1** *the flowers withered in the sun:* **shrivel**, dry up; wilt, droop, fade, perish. **2** *the muscles in his leg withered:* **waste away**, shrivel up, shrink, atrophy. **3** *her confidence withered:* **diminish**, dwindle, shrink, lessen, fade, ebb, wane; evaporate, disappear.
– OPPOSITES thrive, grow.

withering adjective **scornful**, contemptuous, scathing, stinging, devastating; humiliating, mortifying.
– OPPOSITES admiring.

withhold verb **1** *he withheld the information:* **hold back**, keep back, refuse to give; retain, hold on to; hide, conceal, keep secret; informal sit on. **2** *she could not withhold her tears:* **suppress**, repress, hold back, fight back, choke back, control, check, restrain, contain.

within preposition **1** *within the prison walls:* **inside**, in, enclosed by, surrounded by. **2** *within a few hours:* **in less than**, in under.
– OPPOSITES outside.

without preposition *thousands were without food:* **lacking**, short of, deprived of, in need of, wanting, requiring.

withstand verb **resist**, weather, survive, endure, cope with, stand, tolerate, bear, defy, brave, hold out against; stand up to, face, confront.

witness noun **1** *witnesses claimed that he started the fight:* **observer**, onlooker, eyewitness, spectator, viewer, watcher; bystander, passer-by. **2** *a whisky bottle was the only witness of his mood:* **evidence**, indication, proof, testimony.
• verb **1** *who witnessed the incident?* **see**, observe, watch, view, notice, spot; be present at, attend; literary behold. **2** *the will is correctly witnessed:* **countersign**, sign, endorse, validate. **3** *his writings witness an inner toughness:* **attest to**, testify to, confirm, evidence, prove, verify, corroborate, substantiate; show, demonstrate, indicate, reveal, bespeak.

witticism noun **joke**, quip, jest, pun, play on words, bon mot; informal one-liner, gag, funny, crack, wisecrack.

witty adjective **humorous**, amusing, droll, funny, comic; jocular, facetious, waggish; sparkling, scintillating, entertaining; clever, quick-witted.

wizard noun **1** *the wizard cast a spell:* **sorcerer**, warlock, magus, black magician, enchanter. **2** *a financial wizard:* **genius**, expert, master, virtuoso, maestro, marvel, Wunderkind; informal hotshot, demon, whizz-kid, buff, pro, ace; Brit. informal dab hand; N. Amer. informal maven.

wizardry noun **sorcery**, witchcraft, magic, enchantment; spells, charms.

wizened adjective **wrinkled**, lined, creased, shrivelled, withered, weather-beaten, shrunken, gnarled.

wobble verb **1** *the table wobbled:* **rock**, teeter, jiggle, sway, see-saw, shake. **2** *he wobbled across to the door:* **teeter**, totter, stagger, lurch. **3** *her voice wobbled:* **tremble**, shake, quiver, quaver, waver.

wobbly adjective **1** *a wobbly table:* **unsteady**, unstable, shaky, rocky, rickety; unsafe, precarious; informal wonky. **2** *she still felt wobbly:* **shaky**, quivery, weak, unsteady; faint, dizzy, light-headed, giddy, groggy; informal trembly, woozy.
– OPPOSITES stable.

woe noun **1** *a tale of woe:* **misery**, sorrow, distress, wretchedness, sadness, unhappiness, heartache, heartbreak, despondency, despair, depression, gloom, melancholy; adversity, misfortune, disaster, suffering, hardship; literary dolour. **2** *financial woes:* **trouble**, difficulty, problem, trial, tribulation, misfortune, setback, reverse.
– OPPOSITES joy.

woebegone adjective **sad**, unhappy, miserable, dejected, disconsolate, forlorn, crestfallen, downcast, glum, gloomy, doleful, down-hearted, despondent, melancholy,

sorrowful, mournful, woeful, depressed, wretched, desolate; informal down in the mouth, down in the dumps, blue.
– OPPOSITES cheerful.

woeful adjective **1** *a woeful tale:* **tragic**, sad, miserable, cheerless, gloomy, sorry, pitiful, pathetic, traumatic, depressing, heart-breaking, heart-rending, tear-jerking. **2** *the team's woeful performance:* **dreadful**, awful, terrible, atrocious, disgraceful, deplorable, shameful, hopeless, lamentable; informal rotten, appalling, crummy, pathetic, pitiful, lousy, abysmal, dire; Brit. informal duff, chronic, rubbish.
– OPPOSITES cheerful, excellent.

wolf verb **devour**, gobble, guzzle, gulp down, bolt; informal put away, demolish, shovel down, scoff; N. Amer. informal snarf, scarf.

> **WORD LINKS**
> **lupine** relating to wolves

woman noun **1** *a woman got out of the car:* **lady**, female; matron; Scottish & N. English lass; Irish colleen; informal chick; Brit. informal bird; N. Amer. informal sister, dame, broad; Austral./NZ informal sheila; literary damsel. **2** *he found himself a new woman:* **girlfriend**, sweetheart, partner, significant other, lover, mistress; fiancée; wife, spouse; informal missus; Brit. informal trouble and strife; N. Amer. informal squeeze; dated lady friend.

> **WORD LINKS**
> **female**, **feminine** relating to women
> **gynaecology** the branch of medicine concerned with conditions specific to women and girls
> **misogyny** hatred of women

womanhood noun **1** *she was on the brink of womanhood:* **adulthood**, maturity. **2** *she's an ideal of womanhood:* **womanliness**, femininity. **3** *the stereotype of Soviet womanhood:* **women**, womenfolk; womankind; the female sex.

womanizer noun **philanderer**, Casanova, Don Juan, Romeo, Lothario, ladies' man, playboy, seducer; informal skirt-chaser, ladykiller.

womankind noun **women**, the female sex.

womanly adjective **1** *womanly virtues:* **feminine**, female. **2** *her womanly figure:* **voluptuous**, curvaceous, shapely, ample, Junoesque, Rubenesque, buxom, full-figured; informal curvy, busty.
– OPPOSITES manly, boyish.

wonder noun **1** *she was speechless with wonder:* **awe**, admiration, fascination; surprise, astonishment, amazement. **2** *the wonders of nature:* **marvel**, miracle, phenomenon, sensation, spectacle, beauty; curiosity.
• verb **1** *I wondered what was on her mind:* **ponder**, think about, meditate on, reflect on, muse on, speculate about, conjecture.
2 *people wondered at such bravery:* **marvel**, be amazed, be astonished, stand in awe, be dumbfounded, gape, goggle; informal be flabbergasted.

wonderful adjective **marvellous**, magnificent, superb, glorious, sublime, lovely, delightful; informal super, great, fantastic, terrific, tremendous, sensational, incredible, fabulous, awesome, magic, wicked; Brit. informal smashing, brilliant; N. Amer. informal peachy, dandy, neat; Austral./NZ informal beaut, bonzer.

wont (formal) noun *Paul drove fast, as was his wont:* **custom**, habit, way, practice, convention, rule.
• adjective *he was wont to arise at 5.30:* **accustomed**, used, given, inclined.

wonted adjective (literary) **customary**, habitual, usual, accustomed, familiar, normal, conventional, routine, common.

woo verb **1** *he wooed her for several years:* **pursue**, chase; dated court, romance, seek the hand of, set your cap at, make love to. **2** *the party wooed voters with promises:* **seek**, pursue, curry favour with; entice, tempt, coax, persuade, wheedle, seduce; informal sweet-talk.

wood noun **1** *polished wood:* **timber**, planks; logs; N. Amer. lumber. **2** *a walk through the woods:* **forest**, woodland, trees; copse, coppice, grove; Brit. spinney.

> **WORD LINKS**
> **ligneous** relating to wood

wooded adjective **forested**, afforested, tree-covered; literary sylvan.

wooden adjective **1** *a wooden door:* **wood**, timber; technical ligneous. **2** *wooden acting:* **stilted**, stiff, unnatural, awkward, leaden; dry, flat, stodgy, lifeless, passionless, spiritless, soulless. **3** *her face was wooden:* **expressionless**, impassive, poker-faced, emotionless, blank, vacant, unresponsive.

woodland noun **woods**, forest, trees.

woodwork noun **carpentry**, joinery.

wool noun *sheep's wool:* **fleece**, hair, coat.

woolly adjective **1** *a woolly hat:* **woollen**, fleecy. **2** *a sheep's woolly coat:* **fleecy**, shaggy, hairy, fluffy, flocculent. **3** *woolly generalizations:* **vague**, ill-defined, hazy, unclear, fuzzy, blurry, foggy, nebulous, imprecise, inexact, indefinite; confused, muddled.

word noun **1** *the Italian word for 'ham':* **term**, name, expression, designation, locution; formal appellation. **2** *his words were meant kindly:* **remark**, comment, observation, statement, utterance, pronouncement. **3** *I've got three weeks to learn the words:* **script**, lyrics, libretto. **4** *I give you my word:* **promise**, assurance, guarantee, undertaking; pledge, vow, oath, bond; formal troth. **5** *I want a word with you:* **talk**, conversation, chat, tête-à-tête, heart-to-heart, one-to-one; discussion; informal confab, powwow. **6** *there's no word from the hospital:* **news**, information, communication, intelligence; message, report, communiqué, dispatch, bulletin; informal info, gen; literary tidings. **7** *word has it he's turned over a new leaf:* **rumour**, hearsay, talk, gossip; informal the grapevine. **8** *I'm waiting for the word from HQ:* **instruction**, order, command; signal, prompt, cue, tip-off; informal go-ahead, thumbs up, green light. **9** *his word was law:* **command**, order, decree, edict; bidding, will.
• verb *the question was carefully worded:* **phrase**, express, put, couch, frame, formulate, style.
■ **in a word** briefly, in short, in a nutshell, to come to the point, to cut a long story short, not to put too fine a point on it; to sum up. **word for word 1** *they took down the speeches word for word:* verbatim, letter for letter; exactly, faithfully. **2** *a word-for-word translation:* verbatim, literal, exact, direct, accurate, faithful; unadulterated, unabridged.

WORD LINKS
verbal, **lexical** relating to words
semantic relating to the meaning of words

wording noun **phrasing**, phraseology, language, expression, terminology.

wordplay noun **punning**, play on words; wit, witticisms, repartee.

wordy adjective **long-winded**, verbose, prolix, lengthy, protracted, rambling, circumlocutory, periphrastic; loquacious, garrulous, voluble; informal windy; Brit. informal waffly.
– OPPOSITES succinct.

work noun **1** *a day's work in the fields:* **labour**, toil, slog, drudgery, exertion, effort, industry; informal grind, sweat, elbow grease; Brit. informal graft; literary travail. **2** *I'm looking for work:* **employment**, a job, a post, a position, a situation; occupation, profession, career, vocation, calling. **3** *haven't you got any work to do?* **tasks**, jobs, duties, assignments, projects; chores. **4** *works of literature:* **composition**, piece, creation; opus. **5** *this is the work of a radical faction:* **handiwork**, doing, act, deed. **6** *a lifetime spent doing good works:* **deeds**, acts, actions. **7** *the complete works of Shakespeare:* **writings**, oeuvre, canon, output. **8** *a car works:* **factory**, plant, mill, foundry, workshop, shop. **9** *the works of a clock:* **mechanism**, machinery, workings, parts, movement, action; informal insides.
– OPPOSITES leisure.
• verb **1** *staff worked late into the night:* **toil**, labour, exert yourself, slave away; keep at it, keep your nose to the grindstone; informal slog away, beaver away, put your back into it, sweat blood; Brit. informal graft;

literary travail. **2** *farmers worked the land:* **cultivate**, farm, till, plough. **3** *his car was working perfectly:* **function**, go, run, operate, handle; informal behave. **4** *their ploy worked:* **succeed**, get results, be effective; informal come off, pay off, do the trick. **5** *blusher can work miracles:* **bring about**, accomplish, achieve, produce, perform, create, engender, contrive, effect. **6** *he worked the crowd into a frenzy:* **stir**, excite, drive, move, rouse, fire, galvanize; whip up, agitate. **7** *work the mixture into a paste:* **knead**, squeeze, form; mix, stir, blend. **8** *he worked his way through the crowd:* **manoeuvre**, make, thread, wind, weave, wend, elbow.
– OPPOSITES rest, fail.
■ **work on someone** persuade, manipulate, influence; coax, cajole, wheedle, soften up; informal twist someone's arm, lean on. **work out 1** *the bill works out at £50:* amount to, add up to, come to, total; Brit. tot up to. **2** *things didn't work out the way she planned:* end up, turn out, go, come out, develop; happen, occur; informal pan out. **3** *he works out at the local gym:* exercise, train. **work something out 1** *work out what you can afford:* calculate, compute, reckon up, determine. **2** *I'm trying to work out what she meant:* understand, comprehend, puzzle out, sort out, make sense of, get to the bottom of, make head or tail of, unravel, decipher, decode; informal figure out; Brit. informal suss out. **3** *they worked out a plan:* devise, formulate, draw up, put together, develop, construct, arrange, organize, contrive, concoct; hammer out, negotiate. **work something up** stimulate, rouse, raise, arouse, awaken, excite.

workable adjective **practicable**, feasible, viable, possible, achievable; realistic, reasonable, sensible, practical; informal doable.
– OPPOSITES impracticable.

worker noun **1** *a strike by workers:* **employee**, member of staff; workman, labourer, hand, operator; proletarian; wage-earner, breadwinner. **2** (informal) *I got a reputation for being a worker:* **hard worker**, workhorse; informal busy bee, eager beaver, workaholic.

workforce noun **employees**, staff, personnel, workers, labour force, manpower; human resources; informal liveware.

working adjective **1** *child care for working mothers:* **employed**, in work, waged. **2** *a working waterwheel:* **functioning**, operating, running, up and running, active, in working order, operational, functional, serviceable. **3** *a working knowledge of contract law:* **sufficient**, adequate, viable; useful, effective.
– OPPOSITES unemployed, faulty.
• noun **1** *the working of a carburettor:* **functioning**, operation, running, action, performance. **2** *the workings of a watch:* **mechanism**, machinery, parts, movement, action, works; informal insides.

workman noun **worker**, labourer, hand, operative, operator; employee.

workmanship noun **craftsmanship**, artistry, craft, art, artisanship, handiwork; skill, expertise, technique.

workshop noun **1** *a car repair workshop:* **factory**, works, plant; industrial unit, garage. **2** *the craftsmen had a chilly workshop:* **workroom**, studio, atelier. **3** *a workshop on combating stress:* **study group**, discussion group, seminar, forum, class.

world noun **1** *he travelled the world:* **earth**, globe, planet, sphere. **2** *life on other worlds:* **planet**, satellite, moon, star, heavenly body, orb. **3** *the academic world:* **sphere**, society, circle, arena, milieu, province, domain, preserve, realm, field, discipline, area. **4** *she would show the world that she was strong:* **everyone**, people, mankind, humankind, humanity, the public, all and sundry, {every Tom, Dick, and Harry}. **5** *a world of difference:* **huge amount**, abundance, wealth, profusion, mountain; plenty; informal heap, lot, load, ton, masses; Brit. informal shedload.

worldly adjective **1** *worldly pursuits:* **earthly**, terrestrial, temporal, mundane; mortal, human, material, physical, carnal, fleshly, bodily,

W

corporeal, sensual. **2** *a worldly man:* **sophisticated**, experienced, worldly-wise, knowledgeable, knowing, enlightened, shrewd, mature, seasoned, cosmopolitan, urbane, cultured.
– OPPOSITES spiritual, naive.

worldwide adjective **global**, international, intercontinental, universal; ubiquitous, extensive, widespread, far-reaching, wide-ranging.
– OPPOSITES local.

worn adjective *her clothes were worn and faded:* **shabby**, worn out, threadbare, in tatters, holey, falling to pieces, ragged, frayed, moth-eaten, scruffy.
– OPPOSITES smart.

worn out adjective **1** *a worn-out shirt.* See **WORN**. **2** *by evening they were worn out:* **exhausted**, fatigued, tired out, weary, drained, worn, drawn, sapped, spent; informal all in, done in, dog-tired, dead beat, frazzled, shattered; Brit. informal knackered, whacked; N. Amer. informal pooped, tuckered out. **3** *worn-out ideas:* **obsolete**, antiquated, old, stale, hackneyed, trite, overused, overworked, clichéd, unoriginal, commonplace, pedestrian, prosaic, stock, conventional; informal played out, old hat.
– OPPOSITES smart, fresh.

worried adjective **anxious**, perturbed, troubled, bothered, concerned, disquieted, uneasy, fretful, agitated, nervous, edgy, tense, overwrought, worked up, keyed up, jumpy, stressed; apprehensive, fearful, afraid, frightened, scared; informal uptight, a bundle of nerves, on tenterhooks, jittery, twitchy, in a stew, all of a dither, in a flap, in a sweat, het up; Brit. informal having kittens; N. Amer. informal antsy.
– OPPOSITES carefree.

worry verb **1** *she worries about his health:* **fret**, be concerned, be anxious, agonize, brood, panic, lose sleep, get worked up; informal torment yourself. **2** *is something worrying you?* **trouble**, bother, make anxious, disturb, distress, upset, concern, disquiet, fret, agitate, unsettle, perturb, scare, fluster, stress, torment, plague; prey on someone's mind, weigh down, gnaw at; informal bug, get to.
• noun **1** *I'm beside myself with worry:* **anxiety**, perturbation, distress, concern, unease, disquiet, fretfulness, restlessness, nerves, agitation, edginess, tension, stress; apprehension, fear, dread, trepidation, misgiving, angst; informal butterflies (in your stomach), the willies, the heebie-jeebies. **2** *his injury is a worry for the selectors:* **problem**, cause for concern; nuisance, plague, trial, trouble, vexation, bane, bugbear; informal pain, headache, hassle.

worrying adjective **alarming**, worrisome, daunting, perturbing, niggling, bothersome, troublesome, unsettling, nerve-racking; distressing, disquieting, upsetting, traumatic, problematic; informal scary, hairy.

worsen verb **1** *insomnia can worsen a patient's distress:* **aggravate**, exacerbate, compound, add to, intensify, increase, magnify, heighten, inflame, augment; informal add fuel to the fire. **2** *the recession worsened:* **deteriorate**, degenerate, decline; informal go downhill, go to pot, go to the dogs.
– OPPOSITES improve.

worship noun **1** *the worship of saints:* **reverence**, veneration, adoration, glorification, exaltation; devotion, praise, thanksgiving, homage, honour; formal laudation. **2** *morning worship:* **service**, religious rite, prayer, praise, devotion, religious observance; matins, vespers, evensong. **3** *he contemplated her with worship:* **admiration**, adulation, idolization, lionization, hero-worship.
• verb *they worship pagan gods:* **revere**, venerate, pay homage to, honour, adore, praise, pray to, glorify, exalt, extol; hold dear, cherish, treasure, esteem, adulate, idolize, deify, hero-worship, lionize; informal put on a pedestal; formal laud.

worth noun **1** *evidence of the rug's worth:* **value**, price, cost; valuation, quotation, estimate. **2** *the intrinsic worth of education:* **benefit**, advantage, use, value, virtue, utility, service, profit, help, aid; desirability, appeal; significance, sense; informal mileage, percentage. **3** *a sense of personal worth:* **worthiness**, merit, value, excellence, calibre, quality, stature, eminence, consequence, importance, significance, distinction.

worthless adjective **1** *the item was worthless:* **valueless**; inferior, second-rate, low-grade, cheap, shoddy, tawdry; informal ten a penny; N. Amer. informal nickel-and-dime. **2** *a worthless exercise:* **useless**, pointless, meaningless, senseless, fruitless, unproductive. **3** *his worthless son:* **good-for-nothing**, ne'er-do-well, useless, despicable, contemptible, low, ignominious, degenerate; informal no-good, lousy.
– OPPOSITES valuable, useful.

worthwhile adjective **valuable**, useful, of service, beneficial, rewarding, advantageous, positive, helpful, profitable, gainful, fruitful, productive, constructive, effective.

worthy adjective *a worthy citizen:* **virtuous**, righteous, good, moral, ethical, upright, upstanding, high-minded, principled, exemplary; law-abiding, irreproachable, unimpeachable, honest, honourable, reputable, decent, respectable, noble; informal squeaky clean.
– OPPOSITES disreputable.
• noun *local worthies:* **dignitary**, personage, grandee, VIP, notable, notability, pillar of society, luminary, leading light, big name; informal heavyweight, bigwig, top dog, big shot, big cheese.
– OPPOSITES nobody.
■ **be worthy of** deserve, merit, warrant, rate, justify, earn, be entitled to, qualify for.

would-be adjective **aspiring**, budding, promising, prospective, potential, hopeful, keen, eager, ambitious; informal wannabe.

wound noun **1** *a chest wound:* **injury**, lesion, cut, gash, laceration, tear, slash; graze, scratch, abrasion; Medicine trauma. **2** *wounds inflicted by the media:* **insult**, blow, slight, offence, affront; hurt, damage, injury, pain, distress, grief, anguish, torment.
• verb **1** *he was critically wounded:* **injure**, hurt, harm; maim, mutilate, incapacitate; lacerate, cut, graze, gash, stab, slash. **2** *her words had wounded him:* **hurt**, scar, damage, injure; insult, slight, offend, affront, distress, disturb, upset, trouble; grieve, sadden, pain, sting.

wrangle noun *a wrangle over money:* **argument**, dispute, disagreement, quarrel, falling-out, fight, squabble, altercation, war of words, shouting match, tiff; Brit. row; informal set-to, run-in, slanging match; Brit. informal barney, bust-up.
• verb *we wrangled over the details:* **argue**, quarrel, bicker, squabble, fall out, have words, disagree, be at odds, fight, battle, feud, clash; Brit. row; informal scrap.

wrap verb **1** *she wrapped herself in a towel:* **swathe**, bundle, swaddle, muffle, cloak, enfold, envelop, encase, cover, fold, wind. **2** *I wrapped the vase carefully:* **parcel up**, package, pack; gift-wrap.
• noun *he put a wrap round her:* **shawl**, pashmina, stole, cloak, cape, mantle, scarf, poncho, serape.

wrapper noun **1** *a sweet wrapper:* **wrapping**, packaging, paper, cover, covering; jacket, sheath. **2** (N. Amer.) *she wore a cotton wrapper:* **housecoat**, bathrobe, dressing gown, robe, kimono, peignoir.

wrath noun **anger**, rage, fury, outrage, spleen, vexation, exasperation, annoyance; literary ire, choler.

wreak verb **inflict**, bestow, mete out, administer, deliver, impose, exact, create, cause, result in, effect, engender, bring about, perpetrate, unleash, vent; formal effectuate.

wreath noun **garland**, circlet, chaplet, crown, festoon, lei; ring, loop, circle.

wreathe verb **1** *a pulpit wreathed in holly:* **festoon**, garland, drape, cover, deck, decorate, ornament, adorn. **2** *blue smoke wreathed upwards:* **spiral**, coil, loop, wind, curl, twist, snake, curve.

wreck noun **1** *salvage teams landed on the wreck:* **shipwreck**, sunken ship, derelict; shell, hull. **2** *the wreck of a stolen car:* **wreckage**, debris, ruins, remains.
• verb **1** *he had wrecked her car:* **demolish**, crash, smash up, damage, destroy; vandalize, deface, desecrate, write off; N. Amer. informal trash, total. **2** *his ship was wrecked:* **shipwreck**, sink, capsize, run aground. **3** *the*

crisis wrecked his plans: **ruin**, spoil, disrupt, undo, put a stop to, frustrate, blight, crush, quash, dash, destroy, scotch, shatter, devastate, sabotage; informal mess up, screw up, foul up, put paid to, stymie, put the kibosh on; Brit. informal scupper.

wrench noun **1** *she felt a wrench on her shoulders:* **tug**, pull, jerk, jolt, heave; informal yank. **2** *hold the piston with a wrench:* **spanner**. **3** *a wrench in his arm:* **sprain**, twist, strain, rick, crick. **4** *leaving was an immense wrench:* **painful parting**, traumatic event; pang, trauma.
• verb **1** *he wrenched the gun from her:* **tug**, pull, jerk, wrest, heave, twist, pluck, grab, seize, snatch, force, prise; N. Amer. pry; informal yank. **2** *she wrenched her ankle:* **sprain**, twist, turn, strain, rick, crick, pull; injure, hurt.

wrest verb **wrench**, snatch, seize, grab, prise, pluck, tug, pull, jerk, dislodge; N. Amer. pry; informal yank.

wrestle verb **grapple**, fight, struggle, contend, vie, battle, wrangle; scuffle, tussle, brawl; informal scrap.

wretch noun (informal) **scoundrel**, villain, ruffian, rogue, rascal, reprobate, miscreant, good-for-nothing; informal heel, rat, swine; informal, dated rotter, blighter.

wretched adjective **1** *I felt so wretched without you:* **miserable**, unhappy, sad, heartbroken, grief-stricken, sorrowful, distressed, desolate, devastated, despairing, disconsolate, downcast, dejected, crestfallen, cheerless, depressed, melancholy, morose, gloomy, mournful, doleful, dismal, forlorn, woebegone; informal blue; literary dolorous. **2** *I feel wretched:* **ill**, unwell, poorly, sick, below par; Brit. off colour; informal under the weather, out of sorts. **3** *their living conditions are wretched:* **harsh**, hard, grim, stark, difficult; poor, impoverished; pitiful, pathetic, miserable, cheerless, dilapidated; terrible, awful, dire, atrocious, dreadful, lamentable, deplorable; informal God-awful. **4** *the wretched dweller in the shanty town:* **unfortunate**, unlucky, ill-starred, blighted, hapless, poor, pitiable, downtrodden, oppressed.

wriggle verb **1** *she tried to hug him but he wriggled:* **squirm**, writhe, wiggle, jiggle, jerk, thresh, flounder, flail, twitch, twist and turn; snake, worm, slither. **2** *he wriggled out of his responsibilities:* **avoid**, shirk, dodge, evade, elude, sidestep; escape from; informal duck.

wring verb **1** *wring out the clothes:* **twist**, squeeze, screw, scrunch, knead, press, mangle. **2** *concessions were wrung from the government:* **extract**, elicit, force, exact, wrest, wrench, squeeze, milk; informal bleed. **3** *his expression wrung her heart:* **rend**, tear at, harrow, pierce, stab, wound, rack; distress, pain, hurt.

wrinkle noun *fine wrinkles around her mouth:* **crease**, fold, pucker, line, crinkle, furrow, ridge, groove; informal crow's feet.
• verb *his coat tails wrinkled up:* **crease**, pucker, gather, line, crinkle, crumple, rumple, ruck up, scrunch up.

writ noun **summons**, subpoena, warrant, arraignment, indictment, citation, court order.

write verb **1** *he wrote her name in the book:* **note**, jot down, put down, take down, record, register, log, list; inscribe, sign, scribble, scrawl, pencil. **2** *I wrote a poem:* **compose**, draft, think up, formulate, compile, pen, dash off, produce. **3** *he had her address and promised to write:* **correspond**, communicate, get in touch, keep in contact; informal drop someone a line.
■ **write someone/something off** **1** *they have had to write off loans:* forget about, disregard, give up on, cancel, annul, wipe out. **2** *he wrote off his new car:* wreck, smash up, crash, destroy, demolish, ruin; N. Amer. informal total. **3** *who would write off a player of his stature?* disregard, dismiss, ignore.

writer noun **author**, wordsmith, man/woman of letters, penman; novelist, essayist, biographer; journalist, columnist, correspondent; scriptwriter, playwright, dramatist; poet; informal scribbler, scribe, pen-pusher, hack.

writhe verb **squirm**, wriggle, thrash, flail, toss, twist.

writing noun **1** *I can't read his*

writing: **handwriting**, hand, script, print; penmanship, calligraphy, chirography; informal scribble, scrawl. **2** *the writings of Gertrude Stein:* **works**, compositions, books, publications, oeuvre; papers, articles, essays.

WORD LINKS
graphology the study of handwriting
palaeography the study of ancient writing systems

wrong adjective **1** *the wrong answer:* **incorrect**, mistaken, in error, erroneous, inaccurate, inexact, imprecise, fallacious, wide of the mark; informal off beam, out. **2** *he knew he had said the wrong thing:* **inappropriate**, unsuitable, inapt, inapposite, undesirable; ill-advised, ill-considered, ill-judged, impolitic, injudicious, infelicitous, unfitting, improper; informal out of order. **3** *I've done nothing wrong:* **illegal**, unlawful, illicit, criminal, dishonest, dishonourable, corrupt; unethical, immoral, bad, wicked, sinful, iniquitous, nefarious, reprehensible; informal crooked. **4** *there's something wrong with the engine:* **amiss**, awry, out of order, not right, faulty, defective.
– OPPOSITES right, correct, appropriate, legal.
• adverb *she had guessed wrong:* **incorrectly**, wrongly, inaccurately, erroneously, mistakenly.
• noun **1** *the difference between right and wrong:* **immorality**, sin, wickedness, evil; unlawfulness, crime, corruption, villainy, dishonesty, injustice, misconduct, transgression. **2** *an attempt to make up for past wrongs:* **misdeed**, offence, injury, crime, transgression, peccadillo, sin; injustice, outrage, atrocity.
– OPPOSITES right.
• verb *she was determined to forget the man who had wronged her:* **ill-use**, mistreat, do an injustice to, ill-treat, abuse, harm, hurt, injure; informal do the dirty on.
■ **get someone/something wrong** misunderstand, misinterpret, misconstrue, mistake, misread, take amiss; get the wrong idea/impression; informal get the wrong end of the stick, be barking up the wrong tree. **go wrong 1** *I've gone wrong somewhere:* make a mistake, make an error, blunder, miscalculate, trip up; informal slip up, screw up, make a boo-boo; Brit. informal boob. **2** *their plans went wrong:* go awry, go amiss, go off course, fail, be unsuccessful, fall through, come to nothing; backfire, misfire, rebound; informal come to grief, come a cropper, go up in smoke; Brit. informal go adrift. **3** *the radio's gone wrong:* break down, malfunction, fail, stop working, crash, give out; informal be on the blink, conk out, go kaput; Brit. informal play up, pack up. **in the wrong** to blame, at fault, guilty, reprehensible, responsible, culpable, answerable.

wrongdoer noun **offender**, lawbreaker, criminal, felon, delinquent, villain, culprit, evildoer, sinner, transgressor, miscreant, rogue, scoundrel; informal crook; formal malefactor.

wrongdoing noun **crime**, lawbreaking, lawlessness, criminality, misconduct, misbehaviour, malpractice, corruption, immorality, sin, wickedness, evil, vice, iniquity, villainy; offence, felony, misdeed, misdemeanour, fault, peccadillo, transgression.

wrongful adjective **unjustified**, unwarranted, unjust, unfair, undue, undeserved, unreasonable, groundless, indefensible, inappropriate, improper, unlawful, illegal.
– OPPOSITES rightful.

wrought up adjective **agitated**, tense, stressed, overwrought, nervous, edgy, keyed up, worked up, jumpy, anxious, nervy, flustered, fretful; informal in a state, in a stew, het up, wound up, uptight, in a tizz; Brit. informal strung up.
– OPPOSITES calm.

wry adjective **1** *his wry humour:* **ironic**, sardonic, satirical, mocking, sarcastic; dry, droll, witty, humorous. **2** *a wry expression:* **unimpressed**, displeased, annoyed, irritated, irked, vexed, piqued, disgruntled, dissatisfied; informal peeved.

xenophobic adjective **jingoistic,** chauvinistic, flag-waving, nationalistic, isolationist; prejudiced, bigoted, intolerant.

Xerox noun (trademark) **photocopy,** copy, duplicate; trademark photostat.

Xmas noun (informal). See CHRISTMAS.

X-ray noun **radiograph,** radiogram.

WORD LINKS

radiography the medical process of taking X-rays

radiology the science of X-rays and similar radiation

Yy

yank verb (informal) **jerk**, pull, tug, wrench.

yap verb *the dogs yapped about his heels:* **bark**, yelp, snap.

yardstick noun **standard**, measure, gauge, scale, guide, guideline, indicator, test, touchstone, barometer, criterion, benchmark.

yarn noun **thread**, cotton, wool, fibre, filament.

yawning adjective **gaping**, wide, cavernous, deep; huge, great, big.

year noun literary summer, winter; old use twelvemonth.

yearly adjective **annual**.
• adverb **annually**, once a year, per annum, each/every year.

yearn verb **long**, pine, crave, desire, want, wish, hanker, have a yen, covet, hunger, thirst, ache, eat your heart out; informal itch.

yearning noun **longing**, craving, desire, want, wish, hankering, yen, urge, hunger, thirst, ache; informal itch.

yell verb *he yelled in agony:* **cry out**, shout, howl, wail, scream, shriek, screech, yelp, squeal; roar, bawl; informal holler.
• noun *a yell of rage:* **cry**, shout, howl, scream, shriek, screech, yelp, squeal; roar; informal holler.

yellow adjective **flaxen**, golden, gold, blonde, fair.

yelp noun & verb **squeal**, shriek, howl, yell, cry, shout.

yen noun **hankering**, yearning, longing, craving, urge, desire, want, wish, hunger, thirst, ache; informal itch.

yes adverb **all right**, very well, of course, by all means, sure, certainly, absolutely, indeed, affirmative, agreed, roger; Scottish, N. English, & old use aye; Nautical aye aye; informal yeah, yep, uh-huh, okay, OK, okey-dokey; Brit. informal righto, righty-ho; N. Amer. informal surely.
– OPPOSITES no.

yes-man noun (informal) **sycophant**, toady, lickspittle; informal bootlicker, creep.

yet adverb **1** *he hasn't made up his mind yet:* **so far**, as yet, up to now. **2** *he did nothing, yet he seemed happy:* **nevertheless**, nonetheless, even so, but, however, still, notwithstanding, despite that, in spite of that. **3** *yet more advice:* **even**, still.

yield verb **1** *such projects yield poor returns:* **produce**, bear, give, provide, afford, return, bring in, earn, realize, generate, deliver, pay out. **2** *Duke was forced to yield:* **surrender**, capitulate, submit, admit defeat, back down, give in. **3** *he yielded to her demands:* **give in to**, give way to, submit to, comply with, agree to, consent to, go along with; grant, permit, allow; informal cave in to; formal accede to. **4** *the floorboards yielded underfoot:* **bend**, give.
– OPPOSITES withhold, resist, defy.
• noun *we expected a higher yield:* **profit**, gain, return, dividend, earnings.

yob, yobbo noun (Brit. informal). See **HOOLIGAN**.

yokel noun **bumpkin**, peasant, provincial; N. Amer. informal hayseed, hillbilly, hick; Austral. informal bushy.

young adjective **1** *young people:* **youthful**; junior, adolescent, teenage. **2** *she's very young for her age:* **immature**, childish, juvenile, inexperienced, unsophisticated, naive; informal wet behind the ears.

3 *the young microbrewery industry:* **fledgling**, developing, budding, in its infancy, emerging.
– OPPOSITES old, elderly, mature.
• noun **1** *a robin feeding its young:* **offspring**, progeny, family, babies. **2** *the young don't care nowadays:* **young people**, children, boys and girls, youngsters, youth, the younger generation, juveniles, minors; informal kids.

youngster noun **child**, teenager, adolescent, youth, juvenile, minor, junior; boy, girl; Scottish & N. English lass, lassie; informal lad, kid, whipper-snapper, teen.

youth noun **1** *he was a fine athlete in his youth:* **early years**, teens, teenage years, adolescence, boyhood, girlhood, childhood; minority. **2** *she had kept her youth and beauty:* **youthfulness**, freshness, bloom, vigour, energy. **3** *local youths:* **young man**, boy, juvenile, teenager, adolescent, junior, minor; informal lad, kid. **4** *the youth of the nation:* **young people**, young, younger generation, next generation; informal kids.
– OPPOSITES adulthood, old age.

youthful adjective **young-looking**, spry, sprightly, vigorous, active; young, boyish, girlish; fresh-faced.
– OPPOSITES old, elderly.

Zz

zany adjective **eccentric**, odd, unconventional, bizarre, weird; mad, crazy, comic, madcap, funny, quirky, idiosyncratic; informal wacky, screwy, nutty, oddball, off the wall; Brit. informal daft; N. Amer. informal kooky, wacko.
– OPPOSITES conventional, sensible.

zeal noun **passion**, ardour, love, fervour, fire, devotion, enthusiasm, eagerness, keenness, relish, gusto, vigour, energy, intensity; fanaticism.
– OPPOSITES apathy.

zealot noun **fanatic**, enthusiast, extremist, radical, diehard, activist, militant; informal fiend, maniac, nut.

zealous adjective **fervent**, ardent, fanatical, passionate, impassioned, devout, devoted, committed, dedicated, enthusiastic, eager, keen, avid, vigorous, energetic, intense, fierce.
– OPPOSITES apathetic.

zenith noun **high point**, crowning point, height, top, acme, peak, pinnacle, apex, apogee, crown, crest, summit, climax, culmination, prime.
– OPPOSITES nadir.

zero noun **1** *you've left off a zero:* **nought**, nothing, nil, o. **2** *I rated my chances as zero:* **nil**, none; informal zilch, not a dicky bird; Brit. informal not a sausage; N. Amer. informal zip, nada, diddly-squat; old use nought.
■ **zero in on** focus on, focus attention on, centre on, concentrate on, home in on, fix on, pinpoint, highlight, spotlight; informal zoom in on.

zest noun **1** *her zest for life:* **enthusiasm**, gusto, relish, appetite, eagerness, keenness, zeal, fervour, passion. **2** *the zest of an orange:* **rind**, peel, skin.
– OPPOSITES apathy, indifference, blandness.

zigzag verb **twist**, meander, snake, wind.

zip verb (informal). See SPEED verb sense 1.

zone noun **area**, sector, section, belt, stretch, region, territory, district, quarter, precinct, locality, neighbourhood, province.

zoom verb (informal). See SPEED verb sense 1.